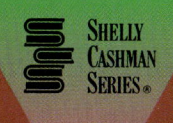

COMPLETE COMPUTER CONCEPTS
and
WINDOWS APPLICATIONS

Microsoft **WORD 2.0 FOR WINDOWS**
Microsoft **EXCEL 4 FOR WINDOWS**
PARADOX 1.0 FOR WINDOWS

Gary B. Shelly
Thomas J. Cashman
Gloria A. Waggoner
William C. Waggoner

Contributing Authors
Misty E. Vermaat
James S. Quasney
Philip J. Pratt
Steven G. Forsythe

SHELLY CASHMAN SERIES®

S0-ENS-643

bf
boyd & fraser
publishing company

Special thanks go to the following reviewers of the Shelly Cashman Series Windows Applications textbooks:

William Dorin, Indiana University Northwest; **Roger Franklin**, The College of William and Mary; **Roy O. Foreman**, Purdue University Calumet; **Patricia Harris**, Mesa Community College; **Cynthia Kachik**, Santa Fe Community College; **Karen Meyer**, Wright State University; **Michael Michaelson**, Palomar College; **John Ross**, Fox Valley Technical College; **Betty Svendsen**, Oakton Community College; **Jeanie Thibault**, Education Dynamics Institute; **Margaret Thomas**, Ohio University; **Melinda White**, Santa Fe Community College; **Eileen Zisk**, Community College of Rhode Island; and **Sue Zulauf**, Sinclair Community College.

© 1994 by boyd & fraser publishing company
A Division of South-Western Publishing Company
One Corporate Place • Ferncroft Village
Danvers, Massachusetts 01923

boyd & fraser publishing company is an ITP Company.
The ITP trademark is used under license.

All rights reserved. No part of this work may be reproduced or used in any form or by any means—graphic, electronic, or mechanical, including photocopying, recording, taping, or information and retrieval systems—without written permission from the publisher.

Manufactured in the United States of America

ISBN 0-87709-145-5

SHELLY CASHMAN SERIES® and **Custom Edition**™ are trademarks of South-Western Publishing Company. Names of all other products mentioned herein are used for identification purposes only and may be trademarks and/or registered trademarks of their respective owners. South-Western Publishing Company and boyd & fraser publishing company disclaim any affiliation, association, or connection with, or sponsorship or endorsement by such owners.

Library of Congress Cataloging-in-Publication Data

Complete computer concepts.
    Complete computer concepts ; and, Learning to use Windows applications. Microsoft Word 2.0 for Windows, Microsoft Excel 4 for Windows, Paradox 1.0 for Windows / Gary B. Shelly ... [et al.].
        p. cm. — (Shelly Cashman series)
    First work originally published: Danvers, MA : Boyd & Fraser, 1993, Second work originally published: Danvers, MA : Boyd & Fraser, 1992.
    Includes index.
    Contents: Complete computer concepts / Gary B. Shelly ... [et al.] — Learning to use Windows applications. Microsoft Word 2.0 for Windows, Microsoft Excel 4 for Windows, Paradox 1.0 for Windows / Gary B. Shelly, Thomas J. Cashman, Misty Vermaat.
    ISBN 0-87709-145-5. — ISBN 0-87709-146-3
    1. Windows (Computer programs), 2. Microsoft Word for Windows. 3. Microsoft Excel 4 for Windows. 4. Paradox for Windows (Computer file) I. Shelly, Gary B. Learning to use Windows applications. Microsoft Word 2.0 for Windows, Microsoft Excel 4 for Windows, Paradox 1.0 for Windows. 1993. II. Title: Learning to use Windows applications. Microsoft Word 2.0 for Windows, Microsoft Excel 4 for Windows, Paradox 1.0 for Windows. III. Series: Shelly, Gary B. Shelly and Cashman series.
QA76.76.W56C655 1993
004—dc20
93-20648
CIP

2 3 4 5 6 7 8 9 10 BC 8 7 6 5 4

Contents

COMPLETE COMPUTER CONCEPTS

▶ **CHAPTER ONE**
An Overview of Computer Concepts   1.1

    OBJECTIVES   1.1
    WHAT IS A COMPUTER?   1.2
    WHAT DOES A COMPUTER DO?   1.2
    WHY IS A COMPUTER SO POWERFUL?   1.3
    HOW DOES A COMPUTER KNOW WHAT TO DO?   1.4
    THE INFORMATION PROCESSING CYCLE   1.4
    WHAT ARE THE COMPONENTS OF A COMPUTER?   1.4
    CATEGORIES OF COMPUTERS   1.6
    COMPUTER SOFTWARE   1.7
    A TYPICAL BUSINESS APPLICATION   1.10
    WHAT ARE THE ELEMENTS OF AN INFORMATION SYSTEM?   1.13
    A TOUR OF AN INFORMATION SYSTEMS DEPARTMENT   1.14
    HOW COMPUTERS ARE USED TODAY   1.19
    SUMMARY OF AN INTRODUCTION TO COMPUTERS   1.20
    CHAPTER SUMMARY   1.20
    KEY TERMS   1.21
    REVIEW QUESTIONS   1.22
    CONTROVERSIAL ISSUES   1.22
    RESEARCH PROJECTS   1.22
    THE EVOLUTION OF THE COMPUTER INDUSTRY   1.23

▶ **CHAPTER TWO**
Microcomputer Applications: User Tools   2.1

    OBJECTIVES   2.1
    AN INTRODUCTION TO GENERAL MICROCOMPUTER APPLICATIONS   2.2
    WORD PROCESSING SOFTWARE: A DOCUMENT PRODUCTIVITY TOOL   2.4
    DESKTOP PUBLISHING SOFTWARE: A DOCUMENT PRESENTATION TOOL   2.8
    ELECTRONIC SPREADSHEET SOFTWARE: A NUMBER PRODUCTIVITY TOOL   2.10
    DATABASE SOFTWARE: A DATA MANAGEMENT TOOL   2.13
    GRAPHICS SOFTWARE: A DATA PRESENTATION TOOL   2.15
    DATA COMMUNICATIONS SOFTWARE: A CONNECTIVITY TOOL   2.18
    INTEGRATED SOFTWARE: A COMBINATION PRODUCTIVITY TOOL   2.18
    OTHER POPULAR MICROCOMPUTER APPLICATIONS   2.20
    GUIDELINES FOR PURCHASING MICROCOMPUTER APPLICATIONS SOFTWARE   2.22
    LEARNING AIDS AND SUPPORT TOOLS FOR APPLICATION USERS   2.23
    SUMMARY OF MICROCOMPUTER APPLICATIONS   2.24
    CHAPTER SUMMARY   2.24
    KEY TERMS   2.25
    REVIEW QUESTIONS   2.26
    CONTROVERSIAL ISSUES   2.26
    RESEARCH PROJECTS   2.26

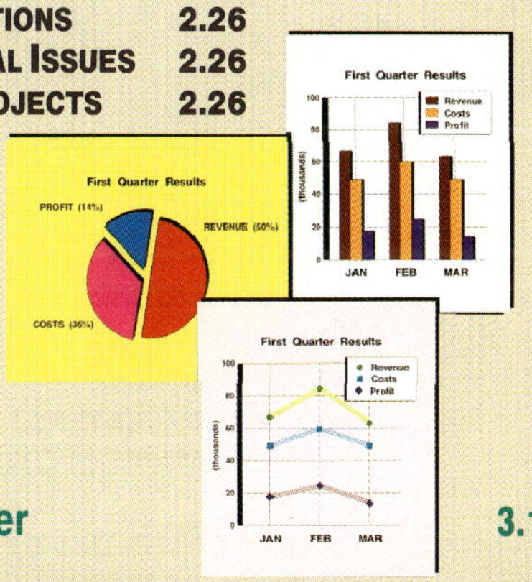

▶ **CHAPTER THREE**
Input to the Computer   3.1

    OBJECTIVES   3.1
    OVERVIEW OF THE INFORMATION PROCESSING CYCLE   3.2
    WHAT IS INPUT?   3.2
    HOW IS DATA ORGANIZED?   3.3
    THE KEYBOARD   3.5
    TERMINALS   3.6
    OTHER INPUT DEVICES   3.8
    INPUT DEVICES DESIGNED FOR SPECIFIC PURPOSES   3.11
    USER INTERFACES   3.17
    GRAPHIC USER INTERFACE   3.21
    FEATURES OF A USER INTERFACE   3.21
    DATA ENTRY   3.22
    DATA ENTRY FOR INTERACTIVE AND BATCH PROCESSING   3.22
    DATA ENTRY PROCEDURES   3.26
    ERGONOMICS   3.28
    SUMMARY OF INPUT TO THE COMPUTER   3.29
    CHAPTER SUMMARY   3.29
    KEY TERMS   3.31
    REVIEW QUESTIONS   3.31
    CONTROVERSIAL ISSUES   3.32
    RESEARCH PROJECTS   3.32

▶ **CHAPTER FOUR**
The Processor Unit   4.1

    OBJECTIVES   4.1
    WHAT IS THE PROCESSOR UNIT?   4.2
    HOW PROGRAMS AND DATA ARE REPRESENTED IN MEMORY   4.4
    PARITY   4.7
    NUMBER SYSTEMS   4.7
    HOW THE PROCESSOR UNIT EXECUTES PROGRAMS AND MANIPULATES DATA   4.10

iv CONTENTS

PROCESSOR SPEEDS	4.11
ARCHITECTURE OF PROCESSOR UNITS	4.13
TYPES OF MEMORY	4.15
SUMMARY	4.17
CHAPTER SUMMARY	4.18
KEY TERMS	4.19
REVIEW QUESTIONS	4.20
CONTROVERSIAL ISSUES	4.20
RESEARCH PROJECTS	4.20
MAKING A CHIP	4.21

▶ CHAPTER FIVE
Output from the Computer — 5.1

OBJECTIVES	5.1
WHAT IS OUTPUT?	5.2
TYPES OF OUTPUT	5.2
PRINTERS	5.5
IMPACT PRINTERS	5.7
NONIMPACT PRINTERS	5.13
CONSIDERATIONS IN CHOOSING A PRINTER	5.15
SCREENS	5.16
OTHER OUTPUT DEVICES	5.20
SUMMARY OF OUTPUT FROM THE COMPUTER	5.24
CHAPTER SUMMARY	5.24
KEY TERMS	5.26
REVIEW QUESTIONS	5.27
CONTROVERSIAL ISSUES	5.27
RESEARCH PROJECTS	5.27

▶ CHAPTER SIX
Auxiliary Storage — 6.1

OBJECTIVES	6.1
WHAT IS AUXILIARY STORAGE?	6.2
MAGNETIC DISK STORAGE	6.3
MAGNETIC TAPE	6.13
OTHER FORMS OF AUXILIARY STORAGE	6.16
SUMMARY OF AUXILIARY STORAGE	6.19
CHAPTER SUMMARY	6.20
KEY TERMS	6.22
REVIEW QUESTIONS	6.22
CONTROVERSIAL ISSUES	6.23
RESEARCH PROJECTS	6.23

▶ CHAPTER SEVEN
File and Database Management — 7.1

OBJECTIVES	7.1
DATA MANAGEMENT	7.2
WHAT IS A FILE?	7.4
TYPES OF FILE ORGANIZATION	7.4
HOW IS DATA IN FILES MAINTAINED?	7.8
DATABASES: A BETTER WAY TO MANAGE AND ORGANIZE DATA	7.12
WHAT IS A DATABASE?	7.12
WHY USE A DATABASE?	7.13
TYPES OF DATABASE ORGANIZATION	7.14
DATABASE MANAGEMENT SYSTEMS	7.17
QUERY LANGUAGES: ACCESS TO THE DATABASE	7.17
DATABASE ADMINISTRATION	7.19
PERSONAL COMPUTER DATABASE SYSTEMS	7.20
SUMMARY OF FILE AND DATABASE MANAGEMENT	7.21
CHAPTER SUMMARY	7.21
KEY TERMS	7.22
REVIEW QUESTIONS	7.23
CONTROVERSIAL ISSUES	7.23
RESEARCH PROJECTS	7.23

▶ CHAPTER EIGHT
Communications — 8.1

OBJECTIVES	8.1
WHAT IS COMMUNICATIONS?	8.2
A COMMUNICATIONS SYSTEM MODEL	8.2
COMMUNICATIONS CHANNELS	8.3
LINE CONFIGURATIONS	8.6
CHARACTERISTICS OF COMMUNICATIONS CHANNELS	8.9
COMMUNICATIONS EQUIPMENT	8.12
COMMUNICATIONS SOFTWARE	8.14
COMMUNICATIONS PROTOCOLS	8.15
COMMUNICATIONS NETWORKS	8.15
NETWORK CONFIGURATIONS	8.18
CONNECTING NETWORKS	8.19
AN EXAMPLE OF A COMMUNICATIONS NETWORK	8.20
SUMMARY OF COMMUNICATIONS	8.21
CHAPTER SUMMARY	8.21
KEY TERMS	8.23
REVIEW QUESTIONS	8.24
CONTROVERSIAL ISSUES	8.24
RESEARCH PROJECTS	8.24

▶ CHAPTER NINE
Operating Systems and Systems Software — 9.1

OBJECTIVES	9.1
WHAT IS SYSTEMS SOFTWARE?	9.2
WHAT IS AN OPERATING SYSTEM?	9.2
LOADING AN OPERATING SYSTEM	9.2
TYPES OF OPERATING SYSTEMS	9.4
FUNCTIONS OF OPERATING SYSTEMS	9.5
POPULAR OPERATING SYSTEMS	9.10
OPERATING ENVIRONMENTS	9.13
UTILITIES	9.13
LANGUAGE TRANSLATORS	9.14
SUMMARY OF OPERATING SYSTEMS AND SYSTEMS SOFTWARE	9.14
CHAPTER SUMMARY	9.14
KEY TERMS	9.16
REVIEW QUESTIONS	9.16
CONTROVERSIAL ISSUE	9.16
RESEARCH PROJECT	9.16

Chapter Ten
Management Information Systems — 10.1

- Objectives — 10.1
- Why Is Information Important to an Organization? — 10.2
- How Do Managers Use Information? — 10.3
- Management Levels in an Organization — 10.4
- Qualities of Information — 10.6
- What Is an Information System? — 10.7
- Integrated Information Systems — 10.11
- The Role of Personal Computers in Management Information Systems — 10.11
- Summary of Management Information Systems — 10.12
- Chapter Summary — 10.12
- Key Terms — 10.13
- Review Questions — 10.13
- Controversial Issue — 10.13
- Research Projects — 10.13

Chapter Eleven
The Information System Life Cycle — 11.1

- Objectives — 11.1
- What Is the Information System Life Cycle? — 11.2
- Analysis Phase — 11.4
- Analysis at Sutherland — 11.9
- Acquisition Phase — 11.10
- Acquisition at Sutherland — 11.14
- Commercial Applications Versus Custom Software — 11.14
- Customizing Phase — 11.15
- Customizing at Sutherland — 11.16
- Design Phase — 11.16
- Design at Sutherland — 11.21
- Development Phase — 11.21
- Development at Sutherland — 11.22
- Implementation Phase — 11.22
- Implementation at Sutherland — 11.23
- Maintenance Phase — 11.24
- Maintenance at Sutherland — 11.25
- Summary of the Information System Life Cycle — 11.25
- Chapter Summary — 11.25
- Key Terms — 11.27
- Review Questions — 11.27
- Controversial Issues — 11.28
- Research Projects — 11.28

Chapter Twelve
Program Development — 12.1

- Objectives — 12.1
- What Is a Computer Program? — 12.2
- What Is Program Development? — 12.2
- Step 1—Reviewing the Program Specifications — 12.3
- Step 2—Designing the Program — 12.3
- Step 3—Coding the Program — 12.9
- Step 4—Testing the Program — 12.9
- Step 5—Finalizing Program Documentation — 12.10
- Program Maintenance — 12.11
- Summary of Program Development — 12.11
- What Is a Programming Language? — 12.12
- Categories of Programming Languages — 12.12
- Programming Languages Used Today — 12.15
- Application Generators — 12.18
- Object-Oriented Programming — 12.19
- How to Choose a Programming Language — 12.20
- Summary of Programming Languages — 12.21
- Chapter Summary — 12.21
- Key Terms — 12.23
- Review Questions — 12.23
- Controversial Issues — 12.24
- Research Projects — 12.24

Chapter Thirteen
Career Opportunities in Information Processing — 13.1

- Objectives — 13.1
- The Information Processing Industry — 13.2
- What Are the Career Opportunities in Information Processing? — 13.3
- Compensation and Growth Trends for Information Processing Careers — 13.5
- Preparing for a Career in Information Processing — 13.7
- Career Development in the Information Processing Industry — 13.8
- Summary of Computer Career Opportunities — 13.10
- Chapter Summary — 13.10
- Key Terms — 13.11
- Review Questions — 13.12
- Controversial Issues — 13.12
- Research Projects — 13.13

Chapter Fourteen
Trends and Issues in the Information Age — 14.1

- Objectives — 14.1
- Information Systems in Business — 14.2
- Bringing the Information Age Home — 14.8
- Social Issues — 14.13
- Summary of Trends and Issues in the Information Age — 14.17
- Chapter Summary — 14.17
- Key Terms — 14.18
- Review Questions — 14.19
- Controversial Issues — 14.19
- Research Projects — 14.19

Index — I.1A

USING MICROSOFT WINDOWS 3.1 — WIN1

▶ PROJECT ONE
An Introduction to Windows — WIN2

OBJECTIVES — WIN2
INTRODUCTION — WIN2
What is a User Interface? — WIN3
MICROSOFT WINDOWS — WIN3
Starting Microsoft Windows — WIN4
COMMUNICATING WITH MICROSOFT WINDOWS — WIN5
The Mouse and Mouse Pointer — WIN5
Mouse Operations — WIN6
The Keyboard and Keyboard Shortcuts — WIN9
Menus and Commands — WIN10
Selecting a Menu — WIN11
Choosing a Command — WIN11
Dialog Boxes — WIN12
USING MICROSOFT WINDOWS — WIN14
Opening a Group Window — WIN14
Correcting an Error While Double-Clicking a Group Icon — WIN16
Starting an Application — WIN16
Correcting an Error While Double-Clicking a Program-Item Icon — WIN18
Maximizing an Application Window — WIN18
Creating a Document — WIN19
Printing a Document by Choosing a Command from a Menu — WIN20
Quitting an Application — WIN21
FILE AND DISK CONCEPTS — WIN22
Naming a File — WIN23
Directory Structures and Directory Paths — WIN23
Saving a Document on Disk — WIN24
Correcting Errors Encountered While Saving a Document File — WIN27
Quitting an Application — WIN28
OPENING A DOCUMENT FILE — WIN28
Starting the Notepad Application and Maximizing the Notepad Window — WIN28
Opening a Document File — WIN29
Editing the Document File — WIN31
Saving the Modified Document File — WIN31
USING WINDOWS HELP — WIN32
Choosing a Help Topic — WIN33
Exiting the Online Help and Paintbrush Applications — WIN35
QUITTING WINDOWS — WIN36
Verify Changes to the Desktop Will Not be Saved — WIN36
Quitting Windows Without Saving Changes — WIN37
PROJECT SUMMARY — WIN38
KEY TERMS — WIN38
QUICK REFERENCE — WIN39
STUDENT ASSIGNMENTS — WIN40
COMPUTER LABORATORY EXERCISES — WIN43

▶ PROJECT TWO
Disk and File Management — WIN47

OBJECTIVES — WIN47
INTRODUCTION — WIN47
STARTING WINDOWS — WIN48
Starting File Manager and Maximizing the File Manager Window — WIN48
FILE MANAGER — WIN49
FORMATTING A DISKETTE — WIN50
Diskette Size and Capacity — WIN50
Formatting a Diskette — WIN51
Correcting Errors Encountered While Formatting a Diskette — WIN54
COPYING FILES TO A DISKETTE — WIN54
Maximizing the Directory Window — WIN55
Selecting a Group of Files — WIN55
Copying a Group of Files — WIN57
Correcting Errors Encountered While Copying Files — WIN59
Replacing a File on Disk — WIN60
Changing the Current Drive — WIN61
Correcting Errors Encountered While Changing the Current Drive — WIN62
RENAMING A FILE — WIN63
DELETING A FILE — WIN65
CREATING A BACKUP DISKETTE — WIN67
Correcting Errors Encountered While Copying a Diskette — WIN71
SEARCHING FOR HELP USING ONLINE HELP — WIN71
Searching for a Help Topic — WIN72
Searching for Help Using a Word or Phrase — WIN75
Quitting File Manager and Online Help — WIN77
SWITCHING BETWEEN APPLICATIONS — WIN77
Verify Changes to the File Manager Window Will Not be Saved — WIN79
Quitting File Manager — WIN79
ADDITIONAL COMMANDS AND CONCEPTS — WIN80
Activating a Group Window — WIN81
Closing a Group Window — WIN82
Resizing a Group Window — WIN83
Arranging Icons — WIN85
Minimizing an Application Window to an Icon — WIN86
PROJECT SUMMARY — WIN86
KEY TERMS — WIN87
QUICK REFERENCE — WIN87
STUDENT ASSIGNMENTS — WIN88
COMPUTER LABORATORY EXERCISES — WIN92

INDEX — WIN96

CONTENTS vii

WORD PROCESSING USING MICROSOFT WORD 2.0 FOR WINDOWS — MSW1

▶ PROJECT ONE
Creating and Editing a Document — MSW2

OBJECTIVES	MSW2
WHAT IS MICROSOFT WORD?	MSW2
PROJECT ONE	MSW2
Document Preparation Steps	MSW4
STARTING WORD	MSW4
THE WORD SCREEN	MSW5
Word Document Window	MSW5
Menu Bar, Toolbar, Ribbon, Ruler, and Status Bar	MSW7
CHANGING THE DEFAULT POINT SIZE	MSW8
ENTERING TEXT	MSW10
Entering Blank Lines into a Document	MSW11
Using the TAB key	MSW12
Displaying Nonprinting Characters	MSW14
Using the Wordwrap Feature	MSW15
Entering Documents Too Long for the Document Window	MSW17
SAVING A DOCUMENT	MSW18
FORMATTING PARAGRAPHS AND CHARACTERS IN A DOCUMENT	MSW21
Selecting Characters to Format	MSW23
CHECKING SPELLING	MSW29
SAVING AN EXISTING DOCUMENT WITH THE SAME FILENAME	MSW31
PRINTING A DOCUMENT	MSW32
QUITTING WORD	MSW34
OPENING A DOCUMENT	MSW35
CORRECTING ERRORS	MSW36
Types of Changes Made to Documents	MSW36
Inserting Text into an Existing Document	MSW37
Deleting Text from an Existing Document	MSW38
Undoing Most Recent Actions	MSW39
Closing the Entire Document	MSW39
WORD'S ONLINE HELP	MSW39
Word's Online Tutorial	MSW40
PROJECT SUMMARY	MSW41
KEY TERMS	MSW41
QUICK REFERENCE	MSW42
STUDENT ASSIGNMENTS	MSW43
COMPUTER LABORATORY EXERCISES	MSW47
COMPUTER LABORATORY ASSIGNMENTS	MSW49

▶ PROJECT TWO
Creating a Research Paper — MSW54

OBJECTIVES	MSW54
INTRODUCTION	MSW54
PROJECT TWO	MSW55
MLA Documentation Style	MSW56
Document Preparation Steps	MSW56
STARTING WORD	MSW57
Displaying Nonprinting Characters	MSW57
CHANGING THE MARGINS	MSW57
ADJUSTING LINE SPACING	MSW59
REDEFINING THE NORMAL STYLE	MSW61
USING A HEADER TO NUMBER PAGES	MSW62
Headers and Footers	MSW63
TYPING THE BODY OF THE RESEARCH PAPER	MSW66
Entering Name and Course Information	MSW67
Centering a Paragraph Before Typing	MSW67
Saving the Research Paper	MSW69
Indenting Paragraphs	MSW69
Adding Footnotes	MSW71
Automatic Page Breaks	MSW75
Viewing Documents in Page Layout	MSW76
CREATING AN ALPHABETICAL WORKS CITED PAGE	MSW78
Switching Back to Normal View	MSW78
Hard Page Breaks	MSW79
Centering the Title of the Works Cited Page	MSW80
Creating a Hanging Indent	MSW81
Sorting Paragraphs	MSW82
Checking Spelling, Saving Again, and Printing the Document	MSW84
REVISING THE RESEARCH PAPER	MSW86
Finding and Replacing Text	MSW86
Finding Text	MSW88
Finding a Specific Page or Footnote	MSW88
Moving Paragraphs	MSW88
Selectively Displaying Nonprinting Characters	MSW91
USING THE THESAURUS	MSW91
DISPLAYING AND PRINTING A DOCUMENT IN PRINT PREVIEW	MSW93
PROJECT SUMMARY	MSW96
KEY TERMS	MSW96
QUICK REFERENCE	MSW97
STUDENT ASSIGNMENTS	MSW98
COMPUTER LABORATORY EXERCISES	MSW103
COMPUTER LABORATORY ASSIGNMENTS	MSW106

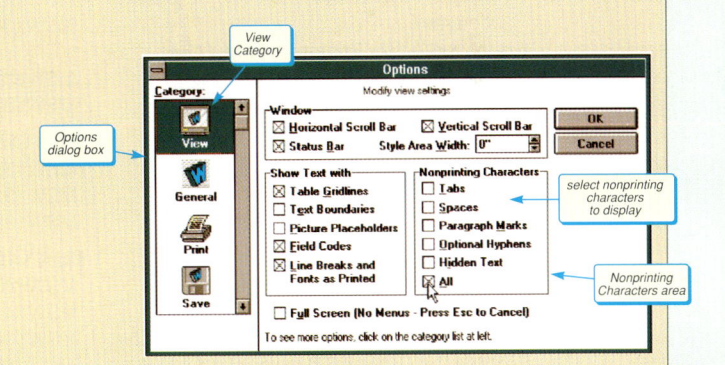

PROJECT THREE
Creating a Proposal Using Tables and Graphics — MSW112

OBJECTIVES	MSW112
INTRODUCTION	MSW112
PROJECT THREE	MSW112
Document Preparation Steps	MSW116
Redefining the Normal Style	MSW116
CREATING A TITLE PAGE	**MSW117**
Entering the First Line of the Title Page	MSW117
Importing a Graphic into the Title Page	MSW118
Entering the Next Lines of Text on the Title Page	MSW121
Importing the Next Graphic	MSW121
Scaling an Imported Graphic	MSW123
Restoring a Scaled Graphic to its Original Size	MSW125
Entering the Next Lines of Text on the Title Page	MSW125
Importing the Final Graphic	MSW126
Changing the Space Between Characters	MSW126
Saving the Title Page	MSW128
INSERTING AN EXISTING DOCUMENT INTO AN OPEN DOCUMENT	**MSW129**
Inserting a Hard Page Break	MSW129
Inserting a Second Document into an Open Document	MSW130
Saving the Active Document with a New Filename	MSW132
Printing the Document	MSW133
SETTING AND USING TABS	**MSW135**
Entering the Table Title	MSW135
Entering Text Using Custom Tab Stops	MSW137
Changing the Alignment of a Tab Stop	MSW138
CREATING A TABLE	**MSW140**
Entering the Title Lines of the Table	MSW140
Inserting an Empty Table	MSW141
To Change the Spacing of Columns in a Table	MSW144
Entering the Column Titles into the Cells of the Table	MSW146
Changing the Alignment of Text within Cells	MSW146
Entering the Data into the Table	MSW148
Summing Rows and Columns in a Table	MSW149
CHARTING A TABLE	**MSW153**
Adding a Title to the Chart	MSW157
ADDING BULLETS TO A LIST	**MSW157**
Finishing the Paper	MSW159
PROJECT SUMMARY	**MSW161**
KEY TERMS	**MSW161**
QUICK REFERENCE	**MSW161**
STUDENT ASSIGNMENTS	**MSW162**
COMPUTER LABORATORY EXERCISES	**MSW166**
COMPUTER LABORATORY ASSIGNMENTS	**MSW169**

PROJECT FOUR
Generating Form Letters and Mailing Labels — MSW179

OBJECTIVES	MSW179
INTRODUCTION	MSW179
PROJECT FOUR	MSW179
Merging	MSW181
Document Preparation Steps	MSW181
Displaying Nonprinting Characters	MSW181
CREATING A DATA FILE	**MSW181**
Field Name Conventions	MSW182
Adjusting Column Widths of a Data File	MSW186
Adding Data Records to the Data File	MSW187
Working with an Existing Data File	MSW188
CREATING THE MAIN DOCUMENT FOR THE FORM LETTER	**MSW190**
Adding the Current Date to the Form Letter	MSW193
Inserting Merge Fields into the Main Document	MSW195
Completing the Inside Address Lines	MSW197
Entering Merge Fields in the Salutation Line	MSW197
Entering the Body of the Form Letter	MSW198
Using an IF Field to Conditionally Print Text in the Form Letter	MSW199
Checking for Errors in the Main Document	MSW203
Printing the Main Document for the Form Letter	MSW204
MERGING THE DOCUMENTS AND PRINTING THE LETTERS	**MSW208**
Selecting Data Records to Merge and Print	MSW210
CREATING AND PRINTING MAILING LABELS	**MSW213**
Printing Mailing Labels	MSW218
PROJECT SUMMARY	**MSW219**
KEY TERMS	**MSW220**
QUICK REFERENCE	**MSW220**
STUDENT ASSIGNMENTS	**MSW221**
COMPUTER LABORATORY EXERCISES	**MSW224**
COMPUTER LABORATORY ASSIGNMENTS	**MSW226**

PROJECT FIVE
Creating a Professional Newsletter — MSW231

OBJECTIVES	MSW231
INTRODUCTION	MSW231
PROJECT FIVE	MSW231
Desktop Publishing Terminology	MSW234
Document Preparation Steps	MSW234
Changing the Default Margins and Redefining the Normal Style	MSW234
CREATING THE NAMEPLATE	**MSW235**
Changing the Font	MSW235
Adding Ruling Lines to Divide Text	MSW237
Adding the Headline with Shading	MSW239
Entering the Issue Information Line	MSW242
CREATING THE FIRST PAGE OF THE BODY OF THE NEWSLETTER	**MSW244**
Formatting a Document into Multiple Columns	MSW245

CONTENTS ix

Entering the Subheads and Article Text	MSW247
Positioning Graphics on the Page	MSW251
Inserting a Column Break	MSW254
Adding a Box Border Around Paragraphs	MSW256
Adding a Vertical Rule Between Columns	MSW258
CREATING THE SECOND PAGE OF THE NEWSLETTER	**MSW262**
Creating the Nameplate on the Second Page	MSW262
Reducing and Magnifying the View of a Document	MSW265
Inserting a Pull-Quote	MSW266
Adding a Shadow Box Border Around Paragraphs	MSW270
ENHANCING THE NEWSLETTER WITH COLOR	**MSW271**
PROJECT SUMMARY	**MSW275**
KEY TERMS	**MSW276**
QUICK REFERENCE	**MSW276**
STUDENT ASSIGNMENTS	**MSW277**
COMPUTER LABORATORY EXERCISES	**MSW281**
COMPUTER LABORATORY ASSIGNMENTS	**MSW283**
INDEX	**MSW286**

SPREADSHEETS USING MICROSOFT EXCEL 4 FOR WINDOWS — E1

▶ PROJECT ONE
Building a Worksheet — E2

OBJECTIVES	**E2**
WHAT IS EXCEL?	**E2**
PROJECT ONE	**E3**
Worksheet Preparation Steps	E3
STARTING EXCEL	**E4**
THE WORKSHEET	**E5**
Cell, Active Cell, and Mouse Pointer	E5
Worksheet Window	E6
Menu Bar, Standard Toolbar, Formula Bar, and Status Bar	E6
SELECTING A CELL	**E8**
ENTERING TEXT	**E8**
Entering the Worksheet Title	E8
Correcting a Mistake While Typing	E10
Entering Column Titles	E10
Entering Row Titles	E12
ENTERING NUMBERS	**E13**
CALCULATING A SUM	**E15**
USING THE FILL HANDLE TO COPY A CELL TO ADJACENT CELLS	**E17**
Summing a Row Total	E19
Copying Cells in a Column	E20
FORMATTING THE WORKSHEET	**E22**
Fonts, Font Size, and Font Style	E22
USING AUTOFORMAT TO FORMAT THE WORKSHEET	**E25**
ADDING A CHART TO THE WORKSHEET	**E28**
SAVING THE WORKSHEET	**E31**
PRINTING THE WORKSHEET	**E35**
EXITING EXCEL	**E37**
OPENING A WORKSHEET	**E38**
CORRECTING ERRORS	**E39**
Correcting Errors Prior to Entering Data into a Cell	E39
Editing Data in a Cell	E39
Undoing the Last Entry — The Undo Command	E40
Clearing a Cell or Range of Cells	E41
Clearing the Entire Worksheet	E41
EXCEL HELP FACILITY	**E42**
Help Tool on the Standard Toolbar	E42
Excel On-line Tutorial	E43
PLANNING A WORKSHEET	**E44**
Define the Problem	E44
Design the Worksheet	E44
Enter the Worksheet	E44
Test the Worksheet	E44
PROJECT SUMMARY	**E45**
KEY TERMS	**E45**
QUICK REFERENCE	**E46**
STUDENT ASSIGNMENTS	**E47**
COMPUTER LABORATORY EXERCISES	**E51**
COMPUTER LABORATORY ASSIGNMENTS	**E53**

▶ PROJECT TWO
Adding Formulas to a Worksheet — E57

OBJECTIVES	**E57**
INTRODUCTION	**E57**
PROJECT TWO	**E57**
ENTERING THE TITLES AND NUMBERS INTO THE WORKSHEET	**E58**
ENTERING FORMULAS	**E59**
Order of Operations	E61
ENTERING FORMULAS USING POINT MODE	**E62**
SUMMING COLUMN TOTALS	**E64**
CALCULATING AN AVERAGE	**E66**
SAVING AN INTERMEDIATE COPY OF THE WORKSHEET	**E69**
FORMATTING TEXT AND DRAWING BORDERS	**E69**
Formatting the Worksheet Title	E70
Formatting the Column Titles	E71
Drawing Borders	E71
Using the Shortcut Menu to Access Excel Commands	E73
Formatting the Row Titles	E74
FORMATTING NUMBERS	**E75**
Formatting Numbers Using the Style Box	E75
Formatting Numbers Using the Number Command	E78
CHANGING THE FONT IN THE WORKSHEET	**E80**

x CONTENTS

CHANGING THE WIDTHS OF COLUMNS AND HEIGHTS OF ROWS	**E82**
Changing the Widths of Columns	E82
Changing the Heights of Rows	E85
SAVING THE WORKSHEET A SECOND TIME USING THE SAME FILE NAME	**E88**
PREVIEWING AND PRINTING THE WORKSHEET	**E88**
PRINTING A SECTION OF THE WORKSHEET	**E90**
DISPLAYING AND PRINTING THE FORMULAS IN THE WORKSHEET	**E92**
Changing the Print Scaling Option Back to 100%	E95
PROJECT SUMMARY	**E95**
KEY TERMS	**E95**
QUICK REFERENCE	**E96**
STUDENT ASSIGNMENTS	**E97**
COMPUTER LABORATORY EXERCISES	**E102**
COMPUTER LABORATORY ASSIGNMENTS	**E104**

▶ PROJECT THREE
Enhancing a Worksheet and Drawing Charts — E109

OBJECTIVES	**E109**
INTRODUCTION	**E109**
PROJECT THREE	**E109**
DELETING AND INSERTING CELLS IN A WORKSHEET	**E112**
Deleting Rows	E112
Deleting Columns	E113
Deleting Individual Cells or a Range of Cells	E113
Inserting Rows	E113
Inserting Columns	E114
Inserting Individual Cells or a Range of Cells	E115
ADDING AND CHANGING DATA IN THE WORKSHEET	**E115**
To Copy a Range of Cells to Adjacent Cells Using the Fill Handle	E115
Adjusting the Ranges in the SUM and AVERAGE Functions	E116
MOVING CELLS	**E117**
Using the Cut and Paste Commands to Move Cells	E119
Moving Cells Versus Copying Cells	E119
THE MAX AND MIN FUNCTIONS	**E120**
COPYING A CELL'S FORMAT	**E124**
ENTERING NUMBERS WITH A FORMAT SYMBOL	**E127**
Summary of Format Symbols	E128
WRAPPING TEXT IN A CELL	**E128**
MAKING DECISIONS — THE IF FUNCTION	**E130**
Absolute Versus Relative References	E131
Copying the IF Function with an Absolute Reference	E133
RECENTERING THE WORKSHEET TITLE	**E134**
ADDING COLOR TO A WORKSHEET	**E134**
Changing the Color of the Font	E135
Changing the Color of the Borders	E137

SAVING A WORKSHEET UNDER A DIFFERENT FILE NAME	**E140**
ADDING A PIE CHART TO THE WORKSHEET	**E141**
Drawing the Pie Chart	E142
ENHANCING THE PIE CHART	**E146**
Opening an Embedded Chart	E147
Bolding and Enlarging the Chart Title	E147
Exploding the Pie Chart	E148
Rotating the Pie Chart	E149
Adding a Chart Arrow	E151
Adding Chart Text	E152
SWITCHING WINDOWS	**E155**
HIDING THE PIE CHART	**E156**
PRINTING THE PIE CHART SEPARATELY FROM THE WORKSHEET	**E158**
THE GALLERY AND CHART MENUS	**E160**
Changing the Preferred Chart	E160
The Chart Menu	E161
PROJECT SUMMARY	**E161**
KEY TERMS	**E161**
QUICK REFERENCE	**E162**
STUDENT ASSIGNMENTS	**E163**
COMPUTER LABORATORY EXERCISES	**E167**
COMPUTER LABORATORY ASSIGNMENTS	**E169**

▶ PROJECT FOUR
Working with Large Worksheets — E175

OBJECTIVES	**E175**
INTRODUCTION	**E175**
PROJECT FOUR	**E176**
Changing the Font of the Entire Worksheet	E177
Entering the Worksheet Title	E177
USING THE FILL HANDLE TO CREATE A SERIES	**E178**
ENTERING THE ROW TITLES AND INCREASING THE COLUMN WIDTHS	**E179**
COPYING A RANGE OF CELLS TO A NONADJACENT PASTE AREA	**E180**
Completing the Entries in the Budget % Expense Table	E182
ENTERING THE REVENUE DATA AND USING THE FORMATTING TOOLBAR	**E183**
Displaying the Formatting Toolbar	E185
Selecting Nonadjacent Cells and Using the Formatting Toolbar	E186
Saving an Intermediate Copy of the Worksheet	E187
FREEZING WORKSHEET TITLES	**E187**
ENTERING AND COPYING THE EXPENSE FORMULAS AND TOTALS	**E188**
Determining and Formatting the Expense Totals and Net Income	E191
HIDING A TOOLBAR	**E192**
FORMATTING THE WORKSHEET, COLUMN, AND ROW TITLES	**E193**
Changing the Font of the Worksheet, Column, and Row Titles	E193
Increasing the Height of Nonadjacent Rows	E194
Drawing Borders in the Worksheet	E195

CONTENTS xi

FORMATTING THE BUDGET % EXPENSES TABLE	**E196**
Shading Cells	E196
Adding a Drop Shadow to a Range of Cells	E197
Changing the Color of the Font in the Budget % Expenses Table	E198
ADDING COMMENTS TO A WORKSHEET	**E198**
DISPLAYING AND DOCKING THE UTILITY TOOLBAR	**E200**
CHECKING SPELLING	**E201**
PRINTING THE WORKSHEET WITH PRINT TITLES	**E203**
Changing the Page Margins and Orientation	E204
MOVING AROUND THE WORKSHEET	**E206**
CHANGING THE VIEW OF THE WORKSHEET	**E206**
Magnifying or Shrinking the View of a Worksheet	E207
Splitting the Window into Panes	E208
OUTLINING A WORKSHEET	**E210**
Creating an Outline	E211
Working with the Visible Cells in an Outlined Worksheet	E214
Expanding Collapsed Rows and Columns	E215
Displaying and Hiding the Outline Symbols	E216
Saving the Worksheet with the Outline	E217
Changing Levels and Clearing the Outline Structure	E217
CHANGING VALUES IN CELLS THAT ARE REFERENCED IN A FORMULA	**E218**
PROJECT SUMMARY	**E220**
KEY TERMS	**E220**
QUICK REFERENCE	**E221**
TOOLBAR REFERENCE	**E222**
STUDENT ASSIGNMENTS	**E223**
COMPUTER LABORATORY EXERCISES	**E226**
COMPUTER LABORATORY ASSIGNMENTS	**E228**

▸ **PROJECT FIVE**
Analyzing Worksheet Data **E233**

OBJECTIVES	**E233**
INTRODUCTION	**E233**
PROJECT FIVE	**E234**
Changing the Font of the Entire Worksheet	E236
Entering the Worksheet Title and Row Titles	E236
Displaying the System Date and System Time	E237
Outlining the Loan Analysis Section of the Worksheet	E239
Entering the Loan Data	E240
CREATING NAMES BASED ON ROW TITLES	**E240**
DETERMINING THE MONTHLY PAYMENT	**E243**
DETERMINING THE TOTAL INTEREST AND TOTAL COST	**E245**
USING A DATA TABLE TO ANALYZE WORKSHEET DATA	**E246**
ENTERING NEW LOAN DATA	**E253**
BUILDING A COMMAND MACRO TO AUTOMATE LOAN DATA ENTRY	**E254**
Planning a Command Macro	E255
Opening a Macro Sheet and Naming the Command Macro	E255

Entering the Command Macro on the Macro Sheet	E257
Adding Overall Documentation to the Macro Sheet	E258
ADDING A BUTTON TO THE WORKSHEET TO PLAY BACK A COMMAND MACRO	**E260**
PLAYING BACK THE COMMAND MACRO	**E263**
GOAL SEEKING TO DETERMINE THE DOWN PAYMENT FOR A SPECIFIC MONTHLY PAYMENT	**E265**
USING SCENARIO MANAGER TO ANALYZE DATA	**E267**
PROTECTING THE WORKSHEET	**E271**
PROJECT SUMMARY	**E273**
KEY TERMS	**E273**
QUICK REFERENCE	**E274**
STUDENT ASSIGNMENTS	**E274**
COMPUTER LABORATORY EXERCISES	**E279**
COMPUTER LABORATORY ASSIGNMENTS	**E282**

▸ **PROJECT SIX**
Sorting and Querying a Worksheet Database **E288**

OBJECTIVES	**E288**
INTRODUCTION	**E288**
PROJECT SIX	**E289**
Setting Up the Worksheet	E290
CREATING A DATABASE	**E290**
Using the Data Form to View Records and Change Data	E295
Printing a Database	E296
SORTING A DATABASE	**E296**
Sorting the Personnel Database by Last Name	E296
Sorting Records Using the Sort Ascending and Sort Descending Tools	E298
Sorting a Personnel Database by Salary within Education within Gender	E298
Sorting with More than Three Fields	E300
FINDING RECORDS THAT PASS THE COMPARISON CRITERIA USING A DATA FORM	**E300**
Using Wildcard Characters in Comparison Criteria	E303
Using Computed Criteria	E303
CREATING A CRITERIA RANGE ON THE WORKSHEET	**E303**
FINDING RECORDS	**E305**
EXTRACTING RECORDS	**E306**
Creating the Extract Range	E306
Extracting Records to an Extract Range	E307
DELETING RECORDS	**E309**
MORE ABOUT COMPARISON CRITERIA	**E309**
A Blank Row in the Criteria Range	E309
Using Multiple Comparison Criteria with the Same Field	E310

xii   CONTENTS

Comparison Criteria in Different Rows and Under Different Fields	E310
USING DATABASE FUNCTIONS	**E310**
USING THE CROSSTAB REPORTWIZARD TO SUMMARIZE DATABASE INFORMATION	**E312**
PROJECT SUMMARY	**E317**
KEY TERMS	**E317**
QUICK REFERENCE	**E318**
STUDENT ASSIGNMENTS	**E318**
COMPUTER LABORATORY EXERCISES	**E323**
COMPUTER LABORATORY ASSIGNMENTS	**E326**
INDEX	**E331**

DATABASE USING PARADOX 1.0 FOR WINDOWS   P1

▶ PROJECT ONE
Creating a Database   P2

OBJECTIVES	**P2**
WHAT IS A DATABASE?	**P2**
WHAT IS PARADOX FOR WINDOWS?	**P4**
DATABASE PREPARATION STEPS	**P4**
STARTING PARADOX	**P5**
THE PARADOX FOR WINDOWS DESKTOP	**P6**
CHANGING THE WORKING DIRECTORY	**P7**
CREATING A TABLE	**P8**
Correcting Errors in the Structure	P15
SAVING A TABLE	**P15**
EXITING PARADOX FOR WINDOWS	**P17**
ADDING RECORDS TO A TABLE	**P17**
ADDING ADDITIONAL RECORDS	**P24**
Correcting Errors in the Data	P27
PRINTING THE CONTENTS OF A TABLE	**P27**
CREATING ADDITIONAL TABLES	**P30**
ADDING RECORDS TO A TABLE	**P32**
USING A FORM TO VIEW DATA	**P33**
CREATING A GRAPH	**P37**
USING THE HELP FACILITY	**P43**
DESIGNING A DATABASE	**P43**
PROJECT SUMMARY	**P45**
KEY TERMS	**P45**
QUICK REFERENCE	**P45**
STUDENT ASSIGNMENTS	**P47**
COMPUTER LABORATORY EXERCISES	**P52**
COMPUTER LABORATORY ASSIGNMENTS	**P53**

▶ PROJECT TWO
Querying a Database   P59

OBJECTIVES	**P59**
INTRODUCTION	**P59**
THE ANSWER TABLE	**P60**
OPENING A NEW QUERY WINDOW	**P61**
INCLUDING ALL FIELDS IN THE ANSWER TABLE	**P62**
RUNNING A QUERY TO CREATE THE ANSWER TABLE	**P64**
Printing the Answer to a Query	P65
Closing the Answer Table	P66
Closing a Query	P67
Clearing a Query Image	P68
DISPLAYING SELECTED FIELDS IN THE ANSWER TABLE	**P68**
ENTERING CONDITIONS	**P70**
Using Character Data in Conditions	P70
Using Special Character Conditions	P72
Querying by Sound Using the LIKE Operator	P73
Using Numeric Data in Conditions	P75
Using Comparison Operators	P77
USING COMPOUND CONDITIONS	**P78**
AND Condition	P78
OR Condition	P79
SORTING DATA IN A QUERY	**P80**
Including Duplicates in the Sorted Data	P82
Sorting Data in a Query in Descending Sequence	P83
Sorting Data in a Query on Multiple Fields	P84
JOINING TABLES	**P86**
Adding a Second Table to the Query	P88
Joining the Tables	P89
Restricting Records in a Join	P90
USING COMPUTED FIELDS	**P92**
CALCULATING STATISTICS	**P94**
Calculating an Average	P94
Grouping Similar Records	P94
GRAPHING THE ANSWER TO A QUERY	**P96**
Changing the Bar Chart	P97
Closing the Graph Window	P100
SAVING A QUERY	**P101**
Using a Query	P101
PROJECT SUMMARY	**P102**
KEY TERMS	**P103**
QUICK REFERENCE	**P103**
STUDENT ASSIGNMENTS	**P104**
COMPUTER LABORATORY EXERCISES	**P109**
COMPUTER LABORATORY ASSIGNMENTS	**P110**

▶ PROJECT THREE
Maintaining a Database   P113

OBJECTIVES	**P113**
INTRODUCTION	**P113**
ADDING, CHANGING AND DELETING RECORDS	**P114**
Adding Records	P114
Searching for a Record	P116
Changing the Contents of a Record	P118
Deleting Records	P119
CHANGING THE STRUCTURE	**P121**
Changing the Size of a Field	P121
Adding a New Field	P122
Updating the Restructured Database	P123
Updating the Contents of a New Field in a Table	P125
CREATING VALIDITY CHECKS	**P127**
Specifying a Required Field	P128
Specifying a Range	P128
Specifying a Default Value	P130

Specifying a Pattern	P131
Specifying a Collection of Legal Values	P133
REFERENTIAL INTEGRITY	**P134**
UPDATING A TABLE THAT CONTAINS VALIDITY CHECKS	**P137**
MASS UPDATES	**P139**
Deleting Groups of Records	P139
Changing Groups of Records	P141
Undoing Mass Changes	P142
CREATING AND USING INDEXES	**P142**
Creating Single-Field Indexes	P145
Creating Multiple-Field Indexes	P148
Using an Index to Order Records	P149
PROJECT SUMMARY	**P152**
KEY TERMS	**P152**
QUICK REFERENCE	**P152**
STUDENT ASSIGNMENTS	**P153**
COMPUTER LABORATORY EXERCISES	**P158**
COMPUTER LABORATORY ASSIGNMENTS	**P159**

▶ **PROJECT FOUR**
Presenting Data: Reports and Forms P163

OBJECTIVES	**P163**
INTRODUCTION	**P163**
CREATING A REPORT	**P166**
Beginning the Report Creation	P166
Selecting the Fields	P168
Report Bands	P170
Changing Column Headings and Widths	P171
Selecting an Area of a Report	P171
Changing Column Headings	P172
Changing the Zoom Factor	P174
Adjusting Column Widths	P175
Resizing Bands	P176
Adding a Field to the Footer	P178
Changing the Label in a Field Object	P180
Saving a Report	P181
Closing a Report	P182
Printing a Report	P182
GROUPING	**P183**
Creating a New Report from an Existing Report	P184
Modifying a Report Design	P184
Adding a Group Band	P184
Adding a Subtotal	P185
Saving the Report with a Different Name	P188
Printing the Report	P188
REPORT DESIGN CONSIDERATIONS	**P188**
CREATING AND USING CUSTOM FORMS	**P188**
Beginning the Form Creation	P189
Selecting Fields for a Form	P191
Using the Grid	P192
Selecting Fields	P193
Moving Fields on a Form	P194
Saving a Form	P195
Viewing Data Using a Form	P195
Adjusting the Position of the Field Edit Region	P195
Adding Boxes to a Form	P197
Adding Text to a Form	P199
Changing Fonts	P200
Removing the Grid	P201
Changing the Background Color	P202
Changing Box Frame Styles	P202
Selecting More than One Object	P203
Changing the Field Frame Styles	P204
Changing the Text Frame Style	P205
Changing the Color of the Field Edit Regions	P206
Closing a Form	P208
Using the Form	P209
FORM DESIGN CONSIDERATIONS	**P209**
PROJECT SUMMARY	**P210**
KEY TERMS	**P210**
QUICK REFERENCE	**P210**
STUDENT ASSIGNMENTS	**P212**
COMPUTER LABORATORY EXERCISES	**P218**
COMPUTER LABORATORY ASSIGNMENTS	**P219**

▶ **PROJECT FIVE**
Advanced Topics P221

OBJECTIVES	**P221**
INTRODUCTION	**P221**
DATE, MEMO, AND OLE FIELDS	**P222**
Graphic Versus OLE Fields	P223
RESTRUCTURING THE SLSREP TABLE	**P223**
UPDATING THE NEW FIELDS	**P225**
Updating Date Fields	P225
Updating Memo Fields	P226
Completing the Display of Memo Fields	P227
Updating OLE Fields	P228
Changing the Magnification of OLE Fields	P231
Entering Additional Graphic Data	P232
Completing the Display of an OLE Field	P233
Saving the Table Properties	P234
ADVANCED FORM TECHNIQUES	**P235**
Creating a Form with a One-To-Many Relationship	P235
Selecting the Fields for the Form	P237
Moving and Resizing Fields	P239
Showing and Working with the Grid	P241
Adding or Removing Scroll Bars	P242
Saving the Form	P243
Viewing Data Using the Form	P243
Changing the Background Color	P243
Changing Frame Styles	P244
Changing Magnification	P245
Resizing a Table Object	P246
Completing the Display of the Note Field and Viewing Records	P246
Changing the Characteristics of Field Labels	P248
Placing a Title on a Form	P249
Changing the Color of the Table Object	P251
Resizing the Table Object	P253
Adding a Scroll Bar to a Note Field	P254
Closing the Form and Saving the Changes	P255
To Open a Form	P255
USING DATE AND MEMO FIELDS IN A QUERY	**P256**
PROJECT SUMMARY	**P258**
KEY TERMS	**P258**
QUICK REFERENCE	**P258**
STUDENT ASSIGNMENTS	**P259**
COMPUTER LABORATORY EXERCISES	**P263**
COMPUTER LABORATORY ASSIGNMENTS	**P265**
INDEX	**P270**

PREFACE

▶ THE WINDOWS ENVIRONMENT

Since the introduction of Microsoft Windows version 3.1, the personal computing industry has moved rapidly toward establishing Windows as the de facto user interface. The majority of software development funds in software vendor companies are devoted to Windows applications. Virtually all PCs purchased today, at any price, come preloaded with Windows and, often, with one or more Windows applications packages. With an enormous installed base, it is clear that Windows is the operating environment for both now and the future.

The Windows environment places the novice as well as the experienced user in the world of the mouse and a common graphical user interface between all applications. An up-to-date educational institution that teaches computer concepts and applications software to students for their immediate use and as a skill to be used within industry must teach Windows-based applications software.

▶ OBJECTIVES OF THIS TEXTBOOK

Complete Computer Concepts and Learning to Use Windows Applications: Microsoft Word 2.0 for Windows, Microsoft Excel 4 for Windows, and Paradox 1.0 for Windows was specifically developed for an introductory computer course with an emphasis on Windows applications software. No previous experience with a computer is assumed, and no mathematics beyond the high school freshman level is required. The objectives of this book are as follows:

- ▶ To present an overview and then a detailed examination of the computer industry, computer hardware, software, and systems available in the mid-1990's
- ▶ To provide an up-to-date and comprehensive course of study in all important aspects of computing for students in all academic disciplines
- ▶ To teach the fundamentals of Windows and Microsoft Word 2.0 for Windows, Microsoft Excel 4 for Windows, and Paradox 1.0 for Windows and acquaint the student with the proper way to solve word processing, spreadsheet, and database problems
- ▶ To use practical problems to illustrate the use of word processing, spreadsheet, and database application software
- ▶ To take advantage of the many new capabilities of applications software in a Windows environment (see Figure P-1)

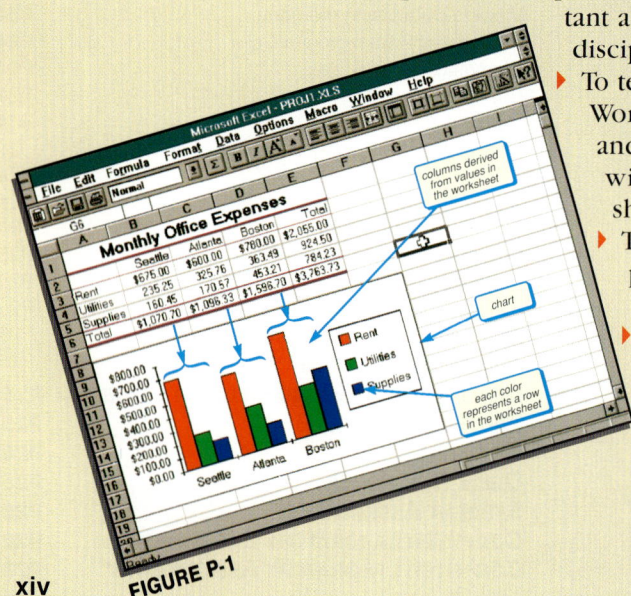

FIGURE P-1

The textbook covers a complete presentation of computer concepts and all essential aspects of Word, Excel, and Paradox for Windows. When students complete a course using this book, they will have a solid understanding of modern computers and their uses together with a firm knowledge of Windows and an ability to solve a variety of applications problems. Further, because they will be learning Windows, students will find the migration to other Windows applications software simple and straightforward.

▸ THE SHELLY CASHMAN APPROACH

The word processing, spreadsheet, database, and Windows software portions of this book are presented by showing the actual screens displayed by Windows and the applications software. Because the student interacts with pictorial displays when using Windows, written words in a textbook substituting for the actual displays the student will see does not suffice. For this reason, the Shelly Cashman Series emphasizes screen displays as the primary means of teaching Windows applications software. Every screen shown in this book appears in color, because the student views color on the screen. In addition, the screens display exactly as the student will see them. The screens in this book were captured while using the software. Nothing has been altered or changed except to highlight portions of the screen when appropriate (see the screens in Figure P-2).

The software section of this book presents the material using a unique pedagogy designed specifically for the graphical environment of Windows. It is primarily designed for a lecture/lab method of presentation, although it is equally suited for a tutorial/hands-on approach wherein the student learns by actually completing each project following the step-by-step instructions. Features of this pedagogy include the following:

- ▸ **Project Orientation:** Each applications software project solves a complete problem, meaning that the student is introduced to a problem to be solved and is then given the step-by-step process to solve the problem.
- ▸ **Step-by-Step Instructions:** Each of the tasks required to complete a project is identified throughout the development of the project. For example, a task might be to change the color of a table object and column headings, and then to view the data in the modified form using Paradox. Then, each step to accomplish the task is specified. The steps are accompanied by screens (Figure P-2). The student is not told to perform a step without seeing the result of the step on a color screen. Hence, students learn from this book the same as if they were using the computer. This attention to detail in accomplishing a task and showing the resulting screen makes the Shelly Cashman Series Windows Applications textbooks unique.
- ▸ **Multiple Ways to Use the Book:** Because each step to accomplish a task is illustrated with a screen, the applications software portion of the book can be used in a number of ways, including: (a) Lecture and textbook approach — The instructor lectures on the material in the book. The student reads and studies the material and then applies the knowledge to an application on a computer; (b) Tutorial approach — The student performs

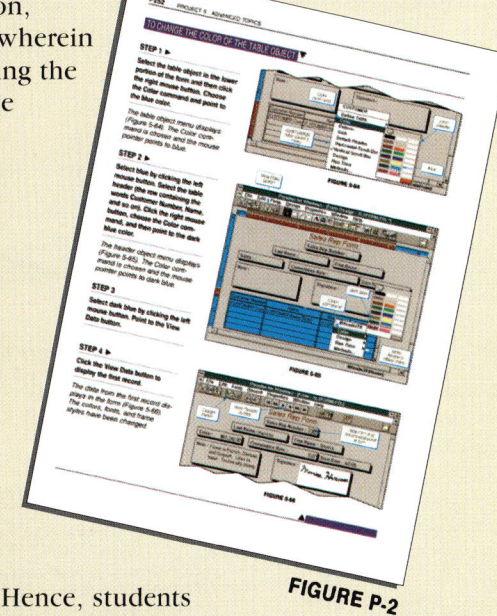

FIGURE P-2

each specified step on a computer. At the end of the project, the student has solved the problem and is ready to solve comparable student assignments; (c) Reference — Each task in a project is clearly identified. Therefore, the material serves as a complete reference because the student can refer to any task to determine how to accomplish it.

▶ **Windows/Graphical User Interface Approach:** Windows provides a graphical user interface. All of the examples in the applications software portion of this book use this interface. Thus, the mouse is used for the majority of control functions and is the preferred user communication tool. When specifying a command to be executed, the sequence is as follows: (a) If a button invokes the command, use the button; (b) If a button is not available, use the command from a menu; (c) If a button or a menu cannot be used, only then is the keyboard used to implement a Windows command.

▶ **Emphasis on Windows techniques:** The most general techniques to implement commands, enter information, and generally interface with Windows are presented. This approach allows the student to move from one application software package to another under Windows with a minimum of relearning with respect to interfacing with the software. An application-specific method is taught only when no other option is available.

▶ **Reference for all techniques:** Even though general Windows techniques are used in all examples in the applications software section, a Quick Reference chart (see Figure P-3) at the end of each project details not only the mouse and menu methods for implementing a command, but also contains the keyboard shortcuts for the commands presented in the project. Therefore, students are exposed to all means for implementing a command.

FIGURE P-3

▶ ORGANIZATION OF THIS TEXTBOOK

*C*omplete Computer Concepts and Learning to Use Windows Applications: Microsoft Word 2.0 for Windows, Microsoft Excel 4 for Windows, and Paradox 1.0 for Windows* consists of *Complete Computer Concepts*, two projects on Microsoft Windows 3.1, five projects on Word for Windows, six projects on Excel for Windows, and five projects on Paradox for Windows.

Complete Computer Concepts

This section of the book covers all important aspects of computing. With more than 400 color pictures and illustrations, the complete computer concepts section presents a thorough, modern coverage of hardware, software, applications, programming, communications, and systems.

Using Microsoft Windows 3.1

To effectively use Windows applications software, students need a practical knowledge of the Microsoft Windows graphical user interface. Thus, two Microsoft Windows projects are included prior to the application software projects.

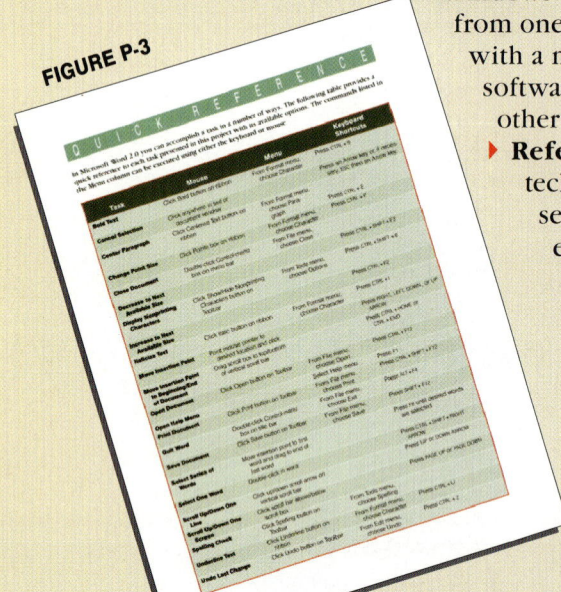

Project 1 — An Introduction to Windows The first project introduces the students to Windows concepts, Windows terminology, and how to communicate with Windows using the mouse and keyboard. Topics include starting and exiting Windows; opening group windows; maximizing windows; scrolling; selecting menus; choosing a command from a menu; starting and exiting Windows applications; obtaining on-line help; and responding to dialog boxes.

Project 2 — Disk and File Management The second project introduces the student to File Manager. Topics include formatting a diskette; copying a group of files; renaming and deleting files; searching for help topics; activating, resizing, and closing a group window; arranging icons in a group window; switching between applications; and minimizing an application window to an application icon.

Word Processing Using Microsoft Word 2.0 for Windows

After presenting the complete computer concepts and Windows concepts, this textbook next provides detailed instruction on how to use Microsoft Word 2.0 for Windows. The material is divided into five projects as follows:

Project 1 — Creating and Editing a Document In Project 1, students are introduced to Word terminology, the Word screen, and a word processing document by creating a business memorandum. Topics include starting and quitting Word; changing the size of displayed and printed characters; entering a document; centering paragraphs; bolding, underlining, italicizing, and enlarging selected text; checking spelling; saving, printing, and opening a document; correcting errors; and obtaining on-line help.

Project 2 — Creating a Research Paper In Project 2, students learn how to create and revise a research paper based on the Modern Language Association (MLA) style of documentation. Topics include changing margin settings; adjusting line spacing; redefining the Normal style; using a header to number pages; indenting paragraphs; adding footnotes; switching from normal to page layout view; inserting hard page breaks; sorting selected paragraphs; finding and replacing text; moving paragraphs with drag and drop and with cut and paste; and using the thesaurus and print preview.

Project 3 — Creating a Proposal Using Tables and Graphics In Project 3, students learn how to create a title page with graphics, insert an existing document beneath the title page, and enhance the document by adding tables and a chart to it. Topics include importing a graphic; scaling an imported graphic; changing the space between characters; saving an active document with a new filename; setting custom tabs; inserting a table; summing the rows and columns in a table; charting a table; and adding bullets to a list.

Project 4 — Generating Form Letters and Mailing Labels In Project 4, students learn how to generate form letters from a data file and a main document and mailing labels from a data file and a document template. Topics include creating a data file and a main document; inserting merge files into the main document; using an IF field; merging and printing the form letters; selectively merging and printing form letters; and creating and printing mailing labels.

Project 5 — Creating a Professional Newsletter In Project 5, students learn how to create a professional looking newsletter with desktop publishing features (see Figure P-4). Topics include changing a character font; adding ruling lines and shading to paragraphs; adding box borders around paragraphs; inserting special characters; formatting a document into multiple columns; inserting a column break; inserting a vertical rule between columns; using a frame to position a graphic; zooming a document; and adding color to characters and lines.

FIGURE P-4

Spreadsheets Using Microsoft Excel 4 for Windows

Following the presentation of Microsoft Word 2.0 for Windows, this textbook provides detailed instruction on how to use Microsoft Excel 4 for Windows. The material is divided into six projects as follows:

Project 1 — Building a Worksheet In Project 1, students are introduced to Excel terminology, the Excel window, and the basic characteristics of a worksheet. Topics include starting and exiting Excel; entering text and numbers; selecting a range; using the AutoSum tool; copying using the fill handle; changing font size; bolding; centering across columns; using the AutoFormat command; charting using the ChartWizard tool; saving and opening a worksheet; editing a worksheet; and obtaining on-line help

Project 2 — Adding Formulas to a Worksheet In Project 2, students use formulas to build a worksheet and learn more about formatting and printing a worksheet. Topics include entering formulas; using the AVERAGE function; formatting text; drawing borders; formatting numbers; changing the width of columns and heights of rows; printing a section of the worksheet; and displaying and printing the formulas in a worksheet.

Project 3 — Enhancing a Worksheet and Drawing Charts In Project 3, students learn how to modify a worksheet, how to use the IF function and absolute references, and how to chart data. Topics include deleting, inserting, copying, and using drag and drop to move cells; copying a cell's format; changing the type, size, and color of fonts; in-depth charting of data (see Figure P-5); previewing a printout; printing in landscape orientation; and printing to fit.

PREFACE xix

Project 4 — Working with Large Worksheets In Project 4, students learn to work with large worksheets. Topics include using the fill handle to create a series; displaying hidden toolbars; freezing titles; adding notes; checking spelling; changing the magnification of worksheets; displaying different parts of the worksheet through panes; creating an outline; and elementary what-if analysis.

Project 5 — Analyzing Worksheet Data In Project 5, students learn more about analyzing data in a worksheet and how to use macros. Topics include applying the PMT function to determine a monthly payment; analyzing data by goal seeking, creating a data table, and creating a Scenario Summary Report worksheet; using macros to automate worksheet activities; creating a button and assigning a macro to it; and protecting a worksheet.

FIGURE P-5

Project 6 — Sorting and Querying a Worksheet Database In Project 6, students learn how to create, sort, and query a database. Topics include using a data form to create and maintain a database; finding, extracting, and deleting records that pass a test; and using the Crosstab ReportWizard to create a crosstab table.

Databases Using Paradox for Windows

The final windows applications software package convered in this book is Paradox for Windows. The material is divided into five projects as follows.

Project 1 — Creating a Database In Project 1, students are introduced to Paradox terminology, the Paradox window, and the basic characteristics of databases. Topics include starting and exiting Paradox; changing the working directory; creating a table; defining fields; opening a table; adding records to an empty table; closing a table; adding records to a non-empty table; and printing the contents of a table. Other topics in this project include using a form to view data; creating and viewing a quick graph; and using the help facility. Students also learn how to design a database to eliminate redundancy.

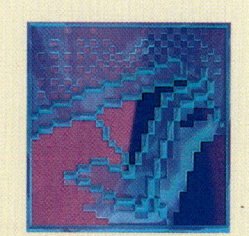

Project 2 — Querying a Database In Project 2, students learn to ask questions concerning the data in their databases by using queries. Topics include creating and running queries and printing the results; displaying only selected fields; using special character conditions; using wildcards and LIKE conditions; using various comparison operators; and creating compound conditions. Other topics include sorting; joining multiple tables; and restricting rows in a join. Students use computed fields, statistics, and grouping and also graph the results of a query.

Project 3 — Maintaining a Database In Project 3, students learn how to maintain a database. Topics include using Table view and Form view to add new records, to change existing records, and to delete records; changing the structure of a table; creating validity checks; and specifying referential integrity. Students perform mass changes and deletes and create and use single-field and multiple-field secondary indexes.

Project 4 — Presenting Data: Reports and Forms In Project 4, students learn to create custom reports. Topics include selecting fields and objects; changing column headings; changing the Zoom factor; adjusting column widths; adding special fields, such as totals, to a report; viewing the report on the screen; saving a report, and printing a report. Other topics include adding group bands and subtotals; creating a form; selecting fields; using a grid to help align objects; moving fields; and adding boxes and text. Students learn to change a variety of special effects such as font sizes, styles, colors, and frame styles.

FIGURE P-6

Project 5 — Advanced Topics In Project 5, students learn to use date, memo, and OLE fields. Topics include incorporating these fields in the structure of a database; updating the data in these fields and changing their display characteristics; creating a form that incorporates a one-to-many relationship between tables; manipulating table objects on a form; incorporating date, memo, graphic, and OLE fields in forms; adding or removing scroll bars; and incorporating various visual effects in forms (Figure P-6). Students learn to use date and memo fields in a query.

▶ END-OF-PROJECT STUDENT ACTIVITIES

Each project in the applications software section of the book ends with a wealth of student activities including these notable features:

FIGURE P-7

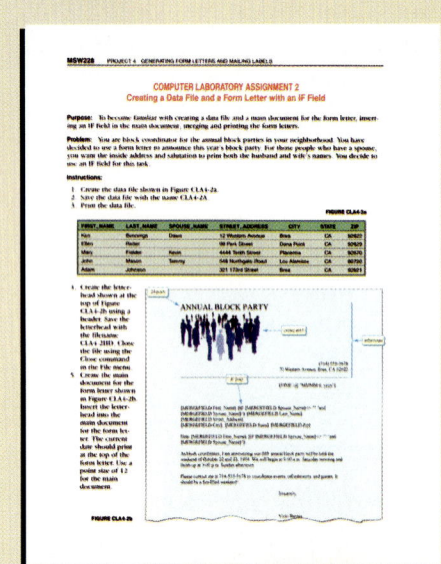

- A list of key terms for review
- A Quick Reference that lists the ways to carry out a task using the mouse, menu, or keyboard shortcuts
- Six Student Assignments for homework and classroom discussion (see Figure P-7)
- Three Computer Laboratory Exercises that usually require the student to load and manipulate a document, spreadsheet, or database from the Student Diskette that accompanies this book
- Four Computer Laboratory Assignments that require the student to develop a complete project assignment; the assignments increase in difficulty from a relatively easy assignment to a case-study

The computer concepts section of the book includes key terms, review questions, controversial issues for classroom discussion or homework assignments, and research projects.

▶ ANCILLARY MATERIALS FOR TEACHING FROM THIS BOOK

A comprehensive instructor's support package accompanies all textbooks in the Shelly Cashman Series.

Annotated Instructor's Edition (AIE) for Windows Applications Software Section The AIE for Windows, Word, Excel, and Paradox is designed to assist you with your lectures by suggesting transparencies to use, summarizing key points, proposing pertinent questions, offering important tips, alerting you to pitfalls, and by incorporating the answers to the Student Assignments. There are over 1,000 annotations for the Windows applications software (see Figure P-8).

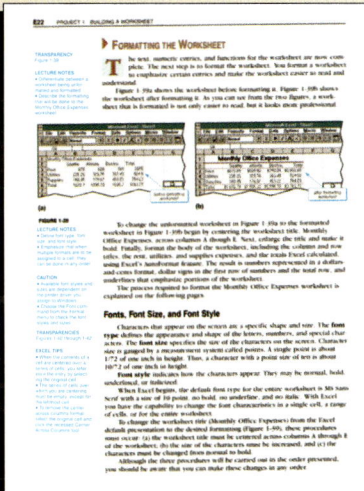

FIGURE P-8

Computer-Based LCD/HyperGraphics Presentations The Shelly Cashman Series proudly presents the finest LCD learning material available in textbook publishing. For the Complete Computer Concepts portion of the book, the HyperGraphics presentation system allows instructors to present much of the content using graphics, color, animation, and instructor-led interactivity. For the Windows applications software section of the book, each project, and each illustrated screen can be shown in a sequenced presentation by the instructor on a classroom computer connected to an LCD. As each step in the book is executed, the events appear one at a time on the screen, showing the student in a precise manner exactly what happens dynamically on the screen. The student and instructor, in the classroom, are able to proceed through each project as though the student were performing the tasks alone on a computer. The instructor need not enter a single piece of data nor choose a single command. The presentation occurs dynamically, under the control of the instructor, by pressing a key or a mouse button or a remote response pad. This presentation software is available without charge.

Instructor's Materials This instructor's ancillary for the concepts and for each of the applications software packages (Figure P-9) contains the following:

- ▶ Detailed lesson plans including project objectives, project overview, and a three-column outline of each project that includes page references and transparency references
- ▶ Answers to all student assignments at the end of the projects
- ▶ A test bank of more than 2,000 True/False, Multiple-Choice, and Fill-In questions for the subjects covered in this book
- ▶ Transparency masters for every screen, diagram, and table in the textbook
- ▶ An Instructor's Diskette that includes the projects and solutions to the Computer Laboratory Assignments at the end of each Windows applications software project

MicroSWAT III MicroSWAT III, a computerized test-generating system, is available free to adopters of any Shelly Cashman Series textbooks. It includes all of the questions from the test bank just described. MicroSWAT III is an easy-to-use, menu-driven software package that provides instructors with testing flexibility and allows customizing of testing documents.

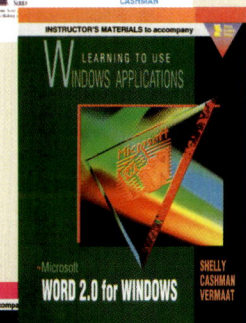

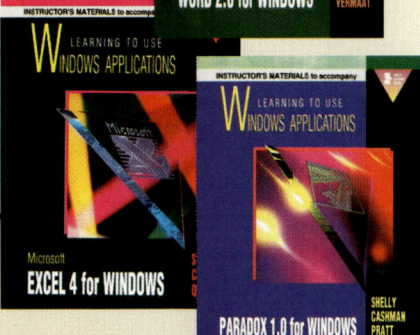

FIGURE P-9

▶ ACKNOWLEDGMENTS

The Shelly Cashman Series would not be the success it is without the contributions of outstanding publishing professionals. First, and foremost, among them is Becky Herrington, director of production and designer. She is the heart and soul of the Shelly Cashman Series, and it is only through her leadership, dedication, and untiring efforts that superior products are produced.

Under Becky Herrington's direction, the following individuals made significant contributions to these books: Virginia Harvey, series coordinator and manuscript editor; Ken Russo, senior illustrator; Anne Craig, Mike Bodnar, John Craig, Greg Herrington, and Greg Archambault, illustrators; Jeanne Black, typographer; Julie Dzigas, manufacturing coordinator; Marilyn Martin, proofreader; and Henry Blackham, cover and opener photography.

Special recognition for a job well done must go to James Quasney, who, together with writing, assumed the responsibilities as series editor. Particular thanks go to Thomas Walker, publisher and vice president of boyd & fraser publishing company, who recognized the need, and provided the support, to produce the full-color Shelly Cashman Series Windows Applications textbooks and encouraged the development of the new, innovative LCD presentation software for teachers.

We hope you will find using the book an enriching and rewarding experience.

Gary B. Shelly
Thomas J. Cashman

PREFACE **xxiii**

▶ SHELLY CASHMAN SERIES—TRADITIONALLY BOUND TEXTBOOKS

The Shelly Cashman Series presents both Windows- and DOS-based personal computer applications in a variety of traditionally bound textbooks, as shown in the table below. For more information, see your South-Western/boyd & fraser representative or call 1-800-543-8444.

COMPUTER CONCEPTS	
Computer Concepts	*Complete Computer Concepts* *Essential Computer Concepts, Second Edition*
Computer Concepts Workbook and Study Guide	*Workbook and Study Guide with Computer Lab Software Projects to accompany Complete Computer Concepts*
Computer Concepts and Windows Applications	*Complete Computer Concepts and Microsoft Works 2.0 for Windows* (also available in spiral bound) *Complete Computer Concepts and Microsoft Word 2.0 for Windows, Microsoft Excel 4 for Windows, and Paradox 1.0 for Windows* (also available in spiral bound)
Computer Concepts and DOS Applications	*Complete Computer Concepts and WordPerfect 5.1, Lotus 1-2-3 Release 2.2, and dBASE IV Version 1.1* (also available in spiral bound) *Complete Computer Concepts and WordPerfect 5.1, Lotus 1-2-3 Release 2.2, and dBASE III PLUS* (also available in spiral bound)
Computer Concepts and Programming	*Complete Computer Concepts and Microsoft BASIC*

WINDOWS APPLICATIONS	
Integrated Package	*Microsoft Works 2.0 for Windows* (also available in spiral bound)
Graphical User Interface	*Microsoft Windows 3.1 Introductory Concepts and Techniques* *Microsoft Windows 3.1 Concepts and Techniques* (Spring 1994)
Windows Applications	*Microsoft Word 2.0 for Windows, Microsoft Excel 4 for Windows, and Paradox 1.0 for Windows* (also available in spiral bound)
Word Processing	*Microsoft Word 2.0 for Windows* *WordPerfect 5.2 for Windows*
Spreadsheets	*Microsoft Excel 4 for Windows* *Lotus 1-2-3 Release 4.0 for Windows* (Spring 1994) *Quattro Pro 5.0 for Windows* (Spring 1994)
Database Management	*Paradox 1.0 for Windows* *Microsoft Access 1.1 for Windows* (Spring 1994)
Presentation Graphics	*Microsoft PowerPoint 3.0 for Windows* (Spring 1994)

DOS APPLICATIONS	
Integrated Package	*Microsoft Works 3.0 for DOS* (Spring 1994)
DOS Applications	*WordPerfect 5.1, Lotus 1-2-3 Release 2.2, and dBASE IV Version 1.1* (also available in spiral bound) *WordPerfect 5.1, Lotus 1-2-3 Release 2.2, and dBASE III PLUS* (also available in spiral bound)
Word Processing	*WordPerfect 6.0* (Spring 1994) *WordPerfect 5.1* *WordPerfect 5.1, Function Key Edition* *WordPerfect 4.2* (with Educational Software) *Microsoft Word 5.0* *WordStar 6.0* (with Educational Software)
Spreadsheets	*Lotus 1-2-3 Release 2.4* *Lotus 1-2-3 Release 2.3* *Lotus 1-2-3 Release 2.2* *Lotus 1-2-3 Release 2.01* *Quattro Pro 5.0* (Spring 1994) *Quattro Pro 3.0* *Quattro with 1-2-3 Menus* (with Educational Software)
Database Management	*dBASE IV Version 1.1* *dBASE III PLUS* (with Educational Software) *Paradox 4.5* (Spring 1994) *Paradox 3.5* (with Educational Software)

PROGRAMMING	
Programming	*Microsoft BASIC* *Microsoft QuickBASIC* *Microsoft Visual Basic 3.0 for Windows* (Spring 1994)

▶ SHELLY CASHMAN SERIES—Custom Edition™ PROGRAM

If you do not find a Shelly Cashman Series traditionally bound textbook to fit your needs, boyd & fraser's unique **Custom Edition** program allows you to choose from a number of options and create a textbook perfectly suited to your course. The customized materials are available in a variety of binding styles, including boyd & fraser's patented **Custom Edition** kit, spiral bound, and notebook bound. Features of the **Custom Edition** program are:

- ▶ Textbooks that match the content of your course
- ▶ Windows- and DOS-based materials for the latest versions of personal computer applications software
- ▶ Shelly Cashman Series quality, with the same full-color materials and Shelly Cashman Series pedagogy found in the traditionally bound texts
- ▶ Affordable pricing so your students receive the **Custom Edition** at a cost similar to that of traditionally bound books

The table on the right summarizes the available materials. For more information, see your South-Western/ boyd & fraser representative or call 1-800-543-8444.

COMPUTER CONCEPTS	
Computer Concepts	Complete Computer Concepts
	Essential Computer Concepts, Second Edition
	Introduction to Computers
OPERATING SYSTEMS	
Graphical User Interface	Microsoft Windows 3.1 Introductory Concepts and Techniques
	Microsoft Windows 3.1 Concepts and Techniques (Spring 1994)
Operating Systems	Introduction to DOS 6.0 (Spring 1994)
	Introduction to DOS 5.0 (using menus)
	Introduction to DOS (all versions using commands)
WINDOWS APPLICATIONS	
Integrated Package	Microsoft Works 2.0 for Windows
Word Processing	Microsoft Word 2.0 for Windows
	WordPerfect 5.2 for Windows
Spreadsheets	Microsoft Excel 4 for Windows
	Lotus 1-2-3 Release 4.0 for Windows (Spring 1994)
	Quattro Pro 5.0 for Windows (Spring 1994)
Database Management	Paradox 1.0 for Windows
	Microsoft Access 1.1 for Windows (Spring 1994)
Presentation Graphics	Microsoft PowerPoint 3.0 for Windows (Spring 1994)
DOS APPLICATIONS	
Integrated Package	Microsoft Works 3.0 for DOS (Spring 1994)
Word Processing	WordPerfect 6.0 (Spring 1994)
	WordPerfect 5.1
	WordPerfect 5.1, Function Key Edition
	Microsoft Word 5.0
	WordPerfect 4.2
	WordStar 6.0
Spreadsheets	Lotus 1-2-3 Release 2.4
	Lotus 1-2-3 Release 2.3
	Lotus 1-2-3 Release 2.2
	Lotus 1-2-3 Release 2.01
	Quattro Pro 5.0 (Spring 1994)
	Quattro Pro 3.0
	Quattro with 1-2-3 Menus
Database Management	dBASE IV Version 1.1
	dBASE III PLUS
	Paradox 4.5 (Spring 1994)
	Paradox 3.5
PROGRAMMING	
Programming	Microsoft BASIC
	Microsoft QuickBASIC
	Microsoft Visual Basic 3.0 for Windows (Spring 1994)

An Overview of Computer Concepts

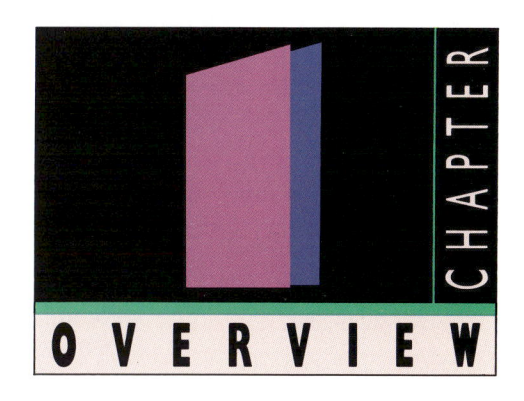

OBJECTIVES

- Explain what a computer is and how it processes data to produce information
- Identify the four operations of the information processing cycle: input, process, output, and storage
- Explain how the operations of the information processing cycle are performed by computer hardware and software
- Identify the major categories of computers
- Describe the six elements of an information system: equipment, software, data, personnel, users, and procedures
- Explain the responsibilities of information system personnel
- Explain the use of computers in our world
- Describe the evolution of the computer industry

Every day computers play a key role in how we work and how we live. Today, even the smallest organizations usually have computers to help them operate more efficiently. Computers also affect our lives in many unseen ways. When we buy groceries at the supermarket, use an automatic teller machine, or make a long-distance phone call, we are also using computers.

As they have for a number or years, personal computers continue to make an increasing impact on our lives. Both at home and at work, these small desktop systems help us do our work faster, more accurately, and in some cases, in ways that previously would not have been possible.

CHAPTER 1 AN OVERVIEW OF COMPUTER CONCEPTS

Today, many people believe that knowing how to use a computer, especially a personal computer, is a basic skill necessary to succeed in business or to function effectively in society. Given the increasing use and availability of computer systems, such knowledge will continue to be an essential skill. The purpose of this book is to give you this knowledge so that you will understand how computers are used today and so that you can adapt to how computers will be used in the future.

In this first chapter we will give you an overview of computer concepts. You will begin to learn what a computer is, how it processes data into information, and what elements are necessary for a successful information system. While you are reading, remember that this chapter is an overview and that many of the terms and concepts that are introduced will be discussed in more detail in later chapters.

WHAT IS A COMPUTER?

The most obvious question related to understanding computers and their impact on our lives is, "What is a computer?". A **computer** is an electronic device, operating under the control of instructions stored in its own memory unit, that can accept data (input), process data arithmetically and logically, produce output from the processing, and store the results for future use. While broader definitions of a computer exist, this definition includes a wide range of devices with various capabilities. For example, the tiny microcomputer chip shown in Figure 1-1 can be called a computer. Generally the term is used to describe a collection of devices that function together to process data. An example of the devices that make up a computer is shown in Figure 1-2.

FIGURE 1-1
Small enough to fit in the palm of a baby's hand, this microcomputer chip contains the electronic circuits that perform the operations of a computer.

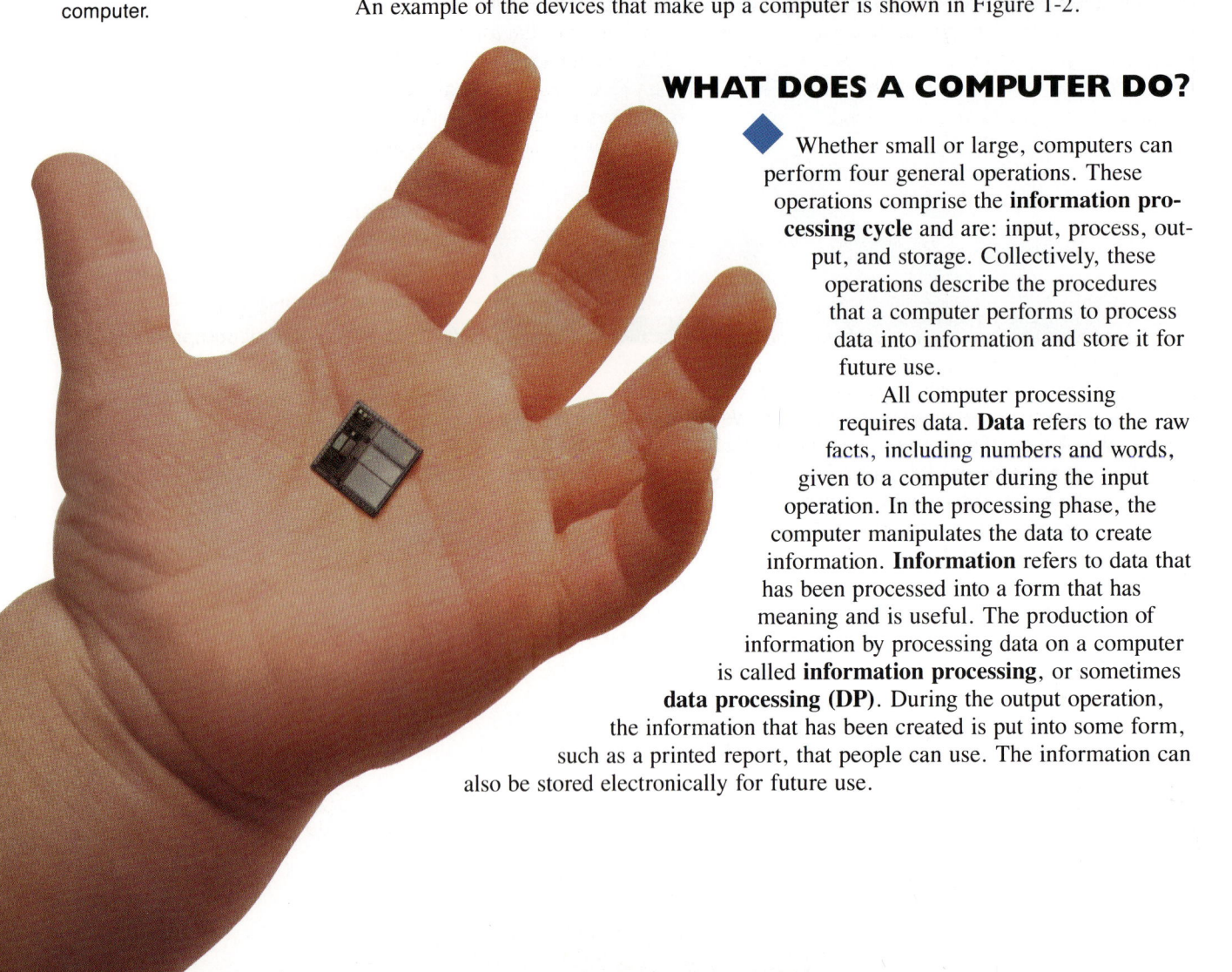

WHAT DOES A COMPUTER DO?

Whether small or large, computers can perform four general operations. These operations comprise the **information processing cycle** and are: input, process, output, and storage. Collectively, these operations describe the procedures that a computer performs to process data into information and store it for future use.

All computer processing requires data. **Data** refers to the raw facts, including numbers and words, given to a computer during the input operation. In the processing phase, the computer manipulates the data to create information. **Information** refers to data that has been processed into a form that has meaning and is useful. The production of information by processing data on a computer is called **information processing**, or sometimes **data processing (DP)**. During the output operation, the information that has been created is put into some form, such as a printed report, that people can use. The information can also be stored electronically for future use.

WHY IS A COMPUTER SO POWERFUL? **1.3**

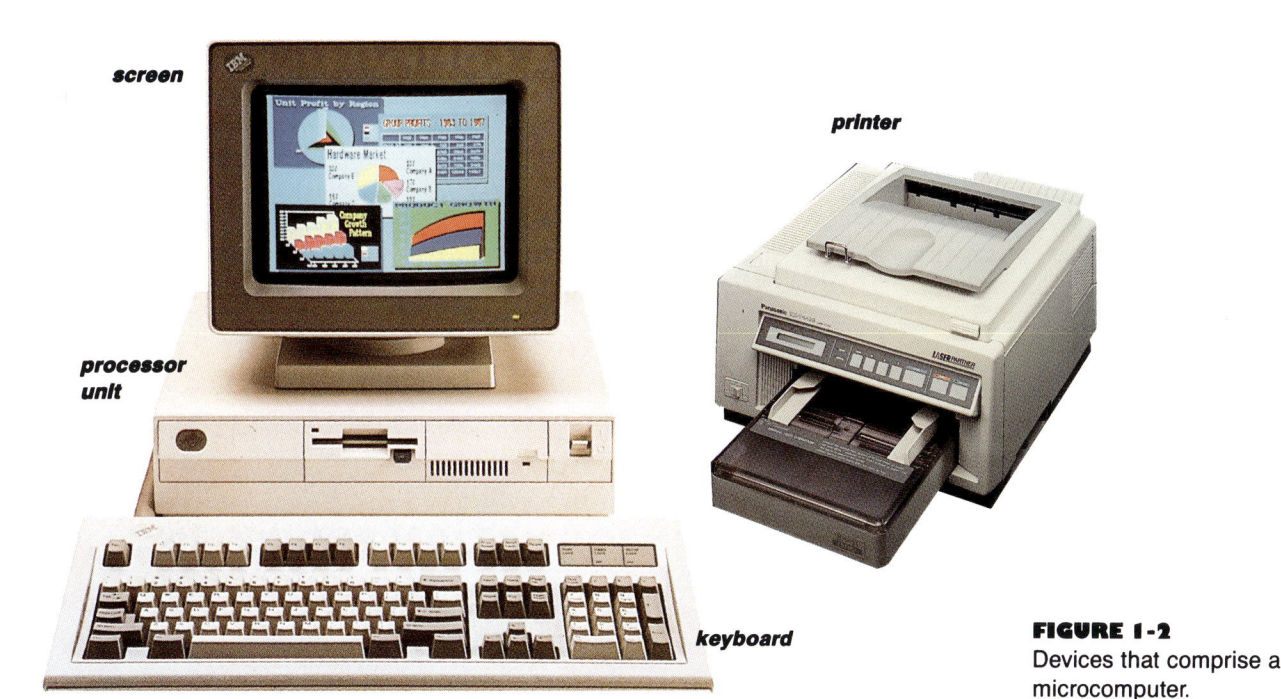

FIGURE 1-2
Devices that comprise a microcomputer.

The people who either use the computer directly or use the information it provides are called **computer users**, **end users**, or sometimes just simply **users**. Figure 1-3 shows a computer user and demonstrates how the four operations of the information processing cycle can occur on a personal computer. ① The computer user inputs data by pressing the keys on the keyboard. ② The data is then processed by the unit called the processor. ③ The output, or results, from the processing are displayed on the screen or printed on the printer, providing information to the user. ④ Finally, the output may be stored on a disk for future reference.

WHY IS A COMPUTER SO POWERFUL?

◆ The input, process, output, and storage operations that a computer performs may seem very basic and simple. However, the computer's power derives from its capability to perform these operations very quickly, accurately, and reliably. In a computer, operations occur through the use of electronic circuits contained on small chips as shown on the next page in Figure 1-4. When data flows along these circuits it travels at close to the speed of light. This allows processing to be accomplished in billionths of a second. The electronic circuits in modern computers are very reliable and seldom fail. Storage capability is another reason why computers are so powerful. They can store enormous amounts of data and keep that data readily available for processing. This capability combined with the factors of speed, accuracy, and reliability are why a computer is considered to be such a powerful tool for information processing.

FIGURE 1-3
The use of this personal computer illustrates the four operations of the information processing cycle: input, process, output, and storage.

CHAPTER 1 AN OVERVIEW OF COMPUTER CONCEPTS

HOW DOES A COMPUTER KNOW WHAT TO DO?

◆ For a computer to perform the operations in the information processing cycle, it must be given a detailed set of instructions that tell it exactly what to do. These instructions are called a **computer program**, **program instructions**, or **software**.

Before the information processing cycle for a specific job begins, the computer program corresponding to that job is stored in the computer. Once the program is stored, the computer can begin to process data by executing the program's first instruction. The computer executes one program instruction after another until the job is complete.

THE INFORMATION PROCESSING CYCLE

◆ Your understanding of the information processing cycle introduced in this chapter is fundamental to understanding computers and how they process data into information. To review, the information processing cycle consists of four operations. They are: input, process, output, storage.

The first three of these operations, **input**, **process**, and **output**, describe the procedures that a computer performs to process data into information. The fourth operation, **storage**, describes a computer's electronic storage capability. As you learn more about computers, you will see that these four operations apply to both the computer equipment and the computer software. The equipment, or devices, of a computer are classified according to the operations that they perform. Computer software is made up of instructions that describe how the operations are to be performed.

FIGURE 1-4
Inside a computer are chips and other electronic components that process data in billionths of a second.

WHAT ARE THE COMPONENTS OF A COMPUTER?

◆ Data is processed by specific equipment that is often called computer **hardware** (Figure 1-5). This equipment consists of: input devices, a processor unit, output devices, and auxiliary storage units.

FIGURE 1-5
A computer is composed of input devices through which data is entered into the computer; the processor that processes data stored in main memory; output devices on which the results of the processing are made available; and auxiliary storage units that store data for future processing.

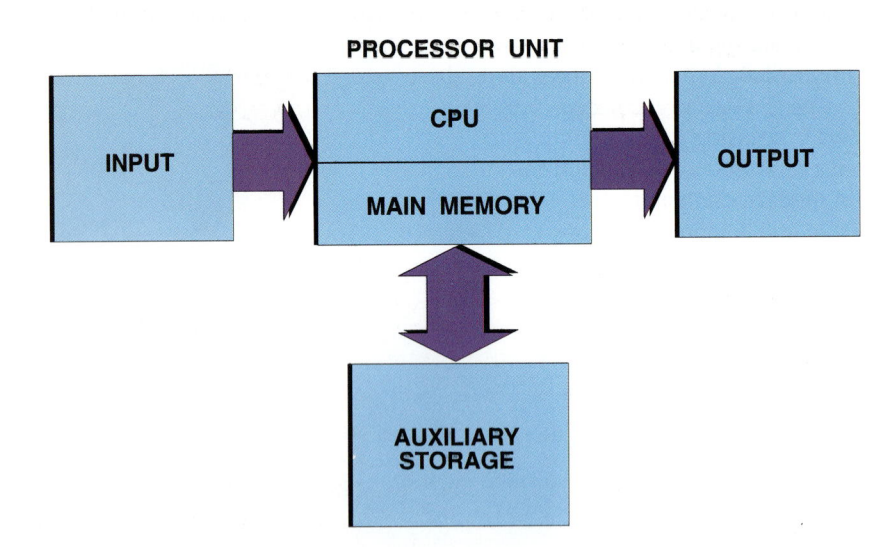

PROCESSOR UNIT

INPUT → CPU / MAIN MEMORY → OUTPUT

AUXILIARY STORAGE

Input Devices

Input devices are used to enter data into a computer. A common input device is the **keyboard**, shown in Figure 1-6⟨a⟩. As the data is entered, or keyed, it is stored in the computer and displayed on a screen.

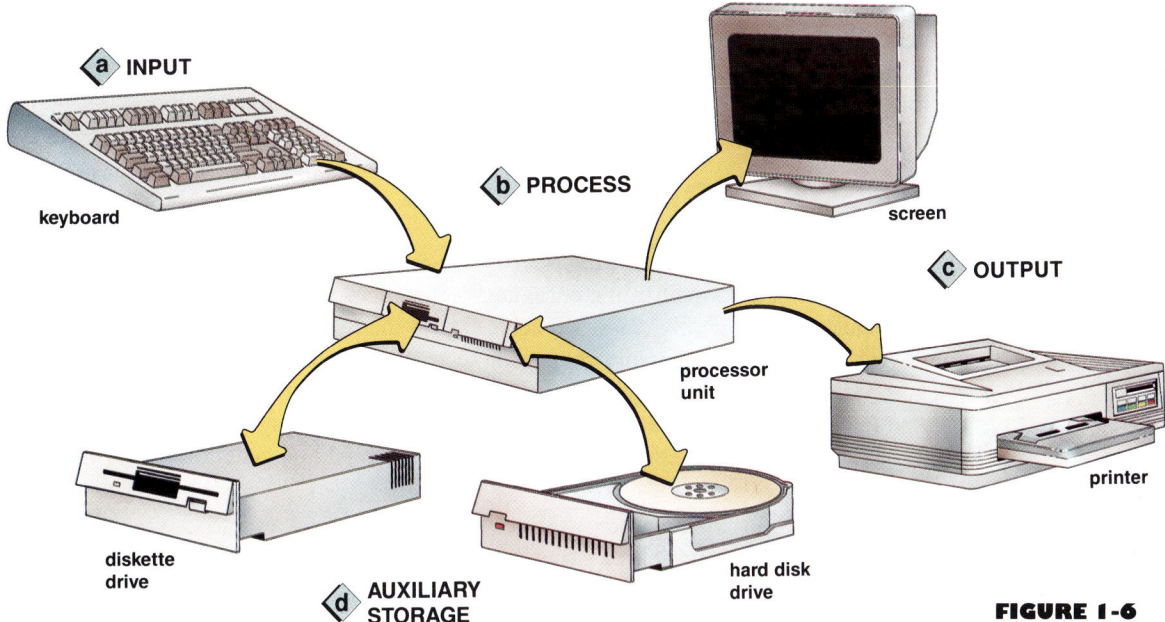

FIGURE 1-6
The components of a computer perform the four operations of the information processing cycle.

Processor Unit

Figure 1-6⟨b⟩ shows the **processor unit** of a computer, which contains the electronic circuits that actually cause the processing of data to occur. The processor unit is divided into two parts, the central processing unit and main memory. The **central processing unit (CPU)** contains a **control unit** that executes the program instructions and an **arithmetic/logic unit (ALU)** that performs math and logic operations. **Arithmetic operations** include numeric calculations such as addition, subtraction, multiplication, and division. Comparisons of data to see if one value is greater than, equal to, or less than another are called **logical operations**.

Main memory, also called **primary storage**, is a part of the processor unit. Main memory electronically stores data and program instructions when they are being processed.

Output Devices

Output from a computer can be presented in many forms. The two most commonly used **output devices** are the **printer** and the computer **screen** shown in Figure 1-6⟨c⟩. Other frequently used names for the screen are the **monitor**, or the **CRT**, which stands for **cathode ray tube**.

Auxiliary Storage Units

Auxiliary storage units, shown in Figure 1-6⟨d⟩, store instructions and data when they are not being used by the processor unit. A common auxiliary storage device on

1.6 CHAPTER 1 AN OVERVIEW OF COMPUTER CONCEPTS

personal computers is a diskette drive, which stores data as magnetic spots on a small plastic disk called a **diskette**. Another auxiliary storage device is called a hard disk drive. **Hard disk** drives contain nonremovable metal disks and provide larger storage capacities than diskettes.

As you can see, each component shown in Figure 1-6 plays an important role in information processing. Collectively, this equipment is called a **computer system**, or simply a computer. The term computer is also used to refer to the processing unit where the actual processing of data occurs. The input devices, output devices, and auxiliary storage units that surround the processing unit are sometimes referred to as **peripheral devices**.

CATEGORIES OF COMPUTERS

Figure 1-7 shows the following four major categories of computers: microcomputers, minicomputers, mainframe computers, and supercomputers.

Computers are generally classified according to their size, speed, processing capabilities, and price. However, rapid changes in technology make firm definitions of these categories difficult. This year's speed, performance, and price classification of a mainframe might fit next year's classification of a minicomputer. Even though they are not firmly defined, the categories are frequently used and should be generally understood.

FIGURE 1-7

ⓐ Microcomputers are small desktop-sized computers. These machines have become so widely used that they are sometimes called desktop appliances. ⓑ Minicomputers can perform many of the functions of a mainframe computer, but on a smaller scale. ⓒ Mainframe computers are large, powerful machines that can handle many users concurrently and process large volumes of data. ⓓ Supercomputers are the most powerful and expensive computers.

Microcomputers, shown in Figure 1-7 ⓐ, also called **personal computers** or **micros**, are the small desktop-sized systems that have become so widely used in recent years. These machines are generally priced under $10,000. This category also includes hand-held, notebook, laptop, portable, and supermicrocomputers.

Minicomputers, shown in Figure 1-7 ⓑ, are more powerful than microcomputers and can support a number of users performing different tasks. Originally developed to perform specific tasks such as engineering calculations, their use grew rapidly as their performance and capabilities increased. These systems can cost from approximately $15,000 up to several hundred thousand dollars. The most powerful minis are called superminicomputers.

Mainframe computers, shown in Figure 1-7 ⓒ, are large systems that can handle hundreds of users, store large amounts of data, and process transactions at a very high rate. Mainframes usually require a specialized environment including separate air conditioning, cooling, and electrical power. Raised flooring is often built to accommodate the many cables connecting the system components underneath. The price range for mainframes is from several hundred thousand dollars to several million dollars.

Supercomputers, shown in Figure 1-7 ⓓ, are the most powerful category of computers and, accordingly, the most expensive. The capability of these systems to process hundreds of millions of instructions per second is used for such applications as weather forecasting, engineering design and testing, space exploration, and other jobs requiring long, complex calculations. These machines cost several million dollars.

Computers of all categories, especially microcomputers, are sometimes wired together to form networks that allow users to share data and computing resources.

COMPUTER SOFTWARE

◆ As we mentioned previously, a computer is directed by a series of instructions called a computer program (Figure 1-8), which specifies the sequence of operations the computer will perform. To do this, the program must be stored in the main memory of the computer. Computer programs are commonly referred to as **computer software**. Many instructions can be used to direct a computer to perform a specific task. For example, some instructions allow data to be entered from a keyboard and stored in main memory; some instructions allow data in main memory to be used in calculations such as adding a series of numbers to obtain a total; some instructions compare two values stored in main memory and direct the computer to perform alternative operations based on the results of the comparison; and some instructions direct the computer to print a report, display information on the screen, draw a color graph on a screen, or store data on a disk.

FIGURE 1-8
A computer program contains instructions that specify the sequence of operations to be performed. This program is written in a language called BASIC. It allows the user to generate a telephone directory of names, area codes, and telephone numbers.

COMPUTER PROGRAM LISTING

```
100 REM TELLIST              SEPTEMBER 22           SHELLY CASHMAN
110                                                               REM
120 REM THIS PROGRAM DISPLAYS THE NAME, TELEPHONE AREA CODE
130 REM AND PHONE NUMBER OF INDIVIDUALS.
140                                                               REM
150 REM VARIABLE NAMES:
160 REM    A.....AREA CODE
170 REM    T$....TELEPHONE NUMBER
180 REM    N$....NAME
190                                                               REM
200 REM ••••• DATA TO BE PROCESSED •••••
210                                                               REM
220 DATA 714, "749-2138", "SAM HORN"
230 DATA 213, "663-1271", "SUE NUNN"
240 DATA 212, "999-1193", "BOB PELE"
250 DATA 312, "979-4418", "ANN SITZ"
260 DATA 999, "999-9999", "END OF FILE"
270                                                               REM
280 REM ••••• PROCESSING •••••                                    REM
290
300 READ A, T$, N$                                                REM
310                                                               REM
320 WHILE N$ <> "END OF FILE"
330    PRINT N$, A, T$
340    READ A, T$, N$
350 WEND
360                                                               REM
370 PRINT " "
380 PRINT "END OF TELEPHONE LISTING"
390 END
```

Most computer programs are written by people with specialized training. They determine the instructions necessary to process the data and place the instructions in the correct sequence so that the desired results will occur. Complex programs may require hundreds or even thousands of program instructions.

Computer software is the key to productive use of computers. With the correct software, a computer can become a valuable tool. Software can be categorized into two types: system software and application software.

System Software and Application Software

System software consists of programs that are related to controlling the actual operations of the computer equipment. An important part of the system software is a set of programs called the operating system. The instructions in the **operating system** tell the computer how to perform functions such as how to load, store, and execute an application program and how to transfer data between the input/output devices and main memory. For a computer to operate, an operating system must be stored in the main memory of the computer. Each time a computer is started, or turned on, the operating system is loaded into the computer and stored in the computer's main memory. Many different operating systems are available for computers. An operating system commonly used on many microcomputers is called DOS. The letters stand for Disk Operating System.

Application software consists of programs that tell a computer how to produce information. When you think of the different ways that people use computers in their careers or in their personal lives, you are thinking of examples of application software. Business, scientific, and educational programs are all examples of application software.

Application Software Packages

Most end users do not write their own programs. In large corporations, the information processing department develops programs for unique company applications. Programs required for common business and personal applications can be purchased from software vendors or stores that sell computer products (Figure 1-9). We often refer to purchased programs as **application software packages**, or simply **software packages**.

FIGURE 1-9
Many programs commonly required for business and personal applications can be purchased from computer stores.

Microcomputer Applications Software Packages

Personal computer users often use applications software packages. Some of the most commonly used packages, shown in Figure 1-10, are: word processing software, electronic spreadsheet software, computer graphics software, and database software.

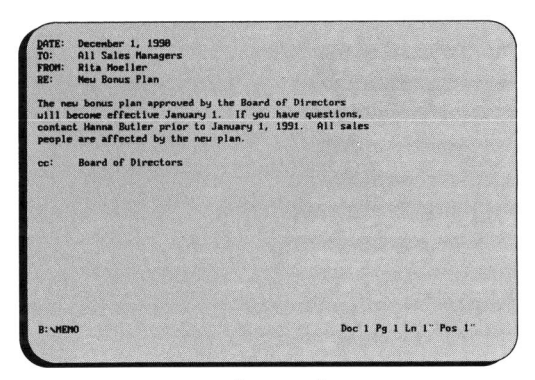

FIGURE 1-10 Commonly used microcomputer applications software packages.

word processing

Word processing is used to write letters, memos, and other documents. As the user keys in words and letters, they display on the screen. The user can easily add, delete, and change any text entered until the document is exactly what he or she wants. The user can then save the document on auxiliary storage and can also print it on a printer.

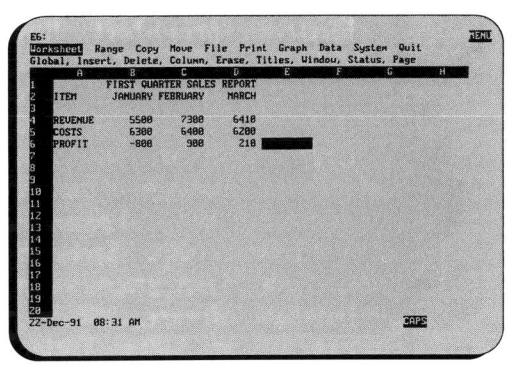

electronic spreadsheet

Electronic spreadsheet software is frequently used by people who work with numbers. The user enters the data and the formulas to be used on the data; then the program applies the formulas to the data and calculates the results. A powerful feature of electronic spreadsheet software is the capability to ask what-if questions by changing the data and quickly recalculating the new results. For example, the user could direct the software to recalculate the total sales based on a percentage increase in the second quarter sales.

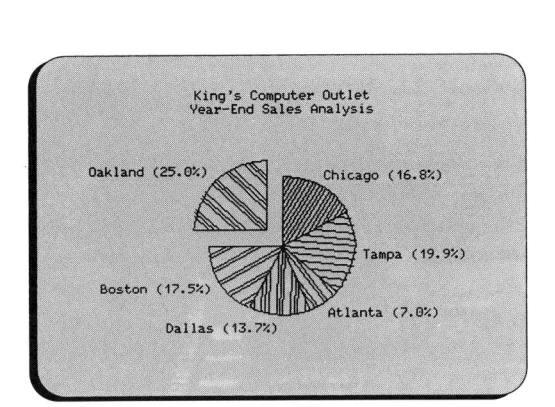

computer graphics

Computer graphics software provides the capability to transform a series of numeric values into graphic form for easier analysis and interpretation. In this example, the sales values from an electronic spreadsheet have been transformed into a pie chart. Using graphics software, these graphs can be produced in seconds instead of the hours that were required for a graphic artist to hand draw each graph.

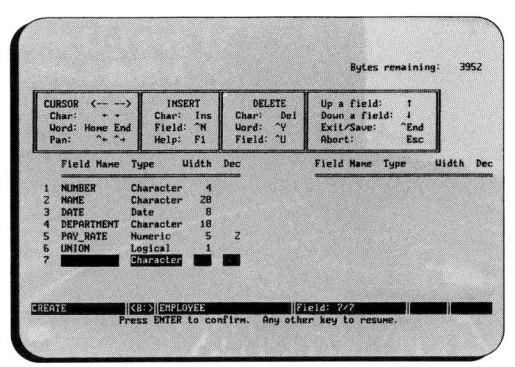

database

Database software allows the user to enter, retrieve, and update data in an organized and efficient manner. This screen shows how a database is created by defining the information that can be stored in each database record. After the database is defined, the user can add, delete, change, display, print, or reorganize the database records.

Word processing software is used to create and print documents that otherwise be prepared on a typewriter. A key advantage of word processing software is its capability to make changes easily in documents, such as correcting spelling, changing margins, and adding, deleting, or relocating entire paragraphs. These changes would be difficult and time consuming to make on a typewriter. With a word processor, documents can be printed quickly and accurately and easily stored on a disk for future use.

Electronic spreadsheet software allows the user to add, subtract, and perform user-defined calculations on rows and columns of numbers. These numbers can be changed and the **spreadsheet** quickly recalculates the new results. Electronic spreadsheet software eliminates the tedious recalculations required with manual methods.

Graphics software converts numbers and text into graphic output that visually conveys the relationships of the data. Some graphics software allows the use of color to further enhance the visual presentation. Line, bar, and pie charts are the most frequent forms of graphics output. Spreadsheet information is frequently converted into a graphic form. In fact, graphics capabilities are included in most spreadsheet packages.

Database software allows the user to enter, retrieve, and update data in an organized and efficient manner. These software packages have flexible inquiry and reporting capabilities that allow users to access the data in different ways and create custom reports.

FIGURE 1-11
After the diskette is inserted in the disk drive, the spreadsheet program is copied into main memory. In this example we use English statements for ease of understanding.

A TYPICAL BUSINESS APPLICATION

◆ Electronic spreadsheets are one of the most widely used software applications. In the following example, a user develops a budget spreadsheet for the first quarter of a year. After loading the operating system and spreadsheet program, the user enters the revenues and the costs for the first three months of the year. The spreadsheet program then calculates the total revenues and total costs, the profit for each month (determined by subtracting costs from revenues), and the profit percentage (obtained by dividing the profit by the revenues). In addition, the spreadsheet program calculates the total profit and the total profit percentage.

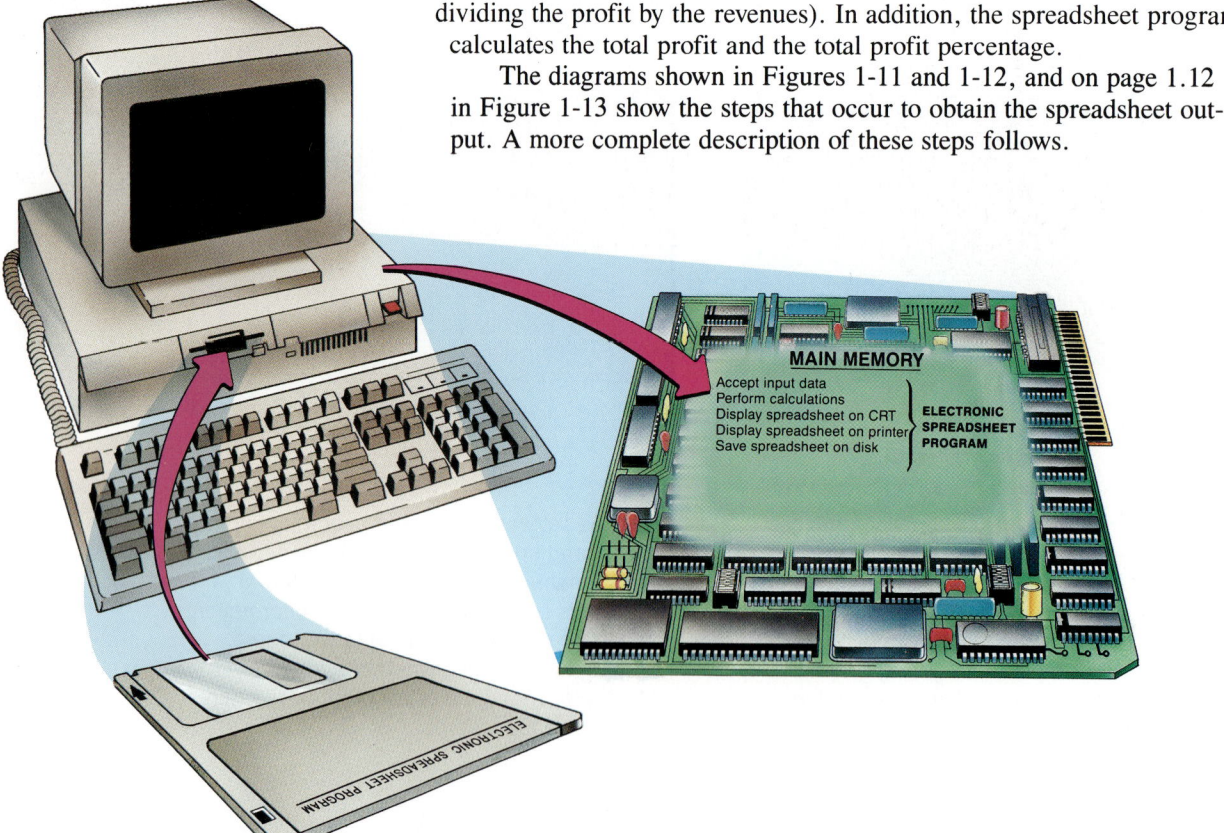

The diagrams shown in Figures 1-11 and 1-12, and on page 1.12 in Figure 1-13 show the steps that occur to obtain the spreadsheet output. A more complete description of these steps follows.

Load the Operating System

When the user turns on the power to the computer, a copy of the operating system is transferred from the hard disk into the main memory of the computer. When this process is complete, the computer is ready to load the application software.

Loading the Application Software

For processing to occur, the application software must also be stored in the main memory of the computer. In this example, the application software is a spreadsheet program that is stored on a diskette. The process of getting the program into the main memory is called loading the program.

In Figure 1-11 the diskette on which the program is stored is inserted into the disk drive. The user then issues a command that instructs the operating system to load a copy of the program from the diskette into main memory. After loading the program, the operating system instructs the computer to begin executing the program.

Input: Enter the Data

The next step is to input the data (Figure 1-12). The user does this by using a keyboard. As the user enters the data on the keyboard ①, the data displays on the screen ②, and it is stored in main memory ③.

The data in this example consists of the words indicating the contents of each of the columns and rows on the screen and the numbers on which the calculations are to be performed.

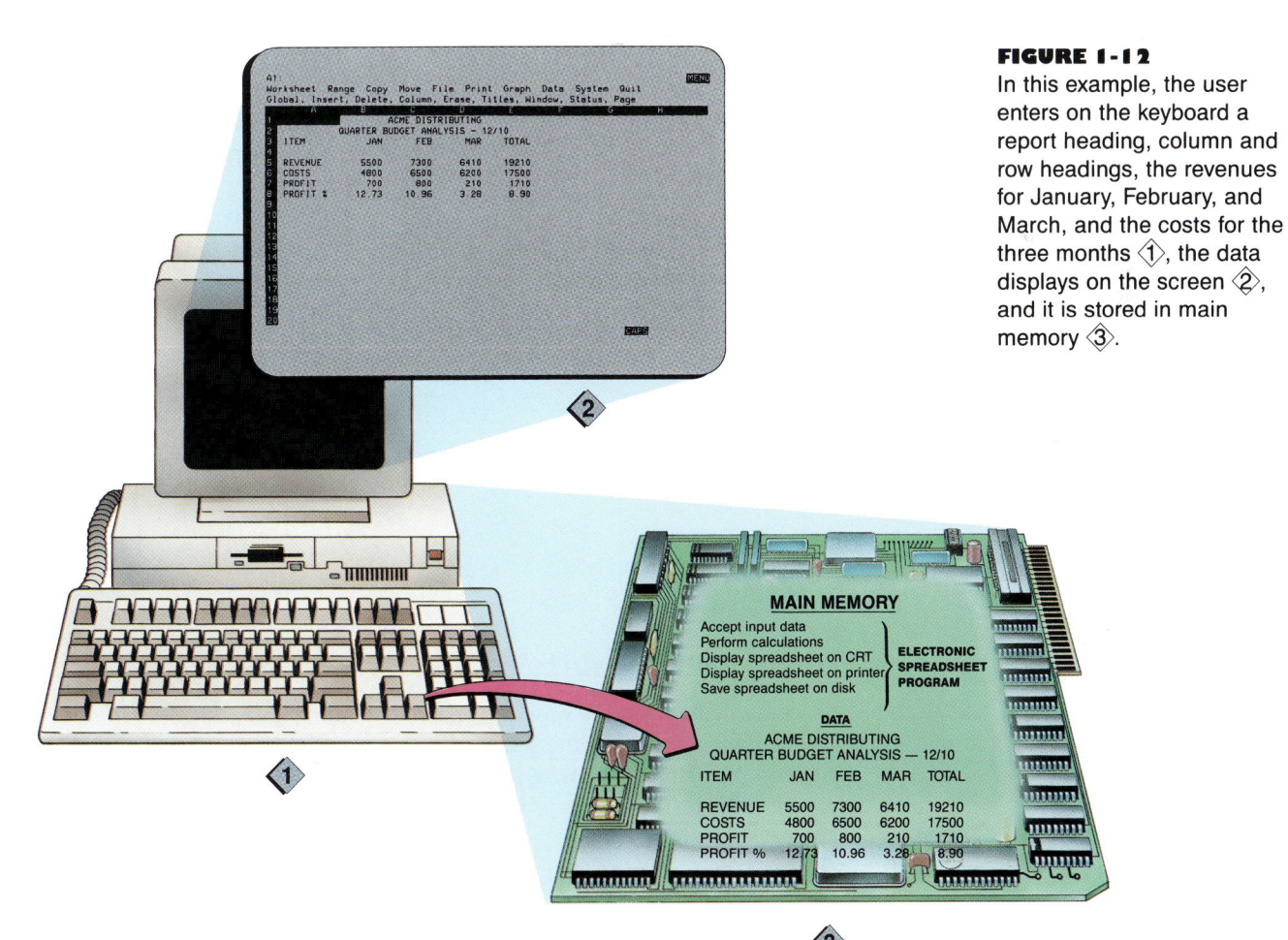

FIGURE 1-12

In this example, the user enters on the keyboard a report heading, column and row headings, the revenues for January, February, and March, and the costs for the three months ①, the data displays on the screen ②, and it is stored in main memory ③.

CHAPTER 1 AN OVERVIEW OF COMPUTER CONCEPTS

FIGURE 1-13
After the data has been entered, the program specifies the following processing steps: ① Perform calculations. ② Display the entire spreadsheet, with the calculation results, on the screen. ③ Print the spreadsheet. ④ Store the spreadsheet data and results on auxiliary storage.

Process: Perform the Calculations

As Figure 1-13 shows, the user has entered the data ①, and the program will direct the processor to perform the required calculations ②. In this example, the program calculates the profit for each month, the total revenue, costs, and profit for the quarter, the profit percent for each month, and the total profit percent.

The preceding operations illustrate the calculating capability of computers. Whenever any calculations are performed on data, the data must be stored in main memory. The results of the calculations are also stored in main memory. If you desire, the program can issue instructions to store the results on an auxiliary storage device such as a hard disk or diskette.

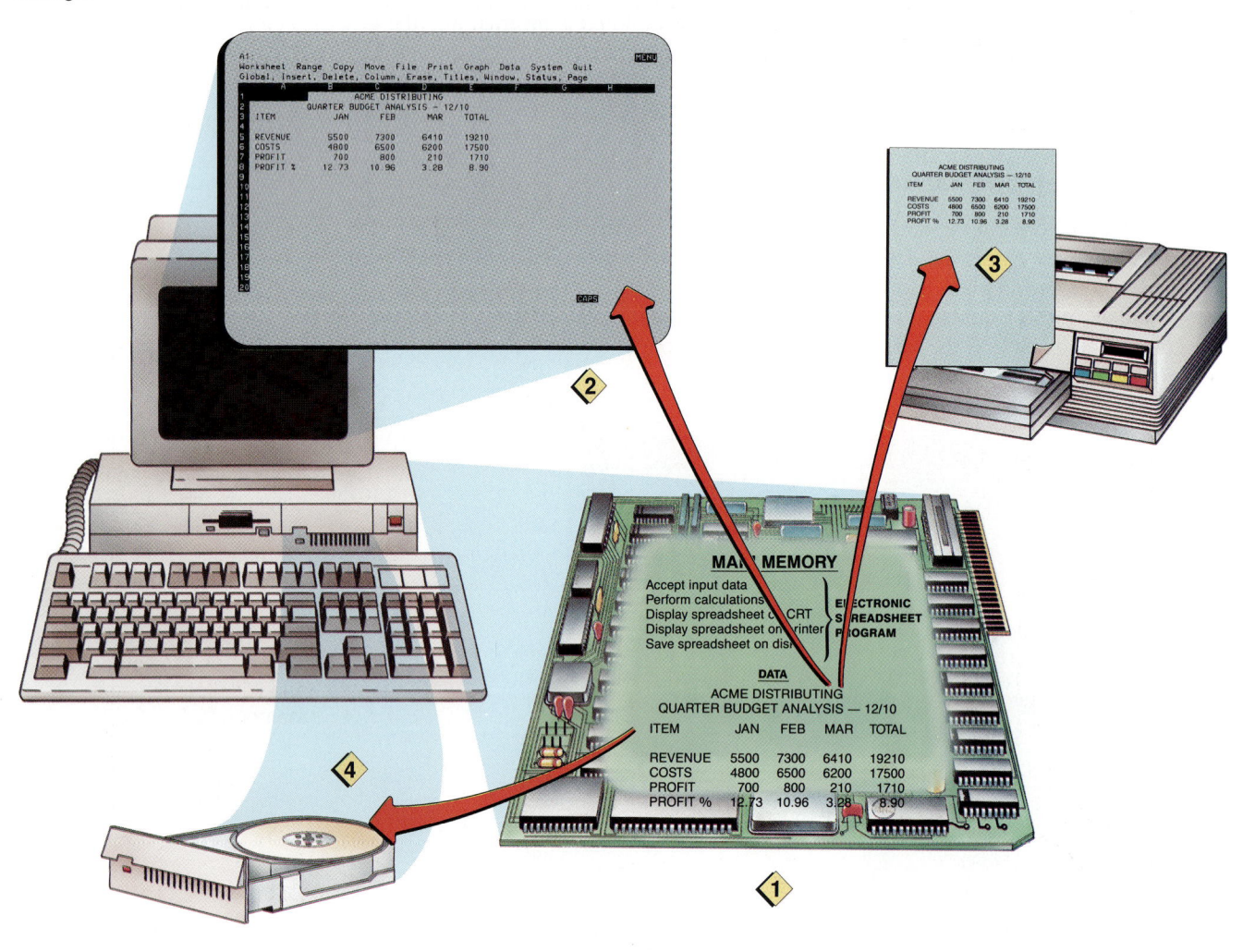

Output: Display the Results

After completing the calculations, the program specifies that the spreadsheet, with the results of the calculations, display on the screen. The program also specifies that the results are printed on the printer ③. When this instruction is executed, the spreadsheet is printed on paper so the results of the processing can be used by someone other than the computer user.

Storage: Save the Results

The spreadsheet is also stored on a disk, in this example a hard disk, so that at a later time it can be retrieved and used again ④.

WHAT ARE THE ELEMENTS OF AN INFORMATION SYSTEM?

◆ Obtaining useful and timely information from computer processing requires more than just the equipment and software we have described so far. Other elements required for successful information processing include accurate data, trained information systems personnel, knowledgeable users, and documented procedures. Together these elements are referred to as an **information system** (Figure 1-14).

FIGURE 1-14
An information system requires computer equipment; software, which runs the equipment; data, which the computer manipulates; people, including both computer personnel who manage the equipment and users who use the information that the equipment produces; and finally procedures, which help the entire system run efficiently.

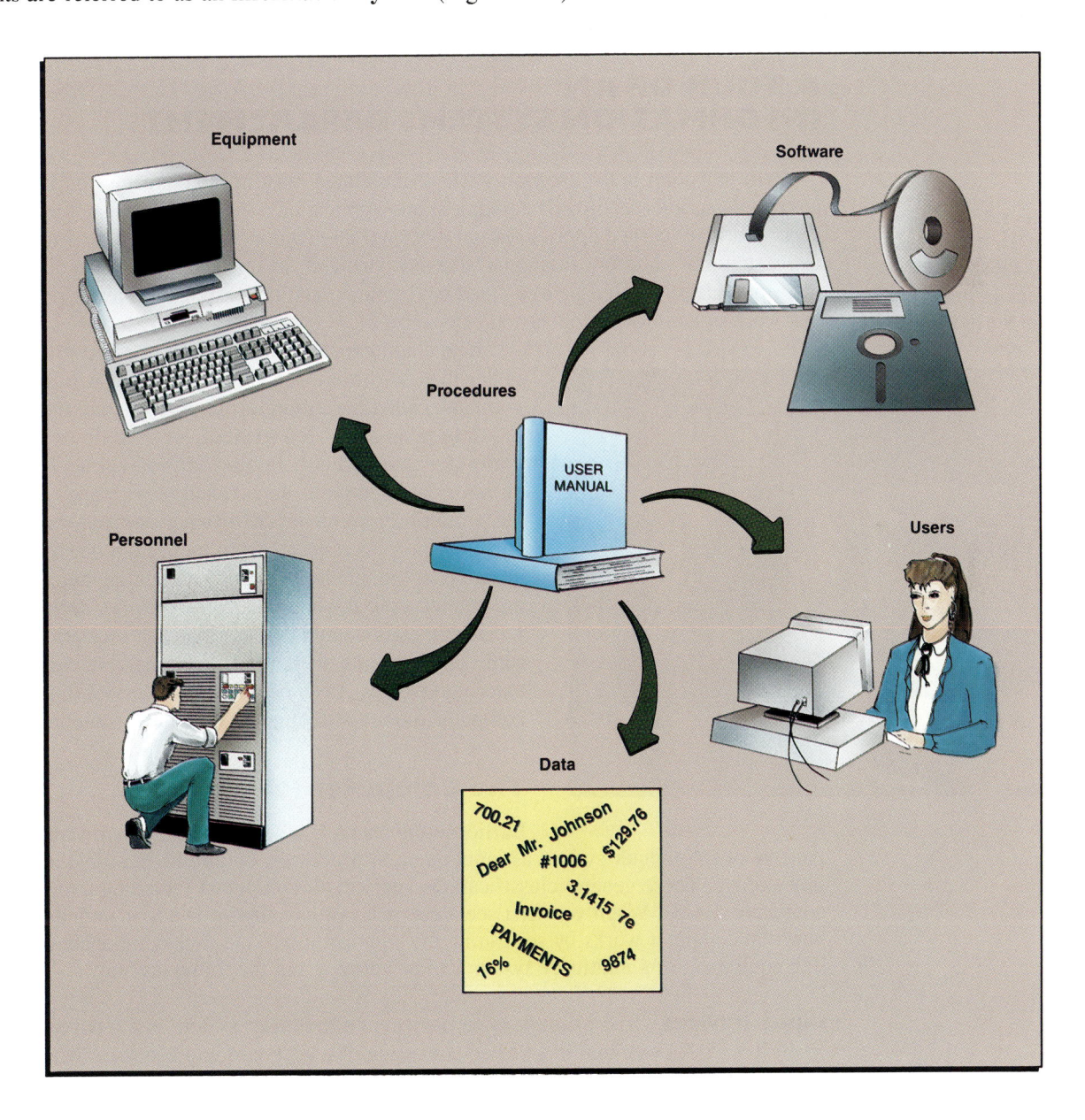

For an information system to provide accurate, timely, and useful information, each element in the system must be strong and all of the elements must work together. The equipment must be reliable and capable of handling the expected work load. The software must have been carefully developed and tested, and the data entered to be processed must be accurate. If the data is incorrect, the resulting information produced from it will be incorrect. Properly trained data processing personnel are required to run most medium and large computer systems. Users are sometimes overlooked as an important element of an information system, but with expanding computer use, users are taking increasing responsibility for the successful operation of information systems. This includes responsibility for the accuracy of both the input and output. In addition, users are taking a more active role in the development of computer applications. They work closely with information systems department personnel in the development of computer applications that relate to their areas of expertise. Finally, all information processing applications should have documented procedures covering not only the computer operations but any other related procedures as well.

A TOUR OF AN INFORMATION SYSTEMS DEPARTMENT

To this point in the chapter, we have illustrated most of the concepts you have learned using microcomputer equipment and applications. To show you how the concepts you have learned apply to larger systems, this section will take you on a narrative and visual tour of an information systems department. In this section we also discuss how computers are used in a business environment and the responsibilities of personnel that work in an information systems department.

FIGURE 1-15
A terminal contains a keyboard and a screen. The screen displays the data entered via the keyboard.

The computers used in a business are generally under the control of a separate department within the company called the **information systems department**, the **data processing department**, or sometimes just the **computer department**. In our tour we will be visiting an information systems department of a company that has a multiuser computer. **Multiuser computers** concurrently process requests from more than one user. For example, if the employees in the accounting department are connected to the computer, one or more accounts receivable clerks could be entering cash receipts at the same time that one or more accounts payable clerks are entering invoices. Let's begin our tour by visiting the computer room and seeing the computer equipment.

The Computer Room

Earlier in the chapter, we identified the hardware components of a computer system as input devices, processor, output devices, and auxiliary storage. These general classifications apply to all computers including a multiuser computer system. When you first see a computer of any size, it is easier to understand how that computer works by separating the equipment into the four component areas. The equipment of a multiuser system can be separated in the following way.

Input Devices The primary input device on a multiuser system is a **terminal** (Figure 1-15). A terminal is a device consisting of a keyboard and a screen, which is connected through a communication line, or cable, to a computer. Sometimes personal computers are used as terminals. While there may be a few terminals in the computer room, most of the terminals are located on the desktops of employees throughout the organization.

A TOUR OF AN INFORMATION SYSTEMS DEPARTMENT   **1.15**

FIGURE 1-16
This mainframe computer processes data for hundreds of users. Such a computer is usually placed in a room designed specifically for the machine. Special air conditioning, humidity control, electrical wiring, and flooring are required for many of these installations.

Processor One of the main pieces of equipment in the computer room is the processor unit (Figure 1-16). The processor unit of a multiuser computer allocates computer resources to the programs that are being processed. Modern computer processors are so fast that they can usually handle numerous users and still provide very quick response time.

Output Devices The most commonly used output devices for a multiuser computer are a printer (Figure 1-17) and a terminal (Figure 1-18). When large volumes of printed output must be produced, high-speed printers are used. Some terminals can display both text material and graphics in either monochrome or color.

Auxiliary Storage The two major types of auxiliary storage for a multiuser computer are magnetic disk and magnetic tape.
   Magnetic disk is the most widely used auxiliary storage on multiuser computers. When using magnetic disk, data is recorded on an oxide coated metal platter (the disk) as a series of magnetic spots. Disk drives can store data on either removable disks or hard disks, sometimes called fixed disks. **Removable disks** refer to disk packs that can be taken out of the disk drive. In Figure 1-19, the containers for the removable disk packs can be seen sitting on the disk drives. Most hard disks contain platters that are enclosed in sealed units to prevent contamination of the disk surface.

FIGURE 1-18
A terminal is both an input and an output device. Here, the user is viewing a color graphics display.

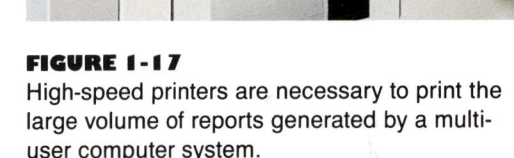

FIGURE 1-17
High-speed printers are necessary to print the large volume of reports generated by a multi-user computer system.

FIGURE 1-19
Removable disk packs are mounted on the disk drives. The multiple disk drives shown here are common in large computer installations.

FIGURE 1-20
This magnetic tape drive uses reels of one-half-inch tape. Tape is often used to backup the data stored on disk drives.

FIGURE 1-21
The console allows the computer operator to monitor the processing.

Magnetic tape (Figure 1-20) stores data as magnetic spots on one-quarter- to one-half-inch tape on cartridges or reels. On systems with disk drives, tape is most often used to store data that does not have to be accessed frequently. Another common use of tape is for backup storage. The contents of the disk drives are regularly copied to tape to provide protection against data loss.

Computer Operators The **computer operator** works in the computer room and is responsible for a number of different tasks. When the computer is running, the operator's console displays messages that indicate the status of the system (Figure 1-21). For example, a message may indicate that a special form, such as a check, must be placed in a printer. The operator responds to these messages to keep the computer running. In many instances, more than one operator is required to run a large computer.

The Data Library

The information systems department keeps its software and data on either disks or tapes. When a disk pack or tape is not in use, it is stored in a **data library** (Figure 1-22). The data library is usually located close to the computer room and is usually staffed by a **data librarian**. The disk packs and tapes in the library must be catalogued so that when they are required, they can be located quickly and taken to the computer room for use.

FIGURE 1-22
The data library stores disk packs and tapes when they are not in use.

Depending on the amount of disk storage available and how frequently it is used, some software applications and data are always available for processing. An example would be order processing software that enters orders into the computer while the sales clerk is on the phone with the customer. Because a phone call can come in at any time, this software application and the data associated with it must always be available for processing.

Offices of Information Systems Personnel

To implement applications on a computer, the information systems department usually employs people who have specialized training in computers and information processing. These employees may include computer operators who work in the computer room and run the equipment; data entry personnel who prepare and enter data into the computer; systems analysts who design the software applications; programmers who write specialized programs; a database administrator who controls and manages data; and managers who oversee the use of the computer.

Data Entry Personnel   **Data entry personnel** (Figure 1-23) are responsible for entering large volumes of data into the computer system. Data is usually entered on terminals from **source documents**, which are original documents such as sales invoices. The accuracy of the data is important because it will affect the usefulness of the resulting information.

FIGURE 1-23
Data entry personnel specialize in entering large amounts of data from source documents.

Systems Analysts   **Systems analysts** review current or proposed applications within a company to determine if the applications should be implemented using a computer. The systems analyst would consider applications for computer implementation if, among other things, productivity can be increased or more timely information can be generated to aid in the management of the company. If an application is to be *computerized*, the systems analyst studies the application to identify what data is used, how the data is processed, and other aspects of the application that are pertinent to the new system. The systems analyst then designs the new system by defining the data required for the computer application, developing the manner in which the data will be processed in the new system, and specifying the associated activities and procedures necessary to implement the application using the computer. Systems analysts work closely with both the people who will be using and benefiting from the new system and the programmers in the information systems department who will be writing the computer programs (Figure 1-24).

FIGURE 1-24
Programmers, systems analysts, and users all work closely in developing new computer applications.

Computer Programmers **Computer programmers** design, write, test, and implement specialized programs that process data on a computer. The design specifications from the systems analyst tell the programmer what processing needs to be accomplished. The programmer develops the specific programs of computer instructions that process the data and create the required information. The systems analyst specifies *what* is to be done; the programmer decides *how* to do it.

Database Administrator An important function within the information systems department is the management of data. In many companies, this task is the responsibility of the **database administrator**. Among other things, the database administrator must develop procedures to ensure that correct data is entered into the system, that confidential company data is not lost or stolen, that access to company data is restricted to those who need the data, and that data is available when it is needed. Data administration is very important. In a business, billions of pieces of data are processed on the computer, and the loss or misappropriation of that data could be extremely detrimental.

Information Systems Department Management Management within an information systems department varies depending on the size and complexity of the department. Most information systems departments have an operations manager, a systems manager, a programming manager, and a manager of the entire department. The **systems manager** oversees the activities in the systems analysis and design area of the department. The **programming manager** is in charge of all programmers within the department. Each of the managers we previously mentioned may also have project managers within their own areas. The **operations manager** oversees the operational aspects of the department such as the scheduling, maintenance, and operation of the equipment. The information systems department manager is in charge of the entire department and may have the title **vice president of information systems**, or **chief information officer (CIO)**.

Summary of the Tour of an Information Systems Department

During the tour of the information systems department we have seen the computer room, data library, and the offices of information systems personnel. You should know more about an information systems department and how a multiuser computer is used in a business.

HOW COMPUTERS ARE USED TODAY

◆ In addition to business, the use of computer technology is widespread in our world. Figure 1-25 shows a variety of computers and their applications. New uses for computers and improvements to existing technology are continually being developed. How do computers affect your life? How will you use computers in the future?

FIGURE 1-25
Here we see computers being used in a wide variety of applications and professions. New applications are being developed every day.

SUMMARY OF AN INTRODUCTION TO COMPUTERS

In this chapter we presented a broad introduction to concepts and terminology that are related to computers. You now have a basic understanding of what a computer is, how it processes data into information, and what elements are necessary for a successful information system. You have also seen some examples of different types of computers and how they are used. The photo essay at the end of the chapter is a time line that shows the evolution of modern computers.

CHAPTER SUMMARY

1. A **computer** is an electronic device, operating under the control of instructions stored in its own memory unit, that can accept data (input), process data arithmetically and logically, produce output from the processing, and store the results for future use.
2. A computer can perform **input**, **process**, **output**, and **storage** operations. These operations are called the **information processing cycle**.
3. **Data** refers to the raw facts, including numbers and words, that are processed on a computer.
4. **Information** is data that has been processed into a meaningful and useful form.
5. The production of information by processing data on a computer is called **information processing**, or **data processing (DP)**.
6. **Computer users** are the people who either directly use the computer or utilize the information it provides.
7. A computer is a powerful tool because it is reliable and can process data quickly and accurately.
8. A **computer program** is a detailed set of instructions that tells the computer exactly what to do.
9. Computer processing can produce many different forms of information from a single set of data.
10. Processing data on a computer is performed by computer equipment including input devices, the processor unit, output devices, and auxiliary storage units. Computer equipment is often referred to as **hardware**.
11. **Input devices** are used to enter data into a computer.
12. The **processor unit** contains the electronic circuits that cause processing to take place.
13. The processor unit contains the central processing unit (CPU) and main memory.
14. The **central processing unit (CPU)** contains the **control unit** and the **arithmetic and logic unit (ALU)**.
15. **Arithmetic operations** are numeric calculations such as addition, subtraction, multiplication, and division that take place in the processor.
16. **Logical operations** are comparisons of data in the processor to see if one value is greater than, equal to, or less than another value.
17. **Main memory** electronically stores data and program instructions.
18. **Output devices** are used to print or display data and information.
19. **Auxiliary storage units** are used to store program instructions and data when they are not being used in the main memory of the computer.
20. The four major categories of computers are microcomputers, minicomputers, mainframes, and supercomputers.
21. Types of **microcomputers** include hand-held, notebook, laptop, portable, desktop, and supermicrocomputers.
22. **Minicomputers** address the needs of users who want more processing power than a microcomputer but do not need the power of a mainframe. Minicomputers can support a number of users performing different tasks.
23. **Mainframe** computers are large systems that can handle hundreds of users, store large amounts of data, and process transactions at a very high rate.
24. **Supercomputers**, the most powerful and expensive category of computers, can process hundreds of millions of instructions per second and perform long, complex calculations.
25. **Computer software** is another name for computer programs.
26. A computer program must first be loaded into main memory before it can be executed.
27. **System software** consists of programs that are related to controlling the actual operations of the computer equipment.

28. An important part of the system software is a set of programs called the **operating system**, which tells the computer how to perform its various functions.
29. **Application software** consists of programs that tell a computer how to produce information.
30. Programs purchased from computer stores or software vendors are called **application software packages**.
31. Commonly used personal computer software packages are word processing, electronic spreadsheet, graphics, and database software.
32. **Word processing software** is used to create and print documents.
33. **Electronic spreadsheet software** performs calculations on rows and columns of numeric data based on formulas entered by the user.
34. **Graphics software** provides the capability to transform numbers and text into a graphic format.
35. **Database software** allows the user to enter, retrieve, and update data efficiently.
36. The elements of an information system are equipment, software, data, personnel, users, and procedures.
37. **Multiuser computers** can concurrently process requests from more than one user.
38. A **terminal**, consisting of a keyboard and screen, is the most commonly used input device for a large computer.
39. Modern computer processors are so fast that they can usually handle numerous users and still provide very quick response time.
40. The most commonly used output devices for large computers are terminals and high-speed printers.
41. Auxiliary storage devices used on a large computer include magnetic disk and magnetic tape.
42. **Computer operators** run the computer equipment and monitor processing operations.
43. A **data library** stores disk packs and tapes when they are not in use.
44. **Source documents** are original documents, such as sales invoices, from which data can be entered.
45. **Data entry personnel** prepare and enter data into the computer.
46. **Systems analysts** review and design computer applications. Systems analysts work closely with users and programmers.
47. **Computer programmers** design, write, test, and implement programs, that process data on a computer.
48. A **database administrator** is responsible for managing an organization's computerized data.
49. Management within an information systems department includes a **systems manager**, **programming manager**, **operations manager**, and a department manager, who is sometimes called the **vice president of information systems**, or **chief information officer (CIO)**.
50. The use of computer technology is widespread in our world.

KEY TERMS

ALU (Arithmetic/Logic Unit) *1.5*
Application software *1.8*
Application software package *1.8*
Arithmetic/Logic Unit (ALU) *1.5*
Arithmetic operation *1.5*
Auxiliary storage unit *1.5*
Cathode ray tube (CRT) *1.5*
Central processing unit (CPU) *1.5*
Chief information officer (CIO) *1.19*
Computer *1.2*
Computer department *1.14*
Computer operator *1.16*
Computer program *1.4*
Computer programmer *1.18*
Computer software *1.7*
Computer system *1.6*
Computer users *1.3*
Control unit *1.5*

CPU (central processing unit) *1.5*
CRT (cathode ray tube) *1.5*
Data *1.2*
Data entry personnel *1.17*
Data librarian *1.16*
Data library *1.16*
Data processing (DP) *1.2*
Data processing department *1.14*
Database administrator *1.18*
Database software *1.10*
Diskette *1.6*
Electronic spreadsheet software *1.10*
End users *1.3*
Graphics software *1.10*
Hard disk *1.6*
Hardware *1.4*
Information *1.2*

Information processing *1.2*
Information processing cycle *1.2*
Information system *1.13*
Information systems department *1.14*
Input *1.4*
Input device *1.5*
Keyboard *1.5*
Logical operation *1.5*
Magnetic disk *1.15*
Magnetic tape *1.16*
Main memory *1.5*
Mainframe *1.7*
Micro *1.7*
Microcomputer *1.7*
Minicomputer *1.7*
Monitor *1.5*
Multiuser computer *1.14*

Operating system *1.8*
Operations manager *1.18*
Output *1.4*
Output device *1.5*
Peripheral device *1.6*
Personal computer *1.7*
Primary storage *1.5*
Printer *1.5*
Process *1.4*

Processor unit *1.5*
Program instruction *1.4*
Programming manager *1.18*
Removable disk *1.15*
Screen *1.5*
Software *1.4*
Software package *1.8*
Source document *1.17*
Spreadsheet *1.10*

Storage *1.4*
Supercomputer *1.7*
Systems analyst *1.17*
Systems manager *1.18*
System software *1.8*
Users *1.3*
Vice president of information systems *1.19*
Word processing software *1.10*

REVIEW QUESTIONS

1. What is the definition of a computer?
2. Define the term computer user.
3. What is the difference between data and information? How is information derived from data?
4. What is the information processing cycle?
5. Describe the four hardware units found on a microcomputer.
6. What is the difference between main memory and auxiliary storage? Why are both necessary?
7. Identify some of the differences among microcomputers, minicomputers, mainframe computers, and supercomputers.
8. What is computer software? How does a computer use software?
9. What is system software? List two functions that the operating system performs.
10. Identify four application software packages often used with personal computers.
11. What are the six elements of an information system?
12. What is the user's role in an information system?
13. Who are some of the personnel who work in an information systems department?
14. What is the role of a systems analyst? How does that position differ from the job of a computer programmer?
15. Describe the key developments in the evolution of the modern computer during the 1960s.

CONTROVERSIAL ISSUES

1. At what grade level should computers be introduced to students? Should all high school or college graduates have a minimum computer skill level? If yes, what should the minimum skill level include?
2. Do computers make mistakes, or is it the humans that program and operate the computers who make the mistakes? Discuss what you think caused recent *computer errors* that you experienced or read about.

RESEARCH PROJECTS

1. Write or call a manufacturer of a minicomputer or mainframe, such as IBM, Bull, DEC, or HP, and ask for a brochure describing one of its popular models. Prepare a report for your class based on what you learned.
2. Prepare a report for your class describing the use of computers at your school. You may focus on a single department or prepare a general report about computer use throughout the school.
3. Prepare a detailed report on an individual who made a contribution to the history of computing.

The Evolution of the Computer Industry

The electronic computer industry began about fifty years ago. This time line summarizes the major events in the evolution of the computer industry.

Dr. John V. Atanasoff and his assistant Clifford Berry designed and began to build the first electronic digital computer during the winter of 1937–38. Their machine, the Atanasoff-Berry-Computer, or ABC, provided the foundation for the next advances in electronic digital computers.

Dr. John von Neumann is credited with writing a brilliant report in 1945 describing several new hardware concepts and the use of stored programs. His breakthrough laid the foundation for the digital computers that have since been built.

1937 **1945** **1951** **1952**

During the years 1943 to 1946, Dr. John W. Mauchly and J. Presper Eckert, Jr. completed the ENIAC (Electronic Numerical Integrator and Computer), the first large-scale electronic digital computer. The ENIAC weighed thirty tons, contained 18,000 vacuum tubes, and occupied a thirty-by-fifty-foot space.

In 1951–52, after much discussion, IBM decided to add computers to their line of business equipment products. This led IBM to become a dominant force in the computer industry.

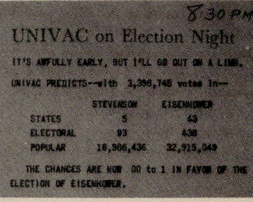

J. Presper Eckert, Jr., standing left, explains the operations of the UNIVAC I, to newsman Walter Cronkite, right. This machine was the first commercially available electronic digital computer.

Public awareness of computers increased when in 1951 the UNIVAC I, after analyzing only 5% of the tallied vote, correctly predicted that Dwight D. Eisenhower would win the presidential election.

1.24 THE EVOLUTION OF THE COMPUTER INDUSTRY

In 1952, Dr. Grace Hopper, a mathematician and commodore in the U.S. Navy, wrote a paper describing how to program a computer with symbolic notation instead of the detailed machine language that had been used.

Dr. Hopper was instrumental in developing high-level languages such as COBOL, a business applications language introduced in 1960. COBOL uses English-like phrases and can be run on most computers, making it one of the most widely used languages in the world.

The IBM model 650 was one of the first widely used computer systems. Originally IBM planned to produce only 50 machines, but the system was so successful that eventually they manufactured over 1,000.

FORTRAN (FORmula TRANslator) was introduced in 1957 proving that efficient, easy-to-use programming languages could be developed. FORTRAN is still in use.

1952   1953   1957   1958   1959   1960

By 1959 over 200 programming languages had been created.

Core memory, developed in the early 1950s, provided much larger storage capacities and greater reliability than vacuum tube memory.

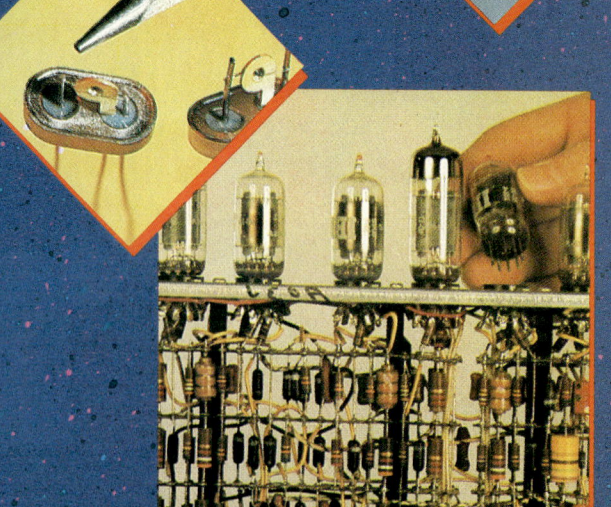

In 1958, computers built with transistors marked the beginning of the second generation of computer hardware. Previous computers built with vacuum tubes were first-generation machines.

THE EVOLUTION OF THE COMPUTER INDUSTRY   1.25

Third-generation computers, with their controlling circuitry stored on chips, were introduced in 1964. The IBM System/360 computers were the first third-generation machines.

From 1958 to 1964, it is estimated, the number of computers in the U.S. grew from 2,500 to 18,000.

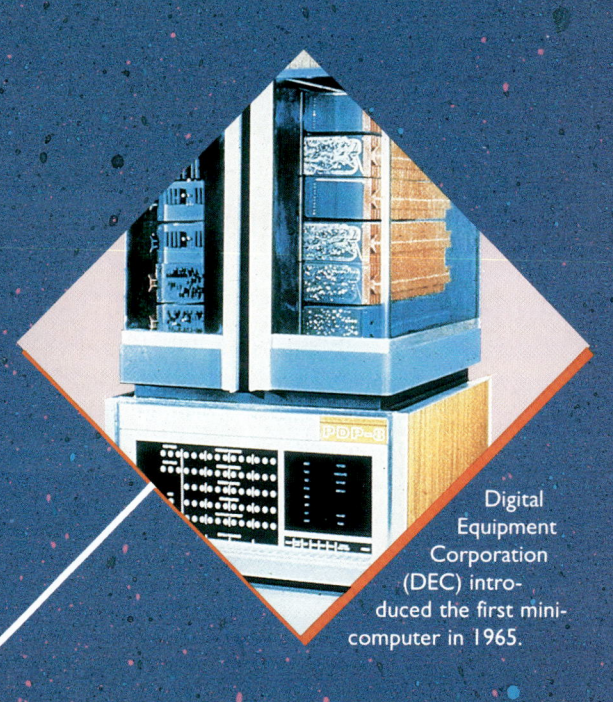

Digital Equipment Corporation (DEC) introduced the first minicomputer in 1965.

1964   **1965**   **1968**   **1969**

In 1965, Dr. John Kemeny of Dartmouth led the development of the BASIC programming language. BASIC is the language most commonly used on microcomputers. More people program in BASIC than any other language.

The software industry emerged in the 1960s. In 1968, Computer Science Corporation became the first software company to be listed on the New York Stock Exchange.

In 1969, under pressure from the industry, IBM announced that some of its software would be priced separately from the computer hardware. This "unbundling" allowed software firms to emerge in the industry.

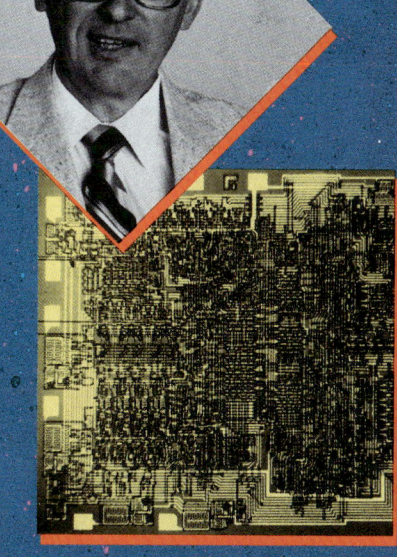

In 1969, Dr. Ted Hoff of Intel Corporation developed a microprocessor, or microprogrammable computer chip, the Intel 4004.

1.26 THE EVOLUTION OF THE COMPUTER INDUSTRY

The fourth-generation computers built with chips that used LSI (large-scale integration) arrived in 1970. The chips used in 1965 contained as many as 1,000 circuits. By 1970, the LSI chip contained as many as 15,000.

The MITS, Inc. Altair computer, sold in kits for less than $400, was the first commercially successful microcomputer.

1970   1975   1976   1979   1980

In 1976, Steve Wozniak and Steve Jobs built the first Apple computer.

The VisiCalc spreadsheet program written by Bob Frankston and Dan Bricklin was introduced in 1979. This product was originally written to run on Apple II computers. Together, VisiCalc and Apple II computers rapidly became successful. Most people consider VisiCalc to be the singlemost important reason why microcomputers gained acceptance in the business world.

THE EVOLUTION OF THE COMPUTER INDUSTRY   1.27

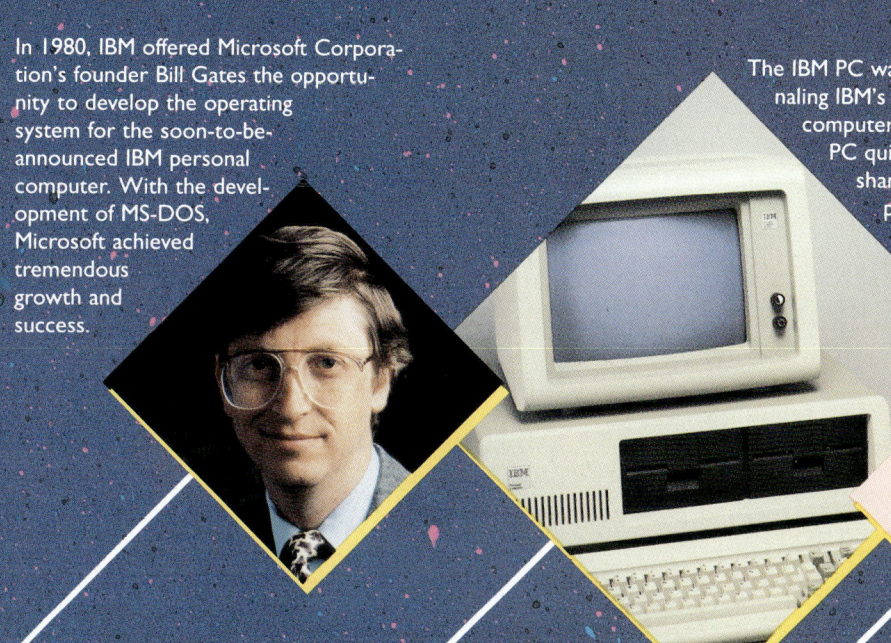

In 1980, IBM offered Microsoft Corporation's founder Bill Gates the opportunity to develop the operating system for the soon-to-be-announced IBM personal computer. With the development of MS-DOS, Microsoft achieved tremendous growth and success.

The IBM PC was introduced in 1981, signaling IBM's entrance into the microcomputer marketplace. The IBM PC quickly garnered the largest share of the personal computer market and became the personal computer of choice in business.

It is estimated that 313,000 microcomputers were sold in 1981. In 1982, the number jumped to 3,275,000.

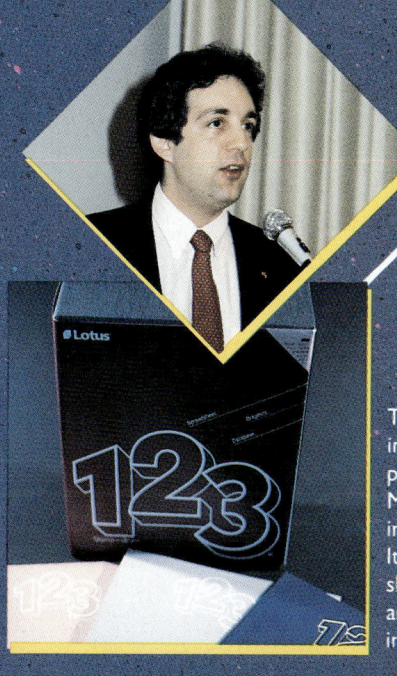

1981　　1982　　1983　　1984

The Lotus 1-2-3 integrated software package, developed by Mitch Kapor, was introduced in 1983. It combined spreadsheet, graphics, and database programs in one package.

Apple introduced the Macintosh computer, which incorporated a unique graphics interface making it easy to learn.

1.28 THE EVOLUTION OF THE COMPUTER INDUSTRY

Several microcomputers using the powerful Intel 80386 microprocessor were introduced in 1987. These machines could handle processing performed previously only by large systems.

The Intel 80486 became the world's first 1,000,000-transistor microprocessor. It crammed 1.2 million transistors on a sliver of silicon that measured .4" × .6" and executed instructions at 15 MIPS (million instructions per second)—four times as fast as its predecessor, the 80386.

In early 1990, estimates indicated that over 54 million computers were in use in the United States.

1987   **1988**   **1989**   **1990**

In October of 1988, former Apple founder Steve Jobs announced his long-awaited NeXT computer. Innovative features included the capability to record and process sound and the use of erasable optical disk storage.

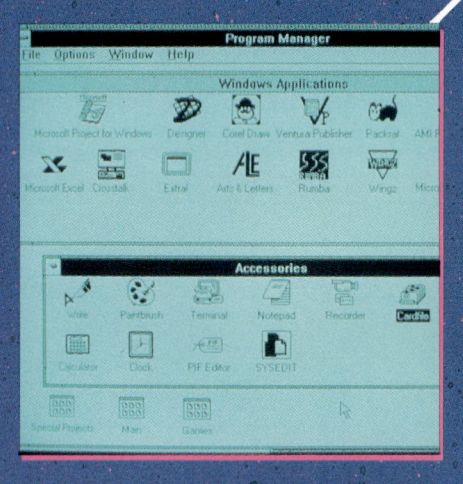

Microsoft released Windows 3.0, a substantially enhanced version of its Windows graphics user interface first introduced in 1985. The software allows users to run multiple applications on a personal computer and more easily move data from one application to another. The package became an instant success selling hundreds of thousands of copies.

The computer industry will continue to evolve as improved technology and innovation lead to a variety of new computer applications.

Microcomputer Applications: User Tools

CHAPTER 2 TOOLS

OBJECTIVES

◆ Identify the most widely used general microcomputer software applications

◆ Describe how each of the applications can help users

◆ Explain the key features of each of the major microcomputer applications

◆ Explain integrated software and its advantages

◆ List and describe six guidelines for purchasing software application packages

◆ List and describe learning aids and support tools that help users to use microcomputer applications

Today, understanding the applications commonly used on microcomputers is considered a part of being computer literate. In fact, a knowledge of these applications is now considered by many educators and employers to be more important than a knowledge of programming. Because of this, we introduce microcomputer applications, focusing on the most widely used applications early in this book. Learning about each application will help you understand how people use microcomputers in our modern world.

2.1

AN INTRODUCTION TO GENERAL MICROCOMPUTER APPLICATIONS

◆ The applications discussed in this chapter are usually called **general microcomputer applications**. This software is called *general* because it is useful to a broad range of users. Word processing is a good example of a general application. Regardless of the type of business a company does, word processing can be used as a tool to help employees generate documents.

An important advantage of general applications is that you do not need any special technical skills or ability to use them. These programs are designed to be **user friendly**, in other words, easy to use. You do not need detailed computer instructions. Instead, you use the software through simple commands. **Commands** are instructions that tell the software what you want to do. For example, when you are finished using an application and you want to save your work, you issue an instruction called a SAVE command. In some applications you must type the command, in other applications the command is entered through a user interface.

User interfaces (Figure 2-1) are methods and techniques that make using an application simpler. They include function keys, screen prompts, menus, icons, and a device called a mouse. To help you understand how to use the software, we include an introduction to these features in this chapter. We present a more thorough discussion in Chapter 3.

FIGURE 2-1
User interfaces.

▲ Function keys — programmed to execute commonly used instructions.

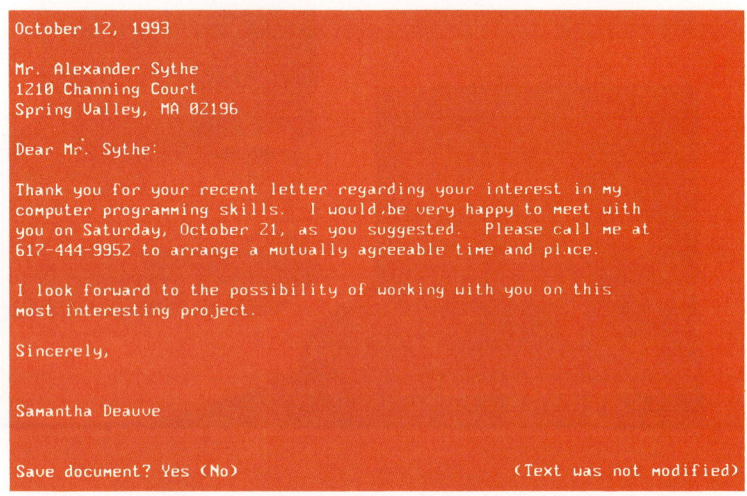

▲ Screen prompts — such as the question in the lower left of this screen — indicate that the software is waiting for the user to respond.

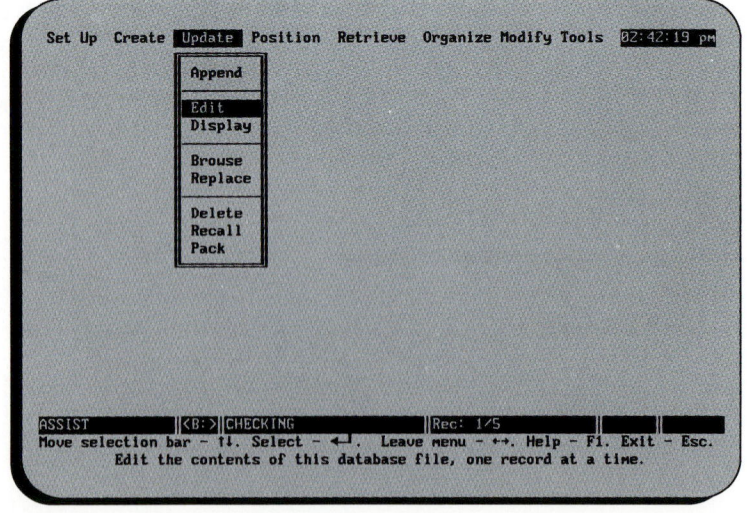

Menus — such as this "pull-down" menu — offer a list of possible processing selections. ▶

The **function keys** that are included on computer keyboards are a type of user interface. Pressing a function key in an applications program is a shortcut that takes the place of entering a command. The software defines exactly what the function key causes to happen. If you used a function key to save your work as we discussed in the previous example, pressing one key instead of several could issue the entire command.

Screen **prompts** are the messages that the program displays to help you while you are using an application. **Menus**, a special kind of screen prompt, are used in applications to provide a list of processing options. You make a selection from the menu by pressing the number or letter key that corresponds with the option you desire. Some applications use a menu called a **pull-down menu**. In this menu style the selections are displayed across the top of the screen. As you use the arrow keys to move from one selection to the next, the options associated with that selection appear to be *pulled down* from the top of the screen like a window shade. **Icons** refer to pictures instead of words that are displayed on the screen to show you various program options. A user interface that extensively uses icons to graphically represent files and processing options is called a **graphic user interface (GUI)**.

A **mouse** is a small input device that is used to move the cursor and input commands. The **cursor** is a symbol, such as an underline character or an arrow, that indicates where you are working on the screen. Many applications require you to move the cursor around on the screen. You do this by using the arrow keys on the keyboard or by moving the mouse. For example, a mouse could be used to move the cursor so that it is pointing to a selection you want to make on a menu. You can then press a button on the mouse to select that menu option.

These are some of the user interfaces that help to make application packages user friendly. User interfaces help minimize the technical computer knowledge you need when you are using general applications packages.

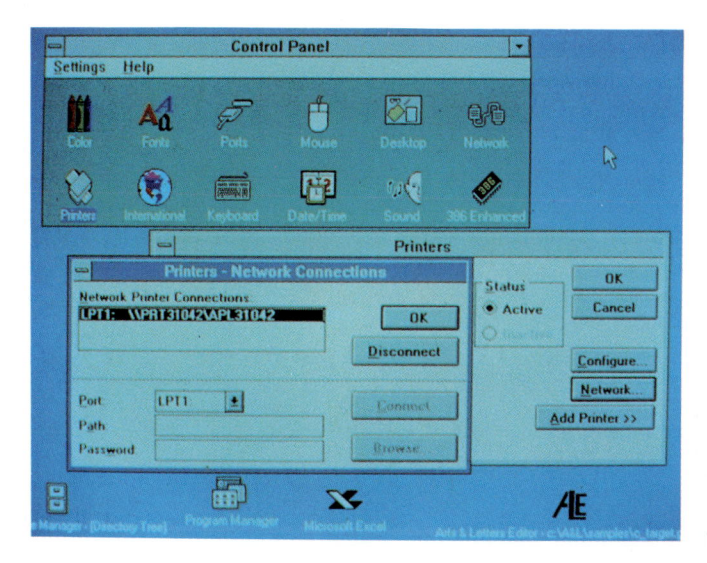

▲ Icons — symbols that represent program options.

Mouse — used to control the movement of the cursor on the screen. By pressing a button on the mouse, menu selections and other processing options can be chosen. ▶

Many kinds of general applications are available. Some of the most widely used software includes:

- Word processing
- Desktop publishing
- Electronic spreadsheet
- Database
- Graphics
- Data communications

Although we will discuss these applications as they are used on microcomputers, they are actually available on computers of all sizes. The concepts you will learn about each application package on microcomputers will also apply if you are working on a larger system.

WORD PROCESSING SOFTWARE: A DOCUMENT PRODUCTIVITY TOOL

The most widely used general application is word processing. If you need to create **documents**, such as letters or memos, you can increase your productivity by learning to use this software tool. Some of the popular packages used today include WordPerfect, Microsoft Word, and WordStar. This section discusses using a word processor to create a document.

Word processing software is used to prepare documents electronically (Figure 2-2). It allows you to enter text on the computer keyboard in the same manner as you create documents on a typewriter. As you enter the characters, they are displayed on the screen and stored in the computer's main memory. Because the document is in an electronic format, you can easily **edit** it by making changes and corrections to the text. You can correct errors and add, move, or delete characters, words, sentences, paragraphs, and large blocks of text. When the document is complete, you enter a command and have the computer send the document to the printer. The document's format is also under your control. You can specify the margins, define the page length, and select the print style. The document can be printed as many times as you like. Each copy is an original and looks the same as the other copies. The computer's storage capability allows you to store your documents so they can be used again. It is an efficient way to file documents because many documents can fit on one disk. If you wish, previously stored documents can be combined to make new documents, and you do not have to reenter the text as you would on a typewriter.

FIGURE 2-2
Word processing using a computer is faster, more accurate, and less tedious than using a typewriter.

The value of word processing is that it reduces the time required to prepare and produce written documents. Any editing you want to do in the document is easy because the software allows you to make changes quickly and efficiently. In addition, you can eliminate the tedious task of typing a final draft.

Most word processing packages include additional support features such as a spelling checker and a thesaurus. In addition, software may be purchased for grammar checking that is designed to work with word processors.

Spelling Checker

Spelling checker software allows you to check individual words or the entire document for correct spelling. To check a document for misspelled words, you enter a command that instructs the software to check the spelling. The words in the text will then be checked against an electronic dictionary stored on a disk that is part of the spelling checker software. If an exact match is not found, the word is highlighted. A menu is then superimposed on the screen, giving you a list of similar words that may be the correct spelling. You can select one of the words displayed on the menu, edit the highlighted word, leave the word unchanged, or add the word to the dictionary.

Some spelling checker dictionaries contain over 120,000 words. Many users customize their software dictionaries by adding company, street, city, and personal names so that the software can check the correct spelling of those words.

While spelling checkers can catch misspelled words and words that are repeated such as the the, they cannot identify words that are used incorrectly. A thesaurus and grammar checker will help you to choose proper words and use them in a correct manner.

Thesaurus

Thesaurus software allows you to look up synonyms for words in a document while you are using your word processor. Using a thesaurus is similar to using a spelling checker. When you want to look up a synonym for a word, you place the cursor on the word that you want to check, enter a command through the keyboard, and the thesaurus software displays a menu of possible synonyms. If you find a word you want to use, you select the desired word from the list and the software automatically incorporates it in the document by replacing the previous word.

Grammar Checker

Grammar checker software is used to check for grammar, writing style, and sentence structure errors (Figure 2-3). This software can check documents for excessive use of a word or phrase, identify sentences that are too long, and find words that are used out of context such as four example.

Whereas many word processors include a spelling checker and a thesaurus, grammar checkers are usually purchased separately. A popular grammar checker that is compatible with many word processing packages is Grammatik.

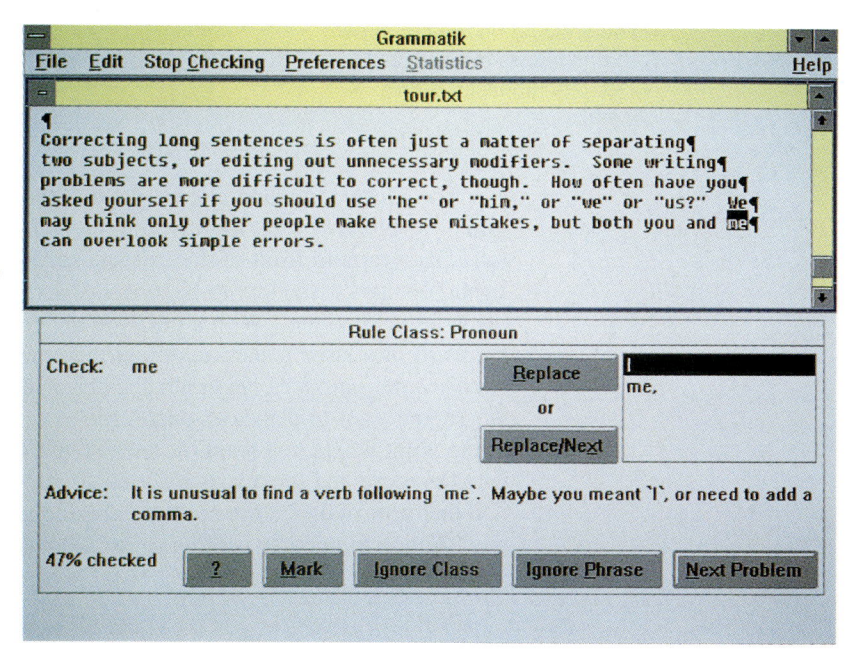

FIGURE 2-3
This grammar checker software is named Grammatik. It can proofread a document for mistakes in grammar, usage, punctuation, and spelling. The document being proofread is shown in the top portion of the screen. The possible problem identified by the software is displayed in the lower portion of the screen.

A Word Processing Example

Figures 2-4 through 2-11 illustrate the following word processing example. Let's say that Julia Broderick, Vice President of Sales of a company, wants to send a memo announcing a meeting of all sales personnel. She remembers that last month she sent a similar memo to just the sales managers. Thus, the first thing she does is load last month's memo into main memory so it will appear on the screen (Figure 2-4). This memo might be stored on a hard disk or on a diskette.

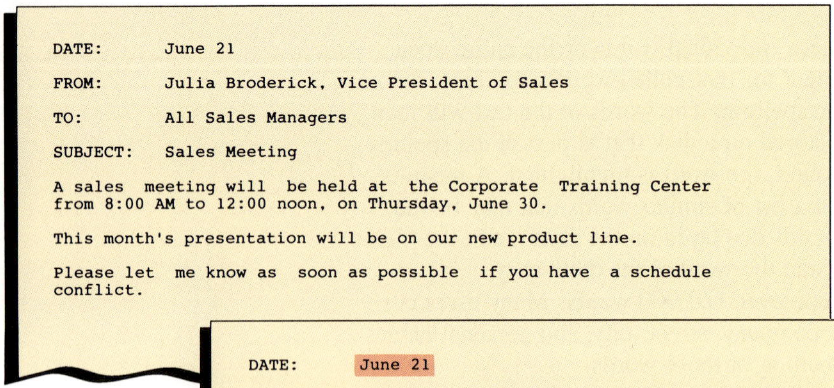

Word processing changes are usually one of three types: inserting text, deleting text, or moving text. When you **insert**, you add characters and words to the existing text in your document. When you **delete**, text is removed from your document. Often it makes sense to do your insertions and deletions at the same time; as you edit your document, you delete the existing word or phrase and insert the new one. Figure 2-5 shows the document with the text to be deleted. Figure 2-6 shows the document after she enters the new text.

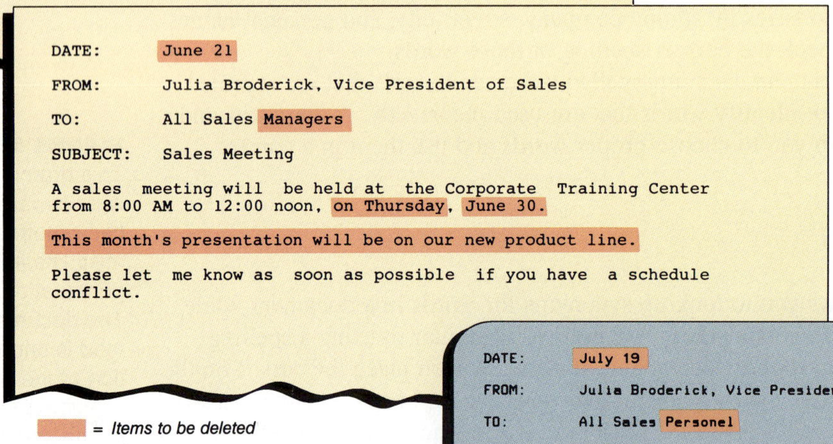

FIGURE 2-4
Last month's memo that will be changed for this month's meeting.

```
DATE:      June 21
FROM:      Julia Broderick, Vice President of Sales
TO:        All Sales Managers
SUBJECT:   Sales Meeting

A sales meeting will be held at the Corporate Training Center
from 8:00 AM to 12:00 noon, on Thursday, June 30.

This month's presentation will be on our new product line.

Please let me know as soon as possible if you have a schedule
conflict.
```

```
DATE:      June 21
FROM:      Julia Broderick, Vice President of Sales
TO:        All Sales Managers
SUBJECT:   Sales Meeting

A sales meeting will be held at the Corporate Training Center
from 8:00 AM to 12:00 noon, on Thursday, June 30.

This month's presentation will be on our new product line.

Please let me know as soon as possible if you have a schedule
conflict.
```

FIGURE 2-5
The shaded areas indicate text to be deleted.

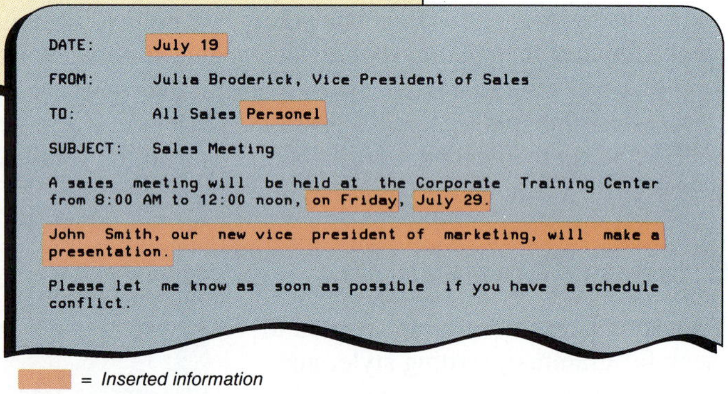

■ = Items to be deleted

FIGURE 2-6
The shading on the computer screen shows the new text inserted into last month's memo.

```
DATE:      July 19
FROM:      Julia Broderick, Vice President of Sales
TO:        All Sales Personel
SUBJECT:   Sales Meeting

A sales meeting will be held at the Corporate Training Center
from 8:00 AM to 12:00 noon, on Friday, July 29.

John Smith, our new vice president of marketing, will make a
presentation.

Please let me know as soon as possible if you have a schedule
conflict.
```

■ = Inserted information

The Move command allows you to either cut (remove) or copy a sentence, paragraph, or block of text. In our example, Julia decides she wants to **move** the existing third paragraph in front of the existing second paragraph (Figure 2-7). First, she highlights, or marks, the text to be moved. Next, she indicates that she wants to *cut* and not *copy* the marked text. With a **cut**, you are removing text from an area. With a **copy**, the word processor makes a copy of the marked text but leaves the marked text where it was. After you perform either the cut or the copy, the word processor needs to know where you want to place, or **paste**, the text. This is usually done by moving the cursor to the point where you want the moved text to begin. You then give a command to execute the move and the text is inserted. Figure 2-8 shows the cut text *pasted* into a position that now makes it the second paragraph. This capability to easily move text from one location to another is often referred to as *cut and paste*.

FIGURE 2-7
The shading shows the text to be moved from the third to the second paragraph.

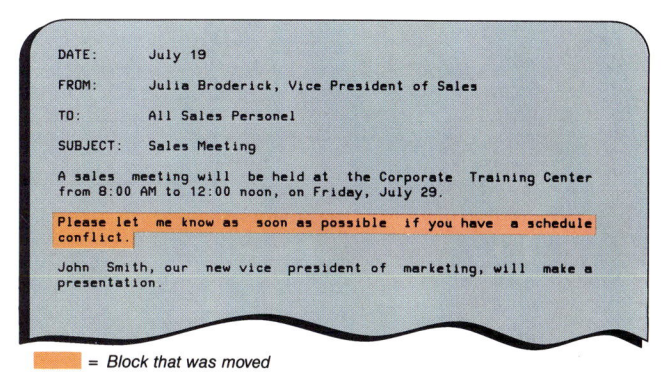

FIGURE 2-8
Memo after the third paragraph was moved to the second paragraph.

After the text changes are made, Julia runs a spelling checker. The spelling checker matches each word in the document against its spelling dictionary and discovers an unrecognized word: personel. Figure 2-9 shows how a spelling checker might present two alternatives for the correct spelling of the word. Julia merely has to enter the letter B and the word processor changes personel to personnel (Figure 2-10).

Before printing the memo, Julia reviews its format. She decides that the length of the lines in the document are too wide and she increases the margins. Figure 2-11 shows the document with the wider, 1 1/2-inch margins.

Now that the text and format are correct, Julia saves the document before printing it in case a system or power failure occurs during printing. Once she saves it, she can print the document as often as necessary. With the document saved, it is readily available to be retrieved by the word processor at any time.

FIGURE 2-9
Spelling checker highlighting unrecognized word and showing two possible spellings.

FIGURE 2-10
Correct spelling of personnel inserted into text by spelling checker.

FIGURE 2-11
Memo after margins are changed.

Word processing software is a productivity tool that allows you to create, edit, format, print, and store documents. Each of the many word processing packages available may have slightly different capabilities, but most have the features summarized in Figure 2-12.

FIGURE 2-12
Common features of word processing software.

WORD PROCESSING FEATURES	
INSERTION AND MOVING Insert character Insert word Insert line Move sentences Move paragraphs Move blocks Merge text **DELETE FEATURES** Delete character Delete word Delete sentence Delete paragraph Delete entire text **SCREEN CONTROL** Scroll up and down by line Scroll by page Word wrap Uppercase and lowercase display Underline display Screen display according to defined format Bold display Superscript display Subscript display	**SEARCH AND REPLACE** Search and replace word Search and replace character strings **PRINTING** Set top and bottom margins Set left and right margins Set tab stops Print columns Single, double, triple space control Variable space control within text Right, left, full justification Center lines Subscripts Superscripts Underline Boldface Condense print Enlarge print Special type fonts Proportional spacing Headers Footers Page numbering Print any page from file

While our discussion of word processing has focused on the creation of documents that contain only text, you should know that some word processing packages now incorporate desktop publishing features that allow graphics to be included with the text. As you will see in the next discussion, the areas of word processing and desktop publishing are closely related.

DESKTOP PUBLISHING SOFTWARE: A DOCUMENT PRESENTATION TOOL

◆ **Desktop publishing (DTP) software** allows users to design and produce professional looking documents that contain both text and graphics (Figure 2-13). Two popular desktop publishing packages are Ventura Publisher and PageMaker. This software produces documents, such as newsletters, marketing literature, technical manuals, and annual reports, that contain art as well as text. Documents of this type were previously created by slower, more expensive traditional publishing methods such as typesetting. With desktop publishing, users can now create professional looking documents on their own computers and produce work that previously could only be done by graphic artists. By using desktop publishing, both the cost and time of producing quality documents is significantly decreased.

As we previously mentioned, some word processing packages now have desktop publishing capabilities. Packages such as WordPerfect and Microsoft Word contain enough features to satisfy the needs of many users. However, most desktop publishing packages still exceed the capabilities of word processing software. On the other hand, the word processing features of many desktop publishing packages are not as complete as those offered by word processing packages. Therefore, text is usually created with a word processor and then transferred into the desktop publishing package.

The graphic art used in the documents created with desktop publishing usually comes from one of three sources:

1. Art can be selected from clip art collections. **Clip art** refers to collections of art that are stored on disks and are designed for use with popular desktop publishing packages (Figure 2-14).
2. Art can be created on the computer with software packages that are specifically designed to create graphics, or through software such as spreadsheet packages that can create pie, line, and bar charts.
3. An input device called a scanner can be connected to the computer and used to electronically capture copies of pictures, photographs, and drawings and store them on a disk for use with desktop publishing software.

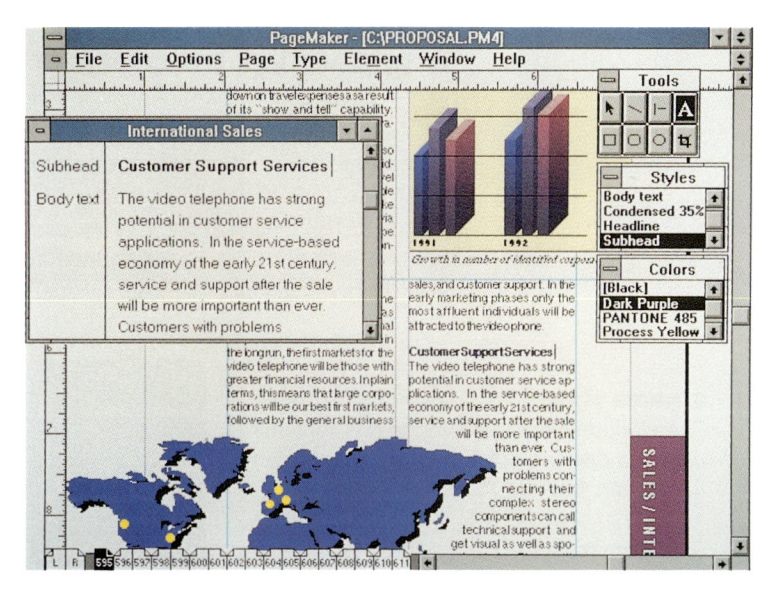

FIGURE 2-13
High-quality printed documents can be produced with desktop publishing software.

FIGURE 2-14
Clip art consists of previously created figures, shapes, and symbols that can be added to documents.

An important feature of desktop publishing is page composition. This means that a user is able to design on the screen an exact image of what a printed page will look like. This capability is called WYSIWYG. **WYSIWYG** is an acronym for What You See Is What You Get. Some of the page composition or layout features that are available include the use of columns for text, the choice of different type sizes and font (type) styles, and the capability to place, edit, enlarge, and reduce the size of charts, pictures, and illustrations in the document. Also, numerous special effects such as borders and backgrounds can be used to enhance the appearance of a document.

As new versions of word processing and desktop publishing software are introduced, the capabilities of both applications will increase and the differences between the two applications will decrease.

ELECTRONIC SPREADSHEET SOFTWARE: A NUMBER PRODUCTIVITY TOOL

Electronic spreadsheet software allows you to organize numeric data in a worksheet or table format called an **electronic spreadsheet** or **spreadsheet**. Manual methods, those done by hand, have long been used to organize numeric data in this manner (Figure 2-15). You will see that the data in an electronic spreadsheet is organized in the same manner as it is in a manual spreadsheet. Within a spreadsheet, data is organized horizontally in **rows** and vertically in **columns**.

FIGURE 2-15
The electronic spreadsheet on the right still uses the row-and-column format of the manual spreadsheet on the left.

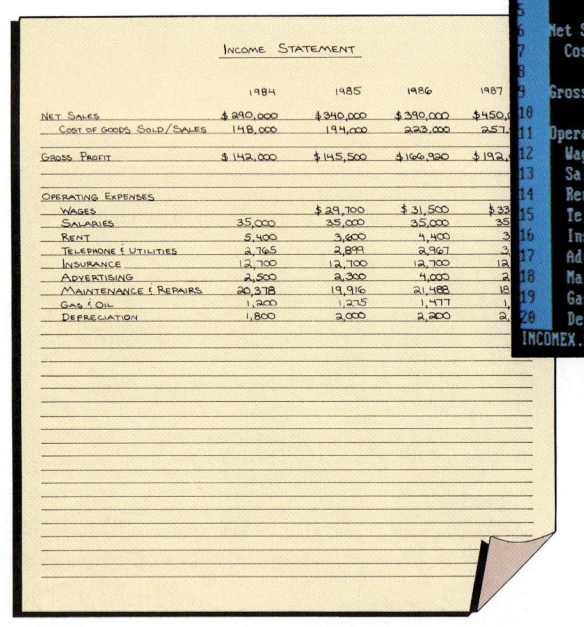

The intersection where a row and column meet is called a **cell** (Figure 2-16). Cells are named by their location in the spreadsheet. In Figure 2-16, the cursor is on cell C2, the intersection of column C and row 2.

Cells may contain three types of data: labels (text), values (numbers), and formulas. The text, or **labels**, as they are called, identify the data and document the worksheet. Good spreadsheets contain descriptive titles. The rest of the cells in a spreadsheet may appear to contain numbers, or **values**. However, some of the cells actually contain formulas. The **formulas** perform calculations on the data in the spreadsheet and display the resulting value in the cell containing the formula.

FIGURE 2-16
In a spreadsheet, rows refer to the horizontal lines of data and columns refer to the vertical lines of data. Rows are identified by numbers and columns are identified by letters. The intersection of a row and column is called a cell. The highlighted cell is the cursor. You can move the cursor by pressing the arrow keys on the keyboard.

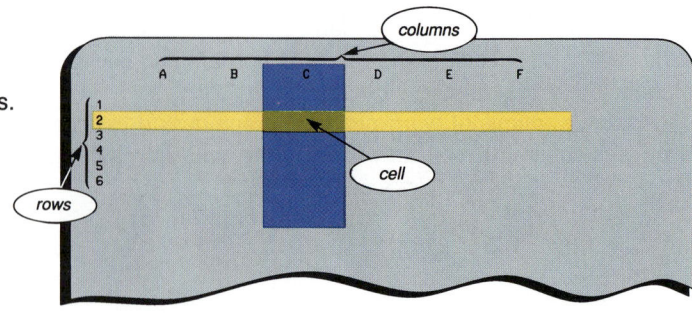

To illustrate this powerful tool, we will show you how to develop the spreadsheet that we used as an example in Chapter 1. Recall that the completed spreadsheet contains revenues, costs, profit, and profit percentage for three months and the totals for the three months. By looking at Figure 2-17, you can see that the first step in creating the spreadsheet is to enter the labels or titles. These should be short but descriptive, to help you organize the layout of the data in your spreadsheet.

The next step is to enter the data or numbers in the body of the spreadsheet (Figure 2-18). The final step is to enter the formulas that calculate the totals. (Some users enter the formulas before they enter the data.)

In a manual spreadsheet, you would have to calculate each of the totals by hand or with your calculator. In an electronic spreadsheet, you simply enter a formula into the cell where the total is to appear. The total is calculated and displayed automatically (Figure 2-19).

Once a formula is entered into a cell, it can be copied to any other cell that requires a similar formula. As the formula is copied, the formula calculations are performed automatically (Figure 2-20). After entering the remaining formulas, the spreadsheet is complete (shown on the next page in Figure 2-21). You can now give the commands to print the spreadsheet and to store it on a disk.

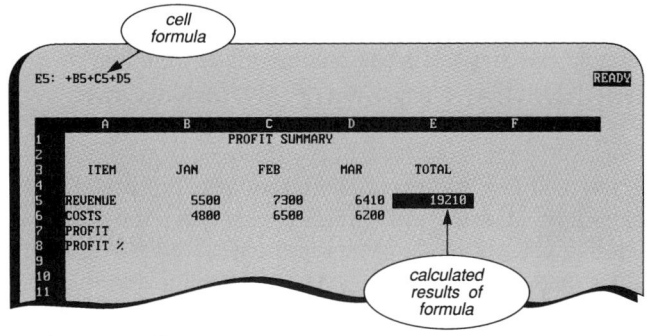

FIGURE 2-17
Labels such as JAN, FEB, REVENUE, and COSTS are entered in the spreadsheet to identify columns and rows of data. The status line shows the address and contents of the current cell. The address of a cell is the intersection of the column letter and row number. Here, the current cell is B5 (column B, row 5). Nothing has been entered for this cell, so the status line shows only the cell address.

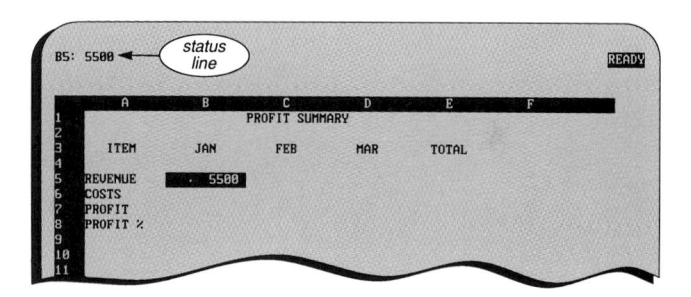

FIGURE 2-18
The value 5500 is entered and stored in cell B5. The status line now displays both the cell address and the cell value.

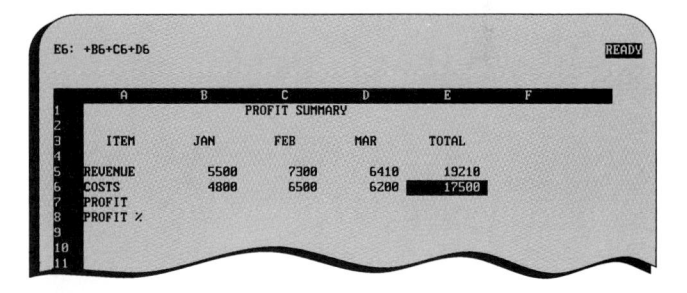

FIGURE 2-19
The remaining values are entered in cells C5, D5, B6, C6, and D6. A formula is entered in cell E5. The formula specifies that cell E5 is to be the sum of the values in cells B5, C5, and D5. Cell E5 displays the numeric sum. The status line at the top of the screen, however, shows the formula that calculates the value in that cell.

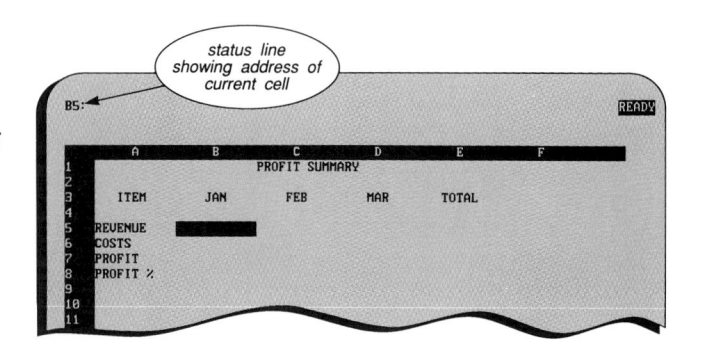

FIGURE 2-20
The formula required for cell E6 is similar to the one for cell E5; it totals the amounts in the three previous columns. When we copy the formula from E5 into E6, the software automatically changes the cell references from B5, C5, and D5 to B6, C6, and D6.

FIGURE 2-21
This screen shows the completed spreadsheet. The value in cell E8 is derived from the formula on the status line, which specifies that the value in cell E7 is to be divided by the value in cell E5 (the slash character indicates division). Since the value in E7 is the total profit and the value in E5 is the total revenue, the result of the division operation is the profit percentage.

FIGURE 2-22
This screen shows the capability of a spreadsheet to recalculate totals when data is changed. This capability gives the user the ability to quickly see the total impact of changing one or more numbers in a spreadsheet. Using the spreadsheet shown in FIGURE 2-21, one number was changed; the REVENUE amount for February. This one change results in five numbers automatically recalculating in the spreadsheet (the recalculated numbers are shown with a check mark). In a manual spreadsheet, each of these five numbers would have to be recalculated separately.

One of the most powerful features of the electronic spreadsheet occurs when the data in a spreadsheet changes. To appreciate the capabilities of spreadsheet software, let's discuss how a change is handled in a manual system. When a value in a manual spreadsheet changes, you must erase it and write a new value into the cell. You must also erase all cells that contain calculations referring to the value that changed and then you must recalculate these cells and enter the new result. For example, the row totals and column totals would be updated to reflect changes to any values within their areas. In large manual spreadsheets, accurately posting changes and updating the values affected can be time consuming and new errors can be introduced. But posting changes on an electronic spreadsheet is easy. You change data in a cell by simply typing in the new value. All other values that are affected are updated automatically. Figure 2-22 shows that if you changed the value in cell C5, the column and row totals that use the value in C5 will automatically change. All other values and totals in the

FIGURE 2-23
The what-if testing capability of electronic spreadsheets is a powerful feature used to aid managers in making decisions.

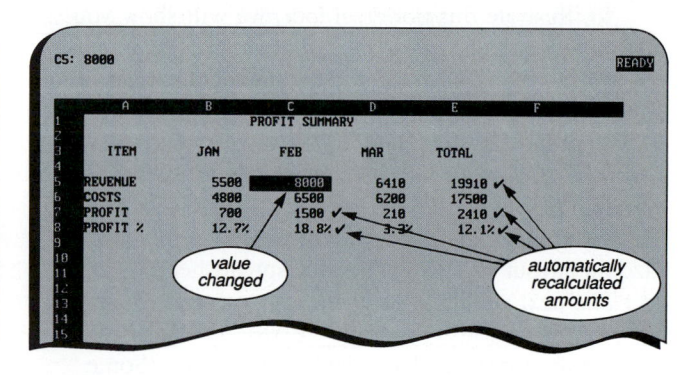

spreadsheet remain unchanged. On a computer, the updating happens very quickly. As row and column totals are recalculated, the changes are said to *ripple* through the spreadsheet.

An electronic spreadsheet's capability to recalculate when data is changed makes it a valuable tool for decision making. This capability allows people to perform what-if testing by changing the numbers in a spreadsheet (Figure 2-23). The resulting values that are calculated by the spreadsheet software provide valuable decision support information based on the alternatives tested.

An electronic spreadsheet is a productivity tool that organizes and performs calculations on numeric data. Spreadsheets are one of the most popular software applications. They have been adapted to a wide range of business and non-business applications. Some of the popular packages used today are Lotus 1-2-3, Excel, and Quattro. Most spreadsheet software has the features shown in Figure 2-24.

DATABASE SOFTWARE: A DATA MANAGEMENT TOOL

A **database** refers to a collection of data that is stored in files. **Database software** allows you to create a database and to retrieve, manipulate, and update the data that you store in it. In a manual system (Figure 2-25), data might be recorded on paper and stored in a filing cabinet. In a database on the computer, the data will be stored in an electronic format on an auxiliary storage device such as a disk.

SPREADSHEET FEATURES

WORKSHEET
Global format
Insert column
Insert row
Delete column
Delete row
Set up titles
Set up windows

RANGE
Format range of data
Erase cells

COPY
Copy from cells
Copy to cells

MOVE
Move from cells
Move to cells

FILE
Save
Retrieve
Erase
List

PRINT
Set up margins
Define header
Define footer
Specify range to print
Define page length
Condense print

FIGURE 2-24
Common features of spreadsheet software.

FIGURE 2-25
An electronic database is similar to a manual system; related data items are stored in files.

When you use a database, you need to be familiar with the terms file, record, and field. Just as in a manual system, the word **file** is a collection of related data that is organized in records. Each **record** contains a collection of related facts called **fields**. For example, a file might consist of records containing information about a checking account. All the data that relates to one check would be considered a record. Each fact, such as the check number or amount, is called a field.

The screens in Figures 2-26 through 2-32 present the development of a database containing personal checking account information using the popular database program dBASE III PLUS. To begin creating the database, you would select the Create menu by moving the cursor until Create was highlighted, as shown in Figure 2-26.

FIGURE 2-26
A menu used to create a file in the popular database program dBASE III PLUS.

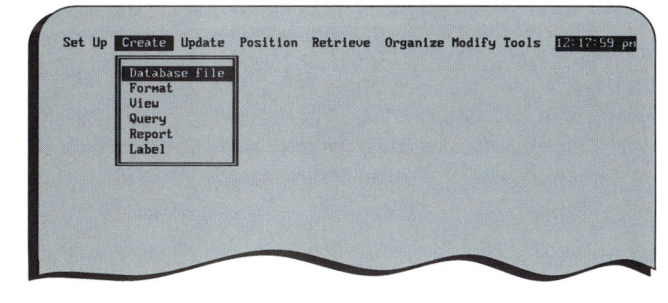

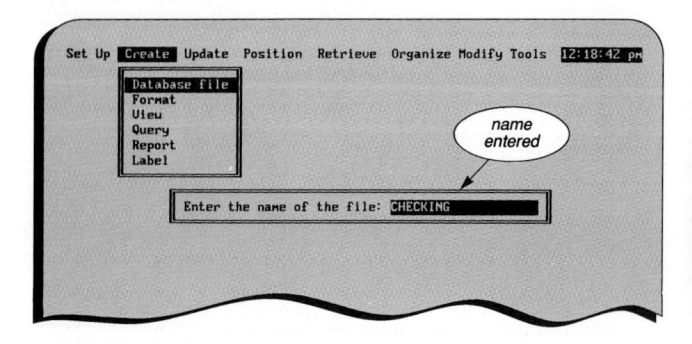

CHAPTER 2 MICROCOMPUTER APPLICATIONS: USER TOOLS

FIGURE 2-27
Screen used to enter the name of the file.

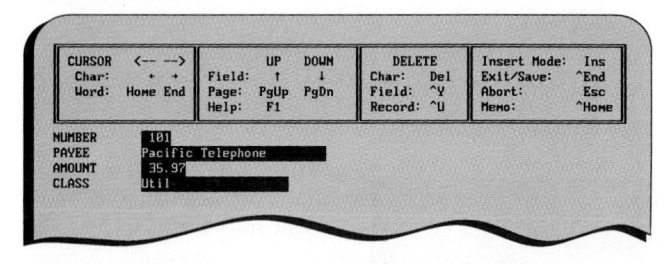

FIGURE 2-28
CREATE FILE screen showing definition of fields for records in the CHECKING file.

Using the pull-down menu displayed under Create, you would select the "Database file" option. After identifying the disk drive to use, the screen would look like Figure 2-27. A prompt asks you to enter a file name, the name under which the file being created will be stored on disk. In this example, you would enter the name "CHECKING".

You are then asked to enter descriptions for each field (Figure 2-28). A field description consists of a field name, the type of data to be stored in the field (C for character, N for numeric data), and the number of characters in the field. In a numeric field, if you want to put digits to the right of the decimal point, you must specify the number of digits to the right. Thus, for the amount field, the designation 6.2 means that the field is six characters wide with two digits to the right of the decimal point. Because the decimal point takes one of the positions, the largest number that can be displayed in this field is 999.99.

Once you have defined the fields in the records, you enter data into the records (Figure 2-29). The software prompts you to enter data for each record. As you type the data into each field it is stored. Thus, after the field name NUMBER, you enter the check number. You complete each field in the same manner, and continue to enter data until all data is entered for the checking account file.

After the file has data stored in it, you can use the file to produce information. For example, suppose you want to display the checks in order by check number. You can use the "Organize" and "Retrieve" options on the menu to enter commands that sort all records by NUMBER and display the sorted list on the screen. Figure 2-30 shows a display of the sorted list. Suppose you also want to display your utility expenses.

FIGURE 2-29
Data entry screen with the word Utility partially entered.

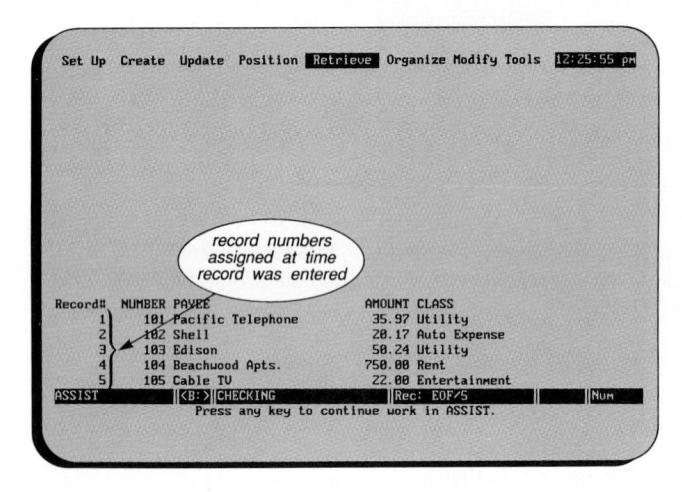

FIGURE 2-30
Display of all records sorted by record number.

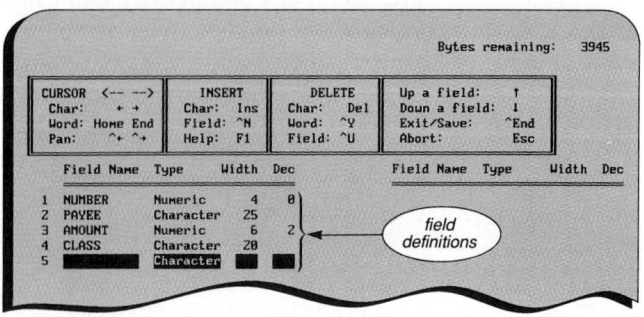

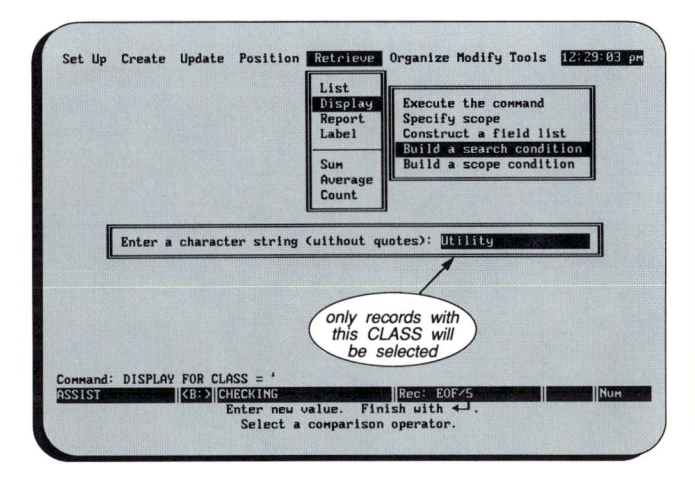

FIGURE 2-31
The software is directed to display only records with a CLASS equal to Utility.

FIGURE 2-32
Display of only the Utility CLASS records.

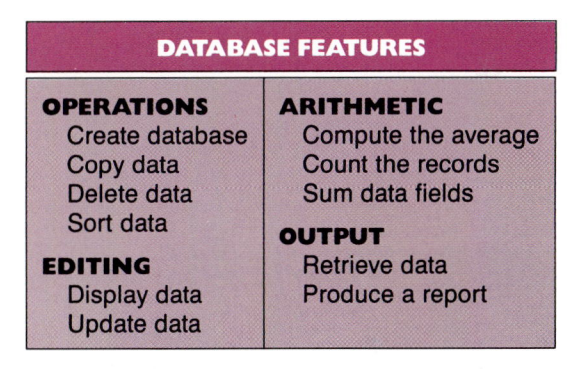

In Figure 2-31, you direct the system to display only those records where the class is equal to Utility. As a result, only those records for which the classification is Utility are retrieved and displayed (Figure 2-32).

As shown in our checkbook example, database software assists users in creating files and storing, manipulating, and retrieving data. Popular software packages that perform these functions include dBASE III PLUS, dBASE IV, R:Base, and Paradox. Figure 2-33 lists some of the common features of these packages.

Recall that when you use a microcomputer database software application, you do not need to have any special technical knowledge. Database software is a general application tool that is designed to help you easily and efficiently manage data electronically.

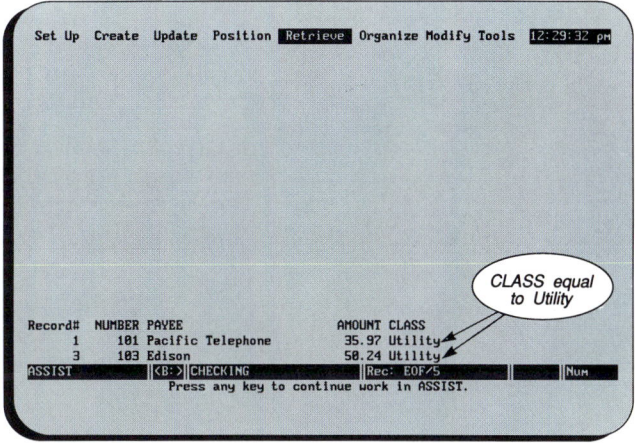

DATABASE FEATURES	
OPERATIONS	**ARITHMETIC**
Create database	Compute the average
Copy data	Count the records
Delete data	Sum data fields
Sort data	**OUTPUT**
EDITING	Retrieve data
Display data	Produce a report
Update data	

FIGURE 2-33
Common features of database software.

GRAPHICS SOFTWARE: A DATA PRESENTATION TOOL

♦ Information presented in the form of a graph or a chart is commonly referred to as **graphics**. Studies have shown that information presented as graphics can be understood much faster than information presented in writing. Three common forms of graphics are **pie charts**, **bar charts**, and **line charts** (on the next page in Figure 2-34).

Today, many software packages can create graphics, including most spreadsheet packages. The graphics capabilities of these packages can be grouped into two categories: analytical graphics and presentation graphics.

CHAPTER 2 MICROCOMPUTER APPLICATIONS: USER TOOLS

Bar charts display blocks, or bars, to show relationships among data clearly.

Pie charts, so called because they look like pies cut into pieces, are particularly effective for showing the relationship of parts to a whole.

FIGURE 2-34

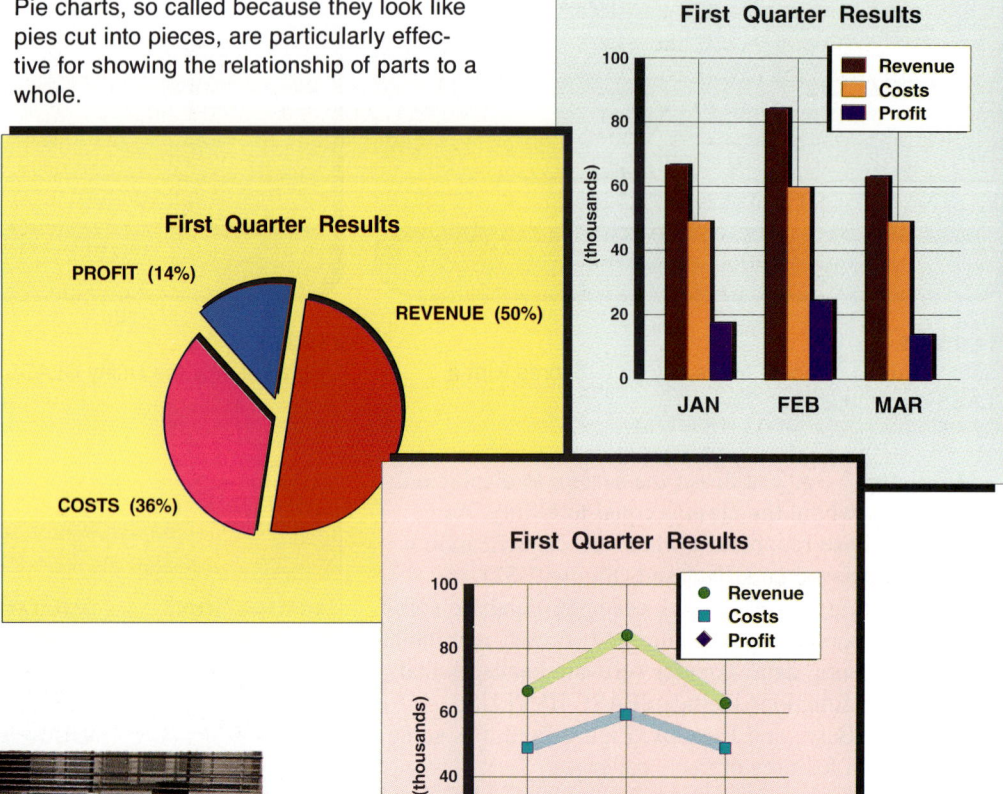

Line charts are effective for showing a trend as indicated by a rising or falling line.

FIGURE 2-35
Color can enhance the presentation of graphic information.

Analytical graphics is widely used by management personnel when they analyze information and when they communicate information to others within their organization (Figure 2-35). For example, a production manager who is planning a meeting with the president of the company may use color graphics to show him the expenses of the production department. This graphic display would have more impact and lead to better understanding than would a printed column of numbers.

GRAPHICS SOFTWARE: A DATA PRESENTATION TOOL   2.17

To create analytical graphics on your computer, you must follow the directions that apply to your graphics software package. Most packages will prompt you to enter the data the graph will represent, and then ask you to select the type of graph you would like. After entering the data, you can select several different graphic forms to see which one will best convey your message. When you decide on a graph, you can print it and also store it for future reference.

As its name implies, **presentation graphics** goes beyond analytical graphics by offering the user a wide choice of presentation effects. These include three-dimensional displays, background patterns, multiple text fonts, and image libraries that contain illustrations of factories, people, coins, dollar signs, and other symbols that can be incorporated into the graphic (Figure 2-36). Figure 2-37 shows an example of presentation graphics projected.

Using graphics software as a presentation tool allows you to efficiently create professional quality graphics that can help you communicate information more effectively. Persuasion and Harvard Graphics are two popular presentation graphics packages.

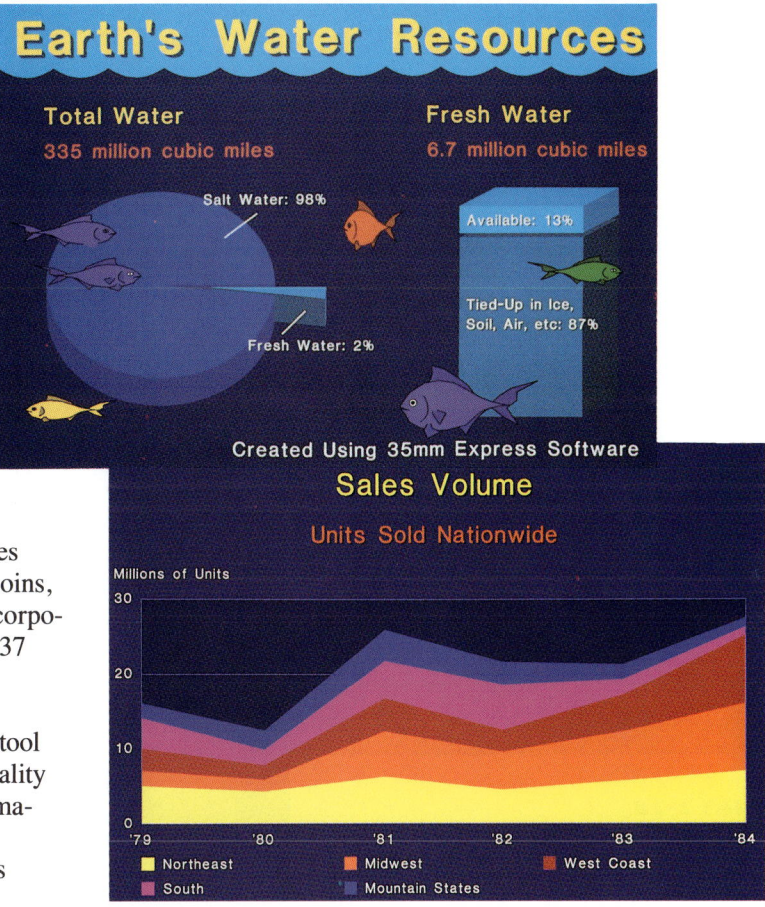

FIGURE 2-36
Examples of presentation graphics.

FIGURE 2-37
Presentation graphics can be an effective way to communicate information to a large group. Presenters can use devices such as the computer projection device shown. When this device is connected to a microcomputer, it can project everything on the microcomputer screen onto a large screen.

DATA COMMUNICATIONS SOFTWARE: A CONNECTIVITY TOOL

◆ **Data communications software** is used to transmit data from one computer to another. It gives users access to databases such as stock prices and airline schedules, and services such as home banking and shopping (Figure 2-38).

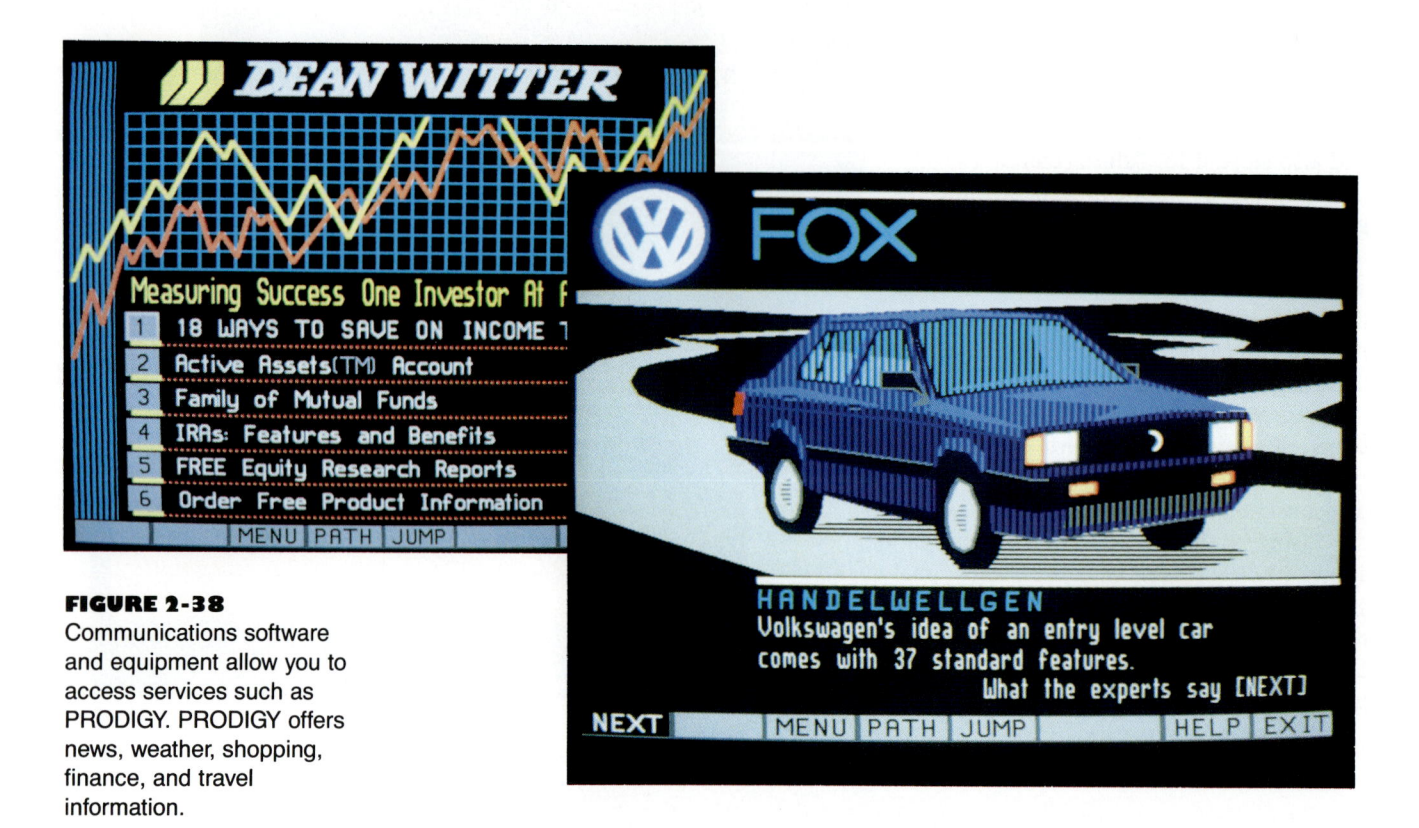

FIGURE 2-38
Communications software and equipment allow you to access services such as PRODIGY. PRODIGY offers news, weather, shopping, finance, and travel information.

For two computers to communicate, they each must have data communications software, data communications equipment, and be connected to a telephone line. To establish a communications link, you would use the data communications software to dial the phone number of the computer you want to call. Once the connection is established, you would enter commands and answer responses to control the transmission of data between the computers. Popular communication software packages include CROSSTALK Communicator and PROCOMM PLUS.

INTEGRATED SOFTWARE: A COMBINATION PRODUCTIVITY TOOL

◆ Software packages such as databases and electronic spreadsheets are generally used independently of each other. But what if you wanted to place information from a database into a spreadsheet? The data in the database would have to be reentered in the spreadsheet. This would be time consuming and errors could be introduced as you reentered the data. The inability of separate programs to communicate with one another and use a common set of data has been overcome through the use of integrated software.

Integrated software refers to packages that combine applications such as word processing, electronic spreadsheet, database, graphics, and data communications into a single, easy-to-use set of programs. The applications that are included in integrated packages are designed to have a consistent command structure; that is, the user can use the same set of common commands such as SAVE or LOAD in all the applications in the package. Besides these consistent commands, a key feature of integrated packages is their capability to pass data quickly and easily from one application to another. For example, revenue and cost information from a database on daily sales could be quickly loaded into a spreadsheet. The spreadsheet could be used to calculate gross profits. Once the calculations are completed, all or a portion of the spreadsheet data can be passed to the graphics program to create pie, bar, line, or other graphs. Finally, the graphic (or the spreadsheet) can be transferred to word processing to create a printed report. A possible disadvantage of an integrated package is that individual integrated programs may not have all the features that are available in nonintegrated packages. Two popular integrated software packages are Microsoft Works and Lotus Works.

Integrated programs frequently use windows. A **window** is a rectangular portion of the screen that is used to display information. They are called *windows* because of their capability to *see* into another part of a program. Many people consider windows to be like multiple sheets of paper on top of a desk. In the same way that each piece of paper on the desk contains different information, each window on the screen contains different information. And just as papers can be moved from the bottom of a pile to the top of the desk when they are needed, windows can be created on a screen and used to show information when it is needed. Windows are used to display a variety of information including: help information about the commands of the program you are using; text from different documents in a word processor and; different parts of a large spreadsheet. With some integrated packages, windows can be used to display data from separate applications such as a spreadsheet and a word processing document. Many programs today use windows and can display multiple windows on the screen at the same time (Figure 2-39). These programs allow you to easily move between applications by moving from one window to another.

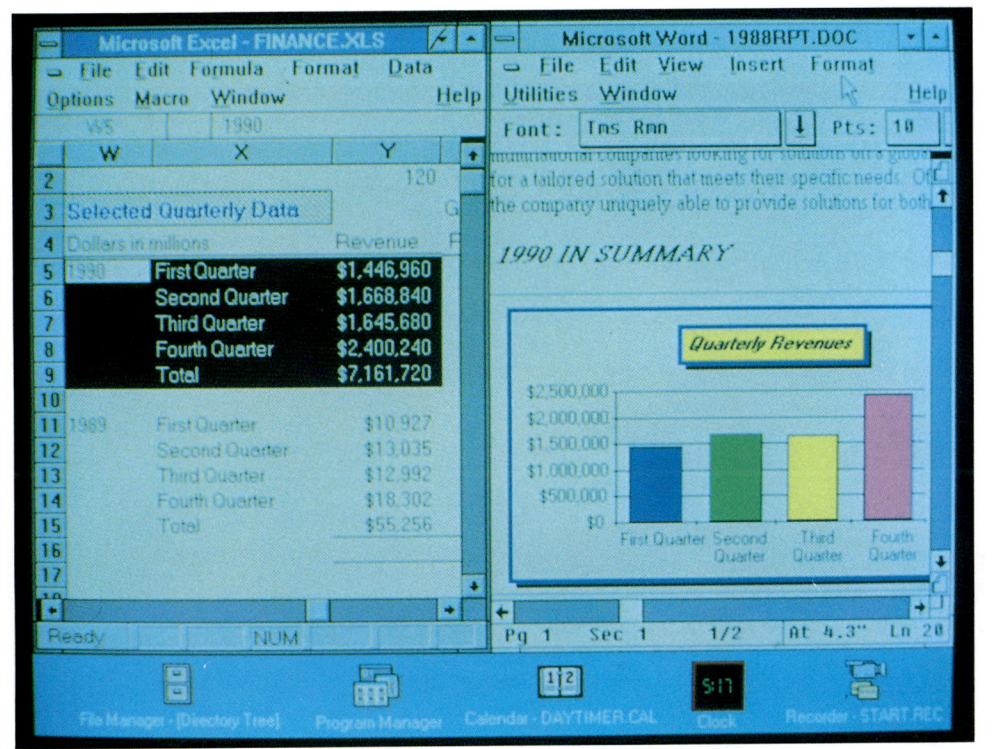

FIGURE 2-39
This screen shows two windows. The window on the left shows a spreadsheet, whereas the window on the right displays a word processing document. The user can work on information displayed in either application.

OTHER POPULAR MICROCOMPUTER APPLICATIONS

◆ The applications we have discussed so far are the most widely used microcomputer applications. Three other application areas that are becoming increasingly popular are software for personal information management, project management, and utilities.

Personal Information Management

Personal information management (PIM) software helps users keep track of the miscellaneous bits of personal information that each of us deals with every day. This information can take many forms: notes to ourselves or from others, phone messages, notes about a current or future project, appointments, and so on. Programs that keep track of this type of information, such as electronic calendars, have been around for some time. In recent years, however, such programs have been combined, or integrated, so that one package can keep track of all of a user's personal information.

Because of the many types of information that these programs can manage, it is difficult to precisely define personal information software. However, the category can be applied to programs that offer any of the following capabilities: appointment calendars, outliners, electronic notepads, data managers, and text retrieval. Some personal information software packages also include communications software capabilities such as phone dialers and electronic mail. Appointment calendars allow you to schedule activities for a particular day and time (Figure 2-40). Most of them will warn you if two activities are scheduled for the same time. Outliners allow you to *rough out* an idea by constructing and reorganizing an outline of important points and subpoints. Electronic notepads allow the user to record comments and assign them to one or more categories that can be used to retrieve the comments. Data managers are simple file management systems that allow the input, update, and retrieval of related records such as name and address lists or phone numbers. Text retrieval provides the capability to search files for specific words or phrases such as Sales Meeting. Two popular personal information management packages are Lotus Agenda and GrandView.

FIGURE 2-40
Personal information management software packages include calendars that help the user schedule and keep track of appointments.

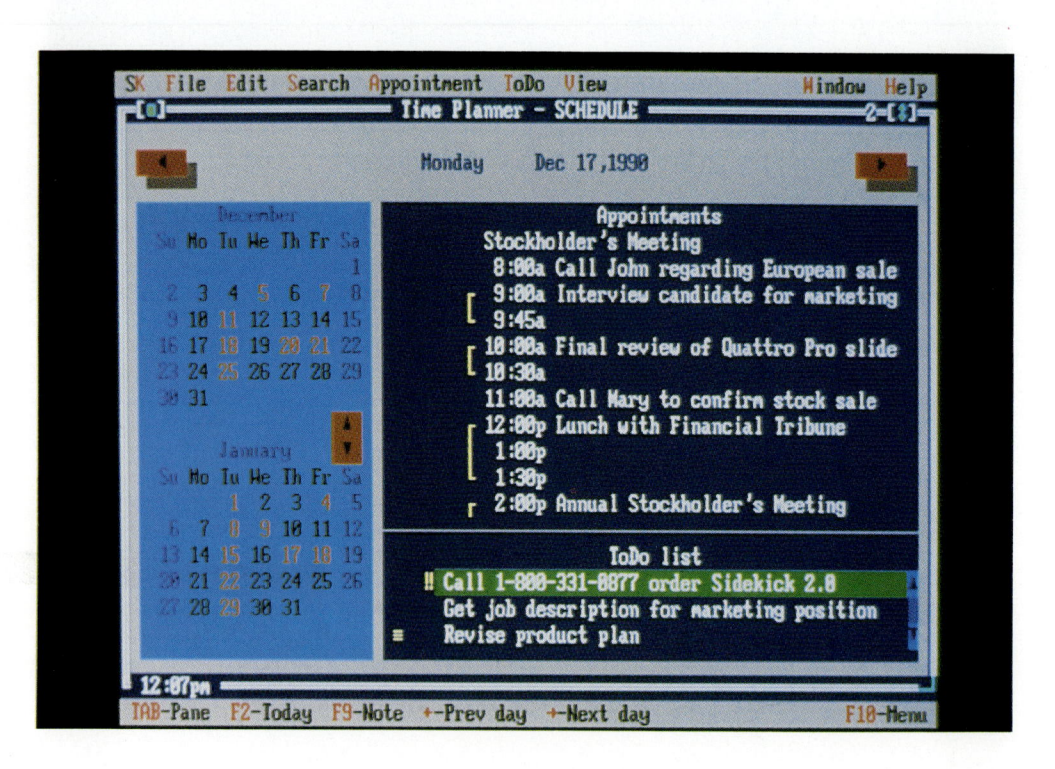

Project Management

Project management software allows users to plan, schedule, track, and analyze the events, resources, and costs of a project (Figure 2-41). For example, a construction company might use this type of software to manage the building of an apartment complex or a campaign manager might use it to coordinate the many activities of a politician running for office. The value of project management software is that it provides a method for managers to control and manage the variables of a project to help ensure that the project will be completed on time and within budget. Popular project management packages include Timeline and Microsoft Project.

FIGURE 2-41
This output was prepared using project management software. It shows the individual tasks that make up the project and the elapsed time that each task is scheduled to take.

Utilities

As its name implies, **utility software** includes a variety of programs to help you manage and maintain the data on your computer system. One of the more valuable utility features is the ability to recover *deleted* files. This is made possible by the fact that when a file is deleted, the data is still on the disk. The process of deletion only modifies the disk directory to indicate that the area of the disk that contains the file information is now available for new data. The disk directory is a special file on a disk that is used to keep track of which files are stored on the disk and where each file is located. If the data has not been overwritten, the utility software can rebuild the disk directory to allow access to the previously deleted file. Another common utility software feature is a defragmenter. When a file is written to the disk it sometimes has to be stored in separate areas because no one area is large enough to hold it all. In such cases, the file is said to be *fragmented*. The **defragmenter** analyzes and reorganizes the disk so that related file information is stored in one continuous area. Other common utility software features include visual directory listings (Figure 2-42), file management capabilities, and disk defect analysis. Popular utility software packages include the Norton Utilities (Advanced Edition), PC Tools Deluxe, and Mace Utilities.

FIGURE 2-42
This visual directory listing, sometimes called a directory tree, makes it easier to see the relationship of the files that are on a disk.

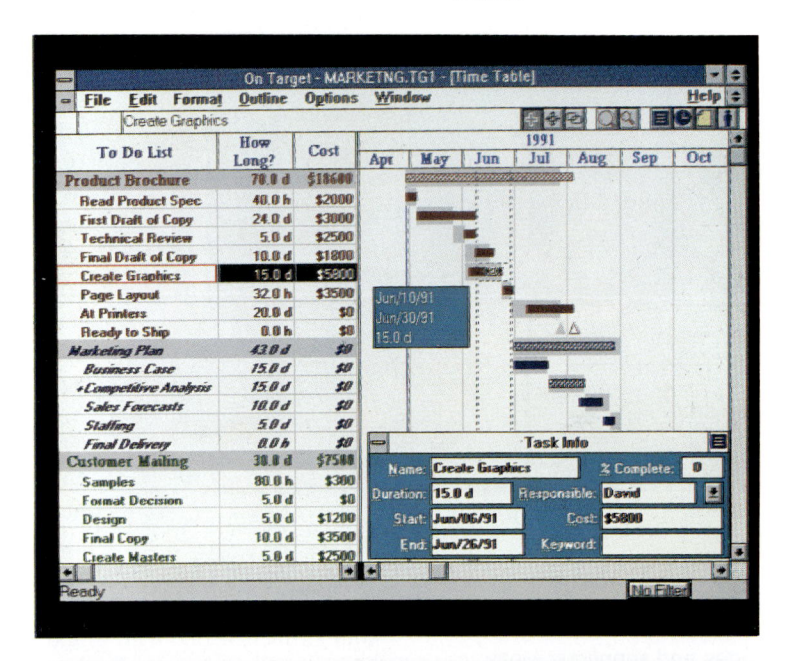

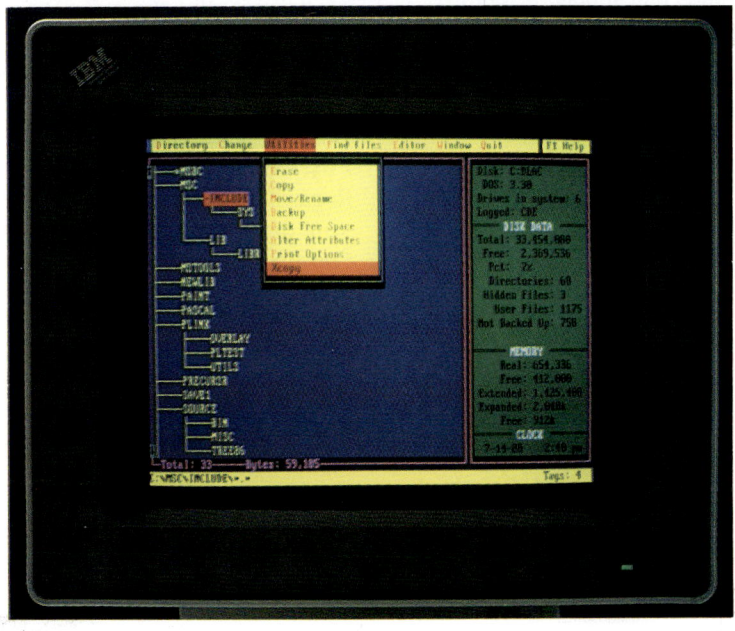

GUIDELINES FOR PURCHASING MICROCOMPUTER APPLICATIONS SOFTWARE

◆ To ensure that applications software will meet your needs, you should follow these six steps when you purchase the software (Figure 2-43).

1. **Read software product reviews.** A good place to start shopping for microcomputer applications software is in computer magazines such as *PC Magazine* and *MACWORLD*. These magazines regularly review applications packages and publish articles and charts to help you choose the package best suited to your needs.
2. **Verify that the software performs the task you desire.** In some cases, software that is supposed to perform particular functions either does not perform the functions or performs them in a manner that will be unacceptable to you. The best method of verifying that the software performs satisfactorily is to try it out prior to purchase. Many computer stores and software vendors will allow you to try software to see if it meets your needs before you purchase it. Some software developers even have special demonstration versions that allow you to try package features on a limited-use basis.
3. **Verify that the software will run on your computer.** The best way to verify this is to run the software on a computer that is the same as yours. Such factors as the number of disk drives, whether the software can run on a computer without a hard disk, main memory requirements, and graphics capabilities or requirements must be evaluated before you buy. For example, it would be unwise to purchase a package that is incompatible with your printer or one with graphics capabilities that your computer cannot handle.
4. **Make sure that the software is adequately documented.** The written material that accompanies the software is known as documentation. Even the best software may be unusable if the documentation does not clearly and completely describe what the software does, how it does it, how to recover from processing errors, and how to back up data.
5. **Purchase software from a reputable software developer or software publisher.** Regardless of the care taken, software sometimes contains errors. A reputable software developer or publisher will correct those errors or replace your software.
6. **Obtain the best value, but keep in mind that value might not mean the lowest price.** Different stores or distributors will sell the same software package for different prices. Be sure to compare prices, but also ask about product support. Sometimes a store will offer training on products that you buy from them; other vendors, such as mail order houses, provide no support or training but offer discount prices. Also, some vendors offer telephone service so that you can call to ask questions about the software.

If you keep these factors in mind when buying application software packages, you are likely to be pleased with the software you buy.

FIGURE 2-43
Shop carefully for software, evaluating the available packages and suppliers. Many people spend more on software than they do on their computer equipment.

LEARNING AIDS AND SUPPORT TOOLS FOR APPLICATION USERS

◆ Learning to use an application software package involves time and practice. In addition to taking a class to learn how to use a software application, several learning aids and support tools are available to help you including: tutorials, online help, trade books, and keyboard templates (Figure 2-44).

FIGURE 2-44
Four ways to learn application software packages are shown here.

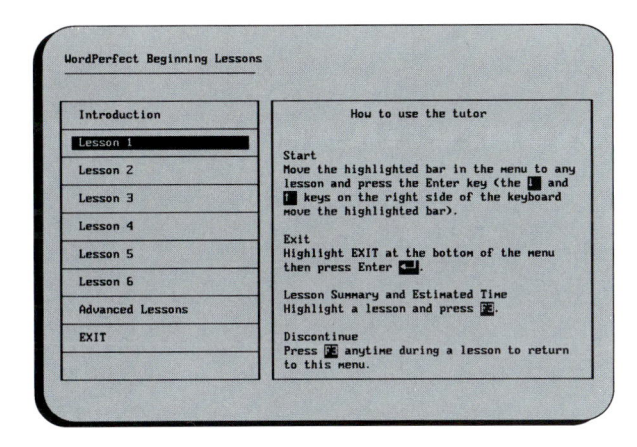

Software tutorials help you learn an application while using the actual software on your computer.

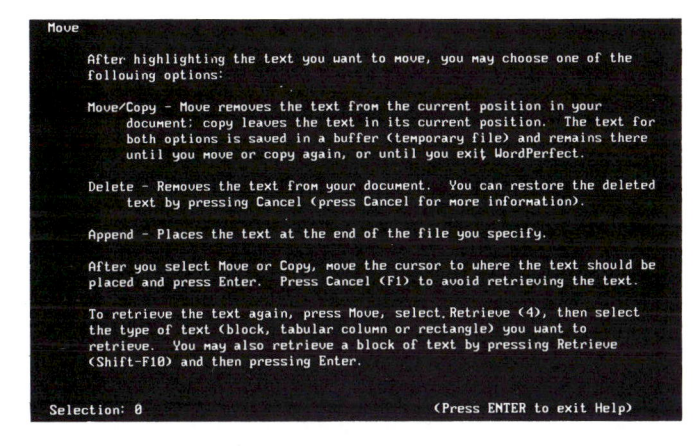

Online help gives you assistance without your having to leave the application.

Trade books are available for the popular software applications.

Keyboard templates give you quick reference to software commands.

Tutorials are step-by-step instructions using real examples that show you how to use an application. Some tutorials are written manuals, but more and more, tutorials are in the software form, allowing you to use your computer to learn about a package.

Online help refers to additional instructions that are available within the application. In most packages, a function key or special combination of keys are reserved for the help feature. When you are using an application and have a question, pressing the designated *help* key will temporarily overlay your work on the screen with information on how to use the package. When you are finished using the help feature, pressing another key allows you to return to your work.

The documentation that accompanies software packages is frequently organized as reference material. This makes it very useful once you know how to use a package, but difficult to use when you are first learning it. For this reason, many **trade books** are available to help users learn to use the features of microcomputer application packages. These books can usually be found where software is sold and are frequently carried in regular bookstores.

Keyboard templates are plastic sheets that fit around a portion of your keyboard. The keyboard commands to select the various features of the application programs are printed on the template. Having a guide to the commands readily available is helpful for both beginners and experienced users.

SUMMARY OF MICROCOMPUTER APPLICATIONS

◆ By reading this chapter, you have learned about several of the commonly used microcomputer applications. You have also learned some guidelines for purchasing microcomputer software and seen some of the learning aids and support tools that are available for applications software. Knowledge about these topics increases your computer literacy and helps you to understand how microcomputers are being used.

CHAPTER SUMMARY

1. Understanding the software applications commonly used on microcomputers is considered a part of being computer literate.
2. Software that is useful to a broad range of users is sometimes referred to as **general microcomputer applications** software.
3. **User interfaces** are methods and techniques including **function keys**, screen **prompts**, **menus**, **icons**, and a device called a **mouse** that make using an application simpler.
4. A **graphic user interface (GUI)** makes extensive use of icons to graphically represent files and processing options.
5. The most widely used microcomputer software applications are word processing, desktop publishing, electronic spreadsheet, database, graphics, and data communications.
6. **Word processing software** is used to prepare documents electronically. With word processing software you **insert**, **delete**, and **move** text.
7. The MOVE command allows you to **cut**, **copy**, and **paste** text.
8. Additional support for a word processing application can include a spelling checker, thesaurus, and grammar checker.
9. **Spelling checker software** allows you to check individual words or an entire document for correct spelling.
10. **Thesaurus software** allows you to look up synonyms for words in a document while you are using your word processor.
11. **Grammar checker software** is usually purchased separately from a word processing package and is used to identify possible grammar, writing style, and sentence structure errors.
12. Word processing software is a document productivity tool that allows you to create, edit, format, print, and store documents.
13. **Desktop publishing software** allows you to design and produce professional looking documents that contain both text and graphics.
14. **WYSIWYG** is an acronym for What You See Is What You Get and describes the capability of a desktop publishing package to display on the screen an exact image of what the printed page will look like.
15. **Electronic spreadsheet software** allows you to organize numeric data in a worksheet or table format.
16. A **spreadsheet** is composed of **rows** and **columns**. Each intersection of a row and column is a **cell**.
17. A spreadsheet cell can contain one of the following: a **label**, a **value**, or a **formula**.

18. The what-if capability of electronic spreadsheet software is a powerful feature that is widely used by management personnel for decision support information.
19. A **database** refers to a collection of data that is stored in files. **Database software** allows you to create a database and to retrieve, manipulate, and update data that you store in it.
20. Just as in a manual system, the word **file** is a collection of related data that is organized in records. Each **record** contains a collection of related facts called **fields**.
21. Information presented in the form of a graph or a chart is commonly referred to as **graphics**. Three popular graphics used to present information include **pie charts**, **bar charts**, and **line charts**.
22. **Analytical graphics** is widely used by management personnel when analyzing information and when communicating information to others within their organization.
23. **Presentation graphics** allows you to create professional quality graphics that can be used to communicate information more effectively.
24. **Data communications software** allows you to transmit data from one computer to another.
25. **Integrated software** packages combine several applications in one package and allow data to be shared between the applications.
26. **Personal information management (PIM) software** packages include capabilities such as appointment calendars, outliners, electronic notepads, data managers, and text retrieval.
27. **Project management software** allows users to plan, schedule, track, and analyze the events, resources, and costs of a project.
28. **Utility software** includes a variety of programs to help you manage and maintain the data on your computer system.
29. When you purchase software, you should follow these six steps: (1) Read software product reviews. (2) Verify that the software performs the task desired. (3) Verify that the software runs on your computer. (4) Make sure the software documentation is adequate. (5) Purchase software from a reputable developer or publisher. (6) Obtain the best value.
30. Aids such as tutorials, online help, trade books, and keyboard templates are useful in learning and using microcomputer applications.

KEY TERMS

Analytical graphics *2.16*
Bar chart *2.15*
Cell *2.10*
Clip art *2.9*
Column *2.10*
Command *2.2*
Copy *2.6*
Cursor *2.3*
Cut *2.6*
Database *2.13*
Database software *2.13*
Data communications software *2.18*
Defragmenter *2.21*
Delete *2.6*
Desktop publishing (DTP) software *2.8*
Document *2.4*
Edit *2.4*
Electronic spreadsheet *2.10*
Electronic spreadsheet software *2.10*
Field *2.13*

File *2.13*
Formula *2.10*
Function keys *2.3*
General microcomputer applications *2.2*
Grammar checker software *2.5*
Graphic user interface (GUI) *2.3*
Graphics *2.4*
Icon *2.3*
Insert *2.6*
Integrated software *2.19*
Keyboard template *2.24*
Label *2.10*
Line chart *2.15*
Menu *2.3*
Mouse *2.3*
Move *2.6*
Online help *2.23*
Paste *2.6*
Personal information management (PIM) software *2.20*
Pie chart *2.15*

Presentation graphics *2.17*
Project management software *2.21*
Prompt *2.3*
Pull-down menu *2.3*
Record *2.13*
Row *2.10*
Spelling checker software *2.5*
Spreadsheet *2.10*
Thesaurus software *2.5*
Trade books *2.24*
Tutorials *2.23*
User friendly *2.2*
User interfaces *2.2*
Utility software *2.21*
Values *2.10*
Window *2.19*
Word processing software *2.4*
WYSIWYG (What You See Is What You Get) *2.9*

REVIEW QUESTIONS

1. What is a user interface? List five examples.
2. What is general microcomputer applications software?
3. List six of the most widely used microcomputer application packages and describe how each application helps users.
4. What is a grammar checker? Give three examples of how a grammar checker works.
5. Describe three sources for art that is used in desktop publishing.
6. What are the three types of data that can be entered into a spreadsheet cell? Explain the purpose of each type of data.
7. Write a definition of the terms database and database software.
8. List the three most commonly used computer graphics. Draw an example of each.
9. Describe the advantage of using integrated software. What is a possible disadvantage? What are windows and how are they used in integrated software packages?
10. Describe how you would make a communications link between your microcomputer and another computer.
11. What is project management software and how is it used?
12. Explain why data files that have been deleted can sometimes be recovered by using a utility software application.
13. List the six steps that should be performed when purchasing software.
14. List and describe four learning aids that can help you use general microcomputer application packages.

CONTROVERSIAL ISSUES

1. As the owner of a small business you are trying to decide whether to purchase a word processor, a desktop publishing software package, or both. Some people have advised you that a word processor is all you need. Other people say you will be disappointed unless you have a desktop publishing package. Discuss the advantages and disadvantages of each option.
2. Some organizations insist that their employees use an integrated package so that data can be easily transferred between users. Other organizations let their users make individual decisions on which package they want to use for a particular application. Discuss the advantages and disadvantages of both policies.

RESEARCH PROJECTS

1. Interview a person who uses a desktop publishing package on a regular basis. Write a report on the types of documents he or she prepares. Include the person's comments on the different desktop publishing features.
2. Find someone who has developed an electronic spreadsheet. Ask him or her to review with you the formulas that he or she used in the spreadsheet.
3. Assume that you have decided to use a database package to keep track of all the members of a ski club. Define the fields that would make up your database record.

Input to the Computer

CHAPTER 3 — INPUT

OBJECTIVES

- Review the four operations of the information processing cycle: input, process, output, and storage
- Define the four types of input and how the computer uses each type
- Define data and explain the terms used to describe data: field, record, file, database
- Describe the standard features of keyboards, and explain how to use the cursor control and function keys
- Explain the three types of terminals and how they are used
- Describe several input devices other than the keyboard and terminal
- Explain user interfaces and list the features that a good user interface should have
- Discuss how data entry differs in interactive and batch processing
- List and explain the systems and procedures associated with data entry
- Explain the term ergonomics and describe some of the important features of good equipment design

The information processing cycle is basic to all computers, large or small. It is important that you understand this cycle, for much of your success in understanding computers and what they do depends on having an understanding or *feeling* for the movement of data as it flows through the information processing cycle and becomes information. In this chapter we discuss the information processing cycle focusing on input operations. We examine the nature of data and how it is organized, describe some of the devices used for input, and explain the ways that both hardware and software are designed to make input operations easier for the user. We also discuss data entry methods and the design, arrangement, and usage of equipment.

OVERVIEW OF THE INFORMATION PROCESSING CYCLE

◆ As we saw in Chapter 1, the information processing cycle consists of four operations: input, processing, output, and storage (Figure 3-1). Regardless of the size and type of computer, these operations process data into a meaningful form called information.

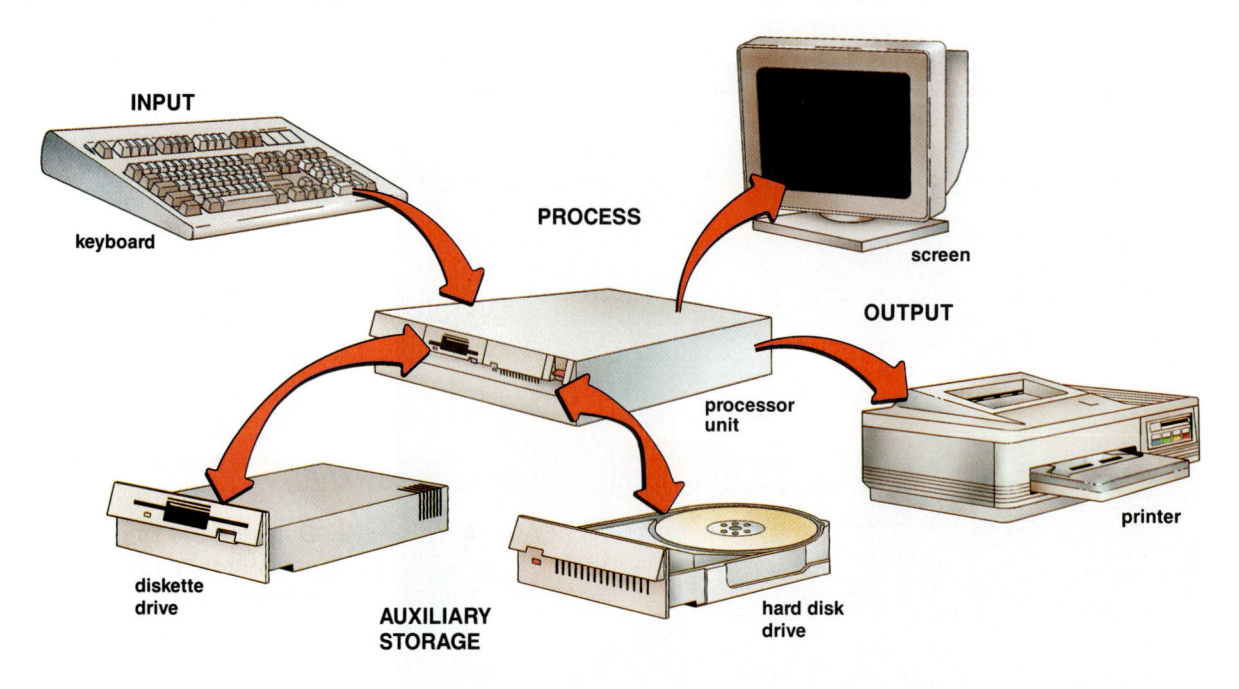

FIGURE 3-1
A computer consists of input devices, the processor unit, output devices, and auxiliary storage units. This equipment, or hardware, is used to perform the operations of the information processing cycle.

The operations in the information processing cycle are carried out through the combined use of computer equipment, also called computer hardware, and computer software. The computer software, or programs, contain instructions that direct the computer equipment to perform the tasks necessary to process data into information. In the information processing cycle, the input operation must take place before any data can be processed and any information produced and stored.

WHAT IS INPUT?

◆ **Input** refers to the process of entering programs, commands, user responses, and data into main memory. Input can also refer to the media (e.g., disks, tapes, documents) that contain these input types. These four types of input are used by a computer in the following ways:

- **Programs** are instructions that direct the computer to perform the necessary operations to process data into information. The program that is loaded and stored in main memory determines the processing that the computer will perform. When a program is first created it is input by using a keyboard. Once the program has been entered and stored on auxiliary storage, it can be transferred to main memory by a command.
- **Commands** are key words and phrases that the user inputs to direct the computer to perform certain activities. For example, if you wanted to use a payroll program, you might issue a command such as LOAD "PAYROLL" to load the program named

PAYROLL into main memory from auxiliary storage. To begin the execution of the program you would enter another command such as RUN (Figure 3-2).

- **User responses** refer to the data that a user inputs to respond to a question or message from the software. Usually these messages appear on a screen and the user responds through a keyboard. One of the most common responses is to answer "Yes" or "No" to a question. Based on the answer, the computer program will perform specific actions. For example, typing the letter Y in response to the message "Do you want to save this file?" will result in the file being saved (written) to the auxiliary storage device.
- **Data** refers to the raw facts, including numbers and words, that a computer receives during the input operation and processes to produce information. Data must be entered and stored in main memory for processing to occur. For example, data entered from sales orders can be processed by a computer program to produce sales reports useful to management. Data is the most common type of input.

Because data is such an important part of the input operation it is important for you to understand what data is and how it is organized.

FIGURE 3-2
In this example, the computer user first entered a command to load the program called "PAYROLL" and then issued the command RUN, which will execute the program.

HOW IS DATA ORGANIZED?

Data is comprised of **characters**. These characters are classified as **alphabetic** (A–Z), **numeric** (0–9), or **special** (all characters other than A–Z and 0–9 such as ()*&%#@,). The raw facts that we refer to as data are made up of a combination of these three kinds of characters. In the monthly sales application example shown in Figure 3-3, the date 01/31 is made up of the numeric characters 0 1 3 and the special character /. In the payroll example (Figure 3-4), the Social Security number contains numeric characters and the special character -. The name Haynes contains only alphabetic characters.

FIGURE 3-3
By itself, the month-ending date, 01/31, is not as useful as when it is related to the monthly sales amount.

```
       MONTHLY SALES

    MONTH        MONTH
    END          SALES
    01/31        $55,273.61
    02/28        $61,177.84
    03/31        $77,143.56

    TOTAL        $193,595.01
```

FIGURE 3-4
The Social Security number becomes more meaningful when it is related to an employee name and pay rate.

```
              PAYROLL REGISTER

    SOCIAL         EMPLOYEE      PAYCHECK
    SECURITY       NAME          AMOUNT

    332-98-8776    HAYNES        $327.00
    776-09-9731    JOHNSON       $265.45
    751-07-3452    RADCLIFFE     $289.67
```

Each fact or unique piece of data is referred to as a **data item**, **data field**, or simply a **field**. Fields are classified by the characters that they contain. For example, a field that contains only alphabetic characters, such as the name field which contains Haynes, is called an **alphabetic field**. A field that contains numeric characters is called a **numeric field**. Numeric fields may also contain some special characters that are commonly used with numbers such as a decimal point (.) and the plus (+) and minus (–) signs. Even with the plus sign (+) and decimal point (.), the number + 500.00 is still called a numeric field. Fields that contain a combination of character types, such as the date 01/31 (numeric and special characters), are called **alphanumeric fields**. Although the word *alphanumeric* implies only alphabetic and numeric characters, it also includes fields that contain special characters. The term alphanumeric is used to describe all fields that do not fall into the alphabetic or numeric classifications.

A field is normally most meaningful when it is combined with related fields. To illustrate, the month and day 01/31 by itself is not as useful as when it is related to monthly sales (Figure 3-3). Also, the Social Security number 332-98-8776 is more useful when it is related to the name HAYNES and to the paycheck amount $327.00 (Figure 3-4). Because related fields are more meaningful if they are together, fields are organized into groups called records.

A **record** is a collection of related fields. Each record normally corresponds to a specific unit of information. For example, a record that could be used to produce the payroll report in Figure 3-4 is illustrated in Figure 3-5. The fields in the record are the Social Security number, employee name, and paycheck amount. This example shows that the data in each record is used to produce a line on the payroll report. The first record contains all the data concerning the employee named HAYNES. The second record contains all the data concerning the employee named JOHNSTON. Each subsequent record also contains all the data for a given employee. Thus, you can see how related data items are grouped together to form a record.

FIGURE 3-5
The records of this payroll file are stored one after another on magnetic tape. The file contains the Social Security number, name, and paycheck amount for all employees.

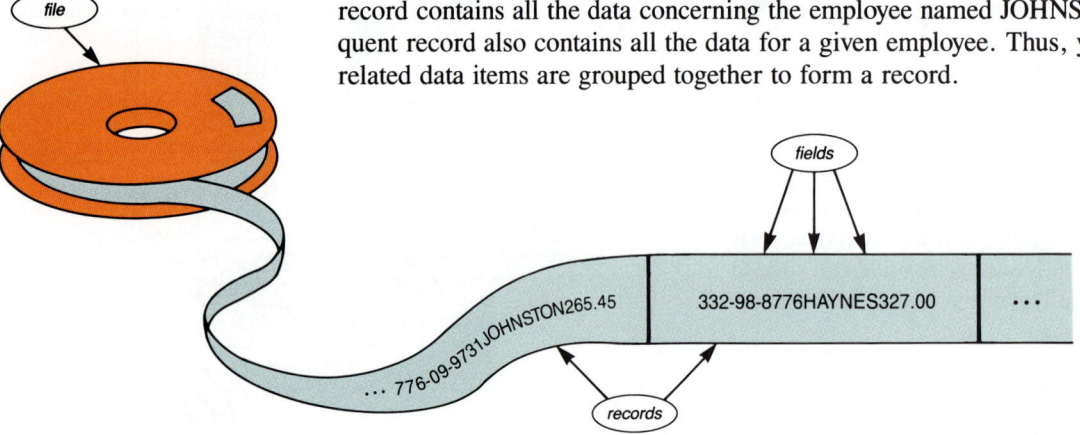

A collection of related records is called a **file**. The payroll file in Figure 3-5, for example, contains all the records required to produce the payroll register report. Files on a computer are usually stored on magnetic tape or magnetic disk.

Data is frequently organized in a **database**. As we discussed in Chapter 2, a database provides an efficient way to establish a relationship between data items and implies that a relationship has been established between multiple files. Data that has been organized in a database can be efficiently manipulated and retrieved by a computer.

In this section we have defined the terms used to describe how data is organized. We have seen that the smallest elements of data are alphabetic, numeric, and special characters and that these characters are used to build the fields, records, files, and databases that are manipulated by an information system to create information.

Data and the other types of input, programs, commands and user responses, will all be entered through an input device. The next section of this chapter discusses the various types of available input devices.

THE KEYBOARD

◆ The **keyboard** is the most commonly used input device. Users input data to a computer by pressing the keys on the keyboard. Keyboards are connected to other devices that have screens, such as a personal computer or a terminal. As the user enters data through the keyboard, the data appears on the screen.

The keyboards used for computer input are very similar to the keyboards used on the familiar office machine, the typewriter. They contain numbers, letters of the alphabet, and some special characters (Figure 3-6). In addition, many computer keyboards are equipped with a **numeric keypad** on the right-hand side of the keyboard. These numeric keys are arranged in an adding machine or calculator format and aid the user with numeric data entry.

Keyboards also contain keys that can be used to position the cursor on the screen. A **cursor** is a symbol, such as an underline character or an arrow, that indicates where on the screen the next character entered will appear. The keys that move the cursor are called **arrow keys** or **cursor control keys**. Cursor control keys have an up arrow, a down arrow, a left arrow, and a right arrow. When you press any of these keys, the cursor moves one space in the same direction as the arrow. In addition, many keyboards contain other cursor control keys such as the Home key, which when you press it can send the cursor to a beginning position such as the upper left position of the screen or document.

Some computer keyboards also contain keys that can alter or edit the text displayed on the screen. For example, the Insert and Delete keys allow characters to be inserted into or deleted from data that appears on the screen.

Function keys are keys that can be programmed to accomplish certain tasks that will assist the user. For example, a function key might be programmed for use as a help key when a terminal is used for word processing. Whenever the key is pressed, messages will appear that give helpful information about how to use the word processing software. Function keys can also save keystrokes. Sometimes several keystrokes

FIGURE 3-6
The IBM PS/2 Model 30 keyboard contains a numeric keypad, cursor control keys, and function keys. The keys on the numeric keypad are arranged in the same order as the keys on an adding machine or a calculator. This arrangement allows people who are skilled in entering numbers to input numeric data at a much faster rate than if the number keys were positioned across the top of the keyboard as they are on a typewriter. The four cursor control keys are identified by up ↑, down ↓, left ←, and right → arrows. When the user presses one of these keys, the cursor moves one position in the direction indicated by the arrow. Function keys are used for specific commands that are either programmed by the user or determined by the application software. Function keys can be in different places, but on most keyboards they are either on the left side or along the top.

are required to accomplish a certain task, for example, printing a document. Some application software packages are written so that the user can either enter the individual keystrokes or press a function key and obtain the same result.

The disadvantage of using a keyboard as an input device is that training is required to use it efficiently. Users who do not know how to type are at a disadvantage because of the time they spend looking for the appropriate keys. While other input devices are appropriate in some situations, users should be encouraged to develop their keyboard skills.

TERMINALS

Terminals, sometimes called **display terminals** or **video display terminals (VDTs)**, consist of a keyboard and a screen. They fall into three basic categories: dumb terminals, intelligent terminals (sometimes called programmable terminals) and special-purpose terminals. We explain the features of each type in the following sections. Figure 3-7 shows a dumb and an intelligent terminal.

FIGURE 3-7
A dumb terminal (left) and a group of intelligent terminals (right). From appearance alone, it is often difficult to tell in which category a terminal belongs. Intelligent terminals have built-in processing capabilities.

Dumb Terminals

A **dumb terminal** consists of a keyboard and a display screen that can be used to enter and transmit data to or receive and display data from a computer to which it is connected. A dumb terminal has no independent processing capability or auxiliary storage and cannot function as a stand-alone device.

Intelligent Terminals

Intelligent terminals have built-in processing capabilities and often contain not only the keyboard and screen, but also disk drives and printers. Because of their built-in capabilities, these terminals can perform limited processing tasks when they are not communicating directly with the central computer. Intelligent terminals are also known as **programmable terminals** or **smart terminals** because they can be programmed by the user to perform many basic tasks, including arithmetic and logic operations. Personal computers are frequently used as intelligent terminals (Figure 3-8).

FIGURE 3-8
This personal computer can function as both a stand-alone computer or as a terminal when it is connected to another computer system.

As the amount of processing power that is incorporated into intelligent terminals increases, more processing can occur at the site of the terminal. This means that the large minicomputer or mainframe at the central site can perform the main processing and serve multiple users faster, rather than having to use its resources to perform tasks that can be performed by the intelligent terminal.

FIGURE 3-9
This point-of-sale terminal has been specifically designed for use in a restaurant. The operator can press separate keys to enter the prices of certain menu items.

Special-Purpose Terminals

Terminals are found in virtually every environment that generates data for processing on a computer. While many are general terminals like those we previously described, others are designed to perform specific jobs and contain features uniquely designed for use in a particular industry.

The terminal shown in Figure 3-9 is called a point-of-sale terminal. **Point-of-sale (POS) terminals** allow data to be entered at the time and place where the transaction with a customer occurs, such as in fast-food restaurants or hotels, for example. Point-of-sale terminals serve as input to either minicomputers located at the place of business or larger computers located elsewhere. The data entered is used to maintain sales records, update inventory, make automatic calculations such as sales tax, verify credit, and perform other activities associated with the sales transactions and critical to running the business. Point-of-sale terminals are designed to be easy to operate, requiring little technical knowledge. As shown in Figure 3-9, the keys are labeled to assist the user.

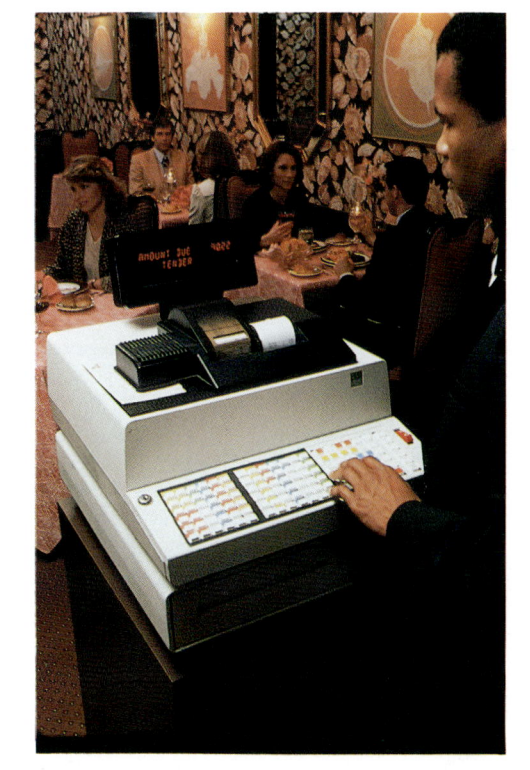

OTHER INPUT DEVICES

Besides keyboards and terminals, there is an increasing variety of other input devices. This section describes some of the devices used for general-purpose applications.

Mouse

The mouse is a unique device used with personal computers and some computer terminals. A **mouse** is a small, lightweight device that easily fits in the palm of your hand. You move it across a flat surface such as a desktop (Figure 3-10) to control the movement of the cursor on a screen.

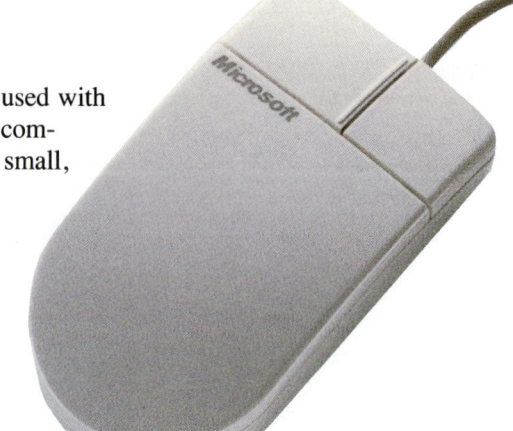

FIGURE 3-10
The mouse can be moved to control the cursor on the screen. You press the button on the top of the mouse to make selections or perform functions, depending on the software you are using. The ball on the underside of the mouse moves as you push the mouse around on a hard, flat surface. The movement of the ball causes the cursor to move correspondingly on the screen.

The mouse is attached to the computer by a cable. On the bottom of the device is a small ball. As the mouse moves across the flat surface, the computer electronically senses the movement of the ball. The movement of the cursor on the screen corresponds to the movement of the mouse (Figure 3-11). When you move the mouse left on the surface of the table or desk, the cursor moves left on the screen. When you move the mouse right, the cursor moves right, and so on.

On top of the mouse are one or more buttons. By using the mouse to move the cursor on the screen and pressing the buttons on the mouse, you can perform many actions such as making menu selections, editing a word processing document, and moving data from one point on the screen to another.

The primary advantage of a mouse is that it is easy to use. Proponents of the mouse say that with a little practice, a person can use a mouse to point to locations on the screen just as easily as using a finger.

There are two major disadvantages of the mouse. The first is that it requires empty desk space where it can be moved about (Figure 3-12). The second disadvantage is that the user must remove a hand from the keyboard and place it on the mouse whenever the cursor is to be moved or a command is to be given. Some keyboard experts have noted that taking hands from the keyboard slows the speed of data entry considerably.

FIGURE 3-11
Here, a mouse is being moved from one side to another. This action will result in the cursor moving from one side of the screen to the other. The buttons on top of the mouse can be used instead of keys on the keyboard.

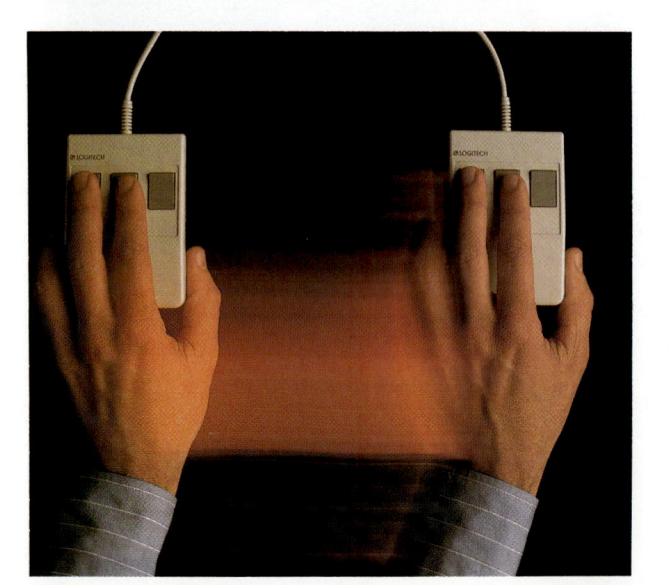

FIGURE 3-12
Notice that some amount of clear desk space is required for moving the mouse.

Thus, some people have said the mouse is not an effective tool in those environments where keying must be performed rapidly, such as in word processing applications. Others, however, say that using a mouse is far superior to using the cursor control keys on a keyboard.

Trackball

A **trackball** is a graphic pointing device like a mouse only with the ball on the top of the device instead of the bottom (Figure 3-13). To move the cursor with a trackball, all you have to do is rotate the ball in the desired direction. With a mouse, you have to move the entire device. To accommodate movement with both the fingers and palms of a hand, the ball on top of a trackball is larger than the ball on the bottom of a mouse. The main advantage of a trackball over a mouse is that it doesn't require the clear desk space.

Touch Screens

Touch screens allow users to touch areas of the screen to enter data. They let the user interact with a computer by the touch of a finger rather than typing on a keyboard or moving a mouse. The user enters data by touching words or numbers or locations identified on the screen (Figure 3-14).

Several electronic techniques change a touch on the screen into electronic impulses that can be interpreted by the computer software. One of the most common techniques uses beams of infrared light that are projected across the surface of the screen. A finger or other object touching the screen interrupts the beams, generating an electronic signal. This signal identifies the location on the screen where the touch occurred. The software interprets the signal and performs the required function.

Touch screens are not used to enter large amounts of data. They are used, however, for applications where the user must issue a command to the software to perform a particular task or must choose from a list of options to be performed.

There are both advantages and disadvantages to touch screens. A significant advantage is that they are very *natural* to use; that is, people are used to pointing to things. With touch screens, users can point to indicate the processing they want performed by the computer. In addition, touch screens are usually easy for the user to learn. As quickly as pointing a finger, the user's request is processed. This is considerably faster than repeatedly pressing arrow keys to move the cursor from one location on the screen to another.

FIGURE 3-13
The trackball is similar to the mouse but does not require the same amount of clear desk space. The user rotates the ball to move the cursor and then presses one of the keys shown at the top of this trackball device.

FIGURE 3-14
Touch screens allow the user to make choices and execute commands by actually touching areas of the screen. Touch screens require special software that determines where the user touched the screen and what action should be taken.

There are some disadvantages to touch screens. First, the resolution of the touching area is not precise. Thus, while a user can point to a box or a fairly large area on the screen and the electronics can determine the location of the touch, it is difficult to point to a single character in a word processing application, for example, and indicate that the character should be deleted. In cases such as these, a keyboard is easier to use. A second disadvantage is that after a period of reaching for the screen, the user's arm might become tired.

Graphic Input Devices

Graphic input devices are used to translate graphic input data, such as photos or drawings, into a form that can be processed on a computer. Three devices that are often used for graphic input are light pens, digitizers, and graphics tablets. A **light pen** is used by touching it on the display screen to create or modify graphics (Figure 3-15). An electronic grid on the screen senses the light generated at the tip of the light pen when it is touched to the screen. A **digitizer** converts points, lines, and curves from a sketch, drawing, or photograph to digital impulses and transmits them to a computer (Figures 3-16 and 3-17). The user indicates the data to be input by pressing one or more buttons on the hand-held digitizer device. A **graphics tablet** works in a manner similar to a digitizer, but it also contains unique characters and commands that can be automatically generated by the person using the tablet (Figure 3-18).

Pen Input Devices

Pen input devices allow the user to input hand-printed letters and numbers to record information. These devices work with a type of hand-held computer sometimes called *scratchpad computers*. These systems consist of a flat screen and the pen device (Figure 3-19). As the characters are printed, special circuitry records the movement of the pen on the screen.

FIGURE 3-15
Placing the light pen at a point on the screen activates a sensing device within the pen. The activated pen transmits the location of the light to the computer, where the program can perform the desired tasks.

FIGURE 3-16
The device in the engineer's hand reads and translates the coordinates on the drawing into data that can be stored in the computer and later used to reproduce the drawing on a screen or a printer.

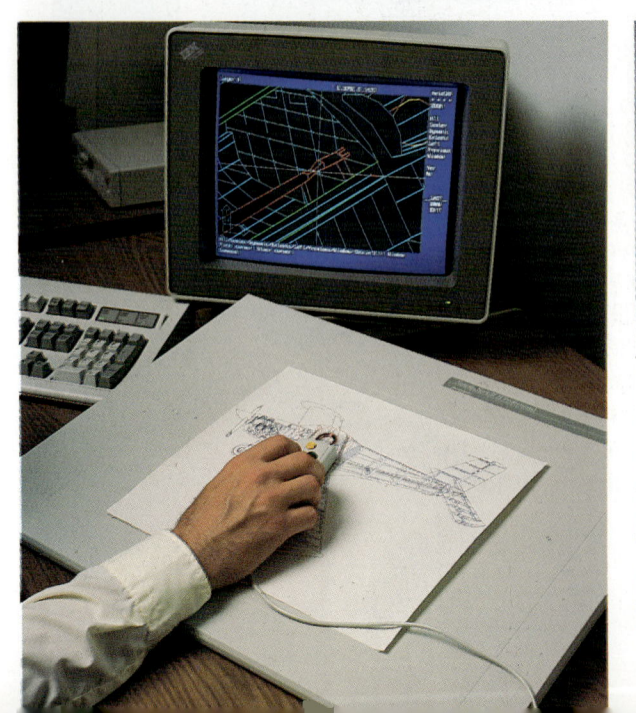

FIGURE 3-17
Digitizers are used to create original drawings or to trace and reproduce existing drawings quickly and accurately.

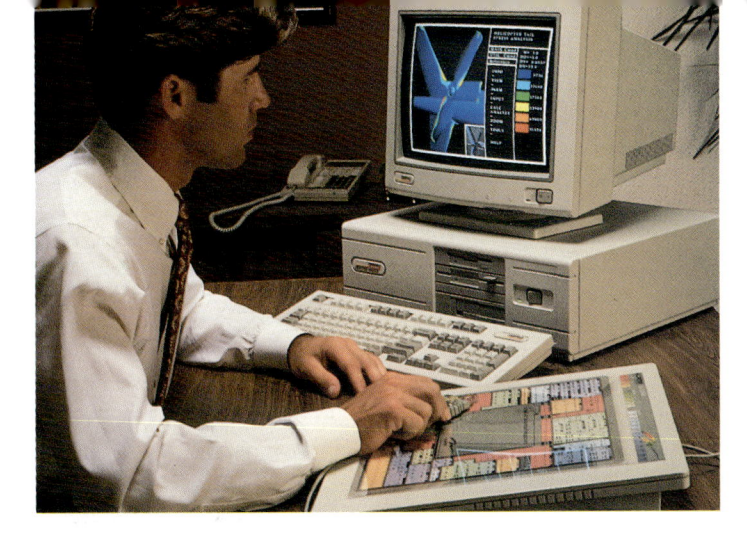

FIGURE 3-18
The color template on the graphics tablet allows the user to select processing options by placing a hand-held device over the appropriate location on the tablet and pressing a button.

The computer translates the pen strokes into characters. The characters are then processed as text or as a user response to a message displayed on the screen. The advantage of pen input systems is that many workers who may have a difficult time using a keyboard can use the more familiar pen to enter data.

FIGURE 3-19
Pen input systems allow the user to use an electronic pen to enter data or select processing options without using a keyboard. This method is easy to learn by individuals who have worked with a pencil and paper.

Voice Input

One of the more exciting recent developments is the use of voice input, sometimes referred to as voice or speech recognition. As the name implies, **voice input** allows the user to enter data and issue commands to the computer with spoken words (Figure 3-20).

Most systems require the user to *train* the system to recognize their voice by first speaking the words that will be used a number of times. As the words are spoken, they are digitized by the system; that is, they are broken down into digital components that the computer can recognize. After each word has been spoken several times, the system develops a digital pattern for the word that can be stored on auxiliary storage. When the user later speaks a word to the system to request a particular action, the system compares the word to words that were previously entered and that it is trained to *understand*. When it finds a match, the software performs the activity associated with the word. For example, in voice-controlled word processing systems, spoken words can control such functions as single- and double-spacing, choosing type styles, and centering text. The major advantage of voice input is that the user does not have to key, move, or touch anything to enter data into the computer. Many experts believe that voice input will be used extensively in the years to come.

FIGURE 3-20
Voice input systems allow the user to enter data without using the keyboard. The microphone headset is attached to the personal computer. Special software and hardware are used to interpret the voice commands.

INPUT DEVICES DESIGNED FOR SPECIFIC PURPOSES

◆ Some input devices are designed to perform specific tasks. Examples are scanners, MICR readers, and data collection devices.

Scanners

Scanners include a variety of devices that *read* printed codes, characters, or images and convert them into a form that can be processed by the computer. This section describes several different types of scanning devices.

Page Scanners A **page scanner** is an input device that can electronically capture an entire page of text or images such as photographs or art work (Figure 3-21). The scanner converts the text or image on the original document into digital information that can be stored on a disk and processed by the computer. The digitized information can be printed or displayed separately or merged into another document such as a newsletter. Hand-held devices that can scan a portion of a page are also available (Figure 3-22) as well as color scanners.

Image Processing Much of the data input to a computer is taken from source documents. Usually, you input only a portion of the data on the source document, but sometimes you might find it necessary to store the entire source document, such as legal document with a signature or a drawing. In these situations, organizations often implement image processing systems. **Image processing systems** use software and special equipment, including scanners, to input and store an actual image of the source document. These systems are like electronic filing cabinets that allow users to rapidly access and review exact reproductions of the original documents (Figure 3-23).

FIGURE 3-21
This scanner can input text, graphics, or photographs for use in word processing or desktop publishing applications.

FIGURE 3-22
A hand-held scanner can enter text or graphics less than a page wide. Software allows you to join separately scanned items to make up a complete page.

FIGURE 3-23
Image processing systems record and store an exact copy of a document. These systems are often used by insurance companies that may need to refer to any of hundreds of thousands of documents.

3.13

FIGURE 3-24
Most modern grocery stores use optical scanning devices such as the one shown here. A laser beam, emitted from the opening on the counter, reads the bar code on the product package. Most retail products have the Universal Product Code (UPC) imprinted somewhere on the label or package (located at the bottom of the can in the photo below). The UPC code uniquely identifies both the manufacturer and the product. The scanning device is connected to a computer system that uses the UPC code to look up the price of the product and add the price into the total sale. A keyboard above the scanner is used to code the numbers for items such as fruit, which do not have UPC labels.

Laser Scanners A scanning device often used by modern grocery stores at checkout counters is a **laser scanner**, also called a **bar code reader** (Figure 3-24). These devices use a laser beam to scan and read the special bar code printed on the products.

Optical Character Readers Optical character recognition (OCR) devices are scanners that read typewritten, computer-printed, and in some cases hand-printed characters from ordinary documents. OCR devices range from large machines that can automatically read thousands of documents per minute to hand-held wands (Figure 3-25).

FIGURE 3-25
This hand-held optical character recognition device is being used to read a typed document one line at a time. Other OCR devices can scan an entire page at one time.

FIGURE 3-26
The full OCR-A standard character set. Characters such as B and 8, S and 5, and 0 and the letter O are designed so the reading device can easily distinguish between them.

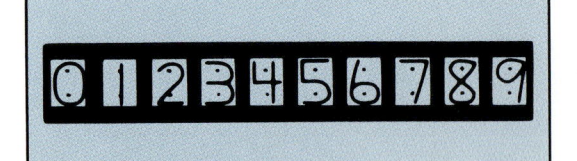

FIGURE 3-27
These hand-printed characters can be read by some types of OCR devices. The two small dots in each square identify where certain portions of each numeric digit must be placed.

An OCR device scans the shape of a character on a document, compares it with a predefined shape stored in memory, and converts the character into the corresponding computer code. The standard OCR typeface, called OCR-A, is illustrated in Figure 3-26. The characters can be read easily by both humans and machines. OCR-B is a set of standard characters widely used in Europe and Japan.

Some optical character readers can read hand-printed characters. Building a machine capable of reading and interpreting hand-printed characters is a challenging task even in this era of high technology. The characters must be carefully printed according to a strict set of rules regarding their shapes. The example in Figure 3-27 illustrates the shape of hand-printed characters that can be read with an OCR device.

The most widespread application of OCR devices is for reading turn-around documents prepared by computer printers. A **turn-around document** is designed to be returned to the organization in which it was originally issued. When the document is returned (*turned around*), the data on it is read by an OCR device. For example, many utility bills, department store bills, insurance premium statements, and so on request that the consumer return the statement with a payment (Figure 3-28). The statement is printed with characters that can be read by OCR devices. When the customer returns it, the machine reads it to give proper credit for the payment received. Some OCR devices, such as the one shown at the bottom of this page in Figure 3-28, are small enough to fit on top of a desk.

Optical Mark Readers An **optical mark reader (OMR)** is a scanning device that can read carefully placed pencil marks on specially designed documents. The pencil marks on the form usually indicate responses to questions and can be read and interpreted by a computer program. Optical mark readers are frequently used to score tests (shown on the next page in Figure 3-29).

FIGURE 3-28
Here, utility company payment receipts are being read by an OCR device. These receipts are examples of turn-around documents because they were designed to be returned to the utility with the customer's payment.

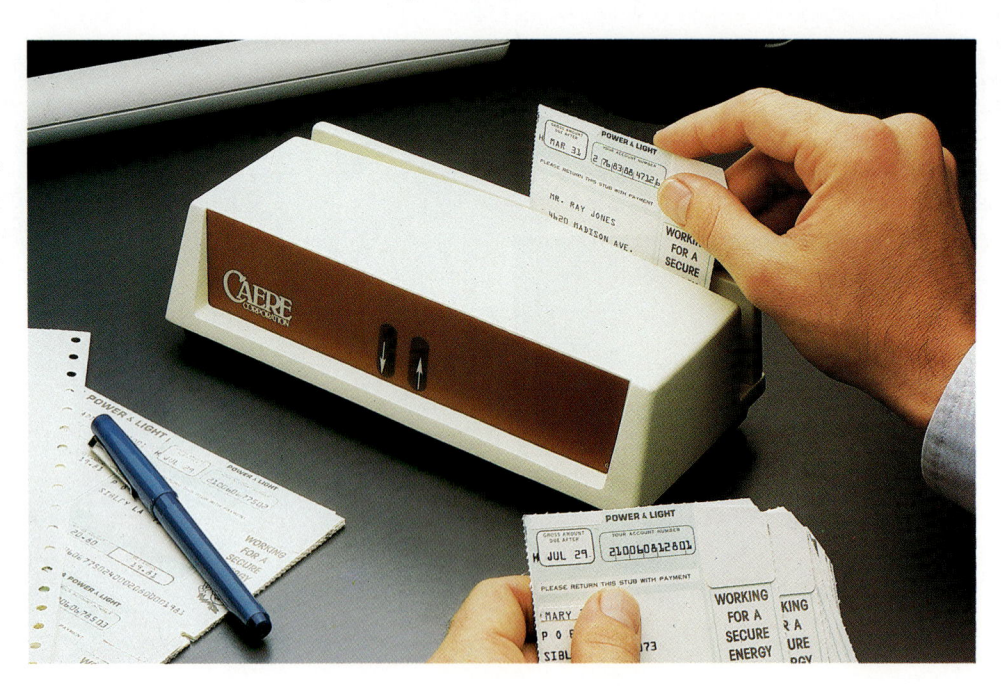

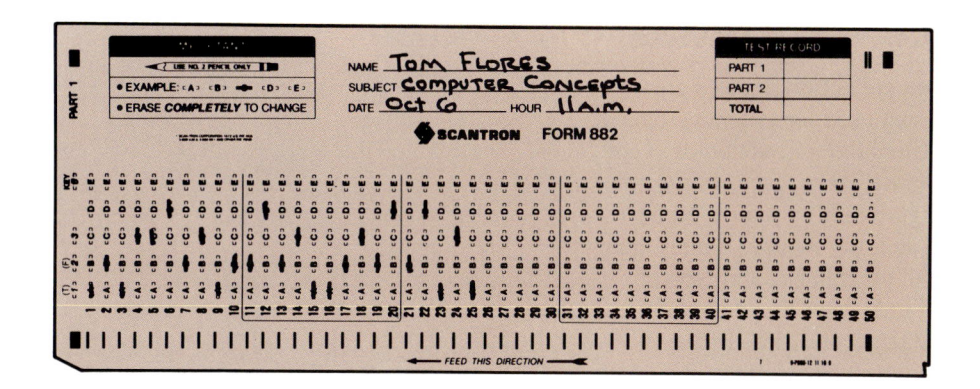

INPUT DEVICES DESIGNED FOR SPECIFIC PURPOSES **3.15**

FIGURE 3-29
The pencil marks made on this test answer sheet can be read by an optical mark reader. The reader can mark the incorrect answers, report the number of correct answers, and report the average score of all tests.

MICR Readers

MICR readers, used almost exclusively in the banking industry for processing checks, are a type of input device. **MICR (magnetic ink character recognition)** is a type of machine-readable data. In the 1950s, the industry chose MICR as the method to be used to encode and read the billions of checks written each year.

When MICR is used, special characters encoded on checks identify such items as the bank number and the account number. When a check is processed, the amount is added to the previously encoded data. The MICR characters (Figure 3-30) use a special ink that can be magnetized during processing. MICR readers interpret the electronic signals generated from the magnetized characters so checks can be sorted and processed to prepare bank statements for customers. MICR devices can process over 1,000 checks per minute (Figure 3-31). MICR also is used in utility companies, credit card companies, and other industries that must process large volumes of data.

FIGURE 3-30
The characters at the bottom of the check are being read by the magnetic ink character recognition (MICR) device. Banks in the United States and in many foreign countries use these codes for checks.

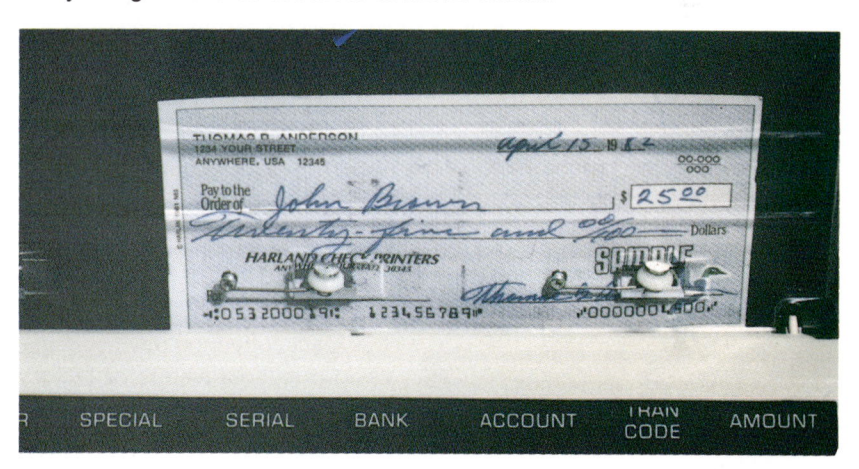

FIGURE 3-31
This MICR reader-sorter can process over a thousand documents per minute. After the documents are read, they are sorted into the vertical bins on the right side of the machine. This device can be connected directly to a computer to allow the documents to be input as they are read.

Data Collection Devices

Many **data collection devices** are designed and used for obtaining data at the site where the transaction or event being reported takes place. For example, in Figure 3-32, a man is taking inventory in a warehouse. Rather than write down the number and type of items and then enter this data, he uses a portable data collection device to record the inventory count in the device's memory. After he takes the inventory, he can transmit the data to a computer for processing.

Sometimes data collection equipment is needed in environments where heat, humidity, and cleanliness are difficult or impossible to control (Figure 3-33). In addition, these devices are often used by people whose primary task is not entering the data. Entering the data is only a small portion of their job duties. Data collection devices used in this manner must be designed and built for use in uncontrolled environments and they must be easy to operate.

Using data collection devices can provide important advantages over alternative methods of input. Because the data is entered as it is collected, clerical costs and transcription errors are reduced or eliminated. If the data collection devices can be connected directly to the computer, the data is immediately available for processing.

Data collection devices range from portable devices that can be carried throughout a store or factory to sophisticated terminal systems with multiple input stations that feed directly into a central computer (Figure 3-34). These devices will continue to improve and find increased use in data entry applications.

FIGURE 3-32
This portable data collection device is being used to take an inventory in a warehouse. The data is stored in memory and can later be transferred to a computer system for processing.

FIGURE 3-33
This data collection terminal has been designed to accommodate the user. Data collection devices should be simple and quick to operate, so that entering the data does not interfere with the main job of the person using the terminal.

FIGURE 3-34
A data collection device located in a production area. Data collected at this station is transferred to the main computer that keeps track of total production.

Figure 3-35 summarizes the most commonly used input devices. Although each device has advantages and disadvantages, each is appropriate for specific applications.

DEVICE	DESCRIPTION
Keyboard	Most commonly used input device. Special keys may include numeric keypad, cursor control keys, and function keys.
Terminal	Can be dumb, intelligent, or special-purpose.
Mouse or Trackball	Input devices used to move the cursor on a screen and select options.
Touch screens	User interacts with the computer by touching the screen.
Graphic input	Light pens, digitizers, and graphics tablets translate graphic data into a form that can be processed by a computer.
Pen	Allows input or hand-printed characters.
Voice input	User enters data and issues commands with spoken words.
MICR reader	Used primarily in banking to read the magnetic ink characters printed on checks.
Scanner	A variety of devices that read printed codes, characters, or images.
Data collection	Used to input data where it is generated.

FIGURE 3-35
This table summarizes some of the more common input devices.

With the widespread use of terminals, personal computers, and other input devices, input operations are performed by many types of users whose computer knowledge and experience varies greatly. Some users have a limited knowledge of computers and others have many years of experience. In addition, some users interact with computers daily, while others use them only occasionally. Information systems need to provide all users with a means of interacting with the computer efficiently. This is accomplished through user interfaces.

USER INTERFACES

◆ A **user interface** is the combination of hardware and software that allows a user to communicate with a computer system. Through a user interface, users are able to input values that (1) respond to messages presented by the computer, (2) control the computer, and (3) request information from the computer. Thus, a user interface provides the means for communication between an information system and the user.

Both the hardware and software working together form a user interface. A terminal is an example of hardware that is frequently part of a user interface. The screen on the terminal displays messages to the user. The devices used for responding to the messages and controlling the computer include the keyboard, the mouse, and other types of input devices. The software associated with an interface are the programs. These programs determine the messages that are given to the user, the manner in which the user can respond, and the actions that will take place based on the user's responses.

In the following sections we discuss two of the most commonly found user interface techniques—prompts and menus—and describe how these interface techniques have improved communication between the user and the computer.

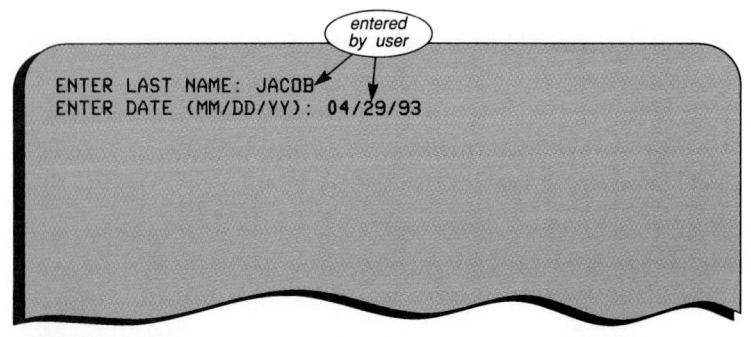

```
                              entered
                              by user
  ENTER LAST NAME: JACOB
  ENTER DATE (MM/DD/YY): 04/29/93
```

FIGURE 3-36
Prompts aid the user in entering data. They can tell the user what data to enter as well as the required format (as shown for the date entry). Prompts were one of the first types of interfaces designed to assist the user in utilizing the computer.

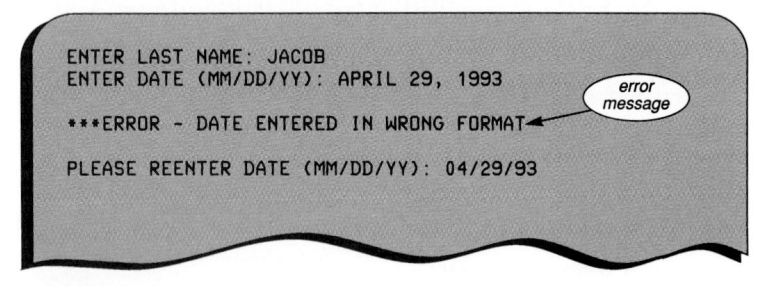

```
  ENTER LAST NAME: JACOB
  ENTER DATE (MM/DD/YY): APRIL 29, 1993
                                              error
  ***ERROR - DATE ENTERED IN WRONG FORMAT    message

  PLEASE REENTER DATE (MM/DD/YY): 04/29/93
```

FIGURE 3-37
The software used for this screen checks the date entered and gives an error message if the date is entered in the wrong format.

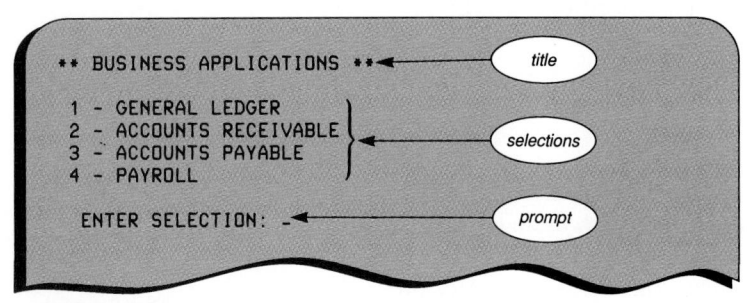

```
  ** BUSINESS APPLICATIONS **              title

  1 - GENERAL LEDGER
  2 - ACCOUNTS RECEIVABLE                selections
  3 - ACCOUNTS PAYABLE
  4 - PAYROLL

    ENTER SELECTION: _                     prompt
```

FIGURE 3-38
A menu consists of a title, the selections that can be made, and a prompt for the user to make an entry.

Prompts

A **prompt** is a message to the user that appears on the screen and provides helpful information or instructions regarding an entry to be made or action to be taken. The example in Figure 3-36 illustrates the use of prompts.

On the first line, the prompt "ENTER LAST NAME:" appears on the screen. This message tells the user to enter his or her last name. After the user enters the last name, a second prompt displays. This prompt, "ENTER DATE (MM/DD/YY):", indicates not only what the user is to enter but also exactly how the user should enter it. MM/DD/YY means to enter the date as a two-digit month number followed by a slash (/), a two-digit day number followed by a slash, and a two-digit year number. Thus, the entry 04/05/93 is valid, but 4/5/93 is not.

To help ensure that the user inputs valid data, the software should use **data editing**, the capability to check the data for proper format and acceptable values. When data is entered incorrectly, a message should appear to identify the error so the user can enter the correct data. The example in Figure 3-37 illustrates what might occur if a user does not enter data in the correct format. An error message appears and requests the user to reenter the date.

Menus

A **menu** is a screen display that provides a list of processing options for the user and allows the user to make a selection. A menu generally consists of three parts: a title, the selections, and a prompt (Figure 3-38). The title identifies the menu and orients the user to the choices that can be made. The selections consist of the words that describe each selection. The prompt asks the user to choose one of the selections.

The user can choose a menu selection in several ways. Figure 3-39 illustrates four common techniques, each of which is described as follows.

1. **Sequential Number**. Numbers are used to identify each of the selections. The user enters the number that corresponds to his or her selection and then presses the Enter key.
2. **Alphabetic Selection**. Letters of the alphabet identify the various processing options. The user enters the letter or letters that correspond to the selection and then presses the Enter key.
3. **Cursor Positioning**. The user presses the arrow or cursor control keys to position the cursor adjacent to the desired selection and then presses the Enter key.

USER INTERFACES **3.19**

4. **Reverse Video**. **Reverse video**, also called **inverse video**, means that the normal screen display, such as amber characters on a black background, is reversed to black characters on an amber background to highlight and draw attention to a certain character, word, or section on the screen. The directions instruct the user to move the reverse video from one selection to another by pressing the Spacebar (or arrow keys). Pressing the Spacebar once moves the reverse video from word processing to graphics; pressing it again highlights the database selection. When the desired selection is highlighted the user presses the Enter key to make that selection.

FIGURE 3-39
This example illustrates four different types of menus and menu selection methods.

⬥ 1

```
** BUSINESS APPLICATIONS **
1 - GENERAL LEDGER
2 - ACCOUNTS RECEIVABLE
3 - ACCOUNTS PAYABLE
4 - PAYROLL

ENTER SELECTION: _
```

⬥ 2

```
** BUSINESS APPLICATIONS **
GL - GENERAL LEDGER
AR - ACCOUNTS RECEIVABLE
AP - ACCOUNTS PAYABLE
PR - PAYROLL

ENTER SELECTION: _
```

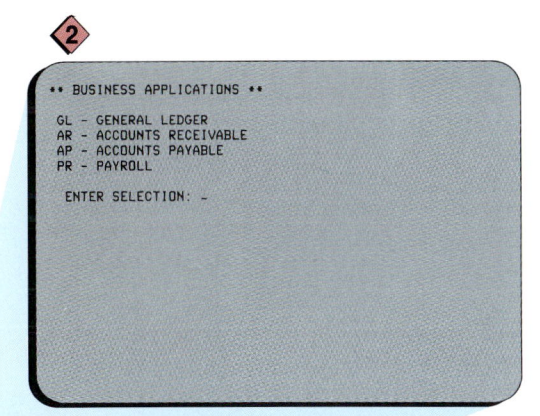

⬥ 3

```
** BUSINESS APPLICATIONS **
   \|/
 -■-GENERAL LEDGER
 /|\ ACCOUNTS RECEIVABLE
    ACCOUNTS PAYABLE
    PAYROLL

POSITION CURSOR TO MAKE SELECTION
THEN PRESS ENTER
```

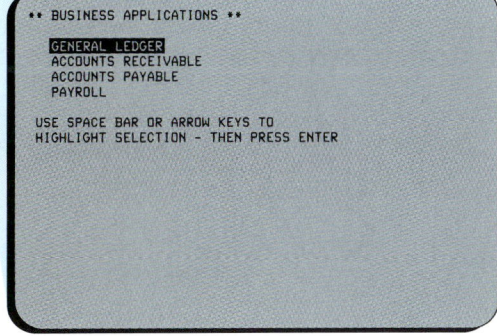

⬥ 4

```
** BUSINESS APPLICATIONS **
GENERAL LEDGER
ACCOUNTS RECEIVABLE
ACCOUNTS PAYABLE
PAYROLL

USE SPACE BAR OR ARROW KEYS TO
HIGHLIGHT SELECTION - THEN PRESS ENTER
```

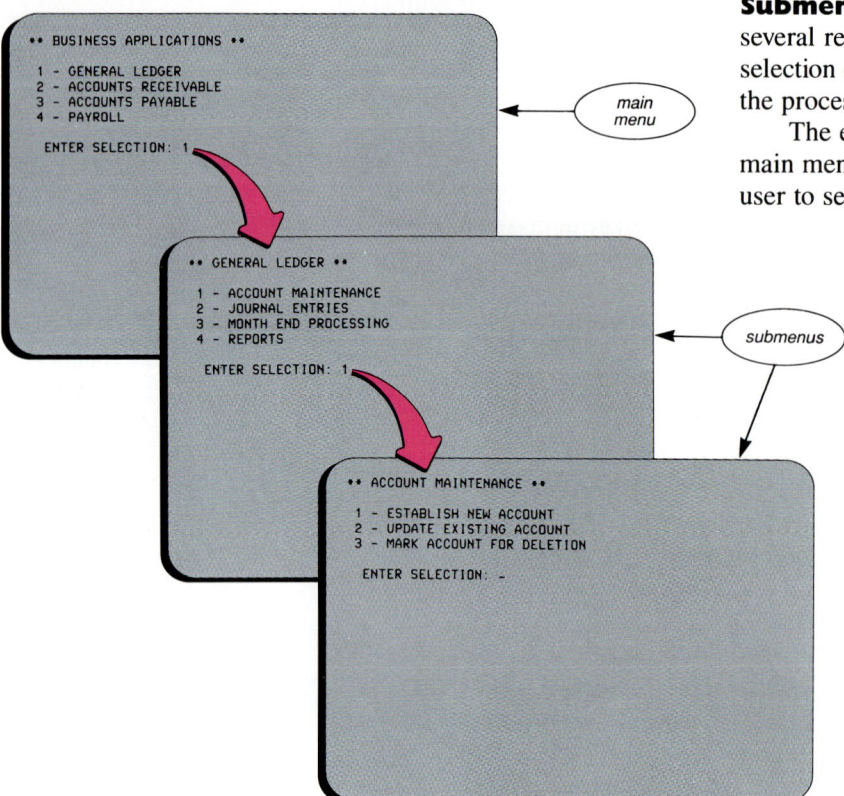

Submenus Some applications require the use of several related menus. When a user chooses a selection on a menu, a **submenu** further defines the processing options that are available.

The example in Figure 3-40 illustrates the main menu from Figure 3-38, which allows the user to select GENERAL LEDGER, ACCOUNTS RECEIVABLE, ACCOUNTS PAYABLE, or PAYROLL. Also shown are two submenus. When the GENERAL LEDGER function is selected, a submenu appears. This submenu contains more detailed functions. Depending on the submenu selection, additional menus could be displayed. For example, if the user selected option 1, ACCOUNT MAINTENANCE, a third menu would appear that displays selections relative to establishing a new account, updating an existing account, or marking an existing account for deletion.

FIGURE 3-40
A submenu is used when additional selections can be made within an application. In this example, the first submenu shows additional General Ledger selections. The second submenu shows General Ledger Account Maintenance options.

Menus: Advantages and Disadvantages Menus are a type of user interface that is used with all sizes and types of computers. There are both advantages and disadvantages to menus. Some of the advantages are:

- The user does not have to remember special commands. He or she merely chooses a selection from a list of possible operations that appear on the menu.
- The user can become productive with minimum training. Instead of having to learn a lot of technical computer information, he or she needs only to learn the application and the results of choosing a particular selection from the menu.
- The user is guided through the application because the selections that are available appear on the menus.

The disadvantage most often associated with menus, according to some experienced users, is that they can be slow and restrictive. For example, the menus illustrated in Figure 3-40 are good for the novice or infrequent computer user because they take him or her step by step through the possible operations that can be performed. The experienced user, however, knows which operations to perform. Therefore, he or she may prefer to enter a few quick commands and immediately begin work instead of having to view and respond to two or more menus. Some menus allow users to go directly to a processing option by entering a code such as the first one or two letters of the processing option name. For example, the user could enter AM to go directly to the Account Maintenance menu.

GRAPHIC USER INTERFACE

◆ A **graphic user interface (GUI)** uses on-screen pictures, called **icons** to represent data or processing options (Figure 3-41). Rather than typing a command to open a file or start a program, with a GUI, the user uses a mouse to select one of the graphic images on the screen. Although they were first developed in the early 1970s by Xerox, GUIs did not become popular until the mid 1980s when Apple introduced the Macintosh computer. Today, many software products offer a GUI. The advantages of a GUI include ease of use, a shorter learning time, and quicker execution of commands.

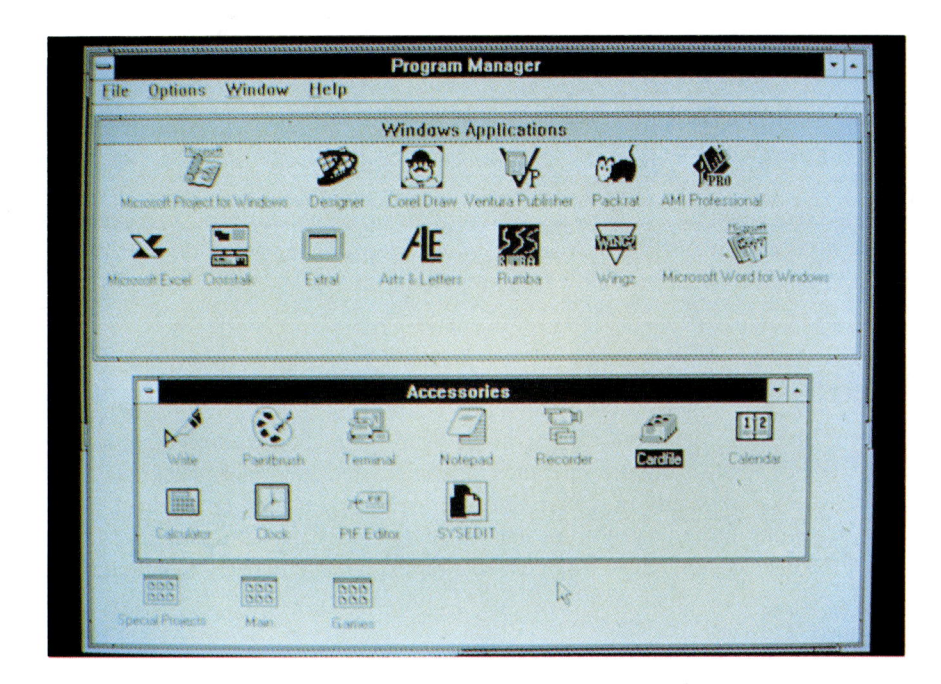

FIGURE 3-41
A graphic user interface (GUI) uses pictures (called icons) to represent data or functions that the user can select. The user selects an icon by using a mouse or similar device to place the cursor on top of the picture and then pressing a button.

FEATURES OF A USER INTERFACE

◆ The following list identifies some features that should be included in a good user interface.

1. Meaningful responses to the user—System responses are the messages a computer displays and the actions the computer takes when a user enters data into the computer. In a well-designed system, the user receives a response for every action he or she takes. Without a response, the user does not know if the computer accepted the input. A system response from the computer avoids user confusion.
2. Good screen design—The design of the messages and pictures that appear on the screen can have a significant impact on the usability of the system. The most important rule is to keep the screen uncluttered and simple. Each message and each action that a user must take should be clear and easily understood. All messages, menus, and prompts within a system should follow a consistent format. This reduces the time needed for users to learn how to use a system and increases ease of use for experienced users.
3. Simple user responses—In general, the simpler the response required from the user, the better the user interface. If the user does not have to enter a large number of characters, data entry will be faster and fewer errors will occur.

4. Error recovery procedures—Errors are inevitable, thus users should be able to easily recover from them. Whenever the user makes an error, three user interface activities should take place: (1) the user should be alerted that an error has been made; (2) the error should be identified as specifically as possible; and (3) the user should be told how to recover from the error.

5. Control and security—Many multiuser computer systems require users to *sign on* to the computer by entering identification such as a name or account number followed by a password. A **password** is a value, such as a word or number, which identifies the user. The computer will only allow a user to sign on if he or she enters the correct password. These procedures help to ensure that only authorized users obtain access to the computer.

Computer professionals should keep these features in mind when they are designing and developing user interfaces. Users should also consider them when they are evaluating software or hardware for purchase.

The question that must be asked when designing or deciding on a user interface is, *Who will be using it and what is their level of computer experience?* A good user interface must be appropriate for the people who are going to use it.

DATA ENTRY

◆ Of the four types of input—program, commands, user responses, and data—the most common type of input is data. Sometimes data is entered by professional data entry operators who are specially trained in data entry procedures and techniques. However, it is becoming more common for data to be entered at its source by users working where the data is generated. The next section explains data entry techniques.

DATA ENTRY FOR INTERACTIVE AND BATCH PROCESSING

◆ Two methods of processing data on a computer are interactive processing and batch processing. **Interactive processing** means that data is processed immediately as it is entered. In **batch processing**, data is collected and, at some later time, all the data that has been gathered is processed as a group or *batch*. As you will see in the following sections, the methods used to enter data for interactive and batch processing differ.

Data Entry for Interactive Processing

Data entered in the interactive processing mode generates immediate output. In most interactive data entry, the person entering the data is communicating directly with the computer that will process the data. Therefore, data entry for interactive processing is said to be **online data entry**, meaning that the device from which the data is being entered is connected directly to the computer.

The output generated from interactive data entry processing is not always produced at the location where the data was entered. In Figure 3-42, for example, the data is entered from a terminal located in the order entry department. The data entered concerns a purchase by a customer. After the data is entered, a picking slip is printed in

DATA ENTRY FOR INTERACTIVE AND BATCH PROCESSING **3.23**

the warehouse. The worker in the warehouse then retrieves the item purchased (in this case, a lawn mower) and packages it for shipping. The terminal operator in the order entry department never sees the output generated, yet this is interactive processing because the data entered is processed immediately.

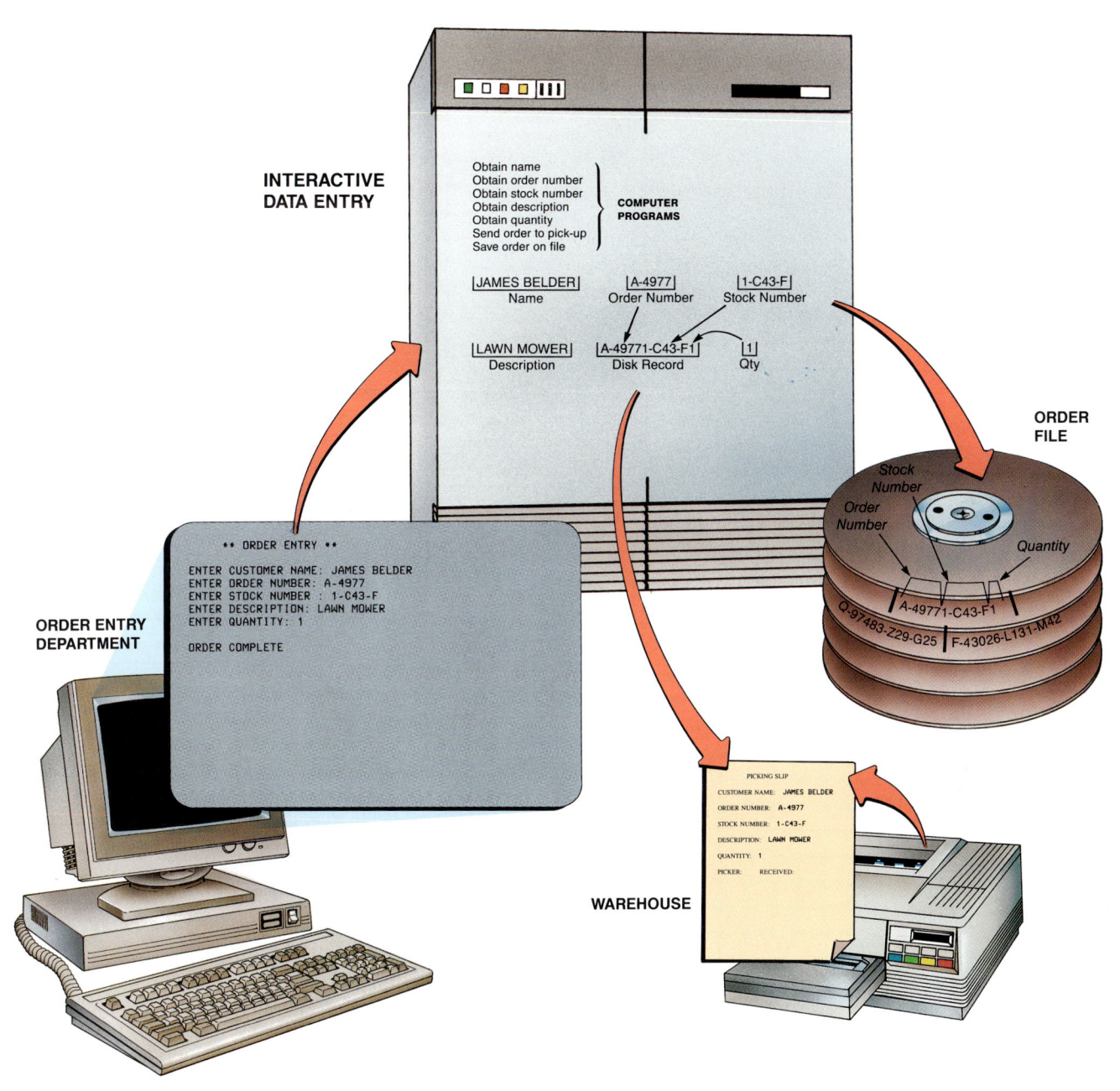

The person entering the order in the order entry department may enter hundreds of such orders each day. When large amounts of data are entered by a terminal operator whose only job is to enter the data, the data entry function is called **production data entry**.

FIGURE 3-42
In this example of data entry for interactive processing, the data is entered by a terminal operator in the order entry department. The output generated, a picking slip, is printed in the warehouse. In addition, a record of the order is stored on disk.

FIGURE 3-43

In online batch data entry, data is input directly to the computer and stored on disk or tape. At a later time, the stored data will be processed as a group by the computer.

Data Entry for Batch Processing

When data is entered for processing in the batch processing mode, it is stored on a storage medium (usually tape or disk) for processing at a later time. Data for batch processing can be entered in either an online or offline manner. As we noted previously, online data entry means that the device from which the data is being entered is connected directly to the computer that will process it (Figure 3-43).

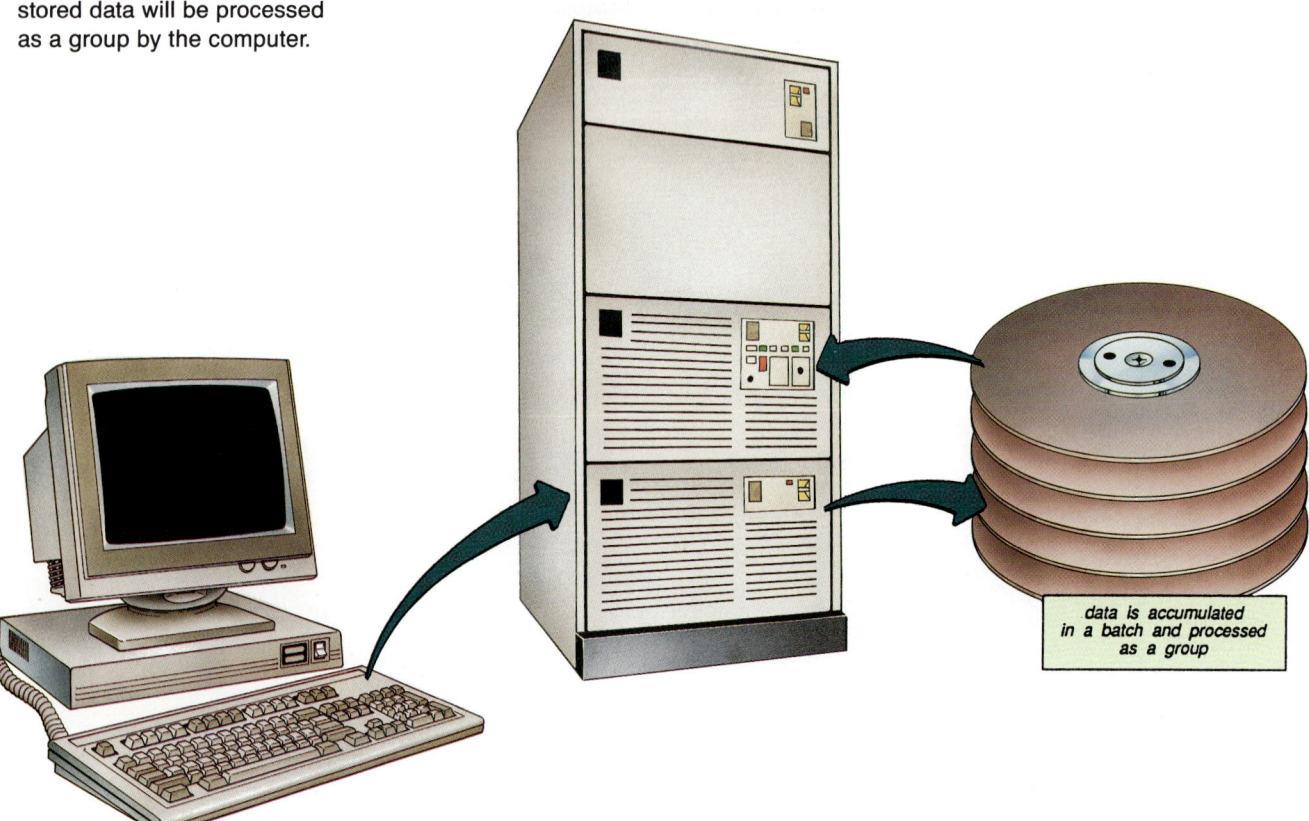

data is accumulated in a batch and processed as a group

Offline data entry means that the device from which the data is being entered is not connected to the computer that will process it (Figure 3-44). Instead, the data is entered using a dedicated computer or other device devoted to the data entry function. This computer or special device accepts the input data and stores it on disk or tape. At a later time, the disk or tape can be transported to the site where the data will be entered for processing in a batch mode to produce information.

When offline data entry is used, source documents are accumulated prior to entering the data. Then the data on these documents is entered into the computer system. For example, in a payroll application, time cards for hourly employees would be the source documents from which data entry operators would enter the hours each employee worked.

To ensure that data is entered and processed accurately, controls are established within applications. Controls are the methods and procedures that ensure the accuracy and reliability of data and processing techniques. In a credit card payment application, for example, payments are usually divided into batches for processing. The payments for each batch are added manually and recorded prior to data entry. When the payment batches are processed on the computer, the total amount of the payments calculated by the computer for each batch is compared to the total determined from the manual addition performed prior to data entry. If the totals are the same, the data was input to the computer accurately. If the totals are not the same, then either the data was entered incorrectly or the manually determined batch total was calculated incorrectly. This technique of balancing to a predetermined total is called a **batch control**.

Summary of Interactive and Batch Data Entry

Entering data to produce information can take place online or offline. Online data entry is always used for interactive processing and often for batch processing as well. Offline data entry is used for batch processing. When using offline data entry, source documents from which the data is obtained must be gathered prior to the data being entered. Regardless of the processing method, producing information often requires a large amount of data entry.

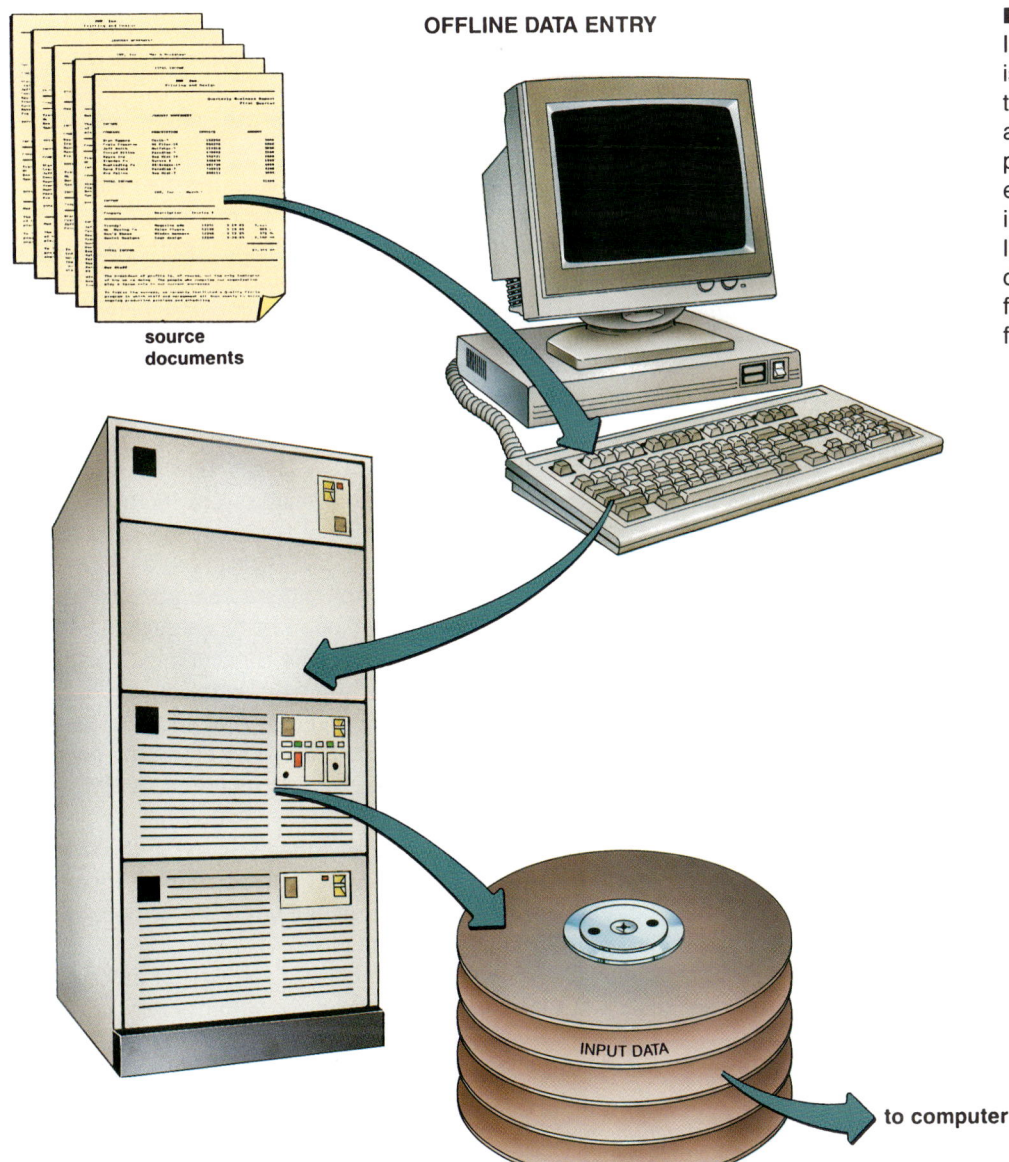

FIGURE 3-44
In offline data entry, the data is input to a computer other than the one that will eventually process it. Often computers used for offline data entry are dedicated to data input functions and perform little if any processing. The data entered is later transferred to another computer for processing.

DATA ENTRY PROCEDURES

The procedures developed for the data entry function are important because accurate data must be entered into a computer to ensure data integrity. In addition, since users are interacting directly with the computer during the data entry function, procedures and documentation must be quite clear. The following questions must be answered in order to implement a data entry application successfully:

- *Who originates the data?* Data entered for processing on a computer is generated from many sources. It is important to identify which people and operations will generate the data so that appropriate procedures can be written to specify what data is to be gathered, how it is to be gathered, and who is to gather it.
- *Where will the data be entered?* Data is generally entered either from the centralized data entry section of the information systems department or from various locations throughout an organization. The hardware, software, and personnel needs vary depending upon which of these two methods is used. In a **centralized data entry** operation, the data is keyed by trained operators from source documents. When data is entered in the centralized data entry section, it is usually processed in a batch processing mode.

    Entering data from various locations in an organization is called **distributed data entry**. Quite often the data entry takes place at the site where the data is generated, for example, sales orders being entered by the sales department. Often, data entered using distributed data entry is processed in an interactive processing mode.
- *How soon will the data be entered?* The amount of time that can elapse between when the event being reported takes place and when the data about that event must be entered should be specified. In some applications, an event can occur but the data need not be entered until hours or even days later. For example, in the payroll application, the time cards are retrieved by a clerk on Monday at 4:00 p.m. These time cards record the workers' time for the previous week. Data entry personnel might not enter this data until Tuesday. Therefore, more than a week might elapse between when the event occurred and when the data about the event was entered. In most cases when entry time is not a critical factor, the data is recorded on source documents and given to data entry personnel to enter at either a centralized or distributed location. In other applications, however, the data must be entered as the event or transaction is occurring and at the location where it is occurring. This process is sometimes called **source data collection**. For example, when a retail sale is made using a point-of-sale terminal, the data must be entered at the moment the sale is made so that the sale can be completed with the customer. Therefore, the documentation for the data entry system should specify the timing requirements for entering data.
- *How will the data be entered?* Based on many of the factors discussed in the first three questions, the procedures must specify how the data will be entered, identifying devices and methods. For example, data will be entered from source documents using terminals in an online, centralized environment.
- *How much data will be entered?* The amount of data entered for a given time period and location must be estimated. Any particularly high or low volumes may require special procedures.
- *How will data errors be identified and corrected?* The documentation must specify the editing for the entered data and the steps to take if the data is not valid. Although different applications will have specific criteria for validating input data, several tests can be performed on input data before the data is processed in a computer. Some of these tests are:
    - Tests for numeric or alphabetic data—For example, in the United States a ZIP code must always be numeric. Therefore, the program performing the editing can

check the values in the ZIP code field. If they are not numeric, the data is incorrect (Figure 3-45).

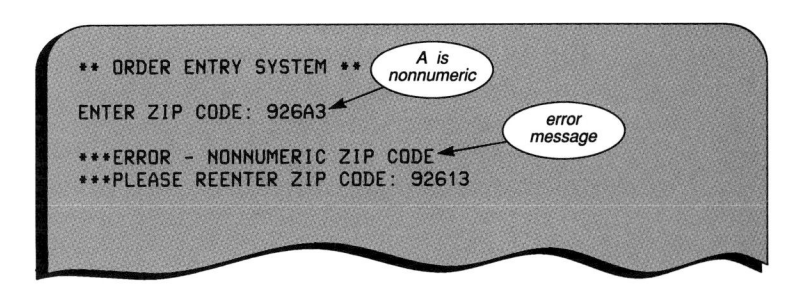

```
** ORDER ENTRY SYSTEM **          (A is nonnumeric)

ENTER ZIP CODE: 926A3

***ERROR - NONNUMERIC ZIP CODE    (error message)
***PLEASE REENTER ZIP CODE: 92613
```

FIGURE 3-45
In this example, a nonnumeric ZIP code is entered and an error message displays. When a numeric ZIP code is entered, the data is accepted and no error message displays. An additional test could be performed to match the entry against a file of valid ZIP codes.

- Tests for data reasonableness—A reasonableness check ensures that the data entered is within normal or accepted boundaries. For example, suppose no employee within a company is authorized to work more than 80 hours per week. If the value entered in the hours worked field is greater than 80, the value in the field would be indicated as a probable error.
- Tests for data consistency—In some cases, data entered cannot, by itself, be found to be invalid. If, however, the data is examined in the context of other data entered for the same record or group of fields, discrepancies might be found. For example, in an airline reservation system, passengers often purchase round-trip tickets (Figure 3-46). If the terminal operator enters the date on which the passenger is leaving, the editing program can only check whether the date entered is valid. Similarly, when the return date is entered, the program can again make sure it is a valid date. The return date can also be compared to the departure date. If the return date is earlier than the departure date, it is likely that an error has been made when entering one of the dates.
- Tests for transcription and transposition errors—There is always a possibility that an operator will make an error when entering data. A **transcription error** occurs when an error is made in copying the values from a source document. For example, if the operator keys the customer number 7165 when the proper number is 7765, the operator has made a transcription error. A **transposition error** happens when the operator switches two numbers. Such an error has occurred when the number 7765 is entered as 7756.
- *How will data be controlled?* The controls and security that will be applied to the data must be defined. This includes what the controls and security measures are, how they are to be implemented, and what action is to be taken if the security of the data is compromised in any way.
- *How many people are needed?* Specifying personnel requirements includes defining who will gather the data, who will enter it, and how many people will be required. Personnel must be educated about gathering and entering the data. They must be trained in using the equipment and software, ensuring reliable data entry, entering the data according to specified procedures, and interpreting any output received from the computer during interactive processing.

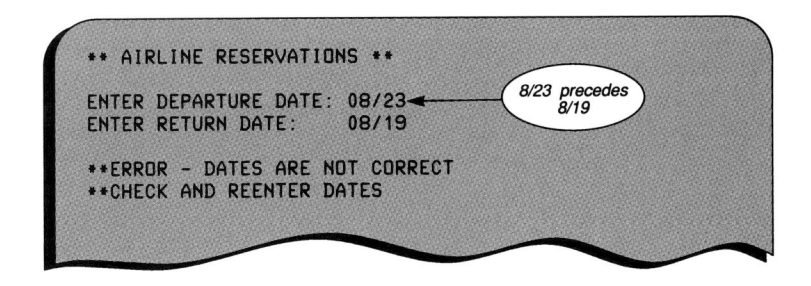

```
** AIRLINE RESERVATIONS **

ENTER DEPARTURE DATE: 08/23        (8/23 precedes 8/19)
ENTER RETURN DATE:    08/19

**ERROR - DATES ARE NOT CORRECT
**CHECK AND REENTER DATES
```

FIGURE 3-46
On this airline reservation screen, the user entered a return date earlier than the departure date and the system displayed an error message.

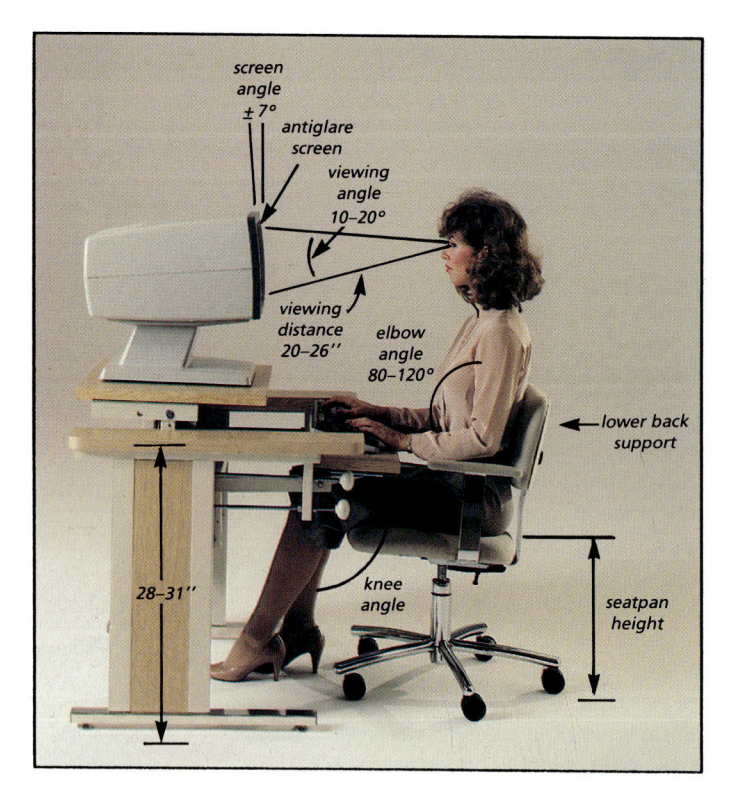

ERGONOMICS

Because of the increased use of computers, many people now spend part or all of their day in front of a computer terminal. In order to make this work environment more comfortable, many equipment manufacturers and users have turned to ergonomics. **Ergonomics** is the study of the design and arrangement of equipment so that people will interact with the equipment in a healthy, comfortable, and efficient manner. As related to computer equipment, ergonomics is concerned with such factors as the physical design of the keyboard, screens, related hardware, computer furniture, and the manner in which people interact with this equipment.

The first computer terminals contained the keyboard and screen as a single unit. The screen frequently displayed white characters on a black background. Early studies found significant user dissatisfaction with these terminals. One study reported that many of the people who used them complained of health problems, including eye fatigue, blurred vision, itching and burning eyes, and back problems. As a result of these and other studies, a number of design recommendations have been made, including the following:

1. Computer keyboards should be detached from the screen so that they can be positioned on a desk for the convenience and comfort of the user.
2. The screen should be movable, and the angle at which the user views the contents of the screen should be adjustable.
3. The screen should be high quality to eliminate any flickering of the image and characters on the screen. The characters displayed on the screen should appear as solid as possible and the images on the screen should be in sharp focus over the entire screen area.
4. The screen should have brightness and contrast adjustments.
5. The screen should have an antiglare coating. Screen glare has been a common complaint of many terminal users, and it is known that glare can be harmful to eyes. A flat screen, now used on some terminals, can also reduce glare.
6. Terminals with screens that display amber or green characters on a black background are preferable to those that display black characters on a white background or white characters on a black background.
7. The screen and keyboard should be positioned at an appropriate height for the user.
8. Users should sit directly in front of the screen and keyboard and use an adjustable chair that has a lower-back support.

Figure 3-47 illustrates some of these recommendations. The keyboard is detachable, the screen is adjustable and has an antiglare coating. The illustration also shows the use of a chair with a lower-back support. Notice the position of the user's body in relation to the terminal.

As more workers use terminals and personal computers, the importance of ergonomically designed equipment increases. Manufacturers are now aware of the importance of ergonomic design and, as a result, are designing and building terminals

FIGURE 3-47
Here, we see some of the ergonomic factors that should be considered when using a terminal for an extended period of time.

SUMMARY OF INPUT TO THE COMPUTER

In this chapter we presented an overview of the information processing cycle and discussed how data is organized. We also discussed the four types of input, a variety of input devices, user interfaces, data entry, and ergonomics. After reading this chapter you should have a better overall understanding of computer input.

CHAPTER SUMMARY

1. In the **information processing cycle** (input, processing, output, and storage), the input operation must take place before any data can be processed and any information produced and stored.
2. **Input** refers to the process of entering programs, commands, user responses, and data into main memory.
3. **Data** refers to the raw facts and consists of the numbers and words that a computer receives and processes to produce information.
4. Data is composed of **characters**. These include **alphabetic** (A–Z), **numeric** (0–9), and **special** characters, such as ()*&%#@,.
5. Individual facts are referred to as **data items**, **data fields**, or **fields**.
6. Fields may be classified as **numeric**, **alphabetic**, or **alphanumeric**.
7. A **record** is a collection of related fields.
8. A collection of related records is called a **file**.
9. Files on a computer are usually stored on magnetic tape or magnetic disk.
10. A **database** provides an efficient way to establish a relationship between data items and implies that a relationship has been established between multiple files.
11. A **cursor** is a symbol, such as an underline character or an arrow, that indicates where on the screen the next character entered will appear.
12. The **keyboard** is the most commonly used input device. Special keys may include the **numeric keypads**, **cursor control keys**, and **function keys**.
13. Terminals may be classified as **dumb terminals**, **intelligent terminals**, and **special-purpose terminals**.
14. A **mouse** is a small input device used to control the movement of the cursor and to select options displayed on the screen.
15. A **trackball** is a graphic pointing device like a mouse only with the ball on the top of the device instead of on the bottom.
16. **Touch screens** allow the user to interact with a computer by merely touching the screen.
17. **Light pens**, **digitizers**, and **graphics tablets** are **graphic input devices** used to translate graphic input data into a form that can be processed by the computer.
18. **Pen input devices** allow the user to input hand-printed letters and numbers to record information.
19. **Voice input** allows the user to enter data and issue commands to a computer with spoken words.
20. **Scanners** are devices that read printed codes, characters, or images and convert them into a form that can be processed by the computer.
21. A **page scanner** is an input device that can electronically capture an entire page of text or images such as photos and art work.
22. **Image processing systems** use software and special equipment, including scanners, to input and store an actual image of a source document.
23. A scanning device called a **laser scanner**, or a **bar code reader**, uses a laser beam to scan and read the special bar code printed on products.

24. **Optical character recognition (OCR)** devices are scanners that read typewritten, computer-printed, and in some cases hand-printed characters from ordinary documents.
25. An **Optical mark reader (OMR)** is a scanning device that can read carefully placed pencil marks on a specially designed form.
26. **Magnetic ink character recognition (MICR)** is a type of machine-readable data. **MICR readers**, used almost exclusively in the banking industry, are a type of input device used to process checks.
27. **Data collection devices** are designed and used for obtaining data at the site where the transaction or event being reported takes place.
28. A **user interface** is the combination of hardware and software that allows a user to communicate with a computer system.
29. A **prompt** is a message to the user that is displayed on the screen and provides information or instructions regarding some entry to be made or action to be taken.
30. **Data editing** is used to check input data for proper format and acceptable values. It helps to ensure that valid data is entered by the user.
31. A **menu** is a screen display that provides a list of processing options for the user and allows the user to make a selection. There are several types of menu-selection techniques including sequential number, alphabetic selection, cursor positioning, and reverse video.
32. **Submenus** are used to further define the processing options that are available.
33. A **graphic user interface (GUI)** uses on-screen pictures, called **icons** to represent data or processing options.
34. Features that relate to good interfaces include: system responses, screen design, user responses, error recovery, and control and security.
35. A **password** is a value, such as a word or number, which identifies the user.
36. **Interactive processing** means that data is processed immediately as it is entered.
37. In **batch processing**, data is collected and, at some later time, all the data that has been gathered is processed as a group or *batch*.
38. Data entry for interactive processing is said to be **online data entry**, meaning that the device from which the data is being entered is connected directly to the computer.
39. Data for batch processing can be entered in either an online or offline manner. **Offline data entry** means that the device from which the data is being entered is not connected to the computer that will process it.
40. Controls are the methods and procedures that ensure the accuracy and reliability of data and processing techniques. For example, balancing to a predetermined total is called a **batch control**.
41. Data entry procedures are important because accurate data must be entered into a computer to ensure data integrity.
42. **Centralized data entry** is performed by trained operators from source documents.
43. **Distributed data entry** often takes place at the site where the data is generated and is input to the computer by a variety of users.
44. **Source data collection** refers to data that is entered as the event or transaction is occurring and at the location where it is occurring.
45. Several tests can be performed on the input prior to processing. Some of these are numeric and alphabetic testing, tests for reasonableness and consistency, and transcription and transposition tests.
46. **Transcription errors** refer to operator errors made at the time of input, such as entering 7165 instead of 7665.
47. **Transposition errors** refer to operator errors where two characters are switched, such as entering 7756 instead of 7765.
48. **Ergonomics** is the study of the design and arrangement of equipment so that people will interact with the equipment in a healthy, comfortable, and efficient manner.

KEY TERMS

Alphabetic character 3.3
Alphabetic field 3.4
Alphanumeric field 3.4
Arrow keys 3.5
Bar code reader 3.13
Batch control 3.25
Batch processing 3.22
Centralized data entry 3.26
Character 3.3
Command 3.2
Cursor 3.5
Cursor control keys 3.5
Data 3.3
Database 3.4
Data collection device 3.16
Data editing 3.18
Data field 3.4
Data item 3.4
Digitizer 3.10
Display terminal 3.6
Distributed data entry 3.26
Dumb terminal 3.6
Ergonomics 3.28
Field 3.4
File 3.4

Function keys 3.5
Graphic input device 3.10
Graphic user interface (GUI) 3.21
Graphics tablet 3.10
Icon 3.21
Image processing system 3.12
Input 3.2
Intelligent terminal 3.6
Interactive processing 3.22
Inverse video 3.19
Keyboard 3.5
Laser scanner 3.13
Light pen 3.10
Magnetic ink character recognition (MICR) 3.15
Menu 3.18
MICR reader 3.15
Mouse 3.8
Numeric character 3.3
Numeric field 3.4
Numeric keypad 3.5
Offline data entry 3.24
Online data entry 3.22
Optical character recognition (OCR) 3.13

Optical mark reader (OMR) 3.14
Page scanner 3.12
Password 3.22
Pen input device 3.10
Point-of-sale (POS) terminal 3.7
Production data entry 3.23
Programmable terminal 3.7
Program 3.2
Prompt 3.18
Record 3.4
Reverse video 3.19
Scanners 3.12
Smart terminal 3.7
Source data collection 3.26
Special character 3.3
Submenu 3.20
Touch screen 3.9
Trackball 3.9
Transcription error 3.27
Transposition error 3.27
Turn-around document 3.14
User interface 3.17
User response 3.3
Video display terminal (VDT) 3.6
Voice input 3.13

REVIEW QUESTIONS

1. List the four operations of the information processing cycle. What types and sizes of computers use the information processing cycle?
2. What is input? What are the four types of input used by a computer?
3. What is data? What terms are used to describe how data is organized for processing?
4. Describe the different types of keys on a keyboard and how they are used.
5. Name three types of terminals. Describe how they are different.
6. How is a mouse used? Describe the advantages and disadvantages of using a mouse. How is a trackball different from a mouse?
7. How does a touch screen work? What are the advantages and disadvantages of a touch screen?
8. Describe three different types of graphic input devices.
9. Describe several applications that use scanners.
10. What types of applications use data collection devices? How do they differ from other input devices?
11. What is the purpose of a user interface?
12. Describe several commonly used user interface techniques.
13. How is a graphic user interface (GUI) different from other interface techniques?
14. Name several features that a good user interface should have.
15. What are the differences between data entry for interactive and batch processing?
16. What are some of the questions that should be answered in order to implement a data entry application?
17. What is ergonomics? Describe several ergonomic features that a terminal or personal computer workplace should have.

CONTROVERSIAL ISSUES

1. Some people believe that the keyboard and the mouse are difficult to learn and use. They believe that voice and pen input systems will someday be the most widely used input devices. Discuss the advantages and disadvantages of each type of device.
2. Some local governments have passed laws regulating the work environment of people who work with terminals. The laws address such issues as proper lighting, furniture, and the amount of time that workers can spend in front of a screen. Other organizations have passed voluntary guidelines. Do you believe that such issues should be regulated?

RESEARCH PROJECTS

1. At school or a local computer store, use a program that allows the use of both function keys and a mouse. Perform several operations using only the function keys or only the mouse. Report on which method you liked best and why.
2. Visit a retail or grocery store in your area that uses laser scanners to check out the merchandise. Ask the clerks what they like and dislike about the system they use. Report back to your class. (You may need to obtain the store manager's approval.)
3. Find a document that is used for input to the computer. Examples might be school registration forms, job applications, or membership applications. Does it appear to be well designed to help both the person completing the document as well as the person who inputs the data to the computer?
4. Visit a fast food franchise that uses point-of-sale terminals. Write a report on how orders are taken, reported to the cooks, and eventually cleared from the system.

The Processor Unit

CHAPTER 4
PROCESS

OBJECTIVES

◆ Identify the components of the processor unit and describe their use

◆ Define a bit and describe how a series of bits in a byte is used to represent characters

◆ Discuss how the ASCII and EBCDIC codes represent characters

◆ Describe why the binary and hexadecimal numbering systems are used with computer systems

◆ List and describe the four steps in a machine cycle

◆ Discuss the three primary factors that affect the speed of the processor unit

◆ Describe the characteristics of RAM and ROM memory, and list several other types of memory

◆ Describe the process of manufacturing integrated circuits

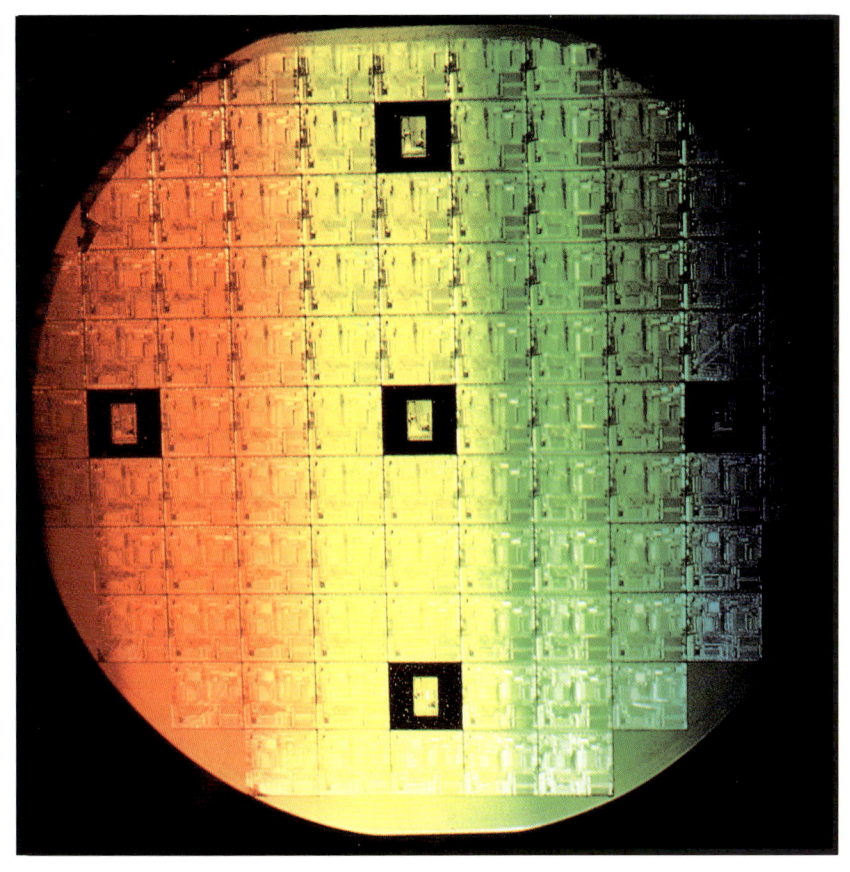

The information processing cycle consists of input, processing, output, and storage operations. When an input operation is completed and both a program and data are stored in main memory, processing operations can begin. During these operations, the processor unit executes, or performs, the program instructions and processes the data into information.

In this chapter we examine the components of the processor unit, describe how main memory stores programs and data, and discuss the sequence of operations that occurs when instructions are executed on a computer.

THE PROCESSOR UNIT

FIGURE 4-1
The processor unit of a computer contains two components: the central processing unit (CPU) and main memory. The CPU includes the control unit and the arithmetic/logic unit.

WHAT IS THE PROCESSOR UNIT?

The term computer is usually used to describe the collection of devices that perform the information processing cycle. This term is also used more specifically to describe the processor unit, because this is where the *computing* actually occurs. It is in the processor unit that the computer programs are executed and the data is manipulated. The main components of the processor unit are the central processing unit, or CPU, and the main memory (Figure 4-1).

The Central Processing Unit

The central processing unit (CPU) contains the control unit and the arithmetic/logic unit. These two components work together using the program and data stored in main memory to perform the processing operations.

The control unit can be thought of as the *brain* of the computer. Just as the human brain controls the body, the control unit *controls* the computer. The **control unit** operates by repeating the following four operations: fetching, decoding, executing, and storing. **Fetching** means obtaining the next program instruction from main memory. **Decoding** is translating the program instruction into the commands that the computer can process. **Executing** refers to the actual processing of the computer commands, and **storing** takes place when the result of the instruction is written to main memory.

The second component of the CPU is the **arithmetic/logic unit (ALU)**. This unit contains the electronic circuitry necessary to perform arithmetic and logical operations on data. **Arithmetic operations** include addition, subtraction, multiplication, and division. Often, the result of one arithmetic calculation is used in a subsequent operation. An example would be a payroll calculation where the gross pay (hours worked times pay rate) is used to calculate the payroll taxes (tax rate times gross pay). **Logical operations** consist of comparing one data item to another to determine if the first data item is *greater than*, *equal to*, or *less than* the other. Based on the result of the comparison, different processing may occur. For example, two part numbers in different records can be compared. If they are equal, the part quantity in one record can be added to the quantity in the other record. If they are not equal, the quantities would not be added.

Both the control unit and the ALU contain **registers**, temporary storage locations for specific types of data. Separate registers exist for the current program instruction, the address of the next instruction, and the values of data being processed.

Main Memory

In addition to the CPU, **main memory**, or **primary storage**, is also contained in the processor unit of the computer. Main memory (Figure 4-2) stores three items: the *operating system* that directs and coordinates the computer equipment; the *application programs* containing the instructions that will direct the work to be done; and the *data* currently being processed by the application programs. Data is stored in areas of main memory referred to as input and output areas and working storage.

The input and output areas receive and send data to the input and output devices. *Working storage* is used to store any other data that is needed for processing.

Within main memory, each storage location is called a **byte**. Just as a house on a street has a unique address that indicates its location on the street, each byte in the main memory of a computer has an address that indicates its location in memory (Figure 4-3). The number that indicates the location of a byte in memory is called a **memory address**. Whenever the computer references a byte, it does so by using the memory address, or location, of that byte.

MEMORY USAGE

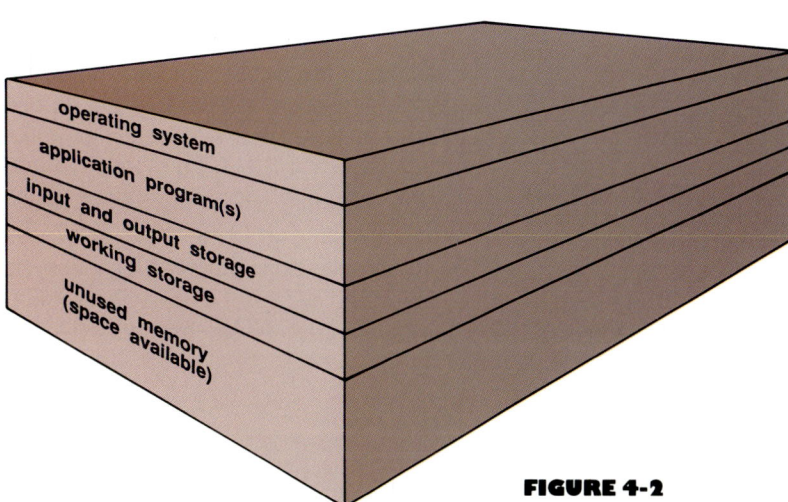

FIGURE 4-2
Main memory is used to store several types of data and programs. The amount of memory space in use changes as program instructions are executed and data is input and output.

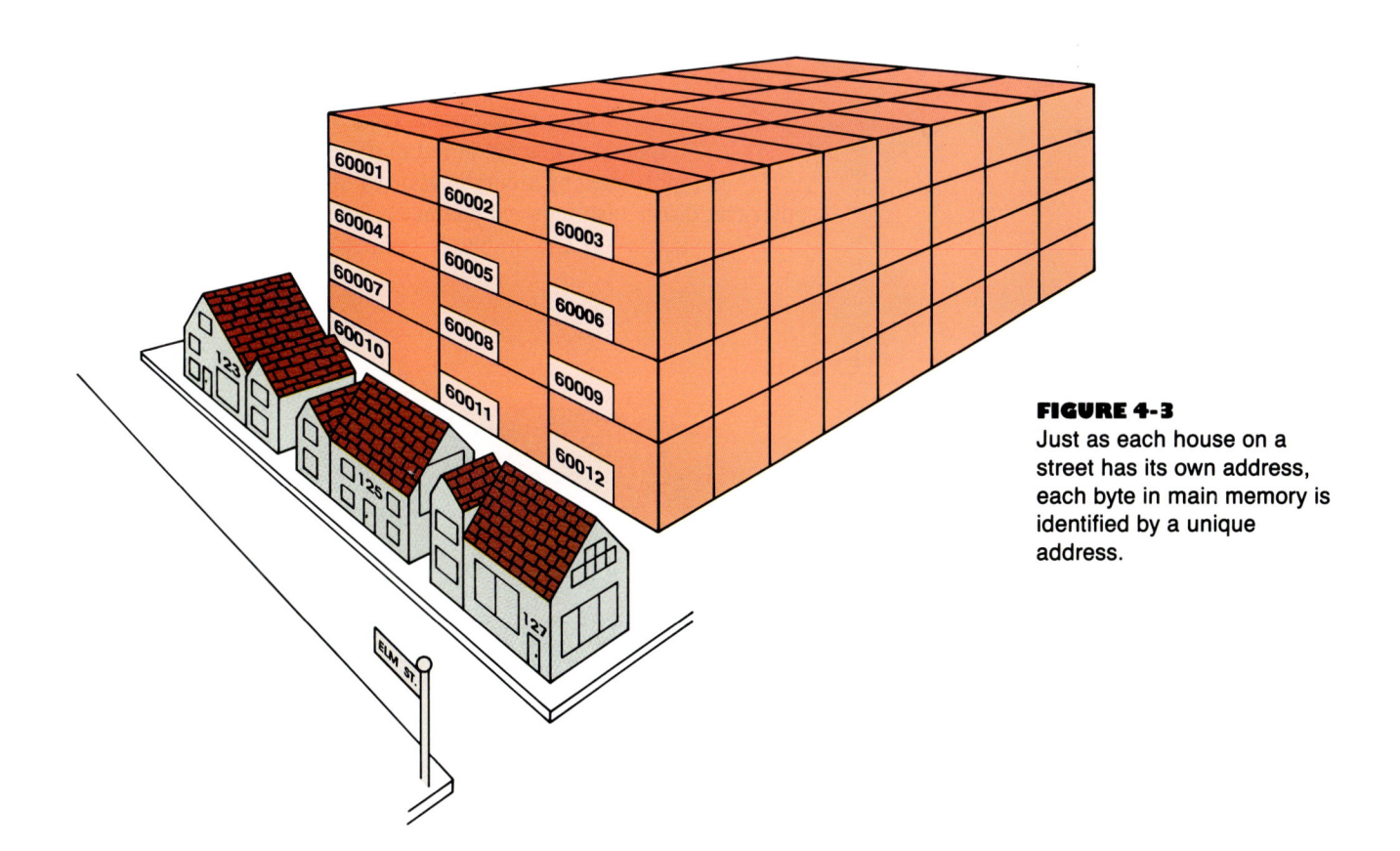

The size of main memory is normally measured in kilobytes. A **kilobyte** (abbreviated as **K** or **KB**) is equal to 1,024 bytes. Often, memory is referred to as if a kilobyte contained only 1,000 bytes. The difference between the actual and the approximate size of memory is usually unimportant and if the exact size of memory is needed, it can be calculated by using the value 1,024. For example, 640K is approximately 640,000 bytes (640 × 1,000). The exact size of 640K is 655,360 bytes (640 × 1,024). When memory exceeds 1,000K or one million bytes, it is referred to in **megabytes**, abbreviated **MB**.

FIGURE 4-3
Just as each house on a street has its own address, each byte in main memory is identified by a unique address.

HOW PROGRAMS AND DATA ARE REPRESENTED IN MEMORY

Program instructions and data are made up of a combination of the three types of characters: alphabetic (A through Z), numeric (0 through 9) and special (all other characters such as *,?/&). To understand how program instructions and data are stored in main memory, it is helpful to think of them as being stored character by character. Generally speaking, when we think of characters being stored in main memory, we think of one character being stored in one memory location, or byte. Thus, the name TOM would take three memory locations, or bytes, because there are three letters in that name. The address 125 Elm St. would take eleven memory locations, or bytes, because it contains eleven characters (including the spaces and .) (Figure 4-4).

FIGURE 4-4
Each character (alphabetic, numeric, or special) requires one memory location (byte) for storage.

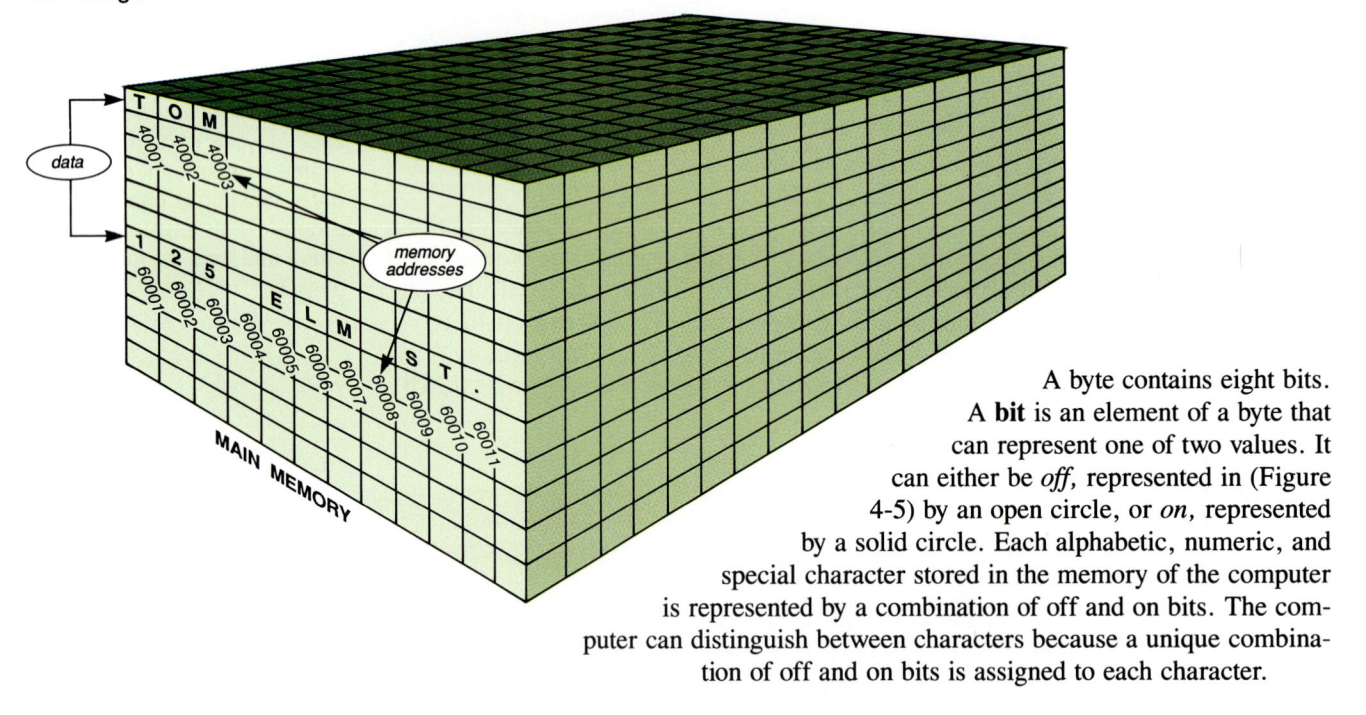

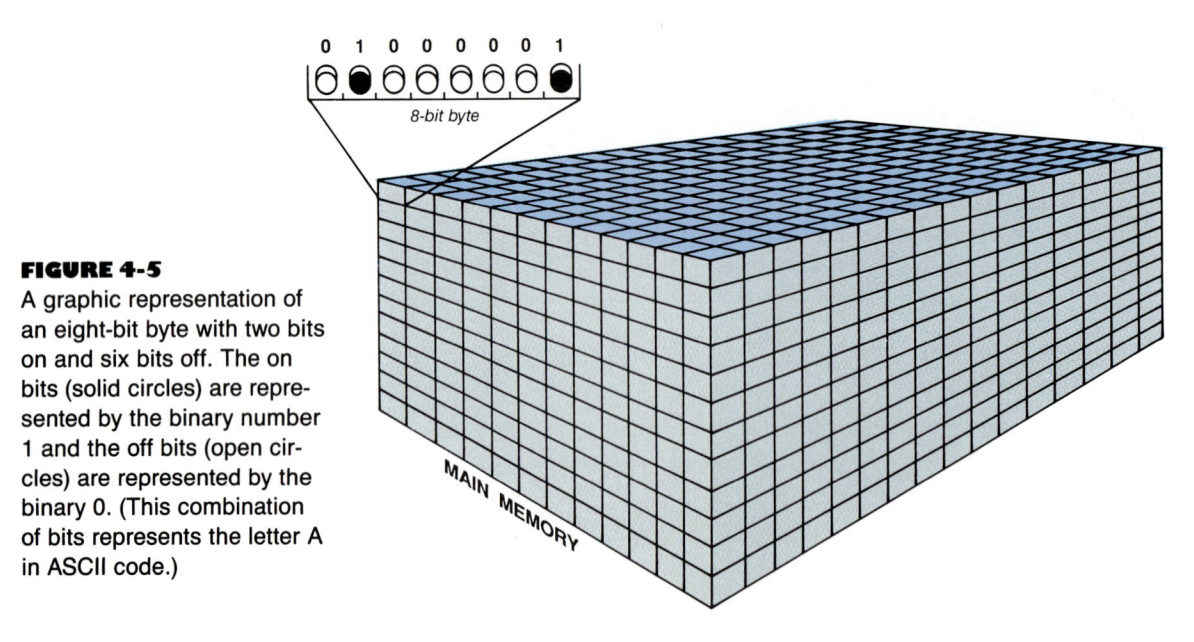

A byte contains eight bits. A **bit** is an element of a byte that can represent one of two values. It can either be *off*, represented in (Figure 4-5) by an open circle, or *on*, represented by a solid circle. Each alphabetic, numeric, and special character stored in the memory of the computer is represented by a combination of off and on bits. The computer can distinguish between characters because a unique combination of off and on bits is assigned to each character.

FIGURE 4-5
A graphic representation of an eight-bit byte with two bits on and six bits off. The on bits (solid circles) are represented by the binary number 1 and the off bits (open circles) are represented by the binary 0. (This combination of bits represents the letter A in ASCII code.)

A mathematical way of representing the off and on conditions of a bit is to use 0 to represent off and 1 to represent on. The **binary** number system (base 2) represents quantities by using only two symbols, 0 and 1. For this reason, binary is used to represent the electronic status of the bits inside the processor unit. The term bit was derived from the a combination of words *b*inary dig*it*.

Two popular codes that use combinations of zeros and ones to represent characters in memory and on auxiliary storage are the ASCII and EBCDIC codes. Figure 4-6 summarizes these codes. Notice how the combination of bits, represented in binary, is unique for each character.

SYMBOL	ASCII	EBCDIC	SYMBOL	ASCII	EBCDIC	SYMBOL	ASCII	EBCDIC
(space)	0100000	01000000	?	0111111	01101111	^	1011110	
!	0100001	01011010	@	1000000	01111100	_	1011111	
"	0100010	01111111	A	1000001	11000001	a	1100001	10000001
#	0100011	01111011	B	1000010	11000010	b	1100010	10000010
$	0100100	01011011	C	1000011	11000011	c	1100011	10000011
%	0100101	01101100	D	1000100	11000100	d	1100100	10000100
&	0100110	01010000	E	1000101	11000101	e	1100101	10000101
'	0100111	01111101	F	1000110	11000110	f	1100110	10000110
(	0101000	01001101	G	1000111	11000111	g	1100111	10000111
)	0101001	01011101	H	1001000	11001000	h	1101000	10001000
*	0101010	01011100	I	1001001	11001001	i	1101001	10001001
+	0101011	01001110	J	1001010	11010001	j	1101010	10010001
,	0101100	01101011	K	1001011	11010010	k	1101011	10010010
-	0101101	01100000	L	1001100	11010011	l	1101100	10010011
.	0101110	01001011	M	1001101	11010100	m	1101101	10010100
/	0101111	01100001	N	1001110	11010101	n	1101110	10010101
0	0110000	11110000	O	1001111	11010110	o	1101111	10010110
1	0110001	11110001	P	1010000	11010111	p	1110000	10010111
2	0110010	11110010	Q	1010001	11011000	q	1110001	10011000
3	0110011	11110011	R	1010010	11011001	r	1110010	10011001
4	0110100	11110100	S	1010011	11100010	s	1110011	10100010
5	0110101	11110101	T	1010100	11100011	t	1110100	10100011
6	0110110	11110110	U	1010101	11100100	u	1110101	10100100
7	0110111	11110111	V	1010110	11100101	v	1110110	10100101
8	0111000	11111000	W	1010111	11100110	w	1110111	10100110
9	0111001	11111001	X	1011000	11100111	x	1111000	10100111
:	0111010	01111010	Y	1011001	11101000	y	1111001	10101000
;	0111011	01011110	Z	1011010	11101001	z	1111010	10101001
<	0111100	01001100	[	1011011	01001010	{	1111011	
=	0111101	01111110	\	1011100		}	1111101	
>	0111110	01101110	]	1011101	01011010			

FIGURE 4-6
This chart shows alphabetic, numeric, and special characters as they are represented in the ASCII and EBCDIC codes. Each character is represented in binary using a unique ordering of zeros and ones.

FIGURE 4-7
Pressing the letter A key on the keyboard sends an electronic signal to the computer ①. Computer circuts convert the signal into a particular combination of bits that are on and off. The combination of bits shown here represents the letter A ②. The character is displayed on the screen ③.

The ASCII Code

The **American Standard Code for Information Interchange**, called **ASCII** (pronounced ask-ee), is the most widely used coding system to represent data. Figure 4-7 illustrates the letter A stored in an eight-bit byte in main memory using the ASCII code. When you type the letter A on the keyboard, the electronic circuitry of the computer interprets the character and stores it in main memory as a series of off and on bits. When the character A appears on the screen or is printed, the ASCII code is converted back into the alphabetic symbol A.

③ Character you enter is displayed on screen

ENTER VALUE: A

MAIN MEMORY

A
0 1 0 0 0 0 0 1
—BYTE—

① Press a key

② Keyboard signal is converted to character

As you can see by looking at Figure 4-6, the ASCII code uses only the rightmost seven bits of the eight bits in a byte to represent characters. These seven bits provide 128 orderings of zeros and ones, enough to represent all the standard characters including numeric, uppercase and lowercase alphabetic, and special. An extended version of the ASCII code has been developed that allows certain foreign alphabetic letters and additional special characters to be stored. This extended version makes use of the eighth bit.

The EBCDIC Code

The ASCII code is widely used on personal computers and many minicomputers. Another common coding scheme used primarily on mainframes is called the **Extended Binary Coded Decimal Interchange Code**, or **EBCDIC** (pronounced eb-see-dick).

Binary Representation of Numbers

When the ASCII or EBCDIC code is used, each character that is represented is stored in one byte of memory. There are other binary formats, however, that the computer sometimes uses to represent numeric data. For example, a computer may store, or *pack* two numeric characters in one byte of memory. These binary formats are used by the computer to increase storage and processing efficiency.

PARITY

◆ Regardless of whether ASCII, EBCDIC, or other binary methods are used to represent characters in main memory, it is important that the characters be stored accurately. For each byte of memory, most computers have at least one extra bit, called a **parity bit**, that is used by the computer for error checking. A parity bit can detect if one of the bits in a byte has been inadvertently changed. Such an error could occur because of voltage fluctuations, static electricity, or a memory chip failure.

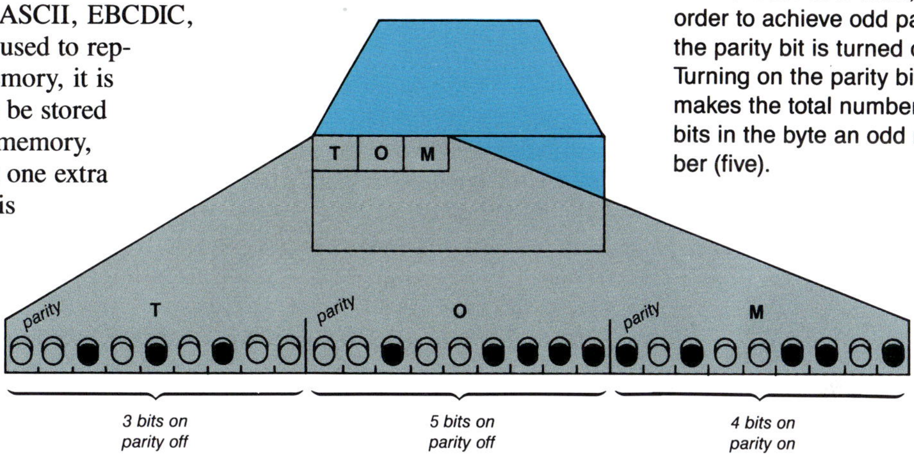

Computers are either odd or even parity machines. In computers with **odd parity**, the total number of *on* bits in the byte (including the parity bit) must be an odd number (Figure 4-8). In computers with **even parity**, the total number of on bits must be an even number. Parity is checked by the computer each time a memory location is used. When data is moved from one location to another in main memory, the parity bits of both the sending and receiving locations are compared to see if they are the same. If the system detects a difference or if the wrong number of bits is on (e.g., an even number in a system with odd parity), an error message displays. Some computers use multiple parity bits that enable them to detect and correct a single-bit error and detect multiple-bit errors.

FIGURE 4-8
In a computer with odd parity, the parity bit is turned on or off in order to make the total number of on bits (including the parity bit) an odd number. Here, the letters T and O have an odd number of bits and the parity bit is left off. However, the number of bits for the letter M is even, so in order to achieve odd parity, the parity bit is turned on. Turning on the parity bit makes the total number of bits in the byte an odd number (five).

3 bits on parity off | 5 bits on parity off | 4 bits on parity on

NUMBER SYSTEMS

◆ This section describes the number systems that are used with computers. Whereas thorough knowledge of this subject is required for technical computer personnel, a general understanding of number systems and how they relate to computers is all most users need.

As you have seen, the binary (base 2) number system is used to represent the electronic status of the bits in main memory. It is also used for other purposes such as addressing the memory locations. Another number system that is commonly used with computers is **hexadecimal** (base 16). Figure 4-9 shows how the decimal values 0 through 15 are represented in binary and hexadecimal.

FIGURE 4-9
The chart shows the binary and hexadecimal representation of decimal numbers 0 through 15. Notice how letters represent the numbers 10 through 15.

DECIMAL	BINARY	HEXADECIMAL
0	0000	0
1	0001	1
2	0010	2
3	0011	3
4	0100	4
5	0101	5
6	0110	6
7	0111	7
8	1000	8
9	1001	9
10	1010	A
11	1011	B
12	1100	C
13	1101	D
14	1110	E
15	1111	F

The mathematical principles that apply to the binary and hexadecimal number systems are the same as those that apply to the decimal number system. To help you better understand these principles, we will start with the familiar decimal system, then progress to the binary and hexadecimal number systems.

The Decimal Number System

The decimal number system is a base 10 number system (*deci* means ten). The *base* of a number system indicates how many symbols are used in it. Decimal uses 10 symbols, 0 through 9. Each of the symbols in the number system has a value associated with it. For example, you know that 3 represents a quantity of three and 5 represents a quantity of five. The decimal number system is also a *positional* number system. This means that in a number such as 143, each position in the number has a value associated with it. When you look at the decimal number 143, you know that the 3 is in the ones, or units, position and represents three ones or (3 × 1); the 4 is in the tens position and represents four tens or (4 × 10); and the 1 is in the hundreds position and represents one hundred or (1 × 100). The number 143 is the sum of the values in each position of the number (100 + 40 + 3 = 143). The chart in Figure 4-10 shows how the positional values (hundreds, tens, and units) for a number system can be calculated. Starting on the right and working to the left, we raise the base of the number system, in this case 10, to consecutive powers (10^2, 10^1, 10^0). These calculations are a mathematical way of determining the place values in a number system.

FIGURE 4-10
This chart shows the positional values in the decimal number 143.

power of 10	10^2	10^1	10^0
positional value	100	10	1
number	1	4	3

$(1 \times 10^2) + (4 \times 10^1) + (3 \times 10^0) =$
$(1 \times 100) + (4 \times 10) + (3 \times 1) =$
$\quad 100 \quad + \quad 40 \quad + \quad 3 \quad = 143$

When you use number systems other than decimal, the same principles apply. The base of the number system indicates the number of symbols that are used, and each position in a number system has a value associated with it. The positional value can be calculated by raising the base of the number system to consecutive powers beginning with zero.

The Binary Number System

As we have discussed, binary is a base 2 number system (*bi* means two), and the symbols that are used are 0 and 1. Just as each position in a decimal number has a place value associated with it, so does each position in a binary number. In binary, the place values are successive powers of two (2^3, 2^2, 2^1, 2^0) or (8 4 2 1). To construct a binary number, you place ones in the positions where the corresponding values add up to the quantity you want to represent; you place zeros in the other positions. For example, the binary place values are 8, 4, 2, and 1, and the binary number 1001 has ones in the positions for the values 8 and 1 and zeros in the positions for 4 and 2. Therefore, the quantity represented by binary 1001 is 9 (8 + 0 + 0 + 1) (Figure 4-11).

power of 2	2^3	2^2	2^1	2^0
positional value	8	4	2	1
binary	1	0	0	1

$(1 \times 2^3) + (0 \times 2^2) + (0 \times 2^1) + (1 \times 2^0) =$
$(1 \times 8) + (0 \times 4) + (0 \times 2) + (1 \times 1) =$
$8 + 0 + 0 + 1 = 9$

FIGURE 4-11
This chart shows how to convert the binary number 1001 to the decimal number 9. Each place in the binary number represents a successive power of 2.

The Hexadecimal Number System

Many computers use a base 16 number system called hexadecimal. The hexadecimal number system uses 16 symbols to represent values. These include the symbols 0 through 9 and A through F (Figure 4-9). The mathematical principles we previously discussed also apply to hexadecimal (Figure 4-12).

power of 16	16^1	16^0
positional value	16	1
hexadecimal	A	5

$(10 \times 16^1) + (5 \times 16^0) =$
$(10 \times 16) + (5 \times 1) =$
$160 + 5 = 165$

FIGURE 4-12
This chart shows how the hexadecimal number A5 is converted into the decimal number 165. Notice that the value 10 is substituted for the A during calculations.

The primary reason why the hexadecimal number system is used with computers is because it can represent binary values in a more compact form and because the conversion between the binary and the hexadecimal number systems is very efficient. An eight-digit binary number can be represented by a two-digit hexadecimal number. For example, in the EBCDIC code, the decimal number 5 is represented as 11110101. This value can be represented in hexadecimal as F5.

One way to convert a binary number to a hexadecimal number is to divide the binary number (from right to left) into groups of four digits; calculate the value of each group; and then change any two-digit values (10 through 15) into the symbols A through F that are used in hexadecimal (Figure 4-13).

positional value	8421	8421
binary	1111	0101
decimal	15	5
hexadecimal	F	5

FIGURE 4-13
This chart shows how the EBCDIC code 11110101 for the value 5 is converted into the hexadecimal value F5. Each group of four binary digits is converted to a hexidecimal symbol.

Summary of Number Systems

As we mentioned at the beginning of the section on number systems, binary and hexadecimal are used primarily by technical computer personnel. A general user does not need a complete understanding of numbering systems. The concepts that you should remember about number systems are that binary is used to represent the electronic status of the bits in main memory and auxiliary storage. Hexadecimal is used to represent binary in a more compact form.

HOW THE PROCESSOR UNIT EXECUTES PROGRAMS AND MANIPULATES DATA

◆ The program instructions that users write are usually in a form similar to English. Before these instructions can be executed, they must be translated by the computer into a form called machine language instructions. A **machine language instruction** is one that the electronic circuits in the CPU can interpret and convert into one or more of the commands in the computer's instruction set. The **instruction set** contains commands, such as ADD or MOVE, that the computer's circuits can directly perform. To help you understand how the processor unit works, let's look at an example of a machine language instruction.

Machine Language Instructions

A machine language instruction is usually composed of three parts: an operation code; values that indicate the number of characters to be processed by the instruction; and the addresses in main memory of the data to be used in the execution of the instruction (Figure 4-14).

FIGURE 4-14
A machine language instruction consists of an operation code, the lengths of the field to be processed, and the main memory addresses of the field.

The **operation code** is a unique value that is typically stored in the first byte in the instruction. This unique value indicates which operation is to be performed. For example, the letter A stored as the operation code might mean *addition*. The letter M might mean *move*.

The number of characters to be processed is included in the machine language instruction so the CPU will manipulate the proper number of bytes. For example, if a four-digit field were to be added to another four-digit field, the number of characters specified in the instruction for each field would be four. The main memory addresses of the fields involved in the operation are also specified in the instruction. This specification of the main memory address enables the CPU to locate where in main memory the data to be processed is stored. The steps involved in executing a computer instruction are illustrated in Figure 4-15. The instruction A44 7000 9000 indicates that the four-digit fields that begin in locations 7000 and 9000 are to be added together. When this instruction is executed, the following steps occur:

FIGURE 4-15
The four steps involved in executing a program instruction.

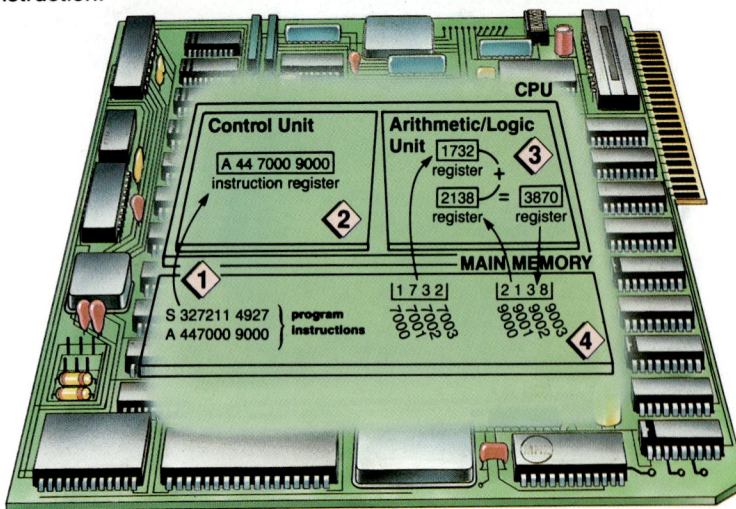

1. The instruction is fetched from main memory and placed in an instruction register. An **instruction register** is an area of memory within the control unit of the CPU that can store a single instruction at a time.
2. The control unit decodes the instruction, and then fetches the data specified by the two addresses in the instruction from main memory.
3. The arithmetic/logic unit executes the instruction by adding the two numbers.
4. The control unit then stores the result of the processing by moving the sum to main memory. This basic sequence of fetch the instruction, decode the instruction, execute the instruction, and store the results, is the way most computers process instructions.

The Machine Cycle

These four steps—fetch, decode, execute, and store—are called the **machine cycle**. As shown in Figure 4-16, the machine cycle is made up of the instruction cycle and the execution cycle. The **instruction cycle** refers to the fetching of the next program instruction and the decoding of that instruction. The **execution cycle** includes the execution of the instruction and the storage of the processing results. One machine cycle is completed when the computer is again ready to fetch the next program instruction.

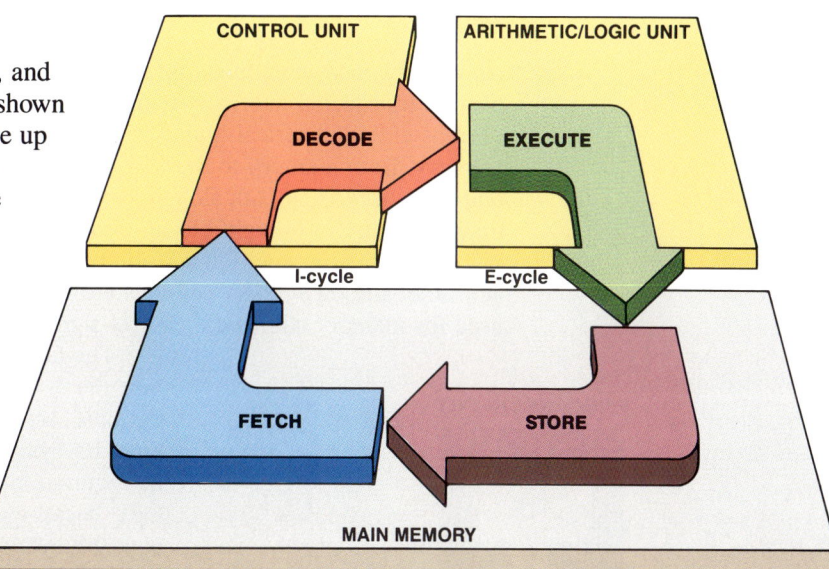

PROCESSOR SPEEDS

◆ Although the machine cycle may appear to be cumbersome and time consuming, computers can perform millions of machine cycles in one second. In fact, the processing speed of computers is often measured in **MIPS**—million instructions per second. A computer with a rating of 1 MIPS can process one million instructions per second. The most powerful personal computers today are rated at between 10 and 15 MIPS. Larger computers can process 75 to 100 MIPS and supercomputers are capable of over 200 MIPS. The speed at which a computer can execute the machine cycle is influenced by three factors: the system clock, the buses, and the word size (Figure 4-17).

FIGURE 4-16
The machine cycle consists of four steps: fetching the next instruction, decoding the instruction, executing the instruction, and storing the result. Fetching and decoding are part of the instruction, or I-cycle. Executing and storing are part of the execution, or E-cycle.

FACTOR	AFFECT ON SPEED
System clock	The system clock generates electronic pulses used to synchronize processing. Faster clock speed results in more operations in a given amount of time.
Bus width	Bus width determines how much data can be transferred at any one time. A 32-bit bus can transfer twice as much data at one time as a 16-bit bus.
Word size	Word size is the number of bits that can be manipulated at any one time. A computer with a 32-bit word size can manipulate twice as much data at one time as a system with a 16-bit word size.

FIGURE 4-17
Factors affecting computer speed.

System Clock

The control unit utilizes the **system clock** to synchronize, or control the timing of, all computer operations. The system clock generates electronic pulses at a fixed rate, measured in **megahertz**. One megahertz equals one million pulses per second. The speed of the system clock varies among computers. Some personal computers can operate at speeds in excess of 30 megahertz.

Buses

As we explained, computers store and process data as a series of electronic bits. These bits are transferred internally within the circuitry of the computer along paths capable of transmitting electrical impulses. The bits must be transferred from input devices to memory, from memory to the CPU, from the CPU to memory, and from memory to output devices. Any path along which bits are transmitted is called a **bus**. Buses can transfer multiples of eight bits at a time. An eight-bit bus has eight lines and can transmit eight bits at a time. On a 16-bit bus, bits can be moved from place to place 16 bits at a time, and on a 32-bit bus, bits are moved 32 bits at a time. Separate buses are used for memory addresses, control signals, and data (Figure 4-18).

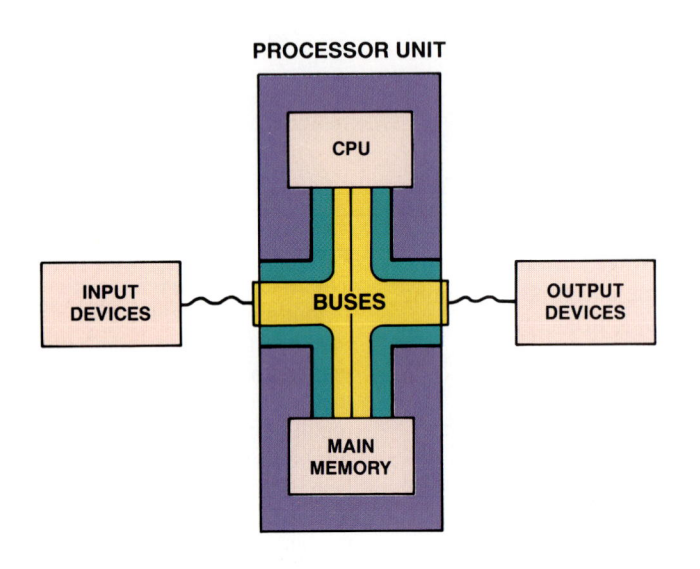

The larger the number of bits that are handled by a bus, the faster the computer can transfer data. For example, assume a number in memory occupies four eight-bit bytes. With an eight-bit bus, four steps would be required to transfer the data from memory to the CPU because on the eight-bit bus, the data in each eight-bit byte would be transferred in an individual step. A 16-bit bus has 16 lines in the bus, so only two transfers would be necessary to move the data in four bytes. And on a 32-bit bus, the entire four bytes could be transferred at one time. The fewer number of transfer steps required, the faster the transfer of data occurs.

FIGURE 4-18
Data is transmitted between computer components via electrical pathways called buses. Separate buses exist for memory addresses, control signals, and data. Input and output devices are connected to the buses by electrical cables.

Word Size

Another factor that affects the speed of a computer is the word size. The **word size** is the number of bits that the CPU can *process* at one time, as opposed to the bus size, which is the number of bits the computer can *transmit* at one time. Like a bus, the word size of a machine is measured in bits. Processors can have 8-bit, 16-bit, 32-bit, or 64-bit word sizes. A processor with an eight-bit word size can manipulate eight bits at a time. If two four-digit numbers are to be added in the ALU of an eight-bit processor, it will take four operations because a separate operation will be required to add each of the four digits. With a 16-bit processor, the addition will take two operations; with a 32-bit processor, only one operation would be required to add the numbers together. Sometimes the word size of a computer is given in bytes instead of bits. For example, a word size of 16 bits may be expressed as a word size of two bytes because there are eight bits in a byte. The larger the word size of the processor, the faster the capability of the computer to process data.

In summary, the speed of a computer is influenced by the system clock, the size of the buses, and the word size. When you purchase a computer, the speed requirements you want should be based on your intended use of the computer. Sixteen-bit computers are widely used today for applications such as word processing, electronic spreadsheets, or database. Thirty-two-bit computers are considered powerful and are useful for applications that require complex and time-consuming calculations such as graphics. The more powerful personal computers, many minicomputers, and most mainframes are 32-bit computers. Most supercomputers are 64-bit computers.

ARCHITECTURE OF PROCESSOR UNITS

◆ The processor unit of a computer can be designed and built in many different ways. For example, the processor for a personal computer may be housed on a single printed circuit board while a larger machine may require a number of circuit boards for the CPU, main memory, and the related electronic circuitry.

Microprocessors

The smallest processor, called a **microprocessor** (Figure 4-19), is a single integrated circuit that contains the CPU and sometimes memory. An **integrated circuit**, also called an **IC**, **chip**, or **microchip**, is a complete electronic circuit that has been etched on a small chip of nonconducting material such as silicon. Microcomputers are built using microprocessors for their CPU.

Figure 4-20 shows the location of the microprocessor chip in the main circuit board, called a **motherboard**, of a personal computer. Some of the microprocessors commonly used in personal computers today are listed on the next page in Figure 4-21.

FIGURE 4-19
The Intel 80486 microprocessor has a word size and bus width of 32 bits and can operate at between 25 and 33 megahertz.

FIGURE 4-20
The main circuit board (motherboard) of an IBM PS/2 personal computer. The microprocessor is shown in the lower left corner.

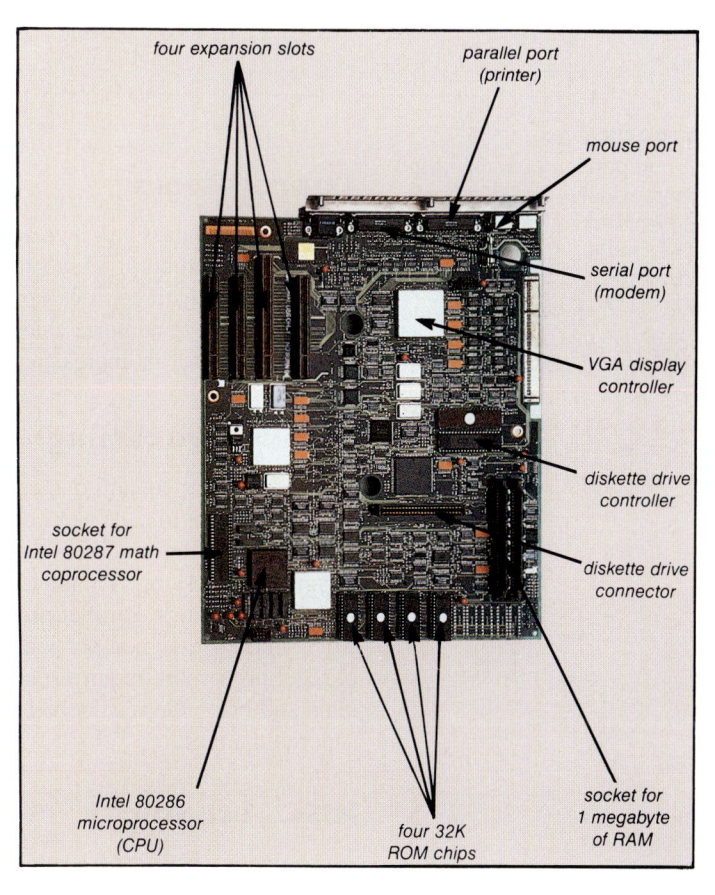

MICROPROCESSOR	MANUFACTURER	WORD SIZE (BITS)	I/O BUS WIDTH (BITS)	CLOCK SPEED (MHz)	MICROCOMPUTERS USING THIS CHIP
6502	MOS Technology	8	8	4	Apple IIe Atari 800
8088	Intel	16	8	8	IBM PC and XT HP 150 Compaq Portable
8086	Intel	16	16	8	Compaq Deskpro Many IBM compatibles
80286	Intel	16	16	8–12	IBM PC/AT Compaq Deskpro 286
68000	Motorola	32	16	12–20	Apple Macintosh SE Commodore Amiga
68020	Motorola	32	32	12–33	Apple Macintosh II
80386	Intel	32	32	16–33	Compaq Deskpro 386 IBM PS/2
68030	Motorola	32	32	16–40	Apple Macintosh SE/30 Apple Macintosh IIfx
68040	Motorola	32	32	25–33	Engineering Workstations
80486	Intel	32	32	25–33	IBM PS/2 Model 70 Compaq Systempro

FIGURE 4-21
A comparison of some of the more widely used microprocessor chips.

Coprocessors

One way computers can increase their productivity is through the use of a **coprocessor**, a special microprocessor chip or circuit board designed to perform a specific task. For example, math coprocessors are commonly added to computers to greatly speed up the processing of numeric calculations. Other types of coprocessors extend the capability of a computer by increasing the amount of software that will run on the computer.

Parallel Processing

Most computers contain one central processing unit (CPU) that processes a single instruction at a time. When one instruction is finished, the CPU begins execution of the next instruction, and so on until the program is completed. This method is known as **serial processing**. **Parallel processing** involves the use of multiple CPUs, each with their own memory. Parallel processors divide up a problem so that multiple CPUs can work on their assigned portion of the problem simultaneously. As you might expect, parallel processors require special software that can recognize how to divide up problems and bring the results back together again. Parallel processors are often used in supercomputers.

RISC Technology

As computers have evolved, more and more commands have been added to hardware instruction sets. In recent years, however, computer designers have reevaluated the need for so many instructions and have developed systems based on RISC technology.

RISC, which stands for reduced instruction set computing (or computers), involves reducing the instructions to only those that are most frequently used. Without the burden of the occasionally used instructions, the most frequently used instructions operate faster and overall processing capability, or throughput, of the system is increased (Figure 4-22).

In summary, you can see that computers have many different types of processor architecture. Regardless of the architecture used, the important concept to remember is that the processor units on all computers perform essentially the same functions.

TYPES OF MEMORY

Recall that electronic components are used to store data in computer memory. The actual materials and devices used for memory have changed throughout the years. The first device used for storing data was the vacuum tube. After the vacuum tube, core memory was used. **Core memory** consisted of small, ring-shaped pieces of material that could be magnetized, or polarized, in one of two directions. The polarity indicated whether the core was on or off. Today, semiconductor memory is used in virtually all computers (Figure 4-23). **Semiconductor memory** is an integrated circuit containing thousands of transistors. A **transistor** is an electronic component that can be either on or off and represents a bit in memory.

When core memory was used as main memory, the time required to access data stored in the memory was measured in microseconds. A **microsecond** is one millionth of a second. Access to data stored in semiconductor memory is measured in nanoseconds. A **nanosecond** is one billionth of a second. In addition, the cost of semiconductor memory is just a fraction of the cost for core memory. Figure 4-24 shows how the storage capacity of semiconductor memory has increased over recent years, while the cost of semiconductor memory has decreased. The trend is expected to continue.

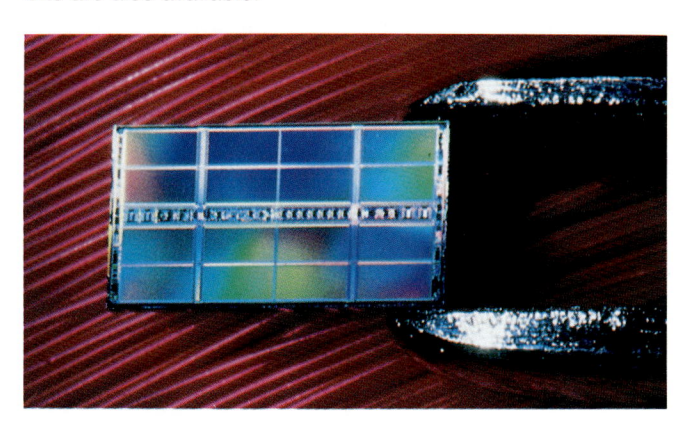

FIGURE 4-22
This IBM computer uses reduced instruction set computer (RISC) technology to obtain performance of over 27 million instructions per second. This level of processing power is best used in applications that require numerous calculations such as computer-aided design (CAD).

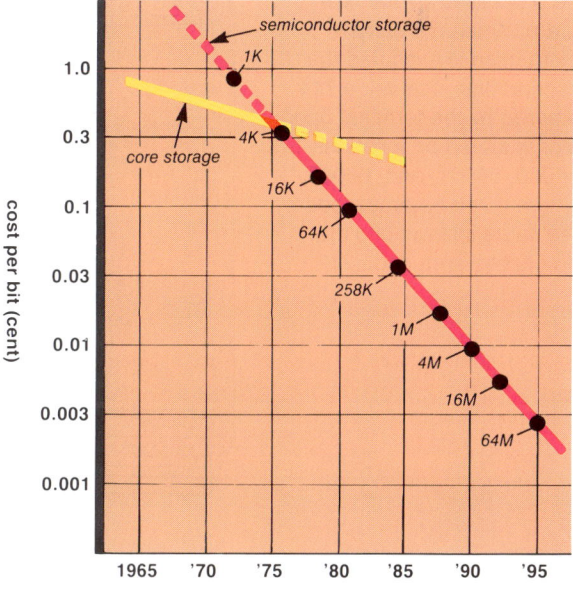

FIGURE 4-23
This semiconductor memory chip can store one million bits of information. Memory chips that can store up to 64 million bits are also available.

FIGURE 4-24
The declining cost and increased storage capacity of semiconductor storage are shown here.

Chip manufacturers say that by the end of the century it will be possible to store over a billion components on a chip. As you can see, semiconductor memory is compact, fast, and inexpensive. Several different types of semiconductor memory chips are used in computers. They are RAM, ROM, PROM, EPROM, and EEPROM chips.

RAM Memory

Random access memory, or **RAM**, is the name given to the integrated circuits, or chips, that are used for main memory. This is the type of memory we have discussed so far in this chapter. Data and programs are transferred into and out of RAM, and data stored in RAM is manipulated by computer program instructions.

There are two types of RAM memory chips: dynamic RAM and static RAM. **Dynamic RAM (DRAM)** chips are smaller and simpler in design than static RAM chips. With dynamic RAM, the current, or charge, on the chip is periodically regenerated by special regenerator circuits, which allow the chip to retain the stored data. **Static RAM** chips are larger and more complicated than dynamic RAM and do not require the current to be periodically regenerated. The main memory of most computers uses dynamic RAM chips.

Figure 4-25 illustrates the processing that could occur as a series of area codes are entered into RAM (computer memory) from a terminal. The first area code, 212, is entered from the keyboard and stored at memory locations 66000, 66001, and 66002. Once in memory, this field can be processed as it is required.

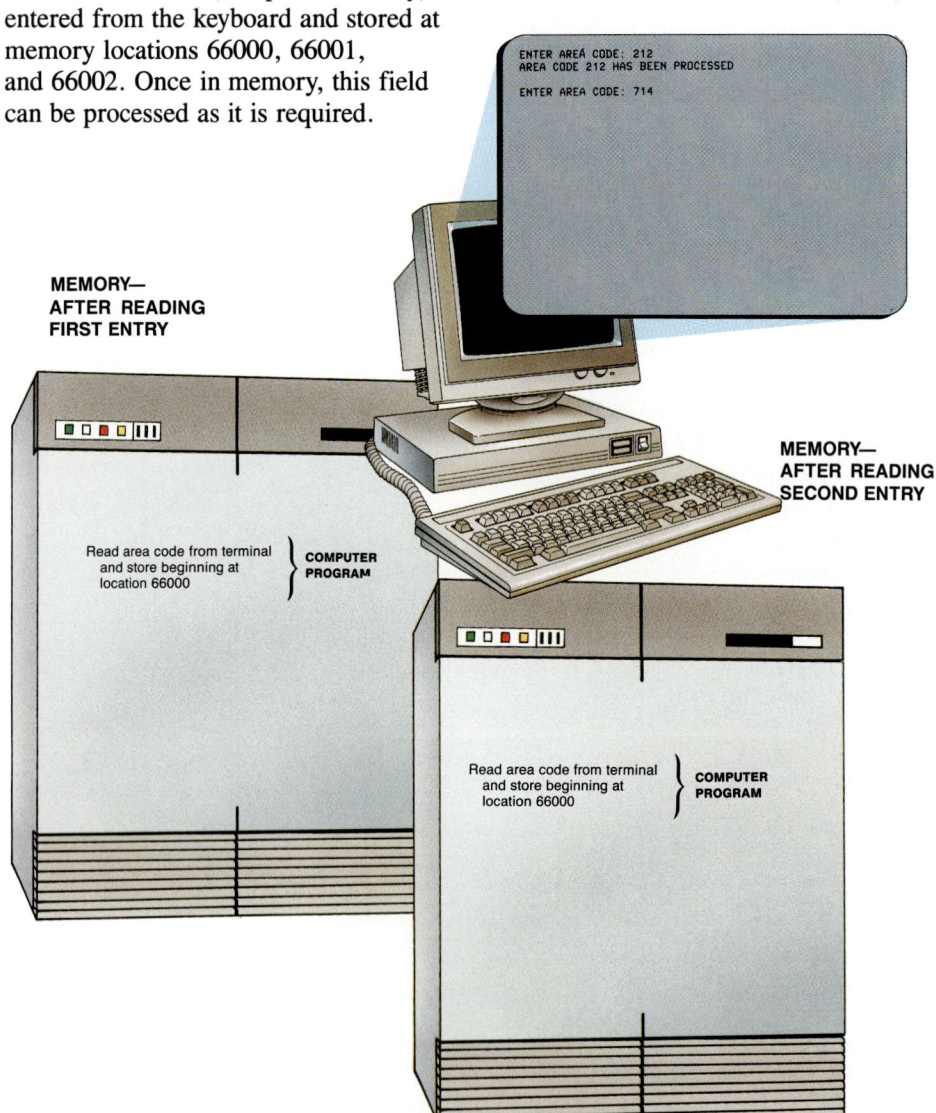

FIGURE 4-25
The instruction in the program specifies that the telephone area code is to be read into adjacent memory locations beginning with location 66000. After the data is placed in the locations, it can be processed by the program. When the same instruction is executed the second time, the value 714 entered by the terminal operator is stored on locations 66000, 66001, and 66002, where it can be processed by the same instructions that processed area code 212.

When the instruction to read (input) data into memory from the keyboard is executed again, the second area code entered from the keyboard, area code 714, would replace the previous value (212) at locations 66000, 66001, and 66002 in memory. Area code 714 could then be processed by the same instructions that processed area code 212.

Some computers improve their processing efficiency by using a limited amount of high-speed RAM memory between the CPU and main memory (Figure 4-26). High-speed memory used in this manner is called **cache memory** (pronounced cash). When the processor needs the next program instruction or data, it first checks the cache memory. If the required instruction or data is present in cache, the processor will execute faster than if the instruction or data had to be retrieved from the slower main memory. Cache memory is used to store the most frequently used instructions and data.

RAM memory is said to be **volatile** because the programs and data stored in RAM are erased when the power to the computer is turned off. As long as the power remains on, the programs and data stored in RAM will remain intact until they are replaced by other programs and data. Programs and data that are needed for future use must be transferred from RAM to auxiliary storage before the power is turned off.

ROM Memory

ROM stands for **read only memory**. With ROM, data is permanently recorded in the memory when it is manufactured. ROM memory retains its contents even when the power is turned off. The data or programs that are stored in ROM can be read and used, but cannot be altered, hence the name *read only*. ROM is used to store items such as the instruction set of the computer. In addition, many of the special-purpose computers used in automobiles, appliances, and so on use small amounts of ROM to store instructions that will be executed repeatedly. Instructions that are stored in ROM memory are called **firmware** or **microcode**.

Other Types of Memory

PROM means **programmable read only memory**. PROM acts the same as ROM when it is part of the computer; that is, it can only be read, and its contents cannot be altered. With PROM, however, the data or programs are not stored in the memory when they are manufactured. Instead, PROM can be loaded with specially selected data or programs prior to installing it in a computer. A variation of PROM is **EPROM** (pronounced ee-prom), which means **erasable programmable read only memory**. In addition to being used in the same way as PROM, EPROM allows the user to erase the data stored in the memory and to store new data or programs in the memory. EPROM is erased through the use of special ultraviolet light devices that destroy the bit settings within the memory.

EEPROM (pronounced double-ee-prom), or **electronically erasable programmable read only memory**, allows the stored data or programs to be erased electronically. The advantage of EEPROM is that it does not have to be removed from the computer to be changed.

FIGURE 4-26
Some computers use an area of high-speed RAM memory, called cache memory, between the CPU and main memory. If the required data or instruction is found in cache, a program will run faster than if the information has to be retrieved from main memory or auxiliary storage.

SUMMARY

◆ In this chapter we examined various aspects of the processor unit including its components, how programs and data are stored, and how the processor executes program instructions to process data into information. Although a detailed understanding of this material is not a prerequisite for computer literacy, understanding these principles will increase your overall comprehension of how processing occurs on a computer.

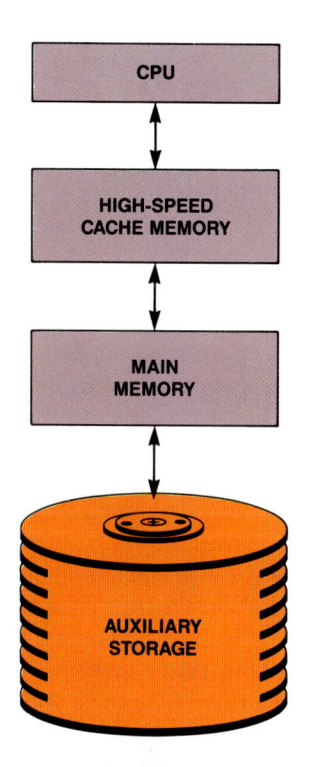

CHAPTER SUMMARY

1. The central processing unit and the main memory are contained in the processor unit.
2. The central processing unit, or CPU, contains the **control unit** and the **arithmetic/logic unit (ALU)**. The control unit directs and coordinates all the activities on the computer. The arithmetic/logic unit performs arithmetic and logic operations.
3. **Arithmetic operations** consist of adding, subtracting, multiplying, and dividing.
4. **Logical operations** consist of comparing one data item to another to determine if the first data item is greater than, equal to, or less than the other.
5. **Registers** are temporary storage locations in the CPU that store specific data such as the address of the next instruction.
6. The **main memory**, also called **primary storage**, stores the operating system, application programs, and data.
7. Each storage location in main memory is called a **byte** and is identified by a **memory address**.
8. The size of main memory is normally expressed in terms of **kilobytes (KB)**. Each kilobyte is equal to 1,024 bytes.
9. A byte consists of eight **bits**. A bit can represent one of two values—off and on.
10. When a letter is entered into main memory from a keyboard, the electronic circuitry interprets the character and stores the character in memory as a series of off and on bits. The computer can distinguish between characters because a unique combination of off and on bits are assigned to each character.
11. One of the most widely used codes to represent characters is the **American Standard Code for Information Interchange**, called the **ASCII code**.
12. A code used for mainframes is the **Extended Binary Coded Decimal Interchange Code (EBCDIC)**.
13. Computers use **parity bits** for error checking.
14. The **binary** (base 2) number system is used by the computer for purposes such as representing memory addresses and the electronic status of the bits in main memory. **Hexadecimal** (base 16) is used to represent binary in a more compact form.
15. A **machine language instruction** can be decoded and executed by the CPU.
16. A machine language instruction is usually composed of an **operation code**; values indicating the number of characters to be processed; and main memory addresses of the data to be processed.
17. Steps in the **machine cycle** consist of: fetch the next instruction; decode the instruction; execute the instruction; and store the results.
18. The speed of a computer is influenced by the system clock, the bus size, and the word size.
19. The **system clock** is used by the control unit to synchronize all computer operations.
20. A **bus** is any line that transmits bits between memory and the input/output devices, and between memory and the CPU.
21. The number of bits that the CPU can process at one time is called the **word size**.
22. Computers can be 8-bit, 16-bit, 32-bit, or 64-bit machines.
23. **Microprocessors** are used for the CPU in microcomputers.
24. **Coprocessors** can be used to enhance and expand the capabilities of a computer.
25. Parallel processors divide up a problem so that multiple CPUs can work on their assigned portion of the problem simultaneously.
26. **RISC** technology involves reducing a computer's instruction set to only those instructions that are the most frequently used.
27. **Core memory** consisted of small, ring-shaped pieces of material that could be magnetized, or polarized, in one of two directions.
28. **Semiconductor memory** is now used in most computers. It consists of transistors etched into a semiconductor material such as silicon.
29. A **microsecond** is a millionth of a second. A **nanosecond** is a billionth of a second. Access to data stored in semiconductor memory is measured in nanoseconds.
30. **RAM**, which stands for **random access memory**, is used for main memory.

31. Some computers improve their processing efficiency by using a limited amount of high-speed memory, called **cache memory**, between the CPU and main memory.
32. RAM memory is said to be **volatile** because the programs and data stored in RAM are erased when the power to the computer is turned off.
33. **ROM** stands for **read only memory**. Data or programs are stored in ROM when the memory is manufactured, and they cannot be altered.
34. **PROM** means **programmable read only memory**. PROM acts the same as ROM except data can be stored into the PROM memory prior to being installed in the computer.
35. **EPROM**, or **erasable programmable read only memory**, can be erased through the use of special ultraviolet devices.
36. **EEPROM**, or **electronically erasable programmable read only memory**, can be electronically erased without being removed from the computer.

KEY TERMS

American Standard Code for Information Interchange (ASCII) *4.6*
Arithmetic/logic unit (ALU) *4.2*
Arithmetic operations *4.2*
ASCII code *4.6*
Binary *4.5*
Bit *4.4*
Bus *4.12*
Byte *4.3*
Cache memory *4.17*
Chip *4.13*
Control unit *4.2*
Coprocessor *4.14*
Core memory *4.15*
Decoding *4.2*
Dynamic RAM (DRAM) *4.16*
EBCDIC *4.6*
EEPROM *4.17*
Electronically erasable programmable read only memory (EEPROM) *4.17*
EPROM *4.17*
Erasable programmable read only memory (EPROM) *4.17*
Even parity *4.7*
Executing *4.2*
Execution cycle *4.11*

Extended Binary Coded Decimal Interchange Code (EBCDIC) *4.6*
Fetching *4.2*
Firmware *4.17*
Hexadecimal *4.7*
IC *4.13*
Instruction cycle *4.11*
Instruction register *4.10*
Instruction set *4.10*
Integrated circuit (IC) *4.13*
K *4.3*
KB *4.3*
Kilobyte (K or KB) *4.3*
Logical operations *4.2*
Machine cycle *4.11*
Machine language instruction *4.10*
Main memory *4.2*
MB *4.3*
Megabyte (MB) *4.3*
Megahertz *4.11*
Memory address *4.3*
Microchip *4.13*
Microcode *4.17*
Microprocessor *4.13*
Microsecond *4.15*
MIPS *4.11*

Motherboard *4.13*
Nanosecond *4.15*
Odd parity *4.7*
Operation code *4.10*
Parallel processing *4.14*
Parity bit *4.7*
Primary storage *4.2*
Programmable read only memory (PROM) *4.17*
PROM *4.17*
RAM *4.16*
Random access memory (RAM) *4.16*
Read only memory (ROM) *4.17*
Registers *4.2*
RISC (reduced instruction set computing) *4.15*
ROM *4.17*
Semiconductor memory *4.15*
Serial processing *4.14*
Static RAM *4.16*
Storing *4.2*
System clock *4.11*
Transistor *4.15*
Volatile *4.17*
Word size *4.12*

REVIEW QUESTIONS

1. Identify the components of the processor unit and describe the functions of each.
2. What are the three items that are stored in main memory? Draw a diagram of main memory and label each of the areas.
3. Define the terms bit and byte. Illustrate how the number 12 is represented in binary, hexadecimal, ASCII, and EBCDIC.
4. What do the letters KB and MB stand for when referring to main memory? What quantity does each represent?
5. Describe how a group of characters entered into the computer as a field are stored in main memory. Draw a diagram to illustrate how the letters in your last name would be stored using the ASCII code. Begin at main memory address 55231.
6. What is parity and how is it used?
7. Why are the binary and hexadecimal number systems used with computers?
8. List and describe the four steps of the machine cycle.
9. What are the three factors that influence the speed of a processor?
10. What is parallel processing and how is it used?
11. Define RAM memory. How is cache memory used by the computer?
12. Describe the process of manufacturing integrated circuits.

CONTROVERSIAL ISSUES

1. Some people feel that industry standards should be set to eliminate the problems caused by incompatibility. For example, unless special enhancements are made, software that is written for an IBM personal computer system will not run on an Apple Macintosh computer. Others feel that standards would restrict competition and product development. Write a paper to discuss your opinions on this topic.
2. The importation of computer goods from foreign manufacturers has affected the computer industry in this country. In addition, the lower cost of producing electronic components outside the United States has caused many U.S. companies to become involved in offshore manufacturing. Discuss whether restrictions should be placed on integrated circuits and other computer goods that are imported or manufactured offshore.

RESEARCH PROJECTS

1. The semiconductor industry continues to develop and introduce new microprocessor and memory chips. Prepare a report on the latest microprocessor and memory chips that are available. Include information on speed and storage capabilities.
2. Research the history of main memory and prepare a report. Include information on the way the data was stored, the speed of the memory, any limitations of the method, the amount of memory that could be used, and the cost of the memory.

MAKING A CHIP

◆ A chip is made by building layers of electronic pathways and connections by using conducting and nonconducting materials on a surface of silicon. The combination of these materials into specific patterns forms microscopic electronic components such as transistors, diodes, and capacitors that make up the integrated chip circuit. The application of the materials to the silicon is done through a series of technically sophisticated chemical and photographic processes. Some of the manufacturing steps are shown in the following photographs.

A chip begins with a design developed by an engineer using a computer-aided circuit design program. Some circuits take only a month or two to design, whereas others may take a year or more. The computer-aided design system allows the engineer to rearrange the design of the circuit pathways and then see them displayed on the screen ◇1. Most chips have at least four to six layers, but some have up to fifteen. A separate design is required for each layer of the chip circuit. To better review the design, greatly enlarged printouts are prepared ◇2. After the design is finalized, a glass photo mask is prepared for each layer ◇3. To provide for mass production of the chips, the design is reduced to the actual size of the circuit, approximately 1/4-inch square, and duplicated over one hundred times on the surface of the photo mask. In a process similar to printing a picture from a negative, the photo mask will be used to project the circuit design onto the material used to make the chips.

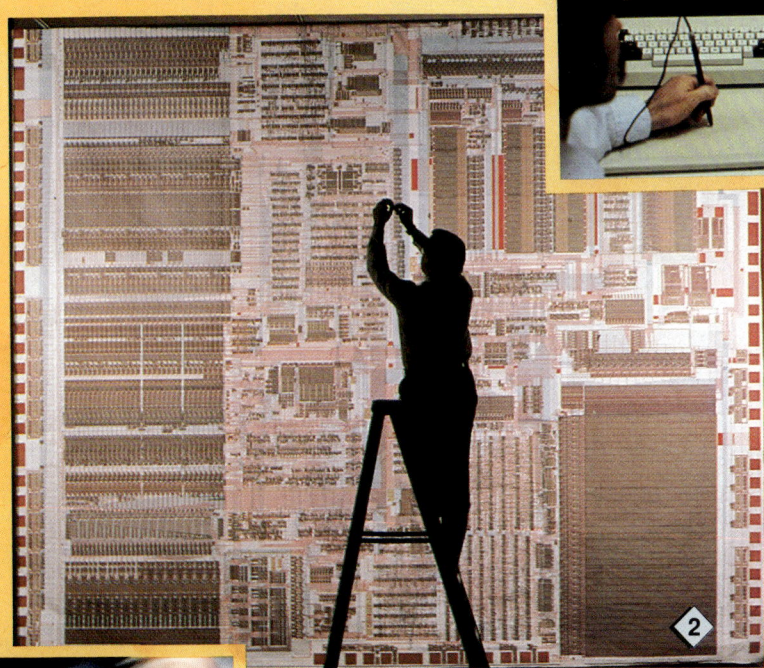

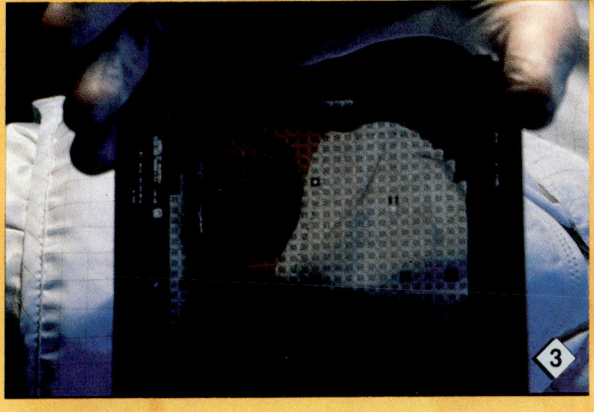

4.21

4.22 MAKING A CHIP

Although other materials can be used, the most common raw material used to make chips is silicon crystals that have been refined from quartz rocks ④. The silicon crystals are melted and *grown* into a cylinder, called an ingot, two to three feet long and eight inches in diameter ⑤. After being smoothed, the silicon ingot is sliced into wafers four to eight inches in diameter and 4/1000 of one inch thick. Much of the chip manufacturing process is performed in special laboratories called clean rooms. Because even the smallest particle of dust can ruin a chip, rooms are kept 1,000 times cleaner than a hospital operating room. People who work in these facilities must wear special protective clothing called bunny suits ⑥. After the wafer has been polished and sterilized, it is placed in a diffusion oven where the first layer of material is added to the wafer surface ⑦. These layers of materials will be etched away to form the circuits.

Before etching, a soft gelatin-like emulsion called photoresist is added to the wafer. During lithography ⟨8⟩, the photoresist is covered by a photo mask and exposed to ultraviolet light. The exposed photoresist becomes hard and the covered photoresist remains soft. The soft photoresist and some of the surface materials are etched away with chemicals or hot gases leaving what will become the circuit pathways. In some facilities, the etching process is done by a robot ⟨9⟩.

The process of adding material and photoresist to the wafer, exposing it to ultraviolet light, and etching away the unexposed surface, is repeated using a different photo mask for each layer of the circuit. After the circuits are tested on the wafer, they are cut into pieces called die by the use of a diamond saw ⟨10⟩ or a laser.

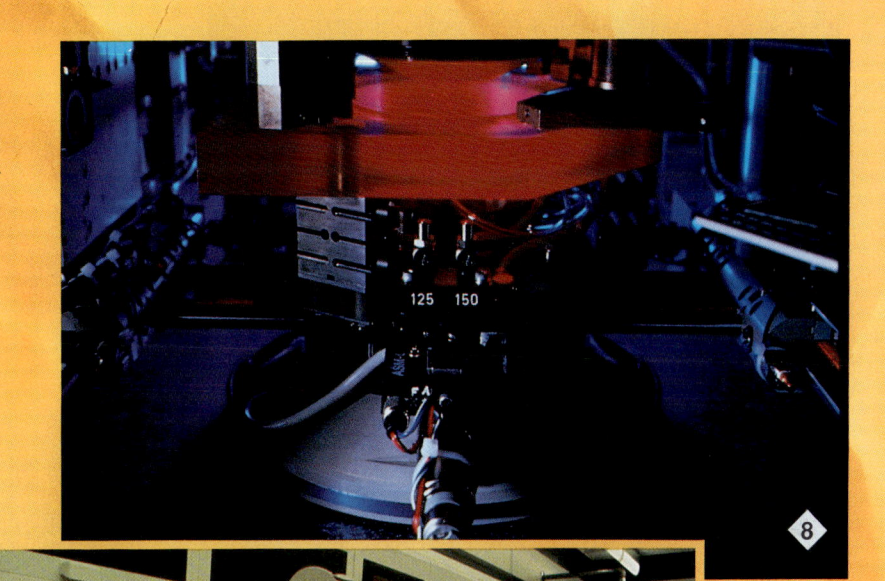

4.24 MAKING A CHIP

The individual chip die ⟨11⟩, approximately 1/4-inch square, are packaged in a hard plastic case ⟨12⟩. This case contains pins that connect the chip to a socket on a circuit board ⟨13⟩.

Output from the Computer

CHAPTER 5 — OUTPUT

OBJECTIVES

- Define the term output
- List the common types of reports that are used for output
- Describe multimedia
- Describe the features and classification of printers
- Identify and explain impact printers
- Identify and explain nonimpact printers
- Describe the types of screens available and list common screen features
- List and describe other types of output devices used with computers

Output is the way the computer communicates with the user; therefore, it is important to know the many forms output can take. In this chapter we discuss the types of output and the devices computers use to produce output.

5.1

FIGURE 5-1
Here, you see the same output in hard-copy and soft-copy form. An advantage of hard copy is that the user can write comments on it and route it to other users.

WHAT IS OUTPUT?

Output is data that has been processed into a useful form called information that can be used by a person or a machine. Output that is used by a machine, such as a disk or tape file, is usually an intermediate result that eventually will be processed into output that can be used by people.

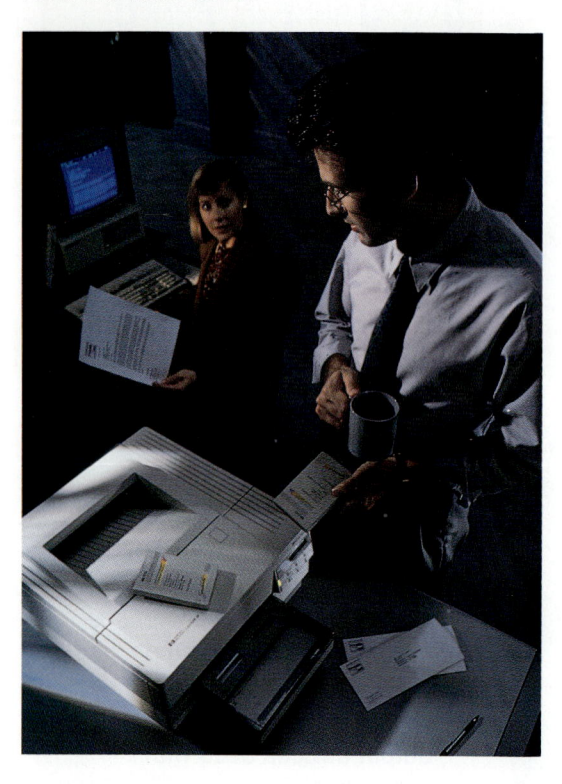

TYPES OF OUTPUT

The type of output generated from the computer depends on the needs of the user and the hardware and software that are used. Two common types of output are reports and graphics. These types of output can be printed on a printer or displayed on a screen. Output that is printed is called **hard copy** and output that is displayed on a screen is called **soft copy** (Figure 5-1). An exciting method of displaying information, called multimedia, combines several types of output on a single screen.

Reports

A **report** is information presented in an organized form. Most people think of reports as items printed on paper or displayed on a screen. For example, word processing documents can be considered reports. Information printed on forms such as invoices or payroll checks can also be considered types of reports. One way to classify reports is by who uses them. An **internal report** is used by individuals in the performance of their jobs. For example, a daily sales report that is distributed to sales personnel is an internal report because it is used only by personnel within the organization. An **external report** is used outside the organization. Sales invoices that are printed and mailed to customers are external reports.

Reports can also be classified by the way they present information. The four types of common reports are: narrative reports, detail reports, summary reports, and exception reports.

Narrative reports may contain some graphic or numeric information, but are primarily text-based reports. These reports, usually prepared with word processing software, include the various types of correspondence commonly used in business such as memos, letters, and sales proposals (Figure 5-2). Detail, summary, and exception reports are primarily used to organize and present numeric-based information.

FIGURE 5-2 ▼
A word processing document is an example of a narrative report.

```
Date:      March 10
To:        Gloria Gilbert
From:      Charlene Kim
Subject:   Electronics Trade Show

The recent Electronics Trade Show was a great success!

At the show, we booked orders of over $2 million.  Most of the
orders were for our new computer product line that was introduced
in January.

In addition to the actual orders, we obtained the names of over
two hundred businesses that are interested in our products.  We
have already added these names to the prospect database and will
be following up with literature and direct phone calls in the
next two weeks.  These names will also be passed along to our
dealers where appropriate.

Based on these successful results, I strongly recommend that we
attend the Computer Products Show next September.  I will obtain
the necessary information and forward it to you as soon as I
receive it.
```

In a **detail report**, each line on the report usually corresponds to one input record that has been read and processed. Detail reports contain a great deal of information and can be quite lengthy. They are usually required by individuals who need access to the day-to-day information that reflects the operating status of the organization. For example, people in the warehouse of a hardware distributor should have access to the location and number of units on hand for each product. The Detail Inventory Report in Figure 5-3 contains a line for each warehouse location for each part number. Separate inventory records exist for each line on the report.

As the name implies, a **summary report** summarizes data. It contains totals for certain values found in the input records. The report shown in Figure 5-4 contains a summary of the total quantity on hand for each part. The information on the summary report consists of totals for each part from the information contained in the detail report in Figure 5-3. Detail reports frequently contain more information than most managers have time to review. With a summary report, however, a manager can quickly review information in summarized form.

An **exception report** contains information that is outside of *normal* user-specified values or conditions, called the exception criteria. Records meeting this criteria are an *exception* to the majority of the data. For example, if an organization wants to know when to reorder inventory items to avoid running out of stock, it would design an exception report. The report would tell which inventory items fell below the reorder points and therefore need to be ordered. An example of such a report is shown in Figure 5-5.

```
              Detail Inventory Report
                 By Part Number
                                              Quantity
 Part #      Description       Location       On  Hand
 1001        claw hammer          W1           1,000
 1001        claw hammer          W2             420
 1001        claw hammer          W3              75
 1049        pipe wrench          W2             725
 1075        gas welder           W1              13
 1075        gas welder           W2               7
 1075        gas welder           W4              11
```

FIGURE 5-3
The data for this detail report was obtained from each input record that was read and processed. A line was printed for each record.

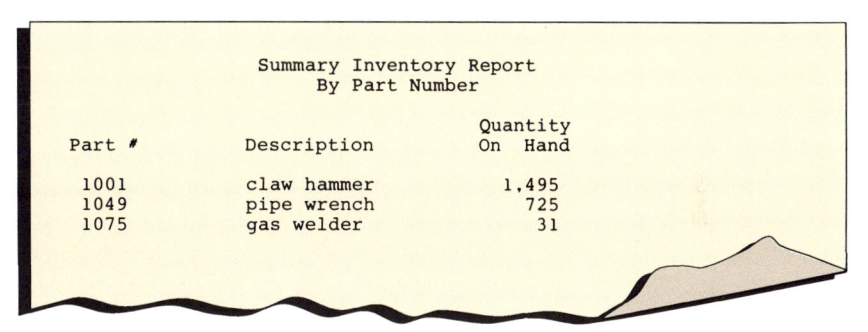

```
             Summary Inventory Report
                 By Part Number
                                  Quantity
 Part #      Description          On  Hand
 1001        claw hammer            1,495
 1049        pipe wrench              725
 1075        gas welder                31
```

FIGURE 5-4
This summary report contains the total on-hand quantity for each part. The report can be prepared using the same data that prepared the report in Figure 5-3.

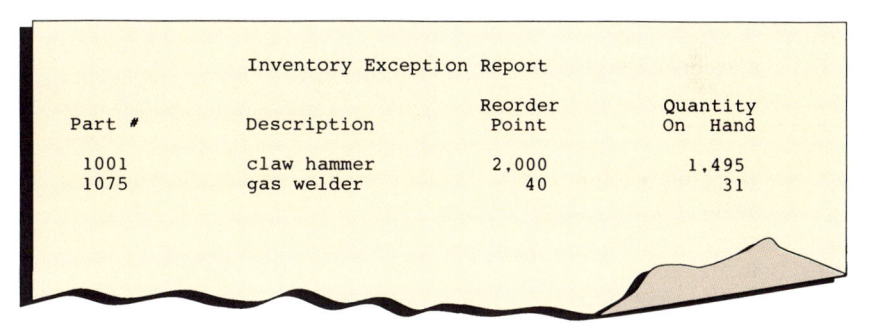

```
             Inventory Exception Report
                                Reorder         Quantity
 Part #      Description         Point          On  Hand
 1001        claw hammer         2,000           1,495
 1075        gas welder             40              31
```

FIGURE 5-5
This exception report lists inventory items with an on-hand quantity below their reorder points. These parts could have been selected from thousands of inventory records. Only these items met the user's exception criteria.

Exception reports help users focus on situations that may require immediate decisions or specific actions. The advantage of exception reports is that they save time and money. In a large department store, for example, there may be over 100,000 inventory items. A detail report containing all inventory items could be longer than 2,000 pages. To search through the report to determine the items whose on-hand quantity was less than the reorder point would be a difficult and time-consuming task. The exception report, however, could select these items, which might number 100 to 200, and place them on a two- to four-page report that could be reviewed in just a few minutes.

Reports are also sometimes classified by how often they are produced. **Periodic reports**, also called **scheduled reports**, are produced on a regular basis such as daily, weekly, or monthly. **On-demand reports** are created for information that is not required on a scheduled basis, but only when it is requested.

Graphics

Another common type of output is computer graphics. In business, **computer graphics** are often used to assist in analyzing data. Computer graphics display information in the form of charts, graphs, or pictures so that the information can be understood easily and quickly (Figure 5-6). Facts contained in a lengthy report and data relationships that are difficult to understand in words can often be summarized in a single chart or graph.

In the past, graphics were not widely used in business because each time data was revised, a graphic artist would have to redraw the chart or graph. Today, relatively inexpensive graphics software makes it possible to redraw a chart, graph, or picture within seconds rather than the hours or days that were previously required. Many application software packages, such as spreadsheets, include graphics capabilities. Analytical and presentation graphics software, discussed in Chapter 2, offer powerful tools for the business user who must present data in a meaningful manner or for the manager who must review, analyze, and make decisions based on data relationships.

FIGURE 5-6
This report lists sales of magazines by school category. With the addition of the pie chart graphic, however, the manager can easily see that colleges account for more than half the sales and that private schools represent a small percentage of the sales. Both the report and the graphic use the same information, but the graphic helps the manager to understand the information more quickly.

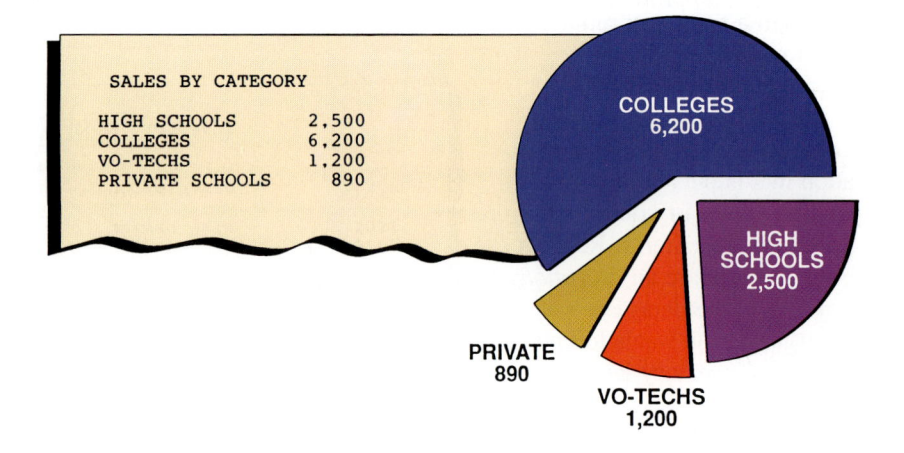

```
SALES BY CATEGORY

HIGH SCHOOLS       2,500
COLLEGES           6,200
VO-TECHS           1,200
PRIVATE SCHOOLS      890
```

COLLEGES 6,200
HIGH SCHOOLS 2,500
PRIVATE 890
VO-TECHS 1,200

Multimedia

Multimedia is the mixing of text, graphics, video (pictures) and audio (sound) output on a screen. An example would be a multimedia encyclopedia where in addition to the standard text, an animated image with sound is displayed (Figure 5-7).

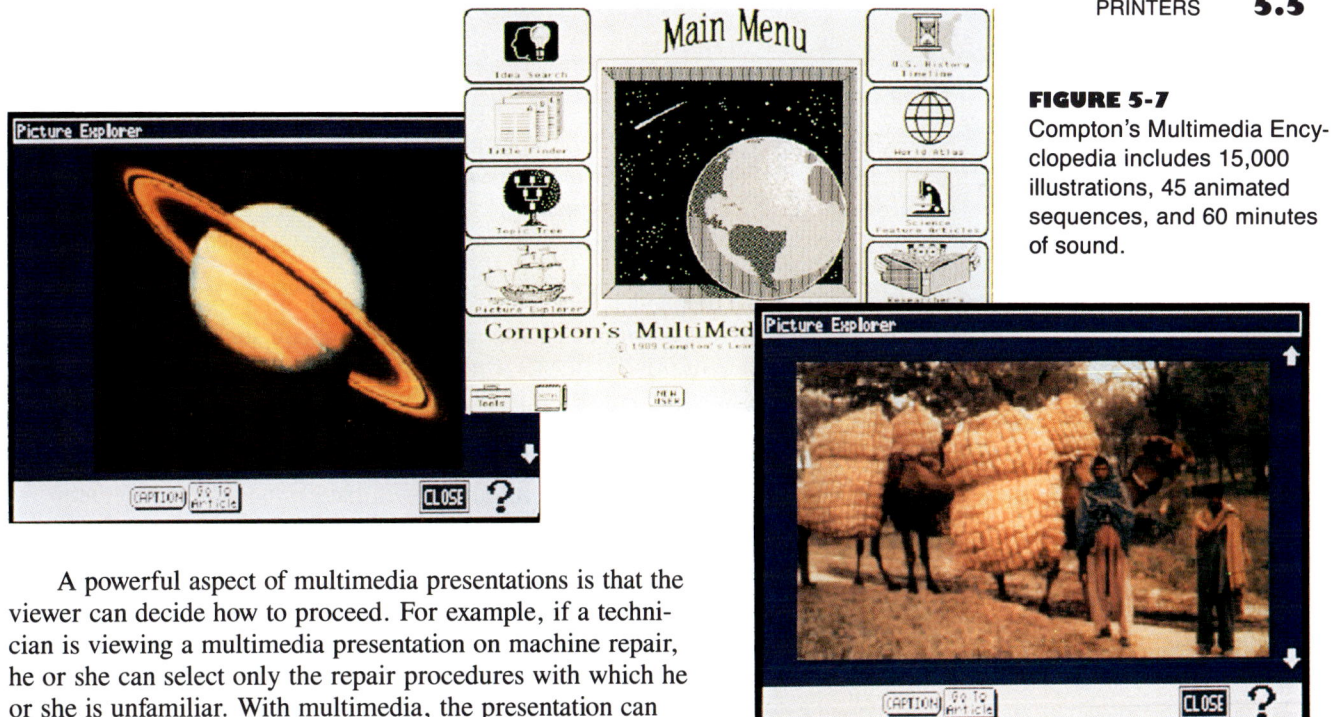

FIGURE 5-7
Compton's Multimedia Encyclopedia includes 15,000 illustrations, 45 animated sequences, and 60 minutes of sound.

A powerful aspect of multimedia presentations is that the viewer can decide how to proceed. For example, if a technician is viewing a multimedia presentation on machine repair, he or she can select only the repair procedures with which he or she is unfamiliar. With multimedia, the presentation can also include sounds that can help the technician identify a specific problem (Figure 5-8).

One of the technical issues that multimedia developers are working on is the tremendous amount of storage required by full-motion video. One minute of full-motion video requires over two billion bytes of storage. Because of this requirement, most multimedia presentations use animation instead of TV-quality video. The key to more widespread use of full motion is **video compression**, making the large amounts of data take up less storage space. One compression technique currently being developed is **digital video interactive (DVI)**. This technique can reduce storage requirements by a factor of 100 or more.

A variety of devices produce the output created in the information processing cycle. The following sections describe the devices most commonly used.

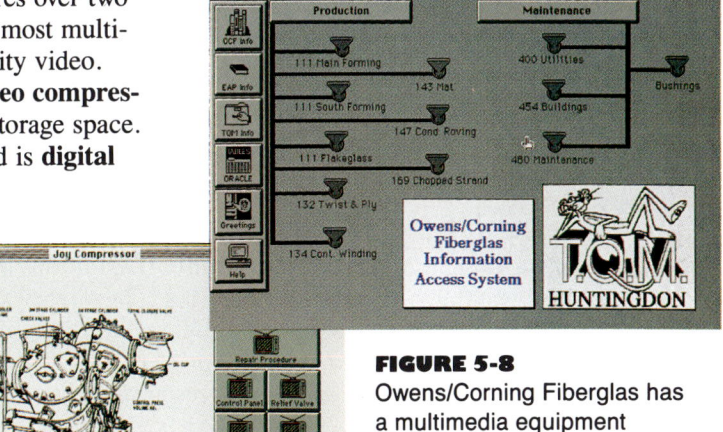

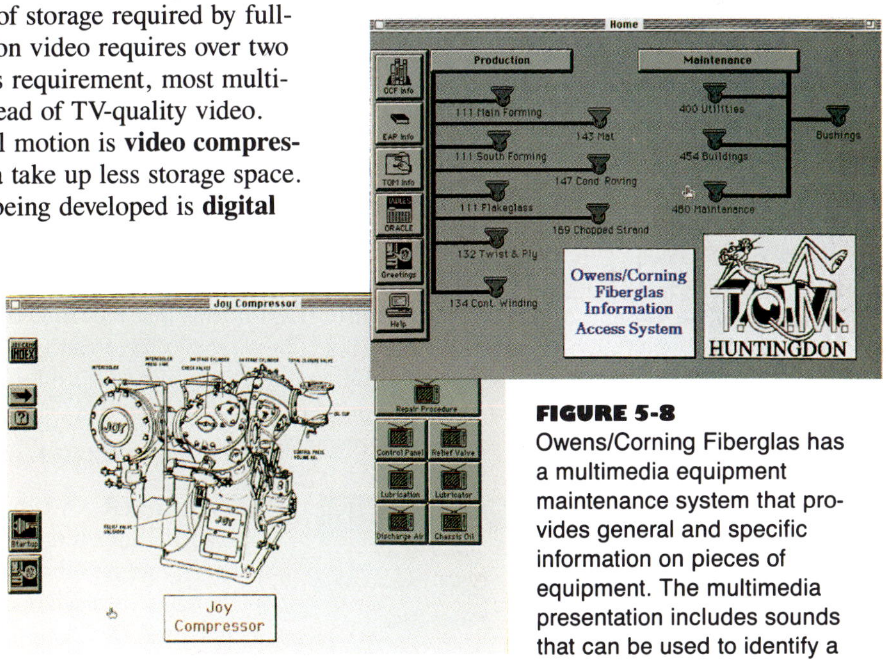

FIGURE 5-8
Owens/Corning Fiberglas has a multimedia equipment maintenance system that provides general and specific information on pieces of equipment. The multimedia presentation includes sounds that can be used to identify a specific repair problem.

PRINTERS

◆ Printing requirements vary greatly among computer users. For example, the user of a personal computer generally uses a printer capable of printing 100 to 200 lines per minute. Users of mainframe computers, such as large utility companies that send printed bills to hundreds of thousands of customers each month, need printers that are capable of printing thousands of lines per minute. These different needs have resulted in the development of printers with varying capabilities. Due to the many choices available and because printed output is so widely used, users must be familiar with printer features and printer technology when choosing a printer.

Printer Features

To decide which printer to choose for a particular application, it is important to know the different features that a printer might have. The main feature choices include speed, paper types and sizes, print quality, and typefaces. Other features include the capability to print color, printer size, and the type of printer interface.

Speed Printers can be rated as low speed, medium speed, high speed, and very high speed. Low-speed printers print one character at a time and are sometimes called character printers. The rate of printing for low-speed printers is expressed in **characters per second (cps)**. Low-speed printers can print from 50 to 400 characters per second. Medium-speed and high-speed printers are called **line printers** because they can print multiple characters on a line at the same time. The rate of printing for these machines is expressed in the number of **lines per minute (lpm)** that can be printed. Medium-speed printers can print from 300 to 600 lines per minute. Printers that can print from 600 to 3,000 lines per minute are classified as high-speed printers. Very high-speed printers can print in excess of 3,000 lines per minute; some, more than 20,000 lines per minute. Some printers produce an entire page at one time. The speed of these printers is rated in **pages per minute (ppm)**.

Paper Types and Sizes Most printers use either continuous-form or single-sheet paper. Some printers can use both. The pages of **continuous-form paper** are connected together for a continuous flow through the printer. The advantage of continuous-form paper is that it doesn't need to be changed frequently; thousands of pages come connected together. A disadvantage of continuous-form paper is that sometimes the individual pages of the report have to be separated. The advantage of using single-sheet printers is that different types of paper, such as letterhead, can be changed quickly.

Continuous-form paper usually has a page size of 8 1/2 by 11 inches or 11 by 14 inches. Single-sheet paper is usually either standard letter size (8 1/2 by 11 inches) or legal size (8 1/2 by 14 inches). Numerous variations on these sizes are available.

Print Quality When users require high-quality printed output, such as for business or legal correspondence, a printer that provides letter-quality output is chosen. The term **letter quality (LQ)** means that the printed character is a fully formed, solid character like those made by a typewriter. Printers that cannot make fully formed characters, but still offer good print quality are said to provide **near letter quality (NLQ)**. **Draft-quality** printers provide output that a business would use for internal purposes and not for correspondence.

FIGURE 5-9
Many printers can now print different typefaces. Here, examples of the Avant Garde, Helvetica, and Times Roman typefaces are shown in regular, italics, and bold type.

REGULAR	ITALIC	BOLD
Avant Garde	*Avant Garde*	**Avant Garde**
Helvetica	*Helvetica*	**Helvetica**
Times Roman	*Times Roman*	**Times Roman**

Typefaces A **typeface** is a set of letters, numbers, and special characters that have a similar design. Commonly used typefaces include Avant Garde, Helvetica, and Times Roman. Each typeface can be printed in a variety of styles and sizes. An example of a different style is *italics* where the characters are slanted or **bold** where the characters are darker (Figure 5-9). Character size is measured in points. A **point** is 1/72 of an inch. Common point sizes for text used in the body of a document are 10 or 12 points. A complete set of characters in the same typeface, style, and size is called a **font**. One feature you should consider when evaluating a printer is the number of fonts it can print. Some printers can print only a limited number of fonts, whereas others are capable of printing numerous fonts.

Other Printer Features Other features that you should consider when you evaluate a printer include color output, the amount of desk space the printer requires (referred to as the *footprint*) and the printer interface, which is the way the printer electronically communicates with the computer to which it is attached. With a **serial interface**, data is sent to the printer a single bit at a time. With a **parallel interface**, an entire byte (eight bits) is sent at the same time. Printers with a parallel interface must be located close to the computer, generally within fifty feet. Serial interface printers can be located up to 1,000 feet away from the computer and can even be used at remote locations where the printed information is transmitted over a communication link such as a phone line.

How Are Printers Classified?

Printers can be classified by how they transfer characters from the printer to the paper, either by impact or nonimpact.

Impact printers transfer the image onto paper by some type of printing mechanism striking the paper, ribbon, and character together. One technique is front striking in which the printing mechanism that forms the character strikes a ribbon against the paper from the front to form an image. This is similar to the method used on typewriters. The second technique utilizes a hammer striking device. The ribbon and paper are struck against the character from the back by a hammer to form the image on the paper (Figure 5-10).

Nonimpact printing means that printing occurs without having a mechanism striking against a sheet of paper. For example, ink is sprayed against the paper or heat is used to fuse a fine black powder into the shape of a character.

Impact and nonimpact methods of printing each have advantages and disadvantages. Impact printing can be noisy because the paper is struck when printing occurs. But because the paper is struck, specially treated multipart paper can be used to create multiple copies of a report at one time, such as an invoice, that is routed to different people. Nonimpact printers are quiet and produce high-quality output. However, they do not strike the paper and can therefore only create one printed copy at a time. If additional copies are needed, they must each be printed separately.

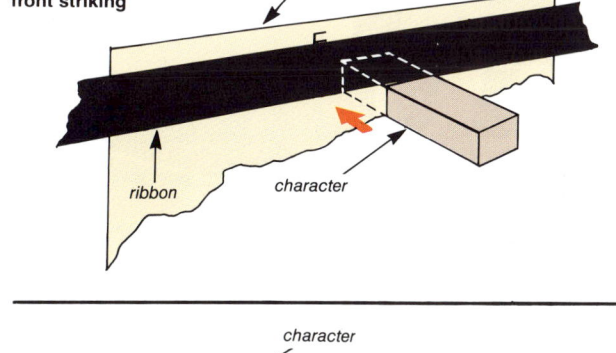

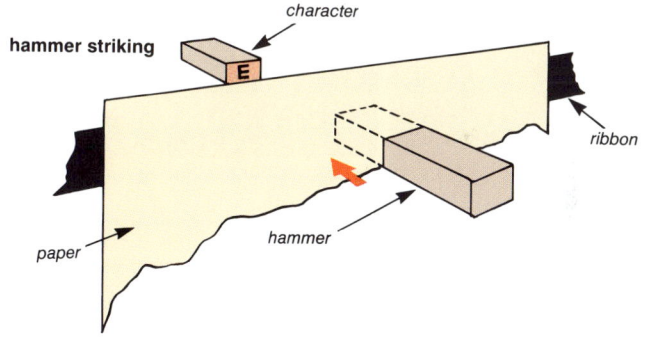

FIGURE 5-10
Impact printers operate in one of two ways: front striking or hammer striking.

IMPACT PRINTERS

◆ The increased use of computers has resulted in the development of a variety of impact printers that vary significantly in speed, quality, and price. Some of these printers, such as dot matrix, daisy wheel, and small page printers, are commonly used on microcomputers or small minicomputers. As the demand for printing information from a computer increases, the use of higher speed printers is required. In industry, minicomputers and mainframes are frequently used to process and print large volumes

FIGURE 5-11 ▼
This Panasonic dot matrix printer is popular for use with personal computers.

of data. The two types of impact printers often used to print large volumes of data are chain printers and band printers. The following sections describe the various types of impact printers.

Dot Matrix Printers

Dot matrix printers are used extensively because they are versatile and relatively inexpensive. The Panasonic printer shown in Figure 5-11 is a well-known dot matrix printer that is used with personal computers. Figure 5-12 shows a popular Printronix dot matrix printer that is frequently used with minicomputers. A **dot matrix printer** is an impact printer. Its print head consists of a series of small tubes containing pins that, when pressed against a ribbon and paper, print small dots. The pins are activated by electromagnets that are arranged in a radial pattern. The combination of small dots printed closely together forms the character (Figure 5-13).

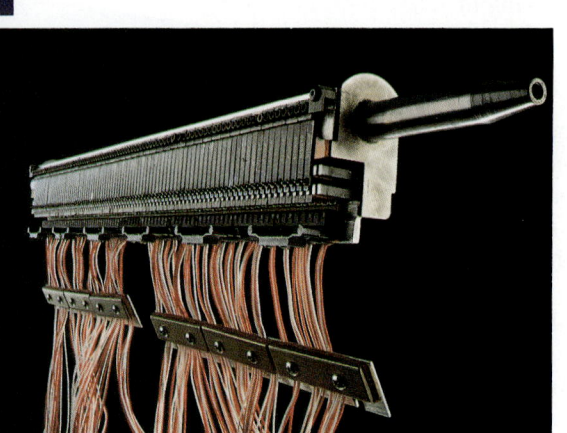

◄ FIGURE 5-12
This dot matrix line printer can print up to 800 lines per minute and is used in many business applications. Print heads at each print position allow this device to print an entire line at one time.

FIGURE 5-13 ▼
The print head assembly for a dot matrix printer consists of a series of pins that are fired at the paper by electromagnets. When activated, the pins strike the ribbon that strikes the paper, creating a dot on the paper.

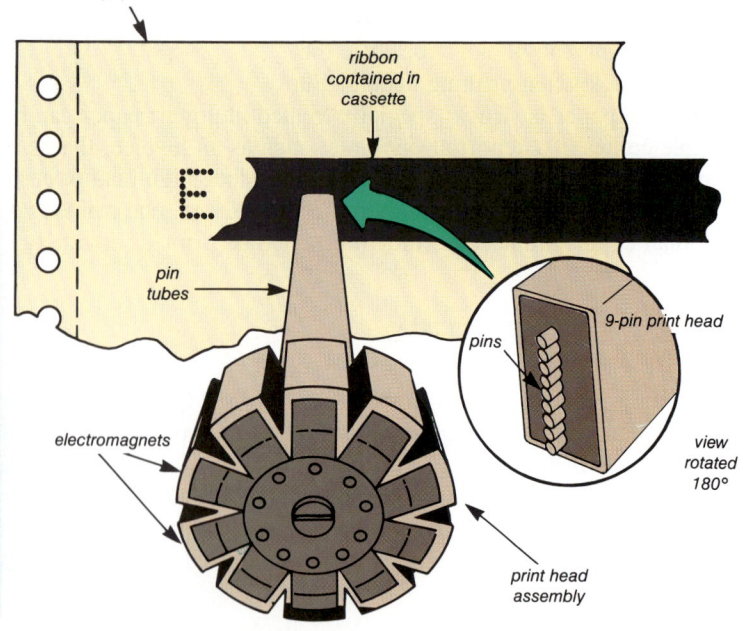

To print a character using a dot matrix printer, the character stored in main memory is sent to the printer's electronic circuitry. The printer circuitry activates the pins in the print head that correspond to the pattern of the character to be printed. The selected pins strike the ribbon and paper and print the character. Most dot matrix printers used with personal computers have a single print head that moves across the page. Dot matrix printers used with larger computers usually have fixed print mechanisms at each print position and can print an entire line at one time.

Dot matrix printers can contain a varying number of pins, depending on the manufacturer and the printer model. Print heads consisting of 9, 18 (two vertical rows of 9), and 24 pins (two vertical rows of 12) are most common. Figure 5-14 illustrates the formation of the letter E using a nine-pin dot matrix printer.

The print quality of dot matrix printers can be improved by overlapping the printed dots. Nine-pin print heads accomplish the overlapping by printing the line twice. The character is slightly offset during the second printing. This results in the appearance of solid characters (Figure 5-15).

Eighteen-pin and 24-pin printers can accomplish the overlapping on a single pass because their multiple rows of pins are slightly offset (Figure 5-16).

FIGURE 5-14
The letter E is formed with seven vertical and five horizontal dots. As the nine-pin print head moves from left to right, it fires one or more pins into the ribbon, which makes a dot on the paper. At print position 1, it fires pins 1 through 7. At print positions 2 through 4, it fires pins 1, 4, and 7. At print position 5, it fires pins 1 and 7. Pins 8 and 9 are used for lowercase characters such as p, q, y, g, and j that extend below the line.

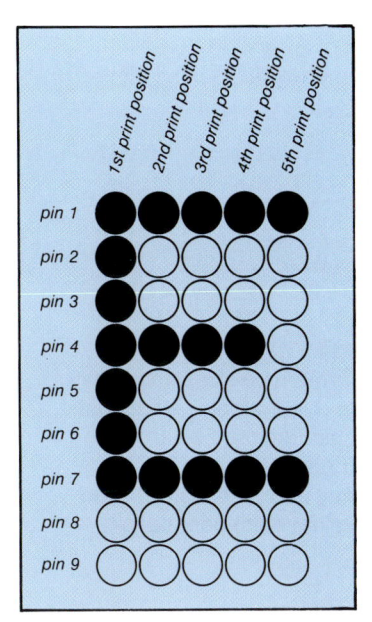

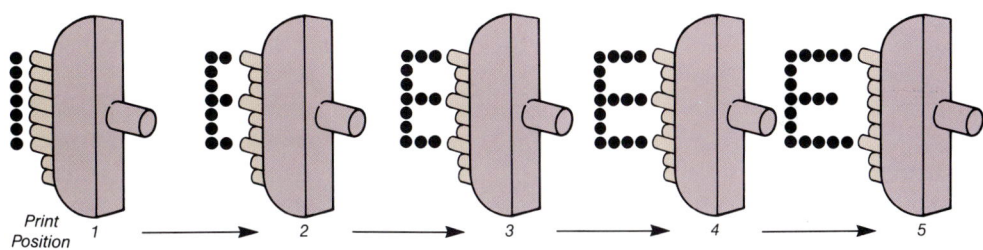

FIGURE 5-15
The letter E in this example is formed by overlapping, or printing the character twice. When it is printed the second time, the character is printed slightly offset so that much of the space between the dots is filled in. This gives the character a better appearance and makes it easier to read.

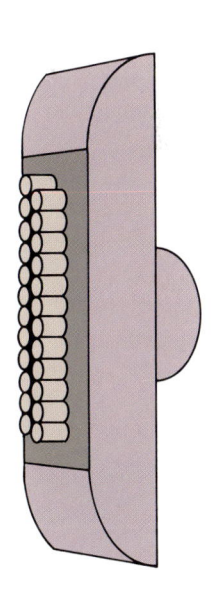

FIGURE 5-16
The two rows of pins on this 24-pin print head are slightly offset (one is higher than the other) so that they will overlap and produce a more solid looking character or a smoother line.

```
CONDENSED PRINT - NORMAL CHARACTERS
CONDENSED PRINT - EMPHASIZED CHARACTERS

STANDARD PRINT - NORMAL CHARACTERS
STANDARD PRINT - EMPHASIZED CHARACTERS

ENLARGED  PRINT  —  NORMAL  CHARACTERS
ENLARGED  PRINT  —  EMPHASIZED  CHARACTERS
```

FIGURE 5-17
Three type sizes are shown in this example—condensed, standard, and enlarged. All three are printed using normal and emphasized (also called bold) print density.

Many dot matrix printers can also print characters in a variety of sizes and densities. Typical sizes include condensed print, standard print, and enlarged print. In addition, each of these print sizes can be printed with increased density or darkness, called bold, or emphasized, print. Figure 5-17 illustrates condensed, condensed bold, standard, standard bold, enlarged, and enlarged bold print.

Dot matrix printers are designed to print in a **bidirectional** manner. That is, the print head, the device that contains the mechanism for transferring the character to the paper, can print as it moves from left to right, and from right to left. The printer does this by storing the next line to be printed in its memory and then printing the line forward or backward as needed. Bidirectional printing greatly increases the speed of the printer.

The feed mechanism determines how the paper moves through the printer. Two types of feed mechanisms found on dot matrix printers are tractor feed and friction feed. **Tractor feed mechanisms** transport continuous-form paper through the printer by using sprockets, small protruding prongs of plastic or metal, which fit into holes on each side of the paper (Figure 5-18). Where it is necessary to feed single sheets of paper into the printer, **friction feed mechanisms** are used. As the name implies, paper is moved through friction feed printers by pressure on the paper and the carriage, as it is on a typewriter. As the carriage rotates, the paper moves through the printer.

FIGURE 5-18
Each sheet of continuous-form paper is connected with the next. A feed mechanism pulls the paper through the printer using the holes on each side of the form. Perforations between each page allow a printed report to be folded to be separated into individual pages.

Dot matrix printers are built with a standard, medium, or wide carriage. A standard carriage printer can accommodate paper up to 8 1/2 inches wide. A medium carriage can accommodate paper up to 11 inches wide, and a wide carriage printer can accommodate paper up to 14 inches wide. Using a normal character size, most printers can print from 80 characters per line on a standard carriage to 132 characters per line on a wide carriage.

Some dot matrix printers can print in multiple colors using ribbons that contain the colors red, yellow, and blue in addition to the standard black. Color output is obtained by repeated printing and repositioning of the paper, print head, and ribbon.

Such printers can be useful in printing graphs and charts, but other types of color printers offer a higher quality of color output.

Most dot matrix printers have a graphics mode that enables them to print pictures and graphs (Figure 5-19). In graphics mode, the individual print head pins can be activated separately or in combination to form unique shapes or continuous lines. The flexibility of the dot matrix printer has resulted in widespread use of this type of printer by all types of computer users.

FIGURE 5-19
Some dot matrix printers can produce color output using multicolor ribbons.

Daisy Wheel Printers

The **daisy wheel printer** is an impact printer. The daisy wheel type element resembles the structure of a flower, with many long, thin petals (Figure 5-20). Each *petal* has a raised character at the tip. When printing occurs, the type element (daisy wheel) rotates so that the character to be printed is in the printing position. A hammer extends, striking the selected character against the ribbon and paper, printing the character. Because of the time required to rotate the daisy wheel, the daisy wheel printer is normally slower than a dot matrix printer; however, the print quality is higher because fully formed characters are printed. Printing speeds vary from 20 to 80 characters per second.

An additional feature of the daisy wheel printer is that the daisy wheel can be easily replaced. Daisy wheels come in a variety of sizes and fonts. Therefore, whenever the user wants to change fonts, he or she can remove one daisy wheel and put another wheel on the printer.

The disadvantage of a daisy wheel printer is that it is capable of printing only the characters that are on the wheel. It cannot, therefore, print graphic output. Although daisy wheel printers are still used, they are being replaced by other letter-quality printers.

FIGURE 5-20
The daisy wheel print element consists of a number of arms, each with a character at the end. When the printer is running, the wheel spins until the desired character is lined up with the hammer. The hammer then strikes against the ribbon and paper, printing the character.

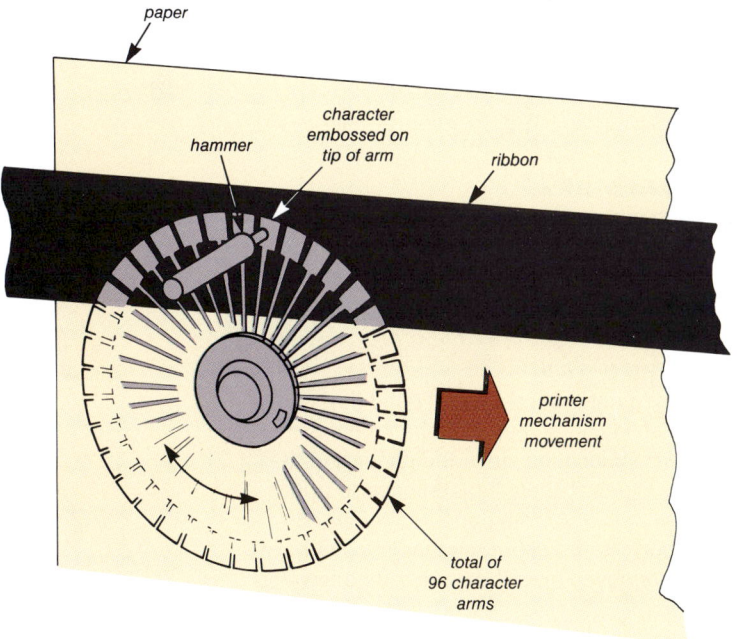

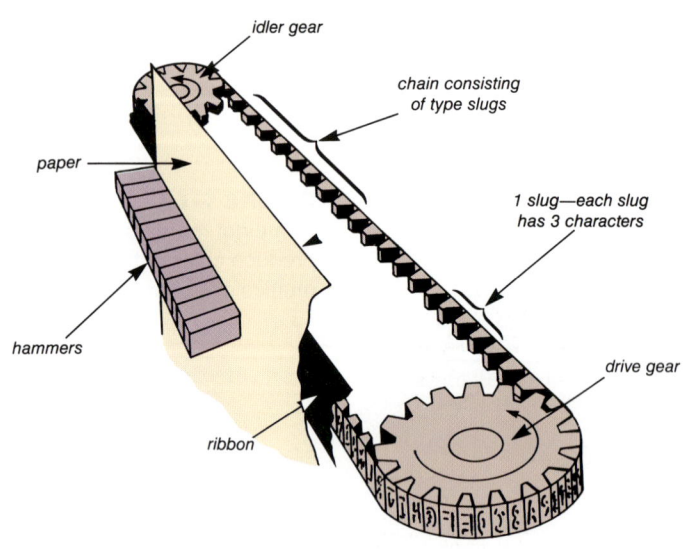

Chain Printers

The **chain printer** is a widely used high-speed printer. It contains numbers, letters of the alphabet, and selected special characters on a rotating chain (Figure 5-21). The chain consists of a series of type slugs that contain the character set. The character set on the type slugs is repeated two or more times on the chain mechanism. The chain rotates at a very high speed. Each possible print position has a hammer that can strike against the back of the paper, forcing the paper and ribbon against the character on the chain. As the chain rotates, the hammer strikes when the character to be printed is in the proper position.

The chain printer has proven to be very reliable. It produces good print quality up to 3,000 lines per minute. The printers in the large computer installation in Figure 5-22 are chain printers.

FIGURE 5-21 ▲
The chain printer contains a complete set of characters on several sections of a chain that rotates at a high, constant rate of speed. Print hammers are located at each horizontal print position. The paper and ribbon are placed between the hammers and the chain. As the chain rotates, the hammers fire when the proper characters are in front of their print positions.

Band Printers

Band printers, similar to chain printers, use a horizontal, rotating band containing characters. The characters are struck by hammers located at each print position behind the paper and ribbon to create a line of print on the paper (Figure 5-23).

FIGURE 5-22 ▲
These high-speed chain printers are used in a large computer installation to produce thousands of lines of printed output per minute.

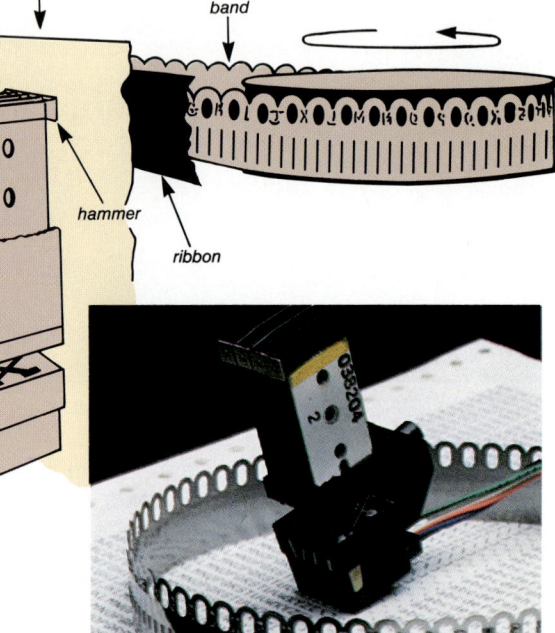

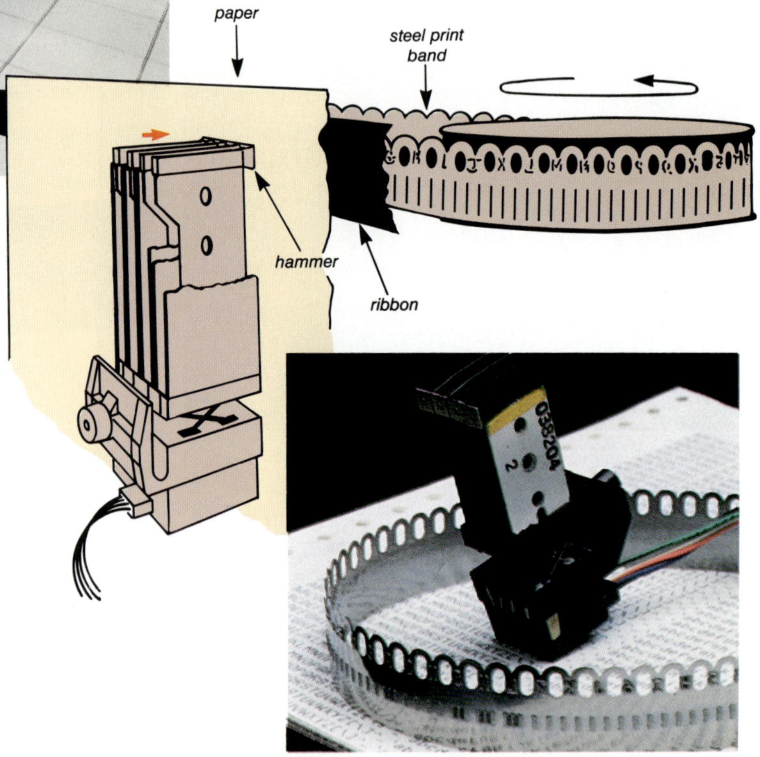

FIGURE 5-23 ▶
A band printer uses a metal band that contains solid characters. Print hammers at each print location strike the paper and the ribbon, forcing them into the band to print the character. A print band and a four-position print hammer mechanism that have been removed from the printer are shown on the right.

Interchangeable type bands can be used on band printers. The different type bands contain many different fonts, or print styles. A band printer can produce up to six carbon copies, has good print quality, high reliability, and depending on the manufacturer and model of the printer, can print in the range of 300 to 2,000 lines per minute.

NONIMPACT PRINTERS

Just as there are a variety of impact printers, there are also a variety of nonimpact printers. Ink jet, thermal, and small page printers are frequently used on microcomputers and small minicomputers. Medium- and high-speed page printers are used on minicomputers, mainframes, and supercomputers. The following sections discuss the various types of nonimpact printers.

Ink Jet Printers

A popular type of nonimpact printer is an **ink jet printer**. To form a character, an ink jet printer uses a nozzle that shoots electronically charged droplets of ink onto the page. The droplets pass between electrically charged deflection plates that guide the droplets to the correct position on the paper (Figure 5-24). Ink jet printers produce high-quality print and graphics and are quiet because the paper is not struck as it is by dot matrix or daisy wheel printers. Disadvantages are that ink jet printers cannot use multipart paper, and the ink sometimes smears on soft, porous paper. Ink jet printers that produce color output are also available (Figure 5-25).

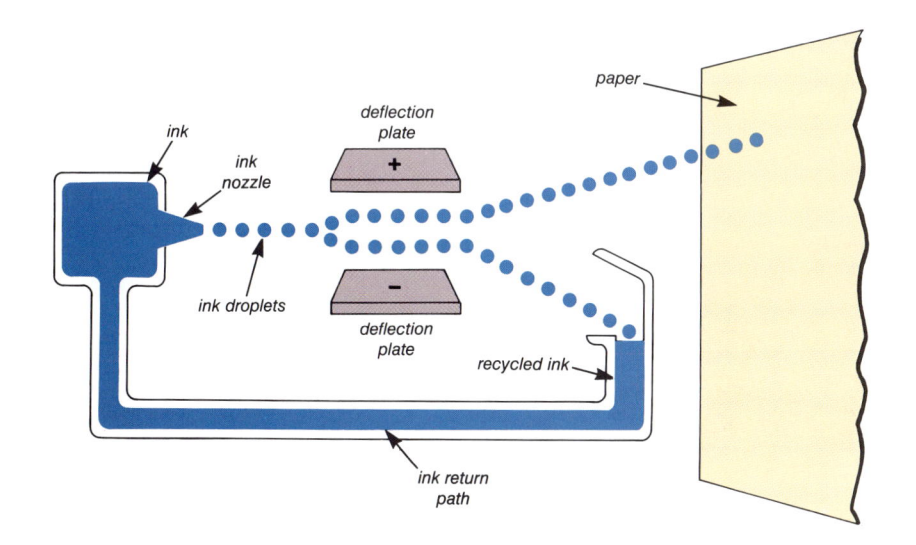

◀ **FIGURE 5-24**
Ink jet printers spray thousands of tiny ink drops toward the paper. The drops are directed to form characters or images by electrically charged deflection plates.

FIGURE 5-25 ▼
An IBM color ink jet printer.

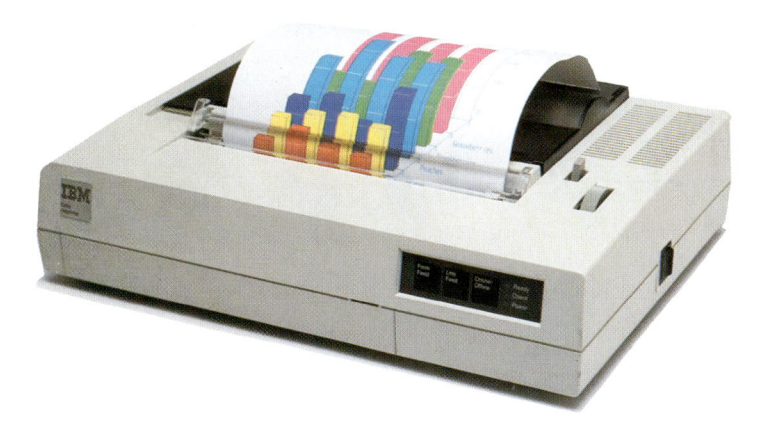

Thermal Printers

Thermal printers use heat to produce fully formed characters and graphic images on special chemically treated paper. Disadvantages of thermal printers are their use of special paper and their relatively slow printing speed. A category of thermal printers called **thermal transfer printers** are used for color printing (Figure 5-26).

Page Printers

The **page printer** is a nonimpact printer that operates similar to a copying machine. The page printer converts data from the computer into light that is directed to a positively charged revolving drum. Each position on the drum touched by the light becomes negatively charged and attracts the toner (powdered ink). The toner is transferred onto the paper and then fused to the paper by heat and pressure. Several methods are used to direct light to the photosensitive drum and create the text or image that will be transferred to the paper. **Laser printers** use a laser beam aimed at the drum by a spinning mirror (Figure 5-27). Other page printers use light emitting diode (LED) arrays or liquid crystal shutters (LCS). With these methods, the light can expose thousands of individual points on the drum. All page printers produce high-quality text and graphics suitable for business correspondence.

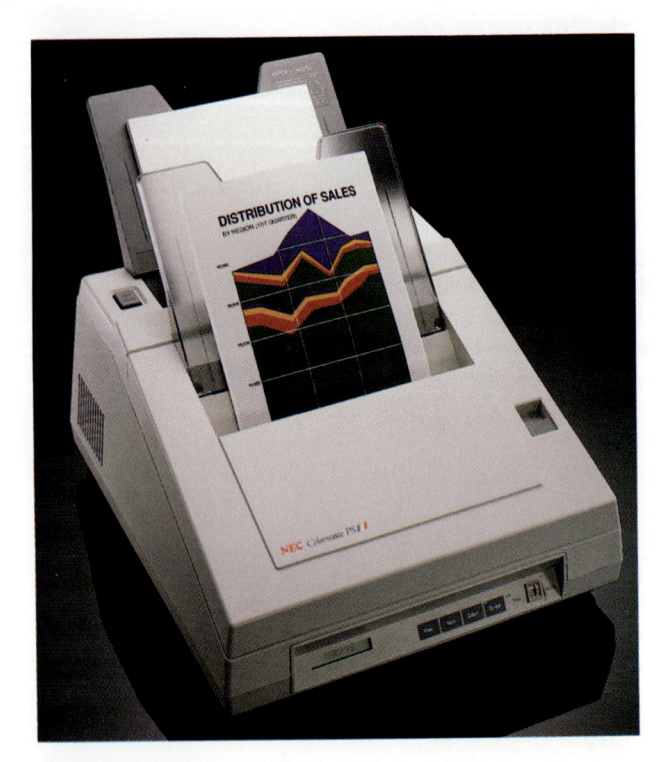

FIGURE 5-26
This thermal transfer printer can produce high-quality color output.

FIGURE 5-27
Laser printers use a process similar to a copying machine. Data from the computer, such as the word SALES ①, is converted into a laser beam ② that is directed by a mirror ③ to a photosensitive drum ④. The sensitized drum attracts toner particles ⑤ that are transferred to the paper ⑥. The toner is fused to the paper with heat and pressure ⑦.

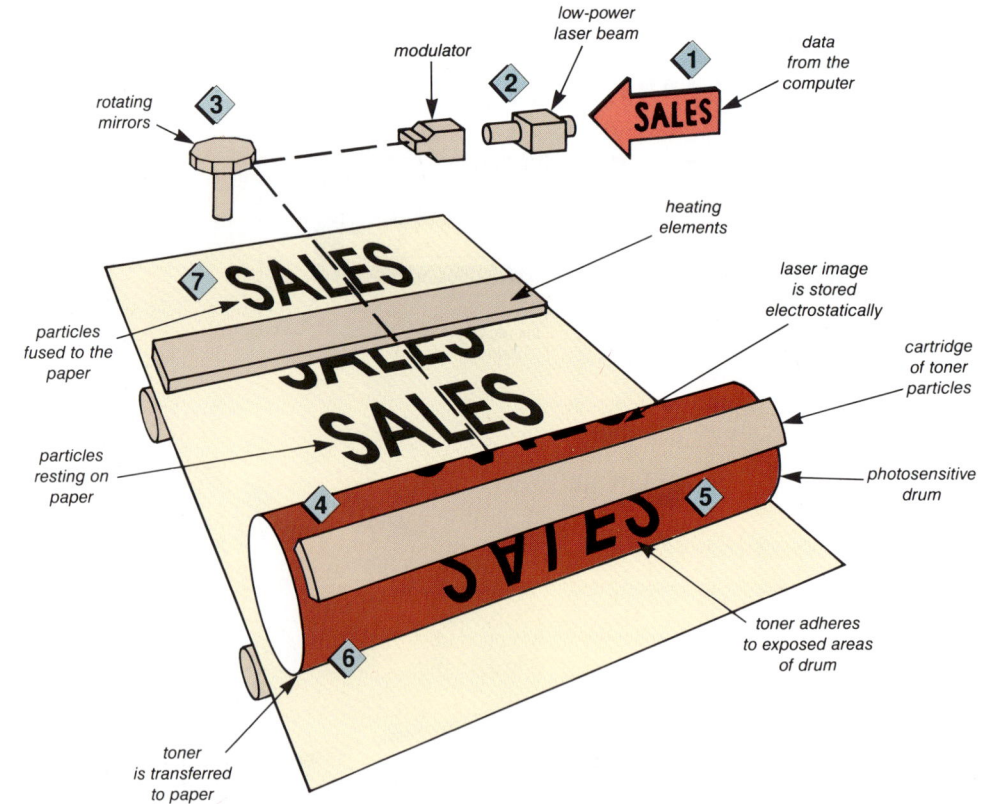

A wide range of page printers are available. Page printers commonly used with personal computers are capable of printing from 4 to 16 pages a minute (Figure 5-28).

Various page printers used with larger computers can print from 20 to 100 pages a minute. **High-speed page printers** can produce printed output at the rate of several hundred pages per minute. As shown in Figure 5-29, these high-speed printers usually consist of a dedicated computer and tape drive to maximize the printing speed.

CONSIDERATIONS IN CHOOSING A PRINTER

In addition to understanding the features and capabilities of the various types of printers that are available, you must consider several other factors before choosing a printer. These include factors such as how much output will be produced and who will use the output. Considering these and the other factors stated in Figure 5-30 will help you to choose a printer that will meet your needs.

FIGURE 5-28
The output shown here was produced by a laser printer. Notice that the output contains a mixture of different sizes and styles of print.

FIGURE 5-29
This laser printer can operate at speeds up to 120 pages per minute. On the left is a tape drive that is used as an input device.

QUESTION	EXPLANATION
How much output will be produced?	Desktop printers are not designed for continuous use. High volume (more than several hundred pages a day) requires a heavy-duty printer.
Who will use the output?	Most organizations want external reports to be prepared on a high-quality printer.
Where will the output be produced?	If the output will be produced at the user's desk, a sound enclosure may be required to reduce the noise of some printers to an acceptable level.
Are multiple copies required?	Some printers cannot use multipart paper.

FIGURE 5-30 Factors that affect the choice of a printer.

SCREENS

The **screen**, also called the **monitor**, **CRT (cathode ray tube)**, or **VDT (video display terminal)**, is another important output device. Screens are used on both personal computers and terminals to display many different types of output. For example, when a user queries a database, the resulting information is frequently displayed on a screen. A screen can also be used to display electronic spreadsheets, electronic mail, and graphs.

Screen Features

Some of the features that should be considered when selecting a screen include size, resolution, and color. A discussion of these and other features follows.

Size The most widely used screens are equivalent in size to a 12- to 16-inch television screen. Although there is no standard number of displayed characters, screens are usually designed to display 80 characters on a line with a maximum of 25 lines displayed at one time. The twenty-fifth line is often reserved for messages or system status reports, not for data. By reducing the character size, some terminals can display up to 132 characters on a single horizontal line. Screens designed for use with desktop publishing or engineering applications come in even larger sizes that can display one or sometimes two 8 1/2 by 11 inch pages of data. One company even makes a screen that can be tilted 90 degrees to display either a long or wide page (Figure 5-31).

FIGURE 5-31
Radius manufactures a screen that can be tilted 90 degrees to display the equivalent of one long or two wide pages.

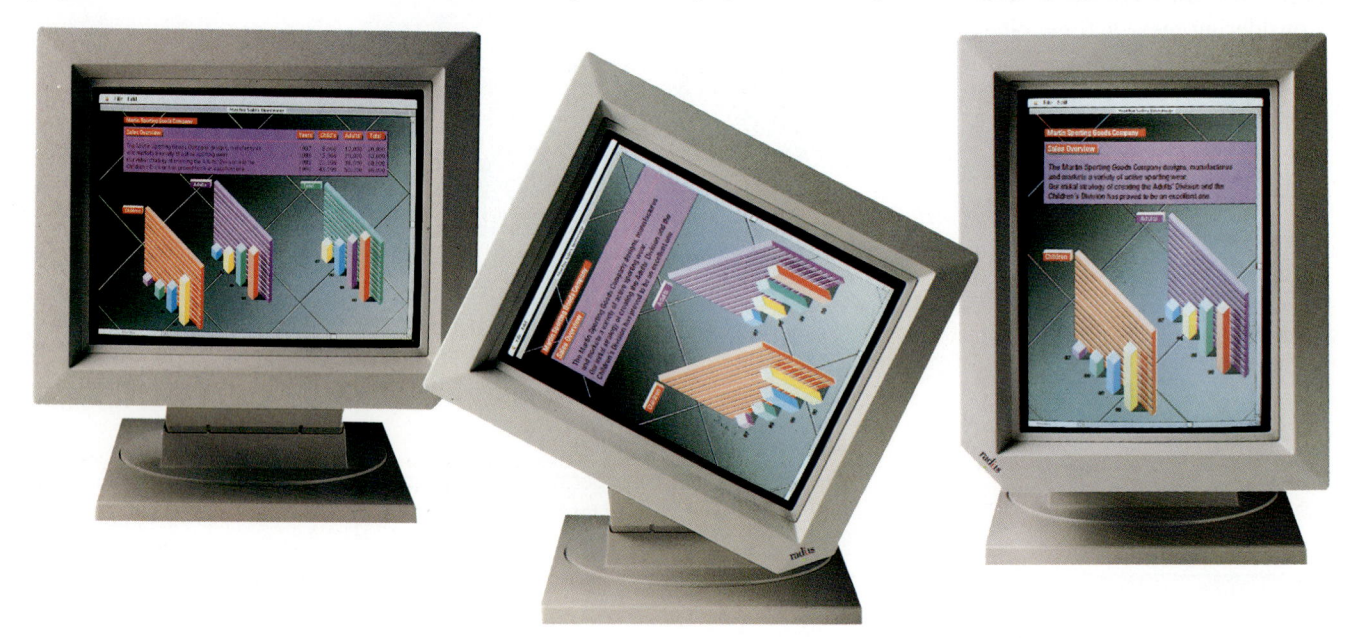

Resolution The **resolution**, or clarity, of the image on the screen depends on the number of individual dots that are displayed on the screen. Each dot that can be illuminated is called a **picture element**, or **pixel** (Figure 5-32). The greater the number of pixels, the better the screen resolution. The resolution of a screen is important, especially when the screen will be used to display graphics or other nontext information.

Screens used for graphics are called **dot-addressable displays**, or sometimes **bit-mapped displays**. On these monitors, the number of addressable locations on the screen corresponds to the number of pixels, or dots, that can be illuminated. The number of pixels on a screen is determined through a combination of the software in the computer, the graphics capability of the computer, and the screen itself.

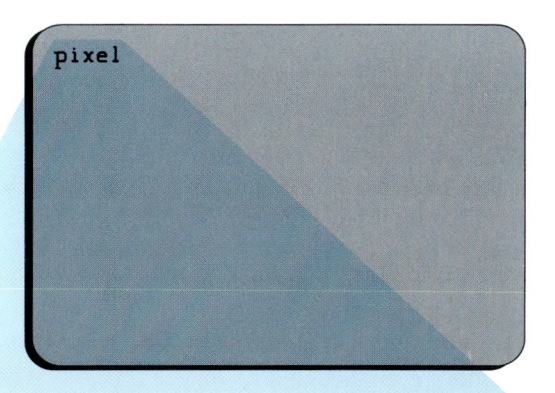

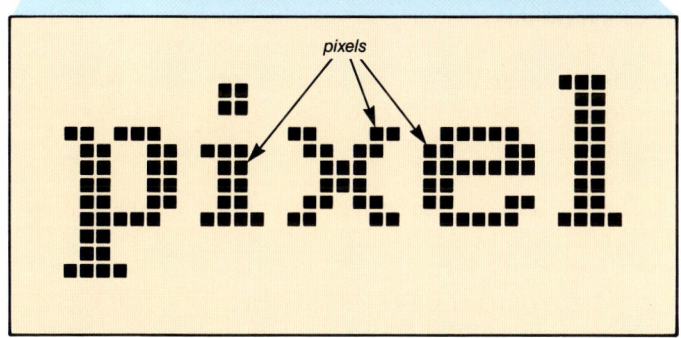

◄ **FIGURE 5-32**
The word pixel shown here is made up of pixels as they would be displayed on a dot-addressable or bit-mapped screen. Each pixel is a small spot of light that appears on the screen at the point where it is activated by an electron beam.

Devices are currently available that offer very high-resolution graphics. The resolution of these devices is high enough to provide an image that is almost equivalent to the quality of a photograph (Figure 5-33). High-resolution graphics require a great deal of storage and are more difficult electronically to maintain as a steady image on the screen. In the past few years, however, picture resolutions have greatly improved. In addition, costs have been reduced so that high-resolution graphics are now widely used.

Several graphics standards have been developed, including CGA (Color Graphics Adapter), EGA (Enhanced Graphics Adapter), VGA (Video Graphics Array), super VGA, and 1024. As shown in Figure 5-34, each standard provides for a different number of pixels and colors. Some manufacturers offer even higher resolution screens.

FIGURE 5-33 ▲
Very high-resolution graphics can depict features such as shading, reflections, and highlights as shown in the top photo. Very high-resolution graphics can also be used for simulation exercises; in this case, a flying situation as shown in the bottom photo. Through the use of the computer, this simulation could be changed quickly to show the plane taking off and landing.

FIGURE 5-34
A summary of the graphics resolution standards for display screens.

STANDARD	CGA	HERCULES	EGA	VGA	SUPER VGA	1024
Year	1981	1982	1984	1986	1988	1989
Resolution (W × H)	640 × 200	720 × 348	640 × 350	640 × 480	800 × 600	1024 × 768
Available Colors	16	None	64	262,144	256	262,144
Maximum Displayed Colors	4	None	16	256	16	256

Color Some screens can display information in color. The range of colors available depends on what software and hardware is being used. Microcomputers are available with screens that can simultaneously display 256 colors.

Cursor A **cursor** is a symbol such as an underline character or an arrow that indicates where you are working on the screen. Most cursors blink when they are on the screen so the user can quickly find their location.

Scrolling **Scrolling** is a method of moving lines displayed on the screen up or down one line at a time. For example, as a new line is added to the bottom of the screen, an existing one, from the top of the screen, is removed. The line removed from the screen remains in the computer's memory even though it no longer appears. When the screen is scrolled in the opposite direction (in this example, down), the line from the top that was removed reappears on the screen and the line at the bottom is removed. In addition to scrolling one line at a time, most screens allow users to scroll forward or backward one full screen at a time. This feature is useful in applications such as word processing when a user wants to move quickly through sections of a long document.

Other Screen Features Screen features also include several options that emphasize characters: reverse video, underlining, bold, and blinking. **Reverse video**, also called **inverse video**, refers to reversing the normal display on the screen. For example, it is possible to display a dark background with light characters or a light background with dark characters. Thus, if the normal screen had amber characters on a black background, reverse video shows black characters on an amber background. This feature permits single characters, whole words or lines, and even the entire screen to be reversed. The **underlining** feature allows characters, words, lines, or paragraphs to be underlined. Another feature used for emphasis is bold. **Bold** means that characters are displayed at a greater brightness level than the surrounding text. The **blinking** feature makes characters or words on a screen blink, thus drawing attention to them.

Types of Screens

Several types of screens are used with computers. The most common types are monochrome screens, color screens, plasma screens, and LCD screens. Plasma and LCD screens, which do not use the conventional cathode ray tube technology, are sometimes called **flat panel display screens** because of their relatively flat screens.

Monochrome screens designed for use with personal computers or as computer terminals usually display a single color such as white, green, or amber characters on a black background (Figure 5-35) or black characters on a white background.

FIGURE 5-35
Many users prefer amber or green characters rather than white characters.

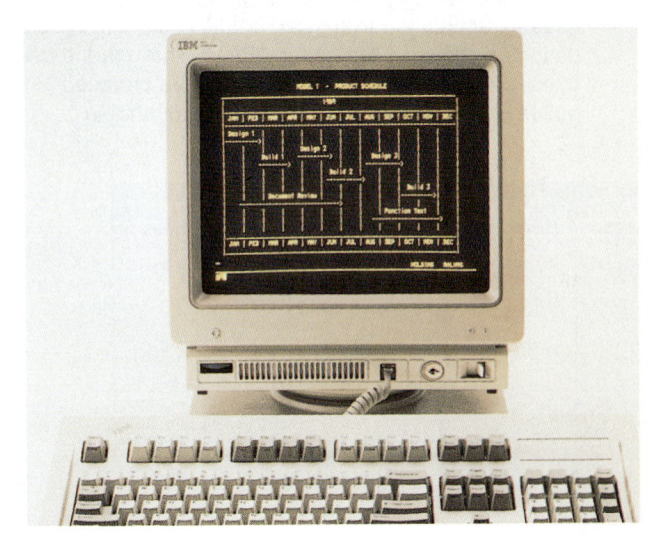

The use of **color screens** is increasing. Although they are more expensive than monochrome, they are desireable because much of today's software uses color. Color enables users to more easily read and understand the information on the screen. When color software is used with a monochrome monitor, the output displays as shades of a single color such as shades of grey.

With the development of truly portable computers, that could be conveniently carried by hand or in a briefcase, came a need for an output display that was equally as portable. **Liquid crystal displays (LCD)** and **plasma screens** are flat screens that are used as output displays for a number of laptop computers (Figure 5-36).

How Images Are Displayed on a CRT Screen

Most screens used with personal computers and terminals use cathode ray tube (CRT) technology. When these screens produce an image, the following four steps occur (Figure 5-37):

1. The image to be displayed on the screen is sent electronically from the CPU to the cathode ray tube.
2. An electron gun generates an electron beam of varying intensity, depending on the electronic data received from the CPU.
3. The yoke, which generates an electromagnetic field, moves the electron beam horizontally and vertically on the phosphor-coated screen.
4. The electron beam causes the desired phosphors to emit light. The higher the intensity of the beam, the brighter the phosphor glows. It is the phosphor-emitted light that produces an image on the screen.

FIGURE 5-36
Toshiba manufactures laptop computers that use liquid crystal display (LCD) screens, such as the model T1000 on the left, and plasma technology, such as the T5200 on the right.

FIGURE 5-37
The process of forming an image on a screen begins when the information to be displayed is sent to the CRT ①. Then the electron gun ② generates an electron beam. The yoke ③ directs the beam to a specific spot on the screen ④, where the phosphors struck by the electron beam begin to glow and form an image on the screen.

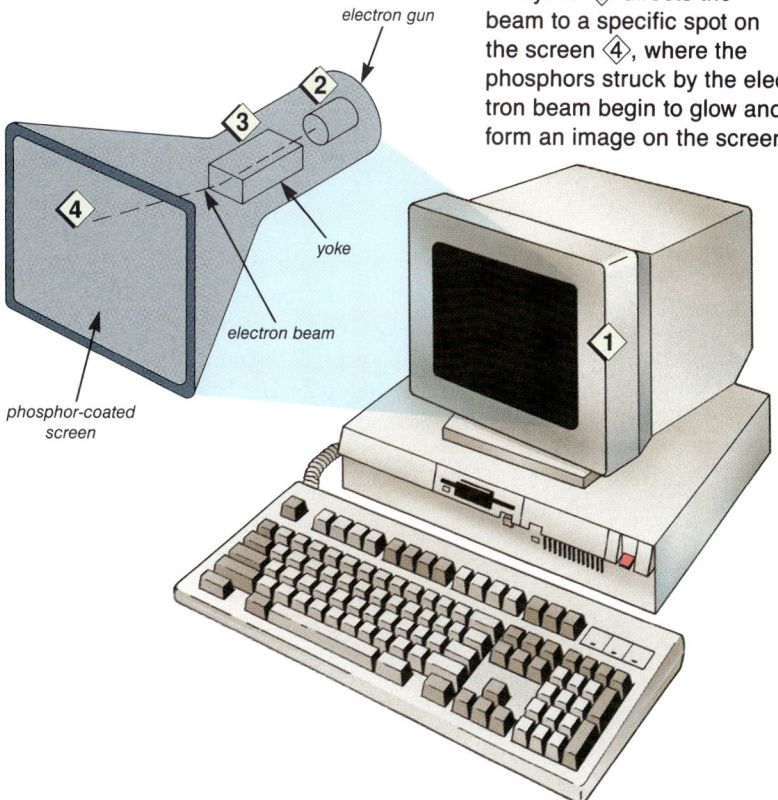

On most screens, the phosphors that emit the light causing the image on the screen do not stay lit very long. They must be refreshed by having the electron beam light them again. If the screen is not scanned enough times per second, the phosphors will begin to lose their light. When this occurs, it appears that the image on the screen is flickering. To eliminate flicker, the entire screen is refreshed 30 times per second.

The brightness of the image on the screen depends on the intensity of the electron beam striking the phosphor, which in turn depends on the voltage applied to the beam. As the beam scans each phosphor dot, the intensity is varied precisely to turn each dot on or off.

How Color Is Produced Color is produced on a screen in several ways. Remember that on a monochrome screen, a single electron beam strikes the phosphor-coated screen, causing the chosen phosphor dot to light. If the characters are green on a black background, the phosphors emit a green light when they are activated. Similarly, if the characters are amber on black, the phosphors emit an amber light.

To show color on a screen, each pixel must have three phosphor dots. These dots are red, blue, and green (Figure 5-38). The electron beam must turn on the desired color phosphors within the pixel to generate an image. In the simplest configuration, eight colors can be generated—no color (black), red only, blue only, green only, red and blue (magenta), red and green (yellow), blue and green (blue-green), and red, blue, and green together (white). By varying the intensity of the electron beam striking the phosphors, many more colors can be generated.

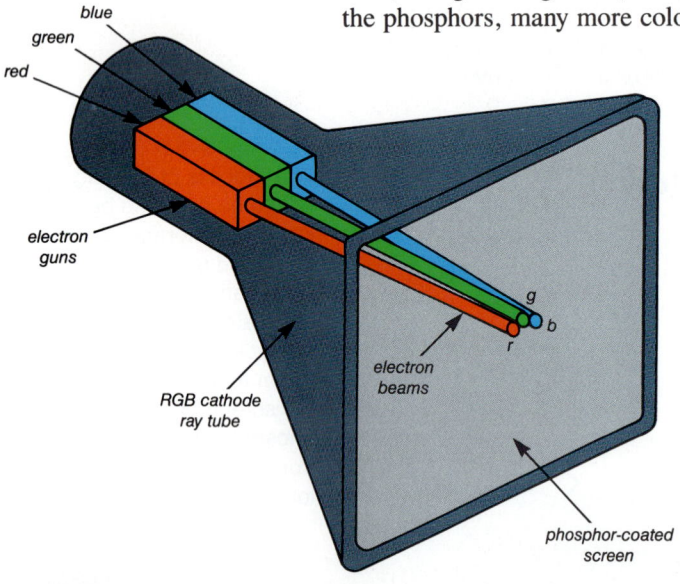

Two types of color screens are composite video monitors and RGB monitors. Both monitors produce color images, and both monitors can be used for color graphics. A **composite video monitor** uses a single electron signal to turn on the color phosphors within the pixel. An **RGB monitor** uses three signals, one for each color, red, green, and blue, to turn on the required phosphors. The difference is that the RGB monitor produces a much clearer display with much better color and character resolution.

FIGURE 5-38
On color monitors, each pixel contains three phosphor dots: one red, one green, and one blue. These dots can be turned on individually or in combinations to display a wide range of colors.

How Flat Panel Displays Work A plasma screen is one type of flat panel display. It consists of a grid of conductors sealed between two flat plates of glass. The space between the glass is filled with neon/argon gas. When the gas at an intersection in the grid is electronically activated, it creates an image. Each intersection of the grid of wires in a plasma screen is addressable. Therefore, this type of screen can display characters in a variety of typefaces and graphics such as line drawings, charts, or even pictures.

In an LCD display, a liquid crystal material is deposited between two sheets of polarizing material. When an electrical current passes between crossing wires, the liquid crystals are aligned so that light cannot shine through, producing an image on the screen.

OTHER OUTPUT DEVICES

Although printers and display devices provide the majority of computer output, other devices are available for particular uses and applications. These include data projectors, plotters, computer output microfilm devices, and voice output devices.

Data Projectors

A variety of devices are available to take the image that appears on a computer screen and project it so that it can be clearly seen by a room full of people. Smaller, lower cost units, called **projection panels**, use liquid crystal display (LCD) technology and are designed to be placed on top of an overhead projector (Figure 5-39).

Larger, more expensive units use technology similar to large screen projection TV sets; separate red, green and blue beams of light are focused onto the screen (Figure 5-40). The projection panels are easily portable and depending on the overhead projector with which they are used, can be located at different distances from the projection screen. The three-beam projectors must be focused and aligned for a specific distance and thus once installed, are usually not moved.

Plotters

A **plotter** is an output device used to produce high-quality line drawings such as building plans, charts, or circuit diagrams. These drawings can be quite large; some plotters are designed to handle paper up to 40 inches by 48 inches, much larger than would fit in a standard printer. Plotters can be classified by the way they create the drawing. The two types are pen plotters and electrostatic plotters.

As the name implies, **pen plotters** create images on a sheet of paper by moving one or more pens over the surface of the paper or by moving the paper under the tip of the pens.

Two different kinds of pen plotters are flatbed plotters and drum plotters. When a **flatbed plotter** is used to plot, or draw, the pen or pens are instructed by the software to move to the down position so the pen contacts the flat surface of the paper. Further instructions then direct the movement of the pens to create the image. Most flatbed plotters have one or more pens of varying colors or widths. The plotter shown in Figure 5-41 is a flatbed plotter that can create color drawings. Another kind of flatbed plotter holds the pen stationary and moves the paper under the pen.

FIGURE 5-39
Projection panels are used together with overhead projectors to display computer screen images to a room full of people.

FIGURE 5-40
This data projector uses three separate red, green, and blue beams to project data onto a screen.

FIGURE 5-41
A color flatbed plotter.

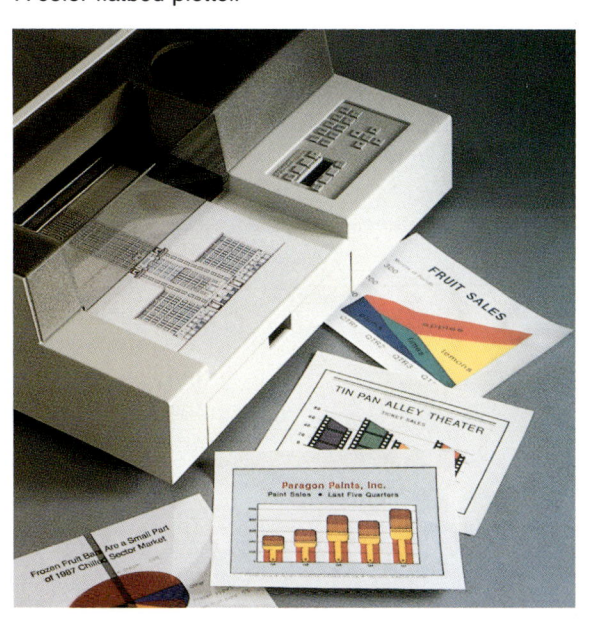

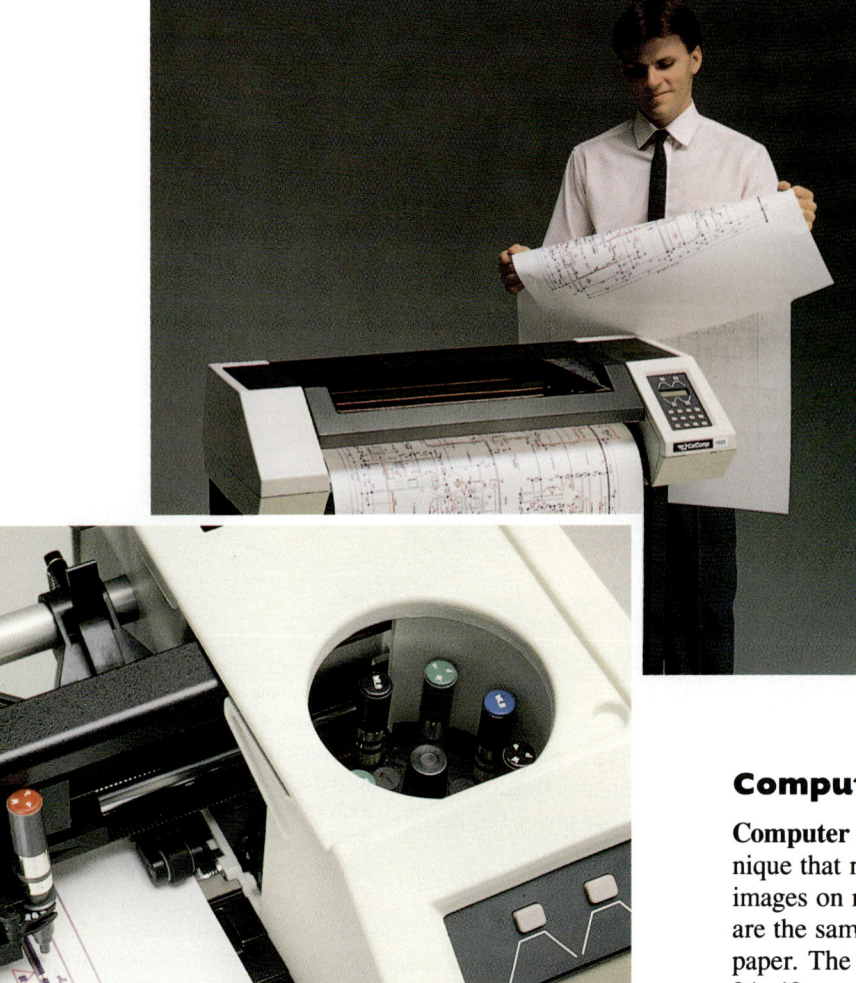

A **drum plotter** uses a rotating drum, or cylinder, over which drawing pens are mounted. The pens can move to the left and right as the drum rotates, creating an image (Figure 5-42). An advantage of the drum plotter is that the length of the plot is virtually unlimited, since roll paper can be used. The width of the plot is limited by the width of the drum.

With an **electrostatic plotter**, the paper moves under a row of wires (called styli) that can be turned on to create an electrostatic charge on the paper. The paper then passes through a developer and the drawing emerges where the charged wires touched the paper. The electrostatic printer image is composed of a series of very small dots, resulting in relatively high-quality output. In addition, the speed of electrostatic plotting is faster than with pen plotters.

Computer Output Microfilm

Computer output microfilm (COM) is an output technique that records output from a computer as microscopic images on roll or sheet film. The images stored on COM are the same as the images that would be printed on paper. The COM recording process reduces characters 24, 42, or 48 times smaller than would be produced on a printer. The information is then recorded on sheet film called **microfiche** or on 16mm, 35mm, or 105mm roll film.

The data to be recorded by the device can come directly from the computer (online) or from a magnetic tape that was previously produced by the computer (offline) (Figure 5-43). After the COM film is processed, the user can view it.

Microfilm has several advantages over printed reports or other storage media for certain applications. Some of these advantages are:

1. Data can be recorded on the film up to 30,000 lines per minute—faster than all but very high-speed printers.
2. Costs for recording the data are lower. The cost of printing a three-part, 1,000-page report is approximately $28, whereas the cost of producing the same report on microfilm is approximately $3.
3. Less space is required to store microfilm than printed materials. Microfilm that weighs one ounce can store the equivalent of 10 pounds of paper.
4. Microfilm provides a less expensive way to store data. For example, the cost per million characters (megabyte) on a disk is approximately $10, whereas the cost per megabyte on microfilm is approximately 65 cents.

FIGURE 5-42
This drum plotter utilizes eight pens of different colors to create diagrams. As the paper moves forward and back, the pens move left and right and, under software control, draw where instructed.

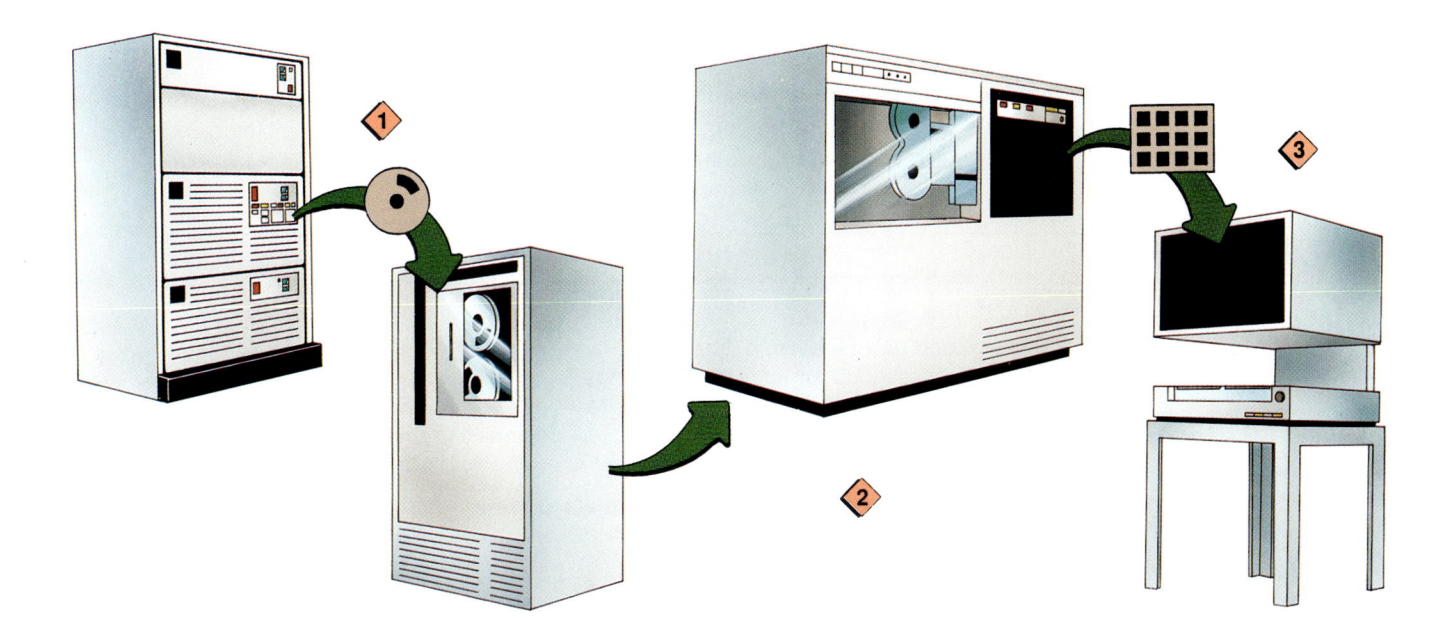

To access data stored on microfilm, a variety of readers are available. They utilize indexing techniques to provide a quick reference to the data. Some microfilm readers can perform automatic data lookup, called **computer-assisted retrieval (CAR)**, under the control of an attached computer. With the powerful indexing software and hardware now available for microfilm, a user can usually locate any piece of data in a 200 million character database in less than 10 seconds, at a far lower cost per inquiry than using an online inquiry system consisting of a computer system that stores the data on a hard disk.

Voice Output

Another important means of generating output from a computer is voice output. **Voice output** consists of spoken words that are conveyed to the user from the computer. Thus, instead of reading words on a printed report or monitor, the user hears the words over earphones, the telephone, or other devices from which sound can be generated.

The data that produces voice output is usually created in one of two ways. First, a person can talk into a device that will encode the words in a digital pattern. For example, the words *The number is* can be spoken into a microphone, and the computer software can assign a digital pattern to the words. The digital data is then stored on a disk. At a later time, the data can be retrieved from the disk and translated back from digital data into voice, so that the person listening will actually hear the words.

A second type of voice generation that holds great promise is called a **voice synthesizer**. It can transform words stored in main memory into speech. The words are analyzed by a program that examines the letters stored in memory and generates sounds for the letter combinations. The software can apply rules of intonation and stress to make it sound as though a person were speaking. The speech is then projected over speakers attached to the computer.

You may have heard voice output used by the telephone company for giving number information. Automobile and vending machine manufacturers are also incorporating voice output into their products. The potential for this type of output is great and it will undoubtedly be used in many products and services in the future.

FIGURE 5-43
The computer output microfilm (COM) process is illustrated here. The computer generates printed images on an output tape that is transferred to the tape drive attached to the COM machine ①. The COM machine reads the tape and produces reduced images of the printed output on the film ②—in this example, microfiche sheet film. Then the film can be viewed using special microfilm reader devices ③.

SUMMARY OF OUTPUT FROM THE COMPUTER

FIGURE 5-44
Some of the more common output devices are summarized in this table.

The output step of the information processing cycle uses a variety of devices to provide users with information. The equipment we discussed in this chapter, including printers, screens, and other output devices are summarized in Figure 5-44.

OUTPUT DEVICE	DESCRIPTION
Printers—Impact	
Dot matrix	Prints text and graphics using small dots.
Daisy wheel	Prints letter-quality documents—no graphics.
Chain	High-speed printer to 3,000 lines per minute—designed to print text.
Band	High-speed printer to 2,000 lines per minute—designed to print text.
Printers—Nonimpact	
Ink jet	Sprays ink onto page to form text and graphic output—prints quietly.
Thermal	Uses heat to produce fully formed characters.
Page	Produces high-quality text and graphics.
Screens	
Monochrome	Displays white, green, or amber images on a black background.
Color	Uses multiple colors to enhance displayed information.
Plasma	A flat screen that produces bright, clear images with no flicker.
LCD	A flat screen used on many laptop computers.
Data Projector	Projects computer screen images to a room full of people.
Plotters	Produces hard-copy graphic output.
COM	Records reduced-size information on sheet film called microfiche or on roll film.
Voice	Conveys information to the user from the computer in the form of speech.

CHAPTER SUMMARY

1. **Output** is data that has been processed into a useful form called information that can be used by a person or a machine.
2. Output that is printed is called **hard copy** and output that is displayed on a screen is called **soft copy**.
3. A **report** is information presented in an organized form.
4. An **internal report** is used within an organization by people performing their jobs.
5. An **external report** is used outside the organization.
6. The major consideration for internal reports is that they are clear and easy to use. For external reports, the quality of the printed output may be important.
7. **Narrative reports** may contain some graphic or numeric information, but are primarily text-based reports.
8. In a **detail report**, each line on the report usually corresponds to one input record.
9. A **summary report** contains summarized data, consisting of totals from detailed input data.
10. An **exception report** contains information that will help users to focus on situations that may require immediate decisions or specific actions.
11. **Periodic reports**, also called **scheduled reports**, are produced on a regular basis such as daily, weekly, or monthly.
12. **On-demand reports** are created for information that is not required on a scheduled basis, but only when it is requested.
13. **Computer graphics** are used to present information so it can be quickly and easily understood.
14. **Multimedia** combines text, graphics, video, and audio output on a screen.

15. The key to use of full-motion video in multimedia is **video compression**, making large amounts of data take up less storage space. **Digital video interactive (DVI)** is one compression technique currently being developed.
16. Computer printer features include speed, paper types and sizes, print quality, typefaces, color capability, size, and interface.
17. The printing rate for low-speed printers is rated in **characters per second (cps)**. The printing rate for medium- and high-speed printers is rated in either **lines per minute (lpm)** or **pages per minute (ppm)**.
18. The pages of **continuous-form paper** are connected for continuous flow through the printer.
19. Print quality is rated as **letter quality (LQ)**, **near letter quality (NLQ)**, or **draft quality**.
20. A **typeface** is a set of letters, numbers, and special characters that have a similar design.
21. Character sizes are measured in points. A **point** is 1/72 of an inch.
22. A complete set of characters in the same typeface, style, and size is called a **font**.
23. Computer printers fall into two broad categories: impact printers and nonimpact printers.
24. **Impact printing** devices transfer the image onto paper by some type of printing mechanism striking the paper, ribbon, and character together.
25. A **nonimpact printer** creates an image without having characters strike against a sheet of paper.
26. Although impact printing is noisy, multiple copies can be made at the same time.
27. Nonimpact printers are quiet and produce high-quality output.
28. **Dot matrix printers** can print text and graphics and are used with more personal computers than any other type of printer.
29. Dot matrix printers have small pins that are contained in a print head. The pins strike the paper and ribbon to print a character.
30. The quality of a dot matrix printer is partly dependent on the number of pins used to form the character.
31. Most dot matrix printers can print condensed print, standard print, and enlarged print.
32. Most dot matrix printers print **bidirectionally**, meaning the print head can print while moving in either direction.
33. **Tractor feed mechanisms** transport continuous-form paper by using sprockets inserted into holes on the sides of the paper.
34. **Friction feed mechanisms** move paper through a printer by pressure between the paper and the carriage.
35. Some dot matrix printers can print in color.
36. **Daisy wheel printers** can print high-quality text, but they cannot print graphics.
37. **Chain printers** use a rotating chain to print up to 3,000 lines per minute.
38. **Band printers** can use interchangeable bands with different fonts.
39. An **ink jet printer** uses a nozzle to spray liquid ink drops onto the page. Some ink jet printers print in color.
40. **Thermal printers** use heat to produce fully formed characters, usually on chemically treated paper.
41. **Page printers** use a process similar to a copying machine to produce high-quality text and graphic output.
42. **High-speed page printers** use a dedicated computer and tape drive and can print several hundred pages per minute.
43. **Screens**, also referred to as **monitors**, **CRTs**, or **VDTs** are used to display data.
44. Most screens are 12 to 16 inches and display 80 characters per line with 25 lines on the screen at one time.
45. The **resolution**, or clarity, of a screen is determined by the number of **pixels** that can be illuminated.
46. The **cursor** is a symbol such as an underline character or an arrow that indicates where you are working on the screen.
47. **Scrolling** refers to the movement of screen data up or down one line or one screen at a time.
48. **Reverse video**, also called **inverse video**, **underlining**, **bold**, and **blinking** are screen features that can be used to emphasize displayed characters.
49. Types of screens include **monochrome screens, color screens, plasma screens,** and **LCD screens**.
50. **Monochrome screens** usually display green, white, or amber images on a black background or black images on a white background.
51. **Color screens** are being used more because color enables the user to more easily read and understand the information displayed on the screen.
52. **Plasma screens** and **liquid crystal display (LCD) screens** are flat screens often used with portable computers.
53. Most screens utilize cathode ray tube (CRT) technology.
54. To display color on a color monitor, three separate dots (red, blue, and green) are turned on by an electron beam.
55. Two types of color monitors are: **composite video monitors** and **RGB monitors**.
56. **Data projectors** can be used to project a screen image so that it can be seen by a room full of people.
57. A **plotter** is an output device that can create line drawings, diagrams, and similar types of output.

58. **Computer output microfilm (COM)** is an output technique that records output from a computer as microscopic images on roll or sheet film.
59. COM offers the advantages of faster recording speed, lower costs of recording the data, less space required for storing the data, and lower costs for storing the data.
60. Some microfilm readers can perform automatic data lookup, called **computer-assisted retrieval (CAR)**.
61. **Voice output** consists of spoken words that are conveyed to the computer user from the computer.
62. A **voice synthesizer** can transform words stored in main memory into human speech.

KEY TERMS

Band printer 5.12
Bidirectional 5.10
Bit-mapped display 5.16
Blinking 5.18
Bold 5.18
Chain printer 5.12
Characters per second (cps) 5.6
Color screen 5.19
Composite video monitor 5.20
Computer-assisted retrieval (CAR) 5.23
Computer graphics 5.4
Computer output microfilm (COM) 5.22
Continuous-form paper 5.6
CRT (cathode ray tube) 5.16
Cursor 5.18
Daisy wheel printer 5.11
Detail report 5.3
Digital video interactive (DVI) 5.5
Dot-addressable display 5.16
Dot matrix printer 5.8
Draft quality 5.6
Drum plotter 5.22
Electrostatic plotter 5.22
Exception report 5.3
External report 5.2

Flatbed plotter 5.21
Flat panel display screen 5.18
Font 5.6
Friction feed mechanism 5.10
Hard copy 5.2
High-speed page printer 5.15
Impact printer 5.7
Ink jet printer 5.13
Internal report 5.2
Inverse video 5.18
Laser printer 5.14
Letter quality (LQ) 5.6
Line printer 5.6
Lines per minute (lpm) 5.6
Liquid crystal display (LCD) 5.19
Microfiche 5.22
Monitor 5.16
Monochrome screen 5.18
Multimedia 5.4
Narrative report 5.2
Near letter quality (NLQ) 5.6
Nonimpact printing 5.7
On-demand report 5.4
Output 5.2
Page printer 5.14
Pages per minute (ppm) 5.6
Parallel interface 5.7

Pen plotter 5.21
Periodic report 5.4
Picture element 5.16
Pixel 5.16
Plasma screen 5.19
Plotter 5.21
Projection panel 5.21
Report 5.2
Resolution 5.16
Reverse video 5.18
RGB monitor 5.20
Scheduled report 5.4
Screen 5.16
Scrolling 5.18
Serial interface 5.7
Soft copy 5.2
Summary report 5.3
Thermal printer 5.14
Thermal transfer printer 5.14
Tractor feed mechanism 5.10
Typeface 5.6
Underlining 5.18
VDT (video display terminal) 5.16
Video compression 5.5
Voice output 5.23
Voice synthesizer 5.23

REVIEW QUESTIONS

1. Name and describe four types of commonly used reports.
2. What is multimedia? Give an example of multimedia.
3. Define the terms typeface, point, and font.
4. Identify the two major classifications of printers and discuss the advantages and disadvantages of each.
5. How does a dot matrix printer produce an image? What techniques are used on dot matrix printers to improve the print quality?
6. What are the two types of impact printers often used to print large volumes of data?
7. How does an ink jet printer produce images?
8. Explain how a page printer works.
9. List four graphics standards that have been developed for screens.
10. List the steps involved in displaying an image on a CRT screen.
11. Identify two types of flat panel display screens that are commonly used with portable computers.
12. What is a projection panel and how is it used?
13. List several advantages of microfilm over printed reports.
14. Describe the two ways of creating voice output.

CONTROVERSIAL ISSUES

1. When computers were first used in business, some people predicted the paperless office; a place where most documents would only exist electronically in the computer database. While some people think this will still happen, others believe that the widespread use of computers, word processing and spreadsheet software, and low-cost printers has actually resulted in an increase in the amount of paperwork. Do you think computers increase or decrease the amount of paper required?
2. Some people believe that multimedia will revolutionize the way information is presented and the way people learn. Others believe multimedia will have only a limited number of successful applications. For which new applications do you think multimedia can be used?

RESEARCH PROJECTS

1. Make a list of the places where you have heard synthesized voice output. Discuss these with others in your class.
2. Visit a computer store and obtain information on the lowest and highest priced printers. Make a presentation explaining the differences between the two printers.

Auxiliary Storage

CHAPTER 6 STORAGE

OBJECTIVES

- Define auxiliary storage
- Identify the primary devices used for auxiliary storage
- Explain how data is stored on diskettes and hard disks
- Describe how data stored on magnetic disks can be protected
- Explain how magnetic tape storage is used with computers
- Describe three other forms of auxiliary storage: optical disks, solid-state devices, and mass storage devices
- Describe how special-purpose storage devices such as smart cards are used

Storage is the fourth and final operation in the information processing cycle. In this chapter we explain storage operations and the various types of auxiliary storage devices that are used with computers. Combining what you learn about storage with your knowledge of input, processing, and output will allow you to complete your understanding of the information processing cycle.

WHAT IS AUXILIARY STORAGE?

◆ It is important to understand the difference between how a computer uses main memory and how it uses auxiliary storage. As you have seen, main memory temporarily stores programs and data that are being processed. **Auxiliary storage**, also called **secondary storage**, stores programs and data when they are not being processed, just as a filing cabinet is used in an office to store records. Records that are not being used are kept in the filing cabinet until they are needed. In the same way, data and programs that are not being used on a computer are kept in auxiliary storage until they are needed. Auxiliary storage devices that are used with computers include devices such as disk and tape drives (Figure 6-1).

FIGURE 6-1
Auxiliary storage is like a filing cabinet in which data is stored until you need it.

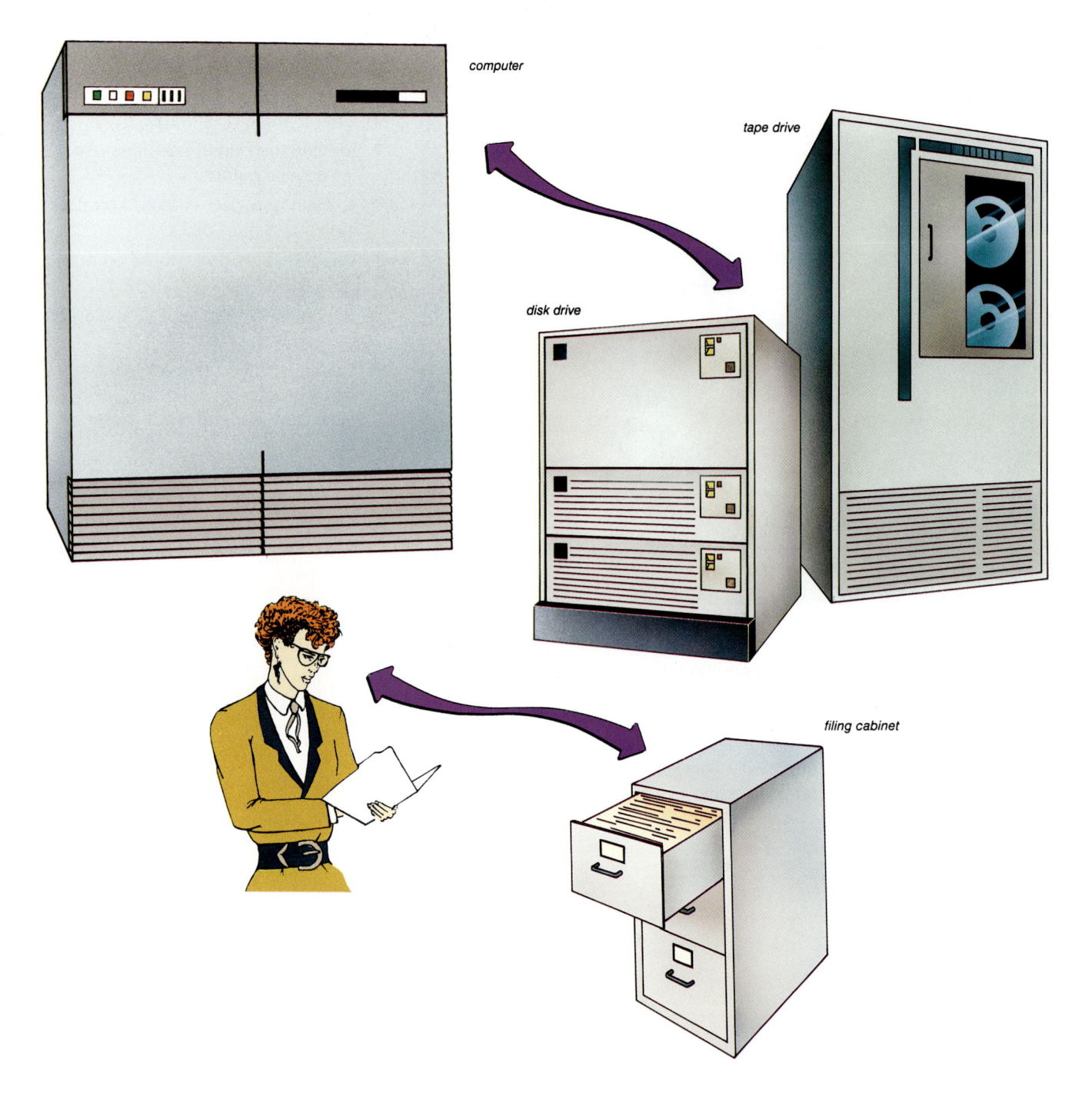

Most auxiliary storage devices provide a more permanent form of storage than main memory because they are **nonvolatile**, that is, data and programs stored on auxiliary storage devices are retained when the power is turned off. Main memory is volatile, which means that when power is turned off, whatever is stored in main memory is erased.

Auxiliary storage devices can be used as both input and output devices. When they are used to receive data that has been processed by the computer, they are functioning as output devices. When some of their stored data is transferred to the computer for processing, they are functioning as input devices.

User auxiliary storage needs can vary greatly. Personal computer users might find the amount of data to be stored to be relatively small. For example, the names, addresses, and telephone numbers of several hundred friends or customers of a small business might require only 20,000 bytes of auxiliary storage (200 records × 100 characters per record). Users of large computers, such as banks or insurance companies, however, might need auxiliary storage devices that can store billions of characters. To meet the different needs of users, a variety of storage devices are available. We discuss magnetic disk, magnetic tape, and other auxiliary storage devices in this chapter.

FIGURE 6-2
Here, a user is inserting a diskette into the disk drive of an IBM personal computer.

MAGNETIC DISK STORAGE

◆ Magnetic disk is the most widely used storage medium for all types of computers. **Magnetic disk** offers high storage capacity, reliability, and the capability to directly access stored data. There are several types of magnetic disk including diskettes, hard disks, and removable disk cartridges.

Diskettes

In the early 1970s, IBM introduced the diskette as a new type of auxiliary storage. These diskettes were eight inches in diameter and were thin and flexible, hence the name **floppy disks**, or *floppies*. Today, **diskettes** are used as a principal auxiliary storage medium for personal computers (Figure 6-2). This type of storage is convenient, reliable, and inexpensive.

Diskettes are available in a number of different sizes. The most common sizes today are 5 1/4" and 3 1/2" diameters (Figure 6-3).

A diskette consists of a circular piece of thin mylar plastic (the actual disk), which is coated with an oxide material similar to that used on recording tape. On a 5 1/4" disk, the circular piece of plastic is enclosed in a flexible square protective jacket. The jacket has an opening so that a portion of the disk's surface is exposed for reading and writing (recording) as shown on the next page in Figure 6-4.

FIGURE 6-3
The most commonly used diskette for personal computers are 5 1/4" and 3 1/2".

FIGURE 6-4
A 5 1/4" diskette consists of the disk itself enclosed within a protective jacket, usually made of vinyl material. The liner of the diskette is essentially friction-free so that the disk can turn freely, but the liner does contact the disk and keep it clean. The magnetic surface of the diskette, which is exposed through the window in the jacket, allows data to be read and stored. The large hole (hub) in the diskette is used to mount the diskette in the disk drive. The small hole is used by some disk drives as an indicator for where to store data.

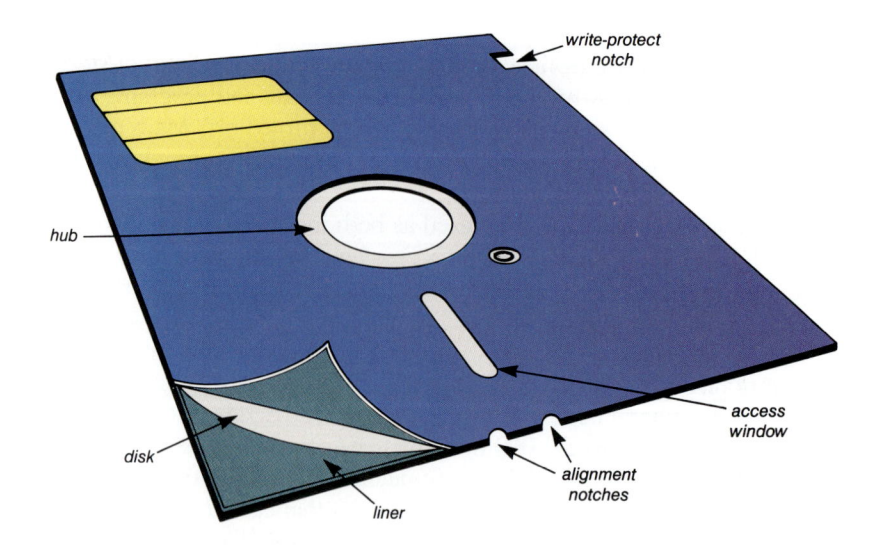

On a 3 1/2" disk, the circular piece of plastic is enclosed in a rigid plastic cover and a piece of metal called the shutter covers the reading and writing area. When the 3 1/2" diskette is inserted into a disk drive, the drive slides the shutter to the side to expose the diskette surface (Figure 6-5).

How Is a Diskette Formatted? Before a diskette can be used for auxiliary storage, it must be formatted. The **formatting** process prepares the diskette so that it can store data and includes defining the tracks, cylinders, and sectors on the surfaces of a diskette (Figure 6-6). A **track** is a narrow recording band forming a full circle around the diskette.

FIGURE 6-5
In a 3 1/2" diskette, the flexible plastic disk is enclosed between two liners that clean the disk surface of any microscopic debris and help to disperse static electricity. The outside cover is made of a rigid plastic material, and the recording window is covered by a metal shutter that slides to the side when the disk is inserted into the disk drive.

FIGURE 6-6
Each track on a diskette is a narrow, circular band. On a diskette containing 40 tracks, the outside track is called track 0 and the inside track is called track 39. The distance between track 0 and track 39 on a 5 1/4" diskette is less that one inch. The disk surface is divided into sectors. This example shows a diskette with nine sectors.

A **cylinder** is defined as all tracks of the same number. For example, track 0 on side 1 of the diskette and track 0 on side 2 of the diskette would be called cylinder 0. The term **sector** is used to refer to a pie-shaped section of the disk. It is also used to refer to a section of a track. When data is read from a diskette, a minimum of one full sector of a track is read. When data is stored on a diskette, at least one full sector of a track is written. The number of tracks and sectors created on a diskette when it is formatted varies based on the capacity of the diskette, the capabilities of the diskette drive being used, and the specifications in the software that does the formatting. Many 5 1/4" diskettes are formatted with 40 tracks and 9 sectors on the surface of the diskette. The 3 1/2" diskettes are usually formatted with 80 tracks and 9 sectors on each side. Even though it is smaller in size, a 3 1/2" diskette has a larger storage capacity than a 5 1/4" diskette.

Formatting is not usually done by the disk manufacturer because different operating systems define the surface of the diskette differently. In addition to defining the disk surface, the formatting process erases any data that is on the disk, analyzes the disk surface for any defective spots, and establishes a directory that will be used to record information about files stored on the diskette.

What Is the Storage Capacity of a Diskette? Knowing the storage capacity of a diskette gives you an idea of how much data or how many programs you can store on the diskette. The amount of data you can store depends on three factors: (1) the number of sides of the diskette used; (2) the recording density of the bits on a track; and (3) the number of tracks on the diskette.

Early diskettes and drives were designed so that data could be recorded on only one side of the diskette. These drives are called **single-sided drives**. Similarly, diskettes on which data can be recorded on one side only are called **single-sided diskettes**. Today, disk drives are designed to record and read data on both sides of the diskette. Drives that can read and write data on both sides of the diskette are called **double-sided drives** and the diskettes are called **double-sided diskettes**. The use of double-sided drives and diskettes *doubles* the amount of data that can be stored on the diskette.

Another factor in determining the storage capacity of a diskette is the recording density provided by the drive. The **recording density** is the number of bits that can be recorded on one inch of the innermost track on the diskette. This measurement is referred to as **bits per inch (bpi)**. The higher the recording density, the higher the storage capacity of the diskette.

The third factor that influences the amount of data that can be stored on a diskette is the number of tracks onto which data can be recorded. This measurement is referred to as **tracks per inch (tpi)**. As we saw earlier in this chapter, the number of tracks depends on the size of the diskette, the drive being used, and how the diskette was formatted.

The capacity of diskettes varies and increases every two or three years as manufacturers develop new ways of recording data more densely. Commonly used diskettes are referred to as either low density or high density. **Low-density diskettes** can store 360K for a 5 1/4" diskette and 720K for a 3 1/2" diskette. Personal computers using **high-density diskettes** (sometimes abbreviated as HD) can store 1.2 megabytes (million characters) on a 5 1/4" diskette and 1.44 megabytes on a 3 1/2" diskette.

How Is Data Stored on a Diskette? Regardless of the type of diskette or how it is formatted, the method of storing data on a diskette is essentially the same. When a 5 1/4" diskette is inserted in a disk drive, the center hole fits over a hub mechanism that positions the diskette in the unit (Figure 6-7). The circular plastic diskette rotates within its cover at approximately 300 revolutions per minute. Data is stored on tracks of the disk, using the same code, such as ASCII, that is used to store the data in main memory. To do this, a recording mechanism in the drive called the **read/write head** rests on the surface of the rotating diskette, generating electronic impulses (Figure 6-8). The electronic impulses change the magnetic polarity, or alignment, of magnetic spots along a track on the disk. The plus or minus polarity represents the 1 or 0 bits being recorded. To access different tracks on the diskette, the drive moves the read/write head from track to track. When reading data from the disk, the read/write head senses the magnetic spots that are recorded on the disk along the various tracks and transfers the data to main memory. When writing, the read/write head transfers data from main memory and stores it as magnetic spots on the tracks on the recording surface.

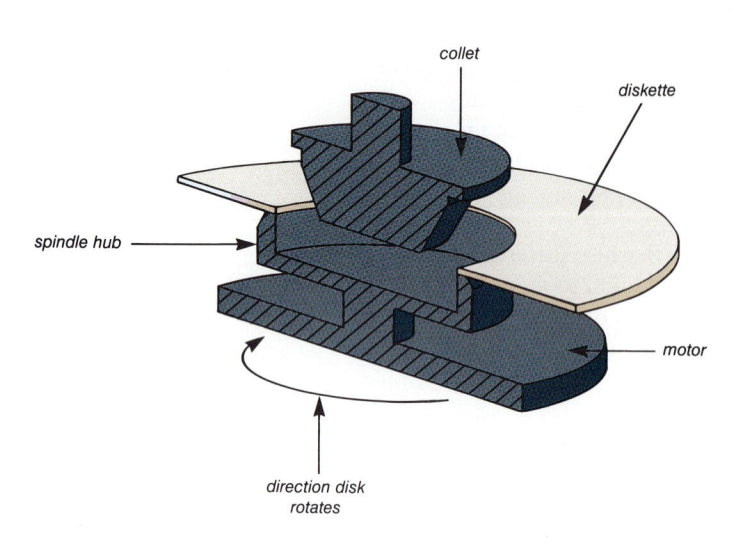

FIGURE 6-7
A cutaway drawing of a 5 1/4" disk drive. When you insert a diskette in a drive, the center hole is positioned between the collet and the hub. After you close the door to the disk drive, the disk is engaged and begins rotating within the protective jacket at approximately 300 RPM.

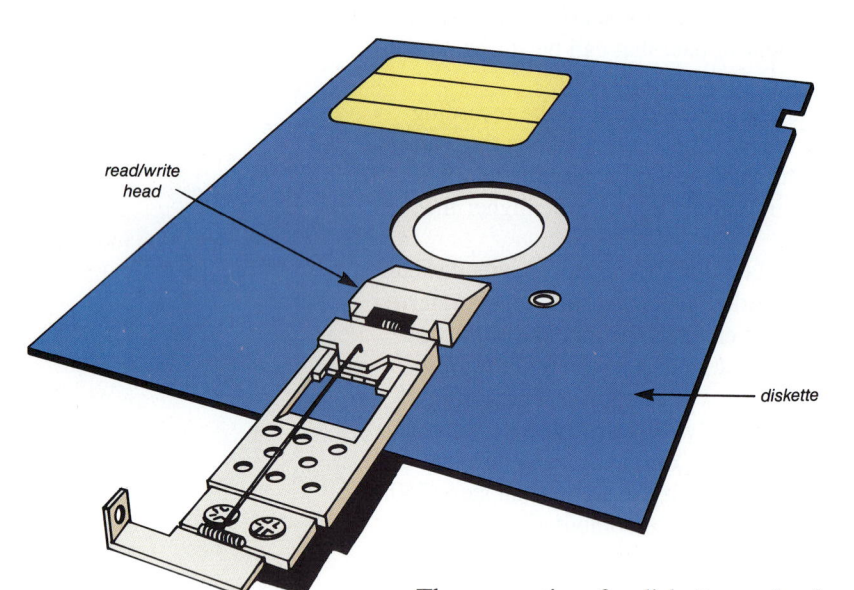

What Is Access Time? Data stored in sectors on a diskette must be retrieved and placed in main memory to be processed. The time required to access and retrieve the data is called the **access time**.

The access time for a diskette drive depends on four factors:

1. **Seek time**, the time it takes to position the read/write head over the proper track.
2. **Rotational delay** (also called **latency**), the time it takes for the sector containing the data to rotate under the read/write head.
3. **Settling time**, the time required for the read/write head to be placed in contact with the disk.
4. **Data transfer rate**, the time required to transfer the data from the disk to main memory.

FIGURE 6-8
The read/write heads move back and forth over the openings on both sides of the protective jacket to read or write data on the disk.

The access time for diskettes varies from about 175 milliseconds (one millisecond equals 1/1000 of one second) to approximately 300 milliseconds. What this means to the user is that, on the average, data stored in a single sector on a diskette can be retrieved in approximately 1/5 to 1/3 of one second.

The Care of Diskettes With reasonable care, diskettes provide an inexpensive and reliable form of storage. In handling diskettes, you should take care to avoid exposing them to heat, magnetic fields, and contaminated environments such as dust, smoke, or salt air. One advantage of the 3 1/2" diskette is that its rigid plastic cover provides more protection for the data stored on the plastic disk inside than the flexible cover on a 5 1/4" diskette. Figure 6-9 shows you ways to properly care for your diskettes. Because the read/write head actually comes in contact with the diskette surface, wear takes place and the diskette will eventually become unreadable. To protect against loss, you should backup or copy data onto other diskettes.

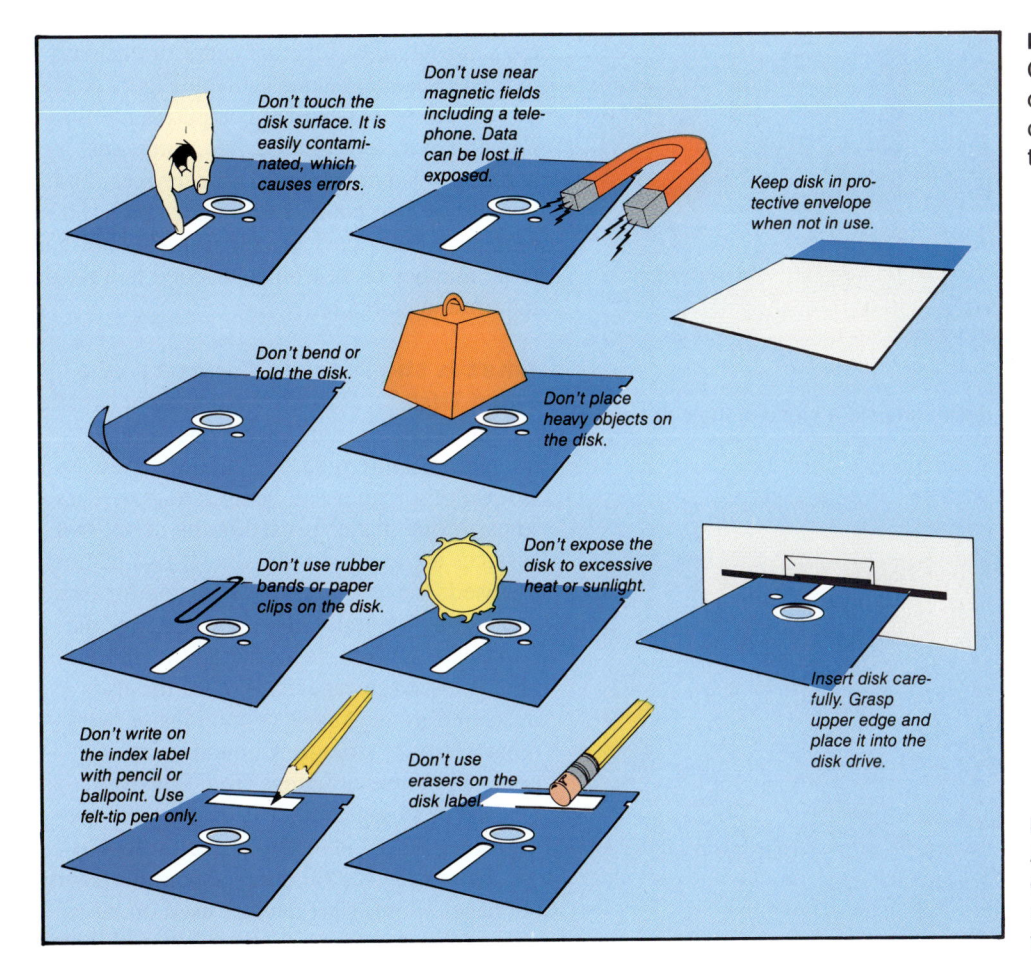

FIGURE 6-9
Guidelines for the proper care of 5 1/4" diskettes. Most of the guidelines also apply to 3 1/2" diskettes.

FIGURE 6-10
A hard disk consists of one or more disk platters. Each side of the platter is coated with an oxide substance that allows data to be magnetically stored.

Hard Disks

Hard disks provide larger and faster auxiliary storage capabilities than diskettes. **Hard disks** consist of one or more rigid metal platters coated with an oxide material that allows data to be magnetically recorded on the surface of the platters (Figure 6-10). These disks are permanently mounted inside the computer and are not removable like diskettes. On hard disks, the metal platters, the read/write heads, and the mechanism for moving the heads across the surface of the disk are enclosed in an airtight, sealed case. This helps to ensure a clean environment for the disk.

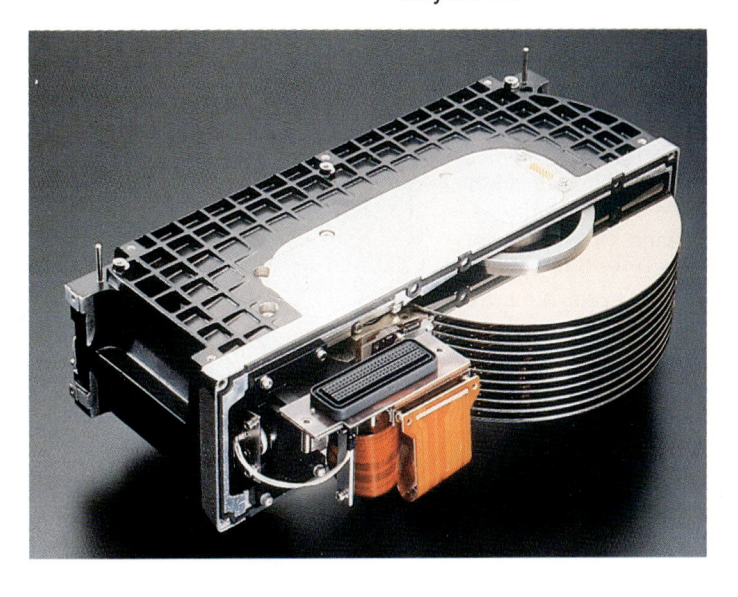

FIGURE 6-11
A high-speed, high-capacity fixed disk drive in a stand-alone cabinet.

FIGURE 6-12
A mainframe computer can have dozens of fixed disk storage devices attached to it.

FIGURE 6-13
This hard disk drive shows the access arm and the read/write heads, which are over the surface of the disks. These heads are extremely stable. They can read and write tracks very close together on the surface of the disk.

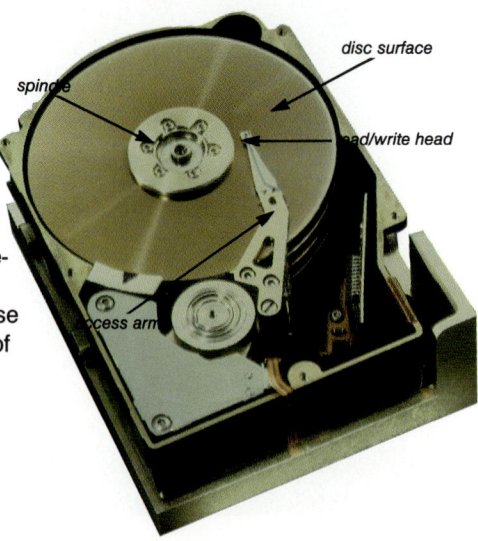

On minicomputers and mainframes, hard disks are sometimes called **fixed disks** because they cannot be removed like diskettes. They are also referred to as **direct-access storage devices (DASD)**. These hard disks are larger versions of the hard disks used on personal computers and can be either mounted in the same cabinet as the computer or enclosed in their own stand-alone cabinet (Figure 6-11).

While most personal computers are limited to two to four disks drives, minicomputers can support 8 to 16 disk devices, and mainframe computers can support over 100 high-speed disk devices. Figure 6-12 shows a large number of disk units attached to a single mainframe computer.

What Is the Storage Capacity of a Hard Disk? Hard drives contain a spindle on which one or more disk platters are mounted (Figure 6-13). On many drives, each surface of a platter can be used to store data. Thus, if one platter is used in the drive, two surfaces are available for data. If two platters are used, four surfaces are available for data, and so on. Naturally, the more platters, the more data that can be stored on the drive.

The storage capacity of hard drives is measured in megabytes or millions of bytes (characters) of storage. Common sizes for personal computers range from 20MB to 100MB of storage and even larger sizes are available; 20MB of storage is equivalent to approximately 10,000 double-spaced typewritten pages. Some disk devices used on large computers can store billions of bytes of information (Figure 6-14). A billion bytes of information is called a **gigabyte**.

FIGURE 6-14
The IBM 3390 disk drive, shown here being assembled, can store 22.7 billion bytes of data.

How Is Data Stored on a Hard Disk? Storing data on hard disks is similar to storing data on diskettes. In order to read or write data on the surface of the spinning disk platter, the disk drives are designed with access arms, or actuators. The **access arms**, or **actuators**, contain one or more read/write heads per disk surface. As the disk rotates at a high rate of speed, usually 3600 revolution per minute, the read/write heads move across its surface. These read/write heads *float* on a cushion of air and do not actually touch the surface of the disk. The distance between the head and the surface varies from approximately ten to twenty millionths of an inch. As shown in Figure 6-15, the close tolerance leaves no room for any type of contamination. If some form of contamination is introduced or if the alignment of the read/write heads is altered by something accidentally jarring the computer, the disk head can collide with and damage the disk surface, causing a loss of data. This event is known as a **head crash**. Because of the time needed to repair the disk and to reconstruct the data that was lost, head crashes can be extremely costly to users in terms of both time and money.

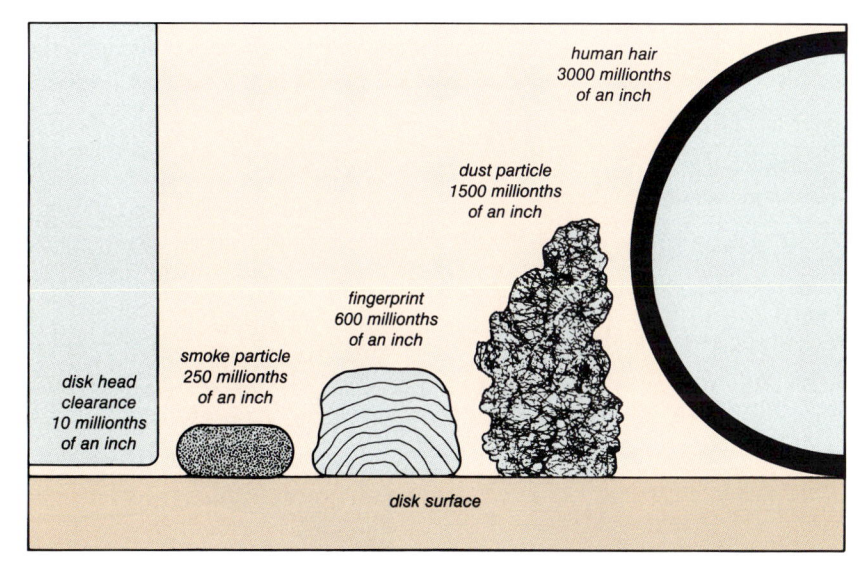

FIGURE 6-15
The clearance between a disk head and the disk surface is about 10 millionths of an inch. With this small difference, contamination such as a smoke particle, fingerprint, dust particle, or human hair could render the drive unusable. Sealed disk drives are designed to minimize contamination.

How Is Data Physically Organized on a Hard Disk? Depending on the type of disk drive, data is physically organized in one of two ways. One way is the sector method and the other is the cylinder method.

The **sector method** for physically organizing data on disks divides each track on the disk surface into individual storage areas called sectors (Figure 6-16). Each sector can contain a specified number of bytes. Data is referenced by indicating the surface, track, and sector where the data is stored.

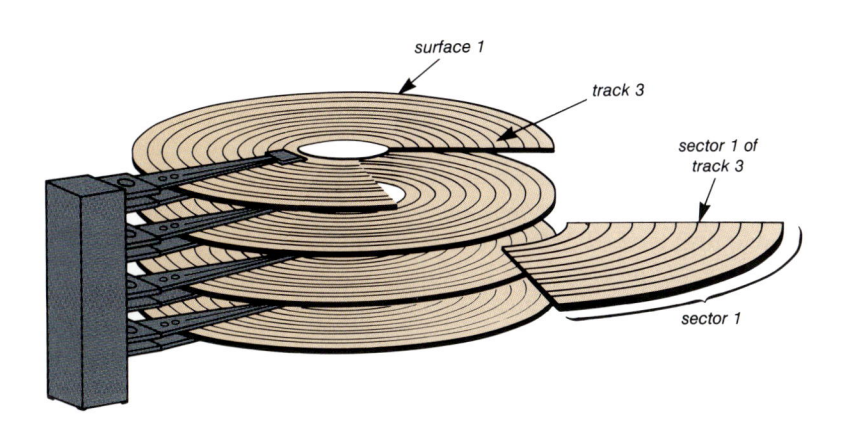

FIGURE 6-16
The sector method of disk addressing divides each track into a number of sectors. To locate data, the surface, track, and sector where the data is stored are specified.

With the **cylinder method**, all tracks of the same number on each recording surface are considered part of the same cylinder (shown on the next page in Figure 6-17). For example, the fifth track on all surfaces would be considered part of cylinder five. All twentieth tracks would be part of cylinder twenty, and so on. When the computer requests data from a disk using the cylinder method, it must specify the cylinder, recording surface, and record number. Because the access arms containing the read/write heads all move together, they are always over the same track on all surfaces. Thus, using the cylinder method to record data *down* the disk surfaces reduces the movement of the read/write head during both reading and writing of data.

FIGURE 6-17
The cylinder method reduces the movement of the read/write head (thereby saving time) by writing information *down* the disk on the same track of successive surfaces.

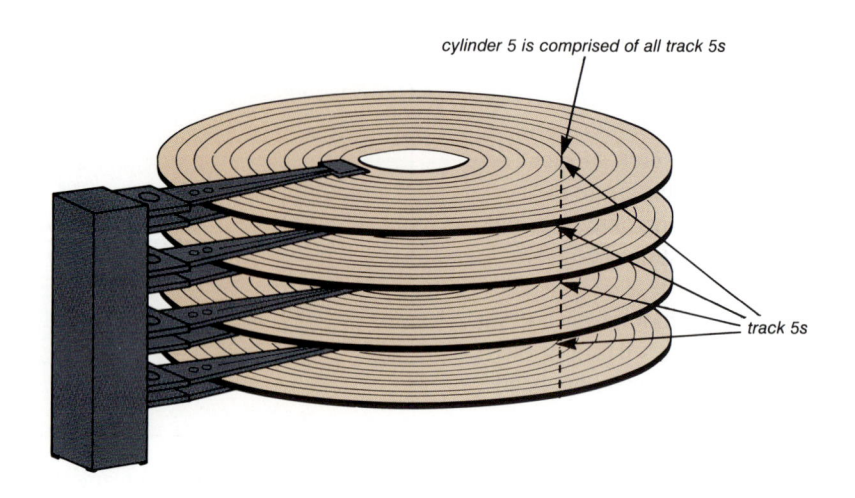

Advantages of Using a Hard Disk on a Personal Computer

A hard disk drive on a personal computer provides many advantages for users. Because of its large storage capacity, a hard disk can store many software application programs and data files. When a user wants to run a particular application or access a particular data file on a hard disk, it is always available. The user does not have to find the appropriate diskette and insert it into the drive. In addition, the faster access time of a hard disk reduces the time needed to load programs and access data. The typical access time of a hard disk for a personal computer is between 15 and 80 milliseconds.

Other Types of Hard Disks

We discuss other devices that use hard disk technology in this section. These include removable disks, hard cards, and disk cartridges.

Removable Disks Removable disk units were introduced in the early 1960s and for nearly 20 years were the most prevalent type of disk storage on minicomputers and mainframes. During the 1980s, however, removable disks began to be replaced by hard fixed disks that offered larger storage capacities and higher reliability.

Removable disk devices consist of the drive unit, which is usually in its own cabinet, and the removable recording media, called a **disk pack**. Removable disk packs consist of five to eleven metal platters that are used on both sides for recording data. The recording capacity of these packs varies from 10 to 300 megabytes of data. One advantage of removable disk packs is that the data on a disk drive can be quickly changed by removing one pack and replacing it with another. This can be accomplished in minutes. When removable disk packs are not mounted in a disk drive they are stored in a protective plastic case. When the packs are being used, the plastic case is usually placed on top of the drive unit. Figure 6-18 shows a large installation of removable disk devices with the empty protective disk pack cases on top of the drives.

MAGNETIC DISK STORAGE **6.11**

FIGURE 6-18
A large installation of removable disk drives showing the protective disk pack cases on top of the drive units.

Hard Cards One option for installing a hard disk in a personal computer is a hard card. The **hard card** is a circuit board that has a hard disk built onto it. Hard cards provide an easy way to expand the storage capacity of a personal computer because the board can be installed into an expansion slot of the computer (Figure 6-19).

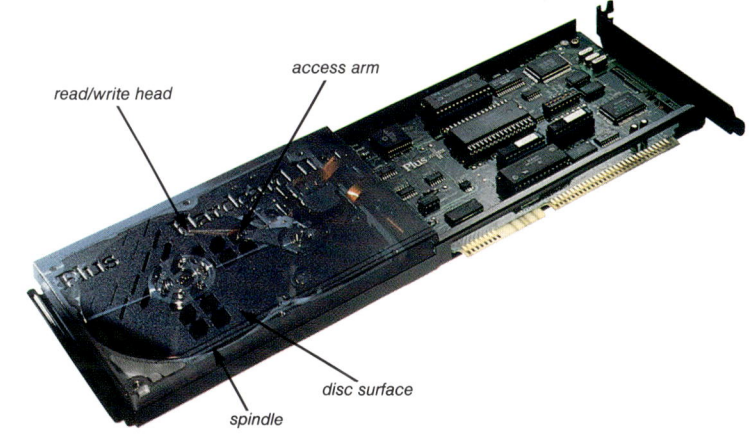

FIGURE 6-19
A hard card is a hard disk on a circuit board that can be mounted in a computer's expansion slot. Notice that a transparent cover (above) allows you to see the disk platter and access arm.

Disk Cartridges Another variation of disk storage available for use with personal computers is the removable disk cartridge. **Disk cartridges**, which can be inserted and removed from a computer (Figure 6-20), offer the storage and fast access features of hard disks and the portability of diskettes. Disk cartridges are often used when data security is an issue. At the end of a work session, the disk cartridge can be removed and locked up, leaving no data on the computer.

Protecting Data Stored on a Disk

Regardless of whether you are using diskettes or hard disks, you must protect the data you store on the disk from being lost. Disk storage is reusable, and data that is stored on a disk may be overwritten and replaced with new data. This is a desirable feature allowing users to remove or replace unwanted files. However, it also raises the possibility of accidentally removing or replacing a file that you wanted to keep. To protect programs and data stored on disks, there are several things you can do.

FIGURE 6-20
A removable hard disk cartridge allows a user to remove and transport the entire hard disk from computer to computer or to lock it up in a safe.

How Is a Diskette Write-Protected? One way to protect the data and programs stored on a 5 1/4" diskette is to use the write-protect notch. This notch is located on the side of the diskette. To prevent writing to a diskette, you cover this notch with a small piece of removable tape. Before writing data onto a diskette, the disk drive checks the notch. If the notch is open, the drive will proceed to write on the diskette. If the notch is covered, the disk drive will not write on the diskette (Figure 6-21).
On 3 1/2" diskettes, the situation is reversed. Instead of a write-protect notch, there is a small window in the corner of the diskette. A piece of plastic in the window can be moved to open and close the window. If the write-protect window is closed, the drive can write on the diskette. If the window is open, the drive will not write on the diskette.

Backup Storage Another way to protect programs and data stored on disks is by creating backup storage. Backup storage means creating a copy of important programs and data. To backup diskettes, simply copy the data on one diskette to another diskette. Diskettes are also commonly used to backup the data stored on a hard disk of a personal computer. Because hard disks can store large quantities of data (20MB, 40MB, or even 100MB) many diskettes are required for backup. For example, approximately thirty 3 1/2" diskettes (720,000 characters each) are required to back up a hard disk containing 20 million characters. Data stored on the hard disks of minicomputers and mainframes must also be backed up. Magnetic tape, another form of auxiliary storage, is commonly used to backup data stored on large-capacity hard disks.

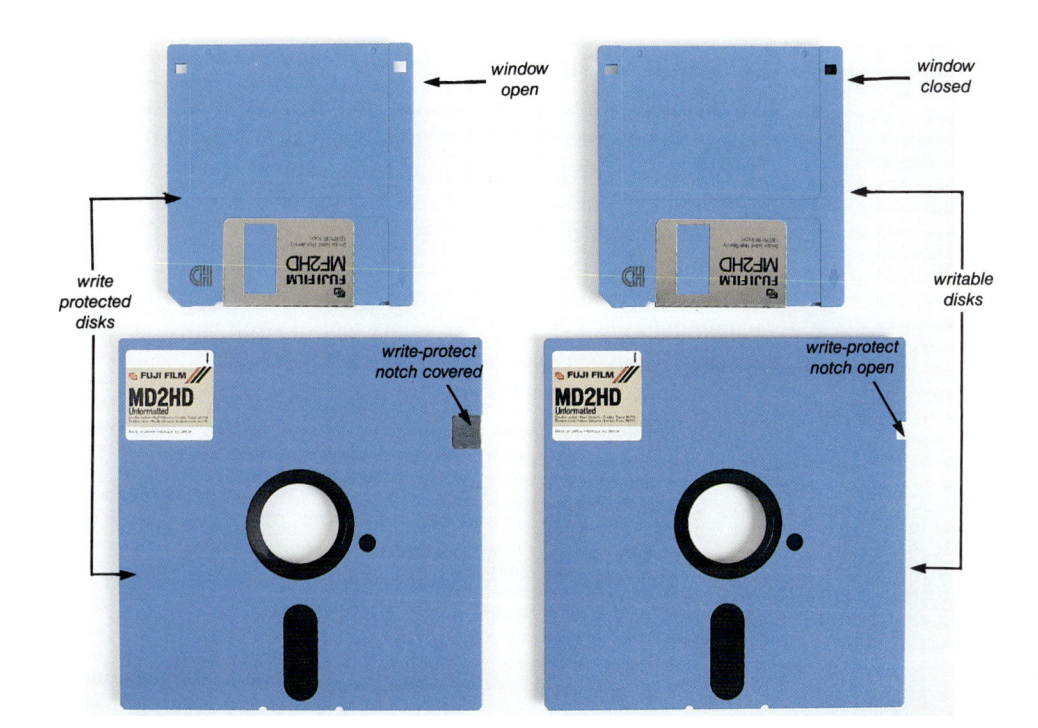

FIGURE 6-21
Data cannot be written on the 3½-inch diskette on the upper left because the window in the corner of the diskette is open. A small piece of plastic covers the window of the 3½-inch diskette on the upper right, so data can be written on this diskette. The reverse situation is true for the 5¼-inch diskettes. The write-protect notch of the 5¼-inch diskette on the lower left is covered and, therefore, data cannot be written to the diskette. The notch of the 5¼-inch diskette on the lower right, however, is open. Data can be written to this diskette.

MAGNETIC TAPE

◆ During the 1950s and early 1960s, prior to the introduction of removable disk pack drives, magnetic tape was the primary method of storing large amounts of data. Today, even though tape is no longer used as the primary method of auxiliary storage, it still functions as a cost-effective way to store data that does not have to be accessed immediately. In addition, tape serves as the primary means of backup for most medium and large systems and is often used when data is transferred from one system to another.

Magnetic tape consists of a thin ribbon of plastic. The tape is coated on one side with a material that can be magnetized to record the bit patterns that represent data. The most common types of magnetic tape devices are reel-to-reel and cartridge. Reel-to-reel tape is usually 1/2-inch wide and cartridge tape is 1/4-inch wide (Figure 6-22).

FIGURE 6-22
A computer operator is positioning a reel of magnetic tape on a tape device (top). A standard 10 1/2-inch reel of magnetic tape (left).

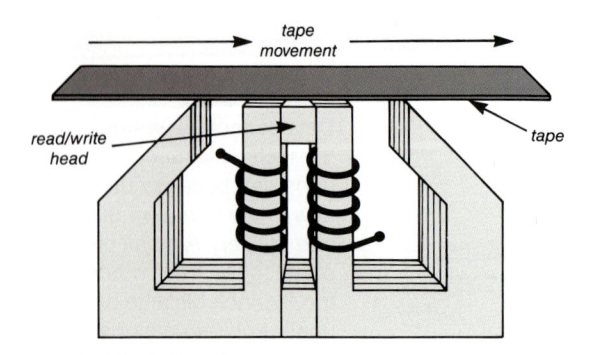

FIGURE 6-23
The tape read/write head senses and records the electronic bits that represent data.

FIGURE 6-24
Older style reel-to-reel magnetic tape storage devices are shown behind newer style tape units.

FIGURE 6-25
Newer style tape drives allow the user to slide the tape into a slot at the front of the unit. The drive automatically threads the tape onto an internal take-up reel.

Reel-to-Reel Tape Devices

Reel-to-reel tape devices use two reels: a supply reel to hold the tape that will be read or written on, and the take-up reel to temporarily hold portions of the supply reel tape as it is being processed. At the completion of processing, tape on the take-up reel is wound back onto the supply reel. As the tape moves from one reel to another, it passes over a read/write head (Figure 6-23), an electromagnetic device that can read or write data on the tape.

Older style tape units (Figure 6-24) are vertical cabinets with vacuum columns that hold five or six feet of slack tape to prevent breaking during sudden start or stop operations.

Newer style tape units (Figure 6-25) allow a tape to be inserted through a slot opening similar to the way videotapes are loaded in a videocassette recorder. This front-loading tape drive takes less space and can be cabinet mounted. The drive automatically threads the end of the tape onto an internal take-up reel. Because of their size and cost, reel-to-reel tape drives are used almost exclusively on minicomputer and mainframe systems.

Reels of tape usually come in lengths of 300, 1,200, 2,400 and 3,600 feet and can store up to 200 megabytes of data.

Cartridge Tape Devices

Cartridge tape is frequently used for backup on personal computers. Faster and higher storage capacity cartridge tapes are also increasingly replacing reel-to-reel tape devices on minicomputers and mainframes. Cartridge tape units are designed to be internally mounted or in a separate external cabinet (Figure 6-26).

How Is Data Stored on Magnetic Tape?

Tape is considered a **sequential storage** media because the computer must record and read tape records one after another. Binary codes, such as ASCII and EBCDIC, are used to represent data stored on magnetic tape. Within a code, each character is represented by a unique combination of bits. The bits are stored on tape in the form of magnetic spots (Figure 6-27). The magnetic spots are organized into rows, called channels, that run the length of the tape. A combination of bits in a vertical column (one from each channel) is used to represent a character. An additional bit is used as a parity bit for error checking.

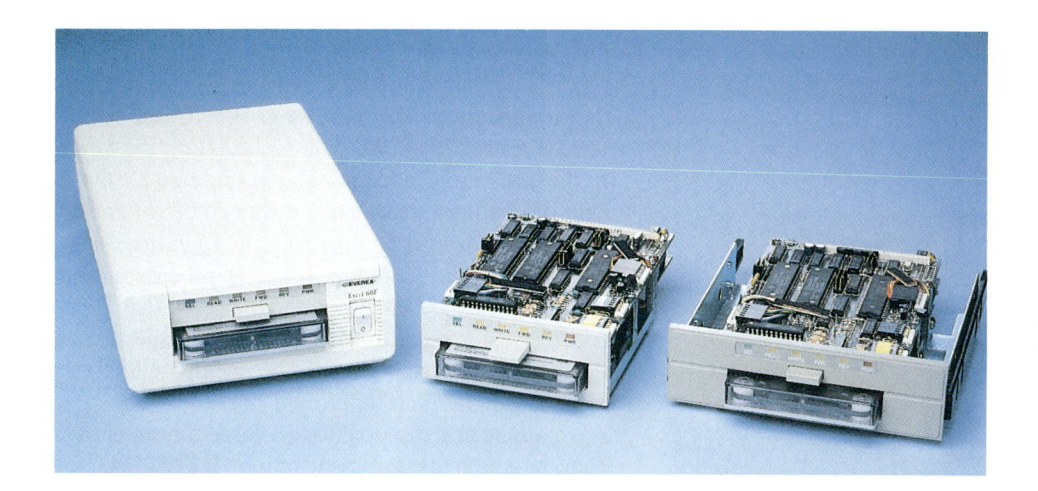

FIGURE 6-26
Cartridge tape drives are an effective way to back up and store data that would otherwise require numerous diskettes.

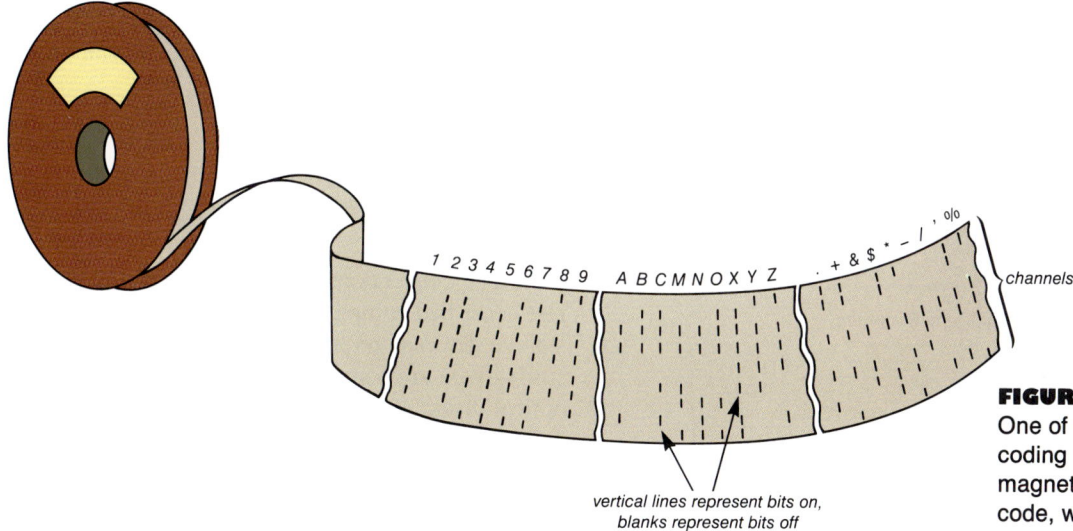

FIGURE 6-27
One of the most common coding structures found on magnetic tape is the EBCDIC code, which is stored in nine channels on the tape. Eight channels are used to store the bits representing a character. The ninth channel is for the error-checking parity bit.

vertical lines represent bits on, blanks represent bits off

Tape density is the number of bits that can be stored on an inch of tape. As on disk drives, tape density is expressed in bits per inch, or bpi. Commonly used tape densities are 800, 1,600, 3,200 and 6,250 bpi. Some of the newer cartridge tape devices can record at densities of over 60,000 bpi. The higher the density, the more data that can be stored on a tape.

Data is recorded on tape in **blocks** which usually consist of two or more records. The individual records are referred to as **logical records**. The group of records making up the block is referred to as a **physical record**. For example, there could be three employee payroll records (three logical records) contained within one block (one physical record) on tape. Each time a tape read or write operation takes place, one physical record is processed. In between each block is a gap of approximately .6 inches called and **interblock gap (IBG)**, or an **interrecord gap (IRG)**. This gap provides room for the tape to slow down and stop after each block has been read. Blocking logical records together has two advantages. First, the space on the tape is used more efficiently than if logical records were written one at a time. Second, because an entire physical record is read into memory each time data is read from tape, reading data takes place faster. A diagram of a section of tape is shown at Figure 6-28.

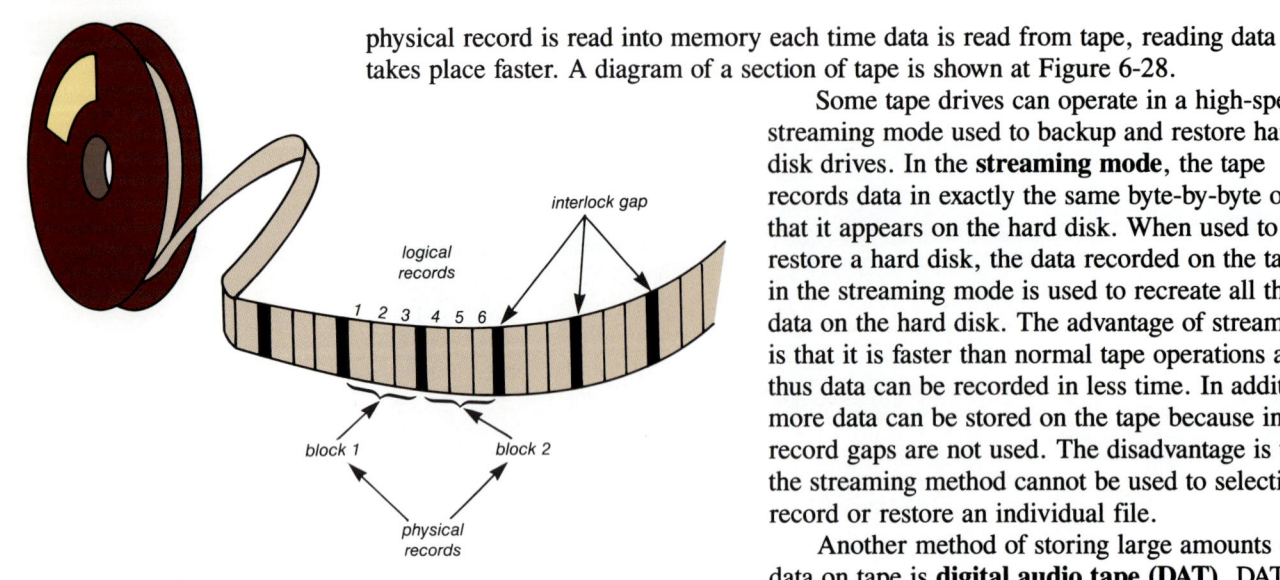

Some tape drives can operate in a high-speed streaming mode used to backup and restore hard disk drives. In the **streaming mode**, the tape records data in exactly the same byte-by-byte order that it appears on the hard disk. When used to restore a hard disk, the data recorded on the tape in the streaming mode is used to recreate all the data on the hard disk. The advantage of streaming is that it is faster than normal tape operations and thus data can be recorded in less time. In addition, more data can be stored on the tape because inter-record gaps are not used. The disadvantage is that the streaming method cannot be used to selectively record or restore an individual file.

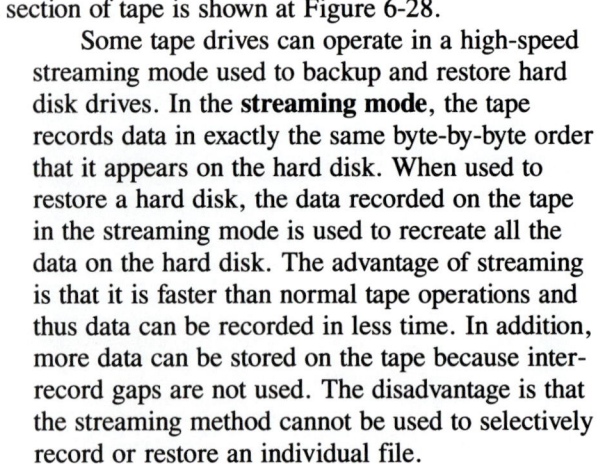

Another method of storing large amounts of data on tape is **digital audio tape (DAT)**. DAT uses **helical scan technology** to write data at much higher densities across the tape at an angle instead of down the length of the tape (Figure 6-29). Using this method, tape densities can be as high as 61,000 bpi.

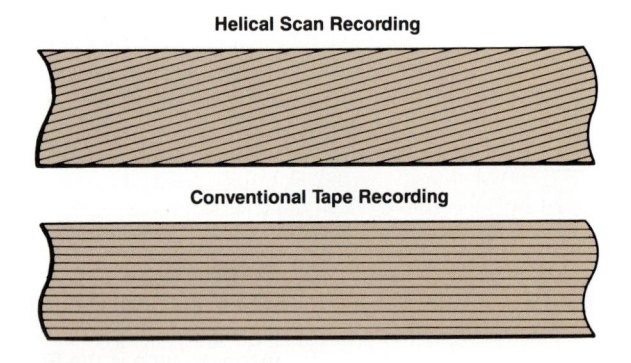

FIGURE 6-28
Three logical records are stored in each block, or physical record, in this diagram. An entire block of records is brought into main memory each time the tape file is read.

OTHER FORMS OF AUXILIARY STORAGE

◆ The conventional disk and tape devices we just described comprise the majority of auxiliary storage devices and media, but other means for storing data are sometimes used. These include optical disks, solid-state devices, and mass storage devices.

Optical Disks

Enormous quantities of information are stored on **optical disks** by using a laser to burn microscopic holes on the surface of a hard plastic disk (Figure 6-30).

FIGURE 6-29
Using helical scan technology, data is recorded at a higher density across the tape at an angle. Conventional tape drives record data in channels running the length of the tape.

FIGURE 6-30
To record data on an optical disk (left), a laser burns microscopic holes on the surface (right).

A lower power laser reads the disk by reflecting light off the disk surface. The reflected light is converted into a series of bits that the computer can process (Figure 6-31).

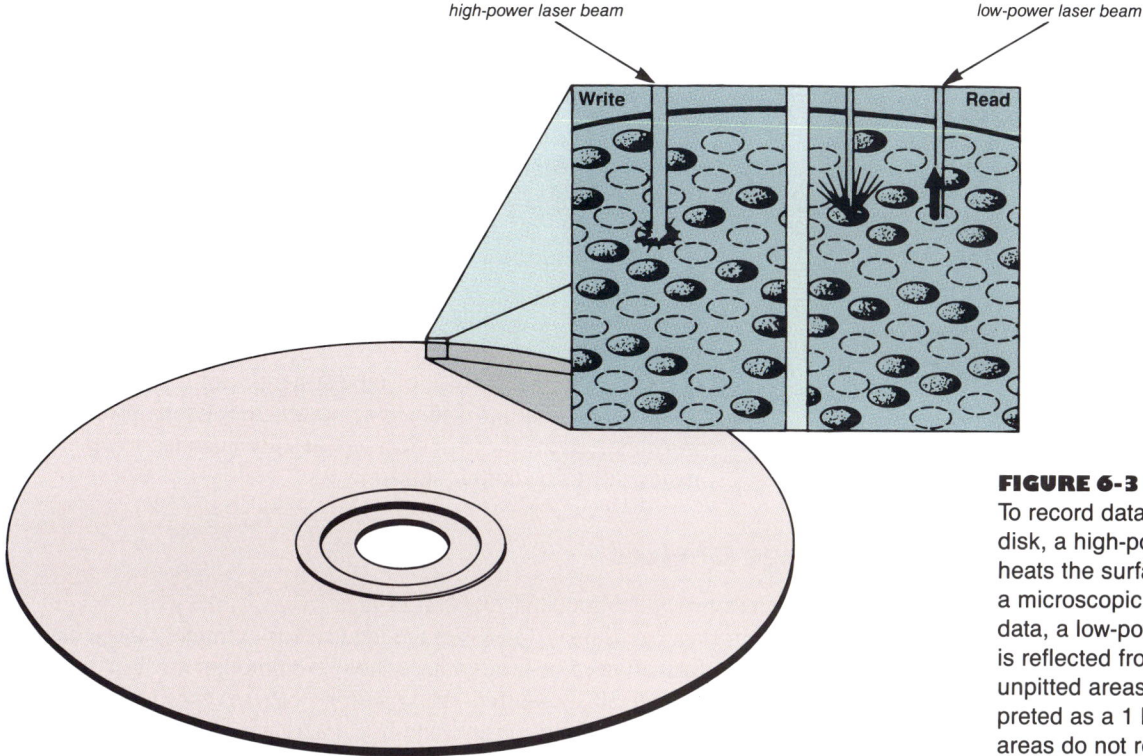

FIGURE 6-31
To record data on an optical disk, a high-power laser heats the surface and makes a microscopic pit. To read data, a low-power laser light is reflected from the smooth unpitted areas and is interpreted as a 1 bit. The pitted areas do not reflect the laser beam and are interpreted as 0 bits.

A full-size, 14-inch optical disk can store 6.8 billion bytes of information. Up to 150 of these disks can be installed in automated disk library systems that provide over one trillion bytes (called a **terabyte**) of online storage. The smaller disks, just under five inches in diameter, can store over 800 million characters, or approximately 1100 times the data that can be stored on a standard density 3 1/2" diskette. That's enough space to store approximately 400,000 pages of typed data. The smaller optical disks are called **CDROM**, an acronym for compact disk read-only memory (Figure 6-32). They use the same laser technology that is used for the CDROM disks that have become popular for recorded music.

Most optical disks are prerecorded and cannot be modified by the user. These disks are used for applications such as an auto parts catalog where the information is changed only occasionally, such as once a year, and a new updated optical disk is created. Optical disk devices that provide for one-time recording are called **WORM** devices, an acronym for write once, read many. Erasable optical disk drives are just starting to be used. The most common erasable optical drives use **magneto-optical technology**, in which a magnetic field changes the polarity of a spot on the disk that has been heated by a laser.

FIGURE 6-32
An optical compact disk can store hundreds of times the data as on a diskette of similar dimensions.

FIGURE 6-33
Solid-state storage devices use rows of RAM chips to emulate a conventional rotating disk drive. This solid-state device, with a RAM memory board shown in front, can transfer data 15 to 20 times faster than a rotating disk system.

Because of their tremendous storage capacities, entire catalogs or reference materials can be stored on a single optical disk. Some people predict that optical disks will someday replace data now stored on film such as microfiche.

Solid-State Devices

To the computer, solid-state storage devices act just like disk drives, only faster. As their name suggests, they contain no moving parts, only electronic circuits. **Solid-state storage** devices use the latest in random access memory (RAM) technology to provide high-speed data access and retrieval. Rows of RAM chips (Figure 6-33) provide megabytes of memory that can be accessed much faster than the fastest conventional disk drives. Solid-state storage devices are significantly more expensive than conventional disk drives offering the same storage capacity. Unlike disk or tape systems, solid-state storage devices are volatile; if they lose power their contents are lost. For this reason, these devices are usually attached to emergency power backup systems.

Mass Storage Devices

Mass storage devices provide automated retrieval of data from a library of storage media such as tape or data cartridges. Mass storage is ideal for extremely large databases that require all information to be readily accessible even though any one portion of the database may be infrequently required. Mass storage systems take less room than conventional tape storage and can retrieve and begin accessing records within seconds. Figure 6-34 shows a mass storage system that uses tape cartridges.

FIGURE 6-34
This is the inside of an automated mass storage system that uses tape cartridges. A robot arm with a camera mounted on top can access and load any one of thousands of tape cartridges in an average of 11 seconds. Each cartridge is a 4 × 4-inch square and about one-inch thick and can hold up to 200 megabytes of data. The tapes are stored in a circular cabinet referred to as a silo.

Special-Purpose Storage Devices

Several devices have been developed for special-purpose storage applications. Two of these are smart cards and optical cards.

Smart cards are the same size and thickness of a credit card and contain a thin microprocessor capable of storing recorded information (Figure 6-35). When it is inserted into compatible equipment, the information on the smart card can be read and if necessary, updated. A current user of smart cards is the U.S. Marine Corps, who issues the cards to recruits instead of cash. Each time a recruit uses the card, the transaction amount is subtracted from the previous balance. Other uses of the card include employee time and attendance tracking (instead of time cards) and security applications where detailed information about the card holder is stored in the card.

Optical cards can store up to 800 pages of text or images on a device the size of a credit card (Figure 6-36). Applications include automobile records and the recording of personal and health-care data.

FIGURE 6-35
Smart cards are credit card-sized devices that contain a microprocessor in the left center of the card. The microprocessor can store up to 64,000 bits of information.

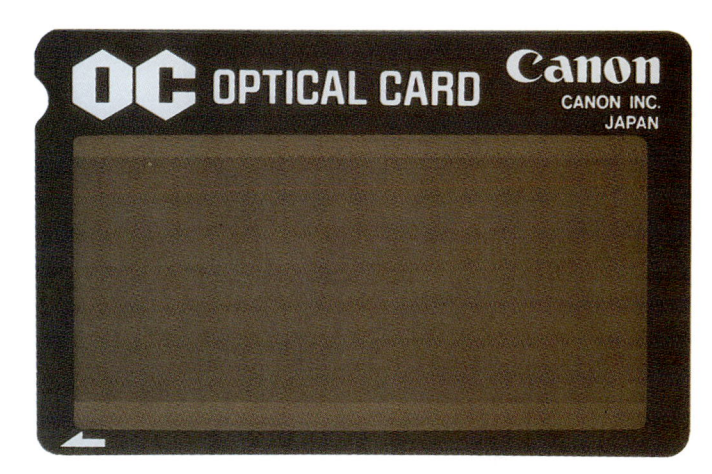

FIGURE 6-36
This optical card can store up to 800 pages of information and images. It is about the size of a credit card.

SUMMARY OF AUXILIARY STORAGE

◆ Auxiliary storage is used to store programs and data that are not currently being processed by the computer. In this chapter, we discussed the various types of auxiliary storage used with computers. The chart on the next page in Figure 6-37 provides a summary of the auxiliary storage devices we covered. What you have learned about

FIGURE 6-37
A summary of the various auxiliary storage devices.

these devices and storage operations in general can now be added to what you have learned about the input, processing, and output operations to complete your understanding of the information processing cycle.

DEVICE	DESCRIPTION
Magnetic Disk	
Diskette	Plastic storage media that is reliable and low in cost.
Hard disk	Fixed metal platter storage media that provides large storage capacity and fast access.
Removable disk	Large disk drives with removable disk packs.
Hard card	Hard disk that is built on a circuit board and installed in an expansion slot of a personal computer.
Disk cartridge	Combines storage and access features of hard disks and portability of diskettes.
Magnetic Tape	
Reel tape	Magnetic tape device using the reel-to-reel method of moving tape.
Tape cartridge	Magnetic tape device using the cartridge method of holding tape.
Other Storage Devices	
Optical storage	Uses lasers to record and read data on a hard plastic disk. Provides high quality and large storage capacity.
Solid-state	Uses RAM chips to provide high-speed data access and retrieval.
Mass storage	Automated retrieval of storage media such as tape or data cartridges.
Special-Purpose Storage Devices	
Smart card	Contains a thin microprocessor capable of storing recorded information.
Optical card	Credit card-sized device that stores text and images.

CHAPTER SUMMARY

1. **Auxiliary storage** is used to store data that is not being processed on the computer.
2. **Magnetic disk** is the most widely used storage medium for all types of computers and offers high storage capacity, reliability, and the capability to directly access stored data.
3. The most common diskette sizes are 5 1/4" and 3 1/2" in diameter.
4. A diskette consists of a plastic disk enclosed within a square protective jacket. A portion of the surface of the disk is exposed so data can be stored on it.
5. The **formatting** process prepares the diskette so that it can store data and includes defining the tracks, cylinders, and sectors on the surfaces of a diskette.
6. Data is stored along the tracks of a diskette. A **track** is a narrow recording band forming a full circle around the diskette.
7. A **cylinder** is defined as all tracks of the same number.
8. The term **sector** is used to refer to a pie-shaped section of the disk. It is also used to refer to a section of a track.
9. When data is read from a diskette, a minimum of one full sector of a track is read. When data is stored on a diskette, at least one full sector of a track is written.
10. The factors affecting disk storage capacity are the number of sides of the disk used; the recording density; and the number of tracks on the disk.
11. The **recording density** is stated as the number of bits that can be recorded on one inch of the innermost track on a disk. The measurement is referred to as **bits per inch (bpi)**.
12. To read or write data on a diskette, it is placed in the disk drive. Within its protective covering the diskette rotates at about 300 revolutions per minute. The **read/write head** rests on the diskette and senses the magnetic spots or generates electronic impulses that represent the bits.

13. The time required to access and retrieve data stored on a diskette is called the **access time**.
14. Access time depends on four factors: (1) **seek time**, the time it takes to position the read/write head on the correct track; (2) **rotational delay time**, or **latency**, the time it takes for the data to rotate under the read/write head; (3) **settling time**, the time required for the head to be placed in contact with the disk; and (4) **data transfer rate**, the amount of data that can be transferred from the disk to main memory.
15. Diskettes should not be exposed to heat or magnetic fields. With proper care, diskettes provide an inexpensive and reliable form of storage.
16. A **hard disk** consists of one or more rigid metal platters coated with an oxide material.
17. On hard disks, the metal platters, read/write heads, and access arm are enclosed in an airtight, sealed case.
18. To read and write data on a hard disk, an **access arm** moves read/write heads in and out. The heads float very close to the surface of the disk, generating or sensing the magnetic spots that represent bits.
19. The **sector method** (identifying the surface, track, and sector number) or the **cylinder method** (identifying the cylinder, recording surface, and record number) can be used to physically organize and address data stored on disk.
20. **Removable disk** devices consist of the drive unit, which is usually in its own cabinet, and the removable recording media, called a **disk pack**.
21. A **hard card** consists of a circuit board that has a hard disk built onto it. The board can be installed into an expansion slot of a personal computer.
22. **Disk cartridges**, which can be inserted and removed from a computer, offer the storage and fast access features of hard disks and the portability of diskettes.
23. The write-protect notch on 5 1/4" diskettes and the window on 3 1/2" diskettes can be used to protect the data stored on a disk from being overwritten.
24. To backup storage means to create a copy of important programs and data on a separate disk or tape.
25. The normal method for diskette backup is to copy the data onto another diskette. For large-capacity hard disks, the data is often copied to magnetic tape.
26. **Magnetic tape** consists of a thin ribbon of plastic. The tape is coated on one side with a material that can be magnetized to record the bit patterns that represent data.
27. The most common types of magnetic tape devices are reel-to-reel and cartridge.
28. Data is recorded on magnetic tape as a series of magnetic spots along a horizontal channel. Each spot represents a bit in a coding scheme.
29. **Tape density** is the number of bits that can be stored on one inch of tape. Common densities are 800, 1,600, 3,200, and 6,520 bytes per inch.
30. Data is recorded on tape in **blocks** which usually consist of two or more records. The individual records are referred to as **logical records**. The group of records making up the block is referred to as a **physical record**.
31. An **interblock gap (IBG)**, also called an **interrecord gap (IRG)**, separates the blocks stored on tape.
32. In the **streaming mode**, a tape records data in exactly the same byte-by-byte order as it appears on the disk.
33. **Digital audio tape (DAT)** uses **helical scan technology** to write data at much higher densities across the tape at an angle instead of down the length of the tape.
34. **Optical disks** use a laser to burn microscopic holes on the surface of a hard plastic disk. Optical disks can store enormous quantities of data.
35. **CDROM** is an acronym for compact disk read-only memory.
36. Optical disks that provide for one-time recording are called **WORM** devices.
37. Most erasable optical disk drives use **magneto-optical technology** that uses a magnetic field to change the polarity of a spot on the disk that has been heated by a laser.
38. RAM chips are used in **solid-state storage** devices to provide fast data access and retrieval. These devices are volatile.
39. Automated retrieval of storage media is provided by **mass storage** devices.
40. **Smart cards** are the same size and thickness of a credit card and contain a thin microprocessor capable of storing recorded information.
41. **Optical cards** can store up to 800 pages of text or images on a device the size of a credit card.

KEY TERMS

Access arm *6.9*
Access time *6.6*
Actuator *6.9*
Auxiliary storage *6.2*
Bits per inch (bpi) *6.5*
Block *6.15*
Cartridge tape *6.14*
CDROM *6.17*
Cylinder *6.5*
Cylinder method *6.9*
Data transfer rate *6.6*
Digital audio tape (DAT) *6.16*
Direct-access storage device (DASD) *6.8*
Disk cartridge *6.12*
Diskette *6.3*
Disk pack *6.10*
Double-sided diskette *6.5*
Double-sided drive *6.5*
Fixed disk *6.8*
Floppy disk *6.3*

Formatting *6.4*
Gigabyte *6.8*
Hard card *6.11*
Hard disk *6.7*
Head crash *6.9*
Helical scan technology *6.16*
High-density diskette *6.5*
Interblock gap (IBG) *6.15*
Interrecord gap (IRG) *6.15*
Latency *6.6*
Logical record *6.15*
Low-density diskette *6.5*
Magnetic disk *6.3*
Magnetic tape *6.13*
Magneto-optical technology *6.17*
Mass storage *6.18*
Nonvolatile *6.3*
Optical card *6.19*
Optical disk *6.16*
Physical record *6.15*
Read/write head *6.6*

Recording density *6.5*
Reel-to-reel *6.14*
Removable disk *6.10*
Rotational delay *6.6*
Secondary storage *6.2*
Sector *6.5*
Sector method *6.9*
Seek time *6.6*
Sequential storage *6.14*
Settling time *6.6*
Single-sided diskette *6.5*
Single-sided drive *6.5*
Smart card *6.19*
Solid-state storage *6.18*
Streaming mode *6.16*
Tape density *6.15*
Terabyte *6.17*
Track *6.4*
Tracks per inch (tpi) *6.5*
WORM *6.17*

REVIEW QUESTIONS

1. Write a definition for auxiliary storage. Explain how auxiliary storage differs from main memory.
2. Draw a diagram of a diskette and label the main parts.
3. Explain the terms track, cylinder, and sector.
4. What are the three factors influencing the storage capacity of a diskette? Briefly describe each of them.
5. What is the difference in storage capacity between low-density and high-density diskettes? Give values for both 5 1/4" and 3 1/2" diskettes.
6. What is access time? List the four factors that influence the access time of a disk drive.
7. Describe how data is stored on a hard disk.
8. What are the advantages of using a hard disk drive on a personal computer?
9. Explain how 5 1/4" and 3 1/2" diskettes may be write-protected.
10. Write a definition for magnetic tape. What are the two most common types of magnetic tape devices?
11. What is the streaming mode of tape operation and how is it used?
12. What is a WORM device? How do they differ from magneto-optical technology?

CONTROVERSIAL ISSUES

1. Some people believe that the increasing capacities and decreasing costs of storage devices such as CDROM will eventually result in the replacement of most books, magazines, and other printed matter. What do you think?
2. Many personal computer users and some businesses do not regularly backup the data on their computer systems. Rather than spending time each day to perform backup, they are willing to take the risk that they may have to spend a considerable amount of time recreating their database if their system should experience a disk failure. Discuss the pros and cons of such a policy.

RESEARCH PROJECTS

1. Visit a computer store and obtain information on the different types of hard disk drives that are available for personal computers. Summarize your findings and include data on price, storage capacity, and access speed. Calculate the cost per megabyte of storage for each drive.
2. Pick several different types of businesses. Write a paper on how their information storage requirements differ. Comment on what types of data should be online and available for immediate access.
3. Write a paper on the possible applications of smart card technology.

File and Database Management

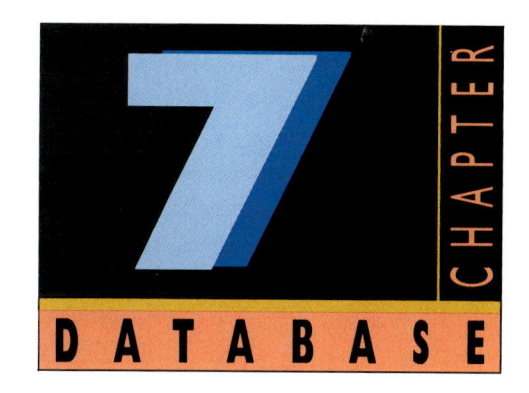

7

DATABASE

OBJECTIVES

- Discuss data management and explain why it is needed
- Describe sequential files, indexed files, and direct (or relative) files
- Explain the difference between sequential retrieval and random retrieval of records from a file
- Describe the data maintenance procedures for updating data including adding, changing, and deleting
- Discuss the advantages of a database management system (DBMS)
- Describe hierarchical, network, and relational database systems
- Explain the use of a query language
- Describe the responsibilities of a database administrator
- Discuss personal computer database systems

In order to provide maximum benefit to a company, data must be carefully managed, organized, and used. The purpose of this chapter is to explain the need for data management, how files on auxiliary storage are organized and maintained (kept current), and the advantages, organization, and use of databases. Learning this information will help you to better understand how data and information is stored and managed on a computer.

DATA MANAGEMENT

◆ For data to be useful, it must be accurate and timely. **Data management** refers to procedures that are used to keep data accurate and timely and provide for the security and maintenance of data. The purpose of data management is to ensure that data required for an application will be available in the correct form and at the proper time for processing. Both data processing professionals and users share the responsibility for data management.

To illustrate the need for data management, we use an example of a credit bureau (Figure 7-1). A summary of the application follows.

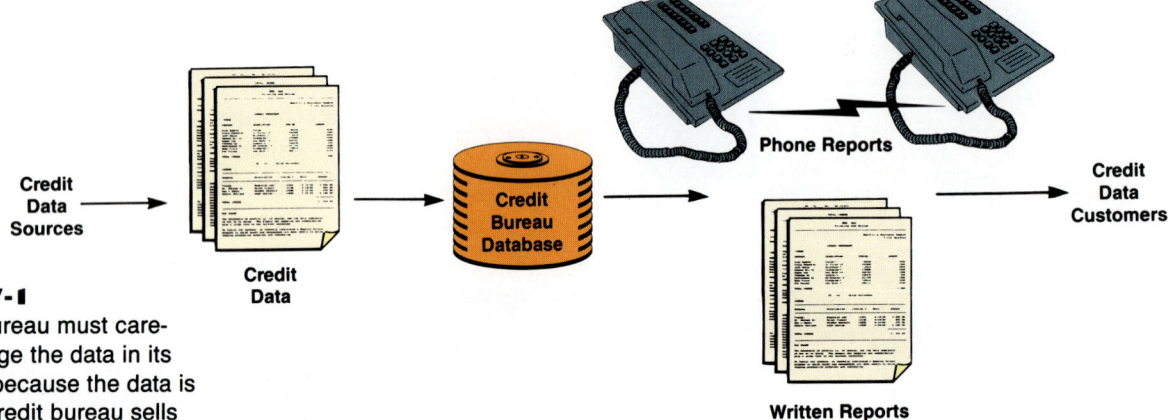

FIGURE 7-1
A credit bureau must carefully manage the data in its database because the data is what the credit bureau sells to its customers. Data management procedures must be in place to make sure the data is accurate and timely and to provide for the proper security and maintenance of the data.

- Data entered into the database of the credit bureau is acquired from numerous sources such as banks and stores. The data includes facts such as income, history of paying debts, bankruptcies, and certain personal information.
- When the data is entered into the computer, it becomes a part of the database. The database is stored on an auxiliary storage device such as a hard disk.
- Customers of the credit bureau can call and request information about an individual. The credit bureau employee uses a terminal to retrieve information from the database and gives the caller a brief credit history of the person in question. The system also generates a record that causes a complete credit history to be printed that night. The credit report will be mailed to the credit bureau customer the following day.

Data Accuracy

For a user, such as a credit bureau customer, to have confidence in the information provided by a computer system, he or she first must be confident that the data used to create the information is accurate. **Data accuracy**, sometimes called **data integrity**, means that the source of the data is reliable and the data is correctly reported and entered. For example, if someone incorrectly reports to the credit bureau that an individual did not pay a bill and this information becomes part of the database, a customer could be denied credit unjustly. Users must be confident that the people and organizations providing data to the credit bureau provide accurate data. In addition, the data they obtain must be entered into the computer correctly. This is called reliable data entry. In the credit bureau example, if a bank reports that the balance on a credit card account is $200.00, but the balance is incorrectly entered as $2,000.00, the information generated would be invalid.

Accurate data must also be timely. Timely data has not lost its usefulness because time has passed. For example, assume that two years ago a salary of $15,000.00 was entered for an individual. Today, that data is not timely because two years have passed and the person may be earning either less or more.

Data Security

Data management also includes managing data security. **Data security** refers to protecting data to keep it from being misused or lost. This is important because misuse or loss of data can have serious consequences. In the credit bureau example, a person's credit rating and history of financial transactions are confidential. People do not want their credit information made available to unauthorized persons. Therefore, the credit bureau must develop systems and procedures that allow only authorized personnel to access the data stored in the database. In addition, if the data in the database should be lost or destroyed, the credit bureau must have a way to recover the correct data. Therefore, data in an information system is periodically copied, or backed up. **Backup** refers to making copies of data files so that if data is lost or destroyed, a timely recovery can be made and processing can continue. Backup copies are normally kept in fireproof safes or in a separate building so that a single disaster, such as a fire, will not destroy both the primary and the backup copy of the data.

Data Maintenance

Data maintenance, another aspect of data management, refers to the procedures used to keep data current. When data is maintained it is called **updating** and includes procedures for **adding** new data, such as creating a record for a new person to include in the credit bureau database; **changing** existing information, such as posting a change of address to an existing record; and **deleting** obsolete information, such as removing inactive records.

Summary of Data Management

Data management includes managing data accuracy, data security, and data maintenance (Figure 7-2). If your attention to data management is inadequate, the information processing system will not perform as intended and the output will have little value.

ACCURACY	SECURITY	MAINTENANCE

Reliable Source Data
Reliable Data Entry
Timeliness
	Authorized Access
	Backup
		Updating:
		  Adding
		  Changing
		  Deleting

FIGURE 7-2
Data management is concerned with data accuracy, data security, and data maintenance.

The data accumulated by companies is stored in files and databases. In the next section we discuss files and how they are organized and maintained. Then we continue with a discussion of databases.

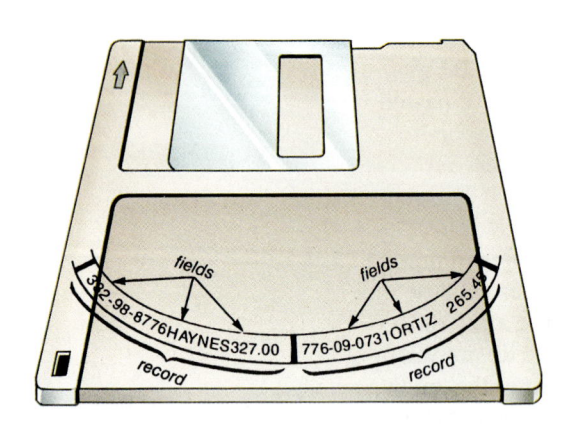

FIGURE 7-3
This payroll file stored on a diskette contains payroll records. Each payroll record contains a social security field, a name field, and a paycheck amount field.

WHAT IS A FILE?

A *file* is a collection of related records that is usually stored on an auxiliary storage device. A *record* is a collection of related fields and a *field*, also called a *data item* or *data element*, is a fact. Figure 7-3 shows a portion of a payroll file that is stored on a diskette. The file contains a separate record for each employee. Each record contains a social security field, a name field and a paycheck amount field. Files contain data that relates to one topic. For example, a business can have separate files that contain data related to payroll, personnel, inventory, customers, vendors, and so forth. Most companies have hundreds, sometimes thousands of files that store the data pertaining to their business. Files that are stored on auxiliary storage devices can be organized in several different ways, and there are advantages and disadvantages to each of these types of file organization.

TYPES OF FILE ORGANIZATION

Three types of file organization are used on auxiliary storage devices. These are sequential, indexed, and direct or relative, file organization.

Sequential File Organization

Sequential file organization means that records are stored one after the other, normally in ascending or descending order, based on a value in each record called the key. The **key** is a field that contains unique data, such as a Social Security number, part number, or customer number that is used to identify the records in a file (Figure 7-4). Files stored on tape are processed as sequential files. Files on disk may be sequential, indexed, or direct.

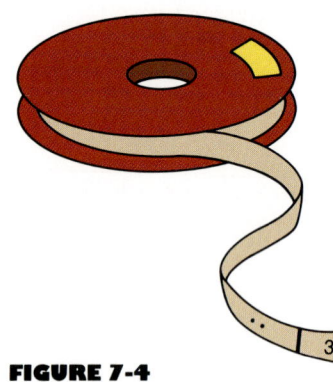

FIGURE 7-4
The student records in this file are stored sequentially in ascending order using the Social Security number as the key field. The records in this file will be retrieved sequentially.

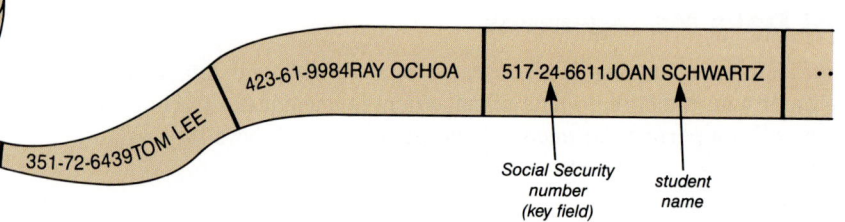

Records stored using sequential file organization are also retrieved sequentially. **Sequential retrieval**, also called **sequential access**, means that the records in a file are retrieved one record after another in the same order that the records are stored. For example, in Figure 7-4, the file contains student records stored in sequence by Social Security number. The data in the file is retrieved one record after another in the same sequence that it is stored in the file.

Sequential retrieval has a major disadvantage — since records must be retrieved one after another in the same sequence as they are stored, the only way to retrieve a record is to read all preceding records first. Therefore, in Figure 7-4, if the record for Joan Schwartz must be retrieved, the records for Tom Lee and Ray Ochoa must be read before retrieving the Joan Schwartz record. Because of this, sequential retrieval is not used when fast access to a particular record is required. However, sequential retrieval is appropriate when records are processed one after another. An example is a weekly payroll application where employee records are processed sequentially.

A common use of sequential files in a computer center is as backup files, where data from a disk is copied onto a tape or another disk so that if the original data becomes unusable, the original file can be restored from the backup file. Sequential files can also be used for batch processing where records are all processed at one time.

Indexed File Organization

A second type of file organization is called **indexed file organization**. Just as in a sequential file, records are stored in an indexed file in an ascending or descending sequence based on the value in the key field of the record.

An indexed file, however, also has an index which itself is a file. An **index** consists of a list containing the values of a key field and the corresponding disk address for each record in a file (Figure 7-5). In the same way that an index for a book points to the page where a particular topic is covered, the index for a file points to the place on a disk where a particular record is located. The index is updated each time a record is added to or deleted from the file. The index is retrieved from the disk and placed in main memory when the file is to be processed.

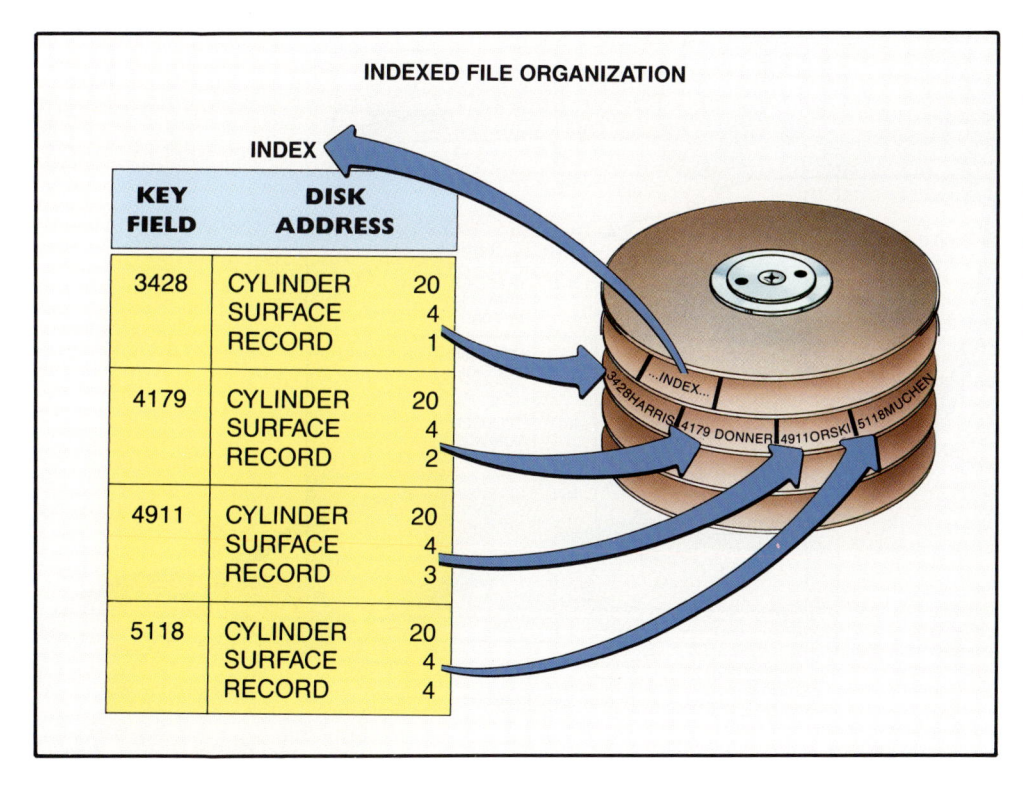

FIGURE 7-5
The index in an indexed file contains the record key and the corresponding disk address for each record in the file. Here, the index contains the employee number, which is the key for the employee file and the disk address for the corresponding employee record.

Records can be accessed in an indexed file both sequentially and randomly. As we previously discussed, sequential retrieval means that the records in a file are retrieved one record after another in the same order that the records are stored. **Random retrieval**, also called **random access** or **direct access**, means the system can go directly to a record without having to read the preceding records. For example, with sequential retrieval, to read the fiftieth record in a file, records 1 through 49 would be read first. With random retrieval, the system can go directly to the fiftieth record. To directly access a record in an indexed file, the index is searched until the key of the record to be retrieved is found. The address of the record (also stored in the index) is then used to retrieve the record directly from the file without reading any other records. For example, if the personnel office asked for the name of employee number 5118, the index could be searched until key 5118 was found (Figure 7-6). The corresponding disk address (cylinder 20, surface 4, record 4) would then be used to read the record directly from the disk into main memory. An advantage of indexed files is that usually more than one index can be maintained. Each index can be used to access or report records in a particular order. For example, an employee file might have three separate indexes; one for employee number, a second for employee name, and a third for Social Security number. A disadvantage of indexed files is that searching an index for a record in a large file can take a long time. In addition, maintaining one or more indexes adds to the processing time whenever a record is added or deleted.

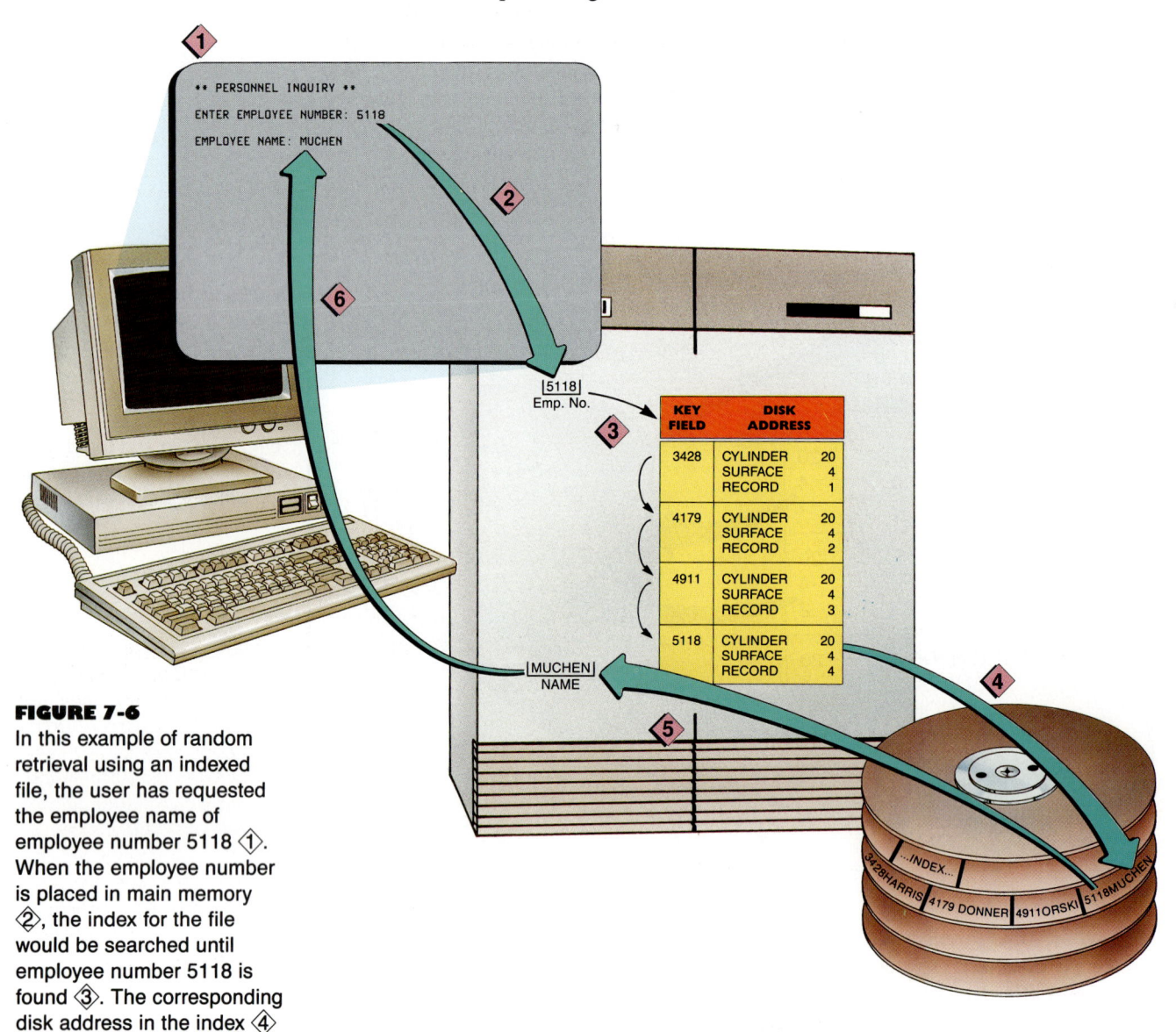

FIGURE 7-6
In this example of random retrieval using an indexed file, the user has requested the employee name of employee number 5118 ①. When the employee number is placed in main memory ②, the index for the file would be searched until employee number 5118 is found ③. The corresponding disk address in the index ④ is then used to access the record stored at that address. Here, the record containing the employee name Muchen is retrieved and placed in main memory ⑤. This name is then sent back to the terminal to answer the user's request ⑥.

Direct or Relative File Organization

A **direct file** or **relative file** (sometimes called a random file) uses the key value of a record to determine the location on the disk where the record is or will be stored. For example, a program could establish a file that has nine locations where records can be stored. These locations are sometimes called **buckets**. A bucket can contain multiple records. If the key in the record is a one-digit value (1–9), then the value in the key would specify the relative location within the file where the record was stored. For example, the record with key 3 would be placed in relative location, or bucket, 3, the record with key 6 would be placed in relative location 6, and so on.

Usually, the storage of records in a file is not so simple. For instance, what if the maximum number of records to be stored in a direct file is 100 and the key for the record is a four-digit number? In this case, the key of the record could not be used to specify the relative or actual location of the record because the four-digit key could result in up to 9,999 records. In cases such as these, an arithmetic formula is used to calculate the relative or actual location in the file where the record is stored. The process of using a formula and performing the calculation to determine the location of a record is called **hashing**.

One hashing method is the division/remainder method. With this method, the computer uses a prime number close to but not greater than the number of records to be stored in the file. A **prime number** is a number divisible by only itself and 1. For example, suppose you have 100 records. The number 97 is the closest prime number to 100 without being greater than 100. The key of the record is then divided by 97 and the remainder from the division operation is the relative location where the record is stored. For example, if the record key is 3428, the relative location where the record will be stored in the file is location 33 (Figure 7-7).

Direct files present one problem you do not encounter with sequential or indexed files. In all three file organization methods, the key in the record must be unique so that it can uniquely identify the record. For example, the employee number, when acting as the key in an employee file, must be unique. No two employees can have the same number. When a hashing technique is used to calculate a disk address, however, it is possible that two different keys could identify the same location on disk. For example, employee number 3331 generates the same relative location (33) as employee number 3428. When the locations generated from the different keys are the same, they are called **synonyms**. The occurrence of this event is called a **collision**. A method that is often used to resolve collisions is to place the record that caused the collision in the next available storage location. This location may be in the same bucket (if multiple records are stored in a bucket) or in the next bucket (Figure 7-8).

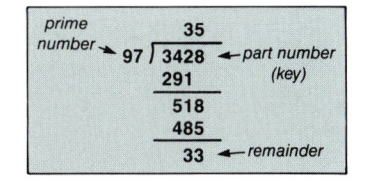

FIGURE 7-7
When the value 3428 is divided by the prime number 97, the remainder is 33. This remainder is used as the bucket where the record with key 3428 is stored in the direct file.

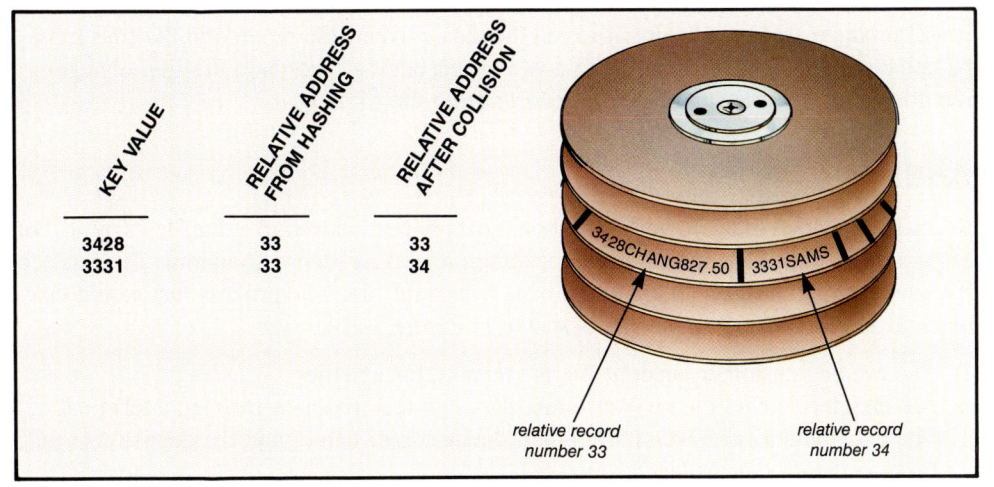

FIGURE 7-8
Sometimes the hashing computation produces synonyms, or records that have the same relative address. In this example, both records have a relative address of 33. When the computer tries to store the second record and finds that location 33 is already full, it stores the second record at the next available location. Here, record 3331 would be stored in location 34.

Once a record is stored in its relative location within a direct file, it can be retrieved either randomly or sequentially. The method normally used with direct files is random retrieval. A record is retrieved from a direct file by performing three steps.

1. The program obtains the key of the record to be retrieved. The value of the key, such as a part number, is entered by the user or is read from another file record such as a sales invoice.

2. The program determines the location of the record to be retrieved by performing the same hashing process as when the record was initially stored. Thus, to retrieve the record with key 3428, the key value would be divided by the prime number 97. The remainder, 33, specifies the location of the bucket where the record is stored.
3. The software directs the computer to bucket 33 to retrieve the record.

Sequential retrieval from a direct file can be accomplished by indicating that the record from the first relative location is to be retrieved, followed by the record from the second relative location, and so on. All the records in the file are retrieved based on their relative location in the file.

Summary of File Organization Concepts

Files are organized as either sequential, indexed, or direct files. Sequential file organization can be used on tape or disk and requires that the records in the file be retrieved sequentially. Indexed files must be stored on disk and the records can be accessed either sequentially or randomly. Direct files are stored on disk and are usually accessed randomly (Figure 7-9).

FIGURE 7-9
The types of storage and the access methods that can be used with each of the three file types.

FILE TYPE	TYPE OF STORAGE	ACCESS METHOD
Sequential	Tape or Disk	Sequential
Indexed	Disk	Random* or Sequential
Direct (Relative)	Disk	Random* or Sequential

Primarily accessed as random files

HOW IS DATA IN FILES MAINTAINED?

Data stored on auxiliary storage must be kept current so that when it is processed it will produce accurate results. To keep the data current, the records in the files must be updated. Updating records within a file means adding records to the file, changing records within the file, and deleting records from the file.

Adding Records

Records are added to a file when additional data is needed to make the file current. For example, if a customer opens a new account at a bank, a record containing the data for the new account must be added to the bank's account file. The process that would take place to add this record to the file is shown in Figure 7-10.

1. The existing customer account file is available for updating.
2. A bank clerk enters the new customer data into the computer through a terminal. The data includes the account number, the customer name, and the deposit that will become the account balance.
3. The update program moves the data entered by the user into the new record area in main memory.
4. The update program writes the new record to the file. The location on the disk where the record is written will be determined by the program that manages the disk. In some cases, a new record will be written between other records in the file. In other cases, such as illustrated in Figure 7-10, the new record will be added to the end of the file.

FIGURE 7-10
In this example of adding records, the file first exists without the new account ①. The bank clerk enters the account number, customer name, and deposit ②. This data is used to create a record ③ that is then added to the file ④.

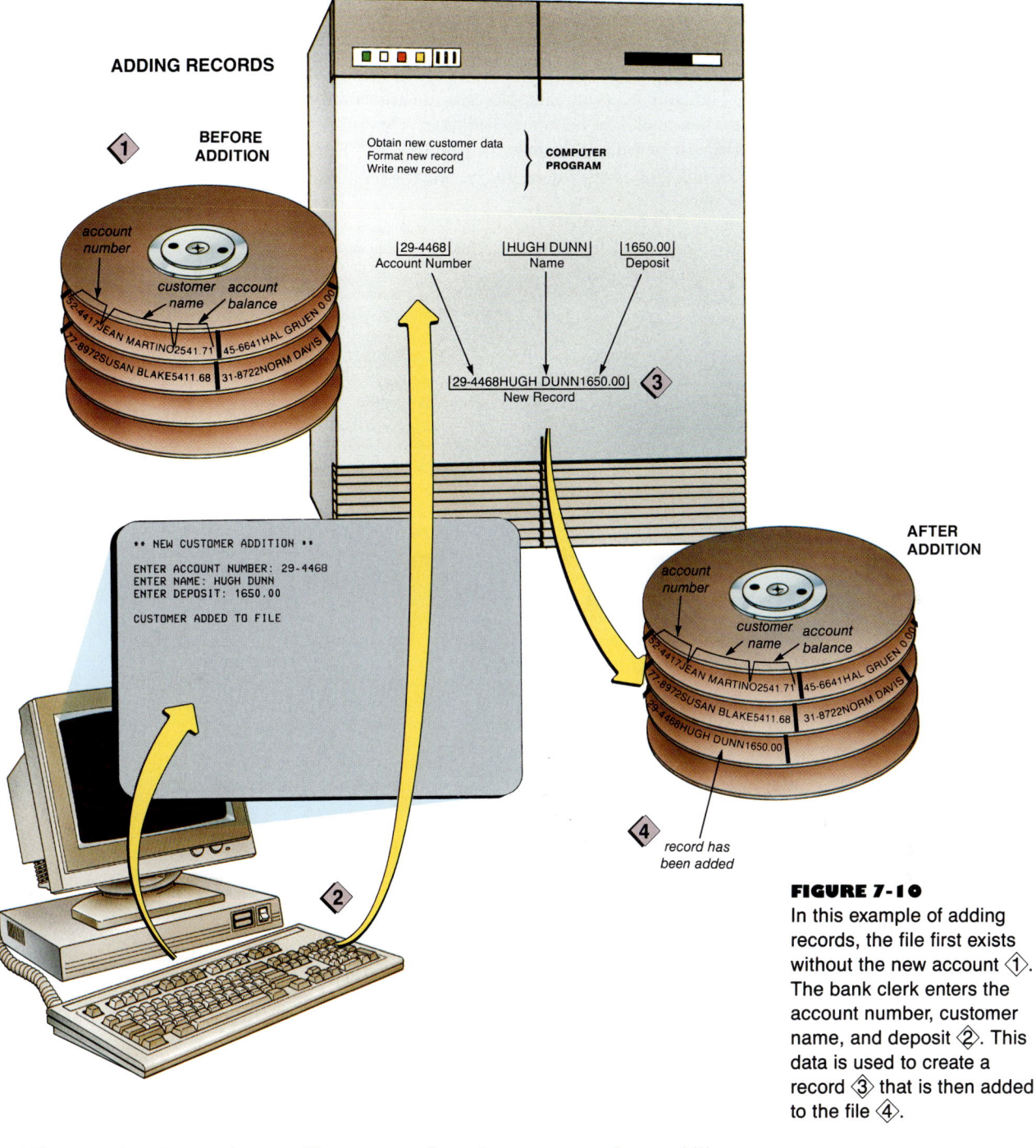

Whenever data is stored on auxiliary storage for subsequent use, the capability to add records must be present in order to keep the data current.

Changing Records

Changing data takes place for two primary reasons: (1) to correct data that is known to be incorrect, and (2) to update data when new data becomes available.

As an example of the first type of change, assume in Figure 7-10 that instead of entering HUGH DUNN as the name for the customer, the bank clerk enters HUGH DONE. The error is not noticed and the customer leaves the bank. When the customer receives his statement he notices the error and contacts the bank to request that the spelling of his name be corrected. To do this, the bank clerk would enter HUGH DUNN as a change to the name field in the record. This change replaces data known to be incorrect with data known to be correct.

The bank account example also illustrates the second reason for change—to update data when new data becomes available. This type of change is made when a customer deposits or withdraws money. In Figure 7-11, Jean Martino withdraws $500.00. The following steps occur when the record for Jean Martino must be changed to reflect her withdrawal.

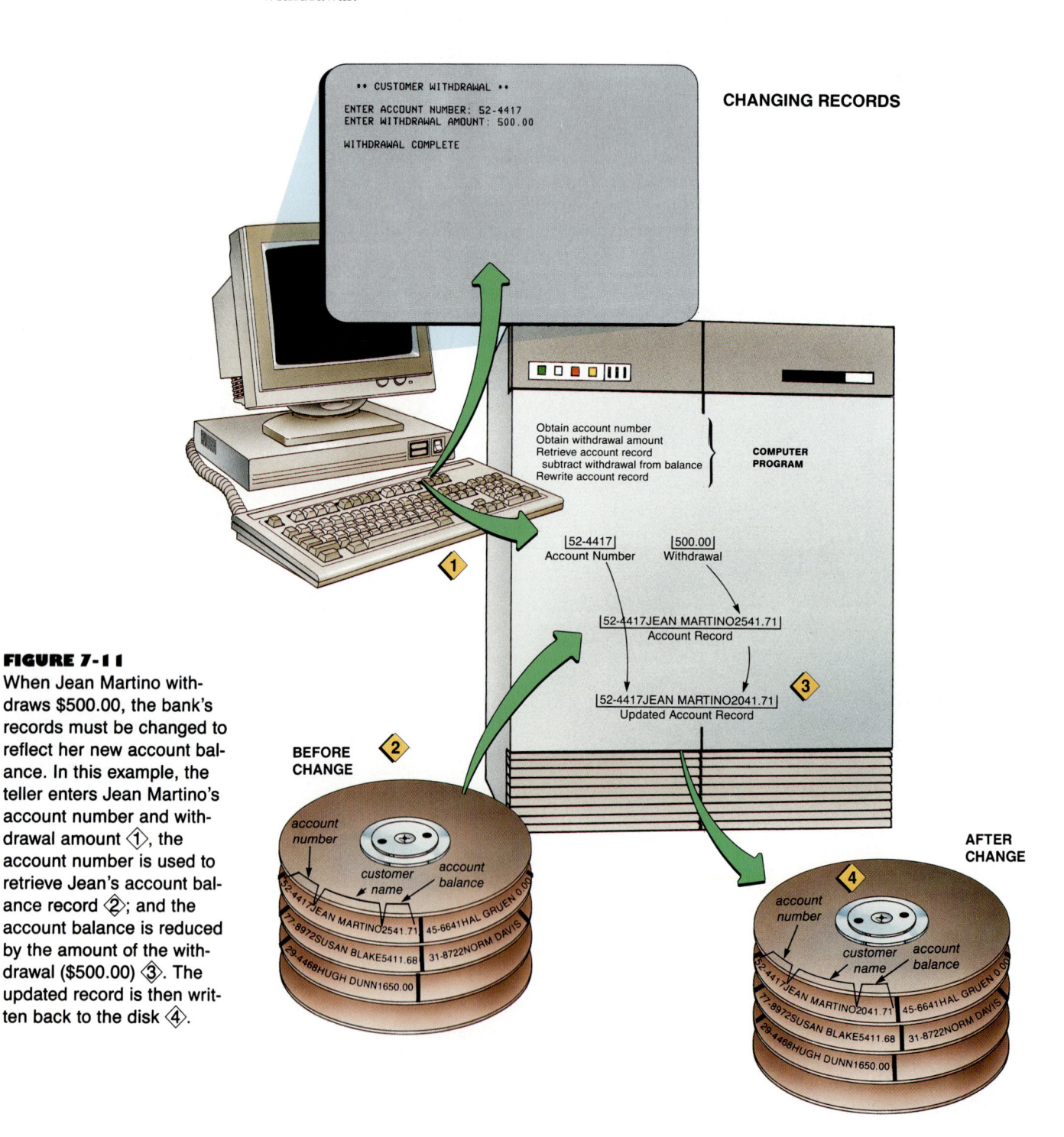

FIGURE 7-11
When Jean Martino withdraws $500.00, the bank's records must be changed to reflect her new account balance. In this example, the teller enters Jean Martino's account number and withdrawal amount ①, the account number is used to retrieve Jean's account balance record ②; and the account balance is reduced by the amount of the withdrawal ($500.00) ③. The updated record is then written back to the disk ④.

1. The bank clerk enters Jean Martino's account number 52-4417 and the amount 500.00.
2. The update program retrieves the record for account number 52-4417 and stores the record in main memory.
3. The program subtracts the withdrawal amount from the account balance in the record. This changes the account balance to reflect the correct balance in the account.
4. After the balance has been changed in memory, the updated record is written back onto the disk. After the change, the account balance has been updated, and the record stored on auxiliary storage contains the new correct account balance.

Changing data stored on auxiliary storage to reflect the correct and current data is an important part of the updating process that is required for data.

Deleting Records

Records are deleted when they are no longer needed as data. Figure 7-12 shows the updating procedures to delete a record for Hal Gruen who has closed his account. The following steps occur to delete the record.

FIGURE 7-12
Here, the account number entered by the teller ① is used to retrieve Hal Gruen's account record ②. The account record is identified as deleted by placing an asterisk in the first position of the record ③. The record is then written back to the file ④. The application software is designed to not process records that begin with an asterisk.

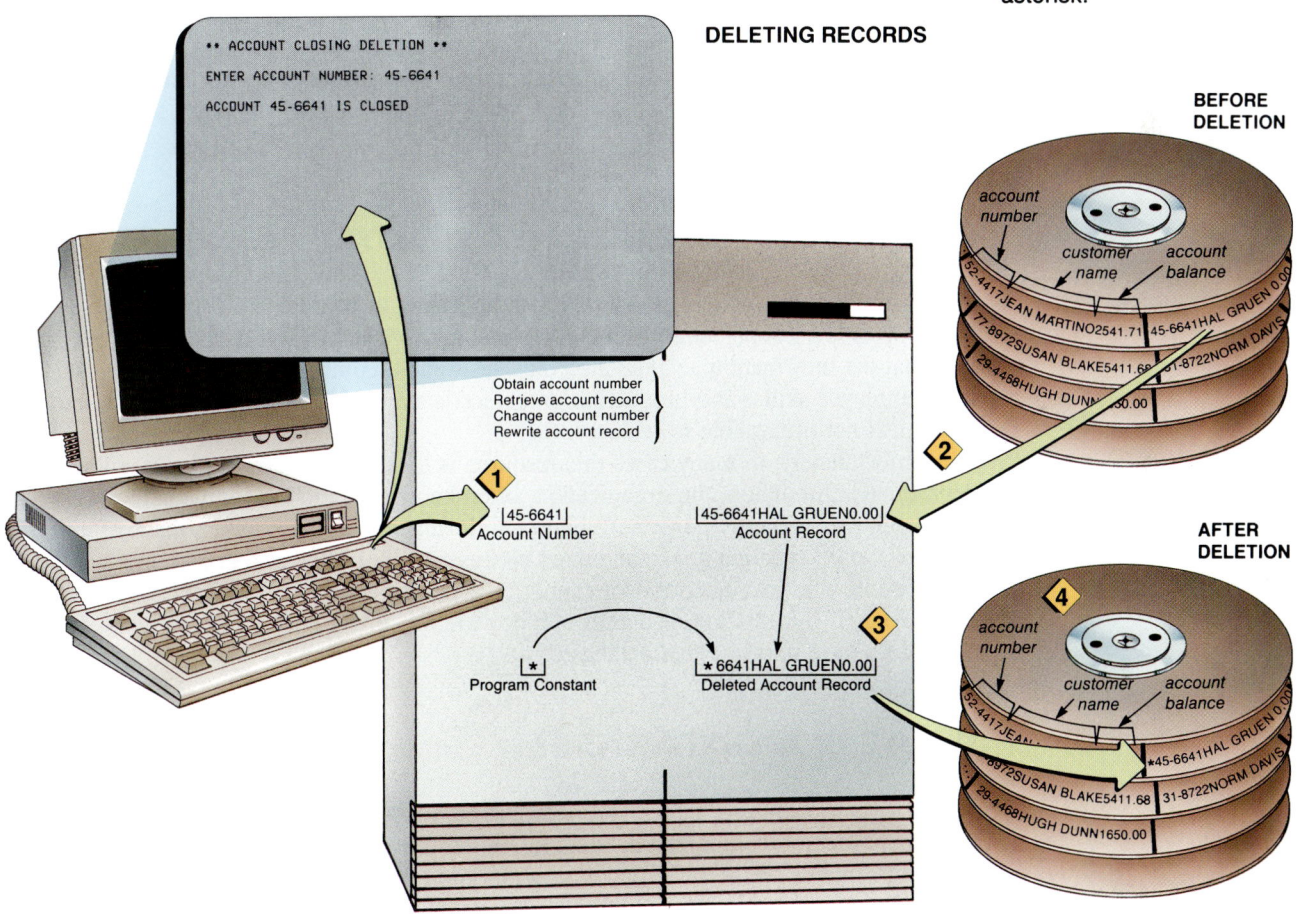

1. The teller enters Hal Gruen's account number (45-6641).
2. The update program retrieves the record from the disk using the account number as the key. The record is placed in main memory.

3. The actual processing that occurs to delete a record from a file depends on the type of file organization being used and the processing requirements of the application. Sometimes the record is removed from the file. Other times, as in this example, the record is not removed from the file. Instead, the record is *flagged*, or marked in some manner, so that it will not be processed again. In this example, an asterisk (*) is added at the beginning of the record.
4. After the asterisk is added, the record is written back to the file. The application program is designed to not process records that begin with an asterisk. Even though the record is still physically stored on the disk, it is effectively deleted because it will not he retrieved for processing.

Flagged records are used in applications where data should no longer be processed but must be maintained for some period of time, such as until the end of the year. Periodically, the user can run a utility program that reorganizes the current records and removes the flagged records. Deleting records from auxiliary storage removes records that are no longer needed and makes additional disk space available.

Summary of How Data Is Maintained

Data maintenance is updating or adding, changing, and deleting data stored on auxiliary storage. The maintenance of data is essential for information derived from the processing of that data to be reliable. When updating data, it does not matter if the data is stored as a single file or if it is part of a series of files organized into a database. The concept of adding, changing, and deleting data to keep it current remains the same.

DATABASES: A BETTER WAY TO MANAGE AND ORGANIZE DATA

◆ Most business people realize that next to the skills of their employees, data (and the information it represents) is one of a company's most valuable assets. They recognize that the information accumulated on sales trends, competitors' products and services, employee skills, and production processes is a valuable resource that would be difficult if not impossible to replace.

Unfortunately, in many cases this resource is located in different files in different departments throughout the organization, often known only to the individuals who work with their specific portion of the total information. In these cases, the potential value of the information goes unrealized because it is not known to people in other departments who may need it or it cannot be accessed efficiently. In an attempt to organize their information resources and provide for timely and efficient access, many companies have implemented databases.

WHAT IS A DATABASE?

◆ Previously in this chapter, we've discussed how data elements (characters, fields, and records) can be organized in files. In file-oriented systems, each file is independent and contains all the information necessary to process the records in that file. In a **database**, the data is organized in multiple related files. Because these files are related, users can access data in multiple files at one time. A **database management system (DBMS)** is the software that allows the user to create, maintain, and report the data and file relationships. By contrast, a **file management system** is software that allows the user to create, maintain, and access one file at a time.

WHY USE A DATABASE?

The following example (Figure 7-13) illustrates some of the advantages of a database system as compared to a file-oriented system. Assume that a business periodically mails catalogs to its customers. If the business is using a file-oriented system, it would probably have a file used for the catalog mailing application that contains information about the catalog plus customer information such as customer account number, name, and address. Files that are used in a file-oriented system are independent of one another. Therefore, other applications such as the sales application, that also need to have customer information would each have files that contain the same customer information stored in the catalog mailing file. Thus, in a file-oriented system, the customer data would be duplicated several times in different files. This duplication of data wastes auxiliary storage space. In addition, it makes maintaining the data difficult because when a customer record must be updated, all files containing that data must be individually updated.

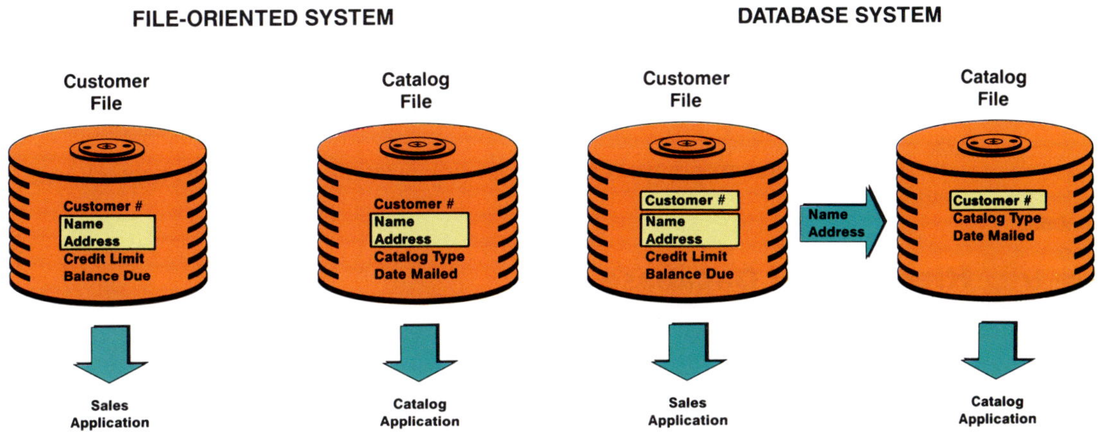

In a database system, however, only one of the applications would have a file containing the customer name and address data. That is because in a database system, files are integrated; that is, related files are linked together by the database software either through predefined relationships or through common data fields. In this example, the link could be the customer account number. If the sales file contained the customer account number, name, and address, the catalog mailing file would only need to contain the customer's account number plus the other catalog information. When the catalog application software is executed, the customer's name and address would be obtained from the sales file. The advantage of the database is that because the files are integrated, the customer name and address would only be stored once. This saves auxiliary storage space. It also allows data to be maintained more easily because update information need only be entered once.

As the previous example illustrates, a database system offers a number of advantages over a file-oriented system. These advantages and several others are summarized as follows:

- **Reduced data redundancy**. Redundant, or duplicate, data is greatly reduced in a database system. Frequently used data elements such as names, addresses, and descriptions are stored in one location. Having such items in one instead of many locations lowers the cost of maintaining the data.
- **Improved data integrity**. Closely related to reduced data redundancy is the database advantage of improved data integrity. Because data is only stored in one place, it is more likely to be accurate. When it is updated, all applications that use the data will be using the most current version.

FIGURE 7-13

In a file-oriented system, each file contains the customer name and address. In the database system, only the customer file contains the name and address. Other files, such as the catalog file, use the customer number to retrieve the customer name and address when it is needed for processing.

- **Integrated files.** As we demonstrated by the catalog mailing example in Figure 7-13, a key advantage of a database management system is its capability to *integrate*, or join together, data from more than one file for inquiry or reporting purposes.
- **Improved data security.** Most database management systems allow the user to establish different levels of security over information in the database. For example, a department manager may have *read only* privileges on certain payroll data: the manager could inquire about the data but not change it. The payroll supervisor would have *full update* privileges: the supervisor could not only inquire about the data but could also make changes. A nonmanagement employee would probably have no access privileges to the payroll data and could neither inquire about nor change the data.
- **Reduced development time.** Because data is better organized in a database, development of programs that use this data is more efficient and takes less time. The need to create new files is reduced. Instead, new attributes are added to existing files.

Now that we've discussed some of their advantages, let's discuss the ways that databases can be organized.

TYPES OF DATABASE ORGANIZATION

There are three major types of database organization: hierarchical, network, and relational.

Hierarchical Database

In a **hierarchical database** (Figure 7-14), data is organized in a series like a family tree or organization chart (the term hierarchy means an organized series). Like a family tree, the hierarchical database has branches made up of parent and child records. Each **parent record** can have multiple child records. However, each **child record** can have only one parent. The parent record at the top of the database is referred to as the **root record**.

FIGURE 7-14
In this hierarchical database, Johnson, Jefferson, and Longtree are the children of Finance, and Finance is their parent. Finance and Accounting are the children of Business, and Business is their parent. These relationships must be established before the database can be used.

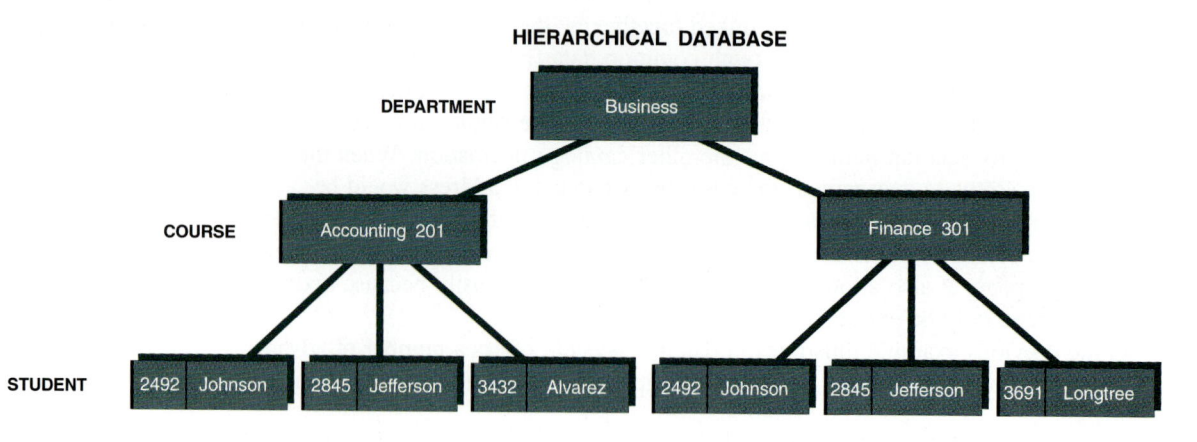

HIERARCHICAL DATABASE

DEPARTMENT: Business

COURSE: Accounting 201, Finance 301

STUDENT: 2492 Johnson, 2845 Jefferson, 3432 Alvarez, 2492 Johnson, 2845 Jefferson, 3691 Longtree

Hierarchical databases are the oldest form of database organization and reflect the fact that they were developed when the disk and memory capacity of computers was limited and most processing was done in batch mode. Data access is sequential in the sense that an inquiry begins at the root record and proceeds down the branch until the requested data is found. All parent-child relationships are established when the database is created in a separate process that is sometimes called *generating the database*.

After the database is created, access must be made through the established relationships. This points out two disadvantages of hierarchical databases. First, records located in separate branches of the database cannot be accessed easily at the same time. Second, adding new fields to database records or modifying existing fields, such as adding the four-digit ZIP code extension, requires the redefinition of the entire database. Depending on the size of the database, this redefinition process can take a considerable amount of time. The advantage of a hierarchical database is that because the data relationships are predefined, access to and updating of data is very fast.

Network Database

A **network database** (Figure 7-15) is similar to a hierarchical database except that each child record can have more than one parent. In network database terminology, a child record is referred to as a **member** and a parent record is referred to as an **owner**. Unlike the hierarchical database, the network database is able to establish relationships between different branches of the data and thus offers increased access capability for the user. However, like the hierarchical database, these data relationships must be established prior to the use of the database and must be redefined if fields are added or modified.

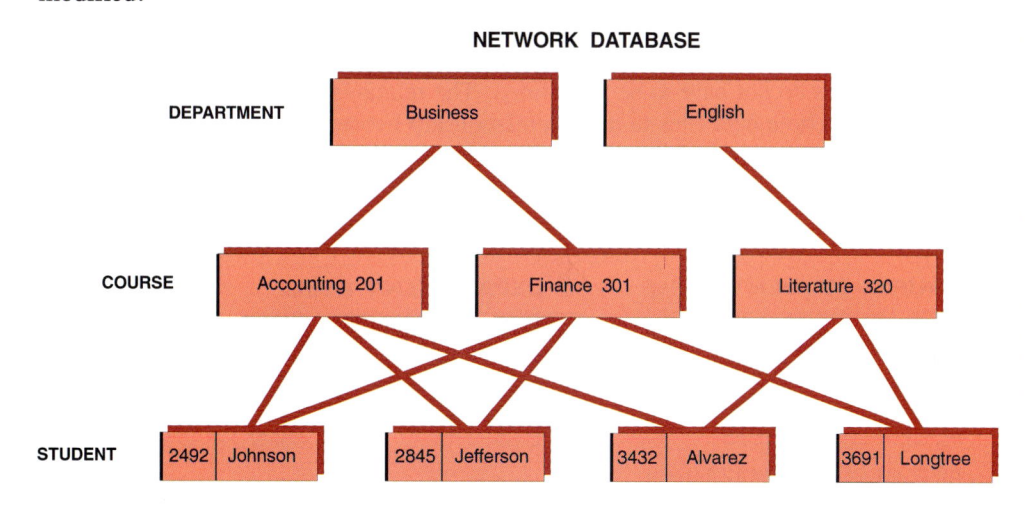

FIGURE 7-15
In a network database, lower level (member) records can be related to more than one higher level (owner) record. For example, Longtree's owners are Finance and Literature. Accounting has three members, Johnson, Jefferson, and Alvarez. As in a hierarchical database, these relationships must be established before the database can be used.

Relational Database

The relational database structure is the most recently developed of the three methods and takes advantage of large-capacity, direct-access storage devices that were not available when the hierarchical and network methods were developed. In a **relational database**, data is organized in tables that in database terminology are called **relations**. The tables are further divided into rows (called **tuples**) and fields (called **attributes**). The tables can be thought of as files and the rows as records. The range of values that an attribute can have is called a **domain**. These terms with a Student Master Table are illustrated on the next page in Figure 7-16.

FIGURE 7-16
In a relational database, the terms used to describe files are called tables.

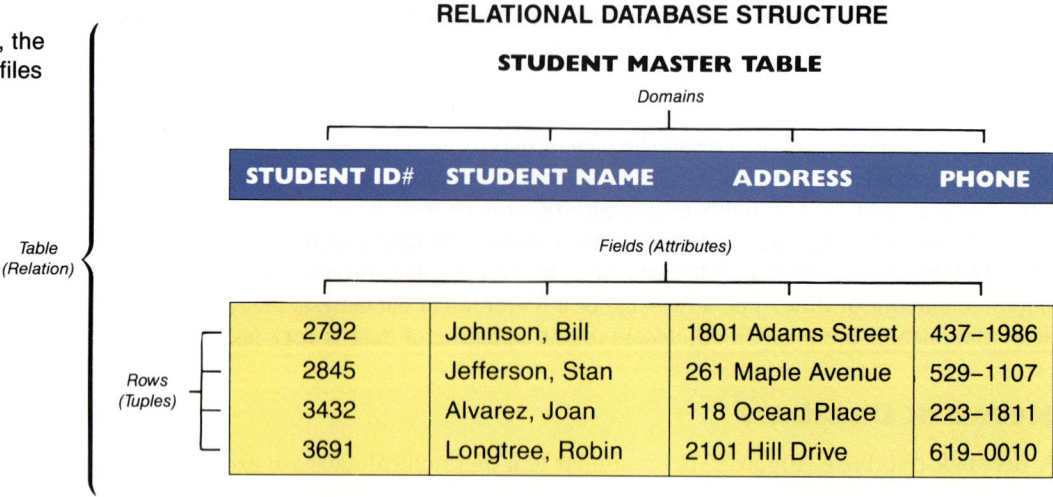

RELATIONAL DATABASE STRUCTURE
STUDENT MASTER TABLE

Domains

Table (Relation):

STUDENT ID#	STUDENT NAME	ADDRESS	PHONE

Fields (Attributes)

Rows (Tuples):

2792	Johnson, Bill	1801 Adams Street	437–1986
2845	Jefferson, Stan	261 Maple Avenue	529–1107
3432	Alvarez, Joan	118 Ocean Place	223–1811
3691	Longtree, Robin	2101 Hill Drive	619–0010

Recall that a key advantage of a database is its capablity to link multiple files together. A relational database accomplishes this by using a common field that exists in each file. For example, in a database for a college, the link between files containing student information could be the student identification number. Hierarchical and network databases can also extract data from multiple files, but in these database structures, the data relationships that will enable the multiple file combination must be defined when the database is created. The advantage of a relational database is that the data relationships do not have to be predefined. The relational database needs only a common field in both data files to make a relationship between them (Figure 7-17). Because it is sometimes difficult to know ahead of time how data will be used, the flexibility provided by a relational database is an important advantage.

FIGURE 7-17
In a relational database, files (called tables) do not require predefined relationships as they do with hierarchal or network databases. Instead, common fields are used to link one table to another. For example, Student ID# could be used to link the Student Master Table in Figure 7-16 above with the Course-Student Table ⓐ. Department ID could be used to link the Department Table ⓑ with the Course-Master Table ⓒ.

ⓐ COURSE-STUDENT TABLE

COURSE #	STUDENT ID#
ACC201	2942
ACC201	2845
ACC201	3432
FIN301	2492
FIN301	2845
FIN301	3691
LIT320	3691

ⓑ DEPARTMENT TABLE

DEPARTMENT ID	DEPARTMENT NAME
BUS	Business
ENG	English

ⓒ COURSE-MASTER TABLE

COURSE #	COURSE NAME	DEPARTMENT ID	UNITS	MAX ENROLLMENT
ACC201	Advanced Accounting	BUS	4	50
FIN301	Investments	BUS	2	30
LIT320	Modern Literature	ENG	3	20

Another advantage of a relational database is its capability to add new fields. All that need be done is to define the fields in the appropriate table. With hierarchical and network database systems, the entire database has to be *redefined*: existing relationships have to be reestablished to include the new fields. A disadvantage of a relational database is that its more complex software requires more powerful computers to provide acceptable performance.

DATABASE MANAGEMENT SYSTEMS

◆ A number of common database management system features are available, including the following described in Figure 7-18.

FEATURE	DESCRIPTION
Data Dictionary	Defines data files and fields.
Utility Program	Creates files and dictionaries, monitors performance, copies data, and deletes unwanted records.
Security	Controls different levels of access to a database.
Query Language	Allows user to specify report content and format.

FIGURE 7-18
A summary of common database management system features.

- **Data dictionary**. The data dictionary defines each data field that will be contained in the database files. The dictionary is used to record the field name, size, description, type of data (e.g., text, numeric, or date), and relationship to other data elements.
- **Utilities**. Database management system utility programs provide for a number of maintenance tasks including creating files and dictionaries, monitoring performance, copying data, and deleting unwanted records.
- **Security**. Most database management systems allow the user to specify different levels of user access privileges. The privileges can be established for each user for each type of access (retrieve, update, and delete) to each data field. Be aware that without some type of access security, the data in a database is more subject to unauthorized access than in a decentralized system of individual files.
- **Query language**. The query language is one of the most valuable features of a database management system. It allows the user to retrieve information from the database based on the criteria and in the format specified by him or her.

QUERY LANGUAGES: ACCESS TO THE DATABASE

◆ A **query language** is a simple English-like language that allows users to specify what data they want to see on a report or screen display. Although each query language has its own grammar, syntax, and vocabulary, these languages can generally be learned in a short time by persons without a programming background.

A Query Example

Figure 7-19 shows how a user might query a relational database. In this example, we illustrate the relational operations that might be performed when a relational database inquiry is made. These three **relational operations** are select, project, and join. They allow the user to manipulate the data from one or more files to create a unique **view**, or subset, of the total data.

FIGURE 7-19
The three relational operations (select, project, and join) that would be used to produce a response to the query. The query response is referred to as a view.

Query: Display customer name and quantity ordered for all sales orders for Part C-143

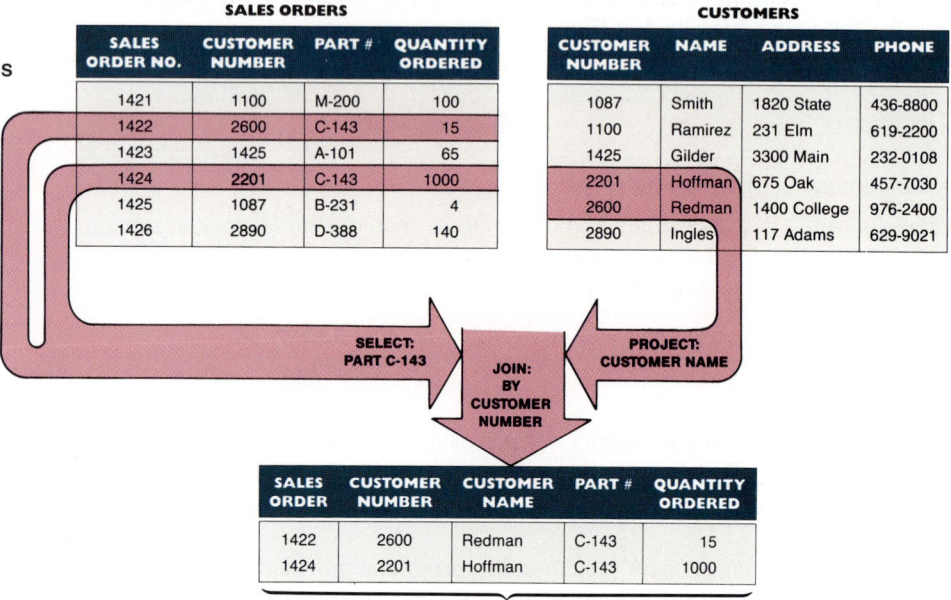

SALES ORDERS

SALES ORDER NO.	CUSTOMER NUMBER	PART #	QUANTITY ORDERED
1421	1100	M-200	100
1422	2600	C-143	15
1423	1425	A-101	65
1424	2201	C-143	1000
1425	1087	B-231	4
1426	2890	D-388	140

CUSTOMERS

CUSTOMER NUMBER	NAME	ADDRESS	PHONE
1087	Smith	1820 State	436-8800
1100	Ramirez	231 Elm	619-2200
1425	Gilder	3300 Main	232-0108
2201	Hoffman	675 Oak	457-7030
2600	Redman	1400 College	976-2400
2890	Ingles	117 Adams	629-9021

SELECT: PART C-143
JOIN: BY CUSTOMER NUMBER
PROJECT: CUSTOMER NAME

SALES ORDER	CUSTOMER NUMBER	CUSTOMER NAME	PART #	QUANTITY ORDERED
1422	2600	Redman	C-143	15
1424	2201	Hoffman	C-143	1000

Response to Query (view)

The **select relational operation** selects certain records (rows or tuples) based on user-supplied criteria. In the example, the user queries the database to select records from the sales order file that contain part number C-143. Selection criteria can be applied to more than one field and can include tests to determine if a field is greater than, less than, equal to, or not equal to a value specified by the user. Connectors such as AND and OR can also be used.

The **project relational operation** specifies the fields (attributes) that appear on the query output. In the example, the user wants to see the names of the customers who placed orders for part number C-143.

The **join relational operation** is used to combine two files (relations or tables). In the example, the customer number, a field contained in each file, is used to join the two files. After the query is executed, most query languages allow the user to give the query a unique name and save it for future use.

Structured Query Language

One of the most widely used query languages is **Structured Query Language**, often referred to as **SQL** or *sequel*. Originally developed during the 1970s by IBM, SQL has been incorporated into a number of relational database software packages including ORACLE by Oracle Corporation and INGRES by Relational Technology. IBM actively supports SQL and incorporates it into their two major relational database system products, SQL/DS and DB2. SQL received increased support as the emerging relational database management system query language when, in 1985, the American National

Standards Institute formed a committee to develop industry standards for SQL. The standards were issued in 1987. Today, most database software vendors have incorporated SQL into their products. The standardization of SQL will further accelerate its implementation on a wide range of computer systems from micros to supercomputers. This fact, coupled with the increasing dominance of relational databases, will mean that SQL will be available to many computer users. Figure 7-20 shows an example of the SQL statements that would be used to create the response (view) shown in Figure 7-19.

```
SELECT ORDNO, CUSTNO, CUSTNAME, PARTNO, QTYORD
FROM SALESORDERS, CUSTOMERS
WHERE SALESORDERS.CUSTNO = CUSTOMERS.CUSTNO
ORDER BY ORDNO
```

FIGURE 7-20
These Structured Query Language (SQL) statements will generate the response (view) shown in Figure 7-19. The statements specify that the sales order number (ORDNO), customer number (CUSTNO), part number (PARTNO), and quantity ordered (QTYORD) appear on the report. This information will be taken from the SALESORDERS and CUSTOMERS files. The report information will be taken from records where the customer number (CUSTNO) in the SALESORDERS file matches the customer number in the CUSTOMERS file. Information on the report will be listed in sales order (ORDNO) sequence.

DATABASE ADMINISTRATION

◆ The centralization of an organization's data into a database requires a great deal of cooperation and coordination on the part of the database users. In file-oriented systems, if a user wanted to keep track of some data, he or she would just create another file, often duplicating some data that was already being tracked by someone else. In a database system, the user must first check to see if some or all of the data is already on file and if not, how it can be added to the system. The role of coordinating the use of the database belongs to the database administrator.

The Database Administrator

The **database administrator**, or **DBA**, is the person responsible for managing all database activities (Figure 7-21). In small organizations, this person usually has other responsibilities such as the overall management of the computer resources. In medium and large organizations, the role of the DBA is a full-time job for one or more people. The job of the DBA usually includes the following responsibilities:

- **Database design**. The DBA determines the design of the database and specifies where to add additional data files and records when they are needed.
- **User coordination**. The DBA is responsible for letting users know what data is available in the database and how the users can retrieve it. The DBA also reviews user requests for additions to the database and helps establish priorities for their implementation.
- **Backup and recovery**. The centralization of data in a database makes an organization particularly vulnerable to a computer system failure. The DBA is often responsible for minimizing this risk, making sure that all data is regularly backed up and preparing (and periodically testing) contingency plans for a prolonged equipment or software malfunction.
- **System security**. The DBA is responsible for establishing and monitoring system access privileges to prevent the unauthorized use of an organization's data.

FIGURE 7-21
The database administrator plays a key role in the managing of a company's data. The DBA should possess good technical and management skills.

- **Performance monitoring.** The performance of the database, usually measured in terms of response time to a user request, can be affected by a number of factors such as file sizes and the types and frequency of inquiries during the day. Most database management systems have utility programs that enable the DBA to monitor these factors and make adjustments to provide for more efficient database use.

In addition to the DBA, the user also has a role in a database management system.

The Responsibility of the User in a Database Management System

One of the user's first responsibilities is to become familiar with the data in the existing database. First-time database users are often amazed at the wealth of information available to help them perform their jobs more effectively.

Another responsibility of the user, in organizations of any size, is to play an active part in the specification of additions to the database. The maintenance of an organization's database is an ongoing task that must be constantly measured against the overall goals of the organization. Therefore, users must participate in designing the database that will be used to help them achieve those goals and measure their progress.

PERSONAL COMPUTER DATABASE SYSTEMS

◆ A variety of software packages are available for personal computers, ranging from simple file management programs to full relational database management systems. Some of the popular database packages designed for personal computer include dBASE III PLUS, dBASE IV, Paradox, Rbase and Foxpro (Figure 7-22).

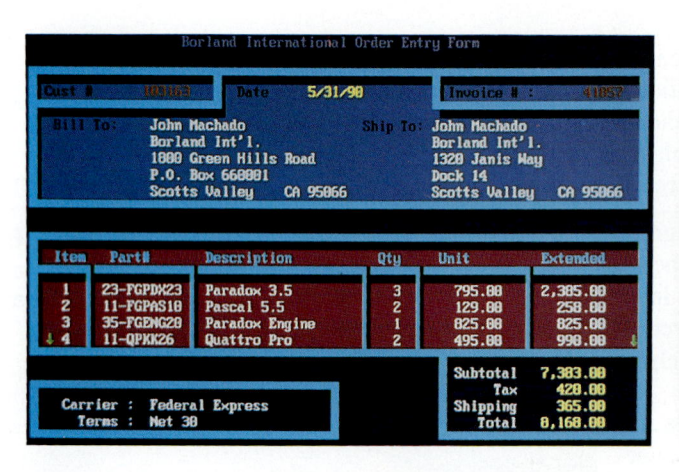

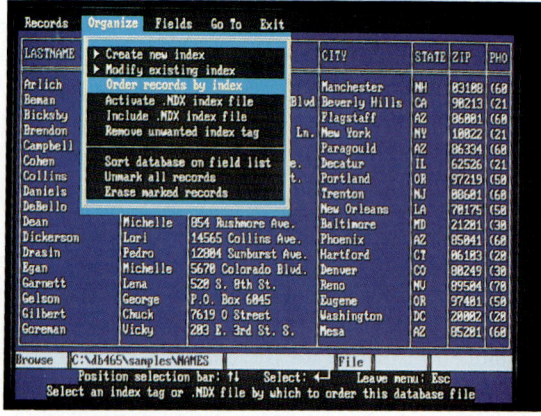

FIGURE 7-22
Paradox and dBASE IV are two of the more popular database software packages. The screen on the left shows an order entry form that was designed with Paradox. The screen on the right shows a name and address file developed using dBASE IV.

As with large system packages, many personal computer software vendors have developed or modified existing packages to support Structured Query Language (SQL). The advantage of SQL packages for personal computers is that they can directly query mainframe databases that support SQL.

The increased computing power of the newest personal computers now allows modified versions of database management packages originally written for mainframe computers to be run on the personal computers. ORACLE (Oracle Corporation) and INFORMIX-SQL (Informix Software) are two SQL-based packages that have been adapted to personal computers.

With so many software packages available (a recent survey included 43), it's difficult to decide which one to choose. If you have simple needs, a file management package is probably all that you need. If you need the capability of a database, one of the more popular database management systems will offer you increased capability and growth potential. For your complex database requirements, the packages originally developed on mainframes should provide all the database resources you require. If you need to select a database software package for your personal computer, you may want to refer to the sections in Chapter 2 that discuss personal computer databases and how to choose software packages for a personal computer.

SUMMARY OF FILE AND DATABASE MANAGEMENT

◆ Understanding the data management, file, and database concepts that we have presented in this chapter gives you a knowledge of how data is stored and managed on a computer. This information will be useful to you, whether you are a home computer user who wants to store personal data on diskettes or a hard drive, or a computer user accessing the database of the company where you are employed.

CHAPTER SUMMARY

1. **Data management** refers to procedures that are used to keep data accurate and timely and provide for the security and maintenance of data.
2. **Data accuracy**, sometimes called **data integrity**, means that the source of the data is reliable and the data is correctly reported and entered.
3. Accurate data must also be timely meaning that it has not lost its usefulness because time has passed.
4. **Data security** refers to protecting data to keep it from being misused or lost.
5. **Backup** procedures provide for maintaining copies of data so that in the event the data is lost or destroyed it can be recovered.
6. Data maintenance refers to **updating** data. This includes **adding**, **changing**, or **deleting** data in order to keep it current.
7. A **file** is a collection of related records that is usually stored on an auxiliary storage device.
8. The three types of file organization are sequential, indexed, and direct or relative.
9. When **sequential file organization** is used, records are stored one after the other, normally in ascending or descending order, based on a value in each record called the key.
10. The **key** is a field that contains unique data, such as a Social Security number, that is used to identify the records in a file.
11. **Sequential retrieval** means that the records on a tape or disk file are retrieved (accessed) one after another in the same order that the records are stored on the tape or disk.
12. With **indexed file organization**, the records are stored on the disk in an indexed file in ascending or descending sequence based on a key field. An index is used to retrieve records.
13. An **index** is a file that consists of a list containing the key field and the corresponding disk address for each record in a file.
14. **Random retrieval**, or **random access**, means the system can go directly to a record without having to read the preceding records.
15. An advantage of indexed files is that usually more than one index can be maintained. Each index can be used to access the records in a file in a particular order.
16. A **direct file**, or **relative file**, uses the key value of a record to determine the location on the disk where the record is or will be stored.
17. The locations on a disk where records in a direct file can be stored are called **buckets**.
18. **Hashing** means the program managing the disk uses a formula or performs a calculation to determine the location (position) where a record will be placed on a disk.
19. A **collision** occurs when the hashing operation generates the same disk location (called **synonyms**) for records with different key values.

20. In a **database**, the data is organized in multiple related files.
21. A **database management system (DBMS)** is the software that allows the user to create, maintain, and report the data and file relationships.
22. By contrast, a **file management system** allows a user to access only one file at a time.
23. The major advantages of using a database include: **reduced data redundancy** (data is not duplicated in several different files); **improved data integrity** (data accuracy); **integrated files** (joining data from more than one file); **improved data security** (ensuring that the data is accessible only to those with the proper authorization); and **reduced development time** (for program development and data preparation).
24. A **hierarchical database** is organized in a top to bottom series of parent-child relationships. Each **parent record** can have multiple child records. However, each **child record** can have only one parent. The parent record at the top of the hierarchy is called the **root record**.
25. A **network database** is organized similar to a hierarchical database except each child record (called a **member**) may have more than one parent record (called an **owner**).
26. Data relationships in both the hierarchical database and the network database must be established prior to the use of the database.
27. A **relational database** is organized into tables called **relations**. The relations are divided into **tuples** (rows) and **attributes** (fields). Each attribute is given a unique name, called the **domain**.
28. In a relational database, a common field is used to connect multiple files.
29. The advantage of a relational database is that the data relationships do not need to be predefined.
30. The database management system (DBMS) consists of a **data dictionary** that defines each data field to be used in the database; **utilities**, or programs, that provide a number of special functions (such as copying data, creating files, and deleting records); **security levels** that control access to the data; and a **query language** that allows users to specify what data they wish to view.
31. When a user queries a relational database, the three **relational operations** are the select, project, and join.
32. The **select relational operation** selects certain records (rows or tuples) based on user-supplied criteria.
33. The **project relational operation** specifies the fields (attributes) that appear on the query output.
34. The **join relational operation** is used to combine two files.
35. A widely used query language is **Structured Query Language (SQL)**.
36. The **database administrator (DBA)** is the person who coordinates all database activities.
37. The database administrator is responsible for database design, user coordination, backup and recovery, database security, and database performance monitoring.
38. Users should become familiar with the data in their organization's database and should actively participate in the specification of additions to the database that will affect their jobs.
39. A variety of data management systems are available for personal computers, ranging from file management programs to full relational database management systems.

KEY TERMS

Adding 7.3
Attribute 7.15
Backup 7.3
Bucket 7.6
Changing 7.3
Child record 7.14
Collision 7.7
Data accuracy 7.2
Data dictionary 7.17
Data integrity 7.2
Data maintenance 7.3
Data management 7.2
Data security 7.3
Database 7.12

Database administrator (DBA) 7.19
Database management system (DBMS) 7.12
Deleting 7.3
Direct access 7.5
Direct file 7.6
Domain 7.15
File management system 7.12
Hashing 7.7
Hierarchical database 7.14
Index 7.5
Indexed file organization 7.5
Join relational operation 7.18
Key 7.4

Member 7.15
Network database 7.15
Owner 7.15
Parent record 7.14
Prime number 7.7
Project relational operation 7.18
Query language 7.17
Random access 7.5
Random retrieval 7.5
Relational database 7.15
Relational operation 7.18
Relation 7.15
Relative file 7.6
Root record 7.14

Security *7.17*
Select relational operation *7.18*
Sequential access *7.4*
Sequential file organization *7.4*
Sequential retrieval *7.4*
Structured Query Language (SQL) *7.18*
Synonym *7.7*
Tuple *7.15*
Updating *7.3*
Utilities *7.17*
View *7.18*

REVIEW QUESTIONS

1. List and describe the three areas of data management.
2. Describe sequential file organization. What is a key?
3. What is an indexed file? Describe how the index is used to retrieve records from an indexed file.
4. Write a definition for a direct file.
5. What is hashing? What are buckets?
6. Write a definition for the term database.
7. Describe what a database management system allows a user to do.
8. What are the advantages of a database management system over a file-oriented system?
9. Draw an example of a hierarchical and network database.
10. Describe how data is organized in a relational database.
11. Discuss two advantages and one disadvantage of a relational database.
12. What are the common features of database management systems?
13. How is a database query used?
14. What are the responsibilities of a database administrator?
15. What are the responsibilities of the user in a database management system?

CONTROVERSIAL ISSUES

1. Database management systems allow the user to establish different levels of security that can be used to restrict access and update privileges. Using a student record file as an example, discuss the different access and update privileges that students, teachers, administrators, and outside organizations should have concerning student file records.
2. Commercial attempts to market databases consisting of personal information on citizens have met strong opposition from critics that contend that the dissemination of such information is an invasion of privacy. Discuss how such a database could be used and misused. What limits, if any, should be placed on the creation of databases that contain information on private citizens?

RESEARCH PROJECTS

1. Visit a local computer store and obtain information on a file management system and a database management system. What features does the database management system have that the file management system does not have?
2. Prepare a report on a database management system that supports Structured Query Language (SQL).

Communications

OBJECTIVES

◆ Define the term communications
◆ Describe the basic components of a communications system
◆ Describe the various transmission media used for communications channels
◆ Describe the different types of line configurations
◆ Describe how data is transmitted
◆ Identify and explain the communications equipment used in a communications system
◆ Describe the functions performed by communications software
◆ Explain the two major categories of networks and describe three common network configurations
◆ Describe how bridges and gateways are used to connect networks

Computers are well recognized as important computing devices. They should also be recognized as important communications devices. It is now possible for a computer to communicate with other computers anywhere in the world. This capability, sometimes referred to as *connectivity*, allows users to quickly and directly access data and information that otherwise would have been unavailable or that probably would have taken considerable time to acquire. Banks, retail stores, airlines, hotels, and many other businesses use computers for communications purposes. Personal computer users communicate with other personal computer users. They can also access special databases available on larger machines to quickly and conveniently obtain information such as weather reports, stock market data, airline schedules, news stories, or even theater and movie reviews.

In this chapter we provide an overview of communications with an emphasis on the communication of data and information. We explain some of the terminology, equipment, procedures, and applications that relate to computers and their use as communications devices. Chapter 14 explains more about some of the specialized communications devices that have been developed for transmitting text, graphics, voice, and video over communications channels.

WHAT IS COMMUNICATIONS?

Communications, sometimes called **data communications**, refers to the transmission of data and information over a communications channel such as a standard telephone line, between one computer or terminal and another computer. Other terms such as telecommunications and teleprocessing are also used to describe communications. **Telecommunications** describes any type of long-distance communications including television signals. **Teleprocessing** refers to the use of telephone lines to transmit data. As communications technology continues to advance, the distinction between these terms is blurred. Therefore, most people refer to the process of transmitting data or information of any type as data communications, or simply communications.

A COMMUNICATIONS SYSTEM MODEL

Figure 8-1 shows the basic model for a communications system. This model consists of the following equipment:

- A computer or a terminal
- Communications equipment that sends (and can usually receive) data
- The communications channel over which the data is sent
- Communications equipment that receives (and can usually send) data
- Another computer

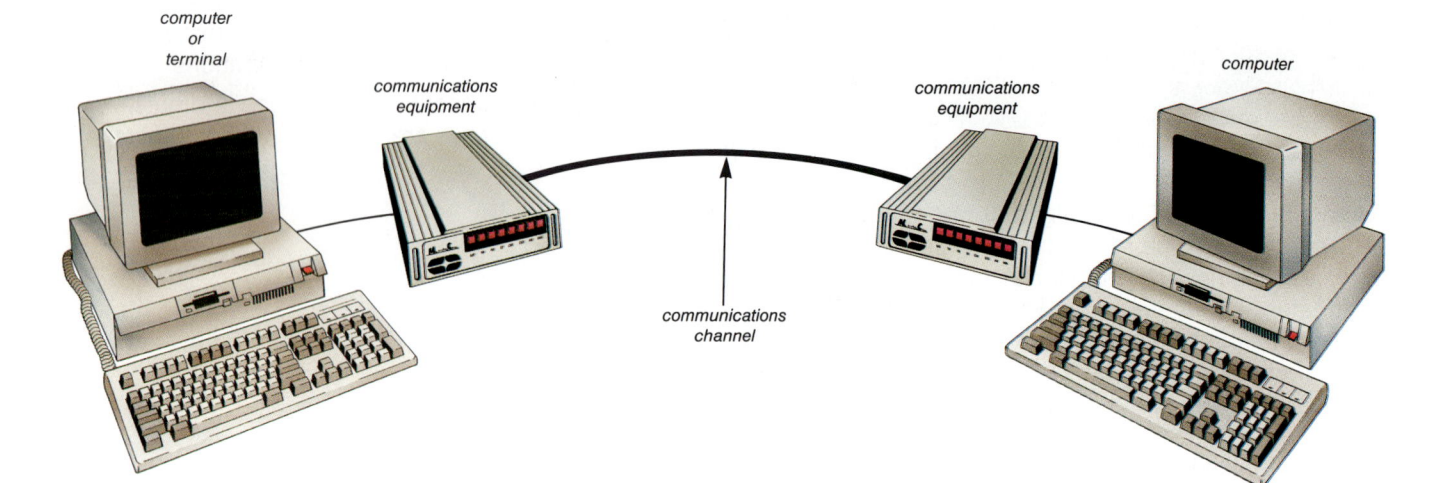

FIGURE 8-1
The basic model of a communications system. In addition to the equipment, communications software is also required.

The basic model also includes communications software. If two computers are communicating with each other, compatible communications software is required on each system. If a computer is communicating with a terminal, communications are directed by either a separate program running on the computer or the computer operating system.

COMMUNICATIONS CHANNELS

◆ A **communications channel**, also called a **communications line** or **communications link**, is the path that the data follows as it is transmitted from the sending equipment to the receiving equipment in a communications system. These channels are made up of one or more **transmission media**, including twisted pair wire, coaxial cable, fiber optics, microwave transmission, satellite transmission, and wireless transmission.

FIGURE 8-2 ▲
Twisted pair wire is most commonly used as telephone wire. It is inexpensive but can be affected by electrical interference that can cause errors in data transmission.

Twisted Pair Wire

Twisted pair wire (Figure 8-2) consists of pairs of copper wires that are twisted together. To insulate and identify the wires, each wire is covered with a thin layer of colored plastic. Twisted pair wire is commonly used for telephone lines. It is an inexpensive transmission medium, and it can be easily strung from one location to another. The disadvantage of twisted pair wire is that it can be affected by outside electrical interference generated by machines such as fans or air conditioners. While this interference might be acceptable on a voice call, it can garble the data as it is sent over the line, causing transmission errors to occur.

FIGURE 8-3 ▼
On coaxial cable, data travels through the copper wire conductor. The outer conductor is made of woven metal mesh that acts as an electrical ground. Coaxial cable can carry up to 100 times as many communication signals as twisted pair wire.

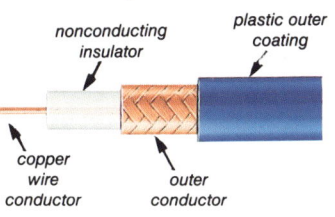

Coaxial Cable

A **coaxial cable** is a high-quality communications line that is used in offices and laid under the ground and under the ocean. Coaxial cable consists of a copper wire conductor surrounded by a nonconducting insulator that is in turn surrounded by a woven metal outer conductor, and finally a plastic outer coating (Figure 8-3). Because of its more heavily insulated construction, coaxial cable is not susceptible to electrical interference and can transmit data at higher data rates over longer distances than twisted pair telephone wire.

There are two types of coaxial cable, named for the transmission techniques they support: baseband and broadband. **Baseband** coaxial cable carries one signal at a time. The signal, however, can travel very fast — in the area of ten million bits per second for the first 1,000 feet. The speed drops significantly as the length of the cable increases, and special equipment is needed to amplify (boost) the signal if it is transmitted more than approximately one mile.

Broadband coaxial cable can carry multiple signals at one time. It is similar to cable TV where a single cable offers a number of channels to the user. A particular advantage of broadband channels is that data, audio, and video transmission can occur over the same line.

FIGURE 8-4 ▼
The two-strand, fiber-optic cable (bottom) can transmit as much information as the 1,500-pair copper cable (top).

Fiber Optics

Fiber optics is a technology that may eventually replace conventional wire and cable in communications systems. This technology is based on the capability of smooth, hair-thin strands of glass to conduct light with high efficiency (Figure 8-4). The major advantages of fiber optics over wire cables include substantial weight and size savings and increased speed of transmission. Another advantage is that fiber-optic cable is not affected by electrical and magnetic fields. A single fiber-optic cable can carry several hundred thousand voice communications simultaneously. The disadvantages of fiber-optic cable are that it is more expensive than twisted pair or coaxial cable and it is more difficult to install and modify than metal wiring. Fiber optics is frequently being used in new voice and data installations.

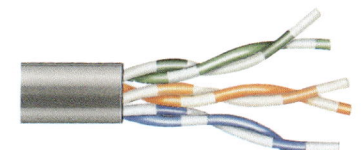

Microwave Transmission

Microwaves are radio waves that can be used to provide high-speed transmission of both voice and data. Data is transmitted through the air from one microwave station to another in a manner similar to the way radio signals are transmitted (Figure 8-5). A disadvantage of microwaves is that they are limited to line-of-sight transmission. This means that microwaves must be transmitted in a straight line and that there can be no obstructions, such as buildings or mountains, between microwave stations. For this reason, microwave stations are characterized by antennas positioned on tops of buildings, towers, or mountains.

Satellite Transmission

Communications satellites receive signals from earth, amplify the signals, and retransmit the signals back to the earth. **Earth stations** (Figure 8-6) are communications facilities that use large, dish-shaped antennas to transmit and receive data from satellites. The transmission *to* the satellite is called an **uplink** and the transmission *from* the satellite to a receiving earth station is called a **downlink**.

Communications satellites are usually placed about 22,300 miles above the earth in a **geosynchronous orbit** (Figure 8-7). This means that the satellite is placed in an orbit where it rotates with the earth, so that the same dish antennas on earth that are used to send and receive signals can remain fixed on the satellite at all times.

FIGURE 8-5 ▲
The round antenna on this tower is used for microwave transmission. Microwave transmission is limited to line-of-sight. Antennas are usually placed 25 to 75 miles apart.

FIGURE 8-6 ▶
Earth stations use large dish antennas to communicate with satellites.

◀ **FIGURE 8-7**
Communications satellites are placed in geosynchronous orbits approximately 22,300 miles above the earth.

Wireless Transmission

Wireless transmission uses one of three techniques to transmit data: light beams, radio waves, or carrier-connect radio, which uses the existing electrical wiring of a building. These methods are sometimes used by companies to connect devices that are in the same general area such as an office or business park. For example, the unit shown in Figure 8-8 uses light beams to transmit or receive data over a distance up to 70 feet. Local wireless systems offer design flexibility and portability, but provide slower transmission speed than wired connections.

For longer distances, radio-wave wireless systems are becoming more widely used. IBM and Motorola combined their private nationwide radio networks and are selling its use to other companies. The combined network contains over 1,100 radio base stations that can serve over 8,000 cities in 50 states. Potential users include companies with large numbers of service personnel who need access to their company's computer data when they are at a customer site. For example, a repair technician may need to know the nearest location of a particular part. Using a portable radio data terminal (Figure 8-9) the technician could access the company's inventory database and obtain information about the availability of the required part.

A wireless device available to the general public that offers many of the same advantages as private radio networks is a cellular telephone. A **cellular telephone** uses radio waves to communicate with a local antenna assigned to a specific geographic area called a cell. Each cell is shaped like a hexagon (Figure 8-10) so that it will precisely fit with adjacent cells. Cellular phones are often used in automobiles. As a cellular telephone user travels from one cell to another, a computer that monitors the activity in each cell switches the conversation from one radio channel to another. By switching channels in this manner, the same channel can be used by another caller in a nonadjacent cell. Individual cells range from one to ten miles in width and use between 50 and 75 radio channels.

FIGURE 8-8
Wireless communications devices are well suited for open office environments where they can be mounted on office partitions. The units work by bouncing light beams off reflective surfaces such as a ceiling or a wall. Multiple terminals or computers can be connected to each device.

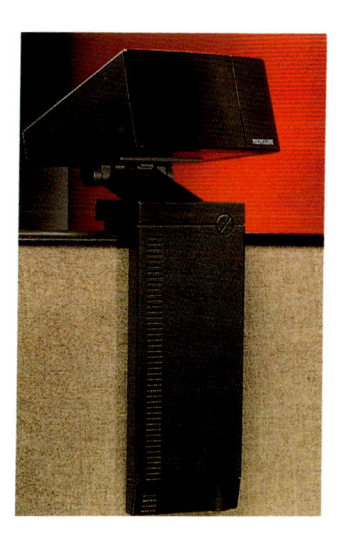

◄ **FIGURE 8-9**
This portable terminal uses radio waves to communicate with a base radio station that is connected to a host computer. Using such a terminal, service technicians can instantly inquire as to the availability of repair parts.

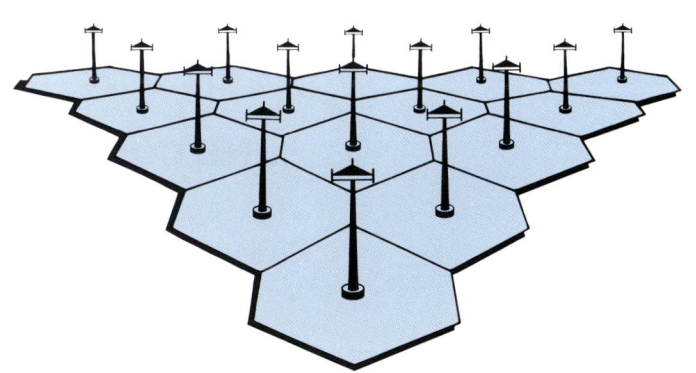

FIGURE 8-10►
Each cell in a cellular phone system is shaped like a hexagon so that it precisely fits with adjacent cells. If a cellular phone user is traveling between cells, such as in a car, a central computer automatically transfers the communication signal from one antenna to another.

An Example of a Communications Channel

When data is transmitted over long distances, several different transmission media are generally used to make a complete communications channel. Figure 8-11 illustrates how some of the various transmission media could be used to transmit data from a personal computer on the west coast of the United States to a large computer on the east coast. An example of the steps that could occur are as follows.

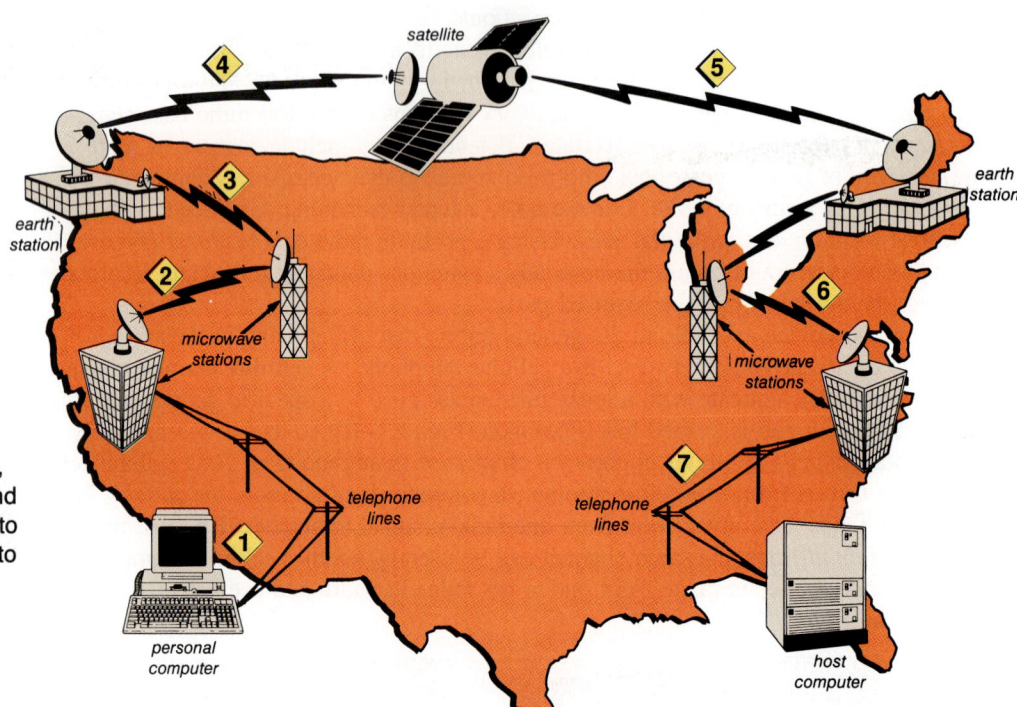

FIGURE 8-11
The use of telephone wires, microwave transmission, and a communications satellite to allow a personal computer to communicate with a large host computer.

① An entry is made on the personal computer. The data is sent over telephone lines from the computer to a microwave station.
② The data is then transmitted from one microwave station to another.
③ The data is transmitted from the last microwave station to an earth station.
④ The earth station transmits the data to the communications satellite.
⑤ The satellite relays the data to another earth station on the other side of the country.
⑥ The data received at the earth station is transmitted to microwave stations.
⑦ The data is sent by the telephone lines to the large computer.

This entire transmission process would take less than one second. Not all data transmission is as complex as this example, but such sophisticated communications systems do exist to meet the needs of some users.

LINE CONFIGURATIONS

Two major **line configurations** (types of line connections) commonly used in communications are: point-to-point lines and multidrop, or multipoint, lines.

Point-to-Point Lines

A **point-to-point line** is a direct line between a sending and a receiving device. It may be one of two types: a switched line or a dedicated line (Figure 8-12).

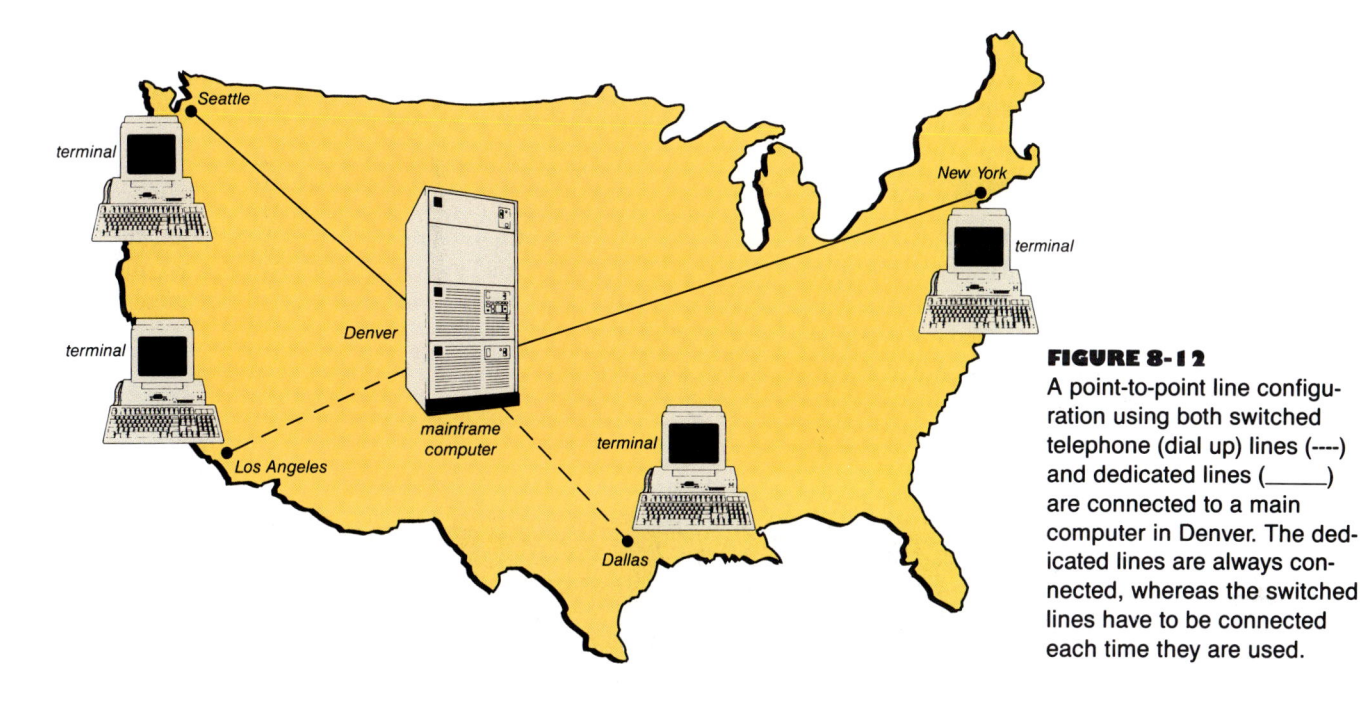

FIGURE 8-12
A point-to-point line configuration using both switched telephone (dial up) lines (----) and dedicated lines (_____) are connected to a main computer in Denver. The dedicated lines are always connected, whereas the switched lines have to be connected each time they are used.

Switched Line A **switched line** uses a regular telephone line to establish a communications connection. Each time a connection is made, the line to be used for the call is selected by the telephone company switching stations (hence the name switched line). Using a switched line for communicating data is the same process as one person using a telephone to call another person. The communications equipment at the sending end dials the telephone number of the communications equipment at the receiving end. When the communications equipment at the receiving end answers the call, a connection is established and data can be transmitted. The process of establishing the communication connection is sometimes referred to as the **handshake**. When the transmission of data is complete, the communications equipment at either end terminates the call by hanging up and the line is disconnected.

An advantage of using switched lines is that a connection can be made between any two locations that have telephone service and communications equipment. For example, a personal computer could dial one computer to get information about the weather and then hang up and place a second call to another computer to get information about the stock market. A disadvantage of a switched line is that the quality of the line cannot be controlled because the line is chosen at random by the telephone company switching equipment. The cost of a switched line is the same for data communications as for a regular telephone call.

Dedicated Line A **dedicated line** is a line connection that is always established (unlike the switched line where the line connection is reestablished each time it is used). The communications device at one end is always connected to the device at the other end. A user can create his or her own dedicated line connection by running a wire or cable between two points, such as between two offices or buildings, or the dedicated line can be provided by an outside organization such as a telephone company or some other communications service company. If the dedicated line is provided by an outside organization, it is sometimes called a **leased line**, or a **private line**. The quality and consistency of the connection is better than on a switched line because a dedicated line is always established. Use of dedicated lines provided by outside organizations are usually charged on a flat-fee basis, a fixed amount each month regardless of how much time the line is actually used to transmit data. The cost of dedicated lines varies based on the distance between the two connected points and, sometimes, the speed at which data will be transmitted.

Multidrop Lines

The second major line configuration is called a **multidrop line**, or **multipoint line**. This type of line configuration is commonly used to connect multiple devices, such as terminals or personal computers, on a single line to a main computer, sometimes called a **host computer** (Figure 8-13).

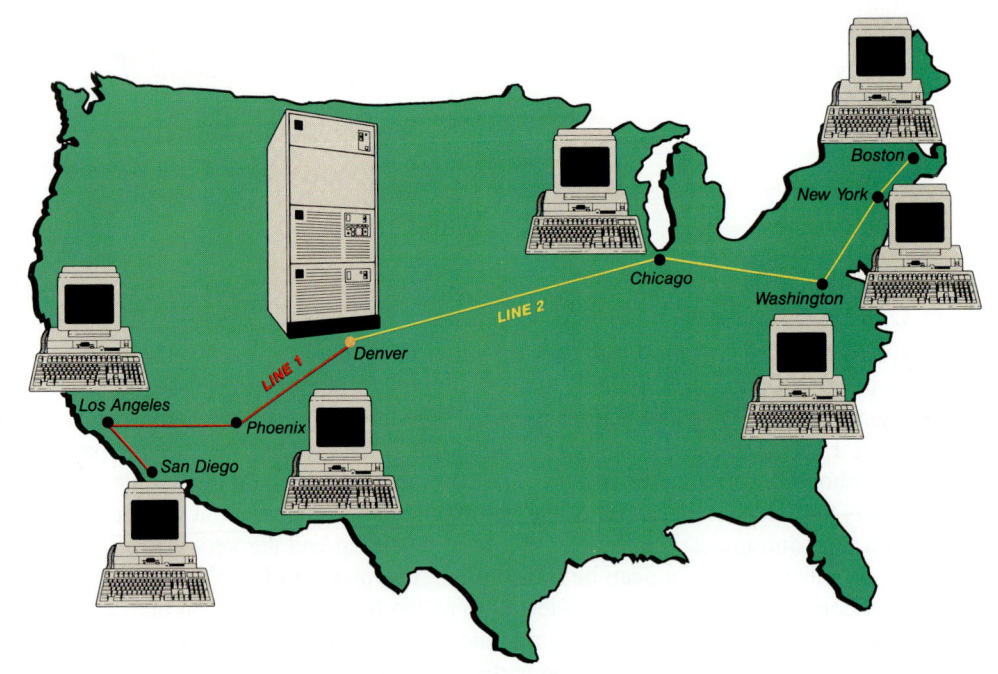

FIGURE 8-13
Two multidrop lines connect several cities with a computer in Denver. Each line is shared by terminals at several locations. Multidrop line configurations are less expensive than individual lines to each remote location.

For example, a ticket agent could use a terminal to enter an inquiry requesting flight information from a database stored on a main computer (Figure 8-14). While the request is being transmitted to the main computer, other terminals on the line are not able to transmit data. The time required for the data to be transmitted to the main computer, however, is short—most likely less than one second. As soon as the inquiry is received by the computer, a second terminal can send an inquiry. With such short delays, it appears to the users that no other terminals are using the line, even though multiple terminals may be sharing the same line.

The number of terminals to be placed on one line is a decision made by the designer of the system based on the anticipated amount of traffic on the line. For example, 100 or more terminals could be contained on a single line, provided each one would send only short messages, such as inquiries, and each terminal would use the communications line only a few hours per day. But if longer messages, such as reports, were required and if the terminals were to be used almost continuously, the number of terminals on one line would have to be smaller.

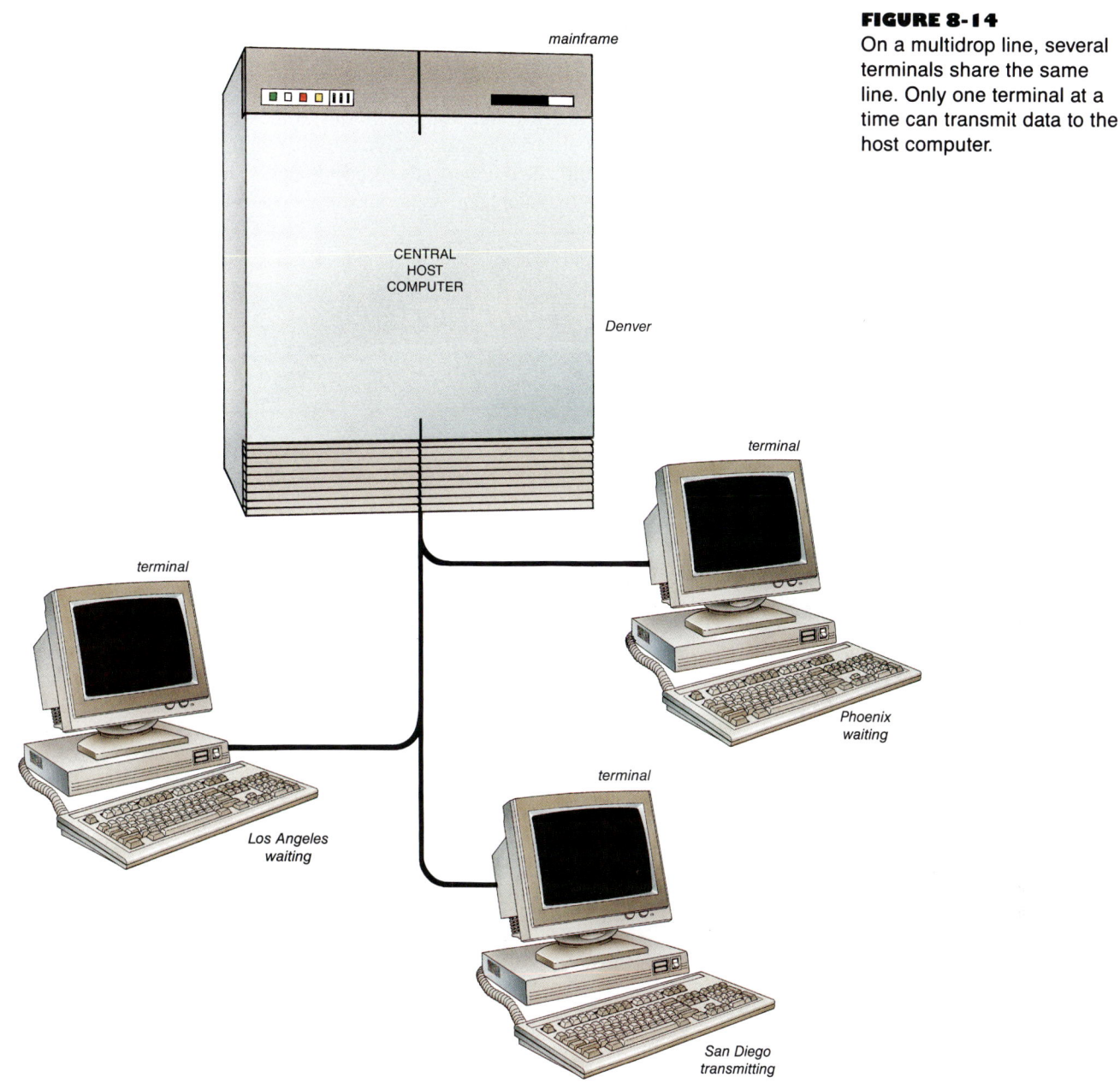

FIGURE 8-14
On a multidrop line, several terminals share the same line. Only one terminal at a time can transmit data to the host computer.

A leased line is almost always used for multidrop line configurations. The use of multidrop lines can decrease line costs considerably because one line is used by many terminals.

CHARACTERISTICS OF COMMUNICATIONS CHANNELS

◆ The communications channels we have just discussed can be categorized by a number of characteristics including the type of signal, transmission mode, transmission direction, and transmission rate.

Types of Signals: Digital and Analog

Computer equipment is designed to process data as **digital signals**, individual electrical pulses that represent the bits that are grouped together to form characters. Telephone equipment was originally designed to carry only voice transmission, which is comprised of a continuous electrical wave called an **analog signal** (Figure 8-15). Thus, a special piece of equipment called a *modem* is used to convert between the digital signals and analog signals so that telephone lines can carry data. We discuss modems in more detail later in this chapter.

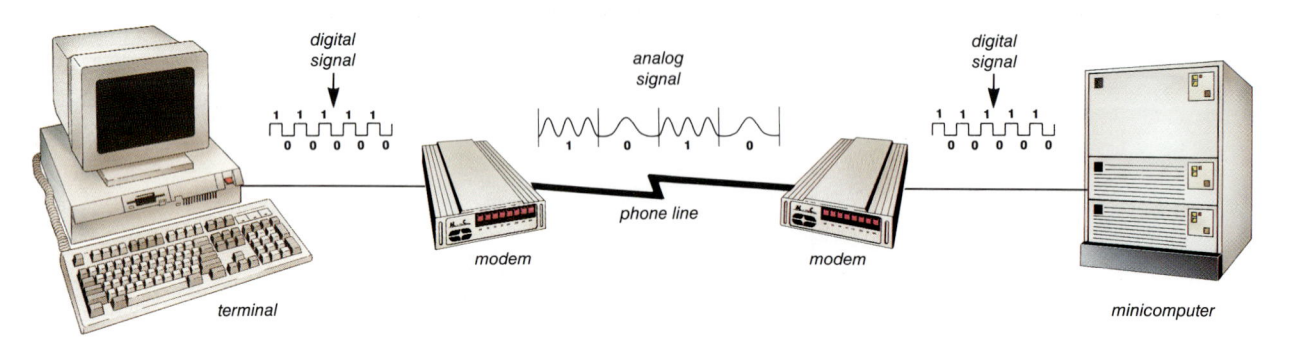

FIGURE 8-15
Individual electrical pulses of the digital signal are converted into analog (electrical wave) signals for transmission over voice telephone lines. The 1s represent ON bits and the 0s represent OFF bits. At the main computer receiving end, another modem converts the analog signals back into digital signals that can be processed by the computer.

To provide better communications services, telephone companies are now offering **digital data service**, communications channels specifically designed to carry digital instead of voice signals. Digital data service is available within and between most major metropolitan areas and provides higher speed and lower error rates than voice lines. Modems are not needed with digital data service; instead, users connect to the communications line through a device called a **data service unit (DSU)**.

Transmission Modes: Asynchronous and Synchronous

In **asynchronous transmission mode** (Figure 8-16), individual characters (made up of bits) are transmitted at irregular intervals, for example, when a user enters data. To distinguish where one character stops and another starts, the asynchronous communication mode uses a start and a stop bit. An additional bit called a *parity bit* is sometimes included at the end of each character. As you learned in our discussion of memory in Chapter 4, parity bits are used for error checking, and they detect if one of the data bits has been changed during transmission. The asynchronous transmission mode is used for lower speed data transmission and is used with most communications equipment designed for personal computers.

FIGURE 8-16
In asynchronous transmission mode, individual characters are transmitted. Each character has start, stop, and error-checking bits. In synchronous transmission mode, multiple characters are sent in a block with start bytes at the beginning of the block and error-checking bits and stop bytes at the end of the block. Synchronous transmission is faster and more accurate.

ASYNCHRONOUS TRANSMISSION MODE

| CHARACTER | IDLE | CHARACTER | IDLE | CHARACTER | IDLE | CHARACTER | IDLE |

SYNCHRONOUS TRANSMISSION MODE

| START BYTES | CHARACTER | CHARACTER | CHARACTER | CHARACTER | ERROR-CHECK BITS | STOP BYTES | IDLE |

In the **synchronous transmission mode** (Figure 8-16), large blocks of data are transmitted at regular intervals. Timing signals synchronize the communications equipment at both the sending and receiving ends and eliminate the need for start and stop bits for each character. Error-checking bits and start and end indicators called sync bytes are also transmitted. Synchronous transmission requires more sophisticated and expensive equipment, but it does give much higher speeds and accuracy than asynchronous transmission.

Direction of Transmission: Simplex, Half-Duplex, and Full-Duplex

The direction of data transmission is classified as either simplex, half-duplex, or full-duplex (Figure 8-17). In **simplex transmission**, data flows in one direction only. Simplex is used only when the sending device, such as a temperature sensor, never requires a response from the computer. For example, if a computer is used to control the temperature of a building, numerous sensors are placed throughout it. Each sensor is connected to the computer with a simplex transmission line because the computer only needs to receive data from the temperature sensors and does not need to send data back to the sensors.

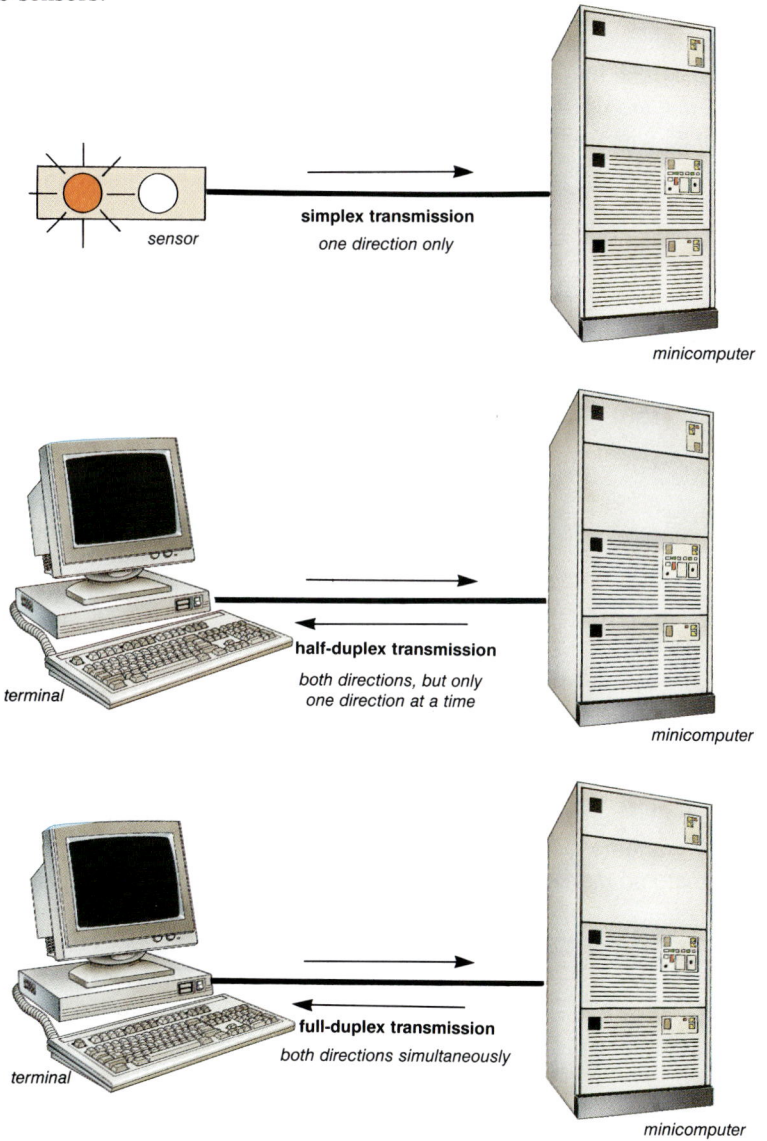

FIGURE 8-17
Simplex transmission allows data to flow in one direction only. Half-duplex transmission allows data to flow in both directions but not at the same time. Full-duplex transmission allows data to flow in both directions simultaneously.

In **half-duplex transmission**, data can flow in both directions but in only one direction at a time. An example is a citizens band radio. The user can talk or listen but not do both at the same time. Half-duplex is often used between terminals and a central computer.

In **full-duplex transmission**, data can be sent in both directions at the same time. A normal telephone line is an example of full-duplex transmission. Both parties can talk at the same time. Full-duplex transmission is used for most interactive computer applications and for computer-to-computer data transmission.

Transmission Rate

The transmission rate of a communications channel is determined by its bandwidth and its speed. The **bandwidth** is the range of frequencies that a channel can carry. Since transmitted data can be assigned to different frequencies, the wider the bandwidth, the more frequencies, and the more data that can be transmitted at the same time.

The speed at which data is transmitted is usually expressed as bits per second or as a baud rate. **Bits per second (bps)** is the number of bits that can be transmitted in one second. Using a 10-bit byte to represent a character (7 data bits, 1 start, 1 stop, and 1 parity bit), a 2,400 bps transmission would transmit 240 characters per second. At this rate, a 20-page, single-spaced report would be transmitted in approximately five minutes. The **baud rate** is the number of times per second that the signal being transmitted changes. With each change, one or more bits can be transmitted. At speeds up to 2,400 bps, usually only one bit is transmitted per signal change and, thus, the bits per second and the baud rate are the same. To achieve speeds in excess of 2,400 bps, more than one bit is transmitted with each signal change and, thus, the bps will exceed the baud rate.

FIGURE 8-18
An external modem is connected to a terminal or computer and to a telephone outlet.

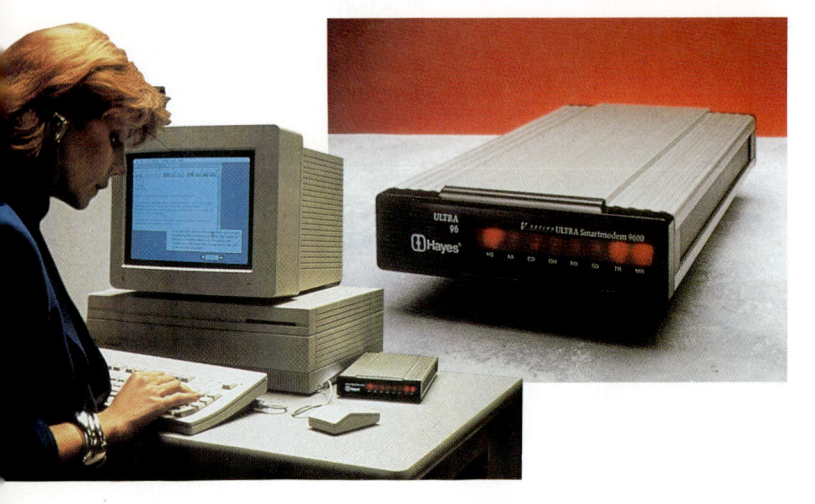

COMMUNICATIONS EQUIPMENT

◆ If a terminal or a personal computer is within approximately 1,000 feet of another computer, the two devices can usually be directly connected by a cable. Over 1,000 feet, however, the electrical signal weakens to the point that some type of special communications equipment is required to increase or change the signal to transmit it farther. A variety of communications equipment exists to perform this task, but the equipment that a user is most likely to encounter is a modem, a multiplexor, and a front-end processor.

Modems

A **modem** converts the digital signals of a terminal or computer to analog signals that are transmitted over a communications channel. It also converts analog signals it receives into digital signals that are used by a terminal or computer. The word modem comes from a combination of the words *mo*dulate, which means to change into a sound or analog signal, and *dem*odulate, which means to convert an analog signal into a digital signal. A modem is needed at both the sending and receiving ends of a communications channel.

FIGURE 8-19
An internal modem is mounted inside a personal computer.

An **external modem** (Figure 8-18) is a separate, or stand-alone, device that is attached to the computer or terminal by a cable and to the telephone outlet by a standard telephone cord. An advantage of an external modem is that it can be easily moved from one terminal or computer to another.

An **internal modem** (Figure 8-19) is a circuit board that is installed inside a computer or terminal. Internal modems are generally less expensive than comparable external modems but once installed, they are not as easy to move.

An **acoustic modem**, also called an **acoustic coupler**, is designed to be used with a telephone handset (Figure 8-20). The acoustic coupler converts the digital signals generated by the terminal or personal computer into a series of audible tones, which are picked up by the mouthpiece in the headset in the same manner that a telephone picks up a person's voice. The analog signals are then transmitted over the communications channel. An acoustic coupler provides portability, but is generally less reliable than an internal or external modem because small outside sounds can be picked up by the acoustic coupler and cause transmission errors. Acoustic couplers are no longer common and are primarily used for special applications, such as with portable computers.

Modems can transmit data at rates from 300 to 38,400 bits per second (bps). Most personal computers would use either a 1,200 or 2,400 bps modem. Business or heavier volume users would use faster and more expensive modems.

FIGURE 8-20
The acoustic coupler (lower left) allows a portable computer user to communicate with another computer over telephone lines. The telephone handset is placed in the molded rubber cups on the acoustic coupler.

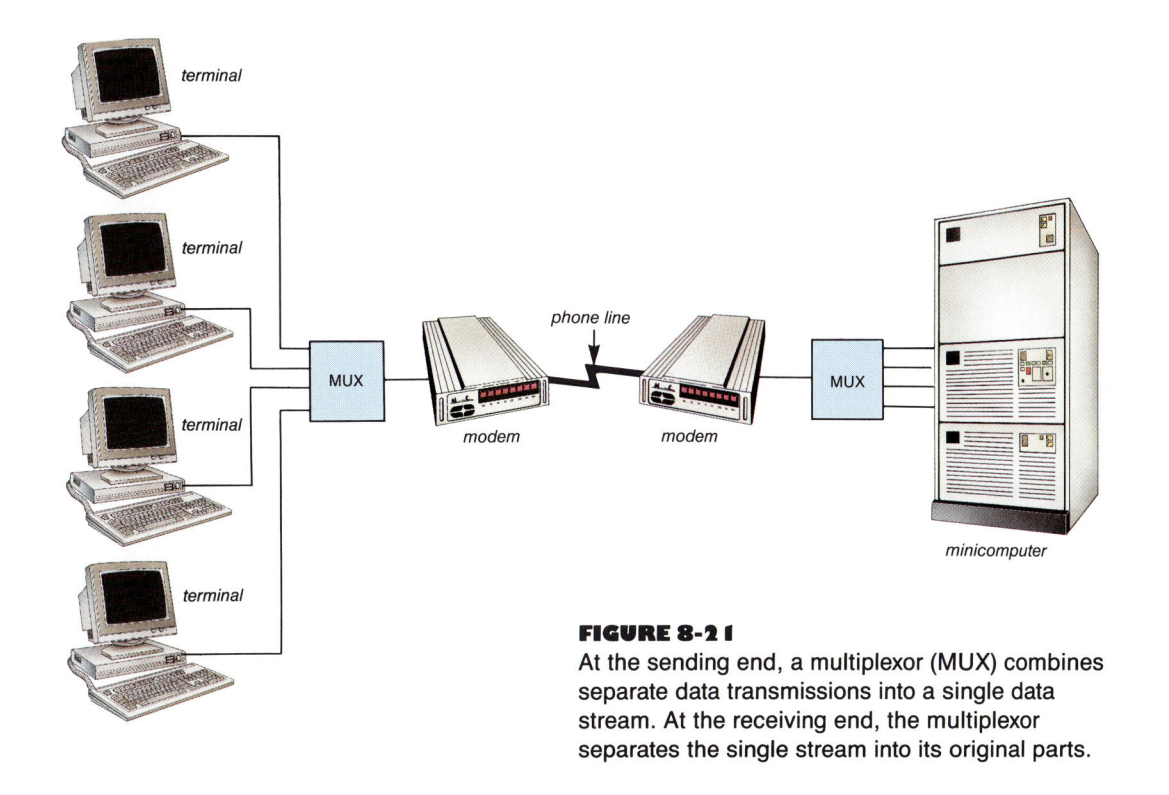

Multiplexors

A **multiplexor**, sometimes referred to as a MUX, combines more than one input signal into a single stream of data that can be transmitted over a communications channel (Figure 8-21). The multiplexor at the sending end codes each character it receives with an identifier that is used by the multiplexor at the receiving end to separate the combined data stream into its original parts. A multiplexor may be connected to a separate modem or may have a modem built in. By combining the individual data streams into one, a multiplexor increases the efficiency of communications and saves the cost of individual communications channels.

FIGURE 8-21
At the sending end, a multiplexor (MUX) combines separate data transmissions into a single data stream. At the receiving end, the multiplexor separates the single stream into its original parts.

FIGURE 8-22
This IBM Series 1 minicomputer is often used as a front-end processor to relieve the main computer of communications tasks.

Front-End Processors

A **front-end processor** (Figure 8-22) is a computer that is dedicated to handling the communications requirements of a larger computer. Relieved of these tasks, the large computer is then dedicated to processing data, while the front-end processor communicates the data. Tasks that the front-end processor would handle include **polling** (checking the connected terminals or computers to see if they have data to send), error checking and correction, and access security to make sure that a connected device or the user of the connected device is authorized to access the computer.

COMMUNICATIONS SOFTWARE

◆ Sometimes communications equipment is preprogrammed to accomplish its designed communications tasks. Other times, the user must load a program before transmitting data. These programs, referred to as **communications software**, can perform a number of tasks including dialing (if a switched telephone line is used), file transfer, terminal emulation, and data encryption (Figure 8-23).

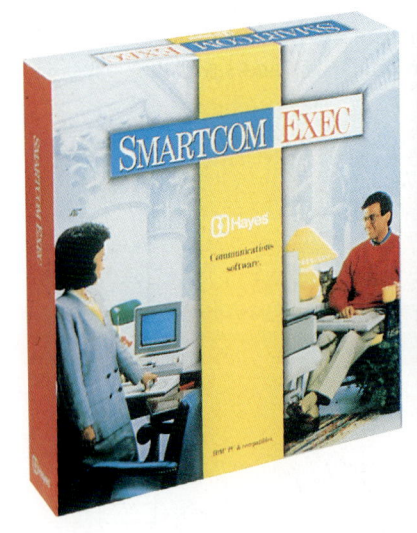

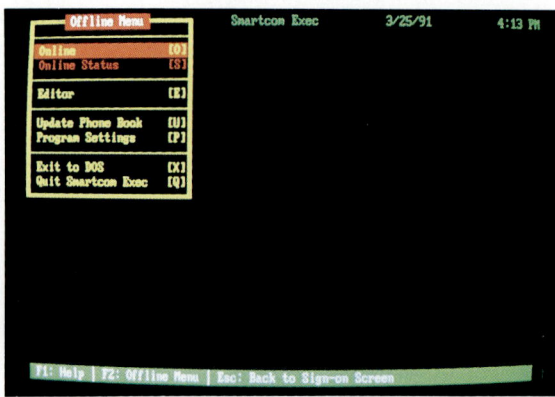

FIGURE 8-23
Communications software performs a variety of tasks that assist the user in operating communications equipment.

Dialing software allows you to store, review, select and dial telephone numbers of computers that can be called (Figure 8-24). The software provides a variety of meaningful messages to assist you in establishing a connection before transmitting data. For example, a person who uses a personal computer at home to communicate with a computer at the office could use dialing software to establish the communications connection. The software would display the office computer's telephone number on the user's personal computer screen. The user would enter the appropriate command for the dialing software, working with a modem, to begin dialing the office computer and to establish a connection. During the 10 or 15 seconds that this process takes, the software would display messages to indicate specifically what was happening, such as "DIALING," "CARRIER DETECT" (which means that the office computer has answered), and "CONNECTED" (to indicate that the communications connection has been established and data transmission can begin).

File transfer software allows you to move one or more files from one system to another. Generally, you have to load the file transfer software on both the sending and receiving computers.

Terminal emulation software allows a personal computer to imitate or appear to be a specific type of terminal, so that the personal computer can connect to another usually larger computer. Most minicomputers and mainframes are designed to work with terminals that have specific characteristics such as speed and parity. Terminal emulation software performs the necessary speed and parity conversion.

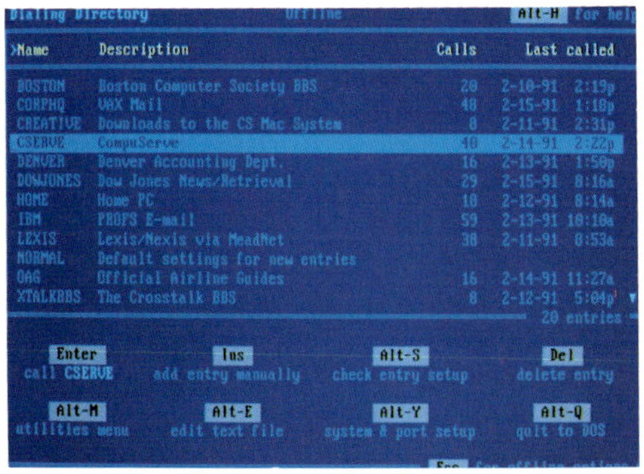

Data encryption protects confidential data during transmission. **Data encryption** is the conversion of data at the sending end into an unrecognizable string of characters or bits and the reconversion of the data at the receiving end. Without knowing how the data was encrypted, someone who intercepted the transmitted data would have a difficult time determining what the data meant.

FIGURE 8-24
This screen from *Crosstalk Communicator* is a popular communications software package for personal computers. The screen shows the information that is displayed when the software is being used to dial the CompuServe Information Service.

COMMUNICATIONS PROTOCOLS

◆ Communications software is written to work with one or more protocols. A **protocol** is a set of rules and procedures for exchanging information between computers. Protocols define how the communications link is established, how information is transmitted, and how errors are detected and corrected. Using the same protocol, different types and makes of computers can communicate with each other. Over the years, numerous protocols have been developed. Today, however, there are strong efforts to establish standards that all computer and communications equipment manufacturers will follow. The International Standards Organization (ISO) based in Geneva, Switzerland has defined a set of communications protocols called the **Open Systems Interconnection (OSI) model**. The OSI model has been endorsed by the United Nations.

COMMUNICATIONS NETWORKS

◆ A communications **network** is a collection of terminals, computers, and other equipment that uses communications channels to share data, information, hardware, and software. Networks can be classified as either local area networks or wide area networks.

Local Area Networks (LANs)

A **local area network**, or **LAN**, is a communications network that is privately owned and that covers a limited geographic area such as an office, a building, or a group of buildings.

The LAN consists of a communications channel that connects either a series of computer terminals together with a minicomputer or, more commonly, a group of personal computers to one another. Very sophisticated LANs can connect a variety of office devices such as word processing equipment, computer terminals, video equipment, and personal computers.

Two common applications of local area networks are hardware resource sharing and information resource sharing. **Hardware resource sharing** allows each personal computer in the network to access and use devices that would be too expensive to provide for each user or would not be justified for each user because of only occasional use. For example, when a number of personal computers are used on the network, each may need to use a laser printer. Using a LAN, a laser printer could be purchased and made a part of the network. Whenever a user of a personal computer on the network needed the laser printer, it could be accessed over the network. Figure 8-25 depicts a simple local area network consisting of four personal computers linked together by a cable. Three of the personal computers (computer 1 in the sales and marketing department, computer 2 in the accounting department, and computer 3 in the personnel department) are available for use at all times. Computer 4 is used as a **server**, sometimes called a **network control unit**, which is dedicated to handling the communications needs of the other computers in the network. The users of this LAN have connected the laser printer to the server. Using the LAN, all computers and the server can use the printer.

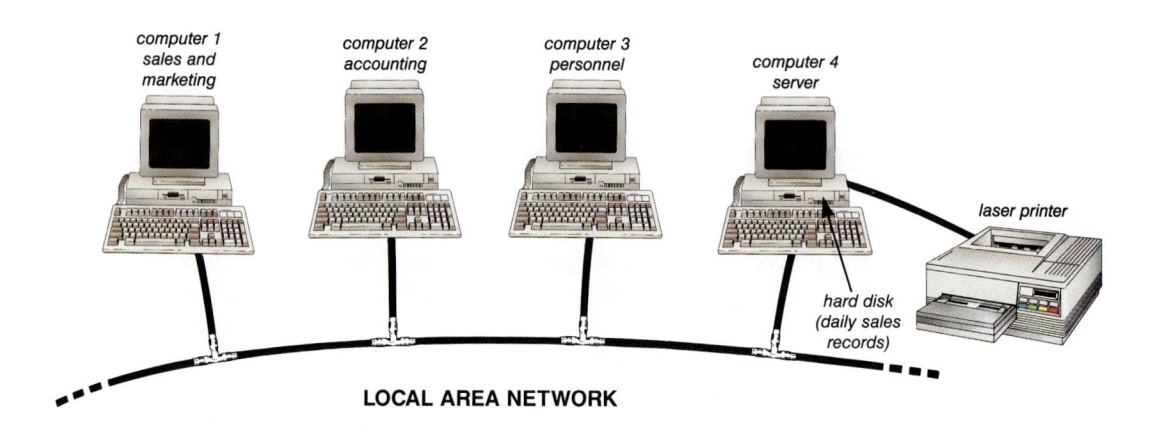

FIGURE 8-25
A local area network (LAN) consists of multiple personal computers or terminals connected to one another. The LAN allows users to share hardware and information.

Information resource sharing allows anyone using a personal computer on the local area network to access data stored on any other computer in the network. In actual practice, hardware resource sharing and information resource sharing are often combined. For example, in Figure 8-25, the daily sales records could be stored on the hard disk associated with the server unit personal computer. Anyone needing access to the sales records could use this information resource. The capability to access and store data on common auxiliary storage is an important feature of many local area networks.

Information resource sharing is usually provided by using either the file-server or client-server method. Using the **file-server** method, the server sends an entire file at a time. The requesting computer then performs the processing. With the **client-server** method, as much processing as possible is done on the server system before data is transmitted. Figure 8-26 illustrates how the two methods would process a request for information stored on the server system for customers with balances over $1,000. With the file-server method, the user transmits a request for the customer file to the server unit ①. The server unit locates the customer file ② and transmits the entire file to the requesting computer ③. The requesting computer selects customers with balances over $1,000 and prepares the report ④. With the client-server method, the user transmits a request for customers with a balance over $1,000 to the server unit ①. The server unit selects the customer records that meet the criteria ② and transmits the selected records to the requesting computer ③. The requesting computer prepares the report ④. The client-server method greatly reduces the amount of data sent over a network but requires a more powerful server system.

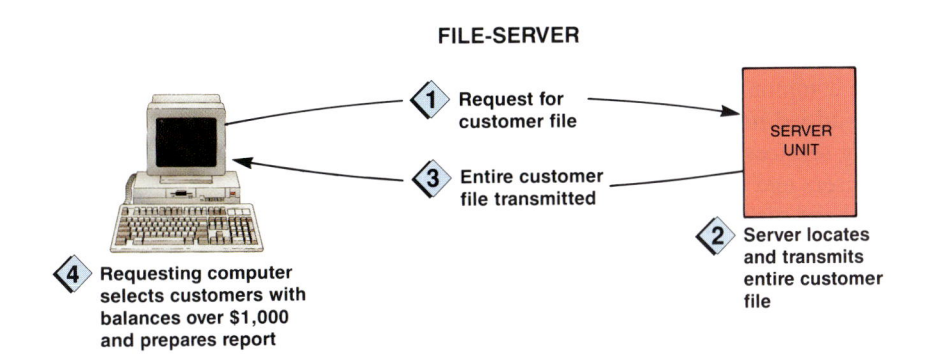

FILE-SERVER

1. Request for customer file
2. Server locates and transmits entire customer file
3. Entire customer file transmitted
4. Requesting computer selects customers with balances over $1,000 and prepares report

CLIENT-SERVER

1. Request for balances over $1,000
2. Server selects customers with balances over $1,000
3. Records of customers with balances over $1,000 transmitted
4. Requesting computer prepares report

FIGURE 8-26
A request for information about customers with balances over $1,000 would be processed differently by file-server and client-server networks.

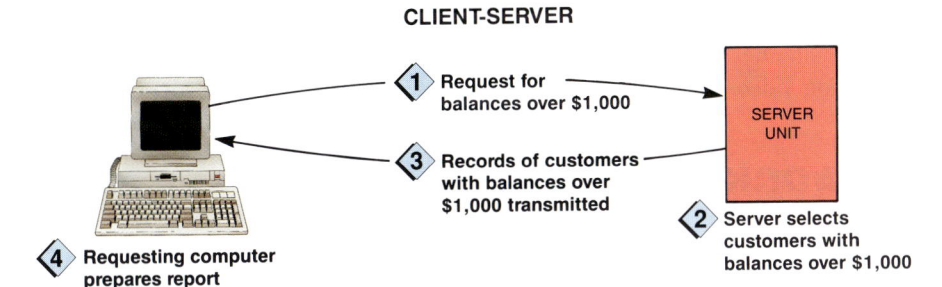

Frequently used software is another type of resource that is often shared on a local area network. For example, if all users need access to word processing software, the software can be stored on the hard disk of the server and accessed by all users as needed. This is much more convenient and faster than having the software stored on a diskette and available at each computer. Sharing software is a common practice for both in-house and commercial software. Many software vendors now sell a network version of their software. When a commercial software package is accessed by many users, it is sometimes necessary to obtain a special agreement from the software vendor, called a **site license**. The site license fee is usually based on the number of computers on the network and is less than if individual copies of the software package were purchased for each computer.

FIGURE 8-27
The control room for EDSNET, the private communications network of Electronic Data Systems Corporation (EDS). The network was built by EDS over a three-year period and a cost of more than $1 billion. The network provides communications for EDS, its computer services customers, and its parent company, General Motors.

Wide Area Networks (WANs)

A **wide area network**, or **WAN**, is geographic in scope (as opposed to local) and uses telephone lines, microwaves, satellites, or a combination of communications channels. Public wide area network companies include so-called **common carriers** such as the telephone companies. Telephone company deregulation has encouraged a number of companies to build their own wide area networks. For example, EDS has built one of the largest private communications network (Figure 8-27) to handle the needs of their computer services business and the needs of their parent company, General Motors.

Communications companies, such as MCI, have built WANs to compete with other communications companies. Companies called **value-added carriers** lease channels from the common carriers to provide specialized communications services referred to as **value-added networks**. For example, Tymnet, Inc. and Telenet provide packet-switching services. **Packet-switching** combines individual packets of information from various users and transmits them together over a high-speed channel. The messages are separated and distributed over lower speed channels at the receiving end. Sharing the high-speed channel is more economical than each user having their own high-speed channel. Most common carriers are now offering **Integrated Services Digital Network (ISDN)** services. ISDN is an international standard for the digital transmission of both voice and data using different channels and communications companies. Using ISDN lines, data can be transmitted over one or more separate channels at 64,000 bits per second. Future plans for ISDN include the use of fiber-optic cable that will allow transmission rates up to 2.2 billion bits per second. These higher speeds will allow full-motion video images to be transmitted.

NETWORK CONFIGURATIONS

The configuration, or physical layout, of the equipment in a communications network is called **topology**. Communications networks are usually configured in one or a combination of three patterns. These configurations are star, bus, and ring networks. Although these configurations can be used with wide area networks, we illustrate them with local area networks. Devices connected to a network, such as terminals, printers, or other computers, are referred to as **nodes**.

FIGURE 8-28
A star network contains a single, centralized host computer with which all the terminals or personal computers in the network communicate. Both point-to-point and multidrop lines can be used in a star network.

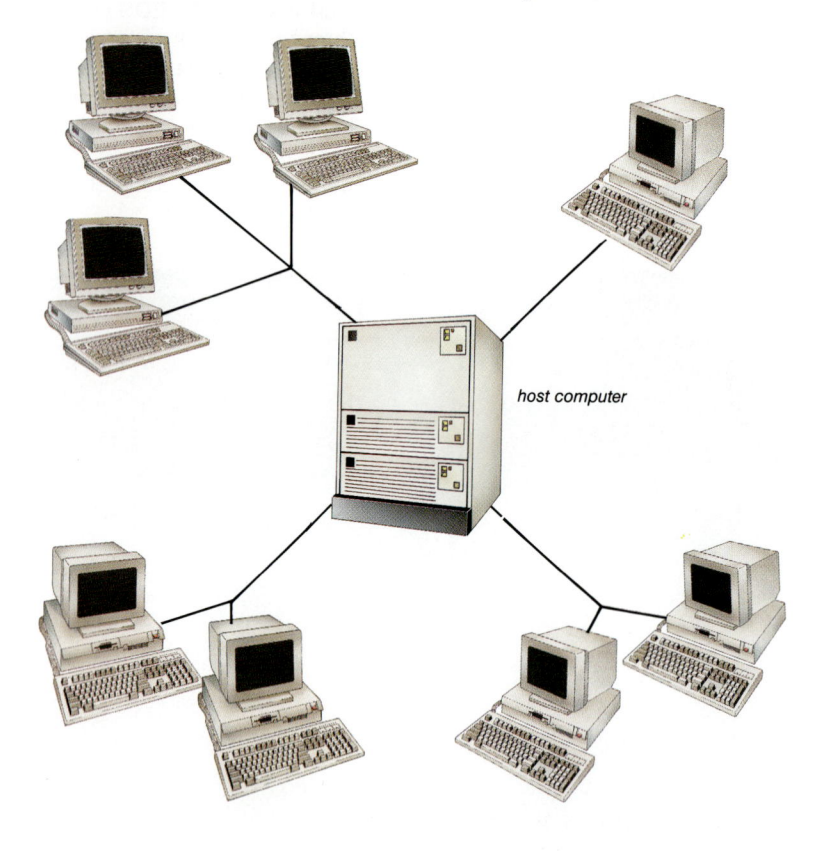

Star Network

A **star network** (Figure 8-28) contains a central computer and one or more terminals or personal computers connected to it, forming a star. A pure star network consists of only point-to-point lines between the terminals and the computer, but most star networks, such as the one shown in Figure 8-28, include both point-to-point lines and multidrop lines. A star network configuration is often used when the central computer contains all the data required to process the input from the terminals, such as an airline reservation system. For example, if inquiries are being processed in the star network, all the data to answer the inquiry would be contained in the database stored on the central computer.

A star network can be relatively efficient, and close control can be kept over the data processed on the network. Its major disadvantage is that the entire network is dependent on the central computer and the associated hardware and software. If any of these elements fail, the entire network is disabled. Therefore, in most large star networks, backup computer systems are available in case the primary system fails.

Bus Network

When a **bus network** is used, all the devices in the network are connected to and share a single cable. Information is transmitted in either direction from any one personal computer to another. Any message can be directed to a specific device. An advantage of the bus network is that devices can be attached or detached from the network at any point without disturbing the rest of the network. In addition, if one computer on the network fails, this does not affect the other users of the network. Figure 8-25 illustrates a simple bus network.

Ring Network

A **ring network** does not use a centralized host computer. Rather, a circle of computers communicate with one another (Figure 8-29). A ring network can be useful when the processing is not done at a central site, but at local sites. For example, computers could be located in three departments: accounting, personnel, and shipping and receiving. The computers in each of these departments could perform the processing required for each of the departments. On occasion, however, the computer in the shipping and receiving department could communicate with the computer in the accounting department to update certain data stored on the accounting department computer. Data travels around a ring network in one direction only and passes through each node. Thus, one disadvantage of a ring network is that if one node fails, the entire network fails because the data does not get past the failed node. An advantage of a ring network is that less cable is usually needed and therefore network cabling costs are lower.

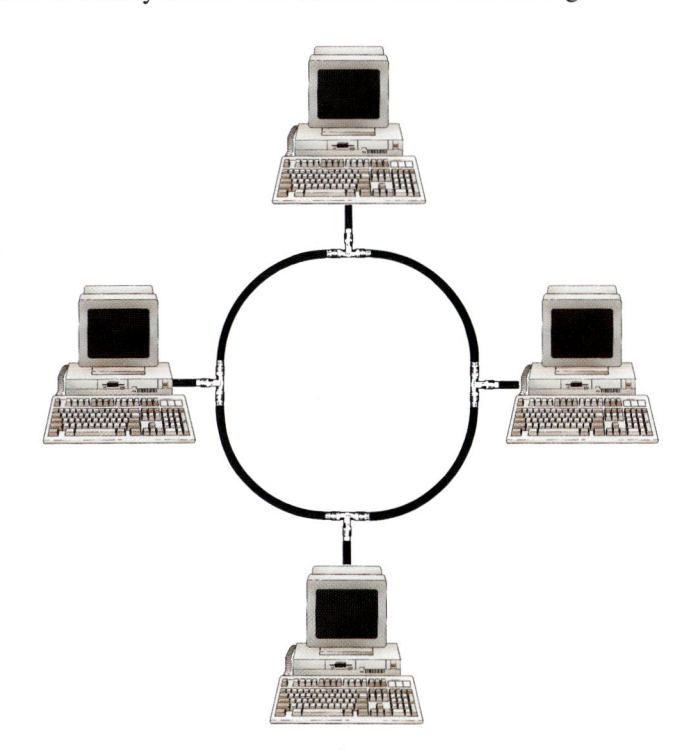

FIGURE 8-29
In a ring network, all computers are connected in a continuous loop. Data flows around the ring in one direction only.

CONNECTING NETWORKS

◆ Sometimes you might want to connect separate networks. You do this by using gateways and bridges. A **gateway** is a combination of hardware and software that allows users on one network to access the resources on a *different* type of network. For example, a gateway could be used to connect a local area network of personal computers to a mainframe computer network. A **bridge** is a combination of hardware and

FIGURE 8-30
These two personal computer networks are connected to a mainframe computer system with a bridge. A gateway is used to connect the personal computer network with the mainframe. All communications with the mainframe are controlled by a separate computer called a front-end processor. Modems are used to connect the networks to leased and dial telephone lines.

software that is used to connect *similar* networks. For example, if a company had similar but separate local area networks of personal computers in their accounting and marketing departments, the networks could be connected with a bridge. In this example, using a bridge makes more sense than joining all the personal computers together in one large network because the individual departments only occasionally need to access information on the other network.

AN EXAMPLE OF A COMMUNICATIONS NETWORK

◆ The diagram in Figure 8-30 illustrates how two personal computer networks and a mainframe computer can be connected to share information with each other and with outside sources.

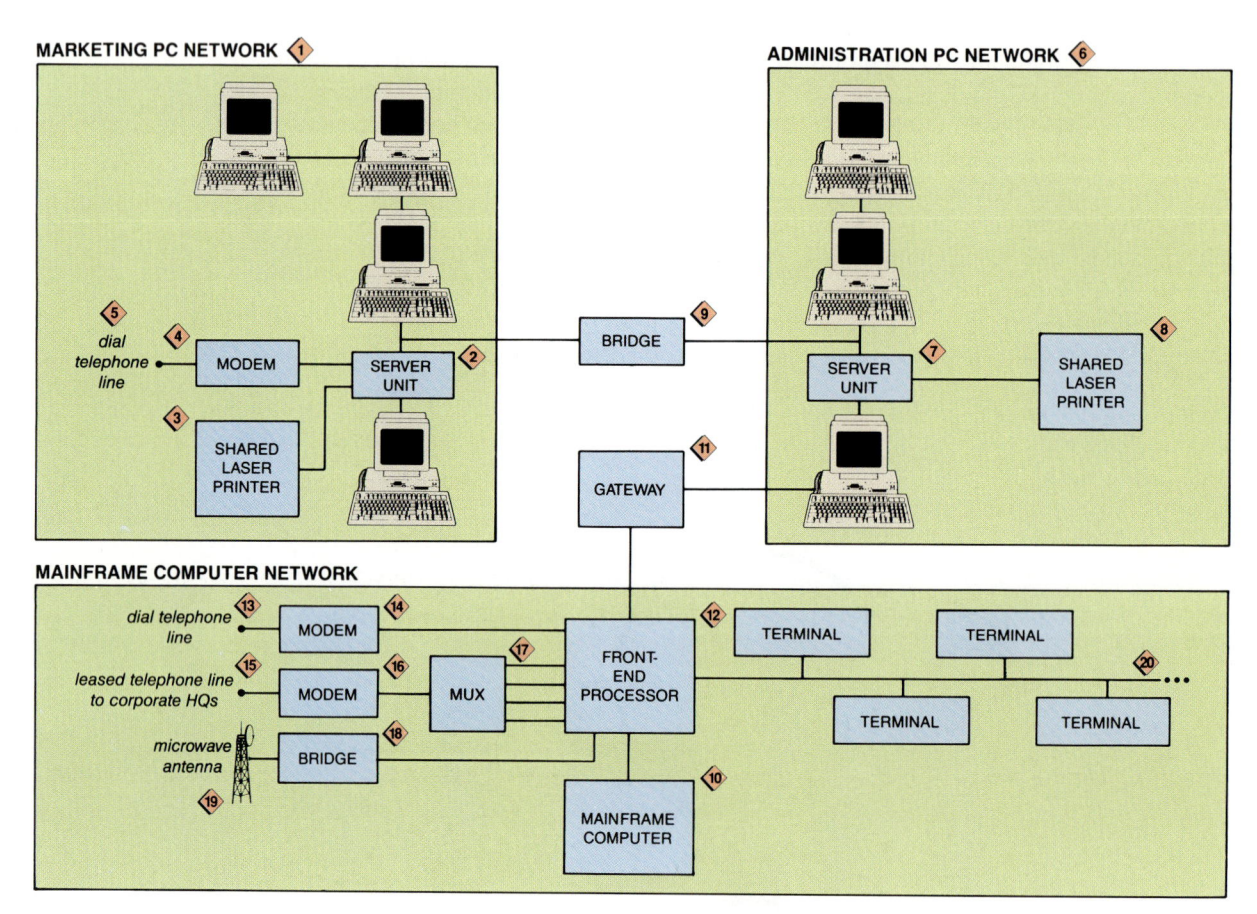

The marketing department operates a bus network of four personal computers ⟨1⟩. Frequently used marketing data and programs are stored in the server unit ⟨2⟩. The personal computers in the marketing department share a laser printer ⟨3⟩. A modem ⟨4⟩ is attached to the marketing server unit so that outside sales representatives can use a dial telephone line ⟨5⟩ to call the marketing system and obtain product price information.

The administration department operates a bus network of three personal computers ⟨6⟩. As with the marketing network, common data and programs are stored on a server unit ⟨7⟩ and the administration personal computers share a laser printer ⟨8⟩. Because the administration department sometimes needs information from the marketing system, the two similar networks are connected with a LAN bridge ⟨9⟩. The bridge allows users on either network to access data or programs on the other network.

Administration department users sometimes need information from the company's mainframe computer system ⟨10⟩. They can access the mainframe through the use of a gateway ⟨11⟩ that allows different types of network systems to be connected. All communications with the mainframe computer are controlled by a front-end processor ⟨12⟩. A dial telephone line ⟨13⟩ connected to a modem ⟨14⟩ allows remote users to call the mainframe and allows mainframe users to call other computers. A leased telephone line ⟨15⟩ and a modem ⟨16⟩ are used for a permanent connection to the computer at the corporate headquarters, several hundred miles away. The leased line can carry the signals of up to four different users. The signals are separated by the use of a multiplexor (MUX) ⟨17⟩. A bridge ⟨18⟩ connects the front-end processor and mainframe system to a microwave antenna ⟨19⟩ on the roof of the building. The microwave antenna sends and receives data from a computer at the manufacturing plant located two miles away. The front-end processor also controls mainframe computer terminals located throughout the company ⟨20⟩.

SUMMARY OF COMMUNICATIONS

◆ Communications will continue to affect how people work and how they use computers. Individuals and organizations are no longer limited to local data resources but instead, with communications capabilities, they can obtain information from anywhere in the world at electronic speed. With communications technology rapidly changing, today's businesses are challenged to find ways to adapt the technology to provide better products and services for their customers and make their operations more efficient. For individuals, the new technology offers increased access to worldwide information and services, and provides new opportunities in business and education.

CHAPTER SUMMARY

1. **Communications**, sometimes called **data communications** refers to the transmission of data or information over a communications channel between one computer or a terminal and another computer.
2. **Telecommunications** describes any type of long-distance communications including television signals.
3. **Teleprocessing** refers to the use of telephone lines to transmit data.
4. The basic components of a communications system are: a personal computer or terminal; communications equipment that sends (and can usually receive) data; the communications channel over which data is sent; communications equipment that receives (and can usually send) data; and a computer. Communications software is also required.
5. A **communications channel**, also called a **communications line** or **communications link** is the link, or path, that the data follows as it is transmitted from the sending equipment to the receiving equipment in a communications system.
6. A communications channel can consist of various **transmission media** including twisted pair wire, coaxial cable, fiber optics, microwave transmission, satellite transmission, and wireless transmission.
7. **Twisted pair wire** is the color-coded copper wires that are twisted together and commonly used as telephone wire.
8. **Coaxial cable** is a high-quality communications line that is used in offices and laid underground and under the ocean. Coaxial cable consists of a copper wire conductor surrounded by a nonconducting insulator that is in turn surrounded by a woven metal mesh outer conductor, and finally a plastic outer coating.
9. Coaxial cable can be either **baseband**, carrying one signal at a time at very high rates of speed, or **broadband**, carrying multiple signals at a time.
10. **Fiber optics** uses technology based on the capability of smooth, hair-thin strands of glass that conduct light waves to rapidly and efficiently transmit data.

11. **Microwaves** are radio waves that can be used to provide high-speed transmissions of voice and data that are sent through the air between microwave stations.
12. **Communications satellites** are man-made space devices that receive, amplify, and retransmit signals from earth.
13. **Earth stations** are communications facilities that contain large, dish-shaped antennas used to transmit data to and receive data from communications satellites.
14. The transmission *to* the satellite is called an **uplink** and the transmission *from* the satellite to a receiving earth station is called a **downlink**.
15. Communications satellites are normally placed about 22,300 miles above the earth in a **geosynchronous orbit**.
16. **Wireless systems** use one of three transmission techniques: light beams, radio waves, or carrier-connect radio.
17. A **cellular telephone** uses radio waves to communicate with a local antenna assigned to a specific geographic area called a cell.
18. **Line configurations** can be either point-to-point lines or multidrop lines.
19. A **point-to-point line** is a direct line between a sending and receiving device. It may be either a **switched line** (a connection established through regular telephone lines) or a **dedicated line** (a line whose connection between devices is always established).
20. If the dedicated line is provided by an outside organization, it is sometimes called a **leased line**, or a **private line**.
21. The process of establishing the communications connection is sometimes referred to as the **handshake**.
22. A **multidrop line**, also known as a **multipoint line**, uses a single line to connect multiple devices to a main computer.
23. A multidrop line, or multipoint line, configuration is commonly used to connect multiple devices, such as terminals or personal computers, on a single line to a main computer sometimes called a **host computer**.
24. Computer equipment processes data as **digital signals**, which are individual electrical pulses representing the bits that are grouped together to form characters.
25. **Analog signals** are continuous electrical waves that are used to transmit data over standard telephone lines.
26. Companies offering **digital data service** provide communications channels specifically designed to carry digital instead of voice signals.
27. Modems are not needed with digital data service; instead, users connect to the communications line through a device called a **data service unit (DSU)**.
28. There are two modes of transmitting data: **asynchronous transmission mode**, which transmits one character at a time at irregular intervals using start and stop bits, and **synchronous transmission mode**, which transmits blocks of data at regular intervals using timing signals to synchronize the sending and receiving equipment.
29. Transmissions may be classified according to the direction in which the data can flow on a line: sending only (**simplex transmission**); sending or receiving but in only one direction at a time (**half-duplex transmission**); and sending and receiving at the same time (**full-duplex transmission**).
30. The transmission rate of a communications channel depends on the **bandwidth** and its speed. The wider the bandwidth, the greater the number of signals that can be carried on the channel at one time and the more data that can be transmitted.
31. **Bits per second (bps)** is the number of bits that can be transmitted in one second.
32. The **baud rate** is the number of times per second that the signal being transmitted changes. With each change, one or more bits can be transmitted.
33. A **modem** converts the digital signals of a terminal or computer to analog signals that are transmitted over a communications channel.
34. There are three basic types of modems: an **external modem**, which is a separate, stand-alone device attached to the computer or terminal by a cable and to the telephone outlet by a standard telephone cable; an **internal modem**, which is a circuit board installed inside a computer or terminal; and an **acoustic modem**, or **acoustic coupler**, which is a device used with a telephone handset.
35. A **multiplexor**, or MUX, combines more than one input signal into a single stream of data that can be transmitted over a communications channel.
36. A **front-end processor** is a computer dedicated to handling the communications requirements of a larger computer.
37. A front-end processor would use **polling** to check the connected terminals or computers to see if they have data to send.
38. **Communications software** consists of programs that perform tasks such as **dialing** (software that stores, selects, and dials telephone numbers); **file transfer**; (moving files from one system to another); **terminal emulation**

(software that allows the personal computer to imitate or appear to be a specific type of terminal, so that the personal computer can connect to specific types of computers); and **data encryption** (software that can code and decode transmitted data for security purposes).

39. A **protocol** is a set of rules and procedures for exchanging information between computers.
40. A **network** is a collection of terminals, computers, and other equipment that use communications channels to share data, information, hardware, and software.
41. A **local area network (LAN)** is a communications network that covers a limited geographic area and is privately owned.
42. Two common uses of local area networks are **hardware resource sharing**, which allows all network users to access a single piece of equipment rather than each user having to be connected to his or her own device, and **information resource sharing**, which allows the network users to access data stored on other computers in the network.
43. A **server**, sometimes called a **network control unit**, is a computer that is dedicated to handling the communications needs of the other computers in a network.
44. Information sharing is usually provided by using either the **file-server** or **client-server** method.
45. When a commercial software package is accessed by many users within the same organization, a special agreement called a **site license** can usually be obtained from the software vendor.
46. A **wide area network (WAN)** is a network that covers a large geographical area.
47. Public wide area network companies include so-called **common carriers** such as the telephone companies.
48. Companies called **value-added carriers** lease channels from the common carriers to provide specialized communications services referred to as **value added networks**.
49. **Packet-switching** combines individual packets of information from various users and transmits them together over a high-speed channel.
50. **Integrated Services Digital Network (ISDN)** services is an international standard for the digital transmission of both voice and data using different channels and communications companies.
51. Network **topology** describes the configuration, or physical layout, of the equipment in a communications network.
52. Devices connected to a network, such as terminals, printers, or other computers, are referred to as **nodes**.
53. A **star network** contains a central computer and one or more terminals or computers connected to it, forming a star.
54. In a **bus network**, all the devices in the network are connected to and share a single cable.
55. A **ring network** has a series of computers connected to each other in a ring.
56. A **gateway** is a combination of hardware and software that allows users on one network to access the resources on a *different* type of network.
57. A **bridge** is a combination of hardware and software that is used to connect *similar* networks.

KEY TERMS

Acoustic coupler *8.13*
Acoustic modem *8.13*
Analog signal *8.10*
Asynchronous transmission mode *8.10*
Bandwidth *8.12*
Baseband *8.3*
Baud rate *8.12*
Bits per second (bps) *8.12*
Bridge *8.19*
Broadband *8.3*
Bus network *8.19*
Cellular telephone *8.5*
Client-server *8.16*
Coaxial cable *8.3*

Common carrier *8.17*
Communications channel *8.3*
Communications line *8.3*
Communications link *8.3*
Communications satellite *8.4*
Communications *8.2*
Communications software *8.14*
Data communications *8.2*
Data encryption *8.15*
Data service unit (DSU) *8.10*
Dedicated line *8.7*
Dialing software *8.14*
Digital data service *8.10*
Digital signal *8.10*

Downlink *8.4*
Earth station *8.4*
External modem *8.12*
Fiber optics *8.3*
File transfer software *8.15*
File-server *8.16*
Front-end processor *8.14*
Full-duplex transmission *8.11*
Gateway *8.19*
Geosynchronous orbit *8.4*
Half-duplex transmission *8.11*
Handshake *8.7*
Hardware resource sharing *8.16*
Host computer *8.8*

Information resource sharing *8.16*
Integrated Services Digital Network (ISDN) *8.18*
Internal modem *8.12*
Leased line *8.8*
Line configuration *8.6*
Local area network (LAN) *8.15*
Microwave *8.4*
Modem *8.12*
Multidrop line *8.8*
Multiplexor *8.13*
Multipoint line *8.8*
Network *8.15*
Network control unit *8.16*
Node *8.18*
Open Systems Interconnection (OSI) model *8.15*
Packet-switching *8.18*
Parity bit *8.10*
Point-to-point line *8.7*
Polling *8.14*
Private line *8.8*
Protocol *8.15*
Ring network *8.19*
Server *8.16*
Simplex transmission *8.11*
Site license *8.17*
Star network *8.18*
Switched line *8.7*
Synchronous transmission mode *8.10*
Telecommunications *8.2*
Teleprocessing *8.2*
Terminal emulation software *8.15*
Topology *8.18*
Transmission media *8.3*
Twisted pair wire *8.3*
Uplink *8.4*
Value-added carrier *8.18*
Value-added network *8.18*
Wide area network (WAN) *8.17*
Wireless transmission *8.5*

REVIEW QUESTIONS

1. Draw and label the basic components of a communications system.
2. List six kinds of transmission media used for communications channels.
3. Describe the two major types of line configurations. What are the advantages and disadvantages of each?
4. List and describe the three types of data transmission (direction) that are used.
5. Why is a modem used? Describe three types of modems that are available.
6. List and explain four tasks that communications software can perform.
7. What is a communications protocol?
8. Discuss the reasons for using a local area network.
9. Name three topologies, or configurations, that are used with networks. Draw a diagram of each.
10. Explain bridges and gateways and how they are used.

CONTROVERSIAL ISSUES

1. Some people believe that better control is maintained if data is stored and processed on a central minicomputer or mainframe. Others believe that personal computer networks that provide decentralized storage and processing are best. Discuss the advantages and disadvantages of both types of systems.
2. Some personal computer users have used communications equipment and software to illegally gain access to private databases. These individuals, known as *hackers*, often claim that their illegal access was only a harmless prank. Do you think this type of computer usage is harmless? Explain your position.

RESEARCH PROJECTS

1. Call or visit a communications company and obtain information relating to the types of services they provide for customers who transmit computer data. Prepare a report on this information for your class.
2. Obtain information about modems for personal computers. Prepare a report for your class that discusses the features and cost of both internal and external models.

Operating Systems and Systems Software

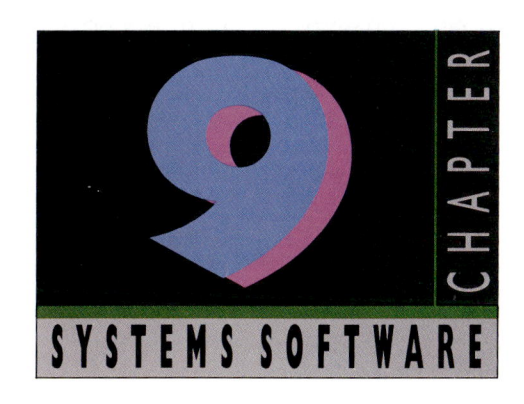

CHAPTER 9
SYSTEMS SOFTWARE

OBJECTIVES

- Describe the three major categories of systems software
- Define the term operating system
- Describe the various types of operating systems and explain the differences in their capabilities
- Describe the functions of an operating system, including allocating system resources, monitoring system activities, and disk and file management
- Explain the difference between proprietary and portable operating systems
- Name and briefly describe the major operating systems that are being used today
- Discuss utilities and language translators

When most people think of software they think of applications software such as word processing, spreadsheet, and database software. For applications software to run on a computer, however, another type of software is needed to interface between the user, the applications software, and the equipment. This software consists of programs that are referred to as the operating system. The operating system is part of what is called systems software.

In this chapter, we discuss operating system features of both large and small computer systems. It is important to understand the features of large computer operating systems because these features are steadily being implemented on small systems such as personal computers.

FIGURE 9-1
The operating system and other systems software programs act as an interface between the user, the applications software, and the computer equipment.

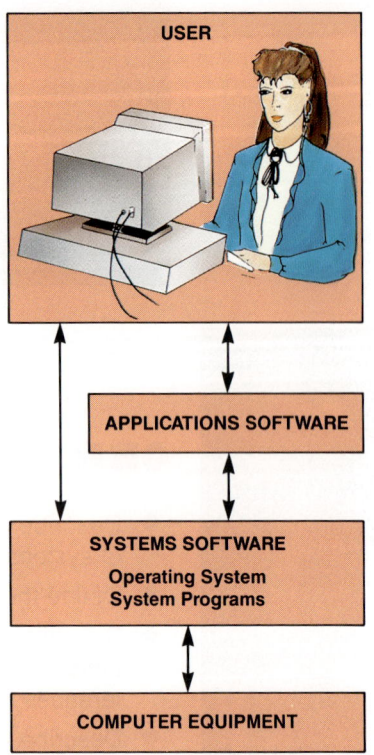

WHAT IS SYSTEMS SOFTWARE?

Systems software consists of all the programs including the operating system that are related to controlling the operations of the computer equipment. Some of the functions that systems software perform include: starting up the computer; loading, executing, and storing applications programs; storing and retrieving files; and performing a variety of functions such as formatting disks, sorting data files, and translating program instructions into machine language. Systems software can be classified into three major categories; operating systems, utilities, and language translators.

WHAT IS AN OPERATING SYSTEM?

An **operating system (OS)** consists of one or more programs that manage the operations of a computer. These programs function as an interface between the user, the applications programs, and the computer equipment (Figure 9-1).

The operating system is usually stored on a disk. For a computer to operate, the essential and most frequently used instructions in the operating system must be copied from the disk and stored in the main memory of the computer. This *resident* portion of the operating system is called by many different names: the **supervisor**, **monitor**, **executive**, **master program**, **control program**, or **kernel**. The *nonresident* portion of the operating system, which consists of the less frequently used instructions, remains stored on a disk and is available to be loaded into main memory whenever it is needed.

LOADING AN OPERATING SYSTEM

The process of loading an operating system into main memory is called **booting** the system. Figure 9-2 shows the steps that occur when an operating system is loaded on a personal computer. This process is not identical to that used on large computers, but it is similar.

1. A diskette that contains the operating system is placed in the disk drive. If the operating system is already stored on a hard disk, the diskette would not be necessary.
2. When the computer is turned on, a series of instructions stored in ROM called the boot routine issue the commands to load the operating system into main memory. To do this, a copy of the operating system is transferred from the diskette or hard disk into main memory.

3. The instructions that loaded the operating system transfer control of the computer to the operating system. In many cases, the operating system displays a message requesting that the user enter the correct date and time, after which the **operating system prompt** appears. This prompt indicates to the user that the operating system has been loaded and is ready to accept a command such as to begin an application program.

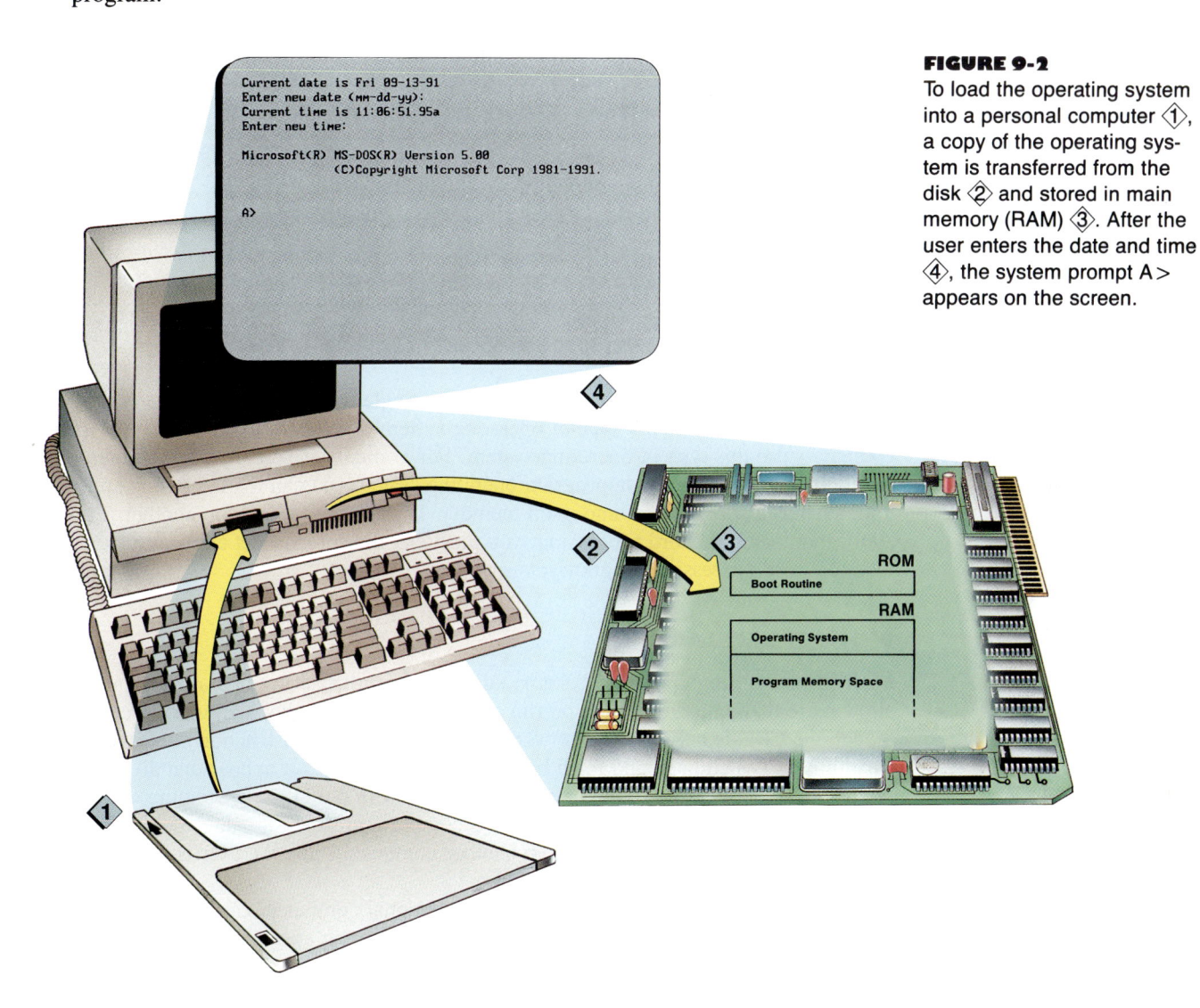

FIGURE 9-2
To load the operating system into a personal computer ①, a copy of the operating system is transferred from the disk ② and stored in main memory (RAM) ③. After the user enters the date and time ④, the system prompt A> appears on the screen.

Once the operating system is loaded into main memory, it usually remains in memory until the computer is turned off. The operating system controls the loading and manages the execution of each application program that is requested by the user. When an application program completes its task or a user finishes using the application program, the operating system displays the system prompt again.

TYPES OF OPERATING SYSTEMS

The types of operating systems include single program, multiprogramming, multiprocessing, and virtual machine operating systems. These operating systems can be classified by two criteria: (1) whether they allow more than one user to use the computer at the same time and (2) whether they allow more than one program to run at the same time (Figure 9-3).

	SINGLE PROGRAM	MULTIPROGRAMMING	MULTIPROCESSING	VIRTUAL MACHINE
NUMBER OF PROGRAMS RUNNING	One	More than one	More than one on each CPU	More than one on each operating system
NUMBER OF USERS	One	One or more than one (Multiuser)	More than one on each CPU	More than one on each operating system

FIGURE 9-3
Operating systems can be classified by whether they allow more than one user and more than one program to be operating at the same time.

Single Program

Single program operating systems allow only a single user to run a single program at one time. This was the first type of operating system developed. Today, many personal computers use this type of operating system. For example, if you are working on a personal computer with a single program operating system you can load only one application, such as a spreadsheet, into main memory. If you want to work on another application, such as word processing, you must exit the spreadsheet application and load the word processing program into memory.

Multiprogramming

Multiprogramming operating systems, also called **multitasking** operating systems, allow more than one program to be run at the same time on one computer. Even though the CPU is only capable of working on one program instruction at a time, its capability to switch back and forth between programs makes it appear that all programs are running at the same time. For example, with a multiprogramming operating system the computer could be performing a complex spreadsheet calculation and at the same time be downloading a file from another computer while the user is writing a memo with the word processing program.

Multiprogramming operating systems on personal computers can usually support a single user running multiple programs. Multiprogramming operating systems on some personal computers and most minicomputers and mainframes can support more than one user running more than one program. This version of a multiprogramming operating system is sometimes called a **multiuser-multiprogramming** operating system. Most of these operating systems also allow more than one user to be running the same program. For example, a wholesale distributor may have dozens of terminal operators entering sales orders using the same order entry program on the same computer.

Multiprocessing

Computers that have more than one CPU are called **multiprocessors**. A **multiprocessing** operating system coordinates the operations of computers with more than one CPU. Because each CPU in a multiprocessor computer can be executing one program instruction, more than one instruction can be executed simultaneously. Besides providing an increase in performance, most multiprocessors offer another advantage. If one CPU fails, work can be shifted to the remaining CPUs. In addition to an extra CPU, some systems, called **fault-tolerant computers**, are built with redundant components such as memory, input and output controllers, and disk drives. If any one of the components fail, the system can continue to operate with the duplicate component. Fault-tolerant systems are used for airline reservation systems, communications networks, bank teller machines, and other applications where it is important to keep the computer operating at all times.

Virtual Machine

A **virtual machine (VM)** operating system allows a single computer to run two or more different operating systems. The VM operating system allocates system resources such as memory and processing time to each operating system. To users it appears that they are working on separate systems, hence the term virtual machine. The advantage of this approach is that an organization can run different operating systems (at the same time) that are best suited to different tasks. For example, some operating systems are best for interactive processing and others are best for batch processing. With a VM operating system both types of operating systems can be run concurrently.

FUNCTIONS OF OPERATING SYSTEMS

◆ The operating system performs a number of functions that allow the user and the applications software to interact with the computer. These functions apply to all operating systems but become more complex for operating systems that allow more than one program to run at a time. The functions can be grouped into three types: allocating system resources, monitoring system activities, and disk and file management (Figure 9-4).

ALLOCATING RESOURCES	MONITORING ACTIVITIES	DISK AND FILE MANAGEMENT
CPU management	System performance	Formatting
Memory management	System security	Copying
Input/output management		Deleting

FIGURE 9-4
Operating system functions.

Allocating System Resources

The primary function of the operating system is to allocate, or assign, the resources of the computer system. That is, like a police officer directing traffic, the operating system decides what resource will currently be used and for how long. These resources include the CPU, main memory, and the input and output devices such as disk and tape drives and printers.

CPU Management Because a CPU can only work on one program instruction at a time, a multiprogramming operating system must keep switching the CPU among the different instructions of the programs that are waiting to be performed. A common way of allocating CPU processing is time slicing. A **time slice** is a fixed amount of CPU processing time, usually measured in milliseconds (thousandths of a second). With this

FIGURE 9-5
With the time slice method of CPU management, each application is allocated one or more fixed amounts of time called slices. Higher priority (more important) applications receive more consecutive slices than lower priority applications. When its processing time has expired, an application goes to the end of the line until all other applications have received at least one time slice. Here, application 2 is the lowest priority and so receives only one time slice. Application 1 is the highest priority and receives three time slices.

technique, each user in turn receives a time slice. Since some instructions take longer to execute than others, some users may have more instructions completed in their time slice than other users. When a user's time slice has expired, the operating system directs the CPU to work on another user's program instructions, and the most recent user moves to the end of the line to await the next time slice (Figure 9-5). Unless the system has a heavy work load, however, users may not even be aware that their program has been temporarily set aside. Before they notice a delay, the operating system has allocated them another time slice and their processing continues.

APPLICATIONS WAITING TO BE PROCESSED

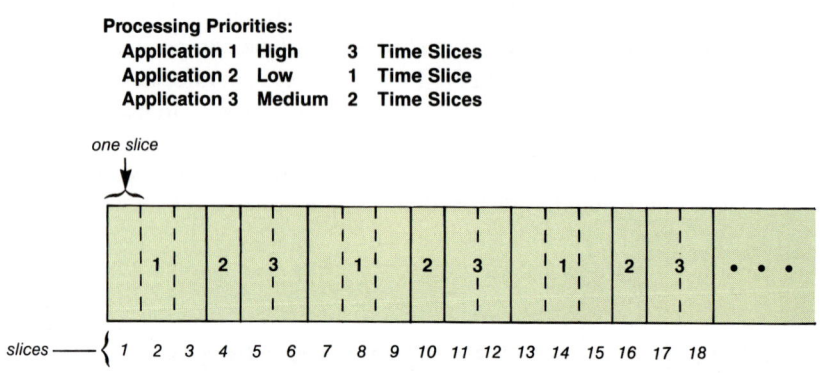

Processing Priorities:
Application 1   High   3 Time Slices
Application 2   Low   1 Time Slice
Application 3   Medium   2 Time Slices

one slice

| 1 | 2 | 3 | 1 | 2 | 3 | 1 | 2 | 3 | ... |

slices — { 1 2 3 4 5 6 7 8 9 10 11 12 13 14 15 16 17 18

Because some work has a higher priority or is more important than other work, most operating systems have ways to adjust the amount of time slices a user receives, either automatically or based on user-specified criteria. One technique for modifying the number of time slices is to have different priorities assigned to each user. For each time slice received by the lowest priority, the highest priority would receive several consecutive time slices. For example, it would be logical to assign a higher priority to a program that processes orders and records sales than to an accounting program that could be run at a later time. Another way to allocate time slices is based on the type of work being performed. For example, some operating systems automatically allocate more time slices to interactive processes such as keyboard entry than they do to CPU-only processes such as calculations or batch processing. This gives a higher priority to users entering data than to a report being output to a printer.

Another way of assigning processing priorities is to designate each job as either foreground or background. **Foreground** jobs receive a higher processing priority and therefore more CPU time. Data entry would be an example of a job that would be classified as a foreground job. **Background** jobs receive a lower processing priority and less CPU time. Printing a report or calculating payroll are examples of jobs that could be classified as background jobs. Background jobs usually involve batch processing or require little or no computer operator intervention.

Memory Management During processing, main memory stores such items as the operating system, application program instructions for one or more programs, data waiting to be processed, and work space used for calculations, sorting, and other temporary tasks. It is the operating system's job to allocate, or assign, each of these items to areas of main memory. Data that has just been read into main memory from an input device or is waiting to be sent to an output device is stored in areas of main memory called **buffers**. The operating system assigns the location of the buffers in main memory and manages the data that is stored in them.

Operating systems allocate at least some portion of memory into fixed areas called partitions (Figure 9-6). Some operating systems allocate all memory on this basis while others use partitions only for the operating system instructions and buffers.

Another way of allocating memory is called virtual memory management, or virtual storage. **Virtual memory management** increases the effective (or *virtual*) limits of memory by expanding the amount of main memory to include disk space. Without virtual memory management, an entire program must be loaded into main memory during execution. With virtual memory management, only the portion of the program that is currently being used is required to be in main memory. Virtual memory management is used with multiprogramming operating systems to maximize the number of programs using memory at the same time. The operating system performs virtual memory management by transferring data and instructions to and from memory and the disk by using one or both of the two methods, segmentation and paging.

In **segmentation**, programs are divided into logical portions called **segments**. For example, one segment of a program might edit data and another segment might perform a calculation. Because the segments are based on logical portions of a program, some segments are larger than others. When a particular program instruction is required, the segment containing that instruction is transferred from the disk into main memory.

In **paging**, a fixed number of bytes is transferred from the disk each time data or program instructions are required. This fixed amount of data is called a **page**, or a **frame**. The size of a page, generally from 512 to 4,000 bytes, is determined by the operating system. Because a page is a fixed number of bytes, it may not correspond to a logical division of a program like a segment.

In both segmentation and paging, a time comes when memory is full but another page or segment needs to be read into memory. When this occurs, the operating system makes room for the new data or instructions by writing back to disk one or more of the pages or segments currently in memory. This process is referred to as **swapping** (Figure 9-7). The operating system usually chooses the least recently used page or segment to transfer back to disk.

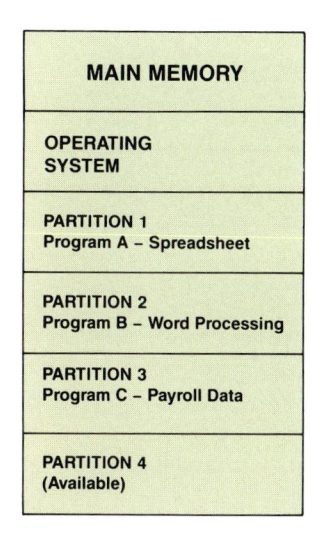

FIGURE 9-6
Some computer systems allocate memory into fixed blocks called partitions. The CPU then keeps track of programs and data by assigning them to a specific partition.

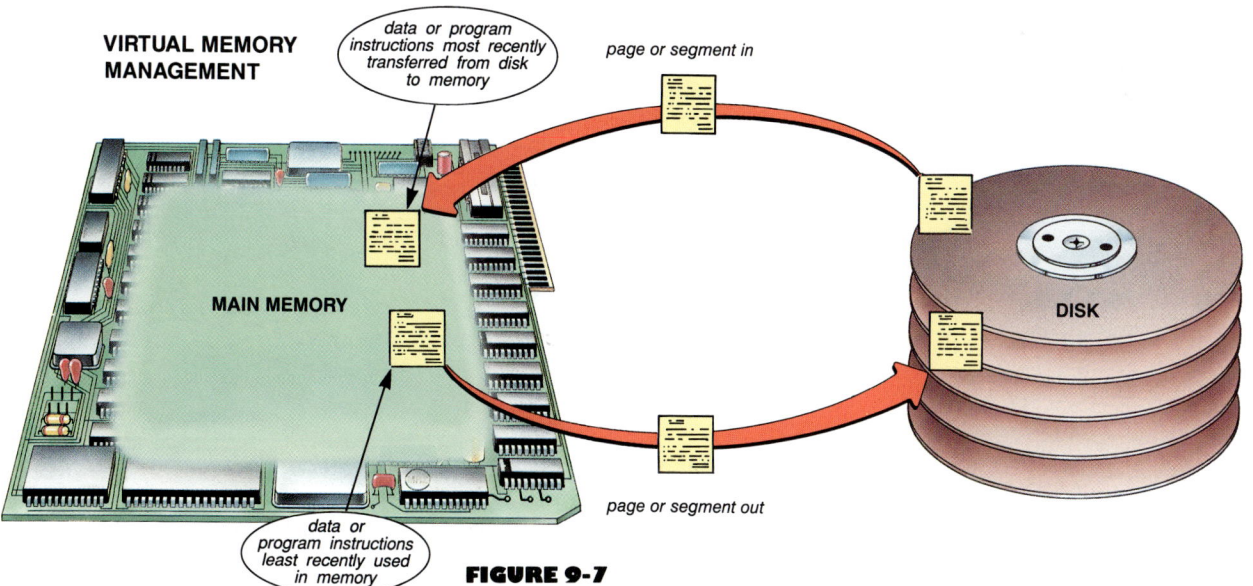

MAIN MEMORY
OPERATING SYSTEM
PARTITION 1 — Program A – Spreadsheet
PARTITION 2 — Program B – Word Processing
PARTITION 3 — Program C – Payroll Data
PARTITION 4 (Available)

FIGURE 9-7
With virtual memory management, the operating system expands the amount of main memory to include available disk space. Data and program instructions are transferred to and from memory and disk as required. The segmentation technique transfers logical portions of programs that might be different sizes. The paging technique transfers pages of the same size. To make room for the new page or segment, the least recently used page or segment is *swapped*, or written back to the disk.

CHAPTER 9 OPERATING SYSTEMS AND SYSTEMS SOFTWARE

Input and Output Management At any given time, more than one input device can be sending data to the computer. At the same time, the CPU could be ready to send data to an output device such as a terminal or printer or a storage device such as a disk. The operating system is responsible for managing these input and output processes.

Some devices, such as a tape drive, are usually allocated to a specific user or application program. This is because tape is a sequential storage medium, and generally it would not make sense to have more than one application writing records to a single tape. Disk drives are usually allocated to all users because the programs and data files that users need are stored on these devices. The operating system keeps track of disk read and write requests, stores these requests in buffers along with the associated data for write requests, and usually processes them sequentially. A printer could be allocated to all users or restricted to a specific user. For example, a printer would be restricted to a specific user if the printer was going to be used with preprinted forms such as payroll checks.

Because the printer is a relatively slow device compared to other computer system devices, the technique of spooling is used to increase printer efficiency and reduce the number of printers required. With **spooling** (Figure 9-8), a report is first written (saved) to the disk before it is printed. Writing to the disk is much faster than writing to the printer. For example, a report that may take one-half hour to print (depending on the speed of the printer) may take only one minute to write to the disk. After the report is written to the disk, the CPU is available to process other programs. The report saved on the disk can be printed at a later time or, on a multiprogramming operating system, a print program can be run (at the same time other programs are running) to process the **print spool** (the reports on the disk waiting to be printed).

FIGURE 9-8
Spooling increases both CPU and printer efficiency by writing reports to the disk before they are printed. After the reports are written to disk, the CPU can begin processing other programs. Writing to the disk is much faster than writing directly to the printer.

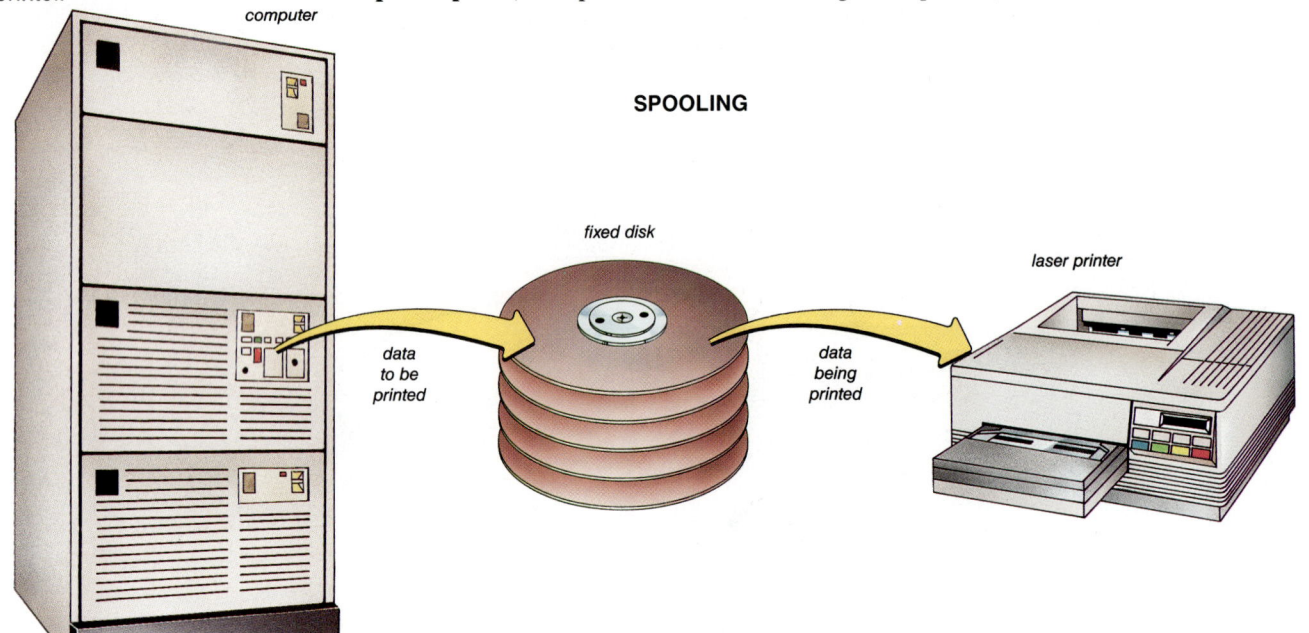

Because many input and output devices use different commands and control codes to transmit and receive data, programs called **device drivers** are used by the operating system to control these devices. For example, a different device driver would be required for a high-resolution color monitor than for a standard-resolution monochrome monitor. Output device drivers for monitors and printers are usually supplied by applications software developers along with their specific application such as word processing or spreadsheet. Input device drivers for equipment such as a mouse or scanner are usually supplied by the equipment manufacturer.

Monitoring System Activities

Another function of the operating system is monitoring the system activity. This includes monitoring system performance and system security.

System Performance System performance can be measured in a number of ways but is usually gauged by the user in terms of response time. **Response time** is the amount of time from the moment a user enters data until the computer responds. Response time can vary based on what the user has entered. If the user is simply entering data into a file, the response time is usually within a second or two. However, if the user has just completed a request for a display of sorted data from several files, the response time could be minutes.

A more precise way of measuring performance is to run a program that is designed to record and report system activity. Among other information, these programs usually report **CPU utilization**, the amount of time that the CPU is working and not idle, waiting for data to process. Figure 9-9 shows a CPU performance measurement report.

Another measure of performance is to compare the CPU utilization with the disk input and output rate, referred to as disk I/O. We previously discussed how a virtual memory management operating system swaps pages or segments from disk to memory as they are needed. Systems with heavy work loads and insufficient memory or CPU power can get into a situation called **thrashing**, where the system is spending more time moving pages to and from the disk than processing the data. System performance reporting can alert the computer operations manager to this problem.

FIGURE 9-9
System performance measurement programs report the amount of time the CPU is actually working and not waiting to process data.

System Security Most multiuser operating systems provide for a logon code, a user ID, and a password that must all be entered correctly before a user is allowed to use an application program (Figure 9-10). Each is a word or series of characters. A **logon code** usually identifies the application that will be used, such as accounting, sales, or manufacturing. A **user ID** identifies the user, such as Jeffrey Ryan or Mary Gonzales. The **password** is usually confidential; often it is known only to the user and the computer system administrator. The logon code, user ID, and password must match entries in an authorization file. If they don't match, the user is denied access to the system. Both successful and unsuccessful logon attempts are often recorded in a file so that management can review who is using or attempting to use the system. These logs can also be used to allocate data processing expenses based on the percentage of system use by an organization's various departments.

FIGURE 9-10
The logon code, user ID, and password must all be entered correctly before the user is allowed to use the computer. Because the password is confidential, it is usually not displayed on the screen when the user enters it.

Disk and File Management

In addition to allocating system resources and monitoring system activities, most operating systems contain programs that can perform functions related to disk and file management. Some of these functions include formatting disks and diskettes, deleting files from a disk, copying files from one auxiliary storage device to another, and renaming stored files.

POPULAR OPERATING SYSTEMS

◆ The first operating systems were developed by manufacturers for the computers in their product line. When the manufacturers came out with another computer or model, they often produced an improved and different operating system. Since programs are designed to be used with a particular operating system, this meant that users who wanted to switch computers, either from one vendor to another or to a different model from the same vendor, would have to convert their existing programs to run under the new operating system. Today, however, the trend is away from operating systems limited to a specific model and toward operating systems that will run on any model by a particular manufacturer. For example, part of Digital Equipment Corporation's success has been attributed to the fact that their VMS operating system is used on all their computer systems.

Going even further, many computer users are supporting the move away from **proprietary operating systems** (meaning privately owned) and toward **portable operating systems** that will run on many manufacturers' computers. The advantage of portable operating systems is that the user is not tied to a particular manufacturer. Using a portable operating system, a user could change computer systems, yet retain existing software and data files, which usually represent a sizable investment in time and money. For example, say a small business purchased a computer system to handle their immediate needs and to provide for several years of anticipated growth. Five years later, the business has reached the capacity of the computer; no more memory or terminals can be added. In addition, the manufacturer of the five-year-old computer does not make a larger or more powerful model. But because they originally chose a computer that used a portable operating system, the business can purchase a more powerful computer from another manufacturer that offers the same portable operating system and continue to use their existing software and data files.

One of the most popular portable operating systems is UNIX, which we will discuss along with the several personal computer operating systems.

UNIX

The **UNIX** operating system was developed in the early 1970s by scientists at Bell Laboratories. It was specifically designed to provide a way to manage a variety of scientific and specialized computer applications. Because of federal regulations, Bell Labs (a subsidiary of AT&T) was prohibited from actively promoting UNIX in the commercial marketplace. Instead, for a low fee Bell Labs licensed UNIX to numerous colleges and universities where it obtained a wide following. With the deregulation of the telephone companies in the 1980s, AT&T was allowed to enter the computer system marketplace. With AT&T's increased promotion and the trend toward portable operating systems, UNIX has aroused tremendous interest. One of the advantages of UNIX is its extensive library of over 400 instruction modules that can be linked together to perform almost any programming task. Today, most major computer manufacturers offer a multiuser version of the UNIX operating system to run on their computers.

With all its strengths, however, UNIX has not yet obtained success in the commercial business systems marketplace. Some people attribute this to the fact that UNIX has never been considered user friendly. For example, most of the UNIX program modules are identified by obscure names such as MAUS, SHMOP, and BRK. Other critics contend that UNIX lacks the file management capabilities to support the online interactive databases that more and more businesses are implementing. With the support of most major computer manufacturers, however, these problems are being worked on and UNIX has a good chance of becoming one of the major operating systems of the coming years.

MS-DOS

The Microsoft Disk Operating System, or **MS-DOS**, was released by Microsoft Corporation in 1981. MS-DOS was originally developed for IBM for their first personal computer system. IBM calls their equivalent version of the operating system **PC-DOS**. Because so many personal computer manufacturers followed IBM's lead and chose MS-DOS for their computers, MS-DOS quickly became an industry standard. Other personal computer operating systems exist, but by far the majority of personal computer software is written for MS-DOS. This single-user operating system is so widely used that it is often referred to simply as DOS.

Macintosh

The Apple **Macintosh** multiprogramming operating system provides a graphic interface that uses icons (figures) and windows (Figure 9-11). Macintosh users interface with the operating system through the use of features called Finder and Multifinder. Finder allows the user to run single programs and perform utility functions such as organizing and finding files.

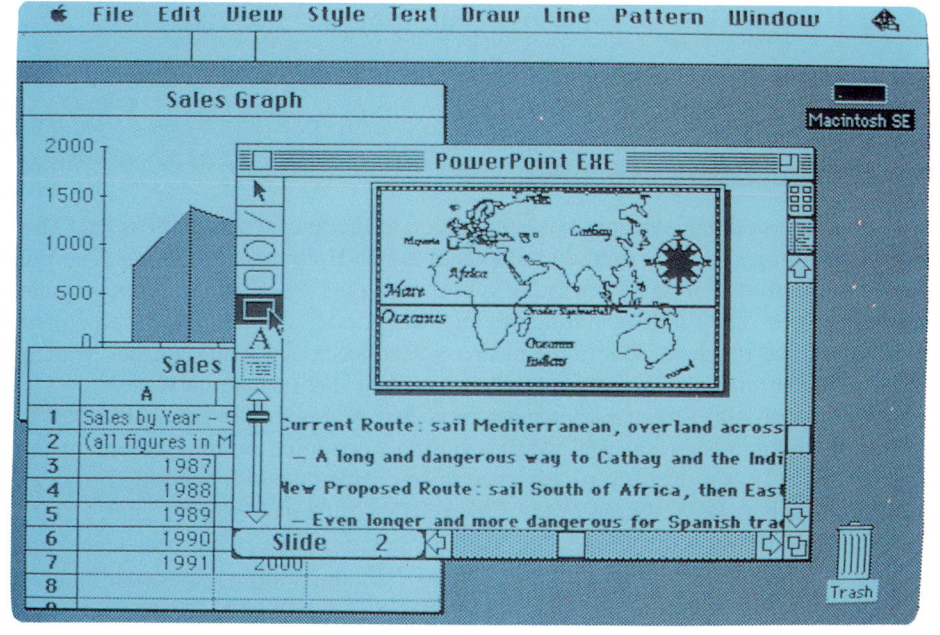

FIGURE 9-11
The Macintosh operating system offers a graphic user interface and the capability to display information in separate windows.

Multifinder allows the user to have certain processes, such as printing a document, run in the background while other processes, such as working on a spreadsheet, are currently being accessed. The Macintosh operating system has set the standard for operating system ease of use and has been the model for most of the new graphic user interfaces developed for non-Macintosh systems.

OS/2

In 1988, IBM released the **OS/2** operating system for its new family of PS/2 personal computers (Figure 9-12). Microsoft Corporation, which developed OS/2 for IBM, also released their equivalent version, called MS-OS/2. OS/2 is designed to take advantage of the increased computing power of the Intel 80286, 80386, and 80486 microprocessors and will run only on systems that use these chips. OS/2 also requires more computing power to operate. For example, OS/2 requires 5MB of hard disk and a minimum of 2MB of main memory just to run the operating system. Additional features offered by OS/2 include the capability to run larger and more complex programs and the capability to do multiprogramming (OS/2 can have up to 12 programs running at the same time).

FIGURE 9-12
IBM's OS/2 operating system takes advantage of the increased processing power of the latest personal computer systems.

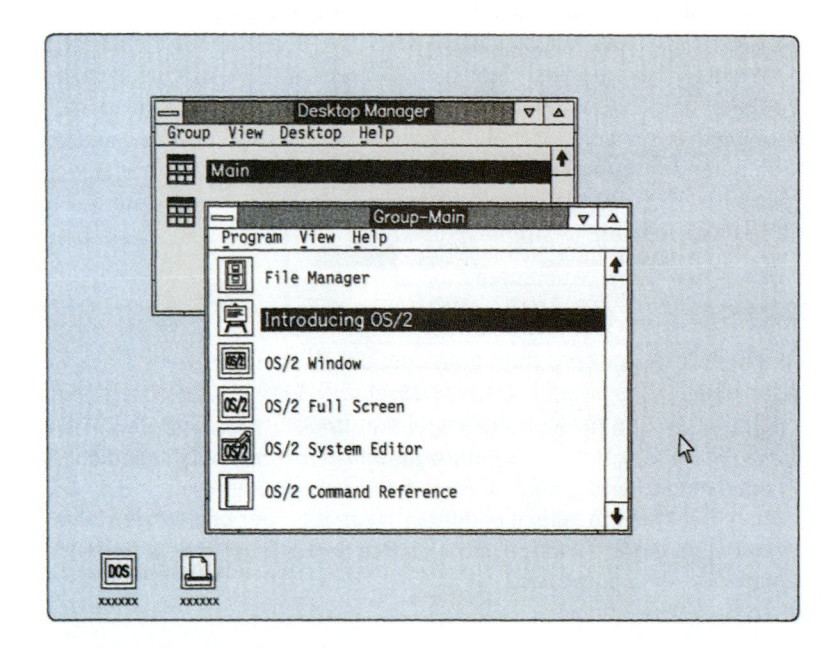

Other Operating Systems

Other popular operating systems exist in addition to the ones we just discussed. The ProDos operating system is used on millions of Apple II computer systems. The PICK operating system is a portable operating system that runs on personal, minicomputers, and mainframes. The PICK operating system incorporates a relational database manager and has had much success in the business data processing marketplace. Minicomputer manufacturers usually provide operating systems that operate only on their equipment. Most minicomputer companies, however, now offer versions of the UNIX and Pick operating systems as well. Most mainframe operating systems are unique to a particular make of computer or are designed to be compatible with one of IBM's operating systems such as DOS/VS, MVS, or VM, IBM's virtual machine operating system.

Although not yet widely used, the MACH operating system has been called a possible replacement for the increasingly popular UNIX operating system and possibly the standard operating system of the future. Considered a streamlined version of UNIX, MACH has the support of several large governmental and educational organizations. Currently being developed by Carnegie Mellon University, MACH has also been chosen by the Open Software Foundation (OSF), a 170 member organization that is trying to establish an industrywide operating system standard.

OPERATING ENVIRONMENTS

◆ Because of the success of the Macintosh operating system, systems software developers have looked for ways to make other operating systems easier to use. One way has been to create an operating environment. An **operating environment**, sometimes called a **windowing environment**, is a graphic interface between the user and the operating system such as DOS, OS/2, or UNIX. Some operating environments, such as Microsoft's Windows (Figure 9-13), are separate software programs that can be added to existing DOS-based systems. Other operating environments, such as IBM's Presentation Manager for OS/2, are included with the operating system. Common features and advantages of an operating environment include use of a mouse, pull-down menus, the capability to have several applications open at the same time, and the capability to easily move data from one application such as a spreadsheet to another application such as a word processing document.

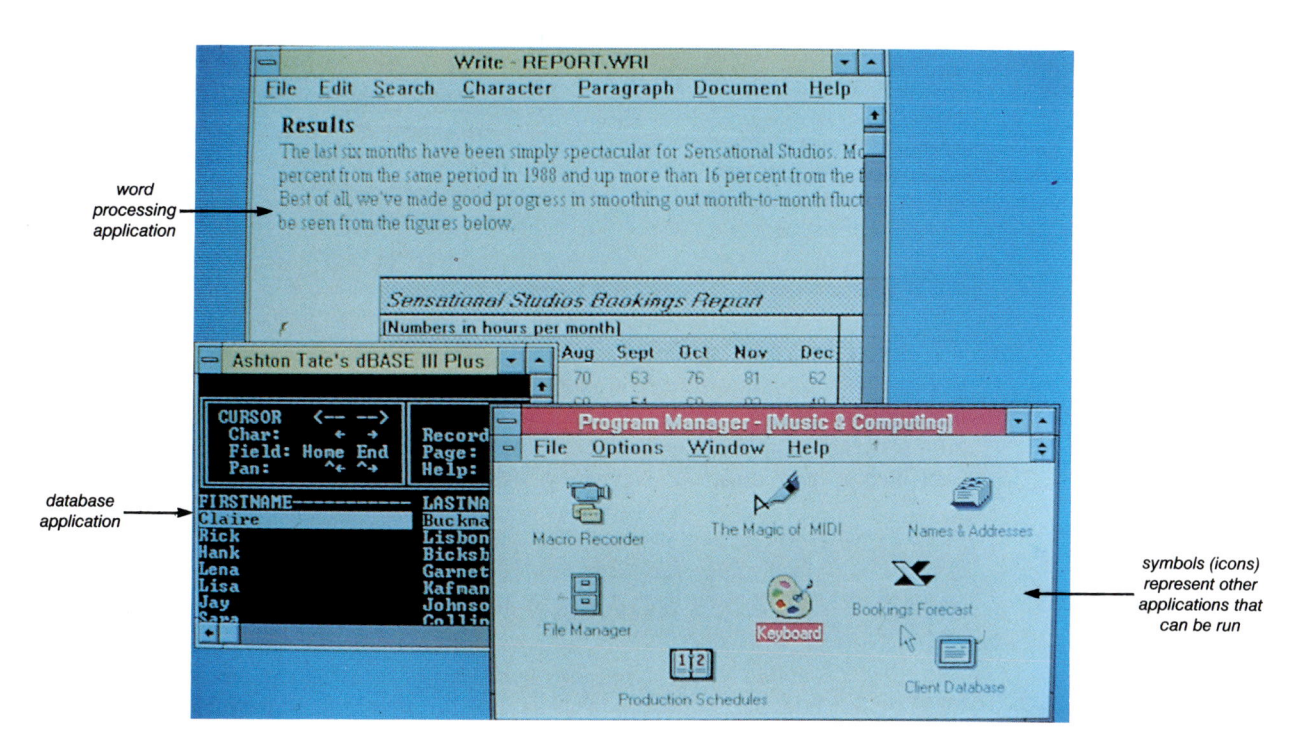

Closely related to operating environments are operating system shell programs. Like an operating environment, a **shell** program acts as an interface between the user and the operating system. Shell programs, however, usually offer a limited number of utility functions such as file maintenance and do not offer applications windowing or graphics.

UTILITIES

◆ In addition to the programs in the operating system, systems software also contains programs called utilities. **Utilities** are programs that provide commonly needed tasks such as file backups, sorting, and editing. Sort utilities place the data stored in files into ascending or descending order based on a value stored in one or more specified fields of each record in a file. For example, a sort utility program could be used

FIGURE 9-13
Microsoft's Windows operating environment provides a graphic user interface for computers that use the DOS operating system. Windows provides the capability to have different applications running in separate windows. The window on the left shows a dBASE III PLUS database application. The window at the top shows a word processing document. The window at the lower right is used to start other application programs represented by the symbols (called icons) shown in the window.

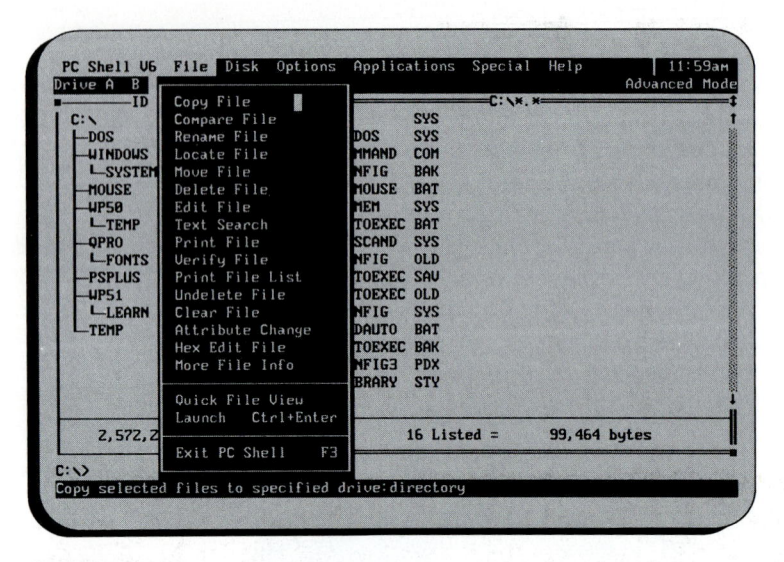

FIGURE 9-14
Utility programs such as PC Tools Deluxe offer a number of functions to help the user perform routine tasks more efficiently. The functions available for maintaining files appear on the screen.

to sort the records in a personnel file in alphabetical order by the employees' last names. An **editor** is a utility program that allows users to make direct changes to programs and data. A programmer can use an editor to change a program instruction that was incorrect or needs to be modified.

Microcomputer operating systems usually contain programs that provide some utility functions such as copying files. In addition, software packages can be purchased to enhance a user's library of systems software. Three popular packages are The Mace Utilities, PC Tools Deluxe, and The Norton Utilities, Advanced Edition. Figure 9-14 shows the file utility functions that are part of PC Tools Deluxe. With larger computer systems, a set of utility programs are usually supplied by the vendor as part of the systems software that is delivered with the computer system.

LANGUAGE TRANSLATORS

◆ Special-purpose systems software programs called **language translators** are used to convert the programming instructions written by programmers into the machine instructions that a computer can understand. Language translators are written for specific programming languages and computer systems. Language translators are explained in more detail in Chapter 12, Program Development.

SUMMARY OF OPERATING SYSTEMS AND SYSTEMS SOFTWARE

◆ Systems software, including the operating system, utilities, and language translators, are essential parts of a computer system and should be understood by users who want to obtain the maximum benefits from their computer. This is especially true for the latest personal computer operating systems that include features such as virtual memory management and multiprogramming. Understanding and being able to use these and other features will give users more control over their computer resources.

CHAPTER SUMMARY

1. **Systems software** consists of all the programs including the operating system that are related to controlling the operations of the computer.
2. An **operating system (OS)** consists of one or more programs that manage the operations of a computer.
3. Operating systems function as an interface between the user, the application programs, and the computer equipment.
4. The essential and most frequently used instructions in an operating system must be stored in main memory for the computer to operate.

5. The *resident* portion of the operating system is called by many different names: the **supervisor, monitor, executive, master program, control program,** or **kernel**.
6. The *nonresident* portion of the operating system, which consists of the less frequently used instructions, remains stored on a disk and is available to be loaded into main memory whenever it is needed.
7. **Booting** the system is the process of loading the operating system into the main memory of a computer.
8. The **operating system prompt** indicates that the operating system has been loaded and is ready to accept a command.
9. **Single program** operating systems allow a single user to run a single program at one time.
10. **Multiprogramming** operating systems, also called **multitasking** operating systems, allow more than one program to be run at the same time.
11. A multiprogramming operating system that allows multiple users is called a **multiuser-multiprogramming** operating system.
12. A **multiprocessor** computer has more than one CPU. **Multiprocessing** operating systems coordinate the operations of these computers.
13. **Fault-tolerant computers** are built with redundant components to allow processing to continue if any single component fails.
14. A **virtual machine (VM)** operating system allows a single computer to run two or more different operating systems.
15. The functions of an operating system include allocating system resources, monitoring system activities, and disk and file management.
16. The system resources that the operating system allocates include the CPU, main memory, and the input/output devices.
17. A **time slice** is a common way for an operating system to allocate CPU processing time.
18. **Foreground** jobs have a higher priority than **background** jobs and thus receive more CPU time.
19. **Buffers** are areas of main memory used to store data that has just been read or is being sent to an output device.
20. **Virtual memory management** increases the effective (or *virtual*) limits of memory by expanding the amount of main memory to include disk space. With virtual memory management, the operating system transfers data and programs between main memory and the disks by segmentation and paging.
21. In **segmentation**, programs are divided into logical portions called **segments**.
22. In **paging**, a fixed number of bytes called a **page**, or **frame**, is transferred from the disk each time data or program instructions are required.
23. The operating system is responsible for managing the input and output processes of the computer.
24. **Spooling** increases printer and computer system efficiency by writing a report to disk before it is printed.
25. The **print spool** refers to reports that have been stored on the disk and are waiting to be printed.
26. **Device drivers** are programs used by the operating system to control different input and output equipment.
27. **Response time** is the amount of time from the moment a user enters data until the computer responds.
28. System performance can be measured by the response time and by comparing the **CPU utilization** with the disk I/O to determine if the system is **thrashing**.
29. Most multiuser operating systems provide for a **logon code**, a **user ID**, and a **password** which all must be entered correctly before a user is allowed to use an application program.
30. Most operating systems contain programs that perform functions that are related to disk and file management.
31. Many computer users are supporting the move away from **proprietary operating systems** and toward **portable operating systems**.
32. Some of the popular operating systems being used today include **UNIX, MS-DOS, PC-DOS, Macintosh,** and **OS/2**.
33. An **operating environment**, sometimes called a **windowing environment**, is a graphic interface between the user and the operating system.
34. A **shell** program acts as an interface between the user and the operating system.
35. **Utilities** are programs that provide commonly needed tasks such as file backups, sorting, and editing.
36. An **editor** is a utility program that allows users to make direct changes to programs and data.
37. **Language translators** are used to convert the programming instructions written by programmers into the machine instructions that a computer can understand.

KEY TERMS

Background 9.6
Booting 9.2
Buffer 9.6
Control program 9.2
CPU utilization 9.9
Device driver 9.8
Editor 9.14
Executive 9.2
Fault-tolerant computer 9.5
Foreground 9.6
Frame 9.7
Kernel 9.2
Language translators 9.14
Logon code 9.9
Macintosh 9.11
Master program 9.2
Monitor 9.2

MS-DOS 9.11
Multiprocessing 9.4
Multiprocessor 9.4
Multiprogramming 9.4
Multitasking 9.4
Multiuser-multiprogramming 9.4
Operating environment 9.13
Operating system (OS) 9.2
Operating system prompt 9.3
OS/2 9.12
Page 9.7
Paging 9.7
Password 9.9
PC-DOS 9.11
Portable operating system 9.10
Print spool 9.8
Proprietary operating system 9.10

Response time 9.9
Segment 9.7
Segmentation 9.7
Shell 9.13
Single program 9.4
Spooling 9.8
Supervisor 9.2
Swapping 9.7
Systems software 9.2
Time slice 9.5
Thrashing 9.9
UNIX 9.10
User ID 9.9
Utilities 9.13
Virtual machine (VM) 9.5
Virtual memory management 9.7
Windowing environment 9.13

REVIEW QUESTIONS

1. How does systems software differ from applications software?
2. Describe how to boot an operating system on a personal computer.
3. What are the different types of operating systems? How are they different?
4. The functions of an operating system can be grouped into which three types?
5. How does an operating system use time slices to assign different processing priorities to jobs?
6. Describe how an operating system uses the disk drive to perform virtual memory management.
7. How does spooling increase printer and computer system efficiency?
8. Discuss several techniques used to measure computer system performance.
9. Describe three types of authorization that an operating system can use to provide system access security.
10. What are the advantages of a portable operating system.
11. List several tasks that the utility programs can perform.

CONTROVERSIAL ISSUE

1. Many people believe that a graphics user interface will eventually be part of all operating systems. Others prefer a nongraphic, command-line operating system. Discuss the advantages and disadvantages of both.

RESEARCH PROJECTS

1. Prepare a paper comparing the MS-DOS and Unix operating systems.

Management Information Systems

CHAPTER 10 — MIS

OBJECTIVES

- Define the term management information systems
- Describe why information is important to an organization
- Discuss the different levels in an organization and how the information requirements differ for each level
- Explain the qualities that all information should have
- Define the term information system and identify the six elements of an information system
- Describe the different types of information systems and the trend toward integration
- Explain how personal computers are used in management information systems

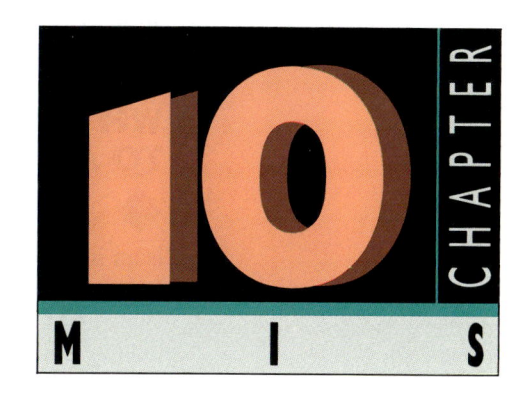

Management information systems, often abbreviated MIS, is a frequently used computer industry term. It is often used, however, to mean different things. It can describe the total system from which information flows to employees of an organization. This could include manual and automated methods as well as computerized systems. The term MIS can also be used to refer to only those portions of a system that provide information to management. Finally, MIS can refer to the department that manages the computer resources of an organization. For the purposes of this chapter, we use a broad definition of **management information systems (MIS)** to mean any computer-based system that provides timely and accurate information for managing an organization. To better understand how a MIS system provides this information, we first need to discuss why information is important to an organization.

WHY IS INFORMATION IMPORTANT TO AN ORGANIZATION?

More and more organizations are realizing that the information in their databases is an important asset that must be protected. Like more tangible assets such as buildings and equipment, an organization's information assets have both a present and future value and have costs associated with their acquisition, maintenance, and storage. Information is no longer thought of as a by-product of doing business, but rather as a key ingredient in both short- and long-range decision making.

Several factors have contributed to the increased need for timely and accurate information. Among these factors are expanded markets, increased competition, shorter product life cycles, and government regulation.

Expanded markets means that to be successful today, many businesses must sell their products in as many markets as possible. Often this means national as well as international distribution of a product. Companies that produce a product for local or regional use are at a disadvantage against companies that produce larger volumes of products for a wider distribution. When companies expand their markets they must have more information about a larger number of potential selling areas (markets) and the different ways of getting their products to those markets. Automobiles are an example of this trend. The number of automobile producers has decreased, and the surviving companies are moving toward worldwide distribution of their products.

Increased competition means that competing companies are financially stronger and better organized. It is, therefore, more important for organizations to have current information on how competitors are selling their products. Many companies now maintain large databases that include information on competitive product features, prices, and methods of distribution. For consumer product companies, this information often includes sales and percent of the total market. This information is important in measuring the impact of advertising campaigns. For example, many companies will measure the impact of a new advertising campaign in a limited geographic area such as a large metropolitan city, before they use the advertising nationwide.

Shorter product life cycles means that companies have less time to perfect a product. More often than not, the product has to be successful when it is first introduced because companies will have less time to make corrections after a product is introduced. This means that before they introduce products, they must have accurate information about what potential customers want. This has led to the increased use of test marketing. Company managers then use the results of tests to decide on advertising, packaging, and product features. Shorter product life cycles also require companies to begin work earlier on the next generation of products. To do this, managers must have information about existing product features that customers want changed and new features they want added.

Government regulation has also contributed to the need for more information. One good example of this is in human resource management. To comply with equal employment opportunity (EEO) guidelines and laws, organizations must keep detailed records on testing, hiring, and promotion practices. The employee database, once used almost exclusively for payroll purposes, has now been expanded to include valuable information on employee skill and education levels as well as the results of performance reviews. With this information companies can document their compliance with government regulations and guidelines.

HOW DO MANAGERS USE INFORMATION?

All employees in an organization need information to effectively perform their jobs; but the primary users of information are managers. **Managers** of an organization are the men and women responsible for directing the use of resources such as people, money, materials, and information so the organization can operate efficiently and prosper. Managers work toward this goal by performing the four management tasks of planning, organizing, directing, and controlling.

1. *Planning* involves establishing goals and objectives. Upper levels of management also plan by establishing the strategies of the organization that will help meet these goals and objectives. For example, upper management often prepares a three- to five-year plan that includes strategies on how to enter new markets or increase existing market share. Lower levels of management plan by establishing specific policies and procedures to implement the strategies. A lower level management plan might include a specific inventory quantity to be maintained for a part.
2. *Organizing* includes identifying and bringing together the resources necessary to achieve the plans of an organization. Resources include people, money, materials (facilities, equipment, raw materials), and information. Organizing also involves establishing the management structure of an organization such as the departments and reporting relationships. For example, to introduce a new product, a company can assign responsibility to an existing department or form a new group whose sole responsibility is the new product.
3. *Directing* involves instructing and authorizing others to perform the necessary work. To direct effectively, managers must be able to communicate what needs to be done and motivate people to do the work. Directing often takes place at daily or weekly meetings where managers meet with their employees to discuss job priorities.
4. *Controlling* involves measuring performance and, if necessary, taking corrective action. Daily production reports are a control device that give managers the information they need to make any necessary adjustments in production rate or product mix.

Figure 10-1 shows how the four management tasks are usually performed in a sequence that becomes a recurring cycle. Actual performance is measured against a previously established plan as part of the control task; this often results in a revised plan. The revised plan may result in additional organizational and directional activities, and so the cycle repeats itself. The four tasks are related and a change in one task usually affects one or more of the other tasks.

All managers perform these management tasks but their area of focus, such as finance or production, and the information they need to perform the tasks is influenced by their level in the organization.

FIGURE 10-1
The four management tasks performed by management are to plan, organize, direct, and control. These tasks are part of a recurring cycle; actions connected with any one task usually affect one or more of the other tasks.

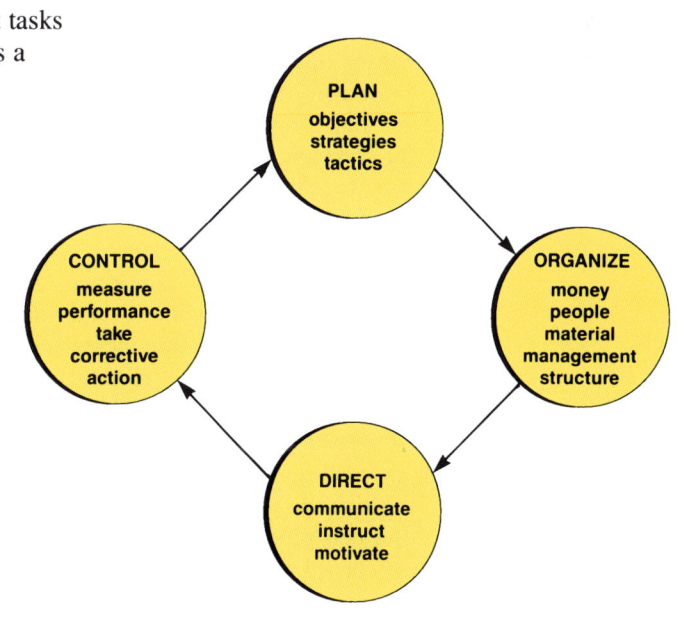

MANAGEMENT LEVELS IN AN ORGANIZATION

◆ Management is usually classified into three levels. The names for these three levels can vary; we call them senior management, middle management and operational management. As shown in Figure 10-2, these three levels of management are above a fourth level of the organization consisting of the production, clerical, and nonmanagement staff. Together, these four levels make up the entire organization. The following sections discuss these levels and their different information requirements.

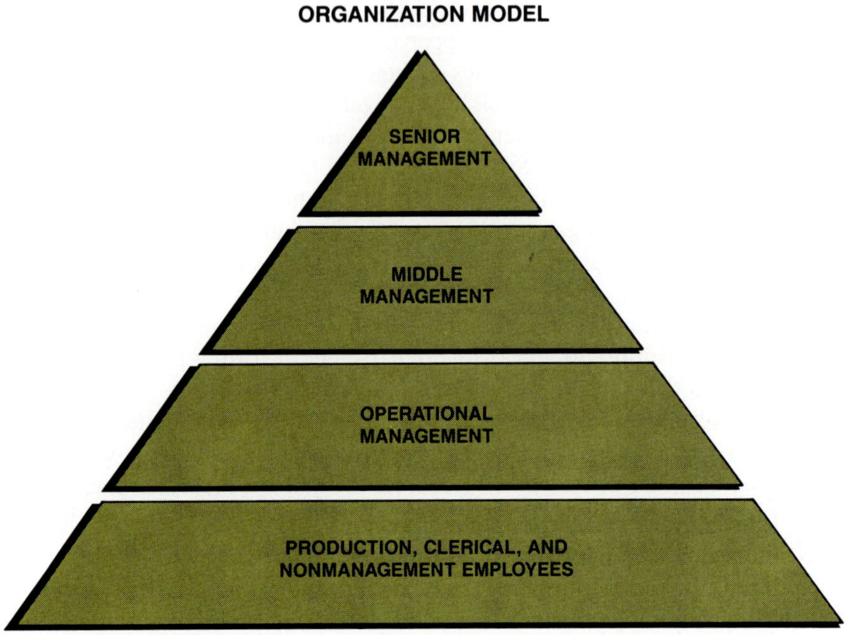

ORGANIZATION MODEL

- SENIOR MANAGEMENT
- MIDDLE MANAGEMENT
- OPERATIONAL MANAGEMENT
- PRODUCTION, CLERICAL, AND NONMANAGEMENT EMPLOYEES

FIGURE 10-2
The model of an organization's management includes three levels with a fourth level made up of the production, clerical, and other nonmanagement employees. Each level makes different types of decisions and requires different types and amounts of information.

Senior Management — Strategic Decisions

Senior management, also referred to as executive or top management, includes the top management positions in an organization. Senior management is concerned with the long-range direction of the organization. Senior managers are primarily responsible for **strategic decisions** that deal with the overall goals and objectives of an organization. Examples of strategic decisions are whether to add or discontinue a product line or whether to diversify into a new business. The time frame for such decisions is usually long-range starting one or more years in the future and continuing for several years or indefinitely. Senior management decisions often involve factors that cannot be directly controlled by the organization such as the changing trends of society. An example of such a trend is the increasing average age of the population. Senior management decisions often require information from outside the company such as industry statistics, consumer surveys, or broad economic indicators such as the change in personal income or the number of new houses being built.

Senior management is also responsible for monitoring how current operations are meeting the objectives of previously made strategic decisions. For example, are sales of a new product meeting previously forecasted levels? Because senior management is concerned with all areas of an organization, it must rely on summarized information to review all operations in a timely manner. Often information on current operations is presented only if it is significantly above or below what was planned. This helps senior management to focus on only the variations that require its involvement.

Another senior management responsibility is to supervise middle management personnel.

Middle Management — Tactical Decisions

Middle management is responsible for implementing the strategic decisions of senior management. To do this, middle managers make **tactical decisions** that implement specific programs and plans necessary to accomplish the stated objectives. Tactical decisions could include how to best advertise and promote a company's products. Such decisions usually involve a shorter time frame than strategic decisions but often cover an entire year. Although they are interested in external events that may influence their work, middle managers are more concerned with the internal operations of the organization and, therefore, rely on information generated by the organization. Middle management also uses summarized and exception-oriented reports although not to the extent of senior management. Middle management sometimes must review detailed information in order to understand performance variances.

Middle management is also responsible for supervising operational management.

Operational Management — Operational Decisions

Operational management supervises the production, clerical, and nonmanagement staff of an organization. In performing their duties, operational managers make **operational decisions** that usually involve an immediate action such as accepting or rejecting an inventory delivery or approving a purchase order. The decision time frame of operational managers tasks is usually very short, such as a day, a week, or a month. Operational managers directly supervise the production and support of an organization's product or service; thus they need detailed information telling them what was produced. Summary and exception reporting, long an important tool for senior and middle level managers, is increasingly being used by operational managers. There are two reasons for this change. First, upper levels of management are allowing lower levels of management to make more decisions. Second, because of computerized systems, the information necessary to make decisions at lower levels is more easily available.

Nonmanagement Employees — On-the-Job Decisions

Nonmanagement employees, which include production, clerical, and staff personnel, also need frequent information to perform their jobs. The trend toward flexible manufacturing systems has increased the need for information to be available to the production worker. Instead of working at the same task all the time, production workers often work as a group on related tasks. Some manufacturing plants allow a group of workers to move with the product from the beginning of production to the end. Such changes require production workers to understand more about the production process than ever before. Often, this information is made available to the workers through the use of production-floor terminals that can be used to inquire on the next production process or tool required. Some systems tell the workers what job they should work on next.

Today, clerical and nonproduction workers also have more information available to them than in the past. For example, more documentation of administrative systems is being placed on-line for immediate access. As we previously mentioned, this is part of a trend toward giving lower level, nonmanagement employees the information they need to make decisions made formerly by managers.

Although we have classified the organization and its corresponding information requirements into four levels as is usually done, in the real world there is often a crossover from one level to another. For example, management and nonmanagement employees frequently join together in committees where all participants have an equal voice. Organizations have realized that formal or informal distinctions between managers and employees hinder communication and can restrict the flow of useful ideas and information. As we will discuss later in this chapter, recent technology, especially the personal computer, has significantly contributed to the flow of timely information to all levels within an organization.

Now that we have discussed why information is important to an organization and how it is used by the various levels, we explain the characteristics, or qualities, that all information should have.

QUALITIES OF INFORMATION

As we have discussed, the purpose of processing data is to create information. Just as data should have certain characteristics, so too should information. These characteristics are often called the qualities of information (Figure 10-3). Terms used to describe these qualities include: accurate, verifiable, timely, organized, meaningful, useful, and cost effective.

Although it may seem obvious, the first quality of information is that it should be *accurate*. Inaccurate information is often worse than no information at all. Accuracy is also a characteristic of data. Although accurate data does not guarantee accurate information, it is impossible to produce accurate information from erroneous data. The computer jargon term **GIGO** states this point very well; it stands for *Garbage In, Garbage Out*.

Closely related to accuracy is that information be *verifiable*. This means that if necessary, the user can confirm the information. For example, before relying on the amounts in a summary report, an accountant would want to know that the totals could be supported by details of the transactions. The accountant could verify the accuracy of the report totals by testing some or all of the totals by adding up the supporting detail records and comparing the results to the report.

QUALITIES OF INFORMATION
☑ Accurate
☑ Verifiable
☑ Timely
☑ Organized
☑ Meaningful
☑ Useful
☑ Cost Effective

FIGURE 10-3
The qualities of information are characteristics that all information should have, whether or not it is produced by a computer.

Another quality of information is that it must be *timely*. Although most information loses its value with time, some information, such as trends, becomes more valuable as time passes and more information is obtained. The point to remember is that the timeliness must be appropriate for any decisions that will be made based on the information. Up-to-the-minute information may be required for some decisions such as the inventory level of a key part, while older information may be satisfactory or more appropriate for other decisions such as the number or employees planning vacations next month.

To be most valuable, information should be *organized* to suit users' requirements. For example, a sales manager that assigns territories on a geographic basis would need prospect lists sorted by ZIP code and not by prospect name.

Meaningful information indicates that the information is relevant to the person who receives it. Certain information is only meaningful to specific individuals or groups within an organization. Management should eliminate extraneous and unnecessary information and always consider the audience when it is accumulating or reporting information.

To be *useful*, information should result in an action being taken or specifically being not taken, depending on the situation. Often, this quality can be improved through exception reporting, which focuses only on the information that exceeds certain limits. An example of exception reporting is an inventory report showing items whose balance on hand is less than a predetermined minimum quantity. Rather than looking through an entire inventory report to find such items, the exception report would quickly bring these items to the attention of the managers responsible for maintaining the inventory.

Last, but not least, information must be *cost effective*. That is, the cost to produce the information must be less than the value of the information. This can sometimes be hard to determine. If the value of the information cannot be determined, perhaps the information should be produced only as managers require it, instead of on a regular basis. Many organizations periodically review the information they produce in reports to determine if the reports maintain the qualities of information we just described. The cost of producing these reports can therefore still be justified or possibly reduced.

Although we have discussed the qualities of information in conjunction with computer systems, these qualities apply to all information regardless of how it is produced. Knowing these qualities will help you evaluate the information you receive and you provide every day, whether or not it is generated by a computer.

The elements of an information system and the general categories of information systems are discussed in the next section.

WHAT IS AN INFORMATION SYSTEM?

◆ An **information system** is a collection of elements that provides accurate, timely, and useful information. As we discussed in Chapter 1, all information systems that are implemented on a computer are comprised of the six elements: equipment, software, accurate data, trained information systems personnel, knowledgeable users, and documented procedures. Each element contributes to a successful information system and conversely, a weakness in any of these elements can cause an information system to fail. People who create, use, or change any type of information system should consider all six elements to ensure success.

Information systems that are implemented on a computer are generally classified into four categories: (1) operational systems; (2) management information systems; (3) decision support systems; and (4) expert systems.

Operational Systems

Operational systems process data generated by the day-to-day transactions of an organization (Figure 10-4). Some examples of operational systems are billing systems, inventory control systems, and order entry systems.

When computers were first used for processing business applications, the information systems developed were primarily operational systems. Usually, the purpose was to computerize an existing manual system. This approach often resulted in faster processing, reduced clerical costs, and improved customer service. Although these operational systems were originally designed to process daily transactions, they were modified over time to provide summaries, trends, and exception data useful to management. Today, operational systems are often a part of management information systems, which we discuss in the next section.

Management Information Systems

In this section we discuss management information systems defined as systems that provide information to management. The concept of management information systems evolved as managers realized that computer processing could be used for more than just day-to-day transaction processing and that the computer's capability to perform rapid calculations and compare data could be used to produce meaningful information

FIGURE 10-4
Operational systems process the day-to-day transactions of an organization.

10.8 CHAPTER 10 MANAGEMENT INFORMATION SYSTEMS

FIGURE 10-5
Management information systems focus on the summary information and exceptions that managers use to perform their jobs.

FIGURE 10-6
Executive information systems (EIS) often use graphics and touch screens to make the systems easier to use by executives who are not familiar with computers.

for management. As we stated at the beginning of the chapter, a management information system (MIS) refers to a computer-based system that generates timely and accurate information for managing an organization. Frequently a management information system is integrated with an operational system. For example, to process a sales order, the operational system would record the sale, update the customer's accounts receivable balance, and make a deduction from the inventory. In the related management information system, reports would be produced that show slow or fast moving items, customers with past due accounts receivable balances, and inventory items that need reordering. In the management information system, the focus is on the information that management needs to do its job (Figure 10-5).

A special type of management information system is the executive information system. **Executive information systems (EIS)** are management information systems that have been designed for the information needs of senior management. Company-wide management information systems usually address the information needs of all levels of management. Because senior managers may not be familiar (or comfortable) working with computer systems, EIS have features that make them easier for executives to use. The EIS user interface often uses a mouse or a touch screen to help executives that are not familiar with using a keyboard. One leading system uses a remote control device similar to those used to control a television set. Another aspect of the EIS user interface is the graphic presentation of information. EIS rely heavily on graphic presentation of both the processing options (Figure 10-6) and data. Again, this is designed to make the system easier to use.

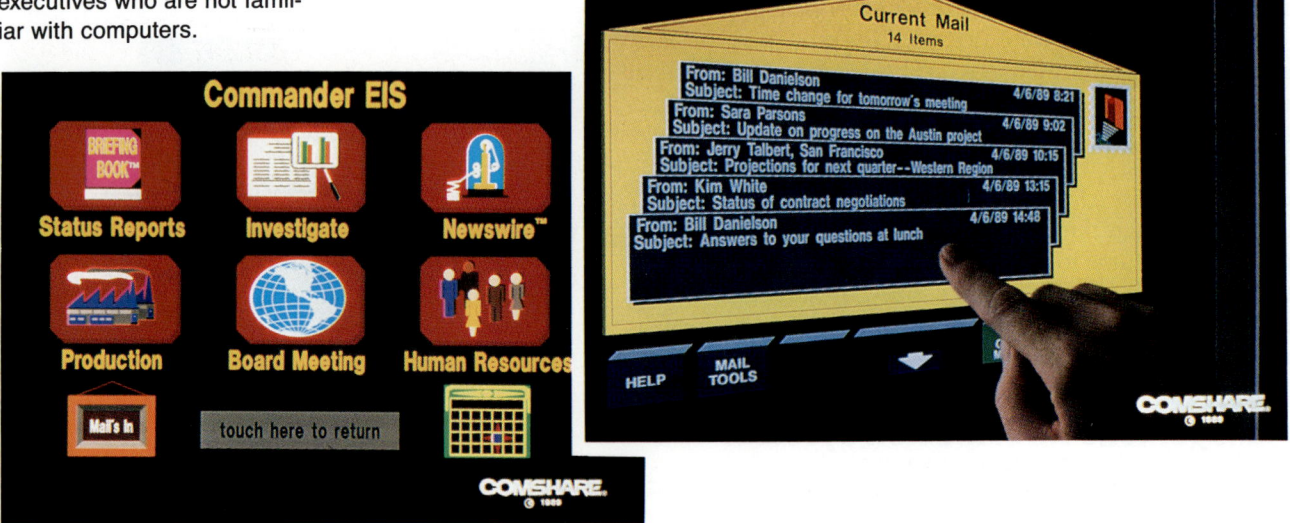

Because executives focus on strategic issues, EIS often have access to external databases such as the Dow Jones News/Retrieval service. Such external sources of information can provide current information on interest rates, commodity prices, and other leading economic indicators.

Although they offer great promise, many EIS have not been successfully implemented and many executives have stopped using them. A common reason cited in several failed attempts is the mistake of not modifying the system to the specific needs of the individual executives who will use the system. For example, many executives prefer to have information presented in a particular sequence with the option of seeing different levels of supporting detail information such as cost data on a spreadsheet. The desired sequence and level of detail varies for each executive. It appears that EIS must be tailored to the executives' requirements or the executives will continue to manage with information they have obtained through previously established methods.

Decision Support Systems

Frequently, management needs information that is not routinely provided by operational and management information systems. For example, a vice president of finance may want to know the net effect on company profits if interest rates on borrowed money increase and raw material prices decrease. Operational or management information systems do not usually provide this type of information. Decision support systems have been developed to provide this information.

A **decision support system (DSS)** is a system designed to help someone reach a decision by summarizing or comparing data from either or both internal and external sources. Internal sources include data from an organization's database such as sales, manufacturing, or financial data. Data from external sources could include information on interest rates, population trends, new housing construction, or raw material pricing. Frito Lay, for example, collects and reports sales data on its own and competitors products every day (Figure 10-7). The information is part of a DSS that allows Frito Lay to analyze important trends in days or weeks instead of the months that it used to take.

FIGURE 10-7
Frito Lay, a major producer of snack foods, has developed a decision support system that uses sales information collected daily on hand-held terminals by over 10,000 salespeople. The system helps Frito Lay spot sales trends in days or weeks instead of the months it used to take.

Decision support systems often include query languages, statistical analysis capabilities, spreadsheets, and graphics to help the user evaluate the decision data. More advanced decision support systems also include capabilities that allow users to create a model of the variables affecting a decision. With a **model**, users can ask *what-if* questions by changing one or more of the variables and seeing what the projected results would be. A simple model for determining the best product price would include factors for the expected sales volume at each price level. Many people use electronic spreadsheets for simple modeling tasks. DSS are sometimes combined with executive information systems (EIS). Generally speaking, DSS are more analytical and are designed

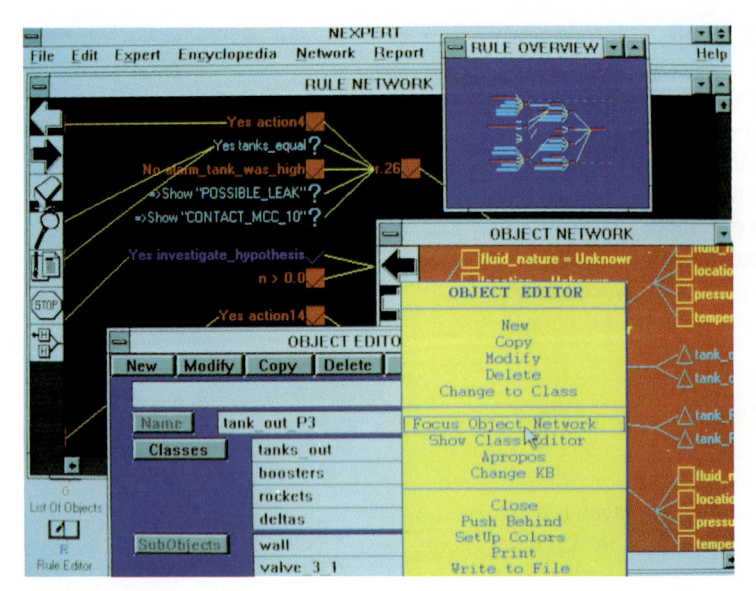

CHAPTER 10 MANAGEMENT INFORMATION SYSTEMS

to work on unstructured problems that do not have a predefined number of variables. For example, a problem involving how to finance a company's growth would involve estimates of sales, income, depreciation, interest rates, and other variables that would best be handled by a DSS. EIS are primarily oriented toward collecting and presenting meaningful information from a variety of sources.

Expert Systems

Expert systems combine the knowledge on a given subject of one or more human experts into a computerized system that simulates the human experts' reasoning and decision making processes (Figure 10-8). Thus, the computer also becomes an *expert* on the subject. Expert systems are made up of the combined subject knowledge of the human experts, called the **knowledge base** and the **inference rules** that determine how the knowledge is used to reach decisions. Although they may appear to *think*, the current expert systems actually operate within narrow preprogrammed limits and cannot make decisions based on common sense or on information outside of their knowledge base. An example of how a simple expert system uses rules to identify an animal is shown in Figure 10-9.

FIGURE 10-8
Nexpert Object is a powerful expert system that provides a highly visual presentation of its data, rules, and conclusions.

FIGURE 10-9
A simulated dialogue between a user and a simple expert system is designed to identify an animal based on observations about the animal provided by the user. Notice how answers to certain questions result in other questions that narrow the possible conclusions. Once a conclusion is reached, the expert system can display or print the rules upon which the conclusion was based.

A more practical application of an expert system has been implemented by Ford Motor Company to help their dealers diagnose engine repair problems. Previously, when they encountered an engine problem that they could not solve, dealers would call Dearborn, Michigan to talk with Ford engine expert Gordy Kujawski. Now dealers can access a nationwide computer system that Ford has developed to duplicate the reasoning that Kujawski uses when troubleshooting a problem (Figure 10-10).

Although expert systems can be used at any level in an organization, to date they have been primarily used by nonmanagement employees for job-related decisions. Expert systems have also been successfully applied to problems as diverse as diagnosing illnesses, searching for oil, and making soup. These systems are part of an exciting branch of computer science called **artificial intelligence**, the application of human intelligence to computer systems.

FIGURE 10-10
Ford Motor Company has developed an expert system that incorporates the knowledge of engine repair expert Gordy Kujawski. Instead of calling Kujawski, Ford dealers can now access the expert system when they are trying to diagnose engine problems.

INTEGRATED INFORMATION SYSTEMS

♦ With today's sophisticated software, it can be difficult to classify a system as belonging uniquely to one of the four types of information systems we have discussed. For example, much of today's application software provides both operational and MIS information and some of the more advanced software even includes some decision support capabilities. Although expert systems still operate primarily as separate systems, the trend is clear: combine all of an organization's information needs into a single, integrated information system.

THE ROLE OF PERSONAL COMPUTERS IN MANAGEMENT INFORMATION SYSTEMS

♦ The personal computer is playing an increasingly significant role in modern management information systems. Some professionals have said that the personal computer is the right tool at the right time. As organizations have moved toward decentralizing decision making, personal computers have given managers access to the information they need to make their decisions. Nonmanagement employees also benefit from having information available through networked personal computers on their desk or in the production area. For many MIS applications, personal computers are more cost effective than larger systems. One study estimated that the cost to process a million transactions on a mainframe is fifty times more expensive than on a personal computer. Flexibility is another advantage of personal computers. Individual or networks of personal computers can often be added more quickly than the corresponding amount of equipment that would be needed with minicomputer or mainframe systems. Many professionals believe that the ideal MIS decision involves a network of personal computers attached to a central mainframe, minicomputer, or file server that stores the common information that many users access. This centralized data and decentralized computing arrangement allow users and organizations the most flexibility over controlling their information resources.

SUMMARY OF MANAGEMENT INFORMATION SYSTEMS

Numerous factors have combined to make information an increasingly important asset for most organizations. Organizations manage this asset through the use of management information systems, computer-based systems that provide the information necessary to manage the activities of the organization. Management information systems provide different types of information based on the users' needs, which is often related to the users' levels in the organization.

The trend of management information systems is to combine and integrate operational, MIS, decision support, and expert systems that previously operated independently.

CHAPTER SUMMARY

1. **Management information system (MIS)** refers to any computer-based system that provides timely and accurate information for managing an organization.
2. Information that is stored in a database is no longer thought of as a by-product of doing business, but rather as a key ingredient in both short- and long-range decision making.
3. Factors that have contributed to the increased need for information include: expanded markets; increased competition; shorter product life cycles; and government regulation.
4. **Managers** of an organization are responsible for performing four different types of tasks: planning, organizing, directing, and controlling.
5. Management is usually divided into three levels: senior management, middle management, and operational management. A fourth level of an organization consists of the production, clerical, and nonmanagement staff.
6. **Senior management** makes strategic decisions and is concerned with the long-range direction of the company.
7. **Strategic decisions** deal with the overall goals and objectives of an organization.
8. **Middle management** makes tactical decisions and is responsible for implementing the strategic decisions of senior management.
9. **Tactical decisions** involve specific programs and plans necessary to accomplish the strategic objectives of an organization.
10. **Operational management** makes operational decisions and provides direct supervision over the production, clerical, and nonmanagement staff of an organization.
11. **Operational decisions** usually involve an immediate action such as accepting or rejecting an inventory delivery or approving a purchase order.
12. The terms used to describe the qualities of information include accurate, verifiable, timely, organized, meaningful, useful, and cost effective.
13. **GIGO** is an acronym that stands for *Garbage In, Garbage Out*.
14. An **information system** is a collection of elements that provide accurate, timely, and useful information. These elements include: equipment, software, accurate data, trained information systems personnel, knowledgeable users, and documented procedures.
15. The types of computer information systems include: (1) operational systems; (2) management information systems; (3) decision support systems; and (4) expert systems.
16. **Operational systems** process data generated by the day-to-day transactions of an organization.
17. **Executive information systems (EIS)** are management information systems that have been designed for the information needs of senior management.
18. A **decision support system (DSS)** is a system designed to help someone reach a decision by summarizing or comparing data from either or both internal and external sources.
19. Some decision support systems allow users to create a **model** where they can ask *what-if* questions by changing one or more of the variables and see what the projected results will be.

20. **Expert systems** combine the knowledge on a given subject of one or more human experts into a computerized system that simulates the human experts' reasoning and decision-making processes.
21. Expert systems are made up of the combined subject knowledge of the human experts, called the **knowledge base** and the **inference rules** that determine how the knowledge is used to reach decisions.
22. An exciting branch of computer science is **artificial intelligence**, the application of human intelligence to computer systems.
23. The trend is to combine all of an organization's information needs into a single, integrated information system.
24. The personal computer is playing an increasingly significant role in modern management information systems.

KEY TERMS

Artificial intelligence *10.11*
Decision support system (DSS) *10.9*
Executive information system (EIS) *10.8*
Expert system *10.10*
GIGO *10.6*
Inference rules *10.10*
Information system *10.7*
Knowledge base *10.10*
Manager *10.2*
Management information system (MIS) *10.1*
Middle management *10.5*
Model *10.9*
Operational decision *10.5*
Operational management *10.5*
Operational system *10.7*
Senior management *10.4*
Strategic decision *10.4*
Tactical decision *10.5*

REVIEW QUESTIONS

1. Define the term management information systems. Discuss three ways that the term is used.
2. List five factors that have contributed to the increased need for organizations to have information.
3. Describe the four different types of tasks that managers perform.
4. Identify the three levels of management in an organization, and describe the types of decisions that are made at each level.
5. What are the six qualities that information should have?
6. List the four general types of information systems.
7. What is an EIS? What are some of the user interfaces frequently used with an EIS?
8. Discuss how the personal computer is being used in management information systems.

CONTROVERSIAL ISSUE

1. Some people are concerned that the increased application of expert systems will lead to real life situations of robots gone wild or uncontrollable computers as they are sometimes portrayed in science fiction. Discuss what limits you think should be placed on computerized decision making.

RESEARCH PROJECTS

1. Think of an application for an expert system. Make a list of the inference rules that would be used.
2. Interview a manager at a local company or your school. Ask him or her what information he or she uses to make decisions. Identify the information that is not provided by the computer system being used at the local company or the school. Could it be provided by the system?

The Information System Life Cycle

ANALYSIS/DESIGN

CHAPTER 11

OBJECTIVES

- Explain the phases and paths of the information system life cycle
- Explain the importance of project management and documentation
- Define commercial applications software and describe the difference between horizontal and vertical applications
- Discuss each of the steps of acquiring commercial applications software
- Discuss the reasons for developing custom software
- Describe how various analysis and design tools, such as data flow diagrams, are used
- Explain how program development is part of the information system life cycle
- Explain several methods that can be used for a conversion to a new system
- Discuss the installation and maintenance of an information system

Every day, competition, government regulations, and other such influences cause people to face new challenges as they try to obtain the information they need to perform their jobs. A new product, a new sales commission plan, or a change in tax rates are just three examples of why an organization must change the way it processes information. Sometimes, these challenges can be met by existing methods but other times, meeting the challenge requires an entirely new way of processing data. In these cases, a new or modified information system is needed. As a computer user, either as an individual or within your organization, it is very likely that someday you will participate in acquiring, developing, or modifying a system. Creating an information system can be described by phases known as the information system life cycle. In this chapter, we illustrate each phase of the system life cycle by using a case study about the wholesale auto parts division of the Sutherland Company.

WHAT IS THE INFORMATION SYSTEM LIFE CYCLE?

The **information system life cycle (ISLC)** is an organized approach to obtaining an information system. Regardless of the type or complexity of an information system, the structured process of the information system life cycle should be followed whenever an information system is acquired or developed. The activities of the information system life cycle can be grouped into distinct phases.

The Phases of the Information System Life Cycle

As shown in Figure 11-1, the phases of the information system life cycle are:

- Analysis
- Acquisition or Design
- Customizing or Development
- Implementation
- Maintenance

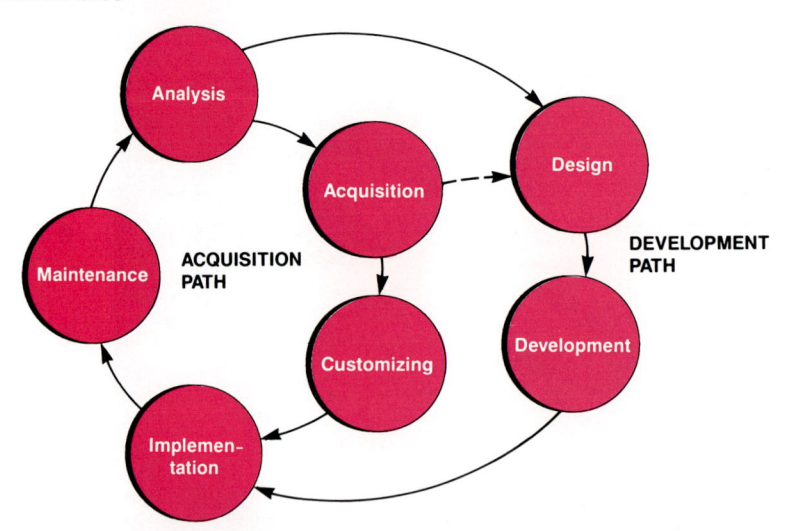

FIGURE 11-1
The information system life cycle consists of several phases. The phases of the acquistion path are analysis, acquisition, customizing, implementation, and maintenance. The phases of the development path include analysis, design, development, implementation, and maintenance.

Each of the phases includes important activities that relate to the acquisition or development of an information system.

As Figure 11-1 also shows, there is an acquisition path and a development path in the information system life cycle. After the analysis phase, an organization can either choose to acquire a system by purchasing software or develop one by writing their own software. If an organization does not find a suitable system during the acquisition phase, it will move to the design phase of the development path. All systems have analysis, implementation, and maintenance phases.

Before explaining each of the phases, we will discuss project management and documentation because these two activities are ongoing processes that are performed throughout the cycle. First, we will identify the information system specialists and users who participate in the various phases of the ISLC.

Project Management

Project management involves planning, scheduling, reporting, and controlling the individual activities that make up the information system development life cycle. These activities are usually recorded in a **project plan** on a week-by-week basis that includes an estimate of the time to complete the activity and the start and finish dates. As you might expect, the start of many activities depends on the successful completion of other activities. For example, implementation activities cannot begin until you have completed at least some, if not all, of the development activities. An effective way of showing the relationship of project activities is with a Gantt chart (Figure 11-2). A Gantt chart usually shows time across the top of the chart and a list of activities to be completed down the left side. Marks on the chart indicate when an activity begins and is completed. Lines or bars between the marks indicate progress toward completing the task.

The importance of maintaining a realistic schedule for project management cannot be overstated. Without a realistic schedule, the success of a development project is in jeopardy from the start. If project members do not believe the schedule is realistic, they may not participate to the full extent of their abilities. Project management is a place for realistic, not wishful, thinking.

Project management should be practiced throughout the development process. In most projects, activities need frequent rescheduling. Some activities will take less time than originally planned and others will take longer. To measure the impact of the actual results and revised estimates, they should be recorded regularly and a revised project plan issued. Project management software provides an efficient method of recording results and revising project plans.

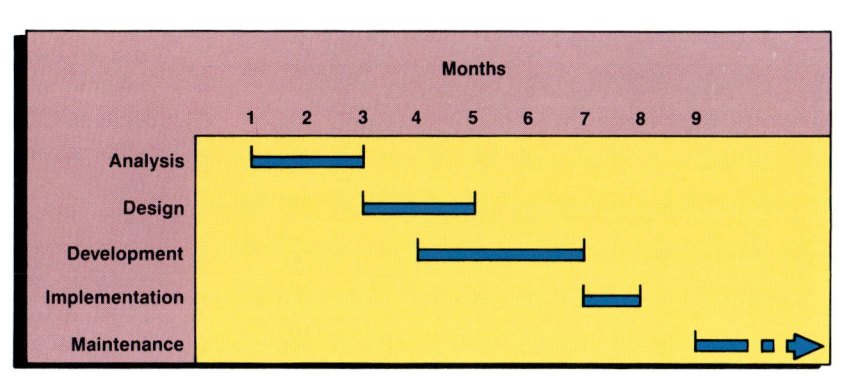

FIGURE 11-2
A Gantt chart is often used in project management to show the time relationships of the project activities.

Documentation

Documentation refers to written materials that are produced as part of the information system development life cycle such as a report describing the overall purpose of the system or layout forms that are used to design reports and screens. Documentation should be identified and agreed on prior to beginning the project. Well-written, thorough documentation makes it easier for users and others to understand why particular decisions are made. Too often, documentation is put off until the completion of a project and is never adequately finished. Documentation should be an ongoing part of the entire development process and should not be thought of as a separate phase. Well-written, thorough documentation can also extend the useful life of a system. Unfortunately, systems are sometimes replaced simply because no one understands how they work.

Who Participates in the Information System Development Life Cycle?

Every person who will be affected by the new system should have the opportunity to participate in its development. The participants fall into two categories: users and information system personnel such as systems analysts and computer programmers. The systems analyst works closely with both the users and the programmers to define the system. The systems analyst's job is challenging, requiring good communication, analytical, and diplomatic skills to keep the development process on track and on schedule. Good communication skills are especially important during analysis, the first phase of the information system life cycle.

ANALYSIS PHASE

Analysis is the separation of a system into its parts to determine how the system works. In addition, the analysis phase of a project also includes the identification of a proposed solution to the problems identified in the current system. A system project can originate in several ways, but a common way is for the manager of a user department, such as accounting or personnel, to contact the information systems department with a request for assistance. The initial request may be oral, but it is eventually written on a standard form that becomes the first item of documentation (Figure 11-3). In most organizations, requests for new system projects exceed the capacity of the information systems department to implement them. Therefore, the manager of the systems department must review each request and make a preliminary determination as to the potential benefit for the company. Requests for large development projects, such as an entirely new system, are often reviewed by committees made up of both user and information systems personnel and representatives of top management. When the managers of both the user and information systems departments determine that a request warrants further review, one or more systems analysts will be assigned to begin a preliminary investigation, the first step in the analysis phase.

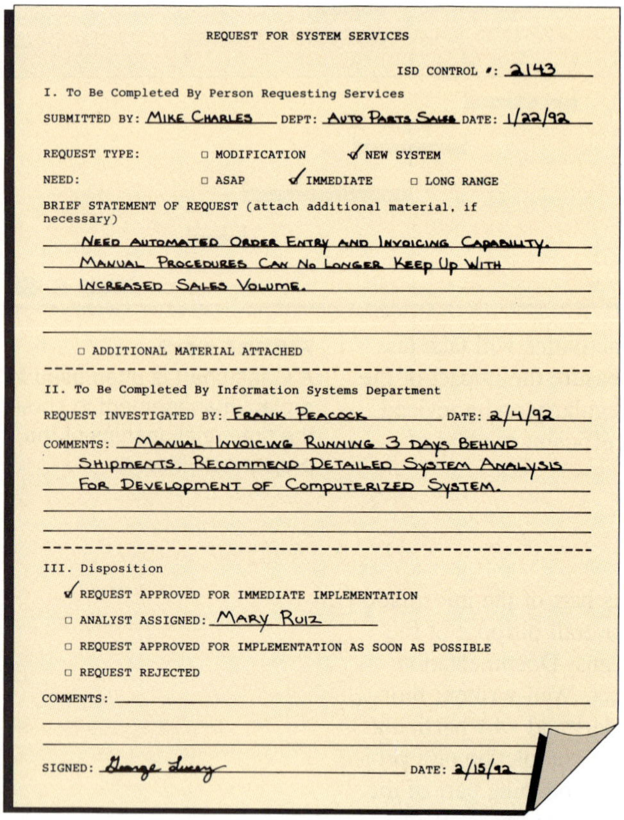
REQUEST FOR SYSTEM SERVICES

ISD CONTROL #: 2143

I. To Be Completed By Person Requesting Services

SUBMITTED BY: MIKE CHARLES DEPT: AUTO PARTS SALES DATE: 1/22/92

REQUEST TYPE: ☐ MODIFICATION ✓ NEW SYSTEM

NEED: ☐ ASAP ✓ IMMEDIATE ☐ LONG RANGE

BRIEF STATEMENT OF REQUEST (attach additional material, if necessary)

NEED AUTOMATED ORDER ENTRY AND INVOICING CAPABILITY. MANUAL PROCEDURES CAN NO LONGER KEEP UP WITH INCREASED SALES VOLUME.

☐ ADDITIONAL MATERIAL ATTACHED

II. To Be Completed By Information Systems Department

REQUEST INVESTIGATED BY: FRANK PEACOCK DATE: 2/4/92

COMMENTS: MANUAL INVOICING RUNNING 3 DAYS BEHIND SHIPMENTS. RECOMMEND DETAILED SYSTEM ANALYSIS FOR DEVELOPMENT OF COMPUTERIZED SYSTEM.

III. Disposition

✓ REQUEST APPROVED FOR IMMEDIATE IMPLEMENTATION

☐ ANALYST ASSIGNED: MARY RUIZ

☐ REQUEST APPROVED FOR IMPLEMENTATION AS SOON AS POSSIBLE

☐ REQUEST REJECTED

COMMENTS:

SIGNED: George Lucey DATE: 2/15/92

FIGURE 11-3
The system development project usually starts with a request from a user. The request should be documented on a form such as this one to provide a record of the action taken.

The Preliminary Investigation

The purpose of the **preliminary investigation** is to determine if a request justifies further detailed investigation and analysis. The most important aspect of the preliminary investigation is **problem definition**, the identification of the true nature of the problem. Often the stated problem and the real problem are not the same. For example, suppose the manager of the accounting department requests a new accounts receivable report that shows recent customer payments. An investigation might reveal that the existing accounts receivable reports would be acceptable if the customer payments were recorded daily instead of once a week. The real problem is that customer payments are being recorded too late to be included in the existing reports. Thus, the preliminary investigation determines the real source of the problem.

The preliminary investigation begins with an interview of the manager who submitted the request. Depending on the request, other users can be interviewed as well. For example, a request might involve data or a process that affects more than one department or clerical workers may have to be interviewed to obtain detail information.

The preliminary investigation is usually quite short when compared to the remainder of the project. At the end of the investigation, the systems analyst presents the findings to both user and information system management and recommends the next action. Sometimes the results of a preliminary investigation indicate an obvious solution that can be implemented at minimal cost. Other times, however, the only thing the preliminary investigation does is confirm that there is a problem that needs further study. In these cases, detailed system analysis is recommended. The user, the information systems management, and the systems analyst work together to decide how to proceed.

Detailed System Analysis

Detailed system analysis involves both a thorough study of the current system and at least one proposed solution to the problems found.

The study of the current system is important for two reasons. First, it helps increase the systems analyst's understanding of the activities that a new system might perform. Second, and perhaps most important, studying the current system builds a relationship between the systems analyst and the user. The systems analyst will have much more credibility with users if he or she understands how the users currently do their job. This may seem an obvious point, but surprisingly, many systems are created or modified without studying the current system or without adequately involving the users.

The basic fact-gathering techniques used during the detailed system analysis are: (1) interviews, (2) questionnaires, (3) reviewing current system documentation, and (4) observing current procedures. During this phase of the system study, the systems analyst must develop a critical, questioning approach to each procedure within the current system to determine what is actually taking place. Often systems analysts find that operations are being performed not because they are efficient or effective, but because they have always been done this way.

Information gathered during this phase includes: (1) the output of the current system, (2) the input to the current system, and (3) the procedures used to produce the output.

An increasingly popular method for documenting this information is called structured analysis. **Structured analysis** is the use of analysis and design tools such as data flow diagrams, data dictionaries, process specifications, structured English, decision tables, and decision trees to document the specifications of an information system.

Data Flow Diagrams One of the difficulties in analyzing any system is how to document the findings in a way that can be understood by users, programmers, and other systems analysts. Structured analysis addresses this problem by using graphics to represent the flow of data. These graphics are called data flow diagrams.

A **data flow diagram (DFD)** graphically shows the flow of data through a system. The key elements of a DFD (Figure 11-4) are arrows, or vectors, called data flows that represent data; circles (also called bubbles) that represent processes such as verifying an order or creating an invoice; parallel lines that represent data files; and squares, called sources, or sinks, that represent either or both an originator or a receiver of data such as a customer.

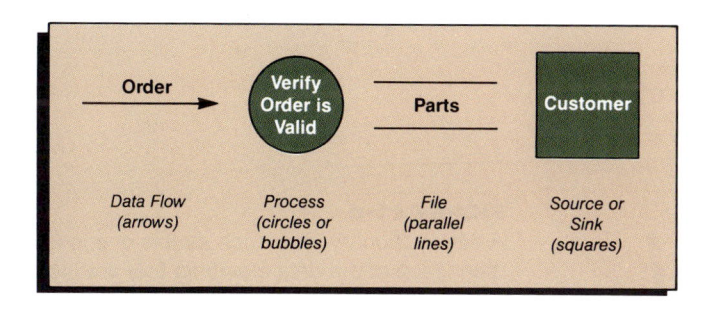

FIGURE 11-4
The symbols used to create data flow diagrams.

Because they are visual, DFDs are particularly useful for reviewing the existing or proposed system with the user (Figure 11-5). One of the features of DFDs is that they are done on a level-by-level basis. The top level would only identify major processes and flows. Lower levels further define the higher levels. For example, in Figure 11-5 the Apply Invoice Payment process in the lower left corner could have its own separate DFD to define subprocesses that take place.

FIGURE 11-5
Data flow diagrams (DFDs) are used to graphically illustrate the flow of information through a system. The customer (box) both originates and receives data (arrows). The circles indicate where actions take place on the data. Files are shown as parallel lines.

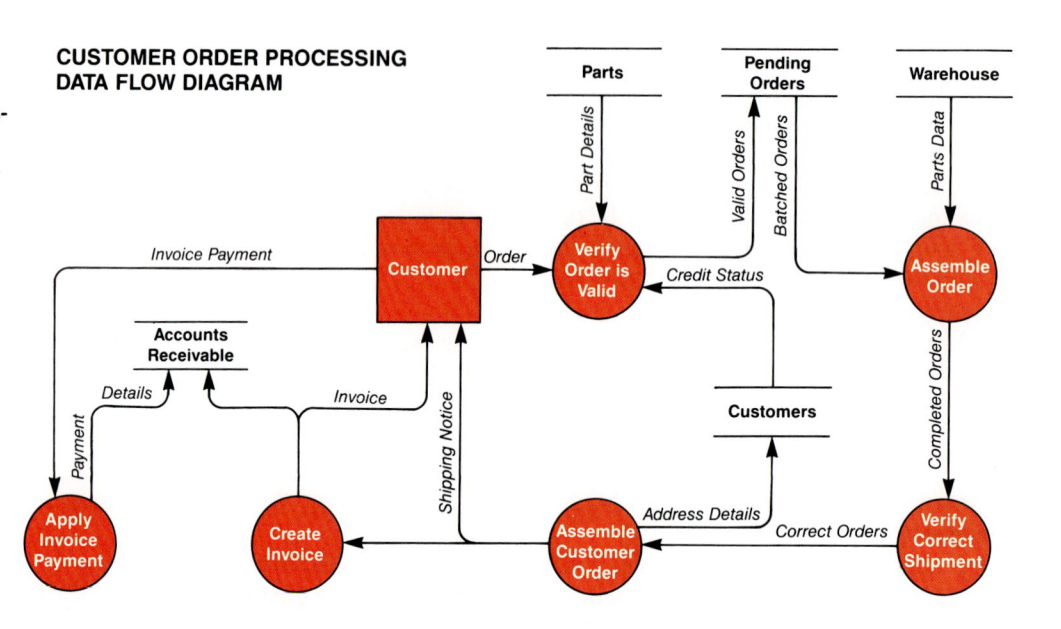

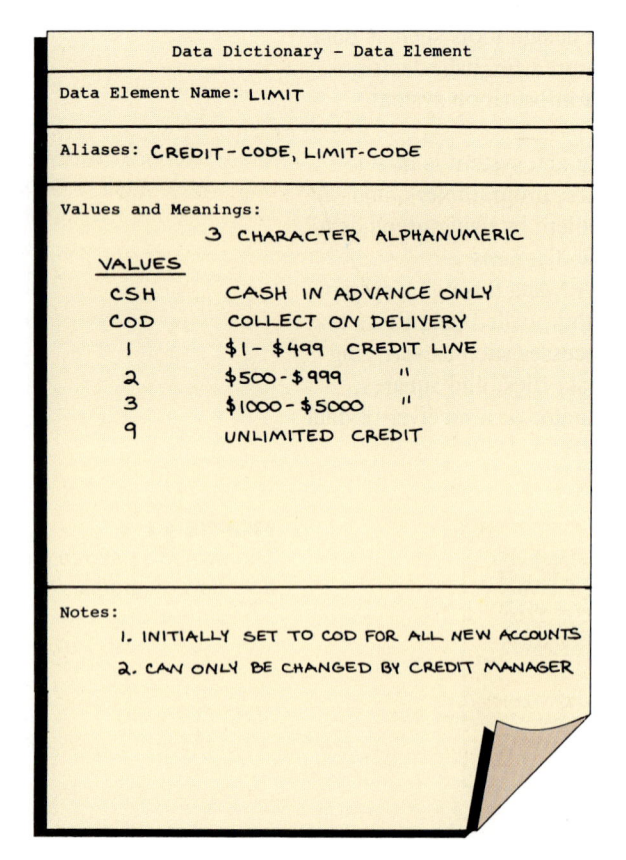

CUSTOMER ORDER PROCESSING DATA FLOW DIAGRAM

Data Dictionaries The **data dictionary** describes the elements that make up the data flow. Each element can be thought of as equivalent to a field in a record. The data dictionary also includes information about the attributes of each element such as length, where the element is used (which files and data flows include the element), and any values or ranges the element might have, such as a value of 2 in Figure 11-6 for a credit limit code to indicate a purchase limit of $1,000.00. The data dictionary is created by the systems analyst in the analysis phase and is used in all subsequent phases of the information system life cycle. Although data dictionaries are often first prepared manually, they are usually entered and maintained on a computer system.

FIGURE 11-6
A data dictionary form such as this one is used to document each of the data elements that are included in the data flows. The form records the length, type of data, and possible values for each data element.

Structured English **Process specifications** describe and document what happens to a data flow when it reaches a process circle. For example in Figure 11-5, process specifications describe what goes on in each of the circles. One way of writing process specifications is to use **structured English**, a style of writing and presentation that highlights the alternatives and actions that are part of the process. Figure 11-7 shows an example of a structured English process specification describing a policy for order processing.

```
If the order amount exceeds $1,000,
    If customer has any unpaid invoices over 90 days old,
        Do not issue order confirmation,
        Write message on order reject report.
    Otherwise (account is in good standing),
        Issue order confirmation.
Otherwise (order is $1,000 or less),
    If customer has any unpaid invoices over 90 days old,
        Issue order confirmation,
        Write message on credit follow-up report.
    Otherwise (account is in good standing),
        Issue order confirmation.
```

FIGURE 11-7
Structured English is an organized way of describing what actions are taken on data. This structured English example describes an order processing policy.

Decision Tables and Decision Trees Another way of documenting the system during the analysis phase is with a decision table or decision tree. A **decision table** or a **decision tree** identifies the actions that should be taken under different conditions. Figures 11-8 and 11-9 show a decision table and decision tree for the order processing policy described with structured English in Figure 11-7. Decision tables and trees are an excellent way of showing the desired action when the action depends on multiple conditions.

	Rules			
	1	2	3	4
Conditions				
1. Order > $1,000	Y	Y	N	N
2. Unpaid invoices over 90 days old	Y	N	Y	N
Actions				
1. Issue confirmation	N	Y	Y	Y
2. Reject order	Y	N	N	N
3. Credit follow-up	N	N	Y	N

FIGURE 11-8
Decision tables help a user quickly determine the course of action based on two or more conditions. This decision table is based on the order processing policy described in Figure 11-7. For example, if an order is $1,000 or less and the customer has an unpaid invoice over 90 days old, the policy (Rule 3) is to issue an order confirmation and perform a credit follow-up on the past due invoice.

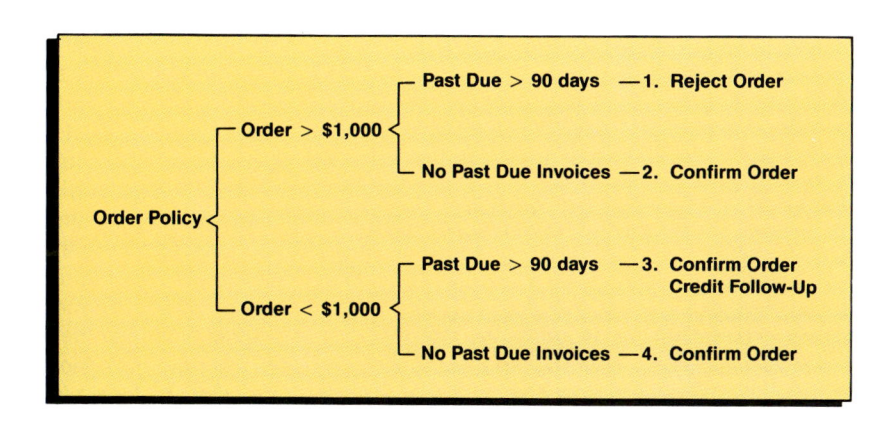

Order Policy
- Order > $1,000
  - Past Due > 90 days — 1. Reject Order
  - No Past Due Invoices — 2. Confirm Order
- Order < $1,000
  - Past Due > 90 days — 3. Confirm Order Credit Follow-Up
  - No Past Due Invoices — 4. Confirm Order

FIGURE 11-9
Like a decision table, a decision tree illustrates the action to be taken based on the given conditions, but presents it graphically. This decision tree is based on the order processing policy described in Figure 11-7.

Making the Decision on How to Proceed

Just as at the completion of the preliminary investigation, at the completion of the analysis phase, the user, systems analyst, and management face another decision on how to proceed. At this point the systems analyst should have completed a study of the current system and, using the same tools and methods, developed one or more proposed solutions to the current system's identified problems. Sometimes, the systems analyst is asked to prepare a feasibility study and a cost/benefit analysis. These two reports are often used together. The **feasibility study** discusses whether the proposed solution is practical and capable of being accomplished. The **cost/benefit analysis** identifies the estimated costs of the proposed solution and the benefits (including potential cost savings) that are expected. If there are strong indications at the beginning of the project that some type of new system will likely be developed, the feasibility study and cost/benefit analysis are sometimes performed as part of the preliminary investigation.

The systems analyst presents the results of his or her work in a written report (Figure 11-10) to both user and information systems management who consider the alternatives and the resources, such as time, people, and money of the organization. The end of the analysis phase is usually when organizations decide either to acquire a commercial software package from an outside source or to develop the software. If a decision is made to proceed, the project enters the acquisition phase if a software package is going to be obtained or the design phase if software is going to be developed. If a suitable software package cannot be found, an organization will start the design phase of the development path.

```
DATE:     April 1, 1992
TO:       Management Review Committee
FROM:     George Lacey, Corporate Systems Manager
SUBJECT:  Detailed Investigation and Analysis of Order Entry System

Introduction

    A detailed system investigation and analysis of the order entry system
was conducted as a result of approval given by the Management Review
Committee on March 1.  The findings of the investigation are presented
below.

Objectives of Detailed Investigation and Analysis

    The study investigated reported problems of the wholesale auto parts
order entry system.  We have received complaints that orders were not being
shipped promptly and that customers were not notified about out-of-stock
parts when they placed their orders.  In addition, invoices are not sent to
customers until twelve to sixteen days after orders are shipped.  The
objective of this study was to determine where the problems existed and to
develop alternative solutions.

Findings of the Detailed Investigation and Analysis

    The following problems appear to exist within the order entry system:
```

```
Possible Solutions:

1.  Acquire a separate minicomputer system and order entry software.
    Estimated costs:  Minicomputer system, $150,000.  Software license,
    $50,000.  Annual maintenance, $20,000.

2.  Investigate commercial applications software for auto parts order entry
    and invoicing that would run on the corporate computer.  Estimated
    costs:  Software license, $50,000 to $100,000.  Annual software
    maintenance, 10% of license fee.  Equipment (four terminals), $6,000.

3.  Internally develop necessary order entry software to run on corporate
    computer.  Estimated costs:  (1) Systems analysis and design, $26,000;
    (2) Programming and implementation, $40,000; (3) Training, new forms,
    and maintenance, $7,000; (4) Equipment (four terminals), $6,000.

Recommended Action

The systems department recommends alternative 2, the investigation of
existing commercial applications software that could run on the corporate
computer.  If suitable software cannot be found, we recommend the design of
a computerized order entry and invoicing system utilizing alternative 3.

George Lacey
```

FIGURE 11-10
Written reports summarizing the systems analyst's work are an important part of the development project. Two portions of such a report are shown. The top portion shows the report introduction that describes why the investigation of the order entry system was performed. The middle portion of the report (not shown) describes the problems that were found during the investigation. The bottom portion shows three possible solutions and the action recommended by the corporate systems manager.

ANALYSIS AT SUTHERLAND

◆ The Sutherland Company is a large corporation with three separate divisions that sell tools, electric motors, and auto parts. Although the tool and electric motor divisions have been computerized for some time, the auto parts division, started just two years ago, has been small enough that it has relied on manual procedures. In the last six months, however, auto parts sales doubled and the manual order entry and invoicing systems are incapable of keeping up with the increased work load.

Mike Charles, the auto parts sales manager, decides to submit a request for system services to the information systems department that provides computer services for all three Sutherland divisions. George Lacey, the head of the Information Systems department assigns Frank Peacock, a senior systems analyst, to investigate Mike's request.

As part of the preliminary investigation, Frank interviews Mike to try to determine the problem. During his interview with Mike and a subsequent tour of the auto parts sales department, Frank discovers that invoices are not being sent to customers until twelve to sixteen days after their parts orders have shipped. In addition, Frank discovers that customers complain about shipments being late and about not being notified when parts they ordered are not available. To quantify the expected increases in sales volume, Frank has Mike prepare the transaction volume summary shown in Figure 11-11. As a result of his preliminary investigation, Frank recommends a detailed system analysis. George Lacey, the corporate systems manager, agrees with Frank's recommendation and assigns systems analyst Mary Ruiz to perform a detailed analysis.

Transaction Volume Summary

	LAST YEAR	CURRENT	1 YEAR	3 YEARS
Number of Customers	175	300	400	600
Orders per Month	525	950	1250	1900
Invoices per Month	600	1100	1375	2100

FIGURE 11-11
A transaction volume summary should be prepared to estimate the projected growth of an application. Systems should be designed to handle the projected volume of transactions, not just the current volume.

Mary reviews Frank's notes and begins to perform a detailed analysis of the auto parts order entry and invoicing systems. As part of her study, Mary interviews several people in the auto parts division and prepares several documents including a data flow diagram (Figure 11-5), a data dictionary definition for the different credit limits assigned to customers (Figure 11-6), and a structured English statement of the order processing policy (Figure 11-7).

After studying the manual procedures for a week, Mary discusses her findings with her supervisor, George Lacey. Based on Mary's work, George writes a report to the management review committee recommending that the order entry and invoicing systems be computerized (Figure 11-10). The report contains three possible solutions; one, obtain a separate minicomputer system; two, obtain a commercial applications software package to run on the corporate computer; and three, internally develop the necessary software for the corporate computer. Before proceeding to develop the necessary software internally, George recommends that Sutherland try to find a suitable commercial software package that would run on Sutherland's central computer. The management review committee meets every month to review requests for additional computer equipment and software. The committee is made up of top management representatives from each division, the finance department, and the information systems department. Based on George's report, the management review committee authorizes the corporate systems department to try and find a commercial package to satisfy the auto parts division's order entry and invoicing requirements.

ACQUISITION PHASE

◆ Once the analysis phase has been completed, the **acquisition** phase begins; it has four steps: (1) summarizing the application requirements, (2) identifying potential software vendors, (3) evaluating software alternatives, and (4) making the purchase. Before we describe these steps, let's discuss commercial applications software.

What is Commercial Applications Software?

Commercial applications software is software that has already been developed and is available for purchase. Prewritten software is available for computers of all sizes. Most users know about the numerous application packages available for microcomputers. In addition, users should be aware that numerous packages are available for larger machines. This section discusses the categories of commercial applications software that are available, how to determine software requirements, and how to acquire the software. This information is important to know because it is very likely that some day you will either acquire applications software for yourself or participate in software selection for your organization.

It's probably safe to say that at least some part of every type of business, government branch, or recreational pastime has been computerized. Figure 11-12 is an excerpt from a category listing from an applications software catalog. Within each category, numerous programs are available to perform different types of tasks. This catalog contains listings for over 20,000 individual software packages. Notice that this list is divided into two parts: nonindustry specific and industry specific. The more commonly used terms are horizontal and vertical applications.

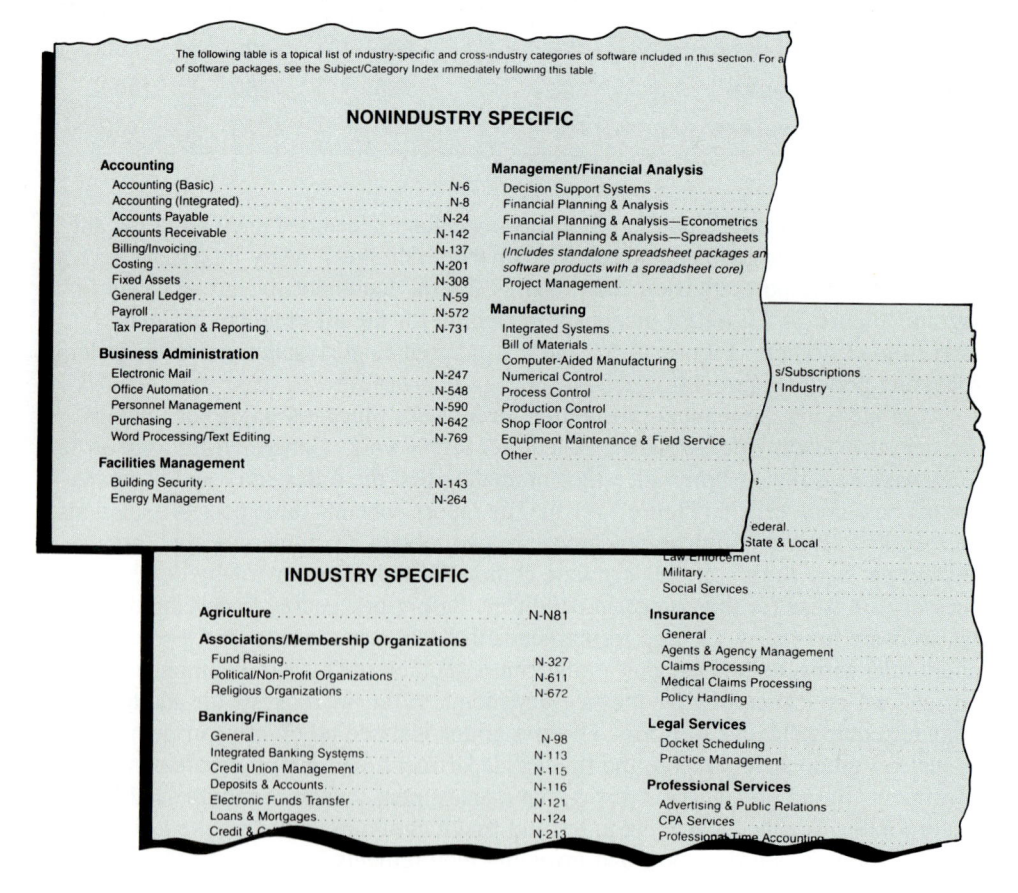

FIGURE 11-12
An excerpt from a category listing in an applications software catalog that contains information on over 20,000 individual software packages.

Horizontal application software is software that can be used by many different types of organizations. Accounting packages are a good example of horizontal applications because they apply to most organizations. If, however, an organization has a unique way of doing business, then it requires a package that has been developed specifically for that job. Software developed for a unique way of doing business, usually within a specific industry, is called **vertical application software**. Examples of specific industries that use vertical software include food service, construction, and real estate. Each of these industries has unique information processing requirements.

The difference between horizontal and vertical application software is important to understand. If you become involved in selecting software, one of the first things you will have to decide is how unique is the task for which you are trying to obtain software. If the task is not unique to your business, you will probably be able to use a horizontal application package. Horizontal application packages tend to be widely available (because they can be used by a greater number of organizations) and less expensive. If your task is unique to your type of organization, you will probably have to search for a vertical software solution. Often an organization's total software requirements are made up of a combination of unique and common requirements.

Now that we understand what commercial applications software is, let's discuss the steps used to acquire it.

FIGURE 11-13
A request for proposal (RFP) documents the key features that a user wants in a software package.

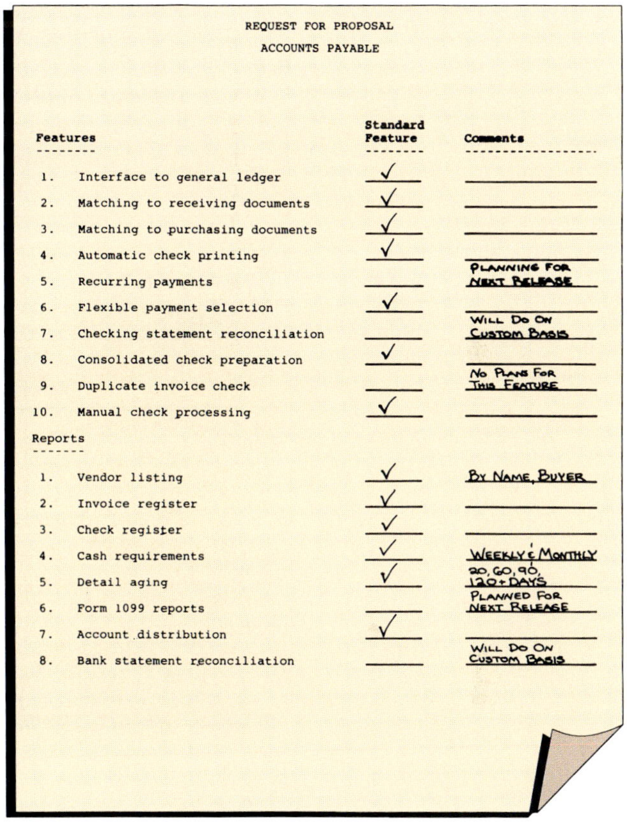
REQUEST FOR PROPOSAL
ACCOUNTS PAYABLE

Features	Standard Feature	Comments
1. Interface to general ledger	✓	
2. Matching to receiving documents	✓	
3. Matching to purchasing documents	✓	
4. Automatic check printing	✓	
5. Recurring payments		PLANNING FOR NEXT RELEASE
6. Flexible payment selection	✓	
7. Checking statement reconciliation		WILL DO ON CUSTOM BASIS
8. Consolidated check preparation	✓	
9. Duplicate invoice check		NO PLANS FOR THIS FEATURE
10. Manual check processing	✓	
Reports		
1. Vendor listing	✓	BY NAME, BUYER
2. Invoice register	✓	
3. Check register	✓	
4. Cash requirements	✓	WEEKLY & MONTHLY
5. Detail aging	✓	20, 60, 90, 120+ DAYS
6. Form 1099 reports		PLANNED FOR NEXT RELEASE
7. Account distribution	✓	
8. Bank statement reconciliation		WILL DO ON CUSTOM BASIS

Summarizing the Application Requirements

One way organizations summarize their software requirements is in a request for proposal. A **request for proposal**, or **RFP**, is a written list of an organization's software requirements. This list is given to prospective software vendors to help the vendors determine if they have a product that is a possible software solution. Just as the depth of application evaluations varies, so do RFPs. RFPs for simple applications might be only a single page consisting of the key features and a transaction volume summary. Other RFPs for large systems might consist of over a hundred pages that identify both key and secondary desired features. An example of a page from an RFP is shown in Figure 11-13.

Identifying Potential Software Vendors

After you have an idea of the software features you want, your next step is to locate potential vendors that sell the type of software you are interested in buying. If the software will be implemented on a personal computer, a good place to start looking for software is a local computer store. Most computer stores have a wide selection of applications software and can suggest several packages for you to consider. If you have prepared an RFP, even a simple one, it will help the store representative to narrow the choices. If you require software for a minicomputer or mainframe, you won't find it at the local personal computer store. For this type of software, which can cost tens to hundreds of thousands of dollars, the best place to start is the computer manufacturer.

In addition to having some software themselves, most manufacturers have a list of software companies with which they work—companies that specialize in developing software for the manufacturer's equipment. **Software houses** are businesses that specialize in developing software for sale. **System houses** not only sell software but also sell the equipment. System houses usually take full responsibility for equipment, software, installation, and training. Sometimes, they even provide equipment maintenance, although this is usually left to the equipment manufacturer. The advantage of dealing with a system house is that the user has to deal with only a single company for the entire system.

Another place to find software suppliers, especially for vertical applications, is to look in trade publications, magazines written for specific businesses or industries. Companies and individuals who have written software for these industries often advertise in the trade publications. Some industry trade groups also maintain lists of companies that provide specific software solutions.

For horizontal applications, many computer magazines publish regular reviews of individual packages and often have annual reviews of several packages of the same type. Figure 11-14 shows a software review of an accounting package.

FIGURE 11-14
Many publications regularly evaluate applications software. This review includes a narrative discussion of the package.

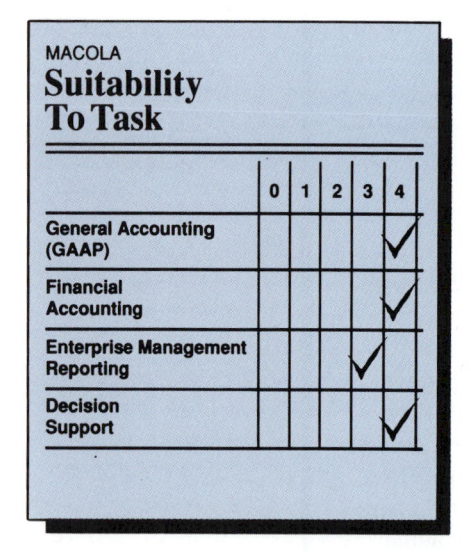

MACOLA Suitability To Task	0	1	2	3	4
General Accounting (GAAP)					✓
Financial Accounting					✓
Enterprise Management Reporting				✓	
Decision Support					✓

PC MAGAZINE FACT FILE — EDITOR'S CHOICE

Macola, Version 4.0
Macola Inc., 333 E. Center St., P.O. Box 485, Marion, OH 43301; (800) 468-0834, (614) 382-5999.
List Price: $795 to $895 per module (for most modules); System Manager: $495 for first 5 users, $995 for each 5-user addition.
Requires: 640K RAM; Novell's *Advanced NetWare/286* 2.0A or later, 3Com's *3+Share*, IBM's *PC LAN*, or most DOS 3.1 standard networks; DOS 3.0 or later.
In Short: A comprehensive, fully integrated, reliable system capable of processing high transaction volumes in both multiuser and standalone environments. A good, easy-to-learn user interface. Source code is available.

Another way to identify software suppliers is to hire a knowledgeable consultant. Although the fee paid to a consultant increases your software costs, it may be worth it, considering the real cost of making a bad decision. Many consultants specialize in assisting organizations of all sizes to identify and implement software packages. A good place to start looking for a consultant would be to contact professional organizations in your industry. Your accountant may also be able to recommend a possible software solution or a consultant.

Evaluating Software Alternatives

After you have identified several possible software solutions, you have to evaluate them and choose one. First, match each choice against your original requirements list. Be as objective as possible—try not to be influenced by the salesperson or representative demonstrating the software or the appeal of the marketing literature. Match each package against your list or RFP and give each package a score. If some key features are more important than others, take that into consideration. Try to complete this rating either during or immediately after a demonstration of the package while the features are still fresh in your mind (Figure 11-15).

The next step is to talk to existing users of the software. For minicomputer and mainframe software packages, software vendors routinely provide user references. User references are important because if a software package does (or doesn't) work for an organization like yours, it probably will (or won't) work for you. For personal computer packages, if the computer store can't provide references, call the software manufacturer directly.

Finally, try the software yourself. For a small application, this may be as simple as entering a few simple transactions using a demonstration copy of the software at the computer store. For large applications, it may require one or more days of testing at the vendor's office or on your existing computer to be sure that the software meets your needs.

If you are concerned about whether the software can handle a certain transaction volume efficiently, you may want to perform a benchmark test. A **benchmark test** measures the time it takes to process a set number of transactions. For example, a benchmark test might consist of measuring the time it takes a particular software package to produce a sales summary report using 1,000 sales transactions. Comparing the time it takes different packages to perform the same task using the same data and the same equipment is one way of measuring the packages' relative performance.

FIGURE 11-15
You should ask to see a demonstration of any program you are considering purchasing. During or after the demonstration, you should rate how well the package meets your requirements.

Making the Purchase

When you purchase software you usually don't own it. What you are actually purchasing is a **software license** (Figure 11-16), the right to use the software under certain terms and conditions. One of the usual terms and conditions of a software license is that you can use the software on a single computer only. In fact, some software is licensed to a specific computer and the serial number of the system is recorded in the license agreement. Other license restrictions include prohibitions against making the software available to others (for example, renting it or leasing it) and modifying or translating the software into another language. These restrictions are designed to protect the rights of the software developer, who doesn't want someone else to benefit unfairly from the developer's work. For personal computer users, software license terms and conditions usually cannot be modified. But for minicomputer and mainframe users, terms of the license agreements can be modified and, therefore, should be carefully reviewed and considered a part of the overall software selection process. Modifications to the software license are generally easier to obtain before the sale is made than after.

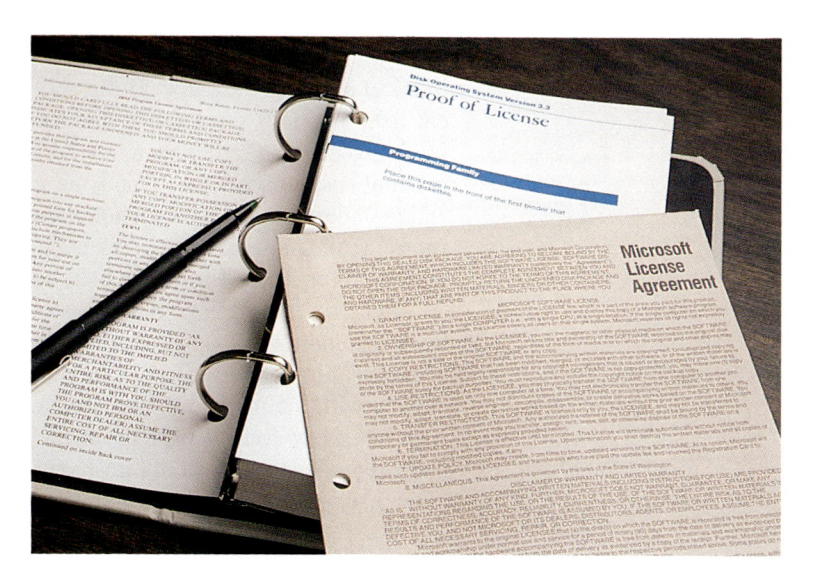

FIGURE 11-16
A software license grants the purchaser the right to use the software but does not include ownership rights.

ACQUISITION AT SUTHERLAND

Based on the directions of the management review committee, a software selection committee is formed with Mike Charles as the chairperson. Mary Ruiz and Frank Peacock from the MIS department are also members as are the order entry and billing supervisors from the auto parts division. Also asked to participate is Bill Comer, computer systems specialist with Sutherland's CPA firm. Mary and Frank take the information developed during the analysis phase and summarize it into a request for proposal (RFP). The RFP is sent to ten software vendors which Bill Comer has identified. Eight of the ten vendors send a response to the RFP within the one month deadline set by Sutherland. Most of the vendors had contacted and visited the auto parts operation to gather information necessary for their responses. Of the eight replies, Sutherland chooses three vendors for further discussions. The committee eliminates five of the vendors because they believe that these systems do not meet the requirements of an auto parts distributor. The software selection committee visits the offices of all three remaining software vendors for a thorough demonstration of their respective packages. In addition, the committee visits a customer of each of the three vendors. The vendor and customer site visits are conducted over a one-month period.

At this point, Sutherland faces a difficult choice. None of the commercial software packages is significantly better than the other and all three have areas that have to be substantially modified to meet Sutherland's way of doing business. The software selection committee summarizes their findings in a report to the management review committee. After discussing the report, the management review committee authorizes the MIS department to begin development of an order entry and invoicing system to run on Sutherland's existing computer system.

COMMERCIAL APPLICATIONS VERSUS CUSTOM SOFTWARE

Each year, the number of applications software packages increases. With all that software available, why would an organization choose to develop its own applications? There could be several reasons. The most common reason is that the organization's software requirements are so unique that it is unable to find a package that will meet its needs. In such a case, the organization would choose to develop the software itself or have it developed specifically for them. Applications software that is developed by the user or at the user's request is called **custom software**. An example of a requirement for custom software might be a government agency that is implementing a new medical assistance service. If the service has new forms and procedures and is different from previous services, it is unlikely that any appropriate software exists. Another reason to develop rather than buy software is that the new software must work with existing custom software. This is an important point to keep in mind; once an organization chooses to use custom software, it will usually choose custom software for future applications as well. This is because it is often difficult to make custom software work with purchased software. The following example illustrates this point.

Let's say a company that has previously developed a custom inventory control software system now wants to computerize their order entry function. Order entry software packages allow the user to sell merchandise from stock and, therefore, must work closely with the inventory files. In fact, many order entry systems are sold together with inventory control systems. If the company wants to retain its existing inventory control application, it would probably have a hard time finding a commercial order entry package that would be able to work with its custom inventory files. This is because the software and the file structures used in the commercial package will not be the same as the existing software. For this reason, the company would probably decide to develop a custom order entry application.

Both custom and commercial software have their advantages and disadvantages. The advantage of custom software is that if it is correctly done, it will match an organization's exact requirements. The disadvantages of custom software are that it is one of a kind, difficult to change, often poorly documented, and usually more expensive than commercial software. In addition, custom software projects are often difficult to manage and complete on time.

The advantage of commercial software is that it's ready to install immediately. After sufficient training, usually provided by the vendor who developed or sold the software, people can begin using the software for productive work. The disadvantage of commercial software is that an organization will probably have to change some of its methods and procedures to adapt to the way the commercial software functions.

A good guideline for evaluating your need for custom or commercial software is to look for a package with an 80% or better fit with your requirements. If there is less than an 80% fit, an organization should either consider custom software or reevaluate its requirements. Figure 11-17 shows the most likely software solutions for different application requirements.

FIGURE 11-17
Software guidelines for different types of applications.

APPLICATION CHARACTERISTICS	APPLICATION EXAMPLE	MOST LIKELY SOFTWARE SOLUTION
Applicable to many different types or organizations	Accounts receivable	Horizontal application package
Specific to a particular type of business or organization	Hotel room reservations	Vertical application package
Unique to a specific organization or business	Space shuttle launch program	Custom software

CUSTOMIZING PHASE

Ideally, acquired commercial applications software will meet 80% or more of an organization's requirements. But what about the other 20% or so? For these requirements, the organization has two choices: change their way of doing business to match the way the software works or modify the way the software works to match their organization. Usually, they will choose a combination of the two alternatives.

Modifying a commercial application package is usually referred to as **customizing**, or **tailoring**. The process of customizing a commercial package involves the following four steps:

1. Identifying potential modifications.
2. Determining the impact of changing current operations to match the software and thus avoiding making a modification.
3. Specifying the amount of work required to make the modifications and the corresponding cost.
4. Choosing which modifications will be made. If possible, the modifications should be made prior to the system being implemented. This avoids users having to relearn how the system works.

Some software vendors do not recommend or support modifications to their packages. Other vendors facilitate modifications by providing copies of the programs or by doing the modifications themselves, usually for a fee. Generally speaking, the larger and more expensive the application package, the more likely that modifications will be required and will be permitted.

CUSTOMIZING AT SUTHERLAND

◆ Because the software selection committee does not choose a commercial applications software package, the customizing phase does not take place at Sutherland.

DESIGN PHASE

◆ The proposed solution developed as part of the analysis phase usually consists of what is called a **logical design**, which means that the design was deliberately developed without regard to a specific computer or programming language and that no attempt was made to identify which procedures should be automated and which procedures should be manual. This approach avoids early assumptions that might limit the possible solutions.

During the **design** phase the logical design will be transformed into a **physical design** that will identify the procedures to be automated, choose the programming language, and specify the equipment needed for the system.

Structured Design Methods

The system design usually follows one of two methods, top-down design or bottom-up design.

Top-Down Design Top-down design, also called **structured design**, focuses on the major functions of the system, such as recording a sale or generating an invoice, and keeps breaking those functions down into smaller and smaller activities, sometimes called modules, that can eventually be programmed. Top-down design is an increasingly popular method because it focuses on the total requirements and helps users and systems analysts reach an early agreement on what the major functions of the new system are.

Bottom-Up Design Bottom-up design focuses on the data, particularly the output of the system. The approach used determines what output is needed and moves *up* to the processes needed to produce the output.

In practice, most systems analysts use a combination of the top-down and bottom-up designs. Some information requirements such as payroll checks, for example, have required data elements that lend themselves to bottom-up design. Other requirements, such as management-oriented exception reports that are based on the needs of a particular user, are better suited to a top-down design. Regardless of the structured design method he or she uses, the systems analyst will eventually need to complete the design activities.

Design Activities

Design activities include individual tasks that a systems analyst performs to design an information system. These include designs for the output, input, database, processes, system controls, and testing.

Output Design The design of the output is critical to the successful implementation of the system. Output provides information to the users, and information is the basis for the justification of most computerized systems. For example, most users don't know (or necessarily care) how the data will be processed, but they usually do have clear ideas on how they want the information output to look. Often, requests for new or modified systems begin with a user-prepared draft of a report that the current system doesn't produce. During **output design**, the systems analyst and the user document specific screen and report layouts for output to display or report information from the new system. The example in Figure 11-18 illustrates a report layout form.

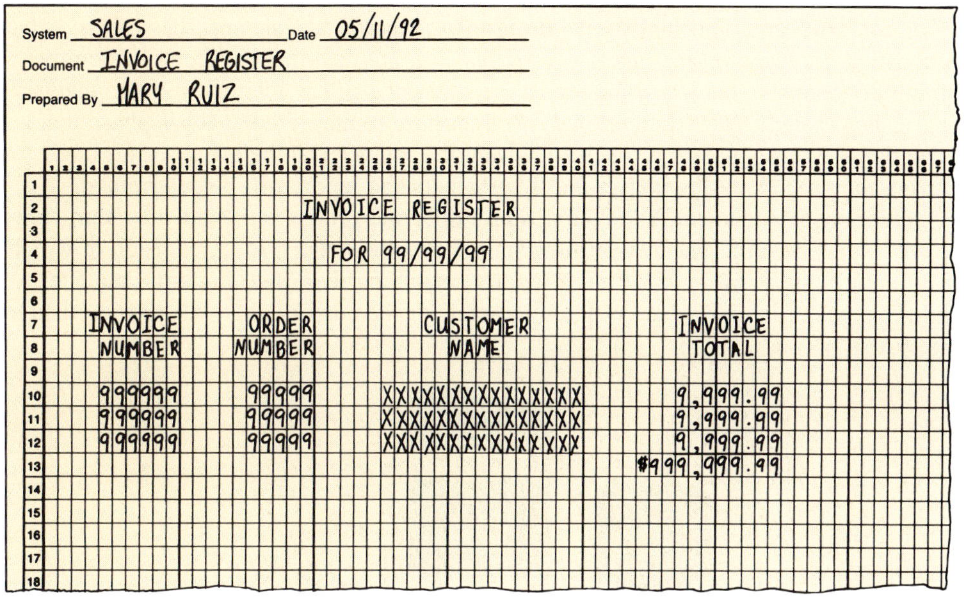

FIGURE 11-18
The report layout form is used to design printed output. Column titles, data width, and report totals are shown on the layout form.

Input Design During **input design** the systems analyst and the user identify what information needs to be entered into the system to produce the desired output, and where and how the data will be entered. With interactive systems, the systems analyst and the user must determine the sequence of inputs and computer responses, called a **dialogue**, that the user will encounter when he or she enters data. Figure 11-19 shows a display screen layout form commonly used to document the format of a screen display.

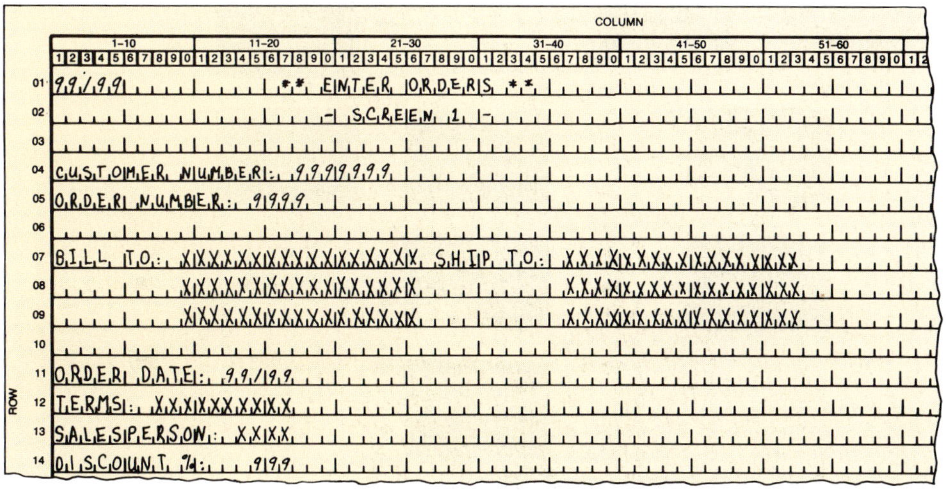

FIGURE 11-19
The display screen layout sheet is similar to the report layout form but is used only for information that will be displayed on a screen. Each row and column corresponds to a row and column on the screen.

Database Design During **database design** the systems analyst uses the data dictionary information developed during the analysis phase and merges it into new or existing system files. During this phase of the design, the systems analyst works closely with the database administrator to identify existing database elements that can be used to satisfy design requirements.

Efficient file design can be a challenging task, especially with relational database systems that stress minimum data redundancy (duplicate data). The systems analyst must also consider the volume of database activity. For example, large files that will be frequently accessed may need a separate index file to allow inquiries to be processed in an amount of time acceptable to the user.

Process Design During **process design**, the systems analyst specifies exactly what actions will be taken on the input data to create output information. Decisions on the timing of actions are added to the logical processes he or she identified in the analysis phase. For example, the systems analyst might have found in the analysis phase that an exception report should be produced if inventory balances fall below a certain level. During the process design phase, the frequency of the report will be determined.

One way to document the relationship of different processes is with a **system flowchart** (Figure 11-20). The system flowchart shows the major processes (each of which may require one or more programs), reports (including their distribution), data files, and the types of input devices such as terminals or tape drives, that will provide data to the system.

FIGURE 11-20
The system flowchart documents the equipment used to enter data, such as the terminals for the salespeople and the order department, the processes that will take place, such as the Verify Customer process, the files that will be used, such as the Parts and Customer files, and the reports that will be produced, such as the Shipping Order. Dotted lines indicate additional copies of reports, such as the copy of the Invoice that is sent to the accounts receivable department.

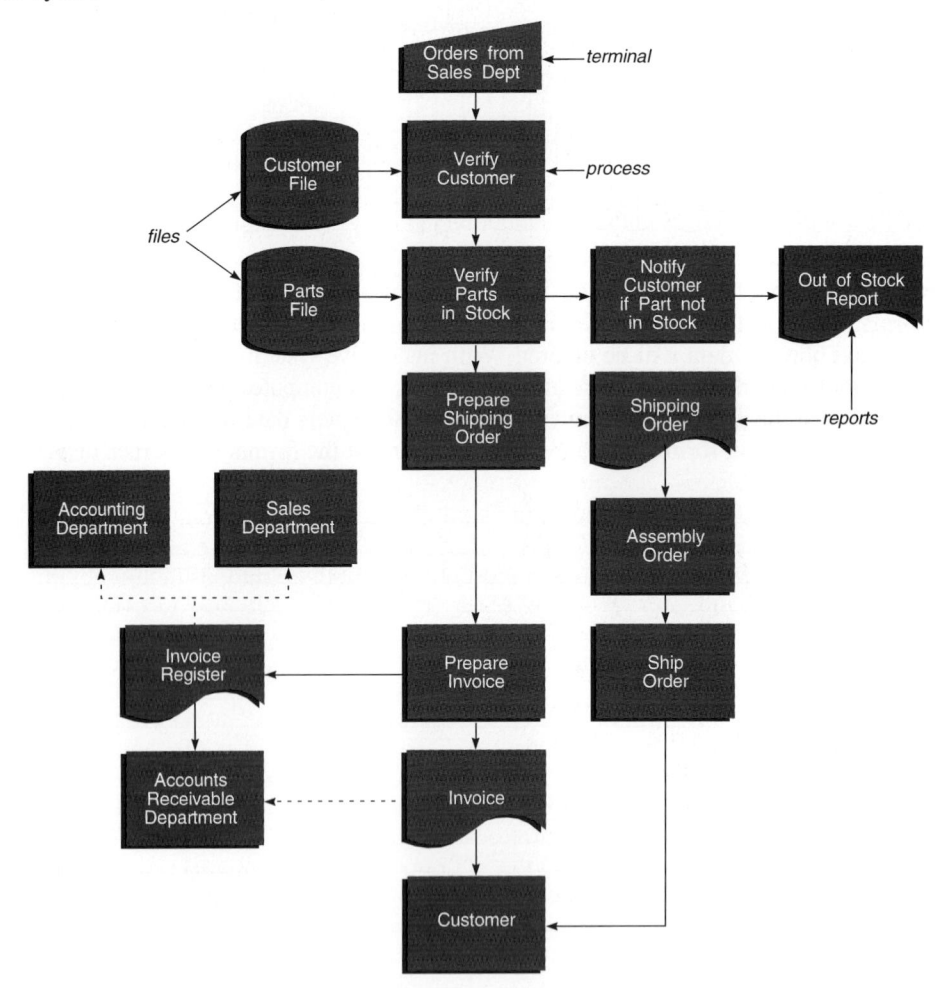

The special symbols used in a system flowchart are shown in Figure 11-21.

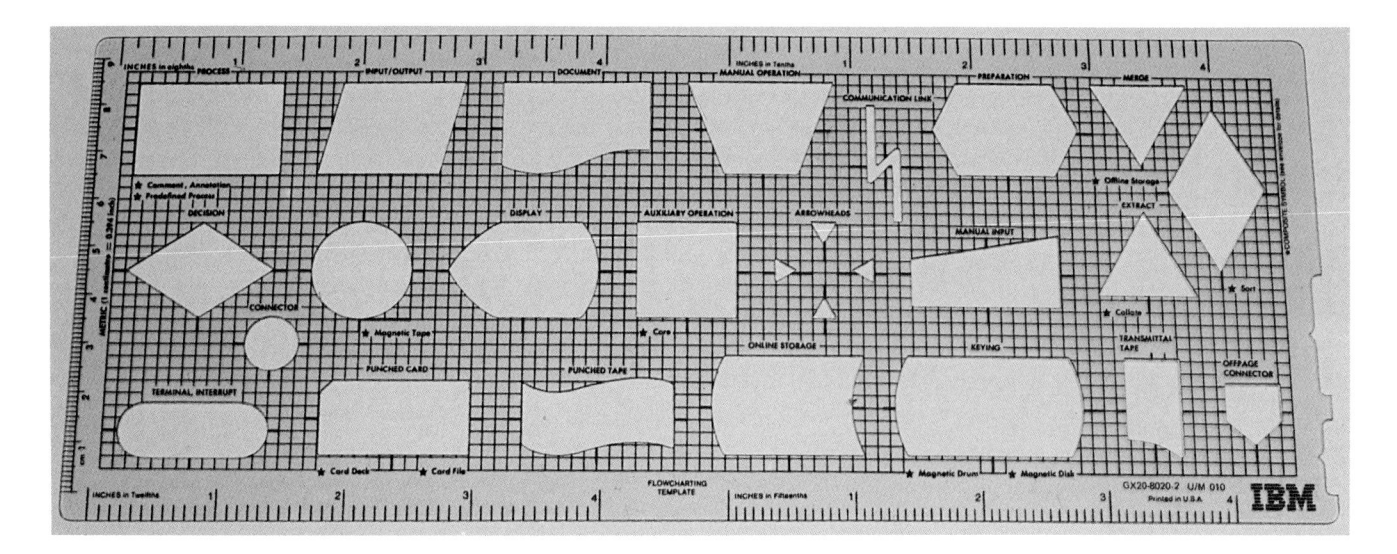

FIGURE 11-21
Symbols used for preparing a system flowchart.

During process design the systems analyst, the user, and the other members of the development project sometimes meet to conduct a **structured walk-through**, a step-by-step review of the process design. The purpose of these sessions is to identify any design logic errors and to continue the communication between the systems analyst and the user.

System Controls An important aspect of the design phase is the establishment of a comprehensive set of system controls. **System controls** ensure that only valid data is accepted and processed. Adequate controls must be established for two reasons: (1) to ensure the accuracy of the processing and the information generated from the system, and (2) to prevent computer-related fraud.

There are four types of controls that must be considered by the systems analyst. These controls are: (1) source document controls, (2) input controls, (3) processing controls, and (4) accounting controls.

1. **Source document controls** include serial numbering of input documents such as invoices and paychecks, document registers in which each input document is recorded and time-stamped as it is received, and batch totaling and balancing to predetermined totals to assure the accuracy of processing.

2. **Input controls** are established to assure the complete and accurate conversion of data from the source documents or other sources to a machine-processable form. Editing data as it enters the system is the most important form of input controls.

3. **Processing controls** refer to procedures that are established to determine the accuracy of information after it has been input to the system. For example, the accuracy of the total accounts receivable could be verified by taking the prior day's total, adding the current day's sales invoices, and subtracting the current day's payments.

4. **Accounting controls** provide assurance that the dollar amounts recorded in the accounting records are correct. One type of accounting control is making sure that detail reports are created to support the summary reports used to make entries in an organization's financial system. For example, many companies record sales by product line based on a summary report showing product line totals. In addition to this summary report, a detail report showing individual product sales should also be prepared and agreed to the summary report.

Testing Design During the design phase, test specifications are developed. The exact tests to be performed should be specified by someone other than the user or the systems analyst, although both should be consulted. Users and systems analysts have a tendency to test only what has been designed. An impartial third party, who has not been actively involved in the design, is more likely to design a test for, and therefore discover, a procedure or type of data that may have been overlooked in the design. Sometimes organizations avoid test design and test their systems with actual transactions. While such *live* testing is valuable, it might not test all conditions that the system is designed to process. This is especially true of error or exception conditions that do not occur regularly. For example, payroll systems are usually designed to reject input for hours worked over some limit, say 60 hours in a week. If only actual data are used to test the system, this limit may not be tested. Thus, it is important to design testing specifications that will test each system control that is part of the system by using both valid and invalid data.

Design Review

At the end of the design phase, management performs a **design review** and evaluates the work completed so far to determine whether to proceed (Figure 11-22). This is a critical point in any development project and all parties must take equal responsibility for the decision.

FIGURE 11-22
The design review is a critical point in the development process. Representatives from the user and information systems departments and top management meet to determine if the system should be developed as designed or if additional design work is necessary.

Usually, the design review will result only in requests for clarification of a few items. But sometimes an entire project will be terminated. Although canceling or restarting a project from the beginning is a difficult decision, in the long run it is less costly than implementing the wrong or an inadequate solution. If management decides to proceed, the project enters the development phase.

Before discussing the development phase, we describe prototyping, a development method that can be used in several phases of a system development project, and computer-aided software engineering, an automated approach to system design.

Prototyping

Prototyping is building a working model of the new system. The advantage of prototyping is that it lets the user actually experience the system before it is completed. Some organizations use prototyping during the analysis phase, others use it during the design phase. Still other companies use prototyping to go directly from the preliminary investigation to an implemented system. These companies just keep refining the prototype until the user says that it is acceptable. A disadvantage of such an accelerated approach is that key features of a new system, especially exception conditions, may be overlooked. Another disadvantage is that documentation, an important part of any system development effort, is usually not as well or as thoroughly prepared. Used as a tool to show the user how the system will operate, prototyping can be an important system development tool.

Computer-Aided Software Engineering (CASE)

Many organizations are now using computer software specifically developed to aid the information system life cycle process. **Computer-aided software engineering (CASE)** refers to the use of automated computer-based tools to design and manage a software system (Figure 11-23). Sometimes these tools, such as a data dictionary, exist separately. Other CASE vendors have combined several tools into an integrated package referred to as a **CASE workbench**. CASE workbench tools might include:

- *Analysis and design tools* such as data dictionaries, decision tables, or data flow diagram builders
- *Prototyping tools* that can be used to create models of the proposed system
- *Code generators* that create actual computer programs
- An *information repository* that cross references and organizes all information about a system
- *Management tools* that assist in the management of a systems project

In addition to the benefits of increased productivity, CASE tools promote the completion of the design work before development begins. Starting the development work before the design is completed often results in work that has to be redone.

FIGURE 11-23
Computer-aided software engineering (CASE) packages help users design complex systems. Excelerator by Index Technologies allows users to create and revise data flow diagrams, data dictionary elements, screens, reports, and process specifications.

DESIGN AT SUTHERLAND

◆ Upon approval by the management review committee, Mary Ruiz begins designing the order entry and invoicing system. After she studies existing manually prepared documents and talks to users, Mary designs printed reports and screen displays. According to Mike Charles, one of the most important reports is the daily invoice register. Using a report layout form (Figure 11-18), Mary shows Mike how the report will look after it is programmed. Using a similar form for screen displays (Figure 11-19), Mary also shows Mike what the order clerks will see when they enter auto parts orders. To graphically show how the overall system will work, Mary prepares a system flowchart (Figure 11-20). The system flowchart shows that auto parts orders will be entered on terminals in the sales department and will use data in the Parts and Customer files to verify that the orders are valid. Shipping orders and invoices are two of the reports produced. An important part of Mary's design time involves specifying the system controls used during processing. These controls include verifying the customer number before processing the order and checking to see if the ordered part is in stock. If the ordered part is not in stock, the customer is notified immediately.

After completing her design work, Mary meets with representatives from the user and information systems departments and top management to review her design. After Mary explains the design, the committee agrees to develop the system.

DEVELOPMENT PHASE

◆ Once the system design phase has been completed, the project enters the system development phase. There are two parts to **development**: program development and equipment acquisition.

Program Development

The process of developing the software, or programs, required for a system is called **program development** and includes the following steps: (1) reviewing the program specifications, (2) designing the program, (3) coding the program, (4) testing the program; and (5) finalizing the program documentation. The primary responsibility for completing these tasks is assumed by computer programmers who work closely with the systems analyst who designed the system. Chapter 12 explains program development in depth. The important concepts to understand now are that this process is a part of the development phase of the information system life cycle and that its purpose is to develop the software required by the system.

Equipment Acquisition

During the development phase, final decisions will be made on what additional equipment, if any, will be required for the new system. A preliminary review of the equipment requirements would have been done during the analysis phase and included in the written report prepared by the systems analyst. Making the equipment acquisition prior to the development phase would be premature because any equipment selected should be based on the requirements specified in the design phase. Equipment selection is affected by factors such as the number of users who will require terminals and the disk storage that will be required for new files and data elements. In some cases, even a new or upgraded CPU is required. If an organization chose to acquire a commercial software package instead of developing software, the equipment acquisition would take place during the acquisition phase.

DEVELOPMENT AT SUTHERLAND

◆ During the development phase, Mary works closely with the two programmers who are assigned to the project. She regularly meets with the programmers to answer questions about the design and to check on the progress of their work. Prior to starting the programming, Mary arranges for the programmers to meet with the auto parts sales employees so that the programmers will have a better understanding of the purpose of the new system.

When the programming is nearly completed, Mary arranges for the terminals to be installed in the sales department.

IMPLEMENTATION PHASE

◆ **Implementation** is the phase of the system development process when people actually begin using the new system. This is a critical phase of the project that usually requires careful timing and the coordination of all the project participants. Important parts of this phase that will contribute to the success of the new system are training and education, conversion, and post-implementation evaluation.

Training and Education

Someone once said, "If you think education is expensive, you should consider the cost without it." The point is that untrained users can prevent the estimated benefits of a new system from ever being obtained or, worse, contribute to less efficiency and more costs than when the old system was operational. Training consists of showing people exactly how they will use the new system (Figure 11-24). This might include classroom-style lectures, but should definitely include hands-on sessions with the equipment they will be using, such as terminals, and realistic sample data. Education consists of learning new principles or theories that help people to understand and use the system. For example, before implementing a modern manufacturing system, many companies now require their manufacturing personnel to attend classes on material requirements planning (MRP), shop floor control, and other essential manufacturing topics.

Conversion

Conversion refers to the process of changing from the old system to the new system. A number of different methods of conversion can be used including direct, parallel, phased, and pilot.

With **direct conversion**, the user stops using the old system one day and begins using the new system the next. The advantage of this approach is that it is fast and efficient. The disadvantage is that it is risky and can seriously disrupt operations if the new system does not work correctly the first time.

Parallel conversion consists of continuing to process data on the old system while some or all of the data is also processed on the new system. Results from both systems are compared, and if they agree, all data is switched to the new system (Figure 11-25).

Phased conversion is used with larger systems that can be broken down into individual modules that can be implemented separately at different times. An example would be a complete business system that could have the accounts receivable, inventory, and accounts payable modules implemented separately in phases. Phased conversions can be direct, parallel, or a combination of both.

Pilot conversion means that the new system will be used first by only a portion of the organization, often at a separate location such as a plant or office.

FIGURE 11-24
All users should be trained on the system before they have to use it to process actual transactions. Training could include both classroom and hands-on sessions.

Post-Implementation Evaluation

After a system is implemented, it is important to conduct a **post-implementation evaluation** to determine if the system is performing as designed, if operating costs are as anticipated, and if any modifications are necessary to make the system operate more effectively.

FIGURE 11-25
During parallel conversion, the user compares results from both the old and the new systems to determine if the new systems is operating properly.

IMPLEMENTATION AT SUTHERLAND

◆ Before they begin to use the new system to enter real transactions, the users participate in several training sessions about the equipment and the software. Because this is the first application in the auto parts division to be computerized, Mary begins the training sessions with an overview of how the central computer system processes data.

She conducts a basic data entry class to teach the employees how to use the terminals (Figure 11-24).

Before the system can be used, the Parts and Customer files have to be created from existing manual records. Temporary employees trained in data entry skills are hired for this task. Their work is carefully reviewed each day by Mike Charles and other permanent department employees.

Although he knows it means extra work, Mike decides that a parallel conversion is the safest way to implement the new system. Using this method, Mike verifies the results of the new system with those of the existing manual system. Actual use of the system begins on the first business day of the month so that transaction totals can be balanced to accounting reports.

Because they are thoroughly trained, the order clerks feel comfortable when they begin entering real orders. They encounter a few minor problems, such as orders for special parts not on the Parts file. These problems become less frequent and at the end of the month, after Mike compares the manual and computerized report totals, he decides to discontinue the use of the manual system.

During the post-implementation review, Mike and Mary discover that nine out of ten customer orders are now shipped the same day as the order is received. Before the new system was implemented, less than half the orders were shipped within two days of receipt. Invoices, which once lagged twelve to sixteen days behind shipments, are now mailed on the same day. Perhaps the most positive benefit of the new system is that customer complaints about order processing are practically eliminated.

MAINTENANCE PHASE

Maintenance is the process of supporting the system after it is implemented. Maintenance consists of three activities: performance monitoring, change management, and error correction.

Performance Monitoring

Performance monitoring is the ongoing process of comparing response times, file sizes, and other system performance measures against the estimates that were prepared during the analysis, design, and implementation phases. Variances from these estimates may indicate that the system requires additional equipment resources, such as more memory or faster disk drives.

Change Management

Change is an inevitable part of any system; thus, all users of the system should be familiar with methods and procedures that provide for change. Sometimes, changes are required because existing requirements were overlooked. Other times, new information requirements caused by external sources such as government regulations will force change. A key part of change management is documentation. The same documentation standards that were followed during the analysis and design phases should also be used to record changes. In fact, in many organizations, the same document that is used to request new systems (Figure 11-3) is used to request changes to an existing system (Figure 11-26). Thus, the information system development cycle continues as the analysis phase begins on the change request.

Error Correction

Error correction deals with problems that are caused by programming and design errors that are discovered after the system is implemented. Often these errors are minor problems, such as the ZIP code not appearing on a name and address report, that can be quickly fixed by a programmer. Other times, however, the error requires more serious investigation by the systems analyst before a correction can be determined. Design errors that are not found until after a system is implemented are much more expensive to correct than had they been found earlier.

MAINTENANCE AT SUTHERLAND

◆ During the months following the system implementation, users discover a number of minor errors in the system. The programming staff quickly corrects most of these errors, but in one case involving special credit terms for a large customer, Mary Ruiz becomes involved and prepares specifications for the necessary program changes.

Approximately one year after Mike Charles submits his original request for a computerized order entry and invoicing system, he submits another request (Figure 11-26) for a change to the system to provide for a new county sales tax. This type of request does not require a preliminary investigation and is assigned to Mary Ruiz as soon as she is available. Mike submits his request five months before the tax is scheduled to go into effect, which allows ample time for the necessary program changes to be implemented.

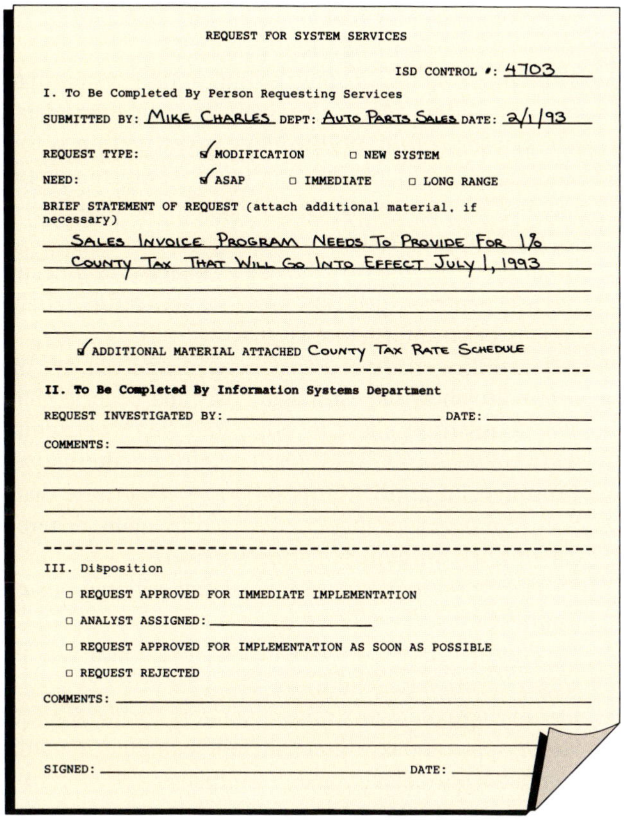

FIGURE 11-26
The same form used to request a new system (Figure 11-3) is also used to request a modification to an existing system.

SUMMARY OF THE INFORMATION SYSTEM LIFE CYCLE

◆ Although the information system development process may appear to be a straightforward series of steps, in practice it is a challenging activity that calls for the skills and cooperation of all involved. New development tools have made the process more efficient but the success of any project always depends on the commitment of the project participants. The understanding you have gained from this chapter will help you participate in information system development projects and give you an appreciation for the importance of each phase.

CHAPTER SUMMARY

1. The **information system life cycle (ISLC)** is an organized approach to obtaining an information system.
2. Planning, scheduling, reporting, and controlling the individual activities that make up the information system development life cycle is called **project management**. These activities are usually recorded in a **project plan**.
3. **Documentation** refers to written materials that are produced throughout the information system development life cycle.

4. All users and information system personnel who will be affected by the new system should have the opportunity to participate in its development.
5. The **analysis** phase is the separation of a system into its parts in order to determine how the system works. This phase consists of the preliminary investigation, detailed system analysis, and making the decision to proceed.
6. The purpose of the **preliminary investigation** is to determine if a request warrants further detailed investigation. The most important aspect of this investigation is **problem definition**.
7. **Detailed system analysis** involves both a thorough study of the current system and at least one proposed solution to any problems found.
8. **Structured analysis** is the use of analysis and design tools such as **data flow diagrams (DFDs)**, **data dictionaries**, **process specifications**, **structured English**, **decision tables**, and **decision trees** to document the specifications of an information system.
9. A **feasibility study** and **cost/benefit analysis** are often prepared to show whether the proposed solution is practical and to show the estimated costs and benefits that are expected.
10. The **acquisition** phase involves four steps: (1) summarizing application requirements, (2) identifying potential software vendors, (3) evaluating software alternatives, and (4) making the purchase.
11. **Commercial applications software** is software that has already been developed and is available for purchase.
12. Software packages that can be used by many different types of organizations, such as accounting packages, are called **horizontal application software**.
13. Software developed for a unique way of doing business, usually within a specific industry, is called **vertical application software**.
14. A **request for proposal (RFP)** is a written list of an organization's software requirements that is given to prospective software vendors.
15. Identifying potential software vendors for personal computers can usually be done at a local computer store. For larger applications sources include computer manufacturers, **software houses**, **system houses**, trade publications, computer periodicals, and consultants.
16. To evaluate software alternatives, match the features of each possible solution against the original requirements list or RFP.
17. A **benchmark test** involves measuring the time it takes to process a set number of transactions.
18. A **software license** is the right to use software under certain terms and conditions.
19. Application software that is developed by a user or at the user's request is called **custom software**.
20. Modifying a commercial applications package is usually referred to as **customizing** or **tailoring**.
21. During the **design** phase the **logical design** that was created in the analysis phase is transformed into a **physical design**.
22. There are two major structured design methods: **top-down design** (or **structured design**) and **bottom-up design**.
23. **Output design**, **input design**, and **database design** all occur during the design phase.
24. A **dialogue** is the sequence of inputs and computer responses that a user will encounter when he or she enters data on an interactive system.
25. During the **process design**, the systems analyst specifies exactly what actions will be taken on the input data to create output information.
26. One method of documenting the relationship of different processes is with a **system flowchart**.
27. A **structured walk-through**, or a step-by-step review, is sometimes performed on the process design.
28. **System controls** are established to (1) ensure that only valid data is accepted and processed and (2) to prevent computer-related fraud. Types of system controls include **source document controls**, **input controls**, **processing controls**, and **accounting controls**.
29. At the end of the design phase, a **design review** is performed to evaluate the work completed so far.
30. **Prototyping** is building a working model of the new system.
31. **Computer-aided software engineering (CASE)** refers to the use of automated computer based tools to design and manage a software system.
32. A **CASE workbench** provides several CASE tools in an integrated package. These tools might include analysis and design tools, prototyping tools, code generators, information repository, and management tools.
33. The **development** phase consists of program development and equipment acquisition.
34. **Program development** includes: (1) reviewing the program specifications, (2) designing the program, (3) coding the program, (4) testing the program, and (5) finalizing the program documentation.
35. The **implementation** phase is when people actually begin using the new system. This phase includes training and education, conversion, and the **post-implementation evaluation**.

36. The process of changing from the old system to the new system is called a **conversion**. The conversion methods that may be used are **direct**, **parallel**, **phased**, and **pilot**.
37. The **maintenance** phase is the process of supporting the information system after it is implemented. It consists of three activities: **performance monitoring**, change management, and error correction.

KEY TERMS

Accounting controls *11.19*
Acquisition *11.10*
Analysis *11.4*
Benchmark test *11.13*
Bottom-up design *11.16*
CASE workbench *11.21*
Commercial applications software *11.10*
Computer-aided software engineering (CASE) *11.21*
Conversion *11.23*
Cost/benefit analysis *11.8*
Custom software *11.14*
Customizing *11.15*
Database design *11.18*
Data dictionary *11.6*
Data flow diagram (DFD) *11.5*
Decision table *11.7*
Decision tree *11.7*
Design *11.16*
Design review *11.20*
Detailed system analysis *11.5*
Development *11.21*

Dialogue *11.17*
Direct conversion *11.23*
Documentation *11.3*
Feasibility study *11.8*
Horizontal application software *11.11*
Implementation *11.22*
Information system life cycle (ISLC) *11.2*
Input controls *11.19*
Input design *11.17*
Logical design *11.16*
Maintenance *11.24*
Output design *11.17*
Parallel conversion *11.23*
Performance monitoring *11.24*
Phased conversion *11.23*
Physical design *11.16*
Pilot conversion *11.23*
Post-implementation evaluation *11.23*
Preliminary investigation *11.4*

Problem definition *11.4*
Process design *11.18*
Processing controls *11.19*
Process specification *11.7*
Program development *11.22*
Project management *11.2*
Project plan *11.2*
Prototyping *11.20*
Request for proposal (RFP) *11.11*
Software house *11.12*
Software license *11.13*
Source document controls *11.19*
Structured analysis *11.5*
Structured design *11.16*
Structured English *11.7*
Structured walk-through *11.19*
System controls *11.19*
System flowchart *11.18*
System house *11.12*
Tailoring *11.15*
Top-down design *11.16*
Vertical application software *11.11*

REVIEW QUESTIONS

1. Draw a diagram showing the phases of the information system life cycle.
2. Describe project management and when it should be performed.
3. What is the preliminary investigation? What is the most important aspect of the preliminary investigation?
4. Briefly describe detailed system analysis. What are the fact-finding techniques used during detailed system analysis?
5. What is commercial applications software? Explain the difference between horizontal and vertical applications.
6. Describe the information that an RFP should contain and how the RFP is used.
7. What is custom software and why is it appropriate for some applications?
8. Describe several things that a user can do to evaluate a software package before purchasing it. What is a benchmark test?
9. What is a software license? Describe some of the terms and conditions that are included in a software license.
10. What are the symbols used in data flow diagrams? Why are data flow diagrams useful?
11. Explain the difference between the logical and physical design of an information system.
12. What are the two methods of structured design? Briefly describe each method.
13. What is prototyping?
14. Write a description of the four types of conversion methods.
15. Describe the three major activities of system maintenance.

CONTROVERSIAL ISSUES

1. Some organizations claim that consultants have saved them considerable sums of money when acquiring applications software. Others say that they would have been better off not using a consultant. What role, if any, do you feel a consultant should play in helping an organization to select applications software?
2. "The difficulty in developing and implementing an information processing system is the user," proclaimed a systems analyst. "Users never know what they want. When they are shown what the system will do, they give their approval, but when the system is implemented they are never happy. They always want changes. It's impossible to satisfy them." How do you feel about these comments? Are the systems analyst's comments about users correct?

RESEARCH PROJECTS

1. Use the yellow pages, computer magazines or newspapers, or computer store references to locate a computer consultant. Interview the consultant over the phone or in person and ask him or her how he or she helps a user choose a computer system. Prepare a report for your class.
2. Prepare a data flow diagram of how you registered for class. Document your work by obtaining copies of any forms that you used during the registration process.

Program Development

CHAPTER 12 PROGRAMS

OBJECTIVES

◆ Define the term computer program
◆ Describe the five steps in program development: review of program specifications, program design, program coding, program testing, and finalizing program documentation
◆ Explain the concepts of structured program design including modules, control structures, and single entry/ single exit
◆ Explain and illustrate the sequence, selection, and iteration control structures used in structured programming
◆ Define the term programming language and discuss the various categories of programming languages
◆ Briefly discuss the programming languages that are commonly used today, including BASIC, COBOL, C, FORTRAN, Pascal, and Ada
◆ Explain and discuss application generators
◆ Explain and discuss object-oriented programming
◆ Explain the factors that should be considered when choosing a programming language

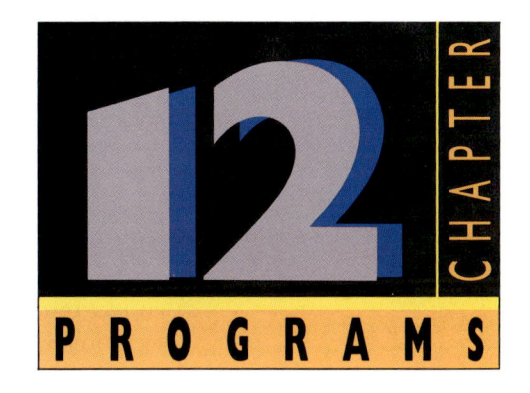

The information system life cycle covers the entire process of taking a plan for processing information through various phases until it becomes a functioning information system. During the development phase of this cycle, computer programs are written. The purpose of these programs is to process data and produce information as specified in the information system design. In this chapter we focus on the steps taken to write a program and the available tools that make the program development process more efficient. Also in this chapter we discuss the different languages used to write programs.

Although you may never write a program yourself, you might someday request information that will require a program to be written or modified; thus, you should understand how a computer program is developed.

WHAT IS A COMPUTER PROGRAM?

A **computer program** is a detailed set of instructions that directs a computer to perform the tasks necessary to process data into information. These instructions, usually written by a computer programmer, can be coded (written) in a variety of programming languages that we discuss later in this chapter. To create programs that are correct (produce accurate information) and maintainable (easy to modify), programmers follow a process called program development.

WHAT IS PROGRAM DEVELOPMENT?

Program development is the process of producing one or more programs to perform specific tasks on a computer. The process of program development has evolved into a series of five steps that most experts agree should take place when any program is developed (Figure 12-1).

FIGURE 12-1
The five steps of program development. Although the process steps are shown sequentially, program development usually requires returning to previous steps to correct errors.

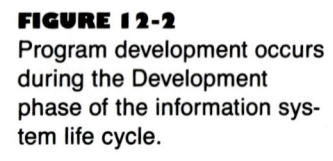

Review Specifications → Design → Code → Test → Finalize Documentation

1. *Review of program specifications.* The programmer reviews the specifications created by the systems analyst during the system design phase.
2. *Program design.* The programmer determines and documents the specific actions the computer will take to accomplish the desired tasks.
3. *Coding.* The programmer writes the actual program instructions.
4. *Testing.* The written programs are tested to make sure they perform as intended.
5. *Finalizing documentation.* Throughout the program development process the programmer documents, or writes, explanatory information about the program. In this final step the documentation produced during steps 1 through 4 is brought together and organized.

Although we list these five steps sequentially, the program development process usually requires returning to previous steps to correct errors that are discovered.

FIGURE 12-2
Program development occurs during the Development phase of the information system life cycle.

To help you to better understand how the steps in the program development process relate to the overall development of an information system, let's review the phases of the information system life cycle. As you can see in Figure 12-2, program development is a phase on the development path of the information system life cycle. If, after the analysis phase, an organization is unable to acquire commercial software that meets its needs, it moves or it proceeds to the design phase. The development phase, which refers to program development, follows the design phase and includes the five steps shown in Figure 12-1.

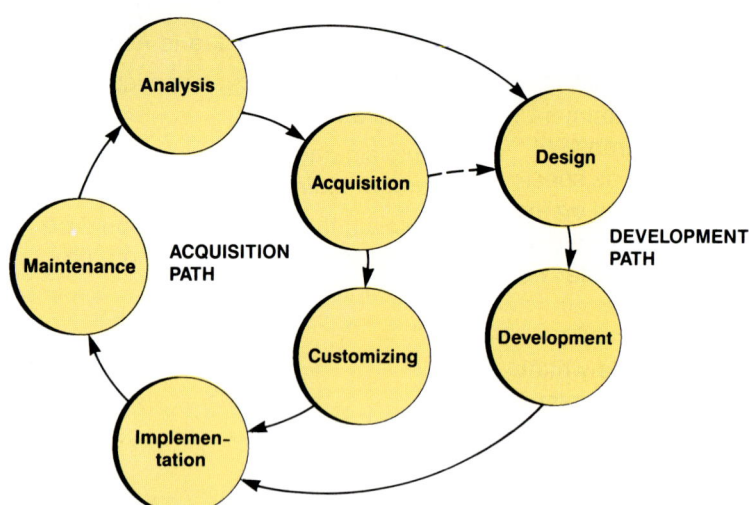

STEP 1—REVIEWING THE PROGRAM SPECIFICATIONS

◆ The first step in the program development cycle is a review of the program specifications. **Program specifications** can consist of data flow diagrams, system flowcharts, process specifications that indicate the action to be taken on the data, a data dictionary identifying the data elements that will be used, screen formats, report layouts, and actual documents such as invoices or checks. These documents help the programmer understand the work that needs to be done by the program. Also, the programmer meets once or more with the user and the systems analyst who designed the system to understand the purpose of the program from the user's point of view.

If the programmer believes some aspect of the design should be changed, such as a screen layout, he or she discusses it with the systems analyst and the user. If the change is agreed on, the written design specification is changed. However, the programmer should not change the specified system without the agreement of the systems analyst and the user. If a change is authorized, it should be recorded in the system design. The systems analyst and the user, through the system design, have specified what is to be done. It is the programmer's job to determine *how* to do it.

Large programming jobs are usually assigned to more than one programmer. In these situations, a good system design is essential so that each programmer can be given a logical portion of the system to be programmed.

STEP 2—DESIGNING THE PROGRAM

◆ After the programmer has carefully reviewed the specifications, program design begins. During **program design** a logical solution to the programming task is developed and documented. The logical solution, or **logic**, for a program is a step-by-step solution to a programming problem. Determining the logic for a computer program can be an extremely complex task. To aid in program design and development, a method called structured program design is commonly used.

Structured Program Design

Structured program design is a methodology that emphasizes three main program design concepts: modules, control structures, and single entry/single exit. Use of these concepts helps to create programs that are easy to write, read, understand, check for errors, and modify.

Modules With structured design, programming problems are *decomposed* (separated) into smaller parts called modules. Each **module**, sometimes referred to as a **subroutine** in programming, performs a given task within the program. The major benefit of this technique is that it simplifies program development because each module of a program can be developed individually. When the modules are combined, they form a complete program that accomplishes the desired result.

Structure charts, also called **hierarchy charts**, are often used to decompose and represent the modules of a program. When the program decomposition is completed, the entire structure of a program is illustrated by the hierarchy chart (on the next page in Figure 12-3), which shows the relationship of the modules within the program.

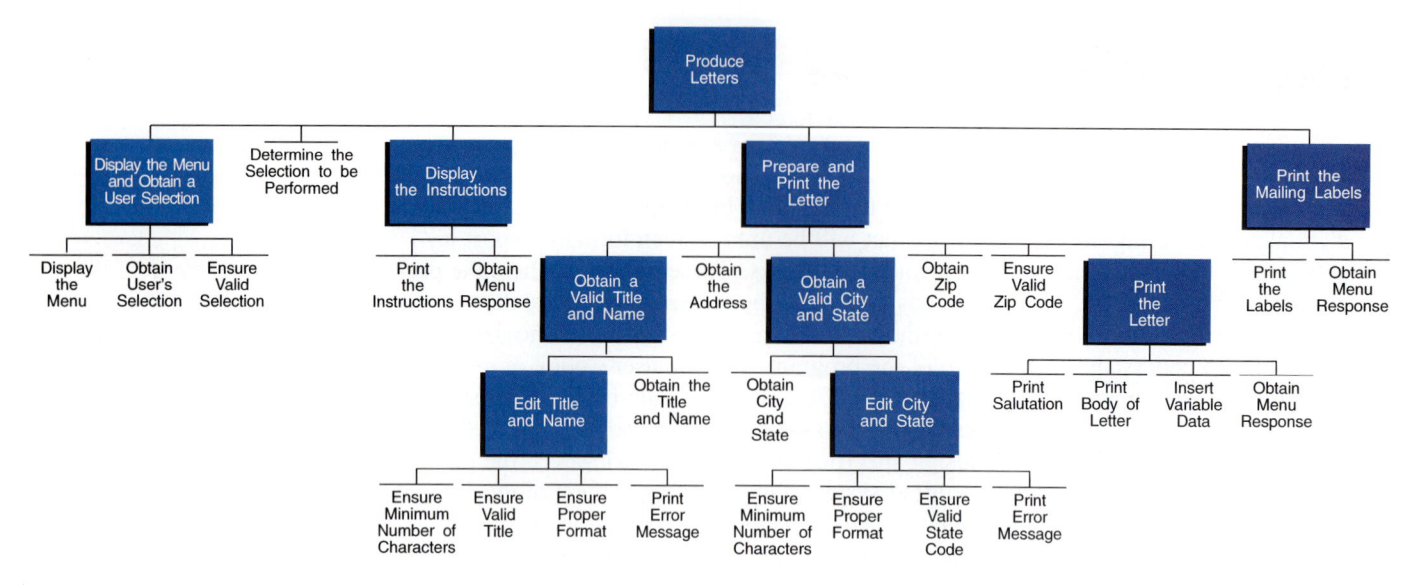

12.4 CHAPTER 12 PROGRAM DEVELOPMENT

FIGURE 12-3
In this structure chart, the relationship of individual program modules are graphically shown as boxes. The text below each box indicates the processing steps that would be performed.

SEQUENCE

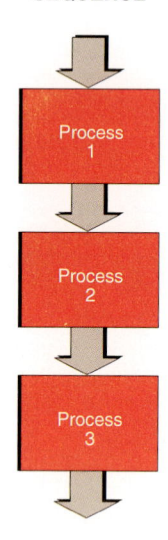

FIGURE 12-4
Each box in the sequence control structure represents a process that will occur immediately after the preceding process.

Control Structures In structured program design three basic **control structures** are used to form the logic of a program. All logic problems can be solved by a combination of these structures. The three basic control structures are: sequence, selection, and iteration.

1. In the **sequence structure**, one process occurs immediately after another. In Figure 12-4, each rectangular box represents a particular process that is to occur. For example, a process could be a computer instruction to move data from one location in main memory to another location. Each process occurs in the exact sequence specified, one process followed by the next.

2. The second control structure, called the **selection structure**, or **if-then-else structure**, gives programmers a way to represent conditional program logic (Figure 12-5). Conditional program logic can be expressed in the following way: *If* the condition is true, *then* perform the true condition processing, *else* perform the false condition processing. When the if-then-else structure is used, the if portion of the structure tests a given condition. The true portion of the statement is executed if the condition tested is true, and the false portion of the statement is executed if the condition is false. An if-then-else structure might be used to determine if an employee is hourly or salaried and then process the employee accordingly. To do this, an employee code might be tested to determine if an employee is hourly. If the employee is hourly, the true portion of the structure would be executed and hourly pay would be calculated. If the employee is not hourly, the false portion of the structure would be executed and salary pay would be calculated. The selection, or if-then-else, structure is used by programmers to represent conditional logic problems.

SELECTION

FIGURE 12-5
The selection, or if-then-else, control structure is used to direct the program to one process or another based on the test of a condition.

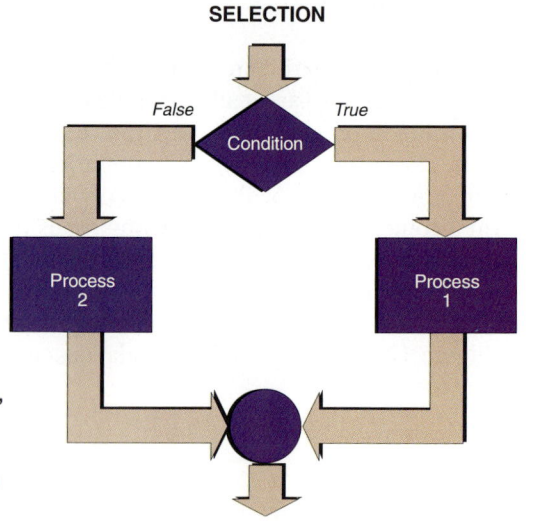

A variation of the selection structure is the case structure. The **case structure** is used when a condition is being tested that can lead to more than two alternatives (Figure 12-6). In a program, a menu is an example of a case structure because it provides multiple processing options.

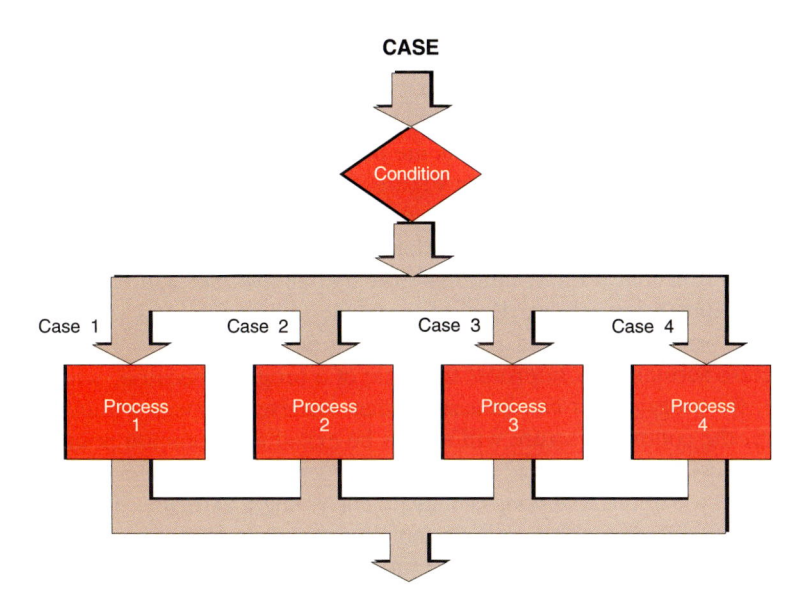

FIGURE 12-6
A case control structure with four possible processing paths is similar to the if-then-else control structure except that it provides for more than two alternatives.

3. The third control structure, called the **iteration structure**, or **looping structure**, means that one or more processes continue to occur as long as a given condition remains true. There are two forms of this control structure: the **do-while structure** and the **do-until structure** (Figure 12-7). In the do-while structure a condition is tested. If the condition is true, the process is performed. The program then *loops* back and tests the condition again. If the condition is still true, the process is performed again. This looping continues until the condition being tested is false. At that time, the program exits the loop, moves to another section of the program, and performs some other processing. An example of this type of testing would be a check to see if all records have been processed. The do-until control structure is similar to the do-while except that the condition tested is at the end instead of the beginning of the loop. Processing continues *until* the condition is met.

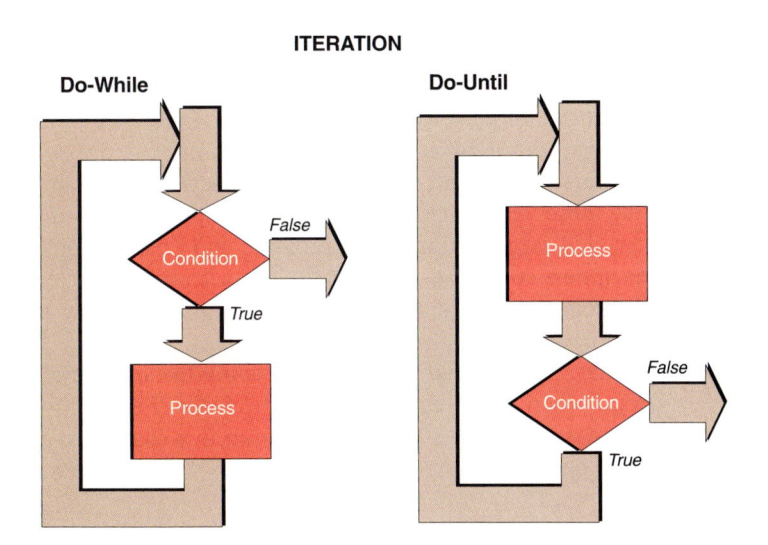

FIGURE 12-7
The iteration control structure has two forms, do-while and do-until. In the do-while structure, the condition is tested before the process. In the do-until structure, the condition is tested after the process.

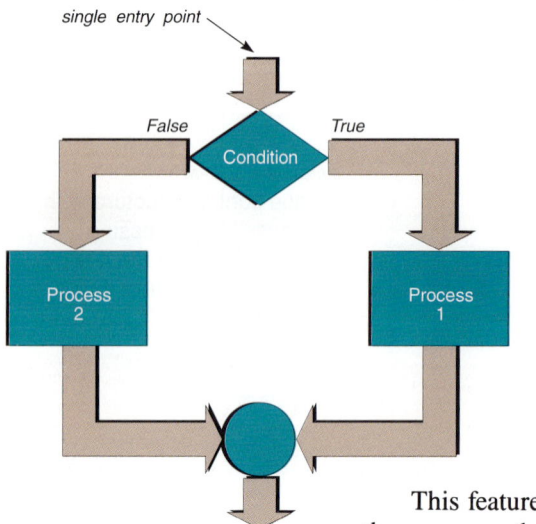

FIGURE 12-8
Structured programming concepts require that all control structures have a single entry point and a single exit point. This contributes to programs that are easier to understand and maintain.

Programmers combine these three control structures—sequence, selection, and iteration—to create program logic solutions. A structured program design rule that applies to these control structures and how they are combined is the single entry/single exit rule.

Single Entry/Single Exit An important concept in structured programming is **single entry/single exit**, meaning that there is only one entry point and one exit point for each of the three control structures. An **entry point** is the point where a control structure is entered. An **exit point** is the point where the control structure is exited. For example, in Figure 12-8, when the if-then-else structure is used, the control structure is entered at the point where the condition is tested. When the condition is tested, one set of instructions will be executed if the condition is true and another set will be executed if the condition is false. Regardless of the result of the test, however, the structure is exited at the single exit point.

This feature substantially improves the logic of a program because, when reading the program, the programmer can be assured that whatever happens within the if-then-else structure, the control structure will always be exited at a common point. Prior to the use of structured programming, many programmers would transfer control to other parts of a program without following the single entry/single exit rule. This practice led to poorly designed programs that were extremely difficult to read, check for errors, and modify. Because the logic path of such programs jumps from one section of the program to another, the programs are sometimes referred to as *spaghetti code*.

Program Design Tools

Programmers use several popular program design tools to develop and document the logical solutions to the problems they are programming. Three commonly used design tools are program flowcharts, pseudocode, and Warnier-Orr diagrams.

Program Flowcharts Program flowcharts were one of the first program design tools. Figure 12-9 shows a flowchart drawn in the late 1940s by Dr. John von Neumann, a computer scientist and one of the first computer programmers. In a **program flowchart** all the logical steps of a program are represented by a combination of symbols and text.

A set of standards for program flowcharts was published in the early 1960s by the American National Standards Institute (ANSI). These standards, which are still used today, specify symbols, such as rectangles and diamonds, that are used to represent the various operations that can be performed on a computer (Figure 12-10). Program flowcharts were used as the primary means of program design for many years prior to the introduction of structured program design. During these years, programmers designed programs by focusing on the detailed steps required for a program and creating logical solutions for each new combination of conditions as it was encountered. Developing programs in this manner led to programs that were poorly designed.

Today, programmers are taught to apply the structured design concepts when they create program flowcharts (Figure 12-11). When they use basic control structures, program flowcharts are a valuable program design tool.

FIGURE 12-9
An example of an early flowchart developed by computer scientist Dr. John von Neumann in the 1940s to solve a problem involving game theory. This flowchart was drawn prior to the standardization of flowchart symbols and the development of structured design techniques.

STEP 2—DESIGNING THE PROGRAM   **12.7**

FIGURE 12-10 ▶
Standard symbols used to create program flowcharts.

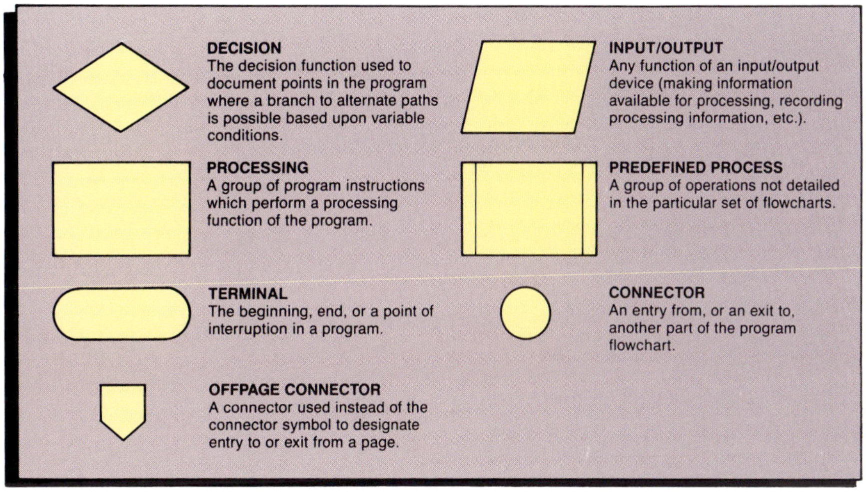

DECISION
The decision function used to document points in the program where a branch to alternate paths is possible based upon variable conditions.

INPUT/OUTPUT
Any function of an input/output device (making information available for processing, recording processing information, etc.).

PROCESSING
A group of program instructions which perform a processing function of the program.

PREDEFINED PROCESS
A group of operations not detailed in the particular set of flowcharts.

TERMINAL
The beginning, end, or a point of interruption in a program.

CONNECTOR
An entry from, or an exit to, another part of the program flowchart.

OFFPAGE CONNECTOR
A connector used instead of the connector symbol to designate entry to or exit from a page.

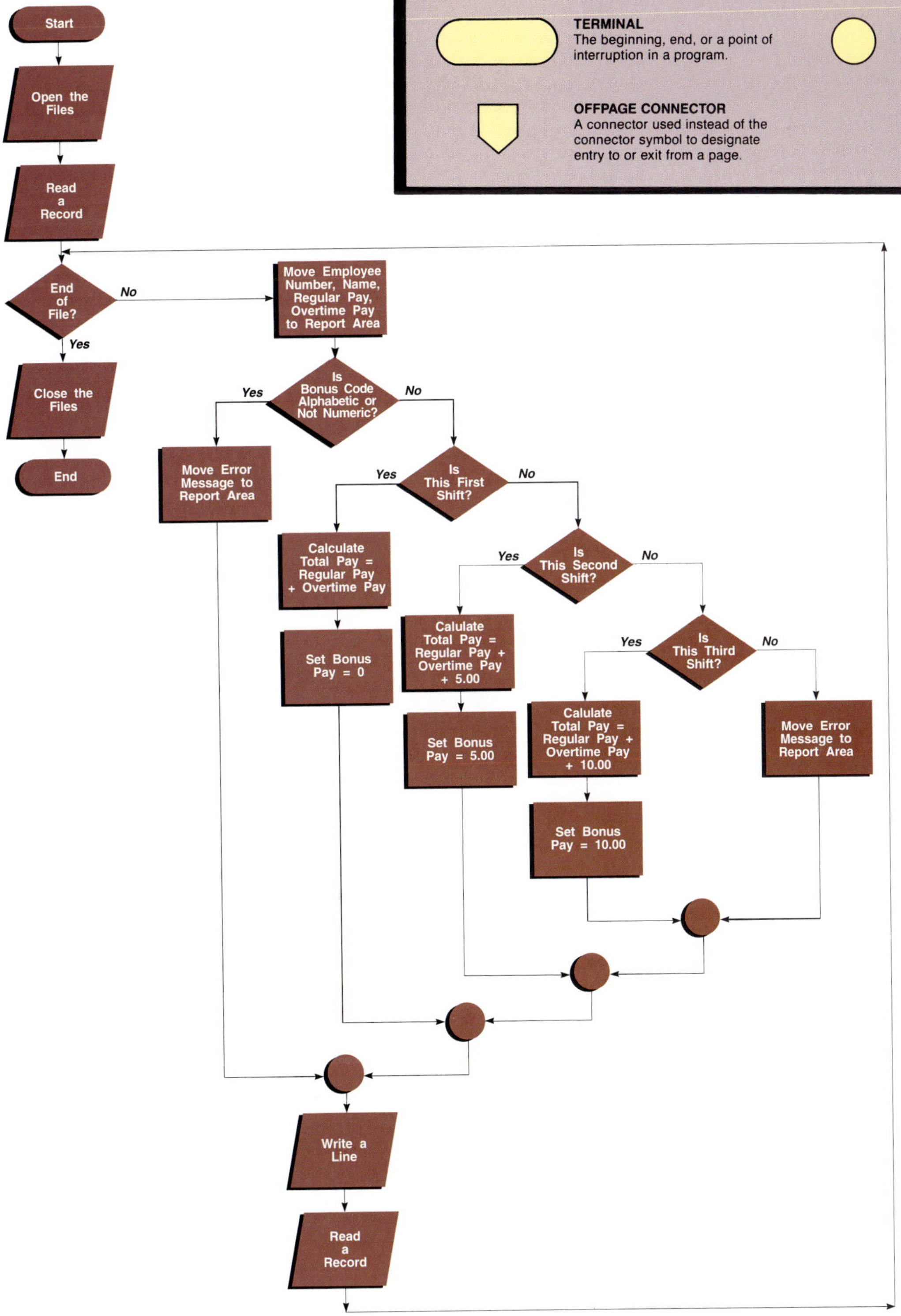

◀ FIGURE 12-11
This flowchart displays the logic required to solve a payroll calculation task using standard flowcharting symbols and the three control structures of structured programming.

```
Open the files
Read a record
PERFORM UNTIL end of file
    Move employee number, name, regular pay, and
        overtime pay to the report area
    IF bonus code is alphabetic or not numeric
        Move error message to report area
    ELSE
        IF first shift
            Calculate total pay = regular pay +
                overtime pay
            Set bonus pay to zero
        ELSE
            If second shift
                Calculate total pay = regular pay +
                    overtime pay + 5.00
                Set bonus pay to 5.00
            ELSE
                If third shift
                    Calculate total pay = regular pay +
                        overtime pay + 10.00
                    Set bonus pay to 10.00
                ELSE
                    Move error message to report area
                ENDIF
            ENDIF
        ENDIF
    ENDIF
    Write a line
    Read a record
ENDPERFORM
Close the files
End the program
```

FIGURE 12-12
This pseudocode is another way of documenting the logic shown in the flowchart in Figure 12-11.

Pseudocode Some experts in program design advocate the use of pseudocode when designing the logic for a program. In **pseudocode**, the logical steps in the solution of a problem are written as English statements and indentations are used to represent the control structures (Figure 12-12). An advantage of pseudocode is that it eliminates the time spent with flowcharting to draw and arrange symbols while attempting to determine the program logic. The major disadvantage is that unlike flowcharting, pseudocode does not provide a graphic representation, which many people find useful and easier to interpret when they examine programming logic.

Warnier-Orr In the **Warnier-Orr technique** (named after Jean Dominique Warnier and Kenneth Orr), the programmer analyzes output to be produced from an application and develops processing modules that are needed to produce the output. The example in Figure 12-13 illustrates a completed Warnier-Orr diagram for the same program as Figures 12-11 and 12-12. Each curly brace ({}) represents a module in the program. The statements within the braces identify the processing that is to occur within the modules.

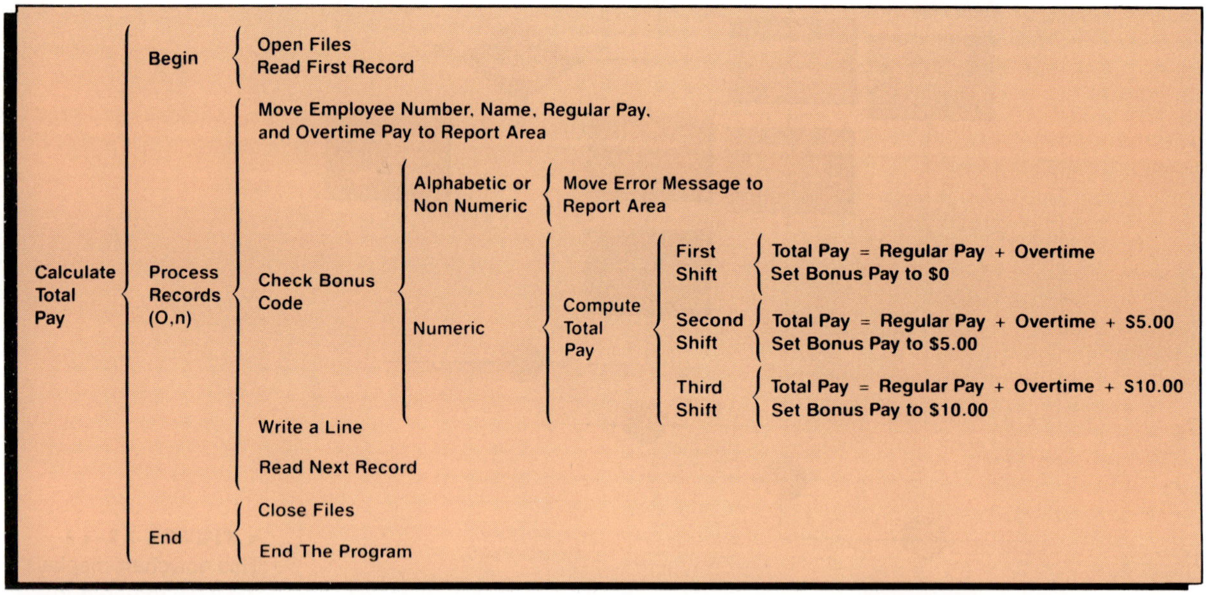

FIGURE 12-13
This Warnier-Orr diagram also illustrates the logic for the payroll calculation problem used for Figures 12-11 and 12-12.

Regardless of the design tool you use, it is important that the program design is efficient and correct. To help ensure this, many organizations use structured walk-throughs.

Structured Walk-Through

After a program has been designed, the programmer schedules a structured walk-through of the program. The programmer, other programmers in the department, and the systems analyst attend. During the walk-through, the programmer who designs the program explains the program logic. The purpose of the design walk-through is to review the logic of the program for errors, and if possible, improve program design. Early detection of errors and approval of program design improvements reduces the overall development time and therefore the cost of the program. It is much better to find errors and make needed changes to the program during the design step than to make them later in the program development process.

Once the program design is complete, the programmer can begin to code the program.

STEP 3—CODING THE PROGRAM

◆ **Coding** the program refers to the process of writing the program instructions that will process the data and produce the output specified in the program design. As we previously mentioned, programs are written in different languages, which each have particular rules on how to instruct the computer to perform specific tasks, such as read a record or multiply two numbers.

If the program design is thorough, logical, and well structured, the coding process is greatly simplified and can sometimes be a one-for-one translation of a design step into a program step. Today, program code, or instructions, are usually entered directly into the computer via a terminal and stored on a disk drive. Using this approach, the programmer can partially enter a program at one time and finish entering it at a later time. Program instructions are added, deleted, and changed until the programmer believes the program design has been fully translated into program instructions and the program is ready for testing.

STEP 4—TESTING THE PROGRAM

◆ Before a program is used to process *real* data and produce information that people rely on, it should be thoroughly tested to make sure it is functioning correctly. A programmer can perform several different types of tests.

Desk checking is the process of reading the program and mentally reviewing its logic. This is a simple process that can be performed by the programmer who wrote the program or by another programmer. This process can be compared to proofreading a letter before you mail it. The disadvantage of this method is that it is difficult to detect other than obvious errors.

Syntax errors are violations of the grammar rules of the language in which the program was written. An example of a syntax error would be the program command READ being misspelled REED. Syntax errors missed by the programmer during desk checking are identified by the computer when it decodes the program instructions.

Logic testing is what most programmers think of when the term testing is used. During **logic testing**, the sequence of program instructions is tested to make sure it provides the correct result. Logic errors may be the result of a programming oversight, such as using the wrong data to perform a calculation, or a design error, such as forgetting to specify that some customers do not have to pay sales tax when they purchase merchandise.

Logic testing is performed with **test data**, data that simulates the type of input that the program will process when it is implemented. To obtain an independent and unbiased test of the program, test data and the review of test results should be the responsibility of someone other than the programmer who wrote the program. The test data should be developed by referring to the system design but it should also try to *break* the program by including data outside the range of data that will be input during normal operations. For example, if the specifications of a payroll program stated that the input for an employee should never exceed 60 hours of work per week, the program should be designed, coded, and tested to properly process transactions in excess of 60 hours. It would do this by displaying an error message or in some other way indicating that an invalid number of hours has been entered. Other similar tests should include alphabetic data when only numeric data is expected, and negative numbers when only positive numbers are normally input.

One of the more colorful terms of the computer industry is **debugging**, which refers to the process of locating and correcting program errors, or **bugs**, found during testing. The term was coined when the failure of one of the first computers was traced to a moth that had become lodged in the electronic components (Figure 12-14).

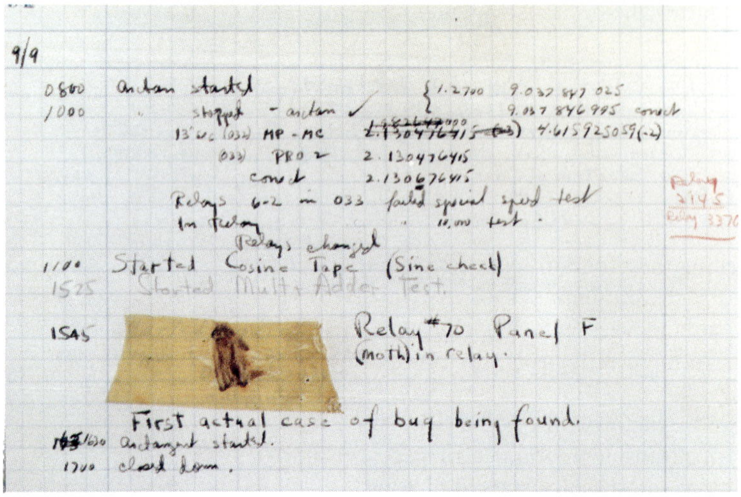

FIGURE 12-14
In 1945, the cause of the temporary failure of the world's first electromechanical computer, the Mark 1, was traced to a dead moth (shown taped to the log book) caught in the electrical components. The term *bug*, meaning a computer error, has been part of computer jargon ever since.

STEP 5—FINALIZING PROGRAM DOCUMENTATION

◆ Documentation, or the preparation of documents, that explains the program is an essential but sometimes neglected part of the programming process. Documentation should be an ongoing part of developing a program and should only be finalized, meaning organized and brought together, after the program is successfully tested and ready for implementation. Documentation developed during the programming process should include a narrative description of the program, program design documents such as flowcharts or pseudocode, program listings, and test results. Comments in the program itself are also an important part of program documentation (Figure 12-15).

Data entry and computer operations procedures should also be documented prior to implementation. Obtaining adequate documentation may be difficult because some programmers can and do develop programs without it; when they have finished coding the program, they have little incentive to go back and complete the documentation after the fact. In addition to helping programmers develop programs, documentation is valuable because it helps the next programmer who, six months or one year later, is asked to make a change to the program. Proper documentation can substantially reduce the amount of time the new programmer will have to spend learning enough about the program to know how best to make the change.

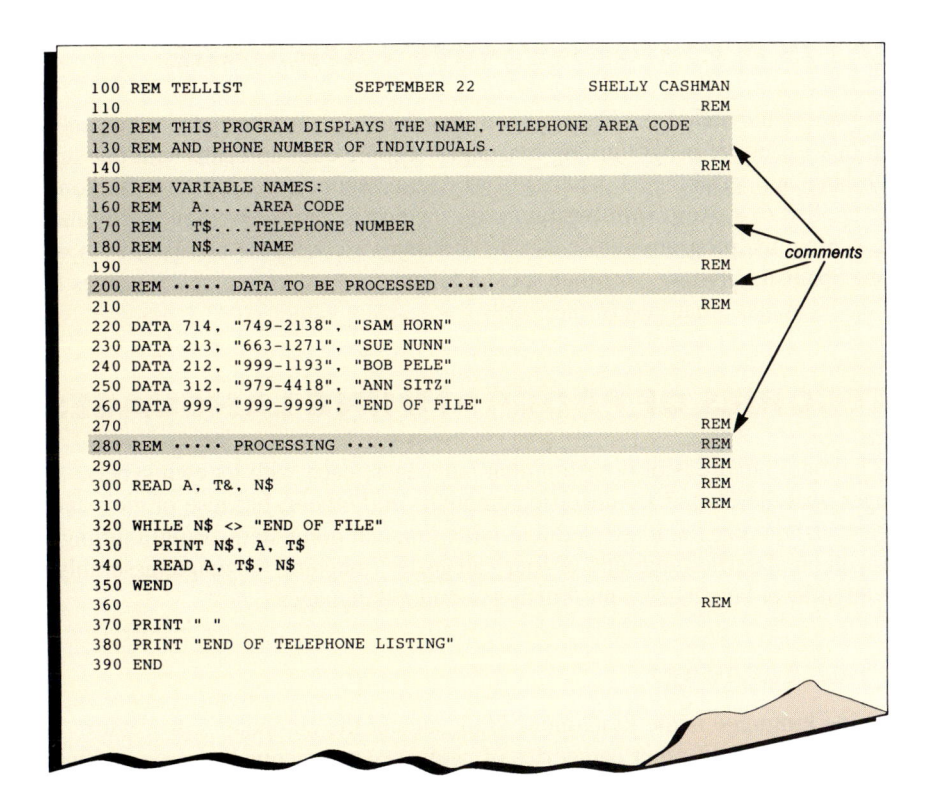

```
100 REM TELLIST          SEPTEMBER 22          SHELLY CASHMAN
110                                                          REM
120 REM THIS PROGRAM DISPLAYS THE NAME, TELEPHONE AREA CODE
130 REM AND PHONE NUMBER OF INDIVIDUALS.
140                                                          REM
150 REM VARIABLE NAMES:
160 REM    A.....AREA CODE
170 REM    T$....TELEPHONE NUMBER
180 REM    N$....NAME
190                                                          REM
200 REM ..... DATA TO BE PROCESSED .....
210                                                          REM
220 DATA 714, "749-2138", "SAM HORN"
230 DATA 213, "663-1271", "SUE NUNN"
240 DATA 212, "999-1193", "BOB PELE"
250 DATA 312, "979-4418", "ANN SITZ"
260 DATA 999, "999-9999", "END OF FILE"
270                                                          REM
280 REM ..... PROCESSING .....                               REM
290                                                          REM
300 READ A, T&, N$                                           REM
310                                                          REM
320 WHILE N$ <> "END OF FILE"
330    PRINT N$, A, T$
340    READ A, T$, N$
350 WEND
360                                                          REM
370 PRINT " "
380 PRINT "END OF TELEPHONE LISTING"
390 END
```

FIGURE 12-15
Most programming languages allow programmers to place explanatory comments directly in the program. This is an effective way of documenting the program. In this program, comment lines are identified by the letters REM, which is an abbreviation for REMARK.

PROGRAM MAINTENANCE

◆ **Program maintenance** includes all changes to a program once it is implemented and processing real transactions. Sometimes, maintenance is required to correct errors that were not found during the testing step. Other times, maintenance is required to make changes that are the result of the users' new information requirements. It may surprise you to learn that the majority of all business programming today consists of maintaining existing programs, not writing new programs.

Because so much time is spent on maintenance programming, it should be subject to the same policies and procedures, such as design, testing, and documentation, that are required for new programs. Unfortunately, this is not always the case. Because maintenance tasks are usually shorter than new programming efforts, they often aren't held to the same standards. The result is that over time, programs can become unrecognizable when compared with their original documentation. Maintaining high standards for program maintenance can not only lower overall programming costs, but also lengthen the useful life of a program.

SUMMARY OF PROGRAM DEVELOPMENT

◆ The key to developing quality programs for an information system is to follow the steps of the program development process. Program specifications must be carefully reviewed and understood. Programmers should use structured concepts to design programs that are modular, use the three control structures, and follow the single entry/single exit rule. Programmers should carefully code and test the program and finalize documentation. If each of these steps is followed, programmers will create quality programs that are correct and that can be easily read, understood, and maintained.

WHAT IS A PROGRAMMING LANGUAGE?

As we mentioned at the beginning of this chapter, computer programs can be written in a variety of programming languages. People communicate with one another through language, established patterns of words and sounds. A similar definition can also be applied to a **programming language**, which is a set of written words and symbols that allow the programmer or user to communicate with the computer. As with English, Spanish, Chinese, or other spoken languages, programming languages have rules, called syntax, that govern their use.

CATEGORIES OF PROGRAMMING LANGUAGES

There are hundreds of programming languages, each with its own syntax. Some languages were developed for specific computers and others, because of their success, have been standardized and adapted to a wide range of computers. Programming languages can be classified into one of four categories: machine language, assembly language, high-level languages, and fourth-generation languages.

Machine Language

A **machine language** is the fundamental language of the computer's processor. Programs written in all other categories of languages are eventually converted into machine language before they are executed. Individual machine language instructions exist for each of the commands in the computer's instruction set, the operations such as add, move, or read that are specific to each computer. Because the instruction set is unique for a particular processor, machine languages are different for computers that have different processors. The advantage of writing a program in machine language is that the programmer can control the computer directly and accomplish exactly what needs to be done. Therefore, well-written machine language programs are very efficient. The disadvantages of machine language programs are that they take a long time to write and they are difficult to review if the programmer is trying to find an error. In addition, because they are written using the instruction set of a particular processor, the programs will only run on computers with the same type of processor. Because they are written for specific processors, machine languages are also called **low-level languages**. Figure 12-16 (a) shows an example of machine language instructions.

FIGURE 12-16

Program instruction chart for: (a) machine language (printed in a hexadecimal form), (b) assembly language, and (c) a high-level language called C. The machine language and assembly language instructions correspond to the high-level instructions and were generated when the high-level language statements were translated into machine language. As you can see, the high-level language requires fewer program instructions and is easier to read.

(a) MACHINE LANGUAGE	(b) ASSEMBLY LANGUAGE	(c) HIGH-LEVEL LANGUAGE

9b df 46 0c
9b d9 c0
9b db 7e f2
9b d9 46 04
9b d8 c9
9b d9 5e fc
	fild WORD PTR [bp+12];qty
	fld ST(0)
	    fstp TBYTE PTR [bp-14]
	    fld DWORD PTR [bp+4];price
	fmul ST(0),ST(1)
	    fstp DWORD PTR [bp-4];gross
		gross = qty * price;

9b d9 c0
9b dc 16 ac 00
9b dd d8
9b dd 7e f0
90 9b
8a 66 f1
9e
9b dd c0
76 19
	fld ST(0)
	    fcom QWORD PTR $T20002
	fstp ST(0)
	    fstsw WORD PTR [bp-16]
	    fwait
	mov ah,BYTE PTR [bp-15]
	    sahf
	ffreeST(0)
	    jbe $I193
		if (qty > ceiling)

9b d9 46 fc
9b dc 0e b4 00
9b de e9
9b d9 5e 08
90 9b
	fld DWORD PTR [bp-4];gross
	    fmul QWORD PTR $T20003
	fsub
	    fstp DWORD PTR [bp+8];net
	    fwait
		net = gross - (gross * discount_rate);

eb 0d 90	jmp SHORT $I194 nop $I193:	else
8b 46 fc 8b 56 fe 89 46 08 89 56 0a	mov ax,WORD PTR [bp-4];gross mov dx,WORD PTR [bp-2] mov WORD PTR [bp+8],ax ;net mov WORD PTR [bp+10],dx $I194:	net = gross;

Assembly Language

To make it easier for programmers to remember the specific machine instruction codes, assembly languages were developed. An **assembly language** is similar to a machine language, but uses abbreviations called **mnemonics** or **symbolic operation code** to represent the machine operation code. Another difference is that assembly languages usually allow **symbolic addressing**, which means that a specific computer memory location can be referenced by a name or symbol, such as TOTAL, instead of by its actual address as it would have to be referenced in machine language. Assembly language programs can also include **macroinstructions** that generate more than one machine language instruction. Assembly language programs are converted into machine language instructions by a special program called an **assembler**. Even though assembly languages are easier to use than machine languages, they are still considered a low-level language because they are so closely related to the specific design of the computer. Figure 12-16 ⓑ shows an example of assembly language instructions.

High-Level Languages

The evolution of computer languages continued with the development of high-level languages in the late 1950s and 1960s. **High-level languages** more closely resemble what most people would think of as a language in that they contain nouns, verbs, and mathematical, relational, and logical operators that can be grouped together to form what appear to be sentences (Figure 12-16 ⓒ). These sentences are called **program statements**. Because of these characteristics, high-level languages can be *read* by programmers and are thus easier to learn and use than machine or assembly languages. Another important advantage over low-level languages is that high-level languages are usually machine independent, which means they can run on different types of computers.

As mentioned previously, all languages must be translated into machine language before they can be executed. High-level languages are translated in one of two ways: with a compiler or an interpreter.

A **compiler** converts an entire program into machine language that is usually stored on a disk for later execution. The program to be converted is called the **source program** and the machine language produced is called the **object program** or **object code**. Compilers check the program syntax, perform limited logic checking, and make sure that data that is going to be used in comparisons or calculations, such as a discount rate, is properly defined somewhere in the program. An important feature of compilers is that they produce an error listing of all program statements that do not meet the program language rules. This listing helps the programmer make the necessary changes to debug or correct the program. Figure 12-17 illustrates the process of compiling a program.

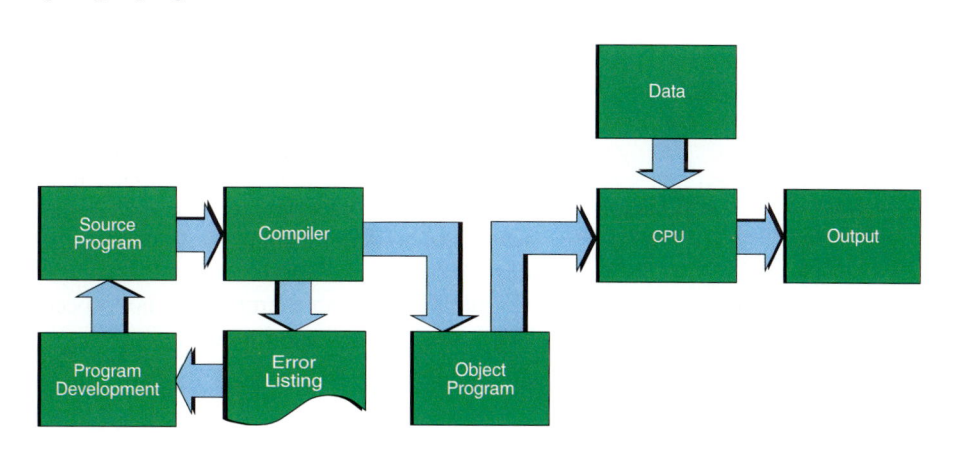

FIGURE 12-17
When a compiler is used, a source language program is compiled into a machine language object program. Usually, both the source and object programs are stored on disk. When the user wants to run the program, the object program is loaded into the main memory of the CPU and the program instructions begin executing. As instructed by the program, the CPU processes data and creates output. Errors in the source program identified during compilation are shown on an error listing that can be used to make the necessary corrections during program development.

Because machine language is unique to each processor, different computers require different compilers for the same language. For example, a mainframe, minicomputer, and personal computer would each have different compilers that would translate the same source language program into the specific machine language for each computer.

While a compiler translates an entire program, an **interpreter** translates one program statement at a time and then executes the resulting machine language before translating the next program statement. When using an interpreter, each time the program is run, the source program is interpreted into machine language and executed. No object program is produced. Figure 12-18 illustrates this process.

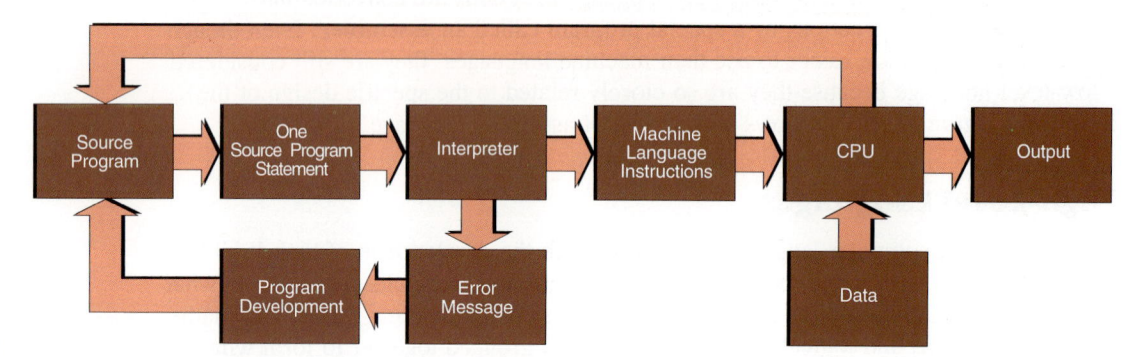

FIGURE 12-18
When an interpreter is used, one source language statement at a time is interpreted into machine language instructions that are executed immediately by the CPU. As instructed by the machine language instructions, the CPU processes data and creates output. Error messages indicating an invalid source language statement are produced as each source program statement is interpreted and are used to make the necessary corrections during program development.

Interpreters are often used with personal computers that do not have the memory or computing power required by compilers. The advantage of interpreters is that the compiling process is not necessary before program changes can be tested. The disadvantage of interpreters is that interpreted programs do not run as fast as compiled programs because the translation to machine language occurs each time the program is run. Compilers for most high-level languages are now available for the newer and more powerful personal computers.

Fourth-Generation Languages

The evolution of computer languages is sometimes described in terms of generations with machine, assembly, and high-level languages considered the first, second, and third generations, respectively. Each generation offered significant improvements in ease of use and programming flexibility over the previous generation. Although a clear definition does not yet exist, **fourth-generation languages (4GLs)**, sometimes called **very high-level languages**, continue the programming language evolution by being even easier to use than high-level languages for both the programmer and the nonprogramming user.

```
LIST CUSTOMERS CUSTOMER.NAME WITH BALANCE.DUE > '1000'
```

FIGURE 12-19
This database query is considered an example of a fourth-generation language because it tells the computer what the user wants, not how to perform the processing.

A term commonly used to describe fourth-generation languages is **nonprocedural**, which means that the programmer does not specify the procedures to be used to accomplish a task as is done with lower procedural language generations. Instead of telling the computer how to do the task, the programmer tells the computer *what* is to be done, usually by describing the desired output. A database query language (Figure 12-19) is an example of a nonprocedural fourth-generation language.

The advantage of fourth-generation languages is that they are *results* oriented (*what* is to be done, not *how*), and they can be used by nonprogramming personnel such as users. The disadvantage of fourth-generation languages is that they do not provide as many processing options to the programmer as other language generations and they require more computer processing power that other language generations. Most experts, however, believe that their ease of use far outweighs these disadvantages and they predict that fourth-generation languages will continue to be more widely used.

An extension of fourth-generation languages, sometimes called the fifth generation, is a natural language. A **natural language** is a type of query language that allows the user to enter a question as if he or she were speaking to another person. For example, a fourth-generation query might be stated as LIST SALESPERSON TOTAL-SALES BY REGION. A natural language version of that same query might be TELL ME THE NAME OF EACH SALESPERSON AND THE TOTAL SALES FOR EACH REGION. The natural language allows the user more flexibility in the structure of the query and can even ask the user a question if it does not understand what is meant by the initial query statement. A few natural languages are available today but they are not yet widely used.

PROGRAMMING LANGUAGES USED TODAY

Although there are hundreds of programming languages, only a few are used extensively enough to be recognized as industry standards. Most of these are high-level programming languages that can be used on a variety of computers. In this section, we discuss the popular programming languages that are commonly used, their origins, and their primary purpose.

To help you understand the differences, we show program code for each of the most popular languages. The code is from programs that solve the same problem. The problem is to compute the net price of a sale. This is done by multiplying the quantity sold times the unit price. A discount of 5% is calculated if the gross sale is over $100.00.

BASIC

BASIC, which stands for **B**eginner's **A**ll-purpose **S**ymbolic **I**nstruction **C**ode, was developed by John Kemeny and Thomas Kurtz in 1964 at Dartmouth College (Figure 12-20). They originally designed BASIC to be a simple, interactive programming language for college students to learn and use. BASIC has become one of the most popular programming languages in use on microcomputers and minicomputers today.

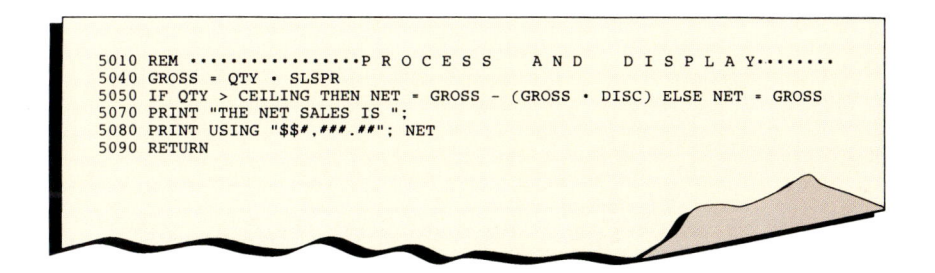

```
5010  REM ••••••••••••••••••P R O C E S S    A N D    D I S P L A Y••••••••
5040  GROSS = QTY * SLSPR
5050  IF QTY > CEILING THEN NET = GROSS - (GROSS * DISC) ELSE NET = GROSS
5070  PRINT "THE NET SALES IS ";
5080  PRINT USING "$$#,###.##"; NET
5090  RETURN
```

FIGURE 12-20
An excerpt from a BASIC program.

COBOL

COBOL (**CO**mmon **B**usiness **O**riented **L**anguage) was introduced in 1960. Backed by the U.S. Department of Defense, COBOL was developed by a committee of representatives from both government and industry. Rear Admiral Grace M. Hopper was a key person on the committee and is recognized as one of the prime developers of the COBOL language. COBOL is one of the most widely used programming languages for business applications (Figure 12-21). Using an English-like format, COBOL instructions are arranged in sentences and grouped into paragraphs. The English format makes COBOL easy to write and read, but also makes it a wordy language that produces lengthy program code. COBOL is very good for processing large files and performing relatively simple business calculations. Other languages are better suited to performing complex mathematical formulas and functions.

FIGURE 12-21
An excerpt from a COBOL program. Notice the additional words in the COBOL program compared to the BASIC program in Figure 12-20. Although the extra words increase the time it takes to write a COBOL program, they also make the program easier to read and understand.

```
00100       016200    C010-PROCESS-AND-DISPLAY.
00101       016400*************************************************
00102       016600*   FUNCTION:            CALCULATE NET SALES AMOUNT    *
00103       016700*                        AND DISPLAY RESULTS           *
00104       016800*   ENTRY/EXIT:          B000-LOOP-CONTROL             *
00105       016900*   CALLS:               NONE                          *
00106       017100*************************************************
00107       017300    COMPUTER GROSS-SALES-WRK = QUANTITY-SOLD-WRK * SALES-PRICE-WRK.
00108       017500    IF QUANTITY-SOLD-WRK IS GREATER THAN CEILING
00109       017600       COMPUTE NET-SALES-WRK = GROSS-SALES-WRK -
00110       017700          <GROSS-SALES-WRK * DISCOUNT-RATE)
00111       017800    ELSE
00112       017900       MOVE GROSS-SALES-WRK TO NET-SALES-WRK.
00113       018100    MOVE NET-SALES-WRK TO NET-SALES-OUTPUT.
00114       018300    DISPLAY CLEAR-SCREEN.
00115       018500    WRITE PRINT-LINE FROM DETAIL-LINE
00116       018600       AFTER ADVANCING 2.
```

C

The C programming language was developed at Bell Laboratories in 1972 by Dennis Ritchie (Figure 12-22). It was originally designed as a programming language for writing systems software, but it is now considered a general-purpose programming language. C is a powerful programming language that requires professional programming skills to be used effectively. The use of C to develop various types of software, including commercial applications, is increasing. C programs are often used with the Unix operating system (most of the Unix operating system is written in C).

FIGURE 12-22
An excerpt from a C program.

```
float gross;
gross = qty * price;
if (qty > ceiling)
    net = gross - (gross * discount_rate);
else
    net = gross;
return(net);
```

FORTRAN

FORTRAN (**FOR**mula **TRAN**slator) was developed by a team of IBM programmers led by John Backus. Released in 1957, FORTRAN was designed as a programming language to be used by scientists, engineers, and mathematicians (Figure 12-23). FORTRAN is considered the first high-level language that was developed and is noted for its capability to easily express and efficiently calculate mathematical equations.

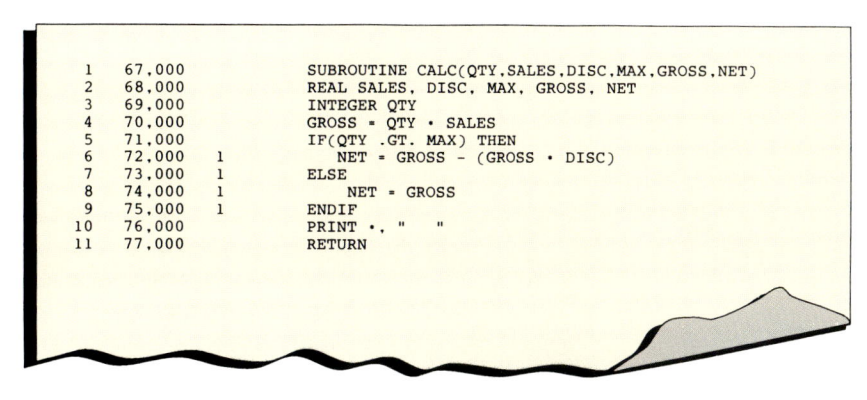

```
 1   67,000           SUBROUTINE CALC(QTY,SALES,DISC,MAX,GROSS,NET)
 2   68,000           REAL SALES, DISC, MAX, GROSS, NET
 3   69,000           INTEGER QTY
 4   70,000           GROSS = QTY * SALES
 5   71,000           IF(QTY .GT. MAX) THEN
 6   72,000  1            NET = GROSS - (GROSS * DISC)
 7   73,000  1        ELSE
 8   74,000  1            NET = GROSS
 9   75,000  1        ENDIF
10   76,000           PRINT *, "    "
11   77,000           RETURN
```

FIGURE 12-23
An excerpt from a FORTRAN program.

Pascal

The **Pascal** language was developed in 1968 by Niklaus Wirth, a computer scientist at the Institut für Informatik in Zurich, Switzerland. It was developed for teaching programming. The name Pascal is not an abbreviation or acronym, but rather the name of a mathematician, Blaise Pascal (1623–1662), who developed one of the earliest calculating machines. Pascal, available for use on both personal and large computers, was one of the first programming languages developed where the instructions in the language were designed and written so that programmers using Pascal would be encouraged to develop programs that follow structured program design (Figure 12-24).

```
BEGIN                              (* Begin procedure *)
    GROSS := SALES * QTY;
    IF QTY > CEILING
        THEN NET := GROSS - (GROSS * DISCOUNT_RATE)
        ELSE NET := GROSS;
    WRITELN('THE NET SALES IS $',NET:6:2)
END;                               (* End of procedure *)
```

FIGURE 12-24
An excerpt from a Pascal program.

Ada

The programming language **Ada** is named for Augusta Ada Byron, Countess of Lovelace, a mathematician in the 1800s, who is thought to have written the first program. The development of Ada was supported by the U. S. Department of Defense and its use is required on all U. S. government military projects. Ada was introduced in 1980 and designed to facilitate the writing and maintenance of large programs that would be used over a long period of time. The language encourages coding of readable programs that are also portable, allowing them to be transferred from computer to computer (Figure 12-25).

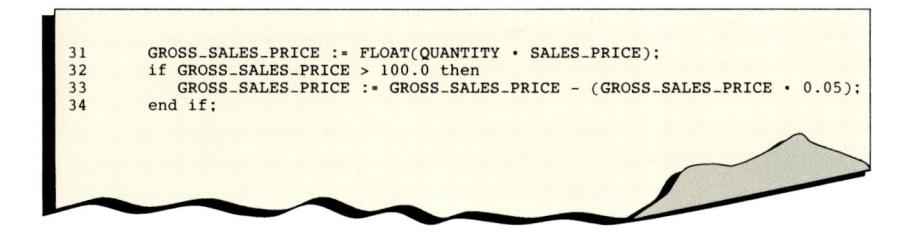

```
31      GROSS_SALES_PRICE := FLOAT(QUANTITY * SALES_PRICE);
32      if GROSS_SALES_PRICE > 100.0 then
33          GROSS_SALES_PRICE := GROSS_SALES_PRICE - (GROSS_SALES_PRICE * 0.05);
34      end if;
```

FIGURE 12-25
An excerpt from an Ada program.

Other Popular Programming Languages

In addition to the commonly used programming languages we just discussed, there are several other popular languages. Figure 12-26 lists some of these languages and their primary uses.

FIGURE 12-26
Other popular computer languages.

ALGOL	**ALGO**rithmetic **L**anguage. Structured programming language used for scientific and mathematical applications.
APL	**A P**rogramming **L**anguage. A powerful, easy-to-learn language that is good for processing data stored in a table (matrix) format.
FORTH	Similar to C. Creates fast and efficient program code. Originally developed to control astronomical telescopes.
LISP	**LIS**t **P**rocessing. Popular artificial intelligence language.
LOGO	Primarily known as an educational tool to teach problem-solving skills.
MODULA-3	Similar to Pascal. Used primarily for developing systems software.
PILOT	**P**rogrammed **I**nquiry **L**earning **O**r **T**eaching. Used by educators to write computer-aided instruction programs.
PL/I	**P**rogramming **L**anguage/One. Business and scientific language that combines many of the features of FORTRAN and COBOL.
PROLOG	**PRO**gramming in **LOG**ic. Used for artificial intelligence.
RPG	**R**eport **P**rogram **G**enerator. Uses special forms to help user specify input, output, and calculation requirements of a program.

APPLICATION GENERATORS

◆ **Application generators**, also called **program generators**, are programs that produce source-language programs, such as BASIC or COBOL, based on input, output, and processing specifications entered by the user. Application generators can greatly reduce the amount of time required to develop a program. They are predicated on the fact that most programs are comprised of standard processing modules, such as routines to read, write, or compare records, that can be combined together to create unique programs. These standard processing modules are stored in a library and are selected and grouped together based on user specifications. Application generators often use menu and screen generators to assist in developing an application.

A **menu generator** lets the user specify a menu (list) of processing options that can be selected. The resulting menu is automatically formatted with heading, footing, and prompt line text (Figure 12-27).

FIGURE 12-27
The left screen is part of a menu generator from ORACLE Corporation that can be used to quickly create professional looking menus on the right screen.

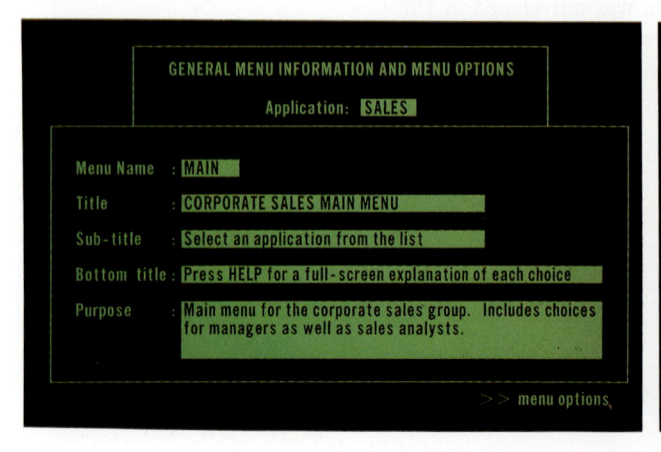

A **screen generator**, sometimes called a **screen painter**, allows the user to design an input or output screen by entering the names and descriptions of the input and output data directly on the screen. The advantage is that the user enters the data exactly as it will appear after the program is created. As each data name, such as Order No., is entered, the screen generator asks the user to specify the length and type of data that will be entered and what processing, if any, should take place before or after the data is entered. The order entry screen shown in Figure 12-28 was created in just one hour using SQL*FORMS, a screen generator product from ORACLE Corporation.

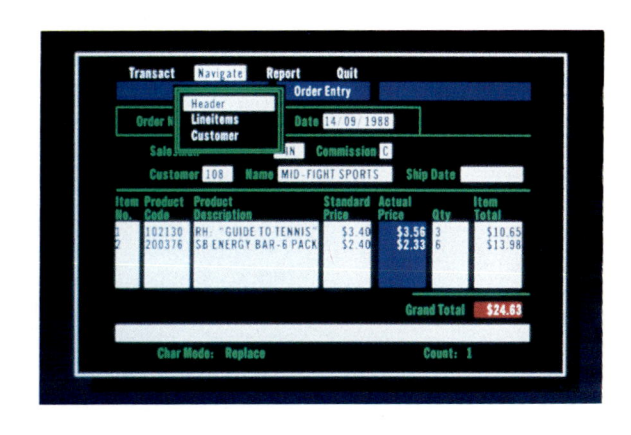

OBJECT-ORIENTED PROGRAMMING

Object-oriented programming (OOP) is a new approach to developing software that allows programmers to create **objects**, a combination of data and program instructions. Traditional programming methods keep data, such as files, independent of the programs that work with the data. Each traditional program, therefore, must define how the data will be used for that particular program. This often results in redundant programming code that must be changed every time the structure of the data is changed, such as when a new field is added to a file. With OOP, the program instructions and data are combined into objects that can be used repeatedly by programmers whenever they need them. Specific instructions, called **methods** define how the object acts when it is used by a program. The following example, illustrated in Figure 12-29, describes how OOP minimizes the number of instructions that must be defined.

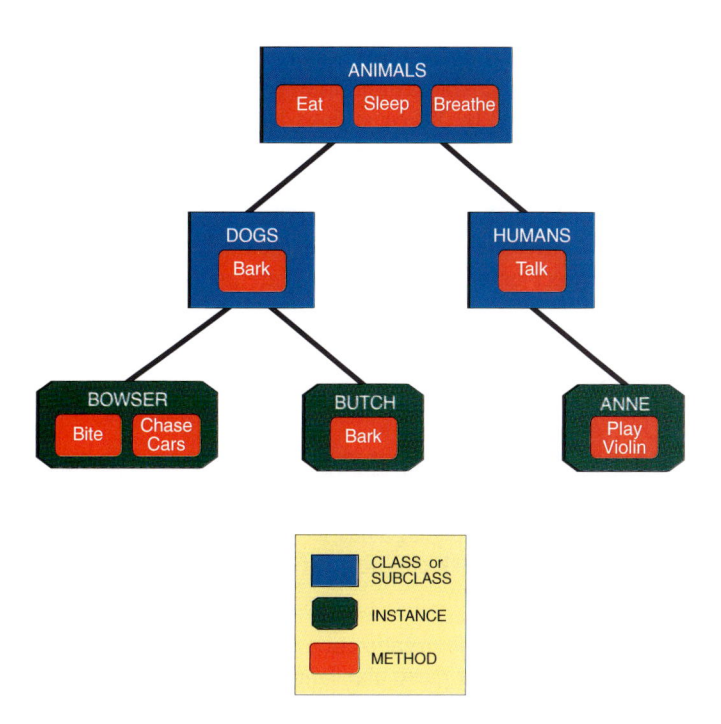

FIGURE 12-28
This order entry screen and the program to process the data were created in one hour using a screen generator from ORACLE Corporation. Using the traditional programming technique of writing individual program instructions would have taken considerably longer.

FIGURE 12-29
Object-oriented programming (OOP) allows procedures (called methods) to be combined with data to form objects. In traditional programming, procedures are defined by the program instructions that are separate from the data. In OOP, the methods define how the object will act when it is referenced and how it can be *inherited* from higher levels, called classes. For example, the method BARK can be inherited by BOWSER from the class DOGS. Objects can also have unique procedures that differ from higher levels. Thus, BUTCH can have a different BARK than BOWSER. The capability to inherit methods from higher levels makes programming more efficient because only methods unique to the specific object need to be defined. A specific occurrence of an object is called an instance.

With OOP, programmers define classes of objects. Each **class** contains the methods that are unique to that class. As shown in Figure 12-29, the class of animals could contain methods on how animals eat, sleep, and breathe. Each class can have one or more subclasses. Each subclass contains the methods of its higher level classes plus whatever methods are unique to the subclass. For example, the subclass Humans contains the method Talk. The subclass Dogs contains the method Bark. Both subclasses, Humans and Dogs, also contain the Eat, Sleep, and Breathe methods of the higher class, Animals. The OOP capability to pass methods to lower levels is called **inheritance**. A specific **instance** of an object contains all methods from its higher level classes plus any methods that are unique to the object. For example, the object Anne contains a method on how to play the violin. The object Bowser contains methods on how Bowser bites and chases cars. Although these methods may be shared by other humans and dogs, respectively, they cannot be placed at higher levels because they are not shared by all humans or dogs. When an OOP object is sent an instruction to do something, called a **message**, unlike a traditional program, the message does not have to tell the OOP object exactly what to do. *What to do* is defined by the methods that the OOP object contains or has inherited. For example, if the object Bowser was sent a message to bark, the method of barking would be defined by the bark method in the subclass Dogs. However, if the object Butch was sent the same message to bark, its actions would be defined by the bark (perhaps a growl) associated with Butch. This illustrates that higher level methods can be overridden to define actions unique to a particular object or class.

A business example of an object would include a class called Invoices. With traditional programming, each time an invoice is displayed on a screen, specific programming instructions are included in the program. With OOP, a method called Display would be part of the object Invoice. An OOP program would only have to send a message identifying the object (Invoice) and stating the desired method (Display). How to display the invoice would be defined as part of the Invoice object.

As OOP is used by an organization, the organization builds a library of OOP objects and classes that can be reused. The more extensive the library, the more powerful and efficient OOP becomes. OOP development systems, such as the Interface Builder used on NeXT computers, allow programmers to access such libraries and link objects to quickly build programs. The programming language most often associated with OOP is Smalltalk, developed by Xerox at their Palo Alto Research Center (PARC) in the 1970s. Versions of several well-known languages, including C and Pascal, also currently offer OOP features.

Closely related to OOP are object-oriented software and object-oriented operating systems. **Object-oriented software** are applications that are developed using OOP programming techniques. **Object-oriented operating systems** are operating systems specifically designed to run OOP applications. Although not widely available, several major companies, including a joint venture of IBM and Apple, are working on versions of object-oriented operating systems.

HOW TO CHOOSE A PROGRAMMING LANGUAGE

◆ Although each programming language has its own unique characteristics, selecting a language for a programming task can be a difficult decision. Factors to be considered include the following:

1. The programming standards of the organization. Many organizations have programming standards that specify that a particular language is used for all applications.
2. The need to interface with other programs. If a program is going to work with other existing or future programs, ideally it should be programmed in the same language as the other programs.

3. The suitability of a language to the application to be programmed. As we discussed, most languages are best suited to a particular type of application. For example, FORTRAN works well with applications requiring many calculations.
4. The expertise of the available programmers. Unless another language is far superior, you should choose the language used by the existing programmers.
5. The availability of the language. Not all languages are available on all machines.
6. The need for the application to be portable. If the application will have to run on different machines, you should choose a common language so the program has to be written only once.
7. The anticipated maintenance requirements. If the user anticipates that the application will have to be modified frequently, consider a language that can be maintained easily and that supports structured programming concepts.

SUMMARY OF PROGRAMMING LANGUAGES

◆ Although procedural languages such as COBOL and BASIC will continue to be used for many years, there is a clear trend toward the creation of programs using nonprocedural tools, such as fourth-generation and natural languages, that allow users to specify what they want accomplished. Your knowledge of programming languages will help you to understand how the computer converts data into information and to obtain better results if you directly participate in the programming process.

CHAPTER SUMMARY

1. A **computer program** is a detailed set of instructions that directs a computer to perform the tasks necessary to process data into information.
2. **Program development** is a series of five steps that take place when a computer program is developed. These steps include: (1) review of the program specifications, (2) program design, (3) program coding, (4) program testing, and (5) finalizing the documentation.
3. In the information system life cycle, program development occurs during the development phase.
4. **Program specifications** can include many documents such as data flow diagrams, system flowcharts, process specifications, a data dictionary, screen formats, and report layouts.
5. During **program design** a logical solution, or **logic**, for a program is developed and documented.
6. **Structured program design** is methodology that emphasizes three main program design concepts: modules, control structures, and single entry/single exit.
7. **Modules**, or **subroutines**, which perform a given task within a program, can be developed individually and then combined to form a complete program.
8. **Structure charts**, or **hierarchy charts**, are used to decompose the modules of a program.
9. The three **control structures** are: the **sequence structure**, where one process occurs immediately after another; the **selection structure**, or **if-then-else structure**, which is used for conditional program logic; and the **iteration structure** or **looping structure**.
10. The **case structure**, which is a variation of the selection structure, is used when a condition is being tested that can lead to more than two alternatives.
11. The two forms of iteration are the **do-while structure** and the **do-until structure**.
12. **Single entry/single exit** means that there is only one **entry point** and one **exit point** from each of the control structures.
13. Three commonly used program design tools are **program flowcharts**, **pseudocode**, and the **Warnier-Orr technique**.
14. Structured walk-throughs are used to review the design and logic of a program.
15. **Coding** is the process of writing the program instructions.

16. Before a program is used to process *real* data it should be thoroughly tested to make sure it is functioning correctly. A simple type of testing is **desk checking**.
17. Programs can be tested for **syntax errors** (grammar). **Logic testing** checks for incorrect results using **test data**.
18. **Debugging** refers to the process of locating and correcting program errors, or **bugs**, found during testing.
19. **Program maintenance** includes all changes to a program once it is implemented and processing real transactions.
20. A **programming language** is a set of written words and symbols that allow a programmer or user to communicate with the computer.
21. Programming languages fit into one of four categories: machine language; assembly language; high-level languages; and fourth-generation languages.
22. Before they can be executed, all programs are converted into **machine language**, the fundamental language of computers, also called **low-level language**.
23. **Assembly language** is a low-level language that is closely related to machine language. It uses **mnemonics** or **symbolic operation code**.
24. Assembly languages use **symbolic addressing** and include **macroinstructions**. Assembly language programs are converted into machine language instructions by an **assembler**.
25. **High-level languages** are easier to learn and use than low-level languages. They use sentences called **program statements**.
26. **Compilers** and **interpreters** are used to translate high-level **source programs** into machine language **object code** or **object programs**.
27. **Fourth-generation languages (4GLs)**, also called **very high-level languages**, are **nonprocedural**, which means that the user tells the computer *what* is to be done, not *how* to do it.
28. A **natural language** allows the user to enter a question as if he or she were speaking to another person.
29. Commonly used programming languages include **BASIC, COBOL, C, FORTRAN, Pascal,** and **Ada**.
30. **BASIC** is one of the most commonly used programming languages on microcomputers and minicomputers.
31. **COBOL** is the most widely used programming language for business applications.
32. **C** is an increasingly popular programming language that requires professional programming skills to be used effectively.
33. **FORTRAN** is noted for its capability to easily express and efficiently calculate mathematical equations.
34. **Pascal** contains programming statements that encourage the use of structured program design.
35. **Ada**, developed and supported by the U.S. Department of Defense, was designed to facilitate the writing and maintenance of large programs that would be used over a long period of time.
36. **Application generators**, or **program generators**, produce source-language programs based on input, output, and processing specifications entered by the user.
37. A **menu generator** lets the user specify a menu of options.
38. A **screen generator**, or **screen painter**, allows the user to design an input or output screen.
39. **Object-oriented programming (OOP)** is a new approach to developing software that allows programmers to create objects.
40. **Objects** are a combination of data and program instructions.
41. **Methods** define how the object acts when it is used by a program.
42. With OOP, each **class** contains the methods that are unique to that class.
43. **Inheritance** is the OOP capability to pass methods to lower levels of classes or objects.
44. A specific **instance** of an object contains all methods inherited from its higher level classes plus and methods that are unique to it.
45. A **message** is an instruction to do something that is sent to an OOP object.
46. **Object-oriented software** are applications that are developed using OOP programming techniques.
47. **Object-oriented operating systems** are operating systems specifically designed to run OOP applications.
48. Some of the factors that you should consider when you choose a programming language are: the programming standards of the organization; the need to interface with other programs; the suitability of a language to the application to be programmed; the expertise of the available programmers; the availability of the language; the need for the application to be portable; and the anticipated maintenance requirements.

KEY TERMS

Ada *12.17*
Application generator *12.18*
Assembler *12.13*
Assembly language *12.13*
BASIC *12.15*
Bugs *12.10*
C *12.16*
Case structure *12.5*
Class *12.20*
COBOL *12.16*
Coding *12.9*
Compiler *12.13*
Computer program *12.2*
Control structure *12.4*
Debugging *12.10*
Desk checking *12.9*
Do-until structure *12.5*
Do-while structure *12.5*
Entry point *12.6*
Exit point *12.6*
FORTRAN *12.17*
Fourth-generation language (4GL) *12.14*
Hierarchy chart *12.3*
High-level language *12.13*
If-then-else structure *12.4*

Inheritance *12.20*
Instance *12.20*
Interpreter *12.14*
Iteration structure *12.5*
Logic *12.3*
Logic testing *12.9*
Looping structure *12.5*
Low-level language *12.12*
Machine language *12.12*
Macroinstruction *12.13*
Menu generator *12.18*
Message *12.20*
Methods *12.19*
Mnemonics *12.13*
Module *12.3*
Natural language *12.15*
Nonprocedural *12.14*
Object *12.19*
Object code *12.13*
Object-oriented operating system *12.20*
Object-oriented programming (OOP) *12.19*
Object-oriented software *12.20*
Object program *12.13*

Pascal *12.17*
Program design *12.3*
Program development *12.2*
Program flowchart *12.6*
Program generator *12.18*
Program maintenance *12.11*
Programming language *12.12*
Program specifications *12.3*
Program statement *12.13*
Pseudocode *12.8*
Screen generator *12.19*
Screen painter *12.19*
Selection structure *12.4*
Sequence structure *12.4*
Single entry/single exit *12.6*
Source program *12.13*
Structure chart *12.3*
Structured program design *12.3*
Subroutine *12.3*
Symbolic addressing *12.13*
Symbolic operation code *12.13*
Syntax error *12.9*
Test data *12.10*
Very high-level language *12.14*
Warnier-Orr technique *12.8*

REVIEW QUESTIONS

1. What is a computer program?
2. List the five steps in program development and give a brief description of each step. Explain how the program development steps relate to the information system life cycle.
3. List at least four types of documents that might be included in the program specifications. Explain the procedures that should be followed if a programmer believes that some aspect of the design should be changed.
4. Draw the three control structures and the two variations that are used in structured program design.
5. Explain the structured programming concept of single entry/single exit. Why is it important?
6. Briefly describe three types of program design tools that are used by programmers.
7. What is desk checking?
8. List at least five types of program documentation. When should documentation be performed?
9. Describe the four categories of programming languages.
10. Explain the advantage of fourth-generation languages.
11. List six commonly used programming languages and explain their primary uses.
12. How do application generators reduce the amount of time required to program?
13. What is object-oriented programming? Explain its advantages over traditional programming methods.
14. List seven factors that you should consider when you choose a programming language.

CONTROVERSIAL ISSUES

1. Although there is a trend toward standardized operating systems, different versions of programming languages are frequently made available. Discuss the advantages and disadvantages of using a single programming language for all applications.
2. Some people believe that programming languages as we know them today will eventually be eliminated. Instead of writing program instructions in a specific computer language, programmers will be able to use a fifth-generation natural language to instruct the computer what to do. Do you think this will happen? If so, when?

RESEARCH PROJECTS

1. Choose a major application at your school or place of work such as registration, payroll, or accounting. Find out what language was used to write the application and why it was chosen. Report to your class.
2. Review the employment advertisements in your local newspaper for computer programming positions. Prepare a report discussing which programming languages are in demand.

Career Opportunities in Information Processing

CHAPTER 13 — CAREERS

OBJECTIVES

- Discuss the three areas that provide the majority of computer-related jobs
- Describe the career positions available in an information systems department
- Describe information processing career opportunities in sales, service and repair, consulting, and education and training
- Discuss the compensation and growth trends for information processing careers
- Discuss the three fields in the information processing industry
- Discuss career development, including professional organizations, certification, and professional growth and continuing education

As society becomes more information oriented, computers are becoming an integral part of most jobs. For this reason, the knowledge you have gained from this text will apply in some way to *any* career you choose. You might, however, want to consider a career in the information processing industry itself.

The purpose of this chapter is to show you the opportunities that exist in the industry, present computer industry career trends, and discuss how to prepare for a career in information systems. Even if you don't choose a computer industry career, you will profit in whatever career you choose if you understand the jobs that computer professionals perform, because any job you choose will likely involve you with one or more of these computer professionals.

THE INFORMATION PROCESSING INDUSTRY

♦ The information processing industry is one of the largest industries in the world with annual sales of well over $100 billion. Job opportunities in the industry come primarily from three areas: the companies that provide the computer equipment; the companies that develop computer software; and the companies that hire information processing professionals to work with these products. As in any major industry, there are also many service companies that support each of these three areas. An example would be a company that sells computer supplies such as printer paper and diskettes.

The Computer Equipment Industry

The computer equipment, or hardware, industry includes all manufacturers and distributors of computers and computer-related equipment such as disk and tape drives, terminals, printers, and communications equipment (Figure 13-1).

The five largest minicomputer and mainframe manufacturers in the United States—IBM, Digital Equipment Corporation, UNISYS, Hewlett-Packard, and NCR— are huge organizations with tens of thousands of employees worldwide. Major microcomputer manufacturers include IBM, Apple, Compaq, and Tandy. The largest company, IBM, has had annual sales of over $70 billion. In addition to the major companies, the computer equipment industry is also known for the many new start-up companies that appear each year. These new companies take advantage of rapid changes in equipment technology, such as laser printers, video disks, and fiber optics, to create new products and new job opportunities. Besides the companies that make end user equipment, thousands of companies make components that most users never see. These companies manufacture chips (processor, memory), power supplies, wiring, and the hundreds of other parts that go into computer equipment.

FIGURE 13-1
Personal-computer keyboards are being assembled and packaged.

The Computer Software Industry

The computer software industry includes all the developers and distributors of applications and system software. Thousands of companies provide a wide range of software from operating systems to complete business systems. The personal computer boom in the early 1980s provided numerous opportunities in the software industry. Thousands of individuals went into business for themselves by creating useful programs for the new microcomputers. Many of these people started by working out of their homes, developing their first software products on their own time while holding other jobs.

Today, software alone is a huge industry that includes leading companies such as MSA, ASK, Microsoft, Lotus, and Borland, with annual sales in the hundreds of millions of dollars. Most of these companies specialize in one particular type of software product such as business application software or productivity tools such as word processing or spreadsheets.

Information Processing Professionals

Information processing professionals are the people who put the equipment and software to work to produce information for the end user (Figure 13-2). This includes people such as programmers and systems analysts who are hired by companies to work in an information systems department. We discuss these and other positions available in the information processing industry in the next section.

WHAT ARE THE CAREER OPPORTUNITIES IN INFORMATION PROCESSING?

◆ The use of computers in so many aspects of life has created thousands of new jobs. Some of these occupations, such as personal computer network sales representative, didn't even exist ten years ago. We describe some of the current career opportunities, and encourage you to consider them as you prepare for your future profession.

FIGURE 13-2
Computer professionals must be able to understand the end user's point of view and often meet with the user to review his or her information processing requirements.

Working in an Information Systems Department

In Chapter 1 we discussed the various jobs within an information systems department. These positions include: data entry personnel, computer operators, computer programmers, systems analysts, database administrator, manager of information systems, and vice president of information systems.

The people in these positions work together as a team to meet the information demands of their organizations. Throughout this book we have discussed the responsibilities associated with many of these positions, including the role of the systems analysts in the information system life cycle (Chapter 11) and the steps programmers perform in program development (Chapter 12). Another way to visualize the positions and their relationships is to look at an organization chart such as the one shown in Figure 13-3. In addition to management, the jobs in an information systems department can be classified into five categories:

1. Operations
2. Data administration
3. Systems analysis and design
4. Programming
5. Information center

FIGURE 13-3
The organization chart shows the many areas within an information systems department that offer employment opportunities.

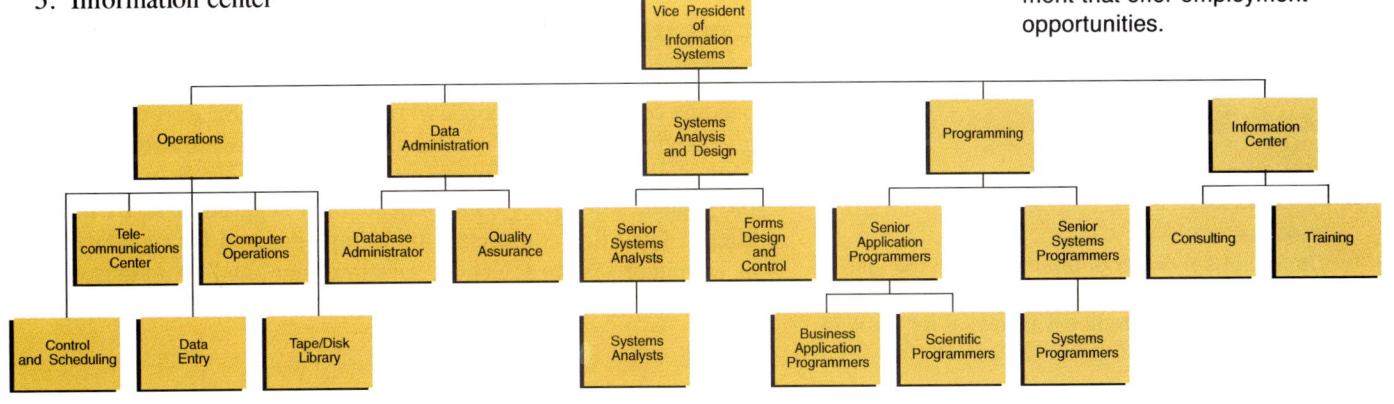

FIGURE 13-4
Computer retailers, such as Computerland, need salespeople who understand personal computers and have good people skills.

Operations personnel are responsible for carrying out tasks such as operating the computer equipment that is located in the computer center. The primary responsibility of data administration is to maintain and control the organization's database. In systems analysis and design, the various information systems needed by an organization are created and maintained. Programming develops the programs needed for the information systems, and the information center provides teaching and consulting services within an organization to help users meet their departmental and individual information processing needs. As you can see, an information systems department provides career opportunities for people with a variety of skills and talents.

Sales

Sales representatives must have a general understanding of computers and a specific knowledge of the product they are selling. Strong interpersonal, or people, skills are important, including listening ability and strong oral and written communication skills. Sales representatives are usually paid based on the amount of product they sell, and top sales representatives are often the most highly compensated employees in a computer company.

Some sales representatives work directly for equipment and software manufacturers and others work for resellers. Most personal computer products are sold through dealers such as Computerland (Figure 13-4). Some dealers, such as Egghead Discount Software, specialize in selling the most popular software products.

Service and Repair

Being a **service and repair technician** is a challenging job for individuals who like to troubleshoot and solve problems and who have a strong background in electronics (Figure 13-5). In the early days of computers, repairs were often made at the site of the computer equipment. Today, however, malfunctioning components, such as circuit boards, are usually replaced and taken back to the service technician's office or sent to a special facility for repair. Many equipment manufacturers are now including special diagnostic software with their computer equipment that helps the service technician identify the problem. Using a modem, some computer systems can automatically telephone another computer at the service technician's office and leave a message that a malfunction has been detected.

Consulting

After building experience in one or more areas, some individuals become **consultants**, people who draw upon their experience to give advice to others. Consultants must have not only strong technical skills in their area of expertise, but must also have the people skills to effectively communicate their suggestions to their clients. Qualified consultants are in high demand for such tasks as computer system selection, system design, and communications network design and installation.

FIGURE 13-5
Computer service and repair is one of the fastest growing computer-related professions. A knowledge of electronics is essential for this occupation.

Education and Training

The increased sophistication and complexity of today's computer products has opened wide opportunities in computer education and training (Figure 13-6). Qualified instructors are needed in schools, colleges, and universities and in private industry as well. In fact, the high demand for teachers has created a shortage at the university level, where many instructors have been lured into private industry because of higher pay. This shortage probably will not be filled in the near future; the supply of Ph.D.s, usually required at the university level, is not keeping up with the demand.

FIGURE 13-6
There is a high demand in schools and industry for qualified instructors who can teach information processing subjects.

COMPENSATION AND GROWTH TRENDS FOR INFORMATION PROCESSING CAREERS

◆ Compensation is a function of experience and demand for a particular skill. Demand is influenced by geographic location, with metropolitan areas usually having higher pay than rural areas. Figure 13-7 shows the result of a salary survey of over 80,000 computer professionals across the United States and Canada.

FIGURE 13-7
Salary levels (in thousands of dollars) for various computer industry positions are based on the number of years of experience. (Source: Source EDP, 1991 Professional Compensation Data, National Statistics).

	YEARS EXP.	MEDIAN SALARY ($1,000)
PROGRAMMING:		
Commercial	<2	27
	2–3	33
	4–6	35
	>6	40
Engineering/Scientific	<2	31
	2–3	35
	4–6	38
	>6	43
Microcomputer/ Minicomputer	<2	27
	2–3	32
	4–6	34
	>6	40
Software Engineer	<2	30
	2–3	36
	4–6	41
	>6	46
Systems Software	<2	32
	2–3	38
	4–6	40
	>6	49
MANAGEMENT:		
Data Center Operations		45
Programming Development		61
Systems Development		58
Technical Services		59
MIS Director/VP		67
BUSINESS SYSTEMS:		
Consultant		45
Project Leader/Sys. Analyst		43

	YEARS EXP.	MEDIAN SALARY ($1,000)
SPECIALISTS:		
Data Base Management Analyst	<4	39
	4–6	41
	>6	49
Information Center Analyst	<4	30
	4–6	33
	>6	43
Office Automation Analyst	<4	30
	4–6	34
	>6	40
Edp Auditor	<4	35
	4–6	38
	>6	44
Technical Writer	<4	30
	4–6	32
	>6	37
Telecommunications (Planning)	<4	35
	>4	45
SALES:		
Hardware		55
Software		57
Services		56
Technical Support	<2	32
	2–3	35
	4–6	38
	>6	45
Management		68
DATA CENTER:		
Computer Operator	<2	20
	2–3	23
	4–6	25
	>6	29
Technical Data Center Analyst	<4	37
	4–6	44
	>6	46
Operations Support Technician	<4	24
	>4	30
Communications/ Network Analyst	<4	26
	>4	34

CHAPTER 13 CAREER OPPORTUNITIES IN INFORMATION PROCESSING

As shown in Figure 13-8, some industries pay higher than others for the same job. According to the survey, the communications, utility, and aerospace industries pay the highest salaries. These industries have many challenging applications and pay the highest rate to obtain the best qualified employees.

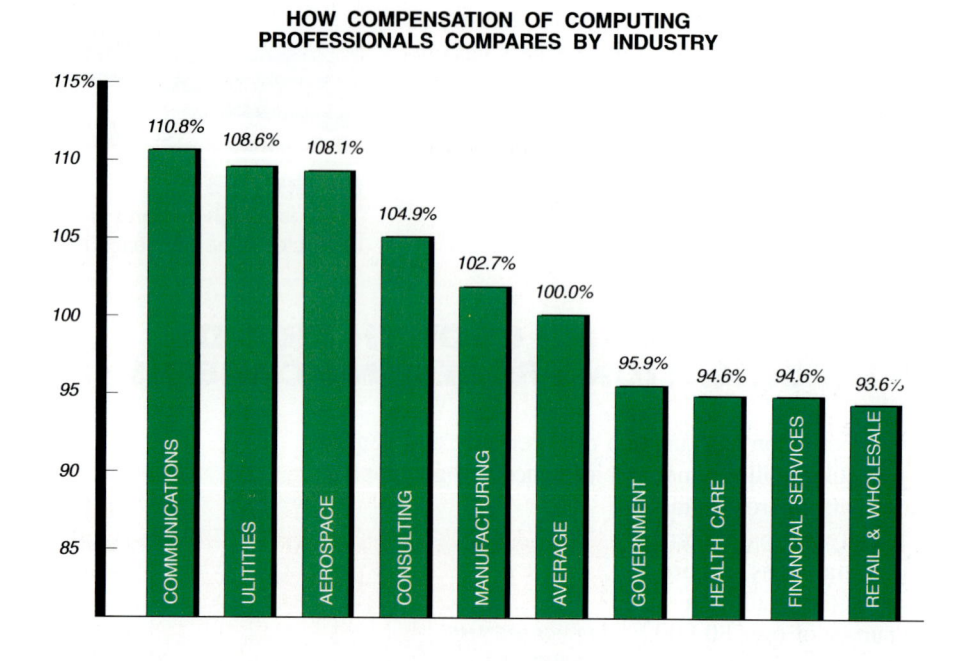

FIGURE 13-8
Some industries pay more for the same job position.

HOW COMPENSATION OF COMPUTING PROFESSIONALS COMPARES BY INDUSTRY

Industry	%
COMMUNICATIONS	110.8%
UTILITIES	108.6%
AEROSPACE	108.1%
CONSULTING	104.9%
MANUFACTURING	102.7%
AVERAGE	100.0%
GOVERNMENT	95.9%
HEALTH CARE	94.6%
FINANCIAL SERVICES	94.6%
RETAIL & WHOLESALE	93.6%

According to the U.S. Bureau of Labor Statistics, the fastest growing computer career positions through 1995 will be systems analyst, applications programmer, machine operator, and computer repair technician (Figure 13-9).

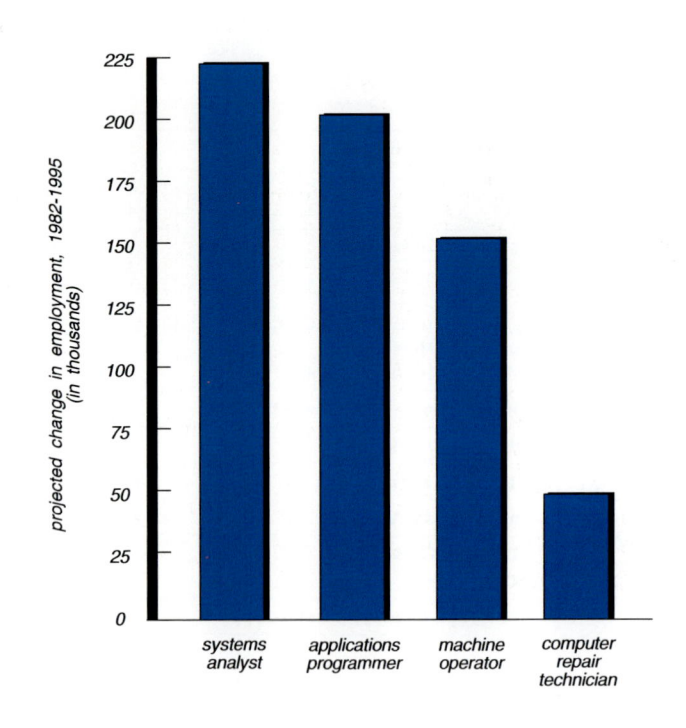

FIGURE 13-9
Computer careers with the highest projected growth, as compiled by the U.S. Bureau of Labor Statistics.

projected change in employment, 1982-1995 (in thousands)

systems analyst	~225
applications programmer	~200
machine operator	~150
computer repair technician	~50

PREPARING FOR A CAREER IN INFORMATION PROCESSING

◆ To prepare for a career in the information processing industry, individuals must decide what computer field they are interested in and obtain education in the field they chose. In this section we discuss the three major computer fields and some of the opportunities for obtaining education in those fields.

What Are the Fields in the Information Processing Industry?

While this book has primarily focused on the use of computers in business, there are actually three broad fields in the information processing industry (Figure 13-10): computer information systems; computer science; and computer engineering. **Computer information systems (CIS)** refers to the use of computers to provide the information needed to operate businesses and other organizations. The field of **computer science** includes the technical aspects of computers such as hardware operation and systems software. **Computer engineering** deals with the design and manufacturing of electronic computer components and computer hardware. Each field provides unique career opportunities and has specialized requirements.

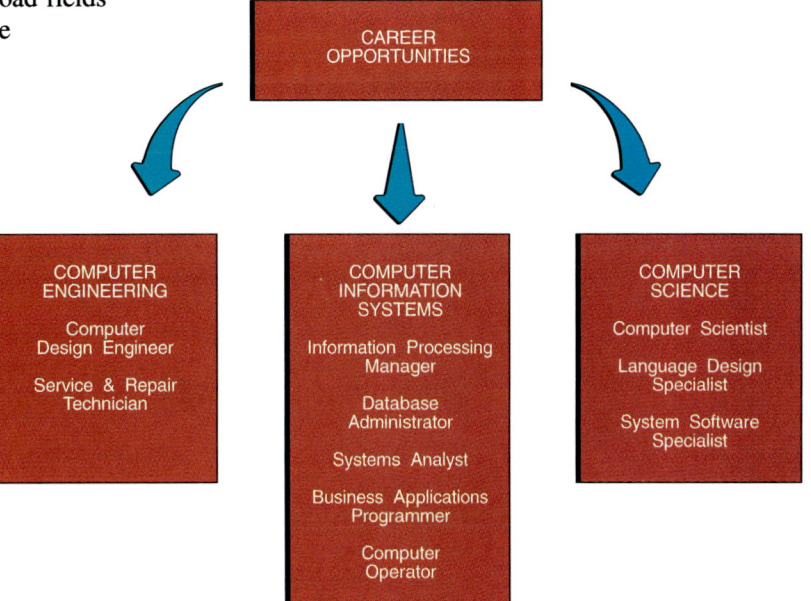

CAREER OPPORTUNITIES

COMPUTER ENGINEERING
Computer Design Engineer
Service & Repair Technician

COMPUTER INFORMATION SYSTEMS
Information Processing Manager
Database Administrator
Systems Analyst
Business Applications Programmer
Computer Operator

COMPUTER SCIENCE
Computer Scientist
Language Design Specialist
System Software Specialist

Obtaining Education for Information Processing Careers

The expanded use of computers in today's world has increased the demand for properly trained computer professionals. Educational institutions have responded to this demand by providing a variety of options for students to study information systems. Trade schools, technical schools, community colleges, colleges, and universities offer formal education and certification or degree programs in computer-related fields. If you are evaluating a program offered by one of these institutions, remember the three areas of information processing: computer information systems, computer science, and computer engineering. Frequently, schools will have separate programs for each area.

Understanding the differences among the three fields will help you to find the courses you want. For example, in a university, courses relating to computer information systems may be listed with the business courses, computer science courses may be with math, and computer engineering may be with electronic technology or electrical engineering. Because schools list and organize their computer courses in different ways, you should carefully read individual course descriptions whenever you are selecting computer education classes.

FIGURE 13-10
There are three broad fields of study in the information processing industry; each with specialized study requirements.

With the wide variety of career opportunities that exist in information processing, it is difficult to make anything other than broad general statements when it comes to discussing degree requirements for employment in the industry. As in most other industries, the more advanced degree an individual has in a chosen field, the better that individual's chances are for success. While not having a degree may limit a person's opportunities for securing a top position, it will neither prevent entry nor preclude success in information processing.

CAREER DEVELOPMENT IN THE INFORMATION PROCESSING INDUSTRY

◆ There are several ways for persons employed in the information processing industry to develop their skills and increase their recognition among their peers. These include professional organizations, certification, and professional growth and continuing education activities.

Professional Organizations

Computer-related organizations have been formed by people who have common interests and a desire to share their knowledge. Some of the organizations that have been influential in the industry include:

1. **Association for Computing Machinery (ACM)**. This association is composed of persons interested in computer science and computer science education. The association has many special interest groups such as computer graphics, database, and business.
2. **Association of Information Systems Professionals (AISP)**. This association was originally aimed at word processing professionals, but now includes a much broader membership, including office automation professionals.
3. **Association of Systems Management (ASM)**. This group is composed of individuals interested in improving the systems analysis and design field.
4. **Data Processing Management Association (DPMA)**. This is a professional association of programmers, systems analysts, and information processing managers.
5. **Institute of Electrical and Electronic Engineers (IEEE) and IEEE Computer Society (IEEE/CS)**. These organizations are primarily composed of computer scientists and engineers.

Each of these organizations has chapters throughout the United States (several have chapters throughout the world), offers monthly meetings, and sponsors periodic workshops, seminars, and conventions. Some organizations have student chapters or offer reduced membership fees for students. Attending professional meetings provides an excellent opportunity for students to learn about the information processing industry and to meet and talk with professionals in the field.

In addition to these and other professional organizations, user groups exist for most makes of computers. A **user group** is a group of people with common computer equipment or software interests that meet regularly to share information. Most metropolitan areas have one or more local computer societies that meet monthly to discuss topics of common interest about personal computers. For anyone employed or simply interested in the computer industry, these groups can be an effective and rewarding way to learn and continue career development.

Certification

Many professions offer certification programs as a way of encouraging and recognizing the efforts of their members to attain a level of knowledge about their profession. The best known certification programs in the information processing industry are administered by the **Institute for the Certification of Computer Professionals (ICCP)**. The ICCP offers four certification designations: Certified Computer Programmer (CCP); Certified Data Processor (CDP); Certified Systems Professional (CSP); and Associate Computer Professional (ACP). The CCP, CDP, and CSP designations are earned by passing three examinations. The ACP designation is obtained by passing a general computer knowledge test and any one of seven programming language tests. A summary of the test requirements for all of the designations is shown in Figure 13-11. To be eligible to take the CCP, CDP, and CSP examinations, a person must have a minimum of five years of experience in the information processing industry. The ACP examination, which is designed for entry level personnel, requires no previous industry experience.

```
                ICCP CERTIFICATION EXAMINATIONS

A.  Examination Requirements for Certified Computer Programmer
    (CCP), Certified Data Processor (CDP), and Certified Systems
    Professional (CSP)

    1.  Core Examination (required for all designations)
        a.  Human and Organization Framework
        b.  Systems Concepts
        c.  Data and Information
        d.  Systems Development
        e.  Technology
        f.  Associated Disciplines
    2.  Professional Designation Examinations
        a.  Certified Computer Programmer (CCP)
            1)  Data and File Organization
            2)  Program Design
            3)  Procedural Program Structure
            4)  Procedural Programming Considerations
            5)  Integration with Hardware and Software
        b.  Certified Data Processor (CDP)
            1)  General Management and Organization Concepts
            2)  Project Management
            3)  Information Systems Management
        c.  Certified Systems Professional (CSP)
            1)  Systems Analysis
            2)  Systems Design and Implementation
            3)  The Systems Analyst as a Professional
    3.  Specialty Examinations (one required)
        a.  Business Information Systems
        b.  Communications
        c.  Office Information Systems
        d.  Scientific Programming
        e.  Software Engineering
        f.  Systems Programming

B.  Associate Computer Professional (ACP) Examination

    1.  Core Examination (same as for CCP, CDP, and CSP)
    2.  Programming Language Examinations (one required)
        a.  FORTRAN
        b.  Pascal
        c.  BASIC
        d.  RPG
        e.  COBOL
        f.  C
        g.  ADA
```

Professional Growth and Continuing Education

Because of rapid changes in technology, staying aware of new products and services in the information processing industry can be a challenging task. One way of keeping up is by participating in professional growth and continuing education activities. This broad category includes events such as workshops, seminars, conferences, conventions, and trade shows that provide both general and specific information on equipment, software, services, and issues affecting the industry, such as computer security. Workshops and seminars usually last a day or two, while conferences, conventions, and trade shows often last a week. The largest trade show in the United States, **COMDEX**, brings together nearly 2,000 vendors to display their newest products and services to over 125,000 attendees (Figure 13-12).

FIGURE 13-11
The subject areas for each of the four certification examinations offered by the Institute for the Certification of Computer Professionals (ICCP). Three of the designations (CCP, CDP, and CSP) are designed for experienced professionals with five or more years of industry experience. The fourth designation (ACP) does not require previous industry experience.

FIGURE 13-12
COMDEX is one of the largest computer product trade shows in the world. Nearly 2,000 vendors come together to demonstrate their new equipment, software, and services to over 125,000 prospective customers.

Another way of keeping informed about what is going on in the computer industry is to regularly read one or more computer industry publications (Figure 13-13). There are hundreds of publications to choose from. Some publications, such as *Computerworld* and *InfoWorld*, are like newspapers and cover a wide range of issues. Other publications are oriented toward a particular topic area such as communications, personal computers, or a specific equipment manufacturer. Many of the more popular publications can be found in public or school libraries.

FIGURE 13-13
Computer industry publications number in the hundreds, with general- and specific-interest topics available to keep you informed.

SUMMARY OF COMPUTER CAREER OPPORTUNITIES

With the increased use of computers, the prospects for computer-related career opportunities are excellent. Not only are the numbers of traditional information processing jobs, such as programmer and systems analyst, expected to increase, but the application of the computer to existing occupations will create additional job opportunities. Regardless of an individual's career choice, a basic understanding of computers should be an essential part of any employee's job skills.

CHAPTER SUMMARY

1. As society becomes more information oriented, computers are becoming an integral part of most jobs.
2. Job opportunities in the information processing industry come from three areas: computer equipment companies, computer software companies, and companies that hire information processing professionals.
3. The computer equipment industry includes all manufacturers and distributors of computers and computer-related equipment.
4. The computer software industry includes all developers and distributors of application and system software.

5. Information processing professionals are the people that put the equipment and software to work to produce information for the end user.
6. Career opportunities in information processing include: working in an information systems department, sales, service and repair, consulting, and education and training.
7. The jobs in an information systems department can be classified into five categories: (1) operations, (2) data administration, (3) systems analysis and design, (4) programming, and (5) information center.
8. **Sales representatives** are often the most highly compensated employees in a computer company.
9. Being a **service and repair technician** is a challenging job for individuals who like to solve problems and who have a strong background in electronics.
10. **Consultants**, people who draw upon their experience to give advice to others, are in high demand for such tasks as computer system selection, system design, and communications network design and installation.
11. According to the U.S. Bureau of Labor Statistics, the fastest growing computer career positions through 1995 will be systems analyst, applications programmer, machine operator, and computer repair technician.
12. The three fields in information processing are computer information systems; computer science; and computer engineering.
13. **Computer information systems (CIS)** refers to the use of computers to provide the information needed to operate businesses and other organizations.
14. **Computer science** includes the technical aspects of computers such as hardware operation and systems software.
15. **Computer engineering** deals with the design and manufacturing of electronic computer components and computer hardware.
16. Trade schools, technical schools, community colleges, colleges, and universities offer formal education and certification or degree programs in computer-related fields.
17. Computer professionals may continue to develop their skills and increase their recognition among their peers through professional organizations, certification, and professional growth and continuing education activities.
18. Professional organizations include the **Association for Computing Machinery (ACM)**, the **Association of Information Systems Professionals (AISP)**, the **Association of Systems Management (ASM)**, the **Data Processing Management Association (DPMA)**, and the **Institute of Electrical and Electronic Engineers (IEEE) and IEEE Computer Society (IEEE/CS)**.
19. A **user group** is a group of people with common computer equipment or software interests that meet regularly to share information.
20. The **Institute for Certification of Computer Professionals (ICCP)** offers four certification programs.
21. Computer professionals stay current by participating in professional growth and continuing education activities such as conferences, workshops, conventions, and trade shows.

KEY TERMS

Association for Computing Machinery (ACM) *13.8*
Association of Information Systems Professionals (AISP) *13.8*
Association of Systems Management (ASM) *13.8*
COMDEX *13.9*
Computer engineering *13.7*

Computer information systems (CIS) *13.7*
Computer science *13.7*
Consultant *13.4*
Data Processing Management Association (DPMA) *13.8*
IEEE Computer Society (IEEE/CS) *13.8*

Institute for the Certification of Computer Professionals (ICCP) *13.9*
Institute of Electrical and Electronic Engineers (IEEE) *13.8*
Sales representative *13.4*
Service and repair technician *13.4*
User group *13.8*

REVIEW QUESTIONS

1. List the three areas that provide the majority of computer related jobs.
2. Identify seven jobs within an information systems department. The jobs in an information systems department can be classified into what five categories?
3. Describe the people skills that are important for a sales representative.
4. What does a consultant do? List three areas of knowledge where consultants are in high demand.
5. What are the four fastest growing computer career positions?
6. Describe the three fields in information processing and list at least two types of jobs in each field.
7. List and describe the purpose of five computer-related professional organizations.
8. What are the four certifications administered by the Institute for the Certification of Computer Professionals (ICCP)?
9. Name two computer industry publications that are like newspapers.

CONTROVERSIAL ISSUES

1. Because the industry is changing so rapidly, computer professionals often disagree as to what should be taught in an introductory computer course. What topics do you think should be included or excluded?
2. Some people believe that computer professions such as programming should be subject to mandatory certification or licensing, like certified public accountants. Others believe that because the industry is changing so rapidly, certification programs should be encouraged but remain voluntary. Discuss the advantages and disadvantages of mandatory programs.

RESEARCH PROJECTS

1. Contact a graduate of your school who is currently working in the computer industry. Write a report on his or her current job responsibilities. Ask the graduate to comment on how his or her education prepared him or her for this current job.
2. Contact a local computer employment specialist. Ask him or her for information on entry level computer positions in your community. Report to your class.

Trends and Issues in the Information Age

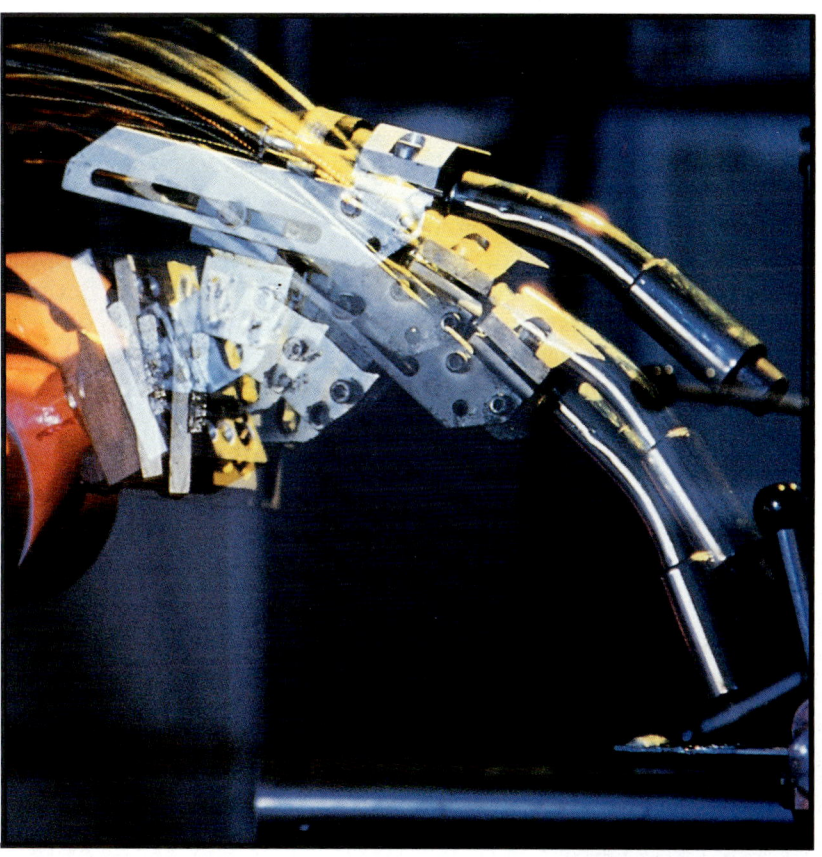

CHAPTER 14
TRENDS/ISSUES

OBJECTIVES

- Discuss the electronic devices and applications that are part of the automated office
- Describe the technologies that are developing for the automated factory, including CAD, CAE, CAM, and CIM
- Discuss the trend toward the computer-integrated enterprise
- Discuss the use of personal computers in the home
- Describe the methods used in computer-aided instruction (CAI)
- Explain guidelines for purchasing personal computers
- Discuss social issues related to computers, such as computer crime and privacy

After reading the preceding chapters, you know what a computer is, what a computer does, how it does it, and why a computer is so powerful. You have learned about computer equipment and software and how the system development process is used to combine these elements with data, personnel, users, and procedures to create a working information system. The purpose of this chapter is to talk about current and future trends, including changes taking place in information systems in the workplace. We also discuss the use of personal computers in the home and some of the social issues related to computers such as security and computer crime, privacy, and ethics.

CHAPTER 14 TRENDS AND ISSUES IN THE INFORMATION AGE

INFORMATION SYSTEMS IN BUSINESS

The largest use of computers is in business. Millions of systems ranging from mainframes to microcomputers are installed and used for applications such as inventory control, billing, and accounting. This section discusses how these traditional applications will be affected by changes in technology and methods. It also covers the automated office, the automated factory, and the computer-integrated enterprise. Although the term automated can be applied to any process or machine that can operate without human intervention, the term is commonly used to describe computer-controlled functions.

How Will Existing Information Systems Change?

Existing business information systems will continue to undergo profound changes as new technology, software, and methods are applied to the huge installed base of traditional business system users. Important overall trends include more online, interactive systems and less batch processing. In addition, the expansion of communications networks and the increased use of relational database systems means that users will have a wider variety of data and information available for decision making, and more flexibility presenting information on reports and displays. The increased number of people using computers will make the computer-user interface even more important. Graphical user interfaces will continue to replace command- and menu-driven interfaces. These and other trends that will affect the information systems of tomorrow are shown in Figure 14-1.

FIGURE 14-1
Trends affecting information systems of tomorrow.

◀ EQUIPMENT

- Increased use of personal computers networked to other personal computers and to central minicomputers or mainframes
- Mainframes and minicomputers used as central storehouses of data with processing done on a decentralized basis by powerful personal computers
- Increased disk storage capacity using new technologies such as laser disks
- High-resolution color graphics screens that can display photo-quality pictures
- Increased use of page printers that can print high-quality graphics and text
- Reduced instruction set computers (RISC) and parallel processing greatly increasing the number of instructions that can be processed at one time
- Increased use of portable computing equipment such as notebook computers
- Handwriting recognition systems allowing users to interact with a computer using a pen-shaped stylus

SOFTWARE ▶

- Fourth-generation and natural languages enabling the user to communicate with the computer in a more conversational manner
- Object orientation combining processes and methods with data
- Computer-aided software engineering (CASE) shortening the system development time frame
- Increased use of decision support and artificial intelligence systems to help users make decisions
- Widespread implementation of graphic user interfaces using icons and symbols to represent information and processes
- Integrated applications to eliminate the need for separate programs for word processing, spreadsheets, graphics, telecommunications, and other applications

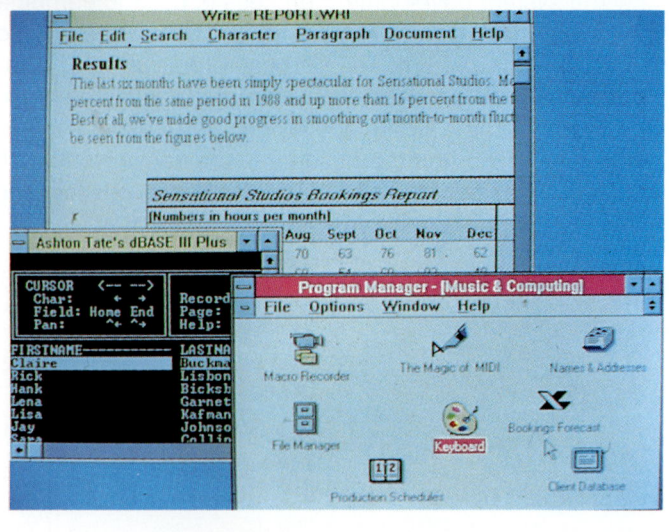

INFORMATION SYSTEMS IN BUSINESS **14.3**

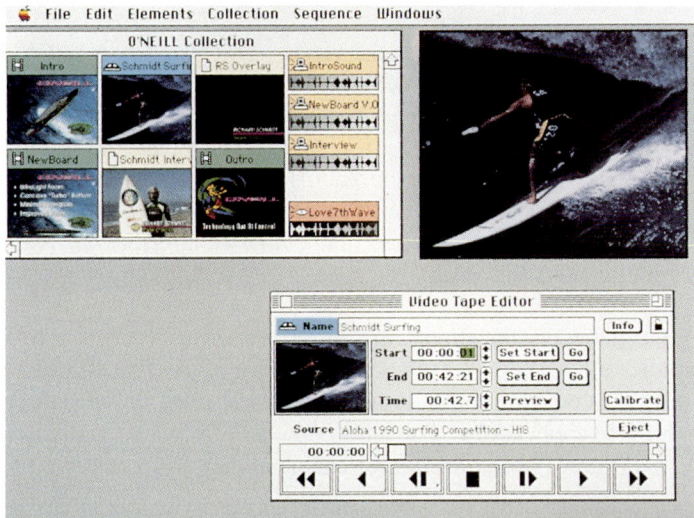

◄ **DATA**

- Automatic input of data at the source where it is created
- Compound documents that combine text, numbers, and nontext data such as voice, image, and full-motion video

USERS ►

- Most people being computer literate, with a basic understanding of how computers work and how to use them in their jobs
- Increased responsibility for design, operation, and maintenance of information processing systems
- Users increasingly relying on computers to manage the continuing proliferation of information (the worldwide volume of printed information doubles every eight years)

◄ **INFORMATION SYSTEMS PERSONNEL**

- Increased interface with users
- Shift from machine and software orientation to user application orientation
- Emphasis from how to capture and process data to how to more effectively use the data available and create information
- Reduced staff levels handling increased processing work loads
- Some processing operations being outsourced to independent contractors
- Continuous need for retraining and education to keep up with new technology

The Automated Office

The **automated office**, sometimes referred to as the **electronic office**, is the term that describes the use of electronic devices such as computers, facsimile machines, and computerized telephone systems to make office work more productive. Automated office applications, such as word processing, electronic mail, voice mail, desktop publishing, facsimile, image processing, and teleconferencing, started out as separate, stand-alone applications. In recent years, however, the trend has been to integrate these applications into a network of devices and services that can share information. A brief review of each of these applications follows.

Word Processing For many organizations, word processing was the first office application to be automated and among all organizations, word processing still ranks as the most widely used office automation technology. Today, most word processing systems are integrated with other applications. This allows the word processing applications to extract data such as names and addresses or financial data from other application files.

Electronic Mail **Electronic mail** is the capability to use computers to transmit messages to and receive messages from other computer users. The other users may be on the same computer network or on a separate computer system reached through the use of a modem or some other communications device. Electronic mail eliminates the need to hand deliver messages or use a delivery service such as the post office or Federal Express. Electronic mail usage will grow as previously separate personal computers are attached to local area networks.

Voice Mail **Voice mail** can be considered verbal electronic mail. Made possible by the latest computerized telephone systems, voice mail reduces the problem of telephone tag, where two people trying to reach each other wind up leaving a series of messages to please call back. With voice mail, the caller can leave a message, similar to leaving a message on an answering machine. The difference is that with a voice mail system, the caller's message is digitized (converted into binary ones and zeros) so that it can be stored on a disk like other computer data. This allows the party who was called to hear the message later (by reconverting it to an audio form) and also, if desired, add a reply or additional comments and forward the message to someone else who has access to the system. Some software applications are now incorporating voice messages as part of stored documents. For example, a budget worksheet could be created with verbal instructions on how it should be completed.

Desktop Publishing Desktop publishing allows the user to control the process of creating high-quality newsletters, brochures, and other documents that previously would had to have been developed by professional artists. Trends in desktop publishing include more sophisticated high-resolution graphics and the increased use of color. More powerful computer systems and the availability of desktop publishing systems for different levels of user sophistication will increase their use in small as well as large organizations.

Facsimile Facsimile, or **FAX**, machines are used to transmit a reproduced image of a document over standard phone lines (Figure 14-2). The document can contain text or graphics, can be hand-written, or be a photograph. FAX machines optically scan the document and convert the image into digitized data that can be transmitted, using a modem, over the phone. A FAX machine at the receiving end converts the digitized data back into its original image. Besides the separate FAX machines, plug-in circuit boards are also available for personal computers. Using either a separate or a built-in modem, these fax boards can directly transmit computer-prepared documents or documents that have been digitized with the use of a scanner. FAX machines are having an increasing impact on the way businesses transmit documents. Many documents that were previously sent through the mail are now sent by FAX. With the speed and convenience of a phone call, a document sent by FAX can be transmitted anywhere in the world.

Image Processing Image processing is the capability to store and retrieve a reproduced image of a document. Image processing is often used when an original document, such as an insurance claim, must be seen to verify data. Image processing and traditional applications will continue to be combined in many areas. For example, in 1988 American Express began sending cardholders copies of the individual charge slips that were related to the charges on their statement. These charge slips were recorded by an image processing system and then merged with the customer statement program.

FIGURE 14-2
A facsimile (FAX) machine can send and receive copies of documents to and from any location where there is phone service and another FAX machine.

Teleconferencing Teleconferencing once meant three or more people sharing a phone conversation. Today, however, teleconferencing usually means **video conferencing**, the use of computers and television cameras to transmit video images and the sound of the conference participants to other participants with similar equipment at a remote location (Figure 14-3). Special software and equipment is used to digitize the video image so that it can be transmitted along with the audio over standard communications channels. Although the video image is not as clear for moving objects as is commercial television, it does contribute to the conference discussion and is adequate for nonmoving objects such as charts and graphs.

FIGURE 14-3
Video conferencing is used to transmit and receive video and audio signals over standard communications channels. This meeting is being transmitted to a video conference center at another location. The people at the other location are also being recorded and transmitted and can be seen on the TV monitor.

Summary of the Automated Office The trend toward integrated automated office capabilities will continue. Currently incompatible devices such as stand-alone FAX machines, copiers, and telephone switches will be standardized or will be provided with software that will enable them to communicate and transfer data with other devices. The higher productivity provided by automated office devices will encourage more organizations to adopt them.

14.6 CHAPTER 14 TRENDS AND ISSUES IN THE INFORMATION AGE

The Automated Factory

As in the automated office, the goal of the **automated factory** is to increase productivity through the use of automated, and often computer-controlled, equipment. Technologies used in the automated factory include computer-aided design, computer-aided engineering, computer-aided manufacturing, and computer-integrated manufacturing.

Computer-Aided Design (CAD) Computer-aided design (CAD) uses a computer and special graphics software to aid in product design (Figure 14-4). The CAD software eliminates the laborious drafting that used to be required and allows the designer to dynamically change the size of some or all of the product and view the design from different angles. The capability to store the design electronically offers several advantages over traditional manual methods. One advantage is that the designs can be changed more easily than before. Another is that the design database can be reviewed more easily by other design engineers. This increases the likelihood that an existing part will be used in a product rather than a new part designed. For example, if a support bracket was required for a new product, the design engineer could review the design database to see if any existing products used a support bracket that would be appropriate for the new product. This not only decreases the overall design time but increases the reliability of the new product by using proven parts.

FIGURE 14-4
Computer-aided design (CAD) is an efficient way to develop plans for new products.

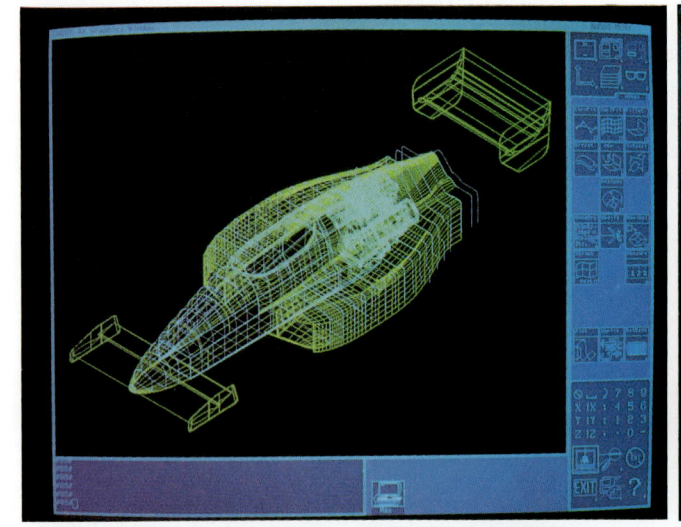

Computer-Aided Engineering (CAE) Computer-aided engineering (CAE) is the use of computers to test product designs. Using CAE, engineers can test the design of an airplane or a bridge before it is built (Figure 14-5). Sophisticated programs simulate the effects of wind, temperature, weight, and stress on product shapes and materials. Before the use of CAE, prototypes of products had to be built and subjected to testing that often destroyed the prototype. CAE allows engineers to create a computer prototype that can be tested under a variety of conditions. CAE allows products to be tested in some conditions, such as earthquakes, that could not previously be simulated.

FIGURE 14-5
Computer-aided engineering (CAE) allows the user to test product designs before they are built and without damaging the product.

Computer-Aided Manufacturing (CAM)
Computer-aided manufacturing (CAM) is the use of computers to control production equipment. CAM production equipment includes software-controlled drilling, lathe, and milling machines as well as robots (Figure 14-6). The use of robots has aroused much interest, partially because of preconceived ideas of robots as intelligent, humanlike machines. In practice, most industrial robots rarely look like a human and can perform only preprogrammed tasks. Robots are often used for repetitive tasks in hazardous or disagreeable environments such as welding or painting areas, or when chemicals that are hazardous to humans are used.

Computer-Integrated Manufacturing (CIM)
Computer-integrated manufacturing (CIM) is the total integration of the manufacturing process using computers (Figure 14-7). Using CIM concepts, individual production processes are linked so that the production flow is balanced and optimized and products flow at an even rate through the factory. In a CIM factory, automated design processes are linked to automated machining processes that are linked to automated assembly processes that are linked to automated testing and packaging. Under ideal CIM conditions, a product will move through the entire production process under computer control. Many companies may never fully implement CIM because it is so complex. But CIM's related concepts of minimum inventory and efficient demand-driven production are valid and will be incorporated into many manufacturers' business plans.

FIGURE 14-6
Computer-aided manufacturing (CAM) is used to control production equipment such as these welding robots on an automobile assembly line.

The Computer-Integrated Enterprise

Although in the previous sections we discuss the automated office and automated factory separately, the long-range trend is the **computer-integrated enterprise**—an organization in which all information storage and processing is performed by a network of computers and intelligent devices. In a computer-integrated enterprise, all office, factory, warehouse, and communications systems are linked using a common interface allowing authorized users in any functional area of the organization to access and use data stored anywhere in the organization. Rather than being machine or software oriented as today's systems, future systems will be document or information oriented. The user won't need to separately start a word processing, spreadsheet, or communications program. Instead, users will be able to create and distribute compound documents that contain text, graphics, numbers, and full-motion video. They will be able to record, in their own voice, comments or questions about the document before it is stored or routed to someone else in the organization. For example, a new product marketing plan could contain a text description of the product, a spreadsheet showing projected sales, and a narrated video showing the product in use. If the president of a company had questions about the plan, he or she could add questions to the plan in his or her own voice, and route the plan to the appropriate person for a response.

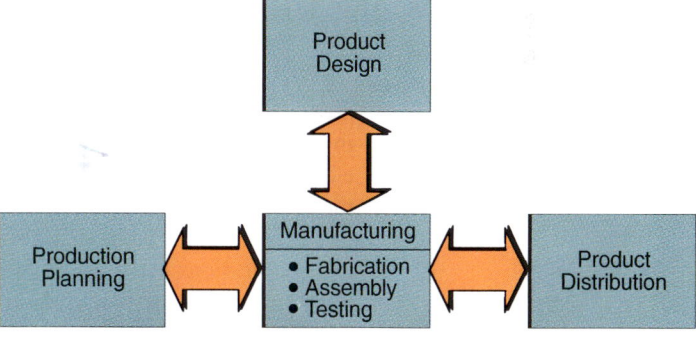

FIGURE 14-7
The concept of computer-integrated manufacturing (CIM) is to use computers to integrate all phases of the manufacturing process from planning and design to manufacturing and distribution.

BRINGING THE INFORMATION AGE HOME

Millions of personal computers have been purchased for home use, and the use of personal computers in the home is expected to increase. Just as the use of computers in the workplace has changed how we work, the use of computers in our homes is changing our personal lives. In the next two sections we discuss how people use personal computers in homes today, how they might use them in the future, and things you should consider when purchasing a personal computer system.

FIGURE 14-8
The Prodigy online information service offers the latest news, weather, sports, and financial information along with shopping, entertainment, and electronic mail.

The Use of Personal Computers in the Home

People use personal computers in their homes in a variety of ways. These ways usually fall into five general categories: (1) personal services, (2) control of home systems, (3) telecommuting, (4) education, and (5) entertainment.

Personal Services In many ways running a home is similar to running a small business. The productivity tools you use in the office, such as word processing, spreadsheet, and database, can also be used in the home to help you with creating documents, with financial planning and analysis, and filing and organizing data. Personal computer software is also available to assist you with home accounting applications such as balancing checkbooks, making household budgets, and preparing tax returns. In addition, using a personal computer to transmit and receive data over telephone lines allows home users to access a wealth of information and services. For example, teleshopping, electronic banking, and airline reservations are services that are becoming more popular, and information such as stock prices, weather reports, and headline news is available to home users who subscribe to online information services such as Prodigy (Figure 14-8), Genie, and CompuServe. The personal services provided by home computer use allows people to perform personal and business-related tasks quickly and conveniently in the comfort of their own homes. Without a personal computer, completing similar activities would take them considerably more time because it would frequently require them to travel to other locations to conduct this business and acquire information.

A different type of service available to users who have personal computers with communications capabilities is the access and use of electronic **bulletin board systems**, called **BBSs**, that allow users to communicate with one another and share information (Figure 14-9). While some bulletin boards provide specific services such as buying and selling used computer equipment, many bulletin boards function as electronic clubs for special-interest groups and are used to share information about hobbies as diverse as stamp collecting, music, genealogy, and astronomy. Some BBSs are strictly social; users meet new friends and conduct conversations by entering messages through their keyboards.

Control of Home Systems Another use of computers in the home is to control home systems such as security, environment, lighting, and landscape sprinkler systems. Personal computers used in this manner are usually linked to special devices such as alarms for security; thermostats for temperature control; and timing devices for lighting and sprinkler systems. For example, if the personal computer system has communications capabilities, a homeowner who is away can use a telephone or another computer to call home and change the operation of one of the control systems. Suppose a homeowner is on vacation in Texas and learns that heavy rains have been falling at home in Pennsylvania. He or she could call the computer and use the keys of a touch-tone telephone to instruct the computer to turn off the garden sprinkler system.

Most existing home control systems were installed after the home was built and often consist of separate systems to control each set of devices. This will change in the future, however. In 1990, the Electronic Industries Association released a new wiring standard called the Consumer Electronics Bus (CEBus). The CEBus sets standards for sending information throughout a home using existing electrical wiring, phone lines, TV cable, and nonwired techniques such as radio waves. In a related effort, Echelon Corporation is designing chips to be used in consumer electronics and building products. The chips will allow appliances, lighting systems, and other home products to be networked together and controlled by a single system using a consistent set of commands. Although they are not yet widely implemented, these changes will result in what many refer to as the intelligent home or smart house.

SAN DIEGO ELECTRONIC BULLETIN BOARDS

1 OMNIBUS BBS	464-6271 ¥
also	280-2696
A&B Express	447-1009 ¥Z
ABC	436-3525 ¥
Adventure Board	224-2636 §
Adventure Games of America	695-3011 •
Adventures In Palancia	222-1785 ¥
Alabaster's cave	528-9218 §
Alcatraz	723-0537 ¥
Amber Knights	460-9762 §
Aquarium BBS	462-1732 8
ARC Modem	589-0339 ¥
Artworld BBS	462-6887 ¥
Ashley's BBS	565-2029 ¥
Astralite	276-7623 ¥
The Asylum	293-0158 ¥
Atari/Amiga	691-7862 ¥
Awesome's Place	482-3025 ¥
The Ballyhoo BBS	447-1008 ¥
The BBS Summit	576-0077 ¥
The Black Box	747-2304 ¥
Bootcamp I	941-0996 8
Border Town BBS	466-3173 ¥
The Bosn's Locker	442-9252 ¥
Brian Smith's BBS	582-0875 ¥
The Bicycle Bulletin Board	720-1830 ¥
Bullit Proof Software	284-6729 Ω
Bytes 'R Us	428-9773 8
California Sands GS	541-7048 8
California Computer Connection	944-1804 8
Camelot 3000	462-0542 ¥
Casa de Cricket	823-1583 ¥
The Chief's Mess	469-1354 8
Christ Line	268-3568 ¥
Classified Connection	566-1745 ¥
The Closet BBS	480-9686 §
also	726-4419
CMS:Lakeside	390-2689 §
CMUG	433-3162 §
Coconet Demo BBS	456-0815 ¥
COM2 (node #1): Remote BBS	471-8730 8
COM2 (node #2): Remote BBS	471-8839 ¥
Commodore Connection	429-6227 ¥
Commodore Edition	575-8364 §
The Commodore Shop	423-7901 §
Commadore User's Network	267-8056 §
Communication link	726-7834 §
Communicore	484-5811 ¥
Computer Buyer's Guide	689-0500 ¥
Computer Outlet, North County	740-0113 ¥Z
The Computer Room	287-6006 ¥
ComputorEdge On-Line	573-1675 ¥
Cornucopia	748-8096 ¥
Cougar Country	480-3056 §Z
Covey's Concepts	439-5131 ¥
Cygnus X-1 BBS	457-2665 ¥
The Crypt BBS	457-1836 ¥
Cuyamaca College	660-2010 §
Data Trax, USRobotics HST	433-8564 8
The Dark Alley	728-5497 ¥
DataWorks BBS	423-9352 Ω
Dave's Place	562-3248 8
Deadwood BBS	598-4088 ¥
dBored	748-3644 8
The Dead Zone BBS/PDSE	755-3350 ¥
also	942-0848
Demon's Den	284-3439 ¥
Digex:SDCS DIGSIG	454-8078 §
DJM BBS	588-6941 8
Dollars and Bytes	483-5477 ¥Z
Don's House	440-6038 ¥
DOOGER'S PLACE	588-8931 8
Dragon's Nest BBS	449-7052 ¥
Dragon's Domain BBS	565-4424 ¥
The Dream Clinic	670-9522 ¥
Eight-Bit Tandy	571-6366 ¥
The Edge Elite	695-6949 ¥
Electro-shok Therapy	723-3065 ¥
Elephant's Graveyard (node #9):	270-3148 ¥
Enigma	453-1819 ¥
Especially Yours	226-3042 ¥
The Evergreen Forest	426-2057 §
Falcon's BBS	726-8001 ¥
Family Historians	297-5746 ¥
Far Star Prev. ST Sig atar	225-1775 ¥
Fax Satellite System	224-3853 ¥
The File Bank	728-4318 8
The File Cabinet	427-5459 Ω
The Final Experience	670-4445 8
The Final Frontier	966-0114 8
Fightertown BBS	537-4217 ¥
The Flare Path	561-2999 Ω
The Forgotten Realm BBS	578-4093 ¥
Foundations Edge	287-2996 ¥
Foy's Trading Post	562-3646 ¥
FSMAO-2	725-6322 ¥
Fuel Dump	390-7896 ¥
The Fun House	697-8714 ¥
The Funny Farm	746-6564 Ω
The Game Board BBS	281-0675 §
Gandalf's	466-9505 ¥
The General	281-4185 ¥
The General	281-5538 Ω
The Ginko BBS	566-4165 ¥
The G.T. Connection	263-0347 ¥
The Hero Network	222-5961 ¥
High Country East	789-4391
Hillcrest Host & BBS	291-0544 ¥
Hog Heaven	561-0058 ¥
The Family Historian	279-5746 ¥
IEEE (San Diego)	452-3131 ¥
I.D.I.C.	461-0982 ¥
Imperial Beach BBS	575-1562 ¥
The Internal Stack II	741-2686 ¥
Inve$tment Club BB$	476-0692 ¥
Jim's BBS of San Diego	492-9714 ¥
Katatania Tales	420-4120 ¥
Key Point BBS	479-8032 Ω
Kit's Hideout	741-0692 §
Knight Shadows' Grotto	792-0455 ¥
Knowledge Works BBS	528-1058 ¥
Lake Murray's Support BBS	460-2292 ¥
Lakeside Wildcat!	390-7328 Ω
The Landing Strip	672-0846 Ω
Launching Acadamy	562-6337 ¥
La Verne & PC Street Again	222-9483 ¥
The Lemonade Stand	941-6158 §
The Lemon Grove BBS	463-9037 ¥
Lips BBS	693-0735 ¥
Light Impressions	538-9131 §
L.O.L.A.	582-6969 §
Longshot	465-9764 ¥√
also	465-0327
The Looney Bin	390-9470 ¥
LoticTek BBS	280-6725 ¥
L.V. Wanderer	560-8203 §
Mac Underground Safehouse	272-2059 ¥
Magic 102 BBS	560-1534 §
Mainstreet Data	439-6624 ¥
Marzland	578-9086 §
MBC Broadcast	422-0239 ¥
MediaLine BBS	298-4027 8
MicroMiga	670-1095 ¥
Milliway's	268-9614 ¥
Mister Rick's Neighborhood	695-1163 8
Molakai Express	462-6319 §
Morning Star	575-3310 Ω
Mount Olympous	465-8236 §
Mousetrap	464-2134 Ω
Multitech PC	578-9221
Mushin BBS	535-9580 8
also	222-3097 8
My House	447-1422 ¥
Mystic Lounge	679-7691 §
Nassau Xpress	433-9777 ¥
The Nesting Ground	484-7283 ¥
New-Ware	455-5226 ¥
NEXUS Z (node #63)	486-0735 ¥
Night Owl, Ham Radio	279-3921 8
Nola's Nemesis	461-1336 ¥
North Clairemont BBS	272-3087 Ω
North San Diego Apple Club	571-9010 ¥
Ocean Beach BBS	224-4878 §
Ocean Sports	558-2691 ¥
Oh No Not Just Another BBS	298-7475 ¥
Orcus's Den BBS	268-4498 ¥
Osborne-CPM User Group	299-1604 §
OtherWorlds	630-1147 §
Outer Limits	596-0667 ¥
PC•LawCom BBS	272-6615 ¥
also	483-1324 •
P-Net (pnet03)	569-9195 ¥
P-Net (pnet01)	444-7006 ¥
Paulette's Playhouse	484-2690 ¥
PD-SIG	749-2741 ¥8$
also	749-2589¥$, 749-3432¥$,
also	749-6222¥8$, 749-6384¥$
People-Net (pnet12)	259-3704 Σ
The Place BBS	479-5244 ¥
Pro-BEAGLE	558-6151 ¥
Pro-Grouch	260-0492 8
ProLine [avalon]	632-7161 8
ProLine [mercury]	697-0261 ¥
ProLine [simasd]	238-2333 8
ProLine [sol]	670-5379 8
The Rabbit Hole	941-3505 §
Radio-Active	268-9625 ¥
The Rasta Think Tank	282-1211 Σ
The Rat's Nest	275-6129 8
The Real Estate BBS	464-4540 ¥
R-n-S Info Foneline	268-0964 ¥
Rogues' Roost C-64	262-6106 §
Rom-Burner	424-7213 ¥
The RPC Library	461-6642 ¥
Rosie's Lair	589-4599 ¥
Rudy's Place BBS	670-3040 ¥
Sabaline	692-1961 8
S.D. Fantasy	476-7733 ¥
San Diego PC Board (node #1)	584-4172 ¥
San Diego PC Board (node #2)	584-1715 ¥
Santee Experiment	562-8758 ¥
Sawyer College of Business BBS	286-8614 ¥Z
Scanline	298-2023 8
SCCG:TIBBS	278-8155 §
SCH Editor's BBS	563-1598 ¥
Scripps Ranch	586-0703 ¥
SDC BBS	754-5425 ¥
S.D. CLIP*BOARD	279-4662 ¥
S.D. Computer Society	549-3788 ¥
The Seaside Connection	481-6479 ¥
Serenity	259-3704 8
Serenity	259-7757 Σ
Serial Port	755-3123 ¥
The Service Center	275-1448 ¥
Sharky's MAChine	747-8719 ¥
S.I.G.H. Amiga	788-0449 ¥
Silver's Cave	561-7206 ¥
Skanked BBS!	480-2441 ¥
SKYNET II	754-1659 ¥
So Cal Graphics BBS	292-0186 ¥
Software Revenge	431-4444 8
The Software Corner	588-6238 ¥
The Software Market Place	669-1581 ¥
SomeWares Bet. Heaven	436-9861 ¥
Sound of Money	461-2521 ¥
ST-NET BBS	268-3996 Ω
ST-SDACE	689-8157 §
also	689-8397
ST SIG Atari ST & Others	726-4419 §
also	726-4419
Star Base 23	560-2996 ¥
Starhelm Graystaff	479-3006 8
Suburbia?	447-5489 Ω
The Surf Shack	967-6017 §
SW/SE Connection	479-0411 8
also	479-3006
Sys-Jam Productions	432-9057 ¥
Tech Pro BBS	755-7357 §
TeleMac	576-1820 √$
The 64 & More Store	258-0951 ¥
Tinker Toys BBS	738-0471 ¥
Trader's World	284-8729 8
The Treehouse	424-6375 ¥
Tunnels of Versarius NODE I	453-1781 √
The Underground Cavern	748-8157 §
The Underground Press	444-4163 §
The VOID! BBS	455-5957 ¥
UN*x Lips Service BBS	693-0735 Ω
USA BBS	443-5968 ¥
USRobotics	286-0841 √
USS Perpetrators	561-4681 ¥
Viking BBS	756-9567 ¥
Waduki's Graphics Pad	425-5831 ¥
The Warezhouse	575-7914 §
The White House	432-0787 §
Willy-NET	535-0816 ¥$
Wisdom BBS	270-3083 ¥
The Wizard's Domain	426-5028 ¥
Xanadu (new users)	287-2044 ¥
Xanadu (validated users)	287-2140 ¥
Zeke	755-5675 ¥

Legend

§ 300/1200 baud, ¥ 300-2400 baud, 8 9600 baud HSTs, Ω 14,400 baud HSTs, √ Dual Standard (14,400 HST and 9600 V.32), Σ V.32 19,200 Telebit Trailblazer, Z After hours or weekends, $ Requires a donation for access.

ComputorEdge acknowledges this is not a complete list of all the BBSs in the San Diego area and reserves the right to reject or cancel, for any reason, any BBS submission for inclusion on this list.

62 October 19, 1990

COMPUTOREDGE

FIGURE 14-9
Some of the bulletin boards available in the San Diego, California area. Bulletin board systems are an excellent source for answers to questions about personal computer equipment and software.

Telecommuting **Telecommuting** refers to the capability of individuals to work at home and communicate with their offices by using personal computers and communications lines. With a personal computer, an employee can access the main computer at the office. He or she can read and answer electronic mail. An employee can access databases, and can transmit completed projects. Some predictions claim that by the end of the 1990s, ten percent of the work force will be telecommuters. Most of these people will probably arrange their business schedules so they can telecommute two or three days a week. Telecommuting provides flexibility, allowing companies and employees to increase productivity and, at the same time, meet the needs of individual employees. Some of the advantages possible with telecommuting include reducing the time needed to commute to the office each week; eliminating the need to travel during poor weather conditions; providing a convenient and comfortable work environment for disabled employees or workers recovering from injuries or illnesses; and allowing employees to combine work with personal responsibilities such as child care.

Education The use of personal computers for education, called **computer-aided instruction (CAI)**, is another rapidly growing area. Whereas CAI is frequently used to describe software that is developed and used in schools, much of the same software is available for home users. CAI software can be classified into three types: drill and practice, tutorials, and simulations.

FIGURE 14-10
Computer-aided instruction (CAI) software provides a structured yet motivating way to learn. This CAI software helps the user to develop deductive reasoning, reference, and research skills while learning geography, history, economics, government, and culture.

FIGURE 14-11
Flight simulators can be both fun and educational. Some simulators offer realistic instrument consoles and flight patterns that help teach the user about flying.

Drill and practice software uses a flash-card approach to teaching by allowing users to practice skills in subjects such as math and language. A problem or word appears on the computer screen and the user enters the answer. The computer accepts the answer and responds by telling the student whether the answer is correct or incorrect. Sometimes the user gets second and third chances to select the correct answer before the computer software reveals the correct answer.

With **tutorial software**, the computer software uses text, graphics, and sometimes sound to teach a user concepts about subjects such as chemistry, music theory, or computer literacy. Following the instruction, tutorial software might present true/false or multiple-choice questions to help the user ensure that he or she understands the concepts. The increased use of optical disk storage provides high-quality graphics and direct access capability; it promises to greatly enhance this type of CAI.

The third type of CAI, **simulation software**, is designed to teach a user by creating a model of a real-life situation. For example, many simulation packages are available to teach business concepts. One program designed for children simulates running a lemonade stand and another program for adults simulates the stock market. In the lemonade simulation, the user makes decisions about *How many quarts of lemonade to make* and *What price to charge customers for a glass of lemonade*. The computer software accepts the user's decisions, performs computations using the software model, and then responds to the user with the amount of profit or loss for the day. Good CAI software is designed to be user friendly and motivate the user to succeed (Figure 14-10).

In addition to CAI software, some trade schools, colleges and universities are now offering students with personal computers a chance to take electronic correspondence courses from their homes. Lessons and assignments for classes are transmitted between the student and the school over communications lines.

Education in the home through CAI or electronic correspondence courses allows home users to learn at their own pace, in the convenience of their home, and at a time that fits into their personal schedule. Well-written educational software can be so entertaining that it is sometimes difficult to distinguish between it and entertainment software.

Entertainment Entertainment software, or game playing, on home computers has always had a large following among the younger members of the family. However, many adults are surprised to find that entertainment software can also provide them with hours of enjoyment. Popular types of entertainment software include arcade games, board games, simulations, and interactive graphics programs. Most people are familiar with the arcade-type games (similar to video games) that are available for computers. A popular board game is computer chess. Simulations include games such as baseball and football and a variety of flight simulators that allow users to pretend they are controlling and navigating different types of aircraft (Figure 14-11).

Also available are a wide variety of interactive graphic adventure games that range from rescuing a princess from a castle's dungeon to solving a murder mystery. People can play many of these games alone or in small groups. The software usually allows players to adjust the level of play to match their abilities, that is, beginner through advanced. With entertainment software, the computer becomes a fun, skillful, and challenging game partner.

In addition to playing games, some personal computer users use their home computer as a tool for personal hobbies. Computers are used by hobbyists to design quilt and stained glass patterns, run model trains, organize stamp, doll, and photography collections, and write, transpose, play, and print musical scores.

Summary of the Use of Personal Computers in the Home   As you can see, personal computers are used in homes in a variety of ways. Whether or not you now use a personal computer in your home, it is very probable that you will at some time in the near future. In fact, it is very possible that within the next decade you will have multiple computers in your home. Because computers can be used in so many different ways and also because computer technology is changing so rapidly, you should carefully choose any computer system you purchase. We discuss some general guidelines for purchasing personal computers in the next section.

Guidelines for Buying a Personal Computer

When you purchase a personal computer, you should make every effort to select a computer system that matches your individual needs as closely as possible. The six steps for purchasing a personal computer system recommend that you:

1. **Become computer literate**. This is truly the first and most important step in making a wise purchase. You might be surprised that many people buy computer equipment without understanding the capability of a personal computer or the tasks it can and cannot perform. Many times these people buy a computer like the one their neighbor or friend purchased, and expect it to meet their needs. Sometimes it does, but frequently they are disappointed. Hopefully, this will not happen to you. You already have an advantage because by reading this book, you now know a great deal about computers and have developed a foundation of knowledge on which you can base your software and equipment decisions. In short, you already are computer literate. But computer technology is changing rapidly, to stay computer literate you will need to stay current with the changes in the field. You can do this by reading periodicals or attending seminars on state-of-the-art computer technology.
2. **Define and prioritize the type of tasks you want to perform on your computer**. This step will help you to see more clearly exactly what you want to do with your computer and will help you select software and equipment that will match these needs. Define your needs in writing. Create a numbered list with the most important application at the top and the least important application at the bottom. General applications such as word processing, spreadsheets, database, and communications are easy to include on the list. You may, however, have a special application in mind such as controlling a household security system. Being computer literate will help you know if a special application is feasible. It will also help you to discuss any special needs you might have with computer professionals who can help you. Once your list is completed you can begin to evaluate the available software.
3. **Select the software packages that best meet your needs**. Publications, computer stores, and user groups are all good resources when it comes to evaluating the available software. For more on evaluating software, review the section in Chapter 2, Guidelines for Purchasing Microcomputer Applications Software.

In addition to purchasing commercial software, you can also consider selecting shareware and public domain software. **Shareware** is software that users may try out on their own systems before paying a fee. If a user decides to keep and use the software, he or she sends a registration fee to the software publisher (Figure 14-12).

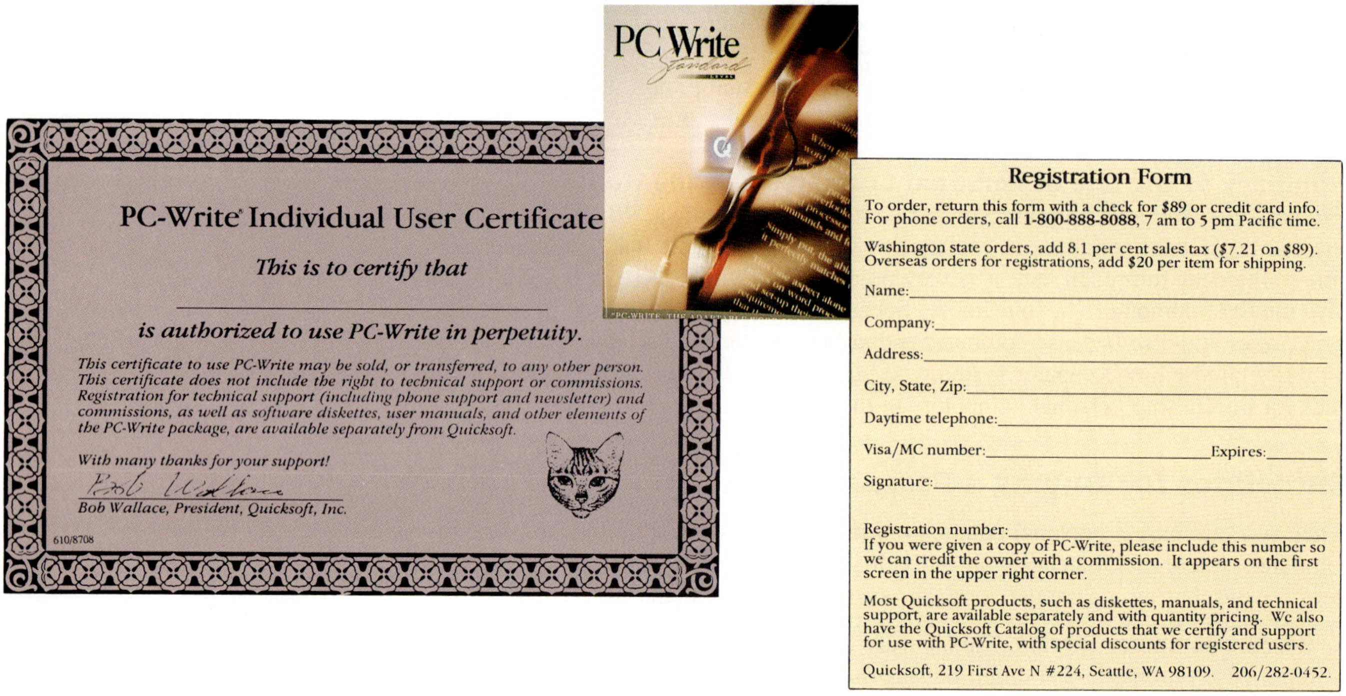

FIGURE 14-12
After trying the PC-Write software, users fill out a registration form and mail it with a fee to Quicksoft, the publisher of PC-Write. A user certificate is then sent to the user.

Public domain software is free software that is not copyrighted and can therefore be distributed among users. While the quality of shareware and public domain software varies greatly, some of the software is quite good. You can obtain this type of software from BBSs and also from public domain software libraries.

4. **Select equipment that will run the software you have selected**. The capabilities of the different types of personal computers vary greatly. For example, some personal computers can perform extensive graphics while others cannot. Selecting the software that meets your needs before selecting your equipment guides you in selecting appropriate equipment. Some software only runs on certain types of personal computers. Also, knowing the software you want to run prevents overbuying (purchasing a machine that is more powerful than you need) or underbuying (purchasing a machine that is not powerful enough). Capabilities to consider when you evaluate equipment include: processing speed of the microprocessor, memory size, system expandability, compatibility of the system with other personal computers, monochrome or color display, graphics capability, amount and type of auxiliary storage, printer type and speed, and communications capabilities. If you can't decide between two configurations, choose the system with more storage and/or processing power. Today's latest software applications require more disk space and CPU speed than applications released in prior years. This trend is expected to continue. Although you don't want to overbuy, you do want to buy a system that will meet your immediate needs and provide room for storage growth and additional applications.

5. **Select the suppliers for the software and equipment**. Your options include used equipment and software, mail order, and computer stores. Price, warranties, training, service, and repair are all details to consider when you select a supplier.

Obtaining the best overall value may not mean paying the lowest price. A store that is willing to provide you with assistance in assembling your system or furnish some training may be well worth a slightly higher price. Student purchasers should always check to see if systems and software are available through their school or if an educational discount is offered.

6. **Purchase the software and equipment**. If you have followed these guidelines you will probably feel both excited and confident with the decisions you have made. Your efforts to define your computing needs and to select software, equipment, and a supplier that will meet those needs should help you to select a personal computer system that is appropriate for you and with which you will be satisfied.

Summary of Bringing the Information Age Home

Personal computers are used in homes to aid in a variety of tasks such as personal services, control of home systems, telecommuting, education, and entertainment. When users purchase a personal computer system for the home, they should first become computer literate and evaluate their computer processing needs, then purchase software and equipment that meets those needs. The trend is clear. Personal computers will continue to bring the information age into our homes.

The changes that accompany the information age raise several issues that are related to society as a whole. We discuss some of these issues in the next section.

SOCIAL ISSUES

◆ Significant inventions such as the automobile and television have always challenged existing values and caused society to think about the right and wrong ways to use the new invention. The computer is no exception; including the social issues related to security and computer crime, privacy, and ethics.

Computer Security and Crime

Computer security and computer crime are closely related topics. **Computer security** refers to the safeguards established to prevent and detect unauthorized use and deliberate or accidental damage to computer systems and data. **Computer crime** is the use of a computer to commit an illegal act. Here we discuss three types of crimes that can be committed and the security measures that can be taken to prevent and detect them.

Software Theft Software theft, often called **software piracy**, became a major problem with the increased use of personal computers. Some people have difficulty understanding why they should pay hundreds, perhaps thousands, of dollars for what appears to be an inexpensive diskette or tape, and instead of paying for an authorized copy of the software they make an illegal copy. Estimates are that for every authorized copy of a commercial program, there is at least one illegal copy. However, it should be stated that software theft is a violation of copyright law and is a crime. Software companies take illegal copying seriously and in some cases offenders who have been caught have been vigorously prosecuted. For large users, the financial incentives for stealing software have been lowered by site licensing and multiple-copy discounts. Site licensing allows organizations to pay a single fee for multiple copies of a program used at a single location. Multiple-copy discounts reduce the fee of each additional copy of a program license.

Unauthorized Access and Use Unauthorized access can be defined as computer trespassing, in other words, being logged on a system without permission. Many so-called computer hackers boast of the number of systems that they have been able to access by using a modem. These hackers usually don't do any damage and merely wander around the accessed system before logging off.

Unauthorized use is the use of a computer system or computer data for unapproved and possibly illegal activities. Unauthorized use may range from an employee using the company computer for keeping his or her child's soccer league scores to someone gaining access to a bank funds system and creating an unauthorized transfer. Unauthorized use could also include the theft of computerized information such as customer lists or product plans. Courts have been taking a harsher view of both unauthorized access and use, and more frequently sentence violators to jail terms and substantial fines.

The key to preventing both unauthorized access and unauthorized use is computer security that controls and monitors an appropriate level of authorization for each user. Authorization techniques range from simple passwords to advanced biometric devices that can identify individuals by their fingerprint, voice, or eye pattern (Figure 14-13). The authorization technique should match the degree of risk associated with unauthorized access. An organization should regularly review the levels of authorization for users to determine if the levels are still appropriate.

FIGURE 14-13
Biometric security devices use biological characteristics to allow or deny access to would-be computer users. A retinal scanner reads a small area of a person's eye (left). An individual's retina pattern is as unique as a fingerprint, which can also be tested by a fingerprint recognition device (right). Other equipment exists to identify people by their voices or by their signatures.

Malicious Damage Malicious or deliberate damage to the data in a computer system is often difficult to detect because the damaged data may not be used or carefully reviewed on a regular basis. A disgruntled employee or an outsider might gain access to the system and delete or alter individual records or an entire file. One of the most potentially dangerous types of malicious damage is done by a **virus**, a computer program designed to copy itself into other software and spread through multiple computer systems. Figure 14-14 shows how a virus can spread from one system to another. Although they have existed for a some time, viruses have become a serious problem only recently.

Organizations have developed specific programs called **vaccines** to locate and remove viruses; in addition organizations are becoming more aggressive in prosecuting persons suspected of planting viruses. In what was described as the first computer virus trial, in 1988 a former programmer was convicted in Texas of planting a program in his employer's computer system that deleted 168,000 sales commission records.

A COMPUTER VIRUS: WHAT IT IS AND HOW IT SPREADS

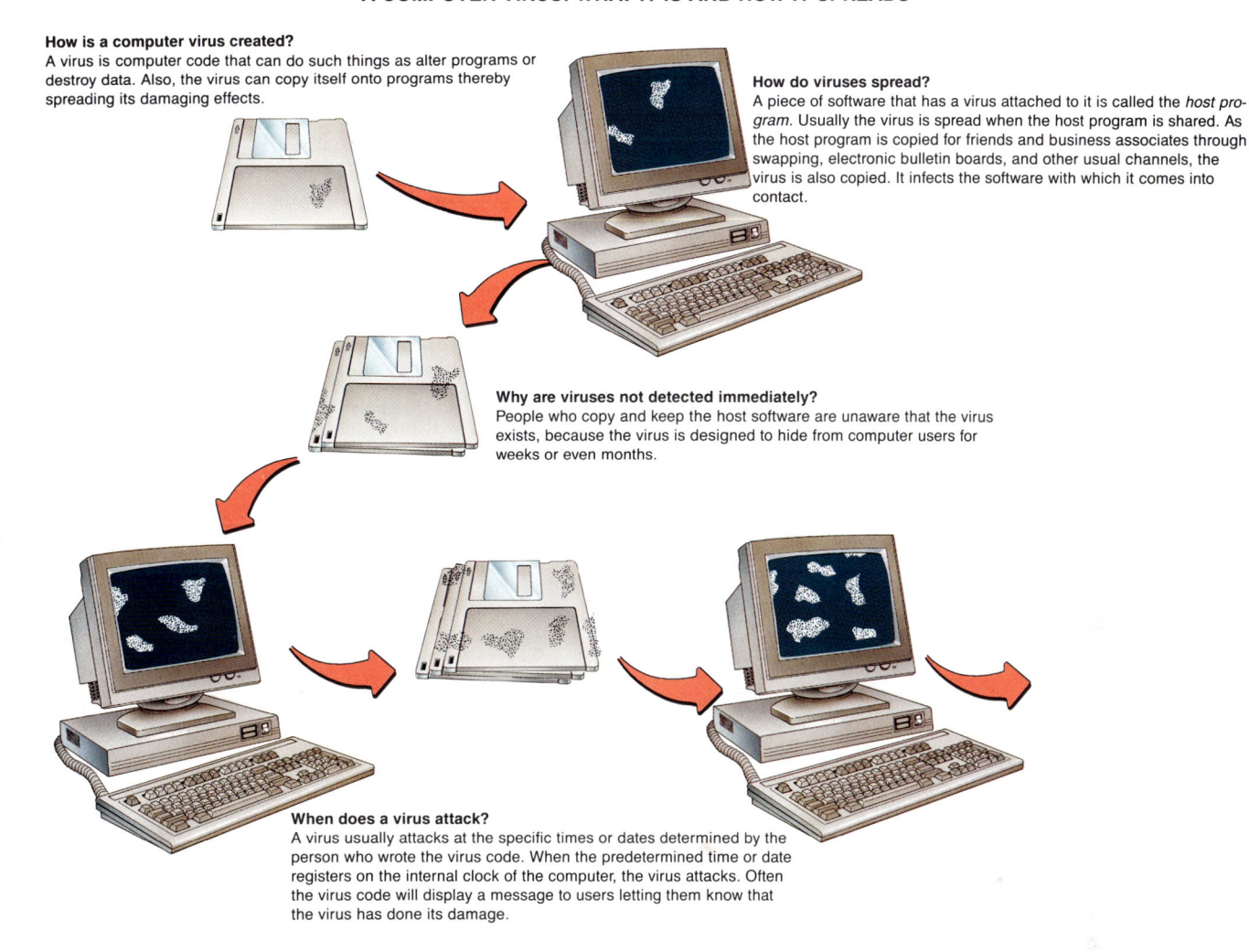

How is a computer virus created?
A virus is computer code that can do such things as alter programs or destroy data. Also, the virus can copy itself onto programs thereby spreading its damaging effects.

How do viruses spread?
A piece of software that has a virus attached to it is called the *host program*. Usually the virus is spread when the host program is shared. As the host program is copied for friends and business associates through swapping, electronic bulletin boards, and other usual channels, the virus is also copied. It infects the software with which it comes into contact.

Why are viruses not detected immediately?
People who copy and keep the host software are unaware that the virus exists, because the virus is designed to hide from computer users for weeks or even months.

When does a virus attack?
A virus usually attacks at the specific times or dates determined by the person who wrote the virus code. When the predetermined time or date registers on the internal clock of the computer, the virus attacks. Often the virus code will display a message to users letting them know that the virus has done its damage.

Single acts of malicious damage, especially when performed by employees with authorized access to the computer system, are very difficult to prevent. The best protection against this type of act remains adequate backup files that enable organizations to restore damaged or lost data.

FIGURE 14-14
How a virus program can be transmitted from one computer system to another.

Privacy

In the past, one way to maintain privacy was to keep information in separate locations—individual stores had their own credit files, government agencies had separate records, doctors had separate files, and so on. However, it is now technically and economically feasible to store large amounts of related data about individuals in one database. Some people believe that this increases the possibility for unauthorized use.

The concern about information privacy has led to federal and state laws regarding the storage and disclosure of personal data. Common points in these laws include: (1) information collected and stored about individuals should be limited to what is necessary to carry out the function of the business or government agency collecting the data. (2) Once collected, provisions should be made to restrict access to the data to those employees within the organization who need access to it to perform their job duties. (3) Personal information should be released outside the organization collecting the data only when the person has agreed to its disclosure. (4) When information is collected about an individual, the individual should know that data is being collected and have the opportunity to determine the accuracy of the data.

Two laws deal specifically with computers. The 1986 Electronic Communications Privacy Act (ECPA) provides the same protection that covers mail and telephone communications to the new forms of electronic communications such as voice mail. The 1988 Computer Matching and Privacy Protection Act regulates the use of government data to determine the eligibility of persons for federal benefits.

Ethics

Society is increasingly concerned about computer ethics and the difference between what is right, what is wrong, and what is criminal. Issues relate to many topics such as software copying, unauthorized access and use of computer systems, and privacy. By studying and learning the information provided in this book, you have become a computer literate member of society. As such, you will be better able to evaluate computer-related issues. The questionnaire in Figure 14-15 presents situations for you to evaluate. How do you feel about each of the questions?

FIGURE 14-15
Ethics questionnaire.

ETHICS OF INFORMATION PROCESSING

1. A computer operator runs a program at work for a friend and uses ten minutes of computer time. The program was run when the computer was idle and not being used for company business.
   Ethical _____ Unethical _____ Computer Crime _____

2. A student gives a password to another student not enrolled in a computer class for which a laboratory fee is charged. The password allows access to the school computer. The student not enrolled uses three hours of computer time in a time-sharing environment.
   Student enrolled in class:
   Ethical _____ Unethical _____ Computer Crime _____
   Student not enrolled in class:
   Ethical _____ Unethical _____ Computer Crime _____

3. A company hires a consultant to develop a payroll program. After completing the project, the consultant gives a copy of the program (without data) to a friend at another company.
   Ethical _____ Unethical _____ Computer Crime _____

4. Using a terminal, an individual breaks a security code and reviews confidential salaries of corporate executives. No use is made of the information. "I was just curious" is the individual's response when caught.
   Ethical _____ Unethical _____ Computer Crime _____

5. A bank employee electronically transfers money from a relatively inactive customer account to his own personal account and then transfers the money to a credit card account to pay current credit card charges. After money is deposited into his personal account on pay day, he electronically transfers the money back to the customer's account. No money physically changes hands, and no interest is lost to the customer's account.
   Ethical _____ Unethical _____ Computer Crime _____

6. While reviewing a list of available programs on a bulletin board, a user notices a title of a program that is the same as a popular spreadsheet package. After downloading the program onto his system, the user discovers that the program appears to be an exact copy of the spreadsheet program that is sold in computer stores for $300.00. The user keeps and uses the program.
   Ethical _____ Unethical _____ Computer Crime _____

7. A programmer is asked to write a program that she knows will generate inaccurate information for stockholders of the company. When she questions her manager about the program, she is told she must write it or lose her job. She writes the program.
   Manager: Ethical _____ Unethical _____ Computer Crime _____
   Programmer: Ethical _____ Unethical _____ Computer Crime _____

8. As a practical joke, a student enters a virus program onto the hard disk of a microcomputer in the school's computer lab. Each time another student uses that machine, the virus program is copied onto that student's diskette. The program is designed so that the first time the disk is used after the first of January a "Happy New Year" message will be displayed on the screen.
   Ethical _____ Unethical _____ Computer Crime _____

9. A photojournalist uses a computer graphics program to retouch the background of a photo that is used on the front page of the newspaper.
   Ethical _____ Unethical _____ Computer Crime _____

10. A company uses software to monitor the productivity of the clerical staff. Supervisors are notified of staff members who fall below what management considers to be the minimum productivity standards.
    Ethical _____ Unethical _____ Computer Crime _____

SUMMARY OF TRENDS AND ISSUES IN THE INFORMATION AGE

Based on current and planned developments, the impact of computers and the information age will be even greater in the future than it has been to date. However, as a society and as individuals, we have an obligation to use the computer responsibly and not abuse the power it provides. This presents constant challenges that sometimes weigh the rights of the individual against increased efficiency and productivity. The computer must be thought of as a tool whose effectiveness is determined by the skill and experience of the user. With the computer knowledge that you have acquired you will be better able to participate in decisions on how to best use computerized information systems.

CHAPTER SUMMARY

1. Existing business information systems will continue to undergo profound changes as new technology, software, and methods become available.
2. Trends will include; more online, interactive systems; less batch processing; expanded communications networks and increased use of relational database systems; and replacing command- and menu-driven interfaces with graphical-user interfaces.
3. The **automated office**, sometimes referred to as the **electronic office**, is the term that describes the use of electronic devices such as computers, facsimile machines, and computerized telephone systems to make office work more productive.
4. Word processing ranks as the most widely used office automation technology.
5. **Electronic mail** is the capability to transmit messages to and receive messages from other computer users.
6. **Voice mail** can be considered verbal electronic mail.
7. Desktop publishing involves the use of computers to produce printed documents that can combine different sizes and styles of text and graphics.
8. **Facsimile**, or **FAX**, machines are used to transmit a reproduced image of a document over standard phone lines.
9. Image processing is the capability to store and retrieve a reproduced image of a document.
10. **Teleconferencing** usually means **video conferencing**, the use of computers and television cameras to transmit video images and the sound of the conference participants to other participants with similar equipment at a remote location.
11. The goal of the **automated factory** is to increase productivity through the use of automated, and often computer-controlled, equipment.
12. **Computer-aided design (CAD)** uses a computer and special graphics software to aid in product design.
13. **Computer-aided engineering (CAE)** is the use of computers to test product designs.
14. **Computer-aided manufacturing (CAM)** is the use of computers to control production equipment.
15. **Computer-integrated manufacturing (CIM)** is the total integration of the manufacturing process using computers.
16. The long-range trend is the **computer-integrated enterprise**; an organization where all information storage and processing is performed by a network of computers and intelligent devices.
17. Personal computers are used in the home in many different ways, including: (1) personal services, (2) control of home systems, (3) telecommuting, (4) education, and (5) entertainment.
18. The personal services provided by home computer use allow people to perform personal and business-related tasks quickly and conveniently in the comfort of their own homes.
19. Electronic **bulletin board systems**, called **BBSs**, allow users to communicate with one another and share information.
20. Another use of computers in the home is to control home systems such as security, environment, lighting, and landscape sprinkler systems.

21. **Telecommuting** refers to the capability of individuals to work at home and communicate with their offices by using personal computers and communication lines.
22. The use of personal computers for education, called **computer-aided instruction (CAI)**, is a rapidly growing area.
23. **Drill and practice software** uses a flash-card approach to teaching by allowing users to practice skills in subjects such as math and language.
24. **Tutorial software** uses text, graphics, and sometimes sound to teach a user concepts about a subject and follows the instruction with questions to help the user ensure that he or she understands the concepts.
25. **Simulation software** is designed to teach a user by creating a model of a real-life situation.
26. Popular types of entertainment software include arcade games, board games, simulations, and interactive graphics programs.
27. The guidelines for purchasing a personal computer recommend that you: (1) become computer literate; (2) define and prioritize the type of tasks you want to perform on your computer; (3) select the software packages that best meet your needs; (4) select equipment that will run the software you have selected; (5) select the suppliers for the software and equipment; and (6) purchase the software and equipment.
28. **Shareware** is software that users may try out on their own systems before paying a fee.
29. **Public domain software** is not copyrighted and can therefore be distributed among users.
30. **Computer security** refers to the safeguards established to prevent and detect unauthorized use and deliberate or accidental damage to computer systems and data.
31. **Computer crime** is the use of a computer to commit an illegal act.
32. Software theft, often called **software piracy**, refers to illegal copying of software.
33. **Unauthorized access** can be defined as computer trespassing, in other words, being logged on a system without permission.
34. **Unauthorized use** is the use of a computer system or computer data for unapproved and possibly illegal activities.
35. The key to preventing both unauthorized access and unauthorized use is computer security that controls and monitors an appropriate level of authorization for each user.
36. One of the most potentially dangerous types of malicious damage is done by a **virus**, a computer program designed to copy itself into other software and spread through multiple computer systems.
37. **Vaccines** are programs that locate and remove viruses.
38. The concern about information privacy has led to federal and state laws regarding the storage and disclosure of personal data.

KEY TERMS

Automated factory *14.6*
Automated office *14.4*
Bulletin board system (BBS) *14.8*
Computer-aided design (CAD) *14.6*
Computer-aided engineering (CAE) *14.6*
Computer-aided instruction (CAI) *14.9*
Computer-aided manufacturing (CAM) *14.7*
Computer crime *14.13*

Computer-integrated enterprise *14.7*
Computer-integrated manufacturing (CIM) *14.7*
Computer security *14.13*
Drill and practice software *14.10*
Electronic mail *14.4*
Electronic office *14.4*
Facsimile (FAX) *14.4*
Public domain software *14.12*
Shareware *14.12*

Simulation software *14.10*
Software piracy *14.13*
Telecommuting *14.9*
Teleconferencing *14.5*
Tutorial software *14.10*
Unauthorized access *14.14*
Unauthorized use *14.14*
Vaccine *14.15*
Video conferencing *14.5*
Virus *14.14*
Voice mail *14.4*

REVIEW QUESTIONS

1. List at least three ways that existing information systems will change.
2. Identify and explain seven automated office applications. What is the trend with these applications?
3. What is the goal of the automated factory? Briefly explain the four technologies that are used.
4. What are some of the personal services available to home computer users?
5. What is CAI? Identify the three categories of CAI an give example of each.
6. List the six guidelines for buying a personal computer. Why is it recommended that you select your software before your equipment?
7. Explain the difference between public domain software and shareware.
8. Write a definition for computer crime. List three types of computer crime.
9. Explain why computer viruses are malicious. What is a vaccine program?
10. Discuss the four common points covered in the state and federal information privacy laws.

CONTROVERSIAL ISSUES

1. Factory and office automation has led to the reduction or elimination of many jobs. What obligation, if any, do you think companies have toward workers that are replaced by automated systems?
2. While most people agree computers can be valuable educational tools there is disagreement about how and when students should be introduced to computers. At what grade level do you think students should begin using computers? What topics should be taught using computers?

RESEARCH PROJECTS

1. Contact your school or a large company in your area and ask to see a copy of their policy on illegally copying software. Compare the policies and discuss them with your class.
2. Contact the person in charge of a computer laboratory at your school and ask him or her about computer viruses. Ask him or her if any viruses have been found in the laboratory. Also find out what procedures or software is being used to protect against viruses.

INDEX

Access arm: Contains the read/write heads and moves the heads across the surface of the disk. **6.9**
Access time: The time required to access and retrieve data stored in sectors on a diskette. **6.6**
Accounting controls: System controls to provide assurance that the dollar amounts recorded in the accounting records are correct. **11.19**
Accounting software packages, 11.11
Acoustic coupler, *See* **Acoustic modem**
Acoustic modem: A communications device used with a telephone handset. Also called acoustic coupler. **8.13**
Acquisition: Phase in the information system life cycle after the analysis phase. The acquisition phase has four steps: (1) summarizing the application requirements, (2) identifying potential software vendors, (3) evaluating software alternatives, and (4) making the purchase. **11.10**–15
Actuator, *See* **Access arm**
Ada: A programming language supported by the U.S. Department of Defense. Its use is required on all U.S. government military projects. Ada was designed to facilitate the writing and maintenance of large programs that would be used over a long period of time. **12.17**
Adding data: Updating data, such as creating a record for a new employee to include in a file or database. **7.3**
Addressing, symbolic, 12.13
Airline reservation system
  data consistency and, 3.27
  fault-tolerant systems, 9.5
ALGOrithmetic Language (ALGOL), 12.18
Alphabetic characters, **3.3**
  memory storage and, 4.4
  tests for, 3.26
Alphabetic characters: Elements that comprise data; specifically, characters A–Z. **3.3**
Alphabetic field: A field that contains only alphabetic characters. **3.4**
Alphanumeric fields: Fields that contain a combination of character types, including alphabetic, numeric, and special characters. **3.4**
Alphanumeric fields, 3.4
Alphabetic menu selection, 3.18
Amber characters, 3.28
American National Standards Institute (ANSI), 7.18–19, 12.6
American Standard Code for Information Interchange (ASCII): The most widely used coding system to represent data, primarily on personal computers and many minicomputers. **4.6**
Analog signal: A signal used on communications lines that consists of a continuous electrical wave. **8.10**
Analysis: Phase in the information system life cycle where the system is separated into its parts in order to determine how the system works. This phase consists of the preliminary investigation, detailed system analysis, and making the decision to proceed. **11.4**–9
  CASE tools and, 11.21
  data dictionary and, 11.6
  data flow diagrams and, 11.5–6
  decision on how to proceed and, 11.8
  detailed, 11.5–7
  preliminary investigation and, 11.4–5
  structured, 11.5–7
  structured English and, 11.7
  at Sutherland, 11.9
Analysis and design tools, 11.5–7
Analytical graphics: Used to selectively examine information and to interpret data through a graphic display. **2.16**
Analytical software, 5.4
Animation, 5.5
ANSI, *See* American National Standards Institute
Apple, 3.21, 9.11, 13.2
Application, computerized, 1.17
Application generators: Programs that produce source-language programs, such as BASIC or COBOL, based on input, output, and processing specifications entered by the user. Also called program generators. **12.18**–19
Application software: Programs that tell a computer how to produce information. **1.8**
  commercial, 11.10, 11.14–15
  custom, 11.14–15
  graphics and, 2.15, 5.4
  horizontal, 11.11
  integrated, 2.18–19
  loading, 1.11
  main memory and, 4.2

microcomputer, 1.9–10
vertical, 11.11
Application software packages: Programs purchased from computer stores or software vendors. **1.8**
Appointment calendars, 2.20
A Programming Language (APL), 12.18
Architecture, of processor units, 4.13-15
Arithmetic/logic unit (ALU): Part of the CPU that performs arithmetic and logical operations. **1.5, 4.2**
  program execution and, 4.10
Arithmetic operations: Numeric calculations performed by the arithmetic/logic unit of the CPU, and include addition, subtraction, multiplication, and division. **1.5, 4.2**
Arrow keys: Keys on a keyboard that move the cursor up, down, left, or right on the screen. 2.3, **3.5**
Art
  desktop publishing and, 2.8–9
  scanners and, 3.12
Artificial intelligence: A branch of computer science applying human intelligence to computer systems. **10.11**
ASCII (American Standard Code for Information Interchange), code, 4.5, **4.6**
ASK, 13.2
Assembler: A special program that converts assembly language programs into machine language instructions. **12.13**
Assembly language: A low-level language that is similar to machine language, but uses abbreviations called mnemonics or symbolic operation code to represent the machine operation code. **12.13**
Associate Computer Professional (ACP), 13.9
Association for Computing Machinery (ACM): Professional organization composed of persons interested in computer science and computer science education. **13.8**
Association of Information Systems Professionals (AISP): Professional organization originally aimed at word processing professionals, but now includes a much broader membership, including office automation professionals. **13.8**
Association of Systems Management (ASM): Professional organization composed of individuals interested in improving the systems analysis and design field. **13.8**
Asynchronous transmission mode: Data communication method which transmits one character at a time at irregular intervals using start and stop bits. **8.10**
Attributes: Fields in a relational database. **7.15**
Automated factory: Factories that have an increase in productivity with the use of automated, and often computer-controlled, equipment. **14.6**–7
Automated office: The use of electronic devices such as computers, facsimile machines, and computerized telephone systems to make office work more productive; also known as electronic office. **14.4**–5
Auto parts sales system, 11.9
Auxiliary storage: Storage of programs and data that are not being processed. Also called secondary storage. **1.5**–6, **6.2**–21
  cartridge devices, 6.14
  disk cartridges, 6.12
  diskettes, 6.3–7
  file organization and, 7.4
  file-oriented versus database system, 7.13
  hard disks, 6.7–11
  magnetic disk, 6.3–12
  magnetic tape, 6.13
  main memory and, 1.12
  mass storage devices, 6.18
  multiuser computers, 1.15–16
  optical cards, 6.19
  optical disks, 6.16–18
  reel-to-reel devices, 6.14
  removable disks, 6.10
  smart cards, 6.19
  solid-state devices, 6.18
  special-purpose devices, 6.19
Avant Garde type, 5.6
Background jobs: Assigned a lower processing priority and less CPU time. Compare with foreground jobs. **9.6**
Back support, 3.28
Backup: Procedures that provide for maintaining copies of program and data files so that in the event the files are lost or destroyed, they can be recovered. 6.12, **7.3**
  database administrator and, 7.19
  sequential files and, 7.5
  tape for, 1.16
  utility programs and, 9.14

Backus, John, 12.17
Band printers: Impact printers that use a horizontal, rotating band, and can print in the range of 300 to 2,000 lines per minute. **5.12**–13
Bandwidth: The range of frequencies that a communications channel can carry. **8.12**
Banking industry, MICR readers and, 3.15
Bar chart: Chart that displays relationships among data with blocks or bars. **2.15**
Bar code reader, *See* **Laser scanners**
Baseband: Coaxial cable that can carry one signal at a time at very high rates of speed. **8.3**
Base 2 number system, 4.7, 4.8
Base 16 number system, 4.7, 4.9
BASIC (Beginner's All-purpose Symbolic Instruction Code): A simple, interactive programming language. BASIC is one of the most commonly used programming languages on microcomputers and minicomputers. **12.15**
Batch control: During batch processing, balancing to a predetermined total, to ensure the accuracy and reliability of data and processing techniques. **3.25**
Batch processing: Data is collected and, at some later time, all the data that has been gathered is processed as a group, or *batch*. **3.22**, 3.23–25
Batch totaling, 11.19
Baud rate: The number of times per second that a data communications signal being transmitted changes; with each change, one or more bits can be transmitted. **8.12**
Bell Laboratories, 9.10, 12.16
Benchmark test: Test on software that measures the time it takes to process a set number of transactions. **11.13**
Bidirectional printing: Printing method of dot matrix printers, in which the print head can print while moving in either direction. **5.10**
Binary number system (base 2): Represents quantities by using only two symbols, 0 and 1, used to represent the electronic status of bits inside the processor unit, and also for addressing the memory locations. **4.5**, 4.7
  magnetic tape, and 6.14
Bit-mapped displays, *See* **Dot-addressable displays**
Bits: An element of a byte that can represent one of two values, on or off. There are 8 bits in a byte. **4.4**, 4.5
  buses and, 4.12
  parity, 4.7, 8.10
Bits per inch (bpi): A measure of the recording density of disk and tape. **6.5**, 6.15
Bits per second (bps): A measure of the speed of data transmission; the number of bits transmitted in one second. **8.12**
Blinking: Screen feature used for emphasis in which characters or words on a screen blink. **5.18**
Blocks: Data is recorded on tape in blocks which usually consist of two or more records. **6.15**
Bold: Screen feature used for emphasis in which characters are displayed at a greater brightness level than the surrounding text. **5.6**, 5.10, **5.18**
Booting: The process of loading an operating system into main memory. **9.2**
Borland, 13.2
Bottom-up design: Design approach that focuses on the data, particularly the output of the system. **11.16**
Bridge: A combination of hardware and software that is used to connect *similar* networks. **8.19**–20
Broadband: Coaxial cable that can carry multiple signals at one time. **8.3**
Bubbles, data flow diagrams and, 11.5
Buckets: The location on a disk where records in a direct file can be stored. **7.6**
Buffers: Areas of main memory used to store data that has been read or is waiting to be sent to an output device. **9.6**
Bugs: Program errors. **12.10**
Bulletin board systems (BBSs): Allow users to communicate electronically with one another and share information, using personal computers. **14.8**
Bunny suit, 4.22
Bus: Any line that transmits bits between memory and the input/output devices, and between memory and the CPU. **4.12**
Business application software industry, 13.2
Business application, typical, 1.10–13
Business systems jobs, salaries and, 13.5
Bus network: A communications network in which all the devices are connected to and share a single cable. **8.19**
Byron, Augusta Ada, 12.17
Byte: Each storage location within main memory, identified by a memory address. **4.3**

I.1A

INDEX

C: A programming language originally designed for writing systems software, but it is now considered a general-purpose programming language. C requires professional programming skills to be used effectively. **12.16**
Cable, 1.14
Cache memory: High-speed RAM memory between the CPU and main memory that increases processing efficiency. **4.17**
Calculations, spreadsheet programs and, 1.12
Capacitors, 4.21
Career development
 certification and, 13.9
 continuing education and, 13.9
 professional organizations and, 13.8
 user groups and, 13.8
Career opportunities, 13.1–11
 career development and, 13.8–10
 compensation and, 13.5
 consulting, 11.12, 13.4
 database administrator, 7.19
 data entry, 1.17, 13.3
 data librarian, 1.16
 data management, 2.20, 7.2
 data processing, 7.2
 education and training, 13.5
 growth trends, 13.5–6
 information systems department and, 13.3–4
 preparing for, 13.7–8
 sales, 13.4
 service and repair, 13.4
Carnegie Mellon University, 9.12
Carriage size, 5.10
Carrier-connect radio, 8.5
Cartridge tape: Frequently used storage medium for backup on personal computers. **6.14**
CASE (computer-aided software engineering): The use of automated computer-based tools to design and manage a software system. **11.21**
Case structure: Variation of the selection structure, used when a condition is being tested that can lead to more than two alternatives. **12.5**
CASE workbench: Integrated package of several CASE tools. These tools might include (1) analysis and design tools, (2) prototyping tools, (3) code generators, (4) information repository, and (5) management tools. **11.21**
Cathode ray tube (CRT): An output device; monitor. 1.5, 5.16
CDROM (compact disk read-only memory): A small optical disk that uses the same laser technology as audio compact disks. **6.17**
Cell: The intersection where a row and column meet on a spreadsheet. **2.10**
Cellular telephone: A wireless telephone available to the general public that uses radio waves to communicate with a local antenna assigned to a specific geographic area call a cell. **8.5**
Centralized data entry: The data is keyed (input) by trained operators from source documents. **3.26**
Central processing unit (CPU): Processing unit containing a control unit that executes program instructions, and an arithmetic/logic unit (ALU) that performs math and logic operations. **1.5, 4.2**
 operating systems and, 9.6–7
 performance measurement and, 9.9
 screen images and, 5.19
Certification, career development and, 13.9
Certified Computer Programmer (CCP), 13.9
Certified Data Processor (CDP), 13.9
CGA (Color Graphics Adapter) monitor, 5.17
Chain printers: High-speed impact printers that use a rotating chain to print up to 3,000 lines per minute, of good print quality. **5.12**
Chair, 3.28
Change management, information system life cycle and, 11.24
Changing data: Updating data, such as posting a change of address to an existing record. **7.3**
Changing existing information, 7.3
Channels, magnetic tape and, 6.14
Character(s): The elements that comprise data, including alphabetic characters (A–Z), numeric characters (0–9), and special characters (punctuation). **3.3**
Character per second (cps): The rating of printing speed for low-speed printers. **5.6**
Charts, 2.9, 2.15–17
Check processing, 3.15
Chief Information Officer (CIO): Title sometimes given to the manager of the information systems department. **1.19**

Child record: In a hierarchical database, a record that is below the parent record. Each child record can have only one parent. **7.14**
Chip, *See* **Integrated circuit**
Class: In object-oriented programming, programmers define classes of objects. Each class contains the methods that are unique to that class. **12.20**
Clean rooms, 4.22
Client-server: In information resource sharing on a network, as much processing as possible is done on the server system before data is transmitted to the requesting computer. **8.16**
Clip art: Collections of art that are stored on disks and are designed for use with popular desktop publishing packages. **2.9**
Coaxial cable: A high-quality communications line that is used in offices and laid underground and under the ocean. Coaxial cable consists of a copper wire conductor surrounded by a nonconducting insulator that is in turn surrounded by a woven metal mesh outer conductor, and finally a plastic outer coating. **8.3**
COBOL (COmmon Business Oriented Language): One of the most widely used programming languages for business applications, which uses an English-like format. **12.16**
Code
 CASE tools and, 11.21
 object, 12.13
 spaghetti, 12.6
Coding: The process of writing the program instructions that will process the data and produce the output specified in the program design. **12.9**
Collision: Occurs with direct files when a hashing operation generates the same disk location (called synonyms) for records with different key values. **7.7**
Color
 dot matrix printers and, 5.10–11
 thermal printers and, 5.14
Color screens: Screens that display information in color and are used because they enable users to more easily read and understand the information on the screen; more expensive than monochrome. 3.28, **5.19**, 5.20
Columns (spreadsheet): Data which is organized vertically on a spreadsheet. **2.10**
COMDEX: The largest computer trade show in the United States. **13.9**
Commands: Key words and phrases that the user inputs to direct the computer to perform certain operations. **2.2, 3.2–3**
 templates and, 2.24
Command structure, integrated software and, 2.19
Commercial applications software: Software that has already been developed and is available for purchase. **11.10**
 advantages and disadvantages of, 11.15
 customizing, 11.15–16
Common carriers: Public wide area network companies such as the telephone companies. **8.17**
Communication line, 1.14
Communications: The transmission of data and information over a communications channel such as a standard telephone line, between one computer or terminal and another computer. **8.2–23**
 dedicated line, 8.7–8
 equipment, 8.12–14
 front-end processors and, 8.14
 line configurations and, 8.6
 modem and, 8.10, 8.12–13
 multidrop lines, 8.8–9
 multiplexor and, 8.13
 networks, *See* **Network**
 point-to-point line, 8.7–8
 protocols, 8.15
 software, 8.14–15
 switched line, 8.7
Communications channel: The link, or path, that the data follows as it is transmitted from the sending equipment to the receiving equipment in a communications system. **8.3–6**
 characteristics of, 8.9–12
 coaxial cable, 8.3
 direction of transmission, 8.11
 example of, 8.6
 fiber optics, 8.3
 satellite transmission, 8.4
 transmission rate and, 8.12
 twisted pair wire, 8.3
 types of signals, 8.10

 wireless transmission, 8.5
Communication skills, information system life cycle and, 11.3
Communications line, *See* **Communications channel**
Communications link, *See* **Communications channel**
Communications network, *See* **Network**
Communications satellites: Man-made space devices that receive, amplify, and retransmit signals from earth. **8.4**
Communications software: Programs that perform data communications tasks such as dialing, file transfer, terminal emulation, and data encryption. **2.18, 8.14**–15
Communications system model, 8.2
Compact disk read-only memory (CDROM), **6.17**
Compaq, 13.2
Compensation, career opportunities and, 13.5–6
Competition, importance of information and, 10.2
Compiler: A program that translates high-level source programs into machine language object code. **12.13**
Components, manufacturers of, 13.2
Composite video monitor: A color screen that uses a single electron signal to turn on the color phosphors within the pixel. **5.20**
Computer(s): An electronic device, operating under the control of instructions stored in its own memory unit, that can accept data (input), process data arithmetically and logically, produce output from the processing, and store the results for future use. **1.2**
 applications, 1.19
 categories of, 1.6–7
 components of, 1.4–6
 functions of, 1.2–3
Computer-aided design (CAD): Design method that uses a computer and special graphics software to aid in product design. **14.6**
Computer-aided engineering (CAE): The use of computers to test product designs. **14.6**
Computer-aided instruction (CAI): The use of personal computers for education. **14.9**–10
Computer-aided manufacturing (CAM): The use of computers to control production equipment. **14.7**
Computer-aided software engineering (CASE), *See* **CASE**
Computer-assisted retrieval (CAR): Process in which microfilm readers perform automatic data lookup. **5.23**
Computer crime: The use of a computer to commit an illegal act. **14.13**
Computer department, **1.14**
Computer engineering: The design and manufacturing of electronic computer components and computer hardware. **13.7**
Computer graphics, *See* **Graphics**
Computer industry publications, 13.10
Computer information systems (CIS): The use of computers to provide the information needed to operate businesses and other organizations. **13.7**
Computer-integrated enterprise: An organization in which all information storage and processing is performed by a network of computers and intelligent devices. **14.7**
Computer-integrated manufacturing (CIM): The total integration of the manufacturing process using computers. **14.7**
Computerland, 13.4
Computer literate, **14.11**
Computer magazines, 13.10
 horizontal application software and, 11.12
Computer manufacturers, 13.2
 software vendors and, 11.11–12
Computer operations procedures, 12.10
Computer operator: Person that works in the computer room and is responsible for running the computer equipment and monitoring processing operations. **1.16,** 13.3
Computer-output microfilm (COM): An output technique that records output from a computer as microscopic images on roll or sheet film. **5.22**–23
Computer program, *See* **Program(s)**
Computer programmers: Persons that design, write, test, and implement programs that process data on a computer. **1.18,** 13.3
 development and, 12.1–22
 expertise in, 12.21
 information system life cycle and, 11.3
 salaries and, 13.5
Computer room, tour of, 1.14–16
Computer science: Includes the technical aspects of computers such as hardware operation and systems software. **13.7**

I.2 INDEX

Computer security, *See* Security
Computer software, *See* Software
Computer stores, 11.11
Computer system: The input, processing, output, and auxiliary storage components of computers. **1.6**
Computer users, *See* User(s)
Computerworld, 13.10
Conditional program logic, 12.4
Consultants: People who draw upon their experience to give advice to others. They must have not only strong technical skills in their area of expertise, but also have the people skills to effectively communicate with clients. **13.4**
 finding, 11.12
 salaries of, 13.5
Consumer product companies, 10.2
Continuing education, career development and, 13.9
Continuous-form paper: A type of paper that is connected together for a continuous flow through the printer. **5.6**
Controlling performance, management and, 10.3
Control program: The resident portion of the operating system. **9.2**
Controls, 3.27
 accounting, 11.19
 credit card payment and, 3.24
 design phase and, 11.19
 input, 11.19
 offline data entry and, 3.24
 processing, 11.19
 source document, 11.19
 user interfaces and, 3.22
Control signals, buses and, 4.12
Control structures: In structured program design, used to form the logic of a program. The three control structures are: the sequence structure, selection structure, and iteration structure. **12.4–6**
Control unit: Part of the CPU that directs and coordinates all the activities on the computer, consisting of four operations: fetching, decoding, executing, and storing. **1.5, 4.2**
 program execution and, 4.10
Conventions, 13.9
Conversion: During the implementation phase of the system development process, conversion refers to the process of changing from the old system to the new system. **11.23**
Coprocessors: A special microprocessor chip or circuit board designed to perform a specific task, such as numeric calculations. **4.14**
Copy text: Makes a copy of the marked text, but leaves marked text where it was. **2.6**
Core memory: Small, ring-shaped pieces of material that could be magnetized, or polarized, in one of two directions. The polarity indicated whether the core was on or off. **4.15**
Cost/benefit analysis: During the analysis phase of the information system life cycle, identifies the estimated costs of the proposed solution and the benefits (including potential cost savings) that are expected. **11.8**
CPU, *See* Central processing unit
CPU utilization: The amount of time that the CPU is working and not idle, waiting for data to process. **9.9**
Credit bureau, example of, 7.2
Credit card payment, controls and, 3.24
CROSSTALK, 2.18
CRT (cathode ray tube), **1.5, 5.16**
Current system, study of, 11.5–7
Cursor: A symbol such as an underline character or an arrow that indicates where you are working on the screen. **2.3, 3.5, 5.18**
Cursor control keys: Keys that move the cursor. Also called arrow keys. **3.5**
Cursor positioning, menu selection and, 3.18
Customizing phase: Modification of a commercial application software package. **11.15–**16
Custom software: Applications software that is developed by the user or at the user's request. **11.14**
 advantages and disadvantages of, 11.15
Cut text: Removing text from an area of a word processing document. **2.6**
Cylinder: All the tracks on a diskette or hard disk that have the same number. **6.5**
Cylinder method: The physical organization of data on a disk where the data is stored *down* the disk surfaces reducing the movement of the read/write head during both reading and writing operations. **6.9–**10
Daisy wheel printers: Impact printers that can print high-quality text, but not graphics. The daisy wheel type element rotates during printing, and a hammer strikes the selected character against the ribbon and paper. Printing speeds range from 20 to 80 characters per second. **5.11**

Data: The raw facts, including numbers and words that a computer receives during the input operation and processes to produce information. **1.2, 3.3**
 accuracy of, *See* Data accuracy
 adding, 7.8–9
 buses and, 4.12
 changing, 7.9–11
 confidential, 8.15
 consistency of, 3.27
 correcting, 7.9–10
 current, 7.8
 future processing of, 14.3
 inputting, *See* Data entry; **Input**
 integrity, 3.26, 7.2
 maintenance of, 7.3, 7.8–12
 memory representation of, 4.4–7
 organization of, 3.3–4
 reasonableness check, 3.27
 redundancy, 7.13, 11.18
 source collection, 3.26
 timely, 7.3
 transfer rate, 6.6
 verifiable, 10.6
Data accuracy: The source of the data is reliable and the data is correctly reported and entered. Also called data integrity. 1.13, **7.2**
 databases and, 7.2–3
 Garbage In, Garbage Out (GIGO) and, 10.6
 processing controls and, 11.19
Database: A collection of data that is organized in multiple related files. **2.13, 3.4, 7.12–**21
 advantages of, 7.13–14
 employee, 10.2
 external, 10.8
 features of, 2.15
 generating, 7.15
 hierarchical, 7.14–15
 mass storage and, 6.18
 network, 7.15
 personal computer systems, 7.20–21
 querying, 7.17–19
 relational, 7.15–17
 types of organization, 7.14–17
 UNIX and, 9.11
 volume of activity, 11.18
Database administrator (DBA): The person responsible for managing an organization's computerized data and all database activities. **1.18, 7.19**
 career opportunity as, 13.3
 database design and, 11.18
 responsibilities of, 7.19–20
Database design: In information system design, the data dictionary information developed during the analysis phase is merged into new or existing system files. **11.18**
 database administrator and, 7.19
Database management system (DBMS): The software that allows the user to create, maintain, and report the data and file relationships. **7.12**
 features of, 7.17
 users and, 7.20
Database software: Software that allows the user to enter, retrieve, and update data in an organized and efficient manner. 1.9, **1.10, 2.13**
Data collection devices: Input devices designed and used for obtaining data at the site where the transaction or event being reported takes place. **3.16**
Data communications, *See* Communications
Data communications software: Used to transmit data from one computer to another. **2.18**
Data dictionary: The data dictionary defines each data field, or element, to be used in the database. **7.17, 11.6**
 CASE tools and, 11.21
 systems analyst and, 11.18
Data editing: Software that has the capability to check data as it is input for proper format and acceptable values. **3.18**
Data element, 7.4
Data encryption: Communications software that protects confidential data during transmission. The data is converted at the sending end into an unrecognizable string of characters or bits and reconverted at the receiving end. **8.15**
Data entry, 3.22–27
 for batch processing, 3.22, 3.24–25
 centralized, 3.26
 distributed, 3.26
 documented, 12.10
 for interactive processing, 3.22–23

 mouse slowing down, 3.8–9
 offline, 3.24
 online, 3.22
 pen input devices and, 3.10–11
 personnel requirements, 3.27
 procedures, 3.26–27
 production, 3.23
 prompts and, 3.18
 reliable, 7.2–3
 touch screens and, 3.9
 volume of, 3.26
Data entry personnel: Persons responsible for entering large volumes of data into the computer system. **1.17,** 13.3
Data field: A fact or unique piece of data. **3.4**
Data flow diagram (DFD): Graphic representation of the flow of data through a system. **11.5–**6
Data integrity, 3.26, **7.2**
Data item: A fact or unique piece of data. **3.4,** 7.4
Data librarian: Person who staffs the data library, and catalogues the disk packs and tapes. **1.16**
Data library: Data stored on disk packs and tapes; when not in use, are kept by the information systems department. **1.16**
Data maintenance: The procedures used to keep data current, called updating. **7.3, 7.8–**12
Data management: Procedures that are used to keep data accurate and timely and provide for the security and maintenance of data. 2.20, **7.2**
 data accuracy and, 7.2–3
 data maintenance and, 7.3, 7.8–12
 data security and, 7.3
Data processing: The production of information by processing data on a computer. Also called information processing. **1.2**
 batch, 3.22, 3.24–25
 interactive, 3.22–23
Data processing department, *See* **Information systems department**
Data Processing Management Association (DPMA): Professional association of programmers, systems analysts, and information processing managers. **13.8**
Data processing professionals, data management and, 7.2
Data redundancy: Data duplicated in several different files. **7.13,** 11.18
Data relationships, graphics and, 5.4
Data security: Protection of data to keep it from being misused or lost. **7.3, 7.14**
Data service unit (DSU): In digital data service, device that connects users to the communications line. **8.10**
Data storage, *See* Storage
Data transfer rate: The time required to transfer data from disk to main memory. **6.6**
dBASE III PLUS, 2.13–15, 7.20
dBASE IV, 2.15, 7.20
Debugging: The process of locating and correcting program errors, or bugs, found during testing. **12.10**
Decimal number system, 4.8
Decimal point (.), 3.4
Decimal values, binary and hexadecimal representation, 4.7
Decisions
 expert, 10.10
 strategic, 10.4
 tactical, 10.5
Decision support system (DSS): A system designed to help someone reach a decision by summarizing or comparing data from either or both internal and external sources. **10.9–**10
Decision tables: A way of documenting the system during the analysis phase; identifies the actions that should be taken under different conditions. **11.7**
Decision trees: Like a decision table, illustrates the action to be taken based on given conditions, but presents it graphically. **11.7**
Decoding: Control unit operation that translates the program instruction into the commands that the computer can process. **4.2,** 12.9
Dedicated computer, 3.24
Dedicated line: A communications line connection between devices that is always established. **8.7**
Defragmenter: Analyzes and reorganizes a disk so that related file information is stored in one continuous area. **2.21**
Delete key, 3.5
Delete text: Removing text from a word processing document. **2.6**

Deleting data: Update procedure for getting rid of obsolete information, such as removing inactive records. **7.3**
Designing program, *See* **Program design**
Design phase: Second phase in the information system life cycle, where the logical design that was created in the analysis phase is transformed into a physical design. **11.16**–20
bottom-up, 11.16
CASE tools and, 11.21
database, 11.18
ergonomics and, 3.28
input, 11.17
logical, 11.16
output, 11.17
physical, 11.16
process, 11.18
structured, 11.16
at Sutherland, 11.21
testing, 11.20
top-down, 11.16
Design review: Performed by management at the end of the design phase to evaluate the work completed thus far to determine whether to proceed. **11.20**
Desk checking: The process of reading the program and mentally reviewing its logic, before the program is used to process real data. **12.9**
Desktop publishing, 2.8–9, 14.4
Desktop publishing software (DTP): Allows users to design and produce professional looking documents that contain both text and graphics. **2.8**
Detailed system analysis: Involves both a thorough study of the current system and at least one proposed solution to any problems found. **11.5**–7
Detail report: A report in which each line usually corresponds to one input record. **5.3**
accounting controls and, 11.19
Development: Phase three in information system life cycle, performed after the design phase. The development phase consists of program development and equipment acquisition. **11.21**–22
Development time, 7.14
Device drivers: Programs used by the operating system to control input and output devices. **9.8**
Diagnostic software, 13.4
Dialing software: Communications software that stores, selects, and dials telephone numbers. **8.14**
Dialogue: The sequence of inputs and computer responses that a user will encounter when he or she enters data on an interactive system. **11.17**
Dictionary
data, *See* **Data dictionary**
spelling checker and, 2.5
Digital audio tape (DAT): A method of storing large amounts of data on tape that uses helical scan technology to write data at much higher densities across the tape at an angle instead of down the length of the tape. **6.16**
Digital data service: Offered by telephone companies, communications channels specifically designed to carry digital instead of voice signals. **8.10**
Digital Equipment Corporation (DEC), 9.10, 13.2
Digital signals: A type of signal for computer processing in which individual electrical pulses represent bits that are grouped together to form characters. **8.10**
Digital video interactive (DVI): A video compression technique that can reduce storage requirements by a factor of 100 or more. **5.5**
Digitizer: Converts points, lines, and curves from a sketch, drawing, or photograph to digital impulses, and transmits them to a computer. **3.10**
Diodes, 4.21
Direct access, 7.5
relational database and, 7.15
Direct-access storage devices (DASD), *See* **Fixed disks**
Direct conversion: The user stops using the old system one day and begins using the new system the next. **11.23**
Direct file: File organization that uses the key value of a record to determine the location on the disk where the record is or will be stored. Also called relative file, or random file. **7.6**–8
Directing activities, management and, 10.3
Directory, formatting process and, 6.5
Directory listings, utilities and, 2.21
Disk cartridges: Disk storage available for use with personal computers, which can be inserted and removed, and offer the storage and fast access features of hard disks with the portability of diskettes. **6.12**

Disk defect analysis, 2.21
Diskettes: Used as a principal auxiliary storage medium for personal computers. **1.6, 6.3**–7
access time, 6.6
backup, 6.12
care of, 6.6–7
formatted, 6.4–5
loading program from, 1.11
method of storing data on, 6.5–6
operating system on, 9.2
write-protected, 6.12
Disk I/O, 9.9
Disk library systems, automated, 6.17
Disk management, operating systems and, 9.10
Disk Operating System (DOS), 1.8
Disk pack: A removable recording media, consisting of five to eleven metal platters that are used on both sides for recording data, used on medium and large computers. 1.15, **6.10**
Display screen layout form, input design and, 11.17
Display terminals: A keyboard and a screen. **3.6**
Distributed data entry: Data entry from various locations in an organization, often at the site where the data is generated. **3.26**
Distribution activities, importance of information and, 10.2
Distributors of computer equipment, 13.2
Division/remainder hashing method, 7.7
Documentation: Written materials that are produced as part of the information system life cycle. 2.24, **11.3**
adequate, 2.22
change management and, 11.24
detailed system analysis and, 11.5
for error correction, 3.26
information system life cycle and, 11.3
program development and, 12.10
prototyping and, 11.20
request for assistance and, 11.4
Documented procedures, 1.13, 1.14
Documents: Letters or memos created on word processing software. **2.4**
controls and, 11.19
turn-around, 3.14
Domain: The range of values an attribute can have in a relational database. **7.15**
DOS, *See* Disk operating system
Dot-addressable displays: Screens used for graphics in which the number of addressable locations corresponds to the number of dots (pixels) that can be illuminated. Also called bit-mapped displays. **5.16**
Dot matrix printers: An impact printer in which the print head consists of a series of small tubes containing pins that, when pressed against a ribbon and paper, print small dots closely together to form characters. **5.8**–11
Double-sided diskettes: Diskettes on which data can be read and written on both sides. **6.5**
Double-sided drives: Disk drives that can read and write data on both sides of a diskette. **6.5**
Do-until structure: Control structure where a condition is tested at the end of a loop. Processing continues until the condition is met. **12.5**
Do-while structure: Control structure where a condition is tested at the beginning of a loop. If the condition is true, the process is performed. The program then loops back and tests the condition again. This looping continues until the condition being tested is false. **12.5**
Dow Jones News/Retrieval service, 10.8
Downlink: The transmission from a satellite to a receiving earth station. **8.4**
Draft quality: Printer output that a business would use for internal purposes and not for correspondence. **5.6**
Drawings, graphic input devices and, 3.10
Drill and practice software: A flash-card approach to teaching by allowing users to practice skills in subjects such as math and language. **14.10**
Drivers, *See* **Device drivers**
Drum plotter: Plotter that uses a rotating drum, or cylinder, over which drawing pens are mounted. **5.22**
Dumb terminal: A keyboard and a display screen that can be used to enter and transmit data to, or receive and display data from a computer to which it is connected. A dumb terminal has no independent processing capability or auxiliary storage. **3.6**
Dynamic RAM (DRAM) chips: A type of RAM memory chip that is small and simple in design, in which the current or charge on the chip is periodically regenerated by special regenerator circuits. **4.16**

Earth stations: Communications facilities that contain large, dish-shaped antennas used to transmit data to and receive data from communications satellites. **8.4**
EBCDIC, *See* **Extended Binary Coded Decimal Interchange Code**
Edit: Make changes and corrections to electronic text. **2.4**
Editing
checking data validity and, 3.18
utility programs and, 9.14
word processing programs and, 2.4
Editor: A utility program that allows users to make direct changes to programs and data. **9.14**
Educating users, information system life cycle and, 11.22–23
Education
for information processing careers, 13.7–8
using personal computers for, 14.9–10
EEPROM, *See* **Electronically erasable programmable read only memory**
EGA (Enhanced Graphics Adapter) monitor, 5.17
Egghead Discount Software, 13.4
Electron beam, screen images and, 5.19
Electronic calendars, 2.20
Electronic circuits, 1.5
Electronic filing cabinets, 3.12
Electronically erasable programmable read only memory (EEPROM): A type of EPROM in which the data or programs can be erased electronically, without being removed from the computer. **4.17**
Electronic mail: The capability to use computers to transmit messages to and receive messages from other computer users. **14.4**
Electronic notepads, 2.20
Electronic office, *See* **Automated office**
Electronics, background in, 13.4
Electronic spreadsheet software: Software that allows the user to add, subtract, and perform user-defined calculations on rows and columns of numbers. **1.10, 2.10**
Electrostatic plotter: Plotter in which the paper moves under a row of wires (styli) that can be turned on to create an electrostatic charge on the paper. **5.22**
Employee database, 10.2
Employees
management, 10.4–5
nonmanagement, 10.5
End users, *See* **User(s)**
English statements, pseudocode and, 12.8
English, structured, 11.7
Entertainment software, 14.10
Entry point: The point where a control structure is entered. **12.6**
EPROM, *See* **Erasable programmable read only memory**
Equal employment opportunity (EEO) guidelines, 10.2
Equipment, *See* **Hardware**
Erasable programmable read only memory (EPROM): A variation of PROM that allows the user to erase the data stored in memory and to store new data or programs in the memory. EPROM is erased with special ultraviolet light devices that destroy the bit settings within the memory. **4.17**
Ergonomics: The study of the design and arrangement of equipment so that people will interact with the equipment in a healthy, comfortable, and efficient manner. **3.28**
Error(s)
logic, 12.9–10
parity bits and, 4.7
transcription, 3.27
transposition, 3.27
Error correction
documentation for, 3.26
information system life cycle and, 11.25
structured walk-through and, 12.9
Error message, 3.18
Error recovery procedures, user interfaces and, 3.22
Etching process, chip manufacture and, 4.23
Ethics, computers and, 14.16
Evaluation, post-implementation, 11.23
Even parity: The total number of on bits in the byte (including the parity bit) must be an even number. **4.7**
Excel, 2.13
Exception conditions, prototyping and, 11.20
Exception report: A report that contains information that will help users to focus on situations that may require immediate decisions or specific actions. **5.3**–4
Executing: Control unit operation that processes the computer commands. **4.2, 4.10**

1.4 INDEX

Execution cycle: Steps in the machine cycle that include the execution of the instruction and the storage of the processing results. **4.11**
Executive: The resident portion of the operating system. **9.2**
Executive information systems (EIS): Management information systems that have been designed for the information needs of senior management. **10.8-10**
Exit point: The point where the control structure is exited. **12.6**
Expert system: Combines the knowledge on a given subject of one or more human experts into a computerized system that simulates the human experts' reasoning and decision-making processes. **10.10-11**
Extended Binary Coded Decimal Interchange Code (EBCDIC): A coding system used to represent data, primarily on mainframes. **4.6-7**
External modem: A separate, or stand-alone, device attached to the computer or terminal by a cable and to the telephone outlet by a standard telephone cord. **8.12**
External report: A report used outside the organization. **5.2**
Facsimile, or **FAX:** Machines used to transmit a reproduced image of a document over standard phone lines. **14.4**
Fact-gathering techniques, detailed system analysis and, 11.5
Fault-tolerant computers: Computers built with redundant components to allow processing to continue if any single component fails. **9.5**
FAX, *See* **Facsimile**
Feasibility study: During the analysis phase of the information system life cycle, the feasibility study discusses whether the proposed solution is practical and capable of being accomplished. **11.8**
Feed mechanism, printer and, 5.10
Fetching: Control unit operation that obtains the next program instruction from main memory. **4.2, 4.10, 4.11**
Fiber optics: A technology based on the capability of smooth, hair-thin strands of glass that conduct light waves to rapidly and efficiently transmit data. **8.3**
Integrated Services Digital Network and, 8.18
Fields (database): A specific item of information, such as a name or Social Security number, in a record of a database file. **2.13, 3.4, 7.4**
  adding, 7.17
  database, **2.13**
  related, 3.4
  See **Attributes; Data field**
Fifth-generation language, 12.15
File(s): A collection of related records, usually stored on an auxiliary storage device. **2.13, 3.4, 7.4**
  adding records to, 7.8-9
  changing records in, 7.9
  database, 2.13
  deleting records, 7.11-12
  direct or relative, 7.6-8
  fragmented, 2.21
  integrated, 7.13, 7.14
  organization, *See* File organization
  recovering deleted, 2.21
File backup, *See* **Backup**
File management
  operating systems and, 9.10
  utilities and, 2.21
File management system: Software that allows the user to create, maintain, and access one file at a time. **7.12**
File organization
  direct or relative, 7.6-8
  sequential, 7.4-5
  types of, 7.4-8
File-oriented system, 7.13
File-server: In information resource sharing on a network, allows an entire file to be sent at a time, on request. The requesting computer then performs the processing. **8.16**
File transfer software: Communications software that allows the user to move one or more files from one system to another. The software generally has to be loaded on both the sending and receiving computers. **8.15**
Firmware: Instructions that are stored in ROM memory. Also called microcode. **4.17**
Fixed disks: Hard disks on minicomputers and mainframes. Also called direct-access storage devices. **6.8**
Flagged records, 7.12
Flatbed plotter: Plotter in which the pens are instructed by the software to move to the down position so the pen contacts the flat surface of the paper. **5.21**
Flat panel display screens: Plasma and LCD screens, which do not use the conventional cathode ray tube technology, and are relatively flat. **3.28, 5.18, 5.20**

Floppy disks, *See* **Diskettes**
Flowcharts, 12.6
Font: A complete set of characters in the same typeface, style, and size. **5.6**
Footprint, 5.7
Ford Motor Company, 10.11
Foreground jobs: Assignment of a higher processing priority and more CPU time. Compare with background jobs. **9.6**
Formatting: Process that prepares a diskette so that it can store data, and includes defining the tracks, cylinders, and sectors on the surfaces of the diskette. **6.4**
Formatting word processing documents, 2.4, 2.7
Formulas (spreadsheet): Perform calculations on the data in a spreadsheet and display the resulting value in the cell containing the formula. **2.10, 2.11**
FORTH, 12.18
FORTRAN (FORmula TRANslator): A programming language designed to be used by scientists, engineers, and mathematicians. FORTRAN is noted for its capability to easily express and efficiently calculate mathematical equations. **12.17**
Fourth-generation languages (4GLs): Programming languages that are easy to use, both for programmers and nonprogrammers, because the user tells the computer *what* is to be done, not *how* to do it. Also called very high-level languages. **12.14-15**
Foxpro, 7.20
Frame, *See* **Page**
Fraud, preventing, 11.19
Friction feed mechanisms: Printing mechanisms that move paper through a printer by pressure between the paper and the carriage. **5.10**
Frito Lay, 10.9
Front-end processor: A computer that is dedicated to handling the communications requirements of a larger computer. **8.14**
Full-duplex transmission: Data transmission method in which data can be sent in both directions at the same time. **8.11**
Full-motion video, storage requirements, 5.5
Function keys: A set of numerical keys preceded by an "F" included on computer keyboards as a type of user interface. Pressing a function key in an applications program is a shortcut that takes the place of entering a command. **2.3, 3.5-6**
Gantt chart, 11.3
Garbage In, Garbage Out, *See* **GIGO**
Gateway: A combination of hardware and software that allows users on one network to access the resources on a *different* type of network. **8.19**
General microcomputer applications: Software that is useful to a broad range of users. **2.2-4**
Generating the database, 7.15
Geosynchronous orbit: Orbit about 22,300 miles above the earth that communications satellites are placed in. The satellite rotates with the earth, so that the same dish antennas on earth that are used to send and receive signals can remain fixed on the satellite at all times. **8.4**
Gigabyte (GB): A measurement of memory space, equal to a billion bytes. **6.8**
GIGO: An acronym that stands for Garbage In, Garbage Out. **10.6**
Glare, screen and, 3.28
Government regulation, human resource management and, 10.2
Grammar checker software: Software used to check for grammar, writing style, and sentence structure errors. **2.5**
Grammatik, 2.5
GrandView, 2.20
Graphics: A type of output used to present information in the form of charts, graphs, or pictures, so it can be quickly and easily understood. **2.15, 5.4**
  analytical, 2.16
  desktop publishing and, 2.8-9
  dot matrix printers and, 5.11
  high-resolution, 5.17
  ink jet printers and, 5.13
  presentation, 2.17
  screens used for, 5.16-17
  structured analysis and, 11.5-6
Graphic input devices: Used to translate graphic input data, such as photos or drawings, into a form that can be processed on a computer. **3.10**
Graphics software: Software that converts numbers and text into graphic output that visually conveys the relationships of the data. **1.10, 2.15-17, 5.4**

Graphics tablet: Converts points, lines, and curves from a sketch, drawing, or photograph to digital impulses and transmits them to a computer. It also contains unique characters and commands that can be automatically generated by the person using the tablet. **3.10**
Graphic User Interface (GUI): A user interface that uses on-screen pictures, called icons to represent data and processing options. **2.3, 3.21**
Green characters, 3.28
Grocery stores, scanning devices and, 3.13 (fig.)
Half-duplex transmission: Data transmission method in which data can flow in both directions, but in only one direction at a time. **8.11**
Hand-held computers, pen input devices and, 3.10
Handshake: The process of establishing the communications connection on a switched line. **8.7**
Hard cards: A circuit board that has a hard disk built onto it. The board can be installed into an expansion slot of a personal computer. **6.11**
Hard copy: Output that is printed. **5.2, 5.5-15**
Hard disks: Auxiliary storage consisting of one or more rigid metal platters coated with an oxide material that allows data to be magnetically recorded on the surface of the platters. These disks are permanently mounted inside the computer. **1.6, 6.7-11**
  advantages of using, 6.10
  backup and, 6.12
  data organization and, 6.9-10
  hard card, 6.11
  method of storing data on, 6.9
  storage capacity of, 6.8
Hardware: Equipment that processes data, consisting of input devices, a processor unit, output devices, and auxiliary storage units. **1.4-6**
  acquisition of, 11.22
  career opportunities and, 13.2-3
  component areas, 1.14
  manufacturers of, 11.11, 13.2
  system house and, 11.12
Hardware resource sharing: Used in local area networks, allowing all network users to access a single piece of equipment rather than each user having to be connected to their own device. **8.16**
Harvard Graphics, 2.17
Hashing: The program managing the disk uses a formula or performs a calculation to determine the location (position) where a record will be placed on a disk. **7.7**
Head crash: The disk head collides with and damages the surface of a hard disk, causing a loss of data. The collision is caused if some form of contamination is introduced, or if the alignment of the read/write heads is altered. **6.9**
Health problems, ergonomics and, 3.28
Helical scan technology: Used by digital audio tape to write data at high densities across the tape at an angle instead of down the length of the tape. **6.16**
Help feature, 2.23
Helvetica type, 5.6
Hewlett-Packard, 13.2
Hexadecimal (base 16): Number system which represents binary in a more compact form. Hexadecimal is used to represent the electronic status of bits in main memory, and addressing the memory locations. **4.7**
Hierarchical database: Database in which data is organized in a top to bottom series like a family tree or organization chart, having branches made up of parent and child records. **7.14**
Hierarchy charts, *See* **Structure charts**
High-density (HD) diskettes: Diskettes that can store 1.2 megabytes on a 5 1/4" diskette and 1.44 megabytes on a 3 1/2" diskette. **6.5**
High-level languages: Computer languages that are easier to learn and use than low-level languages, and contain nouns, verbs, and mathematical, relational, and logical operators that can be grouped together in what appear to be sentences. These sentences are called program statements. **12.13**
High-speed page printers: Nonimpact printers that can produce output at the rate of several hundred pages per minute, and use a dedicated computer and tape drive to maximize printing speed. **5.15**
Home, personal computers in, 14.8-13
Home key, 3.5
Home systems, control of, 14.8-9
Horizontal application software: Software packages that can be used by many different types of organizations, such as accounting packages. **11.11**

INDEX

Host computer: In a data communications system, a main computer that is connected to several devices (such as terminals or personal computers). **8.8**
Human resource management, 10.2
IBM (International Business Machines), 13.2
  OS/2 and, 9.12
  PC-DOS and, 9.11
  PS/2 Model 30 keyboard, 3.5 (fig.)
  radio-wave wireless system and, 8.5
  relational database and, 7.18
IC, *See* **Integrated circuit**
Icons: On-screen pictures that represent data or processing options. **2.3, 3.21**
  Macintosh and, 3.21, 9.11
If-then-else structure, *See* **Selection structure**
Image, scanners and, 3.12
Image libraries, 2.17
Image processing systems: Use software and special equipment, including scanners, to input and store an actual image of the source document. These systems are like electronic filing cabinets. **3.12, 14.5**
Impact printers: Printers that transfer the image onto paper by some type of printing mechanism striking the paper, ribbon, and character together. **5.7–13**
  band, 5.12–13
  chain, 5.12
  daisy wheel, 5.11
  dot matrix, 5.8–11
Implementation: The phase of the system development process when people actually begin using the new system. This phase includes training and education, conversion, and the post-implementation evaluation. **11.22–24**
Index: A file that consists of a list containing the key field and the corresponding disk address for each record in a file. **7.5**
Indexed file organization: Records are stored on disk in an indexed file in ascending or descending sequence based on a key field. An index is used to retrieve records. **7.5–6**
Inference rules: In expert systems, rules that determine how the knowledge is used to reach decisions. **10.10**
Information: Data that has been processed into a form that has meaning and is useful. **1.2**
  accurate, 10.6
  cost effective, 10.6–7
  importance of, 10.2
  managers using, 10.3
  organized, 10.6
  qualities of, 10.6–7
  useful, 10.6
Information age, trends and issues in, 14.1–17
  automated office and, 14.4–7
  home and, 14.8–13
  social issues, 14.13–16
Information processing: The production of information by processing data on a computer, also called data processing (DP). **1.2**
Information processing careers, *See* Career opportunities; Information systems personnel
Information processing cycle: Input, process, output, and storage operations. Collectively, these operations describe the procedures that a computer performs to process data into information and store it for future use. **1.2, 1.4–6**
  overview of, 3.2
  personal computer and, 1.3
Information processing industry, 13.2–3, 13.7–10
Information processing professionals, 13.3
Information repository, CASE tools and, 11.21
Information resource sharing: Allows local area network users to access data stored on any other computer in the network. **8.16**
Information system: A collection of elements that provides accurate, timely, and useful information. These elements include: equipment, software, accurate data, trained information systems personnel, knowledgeable users, and documented procedures. Information systems are classified into four categories: (1) operational systems, (2) management information systems, (3) decision support systems, and (4) expert systems. **1.13, 10.7–11**
  decision support systems, 10.9–10
  expert systems, 10.10–11
  future changes, 14.2–7
  integrated, 10.11
  management information systems, 10.7–9
  operational systems, 10.7
  senior management and, 10.8

Information system life cycle (ISLC): An organized approach to obtaining an information system, grouped into distinct phases: (1) analysis, (2) acquisition or design, (3) customizing or development, (4) implementation, and (5) maintenance. **11.2–27**
  acquisition and, 11.10–15, 11.22
  analysis, 11.4–9
  application requirements, 11.10–11
  change management and, 11.24
  computer-aided software engineering, 11.21
  conversion and, 11.23
  customizing, 11.15–16
  decision on how to proceed and, 11.8
  design and, 11.16–21
  detailed system analysis, 11.5–7
  development, 11.2–3, 11.21–22
  documentation and, 11.3
  education and, 11.22–23
  equipment acquisition and, 11.22
  error correction and, 11.25
  evaluating software alternatives, 11.12–13
  implementation, 11.22–24
  maintenance, 11.24–25
  participants, 11.3
  performance monitoring and, 11.24
  phases of, 11.2
  post-implementation evaluation, 11.23
  preliminary investigation and, 11.4
  program development and, 11.22
  project management and, 11.2–3
  prototyping and, 11.20
  software vendors and, 11.11–12
  training and, 11.22–23
Information systems department: A separate department within an organization that controls the computers. Also called data processing department, or computer department. **1.14**
  career opportunities and, 13.3–4
  management of, 1.18–19
  tour of, 1.14–19
Information systems personnel, 1.13
  career development and, 13.8–10
  compensation and, 13.5
  computer operators, 1.16, 13.3
  computer programmers, 1.18
  consulting, 11.12, 13.4
  database administrator, 1.18, 7.19
  data entry, 1.17, 13.3
  data librarian, 1.16
  data management, 2.20, 7.2
  data processing, 7.2
  department management, 1.18–19
  education and training, 13.5
  future needs, 14.3
  growth trends, 13.5–6
  information systems department and, 13.3–4
  information system life cycle and, 11.3
  offices of, 1.17–19
  preparing for, 13.7–8
  programmers, *See* **Computer programmers**
  sales, 13.4
  service and repair, 13.4
  systems analysts, *See* **Systems analysts**
INFORMIX-SQL, 7.20
InfoWorld, 13.10
Ingot, 4.22
INGRES, 7.18, 7.20
Inheritance: In object-oriented programming, the capability to pass methods to lower levels of classes or objects. **12.20**
Ink jet printer: Nonimpact printer that forms characters by using a nozzle that shoots electronically charged droplets of ink onto the page, producing high-quality print and graphics. **5.13**
Input: The process of entering programs, commands, user responses, and data into main memory. Input can also refer to the media (such as disks, tapes, and documents) that contain these input types. **1.4, 3.2–30**
  auxiliary storage devices and, 6.3
  data collection devices, 3.16
  devices designed for specific purposes, 3.11–17
  graphic devices, 3.10–11
  keyboards, 1.11, 2.3, 3.5–6
  MICR readers, 3.14–15
  mouse, 2.3, 3.8
  multiuser computers and, 1.14
  scanners, 3.12–13
  simulated, 12.10
  terminals and, 3.6–7
  touch screen, 3.9–10
  trackball, 3.9
  user interface and, 3.17–22
  voice, 3.11

Input control: A system control established to assure the complete and accurate conversion of data from the source documents or other sources to a machine-processable form. **11.19**
Input design: The identification of what information needs to be entered into the system to produce the desired output, and where and how the data will be entered. **11.17**
Input device drivers, 9.8
Input devices: Used to enter data into a computer. **1.5**
Input management, operating systems and, 9.8
Insert key, 3.5
Insert text: Add characters to existing text in a word processing document. **2.6**
Installation, system house and, 11.12
Instance: In object-oriented programming, a specific instance of an object contains all methods from its higher level classes plus any methods that are unique to the object. **12.20**
International Business Machines, *See* IBM
Institute for the Certification of Computer Professionals (ICCP): Offers four certification programs, as a way of encouraging and recognizing the efforts of its members to attain a level of knowledge about their profession. **13.9**
Institute of Electrical and Electronic Engineers (IEEE) and IEEE Computer Society (IEEE/CS): Professional organizations that are primarily composed of computer scientists and engineers. **13.8**
Instruction cycle: Steps in the machine cycle that include fetching the next program instruction and the decoding of that instruction. **4.11**
Instruction register: An area of memory within the control unit of the CPU that can store a single instruction at a time. **4.10**
Instructions, prompts and, 3.18
Instruction set: The collection of commands, such as ADD or MOVE, that the computer's circuits can directly perform. **4.10**
  RISC technology and, 4.14–15
  ROM and, 4.17
Instructions per second, 4.11
Integrated circuit (IC): A complete electronic circuit that has been etched on a small chip of nonconducting material such as silicon. Also called chip, or microchip. **4.13, 4.15**
  production of, 4.21–24
Integrated files, 7.14
Integrated Services Digital Network (ISDN): An international standard for the digital transmission of both voice and data using different channels and communications companies. **8.18**
Integrated software: Refers to software packages that combine applications such as word processing, electronic spreadsheet, database, graphics, and data communications into a single, easy-to use set of programs. **2.18–19**
Intel, 9.12
Intelligent terminal: Terminal that contains not only a keyboard and a screen, but also has built-in processing capabilities, disk drives, and printers. **3.6–7**
Interactive processing: Data is processed immediately as it is entered. **3.22–23**
Interblock gap (IBG): A gap of approximately .6 inches that separates the blocks stored on tape. Also called interrecord gap. **6.15**
Interfaces, printers and, 5.7
Interfaces, user, *See* **User interface**
Internal modem: A circuit board containing a modem that is installed inside a computer or terminal. **8.12**
Internal report: A report used by individuals in the performance of their jobs and only by personnel within an organization. **5.2**
Interpreter: Translates a program in a high-level language one program statement at a time into machine language and then executes the resulting machine language before translating the next program statement. **12.14**
Interrecord gap (IRG), *See* **Interblock gap**
Interviews, detailed system analysis and, 11.5
Inventory, 3.16
Inverse video, *See* **Reverse video**
Iteration structure: Control structure where one or more processes continue to occur as long as a given condition remains true, also called looping structure. Two forms of this structure are the do-while structure, and the do-until structure. **12.5**

Join relational operation: In a relational database query, used to combine two files (relations or tables). **7.18**

Kemeny, John, 12.15
Kernel: The resident portion of the operating system. **9.2**

Key: A field that contains unique data, such as a Social Security number, that is used to identify the records in a file. **7.4**
direct files and, 7.7
Keyboard: An input device that contains alphabetic, numeric, cursor control, and function keys. Used to enter data by pressing keys. **1.5**, 1.11, 1.14, **3.5–6**
ergonomics and, 3.28
Keyboard templates: Plastic sheets that fit around a portion of the keyboard. The template details keyboard commands that select various features of the application program. **2.24**
Key terms, 4.19
Kilobyte (K or KB): A measure of memory equal to 1,024 bytes. **4.3**
Knowledge base: In expert systems, the combined subject knowledge of the human experts. **10.10**
Kujawski, Gordy, 10.11
Kurtz, Thomas, 12.15
Labels: Text that is entered in the cell of a spreadsheet. **2.10–11**
Language translators: Special-purpose systems software programs that are used to convert the programming instructions written by programmers into the machine instructions that a computer can understand. **9.14**
Laser printers: Nonimpact page printers that use a laser beam aimed at a photosensitive drum to create the image to be transferred to paper. **5.14**
Laser scanners: Use of a laser beam to scan and read the special bar code printed on products. **3.13**
Latency, *See* **Rotational delay**
Layout, desktop publishing and, 2.9
LCD display, 5.19, 5.20
Learning aids, microcomputer applications and, 2.23–24
Leased line: A dedicated communications line provided by an outside organization. Also called private line. **8.8**, 8.9
Letter quality (LQ): High-quality printer output in which the printed character is a fully formed, solid character like those made by a typewriter, used for business or legal correspondence. **5.6**
License agreement, 11.13
Light beams, 8.5
Light emission, screen images and, 5.19–20
Light emitting diode (LED) arrays, printers and, 5.14
Light pen: A light-emitting pen; used to create or modify graphics by touching it to a screen with an electronic grid. **3.10**
Line chart: Graphic chart that indicates a trend by use of a rising or falling line. **2.15**
Line configurations: The types of line connections used in communications systems. The major line configurations are point-to-point lines and multidrop, or multipoint, lines. **8.6–9**
dedicated line, 8.7–8
multidrop lines, 8.8–9
point-to-point line, 8.7–8
switched line, 8.7
Line printers: Medium- and high-speed printers that print multiple characters on a line at the same time. **5.6**
Lines per minute (lpm): Measurement for the rate of printing of line printers. **5.6**
Liquid crystal displays (LCD): Flat screens often used with portable computers. **5.19**, 5.20
Liquid crystal shutters, 5.14
LISt Processing (LISP), 12.18
Lithography, 4.23
Local area network (LAN): A communications network that is privately owned and covers a limited geographic area such as an office, a building, or a group of buildings. **8.15–17**
Logic: A step-by-step solution to a programming problem. **12.3**
conditional, 12.4
control structures and, 12.4–5
single entry/single exit and, 12.6
testing, **12.9–10**
walk-through and, 12.9
Logical design: In the analysis phase of the information system life cycle, a design that offers a solution to an existing problem without regard to a specific computer or programming language. **11.16**
Logical operations: Comparisons of data by the arithmetic/logic unit of the central processing unit, to see if one value is greater than, equal to, or less than another. **1.5, 4.2**

Logical records: Data is recorded on magnetic tape in blocks which usually consist of two or more records. The individual records are referred to as logical records. **6.15**
Logic testing: The sequence of program instructions is tested for incorrect results using test data. **12.9–10**
LOGO, 12.18
Logon code: In multiuser operating systems, a logon code, consisting of a word or series of characters, must be entered correctly before a user is allowed to use an application program. **9.9**
Looping structure, *See* **Iteration structure**
Lotus, 13.2
Lotus Agenda, 2.20
Lotus 1-2-3, 2.13
Lotus Works, 2.19
Low-density diskettes: Diskettes that can store 360K for a 5 1/4" diskette, and 720K for a 3 1/2" diskette. **6.5**
Low-level language, *See* **Machine language**
Mace Utilities, 2.21, 9.14
MACH operating system, 9.12
Machine cycle: The four steps which the CPU carries out for each machine language instruction: fetch, decode, execute, and store. **4.11**
Machine language: The fundamental language of the computer's processor, also called low-level language. All programs are converted into machine language before they can be executed. **12.12**
languages translated into, 12.13
Machine language instructions: Program instructions written by users are translated into a form that the electronic circuits in the CPU can interpret and convert into one or more of the commands in the computer's instruction set. **4.10**
Macintosh operating system: A multiprogramming operating system developed by Apple Computers, which provides a graphic interface with that uses icons (figures) and windows. 3.21, **9.11**
Macroinstructions: Instructions in assembly language programs that generate more than one machine language instruction. **12.13**
MACWORLD, 2.22
Magazines, 2.22
application software and, 11.12
Magnetic disk storage: The most widely used storage medium for computers, in which data is recorded on a platter (the disk) as a series of magnetic spots. Magnetic disks offer high storage capacity, reliability, and the capability to directly access stored data. **1.15, 6.3**
auxiliary storage, 6.11
disk cartridges, 6.12
diskettes, 6.3–7
hard cards, 6.11
hard disks, 6.7–11
protecting data and, 6.12
removable disks, 6.10
Magnetic ink character recognition, *See* **MICR**
Magnetic polarity, diskettes and, 6.6
Magnetic tape: A thin ribbon of plastic, coated on one side with a material that can be magnetized to record the bit patterns that represent data. The primary means of backup for most medium and large systems. **1.16, 6.13–16**
backup and, 6.12, 6.16
cartridge devices, 6.14
method of storing data on, 6.14–16
reel-to-reel devices, 6.14
Magneto-optical technology: Used by erasable optical disk drives, in which a magetic field changes the polarity of a spot on the disk that is heated by a laser. **6.17**
Mainframe computers: Large systems that can handle hundreds of users, store large amounts of data, and process transactions at a very high rate. **1.7**
EBCDIC and, 4.6
fixed disks and, 6.8
operating systems, 9.12
printers, 5.5
software references and, 11.13
software vendors and, 11.11
Main memory: Contained in the processor unit of the computer, and stores the operating system, application programs, and data. Also called primary storage. **1.5, 1.8, 4.2**
auxiliary storage and, 1.12
calculations and, 1.12
input and output areas, 4.3
operating system and, 9.3, 9.6–7
parity bits and, 4.7

Maintenance: The final phase in the information system life cycle. The process of supporting the system after it is implemented, consisting of three activities: performance monitoring, change management, and error correction. **11.24**
anticipated, 12.21
at Sutherland, 11.25
system house and, 11.12
Management information systems (MIS): Any computer-based system that provides timely and accurate information for managing an organization. **10.1–11**
decision support systems and, 10.9–10
executive information systems and, 10.8–9
expert systems, 10.10–11
importance of information and, 10.2
management levels and, 10.4–6
personal computers and, 10.11
qualities of information and, 10.6–7
use of information and, 10.3
Manager of information systems, 13.3
Managers/management: The men and women responsible for directing the use of resources such as people, money materials, and information so the organization can operate efficiently and prosper. Managers are responsible for the tasks of planning, organizing, directing, and controlling. **10.3**
CASE tools and, 11.21
design review and, 11.20
levels of, 10.4–6
middle, 10.5
operational, 10.5
preliminary investigation and, 11.4
request for assistance and, 11.4
salaries, 13.5
senior, 10.4, 10.8
Manufacturers, *See* Computer manufacturers
Markets, importance of information and, 10.2
Mask, chip production and, 4.21
Mass storage: Storage devices that provide automated retrieval of data from a library of storage media such as tape or data cartridges. **6.18**
Master program: The resident portion of the operating system. **9.2**
Math coprocessors, 4.14
Mathematical equations, FORTRAN and, 12.17
MCI, 8.18
Meaningful information, 10.6
Megabytes (MB): A measure of memory equal to one million bytes. **4.3**
Megahertz: A measurement used to describe the speed of the system clock; it is equal to one million cycles (or pulses) per second. **4.11**
Member: A lower level record in a network database that is related to one or more higher level (owner) records. **7.15**
Memory
cache, 4.17
core, 4.15
EEPROM, 4.17
EPROM, 4.17
how programs and data are represented in, 4.4–7
main, *See* **Main memory**
management of, *See* Memory management
nonvolatile, 6.3
partitions and, 9.7
PROM, 4.17
random access, *See* **Random access memory**
read only memory, *See* **Read only memory**
semiconductor, 4.15
types of, 4.15–17
volatile, 4.17, 6.18
Memory address: The location of a byte in memory. **4.3**
buses and, 4.12
Memory management
operating systems and, 9.6–7
storage, 9.7
virtual, 9.7
Menu(s): A screen display that provides a list of processing options for the user and allows the user to make a selection. **2.3, 3.18–20**
advantages and disadvantages of, 3.20
case structure and, 12.5
pull-down, 2.3
sub-, 3.20

INDEX **I.7**

Menu generator: Software that lets the user specify a menu (list) of processing options that can be selected. The resulting menu is automatically formatted. **12.18**
Message: In object-oriented programming, the instruction to do something that is sent to an object. **12.20**
Methods: In object-oriented programming, specific instructions that define how the object acts when it is used by a program. **12.19**
MICR (magnetic ink character recognition): A type of machine-readable data. **3.15**
MICR (magnetic ink character recognition) readers: A type of input device that reads characters encoded with a special magnetized ink. **3.15**
Microchip, *See* **Integrated circuit**
Microcode, *See* **Firmware**
Microcomputer(s), *See* **Personal computers**
Microcomputer applications, 1.9–10, 2.1–25
 database, 2.13–15
 desktop publishing, 2.8–9
 general, 2.2–24
 graphics, 2.15–17
 introduction to, 2.2–4
 learning aids and, 2.23–24
 support tools and, 2.23–24
 word processing software, 2.4–8
Microcomputer chip, 1.2
Microfiche: The sheet film used by computer output microfilm. **5.22**
Microprocessors: The smallest processor, which is a single integrated circuit that contains the CPU and sometimes memory. **4.13**
Microsecond: Measure of time equal to one millionth of a second. **4.15**
Microsoft Corporation, 9.11, 9.12, 13.2
Microsoft Project, 2.21
Microsoft Word, 2.4
Microsoft Works, 2.19
Microwaves: Radio waves that can be used to provide high-speed transmission of both voice and data. **8.4**
Middle management: Makes tactical decisions and is responsible for implementing the strategic decisions of senior management. **10.5**
Minicomputers: More powerful than microcomputers and can support a number of users performing different tasks. **1.7**
 fixed disks and, 6.8
 operating systems, 9.12
 software references and, 11.13
 software vendors and, 11.11
Minus (–) sign, numeric fields and, 3.4
MIPS (million instructions per second): Measure of the processing speed of computers. **4.11**
Mnemonic: A simple, easily remembered abbreviation used in assembly language programming to represent a machine operation code. Also called symbolic operation code. **12.13**
Models: In decision support systems, models allow users to ask *what-if* questions by changing one or more of the variables and seeing what the projected results would be. **10.9**
Modem (*mo*dulate-*dem*odulate): A communications device that converts data between the digital signals of a terminal or computer and the analog signals that are transmitted over a communications channel. 8.10, **8.12–13**
 service technician and, 13.4
MODULA-3, 12.18
Module: Performs a given task within a program, and can be developed individually and then combined to form a complete program; sometimes called subroutine. **12.3**
Monitor: The resident portion of the operating system. **9.2**
Monitor: The screen (terminal) portion of the computer system; can be color or monochrome. **1.5, 5.16**
 color, 5.18
 device drivers and, 9.8
 monochrome, 5.18
Monochrome screens: Screens that display a single color such as white, green, or amber characters on a black background, or black characters on a white background. **5.18**
Motherboard: The main circuit board of a personal computer. **4.13**
Motorola, 8.5
Mouse: A small input device that is used to move the cursor, and input commands. **2.3, 3.8**
 graphic user interface and, 3.21
 operating environment and, 9.13
Move text: A command the enables the user to either cut (remove) or copy a sentence, paragraph, or block of text in a word processing document. **2.6**

MSA, 13.2
MS-DOS (Microsoft Disk Operating System): A single-user operating system originally developed by Microsoft Corporation for IBM personal computers. The IBM version is called PC-DOS. MS-DOS quickly became an industry standard for personal computer operating systems. **9.11**
Multidrop line: A communications line configuration using a single line to connect multiple devices, such as terminals or personal computers, to a main computer. Also called multipoint line. **8.8**
Multimedia: The mixing of text, graphics, video (pictures), and audio (sound) output on a screen. **5.4–5**
Multiplexor (MUX): An electronic device that converts multiple input signals into a single stream of data that can be efficiently transmitted over a communication channel. **8.13**
Multipoint line, *See* **Multidrop line**
Multiprocessing operating system: Coordinates the operations of computers with more than one CPU. **9.4**
Multiprocessors: Computers that have more than one CPU. **9.4**
Multiprogramming operating systems: Allow more than one program to be run at the same time. Also called multitasking operating systems. **9.4,** 9.12
Multitasking operating systems, *See* **Multiprogramming operating systems**
Multiuser computers: Computers that can concurrently process requests from more than one user. **1.14**
Multiuser-multiprogramming operating systems: A multiprogramming operating system that supports more than one user running more than one program. **9.4**
MUX, *See* **Multiplexor**
Nanosecond: Measure of time equal to one billionth of a second. **4.15**
Narrative reports: Reports that are primarily text-based, but may contain some graphic or numeric information. **5.2**
Natural language: A type of query language that allows the user to enter a question as if he or she were speaking to another person. **12.15**
NCR, 13.2
Near letter quality (NLQ): Printer output that is not fully formed characters, but still offers good print quality. **5.6**
Neon-argon gas, 5.20
Network: In data communications, a collection of terminals, computers, and other equipment that use communications channels to share data, information, hardware, and software. 1.7, **8.15–21**
 bus, 8.19
 configurations, 8.18–19
 connecting, 8.19–20
 example of, 8.20–21
 fault-tolerant systems, 9.5
 local area, 8.15–17
 managemet information systems and, 10.11
 radio, 8.5
 ring, 8.19
 star, 8.18
 wide area, 8.17–18
Network control unit, *See* **Server**
Network database: Similar to a hierarchical database except that each member, can have more than one owner. **7.15**
Network design, consultants and, 13.4
Nodes: Devices connected to a network, such as terminals, printers, or other computers. **8.18**
Nonimpact printers: Printers that create an image without having a mechanism striking against a sheet of paper. **5.7,** 5.13–15
 ink jet, 5.13
 laser, 5.14
 page, 5.14–15
 thermal, 5.14
Nonprocedural: Said of fourth-generation languages, because the programmer does not specify the actual procedures that the program must use to solve a problem. **12.14**
Nonvolatile: Data and programs are retained when the power is turned off. **6.3**
Norton Utilities, 2.21, 9.14
Number systems, 4.7–9
 binary, 4.7, 4.8
 decimal, 4.8
 hexadecimal, 4.9
Numeric calculations, math coprocessors and, 4.14

Numeric characters: The elements that comprise data; specifically, the numbers 0–9. **3.3**
 memory storage and, 4.4
Numeric data, tests for, 3.26
Numeric field: A field that contains numeric characters and some special characters. **3.4**
Numeric keypad: Numeric keys arranged in an adding machine or calculator format to aid the user with numeric data entry. **3.5**
Object code, *See* **Object program**
Object-oriented operating systems: Operating systems specifically designed to run object-oriented programming applications. **12.20**
Object-oriented programming (OOP): A new approach to developing software that allows programmers to create objects, which can be used repeatedly by programmers whenever they need them. **12.19**
Object-oriented software: Applications that are developed using object-oriented programming techniques. **12.20**
Object program: The machine instructions produced by a compiler from a program originally written in a high-level language. Also called object code. **12.13**
Objects: A combination of data and program instructions, used in object-oriented programming. **12.19**
 library of, 12.20
OCR, *See* **Optical character recognition**
OCR typeface (OCR-A), 3.14
Odd parity: The total number of on bits in the byte (including the parity bit) must be an odd number. **4.7**
Offline data entry: The device from which the data is being entered is not connected to the computer that will process it; used for batch processing. **3.24**
On-demand reports: Reports created for information that is not required on a scheduled basis, but only when it is requested. **5.4**
Online data entry: Data entry for interactive processing; the device from which the data is being entered is connected directly to the computer. **3.22**
Online help: Instructions within an application showing how to use an application. A function key or special combination of keys are reserved for the help feature. **2.23**
Open Software Foundation, 9.12
Open Systems Interconnection (OSI) model: A set of communications protocols defined by the International Standards Organization based in Geneva, Switzerland. **8.15**
Operating environment: A graphic interface between the user and the operating system. Also called windowing environment. **9.13**
Operating system (OS): One or more programs that manage the operations of a computer, and function as an interface between the user, the application programs, and the computer equipment. **1.7, 1.8, 9.2–13**
 allocating system resources, 9.5–8
 Apple Macintosh, 9.11, 9.13
 buffers and, 9.6
 CPU management and, 9.6–7
 disk management and, 9.10
 DOS, 1.8
 file management and, 9.10
 formatting process and, 6.5
 functions of, 9.5–10
 input management and, 9.8
 loading, 1.11, 9.2–3
 MACH, 9.12
 main memory and, 4.2
 memory management and, 9.6–7
 monitoring system activities and, 9.9
 MS-DOS, 9.11
 multiprocessors and, 9.4–5
 multiprogramming and, 9.4
 object-oriented, 12.20
 OS/2, 9.12
 output management and, 9.8
 PC-DOS, 9.11
 personal computers and, 9.2, 9.4
 PICK, 9.12
 popular, 9.10–12
 ProDos, 9.12
 proprietary versus portable, 9.10
 security and, 9.9
 shell programs, 9.13
 single program, 9.4
 system performance and, 9.9
 types of, 9.4–5
 UNIX, 9.10

Operating system prompt: Indicates to the user that the operating system has been loaded and is ready to accept a command. **9.3**
Operational decisions: Decisions made by operational management that involve an immediate action such as accepting or rejecting an inventory delivery or approving a purchase order. **10.5**
Operational management: Management level that makes operational decisions and provides direct supervision over the production, clerical, and nonmanagement staff of an organization. **10.5**
Operational systems: Information systems that process data generated by the day-to-day transactions of an organization. **10.7**
Operation code: A unique value typically stored in the first byte in a machine language instruction that indicates which operation is to be performed. **4.10**
Operations manager: Manager in the information systems department who oversees the operational aspects, such as scheduling, maintenance, and operation of the equipment. **1.19**
Optical cards: Special-purpose storage device that store up to 800 pages of text or images on a device the size of a credit card. **6.19**
Optical character recognition (OCR): Scanners that read typewritten, computer printed, and in some cases handprinted characters from ordinary documents. These devices range from large machines that can automatically read thousands of documents per minute, to hand held wands. **3.13**
Optical disks: Storage medium that uses lasers to burn microscopic holes on the surface of a hard plastic disk; able to store enormous quantities of information. **6.16**–18
   erasable, 6.17
Optical mark reader (OMR): A scanning device that can read carefully placed pencil marks on specially designed documents. **3.14**
ORACLE, 7.17, 7.20
Oracle Corporation, 7.18, 12.19 (fig.)
Order processing software, 1.17
Organization
   management levels in, 10.4–6
   programming standards of, 12.20
Organizing, information used by management and, 10.3
OS/2: The operating system released by IBM for its family of PS/2 personal computers, developed by Microsoft Corporation. **9.12**
Outliners, 2.20
Output: The data that has been processed into a useful form called information that can be used by a person or machine. 1.2, **1.4, 1.5**, 1.12, **5.2**–26
   auxiliary storage devices and, 6.3
   computer graphics, 5.4
   computer output microfilm, 5.22–23
   data projectors, 5.21
   draft, 5.6
   impact printers and, 5.7–13
   letter-quality, 5.6
   multimedia, 5.4–5
   multiuser computer, 1.15
   nonimpact printers and, 5.13–15
   plotters, 5.21–22
   printers, *See* **Printers/printing**
   reports, 5.2–4
   screen, 5.16–20
   types of, 5.2–5
   voice, 5.23
Output design: The design of specific screen and report layouts that will be used for output to display or report information from the new system. **11.17**
Output device drivers, 9.8
Output devices: Most commonly used devices are the printer and the computer screen. **1.5, 5.24**
Output management, operating systems and, 9.8
Output multimedia, 5.4–5
Owner: The higher level record in a network database. **7.15**

Packet switching: In communications networks, individual packets of information from various users are combined and transmitted over a high-speed channel. **8.18**
Page: In virtual memory management, the fixed number of bytes that are transferred from disk to memory each time new data or program instruction are required. **9.7**
Page composition, desktop publishing and, 2.9
PageMaker, 2.8
Page(s) per minute (ppm): Measure of the speed of printers that can produce an entire page at one time. **5.6**

Page printers: Nonimpact printers that operate similar to a copying machine to produce high-quality text and graphic output. **5.14**
Page scanner: An input device that can electronically capture an entire page of text or images such as photographs or art work. The scanner converts the text or image on the original document into digital information that can be stored, printed, or displayed. **3.12**
Paging: In virtual memory management, a fixed number of bytes (a *page*) is transferred from disk to memory each time new data or program instructions are required. **9.7**
Palo Alto Research Center, 12.20
Panasonic printer, 5.8
Paper, types and sizes of, 5.6
Paradox, 2.15, 7.20
Parallel conversion: Continuing to process data on the old system while some or all of the data is also processed on the new system. **11.23**
Parallel interface: The computer communication with the printer, in which an entire byte (eight bits) is sent at the same time. **5.7**
Parallel processing: The use of multiple CPUs, each with their own memory, that work on their assigned portion of a problem simultaneously. **4.14**
Parent-child relationships, 7.15
Parent record: In a hierarchical database, a record that has one or more child records. **7.14**
Parity bit: One extra bit for each byte that is used for error checking. **4.7**, 8.10
Partitions, memory and, 9.7
Pascal: A programming language developed for teaching programming. Pascal contains programming statements that encourage the use of structured program design. **12.17**
Password: A value, such as a word or number, which identifies the user. In multiuser operating systems, the password must be entered correctly before a user is allowed to use an application program. The password is usually confidential. **3.22, 9.9**
Paste text: An option used after performing either the cut or the copy command, where the text is placed elsewhere in a word processing document. **2.6**
PC-DOS: The IBM single-user operating system developed by Microsoft Corporation for personal computers. **9.11**
PC Magazine, 2.22
PC Tools Deluxe, 2.21, 9.14
Pen input devices: Allows the user to input hand-printed letters and numbers to record information. **3.10–11**
Pen plotters: Plotters used to create images on a sheet of paper by moving one or more pens over the surface. **5.21**
Performance, management controlling, 10.3
Performance monitoring: During the maintenance phase of the information system life cycle, the ongoing process of comparing response times, file sizes, and other system performance measures against the values that were estimated when the system was designed. **11.24**
   database administrator and, 7.20
Periodic reports: Reports that are produced on a regular basis such as daily, weekly, or monthly. Also called scheduled reports. **5.4**
Peripheral devices: The input devices, output devices, and auxiliary storage units that surround the processing unit. **1.6**
Personal computers: The small desktop-sized systems that are widely used, and generally priced under $10,000. Also called personal computers, or micros. **1.7**
   auxiliary storage, 1.6, 6.3
   database systems, 7.20–21
   hard cards and, 6.11
   home use, 14.8–13
   information processing cycle and, 1.3
   interpreters and, 12.14
   loading operating system, 9.2
   management information systems and, 10.11
   microprocessors, 4.13–14
   operating system and, 9.2, 9.4
   printers, 5.5
   purchasing guidelines, 14.11–13
   software references and, 11.13
   software vendors and, 11.11
   utility functions, 9.14
Personal information management (PIM) software: Helps users keep track of miscellaneous bits of personal information. Notes to self, phone messages, and appointment scheduling are examples of this type of software. **2.20**
Personal services, 14.8
Personnel, *See* **Career opportunities**; **Information systems personnel**
Persuasion, 2.17

Phased conversion: Used with larger systems that can be broken down into individual modules that can be implemented separately at different times. **11.23**
Ph.D.s, demand for, 13.5
Phosphor-coated screen, 5.19–20
Photo mask, 4.21
Photographs
   graphic input devices and, 3.10
   scanners and, 3.12
Photoresist, 4.23
Physical design: In the information system life cycle, the logical design that was created during the analysis phase is transformed into physical design, identifying the procedures to be automated, choosing the programming language, and specifying the equipment needed for the system. **11.16**
Physical record: The group of records making up a block of data recorded on tape. **6.15**
PICK operating system, 9.12
Pie chart: A graphic representation of proportions depicted as slices of a *pie*. **2.15**
Pilot conversion: The new system will be used first by only a portion of the organization, often at a separate location. **11.23**
Pins, dot matrix printers and, 5.8–9
Pixels (picture elements): On screens, the dots that can be illuminated. **5.16**
Planning
   information used by management and, 10.3
   project management and, 11.3
Plasma screens: Flat screens often used with portable computers. **5.19, 5.20**
PL/I (Programming Language/One), 12.18
Plotters: An output device used to produce high-quality line drawings and diagrams. **5.21**
Plus (+) sign, 3.4
Point: Measure of character size, equal to 1/72 of one inch. **5.6**
Point-of-sale (POS) terminals: Allow data to be entered at the time and place where the transaction with the consumer occurs, such as in fast-food restaurants or hotels. **3.7**, 3.26
Point-to-point line: A line configuration used in communications which is a direct line between a sending and a receiving device. It may be either a switched line or a dedicated line. **8.7**
Polling: Used by a front-end processor to check the connected terminals or computers to see if they have data to send. **8.14**
Portable operating systems: Operating systems that will run on many manufacturers' computers. **9.10**
Positional decimal system, 4.8
Post-implementation evaluation: Conducted after a system is implemented to determine if the system is performing as designed, if operating costs are as anticipated, and if any modifications are necessary to make the system operate more effectively. **11.23**
Preliminary investigation: Determines if a request for development or modification of an information system justifies further detailed investigation. **11.4**, 11.8
Presentation graphics: Graphics that offer the user a wide range of presentation effects. These include three-dimensional displays, background patterns, multiple text fonts, and image libraries. **2.17**, 5.4
Presentation Manager, 9.13
Presentations, multimedia, 5.4–5
Primary storage, *See* **Main memory**
Prime numbers: A number divisible by only itself and 1, used in a hashing operation. **7.7**
Printers/printing: Output device. **1.5,** 1.12, **5.5**–15
   band, 5.12–13
   bidirectional, 5.10
   chain, 5.12
   classification of, 5.7
   considerations in choosing, 5.15
   daisy wheel, 5.11
   device drivers and, 9.8
   features of, 5.6–7
   impact, 5.7–13
   interfaces and, 5.7
   laser, 5.14
   line, 5.6
   multiuser computer, 1.15
   nonimpact, 5.7, 5.13–15
   page, 5.14–15
   paper and, 5.6
   speed, 5.6
   spooling and, 9.8
   word processing and, 2.7, 2.8
Print head, 5.10

Print quality, 5.6
Printronix printer, 5.8
Print spool: The reports stored on disk that are waiting to be printed. **9.8**
Privacy, computers and, 14.15–16
Private line, *See* **Leased line**
Problem definition: Aspect of preliminary investigation, where the true nature of the problem is identified. **11.4**
Process: Part of the information processing cycle; the procedures a computer performs to process data into information. **1.4**
 data flow diagrams and, 11.5
 sequence structure, 12.4
 specifications, 11.7
Process circle, structured English and, 11.7
Process design: In information systems design, the systems analyst specifies exactly what actions will be taken on the input data to create output information. **11.18**
Processing
 parallel, 4.14
 serial, 4.14
 speed of, 1.3
Processing control: Procedures that are established to determine the accuracy of information after it has been input to the system. **11.19**
Processing data, *See* **Data processing**
Processor
 front-end, 8.14
 fundamental language of, 12.12
 instruction set of, 12.12
 multiuser computer, 1.15
Processor unit: Contains the electronic circuits that cause the processing of data to occur, and is divided into two parts, the central processing unit (CPU), and main memory. **1.5**, **4.1–24**
 architecture of, 4.13–15
 ASCII code and, 4.5–6
 buses and, 4.12
 central processing unit and, 4.2
 EBCDIC and, 4.5, 4.6
 machine language instructions and, 4.10
 main memory, 4.2–3
 speed of, 4.11–12
 system clock and, 4.11
 word size and, 4.12
Process specifications: Describe and document what happens to a data flow when it reaches a process circle. **11.7**
PROCOMM PLUS, 2.18
Production data entry: Large amounts of data are entered by a terminal operator whose only job is to enter the data. **3.23**
Product life cycles, importance of information and, 10.2
Product support, 2.22
Professional growth, 13.9
Professional organizations, 13.8
Program(s): The detailed set of instructions that tells the computer exactly what to do, so it can perform the operations in the information processing cycle. Also called program instructions, or software. **1.3–4, 1.7–10, 3.2, 12.2**
 benchmark test, 11.13
 career opportunities and, 13.2–3
 changes to, 12.11
 comments in, 12.10
 demonstration of, 2.22, 11.13
 designing, *See* **Program design**
 development, *See* **Program development**
 evaluating alternatives, 11.12–13
 existing users of, 11.13
 interface with, 12.20
 loading, 1.11
 making the purchase, 11.13
 memory representation of, 4.4–7
 narrative description of, 12.10
 object, 12.13
 object-oriented, 12.20
 organizational standards, 12.20
 product reviews, 2.22
 reputable publisher, 2.22
 sharing on network, 8.17
 source, 12.13
 standard processing modules, 12.18
 subroutine, 12.3
 system house and, 11.12
 trying out, 2.22
 vendors, 11.11–12
Program decomposition, 12.3
Program design: A logical solution, or logic, for a program is developed and documented. 11.22, 12.2, **12.3–9**
 pseudocode and, 12.8

 structured, 12.3–6
 tools for, 12.6–8
 Warnier-Orr, 12.8
Program development: The process of developing the software, or programs, required for a system. Program development includes the following steps: (1) review of the program specifications, (2) program design, (3) program coding, (4) program testing, and (5) finalizing the documentation. **11.22, 12.2**
 application generators and, 12.18–19
 coding and, 12.9
 designing the program and, 12.2, 12.3–9
 finalizing program documentation and, 12.10
 maintenance and, 12.11
 object-oriented programming and, 12.19–20
 programming languages and, 12.12–18
 reputable developer and, 2.22
 reviewing the program specifications, 12.2, 12.3
 steps in, 12.2
 structured walk-through and, 12.9
 summary of, 12.11
 testing, 12.9–10
Program flowchart: A program design tool in which the logical steps of a program are represented by a combination of symbols and text. **12.6**
Program generators, *See* **Application generators**
Program instructions: The detailed set of instructions that tell a computer which operations to perform. **1.4**
 steps involved in executing, 4.10
 time slice and, 9.5–6
Programmable read only memory (PROM): Acts the same as ROM except the data can be stored into the PROM memory prior to being installed in the computer. **4.17**
Programmable terminals, *See* **Intelligent terminals**
Program maintenance: Includes all changes to a program once it is implemented and processing real transactions. **12.11**
Programmed Inquiry Learning or Teaching (PILOT), 12.18
Programmers, *See* **Computer programmers**
Programming
 maintenance, 12.11
 object-oriented, 12.19–20
Programming language: A set of written words and symbols that allow a programmer or user to communicate with the computer. **12.12–18**
 Ada, 12.17
 assembly, 12.13
 BASIC, 12.15
 C, 12.16
 categories of, 12.12–15
 COBOL, 12.16
 fifth generation, 12.15
 FORTRAN, 12.17
 fourth-generation, 12.14–15
 high-level, 12.13–14
 low-level, 12.12
 machine, 12.12
 Pascal, 12.17
 rational, 12.15
 translators, 9.14
 used today, 12.15–18
Programming manager: Manager in the information systems department who is in charge of all programmers. **1.18**
Program specifications: Can include many documents such as data flow diagrams, system flowcharts, process specifications, a data dictionary, screen formats, and report layouts. 11.2, **12.3**
Program statements: The *sentences* of a high-level programming language. **12.13**
Projection panels: Projection of the computer screen image that can be clearly seen by a room full of people, using liquid crystal display technology, designed to be placed on top of an overhead projector. **5.21**
Project management: Involves planning, scheduling, reporting, and controlling the individual activities that make up the information system life cycle. **11.2–3**
Project management software: Allows users to plan, schedule, track, and analyze the events, resources, and costs of a project. **2.21**
Project plan: Week-by-week record of individual activities that make up the information system life cycle, and includes an estimate of the time to complete the activity and the start and finish dates. **11.2–3**
Project relational operation: In a relational database query, specifies the fields (attributes) that appear on the query output. **7.18**

PROLOG (PROgramming in LOGic), 12.18
PROM, *See* **Programmable read only memory**
Prompts: Messages to the user that are displayed on screen and provide information or instructions regarding an entry to be made or action to be taken. **2.3, 3.18**
 operating system, 9.3
Proprietary operating systems: Operating systems that are privately owned, and limited to a specific computer model. **9.10**
Protocols: In data communications, a set of rules and procedures for exchanging information between computers. **8.15**
Prototyping: In information system development, building a working model of the new system. **11.20**
 CASE tools and, 11.21
Pseudocode: The logical steps in the solution of a problem are written as English statements and indentations are used to represent the control structures. **12.8**
Public domain software: Free software that is not copyrighted and can therefore be distributed among users. **14.12**
Pull-down menu: A menu style wherein the selections are displayed across the screen. As the user makes a selection, the options associated with that selection appear to be *pulled down* from the top of the screen like a window shade. **2.3, 9.13**
Pulses per second, 4.11

Quattro, 2.13
Query language: A simple English-like language that allows users to retrieve information from the database based on the criteria and in the format specified by the user. **7.17–19, 12.15**
Questionnaires
 detailed system analysis and, 11.5
 ethics and, 14.16 (fig.)

Radio-wave wireless systems, 8.5
RAM, *See* **Random access memory**
RAM chips, solid-state storage and, 6.18
Random access, *See* **Random retrieval**
Random access memory (RAM): The name given to integrated circuits, or chips, that are used for main memory. **4.16**
Random file, *See* **Direct file**
Random retrieval: A retrieval method in which the system can go directly to a record without having to read the preceding records. Also called random access, or direct access. **7.5**
R:Base, 2.15, 7.20
Read only memory (ROM): Memory in which data or programs are written to it once at the time of manufacture, and always retained thereafter, even when the computer's power is turned off. **4.17**
Read/write head: A recording mechanism in the drive that rests on or floats above the surface of the rotating disk, generating electronic impulses to record bits, or reading bits previously recorded. **6.6, 6.9**
 diskettes and, 6.6
 hard disks and, 6.7, 6.9–10
Recalculations, spreadsheets and, 2.12
Record(s): A collection of related data items or fields. **2.13, 3.4**
 changing, 7.9–11
 child, 7.14–15
 data, 7.11–12
 database, 2.13
 deleting, 7.11–12
 file organization and, 7.4
 flagged, 7.12
 logical, 6.15
 parent, 7.14–15
 physical, 6.15
 related, 3.4
 root, 7.14
Recording density: The number of bits that can be recorded on one inch of the innermost track on a disk, referred to as bits per inch. **6.5**
Recovery
 database administrator and, 7.19
 utilities and, 2.21
Reel-to-reel tape devices: Tape devices that use two reels: a supply reel to hold the tape that will be read or written on, and a take-up reel to temporarily hold portions of the supply reel tape as it is being processed. As the tape moves from one reel to another, it passes over a read/write head. **6.14**

INDEX

Registers: Storage locations in the CPU that temporarily store specific data such as the address of the next instruction. **4.2**
Relational database: Database in which data is organized in tables called relations. **7.15**,
   PICK operating system and, 9.12
   querying, 7.18
Relational operations: When a user queries a relational database, the three relational operations are select, project, and join. **7.18**
Relational Technology, 7.18
Relations: Tables in a relational database. **7.15**
Relationships, 3.4, 7.13
Relative file, *See* **Direct file**
Remote locations, serial interface printers and, 5.7
Removable disks: Consist of the drive unit, which is usually in its own cabinet, and the removable recording media, called a disk pack. **1.15, 6.10**
Report: Information presented in an organized form. **5.2**
   cost of producing, 10.6-7
   detail, 5.3
   exception, 5.3-4
   external, 5.2
   internal, 5.2
   narrative, 5.2
   on-demand, 5.4
   periodic, 5.4
   scheduled, 5.4
   summary, 5.3
Report layout form, 11.17
Request for proposal (RFP): A written list of an organization's software requirements that is given to prospective software vendors. **11.11**
Resolution: Measure of a screen's image clarity, and depends on the number of individual dots displayed that can be illuminated, called pixels. **5.16-17**
Resource sharing, LANs and, 8.16
Response time: The amount of time from the moment a user enters data until the computer responds. **1.15, 9.9**
Restaurants, point-of-sale terminals and, 3.7
Retrieval
   databases and, 2.14-15, 3.4
   direct file, 7.6-8
   file organization and, 7.4-8
   index and, 7.5
   microfilm and, 5.23
   query language and, 7.17-19
   random, 7.5, 7.7
   sequential, 7.4
Reverse video: Screen feature used to emphasize characters in which the normal display on the screen is reversed, such as a dark background with light characters. Also called inverse video. **3.19, 5.18**
RGB (red, green, blue) monitor: A color screen that uses three signals, one for each color, red, green, and blue, to turn on the required phosphors. **5.20**
Ring network: A communications network that has a series of computers connected to each other in a ring. **8.19**
RISC (reduced instruction set computing): Technology that involves reducing the computer's instruction set to only those instructions that are most frequently used, which allows the computer to operate faster. **4.14-15**
Ritchie, Dennis, 12.16
ROM, *See* **Read only memory**
Root record: In a hierarchical database, the parent record at the top of the hierarchy. **7.14**
Rotational delay: The time it takes for the sector containing the data to rotate under the read/write head. Also called latency. **6.6**
Rows (spreadsheet): Data which is organized horizontally on a spreadsheet. **2.10**
RPG (Report Program Generator), 12.18
Salaries, *See* **Compensation**
Sales information, 10.2
Sales representatives: Persons that must have a general understanding of computers and a specific knowledge of the product they are selling; often the most highly compensated employees in a computer company. **13.4**
   salaries and, 13.5
Satellites, 8.4
Saving, 2.2, 2.7
Scanners: Include a variety of devices that read printed codes, characters, or images and convert them into a form that can be processed by the computer. 2.9, **3.12-13**
   image processing and, 3.12
   laser, 3.13
   optical character reader, 3.13

optical mark readers, 3.14
   page, 3.12
Scheduled reports, *See* **Periodic reports**
Scheduling, project management and, 11.3
Scratchpad computers, 3.10
Screen(s): Output device used to display data on both personal computers and terminals. Also called a monitor, CRT (cathode ray tube), or VDT (video display terminal). **1.5, 1.11, 1.14, 5.16-20**
   antiglare coating, 3.28
   brightness and contrast adjustments, 3.28
   color and, 5.18, 5.19, 5.20
   cursor and, 2.3, 5.18
   ergonomics and, 3.28
   features of, 5.16-18
   how images are displayed on, 5.19-20
   LCD, 5.19
   monochrome, 5.18
   plasma, 5.19-20
   prompts and, 3.18
   refreshed, 5.20
   resolution of, 5.16-17
   scrolling and, 5.18
   size, 5.16
   touch, 3.9-10
   types of, 5.18-19
   user interface, 3.17
Screen control, word processing and, 2.8
Screen design, 3.21, 11.17
Screen generator: Software that allows the user to design an input or output screen by entering the names and descriptions of the input and output data directly on the screen. **12.19**
Screen painter, *See* **Screen generator**
Scrolling: The movement of screen data up or down one line or one screen at a time. **5.18**
Search and replace, word processing and, 2.8
Seating, ergonomics and, 3.28
Secondary storage, *See* **Auxiliary storage**
Sector: A pie-shaped section of the disk, also a section of a track; the basic storage unit of floppy disks. **6.5**
Sector method: Physical organization and addressing of data stored on disk which divides each track on the disk surface into individual storage areas called sectors. **6.9**
Security: The safeguards established to prevent and detect unauthorized use and deliberate or accidental damage to computer systems and data. In a DBMS, the control of access to data. Usually the user can specify different levels of user access privileges. **7.17, 14.13**
   database mamangement systems and, 7.17, 7.19
   data management and, 7.3, 7.14
   data entry procedures and, 3.27
   operating systems and, 9.9
   user interfaces and, 3.22
Seek time: The time it takes to position the read/write head over the proper track. **6.6**
Segmentation: In virtual memory management, programs are divided into logical portions called segments, which are brought into main memory from disk only when needed. **9.7**
Segments: In virtual memory management, programs that are divided into logical portions. **9.7**
Selection structure: Control structure used for conditional program logic, also called if-then-else structure. **12.4**
Select relational operation: In a relational database query, selects certain records (rows or tuples) based on user-supplied criteria. **7.18**
Semiconductor memory: An integrated circuit containing thousands of transistors etched into a semiconductor material such as silicon. **4.15**
Senior management: The top managers in an organization, who make strategic decisions and are concerned with the long-range direction of the organization. Also called executive or top management. **10.4, 10.8**
Sequence structure: Control structure where one process occurs immediately after another. **12.4**
Sequential access, *See* **Sequential retrieval**
Sequential file organization: A file organization process in which records are stored one after the other, normally in ascending or descending order, based on a value in each record called the key. **7.4-5**
Sequential number, menu selection and, 3.18
Sequential retrieval: The records on a tape or disk are retrieved (accessed) one after another in the same order that the records are stored. Also called sequential access. **7.4**
Sequential storage: Magnetic tape is considered a sequential storage media because the computer must record and read tape records one after another. **6.14**

Serial interface: The computer communication with the printer, in which data is sent to the printer a single bit at a time. **5.7**
Serial processing: Computers that contain one CPU that processes a single instruction at a time. **4.14**
Server: In local area networks, a computer that is dedicated to handling the communications needs of the other computers in the network. Also called network control unit. **8.16**
Service and repair technician: A challenging job for individuals who like to troubleshoot and solve problems, and who have a strong background in electronics. **13.4**
Settling time: The time required for the read/write head to be placed in contact with the disk. **6.6**
Shareware: Software that users may try out on their own systems before paying a fee. **14.12**
Shell programs: Act as an interface between the user and the operating system, and offer a limited number of utility functions such as file maintenance, but not applications windowing or graphics. **9.13**
Shutter, diskette and, 6.4
Signal type, communication channels and, 8.10
Sign on, 3.22
Silicon, 4.13, 4.21, 4.22
Simplex transmission: Data transmission method in which data flows in only one direction. **8.11**
Simulation software: Software designed to teach a user by creating a model of a real-life situation. **14.10**
Single entry/single exit: Means there is only one entry point and one exit point from each of the control structures. **12.6**
Single program operating systems: Allow only a single user to run a single program at one time. **9.4**
Single-sided diskettes: Diskettes on which data can be read and written on only one side. **6.5**
Single-sided drives: Disk drives that can read and write data on only one side. **6.5**
Sinks, data flow diagrams and, 11.5
Site license: A special agreement, obtained from the software vendor, that allows a commercial software package to be shared by many users within the same organization. **8.17**
Sixteen-bit computers, 4.12
Smalltalk, 12.20
Smart cards: Special purpose storage devices about the same size and thickness of a credit card that contain a thin microprocessor capable of storing recorded information. **6.19**
Smart terminals, *See* **Intelligent terminals**
Social issues, computer use and, 14.13-16
Soft copy: Output displayed on a screen. **5.2, 5.16-20**
Software, *See* **Program(s)**
Software houses: Businesses that specialize in developing software for sale. **11.12**
Software industry, 13.2
Software license: A license from the software manufacturer to the buyer that describes the right to use software under certain terms and conditions. **11.13**
Software packages, *See* **Application software packages**
Software piracy: Illegal copying of software, also called software theft. **14.13**
Solid-state storage: Use RAM chips to provide fast data access and retrieval. These devices are volatile. **6.18**
Sort utilities, 9.13-14
Source data collection: Data that is entered as the event or transaction is occurring and at the location where it is occurring. **3.26**
Source document(s): Original documents, such as sales invoices, from which data can be entered. **1.17, 3.12**
   accurate conversion from, 11.19
   offline data entry and, 3.24
Source document control: A system control that includes serial numbering of input documents such as invoices and paychecks, document registers in which each input document is recorded and time-stamped as it is received, and batch totaling and balancing to predetermined totals to assure the accuracy of processing. **11.19**
Source program: A program written in high-level language, and later converted by a compiler, or interpreter, to machine language. **12.13-14**
Sources, data flow diagrams and, 11.5
Spacebar, menu selection and, 3.19
Spaghetti code, 12.6
Special characters: All characters other than A-Z and 0-9; specifically, punctuation and symbols. **3.3**
   memory storage and, 4.4
Special-purpose terminals, 3.7

Spelling checker software: Allows the user to enter a command that tells the software to check individual words or entire documents for correct spelling. **2.5**, 2.7
Spooling: A report is first written (saved) to the disk before it is printed; used to increase printer efficiency. **9.8**
Spreadsheet: Organization of numeric data in a worksheet or table format, by electronic spreadsheet software. Data is organized horizontally in rows, and vertically in columns. 1.9, **1.10**–13, **2.10**–13
  changes rippling through, 2.12
  features of, 2.13
  graphics capabilities, 5.4
  recalculations and, 2.12
SQL, *See* **Structured Query Language**
Star network: A communications network that contains a central computer and one or more terminals or computers connected to it, forming a star. **8.18**
Static RAM chip: A type of RAM memory chip that is larger and more complicated than dynamic RAM and does not require the current to be periodically regenerated. **4.16**
Storage, 1.4, 1.13
  auxiliary, *See* **Auxiliary storage**
  backup, 6.12
  batch processing and, 3.24
  capability, 1.3
  direct access, 6.8, 7.15
  main memory and, 4.2
  primary, *See* **Primary storage**
  of processing results, 4.10. 4.11
  temporary, 4.2
Storage location, 4.3
Storing: Control unit operation that takes place when the result of the instruction is written to main memory. **4.2**
Strategic decisions: Decisions made by senior management that deal with the overall goals and objectives of an organization. **10.4**
Streaming mode: The magnetic tape records data in exactly the same byte-by-byte order that it appears on the hard disk. **6.16**
Structure charts: Charts used to decompose and represent the modules of a program; also called hierarchy charts. **12.3**
Structured analysis: The use of analysis and design tools such as data flow diagrams, data dictionaries, process specifications, structured English, decision tables, and decision trees to document the specifications of an information system. **11.5**
Structured design, *See* **Top-down design**
Structured English: One way of writing process specifications; a style of writing and presentation that highlights the alternatives and actions that are part of the process. **11.7**
Structured program design: A methodology that emphasizes three main program design concepts: modules, control structures, and single entry/single exit. **12.3**
Structured Query Language (SQL): A widely used query language. **7.18**–19, 7.20
Structured walk-through: A step-by-step review performed on the process design to identify any design logic errors, and to continue the communication between the systems analyst and the user. Also used during program development. **11.19**, 12.9
Submenus: Menus that are used to further define the processing options that are available. **3.20**
Subroutine, *See* **Module**
Summary report: A report which summarizes data, containing totals from detailed input data. **5.3**
  accounting controls and, 11.19
Supercomputers: The most powerful category of computers, and the most expensive. They can process hundreds of millions of instructions per second. **1.7**
  MIPS, 4.11
  parallel processors and, 4.14
Supermicrocomputers, 1.7
Super VGA monitor, 5.17
Supervisor: The resident portion of the operating system. **9.2**
Support tools, microcomputer applications and, 2.23–24
Swapping: When using paging or segmentation, the operating system sometimes needs to *swap* data in memory with new data on disk. **9.7**
Switched line: A point-to-point line using a regular telephone line to establish a communications connection. **8.7**
Symbolic addressing: Assembly language allows a specific computer memory location to be referenced by a name or symbol. **12.13**
Symbolic operation code, *See* **Mnemonic**

Symbols, flowcharts and, 12.6
Synchronous transmission: Data communication method which transmits blocks of data at regular intervals using timing signals to synchronize the sending and receiving equipment. **8.10**
Synonyms: The same disk location for records with different key values, in a hashing operation. **7.7**
Synonyms, word processing programs and, 2.5
Syntax errors: Violations of the grammar rules of the language in which the program was written. **12.9**
System clock: Used by the control unit to synchronize, or control the timing of, all computer operations, generating electronic pulses at a fixed rate, measured in megahertz. **4.11**
System activities, operating systems monitoring, 9.9
System controls: During the design phase, system controls are established to (1) ensure that only valid data is accepted and processed, and (2) to prevent computer-related fraud. **11.19**
System design, consultants and, 13.4
System flowchart: A graphical depiction of the major processes, reports, data files, and types of input devices that provide data to the system. **11.18**
System houses: Software companies that not only sell software but also sell the equipment. **11.12**
System performance, operating systems and, 9.9
System resources, allocation of, 9.5–8
System responses, meaningful, 3.21
Systems analysis, information system life cycle and, 11.3–9
Systems analysts: Persons that review and design computer applications. **1.17**–18, 13.3
  database design and, 11.18
  input design and, 11.17
  output design and, 11.17
  process design and, 11.18
  testing design and, 11.20
  written report from, 11.8
System selection, consultants and, 13.4
Systems manager: Manager in the information systems department who oversees the activities in the systems analysis and design area. **1.18**
Systems software: All the programs including the operating system that are related to controlling the operations of the computer equipment, classified into three major categories: operating systems, utilities, and language translators. **1.8**, **9.2**–15
  language translators, 9.14
  operating system and, 9.3–13
  utilities, 9.13–14

Tables, decision, 11.7
Tactical decisions: The decisions made by middle management, implementing specific programs and plans necessary to accomplish the strategic objectives of an organization. **10.5**
Tailoring software, *See* **Customizing phase**
Tandy, 13.2
Tape cartridges, mass storage and, 6.18
Tape density: The number of bits that can be stored on one inch of tape. Commonly used densities are 800, 1,600, 3,200, and 6,250 bpi. **6.15**
Teachers, demand for, 13.5
Teamwork, 13.3
Technology, rapid changes in, 13.2, 14.2
Telecommunications: Any type of long-distance communications including television signals. **8.2**
Telecommuting: The capability of individuals to work at home and communicate with their offices by using personal computers and communications lines. **14.9**
Teleconferencing: Usually means video conferencing, the use of computers and television cameras to transmit video images and the sound of the conference participants to other participants with similar equipment at a remote location. **14.5**
Telephone, cellular, 8.5
Telephone companies
  deregulation of, 9.10
  digital data service, 8.10
  switching systems, 8.7
Telephone line, 8.2
  data communications and, 2.18
  switched line and, 8.7
Teleprocessing: The use of telephone lines to transmit data. **8.2**
1024 screens, 5.17
Terabyte: One trillion bytes. **6.17**
Terminal: The primary input device on a multiuser system consisting of a keyboard and a screen, which is connected through a communication line, or cable, to a computer. **1.14**, 3.6–7

  dumb, 3.6
  ergonomics and, 3.28
  intelligent, 3.6
  multidrop lines and, 8.8
  multiuser computer, 1.15
  point-of-sale, 3.7, 3.26
  smart, 3.7
  special-purpose, 3.7
  user interface, 3.17
Terminal emulation software: Communications software that allows a personal computer to imitate or appear to be a specific type of terminal, so that the personal computer can connect to another usually larger computer. **8.15**
Test data: Data that simulates the type of input that the program will process when it is implemented; used during logic testing. **12.10**
Testing
  design phase and, 11.20
  desk checking, 12.9
  live, 11.20
  logic, 12.9–10
  looping structure and, 12.5
Text
  inserting and deleting, 2.6
  retrieval, 2.20
Text-based reports, 5.2
Thermal printers: Nonimpact printers that use heat to produce fully formed characters and graphics on chemically treated paper. **5.14**
Thermal transfer printers: Thermal printers used for color printing. **5.14**
Thesaurus software: Allows the user to look up synonyms for words in a document while the word processor is in use. **2.5**
32-bit computers, 4.12
Thrashing: A condition where the operating system is spending more time swapping pages to and from the disk than processing data. **9.9**
Timeline, 2.21
Time slice: A common way for an operating system to allocate CPU processing time. **9.5**
Times Roman, 5.6
Time-stamped, 11.19
Titles, spreadsheet, 2.10–11
Top-down design: A design approach that focuses on the major functions of an information system, and keeps breaking those functions down into smaller and smaller activities, sometimes called modules, that can eventually be programmed. Also called structured design. **11.16**, **12.3**–6
  modules and, 12.3
  control structures and, 12.4–6
  flowcharts and, 12.6
  Pascal and, 12.17
  single entry/single exit and, 12.6
Topology: The configuration, or physical layout, of the equipment in a communications network. **8.18**
Touch screens: Allow users to touch areas of the screen to enter data. They let the user interact with the computer by the touch of a finger rather than typing on a keyboard or moving a mouse. **3.9**–10
Track: A narrow recording band forming a full circle around the diskette. **6.4**
Trackball: A graphic pointing device like a mouse. To move the cursor with a trackball, the user simply rotates the top mounted ball in the desired direction. **3.9**
Tracks per inch (tpi): A measure of the amount of data that can be stored on a diskette. **6.5**
Tractor feed mechanisms: Printer mechanisms that transport continuous-form paper by using sprockets inserted into holes on the sides of the paper. **5.10**
Trade books: Books to help users learn to use the features of a microcomputer application package. These books are usually found where software is sold, and are frequently carried in regular bookstores. **2.24**
Trade publications, vertical application software and, 11.12
Trade shows, 13.9
Training, 2.22
  information system life cycle and, 11.22–23
  learning aids and, 2.23–24
  system house and, 11.12
Transcription error: During data entry, operator error made in copying the values from a source document. **3.27**
Transistor: An electronic component etched into a semiconductor material such as silicon. The transistor can be either on or off and represents a bit in memory. **4.15**, 4.21

INDEX

Transmission
 direction of, 8.11
 rate of, 8.12
 types of, 8.11
Transmission media: Communications channels are made up of one or more transmission media, including twisted pair wire, coaxial cable, fiber optics, microwave transmission, satellite transmission, and wireless transmission. **8.3**
Transmission modes, communications channels, 8.10
Transposition error: During data entry, operator error made by switching two characters. **3.27**
Trees, decision, 11.7
Tuples: Rows in a relational database. **7.15**
Turn-around document: A document designed to be returned to the organization in which is was originally issued. When it is returned (turned around), the data on it is read by an OCR device. **3.14**
Tutorial software: Software that uses text, graphics, and sometimes sound to teach users concepts about a subject and follows the instruction with questions to help the user ensure that he or she understands the concepts. **2.23, 14.10**
Twisted pair wire: Color-coded pairs of copper wires that are twisted together, commonly used for telephone lines. **8.3**
Type element, daisy wheel, 5.11
Typeface: A set of letters, numbers, and special characters that have a similar design. **5.6**
Unauthorized access: Computer trespassing, in other words, being logged on a system without permission. **14.14**
Unauthorized use: The use of a computer system or computer data for unapproved and possibly illegal activities. **14.14**
Underlining: Screen feature for emphasis that allows characters, words, lines, or paragraphs to be underlined. **5.18**
UNISYS, 13.2
Universal Product Code (UPC), 3.13 (fig.)
UNIX operating system: A popular operating system from AT&T that was originally developed to manage a variety of scientific and specialized computer applications. With the deregulation of the telephone companies in the 1980s, a multiuser version of UNIX has become available to run on most major computers. **9.10**–11, 12.16
Updating: Data maintenance procedures for adding new data, changing existing information, and deleting obsolete information. **7.3, 7.8**–12
 file-oriented versus database system, 7.13, 7.14
Uplink: The transmission to a satellite. **8.4**
User(s): The people who either use the computer directly or use the information it provides, also called computer users, or end users. **1.2, 1.3**
 coordination and, 7.19
 database management system and, 7.20
 data management and, 7.2
 future trends and, 14.3
 information system life cycle and, 11.3
 input design and, 11.17
 knowledgeable, 1.13
 meaningful responses to, 3.21
 output design and, 11.17
 preliminary investigation and, 11.4
 priorities assigned to, 9.6
 process design and, 11.19
 responsibility of, 1.14
 software references and, 11.13
 testing design and, 11.20
 UNIX and, 9.11
User friendly: Not requiring any special technical skills or ability to use. **2.2**
User group: A group of people with common computer equipment or software interests that meet regularly to share information. **13.8**
User ID: In multiuser operating systems, a user ID identifies the user, and must be entered correctly before a user is allowed to use an application program. **9.9**
User interface: A combination of hardware and software that allows a user to communicate with a computer system. **2.2**–3, **3.17**–22
 features of, 3.21–22
 future changes, 14.2
 graphic, 3.21, 14.2
 menus and, 3.18
 prompts and, 3.18
User responses: The data that a user inputs to respond to a question or message from the software. **3.3**
 simple, 3.21
U.S. government military projects, Ada and, 12.17
Utilities: In a DBMS, programs that provide for a number of maintenance tasks including creating files and dictionaries, monitoring performance, copying data, and deleting unwanted records. **7.17**
Utilities: Programs that provide commonly needed tasks such as file backups, sorting, and editing. **9.13**–14
Utility bills, 3.14
Utility software: Includes a variety of programs to help manage and maintain the data on the computer system. **2.21**
Vaccines: Programs that locate and remove viruses. **14.14**
Vacuum tube, 4.15
Value-added carriers: Companies that lease channels from common carriers to provide specialized communications services. **8.18**
Value-added networks: Networks provided by companies that lease channels from common carriers to provide specialized communications services. **8.18**
Values (spreadsheet): Numerical data contained in the cells of a spreadsheet. **2.10**
Vendors, 2.22
Ventura Publisher, 2.8
Vertical application software: Software developed for a unique way of doing business, usually within a specific industry. **11.11**, 11.12
Very high-level languages, See **Fourth-generation languages**
VGA (Video Graphics Array) monitor, 5.17
Vice President of Information Systems: The information systems manager may have this title. **1.19**, 13.3
Video compression: The key to use of full-motion video in multimedia, that makes large amounts of data take up less storage space. **5.5**
Video conferencing, See **Teleconferencing**
Video display terminals (VDT), See **Display terminals; Screen(s)**
View: In a relational database, the data from one or more files the user manipulates for a query. **7.18**
Virtual machine (VM) operating system: Allows a single computer to run two or more different operating systems. **9.5**
Virtual memory management: Increases the effective (or *virtual*) limits of memory by expanding the amount of main memory to include disk space. **9.7**
Virus: A computer program designed to copy itself into other software and spread through multiple computer systems. **14.14**
VMS operating system, 9.10
Voice input: Allows the user to enter data and issue commands to the computer with spoken words. **3.11**
Voice mail: Verbal electronic mail, made possible by the latest computerized telephone systems. **14.4**
Voice output: Spoken words that are conveyed to the user from the computer. **5.23**
Voice synthesizer: A type of voice generation that can transform words stored in main memory into speech. **5.23**
Volatile memory: RAM memory is said to be volatile because the programs and data stored in RAM are erased when the power to the computer is turned off. **4.17**
Warnier-Orr technique: (named after Jean Dominique Warnier and Kenneth Orr) The programmer analyzes output to be produced from an application and develops processing modules that are needed to produce the output. **12.8**
What-if questions, 10.9
Wide area network (WAN): A communications network that covers a large geographic area, and uses telephone lines, microwaves, satellites, or a combination of communications channels. **8.17**-18
Window: A rectangular portion of the screen that is used to display information. **2.19**
Windowing environment, See **Operating environment**
Wireless transmission: Used to connect devices that are in the same general area such as an office or business park, using one of three transmission techniques: light beams, radio waves, or carrier-connect radio. **8.5**
Wirth, Niklaus, 12.17
WordPerfect, 2.4
Word processing software: Used to prepare documents electronically. It allows text to be entered on the computer keyboard in the same manner as on a typewriter. Characters are displayed on a screen and stored in the computer's main memory for ease of editing. 1.9, **1.10**, 2.2, **2.4**, 14.4
 common features of, 2.8
 desktop publishing and, 2.8
 example, 2.6–8
 grammar checker and, 2.5
 mouse and, 3.9
 spelling checker and, 2.5
 thesaurus and, 2.5
Word processing systems, voice-controlled, 3.11
Word size: The number of bits that the CPU can process at one time. **4.12**
WordStar, 2.4
Work environment, ergonomics and, 3.28
Working storage, 4.3
WORM (write once, read many): Optical disk devices that provide for one-time recording. **6.17**
WYSE pc 286 personal computer, 3.7 (fig.)
WYSIWYG: An acronym for What You See Is What You Get. A feature that allows the user to design on screen an exact image of what a printed page will look like. **2.9**
Write-protect notch, 6.12

Xerox, 3.21, 12.20

Yoke, screen images and, 5.19

WINDOWS

USING MICROSOFT WINDOWS 3.1

▶ PROJECT ONE

AN INTRODUCTION TO WINDOWS

Objectives **WIN2**
Introduction **WIN2**
Microsoft Windows **WIN3**
Communicating with Microsoft
 Windows **WIN5**
Using Microsoft
 Windows **WIN14**
File and Disk Concepts **WIN22**
Opening a Document
 File **WIN28**
Using Windows Help **WIN32**
Quitting Windows **WIN36**
Project Summary **WIN38**
Key Terms **WIN38**
Quick Reference **WIN39**
Student Assignments **WIN40**
Computer Laboratory
 Exercises **WIN43**

▶ PROJECT TWO

FILE AND DISK OPERATIONS

Objectives **WIN47**
Introduction **WIN47**
Starting Windows **WIN48**
File Manager **WIN49**
Formatting a Diskette **WIN50**
Copying Files to a
 Diskette **WIN54**
Renaming a File **WIN63**
Deleting a File **WIN65**
Creating a Backup
 Diskette **WIN67**
Searching for Help Using Online
 Help **WIN71**
Additional Commands and
 Concepts **WIN80**
Project Summary **WIN86**
Key Terms **WIN87**
Quick Reference **WIN87**
Student Assignments **WIN88**
Computer Laboratory
 Exercises **WIN92**

INDEX **WIN96**

Microsoft Windows 3.1
PROJECT ONE

An Introduction to Windows

OBJECTIVES You will have mastered the material in this project when you can:

- Describe a user interface
- Describe Microsoft Windows
- Identify the elements of a window
- Perform the four basic mouse operations of pointing, clicking, double-clicking, and dragging
- Correct errors made while performing mouse operations
- Understand the keyboard shortcut notation
- Select a menu
- Choose a command from a menu
- Respond to dialog boxes
- Start and exit an application
- Name a file
- Understand directories and subdirectories
- Understand directory structures and directory paths
- Create, save, open, and print a document
- Open, enlarge, and scroll a window
- Obtain online Help while using an application

▶ INTRODUCTION

The most popular and widely used graphical user interface available today is **Microsoft Windows**, or **Windows**. Microsoft Windows allows you to easily communicate with and control your computer. In addition, Microsoft Windows makes it easy to learn the application software installed on your computer, transfer data between the applications, and manage the data created while using an application.

In this project, you learn about user interfaces, the computer hardware and computer software that comprise a user interface, and Microsoft Windows. You use Microsoft Windows to perform the operations of opening a group window, starting and exiting an application, enlarging an application window, entering and editing data within an application, printing a document on the printer, saving a document on disk, opening a document, and obtaining online Help while using an application.

What Is a User Interface?

A **user interface** is the combination of hardware and software that allows the computer user to communicate with and control the computer. Through the user interface, you are able to control the computer, request information from the computer, and respond to messages displayed by the computer. Thus, a user interface provides the means for dialogue between you and the computer.

Hardware and software together form the user interface. Among the hardware associated with a user interface are the CRT screen, keyboard, and mouse (Figure 1-1). The CRT screen displays messages and provides information. You respond by entering data in the form of a command or other response using the keyboard or mouse. Among the responses available to you are responses that specify what application software to run, when to print, and where to store the data for future use.

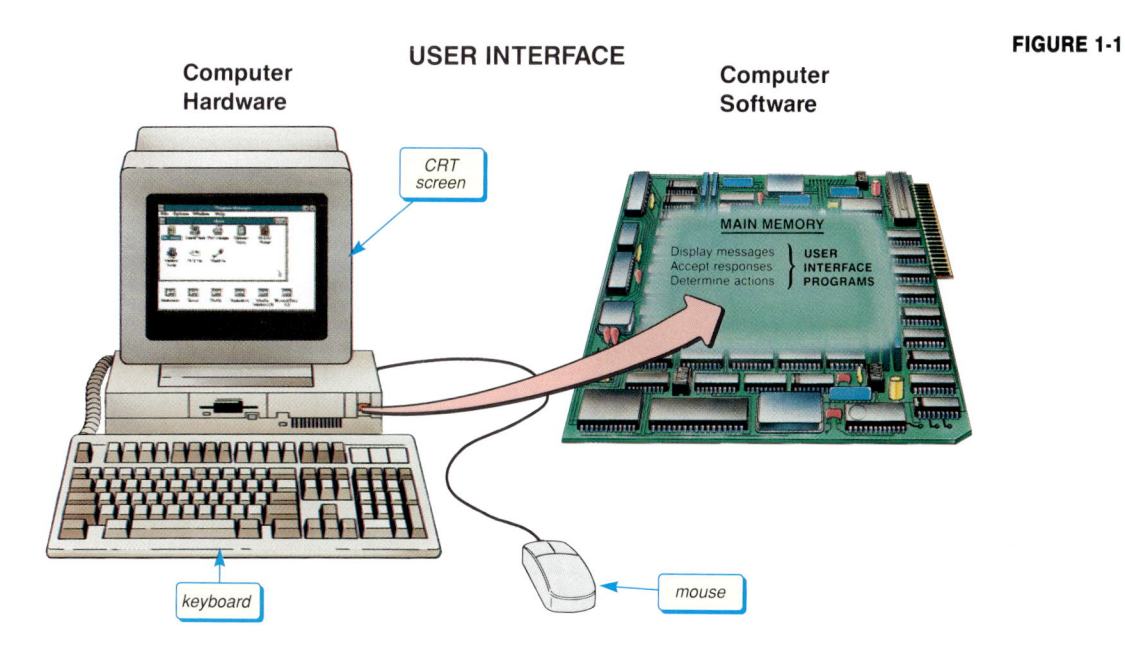

FIGURE 1-1

The computer software associated with the user interface are the programs that engage you in dialogue (Figure 1-1). The computer software determines the messages you receive, the manner in which you should respond, and the actions that occur based on your responses. The goal of an effective user interface is to be **user friendly**, meaning the software can be easily used by individuals with limited training. Research studies have indicated that the use of graphics can play an important role in aiding users to effectively interact with a computer. A **graphical user interface**, or **GUI**, is a user interface that displays graphics in addition to text when it communicates with the user.

▶ MICROSOFT WINDOWS

Microsoft Windows, or Windows, the most popular graphical user interface, makes it easy to learn and work with **application software**, which is software that performs an application-related function, such as word processing. Numerous application software packages are available for purchase from retail computer stores, and several applications are included with the Windows interface software. In Windows terminology, these application software packages are referred to as **applications**.

WIN4   PROJECT 1   AN INTRODUCTION TO WINDOWS

Starting Microsoft Windows

When you turn on the computer, an introductory screen consisting of the Windows logo, Windows name, version number (3.1), and copyright notices displays momentarily (Figure 1-2). Next, a blank screen containing an hourglass icon (⧗) displays (Figure 1-3). The **hourglass icon** indicates that Windows requires a brief interval of time to change the display on the screen, and you should wait until the hourglass icon disappears.

FIGURE 1-2

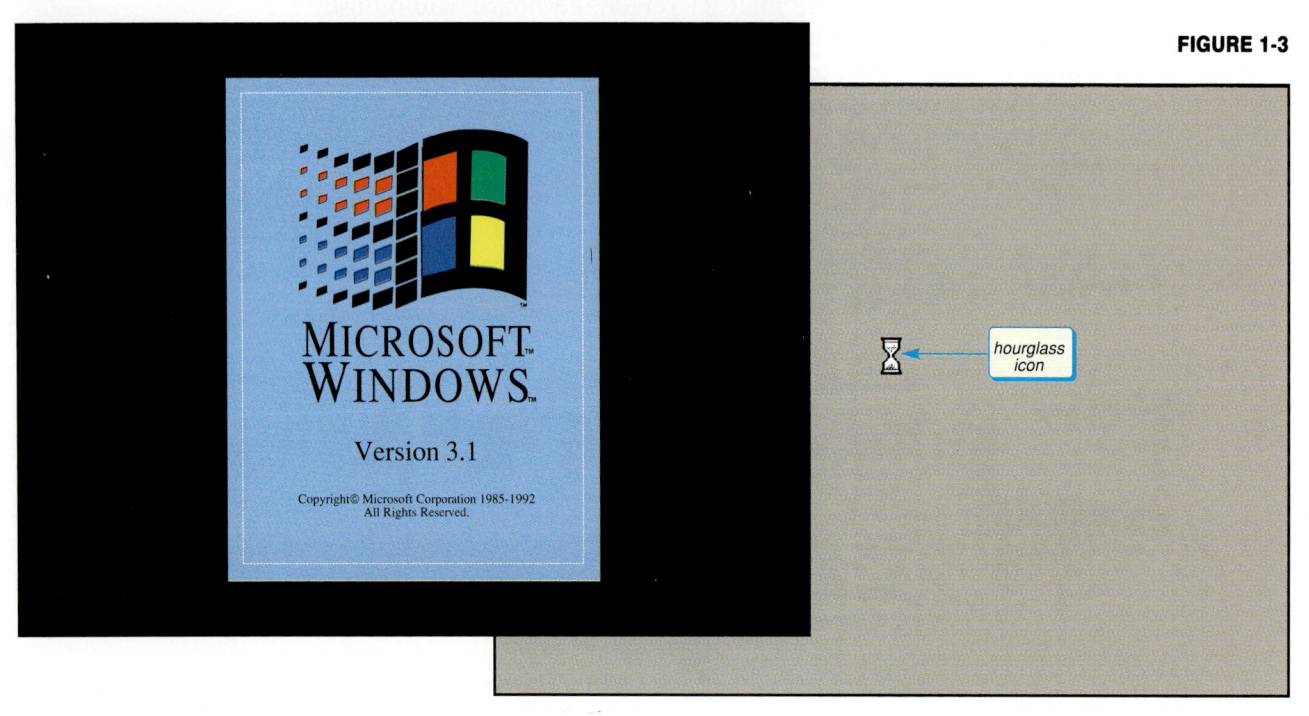

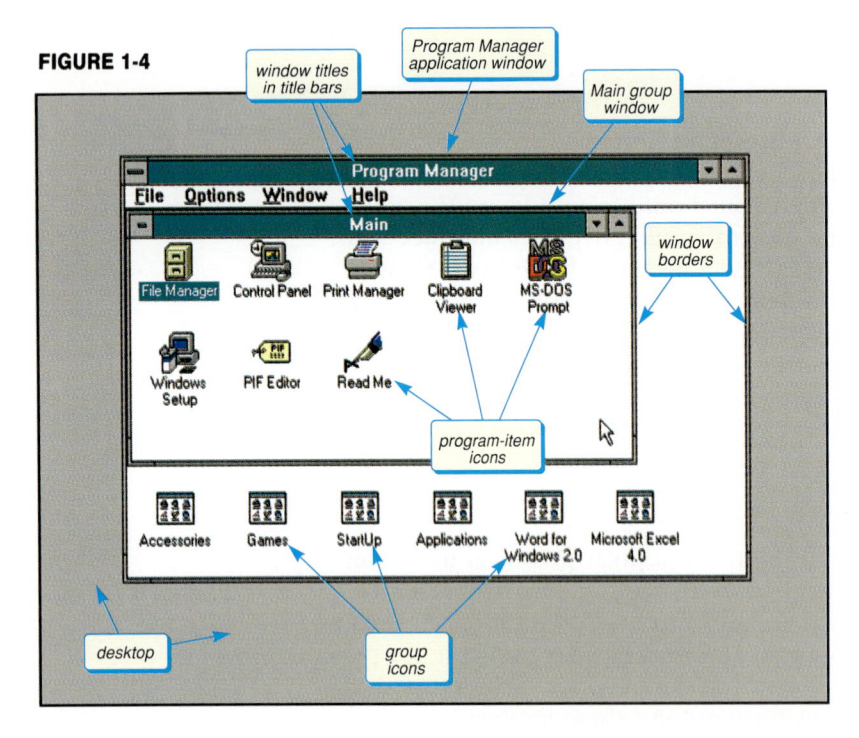

FIGURE 1-3

FIGURE 1-4

Finally, two rectangular areas, or **windows**, display (Figure 1-4). The double-line, or **window border**, surrounding each window determines their shape and size. The horizontal bar at the top of each window, called the **title bar**, contains a **window title** that identifies each window. In Figure 1-4, the Program Manager and Main titles identify each window.

The screen background on which the windows display is called the **desktop**. If your desktop does not look similar to the desktop in Figure 1-4, your instructor will inform you of the modifications necessary to change your desktop.

The Program Manager window represents the **Program Manager** application. The Program Manager application starts when you start Windows and is central to the operation of Windows. Program Manager organizes related applications into groups and displays the groups in the Program Manager window. A window that represents an application, such as the Program Manager window, is called an **application window**.

Small pictures, or **icons**, represent an individual application or groups of applications. In Figure 1-4 on the previous page, the Main window contains a group of eight icons (File Manager, Control Panel, Print Manager, Clipboard Viewer, MS-DOS Prompt, Windows Setup, PIF Editor, and Read Me). A window that contains a group of icons, such as the Main window, is called a **group window**. The icons in a group window, called **program-item icons**, each represent an individual application. A name below each program-item icon identifies the application. The program-item icons are unique and, therefore, easily distinguished from each other.

The six icons at the bottom of the Program Manager window in Figure 1-4 on the previous page, (Accessories, Games, StartUp, Applications, Word for Windows 2.0, and Microsoft Excel 4.0), called **group icons**, each represent a group of applications. Group icons are similar in appearance and only the name below the icon distinguishes one icon from another icon. Although the program-item icons of the individual applications in these groups are not visible in Figure 1-4, a method to view these icons will be demonstrated later in this project.

▶ COMMUNICATING WITH MICROSOFT WINDOWS

The Windows interface software provides the means for dialogue between you and the computer. Part of this dialogue involves requesting information from the computer and responding to messages displayed by the computer. You can request information and respond to messages using either the mouse or keyboard.

The Mouse and Mouse Pointer

A **mouse** is a pointing device commonly used with Windows that is attached to the computer by a cable and contains one or more buttons. The mouse in Figure 1-5 contains two buttons, the left mouse button and the right mouse button. On the bottom of this mouse is a ball (Figure 1-6).

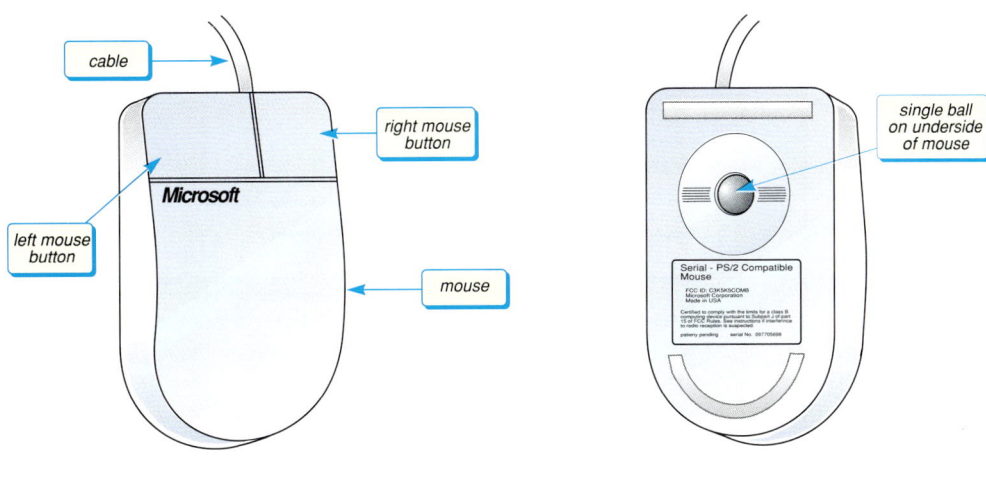

FIGURE 1-5   **FIGURE 1-6**

As you move the mouse across a flat surface (Figure 1-7), the movement of the ball is electronically sensed, and a **mouse pointer** in the shape of a block arrow (▷) moves across the desktop in the same direction.

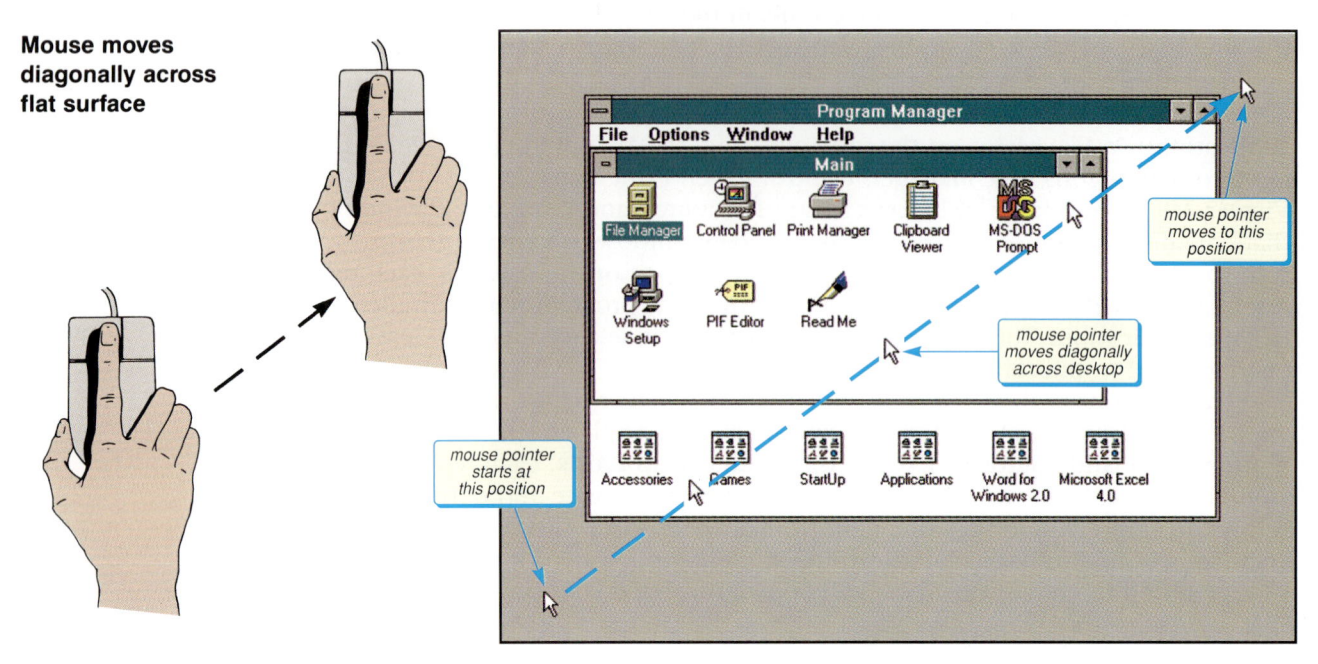

FIGURE 1-7

Mouse Operations

You use the mouse to perform four basic operations: (1) pointing; (2) clicking; (3) double-clicking; and (4) dragging. **Pointing** means moving the mouse across a flat surface until the mouse pointer rests on the item of choice on the desktop. In Figure 1-8, you move the mouse diagonally across a flat surface until the tip of the mouse pointer rests on the Print Manager icon.

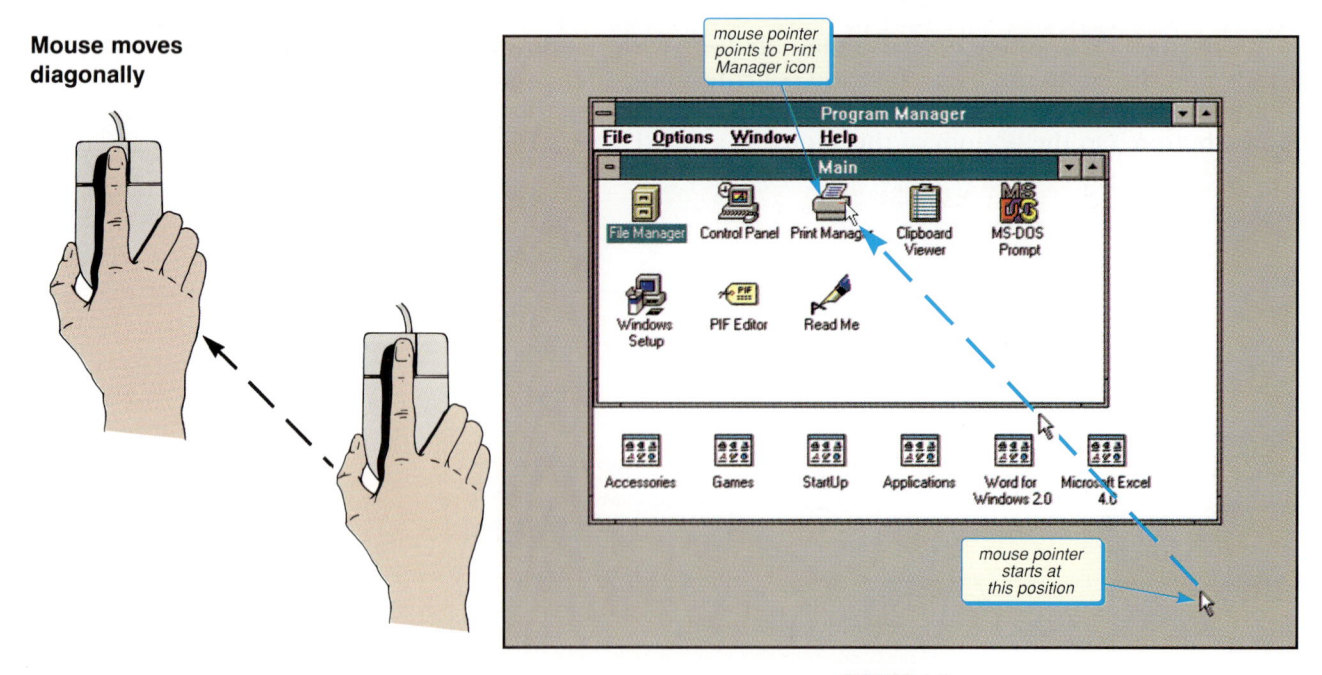

FIGURE 1-8

COMMUNICATING WITH MICROSOFT WINDOWS   **WIN7**

Clicking means pressing and releasing a mouse button. In most cases, you must point to an item before pressing and releasing a mouse button. In Figure 1-9, you highlight the Print Manager icon by pointing to the Print Manager icon (Step 1) and pressing and releasing the left mouse button (Step 2). These steps are commonly referred to as clicking the Print Manager icon. When you click the Print Manager icon, Windows highlights, or places color behind, the name below the Print Manager icon (Step 3).

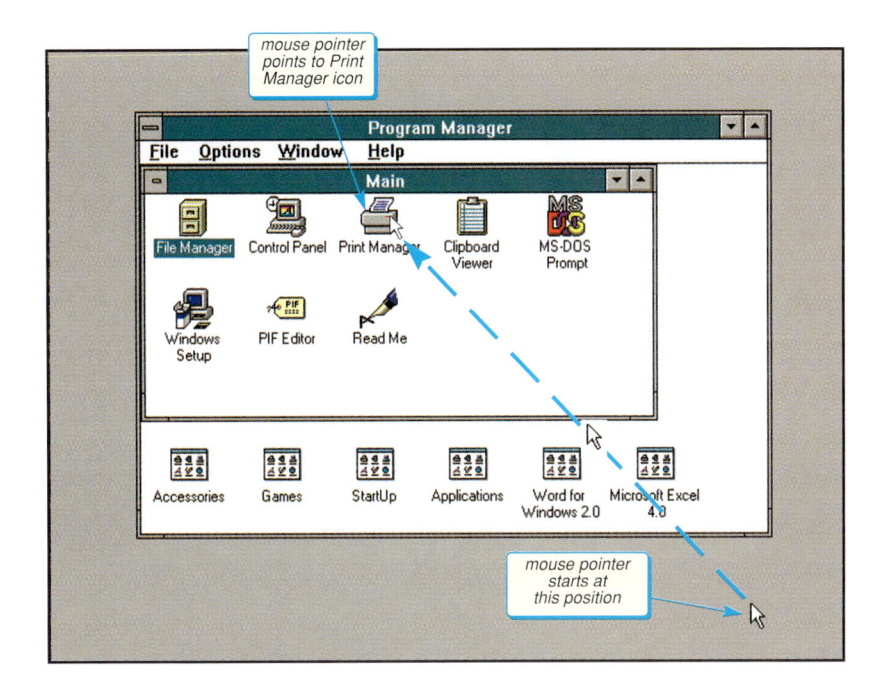

Step 1: Point to the Print Manager icon.

Step 2: Press and release the left mouse button.

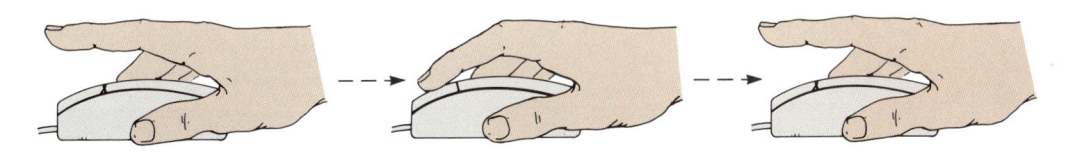

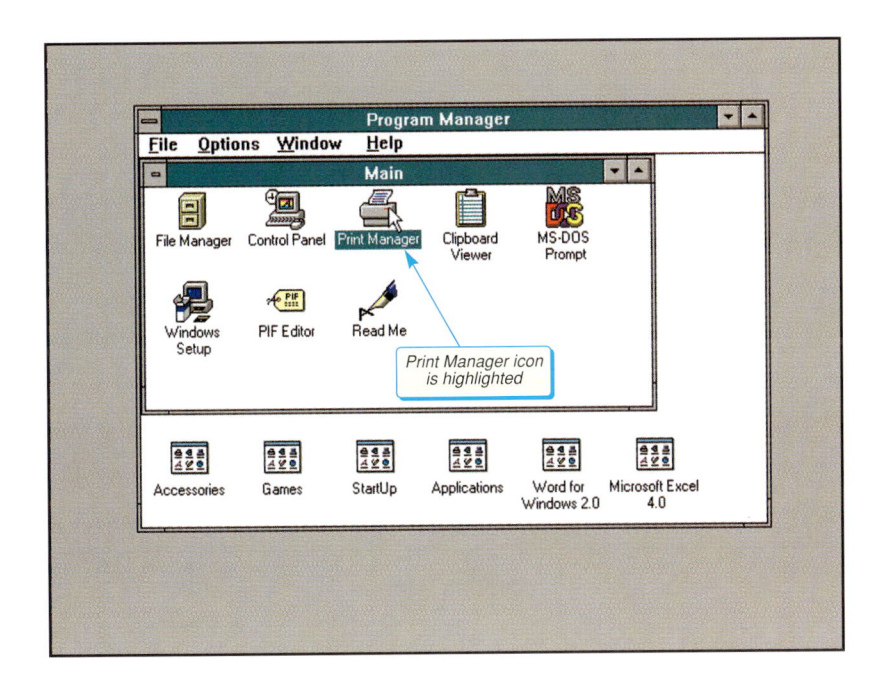

Step 3: Windows highlights the Print Manager name.

FIGURE 1-9

Double-clicking means quickly pressing and releasing a mouse button twice without moving the mouse. In most cases, you must point to an item before quickly pressing and releasing a mouse button twice. In Figure 1-10, to open the Accessories group window, point to the Accessories icon (Step 1), and quickly press and release the left mouse button twice (Step 2). These steps are commonly referred to as double-clicking the Accessories icon. When you double-click the Accessories icon, Windows opens a group window with the same name (Step 3).

Step 1: Point to the Accessories icon.

Step 2: Quickly press and release the left mouse button twice.

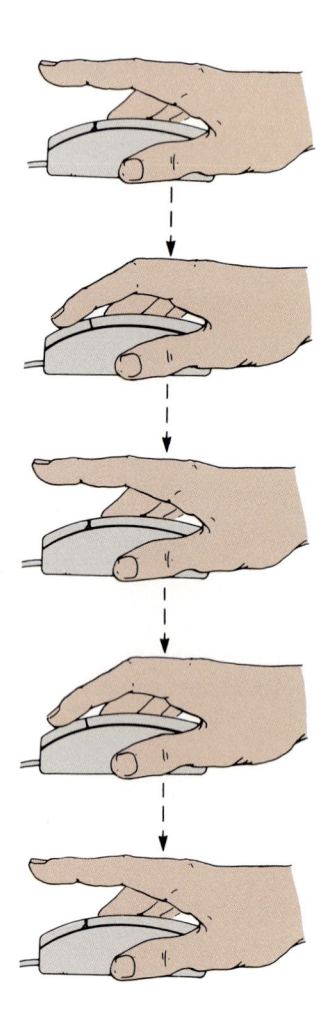

Step 3: Windows opens the Accessories group window.

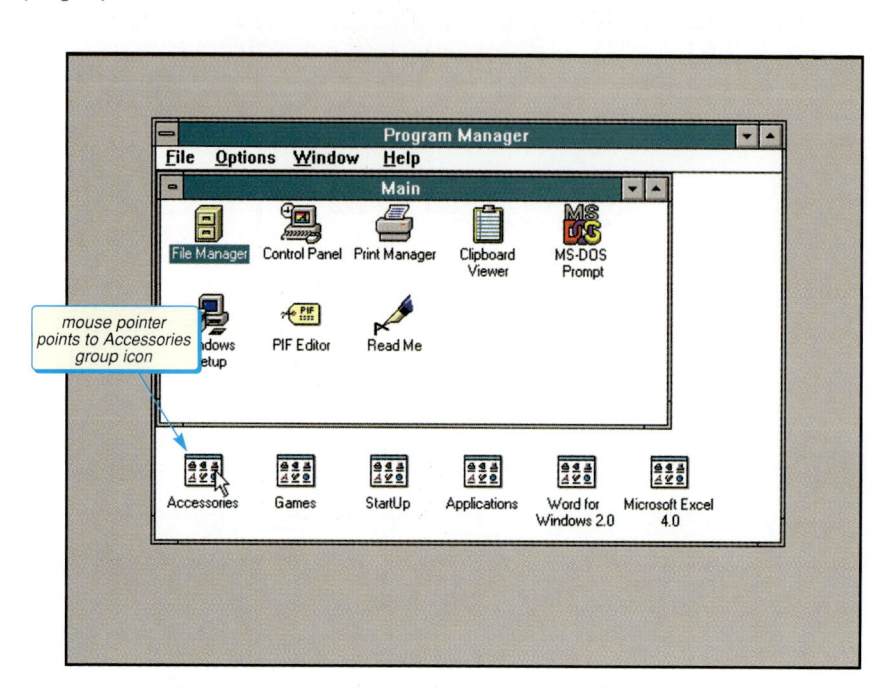

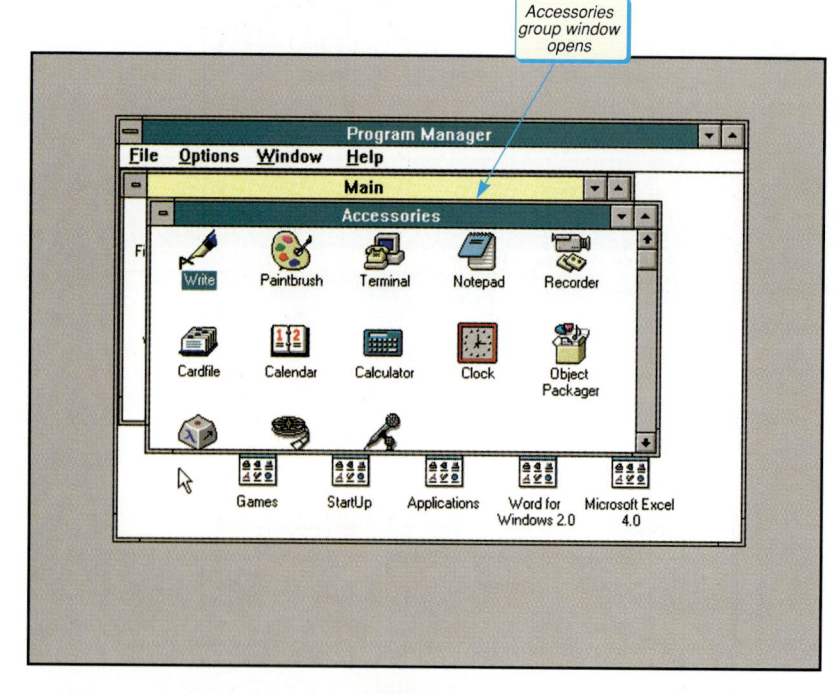

FIGURE 1-10

Dragging means holding down the left mouse button, moving an item to the desired location, and then releasing the left mouse button. In most cases, you must point to an item before doing this. In Figure 1-11, you move the Control Panel program-item icon by pointing to the Control Panel icon (Step 1), holding down the left mouse button while moving the icon to its new location (Step 2), and releasing the left mouse button (Step 3). These steps are commonly referred to as dragging the Control Panel icon.

In Figure 1-11, the location of the Control Panel program-item icon was moved to rearrange the icons in the Main group window. Dragging has many uses in Windows, as you will see in subsequent examples.

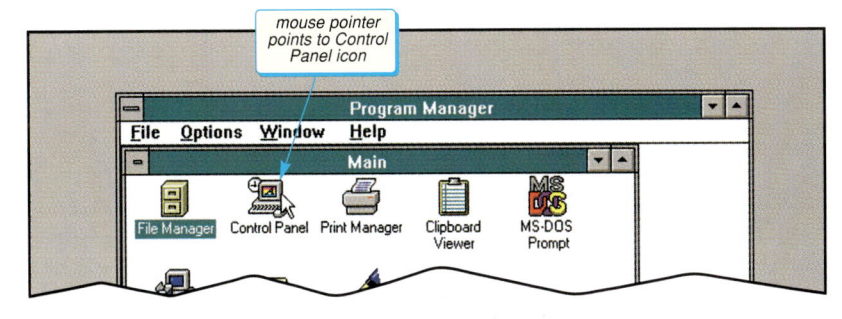

Step 1: Point to the Control Panel icon.

Step 2: Hold down the left mouse button and move the icon to its new location.

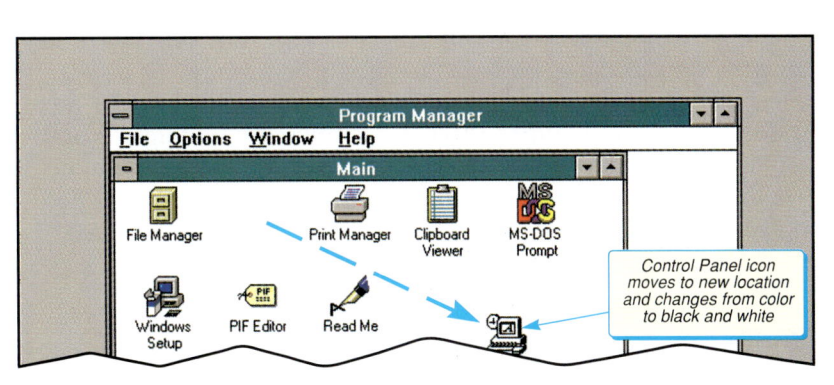

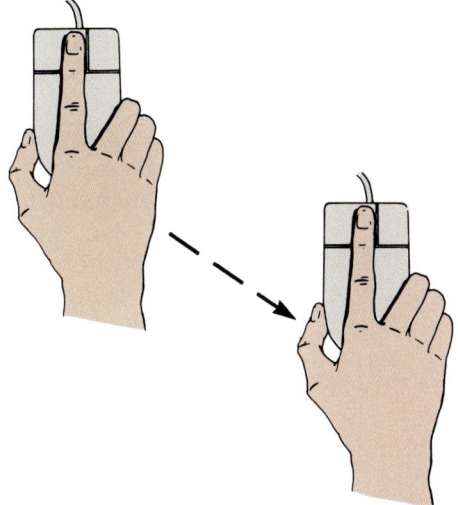

Step 3: Release the left mouse button.

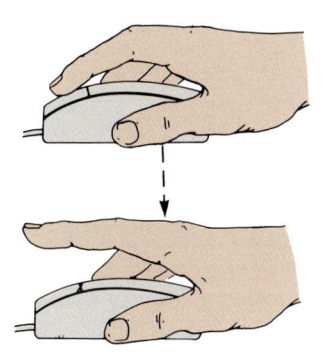

FIGURE 1-11

The Keyboard and Keyboard Shortcuts

The **keyboard** is an input device on which you manually key, or type, data. Figure 1-12 on the next page shows the enhanced IBM PS/2 keyboard. Any task you accomplish with a mouse you can also accomplish with the keyboard. Although the choice of whether you use the mouse or keyboard is a matter of personal preference, the mouse is strongly recommended.

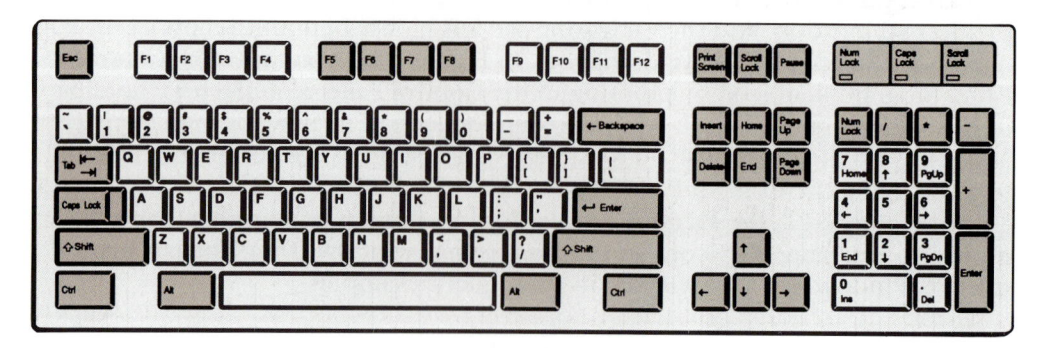

FIGURE 1-12

The Quick Reference at the end of each project provides a list of tasks presented and the manner in which to complete them using a mouse, menu, or keyboard.

To perform tasks using the keyboard, you must understand the notation used to identify which keys to press. This notation is used throughout Windows to identify **keyboard shortcuts** and in the Quick Reference at the end of each project. Keyboard shortcuts can consist of pressing a single key (RIGHT ARROW), pressing two keys simultaneously as shown by two key names separated by a plus sign (CTRL + F6), or pressing three keys simultaneously as shown by three key names separated by plus signs (CTRL + SHIFT + LEFT ARROW).

For example, to move the highlight from one program-item icon to the next you can press the RIGHT ARROW key (RIGHT ARROW). To move the highlight from the Main window to a group icon, hold down the CTRL key and press the F6 key (CTRL + F6). To move to the previous word in certain Windows applications, hold down the CTRL and SHIFT keys and press the LEFT ARROW key (CTRL + SHIFT + LEFT ARROW).

Menus and Commands

A **command** directs the software to perform a specific action, such as printing on the printer or saving data for use at a future time. One method in which you carry out a command is by choosing the command from a list of available commands, called a menu.

Windows organizes related groups of commands into **menus** and assigns a menu name to each menu. The **menu bar**, a horizontal bar below the title bar of an application window, contains a list of the menu names for that application. The menu bar for the Program Manager window in Figure 1-13 contains the following menu names: File, Options, Window, and Help. One letter in each name is underlined.

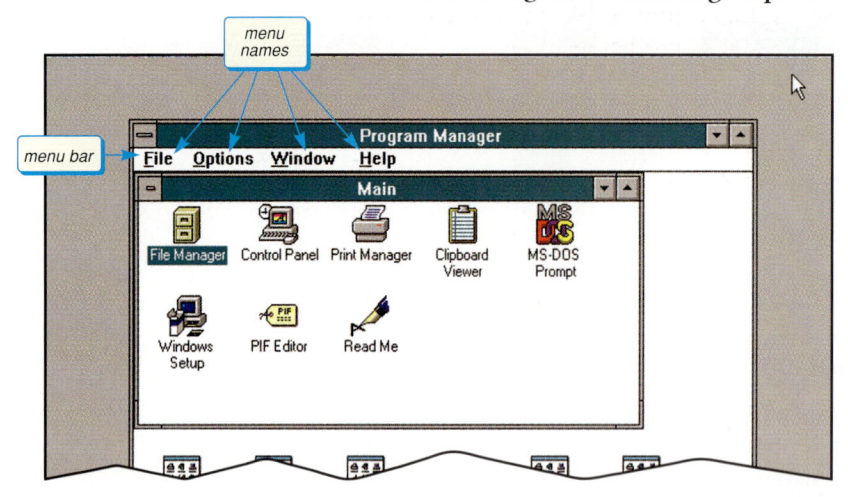

FIGURE 1-13

Selecting a Menu

To display a menu, you select the menu name. **Selecting** means marking an item. In some cases, when you select an item, Windows marks the item with a highlight by placing color behind the item. You select a menu name by pointing to the menu name in the menu bar and pressing the left mouse button (called clicking) or by using the keyboard to press the ALT key and then the keyboard key of the underlined letter in the menu name. Clicking the menu name File in the menu bar or pressing the ALT key and then the F key opens the File menu (Figure 1-14).

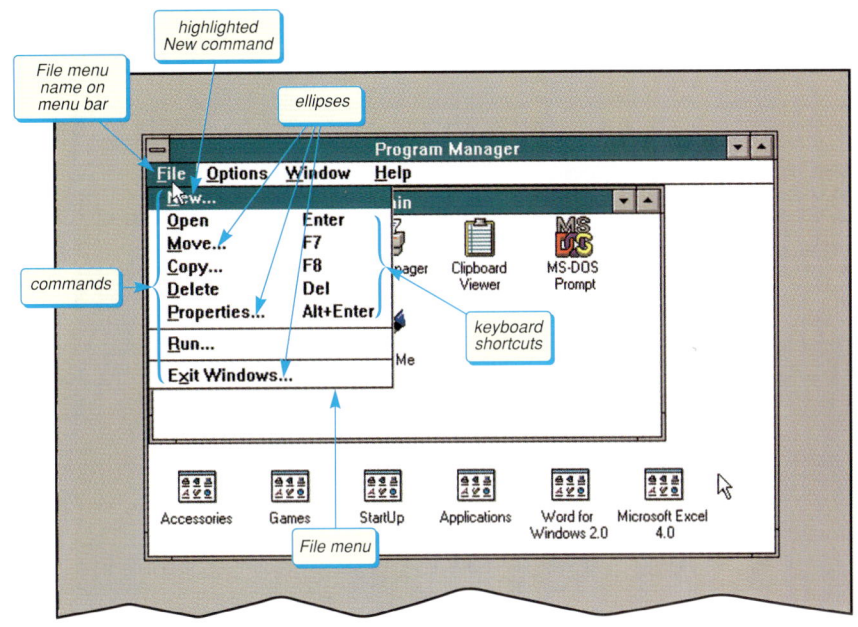

FIGURE 1-14

The File menu in Figure 1-14 contains the following commands: New, Open, Move, Copy, Delete, Properties, Run, and Exit Windows. The first command in the menu (New) is highlighted and a single character in each command is underlined. Some commands (New, Move, Copy, Properties, Run, and Exit Windows) are followed by an ellipsis (...). An **ellipsis** indicates Windows requires more information before executing the command. Commands without an ellipsis, such as the Open command, execute immediately.

Choosing a Command

You **choose** an item to carry out an action. You can choose using a mouse or keyboard. For example, to choose a command using a mouse, either click the command name in the menu or drag the highlight to the command name. To choose a command using the keyboard, either press the keyboard key of the underlined character in the command name or use the Arrow keys to move the highlight to the command name and press the ENTER key.

Some command names are followed by a keyboard shortcut. In Figure 1-14, the Open, Move, Copy, Delete, and Properties command names have keyboard shortcuts. The keyboard shortcut for the Properties command is ALT+ENTER. Holding down the ALT key and then pressing the ENTER key chooses the Properties command without selecting the File menu.

Dialog Boxes

When you choose a command whose command name is followed by an ellipsis (...), Windows opens a dialog box. A **dialog box** is a window that appears when Windows needs to supply information to you or wants you to enter information or select among options.

For example, Windows may inform you that a document is printing on the printer through the use of dialog box; or Windows may ask you whether you want to print all the pages in a printed report or just certain pages in the report.

A dialog box contains a title bar that identifies the name of the dialog box. In Figure 1-15, the name of the dialog box is Print.

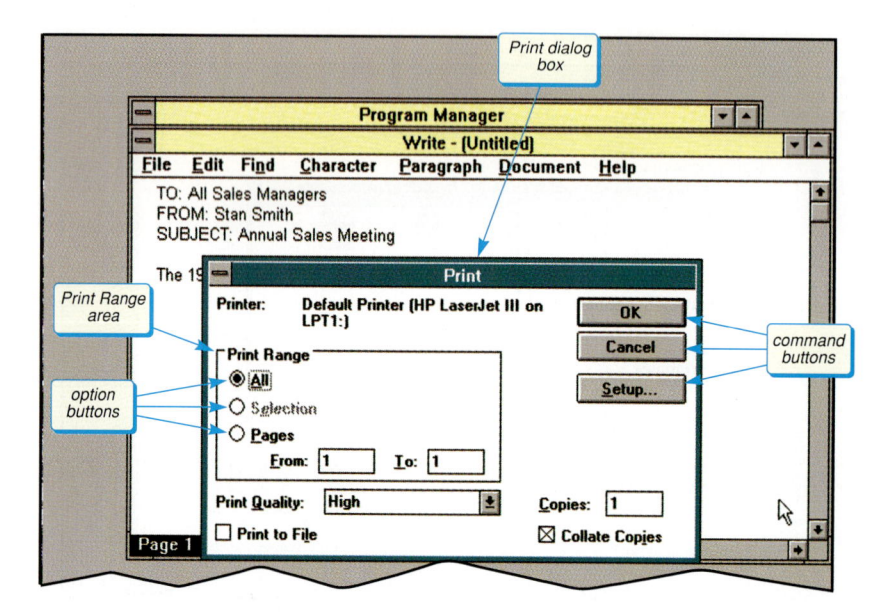

FIGURE 1-15

The types of responses Windows will ask for when working with dialog boxes fall into five categories: (1) Selecting mutually exclusive options; (2) Selecting one or more multiple options; (3) Entering specific information from the keyboard; (4) Selecting one item from a list of items; (5) Choosing a command to be implemented from the dialog box.

Each of these types of responses is discussed in the following paragraphs, together with the method for specifying them.

The Print dialog box in Figure 1-15 opens when you choose the Print command from the File menu of some windows. The Print Range area, defined by the name Print Range and a rectangular box, contains three option buttons.

The **option buttons** give you the choice of printing all pages of a report (All), selected parts of a report (Selection), or certain pages of a report (Pages). The option button containing the black dot (All) is the **selected button**. You can select only one option button at a time. A dimmed option, such as the Selection button, cannot be selected. To select an option button, use the mouse to click the option button or press the TAB key until the area containing the option button is selected and press the Arrow keys to highlight the option button.

The Print dialog box in Figure 1-15 on the previous page also contains the OK, Cancel, and Setup command buttons. **Command buttons** execute an action. The OK button executes the Print command, and the Cancel button cancels the Print command. The Setup button changes the setup of the printer by allowing you to select a printer from a list of printers, select the paper size, etc.

Figure 1-16 illustrates text boxes and check boxes. A **text box** is a rectangular area in which Windows displays text or you enter text. In the Print dialog box in Figure 1-16, the Pages option button is selected, which means only certain pages of a report are to print. You select which pages by entering the first page in the From text box (1) and the last page in the To text box (4). To enter text into a text box, select the text box by clicking it or by pressing the TAB key until the text in the text box is highlighted, and then type the text using the keyboard. The Copies text box in Figure 1-16 contains the number of copies to be printed (3).

Check boxes represent options you can turn on or off. An X in a check box indicates the option is turned on. To place an X in the box, click the box, or press the TAB key until the Print To File check box is highlighted, and then press SPACEBAR. In Figure 1-16, the Print to File check box, which does not contain an X, indicates the Print to File option is turned off and the pages will print on the printer. The Collate Copies check box, which contains an X, indicates the Collate Copies feature is turned on and the pages will print in collated order.

The Print dialog boxes in Figure 1-17 and Figure 1-18 on the next page, illustrate the Print Quality drop-down list box. When first selected, a **drop-down list box** is a rectangular box containing highlighted text and a down arrow box on the right. In Figure 1-17, the highlighted text, or **current selection**, is High.

FIGURE 1-16

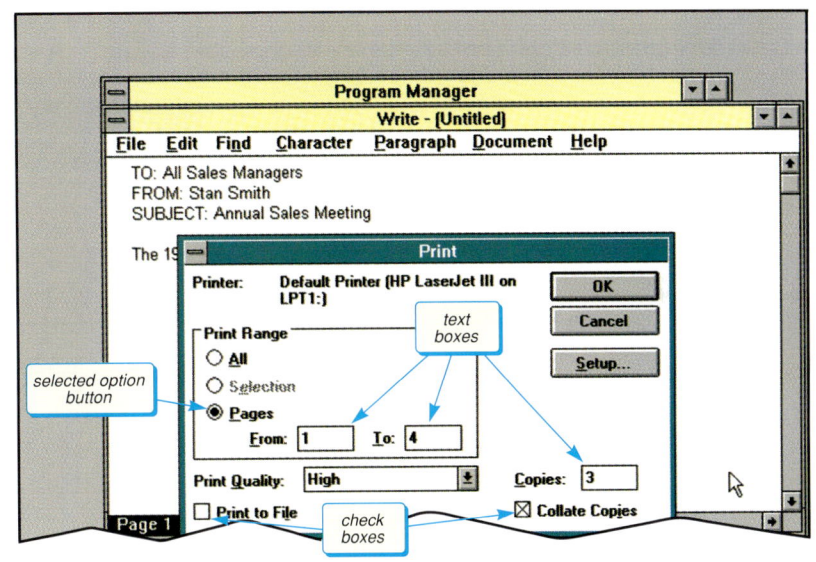

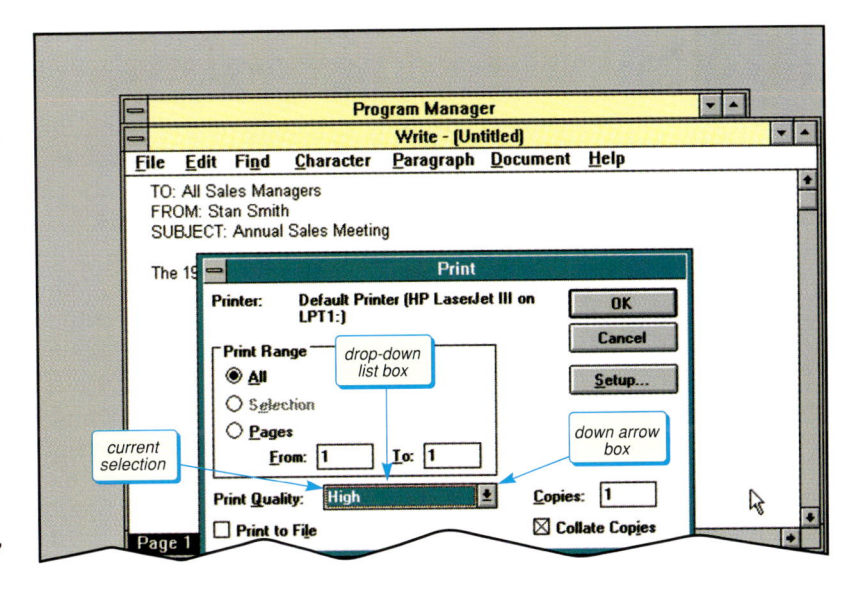

FIGURE 1-17

When you click the down arrow button, the drop-down list in Figure 1-18 appears. The list contains three choices (High, Medium, and Low). The current selection, High, is highlighted. To select from the list, use the mouse to click the selection or press the TAB key until the Print Quality drop-down list box is highlighted, press the DOWN ARROW key to highlight the selection, and then press ALT + UP ARROW or ALT + DOWN ARROW to make the selection.

Windows uses drop-down list boxes when a list of options must be presented but the dialog box is too crowded to contain the entire list. After you make your selection, the list disappears and only the current selection displays.

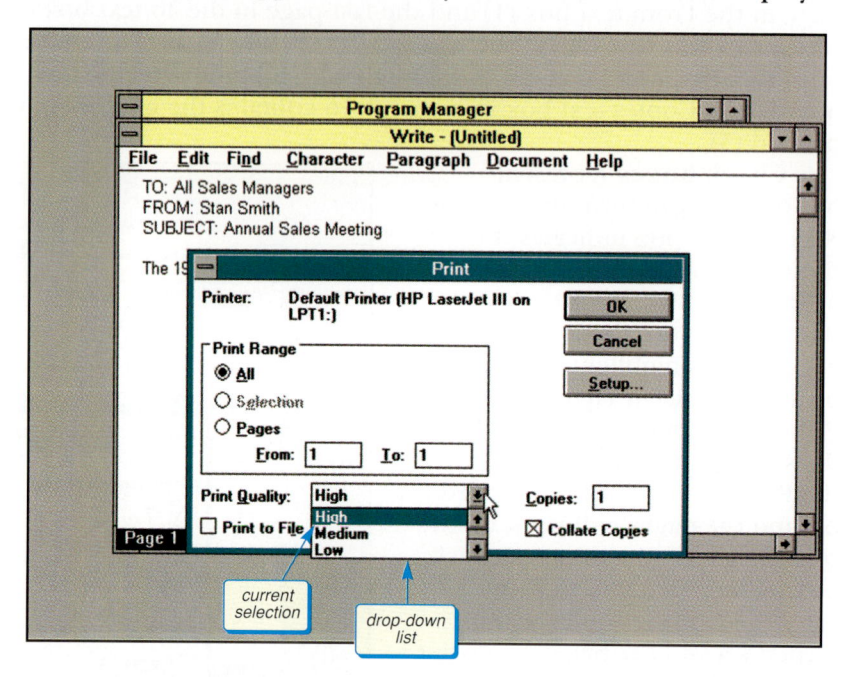

FIGURE 1-18

USING MICROSOFT WINDOWS

The remainder of this project illustrates how to use Windows to perform the operations of starting and quitting an application, creating a document, saving a document on disk, opening a document, editing a document, printing a document and using the Windows help facility. Understanding how to perform these operations will make completing the remainder of the projects in this book easier. These operations are illustrated by the use of the Notepad and Paintbrush applications.

One of the many applications included with Windows is the Notepad application. **Notepad** allows you to enter, edit, save, and print notes. Items that you create while using an application, such as a note, are called **documents**. In the following section, you will use the Notepad application to learn to (1) open a group window, (2) start an application from a group window, (3) maximize an application window, (4) create a document, (5) select a menu, (6) choose a command from a menu, (7) print a document, and (8) quit an application. In the process, you will enter and print a note.

Opening a Group Window

Each group icon at the bottom of the Program Manager window represents a group window that may contain program-item icons. To open the group window and view the program-item icons in that window use the mouse to point to the group icon and then double-click the left mouse button, as shown in the steps on the next page.

USING THE MICROSOFT WINDOWS INTERFACE   WIN15

TO OPEN A GROUP WINDOW

STEP 1 ▶

Point to the Accessories group icon at the bottom of the Program Manager window.

The mouse pointer points to the Accessories icon (Figure 1-19).

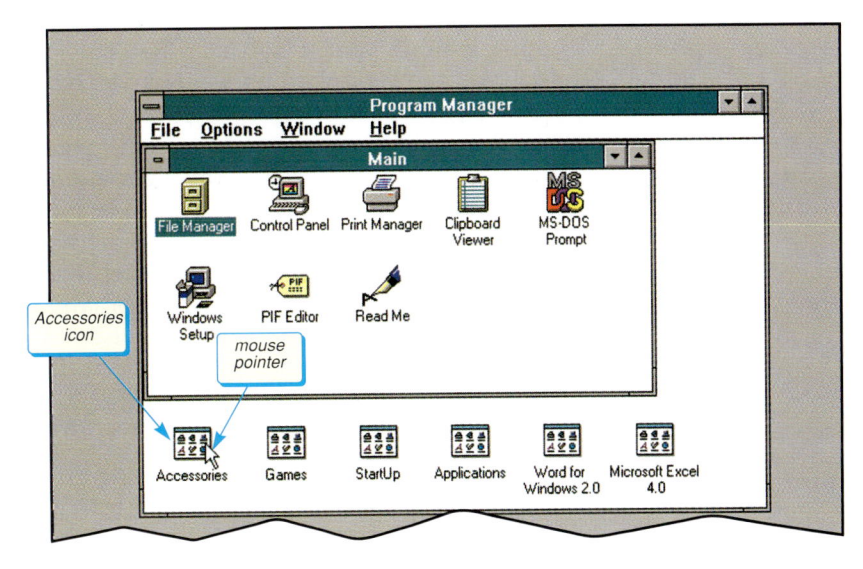

FIGURE 1-19

STEP 2 ▶

Double-click the left mouse button.

Windows removes the Accessories icon from the Program Manager window and opens the Accessories group window on top of the Program Manager and Main windows (Figure 1-20). The Accessories window contains the Notepad icon.

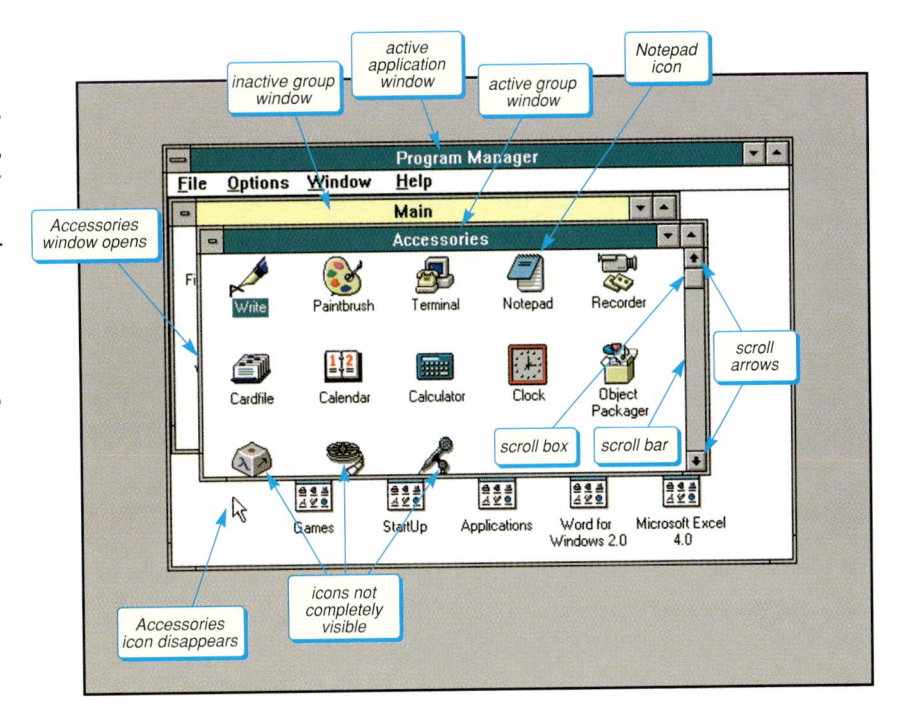

FIGURE 1-20

Opening a group window when one or more group windows are already open in the Program Manager window causes the new group window to display on top of the other group windows. The title bar of the newly opened group window is a different color or intensity than the title bars of the other group windows. This indicates the new group window is the active window. The **active window** is the window currently being used. Only one application window and one group window can be active at the same time. In Figure 1-20 on the previous page, the colors of the title bars indicate that Program Manager is the active application window (green title bar) and the Accessories group window is the active group window (green title bar). The color of the Main window title bar (yellow) indicates the Main window is inactive. The colors may not be the same on the computer you use.

A scroll bar appears on the right edge of the Accessories window. A **scroll bar** is a bar that appears at the right and/or bottom edge of a window whose contents are not completely visible. In Figure 1-20 on the previous page, the third row of program-item icons in the Accessories window is not completely visible. A scroll bar contains two **scroll arrows** and a **scroll box** which enable you to view areas of the window not currently visible. To view areas of the Accessories window not currently visible, you can click the down scroll arrow repeatedly, click the scroll bar between the down scroll arrow and the scroll box, or drag the scroll box toward the down scroll arrow until the area you want to view is visible in the window.

Correcting an Error While Double-Clicking a Group Icon

While double-clicking, it is easy to mistakenly click once instead of double-clicking. When you click a group icon such as the Accessories icon once, the **Control menu** for that icon opens (Figure 1-21). The Control menu contains the following seven commands: Restore, Move, Size, Minimize, Maximize, Close, and Next. You choose one of these commands to carry out an action associated with the Accessories icon. To remove the Control menu and open the Accessories window after clicking the Accessories icon once, you can choose the Restore command; or click any open area outside the menu to remove the Control menu and then double-click the Accessories icon; or simply double-click the Accessories icon as if you had not clicked the icon at all.

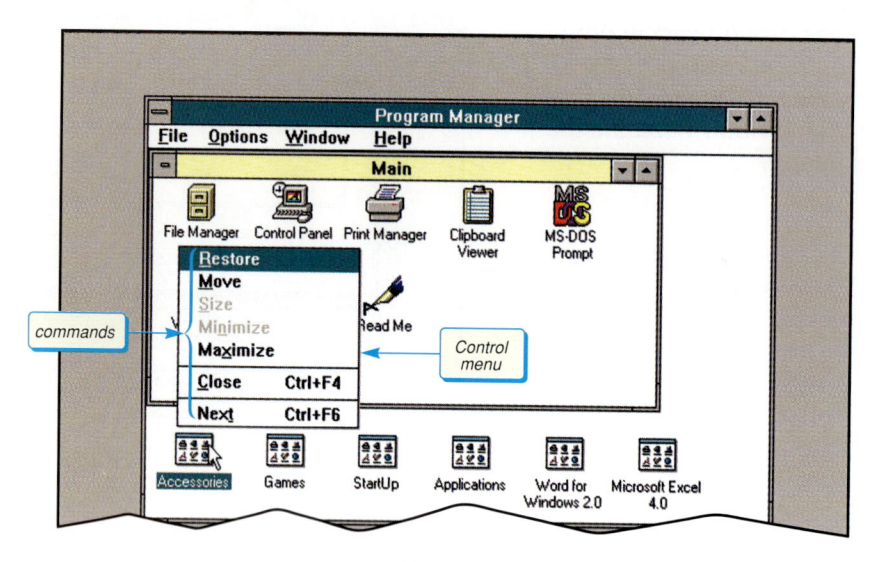

FIGURE 1-21

Starting an Application

Each program-item icon in a group window represents an application. To start an application, double-click the program-item icon. In this project, you want to start the Notepad application. To start the Notepad application, perform the steps on the next page.

USING THE MICROSOFT WINDOWS INTERFACE   WIN17

TO START AN APPLICATION

STEP 1 ▶

Point to the Notepad icon (Figure 1-22).

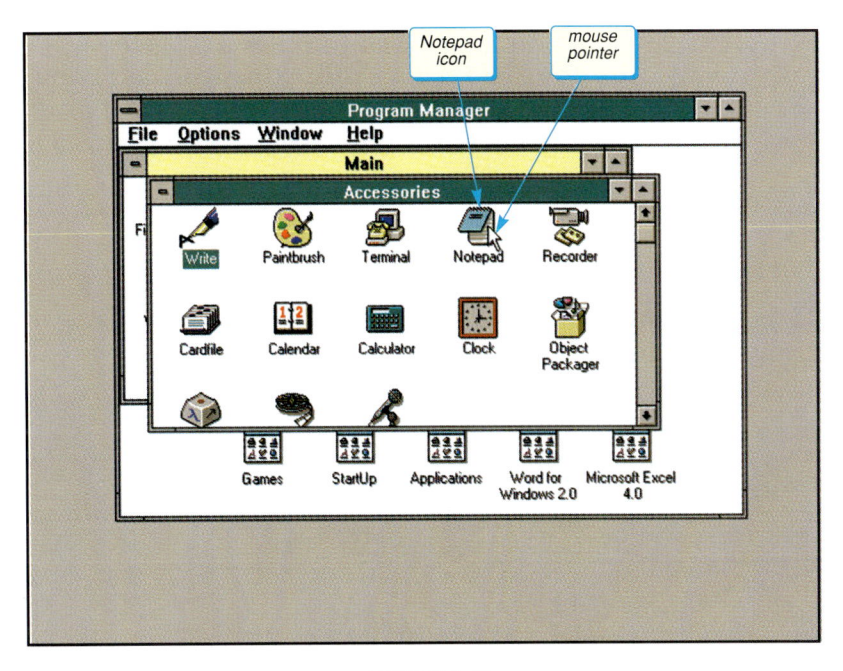

FIGURE 1-22

STEP 2 ▶

Double-click the left mouse button.

*Windows opens the Notepad window on the desktop (Figure 1-23). Program Manager becomes the inactive application (yellow title bar) and Notepad is the active application (green title bar). The word Untitled in the window title (Notepad — [Untitled]) indicates a document has not been created and saved on disk. The menu bar contains the following menus: File, Edit, Search, and Help. The area below the menu bar contains an insertion point, mouse pointer, and two scroll bars. The **insertion point** is a flashing vertical line that indicates the point at which text entered from the keyboard will be displayed. When you point to the interior of the Notepad window, the mouse pointer changes from a block arrow to an I-beam (I).*

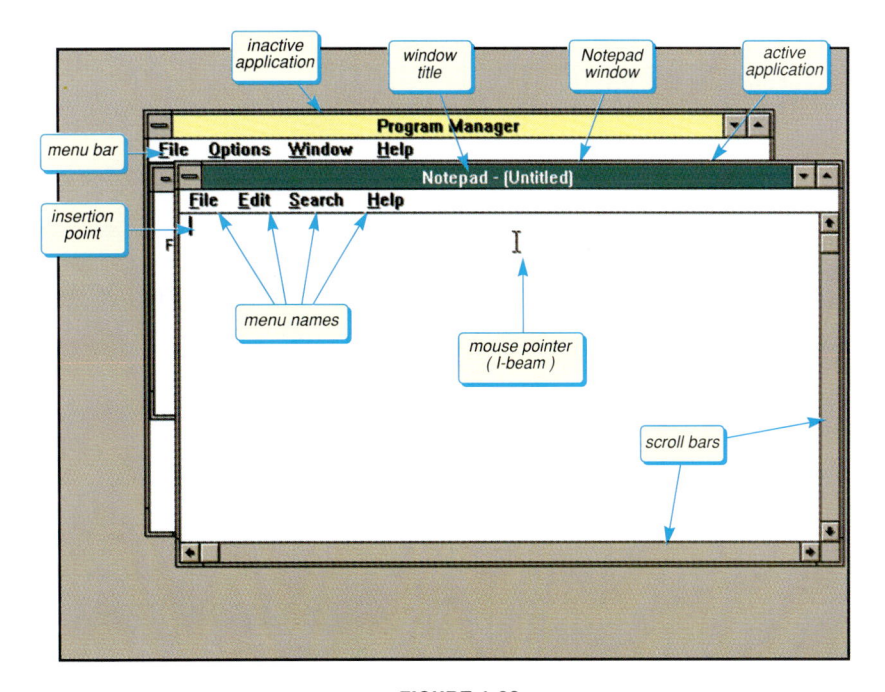

FIGURE 1-23

Correcting an Error While Double-Clicking a Program-Item Icon

While double-clicking a program-item icon you can easily click once instead. When you click a program-item icon such as the Notepad icon once, the icon becomes the **active icon** and Windows highlights the icon name (Figure 1-24). To start the Notepad application after clicking the Notepad icon once, double-click the Notepad icon as if you had not clicked the icon at all.

Maximizing an Application Window

Before you work with an application, maximizing the application window makes it easier to see the contents of the window. You can maximize an application window so the window fills the entire desktop. To maximize an application window to its maximum size, choose the **Maximize button** (▲) by pointing to the Maximize button and clicking the left mouse button. Complete the following steps to maximize the Notepad window.

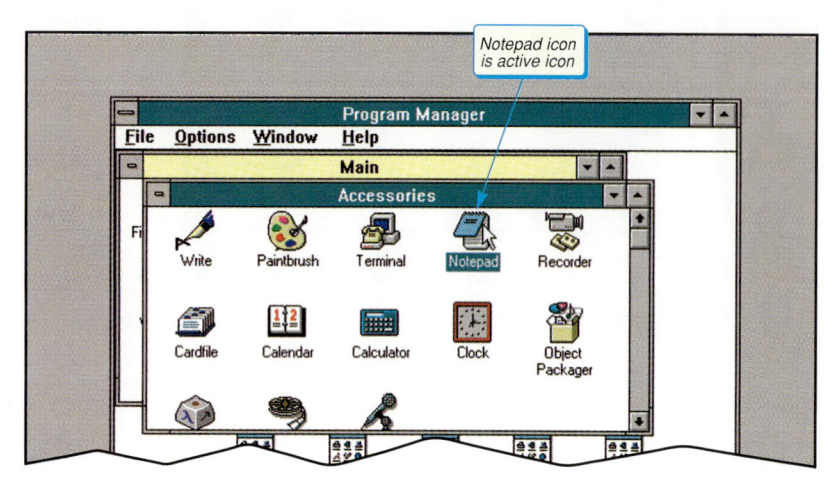

FIGURE 1-24

TO MAXIMIZE AN APPLICATION WINDOW

STEP 1 ▶

Point to the Maximize button in the upper right corner of the Notepad window.

The mouse pointer becomes a block arrow and points to the Maximize button (Figure 1-25).

FIGURE 1-25

STEP 2 ▶

Click the left mouse button.

*The Notepad window fills the desktop (Figure 1-26). The **Restore button** (◆) replaces the Maximize button at the right side of the title bar. Clicking the Restore button will return the window to its size before maximizing.*

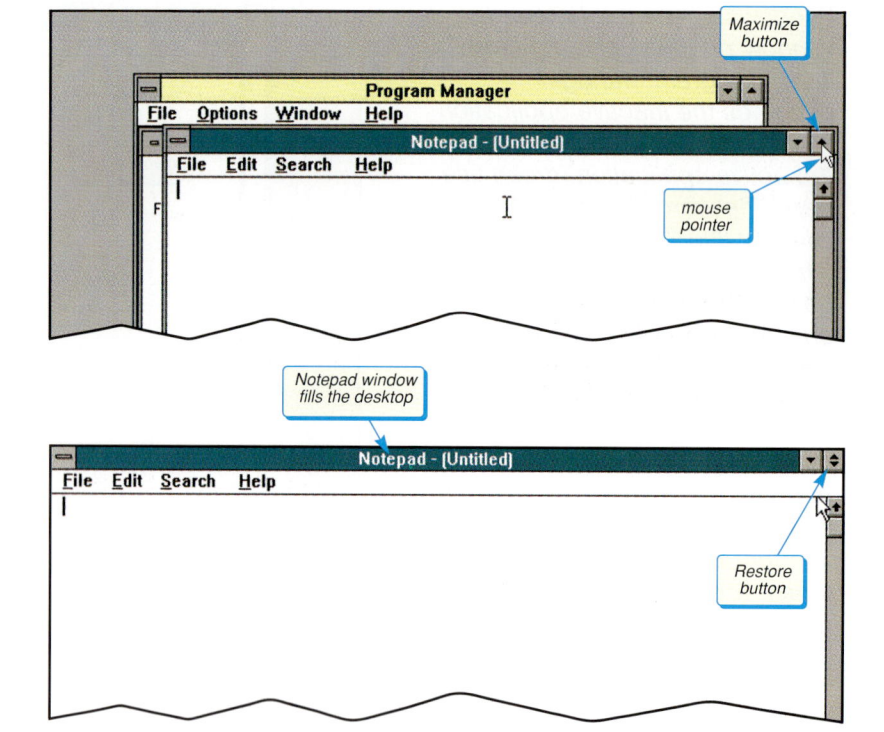

FIGURE 1-26

Creating a Document

To create a document in Notepad, type the text you want to display in the document. After typing a line of text, press the ENTER key to terminate the entry of the line. To create a document, enter the note to the right by performing the steps below.

> Things to do today —
> 1) Take fax\phone to Conway Service Center
> 2) Pick up payroll checks from ADM
> 3) Order 3 boxes of copier paper

TO CREATE A NOTEPAD DOCUMENT ▼

STEP 1 ▶

Type Things to do today - **and press the ENTER key.**

The first line of the note is entered and the insertion point appears at the beginning of the next line (Figure 1-27).

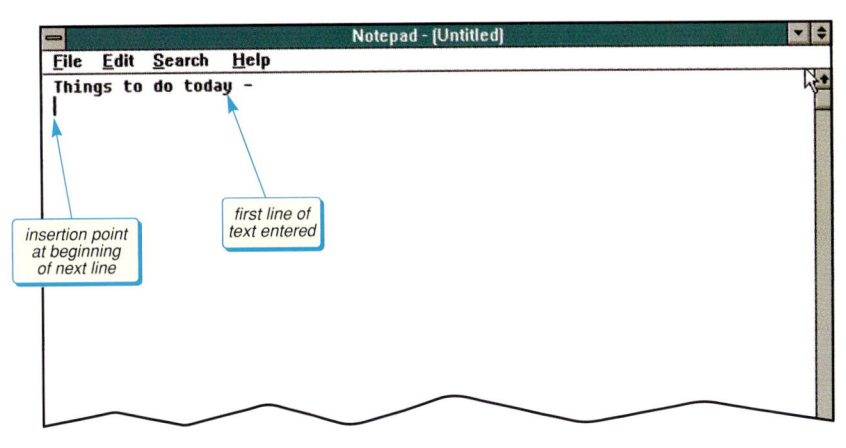

FIGURE 1-27

STEP 2 ▶

Type the remaining lines of the note. Press the ENTER key after typing each line.

The remaining lines in the note are entered and the insertion point is located at the beginning of the line following the note (Figure 1-28).

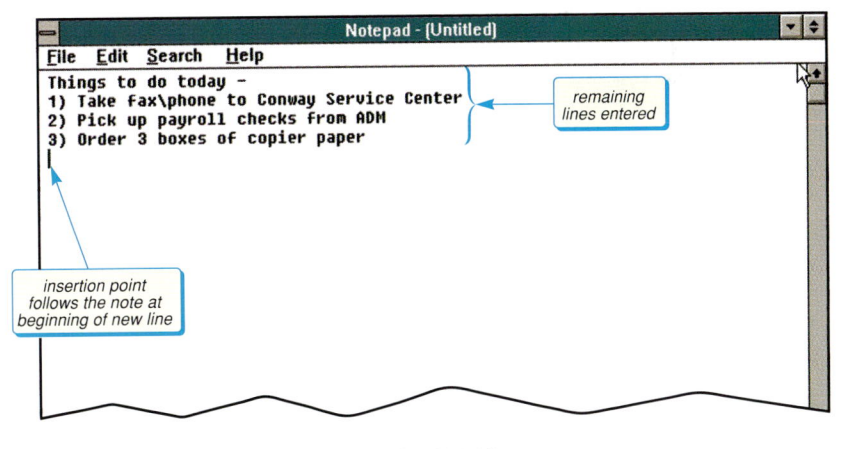

FIGURE 1-28

Printing a Document by Choosing a Command from a Menu

After creating a document, you often print the document on the printer. To print the note, complete the following steps.

TO PRINT A DOCUMENT

STEP 1 ▶

Point to File on the Notepad menu bar (Figure 1-29).

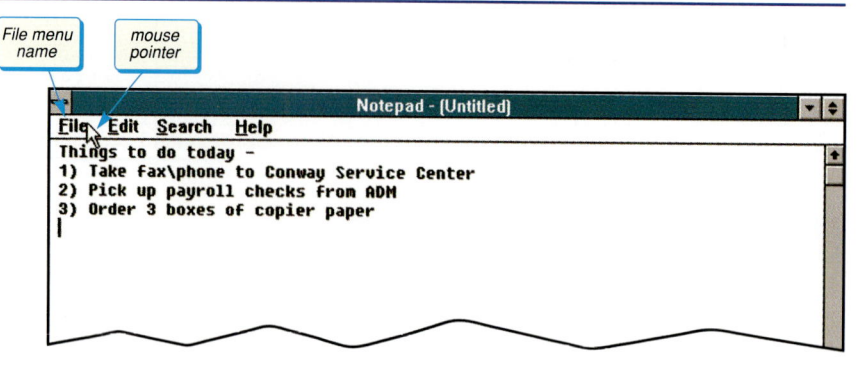

FIGURE 1-29

STEP 2 ▶

Select File by clicking the left mouse button.

Windows opens the File menu in the Notepad window (Figure 1-30). The File menu name is highlighted and the File menu contains the following commands: New, Open, Save, Save As, Print, Page Setup, Print Setup, and Exit. Windows highlights the first command in the menu (New). Notice the commands in the Notepad File menu are different than those in the Program Manager File menu (see Figure 1-14 on page WIN11). The commands in the File menu will vary depending on the application you are using.

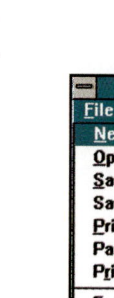

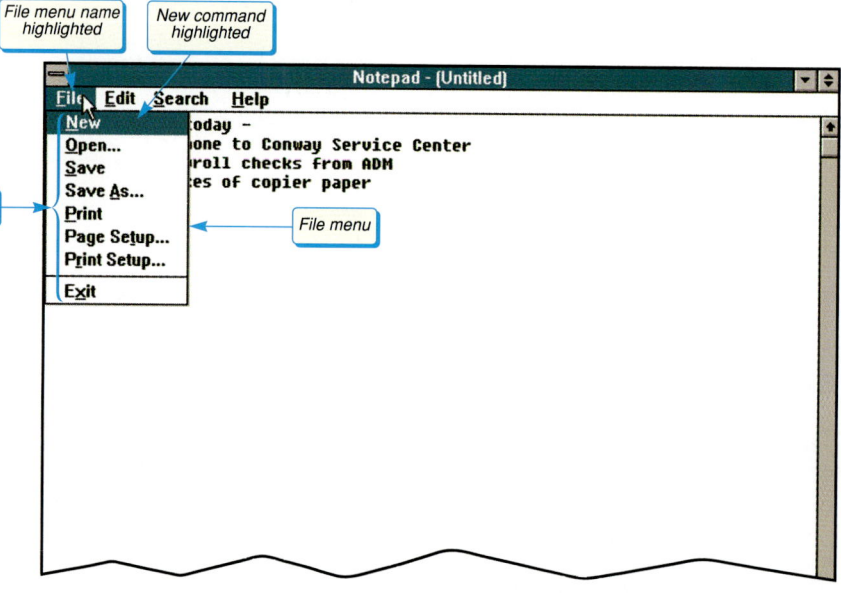

FIGURE 1-30

STEP 3 ▶

Point to the Print command.

The mouse pointer points to the Print command (Figure 1-31).

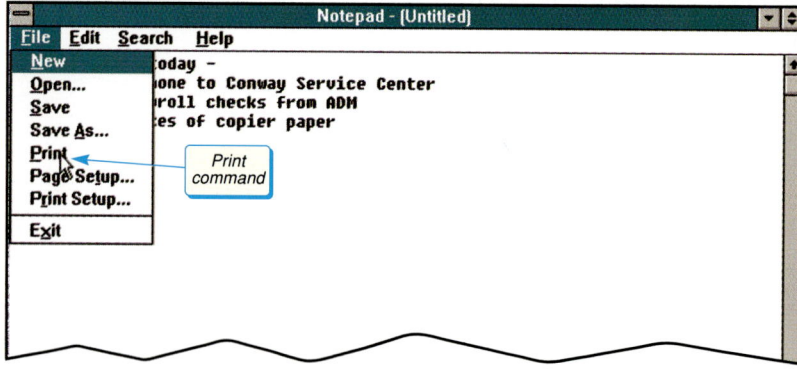

FIGURE 1-31

USING THE MICROSOFT WINDOWS INTERFACE **WIN21**

STEP 4 ▶

Choose the Print command from the File menu by clicking the left mouse button.

Windows momentarily opens the Notepad dialog box (Figure 1-32). The dialog box contains the Now Printing text message and the Cancel command button (Cancel). When the Notepad dialog box closes, Windows prints the document on the printer (Figure 1-33).

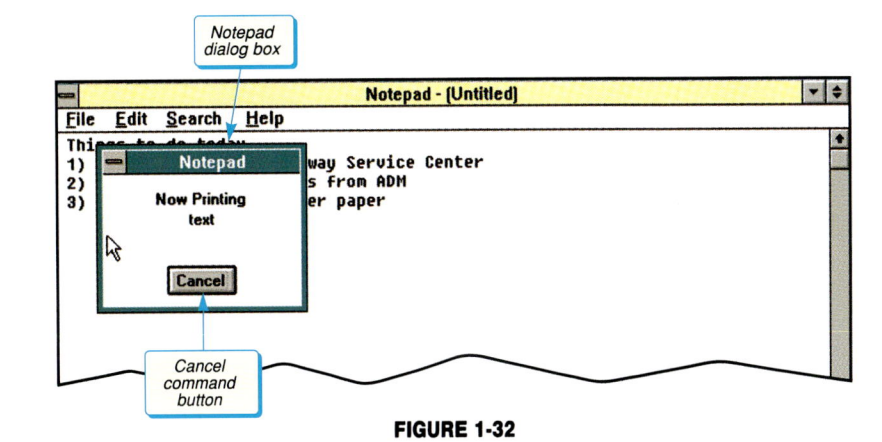

FIGURE 1-32

FIGURE 1-33

Quitting an Application

When you have finished creating and printing the document, quit the application by following the steps below and on the next page.

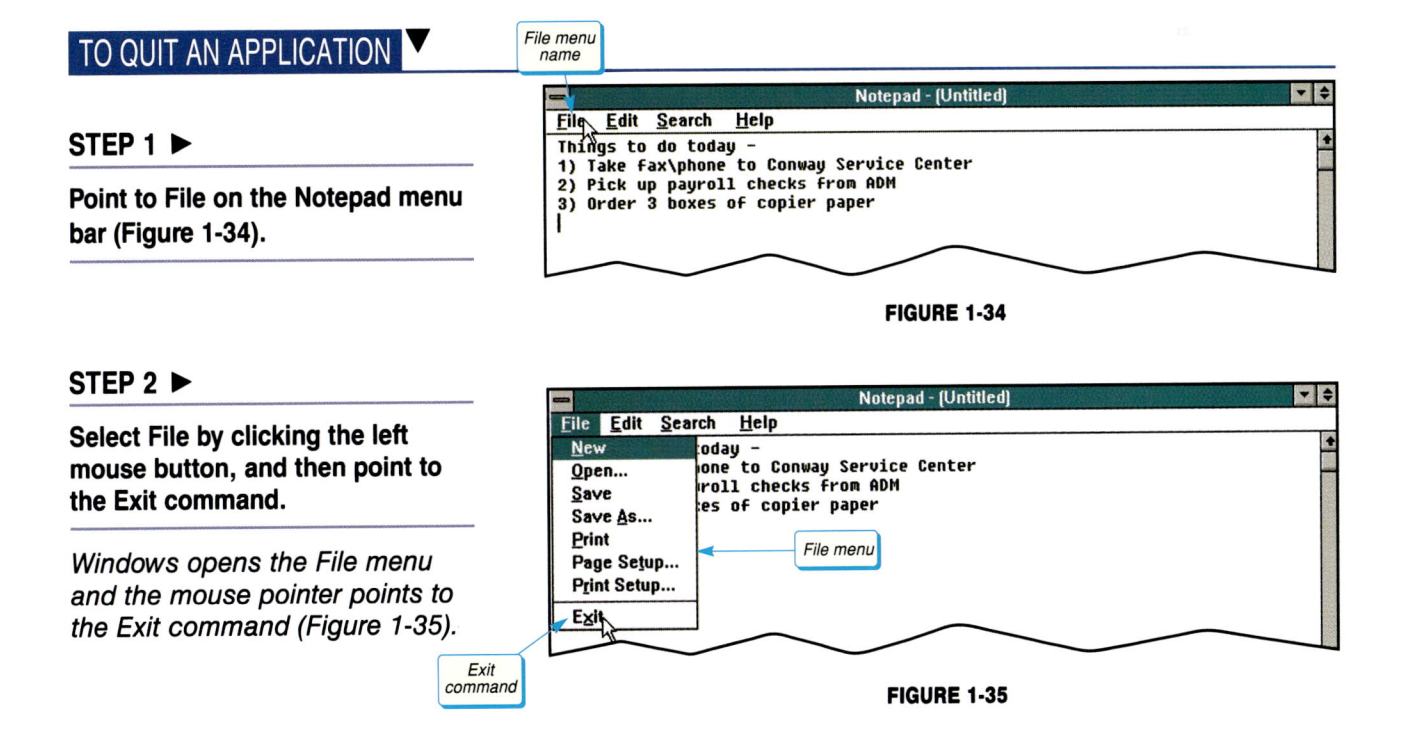

TO QUIT AN APPLICATION ▼

STEP 1 ▶

Point to File on the Notepad menu bar (Figure 1-34).

FIGURE 1-34

STEP 2 ▶

Select File by clicking the left mouse button, and then point to the Exit command.

Windows opens the File menu and the mouse pointer points to the Exit command (Figure 1-35).

FIGURE 1-35

STEP 3 ▶

Choose the Exit command from the File menu by clicking the left mouse button, and then point to the No button.

Windows opens the Notepad dialog box (Figure 1-36). The dialog box contains the following: The message, The text in the [Untitled] file has changed., the question, Do you want to save the changes?, and the Yes, No, and Cancel command buttons. The mouse pointer points to the No button (Yes). You choose the Yes button (No) to save the document on disk and exit Notepad. You choose the No button if you do not want to save the document and want to exit Notepad. You choose the Cancel button to cancel the Exit command.

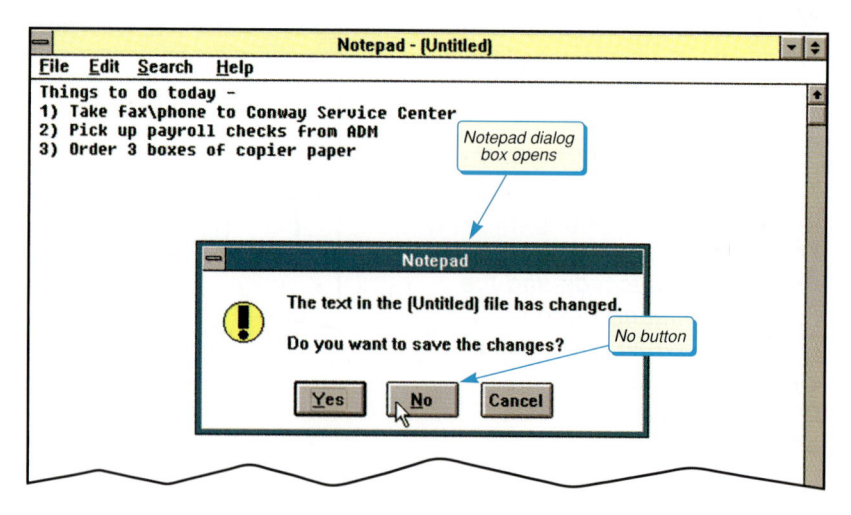

FIGURE 1-36

STEP 4 ▶

Choose the No button by clicking the left mouse button.

Windows closes the Notepad dialog box and Notepad window and exits the Notepad application (Figure 1-37).

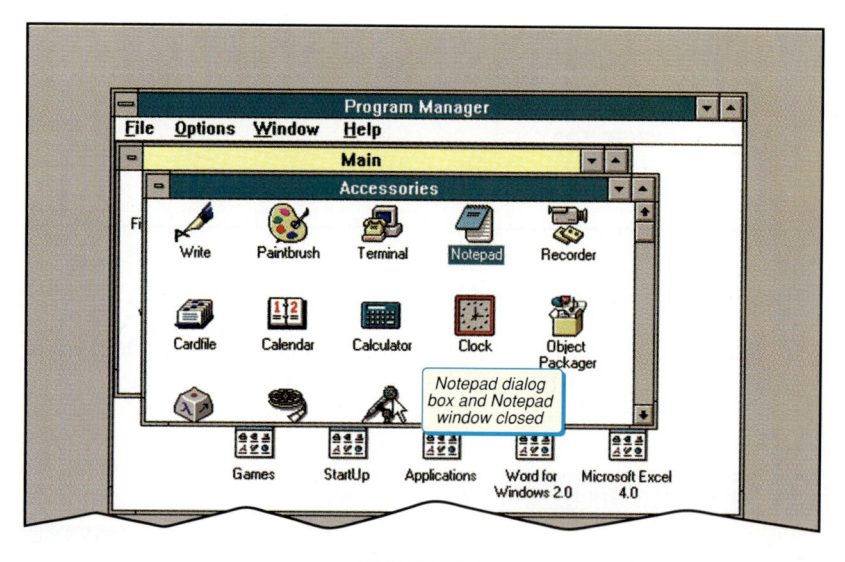

FIGURE 1-37

In the preceding example, you used the Microsoft Windows graphical user interface to accomplish the tasks of opening the Accessories group window, starting the Notepad application from the Accessories group window, maximizing the Notepad application window, creating a document in the Notepad application window, printing the document on the printer, and quitting the Notepad application.

▶ FILE AND DISK CONCEPTS

To protect against the accidental loss of a document and to save a document for use in the future, you should save a document on disk. Before saving a document on disk, however, you must understand the concepts of naming a file, directories, subdirectories, directory structures, and directory paths. The following section explains these concepts.

Naming a File

When you create a document using an application, the document is stored in main memory. If you quit the application without saving the document on disk, the document is lost. To save the document for future use, you must store the document in a **document file** on the hard disk or on a diskette before quitting the application. Before saving a document, you must assign a name to the document file.

All files are identified on disk by a **filename** and an **extension**. For example, the name SALES.TXT consists of a filename (SALES) and an extension (.TXT). A filename can contain from one to eight characters and the extension begins with a period and can contain from one to three characters. Filenames must start with a letter or number. Any uppercase or lowercase character is valid except a period (.), quotation mark (''), slash (/), backslash (\), brackets ([]), colon (:), semicolon (;), vertical bar (|), equal sign (=), comma (,), or blank space. Filenames cannot be CON, AUX, COM1, COM2, COM3, COM4, LPT1, LPT2, LPT3, PRN, and NUL.

To more easily identify document files on disk, it is convenient to assign the same extension to document files you create with a given application. The Notepad application, for instance, automatically uses the .TXT extension for each document file saved on disk. Typical filenames and extensions of document files saved using Notepad are: SHOPPING.TXT, MECHANIC.TXT, and 1994.TXT.

You can use the asterisk character (*) in place of a filename or extension to refer to a group of files. For example, the asterisk in the expression *.TXT tells Windows to reference any file that contains the .TXT extension, regardless of the filename. This group of files might consist of the HOME.TXT, AUTOPART.TXT, MARKET.TXT, JONES.TXT, and FRANK.TXT files.

The asterisk in MONTHLY.* tells Windows to reference any file that contains the filename MONTHLY, regardless of the extension. Files in this group might consist of the MONTHLY.TXT, MONTHLY.CAL, and MONTHLY.CRD files.

Directory Structures and Directory Paths

After selecting a name and extension for a file, you must decide which auxiliary storage device (hard disk or diskette) to use and in which directory you want to save the file. A **directory** is an area of a disk created to store related groups of files. When you first prepare a disk for use on a computer, a single directory, called the **root directory**, is created on the disk. You can create **subdirectories** in the root directory to store additional groups of related files. The hard disk in Figure 1-38 contains the root directory and the WINDOWS, MSAPPS, and SYSTEM subdirectories. The WINDOWS, MSAPPS, and SYSTEM subdirectories are created when Windows is installed and contain files related to Windows.

HARD DISK

FIGURE 1-38

Directory Structure	Directory Path
📂 c:\	C:\
📂 windows	C:\WINDOWS
📁 msapps	C:\WINDOWS\MSAPPS
📁 system	C:\WINDOWS\SYSTEM

▶ **TABLE 1-1**

The relationship between the root directory and any subdirectories is called the **directory structure**. Each directory or subdirectory in the directory structure has an associated directory path. The **directory path** is the path Windows follows to find a file in a directory. Table 1-1 contains a graphic representation of the directory structure and the associated paths of drive C.

Each directory and subdirectory on drive C is represented by a file folder icon in the directory structure. The first file folder icon, an unshaded open file folder (📂), represents the root directory of the current drive (drive C). The c:\ entry to the right of the icon symbolizes the root directory (identified by the \ character) of drive C (c:). The path is C:\. Thus, to find a file in this directory, Windows locates drive C (C:) and the root directory (\) on drive C.

The second icon, a shaded open file folder (📂), represents the current subdirectory. This icon is indented below the first file folder icon because it is a subdirectory. The name of the subdirectory (windows) appears to the right of the shaded file folder icon. Because the WINDOWS subdirectory was created in the root directory, the path for the WINDOWS subdirectory is C:\WINDOWS. To find a file in this subdirectory, Windows locates drive C, locates the root directory on drive C, and then locates the WINDOWS subdirectory in the root directory.

Because the current path is C:\WINDOWS, the file folder icons for both the root directory and WINDOWS subdirectory are open file folders. An open file folder indicates the directory or subdirectory is in the current path. Unopened file folders represent subdirectories not in the current path.

The third and fourth icons in Table 1-1, unopened file folders (📁), represent the MSAPPS and SYSTEM subdirectories. The unopened file folders indicate these subdirectories are not part of the current path. These file folder icons are indented below the file folder for the WINDOWS subdirectory which means they were created in the WINDOWS subdirectory. The subdirectory names (msapps and system) appear to the right of the file folder icons.

Since the MSAPPS and SYSTEM subdirectories were created in the WINDOWS subdirectory, the paths for these subdirectories are C:\WINDOWS\MSAPPS and C:\WINDOWS\SYSTEM. The second backslash (\) in these paths separates the two subdirectory names. To find a file in these subdirectories, Windows locates drive C, locates the root directory on drive C, then locates the WINDOWS subdirectory in the root directory, and finally locates the MSAPPS or SYSTEM subdirectory in the WINDOWS subdirectory.

Saving a Document on Disk

After entering data into a document, you will often save it on the hard disk or a diskette to protect against accidental loss and to make the document available for use later. In the previous example using the Notepad application, the note was not saved prior to exiting Notepad. Instead of exiting, assume you want to save the document you created. The screen before you begin to save the document is shown in Figure 1-39. To save the document on a diskette in drive A using the filename, agenda, perform the steps that begin at the top of the next page.

FIGURE 1-39

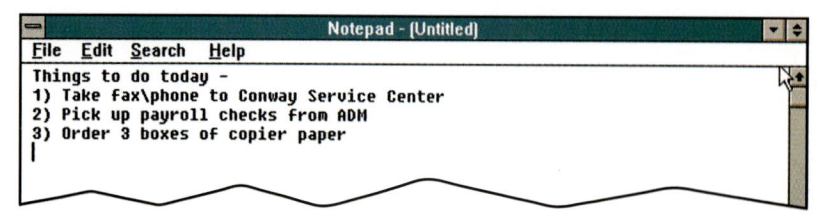

```
Notepad - [Untitled]
File  Edit  Search  Help
Things to do today -
1) Take fax\phone to Conway Service Center
2) Pick up payroll checks from ADM
3) Order 3 boxes of copier paper
```

TO SAVE A FILE ▼

STEP 1 ▶

Insert a formatted diskette into drive A (Figure 1-40).

The diskette must be properly formatted before being used to save data. To learn the technique for formatting a diskette see Project 2.

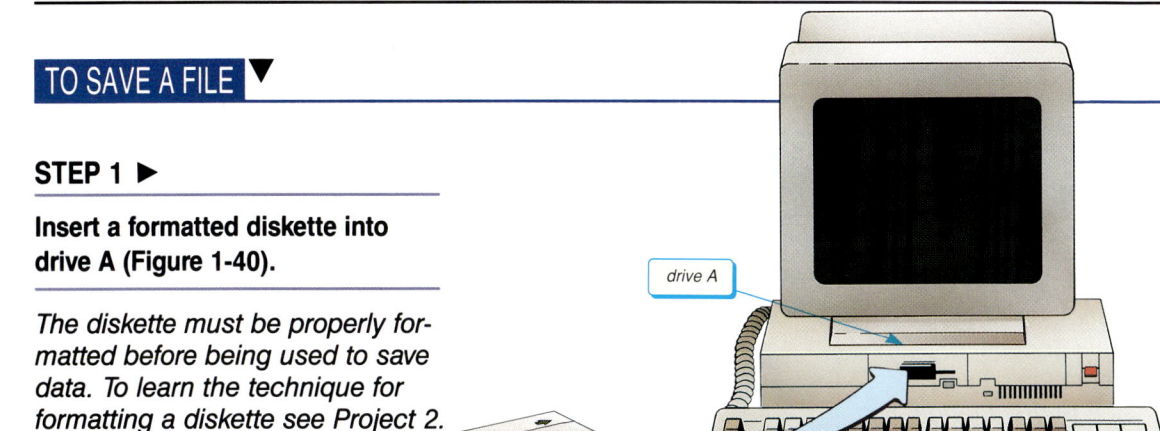

FIGURE 1-40

STEP 2 ▶

Select File on the Notepad menu bar, and then point to the Save As command.

Windows opens the File menu in the Notepad window and the mouse pointer points to the Save As command (Figure 1-41). The ellipsis (...) following the Save As command indicates Windows will open a dialog box when you choose this command.

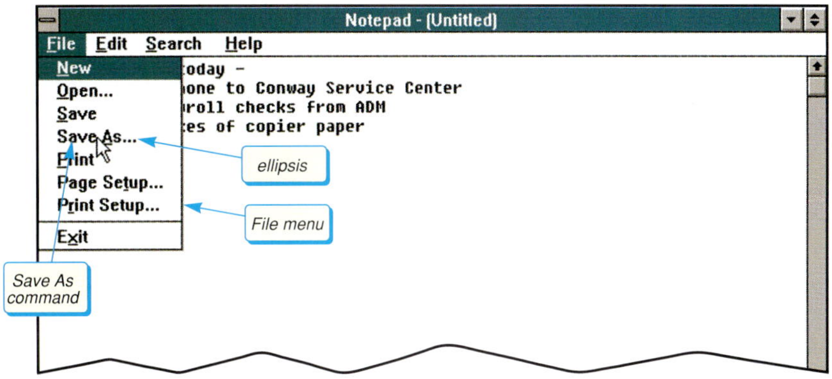

FIGURE 1-41

STEP 3 ▶

Choose the Save As command from the File menu by clicking the left mouse button.

The Save As dialog box opens (Figure 1-42). The File Name text box contains the highlighted *.txt entry. Typing a filename from the keyboard will replace the entire *.txt entry with the filename entered from the keyboard. The current path is c:\windows and the Directories list box contains the directory structure of the current subdirectory (windows). The drive selection in the Drives drop-down list box is c:. The dialog box contains the OK (OK) and Cancel (Cancel) command buttons.

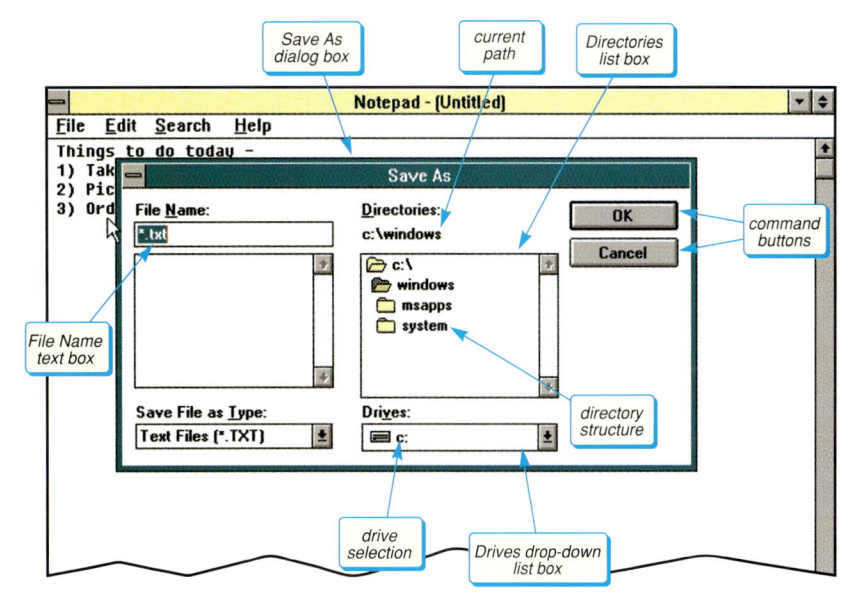

FIGURE 1-42

STEP 4 ▶

Type agenda **in the File Name text box, and then point to the Drives drop-down list box arrow.**

The filename, agenda, and an insertion point display in the File Name text box (Figure 1-43). When you save this document, Notepad will automatically add the .TXT extension to the agenda filename and save the file on disk using the name AGENDA.TXT. The mouse pointer points to the Drives drop-down list box arrow.

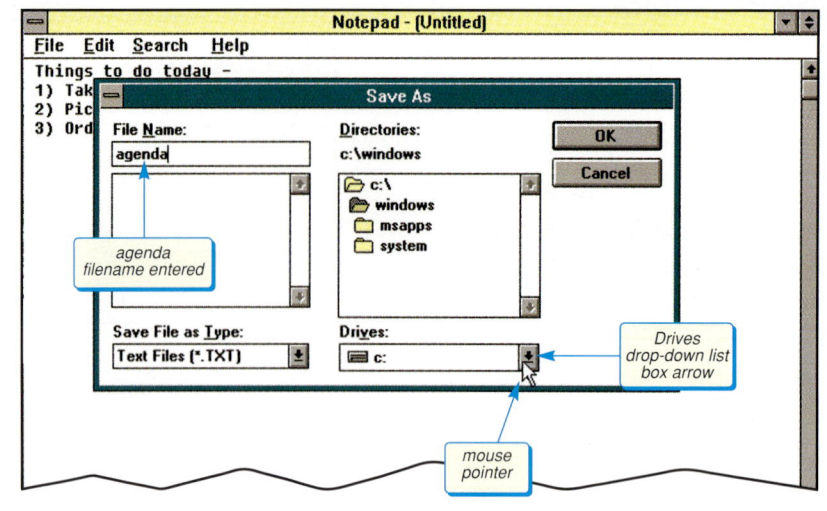

FIGURE 1-43

STEP 5 ▶

Choose the Drives drop-down list box arrow by clicking the left mouse button, and then point to the drive a: icon ( ) in the Drives drop-down list.

Windows displays the Drives drop-down list (Figure 1-44). The drive a: icon and drive c: icon appear in the drop-down list. The mouse pointer points to the drive a: icon.

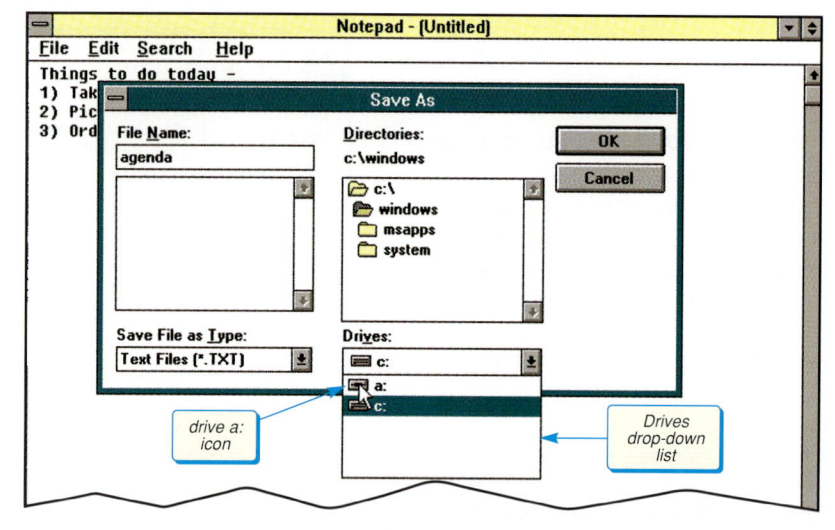

FIGURE 1-44

STEP 6 ▶

Select the drive a: icon by clicking the left mouse button, and then point to the OK button.

The selection is highlighted and the light on drive A turns on while Windows checks for a diskette in drive A (Figure 1-45). The current path changes to a:\ and the Directories list box contains the directory structure of the diskette in drive A.

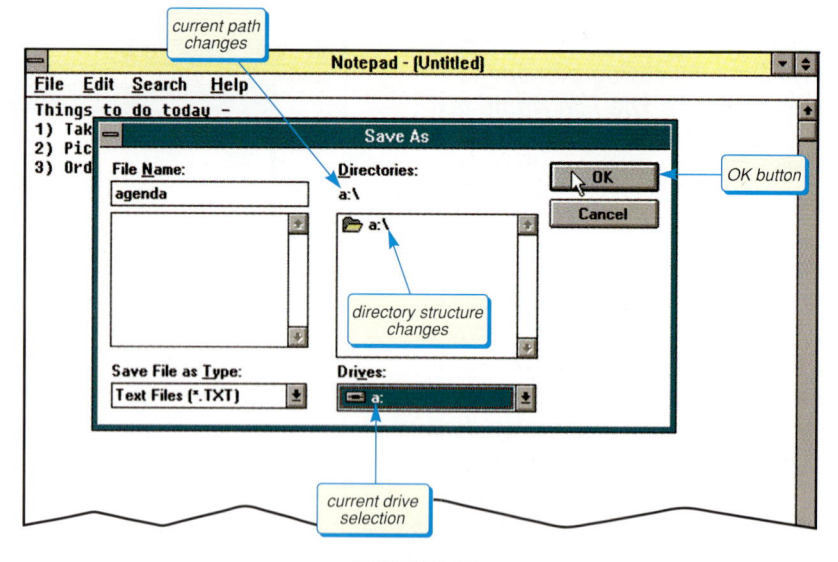

FIGURE 1-45

FILE AND DISK CONCEPTS **WIN27**

STEP 7 ▶

Choose the OK button in the Save As dialog box by clicking the left mouse button.

Windows closes the Save As dialog box and displays an hourglass icon while saving the AGENDA.TXT document file on the diskette in drive A. After the file is saved, Windows changes the window title of the Notepad window to reflect the name of the AGENDA.TXT file (Figure 1-46).

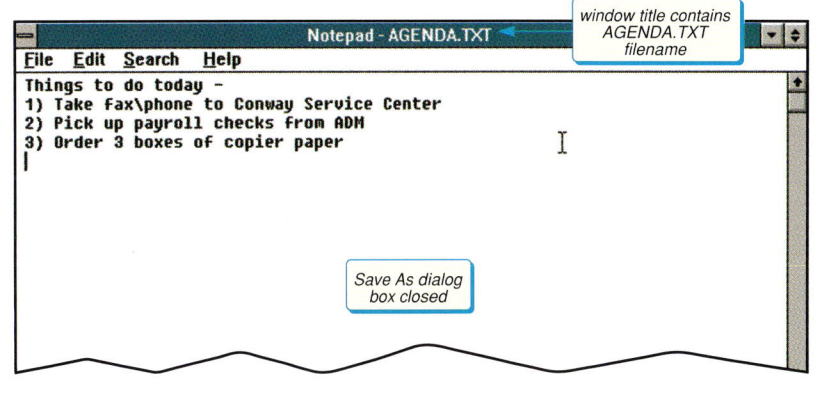

FIGURE 1-46

Correcting Errors Encountered While Saving a Document File

Before you can save a document file on a diskette, you must insert a formatted diskette into the diskette drive. **Formatting** is the process of preparing a diskette for use on a computer by establishing the sectors and cylinders on a disk, analyzing the diskette for defective cylinders, and establishing the root directory. The technique for formatting a diskette is shown in Project 2. If you try to save a file on a diskette and forget to insert a diskette, forget to close the diskette drive door after inserting a diskette, insert an unformatted diskette, or insert a damaged diskette, Windows opens the Save As dialog box in Figure 1-47.

The dialog box contains the messages telling you the condition found and the Retry (Retry) and Cancel buttons. To save a file on the diskette in drive A after receiving this message, insert a formatted diskette into the diskette drive, point to the Retry button, and click the left mouse button.

In addition, you cannot save a document file on a write-protected diskette. A **write-protected diskette** prevents accidentally erasing data stored on the diskette by not letting the disk drive write new data or erase existing data on the diskette. If you try to save a file on a write-protected diskette, Windows opens the Save As dialog box shown in Figure 1-48.

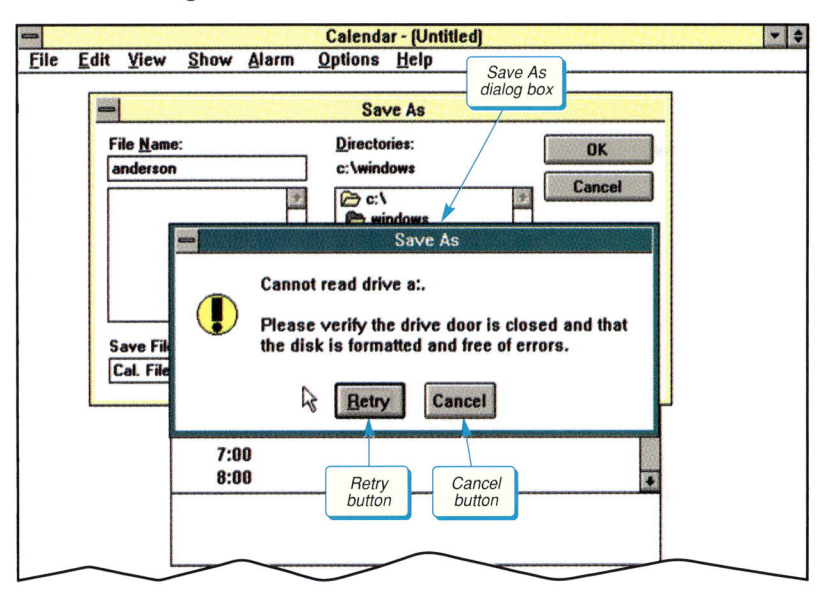

FIGURE 1-47

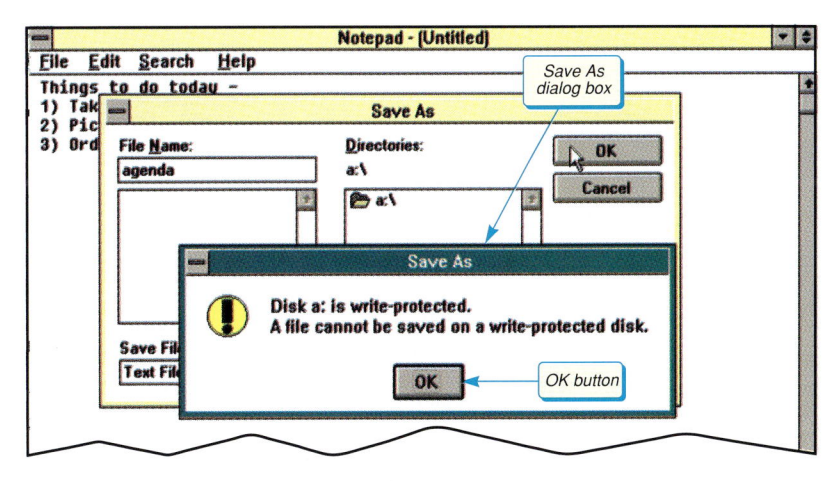

FIGURE 1-48

The Save As dialog box in Figure 1-48 on the previous page contains the messages, Disk a: is write-protected., and, A file cannot be saved on a write-protected disk., and the OK button. To save a file on diskette after inserting a write-protected diskette into drive A, remove the diskette from the diskette drive, remove the write-protection from the diskette, insert the diskette into the diskette drive, point to the OK button, and click the left mouse button.

Quitting an Application

When you have finished saving the AGENDA.TXT file on disk, you can quit the Notepad application as shown in Figure 1-34 through Figure 1-37 on pages WIN21 and WIN22. The steps are summarized below.

TO QUIT AN APPLICATION

Step 1: Point to File on the Notepad menu bar.
Step 2: Select File by clicking the left mouse button, and then point to the Exit command.
Step 3: Choose the Exit command by clicking the left mouse button.

If you have made changes to the document since saving it on the diskette, Notepad will ask if you want to save the changes. If so, choose the Yes button in the dialog box; otherwise, choose the No button.

▶ OPENING A DOCUMENT FILE

Changes are frequently made to a document saved on disk. To make these changes, you must first open the document file by retrieving the file from disk using the Open command. After modifying the document, you save the modified document file on disk using the Save command. Using the Notepad application, you will learn to (1) open a document file and (2) save an edited document file on diskette. In the process, you will add the following line to the AGENDA.TXT file: 4) Buy copier toner.

Starting the Notepad Application and Maximizing the Notepad Window

To start the Notepad application and maximize the Notepad window, perform the following step.

TO START AN APPLICATION AND MAXIMIZE ITS WINDOW ▼

STEP 1 ▶

Double-click the Notepad icon in the Accessories group window. When the Notepad window opens, click the Maximize button.

Double-clicking the Notepad icon opens the Notepad window. Clicking the Maximize button maximizes the Notepad window (Figure 1-49).

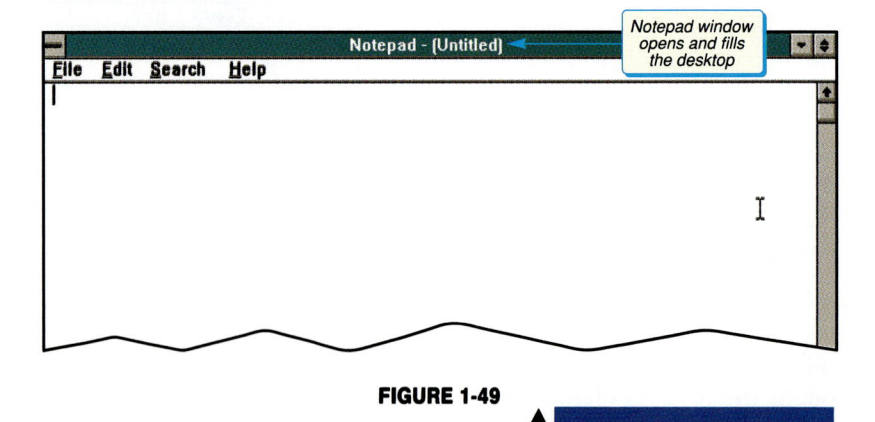

FIGURE 1-49

OPENING A DOCUMENT FILE   WIN29

Opening a Document File

Before you can modify the AGENDA.TXT document, you must open the file from the diskette on which it was stored. To do so, ensure the diskette containing the file is inserted into drive A, then perform the following steps.

TO OPEN A DOCUMENT FILE ▼

STEP 1 ▶

Select File on the menu bar, and then point to the Open command.

Windows opens the File menu and the mouse pointer points to the Open command (Figure 1-50).

FIGURE 1-50

STEP 2 ▶

Choose the Open command from the File menu by clicking the left mouse button, and then point to the Drives drop-down list box arrow.

*The Open dialog box opens (Figure 1-51). The File Name text box contains the *.txt entry and the File Name list box is empty because no files with the .TXT extension appear in the current directory. The current path is c:\windows. The Directories list box contains the directory structure of the current subdirectory (WINDOWS). The selected drive in the Drives drop-down list box is c:. The mouse pointer points to the Drives drop-down list box arrow.*

FIGURE 1-51

STEP 3 ▶

Choose the Drives drop-down list box arrow by clicking the left mouse button, and then point to the drive a: icon.

Windows displays the Drives drop-down list (Figure 1-52). The drive a: icon and drive c: icon appear in the drop-down list. The current selection is c:. The mouse pointer points to the drive a: icon.

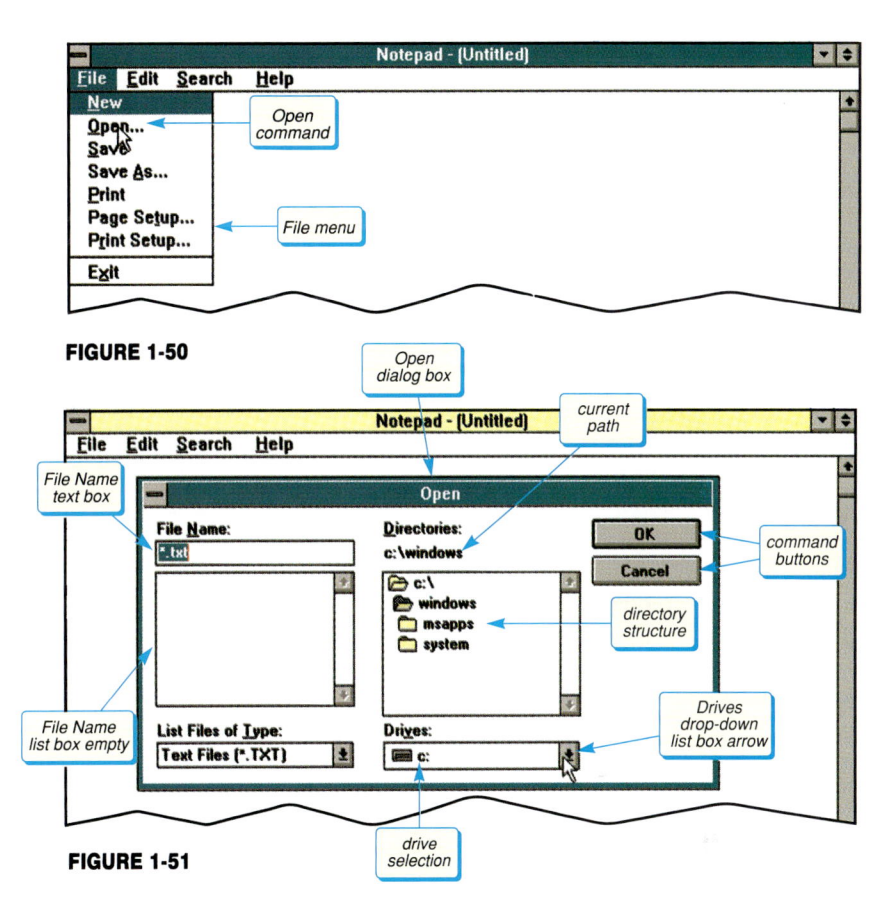

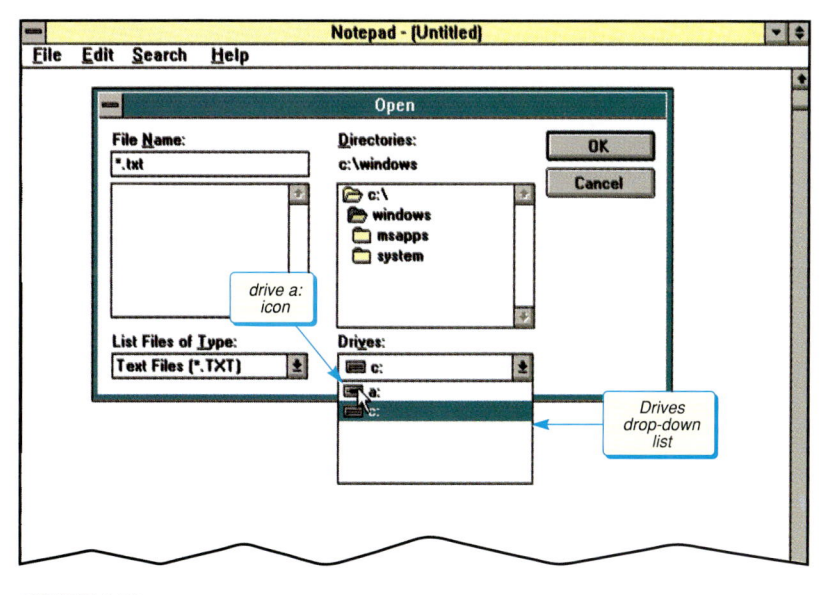

FIGURE 1-52

STEP 4 ▶

Select the drive a: icon by clicking the left mouse button, and then point to the agenda.txt entry in the File Name list box.

The light on drive A turns on, and Windows checks for a diskette in drive A. If there is no diskette in drive A, a dialog box opens to indicate this fact. The current selection in the Drives drop-down list box is highlighted (Figure 1-53). The File Name list box contains the filename agenda.txt, the current path is a:\, and the Directories list box contains the directory structure of drive A. The mouse pointer points to the agenda.txt entry.

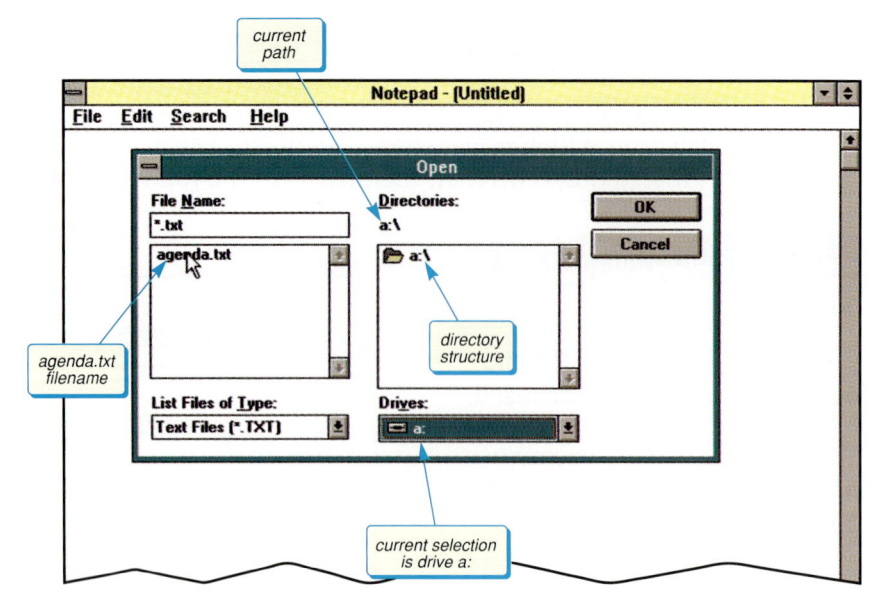

FIGURE 1-53

STEP 5 ▶

Select the agenda.txt file by clicking the left mouse button, and then point to the OK button.

Notepad highlights the agenda.txt entry in the File Name text box, and the agenda.txt filename appears in the File Name text box (Figure 1-54). The mouse pointer points to the OK button.

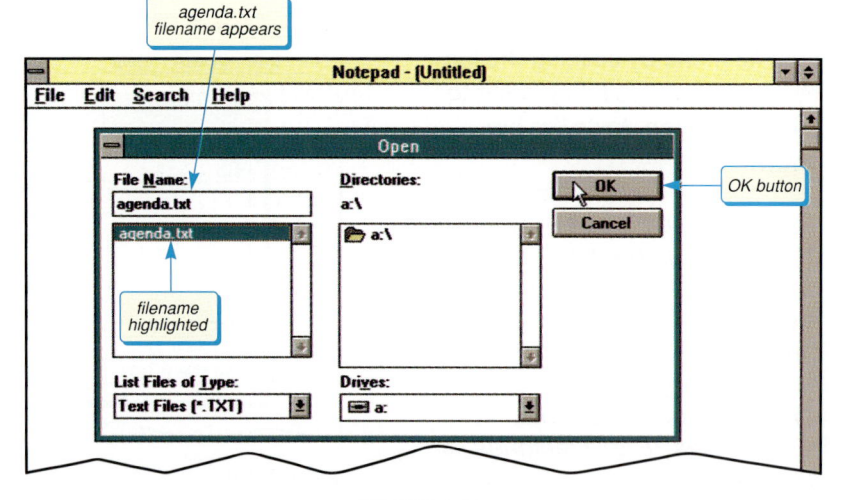

FIGURE 1-54

STEP 6 ▶

Choose the OK button from the Open dialog box by clicking the left mouse button.

Windows retrieves the agenda.txt file from the diskette in drive A and opens the AGENDA.TXT document in the Notepad window (Figure 1-55).

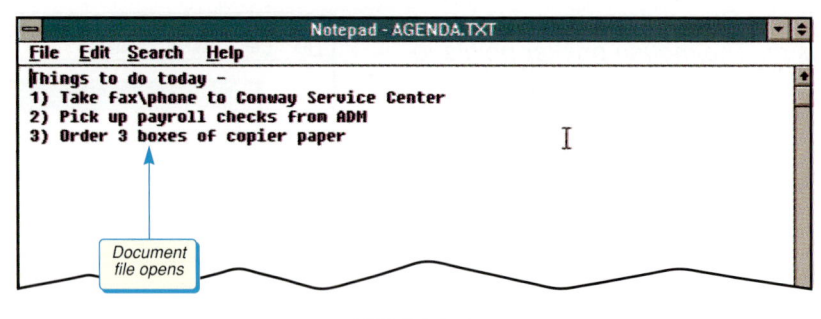

FIGURE 1-55

Editing the Document File

You edit the AGENDA.TXT document file by entering the fourth line of text.

TO EDIT THE DOCUMENT ▼

STEP 1 ▶

Press the DOWN ARROW key four times to position the insertion point, and then type the new line, 4) Buy Copier toner.

The new line appears in the Notepad document (Figure 1-56).

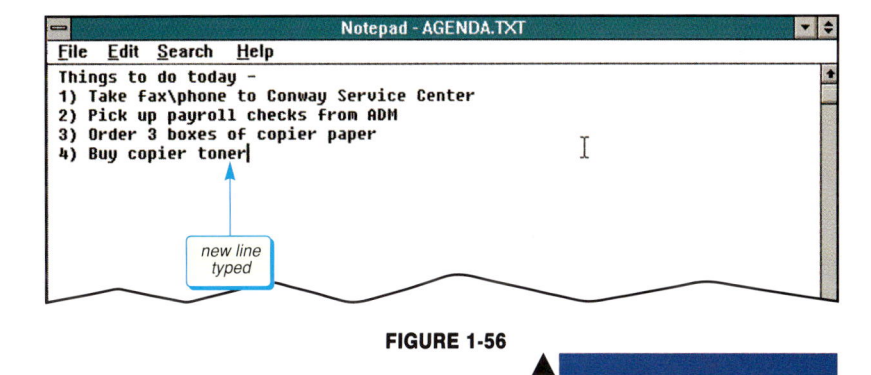

FIGURE 1-56

Saving the Modified Document File

After modifying the AGENDA.TXT document, you should save the modified document on disk using the same AGENDA.TXT filename. To save a modified file on disk, choose the Save command. The Save command differs from the Save As command in that you choose the Save command to save changes to an existing file while you choose the Save As command to name and save a new file or to save an existing file under a new name.

TO SAVE A MODIFIED DOCUMENT FILE ▼

STEP 1 ▶

Select File on the Notepad menu bar, and then point to the Save command.

Windows opens the File menu and the mouse pointer points to the Save command (Figure 1-57).

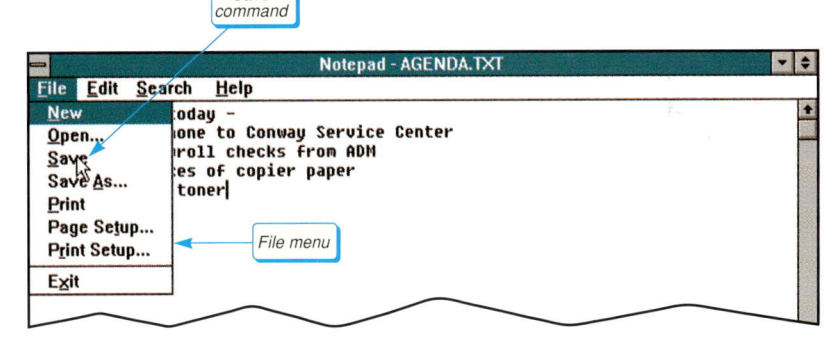

FIGURE 1-57

STEP 2 ▶

Choose the Save command from the File menu by clicking the left mouse button.

Windows closes the File menu, displays the hourglass icon momentarily, and saves the AGENDA.TXT document on the diskette in drive A (Figure 1-58).

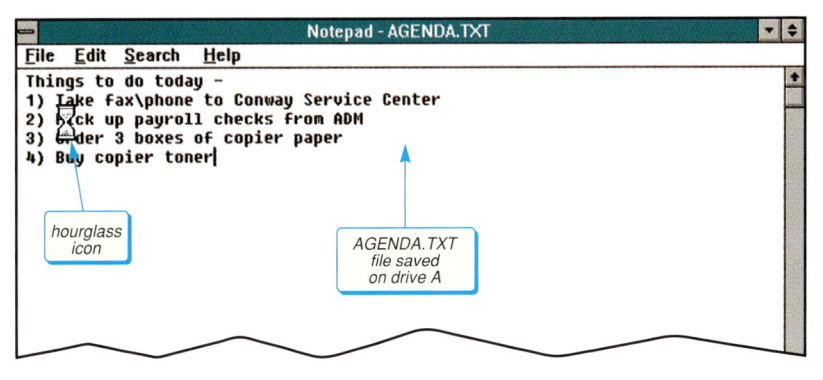

FIGURE 1-58

WIN32   PROJECT 1   AN INTRODUCTION TO WINDOWS

STEP 3 ▶

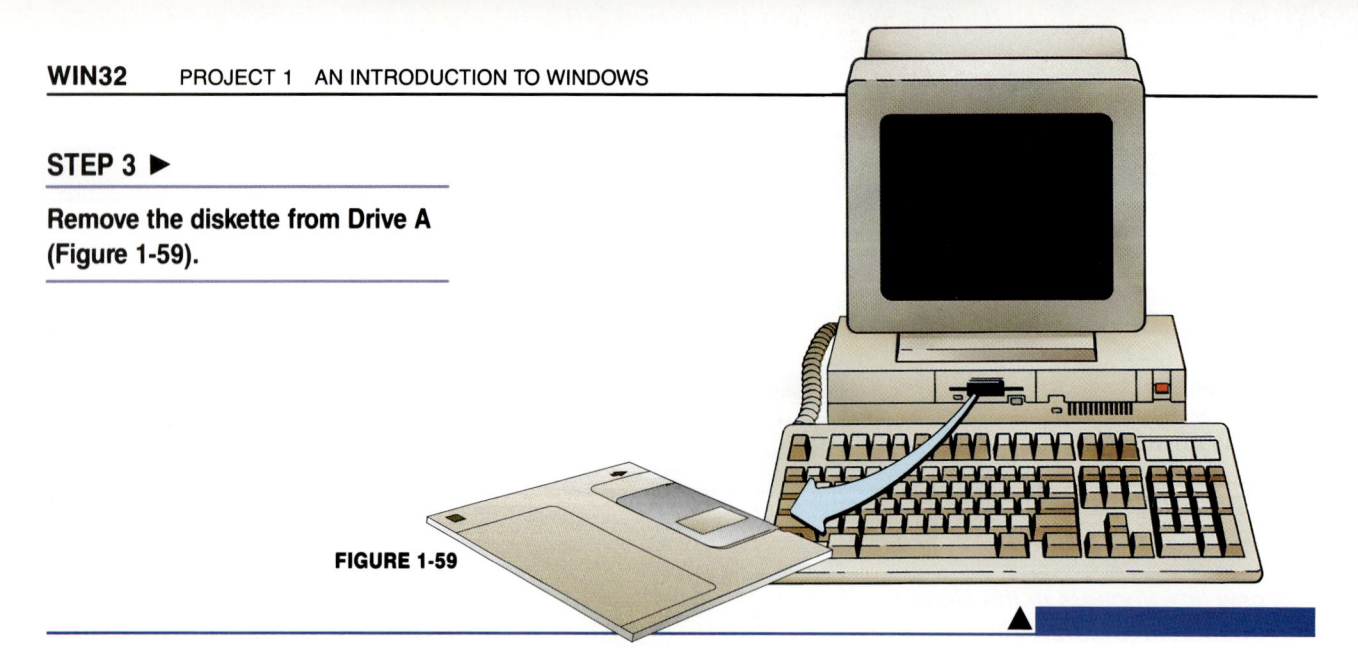

Remove the diskette from Drive A (Figure 1-59).

FIGURE 1-59

When you have finished saving the modified AGENDA.TXT file, quit the Notepad application by performing the following steps.

TO QUIT NOTEPAD

Step 1: Select File on the Notepad menu bar.
Step 2: Choose the Exit command.

▶ USING WINDOWS HELP

I f you need help while using an application, you can use Windows online Help. **Online Help** is available for all applications except Clock. To illustrate Windows online Help, you will start the Paintbrush application and obtain help about the commands on the Edit menu. **Paintbrush** is a drawing program that allows you to create, edit, and print full-color illustrations.

TO START AN APPLICATION

STEP 1 ▶

Double-click the Paintbrush icon (🖌) in the Accessories group window in Program Manager, and then click the Maximize button on the Paintbrush — [Untitled] window.

Windows opens and maximizes the Paintbrush window (Figure 1-60).

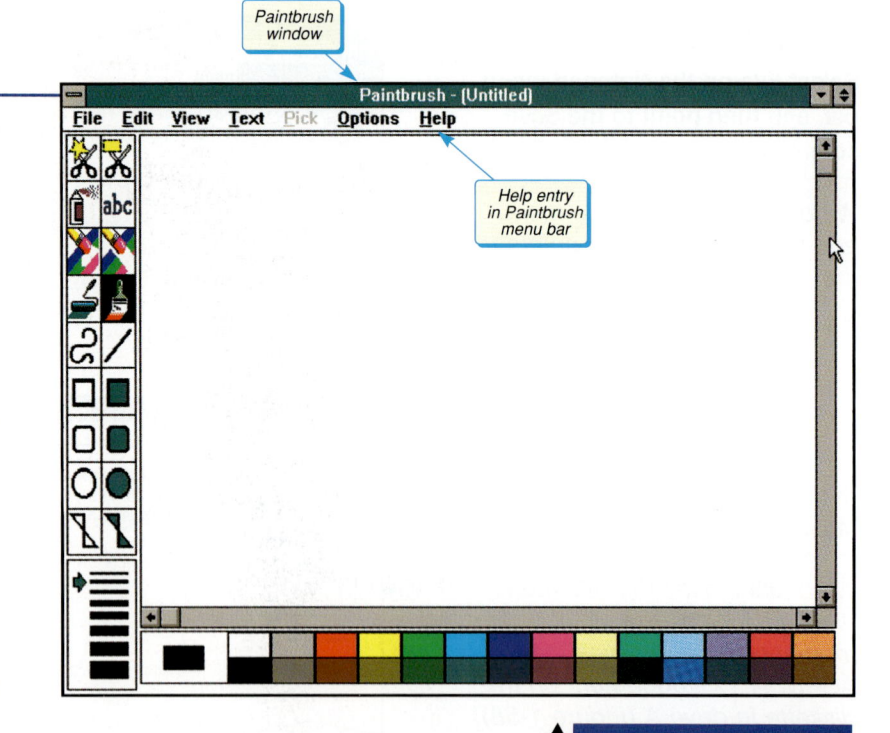

FIGURE 1-60

USING WINDOWS HELP   **WIN33**

TO OBTAIN HELP ▼

STEP 1 ▶

Select Help on the Paintbrush menu bar, and then point to the Contents command.

Windows opens the Help menu (Figure 1-61). The Help menu contains four commands. The mouse pointer points to the Contents command.

FIGURE 1-61

STEP 2 ▶

Choose the Contents command from the Help menu by clicking the left mouse button. Then click the Maximize button on the Paintbrush Help window.

Windows opens the Paintbrush Help window (Figure 1-62), and when you click the Maximize button, it maximizes the window.

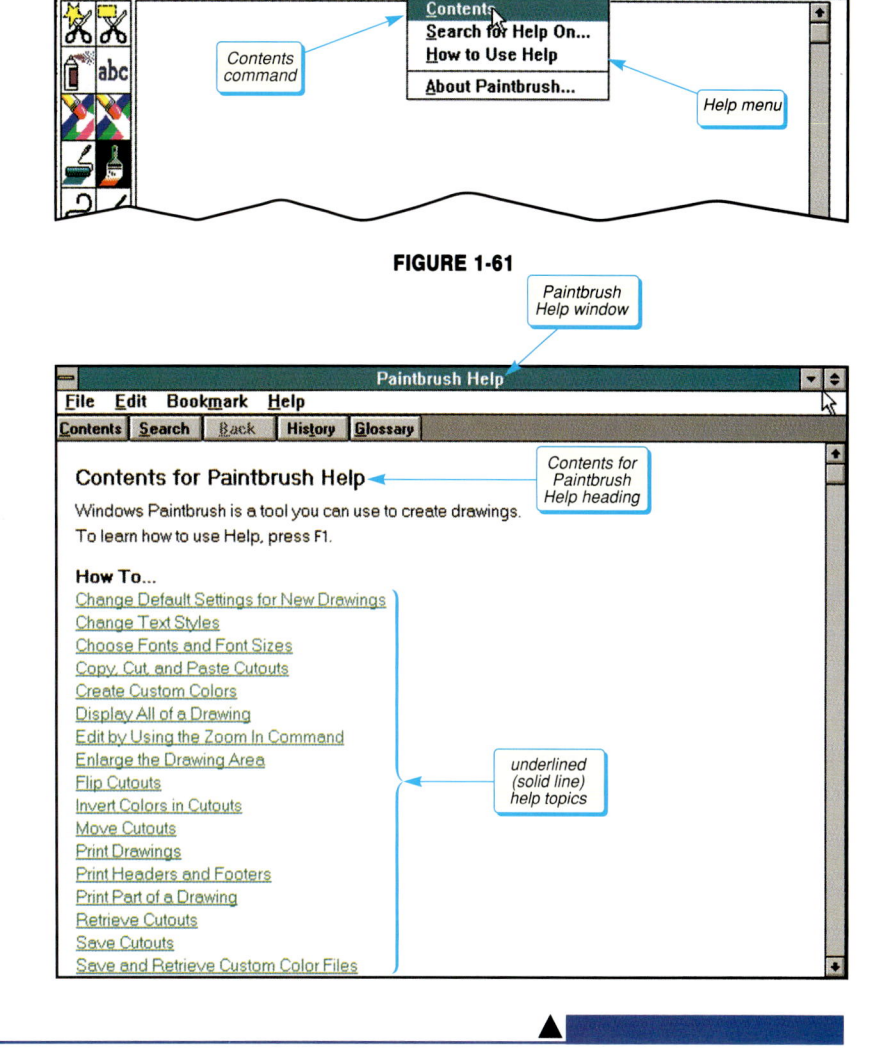

FIGURE 1-62

The Contents for Paintbrush Help screen appears in the window. This screen contains information about the Paintbrush application, how to learn to use online Help (press F1), and an alphabetical list of all help topics for the Paintbrush application. Each **help topic** is underlined with a solid line. The solid line indicates additional information relating to the topic is available. Underlined help topics are called jumps. A **jump** provides a link to viewing information about another help topic or more information about the current topic. A jump may be either text or graphics.

Choosing a Help Topic

To choose an underlined help topic, scroll the help topics to make the help topic you want visible, then point to the help topic and click the left mouse button. When you place the mouse pointer on a help topic, the mouse pointer changes to a hand ( ). To obtain help about the Edit menu, perform the steps on the next page.

TO CHOOSE A HELP TOPIC ▼

STEP 1 ▶

Point to the down scroll arrow (Figure 1-63).

FIGURE 1-63

STEP 2 ▶

Hold down the left mouse button (scroll) until the Edit Menu Commands help topic is visible, and then point to the Edit Menu Commands topic.

The Commands heading and the Edit Menu Commands topic are visible (Figure 1-64). The mouse pointer changes to a hand icon and points to the Edit Menu Commands topic.

FIGURE 1-64

STEP 3 ▶

Choose the Edit Menu Commands topic by clicking the left mouse button.

The Edit Menu Commands screen contains information about each of the commands in the Edit menu (Figure 1-65). Two terms (scroll bar and cutout) are underlined with a dotted line. Terms underlined with a dotted line have an associated glossary definition. To display a term's glossary definition, point to the term and click the left mouse button.

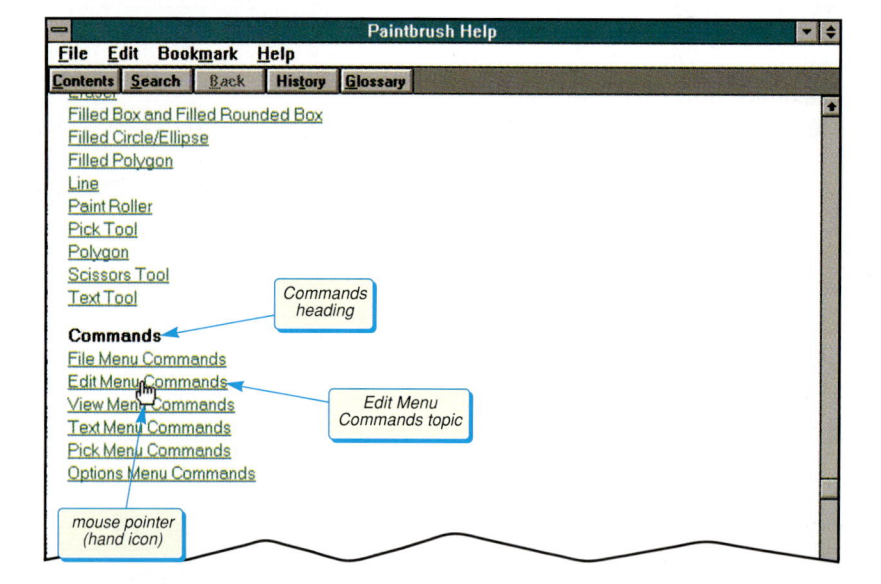

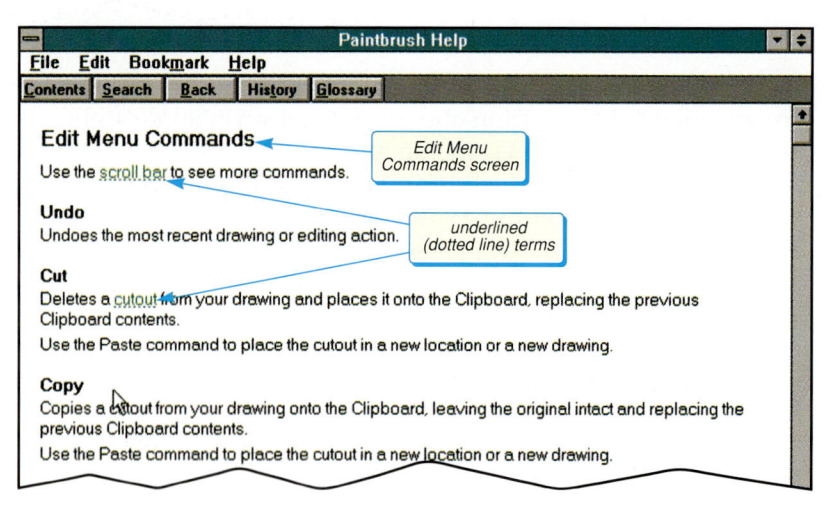

FIGURE 1-65

TO DISPLAY A DEFINITION ▼

STEP 1 ►

Point to the term, scroll bar.

The mouse pointer changes to a hand and points to the term, scroll bar (Figure 1-66).

FIGURE 1-66

STEP 2 ►

Choose the term, scroll bar, by clicking the left mouse button.

Windows opens a **pop-up window** *containing the glossary definition of the term, scroll bar (Figure 1-67).*

FIGURE 1-67

STEP 3 ►

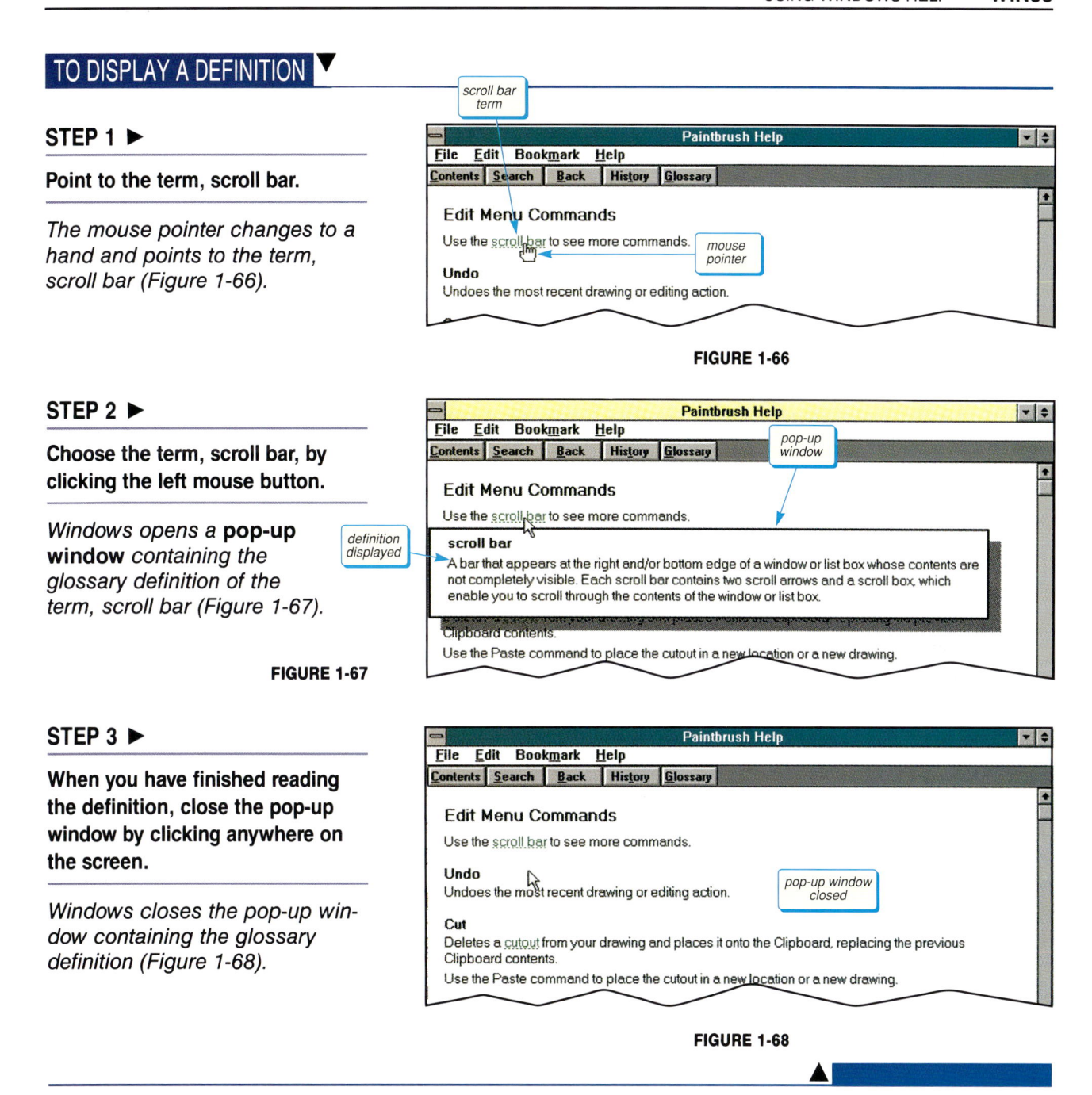

When you have finished reading the definition, close the pop-up window by clicking anywhere on the screen.

Windows closes the pop-up window containing the glossary definition (Figure 1-68).

FIGURE 1-68

Exiting the Online Help and Paintbrush Applications

After obtaining help about the Edit Menu commands, quit Help by choosing the Exit command from the Help File menu. Then, quit Paintbrush by choosing the Exit command from the Paintbrush File menu. The steps are summarized below.

TO QUIT PAINTBRUSH HELP

Step 1: Select File on the Paintbrush Help menu bar.
Step 2: Choose the Exit command.

TO QUIT PAINTBRUSH

Step 1: Select File on the Paintbrush menu bar.
Step 2: Choose the Exit command.

▶ QUITTING WINDOWS

You always want to return the desktop to its original state before beginning your next session with Windows. Therefore, before exiting Windows, you must verify that any changes made to the desktop are not saved when you quit windows.

Verify Changes to the Desktop Will Not be Saved

Because you want to return the desktop to its state before you started Windows, no changes should be saved. The Save Settings on Exit command on the Program Manager Options menu controls whether changes to the desktop are saved or are not saved when you quit Windows. A check mark (✓) preceding the Save Settings on Exit command indicates the command is active and all changes to the layout of the desktop will be saved when you quit Windows. If the command is preceded by a check mark, choose the Save Settings from Exit command by clicking the left mouse button to remove the check mark, so the changes will not be saved. Perform the following steps to verify that changes are not saved to the desktop.

TO VERIFY CHANGES ARE NOT SAVED TO THE DESKTOP ▼

STEP 1 ▶

Select Options on the Program Manager menu bar, and then point to the Save Settings on Exit command.

The Options menu opens (Figure 1-69). A check mark (✓) precedes the Save Settings on Exit command.

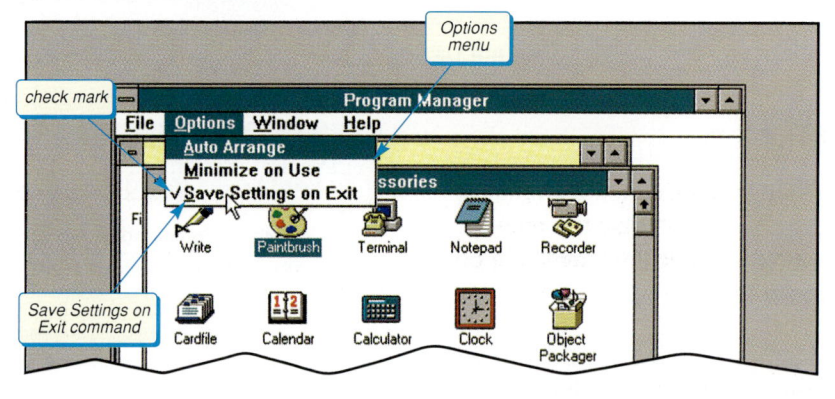

FIGURE 1-69

STEP 2 ▶

To remove the check mark, choose the Save Settings on Exit command from the Options menu by clicking the left mouse button.

Windows closes the Options menu (Figure 1-70). Although not visible in Figure 1-70, the check mark preceding the Save Settings from Exit command has been removed. This means any changes made to the desktop will not be saved when you exit Windows.

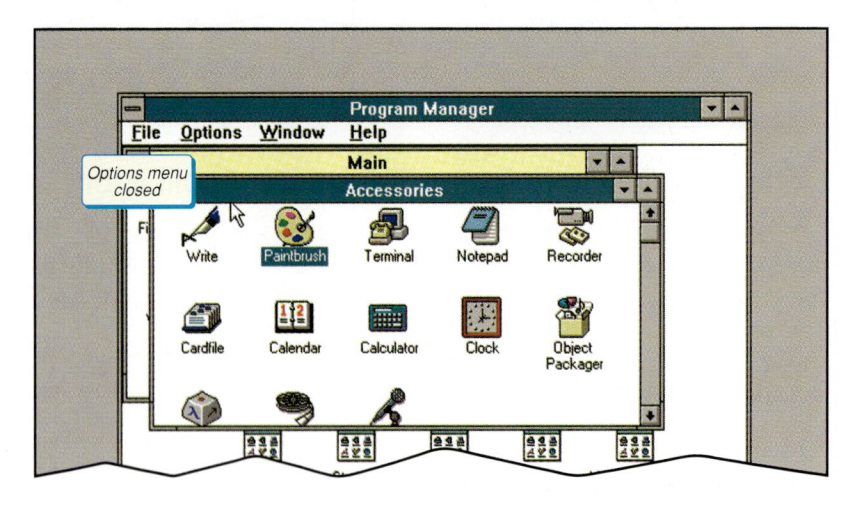

FIGURE 1-70

QUITTING WINDOWS **WIN37**

Quitting Windows Without Saving Changes

After verifying the Save Settings on Exit command is not active, quit Windows by choosing the Exit Windows command from the File menu, as shown below.

TO QUIT WINDOWS ▼

STEP 1 ▶

Select File on the Program Manager menu bar, and then point to the Exit Windows command.

Windows opens the File menu and the mouse pointer points to the Exit Windows command (Figure 1-71).

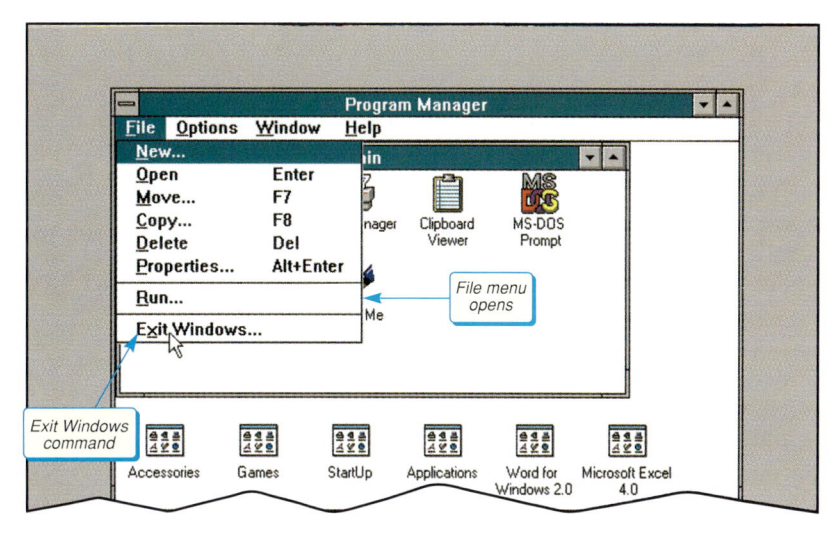

FIGURE 1-71

STEP 2 ▶

Choose the Exit Windows command from the File menu by clicking the left mouse button and point to the OK button.

The Exit Windows dialog box opens and contains the message, This will end your Windows session., and the OK and Cancel buttons (Figure 1-72). Choosing the OK button exits Windows. Choosing the Cancel button cancels the exit from Windows and returns you to the Program Manager window. The mouse pointer points to the OK button.

STEP 3 ▶

Choose the OK button by clicking the left mouse button.

When you quit Windows, all windows are removed from the desktop and control is returned to the DOS operating system.

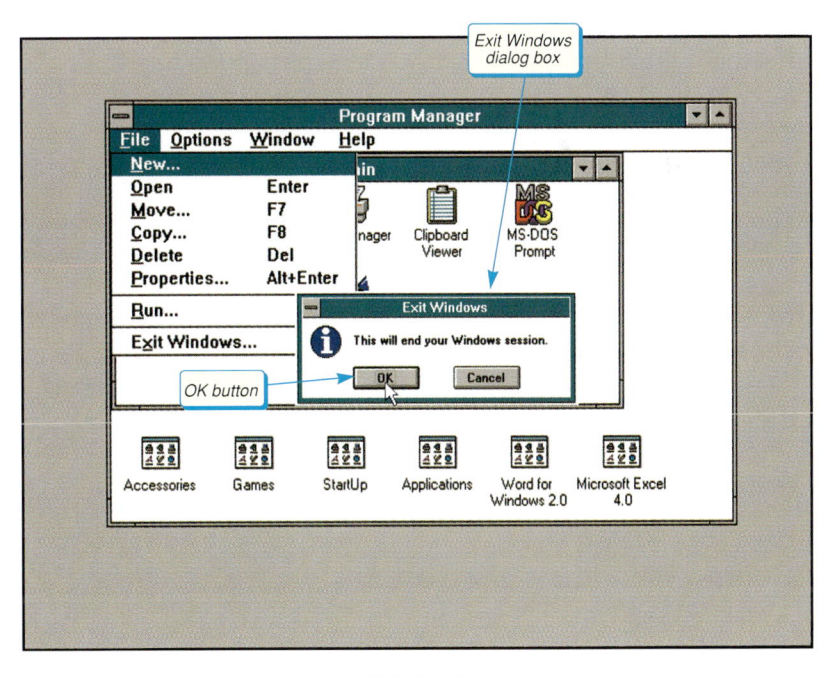

FIGURE 1-72

▶ Project Summary

In this project you learned about user interfaces and the Microsoft Windows graphical user interface. You started and exited Windows and learned the parts of a window. You started Notepad, entered and printed a note, edited the note, opened and saved files, and exited the applications. You opened group windows, maximized application windows, and scrolled the windows. You used the mouse to select a menu, choose a command from a menu, and respond to dialog boxes. You used Windows online Help to obtain help about the Paintbrush application.

▶ Key Terms

active icon (*WIN18*)
active window (*WIN15*)
application (*WIN3*)
application software (*WIN3*)
application window (*WIN5*)
check box (*WIN13*)
choosing (*WIN11*)
choosing a command (*WIN11*)
choosing a help topic (*WIN33*)
clicking (*WIN7*)
command (*WIN10*)
command button (*WIN13*)
Control menu (*WIN16*)
creating a document (*WIN19*)
current selection (*WIN13*)
desktop (*WIN4*)
dialog box (*WIN12*)
directory (*WIN23*)
directory path (*WIN24*)
directory structure (*WIN24*)
displaying a definition (*WIN35*)
document (*WIN14*)
document file (*WIN23*)
double-clicking (*WIN8*)
dragging (*WIN9*)
drop-down list box (*WIN13*)
ellipsis (*WIN11*)
edit a document file (*WIN31*)
error correction (*WIN16, WIN18, WIN27*)
extension (*WIN23*)
file and disk concepts (*WIN22–WIN24*)

filename (*WIN23*)
formatting (*WIN27*)
graphical user interface (GUI) (*WIN3*)
group icons (*WIN5*)
group window (*WIN5*)
GUI (*WIN3*)
help topic (*WIN33*)
hourglass icon (*WIN4*)
icons (*WIN5*)
insertion point (*WIN17*)
jump (*WIN33*)
keyboard (*WIN9*)
keyboard shortcuts (*WIN10*)
Maximize button (*WIN18*)
maximizing a window (*WIN18*)
menu (*WIN10*)
menu bar (*WIN10*)
Microsoft Windows (*WIN2*)
mouse (*WIN5*)
mouse operations (*WIN6–WIN9*)
mouse pointer (*WIN6*)
naming a file (*WIN23*)
Notepad (*WIN14*)
online Help (*WIN32*)
opening a document file (*WIN28*)
opening a window (*WIN14*)
option button (*WIN12*)
Paintbrush (*WIN32*)
pointing (*WIN6*)
pop-up window (*WIN35*)

printing a document (*WIN20*)
Program Manager (*WIN5*)
program-item icons (*WIN5*)
quitting an application (*WIN21, WIN28*)
quitting Windows (*WIN36*)
Restore button (*WIN18*)
root directory (*WIN23*)
saving a document (*WIN24*)
saving a modified document file (*WIN31*)
scroll arrows (*WIN16*)
scroll bar (*WIN16*)
scroll box (*WIN16*)
selected button (*WIN12*)
selecting (*WIN11*)
selecting a menu (*WIN11*)
starting an application (*WIN16*)
starting Microsoft Windows (*WIN4*)
subdirectory (*WIN23*)
text box (*WIN13*)
title bar (*WIN4*)
user friendly (*WIN3*)
user interface (*WIN3*)
using Windows help (*WIN32*)
window (*WIN4*)
window border (*WIN4*)
window title (*WIN4*)
Windows (*WIN2*)
write-protected diskette (*WIN27*)

QUICK REFERENCE

In Microsoft Windows you can accomplish a task in a number of ways. The following table provides a quick reference to each task presented in this project with it available options. The commands listed in the Menu column can be executed using either the keyboard or mouse.

Task	Mouse	Menu	Keyboard Shortcuts
Choose a Command from a menu	Click command name, or drag highlight to command name and release mouse button		Press underlined character; or press arrow keys to select command, and press ENTER
Choose a Help Topic	Click Help topic		Press TAB, ENTER
Display a Definition	Click definition		Press TAB, ENTER
Enlarge an Application Window	Click Maximize button	From Control menu, choose Maximize	
Obtain Online Help		From Help menu, choose Contents	Press F1
Open a Document		From File menu, choose Open	
Open a Group Window	Double-click group icon	From Window menu, choose group window name	Press CTRL+F6 (or CTRL+TAB) to select group icon, and press ENTER
Print a File		From File menu, choose Print	
Quit an Application	Double-click control menu box, click OK button	From File menu, choose Exit	
Quit Windows	Double-click Control menu box, click OK button	From File menu, choose Exit Windows, choose OK button	
Remove a Definition	Click open space on desktop		Press ENTER
Save a Document on Disk		From File menu, choose Save As	
Save an Edited Document on Disk		From File menu, choose Save	
Save Changes when Quitting Windows		From Options menu, choose Save Settings on Exit if no check mark precedes command	
Save No Changes when Quitting Windows		From Options menu, choose Save Settings on Exit if check mark precedes command	
Scroll a Window	Click up or down arrow, drag scroll box, click scroll bar		Press UP or DOWN ARROW
Select a Menu	Click menu name on menu bar		Press ALT+underlined character (or F10+underlined character)
Start an Application	Double-click program-item icon	From File menu, choose Open	Press arrow keys to select program-item icon, and press ENTER

WIN39

STUDENT ASSIGNMENTS

STUDENT ASSIGNMENT 1
True/False

Instructions: Circle T if the statement is true or F if the statement is false.

T F 1. A user interface is a combination of computer hardware and computer software.
T F 2. Microsoft Windows is a graphical user interface.
T F 3. The Program Manager window is a group window.
T F 4. The desktop is the screen background on which windows are displayed.
T F 5. A menu is a small picture that can represent an application or a group of applications.
T F 6. Clicking means quickly pressing and releasing a mouse button twice without moving the mouse.
T F 7. CTRL + SHIFT + LEFT ARROW is an example of a keyboard shortcut.
T F 8. You can carry out an action in an application by choosing a command from a menu.
T F 9. Selecting means marking an item.
T F 10. Windows opens a dialog box to supply information, allow you to enter information, or select among several options.
T F 11. A program-item icon represents a group of applications.
T F 12. You open a group window by pointing to its icon and double-clicking the left mouse button.
T F 13. A scroll bar allows you to view areas of a window that are not currently visible.
T F 14. Notepad and Paintbrush are applications.
T F 15. Choosing the Restore button maximizes a window to its maximize size.
T F 16. APPLICATION.TXT is a valid name for a document file.
T F 17. The directory structure is the relationship between the root directory and any subdirectories.
T F 18. You save a new document on disk by choosing the Save As command from the File menu.
T F 19. You open a document by choosing the Retrieve command from the File menu.
T F 20. Help is available while using Windows only in the *User's Guide* that accompanies the Windows software.

STUDENT ASSIGNMENT 2
Multiple Choice

Instructions: Circle the correct response.

1. Through a user interface, the user is able to _____.
   a. control the computer
   b. request information from the computer
   c. respond to messages displayed by the computer
   d. all of the above
2. _____ is quickly pressing and releasing a mouse button twice without moving the mouse.
   a. Double-clicking
   b. Clicking
   c. Dragging
   d. Pointing

WIN40

3. To view the commands in a menu, you _____ the menu name.
   a. choose
   b. maximize
   c. close
   d. select
4. A _____ is a window that displays to supply information, allow you to enter information, or choose among several options.
   a. group window
   b. dialog box
   c. application window
   d. drop-down list box
5. A _____ is a rectangular area in which Windows displays text or you enter text.
   a. dialog box
   b. text box
   c. drop-down list box
   d. list box
6. The title bar of one group window that is a different color or intensity than the title bars of the other group windows indicates a(n) _____ window.
   a. inactive
   b. application
   c. group
   d. active
7. To view an area of a window that is not currently visible in a window, use the _____.
   a. title bar
   b. scroll bar
   c. menu bar
   d. Restore button
8. The _____ menu in the Notepad application contains the Save, Open, and Print commands.
   a. Window
   b. Options
   c. Help
   d. File
9. Before exiting Windows, you should check the _____ command to verify that no changes to the desktop will be saved.
   a. Open
   b. Exit Windows
   c. Save Settings on Exit
   d. Save Changes
10. Online Help is available for all applications except _____.
    a. Program Manager
    b. Calendar
    c. Clock
    d. File Manager

WIN42   PROJECT 1   AN INTRODUCTION TO WINDOWS

STUDENT ASSIGNMENT 3
Identifying Items in the Program Manager Window

Instructions: On the desktop in Figure SA1-3, arrows point to several items in the Program Manager window. Identify the items in the space provided.

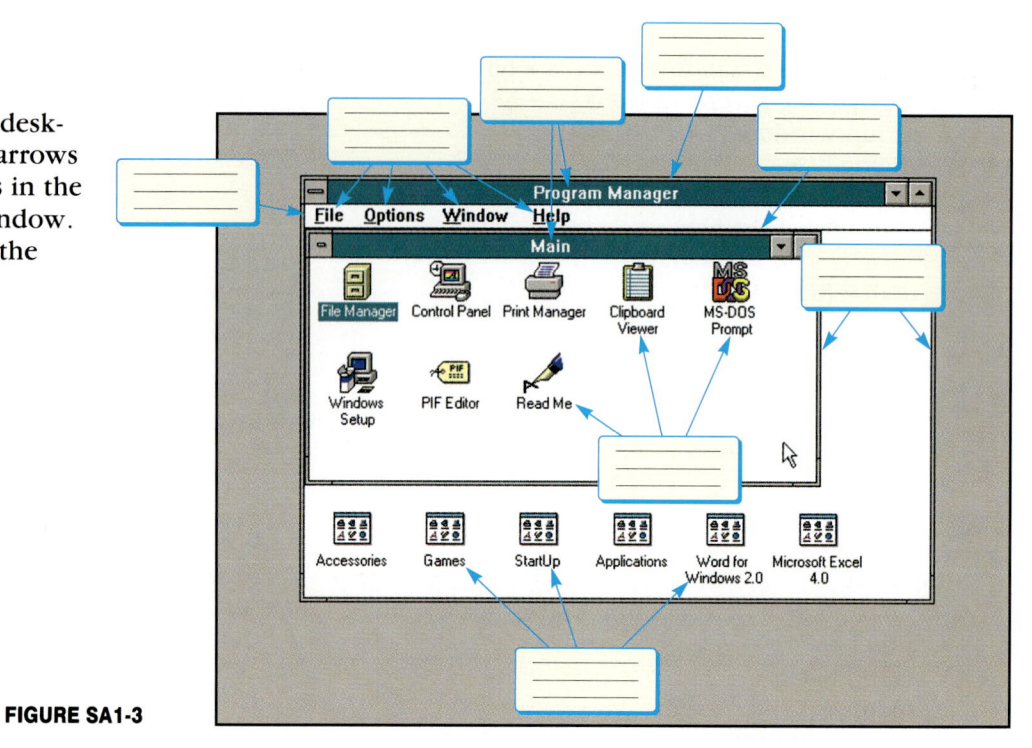

FIGURE SA1-3

STUDENT ASSIGNMENT 4
Starting an Application

Instructions: Using the desktop shown in Figure SA1-4, list the steps in the space provided to open the Accessories window and start the Notepad application.

Step 1: _____

Step 2: _____

Step 3: _____

Step 4: _____

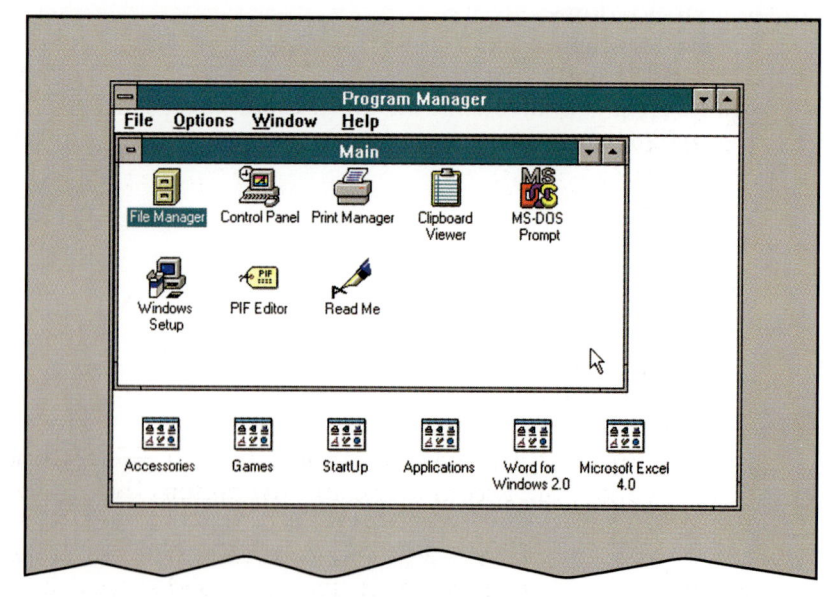

FIGURE SA1-4

COMPUTER LABORATORY EXERCISES

COMPUTER LABORATORY EXERCISE 1
Improving Your Mouse Skills

Instructions: Use a computer to perform the following tasks.

1. Start Microsoft Windows.
2. Double-click the Games group icon ( ) to open the Games window if necessary.
3. Double-click the Solitaire program-item icon ( ).
4. Click the Maximize button to maximize the Solitaire window.
5. From the Help menu in the Solitaire window (Figure CLE1-1), choose the Contents command. One-by-one click on the help topics in green. Double-click on the Control-menu box in the title bar of the Solitaire Help window to close it.
6. Play the game of Solitaire.
7. To quit Solitaire choose the Exit command from the Game menu.

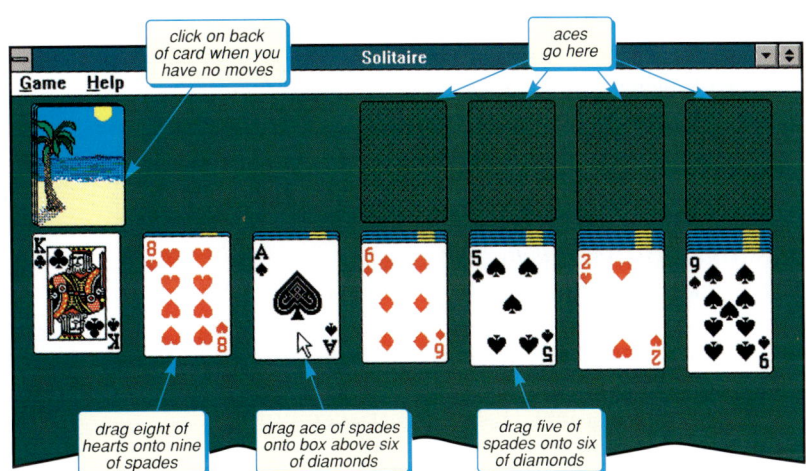

FIGURE CLE1-1

COMPUTER LABORATORY EXERCISE 2
Windows Tutorial

Instructions: Use a computer to perform the following tasks.

1. Start Microsoft Windows.
2. From the Help menu in the Program Manager window, choose the Windows Tutorial command.
3. Type the letter M. Follow the instructions (Figure CLE1-2) to step through the mouse practice lesson. Press the ESC key to exit the tutorial.
4. From the Help menu in the Program Manager window, choose the Windows Tutorial command.
5. Type the letter W. Click the Instructions button (Instructions) and read the information. When you are finished, choose the Return to the Tutorial button (Return to the Tutorial). Next choose the Contents button (Contents) in the lower right corner of the screen.
6. Choose the second item (Starting an Application) from the Contents list. The Windows tutorial will step you through the remaining lessons. Respond as needed to the questions and instructions. Press the ESC key to exit the tutorial.

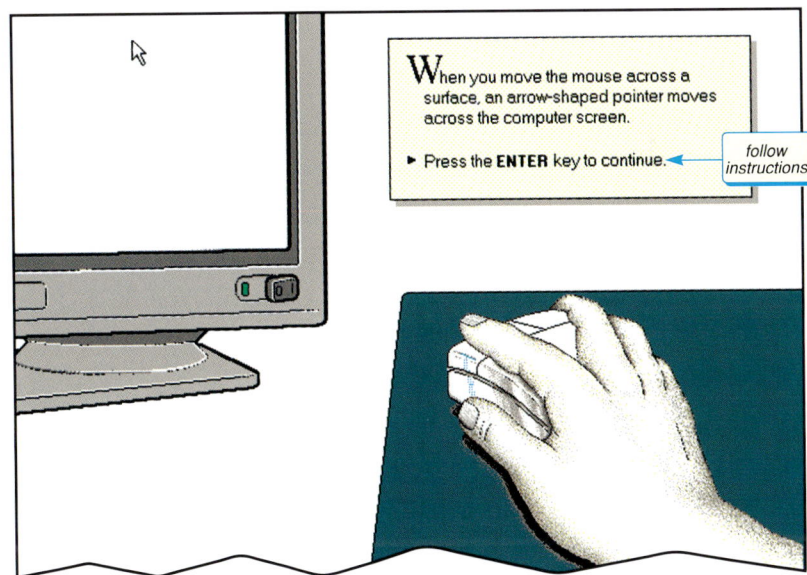

FIGURE CLE1-2

COMPUTER LABORATORY EXERCISE 3
Creating, Saving, and Printing Documents

Instructions: Use a computer to perform the following tasks.

1. Start Microsoft Windows if necessary.
2. Double-click the Accessories icon to open the Accessories window.
3. Double-click the Notepad icon to start the Notepad application.
4. Click the Maximize button to maximize the Notepad window.
5. Enter the note shown at the right at the insertion point on the screen.
6. Insert the Student Diskette that accompanies this book into drive A.
7. Select the File menu on the Notepad menu bar.
8. Choose the Save As command.
9. Enter grocery in the File Name text box.
10. Change the current selection in the Drives drop-down list box to a:.
11. Click the OK button to save the document on drive A.
12. Select the File menu on the Notepad menu bar.
13. Choose the Print command to print the document on the printer (Figure CLE1-3).
14. Remove the Student Diskette from drive A.
15. Select the File menu on the Notepad menu bar.
16. Choose the Exit command to quit Notepad.

Grocery List —
1/2 Gallon of Low Fat Milk
1 Dozen Medium Size Eggs
1 Loaf of Wheat Bread

```
                        GROCERY.TXT


    Grocery List -
    1/2 Gallon of Low Fat Milk
    1 Dozen Medium Size Eggs
    1 Loaf of Wheat Bread
```

FIGURE CLE1-3

COMPUTER LABORATORY EXERCISE 4
Opening, Editing, and Saving Documents

Instructions: Use a computer to perform the following tasks. If you have questions on how to procede, use the Calendar Help menu.

1. Start Microsoft Windows if necessary.
2. Double-click the Accessories icon to open the Accessories window.
3. Double-click the Calendar icon ( ) to start the Calendar application.
4. Click the Maximize button to maximize the Calendar window.
5. Insert the Student Diskette that accompanies this book into drive A.
6. Select the File menu on the Calendar menu bar.

7. Choose the Open command.
8. Change the current selection in the Drives drop-down list box to a:.
9. Select the thompson.cal filename in the File Name list box. The THOMPSON.CAL file contains the daily appointments for Mr. Thompson.
10. Click the OK button in the Open dialog box to open the THOMPSON.CAL document. The document on your screen is shown in Figure CLE1-4a.
11. Click the Left or Right Scroll arrow repeatedly to locate the appointments for Thursday, September 29, 1994.
12. Make the changes shown below to the document.

TIME	CHANGE
11:00 AM	Stay at Auto Show one more hour
2:00 PM	Change the Designer's Meeting from 2:00 PM to 3:00 PM
4:00 PM	Remove the Quality Control Meeting

13. Select the File menu on the Calendar menu bar.
14. Choose the Save As command to save the document file on drive A. Use the filename PETER.CAL.
15. Select the File menu on the Calendar menu bar.
16. Choose the Print command.
17. Choose the OK button to print the document on the printer (Figure CLE1-4b).
18. Remove the Student Diskette from drive A.
19. Select the File menu on the Calendar menu bar.
20. Choose the Exit command to quit Calendar.

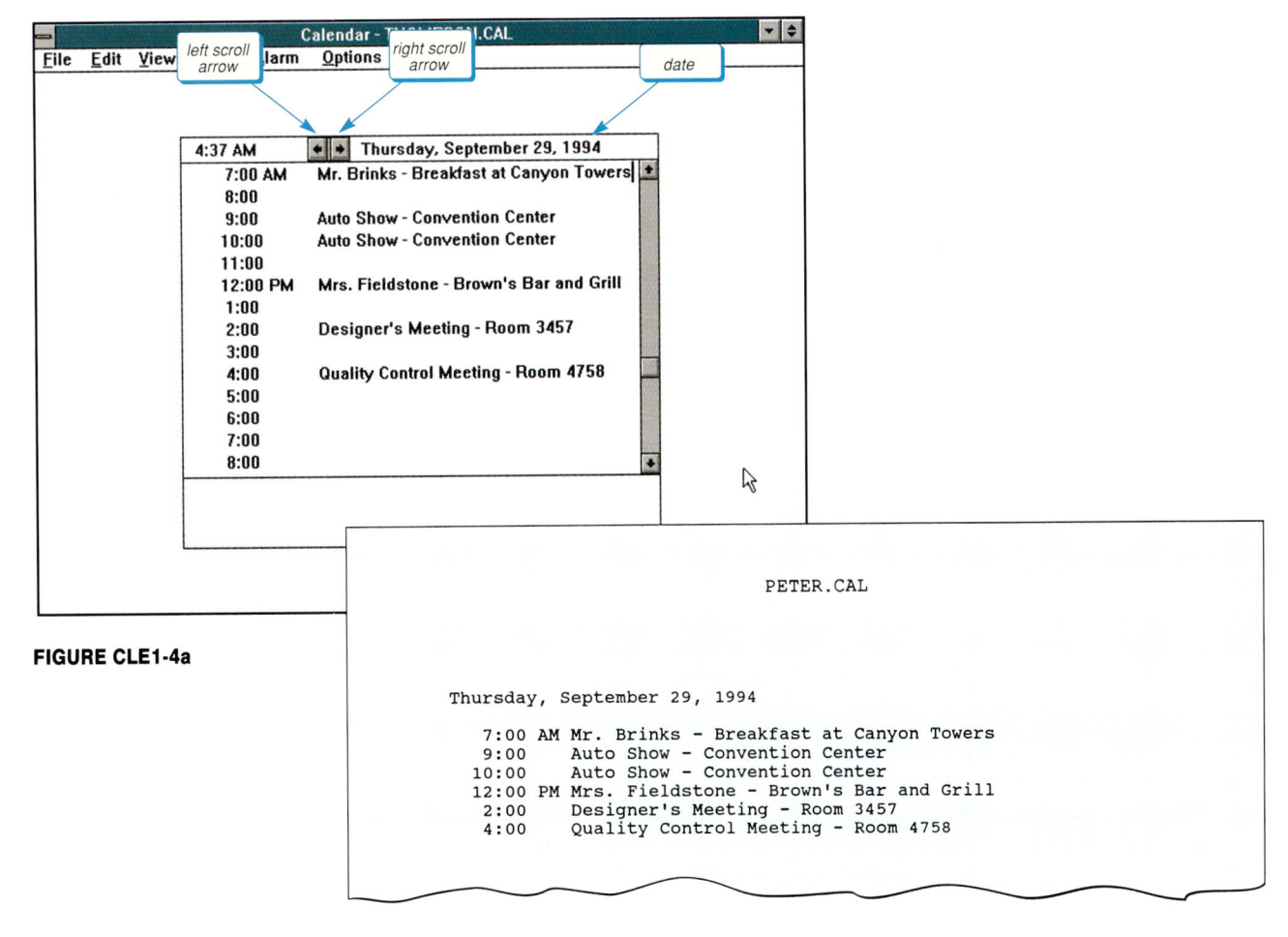

FIGURE CLE1-4a

FIGURE CLE1-4b

COMPUTER LABORATORY EXERCISE 5
Using Online Help

Instructions: Use a computer to perform the following tasks.

1. Start Microsoft Windows if necessary.
2. Double-click the Accessories icon to open the Accessories window.
3. Double-click the Cardfile icon ( ) to start the Cardfile application.
4. Select the Help menu.
5. Choose the Contents command.
6. Click the Maximize button to maximize the Cardfile Help window.
7. Choose the Add More Cards help topic.
8. Select the File menu on the Cardfile Help menu bar.
9. Choose the Print Topic command to print the Adding More Cards help topic on the printer (Figure CLE1-5a).
10. Display the definition of the term, index line.
11. Remove the index line definition from the desktop.
12. Choose the Contents button.
13. Choose the Delete Cards help topic.
14. Choose the Selecting Cards help topic at the bottom of the Deleting Cards screen.

Adding More Cards

Cardfile adds new cards in the correct alphabetic order and scrolls to display the new card at the front.

To add a new card to a file
1 From the Card menu, choose Add.
2 Type the text you want to appear on the index line.
3 Choose the OK button.
4 In the information area, type text.

FIGURE CLE1-5a

15. Select the File menu on the Cardfile Help menu bar.
16. Choose the Print Topic command to print the Selecting Cards help topic (Figure CLE 1-5b).
17. Select the File menu on the Cardfile Help menu bar.
18. Choose the Exit command to quit Cardfile Help.
19. Select the File menu on the Cardfile window menu bar.
20. Choose the Exit command to quit Cardfile.

Selecting Cards

To select a card in Card view
▶ Click the card's index line if it is visible.
  Or click the arrows in the status bar until the index line is visible, and then click it.
  If you are using the keyboard, press and hold down CTRL+SHIFT and type the first letter of the index line.

To select a card by using the Go To command
1 From the Search menu, choose Go To.
2 Type text from the card's index line.
3 Choose the OK button.

To select a card in List view
▶ Click the card's index line.
  Or use the arrow keys to move to the card's index line.

See Also
Moving Through a Card File

FIGURE CLE1-5b

Microsoft Windows 3.1
PROJECT TWO

DISK AND FILE MANAGEMENT

OBJECTIVES You will have mastered the material in this project when you can:

- Identify the elements of the directory tree window
- Understand the concepts of diskette size and capacity
- Format and copy a diskette
- Select and copy one file or a group of files
- Change the current drive
- Rename or delete a file
- Create a backup diskette
- Search for help topics using Windows online Help
- Switch between applications
- Activate, resize, and close a group window
- Arrange the icons in a group window
- Minimize an application window to an icon

INTRODUCTION

File Manager is an application included with Windows that allows you to organize and work with your hard disk and diskettes and the files on those disks. In this project, you will use File Manager to (1) format a diskette; (2) copy files between the hard disk and a diskette; (3) copy a diskette; (4) rename a file on diskette; and (5) delete a file from diskette.

Formatting a diskette and copying files to a diskette are common operations illustrated in this project that you should understand how to perform. While performing the Computer Laboratory Exercises and the Computer Laboratory Assignments at the end of each application project, you will save documents on a diskette that accompanies this textbook. To prevent the accidental loss of stored documents on a diskette, it is important to periodically make a copy of the entire diskette. A copy of a diskette is called a **backup diskette**. In this project, you will learn how to create a backup diskette to protect against the accidental loss of documents on a diskette.

You will also use Windows online Help in this project. In Project 1, you obtained help by choosing a topic from a list of help topics. In this project, you will use the Search feature to search for help topics.

WIN48　PROJECT 2　DISK AND FILE MANAGEMENT

Starting Windows

As explained in Project 1, when you turn on the computer, an introductory screen consisting of the Windows logo, Windows name, version number, and copyright notices displays momentarily. Next, a blank screen containing an hourglass icon displays. Finally, the Program Manager and Main windows open on the desktop (Figure 2-1). The File Manager program-item icon displays in the Main window. If your desktop does not look similar to the desktop in Figure 2-1, your instructor will inform you of the modifications necessary to change your desktop.

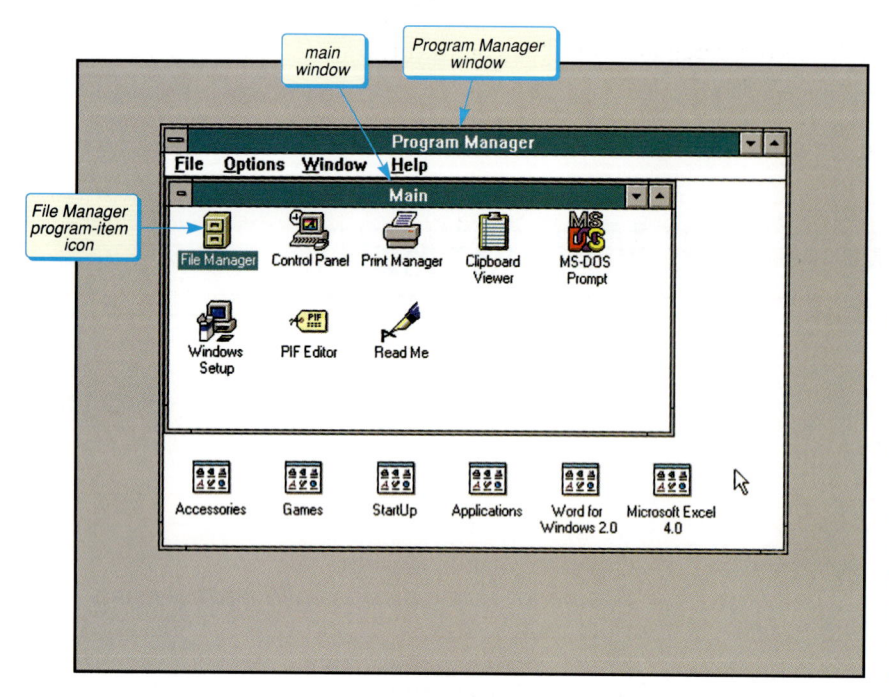

FIGURE 2-1

Starting File Manager and Maximizing the File Manager Window

To start File Manager, double-click the File Manager icon (📁) in the Main window. To maximize the File Manager window, choose the Maximize button on the File Manager window by pointing to the Maximize button and clicking the left mouse button.

TO START AN APPLICATION AND MAXIMIZE ITS WINDOW ▼

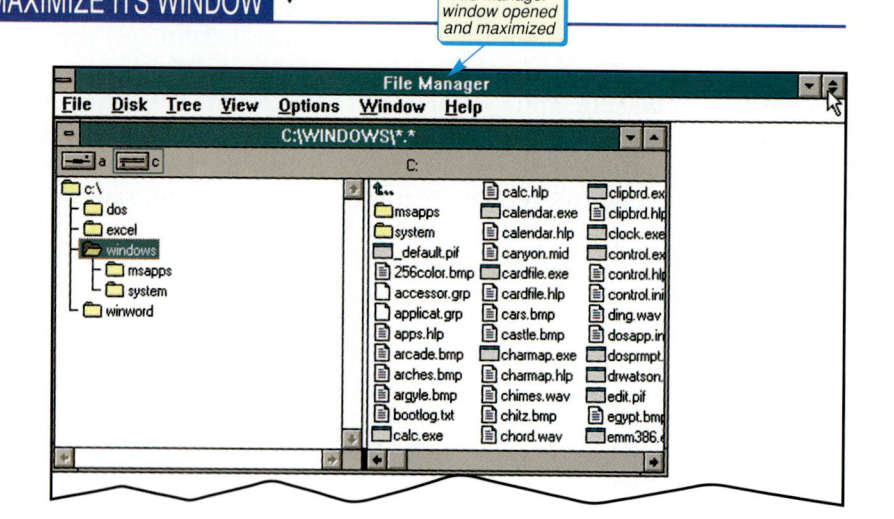

STEP 1 ▶

Double-click the File Manager icon in the Main window (see Figure 2-1), then click the Maximize button on the File Manager title bar.

Windows opens and maximizes the File Manager window (Figure 2-2).

FIGURE 2-2

► FILE MANAGER

When you start File Manager, Windows opens the File Manager window (Figure 2-3). The menu bar contains the File, Disk, Tree, View, Options, Window, and Help menus. These menus contain the commands to organize and work with the disks and the files on those disks.

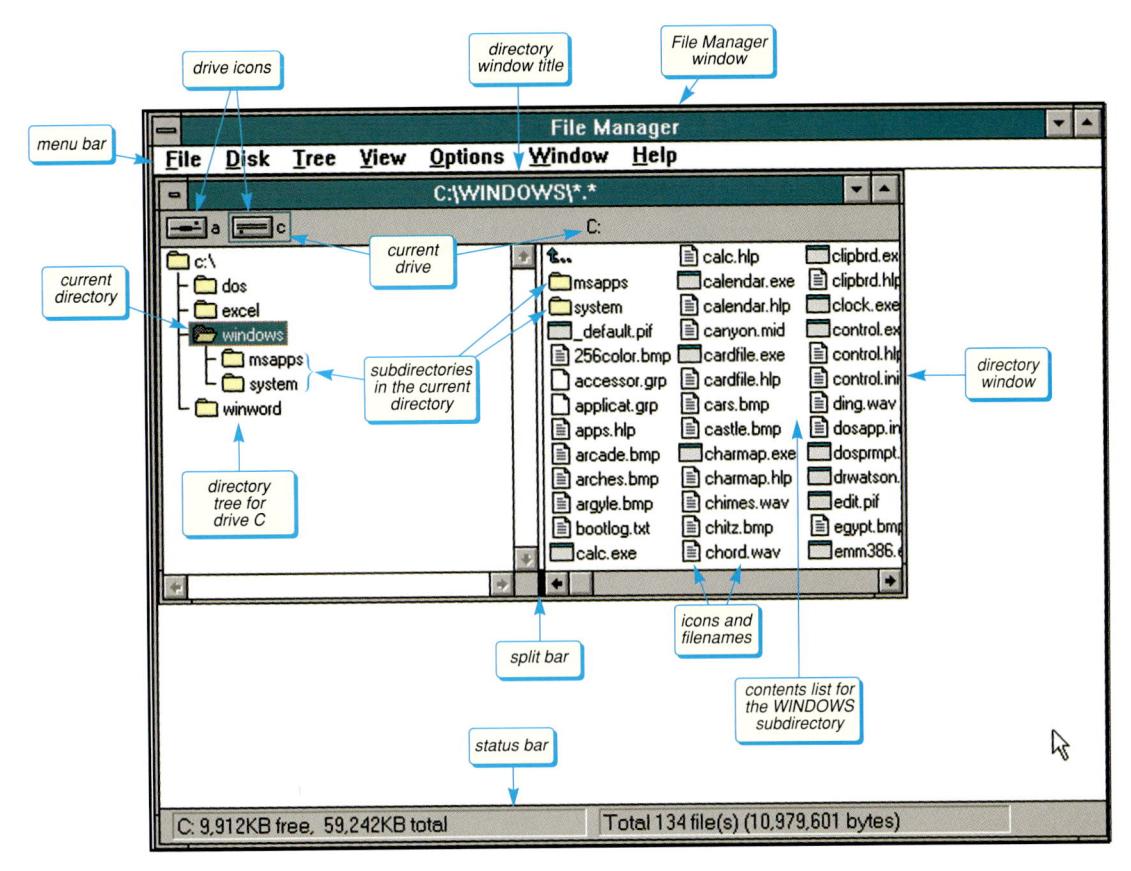

FIGURE 2-3

Below the menu bar is a **directory window** titled C:\WINDOWS*.*. The window title consists of a directory path (C:\WINDOWS), backslash (\), and filename (*.*). The directory path is the path of the current directory on drive C (WINDOWS subdirectory). The backslash separates the path and filename. The filename (*.*) references a group of files whose filename and extension can be any valid filename and extension.

Below the title bar is a horizontal bar that contains two **drive icons**. The drive icons represent the disk drives attached to the computer. The first drive icon (a:) represents drive A (diskette drive) and the second drive icon (c:) represents drive C (hard drive). Depending upon the number of disk drives attached to your computer, there may be more than two drive icons in the horizontal bar. A rectangular box surrounding the drive C icon indicates drive C is the **current drive**. The entry to the right of the icons (C:) also indicates drive C is the current drive.

The directory window is divided into two equal-sized areas. Each area is separated by a split bar. The **directory tree** in the area on the left contains the directory structure. The **directory tree** in the **directory structure** shows the relationship between the root directory and any subdirectories on the current drive (drive C). You can drag the **split bar** to the left or right to change the size of the two areas.

In the left area, a file folder icon represents each directory or subdirectory in the directory structure (see Figure 2-3). The shaded open file folder (📂) and subdirectory name for the current directory (WINDOWS subdirectory) are highlighted. The unopened file folder icons (📁) for the two subdirectories in the WINDOWS subdirectory (MSAPPS and SYSTEM) are indented below the icon for the WINDOWS subdirectory.

The area on the right contains the contents list. The **contents list** is a list of the files in the current directory (WINDOWS subdirectory). Each entry in the contents list consists of an icon and name. The shaded file folder icons for the two subdirectories in the current directory (MSAPPS and SYSTEM) display at the top of the first column in the list.

The status bar at the bottom of the File Manager window indicates the amount of unused disk space on the current drive (9,912KB free), amount of total disk space on the current drive (59,242KB total), number of files in the current directory (134 files), and the amount of disk space the files occupy (10,979,601 bytes).

▶ FORMATTING A DISKETTE

Before saving a document file on a diskette or copying a file onto a diskette, you must format the diskette. **Formatting** prepares a diskette for use on a computer by establishing the sectors and cylinders on the diskette, analyzing the diskette for defective cylinders, and establishing the root directory. To avoid errors while formatting a diskette, you should understand the concepts of diskette size and capacity that are explained in the following section.

Diskette Size and Capacity

How a diskette is formatted is determined by the size of the diskette, capacity of the diskette as established by the diskette manufacturer, and capabilities of the disk drive you use to format the diskette. **Diskette size** is the physical size of the diskette. Common diskette sizes are 5 1/4-inch and 3 1/2-inch.

Diskette capacity is the amount of space on the disk, measured in kilobytes (K) or megabytes (MB), available to store data. A diskette's capacity is established by the diskette manufacturer. Common diskette capacities are 360K and 1.2MB for a 5 1/4-inch diskette and 720K and 1.44MB for a 3 1/2-inch diskette.

A diskette drive's capability is established by the diskette drive manufacturer. There are 3 1/2-inch diskette drives that are capable of formatting a diskette with a capacity of 720K or 1.44MB and there are 5 1/4-inch diskette drives capable of formatting a diskette with a capacity of 360K or 1.2MB.

Before formatting a diskette, you must consider two things. First, the diskette drive you use to format a diskette must be capable of formatting the size of diskette you want to format. You can use a 3 1/2-inch diskette drive to format a 3 1/2-inch diskette, but you cannot use a 3 1/2-inch diskette drive to format a

FORMATTING A DISKETTE   WIN51

5 1/4-inch diskette. Similarly, you can use a 5 1/4-inch diskette drive to format a 5 1/4-inch diskette, but you cannot use a 5 1/4-inch diskette drive to format a 3 1/2-inch diskette.

Second, the diskette drive you use to format a diskette must be capable of formatting the capacity of the diskette you want to format. A 5 1/4-inch diskette drive capable of formatting 1.2MB diskettes can be used to either format a 360K or 1.2MB diskette. However, because of the differences in the diskette manufacturing process, you cannot use a diskette drive capable of formatting 360K diskettes to format a 1.2MB diskette. A 3 1/2-inch diskette drive capable of formatting 1.44MB diskettes can be used to format either a 720K or 1.44MB diskette. Since the 1.44 MB diskette is manufactured with two square holes in the plastic cover and the 720K diskette is manufactured with only one square hole, you cannot use a diskette drive capable of formatting 720K diskette to format a 1.44MB diskette.

The computer you use to complete this project should have a 3 1/2-inch diskette drive capable of formatting a diskette with 1.44MB of disk storage. Trying to format a 3 1/2-inch diskette with any other diskette drive may result in an error. Typical errors encountered because of incorrect diskette capacity and diskette drive capabilities are explained later in this project. For more information about the diskette drive you will use to complete the projects in this textbook, contact your instructor.

Formatting a Diskette

To store a file on a diskette, the diskette must already be formatted. If the diskette is not formatted, you must format the diskette using File Manager. When formatting a diskette, use either an unformatted diskette or a diskette containing files you no longer need. Do not format the Student Diskette that accompanies this book.

To format a diskette using File Manager, you insert the diskette into the diskette drive, and then choose the **Format Disk command** from the Disk menu. Perform the following steps to format a diskette.

TO FORMAT A DISKETTE ▼

STEP 1

Insert an unformatted diskette or a formatted diskette containing files you no longer need into drive A.

STEP 2 ▶

Select the Disk menu, and then point to the Format Disk command.

Windows opens the Disk menu (Figure 2-4). The mouse pointer points to the Format Disk command.

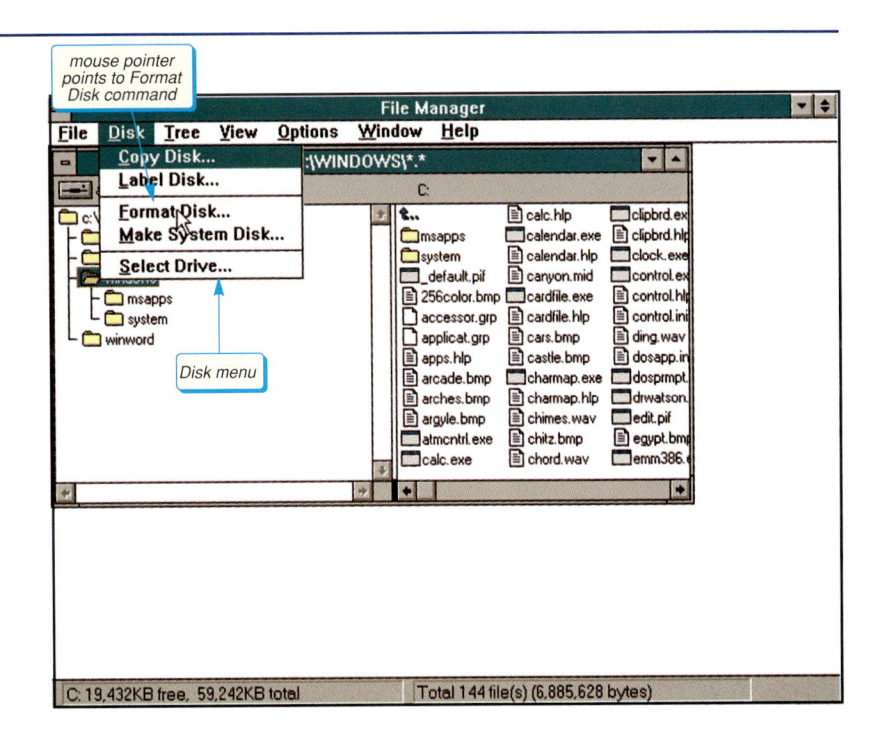

FIGURE 2-4

WIN52 PROJECT 2 DISK AND FILE MANAGEMENT

STEP 3 ▶

Choose the Format Disk command from the Disk menu, and then point to the OK button.

Windows opens the Format Disk dialog box (Figure 2-5). The current selections in the Disk In and Capacity boxes are Drive A: and 1.44 MB, respectively. With these selections, the diskette in drive A will be formatted with a capacity of 1.44MB. The Options list box is not required to format a diskette in this project. The mouse pointer points to the OK button.

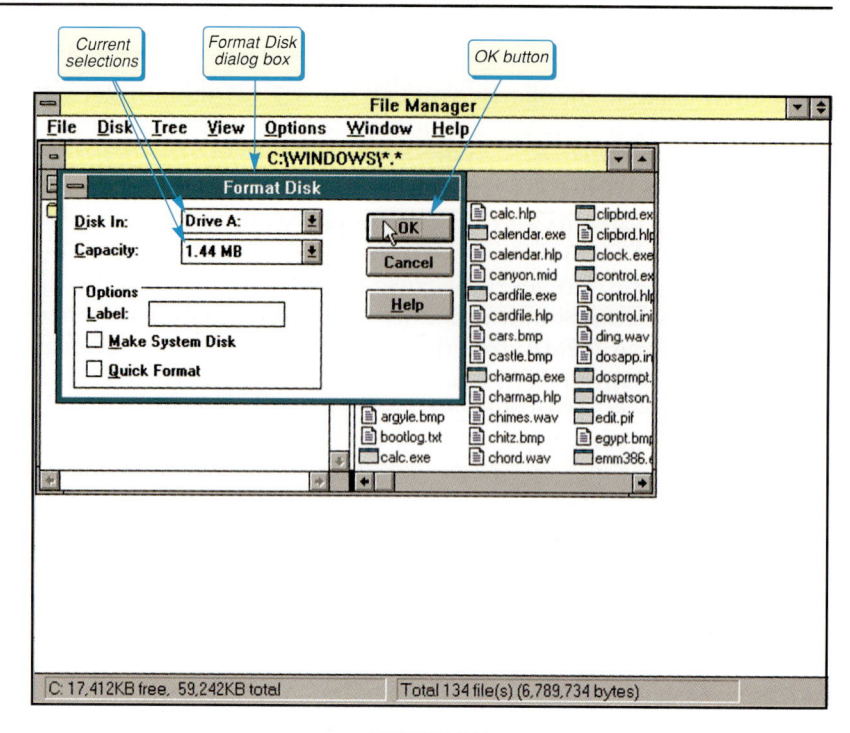

FIGURE 2-5

STEP 4 ▶

Choose the OK button by clicking the left mouse button, and then point to the Yes button.

Windows opens the Confirm Format Disk dialog box (Figure 2-6). This dialog box reminds you that if you continue, Windows will erase all data on the diskette in drive A. The mouse pointer points to the Yes button.

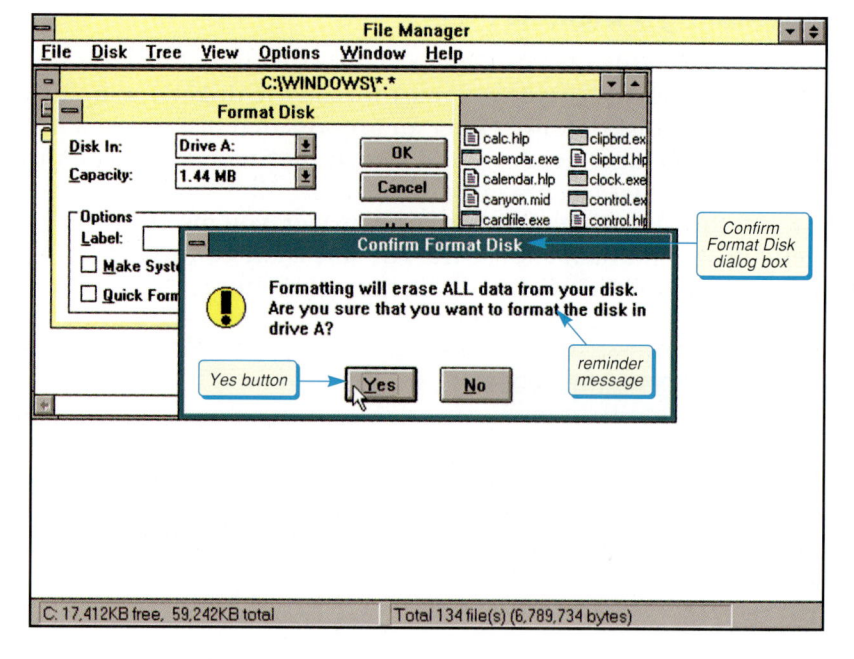

FIGURE 2-6

STEP 5 ▶

Choose the Yes button by clicking the left mouse button.

Windows opens the Formatting Disk dialog box (Figure 2-7). As the formatting process progresses, a value from 1 to 100 indicates what percent of the formatting process is complete. Toward the end of the formatting process, the creating root directory message replaces the 1% completed message to indicate Windows is creating the root directory on the diskette. The formatting process takes approximately two minutes.

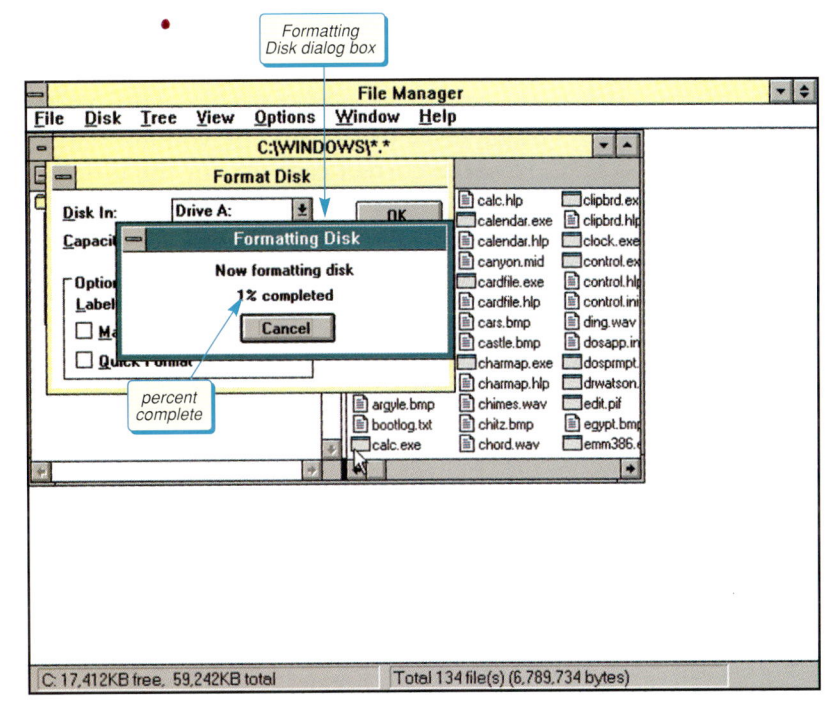

FIGURE 2-7

When the formatting process is complete, Windows opens the Format Complete dialog box (Figure 2-8). The dialog box contains the total disk space (1,457,664 bytes) and available disk space (1,457,664 bytes) of the newly formatted diskette. The values for the total disk space and available disk space in the Format Complete dialog box may be different for your computer.

STEP 6 ▶

Choose the No button by pointing to the No button, and then clicking the left mouse button.

Windows closes the Format Disk and Format Complete dialog boxes.

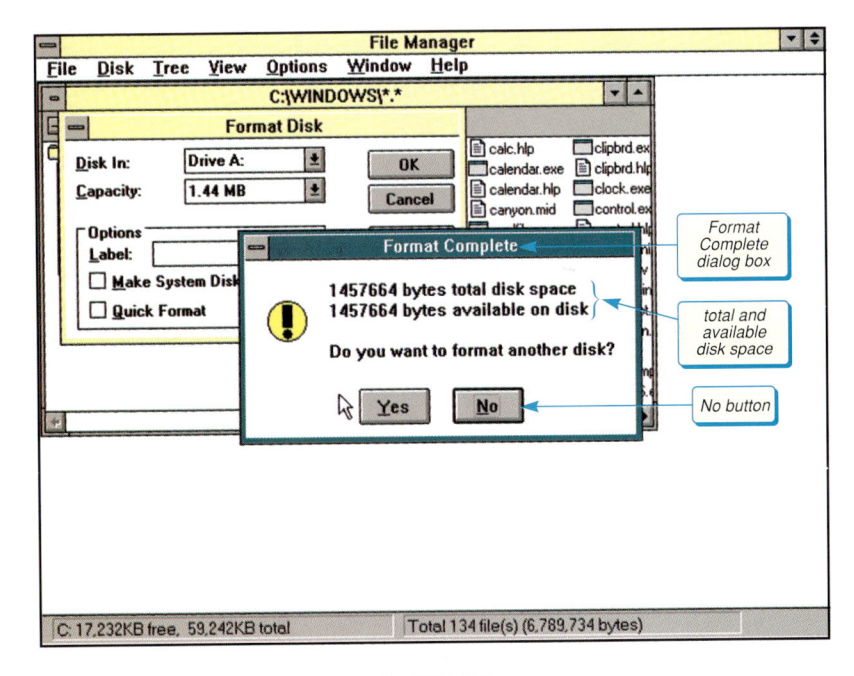

FIGURE 2-8

Correcting Errors Encountered While Formatting a Diskette

When you try to format a diskette but forget to insert a diskette into the diskette drive or the diskette you inserted is write-protected, damaged, or does not have the correct capacity for the diskette drive, Windows opens the Format Disk Error dialog box shown in Figure 2-9. The dialog box contains an error message (Cannot format disk.), a suggested action (Make sure the disk is in the drive and not write-protected, damaged, or of wrong density rating.), and the OK button. To format a diskette after forgetting to insert the diskette into the diskette drive, insert the diskette into the diskette drive, choose the OK button, and format the diskette.

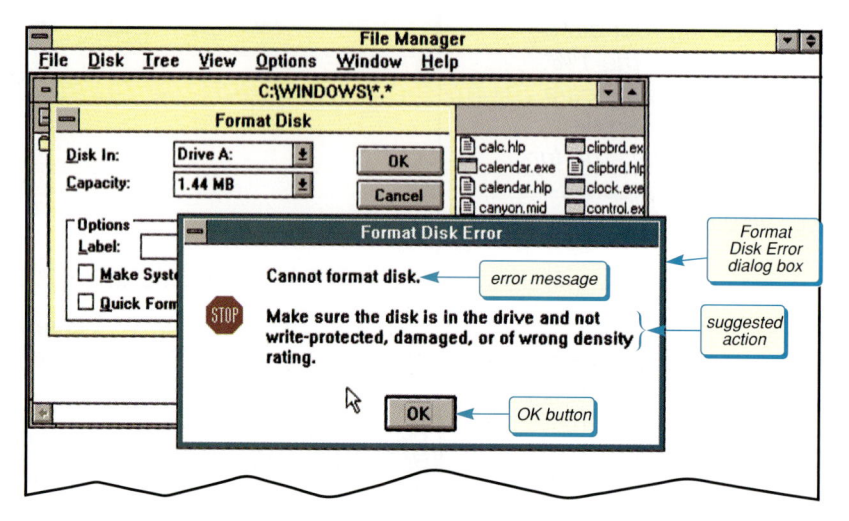

FIGURE 2-9

If the same dialog box opens after inserting a diskette into drive A, remove the diskette and determine if the diskette is write-protected, not the correct capacity for the diskette drive, or damaged. If the diskette is write-protected, remove the write-protection from the diskette, choose the OK button and format the diskette. If the diskette is not write-protected, check the diskette to determine if the diskette is the same capacity as the diskette drive. If it is not, insert a diskette with the correct capacity into the diskette drive, choose the OK button and format the diskette. If the diskette is not write-protected and the correct capacity, throw the damaged diskette away and insert another diskette into drive A, choose the OK button, and format the new diskette.

▶ COPYING FILES TO A DISKETTE

After formatting a diskette, you can save files on the diskette or copy files to the diskette from the hard drive or another diskette. You can easily copy a single file or group of files from one directory to another directory using File Manager. When copying files, the drive and directory containing the files to be copied are called the **source drive** and **source directory**, respectively. The drive and directory to which the files are copied are called the **destination drive** and **destination directory**, respectively.

To copy a file, select the filename in the contents list and drag the highlighted filename to the destination drive icon or destination directory icon. Groups of files are copied in a similar fashion. You select the filenames in the contents list and drag the highlighted group of filenames to the destination drive or destination directory icon. In this project, you will copy a group of files consisting of the ARCADE.BMP, CARS.BMP, and EGYPT.BMP files from the WINDOWS subdirectory of drive C to the root directory of the diskette that you formatted earlier in this project. Before copying the files, maximize the directory window to make it easier to view the contents of the window.

Maximizing the Directory Window

To enlarge the C:\WINDOWS*.* window, click the Maximize button on the right side of the directory window title bar. When you maximize a directory window, the window fills the File Manager window.

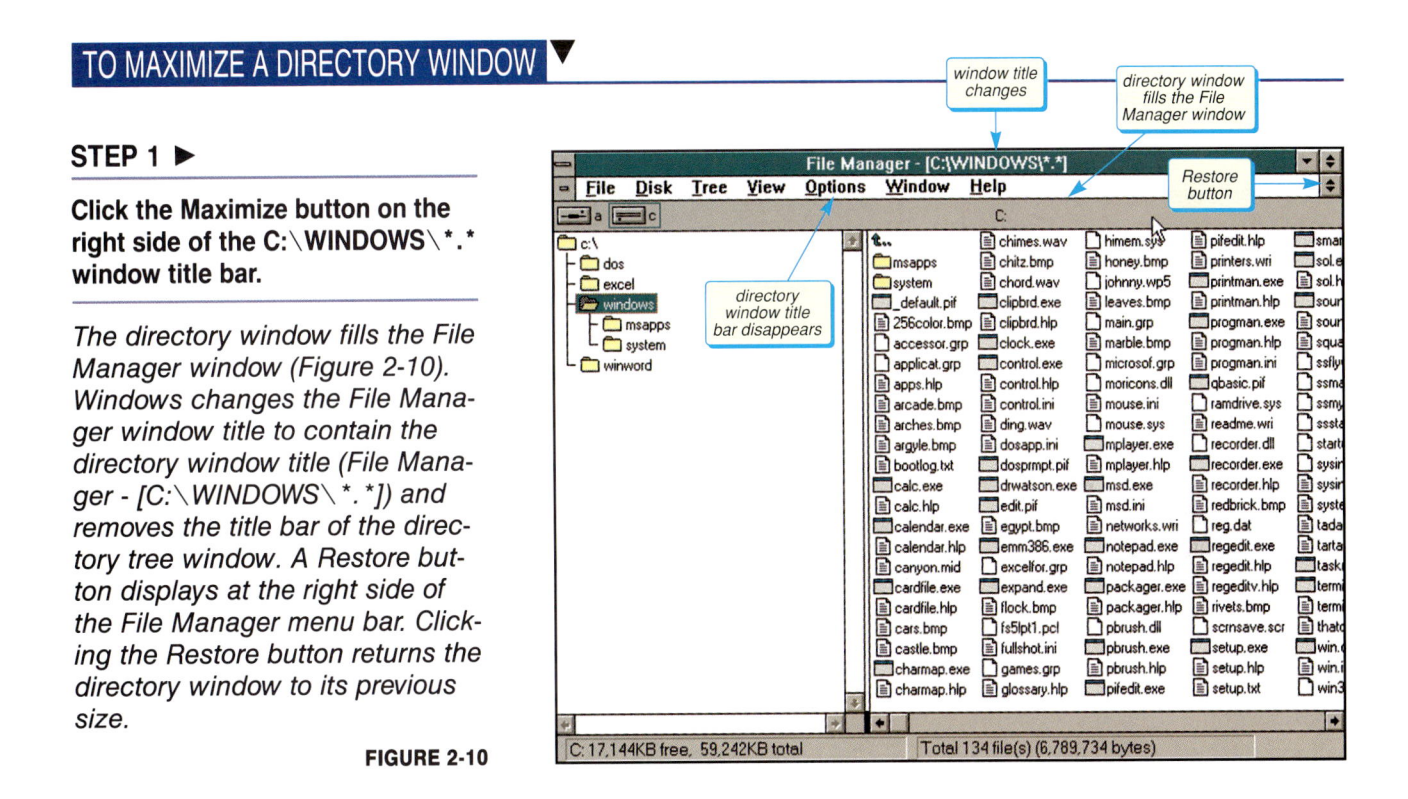

TO MAXIMIZE A DIRECTORY WINDOW

STEP 1 ▶

Click the Maximize button on the right side of the C:\WINDOWS*.* window title bar.

The directory window fills the File Manager window (Figure 2-10). Windows changes the File Manager window title to contain the directory window title (File Manager - [C:\WINDOWS*.]) and removes the title bar of the directory tree window. A Restore button displays at the right side of the File Manager menu bar. Clicking the Restore button returns the directory window to its previous size.*

FIGURE 2-10

Selecting a Group of Files

Before copying a group of files, you must select (highlight) each file in the contents list. You select the first file in a group of files by pointing to its icon or filename and clicking the left mouse button. You select the remaining files in the group by pointing to each file icon or filename, holding down the CTRL key, clicking the left mouse button, and releasing the CTRL key. The steps on the following pages show how to select the group of files consisting of the ARCADE.BMP, CARS.BMP, and EGYPT.BMP files.

TO SELECT A GROUP OF FILES

STEP 1 ▶

Point to the ARCADE.BMP filename in the contents list (Figure 2-11).

FIGURE 2-11

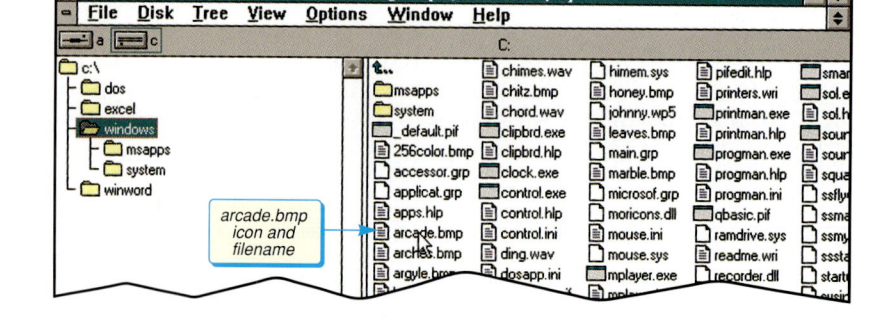

STEP 2 ▶

Select the ARCADE.BMP file by clicking the left mouse button, and then point to the CARS.BMP filename.

When you select the first file, the highlight on the current directory (WINDOWS) in the directory tree changes to a rectangular box (Figure 2-12). The ARCADE.BMP entry is highlighted, and the mouse pointer points to the CARS.BMP filename.

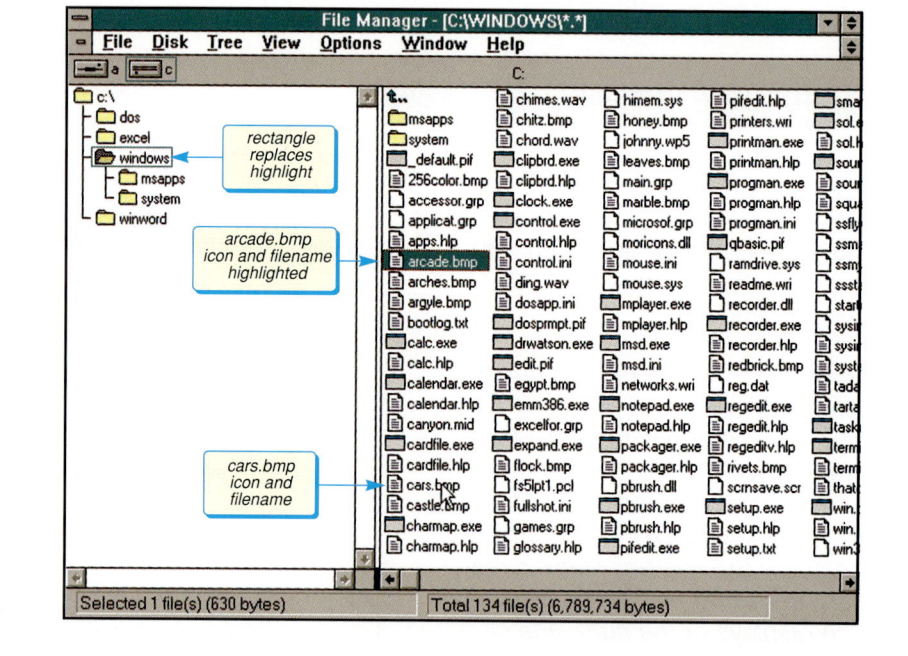

FIGURE 2-12

STEP 3 ▶

Hold down the CTRL key, click the left mouse button, release the CTRL key, and then point to the EGYPT.BMP filename.

Two files, ARCADE.BMP and CARS.BMP are highlighted (Figure 2-13). The mouse pointer points to the EGYPT.BMP filename.

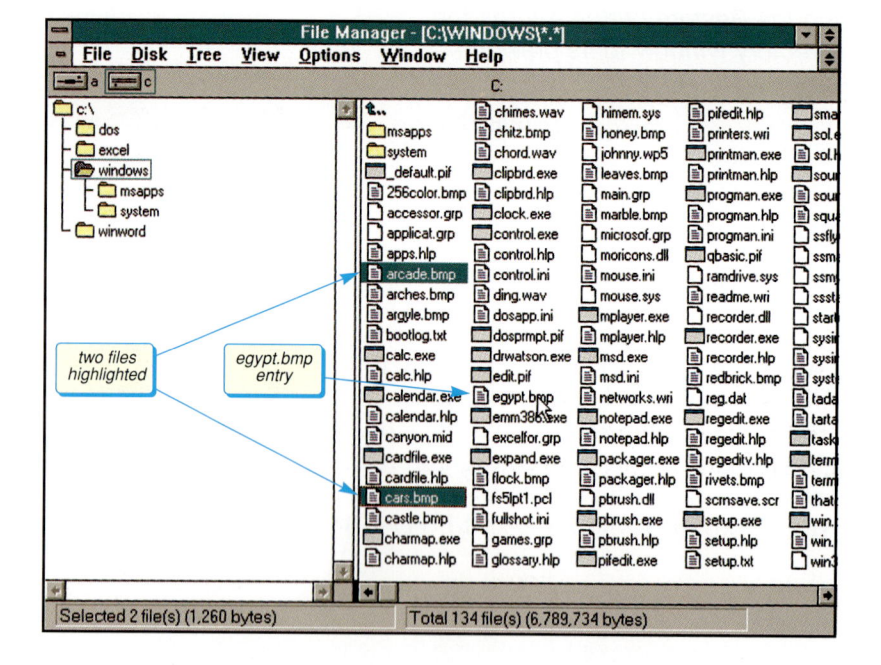

FIGURE 2-13

COPYING FILES TO A DISKETTE WIN57

STEP 4 ▶

Hold down the CTRL key, click the left mouse button, and then release the CTRL key.

The group of files consisting of the ARCADE.BMP, CARS.BMP, and EGYPT.BMP files is highlighted (Figure 2-14).

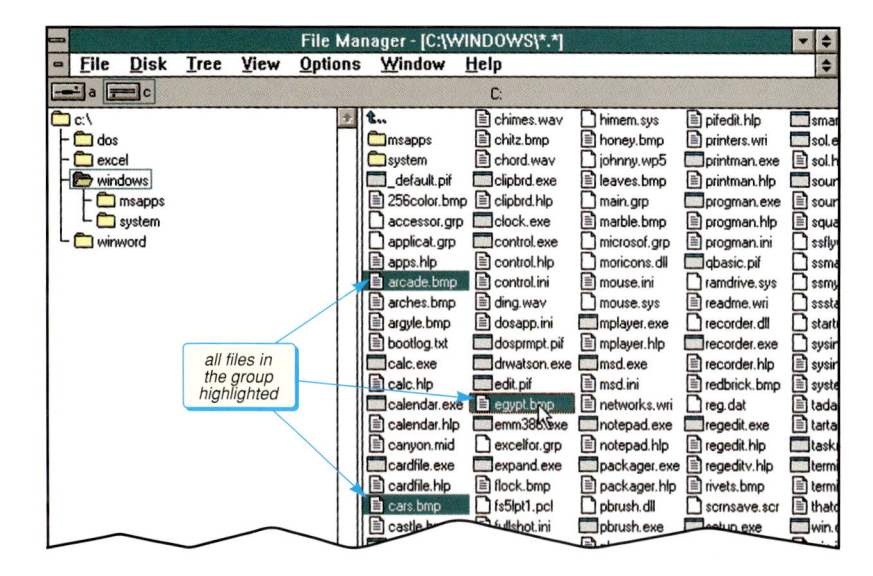

FIGURE 2-14

The ARCADE.BMP, CARS,BMP, and EGYPT.BMP files in Figure 2-14 are not located next to each other (sequentially) in the contents list. To select this group of files you selected the first file by pointing to its filename and clicking the left mouse button. Then, you selected each of the other files by pointing to their filenames, holding down the CTRL key, and clicking the left mouse button. If a group of files is located sequentially in the contents list, you select the group by pointing to the first filename in the list and clicking the left mouse button, and then hold down the SHIFT key, point to the last filename in the group and click the left mouse button.

Copying a Group of Files

After selecting each file in the group, insert the formatted diskette into drive A, and then copy the files to drive A by pointing to any highlighted filename and dragging the filename to the drive A icon.

TO COPY A GROUP OF FILES ▼

STEP 1

Verify that the formatted diskette is in drive A.

STEP 2 ▶

Point to the highlighted ARCADE.BMP entry (Figure 2-15).

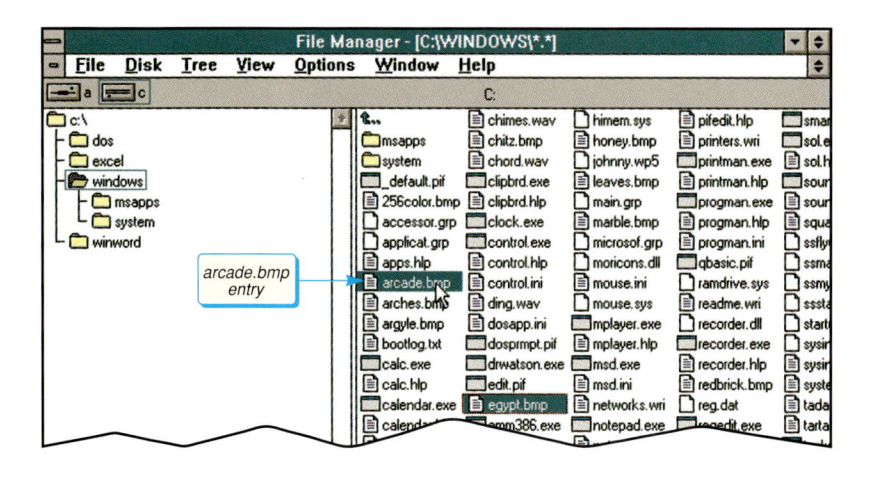

FIGURE 2-15

WIN58   PROJECT 2   DISK AND FILE MANAGEMENT

STEP 3 ▶

Drag the ARCADE.BMP filename over to the drive A icon.

As you drag the entry, the mouse pointer changes to an outline of a group of documents (📄) (Figure 2-16). The outline contains a plus sign to indicate the group of files is being copied, not moved.

FIGURE 2-16

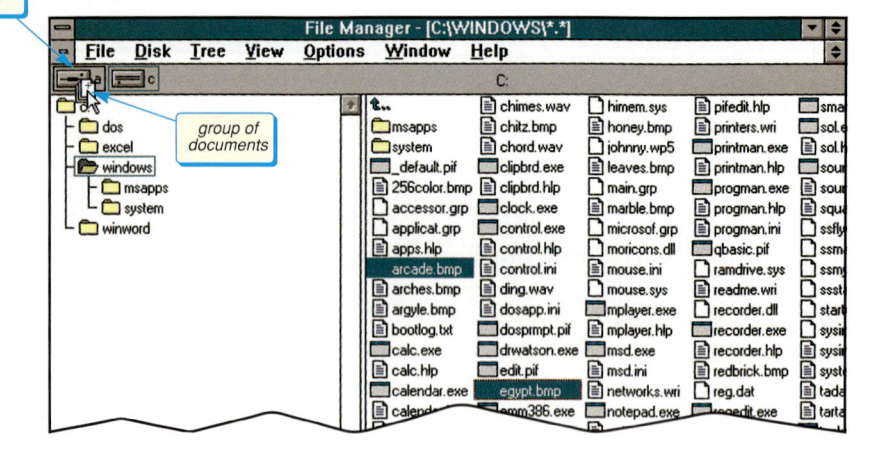

STEP 4 ▶

Release the mouse button, and then point to the Yes button.

Windows opens the Confirm Mouse Operation dialog box (Figure 2-17). The dialog box opens to confirm that you want to copy the files to the root directory of drive A (A:\). The highlight over the CARS.BMP entry is replaced with a dashed rectangular box. The mouse pointer points to the Yes button.

FIGURE 2-17

STEP 5 ▶

Choose the Yes button by clicking the left mouse button.

Windows opens the Copying dialog box, and the dialog box remains on the screen while Windows copies each file to the diskette in drive A (Figure 2-18). The dialog box in Figure 2-18 indicates the EGYPT.BMP file is currently being copied.

FIGURE 2-18

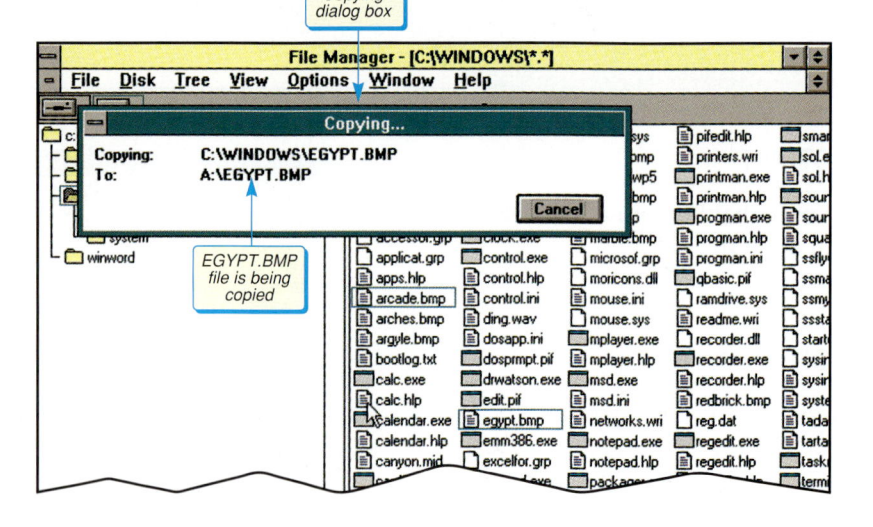

Correcting Errors Encountered While Copying Files

When you try to copy a file to an unformatted diskette, Windows opens the Error Copying File dialog box illustrated in Figure 2-19. The dialog box contains an error message (The disk in drive A is not formatted.), a question (Do you want to format it now?), and the Yes and No buttons. To continue the copy operation, format the diskette by choosing the Yes button. To cancel the copy operation, choose the No button.

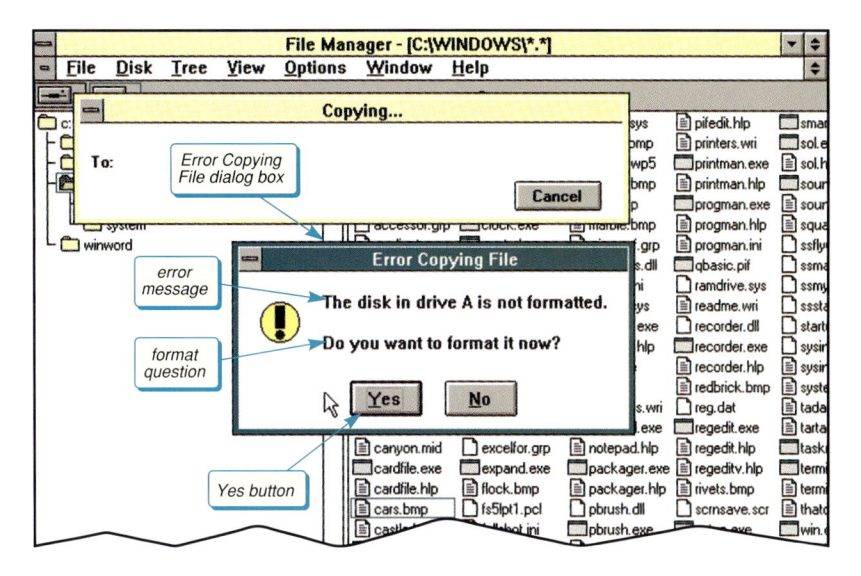

FIGURE 2-19

When you try to copy a file to a diskette but forget to insert a diskette into the diskette drive, Windows opens the Error Copying File dialog box shown in Figure 2-20. The dialog box contains an error message (There is no disk in drive A.), a suggested action (Insert a disk, and then try again.), and the Retry and Cancel buttons. To continue the copy operation, insert a diskette into drive A, and then choose the Retry button.

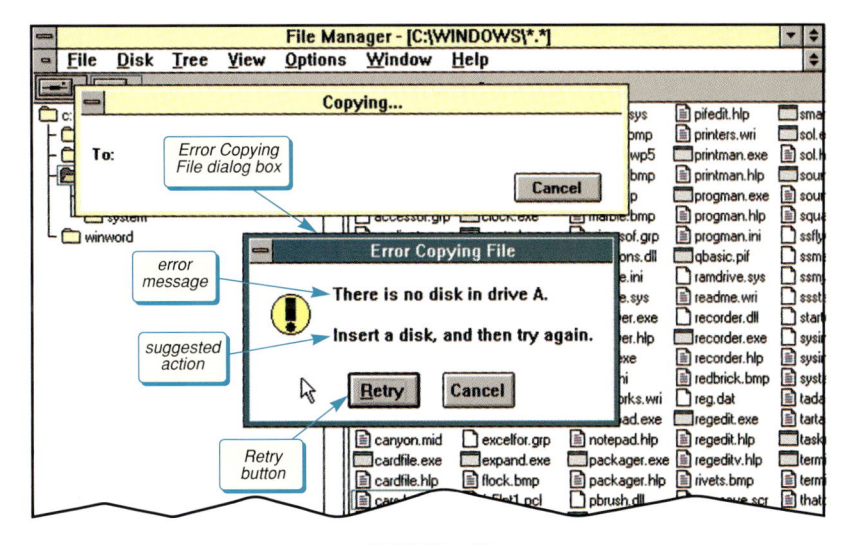

FIGURE 2-20

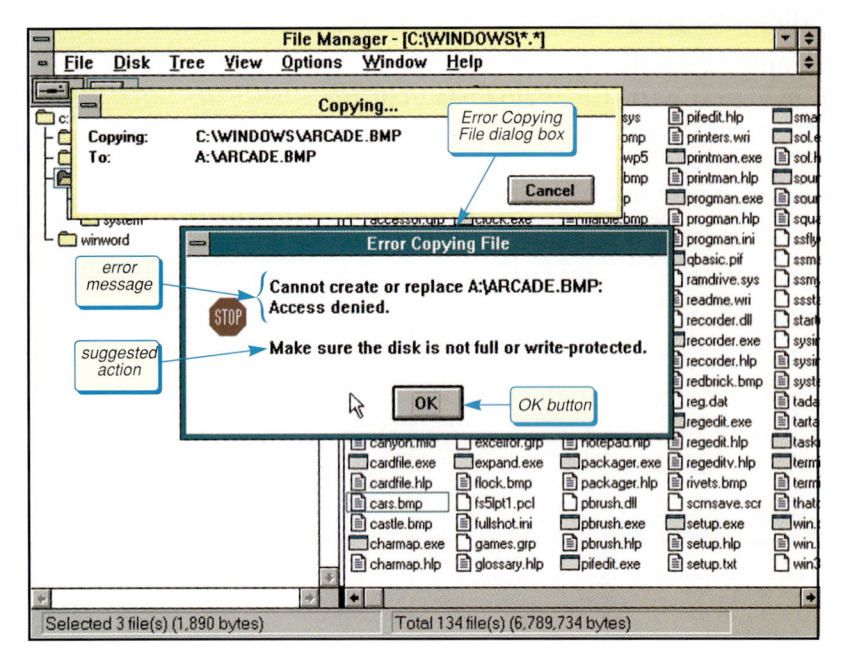

FIGURE 2-21

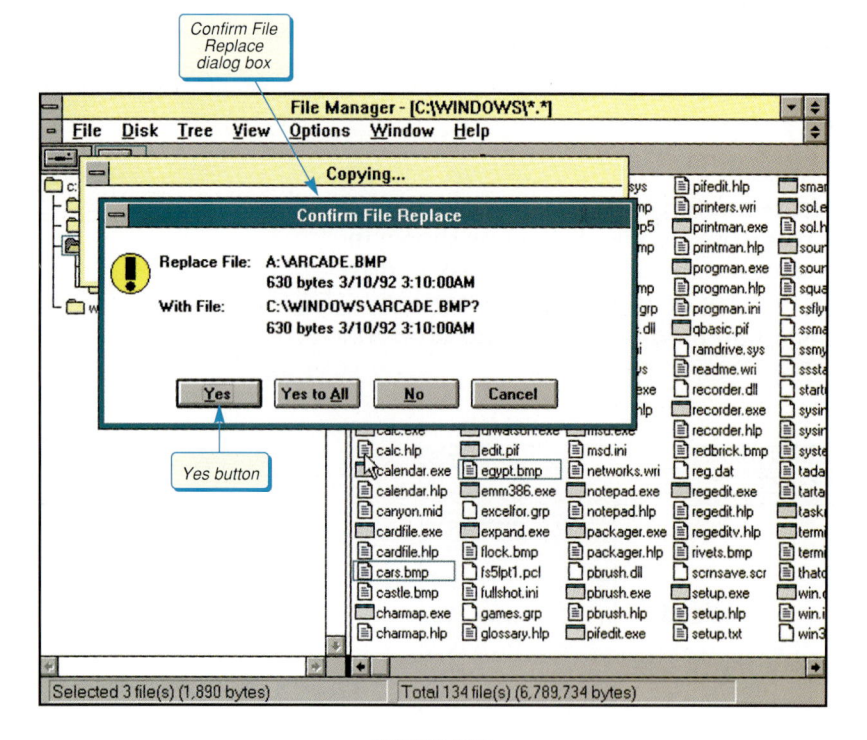

FIGURE 2-22

If you try to copy a file to a diskette that does not have enough room for the file, or you have inserted a write-protected diskette into the diskette drive, Windows opens the Error Copying File dialog box in Figure 2-21. The dialog box contains an error message (Cannot create or replace A:\ARCADE.BMP: Access denied.), a suggested action (Make sure the disk is not full or write-protected.), and the OK button. To continue with the copy operation, first remove the diskette from the diskette drive. Next, determine if the diskette is write-protected. If it is, remove the write-protection from the diskette, insert the diskette into the diskette drive, and then choose the OK button. If you determine the diskette is not write-protected, insert a diskette that is not full into the diskette drive, and then choose the OK button.

Replacing a File on Disk

If you try to copy a file to a diskette that already contains a file with the same filename and extension, Windows opens the Confirm File Replace dialog box (Figure 2-22). The Confirm File Replace dialog box contains information about the file being replaced (A:\ARCADE.BMP), the file being copied (C:\WINDOWS\ARCADE.BMP), and the Yes, Yes to All, No, and Cancel buttons. If you want to replace the file, on the diskette with the file being copied, choose the Yes button. If you do not want to replace the file choose the No button. If you want to cancel the copy operation, choose the Cancel button.

COPYING FILES TO A DISKETTE   WIN61

Changing the Current Drive

After copying a group of files, you should verify the files were copied onto the correct drive and into the correct directory. To view the files on drive A, change the current drive to drive A by pointing to the drive A icon and clicking the left mouse button.

TO CHANGE THE CURRENT DRIVE ▼

STEP 1 ▶

Point to the drive A icon.

The mouse pointer points to the drive A icon and the current drive is drive C (Figure 2-23).

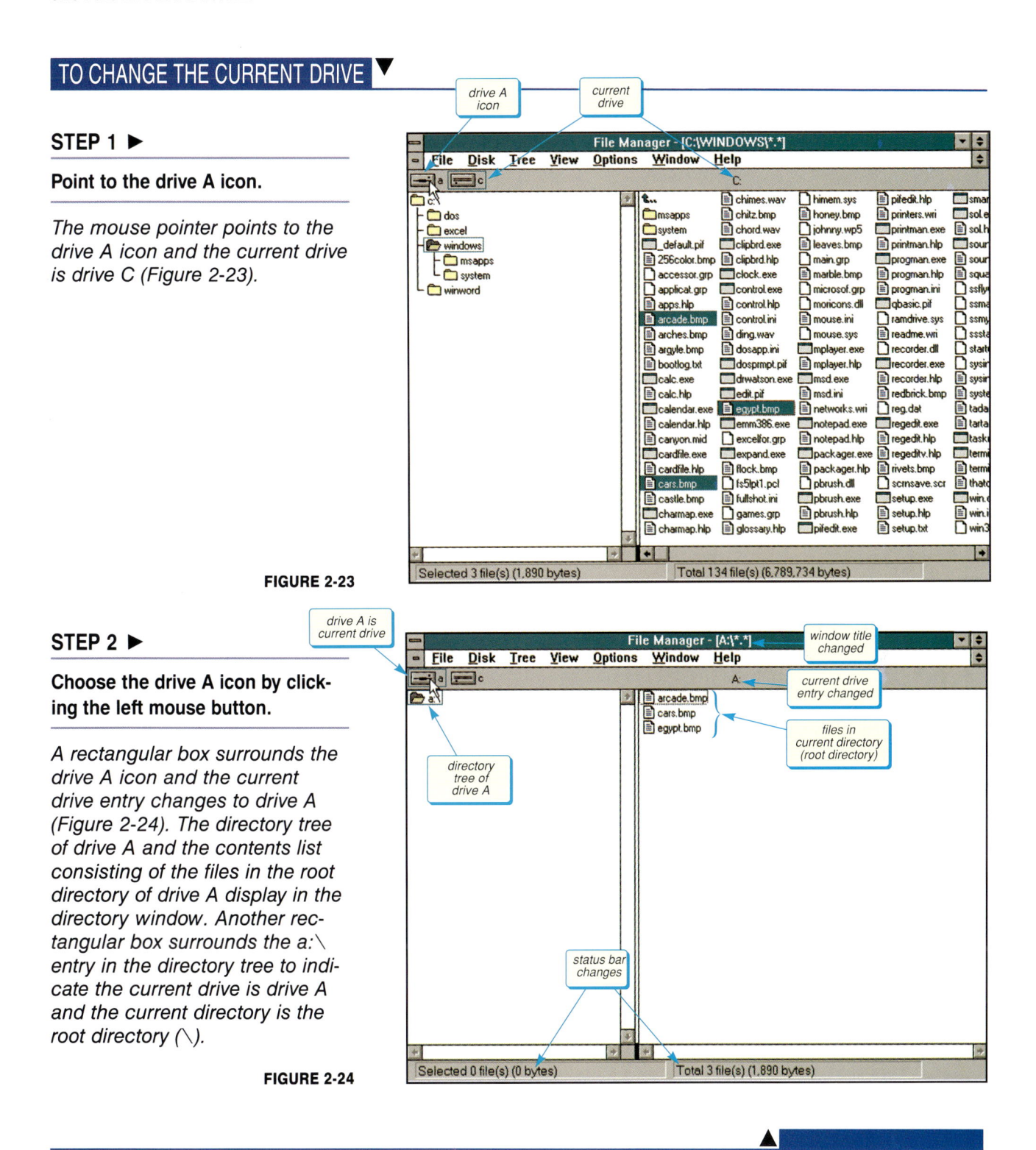

FIGURE 2-23

STEP 2 ▶

Choose the drive A icon by clicking the left mouse button.

A rectangular box surrounds the drive A icon and the current drive entry changes to drive A (Figure 2-24). The directory tree of drive A and the contents list consisting of the files in the root directory of drive A display in the directory window. Another rectangular box surrounds the a:\ entry in the directory tree to indicate the current drive is drive A and the current directory is the root directory (\).

FIGURE 2-24

Correcting Errors Encountered While Changing the Current Drive

When you try to change the current drive before inserting a diskette into the diskette drive, Windows opens the Error Selecting Drive dialog box illustrated in Figure 2-25. The dialog box contains an error message (There is no disk in drive A.), a suggested action (Insert a disk, and then try again.), and the Retry and Cancel buttons. To change the current drive after forgetting to insert a diskette into drive A, insert a diskette into drive A, and choose the Retry button.

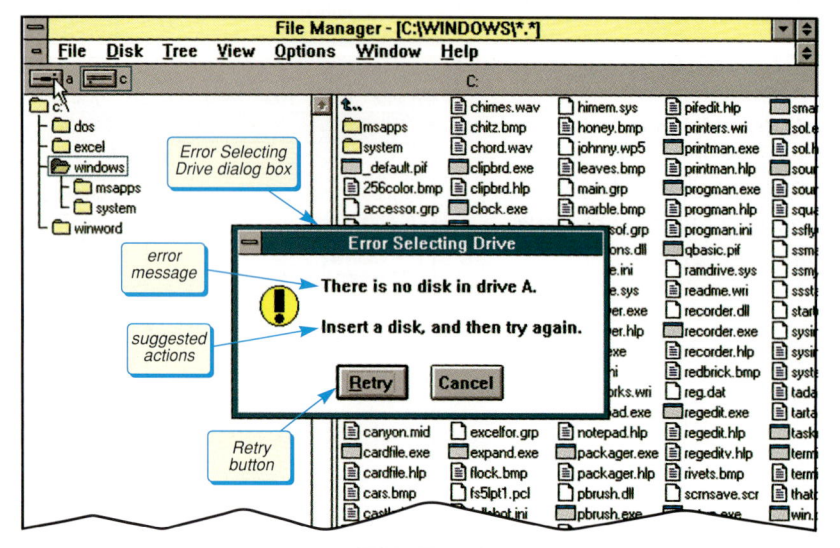

FIGURE 2-25

When you try to change the current drive and there is an unformatted diskette in the diskette drive, Windows opens the Error Selecting Drive dialog box shown in Figure 2-26. The dialog box contains an error message (The disk in drive A is not formatted.), a suggested action (Do you want to format it now?), and the Yes and No buttons. To change the current drive after inserting an unformatted diskette into drive A, choose the Yes button to format the diskette and change the current drive. Choose the No button to cancel the change.

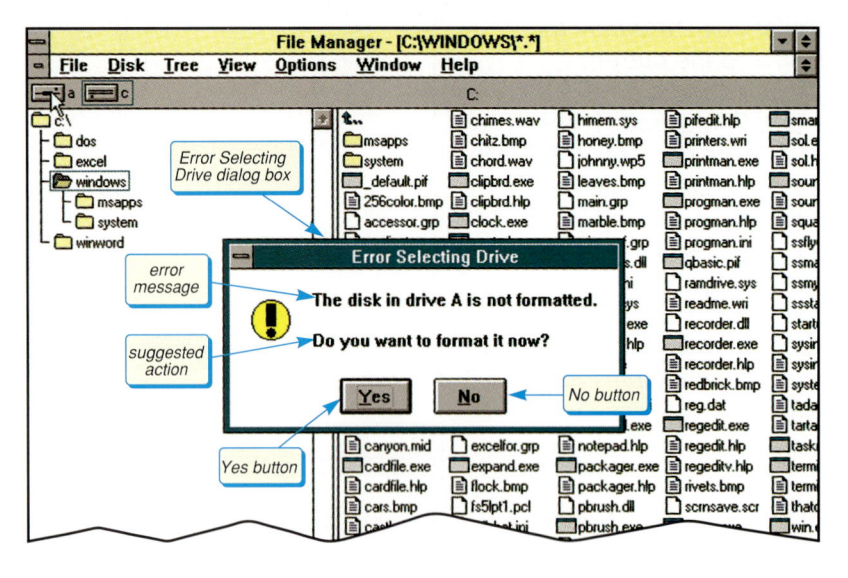

FIGURE 2-26

▶ Renaming a File

Sometimes you may want to rename a file by changing its name or filename extension. You change the name or extension of a file by selecting the filename in the contents list, choosing the **Rename command** from the File menu, entering the new filename, and choosing the OK button. In this project, you will change the name of the CARS.BMP file on the diskette in drive A to AUTOS.BMP.

TO RENAME A FILE ▼

STEP 1 ▶

Select the CARS.BMP entry by clicking the CARS.BMP filename in the contents list.

The CARS.BMP entry is highlighted (Figure 2-27).

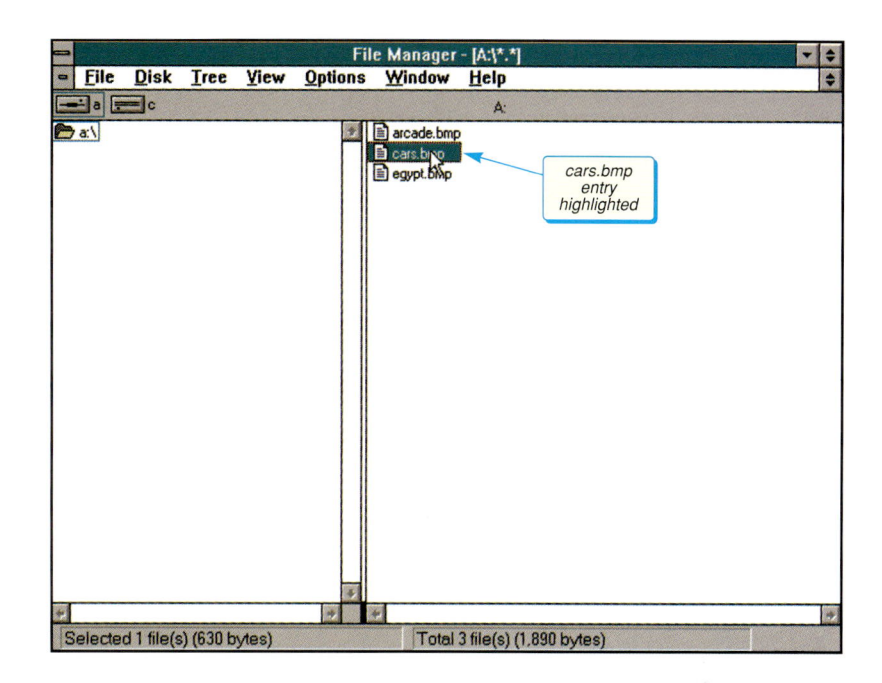

FIGURE 2-27

STEP 2 ▶

Select the File menu, and then point to the Rename command.

Windows opens the File menu (Figure 2-28). The mouse pointer points to the Rename command.

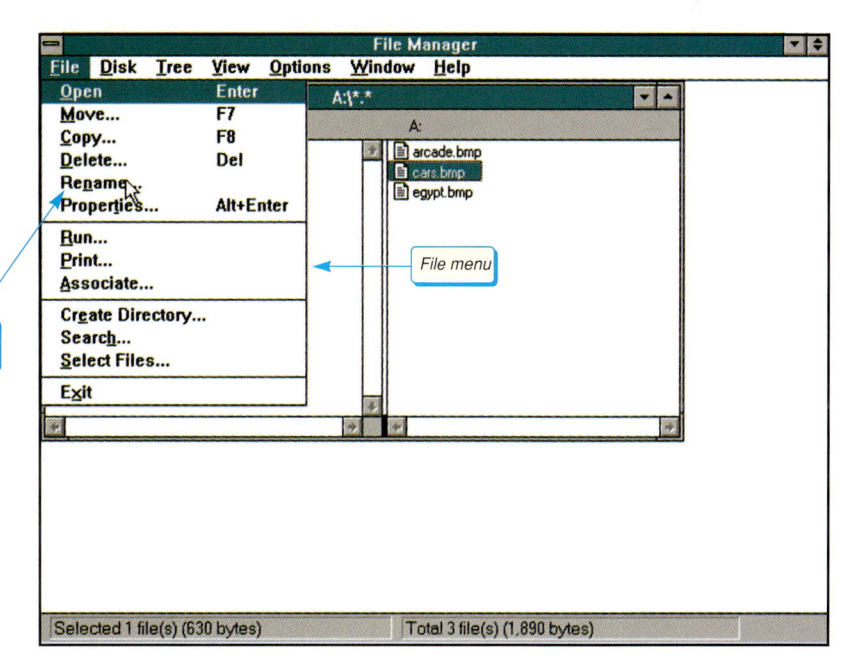

FIGURE 2-28

STEP 3 ▶

Choose the Rename command from the File menu by clicking the left mouse button.

Windows opens the Rename dialog box (Figure 2-29). The dialog box contains the Current Directory : A:\ message, the From and To text boxes, and the OK, Cancel, and Help buttons. The From text box contains the CARS.BMP filename and To text box contains an insertion point.

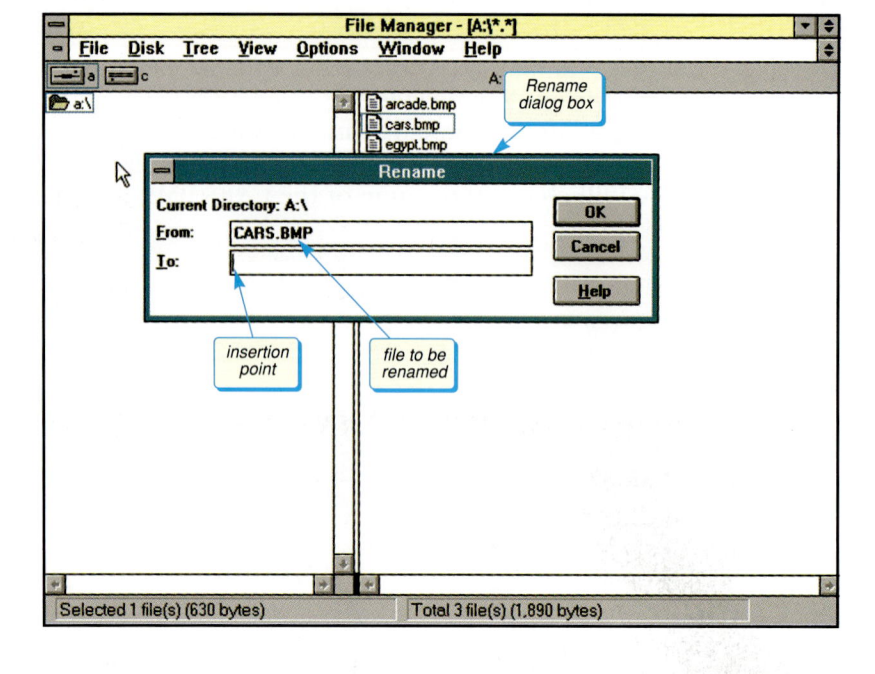

FIGURE 2-29

STEP 4 ▶

Type `autos.bmp` in the To text box, and then point to the OK button.

The To text box contains the AUTOS.BMP filename and the mouse points to the OK button (Figure 2-30).

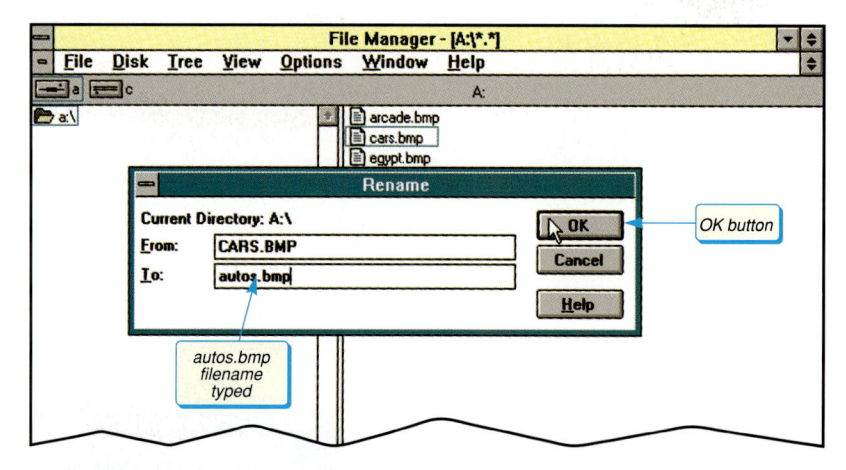

FIGURE 2-30

STEP 5 ▶

Choose the OK button by clicking the left mouse button.

The filename in the cars.bmp entry changes to autos.bmp (Figure 2-31).

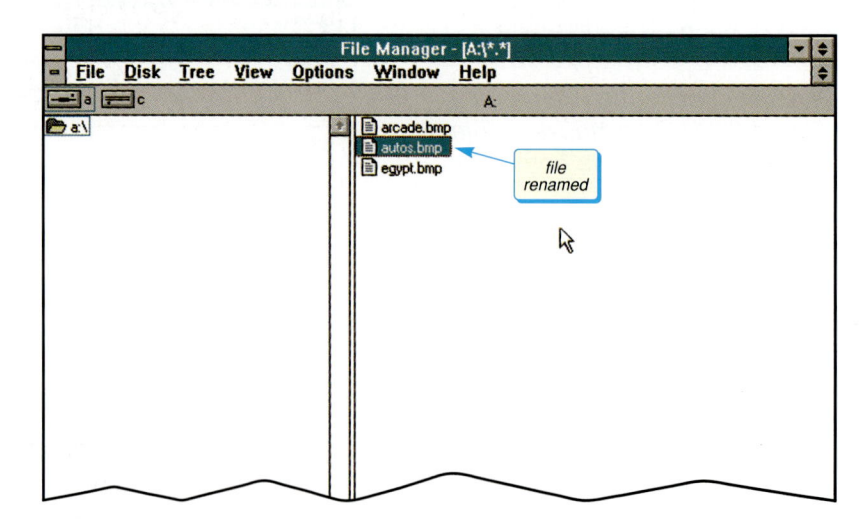

FIGURE 2-31

▶ Deleting a File

When you no longer need a file, you can delete it by selecting the filename in the contents list, choosing the **Delete command** from the File menu, choosing the OK button, and then choosing the Yes button. In this project, you will delete the EGYPT.BMP file from the diskette in drive A.

TO DELETE A FILE ▼

STEP 1 ▶

Select the EGYPT.BMP entry.

The EGYPT.BMP entry is highlighted (Figure 2-32).

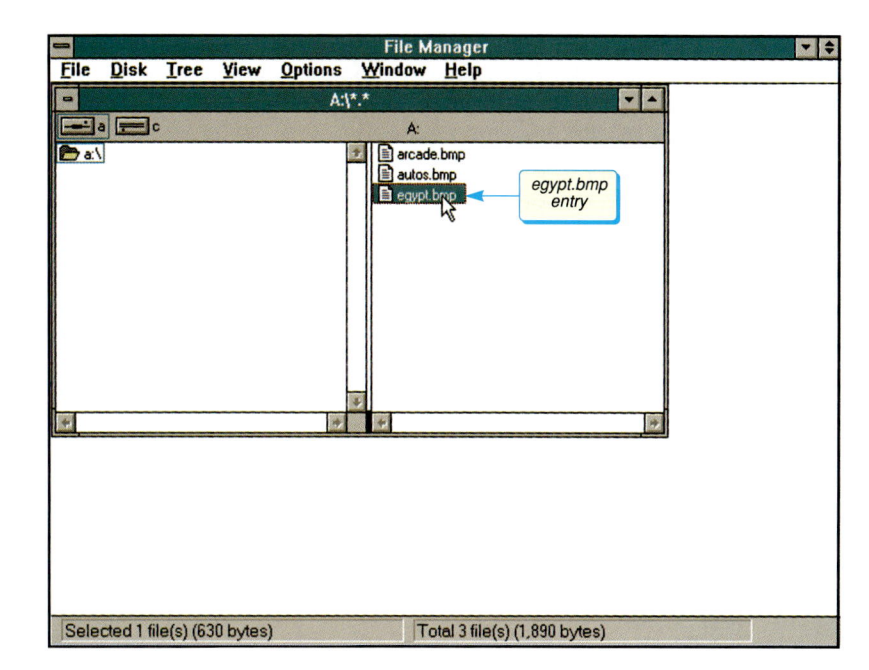

FIGURE 2-32

STEP 2 ▶

Select the File menu from the menu bar, and then point to the Delete command.

Windows opens the File menu (Figure 2-33). The mouse pointer points to the Delete command.

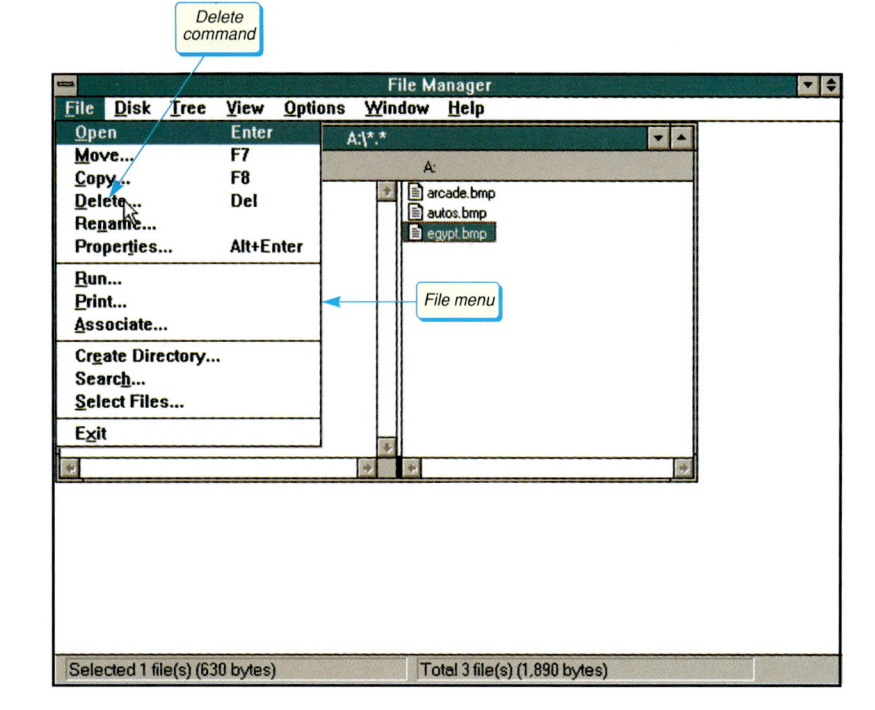

FIGURE 2-33

STEP 3 ▶

Choose the Delete command from the File menu by clicking the left mouse button, and then point to the OK button.

Windows opens the Delete dialog box (Figure 2-34). The dialog box contains the Current Directory: A:\ message, Delete text box, and the OK, Cancel, and Help buttons. The Delete text box contains the name of the file to be deleted (EGYPT.BMP), and the mouse pointer points to the OK button.

FIGURE 2-34

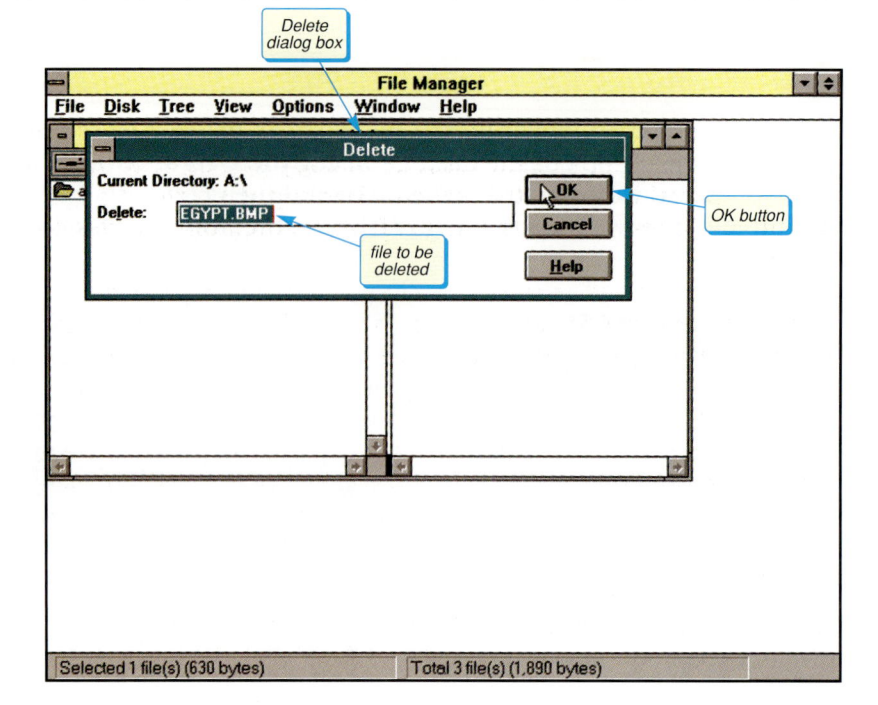

STEP 4 ▶

Choose the OK button by clicking the left mouse button, and then point to the Yes button.

Windows opens the Confirm File Delete dialog box (Figure 2-35). The dialog box contains the Delete File message and the path and filename of the file to delete (A:\EGYPT.BMP). The mouse pointer points to the Yes button.

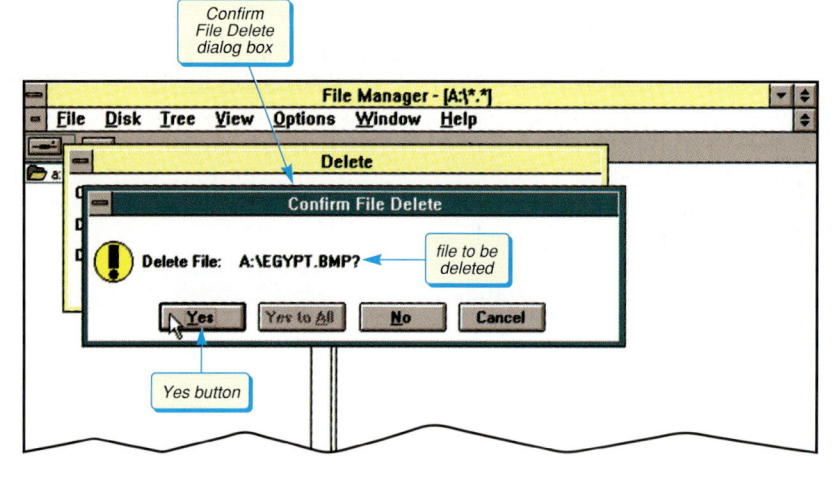

FIGURE 2-35

STEP 5 ▶

Choose the Yes button by clicking the left mouse button.

Windows deletes the EGYPT.BMP file from the diskette on drive A, removes the EGYPT.BMP entry from the contents list, and highlights the AUTOS.BMP file (Figure 2-36).

STEP 6

Remove the diskette from drive A.

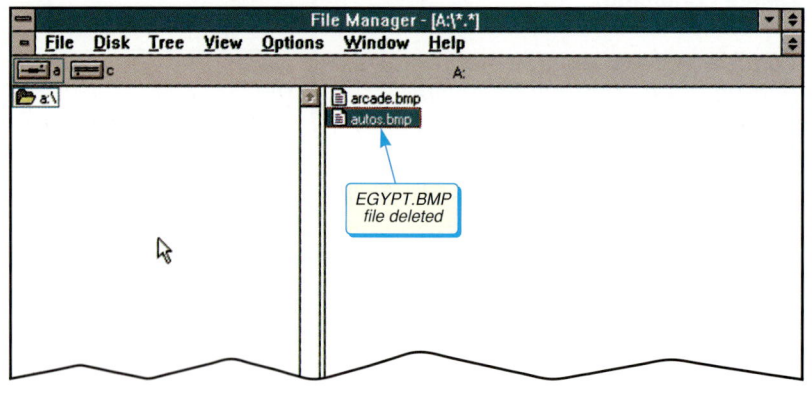

FIGURE 2-36

▶ Creating a Backup Diskette

To prevent accidental loss of a file on a diskette, you should make a backup copy of the diskette. A copy of a diskette made to prevent accidental loss of data is called a **backup diskette**. Always be sure to make backup diskettes before installing software stored on diskettes onto the hard drive.

The first step in creating a backup diskette is to protect the diskette to be copied, or **source diskette**, from accidental erasure by write-protecting the diskette. After write-protecting the source diskette, choose the **Copy Disk command** from the Disk menu to copy the contents of the source diskette to another diskette, called the **destination diskette**. After copying the source diskette to the destination diskette, remove the write-protection from the source diskette and identify the destination diskette by writing a name on the paper label supplied with the diskette and affixing the label to the diskette.

In this project, you will use File Manager to create a backup diskette for a diskette labeled Business Documents. The Business Documents diskette contains valuable business documents that should be backed up to prevent accidental loss. The source diskette will be the Business Documents diskette and the destination diskette will be a formatted diskette that will later be labeled Business Documents Backup. To create a backup diskette, both the Business Documents diskette and the formatted diskette must be the same size and capacity.

File Manager copies a diskette by asking you to insert the source diskette into drive A, reading data from the source diskette into main memory, asking you to insert the destination disk, and then copying the data from main memory to the destination disk. Depending on the size of main memory on your computer, you may have to insert and remove the source and destination diskettes several times before the copy process is complete. The copy process takes about three minutes to complete.

TO COPY A DISKETTE ▼

STEP 1 ▶

Write-protect the Business Documents diskette by opening the write-protect window (Figure 2-37).

FIGURE 2-37

STEP 2 ▶

Select the Disk menu from the menu bar, and then point to the Copy Disk command.

Windows opens the Disk menu (Figure 2-38). The mouse pointer points to the Copy Disk command.

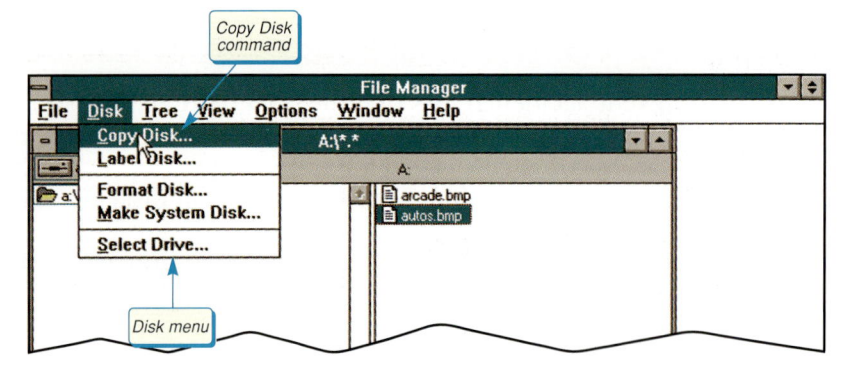

FIGURE 2-38

STEP 3 ▶

Choose the Copy Disk command from the Disk menu by clicking the left mouse button, and then point to the Yes button.

Windows opens the Confirm Copy Disk dialog box (Figure 2-39). The dialog box reminds you that the copy process will erase all data on the destination disk. The mouse pointer points to the Yes button.

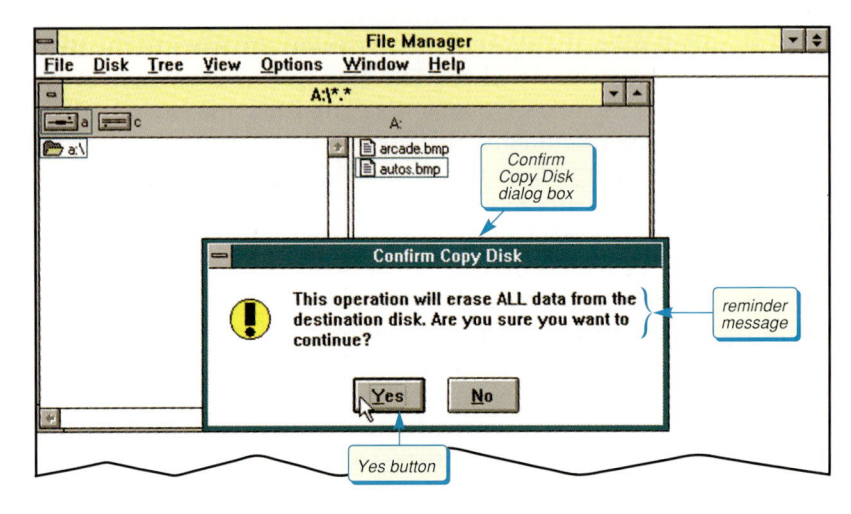

FIGURE 2-39

STEP 4 ▶

Choose the Yes button by clicking the left mouse button, and then point to the OK button.

Windows opens the Copy Disk dialog box (Figure 2-40). The dialog box contains the Insert source disk message and the mouse pointer points to the OK button.

STEP 5 ▶

Insert the source diskette, the Business Documents diskette, into drive A.

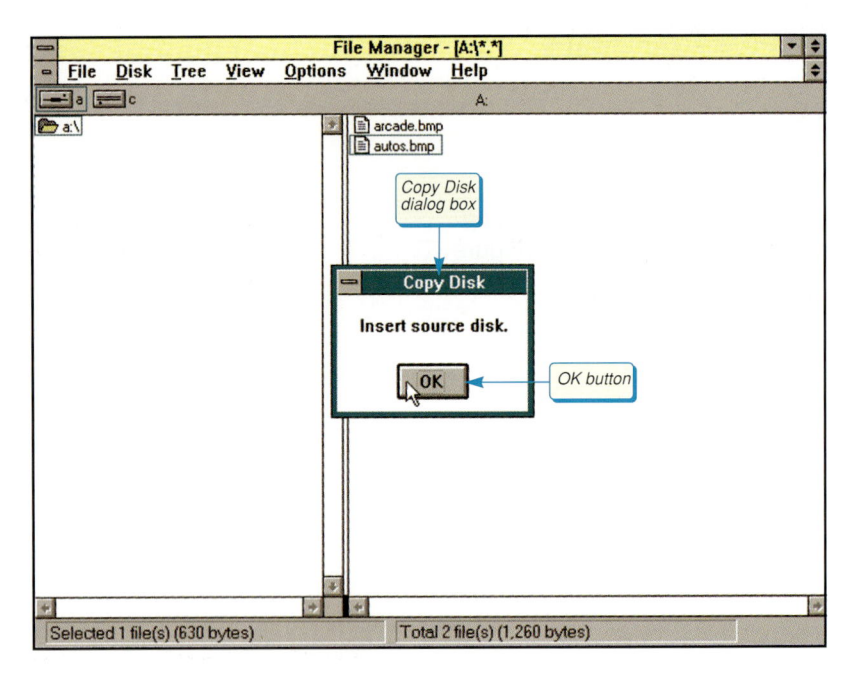

FIGURE 2-40

CREATING A BACKUP DISKETTE **WIN69**

STEP 6 ▶

Choose the OK button in the Copy Disk dialog box by clicking the left mouse button.

Windows opens the Copying Disk dialog box (Figure 2-41). The dialog box contains the messages, Now Copying disk in Drive A:. and 1% completed. As the copy process progresses, a value from 1 to 100 indicates what percent of the copy process is complete.

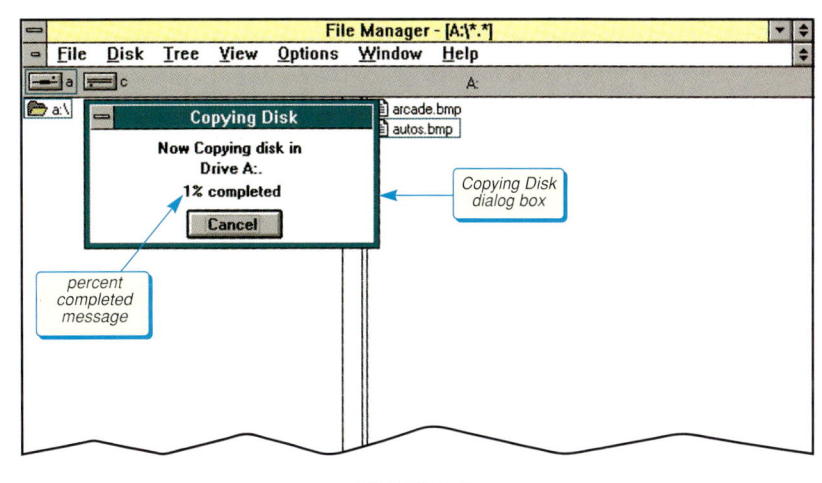

FIGURE 2-41

When as much data from the source diskette as will fit in main memory is copied to main memory, Windows opens the Copy Disk dialog box (Figure 2-42). The dialog box contains the message, Insert destination disk, and the OK button.

STEP 7 ▶

Remove the source diskette (Business Documents diskette) from drive A and insert the destination diskette (Business Documents Backup diskette) into drive A.

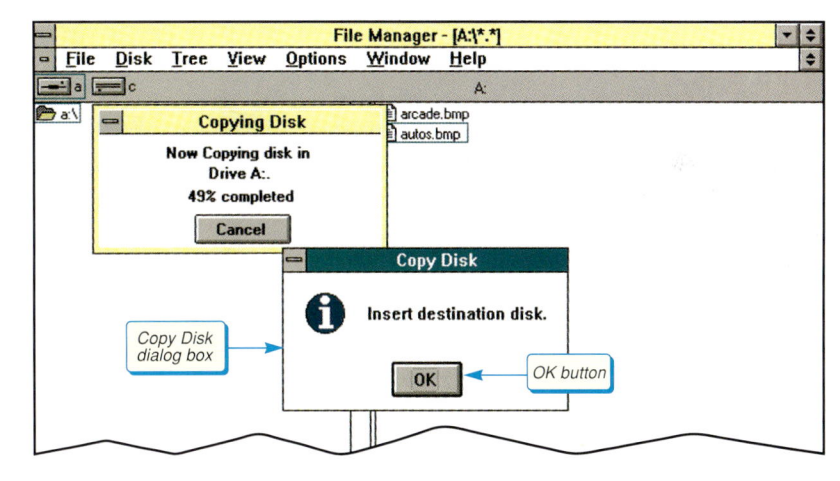

FIGURE 2-42

STEP 8 ▶

Choose the OK button from the Copy Disk dialog box.

Windows opens the Copying Disk dialog box (Figure 2-43). A value from 1 to 100 displays as the data in main memory is copied to the destination disk.

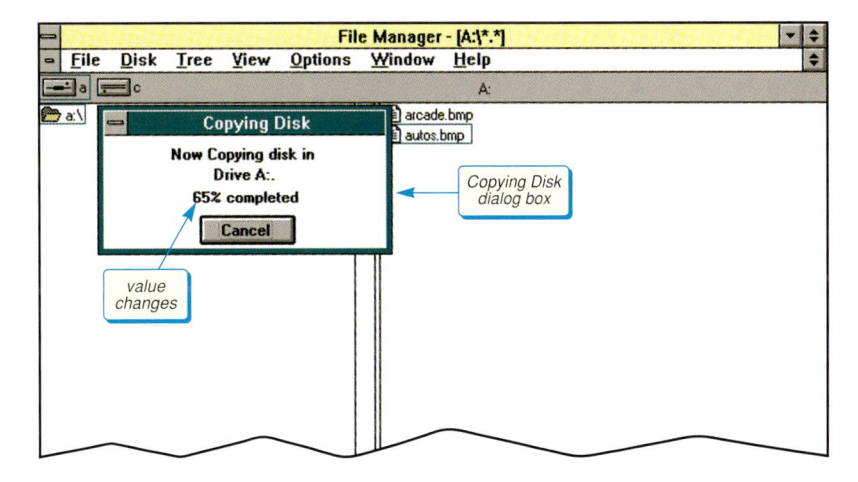

FIGURE 2-43

STEP 9 ▶

Remove the Business Documents Backup diskette from drive A and remove the write-protection from the Business Documents diskette by closing the write-protect window.

The write-protection is removed from the 3 1/2—inch Business Documents diskette (Figure 2-44).

write-protect window closed means you can write to this diskette

FIGURE 2-44

STEP 10 ▶

Identify the Business Documents Backup diskette by writing the words Business Documents Backup on the paper label supplied with the diskette and then affix the label to the diskette (Figure 2-45).

FIGURE 2-45

Depending on the size of main memory on your computer, you may have to insert and remove the source and destination diskettes several times before the copy process is complete. If prompted by Windows to insert the source diskette, remove the destination diskette (Business Documents Backup diskette) from drive A, insert the source diskette (Business Documents diskette) into drive A, and then choose the OK button. If prompted to insert the destination diskette, remove the source diskette (Business Documents diskette) from drive A, insert the destination diskette (Business Documents Backup diskette) into drive A, and then choose the OK button.

In the future if you change the contents of the Business Documents diskette, choose the Copy Disk command to copy the contents of the Business Documents diskette to the Business Documents Backup diskette. If the Business Documents diskette becomes unusable, you can format a diskette, choose the Copy Disk command to copy the contents of the Business Documents Backup diskette (source diskette) to the formatted diskette (destination diskette), label the formatted diskette, Business Documents, and use the new Business Documents diskette in place of the unusable Business Documents diskette.

Correcting Errors Encountered While Copying A Diskette

When you try to copy a disk and forget to insert the source diskette when prompted, insert an unformatted source diskette, forget to insert the destination diskette when prompted, or insert a write-protected destination diskette, Windows opens the Copy Disk Error dialog box illustrated in Figure 2-46. The dialog box contains the Unable to copy disk error message and OK button. To complete the copy process after forgetting to insert a source diskette or inserting an unformatted source diskette, choose the OK button, insert the formatted source diskette into the diskette drive, and choose the **Disk Copy command** to start over the disk copy process. To complete the copy process after forgetting to insert a destination diskette or inserting a write-protected destination diskette, choose the OK button, insert a nonwrite-protected diskette in the diskette drive, and choose the Disk Copy command to start over the disk copy.

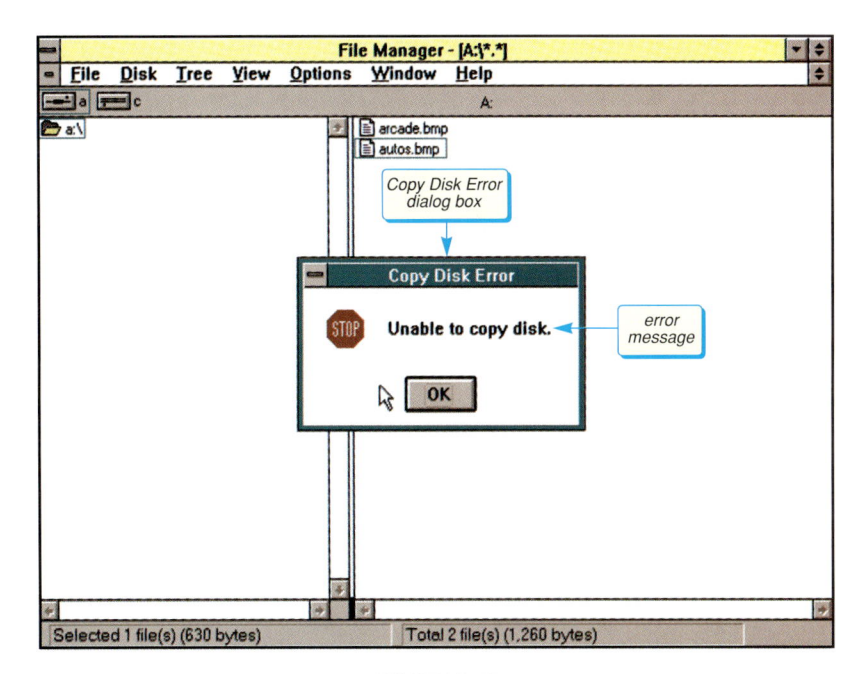

FIGURE 2-46

▶ SEARCHING FOR HELP USING ONLINE HELP

In Project 1, you obtained help about the Paintbrush application by choosing the Contents command from the Help menu of the Paintbrush window (see pages WIN32 through WIN35). You then chose a topic from a list of help topics on the screen. In addition to choosing a topic from a list of available help topics, you can use the Search feature to search for help topics. In this project, you will use the Search feature to obtain help about copying files and selecting groups of files using the keyboard.

Searching for a Help Topic

In this project, you used a mouse to select and copy a group of files. If you want to obtain information about how to select a group of files using the keyboard instead of the mouse, you can use the Search feature. A search can be performed in one of two ways. The first method allows you to select a search topic from a list of search topics. A list of help topics associated with the search topic displays. You then select a help topic from this list. To begin the search, choose the **Search for Help on command** from the Help menu.

TO SEARCH FOR A HELP TOPIC

STEP 1 ▶

Select the Help menu from the File Manager window menu bar, and then point to the Search for Help on command.

Windows opens the Help menu (Figure 2-47). The mouse pointer points to the Search for Help on command.

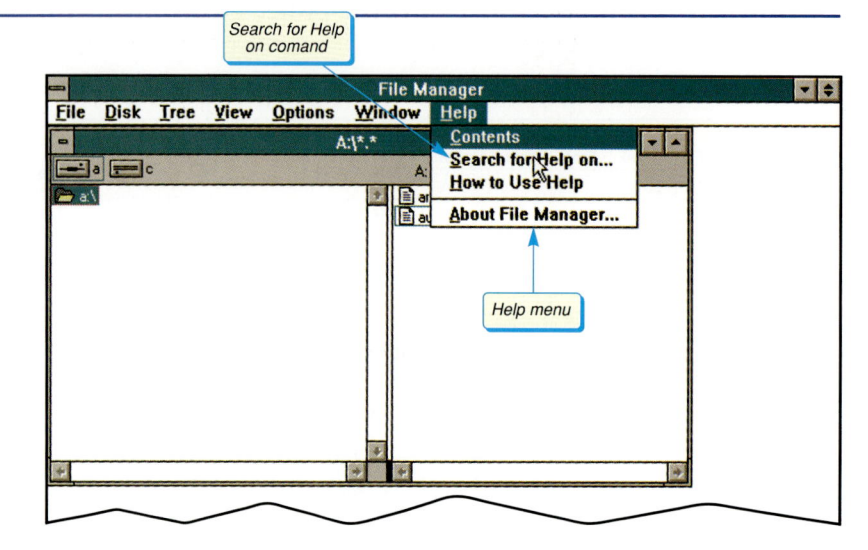

FIGURE 2-47

STEP 2 ▶

Choose the Search for Help on command from the Help menu by clicking the left mouse button.

Windows opens the Search dialog box (Figure 2-48). The dialog box consists of two areas separated by a horizontal line. The top area contains the Search For text box, Search For list box, and Cancel and Show Topics buttons. The Search For list box contains an alphabetical list of search topics. A vertical scroll bar indicates there are more search topics than appear in the list box. The Cancel button cancels the Search operation. The Show Topics button is dimmed and cannot be chosen. The bottom area of the dialog box contains the empty Help Topics list box and the dimmed Go To button.

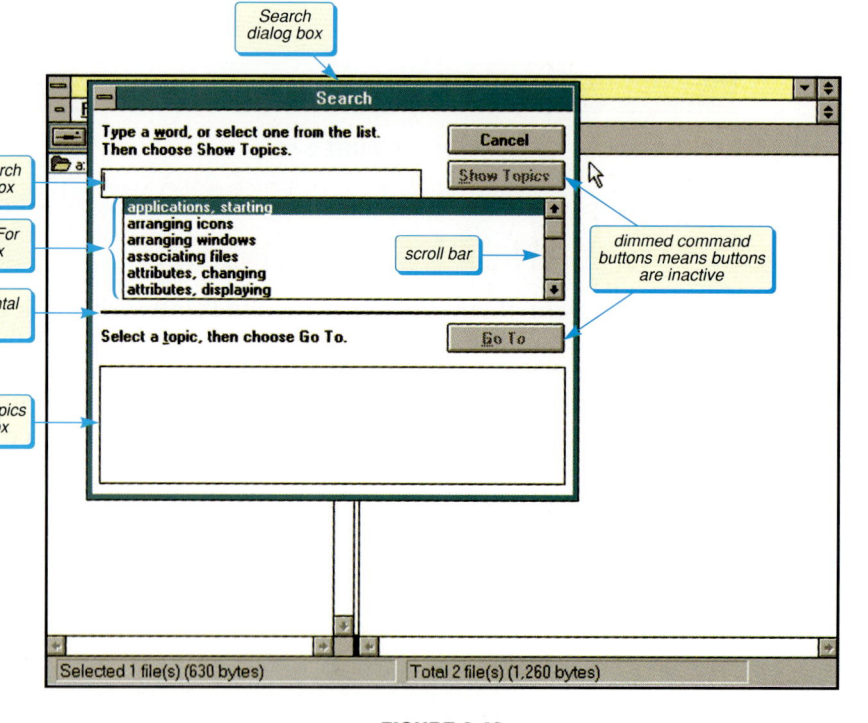

FIGURE 2-48

SEARCHING FOR HELP USING ONLINE HELP   WIN73

STEP 3 ▶

Point to the down scroll arrow in the Search For list box (Figure 2-49).

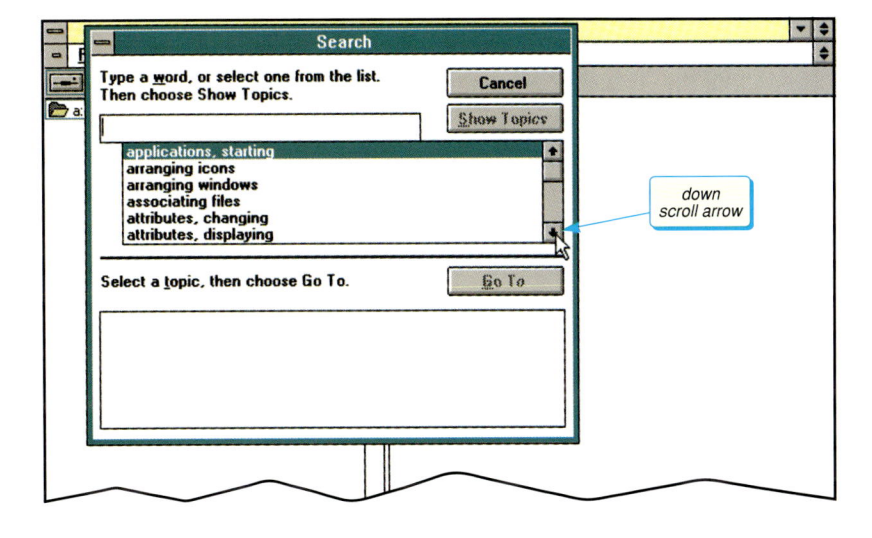

FIGURE 2-49

STEP 4 ▶

Hold down the left mouse button until the selecting files search topic is visible, and then point to the selecting files search topic (Figure 2-50).

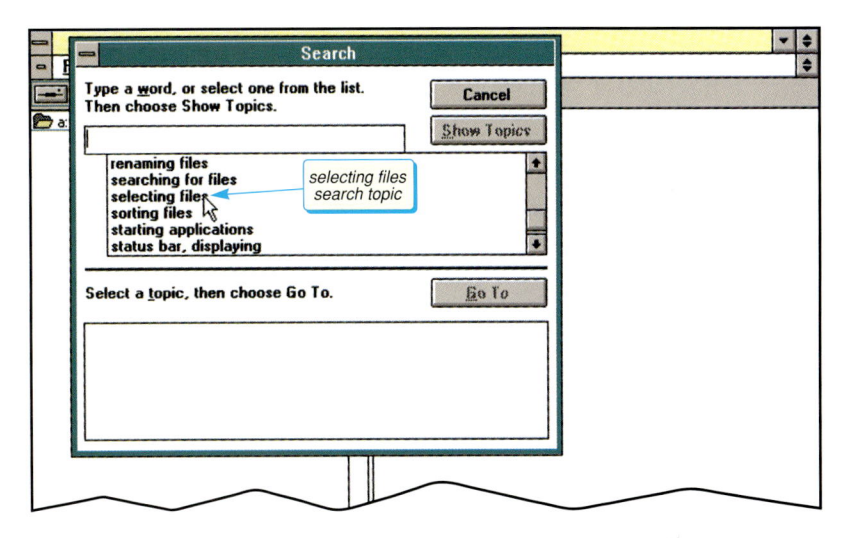

FIGURE 2-50

STEP 5 ▶

Select the selecting files search topic by clicking the left mouse button, and then point to the Show Topics button (Show Topics).

The selecting files search topic is highlighted in the Search For list box and displays in the Search For text box (Figure 2-51). The Show Topics button is no longer dimmed and the mouse pointer points to the Show Topics button.

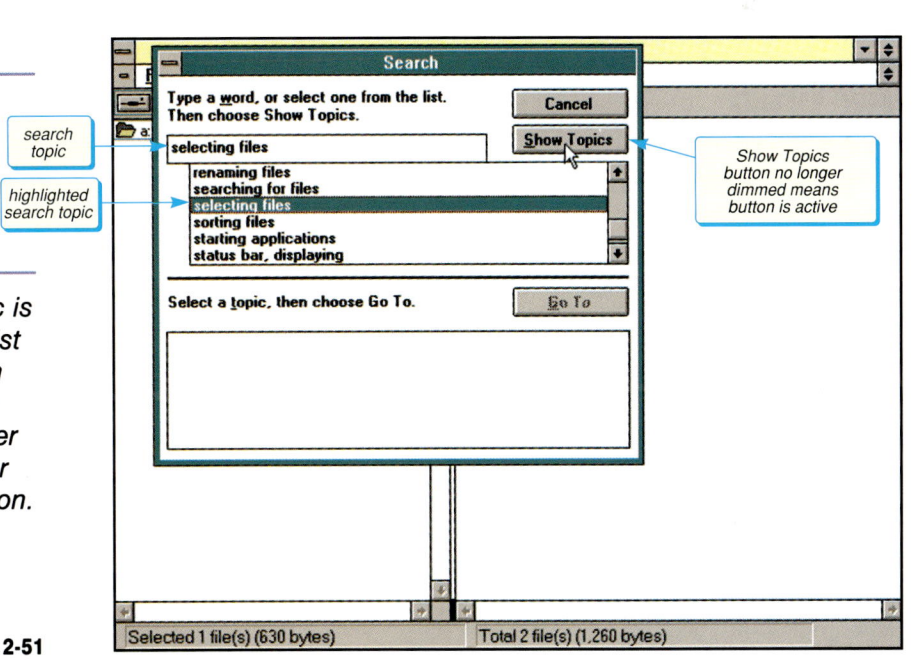

FIGURE 2-51

STEP 6 ▶

Choose the Show Topics button by clicking the left mouse button, and then point to the Using the Keyboard to Select Files help topic.

The Help Topics list box contains four help topics (Figure 2-52). The Go To button (Go To) is no longer dimmed, and the mouse pointer points to the Using the Keyboard to Select Files help topic.

FIGURE 2-52

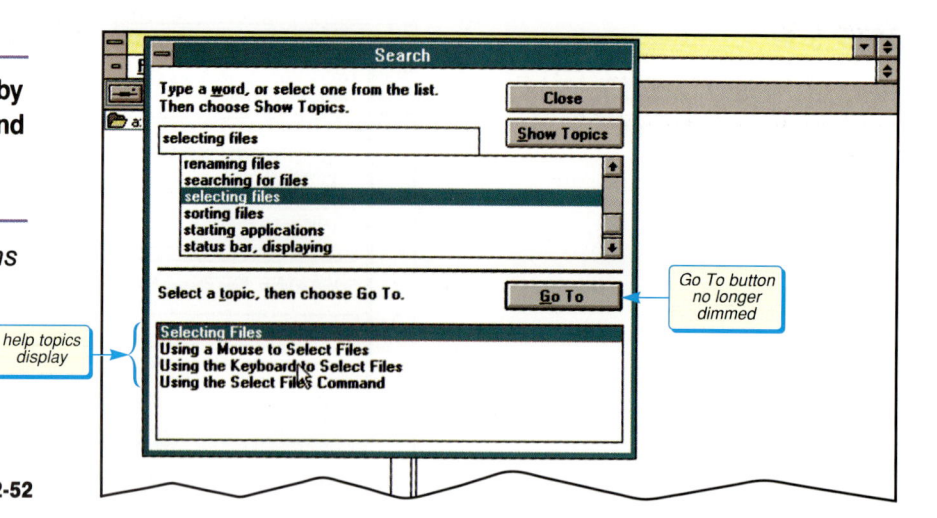

STEP 7 ▶

Select the Using the Keyboard to Select Files help topic by clicking the left mouse button, and then point to the Go To button.

The Using the Keyboard to Select Files help topic is highlighted in the Help Topics list box and the mouse pointer points to the Go To button (Figure 2-53).

FIGURE 2-53

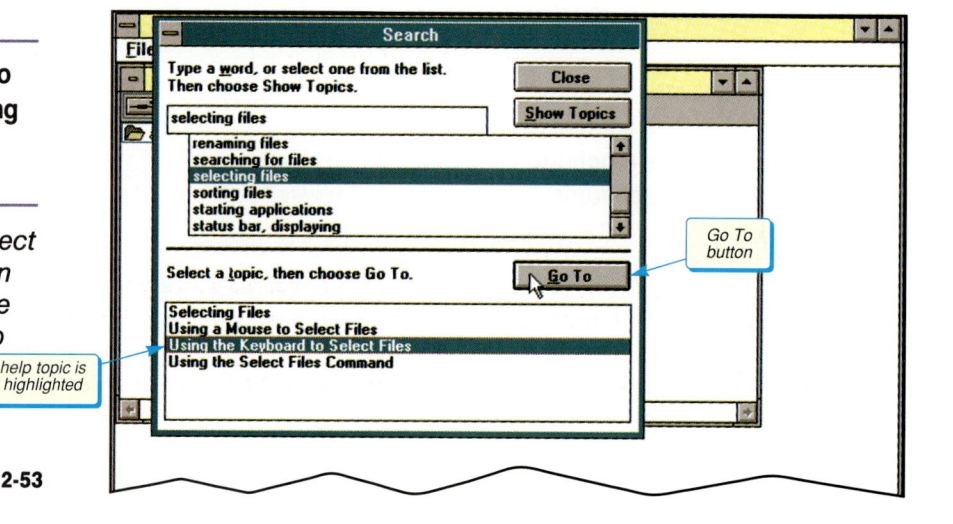

STEP 8 ▶

Choose the Go To button by clicking the left mouse button.

Windows closes the Search dialog box and opens the File Manager Help window (Figure 2-54). The Using the Keyboard to Select Files screen displays in the window.

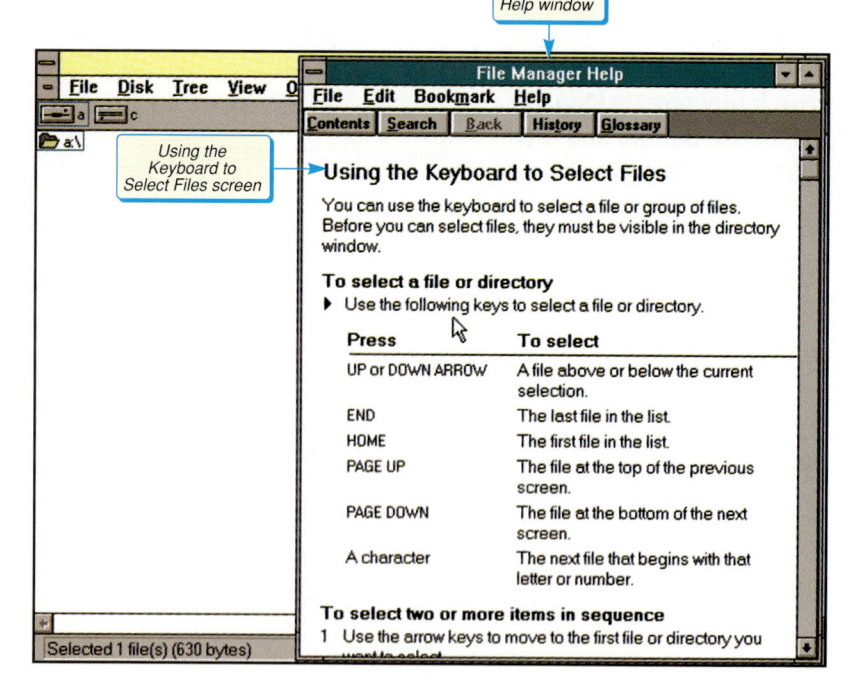

FIGURE 2-54

SEARCHING FOR HELP USING ONLINE HELP **WIN75**

STEP 9 ▶

Click the Maximize button ( ) to maximize the File Manager Help window (Figure 2-55).

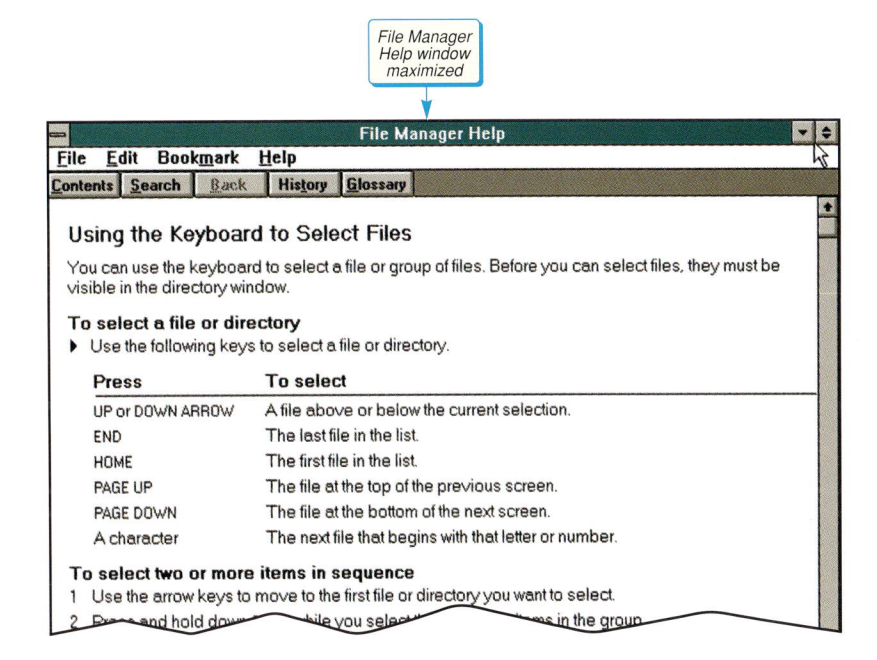

FIGURE 2-55

Searching for Help Using a Word or Phrase

The second method you can use to search for help involves entering a word or phrase to assist the Search feature in finding help related to the word or phrase. In this project, you copied a group of files from the hard disk to a diskette. To obtain additional information about copying files, choose the Search button and type copy from the keyboard.

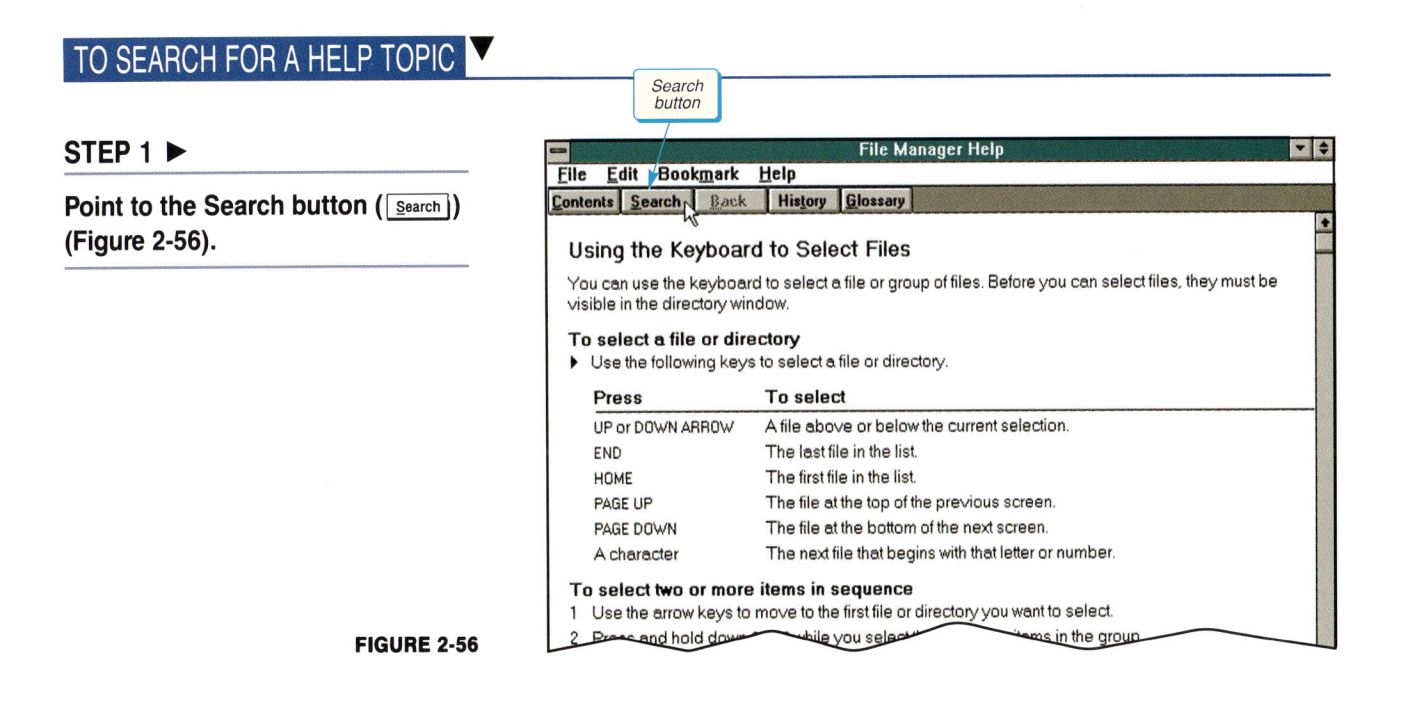

TO SEARCH FOR A HELP TOPIC ▼

STEP 1 ▶

Point to the Search button (Search) (Figure 2-56).

FIGURE 2-56

WIN76　PROJECT 2　DISK AND FILE MANAGEMENT

STEP 2 ▶

Choose the Search button by clicking the left mouse button, and then type `copy`.

Windows opens the Search dialog box (Figure 2-57). As you type the word copy, each letter of the word displays in the Search For text box and the Search For Topics in the Search For Topics list box change. When the entry of the word is complete, the word copy displays in the Search For text box and the Search For topics beginning with the four letters c-o-p-y display first in the Search For list box.

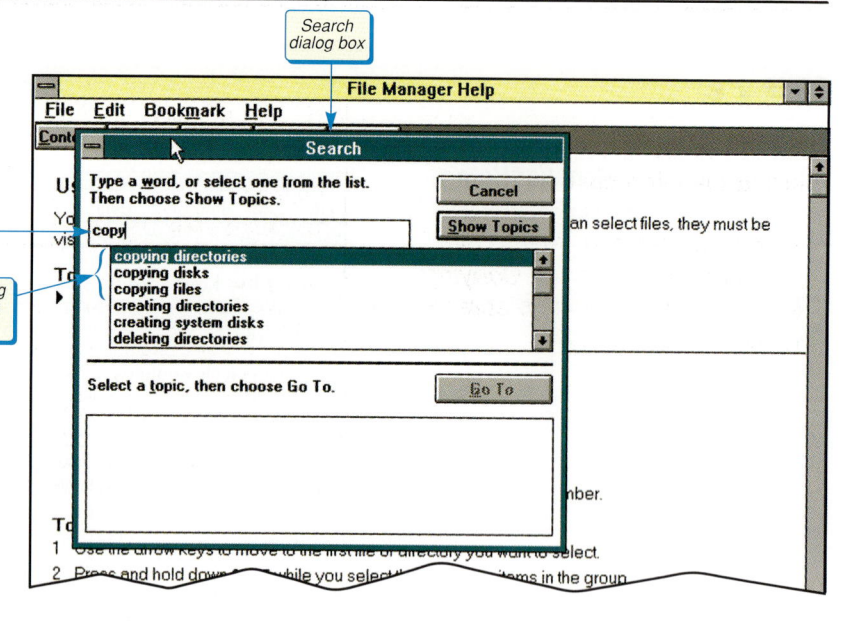

FIGURE 2-57

STEP 3 ▶

Select the copying files search topic by pointing to the topic and clicking the left mouse button, and then point to the Show Topics button.

The copying files search topic is highlighted in the Search For list box and displays in the Search For text box (Figure 2-58).

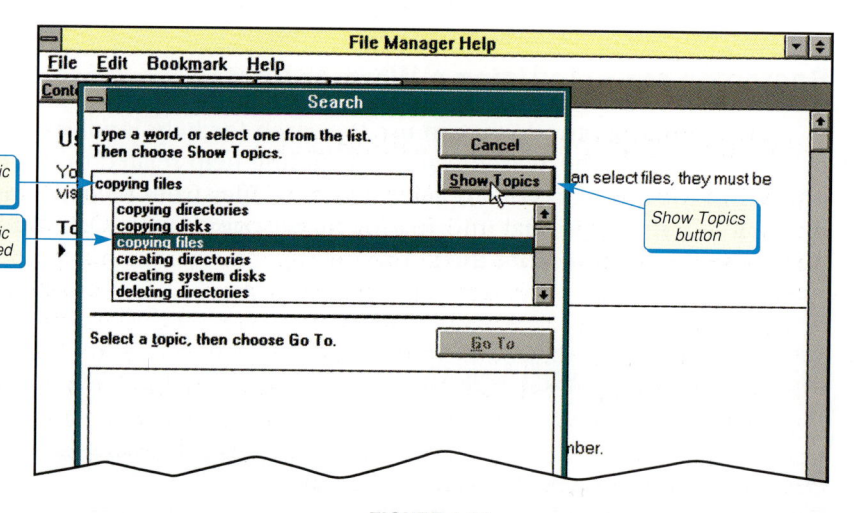

FIGURE 2-58

STEP 4 ▶

Choose the Show Topics button by clicking the left mouse button, and then point to the Go To button.

Only the Copying Files and Directories help topic display in the Help Topic list box (Figure 2-59).

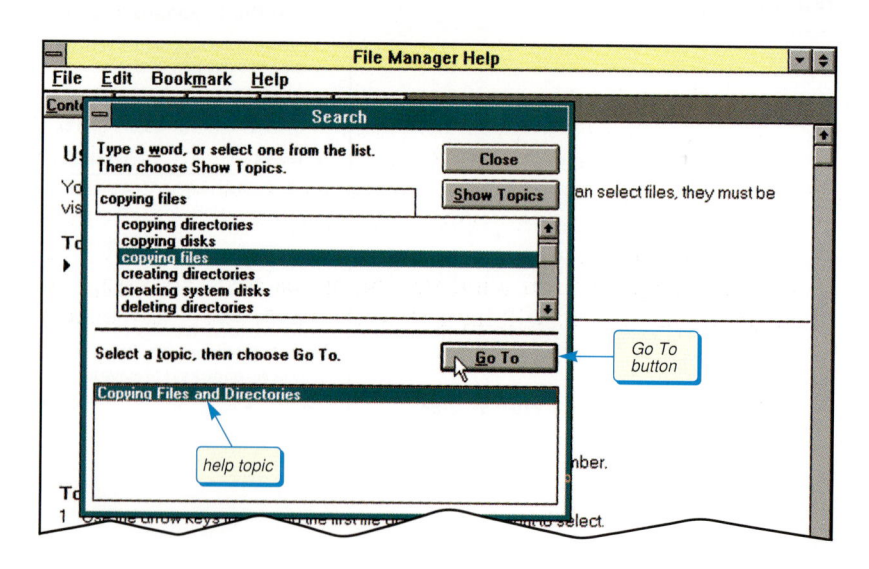

FIGURE 2-59

SEARCHING FOR HELP USING ONLINE HELP **WIN77**

STEP 5 ▶

Choose the Go To button by clicking the left mouse button.

Windows closes the Search dialog box and displays the Copying Files and Directories help screen (Figure 2-60).

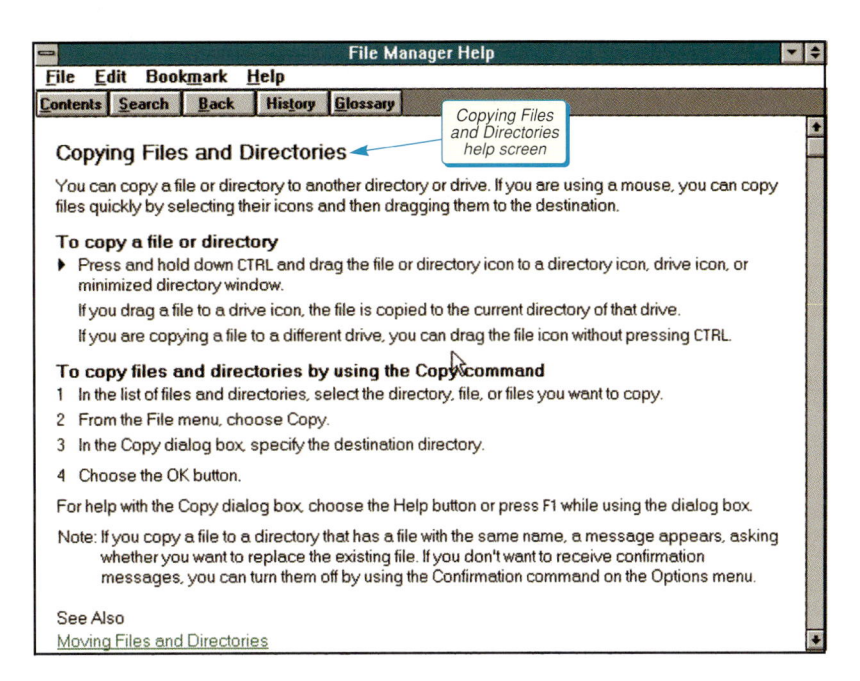

FIGURE 2-60

Quitting File Manager and Online Help

When you finish using File Manager and Windows online Help, you should quit the File Manager Help and File Manager applications. One method of quitting these applications is to first quit the File Manager Help application, and then quit the File Manager application. However, because quitting an application automatically quits the help application associated with that application, you can simply quit the File Manager application to quit both applications. Because the Program Manager and File Manager windows are hidden behind the File Manager Help window (see Figure 2-60), you must move the File Manager window on top of the other windows before quitting File Manager. To do this, you must switch to the File Manager application.

▶ SWITCHING BETWEEN APPLICATIONS

Each time you start an application and maximize its window, its application window displays on top of the other windows on the desktop. To display a hidden application window, you must switch between applications on the desktop using the ALT and TAB keys. To switch to another application, hold down the ALT key, press the TAB key one or more times, and then release the ALT key. Each time you press the TAB key, a box containing an application icon and application window title opens on the desktop. To display the File Manager window, you will have to press the TAB key only once.

TO SWITCH BETWEEN APPLICATIONS

STEP 1 ▶

Hold down the ALT key, and then press the TAB key.

A box containing the File Manager application icon and window title (File Manager) displays (Figure 2-61).

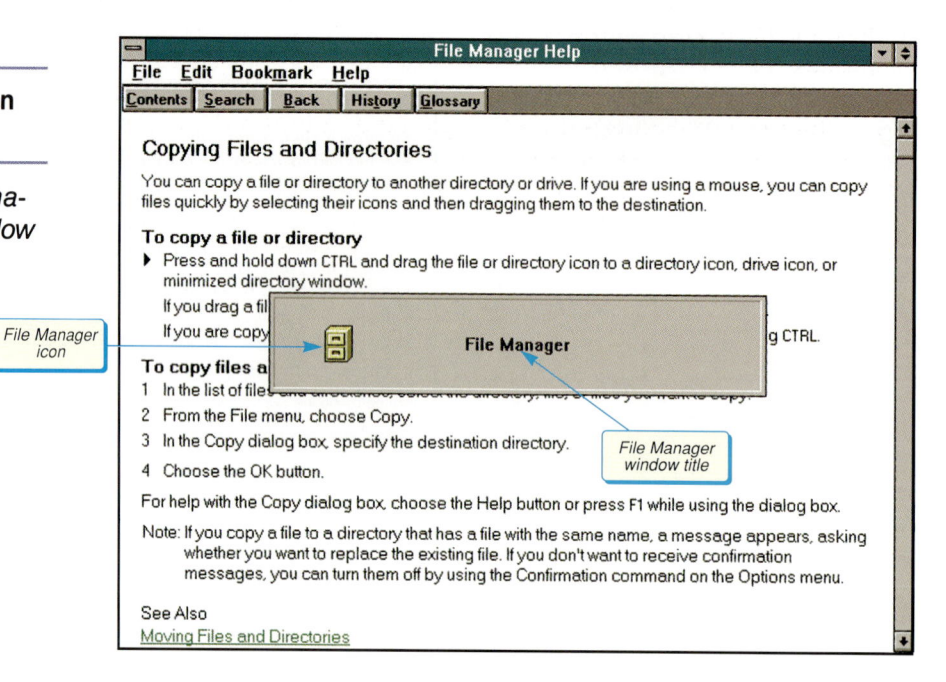

FIGURE 2-61

STEP 2 ▶

Release the ALT key.

The File Manager window moves on top of the other windows on the desktop (Figure 2-62).

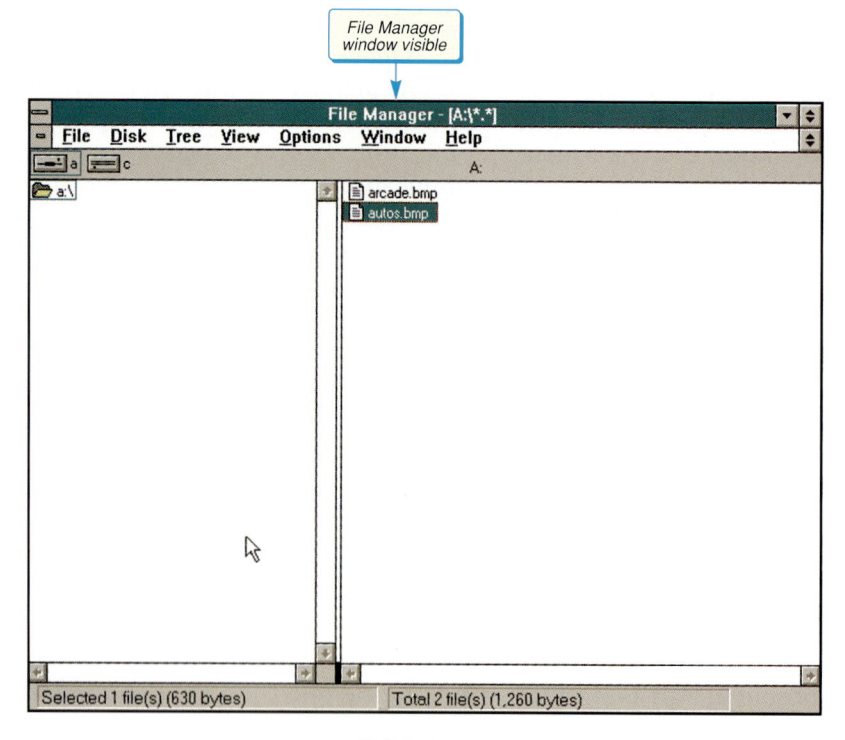

FIGURE 2-62

SEARCHING FOR HELP USING ONLINE HELP **WIN79**

Verify Changes to the File Manager Window Will Not Be Saved

Because you want to return the File Manager window to its state before you started the application, no changes should be saved. The **Save Settings on Exit command** on the Options menu controls whether changes to the File Manager window are saved or not saved when you quit File Manager. A check mark (✓) preceding the Save Settings on Exit command indicates the command is active and all changes to the layout of the File Manager window will be saved when you quit File Manager. If the command is preceded by a check mark, choose the Save Settings on Exit command by clicking the left mouse button to remove the check mark, so the changes will not be saved. Perform the following steps to verify that changes are not saved to the File Manager window.

TO VERIFY CHANGES WILL NOT BE SAVED ▼

STEP 1 ▶

Select the Options menu from the File Manager menu bar.

The Options menu opens (Figure 2-63). A check mark (✓) precedes the Save Settings on Exit command.

STEP 2 ▶

To remove the check mark, choose the Save Settings on Exit command from the Options menu by pointing to the Save Settings on Exit command and clicking the left mouse button.

Windows closes the Options menu. Although not visible, the check mark preceding the Save Settings on Exit command has been removed. This means any changes made to the desktop will not be saved when you exit File Manager.

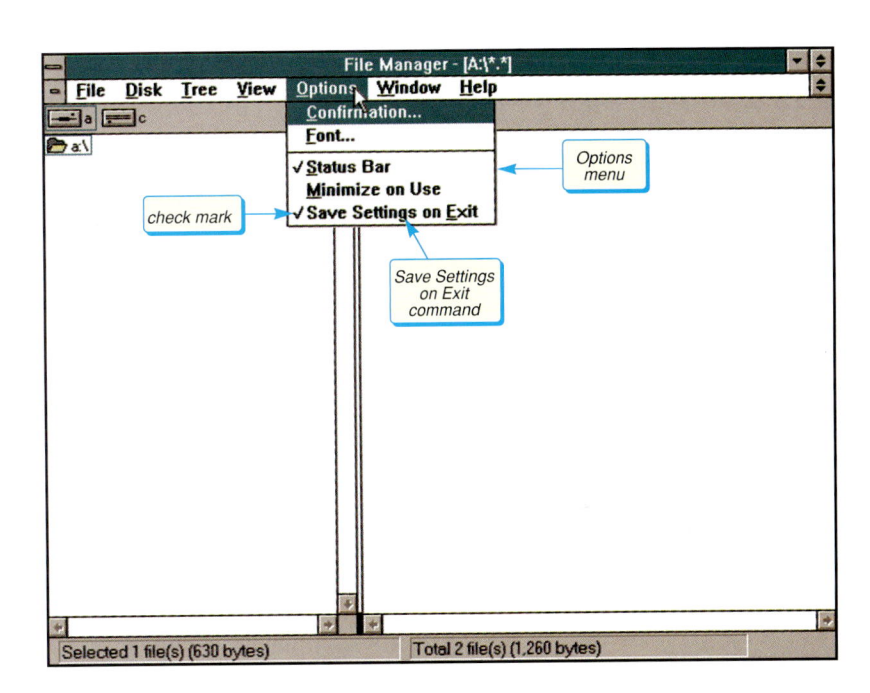

FIGURE 2-63

Quitting File Manager

After verifying no changes to the File Manager window will be saved, the Save Settings on Exit command is not active, so you can quit the File Manager application. In Project 1 you chose the Exit command from the File menu to quit an application. In addition to choosing a command from a menu, you can also quit an application by pointing to the **Control-menu box** in the upper left corner of the application window and double-clicking the left mouse button, as shown in the steps on the next page.

TO QUIT AN APPLICATION ▼

STEP 1 ▶

Point to the Control-menu box in the upper left corner of the File Manager window (Figure 2-64).

STEP 2 ▶

Double-click the left mouse button to exit the File Manager application.

Windows closes the File Manager and File Manager Help windows, causing the Program Manager window to display.

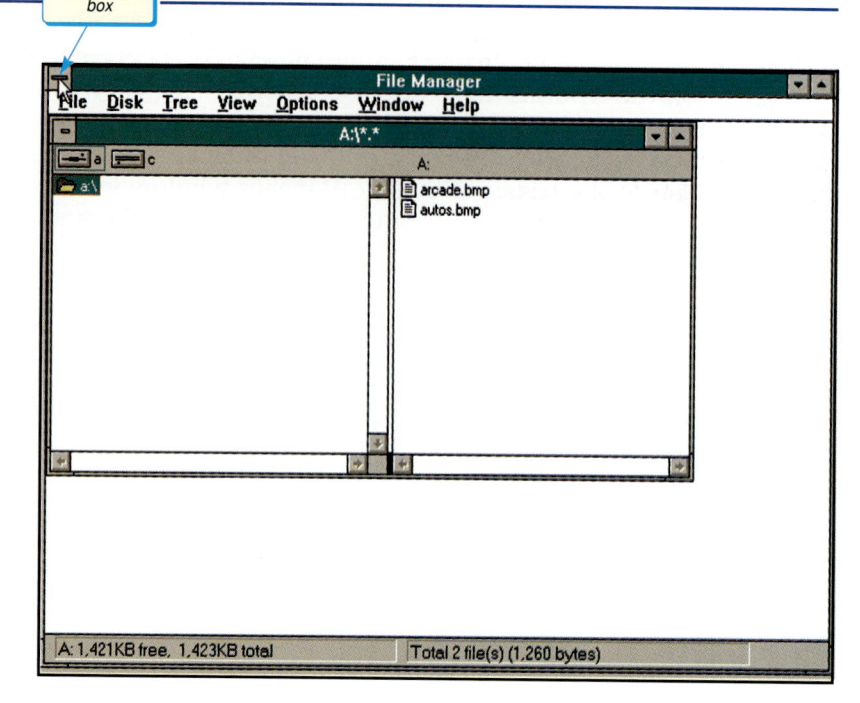

FIGURE 2-64

TO QUIT WINDOWS

Step 1: Select the Options menu from the Program Manager menu bar.
Step 2: If a check mark precedes the Save Settings on Exit command, choose the Save Settings on Exit command.
Step 3: Point to the Control-menu box in the upper left corner of the Program Manager window.
Step 4: Double-click the left mouse button.
Step 5: Choose the OK button to exit Windows.

▶ ADDITIONAL COMMANDS AND CONCEPTS

In addition to the commands and concepts presented in Project 1 and this project, you should understand how to activate a group window, arrange the program-item icons in a group window, and close a group window. These topics are discussed on the following pages. In addition, methods to resize a window and minimize an application window to an application icon are explained.

ADDITIONAL COMMANDS AND CONCEPTS   WIN81

Activating a Group Window

Frequently, several group windows are open in the Program Manager window at the same time. In Figure 2-65, two group windows (Main and Accessories) are open. The Accessories window is the active group window, and the inactive Main window is partially hidden behind the Accessories window. To view a group window that is partially hidden, activate the hidden window by selecting the Window menu and then choosing the name of the group window you wish to view.

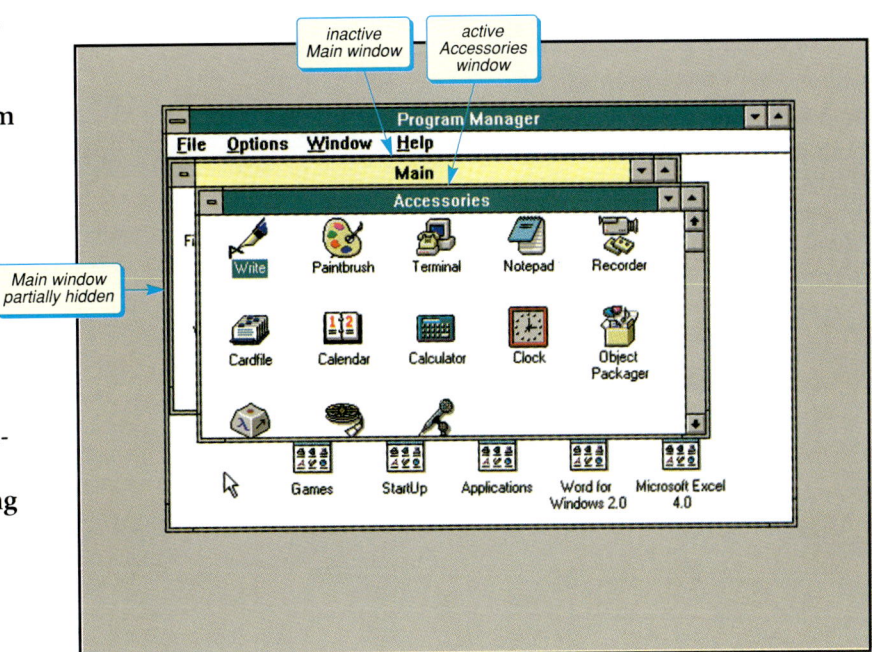

FIGURE 2-65

TO ACTIVATE A GROUP WINDOW ▼

STEP 1 ▶

Select the Window menu from the Program Manager menu bar, and then point to the Main group window name.

The Window menu consists of two areas separated by a horizontal line (Figure 2-66). Below the line is a list of the group windows and group icons in the Program Manager window. Each entry in the list is preceded by a value from one to seven. The number of the active window (Accessories) is preceded by a check mark and the mouse pointer points to the Main group window name.

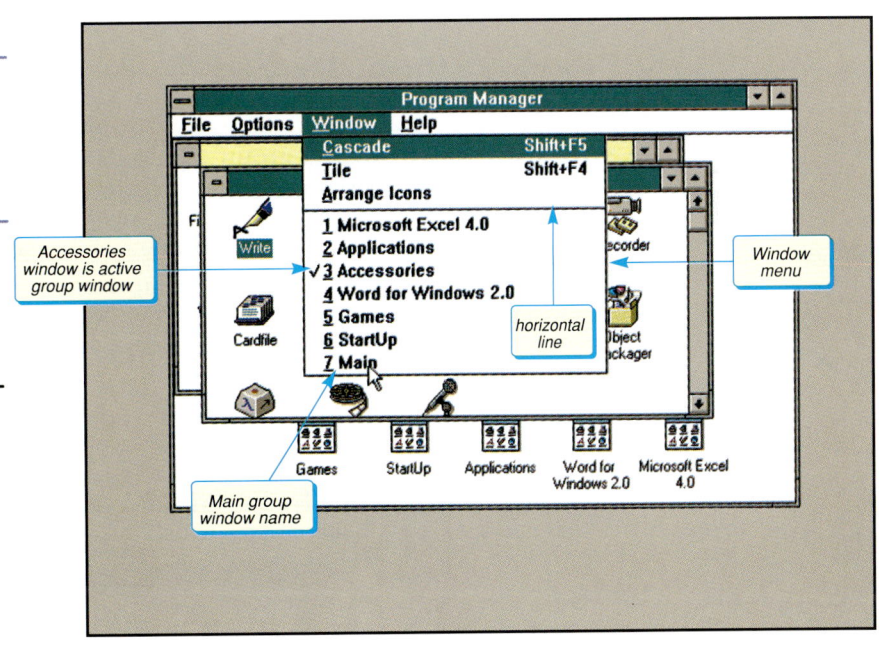

FIGURE 2-66

STEP 2 ▶

Choose the Main group window name by clicking the left mouse button.

The Main window moves on top of the Accessories window (Figure 2-67). The Main window is now the active window.

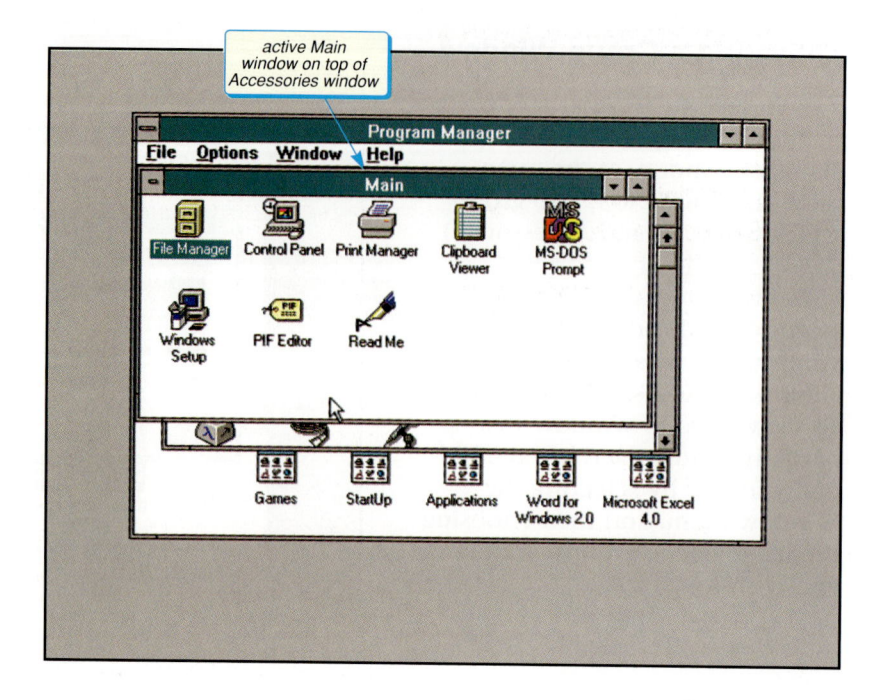

FIGURE 2-67

An alternative method of activating an inactive window is to point to any open area of the window and click the left mouse button. This method cannot be used if the inactive window is completely hidden behind another window.

Closing a Group Window

When several group windows are open in the Program Manager window, you may want to close a group window to reduce the number of open windows. In Figure 2-68, the Main, Accessories, and Games windows are open. To close the Games window, choose the Minimize button on the right side of the Games title bar. Choosing the Minimize button removes the group window from the desktop and displays the Games group icon at the bottom of the Program Manager window.

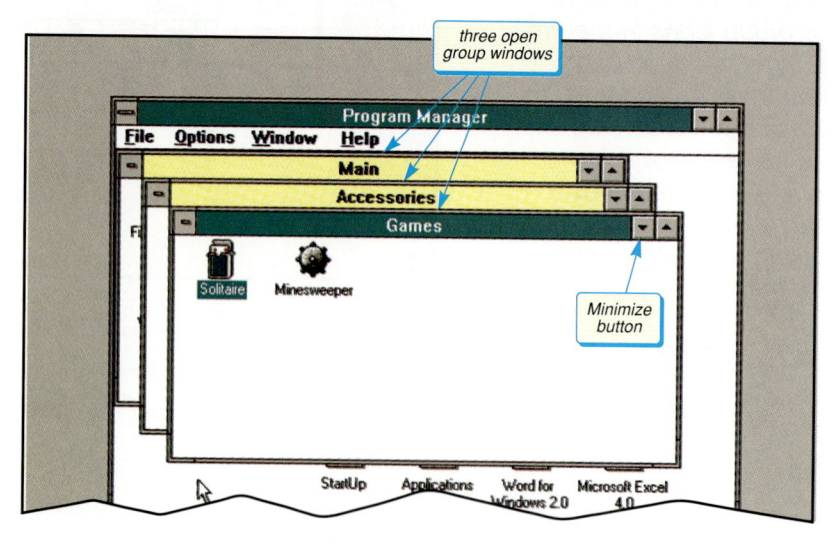

FIGURE 2-68

ADDITIONAL COMMANDS AND CONCEPTS WIN83

TO CLOSE A GROUP WINDOW

STEP 1 ▶

Choose the Minimize button (▼) on the Games title bar.

The Games window closes and the Games icon displays at the bottom edge of the Program Manager window (Figure 2-69).

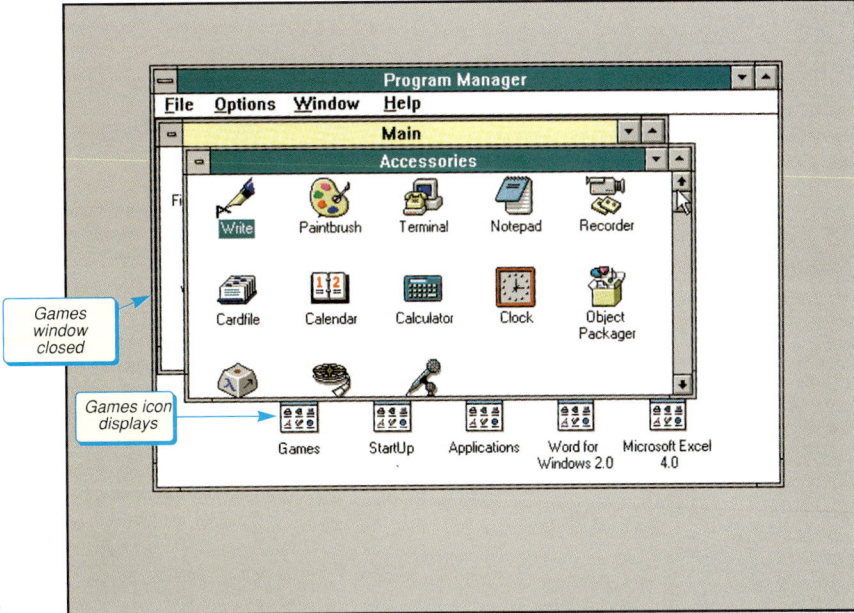

FIGURE 2-69

Resizing a Group Window

When more than six group icons display at the bottom of the Program Manager window, some group icons may not be completely visible. In Figure 2-70, the name of the Microsoft SolutionsSeries icon is partially visible. To make the icon visible, resize the Main window by dragging the bottom window border toward the window title.

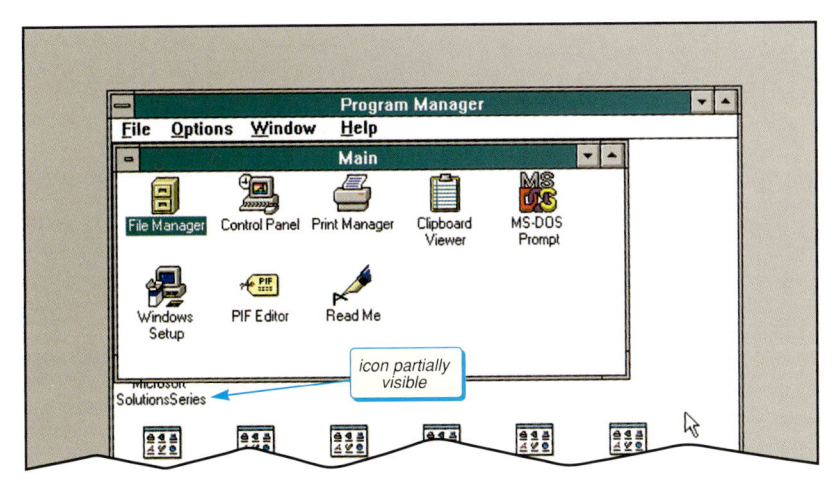

FIGURE 2-70

TO RESIZE A WINDOW

STEP 1 ▶

Point to the bottom border of the Main window.

As the mouse pointer approaches the window border, the mouse pointer changes to a double-headed arrow icon (↕) (Figure 2-71).

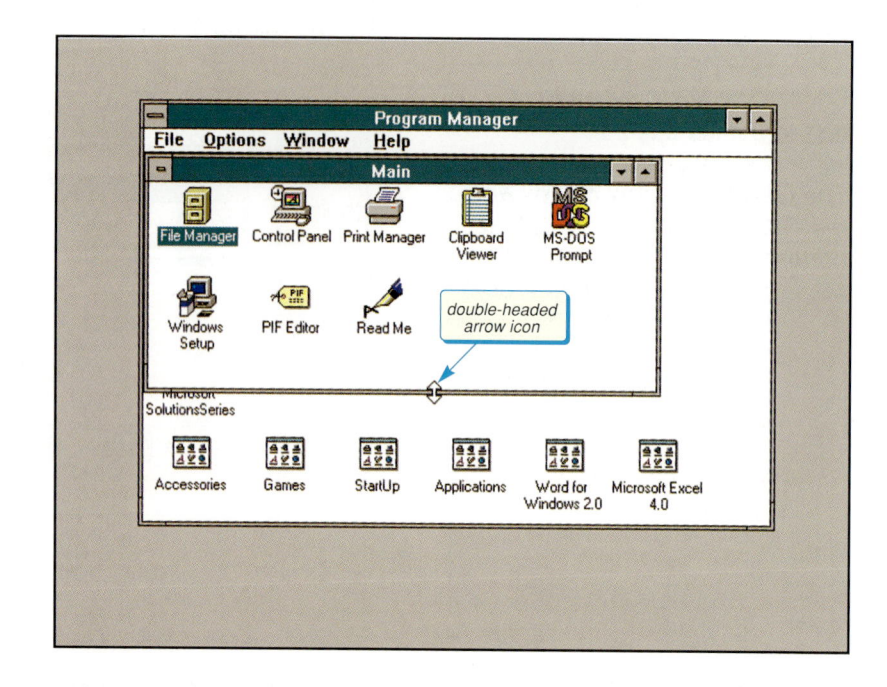

FIGURE 2-71

STEP 2 ▶

Drag the bottom border toward the window title until the Microsoft SolutionsSeries icon is visible.

The Main window changes shape, and the Microsoft SolutionsSeries icon is visible (Figure 2-72).

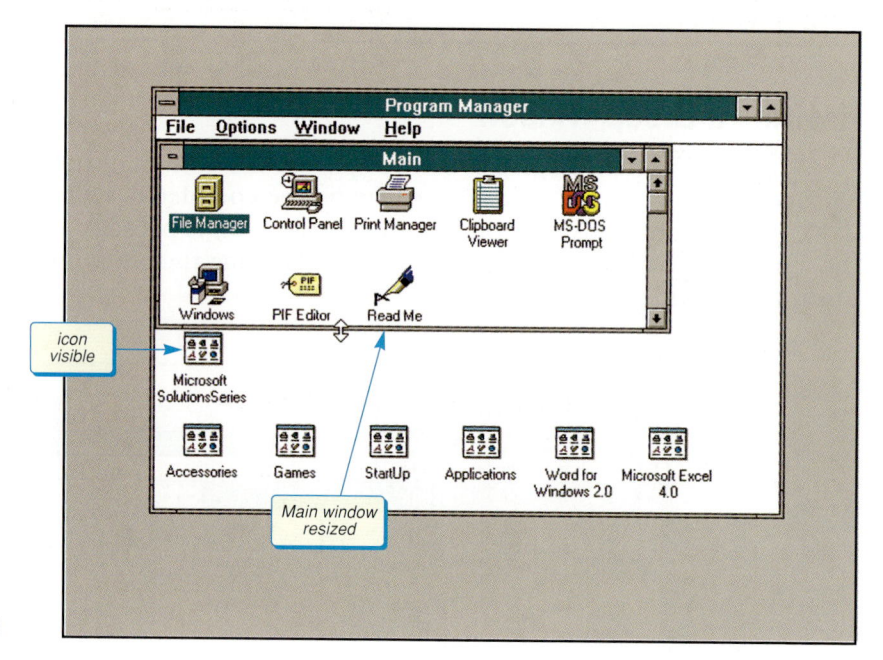

FIGURE 2-72

In addition to dragging a window border to resize a window, you can also drag a window corner to resize the window. By dragging a corner, you can change both the width and length of a window.

Arranging Icons

Occasionally, a program-item icon is either accidentally or intentionally moved within a group window. The result is that the program-item icons are not arranged in an organized fashion in the window. Figure 2-73 shows the eight program-item icons in the Main window. One icon, the File Manager icon, is not aligned with the other icons. As a result, the icons in the Main window appear unorganized. To arrange the icons in the Main window, choose the **Arrange Icons command** from the Window menu.

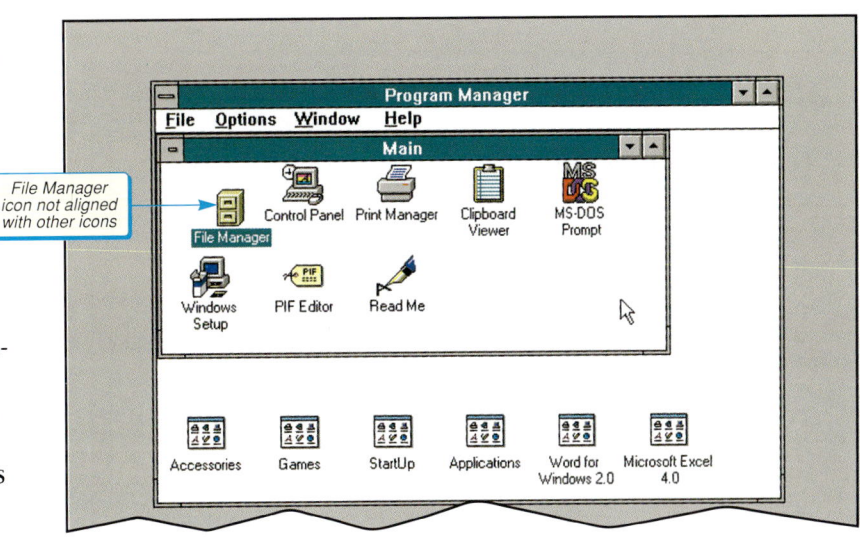

FIGURE 2-73

TO ARRANGE PROGRAM-ITEM ICONS

STEP 1 ▶

Select the Window menu from the Program Manager menu bar, and then point to the Arrange Icons command.

Windows opens the Window menu (Figure 2-74). The mouse pointer points to the Arrange Icons command.

FIGURE 2-74

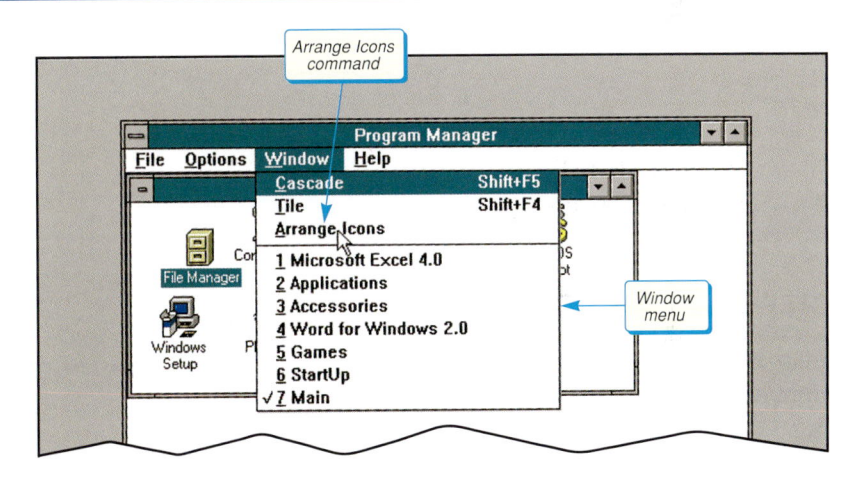

STEP 2 ▶

Choose the Arrange Icons command by clicking the left mouse button.

The icons in the Main window are arranged (Figure 2-75).

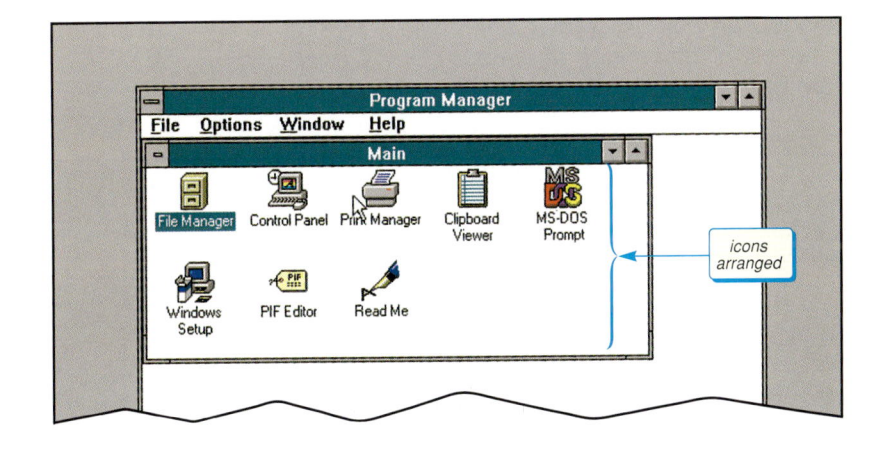

FIGURE 2-75

Minimizing an Application Window to an Icon

When you finish work in an application and there is a possibility of using the application again before quitting Windows, you should minimize the application window to an application icon instead of quitting the application. An **application icon** represents an application that was started and then minimized. Minimizing a window to an application icon saves you the time of starting the application and maximizing its window if you decide to use the application again. In addition, you free space on the desktop without quitting the application. The desktop in Figure 2-76 contains the Paintbrush window. To minimize the Paintbrush window to an application icon, click the Minimize button on the right side of the Paintbrush title bar.

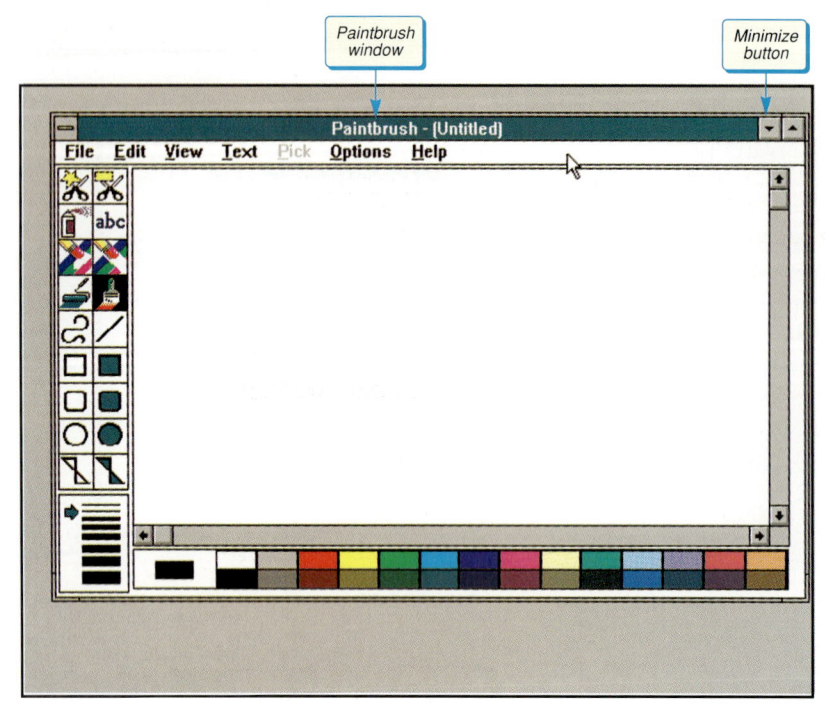

FIGURE 2-76

TO MINIMIZE AN APPLICATION WINDOW TO AN ICON ▼

STEP 1 ▶

Click the Minimize button on the right side of the Paintbrush title bar.

Windows closes the Paintbrush window and displays the Paintbrush application icon at the bottom of the desktop (Figure 2-77).

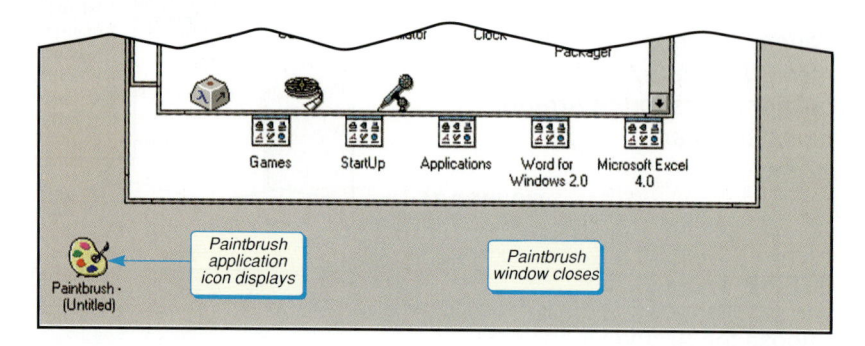

FIGURE 2-77

After minimizing an application window to an application icon, you can start the application again by double-clicking the application icon.

▶ PROJECT SUMMARY

In this project, you used File Manager to format and copy a diskette, copy a group of files, and rename and delete a file. You searched for help about File Manager using the Search feature of online Help, and you switched between applications on the desktop. In addition, you activated, resized, and closed a group window, arranged the icons in a group window, and minimized an application window to an application icon.

▶ Key Terms

application icon (*WIN86*)
Arrange Icons command (*WIN85*)
backup diskette (*WIN47*)
Cascade command (*WIN94*)
contents list (*WIN49*)
Control-menu box (*WIN79*)
Copy Disk command (*WIN67*)
current drive (*WIN48*)
Delete command (*WIN65*)
destination directory (*WIN54*)
destination diskette (*WIN67*)
destination drive (*WIN54*)

directory structure (*WIN49*)
directory tree (*WIN49*)
directory window (*WIN48*)
Disk Copy command (*WIN71*)
Disk menu (*WIN51*)
diskette capacity (*WIN50*)
diskette size (*WIN50*)
drive icon (*WIN48*)
File Manager (*WIN48*)
Format Disk command (*WIN51*)
formatting (*WIN50*)
Help menu (*WIN72*)

Options menu (*WIN79*)
Rename command (*WIN63*)
Save Settings on Exit command (*WIN79*)
Search for Help on command (*WIN72*)
source directory (*WIN54*)
source diskette (*WIN67*)
source drive (*WIN54*)
split bar (*WIN49*)
Tile command (*WIN94*)
Window menu (*WIN81*)

QUICK REFERENCE

In Windows you can accomplish a task in a number of ways. The following table provides a quick reference to each task presented in the project with its available options. The commands listed in the Menu column can be executed using either the keyboard or mouse.

Task	Mouse	Menu	Keyboard Shortcuts
Activate a Group Window	Click group window	From Window menu, choose window title	
Arrange Program-Item Icons in a Group Window		From Window menu, choose Arrange Icons	
Change the Current Drive	Click drive icon		Press TAB to move highlight to drive icon area, press arrow keys to outline drive icon, and press ENTER
Close a Group Window	Click Minimize button or double-click control-menu box	From Control menu, choose Close	Press CTRL + F4
Copy a Diskette		From Disk menu, choose Copy Disk	
Copy a File or Group of Files	Drag highlighted filename(s) to destination drive or directory icon	From File menu, choose Copy	
Delete a File		From File menu, choose Delete	Press DEL
Format a Diskette		From Disk menu, choose Format Disk	

(continued)

QUICK REFERENCE (continued)

Task	Mouse	Menu	Keyboard Shortcuts
Maximize a Directory Window	Click Maximize button	From Control menu, choose Maximize	
Minimize an Application Window	Click Minimize button	From Control menu, choose Minimize	Press ALT, SPACE BAR, N
Rename a File		From File menu, choose Rename	
Resize a Window	Drag window border or corner	From Control menu, choose Size	
Save Changes when Quitting File Manager		From Options menu, choose Save Settings on Exit if no check mark precedes command	
Save No Changes when Quitting Windows		From Options menu, choose Save Settings on Exit if check mark precedes command	
Search for a Help Topic		From Help menu, choose Search for Help on	
Select a File in the Contents List	Click the filename		Press arrow keys to outline filename, press SHIFT+F8
Select a Group of Files in the Contents List	Select first file, hold down CTRL key and select other files		Press arrow keys to outline first file, press SHIFT+F8, press arrow keys to outline each additional filename, and press SPACEBAR
Switch between Applications	Click application window		Hold down ALT, press TAB (or ESC), release ALT

STUDENT ASSIGNMENTS

STUDENT ASSIGNMENT 1
True/False

Instructions: Circle T if the statement is true or F if the statement if false.

T F 1. Formatting prepares a diskette for use on a computer.
T F 2. It is not important to create a backup diskette of the Business Documents diskette.
T F 3. Program Manager is an application you can use to organize and work with your hard disk and diskettes and the files on those disks.
T F 4. A directory window title bar usually contains the current directory path.
T F 5. A directory window consists of a directory tree and contents list.
T F 6. The directory tree contains a list of the files in the current directory.
T F 7. The disk capacity of a 3 1/2-inch diskette is typically 360K or 1.2MB.
T F 8. The source drive is the drive from which files are copied.
T F 9. You select a single file in the contents list by pointing to the filename and clicking the left mouse button.

T F 10. You select a group of files in the contents list by pointing to each filename and clicking the left mouse button.
T F 11. Windows opens the Error Copying File dialog box if you try to copy a file to an unformatted diskette.
T F 12. You change the filename or extension of a file using the Change command.
T F 13. Windows opens the Confirm File Delete dialog box when you try to delete a file.
T F 14. When creating a backup diskette, the disk to receive the copy is the source disk.
T F 15. The first step in creating a backup diskette is to choose the Copy Disk command from the Disk menu.
T F 16. On some computers, you may have to insert and remove the source and destination diskettes several times to copy a diskette.
T F 17. Both the Search for Help on command and the Search button initiate a search for help.
T F 18. An application icon represents an application that was started and then minimized.
T F 19. You hold down the TAB key, press the ALT key, and then release the TAB key to switch between applications on the desktop.
T F 20. An application icon displays on the desktop when you minimize an application window.

STUDENT ASSIGNMENT 2
Multiple Choice

Instructions: Circle the correct response.

1. The _____ application allows you to format a diskette.
   a. Program Manager
   b. File Manager
   c. online Help
   d. Paintbrush
2. The _____ contains the directory structure of the current drive.
   a. contents list
   b. status bar
   c. split bar
   d. directory tree
3. The _____ key is used when selecting a group of files.
   a. CTRL
   b. ALT
   c. TAB
   d. ESC
4. After selecting a group of files, you _____ the group of files to copy the files to a new drive or directory.
   a. click
   b. double-click
   c. drag
   d. none of the above
5. The commands to rename and delete a file are located on the _____ menu.
   a. Window
   b. Options
   c. Disk
   d. File
6. The first step in creating a backup diskette is to _____.
   a. write-protect the destination diskette
   b. choose the Copy command from the Disk menu
   c. write-protect the source diskette
   d. label the destination diskette

STUDENT ASSIGNMENT 2 (continued)

7. When searching for help, the _____ button displays a list of Help topics.
   a. Go To
   b. Topics
   c. Show Topics
   d. Search
8. You use the _____ and _____ keys to switch between applications on the desktop.
   a. ALT, TAB
   b. SHIFT, ALT
   c. ALT, CTRL
   d. ESC, CTRL
9. When you choose a window title from the Window menu, Windows _____ the associated group window.
   a. opens
   b. closes
   c. enlarges
   d. activates
10. To resize a group window, you can use the _____.
    a. title bar
    b. window border
    c. resize command on the Window menu
    d. arrange Icons command on the Options menu

STUDENT ASSIGNMENT 3
Identifying the Parts of a Directory Window

Instructions: On the desktop in Figure SA2-3, arrows point to several items in the C:\WINDOWS*.* directory window. Identify the items in the space provided.

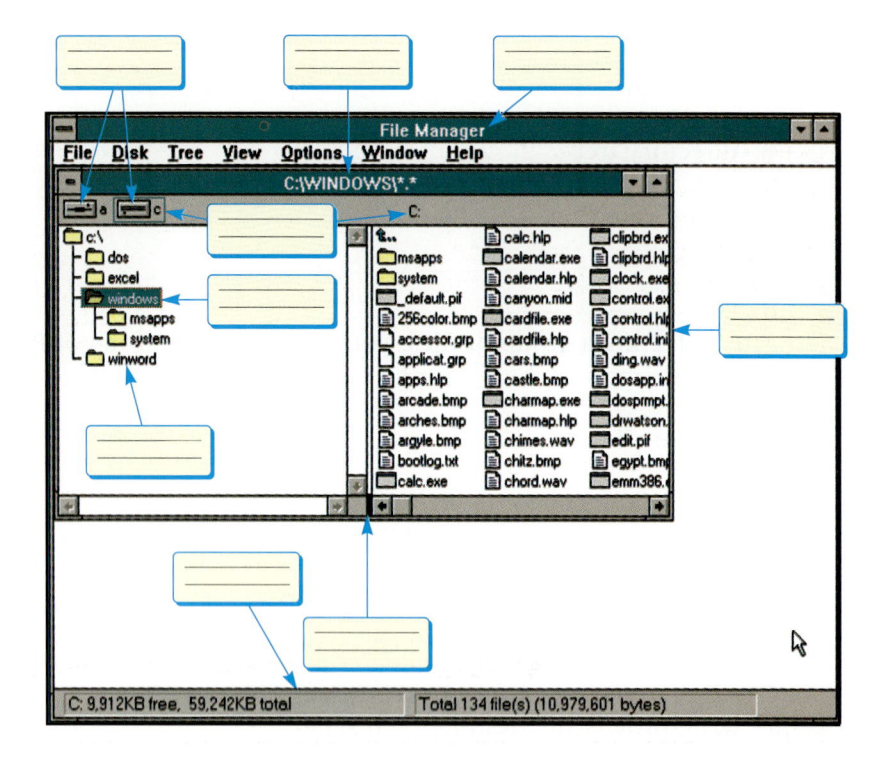

FIGURE SA2-3

STUDENT ASSIGNMENTS   WIN91

STUDENT ASSIGNMENT 4
Selecting a Group of Files

Instructions: Using the desktop in Figure SA2-4, list the steps to select the group of files consisting of the ARCADE.BMP, CARS.BMP, and EGYPT.BMP files in the space provided.

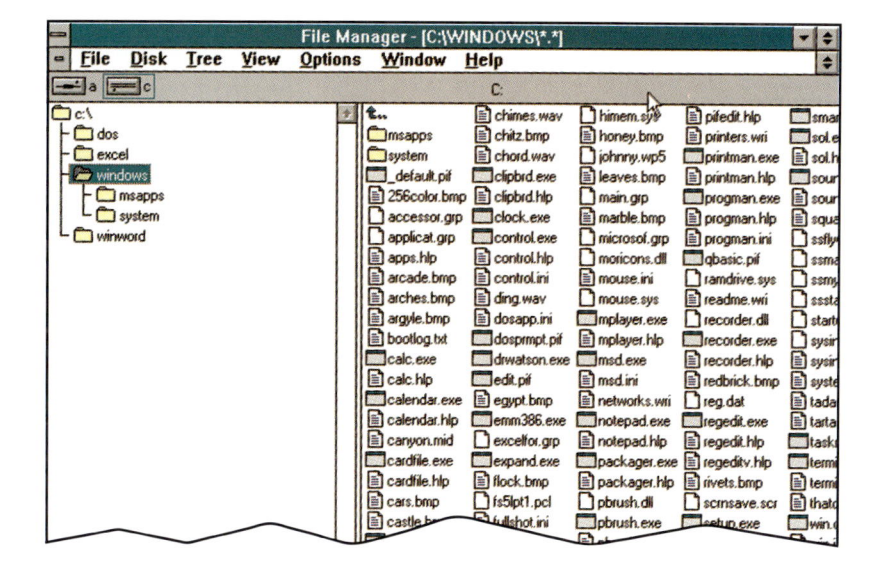

FIGURE SA2-4

Step 1: _____

Step 2: _____

Step 3: _____

Step 4: _____

STUDENT ASSIGNMENT 5
Copying a Group of Files

Instructions: Using the desktop in Figure SA2-5, list the steps to copy the group of files selected in Student Assignment 4 to the root directory of drive A. Write the steps in the space provided.

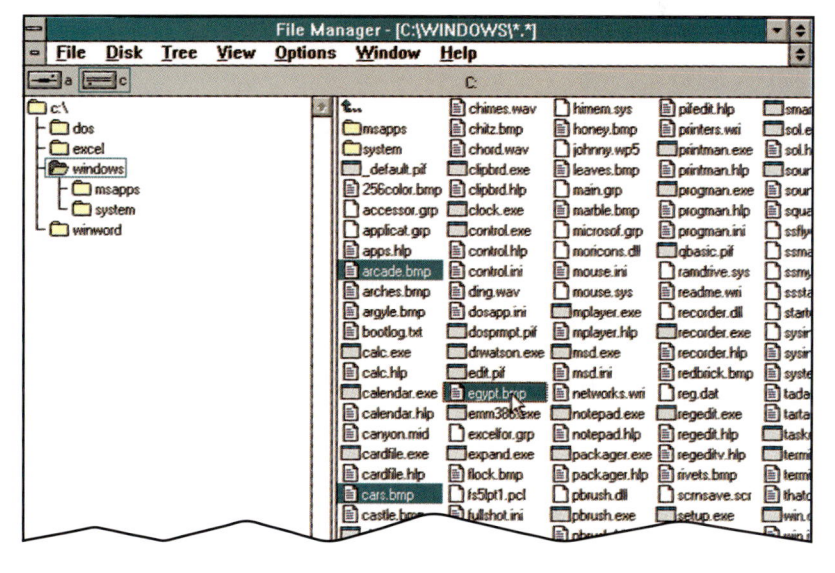

FIGURE SA2-5

Step 1: _____

Step 2: _____

Step 3: _____

Step 4: _____

WIN92   PROJECT 2   DISK AND FILE MANAGEMENT

STUDENT ASSIGNMENT 6
Searching for Help

Instructions: Using the desktop in Figure SA2-6, list the steps to complete the search for the Using the Keyboard to Select Files help topic. The mouse pointer points to the down scroll arrow. Write the steps in the space provided.

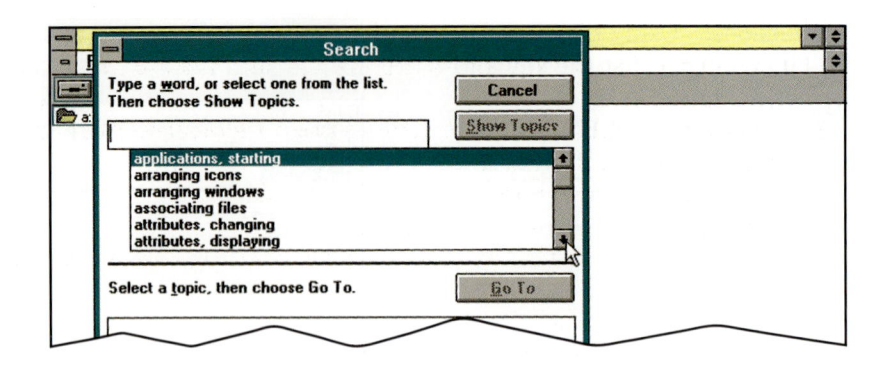

FIGURE SA2-6

Step 1: _____

Step 2: _____

Step 3: _____

Step 4: _____

Step 5: _____

Step 6: _____

COMPUTER LABORATORY EXERCISES

COMPUTER LABORATORY EXERCISE 1
Selecting and Copying Files

Instructions: Perform the following tasks using a computer.

Part 1:

1. Start Windows.
2. Double-click the File Manager icon to start File Manager.
3. Click the Maximize button on the File Manager window to enlarge the File Manager window.
4. Click the Maximize button on the C:\WINDOWS*.* window to enlarge the C:\WINDOWS*.* window.
5. Select the CHITZ.BMP file.
6. Hold down the CTRL key and click the LEAVES.BMP filename to select the LEAVES.BMP file. The CHITZ.BMP and LEAVES.BMP files should both be highlighted.
7. Insert the Student Diskette into drive A.
8. Drag the group of files to the drive A icon.
9. Choose the Yes button in the Confirm Mouse Operation dialog box.
10. Choose the drive A icon to change the current drive to drive A.
11. Select the CHITZ.BMP file.
12. Choose the Delete command from the File menu.
13. Choose the OK button in the Delete dialog box.
14. Choose the Yes button in the Confirm File Delete dialog box.
15. If the LEAVES.BMP file is not highlighted, select the LEAVES.BMP file.

16. Choose the Rename command from the File menu.
17. Type AUTUMN.BMP in the To text box.
18. Choose the OK button in the Rename dialog box to rename the LEAVES.BMP file.

Part 2:

1. Hold down the ALT key, press the TAB key, and release the ALT key to switch to the Program Manager application.
2. Double-click the Accessories icon to open the Accessories window.
3. Double-click the Paintbrush icon to start Paintbrush.
4. Click the Maximize button on the Paintbrush window to enlarge the Paintbrush window.
5. Choose the Open command from the File menu.
6. Click the Down Arrow button in the Drives drop down list box to display the Drives drop down list.
7. Select the drive A icon.
8. Select the AUTUMN.BMP file in the File Name list box.
9. Choose the OK button to retrieve the AUTUMN.BMP file into Paintbrush.
10. Choose the Print command from the File menu.
11. Click the Draft option button in the Print dialog box.
12. Choose the OK button in the Print dialog box to print the contents of the AUTUMN.BMP file.
13. Remove the Student Diskette from drive A.
14. Choose the Exit command from the File menu to quit Paintbrush.
15. Hold down the ALT key, press the TAB key, and release the ALT key to switch to the File Manager application.
16. Select the Options menu.
17. If a check mark precedes the Save Settings on Exit command, choose the Save Settings on Exit command.
18. Choose the Exit command from the File menu of the File Manager window to quit File Manager.
19. Choose the Exit Windows command from the File menu of the Program Manager window.
20. Click the OK button to quit Windows.

COMPUTER LABORATORY EXERCISE 2
Searching with Online Help

Instructions: Perform the following tasks using a computer.

1. Start Microsoft Windows.
2. Double-click the Accessories icon to open the Accessories window.
3. Double-click the Write icon to start the Write application.
4. Click the Maximize button on the Write window to enlarge the Write window.
5. Choose the Search for Help on command from the Help menu.
6. Scroll the Search For list box to make the cutting text topic visible.
7. Select the cutting text topic.
8. Choose the Show Topics button.
9. Choose the Go To button to display the Copying, Cutting, and Pasting Text topic.
10. Click the Maximize button on the Write Help window to enlarge the window.
11. Choose the Print Topic command from the File menu to print the Copying, Cutting, and Pasting Text topic on the printer.
12. Choose the Search button.
13. Enter the word paste in the Search For list box.
14. Select the Pasting Pictures search topic.
15. Choose the Show Topics button.
16. Choose the Go To button to display the Copying, Cutting, and Pasting Pictures topic.
17. Choose the Print Topic command from the File menu to print the Copying, Cutting, and Pasting Pictures topic on the printer.

COMPUTER LABORATORY EXERCISE 2 (continued)

18. Choose the Exit command from the File menu to quit Write Help.
19. Choose the Exit command from the File menu to quit Write.
20. Select the Options menu.
21. If a check mark precedes the Save Settings on Exit command, choose the Save Settings on Exit command.
22. Choose the Exit Windows command from the File menu.
23. Click the OK button to quit Windows.

COMPUTER LABORATORY EXERCISE 3
Working with Group Windows

Instructions: Perform the following tasks using a computer.

1. Start Windows. The Main window should be open in the Program Manger window.
2. Double-click the Accessories icon to open the Accessories window.
3. Double-click the Games icon to open the Games window.
4. Choose the Accessories window title from the Window menu to activate the Accessories window.
5. Click the Minimize button on the Accessories window to close the Accessories window.
6. Choose the **Tile command** from the Window menu. The Tile command arranges a group of windows so no windows overlap, all windows are visible, and each window occupies an equal portion of the screen.
7. Move and resize the Main and Games windows to resemble the desktop in Figure CLE2-3. To resize a window, drag the window border or corner. To move a group window, drag the window title bar. Choose the Arrange Icons command from the Window menu to arrange the icons in each window.

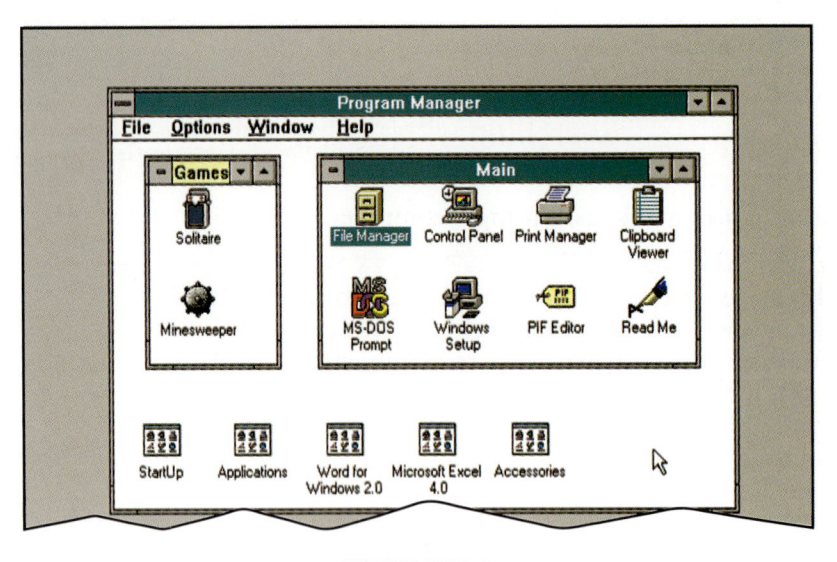

FIGURE CLE2-3

8. Press the PRINTSCREEN key to capture the desktop.
9. Open the Accessories window.
10. Choose the **Cascade command** from the Window menu. The Cascade command arranges a group of windows so the windows overlap and the title bar of each window is visible.
11. Double-click the Paintbrush icon to start Paintbrush.
12. Click the Maximize button on the Paintbrush window to enlarge the Paintbrush window.
13. Choose the Paste command from the Edit menu to place the picture of the desktop in the window.
14. Choose the Print command from the File menu.

15. Click the Draft option button.
16. Choose the OK button in the Print dialog box to print the desktop.
17. Choose the Exit command from the File menu of the Paintbrush window.
18. Choose the No button to not save current changes and quit Paintbrush.
19. Select the Options menu.
20. If a check mark precedes the Save Settings on Exit command, choose the Save Settings on Exit command.
21. Choose the Exit Windows command from the File menu.
22. Click the OK button.

COMPUTER LABORATORY EXERCISE 4
Backing Up Your Student Diskette

Instructions: Perform the following tasks using a computer to back up your Student Diskette.

Part 1:

1. Start Windows.
2. Double-click the File Manager icon to start the File Manager application.
3. Click the Maximize button on the File Manager window to enlarge the File Manager window.
4. Write-protect the Student Diskette.
5. Choose the Copy Disk command from the Disk menu.
6. Choose the Yes button in the Confirm Copy Disk dialog box.
7. Insert the source diskette (Student Diskette) into drive A.
8. Choose the OK button in the Copy Disk dialog box.
9. When prompted, insert the destination diskette (the formatted diskette created in this project) into drive A.
10. Choose the OK button in the Copy Disk dialog box.
11. Insert and remove the source and destination diskette until the copy process is complete.
12. Click the drive A icon to change the current drive to drive A.
13. Press the PRINTSCREEN key to capture the desktop.
14. Select the Options menu on the File Manager menu bar.
15. If a check mark precedes the Save Settings on Exit command, choose the Save Settings on Exit command.
16. Choose the Exit command from the File menu on the File Manager menu bar to quit File Manager.

Part 2:

1. Double-click the Accessories icon to open the Accessories window.
2. Double-click the Paintbrush icon to start Paintbrush.
3. Click the Maximize button to enlarge the Paintbrush window.
4. Choose the Paste command from the Edit menu to place the picture of the desktop in the window.
5. Choose the Print command from the File menu.
6. Click the Draft option button.
7. Choose the OK button in the Print dialog box to print the picture of the desktop on the printer.
8. Choose the Exit command from the File menu.
9. Choose the No button to not save current changes and quit Paintbrush.
10. Select the Options menu.
11. If a check mark precedes the Save Settings on Exit command, choose the Save Settings on Exit command.
12. Choose the Exit Windows command from the File menu of the Program Manager menu bar.
13. Click the OK button to quit Windows.
14. Remove the diskette from drive A.
15. Remove the write-protection from the Student Diskette.

Index

Active command, WIN36, WIN79
Active icon, **WIN18**
Active window, **WIN15**–16, WIN81–82
ALT key, switching between applications and, WIN77–78
Application(s), **WIN3**
 inactive, WIN17
 quitting, WIN21–22, WIN28, WIN32, WIN79–80
 starting, WIN16–17
 switching between, WIN77–78
Application icon, **WIN86**
Application software, **WIN3**
Application window
 displaying hidden, WIN77–80
 maximizing, WIN18
Arrange Icons command, WIN85
Asterisk (*), group of files and, WIN23
Auxiliary storage device, WIN23

Backslash (\), directory and, WIN24, WIN48
Backup diskette, **WIN47, WIN67**–71, WIN95
Bottom window border, WIN83–84
Buttons, WIN12, WIN13

Calendar application, WIN44–45
Cancel command button, WIN21
Cancel copy operation, WIN60
Cardfile application, WIN46
Cascade command, **WIN94**
Check boxes, **WIN13**
Check mark, active command and, WIN36, WIN79
Choosing a command, **WIN11**
Close, WIN16
Closing
 group window, WIN82–83
 pop-up window, WIN35
Command, **WIN10**
 active, WIN36, WIN79
Command buttons, **WIN13**
Confirm Copy Disk dialog box, WIN68
Confirm File Delete dialog box, WIN66
Confirm File Replace dialog box, WIN60
Confirm Format Disk dialog box, WIN52
Confirm Mouse Operation dialog box, WIN58
Contents command, WIN33
Contents list, **WIN49,** WIN61, WIN63
Control menu, **WIN16**
Control-menu box, **WIN79**–80
Copy Disk command, **WIN67,** WIN68, WIN70
Copy Disk dialog box, WIN68–69
Copy Disk Error dialog box, WIN71
Copying Disk dialog box, WIN69
Copying dialog box, WIN58
Copying files, WIN54–62, WIN71, WIN92–93
 searching for help about, WIN75–77
CRT screen, WIN3
CTRL key, selecting files and, WIN55–57
Current directory, number of files in, WIN49
Current drive, **WIN48**
 changing, WIN61–62
 disk space on, WIN49
Current path, WIN24
Current selection, **WIN13**

Delete command, **WIN65**–66
Delete dialog box, WIN66
Delete text box, WIN66
Desktop, **WIN4,** WIN18, WIN49
Destination directory, **WIN54**
Destination directory icon, WIN55
Destination diskette, **WIN67,** WIN69, WIN70
Destination drive, **WIN54**
Destination drive icon, WIN55
Dialog boxes, **WIN12**–14
Directory, **WIN23,** WIN54–55
Directory path, **WIN24,** WIN48
Directory structure, **WIN24, WIN49**
Directory tree, **WIN49,** WIN61
Directory window, **WIN48**–49
 maximizing, WIN55
Disk, replacing file on, WIN60

Disk Copy command, **WIN71**
Disk drives, WIN48
Disk management, WIN47–71
Disk menu
 Copy Disk, WIN67, WIN68, WIN70
 Format Disk, WIN51–53
Diskette, WIN23
 protecting, WIN67
 saving document on, WIN24–28
Diskette capacity, **WIN50**–51
Diskette drive, WIN48, WIN50–51
Diskette size, **WIN50**–51
Document(s), **WIN14**
 creating, WIN19, WIN44
 printing, WIN20–21, WIN44
Document file, **WIN23**
Dragging window border to resize window, WIN83–84
Drive, WIN23, WIN48, WIN50–51, WIN54, WIN61–62
Drive icons, **WIN48**
Drives drop-down list box, WIN29
Drop-down list box, **WIN13**–14

Editing document file, WIN31, WIN44–45
Edit menu, help and, WIN32–34
Ellipsis, commands and, **WIN11,** WIN12, WIN25
Error Copying File dialog box, WIN59
Error correction
 changing current drive and, WIN62
 copying files and, WIN59–60, WIN71
 double-clicking group icon and, WIN16
 double-clicking program-item icon and, WIN18
 saving document file and, WIN27–28
Error Selecting Drive dialog box, WIN62
Exit command, WIN21–22, WIN28, WIN37
Exiting
 online help, WIN35
 Windows, WIN36–37
Extension, file, **WIN23**

File(s)
 copying to a diskette, WIN54–62
 in current directory, WIN49
 deleting, WIN65–66
 disk space occupied by, WIN49
 editing, WIN31
 naming, WIN23
 opening, WIN28–32
 renaming, WIN63–64
 replacing on disk, WIN60
 saving, WIN31–32
 selecting group of, WIN55–57, WIN92–93
File management, WIN47–80
 deleting files, WIN65–66
 formatting diskettes, WIN50–54
File Manager, **WIN47**–49
 quitting, WIN77, WIN79–80
 starting, WIN50
File Manager Help applications, quitting, WIN77
File Manager Help window, WIN74–75
File Manager icon, WIN50
File Manager menu bar, WIN48
File Manager window, WIN48, WIN55
 maximizing, WIN50
 saving changes to, WIN79
File menu, WIN11
Filename, **WIN23,** WIN48
 changing, WIN63–64
Filename extension, changing, WIN63
File Name list box, WIN30
File Name text box, WIN25
Format Disk command, **WIN51**–53
Format Disk dialog box, WIN52
Format Disk Error dialog box, WIN54
Formatting a diskette, **WIN27, WIN50**–54
 error correction and, WIN54
Formatting Complete dialog box, WIN53
Formatting Disk dialog box, WIN53
Games, Solitaire, WIN43
Glossary definition, help and, WIN34
Go To button, WIN74
Graphical user interface (GUI), **WIN3**
Group icons, WIN14

error correction while double-clicking, WIN16
Group of files
 copying, WIN57–58, WIN92–93
 selecting, WIN55–57, WIN92–93
Group window(s), WIN81–85, WIN94–95
 activating, WIN81–82
 active window, WIN15–16
 closing, WIN82–83
 hidden, WIN81
 opening, WIN14–15
 resizing, WIN83–84
Hard disk, WIN23
Hard drive, WIN48
Help, online, **WIN32**–35, WIN46, WIN71–77, WIN93–94
 exiting, WIN35, WIN77
 searching with, WIN71–77, WIN93–94
Help menu, WIN33
 Search for Help, WIN72
 Windows Tutorial, WIN43
Help topic, **WIN33**–35
 searching for, WIN47, WIN72–75
Help Topics list box, WIN74

Icon(s)
 active, WIN18
 arranging, WIN85
 Control menu for, WIN16
 drive, **WIN48**
 file folder, WIN24
 minimizing application window to, WIN86
Insertion point, **WIN17,** WIN19

Jump, **WIN33**

Keyboard, WIN3, **WIN9**–10
Keyboard shortcuts, **WIN10,** WIN11

Main memory, copying disks and, WIN69, WIN70
Maximize, WIN16
 application window, WIN18
 directory window, WIN55
 File Manager Help window, WIN75
 File Manager window, WIN55
 Help window, WIN33
 Notepad window, WIN28
Maximize button, **WIN18,** WIN50, WIN55
Menu(s), **WIN10**–11, WIN20–21
Menu bar, **WIN10**
Microsoft Windows, see Windows, Microsoft
Minimize, WIN16
 application window to an icon, WIN86
Minimize button, WIN83, WIN86
Mouse, WIN3, **WIN5**–9
 clicking, WIN7
 double-clicking, WIN8
 double-clicking and error correction, WIN16–18
 dragging, WIN9
 pointing with, WIN6
Mouse pointer, **WIN6**
 block arrow, WIN6
 double-headed arrow icon, WIN84
 hand, WIN33
 I-beam, WIN17
Mouse skills exercise, WIN43
Move, WIN16

Naming files, WIN23
Next, WIN16
Notepad application, **WIN14**–22
 quitting, WIN32
 starting, WIN28
Notepad dialog box, WIN21, WIN22
Notepad menu, File, WIN25

Open command, WIN29, WIN44–45
Opening file, WIN28–32
Option(s), turning on or off, WIN13
Option buttons, **WIN12**
Options menu, Save Settings on Exit, WIN36, WIN79, WIN80

Paintbrush application, **WIN32**–34, WIN93, WIN94, WIN95
 quitting, WIN35
Phrase, searching for help using, WIN75–77

Pop-up window, **WIN35**
Print command, WIN20–21
Print dialog box, WIN12–14
Printing, WIN44
 by choosing command from menu, WIN20–21
Program Manager menu, WIN10
Program Manager window, WIN80
 activating group window, WIN81
Program-item icons, WIN14
 double-clicking, WIN16–17
 error correction while double-clicking, WIN18

Quitting, without saving changes, WIN37

Rename command, **WIN63**–64
Rename dialog box, WIN64
Resizing group window, WIN83–84
Restore, WIN16
Restore button, **WIN18,** WIN55
Retrieving files, WIN29–30
Retry button, WIN59, WIN62
Root directory, **WIN23,** WIN24, WIN49

Save As command, WIN25
Save As dialog box, WIN25, WIN27–29
Save command, WIN31
Save Settings on Exit command, WIN36, **WIN79,** WIN80
Saving, WIN24–28, WIN44
 modified document file, WIN31–32
Screen, WIN3, WIN4
Scroll arrows, **WIN16**
Scroll bar, **WIN16**
Scroll box, **WIN16**
Search dialog box, WIN72, WIN76
Search feature, help and, WIN47, WIN71–77, WIN93–94
Search for Help on command, **WIN72**
Search topics, WIN72
Selected button, **WIN12**
Selecting a menu, **WIN11**
Selecting files search topic, WIN73
Selection, current, **WIN13**
SHIFT key, selecting group of files and, WIN57
Show Topics button, WIN73–74, WIN76
Size, Control menu and, WIN16
Size, group window, WIN83–84
Software, user interface and, WIN3
Source directory, **WIN54**
Source diskette, **WIN67,** WIN68–69
Source drive, **WIN54**
Split bar, directory window and, **WIN49**
Status bar, WIN49
Subdirectories, **WIN23,** WIN49

Text box, **WIN13**
Tile command, **WIN94**
Title bar, **WIN4**
 dialog box and, WIN12
Tutorial, WIN43
TXT extension, WIN25–26

User friendly, **WIN3**
User interface, WIN3

Window border, **WIN4**
 dragging to resize window, WIN83–84
Window corner, dragging, WIN84
Window menu, WIN81, WIN85, WIN94
Window title, **WIN4**
Windows, **WIN4**
 activating group, WIN81–82
 dialog box and, WIN12
 directory, WIN48–49
 minimizing to icon, WIN86
Windows, Microsoft, **WIN2,** WIN3
 communicating with, WIN5–14
 mouse operations and, WIN5–9
 quitting, WIN36–37
 starting, WIN4–5, WIN49–50
 tutorial, WIN43
 using, WIN14–22
Word, searching for help using, WIN75–77
Write application, WIN93
Write-protect window, WIN70
Write-protected diskette, **WIN27,** WIN28, WIN54, WIN60, WIN67, WIN70

WIN96

WORD PROCESSING
USING MICROSOFT WORD 2.0 FOR WINDOWS

▶ PROJECT ONE
CREATING AND EDITING A DOCUMENT
Objectives **MSW2**
What Is Microsoft Word? **MSW2**
Project One **MSW2**
Starting Word **MSW4**
The Word Screen **MSW5**
Changing the Default Point Size **MSW8**
Entering Text **MSW10**
Saving a Document **MSW18**
Formatting Paragraphs and Characters in a Document **MSW21**
Checking Spelling **MSW29**
Saving an Existing Document with the Same Filename **MSW31**
Printing a Document **MSW32**
Quitting Word **MSW34**
Opening a Document **MSW35**
Correcting Errors **MSW36**
Word's Online Help **MSW39**
Project Summary **MSW41**
Key Terms **MSW41**
Quick Reference **MSW42**
Student Assignments **MSW43**
Computer Laboratory Exercises **MSW47**
Computer Laboratory Assignments **MSW49**

▶ PROJECT TWO
CREATING A RESEARCH PAPER
Objectives **MSW54**
Introduction **MSW54**
Project Two **MSW55**
Starting Word **MSW57**
Changing the Margins **MSW57**
Adjusting Line Spacing **MSW59**
Redefining the Normal Style **MSW61**
Using a Header To Number Pages **MSW62**
Typing the Body of the Research Paper **MSW66**
Creating An Alphabetical Works Cited Page **MSW78**
Revising the Research Paper **MSW86**
Using the Thesaurus **MSW91**
Displaying and Printing a Document in Print Preview **MSW93**
Project Summary **MSW96**
Key Terms **MSW96**
Quick Reference **MSW97**
Student Assignments **MSW98**
Computer Laboratory Exercises **MSW103**
Computer Laboratory Assignments **MSW106**

▶ PROJECT THREE
CREATING A PROPOSAL USING TABLES AND GRAPHICS
Objectives **MSW112**
Introduction **MSW112**
Project Three **MSW112**
Creating a Title Page **MSW117**
Inserting an Existing Document Into an Open Document **MSW129**
Setting and Using Tabs **MSW135**
Creating a Table **MSW140**
Charting a Table **MSW153**
Adding Bullets to a List **MSW157**
Project Summary **MSW161**
Key Terms **MSW161**
Quick Reference **MSW161**
Student Assignments **MSW162**
Computer Laboratory Exercises **MSW166**
Computer Laboratory Assignments **MSW169**

▶ PROJECT FOUR
GENERATING FORM LETTERS AND MAILING LABELS
Objectives **MSW179**
Introduction **MSW179**
Project Four **MSW179**
Creating a Data File **MSW181**
Creating the Main Document for the Form Letter **MSW190**
Merging the Documents and Printing the Letters **MSW208**
Creating and Printing Mailing Labels **MSW213**
Project Summary **MSW219**
Key Terms **MSW220**
Quick Reference **MSW220**
Student Assignments **MSW221**
Computer Laboratory Exercises **MSW224**
Computer Laboratory Assignments **MSW226**

▶ PROJECT FIVE
CREATING A PROFESSIONAL NEWSLETTER
Objectives **MSW231**
Introduction **MSW231**
Project Five **MSW231**
Creating the Nameplate **MSW235**
Creating the First Page of the Body of the Newsletter **MSW244**
Creating the Second Page of the Newsletter **MSW262**
Enhancing the Newsletter with Color **MSW271**
Project Summary **MSW275**
Key Terms **MSW276**
Quick Reference **MSW276**
Student Assignments **MSW277**
Computer Laboratory Exercises **MSW281**
Computer Laboratory Assignments **MSW283**
INDEX MSW286

MICROSOFT WORD 2.0 FOR WINDOWS
PROJECT ONE

CREATING AND EDITING A DOCUMENT

OBJECTIVES You will have mastered the material in this project when you can:

- Start Word
- Describe the Word screen
- Change the default point size of all text
- Enter text into a document
- Save a document
- Select a single word or series of words
- Center a paragraph
- Underline selected text
- Bold selected text
- Italicize selected text
- Change the point size of selected text
- Print a document
- Use Word's Spelling feature
- Correct errors in a document
- Use Word's online Help
- Quit Word

▶ WHAT IS MICROSOFT WORD?

Microsoft Word is a full-featured **word processing program** that allows you to efficiently and economically create professional looking documents such as memoranda, letters, reports, and resumes, and revise them easily. To improve the accuracy of your writing, Word can check your spelling and grammar. You can use Word's thesaurus to add variety and precision to your writing. With Word, you can easily include tables and graphics in your documents. You can also use Word's desktop publishing features to create brochures, advertisements, and newsletters.

▶ PROJECT ONE

To illustrate the features of Word, this book presents a series of projects that use Word to create documents similar to those you will encounter in the academic and business environments. Project 1 uses Word to produce the memorandum shown in Figure 1-1. The memorandum notifies employees of upcoming training seminars on new versions of word processing and electronic spreadsheet software.

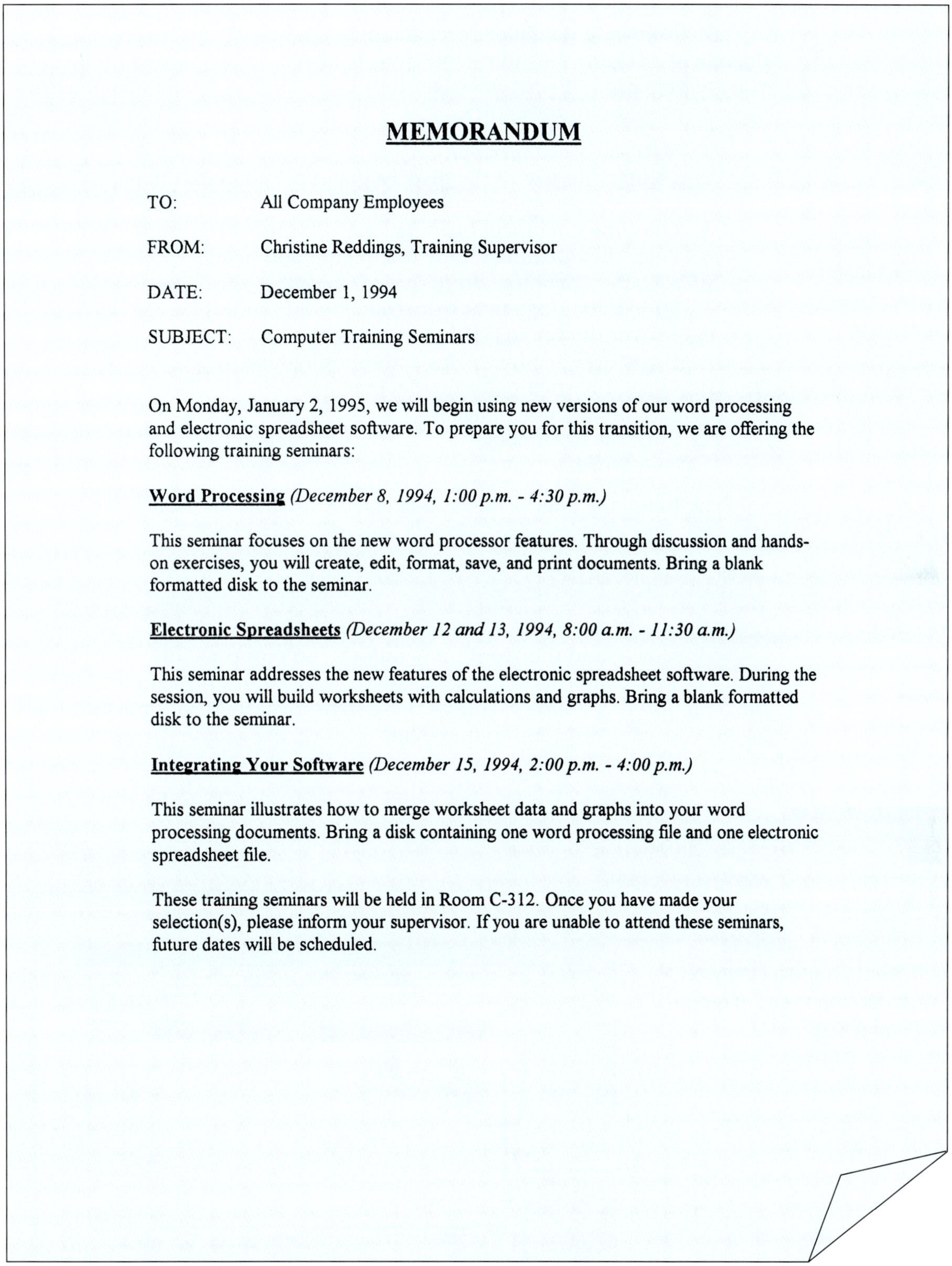

MEMORANDUM

TO: All Company Employees

FROM: Christine Reddings, Training Supervisor

DATE: December 1, 1994

SUBJECT: Computer Training Seminars

On Monday, January 2, 1995, we will begin using new versions of our word processing and electronic spreadsheet software. To prepare you for this transition, we are offering the following training seminars:

Word Processing *(December 8, 1994, 1:00 p.m. - 4:30 p.m.)*

This seminar focuses on the new word processor features. Through discussion and hands-on exercises, you will create, edit, format, save, and print documents. Bring a blank formatted disk to the seminar.

Electronic Spreadsheets *(December 12 and 13, 1994, 8:00 a.m. - 11:30 a.m.)*

This seminar addresses the new features of the electronic spreadsheet software. During the session, you will build worksheets with calculations and graphs. Bring a blank formatted disk to the seminar.

Integrating Your Software *(December 15, 1994, 2:00 p.m. - 4:00 p.m.)*

This seminar illustrates how to merge worksheet data and graphs into your word processing documents. Bring a disk containing one word processing file and one electronic spreadsheet file.

These training seminars will be held in Room C-312. Once you have made your selection(s), please inform your supervisor. If you are unable to attend these seminars, future dates will be scheduled.

FIGURE 1-1

Document Preparation Steps

The following document preparation steps give you an overview of how the document in Figure 1-1 on the previous page will be developed in this project. If you are preparing the document in this project on a personal computer, read these steps without doing them.

1. Start the Word program.
2. Change the size of the displayed and printed characters.
3. Enter the document title (MEMORANDUM).
4. Enter the document heading (TO:, FROM:, DATE:, and SUBJECT: lines).
5. Enter the document body (the memorandum).
6. Save the document on disk.
7. Format the document title (center, bold, underline, and enlarge).
8. Format the seminar titles (bold and underline).
9. Format the seminar dates and times (italicize).
10. Check the spelling of the document.
11. Save the document again.
12. Print the document.
13. Quit Word.

The following pages contain a detailed explanation of each of these steps.

▶ STARTING WORD

To start Word, the Windows Program Manager must display on the screen, and the Word for Windows 2.0 group window must be open. To accomplish these tasks, use the procedures presented earlier in *Introduction to Windows*. Follow these steps to start Word, or ask your instructor how to start Word for your system.

TO START WORD ▼

STEP 1 ▶

Use the mouse to point to the Microsoft Word program-item icon in the Word for Windows 2.0 group window (Figure 1-2).

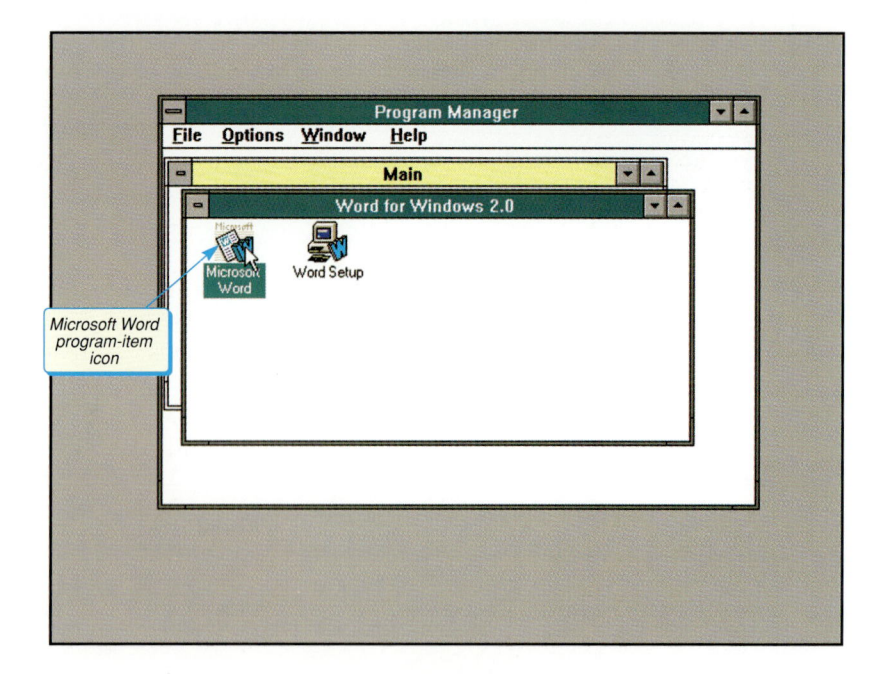

FIGURE 1-2

STEP 2 ▶

Double-click the left mouse button.

Word displays an empty document titled Document1 (Figure 1-3).

FIGURE 1-3

▶ THE WORD SCREEN

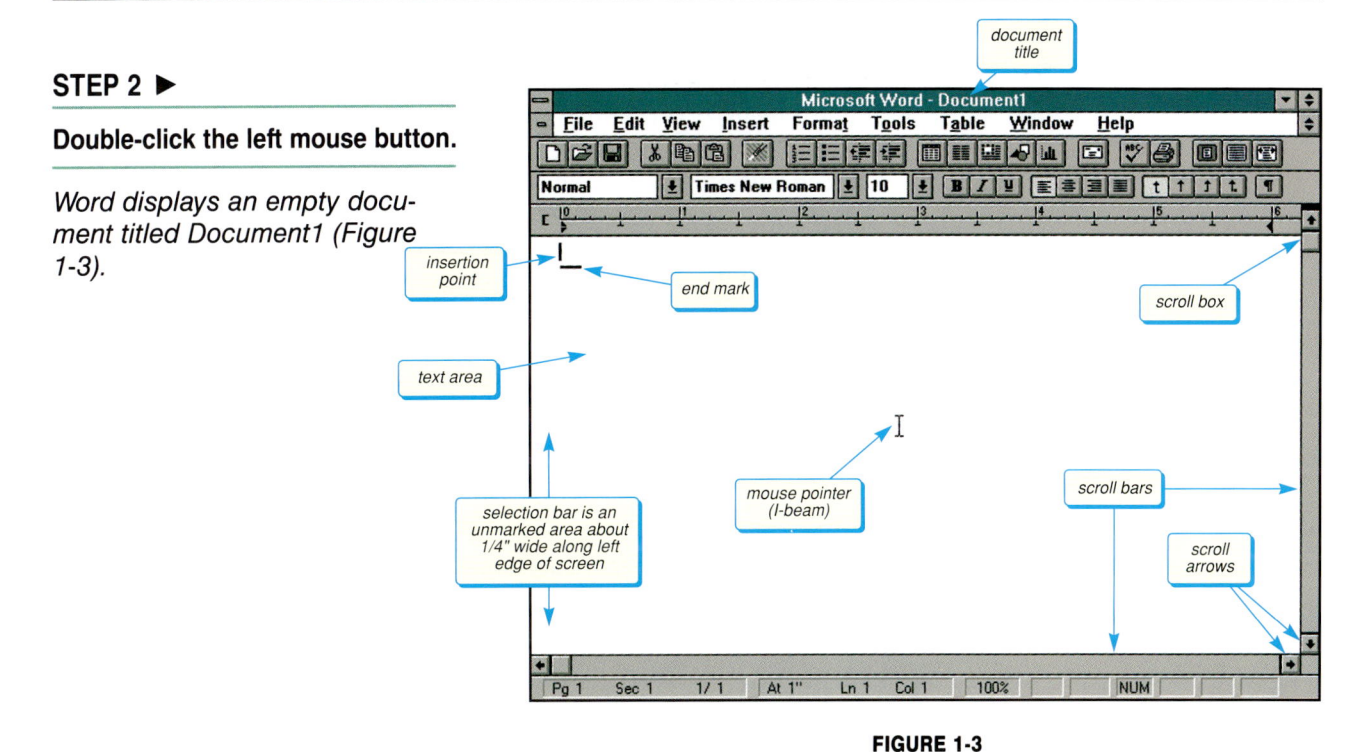

The **Word screen** (Figure 1-3), also called the **workplace**, consists of a variety of features to make your work more efficient and results more professional. (If you are following along on a personal computer and your screen differs from Figure 1-3, select the View menu and choose the Normal command.)

Word Document Window

The **Word document window** contains several elements similar to the document windows in other applications, as well as some elements unique to Word. The main elements of the Word document window are the text area, insertion point, end mark, mouse pointer, scroll bars, and selection bar (Figure 1-3).

TEXT AREA As you type or insert graphs, your text and graphics display in the **text area**.

INSERTION POINT The **insertion point** is a blinking vertical bar that indicates where the text will be inserted when you type. As you type, the insertion point moves to the right and, when you reach the end of a line, downward to the next line. You also insert graphs at the location of the insertion point.

END MARK The **end mark** indicates the end of your document. Each time you begin a new line as you type, the end mark moves downward.

MOUSE POINTER The **mouse pointer** can become one of seventeen different shapes, depending on the task you are performing in Word and the pointer's location on the screen. The mouse pointer in Figure 1-3 on the previous page has the shape of an I-beam (I). The mouse pointer displays as an I-beam when it is in the text area. The other mouse pointer shapes are described when they appear on the screen during this and subsequent projects.

SCROLL BARS You can use the **scroll bars** to display different portions of your document in the document window. The **scroll box** indicates your current location in the document.

SELECTION BAR The **selection bar** is an unmarked area about 1/4" wide along the left edge of the text area that is used to select text with the mouse.

Word is preset to use standard 8 1/2 by 11-inch paper, with 1.25" left and right margins and 1" top and bottom margins. Only a portion of your document, however, displays on the screen at one time. You view the portion of the document displayed on the screen through the **document window** (Figure 1-4).

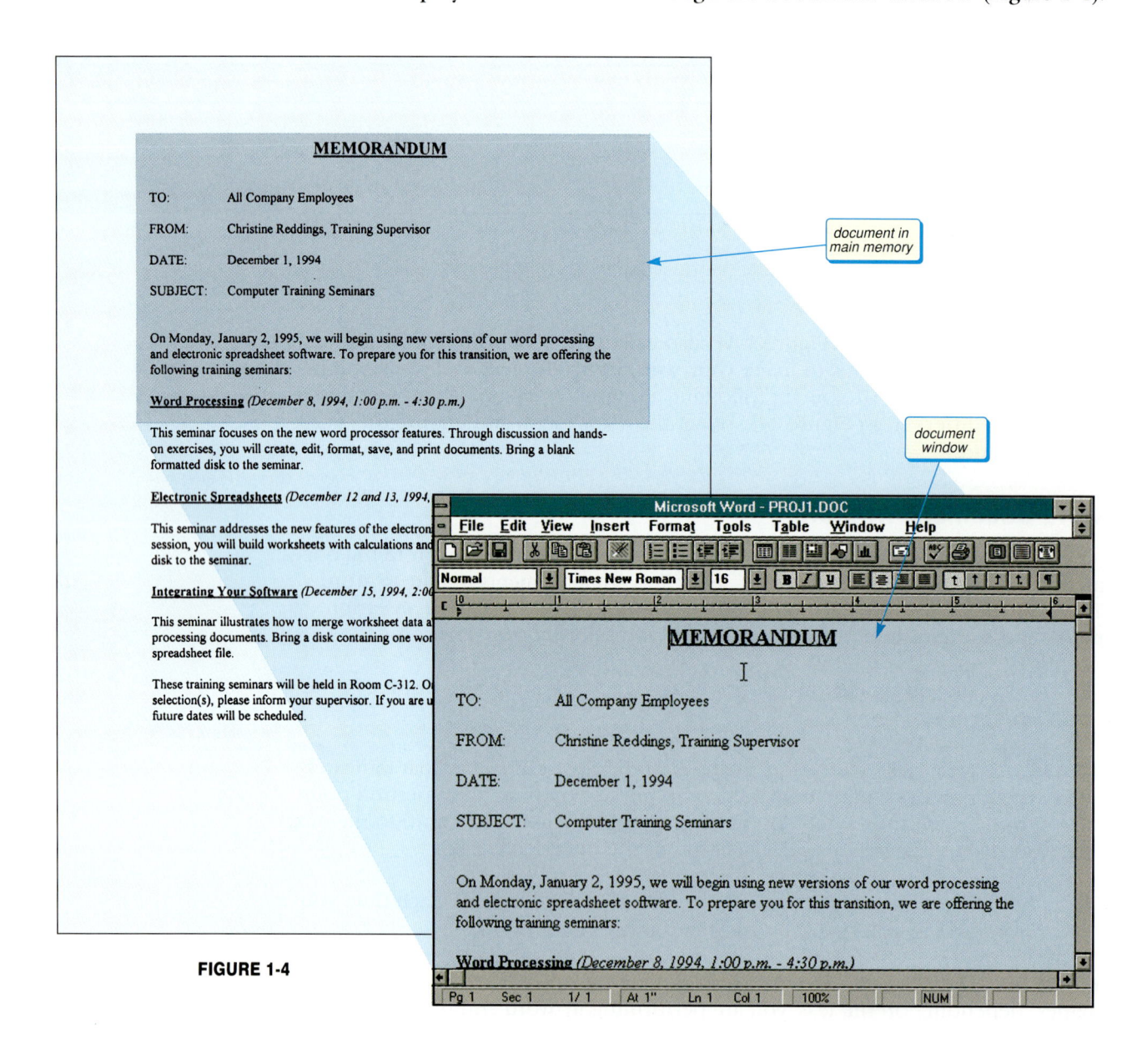

FIGURE 1-4

Menu Bar, Toolbar, Ribbon, Ruler, and Status Bar

The menu bar, Toolbar, ribbon, and ruler appear at the top of the screen just below the title bar (Figure 1-5). The status bar appears at the bottom of the screen.

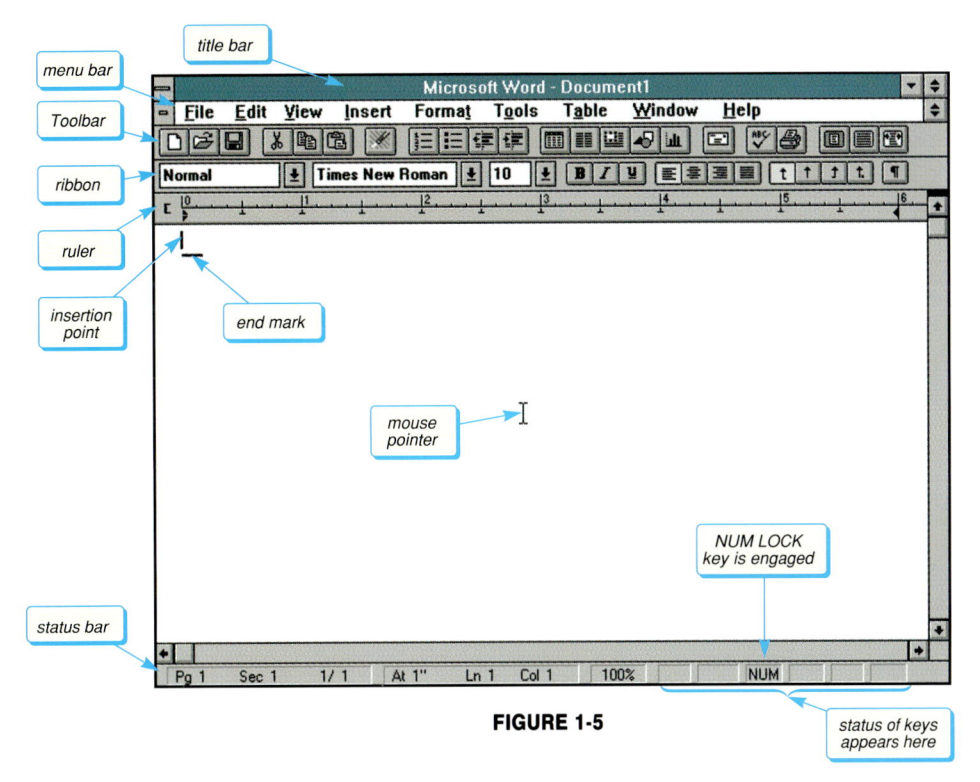

FIGURE 1-5

MENU BAR The **menu bar** displays the Word menu names. Each menu name represents a menu of commands which you can use to retrieve, store, print, and format data in your document. To display a menu such as the File menu, select the menu name in the manner you learned in *Introduction to Windows*.

TOOLBAR The **Toolbar** contains buttons that allow you to perform tasks more quickly than using the menu bar. For example, to print you point to the Print button ( ) and press the left mouse button (called clicking the Print button on the Toolbar). Each button has a picture on the face that helps you remember its function. Figure 1-6 illustrates the Toolbar and identifies its buttons. Each button will be explained in detail when it is used in the projects.

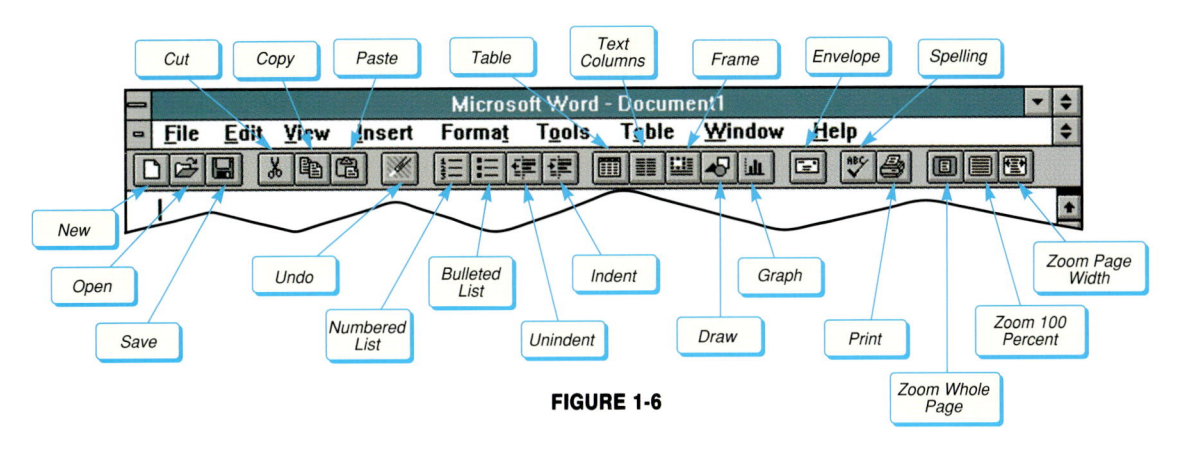

FIGURE 1-6

RIBBON The **ribbon** is located just below the Toolbar. With the ribbon, you can change the appearance of selected text. For example, to underline a selected word, you click the Underline button ([U]) by pointing to the button and pressing the left mouse button. Figure 1-7 illustrates the ribbon and describes the different areas on it. Notice the preset style is Normal, preset character type is Times New Roman, and preset character size is 10. Each of the areas on the ribbon will be explained in detail when it is used in the projects.

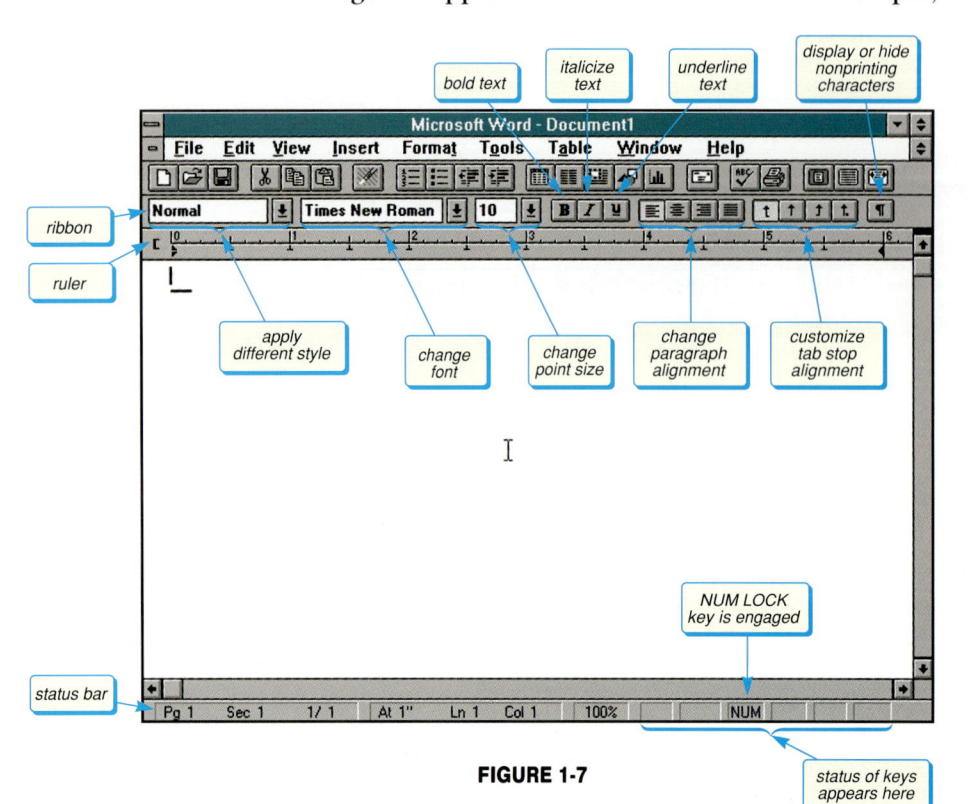

FIGURE 1-7

RULER Below the ribbon is the **ruler** (Figure 1-7). You use the ruler to change paragraph indentation and margin settings.

STATUS BAR The **status bar** is located at the bottom of the screen. From left to right the following information displays about the page shown in Figure 1-7: the page number, the section number, the number of pages through the current page followed by the total number of pages in the document, the position of the insertion point in inches from the top of the page, the line number and column number of the insertion point, the level of magnification, and the status of several keys such as NUM, which indicates the NUM LOCK key is engaged.

When you have selected a command from a menu, the status bar displays a brief description of the currently selected command.

▶ CHANGING THE DEFAULT POINT SIZE

Characters that display on the screen are a specific shape and size. The **font** defines the appearance and shape of the letters, numbers, and special characters. The preset, or default, font is Times New Roman (Figure 1-7). The **point size** specifies the size of the characters on the screen. Character size is gauged by a measurement system called points. A single point is about 1/72 of an inch in height. Thus, a character with a point size of ten is about 10/72 of an inch in height. The default point size in some versions of Word is 10. Many business documents use a point size of 12 as illustrated in Figure 1-1 on page MSW3. If necessary, you can easily change the default point size before you type as shown in the steps on the following page.

THE WORD SCREEN **MSW9**

TO CHANGE THE DEFAULT POINT SIZE BEFORE TYPING ▼

STEP 1 ▶

Point to the Points box arrow.

The mouse pointer changes to a left-pointing block arrow ( ) (Figure 1-8).

FIGURE 1-8

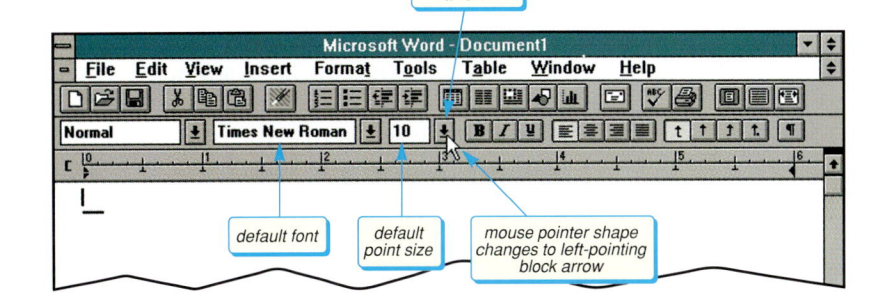

STEP 2 ▶

Click the Points box arrow.

A list of available point sizes displays in the Points drop-down list box (Figure 1-9).

FIGURE 1-9

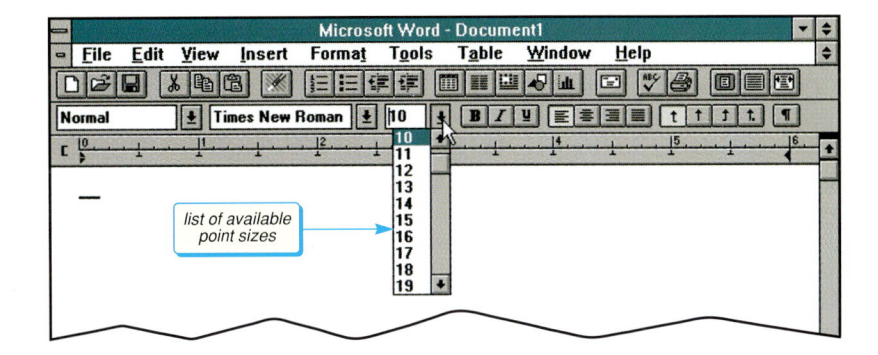

STEP 3 ▶

Point to point size 12 (Figure 1-10).

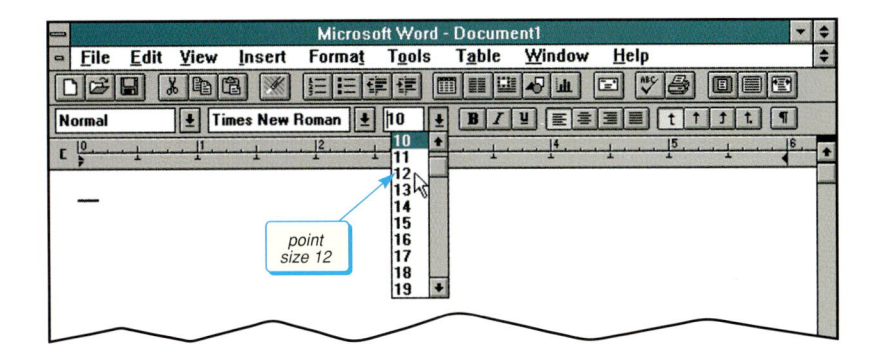

FIGURE 1-10

STEP 4 ▶

Select point size 12 by clicking the left mouse button.

The point size for this document changes to 12 (Figure 1-11).

FIGURE 1-11

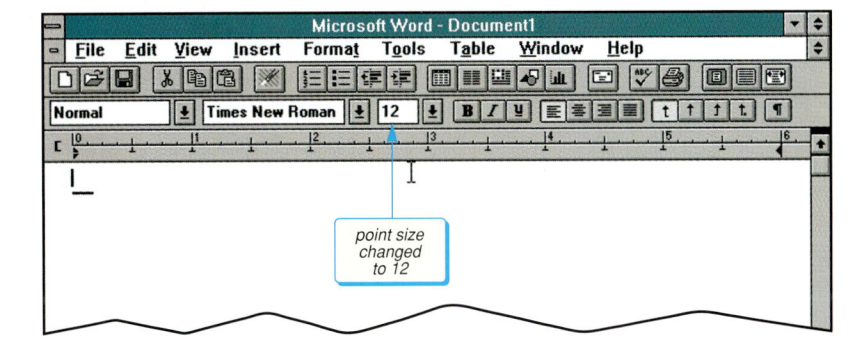

The new default point size takes effect immediately in your document. Word uses this point size for the remainder of this memorandum.

▶ ENTERING TEXT

To prepare a document in Word, you enter text by typing on the keyboard. In Project 1, the title MEMORANDUM appears capitalized on the first line of the document. The following example explains the steps to enter the title in all capital letters at the left margin. Later in the project, the title will be centered across the top of the document, formatted in bold, underlined, and enlarged.

TO ENTER A CAPITALIZED WORD INTO A DOCUMENT ▼

STEP 1 ▶

Press the CAPS LOCK key.

The CAPS indicator appears in the status bar, indicating the CAPS LOCK key has been pressed (Figure 1-12).

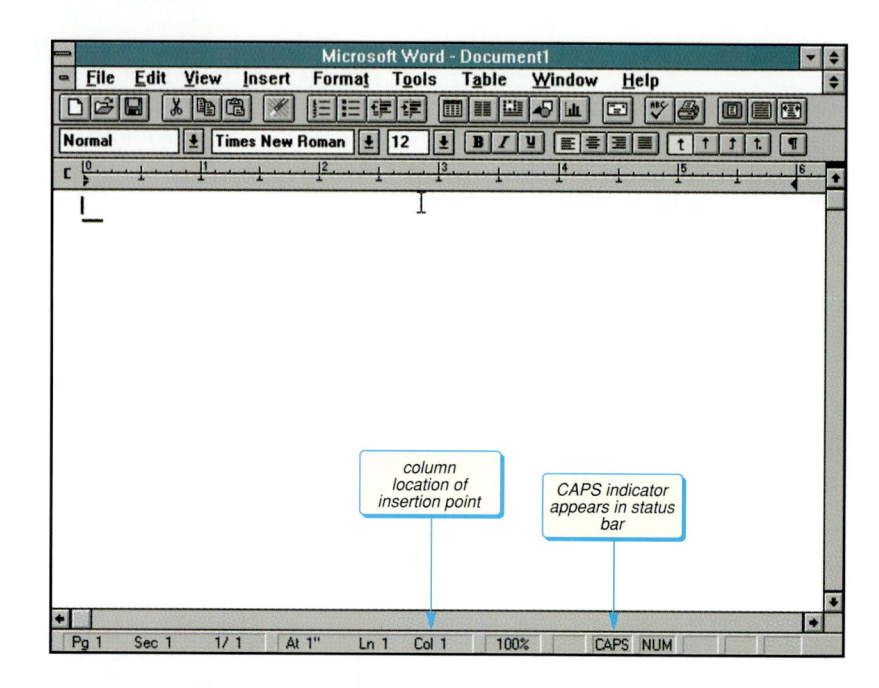

FIGURE 1-12

STEP 2 ▶

Type the title MEMORANDUM.

Word places the M in MEMORANDUM at the location of the insertion point. As you continue typing the title, the insertion point moves to the right (Figure 1-13). If at any time during typing you make an error, press the BACKSPACE key until you have deleted the text in error and then retype text correctly.

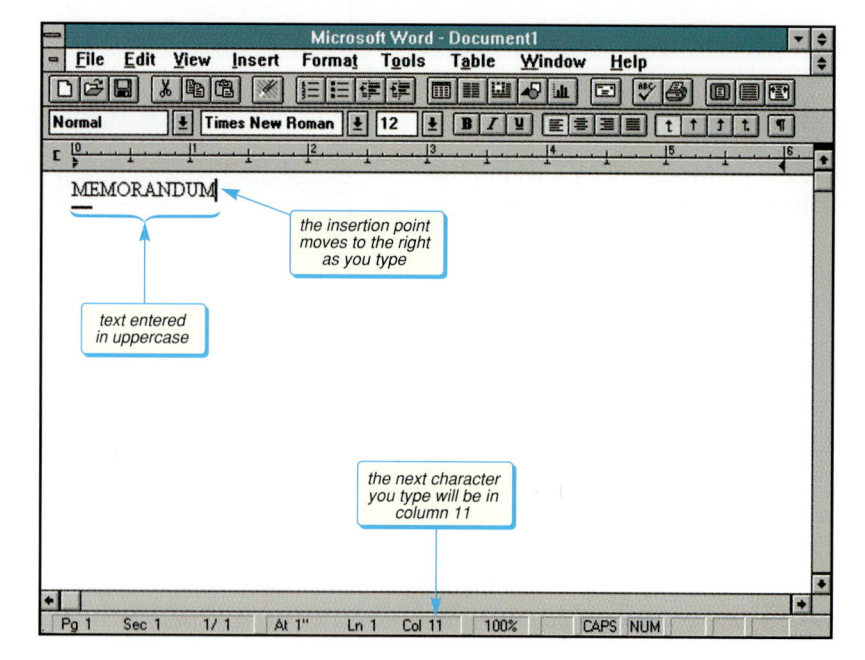

FIGURE 1-13

ENTERING TEXT **MSW11**

STEP 3 ▶

Press the CAPS LOCK key.

The CAPS indicator disappears from the status bar (Figure 1-14). Any subsequent text you type will not be capitalized unless you hold down the SHIFT key or engage CAPS LOCK again.

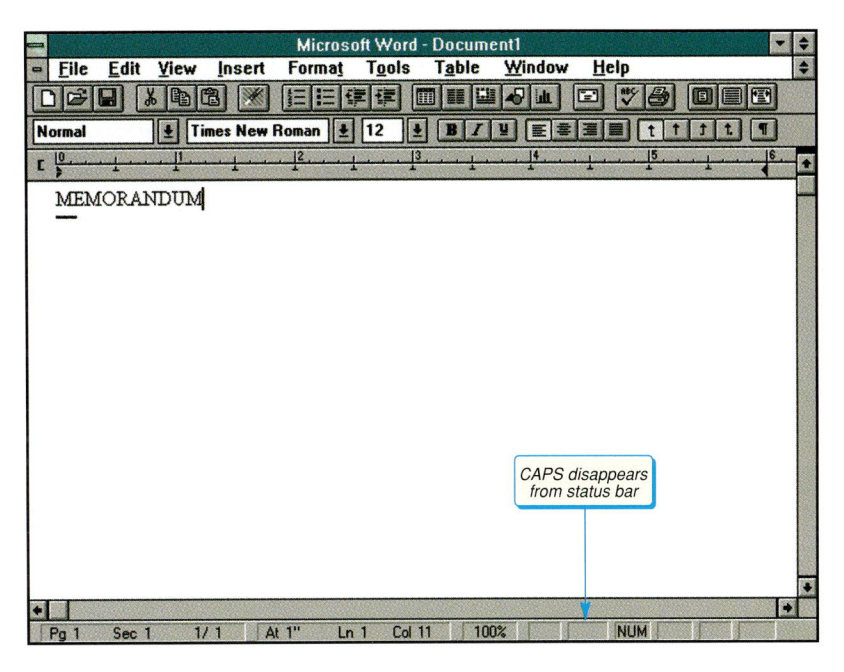

FIGURE 1-14

STEP 4 ▶

Press the ENTER key.

Word creates a new paragraph by moving the insertion point to the beginning of the next line (Figure 1-15). Whenever you press the ENTER key, Word considers the previous line and the next line to be different paragraphs. Notice the status bar indicates the current position of the insertion point.

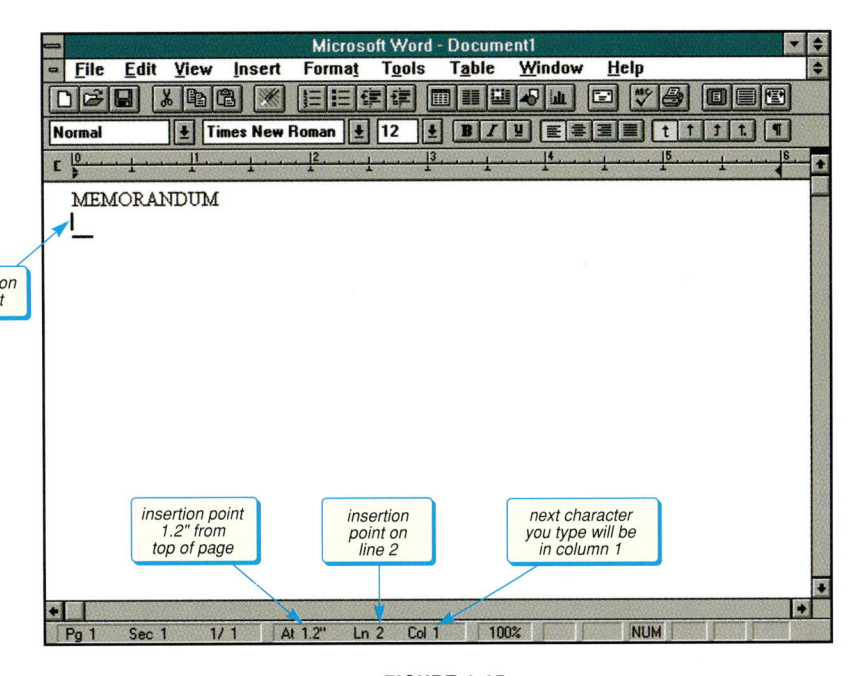

FIGURE 1-15

Entering Blank Lines into a Document

To enter a blank line into a document, press the ENTER key without typing anything on the line. The example on the next page explains how to enter two blank lines after the title MEMORANDUM.

TO ENTER BLANK LINES INTO A DOCUMENT ▼

STEP 1 ▶

Press the ENTER key twice.

Word inserts two blank lines into your document, one for each time you pressed the ENTER key (Figure 1-16).

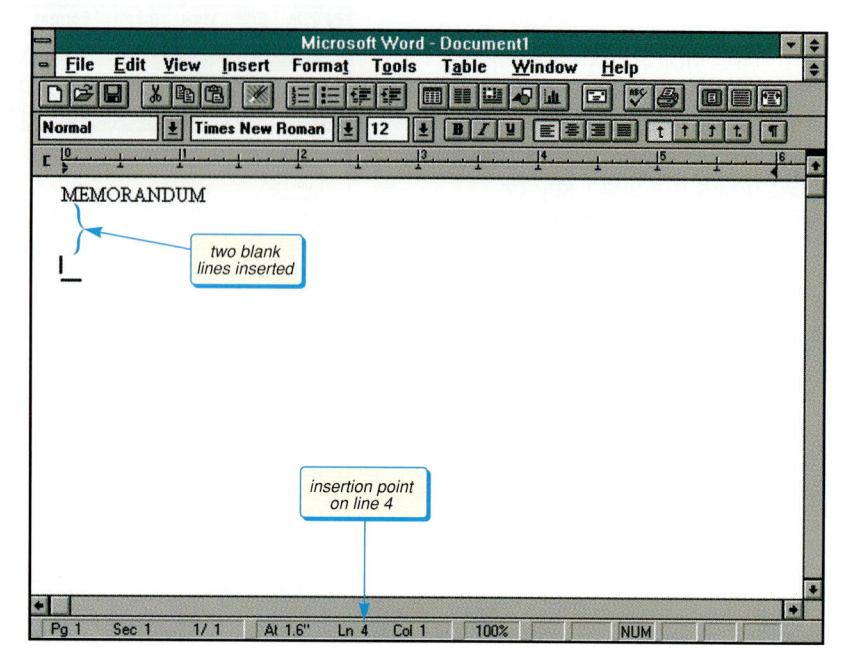

FIGURE 1-16

Using the TAB Key

The next step in creating the memorandum in Project 1 is to enter the heading lines. Notice in Figure 1-17 that the names, date, and subject are vertically aligned. That is, the A in All is directly above the C in Christine, which is directly above the D in December, and so on. You press the TAB key to vertically align text in a document.

Word presets tab stops at every one-half inch. These preset, or default, tabs are indicated on the ruler by inverted Ts (Figure 1-17). In a later project, you will learn how to change the preset tab stops.

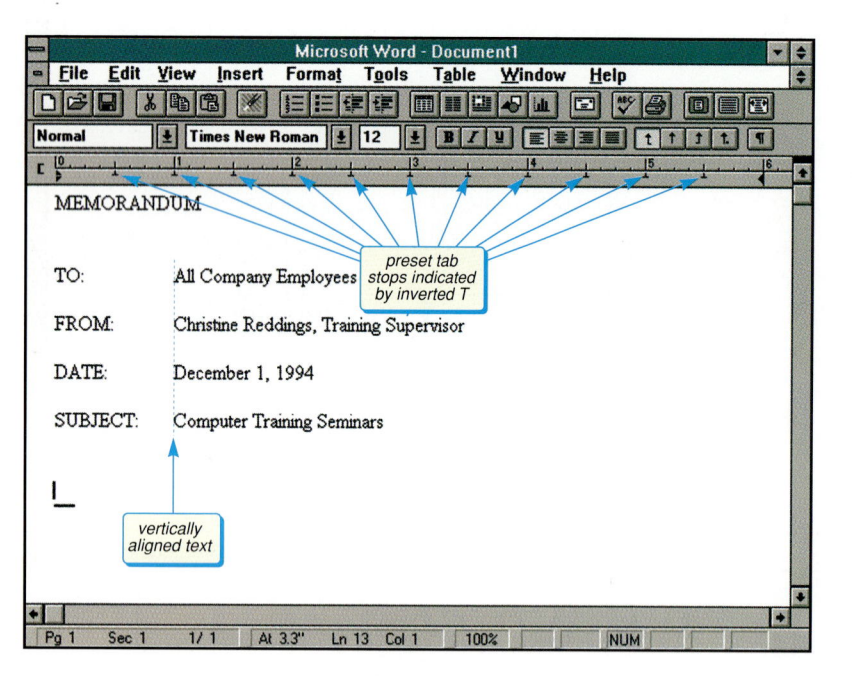

FIGURE 1-17

ENTERING TEXT **MSW13**

TO VERTICALLY ALIGN TEXT WITH THE TAB KEY ▼

STEP 1 ▶

Type the text TO: and press the TAB key twice.

The text displays as you type and the insertion point moves two tab stops to the right, which is one inch from the left margin (Figure 1-18).

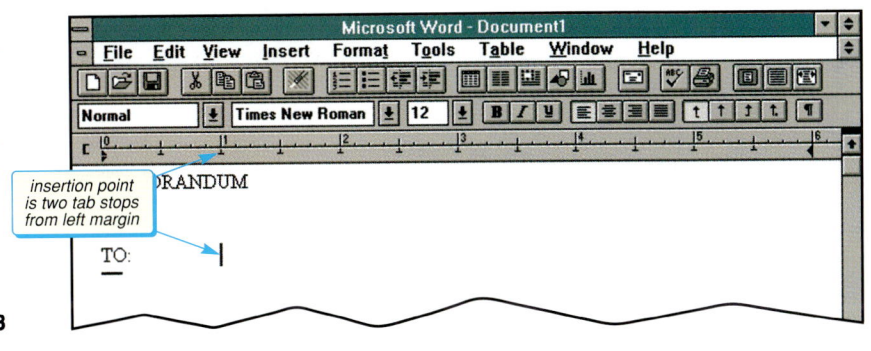

FIGURE 1-18

insertion point is two tab stops from left margin

MEMORANDUM

TO:

STEP 2 ▶

Type the text All Company Employees and press the ENTER key twice.

The text you type is entered into the document and a blank line follows the text (Figure 1-19).

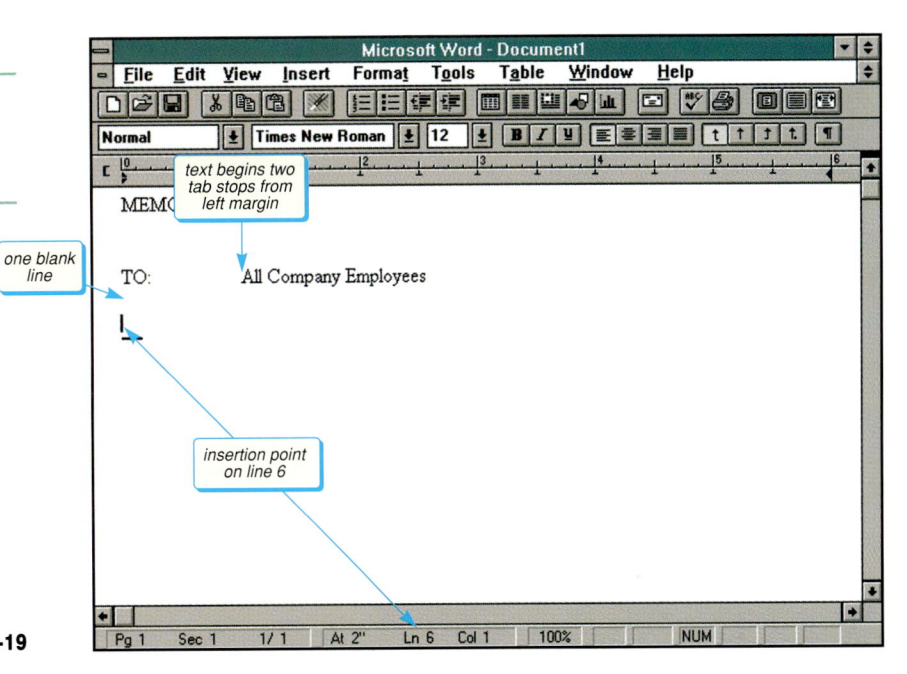

text begins two tab stops from left margin

MEMO

one blank line

TO: All Company Employees

insertion point on line 6

FIGURE 1-19

STEP 3 ▶

Type the text FROM: and press the TAB key once. Type the text Christine Reddings, Training Supervisor and press the ENTER key twice.

The FROM: line is entered followed by a blank line (Figure 1-20). Notice you pressed the TAB key only once to advance to the second tab because the text FROM: extended beyond the first tab stop.

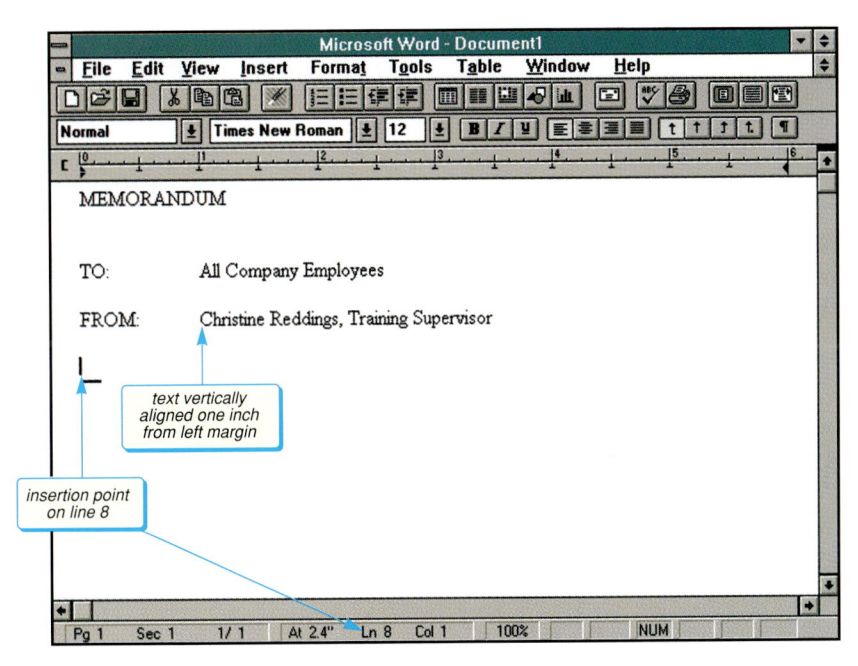

MEMORANDUM

TO: All Company Employees

FROM: Christine Reddings, Training Supervisor

text vertically aligned one inch from left margin

insertion point on line 8

FIGURE 1-20

STEP 4 ▶

Type the text DATE: **and press the** TAB **key twice. Type the text** December 1, 1994 **and press the** ENTER **key twice. Type the text** SUBJECT: **and press the** TAB **key once. Type the text** Computer Training Seminars **and press the** ENTER **key three times.**

The memorandum heading lines display as shown in Figure 1-21.

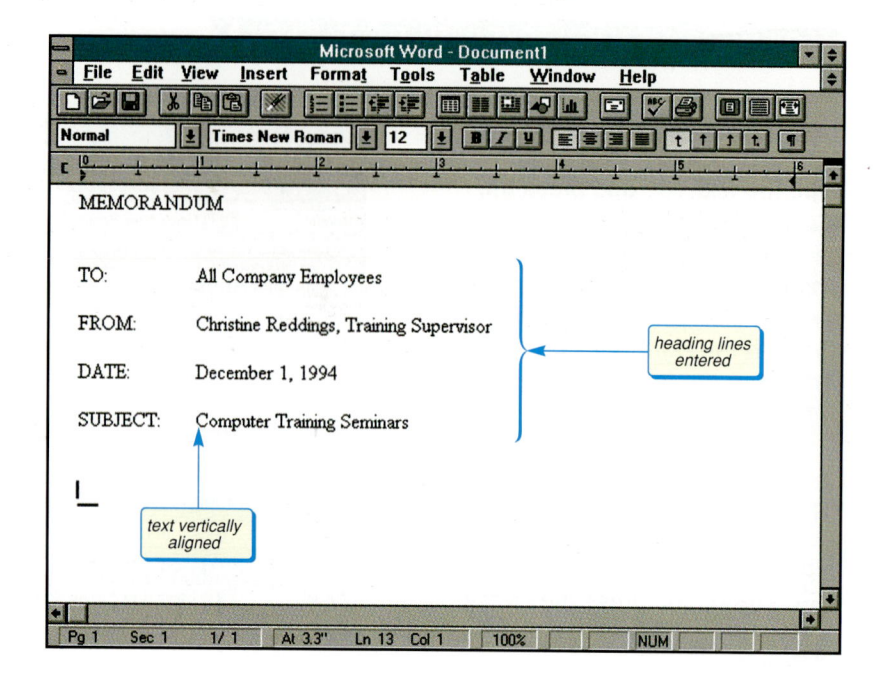

FIGURE 1-21

Displaying Nonprinting Characters

You will find it helpful to display nonprinting characters that indicate where in the document you pressed the ENTER key, SPACEBAR, or TAB key. The paragraph mark (¶) is a **nonprinting character** that indicates where you pressed the ENTER key. A raised dot (•) shows where you pressed the SPACEBAR. A right-pointing arrow (→) indicates where you pressed the TAB key. Nonprinting characters display *only* on the screen. They do not appear in printed documents. Other nonprinting characters are discussed when they display on the screen during subsequent projects. The following steps illustrate how to display nonprinting characters.

TO DISPLAY NONPRINTING CHARACTERS ▼

STEP 1 ▶

Point to the Show/Hide Nonprinting Characters button (¶) on the ribbon (Figure 1-22).

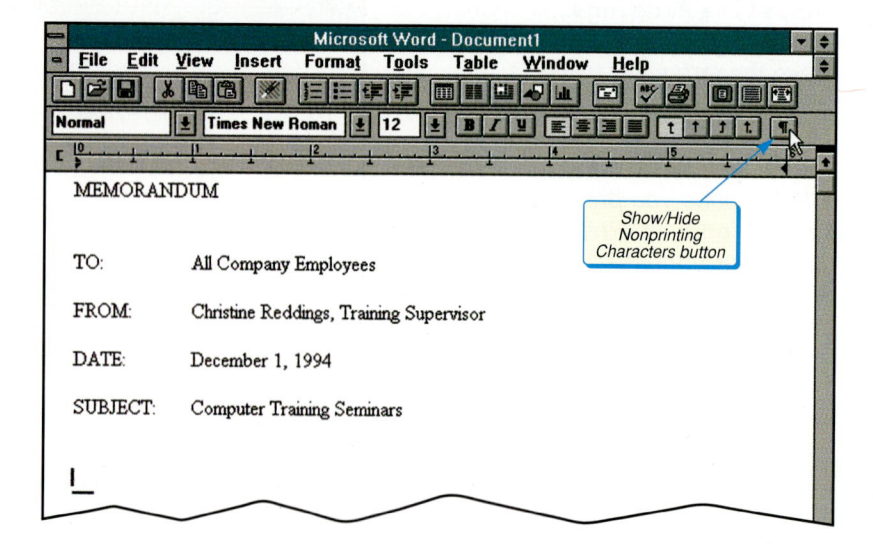

FIGURE 1-22

ENTERING TEXT **MSW15**

STEP 2 ▶

Click the Show/Hide Nonprinting Characters button.

Word displays nonprinting characters on the screen and the Show/Hide Nonprinting Characters button on the ribbon is recessed (Figure 1-23).

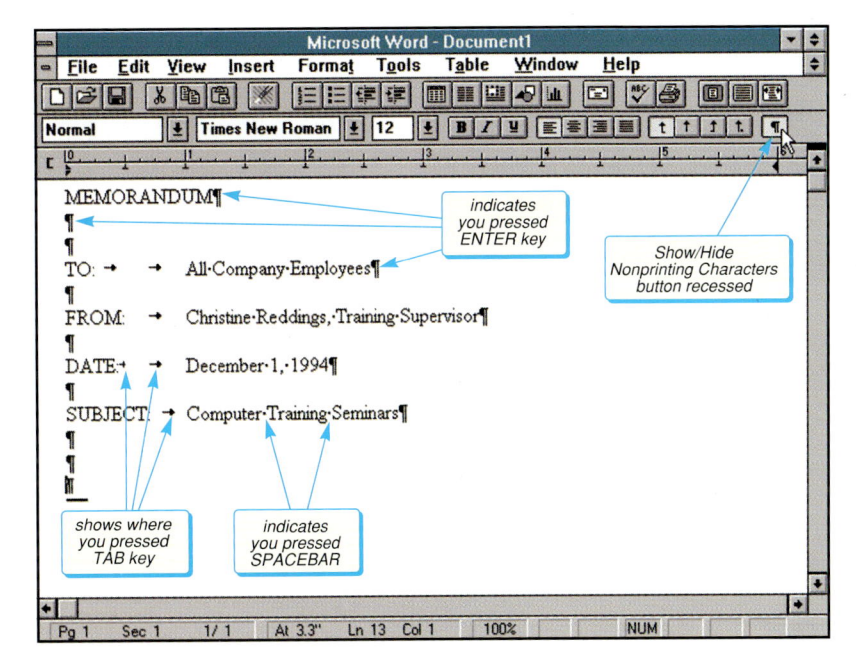

FIGURE 1-23

Notice several changes to your screen display (Figure 1-23). The paragraph symbol appears at the end of each line, which indicates you pressed the ENTER key. Between each word, a raised dot appears indicating you pressed the SPACEBAR. Six right-pointing arrows show where you pressed the TAB key. Finally, the Show/Hide Nonprinting Characters button is recessed, which indicates it is selected.

If you feel the nonprinting characters clutter your screen, you can hide them by clicking the Show/Hide Nonprinting Characters button again.

Using the Wordwrap Feature

Wordwrap allows you to type words in a paragraph continually without pressing the ENTER key at the end of each line. When the insertion point moves beyond the right margin, Word automatically positions it at the beginning of the next line. As you type, if a word extends beyond the right margin, Word also automatically positions the word on the next line with the insertion point. Thus, as you enter text using Word, do not press the ENTER key when the insertion point reaches the right margin. Press the ENTER key only in these circumstances:

1. to insert blank lines into a document.
2. to begin a new paragraph.
3. to terminate a short line of text and advance to the next line.
4. in response to certain Word commands.

TO USE THE WORDWRAP FEATURE

STEP 1 ▶

Type the first sentence in the body of the document: On Monday, January 2, 1995, we will begin using new versions of our word processing and electronic spreadsheet software.

Word automatically wraps the word and *to the beginning of line 14 because it is too long to fit on line 13 (Figure 1-24). Notice that you only press the* SPACEBAR *one time following the end of the sentence. It is standard practice to type one space after periods and colons when using variable character fonts such as Times New Roman. (Your document may wordwrap on a different word depending on the type of printer you are using.)*

[Screenshot callouts: ENTER key not pressed when right margin reached; press SPACEBAR only once after period; word and could not fit on line 13, so Word wrapped it around to beginning of line 14]

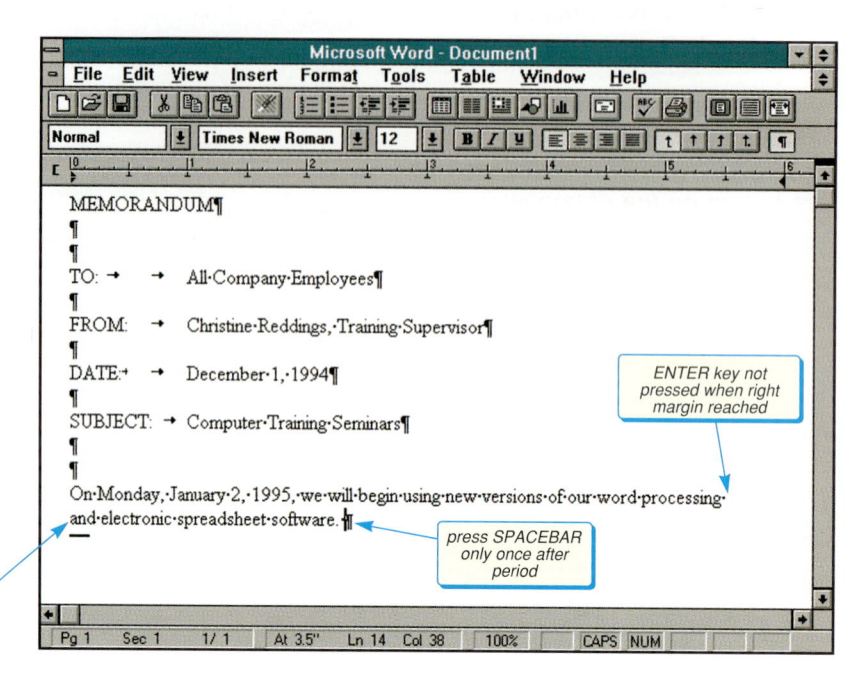

FIGURE 1-24

STEP 2 ▶

Type the second sentence: To prepare you for this transition, we are offering the following training seminars: **and press the** ENTER **key twice.**

Word automatically wraps the word following *to line 15 because it is too long to fit on line 14. The second sentence is followed by a paragraph symbol and a blank line (Figure 1-25).*

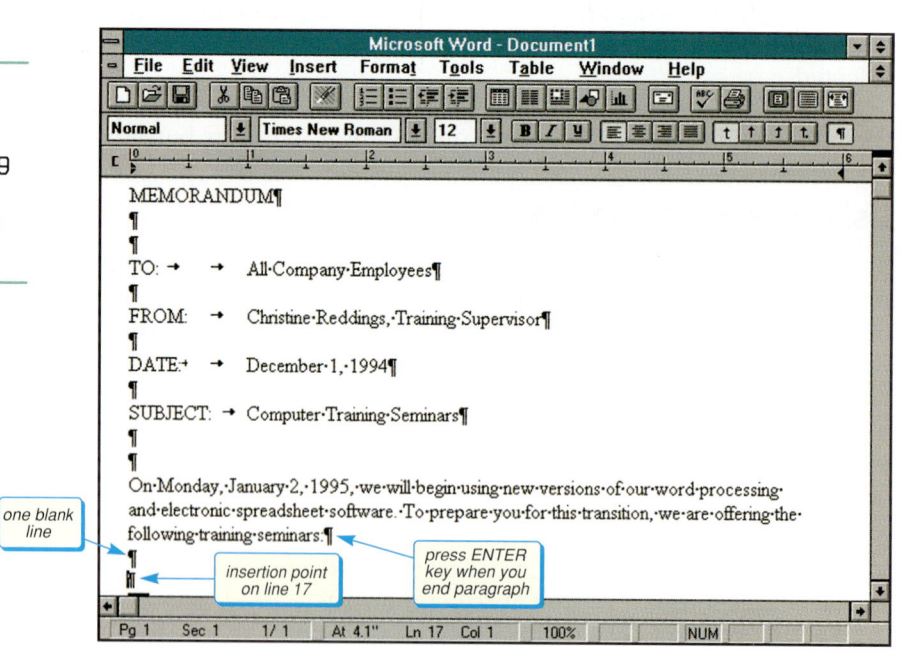

[Screenshot callouts: one blank line; insertion point on line 17; press ENTER key when you end paragraph]

FIGURE 1-25

ENTERING TEXT **MSW17**

Entering Documents Too Long for the Document Window

As you type more lines of text than Word can display in the text area, Word **scrolls** the top portion of the document upward off of the screen. Although you cannot see the text once it scrolls off the screen, it still remains in the document. Recall that the document window allows you to view only a portion of your document at one time (Figure 1-4 on page MSW6).

TO ENTER A DOCUMENT TOO LONG FOR THE DOCUMENT WINDOW ▼

STEP 1 ▶

Type the word processing paragraphs into the memorandum as shown in Figure 1-26.

Word scrolls the title and the lines TO: and FROM: off the top of the screen. (Your screen may scroll differently depending on the type of monitor or printer you are using.)

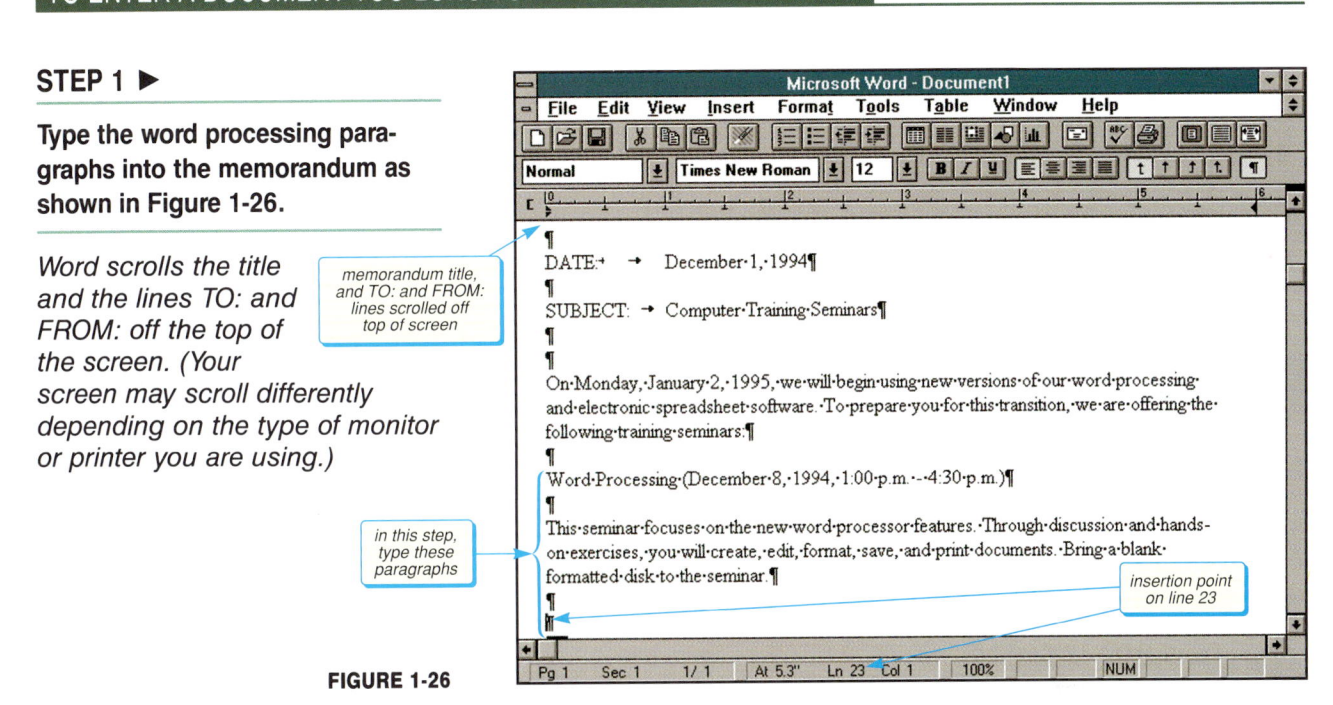

FIGURE 1-26

STEP 2 ▶

Type the remainder of the paragraphs into the memorandum as shown in Figure 1-27.

Word scrolls most of the word processing paragraphs off of the screen. The document, without formatting, is now complete (Figure 1-27).

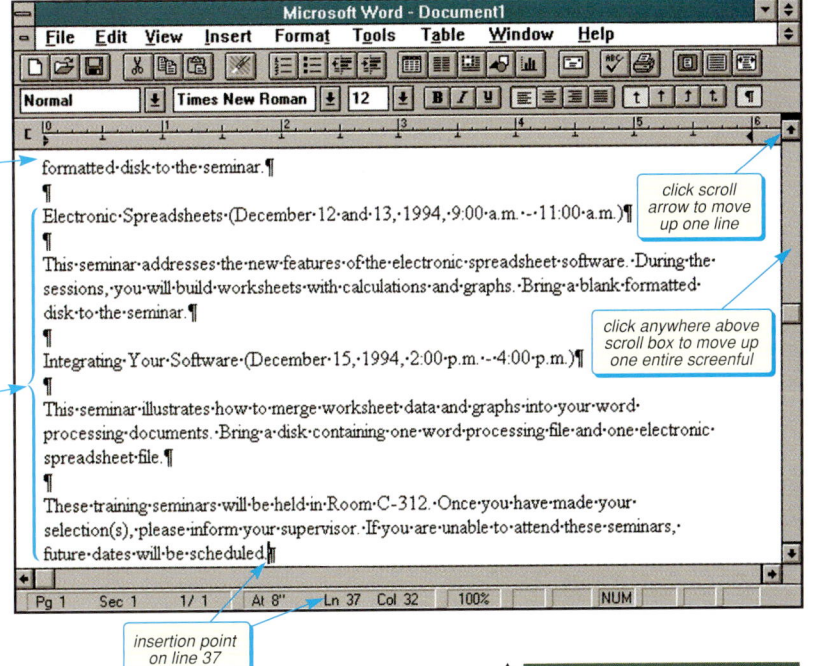

FIGURE 1-27

When Word scrolls text off the top of the screen, the scroll box on the scroll bar at the right edge of the document window moves downward. The scroll box indicates the current relative location of the insertion point in the document. To move the insertion point to a portion of the document that has scrolled off the screen, you can drag the scroll box upward or downward. To move the document up or down one entire screenful at a time, you can click anywhere above or below the scroll box on the scroll bar or press PAGE UP or PAGE DOWN on the keyboard. To move the document up or down one line at a time in the window, you can click the scroll arrow at the top or bottom of the scroll bar. To move to the top of the document using the keyboard, press CTRL + HOME.

▶ SAVING A DOCUMENT

When you are creating a document in Word, the computer stores it in main memory. If the computer is turned off or if you lose electrical power, the document is lost. Hence, it is mandatory to save on disk any document that you will use later. The following steps illustrate how to save a document on a diskette inserted in drive A using the Save button on the Toolbar.

TO SAVE A NEW DOCUMENT ▼

STEP 1 ▶

Insert a formatted disk into drive A. Point to the Save button (🖫) on the Toolbar and click.

Word responds by displaying the Save As dialog box with the insertion point in the File Name box (Figure 1-28).

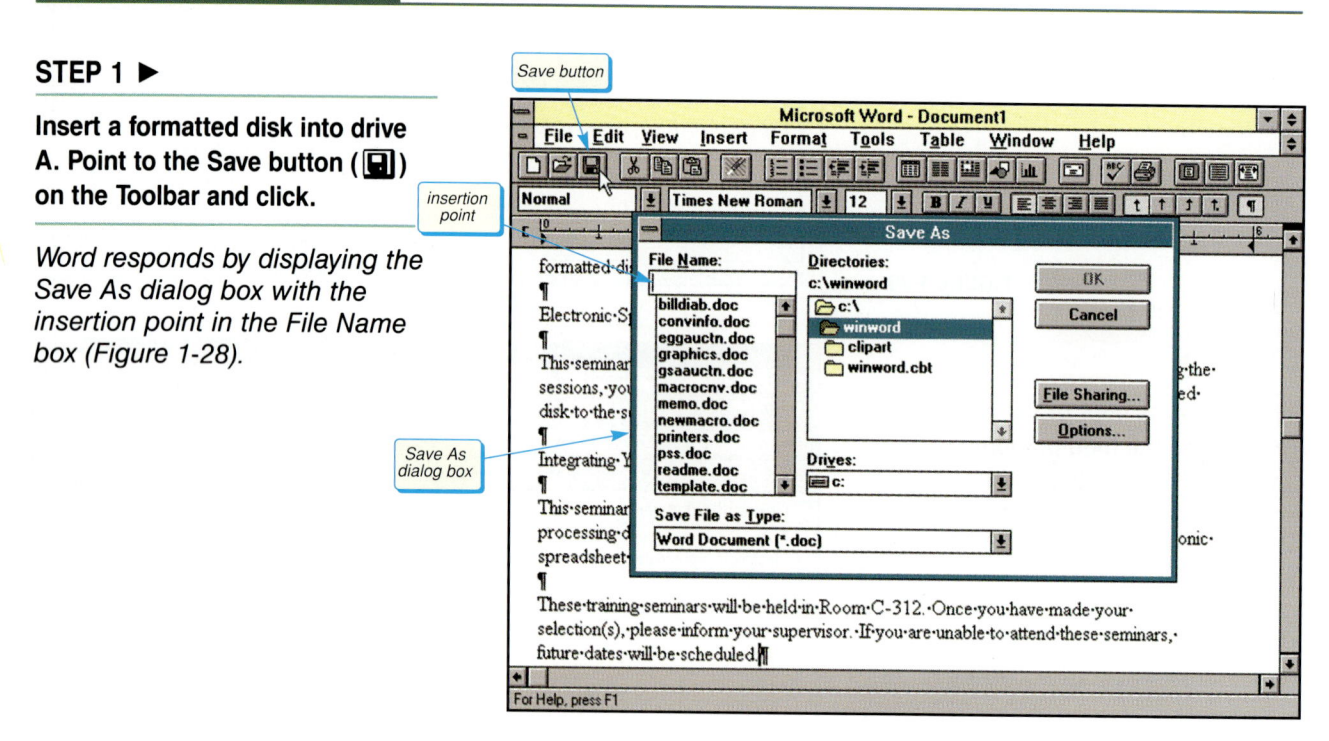

FIGURE 1-28

SAVING A DOCUMENT **MSW19**

STEP 2 ▶

Type the filename `proj1` in the File Name box. Do not press the ENTER key after typing the filename.

The filename proj1 displays in the File Name box (Figure 1-29).

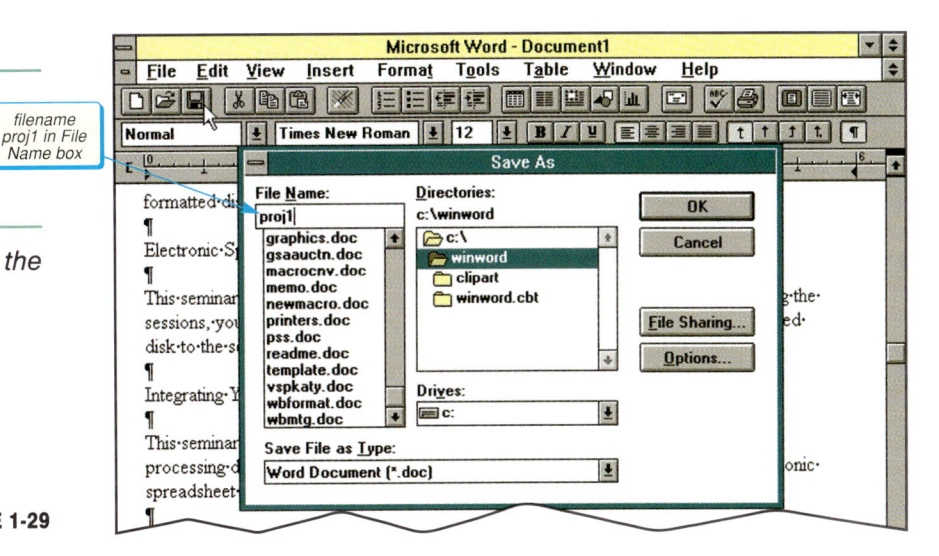

FIGURE 1-29

STEP 3 ▶

Click the Drives drop-down list box arrow and point to (a:).

A list of the available drives appears (Figure 1-30).

FIGURE 1-30

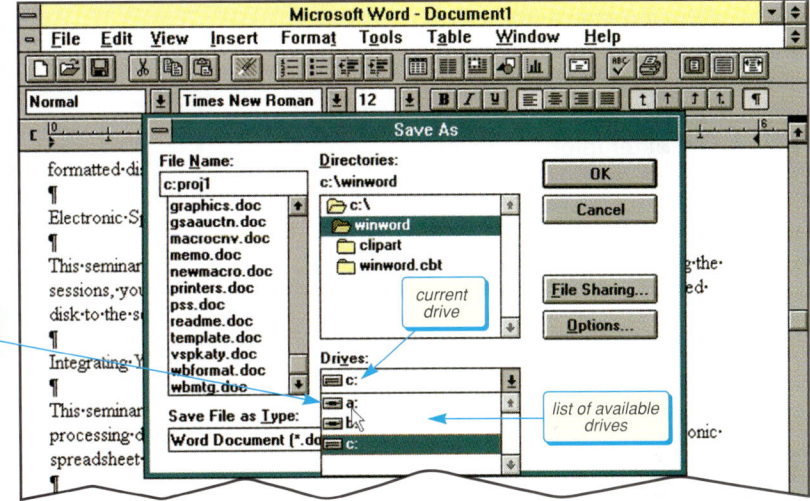

STEP 4 ▶

Select drive a: by clicking it. Point to the OK button.

Drive a: becomes the selected drive (Figure 1-31). The names of existing files stored on the diskette in drive a: appear in the File Name list box. In Figure 1-31 no files are stored on the diskette in drive A.

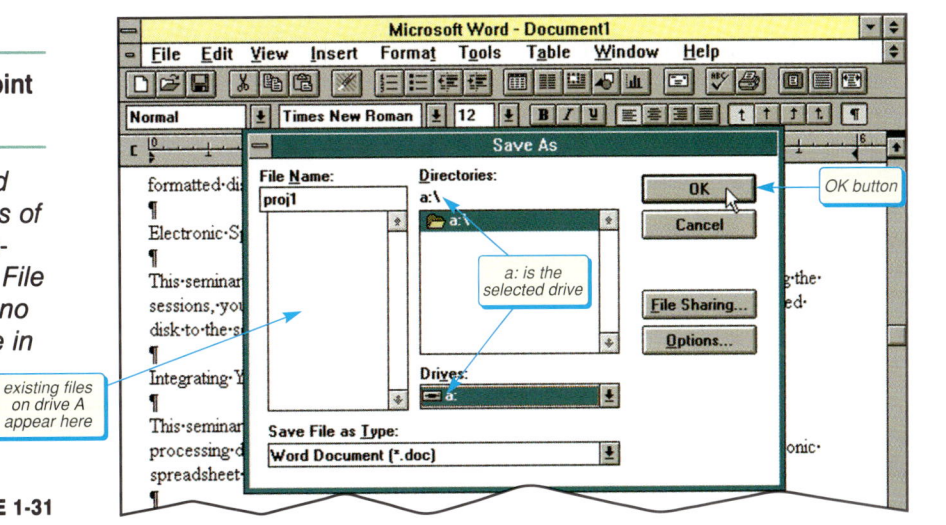

FIGURE 1-31

MSW20　PROJECT 1　CREATING AND EDITING A DOCUMENT

STEP 5 ▶

Choose the OK button in the Save As dialog box.

Word displays a Summary Info dialog box (Figure 1-32).

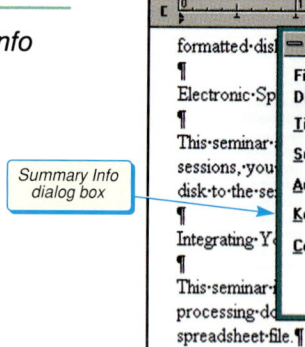

FIGURE 1-32

STEP 6 ▶

If you wish, you may enter information in the Summary Info dialog box to further identify your document, as shown in Figure 1-33. If you enter information into the text boxes, be sure to press the TAB key when advancing from one text box to the next.

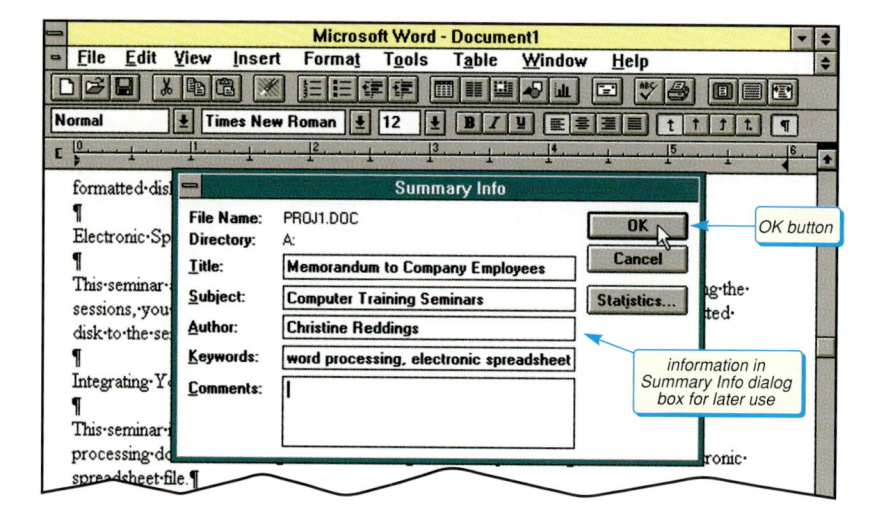

FIGURE 1-33

STEP 7 ▶

Choose the OK button in the Summary Info dialog box. Then press CTRL + HOME.

*Word saves the document on the diskette in drive A under the name proj1.doc. Word automatically appends the extension **.doc** (which stands for Word document) to the file name proj1. Although the memorandum is saved on disk, it also remains in main memory and displays on the screen. As a result of pressing CTRL + HOME, the insertion point is at the top of your document (Figure 1-34).*

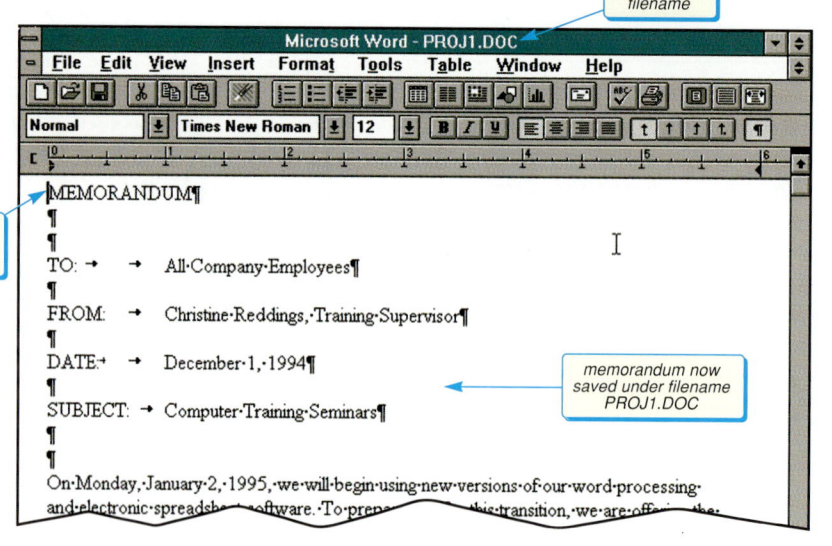

FIGURE 1-34

▶ FORMATTING PARAGRAPHS AND CHARACTERS IN A DOCUMENT

The text for Project 1 is now complete. The next step is to format the characters and paragraphs within the memorandum. Paragraphs encompass the text up to and including the paragraph mark (¶). **Paragraph formatting** is the process of changing the appearance of a paragraph. For example, you can center or indent a paragraph.

Characters include letters, numbers, punctuation marks, and symbols. **Character formatting** is the process of changing the way characters appear on the screen and in print. You use character formatting to emphasize certain words and improve readability of a document. With Word, you can format before you type or apply new formats after you type. Earlier, you changed the point size before you typed any text. Then, you entered the text. Now, you will format existing text.

Figure 1-35a shows the memorandum before formatting the characters in it. Figure 1-35b on the next page shows the memorandum after formatting it. As you can see from the two figures, a document that is formatted is not only easier to read, but it looks more professional.

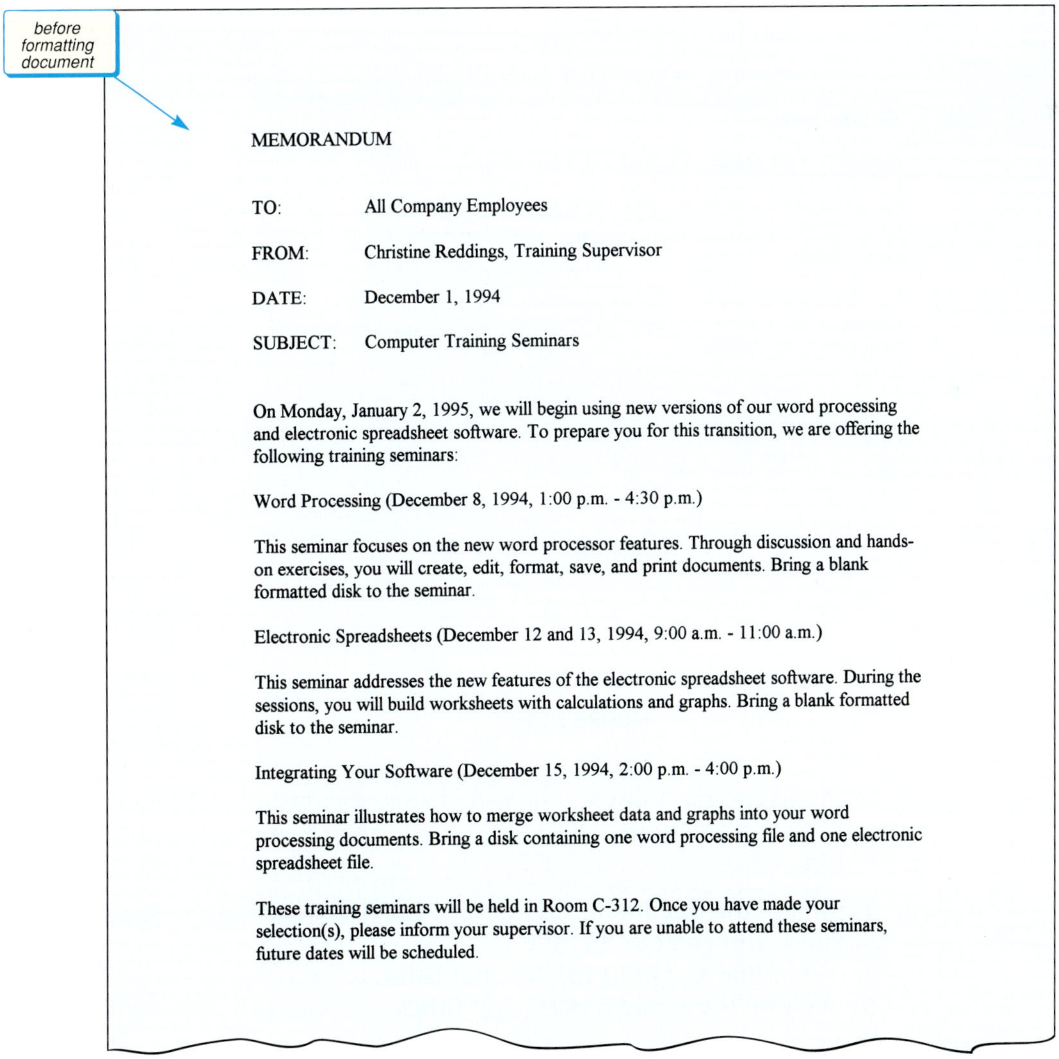

before formatting document

MEMORANDUM

TO: All Company Employees

FROM: Christine Reddings, Training Supervisor

DATE: December 1, 1994

SUBJECT: Computer Training Seminars

On Monday, January 2, 1995, we will begin using new versions of our word processing and electronic spreadsheet software. To prepare you for this transition, we are offering the following training seminars:

Word Processing (December 8, 1994, 1:00 p.m. - 4:30 p.m.)

This seminar focuses on the new word processor features. Through discussion and hands-on exercises, you will create, edit, format, save, and print documents. Bring a blank formatted disk to the seminar.

Electronic Spreadsheets (December 12 and 13, 1994, 9:00 a.m. - 11:00 a.m.)

This seminar addresses the new features of the electronic spreadsheet software. During the sessions, you will build worksheets with calculations and graphs. Bring a blank formatted disk to the seminar.

Integrating Your Software (December 15, 1994, 2:00 p.m. - 4:00 p.m.)

This seminar illustrates how to merge worksheet data and graphs into your word processing documents. Bring a disk containing one word processing file and one electronic spreadsheet file.

These training seminars will be held in Room C-312. Once you have made your selection(s), please inform your supervisor. If you are unable to attend these seminars, future dates will be scheduled.

FIGURE 1-35a

<u>**MEMORANDUM**</u> ← centered, bold, and underlined

(after formatting document)

TO: All Company Employees

FROM: Christine Reddings, Training Supervisor

DATE: December 1, 1994

SUBJECT: Computer Training Seminars

On Monday, January 2, 1995, we will begin using new versions of our word processing and electronic spreadsheet software. To prepare you for this transition, we are offering the following training seminars:

<u>**Word Processing**</u> *(December 8, 1994, 1:00 p.m. - 4:30 p.m.)*

This seminar focuses on the new word processor features. Through discussion and hands-on exercises, you will create, edit, format, save, and print documents. Bring a blank formatted disk to the seminar.

<u>**Electronic Spreadsheets**</u> *(December 12 and 13, 1994, 8:00 a.m. - 11:30 a.m.)*

This seminar addresses the new features of the electronic spreadsheet software. During the session, you will build worksheets with calculations and graphs. Bring a blank formatted disk to the seminar.

<u>**Integrating Your Software**</u> *(December 15, 1994, 2:00 p.m. - 4:00 p.m.)*

This seminar illustrates how to merge worksheet data and graphs into your word processing documents. Bring a disk containing one word processing file and one electronic spreadsheet file.

These training seminars will be held in Room C-312. Once you have made your selection(s), please inform your supervisor. If you are unable to attend these seminars, future dates will be scheduled.

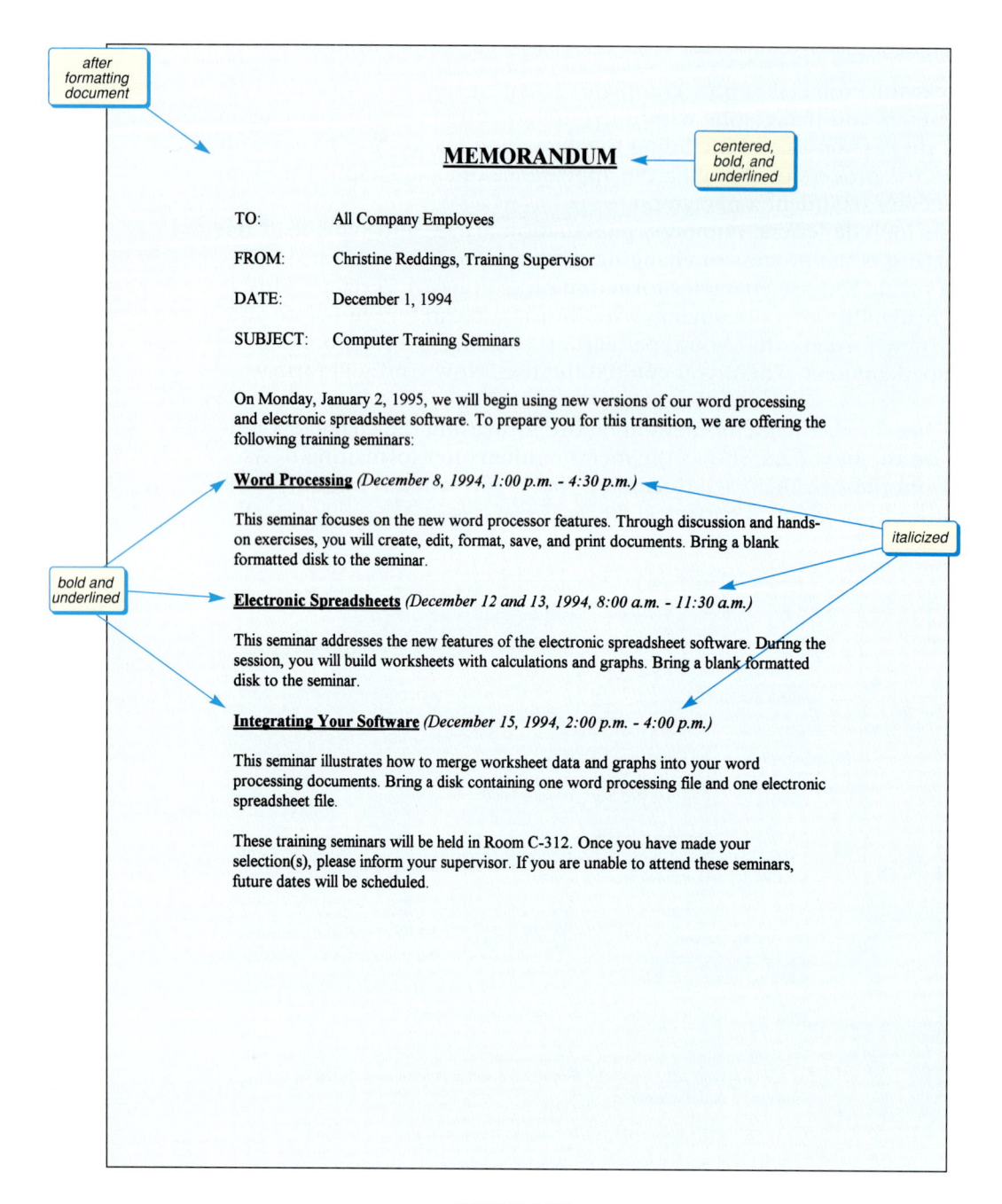

(bold and underlined; italicized)

FIGURE 1-35b

In the pages that follow, you will change the unformatted memorandum in Figure 1-35a, on the previous page, to the formatted memorandum in Figure 1-35b using these steps:

1. Center the document title, MEMORANDUM, across the page. Underline, bold, and enlarge the title.
2. Underline and bold the seminar titles.
3. Italicize the seminar dates and times.

The process required to format the memorandum is explained on the following pages. The first formatting step is to center the title MEMORANDUM between the margins.

FORMATTING PARAGRAPHS AND CHARACTERS IN A DOCUMENT **MSW23**

TO CENTER A PARAGRAPH ▼

STEP 1 ▶

Position the insertion point anywhere in the paragraph to be centered and point to the Centered Text button (☰) on the ribbon (Figure 1-36).

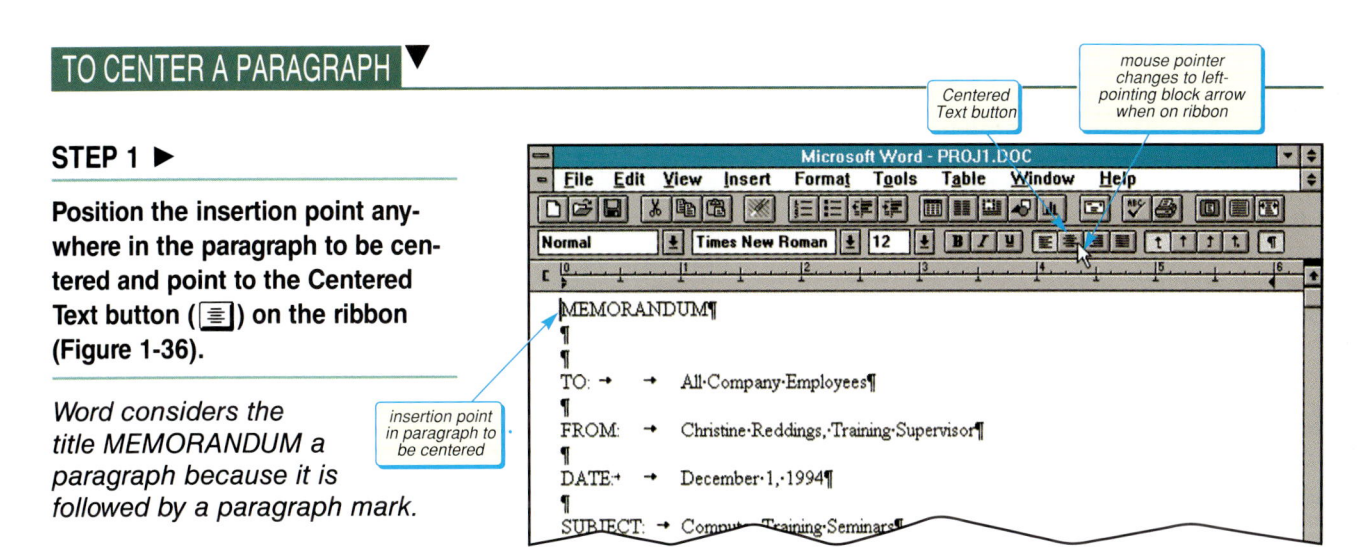

Word considers the title MEMORANDUM a paragraph because it is followed by a paragraph mark.

FIGURE 1-36

STEP 2 ▶

Click the Centered Text button on the ribbon.

Word centers the title MEMORANDUM between the left and right margins on line one (Figure 1-37). The Centered Text button on the ribbon is recessed, indicating the paragraph is centered.

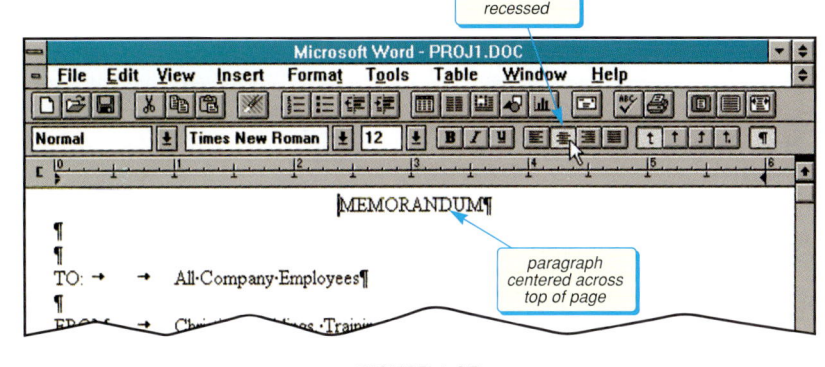

FIGURE 1-37

Selecting and Formatting Characters

To format characters in a document, you must first **select** the characters you want to format. Selected text is highlighted. For example, if your screen normally displays dark letters on a light background, then selected text appears as light letters on a dark background.

To underline, bold, and enlarge the title MEMORANDUM in Project 1, you must first select it as described in the following steps.

TO SELECT A SINGLE WORD ▼

STEP 1 ▶

Position the mouse pointer somewhere in the word MEMORANDUM.

The I-beam rests in the word MEMORANDUM (Figure 1-38).

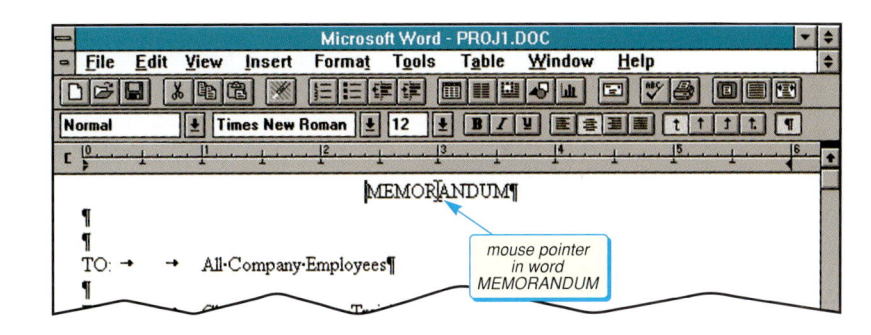

FIGURE 1-38

MSW24   PROJECT 1   CREATING AND EDITING A DOCUMENT

STEP 2 ▶

Double-click the left mouse button.

A highlight appears on the title MEMORANDUM and the mouse pointer changes to a left-pointing block arrow (Figure 1-39).

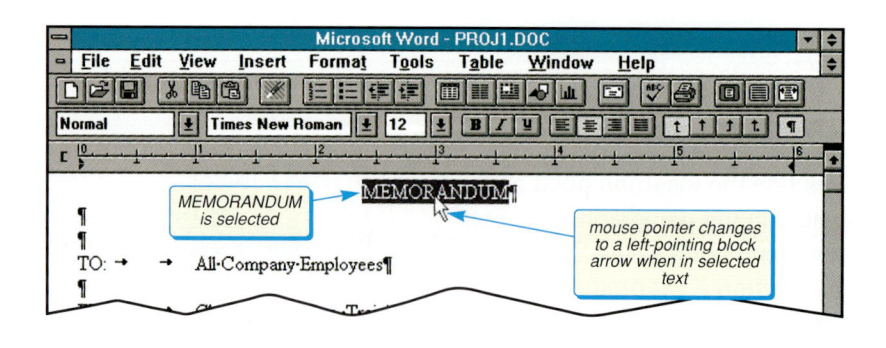

FIGURE 1-39

After you have selected the text, the next step is to underline the title MEMORANDUM.

TO UNDERLINE SELECTED TEXT ▼

STEP 1 ▶

Point to the Underline button (U) on the ribbon and click.

Word underlines the title MEMO-RANDUM (Figure 1-40).

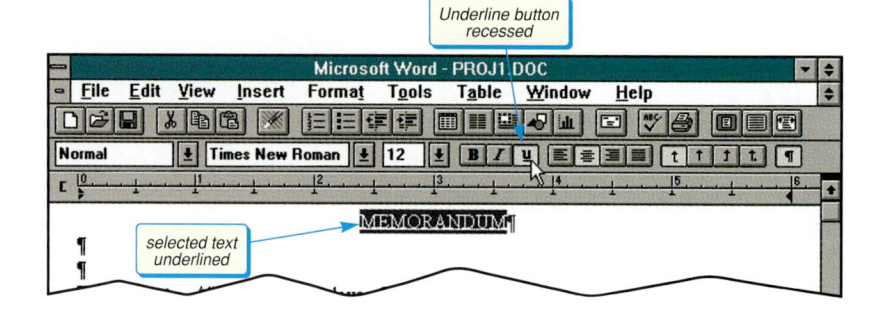

FIGURE 1-40

When the selected text is underlined, the Underline button on the ribbon is recessed (Figure 1-40). Clicking the Underline button a second time removes the underline format.

You can perform further formatting on the selected text or remove the selection by clicking anywhere in the text area. Because you will also bold and enlarge the title, leave the selection on. The next formatting step is to bold the title MEMORANDUM.

TO BOLD SELECTED TEXT ▼

STEP 1 ▶

Point to the Bold button (B) on the ribbon and click.

Word formats the title MEMO-RANDUM in bold (Figure 1-41).

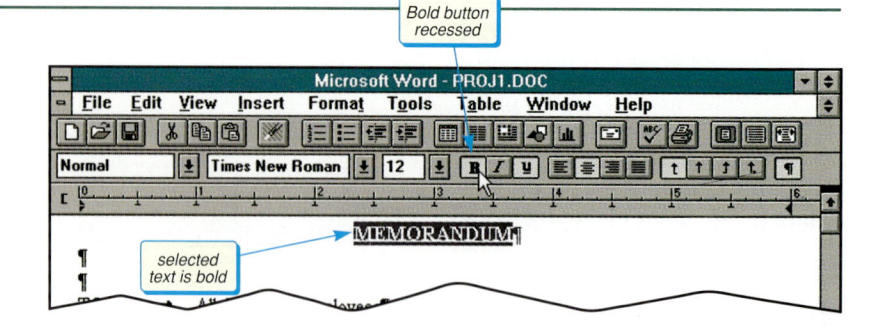

FIGURE 1-41

FORMATTING PARAGRAPHS AND CHARACTERS IN A DOCUMENT MSW25

When the selected text is bold, the Bold button on the ribbon is recessed (Figure 1-41 on the previous page). Clicking the Bold button a second time removes the bold format.

The final step in formatting the title is to increase its point size. Recall that the point size specifies the size of the characters on the screen. Earlier in this project you changed the point size for the entire memorandum from 10 to 12. The title, however, requires a larger point size than the rest of the document.

TO CHANGE THE POINT SIZE OF SELECTED TEXT

STEP 1 ▶

Point to the Points box arrow on the ribbon and click. Then, point to 16.

A list of the available point sizes appears (Figure 1-42). The mouse pointer points to point size 16.

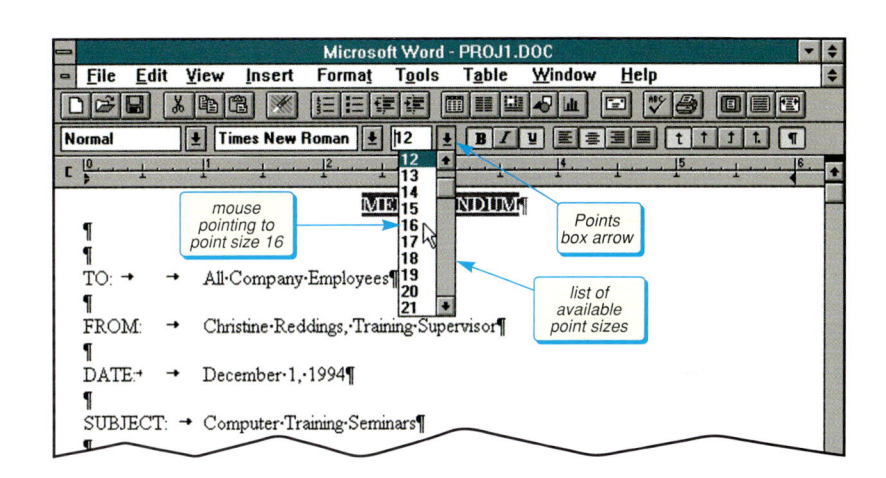

FIGURE 1-42

STEP 2 ▶

Select point size 16 by clicking the left mouse button.

Word increases the point size of the title MEMORANDUM from 12 to 16 (Figure 1-43). The Points box on the ribbon displays 16, indicating the selected text has a point size of 16.

FIGURE 1-43

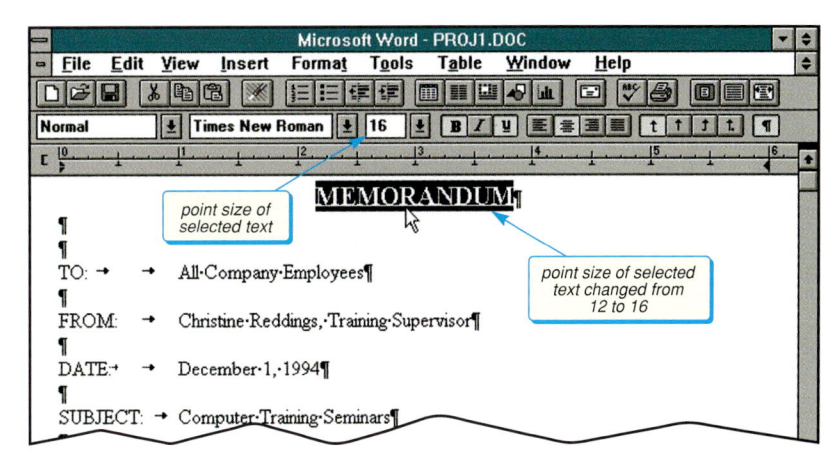

The title MEMORANDUM remains selected until you click anywhere outside the selected text.

Formatting the title MEMORANDUM is now complete. The next step is to format the three seminar titles, dates, and times. The seminar titles are to be bold and underlined; the seminar dates and times should be italicized. The seminar titles contain multiple words. Thus, you must select the entire group of words prior to formatting them. Perform the steps on the next page to select a group of words and format them.

TO SELECT A GROUP OF WORDS AND BOLD THEM

STEP 1 ▶

Press the PAGE DOWN key and position the mouse pointer on the W in Word Processing.

The document scrolls down one screenful and the mouse pointer is at the beginning of the words to select (Figure 1-44).

FIGURE 1-44

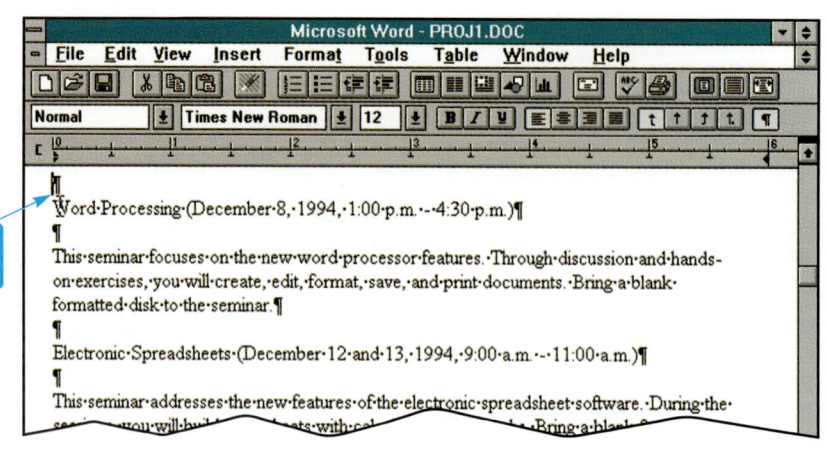

STEP 2 ▶

Drag the pointer through the g in Word Processing.

Word highlights the text Word Processing (Figure 1-45).

FIGURE 1-45

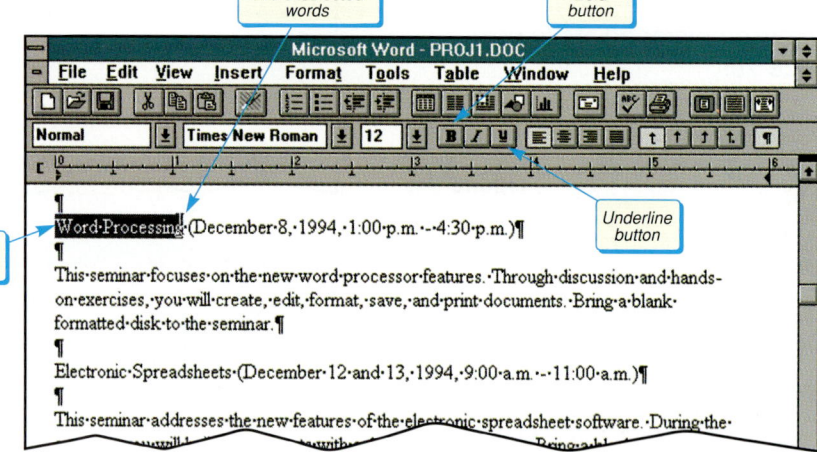

STEP 3 ▶

With the text selected, point to the Bold button on the ribbon and click. Then, point to the Underline button and click. Click anywhere in the selected text to remove the highlight.

The text, Word Processing, is bold and underlined, and the insertion point is blinking in the text, Word Processing (Figure 1-46). The Bold and Underline buttons are recessed, indicating the text, Word Processing, is bold and underlined.

FIGURE 1-46

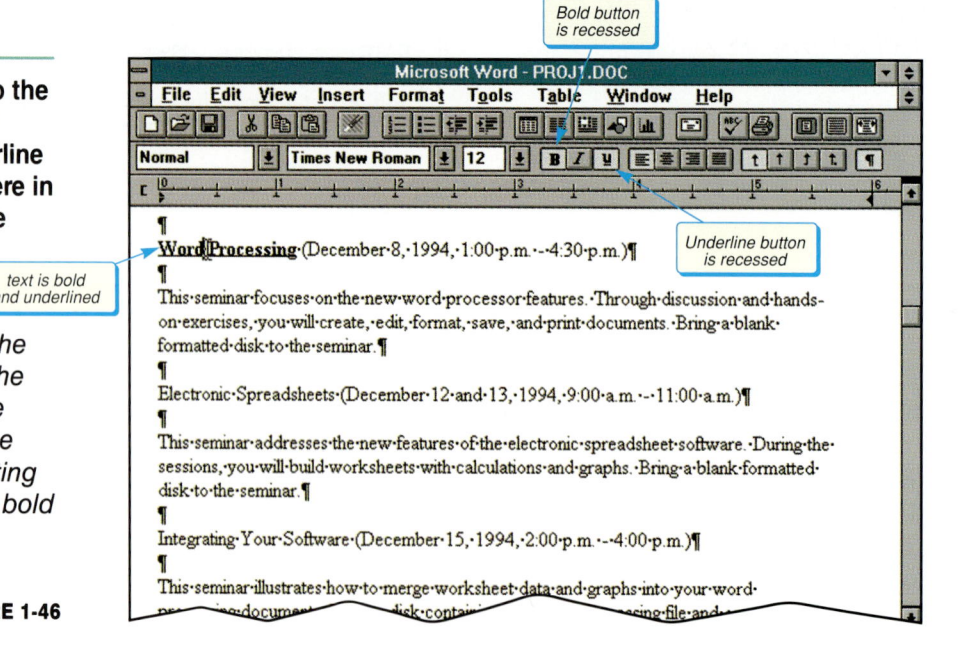

FORMATTING PARAGRAPHS AND CHARACTERS IN A DOCUMENT   MSW27

STEP 4 ▶

Repeat the procedures in Step 1 through Step 3 for the titles Electronic Spreadsheets and Integrating Your Software.

The seminar titles display as shown in Figure 1-47.

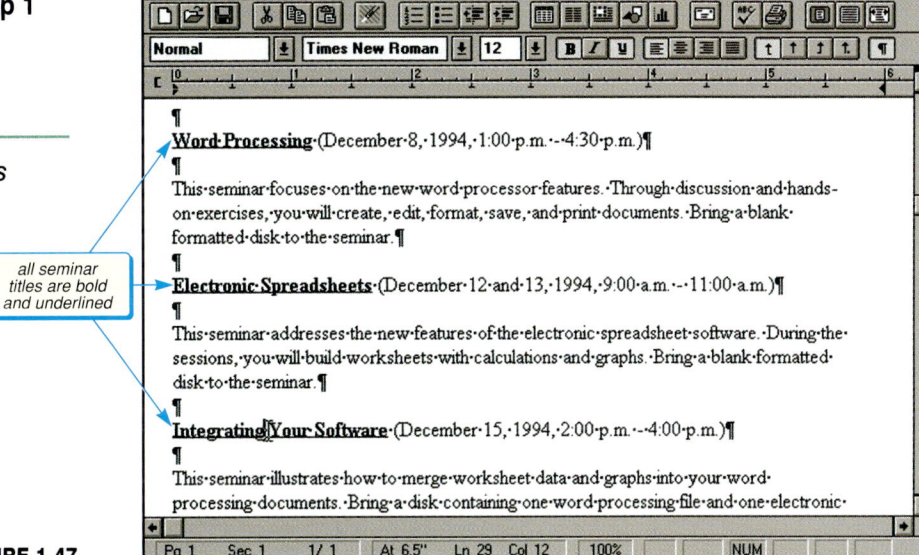

FIGURE 1-47

When the selected text is bold and underlined, the Bold and Underline buttons on the ribbon are recessed. Clicking the Bold and Underline buttons a second time removes the bold and underline formats. Perform the following steps to italicize the seminar dates and times.

TO ITALICIZE TEXT ▼

STEP 1 ▶

Position the mouse pointer on the left parenthesis in (December and drag the pointer through the right parenthesis in p.m.) as shown in Figure 1-48.

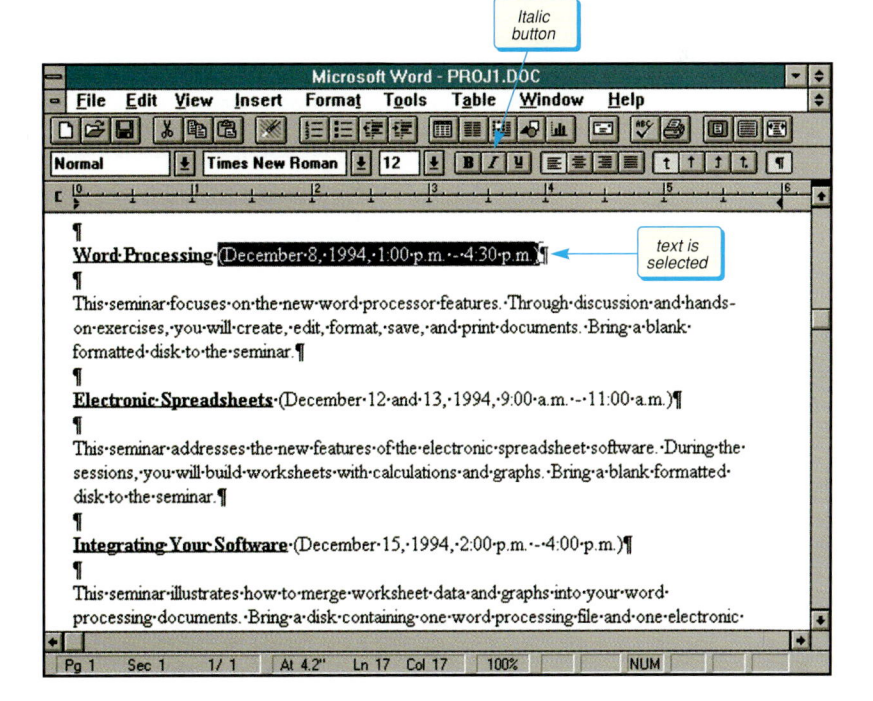

FIGURE 1-48

MSW28   PROJECT 1   CREATING AND EDITING A DOCUMENT

STEP 2 ▶

With the text highlighted, point to the Italic button (*I*) on the ribbon and click. Then, click in the selected text to remove the highlight.

The phrase (December 8, 1994, 1:00 p.m. – 4:30 p.m.) is italicized (Figure 1-49).

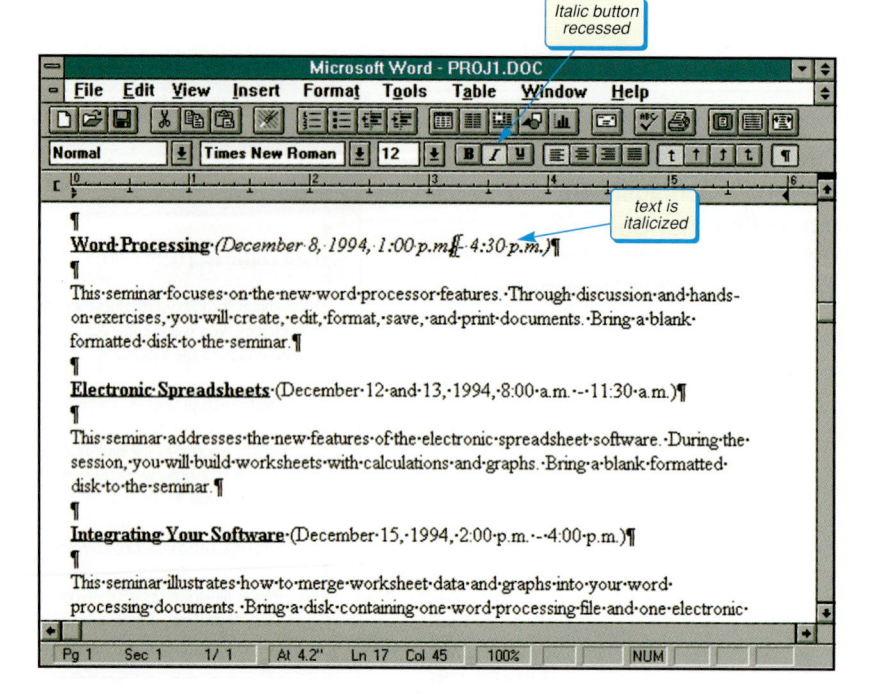

FIGURE 1-49

STEP 3 ▶

Repeat the procedures in Step 1 and Step 2 for the Electronic Spreadsheets and Integrating Your Software seminar dates and times. Click in the selected text to remove the highlight.

The italicized text appears as shown in Figure 1-50.

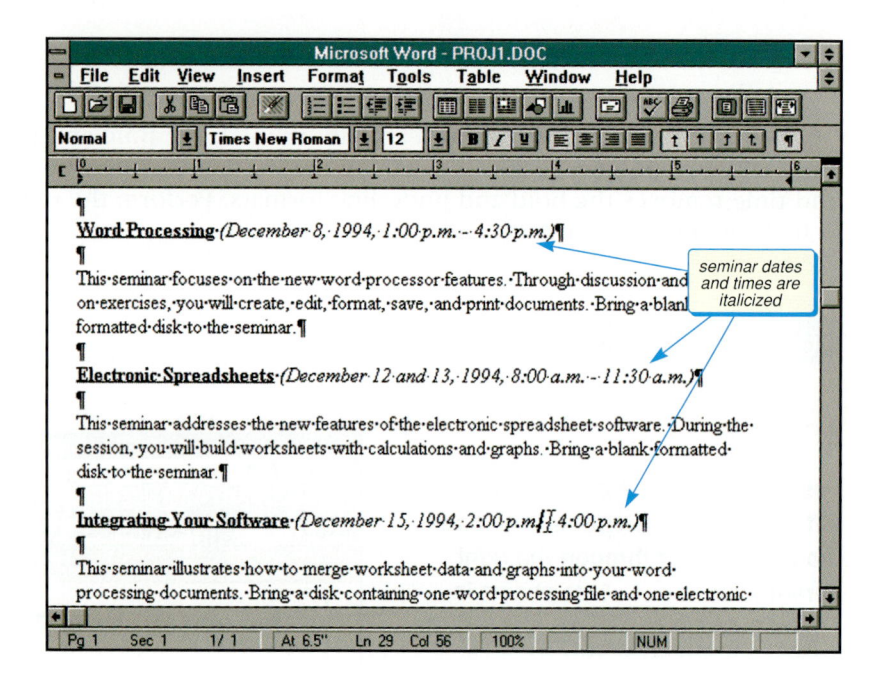

FIGURE 1-50

When the selected text is italicized, the Italic button on the ribbon is recessed. Clicking the Italic button a second time removes the italic format.

The formatting for Project 1 is now complete. After you have entered and formatted a document, you should ensure that no typographical errors have occurred by checking the spelling of the words in your document.

▶ CHECKING SPELLING

Word checks your document for spelling errors using a standard dictionary contained in the Word program. If a word is not found in the dictionary, the word is displayed in the Spelling dialog box with a message indicating the word is not in the Word dictionary. From the Spelling dialog box, you may correct the word. Sometimes, however, the word is spelled correctly. For example, many names, abbreviations, and specialized terms are not in the standard dictionary. In these cases, you ignore the message and continue the spelling check.

When you invoke the Word **spell checker**, it checks all of your document beginning at the insertion point. Thus, you should position the insertion point at the top of your document before beginning the spelling check. To position the insertion point in column one, line one of the document, press the keys CTRL+HOME. The following steps illustrate how to spell check PROJ1.DOC. (Notice in the following example, the word inform has intentionally been misspelled to illustrate the use of Word's spell checker. If you are doing this project on a personal computer, your memorandum may have different misspelled words, depending on the accuracy of your typing.)

TO CHECK THE SPELLING OF A DOCUMENT ▼

STEP 1 ▶

Point to the Spelling button (🔲) on the Toolbar as shown in Figure 1-51.

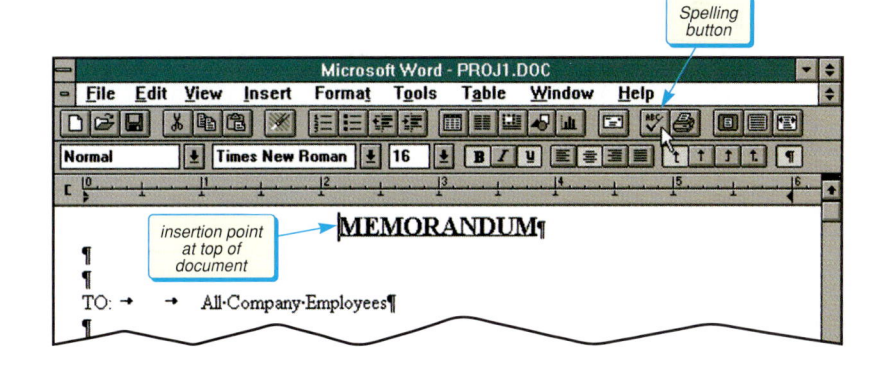

FIGURE 1-51

STEP 2 ▶

Click the Spelling button on the Toolbar.

Word begins the spelling check at the top of your document. When Word finds a word not in the dictionary, it displays the Spelling: English [US] dialog box (Figure 1-52). Word did not find the word Reddings in its standard dictionary. Reddings is a proper name and is spelled correctly.

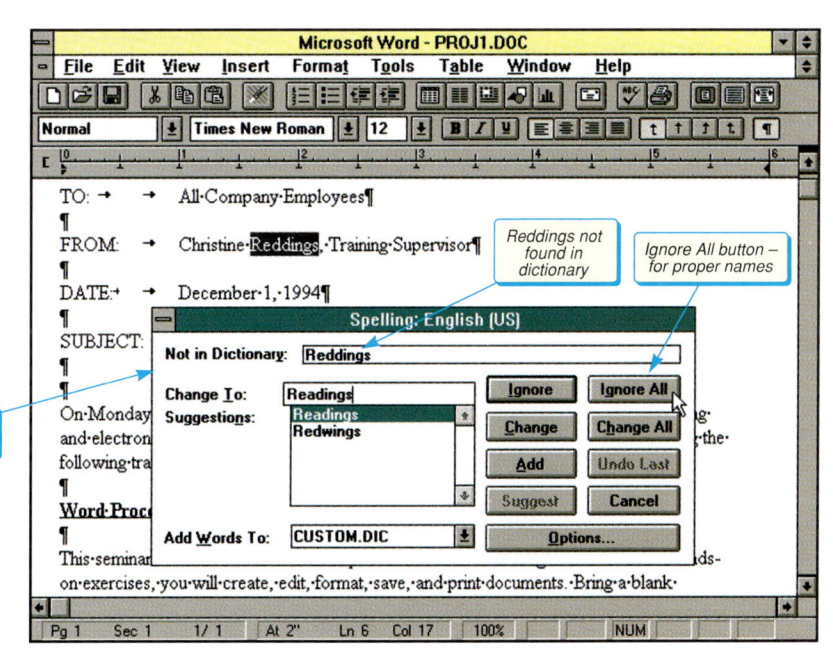

FIGURE 1-52

MSW30   PROJECT 1   CREATING AND EDITING A DOCUMENT

STEP 3 ▶

Choose the Ignore All button (Ignore All) in the Spelling dialog box.

The spelling check ignores all future occurrences of the word Reddings. Word continues the spelling check until it finds the next error or reaches the end of the document. The spelling check did not find the word infrom in its standard dictionary. The spelling check lists suggested corrections in the Suggestions list box and places its choice (inform) in the Change To text box (Figure 1-53).

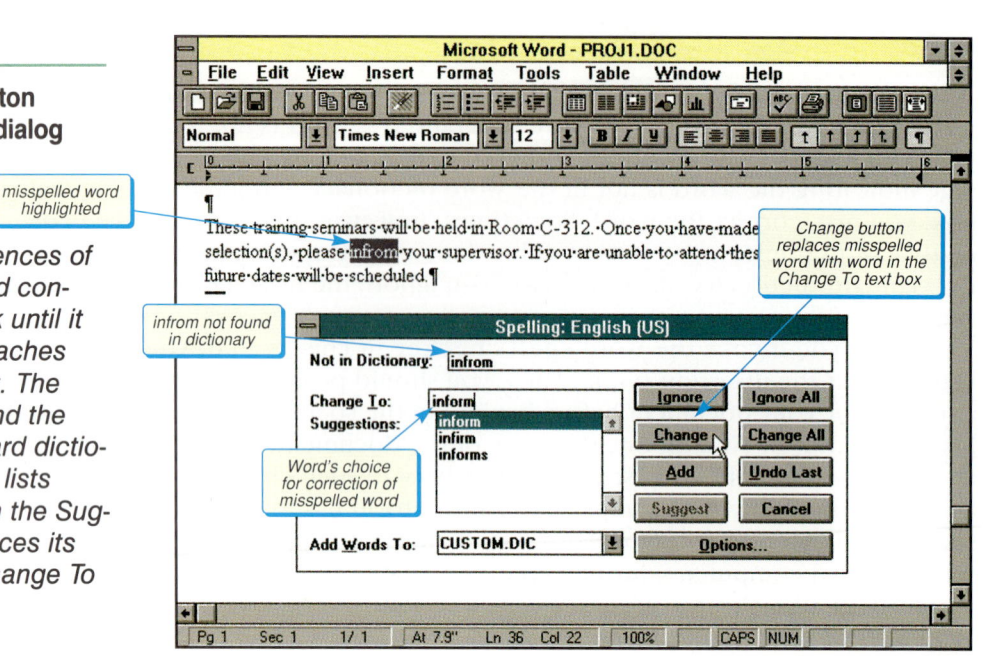

FIGURE 1-53

STEP 4 ▶

Choose the Change button (Change) in the Spelling dialog box.

The spelling check changes the misspelled word (infrom) to its suggestion (inform). Word continues to check spelling until it finds the next error or reaches the end of the document. Word displays a message that it has checked the entire document (Figure 1-54).

STEP 5

Choose the OK button (OK).

Word returns to your document.

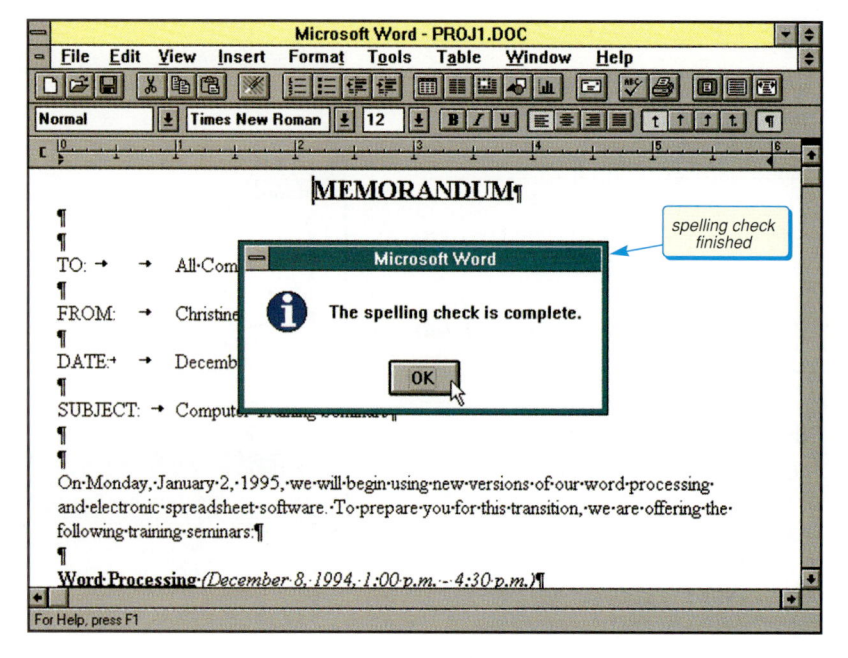

FIGURE 1-54

If the suggested change made by the spelling check is not your choice, you can select any of the other words in the list of suggested words by clicking the desired word. The word you click appears in the Change To text box. If your choice is not in the list of suggested words, you may type your desired word directly into the Change To text box. When you choose the Change button, the word in the Change To text box will replace the misspelled word.

SAVING AN EXISTING DOCUMENT WITH THE SAME FILENAME   MSW31

If the insertion point is not positioned at the top of the document when you invoke the spelling check, Word checks your spelling beginning at the insertion point. When the spelling check reaches the end of the document, a Word message asks if you want to continue checking at the beginning of the document. If you want to check the spelling of the entire document, click the Yes button (Yes).

▶ SAVING AN EXISTING DOCUMENT WITH THE SAME FILENAME

The memorandum for Project 1 is now complete. To transfer the formatting changes and spelling corrections to your diskette in drive A, you must save the document again. When you saved the document the first time, you assigned a filename to it (PROJ1). Word automatically assigns this filename to the document each time you subsequently save it if you use the following procedure.

TO SAVE AN EXISTING DOCUMENT WITH THE SAME FILENAME ▼

STEP 1 ▶

Point to the Save button on the Toolbar and click.

Word saves the document on a diskette inserted in drive A using the currently assigned filename, PROJ1. When the save is finished, the document remains in main memory and displays on the screen (Figure 1-55).

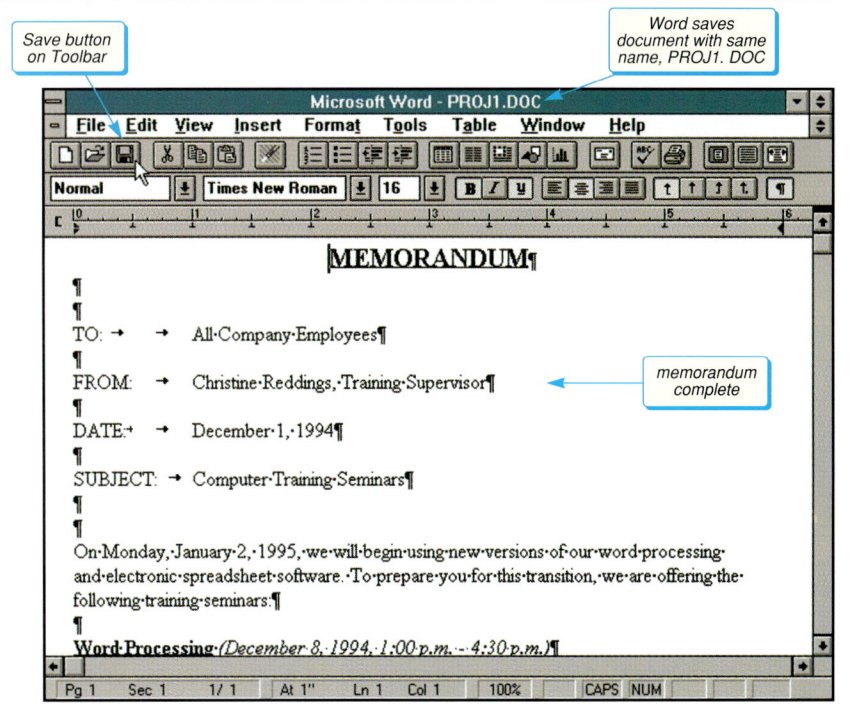

FIGURE 1-55

MSW32   PROJECT 1   CREATING AND EDITING A DOCUMENT

▸ PRINTING A DOCUMENT

The next step is to print the document you created. A printed version of the document is called a **hard copy** or **printout**.

Perform the following steps to print the memorandum created in Project 1.

TO PRINT A DOCUMENT ▼

STEP 1 ▶

Ready the printer according to the printer instructions. Point to the Print button (🖨) on the Toolbar as shown in Figure 1-56.

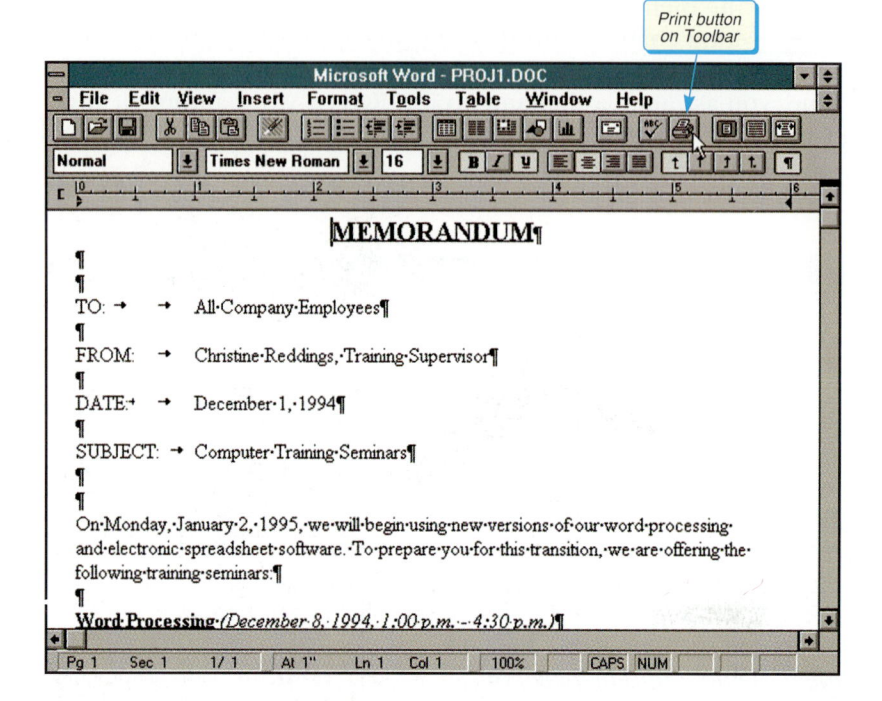

FIGURE 1-56

STEP 2 ▶

Click the Print button on the Toolbar.

The mouse pointer changes to an hourglass shape (⌛) for a few moments, and then Word displays the Printing dialog box (Figure 1-57). The document then begins printing on the printer.

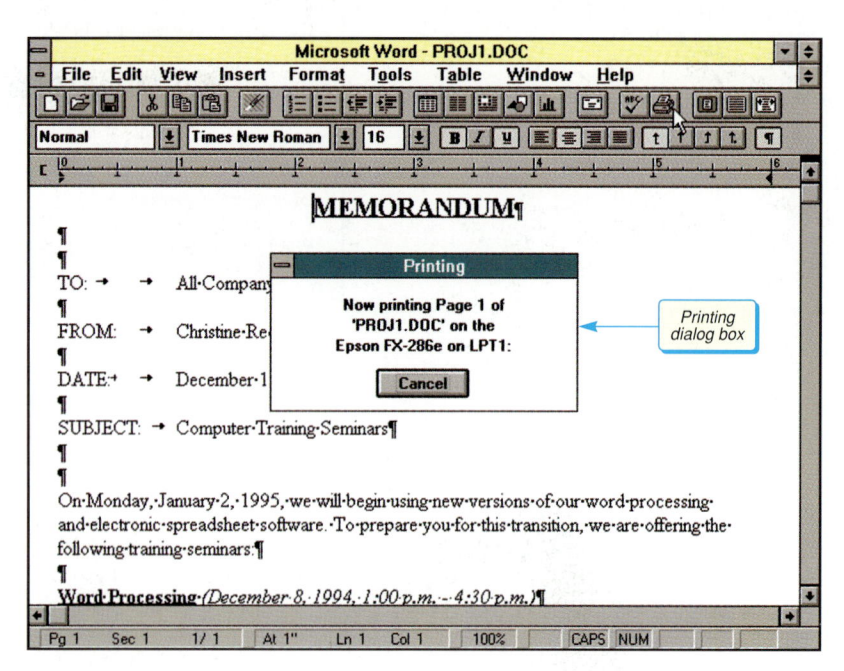

FIGURE 1-57

STEP 3 ▼

When the printer stops, retrieve the printout (Figure 1-58).

MEMORANDUM

TO: All Company Employees

FROM: Christine Reddings, Training Supervisor

DATE: December 1, 1994

SUBJECT: Computer Training Seminars

On Monday, January 2, 1995, we will begin using new versions of our word processing and electronic spreadsheet software. To prepare you for this transition, we are offering the following training seminars:

Word Processing *(December 8, 1994, 1:00 p.m. - 4:30 p.m.)*

This seminar focuses on the new word processor features. Through discussion and hands-on exercises, you will create, edit, format, save, and print documents. Bring a blank formatted disk to the seminar.

Electronic Spreadsheets *(December 12 and 13, 1994, 8:00 a.m. - 11:30 a.m.)*

This seminar addresses the new features of the electronic spreadsheet software. During the session, you will build worksheets with calculations and graphs. Bring a blank formatted disk to the seminar.

Integrating Your Software *(December 15, 1994, 2:00 p.m. - 4:00 p.m.)*

This seminar illustrates how to merge worksheet data and graphs into your word processing documents. Bring a disk containing one word processing file and one electronic spreadsheet file.

These training seminars will be held in Room C-312. Once you have made your selection(s), please inform your supervisor. If you are unable to attend these seminars, future dates will be scheduled.

FIGURE 1-58

When you use the Print button to print a document, Word automatically prints the entire document. You may then distribute the hard copy or keep it as a permanent record of the document.

MSW34 PROJECT 1 CREATING AND EDITING A DOCUMENT

▶ QUITTING WORD

After you create, save, and print the memorandum, Project 1 is complete. To quit Word and return control to Program Manager, perform the following steps.

TO QUIT WORD ▼

STEP 1 ▶

Select the File menu and point to the Exit command (Figure 1-59).

Exit command

mouse shape is left-pointing block arrow when in menu

File menu

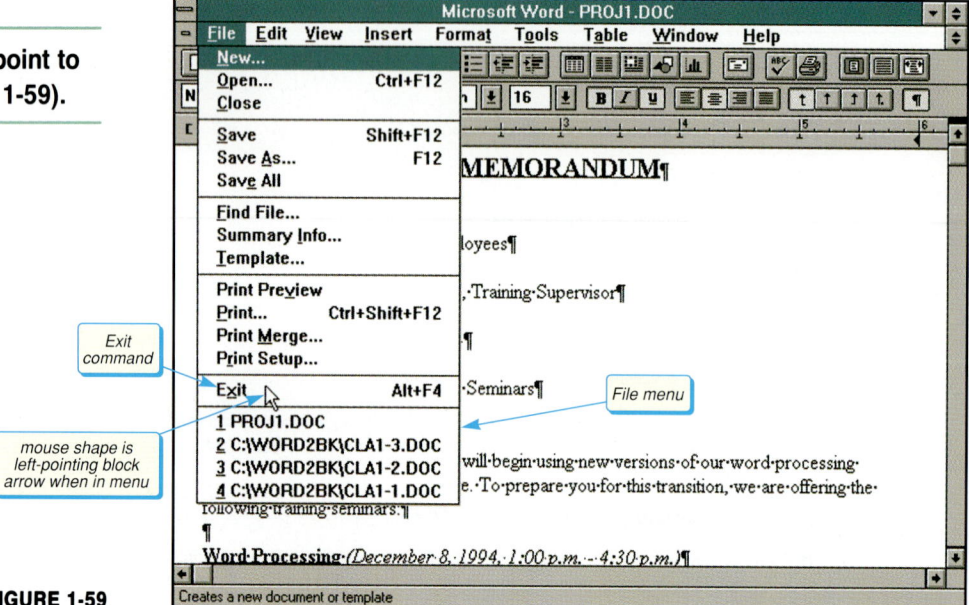

FIGURE 1-59

STEP 2 ▶

Choose the Exit command.

If you made changes to the document since the last save, Word displays a message asking if you want to save the changes (Figure 1-60). Choose the Yes button to save changes; choose the No button (No) to ignore the changes; or choose the Cancel button (Cancel) to return to the document. If you made no changes since saving the document, this dialog box does not display.

Yes to save changes before exiting

FIGURE 1-60

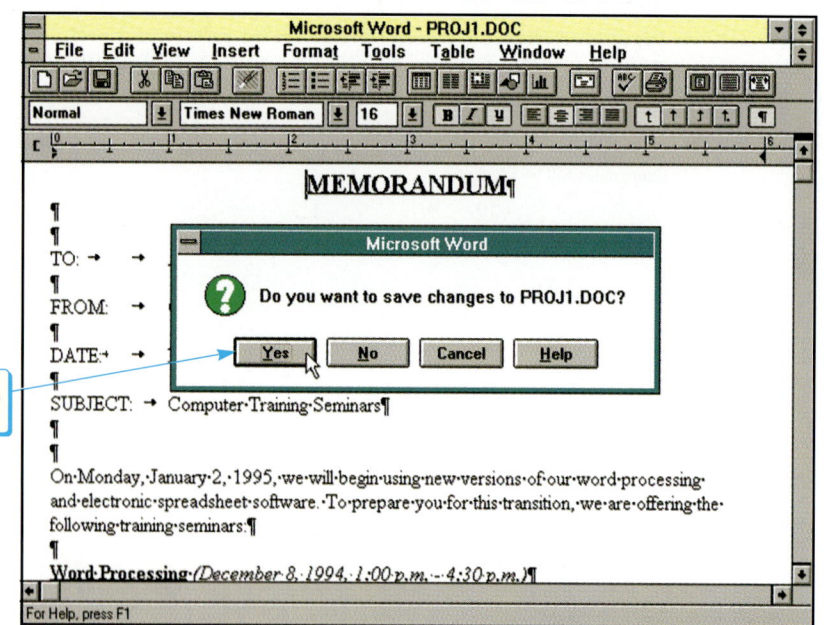

OPENING A DOCUMENT   MSW35

You can also quit Word by double-clicking the Control-menu box on the left edge of the title bar.

Project 1 is now complete. You created, formatted, checked spelling, and printed it. You might, however, decide to change the memorandum at a later date. To do this, you must start Word and then as shown in the following steps retrieve your document from the disk in drive A.

▶ OPENING A DOCUMENT

Earlier, you saved on disk the document built in Project 1 using the filename PROJ1.DOC. Once you have created and saved a document, you will often have reason to retrieve it from disk. For example, you might want to revise the document or print another copy of it. You can use the following steps to open the file PROJ1.DOC using the Open button (📂) on the Toolbar.

TO OPEN A DOCUMENT ▼

STEP 1 ▶

Point to the Open button on the Toolbar and click.

Word displays the Open dialog box (Figure 1-61).

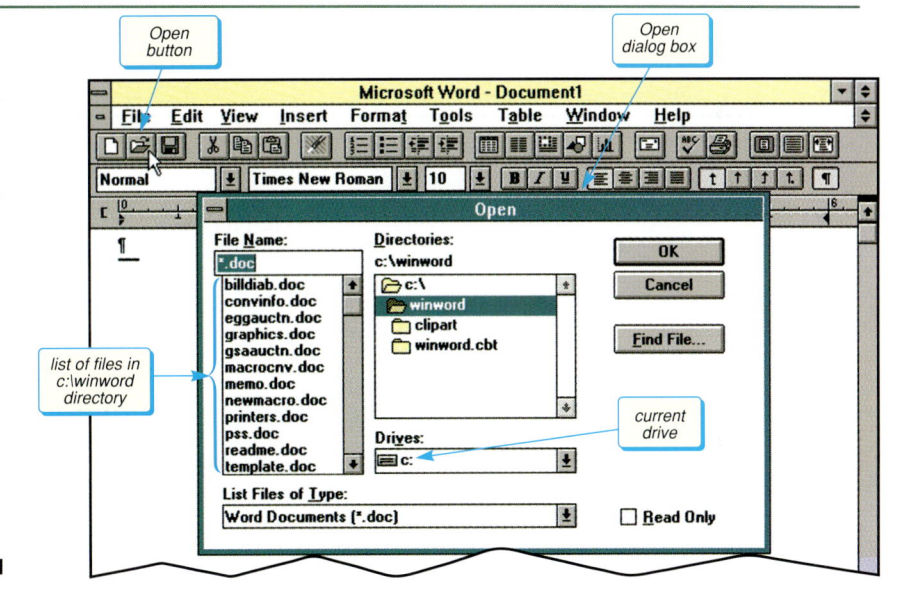

FIGURE 1-61

STEP 2 ▶

If drive A is not the selected drive, select a: in the Drives drop-down list box (refer to Figures 1-30 and 1-31 on page MSW19 to review this technique). Then, select the filename proj1.doc by clicking the filename in the File Name list box, and point to the OK button (Figure 1-62).

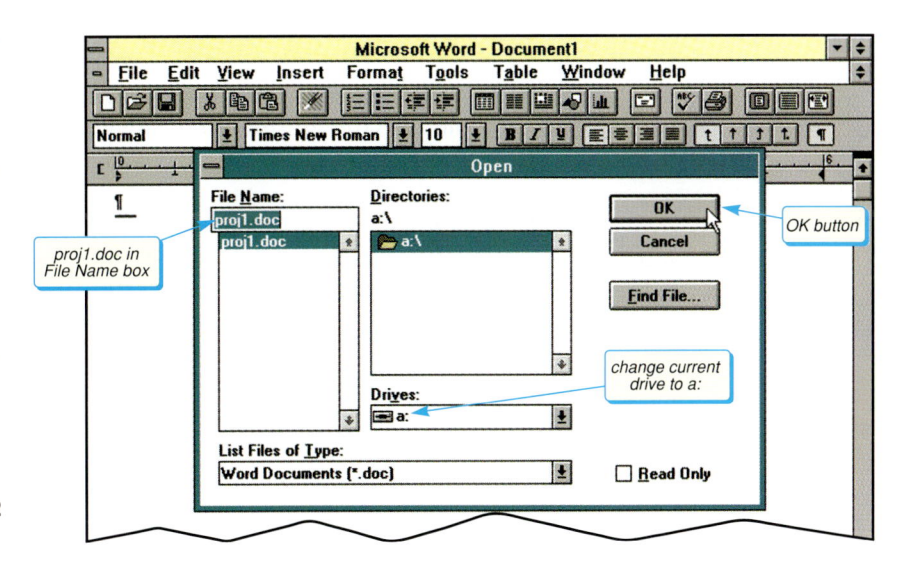

FIGURE 1-62

STEP 3 ▶

Choose the OK button in the Open dialog box.

Word opens the document PROJ1.DOC from drive A and displays it on the screen (Figure 1-63).

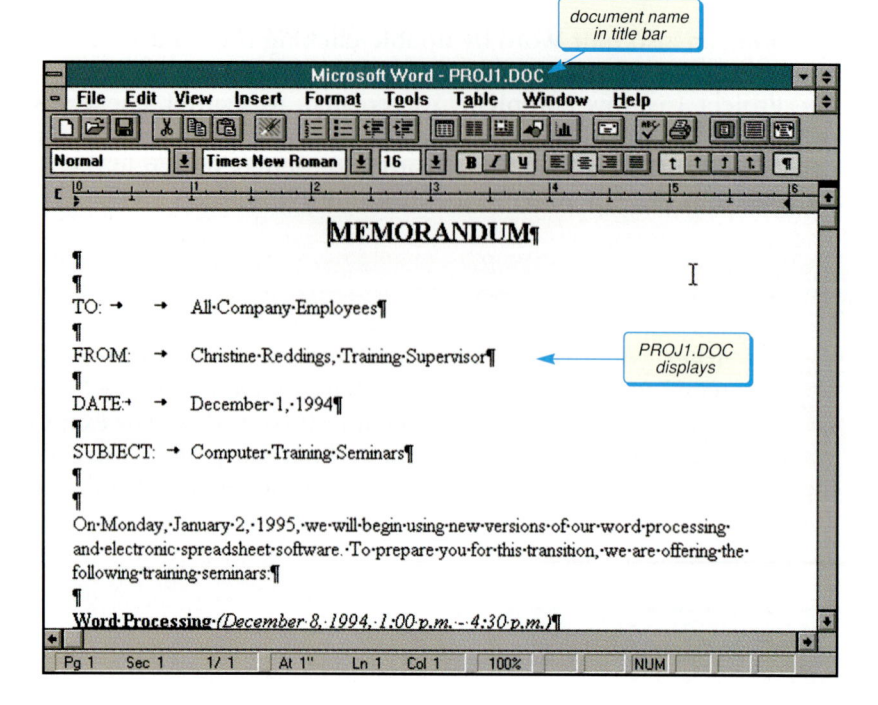

FIGURE 1-63

▶ **CORRECTING ERRORS**

After creating a document, you will often find you must make changes to the document. Changes can be required because the document contains an error or because of new circumstances.

Types of Changes Made to Documents

The types of changes normally fall into one of the three following categories: additions, deletions, or modifications.

ADDITIONS You might have to place additional words, sentences, or paragraphs in the document. Additions occur when you omit text from a document and are required to add it later. For example, you might accidentally forget to put the word Computer in the SUBJECT line in Project 1.

DELETIONS Sometimes text in a document is incorrect or is no longer needed. For example, the Integrating Your Software seminar in Project 1 could be canceled. In this case, you would delete the seminar text from the memorandum.

MODIFICATIONS If an error is made in a document, you might have to revise the word(s) in the text. For example, the date of the Word Processing seminar in Project 1 might change to December 14.

Word provides several methods for correcting errors in a document. For each of the error correction techniques, you must first move the insertion point to the error.

Inserting Text into an Existing Document

If you leave a word or phrase out of a sentence, you can insert it into the sentence by positioning the insertion point where you would like the text inserted. Word always inserts the text to the *left* of the insertion point. The text to the right of the insertion point moves to the right and downward to accommodate the added text. The following steps illustrate adding the word help before the word prepare in the first paragraph of the text in Project 1.

TO INSERT TEXT INTO AN EXISTING DOCUMENT ▼

STEP 1 ▶

Point the mouse pointer immediately to the left of the p in prepare (Figure 1-64).

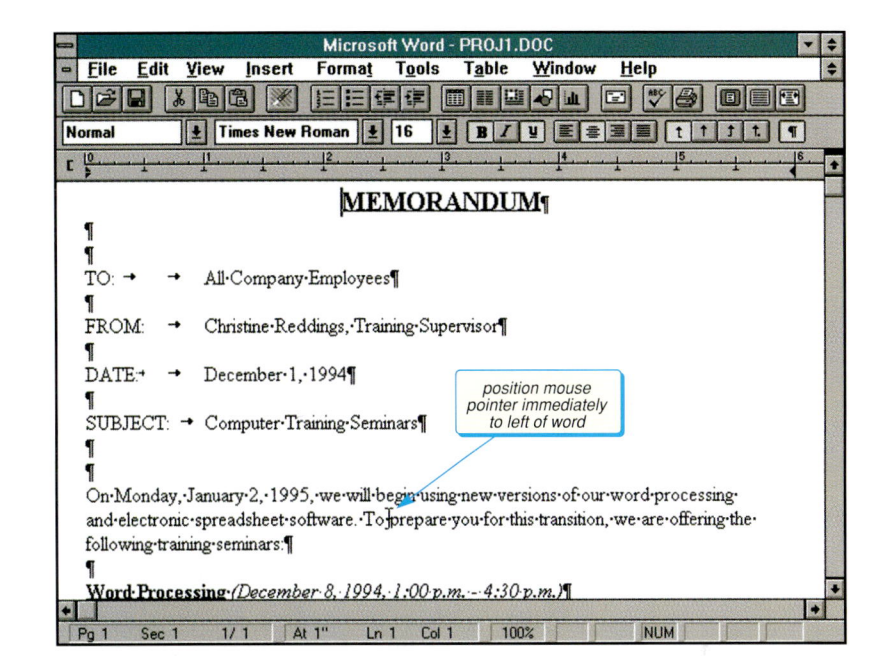

FIGURE 1-64

STEP 2 ▶

Click the left mouse button.

The insertion point displays immediately to the left of the p in prepare (Figure 1-65).

FIGURE 1-65

STEP 3 ▶

Type the word `help` **followed by a space.**

The word help is now inserted between the words To and prepare in the memorandum for Project 1 (Figure 1-66).

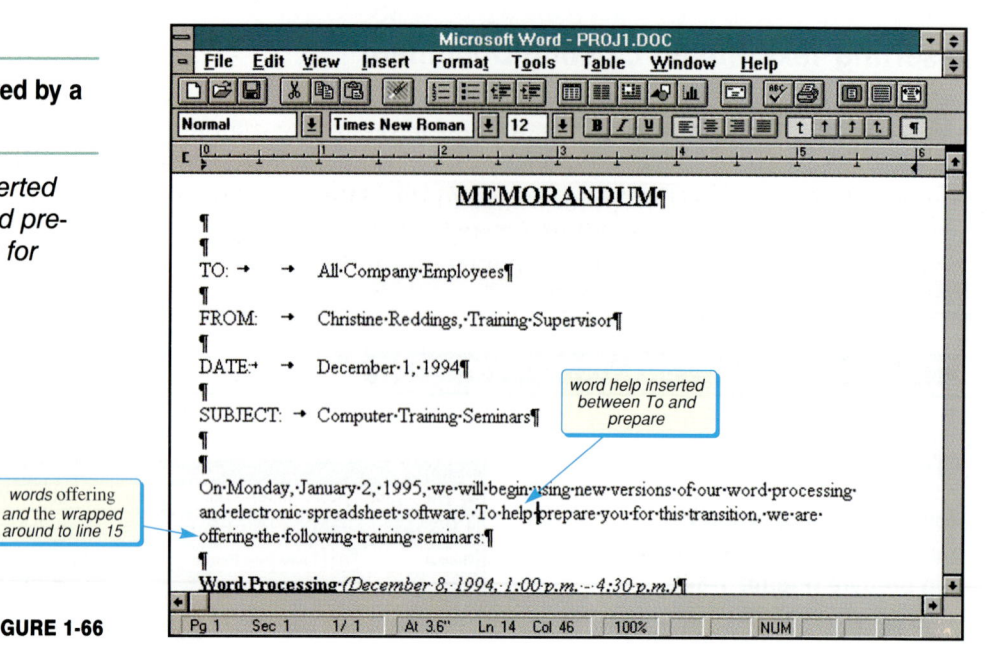

FIGURE 1-66

Notice in Figure 1-66 that the text to the right of the word prepare moved to the right and downward to accommodate the insertion of the word help. That is, the words *offering* and *the* moved down to line 15.

In Word, the default typing mode is **insert mode**. In insert mode, as you type a character, Word inserts the character and moves all the characters to the right of the typed character one position to the right. You can change to **overtype mode** by pressing the INSERT key. In overtype mode, Word overtypes characters to the right of the insertion point. The INSERT key toggles the keyboard between insert mode and overtype mode.

Deleting Text from an Existing Document

It is not unusual to type incorrect characters or words in a document. In such a case, to correct the error, you might want to delete certain letters or words. Perform the following steps to delete an incorrect character or word.

TO DELETE AN INCORRECT CHARACTER IN A DOCUMENT

Step 1: Position the insertion point next to the incorrect character.
Step 2: Press the BACKSPACE key to erase to the left of the insertion point; or press the DELETE key to erase to the right of the insertion point.

TO DELETE AN INCORRECT WORD OR PHRASE IN A DOCUMENT

Step 1: Select the word or phrase you want to erase.
Step 2: Press the DELETE key or the BACKSPACE key.

Undoing Most Recent Actions

Word provides an Undo button (▓) on the Toolbar that you can use to cancel your most recent command or action. If you accidentally delete some text, point to the Undo button and click. Some actions, like saving a document, cannot be undone. In these cases, Word will beep when you click the Undo button to signal the action you just performed cannot be reversed.

Closing the Entire Document

Sometimes, everything goes wrong. If this happens, you may want to **close the document** entirely and start over. You may also want to close a document when you are finished with it so you can begin your next document. To close the document, follow these steps.

TO CLOSE THE ENTIRE DOCUMENT AND START OVER

Step 1: Select the File menu.
Step 2: Choose the Close command.
Step 3: When Word displays the dialog box, choose the No button to ignore the changes.
Step 4: Point to the New button (▣) on the Toolbar and click.

You can also close the document by double-clicking on the Control-menu box on the left edge of the menu bar.

▶ WORD'S ONLINE HELP

At any time while you are using Word, you can select the Help menu to gain access to **Online Help** (Figure 1-67). The Word Help menu provides an index for navigating around the Help facility. Pressing function key F1 allows you to obtain **context sensitive** help on various topics. The term context-sensitive help means that Word will display immediate information on the activity you are performing when you press function key F1. For example, if you have clicked the Points box arrow on the ribbon and are not sure what to do next, press function key F1. The Points list box disappears and a window displaying help about the Ribbon appears as shown in Figure 1-68 on the next page.

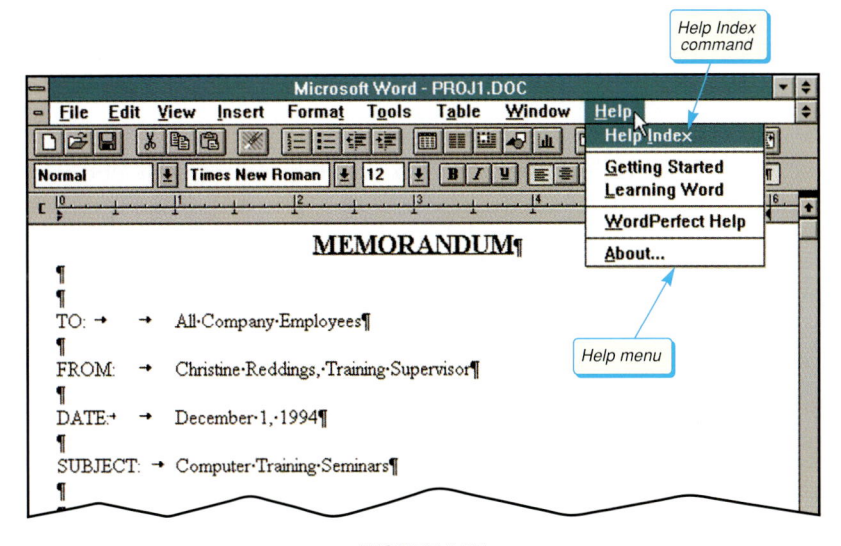

FIGURE 1-67

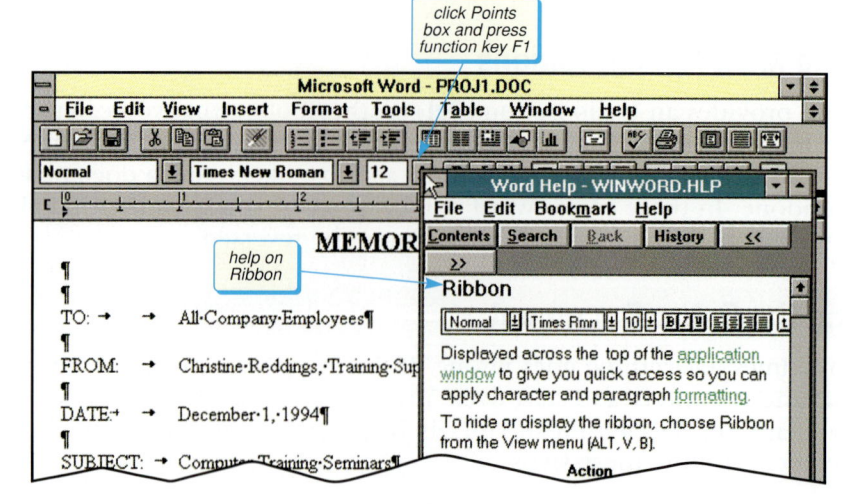

MSW40   PROJECT 1   CREATING AND EDITING A DOCUMENT

FIGURE 1-68

In many Word dialog boxes, you can click a Help button to obtain help about the current activity on which you are working. If there is no Help button in a dialog box, press function key F1 while the dialog box appears on the screen.

You may also obtain help about any item on the Word screen by pressing SHIFT+F1 and clicking on the item. When you press SHIFT+F1, the mouse pointer shape changes to a left-pointing arrow with a question mark ( ) beside it (Figure 1-69). Next, point to any item on the Word screen and click to display help about the item you clicked. For example, to obtain help about the ruler, press SHIFT+F1, and then click anywhere in the ruler.

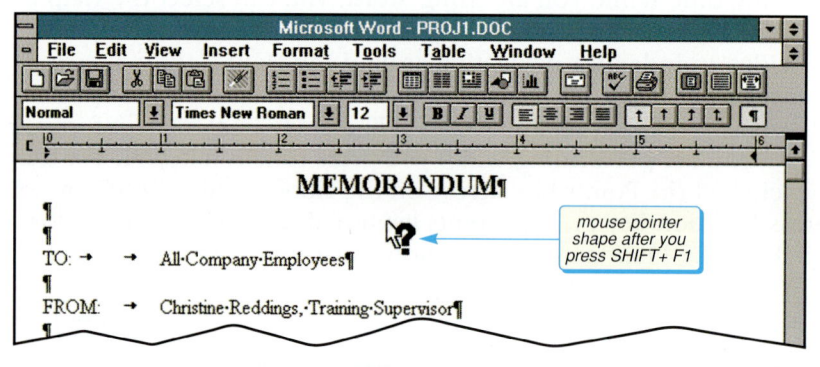

FIGURE 1-69

You can print the Help information in the Help window by choosing the Print Topic command from the File menu in the Help window. You close a Help window by choosing Exit from the File menu in the Help window or by double-clicking the Control-menu box in the title bar on the Help window.

Word's Online Help has features that make it powerful and easy to use. The best way to familiarize yourself with Online Help is to use it.

Word's Online Tutorial

You can improve your Word skills by stepping through the on-line **tutorial**. Before you begin the tutorial, point to the Save button on the Toolbar and click to save the document with your latest changes. Next, choose Learning Word from the Help menu (Figure 1-67 on the previous page). Word responds by displaying a welcome screen. When you press the left mouse button, Word responds by displaying the screen shown in Figure 1-70. Select any of the six lessons. When you select a lesson, Word displays another menu so you can customize your lessons.

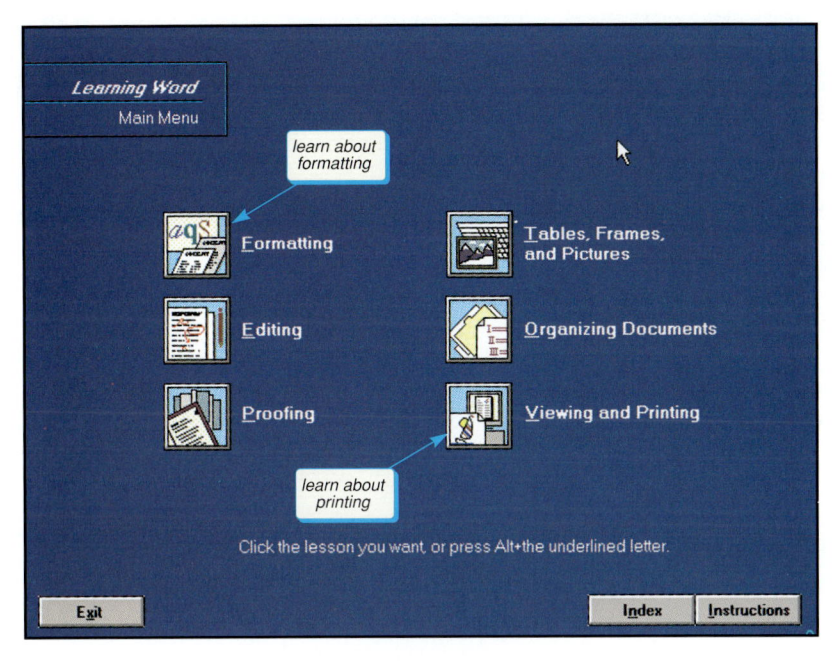

FIGURE 1-70

▶ Project Summary

Project 1 introduced you to starting Word and creating a document. You learned how to change the point size before entering any text in the document. You also learned how to save and print a document. Once you saved the document, you learned how to center paragraphs and select words and bold, underline, and italicize them. You then used the spelling check to check the document for typographical errors. You learned to move the insertion point so you could insert, delete, and modify text. Finally, you learned to use the Online Help.

▶ Key Terms

Bold button (*MSW24*)
Center button (*MSW23*)
character formatting (*MSW21*)
close a document (*MSW39*)
context-sensitive (*MSW39*)
.doc (*MSW20*)
document window (*MSW5*)
end mark (*MSW5*)
exiting Word (*MSW34*)
filename (*MSW19*)
font (*MSW8*)
font size (*MSW8*)
font type (*MSW8*)
formatting characters (*MSW21*)
hard copy (*MSW32*)
insert mode (*MSW38*)
insertion point (*MSW5*)

Italic button (*MSW28*)
menu bar (*MSW7*)
moving the insertion point (*MSW37*)
mouse pointer (*MSW5*)
nonprinting character (*MSW14*)
Online Help (*MSW39*)
opening a document (*MSW35*)
overtype mode (*MSW38*)
paragraph formatting (*MSW21*)
point size (*MSW8*)
Print button (*MSW32*)
printout (*MSW32*)
Quit Word (*MSW33*)
ribbon (*MSW8*)
ruler (*MSW8*)
saving a document (*MSW18*)

scroll bars (*MSW6*)
scroll box (*MSW6*)
scrolling (*MSW17*)
select (*MSW23*)
selection bar (*MSW6*)
spell checker (*MSW28*)
starting Word (*MSW4*)
status bar (*MSW8*)
text area (*MSW5*)
Toolbar (*MSW7*)
tutorial (*MSW40*)
Underline button (*MSW24*)
word processing program (*MSW2*)
Word screen (*MSW5*)
wordwrap (*MSW15*)
workplace (*MSW5*)

QUICK REFERENCE

In Microsoft Word 2.0 you can accomplish a task in a number of ways. The following table provides a quick reference to each task presented in this project with its available options. The commands listed in the Menu column can be executed using either the keyboard or mouse.

Task	Mouse	Menu	Keyboard Shortcuts
Bold Text	Click Bold button on ribbon	From Format menu, choose Character	Press CTRL + B
Cancel Selection	Click anywhere in text of document window		Press an Arrow key or, if necessary, ESC then an Arrow key.
Center Paragraph	Click Centered Text button on ribbon	From Format menu, choose Paragraph	Press CTRL + E
Change Point Size	Click Points box on ribbon	From Format menu, choose Character	Press CTRL + P
Close Document	Double-click Control-menu box on menu bar	From File menu, choose Close	
Decrease to Next Available Size			Press CTRL + SHIFT + F2
Display Nonprinting Characters	Click Show/Hide Nonprinting Characters button on Toolbar	From Tools menu, choose Options	Press CTRL + SHIFT + 8
Increase to Next Available Size			Press CTRL + F2
Italicize Text	Click Italic button on ribbon	From Format menu, choose Character	Press CTRL + I
Move Insertion Point	Point mouse pointer to desired location and click		Press RIGHT, LEFT, DOWN, or UP ARROW
Move Insertion Point to Beginning/End of Document	Drag scroll box to top/bottom of vertical scroll bar		Press CTRL + HOME or CTRL + END
Open Document	Click Open button on Toolbar	From File menu, choose Open	Press CTRL + F12
Open Help Menu		Select Help menu	Press F1
Print Document	Click Print button on Toolbar	From File menu, choose Print	Press CTRL + SHIFT + F12
Quit Word	Double-click Control-menu box on title bar	From File menu, choose Exit	Press ALT + F4
Save Document	Click Save button on Toolbar	From File menu, choose Save	Press SHIFT + F12
Select Series of Words	Move insertion point to first word and drag to end of last word		Press F8 until desired words are selected
Select One Word	Double-click in word		Press CTRL + SHIFT + RIGHT ARROW
Scroll Up/Down One Line	Click up/down scroll arrow on vertical scroll bar		Press UP or DOWN ARROW
Scroll Up/Down One Screen	Click scroll bar above/below scroll box		Press PAGE UP or PAGE DOWN
Spelling Check	Click Spelling button on Toolbar	From Tools menu, choose Spelling	
Underline Text	Click Underline button on ribbon	From Format menu, choose Character	Press CTRL + U
Undo Last Change	Click Undo button on Toolbar	From Edit menu, choose Undo	Press CTRL + Z

STUDENT ASSIGNMENTS

STUDENT ASSIGNMENT 1
True/False

Instructions: Circle T if the statement is true or F if the statement is false.

T F 1. Word is a word processing program that allows you to create and revise documents.
T F 2. The status bar is used to retrieve a document and display it in the document window.
T F 3. To create a new paragraph, press the ENTER key.
T F 4. To enter a blank line into a document, click the Blank Line button on the Toolbar.
T F 5. The TAB key is used to horizontally align text in a document.
T F 6. You should always hide nonprinting characters before printing a document because nonprinting characters can make your printed document difficult to read.
T F 7. Wordwrap allows you to type continually without pressing the ENTER key at the end of each line.
T F 8. To save a document, click the Save button on the Toolbar.
T F 9. When you select a word, it appears on the status bar.
T F 10. The Underline button is located on the Toolbar.
T F 11. When you check spelling of a document, Word displays a list of suggestions for the misspelled word(s).
T F 12. When you save a document, it disappears from the screen.
T F 13. A printed version of a document is called a hardcopy, or printout.
T F 14. Click the Exit button on the Toolbar to quit Word.
T F 15. Word always inserts text to the left of the insertion point.
T F 16. To open a document, click the New tool.
T F 17. If you don't assign a filename when you save a document, Word automatically assigns one for you.
T F 18. When selected text has been centered, the Centered Text button appears recessed.
T F 19. If you accidentally delete a word, you can bring it back by clicking the Undo button.
T F 20. To select a single word, click anywhere inside the word.

STUDENT ASSIGNMENT 2
Multiple Choice

Instructions: Circle the correct response.

1. Word is preset to use standard 8 1/2 by 11-inch paper, with _____ inch left and right margins and _____ inch top and bottom margins.
   a. 1 1/4, 1
   b. 1 1/2, 1 1/4
   c. 1, 1 1/2
   d. 1, 1 1/4
2. As you type or insert graphs, your text and graphics display in the _____.
   a. scroll bars
   b. text area
   c. insertion area
   d. selection bar

(continued)

STUDENT ASSIGNMENT 2 (continued)

3. When the mouse pointer is in an open menu, it has the shape of a(n) _____.
   a. I-beam
   b. hourglass
   c. left-pointing block arrow
   d. vertical bar
4. To move the document up one entire screenful at a time, _____.
   a. click the scroll box
   b. click anywhere on the scroll bar above the scroll box
   c. click the up scroll button at the top of the scroll bar
   d. both b and c
5. Word automatically adds the extension of _____ to a filename when you save a document.
   a. .DOC
   b. .TXT
   c. .WRD
   d. .MWD
6. To erase the character to the left of the insertion point, press the _____ key.
   a. DELETE
   b. INSERT
   c. BACKSPACE
   d. both a and c
7. Which key gives you context-sensitive help?
   a. HELP
   b. F9
   c. SHIFT-F9
   d. F1
8. Tabs are indicated on the ruler by _____.
   a. capital Ts
   b. inverted Ts
   c. the word Tab
   d. right-pointing arrows
9. The _____ key toggles between insert and overtype mode.
   a. OVERTYPE
   b. TOGGLE
   c. CAPS LOCK
   d. INSERT
10. When you close a document, _____.
    a. it is erased from disk
    b. it is removed from the screen
    c. control is returned to Program Manager
    d. both a and c

STUDENT ASSIGNMENTS   MSW45

STUDENT ASSIGNMENT 3
Understanding the Word Screen

Instructions: In Figure SA1-3, arrows point to major components of the Word screen. Identify the various parts of the screen in the space provided.

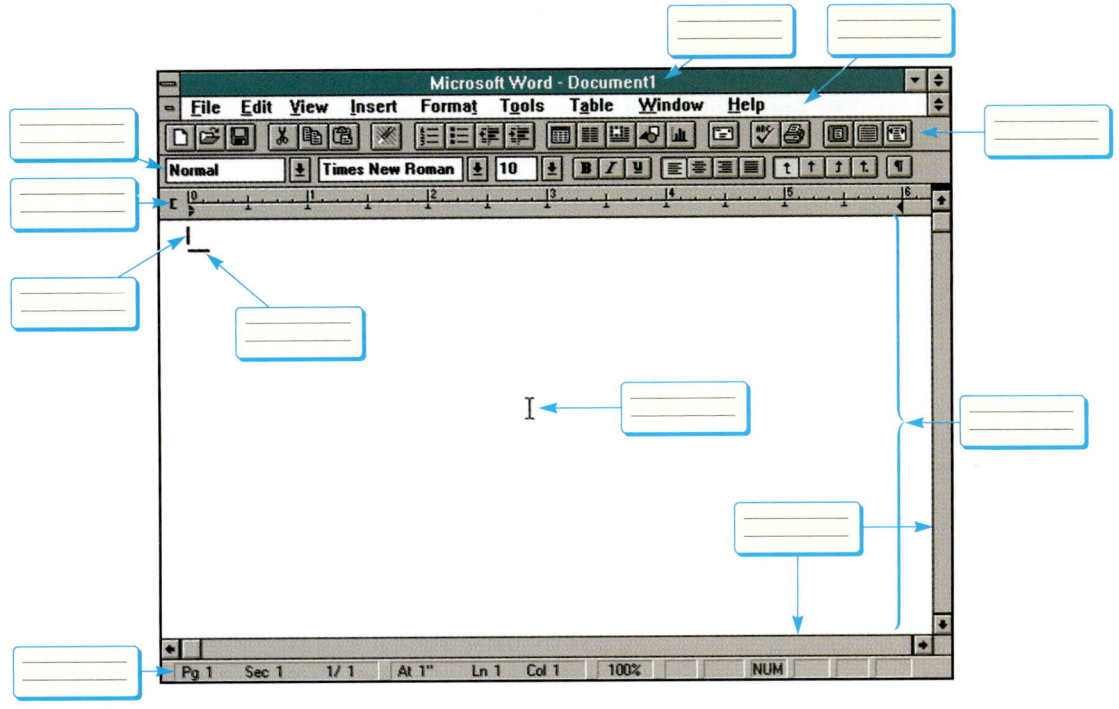

FIGURE SA1-3

STUDENT ASSIGNMENT 4
Understanding the Toolbar

Instructions: In Figure SA1-4, arrows point to several of the buttons on the Toolbar. In the space provided, briefly explain the purpose of each button.

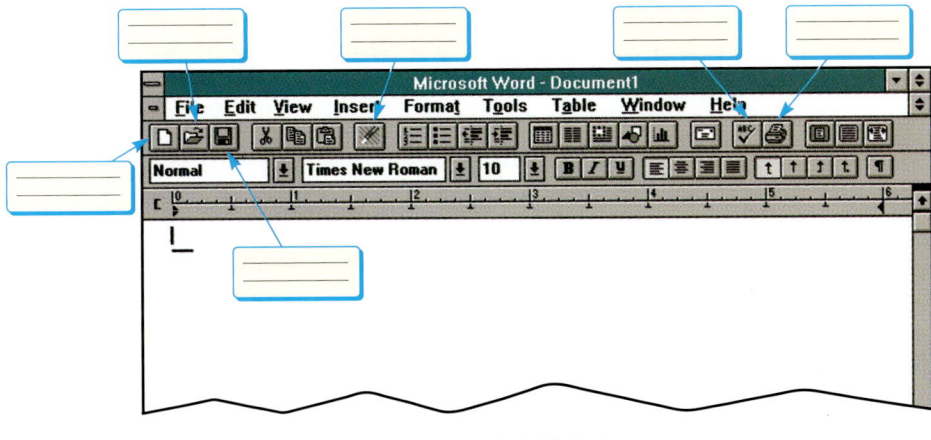

FIGURE SA1-4

MSW46   PROJECT 1   CREATING AND EDITING A DOCUMENT

STUDENT ASSIGNMENT 5
Understanding the Ribbon

Instructions: Answer the following questions concerning the contents of the ribbon in Figure SA1-5.

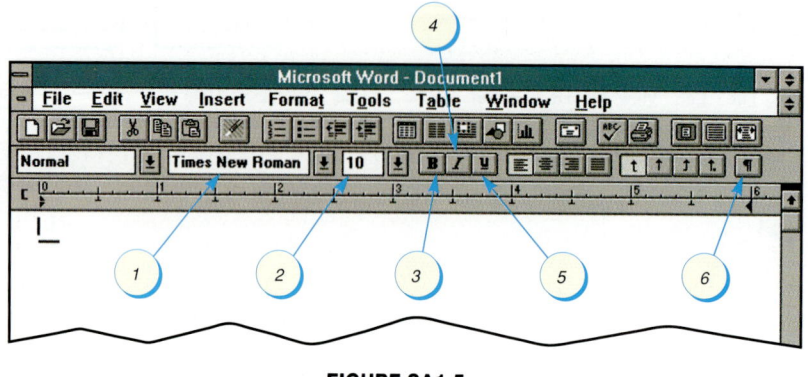

FIGURE SA1-5

1. What do the Words Times New Roman indicate?

2. What does the 10 indicate?

3. What is the purpose of the button that contains the dark capital B?

4. What is the purpose of the button that contains the slanted capital I?

5. What is the purpose of the button that contains the lowercase u?

6. What is the purpose of the button at the far right edge of the ribbon?

STUDENT ASSIGNMENT 6
Understanding Methods of Deleting Text

Instructions: Describe the result of various methods of deleting text in the space provided.

METHOD	RESULT
Position the insertion point and press the DELETE key.	
Position the insertion point and press the BACKSPACE key.	
Select a word or phrase and press the DELETE key.	

COMPUTER LABORATORY EXERCISES

COMPUTER LABORATORY EXERCISE 1
Using the Help Menu and Tutorial

Instructions: Perform the following tasks using a computer.

1. Start Word.
2. Select Help from the menu bar by pointing to Help and clicking the left mouse button.
3. Choose the Help Index command by pointing to the Help Index command and clicking the left mouse button. A screen with the title, Word Help Index, displays.
4. Choose the Instructions button by pointing to the Instructions button and clicking the left mouse button. What shape does the mouse pointer become when you point to the Instructions button? _____
5. A screen with the title, Help Instructions, displays. Read the contents of the screen.
6. Select File from the Help window by pointing to File and clicking the left mouse button.
7. Ready the printer and choose the Print Topic command by pointing to the Print Topic command and clicking the left mouse button. Word produces a hardcopy of the Help Instructions screen.
8. To return to the Word Help Index, choose the Contents button by pointing to Contents and clicking the left mouse button.
9. To close the Help window, choose the Exit command from the File menu in the Help window.
10. Choose Getting Started from the Help menu.
11. Press the left mouse button when the Welcome screen displays.
12. Select and read all three lessons: The Word Screen, Basic Skills, and Five Minutes to Productivity.
13. When you have completed reading the three lessons, return to the Word text screen by choosing the Exit button from the controls menu on the Word Screen Lesson menu.

COMPUTER LABORATORY EXERCISE 2
Formatting a Word Processing Document

Instructions: Start word. Open the document CLE1-2.DOC from the Word subdirectory on the Student Diskette that accompanies this book. The document CLE1-2.DOC is shown in Figure CLE1-2. The document resembles the memorandum created in Project 1.

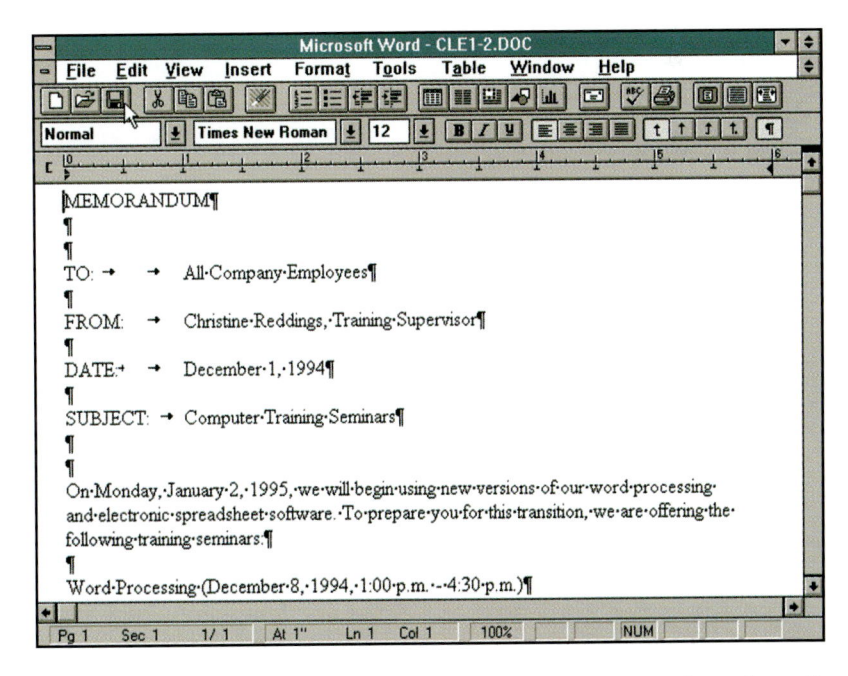

FIGURE CLE1-2

(continued)

MSW47

MSW48   PROJECT 1   CREATING AND EDITING A DOCUMENT

COMPUTER LABORATORY EXERCISE 2 (continued)

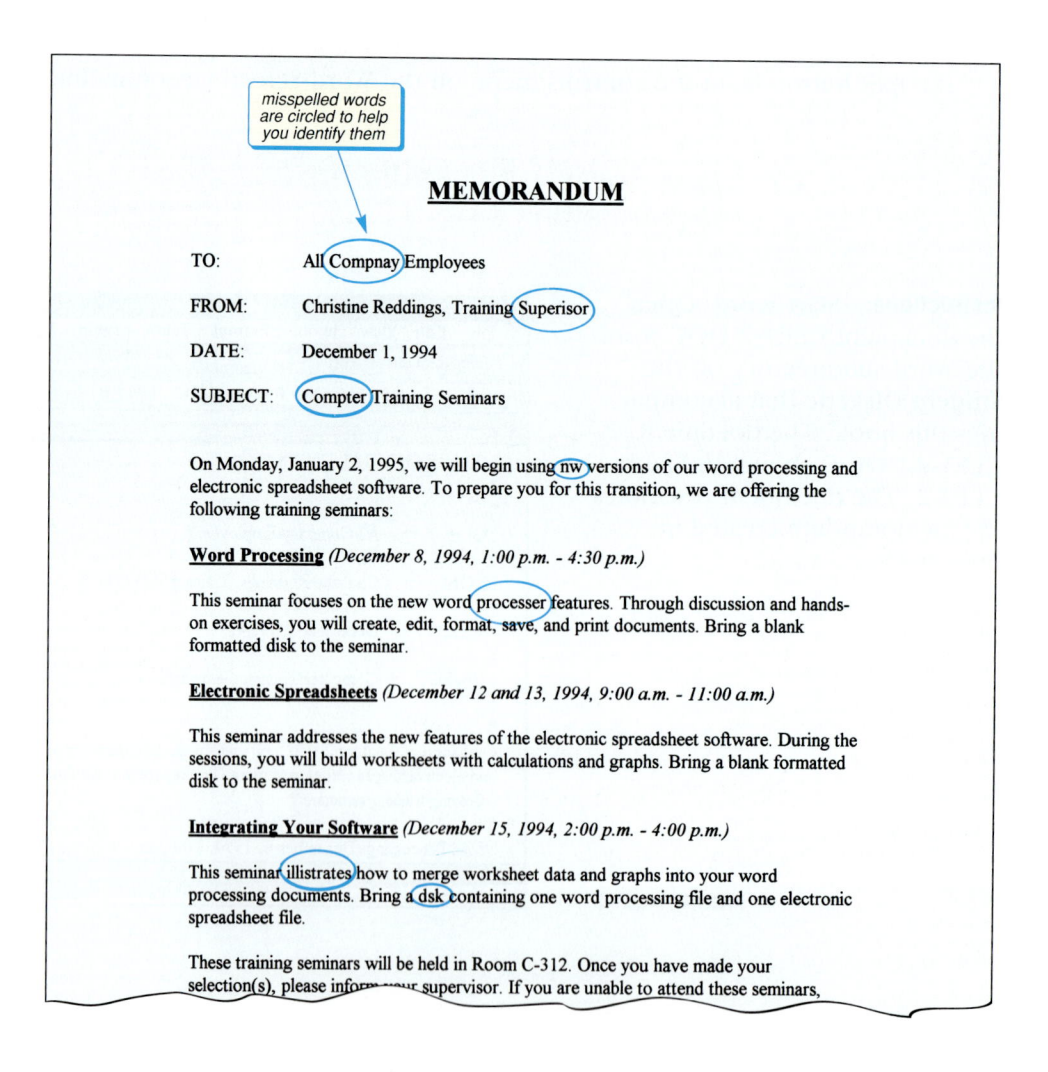

Perform the following tasks:

1. Position the insertion point in the title MEMORANDUM and center it.
2. Select the title MEMORANDUM.
3. Bold the title.
4. Underline the title.
5. Increase the point size of the title from 12 to 16.
6. Select the seminar title Word Processing.
7. Bold the seminar title.
8. Underline the seminar title.
9. Select the seminar time.
10. Italicize the seminar time.
11. Insert the word help between the words To and prepare in the second sentence of the memorandum.
12. Save the formatted document on your data disk. Be sure to replace the Student Diskette that accompanies this book with your data disk before saving the document.
13. Print the document by pointing to the Print button on the Toolbar and clicking.
14. Choose the Close command from the File menu to close the document.

COMPUTER LABORATORY EXERCISE 3
Checking Spelling of a Document

Instructions:

Start Word. Open the document CLE1-3.DOC from the Word sub-directory on the Student Diskette that accompanies this book. As shown in Figure CLE1-3, the document resembles the memorandum created in Project 1, except it contains many typographical errors.

misspelled words are circled to help you identify them

MEMORANDUM

TO: All Compnay Employees

FROM: Christine Reddings, Training Superisor

DATE: December 1, 1994

SUBJECT: Compter Training Seminars

On Monday, January 2, 1995, we will begin using nw versions of our word processing and electronic spreadsheet software. To prepare you for this transition, we are offering the following training seminars:

Word Processing *(December 8, 1994, 1:00 p.m. - 4:30 p.m.)*

This seminar focuses on the new word processer features. Through discussion and hands-on exercises, you will create, edit, format, save, and print documents. Bring a blank formatted disk to the seminar.

Electronic Spreadsheets *(December 12 and 13, 1994, 9:00 a.m. - 11:00 a.m.)*

This seminar addresses the new features of the electronic spreadsheet software. During the sessions, you will build worksheets with calculations and graphs. Bring a blank formatted disk to the seminar.

Integrating Your Software *(December 15, 1994, 2:00 p.m. - 4:00 p.m.)*

This seminar illustrates how to merge worksheet data and graphs into your word processing documents. Bring a dsk containing one word processing file and one electronic spreadsheet file.

These training seminars will be held in Room C-312. Once you have made your selection(s), please inform your supervisor. If you are unable to attend these seminars,

FIGURE CLE1-3

Perform the following tasks:

1. Position the insertion point at the beginning of the document and start the spelling checker by clicking the Spelling button on the Toolbar.
2. Change the incorrect word Compnay to Company by clicking the Change button.
3. Ignore the spelling checker's message on Reddings by clicking the Ignore All button.
4. Change the incorrect word Superisor to Supervisor by pointing to Supervisor in the suggested list of words and clicking. Then, click the Change button.
5. Change the incorrect word Comptr to Computer by clicking the Change button
6. Change the incorrect word nw to new by pointing to new in the suggested list of words and clicking. Then, click the Change button.
7. Change the incorrect word processer to processor by clicking the Change button.
8. Change the incorrect word illistrates to illustrates by clicking the Change button.
9. Change the incorrect word dsk to disk by erasing Ds from the Correct To box and typing in disk. Then, click the Change button.
10. Save the document on your data disk. Be sure to replace the Student Diskette that accompanies this book with your data disk before saving the document.
11. Print the spelling checked document.

COMPUTER LABORATORY ASSIGNMENTS

COMPUTER LABORATORY ASSIGNMENT 1
Creating a Memorandum

Purpose: To become familiar with creating a document, saving and printing a document, and formatting and spell checking a document.

Problem: You are the Director of Personnel Services for a medium-sized company. Your main responsibility is the company insurance plan. You have heard many employees complaining about the current insurance plan. You would like their feedback so next year's plan will be more successful. You decide to schedule a meeting with all full-time employees to openly discuss this matter.

Instructions:

1. Change the point size from 10 to 12 by clicking the Points box arrow and selecting 12.
2. Click the Show/Hide Nonprinting Characters button on the ribbon to display paragraph marks, tabs, and spaces.
3. Create the memorandum shown in Figure CLA1-1 on the next page. Enter the document unformatted, that is without any bolding, underlining, italicizing, or centering.
4. Save the document on a diskette with the filename CLA1-1.
5. Center the title MEMORANDUM.
6. Select the title MEMORANDUM. Bold and underline it. Change its font size from 12 to 16.
7. Select the sentence, We want your feedback. Italicize it.
8. Select the topic, Current Plan. Bold and underline it.
9. Select the phrase, pros and cons. Italicize it.
10. Select the topic, 1995 Plan Alternatives. Bold and underline it.
11. Select the date, September 9, and underline it.
12. Check the spelling of the memorandum.
13. Save the memorandum again.
14. Print the memorandum.

MEMORANDUM

TO:　　　　All Full-Time Employees

FROM:　　　Cathy Ackerman, Personnel Services

DATE:　　　August 10, 1994

SUBJECT:　　Insurance Plan

How do you feel about our current insurance plan? Does it meet your needs? What benefits do you find valuable? Are there any benefits you do not use? Would you like any benefits added to the plan? *We want your feedback.*

Please be advised we will hold an insurance meeting in Lunchroom A on August 17 from 9:00 a.m. to 11:00 a.m. covering the topics listed below:

Current Plan

Please be prepared to discuss the *pros and cons* of our current insurance plan.

1995 Plan Alternatives

We will discuss alternative plans available for 1995.

Following the meeting, we will prepare and distribute a list of alternative insurance plans to all full-time employees. We must decide on a benefit package by September 16. Please be sure to return your choice to us no later than September 9.

FIGURE CLA1-1

COMPUTER LABORATORY ASSIGNMENT 2
Creating a Schedule

Purpose: To become familiar with creating a document, saving and printing a document, and formatting and spell checking a document.

Problem: You are the Manager of the Secretarial Staff and your company has just purchased a word processing system. You hired Ameritel Training Corporation to train your secretarial staff on October 5, 1994. You plan on sending a schedule of events to the coordinator at Ameritel. Create this document by following the steps on the next page.

WORD PROCESSING WORKSHOP

Ameritel Training Corporation

October 5, 1994

SCHEDULE

8:00 a.m.	Arrive Ameritel Training Corporation	
8:15 a.m.	Breakfast	Conference Room C
9:00 a.m.	*Session 1:* Create a Document	Room 2219
10:30 a.m.	Break	
10:45 a.m.	*Resume Session 1:* Format a Document	Room 2219
Noon	End Session 1	
12:15 p.m.	Lunch	Conference Room B
1:30 p.m.	*Session 2:* Create a Document	Room 1343
3:00 p.m.	Break	
3:15 p.m.	*Resume Session 2:* Format a Document	Room 1343
4:45 p.m.	End Session 2	
5:00 p.m.	Ameritel Training Corporation departure	

FIGURE CLA1-2

(continued)

COMPUTER LABORATORY ASSIGNMENT 2 (continued)

Instructions:

1. Change the point size from 10 to 12 by clicking the Points box arrow and selecting 12.
2. Click the Show/Hide Nonprinting Characters button on the ribbon to display paragraph marks, tabs, and spaces.
3. Create the schedule shown in Figure CLA1-2 on the previous page. Enter the schedule unformatted, that is without any bold, underlining, italicizing, or centering. Use the TAB key to vertically align the activities and locations. Tab to the 1'' mark on the ruler before typing the activities; tab to the 4'' mark on the ruler before typing the locations.
4. Save the document with the filename CLA1-2.
5. Center the title Word Processing Workshop. Select the title. Bold it and increase its point size from 12 to 16.
6. Center the subtitle Ameritel Training Corporation. Select the subtitle. Bold it and increase its point size from 12 to 14.
7. Center the subtitle October 5, 1994. Select it and bold it.
8. Select the heading SCHEDULE. Bold and underline it.
9. Select and italicize the following phrases in the schedule: Session 1:, Resume Session 1:, Session 2:, and Resume Session 2:.
10. Check the spelling of the schedule.
11. Save the schedule again.
12. Print the schedule.

COMPUTER LABORATORY ASSIGNMENT 3
Creating a Memorandum

Purpose: To become familiar with creating a document, saving and printing a document, and formatting and spell checking a document.

Problem: You are the Regional Sales Director for a cable television company. You wish to inform your sales representatives of three new cable channels being added to the network beginning in December. Two of the channels will be included in basic service, and one will be a pay channel.

Instructions:

1. Change the point size from 10 to 12 by clicking the Points box and selecting 12.
2. Click the Show/Hide Nonprinting Characters button on the ribbon to display paragraph marks, tabs, and spaces.
3. Create the memorandum shown in Figure CLA1-3 on the next page. Enter the memorandum unformatted, that is without any bolding, underlining, italicizing, or centering.
4. Save the document with the filename CLA1-3.
5. Center the title MEMORANDUM. Select the title. Bold it and increase its font size from 12 to 16.
6. Select the heading Direct Network Shopping Club. Bold and underline it.
7. Select the phrase (Channel 47). Italicize it.
8. Select the heading Learning Made Easy. Bold and underline it.
9. Select the phrase (Channel 53). Italicize it.
10. Select the heading Movies, Movies, Movies. Bold and underline it.
11. Select the phrase (Channel 24). Italicize it.
12. Check the spelling of the memorandum.
13. Save the memorandum again.
14. Print the memorandum.

> # **MEMORANDUM**
>
> TO: Cable Television Sales Representatives
>
> FROM: Sam Conners, Regional Sales Director
>
> DATE: November 2, 1994
>
> SUBJECT: New Cable Channels
>
> During the month of December, we will be adding three new channels to our cable network. The first two are included in the basic service package; the third is a pay channel. Please inform all current and potential customers of these new upcoming cable channels:
>
> **Direct Network Shopping Club** *(Channel 47)*
>
> This is a twenty-four hour home shopping club. Merchandise includes clothing, jewelry, collectibles, antiques, and electronics. Viewers simply call a toll-free number to place an order. All goods are guaranteed to ship within 48 hours.
>
> **Learning Made Easy** *(Channel 53)*
>
> This is a twenty-four hour education channel. Topics taught range from the basics of reading, writing, and arithmetic to more complex areas like science, computers and electronics. Daytime broadcasting is designed for the younger audiences, while evening programs are geared toward the adult learner.
>
> **Movies, Movies, Movies** *(Channel 24)*
>
> This pay channel provides a variety of movies from the latest box office hits to old-time favorites. Additionally, one day per week will be reserved for viewer requests. With this feature, viewers can customize the Movies, Movies, Movies channel to enhance their viewing pleasure.

FIGURE CLA1-3

COMPUTER LABORATORY ASSIGNMENT 4
Designing and Creating a Movie Evaluation Memorandum

Purpose: To provide practice in planning and building a document.

Problem: You have been hired by Videos Are Us as a part-time evaluator. Your job responsibilities are to watch three movies per week and evaluate them. You must develop a rating system by which you will evaluate the movies. Your written evaluation must be a memorandum which explains your rating system and includes the name of each movie reviewed, the date you viewed it, a brief description of your evaluation, and your rating of the movie.

Instructions: Design and create a movie evaluation memorandum. Develop a rating system that is easy to understand. Be sure to clearly explain it in the memorandum. Use three movies you have recently viewed for your evaluation. Use the techniques you learned in this project to format the memorandum.

MICROSOFT WORD 2.0 FOR WINDOWS
PROJECT TWO

CREATING A RESEARCH PAPER

OBJECTIVES You will have mastered the material in this project when you can:

- Describe the MLA documentation style for research papers
- Change the margin settings in a document
- Adjust line spacing in a document
- Redefine the Normal style for a document
- Use a header to number pages of a document
- Indent paragraphs
- Add footnotes to a research paper
- Switch from normal to page layout view
- Insert hard page breaks
- Select multiple paragraphs
- Sort selected paragraphs
- Find and replace specified text
- Drag and drop a paragraph
- Cut and paste a paragraph
- Selectively display nonprinting characters
- Use the thesaurus
- Display a document in print preview

▶ INTRODUCTION

In both the academic and business environments, you will be asked to write reports. Business reports range from proposals to cost justifications to five-year plans to research findings. Academic reports focus mostly on research findings. Whether you are writing a business report or an academic report, you should follow a standard style when preparing it.

Many different styles of documentation exist for report preparation, depending on the nature of the report. Each style requires the same basic information; the differences among styles appear in the manner of presenting the information. For example, one documentation style may use the term *bibliography*; whereas, another uses *references*, and yet a third prefers *works cited*. A popular documentation style used today for research papers is presented by the **Modern Language Association** (MLA). Thus, this project uses the **MLA style of documentation**.

MSW54

▶ PROJECT TWO

Project Two illustrates the creation of a short research paper describing power disturbances that can damage a computer and its peripherals. As depicted in Figure 2-1, the paper follows the MLA style of documentation. The first two pages present the research paper and the third page alphabetically lists the works cited.

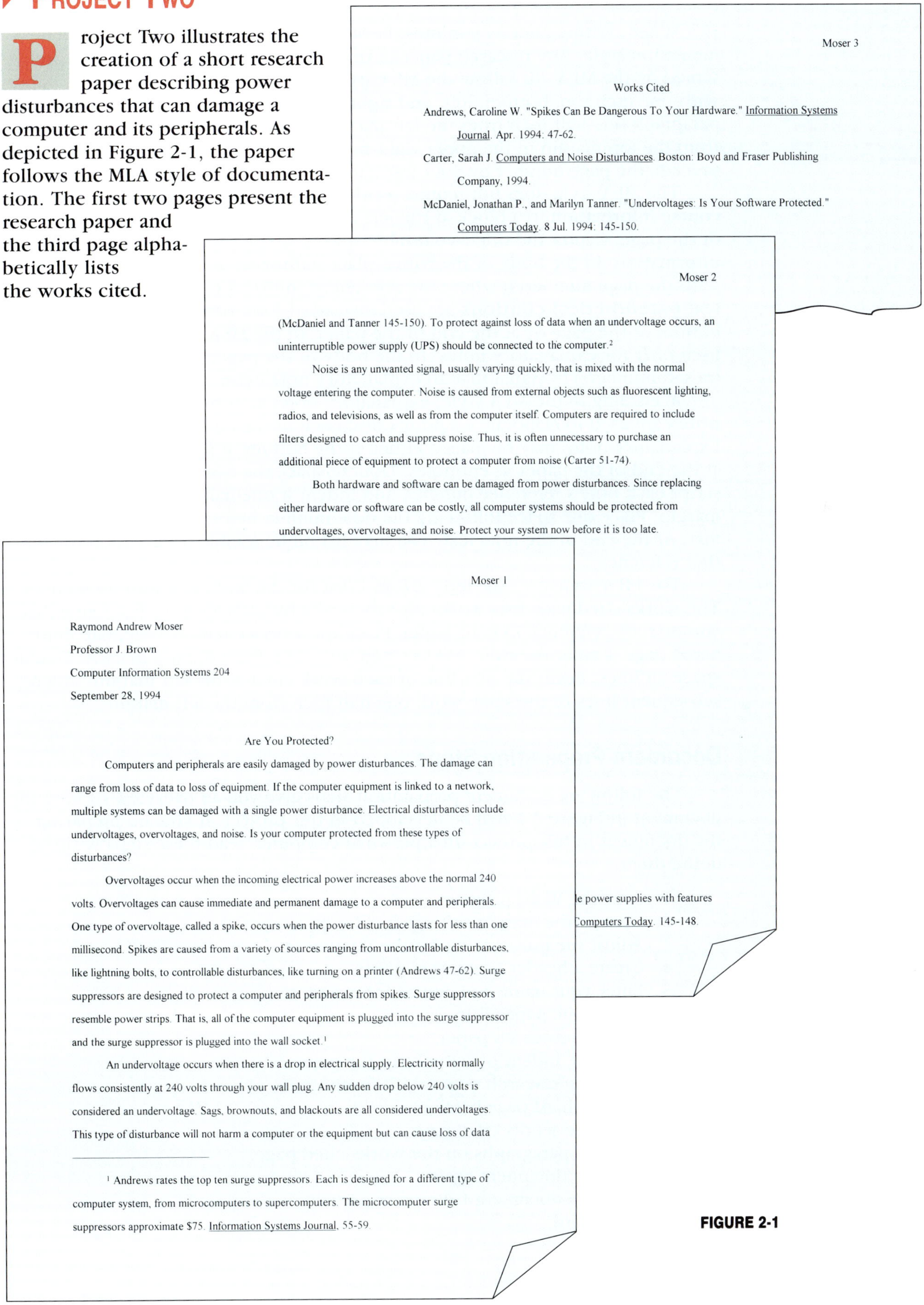

Moser 3

Works Cited

Andrews, Caroline W. "Spikes Can Be Dangerous To Your Hardware." <u>Information Systems Journal</u>. Apr. 1994: 47-62.

Carter, Sarah J. <u>Computers and Noise Disturbances</u>. Boston: Boyd and Fraser Publishing Company, 1994.

McDaniel, Jonathan P., and Marilyn Tanner. "Undervoltages: Is Your Software Protected." <u>Computers Today</u>. 8 Jul. 1994: 145-150.

Moser 2

(McDaniel and Tanner 145-150). To protect against loss of data when an undervoltage occurs, an uninterruptible power supply (UPS) should be connected to the computer.[2]

Noise is any unwanted signal, usually varying quickly, that is mixed with the normal voltage entering the computer. Noise is caused from external objects such as fluorescent lighting, radios, and televisions, as well as from the computer itself. Computers are required to include filters designed to catch and suppress noise. Thus, it is often unnecessary to purchase an additional piece of equipment to protect a computer from noise (Carter 51-74).

Both hardware and software can be damaged from power disturbances. Since replacing either hardware or software can be costly, all computer systems should be protected from undervoltages, overvoltages, and noise. Protect your system now before it is too late.

Moser 1

Raymond Andrew Moser
Professor J. Brown
Computer Information Systems 204
September 28, 1994

Are You Protected?

Computers and peripherals are easily damaged by power disturbances. The damage can range from loss of data to loss of equipment. If the computer equipment is linked to a network, multiple systems can be damaged with a single power disturbance. Electrical disturbances include undervoltages, overvoltages, and noise. Is your computer protected from these types of disturbances?

Overvoltages occur when the incoming electrical power increases above the normal 240 volts. Overvoltages can cause immediate and permanent damage to a computer and peripherals. One type of overvoltage, called a spike, occurs when the power disturbance lasts for less than one millisecond. Spikes are caused from a variety of sources ranging from uncontrollable disturbances, like lightning bolts, to controllable disturbances, like turning on a printer (Andrews 47-62). Surge suppressors are designed to protect a computer and peripherals from spikes. Surge suppressors resemble power strips. That is, all of the computer equipment is plugged into the surge suppressor and the surge suppressor is plugged into the wall socket.[1]

An undervoltage occurs when there is a drop in electrical supply. Electricity normally flows consistently at 240 volts through your wall plug. Any sudden drop below 240 volts is considered an undervoltage. Sags, brownouts, and blackouts are all considered undervoltages. This type of disturbance will not harm a computer or the equipment but can cause loss of data

---

[1] Andrews rates the top ten surge suppressors. Each is designed for a different type of computer system, from microcomputers to supercomputers. The microcomputer surge suppressors approximate $75. <u>Information Systems Journal</u>, 55-59.

FIGURE 2-1

MLA Documentation Style

When writing papers, you must be sure to adhere to some form of documentation style. The research paper in this project follows the guidelines presented by the MLA. To follow the MLA style, double-space all pages of the paper with one-inch top, bottom, left, and right margins. Indent the first word of each paragraph one-half inch from the left margin. Place a page number one-half inch from the top margin in the upper right-hand corner of each page. On each page, precede the page number by your last name.

The MLA style does not require a title page; rather place your name and course information in a block at the left margin beginning one inch from the top of the page. Center the title two double-spaces below your name and course information. In the body of the paper, place author references in parentheses with the page number(s) where the referenced information is located. These in-text **parenthetical citations** are used instead of footnoting each source at the bottom of the page or at the end of the paper. In the MLA style, footnotes are used *only* for explanatory notes. In the body of the paper, use **superscripts** (raised numbers) to signal that an explanatory note exists.

According to the MLA style, explanatory notes are optional. **Explanatory notes** are used to elaborate on points discussed in the body of the paper. Explanatory notes may be placed either at the bottom of the page as footnotes or at the end of the paper as endnotes. Double-space the explanatory notes. Superscript each note's reference number, and indent it one-half inch from the left margin. Place one space following the note number before beginning the note text. At the end of the note text, you may list bibliographic information for further reference.

The MLA style uses the term *works cited* for the bibliographical references. The works cited page lists works alphabetically by each author's last name that you directly reference in your paper. Place the works cited on a separate numbered page. Center the title, Works Cited, one inch from the top margin. Double-space all lines. Begin the first line of each work cited at the left margin; indent subsequent lines of the same work one-half inch from the left margin.

Document Preparation Steps

The following document preparation steps give you an overview of how the document in Figure 2-1 will be developed in this project. If you are preparing the document in this project on a personal computer, read these steps without doing them.

1. Start the Word program.
2. Change the margin settings for the document.
3. Adjust the line spacing for the document.
4. Create a header to number pages.
5. Enter your name and course information.
6. Center the paper title.
7. Save the research paper.
8. First-line indent paragraphs in the paper.
9. Enter the research paper with footnotes.
10. Insert a hard page break.
11. Enter the works cited page.
12. Sort the paragraphs on the works cited page.
13. Save the document again.
14. Print the document from print preview.
15. Quit Word.

CHANGING THE MARGINS MSW57

▶ STARTING WORD

To start Word, the Windows Program Manager must display on the screen, and the Word for Windows 2.0 group window must be open. Then, you double-click on the Microsoft Word program-item icon in the Word for Windows 2.0 group window.

Displaying Nonprinting Characters

As discussed in Project 1, it is helpful to display nonprinting characters that indicate where in the document you pressed the ENTER key, SPACEBAR, or TAB key. Thus, you should display the nonprinting characters by clicking the Show/Hide Nonprinting Characters button on the ribbon, as illustrated in Project 1 on pages MSW14 and MSW15, if it is not already recessed. Later in this project you will see how to selectively display nonprinting characters. For example, you may only want to display the paragraph marks, hiding the raised dots and right-pointing arrows.

▶ CHANGING THE MARGINS

Word is preset to use standard 8.5 by 11-inch paper, with 1.25-inch left and right margins and 1-inch top and bottom margins. These margin settings affect every paragraph in the document. Often, you may want to change these default margin settings. For example, the MLA documentation style requires one-inch top, bottom, left, and right margins throughout the paper. The following steps illustrate how to change the default margin settings for a document.

TO CHANGE THE DEFAULT MARGIN SETTINGS ▼

STEP 1 ▶

Select the Format menu, and point to the Page Setup command (Figure 2-2).

FIGURE 2-2

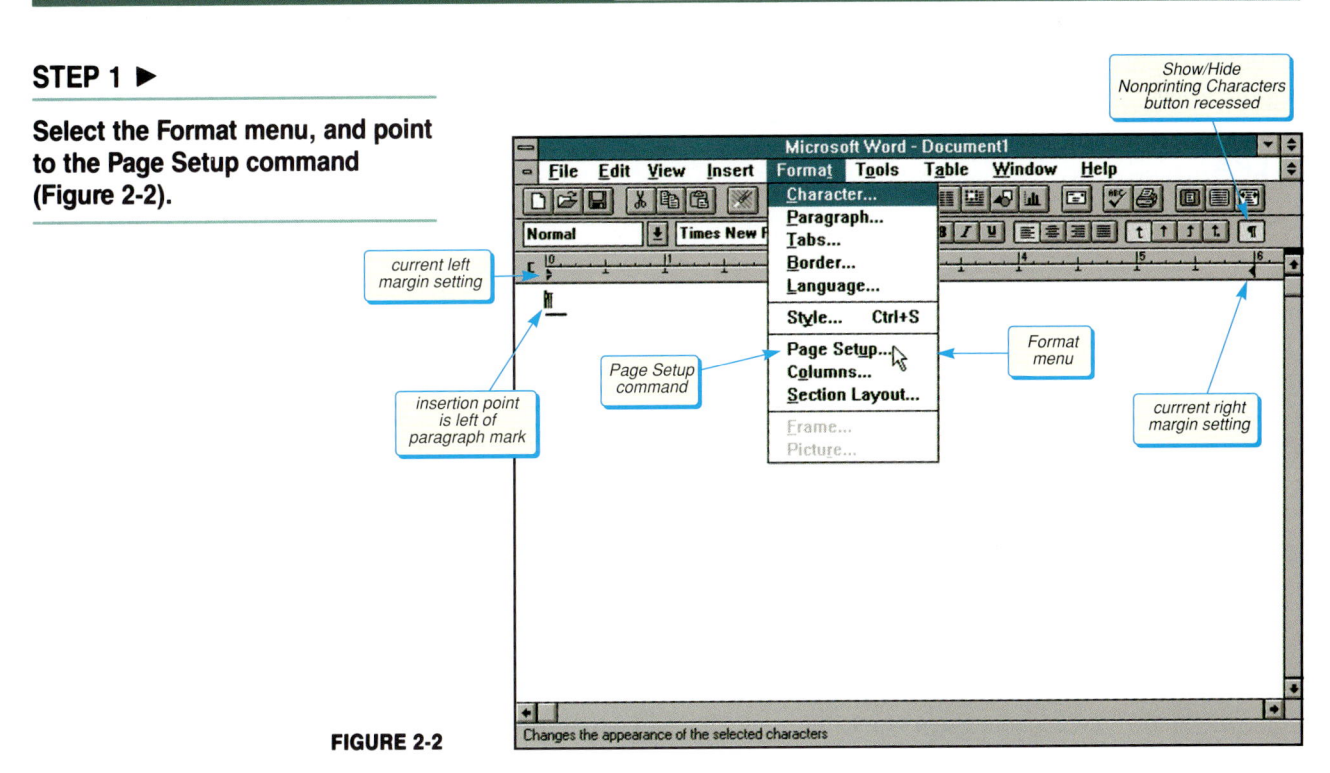

STEP 2 ▶

Choose the Page Setup command. Point to the down arrow box next to the Left text box.

Word displays the Page Setup dialog box with the Margins option button selected. (If your Margins option button is not selected, click it.) Word lists the current margin settings in the respective text boxes and displays them graphically in the Sample area (Figure 2-3). Use the up and down arrow boxes next to the Top, Bottom, Left, and Right text boxes to change the margin settings by clicking them.

STEP 3 ▶

Repeatedly click the down arrow box next to the Left text box until the text box displays 1". Click the down arrow box next to the Right text box until the text box displays 1".

The current left and right margin settings decrease from 1.25 inches to 1 inch, and the Sample area adjusts accordingly to reflect the new margin settings (Figure 2-4).

STEP 4

Choose the OK button.

Word returns you to the document with the left and right margins changed (Figure 2-5 on the next page).

FIGURE 2-3

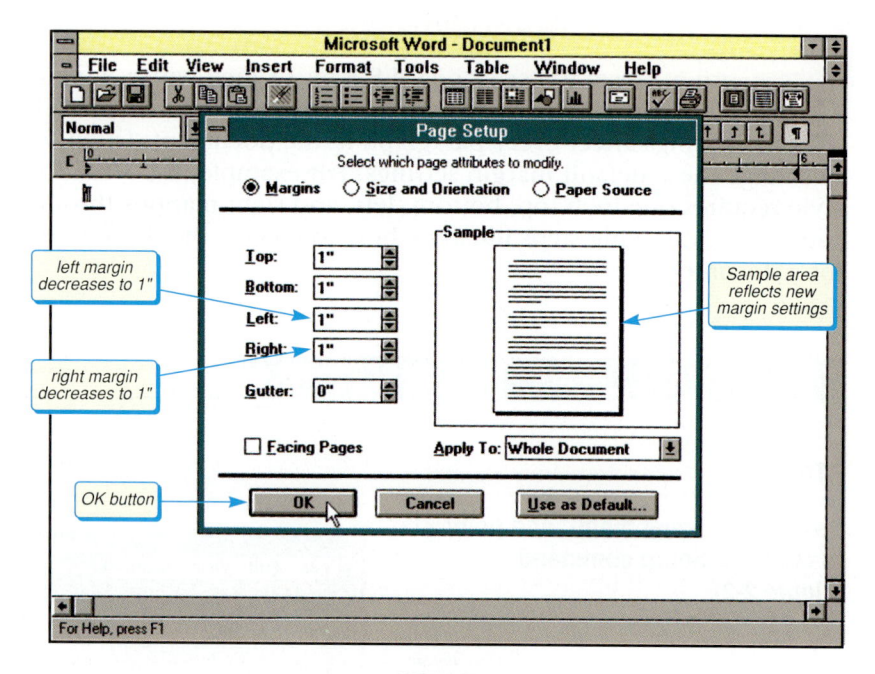

FIGURE 2-4

▲

If the desired margin settings do not appear as you click the up and down arrow boxes in the Page Setup dialog box, you can tab from one text box to another and type specific margin settings. The new margin settings take effect in the document immediately. Word uses these margins for the entire document.

In some versions of Word for Windows, when the body of your paper is double-spaced, the top margin may include an extra blank line. Thus, the top margin may actually print 1.17 inches from the top of your page. Later when you print the document, if you notice the top margin is greater than one inch, enter .83 in the Top text box of the Page Setup dialog box shown in Figure 2-4.

▶ Adjusting Line Spacing

Word, by default, single-spaces between lines of text and automatically adjusts line height to accommodate various font sizes and graphics. The MLA documentation style requires that you double-space the entire paper. Thus, you must adjust the line spacing as described in the following steps.

TO ADJUST LINE SPACING ▼

STEP 1 ▶

Select the Format menu and point to the Paragraph command (Figure 2-5).

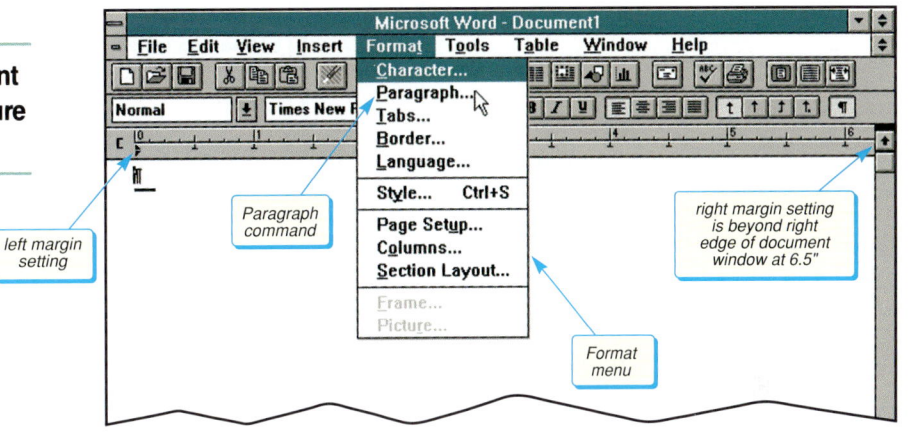

FIGURE 2-5

STEP 2 ▶

Choose the Paragraph command. Point to the Line Spacing box arrow.

Word displays the Paragraph dialog box, listing the current settings in the text boxes and displaying them graphically in the Sample area (Figure 2-6).

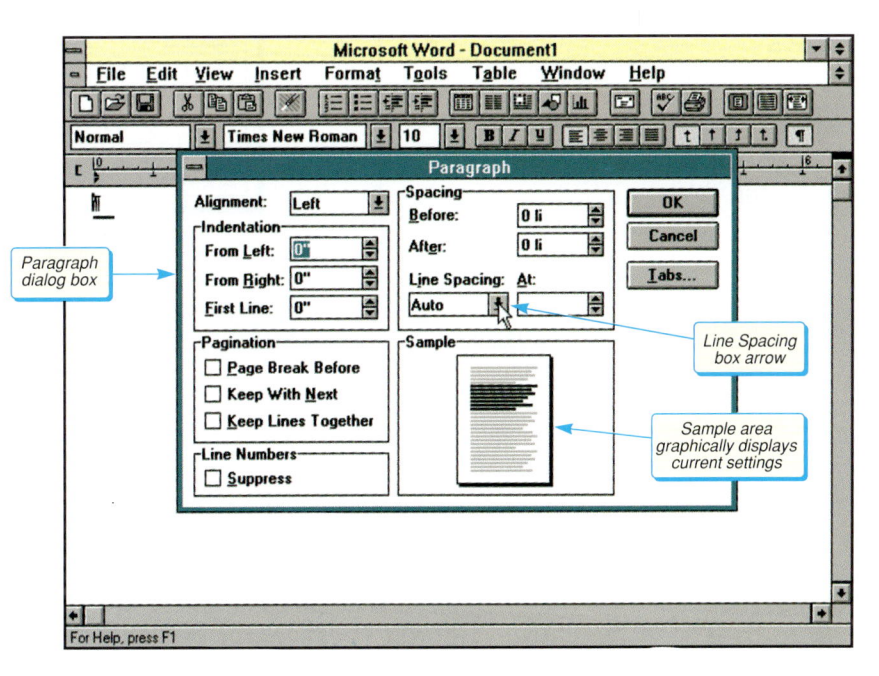

FIGURE 2-6

MSW60 PROJECT 2 CREATING A RESEARCH PAPER

STEP 3 ▶

Click the Line Spacing box arrow and point to Double.

A list of available line spacing options displays (Figure 2-7).

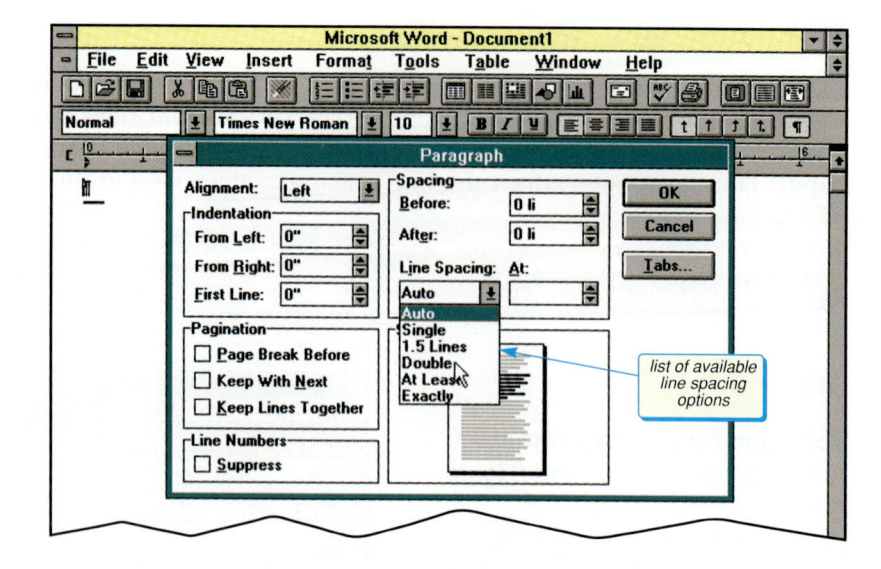

FIGURE 2-7

STEP 4 ▶

Select Double by clicking it.

Word displays Double in the Line Spacing text box and graphically portrays the new line spacing in the Sample area (Figure 2-8).

STEP 5

Choose the OK button.

Word returns you to the document.

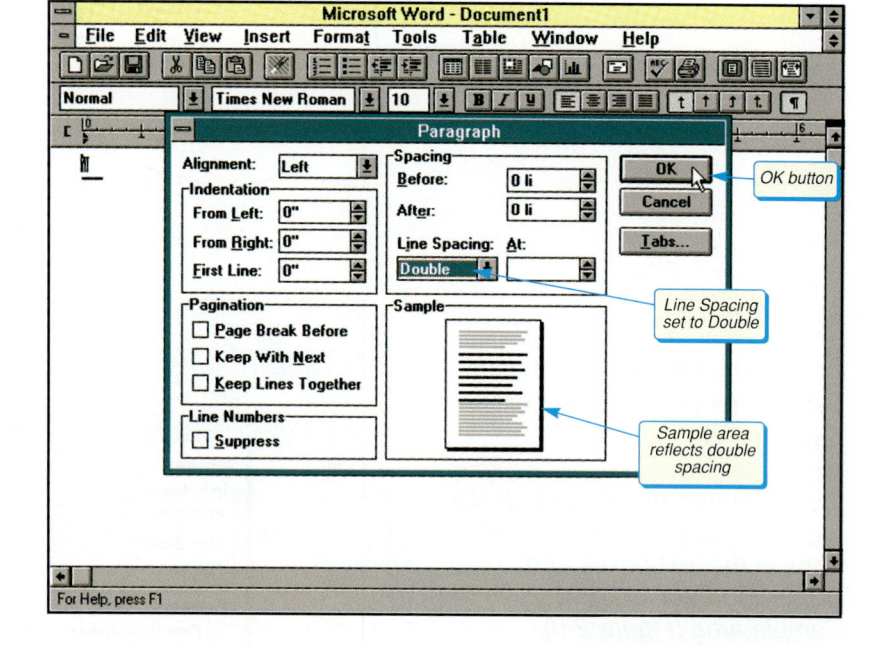

FIGURE 2-8

In the Line Spacing drop-down list box, you have a variety of options for the line spacing settings (Figure 2-7). The default, Auto, allows Word to automatically adjust line spacing to accommodate the largest font or graphic on a line. The options Single, 1.5 Lines, and Double each adjust spacing as specified, allowing Word to increase the designated line spacing if necessary to accommodate fonts or graphics. The last two options, At Least and Exactly, enable you to specify a line spacing not provided in the first four options. The difference is that the At Least option allows Word to increase the designation if necessary; whereas, the Exactly option does not enable Word to increase the specification.

▶ Redefining the Normal Style

In Project 1 you created a memorandum that was single-spaced with 1.25 inch left and right margins. Thus, in Project 1 you used the default Normal style when typing the document. The **Normal style** specifies the document's default formats, such as line spacing, margins, font, and point size. You apply the Normal style for day-to-day word processing usage. Thus far in this project, you have changed the line spacing to double and all margins to one inch. You would also like this document to be typed in 12 point so it is easier to read. Once you have changed text formats for a document, you should redefine the Normal style to reflect these changes. By redefining the Normal style, all text you type in the document will be formatted according to Normal style specifications. To redefine the Normal style to include the new line spacing, margin settings and point size, follow these steps.

TO REDEFINE NORMAL STYLE ▼

STEP 1 ▶

Position the mouse pointer in the selection bar to the left of the paragraph mark on line 1 of the document window.

The mouse pointer changes to a right-pointing block arrow ( ) in the selection bar (Figure 2-9). The selection bar is an unmarked area about 1/4 inch wide along the left edge of the screen.

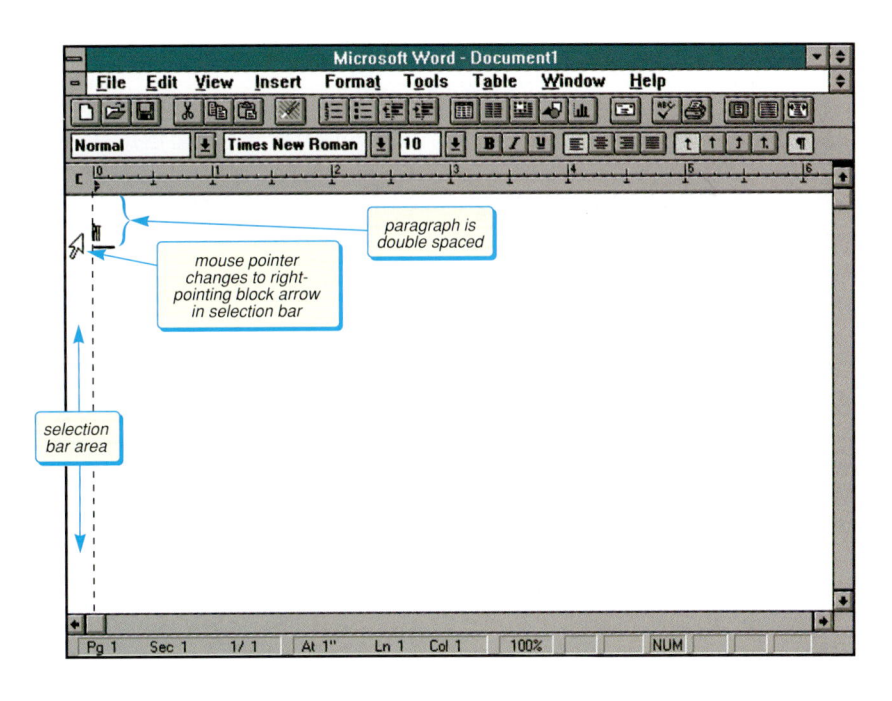

FIGURE 2-9

STEP 2 ▶

Click the mouse.

Word selects the line to the right of the mouse pointer (Figure 2-10). Recall that selected text is highlighted. In this case, the paragraph mark is highlighted.

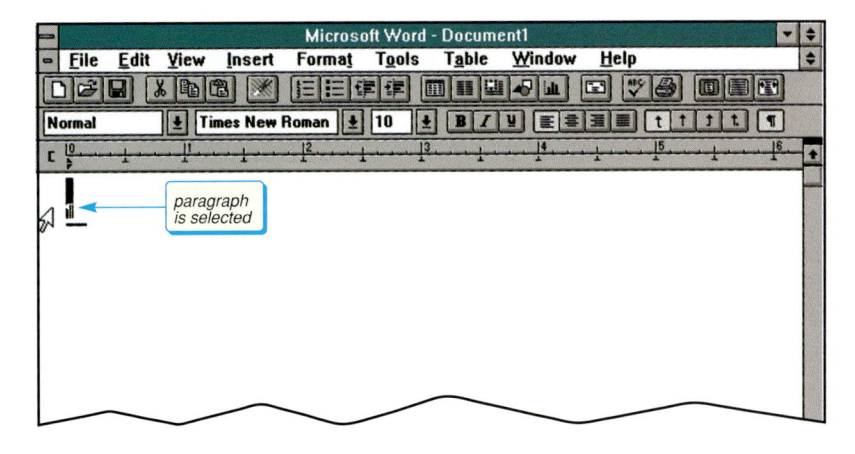

FIGURE 2-10

MSW62   PROJECT 2   CREATING A RESEARCH PAPER

STEP 3 ▶

Change the point size to 12 by clicking the Points box arrow on the ribbon and selecting point size 12 (Figure 2-11).

STEP 4 ▶

Position the mouse pointer in the Style box on the ribbon and double-click.

Word selects the word Normal in the Style box on the ribbon (Figure 2-11).

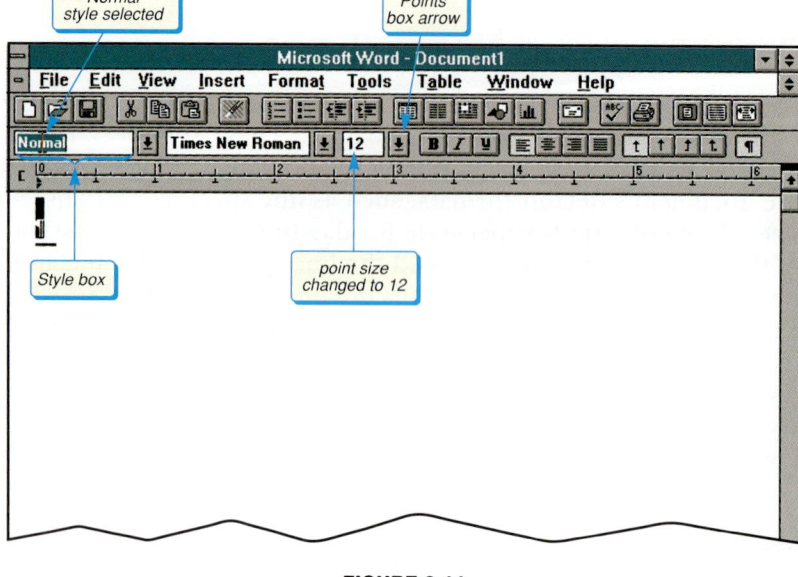

FIGURE 2-11

STEP 5 ▶

Press the ENTER key and point to the Yes button.

A Microsoft Word dialog box displays asking if you want to redefine the Normal style based on the current selection (Figure 2-12).

STEP 6

Choose the Yes button. Click outside the selected paragraph to remove the highlight.

Word redefines the Normal style to be double-spacing, all margins at one inch, and a point size of 12.

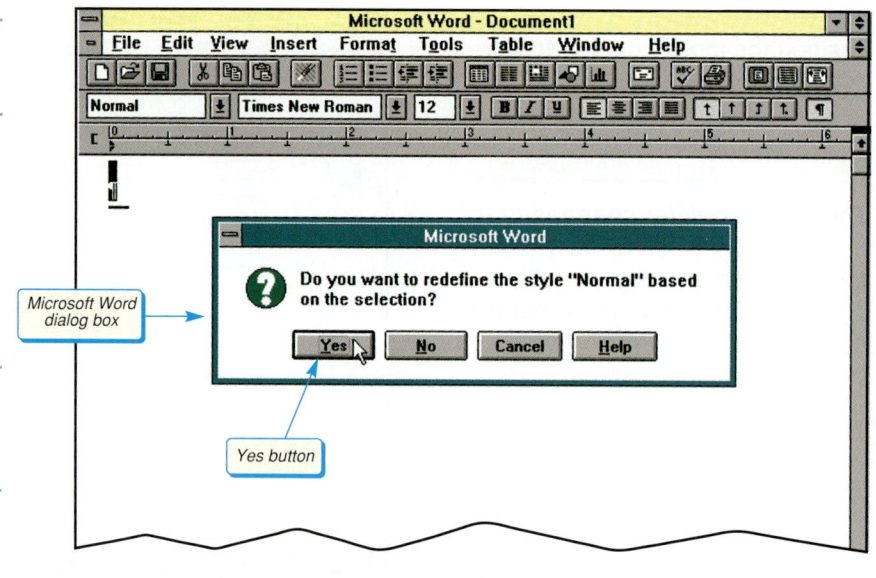

FIGURE 2-12

When you redefine the Normal style, the new definition applies *only* to the current document. That is, if you close this document and begin a new document, the default Normal style (1.25 inch left and right margins, single spacing, and point size of 10) will be in effect.

▶ USING A HEADER TO NUMBER PAGES

In Word, you can easily number pages by choosing the Page Numbers command from the Insert menu. Once chosen, this command places page numbers on every page after the first. You cannot, however, place your name as required by the MLA in front of the page number with the Page Numbers command. To do this, you must create a header that contains the page number.

Headers and Footers

A **header** is text you want printed at the top of each page in the document. A **footer** is text you want printed at the bottom of every page. In Word, headers are printed in the top margin one-half inch from the top of every page, and footers are printed in the bottom margin one-half inch from the bottom of each page, which meets the MLA style. Headers and footers can include both text and graphics, as well as the page number, current date, and current time.

In this project, you are to precede the page number with your last name placed one-half inch from the top of each page. Your name and page number should print **right-aligned**; that is, at the right margin. Use the procedures in the following steps to create the header with page numbers according to the MLA style.

TO CREATE A HEADER ▼

STEP 1 ▶

Select the View menu and point to the Header/Footer command (Figure 2-13).

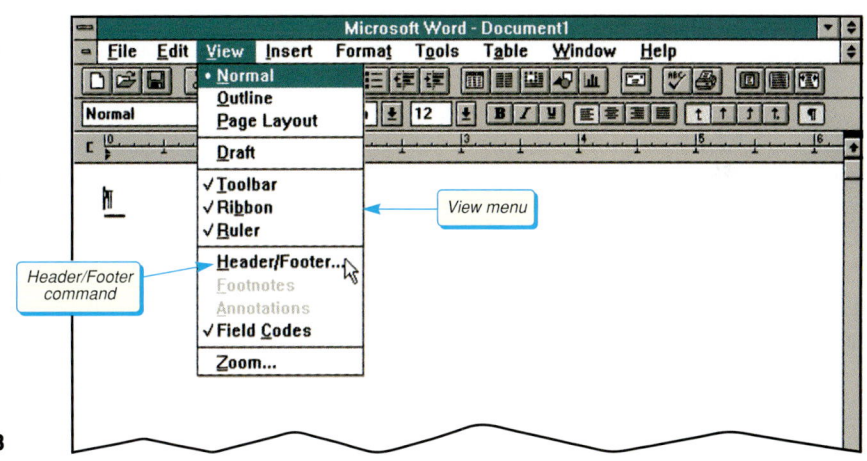

FIGURE 2-13

STEP 2 ▶

Choose the Header/Footer command, and then point to the OK button.

Word displays the Header/Footer dialog box (Figure 2-14). Header is the default selection in the Header/Footer list box.

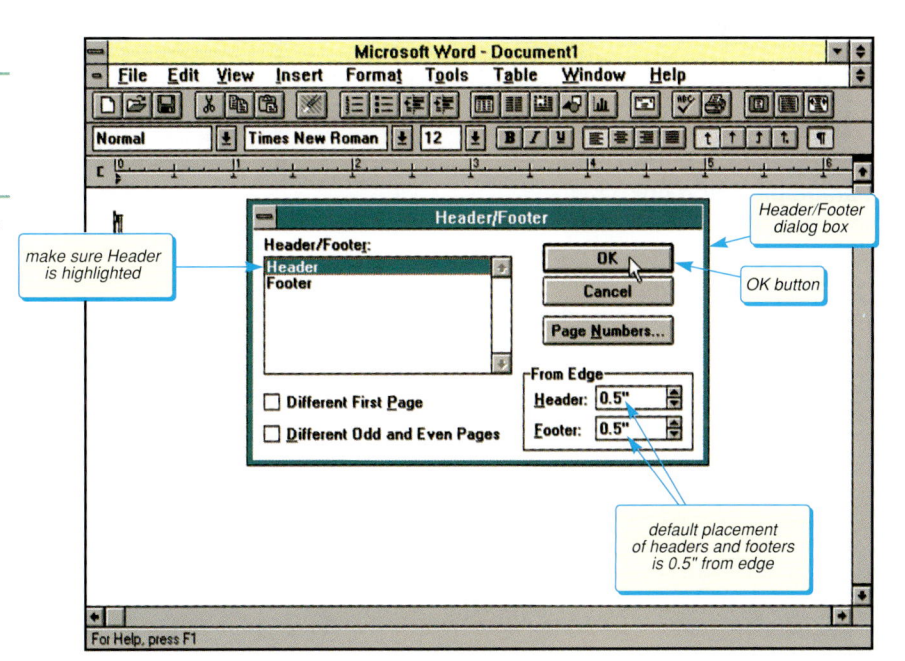

FIGURE 2-14

MSW64   PROJECT 2   CREATING A RESEARCH PAPER

STEP 3 ▶

Choose the OK button.

*Word opens a header pane in the lower portion of the screen with the insertion point at the left margin (Figure 2-15a). The **header pane** is an area at the bottom of the screen, which contains an option bar, a text area, and scroll bars.*

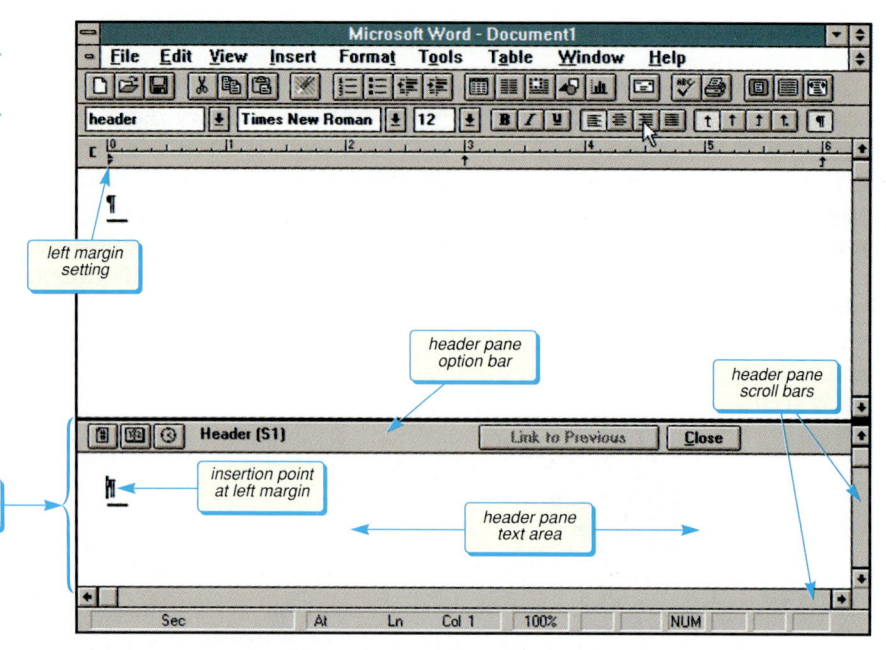

FIGURE 2-15a

STEP 4 ▶

Choose the Paragraph command from the Format menu. Click the Line Spacing box arrow and point to Single.

Word displays the Paragraph dialog box (Figure 2-15b). The mouse pointer points to Single.

STEP 5

Select Single by clicking it and choose the OK button in the Paragraph dialog box.

The insertion point and paragraph mark are single spaced in the header pane (Figure 2-16 on the next page).

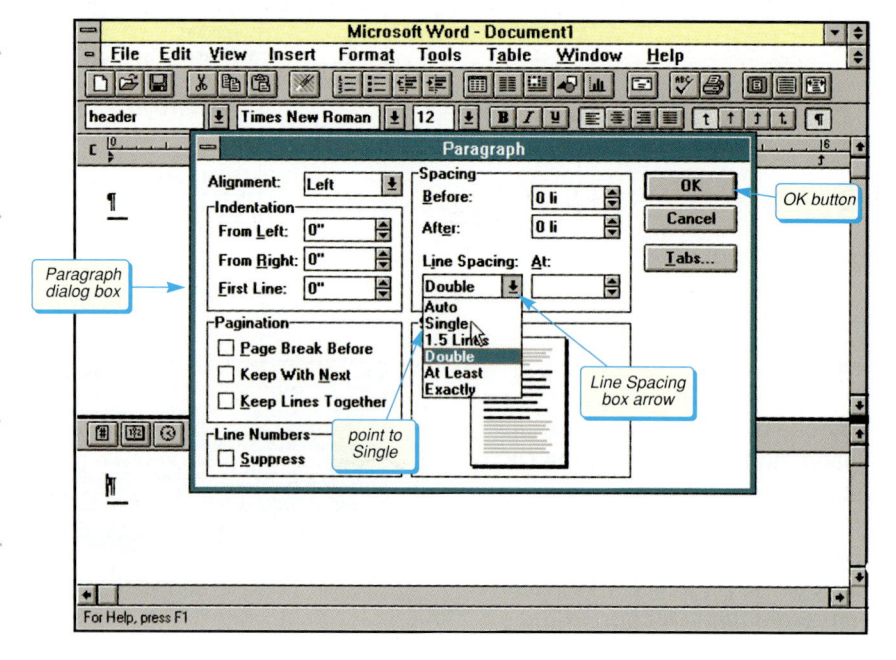

FIGURE 2-15b

USING A HEADER TO NUMBER PAGES **MSW65**

STEP 6 ▶

Click the Right-Aligned Text button (▤) on the ribbon.

The paragraph mark and insertion point in the header pane are positioned at the right margin, and the Right-Aligned Text button is recessed (Figure 2-16). Notice that the document window and the header pane have scrolled to the right so the right margin on the ruler is visible.

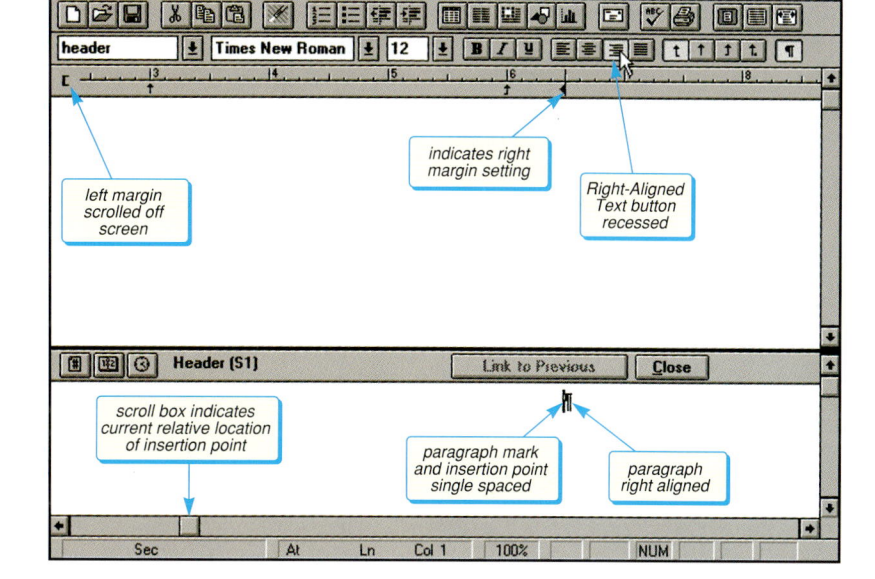

FIGURE 2-16

STEP 7 ▶

Type Moser followed by a space. Click the Page Number button (▣) on the header pane option bar.

The last name Moser followed by the page number 1 appears right-aligned in the text area of the header pane (Figure 2-17). If your screen does not display the page number, choose the Field Codes command from the View menu.

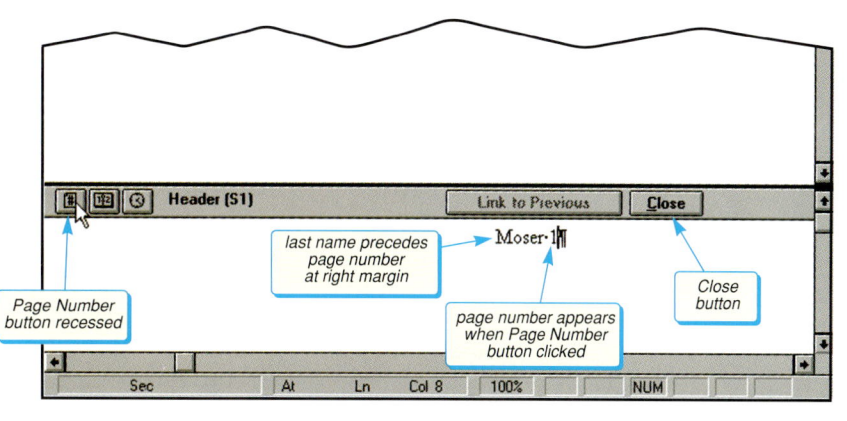

FIGURE 2-17

STEP 8 ▶

Choose the Close button (Close) on the header pane option bar. Point to the left of the scroll box on the horizontal scroll bar at the bottom of the document window.

Word closes the header pane and returns you to the document window. Notice the document window is still positioned at the right margin (Figure 2-18).

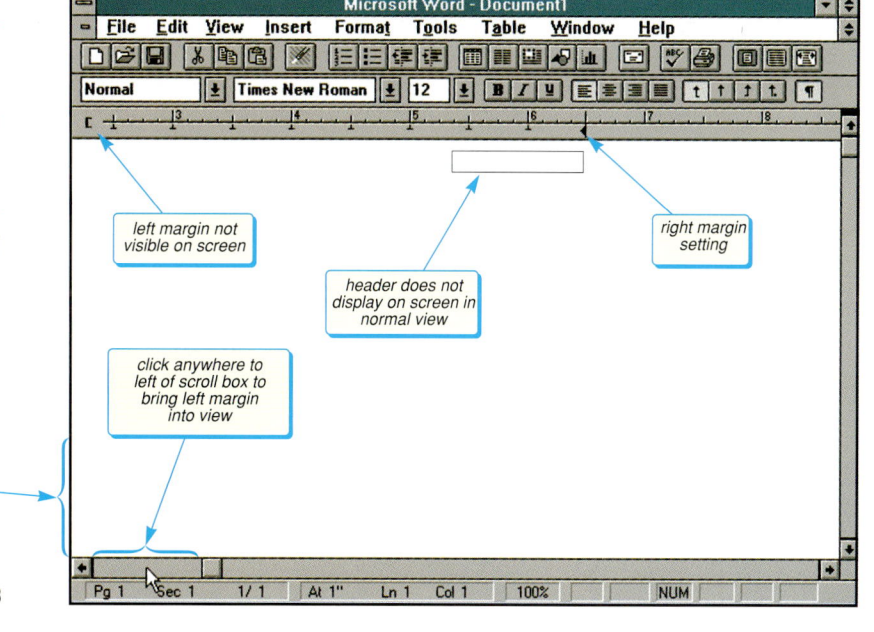

FIGURE 2-18

STEP 9 ▶

Click the left mouse button.

The document window scrolls one screen to the left. The scroll box is positioned at the left margin on the horizontal scroll bar (Figure 2-19).

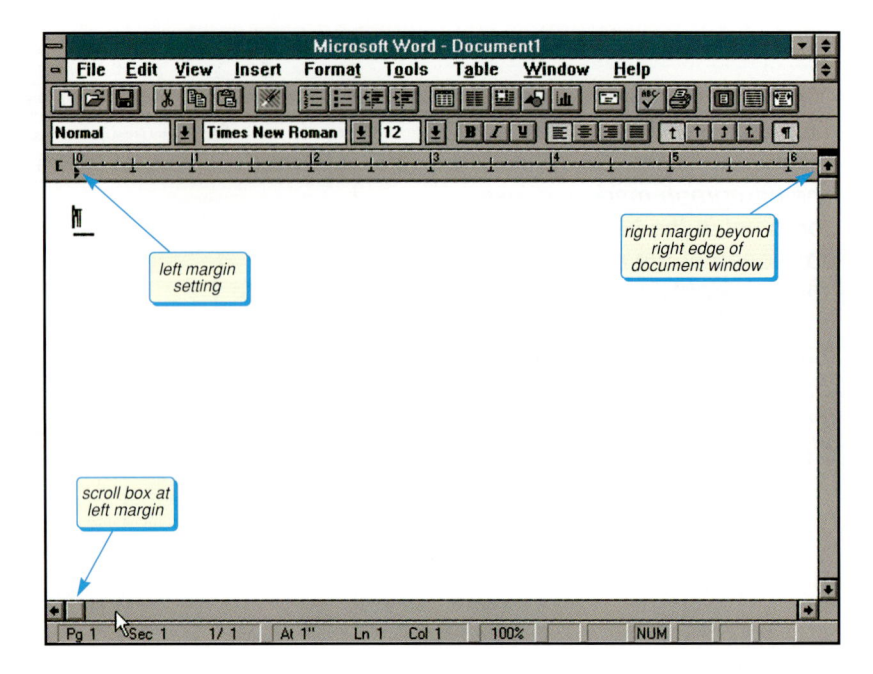

FIGURE 2-19

The header does not display on the screen when the document window is in **normal view** because it tends to clutter the screen. You will, however, want to verify that the header will print correctly. Later in this project you will view the document in both page layout view and print preview. These views display the header on the screen with the rest of the text.

Just as the Page Number button on the header pane option bar inserts the page number into the document, you can use two other buttons on the header pane option bar to insert items into the document. The Current Date button (▦) inserts the current date into the document (Figure 2-17 on the previous page). In the same manner, the Current Time button (◯) inserts the current time (Figure 2-17 on the previous page).

▶ TYPING THE BODY OF THE RESEARCH PAPER

The body of the research paper encompasses the first two pages in Figure 2-1 on page MSW55. The steps on the following pages illustrate how to enter the body of the research paper.

TYPING THE BODY OF THE RESEARCH PAPER   **MSW67**

Entering Name and Course Information

Recall that the MLA style does not require a separate title page for research papers. Instead, you place your name and course information in a block at the top of the page at the left margin. Thus, follow the step below to begin the body of the research paper.

TO ENTER NAME AND COURSE INFORMATION ▼

STEP 1 ▶

Type Raymond Andrew Moser **and press the ENTER key. Type** Professor J. Brown **and press the ENTER key. Type** Computer Information Systems 204 **and press the ENTER key. Type** September 28, 1994 **and press the ENTER key twice.**

The student name appears on line 1, the professor name on line 2, the course name on line 3, and the paper due date on line 4 (Figure 2-20). Each time you press the ENTER key, Word advances two lines on the screen, but increments the line counter by only one because earlier you set line spacing to double.

one blank line automatically appears each time the ENTER key is pressed because the text is double-spaced

insertion point on line 6

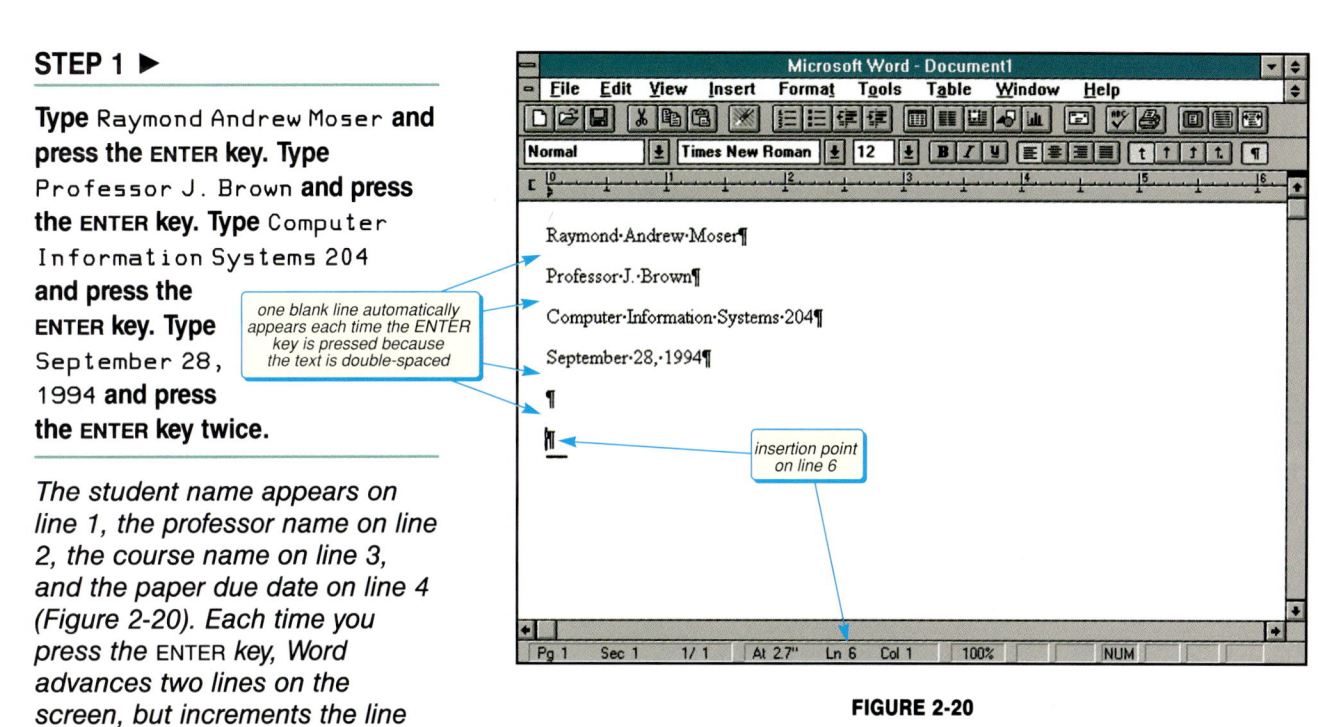

FIGURE 2-20

Centering a Paragraph Before Typing

In Project 1, you learned how to center a paragraph after you typed it. You can also center a paragraph before you type it by following the steps on the next page.

TO CENTER A PARAGRAPH BEFORE TYPING

STEP 1 ▶

Position the insertion point on the paragraph mark to be centered and click the Centered Text button on the ribbon.

Word centers the paragraph mark and the insertion point between the left and right margins (Figure 2-21). The Centered Text button on the ribbon is recessed, indicating the text you type will be centered.

FIGURE 2-21

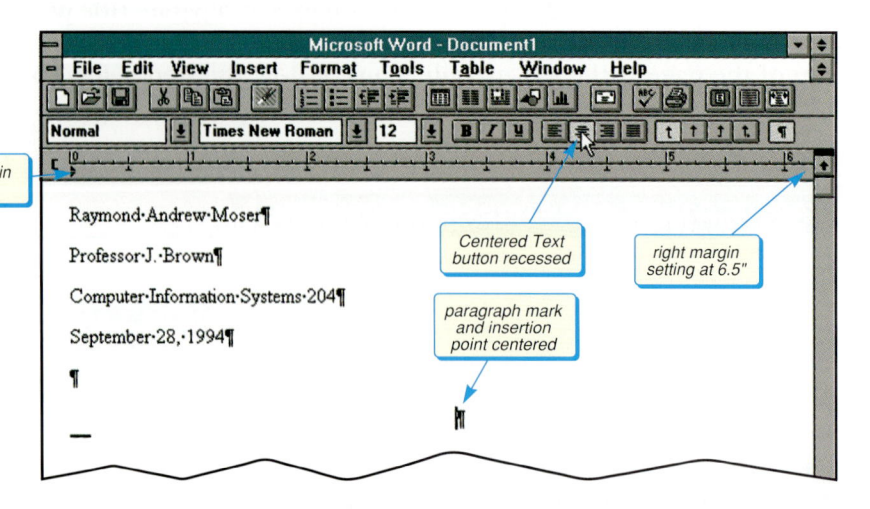

STEP 2 ▶

Type the text `Are You Protected?` **and press the ENTER key.**

The text is centered on line 6 and the insertion point advances to line 7 (Figure 2-22). Notice the paragraph mark and insertion point on line 7 are centered because the formatting specified in the prior paragraph (line 6) is carried forward to the next paragraph (line 7).

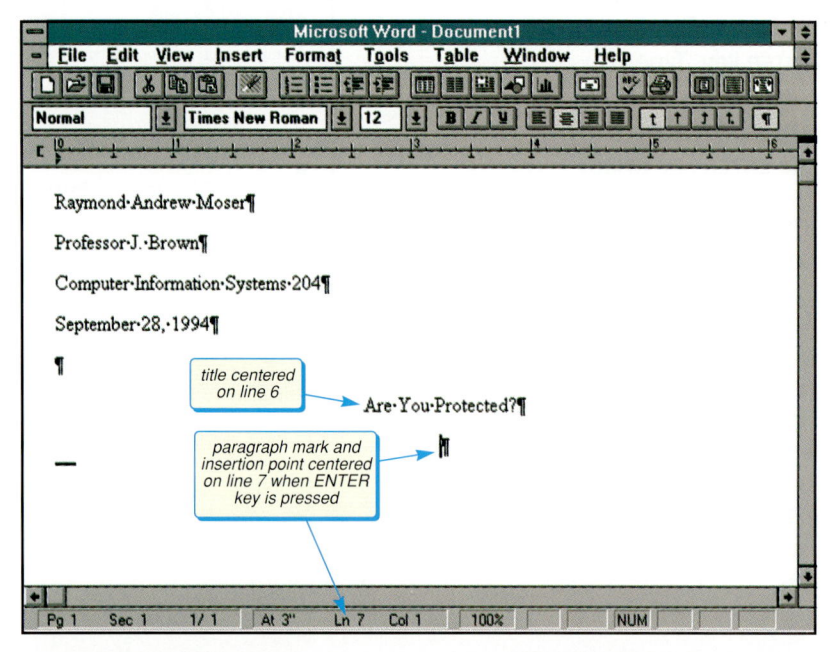

FIGURE 2-22

STEP 3 ▶

Click the Left-Aligned Text button (☰) on the ribbon.

Word positions the paragraph mark and the insertion point at the left margin (Figure 2-23). The next material you type will be left-aligned.

FIGURE 2-23

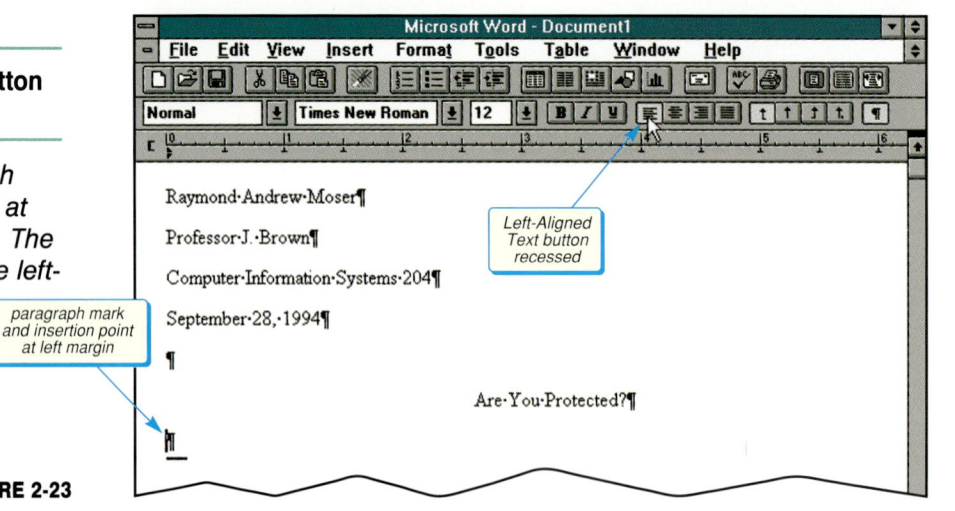

TYPING THE BODY OF THE RESEARCH PAPER   **MSW69**

Saving the Research Paper

Recall from Project 1 that it is prudent to save your work on disk at regular intervals. Because you have performed several tasks thus far, you should save your research paper. For a detailed example of the procedure summarized below, refer to pages MSW18 through MSW20 in Project 1.

TO SAVE A DOCUMENT

Step 1: Click the Save button on the Toolbar.
Step 2: Type the filename `proj2` in the File Name text box. Do not press the ENTER key.
Step 3: Click the Drives drop-down list box and select drive A.
Step 4: Choose the OK button in the Save As dialog box.
Step 5: If you desire, enter information in the Summary Info dialog box.
Step 6: Choose the OK button in the Summary Info dialog box.

Indenting Paragraphs

According to the MLA, the first line of each paragraph in the research paper is to be indented one-half inch from the left margin. This procedure, called **first-line indent** can be accomplished using the ruler as shown in the following steps.

TO FIRST-LINE INDENT PARAGRAPHS

STEP 1 ▶

Point to the First-Line Indent marker on the ruler (Figure 2-24).

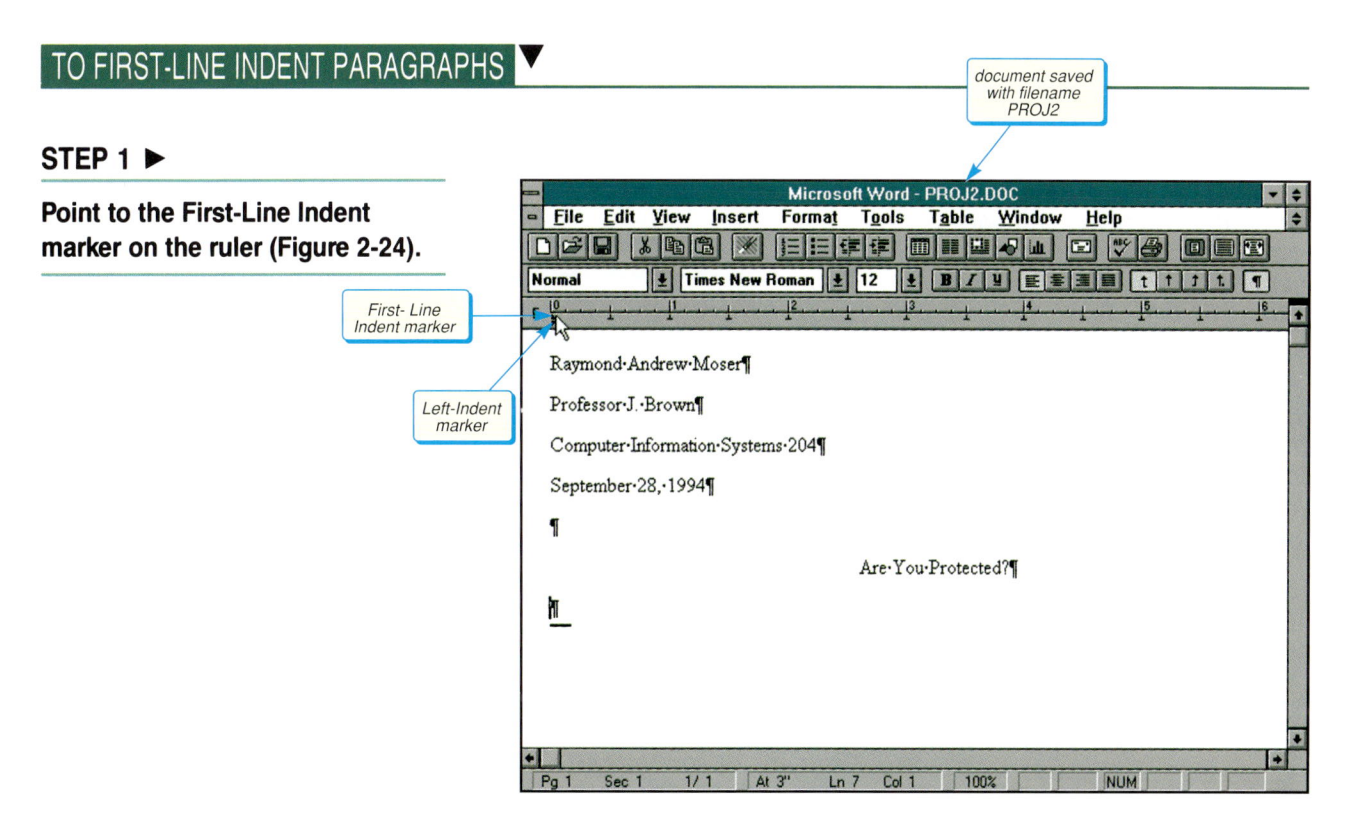

FIGURE 2-24

STEP 2 ▶

Drag the First-Line Indent marker to the 1/2" mark on the ruler.

The First-Line Indent marker appears at the location of the first tab stop, one-half inch from the left margin. The paragraph mark containing the insertion point in the document window also moves one-half inch to the right (Figure 2-25).

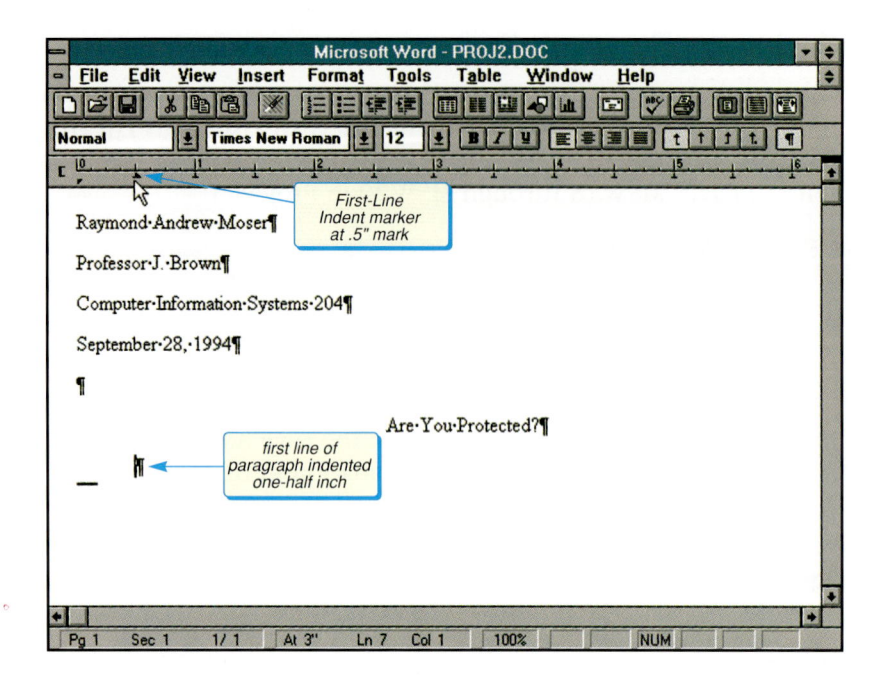

FIGURE 2-25

STEP 3 ▶

Type the first paragraph and first two lines of the second paragraph as shown in Figure 2-26.

Notice when you press the ENTER key at the end of the first paragraph of text, the insertion point automatically indents the first line of the second paragraph by one-half inch. Each time you press the ENTER key, the paragraph formatting in the prior paragraph is carried forward to the next paragraph.

FIGURE 2-26

You might be tempted to use the TAB key to indent the first line of each paragraph in your research paper. Using the TAB key for this task is inefficient because you must press it each time you begin a new paragraph. By setting the first-line indent with the ruler, the first-line indent format is automatically carried to each subsequent paragraph.

Adding Footnotes

Recall that explanatory notes are optional in the MLA style of documentation. They are used primarily to elaborate on points discussed in the body of the paper. The style specifies to use superscripts (raised numbers) to signal that an explanatory note exists either at the bottom of the page as a **footnote** or at the end of the document as an **endnote**.

Word, by default, places footnotes at the bottom of each page. In Word, **footnote text** can be of any length and format. Word automatically sequentially numbers footnotes for you by placing a **footnote reference mark** in the body of the document and in front of the footnote text. If, however, you rearrange, insert, or remove footnotes, the remaining footnote text and reference marks are renumbered according to their new sequence in the document. Follow these steps to add a footnote to the research paper (see Figure 2-33 on page MSW74).

TO ADD A FOOTNOTE ▼

STEP 1 ▶

Type the remainder of the second paragraph (see Figure 2-1 on page MSW55). Position the insertion point in the document where you want the footnote reference mark to appear (immediately after the period at the end of paragraph 2). Select the Insert menu and point to the Footnote command.

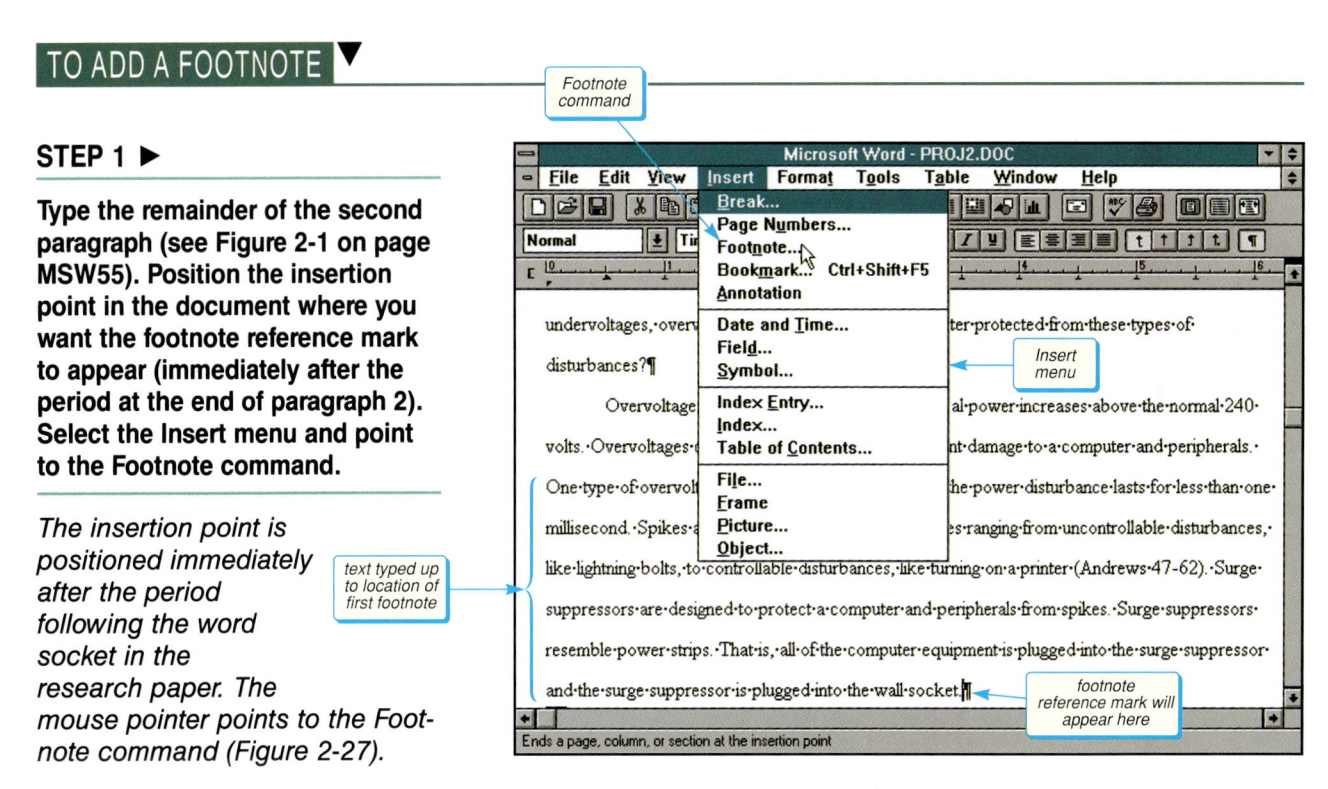

The insertion point is positioned immediately after the period following the word socket in the research paper. The mouse pointer points to the Footnote command (Figure 2-27).

FIGURE 2-27

MSW72   PROJECT 2   CREATING A RESEARCH PAPER

STEP 2 ▶

Choose the Footnote command. Point to the OK button in the Footnote dialog box.

Word displays the Footnote dialog box (Figure 2-28).

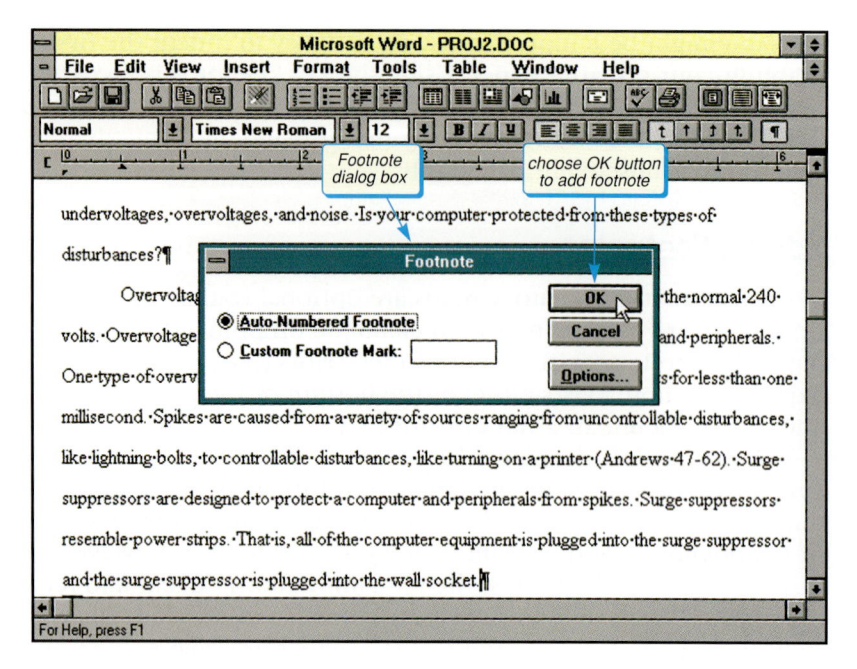

FIGURE 2-28

STEP 3 ▶

Choose the OK button in the Footnote dialog box.

Word opens a **footnote pane** *in the lower portion of the window with the footnote reference mark (a superscripted 1) positioned at the left margin (Figure 2-29). The footnote reference mark also appears in the document window at the location of the insertion point. Footnote reference marks are, by default, superscripted; that is, raised above other letters.*

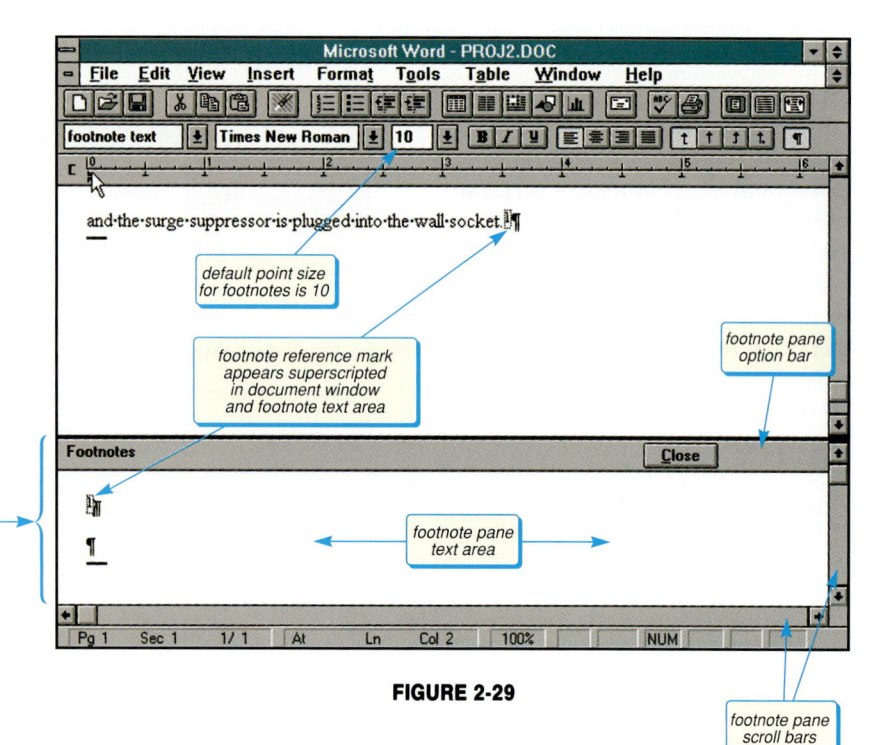

FIGURE 2-29

TYPING THE BODY OF THE RESEARCH PAPER **MSW73**

STEP 4 ▶

Indent the first line of the footnote one-half inch by dragging the First-Line Indent marker to the .5 inch mark on the ruler (Figure 2-30).

STEP 5 ▶

Change the point size to 12 by clicking the Points box arrow and selecting point size 12 (Figure 2-30).

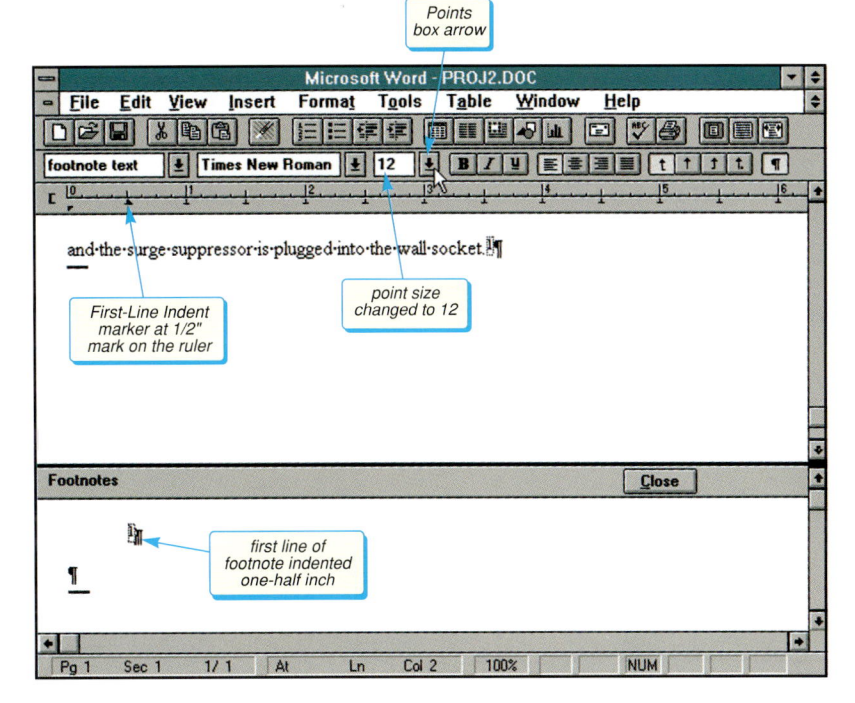

FIGURE 2-30

STEP 6 ▶

Press the SPACEBAR once and type the footnote text Andrews rates the top ten surge suppressors. Each is designed for a different type of computer system, from microcomputers to supercomputers. The microcomputer surge suppressors approximate $75. **followed by a space.**

The typed text displays in the footnote pane (Figure 2-31).

STEP 7 ▶

Click the Underline button on the ribbon.

The Underline button appears recessed on the ribbon (Figure 2-31). According to MLA style, the book title should be underlined.

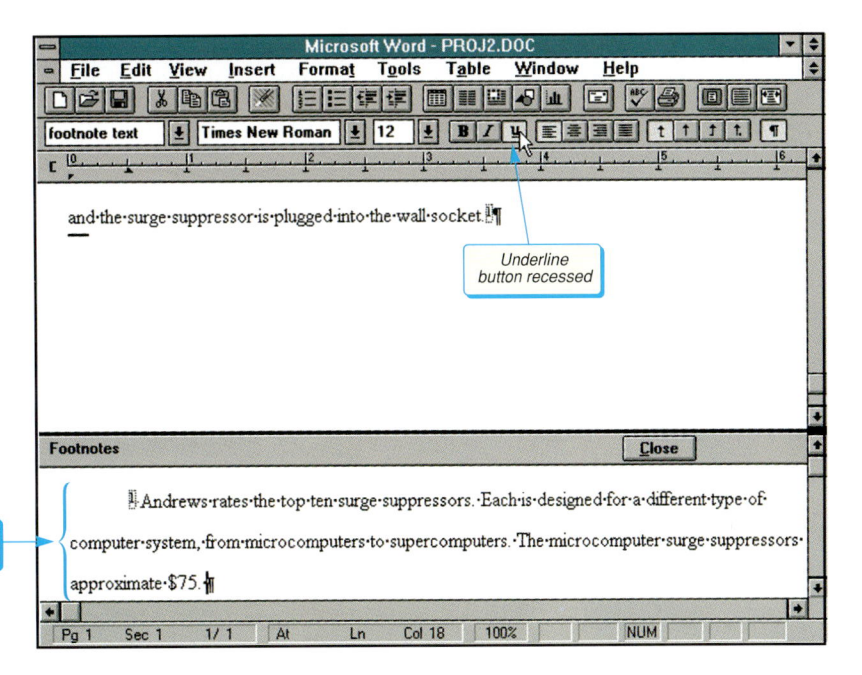

FIGURE 2-31

MSW74   PROJECT 2   CREATING A RESEARCH PAPER

STEP 8 ▶

Type `Information Systems Journal` **and click the Underline button again.**

The book name, Information Systems Journal, displays underlined in the footnote pane. The Underline button is no longer recessed (Figure 2-32).

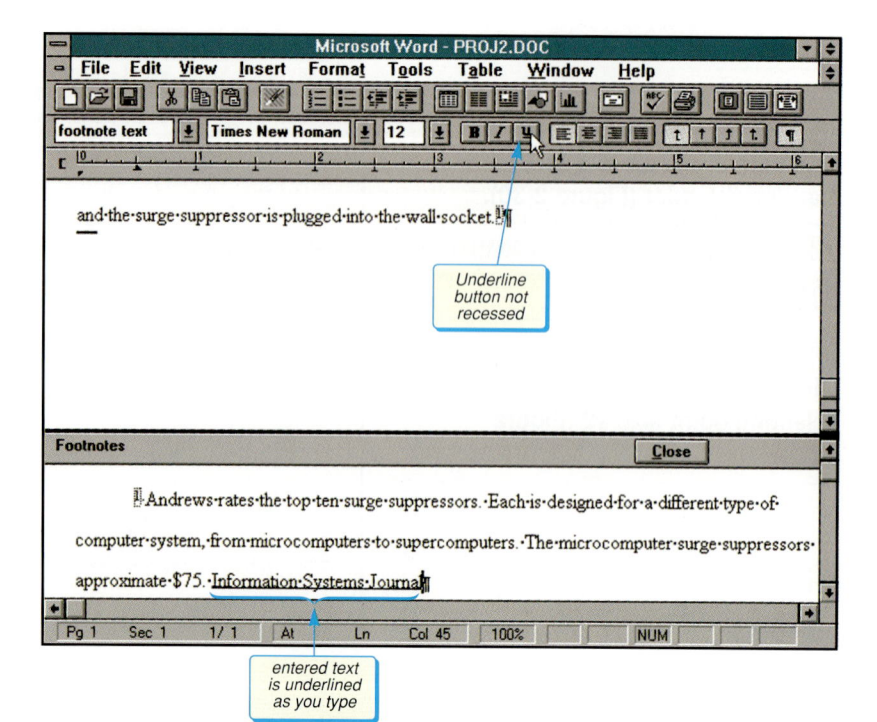

FIGURE 2-32

STEP 9 ▶

Type `,55-59.` **and point to the Close button on the footnote pane option bar.**

The complete footnote displays in the footnote pane (Figure 2-33).

STEP 10

Choose the Close button.

Word closes the footnote pane and returns to the document.

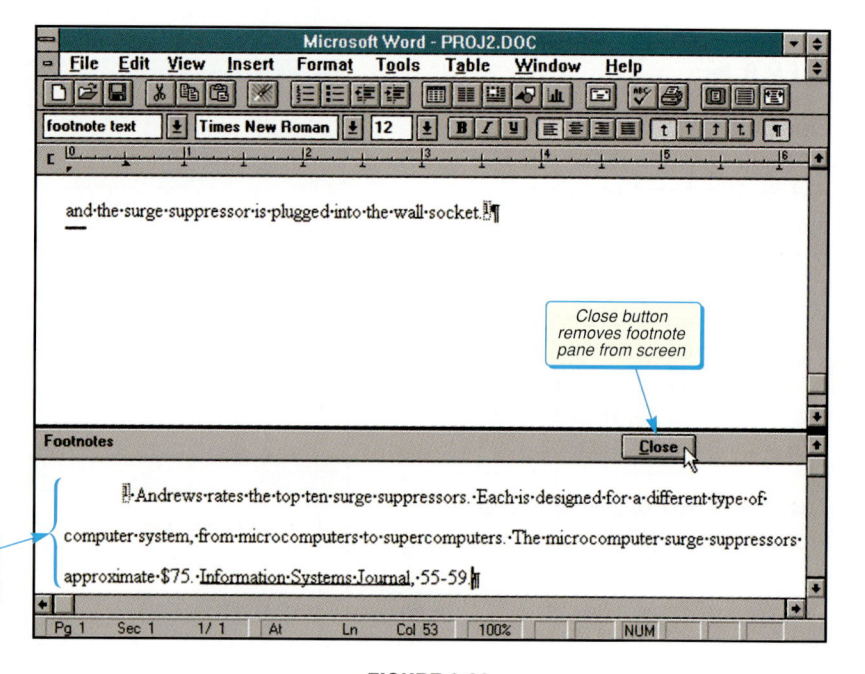

FIGURE 2-33

When Word closes the footnote pane and returns you to the document, the footnote text disappears from the screen. The footnote text still exists; however, it is not visible in normal view. Later in this project, you will change the document window from normal view to page layout view, where you will be able to see the footnote text on the screen.

TYPING THE BODY OF THE RESEARCH PAPER   **MSW75**

Automatic Page Breaks

As you type documents that exceed one page, Word automatically inserts page breaks when it determines the text has filled one page according to paper size, margin settings, line spacing, and other settings. These **automatic page breaks** are often referred to as **soft page breaks**. If you add text, delete text, or modify text on a page, Word recomputes the position of soft page breaks and adjusts them accordingly. Word performs page recomputation between the keystrokes; that is, in between the pauses in your typing. Thus, Word refers to the automatic page break task as **background repagination**. In normal view, soft page breaks appear on the Word screen as a single horizontal thinly dotted line. Word's automatic page break feature is illustrated below.

TO USE AUTOMATIC PAGE BREAK ▼

STEP 1 ▶

Type the next paragraph of the research paper as shown in Figure 2-34.

Word automatically inserts a soft page break following the line beginning This type of disturbance will not harm... *(Figure 2-34). The status bar now displays Pg 2 as the current page.*

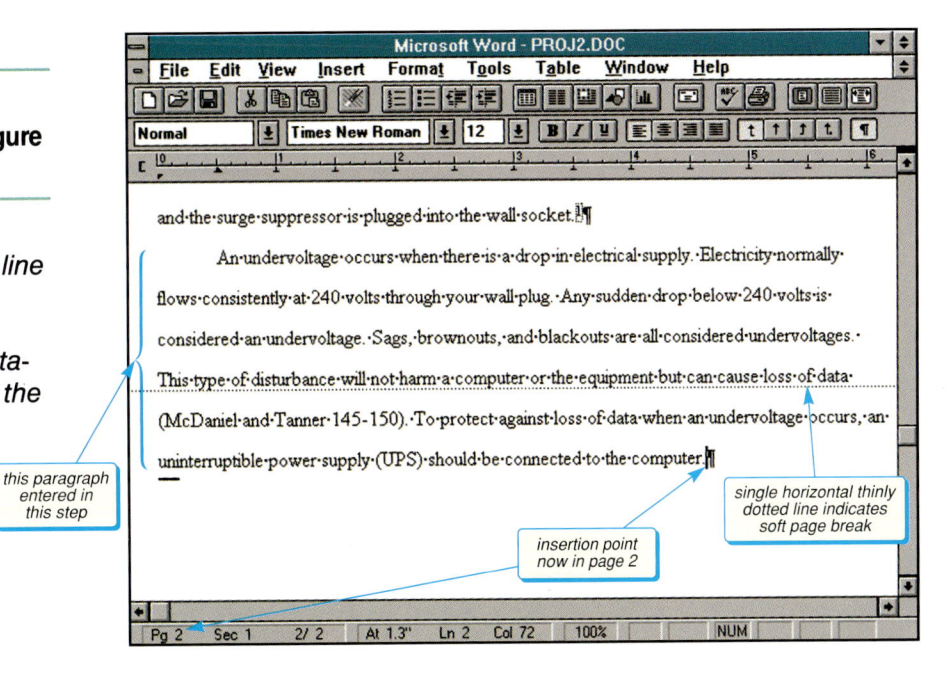

FIGURE 2-34

The next step in Project 2 is to add a second footnote at the end of the paragraph entered in Figure 2-34 and type the last two paragraphs of the research paper.

MSW76   PROJECT 2   CREATING A RESEARCH PAPER

TO ADD ANOTHER FOOTNOTE AND FINISH THE PAPER ▼

STEP 1

From the Insert menu, choose the Footnote command. Choose the OK button in the Footnote dialog box. Indent the first line of the footnote one-half inch by dragging the First-Line Indent marker to the .5 inch mark on the ruler. Change the point size to 12.

STEP 2 ▶

Type the footnote text as shown in Figure 2-35. Point to the Close button on the footnote pane option bar.

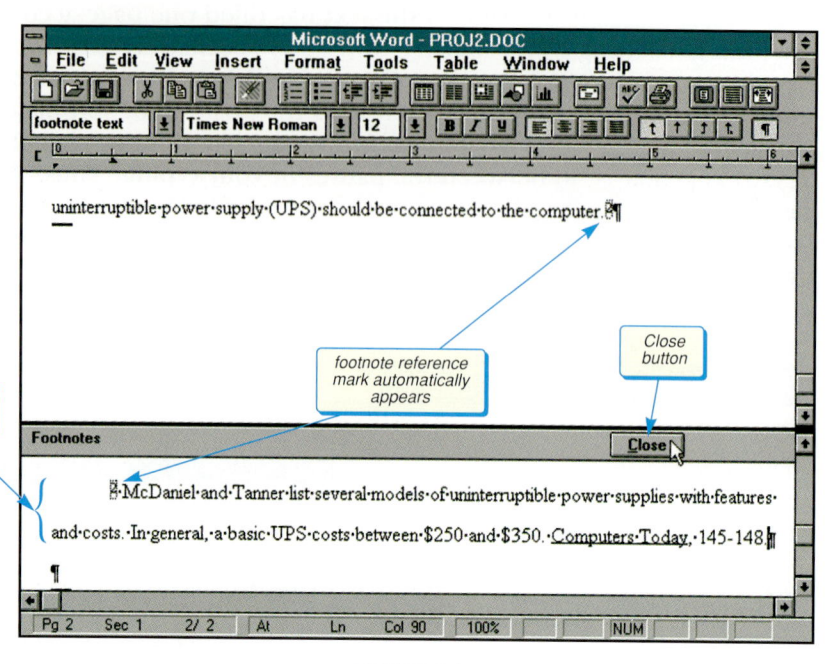

FIGURE 2-35

STEP 3

Choose the Close button.

Word closes the footnote pane and returns you to the document.

STEP 4 ▶

Enter the last two paragraphs of the research paper as shown in Figure 2-36.

The body of the research paper is complete.

FIGURE 2-36

Viewing Documents in Page Layout

As illustrated in Figures 2-35 and 2-36, the footnotes you entered do not appear at the bottom of the page in normal view. In normal view, Word does not display headers, footers, or footnotes. Often, you like to verify the content of the footnote or header text. In order to illustrate how to display headers, footers, and footnotes on the screen, switch to **page layout view** as shown on the next page.

TO SWITCH TO PAGE LAYOUT VIEW

STEP 1 ▶

Click the up arrow on the vertical scroll bar four times. Select the View menu and point to the Page Layout command.

The soft page break is in the document window and the mouse pointer points to the Page Layout command (Figure 2-37).

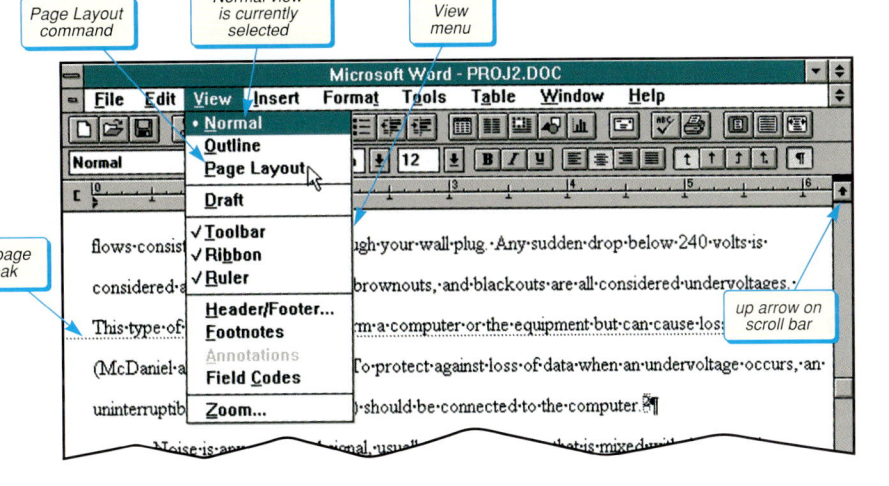

FIGURE 2-37

STEP 2 ▶

Choose the Page Layout command. Point beneath the scroll box on the vertical scroll bar.

*Word switches from normal to page layout view (Figure 2-38). The footnotes display in position on the screen in page layout view. The footnotes are separated from the text by a **footnote separator** which is a solid line two inches long beginning at the left margin.*

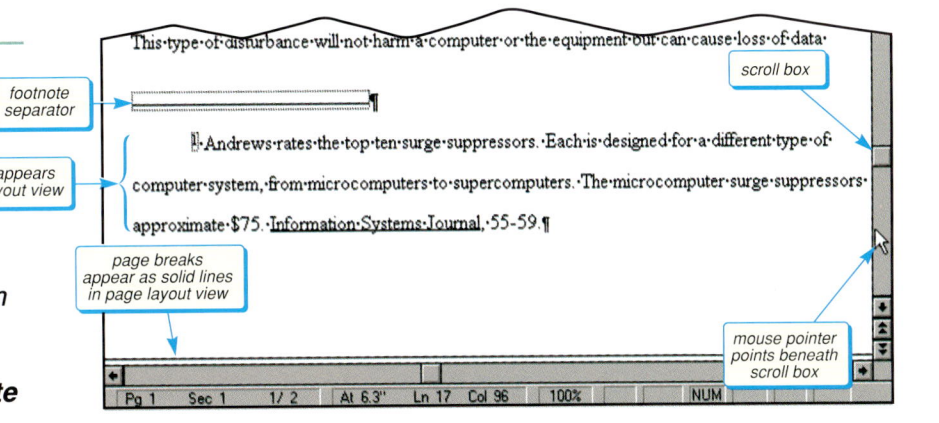

FIGURE 2-38

STEP 3 ▶

Click twice beneath the scroll box on the vertical scroll bar. Point to the right of the scroll box on the horizontal scroll bar.

The header on page 2 appears on the screen in page layout view (Figure 2-39a).

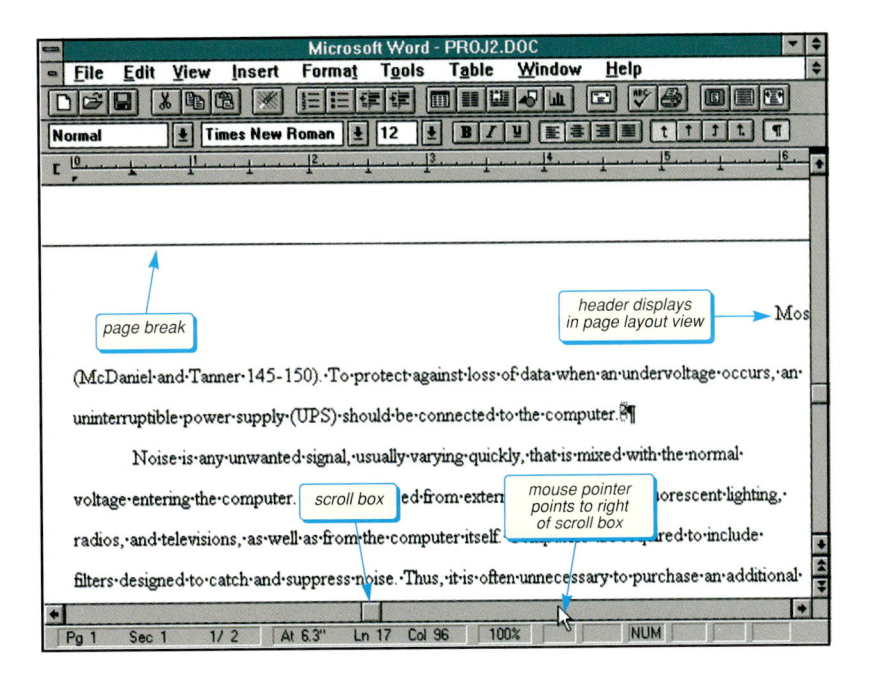

FIGURE 2-39a

STEP 4 ▶

Click to the right of the scroll box on horizontal scroll bar.

The document window scrolls one screen to the right (Figure 2-39b).

STEP 5

Click to the left of the scroll box on horizontal scroll bar.

The document window scrolls one screen to the left.

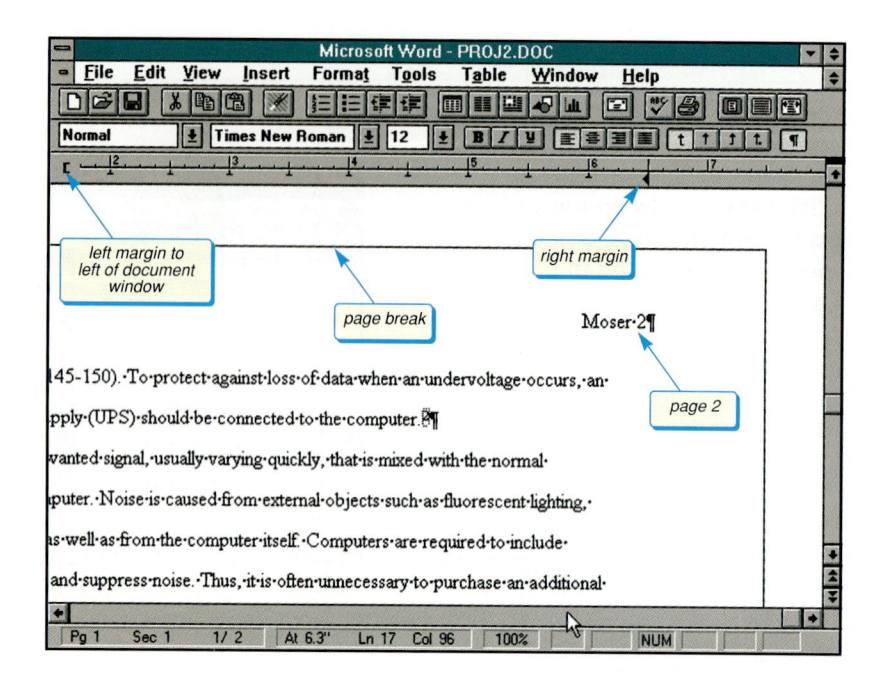

FIGURE 2-39b

In page layout view, you can type and edit text in the same manner as in normal view. The only difference is that the headers, footers, and footnotes display properly positioned in the document in page layout view.

▶ CREATING AN ALPHABETICAL WORKS CITED PAGE

According to the MLA style, the works cited page is a bibliographical list of works you directly reference in your paper. The list is placed on a separate page with the title, Works Cited, centered one inch from the top margin. The works cited are to be alphabetized by author's last name. The first line of each work cited begins at the left margin; with subsequent lines of the same work indented one-half inch from the left margin.

Because page layout view clutters the screen and is unnecessary for the works cited page, the next step is to return to normal view.

Switching Back to Normal View

When you switch back to normal view, the header and footnotes disappear from the screen. They are still part of the document and will print. The steps to switch back to normal view are summarized below.

TO SWITCH TO NORMAL VIEW

Step 1: Select the View menu.
Step 2: Choose the Normal command.

The next step is to force a page break so the works cited display on a separate page.

CREATING AN ALPHABETICAL WORKS CITED PAGE   MSW79

Hard Page Breaks

Because the works cited are to display on a separate numbered page, you need to insert a hard page break following the body of the research paper. A **hard page break** is one that you force into the document at a specific location. Hard page breaks appear on the screen as thickly dotted horizontal lines. Word never moves or adjusts hard page breaks. When you insert hard page breaks, however, Word does adjust any soft page breaks that follow in the document. Word inserts hard page breaks just before the insertion point. Follow these steps to insert a hard page break following the body of the research paper.

TO INSERT A HARD PAGE BREAK ▼

STEP 1 ▶

Click the up arrow on the vertical scroll bar seven times. Press the ENTER key once. Select the Insert menu and point to the Break command.

The last paragraph of the research paper appears at the top of document window. The insertion point is positioned one line below the body of the research paper. The mouse pointer points to the Break command (Figure 2-40).

FIGURE 2-40

STEP 2 ▶

Choose the Break command.

Word displays the Break dialog box (Figure 2-41). The default option button is Page Break in the Break dialog box.

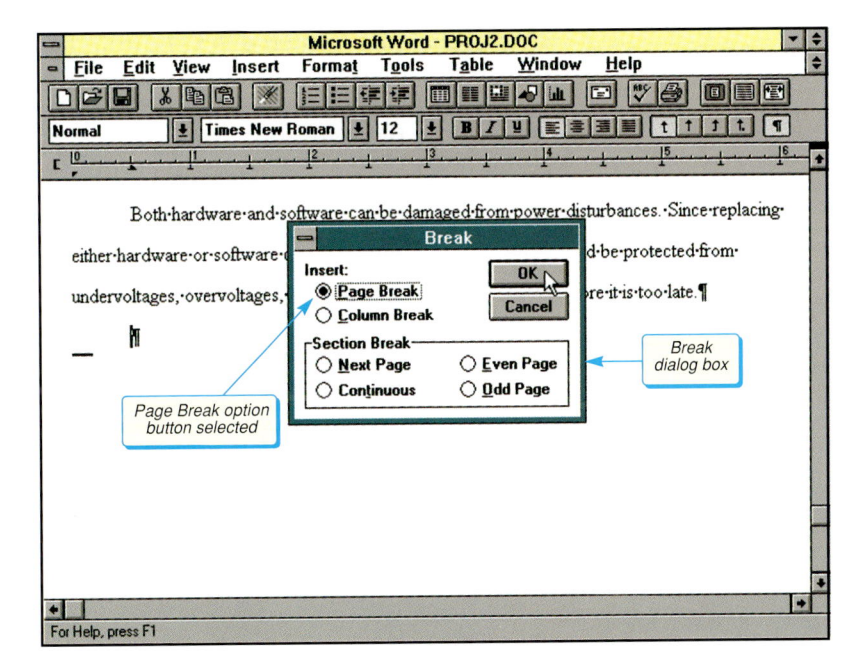

FIGURE 2-41

STEP 3 ▶

Choose the OK button in the Break dialog box.

Word inserts a hard page break immediately before the insertion point and positions the insertion point immediately below the hard page break (Figure 2-42). The hard page break appears as a thickly dotted horizontal line on the screen. The status bar indicates the insertion point is located on page 3.

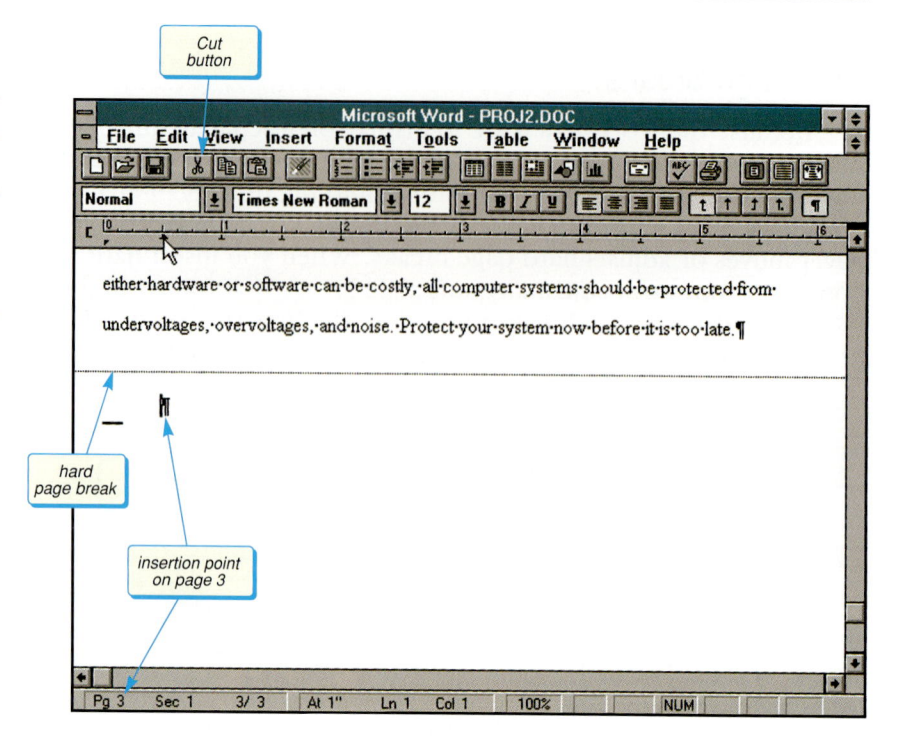

FIGURE 2-42

To remove a hard page break from your document, you must select it first by pointing to it and clicking. Then, click the **Cut button** ( ) on the Toolbar or press the DELETE key.

Centering the Title of the Works Cited Page

As with the previous titles, the works cited title is to be centered. If you simply click the Centered Text button, however, the title will not be properly centered; rather, it will be one-half inch to the right of the center point. Recall earlier you set first-line indent by dragging the First-Line Indent marker on the ruler to the first tab stop. Thus, the left margin for the first line of every paragraph is set at one-half inch. You must move the First-Line Indent marker to the left margin prior to clicking the Centered Text button. The steps to center this title are summarized as follows.

TO CENTER THE TITLE OF THE WORKS CITED PAGE

Step 1: Drag the First-Line Indent marker to the 0" mark on the ruler.
Step 2: Click the Centered Text button on the ribbon.
Step 3: Type Works Cited and press the ENTER key.
Step 4: Click the Left-Aligned Text button on the ribbon.

The title displays properly centered as shown in Figure 2-43.

CREATING AN ALPHABETICAL WORKS CITED PAGE   **MSW81**

FIGURE 2-43

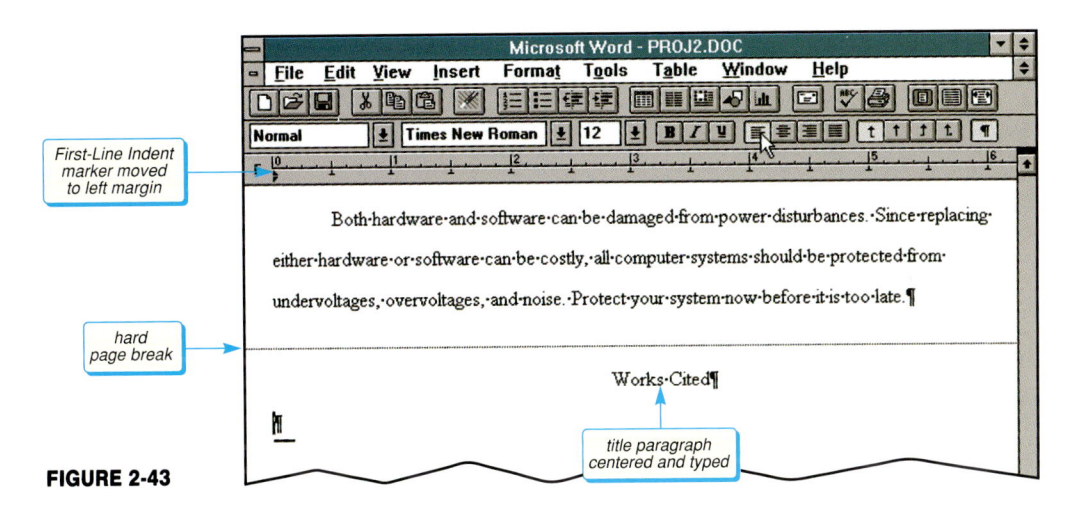

Creating a Hanging Indent

On the works cited page, the paragraphs begin at the left margin. Subsequent lines in the same paragraph are indented one-half inch from the left margin. In essence, the first line *hangs* to the left of the rest of the paragraph; thus, this type of paragraph formatting is called a **hanging indent**. Follow these steps to create a hanging indent.

TO CREATE A HANGING INDENT ▼

STEP 1 ▶

Press and hold down the SHIFT key while dragging the Left-Indent marker to the one-half inch mark on the ruler.

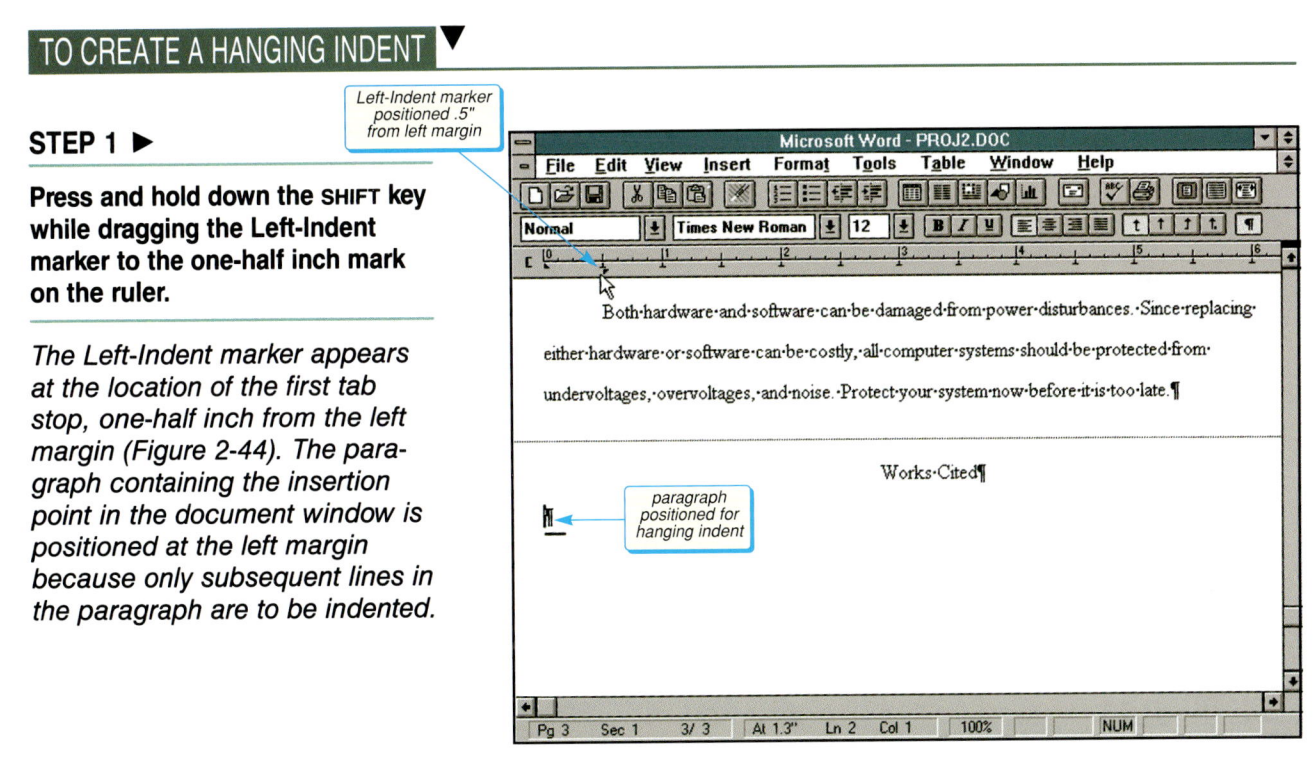

The Left-Indent marker appears at the location of the first tab stop, one-half inch from the left margin (Figure 2-44). The paragraph containing the insertion point in the document window is positioned at the left margin because only subsequent lines in the paragraph are to be indented.

FIGURE 2-44

MSW82   PROJECT 2   CREATING A RESEARCH PAPER

STEP 2 ▶

Type the Works Cited paragraphs as shown in Figure 2-45.

Notice when Word wraps the text in each works cited paragraph, it automatically indents the second line of the paragraph by one-half inch. When you press the ENTER key at the end of the first paragraph of text, the insertion point automatically returns to the left margin for the next paragraph (Figure 2-45). Recall that each time you press the ENTER key, the paragraph formatting in the prior paragraph is carried forward to the next paragraph.

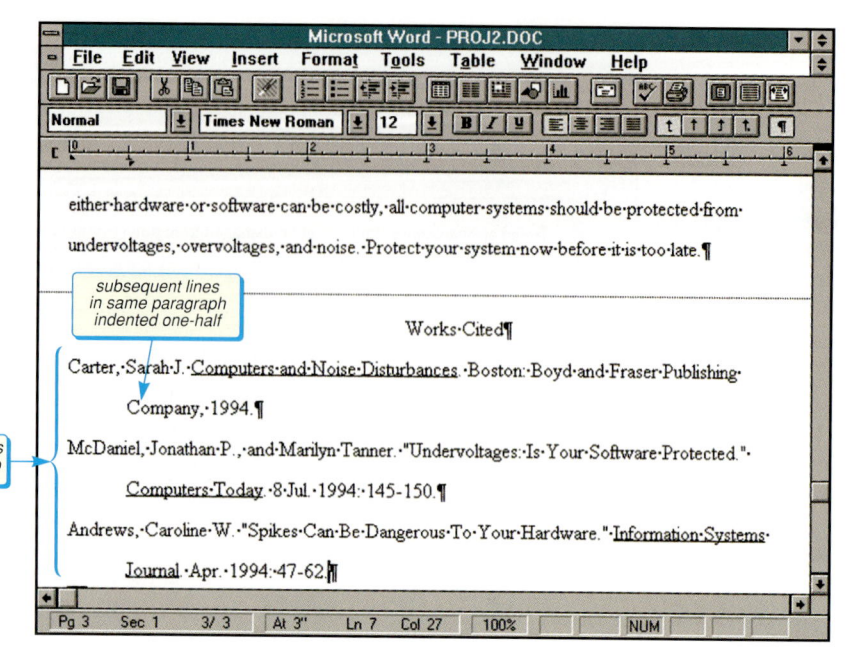

callouts: subsequent lines in same paragraph indented one-half; these paragraphs typed in this step

FIGURE 2-45

Sorting Paragraphs

The MLA style requires that the works cited be listed in alphabetical order by author's last name. With Word, you can arrange paragraphs in alphabetic, numeric, or date order based on the first character in each paragraph. Ordering characters in this manner is called **sorting**. Arrange the works cited paragraphs in alphabetic order as illustrated in the following steps (see Figure 2-50 on page MSW84).

TO SORT PARAGRAPHS ▼

STEP 1 ▶

Position the mouse pointer in the selection bar to the left of the first paragraph to be sorted. Press and hold down the left mouse button.

The mouse pointer changes to a right-pointing block arrow when in the selection bar. The first line of text is selected (Figure 2-46).

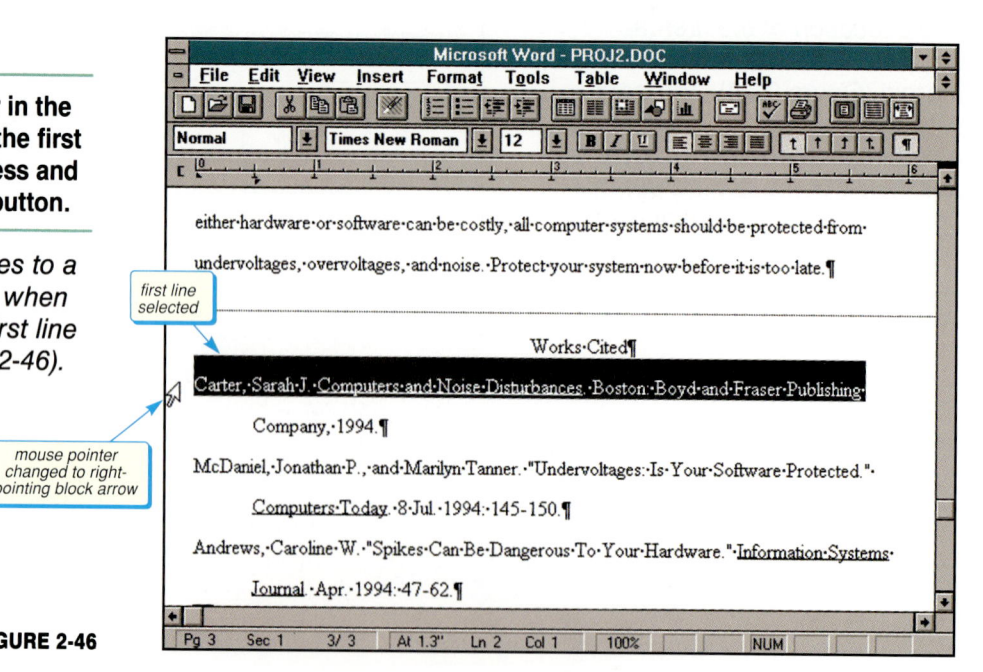

callouts: first line selected; mouse pointer changed to right-pointing block arrow

FIGURE 2-46

CREATING AN ALPHABETICAL WORKS CITED PAGE **MSW83**

STEP 2 ▶

Drag the mouse pointer to the last line of the last paragraph to be sorted. Release the mouse button.

All of the paragraphs to be sorted are selected (Figure 2-47).

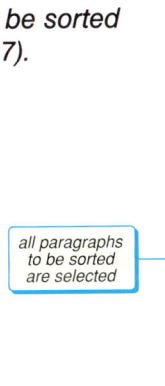

FIGURE 2-47

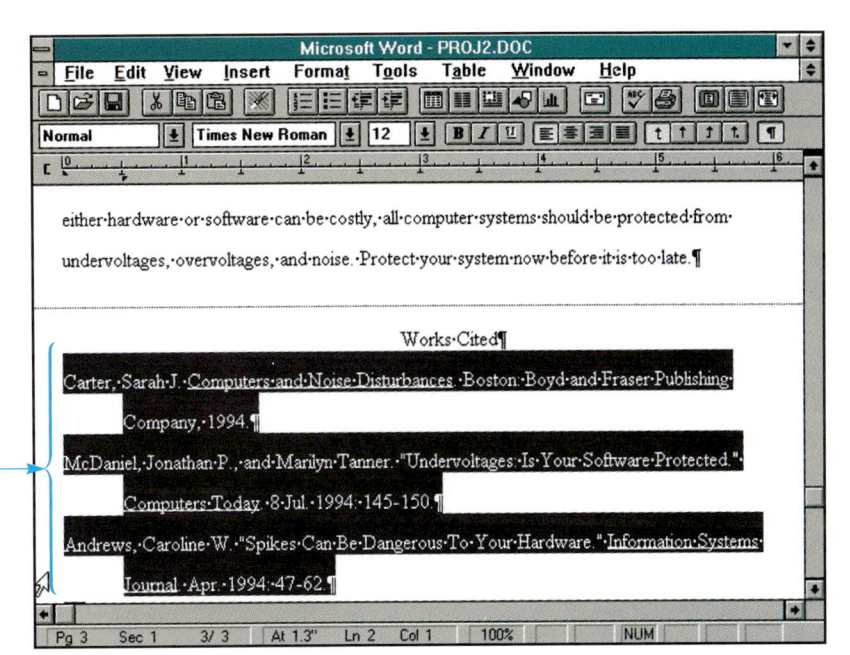

STEP 3 ▶

Select the Tools menu and point to the Sorting command (Figure 2-48).

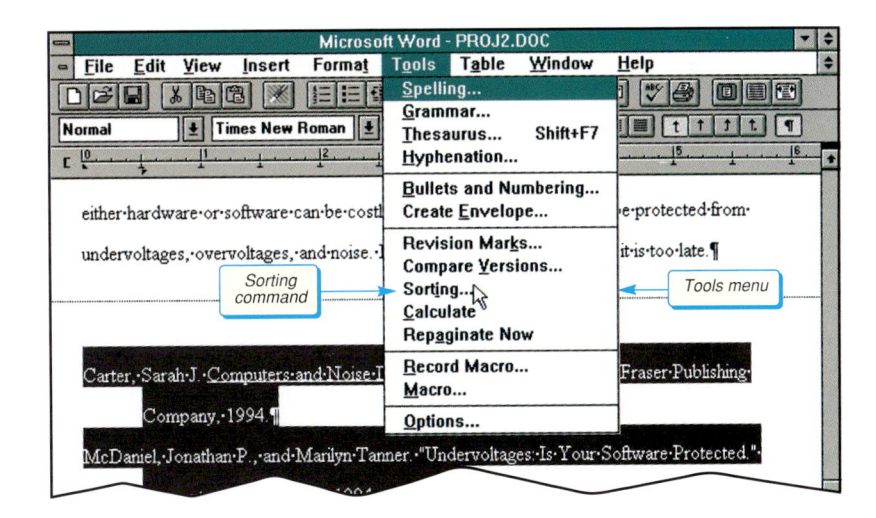

FIGURE 2-48

STEP 4 ▶

Choose the Sorting command.

Word displays a Sorting dialog box (Figure 2-49). In the Sorting Order area, Ascending is selected. Ascending sorts in alphabetic or numeric order.

FIGURE 2-49

MSW84 PROJECT 2 CREATING A RESEARCH PAPER

STEP 5 ▶

Choose the OK button in the Sorting dialog box. Click outside of the selection to remove the highlight.

Word alphabetically sorts the works cited paragraphs (Figure 2-50).

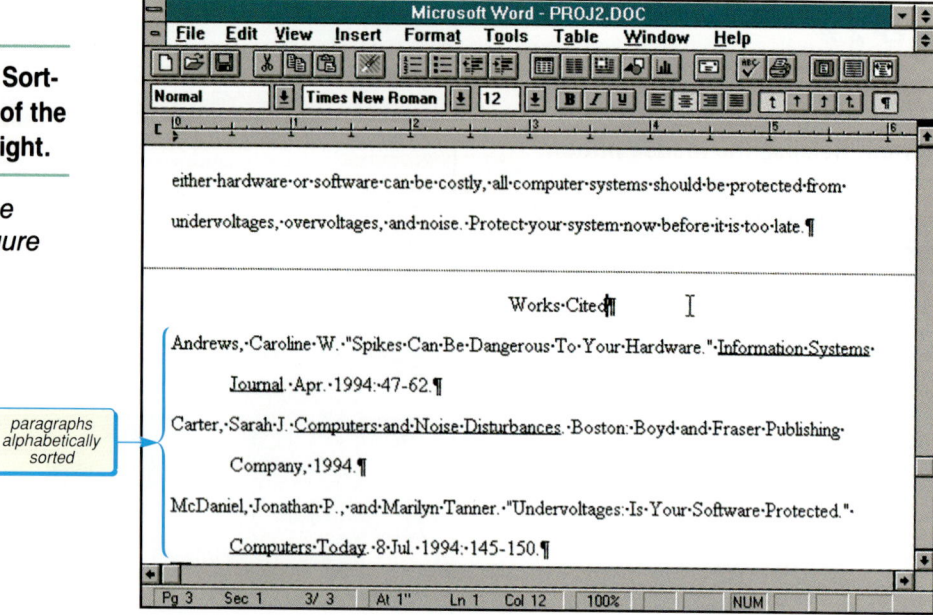

FIGURE 2-50

If you accidentally sort the wrong paragraphs, you can undo a sort by clicking the Undo button on the Toolbar.

In the Sorting dialog box (Figure 2-49 on the previous page), the default key type is Alphanumeric, which means the first character in each paragraph may be a letter, number, or date. If it is a letter, word sorts alphabetically on the first letter of the paragraph. Word by default, orders in **ascending sort order**, which means from the beginning of the alphabet, lowest number, or earliest date. If the first character of the paragraphs contain a mixture of letters, numbers, and dates, then the numbers appear first and letters appear last. Uppercase letters appear before lowercase letters. In case of ties, Word looks to the first character with a non-identical letter and sorts on that character for the paragraphs where the tie occurs.

You can also sort in descending order by choosing the Descending option button in the Sorting dialog box. **Descending sort order** begins sorting from the end of the alphabet, the highest number, or the most recent date.

The research paper is now complete and ready for proofing.

Checking Spelling, Saving Again, and Printing the Document

The document is now complete (see Figure 2-1 on MSW55). After completing the document, you should check the spelling of the document by clicking the Spelling button on the Toolbar. Because you have performed several tasks since the last save, you should save the research paper again by clicking the Save button on the Toolbar. Finally, you should print the research paper by clicking the Print button on the Toolbar. When you remove the document from the printer, proofread it carefully and mark anything that needs to be changed(Figure 2-51).

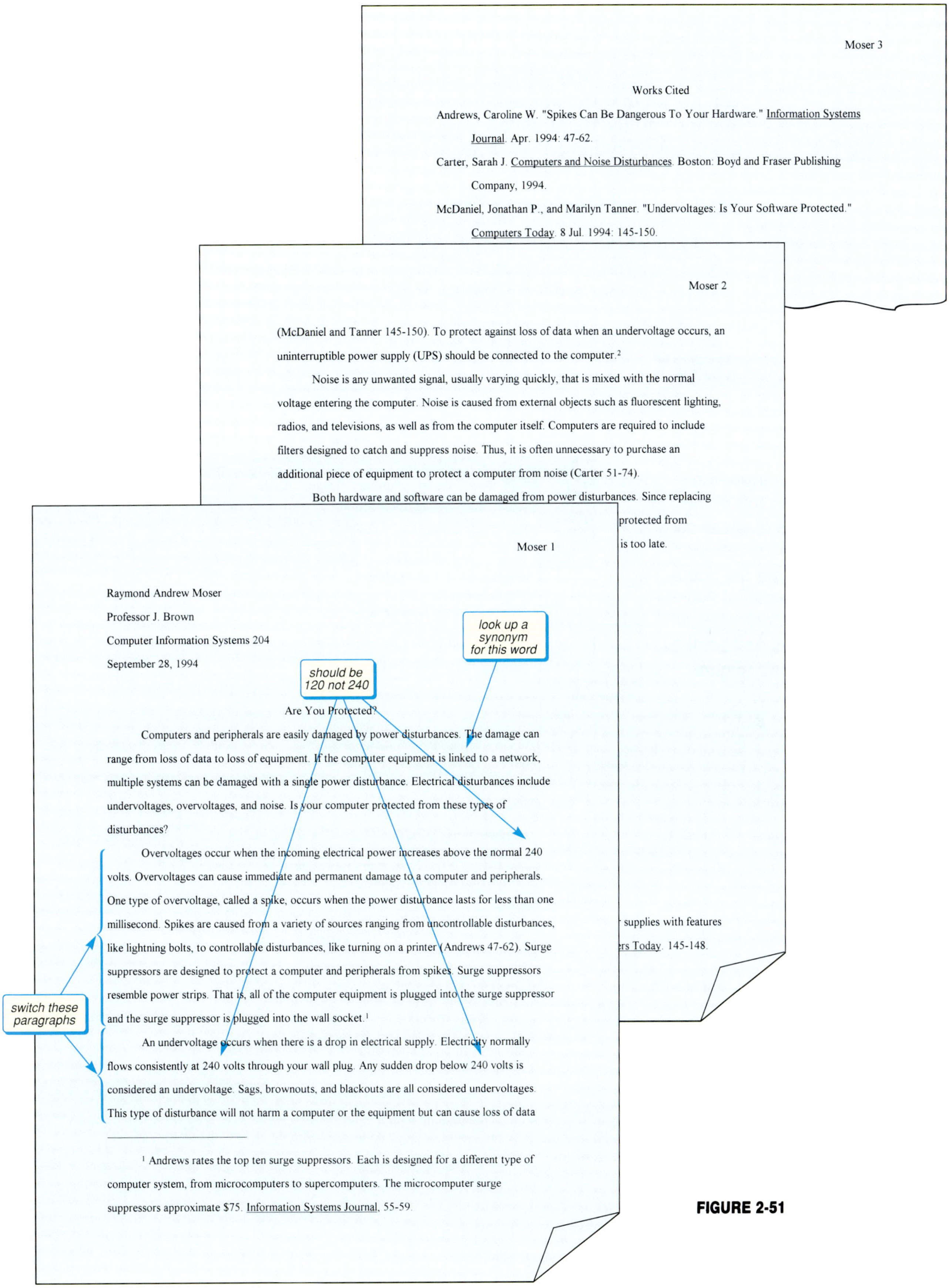

CREATING AN ALPHABETICAL WORKS CITED PAGE   MSW85

Moser 3

Works Cited

Andrews, Caroline W. "Spikes Can Be Dangerous To Your Hardware." Information Systems
    Journal. Apr. 1994: 47-62.

Carter, Sarah J. Computers and Noise Disturbances. Boston: Boyd and Fraser Publishing
    Company, 1994.

McDaniel, Jonathan P., and Marilyn Tanner. "Undervoltages: Is Your Software Protected."
    Computers Today. 8 Jul. 1994: 145-150.

Moser 2

(McDaniel and Tanner 145-150). To protect against loss of data when an undervoltage occurs, an uninterruptible power supply (UPS) should be connected to the computer.[2]

Noise is any unwanted signal, usually varying quickly, that is mixed with the normal voltage entering the computer. Noise is caused from external objects such as fluorescent lighting, radios, and televisions, as well as from the computer itself. Computers are required to include filters designed to catch and suppress noise. Thus, it is often unnecessary to purchase an additional piece of equipment to protect a computer from noise (Carter 51-74).

Both hardware and software can be damaged from power disturbances. Since replacing
protected from
is too late.

Moser 1

Raymond Andrew Moser
Professor J. Brown
Computer Information Systems 204
September 28, 1994

[look up a synonym for this word]

[should be 120 not 240]

Are You Protected?

Computers and peripherals are easily damaged by power disturbances. The damage can range from loss of data to loss of equipment. If the computer equipment is linked to a network, multiple systems can be damaged with a single power disturbance. Electrical disturbances include undervoltages, overvoltages, and noise. Is your computer protected from these types of disturbances?

Overvoltages occur when the incoming electrical power increases above the normal 240 volts. Overvoltages can cause immediate and permanent damage to a computer and peripherals. One type of overvoltage, called a spike, occurs when the power disturbance lasts for less than one millisecond. Spikes are caused from a variety of sources ranging from uncontrollable disturbances, like lightning bolts, to controllable disturbances, like turning on a printer (Andrews 47-62). Surge suppressors are designed to protect a computer and peripherals from spikes. Surge suppressors resemble power strips. That is, all of the computer equipment is plugged into the surge suppressor and the surge suppressor is plugged into the wall socket.[1]

[switch these paragraphs]

An undervoltage occurs when there is a drop in electrical supply. Electricity normally flows consistently at 240 volts through your wall plug. Any sudden drop below 240 volts is considered an undervoltage. Sags, brownouts, and blackouts are all considered undervoltages. This type of disturbance will not harm a computer or the equipment but can cause loss of data

---

[1] Andrews rates the top ten surge suppressors. Each is designed for a different type of computer system, from microcomputers to supercomputers. The microcomputer surge suppressors approximate $75. Information Systems Journal, 55-59.

supplies with features
rs Today. 145-148.

FIGURE 2-51

MSW86 PROJECT 2 CREATING A RESEARCH PAPER

▶ REVISING THE RESEARCH PAPER

As discussed in Project 1, once you complete a document, you might find it necessary to make changes to it. For example, when reviewing the printout of the research paper (Figure 2-51 on the previous page), you notice that the normal flow of electricity should be 120 volts, not 240 volts. You also notice that the paper would read better if the second and third paragraphs were switched. With Word, you can easily accomplish these editing tasks.

Finding and Replacing Text

Throughout the research paper, the number, 240, appears for the voltage in several locations. You want to change each occurrence of 240 to 120. To accomplish this, perform the following steps.

TO FIND AND REPLACE TEXT ▼

STEP 1 ▶

Press CTRL + HOME to move the insertion point to the top of the document. Click the down arrow on the vertical scroll bar eleven times to scroll through the document so all occurrences of 240 appear in the document window. Select the Edit menu and point to the Replace command (Figure 2-52).

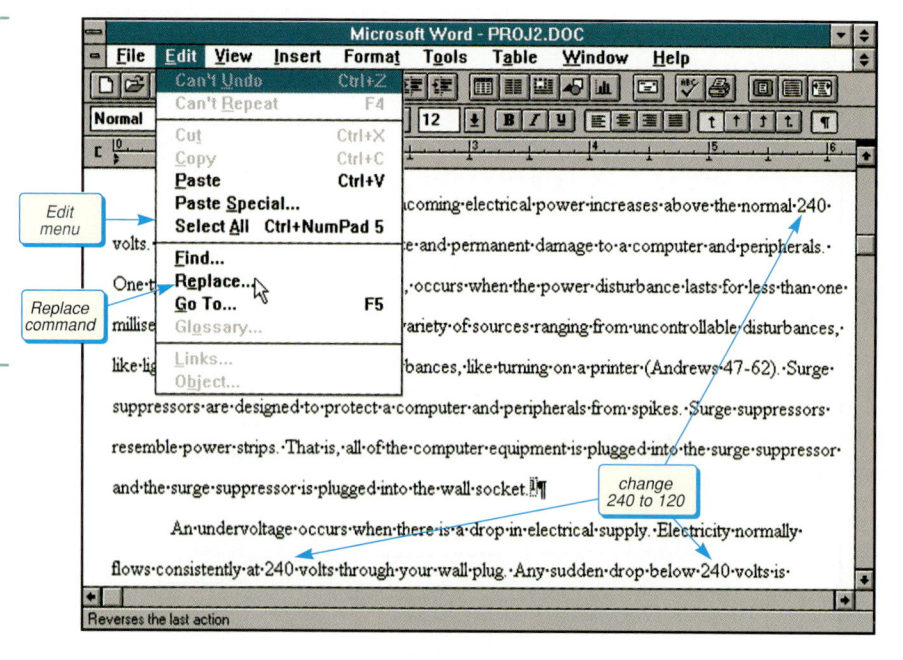

FIGURE 2-52

REVISING THE RESEARCH PAPER **MSW87**

STEP 2 ▶

Choose the Replace command.

Word displays the Replace dialog box (Figure 2-53a).

STEP 3 ▶

Type the text 240 **in the Find What text box. Press the TAB key to advance to the Replace With text box. Type the text** 120 **and point to the Replace All button (Replace All).**

The Find What text box displays 240 and the Replace With text box displays 120 (Figure 2-53a).

STEP 4

Choose the Replace All button in the Replace dialog box.

Word replaces all occurrences of the text 240 with the text 120.

STEP 5

Choose the Close button in the Replace dialog box.

Word removes the Replace dialog box from the screen.

STEP 6 ▶

Click the down arrow on the vertical scroll bar eleven times.

All occurrences of 240 have been changed to 120 (Figure 2-53b).

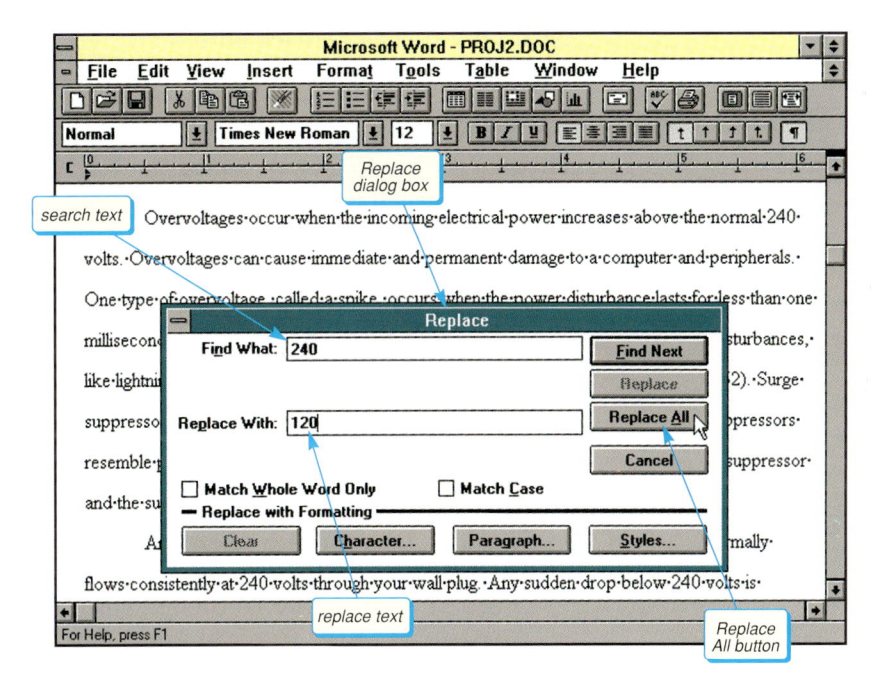

FIGURE 2-53a

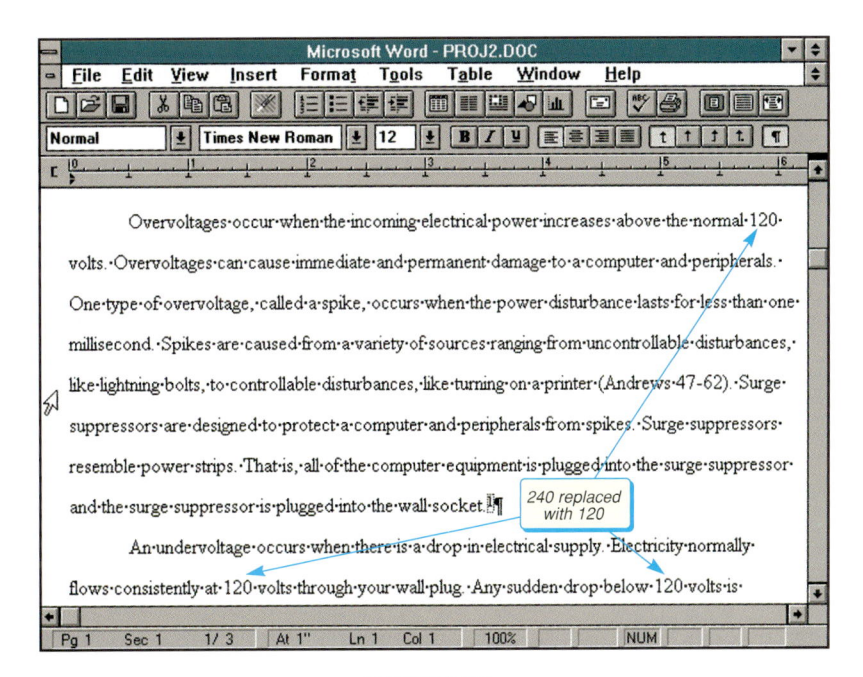

FIGURE 2-53b

In some cases, you may want to only replace certain occurrences of the text, not all of them. To instruct Word to confirm each change, choose the Find Next button (Find Next) in the Replace dialog box, rather than the Replace All button. When Word finds an occurrence of the text in the Find What text box, it pauses and waits for you to choose either the Replace button (Replace) or the Find Next button. The Replace button changes the text; the Find Next button instructs Word to disregard the replacement and look for the next occurrence of the search text.

If you accidentally replace the wrong text, you can undo a replacement by clicking the Undo button on the Toolbar. If you used the Replace All button, Word undoes all replacements. If you used the Replace button, Word only undoes the most recent replacement.

Finding Text

Sometimes you may want to only find text, rather than find and replace text. To just search for an occurrence of text, follow the steps summarized below.

TO FIND TEXT

Step 1: Position the insertion point where you want to begin the search.
Step 2: Select the Edit menu.
Step 3: Choose the Find command. Word displays the Find dialog box.
Step 4: Type the text you want to locate in the Find What text box.
Step 5: Choose the Find Next button.
Step 6: To edit the text and close the Find dialog box, choose the Close button; to continue searching for the next occurrence of the text, choose the Find Next button.

Finding a Specific Page or Footnote

Often you will want to advance directly to a certain page in a document or quickly locate a particular footnote in a document. To go directly to either a page or footnote, follow these steps.

TO LOCATE A PAGE OR FOOTNOTE

Step 1: Select the Edit menu.
Step 2: Choose the Go To command.
Step 3: In the Go To text box, type the desired page number or type f followed by the desired footnote number.
Step 4: Choose the OK button.

Moving Paragraphs

To move paragraphs, you can either **drag and drop** one of the paragraphs or **cut and paste** one of the paragraphs. Both techniques require you to first select the paragraph to be moved. With dragging and dropping, you then drag the selected paragraph to its new location and insert, or drop, it there. Cutting involves removing selected text from the document and placing it on the **clipboard**, a temporary storage area. Pasting is the process of copying an item from the Clipboard into the document at the location of the insertion point.

You should use the drag and drop technique to move paragraphs a short distance. When you are moving between several pages, however, the cut and paste technique is more efficient. Thus, use the drag and drop technique to switch the second and third paragraphs as shown in the following steps (see Figure 2-57 on page MSW90).

REVISING THE RESEARCH PAPER   **MSW89**

TO DRAG AND DROP PARAGRAPHS

STEP 1 ▶

Position the mouse pointer in the selection bar to the left of the paragraph to be moved.

The mouse pointer changes to a right-pointing block arrow when in the selection bar (Figure 2-54).

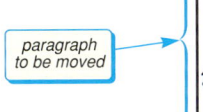

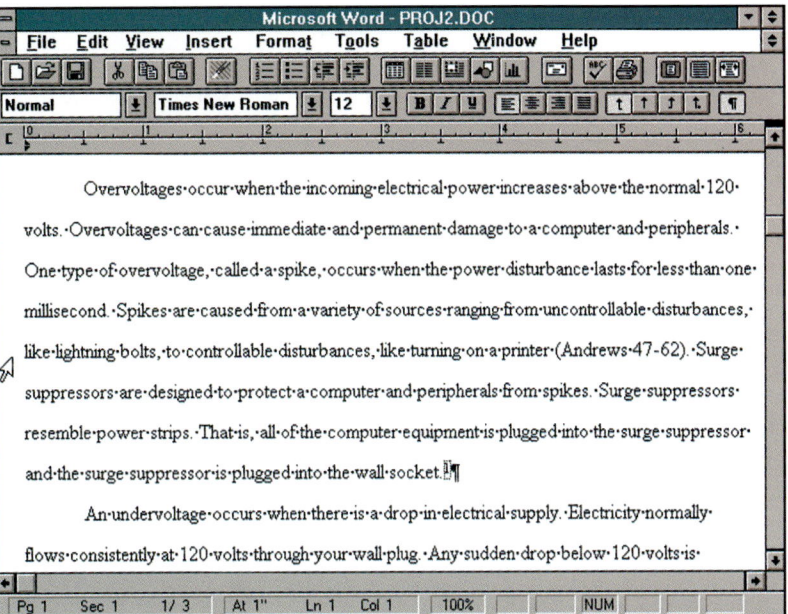

FIGURE 2-54

STEP 2 ▶

Double-click the mouse. Move the mouse pointer into the selection.

Word selects the entire paragraph and the mouse pointer changes to a left-pointing block arrow in the selected paragraph (Figure 2-55).

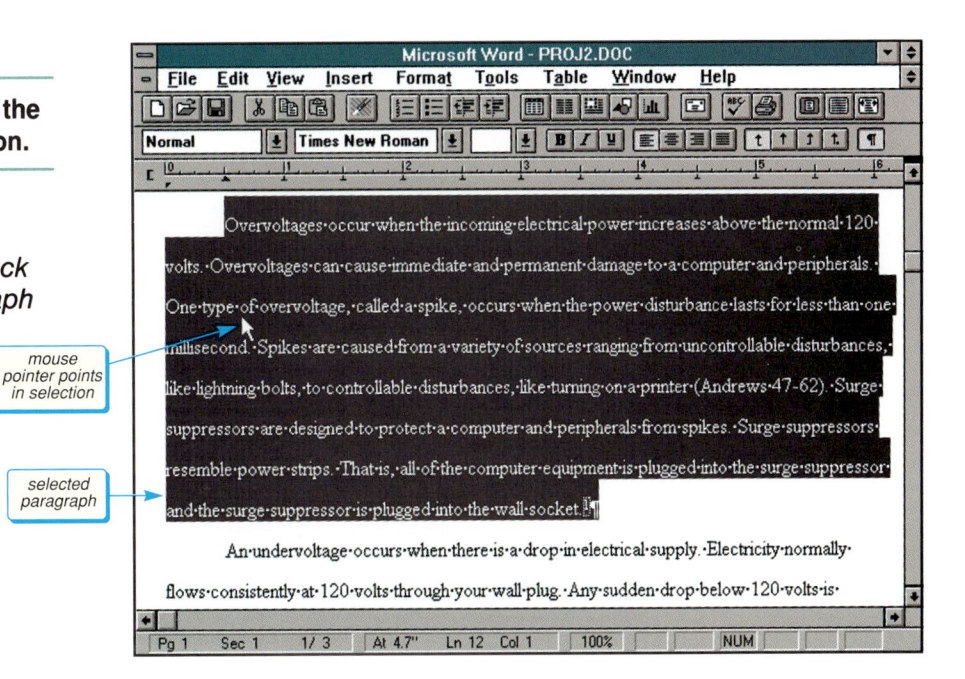

FIGURE 2-55

MSW90 PROJECT 2 CREATING A RESEARCH PAPER

STEP 3 ▶

Press and hold the left mouse button.

The insertion point changes to a dotted insertion point and the mouse pointer has a small dotted box beneath it (Figure 2-56).

STEP 4 ▶

Drag the dotted insertion point to the location where the paragraph is to be moved.

The dotted insertion point is positioned beneath the original third paragraph (Figure 2-56).

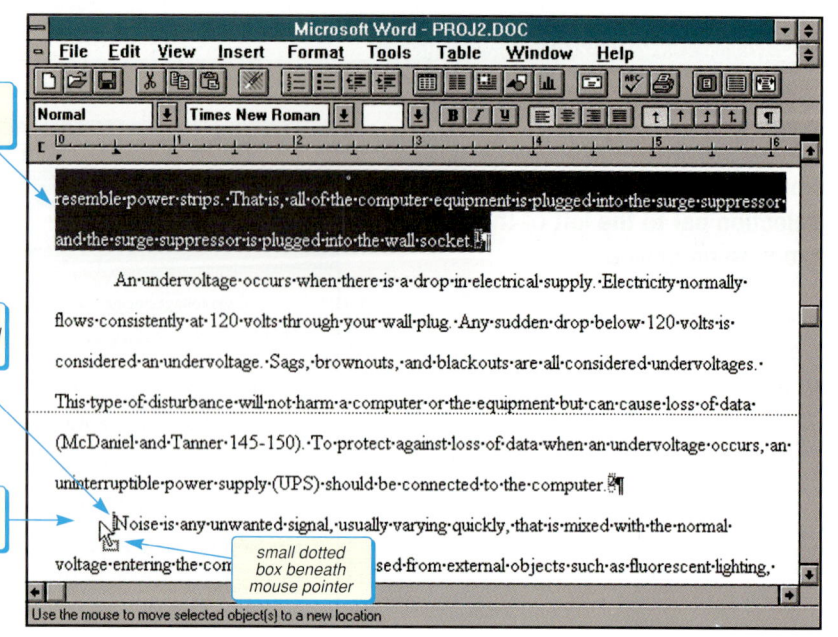

FIGURE 2-56

STEP 5 ▶

Release the mouse button.

The selected paragraph is moved to the location of the dotted insertion point in the document (Figure 2-57). The second and third paragraphs are switched.

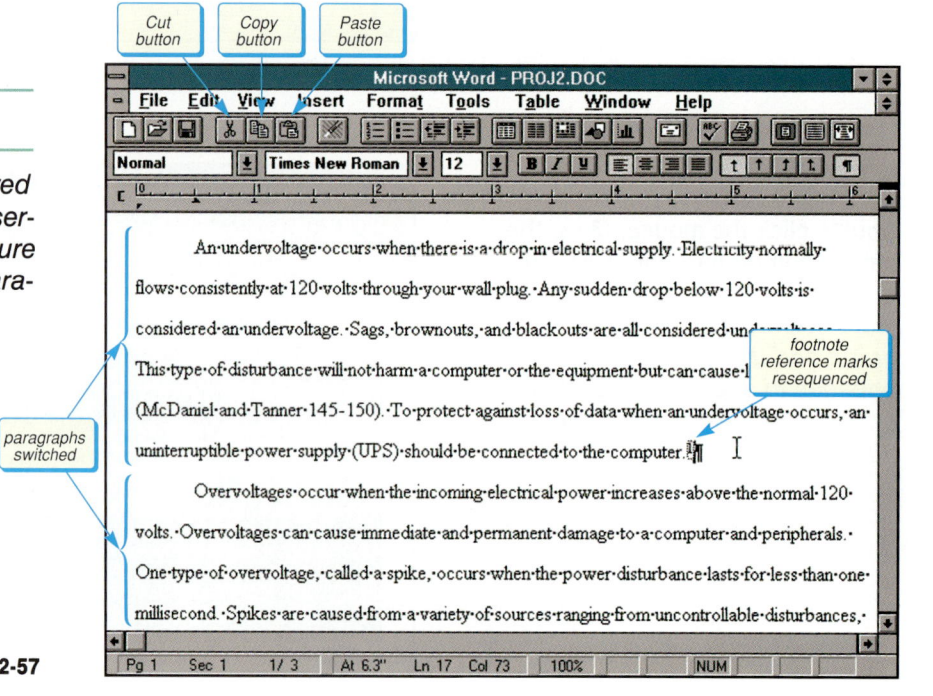

FIGURE 2-57

TO CUT AND PASTE A PARAGRAPH

Step 1: Position the mouse pointer in the selection bar to the left of the paragraph to be cut.
Step 2: Double-click the mouse.
Step 3: Click the Cut button ( ) on the Toolbar. Word removes the selected paragraph from the screen and places it on the Clipboard.
Step 4: Move the insertion point to the location where the paragraph on the Clipboard is to be pasted.
Step 5: Click the Paste button ( ) on the Toolbar.

You may also want to copy text onto the Clipboard, without cutting it from the document. To copy selected text, leaving the selected text in place, click the Copy button ( ) instead of the Cut button. Whether you click the Copy button or the Cut button, when you click the Paste button, the text on the Clipboard is placed at the location of the insertion point. When you paste, the text on the Clipboard is not erased. That is, you can paste the text on the Clipboard in as many locations as you desire. The only time the Clipboard text is erased is when you cut or copy again, which replaces the old text on Clipboard with the new selected text.

If you accidentally cut or copy, you can undo these activities by clicking the Undo button on the Toolbar.

Selectively Displaying Nonprinting Characters

Word displays nonprinting characters on the screen when you click the Show/Hide Nonprinting Characters button on the ribbon. Recall that the paragraph mark indicates you pressed the ENTER key; the raised dot shows where you pressed the SPACEBAR; and so on. If you feel all these nonprinting characters clutter your screen, you can choose which nonprinting characters will display when you click the Show/Hide Nonprinting Characters button by following these steps (see Figure 2-58).

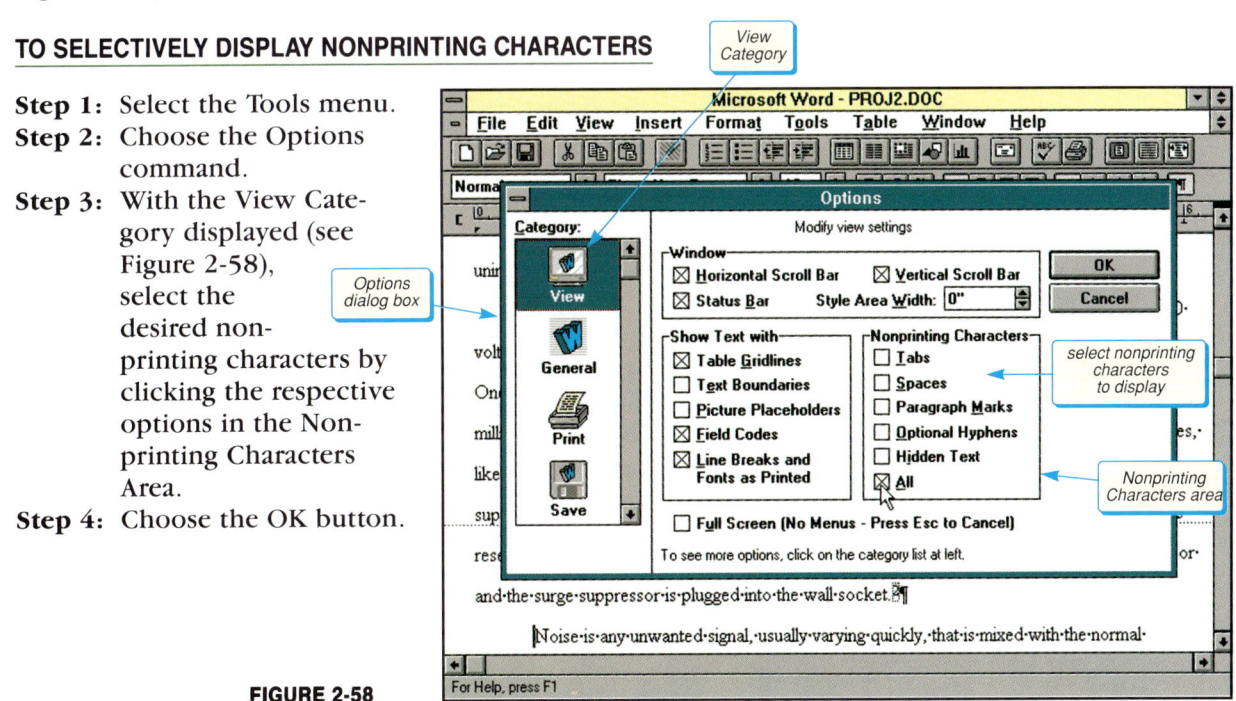

TO SELECTIVELY DISPLAY NONPRINTING CHARACTERS

Step 1: Select the Tools menu.
Step 2: Choose the Options command.
Step 3: With the View Category displayed (see Figure 2-58), select the desired nonprinting characters by clicking the respective options in the Nonprinting Characters Area.
Step 4: Choose the OK button.

FIGURE 2-58

▶ USING THE THESAURUS

When writing papers, you may find that you used the same word in multiple locations or that a word you used was not quite appropriate. In these instances, you will want to look up a word similar in meaning to the duplicate or inappropriate word. These similar words are called **synonyms**. A book of synonyms is referred to as a **thesaurus**. Word provides an on-line thesaurus for your convenience. The steps on the next page illustrate how to use Word's thesaurus to locate a synonym for the word *linked* in the first paragraph of Project 2.

TO USE WORD'S THESAURUS

STEP 1 ▶

Select the word for which you want to look up a synonym by double-clicking in it.

The word linked *is highlighted in the document (Figure 2-59).*

STEP 2 ▶

Select the Tools menu and point to the Thesaurus command (Figure 2-59).

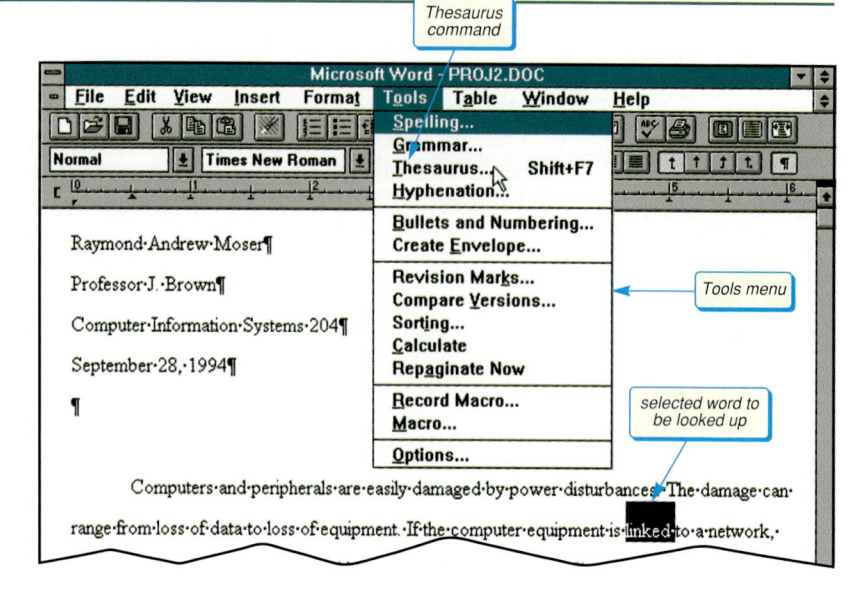

FIGURE 2-59

STEP 3 ▶

Choose the Thesaurus command.

Word displays the Thesaurus: English [US] dialog box (Figure 2-60). The Meanings area displays the definition of the selected word, and the Synonyms area displays a variety of words with similar meanings.

STEP 4 ▶

Select the synonym you want (connected) by clicking it. Point to the Replace button.

The word connected *is highlighted (Figure 2-60).*

STEP 5

Choose the Replace button. Press **CTRL + HOME**.

Word replaces the word linked with connected and returns you to the top of your document (Figure 2-61 on the next page).

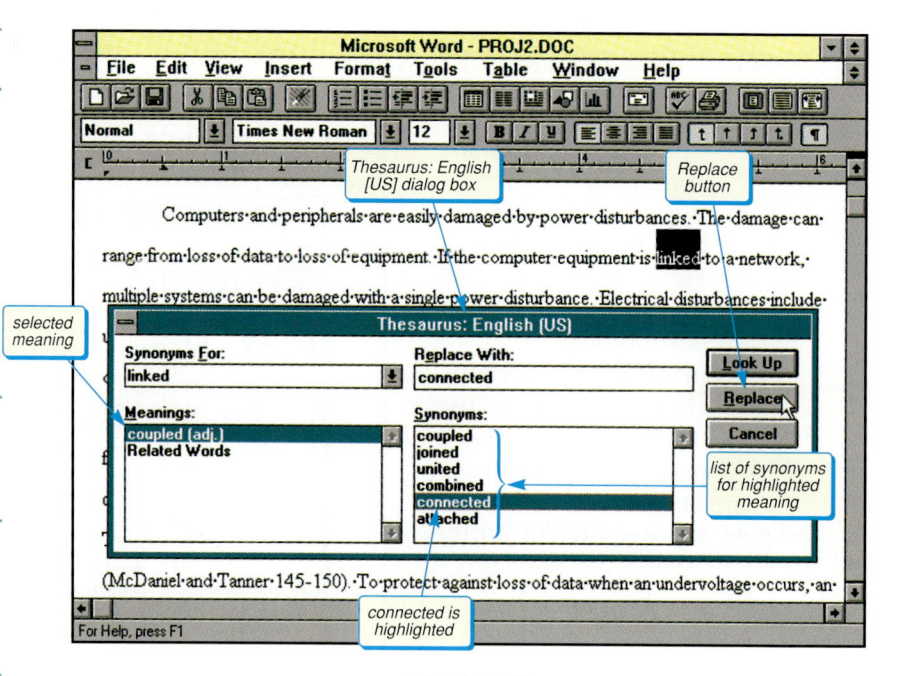

FIGURE 2-60

If multiple meanings are listed in the Meanings area, select the appropriate meaning by clicking it. The Synonyms area will change based on the meaning you select. The research paper is now complete. Be sure to save your research paper one final time before printing it. The next step is to display and print the document in print preview.

DISPLAYING AND PRINTING A DOCUMENT IN PRINT PREVIEW   MSW93

▶ DISPLAYING AND PRINTING A DOCUMENT IN PRINT PREVIEW

Earlier in this project you learned how to switch from normal to page layout view. In page layout view, you viewed the *printed* page on the screen. That is, headers, footers, and footnotes displayed in their proper positions. To see exactly how a document will look when you print it, you should display it in **print preview**. In print preview, headers, footers, and footnotes display. Once you preview the document, you can print it directly from within print preview.

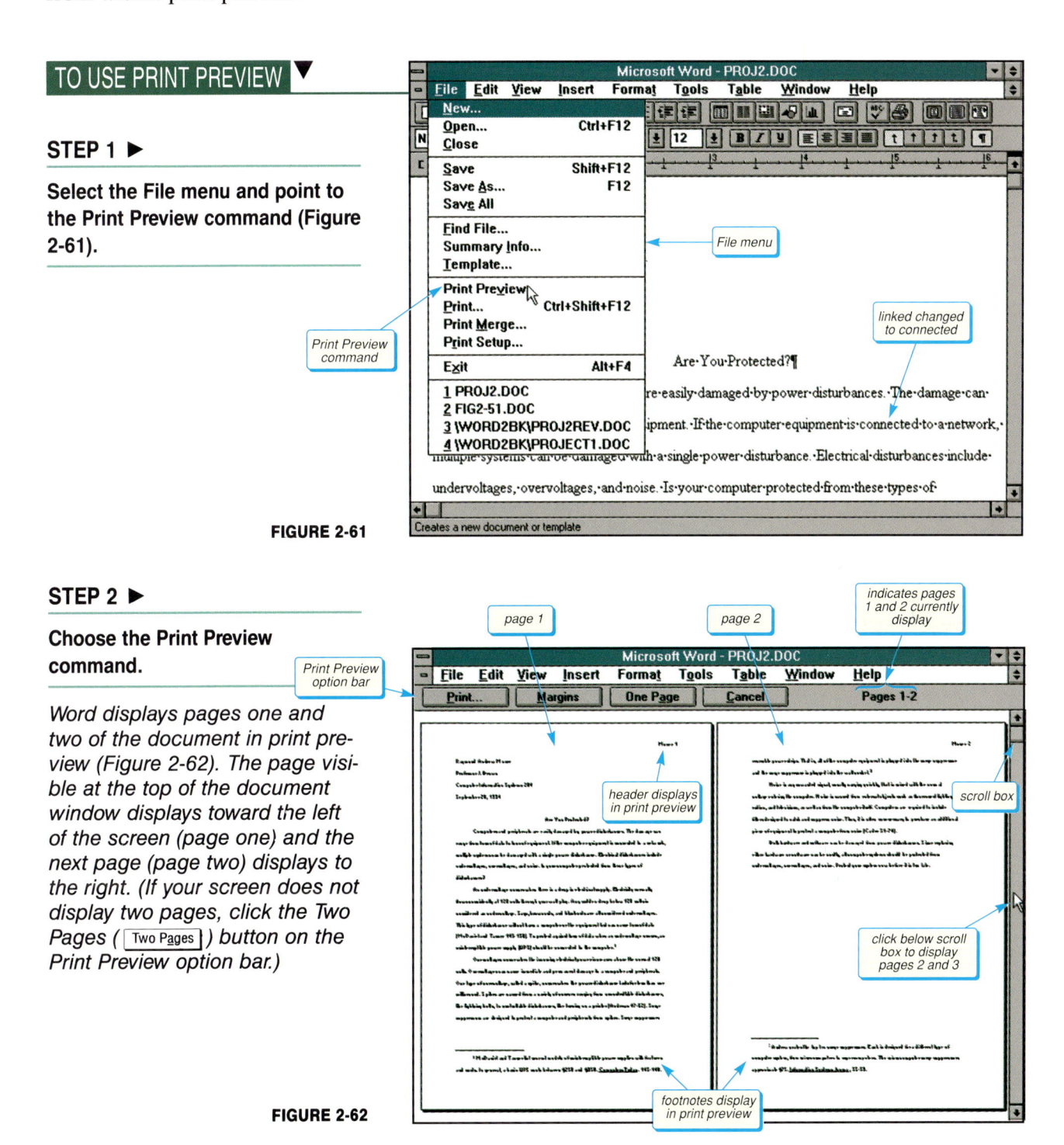

TO USE PRINT PREVIEW ▼

STEP 1 ▶

Select the File menu and point to the Print Preview command (Figure 2-61).

FIGURE 2-61

STEP 2 ▶

Choose the Print Preview command.

Word displays pages one and two of the document in print preview (Figure 2-62). The page visible at the top of the document window displays toward the left of the screen (page one) and the next page (page two) displays to the right. (If your screen does not display two pages, click the Two Pages (Two Pages) button on the Print Preview option bar.)

FIGURE 2-62

MSW94 PROJECT 2 CREATING A RESEARCH PAPER

STEP 3 ▶

Click below the scroll box on the scroll bar to see the next two pages in the document.

Pages two and three display in print preview (Figure 2-63).

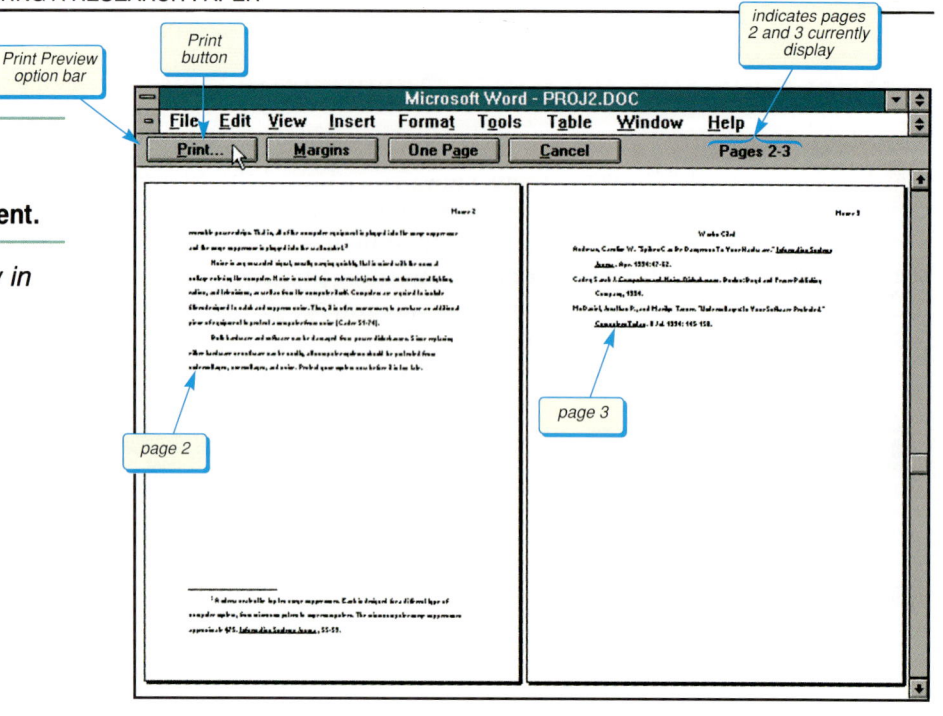

FIGURE 2-63

STEP 4 ▶

Click the Print button (Print...) on the Print Preview option bar.

Word displays the Print dialog box (Figure 2-64).

STEP 5 ▶

Ready the printer. Click the OK button in the Print dialog box.

Word prints the document on the printer.

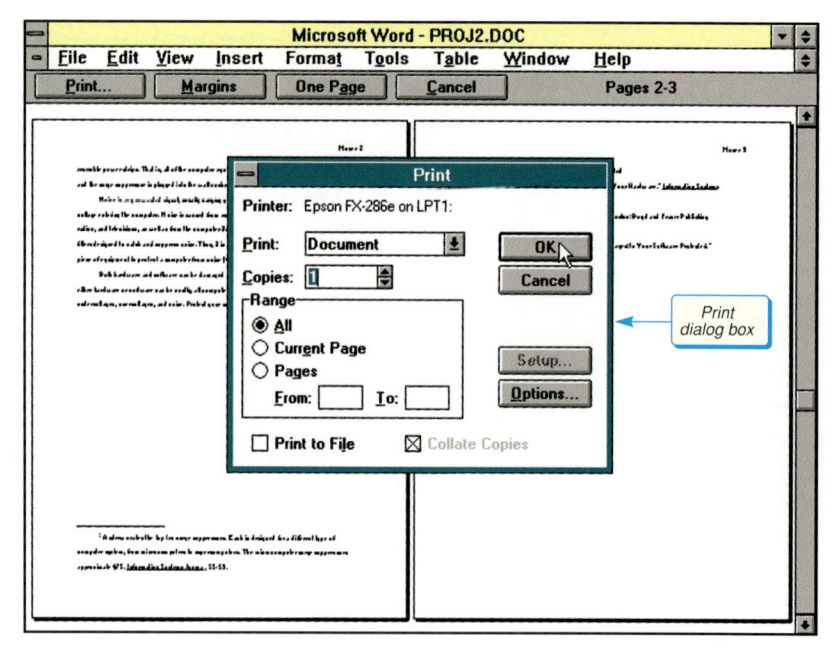

FIGURE 2-64

STEP 6 ▶

When the printer stops, retrieve the printout (Figure 2-65).

STEP 7 ▶

Choose the Close button (Close) on the Print Preview option bar.

After the document prints, the Cancel button (Cancel) on the option bar changes to the Close button. Word then returns you to the document in normal view.

Moser 3

Works Cited

Andrews, Caroline W. "Spikes Can Be Dangerous To Your Hardware." Information Systems Journal. Apr. 1994: 47-62.

Carter, Sarah J. Computers and Noise Disturbances. Boston: Boyd and Fraser Publishing Company, 1994.

McDaniel, Jonathan P., and Marilyn Tanner. "Undervoltages: Is Your Software Protected." Computers Today. 8 Jul. 1994: 145-150.

Moser 2

resemble power strips. That is, all of the computer equipment is plugged into the surge suppressor and the surge suppressor is plugged into the wall socket.[2]

Noise is any unwanted signal, usually varying quickly, that is mixed with the normal voltage entering the computer. Noise is caused from external objects such as fluorescent lighting, radios, and televisions, as well as from the computer itself. Computers are required to include filters designed to catch and suppress noise. Thus, it is often unnecessary to purchase an mputer from noise (Carter 51-74).

amaged from power disturbances. Since replacing computer systems should be protected from ct your system now before it is too late.

Moser 1

Raymond Andrew Moser
Professor J. Brown
Computer Information Systems 204
September 28, 1994

Are You Protected?

Computers and peripherals are easily damaged by power disturbances. The damage can range from loss of data to loss of equipment. If the computer equipment is connected to a network, multiple systems can be damaged with a single power disturbance. Electrical disturbances include undervoltages, overvoltages, and noise. Is your computer protected from these types of disturbances?

An undervoltage occurs when there is a drop in electrical supply. Electricity normally flows consistently at 120 volts through your wall plug. Any sudden drop below 120 volts is considered an undervoltage. Sags, brownouts, and blackouts are all considered undervoltages. This type of disturbance will not harm a computer or the equipment but can cause loss of data (McDaniel and Tanner 145-150). To protect against loss of data when an undervoltage occurs, an uninterruptible power supply (UPS) should be connected to the computer.[1]

Overvoltages occur when the incoming electrical power increases above the normal 120 volts. Overvoltages can cause immediate and permanent damage to a computer and peripherals. One type of overvoltage, called a spike, occurs when the power disturbance lasts for less than one millisecond. Spikes are caused from a variety of sources ranging from uncontrollable disturbances, like lightning bolts, to controllable disturbances, like turning on a printer (Andrews 47-62). Surge suppressors are designed to protect a computer and peripherals from spikes. Surge suppressors

pressors. Each is designed for a different type of percomputers. The microcomputer surge stems Journal, 55-59.

---

[1] McDaniel and Tanner list several models of uninterruptible power supplies with features and costs. In general, a basic UPS costs between $250 and $350. Computers Today. 145-148.

FIGURE 2-65

When in print preview, you can also click the up or down arrows on the scroll bar, drag the scroll box, or press the PAGE UP key or PAGE DOWN key to bring different pages into the window area. To return to the document window without printing the document, choose the Close or Cancel button on the Print Preview option bar.

Your research paper is now complete. You may quit Word.

TO QUIT WORD

Step 1: Select the File menu.
Step 2: Choose the Exit command.

▶ Project Summary

Project 2 introduced you to creating and revising a research paper in Word. You used the MLA style of documentation to create the paper. You learned how to change margin settings, adjust line spacing, create headers with page numbers, and indent paragraphs. Then you added footnotes to the research paper. You alphabetized the works cited page by sorting its paragraphs. Next, you revised the research paper by finding and replacing text and switching paragraphs. Finally, you used Word's thesaurus to look up synonyms.

▶ Key Terms

adjusting line spacing (*MSW59*)
ascending sort order (*MSW84*)
automatic page break (*MSW75*)
background repagination (*MSW75*)
changing margins (*MSW57*)
Clipboard (*MSW88*)
Cut button (*MSW90*)
cut and paste (*MSW88*)
descending sort order (*MSW84*)
drag and drop (*MSW88*)
endnote (*MSW71*)
explanatory note (*MSW56*)
first-line indent (*MSW69*)
footer (*MSW63*)

footnote (*MSW71*)
footnote pane (*MSW72*)
footnote reference mark (*MSW71*)
footnote separator (*MSW77*)
footnote text (*MSW71*)
hanging indent (*MSW81*)
hard page break (*MSW79*)
header (*MSW63*)
header pane (*MSW64*)
Left-Aligned Text button (*MSW68*)
MLA style of documentation (*MSW54*)

Modern Language Association (MLA) (*MSW54*)
Normal style (*MSW61*)
normal view (*MSW66*)
page layout view (*MSW76*)
parenthetical citation (*MSW56*)
print preview (*MSW93*)
right-aligned (*MSW63*)
Right-Aligned Text button (*MSW65*)
soft page break (*MSW75*)
Sorting (*MSW82*)
superscripts (*MSW56*)
synonyms (*MSW91*)
thesaurus (*MSW91*)

QUICK REFERENCE

In Microsoft Word you can accomplish a task in a number of ways. The following table provides a quick reference to each task presented in this project with its available options. The commands listed in the menu column can be executed using either the keyboard or mouse.

Task	Mouse	Menu	Keyboard Shortcuts
Add Footnotes		From Insert menu, choose Footnote	
Adjust Line Spacing		From Format menu, choose Paragraph	
Change Margins		From Format menu, choose Page Setup	
Close a Pane	Click Close button on option bar		Press ALT + SHIFT + C
Copy Selected Text	Click Copy button on Toolbar	From Edit menu, choose Copy	Press CTRL + C
Create a Header		From View menu, choose Header/Footer	
Create Hanging Indent	Hold SHIFT and drag Left-Indent marker on ruler	From Format menu, choose Paragraph	Press CTRL + T
Cut Selected Text	Click Cut button on Toolbar	From Edit menu, choose Cut	Press CTRL + X
Display Document in Print Preview		From File menu, choose Print Preview	
Find Text		From Edit menu, choose Find	
First-Line Indent Paragraphs	Drag First-Line Indent marker on ruler	From Format menu, choose Paragraph	
Go to Page or Footnote		From Edit menu, choose Go To	Press F5 twice.
Indent Paragraph	Drag Right- or Left-Indent marker on ruler	From Format menu, choose Paragraph	Press CTRL + N
Insert Current Date	Click Current Date button on option bar		Press ALT + SHIFT + D
Insert Current Time	Click Current Time button on option bar		Press ALT + SHIFT + T
Insert Hard Page Break		From Insert menu, choose Break	Press CTRL + ENTER
Insert Page Number	Click Page Number button on option bar	From Insert menu, choose Page Numbers	Press ALT + SHIFT + P
Left-Align a Paragraph	Click Left-Aligned Text button on ribbon	From Format menu, choose Paragraph	Press CTRL + L
Paste from Clipboard	Click Paste button on Toolbar	From Edit menu, choose Paste	Press CTRL + V
Remove Selected Hard Page Break	Click Cut button on Toolbar	From Edit menu, choose Cut	Press DEL

(continued)

MSW97

QUICK REFERENCE (continued)

Task	Mouse	Menu	Keyboard Shortcuts
Replace Text		From Edit menu, choose Replace	
Right-Align a Paragraph	Click Right-Aligned Text button on ribbon	From Format menu, choose Paragraph	Press CTRL + R
Select a Line	Click to left of line in selection bar		With insertion point at column 1, press SHIFT + END
Select a Paragraph	Double-click to left of paragraph in selection bar		With insertion point at start of paragraph, press CTRL + SHIFT + DOWN ARROW
Select a Sentence	Press CTRL and click in sentence		
Sorting Paragraphs		From Tools menu, choose Sorting	
Switch to Normal View		From View menu, choose Normal	
Switch to Page Layout View		From View menu, choose Page Layout	
Use Thesaurus		From Tools menu, choose Thesaurus	Press SHIFT + F7

STUDENT ASSIGNMENTS

STUDENT ASSIGNMENT 1
True/False

Instructions: Circle T if the statement is true or F if the statement is false.

T F   1. A popular documentation style used today for research papers is presented by the Modern Language Association (MLA).
T F   2. The MLA style uses the term *references* rather than *bibliography*.
T F   3. To change margin settings, choose the Margins command from the Format menu.
T F   4. Word, by default, single-spaces between lines of text and automatically adjusts line height to accommodate various font sizes and graphics.
T F   5. A header is text you want to print at the top of each page in a document.
T F   6. A header displays on the screen in normal view.
T F   7. Type the words PAGE NUMBER HERE wherever you want the page number to appear in the document.
T F   8. Superscripted numbers are those that appear raised above other text in a document.
T F   9. When you change the Normal style in a document, all future documents will use the new style.
T F 10. Word, by default, prints footnotes at the bottom of the page on which the footnote reference mark appears.
T F 11. In page layout view, Word displays headers, footers, and footnotes properly positioned in the document on the screen.
T F 12. Hard page breaks display on the screen as a single horizontal thickly dotted line.
T F 13. The default footnote separator in Word is a two-inch solid line placed at the left margin of the document.

T F 14. A hanging indent indents the first line of each paragraph one-half inch from the left margin.
T F 15. To sort selected paragraphs, click the Sort button on the Toolbar.
T F 16. To find and replace text in a document, choose the Find command from the Edit menu.
T F 17. Dragging and dropping involves removing selected text from the document and placing it on the Clipboard, a temporary storage area.
T F 18. When you paste text, the Clipboard contents are erased.
T F 19. Word's thesaurus enables you to look up homonyms for a selected word.
T F 20. To selectively display nonprinting characters, choose the Options command from the Tools menu.

STUDENT ASSIGNMENT 2
Multiple Choice

Instructions: Circle the correct response.

1. The MLA documentation style suggests all pages of a research paper should be _____ -spaced with _____ inch top, bottom, left, and right margins.
   a. single, 1
   b. double, 1
   c. single, 1 1/4
   d. double, 1 1/4
2. Which command can you use to insert page numbers into a document?
   a. Page Numbers command from the Insert menu
   b. Header/Footer command from the View menu
   c. either a or b
   d. neither a nor b
3. The drag and drop technique is best used _____.
   a. to move text short distances
   b. to move text long distances
   c. to copy text long distances
   d. both b and c
4. To efficiently indent the first line of each paragraph in a document, _____.
   a. press the TAB key at the beginning of each paragraph
   b. drag the First-Line Indent marker on the ruler
   c. click the First-Line button on the Toolbar
   d. choose the Indent Paragraph command from the Format menu
5. When Word automatically inserts page breaks, these page breaks are called _____.
   a. automatic page breaks
   b. soft page breaks
   c. hard page breaks
   d. both a and b
6. If the screen displays a horizontal thickly dotted line completely across the screen, you have a _____ in the document.
   a. soft page break
   b. hard page break
   c. footnote separator
   d. automatic page break
7. To sort selected paragraphs in alphabetical order, choose the _____ option button in the Sorting dialog box.
   a. Alphabetical
   b. Ascending
   c. Descending
   d. either a or b

(continued)

MSW100   PROJECT 2   CREATING A RESEARCH PAPER

STUDENT ASSIGNMENT 2 (continued)

8. When the mouse pointer is in the selection bar, it has a shape of a(n) _____.
   a. I-beam (I)
   b. left-pointing arrow (▨)
   c. right-pointing arrow (▨)
   d. hourglass (⧗)
9. To view different pages in print preview, _____.
   a. press the PAGE UP or PAGE DOWN key
   b. click the up or down arrow on the scroll bar
   c. drag the scroll box on the scroll bar
   c. all of the above
10. Headers, footers, and footnotes appear when Word is in _____.
    a. normal view
    b. page layout view
    c. print preview
    d. both b and c

STUDENT ASSIGNMENT 3
Understanding the Ruler

Instructions: Answer the following questions concerning the ruler in Figure SA2-3. The numbers in the figure correspond to the numbers of the questions below.

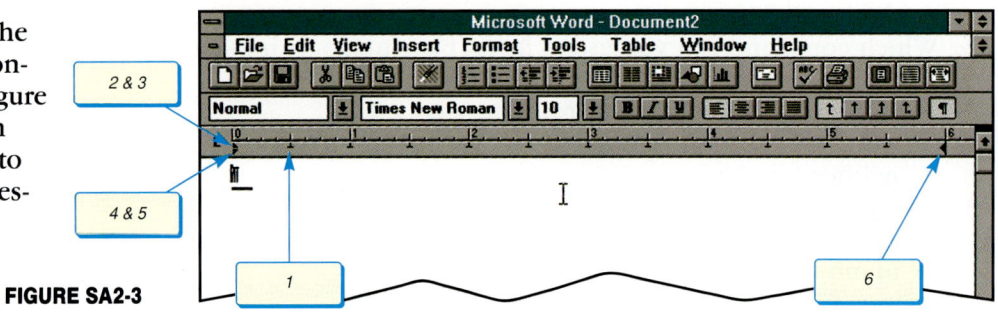

FIGURE SA2-3

1. How many inches from the left margin is the first tab stop?
   _____

2. What is the name of the top triangle at the left margin?
   _____

3. What is the purpose of dragging the top triangle to the first tab stop?
   _____

4. What is the name of the bottom triangle at the left margin?
   _____

5. What is the purpose of dragging the bottom triangle to the first tab stop?
   _____

6. What is the significance of the triangle just beneath the 6 at the right edge of the ruler?
   _____

STUDENT ASSIGNMENT 4
Understanding the Drag and Drop Procedure

Instructions: Fill in the step numbers below to correctly order the process of switching two paragraphs around.

Step _____: Drag the dotted insertion point to the location where the paragraph is to be moved.

Step _____: Double-click the mouse. Move the mouse pointer into the selected text.

Step _____: Press and hold down the mouse button.

Step _____: Position the mouse pointer in the selection bar to the left of the paragraph to be moved.

Step _____: Release the mouse button.

STUDENT ASSIGNMENT 5
Understanding Commands in Menus

Instructions: Write the appropriate command name to accomplish each task and the menu in which each command is located.

TASK	COMMAND NAME	MENU NAME
Add Footnotes		
Adjust Line Spacing		
Change Margins		
Create a Header		
Display Document in Print Preview		
Insert Hard Page Break		
Sort Paragraphs		
Switch to Page Layout View		
Use Thesaurus		

MSW102   PROJECT 2   CREATING A RESEARCH PAPER

STUDENT ASSIGNMENT 6
Understanding the Header Pane

Instructions: Answer the following questions concerning the header pane in Figure SA2-6. The numbers in the figure correspond to the numbers of the questions below.

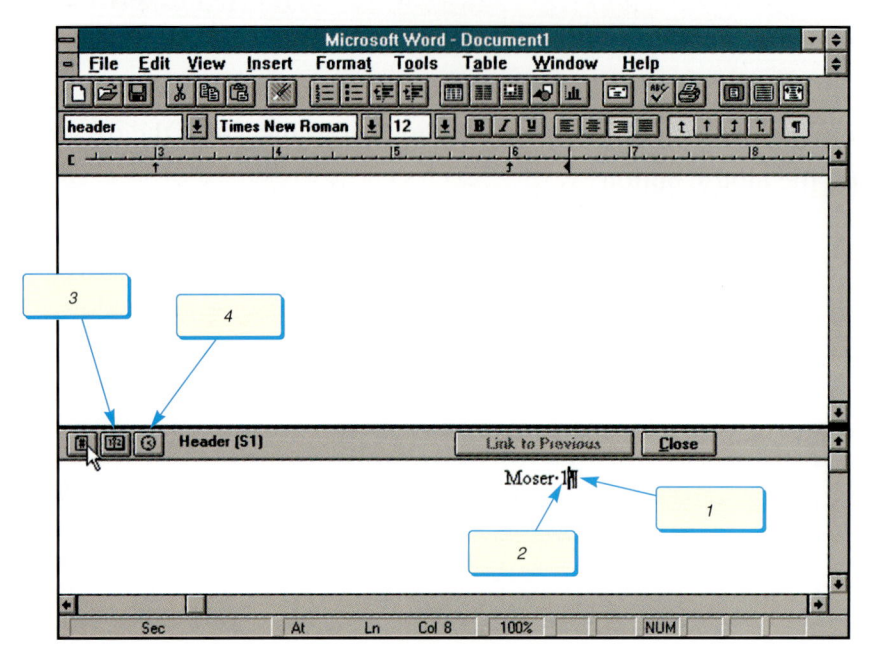

FIGURE SA2-6

1. What button on the ribbon caused the entry, Moser 1, to be placed at the right margin?

2. How did the page number 1 display in the header pane?

3. What is the purpose of the second button from the left on the header pane option bar?

4. What is the purpose of the third button from the left on the header pane option bar?

5. Once you close the header pane option bar, what will you click to bring the left margin of the document window into view?

COMPUTER LABORATORY EXERCISES

COMPUTER LABORATORY EXERCISE 1
Using Word's Thesaurus and Print Preview

Instructions: Start Word. Open the document CLE2-1 from the Word subdirectory on the Student Diskette that accompanies this book. A portion of the document is shown in Figure CLE2-1. The document resembles the research paper created in Project 2.

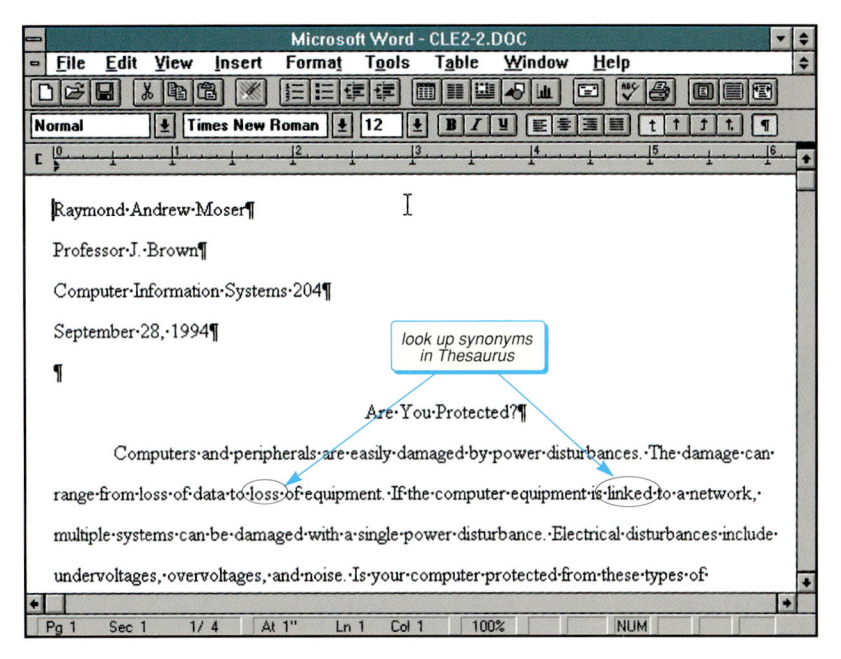

FIGURE CLE2-1

Perform the following tasks:

1. Choose the Help Index command from the Help menu. Choose the Search button. Type THESAURUS and press the ENTER key. Choose the Go To button. Read and print the information. Choose the Back button. Choose the Search button. Type PRINT PREVIEW and press the ENTER key. Select Previewing a document before printing. Choose the Go To button. Read and print the information. Close the Help window.
2. Select the word linked in the first paragraph of the research paper.
3. Choose the Thesaurus command from the Tools menu to display the Thesaurus dialog box.
4. Select the synonym connected by clicking it.
5. Choose the Replace button to replace the word linked with the word connected.
6. Select the second occurrence of the word loss in the first paragraph.
7. Choose the Thesaurus command from the Tools menu.
8. Select the synonym destruction and choose the Replace button.
9. Replace the Student Diskette that accompanies this book with your data disk before saving the document. Save the revised document on your data disk.
10. Choose the Print Preview command from the File menu.
11. Click the up arrow and down arrow on the scroll bar to display various pages of the document on the screen.
12. Click the Print button on the Print Preview option bar.
13. Click the OK button in the Print dialog box.
14. Choose the Close command on the Print Preview option bar to return to the document window.
15. Choose the Close command from the File menu to close the document.

MSW103

COMPUTER LABORATORY EXERCISE 2
Revising a Word Processing Document

Instructions: Start Word. Open the document CLE2-2 from the Word subdirectory on the Student Diskette that accompanies this book. A portion of the document is shown in Figure CLE2-2. The document resembles the research paper created in Project 2. By following the steps below, you are to replace all occurrences of the text 240 with the text 120, switch the second and third paragraphs in the research paper, and experiment with cut and paste.

Perform the following tasks:

1. Choose the Replace command from the Edit menu to open the Replace dialog box.
2. Type 240 in the Find What text box. Press the TAB key to advance to the Replace With text box. Type 120 in the Replace With text box.
3. Choose the Replace All button in the Replace dialog box to replace all occurrences of 240 with 120. Choose the Close button.
4. Position the mouse pointer in the selection bar to the left of the paragraph beginning, Overvoltages occur when the ... .
5. Double-click the mouse to select the paragraph.
6. Press and hold down the left mouse button. Drag the insertion point to page 2 to the left of the N in the paragraph beginning, Noise is any unwanted signal, usually... . Release the left mouse button.
7. Replace the Student Diskette that accompanies this book with your data disk before saving the document. Save the revised document on your data disk.
8. Print the document by clicking the Print button on the Toolbar.
9. Position the insertion point to the left of the first paragraph.
10. Double-click the mouse to select the paragraph. Click the Cut button to remove the selected paragraph from the screen and place it on the Clipboard.
11. Position the insertion point after the last paragraph in the document (before the Works Cited page). Press the ENTER key. Click the Paste button twice to copy the paragraph from the Clipboard to the end of the document twice.
12. Print the document.
13. Choose the Close command from the File menu to close the document.

FIGURE CLE2-2

COMPUTER LABORATORY EXERCISE 3
Sorting Paragraphs

Instructions: Start Word. Open the document CLE2-3 from the Word subdirectory on the Student Diskette that accompanies this book. A portion of the document is shown in Figure CLE2-3. The document resembles the Works Cited page of the research paper created in Project 2.

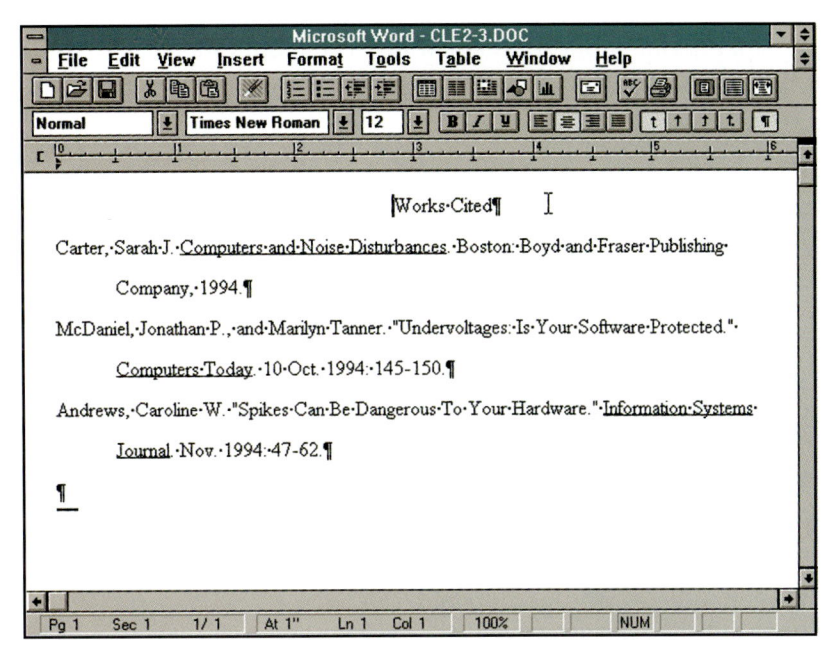

FIGURE CLE2-3

Perform the following tasks:

1. Position the mouse pointer in the selection bar to the left of the first works cited paragraph.
2. Drag the mouse pointer through the last works cited paragraph.
3. Choose the Sorting command from the Tools menu.
4. Select the Descending option button in the Sorting dialog box.
5. Choose the OK button in the Sorting dialog box.
6. Position the mouse pointer in the selection bar to the left of the title, Works Cited, and click to select it.
7. Type the new title, Works Cited in Descending Order.
8. Print the works cited page by clicking the Print button on the Toolbar.
9. Select the works cited paragraphs again (repeat Steps 1 and 2).
10. Choose the Sorting command from the Tools menu.
11. Select the Ascending option button in the Sorting dialog box, and then choose the OK button.
12. Select the title and type a new title, Works Cited in Ascending Order.
13. Replace the Student Diskette that accompanies this book with your data disk before saving the document. Save the revised document on your data disk.
14. Print the Works Cited page by clicking the Print button on the Toolbar.
15. Choose the Close command from the File menu to close the document.

COMPUTER LABORATORY ASSIGNMENTS

COMPUTER LABORATORY ASSIGNMENT 1
Preparing a Research Report and Works Cited Page

Purpose: To become familiar with creating a research report according to the MLA style of documentation.

Problem: You are a college student currently enrolled in a computer class. Your assignment is to prepare a short research paper about application software. The requirements are that the paper be presented according to the MLA documentation style and have three references (Figure CLA2-1).

Instructions: Perform the following tasks:

1. Click the Show/Hide Nonprinting Characters button on the ribbon.
2. Change all margin settings to one inch.
3. Adjust line spacing to double.
4. Change the Normal style by clicking the paragraph mark. Then, change the point size to 12 and click the Normal style. Press the ENTER key and click the Yes button.
5. Create a header to number pages.
6. Type the name and course information at the left margin.
7. Center and type the title.
8. First-line indent all paragraphs in the paper.
9. Type the body of the paper as shown in Figure CLA2-1. At the end of the body of the research paper, press the ENTER key once and insert a hard page break.
10. Create the works cited page. Be sure to alphabetize the works.
11. Check the spelling of the document.
12. Save the document on a disk with the filename CLA2-1.
13. View the document in print preview.
14. Print the document from within print preview.

Parker 3

Works Cited

Aldrin, James F. "A Discussion of Database Management Systems," Database Monthly. May
1994: 25-37.

Little, Karen A. and Jeffrey W. Benson. Word Processors. Boston: Boyd and Fraser Publishing
Company, 1994.

Wakefield, Sheila A. "What Can An Electronic Spreadsheet Do For You," PC Analyzer. Apr.
1994: 98-110.

Parker 2

resources to any organizations. For this reason, users desire data be organized and readily accessible in a variety of formats. With a DBMS, a user can then easily store data, retrieve data, modify data, analyze data, and create a variety of reports from the data (Aldrin 25-37).

Many organizations today have all three of these types of application software packages installed on their personal computers. Word processors, electronic spreadsheets, and database management systems make users' tasks more efficient. When users are more efficient, the company as a whole operates more economically and efficiently.

Parker 1

Gerald Charles Parker
Professor C. Mason
Computer Information Systems 204
September 13, 1994

Application Software

Computer systems contain both hardware and software. Hardware is any tangible item in a computer system, like the system unit, keyboard, or printer. Software, or a computer program, is the set of instructions that direct the computer to perform a task. Software falls into one of two categories: system software and application software. System software controls the operation of the computer hardware; whereas, application software enables a user to perform tasks. Three major types of application software on the market today for personal computers are word processors, electronic spreadsheets, and database management systems (Little and Benson 10-42).

A word processing program allows a user to efficiently and economically create professional looking documents such as memoranda, letters, reports, and resumes. With a word processor, one can easily revise a document. To improve the accuracy of one's writing, word processors can check the spelling and grammar in a document. They also provide a thesaurus to enable a user to add variety and precision to his or her writing. Many word processing programs also provide desktop publishing features to create brochures, advertisements, and newsletters.

An electronic spreadsheet program enables a user to organize data in a fashion similar to a paper spreadsheet. The difference is the user need not perform calculations manually; electronic spreadsheets can be instructed to perform any computation desired. The contents of an electronic spreadsheet can be easily modified by a user. Once the data is modified, all calculations in the spreadsheet are recomputed automatically. Many electronic spreadsheet packages also enable a user to graph the data in his or her spreadsheet (Wakefield 98-110).

A database management system (DBMS) is a software program that allows a user to efficiently store a large amount data in a centralized location. Data is one of the most valuable

FIGURE CLA2-1

COMPUTER LABORATORY ASSIGNMENT 2
Preparing a Research Report with Footnotes

Purpose: To become familiar with creating a research report according to the MLA style of documentation.

Problem: You are a college student currently enrolled in an English class. Your assignment is to prepare a short research paper in any area of interest to you. The only requirements are that the paper be presented according to the MLA documentation style and have three references. You decide to prepare a paper discussing upper and lower respiratory infections (Figure CLA2-2).

Part 1 Instructions: Perform the following tasks:

1. Click the Show/Hide Nonprinting Characters button on the ribbon.
2. Change all margin settings to one inch.
3. Adjust line spacing to double.
4. Change the Normal style by clicking the paragraph mark. Then, change the point size to 12 and click the Normal style. Press the ENTER key and click the Yes button.
5. Create a header to number pages.
6. Type the name and course information at the left margin.
7. Center and type the title.
8. First-line indent all paragraphs in the paper.
9. Type the body of the paper as shown in Figure CLA2-2 with appropriate footnotes. At the end of the body of the research paper, press the ENTER key once and insert a hard page break.
10. Create the works cited page. Be sure to alphabetize the works.
11. Check the spelling of the document.
12. Save the document on a disk with the filename CLA2-2a.
13. View the document in print preview.
14. Print the document from within print preview.

FIGURE CLA2-2a

Kramer 1

Mary Ann Kramer
Professor S. Barrington
English 104
October 17, 1994

Commonly Confused Infections

Throughout the course of your life, you will experience many upper and lower respiratory infections. Common names used to refer to these infections include influenza, pneumonia, and the common cold. Some of these infections have similar symptoms, like coughing. Each, however, has unique symptoms to differentiate it from the others. Successful treatment of these types of infections depends on correct identification of the virus.

Viruses that affect the lungs are called lower respiratory tract infections. Pneumonia is an infection that attacks the lungs. Pneumonia can be caused by either a virus or bacteria. Influenza is one type of viral pneumonia, commonly called the flu[1]. Patients with a flu virus often experience sudden weakness and severe fatigue, as well as upper respiratory symptoms like sore throat, watery eyes, muscle aches, headache, and nasal stuffiness. Following these ailments, the patient suffers from fever, a dry cough, and chest pain. Treatment of the flu virus includes bed rest, plenty of fluids, and aspirin (Jones 68-75).

Bacterial pneumonia, on the other hand, is more severe than viral pneumonia. Bacteria enters the lungs from many sources, ranging from normal breathing to infection in another part of the body. Bacterial pneumonia inflames the lungs, and the air space begins to fill with fluid. Symptoms the patient experiences are deep cough, fever, chest pain, and chills. Treatment includes ridding the lungs of these fluids and reducing the inflammation with antibiotics.

---

[1] Jones states other types of lower respiratory tract diseases include epiglottitis, laryngitis, and tracheobronchitis. *Medical Journal*, 70.

Part 2 Instructions: Perform the following tasks to modify the research paper:

1. Move the fourth paragraph so it is the second paragraph. That is, the paragraph discussing the common cold should appear immediately beneath the introductory paragraph.
2. Use Word's thesaurus to change the word differentiate in the first paragraph to a word of your choice. Be sure you have the proper meaning highlighted when looking for a synonym.
3. Use Word's thesaurus to change the word similar in the last paragraph to a word of your choice.
4. Change all occurrences of the word patient(s) to victim(s).
5. Save the document on a disk with the filename CLA2-2b.
6. View the document in print preview.
7. Print the document from within print preview.

COMPUTER LABORATORY ASSIGNMENT 3
Composing a Research Report with Footnotes

Purpose: To become familiar with composing a research report from your notes according to the MLA style of documentation.

Problem: You have drafted the notes shown in Figure CLA2-3. Your assignment is to prepare a short research paper based on these notes. You are to review the notes and then rearrange and reword. Embellish the paper as you deem necessary. Add two footnotes elaborating on personal experiences you have had. The requirements are that the paper be presented according to the MLA documentation style.

Instructions: Perform the following tasks:

1. Click the Show/Hide Nonprinting Characters button on the ribbon.
2. Change all margin settings to one inch.
3. Adjust line spacing to double.
4. Change the Normal style by clicking the paragraph mark. Then, change the point size to 12 and click the Normal style. Press the ENTER key and click the Yes button.
5. Create a header to number pages.
6. Type the name and course information at the left margin.
7. Center and type the title.
8. First-line indent all paragraphs in the paper.
9. Compose the body of the paper from the notes in Figure CLA2-3 with footnotes as specified above. At the end of the body of the research paper, press the ENTER key once and insert a hard page break.
10. Create the works cited page from the listed sources. Be sure to alphabetize the works.
11. Check the spelling of the document.
12. Save the document on a disk with the filename CLA2-3.
13. View the document in print preview.
14. Print the document from within print preview.

> Computers perform three basic activities: input, processing, and output.
>
> The processor transforms input into output.
> The processor contains one or more small semiconductor circuits on a piece of silicon, called an integrated circuit or computer chip.
> Types of processing include adding, subtracting, multiplying, dividing, organizing and sorting.
> Source: Computers Today, a book published by Boyd and Fraser Publishing Company in Boston, 1994, pages 45-55, author Kathy L. Stinson.
>
> Input devices send data into the computer.
> Examples of input devices are a keyboard, mouse, joystick, and light pen.
> Data is input into a computer.
> Examples of data include employee timecards, debits and credits, and student grades.
> Input and output devices are often referred to as peripheral devices because they are attached to the main unit of the computer.
> Source: "Input Data", an article in Peripherals Today, April 1994 issue, pages 109-118, author William E. Trainor.
>
> Output devices receive information from the computer.
> Information is processed data. Information is output from a computer.
> Output can be hardcopy or softcopy.
> Printers and plotters are examples of hardcopy output devices.
> A monitor is an example of a softcopy output device.
> Examples of information include employee paychecks, balance sheets, and report cards.
> Source: "Information is Output", an article in Information Magazine, June 1994 issue, pages 80-97, author Nancy C. Walters.

FIGURE CLA2-3

COMPUTER LABORATORY ASSIGNMENT 4
Creating A Research Report

Purpose: To become familiar with researching a topic of interest and preparing a research report that conforms to the MLA style of documentation.

Problem: You are to visit a library and research a topic of interest to you that relates to a current event in the computer industry. You are to obtain a minimum of two references dated sometime within the past two years. Prepare a research report based on your findings.

Instructions: Create your research report according to the MLA documentation style. Your report should be at least one and one-fourth pages in length and contain a minimum of five paragraphs: introduction, three supporting, and conclusion. Use complete sentences, proper punctuation, and good grammar. Place at least one explanatory note in your paper and include both of your references in the works cited. Be sure to check the spelling of your document before printing it. Save your document with the filename CLA2-4.

MICROSOFT WORD 2.0 FOR WINDOWS
PROJECT THREE

CREATING A PROPOSAL USING TABLES AND GRAPHICS

OBJECTIVES You will have mastered the material in this project when you can:

- Import a graphic
- Scale an imported graphic
- Change the spacing between document characters
- Insert an existing document into an open document
- Save an active document with a new filename
- Set custom tabs
- Change alignment of tab stops
- Insert a table into a document
- Change spacing between table columns
- Change alignment in table cells
- Sum the rows and columns in a table
- Chart a table
- Add bullets to a list

▶ INTRODUCTION

In all liklihood, sometime during your professional life you will find yourself placed in a sales role. You might be selling a tangible product like plastic, or a service like interior decorating, to a customer or client. Within the organization, you might be selling an idea, such as a benefits package, to company employees or a budget plan to upper management. To sell an item, whether tangible or intangible, you will often find yourself writing a proposal. Proposals vary in length, style, and formality, but all are designed to elicit acceptance from the reader.

▶ PROJECT THREE

Project 3 uses Word to produce the proposal shown in Figure 3-1 on the next three pages. The proposal is designed to persuade prospective students to choose Blue Lake Institute of Technology for a college education. The proposal has a colorful title page to grasp the attention of the reader. The body of the proposal uses tables and graphs to pictorially present numeric data.

MSW112

GET A RUNNING START ON A NEW CAREER!

Prepared for

New Career Seekers   Single Parents   High School Students

By

BLUE LAKE
INSTITUTE OF TECHNOLOGY

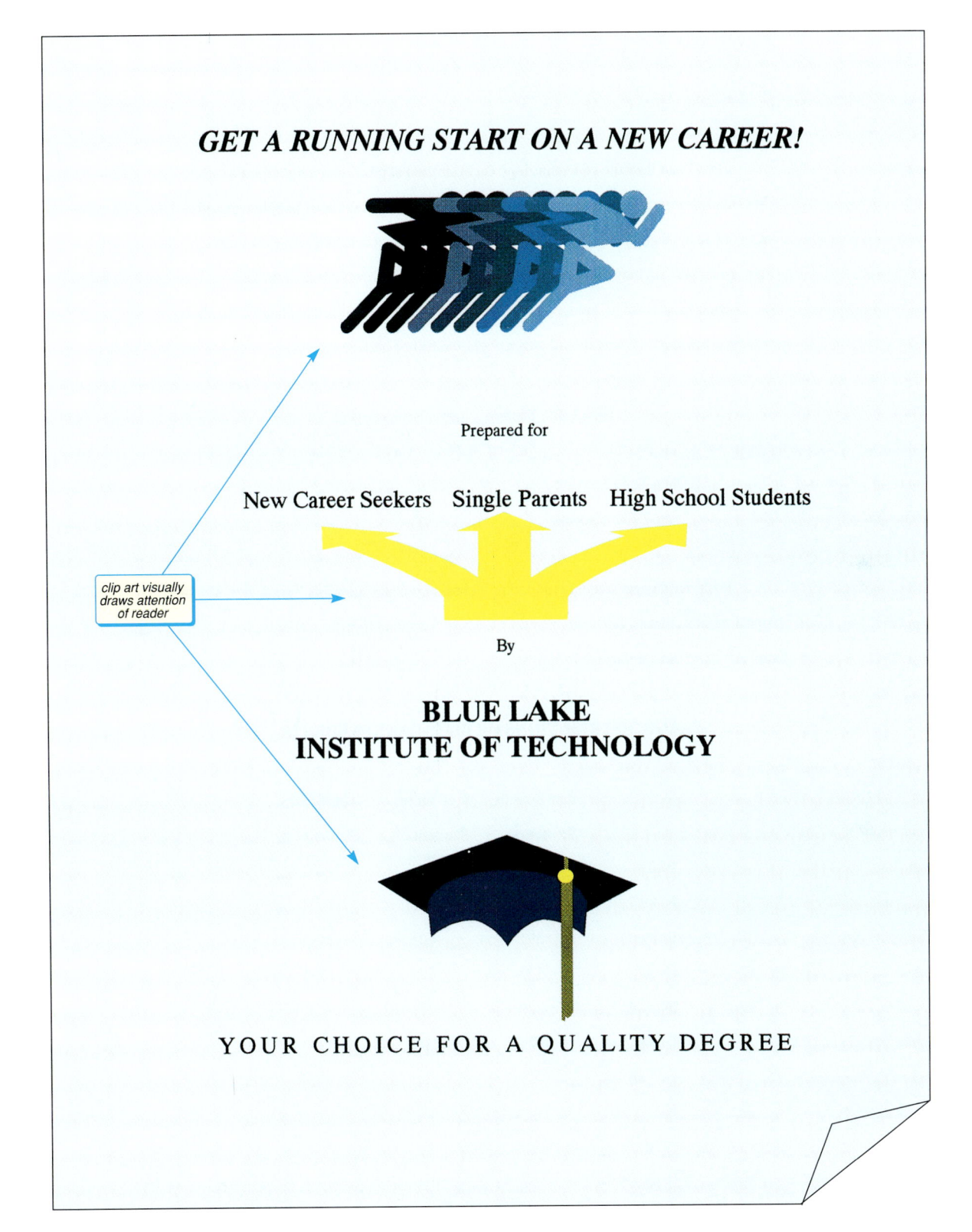

YOUR CHOICE FOR A QUALITY DEGREE

clip art visually draws attention of reader

FIGURE 3-1a

Blue Lake Institute of Technology is committed to providing a high quality education for the people of its surrounding communities. Thousands of people from all walks of life have graduated from Blue Lake and are now successfully achieving their career goals. We invite you to join our student body and realize your dreams too.

Blue Lake is small enough to give you personalized attention, yet large enough to meet your needs. Choose to attend our school on a full or part-time basis.

Blue Lake Student Status Breakdown

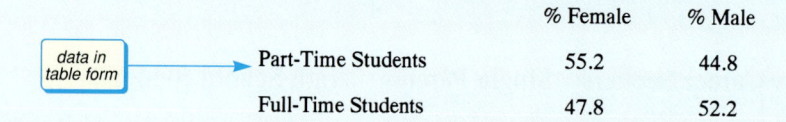

	% Female	% Male
Part-Time Students	55.2	44.8
Full-Time Students	47.8	52.2

With our diverse student population including recent high school graduates, single parents, senior citizens, housewives, new career seekers, and transfer students, you'll feel comfortable in our campus environment.

AGE DISTRIBUTIONS OF BLUE LAKE STUDENTS
(in table form)

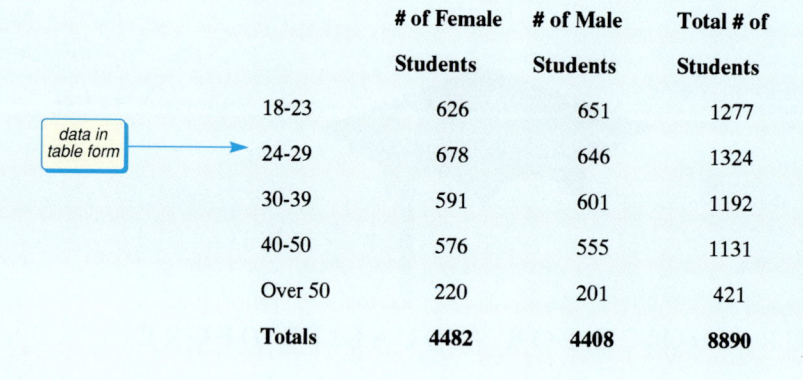

	# of Female Students	# of Male Students	Total # of Students
18-23	626	651	1277
24-29	678	646	1324
30-39	591	601	1192
40-50	576	555	1131
Over 50	220	201	421
Totals	**4482**	**4408**	**8890**

FIGURE 3-1b

AGE DISTRIBUTIONS OF BLUE LAKE STUDENTS
(in graph form)

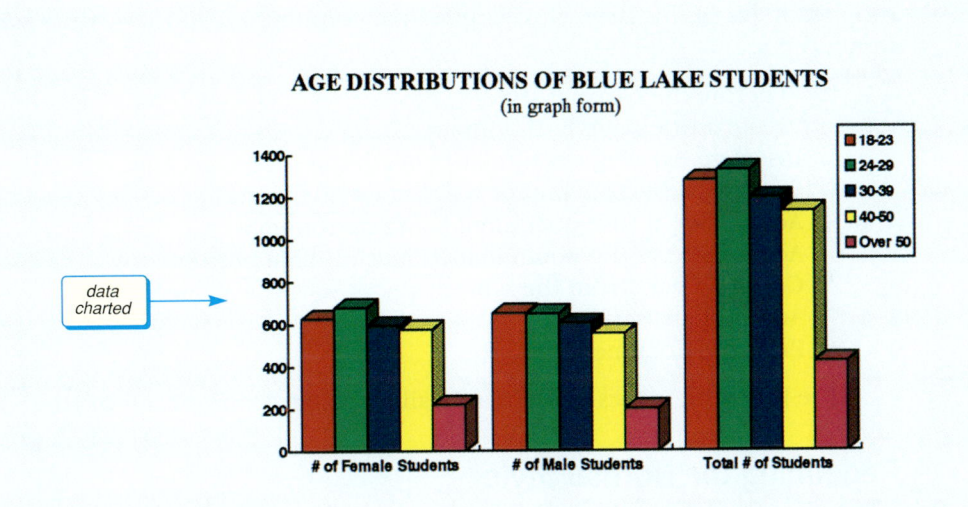

data charted

Your decision to pursue a college education and subsequently choose a college requires careful thought and planning. We at Blue Lake have attempted to address your wants and desires. We offer the following conveniences to make your experiences at Blue Lake more rewarding:

bulleted list highlights important points

- two-year degrees and four-year degrees
- adequate parking facilities
- readily available advising and counseling services
- high frequency of course offerings
- professors with practical field experience
- life experience credit
- campus clubs and school sponsored activities

Obtaining a college degree is a personal decision, which could dramatically change your life. Blue Lake Institute of Technology would like to help you make your dream a reality. Call our Department of Admissions at 555-3456 today and take advantage of our 'first class free of charge' program so you can begin to experience the benefits of earning a college degree.

PROPOSAL DESIGN BY THE JUNIOR AND SENIOR STUDENTS OF BLUE LAKE INSTITUTE OF TECHNOLOGY

FIGURE 3-1c

Document Preparation Steps

The following document preparation steps give you an overview of how the document in Figure 3-1 will be developed in this project. If you are preparing the document in this project on a personal computer, read these steps without doing them.

1. Redefine the Normal style.
2. Create a title page with clip art.
3. Insert an existing document beneath the title page.
4. Save the active document with a new filename.
5. Add a table to the document using custom tabs.
6. Add a table to the document using the Table button.
7. Create a chart from the table.
8. Add bullets to a list.
9. Print the document.

The following pages contain a detailed explanation of each of these steps.

Redefining the Normal Style

Recall from Project 2 that your desired document settings may differ from Word's default settings. In these cases, it is good practice to define your document settings and save these settings in the Normal style to ensure that your entire document follows the same style. The proposal in this project should be double-spaced with a point size of 12. Word's defaults are single-spacing with a point size of 10. Follow these steps to redefine the Normal style.

TO REDEFINE THE NORMAL STYLE

Step 1: If it is not already recessed, click the Show/Hide Nonprinting Characters button on the ribbon (see Figure 3-2).

Step 2: From the Format menu, choose the Paragraph command. Choose the Line Spacing drop-down list box arrow and select Double. Choose the OK button.

Step 3: Select the paragraph mark in the top left corner of the document window by clicking in the selection bar to the left of the paragraph mark. Choose the Points box arrow on the ribbon and select 12 (see Figure 3-2). Select the word Normal in the Style box on the ribbon by double-clicking it (see Figure 3-2). Press the ENTER key to display the dialog box and choose the Yes button. Click anywhere outside of the highlighted paragraph to remove the selection.

The Word workplace now displays as shown in Figure 3-2. The Normal style includes the display of nonprinting characters, double-spacing, and point size of 12.

CREATING A TITLE PAGE   **MSW117**

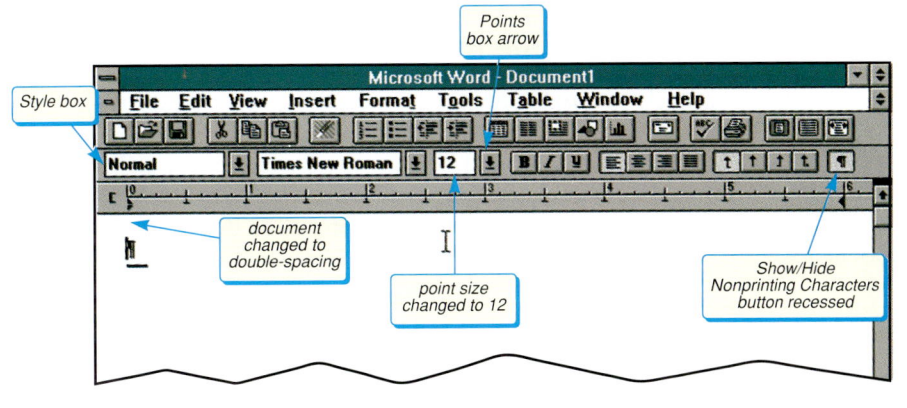

FIGURE 3-2

▶ CREATING A TITLE PAGE

A title page should be designed to catch the attention of the reader. Therefore, the title page of the proposal in Project 3 (Figure 3.1a on page MSW113) uses three graphics and a variety of fonts and point sizes. The steps on the following pages outline how to create the title page in Project 3.

Entering the First Line of the Title Page

The first step in creating the title page is to enter the top line of the title page, which is centered, italicized, and has a point size of 20 (see Figure 3-3).

TO ENTER THE FIRST LINE OF THE TITLE PAGE

Step 1: Click the Centered Text button on the ribbon.
Step 2: Type GET A RUNNING START ON A NEW CAREER and press the ENTER key twice.
Step 3: Select the paragraph containing the text typed in Step 2.
Step 4: Click the Italic button on the ribbon.
Step 5: Change the point size to 20 by clicking the Points box arrow on the ribbon and selecting point size 20.
Step 6: Click on the paragraph mark in line 3 to remove the selection from the paragraph typed in Step 2.

The title page now displays as shown in Figure 3-3.

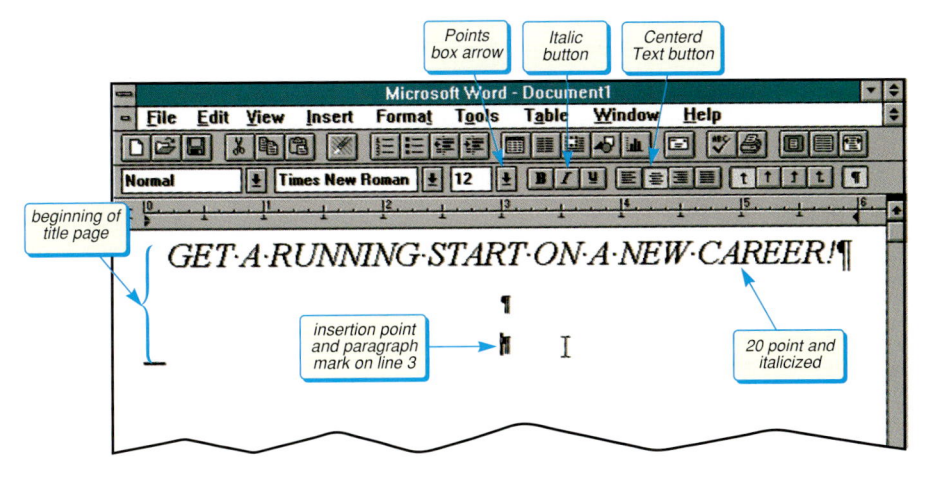

FIGURE 3-3

Importing a Graphic into the Title Page

Word for Windows software includes a series of predefined graphics called **Windows Metafiles**. You can insert, or **import**, these graphics into a Word document by choosing the Picture command from the Insert menu. **Microsoft Draw**, a drawing software package included with Word for Windows, allows you to design your own graphics and import them into your document. Word also supports a variety of graphic formats from other applications, such as PC Paintbrush.

In Project 3, you will import graphics contained in the Windows Metafiles. The first graphic on the title page is a picture of runner in motion. Follow these steps to import the Windows Metafile called running.wmf into your document (see Figure 3-10 on page MSW120). Windows Metafiles have an extension of .wmf.

TO IMPORT A GRAPHIC ▼

STEP 1 ▶

Position the insertion point where you want the graphic to be inserted.

The insertion point is centered on line 3 of the title page.

STEP 2 ▶

Select the Insert menu and point to the Picture command (Figure 3-4).

FIGURE 3-4

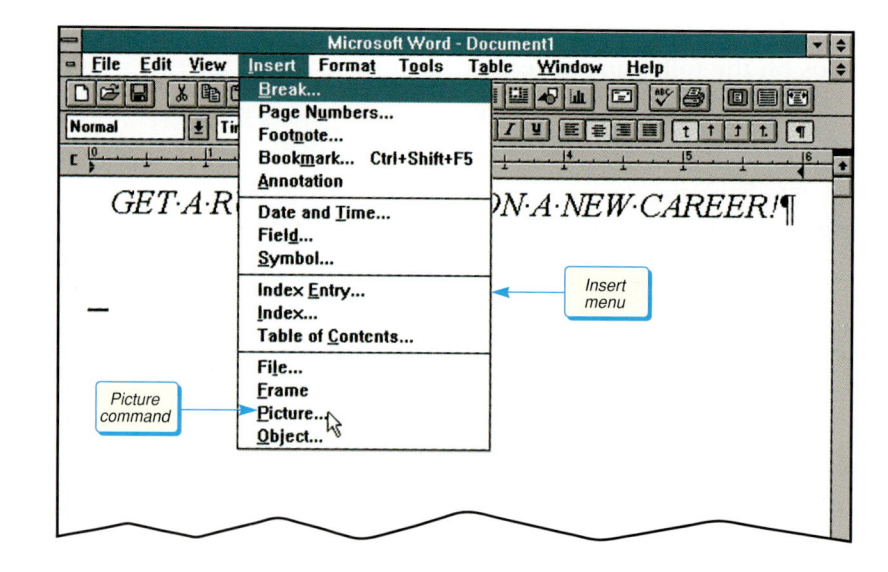

STEP 3 ▶

Choose the Picture command. Point to the subdirectory called Clipart.

Word displays the Picture dialog box (Figure 3-5). The current directory is winword on drive C. The Windows Metafiles are located in the subdirectory called clipart.

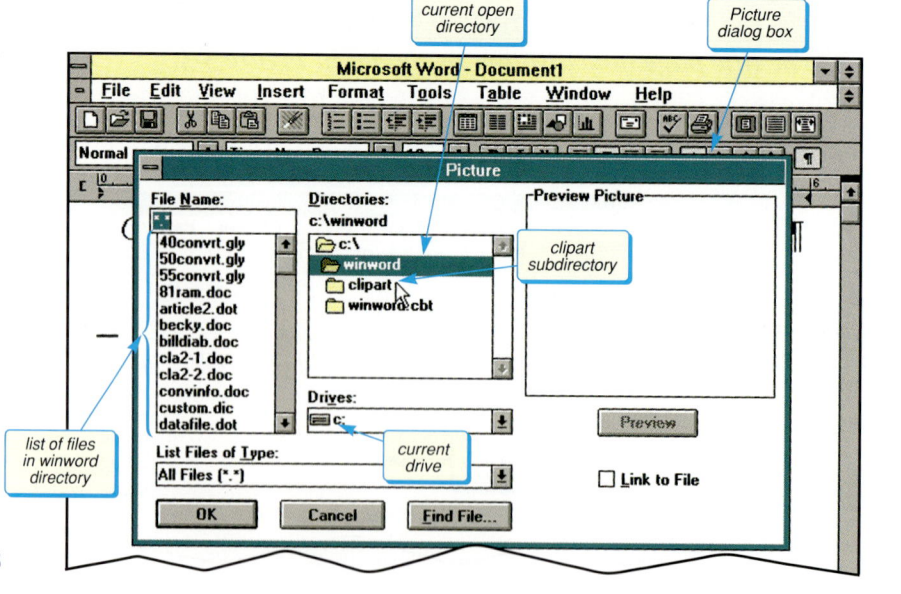

FIGURE 3-5

CREATING A TITLE PAGE   **MSW119**

STEP 4 ▶

Open the subdirectory by double-clicking it. Point to the down scroll arrow on the File Name scroll bar.

Word displays the Windows Metafiles in the File Name list box (Figure 3-6). The file running.wmf is not in view in the File Name list box.

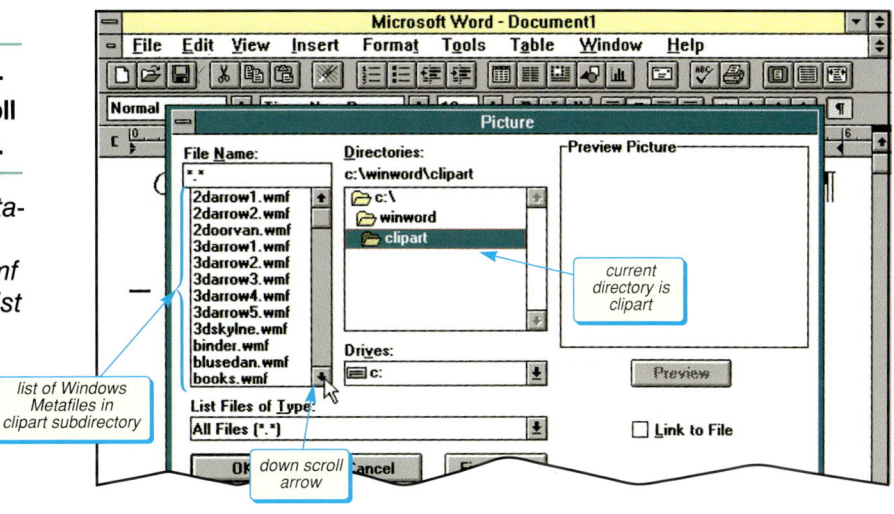

FIGURE 3-6

STEP 5 ▶

Hold down the left mouse button until the file running.wmf appears in the File Name list box. Point to the file running.wmf (Figure 3-7).

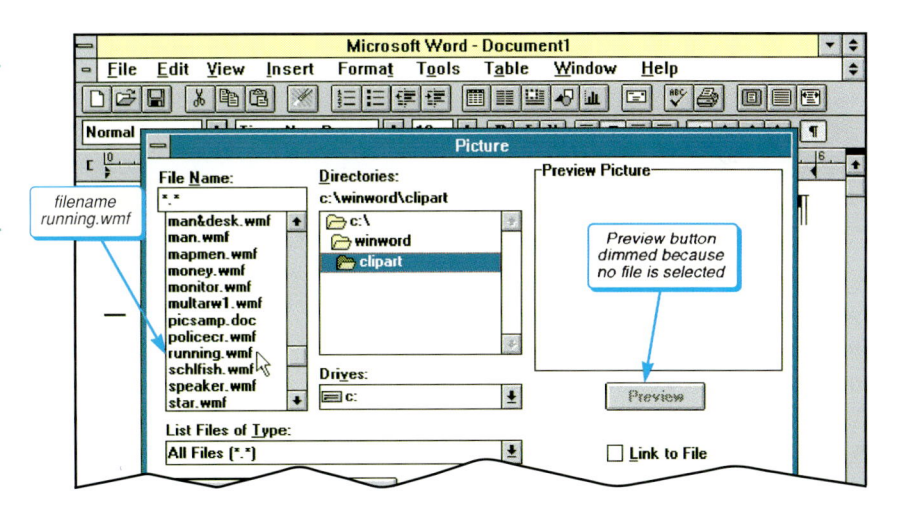

FIGURE 3-7

STEP 6 ▶

Select the file running.wmf by clicking it.

Word highlights the filename and places it in the File Name text box (Figure 3-8). The Preview button (Preview) is now available so you can view the Windows Metafile prior to inserting it into the document.

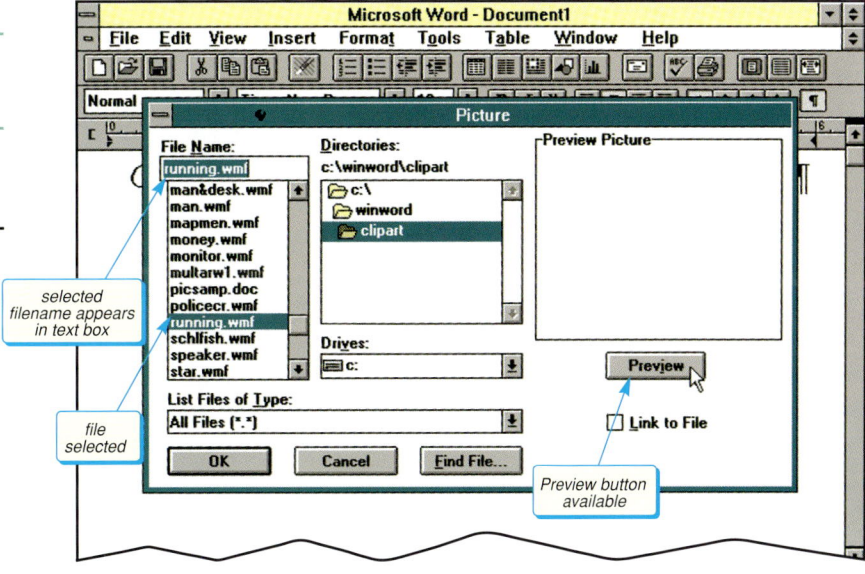

FIGURE 3-8

STEP 7 ▶

Choose the Preview button.

Word displays a preview of running.wmf, the selected Windows Metafile, in the Preview Picture area (Figure 3-9).

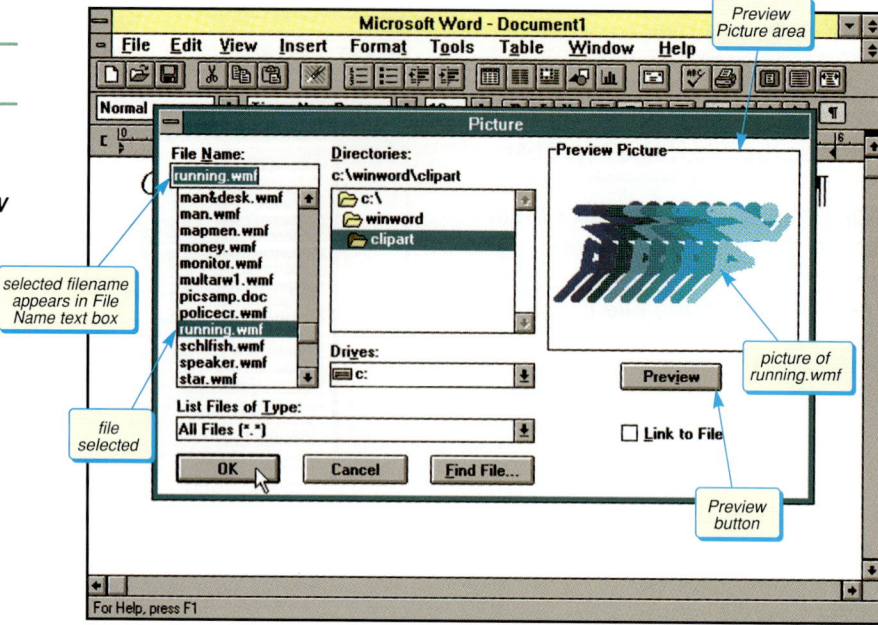

FIGURE 3-9

STEP 8 ▶

Choose the OK button.

Word inserts the graphic into your document at the location of the insertion point (Figure 3-10). The insertion point size changes to reflect the size of the graphic.

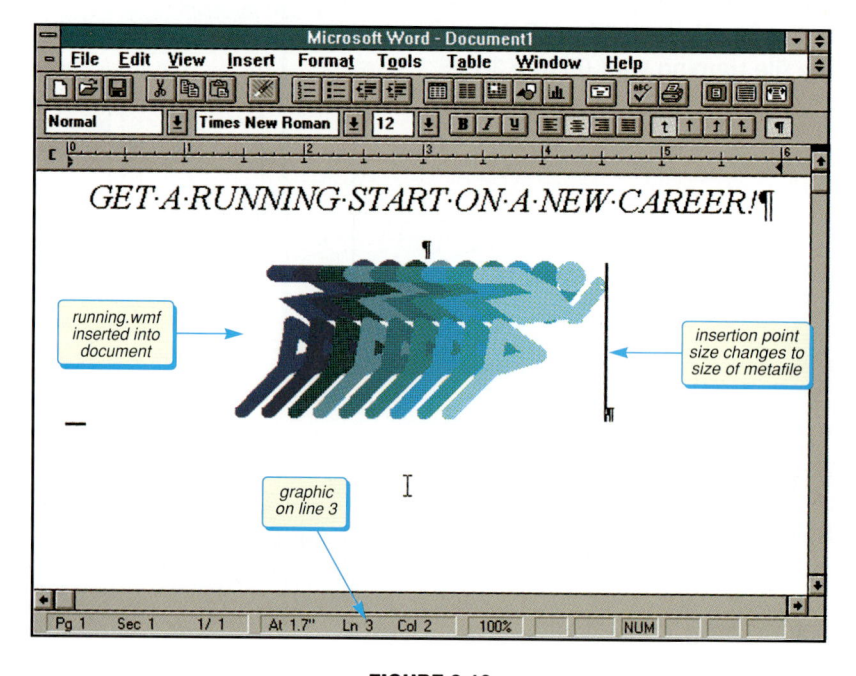

FIGURE 3-10

The graphic in the document is part of a paragraph. Therefore, you can use any of the paragraph alignment buttons on the ribbon to reposition the graphic.

Entering the Next Lines of Text on the Title Page

The next step in Project 3 is to enter the two lines of text between the first and second graphics. The steps to accomplish this are summarized below.

TO ENTER THE NEXT LINES OF TEXT

Step 1: Press the ENTER key twice.
Step 2: Type Prepared for and press the ENTER key twice.
Step 3: Type New Career Seekers and press the TAB key. Type Single Parents and press the TAB key. Type High School Students and press the ENTER key.
Step 4: Select the paragraph typed in Step 3 by clicking in the selection bar to the left of the text.
Step 5: Change the point size of the selected text to 16 by clicking the Points box arrow on the ribbon and selecting 16.
Step 6: Click the paragraph mark in line 8 to remove the selection.

The title page now displays as shown in Figure 3-11.

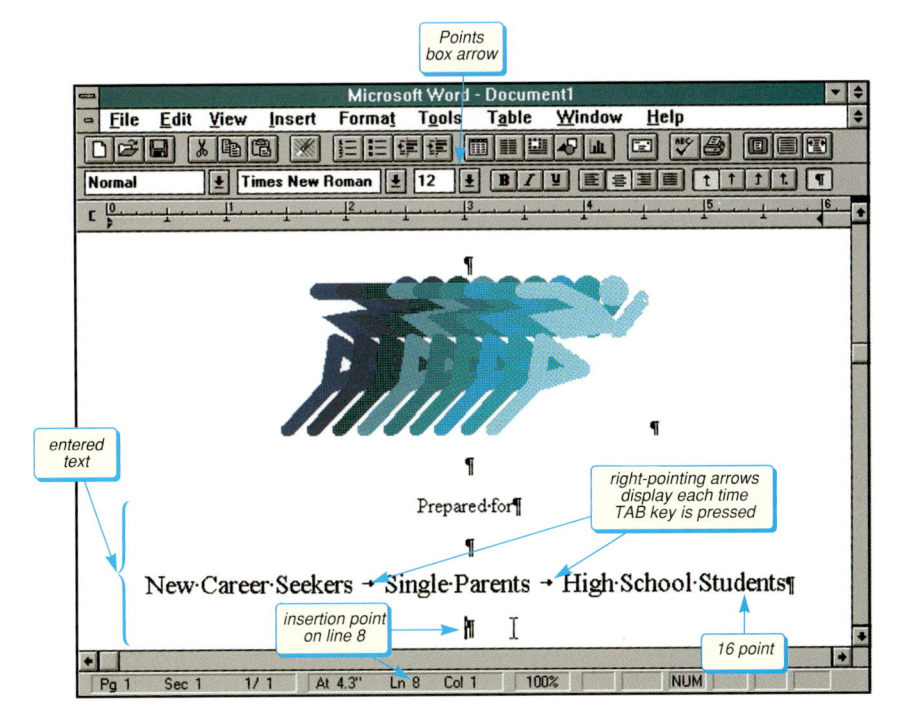

FIGURE 3-11

Importing the Next Graphic

The next step is to import the three-way arrow into the document (see Figure 3-13 on the next page).

TO IMPORT THE NEXT GRAPHIC

STEP 1

Position the insertion point where you want the graphic inserted. From the Insert menu, choose the Picture command. Hold down the left mouse button on the down scroll arrow on the File Name scroll bar until the filename multarw1.wmf appears in the File Name list box.

STEP 2 ▶

Select the file multarw1.wmf by clicking it. Then click the Preview button.

Word displays the selected graphic, multarw1.wmf, in the Preview Picture area (Figure 3-12).

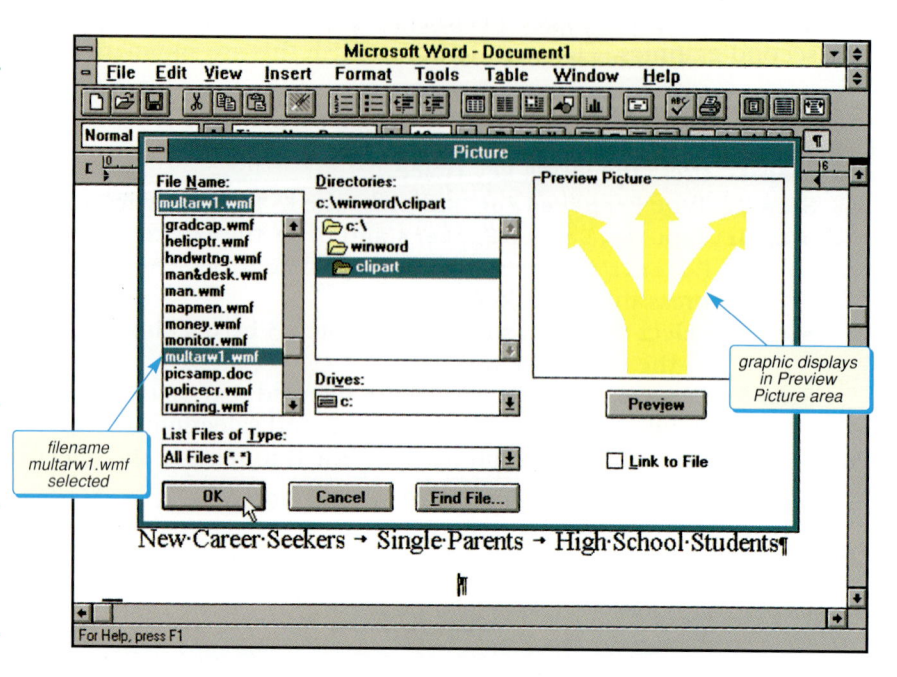

FIGURE 3-12

STEP 3 ▶

Choose the OK button.

Word inserts the graphic into your document (Figure 3-13).

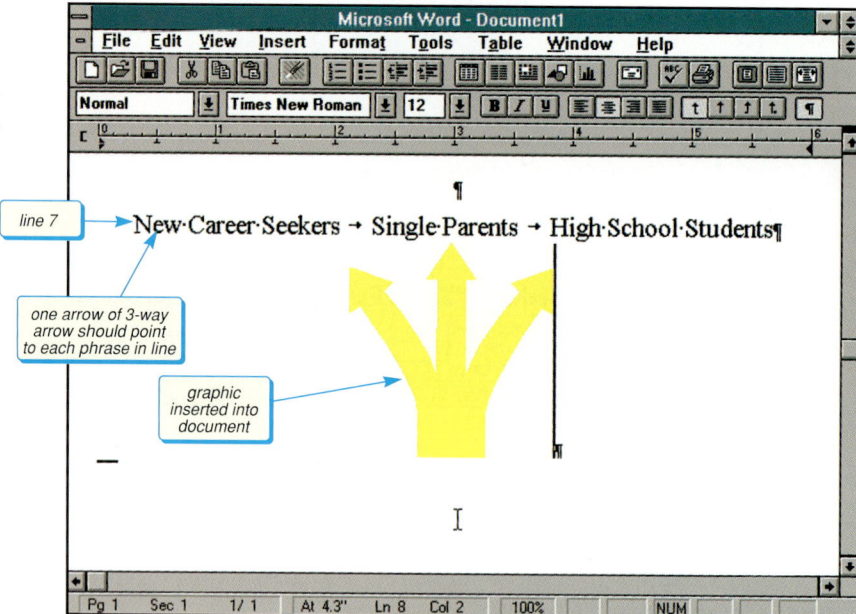

FIGURE 3-13

CREATING A TITLE PAGE   **MSW123**

Compare the graphic in Figure 3-13 to the one in Figure 3-1a on page MSW113. Notice the one in Figure 3-1a is wider and flatter, so each arrow points to a different phrase on line 7. The next step is to resize the imported graphic.

Scaling an Imported Graphic

Once a graphic has been imported into a document, you can easily change its size, or **scale** it. Scaling includes both enlarging and reducing the size of a graphic. To scale a graphic, you must first select it. The following steps show how to select and scale the yellow three-way arrow just imported into the title page (see Figure 3-18 on the next page).

TO SCALE A GRAPHIC ▼

STEP 1 ▶

Click anywhere in the yellow three-way arrow graphic.

*Word selects the graphic (Figure 3-14). Selected graphics display surrounded by a box with small black squares, called **sizing handles**, at each corner and center locations.*

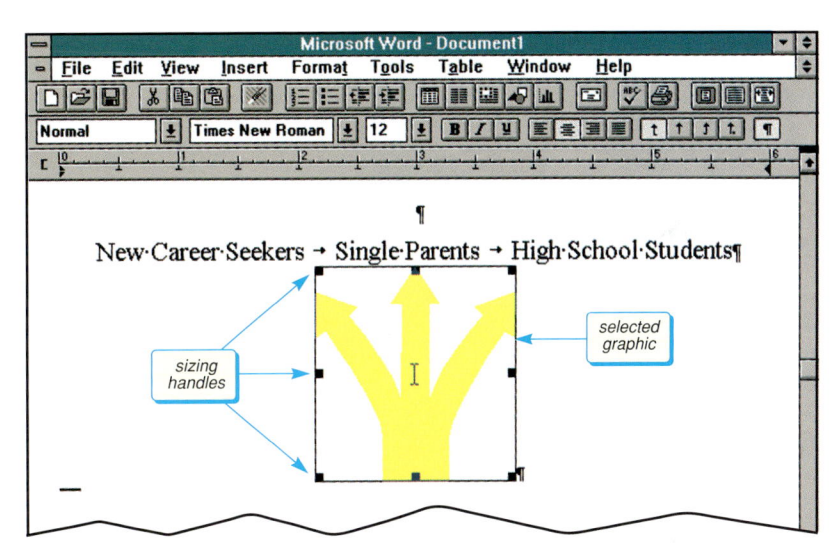

FIGURE 3-14

STEP 2 ▶

Select the Format menu and point to the Picture command (Figure 3-15).

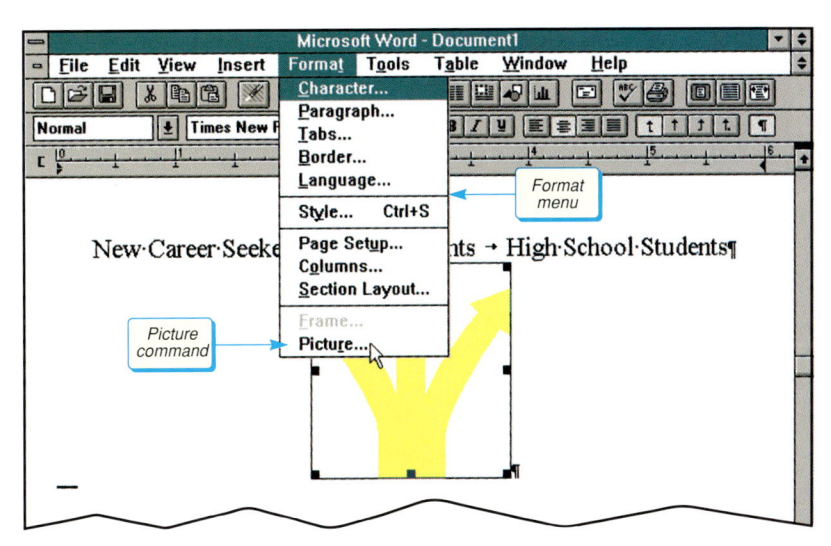

FIGURE 3-15

STEP 3 ▶

Choose the Picture command.

Word displays the Picture dialog box.

STEP 4 ▶

Double-click in the Width text box in the Size area.

Word selects the current width of 1.73" (Figure 3-16).

FIGURE 3-16

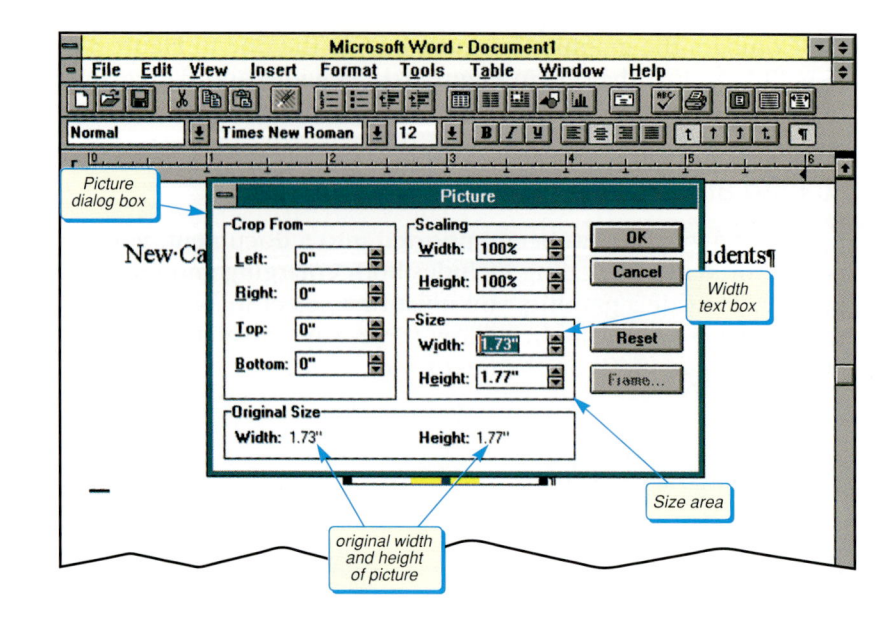

STEP 5 ▶

Type 3.5 (new width) and press the TAB key. Type 1 (new height) and point to the OK button.

The width and height have been changed to 3.5" and 1", respectively (Figure 3-17).

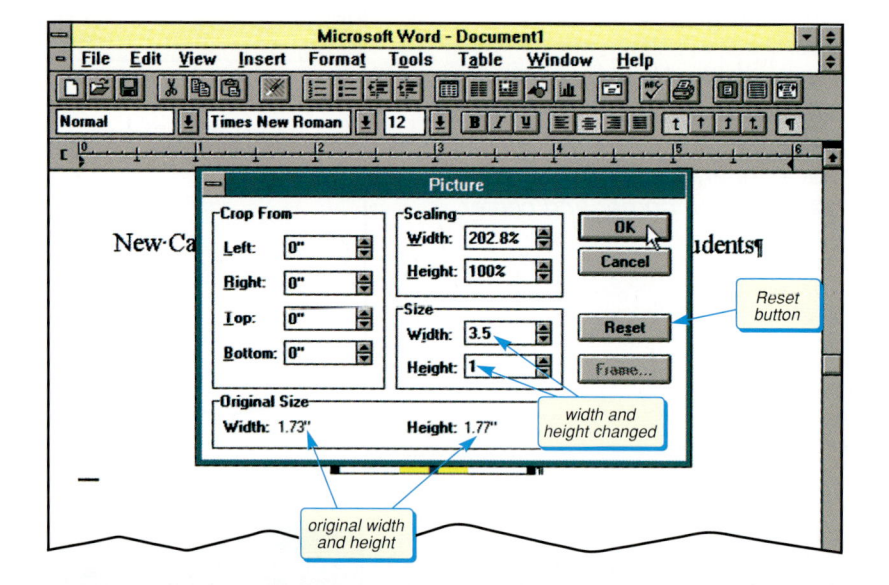

FIGURE 3-17

STEP 6 ▶

Choose the OK button in the Picture dialog box. Click to the right of the graphic to remove the selection.

Word resizes the graphic in the document (Figure 3-18).

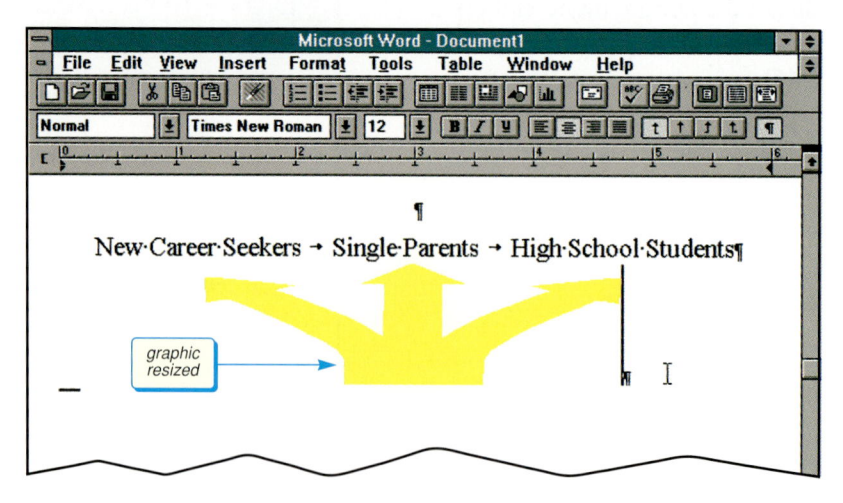

FIGURE 3-18

Rather than scaling a graphic with the Picture command, you can also use the mouse to drag the sizing handles on the selected graphic. If you have a precise measurement for the graphic, use the Picture command; otherwise, drag the sizing handles until the graphic appears the right size to you.

Restoring a Scaled Graphic to its Original Size

Sometimes you scale a graphic and realize it is the wrong size. In these cases, you might want to return the graphic to its original size and start over. To return a scaled graphic to its original size, select the graphic and choose the Picture command from the Format menu. Then choose the Reset button in the Picture dialog box (see Figure 3-17). Finally, choose the OK button in the Picture dialog box.

Entering the Next Lines of Text on the Title Page

The next step in Project 3 is to enter the two lines of text between the second and third graphics. The following steps explain how to accomplish this.

TO ENTER THE NEXT LINES OF TEXT

Step 1: Press the ENTER key. Type By and press the ENTER key twice.
Step 2: Type BLUE LAKE and press the ENTER key.
Step 3: Type INSTITUTE OF TECHNOLOGY and press the ENTER key twice.
Step 4: Select the paragraphs typed in Steps 2 and 3 by dragging the mouse in the selection bar to the left of the text.
Step 5: Click the Bold button on the ribbon.
Step 6: Change the point size of the selected text to 20 by clicking the Points box arrow on the ribbon and selecting 20.
Step 7: Click the paragraph mark in line 14 to remove the selection.

The title page now displays as shown in Figure 3-19.

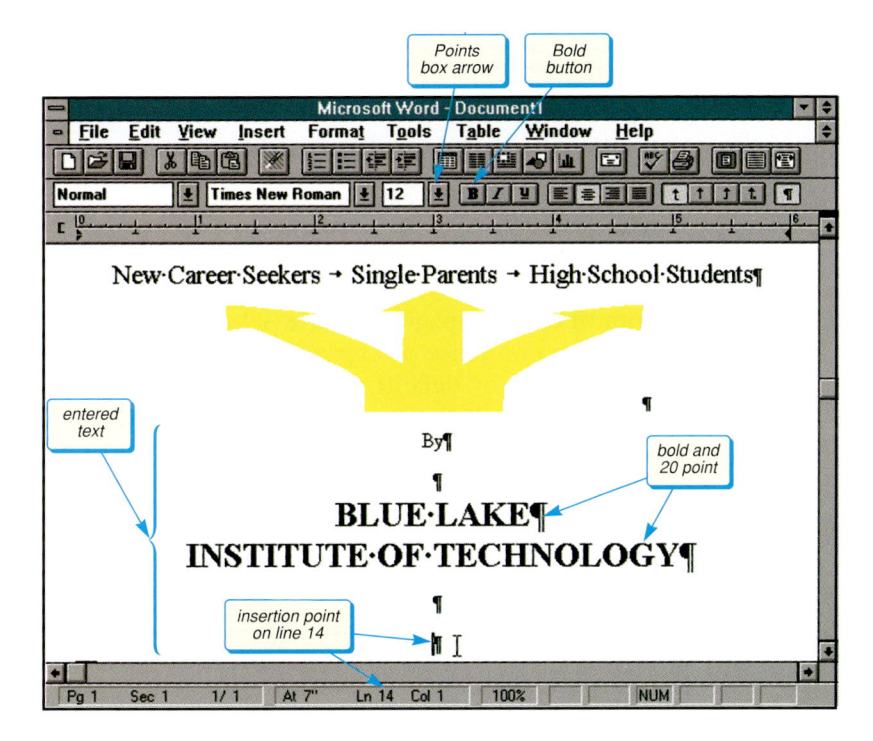

FIGURE 3-19

Importing the Final Graphic

The next step is to import the graduation cap into the document (see Figure 3-20). Follow these steps to import the graphic.

TO IMPORT A GRADUATION CAP INTO THE DOCUMENT

Step 1: From the Insert menu, choose the Picture command.
Step 2: In the Picture dialog box, hold down the left mouse button on the down scroll arrow on the File Name scroll bar until the filename gradcap.wmf appears in the File Name text box.
Step 3: Select the file gradcap.wmf by clicking it.
Step 4: Click the Preview button to view the graduation cap.
Step 5: Choose the OK button.

Word inserts the graduation cap into the document as shown in Figure 3-20.

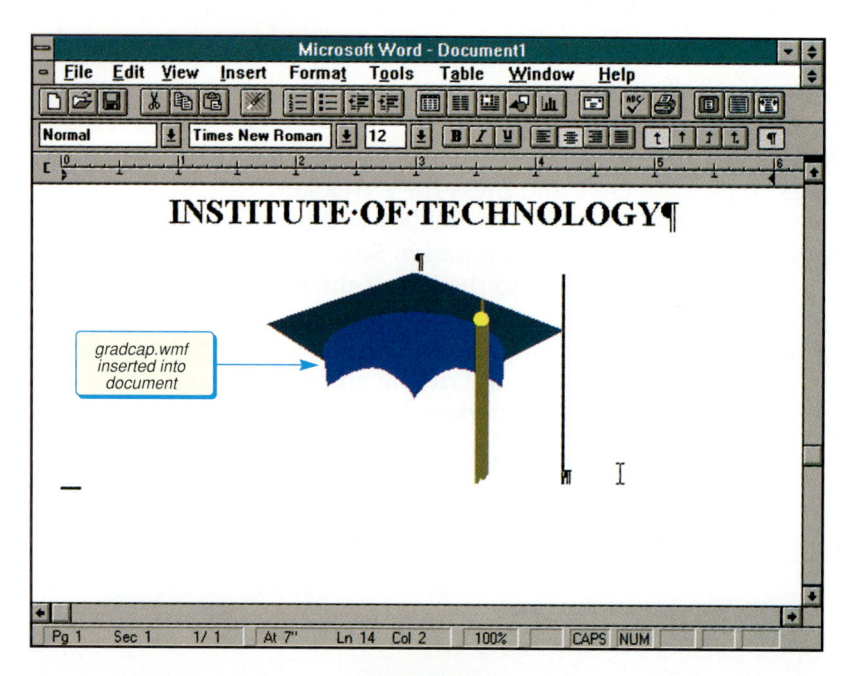

FIGURE 3-20

Changing the Space Between Characters

The text at the bottom of the title page in Figure 3-1a on page MSW113 is expanded. With Word, you can condense or expand the spacing between characters to create special effects. Word, by default, condenses the space between characters by 1.75 points and expands the space between characters by 3 points. Follow the steps on the next two pages to enter the final line of text on the title page and expand the space between characters (see Figure 3-24).

CREATING A TITLE PAGE   **MSW127**

TO CHANGE THE SPACE BETWEEN CHARACTERS ▼

STEP 1 ▶

Press the ENTER key. Type YOUR CHOICE FOR A QUALITY DEGREE and press the ENTER key. Select the text typed in Step 1 by clicking in the selection bar to the left of the text.

STEP 2 ▶

Change the point size of the selected text to 16 by clicking the Points box arrow on the ribbon and selecting 16. Select the Format menu and point to the Character command (Figure 3-21).

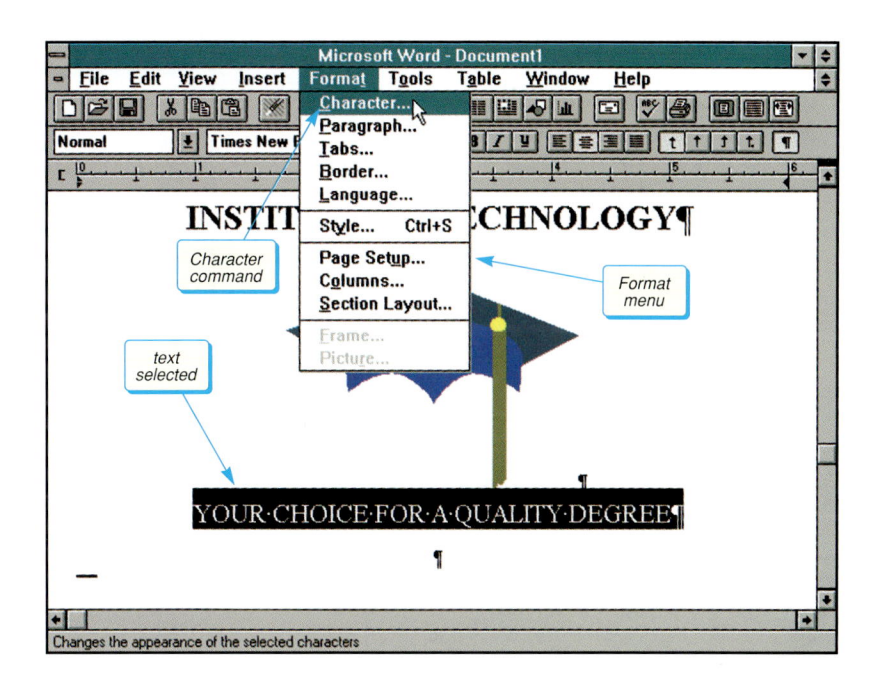

FIGURE 3-21

STEP 3 ▶

Choose the Character command.

Word displays the Character dialog box.

STEP 4 ▶

Choose the Spacing box arrow by clicking it and point to Expanded.

A drop-down list of available spacing options displays (Figure 3-22).

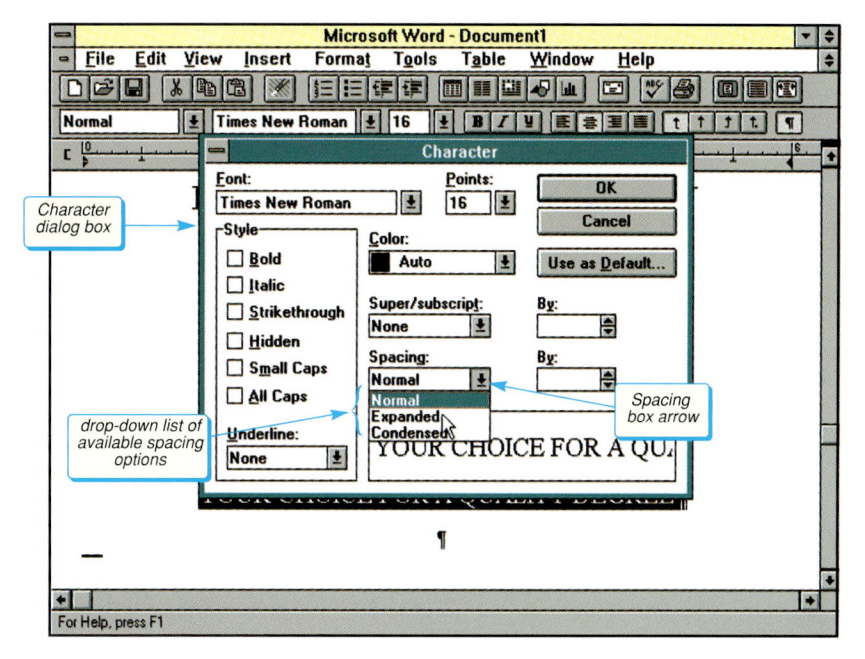

FIGURE 3-22

STEP 5 ▶

Select Expanded by clicking it. Point to the OK button.

Expanded becomes the selected spacing (Figure 3-23). The Sample area displays the selected text in expanded print.

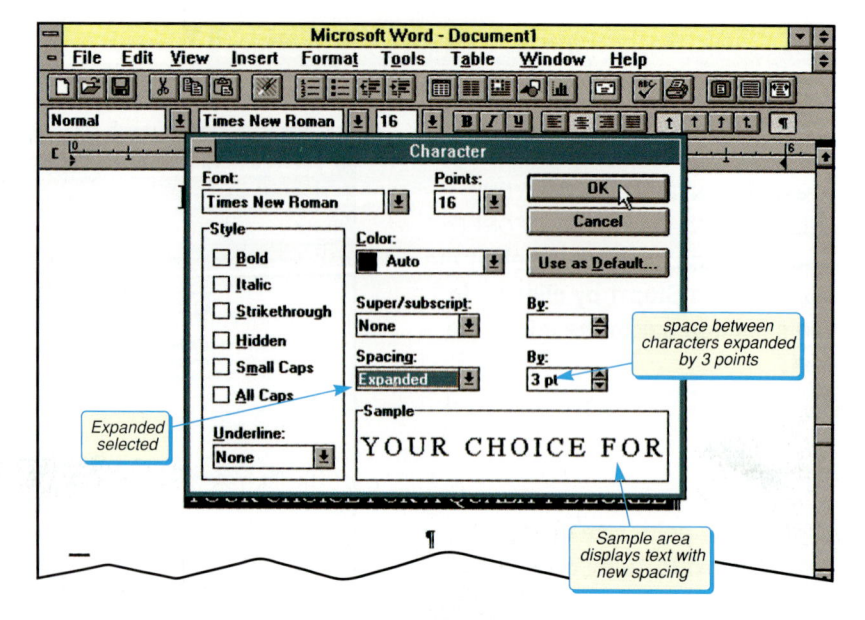

FIGURE 3-23

STEP 6 ▶

Choose the OK button. Click the paragraph mark in line 16 to remove the highlight.

Word expands the selected text and returns you to the document (Figure 3-24).

FIGURE 3-24

Saving the Title Page

Because you have finished the title page, you should save it by performing the following steps.

TO SAVE A DOCUMENT

Step 1: Insert the data diskette into drive A. Click the Save button on the Toolbar.
Step 2: Type the filename, `proj3ttl`, in the File Name text box. Do not press the ENTER key.
Step 3: Click the Drives drop-down list box and select drive A.
Step 4: Choose the OK button in the Save As dialog box.
Step 5: If you desire, enter information in the Summary Info dialog box.
Step 6: Choose the OK button in the Summary Info dialog box.

The title page for the proposal is now complete. The next step is to insert a draft of the proposal beneath the title page.

▶ INSERTING AN EXISTING DOCUMENT INTO AN OPEN DOCUMENT

Assume you have already prepared a draft of the body of the proposal and saved it with the filename PROJ3PRO. You would like the draft to display on a separate page beneath the title page. Once the two documents appear on the screen together as one document, you would like to save this active document with a new name so each of the original documents remains intact.

Inserting a Hard Page Break

The draft should appear on a separate page beneath the title page. Thus, you must insert a hard page break beneath the title page (see Figure 3-25). Use the following steps to insert the hard page break.

TO INSERT A HARD PAGE BREAK

Step 1: Position the insertion point on line 16.
Step 2: From the Insert menu, choose the Break command.
Step 3: Choose the OK button.

Word inserts a hard page break immediately before the insertion point and positions the insertion point immediately below the hard page break as shown in Figure 3-25.

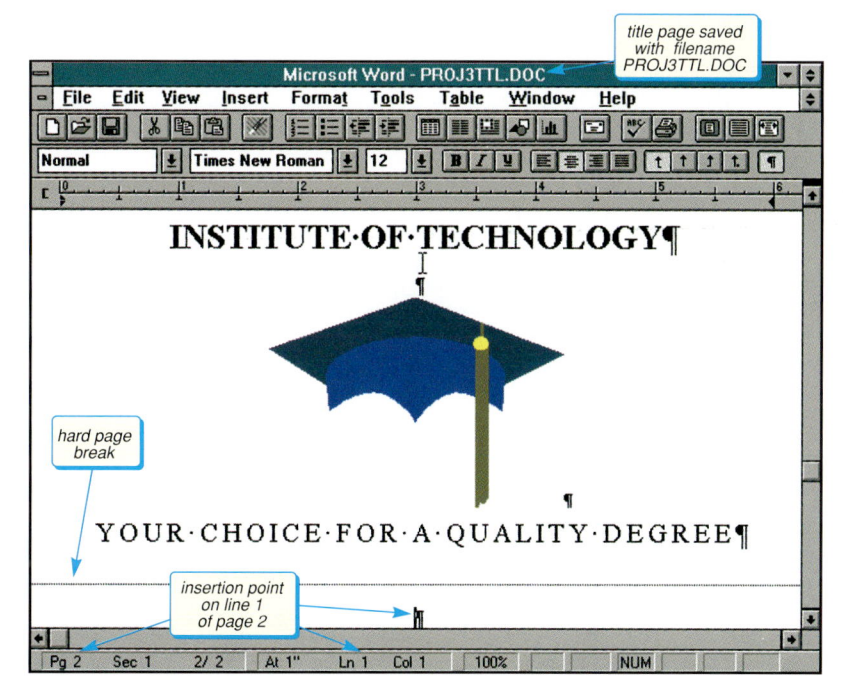

FIGURE 3-25

MSW130   PROJECT 3   CREATING A PROPOSAL USING TABLES AND GRAPHICS

Inserting a Second Document into an Open Document

The next step is to insert the draft of the proposal beneath the hard page break. If you created the draft at an earlier time, you may have forgotten its name. Thus, you can display the contents of, or **preview**, any file before inserting it. Follow these steps to insert the draft of the proposal into the open document.

TO INSERT A SECOND DOCUMENT INTO AN OPEN DOCUMENT ▼

STEP 1 ▶

Insert into drive A the Student Diskette that accompanies this book. Be sure the insertion point is positioned on the paragraph mark immediately below the hard page break. Select the Insert menu and point to the File command (Figure 3-26).

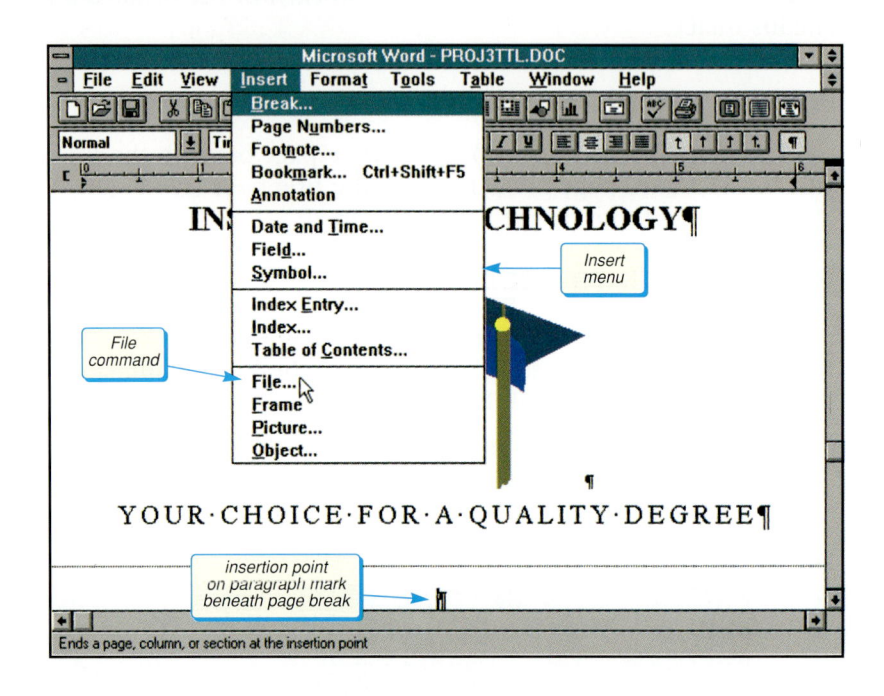

FIGURE 3-26

STEP 2 ▶

Choose the File command. Click the Drives drop-down list box and select a:. Double-click the WORD subdirectory in the Directories list box.

Word displays the File dialog box (Figure 3-27). A list of available files in the WORD subdirectory on drive A displays in the File Name list box.

STEP 3 ▶

Point to the Find File button (Find File...) as shown in Figure 3-27.

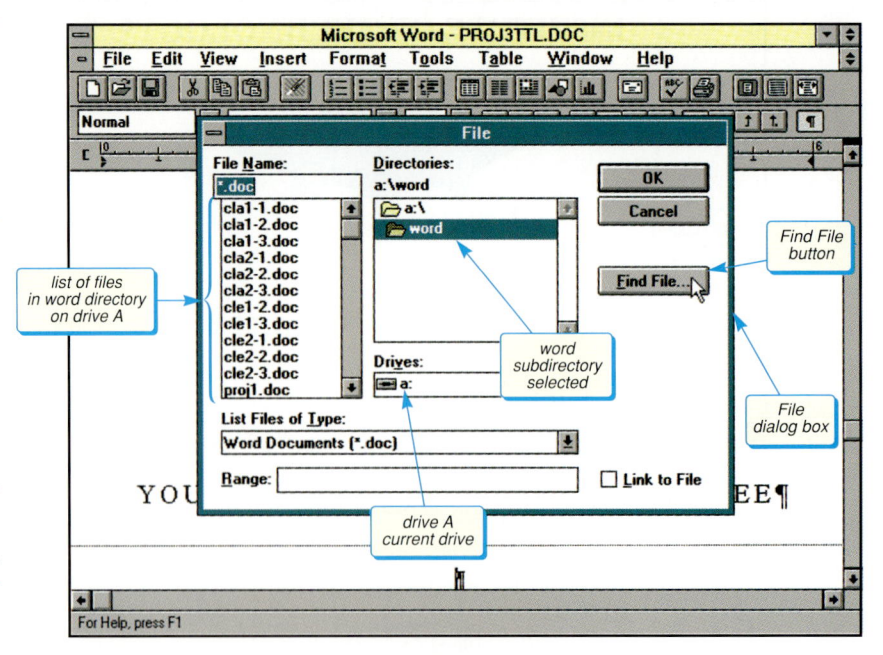

FIGURE 3-27

INSERTING AN EXISTING DOCUMENT INTO AN OPEN DOCUMENT   **MSW131**

STEP 4 ▶

Choose the Find File button.

Word displays the Find File dialog box (Figure 3-28). A list of files on the default drive displays in the File Name list box. The first file in the File Name list box is highlighted and its contents display in the Content area. (If your screen does not display file contents, choose the Options button in the Find File dialog box. Then select the Content Option and choose the OK button in the Options dialog box.)

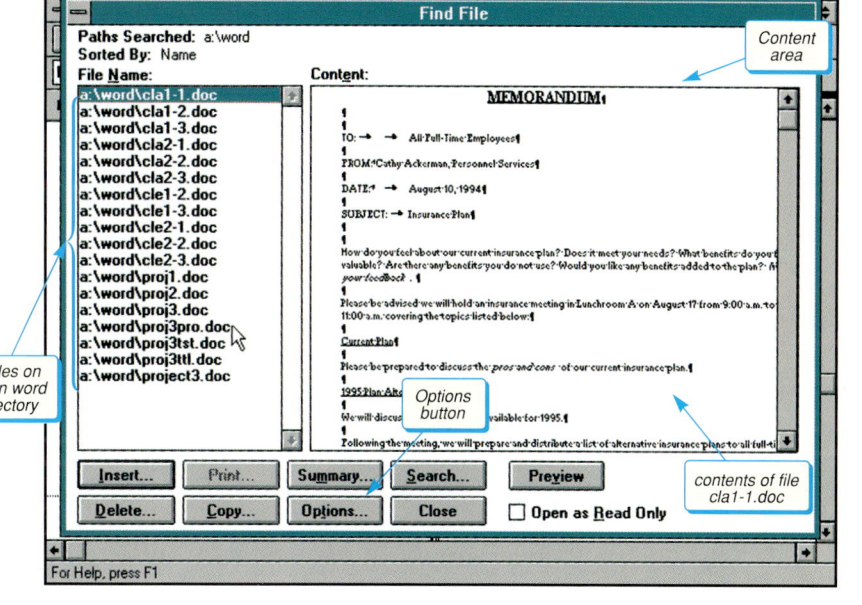

FIGURE 3-28

STEP 5 ▶

Select the filename PROJ3PRO by pointing to a:\word\proj3pro.doc and clicking it. Point to the Insert button (Insert).

Word displays the contents of PROJ3PRO in the Content area (Figure 3-29).

STEP 6 ▶

Choose the Insert button.

Word returns you to the File dialog box.

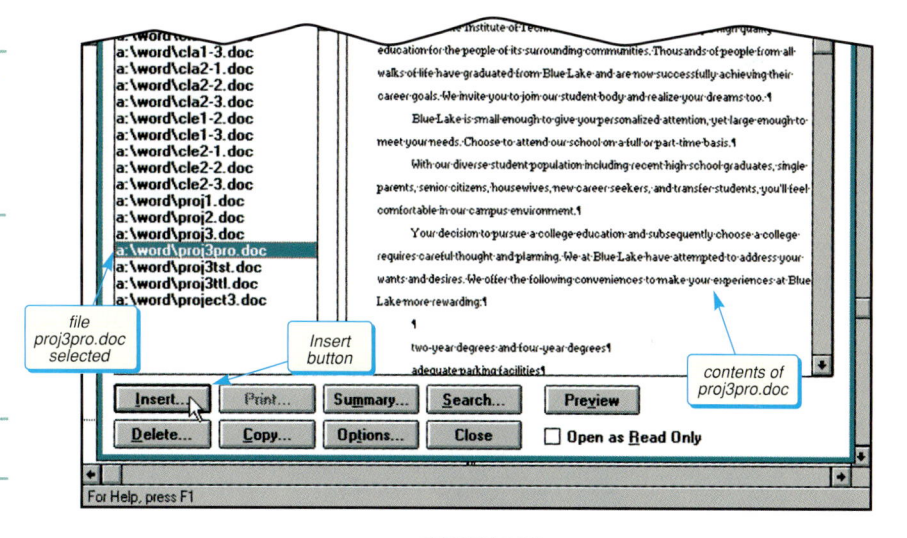

FIGURE 3-29

STEP 7 ▶

Choose the OK button in the File dialog box. Repeatedly click above the scroll box on the vertical scroll bar or click the up arrow on the scroll bar to bring the top of the inserted document into view.

Word inserts the file PROJ3PRO into the open document above the insertion point (Figure 3-30).

FIGURE 3-30

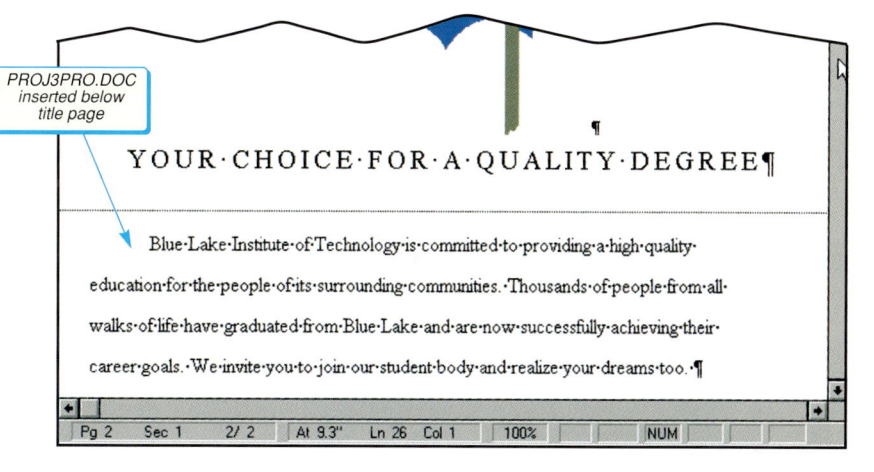

Word inserts the complete document immediately above the insertion point and positions the insertion point beneath the inserted document. If the insertion point is positioned in the middle of the first document, the first document continues after the end of the inserted document.

Previewing files before opening them is very useful if you have forgotten the name of a particular file. For this reason, you can choose the Find File command directly from the File menu. Once chosen, the Find File dialog box displays as shown in Figure 3-28 on the previous page. The only difference is the Insert button is an Open button. Thus, you can open a file directly from the Find File command on the File menu, rather than using the File command on the Insert menu.

Saving The Active Document with a New Filename

The current filename in the title bar is PROJ3TTL.DOC, yet the active document contains both the title page and the draft of the proposal. Because you might want to keep the title page as a separate document called PROJ3TTL, you should save the active document with a new file name. If you save the active document by clicking the Save button on the Toolbar, Word will assign it the current filename. Thus, use the following steps to save the active document with a new filename.

TO SAVE AN ACTIVE DOCUMENT WITH A NEW FILENAME ▼

STEP 1 ▶

Insert the data disk into drive A. Select the File menu and point to the Save As command (Figure 3-31).

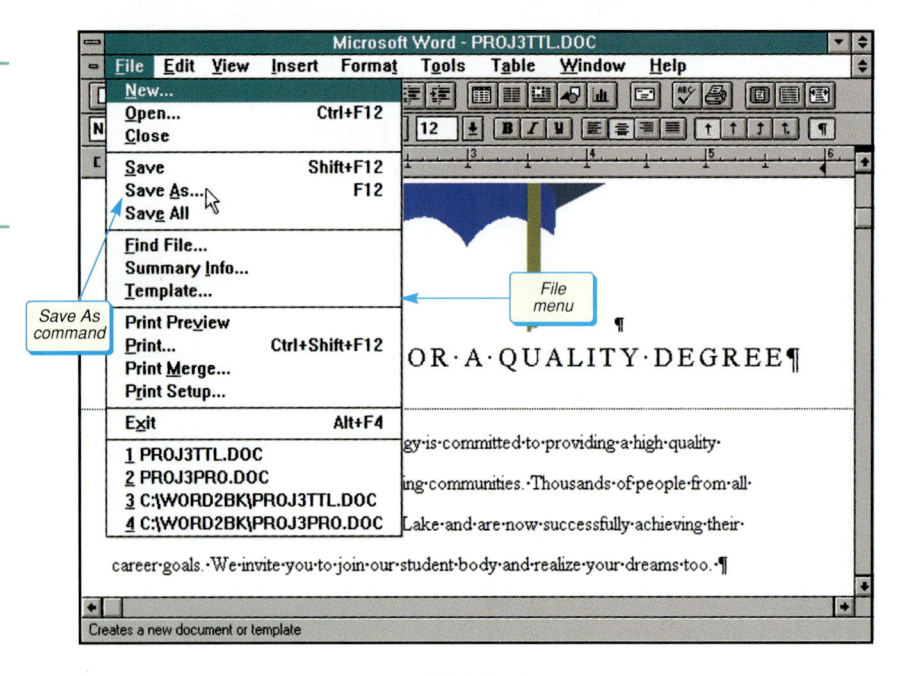

FIGURE 3-31

STEP 2 ▶

Choose the Save As command. Type the filename, `proj3`, in the File Name text box. Do not press the ENTER key after typing the filename. If drive A is not the current drive, select it by clicking the Drives drop-down box arrow and selecting a:.

Word displays the Save As dialog box with drive A selected and the filename proj3 entered in the File Name text box (Figure 3-32).

STEP 3

Choose the OK button in the Save As dialog box.

Word saves the document with a filename of PROJ3.DOC.

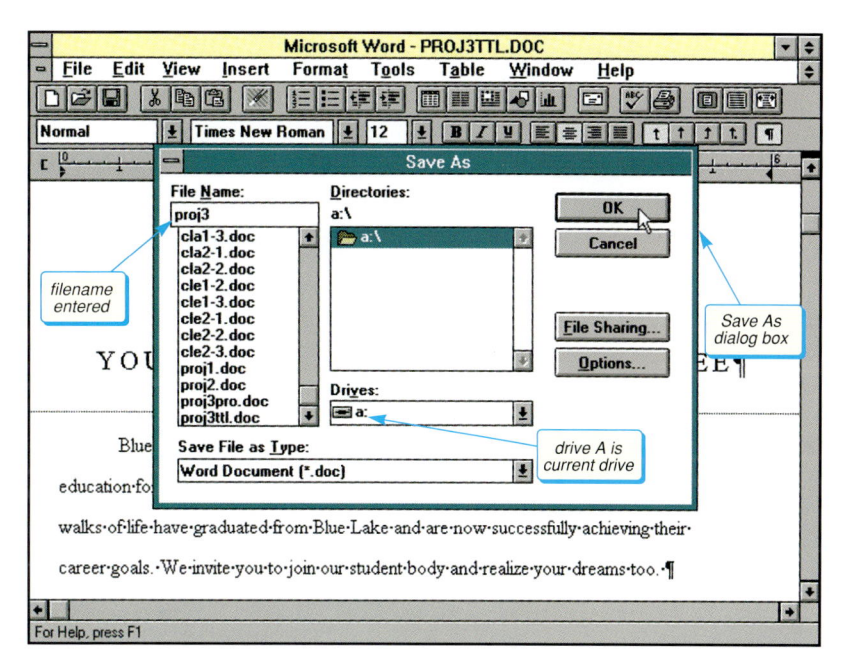

FIGURE 3-32

Printing the Document

To see a hard copy of the newly formed file PROJ3, perform the following steps:

TO PRINT THE DOCUMENT

Step 1: Ready the printer.
Step 2: Click the Print button on the Toolbar.

When you remove the document from the printer, review it carefully (Figure 3-33 on the next page).

To make the body of the proposal more pleasing to the eye, you could add one or two tables, a graph, and a bulleted list. These enhancements to Project 3 are discussed in the following pages.

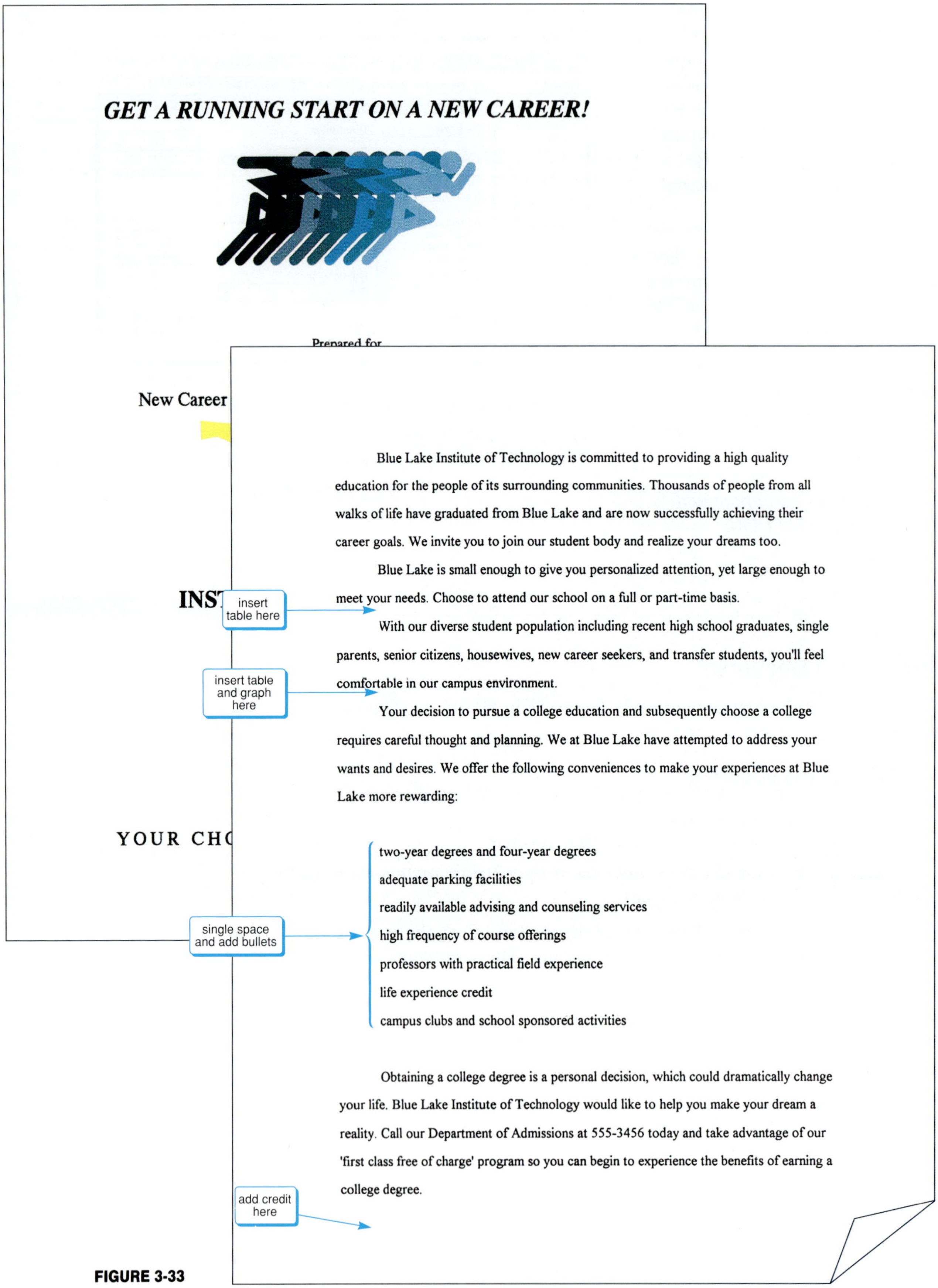

MSW134   PROJECT 3   CREATING A PROPOSAL USING TABLES AND GRAPHICS

GET A RUNNING START ON A NEW CAREER!

Prepared for

New Career

Blue Lake Institute of Technology is committed to providing a high quality education for the people of its surrounding communities. Thousands of people from all walks of life have graduated from Blue Lake and are now successfully achieving their career goals. We invite you to join our student body and realize your dreams too.

Blue Lake is small enough to give you personalized attention, yet large enough to meet your needs. Choose to attend our school on a full or part-time basis.

INS*[insert table here]*

With our diverse student population including recent high school graduates, single parents, senior citizens, housewives, new career seekers, and transfer students, you'll feel comfortable in our campus environment.

[insert table and graph here]

Your decision to pursue a college education and subsequently choose a college requires careful thought and planning. We at Blue Lake have attempted to address your wants and desires. We offer the following conveniences to make your experiences at Blue Lake more rewarding:

YOUR CHO

[single space and add bullets]

- two-year degrees and four-year degrees
- adequate parking facilities
- readily available advising and counseling services
- high frequency of course offerings
- professors with practical field experience
- life experience credit
- campus clubs and school sponsored activities

Obtaining a college degree is a personal decision, which could dramatically change your life. Blue Lake Institute of Technology would like to help you make your dream a reality. Call our Department of Admissions at 555-3456 today and take advantage of our 'first class free of charge' program so you can begin to experience the benefits of earning a college degree.

[add credit here]

FIGURE 3-33

▶ Setting and Using Tabs

Beneath the second paragraph of the proposal, you decide to add a table that displays the number of full-time and part-time students by gender at Blue Lake Institute of Technology. With Word, you can create tables by setting tab stops (like on a typewriter) or by using the Table button on the Toolbar. For this first table, you will set tab stops; for the second table that will be added later, you will use the Table button.

Recall that Word, by default, places tab stops at every .5-inch mark on the ruler. You can use these default tab stops or set your own custom tab stops. When you set a custom tab stop, Word clears all default tab stops to the left of the custom tab stop. You can also specify how the text will align at a tab stop: left, centered, right, or decimal. Tab settings are stored in the paragraph mark at the end of each paragraph. Thus, each time you press the ENTER key, the custom tab stops are carried forward to the next paragraph. The first step in creating the table is to enter its title.

Entering the Table Title

The title of the table should be bold and underlined as described in the following steps.

TO ENTER THE TABLE TITLE

Step 1: Position the insertion point at the end of the second paragraph and press the ENTER key twice.
Step 2: If the First-Line Indent marker is not at the 0-inch mark on the ruler, drag it to the left margin (0-inch mark on ruler).
Step 3: Click the Centered Text, Bold, and Underline buttons on the ribbon.
Step 4: Type Blue Lake Student Status Breakdown and click the Bold and Underline buttons on the ribbon.
Step 5: Press the ENTER key.
Step 6: Click the Left-Aligned Text button on the ribbon.

The title for the table displays as shown in Figure 3-34 on the next page.

The next step in creating the table is to set custom tab stops for the heading lines in the table. The text in the first tab stop should be left-justified, the default; and the text in the last two tab stops should be centered. The steps on the following pages show how to set custom tab stops for the paragraph at the location of the insertion point.

TO SET CUSTOM TAB STOPS

STEP 1 ▶

Point to the location on the ruler where you want the custom tab stop to be set.

The mouse points to the 1-inch mark on the ruler (Figure 3-34).

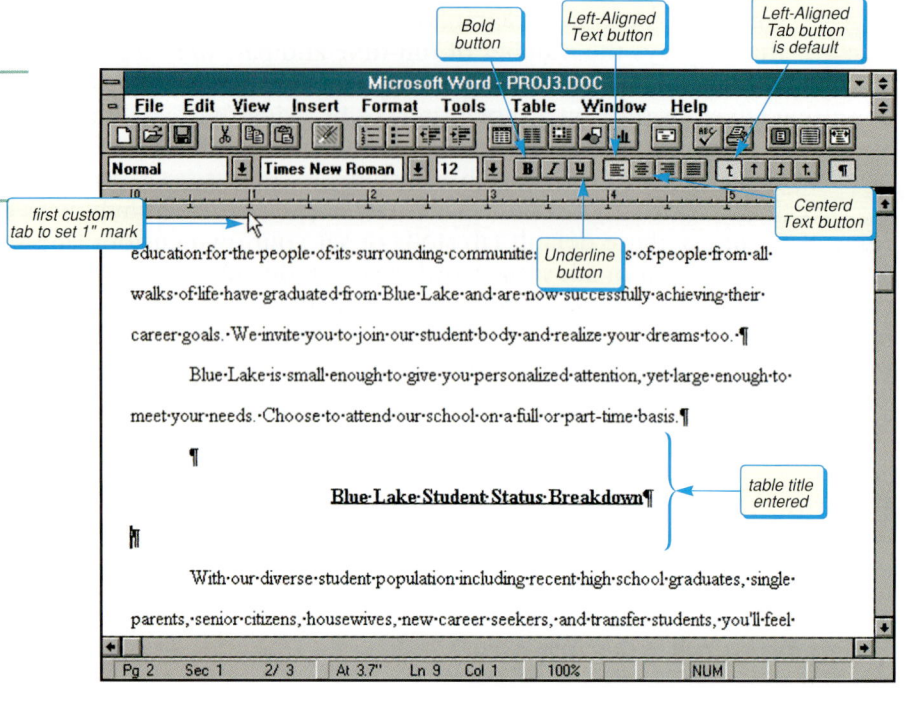

FIGURE 3-34

STEP 2 ▶

Click the left mouse button.

Word places a custom tab stop at the 1-inch mark on the ruler and removes the default tab stop at the .5-inch mark (Figure 3-35). The custom tab stop appears with a right-pointing tail, indicating the text entered at the tab stop will be left-justified. The next tab stop is to be centered.

STEP 3 ▶

Point to the Centered Tab (↑) button on the ruler. Click the Centered Tab button.

The Centered Tab button appears recessed on the ribbon.

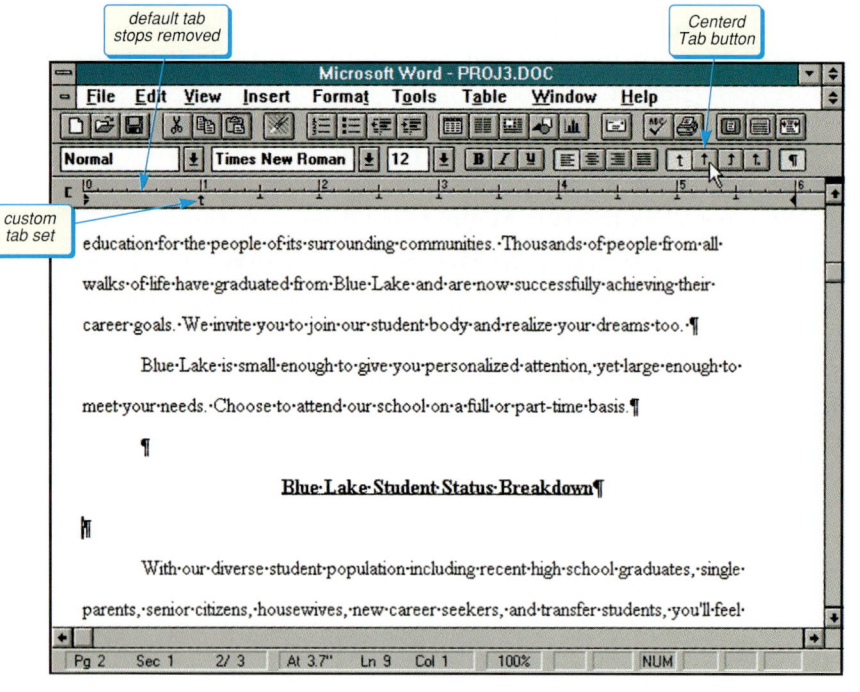

FIGURE 3-35

SETTING AND USING TABS   MSW137

STEP 4 ▶

Click the 3.5-inch mark on the ruler.

Word places a custom tab stop at the 3.5-inch mark on the ruler and removes the default tab stops to the left of the 3.5-inch mark. The custom tab stop appears as a vertical line, indicating text typed at the tab stop will be centered.

STEP 5 ▶

Click the 4.5-inch mark on the ruler.

Word places a custom tab stop at the 4.5-inch mark on the ruler and removes the default tab stops to the left of the 4.5-inch mark (Figure 3-36).

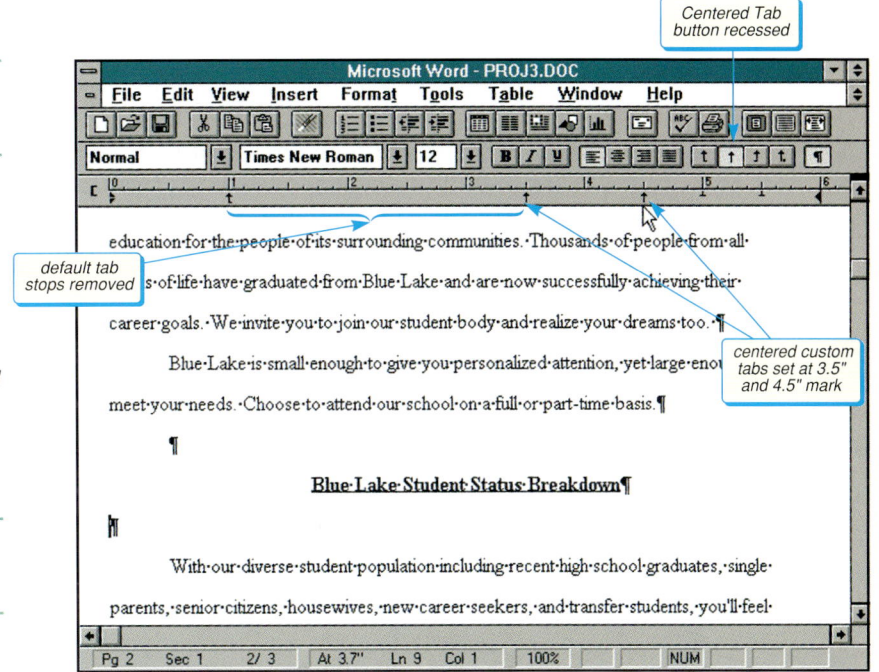

FIGURE 3-36

If necessary, to move a custom tab stop drag it to the new location on the ruler. The next step in creating the table with tabs is to begin typing the text in the table.

Entering Text Using Custom Tab Stops

As described below, to move from one tab stop to another, you press the TAB key. A tab character (→) appears in the empty space and the insertion point moves to the next custom tab stop.

TO ENTER TEXT USING CUSTOM TAB STOPS

Step 1: Position the insertion point on the paragraph mark just beneath the title of the table. Press the TAB key twice.
Step 2: Type % Female and press the TAB key.
Step 3: Type % Male and press the ENTER key.
Step 4: Press the TAB key and type Part-Time Students.

The document window displays as shown in Figure 3-37.

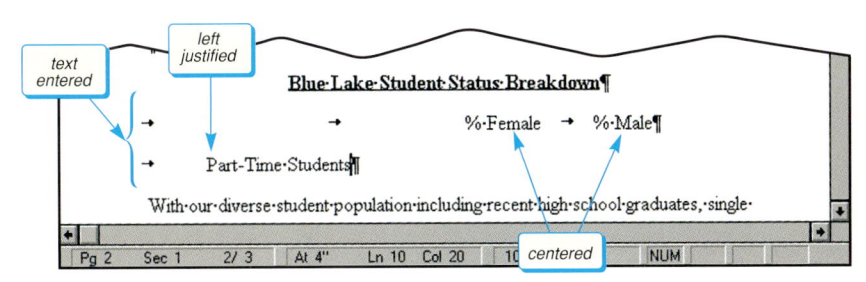

FIGURE 3-37

Changing the Alignment of a Tab Stop

On the previous two pages, you defined the tab stops at the 3.5-inch and 4.5-inch mark as centered tabs. The actual percentage values, however, have decimal points in the numbers. Typically, you align values such as these on the decimal point. To change the tab stops from centered tabs to decimal tabs, you must first clear the existing custom tabs and reset them. Then, you can finish the remaining entries in the table as shown in the following steps (see Figure 3-41).

TO CHANGE THE ALIGNMENT OF TAB STOPS

STEP 1 ▶

Point to the 3.5-inch custom tab stop marker on the ruler (Figure 3-38).

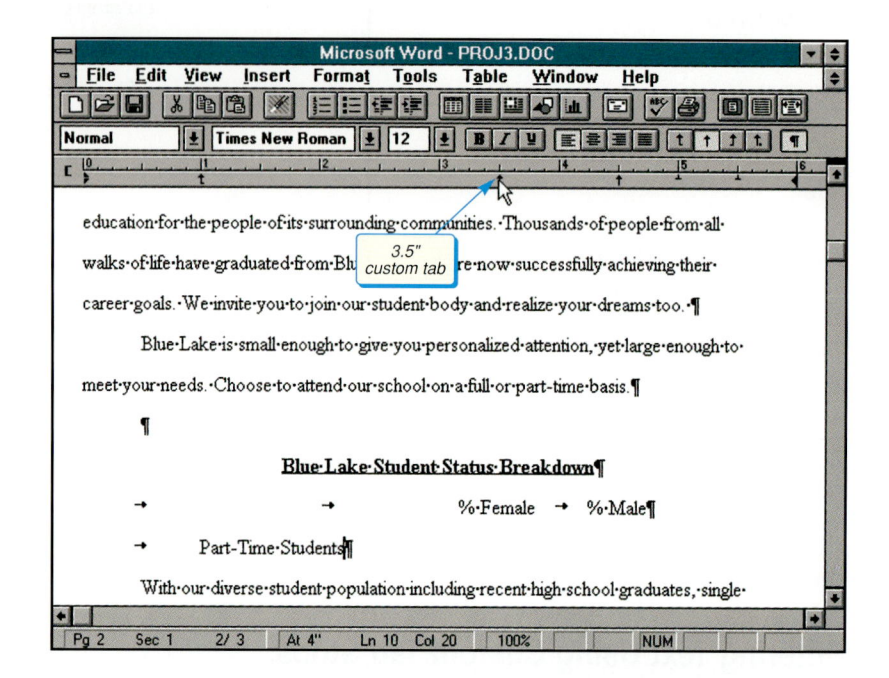

FIGURE 3-38

STEP 2 ▶

Drag the 3.5-inch custom tab stop marker down and out of the ruler. Point to the 4.5-inch custom tab stop marker on the ruler.

Word removes the 3.5-inch custom tab stop (Figure 3-39).

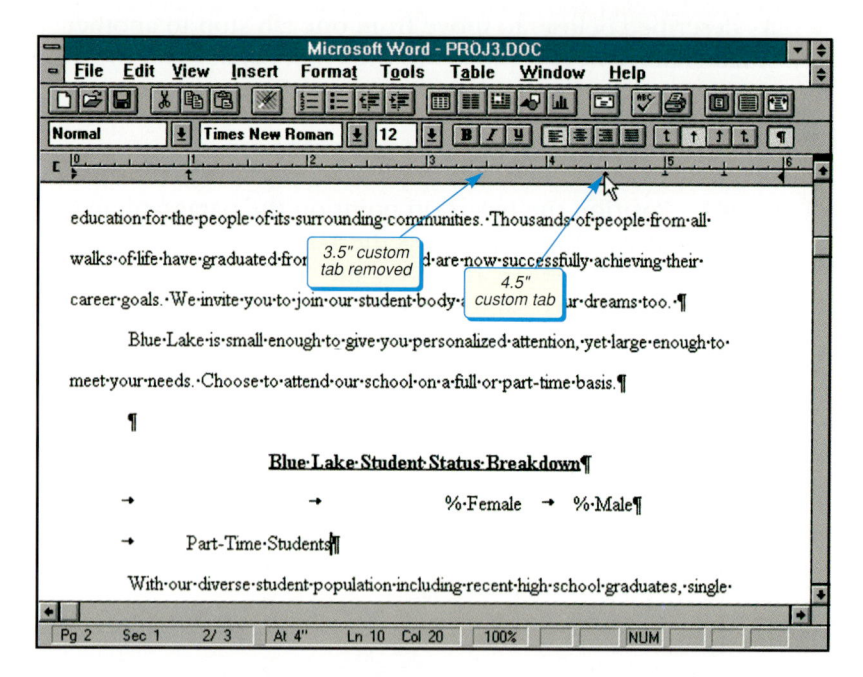

FIGURE 3-39

SETTING AND USING TABS **MSW139**

STEP 3 ▶

Drag the 4.5-inch custom tab stop marker down and out of the ruler. Point to the Decimal Tab button ( ) on the ruler.

Word removes the 4.5-inch custom tab stop and fills to the right of the 1-inch mark with default tab stops (Figure 3-40).

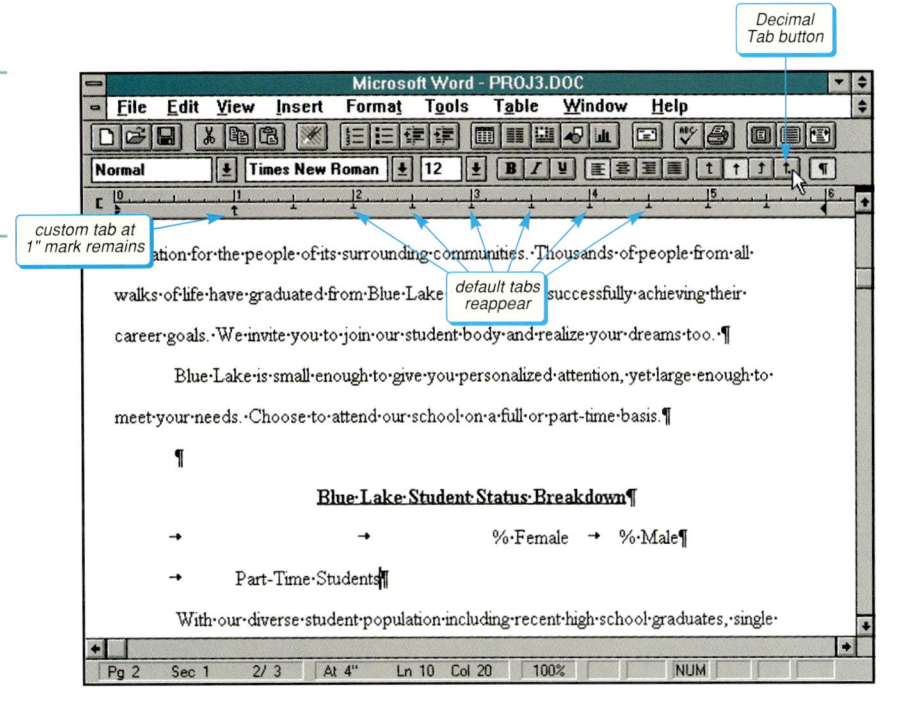

FIGURE 3-40

STEP 4 ▶

Click the Decimal Tab button. Click the 3.5-inch mark on the ruler. Click the 4.5-inch mark on the ruler.

Word places custom tab stops at the 3.5-inch and 4.5-inch mark on the ruler. The custom tab stop appears as a vertical line with a decimal point beside it, indicating text typed at the tab stop will be decimal-aligned.

STEP 5 ▶

Press the TAB key, type `55.2` **and press the TAB key. Type** `44.8` **and press the ENTER key. Press the TAB key, type** `Full-Time Students` **and press the TAB key. Type** `47.8` **and press the TAB key. Type** `52.2` **and press the ENTER key.**

The first table in the proposal displays as shown in Figure 3-41.

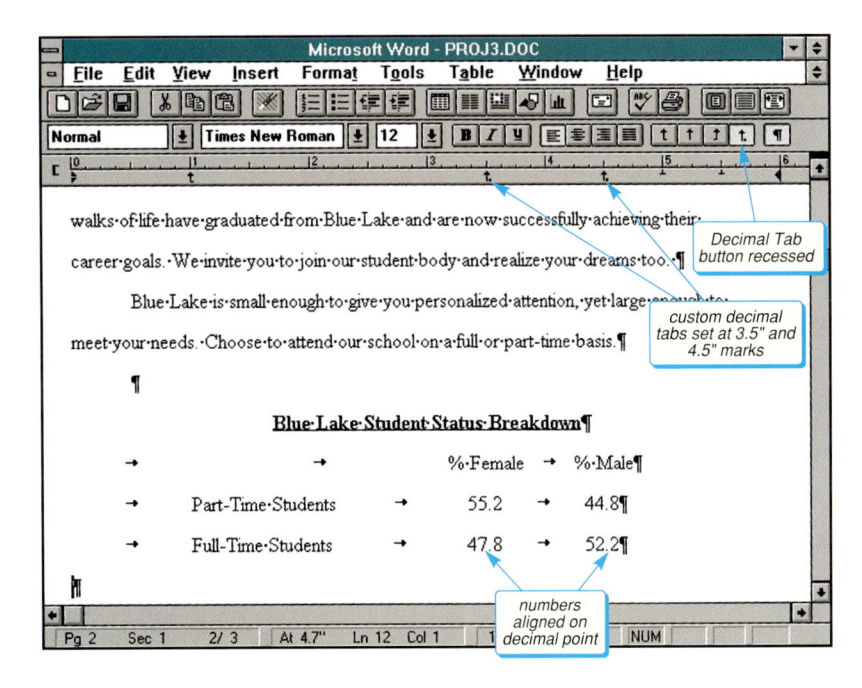

FIGURE 3-41

▶ CREATING A TABLE

Beneath the third paragraph of the proposal draft (see Figure 3-33 on page MSW134), you decide to add another table. This time, however, you want to place a chart of the table data immediately below the table. One easy way to chart data is to enter the data into a Word table. Thus, you will use the Table button (▦) to create this second table.

A Word **table** is a collection of rows and columns. The intersection of a row and a column is called a **cell**. Cells are filled with data. The data you enter within a cell wordwraps just as the text does between the margins of a document.

Within a table, you can easily rearrange rows and columns, change column widths, sort rows and columns, and sum the contents of rows and columns. You can also perform all character formatting and paragraph formatting to table data. For these reasons, many Word users create tables with the Table button, rather than using tabs as discussed in the prior section.

The first step in creating a table using the Table button is to enter the title lines.

Entering the Title Lines of the Table

The title of the second table spans two lines. The first line is centered and bold. The second line is single-spaced beneath the first and typed in a point size of 10.

TO ENTER THE TITLE LINES OF THE TABLE

Step 1: Position the insertion point at the end of the third paragraph (after the period following the word environment) and press the ENTER key twice.

Step 2: To properly center the title between the left and right margins, drag the First-Line Indent marker to the left margin. Click the Centered Text button.

Step 3: Click the Bold button. Type AGE DISTRIBUTIONS OF BLUE LAKE STUDENTS and press the ENTER key twice.

Step 4: Position the insertion point on the paragraph mark just beneath the title typed in Step 3. From the Format menu, choose the Paragraph command.

Step 5: Click the Line Spacing box arrow and select Single. Choose the OK button.

Step 6: Change the point size to 10 by clicking the Points box arrow and selecting 10.

Step 7: Type (in table form).

The title lines of the table display as shown in Figure 3-42.

CREATING A TABLE   MSW141

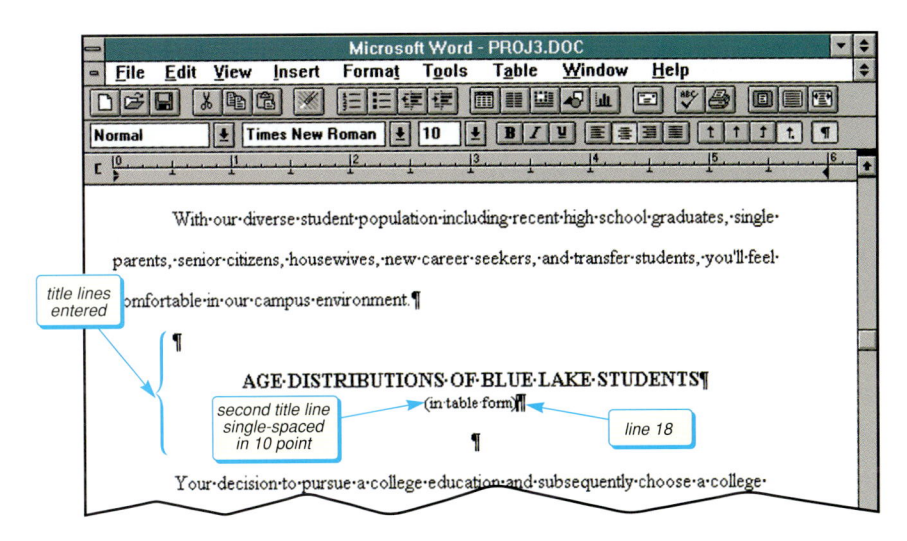

FIGURE 3-42

Inserting an Empty Table

The next step is to insert an empty table into the document. When inserting a table, you must specify the total number of rows and columns. Referring to Figure 3-43, this table contains seven rows and four columns, called a 7 × 4 table. If you initially insert a table with too few or too many rows and/or columns, you can easily add or delete rows and/or columns to or from the table.

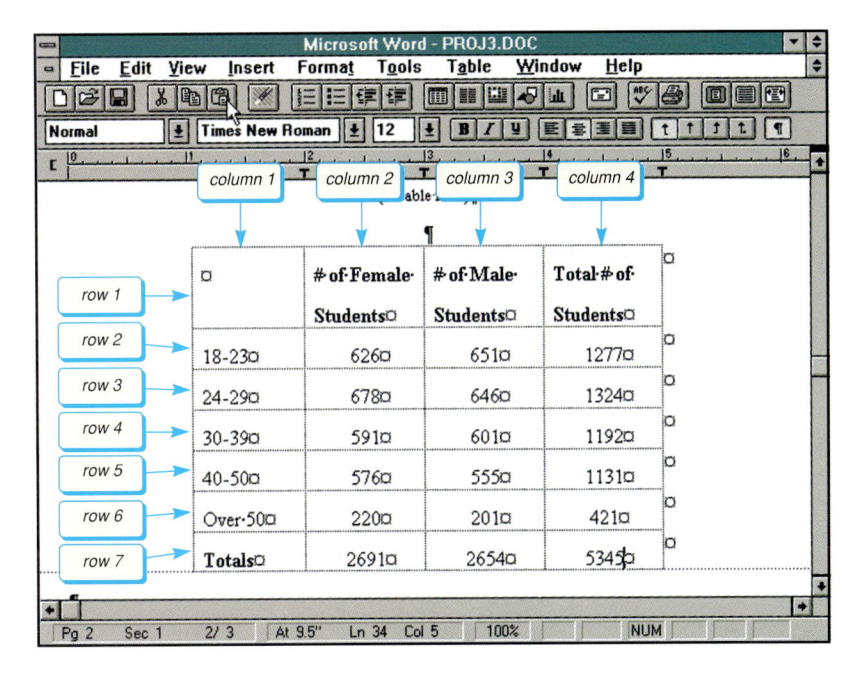

FIGURE 3-43

Word inserts the table above the insertion point. Follow the steps on the next two pages to insert a 7 × 4 table into Project 3 (see Figure 3-47 on page MSW143).

TO INSERT AN EMPTY TABLE

STEP 1

Position the insertion point on the paragraph mark beneath the text, (in table form), and press the ENTER key. Click the Left-Aligned Text button. Click the Table button on the Toolbar.

Word will insert the table immediately above the insertion point, which is in line 20. The data in the table cells will be left aligned. The Table button appears recessed, and Word displays a Table button grid.

STEP 2 ▶

Point to the upper left cell in the Table button grid. Press and hold the left mouse button.

Word selects the upper left cell and displays the current table dimension (1 × 1 Table) at the base of the Table button grid (Figure 3-44).

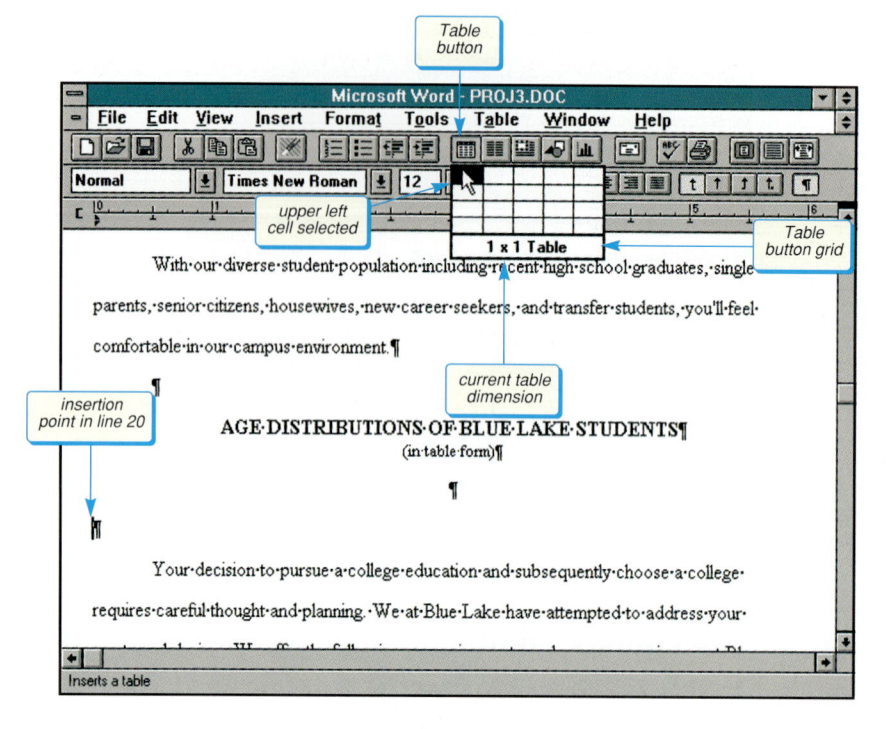

FIGURE 3-44

STEP 3 ▶

While still holding the left mouse button, drag the mouse to the right until the first four columns in the first row are selected. Continue holding the left mouse button.

Word selects the first four columns in the first row and displays the current table dimension of 1 × 4 Table (Figure 3-45).

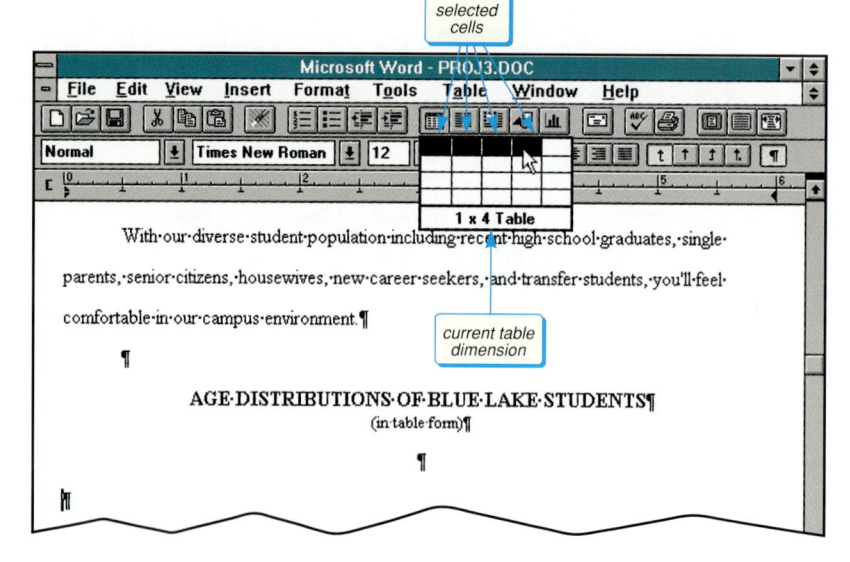

FIGURE 3-45

CREATING A TABLE **MSW143**

STEP 4 ▶

While still holding the left mouse button, drag the mouse down until the first seven rows are selected.

Word selects a rectangular area of seven rows and four columns and displays the current table dimension of 7 × 4 Table (Figure 3-46).

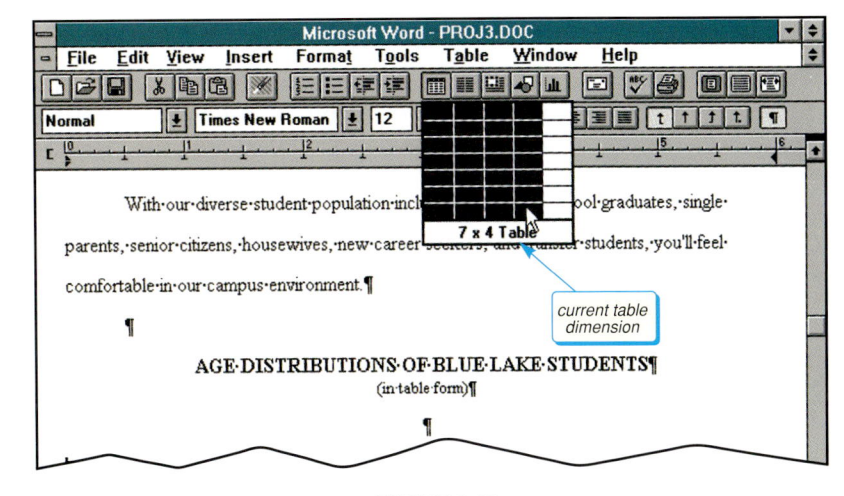

FIGURE 3-46

STEP 5 ▶

Release the mouse button.

Word inserts an empty 7 × 4 table into the document (Figure 3-47). The insertion point is in the first cell (row 1 column 1) of the table.

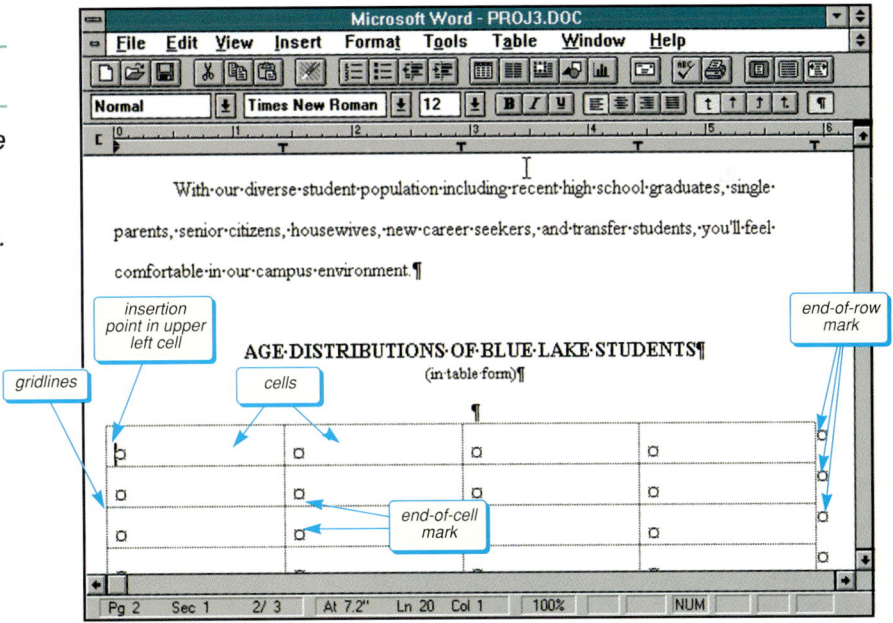

FIGURE 3-47

The table displays on the screen with dotted **gridlines**. If your table does not have gridlines, choose the Gridlines command from the Table menu. Word does not print the table with gridlines; rather the gridlines display to help you identify in which row and column you are working. Each row has an **end-of-row mark**, which is used to add columns to the right of a table. Each cell has an **end-of-cell** mark, which is used to select a cell. Recall that a cell is the intersection of a row and a column. Notice the end-of-cell marks are currently left-justified within each cell.

The default column widths are too large for the needs of this table. Thus, the next step is to change the spacing of the columns in the table.

To Change the Spacing of Columns in a Table

When the insertion point is in a cell of a table, the ruler changes to reflect table columns. Table columns are identified by dark Ts (T) on the ruler, called **column markers**. These column markers are similar to tab stops. To move from one column to the next in a table, you press the TAB key. You can also adjust the spacing between columns in a table by dragging these column markers along the ruler. The marks on the ruler are evenly spaced every .125th of one inch (eighth of an inch). The following steps show how to change the spacing between columns in a table (see Figure 3-51).

TO CHANGE THE SPACING BETWEEN COLUMNS IN A TABLE ▼

STEP 1 ▶

Point to the Left-Indent marker on the ruler (Figure 3-48).

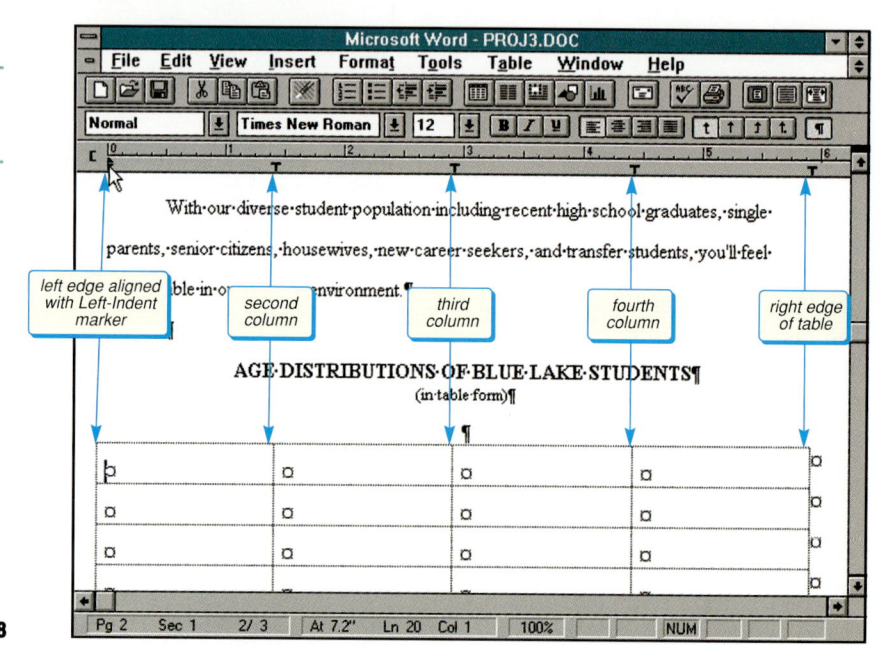

FIGURE 3-48

STEP 2 ▶

Drag the Left-Indent marker to the 1.125-inch mark on the ruler.

The left edge of the table moves to the right 1.125 inches (Figure 3-49).

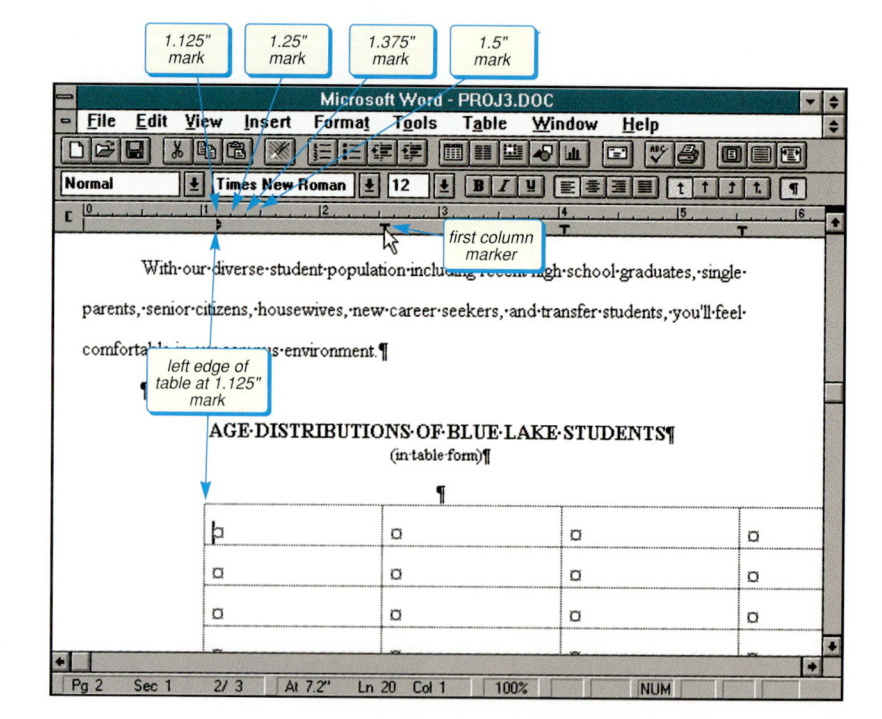

FIGURE 3-49

CREATING A TABLE **MSW145**

STEP 3 ▶

Point to the first column marker on the ruler. Drag the column marker to the 2-inch mark on the ruler.

The beginning of the second column is aligned at the 2-inch mark on the ruler (Figure 3-50). The width of the first column is reduced.

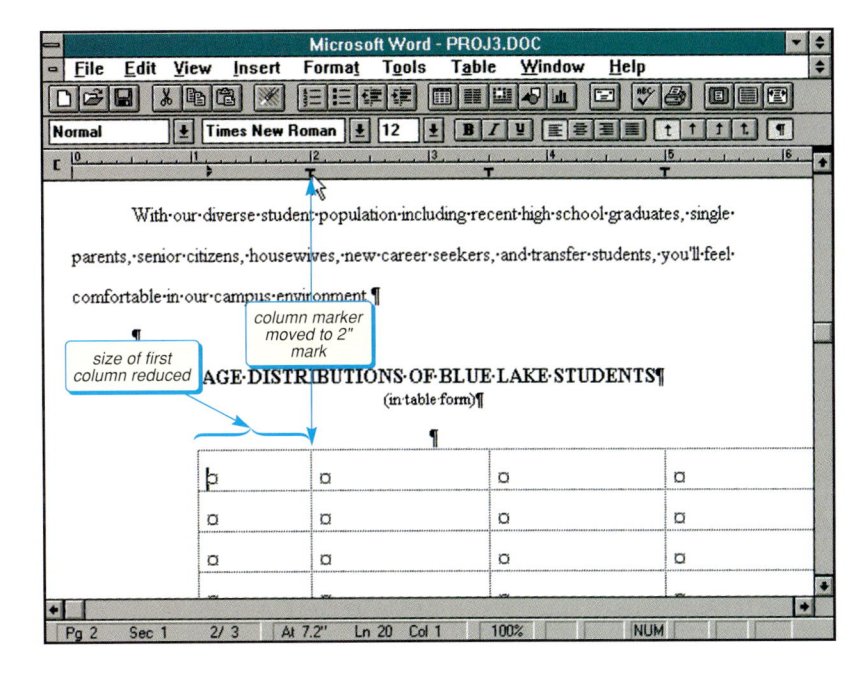

FIGURE 3-50

STEP 4 ▶

Point to the second column marker on the ruler and drag it to the 3-inch mark. Point to the third column marker on the ruler and drag it to the 4-inch mark. Point to the fourth column marker on the ruler and drag it to the 5-inch mark.

All of the columns in the table are resized (Figure 3-51).

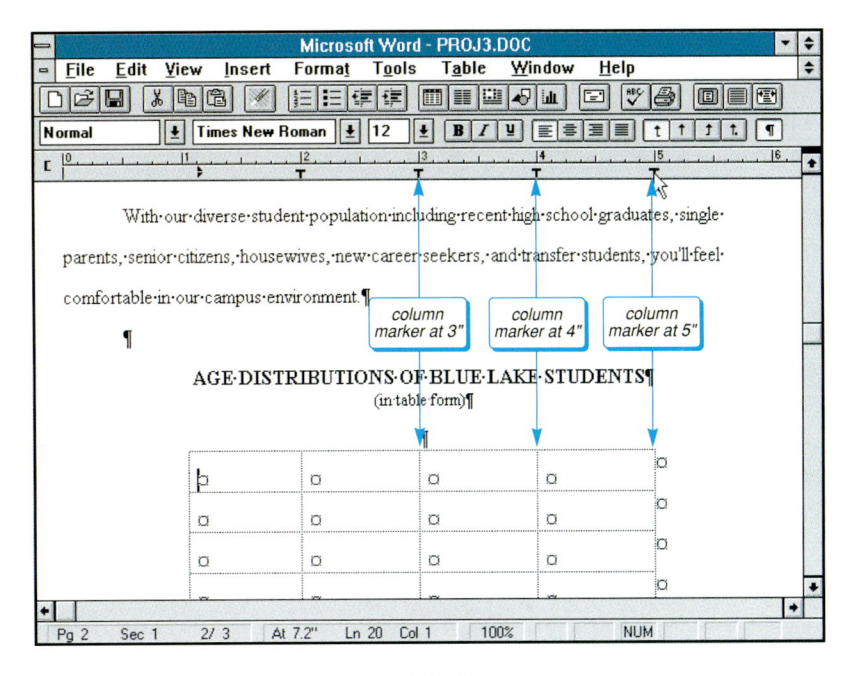

FIGURE 3-51

Entering the Column Titles into the Cells of the Table

Entering data into cells is as easy as tabbing from one cell to the next. The steps to enter the data are shown below.

TO ENTER COLUMN TITLES INTO THE TABLE

STEP 1 ▶

Press the TAB key. Click the Bold button on the ribbon. Type `# of Female Students` **and press the TAB key.**

The word Students automatically wraps around in the second cell in row one.

STEP 2 ▶

Click the Bold button. Type `# of Male Students` **and press the TAB key. Click the Bold button. Type** `Total # of Students` **and press the TAB key.**

The title lines are entered and the insertion point is positioned in the first column of the second row (Figure 3-52).

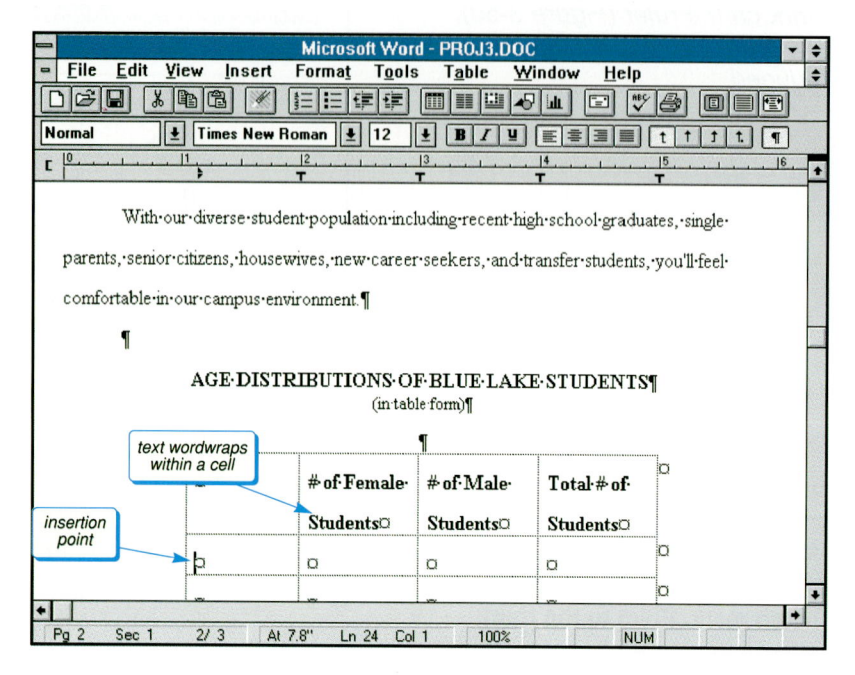

FIGURE 3-52

Changing the Alignment of Text within Cells

The data you enter into the cells is by default left-aligned. You can change the alignment just as you would for a paragraph. You must first select the cell(s) before changing its alignment. You select a cell by pointing to the **cell selection bar** at the left edge of the cell and clicking the left mouse button. When the mouse pointer is in the cell selection bar, it changes to a right-pointing block arrow. Follow the steps on the next two pages to center the end-of-cell marks for cells that will contain numeric values (see Figure 3-55 on page MSW148).

TO CENTER END-OF-CELL MARKS

STEP 1 ▶

Point to the first end-of-cell mark to be centered (row 2 column 2).

The mouse pointer points to column 2 of the second row (Figure 3-53).

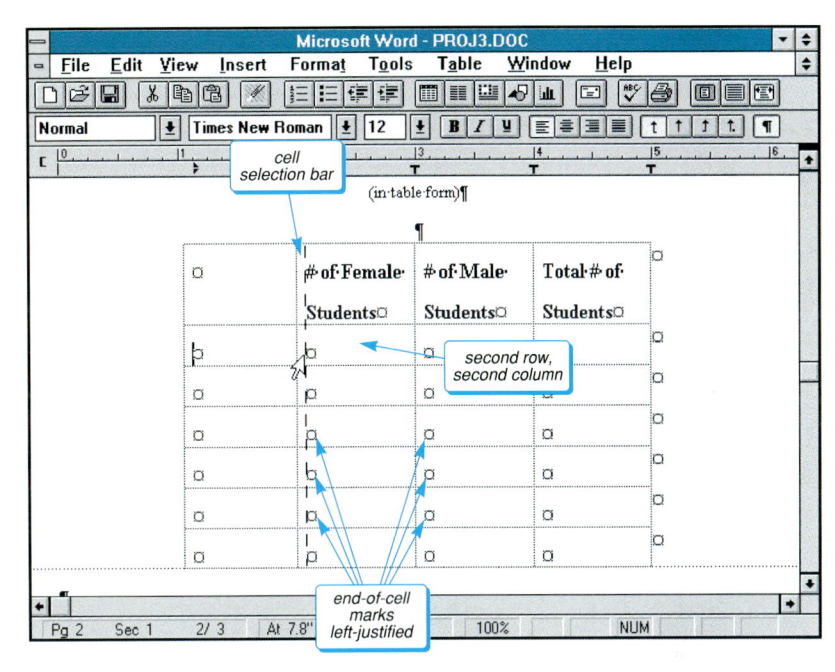

FIGURE 3-53

STEP 2 ▶

Drag the mouse to highlight all the cells to be centered (columns 2, 3, and 4 of rows 2 through 7).

Word selects columns 2, 3, and 4 of the last six rows in the table (Figure 3-54). The mouse pointer points to the bottom right cell in the table (row 7 column 4)

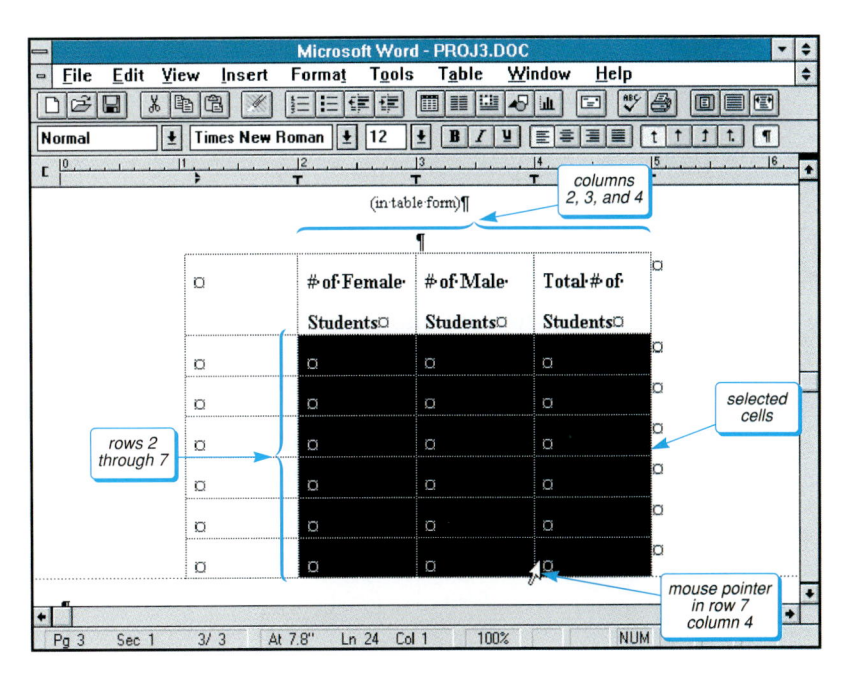

FIGURE 3-54

CREATING A TABLE   MSW147

MSW148   PROJECT 3   CREATING A PROPOSAL USING TABLES AND GRAPHICS

STEP 3 ▶

Click the Centered Text button on the ribbon.

Word centers the end-of-cell marks in the selected area (Figure 3-55). The Centered Text button appears recessed.

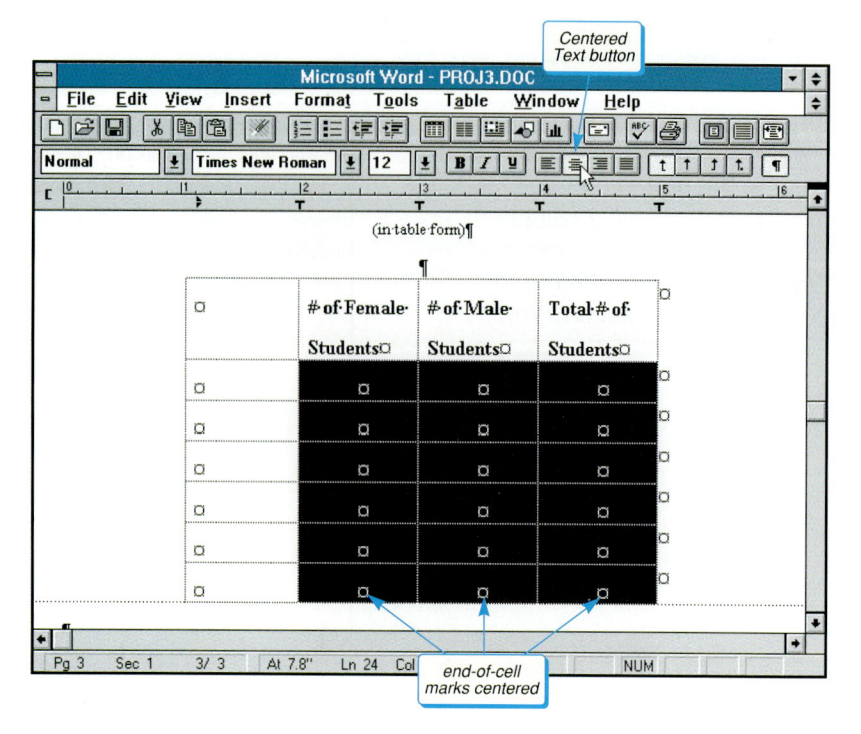

FIGURE 3-55

Just as with paragraphs, you can left-align, center, or right-align the end-of-cell marks in a table.

Entering the Data into the Table

The next step is to insert the data within the table. To advance from one row to the next, press the TAB key; do not press the ENTER key. The ENTER key is used to begin new paragraphs *within* a cell. Perform the following steps to enter the data into the table.

TO ENTER DATA INTO THE TABLE

Step 1: Click in the cell at the intersection of row 2 and column 1.
Step 2: Type 18-23 and press the TAB key. Type 626 and press the TAB key. Type 651 and press the TAB key twice.
Step 3: Type 24-29 and press the TAB key. Type 678 and press the TAB key. Type 646 and press the TAB key twice.
Step 4: Type 30-39 and press the TAB key. Type 591 and press the TAB key. Type 601 and press the TAB key twice.
Step 5: Type 40-50 and press the TAB key. Type 576 and press the TAB key. Type 555 and press the TAB key twice.
Step 6: Type Over 50 and press the TAB key. Type 220 and press the TAB key. Type 201 and press the TAB key twice.
Step 7: Click the Bold button on the ribbon. Type Totals.

The table data displays as shown in Figure 3-56.

CREATING A TABLE   MSW149

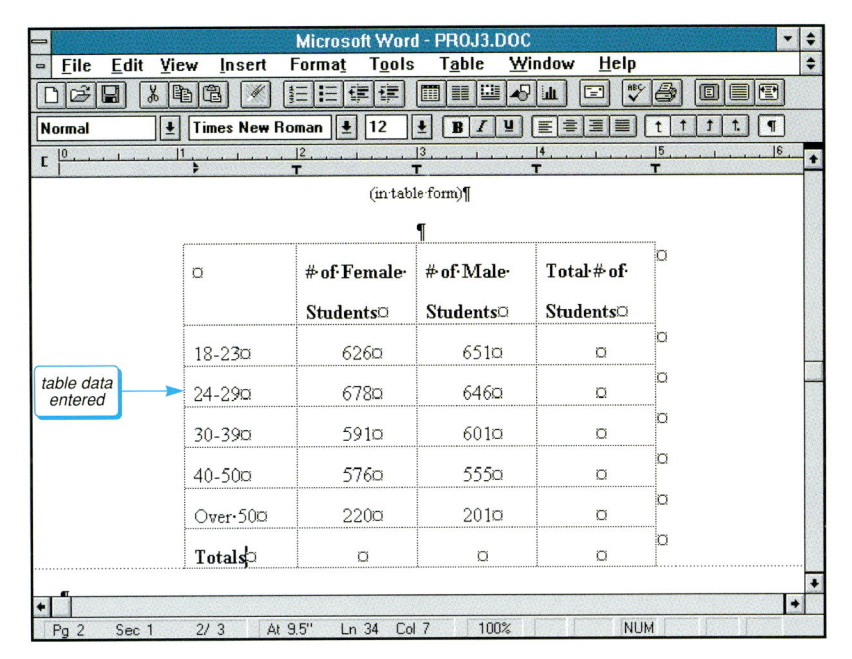

FIGURE 3-56

You modify the contents of cells just as you modify text in a document. To delete the contents of a cell, select the cell and press the DELETE key. To modify text within a cell, position the insertion point in the cell and correct the entry. You can use the INSERT key to toggle between insert and overtype modes. You may also cut and paste the contents of cells.

Summing Rows and Columns in a Table

Word can add together the contents of cells in a table. Once computed, Word places the result on the Clipboard. You can then paste the contents (the calculation result) into another cell in the table. Follow these steps to add up the contents of rows 2 through 6 (see Figure 3-61 on page MSW151).

TO ADD THE CONTENTS OF CELL ROWS ▼

STEP 1 ▶

Select the cells to be added together by clicking in the cell selection bar of the first cell (row 2 column 2) and dragging the mouse pointer into the second cell (row 2 column 3).

Word highlights the number of female and male students in the 18-23 range (Figure 3-57).

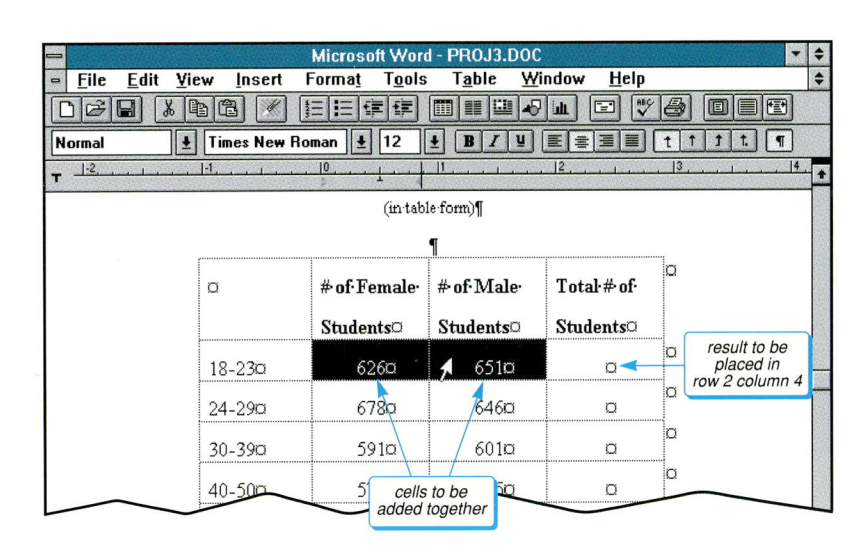

FIGURE 3-57

MSW150   PROJECT 3   CREATING A PROPOSAL USING TABLES AND GRAPHICS

STEP 2 ▶

Select the Tools menu and point to the Calculate command (Figure 3-58).

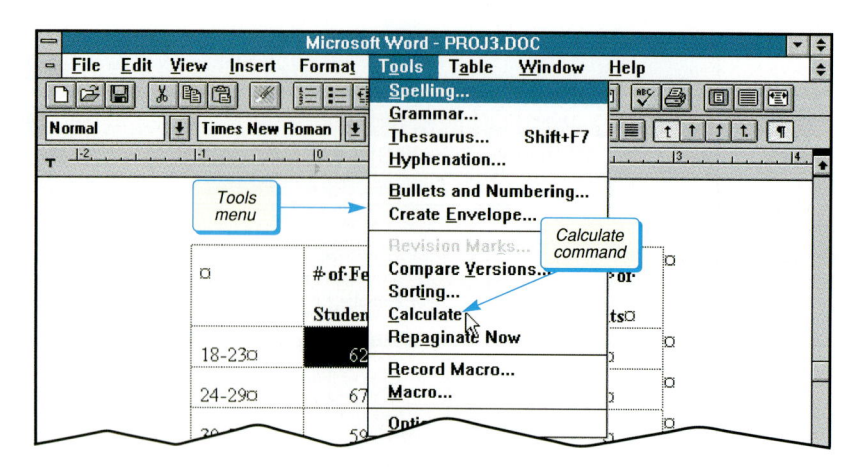

FIGURE 3-58

STEP 3 ▶

Choose the Calculate command.

Word adds the contents of the selected cells and displays the result on the status bar (Figure 3-59). Word places the result of the calculation on the Clipboard so you can paste it into the document.

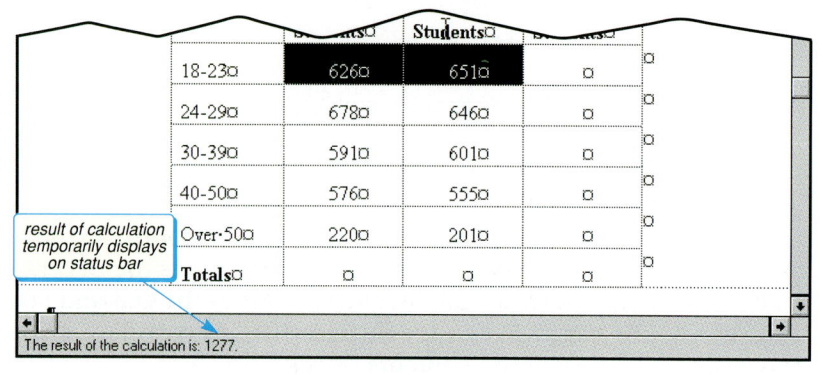

FIGURE 3-59

STEP 4 ▶

Click in the cell into which you want the result pasted (row 2 column 4). Then, click the Paste button on the Toolbar.

Word places the sum, 1277, in the total number of students column (Figure 3-60).

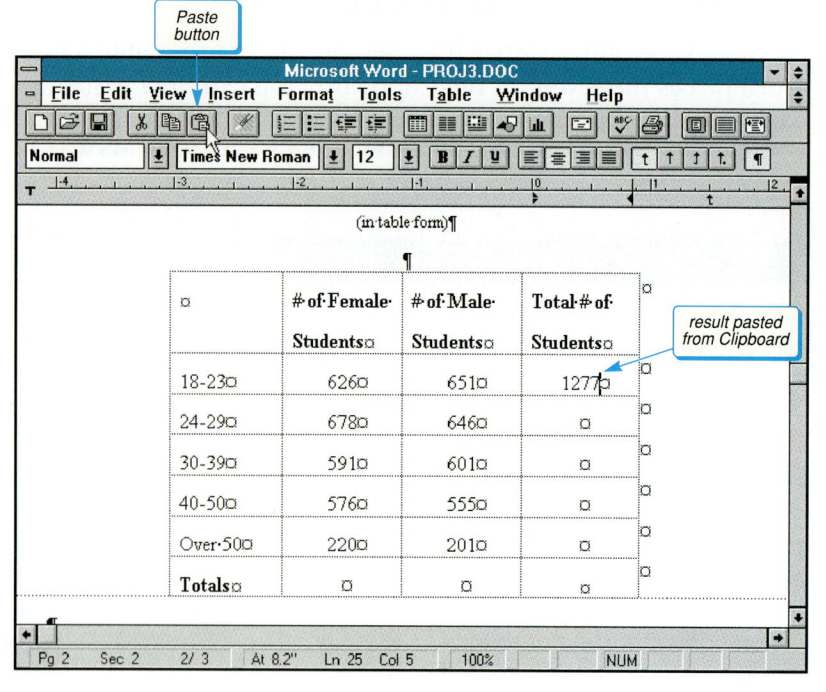

FIGURE 3-60

CREATING A TABLE **MSW151**

STEP 5 ▶

Repeat the procedure in Step 1 through Step 4 for the total number of students column in rows 3 through 6.

The totals display as shown in Figure 3-61.

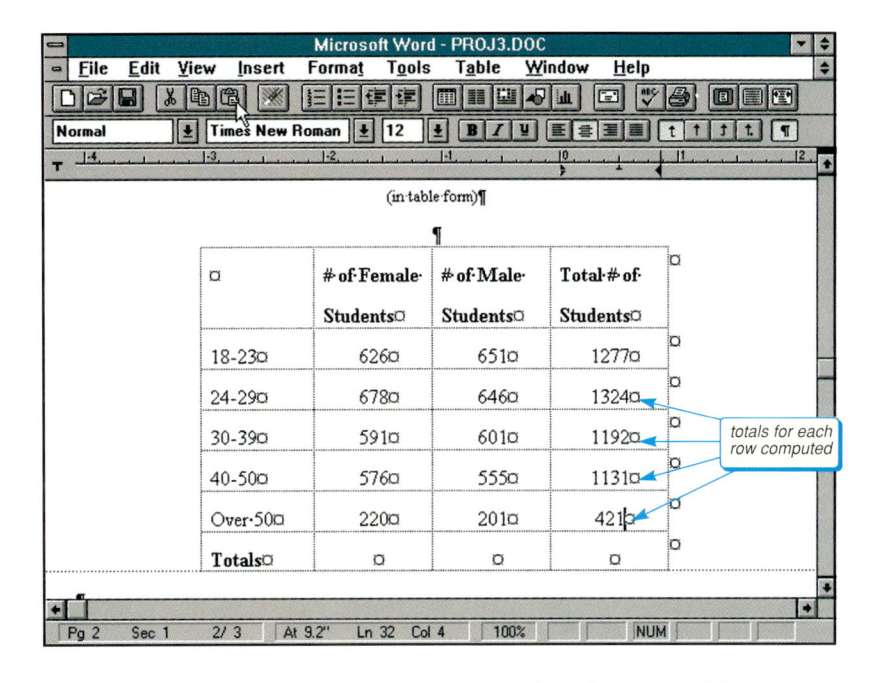

FIGURE 3-61

(totals for each row computed)

	# of Female Students	# of Male Students	Total # of Students
18-23	626	651	1277
24-29	678	646	1324
30-39	591	601	1192
40-50	576	555	1131
Over-50	220	201	421
Totals			

The next step is to add up the contents of columns 2, 3, and 4 as shown in Figure 3-64 on the next page.

To select an entire column, you click in the **column selection bar**, which is located at the top of a column. The mouse pointer changes to a solid down-pointing arrow (↓) when in the column selection bar. To select an entire row, you click in the **row selection bar**, which is located to the left of a row. The mouse pointer changes to a right-pointing arrow in the row selection bar.

TO ADD THE CONTENTS OF COLUMNS ▼

STEP 1 ▶

Click in the column selection bar of the column to be totaled.

The mouse pointer changes to a down-pointing arrow, and Word selects the entire column (Figure 3-62).

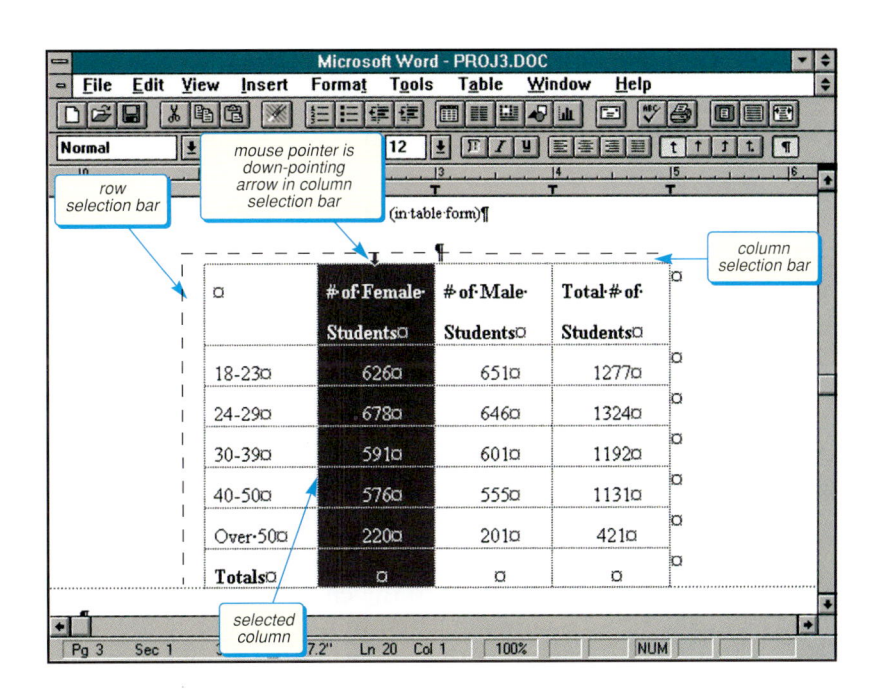

FIGURE 3-62

STEP 2 ▶

From the Tools menu, choose the Calculate command. Click in the cell into which you want the results pasted. Click the Paste button on the Toolbar.

Word displays the total 2691 in the second column of row 7 (Figure 3-63).

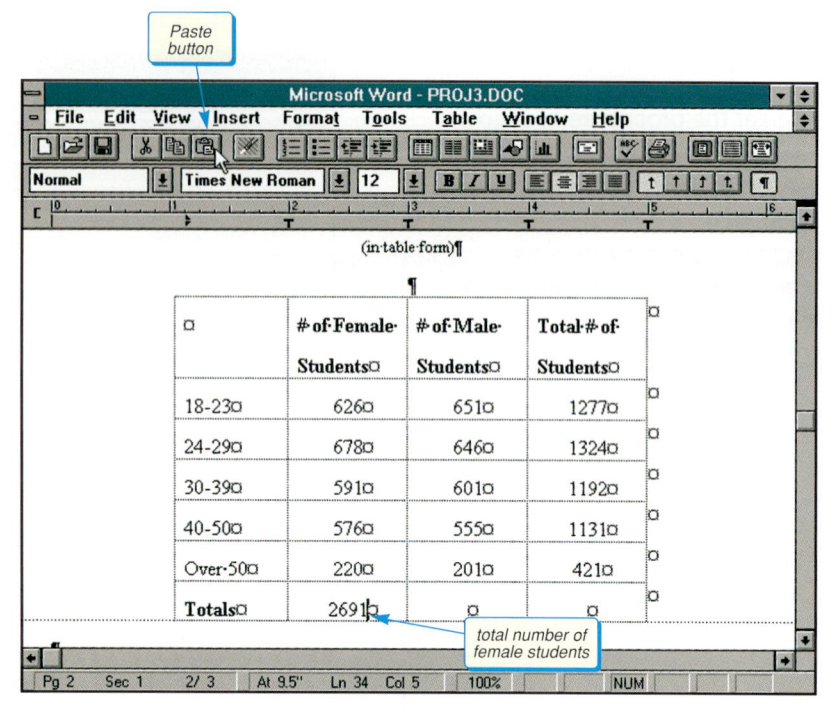

FIGURE 3-63

STEP 3 ▶

Repeat the procedure in Step 1 and Step 2 for the last two columns in the table.

The table entries are complete (Figure 3-64).

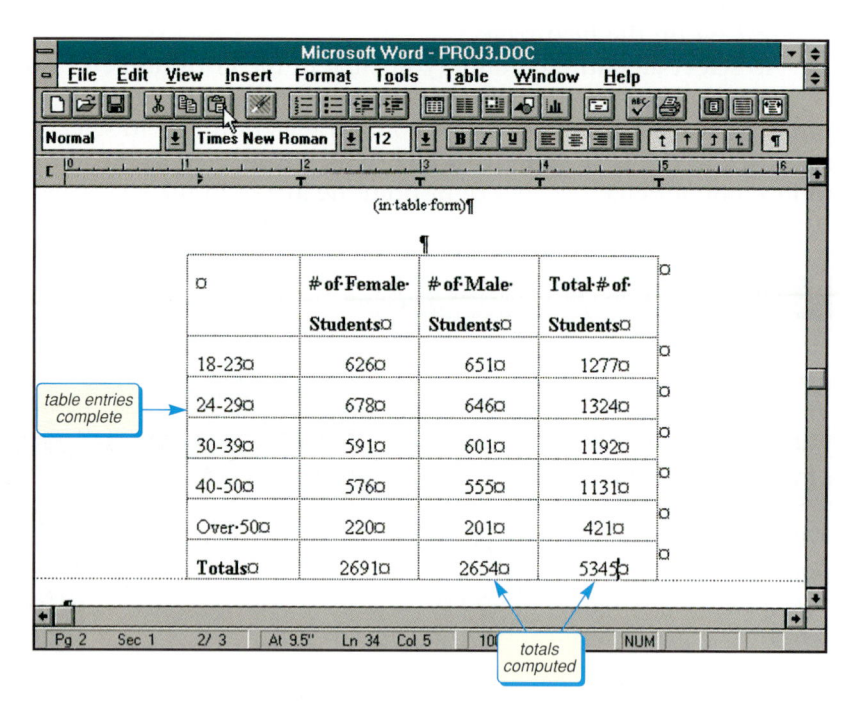

FIGURE 3-64

At times you might want to add additional rows or columns to a table. To add a row to the end of a table, position the insertion point in the bottom right corner cell and press the TAB key. Depending on the task you want to perform in a table, the commands in the Table menu change. To add rows in the middle of a

CHARTING A TABLE **MSW153**

table, select the row below where you want to insert a row and choose the **Insert Rows command** from the Table menu. To add a column in the middle of a table, select the column to the right of where you want to insert a column and choose the **Insert Columns command** from the Table menu. To add a column to the right of a table, select the end-of-row marks by pointing to the right edge of the table and clicking the right mouse button. Then choose the Insert Columns command from the Table menu.

If you want to delete rows or columns from a table, select the rows or columns to delete and choose the Delete Rows or Delete Columns command from the Table menu.

▶ CHARTING A TABLE

When you use the Table button to create a table, Word can easily convert the data you enter in the table into a chart by using an embedded charting application called **Microsoft Graph**. With Microsoft Graph you can chart all or part of a table. Because Microsoft Graph is an embedded application, it has its own menus and commands. With these commands, you easily change the appearance of any chart.

The table you want to chart cannot exceed the 4.75-inch mark on the ruler. If it does, you must move the chart to the left before opening Microsoft Graph. The following steps illustrate how to chart the Age Distributions table just created (see Figure 3-72 on page MSW156).

TO CHART A TABLE ▼

STEP 1 ▶

With the insertion point in the table, drag the Left-Indent marker to the .875-inch mark on the ruler.

The entire table shifts from the 1.125-inch mark to the .875-inch mark.

STEP 2 ▶

Select the first six rows of the table by dragging the mouse pointer through the row selection bar to the left of each of the first six rows. Point to the Graph button (📊) on the Toolbar.

Word highlights the first six rows in the table (Figure 3-65).

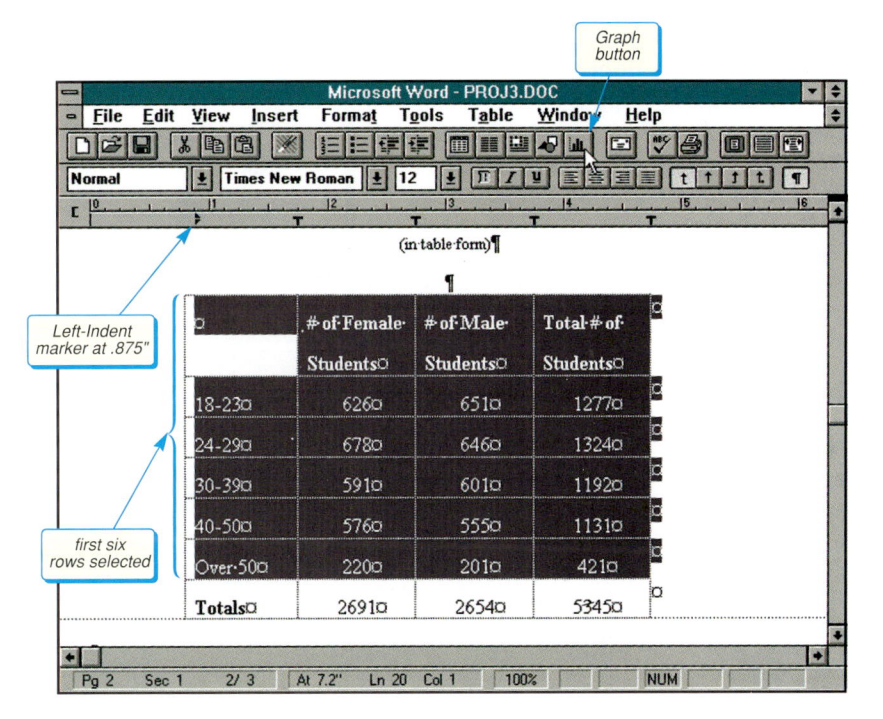

FIGURE 3-65

STEP 3 ▶

Choose the Graph button.

*Word opens the Microsoft Graph application. The selected rows in the table display in a **Datasheet window**, and the chart of the datasheet displays in a **Chart window**. The document window displays in a window behind Microsoft Graph.*

STEP 4 ▶

Move the mouse pointer to the left border of the Chart window.

The mouse pointer changes to a double-headed arrow (⇔) when on the border of a window (Figure 3-66).

FIGURE 3-66

STEP 5 ▶

Drag the mouse to the left edge of the Microsoft Graph window. Move the mouse pointer to the right edge of the Chart window and drag the mouse to the right edge of the Microsoft Graph window.

The chart width is now the same as the Microsoft Graph window (Figure 3-67).

STEP 6 ▶

Move the mouse pointer to the top edge of the Chart window.

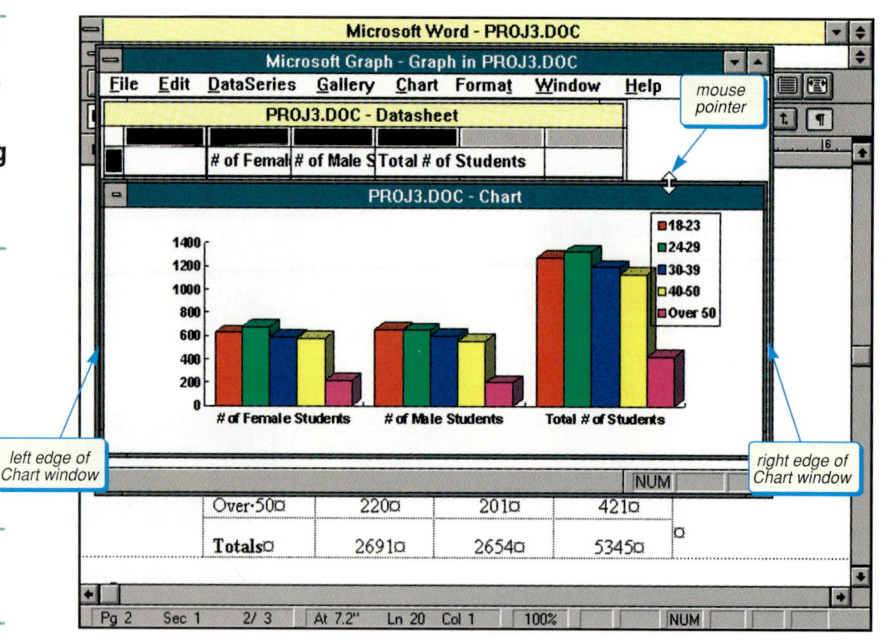

FIGURE 3-67

CHARTING A TABLE   MSW155

STEP 7 ▶

Drag the mouse to the top edge of the Datasheet window. Move the mouse pointer into the legend in the Chart window (Figure 3-68).

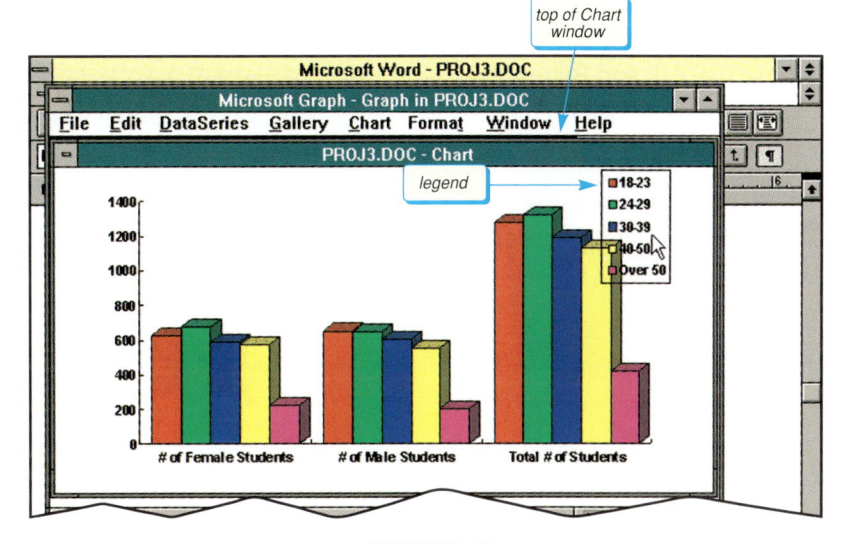

FIGURE 3-68

STEP 8 ▶

Drag the legend to the upper right corner of the Chart window.

The legend moves to the right (Figure 3-69). When the legend is selected, it displays sizing handles, which are used to resize it.

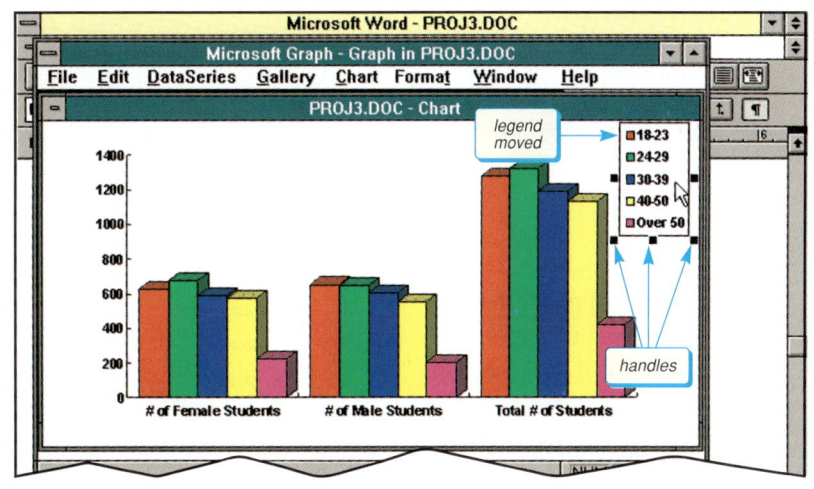

FIGURE 3-69

STEP 9 ▶

Select the File menu and point to the Exit and Return to PROJ3.DOC command (Figure 3-70).

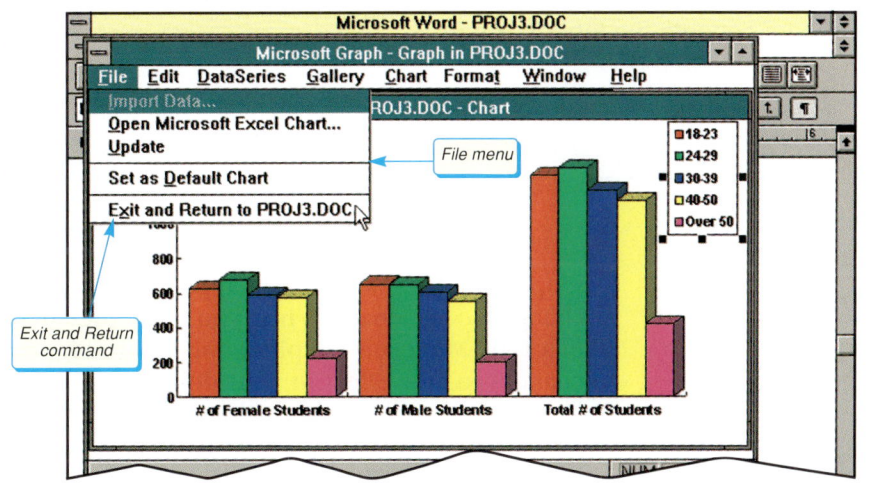

FIGURE 3-70

STEP 10 ▶

Choose the Exit and Return to PROJ3.DOC command. Point to the Yes button.

Word displays a Microsoft Graph dialog box asking if you want to place the chart into PROJ3.DOC (Figure 3-71).

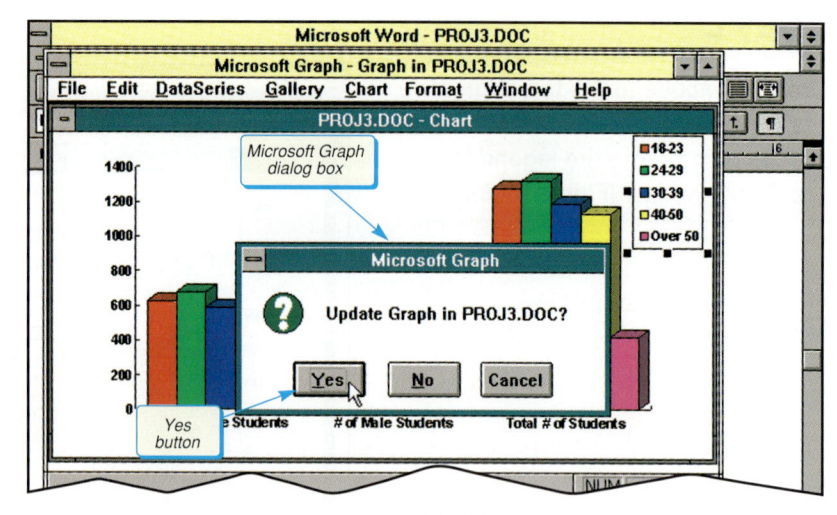

FIGURE 3-71

STEP 11

Choose the Yes button.

Word closes the Microsoft Graph application and places the chart beneath the table in PROJ3.DOC.

STEP 12 ▶

Click to the right of row 7 in the table and drag the Left-Indent marker back to the 1.125-inch on the ruler. Click the down arrow on the vertical scroll bar nine times.

The table is moved back to its original position before opening Microsoft Graph, and the chart appears beneath the table in the document (Figure 3-72).

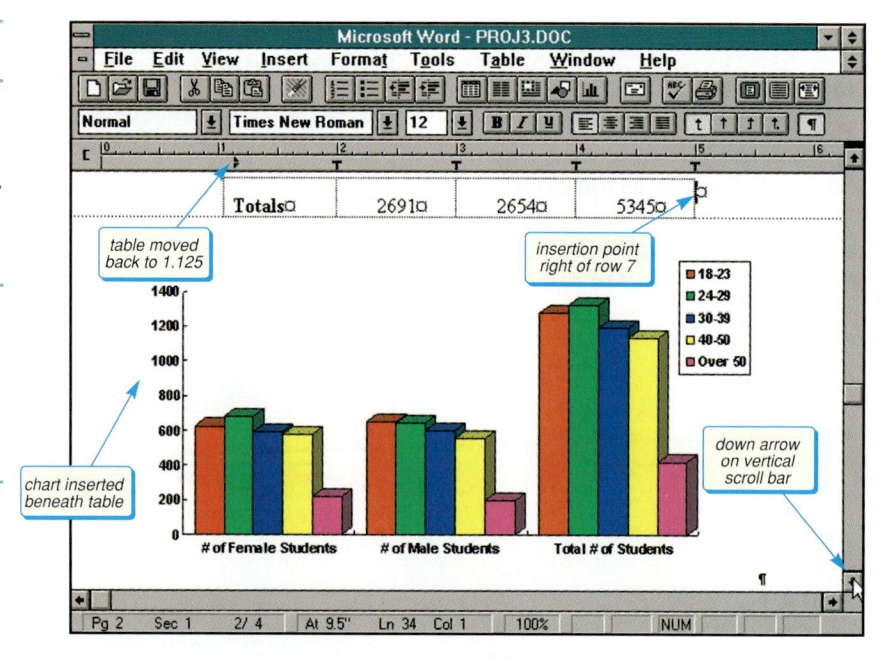

FIGURE 3-72

To modify an existing chart in the document, double-click on the chart to reopen the Microsoft Graph application. Then, you can make any necessary changes to the chart. When you close the Microsoft Graph window, Word displays the Microsoft Graph dialog box in Figure 3-71 to confirm you want the changes to take effect in your document.

Adding a Title to the Chart

Because the title of the table and chart are essentially the same, follow these steps to copy the table title to the graph title by holding down the CONTROL key while you drag and drop the title.

TO COPY A TITLE AND MODIFY IT

Step 1: Click the paragraph mark between the table and chart. From the Insert menu, choose the Break command. Choose the OK button to insert a hard page break beneath the table.

Step 2: Click above the scroll box on the vertical scroll bar and select the two title lines above the table.

Step 3: Hold down the CONTROL key and drag the selection to the paragraph mark above the chart. Release the mouse button.

Step 4: Select the word table in the second title line and type graph. Click outside the selection to remove the highlight.

The chart title displays as shown in Figure 3-73.

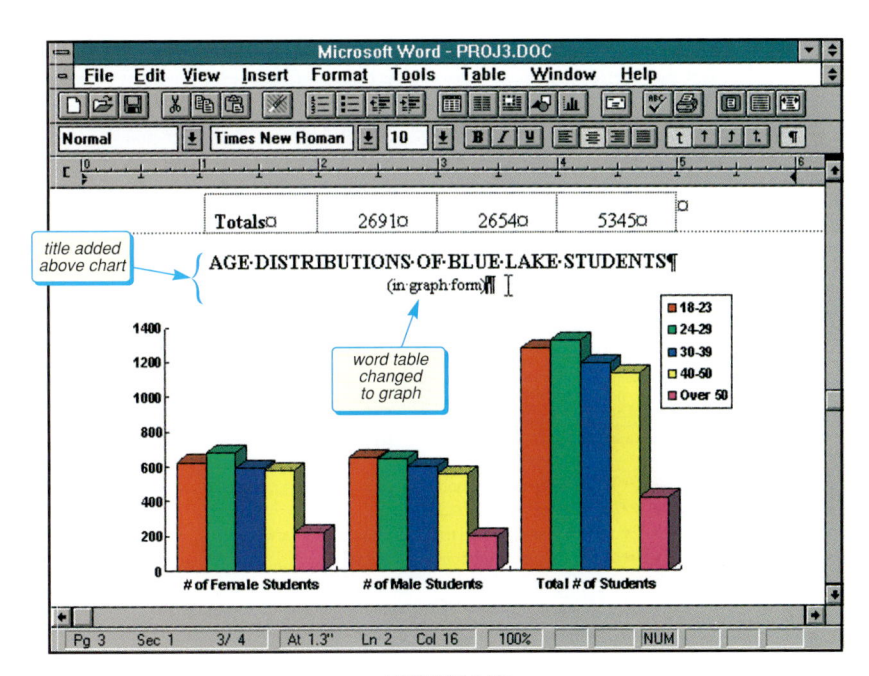

FIGURE 3-73

▶ ADDING BULLETS TO A LIST

Often you want to emphasize a list of items by either placing dots, called **bullets**, to the left of each item or numbering each item in the list. In Project 3, the list of conveniences at Blue Lake Institute of Technology should be emphasized with a single-spaced bulleted list. Because the paragraphs are all double-spaced in the document, you must change the spacing to single and then add the bullets as shown in the following steps (see Figure 3-75 on the next page).

TO ADD BULLETS TO A LIST

STEP 1 ▶

Select the paragraphs to be single-spaced. From the Format menu, choose the Paragraph command. Choose the Line Spacing box arrow and select Single by clicking it. Choose the OK button in the Paragraph dialog box. Point to the Bulleted List button (📋) on the Toolbar.

The paragraphs are single-spaced and highlighted (Figure 3-74).

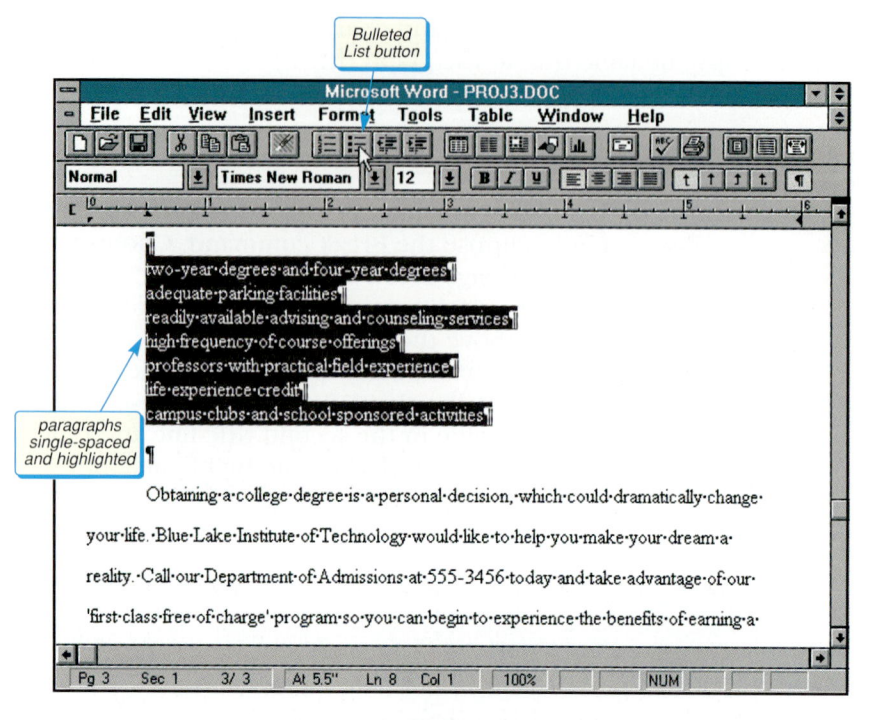

FIGURE 3-74

STEP 2 ▶

Choose the Bulleted List button. Click outside the selected paragraphs to remove the highlight.

Word places bullets to the left of each paragraph and moves each paragraph to the right one tab stop (Figure 3-75).

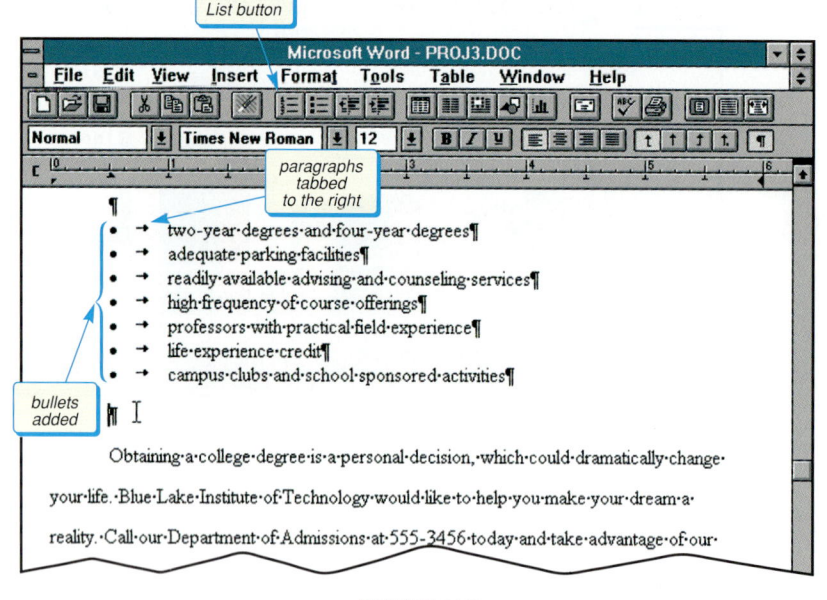

FIGURE 3-75

To add numbers to the front of a list rather than bullets, click the Numbered List button ( ) instead of the Bulleted List button. To remove bullets or numbers from a list, select the list and choose the Bullets and Numbering command from the Tools menu. Then choose the Remove button in the Bullets and Numbering dialog box.

Finishing the Paper

Give yourself credit for making the proposal so visually pleasing. At the very bottom of the proposal, perform these steps to enter the following information.

TO ENTER IDENTIFICATION INFORMATION

Step 1: Move the insertion point to the last paragraph mark in the document. Press the ENTER key once and change the point size to 8.

Step 2: Click the Centered Text button, type PROPOSAL DESIGN BY THE JUNIOR AND SENIOR STUDENTS OF BLUE LAKE INSTITIUTE OF TECHNOLOGY and click the Centered Text button again.

The credit line displays as shown in Figure 3-76.

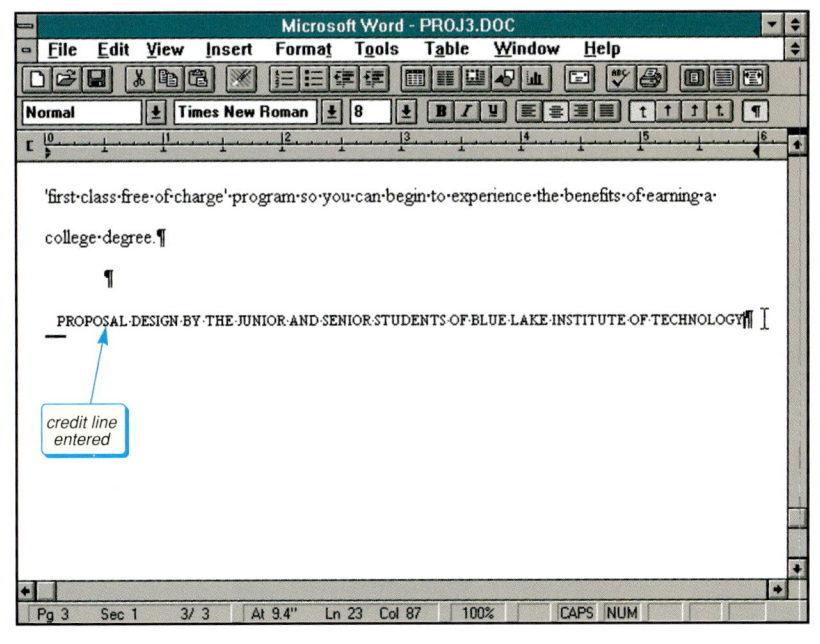

FIGURE 3-76

Check the spelling of the document by clicking the Spelling button on the Toolbar. Save the document one final time by clicking the Save button on the Toolbar, and print the proposal by clicking the Print button. The printed document displays as shown in Figure 3-77 on the next page. You have now finished Project 3. You can quit Word by choosing the Exit command from the File menu.

MSW160   PROJECT 3   CREATING A PROPOSAL USING TABLES AND GRAPHICS

GET A RUNNING START ON A NEW CAREER!

New Care

INS

YOUR CH

AG

18-
24-
30-
40-
Ov
To

Blue Lake Institute of Technology is committed to providing a high quality education for the people of its surrounding communities. Thousands of people from all walks of life have graduated from Blue Lake and are now successfully achieving their career goals. We invite you to join our student body and realize your dreams too.

Blue Lake is small enough to give you personalized attention, yet large enough to meet your needs. Choose to attend our school on a full or part-time basis.

Blue Lake Student Status Breakdown

Part
Full

With our di
parents, senior citiz
comfortable in our

AGE DISTRIBUTIONS OF BLUE LAKE STUDENTS
(in graph form)

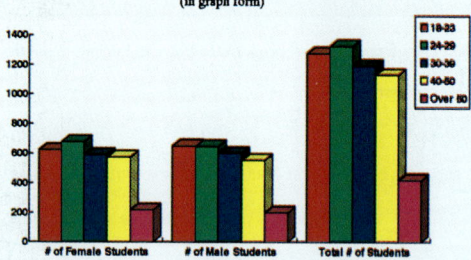

Your decision to pursue a college education and subsequently choose a college requires careful thought and planning. We at Blue Lake have attempted to address your wants and desires. We offer the following conveniences to make your experiences at Blue Lake more rewarding:

- two-year degrees and four-year degrees
- adequate parking facilities
- readily available advising and counseling services
- high frequency of course offerings
- professors with practical field experience
- life experience credit
- campus clubs and school sponsored activities

Obtaining a college degree is a personal decision, which could dramatically change your life. Blue Lake Institute of Technology would like to help you make your dream a reality. Call our Department of Admissions at 555-3456 today and take advantage of our 'first class free of charge' program so you can begin to experience the benefits of earning a college degree.

PROPOSAL DESIGN BY THE JUNIOR AND SENIOR STUDENTS OF BLUE LAKE INSTITUTE OF TECHNOLOGY

FIGURE 3-77

QUICK REFERENCE   MSW161

▶ PROJECT SUMMARY

Project 3 introduced you to creating a proposal using tables and graphics. First, you created a title page with three graphics and characters in a variety of point sizes. You learned how to insert an existing document into the active document. Then, you saved the active document with a new filename. Next, you set custom tabs and used them to create a table. Then, you used the Table button to create a second table. You opened Microsoft Graph to chart the second table. Finally, you added bullets to a list of items.

▶ KEY TERMS

bullets (*MSW157*)
Calculate command (*MSW150*)
cell (*MSW140*)
cell selection bar (*MSW146*)
Character command (*MSW127*)
Chart window (*MSW154*)
column markers (*MSW144*)
column selection bar (*MSW151*)
Datasheet window (*MSW154*)

end-of-cell mark (*MSW143*)
end-of-row mark (*MSW143*)
gridlines (*MSW143*)
import (*MSW118*)
Insert Columns command (*MSW153*)
Insert Rows command (*MSW153*)
Microsoft Draw (*MSW118*)

Microsoft Graph (*MSW153*)
Picture command (*MSW118*)
preview (*MSW130*)
row selection bar (*MSW151*)
scale (*MSW123*)
sizing handles (*MSW123*)
table (*MSW140*)
Windows Metafiles (*MSW118*)

QUICK REFERENCE

In Microsoft Word you can accomplish a task in a number of ways. The following table provides a quick reference to each task presented in this project with its available options. The commands listed in the Menu column can be executed using either the keyboard or mouse.

Task	Mouse	Menu	Keyboard Shortcuts
Changing Space Between Characters		From Format menu, choose Character	
Clear Custom Tab Stops	Drag tab stop marker down out of ruler	From Format menu, choose Tabs	
Delete Selected Table Row or Column		From Table menu, choose Delete Rows or Delete Columns	
Find a File		From File menu, choose Find File	
Import a Graphic		From Insert menu, choose Picture	
Insert Empty Table	Click Table button on Toolbar	From Table menu, choose Insert Table	
Insert Selected Table Column		From Table menu, choose Insert Column	

(continued)

QUICK REFERENCE (continued)

Task	Mouse	Menu	Keyboard Shortcuts
Insert Selected Table Row		From Table menu, choose Insert Rows	
Insert a Second Document into an Open Document		From Insert menu, choose File	
Restore Scaled Graphic		From Format menu, choose Picture	
Save a Document with New Filename		From File menu, choose Save As	Press F12
Scale Selected Graphic	Drag sizing handles	From Format menu, choose Picture	
Select a Graphic	Click graphic		Press SHIFT + RIGHT ARROW
Select a Table Cell	Click in cell selection bar		Press SHIFT + END
Select a Table Column	Click in column selection bar	From Table menu, choose Select Column	Press ALT + SHIFT + PAGE DOWN
Select a Table Row	Click in row selection bar	From Table menu, choose Select Row	
Set Tab Stops	Click on desired location on ruler	From Format menu, choose Tabs	

STUDENT ASSIGNMENTS

STUDENT ASSIGNMENT 1
True/False

Instructions: Circle T if the statement is true or F if the statement is false.

T F 1. Word for Windows software contains a series of predefined graphic files called Windows Graphics.
T F 2. To import graphics into a Word document, choose the Picture command from the Insert menu.
T F 3. Windows Metafiles are located in a subdirectory called METAFILES.
T F 4. You select a graphic by clicking it.
T F 5. Sizing handles are small triangles at the center and corners of a selected graphic.
T F 6. To expand the spacing between characters, click the Expand button on the Toolbar.
T F 7. In the Find File dialog box, you can preview the contents of files.
T F 8. To save an active file with a new filename, click the Save As button on the Toolbar.
T F 9. When you set a custom tab stop, Word clears all default tabs to the left of the custom tab stop.
T F 10. To center text at a custom tab stop, click the Centered Text button before entering the text.
T F 11. To clear a custom tab stop, drag the tab stop down and out of the ruler.
T F 12. A Word table is a collection of rows and columns.
T F 13. The intersection of a table row and table column is called a cell.
T F 14. You should turn off the gridlines before printing a table if you do not want the gridlines in your hardcopy.

T F 15. To move from one table column to the next, press the TAB key.
T F 16. To delete the contents of a cell, select the cell and press the DELETE key.
T F 17. Once the Calculate command is chosen, its results are placed at the location of the insertion point.
T F 18. To delete a row from a table, select the row and choose the Delete Rows command from the Table menu.
T F 19. Microsoft Graph is an embedded charting application that enables you to chart the data in a table.
T F 20. You add bullets to a list by selecting the list and clicking the Bulleted List button on the Toolbar.

STUDENT ASSIGNMENT 2
Multiple Choice

Instructions: Circle the correct response.

1. A drawing software package included with Word for Windows that allows you to design your own graphics is called _____.
   a. Microsoft Graphics
   b. Microsoft Draw
   c. Microsoft Write
   d. Microsoft Paint
2. Windows Metafiles have an extension of _____.
   a. .DOC   c. .WMF
   b. .MET   d. .MWM
3. Scaling is the process of _____ the size of a graphic.
   a. enlarging
   b. reducing
   c. both a and b
   d. neither a nor b
4. With Word, you can insert a second document _____.
   a. at the beginning of an active document
   b. in the middle of an active document
   c. at the end of an active document
   d. all of the above
5. To set a custom tab stop in Word, _____.
   a. click the Tab button on the Toolbar
   b. click on the desired tab stop location on the ruler
   c. choose the Custom command from the Tab menu
   d. click the Set Tab button on the ribbon
6. A table with 9 rows and 3 columns is referred to as a _____ table.
   a. 3 × 9   c. 27
   b. 9 × 3   d. 12
7. When the insertion point is in a table, the ruler identifies table columns with _____.
   a. the letters TC
   b. an up-pointing arrow
   c. a dark letter T
   d. a small plus sign
8. In a table, the cell selection bar is located _____.
   a. at the left edge of a cell
   b. at the right edge of a cell
   c. at the bottom edge of a cell
   d. at the top edge of a cell

(continued)

PROJECT 3   CREATING A PROPOSAL USING TABLES AND GRAPHICS

STUDENT ASSIGNMENT 2 (continued)

9. When in the column selection bar, the mouse pointer changes to a(n) _____.
   a. left-pointing arrow (▨)
   b. right-pointing arrow (▧)
   c. up-pointing arrow (↑)
   d. down-pointing arrow (↓)
10. To open the Microsoft Graph application, _____.
    a. click the Graph button on the Toolbar
    b. choose the Microsoft Graph command from the Tools menu
    c. exit Word for Windows and double-click the Microsoft Graph program-item icon
    d. none of the above

STUDENT ASSIGNMENT 3
Understanding the Steps to Import a Graphic

Instructions: Fill in the Step numbers below to correctly order the process of importing a graphic.

Step _____: Choose the Preview button in the Picture dialog box.

Step _____: From the Insert menu, choose the Picture command.

Step _____: Position the insertion point where you want the graphic to be inserted.

Step _____: Choose the OK button in the Picture dialog box.

Step _____: Select the desired Windows Metafile.

Step _____: Open the subdirectory clipart in the Picture dialog box.

STUDENT ASSIGNMENT 4
Understanding Custom Tab Stops

Instructions: Answer the questions on the next page concerning Figure SA3-4. The numbers in the figure correspond to question numbers.

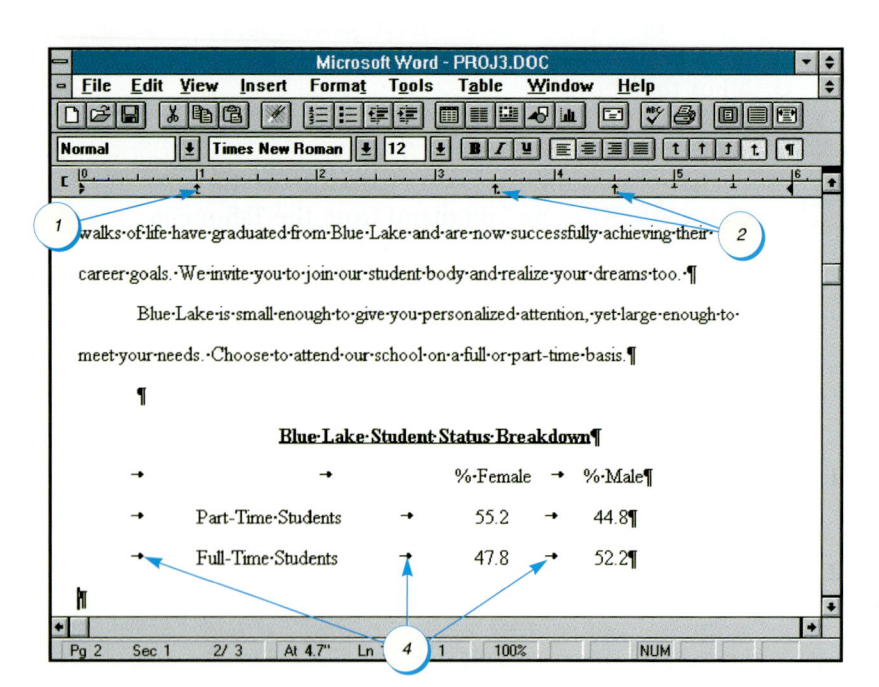

FIGURE SA3-4

1. What is the alignment of the tab stop at the 1-inch mark?

2. What is the alignment of the tab stops at the 3.5-inch and 4.5-inch marks?

3. What key do you press to move from one tab stop to the next?

4. Why do the dark right-pointing arrows appear between the tab stops in the table?

5. How would you remove the tab stop at the 4.5-inch mark on the ruler?

STUDENT ASSIGNMENT 5
Understanding Tables

Instructions: In Figure SA3-5, arrows point to several items on the table. In the space provided, briefly identify each area. Then answer the questions concerning the table.

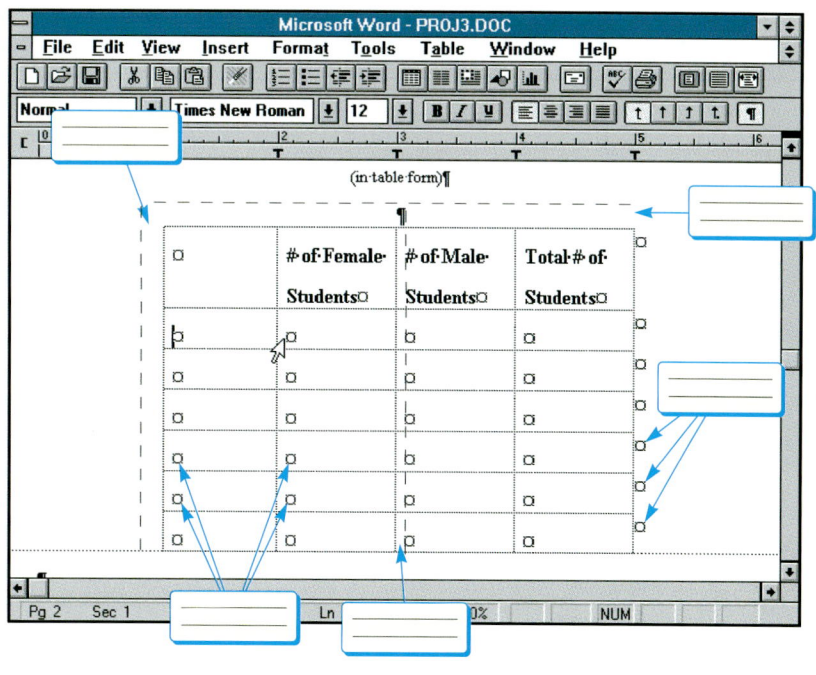

FIGURE SA3-5

1. How many rows and columns does this table have?

2. How do you advance from one table cell to the next?

STUDENT ASSIGNMENT 6
Understanding the Microsoft Graph Window

Instructions: In Figure SA3-6, arrows point to several areas of the Microsoft Graph window. In the space provided, briefly identify each area.

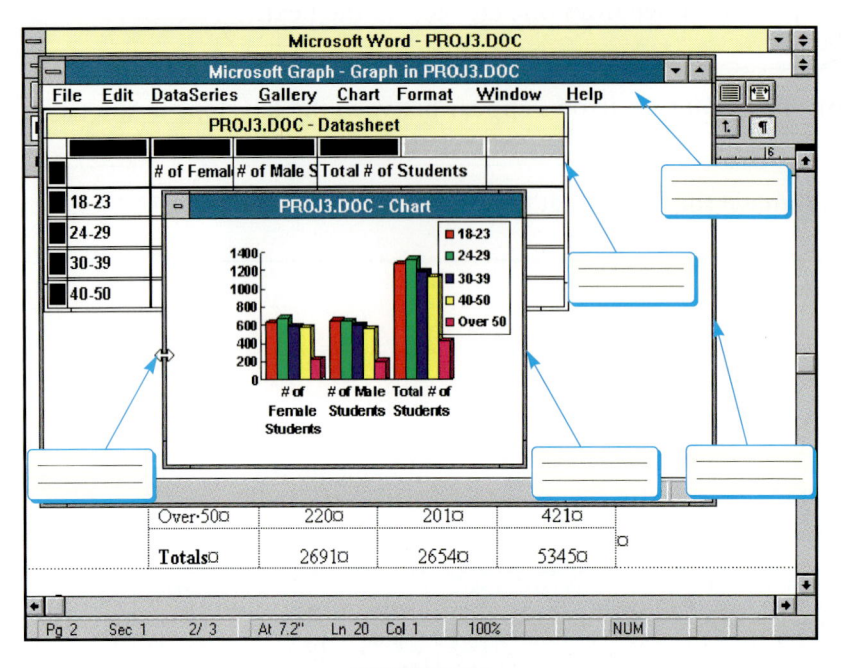

FIGURE SA3-6

COMPUTER LABORATORY EXERCISES

COMPUTER LABORATORY EXERCISE 1
Adding Bullets to a List

Instructions: Start Word. Open the document CLE3-1 from the Word subdirectory on the Student Diskette that accompanies this book. A portion of document is shown in Figure CLE3-1. The document resembles the body of the proposal in Project 3. By following the steps below, you are to change the spacing of the conveniences and add bullets to them.

Perform the following tasks:

1. From the Help menu, choose the Help Index command. Choose the Search button. Type bullets and press the ENTER key. Select Adding bullets to a list. Choose the Go To button. Read and print the information. Choose the Back button. Choose the Search button. Type saving and press the ENTER key. Select Making a copy of the active document. Choose the Go To button. Read and print the information. Close the Help window.
2. Use the scroll bar to position the insertion point on the paragraph mark just above the list as shown in Figure CLE3-1.
3. Select the paragraphs to be bulleted by dragging the mouse down through the selection bar.
4. From the Format menu, choose the Paragraph command. Choose the Line Spacing box arrow by clicking it and select Single by clicking it. Choose the OK button in the Paragraph dialog box.

5. Choose the Bulleted List button on the Toolbar. Click outside the selection to remove the highlight.
6. Save the active document with a new filename by choosing the Save As command from the File menu. Enter the filename CLE3-1A.
7. Print the document by clicking the Print button on the Toolbar.
8. From the File menu, choose the Close command to close the document.

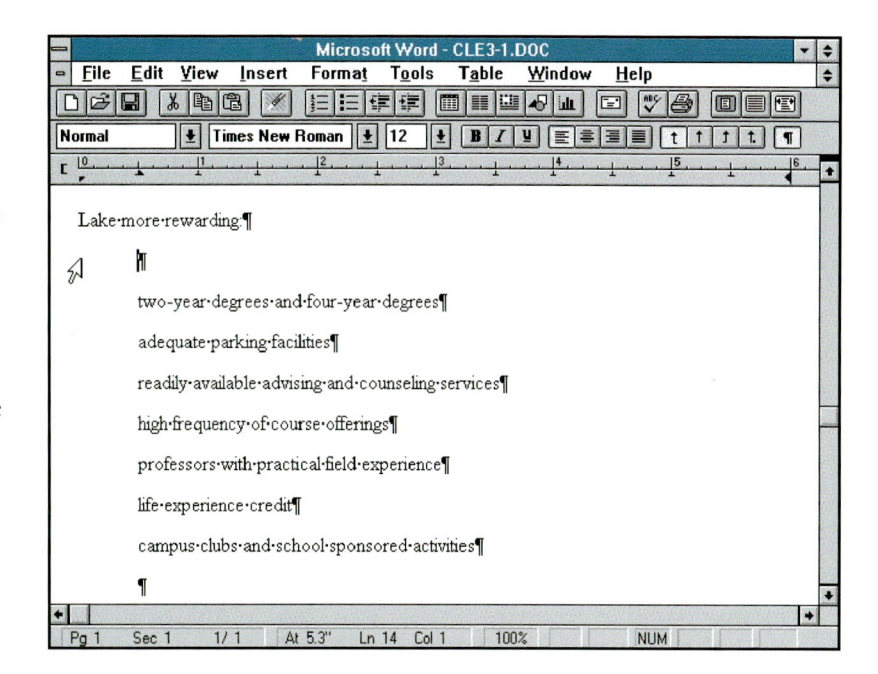

FIGURE CLE3-1

COMPUTER LABORATORY EXERCISE 2
Summing the Rows and Columns in a Table

Instructions: Start Word. Open the document CLE3-2 from the Word subdirectory on the Student Diskette that accompanies this book. The document is shown in Figure CLE3-2. The document resembles a table created in Project 3.

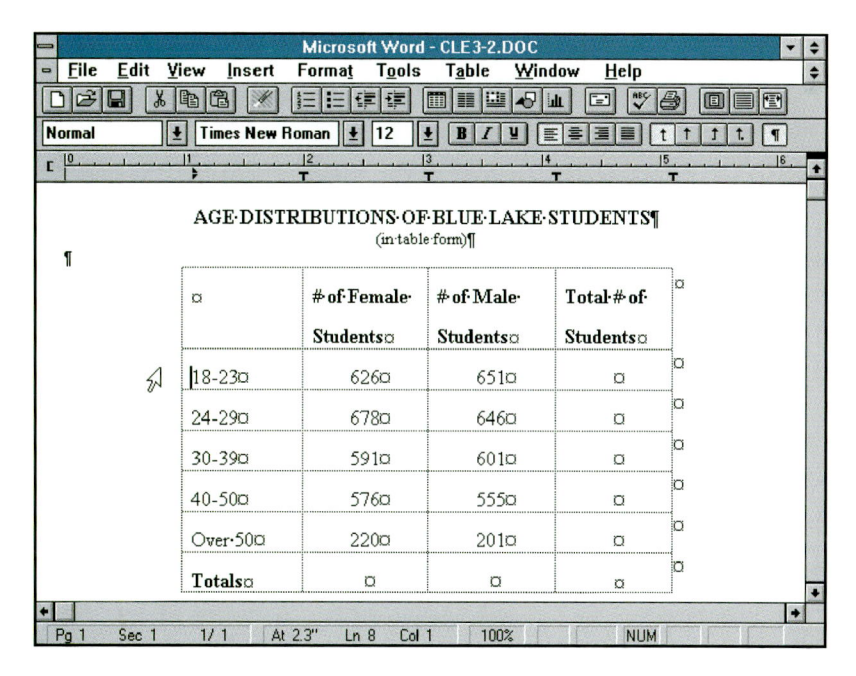

FIGURE CLE3-2

(continued)

COMPUTER LABORATORY EXERCISE 2 (continued)

Perform the following tasks:

1. Position the mouse pointer in the second row of the second column.
2. Drag the mouse through the third column of the second row.
3. From the Tools menu, choose the Calculate command.
4. Click in the cell intersecting the Total # of Students column and the 18-23 row.
5. Click the Paste button on the Toolbar.
6. Repeat the procedure in Step 1 through Step 5 for the 24-29, 30-39, 40-50, and Over 50 rows.
7. Position the mouse pointer in the column selection bar above the # of Female Students column.
8. Click the mouse to select the entire column.
9. From the Tools menu, choose the Calculate command.
10. Click in the cell intersecting the Totals row and # of Female Students column.
11. Click the Paste button on the Toolbar.
12. Repeat the procedure in Step 7 through Step 11 for the # of Male Students and Total # of Students columns.
13. Save the revised document with the filename CLE3-2A using the Save As command on the File menu.
14. Print the document by clicking the Print button on the Toolbar.
15. From the File menu, choose the Close command to close the document.

COMPUTER LABORATORY EXERCISE 3
Importing a Graphic

Instructions: Start Word. Open the document CLE3-3 from the Word subdirectory on the Student Diskette that accompanies this book. The document is shown in Figure CLE3-3. The document resembles the title page of the proposal created in Project 3.

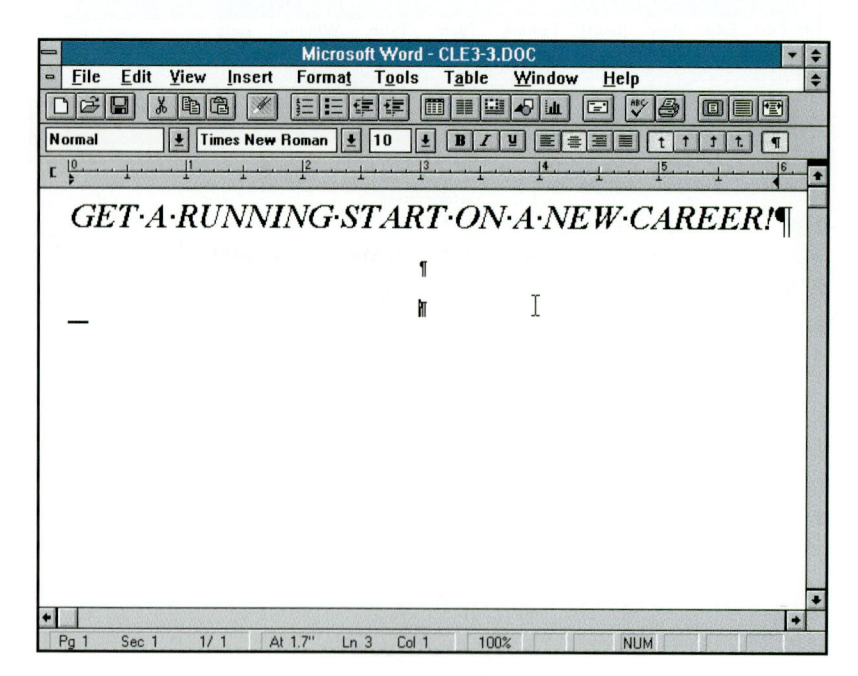

FIGURE CLE3-3

Perform the following tasks:

1. Position the insertion point on the last paragraph mark in the document.
2. From the Insert menu, choose the Picture command.
3. Open the subdirectory clipart in the winword directory on drive C by double-clicking it.
4. Repeatedly click the down arrow at the bottom of the scroll bar in the File Name list box until the filename running.wmf displays. Select this file by clicking it.
5. Choose the Preview button to display the Windows Metafile.
6. Choose the OK button.
7. Save the revised document with the filename CLE3-3A using the Save As command on the File menu.
8. Print the document by clicking the Print button on the Toolbar.
9. From the File menu, choose the Close command to close the document.

COMPUTER LABORATORY ASSIGNMENTS

COMPUTER LABORATORY ASSIGNMENT 1
Creating a Proposal Using Tabs

Purpose: To become familiar with importing and scaling graphics, creating a bulleted list, and using tabs to create a table.

Problem: You are on the town board of Clifton Heights. The board has recently funded the construction of a new public library. As a recent graduate in the field of Creative Arts, you have been asked to write an informal proposal to be sent to all community residents announcing the new public library and explaining its benefits.

Instructions:

1. Click the Show/Hide Nonprinting Characters button on the ribbon.
2. Adjust line spacing to double.
3. Change the Normal style by clicking the paragraph mark. Then change the point size to 12 and double-click the word Normal in the Style box. Press the ENTER key and click the Yes button.
4. Create the title page as shown in Figure CLA3-1a on the next page.
5. Create the body of the proposal as shown in Figure CLA3-1b on MSW171. The body of the proposal has a single-spaced bulleted list and a table created with tabs. The tabs are set at .875-inches, 2-inches, 3.125-inches, and 4.375-inches.
6. Spell check the document.
7. Save the document with the filename CLA3-1.
8. View the document in print preview.
9. Print the document from within print preview.

(continued)

MSW170   PROJECT 3   CREATING A PROPOSAL USING TABLES AND GRAPHICS

COMPUTER LABORATORY ASSIGNMENT 1 (continued)

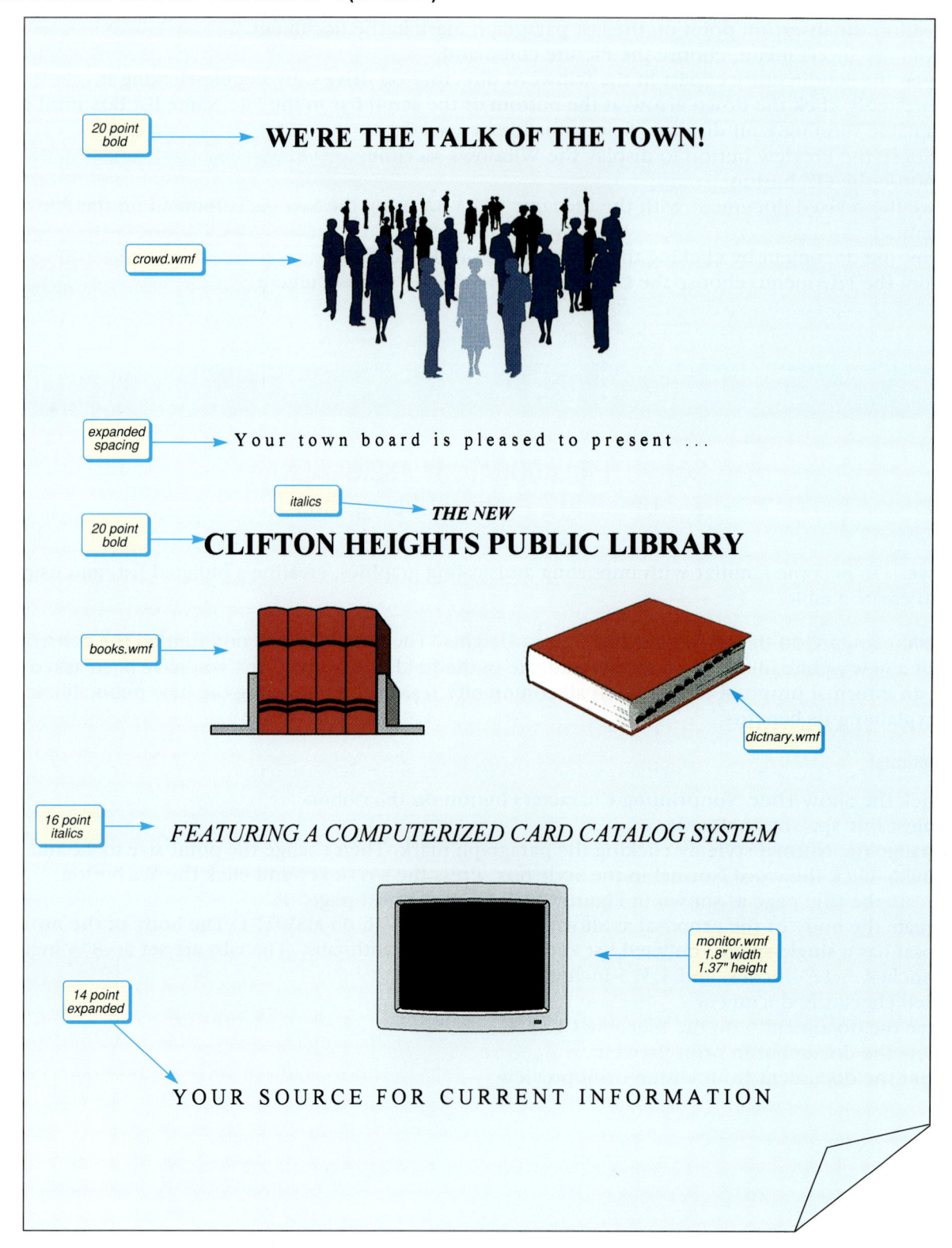

20 point bold → **WE'RE THE TALK OF THE TOWN!**

crowd.wmf →

expanded spacing → Your town board is pleased to present ...

italics → *THE NEW*

20 point bold → **CLIFTON HEIGHTS PUBLIC LIBRARY**

books.wmf →

dictnary.wmf ←

16 point italics → *FEATURING A COMPUTERIZED CARD CATALOG SYSTEM*

monitor.wmf 1.8" width 1.37" height ←

14 point expanded → YOUR SOURCE FOR CURRENT INFORMATION

FIGURE CLA3-1a

Clifton Heights Public Library is conveniently located near you and has been designed to provide our community with a variety of information.

Our shelves are stocked with materials for your reading pleasure, as well as for your reference. We have a huge selection of each of the following:

- non-fiction books
- fiction books
- reference materials
- periodicals
- newspapers
- pamphlets
- video tapes
- compact discs and cassettes
- childrens books, magazines, and tapes

You may check availability, as well as check out any, of these items directly through our computerized card catalog system. For demonstrations of how to use our computerized card catalog system, stop by the library at any of the times listed below:

COMPUTERIZED CARD CATALOG DEMONSTRATIONS

When?	Where?	A.M. Times?	P.M. Times?
Weekdays	Room A	9, 10, 11	2, 3, 4, 6, 7
Weekends	Room B	8, 9, 10,11	1, 2, 3, 4

We also have four personal computers and six typewriters in our library for your use at any time.

We are open on weekdays from 8:30 a.m. to 8:30 p.m. and on weekends from 7:30 a.m. to 5:30 p.m. We are located at 1029 South Western Boulevard in Clifton Heights. Our telephone number is 717 555-1234.

VISIT YOUR SOURCE FOR INFORMATION TODAY!

FIGURE CLA3-1b

COMPUTER LABORATORY ASSIGNMENT 2
Creating a Proposal Using the Table and Graph Buttons

Purpose: To become familiar with importing and scaling graphics, creating a table, and graphing the table.

Problem: You are director of the Placement Office at The Computer Institute (TCI). You are currently on a campaign to recruit new students. Your major theme is guaranteed job placement for all graduates. You have been assigned the task of developing the proposal in Figure CLA3-2 for prospective students.

Instructions:

1. Click the Show/Hide Nonprinting Characters button on the ribbon.
2. Adjust line spacing to double.
3. Change the Normal style by clicking the paragraph mark. Then change the point size to 12 and double-click the word Normal in the Style box. Press the ENTER key and click the Yes button.
4. Create the title page as shown in Figure CLA3-2a.
5. Create the body of the proposal as shown in Figure CLA3-2b on MSW174. The body of the proposal has a table created with the Table button. The first four rows of the table are charted with the Graph button.
6. Spell check the document.
7. Save the document with the filename CLA3-2.
8. View the document in print preview.
9. Print the document from within print preview.

COMPUTER LABORATORY ASSIGNMENTS   **MSW173**

DO YOU WANT TO EARN BIG BUCKS?

Join thousands of graduates from

THE COMPUTER INSTITUTE

with jobs in

Computer Programming   Office Automation   Systems Analysis & Design

WE ARE SO CONFIDENT IN OUR EDUCATIONAL PROGRAM THAT

OUR GRADUATES ARE <u>GUARANTEED</u> JOB PLACEMENT!

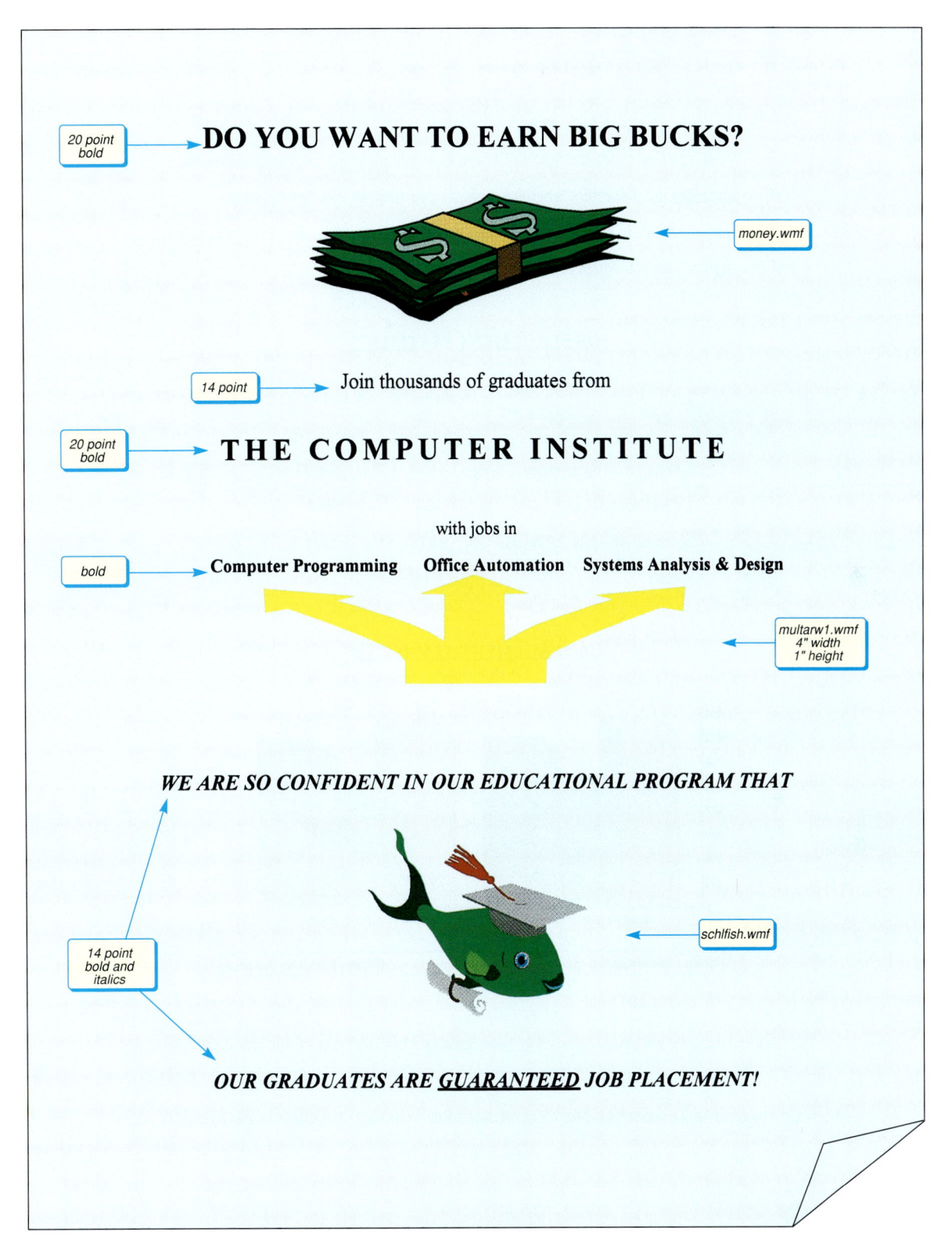

FIGURE CLA3-2a

(continued)

MSW174   PROJECT 3   CREATING A PROPOSAL USING TABLES AND GRAPHICS

COMPUTER LABORATORY ASSIGNMENT 2 (continued)

We at The Computer Institute (TCI) are so confident in our educational process that we <u>guarantee</u> job placement when you acquire your degree. We have placed thousands of graduates in computer programming, office automation, and systems analysis and design jobs. Our placement reputation speaks for itself.

JOB PLACEMENT STATISTICS
(in table form)

	Number of Graduates	Number of Placements
Computer Programming	1438	1429
Office Automation	954	954
Systems Analysis & Design	1276	1273
Totals	3668	3656

JOB PLACEMENT STATISTICS
(in graph form)

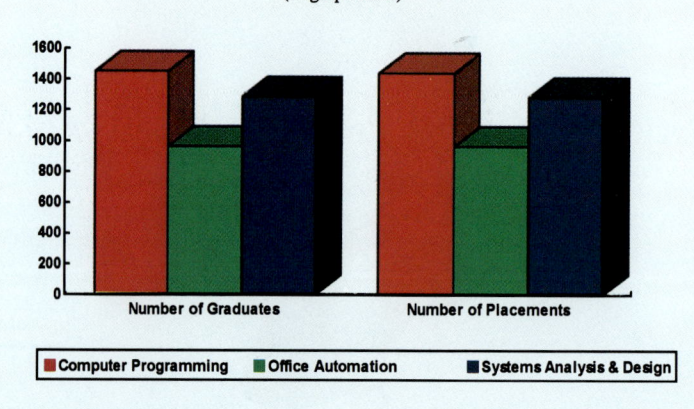

As you can see, we have a nearly **100%** success rate in placement of our graduates!

CONTACT OUR ADMISSIONS OFFICE AT 803-555-2020 FOR DETAILS ON OUR PROGRAMS

FIGURE CLA3-2b

COMPUTER LABORATORY ASSIGNMENT 3
Enhancing a Draft of a Proposal

Purpose: To become familiar with importing and scaling graphics, inserting an existing document into an active document, saving an active document with a new filename, creating a table with tabs, creating a table with the Table button and graphing the table, and adding a single-spaced bulleted list.

Problem: You are the owner of Star Realty. One of your employees has drafted an informal proposal to be sent to prospective clients in the downtown area. You decide to add pizzazz to the proposal by creating a title page. You also add a couple of tables and a graph to the body of the proposal.

Instructions:

1. Click the Show/Hide Nonprinting Characters button on the ribbon.
2. Adjust line spacing to double.
3. Change the Normal style by clicking the paragraph mark. Then change the point size to 12 and double-click the word Normal in the Style box. Press the ENTER key and click the Yes button.
4. Create the title page as shown in Figure CLA3-3a on the next page.
5. Insert the draft of the body of the proposal beneath the title page using the File command from the Insert menu. The draft is called CLA3-3B in the WORD subdirectory on the Student Diskette that accompanies this book. The draft of the body of the proposal is shown in Figure CLA3-3b on page MSW177.
6. Add the following table created with tabs below the first paragraph in the proposal. Double space the table and set custom tabs at 1-inch, 2.5-inches, and 4-inches. Above the table, center, bold, and underline the title, Star Realty Condominium Sales.

	# of Prospects	# of Units Sold
This Year	2230	2039
Last Year	2098	1892

7. Use the Table button to create the following table below the second paragraph in the proposal. Double-space the table. Above the table, center and bold the first line of the title, AVERAGE CONDOMINIUM PRICES. Single-spaced below the first title line, in 10-point type, (in table form).

	Lower Floors of Building	**Upper Floors of Building**
2 Rooms	$100,000	$175,000
3 Rooms	$120,000	$235,000
4 Rooms	$135,000	$265,000
5 Rooms	$155,000	$300,000
6 Rooms	$195,000	$345,000
7 Rooms	$210,000	$365,000

8. Select all rows in the table and chart the table using the Graph button. In the Microsoft Graph application, resize the chart so it is easy to read. Use the same title as for the table, except change the word table to graph.
9. Single-space and add bullets to the list of items beneath the third paragraph.
10. Save the active document with the filename CLA3-3 using the Save As command in the File menu.
11. View the document in print preview.
12. Print the document from within print preview.

(continued)

MSW176   PROJECT 3   CREATING A PROPOSAL USING TABLES AND GRAPHICS

COMPUTER LABORATORY ASSIGNMENT 3 (continued)

18 point bold and italics

LOOKING FOR YOUR DREAM CONDOMINIUM?

cityview.wmf
2" width
2.75" height

16 point bold and italics

OVERLOOKING OUR BEAUTIFUL DOWNTOWN SKYLINE?

bold

CALL US!

bold and expanded spacing

STAR REALTY

star.wmf

bold

bold and expanded spacing

965-555-2098

STAR REALTY

3darrow4.wmf
4.5" width
.75" height

Serving Satisfied Customers Since 1942

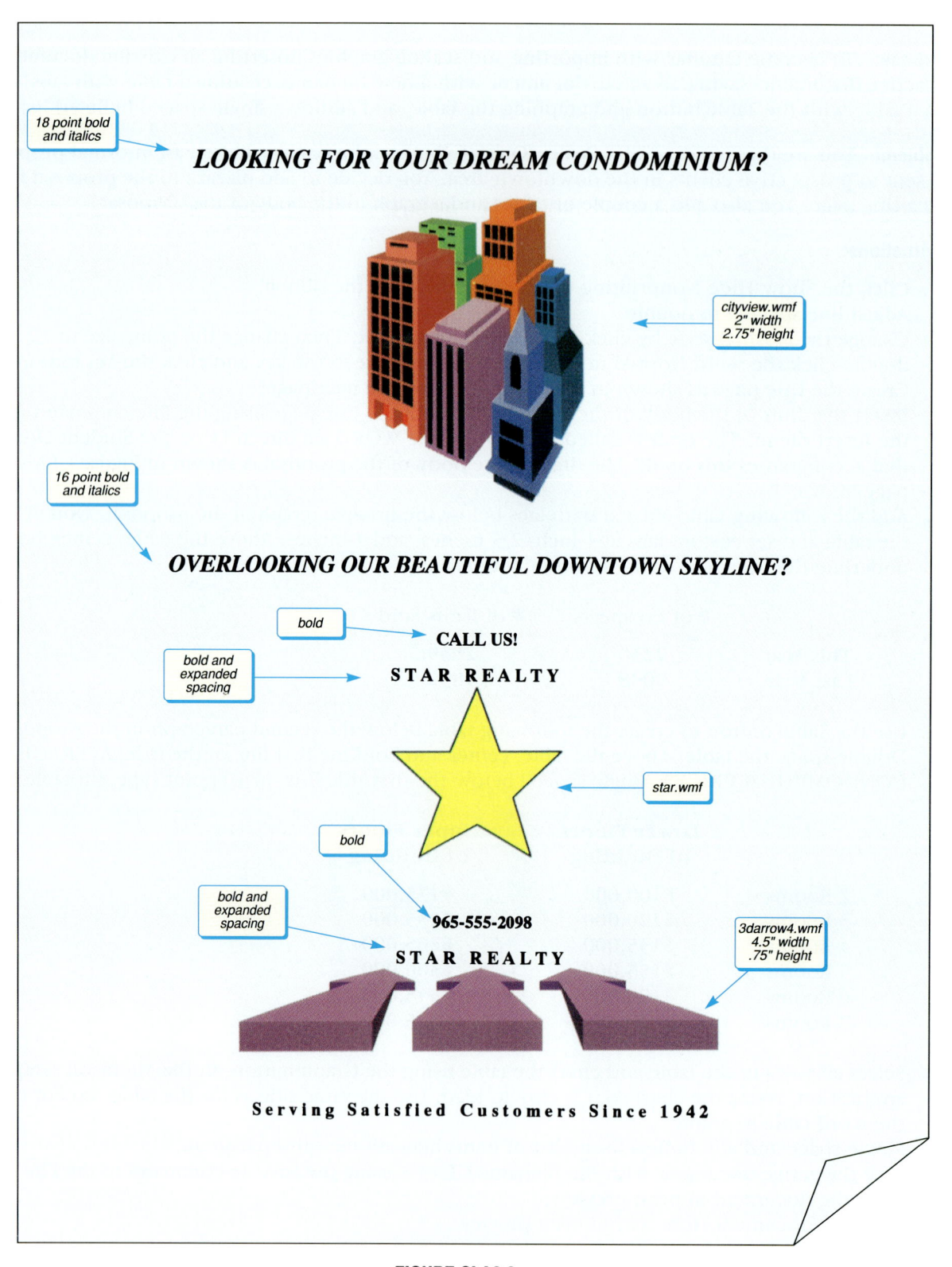

FIGURE CLA3-3a

At Star Realty we take pride in our record of serving satisfied customers. We specialize in locating prime condominiums in the downtown area. We have successfully located thousands of prime units for prospective clients. If you are in the market for a condominium, then Star Realty is the real estate office for you.

With our long history and reputation, we are able to negotiate the most affordable prices for our clients and seek loan arrangements that are best suited to their needs. Depending on the placement of the condominium in the building and the number of rooms, prices vary as shown below.

At Star Realty, we offer a wide variety of services to make your condomium search a pleasant and rewarding experience. Star Realty is committed to giving you red carpet treatment:

prime condominiums in beautiful downtown

well-trained, friendly real estate agents

no-hassle pre-purchase qualification

flexible hours

24-hour paging service

Star Realty would like to help you find the condominium of your dreams. Our office is conveniently located at 12 Michigan Avenue in Suite 44A. Stop by at your convenience or call us at 965 555-2098 for an appointment.

WE LOOK FORWARD TO SERVING YOU

FIGURE CLA3-3b

COMPUTER LABORATORY ASSIGNMENT 4
Creating a Proposal

Purpose: To become familiar with designing a title page and preparing a proposal including tables and graphs.

Problem: You are to scan through the list of available Windows Metafiles in the clipart directory and select an area of interest to you. Assume you are the owner of a company that sells your selected product or service. Then research the area obtaining prices and other pertinent information to enhance your sale.

Instructions: Create a title page with multiple Windows Metafiles, including the one you selected earlier. Be sure the color of each one blends nicely together. Use a variety of point sizes, spacing between characters, italics, bold, and underlining on your title page. Be creative. Then enter the proposal. Include one table created with tabs and another created with the Table button. Graph the table created with the Table button. Be sure to check the spelling of your proposal before printing it. Save your proposal with the filename CLA3-4.

MICROSOFT WORD 2.0 FOR WINDOWS
PROJECT FOUR

GENERATING FORM LETTERS AND MAILING LABELS

OBJECTIVES You will have mastered the material in this project when you can:

- Explain the merging process
- Explain the terms, field and record
- Create a data file
- Switch from a data file to the main document
- Insert merge fields into the main document
- Use an IF field in the main document
- Merge and print form letters
- Selectively merge and print form letters
- Create and print mailing labels

▶ INTRODUCTION

Form letters are used regularly in both business and personal correspondence. The basic contents of a group of form letters are similar; however, items like name, address, city, state, and zip code change from one letter to the next. Thus, form letters are personalized to the addressee. An individual is more likely to open and read a personalized letter than a standard Dear Sir or Madam letter. Form letters are usually sent to a group of people. Business form letters include announcements of sales to customers or introduction of company benefits to employees. Personal form letters include letters of application for a job or invitations to participate in a sweepstakes giveaway. Once form letters are generated, mailing labels must be created for the envelopes.

▶ PROJECT FOUR

Project Four illustrates the generation of a business form letter and corresponding mailing labels. The form letter is sent to all new customers at Peripherals Plus, thanking them for their recent order and informing them of their customer service representative's name. The customer service representative's name varies, depending on the location of the customer. As shown in Figure 4-1 on the next page, the process of generating form letters involves creating a main document for the form letter and a data file, and merging, or *blending*, the two together into a series of individual letters.

MSW179

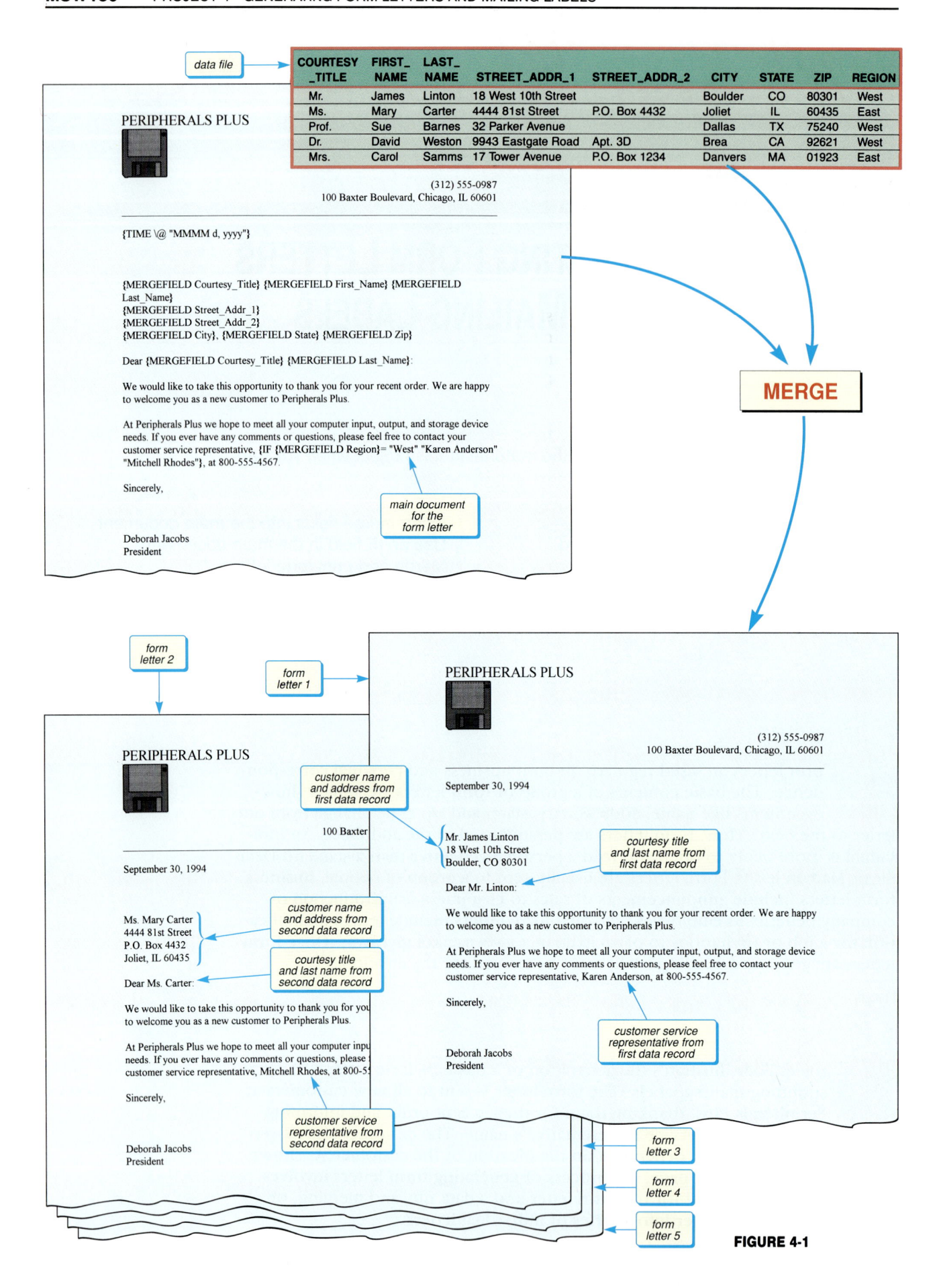

MSW180 PROJECT 4 GENERATING FORM LETTERS AND MAILING LABELS

	COURTESY _TITLE	FIRST_ NAME	LAST_ NAME	STREET_ADDR_1	STREET_ADDR_2	CITY	STATE	ZIP	REGION
data file →	Mr.	James	Linton	18 West 10th Street		Boulder	CO	80301	West
	Ms.	Mary	Carter	4444 81st Street	P.O. Box 4432	Joliet	IL	60435	East
	Prof.	Sue	Barnes	32 Parker Avenue		Dallas	TX	75240	West
	Dr.	David	Weston	9943 Eastgate Road	Apt. 3D	Brea	CA	92621	West
	Mrs.	Carol	Samms	17 Tower Avenue	P.O. Box 1234	Danvers	MA	01923	East

PERIPHERALS PLUS

(312) 555-0987
100 Baxter Boulevard, Chicago, IL 60601

{TIME \@ "MMMM d, yyyy"}

{MERGEFIELD Courtesy_Title} {MERGEFIELD First_Name} {MERGEFIELD Last_Name}
{MERGEFIELD Street_Addr_1}
{MERGEFIELD Street_Addr_2}
{MERGEFIELD City}, {MERGEFIELD State} {MERGEFIELD Zip}

Dear {MERGEFIELD Courtesy_Title} {MERGEFIELD Last_Name}:

We would like to take this opportunity to thank you for your recent order. We are happy to welcome you as a new customer to Peripherals Plus.

At Peripherals Plus we hope to meet all your computer input, output, and storage device needs. If you ever have any comments or questions, please feel free to contact your customer service representative, {IF {MERGEFIELD Region}= "West" "Karen Anderson" "Mitchell Rhodes"}, at 800-555-4567.

Sincerely,

Deborah Jacobs
President

main document for the form letter

MERGE

---

form letter 2

PERIPHERALS PLUS

100 Baxter

September 30, 1994

Ms. Mary Carter
4444 81st Street
P.O. Box 4432
Joliet, IL 60435

Dear Ms. Carter:

We would like to take this opportunity to thank you for you
to welcome you as a new customer to Peripherals Plus.

At Peripherals Plus we hope to meet all your computer inpu
needs. If you ever have any comments or questions, please
customer service representative, Mitchell Rhodes, at 800-5

Sincerely,

Deborah Jacobs
President

customer name and address from second data record

courtesy title and last name from second data record

customer service representative from second data record

---

form letter 1

PERIPHERALS PLUS

(312) 555-0987
100 Baxter Boulevard, Chicago, IL 60601

September 30, 1994

Mr. James Linton
18 West 10th Street
Boulder, CO 80301

Dear Mr. Linton:

We would like to take this opportunity to thank you for your recent order. We are happy to welcome you as a new customer to Peripherals Plus.

At Peripherals Plus we hope to meet all your computer input, output, and storage device needs. If you ever have any comments or questions, please feel free to contact your customer service representative, Karen Anderson, at 800-555-4567.

Sincerely,

Deborah Jacobs
President

customer name and address from first data record

courtesy title and last name from first data record

customer service representative from first data record

form letter 3
form letter 4
form letter 5

FIGURE 4-1

Merging

Merging is the process of combining the contents of a data file with a main document. The **main document** contains the constant, or unchanging, text, punctuation, spaces, and graphics. In Figure 4-1, the main document represents the portion of the form letters that is identical from one merged letter to the next. Conversely, the **data file** contains the variable, or changing, values in each letter. In Figure 4-1, the data file contains five different customers. One form letter is generated for each customer listed in the data file.

Document Preparation Steps

The following document preparation steps give you an overview of how the form letters in Figure 4-1 and corresponding mailing labels will be developed in this project. If you are preparing the documents in this project on a personal computer, read these steps without doing them.

1. Create a data file.
2. Create the main document for the form letter.
3. Merge and print the form letters.
4. Create mailing labels.
5. Print the mailing labels.

The following pages contain a detailed explanation of each of these steps.

Displaying Nonprinting Characters

As discussed in earlier projects, it is helpful to display nonprinting characters that indicate where in the document you pressed the ENTER key, SPACEBAR, or TAB key. Thus, you should display the nonprinting characters by clicking the Show/Hide Nonprinting Characters button on the ribbon.

▶ Creating a Data File

A data file is a Word table (Figure 4-2). Recall from Project 3 that a Word table is a series of rows and columns. Each row in a data file is called a **record**. A record contains a set of related data values. Two types of records can exist in a data file: data records and a header record. **Data records** contain the text that varies from one merged document to the next. The data file for this project contains five data records. In this project, each data record identifies a different customer. Thus, five form letters are to be generated from this data file.

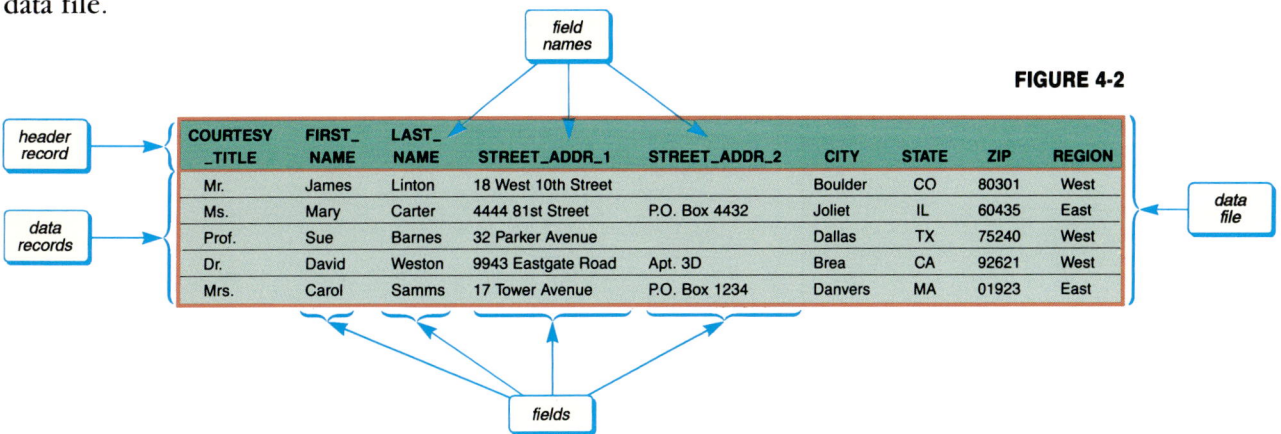

FIGURE 4-2

COURTESY_TITLE	FIRST_NAME	LAST_NAME	STREET_ADDR_1	STREET_ADDR_2	CITY	STATE	ZIP	REGION
Mr.	James	Linton	18 West 10th Street		Boulder	CO	80301	West
Ms.	Mary	Carter	4444 81st Street	P.O. Box 4432	Joliet	IL	60435	East
Prof.	Sue	Barnes	32 Parker Avenue		Dallas	TX	75240	West
Dr.	David	Weston	9943 Eastgate Road	Apt. 3D	Brea	CA	92621	West
Mrs.	Carol	Samms	17 Tower Avenue	P.O. Box 1234	Danvers	MA	01923	East

Each column in the data file is called a **field**. A field represents a group of similar data. In this project, the data file contains nine fields. For example, courtesy title, first name, last name, street address, city, state, zip, and region are fields.

Each field must be uniquely identified with a name, called a **field name**. For example, the name First_Name represents the field (column) containing the first names of the customers. These field names are placed in the first row of the data file to identify the name of each column. Thus, the first record of the data file is called the **header record**.

Field Name Conventions

The first step in creating a data file is to decide which fields it will contain. That is, you must identify the information varying from one merged document to the next. In Project 4, each record contains up to nine different fields for each customer: a courtesy title, first name, last name, first line of street address, second line of street address (optional), city, state, zip code, and region. Regions are divided into East and West, depending on the customer's state. The customer service representative is determined based on the customer's region.

For each field, you must decide on a field name. Field names must be unique. That is, no two field names may be the same. Field names cannot exceed 32 characters. The first character of a field name must be a letter; the remaining 31 characters can be either letters, numbers, or the underscore (_) character. Because spaces are not allowed in field names, use the underscore character to separate words in field names. Thus, the field names for the data file in Project 4 are as follows: Courtesy_Title, First_Name, Last_Name, Street_Addr_1, Street_Addr_2, City, State, Zip, and Region. Notice the first letter of each word in the field names is capitalized to make them easier to read.

Fields and related field names may be listed in any order in the data file. The order of fields has no effect on the order they will print in the main document.

The following steps illustrate how to create a new data file.

TO CREATE A DATA FILE ▼

STEP 1 ▶

Select the File menu and point to the Print Merge command (Figure 4-3).

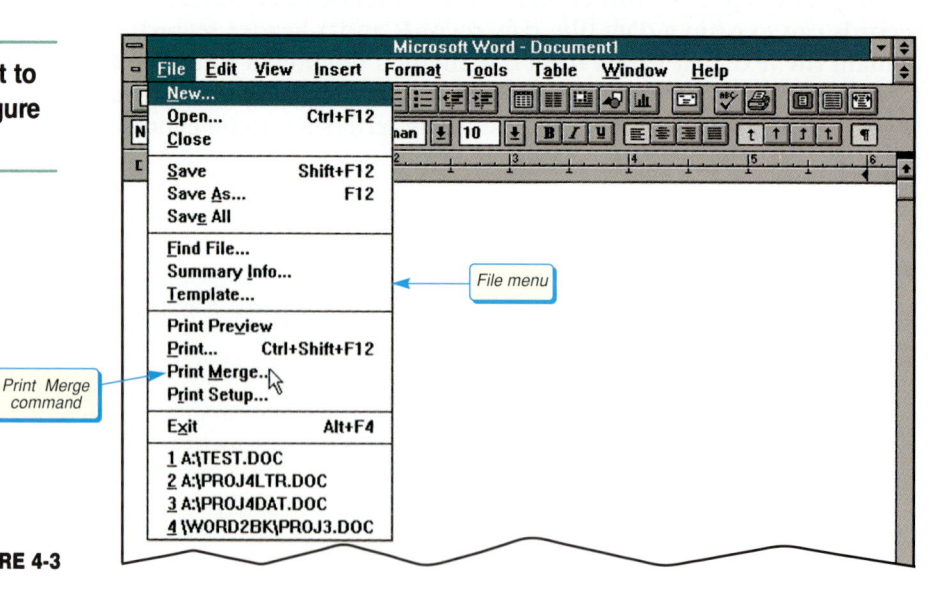

FIGURE 4-3

CREATING A DATA FILE   **MSW183**

STEP 2 ▶

Choose the Print Merge command. When the Print Merge Setup dialog box displays, point to the Attach Data File button (Attach Data File...).

Word displays the Print Merge Setup dialog box (Figure 4-4). The Print Merge Setup dialog box pictorially represents the merge process. That is, a data file and a main document are merged together into a series of resulting documents.

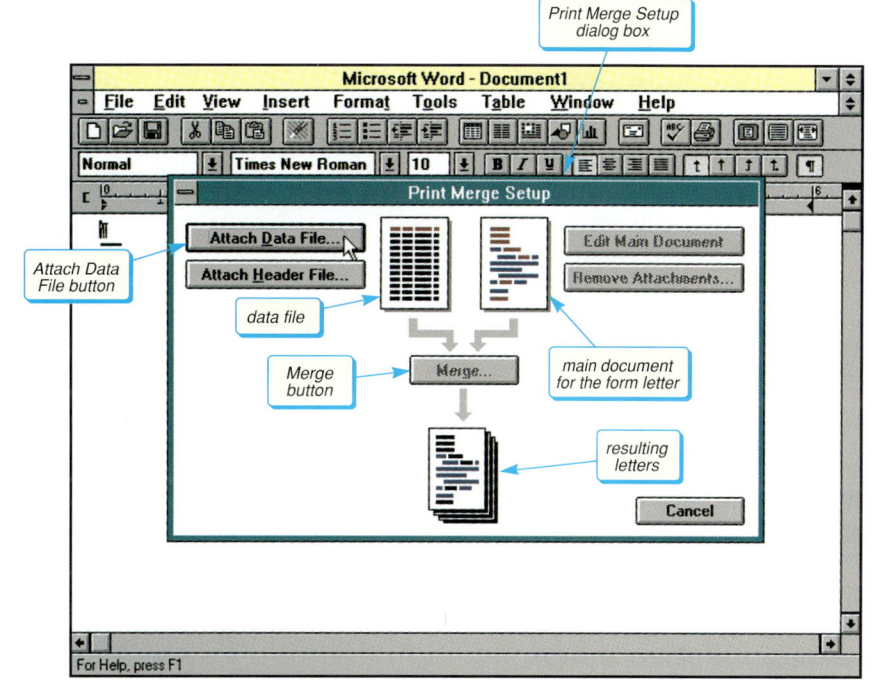

FIGURE 4-4

STEP 3 ▶

Choose the Attach Data File button. When the Attach Data File dialog box displays, click the Drives drop-down list box arrow and select drive A. Point to the Create Data File button (Create Data File).

Word displays the Attach Data File dialog box (Figure 4-5). If the data file already existed, you would select it from the File Name list box and choose the OK button. To create a new data file, you will choose the Create Data File button.

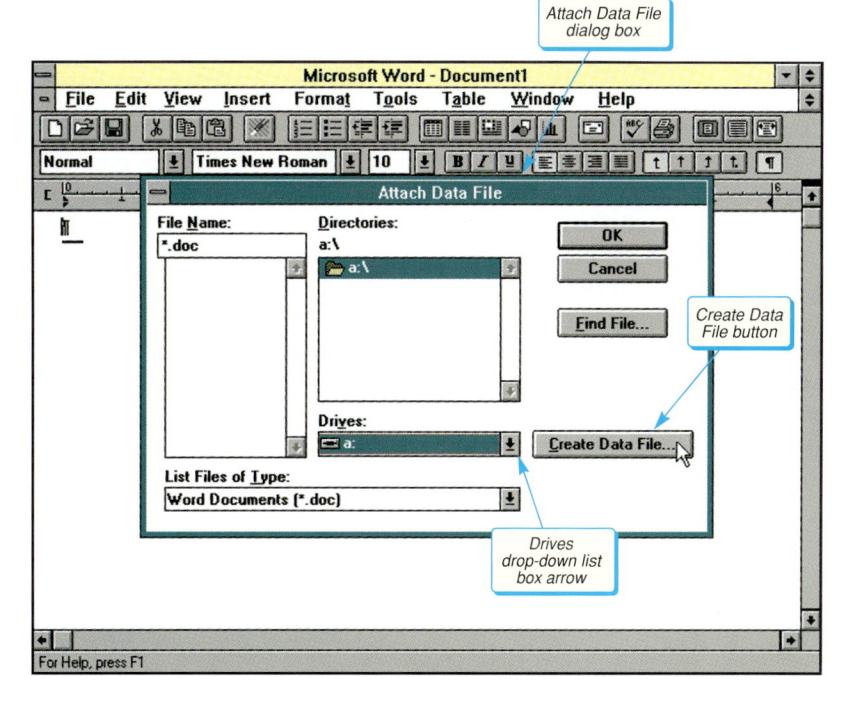

FIGURE 4-5

MSW184   PROJECT 4   GENERATING FORM LETTERS AND MAILING LABELS

STEP 4 ▶

Choose the Create Data File button.

Word displays the Create Data File dialog box. You enter field names in the Field Name text box of the Create Data File dialog box. Word uses these field names to create the header record in the data file you create.

STEP 5 ▶

Type `Courtesy_Title` **and point to the Add button (** Add... **).**

The first field name, Courtesy_Title, displays in the Field Name text box. The mouse pointer points to the Add button (Figure 4-6).

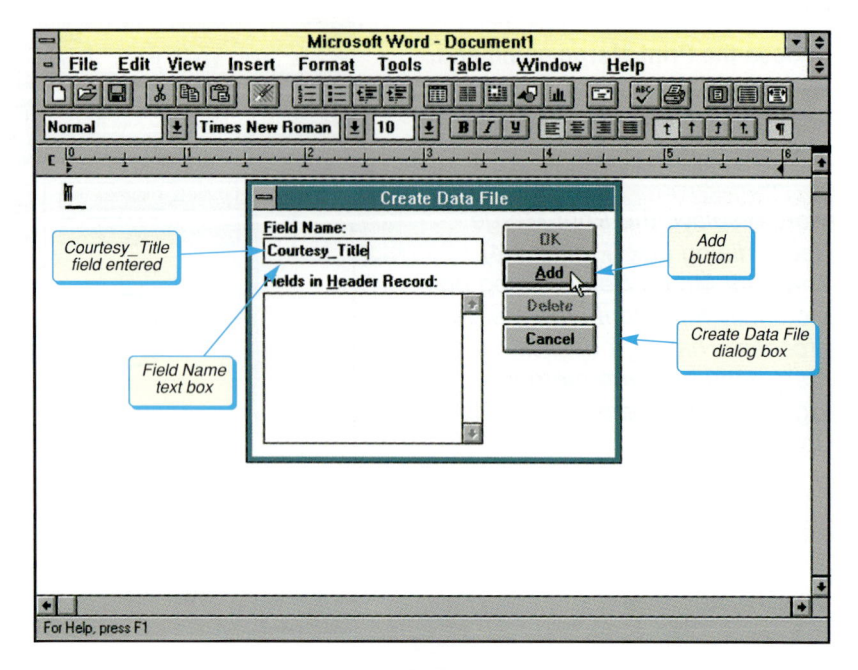

FIGURE 4-6

STEP 6 ▶

Choose the Add button in the Create Data File dialog box.

Word places the field name, Courtesy_Title, in the Fields in Header Record list box (Figure 4-7). The insertion point is placed in the Field Name text box, ready for the next field name to be entered. The Add button is dimmed because the Field Name text box is empty.

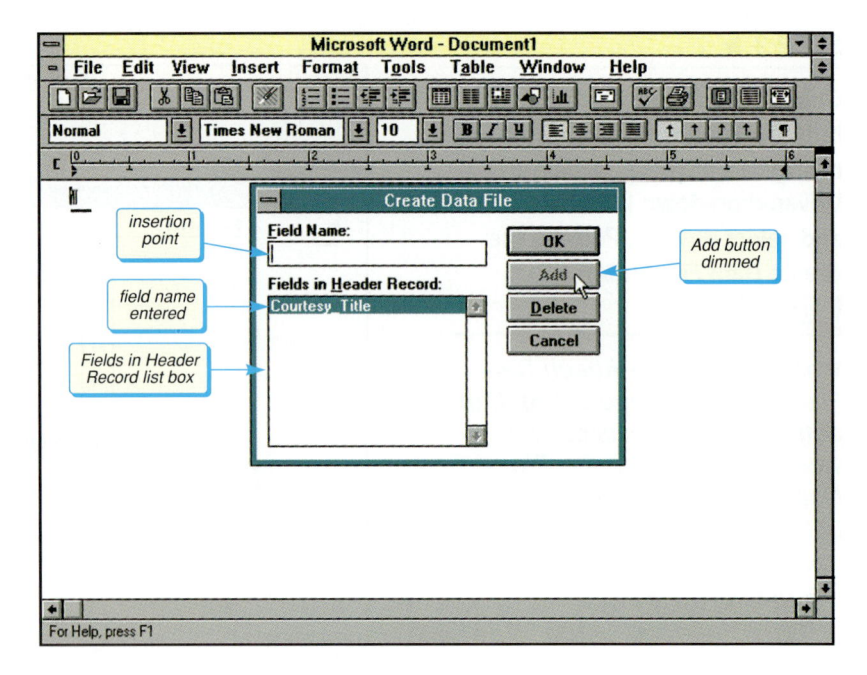

FIGURE 4-7

CREATING A DATA FILE **MSW185**

STEP 7 ▶

Type `First_Name` and choose the Add button. Type `Last_Name` and choose the Add button. Type `Street_Addr_1` and choose the Add button. Type `Street_Addr_2` and choose the Add button. Type `City` and choose the Add button. Type `State` and choose the Add button. Type `Zip` and choose the Add button. Type `Region` and choose the Add button. Point to the OK button.

The field names have all been entered into the Create Data File dialog box (Figure 4-8).

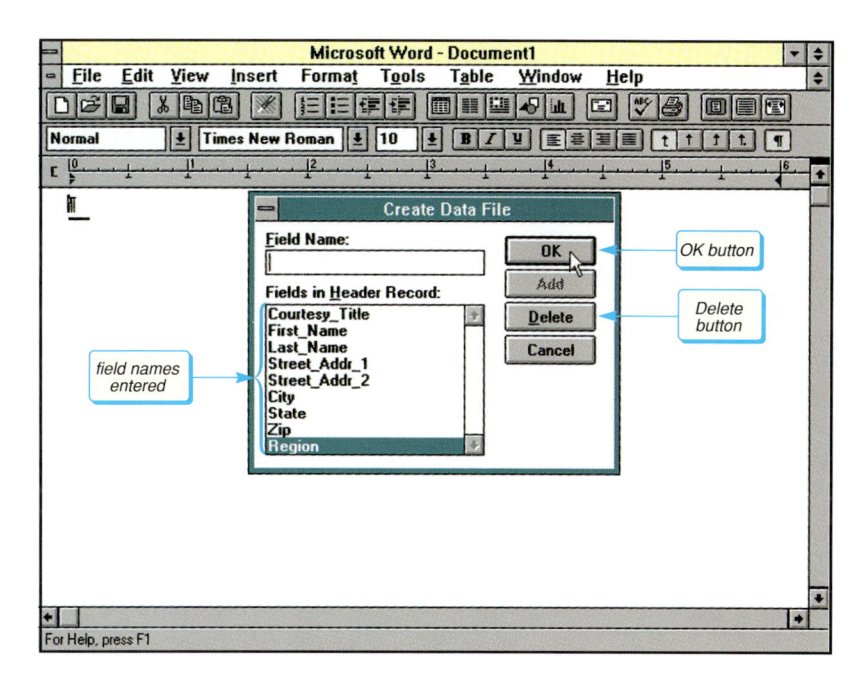

FIGURE 4-8

STEP 8 ▶

Choose the OK button in the Create Data File dialog box. When the Save As dialog box displays, type `proj4dat` and point to the OK button.

Word displays the Save As dialog box (Figure 4-9). You assign the file name, proj4dat, to the data file in the Save As dialog box.

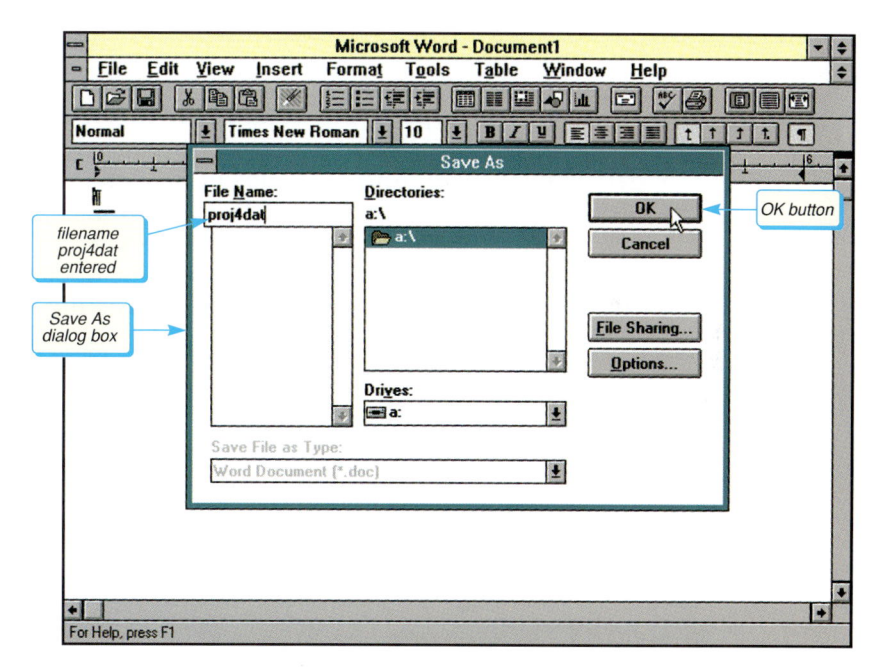

FIGURE 4-9

MSW186   PROJECT 4   GENERATING FORM LETTERS AND MAILING LABELS

STEP 9 ▶

Choose the OK button in the Save As dialog box.

Word opens a new document window, creates a table for the data file, and saves the data file with the filename PROJ4DAT.DOC (Figure 4-10). Recall that the first record in the data file, the header record, contains field names. Word places the field names you defined in the Create Data File dialog box as the first record in the data file. Each field you defined represents one column in the data file.

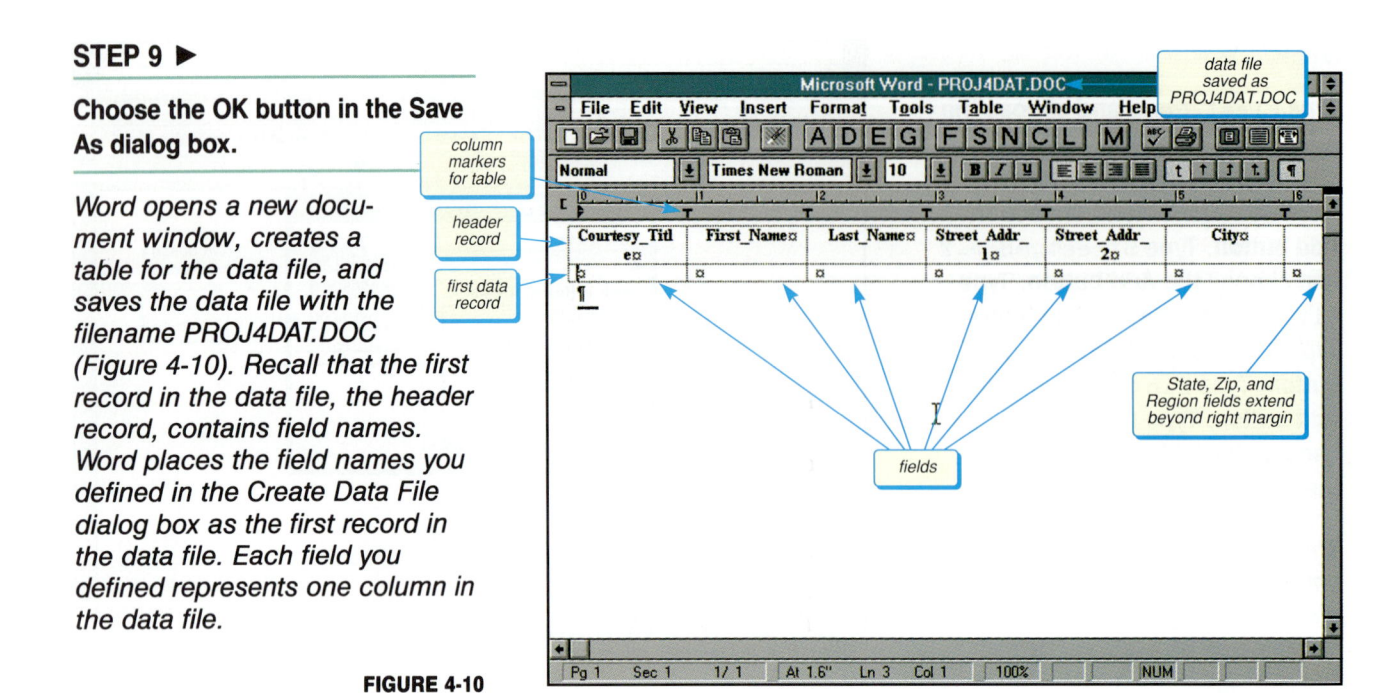

FIGURE 4-10

When specifying fields in the Create Data File dialog box (Figure 4-8 on the previous page), you may notice a misspelled field name or extra field. To remove a field name from the Fields in Header Record list box, select the field name by clicking it and choose the Delete button.

In the data file in Figure 4-10, some of the fields (State, Zip, and Region) extend beyond the right margin of the document window. Thus, the next step is to adjust the column widths of the data file so they all display in the document window.

Adjusting Column Widths of a Data File

Recall that a data file is a Word table. Thus, you adjust the column widths of a data file using the procedure you used to change the spacing between columns of a table in Project 3. When the insertion point is in the cell of a table, the ruler changes to reflect the table columns. Recall that table columns are identified by dark Ts (**T**) on the ruler, called column markers. To adjust the column widths of a data file, drag the column markers to the desired location. The following steps explain how to adjust column widths of the data file used in this project (Figure 4-11).

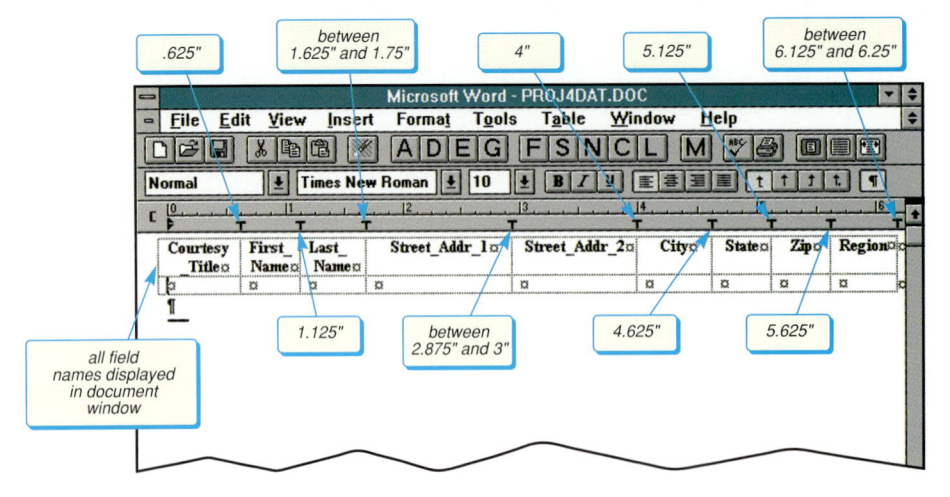

FIGURE 4-11

CREATING A DATA FILE **MSW187**

TO ADJUST COLUMN WIDTHS OF A DATA FILE

Step 1: Drag the first column marker to the .625-inch mark on the ruler.
Step 2: Drag the second column marker to the 1.125-inch mark on the ruler.
Step 3: Drag the third column marker so it is positioned between the 1.625-inch and 1.75-inch marks on the ruler.
Step 4: Drag the fourth column marker so it is positioned between the 2.875-inch and 3-inch marks on the ruler.
Step 5: Drag the fifth column marker to the 4-inch mark on the ruler.
Step 6: Drag the sixth column marker to the 4.625-inch mark on the ruler.
Step 7: Drag the seventh column marker to the 5.125-inch mark on the ruler.
Step 8: Drag the eighth column marker to the 5.625-inch mark on the ruler.
Step 9: Click to the right of the scroll box on the horizontal scroll bar to bring the Region field name into the document window. Drag the ninth column marker so it is positioned between the 6.125-inch and 6.25-inch marks on the ruler. Click to the left of the scroll box on the horizontal scroll bar.

All fields in the data file now display in the document window as shown in Figure 4-11. (Depending on your printer driver, you may need to drag the column markers to different locations to make your screen look like Figure 4-11.)

Adding Data Records to the Data File

Because a data file is a Word table, you add records to a data file the same way you add rows to a table. To move from one field to the next, press the TAB key. Follow these steps to add the five data records to the data file in Project 4.

TO ADD DATA RECORDS TO THE DATA FILE ▼

STEP 1 ▶

Type Mr. and press the TAB key.
Type James and press the TAB key.
Type Linton and press the TAB key. Type 18 West 10th Street and press the TAB key twice. Type Boulder and press the TAB key. Type CO and press the TAB key. Type 80301 and press the TAB key. Type West.

The first data record is added to the data file (Figure 4-12). Notice the Street_Addr_2 field is empty because James Linton does not have a second street address, such as a post office box.

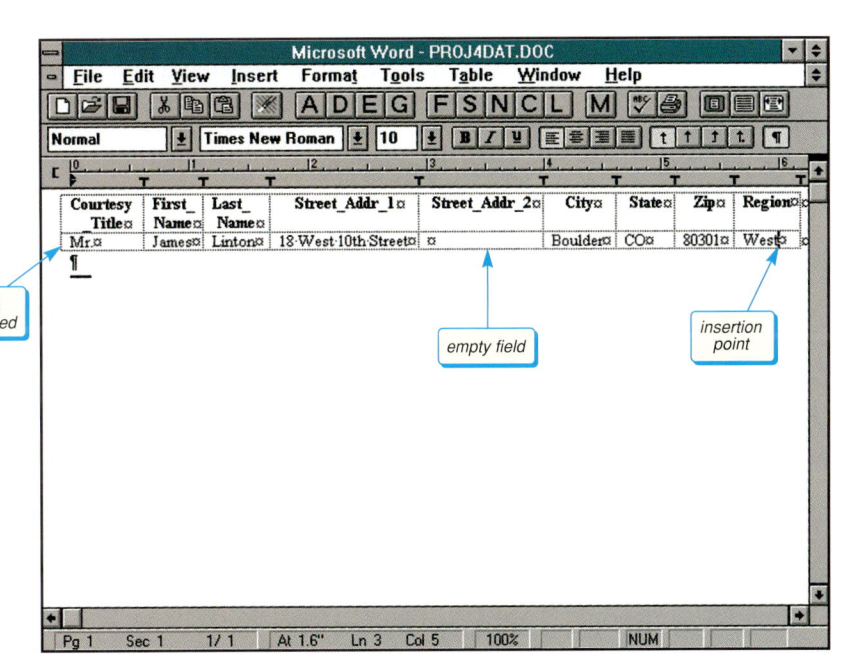

FIGURE 4-12

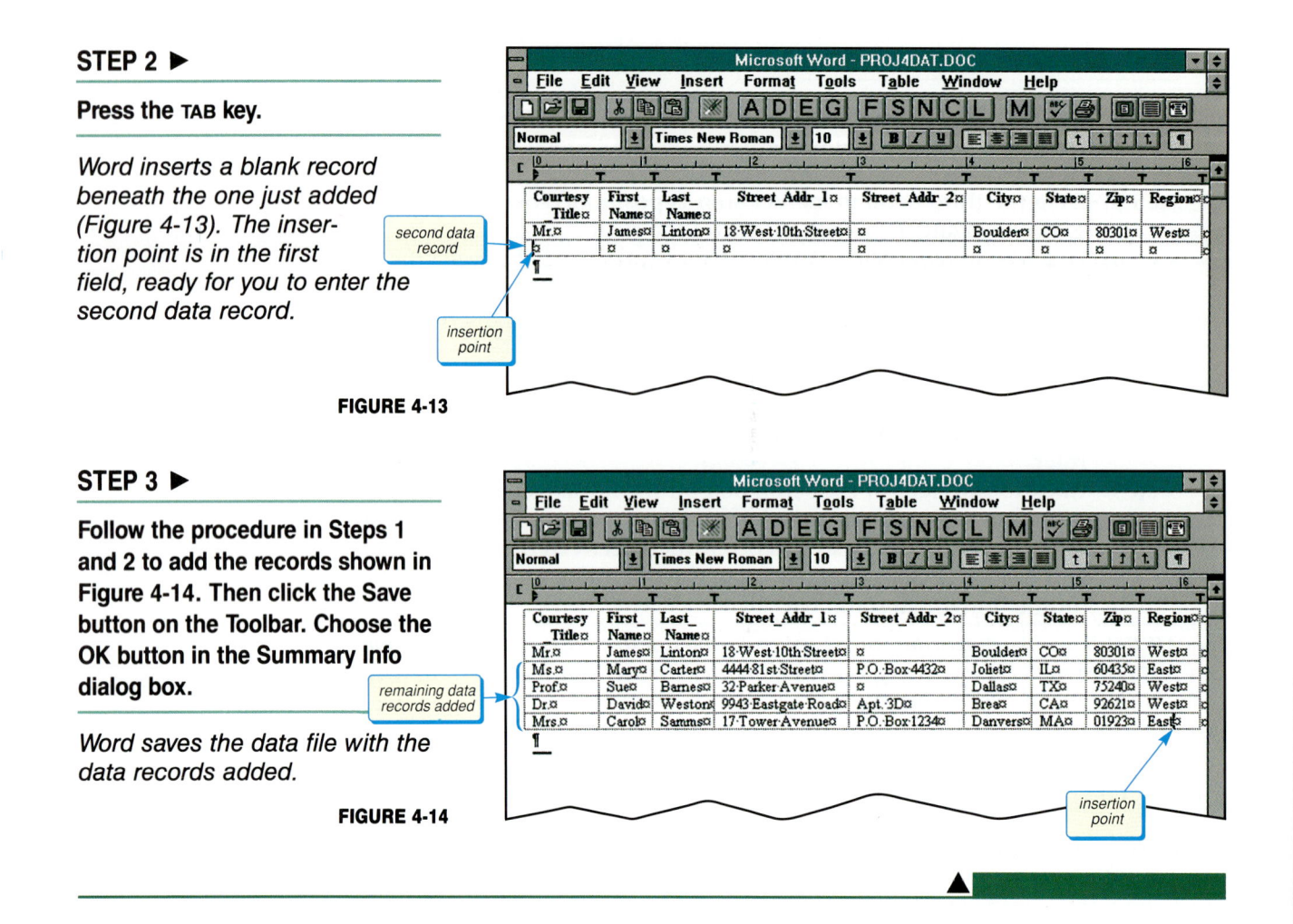

STEP 2 ▶

Press the TAB key.

Word inserts a blank record beneath the one just added (Figure 4-13). The insertion point is in the first field, ready for you to enter the second data record.

FIGURE 4-13

STEP 3 ▶

Follow the procedure in Steps 1 and 2 to add the records shown in Figure 4-14. Then click the Save button on the Toolbar. Choose the OK button in the Summary Info dialog box.

Word saves the data file with the data records added.

FIGURE 4-14

The data file is now complete. If you wish, you can print the data file by clicking the Print button on the Toolbar.

Working with an Existing Data File

When the data file is the current active document, Word changes the buttons on the Toolbar to reflect actions you may take regarding the data file (Figure 4-15). The buttons on the Toolbar are divided into three major categories: **Record Management Tools**, **Database Management Tools**, and **Main Document Tool**.

RECORD MANAGEMENT TOOLS Using these buttons, you can add a new data record, delete a record, edit data about an existing record, or locate a record based on its location.

DATABASE MANAGEMENT TOOLS Using these buttons, you can add a new field, sort the data file records, insert record numbers for each record, clean up a data file converted from another application (like Microsoft Excel), or link the data file to another application (like Microsoft Excel).

MAIN DOCUMENT TOOL Using this button, you can switch from the data file to the main document.

CREATING A DATA FILE **MSW189**

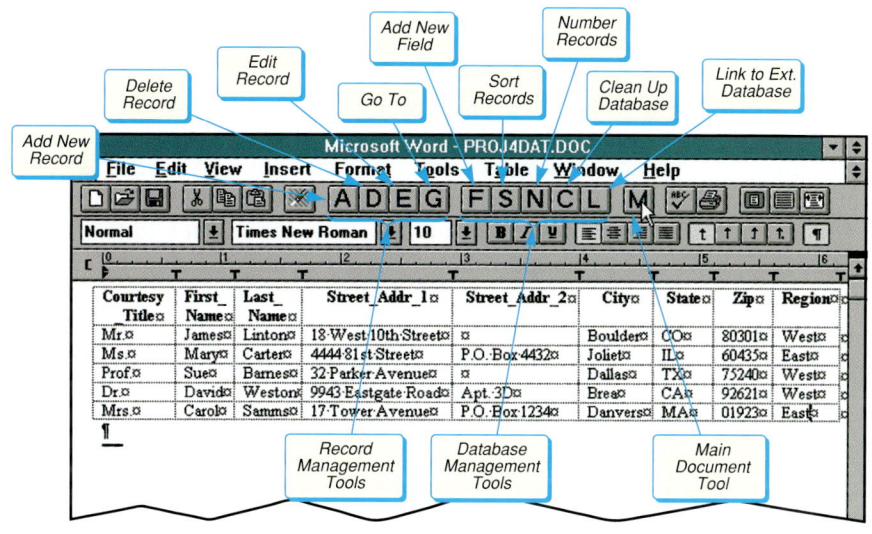

FIGURE 4-15

To use any of these tools, click the appropriate button on the Toolbar. The next step in Project 4 is to switch to the main document to create the form letter.

TO SWITCH FROM THE DATA FILE TO THE MAIN DOCUMENT ▼

STEP 1 ▶

Point to the Main Document button (M) on the Toolbar (see Figure 4-15 above).

STEP 2 ▶

Click the left mouse button.

*Word opens the main document (Figure 4-16). A **print merge bar** displays between the ribbon and ruler. The name of the attached data file displays at the right edge of the print merge bar.*

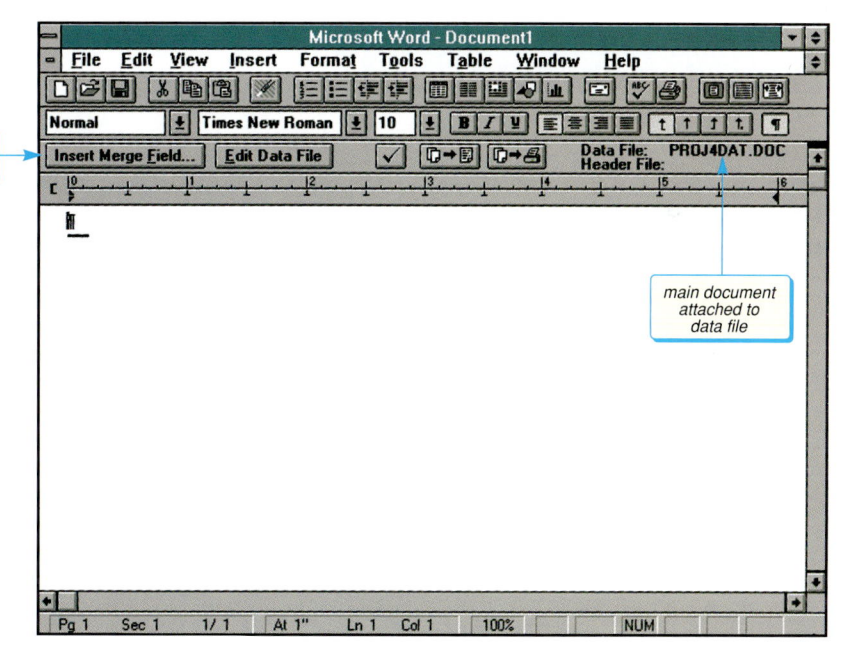

FIGURE 4-16

▶ CREATING THE MAIN DOCUMENT FOR THE FORM LETTER

The next step is to create the main document for the form letter (see Figure 4-1 on page MSW180). In Project 4, the letterhead at the top of the main document is created with a header. The form letter is based on a block style letter. That is, all paragraphs are left-justified. The current date displays in the upper left corner of the form letter. Because a block letter is a very common letter style, Word provides a block letter document template. A **document template** is like a blueprint of a document. It specifies formatting for a document and any preprinted text to appear in a document. Word has templates for a variety of styles of documents, ranging from memos to letters to fax cover sheets. The document templates, however, are designed for single-user workstations. That is, if many people share a computer and one person changes the contents of a template, it is changed for all future users. Thus, in a multiuser environment, document templates should be avoided.

The following sections illustrate how to create the main document for the form letter.

Creating Letterhead for the Form Letter

In large businesses, letterhead is preprinted on stationery used by everyone throughout the organization. In smaller organizations, however, preprinted letterhead may not be purchased because of its expense. An alternative for smaller businesses is to create their own letterhead and save it in a file. Then, everyone can insert this file with the letterhead into their documents as needed. The following steps illustrate how to create company letterhead using a header.

TO CREATE COMPANY LETTERHEAD ▼

STEP 1 ▶

Point to the New button ( ) on the Toolbar (Figure 4-17).

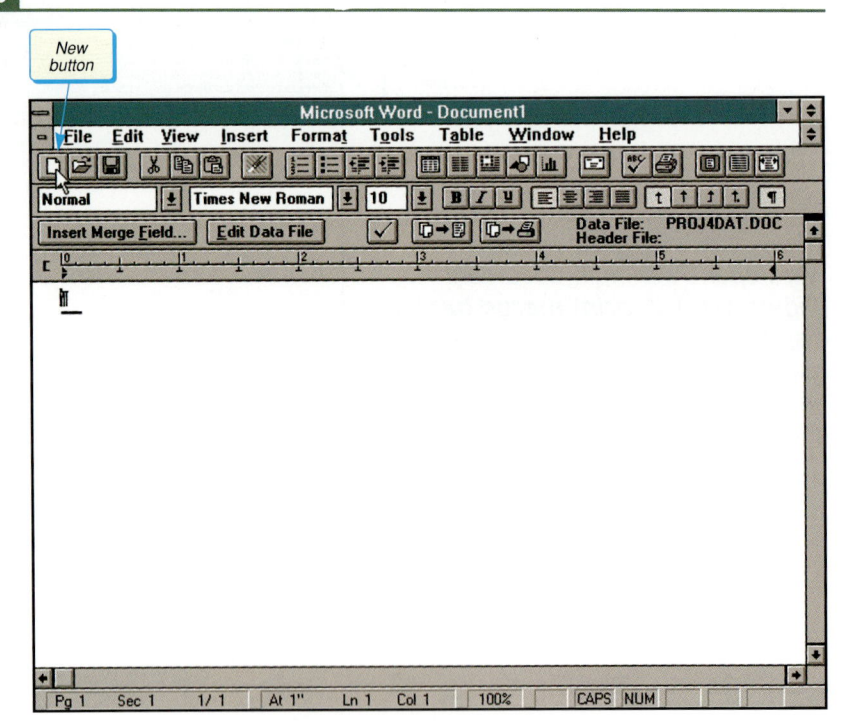

FIGURE 4-17

CREATING THE MAIN DOCUMENT FOR THE FORM LETTER **MSW191**

STEP 2 ▶

Click the left mouse button. From the View menu, choose the Header/Footer command. When the Header/Footer dialog box displays, choose the OK button. Change the point size to 16 by clicking the Points box arrow and selecting 16. Type PERIPHERALS PLUS and press the ENTER key. From the Insert menu, choose the Picture command. Open the clipart subdirectory in the winword directory on drive C by double-clicking it. Select the metafile called disk35.wmf by clicking it. Choose the OK button in the Picture dialog box.

Word displays the company name, PERIPHERALS PLUS, and a graphic of a 3 1/2" diskette in the header pane (Figure 4-18).

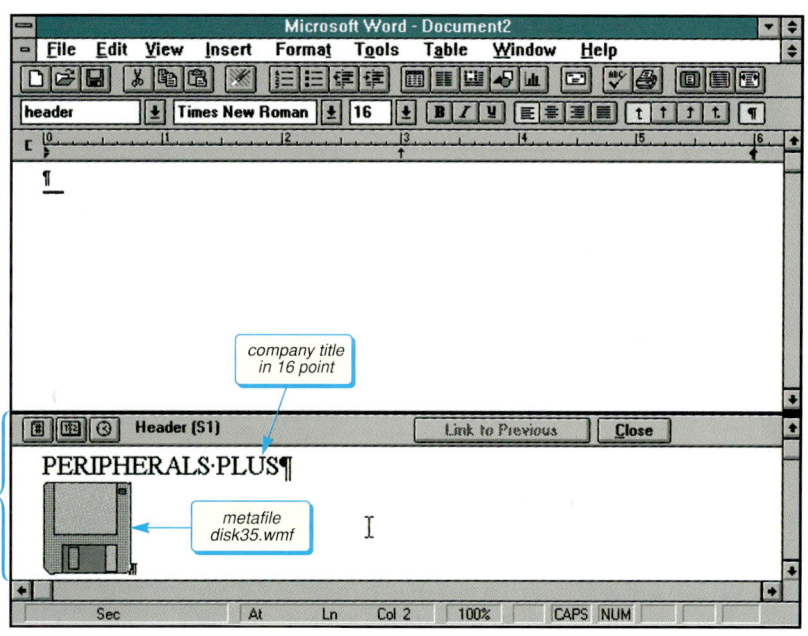

FIGURE 4-18

STEP 3 ▶

Press the ENTER key. Change the point size to 12. Click the Right-Aligned Text button on the Toolbar. Type (312) 555-0987 and press the ENTER key. Type 100 Baxter Boulevard, Chicago, IL 60601 and press the ENTER key. Click the Left-Aligned Text button. Type the underscore character (_) enough times to fill an entire line and press the ENTER key.

The letterhead is complete (Figure 4-19).

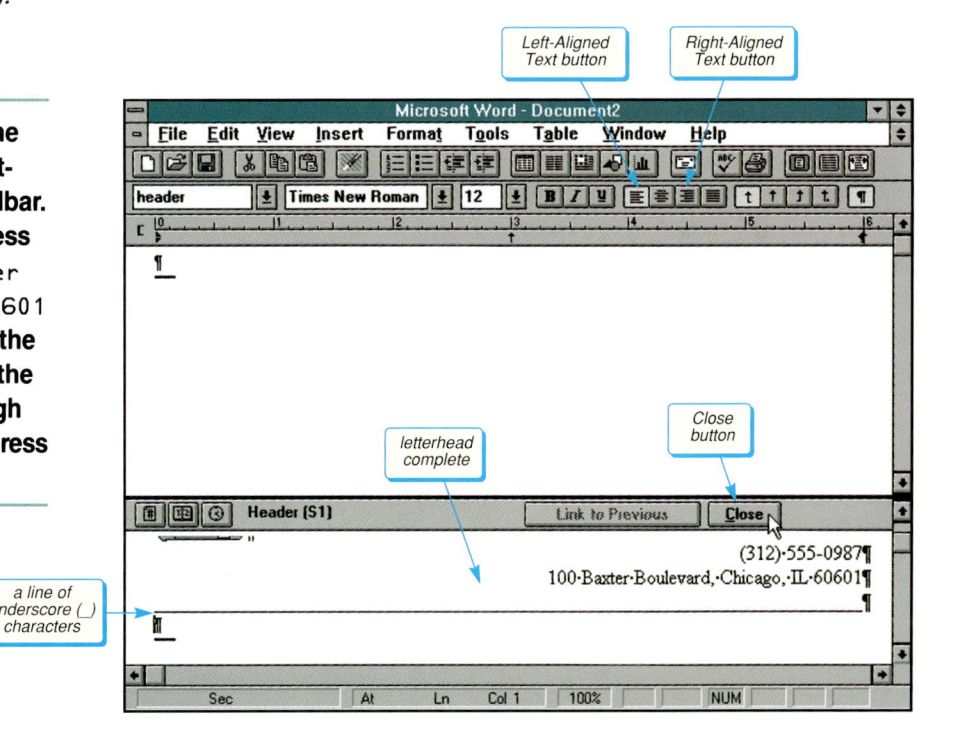

FIGURE 4-19

MSW192   PROJECT 4   GENERATING FORM LETTERS AND MAILING LABELS

STEP 4 ▶

Choose the Close button (Close) on the header pane option bar.

Word closes the header pane and returns to the document window (Figure 4-20a). Recall that a header does not display on the screen in normal view.

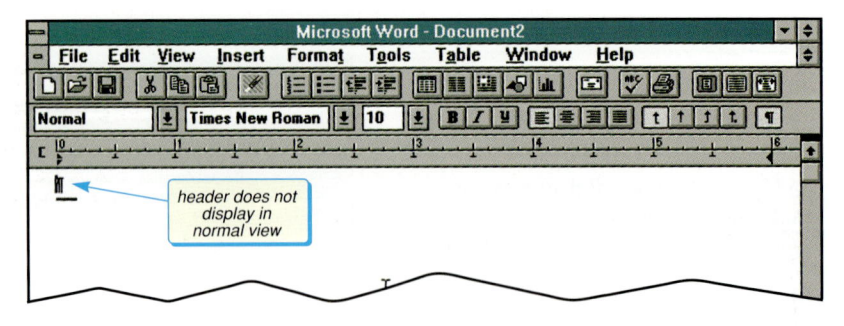

FIGURE 4-20a

STEP 5 ▶

From the File menu, choose the Save As command. When the Save As dialog box displays, type `ppltrhd` **in the File Name text box. Do not press the ENTER key. If drive A is not the current drive, select it by clicking the Drives drop-down list box arrow and selecting a:. Point to the OK button.**

The letterhead will be saved with the filename PPLTRHD.DOC (Figure 4-20b).

STEP 6

Choose the OK button in the Save As dialog box. Choose the OK button in the Summary Info dialog box. From the File menu, choose the Close command.

Word saves the letterhead with the filename PPLTRHD.DOC and returns you to the main document.

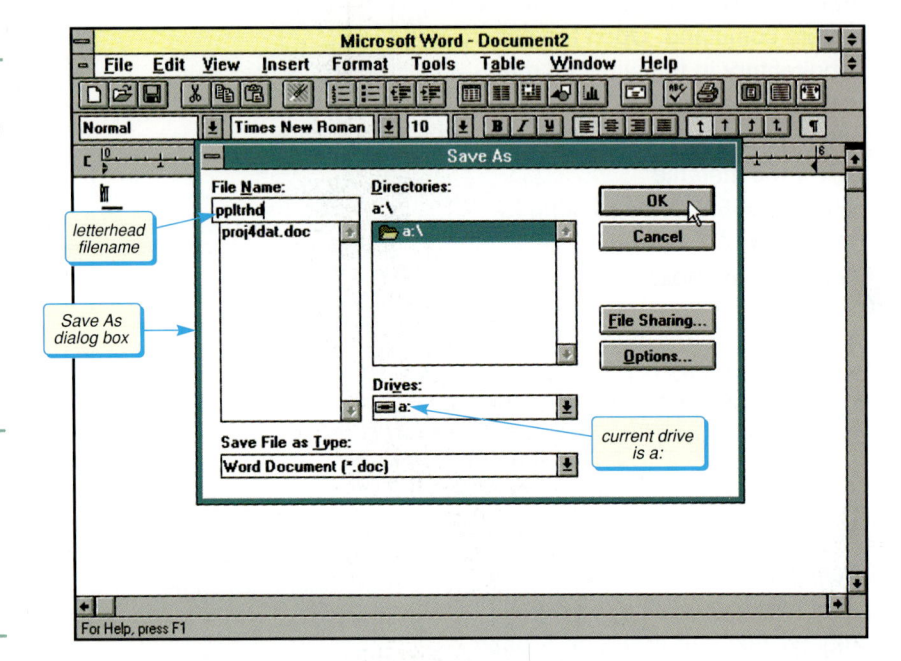

FIGURE 4-20b

The company letterhead is saved in a file called PPLTRHD.DOC. Anyone in the organization who wants to create a letter with the letterhead simply needs to insert the letterhead file into his or her document as shown in the following steps.

TO INSERT THE LETTERHEAD FILE INTO THE MAIN DOCUMENT ▼

STEP 1 ▶

From the Insert menu, choose the File command. When the File dialog box displays, choose the file ppltrhd.doc by clicking it.

Word displays the File dialog box with the current files on drive A (Figure 4-21). (If drive A is not the current drive, select it by clicking the Drives drop-down list box arrow and selecting a:.)

STEP 2

Choose the OK button in the File dialog box. Press the DELETE key once.

Word returns to the main document. Recall that the letterhead does not display on the screen in normal view because it is in a header. When you insert a document into an open document, Word places a paragraph mark at the location of the insertion. Pressing the DELETE key removes the extra paragraph mark.

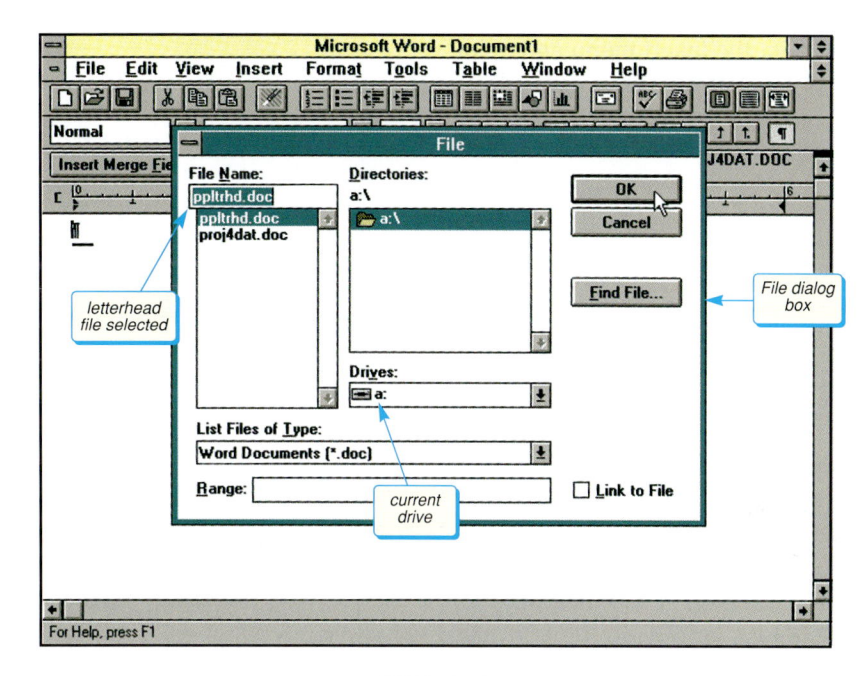

FIGURE 4-21

Adding the Current Date to the Form Letter

When sending letters to customers, you want the current date to print at the top of the letter. Word provides a method of inserting the computer's system date into a document. In this way, if you type the letter today and print it at a later date, it will print the correct date. Follow the steps on the next page to insert the current date at the top of the main document.

TO INSERT THE CURRENT DATE IN A DOCUMENT

STEP 1 ▶

Change the point size for the main document to 12 by clicking the Points box arrow and selecting 12. Select the Insert menu and point to the Date and Time command (Figure 4-22).

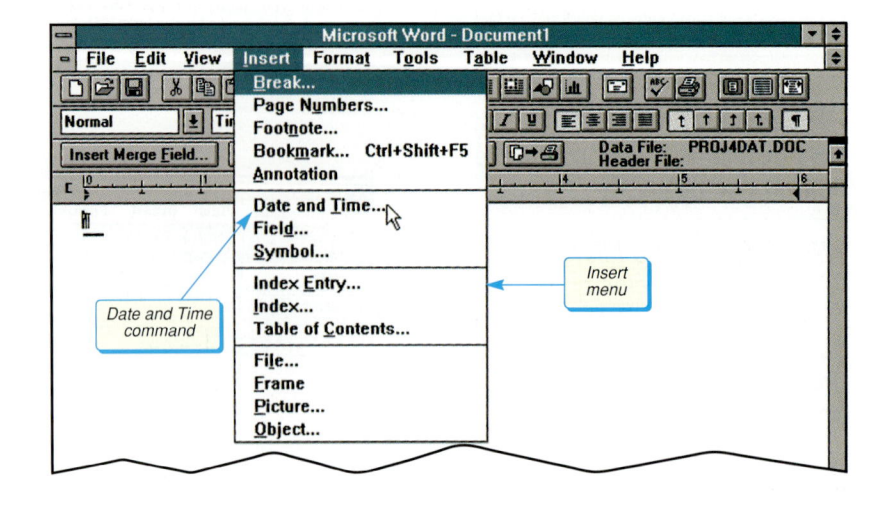

FIGURE 4-22

STEP 2

Choose the Date and Time command.

Word displays the Date and Time dialog box. A list of available formats for displaying the current date and time appear.

STEP 3 ▶

Select the format September 30, 1994 (the current date on your screen) by clicking it and point to the OK button.

Word highlights the selected format (Figure 4-23). The current date will display in the main document according to the selected format.

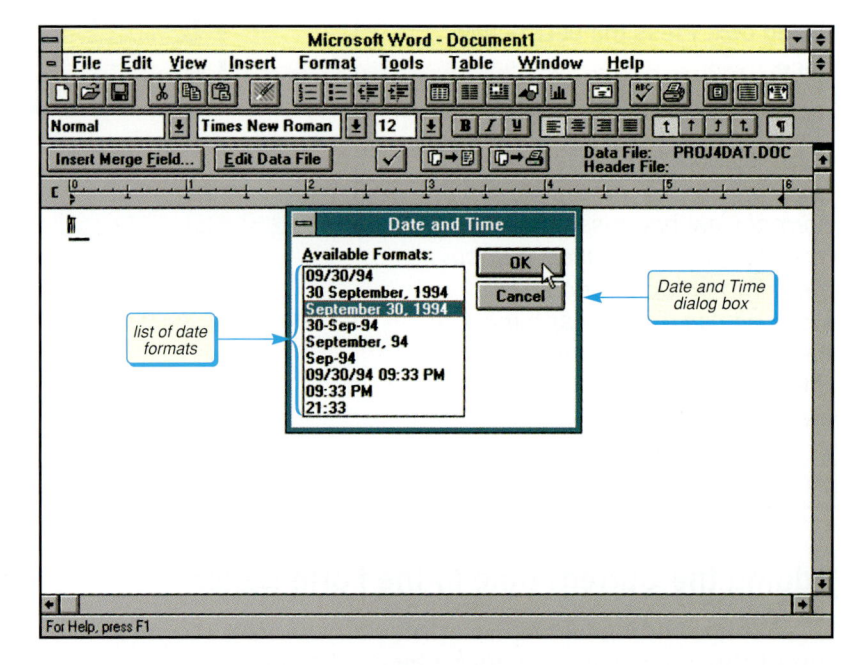

FIGURE 4-23

STEP 4 ▶

Choose the OK button.

Word displays the current date in the main document (Figure 4-24).

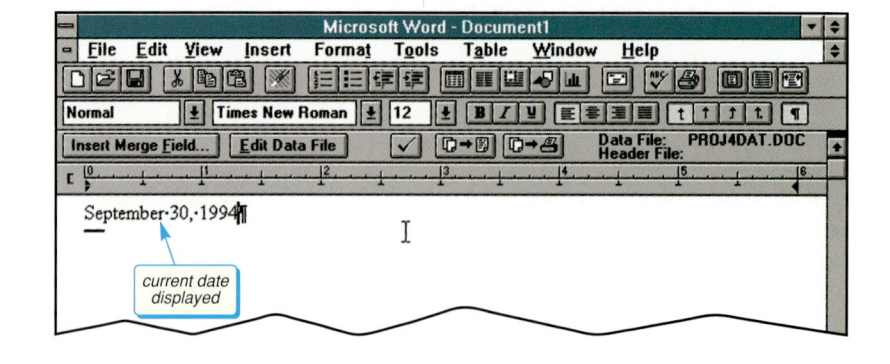

FIGURE 4-24

The current date is actually a field that Word updates when it prints the document. If you would like to update the field on the screen, position the insertion point in the date and press the Update Field key (F9). If for some reason you need to delete the date field from the main document, select it and press the DELETE key.

The next step is to enter the inside address on the letter. The contents of the inside address are located in the data file. Thus, you insert fields from the data file into the main document.

Inserting Merge Fields into the Main Document

Earlier in this project you created the data file for the form letter. The first record in the data file, the header record, contains the field names of each field in the data file. To link the data file to the main document, you must also insert these fields into the main document. In the main document, these field names are called **merge fields** because they merge, or combine, the main document with the contents of the data file. When a field is inserted into the main document from the data file, it is surrounded by merge characters. **Merge characters** mark the beginning («) and ending (») of a merge field. The merge characters are not on the keyboard; therefore, you cannot type them directly into the document. They appear as a result of inserting a merge field with the Insert Merge Field button on the print merge bar.

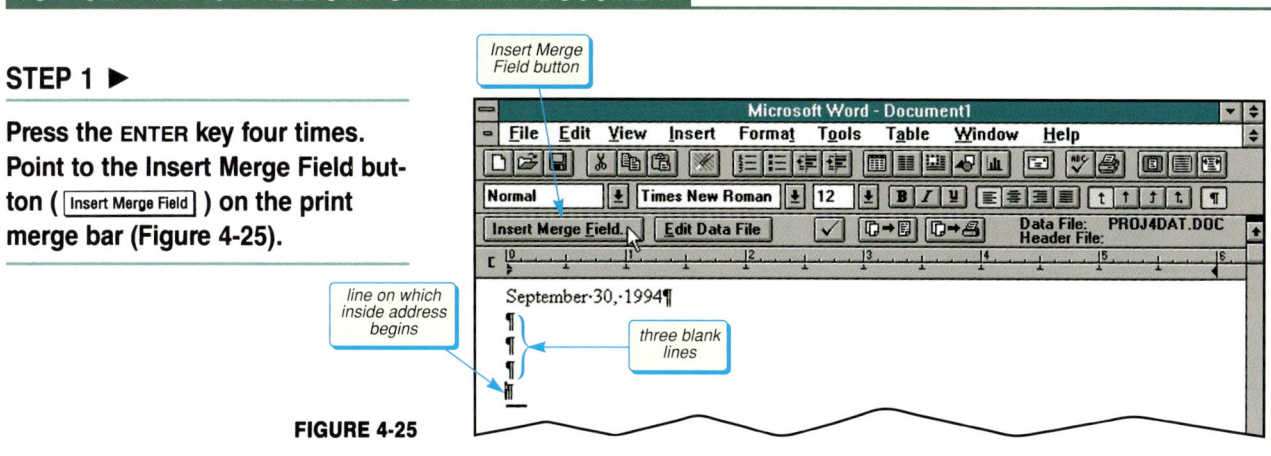

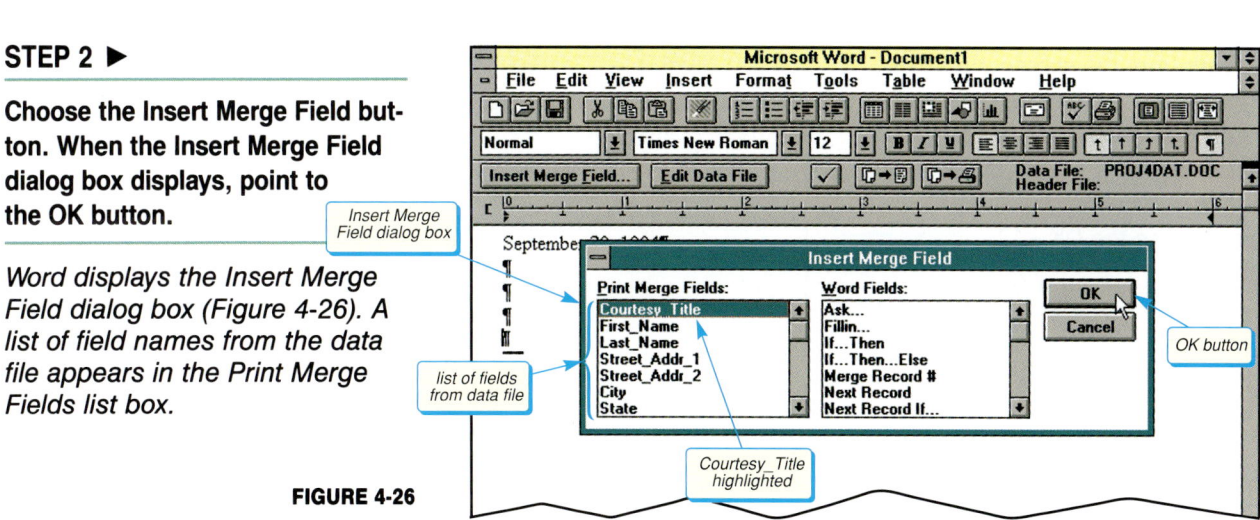

TO INSERT MERGE FIELDS INTO THE MAIN DOCUMENT ▼

STEP 1 ▶

Press the ENTER key four times. Point to the Insert Merge Field button ([Insert Merge Field]) on the print merge bar (Figure 4-25).

FIGURE 4-25

STEP 2 ▶

Choose the Insert Merge Field button. When the Insert Merge Field dialog box displays, point to the OK button.

Word displays the Insert Merge Field dialog box (Figure 4-26). A list of field names from the data file appears in the Print Merge Fields list box.

FIGURE 4-26

STEP 3 ▶

Choose the OK button. When the Insert Merge Field dialog box disappears from the screen, press the SPACEBAR once.

Word displays the field name, Courtesy_Title, enclosed in merge characters in the main document (Figure 4-27). When you merge the data file with the main document, the customer's courtesy title will print in the location of the merge field Courtesy_Title. One space follows the ending merge character in the Courtesy_Title merge field.

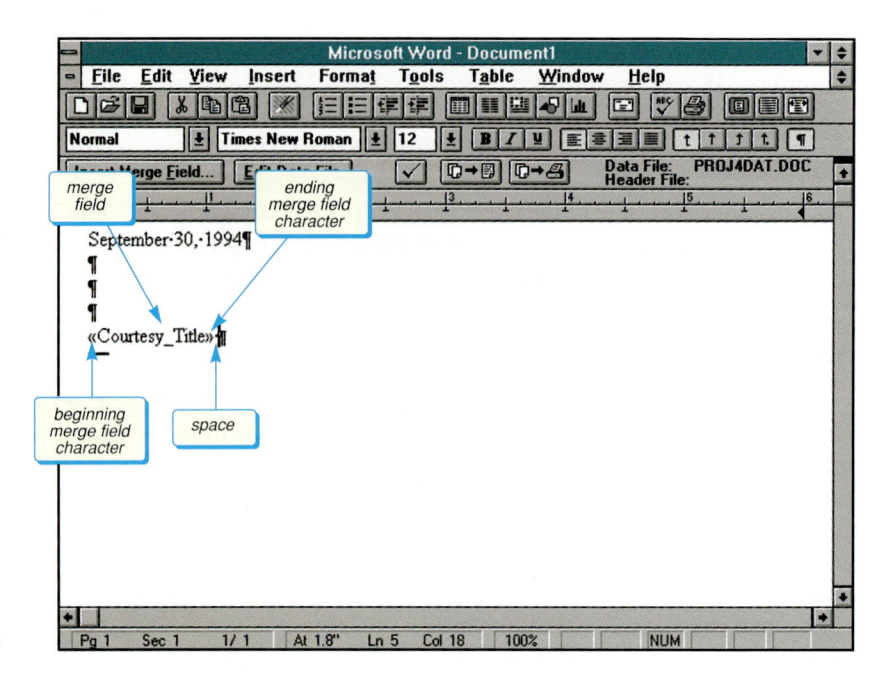

FIGURE 4-27

STEP 4 ▶

Choose the Insert Merge Field button. Select the First_Name field in the Print Merge Fields list box by clicking it. Point to the OK button.

Word selects the First_Name field in the Print Merge Fields list (Figure 4-28).

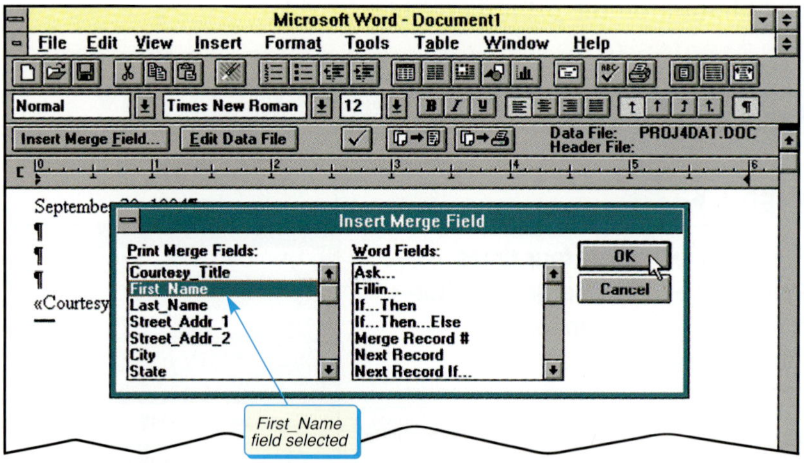

FIGURE 4-28

STEP 5 ▶

Choose the OK button. When the Insert Merge Field dialog box disappears from the screen, press the SPACEBAR once. Choose the Insert Merge Field button. Select the Last_Name field in the Print Merge Fields list box. Choose the OK button.

The first line of the inside address is complete (Figure 4-29).

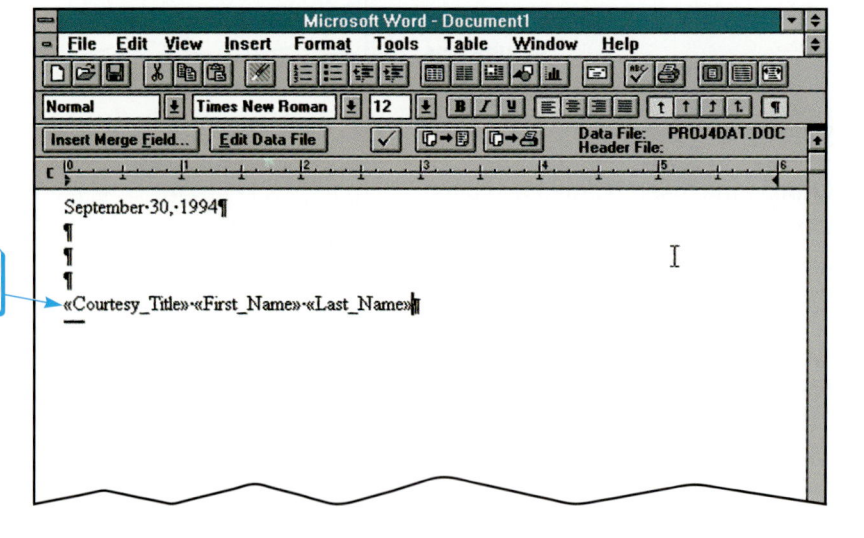

FIGURE 4-29

CREATING THE MAIN DOCUMENT FOR THE FORM LETTER **MSW197**

Completing the Inside Address Lines

The next step is to enter the remaining merge fields in the inside address lines.

TO COMPLETE THE INSIDE ADDRESS

Step 1: Press the ENTER key. Choose the Insert Merge Field button. Select the Street_Addr_1 field. Choose the OK button.

Step 2: Press the ENTER key. Choose the Insert Merge Field button. Select the Street_Addr_2 field. Choose the OK button.

Step 3: Press the ENTER key. Choose the Insert Merge Field button. Select the City field. Choose the OK button. Type , followed by a space. Choose the Insert Merge Field button. Select the State field. Choose the OK button. Press the SPACEBAR once. Choose the Insert Merge Field button. Select the Zip field. Choose the OK button.

The inside address lines are complete as shown in Figure 4-30.

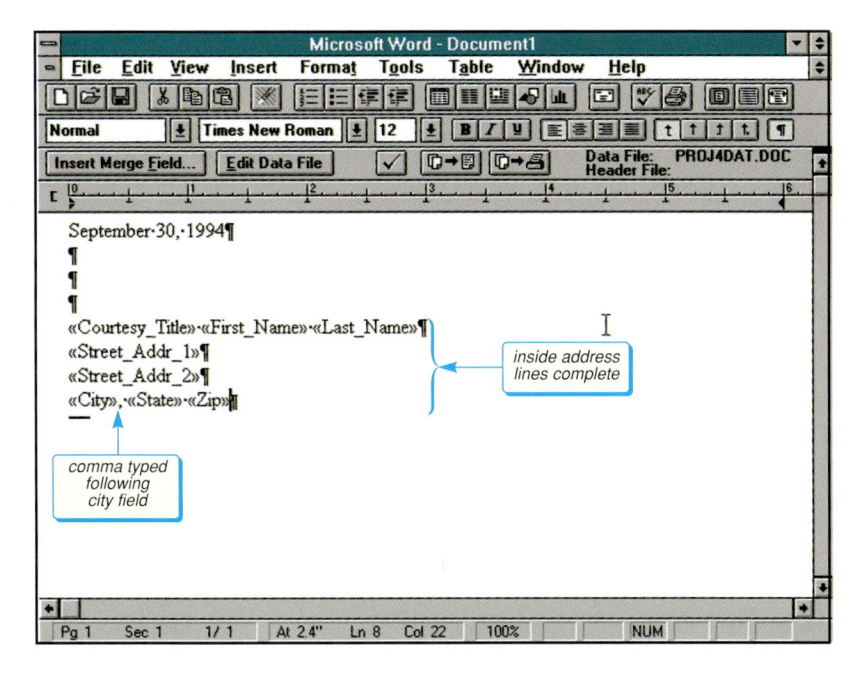

FIGURE 4-30

Entering Merge Fields in the Salutation Line

The salutation in Project 4 begins with the word Dear placed at the left margin followed by the courtesy title and the customer's last name. You are to insert the appropriate merge fields after the word Dear as shown in the steps on the next page.

MSW198   PROJECT 4   GENERATING FORM LETTERS AND MAILING LABELS

TO ENTER MERGE FIELDS IN THE SALUTATION ▼

STEP 1 ▶

Press the ENTER key twice. Type Dear followed by a space. Choose the Insert Merge Field button on the print merge bar. If it is not already highlighted, select the Courtesy_Title field by clicking it. Point to the OK button.

Word displays the Insert Merge Field dialog box (Figure 4-31). The selected field will be added at the location of the insertion point in the document.

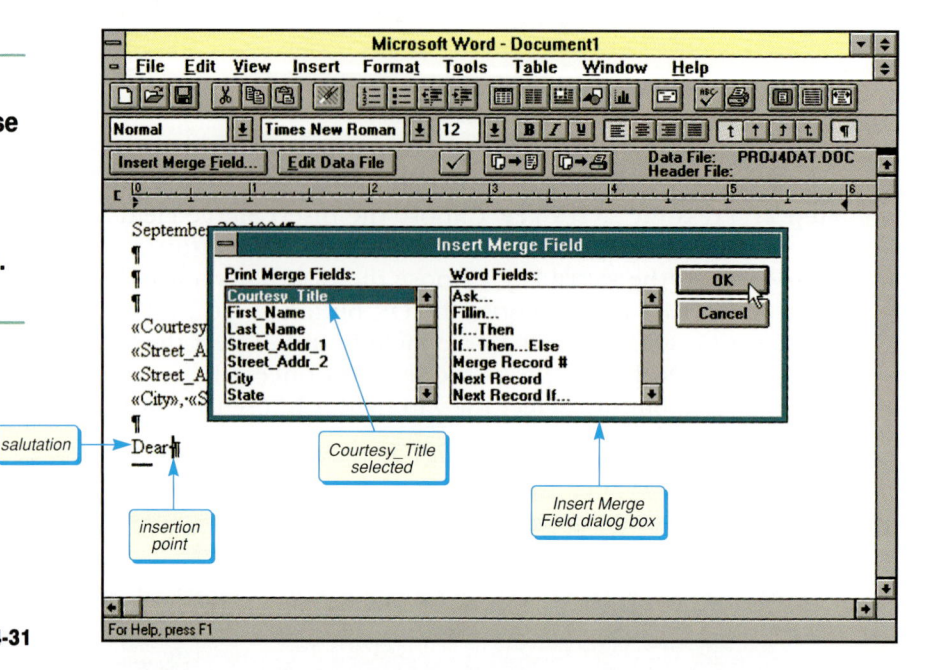

FIGURE 4-31

STEP 2 ▶

Choose the OK button. Press the SPACEBAR once. Choose the Insert Merge Field button. Select the Last_Name field by clicking it. Choose the OK button in the Insert Merge Field dialog box. Press the COLON key.

The salutation line is complete (Figure 4-32).

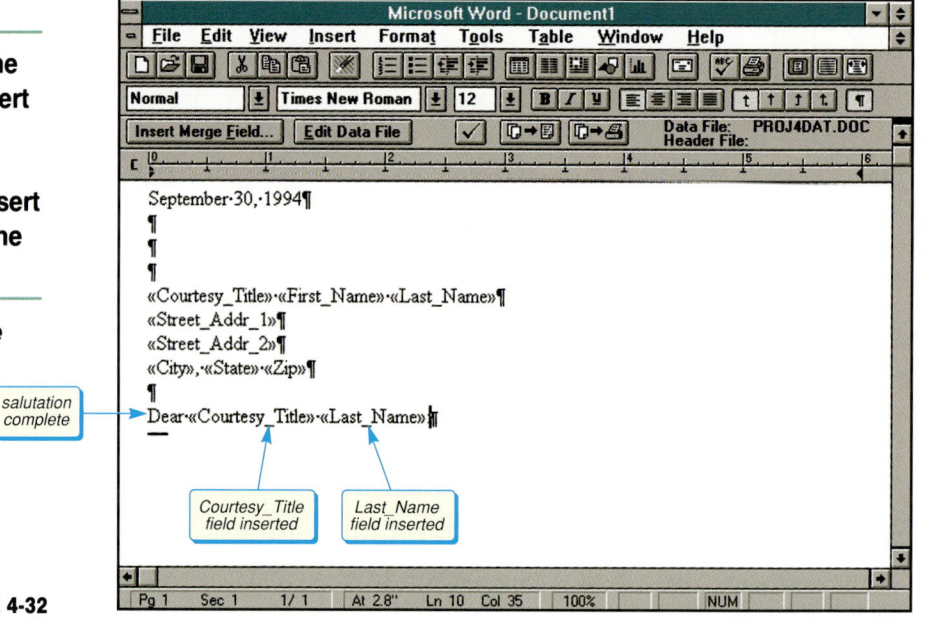

FIGURE 4-32

Entering the Body of the Form Letter

The next step is to enter the text in the body of the form letter. The entire first paragraph and the beginning of the second paragraph contain constant, or unchanging, text to be printed in each form letter. To enter the text in the body of the form letter, type the text as shown in Figure 4-33.

TO BEGIN ENTERING THE BODY OF THE FORM LETTER

Step 1: Press the ENTER key twice. Type We would like to take this opportunity to thank you for your recent order. We are happy to welcome you as a new customer to Peripherals Plus.

Step 2: Press the ENTER key twice. Type At Peripherals Plus we hope to meet all your computer input, output, and storage device needs. If you ever have any comments or questions, please feel free to contact your customer service representative, followed by a space.

The body of the form letter displays as shown in Figure 4-33.

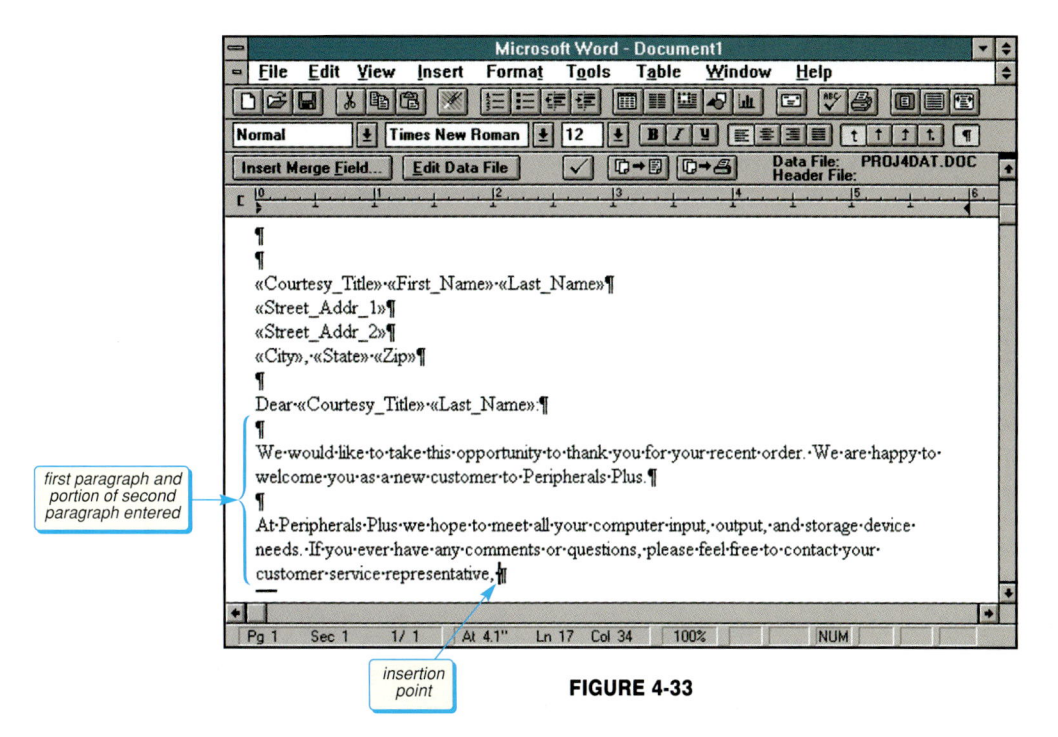

FIGURE 4-33

Using an IF Field to Conditionally Print Text in the Form Letter

In addition to merge fields, you can insert other types of fields in your main document. One type of field is called an **IF field**. One form of the IF field is: If a condition is true, then perform an action. For example, If Mary is a student, then inform her of the good student discount program for car insurance. This type of IF field is called **If...Then**. Another form of the IF field is: If a condition is true, then perform an action; else perform a different action. For example, If the weather is sunny, we'll go to the beach; else we'll go the movies. This type of IF field is called **If...Then...Else**.

In Project 4, the form letter checks the customer's region to determine the customer service representative. If the region is equal to West, then Karen Anderson is the customer service representative. If the region is equal to East, then Mitchell Rhodes is the customer service representative. To determine the customer service representative, use the If...Then...Else: If the region is equal to West, then print Karen Anderson's name, else print Mitchell Rhodes' name.

The phrase that appears after the word If is called a condition. A **condition** is composed of an expression, followed by a mathematical operator, followed by a final expression.

EXPRESSIONS The expression in a condition can be either a merge field, a number, or a text of characters. Text of characters must be enclosed in double quotation marks (''). Place two double quotation marks together ('''') to indicate an empty, or **null**, expression.

MATHEMATICAL OPERATORS The **mathematical operator** in a condition must be one of six characters: = (for equal to or matches the text), < (for less than), < = (for less than or equal to), > (for greater than), > = (for greater than or equal to), or < > (for not equal to or does not match text).

In Project 4, the first expression is a merge field (Region); the operator is an equal sign (=); and the second expression is the text ''West''. If the condition is true, print Karen Anderson, else print Mitchell Rhodes. That is, If Region = ''West'' ''Karen Anderson'' ''Mitchell Rhodes''.

Follow these steps to insert the IF field into the form letter.

TO INSERT AN IF FIELD INTO THE MAIN DOCUMENT ▼

STEP 1 ▶

Choose the Insert Merge Field button on the print merge bar. When Word displays the Insert Merge Field dialog box, select the If...Then...Else field from the Word Fields list box. Point to the OK button.

Word displays the Insert Merge Field dialog box and highlights If...Then...Else in the Word Fields list box (Figure 4-34).

FIGURE 4-34

STEP 2 ▶

Choose the OK button in the Insert Merge Field dialog box.

Word inserts the IF field into the document at the location of the insertion point (Figure 4-35). The IF field contains generic abbreviations like Exp for expression and Op for mathematical operator. You must replace these generic abbreviations with actual expressions and operators.

FIGURE 4-35

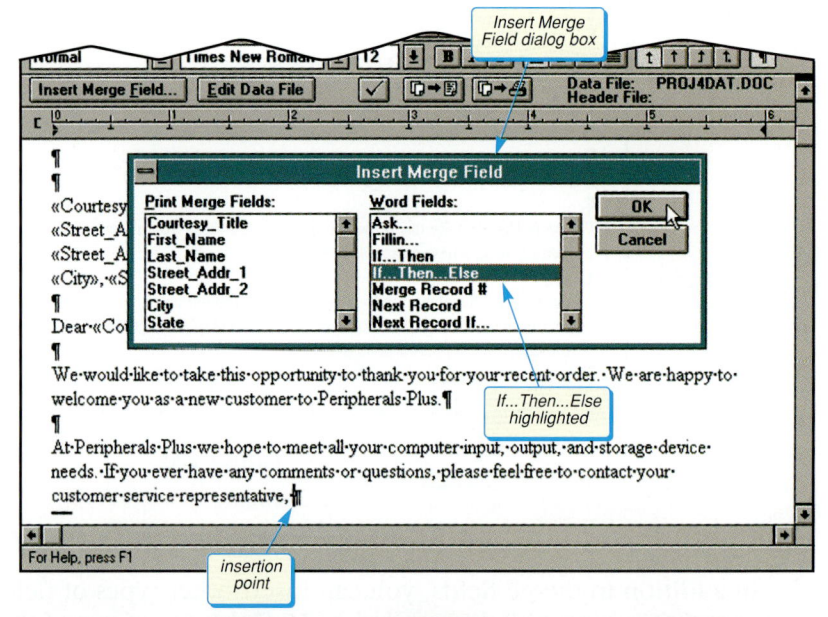

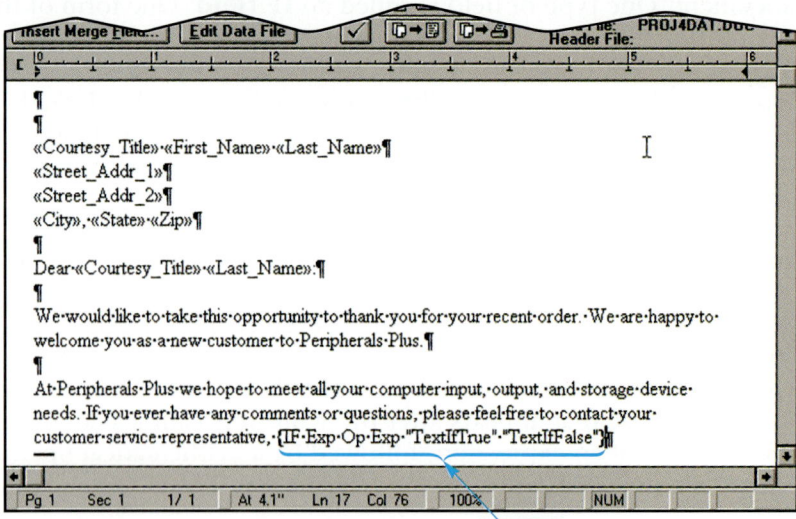

CREATING THE MAIN DOCUMENT FOR THE FORM LETTER **MSW201**

STEP 3 ▶

Point to the abbreviation Exp in the IF field and double-click. Choose the Insert Merge Field button on the print merge bar.

Word selects the abbreviation Exp in the IF field and displays the Insert Merge Field dialog box.

STEP 4 ▶

Select the merge field Region by clicking the down arrow on the Print Merge Fields scroll bar twice and clicking on the field Region. Point to the OK button.

Word highlights the Region field in the Print Merge Fields list box (Figure 4-36).

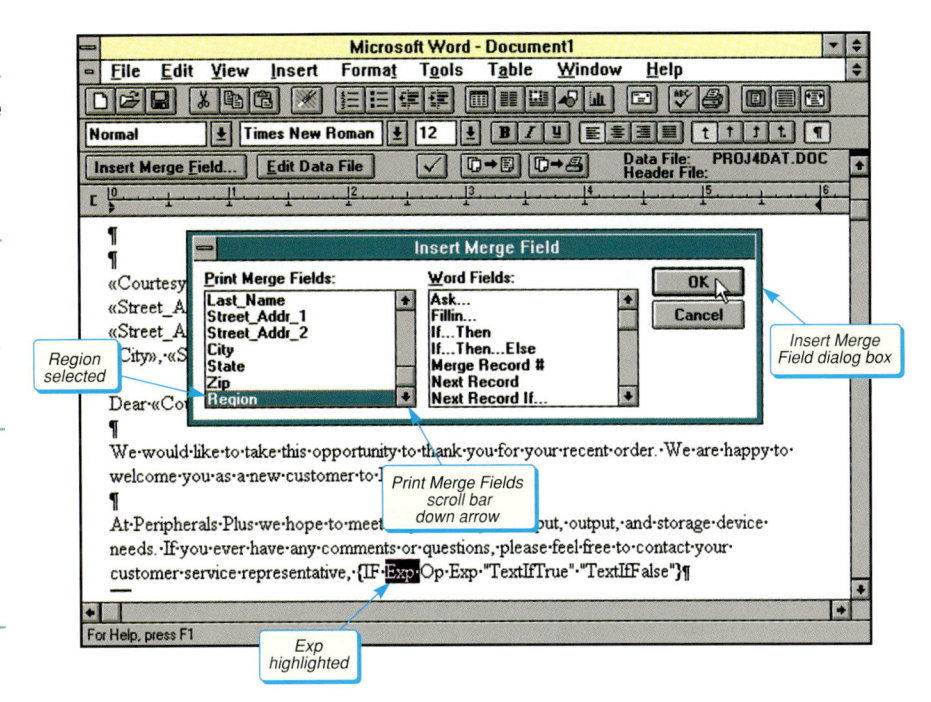

FIGURE 4-36

STEP 5 ▶

Choose the OK button.

Word replaces the selection Exp with the merge field Region in the main document.

STEP 6 ▶

Point to the abbreviation Op in the IF field and double-click.

Word highlights the abbreviation Op in the IF field (Figure 4-37).

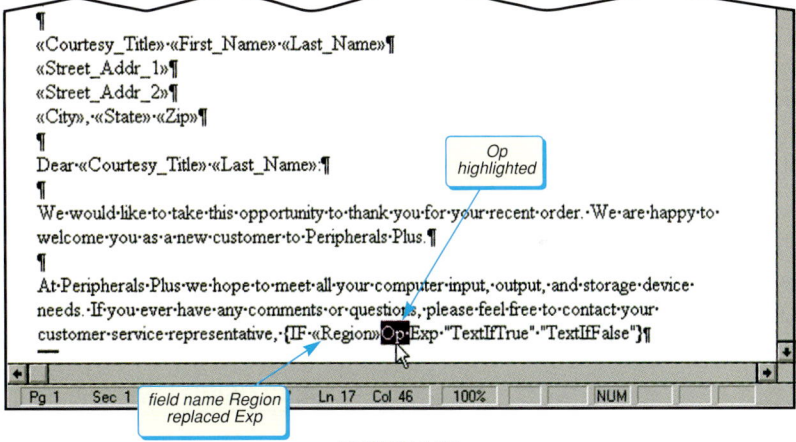

FIGURE 4-37

STEP 7 ▶

Type =.

Word replaces the selection Op with an equal sign (Figure 4-38).

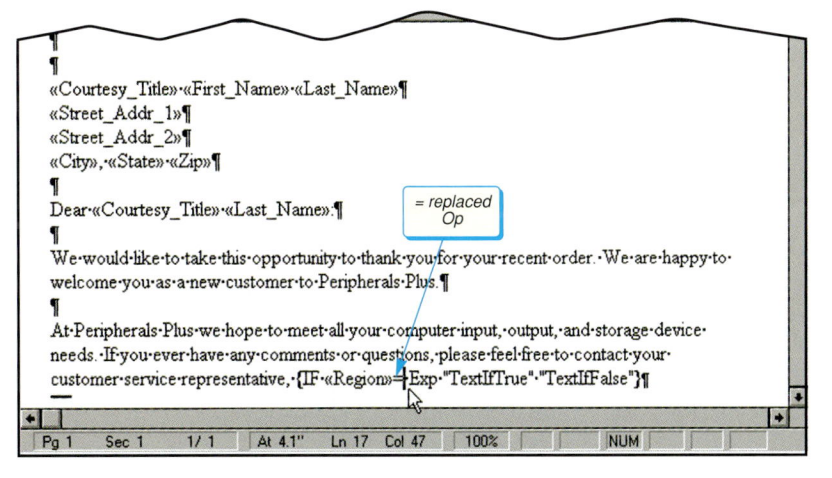

FIGURE 4-38

STEP 8 ▶

Point to the abbreviation Exp in the IF field and double-click. Type `"West"`. **Point to the phrase TextIfTrue in the IF field and double-click. Type** `Karen Anderson`. **Point to the phrase TextIfFalse in the IF field and double-click. Type** `Mitchell Rhodes`.

The IF field replacements are complete (Figure 4-39).

FIGURE 4-39

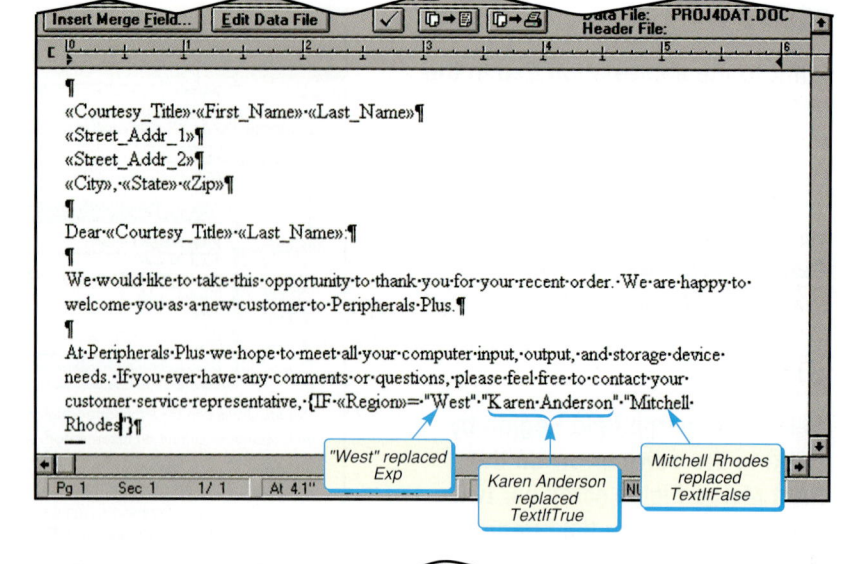

STEP 9 ▶

Press the END key to move to the insertion point to end of the line and type `, at 800-555-4567`.

The body of the form letter is complete (Figure 4-40).

FIGURE 4-40

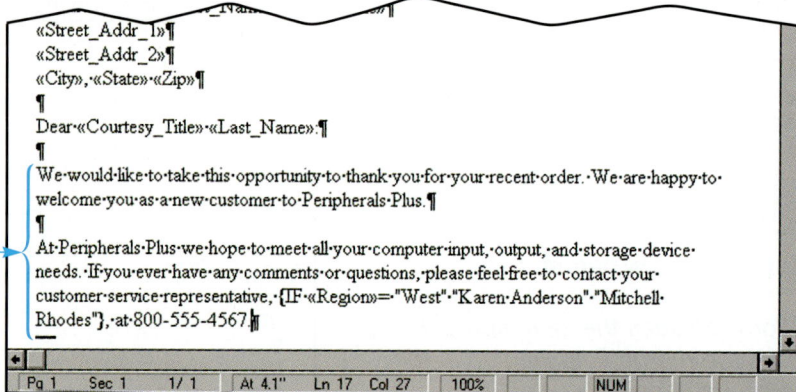

The next step is to enter the closing line and signature block in the form letter.

TO ENTER THE CLOSING LINE AND SIGNATURE BLOCK

Step 1: Press the ENTER key twice. Type `Sincerely,` and press the ENTER key four times.

Step 2: Type `Deborah Jacob` and press the ENTER key. Type `President`.

The form letter is complete (Figure 4-41).

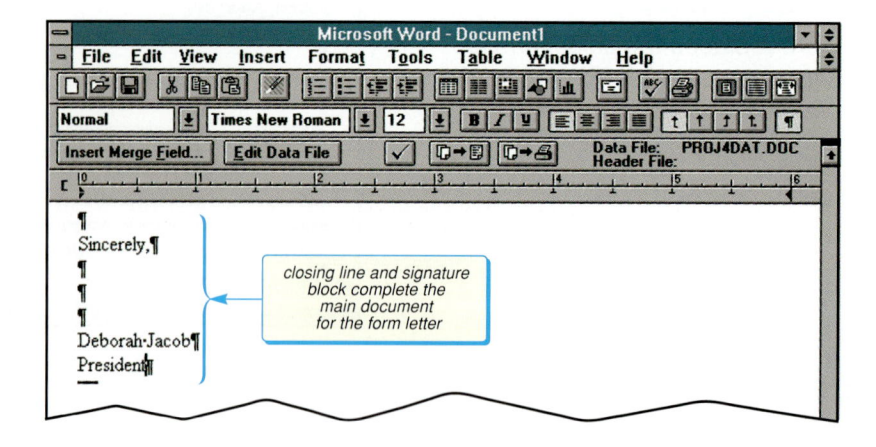

FIGURE 4-41

CREATING THE MAIN DOCUMENT FOR THE FORM LETTER **MSW203**

The main document for the form letter is now complete, and you should save it by clicking the Save button on the Toolbar. Use the filename PROJ4LTR for the main document.

Checking for Errors in the Main Document

When you add fields to a main document, it is possible you may make a mistake. For this reason, it is always a good idea to check the main document for errors before printing and merging it with the data file. Follow the steps below to perform the error checking process.

TO CHECK FOR ERRORS IN THE MAIN DOCUMENT ▼

STEP 1 ▶

Press CTRL+HOME to position the insertion point at the top of the document. Point to the Only Check For Errors button (✓) on the print merge bar. Click the left mouse button.

Word checks the main document for merge errors and displays a Microsoft Word dialog box (Figure 4-42). This dialog box indicates whether Word located any errors so you can correct them before merging the main document to the data file.

STEP 2

Choose the OK button in the Microsoft Word dialog box.

Word returns to the main document.

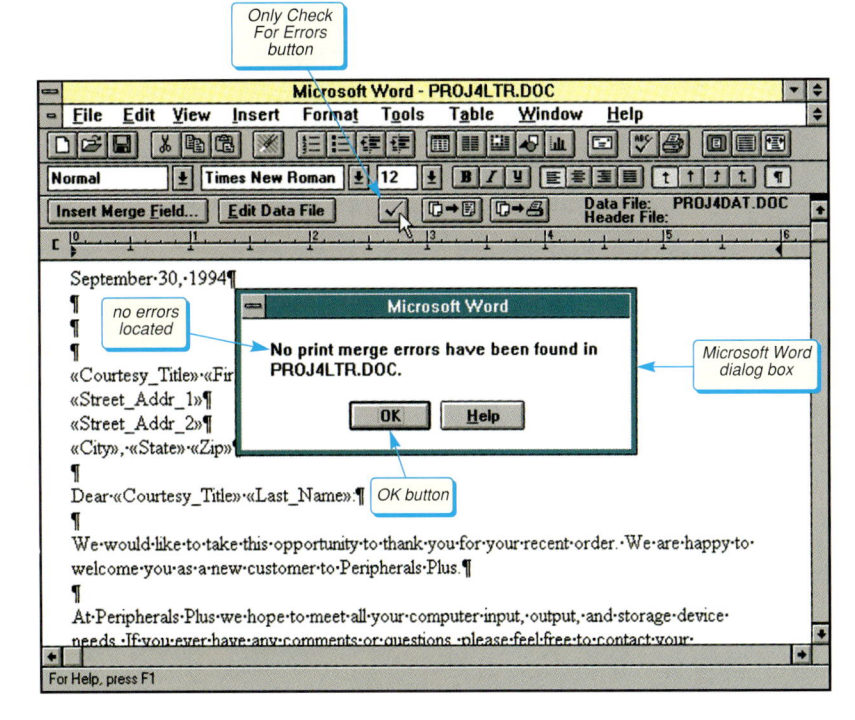

FIGURE 4-42

MSW204   PROJECT 4   GENERATING FORM LETTERS AND MAILING LABELS

Printing the Main Document for the Form Letter

Because you may want a hardcopy of the form letter as it currently displays in the document window, follow these steps to print the main document for the form letter.

TO PRINT THE MAIN DOCUMENT ▼

STEP 1 ▶

Click the Print button on the Toolbar.

Word sends the main document for the form letter to the printer (Figure 4-43).

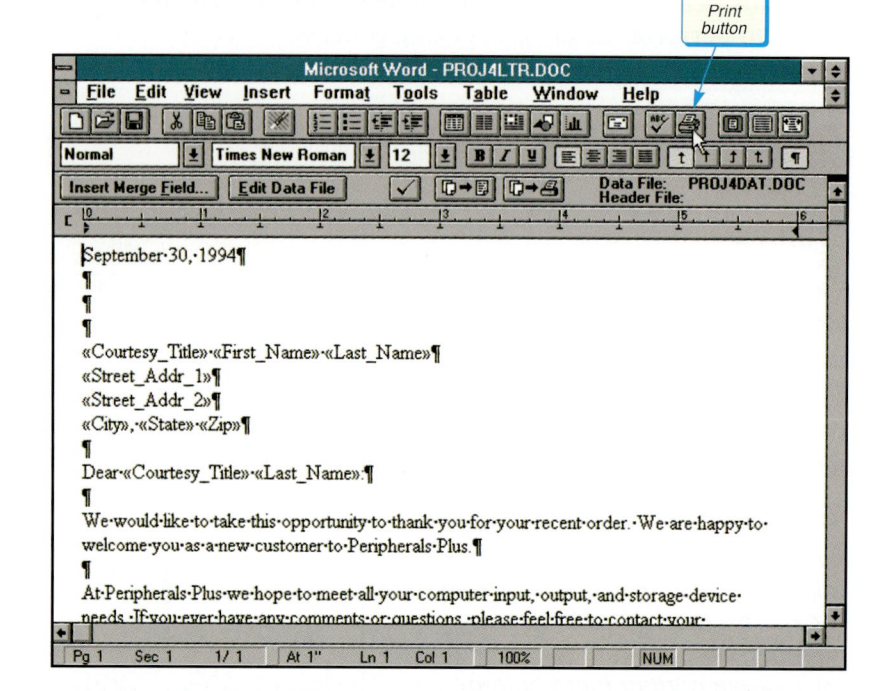

FIGURE 4-43

STEP 2 ▶

Click below the scroll box on the vertical scroll bar.

Notice the IF field does not display in the main document on the screen any more (Figure 4-44).

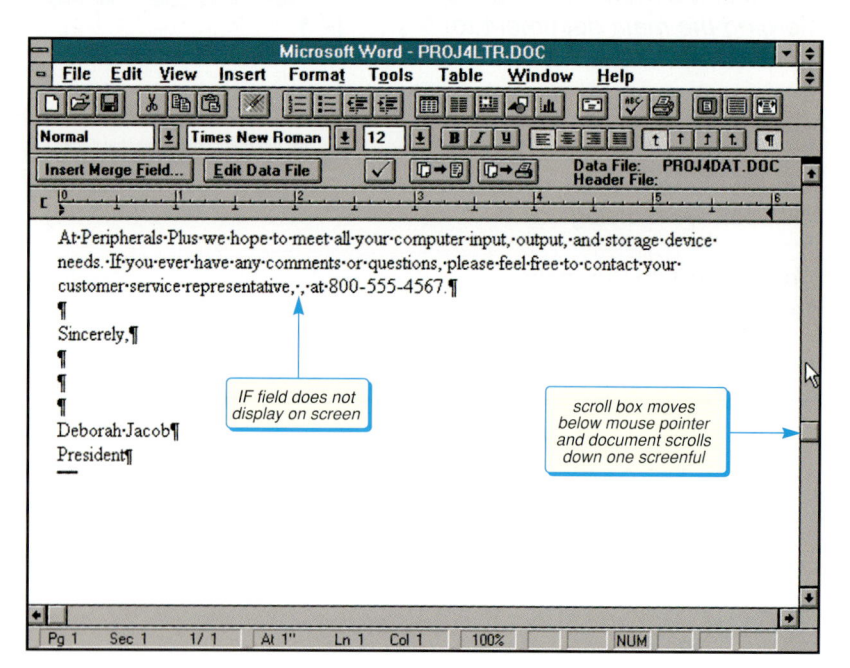

FIGURE 4-44

CREATING THE MAIN DOCUMENT FOR THE FORM LETTER   MSW205

STEP 3 ▶

Remove the hardcopy from the printer.

Notice the IF field does not display in the printed main document for the form letter (Figure 4-45).

STEP 4

Click above the scroll box on the vertical scroll bar.

Word returns to the top of the main document.

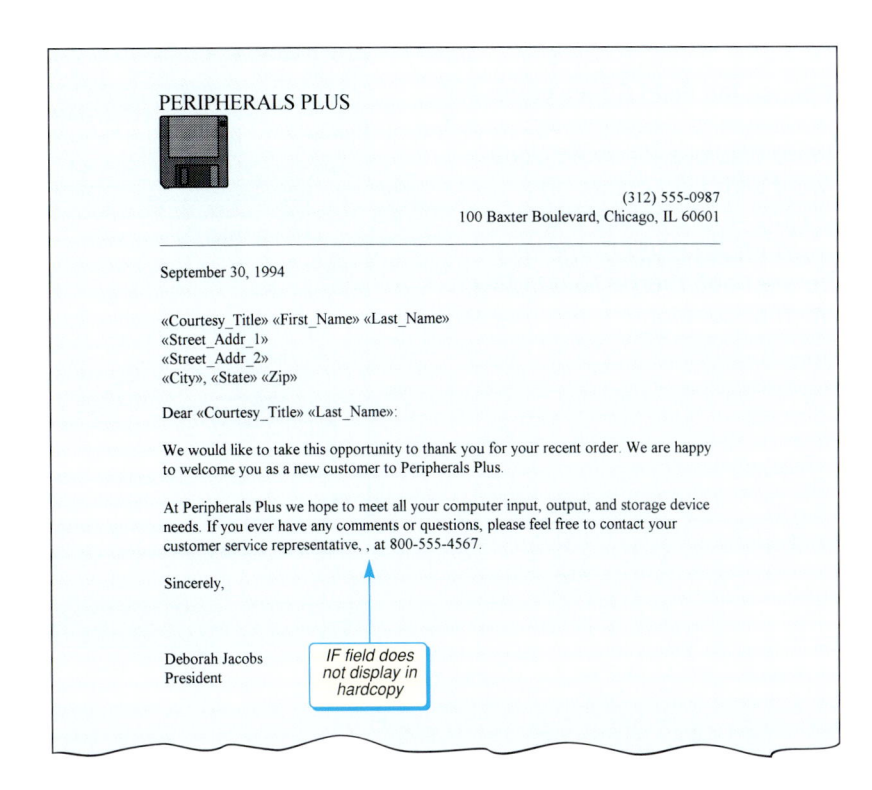

FIGURE 4-45

The IF field is referred to as a field code, and the default mode for Microsoft Word is field codes off. Thus, field codes will not print or display unless you turn them on. You use one procedure to display field codes on the screen and a different procedure to print them on a hardcopy. Whether field codes are on or off on your screen has no effect on the print merge process. The following steps illustrate how to turn on field codes so you may see them on the screen. Most Word users only turn on field codes to verify their accuracy. Because field codes tend to clutter the screen, you may want to turn them off after checking their accuracy.

TO TURN FIELD CODES ON OR OFF FOR DISPLAY ▼

STEP 1 ▶

Select the View menu and point to the Field Codes command (Figure 4-46).

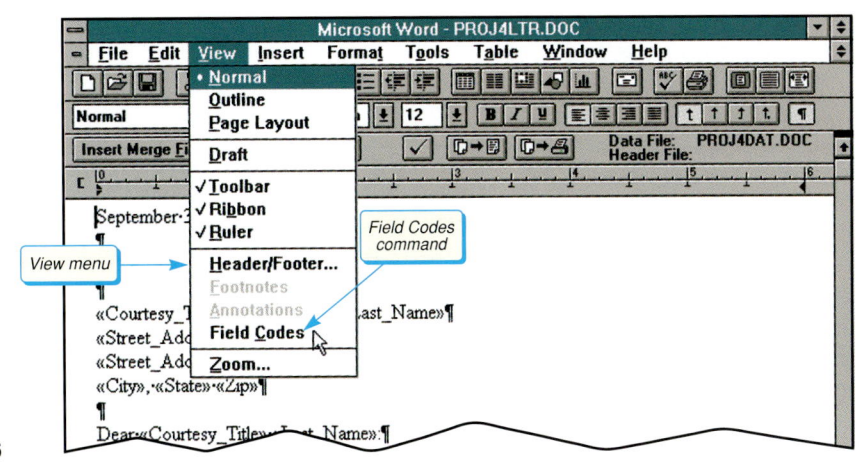

FIGURE 4-46

STEP 2 ▶

Choose the Field Codes command.

Word displays the main document with field codes on (Figure 4-47). Notice the word MERGEFIELD appears before each merge field in the main document.

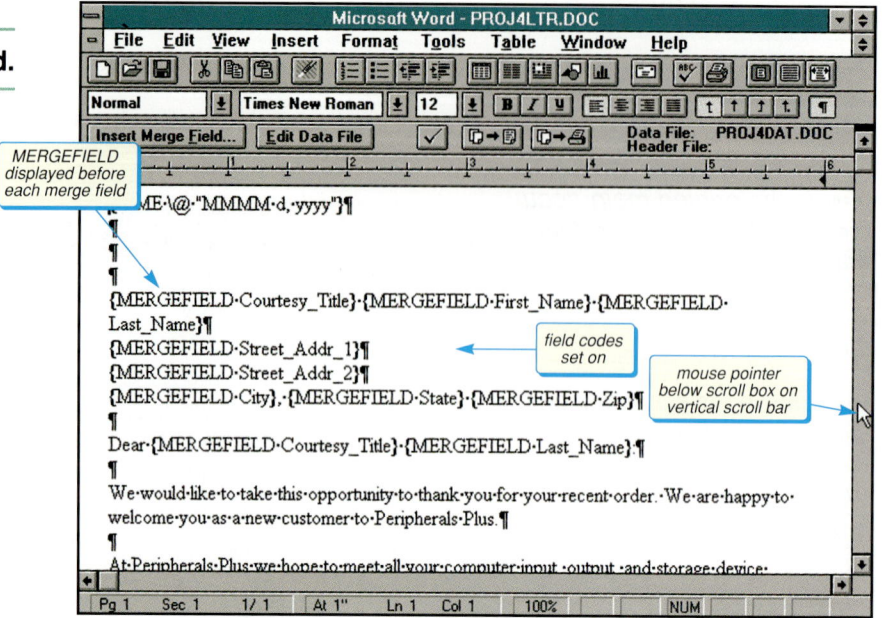

FIGURE 4-47

STEP 3 ▶

Click below the scroll box on the vertical scroll bar.

Word scrolls down one screenful (Figure 4-48). The IF field now displays on the screen.

STEP 4

Click above the scroll box on the vertical scroll bar. From the View menu, choose the Field Codes command.

Word scrolls up one screenful to the top of the main document. Word turns field codes off and returns to the screen displayed in Figure 4-43 on MSW204.

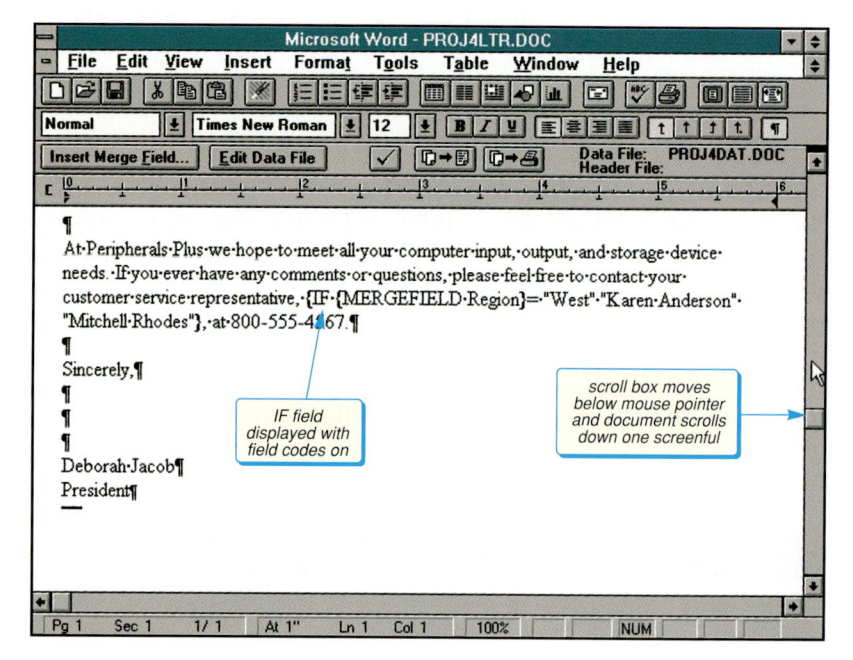

FIGURE 4-48

You may also choose to print the field-codes-on version of the form letter (see Figure 4-52 on page MSW208). Field codes can be printed only through the Print dialog box. You must remember to turn off the field codes option before merging the form letters; otherwise, all of your form letters will display field codes instead of data.

CREATING THE MAIN DOCUMENT FOR THE FORM LETTER   MSW207

TO PRINT FIELD CODES IN THE MAIN DOCUMENT ▼

STEP 1 ▶

Select the File menu and point to the Print command (Figure 4-49).

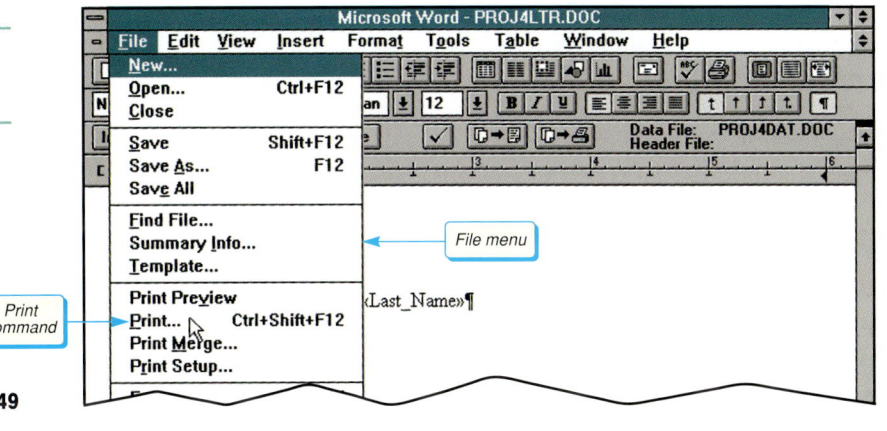

FIGURE 4-49

STEP 2 ▶

Choose the Print command. When the Print dialog box displays, point to the Options button (Options...).

Word displays the Print dialog box (Figure 4-50).

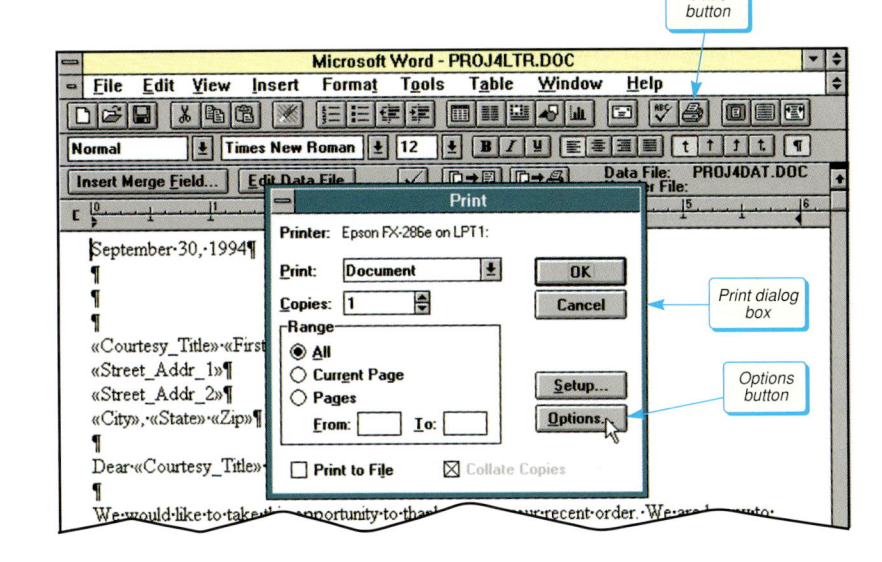

FIGURE 4-50

STEP 3 ▶

Choose the Options button. Select the Field Codes check box by clicking it. Point to the OK button.

Word displays the Options dialog box. Word places an X in the Field Codes check box (Figure 4-51).

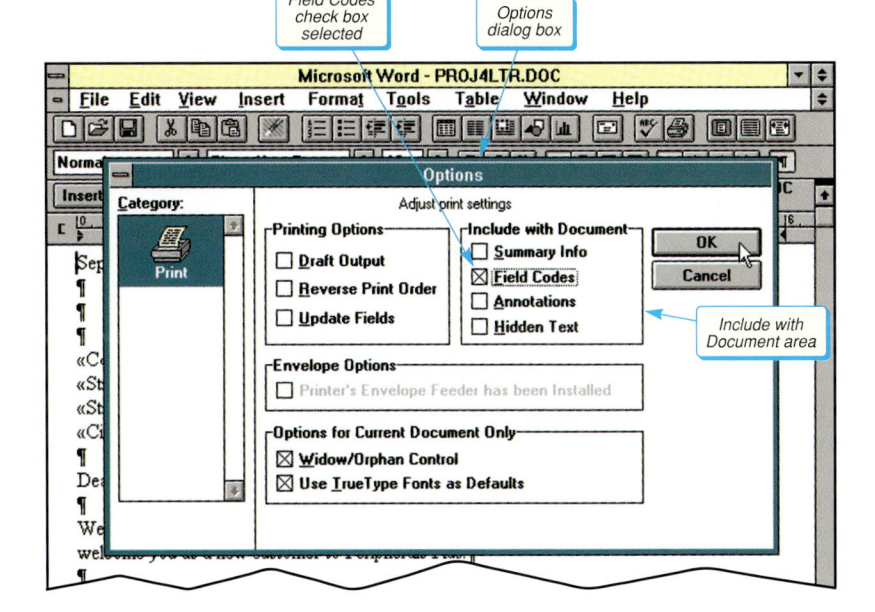

FIGURE 4-51

STEP 4

Choose the OK button in the Options dialog box. When Word displays the Print dialog box, choose the OK button.

Word sends the main document with field codes to the printer.

STEP 5

From the File menu, choose the Print command. Choose the Options button in the Print dialog box. Turn off field codes by clicking the Field Codes check box. Choose the OK button in the Options dialog box. Choose the Close button in the Print dialog box.

The field codes have been turned off. No future documents will print field codes.

STEP 6 ▶

Remove the document from the printer.

Word printed the main document with field codes on (Figure 4-52).

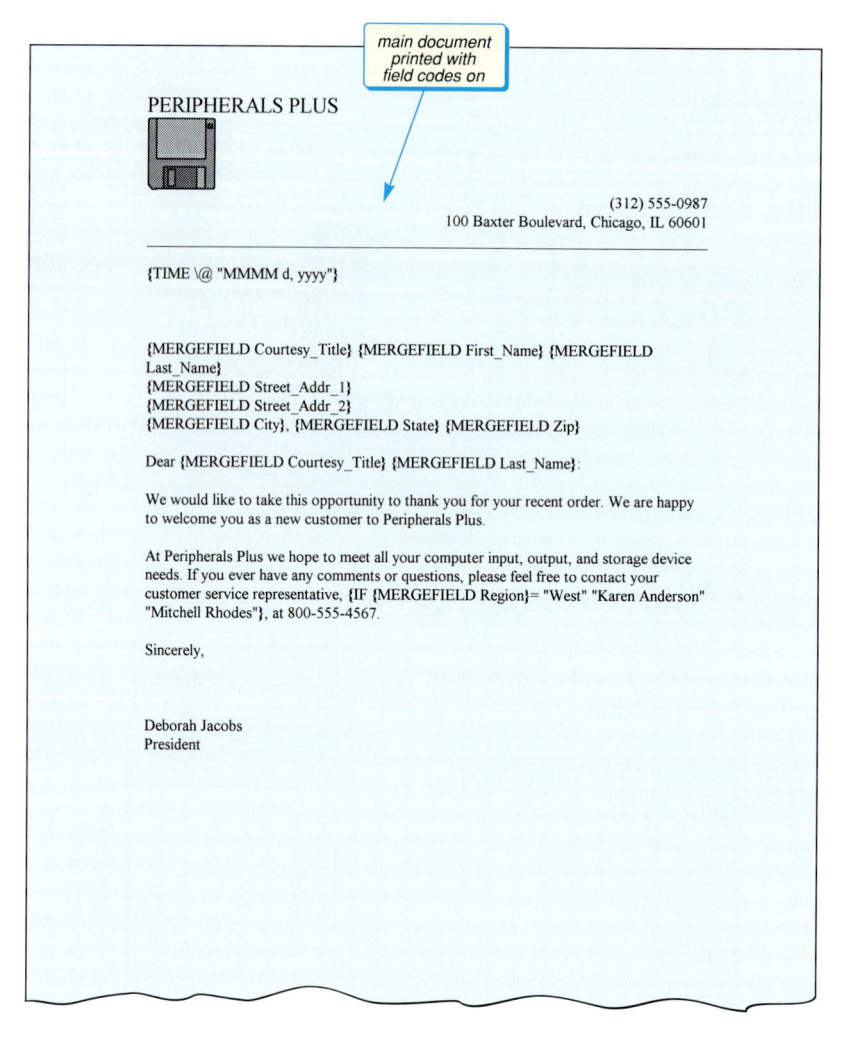

FIGURE 4-52

▶ MERGING THE DOCUMENTS AND PRINTING THE LETTERS

T he data file and form letter are complete. The next step is to merge them together to generate the individual form letters as shown in the following steps.

TO MERGE THE DOCUMENTS AND PRINT THE FORM LETTERS ▼

STEP 1 ▶

Point to the Merge To Printer button ( ) on the print merge bar.

The mouse pointer points to the Merge To Printer button (Figure 4-53).

FIGURE 4-53

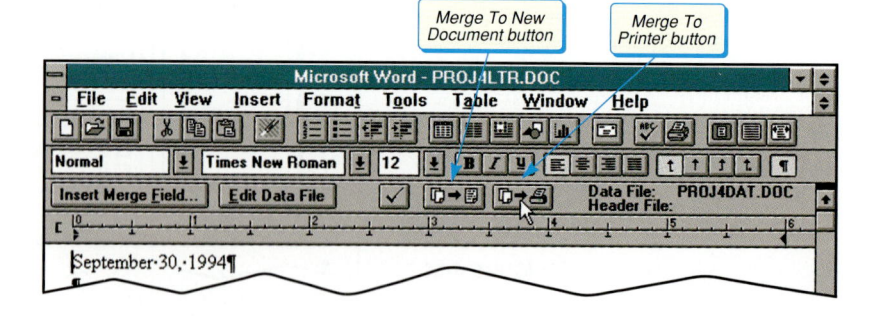

MERGING THE DOCUMENTS AND PRINTING THE LETTERS   **MSW209**

STEP 2

Click the left mouse button. When the Print dialog box displays, choose the OK button.

Word displays the Print dialog box and then sends the form letters to the printer.

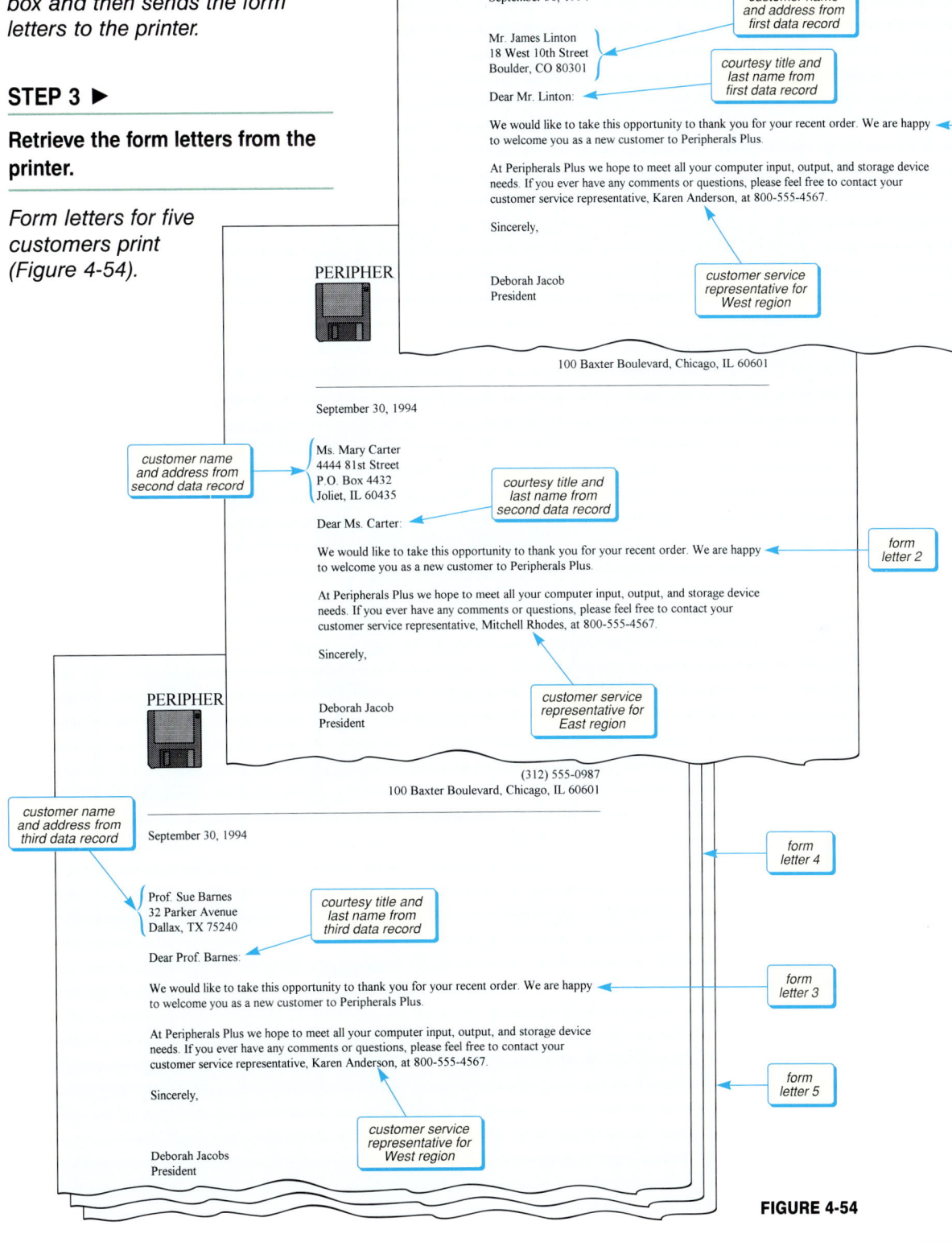

STEP 3 ▶

Retrieve the form letters from the printer.

Form letters for five customers print (Figure 4-54).

PERIPHERALS PLUS

(312) 555-0987
100 Baxter Boulevard, Chicago, IL 60601

September 30, 1994

Mr. James Linton
18 West 10th Street
Boulder, CO 80301

Dear Mr. Linton:

We would like to take this opportunity to thank you for your recent order. We are happy to welcome you as a new customer to Peripherals Plus.

At Peripherals Plus we hope to meet all your computer input, output, and storage device needs. If you ever have any comments or questions, please feel free to contact your customer service representative, Karen Anderson, at 800-555-4567.

Sincerely,

Deborah Jacob
President

— customer name and address from first data record
— courtesy title and last name from first data record
— form letter 1
— customer service representative for West region

---

100 Baxter Boulevard, Chicago, IL 60601

September 30, 1994

Ms. Mary Carter
4444 81st Street
P.O. Box 4432
Joliet, IL 60435

Dear Ms. Carter:

We would like to take this opportunity to thank you for your recent order. We are happy to welcome you as a new customer to Peripherals Plus.

At Peripherals Plus we hope to meet all your computer input, output, and storage device needs. If you ever have any comments or questions, please feel free to contact your customer service representative, Mitchell Rhodes, at 800-555-4567.

Sincerely,

Deborah Jacob
President

— customer name and address from second data record
— courtesy title and last name from second data record
— form letter 2
— customer service representative for East region

---

(312) 555-0987
100 Baxter Boulevard, Chicago, IL 60601

September 30, 1994

Prof. Sue Barnes
32 Parker Avenue
Dallax, TX 75240

Dear Prof. Barnes:

We would like to take this opportunity to thank you for your recent order. We are happy to welcome you as a new customer to Peripherals Plus.

At Peripherals Plus we hope to meet all your computer input, output, and storage device needs. If you ever have any comments or questions, please feel free to contact your customer service representative, Karen Anderson, at 800-555-4567.

Sincerely,

Deborah Jacobs
President

— customer name and address from third data record
— courtesy title and last name from third data record
— form letter 4
— form letter 3
— form letter 5
— customer service representative for West region

FIGURE 4-54

The contents of the data file merge with the merge fields in the main document to generate the form letters. One form letter for each customer is generated because each customer is a separate record in the data file. Notice that the address lines suppress blanks. That is, customers without a second address line begin the city on the line immediately below the first address line. Also notice that the customer service representative changes from one letter to the next based on the region of the customer.

Instead of printing the form letters, you can send them into a new document by clicking the Merge To New Document button ( ) on the print merge bar. With this button, you can then save the form letters in a file and print them later.

Selecting Data Records to Merge and Print

Instead of merging and printing all of the records in the data file, you can choose which records will merge based on a record selection rule. A **record selection rule** is essentially a condition you specify. For example, to merge and print only those customers whose region is East, perform the following steps.

TO SELECTIVELY PRINT RECORDS ▼

STEP 1 ▶

From the File menu, choose the Print Merge command. When Word displays the Print Merge Setup dialog box, point to the Merge button (Merge...).

Word displays the Print Merge Setup dialog box (Figure 4-55).

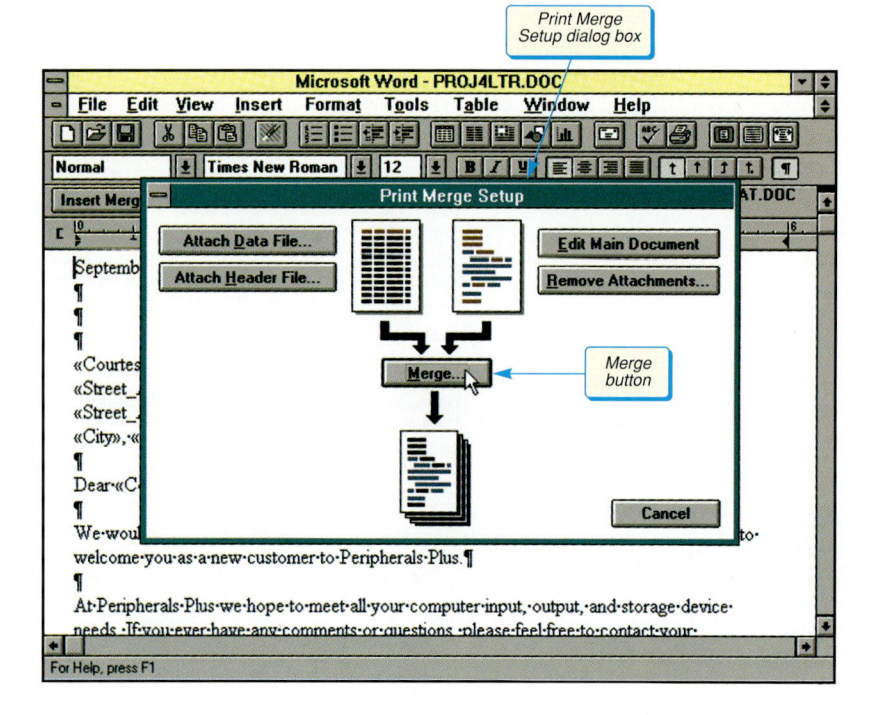

FIGURE 4-55

MERGING THE DOCUMENTS AND PRINTING THE LETTERS **MSW211**

STEP 2 ▶

Choose the Merge button. When Word displays the Print Merge dialog box, point to the Record Selection button (Record Selection).

Word displays the Print Merge dialog box (Figure 4-56).

FIGURE 4-56

STEP 3 ▶

Choose the Record Selection button in the Print Merge dialog box.

Word displays the Record Selection dialog box (Figure 4-57).

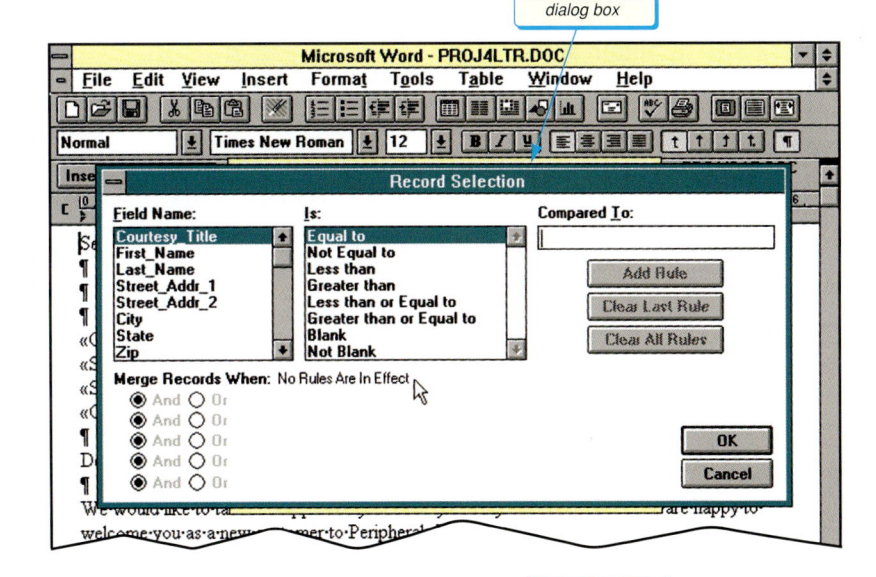

FIGURE 4-57

STEP 4 ▶

Click the down arrow on the Field Name scroll bar once. Select Region in the Field Name list box by clicking it. If Equal to is not highlighted in the Is list box, click it. Click in the Compared To text box and type `East` **in the text box. Point to the Add Rule button (Add Rule).**

Word highlights Region in the Field Name list box, Equal to in the Is list box, and displays East in the Compared To text box (Figure 4-58).

FIGURE 4-58

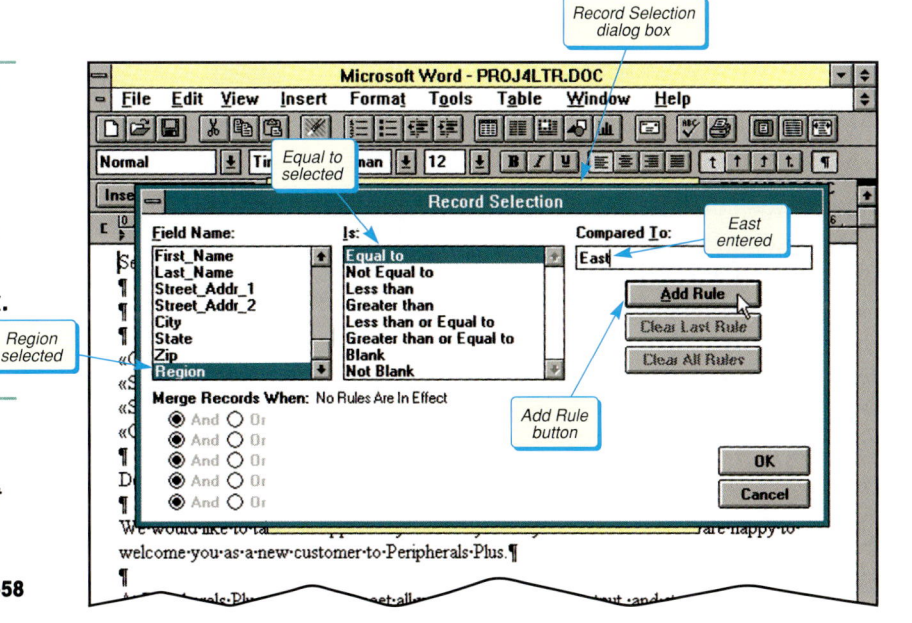

STEP 5 ▶

Choose the Add Rule button. Point to the OK button.

Word displays the rule, Region is Equal to East, in the Merge Records When area (Figure 4-59).

STEP 6

Choose the OK button in the Record Selection dialog box.

Word returns to the Print Merge dialog box.

STEP 7

Choose the OK button in the Print Merge dialog box.

Word displays the Print dialog box.

STEP 8 ▶

Choose the OK button in the Print dialog box.

Word prints the form letters (Figure 4-60) that match the specified rule: Region is Equal to East. Two form letters print because two customers are in the East region.

STEP 9

From the File menu, choose the Print Merge command. Choose the Merge button in the Print Merge Setup dialog box. Choose the Record Selection button in the Print Merge dialog box. Choose the Clear All Rules button. Choose the OK button in the Record Selection dialog box. Choose the Close button in the Print Merge dialog box.

Word removes the specified rule.

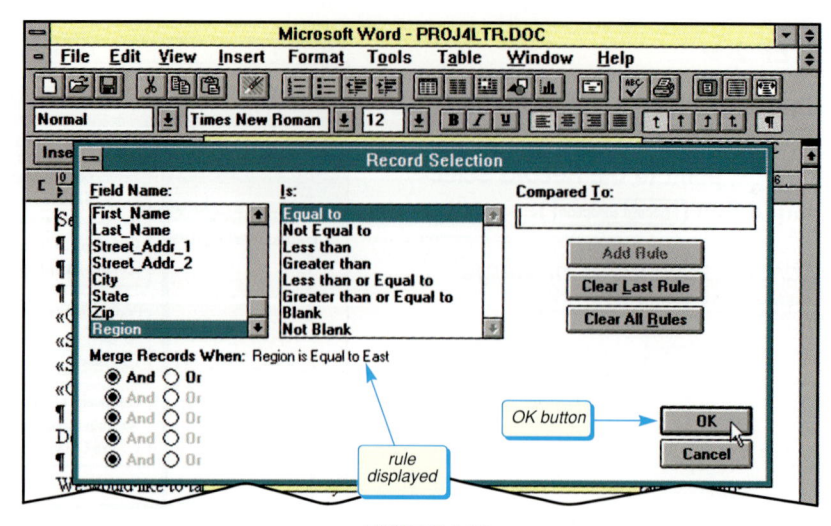

FIGURE 4-59

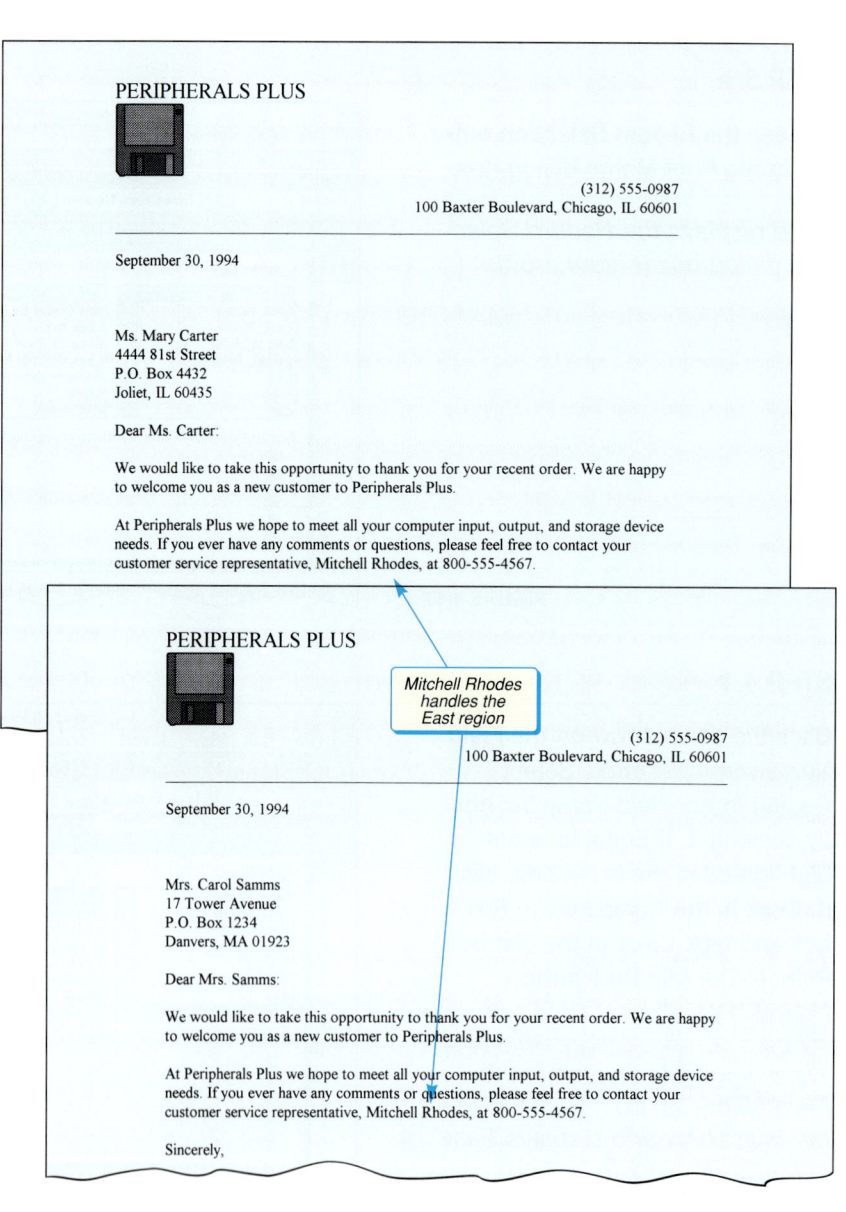

FIGURE 4-60

▶ CREATING AND PRINTING MAILING LABELS

Now that you have printed the form letters, the next step is to create mailing labels for the envelopes of the form letters. Just as Word provides a predefined template for letters and faxes, Word also has a template for the mailing labels. The mailing labels will use the same data file as the form letter, PROJ4DAT.DOC. The mailing labels will be laid out exactly the same way as the inside address in the form letter. That is, the first line will contain the courtesy title, followed by the customer's first name, followed by the customer's last name. The second line will contain the customer's street address, and so on. Follow these steps to create the mailing labels.

TO CREATE MAILING LABELS FROM A DATA FILE ▼

STEP 1 ▶

Select the File menu and point to the New command (Figure 4-61).

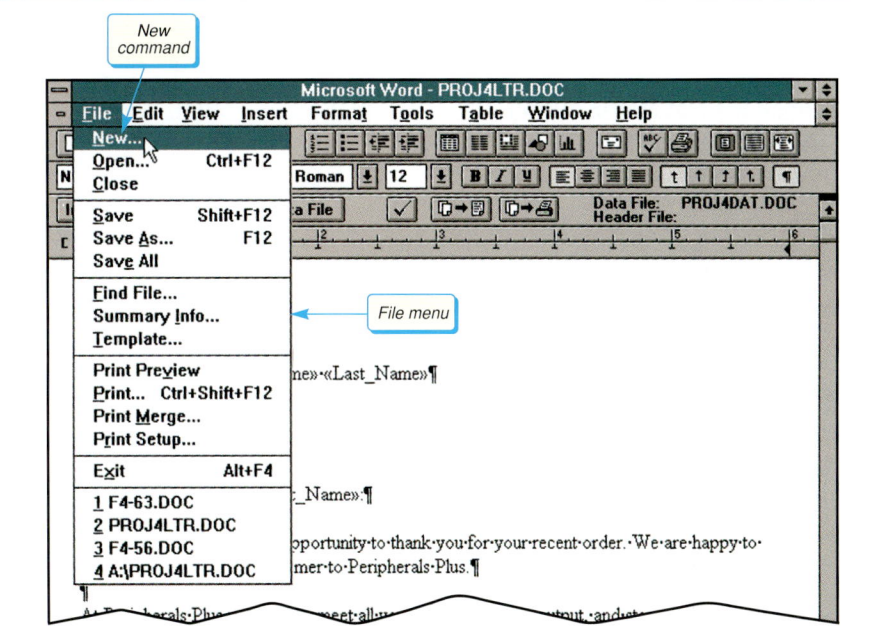

FIGURE 4-61

STEP 2 ▶

Choose the New command. When Word displays the New dialog box, select the MAILLABL template in the Use Template list box by clicking it. Point to the OK button.

Word displays the New dialog box and highlights the MAILLABL template in the Use Template list box (Figure 4-62). The template name MAILLABL also displays in the Use Template text box.

FIGURE 4-62

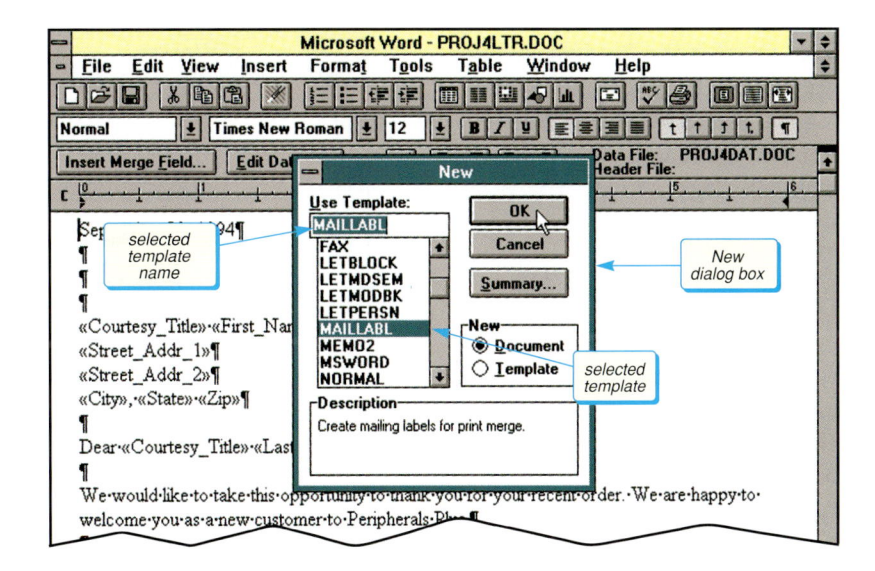

MSW214 PROJECT 4 GENERATING FORM LETTERS AND MAILING LABELS

STEP 3 ▶

Choose the OK button in the New dialog box.

Word displays a Mailing Labels dialog box requesting a printer type (Figure 4-63).

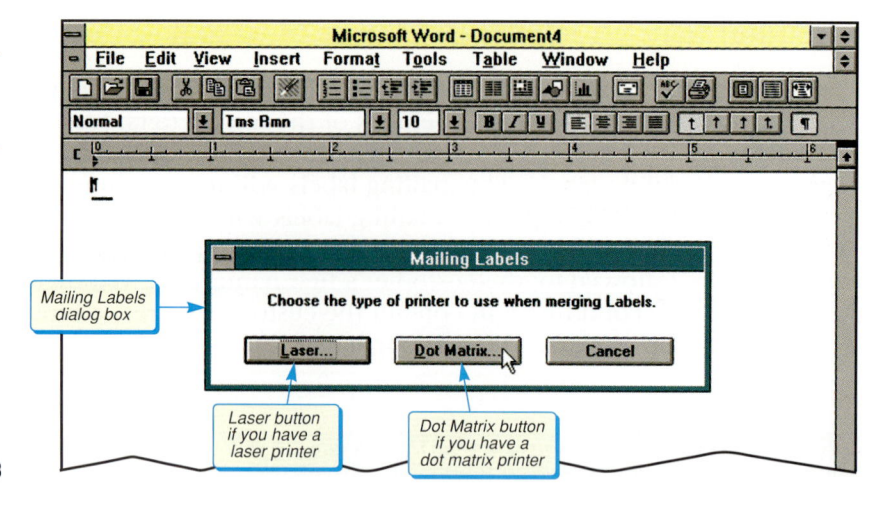

FIGURE 4-63

STEP 4 ▶

Choose the Dot Matrix button (Dot Matrix...). (If you have a laser printer, choose the Laser button (Laser...).

Word displays the Dot Matrix Printer Label Sizes dialog box (Figure 4-64). (If you have a laser printer, Word displays the Laser Printer Label Sizes dialog box). The Product Number list box lists the product numbers for all possible Avery mailing label sheets compatible with the printer.

FIGURE 4-64

STEP 5 ▶

Choose the desired Avery mailing label sheet in the Product Number list box by clicking it and choose the OK button in the Dot Matrix Printer Label Sizes dialog box.

Word outlines the label roll in the document window and displays a Microsoft Word dialog box requesting single or multiple labels (Figure 4-65). To link a data file to the mailing label template, choose the Multiple Labels button (Multiple Labels).

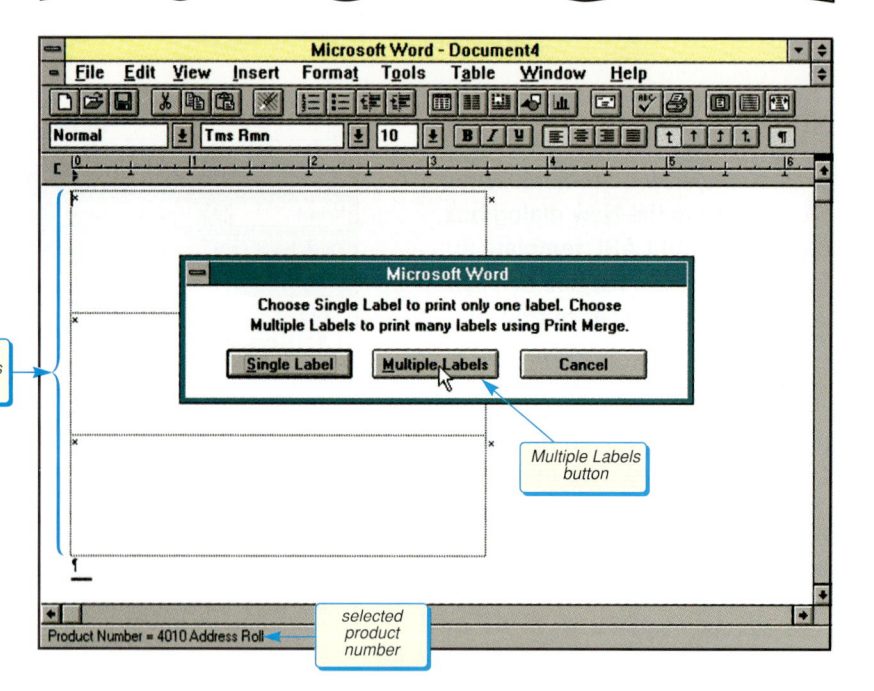

FIGURE 4-65

CREATING AND PRINTING MAILING LABELS **MSW215**

STEP 6 ▶

Choose the Multiple Labels button.

Word displays a Microsoft Word dialog box asking if the data file and header file are in two separate files (Figure 4-66).

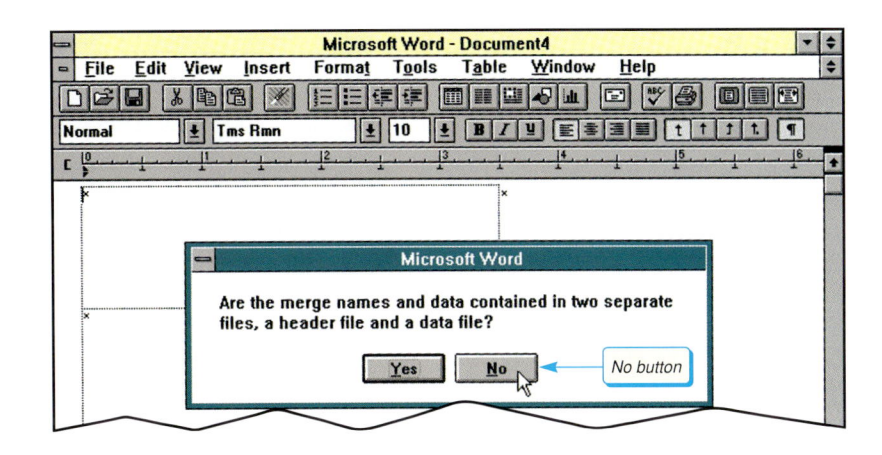

FIGURE 4-66

STEP 7 ▶

Choose the No button in the Microsoft Word dialog box. When Word displays the Attach Data File dialog box, if drive A is not the current drive, select it by clicking the Drives drop-down list box arrow and selecting a:. Then click the filename proj4dat.doc in the File Name list box.

Word displays the Attach Data File dialog box with the filename proj4dat.doc in the File Name text box (Figure 4-67). You are attaching data file, proj4dat.doc, to the mailing label template.

FIGURE 4-67

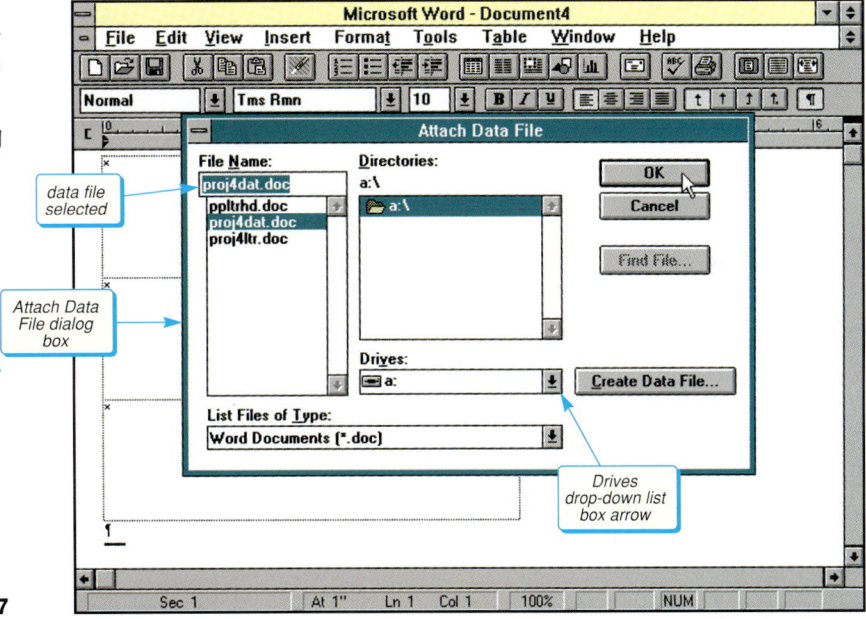

STEP 8 ▶

Choose the OK button in the Attach Data File dialog box. Select Courtesy_Title in the Field Names list box by clicking it. Select (space) in the Special Character list box by clicking it. Point to the Add To Label button (Add to Label).

Word displays the Layout Mailing Labels dialog box and highlights the field Courtesy_Title and the space special character (Figure 4-68). The customer's courtesy title will appear first in the mailing label followed by a space.

FIGURE 4-68

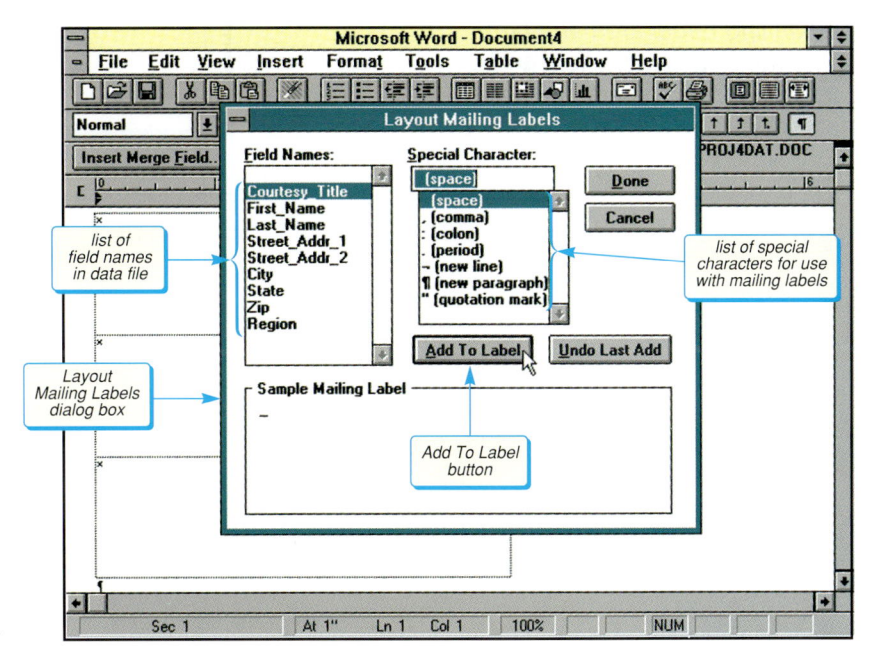

MSW216   PROJECT 4   GENERATING FORM LETTERS AND MAILING LABELS

STEP 9 ▶

Choose the Add To Label button. Select the First_Name field by clicking it. Select the Special Character (space) by clicking it.

Word places the highlighted field and special character in the Sample Mailing Label area of the Layout Mailing Labels dialog box (Figure 4-69). The First_Name field and space special character are highlighted.

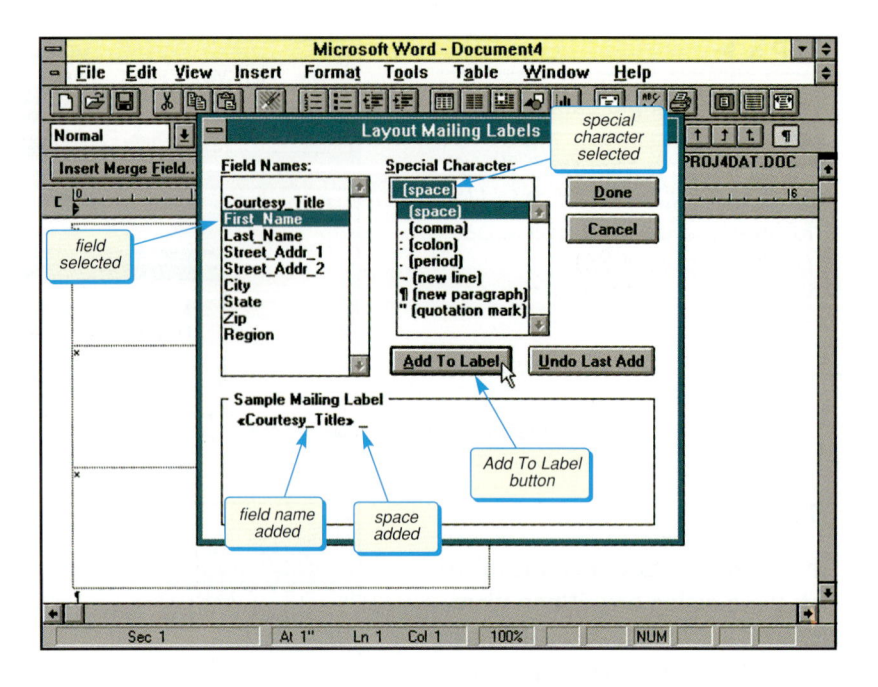

FIGURE 4-69

STEP 10 ▶

Choose the Add To Label button. Select Last_Name in the Field Names list box by clicking it. Select ¶ (new paragraph) in the Special Character list box by clicking it. Point to the Add To Label button.

Word places the First_Name field followed by a space in the Sample Mailing Label area and highlights the Last_Name field and the new paragraph special character (Figure 4-70).

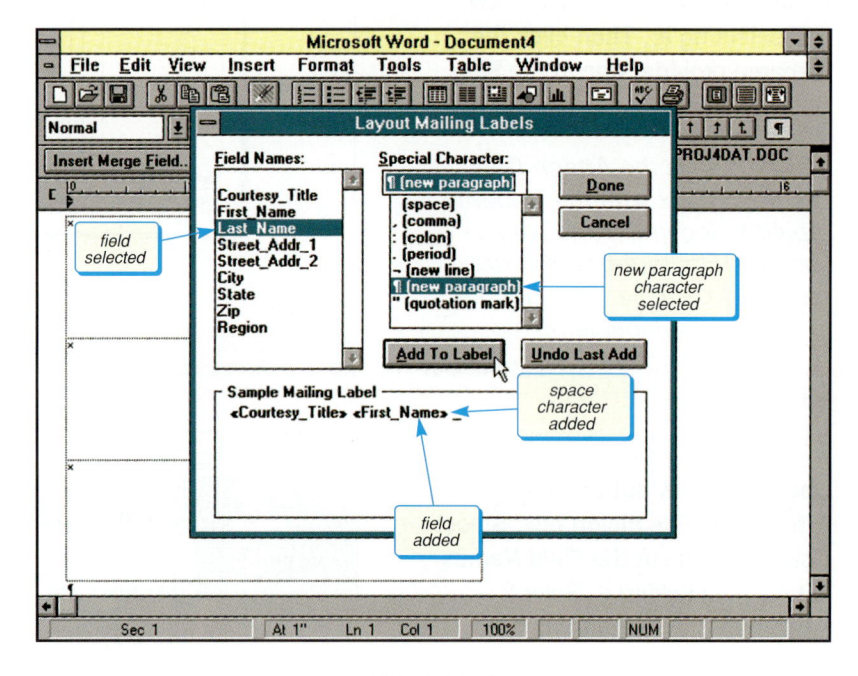

FIGURE 4-70

CREATING AND PRINTING MAILING LABELS **MSW217**

STEP 11 ▶

Choose the Add To Label button. Select the Street_Addr_1 field. Select the Special Character ¶ (new paragraph). Choose the Add To Label button. Select the Street_Addr_2 field. Select the Special Character ¶ (new paragraph). Choose the Add To Label button. Select the City field. Select the Special Character , (comma). Choose the Add To Label button. Select the Special Character (space). Choose the Add To Label button. Select the State field. Select the Special Character (space). Choose the Add To Label button. Select the Zip field. Choose the Add To Label button. Point to the Done button (Done).

The mailing label layout is complete (Figure 4-71).

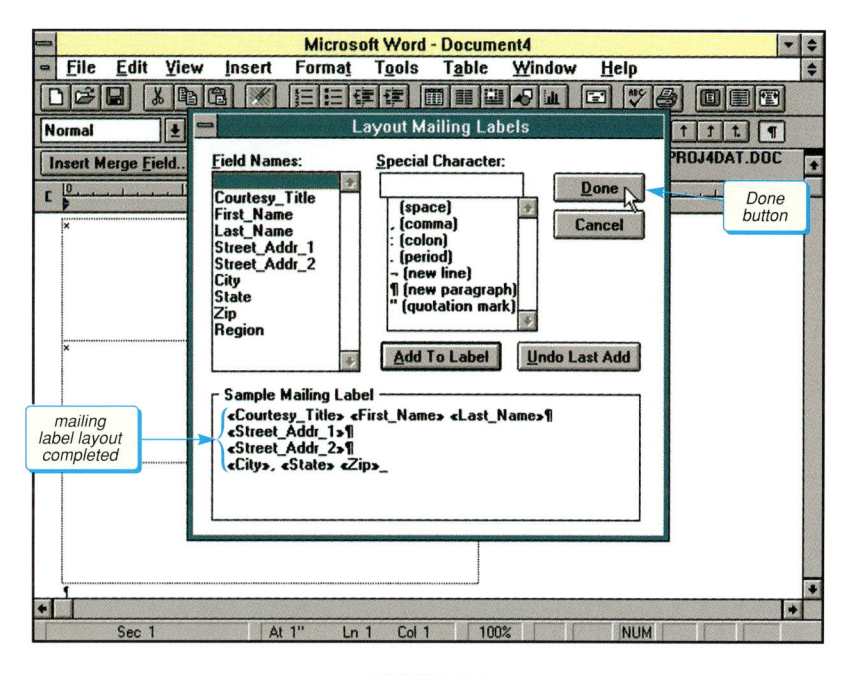

FIGURE 4-71

STEP 12 ▶

Choose the Done button in the Layout Mailing Labels dialog box.

Word displays a Mailing Label dialog box informing you the mailing labels are complete (Figure 4-72). Because the mailing labels are attached to a data file, the print merge bar displays between the ribbon and ruler. Thus, mailing labels are merged and printed the same way the form letters were merged and printed.

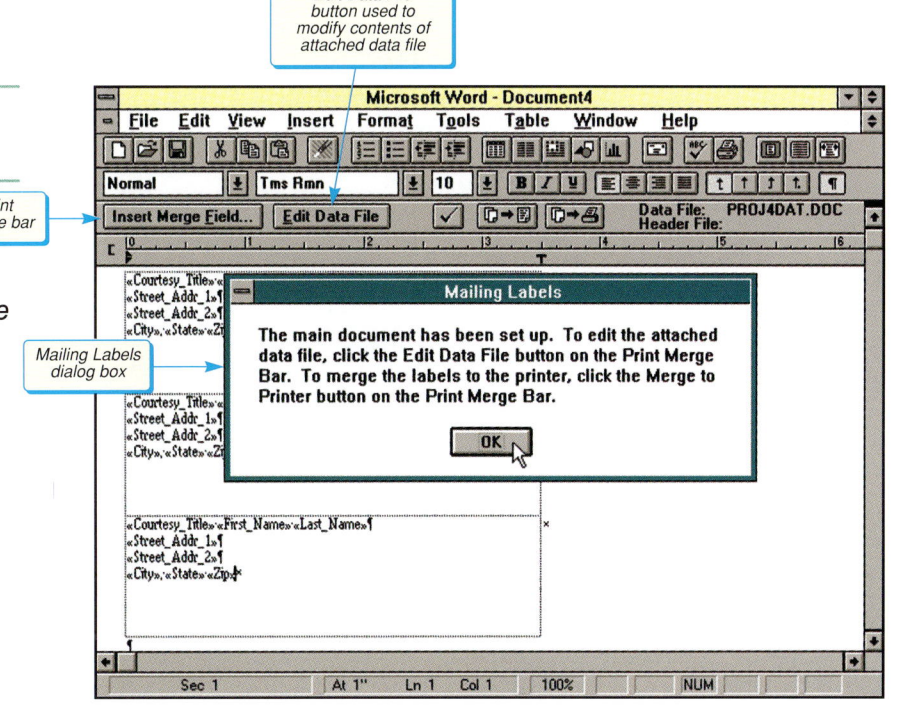

FIGURE 4-72

MSW218   PROJECT 4   GENERATING FORM LETTERS AND MAILING LABELS

STEP 13 ▶

Choose the OK button in the Mailing Labels dialog box.

Word displays a Microsoft Word dialog box instructing you how to position mailing labels in your printer (Figure 4-73).

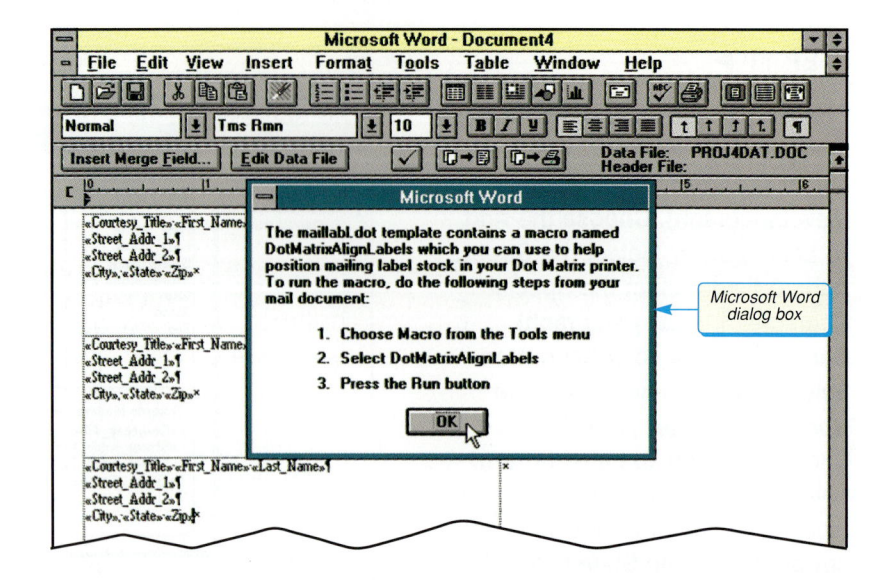

FIGURE 4-73

STEP 14 ▶

Choose the OK button in the Microsoft Word dialog box.

Word returns to the document window with the mailing label layout on the screen (Figure 4-74).

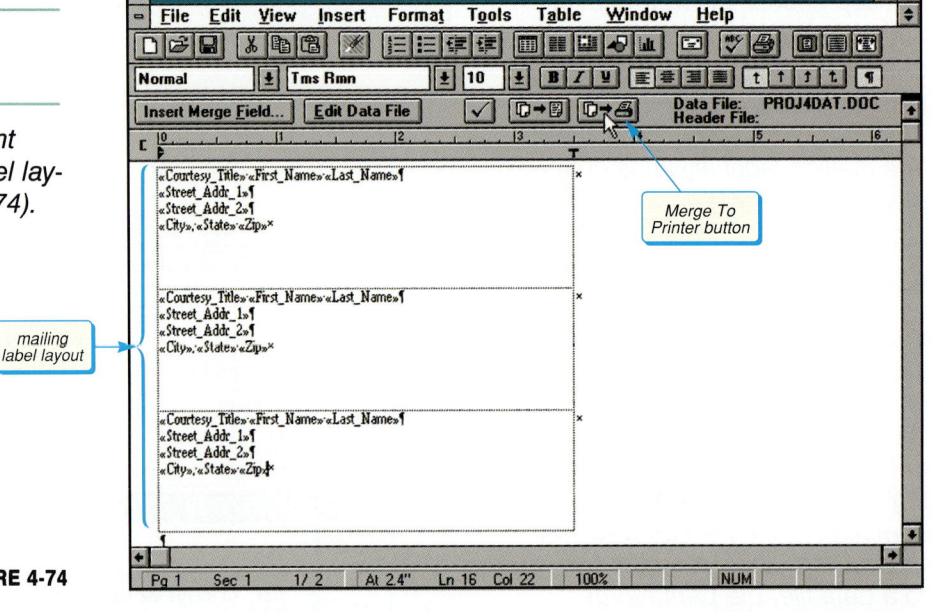

FIGURE 4-74

The mailing label layout is now complete. Save the layout by clicking the Save button on the Toolbar. Use the filename PROJ4LBL.

Printing Mailing Labels

The mailing labels are merged and printed the same way the form letters were merged and printed.

TO PRINT THE MAILING LABELS

Step 1: Click the Merge To Printer button on the print merge bar.
Step 2: Choose the OK button in the Print dialog box.
Step 3: Retrieve the mailing labels from the printer.

The mailing labels print as shown in Figure 4-75.

Before printing the mailing labels, you may want to align your mailing labels properly in the printer. To do this, choose the Macro command from the Tools menu. Then select DotMatrixAlignLabels in the Macro Name list box and choose the Run button (Run). Sample labels print so you can determine if your labels are properly aligned.

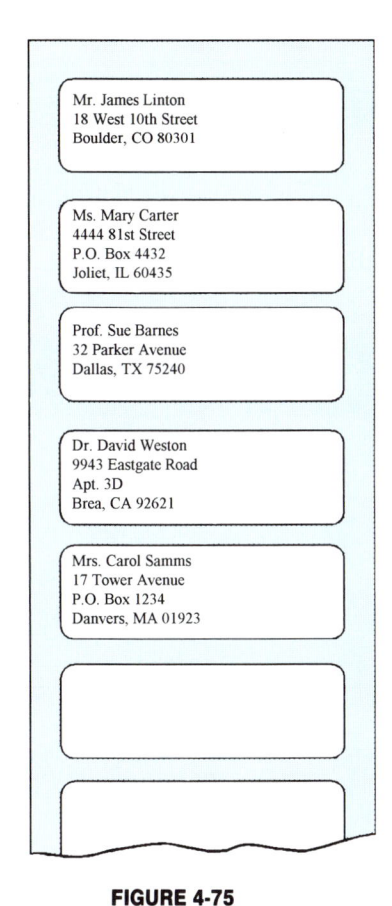

```
Mr. James Linton
18 West 10th Street
Boulder, CO 80301

Ms. Mary Carter
4444 81st Street
P.O. Box 4432
Joliet, IL 60435

Prof. Sue Barnes
32 Parker Avenue
Dallas, TX 75240

Dr. David Weston
9943 Eastgate Road
Apt. 3D
Brea, CA 92621

Mrs. Carol Samms
17 Tower Avenue
P.O. Box 1234
Danvers, MA 01923
```

FIGURE 4-75

Project 4 is now complete. You may close all the files and quit Word.

▶ PROJECT SUMMARY

Project 4 introduced you to generating form letters and corresponding mailing labels. First, you created a data file. Next, you created the main document for the form letter. The form letter included merge fields and the IF field. In this project, you learned how to merge and print all the form letters, as well as only certain records in the data file. Finally, you created and printed mailing labels to correspond with the form letters.

MSW220 PROJECT 4 GENERATING FORM LETTERS AND MAILING LABELS

▶ Key Terms

condition (*MSW199*)
data file (*MSW181*)
data record (*MSW181*)
Database Management Tools (*MSW188*)
document template (*MSW190*)
expression (*MSW200*)
field (*MSW182*)
field name (*MSW182*)
header record (*MSW182*)

IF field (*MSW199*)
If...Then (*MSW199*)
If...Then...Else (*MSW199*)
main document (*MSW181*)
Main Document Tool (*MSW188*)
mathematical operator (*MSW200*)
merge characters (*MSW195*)
merge fields (*MSW195*)
merging (*MSW181*)

null (*MSW200*)
print merge bar (*MSW189*)
Print Merge command (*MSW210*)
record (*MSW181*)
Record Management Tools (*MSW188*)
record selection rule (*MSW210*)

QUICK REFERENCE

In Microsoft Word you can accomplish a task in a number of ways. The following table provides a quick reference to each task presented in this project with its available options. The commands listed in the Menu column can be executed using either the keyboard or the mouse.

Task	Mouse	Menu	Keyboard Shortcuts
Change Template Paragraph Style		From Format menu, choose Paragraph	
Create Data File		From File menu, choose Print Merge	
Create Mailing Labels		From File menu, choose New	
Insert Current Date		From Insert menu, choose Date and Time	Press ALT + SHIFT + D
Insert Merge Field	Click Insert Merge Field button on print merge bar	From Insert menu, choose Field	Press CTRL + F9
Merging and Printing	Click Merge To Printer button on print merge bar	From File menu, choose Print Merge	
Merging to a File	Click Merge To New Document button on print merge bar	From File menu, choose Print Merge	
Move Insertion Point to End of Line			Press END
Print Document with Field Codes		From File menu, choose Print	
Switch from Data File to Main Document	Click Main Document button on Toolbar	From Window menu, choose main document name	
Turn On/Off Field Code Display		From View menu, choose Field Codes	

STUDENT ASSIGNMENTS

STUDENT ASSIGNMENT 1
True/False

Instructions: Circle T if the statement is true or F if the statement is false.

T F 1. Merging is the process of blending a data file into a main document.
T F 2. A data file contains the constant, or unchanging, text in a form letter.
T F 3. Each row in a data file is called a field.
T F 4. Data records contain the text that varies from one merged document to the next.
T F 5. The header record contains the field names.
T F 6. A data file is a Word table.
T F 7. When your data file is the current active document, the buttons on the Toolbar change.
T F 8. To switch from the data file to the main document, click the Main Document button on the Toolbar.
T F 9. Click the Current Date button on the Toolbar to place the current date at the top of a document.
T F 10. To insert a merge field into the main document, type the beginning merge character, followed by the field name, followed by the ending merge character.
T F 11. A null expression is indicated by the text "NULL".
T F 12. A condition is composed of two expressions separated by a mathematical operator.
T F 13. The Check For Errors button on the print merge bar checks the form letter for spelling errors.
T F 14. When field codes are off, the IF field displays on the screen.
T F 15. To merge and print, click the Merge To Printer button on the Toolbar.
T F 16. You can add a field selection rule when merging and printing so only certain fields print from the data file.
T F 17. Word provides a predefined template for mailing labels.
T F 18. To add merge fields to a mailing label, choose the Insert Merge Field button from the print merge bar.
T F 19. When field codes are on, the word MERGEFIELD displays in front of every merge field in the main document.
T F 20. When merging a data file to a main document, Word by default suppresses empty fields in the data file.

STUDENT ASSIGNMENT 2
Multiple Choice

Instructions: Circle the correct response.

1. Each column in a data file is called a _____.
   a. character
   b. field
   c. record
   d. file
2. The first record in a data file is called the _____.
   a. initial record
   b. data record
   c. header record
   d. start record

(continued)

STUDENT ASSIGNMENT 2 (continued)

3. In a data file, field names _____.
   a. can be duplicated
   b. have a maximum length of 50 characters
   c. must begin with a letter
   d. all of the above
4. Which of the following is a valid field name?
   a. First Name
   b. 1st_Name
   c. First_Name
   d. both b and c
5. Database Management Tools allow you to _____.
   a. add a new field
   b. sort the data records
   c. insert record numbers
   d. all of the above
6. In the main document, the print merge bar is located between the _____ and the _____.
   a. title bar, menu bar
   b. menu bar, Toolbar
   c. Toolbar, ribbon
   d. ribbon, ruler
7. Which of the following mathematical operators stands for not equal to or does not match?
   a. ! =
   b. < =
   c. > =
   d. < >
8. Text expressions in an IF field must be surrounded by _____.
   a. equal signs (=)
   b. apostrophes (')
   c. quotation marks ('')
   d. hyphens (–)
9. To use the mailing label template, _____.
   a. click the New button on the Toolbar
   b. choose the New command from the File menu
   c. either a or b
   c. neither a nor b
10. To move the insertion point to the end of a line, press _____.
    a. ENTER
    b. END
    c. CTRL + ENTER
    d. CTRL + END

STUDENT ASSIGNMENTS **MSW223**

STUDENT ASSIGNMENT 3
Understanding the Toolbar in a Data File

Instructions: In Figure SA4-3, arrows point to various buttons on the Toolbar when a data file is the active document. In the space provided, briefly explain the purpose of each button.

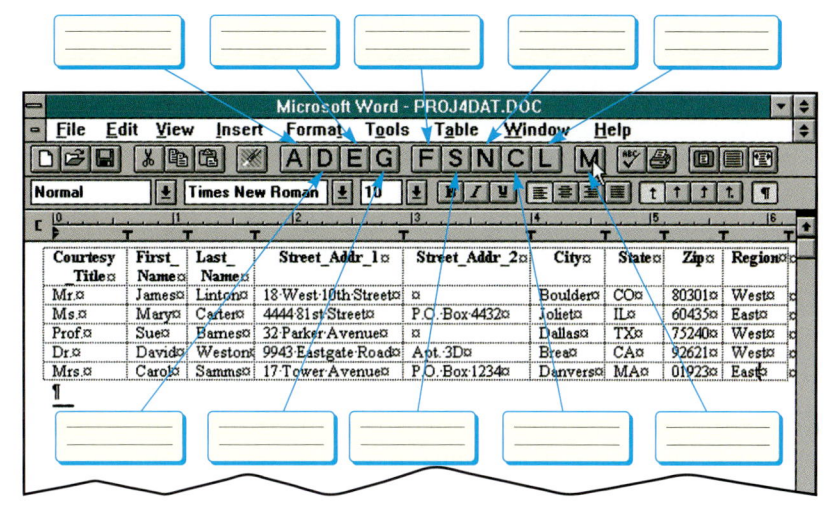

FIGURE SA4-3

STUDENT ASSIGNMENT 4
Understanding the Print Merge Bar

Instructions: In Figure SA4-4, arrows point to various buttons and one filename on the print merge bar. In the space provided, briefly explain the purpose of each button and the filename.

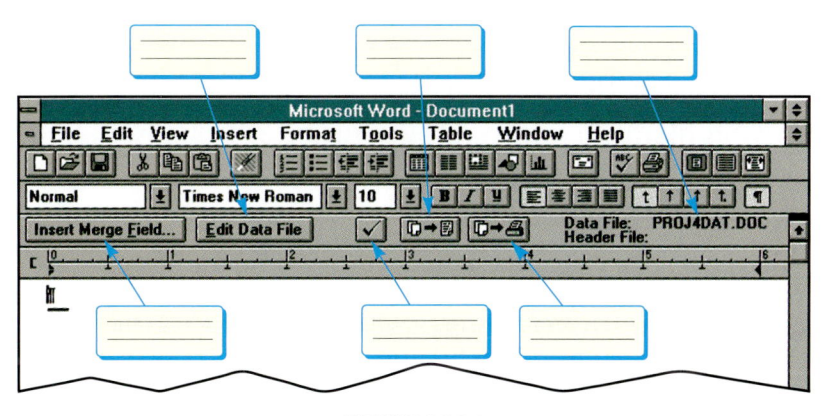

FIGURE SA4-4

STUDENT ASSIGNMENT 5
Understanding Field Name Rules

Instructions: Each field name listed below is invalid. In the space provided, briefly explain why each field name is invalid.

FIELD NAME	EXPLANATION WHY FIELD NAME IS INVALID
1. Street Address	_____
2. Customer_Service_Representative_Name	_____
3. 1st_Name	_____
4. P.O.Box	_____
5. Middle-Initial	_____

STUDENT ASSIGNMENT 6
Understanding IF fields

Instructions: The following is a generic IF field inserted into a main document with the Insert Merge Field button. Below the IF Field is the condition to be placed in the main document. In the space provided, rewrite the IF field so it meets the criteria.

Generic IF Field: {IF Exp Op Exp ''TextIfTrue'' ''TextIfFalse''}
Criteria: If Region is equal to East, then print the name Mitchell Rhodes; otherwise print the name Karen Anderson.

Completed IF Field: _____

COMPUTER LABORATORY EXERCISES

COMPUTER LABORATORY EXERCISE 1
Using the Help Menu to Learn about Form Letters and Mailing Labels

Instructions: Start Word and perform the following tasks.

1. Choose the Help Index command from the Help menu. Choose the Search button. Type `form letters` and press the ENTER key. Select Overview of Form Letters, Mailing Labels, and Other Merged Documents. Choose the GOTO button. Read and print the information.
2. Choose the Back button. Choose the Search button. Type `form letters: merging and printing` and press the ENTER key. Select Printing form letters, mailing labels, or other merged documents. Choose the GOTO button. Read and print the information.
3. Choose the Back button. Choose the Search button. Type `form letters: print merge bar` and press the ENTER key. Choose the GOTO button. Read and print the information.

COMPUTER LABORATORY EXERCISE 2
Printing the Main Document with and without Field Codes

Instructions: Start Word. Open the document CLE4-2 from the Word subdirectory on the Student Diskette that accompanies this book. A portion of the document is shown in Figure CLE4-2. The document resembles the form letter created in Project 4. By following the steps below, you are to print the document both with and without field codes.

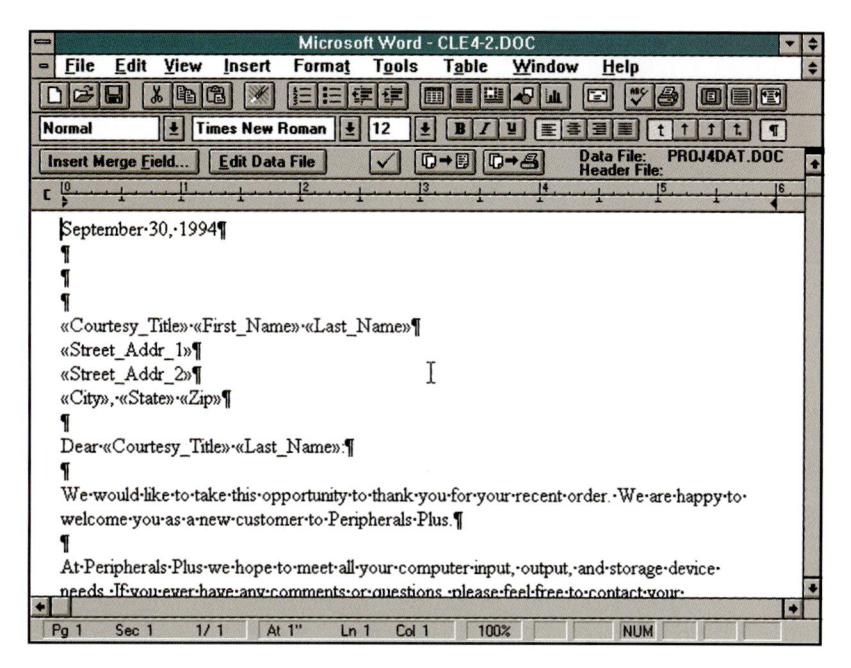

FIGURE CLE4-2

Perform the following tasks:

1. Click the Print button on the Toolbar.
2. Retrieve the printout from the printer.
3. From the File menu, choose the Print command.
4. Choose the Options button in the Print dialog box.
5. Turn on field codes by clicking the Field Codes check box in the Options dialog box.
6. Choose the OK button in the Options dialog box.
7. Choose the OK button in the Print dialog box. Retrieve the printout from the printer.
8. From the File menu, choose the Print command.
9. Choose the Options button in the Print dialog box.
10. Turn off the field codes by clicking the Field Codes check box in the Options dialog box.
11. Choose the OK button in the Options dialog box.
12. Choose the Close button in the Print dialog box.
13. Choose the Close command from the File menu.

COMPUTER LABORATORY EXERCISE 3
Selecting Data Records to Merge

Instructions: Start Word. Open the document CLE4-3 from the Word subdirectory on the Student Diskette that accompanies this book. A portion of the document is shown in Figure CLE4-3. The document resembles the data file created in Project 4.

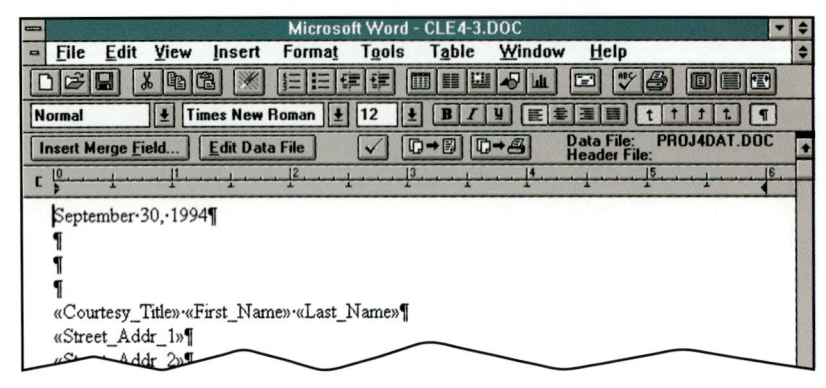

FIGURE CLE4-3

Perform the following tasks:

1. From the File menu, choose the Print Merge command.
2. Choose the Merge button in the Print Merge Setup dialog box.
3. Choose the Record Selection button in the Print Merge dialog box.
4. Click the down arrow on the Field Name scroll bar once and select Region.
5. Select Equal to in the To list box.
6. Click in the Compared To text box and type West.
7. Choose the Add Rule button in the Record Selection dialog box.
8. Choose the OK button in the Record Selection dialog box.
9. Choose the OK button in the Print dialog box. Retrieve the printout from the printer.
10. Choose the Close command from the File menu.

COMPUTER LABORATORY ASSIGNMENTS

COMPUTER LABORATORY ASSIGNMENT 1
Creating a Data File, Form Letter, and Mailing Labels

Purpose: To become familiar with creating a data file and a main document for a form letter, merging and printing the form letters, and generating mailing labels.

Problem: Riverton University is holding its annual computer conference. As a professor in the CIS Department, you have been assigned the task of recruiting local vendors to participate in the vendor display. You decide to send a form letter to all vendors that participated last year.

Instructions:

1. Create the data file shown in Figure CLA4-1a.
2. Save the data file with the name CLA4-1A.

Peripherals Plus	Ms. Jane Sperry	70 River Road	P.O. Box 1234	Hammond	IN	46323
Hardware, Inc.	Mr. Al Krammer	P.O. Box 4567		Munster	IN	46321
SoftWarehouse	Mr. Jerry Jones	P.O. Box 9807		Highland	IN	46322
Computers R Us	Mrs. Karen Clarkl	5555 East Avenue		Hobart	IN	46324
Printers, Etc.	Ms. Betty Vaughn	4321 81st Street	P.O. Box 8102	Highland	IN	46322

FIGURE CLA4-1a

3. Print the data file.
4. Create the letterhead shown at the top of Figure CLA4-1b using a header. Save the letterhead with the filename CLA4-1HD. Close the file using the Close command in the File menu.
5. Create the main document for the form letter shown in Figure CLA4-1b. Insert the letterhead into the main document for the form letter. The current date should print at the top of the form letter. Use a point size of 12 for the main document.
6. Save the main document for the form letter with the name CLA4-1B.
7. Print the main document.
8. Merge and print the form letters.
9. Create mailing labels using the mailing label template.
10. Save the mailing label layout with the name CLA4-1C.
11. Print the mailing labels.

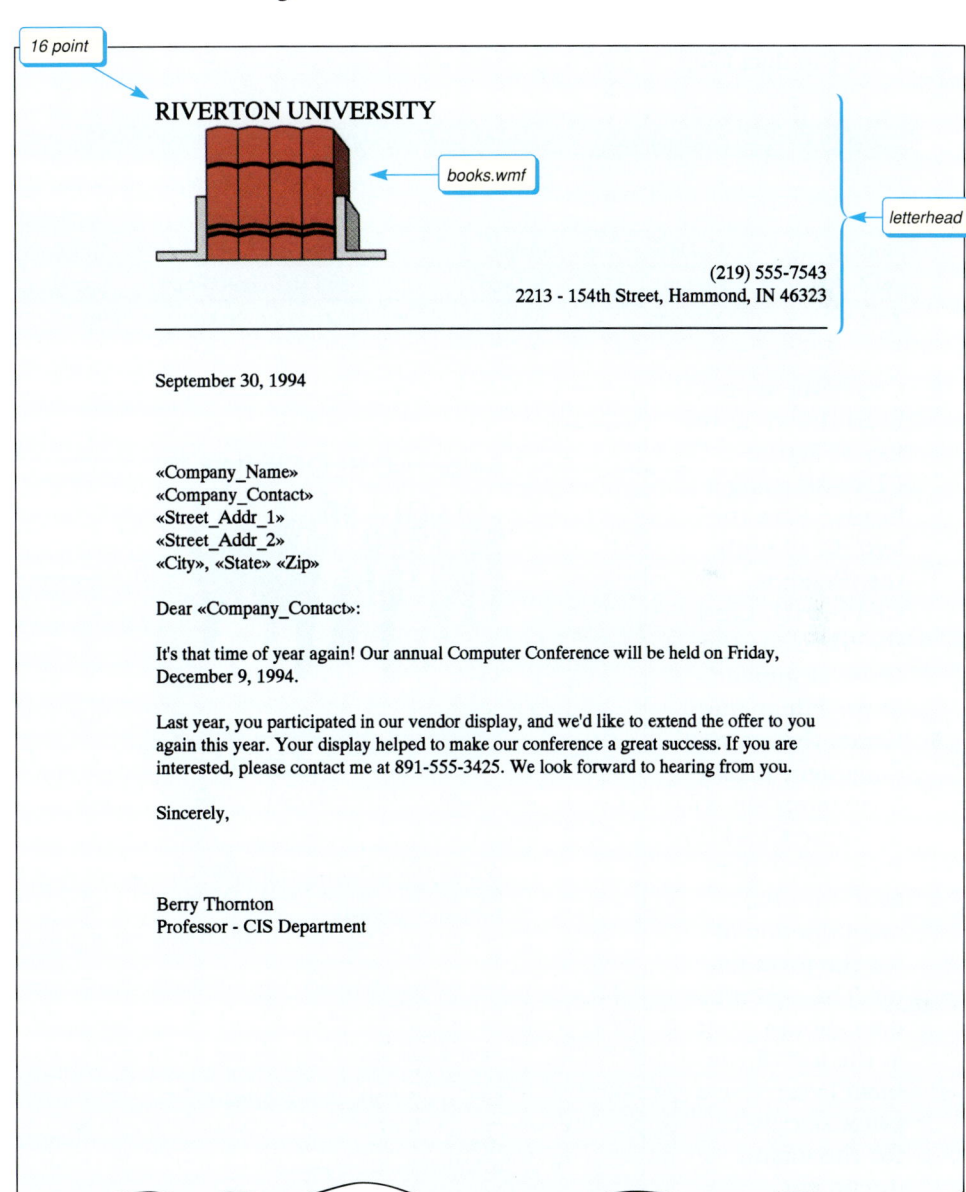

16 point

RIVERTON UNIVERSITY

books.wmf

letterhead

(219) 555-7543
2213 - 154th Street, Hammond, IN 46323

September 30, 1994

«Company_Name»
«Company_Contact»
«Street_Addr_1»
«Street_Addr_2»
«City», «State» «Zip»

Dear «Company_Contact»:

It's that time of year again! Our annual Computer Conference will be held on Friday, December 9, 1994.

Last year, you participated in our vendor display, and we'd like to extend the offer to you again this year. Your display helped to make our conference a great success. If you are interested, please contact me at 891-555-3425. We look forward to hearing from you.

Sincerely,

Berry Thornton
Professor - CIS Department

FIGURE CLA4-1b

COMPUTER LABORATORY ASSIGNMENT 2
Creating a Data File and a Form Letter with an IF Field

Purpose: To become familiar with creating a data file and a main document for the form letter, inserting an IF field in the main document, merging and printing the form letters.

Problem: You are block coordinator for the annual block parties in your neighborhood. You have decided to use a form letter to announce this year's block party. For those people who have a spouse, you want the inside address and salutation to print both the husband and wife's names. You decide to use an IF field for this task.

Instructions:

1. Create the data file shown in Figure CLA4-2a.
2. Save the data file with the name CLA4-2A.
3. Print the data file.

FIGURE CLA4-2a

FIRST_NAME	LAST_NAME	SPOUSE_NAME	STREET_ADDRESS	CITY	STATE	ZIP
Ken	Bennings	Dawn	12 Western Avenue	Brea	CA	92622
Ellen	Reiter		98 Park Street	Dana Point	CA	92629
Mary	Fielder	Kevin	4444 Tenth Street	Placentia	CA	92670
John	Mason	Tammy	546 Northgate Road	Los Alamitos	CA	90720
Adam	Johnson		321 173rd Street	Brea	CA	92621

4. Create the letterhead shown at the top of Figure CLA4-2b using a header. Save the letterhead with the filename CLA4-2HD. Close the file using the Close command in the File menu.

5. Create the main document for the form letter shown in Figure CLA4-2b. Insert the letterhead into the main document for the form letter. The current date should print at the top of the form letter. Use a point size of 12 for the main document.

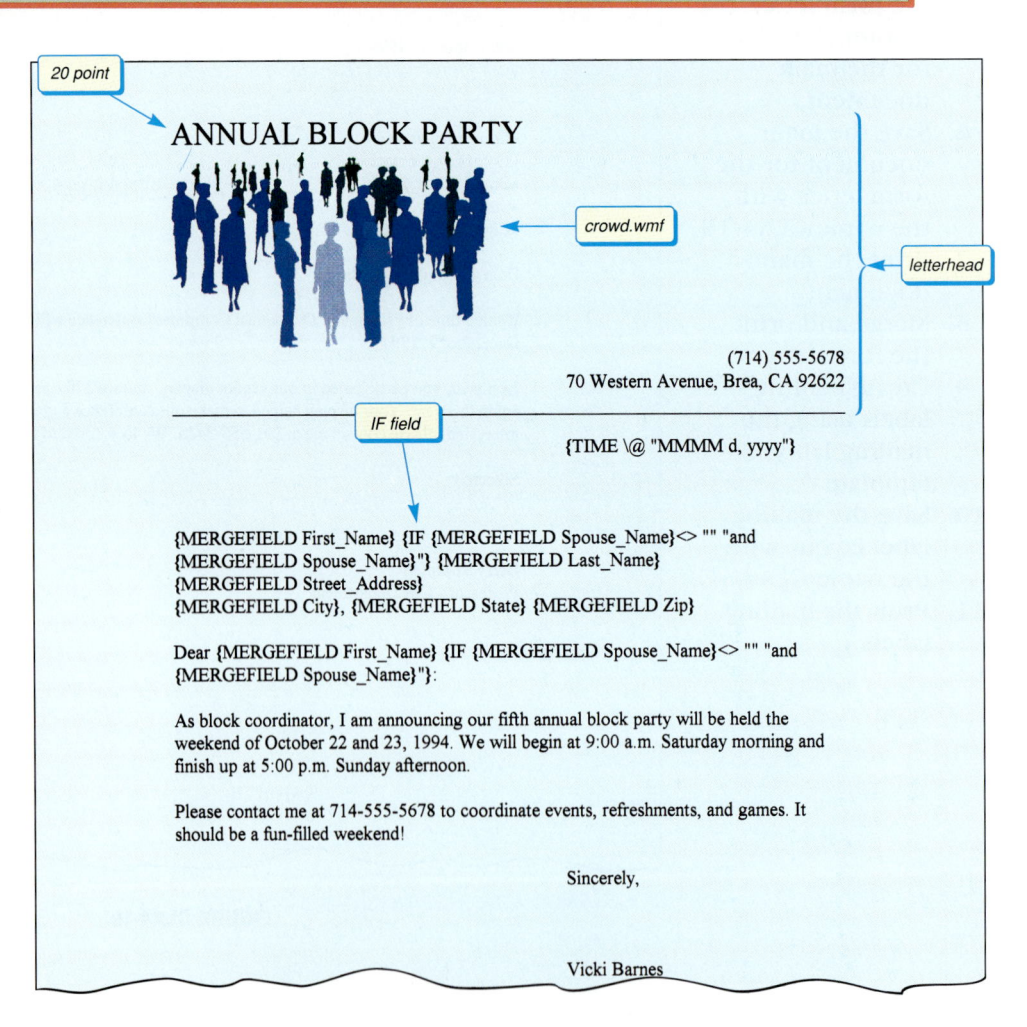

ANNUAL BLOCK PARTY *(20 point)*

crowd.wmf

letterhead

(714) 555-5678
70 Western Avenue, Brea, CA 92622

{TIME \@ "MMMM d, yyyy"}

IF field

{MERGEFIELD First_Name} {IF {MERGEFIELD Spouse_Name}<> "" "and {MERGEFIELD Spouse_Name}"} {MERGEFIELD Last_Name}
{MERGEFIELD Street_Address}
{MERGEFIELD City}, {MERGEFIELD State} {MERGEFIELD Zip}

Dear {MERGEFIELD First_Name} {IF {MERGEFIELD Spouse_Name}<> "" "and {MERGEFIELD Spouse_Name}"}:

As block coordinator, I am announcing our fifth annual block party will be held the weekend of October 22 and 23, 1994. We will begin at 9:00 a.m. Saturday morning and finish up at 5:00 p.m. Sunday afternoon.

Please contact me at 714-555-5678 to coordinate events, refreshments, and games. It should be a fun-filled weekend!

Sincerely,

Vicki Barnes

FIGURE CLA4-2b

6. Save the main document for the form letter with the name CLA4-2B.
7. Print the main document with field codes on.
8. Merge and print the form letters.
9. Create mailing labels using the mailing label template.
10. Save the mailing label layout with the name CLA4-2C.
11. Print the mailing labels.

COMPUTER LABORATORY ASSIGNMENT 3
Designing a Data File, Form Letter, and Mailing Labels from Sample Letters

Purpose: To become familiar with designing a data file, form letter, and mailing labels from sample drafted letters.

Problem: As staff benefits coordinator, your boss has asked you to schedule a meeting with all company employees to discuss the new benefits package. She drafted two sample finished letters for you and suggested you design a data file and form letter to generate similar letters for all company employees. The sample drafted letters are shown in Figure CLA4-3.

Instructions:

1. Decide on field names to be used in the data file.
2. Create a data file with five sample employees.
3. Save the data file with the name CLA4-3A.
4. Print the data file.
5. Design the layout of the form letter from the sample letters.
6. Create the letterhead shown at the top of Figure CLA4-3 using a header. Save the letterhead with the filename CLA4-3HD. Close the file using the Close command from the File menu.
7. Create the main document for the form letter. Insert the letterhead into the main document for the form letter. The current date should print at the top of the form letter. Use a point size of 12 for the main document.

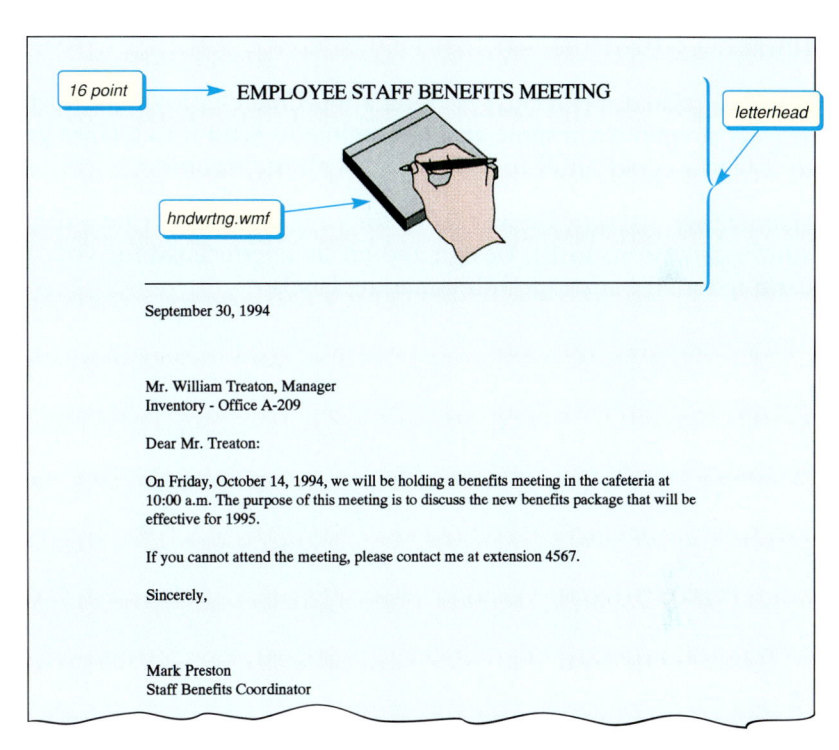

FIGURE CLA4-3

(continued)

COMPUTER LABORATORY ASSIGNMENT 3 (continued)

8. Save the main document with the name CLA4-3B.
9. Print the main document.
10. Merge and print the form letters.
11. Create mailing labels using the mailing label template.
12. Save the mailing label layout with the name CLA4-3C.
13. Print the mailing labels.

COMPUTER LABORATORY ASSIGNMENT 4
Designing and Creating a Cover Letter

Purpose: To provide practice in planning, designing, and creating a data file, form letters, and mailing labels.

Problem: You are currently seeking a full-time employment position in your area of expertise. You have already prepared a resume and would like to send it to a large group of potential employers. You decide to design a cover letter to send along with the resume.

Instructions: Design a cover letter for your resume. Create a data file with potential employers' names, addresses, and so forth. Design and create a letterhead for your cover letter using a header. Create the form letter and corresponding mailing labels.

MICROSOFT WORD 2.0 FOR WINDOWS
PROJECT FIVE

CREATING A PROFESSIONAL NEWSLETTER

OBJECTIVES You will have mastered the material in this project when you can:

- Define desktop publishing terminology
- Change a character font
- Add ruling lines to paragraphs
- Add shading to selected paragraphs
- Insert special characters in a document
- Format a document into multiple columns
- Use a frame to position a graphic
- Insert a column break
- Add box borders around paragraphs
- Insert a vertical rule between columns
- Zoom a document
- Add color to characters and lines

▶ INTRODUCTION

Professional looking documents, such as newsletters and brochures, are often created using desktop publishing software. With **desktop publishing software**, you can divide a document into multiple columns, insert pictures and wrap text around them, change fonts and point sizes, add color and lines, and so on, to make the document more professional and attractive. A traditional viewpoint of desktop publishing software, such as PageMaker or Ventura, is that it enables you to load an existing word processing document and enhance it through formatting not provided in your word processor. Word for Windows, however, provides you with all of the desktop publishing formatting features that you would find in a specialized package. Thus, you can create professional newsletters and brochures from directly within Word for Windows.

▶ PROJECT FIVE

Project 5 uses Word to produce the monthly newsletter shown in Figure 5-1 on the next two pages. The newsletter is a monthly publication for members of the Home Buyers' Club. Notice that it incorporates the desktop publishing features of Word for Windows. The newsletter is divided into three columns; includes a picture of a Victorian house and a pull-quote with text wrapped around it; has both horizontal and vertical lines to separate distinct areas; and uses different fonts, point sizes, shading, and color for various characters.

MSW231

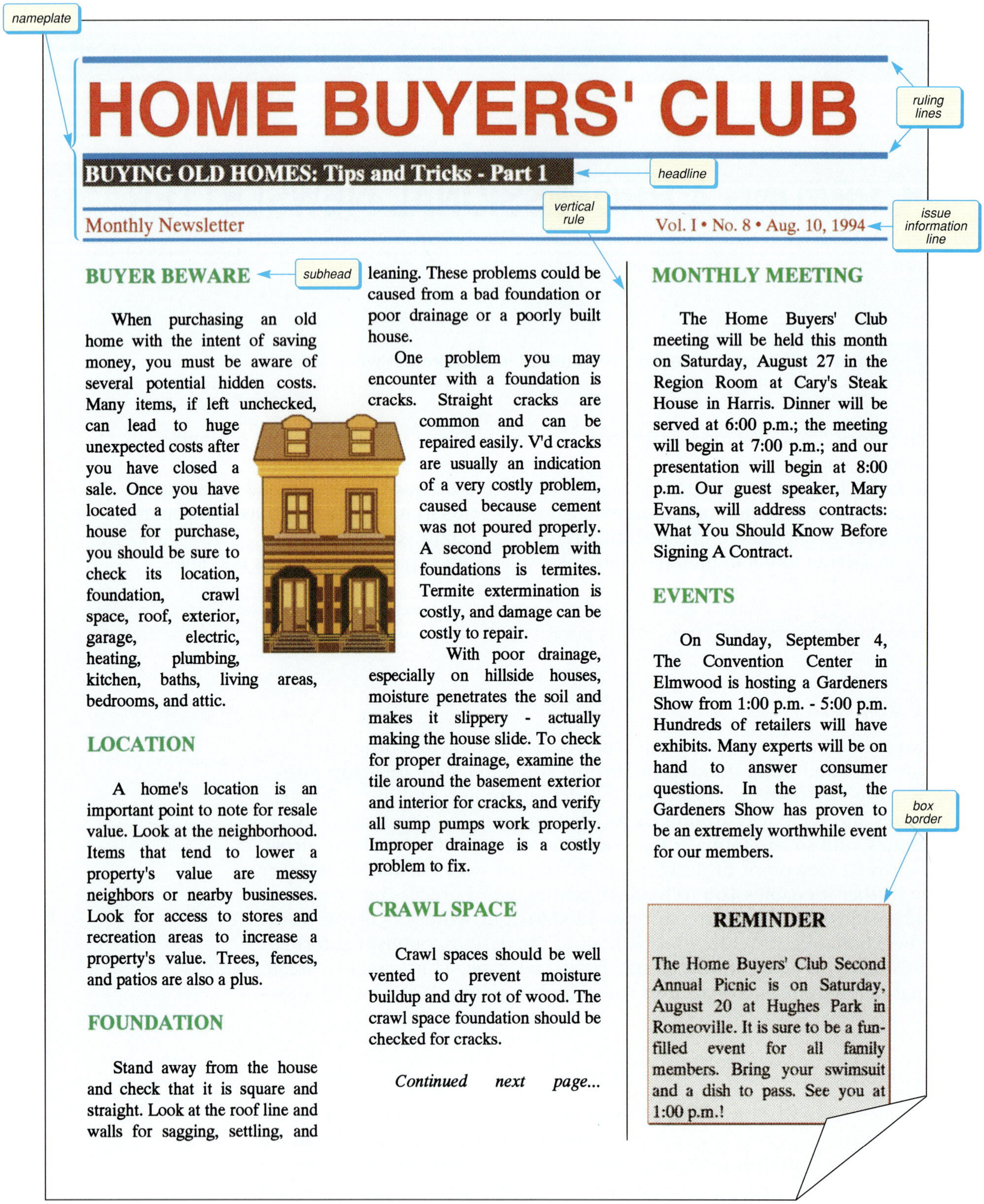

HOME BUYERS' CLUB

BUYING OLD HOMES: Tips and Tricks - Part 1

Monthly Newsletter　　　　　　　　　　　　　　　　Vol. I • No. 8 • Aug. 10, 1994

BUYER BEWARE

When purchasing an old home with the intent of saving money, you must be aware of several potential hidden costs. Many items, if left unchecked, can lead to huge unexpected costs after you have closed a sale. Once you have located a potential house for purchase, you should be sure to check its location, foundation, crawl space, roof, exterior, garage, electric, heating, plumbing, kitchen, baths, living areas, bedrooms, and attic.

LOCATION

A home's location is an important point to note for resale value. Look at the neighborhood. Items that tend to lower a property's value are messy neighbors or nearby businesses. Look for access to stores and recreation areas to increase a property's value. Trees, fences, and patios are also a plus.

FOUNDATION

Stand away from the house and check that it is square and straight. Look at the roof line and walls for sagging, settling, and leaning. These problems could be caused from a bad foundation or poor drainage or a poorly built house.

One problem you may encounter with a foundation is cracks. Straight cracks are common and can be repaired easily. V'd cracks are usually an indication of a very costly problem, caused because cement was not poured properly. A second problem with foundations is termites. Termite extermination is costly, and damage can be costly to repair.

With poor drainage, especially on hillside houses, moisture penetrates the soil and makes it slippery - actually making the house slide. To check for proper drainage, examine the tile around the basement exterior and interior for cracks, and verify all sump pumps work properly. Improper drainage is a costly problem to fix.

CRAWL SPACE

Crawl spaces should be well vented to prevent moisture buildup and dry rot of wood. The crawl space foundation should be checked for cracks.

Continued next page...

MONTHLY MEETING

The Home Buyers' Club meeting will be held this month on Saturday, August 27 in the Region Room at Cary's Steak House in Harris. Dinner will be served at 6:00 p.m.; the meeting will begin at 7:00 p.m.; and our presentation will begin at 8:00 p.m. Our guest speaker, Mary Evans, will address contracts: What You Should Know Before Signing A Contract.

EVENTS

On Sunday, September 4, The Convention Center in Elmwood is hosting a Gardeners Show from 1:00 p.m. - 5:00 p.m. Hundreds of retailers will have exhibits. Many experts will be on hand to answer consumer questions. In the past, the Gardeners Show has proven to be an extremely worthwhile event for our members.

REMINDER

The Home Buyers' Club Second Annual Picnic is on Saturday, August 20 at Hughes Park in Romeoville. It is sure to be a fun-filled event for all family members. Bring your swimsuit and a dish to pass. See you at 1:00 p.m.!

FIGURE 5-1a

Aug. 10, 1994 — Home Buyers' Club — 2

BUYING OLD HOMES: Tips and Tricks - Part 1 (Continued...)

ROOF

You may encounter four types of roofs on a house: wood shake, wood shingles, asphalt shingles, or fiberglass shingles. The life expectancy of wood roofs is 20-25 years, asphalt is 15 years, and fiberglass is 15-20 years. Be sure to ask the current homeowner how many layers of shingles are on the roof. If there is one, the roof is probably the same age as the house. To determine the remaining life of the shingles, simply subtract the age of the house from the life expectancy of the shingles. If the owner doesn't know or you are not convinced, you can contact the city or county for the permit issued to the house.

Roofs also need proper drainage through gutters and down spouts. Be sure the water runs away from the house and not into the foundation. All types of gutters should be checked for leaky joints. Aluminum gutters are usually the best type. Wood gutters have to be oiled every year. Steel galvanized gutters should also be checked for rust.

EXTERIOR

Four basic home exteriors are paint, brick, stone, and stucco. If the house is painted, look for peeling, checking, and chalking. Peeling is when the paint has lifted from the wall (like orange peels). Peeling is usually caused from old paint or poor insulation. If the paint is older than seven years, peeling is natural. When a house is poorly insulated, heat escapes and moisture develops.

"If there is only one layer of shingles, the roof is probably the same age as the house."

The moisture saturates the wood while trying to escape. In these cases, the house has to be re-insulated by either removing the outside or inside walls to make the paint stick.

Painted houses must also be looked at for checking and chalking. Checking is when the paint has little cracks on its surface with a rough-looking finish. Checking is caused by insufficient drying time between coats or poor quality paint. To correct this problem, you have to remove the paint by stripping or sandblasting it and then re-paint.

Chalking is when the paint surface is dull and powdery. It is caused by oil-based paints. To correct this problem, simply wash the wall surface. Be aware, though, that each time the surface is washed, the paint becomes thinner.

If a house has brick siding, check if it is a solid brick wall or a veneer brick. Solid brick walls usually have a header brace every third or fourth row with full bricks in the wall. A header brace is full bricks laid the opposite direction. Veneer brick, the most common today, is an outside layer of brick attached to an existing studded wall, giving the appearance of an all-brick home. Although these homes look fine, look for these side effects: moisture in the wood, termites, and poor insulation.

Stone houses are a lot like veneer brick houses in their construction and problems. The major difference is stone houses are much more expensive because of construction methods.

Houses with a stucco exterior attract a lot of moisture. Stucco is mortar attached to a screening. The screening is then attached to an existing wood wall. The moisture produces dry-rotting of the wood wall. Stucco is also prone to cracks. Avoid stucco, if possible.

Be sure to check all exterior windows. They should be painted with no signs of rotting. Older homes should have proper storm windows, and newer homes should have clear thermal panes.

This concludes Part 1 of Buying Old Homes: Tips and Tricks.

NEXT MONTH...

Next month's issue of Home Buyers' Club will cover items to look for in a home's garage, electric, heating, plumbing, kitchen, baths, living areas, bedrooms, and attic.

FIGURE 5-1b

Desktop Publishing Terminology

As you create professional looking newsletters and brochures you should be aware of several desktop publishing terms. In Project 5 (Figure 5-1 on the previous two pages), the **nameplate**, or **banner**, is the top portion of the newsletter above the three columns. It contains the name of the newsletter; the **headline**, or subject, of the newsletter; and the **issue information line**. The horizontal lines in the nameplate are called **rules**, or **ruling lines**.

Within the body of the newsletter, a heading, like BUYER BEWARE, is called a **subhead**. The vertical line dividing the second and third columns is a **vertical rule**. The text that wraps around the Victorian house is referred to as **wraparound text**, and the space between the house and the words is called the **runaround**. The REMINDER notice in the lower right corner of the first page has a **box border**, and the NEXT MONTH notice in the lower right corner of the second page has a **shadow box border**, with a shadow appearing on the right and bottom edges of the box.

Document Preparation Steps

The following document preparation steps give you an overview of how the document in Figure 5-1 on the previous two pages will be developed in this project. If you are preparing the document in this project on a personal computer, read these steps without doing them.

1. Create the nameplate.
2. Create the first page of the body of the newsletter.
3. Create the second page of the newsletter.
4. Add color to the newsletter.

Because this project involves several steps requiring you to drag the mouse, you may want to cancel an action if you drag to the wrong location. Remember that you can always click the Undo button on the Toolbar to cancel your most recent action.

Changing the Default Margins and Redefining the Normal Style

Recall from earlier projects that your desired document settings may differ from Word's default settings. In these cases, it is good practice to define your document settings and save these settings in the Normal style to ensure that the entire document follows the same style. Much of the text in the newsletter in Project 5 has a point size of 12. Desktop publishers recommend this point size because people of all ages can easily read it.

The margins in the newsletter in this project are all set at one-half inch. Depending on the printer you are using, you may need to set the margins differently. For example, an HP Laserjet III requires margin settings of four-tenths of an inch for this project.

Use the following steps to change the margins and redefine the Normal style.

TO CHANGE THE DEFAULT MARGINS AND REDEFINE THE NORMAL STYLE

Step 1: If it is not already recessed, click the Show/Hide Nonprinting Characters button on the ribbon.

Step 2: From the Format menu, choose the Page Setup command. Change all of the margins to .5 inch by clicking the down arrow next to the Top, Bottom, Left, and Right text boxes until each text box displays .5". Choose the OK button.

Step 3: Select the paragraph mark in the top left corner of the document window by clicking in the selection bar to the left of the paragraph mark. Choose the Points box arrow on the ribbon and select 12. Select the word Normal in the Style box on the ribbon by double-clicking it. Press the ENTER key to display the Microsoft Word dialog box and choose the Yes button. Click anywhere outside the highlighted paragraph to remove the selection.

▶ CREATING THE NAMEPLATE

The nameplate in Project 5 consists of all the text above the multiple columns (see Figure 5-1a on page MSW232). The nameplate consists of the newsletter title, HOME BUYERS' CLUB; the headline, BUYING OLD HOMES: Tips and Tricks - Part 1; and the issue information line. The steps on the following pages illustrate how to create the nameplate for the first page of the newsletter in Project 5.

Changing the Font

The default **font**, or type style, in Word is **Times New Roman**. Fonts, along with point sizes, establish the look of characters in a document. **Screen fonts** display characters on the screen and are installed with Microsoft Windows. **Printer fonts** are used to print documents and are based on the printer driver you are using. Printer fonts are identified with a printer symbol in the Font box. Because of differences between screen and printer technology, screen fonts and printer fonts may not match exactly. To see exactly how the fonts will print in a document, you should choose the Page Layout command from the View menu.

In Project 5, the newsletter title uses the Arial font in a point size of 50. Follow the steps on the next page to change the font and point size of the characters in the newsletter title.

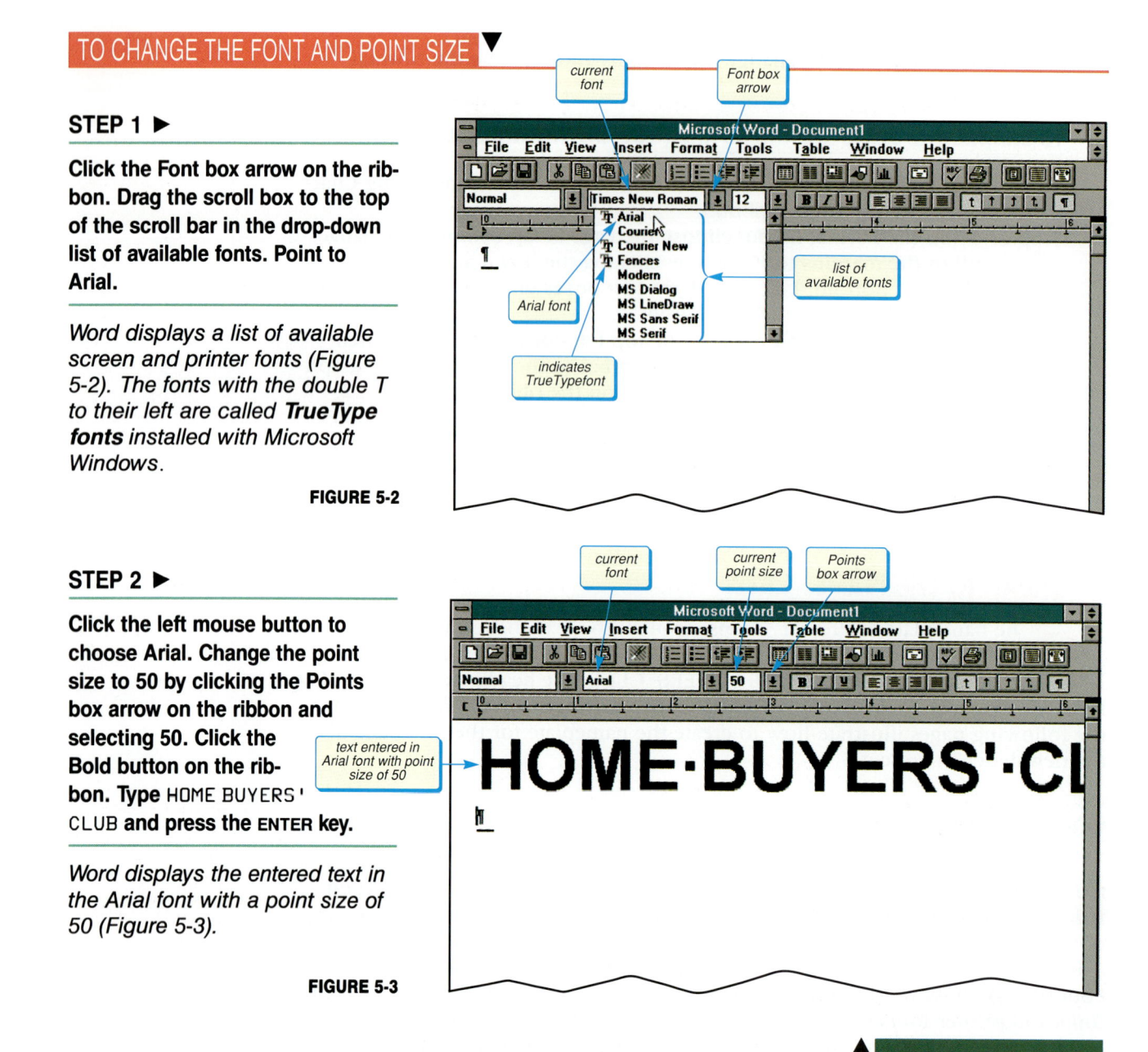

MSW236   PROJECT 5   CREATING A PROFESSIONAL NEWSLETTER

TO CHANGE THE FONT AND POINT SIZE

STEP 1 ▶

Click the Font box arrow on the ribbon. Drag the scroll box to the top of the scroll bar in the drop-down list of available fonts. Point to Arial.

*Word displays a list of available screen and printer fonts (Figure 5-2). The fonts with the double T to their left are called **TrueType fonts** installed with Microsoft Windows.*

FIGURE 5-2

STEP 2 ▶

Click the left mouse button to choose Arial. Change the point size to 50 by clicking the Points box arrow on the ribbon and selecting 50. Click the Bold button on the ribbon. Type HOME BUYERS' CLUB and press the ENTER key.

Word displays the entered text in the Arial font with a point size of 50 (Figure 5-3).

FIGURE 5-3

The point sizes that display in the Points drop-down list box are those available for the selected font. Thus, available point sizes may change depending on the selected font.

The next step is to add rules, or ruling lines, above and below the newsletter title.

CREATING THE NAMEPLATE   MSW237

Adding Ruling Lines to Divide Text

In Word, ruling lines are created through the Border command. Borders can be applied to graphics, paragraphs, and tables. Borders can completely surround the selected text or appear only on specified edges. With respect to ruling lines, the borders appear either above or below a selected paragraph or above and below it. Use the following steps to add ruling lines above and below the newsletter title.

TO ADD RULING LINES TO A DOCUMENT ▼

STEP 1 ▶

Select the newsletter title by clicking in the selection bar to the left of the text. Select the Format menu and point to the Border command (Figure 5-4).

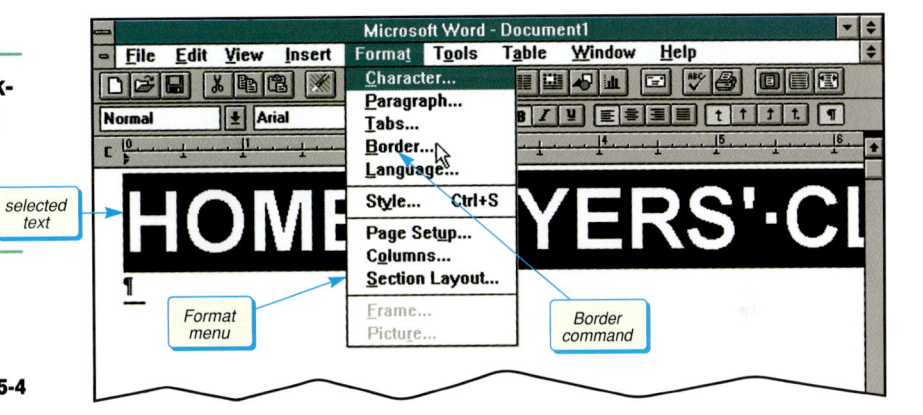

FIGURE 5-4

STEP 2 ▶

Choose the Border command. When the Border Paragraphs dialog box displays, point between the two horizontal border markers above the paragraphs in the Border area.

Word displays the Border Paragraphs dialog box (Figure 5-5). The Border area displays a diagram that indicates where borders will display based on the **border markers**, *or small dark triangles (▶). Initially, eight border markers display in the Border area. The border markers that point toward each other will be connected with a line in the document. Thus, the default border markers will form a box.*

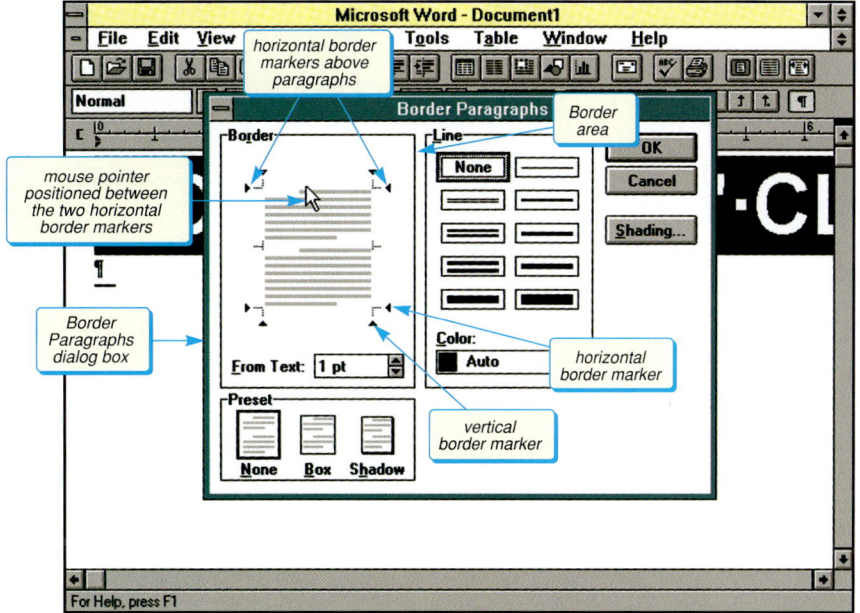

FIGURE 5-5

STEP 3 ▶

Click the left mouse button. Point below the paragraphs in the Border area.

Word removes all border markers except for the two horizontal ones above the paragraphs in the Border area (Figure 5-6). These two markers will display one ruling line above the newsletter title.

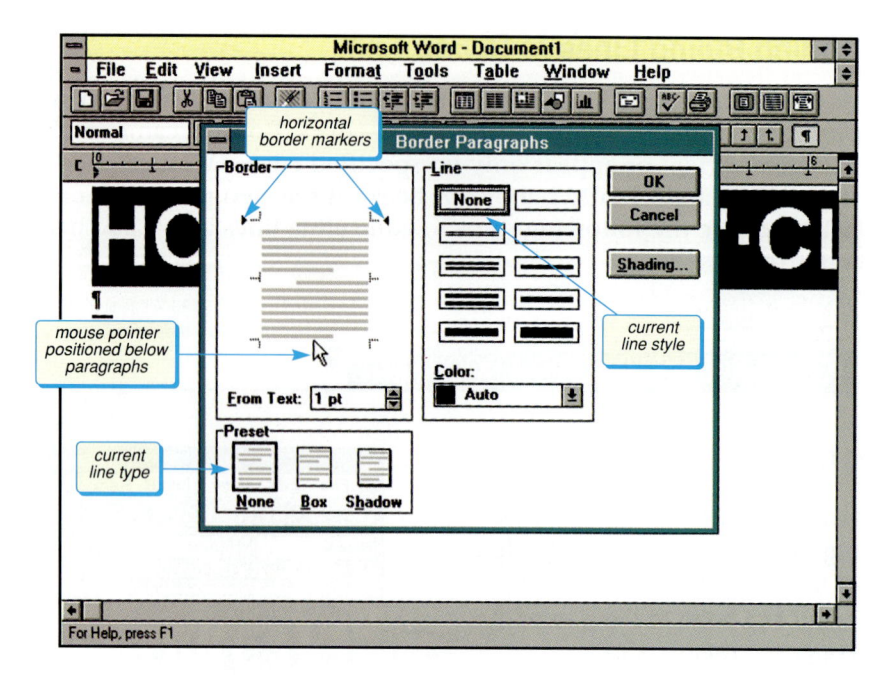

FIGURE 5-6

STEP 4

Hold down the CTRL key while clicking the left mouse button.

Word adds two border markers below the paragraphs in the Border area.

STEP 5 ▶

Click the 4.5-point border line style at the bottom of the first column in the Line area. Point to the OK button.

Word draws a box around the selected line style (Figure 5-7). The selected line style appears in the diagram in the Border area according to the displayed border markers. Word provides ten line styles for borders, ranging from a 0.75-point border to a 6-point border. The default line style is None.

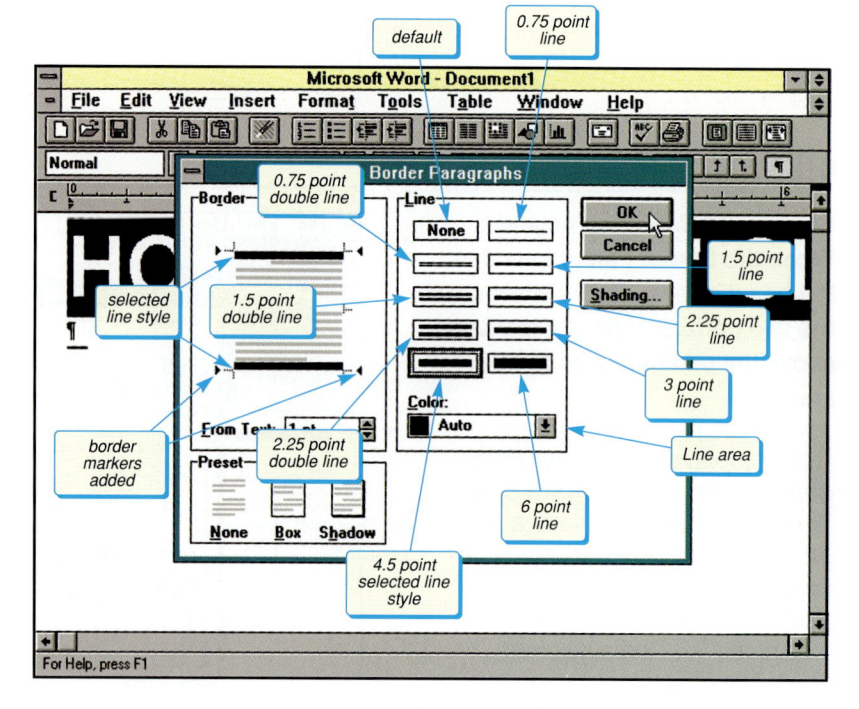

FIGURE 5-7

CREATING THE NAMEPLATE   MSW239

STEP 6 ▶

Choose the OK button. Click the paragraph mark in line 2 to remove the selection.

Word places ruling lines both above and below the newsletter title (Figure 5-8).

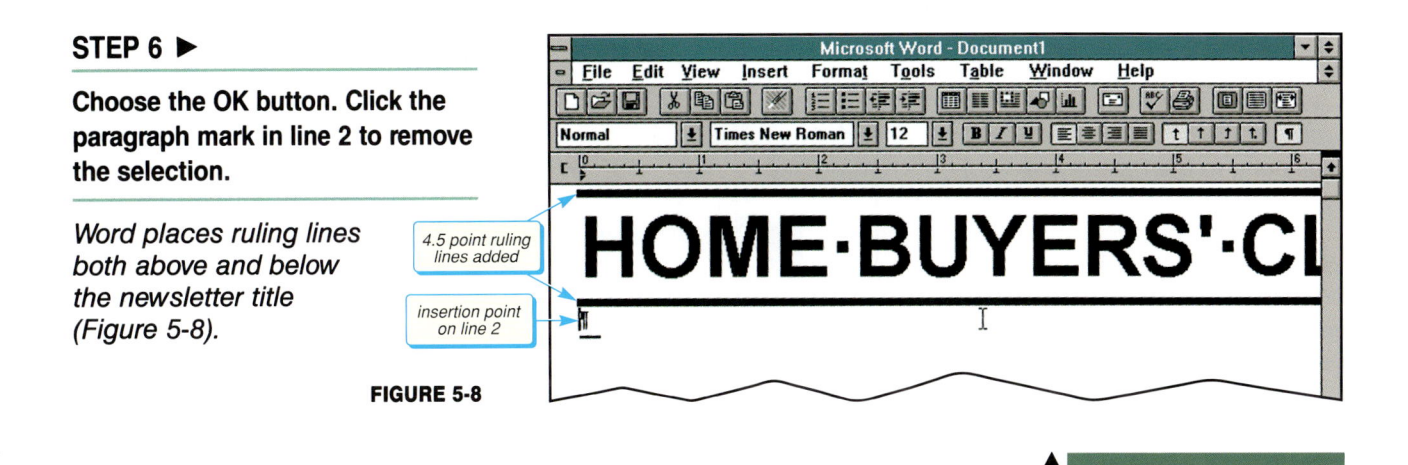

4.5 point ruling lines added

insertion point on line 2

FIGURE 5-8

Borders are part of paragraph formatting. If you press the ENTER key in a bordered paragraph, the border will carry forward to the next paragraph. To avoid this, move the insertion point outside of the bordered paragraph before pressing the ENTER key.

The next step is to enter the headline in the nameplate.

Adding the Headline with Shading

Shading is often used by desktop publishers to emphasize text. In Word, you can shade both paragraphs and tables. By default, the shading begins at the left margin and extends to the right margin. Because shading tends to reduce the legibility of text, the characters in the shading should have a larger point size and be bold.

In this project, the headline, BUYING OLD HOMES: Tips and Tricks - Part 1, is shaded. When adding shading in Word, you can specify the pattern of the shading. Use 50% shading for the headline paragraph as shown in the following steps.

TO SHADE A HEADLINE PARAGRAPH ▼

STEP 1 ▶

Change the point size to 15 by clicking the Points box arrow on the ribbon and selecting 15. Click the Bold button on the ribbon. Type BUYING OLD HOMES: Tips and Tricks - Part 1 **and press the ENTER key. Select the entered text by clicking in the selection bar to the left of the text. From the Format menu, choose the Border command. Point to the Shading (Shading...) button.**

Word highlights the selected text and displays the Border Paragraphs dialog box (Figure 5-9).

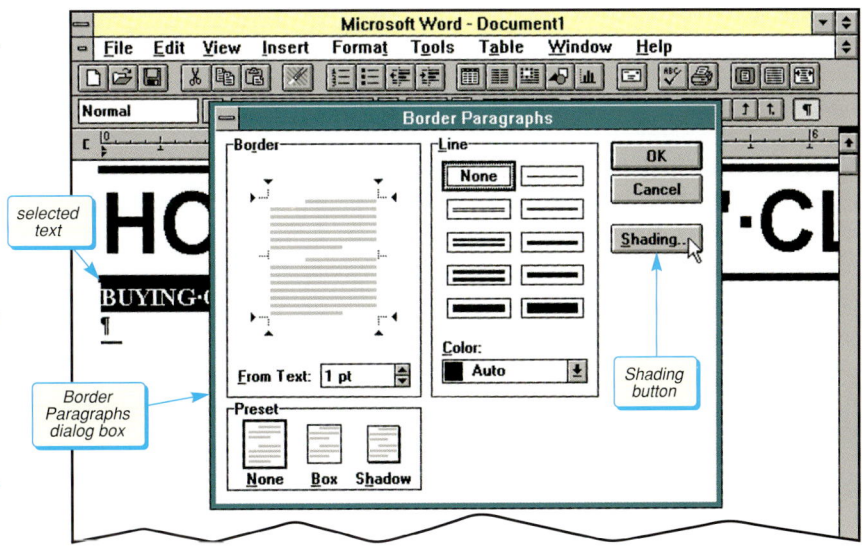

selected text

Border Paragraphs dialog box

Shading button

FIGURE 5-9

STEP 2 ▶

Choose the Shading button. When Word displays the Shading dialog box, point to the Pattern box arrow.

Word displays the Shading dialog box (Figure 5-10). You specify the shading pattern in the Pattern list box in the Fill area.

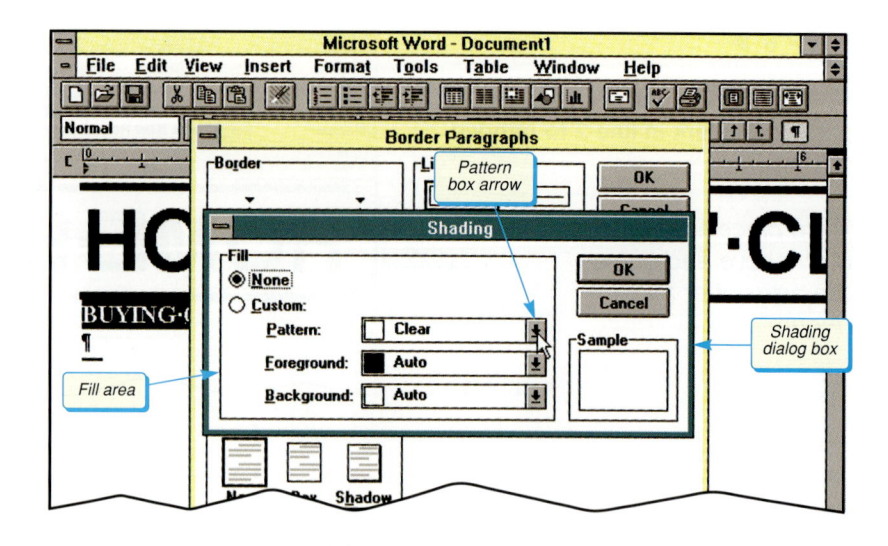

FIGURE 5-10

STEP 3 ▶

Click the Pattern box arrow. Point to 50%.

Word displays a list of available shading patterns (Figure 5-11).

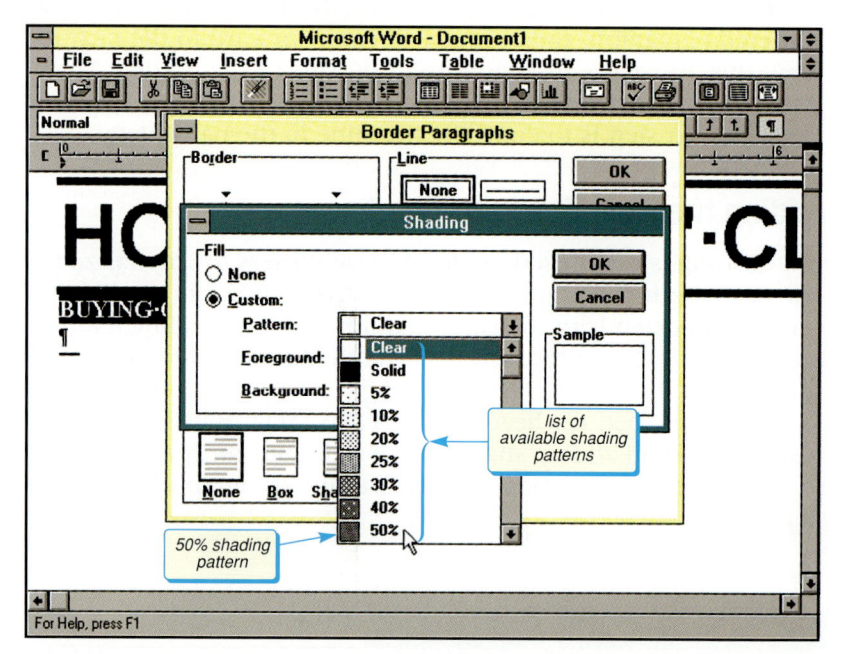

FIGURE 5-11

STEP 4 ▶

Select 50% by clicking it. Point to the OK button.

Word displays 50% in the Pattern box (Figure 5-12). The Sample area graphically displays the 50% pattern.

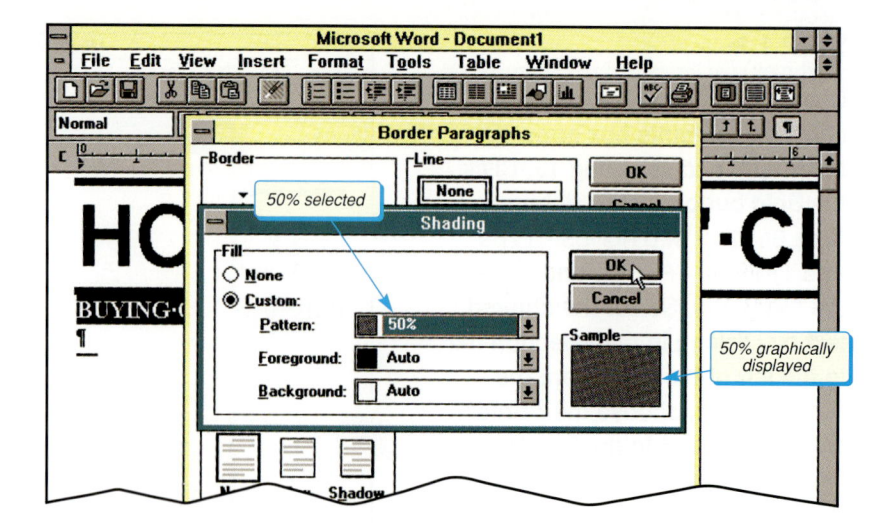

FIGURE 5-12

CREATING THE NAMEPLATE   MSW241

STEP 5 ▶

Choose the OK button in the Shading dialog box. Choose the OK button in the Border Paragraphs dialog box. Point to the right of the scroll box on the horizontal scroll bar at the bottom of the document window.

Word adds shading to the selected text between the left and right margins (Figure 5-13). Because the shading should end when the text does, you must drag the right margin for this line to the 4.5" mark on the ribbon.

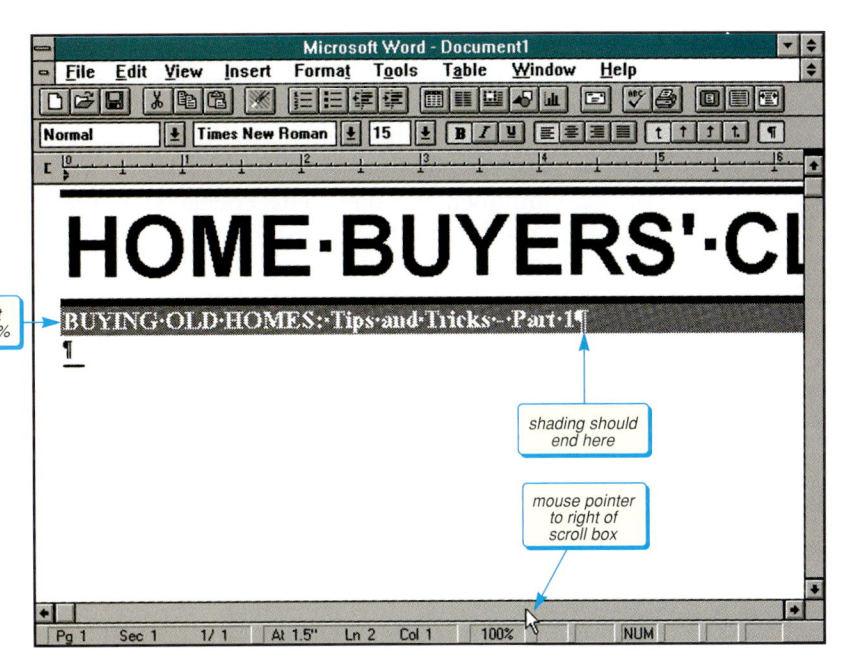

FIGURE 5-13

STEP 6 ▶

Click the mouse. Point to the right margin marker at the 7.5-inch mark on the ruler.

Word scrolls to the right to display the right margin in the document window (Figure 5-14).

FIGURE 5-14

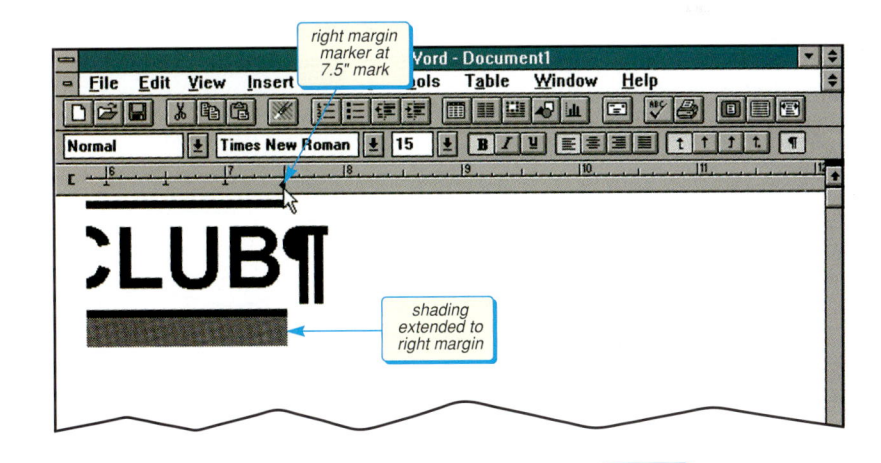

STEP 7 ▶

Drag the right margin marker left to the 4.5-inch mark on the ruler. Click to the left of the scroll box on the horizontal scroll bar at the bottom of the document window.

Word moves the shading from the 7.5-inch mark to the 4.5-inch mark (Figure 5-15).

STEP 8

Click the paragraph mark in line 3 to remove the highlight from line 2.

FIGURE 5-15

The next step is to add the issue information line.

Entering the Issue Information Line

The issue information line in this project contains the volume, number, and date of the newsletter. It also displays a large round dot between the volume, number, and date. This special symbol, called a **bullet**, is not on the keyboard. You insert bullets and other special symbols, like the Greek alphabet and mathematical characters, through the Symbol font supplied with standard fonts. Follow these steps to add a bullet in the issue information line.

TO ADD A BULLET TO TEXT ▼

STEP 1 ▶

Press the ENTER key. Change the point size to 14. Type `Monthly Newsletter` **and press the TAB key eight times. Change the point size to 12. Type** `Vol. I` **followed by a space.**

The first part of the issue information line is entered (Figure 5-16).

FIGURE 5-16

STEP 2 ▶

Select the Insert menu and point to the Symbol command (Figure 5-17).

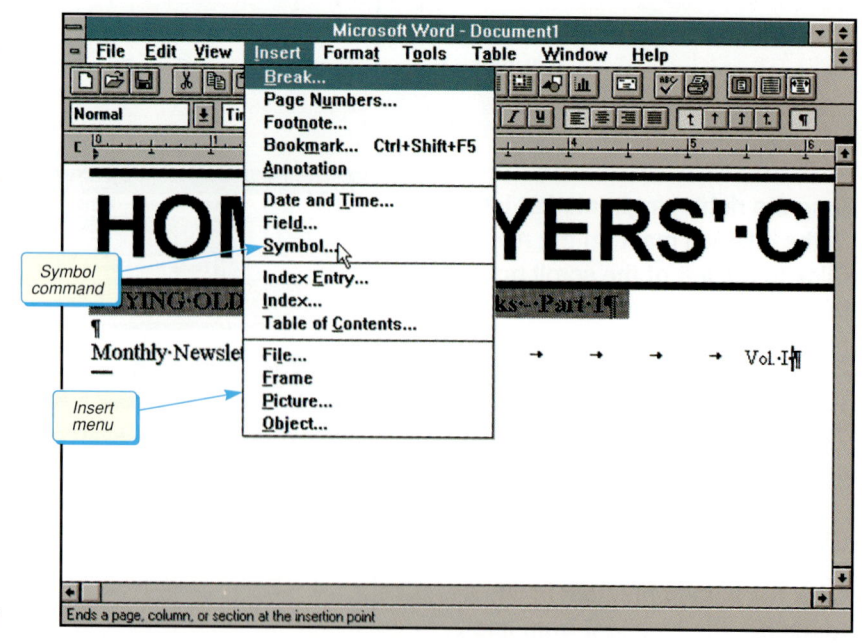

FIGURE 5-17

CREATING THE NAMEPLATE **MSW243**

STEP 3 ▶

Choose the Symbol command. Click the bullet symbol if it is not selected. Point to the OK button.

Word displays the Symbol dialog box (Figure 5-18). If the Symbols From text box does not display (Normal Text), click the Symbols From box down arrow and select (Normal Text). Selected symbols display with a box around the symbol.

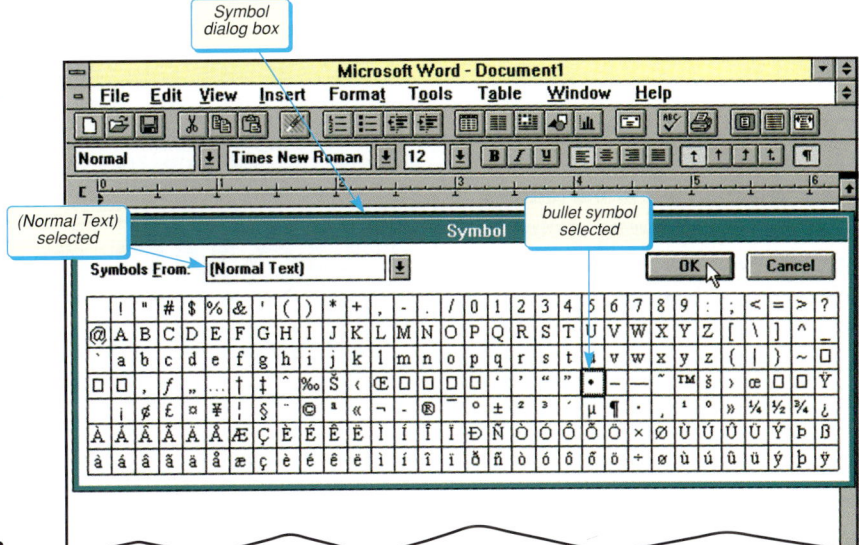

FIGURE 5-18

STEP 4 ▶

Choose the OK button.

Word inserts the bullet character to the left of the insertion point (Figure 5-19).

FIGURE 5-19

STEP 5 ▶

Press the SPACEBAR once. Type `No. 8` **followed by a space. From the Insert menu, choose the Symbol command. Choose the OK button in the Symbol dialog box. Press the SPACEBAR once. Type** `Aug. 10, 1994`.

The issue information line displays as shown in Figure 5-20.

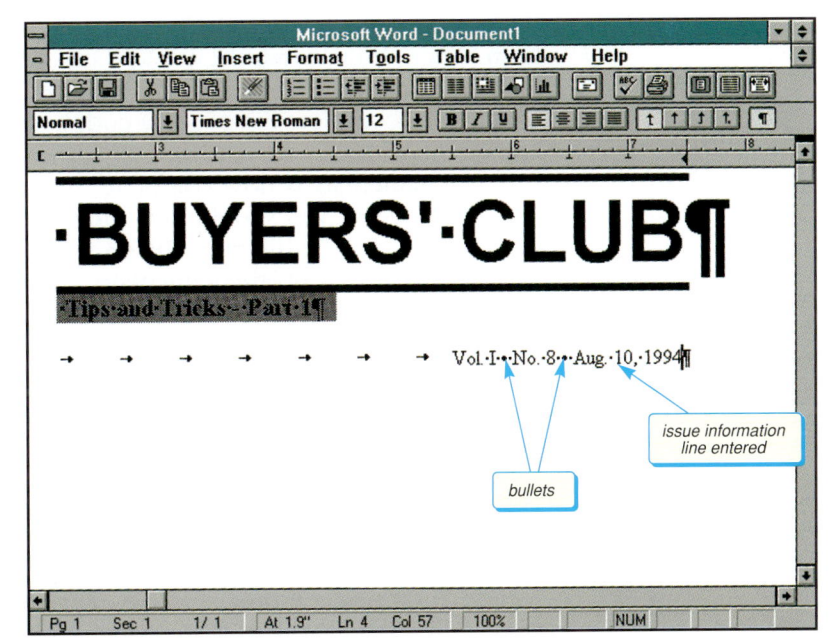

FIGURE 5-20

STEP 6 ▶

Press the ENTER key. Select the issue information line by clicking in the selection bar to the left of it. From the Format menu, choose Border. When the Border Paragraphs dialog box displays, click between the horizontal border markers above the paragraphs in the Border area. Hold down the CTRL key while clicking between the horizontal border markers below the paragraphs in the Border area. Click the 2.25-point border in the Line area (see Figure 5-7 on page MSW238). Choose the OK button in the Border Paragraphs dialog box. Click line 5 to remove the selection from the text.

The issue information line is complete (Figure 5-21).

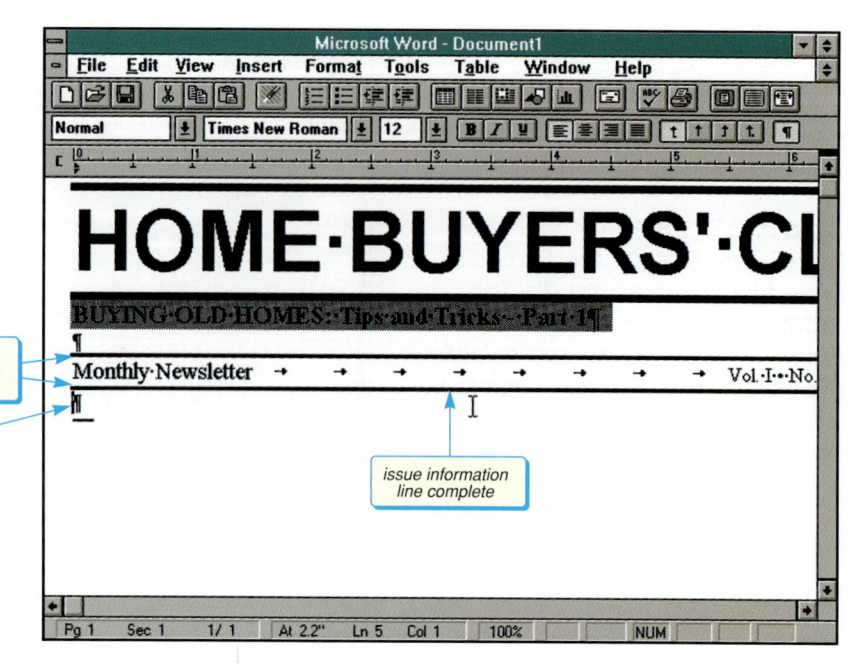

FIGURE 5-21

You can also insert **ANSI characters** into a document by entering the ANSI code directly into the document. The ANSI characters are a predefined set of characters, including both characters on the keyboard and special characters, such as the bullet character. To enter the ANSI code, make sure the NUM LOCK key is on. Then, hold down the ALT key and type a zero followed by the ANSI code for the character. You *must* use the numeric keypad when entering the ANSI code. For a complete list of ANSI codes, see your Microsoft Windows documentation.

The nameplate is now complete. Because you have completed a significant portion of work, you should save the newsletter by clicking the Save button on the Toolbar. Use the filename PROJ5.DOC. It is also a good idea to save this portion of the document, the nameplate, under a different name like NAMEPLAT so you can load just the nameplate for future issues of the newsletter.

The next step is to enter the body of the first page of the newsletter.

▶ CREATING THE FIRST PAGE OF THE BODY OF THE NEWSLETTER

The body of the newsletter in this project is divided into three columns (see Figure 5-1a on page MSW232). A Victorian house displays between the first and second columns on page one. A vertical rule separates the second and third columns on page one. A box border surrounds the REMINDER notice. The steps on the following pages illustrate how to enter the first page of the body of the newsletter with these desktop publishing features.

CREATING THE FIRST PAGE OF THE BODY OF THE NEWSLETTER **MSW245**

Formatting a Document into Multiple Columns

With Word, you can create two types of columns: parallel columns and snaking columns. **Parallel columns**, or table columns, are created with the Table button. You created parallel columns in Project 3. The text in **snaking columns**, or newspaper-style columns, flows from the bottom of one column to the top of the next. The body of the newsletter in Project 5 uses snaking columns.

When you begin a document in Word, it has one column. You can specify up to 100 columns across a document. Within each column, you can type, modify, or format text. Follow these steps to divide the body of the newsletter into three columns. The multi-column layout begins above the insertion point.

TO CREATE COLUMNS IN A DOCUMENT ▼

STEP 1 ▶

Press the ENTER key. Select the Format menu and point to the Columns command (Figure 5-22).

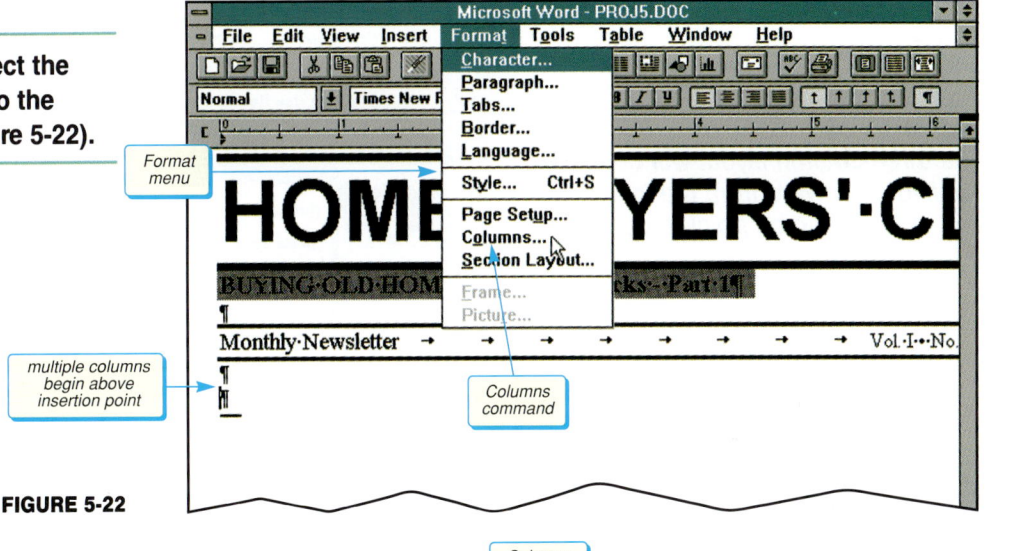

FIGURE 5-22

STEP 2 ▶

Choose the Columns command.

Word displays the Columns dialog box (Figure 5-23). The default number of columns is one, which is graphically presented in the Sample area.

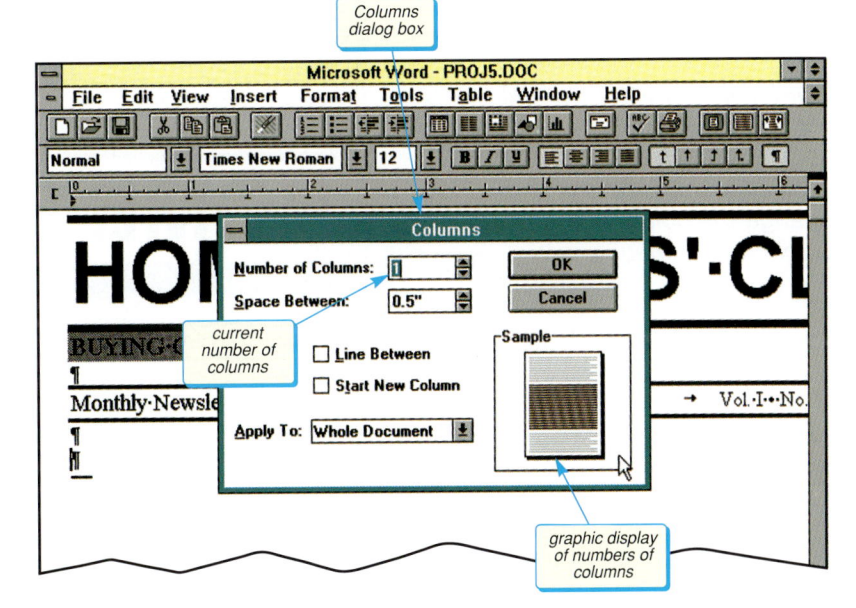

FIGURE 5-23

STEP 3 ▶

Type 3 **in the Number of Columns text box. Click the Apply To down arrow and point to This Point Forward.**

Word changes the number of columns to 3 (Figure 5-24). The Sample area graphically displays three columns. You can format the whole document or start from this point forward to three columns.

FIGURE 5-24

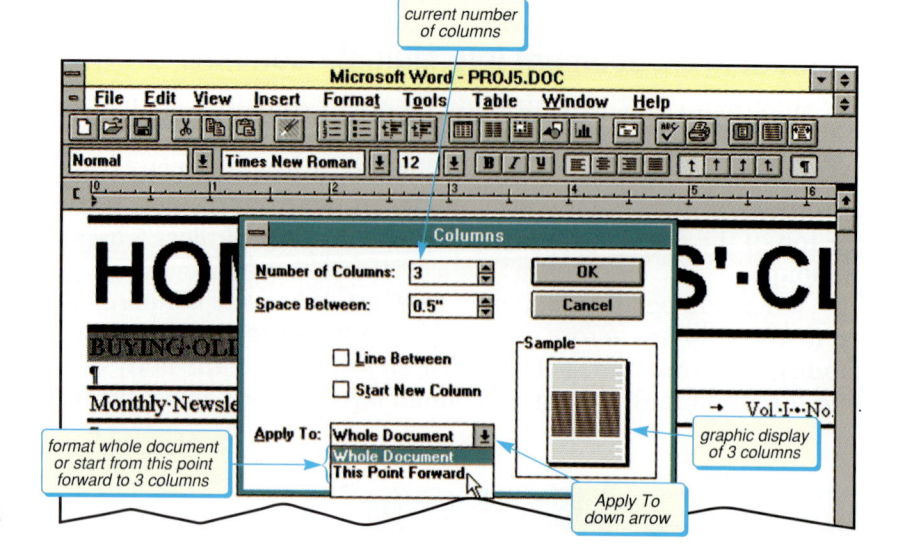

STEP 4 ▶

Select This Point Forward by clicking it. Point to the OK button.

The three-column layout will be applied downward from the location of the insertion point (Figure 5-25).

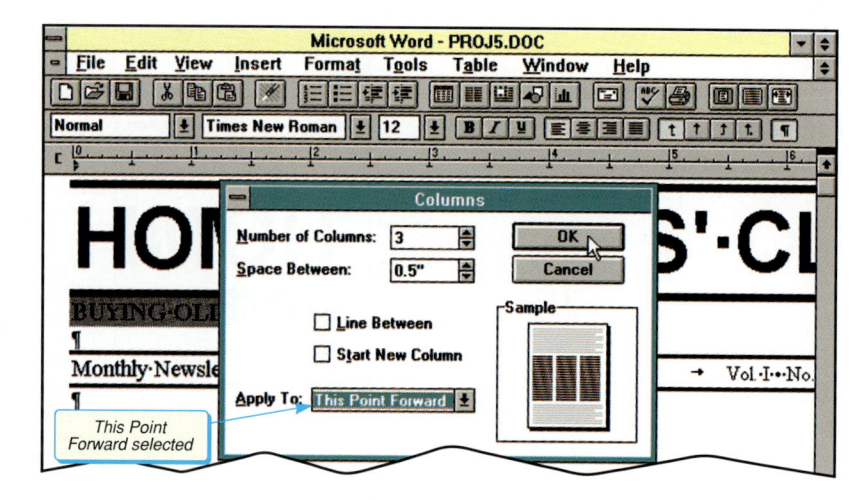

FIGURE 5-25

STEP 5 ▶

Choose the OK button.

Word inserts a section break immediately above the insertion point (Figure 5-26). A section break occurs whenever you change the column layout within a document.

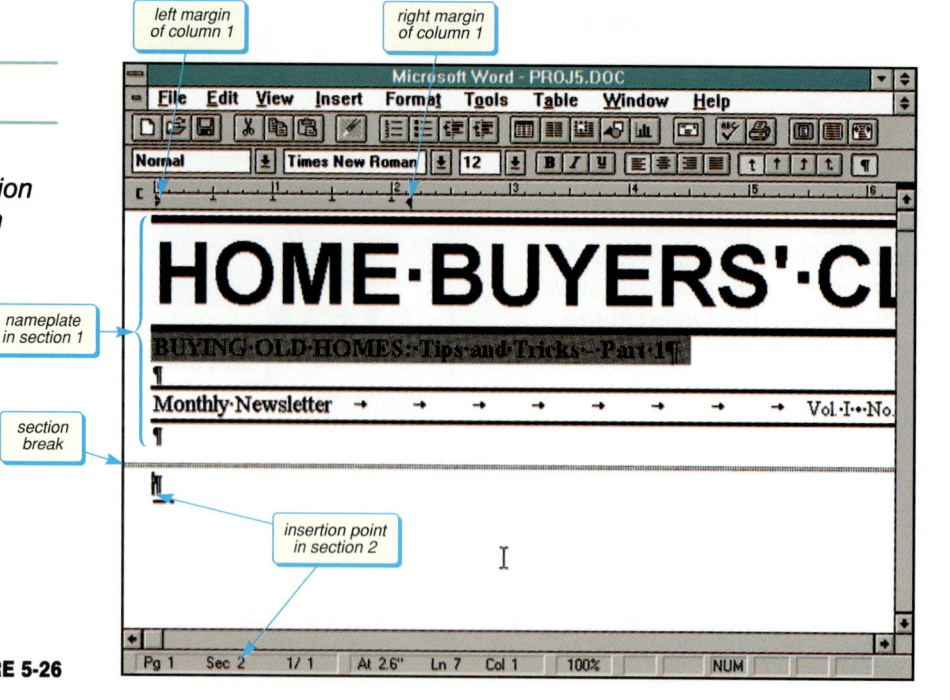

FIGURE 5-26

A Word document can be divided into any number of **sections**. All documents have at least one section. If during the course of creating a document, you would like to change the margins, paper size, page orientation, number of columns, page number position, contents or position of headers or footers, or footnotes, you must create a new section. Thus, each section may be formatted differently from the others.

When you create a new section, a **section break** displays on the screen as a horizontal double-dotted line (Figure 5-26). Section breaks do not print. All section formatting is stored in the section break. You can delete a section break and all the section formatting by selecting the section break and pressing the DELETE key. If you accidentally delete a section break, you can bring it back by clicking the UNDO button (▨).

When changing the number of columns within a document, Word automatically inserts a section break above the insertion point. To manually insert a section break, choose the Break command from the Insert menu.

Notice in Figure 5-26 that the ruler indicates the current column and its size. The 0-inch mark indicates the current column's left boundary and left and right markers indicate column margin settings.

Entering the Subheads and Article Text

Subheads are headings placed throughout the body of the newsletter, such as BUYER BEWARE. In this project, the subheads are bold and have a point size of 14. The text beneath the subheads is justified. **Justified** means that the left and right margins are aligned, like newspaper columns. The first line of each paragraph is indented .25 inch. Follow these steps to enter the first two columns of the first page of the newsletter.

TO ENTER SUBHEADS AND ASSOCIATED TEXT ▼

STEP 1 ▶

Change the point size to 14. Click the Bold button. Type BUYER BEWARE **and click the Bold button. Change the point size back to 12 and press the** ENTER **key twice. Drag the First-Line Indent marker on the ruler to the .25-inch mark.**

The first subhead is entered and the insertion point is indented .25 inch (Figure 5-27).

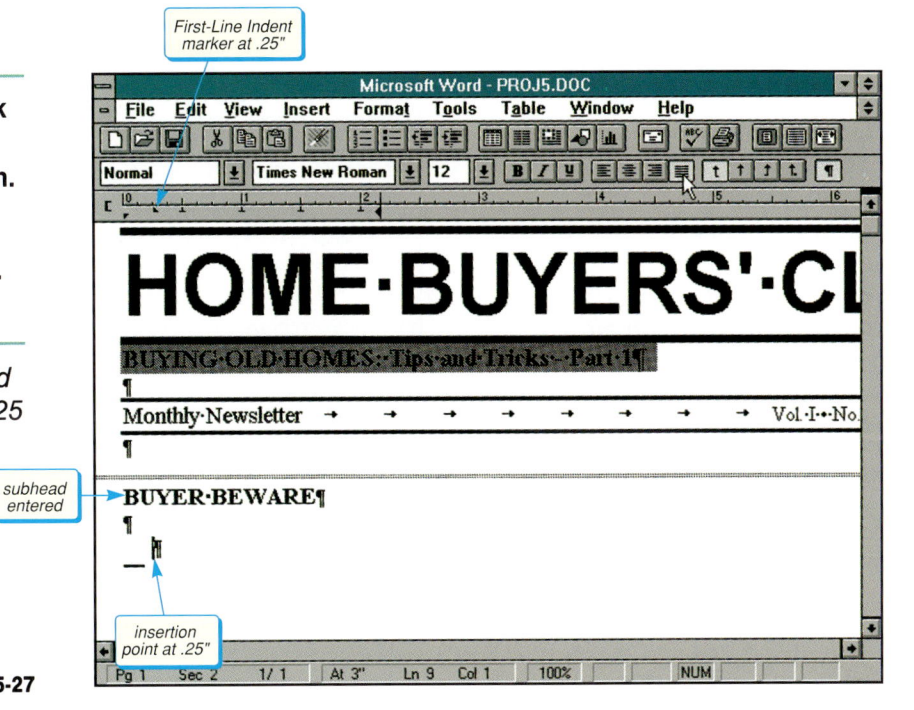

FIGURE 5-27

STEP 2 ▶

Click the Justified Text button (≡) on the ribbon. Type the paragraph beneath the BUYER BEWARE subhead.

Word automatically aligns both the left and right edges of the paragraph like newspaper columns (Figure 5-28). Notice that extra space is placed between some words when you justify text.

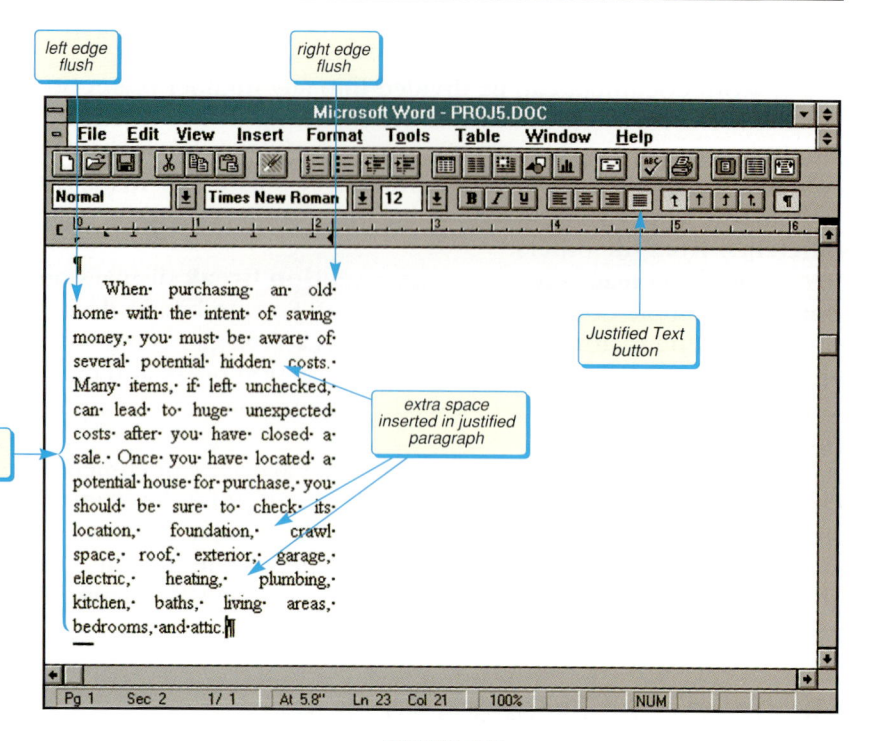

FIGURE 5-28

STEP 3 ▶

Press the ENTER key twice. Drag the First-Line Indent marker back to the 0-inch mark on the ruler. Change the point size to 14. Click the Bold button. Type LOCATION and click the Bold button. Change the point size back to 12. Press the ENTER key twice. Drag the First-Line Indent marker to the .25-inch mark on the ruler. Type the paragraph beneath the LOCATION subhead.

The LOCATION subhead and associated paragraph are entered (Figure 5-29).

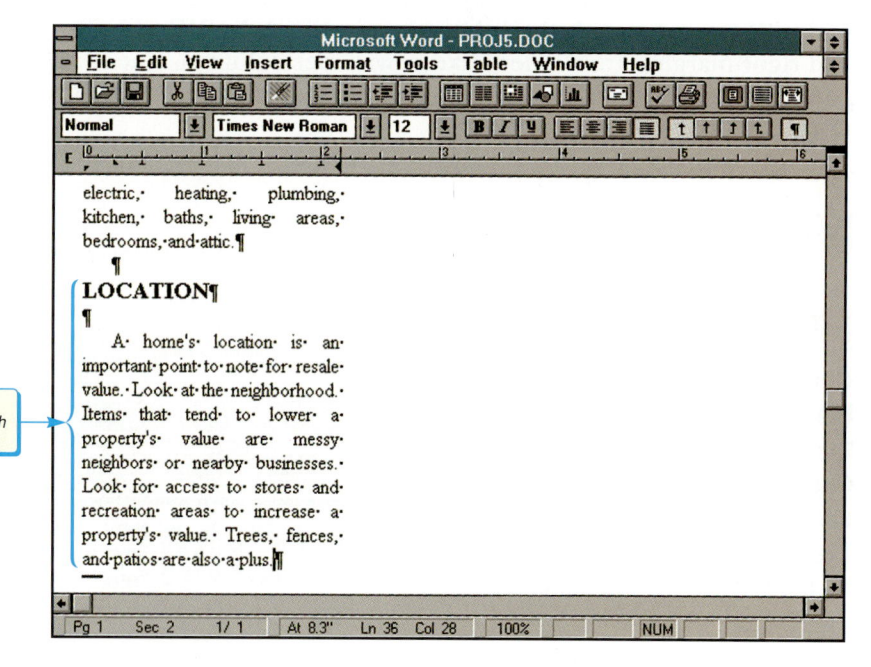

FIGURE 5-29

CREATING THE FIRST PAGE OF THE BODY OF THE NEWSLETTER MSW249

STEP 4 ▶

Press the ENTER key twice. Drag the First-Line Indent marker to the 0-inch mark on the ruler. Change the point size to 14. Click the Bold button. Type FOUNDATION and click the Bold button. Change the point size back to 12. Press the ENTER key twice. Drag the First-Line Indent marker to the .25-inch mark on the ruler. Type the first two paragraphs beneath the LOCATION subhead as shown in Figures 5-30a and 5-30b.

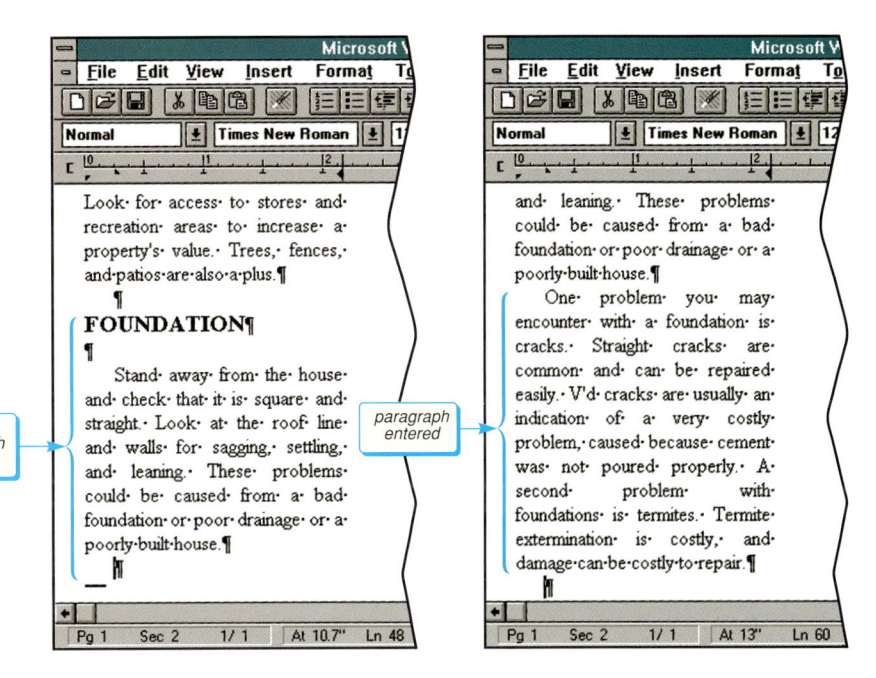

FIGURE 5-30a

FIGURE 5-30b

STEP 5 ▶

Type the third paragraph beneath the LOCATION subhead as shown in Figure 5-30c. Press the ENTER key twice. Drag the First-Line Indent marker to the 0-inch mark on the ruler. Change the point size to 14. Click the Bold button. Type CRAWL SPACE and click the Bold button. Change the point size back to 12. Press the ENTER key twice. Drag the First-Line Indent marker to the .25-inch mark on the ruler. Type the paragraph beneath the CRAWL SPACE subhead as shown in Figure 5-30d.

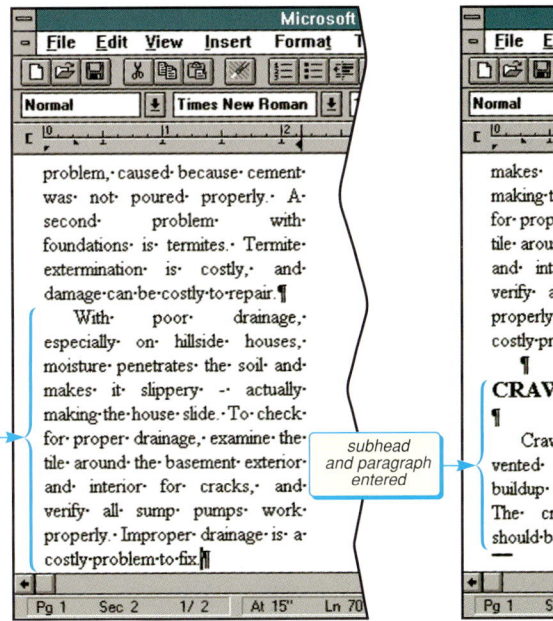

FIGURE 5-30c

FIGURE 5-30d

Notice in Figure 5-30d on the previous page that you are on line 78 in this section. Because a page is only 66 lines long, some of this column should actually be in the second column. In normal view, the columns do not display side by side; instead, they display in one long column at the left margin. To see the columns side by side, you can display the document in print preview or page layout view. Recall from Project 2 that in print preview you cannot edit the document. Thus, the next step is to change to page layout view so the columns display side by side.

TO CHANGE TO PAGE LAYOUT VIEW

STEP 1 ▶

Select the View menu and point to the Page Layout command (Figure 5-31).

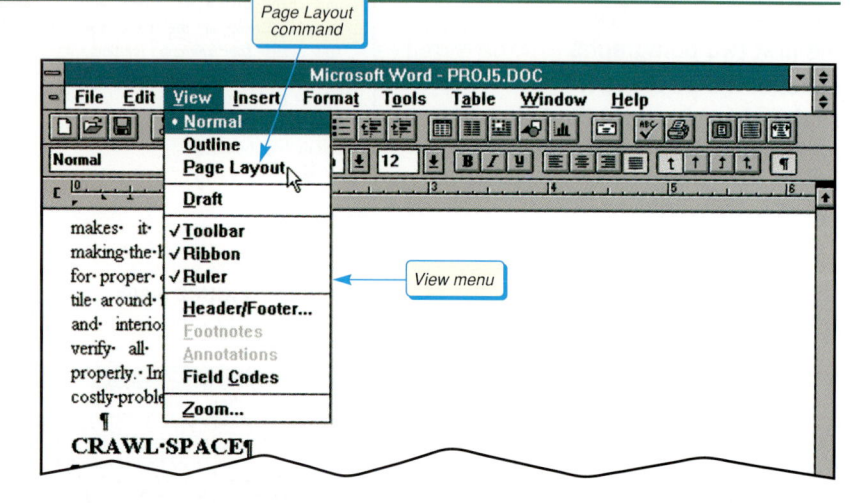

FIGURE 5-31

STEP 2 ▶

Choose the Page Layout command.

Word switches from normal to page layout view and displays the columns side by side (Figure 5-32).

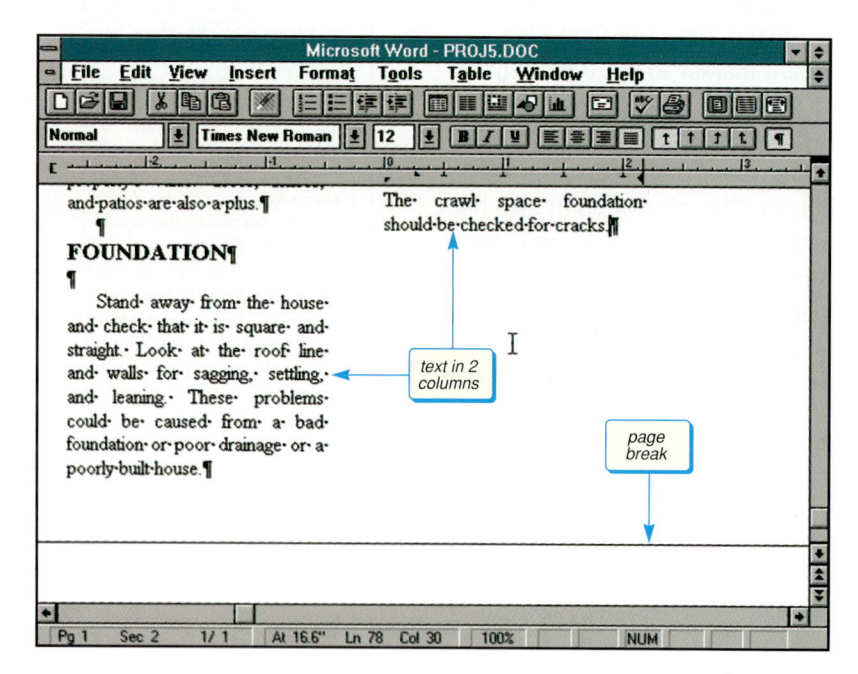

FIGURE 5-32

CREATING THE FIRST PAGE OF THE BODY OF THE NEWSLETTER   MSW251

STEP 3 ▶

Scroll the top of the newsletter into view by clicking the up arrow on the vertical scroll bar.

Two columns display on the screen beneath the nameplate (Figure 5-33).

FIGURE 5-33

The next step is to insert the Victorian house graphic and position it between the first and second columns.

Positioning Graphics on the Page

In Project 3, you learned how to insert a graphic into a document with the Picture command on the Insert menu. With this command, the graphic displays in the column that contains the insertion point. If you select the graphic and move it, it can only be moved into another column, not between columns. To move the graphic *between* columns, you must first enclose it in a **frame**. When you position a graphic in a frame, everything in the frame moves as one unit. You can resize a frame by dragging the sizing handles and position a frame anywhere on the page by dragging the frame itself. When you move the frame, its contents move. Follow these steps to position a Victorian house between the first and second columns of page one in the newsletter (see Figure 5-38 on page MSW253).

TO POSITION A GRAPHIC ON THE PAGE ▼

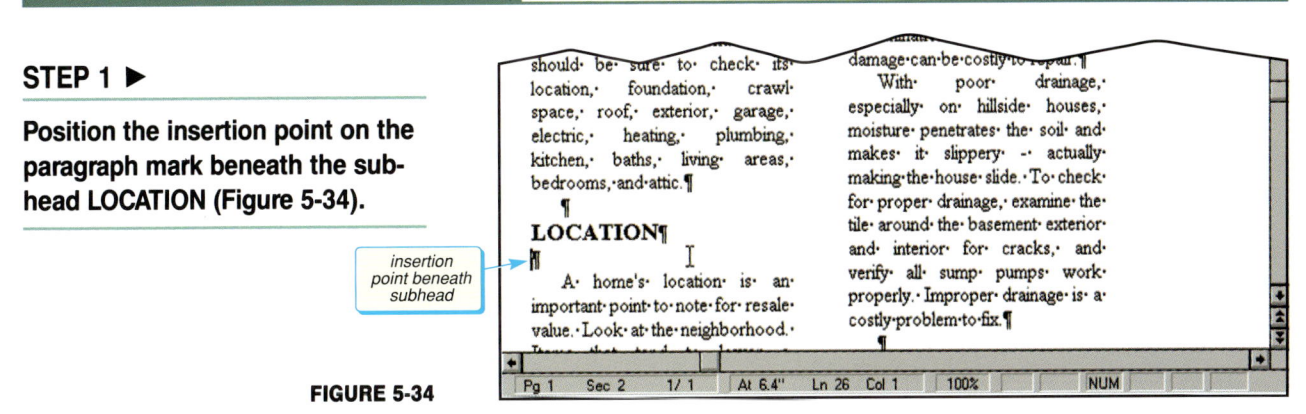

STEP 1 ▶

Position the insertion point on the paragraph mark beneath the subhead LOCATION (Figure 5-34).

FIGURE 5-34

STEP 2 ▶

From the Insert menu, choose the Picture command. In the winword directory on drive C, select the clipart subdirectory by double-clicking it. Select the metafile vichouse.wmf by scrolling through the File Name list and clicking vichouse.wmf. Choose the Preview button to display the Victorian house. Point to the OK button.

Word displays the Picture dialog box with the metafile vichouse.wmf selected and displayed in the Preview Picture area (Figure 5-35).

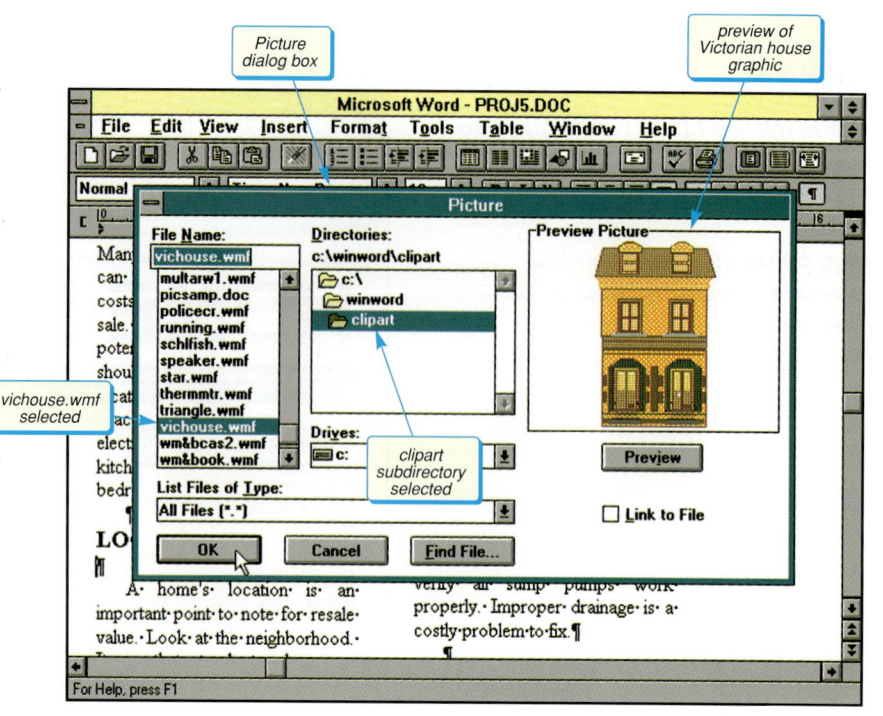

FIGURE 5-35

STEP 3

Choose the OK button.

Word inserts the Victorian house at the location of the insertion point.

STEP 4 ▶

Click the Victorian house. Point to the Frame button ( ) on the Toolbar.

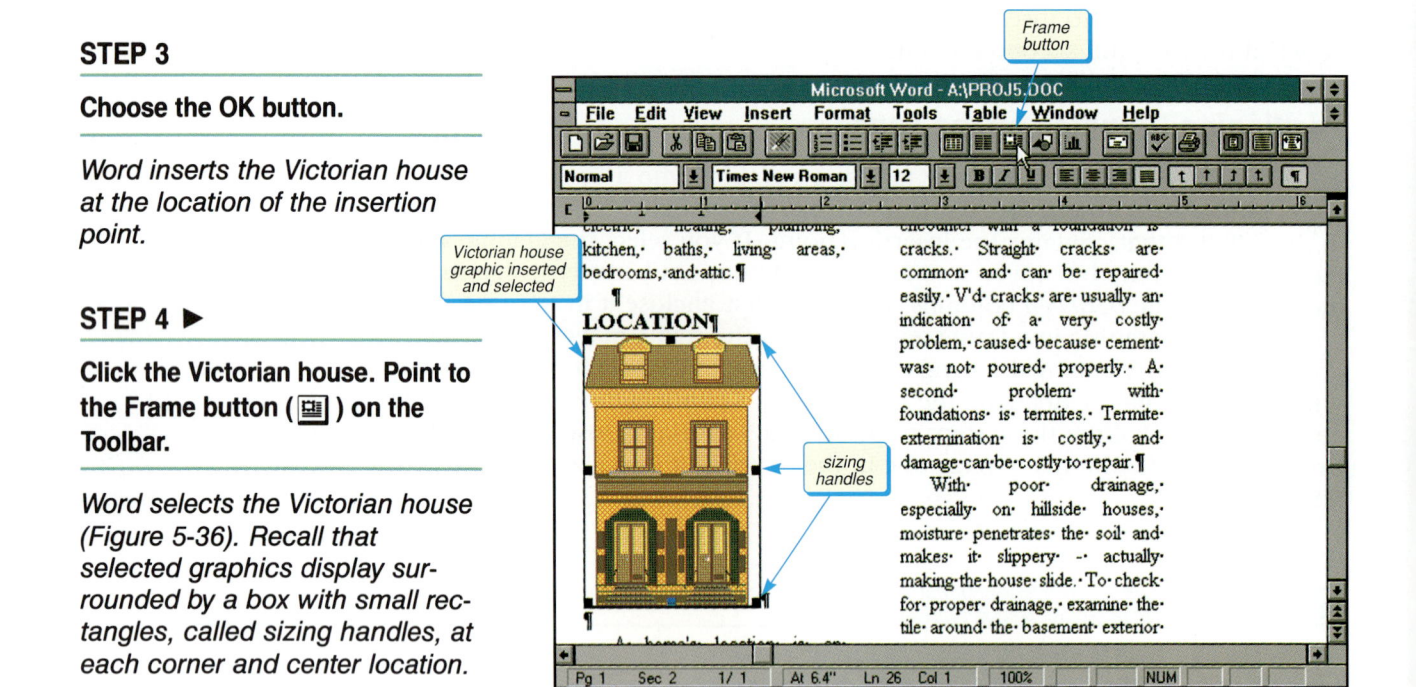

Word selects the Victorian house (Figure 5-36). Recall that selected graphics display surrounded by a box with small rectangles, called sizing handles, at each corner and center location.

FIGURE 5-36

CREATING THE FIRST PAGE OF THE BODY OF THE NEWSLETTER   MSW253

STEP 5 ▶

Click the Frame button. Point inside the graphic.

Word frames the Victorian house (Figure 5-37). When inside a frame, the mouse pointer changes to a four-headed arrow (✥). A frame does not actually display on the screen. Rather, the selection surrounding the house is now the frame.

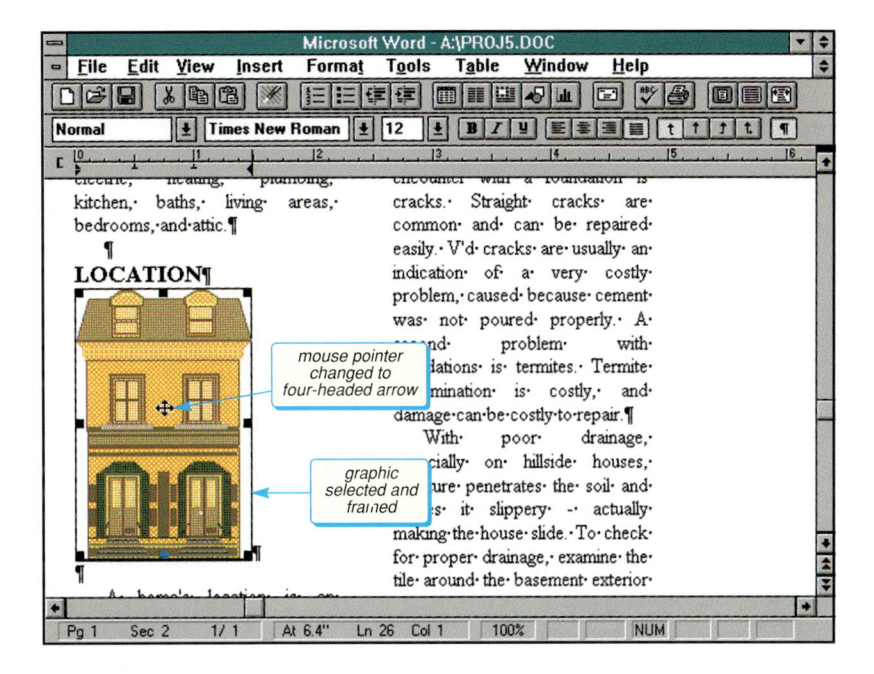

FIGURE 5-37

STEP 6 ▶

Drag the graphic to the desired location. Click outside the graphic to remove the selection.

As you drag the graphic, the frame moves to show its location. When you release the mouse button, the graphic is positioned at the location of the moved frame (Figure 5-38). (You may have to drag the house a couple of times to position it properly.)

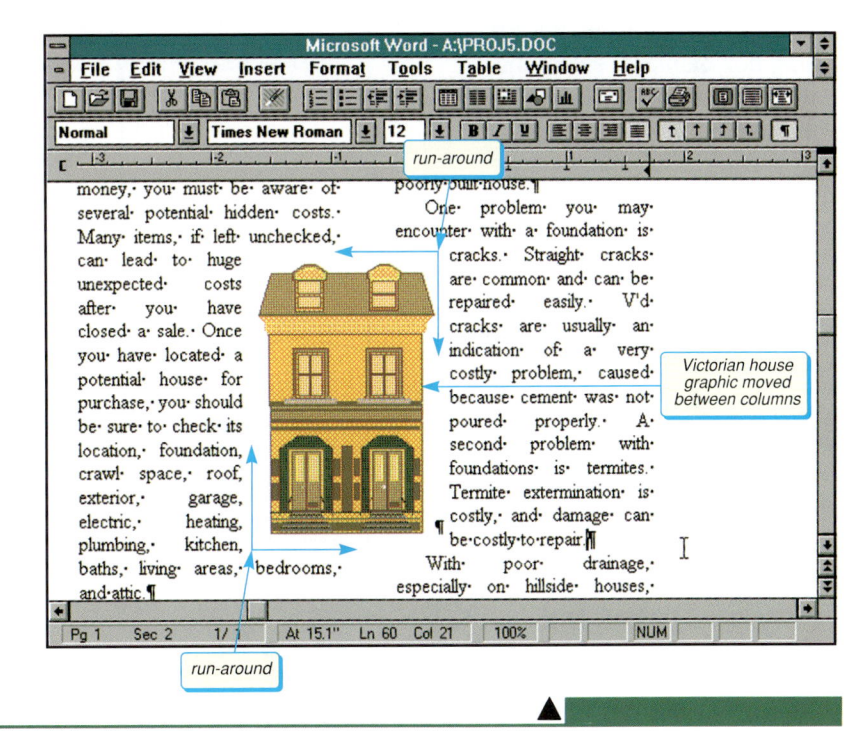

FIGURE 5-38

Notice in Figure 5-38 that the text in columns one and two wrap around the Victorian house. Thus, it is called wrap-around text. The space between the house and the wrap-around text is called the run-around.

The next step is to insert a column break.

Inserting a Column Break

Notice in Figure 5-1a on page MSW232 that the third column is *not* a continuation of the article. The third column contains several announcements. The Buying Old Homes article is actually continued on the second page of the newsletter. If you continue typing, the new text will fill in the bottom of the second column and continue at the top of the third column. You want the announcements, however, to be separated into the third column. Thus, you must force a **column break** at this point. Word inserts column breaks at the location of the insertion point.

TO INSERT A COLUMN BREAK

STEP 1 ▶

Press CTRL + END to move the insertion point to the end of the document. Press the ENTER key twice. From the Insert menu, choose the Break command. When the Break dialog box displays, select the Column Break option by clicking it. Point to the OK button.

Word displays the Break dialog box (Figure 5-39). The Column Break option is selected.

FIGURE 5-39

STEP 2 ▶

Choose the OK button in the Break dialog box. Position the insertion point at the bottom of column two. Press the ENTER key. Click the Italic button on the ribbon. Type `Continued next page...` and click the Italic button again.

Word inserts a column break and advances the insertion point to the top of column three. A continued message displays beneath column two (Figure 5-40).

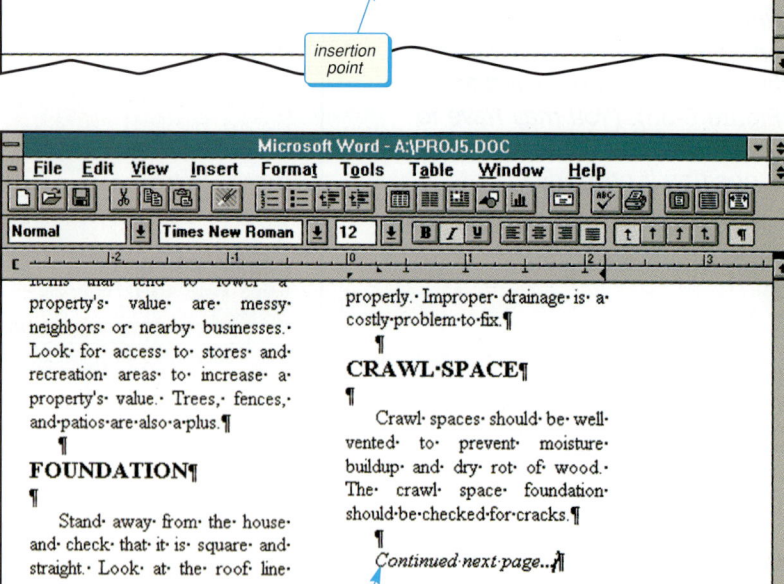

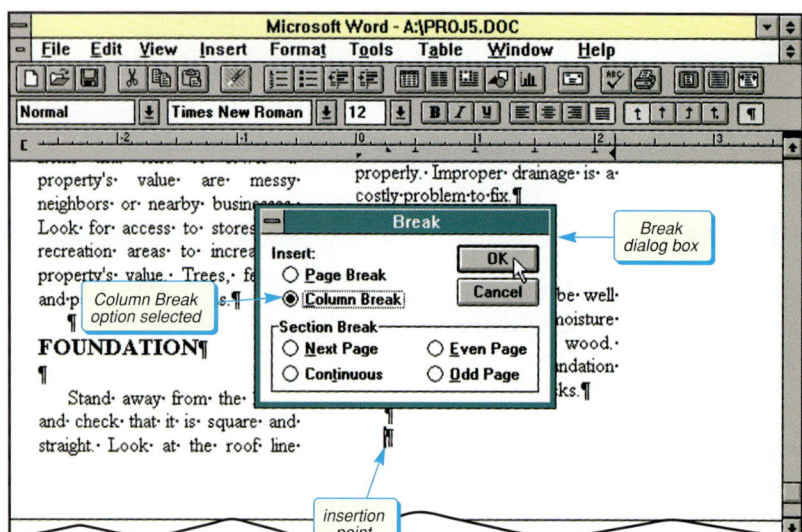

FIGURE 5-40

The next step is to enter the announcements in the third column of the newsletter.

TO ENTER THE MONTHLY MEETING ANNOUNCEMENT

Step 1: Press the CTRL + END to advance to column three (the end of the document). Click to the right of the scroll box on the horizontal scroll bar to bring the entire third column into view in the document window.

Step 2: Drag the First-Line Indent marker on the ruler to the 0-inch mark. Change the point size to 14. Click the Bold button. Type MONTHLY MEETING and click the Bold button. Change the point size back to 12 and press the ENTER key twice. Drag the First-Line Indent marker on the ruler to the .25-inch mark.

Step 3: Enter the paragraph beneath the subhead.

The MONTHLY MEETING announcement displays as shown in Figure 5-41.

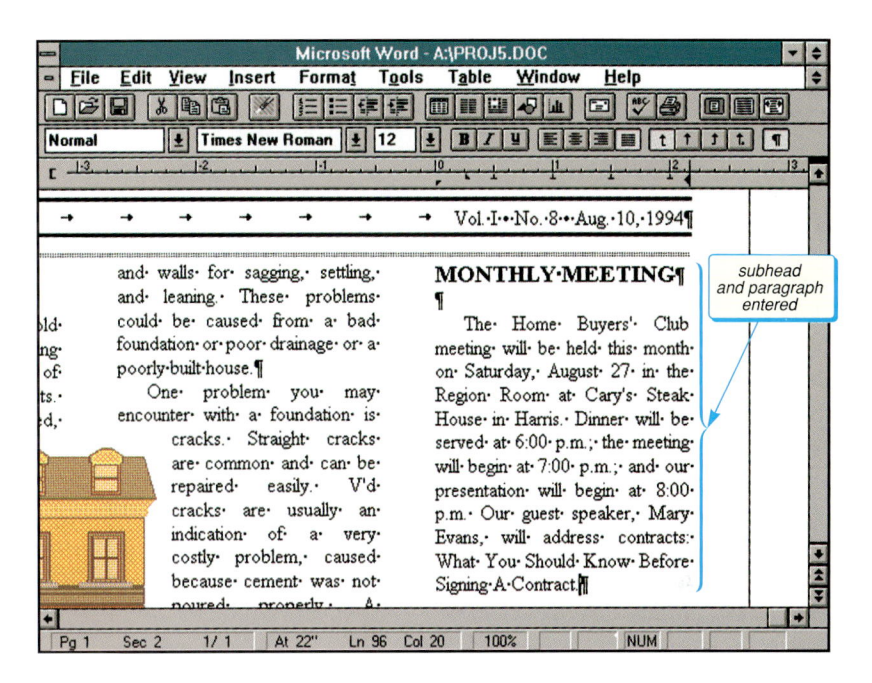

FIGURE 5-41

TO ENTER THE EVENTS ANNOUNCEMENT

Step 1: Press the ENTER key twice. Drag the First-Line Indent marker on the ruler to the 0-inch mark on the ruler. Change the point size to 14. Click the Bold button. Type EVENTS and click the Bold button. Change the point size back to 12 and press the ENTER key twice. Drag the First-Line Indent marker on the ruler to the .25-inch mark.

Step 2: Enter the paragraph beneath the subhead.

The EVENTS announcement displays as shown in Figure 5-42.

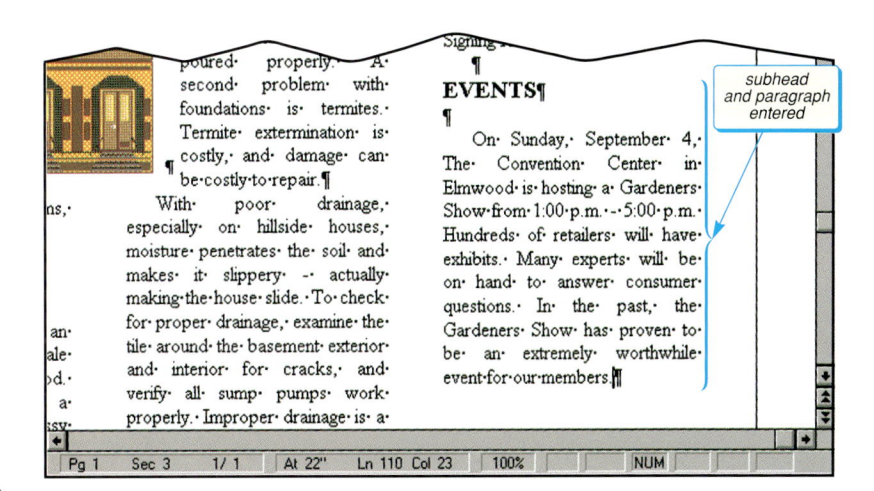

FIGURE 5-42

Adding a Box Border Around Paragraphs

The REMINDER notice at the bottom of the third column is shaded and has a box border around it. Box borders are placed around paragraphs the same way ruling lines are added above and/or below paragraphs. Follow these steps to shade and add a box border to the REMINDER notice paragraphs.

TO ADD A BOX BORDER AROUND PARAGRAPHS ▼

STEP 1 ▶

Press the ENTER key three times. Drag the First-Line Indent marker on the ruler to the 0-inch mark. Change the point size to 14. Click the Bold button. Click the Centered Text button. Type REMINDER and click the Bold button. Change the point size back to 12 and press the ENTER key twice. Click the Justified Text button. Type the paragraph beneath the subhead. Press the ENTER key at the end of the paragraph. Select the REMINDER notice by dragging the mouse in the selection bar to the left of the third column. Do not select the paragraph mark below the REMINDER paragraph. Select the Format menu and point to the Border command.

Word selects the entered paragraph (Figure 5-43). When the screen is divided into multiple columns, each column has its own selection bar immediately to its left.

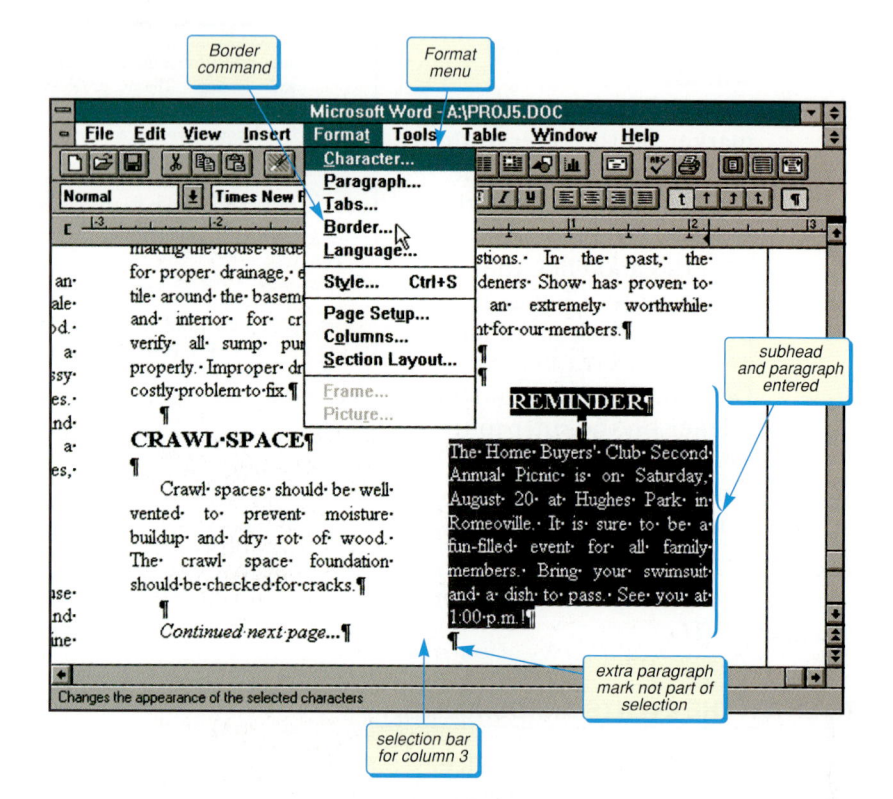

FIGURE 5-43

CREATING THE FIRST PAGE OF THE BODY OF THE NEWSLETTER **MSW257**

STEP 2 ▶

Choose the Border command. When the Border Paragraphs dialog box displays, select the Box option in the Preset area. Then choose the Shading button. When the Shading dialog box displays, change the Pattern to 10% by clicking the Pattern box down arrow and selecting 10%. Point to the OK button.

The Shading dialog box displays over the Border Paragraphs dialog box (Figure 5-44).

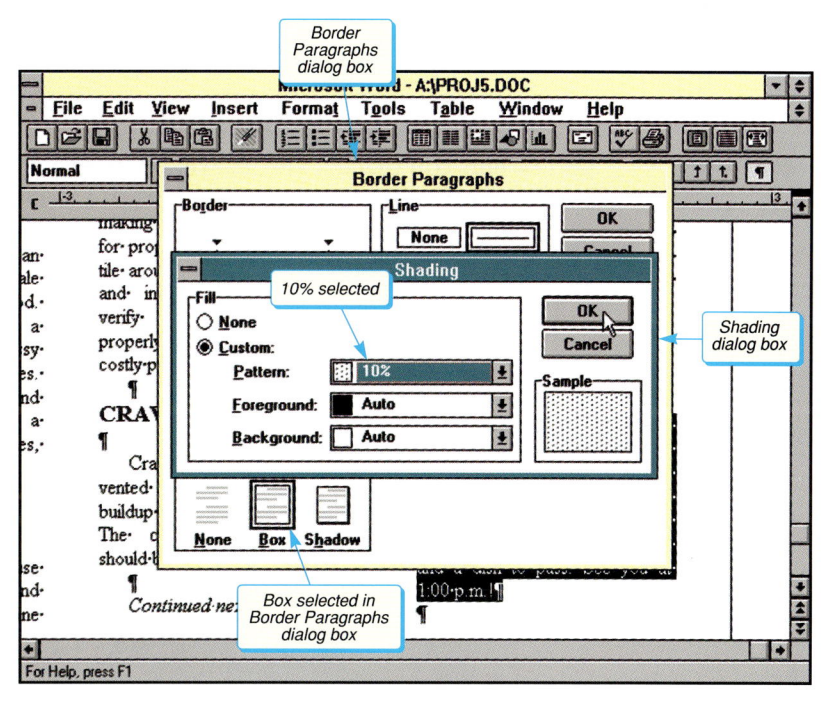

FIGURE 5-44

STEP 3 ▶

Choose the OK button in the Shading dialog box. Choose the OK button in the Border Paragraphs dialog box. Click outside the selection to remove the highlight.

Word shades the selected paragraphs and places a box around them (Figure 5-45). The extra paragraph mark will not fit on the page with the box border so it advances to the next page. If you had not placed the extra paragraph mark beneath your selection, the last paragraph mark would have been in the box border. When you wanted to advance to page two and pressed the ENTER *key from within the box border, the box border would have continued to the next page. Thus, the extra paragraph mark eliminates this problem.*

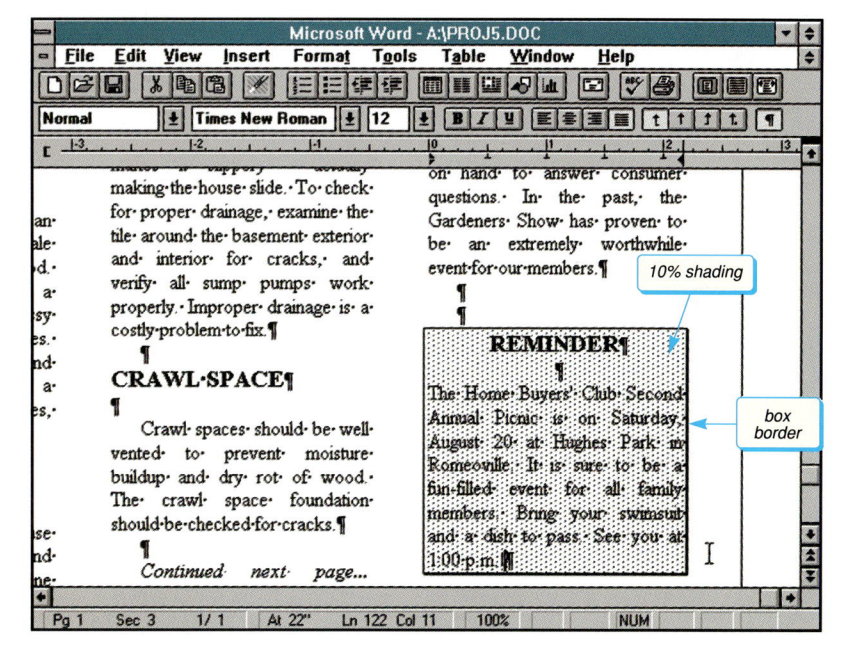

FIGURE 5-45

▲

The next step is to place a vertical rule between the second and third columns in the newsletter.

Adding a Vertical Rule Between Columns

In newsletters, you often see vertical rules separating columns. With Word, you can place a vertical rule between all columns or between selected columns. When you place a vertical rule between selected columns, your selection becomes a separate section beneath the existing columns. Therefore, you must format the new section to begin in a new column. Because this creates an extra blank column, you must then delete the blank column. Follow these steps to add a vertical rule between the second and third column in the newsletter (see Figure 5-54 on page MSW261).

TO ADD A VERTICAL RULE

STEP 1 ▶

Position the insertion point at the end of the second column.

The insertion point is in column 23 of line 81 (Figure 5-46).

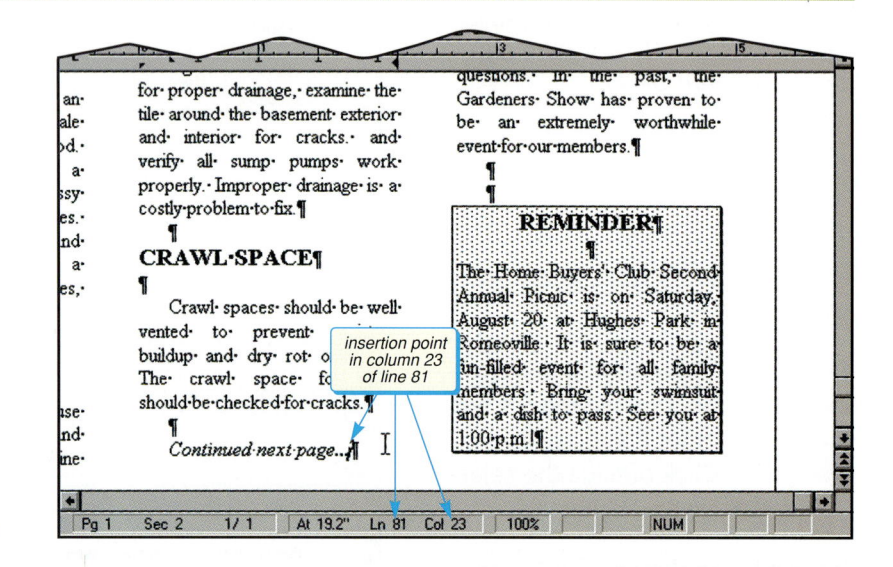

FIGURE 5-46

STEP 2 ▶

Drag the mouse to the right to highlight all of the third column (Figure 5-47).

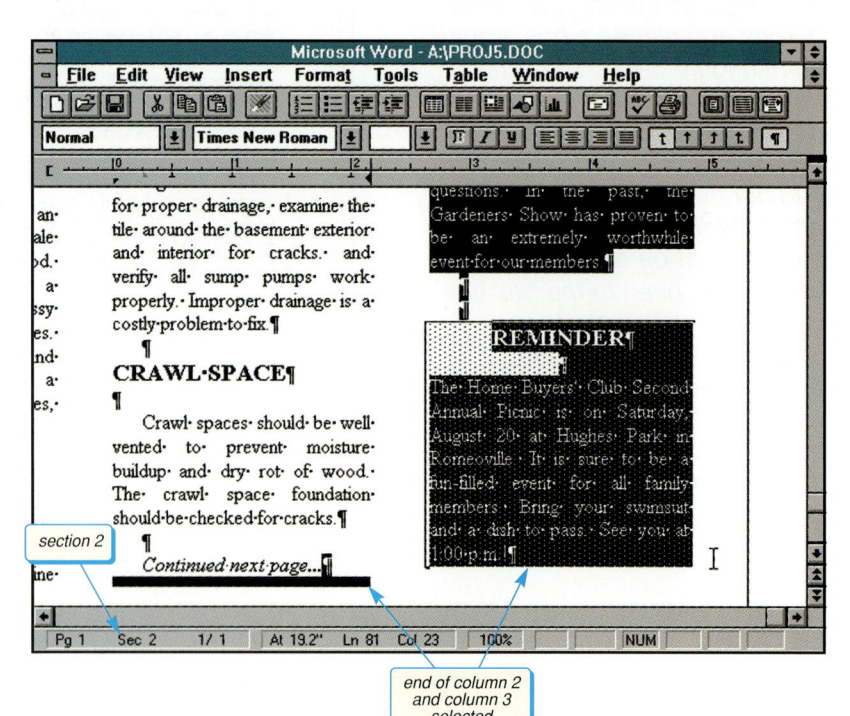

FIGURE 5-47

CREATING THE FIRST PAGE OF THE BODY OF THE NEWSLETTER   **MSW259**

STEP 3 ▶

From the Format menu, choose the Columns command. When the Columns dialog box displays, select the Line Between check box by clicking it. Click the Apply To box arrow and select Selected Text. Point to the OK button.

Word displays the Columns dialog box (Figure 5-48). The Line Between check box is selected. Because the Apply To text box displays Selected Text, a line will be placed between only the selected columns.

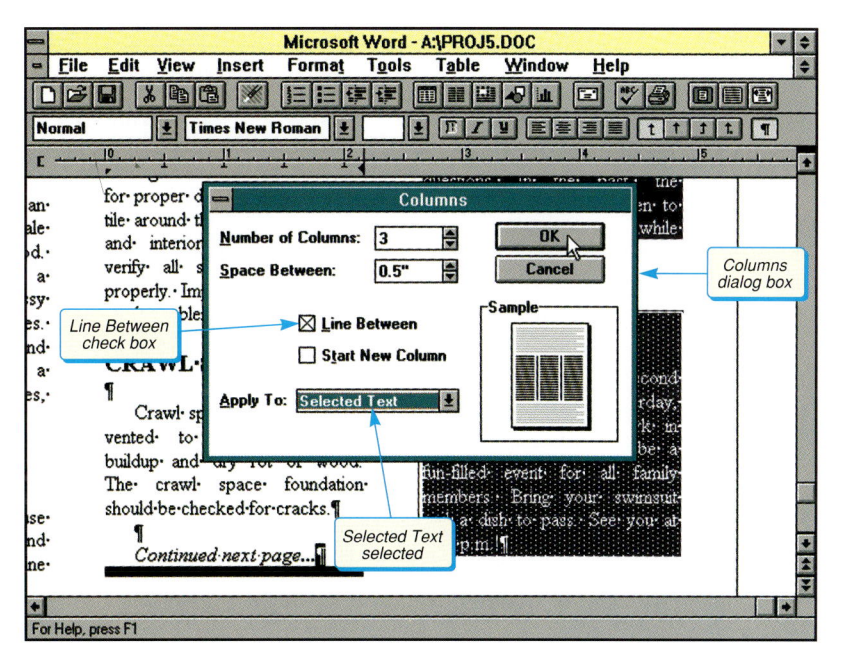

FIGURE 5-48

STEP 4 ▶

Choose the OK button.

Word moves the selection beneath the existing columns in a new section. You need to format the new section to begin in a new column.

STEP 5 ▶

Select the Format menu and point to the Section Layout command (Figure 5-49).

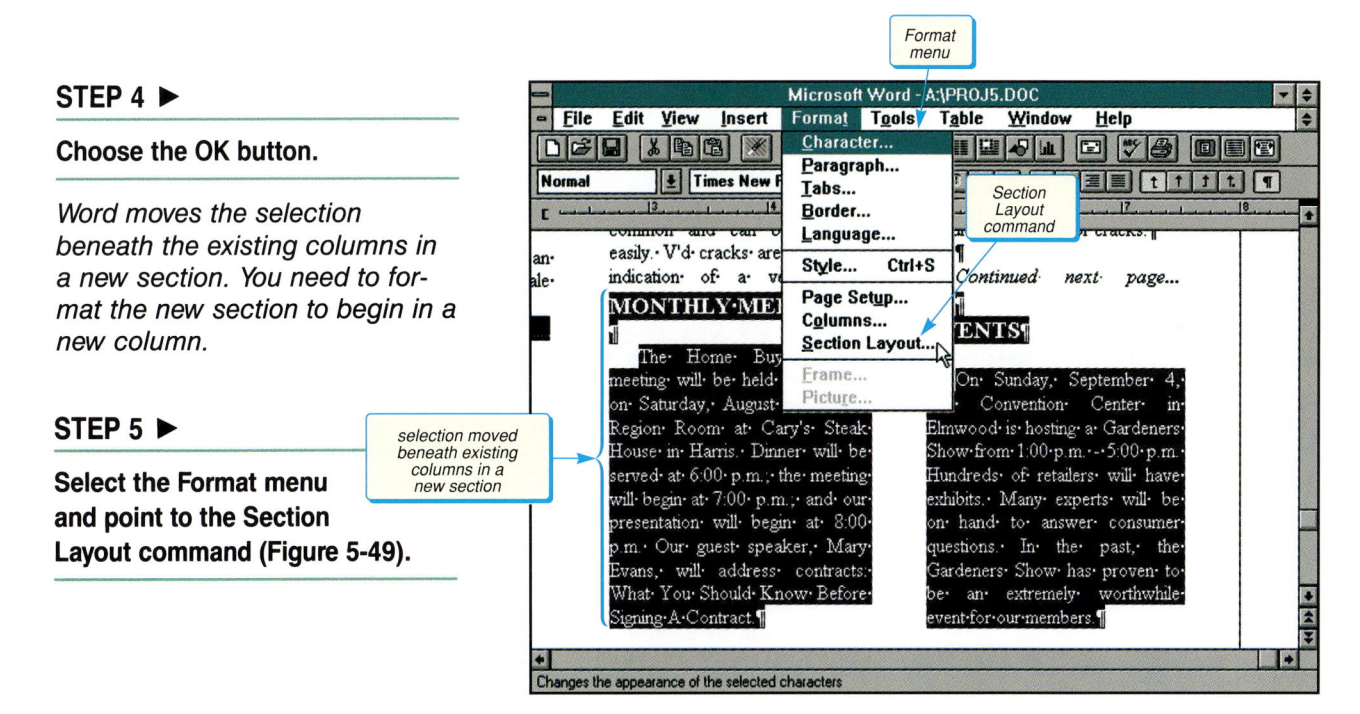

FIGURE 5-49

STEP 6 ▶

Choose the Section Layout command. When Word displays the Section Layout dialog box, click the Section Start box arrow. Point to New Column.

Word displays the Section Layout dialog box (Figure 5-50). A list of available places to begin the selected section displays. Notice the selection is in section 3.

FIGURE 5-50

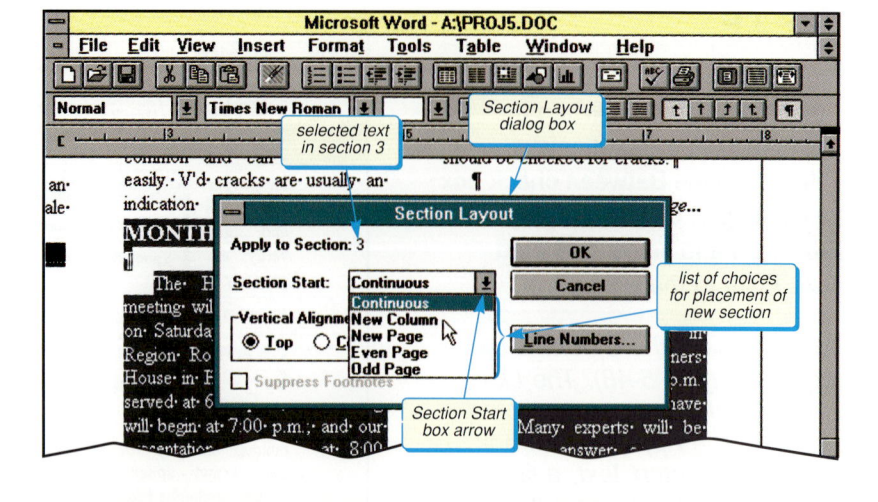

STEP 7 ▶

Choose New Column by clicking it. Point to the OK button.

Word displays New Column in the Section Start text box (Figure 5-51).

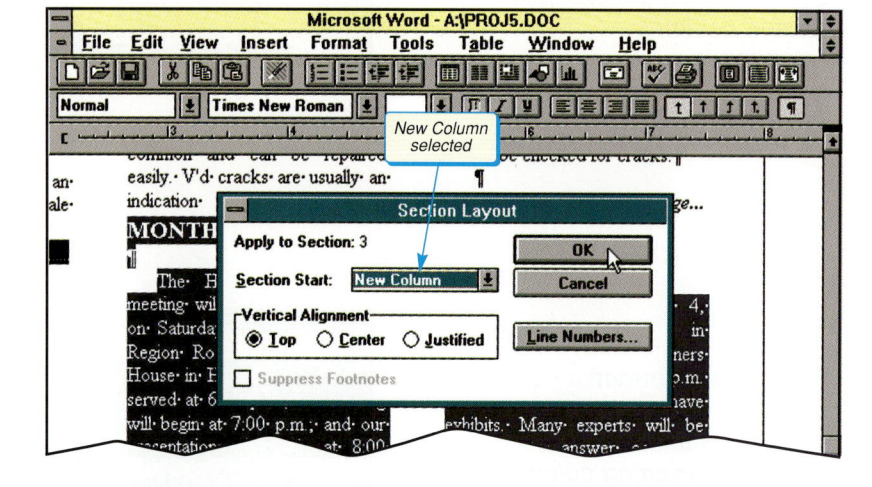

FIGURE 5-51

STEP 8

Choose the OK button in the Section Layout dialog box. Click outside the selection.

Word places the selected section in a new column on the next page. The third column on page one is blank.

STEP 9 ▶

Scroll up to page one to display the top of the third column. Select the paragraph mark and column break by dragging the mouse in the selection bar to the left of the paragraph mark and column break.

Word selects the paragraph mark and column break in the third column of page one (Figure 5-52).

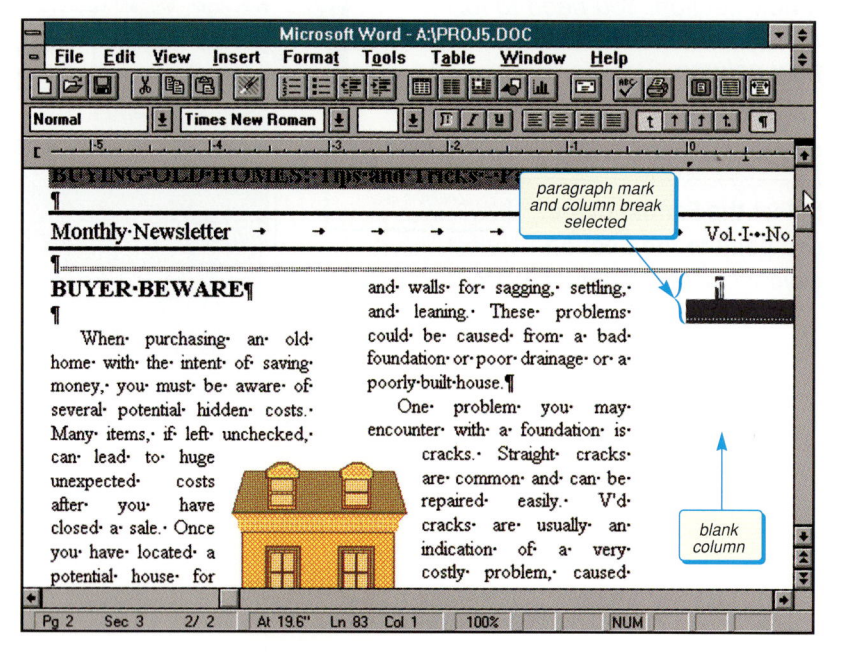

FIGURE 5-52

CREATING THE FIRST PAGE OF THE BODY OF THE NEWSLETTER MSW261

STEP 10 ▶

Press the DELETE key.

Word removes the blank column, which moves the column on page two to page one (Figure 5-53). Notice the vertical rule does not display on the screen in page layout view.

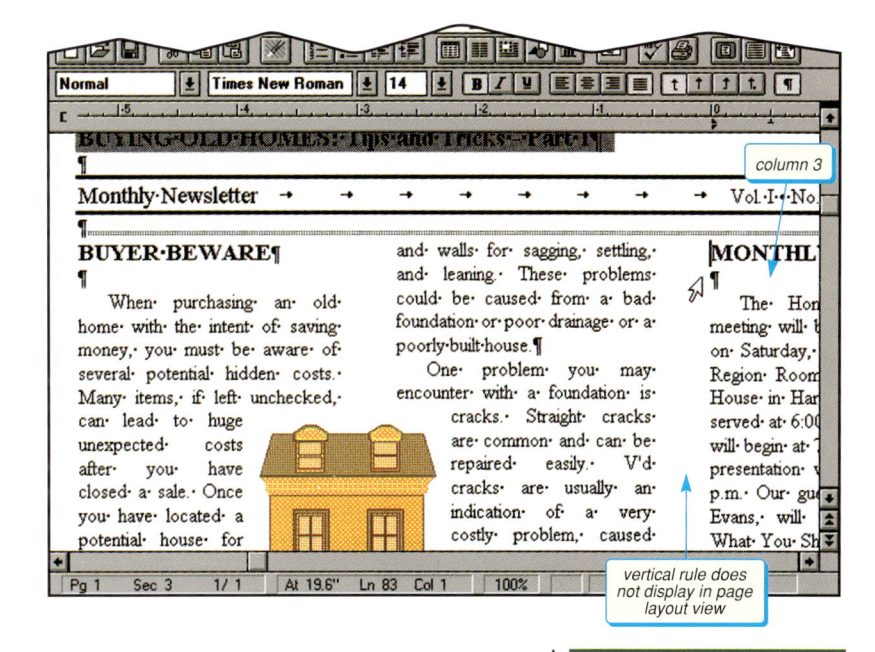

FIGURE 5-53

Vertical rules are not displayed in normal or page layout view. To see the vertical rule as it will print, you must be in print preview.

TO VIEW A DOCUMENT IN PRINT PREVIEW

Step 1: From the File menu, choose the Print Preview command.
Step 2: When finished viewing the document, choose the Cancel button.

Page one of the newsletter is complete as shown in Figure 5-54.

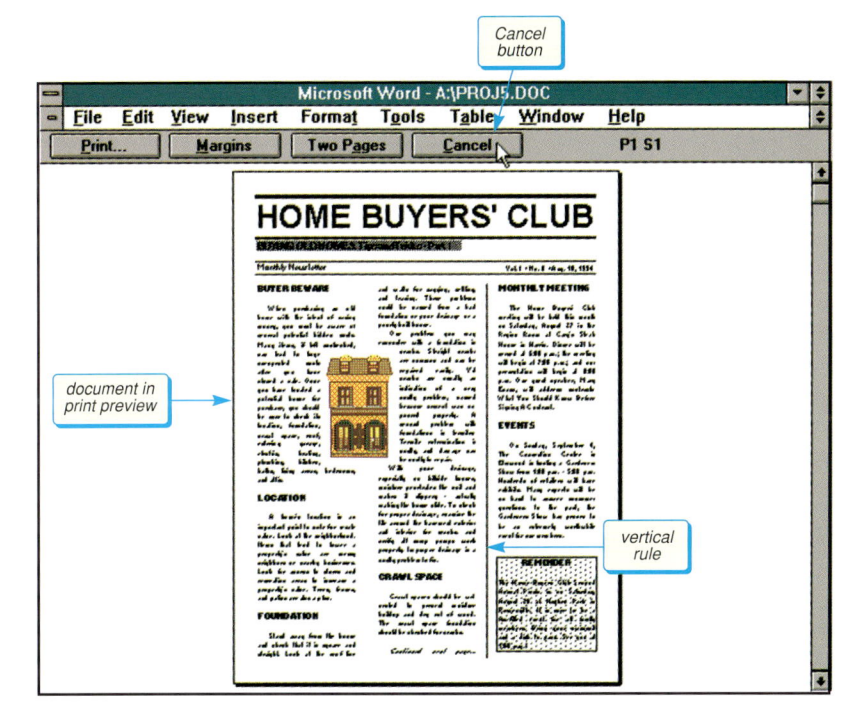

FIGURE 5-54

▶ Creating the Second Page of the Newsletter

The second page of the newsletter continues the article that began in the first two columns of page one (see Figure 5-1b on page MSW233). The nameplate on the second page is much more brief than on page one. In addition to the text in the article, page two contains a pull-quote and a shadow box border around the NEXT MONTH notice. The following pages illustrate how to create the second page of the newsletter in this project.

Creating the Nameplate on the Second Page

Because the document is currently formatted into three columns and the nameplate is a single column, the next step is to change the number of columns to one. Recall each time you change the number of columns in a document, you must create a new section. Earlier you accomplished this through the Columns command on the Format menu. Here you will use the Text Columns button (🔲) on the Toolbar. When you use the Text Columns button, you must first insert a section break; otherwise, Word will change the columns in the current section to the new choice. Follow these steps to format the top of page two to one column.

TO FORMAT COLUMNS WITH THE TEXT COLUMNS BUTTON ▼

STEP 1 ▶

Press CTRL + END to move to the end of the document (the top of page two). From the Insert menu, choose the Break command. When the Break dialog box displays, click the Continuous button in the Section Break area. Point to the OK button.

Word displays the Break dialog box (Figure 5-55). The bullet in the Continuous option indicates it is currently selected.

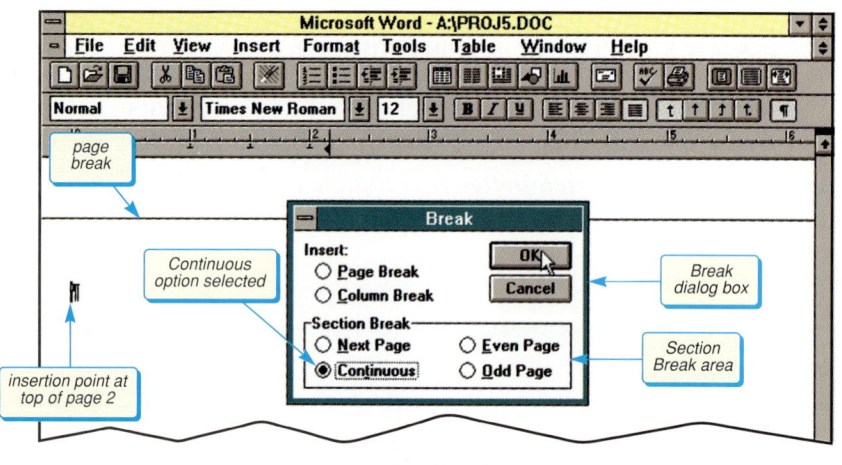

FIGURE 5-55

STEP 2 ▶

Choose the OK button.

Word creates a new section at the location of the insertion point. You are now in section 5.

STEP 3 ▶

Click the Text Columns button on the Toolbar.

Word displays a graphic of multiple columns (Figure 5-56).

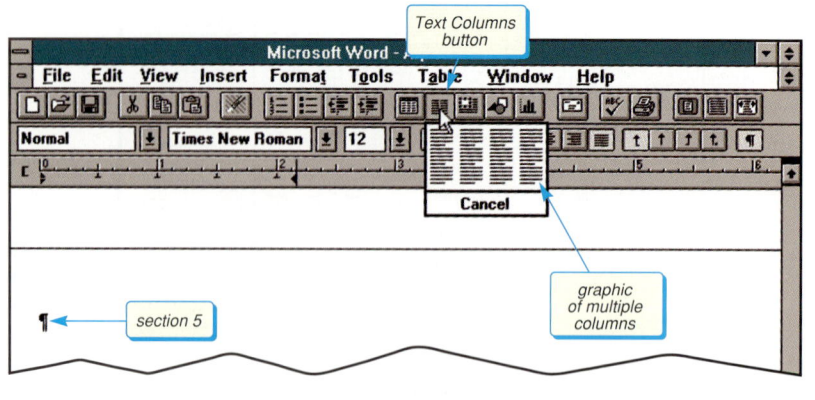

FIGURE 5-56

CREATING THE SECOND PAGE OF THE NEWSLETTER   MSW263

STEP 4 ▶

Press and hold the left mouse button in the first column of the column graphic.

Word highlights the first column in the column graphic and displays 1 Column beneath the graphic (Figure 5-57). The current section will be formatted to one column.

STEP 5

Release the mouse button.

Word formats the current section to one column.

FIGURE 5-57

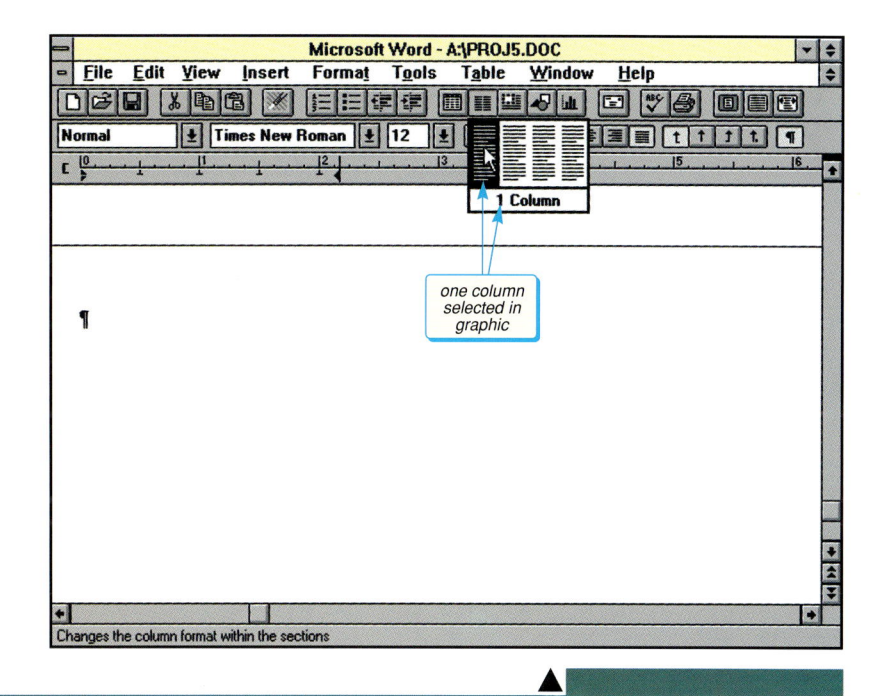

The next step is the enter the nameplate for the second page of the newsletter.

TO ENTER THE NAMEPLATE ON THE SECOND PAGE

Step 1: Type Aug. 10, 1994 and press the TAB key four times. Press the SPACEBAR four times. Change the point size to 19. Type Home Buyers' Club and press the TAB key five times. Press the SPACEBAR five times and change the point size back to 12. Type 2. Press the ENTER key.

Step 2: Select the line typed in Step 1 by clicking in the selection bar to the left of the line. From the Format menu, choose the Border command. When the Border Paragraphs dialog box displays, click above and below the paragraphs in the Border area to add ruling lines to the nameplate. Select the 2.25-point border in the Line area. Choose the OK button. Click the paragraph mark in line two.

Step 3: Change the point size to 15. Click the Bold button. Type BUYING OLD HOMES: Tips and Tricks - Part 1 and press the TAB key four times. Press the SPACEBAR five times. Type (Continued...) and change the point size back to 12. Click the Bold button. Press the ENTER key three times.

Step 4: Select the line typed in Step 3. From the Format menu, choose the Border command. When the Border Paragraphs dialog box displays, choose the Shading button. When the Shading dialog box displays, select a pattern of 50%. Choose the OK button in the Shading dialog box. Choose the OK button in the Border Paragraphs dialog box.

Step 5: Position the insertion point on the last paragraph mark on page 2. From the Format menu, choose the **Columns command**. Type 3 in the Number of Columns text box. Change the Apply To text box to This Point Forward by clicking the Apply To box arrow and selecting This Point Forward. Choose the OK button.

Word displays the nameplate on page two as shown in Figure 5-58 on the next page.

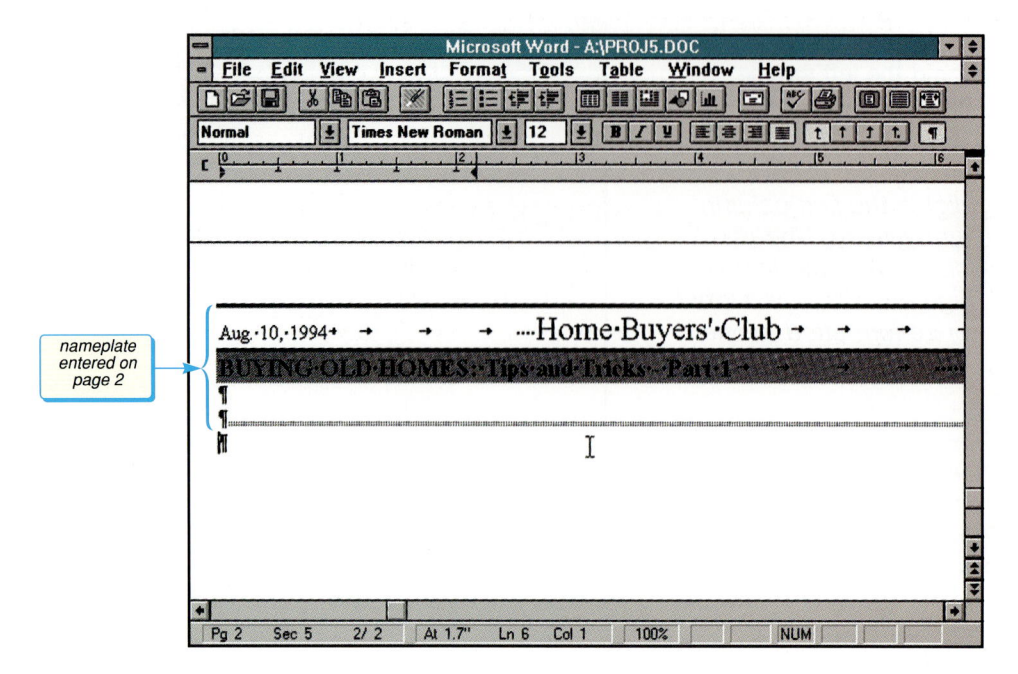

MSW264　PROJECT 5　CREATING A PROFESSIONAL NEWSLETTER

FIGURE 5-58

Now, type the rest of the text for the article (see Figure 5-1b on page MSW233). The end of the article, up to but not including the NEXT MONTH announcement, displays as shown in Figure 5-59.

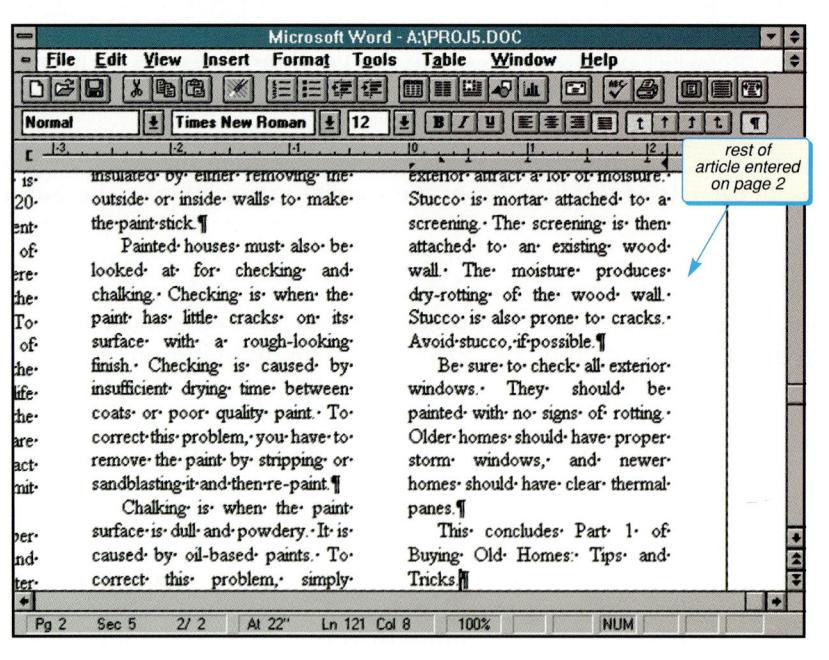

FIGURE 5-59

CREATING THE SECOND PAGE OF THE NEWSLETTER **MSW265**

Reducing and Magnifying the View of a Document

With Word, you can reduce or magnify a document on your screen. This process is called **zooming**. In page layout view, you cannot see both the left and right margins of this project in the document window at the same time. You have to click to the right of the scroll box on the horizontal scroll bar to bring the right margin into view or to the left of the scroll box to bring the left margin into view. If you would like to see both margins on the screen at the same time, you can reduce the size of the document to fit in the document window. If you would like to see the layout of an entire page on the screen, you can reduce the size of the entire page to fit in the document window. The following steps illustrate how to reduce and magnify the view of a document using buttons on the Toolbar.

TO VIEW AN ENTIRE PAGE IN THE DOCUMENT WINDOW ▼

STEP 1 ▶

Click the Zoom Whole Page button (▣) on the Toolbar.

Word displays page two of the newsletter in the document window (Figure 5-60). Because the text is illegible, use this view to check column lengths, picture position, and so on.

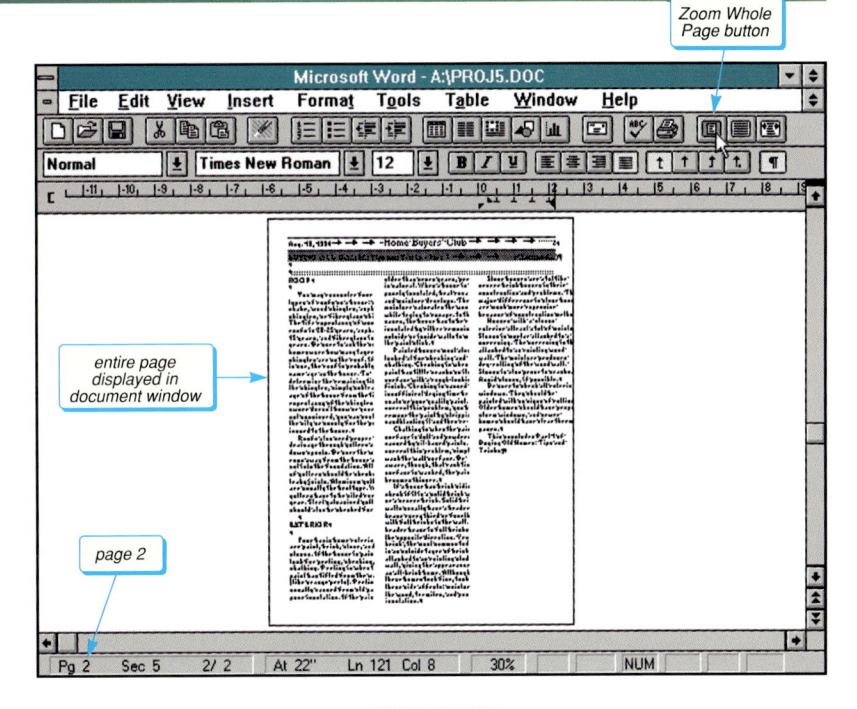

FIGURE 5-60

TO VIEW THE LEFT AND RIGHT MARGINS IN THE DOCUMENT WINDOW

STEP 1 ▶

Click the Zoom Page Width button (📄) on the Toolbar.

Word displays page two on the screen so both the right and left margins are visible in the document window (Figure 5-61).

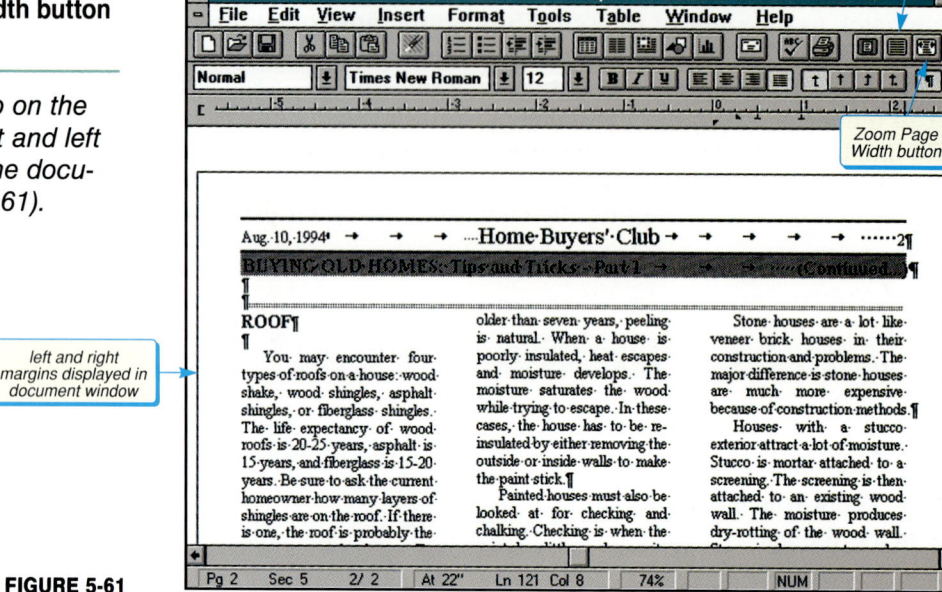

left and right margins displayed in document window

FIGURE 5-61

Zoom 100 Percent button

Zoom Page Width button

To return to the original page layout view, you must first choose the Zoom 100 Percent button (📄) on the Toolbar. This button returns you to the original screen display in normal view. Then, you change back to page layout view.

TO VIEW THE DOCUMENT AT 100 PERCENT MAGNIFICATION

Step 1: Click the Zoom 100 Percent button on the Toolbar.
Step 2: From the View menu, choose the Page Layout command.

Zooming in or out on the screen has no effect on the printed document. Zooming is strictly for your convenience while looking at the screen display. While zooming, you can edit any portion of the document. If you want to specify a zoom percentage, you can choose the Zoom command on the View menu and specify a zoom percentage ranging from 25 to 200 percent magnification.

The next step is to insert a pull-quote between the first and second columns on page two of the newsletter.

Inserting a Pull-Quote

A **pull-quote** is a quotation *pulled* from the text of the document and given graphic emphasis so it stands apart and grasps the attention of the reader. Because of their bold emphasis, pull-quotes should be used sparingly in documents. The newsletter in this project has a pull-quote on the second page between the first and second columns (see Figure 5-1b on page MSW233). To give more emphasis to the pull-quote, the left and right quotation marks from the **Symbol font** surround the quote, instead of the vertical quotation marks on the keyboard.

CREATING THE SECOND PAGE OF THE NEWSLETTER   MSW267

To create a pull-quote, you first type the quotation with the rest of the text. To position it between columns, you frame it and move it to the desired location. Follow these steps to create the pull-quote in Project 5 (see Figure 5-68 on page MSW269).

TO CREATE A PULL-QUOTE ▼

STEP 1 ▶

Position the insertion point on the paragraph mark below the ROOF subhead on page two of the newsletter. Press the ENTER key. Drag the First-Line Indent marker to the 0-inch mark on the ruler. Change the point size to 16. From the Insert menu, choose the Symbol command. When the Symbol dialog box displays, click the left quotation marks. Point to the OK button.

Word displays the Symbol dialog box (Figure 5-62). The left quotation marks symbol is selected.

FIGURE 5-62

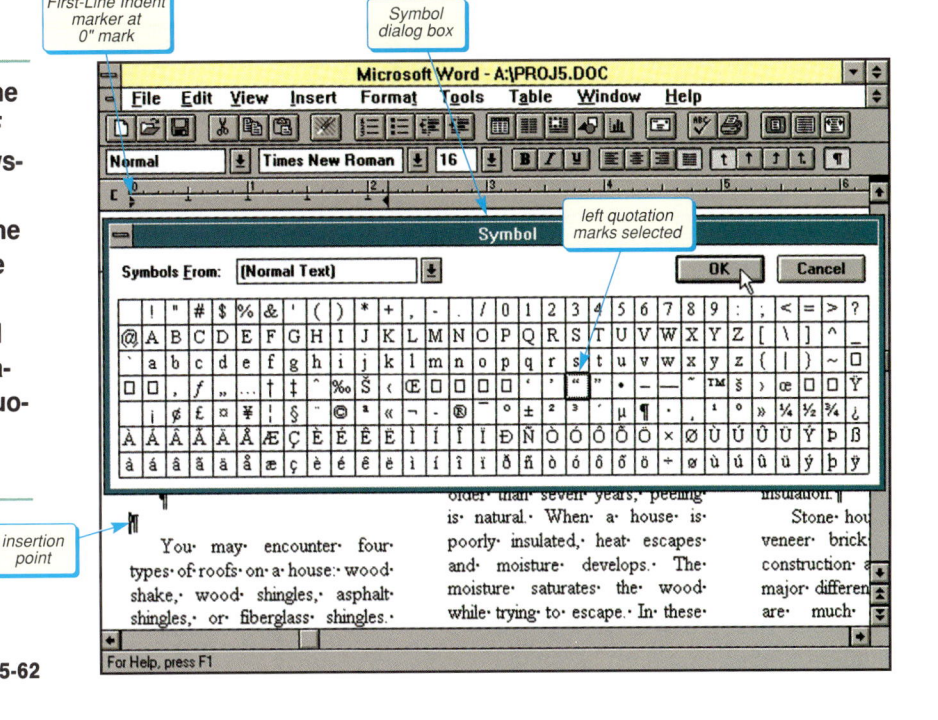

STEP 2 ▶

Choose the OK button. Change the point size to 14. Click the Bold and Italic buttons on the ribbon. Type `If there is only one layer of shingles, the roof is probably the same age as the house.` and click the Bold and Italic buttons on the ribbon. Change the point size to 16. From the Insert menu, choose the Symbol command. When the Symbol dialog box displays, click the right quotation marks. Choose the OK button. Select the pull-quote by positioning the mouse pointer in the selection bar to the left of the pull-quote and double-clicking.

The pull-quote is highlighted beneath the ROOF subhead (Figure 5-63).

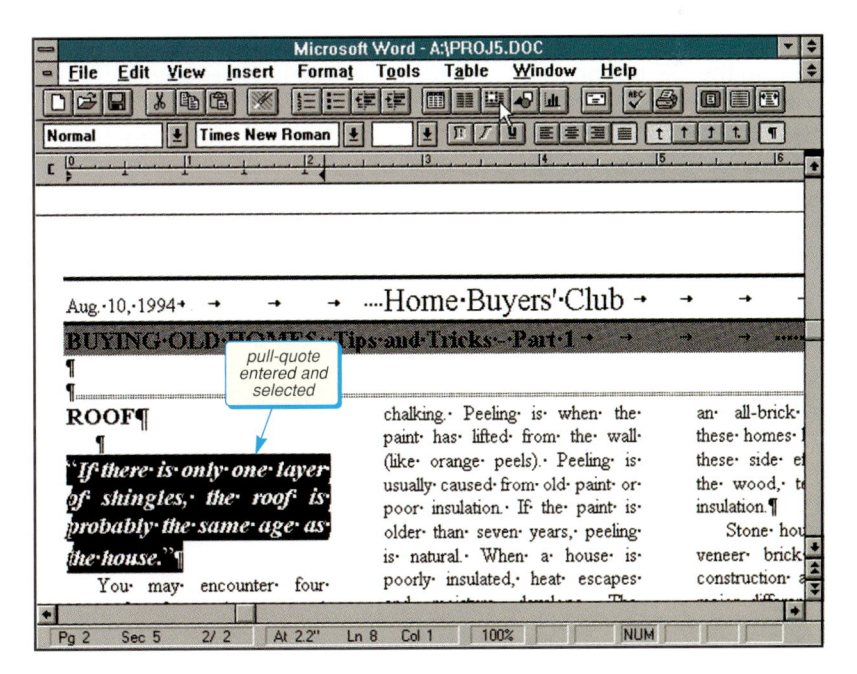

FIGURE 5-63

MSW268   PROJECT 5   CREATING A PROFESSIONAL NEWSLETTER

STEP 3 ▶

Click the Frame button on the Toolbar.

Word places a frame around the selected text (Figure 5-64). As discussed earlier, the frame can be moved or resized.

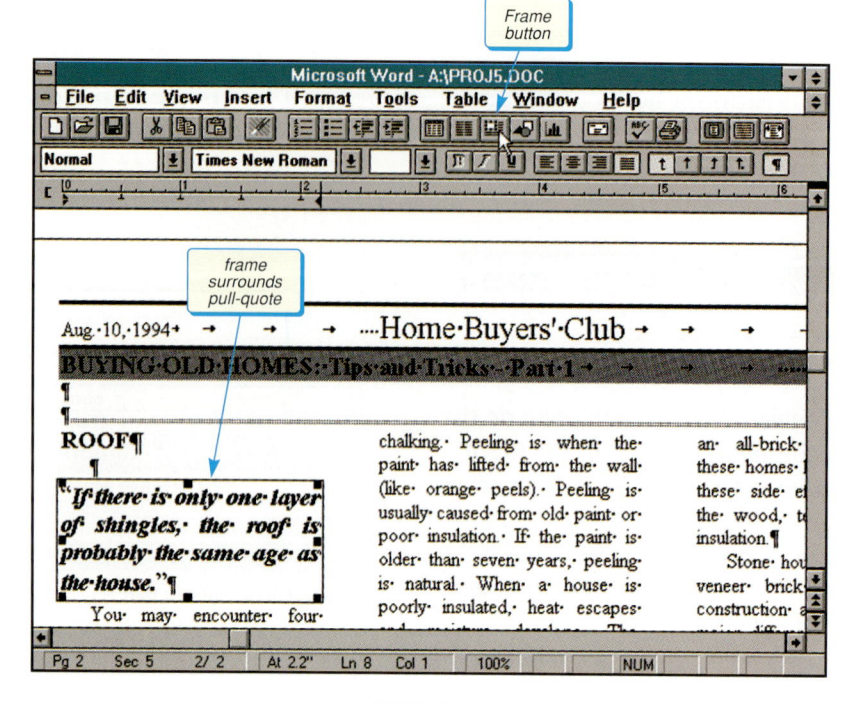

FIGURE 5-64

STEP 4 ▶

From the Format menu, choose the Paragraph command. When the Paragraph dialog box displays, change Alignment to Left, Indentation From Left to 0.4", Indentation From Right to 0.4", Spacing Before to 1 li, and Spacing After to 1 li. Point to the OK button.

Word displays the Paragraph dialog box (Figure 5-65). The pull-quote will be left-aligned with a 0.4-inch space on the left and right edges and one blank line above and below it.

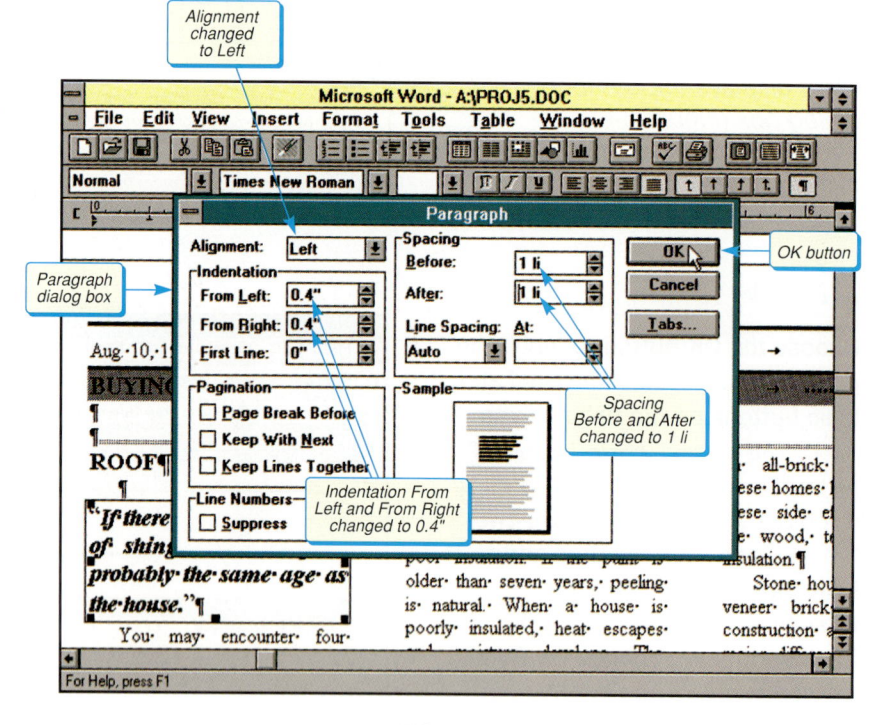

FIGURE 5-65

CREATING THE SECOND PAGE OF THE NEWSLETTER MSW269

STEP 5 ▶

Choose the OK button in the Paragraph dialog box. Position the mouse pointer on the frame so it changes to the four-headed arrow.

Word displays the pull-quote left aligned with a 0.4" space between the border and the frame on the left and right sides. One blank line displays between the border and frame on the top and bottom sides (Figure 5-66). Notice that Word places a border around the pull-quote. When you add a frame to a paragraph, Word automatically places a border around it.

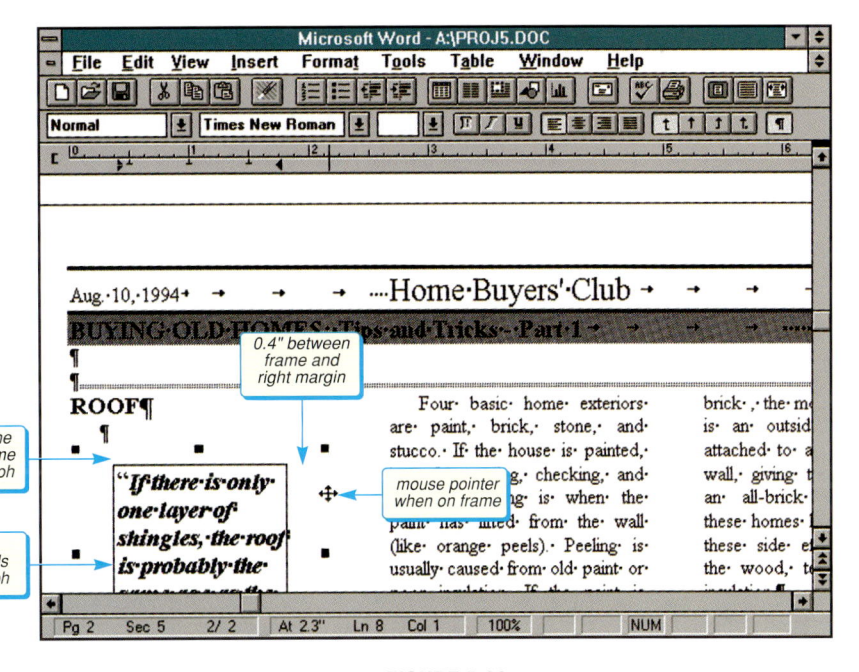

FIGURE 5-66

STEP 6 ▶

Drag the frame to its new position (Figure 5-67).

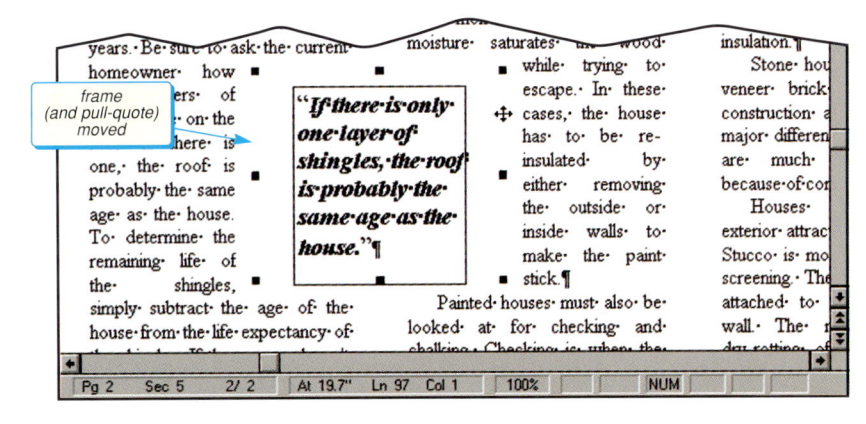

FIGURE 5-67

STEP 7 ▶

From the Format menu, choose the Border command. When the Border Paragraphs dialog box displays, click None in the Line area to remove the border. Choose the OK button. Click outside the pull-quote to remove the frame.

The pull-quote is complete (Figure 5-68).

FIGURE 5-68

Adding a Shadow Box Border Around Paragraphs

The NEXT MONTH notice at the bottom of the third column on page two is shaded and has a shadow box border around it (Figure 5-69). That is, a shadow appears on the bottom and right sides, giving a three-dimensional appearance. Shadow box borders are placed around paragraphs the same way box borders are added. Follow these steps to shade and add a shadow box border to the NEXT MONTH notice paragraphs.

TO ADD A SHADOW BOX BORDER AROUND PARAGRAPHS

Step 1: Press CTRL+END. Press the ENTER key three times. Drag the First-Line Indent marker on the ruler to the 0-inch mark on the ruler. Change the point size to 14. Click the Bold button. Type NEXT MONTH... and click the Bold button. Change the point size back to 12 and press the ENTER key twice. Type the paragraph beneath the subhead.

Step 2: Select the paragraphs in the NEXT MONTH notice by dragging the mouse in the selection bar to the left of them. From the Format menu, choose the Border command.

Step 3: When the Border Paragraphs dialog box displays, select the Shadow option in the Preset area. Select the 2.25-point border in the Line area. Choose the OK button. Click outside the shadow box border to remove the selection.

The shadow box border appears around the NEXT MONTH notice as shown in Figure 5-69.

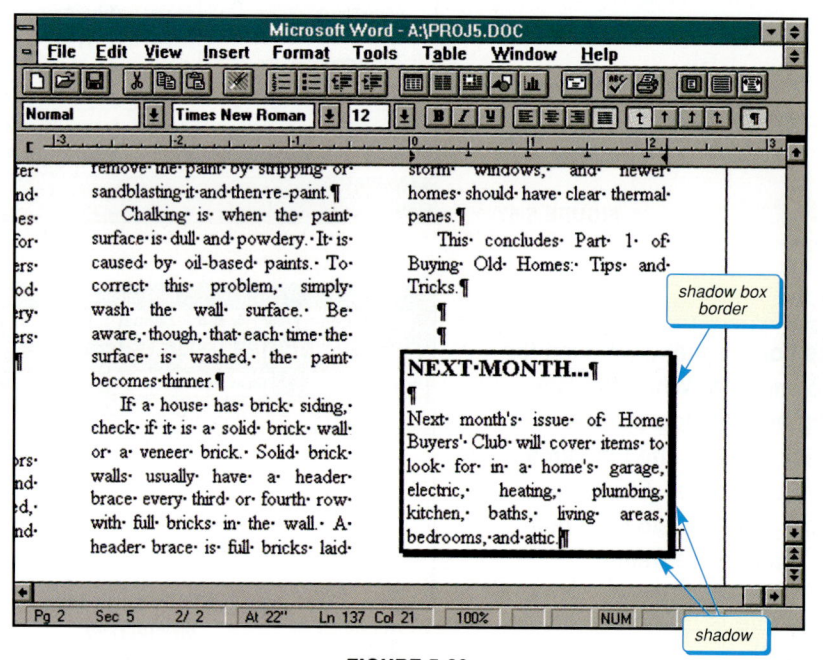

FIGURE 5-69

ENHANCING THE NEWSLETTER WITH COLOR **MSW271**

▶ ENHANCING THE NEWSLETTER WITH COLOR

Many of the characters and lines in the newsletter in Project 5 are colored (see Figure 5-75 on pages MSW274 and MSW275). Word provides 16 colors from which you can choose to enhance the appearance of characters and lines. The default is Auto, which displays and prints as black. Follow these steps to change the color of the title and surrounding ruling lines in the nameplate on page 1 of the newsletter. The title is red and the ruling lines are cyan.

TO CHANGE COLORS OF CHARACTERS AND LINES ▼

STEP 1 ▶

Press CTRL + HOME. Select the title by clicking in the selection bar to the left of it. Select the Format menu and point to the Character command.

The top of the document displays in the document window and the title is highlighted (Figure 5-70). The mouse pointer points to the Character command.

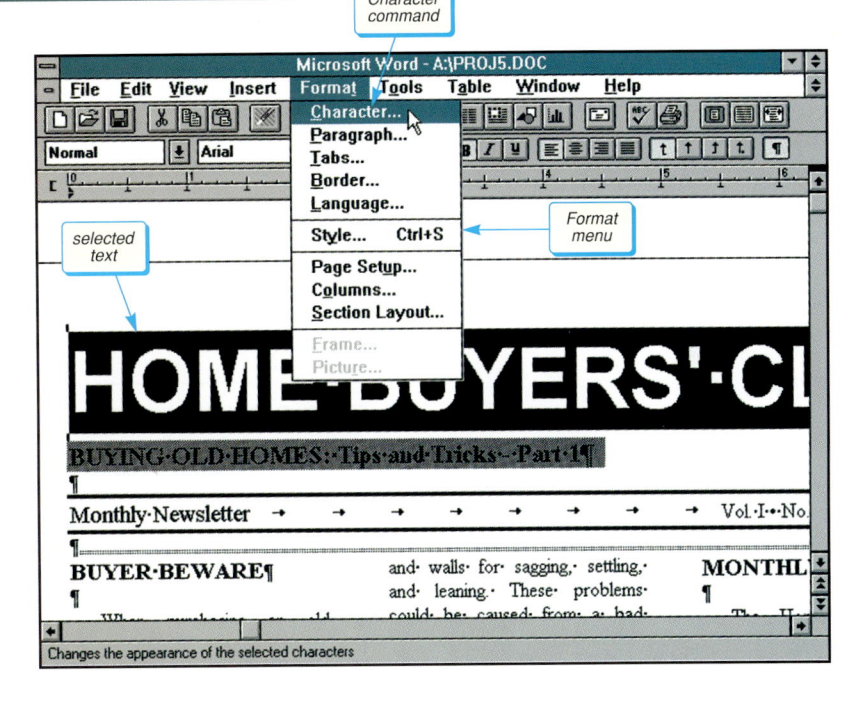

FIGURE 5-70

STEP 2 ▶

Choose the Character command. When the Character dialog box displays, click the Color box arrow. Point to Red.

Word displays the Character dialog box (Figure 5-71). A list of available colors displays in the Color list box.

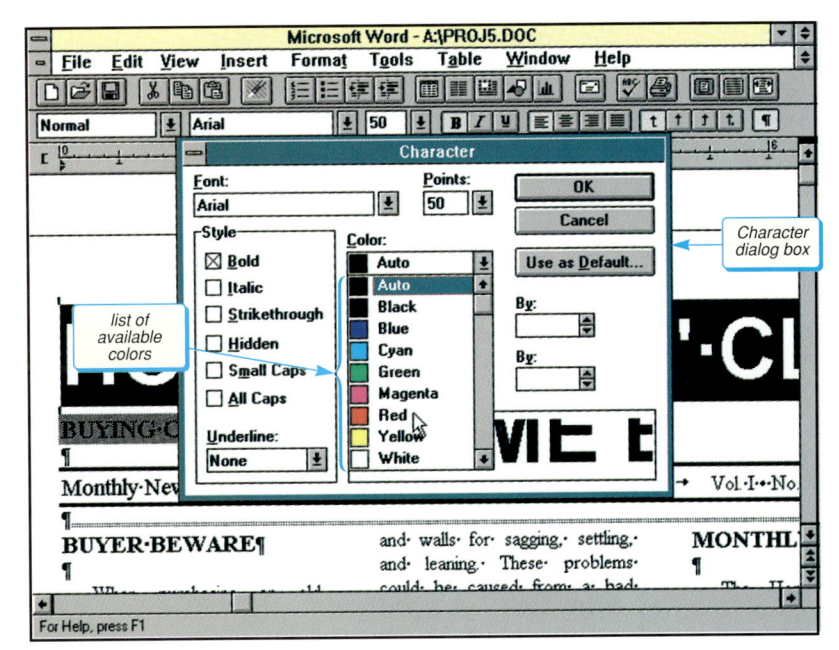

FIGURE 5-71

STEP 3 ▶

Select Red by clicking it. Point to the OK button.

Word displays Red in the Color text box (Figure 5-72). The sample area displays the selected text in red.

STEP 4

Choose the OK button in the Character dialog box.

Word changes the selected characters to red.

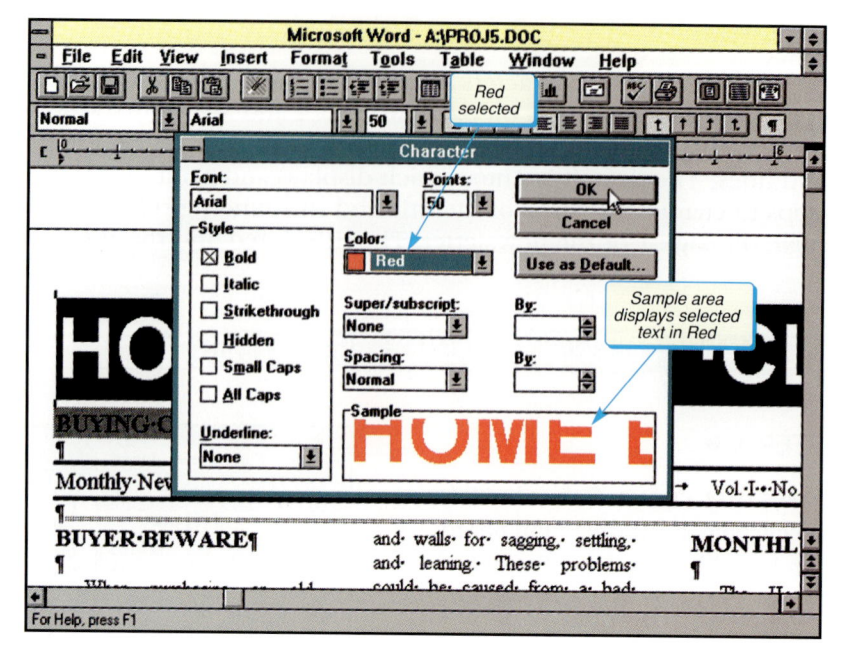

FIGURE 5-72

STEP 5 ▶

From the Format menu, choose the Border command. When the Border Paragraphs dialog box displays, click the Color box arrow and select Cyan. Point to the OK button.

Word displays the Border Paragraphs dialog box (Figure 5-73). Cyan displays in the Color text box, and all of the lines in the dialog box display in cyan.

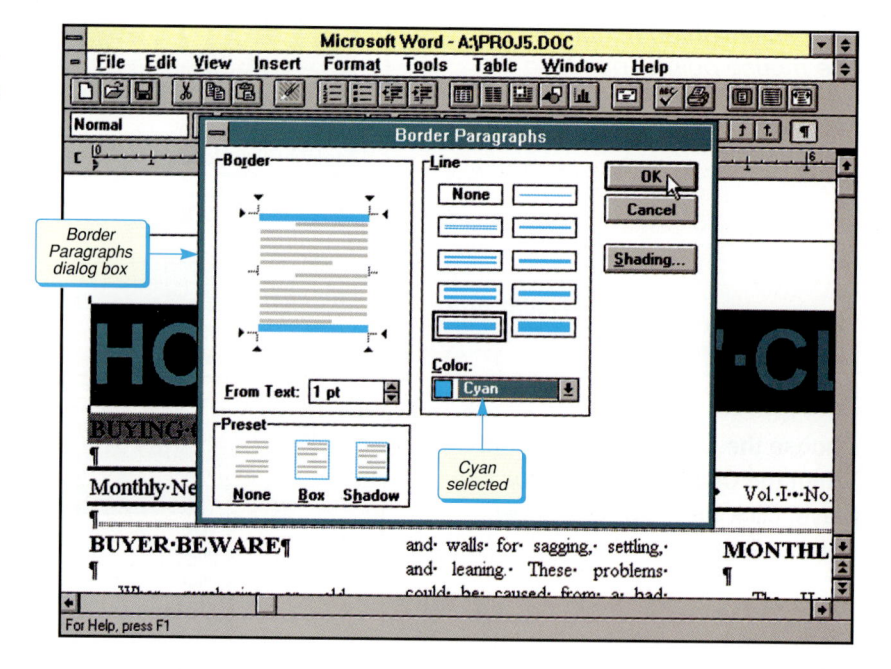

FIGURE 5-73

STEP 6 ▶

Choose the OK button in the Border Paragraphs dialog box. Click outside the selection to remove the highlight.

The title characters are colored in red with cyan ruling lines (Figure 5-74).

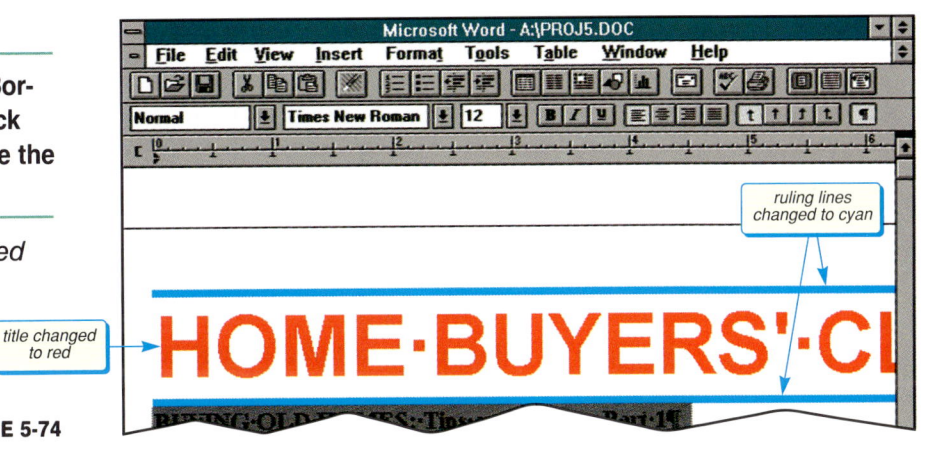

FIGURE 5-74

The next step is to color the headline in white.

TO COLOR THE HEADLINE CHARACTERS IN WHITE

Step 1: Select the headline. From the Format menu, choose the Character command.
Step 2: Click the Color box arrow and select White.
Step 3: Choose the OK button in the Character dialog box. Click outside the selection to remove the highlight.

The issue information line is red with cyan ruling lines.

TO COLOR THE ISSUE INFORMATION LINE

Step 1: Select the issue information line. From the Format menu, choose the Character command.
Step 2: Click the Color box arrow and select Red.
Step 3: Choose the OK button in the Character dialog box.
Step 4: From the Format menu, choose the Border command.
Step 5: Click the Color box arrow and select Cyan.
Step 6: Choose the OK button in the Border Paragraphs dialog box. Click outside the selection to remove the highlight.

Each of the subheads in the newsletter are colored in green.

TO COLOR THE SUBHEADS

Step 1: Select the first subhead, BUYER BEWARE. From the Format menu, choose the Character command.
Step 2: Click the Color box arrow and select Green.
Step 3: Choose the OK button in the Character dialog box. Click outside the selection to remove the highlight.
Step 4: Repeat the procedure in Steps 1 through 3 for each of these subheads: LOCATION, FOUNDATION, CRAWL SPACE, MONTHLY MEETING, EVENTS, ROOF, EXTERIOR, and NEXT MONTH...

The border on the each of the boxes is red.

TO COLOR THE BORDER OF THE BOXES

Step 1: Select the first box, REMINDER, by dragging the mouse through the text in the box. From the Format menu, choose the Border command.
Step 2: Click the Color box arrow and select Red.
Step 3: Choose the OK button in the Border Paragraphs dialog box. Click outside the selection to remove the highlight.
Step 4: Repeat the procedure in Steps 1 through 3 for the NEXT MONTH box on page two of the newsletter.

The pull-quote is colored in dark magenta.

TO COLOR THE PULL-QUOTE

Step 1: Select the pull-quote by dragging the mouse from the left quotation mark through the right quotation mark. From the Format menu, choose the Character command.
Step 2: Click the Color box arrow and select Dk Magenta.
Step 3: Choose the OK button in the Character dialog box. Click outside the selection to remove the highlight.

The newsletter is now complete. Save it one final time by clicking the Save button on the Toolbar. Spell check it by clicking the Spelling button. Then, print it by clicking the Print button. If you have a color printer, it will print in color as shown in Figure 5-75a and Figure 5-75b.

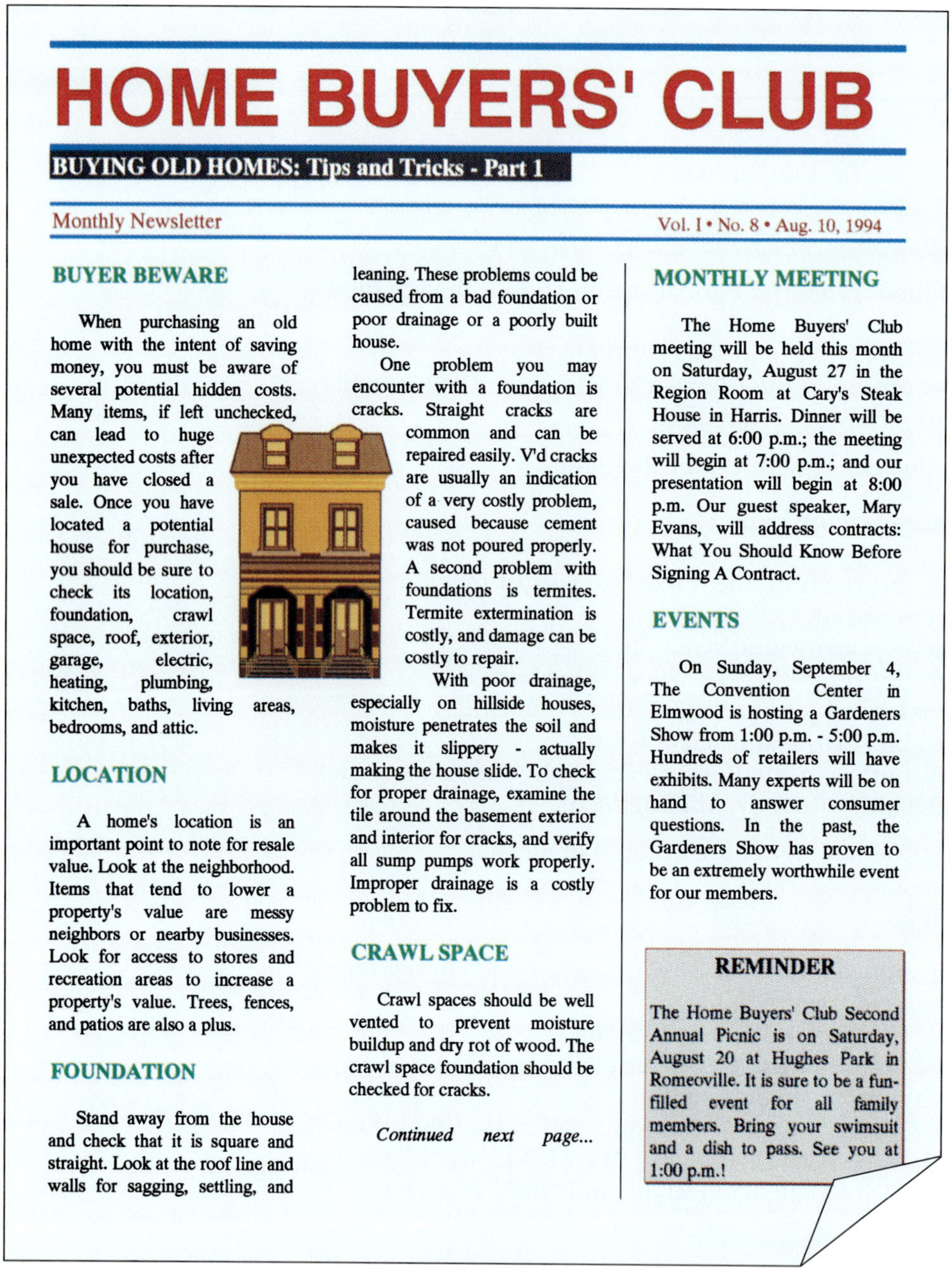

HOME BUYERS' CLUB

BUYING OLD HOMES: Tips and Tricks - Part 1

Monthly Newsletter Vol. I • No. 8 • Aug. 10, 1994

BUYER BEWARE

When purchasing an old home with the intent of saving money, you must be aware of several potential hidden costs. Many items, if left unchecked, can lead to huge unexpected costs after you have closed a sale. Once you have located a potential house for purchase, you should be sure to check its location, foundation, crawl space, roof, exterior, garage, electric, heating, plumbing, kitchen, baths, living areas, bedrooms, and attic.

LOCATION

A home's location is an important point to note for resale value. Look at the neighborhood. Items that tend to lower a property's value are messy neighbors or nearby businesses. Look for access to stores and recreation areas to increase a property's value. Trees, fences, and patios are also a plus.

FOUNDATION

Stand away from the house and check that it is square and straight. Look at the roof line and walls for sagging, settling, and leaning. These problems could be caused from a bad foundation or poor drainage or a poorly built house.

One problem you may encounter with a foundation is cracks. Straight cracks are common and can be repaired easily. V'd cracks are usually an indication of a very costly problem, caused because cement was not poured properly. A second problem with foundations is termites. Termite extermination is costly, and damage can be costly to repair.

With poor drainage, especially on hillside houses, moisture penetrates the soil and makes it slippery - actually making the house slide. To check for proper drainage, examine the tile around the basement exterior and interior for cracks, and verify all sump pumps work properly. Improper drainage is a costly problem to fix.

CRAWL SPACE

Crawl spaces should be well vented to prevent moisture buildup and dry rot of wood. The crawl space foundation should be checked for cracks.

Continued next page...

MONTHLY MEETING

The Home Buyers' Club meeting will be held this month on Saturday, August 27 in the Region Room at Cary's Steak House in Harris. Dinner will be served at 6:00 p.m.; the meeting will begin at 7:00 p.m.; and our presentation will begin at 8:00 p.m. Our guest speaker, Mary Evans, will address contracts: What You Should Know Before Signing A Contract.

EVENTS

On Sunday, September 4, The Convention Center in Elmwood is hosting a Gardeners Show from 1:00 p.m. - 5:00 p.m. Hundreds of retailers will have exhibits. Many experts will be on hand to answer consumer questions. In the past, the Gardeners Show has proven to be an extremely worthwhile event for our members.

REMINDER

The Home Buyers' Club Second Annual Picnic is on Saturday, August 20 at Hughes Park in Romeoville. It is sure to be a fun-filled event for all family members. Bring your swimsuit and a dish to pass. See you at 1:00 p.m.!

FIGURE 5-75a

Aug. 10, 1994 Home Buyers' Club 2

BUYING OLD HOMES: Tips and Tricks - Part 1 (Continued...)

ROOF

You may encounter four types of roofs on a house: wood shake, wood shingles, asphalt shingles, or fiberglass shingles. The life expectancy of wood roofs is 20-25 years, asphalt is 15 years, and fiberglass is 15-20 years. Be sure to ask the current homeowner how many layers of shingles are on the roof. If there is one, the roof is probably the same age as the house. To determine the remaining life of the shingles, simply subtract the age of the house from the life expectancy of the shingles. If the owner doesn't know or you are not convinced, you can contact the city or county for the permit issued to the house.

Roofs also need proper drainage through gutters and down spouts. Be sure the water runs away from the house and not into the foundation. All types of gutters should be checked for leaky joints. Aluminum gutters are usually the best type. Wood gutters have to be oiled every year. Steel galvanized gutters should also be checked for rust.

EXTERIOR

Four basic home exteriors are paint, brick, stone, and stucco. If the house is painted, look for peeling, checking, and chalking. Peeling is when the paint has lifted from the wall (like orange peels). Peeling is usually caused from old paint or poor insulation. If the paint is older than seven years, peeling is natural. When a house is poorly insulated, heat escapes and moisture develops. The moisture saturates the wood while trying to escape. In these cases, the house has to be re-insulated by either removing the outside or inside walls to make the paint stick.

> *"If there is only one layer of shingles, the roof is probably the same age as the house."*

Painted houses must also be looked at for checking and chalking. Checking is when the paint has little cracks on its surface with a rough-looking finish. Checking is caused by insufficient drying time between coats or poor quality paint. To correct this problem, you have to remove the paint by stripping or sandblasting it and then re-paint.

Chalking is when the paint surface is dull and powdery. It is caused by oil-based paints. To correct this problem, simply wash the wall surface. Be aware, though, that each time the surface is washed, the paint becomes thinner.

If a house has brick siding, check if it is a solid brick wall or a veneer brick. Solid brick walls usually have a header brace every third or fourth row with full bricks in the wall. A header brace is full bricks laid the opposite direction. Veneer brick , the most common today, is an outside layer of brick attached to an existing studded wall, giving the appearance of an all-brick home. Although these homes look fine, look for these side effects: moisture in the wood, termites, and poor insulation.

Stone houses are a lot like veneer brick houses in their construction and problems. The major difference is stone houses are much more expensive because of construction methods.

Houses with a stucco exterior attract a lot of moisture. Stucco is mortar attached to a screening. The screening is then attached to an existing wood wall. The moisture produces dry-rotting of the wood wall. Stucco is also prone to cracks. Avoid stucco, if possible.

Be sure to check all exterior windows. They should be painted with no signs of rotting. Older homes should have proper storm windows, and newer homes should have clear thermal panes.

This concludes Part 1 of Buying Old Homes: Tips and Tricks.

NEXT MONTH...

Next month's issue of Home Buyers' Club will cover items to look for in a home's garage, electric, heating, plumbing, kitchen, baths, living areas, bedrooms, and attic.

FIGURE 5-75b

Project Summary

Project 5 introduced you to creating a professional looking newsletter with desktop publishing features. You created nameplates with ruling lines and shading. You formatted the body of the newsletter into three columns and added a vertical rule between the second and third columns. You learned how to frame both graphics and paragraphs and move them between columns. In the newsletter, you added box borders and shadow box borders around paragraphs. Finally, you colored a variety of characters and lines in the document.

▶ Key Terms

ANSI characters (*MSW244*)
banner (*MSW234*)
Border command (*MSW269*)
border markers (*MSW237*)
box border (*MSW234*)
Break command (*MSW262*)
bullet (*MSW242*)
Character command (*MSW271*)
column break (*MSW254*)
Columns command (*MSW245*)
desktop publishing software (*MSW231*)
font (*MSW235*)
frame (*MSW251*)
Frame button (*MSW268*)
headline (*MSW234*)
issue information line (*MSW234*)
justified (*MSW247*)
Justified Text button (*MSW248*)
nameplate (*MSW234*)
Paragraph command (*MSW268*)
parallel columns (*MSW245*)
printer fonts (*MSW235*)
pull-quote (*MSW266*)
rule (*MSW234*)
ruling line (*MSW234*)
run-around (*MSW234*)
screen fonts (*MSW235*)
sections (*MSW247*)
section break (*MSW247*)
Section Layout command (*MSW260*)
shadow box border (*MSW234*)
snaking columns (*MSW245*)
subhead (*MSW234*)
Symbol command (*MSW267*)
Symbol font (*MSW266*)
Text Columns button (*MSW262*)
Times New Roman (*MSW235*)
TrueType font (*MSW236*)
vertical rule (*MSW234*)
wrap-around text (*MSW234*)
zooming (*MSW265*)
Zoom Page Width button (*MSW266*)
Zoom Whole Page button (*MSW265*)

QUICK REFERENCE

In Microsoft Word you can accomplish a task in a number of ways. The following table provides a quick reference to each task presented in this project with its available options. The commands listed in the Menu column can be executed using either the keyboard or mouse.

Task	Mouse	Menu	Keyboard Shortcuts
Add Box Border to Selected Paragraphs		From Format menu, choose Border	
Add Color to Characters		From Format menu, choose Character	
Add Color to Ruling Lines		From Format menu, choose Border	
Add Ruling Lines		From Format menu, choose Border	
Add Vertical Rule Between Columns		From Format menu, choose Columns	
Change Font	Click Font box arrow on ribbon	From Format menu, choose Character	Press CTRL + F
Create Multiple Columns	Click Text Columns button on Toolbar	From Format menu, choose Columns	
Insert a Frame	Click Frame button on Toolbar	From Insert menu, choose Frame	
Insert Bullet Symbol		From Format menu, choose Symbol	
Insert Column Break		From Insert menu, choose Break	Press CTRL + SHIFT + ENTER

Task	Mouse	Menu	Keyboard Shortcuts
Insert Section Break		From Insert menu, choose Break	
Justify Text	Click Justified Text button on ribbon	From Format menu, choose Paragraph	Press CTRL + J
Remove Selected Section Break	Click the Cut button on Toolbar		Press DELETE
Shade Selected Paragraphs		From Format menu, choose Border	
Switch to Page Layout View		From View menu, choose Page Layout	
Zoom the Screen	Click desired Zoom button on Toolbar	From View menu, choose Zoom	

STUDENT ASSIGNMENTS

STUDENT ASSIGNMENT 1
True/False

Instructions: Circle T if the statement is true or F if the statement is false.

T F 1. Word for Windows provides you with all of the desktop publishing features you would find in a specialized package.

T F 2. The space between a framed object and the text that wraps around the framed object is called wrap-around text.

T F 3. The default font in Word is Arial.

T F 4. In the desktop publishing field, ruling lines, or rules, are vertical lines that separate columns.

T F 5. To shade a selected paragraph, choose the Shade command from the Format menu.

T F 6. When inserting special characters by typing their ANSI code, you must use the numeric keypad to type the code.

T F 7. Snaking columns are created with the Table button on the Toolbar.

T F 8. All Word documents have at least one section.

T F 9. Columns display side by side in the document window in normal view.

T F 10. To move a graphic between columns, you must first enclose it in a frame.

T F 11. To insert a column break, click the Text Columns button on the Toolbar.

T F 12. To view an entire page in the document window, click the Zoom Whole Page button.

T F 13. A pull-quote is a quotation mark displayed in a point size larger than 40 points.

T F 14. To change the color of characters, choose the Color command from the Format menu.

T F 15. Word provides 16 colors for characters and lines.

T F 16. Word provides 25 line styles for borders.

T F 17. When shading a paragraph, the shading begins at the left margin and stops at the paragraph mark.

T F 18. The default number of columns in a document is three.

T F 19. If you zoom a document on the screen, it will print just as it displays on the screen.

T F 20. When you place a frame around a picture, Word automatically places a border around the picture.

STUDENT ASSIGNMENT 2
Multiple Choice

Instructions: Circle the correct response.

1. In the desktop publishing field, the _____ is located at the top of a newsletter.
   a. box border
   b. nameplate
   c. wrap-around text
   d. pull-quote
2. To add ruling lines to a selected paragraph, _____.
   a. choose the Border command from the Format menu
   b. choose the Ruling Lines command from the Format menu
   c. click the ruler
   d. click the Ruler button on the Toolbar
3. To insert special characters and symbols into a document, _____.
   a. choose the Symbol command from the Insert menu
   b. hold down the ALT key and type 0 followed by the ANSI character code
   c. either a or b
   d. neither a nor b
4. Each section in a document can have its own _____.
   a. number of columns
   b. margins settings
   c. headers
   d. all of the above
5. To enclose a selected graphic or paragraph in a frame, _____.
   a. choose the Frame command from the Tools menu
   b. click the Frame button on the Toolbar
   c. choose the Border command from the Format menu
   d. none of the above
6. To display paragraphs so the left and right margins are flush, like newspaper print, click the _____ button on the ribbon.
   a. Left-Aligned Text
   b. Centered Text
   c. Right-Aligned Text
   d. Justified Text
7. To view both the left and right margins of a document in the document window, click the _____ button on the Toolbar.
   a. Zoom Whole Page
   b. Zoom 100 Percent
   c. Zoom Page Width
   d. both b and c
8. A border surrounding a paragraph that appears three-dimensional is called a _____.
   a. 3-D border
   b. box border
   c. shadow box border
   d. surrounding border
9. You can specify a zoom percentage of _____ to _____ percent magnification by choosing the Zoom command from the View menu.
   a. 10, 100
   b. 0, 1000
   c. 50, 500
   d. 25, 200
10. To add color to a selected paragraph's ruling lines, _____.
    a. choose the Color command from the Format menu
    b. choose the Border command from the Format menu
    c. choose the Ruling Lines command from the Format menu
    d. none of the above

STUDENT ASSIGNMENTS **MSW279**

STUDENT ASSIGNMENT 3
Understanding the Toolbar

Instructions: In Figure SA5-3, arrows point to several of the buttons on the Toolbar. In the space provided, briefly explain the purpose of each button.

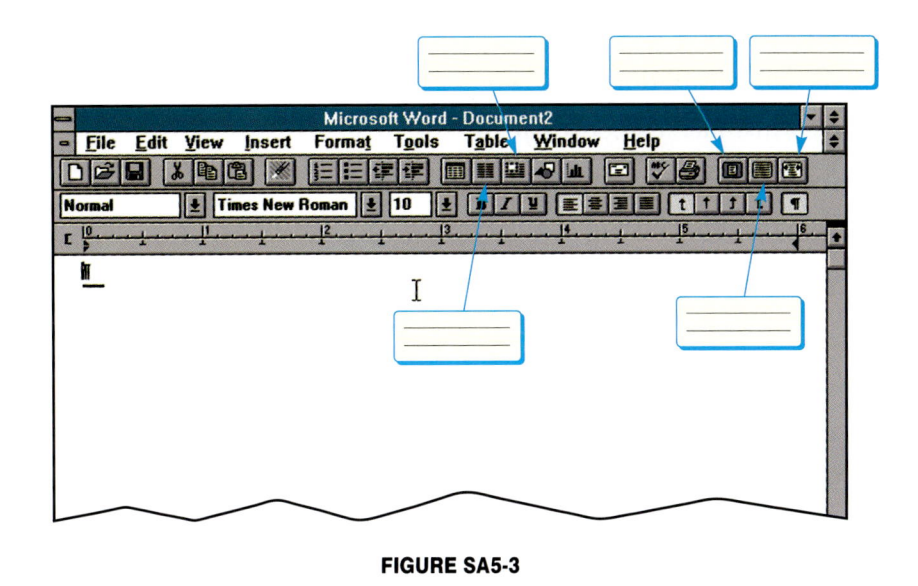

FIGURE SA5-3

STUDENT ASSIGNMENT 4
Understanding Desktop Publishing Terminology

Instructions: In the space provided, briefly define each of the desktop publishing terms listed.

TERM	DEFINITION
1. nameplate	_____
2. ruling line	_____
3. vertical rule	_____
4. issue information line	_____
5. subhead	_____
6. wrap-around text	_____
7. run-around	_____
8. box border	_____
9. shadow box border	_____
10. pull-quote	_____

STUDENT ASSIGNMENT 5
Understanding the Steps to Shade a Paragraph

Instructions: Fill in the step numbers below to correctly order the process of shading a paragraph.

Step _____: Choose the OK button in the Border Paragraphs dialog box.

Step _____: Select the paragraph.

Step _____: Choose the Shading button in the Border Paragraphs dialog box.

Step _____: From the Format menu, choose the Border command.

Step _____: Choose the OK button in the Shading dialog box.

Step _____: Select a pattern in the Shading dialog box.

STUDENT ASSIGNMENT 6
Understanding Commands in Menus

Instructions: Write the appropriate command name to accomplish each task and the menu in which each command is located.

TASK	COMMAND NAME	MENU NAME
Add Box Border	_____	_____
Add Color to Characters	_____	_____
Add Color to Ruling Lines	_____	_____
Add Ruling Lines	_____	_____
Add Vertical Rule Between Columns	_____	_____
Create Multiple Columns	_____	_____
Insert Bullet Symbol	_____	_____
Insert Column Break	_____	_____
Insert Section Break	_____	_____
Shade Selected Paragraph	_____	_____

COMPUTER LABORATORY EXERCISES

COMPUTER LABORATORY EXERCISE 1
Using the Help Menu to Learn about Word's Desktop Publishing Features

Instructions: Start Word and perform the following tasks.

1. Choose the Help Index command from the Help menu. Choose the Search button. Type `shading` and press the ENTER key. Select Shading paragraphs or table cells. Choose the Go To button. Read and print the information.
2. Choose the Back button. Choose the Search button. Type `borders: applying` and press the ENTER key. Select Applying borders to paragraphs, tables, or graphics. Choose the Go To button. Read and print the information.
3. Choose the Back button. Choose the Search button. Type `frames: adding` and press the ENTER key. Select Framing a paragraph, graphic, or table. Choose the Go To button. Read and print the information.
4. Choose the Back button. Choose the Search button. Type `columns (newspaper): creating` and press the ENTER key. Select Setting up newspaper-style columns. Choose the Go To button. Read and print the information.

COMPUTER LABORATORY EXERCISE 2
Adding Ruling Lines to a Paragraph

Instructions: Start Word. Open the document CLE5-2 from the Word subdirectory on the Student Diskette that accompanies this book. The document is shown in Figure CLE5-2. The document resembles the nameplate created in Project 5. By following the steps below, you are to add ruling lines to the title of the newsletter and print it.

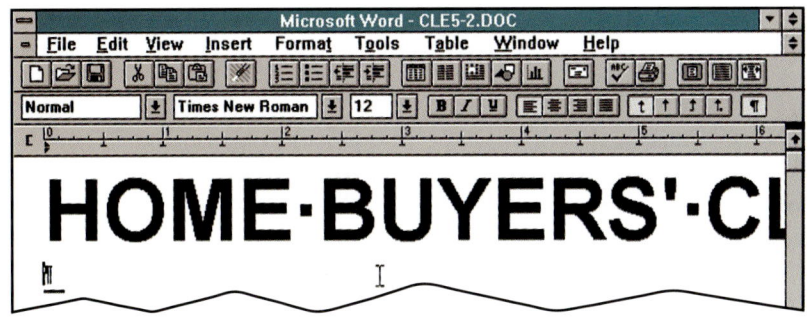

FIGURE CLE5-2

Perform the following tasks:

1. Select the newsletter title by clicking in the selection bar to the left of it.
2. From the Format menu, choose the Border command.
3. Click between the horizontal border markers above the paragraphs in the Border area of the Border Paragraphs dialog box.
4. Hold down the CTRL key while clicking between the horizontal border markers below the paragraphs in the Border area of the Border Paragraphs dialog box.
5. Click the 4.5-point border in the Line area of the Border Paragraphs dialog box.
6. Choose the OK button in the Border Paragraphs dialog box.
7. Click outside the selection to remove the highlight.
8. Print the title with ruling lines by clicking the Print button on the Toolbar.

MSW281

MSW282   PROJECT 5   CREATING A PROFESSIONAL NEWSLETTER

COMPUTER LABORATORY EXERCISE 3
Adding Color to Characters and Lines

Instructions: Start Word. Open the document CLE5-3 from the Word subdirectory on the Student Diskette that accompanies this book. The document is shown in Figure CLE5-3. The document resembles the newsletter title created in Project 5. By performing the steps below Figure CLE5-3, you are to add color to the characters and lines in the newsletter title.

FIGURE CLE5-3

Perform the following tasks:

1. Select the title of the newsletter by clicking in the selection bar to the left of it.
2. From the Format menu, choose the Character command. Click the Color box arrow in the Character dialog box and select Red. Choose the OK button in the Character dialog box.
3. From the Format menu, choose the Border command. Click the Color box arrow in the Border dialog box and select Cyan. Choose the OK button in the Border dialog box.
4. Print the nameplate with the new colors.

COMPUTER LABORATORY ASSIGNMENTS

COMPUTER LABORATORY ASSIGNMENT 1
Creating the First Page of a Newsletter

Purpose: To become familiar with creating a newsletter with desktop publishing features such as multiple columns, graphics, fonts, ruling lines, and vertical rules.

Problem: You are an associate editor of the Home Buyers' Club monthly newsletter. The September edition is due out in three weeks. You have been assigned the task of preparing the the first page of the newsletter.

Instructions:

1. Change the margins to .5 inch on all sides. (Depending on your printer, you may need different margin settings.)
2. Redefine the Normal style to a point size of 12.
3. Create page one of the newsletter shown in Figure CLA5-1. Use the following formats: a) title—Arial font, 50 point bold; b) headline—15 point bold; c) text at left margin of issue information line—14 point; d) graphic—checkmark.wmf (resized); e) subheads—14 point bold; f) all other text is 12 point.
4. Save the document with the filename CLA5-1.
5. Print the document.

FIGURE CLA5-1

HOME BUYERS' CLUB
BUYING OLD HOMES: Tips and Tricks - Part 2

Monthly Newsletter   Vol. I • No. 9 • Sep. 14, 1994

Last month's Home Buyers' Club discussed how to check a home's location, foundation, crawl space, roof, and exterior before making a purchase. This month's issue discusses the garage, electric, plumbing, heating, kitchen, baths, living areas, bedrooms, and attic.

GARAGE

If the house has a garage, check its exterior, foundation, and roof as discussed in last month's newsletter. In addition, check the door operation.

ELECTRIC

Ask the current owner the amount of voltage and ampere service coming into the house - 240 volts and 200 amp are desirable. If the owner is unsure, you may be able to check yourself. In an older house, look at the number of wires coming into the house from above. Two wires means 120 volts and three wires means 240 volts, which is usually 200 amp service. Newer houses are always wired with 240 volts.

Check in the basement for fuses or circuit breakers. Check the condition of Romex wiring or conduit. Look upstairs for the number of outlets on one circuit breaker, number of outlets in the rooms, size of the wires, condition of wires inside the walls, and so on.

PLUMBING

Plumbing can be very costly, especially in older houses. Look in the basement at whether the pipes are copper, cast-iron, or old lead. Newer homes almost always have copper.

Check all sinks for dripping (cold and hot) and leaking below cabinets. Check the toilets for leaking around the floor board. These are not costly problems to fix.

Check the bathtub and showers for leaking (cold and hot). Usually these have hidden leaks, which can be found under the floor below. In the room below, check the dry wall for signs of leaks, like water stains.

Check the water pressure. In older houses, cast iron pipes tend to rust and restrict flow. Copper pipe does not have this problem. Turn all faucets on at once, and flush the toilets. Then take note of the pressure. Low pressure could be a costly problem. Be aware that in some cases city water is restricted before coming into the house.

Continued next page...

MONTHLY MEETING

The Home Buyers' Club meeting will be held this month on Saturday, September 24 in the Banquet Room at Geeno's Surf & Turf in Bellview. Dinner will be served at 6:00 p.m.; the meeting will begin at 7:00 p.m.; and our presentation will begin at 8:00 p.m. Our guest speaker, Tim Zimmerman, will address plumbing: Does Your Water Pressure Measure Up?

ELECTIONS

During our November meeting, we will be electing new officers for our Home Buyers' Club. Officer terms run for one year. Officers meet twice a month. Member dues are waived for officers during their term. If you are interested in serving as either President, Vice President, Secretary, or Treasurer, contact Joe Deevers at (737) 555-9623 by the end of September.

NEXT MONTH...

Next month's issue of Home Buyers' Club will cover renting houses for profit. Topics covered will include taxes, insurance, tenants, landlord responsibilities, revenues and expenses, and maintenance.

MSW283

MSW284   PROJECT 5   CREATING A PROFESSIONAL NEWSLETTER

COMPUTER LABORATORY ASSIGNMENT 2
Creating the Second Page of a Newsletter

Purpose: To become familiar with creating a newsletter with desktop publishing features such as multiple columns, graphics, fonts, ruling lines, and vertical rules.

Problem: You are an associate editor of the Home Buyers' Club monthly newsletter. The October edition is due out in three weeks. You have been assigned the task of preparing the the second page of the newsletter.

Instructions:

1. Open the file CLA5-1 from your data disk.
2. Save it with the filename CLA5-2.
3. Create page two of the newsletter shown in Figure CLA5-2. Use the following formats: a) Home Buyers' Club in nameplate—19 point; b) headline—15 point bold; c) subheads—14 point bold; d) all other text is 12 point.
4. Save the document again.
5. Print the document.

Sep. 14, 1994   **Home Buyers' Club**   2

BUYING OLD HOMES: Tips and Tricks - Part 2   (Continued...)

PLUMBING (Cont'd)

Check the hot water heater by turning on the hot water in the kitchen. Note the time it takes to turn hot and its temperature. Ask the owner the age of the hot water heater. Life expectancy of hot water heaters is 15 years; copper lined tanks last 20 years.

If you are looking at a country home, check the type of well and pump. Older homes have old wells. Have the water checked and the condition of the well. New wells are costly.

HEATING

Gas and electric forced air heat are the most common and are very good. Check for their age, duct work, and the number of supplies throughout the house. Turn the unit on and check its operation. These units are also good for central air conditioning because they adapt directly to it.

Hot water baseboard heat is another good, clean way to heat a home; but it can cause water leaks, takes up space along walls, is slow for recovery, and cannot accommodate central air conditioning. Stay away from old gravity-fed furnaces. In older houses, count on replacing this type of furnace.

Floor electric heaters and electric baseboard heaters are usually found in additions and are dangerous. They are not recommended and could be costly to add on to the regular heating system.

KITCHEN

In a kitchen, you should check the cabinets for door operation, space, etc. Count the number of outlets. See if there is enough light from the light fixtures. If appliances are included, be sure they work. Check if exhaust fan is vented outside. Check if the sink is chipped, scratched, or cracked. If the sink has a garbage disposal, be sure it works.

BATHROOM

Bathrooms can be very costly to redo and/or recondition. Check if fixtures are modern or are chipped and cracked. Check if walls are solid, not rotted. If tiled, check the condition of the grout. Bad grout can be expensive to repair.

LIVING AREAS & BEDROOM

Check for insulation in walls by taking a light switch cover off of an inside wall. Look at the insulation with a flashlight. If no sign of insulation, the outside wall usually must be removed, which is costly.

Check all doors for operation, not sticking or scraping the floor. These are easy and inexpensive to repair.

Jump up and down on the floors. They will squeak if loose. If joists are properly built, squeaking is caused from the house settling and can be easily fixed. If the walls shake and the floor acts like a spring, floor joists are poorly built; this house should be avoided.

Look for moisture, especially in the ceiling area. It could be caused from a leaking roof or a bathroom above.

Check hardwood floors for scratching. This can be costly to repair. Check walls for paint, wall paper, or paneling condition.

Make sure all switches and lights work. Check for lights in closets.

ATTIC

Check that the attic is insulated properly with at least 10 inches thick of insulation. Check for water leaks with a flashlight. When dry, you will see where water has been running down. Check for proper ventilation: vents at soffit (where the roof meets the house) and the top roof ridge. Rafters should be contructed in this area with 2 x 6 boards 16 inches apart and cross braced. Older homes and some pre-fab houses are usually not cross braced.

This concludes Buying Old Homes: Tips and Tricks. The checks presented in this article are designed to save you time and money before your purchase. If you are in doubt, have your chosen house checked by a professional before you sign a contract.

FIGURE CLA5-2

COMPUTER LABORATORY ASSIGNMENT 3
Creating a Newsletter

Purpose: To become familiar with creating a newsletter with desktop publishing features such as multiple columns, graphics, fonts, ruling lines, and vertical rules.

Problem: As senior marketing representative for All-Aboard Cruiselines, you send a monthly newsletter to all people signed up for a cruise with your organization. These newsletters are designed to inform the upcoming passengers of ship procedures, policies, and so on. The subject of this month's newsletter is What To Pack.

Instructions:

1. Change the margins to .5 inch on all sides. (Depending on your printer, you may need different margin settings.)
2. Redefine the Normal style to a point size of 12.
3. Create page one of the newsletter shown in Figure CLA5-3. Use the following formats: a) title—Arial font, 39 point bold; b) text at left margin of issue information line—14 point; c) headlines—bold; d) subheads—14 point bold; e) graphic—yacht.wmf; f) pull-quote—16 point bold; g) shadow box text—14 point bold; h) all other text is 12 point.
4. Save the document with the filename CLA5-3.
5. Print the document.

FIGURE CLA5-3

COMPUTER LABORATORY ASSIGNMENT 4
Designing and Creating a Newsletter

Purpose: To provide practice in planning, designing, and creating a newsletter.

Problem: You work in the Media Services department for your school. You have been assigned the task of designing a newsletter to be sent to all houses in a 30-miles radius of the school. The newsletter is to inform the community of the campus, its people, and its events.

Instructions: Design a two-page newsletter for your school. Use all of the desktop publishing features presented in this project. Be sure the colors and graphics work well together.

Index

Add button, MSW184
Add Rule, MSW211–212
Add to Label, MSW215–217
Alignment
  justified text, MSW247–248
  tabs stops, MSW138–139
  text in tables, MSW146–148
  wordwrap, **MSW15**
Alphabetization, MSW78, MSW82–84
Alphanumeric type, MSW84
ANSI characters, MSW244
Arial font, MSW235, MSW236
Ascending sort order, MSW83, **MSW84**
At Least option, MSW60
Attach Data File, MSW183, MSW215
Author references, MSW56, MSW78–79
Automatic page breaks, **MSW75**
Avery mailing label sheets, MSW214

Background repagination, MSW75
BACKSPACE key, MSW10, MSW38
Banner, **MSW234**
Bibliographical list, MSW56, MSW78
Blank lines, MSW11–12
Block style letter, MSW190
Bold, MSW24–25, MSW26–27, MSW135
Border
  box, **MSW234**, MSW256–257, MSW270, MSW274
  color, MSW274
  line styles, MSW238
  paragraph, MSW256–257, MSW269
  ruling lines, MSW237–239
  shadow box, **MSW234**, MSW270
Border command, MSW237, MSW257, MSW269, MSW272
Border markers, **MSW237**–238
Border Paragraphs dialog box, MSW237, MSW257, MSW270, MSW272–273
Box border, **MSW234**, MSW256–257, MSW270
  color, MSW274
Break, MSW79–80, MSW129, MSW254, MSW262
Brochures, MSW231
Bullet, **MSW157**–158, **MSW242**–243
Bulleted List button, MSW158

Calculate
  column sums, MSW151–152
  row sums, MSW149–151
CAPS indicator, MSW10–11
Cell, **MSW140**
  end-of-cell mark, **MSW143**, MSW147
  selection bar, **MSW146**
Center button, MSW23
Centered Tab, MSW136
Centered Text, MSW68, MSW80
Centering, MSW21, MSW23
  end-of-cell mark, MSW147
  paragraph, MSW67–68
  title, MSW80
Change button, MSW30
Character, MSW127, MSW271–272, MSW274
Character formatting, **MSW21**. *See also specific formats*
Character spacing, MSW126–128
Character type, MSW8. *See also* Font

Charts, MSW155–157
Chart window, **MSW154**–155
Clear All Rules, MSW212
Clipart subdirectory, MSW118
Clipboard, **MSW88**, MSW90–91
  calculation results, MSW149–150
Close button, MSW65
Closing and starting over, MSW39
Color, MSW271–274
Column(s), MSW140, MSW141
  adding to table, MSW152–153
  deleting, MSW153, MSW261
  multiple column format, MSW245–246
  page layout view, MSW250
  parallel, **MSW245**
  single column formatting, MSW262–263
  snaking, **MSW245**
  spacing, MSW144–145
  summing, MSW151–152
  titles, MSW146
  vertical rule separation, MSW258–261
  width adjustment, MSW186–187
Column break, **MSW254**, MSW260
Column markers, **MSW144**
Columns dialog box, MSW245, MSW259
Column selection bar, **MSW151**
Condition, **MSW199**–200
Context sensitive help, MSW39
Copy button, MSW91
Corrections, *see* Error correction
Create Data File, MSW183–186
CTRL + HOME, MSW18
Current date, MSW66, MSW193–195
Current Time, MSW66
Cursor, *see* Insertion point
Custom tab settings, MSW135–137
Cut and paste, **MSW88**, MSW89–90
Cut button, **MSW80**, MSW90

Database Management Tools, **MSW188**
Data file, MSW179, **MSW181**
  adding data records, MSW187–188
  column width adjustments, MSW186–187
  creating, MSW181–186
  field specification, MSW182
  mailing labels, MSW213, MSW215–217
  merging and printing, MSW208–212
  switching to main document, MSW188–189
  Toolbar features, MSW188-189
Data records, **MSW181**
  adding to data file, MSW187–188
  selective printing, MSW210–212
Datasheet window, **MSW154**–155
Date, MSW66, MSW193–195
Decimal tabs, MSW138–139
Default
  color, MSW271
  field code display, MSW205
  fonts, MSW8, **MSW235**
  margin settings, MSW57
  Normal style redefinition, MSW61–62, MSW234–235
  paper size, MSW6
  sort settings, MSW84
  tab setting, MSW12, MSW135
DELETE key, MSW38
Deletion, MSW36, MSW38
  BACKSPACE key, MSW10, MSW38

columns, MSW261
  field names, MSW186
  hard page breaks, MSW80
  rows or columns, MSW153
Descending sort order, **MSW84**
Desktop publishing
  software, **MSW231**
  terminology, MSW234
Disk drive, MSW19, MSW35
doc extension, MSW20
Document
  closing and starting over, MSW39
  insertion into existing document, MSW129–132
  opening, MSW35–36
  printing, MSW32–33. *See also* Printing
  reduced and magnified views, MSW265–266
  saving, MSW18–19, MSW31, MSW69
Documentation styles, MSW54–56
Document template, **MSW190**
Document window, **MSW5, MSW6**
  document length limitations, MSW17–18
Dot Matrix button, MSW214
Double-spacing, MSW59–60
Drag and drop, **MSW88**–90
Draw, **MSW118**
Drives drop-down list, MSW19, MSW35, MSW130

End mark, **MSW5**
Endnote, **MSW71**
End-of-cell mark, **MSW143**, MSW147
End-of-row mark, **MSW143**
Entering text, MSW10–11, MSW121
  blank lines, MSW11–12
  custom tab stops, MSW137
  in tables, MSW148–149
ENTER key
  blank line insertion, MSW11–12
  double spacing, MSW67
  first-line indent, MSW70
  new paragraph creation, MSW11
  nonprinting character, MSW14, MSW15, MSW57
Equal (=), MSW200
Error correction, MSW36
  using BACKSPACE, MSW10, MSW38
  form letter main document, MSW203
  spell checker, **MSW29**–31, MSW84
Exactly, MSW60
Exit, MSW34–35
Exit and Return, MSW155–156
Exp, MSW200, MSW202
Expanded spacing, MSW128
Explanatory notes, **MSW56**, MSW71–74
Expression, MSW199–200

F1, MSW39, MSW40
F9, MSW195
Field(s), **MSW182**
  IF field, **MSW199**–202
  merge fields, **MSW195**–198
  names, **MSW182**, MSW185–186
Field codes, MSW65
  displaying, MSW205–206
  printing, MSW207–208
File, MSW130
File Name, MSW18–19, MSW131

Find
 and replace, MSW86–88
 specific page or footnote, MSW88
 text, MSW88
Find File, MSW130–131, MSW132
Find Next button, MSW87–88
First-line indent, **MSW69**–71
 and centering text, MSW80
Font, **MSW8**, **MSW235**
 default, MSW8
 newsletter nameplate, MSW235–236
 printer, **MSW235**
 screen, **MSW235**
Footer, **MSW63**
Footnote, **MSW71**–74, MSW76
 dialog box, MSW72, MSW76
 finding, MSW88
 MLA style, MSW565
 pane, **MSW72**
 reference mark, **MSW71**
 separator, **MSW77**
 text, **MSW71**
 viewing, MSW74, MSW76–78
Format menu, MSW259
Formatting, MSW21–28. *See also* Character formatting; Paragraph formatting
Form letter, MSW179
 closing line, MSW202
 conditional printing (IF field), **MSW199**–202
 current date, MSW193–195
 data file creation, MSW181–189
 document preparation steps, MSW181
 error checking, MSW203
 inside address lines, MSW197
 letterhead, MSW190–193
 main document, MSW190–203
 merging, MSW179–181, MSW208–212
 printing, MSW204–205, MSW208–212
 salutation line, MSW197–198
Frame, **MSW251**, MSW252–253, MSW268–269

Graph button, MSW153–154
Graphics
 importing, MSW118–123, MSW126
 positioning, MSW251–253
 pull-quotes, **MSW266**–269
 scaling, **MSW123**–125
 table charting, MSW153–156
 viewing, MSW119–120
Greater than, (>), MSW200
Greater than or equal to (> =), MSW200
Gridlines, **MSW143**

Handles, **MSW123**, MSW125, **MSW155**, MSW251, MSW252
Hanging indent, **MSW81**–82
Hard copy, **MSW32**
Hard page break, **MSW79**–80, MSW129
Header, **MSW63**
 letterhead, MSW190–192
 page numbering with, MSW62–66
 viewing, MSW77
Header/Footer, MSW63, MSW191
Header pane, **MSW64**, MSW192
Header records, MSW181, **MSW182**, MSW186
Heading, MSW234
Headline, **MSW234**, MSW239–241
 color, MSW273
Help, **MSW39**–40
Highlight, MSW23–24

IF field, **MSW199**
 displaying field codes, MSW205–206
 inserting into main document, MSW200–202
 printing field codes, MSW206–208
If...Then, **MSW199**
If...Then...Else, **MSW199**, MSW200
Ignore All, MSW30
Import graphics, **MSW118**–123, MSW126
Indentation, MSW8, MSW21, MSW69–71
 centered text and, MSW80
 first-line, **MSW69**–71, MSW80
 footnotes, MSW73
 hanging indent, **MSW81**–82
Insert
 ANSI characters, MSW244
 documents, MSW129–132
 empty tables, MSW141–143
 hard page break, MSW129
 key, MSW38
 letterhead, MSW193
 mode, **MSW38**
 text, MSW37–38
Insert button, MSW131
Insert Columns command, **MSW153**
Insertion point, **MSW5**, MSW10
 repositioning, MSW29, MSW37–38
Insert Merge Field, MSW195–198, MSW200
Insert Rows command, **MSW153**
Issue information line, **MSW234**, MSW242–244, MSW273
Italic button, MSW28, MSW254

Justified text, **MSW247**–248

Label(s), *see* Mailing labels
Label sizes, MSW214
Laser button, MSW214
Layout Mailing Labels, MSW215–217
Less than (<), MSW200
Less than or equal to (< =), MSW200
Letterhead, MSW190–193
Line spacing, MSW59–60, MSW158

Mailing labels, MSW179, MSW213–218
 data file, MSW213, MSW215–217
 printing, MSW218–219
Main document, **MSW181**, MSW190
 error checking, MSW203
 field codes, MSW206–208
 letterhead insertion, MSW193
 merging and printing, MSW208–212
 printing without merging, MSW204–208
 switching from data file, MSW188–189
Main Document tools, **MSW188**–189
Margins, MSW8
 changing default, MSW57–58, MSW234–235
 MLA style, MSW56, MSW57–58
 viewing using Zoom feature, MSW265, MSW266
 wordwrap, **MSW15**
Mathematical operator, MSW200
Memorandum, MSW2
 document preparation steps, MSW4
 formatting, MSW21–28
Menu bar, **MSW7**
Merge button, MSW210–211
Merge field, **MSW195**–198
MERGEFIELD, MSW206
Merging, MSW179–181, MSW208–212
Metafiles, **MSW118**
Microsoft Draw, **MSW118**

Microsoft Graph, **MSW153**–156
Microsoft Word, *see* Word
Microsoft Word dialog box, MSW62, MSW203
MLA style of documentation, **MSW54**–56
Modern Language Association (MLA), **MSW54**–56
Modifying text, MSW36
Mouse pointer, **MSW5**–6
Multarw1.wmf, MSW122
Multiple Labels, MSW214–215

Nameplate, **MSW234**, MSW262–264
 borders, MSW237–239
 color, MSW271
 font and point size, MSW235–236
 headline, MSW239–241
 issue information line, MSW242–244
Naming
 fields, MSW182, MSW185–186
 saved documents, MSW31, MSW132–133
New, MSW190, MSW213
Newsletter, MSW231–233
 color enhancement, MSW271–274
 document preparation steps, MSW234
 first page, MSW244–261
 graphics, MSW251–253
 issue information line, MSW242–244
 nameplate, MSW235–244, MSW262–264
 pull-quotes, **MSW266**–269
 second page, MSW262–270
 subheads, MSW247–249
Nonprinting characters, **MSW14**
 general display of, MSW14–15, MSW57
 selective display, MSW91
Normal style, redefining, **MSW61**–62, MSW116, MSW234–235
Normal view, **MSW66**, MSW79
Null expression (" "), MSW200
Numbered List button, MSW159
Numeric keypad, MSW244

Online Help, **MSW39**–40
Online tutorial, **MSW40**–41
Only Check for Errors, MSW203
Op, MSW200, MSW201
Opening document, MSW35–36
Overtype mode, **MSW38**

Page(s), finding, MSW88
Page breaks
 automatic (soft), MSW75
 hard, **MSW79**–80, MSW129
PAGE DOWN, MSW18
Page Layout, MSW77
Page layout view, MSW74, **MSW76**–78, MSW93
 column display, MSW250
Page Number button, MSW65
Page numbering, MSW62
 headers, MSW62–66
 MLA style, MSW56
Page Setup, MSW58, MSW235
PAGE UP, MSW18
Paper size, default mode, MSW6
Paragraph
 borders, MSW239, MSW256–257, MSW270
 centering, MSW21, MSW23, MSW67–68
 ENTER key and, MSW11
 formatting, **MSW21**, MSW23
 frames, MSW269
 graphics, MSW120
 indenting, MSW69–71

INDEX

shading, MSW239–241
sorting, **MSW82–84**
Paragraph command, MSW59, MSW64
Paragraph dialog box, MSW59, MSW64, MSW158, MSW268–269
Paragraph mark, MSW14–15
Parallel columns, **MSW245**
Parenthetical citations, **MSW56**
Paste, MSW90–91, MSW150
Pattern box arrow, MSW240
Picture command, MSW118, MSW123–124, MSW191, MSW252
Points box arrow, MSW9, MSW25, MSW62
Point size, **MSW8**–9
 changing, MSW25, MSW62
 default, MSW8
 desktop publisher recommendations, MSW234
 newsletter nameplate, MSW235–236
Preview, **MSW93–94**, MSW119–120, **MSW130**, MSW132
Print button, MSW7, MSW32, MSW204
Print dialog box, MSW94, MSW206, MSW208, MSW209
Printer type selection, MSW214
Printing, MSW32–33, MSW133
 field codes, MSW206–208
 form letter main document, MSW204–208
 Help information, MSW40
 mailing labels, MSW218–219
 merged document, MSW208–212
 selected data records, MSW210–212
Print Merge, MSW183, MSW210–212
Print merge bar, **MSW189**
Print Merge Fields list box, MSW195–196
Printout, **MSW32**
Print preview, **MSW93–94**, MSW261
Print topic command, MSW40
Proposal, MSW112–115
 document preparation steps, MSW116
 printing, MSW133
 saving, MSW132–133
 title page, MSW117–129
Pull-quotes, **MSW266**–269
 color, MSW274

Quitting Word, MSW34–35
Quotation marks, MSW200, MSW266, MSW267

Record(s), **MSW181**
 data, **MSW181**, MSW187–188, MSW210–212
 header, **MSW182**, MSW186
Record Management Tools, **MSW188**
Record Selection button, MSW211
Record selection rule, **MSW210**–212
References, MSW56
Replace, MSW86–88
Replace All, MSW87
Reports, MSW54–55
Research paper, MSW54–55
 document preparation steps, MSW56
 footnotes, **MSW71**–74
 page numbering, MSW62–66
 revisions, MSW86–91
 saving, MSW69
 works cited page, MSW78–79
Ribbon, MSW7, **MSW8**
Right-aligned text, **MSW63**, MSW65
Rows, MSW140, **MSW141**
 adding to table, MSW152–153
 in data file, MSW181
 deleting, MSW153

end-of-row mark, **MSW143**
summing, MSW149–151
Row selection bar, **MSW151**
Ruler, MSW7, **MSW8**
 custom tab settings, MSW136
 first-line indent marker, MSW69
 table columns, MSW144
Rules, **MSW234**
Ruling lines, **MSW234**, MSW237–239
 vertical between columns, MSW258–261
Run-around, **MSW234**, MSW253
Running.wmf, MSW118

Salutation line, MSW197–198
Save As, MSW18, MSW133, MSW192
Save button, MSW18, MSW31
Saving, MSW69
 existing document, MSW31
 new documents, MSW18–19
 new filename, MSW132–133
 and quitting Word, MSW34
 title page, MSW128
Scale, **MSW123**–125
Screen, **MSW5**
Scroll bars, **MSW6**
Scroll box, **MSW6**, MSW18
Scrolling, **MSW17**–18
Section, **MSW247**
Section break, **MSW247**, MSW262
Section Layout, MSW259–260
Select, **MSW23**
Selection bar, **MSW6**, MSW61
Shading, MSW239–241, MSW257
Shadow box border, **MSW234**, MSW270
Show/Hide Nonprinting Characters, MSW14–15, MSW57, MSW91
Sizing handles, **MSW123**, MSW125, **MSW155**, MSW251, MSW252
Snaking columns, **MSW245**
Soft page breaks, **MSW75**
Sorting, **MSW82**–84
SPACEBAR, nonprinting character, MSW14, MSW15, MSW57
Spacing
 between characters, MSW126–128
 lines, MSW159
 table columns, MSW144–145
Spell checker, **MSW29**–31, MSW84
Starting Word, MSW4–5, MSW57
Status bar, **MSW8**
Student diskette, MSW130
Style redefinition, MSW61–62, MSW116, MSW234–235
Subhead, **MSW234**, MSW247–249
 color, MSW274
Summary Info dialog box, MSW20
Summing columns, MSW151–152
Summing rows, MSW149–151
Superscripts, **MSW56**, MSW72
Symbol command, MSW242–243, MSW266, MSW267
Synonyms, **MSW91**

Tab, MSW12–14, MSW137
 changing alignment, MSW138–139
 custom settings for tables, MSW135–137
 default, MSW12, MSW135
 entering text with, MSW137
 nonprinting character, MSW14, MSW15, MSW57, MSW137
Table(s), **MSW140**
 adding new rows or columns, MSW152–153

calculations, MSW149–152
charting, MSW153–156
custom tab settings, MSW135–137
data files as, MSW181, MSW187
deleting rows or columns, MSW153
entering text in, MSW148–149
inserting, MSW141–143
shading, MSW239
text alignment, MSW146–148
titles, MSW140, MSW157
See also Column(s); Rows
Table button grid, MSW142
Template
 document, **MSW190**
 mailing labels, MSW213
Text areas, **MSW5**
Text Columns, MSW262
Thesaurus, **MSW91**–92
Time, MSW66
Times New Roman font, MSW8
Title
 centering, MSW80
 for charts, MSW157
 color, MSW271
 newsletter nameplate, **MSW234**, MSW235–241
 table, MSW140
 table columns, MSW146
Title page
 character spacing, MSW126–128
 first line, MSW117
 graphics, MSW118–120, MSW121–125, MSW126
 MLA style, MSW56
 saving, MSW128
 text, MSW117, MSW121, MSW125
Toolbar, **MSW7**
True Type fonts, **MSW236**
Tutorial, **MSW40**–41
Two Pages button, MSW93
Type style, MSW235

Underline, MSW8, MSW24, MSW26, MSW73, MSW135
Undo, MSW39
 replacements, MSW88
 sort, MSW84
Update Field key, MSW195
Use Template text box, MSW213

Vertical rule, **MSW234**, MSW258–259
Vichouse.wmf, MSW252
Victorian house graphic, MSW251–253
View, MSW77, MSW250

Windows Metafiles, **MSW118**–119
wmf extension, MSW118
Word, MSW2
 document window, **MSW5**
 quitting, MSW34–35
 screen, MSW5
 starting, MSW4–5, MSW57
Word processing program, MSW2
WORD subdirectory, MSW130
Wordwrap, **MSW15**–16
Workplace, MSW5
Works cited page, MSW56, MSW78–79
Wrap-around text, **MSW234**, MSW253

Zooming, **MSW265**–266
Zoom Page Width button, MSW266
Zoom Whole Page button, MSW265

SPREADSHEETS
USING MICROSOFT EXCEL 4 FOR WINDOWS

▶ PROJECT ONE
BUILDING A WORKSHEET
Objectives **E2**
What Is Excel? **E2**
Project One **E3**
Starting Excel **E4**
The Worksheet **E5**
Selecting a Cell **E8**
Entering Text **E8**
Entering Numbers **E13**
Calculating a Sum **E15**
Using the Fill Handle to Copy a Cell to Adjacent Cells **E17**
Formatting the Worksheet **E22**
Using Autoformat to Format the Worksheet **E25**
Adding a Chart to the Worksheet **E28**
Saving the Worksheet **E31**
Printing the Worksheet **E35**
Exiting Excel **E37**
Opening a Worksheet **E38**
Correcting Errors **E39**
Excel Help Facility **E42**
Planning a Worksheet **E44**
Project Summary **E45**
Key Terms **E45**
Quick Reference **E46**
Student Assignments **E47**
Computer Laboratory Exercises **E51**
Computer Laboratory Assignments **E53**

▶ PROJECT TWO
ADDING FORMULAS TO A WORKSHEET
Objectives **E57**
Introduction **E57**
Project Two **E57**
Entering the Titles and Numbers into the Worksheet **E58**
Entering Formulas **E59**
Entering Formulas Using Point Mode **E62**
Summing Column Totals **E64**
Calculating an Average **E66**
Saving an Intermediate Copy of the Worksheet **E69**
Formatting Text and Drawing Borders **E69**
Formatting Numbers **E75**
Changing the Font in the Worksheet **E80**
Changing the Widths of Columns and Heights of Rows **E82**
Saving the Worksheet a Second Time Using the Same File Name **E88**
Previewing and Printing the Worksheet **E88**
Printing a Section of the Worksheet **E90**
Displaying and Printing the Formulas in the Worksheet **E92**
Project Summary **E95**
Key Terms **E95**
Quick Reference **E96**
Student Assignments **E97**
Computer Laboratory Exercises **E102**
Computer Laboratory Assignments **E104**

▶ PROJECT THREE
ENHANCING A WORKSHEET AND DRAWING CHARTS
Objectives **E109**
Introduction **E109**
Project Three **E109**
Deleting and Inserting Cells in a Worksheet **E112**
Adding and Changing Data in the Worksheet **E115**
Moving Cells **E117**
The MAX and MIN Functions **E120**
Copying a Cell's Format **E124**
Entering Numbers with a Format Symbol **E127**
Wrapping Text in a Cell **E128**
Making Decisions—The IF Function **E130**
Recentering the Worksheet Title **E134**
Adding Color to a Worksheet **E134**
Saving a Worksheet Under a Different File Name **E140**
Adding a Pie Chart to the Worksheet **E141**
Enhancing the Pie Chart **E146**
Switching Windows **E155**
Hiding the Pie Chart **E156**
Printing the Pie Chart Separately from the Worksheet **E158**
The Gallery and Chart Menus **E160**
Project Summary **E161**
Key Terms **E161**
Quick Reference **E162**
Student Assignments **E163**
Computer Laboratory Exercises **E167**
Computer Laboratory Assignments **E169**

▶ PROJECT FOUR
WORKING WITH LARGE WORKSHEETS
Objectives **E175**
Introduction **E175**
Project Four **E176**
Using the Fill Handle to Create a Series **E178**
Entering the Row Titles and Increasing the Column Widths **E179**
Copying a Range of Cells to a Nonadjacent Paste Area **E180**
Entering the Revenue Data and Using the Formatting Toolbar **E183**
Freezing Worksheet Titles **E187**
Entering and Copying the Expense Formulas and Totals **E188**
Hiding a Toolbar **E192**
Formatting the Worksheet, Column, and Row Titles **E193**
Formatting the Budget % Expenses Table **E196**
Adding Comments to a Worksheet **E198**
Displaying and Docking the Utility Toolbar **E200**
Checking Spelling **E201**
Printing the Worksheet with Print Titles **E203**
Moving Around the Worksheet **E206**
Changing the View of the Worksheet **E206**
Outlining a Worksheet **E210**
Changing Values in Cells that Are Referenced in a Formula **E218**
Project Summary **E220**
Key Terms **E220**
Quick Reference **E221**
Toolbar Reference **E222**
Student Assignments **E223**
Computer Laboratory Exercises **E226**
Computer Laboratory Assignments **E228**

▶ PROJECT FIVE
ANALYZING WORKSHEET DATA
Objectives **E233**
Introduction **E233**
Project Five **E234**
Creating Names Based on Row Titles **E240**
Determining the Monthly Payment **E243**
Determining the Total Interest and Total Cost **E245**
Using a Data Table to Analyze Worksheet Data **E246**
Entering New Loan Data **E253**
Building a Command Macro to Automate Loan Data Entry **E254**
Adding a Button to the Worksheet to Play Back a Command Macro **E260**
Playing Back the Command Macro **E263**
Goal Seeking to Determine the Down Payment for a Specific Monthly Payment **E265**
Using Scenario Manager to Analyze Data **E267**
Protecting the Worksheet **E271**
Project Summary **E273**
Key Terms **E273**
Quick Reference **E274**
Student Assignments **E274**
Computer Laboratory Exercises **E279**
Computer Laboratory Assignments **E282**

▶ PROJECT SIX
SORTING AND QUERYING A WORKSHEET DATABASE
Objectives **E288**
Introduction **E288**
Project Six **E289**
Creating a Database **E290**
Sorting a Database **E296**
Finding Records that Pass the Comparison Criteria Using a Data Form **E300**
Creating a Criteria Range on the Worksheet **E303**
Finding Records **E305**
Extracting Records **E306**
Deleting Records **E309**
More About Comparison Criteria **E309**
Using Database Functions **E310**
Using the Crosstab ReportWizard to Summarize Database Information **E312**
Project Summary **E317**
Key Terms **E317**
Quick Reference **E318**
Student Assignments **E318**
Computer Laboratory Exercises **E323**
Computer Laboratory Assignments **E326**

INDEX E331

Microsoft Excel 4 for Windows

PROJECT ONE

BUILDING A WORKSHEET

OBJECTIVES You will have mastered the material in this project when you can:

- Start Excel
- Describe the Excel worksheet
- Select a cell or range of cells
- Enter text and numbers
- Use the AutoSum tool to sum a range of cells
- Copy a cell to a range of cells using the fill handle
- Increase the size and decrease the size of the font in a cell
- Bold entries on a worksheet
- Center cell contents over a series of columns
- Apply the AutoFormat command to format a range
- Create a column chart using the ChartWizard
- Save a worksheet
- Print a worksheet
- Open a worksheet
- Exit Excel
- Correct errors on a worksheet
- Use the Excel Help facility
- Use the Excel tutorial
- Planning a worksheet

▶ WHAT IS EXCEL?

Excel is a spreadsheet program that allows you to organize data, complete calculations, make decisions, graph data, and develop professional looking reports. The three major parts of Excel are:

- ▶ *Worksheets* Worksheets allow you to enter, calculate, manipulate, and analyze data such as numbers and text.
- ▶ *Charts* Charts pictorially represent data. Excel can draw two-dimensional and three-dimensional column charts, pie charts, and other types of charts.
- ▶ *Databases* Databases manage data. For example, once you enter data onto a worksheet, Excel can sort the data, search for specific data, and select data that meets a criteria.

▶ Project One

To illustrate the features of Microsoft Excel, this book presents a series of projects that use Excel to solve typical business problems. Project 1 uses Excel to produce the worksheet and column chart shown in Figure 1-1.

The worksheet contains a company's monthly office expenses (rent, utilities, and supplies) for three locations — Seattle, Atlanta, and Boston. The worksheet also includes expense totals for each city, each type of expense, and a total of all expenses. Excel calculates the totals by summing the appropriate numbers.

Beneath the worksheet, Excel displays a column chart that it easily creates from the data contained in the worksheet. The **column chart** compares the expenses for each of the three cities. For example, you can see from the column chart that the greatest expense in all three cities is rent.

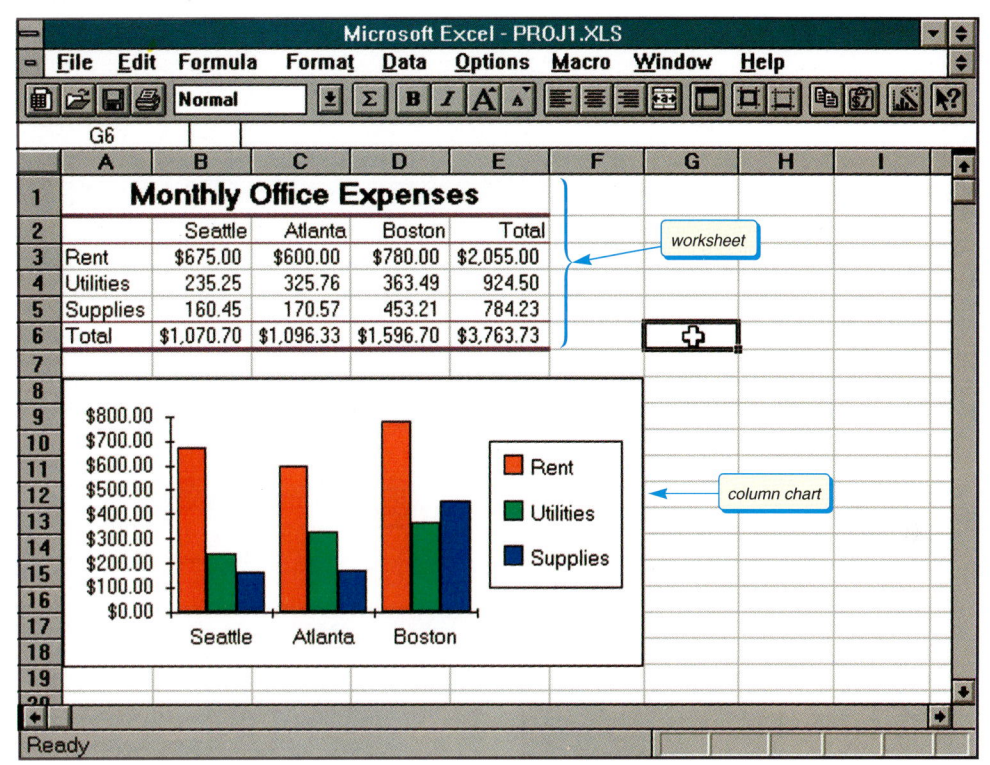

FIGURE 1-1

Worksheet Preparation Steps

The worksheet preparation steps give you an overview of how the worksheet and chart in Figure 1-1 will be built in this project. If you are building the worksheet and chart in this project on a personal computer, read these ten steps without doing them.

1. Start the Excel program.
2. Enter the worksheet title (Monthly Office Expenses), the column titles (Seattle, Atlanta, Boston, and Total), and the row titles (Rent, Utilities, Supplies, and Total).
3. Enter the monthly office expenses (rent, utilities, and supplies) for Seattle, Atlanta, and Boston.
4. Use the SUM function to calculate the monthly expense totals for each city, for each type of expense, and for all the expenses.
5. Format the worksheet title (center it across the five columns, enlarge it, and make it bold).
6. Format the body of the worksheet (add underlines, display the numbers in dollars and cents, and add dollar signs).
7. Direct Excel to create the chart.
8. Save the worksheet and chart on disk.
9. Print the worksheet and chart.
10. Quit Excel.

The following pages contain a detailed explanation of each of these steps.

▶ Starting Excel

To start Excel, the Windows Program Manager must appear on the screen and the Microsoft Excel 4.0 group window must be open. To accomplish these tasks, use the procedures presented earlier in *Introduction to Windows*. Perform the following steps to start Excel.

TO START EXCEL ▼

STEP 1 ▶

Use the mouse to point to the Microsoft Excel program-item icon in the Microsoft Excel 4.0 group window (Figure 1-2).

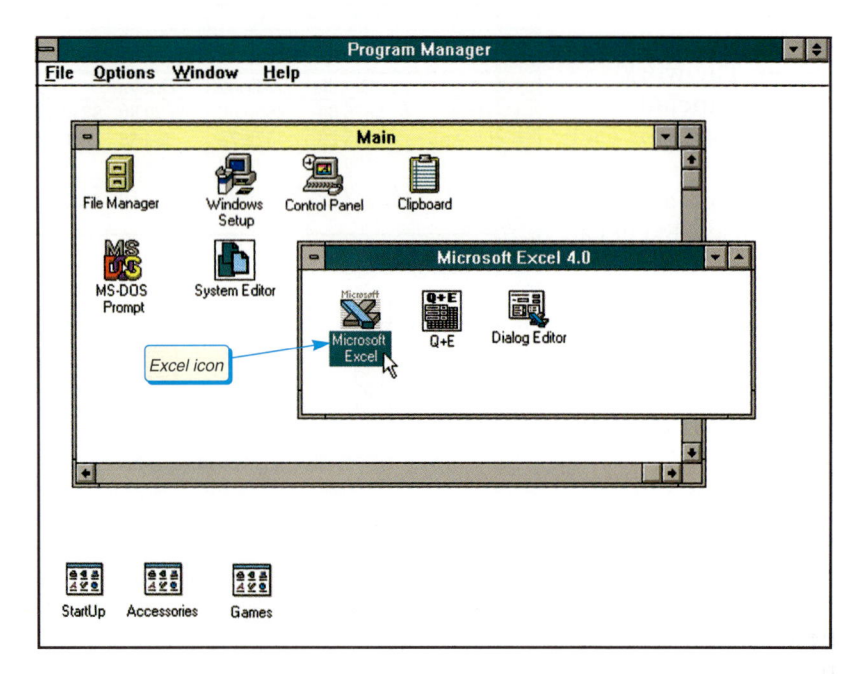

FIGURE 1-2

STEP 2

Double-click the left mouse button.

Excel displays an empty worksheet titled Sheet1 (Figure 1-3).

STEP 3 ▶

Point to the Sheet1 Maximize button (▲) (Figure 1-3).

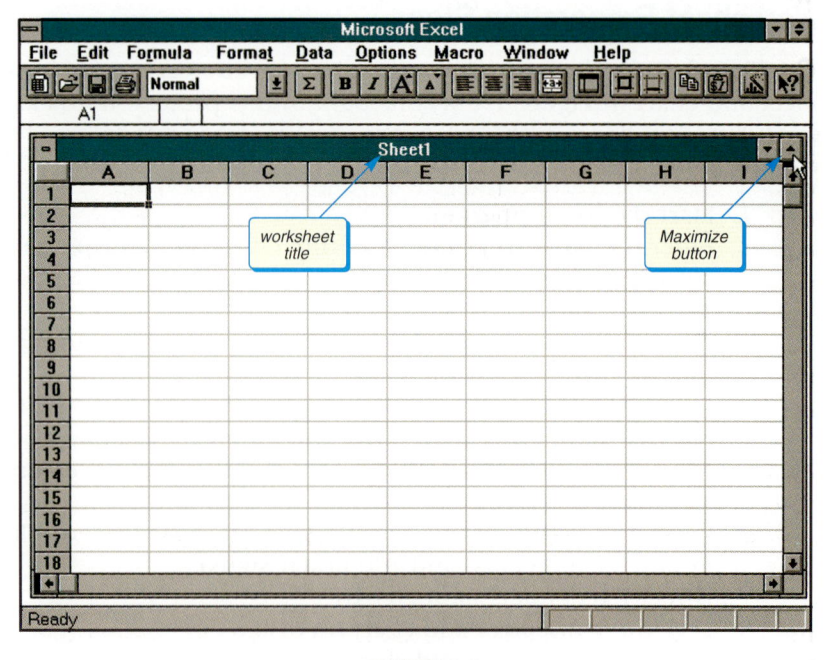

FIGURE 1-3

STEP 4 ▶

Click the left mouse button.

Excel maximizes Sheet1 and places the title Sheet1 on the title bar (Figure 1-4).

FIGURE 1-4

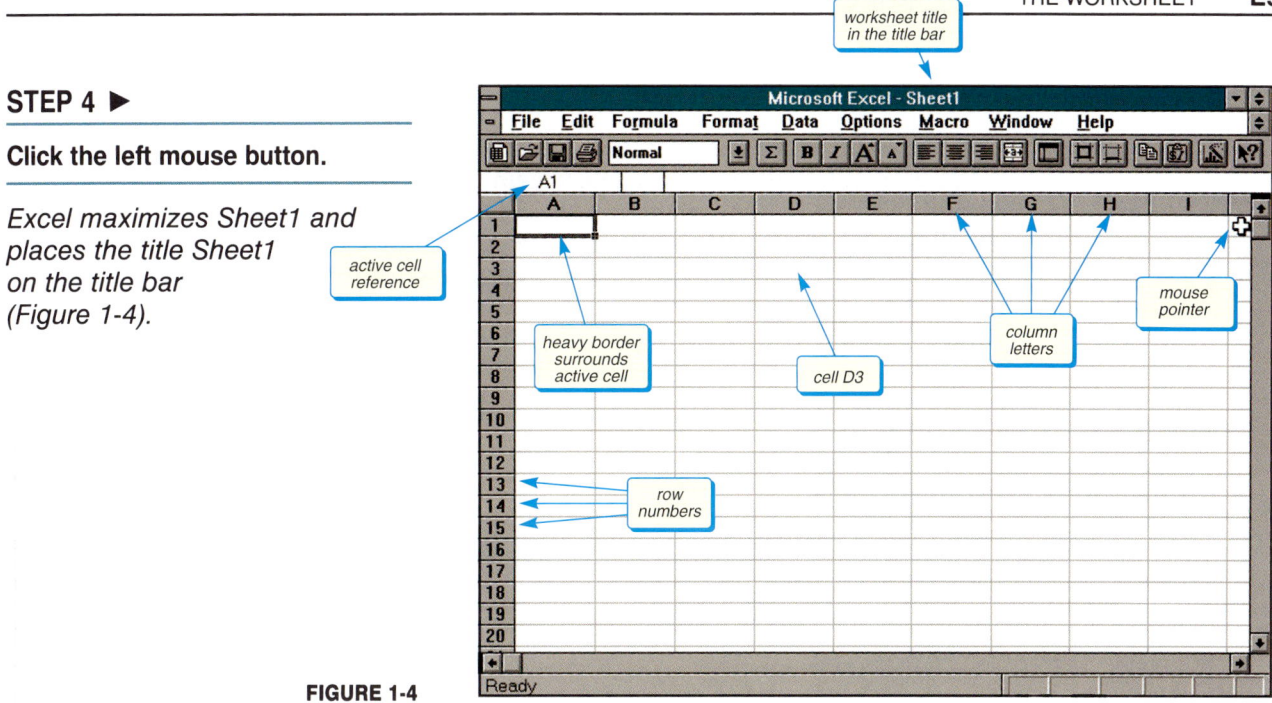

▶ THE WORKSHEET

The **worksheet** (Figure 1-4), also called a spreadsheet, is organized into a rectangular grid containing columns (vertical) and rows (horizontal). A column letter above the grid, also called the column heading, identifies each **column**. A row number on the left side of the grid, also called the row title, identifies each **row**. Nine complete columns (A through I) and twenty complete rows (1 through 20) of the worksheet appear on the screen when the worksheet is maximized (Figure 1-4).

Cell, Active Cell, and Mouse Pointer

The intersection of each column and row is a **cell**. A cell is the basic unit of a worksheet into which you enter data. A cell is referred to by its **cell reference**, the coordinates of the intersection of a column and a row. To identify a cell, specify the column letter first, followed by the row number. For example, cell reference D3 refers to the cell located at the intersection of column D and row 3 (Figure 1-4).

One cell on the worksheet, designated the **active cell**, is the one in which you can enter data. The active cell in Figure 1-4 is A1. Cell A1 is identified in two ways. First, a heavy border surrounds the cell. Second, the **active cell reference** displays immediately above column A.

The mouse pointer can become one of fourteen different shapes, depending on the task you are performing in Excel and the pointer's location on the screen. The mouse pointer in Figure 1-4 has the shape of a block plus sign (✥). The mouse pointer displays as a block plus sign whenever it is located in a cell in the worksheet.

Another common shape of the mouse pointer is the block arrow (▨). The mouse pointer turns into the block arrow whenever you move it outside the window or when you drag cell contents between rows or columns.

The other **mouse pointer shapes** are described when they appear on the screen during this and subsequent projects.

Worksheet Window

The Excel worksheet has 256 columns and 16,384 rows for a total of 4,194,304 cells. The column names begin with A and end with IV. The row names begin with 1 and end with 16,384. Only a small fraction of the worksheet displays on the screen at one time. You view the portion of the worksheet displayed on the screen through a **worksheet window** (Figure 1-5). Below and to the right of the worksheet window are **scroll bars**, **scroll arrows**, and **scroll boxes** which you can use to move the window around the worksheet.

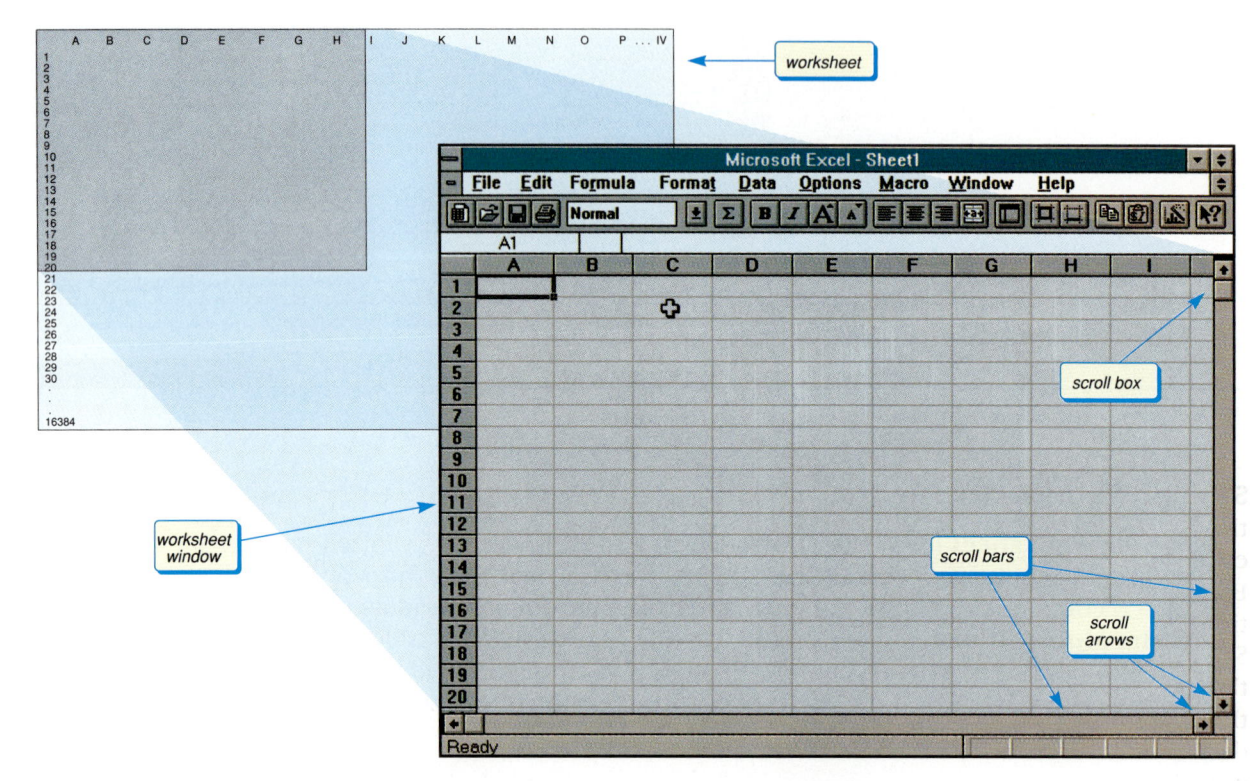

FIGURE 1-5

Menu Bar, Standard Toolbar, Formula Bar, and Status Bar

The menu bar, Standard toolbar, and formula bar appear at the top of the screen just below the title bar (Figure 1-6). The status bar appears at the bottom of the screen.

MENU BAR The **menu bar** displays the Excel menu names (Figure 1-6). Each menu name represents a pull-down menu of commands which you can use to retrieve, store, print, and manipulate data in the worksheet. To pull down a menu such as the File menu, select the menu name in the manner you learned in *Introduction to Windows*.

The menu bar can change to include other menu names depending on the type of work you are doing in Excel. For example, if you are working with a chart rather than a worksheet, the menu bar consists of a menu of names for use specifically with charts.

THE WORKSHEET **E7**

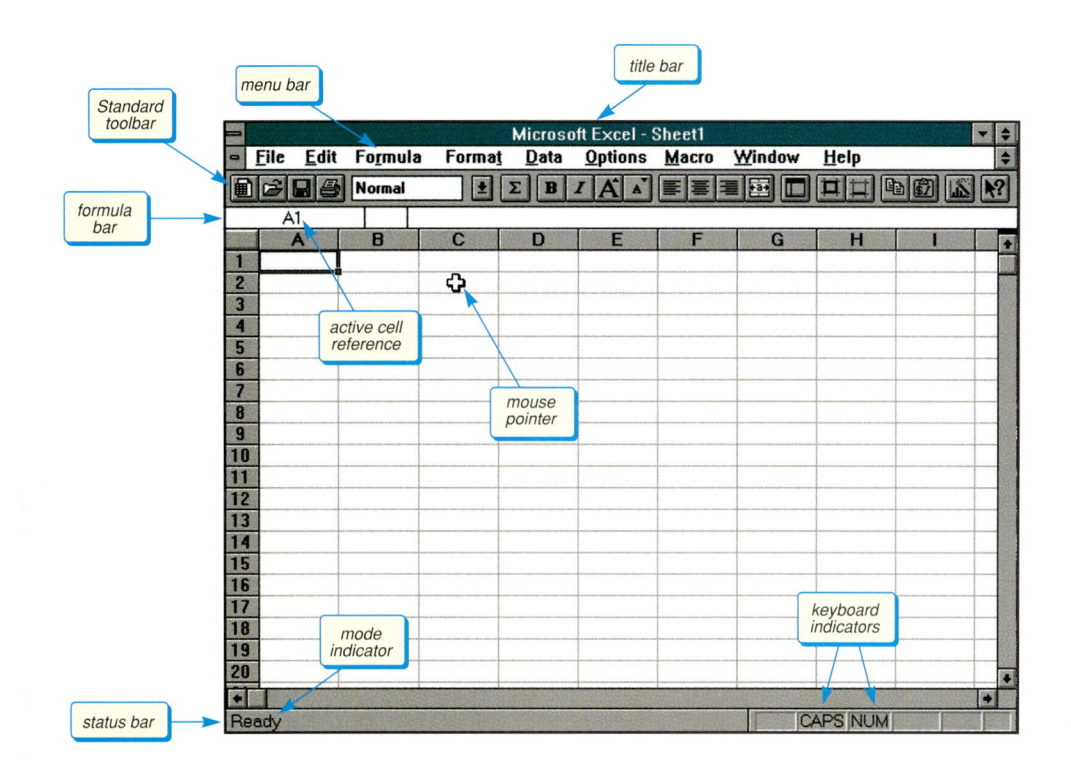

FIGURE 1-6

STANDARD TOOLBAR The **Standard toolbar** (Figure 1-6) contains tools (buttons) that allow you to perform frequent tasks quicker than using the menu bar. For example, to print you point to the Print tool and press the left mouse button. Each tool has a picture on the tool face that helps you remember the tool's function. Figure 1-7 illustrates the Standard toolbar and describes the functions of the tools. Each of the tools will be explained in detail when they are used in the projects.

Excel has several additional toolbars you can activate through the Options menu on the menu bar. In some cases, when you initiate an activity, Excel automatically displays a corresponding toolbar at the bottom of the screen.

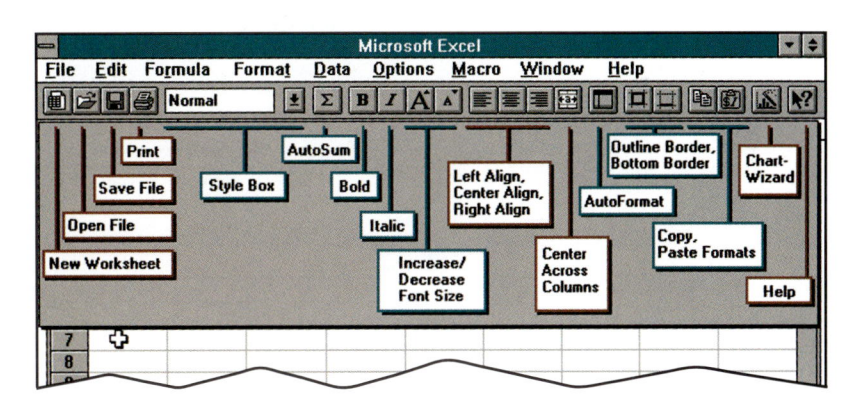

FIGURE 1-7

FORMULA BAR Below the Standard toolbar is the **formula bar** (Figure 1-6). As you type, the data appears in the formula bar. Excel also displays the active cell reference in the left side of the formula bar.

STATUS BAR The left side of the **status bar** at the bottom of the screen displays a brief description of the currently selected command or the current activity (mode) in progress (Figure 1-6). **Mode indicators**, such as Enter and Ready, specify the current mode of Excel. When the mode is Ready, as shown in Figure 1-6, Excel is ready to accept the next command or data entry. When the mode indicator is Enter, Excel is in the process of accepting data for the active cell.

SELECTING A CELL

To enter data into a cell, you must first select it. The easiest way to **select a cell** (make active) is to use the mouse to move the block plus sign to the cell and click the left mouse button.

An alternative method is to use the arrow keys that are located just to the right of the typewriter keys on the keyboard. An **arrow key** selects the cell adjacent to the active cell in the direction of the arrow on the key.

You know a cell is selected (active) when a heavy border surrounds the cell and the desired cell reference displays in the active cell reference in the formula bar.

ENTERING TEXT

In Excel, any set of characters containing a letter is considered **text**. Text is used to place titles on the worksheet, such as worksheet titles, column titles, and row titles. In Project 1 (Figure 1-8), the centered worksheet title Monthly Office Expenses identifies the worksheet. The column titles are the names of cities (Seattle, Atlanta, Boston) and Total. The row titles (Rent, Utilities, Supplies, and Total) identify the data in each row.

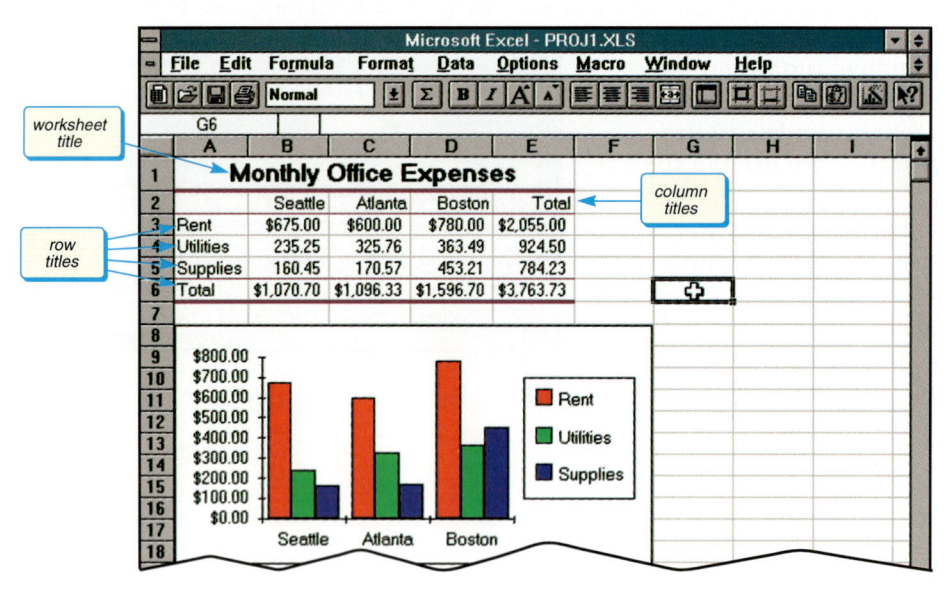

FIGURE 1-8

Entering the Worksheet Title

The following example explains the steps to enter the worksheet title into cell A1. Later in this project, the worksheet title in cell A1 will be centered over the column titles.

ENTERING TEXT **E9**

TO ENTER THE WORKSHEET TITLE ▼

STEP 1 ▶

Select cell A1 by pointing to cell A1 and clicking the left mouse button.

Cell A1 becomes the active cell and a heavy border surrounds it (Figure 1-9).

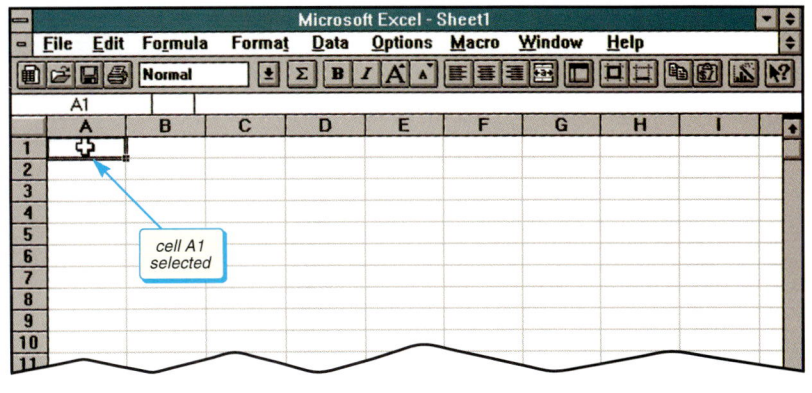

FIGURE 1-9

STEP 2 ▶

Type the text `Monthly Office Expenses`.

*When you type the first character, the mode indicator in the status bar changes from Ready to Enter and Excel displays two boxes: one called the **cancel box** (☒) and the other called the **enter box** (☑) in the formula bar (Figure 1-10). The entire title displays in the formula bar, followed immediately by the insertion point. The **insertion point** is a blinking vertical line that indicates where the next character typed will appear. The last few characters of the title display in the active cell. The text also appears in cell A1.*

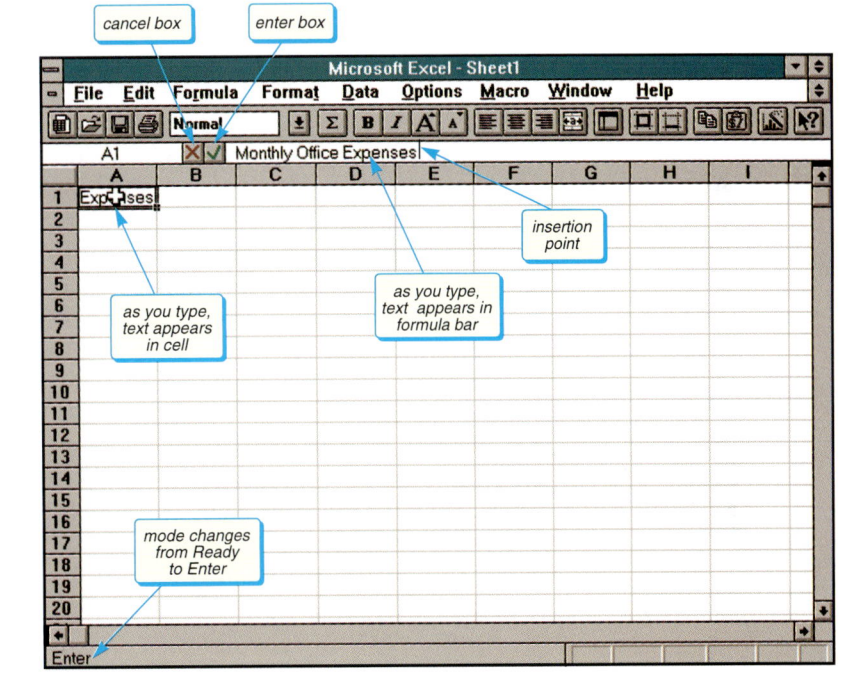

FIGURE 1-10

STEP 3 ▶

After you type the text, point to the enter box (Figure 1-11).

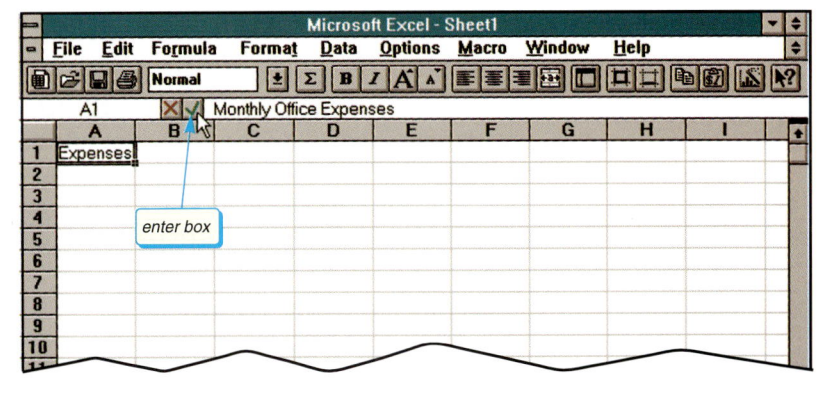

FIGURE 1-11

STEP 4 ▶

Click the left mouse button to complete the entry.

Excel enters the worksheet title in cell A1 (Figure 1-12).

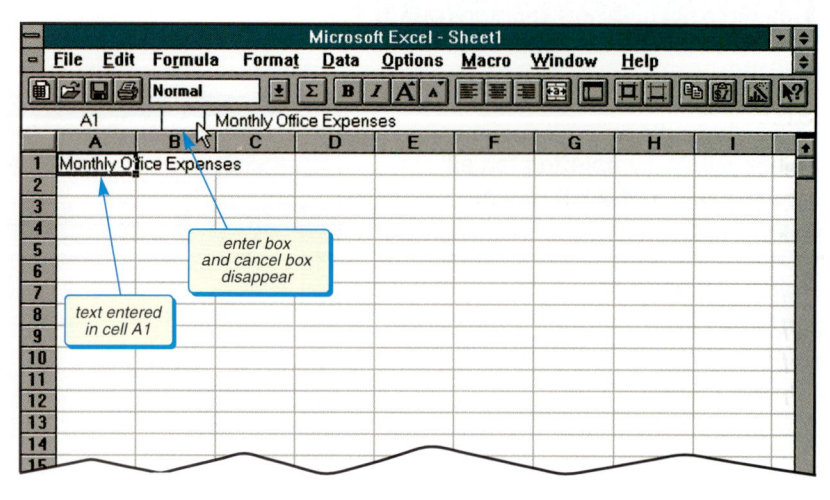

FIGURE 1-12

In the previous example, instead of using the mouse to complete an entry, you can press the ENTER **key** after typing the text. Pressing the ENTER key replaces Steps 3 and 4.

When you complete a text entry into a cell, a series of events occurs. First, Excel positions the text **left-justified** in the active cell. Therefore, the M in the word Monthly begins in the leftmost position of cell A1.

Second, when the text is longer than the width of a column, Excel displays the overflow characters in adjacent cells to the right as long as these adjacent columns contain no data. In Figure 1-12, the width of cell A1 is approximately nine characters. The text entered consists of 23 characters. Therefore, Excel displays the overflow characters in cells B1 and C1, since both cells are empty.

If cell B1 contained data, only the first nine characters of cell A1 would display on the worksheet. Excel would hide the overflow characters, but they would still remain stored in cell A1 and would display in the formula bar whenever cell A1 is the active cell.

Third, when you complete an entry into a cell by clicking the enter box or pressing the ENTER key, the cell in which the text is entered remains the active cell.

Correcting a Mistake While Typing

If you type the wrong letter and notice the error before clicking the enter box or pressing the ENTER key, use the **BACKSPACE key** to erase all the characters back to and including the ones that are wrong. To cancel the entire entry before entering it into the cell, click the cancel box in the formula bar or press the **ESC key**. If you see an error in a cell, select the cell and retype the entry. Later in this project, additional error-correction techniques are covered.

Entering Column Titles

To enter the column titles, select the appropriate cell and then enter the text, as described in the steps on the next two pages.

ENTERING TEXT **E11**

TO ENTER THE COLUMN TITLES

STEP 1 ▶

Select cell B2 by pointing to cell B2 and clicking the left mouse button.

Cell B2 becomes the active cell (Figure 1-13). The active cell reference in the formula bar changes from A1 to B2.

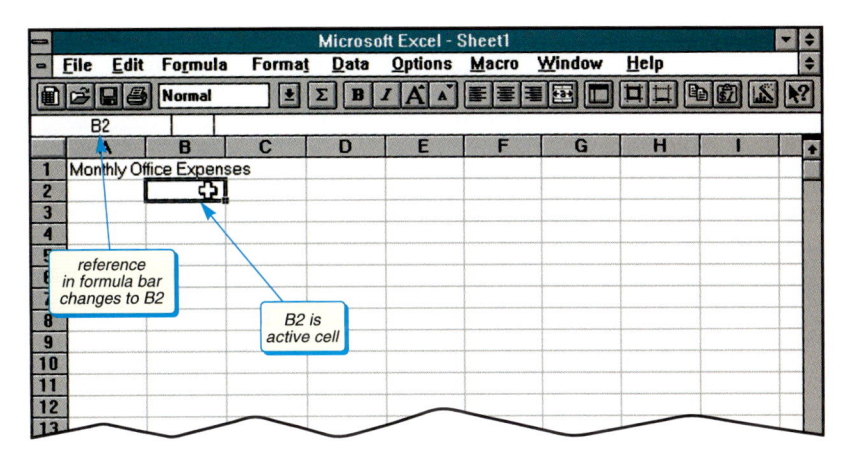

FIGURE 1-13

STEP 2 ▶

Type the column title `Seattle`**.**

Excel displays Seattle in the formula bar and in cell B2 (Figure 1-14).

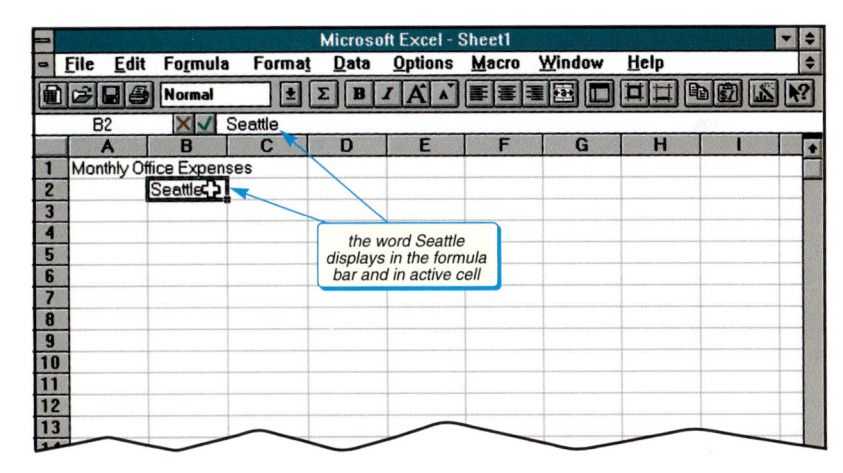

FIGURE 1-14

STEP 3 ▶

Press the RIGHT ARROW key.

Excel enters the column title, Seattle, in cell B2 and makes cell C2 the active cell (Figure 1-15). When you press an arrow key to complete an entry, the adjacent cell in the direction of the arrow (up, down, left, or right) becomes the active cell.

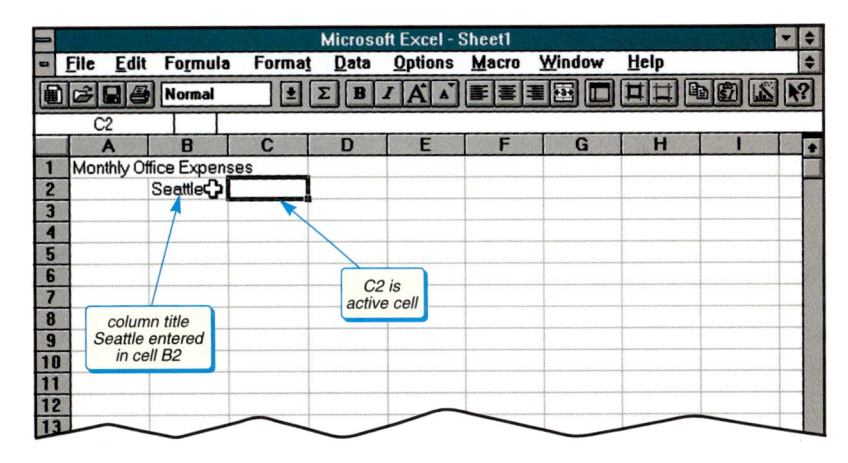

FIGURE 1-15

E12 PROJECT 1 BUILDING A WORKSHEET

STEP 4 ▶

Repeat Step 2 and Step 3 for the remaining column titles in row 2. That is, enter `Atlanta` in cell C2, `Boston` in cell D2, and `Total` in cell E2. Complete the last column title entry in cell E2 by clicking the enter box or by pressing the ENTER key.

The column titles display as shown in Figure 1-16.

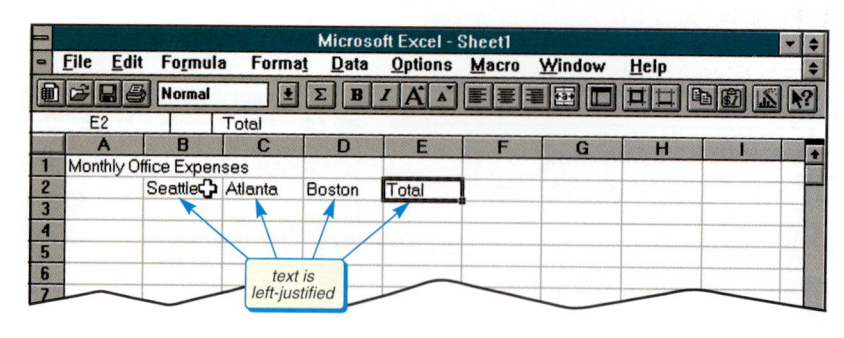

FIGURE 1-16

To complete an entry in a cell, use the arrow keys if the next entry is in an adjacent cell. If the next entry is not in an adjacent cell, click the enter box in the formula bar or press the ENTER key and then use the mouse to select the appropriate cell for the next entry.

Entering Row Titles

The next step in developing the worksheet in Project 1 is to enter the row titles in column A. This process is similar to entering the column titles and is described below.

TO ENTER ROW TITLES ▼

STEP 1 ▶

Select cell A3 by pointing to cell A3 and clicking the left mouse button.

Cell A3 becomes the active cell (Figure 1-17). The active cell reference in the formula bar changes from E2 to A3.

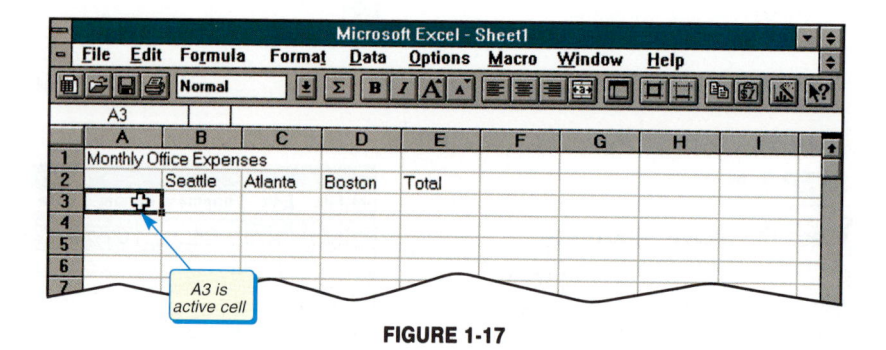

FIGURE 1-17

STEP 2 ▶

Type the row title `Rent` and press the DOWN ARROW key.

Excel enters the row title Rent in cell A3 and cell A4 becomes the active cell (Figure 1-18).

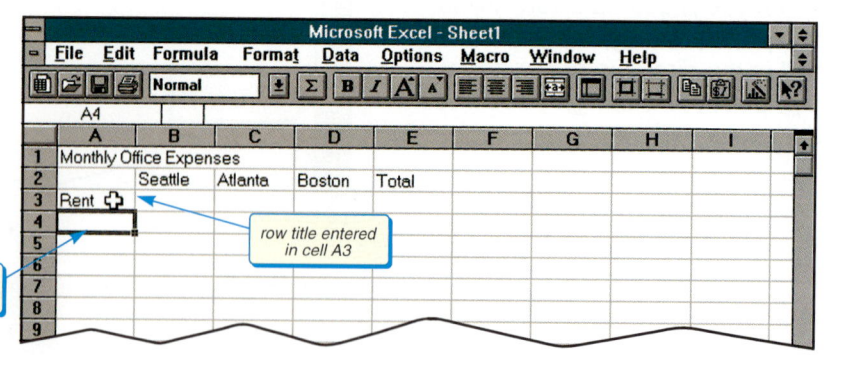

FIGURE 1-18

ENTERING NUMBERS E13

STEP 3 ▶

Repeat Step 2 for the remaining row titles in column A. Enter `Utilities` in cell A4, `Supplies` in cell A5, and `Total` in cell A6. Complete the last row title in cell A6 by clicking the enter box or by pressing the ENTER key.

The row titles display as shown in Figure 1-19.

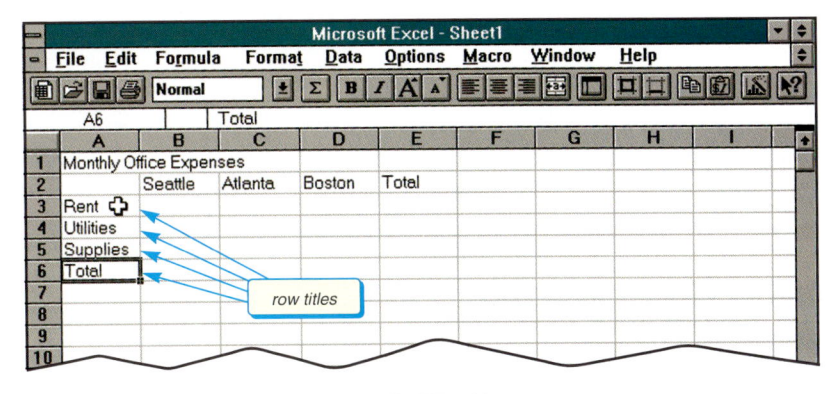

FIGURE 1-19

▶ ENTERING NUMBERS

In Excel you can enter **numbers** into cells to represent amounts. Numbers can include the digits zero through nine and any one of the following special characters:

+ − ( ) , / . $ % E e

If a cell entry contains any other character from the keyboard, Excel interprets the entry as text and treats it accordingly. The use of the special characters is explained when they are required in a project.

In Project 1, the expense amounts for Rent, Utilities, and Supplies for each of the three cities (Seattle, Atlanta, and Boston) must be entered in rows three, four, and five. The following steps illustrate how to enter these values one row at a time.

TO ENTER NUMERIC DATA ▼

STEP 1 ▶

Select cell B3 by pointing to cell B3 and clicking the left mouse button.

Cell B3 becomes the active cell (Figure 1-20).

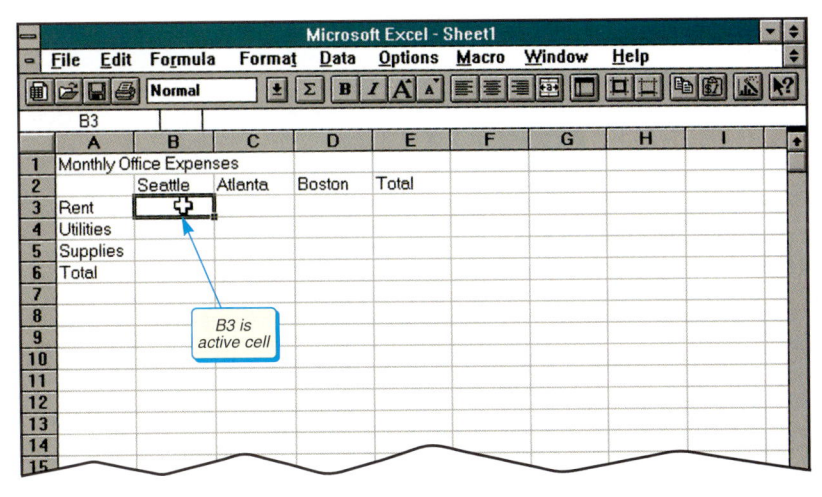

FIGURE 1-20

E14 PROJECT 1 BUILDING A WORKSHEET

STEP 2 ▶

Type the number 675.

When you type the first digit, the mode indicator in the status bar changes from Ready to Enter (Figure 1-21). The number 675 displays in the formula bar and in the active cell. Enter whole numbers like 675 without a dollar sign, decimal point, or trailing zeros. The numbers on the worksheet are formatted with dollar signs and cents later in this project.

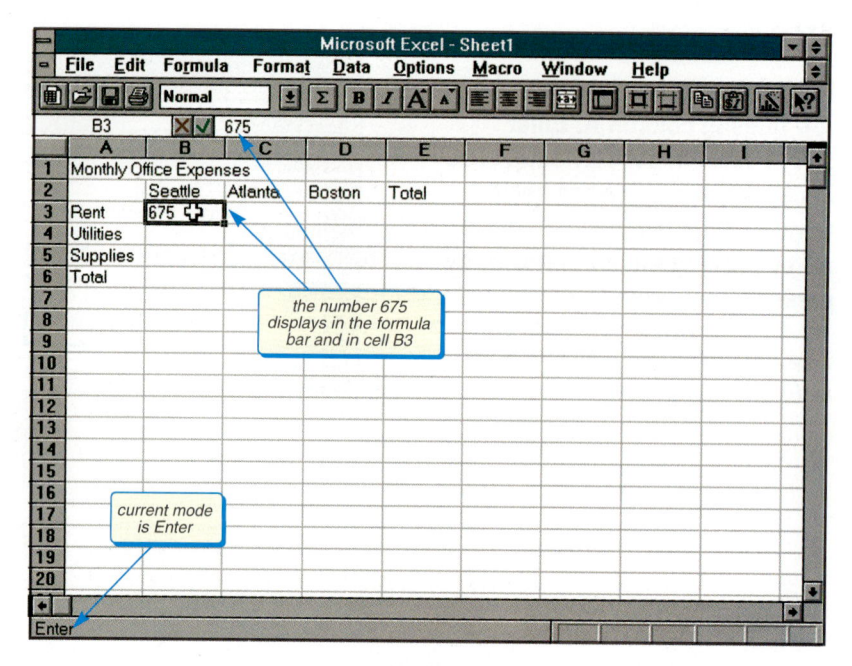

FIGURE 1-21

STEP 3 ▶

Press the RIGHT ARROW key.

Excel enters the number 675 right-justified in cell B3 and changes the active cell to cell C3 (Figure 1-22).

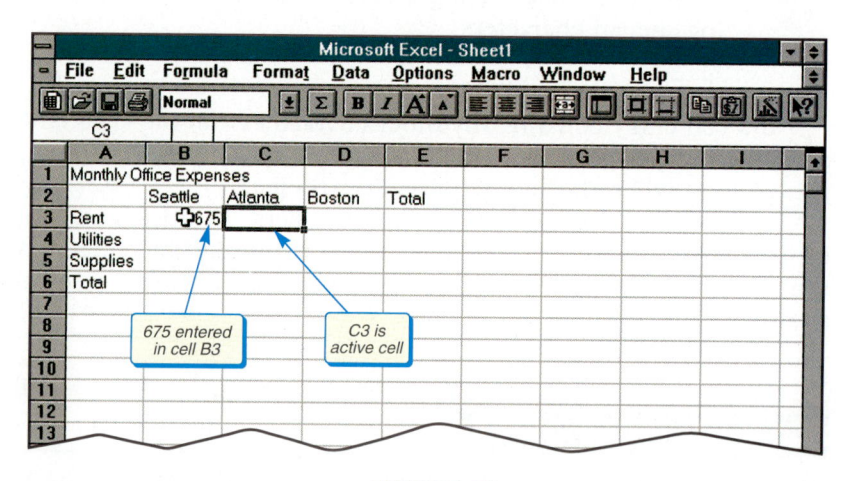

FIGURE 1-22

STEP 4 ▶

Enter 600 in cell C3 and 780 in cell D3.

Row 3 now contains the rent expenses all right-justified (Figure 1-23).

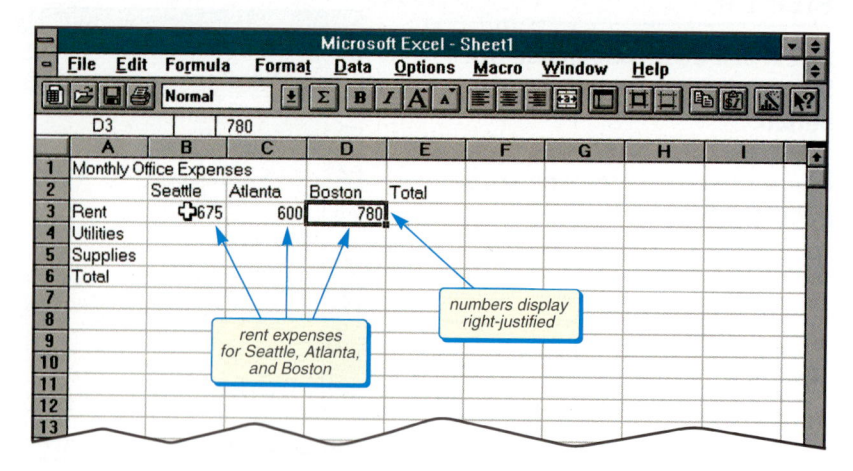

FIGURE 1-23

CALCULATING A SUM   E15

STEP 5 ▶

Select cell B4 by pointing to cell B4 and clicking the left mouse button.

Cell B4 becomes the active cell (Figure 1-24).

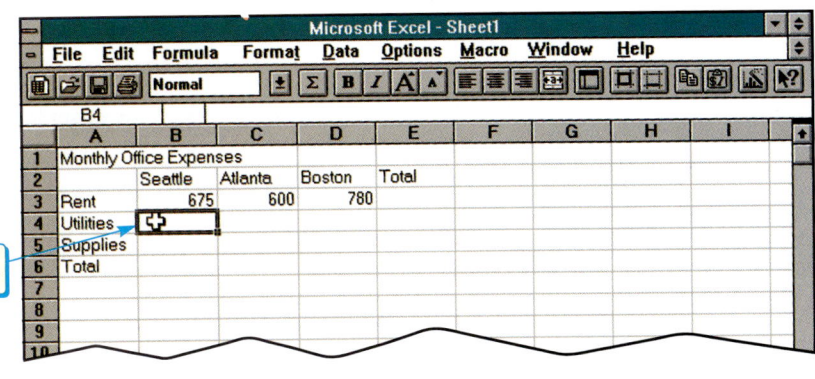

FIGURE 1-24

STEP 6 ▶

Repeat Steps 2 through 5 to enter the utility expenses for the three cities (235.25 for Seattle, 325.76 for Atlanta, and 363.49 for Boston) and the supplies expenses for the three cities (160.45 for Seattle, 170.57 for Atlanta, and 453.21 for Boston).

The utility and supplies expenses for the three cities display in row 4 and row 5 (Figure 1-25).

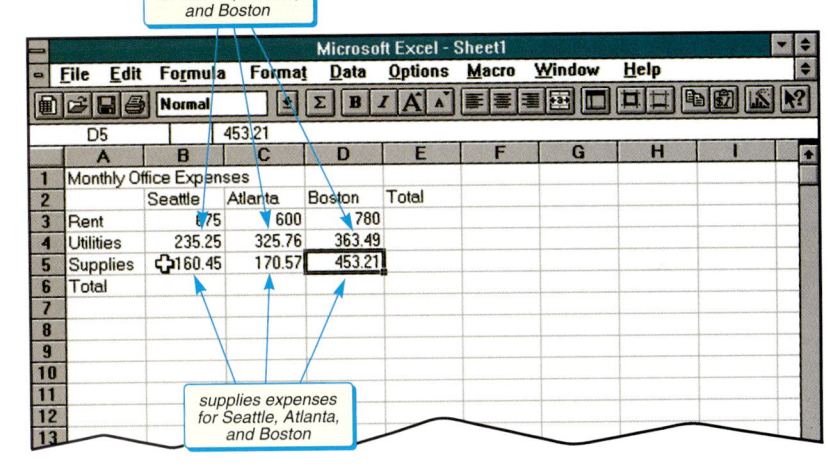

FIGURE 1-25

Steps 1 through 6 complete the numeric entries. Notice several important points. First, you are not required to type dollar signs and trailing zeros. Later, dollar signs will be added as previously described in Figure 1-1 on page E3. However, when you enter a number that has cents, you must add the decimal point and the numbers representing the cents when you enter the number.

Second, Excel stores numbers right-justified in the cells which means they occupy the rightmost positions in the cells.

Third, Excel will calculate the totals in row 6 and in column E in Figure 1-1. Indeed, the capability of Excel to perform calculations is one of its major features.

▶ CALCULATING A SUM

The next step in creating the Monthly Office Expenses worksheet is to determine the total expenses for the Seattle office. To calculate this value in cell B6, Excel must add the numbers in cells B3, B4, and B5. Excel's **SUM function** provides a convenient means to accomplish this task.

To use the SUM function, you must first identify the cell in which the sum will be stored after it is calculated. Then, you can use the **AutoSum tool** (Σ) on the Standard toolbar.

The following steps illustrate how to use the AutoSum tool to sum (add) the expenses for Seattle in cells B3, B4, and B5 and enter the result in B6.

TO SUM A COLUMN OF NUMBERS

STEP 1 ▶

Select cell B6 by pointing to cell B6 and clicking the left mouse button.

Cell B6 becomes the active cell (Figure 1-26).

FIGURE 1-26

STEP 2 ▶

Point to the AutoSum tool on the Standard toolbar and click.

Excel responds by displaying =SUM(B3:B5) in the formula bar and in the active cell B6 (Figure 1-27). The =SUM entry identifies the SUM function. The B3:B5 within parentheses following the function name SUM is Excel's way of identifying the cells B3, B4, and B5. Excel also surrounds the proposed cells to sum with a moving border.

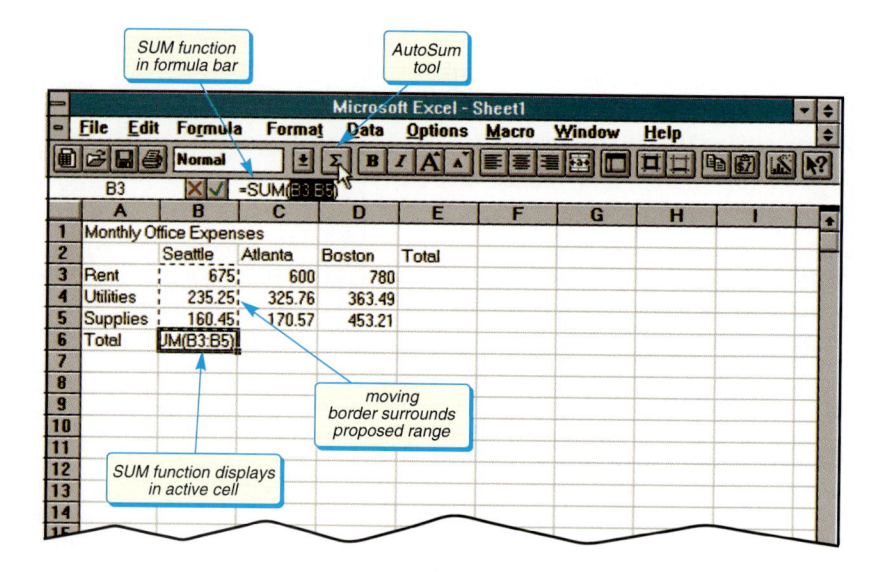

FIGURE 1-27

STEP 3 ▶

Point to the enter box in the formula bar (Figure 1-28).

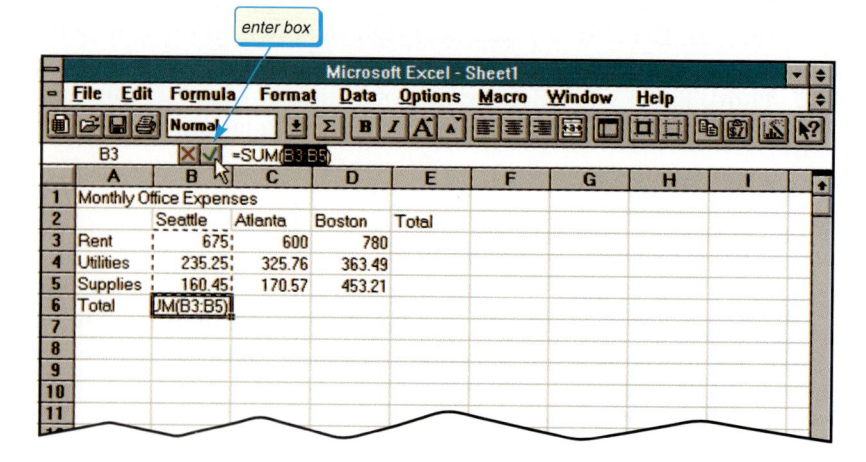

FIGURE 1-28

STEP 4 ▶

Click the enter box in the formula bar.

Excel enters the sum of the expenses for Seattle (1070.7 = 675 + 235.25 + 160.45) in cell B6 (Figure 1-29). The function assigned to cell B6 displays in the formula bar when B6 is the active cell.

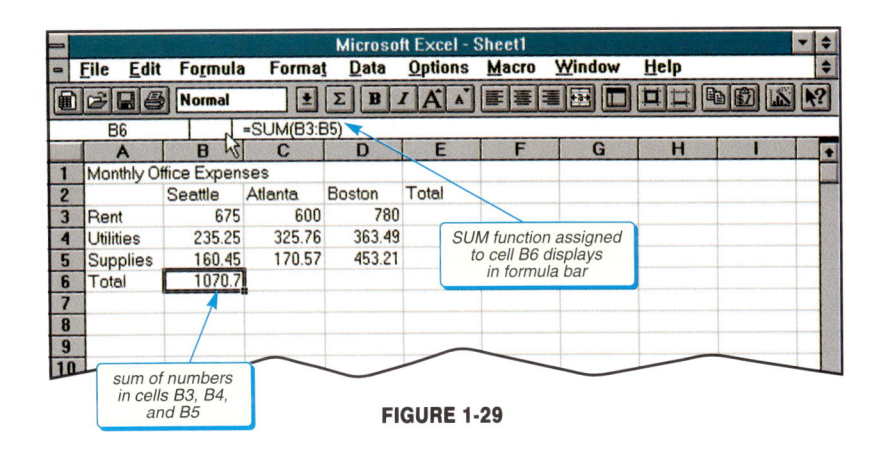

FIGURE 1-29

When you enter the SUM function using the AutoSum tool, Excel automatically selects what it considers to be your choice of the group of cells to sum. The group of cells B3, B4, and B5 is called a range. A **range** is a series of two or more adjacent cells in a column or row, or a rectangular group of cells. Many Excel operations, such as summing numbers, take place on cells within a range.

In proposing the range to sum, Excel first looks for a range of cells with numbers above the active cell and then to the left. If Excel proposes the wrong range, you can use the mouse to drag the correct range anytime prior to clicking the enter box or pressing the ENTER key. You can also enter the correct range in the formula bar by typing the beginning cell reference, a colon (:), and the ending cell reference.

You can speed up the entry of the SUM function by clicking the AutoSum tool a second time instead of moving the pointer and clicking the enter box. After clicking once and ensuring the correct range is selected, clicking the AutoSum tool a second time will perform the same task as clicking the enter box.

▶ USING THE FILL HANDLE TO COPY A CELL TO ADJACENT CELLS

On the Monthly Office Expenses worksheet, Excel must also calculate the totals for Atlanta in cell C6 and the totals for Boston in cell D6. Table 1-1 illustrates the similarity between the entry in B6 and the entries required for the totals in cells C6 and D6.

▶ **TABLE 1-1**

CELL	SUM FUNCTION ENTRIES	REMARK
B6	= SUM(B3:B5)	Sums cells B3, B4, and B5
C6	= SUM(C3:C5)	Sums cells C3, C4, and C5
D6	= SUM(D3:D5)	Sums cells D3, D4, and D5

To place the SUM functions in cell C6 and cell D6, you can follow the same steps shown in Figures 1-26 through 1-29. A second, more efficient method is to copy the SUM function from cell B6 to the range C6:D6. The range of cells receiving the copy is called the **paste area**.

E18 PROJECT 1 BUILDING A WORKSHEET

Notice from Table 1-1 that although the SUM function entries are similar, they are not exact copies. Each cell to the right of cell B6 has a range that is one column to the right of the previous column. When you copy cell addresses, Excel adjusts them for each new position, resulting in the SUM entries illustrated in Table 1-1. Each adjusted cell reference is called a **relative reference**.

The easiest way to copy the SUM formula from cell B6 to cells C6 and D6 is to use the fill handle. The **fill handle** is the small rectangular dot located in the lower right corner of the heavy border around the active cell (Figure 1-30). The following steps show how to use the fill handle to copy one cell to adjacent cells.

TO COPY ONE CELL TO ADJACENT CELLS IN A ROW ▼

STEP 1 ▶

Select cell B6, the cell to copy and point to the fill handle.

The mouse pointer changes from the block plus sign to the small, dark plus sign (+) (Figure 1-30).

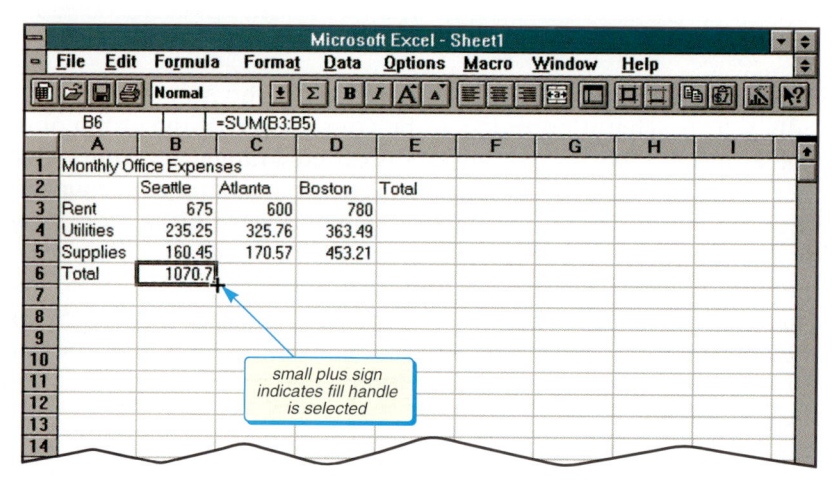

FIGURE 1-30

STEP 2 ▶

Drag the fill handle to select the paste area C6:D6.

Excel shades the border of the paste area C6:D6 (Figure 1-31).

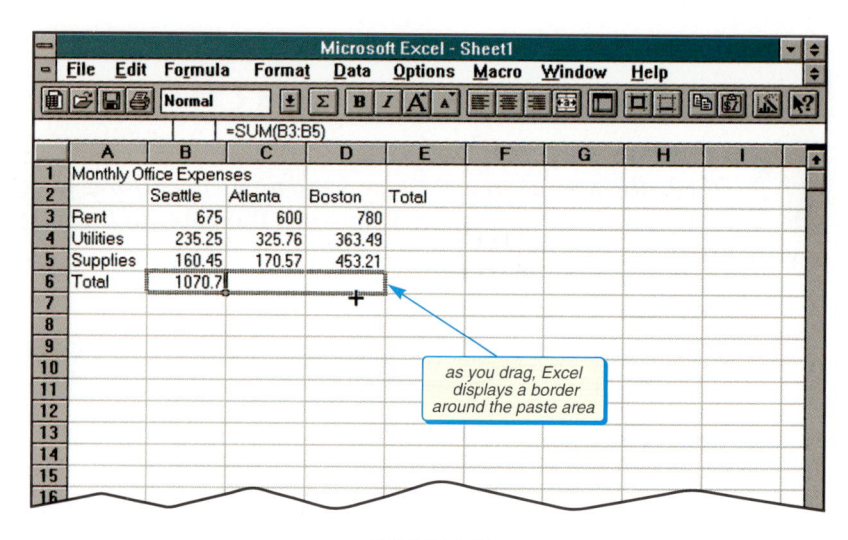

FIGURE 1-31

USING THE FILL HANDLE TO COPY A CELL TO ADJACENT CELLS   **E19**

STEP 3 ▶

Release the left mouse button.

Excel copies the SUM function in cell B6 to the range C6:D6 (Figure 1-32). In addition, Excel calculates the sums and enters the results in cells C6 and D6.

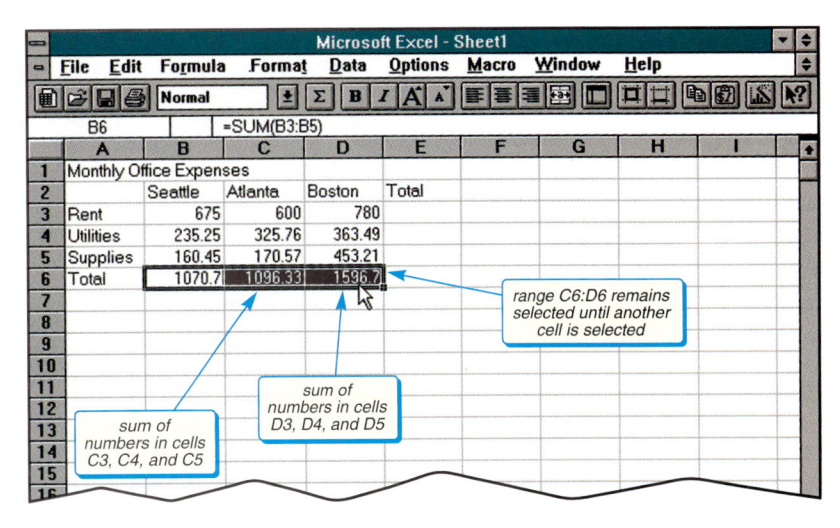

FIGURE 1-32

After the copy is complete, the range remains selected. To remove the range selection, select any cell.

Summing a Row Total

The next step in building the Monthly Office Expenses worksheet is to total the rent expenses, utilities expenses, supplies expenses, and the total of all expenses and place the sums in column E. The SUM function is used in the same manner as totaling the expenses by city in row 6. The following steps illustrate this process.

TO SUM A ROW OF VALUES ▼

STEP 1 ▶

Select cell E3 by pointing to cell E3 and clicking the left mouse button.

Cell E3 becomes the active cell (Figure 1-33).

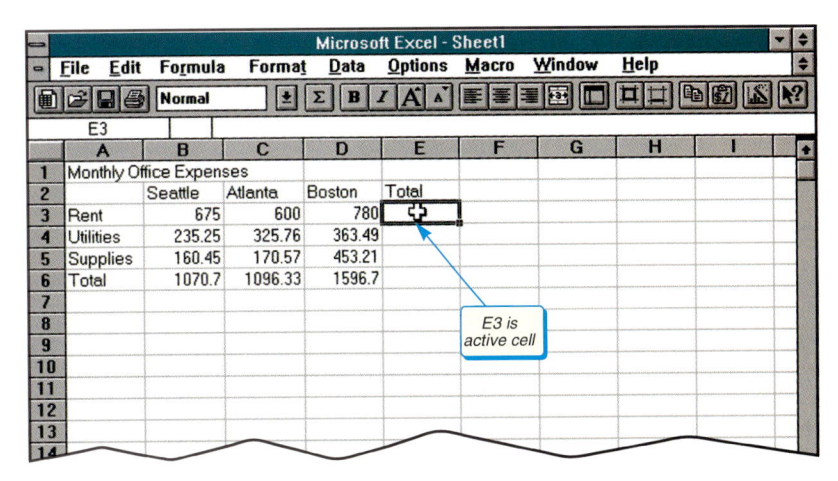

FIGURE 1-33

E20 PROJECT 1 BUILDING A WORKSHEET

STEP 2 ▶

Point to the AutoSum tool on the Standard toolbar and click.

Excel displays the SUM function in the formula bar and in cell E3 (Figure 1-34). The proposed range B3:D3 is surrounded by a moving border.

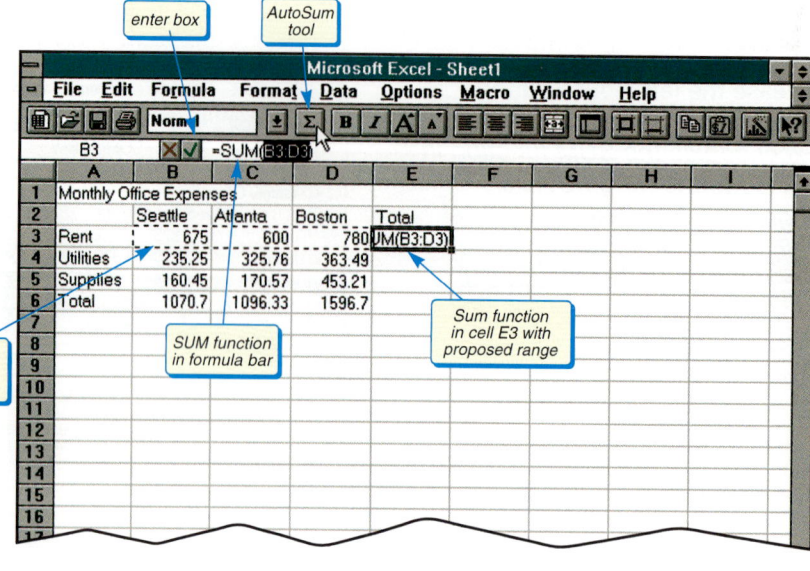

FIGURE 1-34

STEP 3 ▶

Point to the enter box in the formula bar and click.

Excel calculates the sum of the numbers in the range B3:D3 and stores the result in cell E3 (Figure 1-35).

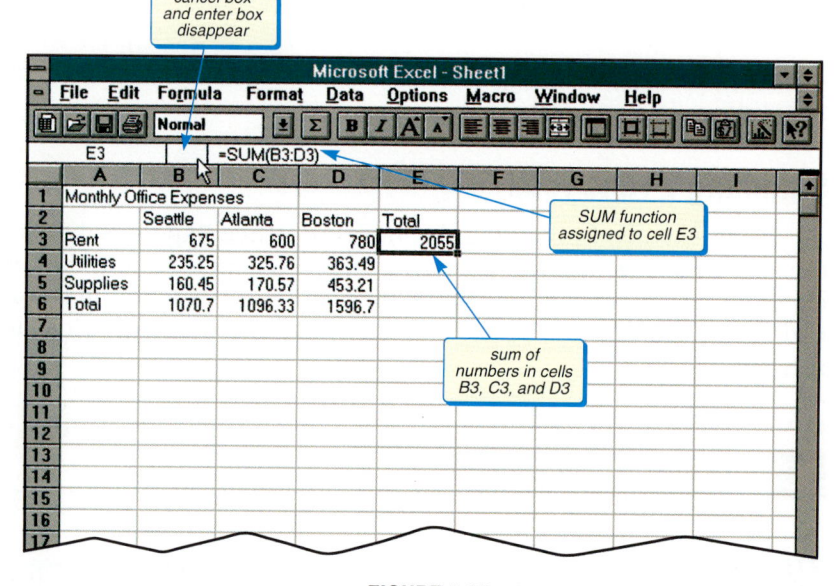

FIGURE 1-35

As discussed previously, you can accomplish Step 3 by clicking the AutoSum tool a second time instead of clicking the enter box.

Copying Cells in a Column

The next step is to copy the SUM function in cell E3 to the range E4:E6 to obtain the total expenses for the utilities, supplies, and the total of all expenses. Use the fill handle to accomplish this task.

TO COPY ONE CELL TO ADJACENT CELLS IN A COLUMN

STEP 1 ▶

Point to the fill handle in the active cell E3.

When you point to the fill handle, the mouse pointer changes from a block plus sign to a small, dark plus sign (Figure 1-36).

FIGURE 1-36

STEP 2 ▶

Drag the fill handle to select the paste area E4:E6.

Excel shades the border of the paste area E4:E6 (Figure 1-37).

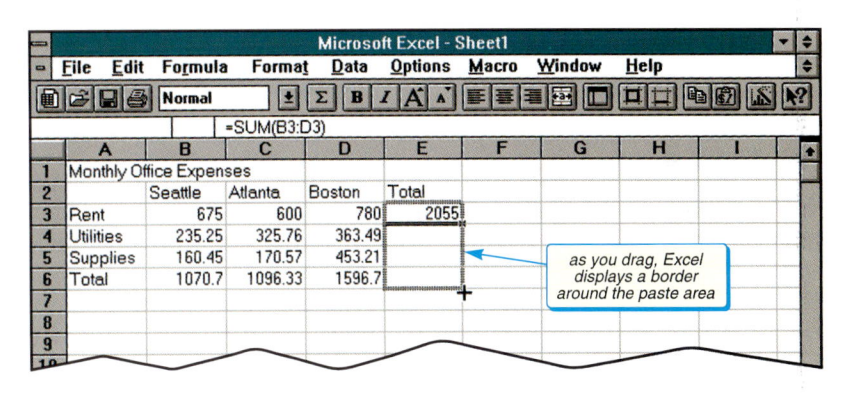

FIGURE 1-37

STEP 3 ▶

Release the left mouse button.

Excel copies the SUM function in cell E3 to the range E4:E6 and calculates the totals (Figure 1-38).

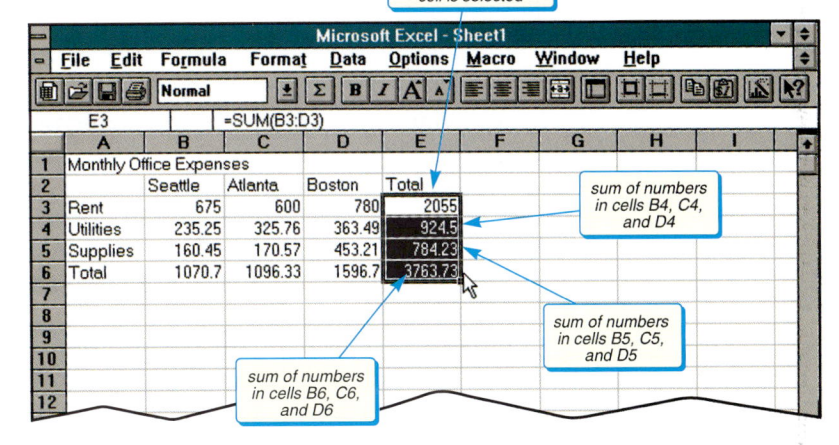

FIGURE 1-38

After Excel copies the cell contents, the range E4:E6 remains selected. Select any cell to remove the range selection.

FORMATTING THE WORKSHEET

The text, numeric entries, and functions for the worksheet are now complete. The next step is to format the worksheet. You format a worksheet to emphasize certain entries and make the worksheet easier to read and understand.

Figure 1-39a shows the worksheet before formatting it. Figure 1-39b shows the worksheet after formatting it. As you can see from the two figures, a worksheet that is formatted is not only easier to read, but it looks more professional.

(a)

(b)

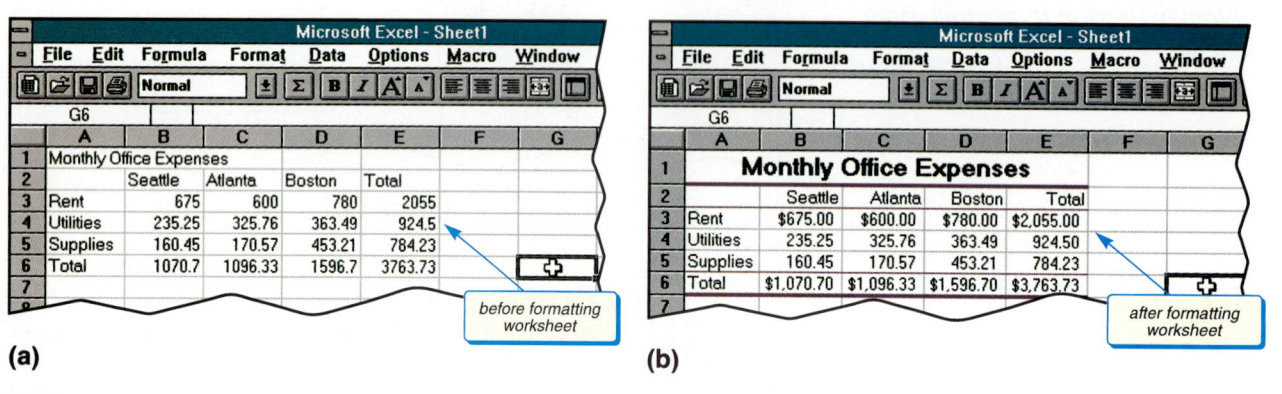

FIGURE 1-39

To change the unformatted worksheet in Figure 1-39a to the formatted worksheet in Figure 1-39b begin by centering the worksheet title, Monthly Office Expenses, across columns A though E. Next, enlarge the title and make it bold. Finally, format the body of the worksheet, including the column and row titles, the rent, utilities, and supplies expenses, and the totals Excel calculated, using Excel's AutoFormat feature. The result is numbers represented in a dollars-and-cents format, dollar signs in the first row of numbers and the total row, and underlines that emphasize portions of the worksheet.

The process required to format the Monthly Office Expenses worksheet is explained on the following pages.

Fonts, Font Size, and Font Style

Characters that appear on the screen are a specific shape and size. The **font type** defines the appearance and shape of the letters, numbers, and special characters. The **font size** specifies the size of the characters on the screen. Character size is gauged by a measurement system called points. A single point is about 1/72 of one inch in height. Thus, a character with a point size of ten is about 10/72 of one inch in height.

Font style indicates how the characters appear. They may be normal, bold, underlined, or italicized.

When Excel begins, the default font type for the entire worksheet is MS Sans Serif with a size of 10 point, no bold, no underline, and no italic. With Excel you have the capability to change the font characteristics in a single cell, a range of cells, or for the entire worksheet.

To change the worksheet title (Monthly Office Expenses) from the Excel default presentation to the desired formatting (Figure 1-39), these procedures must occur: (a) the worksheet title must be centered across columns A through E of the worksheet; (b) the size of the characters must be increased; and (c) the characters must be changed from normal to bold.

Although the three procedures will be carried out in the order presented, you should be aware that you can make these changes in any order.

FORMATTING THE WORKSHEET   **E23**

TO CENTER A CELL'S CONTENTS ACROSS COLUMNS

STEP 1 ▶

Select cell A1 by pointing to cell A1 and clicking the left mouse button.

Cell A1 becomes the active cell (Figure 1-40).

FIGURE 1-40

STEP 2 ▶

Drag the block plus sign from the active cell (A1) to the rightmost cell (E1) in the range over which to center.

When you drag the mouse pointer over the range A1:E1, Excel highlights the cells (Figure 1-41).

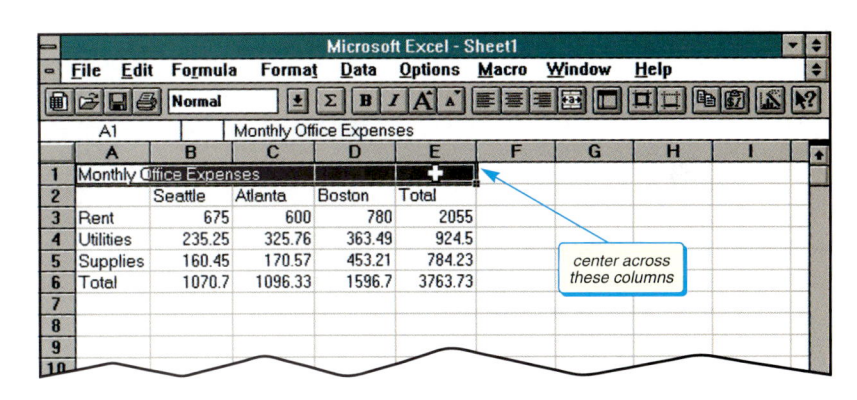

FIGURE 1-41

STEP 3 ▶

Click the Center Across Columns tool ( ) on the Standard toolbar.

*Excel centers the contents of cell A1 across columns A through E (Figure 1-42). For the **Center Across Columns tool** to work properly, all the cells except the leftmost cell in the range of cells must be empty.*

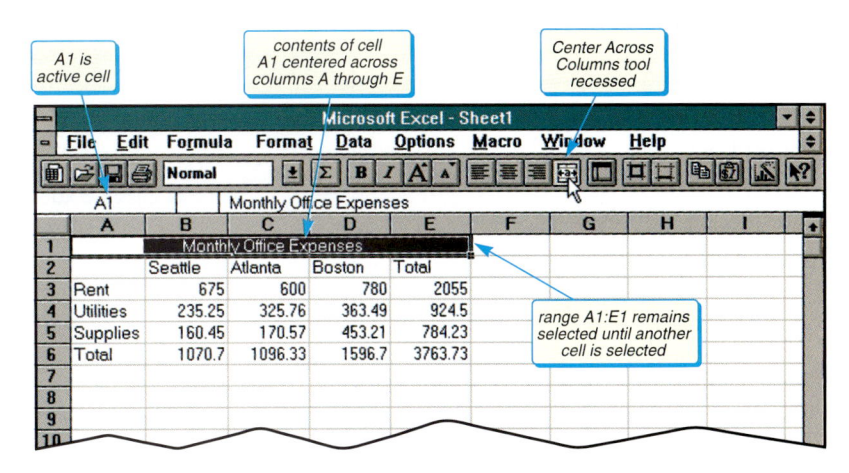

FIGURE 1-42

To remove the selection from range A1:E1, select any cell in the worksheet. Increasing the font size is the next step in formatting the worksheet title.

TO INCREASE THE FONT SIZE

STEP 1 ▶

Select cell A1 by pointing to cell A1 and clicking the left mouse button.

Cell A1 becomes the active cell (Figure 1-43).

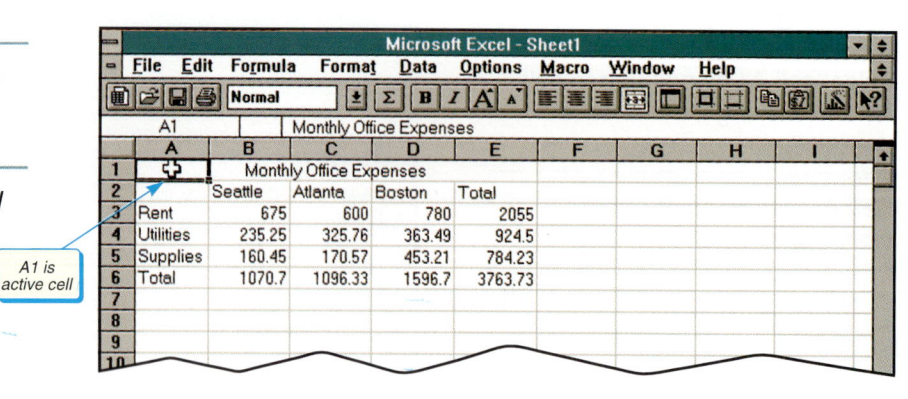

FIGURE 1-43

STEP 2 ▶

Point to the Increase Font Size tool (A) on the Standard toolbar and click.

The letters in the selected cell increase in size by two points (Figure 1-44). The characters in cell A1 now have a size of 12 points.

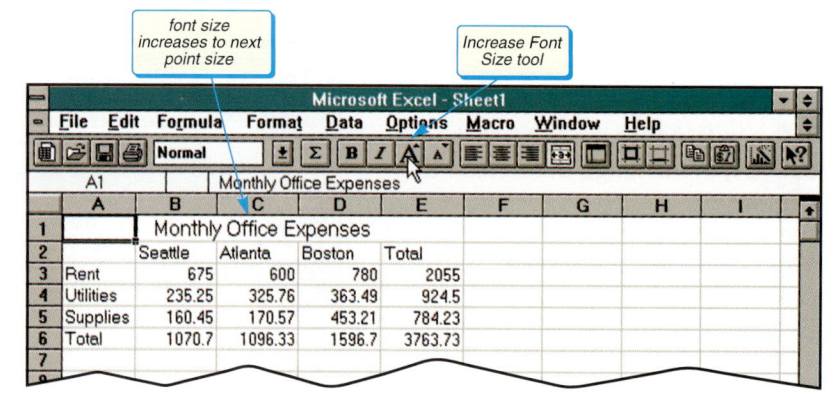

FIGURE 1-44

STEP 3 ▶

Click the Increase Font Size tool a second time.

The letters in the selected cell once again increase in size by two points (Figure 1-45). The characters in cell A1 now have a size of 14 points. This is the desired size for the worksheet title.

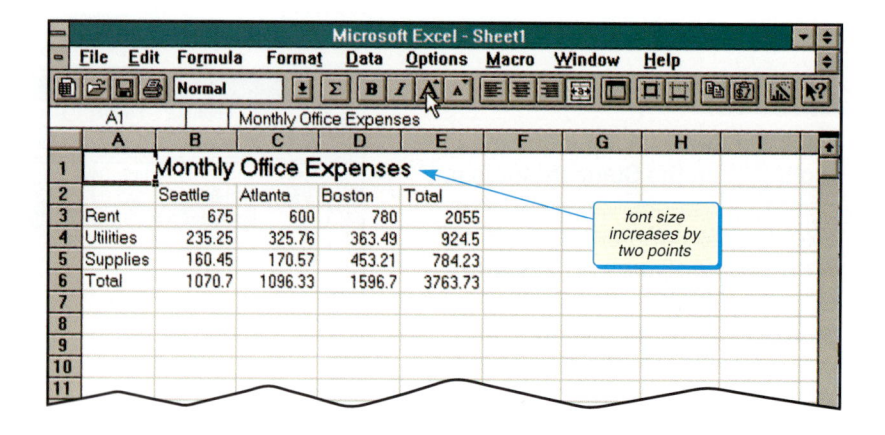

FIGURE 1-45

The tool just to the right of the Increase Font Size tool is the **Decrease Font Size tool**. To decrease the font size of a cell entry, click the Decrease Font Size tool instead of the Increase Font Size tool, using the same procedure as for increasing the font size.

USING AUTOFORMAT TO FORMAT THE WORKSHEET **E25**

The final step in formatting the worksheet title is to change the cell format to bold.

TO CHANGE THE CELL FORMAT TO BOLD

STEP 1

Select cell A1 by pointing to cell A1 and clicking the left mouse button.

STEP 2 ▶

Point to the Bold tool (**B**) on the Standard toolbar and click.

Excel changes the worksheet title Monthly Office Expenses to a bold format (Figure 1-46).

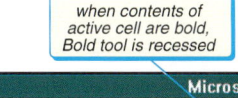

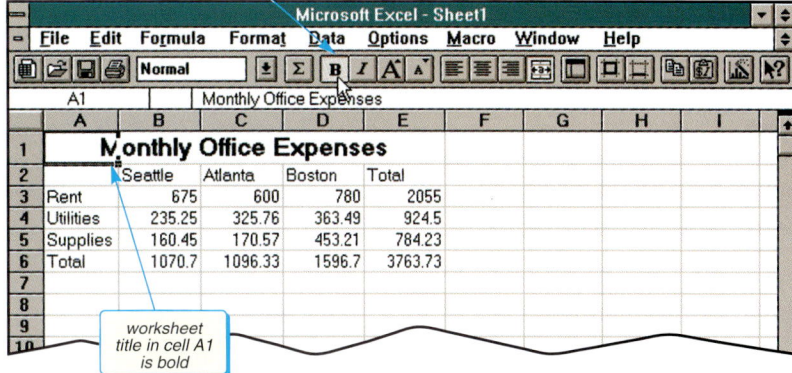

FIGURE 1-46

When the active cell is bold, the **Bold tool** is recessed (Figure 1-46). Clicking the Bold tool a second time removes the bold format.

▶ USING AUTOFORMAT TO FORMAT THE WORKSHEET

Excel has several customized format styles called **table formats** that allow you to format the body of the worksheet. The table formats can be used to give your worksheet a professional appearance. Follow these steps to automatically format the range A2:E6 on the Monthly Office Expenses worksheet.

TO USE THE AUTOFORMAT COMMAND

STEP 1 ▶

Select cell A2, the upper left corner cell of the rectangular range to format (Figure 1-47).

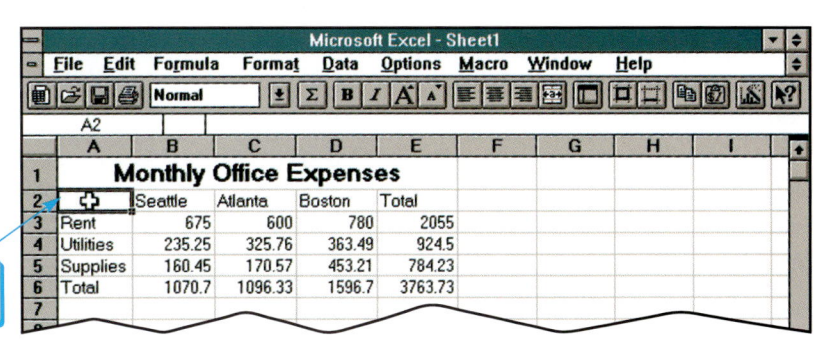

FIGURE 1-47

E26 PROJECT 1 BUILDING A WORKSHEET

STEP 2 ▶

Drag the mouse pointer to cell E6, the lower right corner cell of the range to format, and release the left mouse button.

Excel highlights the range to format (Figure 1-48).

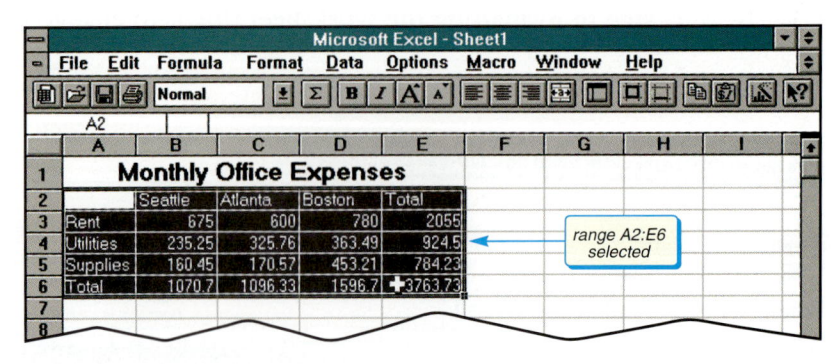

FIGURE 1-48

STEP 3 ▶

Select the Format menu and point to the AutoFormat command.

Excel pulls down the Format menu (Figure 1-49).

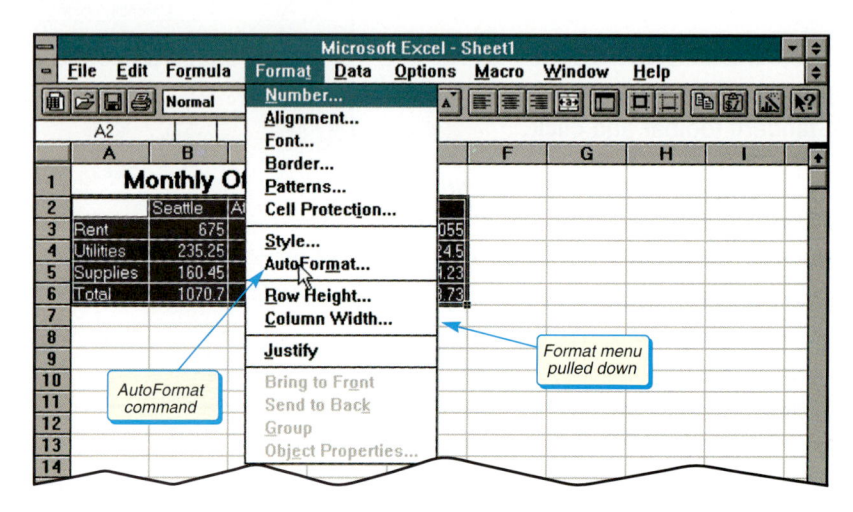

FIGURE 1-49

STEP 4 ▶

Choose the AutoFormat command.

Excel displays the AutoFormat dialog box (Figure 1-50). On the left side of the dialog box is a list of Table Format names. In Figure 1-50, the Table Format name, Classic 1, is highlighted. In the middle of the dialog box is a sample of the format that corresponds to the highlighted Table Format name, Classic 1.

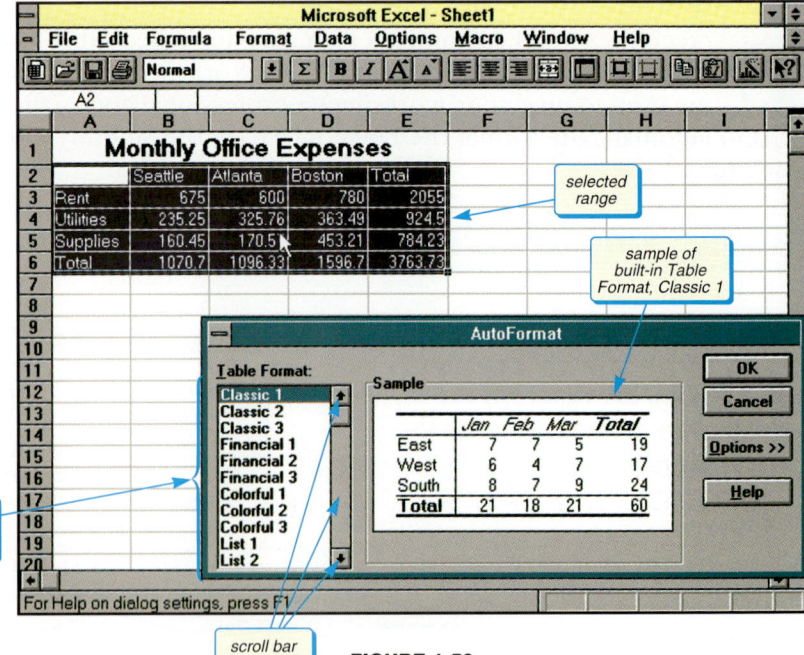

FIGURE 1-50

USING AUTOFORMAT TO FORMAT THE WORKSHEET   **E27**

STEP 5 ▶

Point to the Table Format name Financial 2 and click.

The sample in the dialog box now shows the Financial 2 format selected (Figure 1-51).

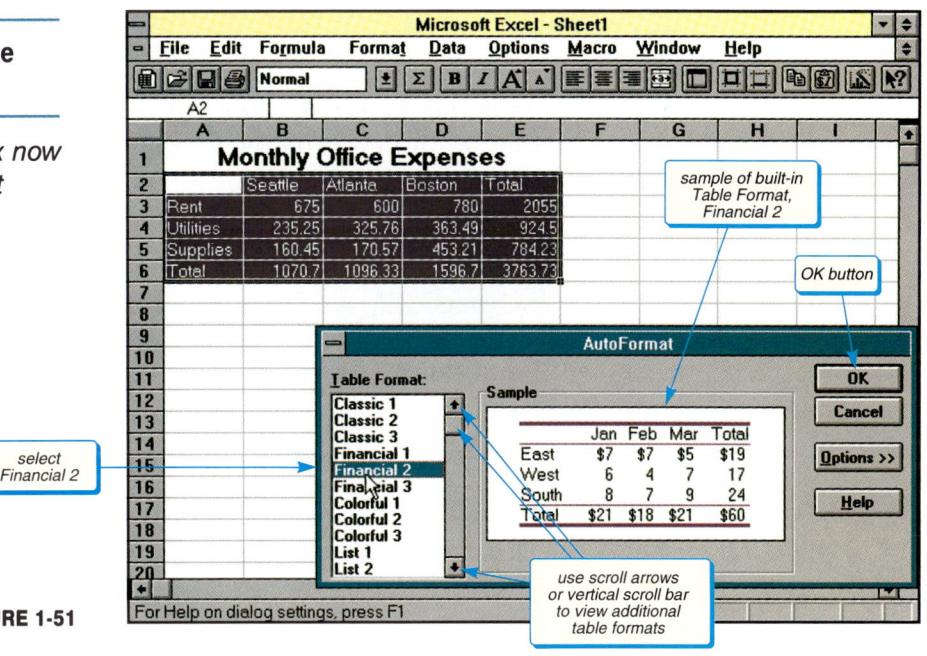

FIGURE 1-51

STEP 6 ▶

Choose the OK button (OK) from the AutoFormat dialog box. Select any cell in the worksheet outside the range A2:E6.

Excel displays the worksheet with the range A2:E6 using the customized format, Financial 2 (Figure 1-52).

FIGURE 1-52

Excel provides fourteen customized format styles from which to choose. Each format style has different characteristics. The format characteristics associated with the customized format, Financial 2 (Figure 1-52), include right-justification of column titles, numeric values displayed as dollars and cents, comma placement, numbers aligned on the decimal point, dollar signs in the first row of numbers and in the total row, and top and bottom borders emphasized.

Excel includes an **AutoFormat tool** ( ) on the Standard toolbar (Figure 1-52). If you select a range and click the AutoFormat tool, Excel uses the last format style selected. Hence, if you frequently use the same format style, select the range to format and click the AutoFormat tool instead of using the AutoFormat command on the Format menu.

The worksheet is now complete. The next step is to chart the monthly office expenses for the three offices.

▶ ADDING A CHART TO THE WORKSHEET

The column chart drawn by Excel in this project is based on the data in the Monthly Office Expenses worksheet (Figure 1-53). It is called an **embedded chart** because it is part of the worksheet and displays whenever the worksheet is on the screen.

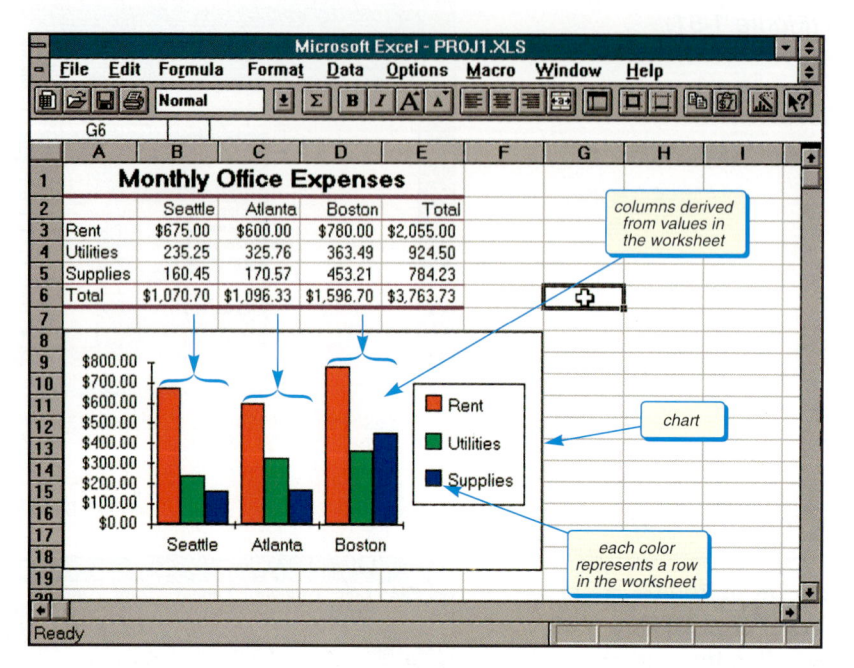

FIGURE 1-53

For Seattle, the red column represents the rent expense ($675.00), the green column represents the utilities expense ($235.25), and the blue column represents the supplies expense ($160.45). For Atlanta and Boston, the same color columns represent the comparable expenses. Notice in this chart that the totals from the worksheet are not represented because the totals were not in the range specified for charting.

Excel derived the dollar values along the Y-axis of the chart on the basis of the values in the worksheet. The value $800.00 is greater than any value in the worksheet, so it is the maximum value Excel included on the chart.

To draw a chart like the one in Figure 1-53, select the range to chart, click the **ChartWizard tool** ( ) on the Standard toolbar, and select the area on the worksheet where you want the chart drawn. In Figure 1-53, the chart is located immediately below the worksheet. When you determine the location of the chart on the worksheet, you also determine its size by dragging the mouse pointer from the upper left corner of the chart location to the lower right corner of the chart location.

Follow these detailed steps to draw a column chart that compares the monthly office expenses for the three cities.

ADDING A CHART TO THE WORKSHEET **E29**

TO DRAW AN EMBEDDED COLUMN CHART ▼

STEP 1 ▶

Select cell A2, the upper left corner of the range to chart (Figure 1-54).

FIGURE 1-54

STEP 2 ▶

Drag the mouse pointer to the lower right corner cell (cell D5) of the range to chart.

Excel highlights the range to chart (Figure 1-55).

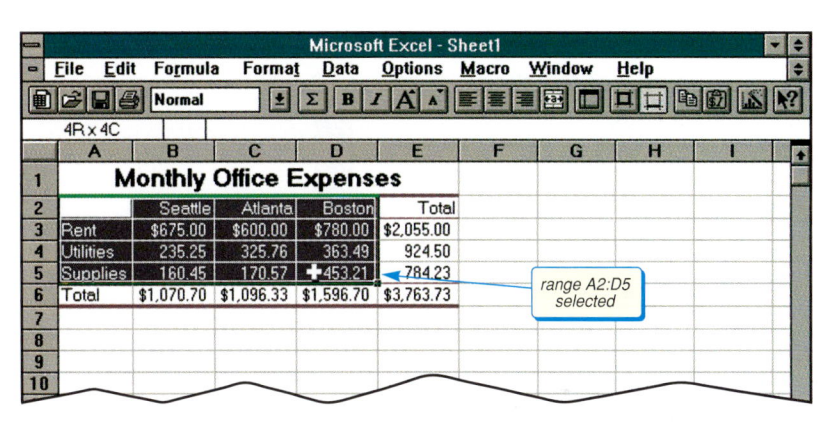

FIGURE 1-55

STEP 3 ▶

Click the ChartWizard tool on the Standard toolbar and move the mouse pointer into the window (Figure 1-56).

The mouse pointer changes to a cross hair (+).

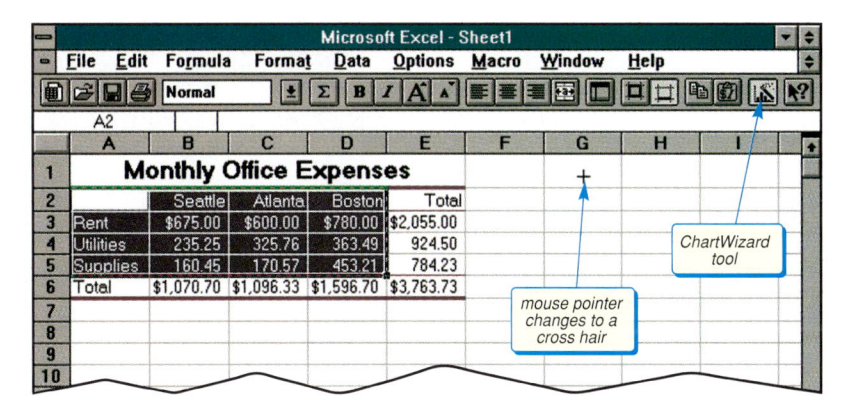

FIGURE 1-56

E30 PROJECT 1 BUILDING A WORKSHEET

STEP 4 ▶

Move the mouse pointer to the upper left corner of the chart location (cell A8) immediately below the worksheet.

A moving border surrounds the range to chart A2:D5. (Figure 1-57).

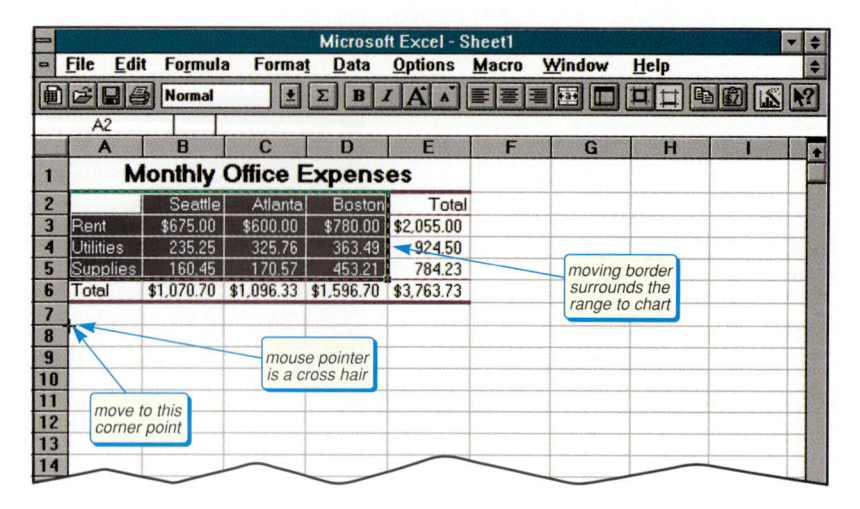

FIGURE 1-57

STEP 5 ▶

Drag the mouse pointer to the lower right corner of the chart location (cell F18).

The mouse pointer is positioned at the lower right corner of cell F18, and the chart location is surrounded by a dashed rectangle (Figure 1-58).

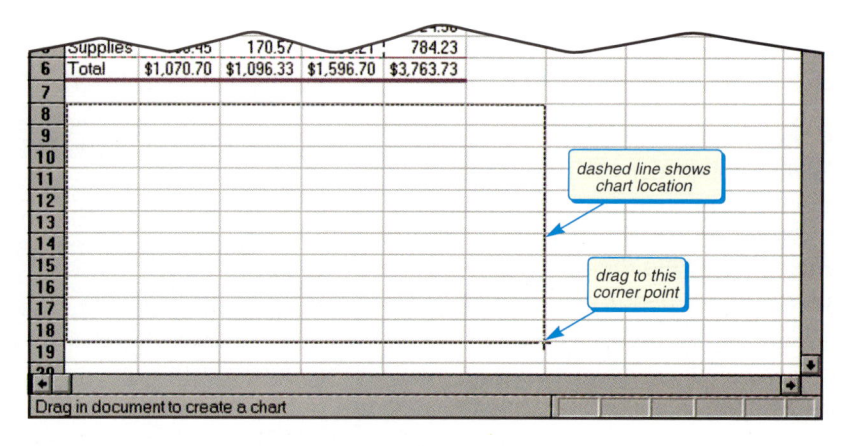

FIGURE 1-58

STEP 6 ▶

Release the left mouse button.

Excel responds by displaying the ChartWizard dialog box (Figure 1-59).

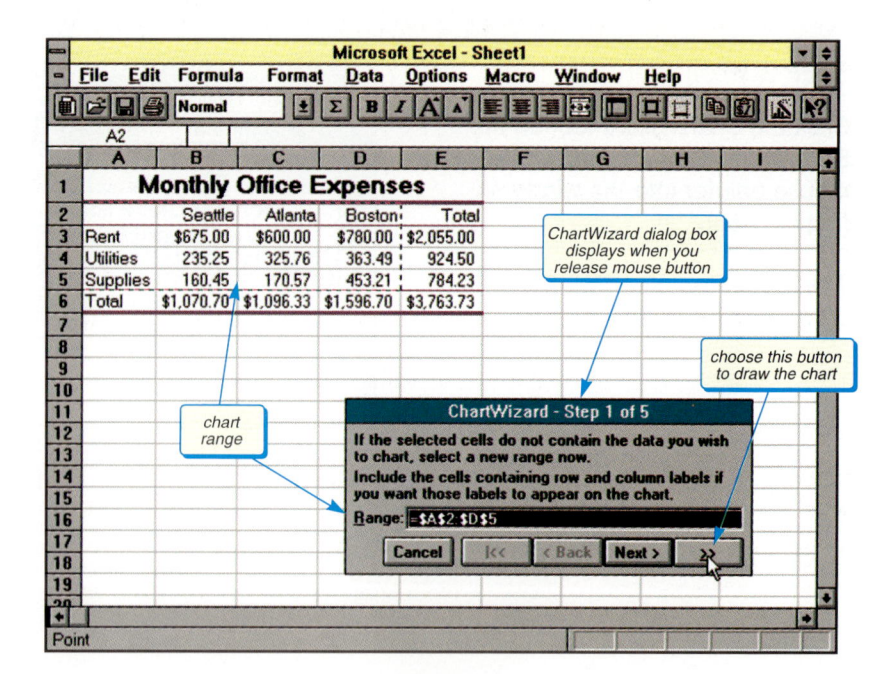

FIGURE 1-59

STEP 7 ▶

In the ChartWizard dialog box, choose the rightmost button with the two greater than signs (>>).

A column chart comparing the monthly office expenses for the three cities is drawn over the chart location (Figure 1-60). The small selection squares, or handles, on the border of the chart location indicate that the chart is selected. While the chart is selected, you can drag the chart to any location on the worksheet. You can also resize the chart by dragging on the handles.

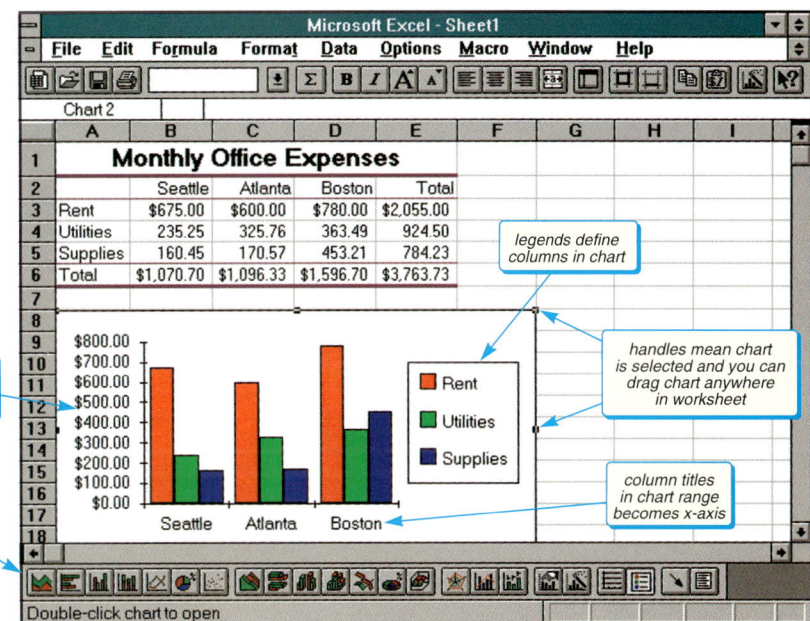

FIGURE 1-60

Select a cell outside the chart location to remove the chart selection.

The embedded column chart in Figure 1-60 compares the monthly office expenses for each city. It also allows you to compare the expenses between the cities. Notice that Excel automatically selects the entries in the row at the top of the range (row 2) as the titles for the x-axis and draws a column for each of the nine cells containing numbers in the range. The small box to the right of the column chart in Figure 1-60 contains the legends. The **legend** identifies each column in the chart. Excel automatically selects the leftmost column of the range (column A) as titles for the explanations. Excel also automatically scales the y-axis on the basis of the magnitude of the numbers in the graph range.

You can use the Chart toolbar that displays at the bottom of the screen while the chart is selected (Figure 1-60) to select different types of charts. Subsequent projects will discuss changing charts, sizing charts, adding text to charts, and why Excel initially draws a column chart rather than some other type of chart.

▶ SAVING THE WORKSHEET

While you are building a worksheet, the computer stores it in main memory. If the computer is turned off or if you lose electrical power, the worksheet is lost. Hence, it is mandatory to save on disk any worksheet that you will use later. The steps on the next three pages illustrate how to save a worksheet to drive A using the Save File tool on the Standard toolbar. It is assumed that you have a formatted disk in drive A.

E32 PROJECT 1 BUILDING A WORKSHEET

TO SAVE THE WORKSHEET

STEP 1 ▶

Point to the Save File tool (▫) on the Standard toolbar and click.

Excel responds by displaying the Save As dialog box (Figure 1-61).

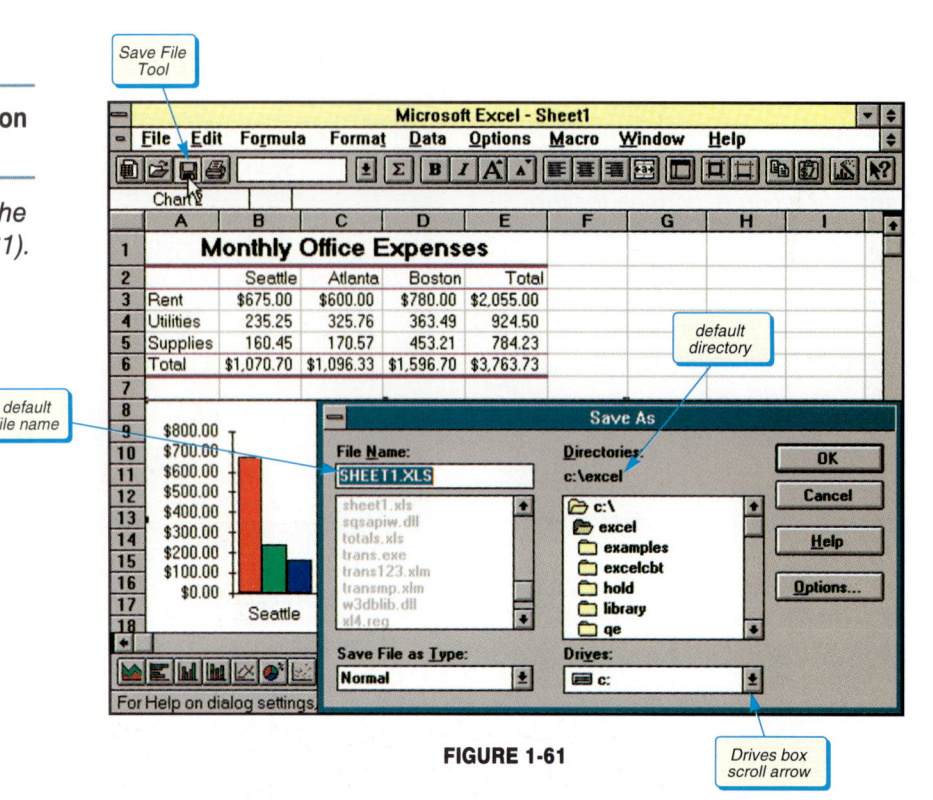

FIGURE 1-61

STEP 2 ▶

Type the file name `proj1` in the File Name box.

Thus, proj1 replaces SHEET1.XLS in the File name Box (Figure 1-62).

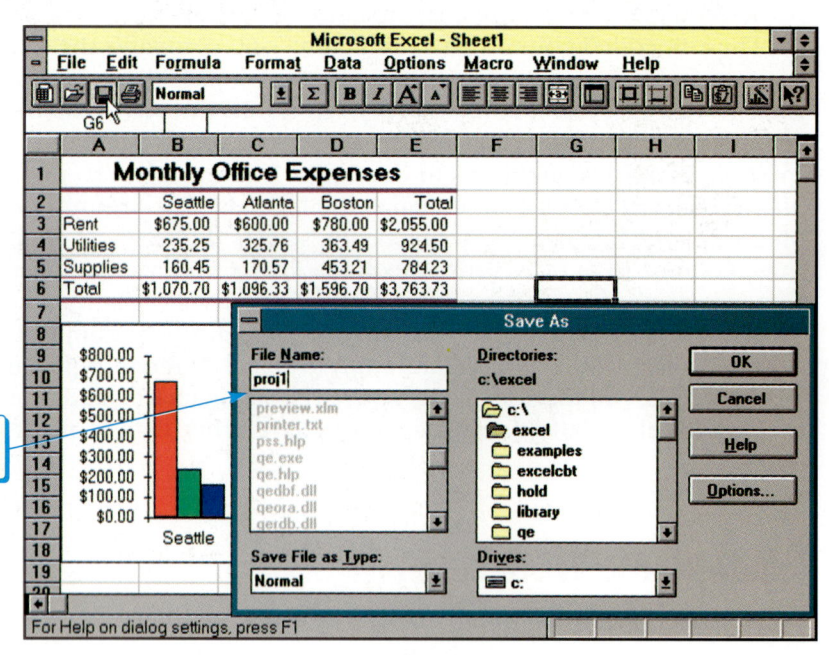

FIGURE 1-62

STEP 3 ▶

Click the Drives drop-down list box scroll arrow and point to a:.

A list of the available drives appears (Figure 1-63).

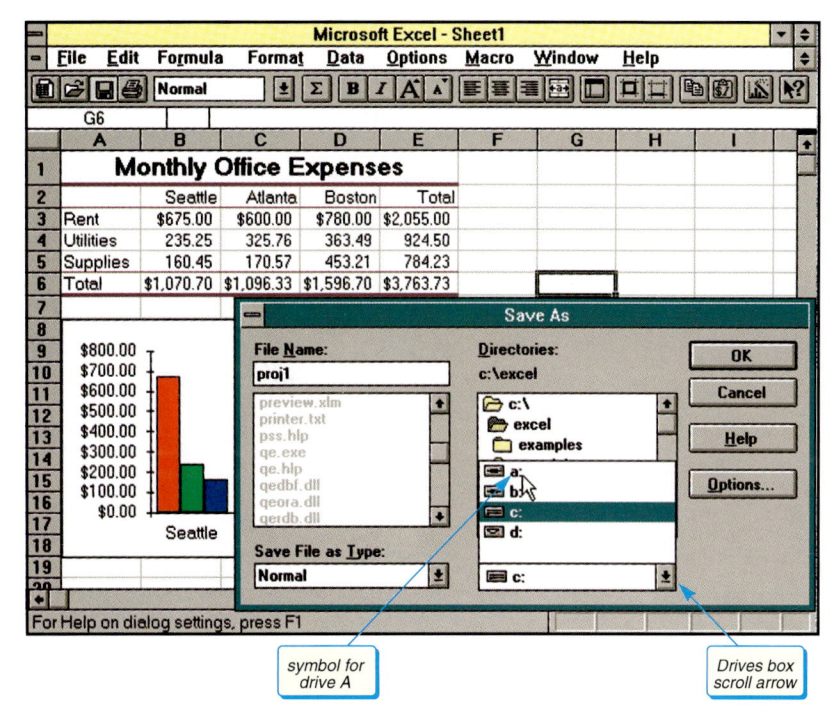

FIGURE 1-63

STEP 4 ▶

Select the drive name a:.

Drive A becomes the selected drive (Figure 1-64).

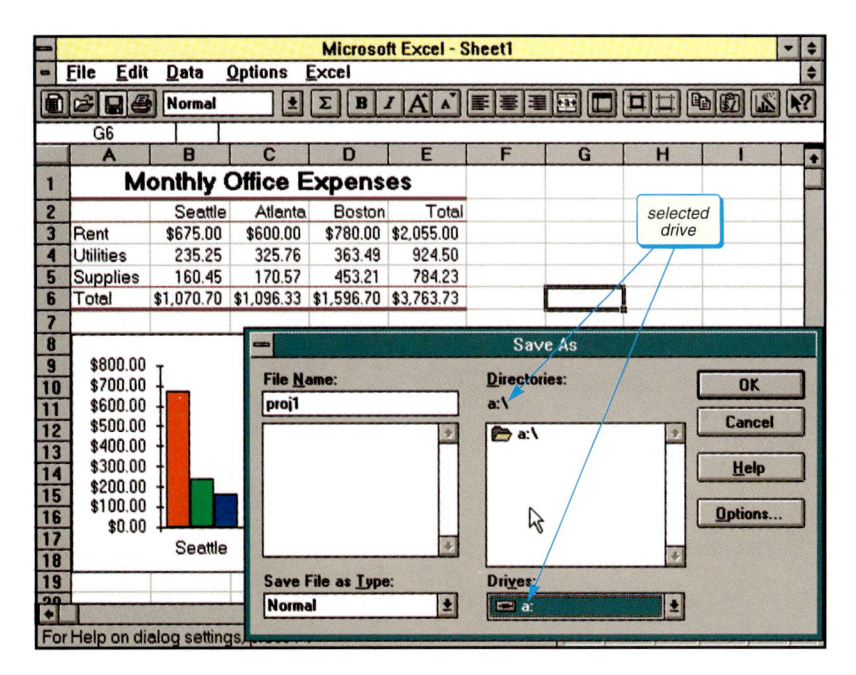

FIGURE 1-64

E34   PROJECT 1   BUILDING A WORKSHEET

STEP 5 ▶

Point to the OK button in the Save As dialog box (Figure 1-65).

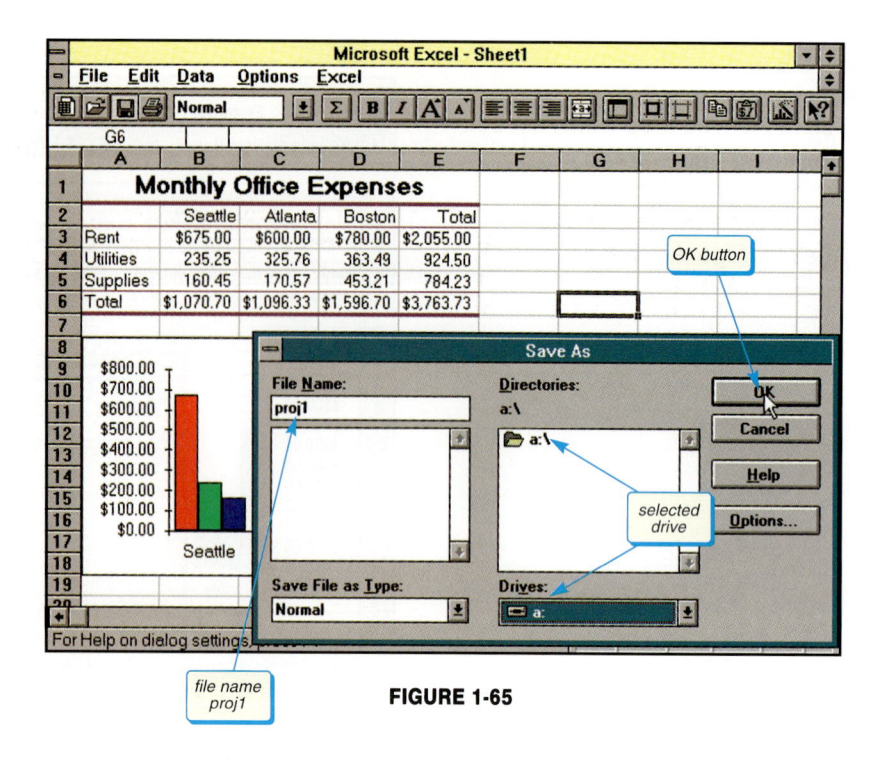

FIGURE 1-65

STEP 6 ▶

Choose the OK button from the Save As dialog box.

The worksheet is saved to drive A under the name proj1.xls. Excel automatically appends to the file name proj1 the extension .xls, which stands for Excel spreadsheet. Although the Monthly Office Expenses worksheet is saved on disk, it also remains in main memory and displays on the screen (Figure 1-66).

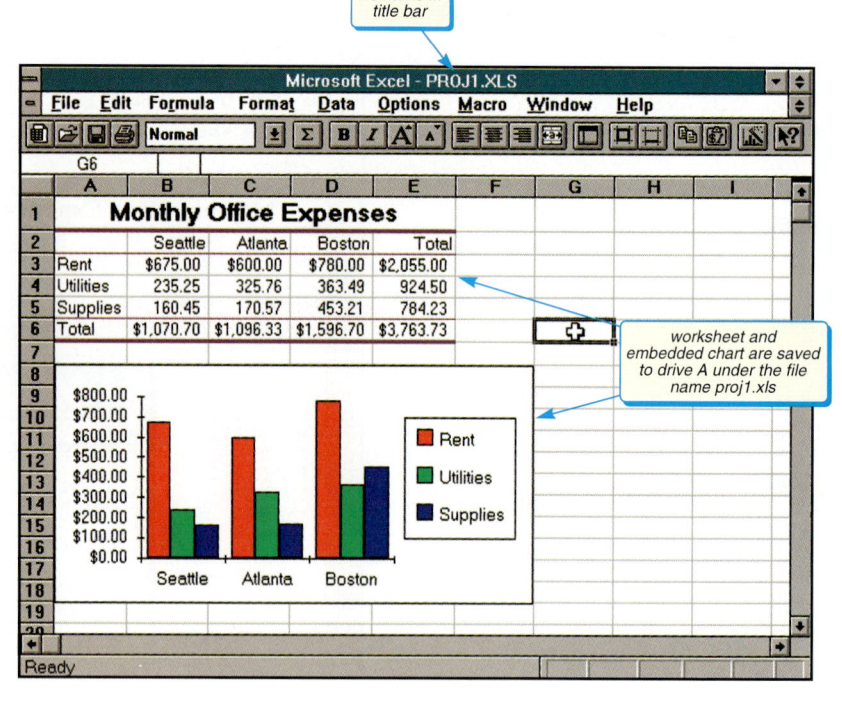

FIGURE 1-66

While Excel is saving the worksheet, it momentarily displays the percent saved in place of the active cell reference on the left side of the formula bar. After the save operation is complete, Excel changes the name of the worksheet in the title bar from Sheet1 to PROJ1.XLS (Figure 1-66).

Printing the Worksheet

Once you have created a worksheet and saved it on disk, you might want to print it. A printed version of the worksheet is called a **hard copy** or **printout**.

There are several reasons why you would want a printout. First, to present the worksheet to someone who does not have access to your computer, it must be in printed form. In addition, worksheets and charts are often kept for reference by persons other than those who prepare them. In many cases, the worksheets are printed and kept in binders for use by others. This section describes how to print a worksheet and the embedded chart.

TO PRINT A WORKSHEET

STEP 1

Ready the printer according to the printer instructions.

STEP 2 ▶

Select the File menu and point to the Page Setup command.

Excel displays the File menu (Figure 1-67).

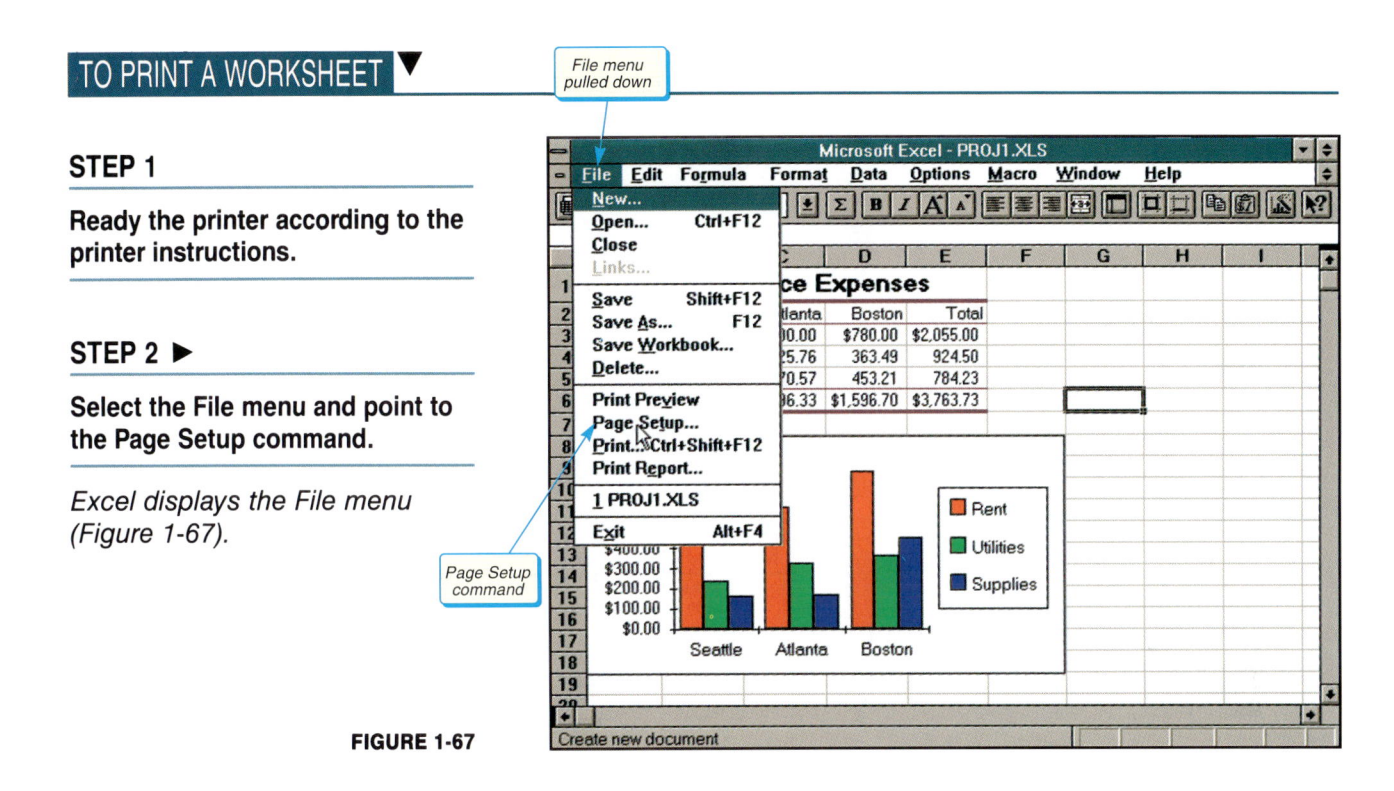

FIGURE 1-67

STEP 3 ▶

Choose the Page Setup command.

Excel displays the Page Setup dialog box (Figure 1-68).

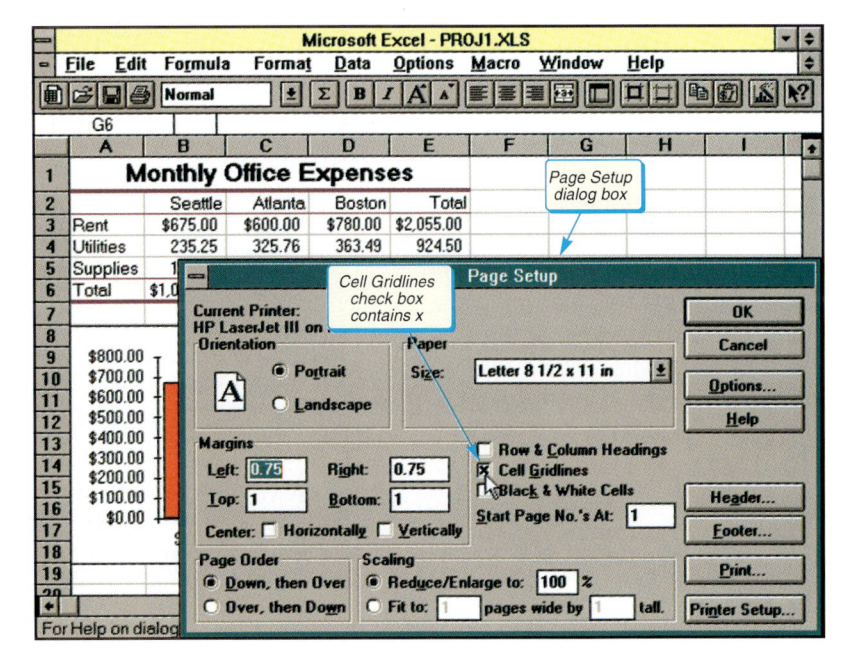

FIGURE 1-68

STEP 4 ▶

If an x appears in the Cell Gridlines check box in the middle of the Page Setup dialog box, select the check box by clicking it so that the x disappears.

The Cell Gridlines check box is empty (Figure 1-69). The gridlines on the screen will not print.

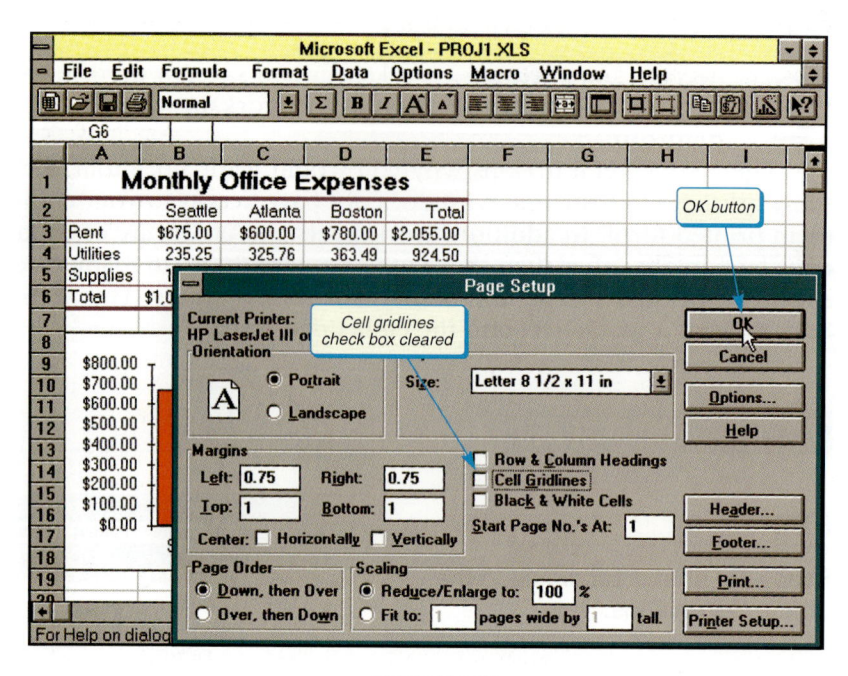

FIGURE 1-69

STEP 5 ▶

Choose the OK button from the Page Setup dialog box.

The Page Setup dialog box disappears and the worksheet reappears with a dashed line showing the right boundary of the page that Excel will print (Figure 1-70)

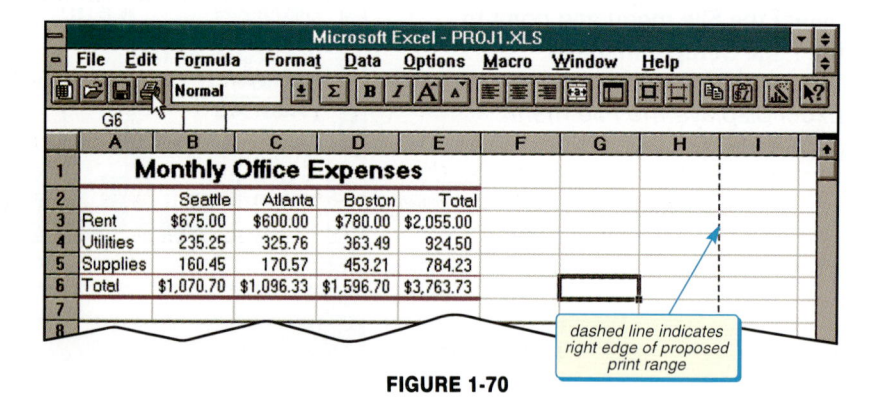

FIGURE 1-70

STEP 6 ▶

Point to the Print tool (🖨) on the Standard toolbar and click.

Excel displays the Printing dialog box (Figure 1-71) that allows you to cancel the print job at any time while the system is internally creating the worksheet image to send to the printer. When the Printing dialog box disappears, the printing begins.

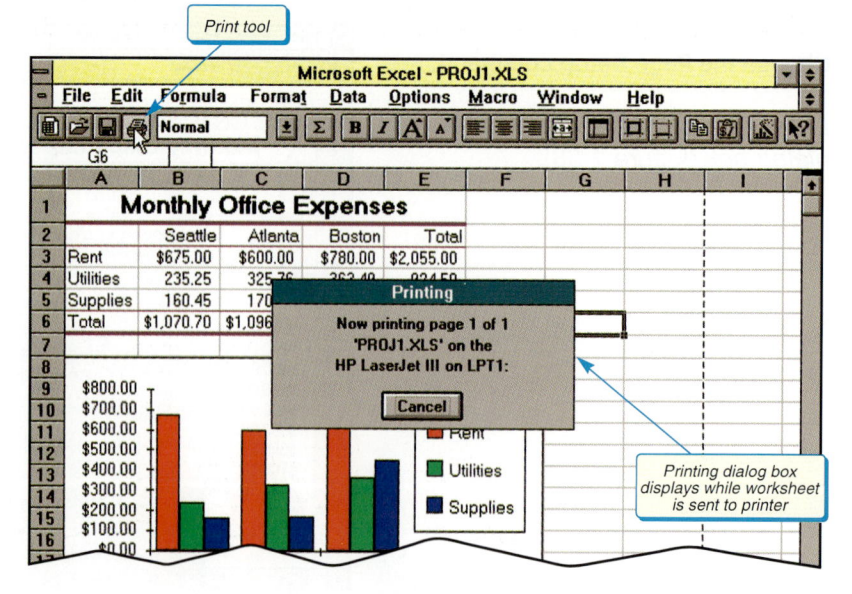

FIGURE 1-71

EXITING EXCEL **E37**

STEP 7 ▶

When the printer stops, retrieve the printout (Figure 1-72).

STEP 8

Point to the Save File tool on the Standard toolbar and click.

Excel saves the worksheet with the page setup characteristics shown in Figure 1-69. Saving the worksheet after changing the page setup means that you do not have to do Steps 2 through 5 the next time you print the worksheet unless you want to make other page setup changes.

FIGURE 1-72

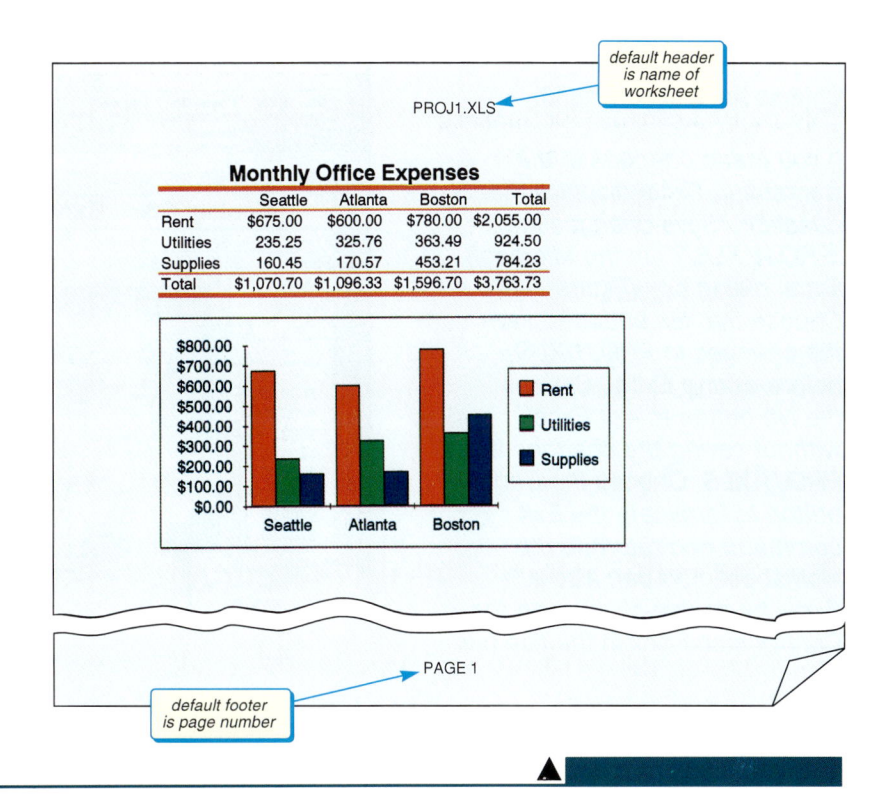

[Printout showing PROJ1.XLS header, Monthly Office Expenses table and bar chart, with PAGE 1 footer. Annotations: "default header is name of worksheet" and "default footer is page number".]

	Seattle	Atlanta	Boston	Total
Rent	$675.00	$600.00	$780.00	$2,055.00
Utilities	235.25	325.76	363.49	924.50
Supplies	160.45	170.57	453.21	784.23
Total	$1,070.70	$1,096.33	$1,596.70	$3,763.73

Notice in Figure 1-72 that Excel adds a header and footer. A **header** is a line of text that prints at the top of each page. A **footer** is a line of text that prints at the bottom of each page. By default, Excel prints the worksheet name as the header and the page number as the footer.

If you already know that the Cell Gridlines check box is clear, then you can skip Steps 2 through 5 in the previous list. In other words, if the printer is ready, click the Print tool to print the worksheet.

▶ EXITING EXCEL

After you build, save, and print the worksheet, Project 1 is complete. To exit Excel and return control to Program Manager, do the following:

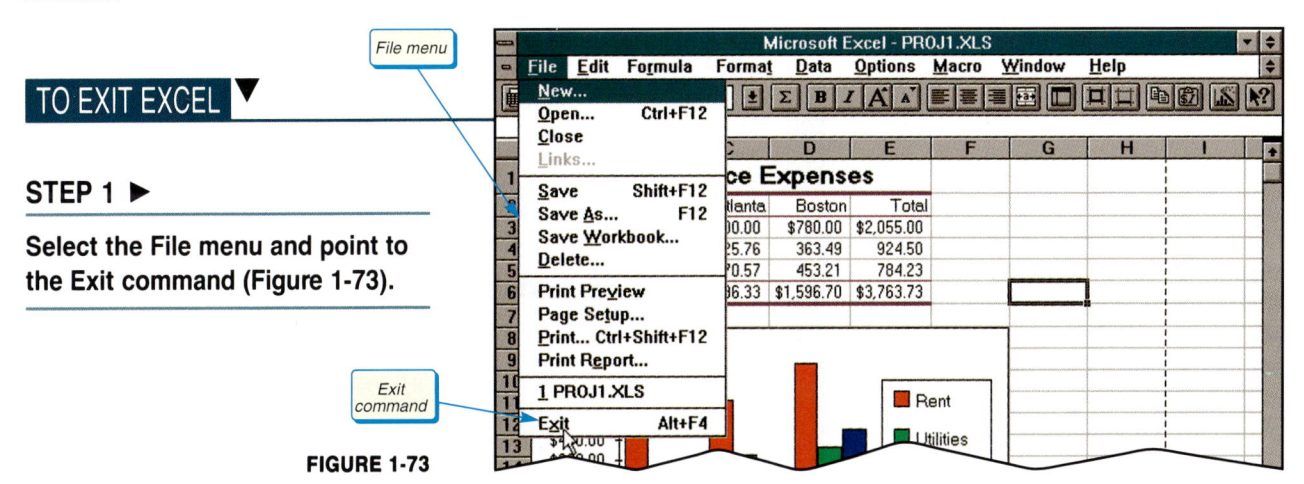

TO EXIT EXCEL ▼

STEP 1 ▶

Select the File menu and point to the Exit command (Figure 1-73).

FIGURE 1-73

[Screenshot of Microsoft Excel - PROJ1.XLS showing the File menu open with commands: New..., Open... Ctrl+F12, Close, Links..., Save Shift+F12, Save As... F12, Save Workbook..., Delete..., Print Preview, Page Setup..., Print... Ctrl+Shift+F12, Print Report..., 1 PROJ1.XLS, Exit Alt+F4. Annotations point to "File menu" and "Exit command".]

STEP 2 ▶

Choose the Exit command.

If you made changes to the worksheet, Excel displays the question "Save changes in 'PROJ1.XLS'?" in the Microsoft Excel dialog box (Figure 1-74). Choose the Yes button to save the changes to PROJ1.XLS before exiting Excel. Choose the No button to exit Excel without saving the changes to PROJ1.XLS. Choose the Cancel button to terminate the Exit command and return to the worksheet. You can also exit Excel by double-clicking on the Control-menu box in the title bar.

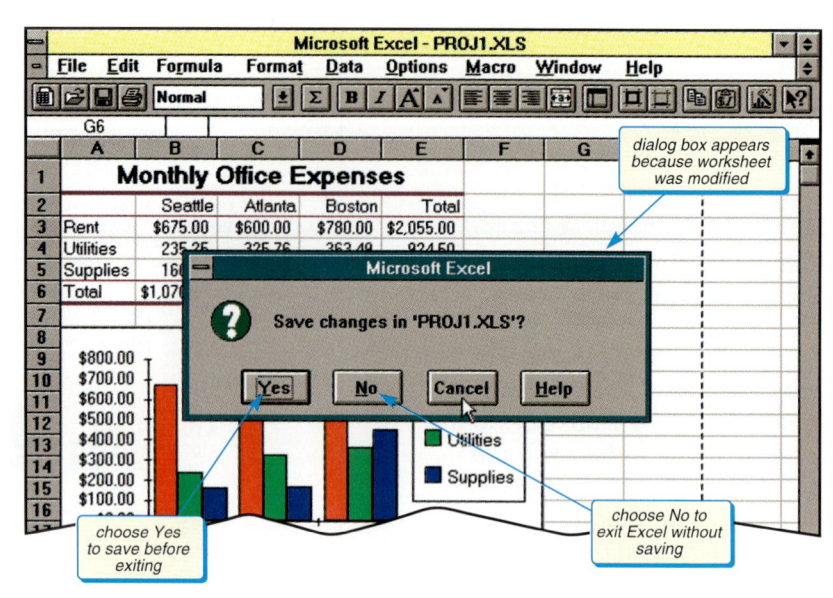

FIGURE 1-74

▶ OPENING A WORKSHEET

Earlier, you saved on disk the worksheet built in Project 1 using the filename PROJ1.XLS. Once you have created and saved a worksheet, you will often have reason to retrieve it from disk. For example, you might want to enter revised data, review the calculations on the worksheet, or add more data to the worksheet. After starting Excel (see page E4), you can use the following steps to open PROJ1.XLS using the Open File tool ( ).

TO OPEN A WORKSHEET ▼

STEP 1

Point to the Open File tool on the Standard toolbar and click.

Excel displays the Open dialog box.

STEP 2 ▶

If Drive A is not the selected drive, select a: in the Drives drop-down list box (refer to Figures 1-63 and 1-64 on page E33 to review this technique). Select the file name proj1.xls by clicking the file name in the File Name list box (Figure 1-75).

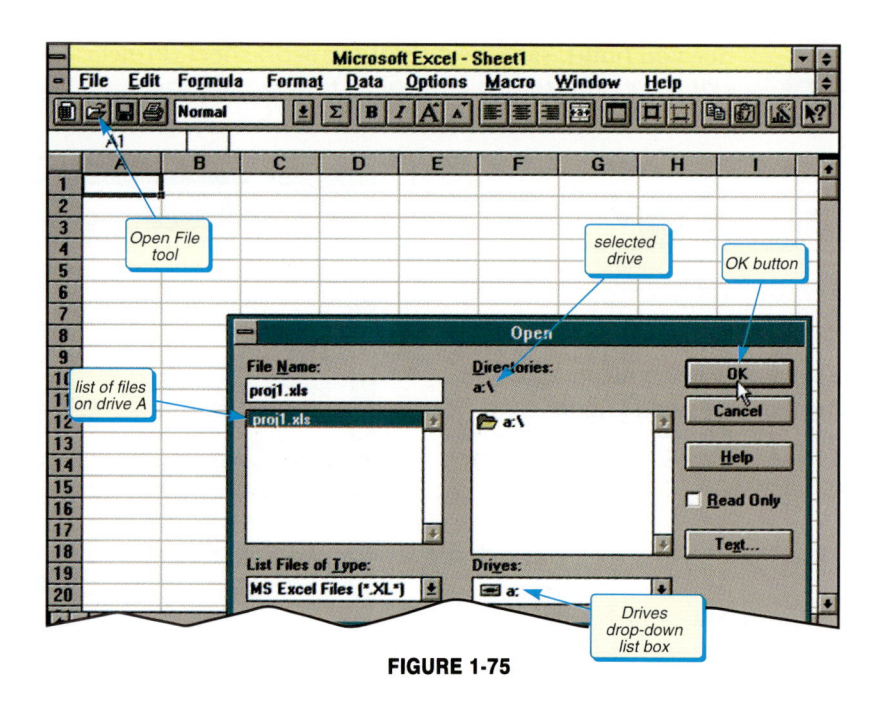

FIGURE 1-75

STEP 3 ▶

Choose the OK button from the Open dialog box.

Excel loads the worksheet PROJ1.XLS from drive A into main memory, and displays it on the screen (Figure 1-76).

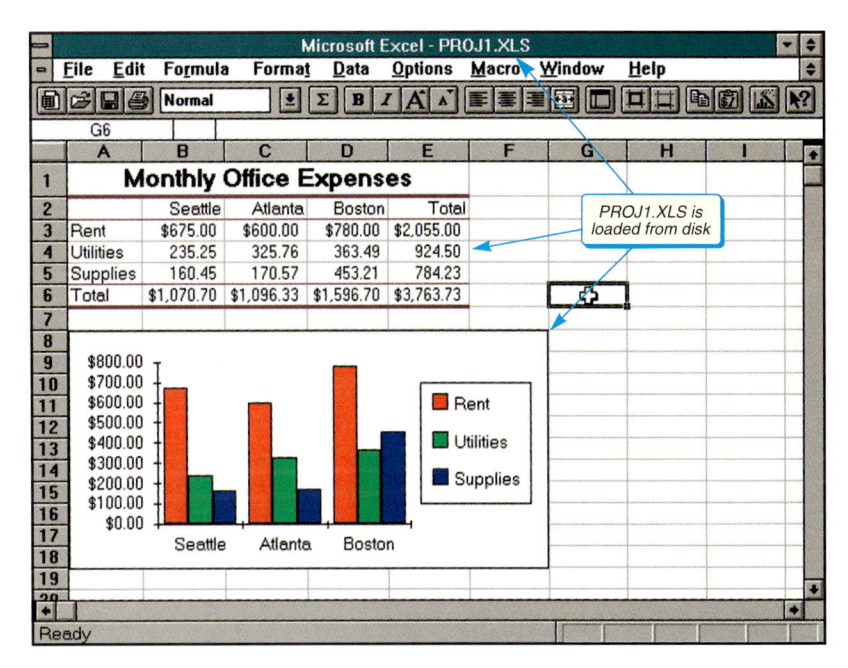

FIGURE 1-76

▶ CORRECTING ERRORS

Several methods are available for correcting errors on a worksheet. The one you choose will depend on the severity of the error and whether you notice it while typing the data in the formula bar or after you have entered the incorrect data into the cell.

Correcting Errors Prior to Entering Data into a Cell

If you notice an error prior to entering data into a cell, do one of the following:

1. Use the BACKSPACE key to erase the portion in error and then type the correct characters; or
2. If the error is too severe, click the cancel box or press the ESC key to erase the entire entry in the formula bar and reenter the data from the beginning.

Editing Data in a Cell

If you spot an error in the worksheet after entering the data, select the cell with the error. You can correct the error in one of two ways:

1. If the entry is short, simply retype it and click the enter box or press the ENTER key. The new entry will replace the old entry. Remember, the heavy border must be around the cell with the error before you begin typing.
2. If the entry in the cell is long and the errors are minor, the **Edit mode** may be a better choice. Use the Edit mode described in the list that follows on the next page.

a. Select the cell with the error.
b. Click the first character in error in the formula line (or press function key F2). Excel displays Edit in the status bar at the bottom of the screen and activates the insertion point in the formula bar.
c. Make your changes.

When Excel enters the Edit mode, the keyboard is normally in Insert mode (OVR displays in the status bar if it is NOT in Insert mode). In **Insert mode**, as you type a character Excel inserts the character and moves all characters to the right of the typed character one position to the right.

You can change to Overtype mode (OVR) by pressing the INSERT key. In **Overtype mode**, Excel overtypes characters to the right of the edit cursor. The INSERT key toggles the keyboard between Insert mode and Overtype mode.

To delete a character in the formula bar, place the edit cursor to the left of the character you want to delete and press the DELETE key.

When you're finished editing an entry, click the enter box or press the ENTER key. It is common to make keyboard and grammatical errors. Understanding how to use Edit mode will allow you to correct mistakes easily.

Undoing the Last Entry — The Undo Command

Excel provides an **Undo command** that you can use to erase the most recent cell entry. If you enter the wrong data in a cell, from the Edit menu, choose the Undo command (Figure 1-77). Excel changes the cell contents to what they were prior to entering the incorrect data.

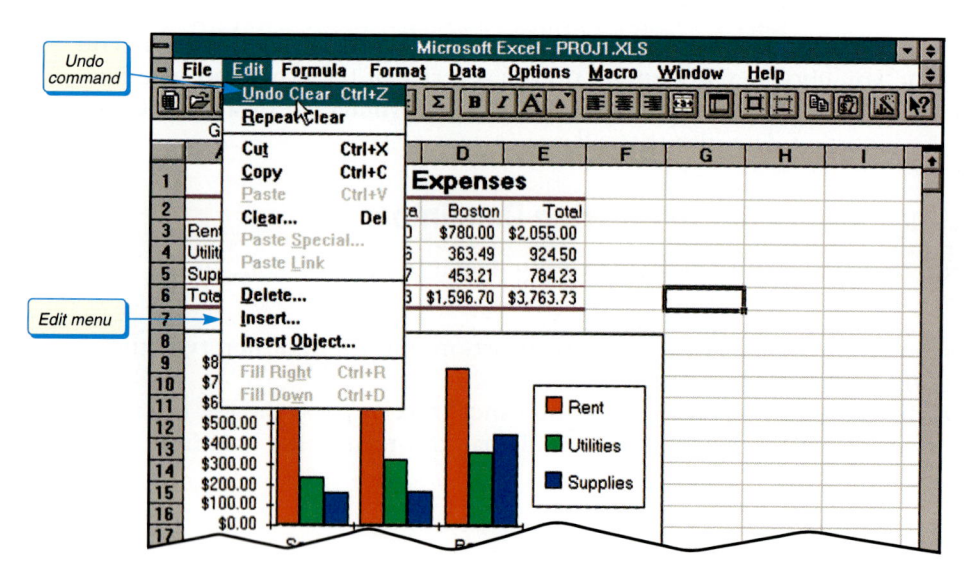

FIGURE 1-77

You can use the Undo command to undo more complicated worksheet activities than a single cell entry. For example, most commands you issue can be undone if you choose the Undo command before making another entry. The general rule is that the Undo command can restore the worksheet data and settings to what they were the last time Excel was in Ready mode. If Excel cannot undo an operation, then the words "Can't Undo" appear dimmed at the top of the Edit menu in place of Undo.

Clearing a Cell or Range of Cells

It is not unusual to enter data into the wrong cell or range of cells. In such a case, to correct the error, you might want to erase or clear the data. *Never select a cell and press the* SPACEBAR *to enter a blank character to clear a cell.* A blank character is text and is different than an empty cell, even though the cell may appear empty.

Excel provides three methods to clear the contents of a cell or a range of cells.

TO CLEAR CELL CONTENTS USING THE FILL HANDLE

Step 1: Select the cell or range of cells and point at the fill handle so the mouse pointer changes to a small dark plus sign.
Step 2: Drag the fill handle into the cell or range until a shadow covers the cell or cells you want to erase.
Step 3: Release the left mouse button.

TO CLEAR CELL CONTENTS USING THE DELETE KEY

Step 1: Select the cell or range of cells to be cleared.
Step 2: Press the DELETE key.
Step 3: When Excel displays the Delete dialog box, select the All option button.
Step 4: Choose OK from the Delete dialog box.

TO CLEAR CELL CONTENTS USING THE CLEAR COMMAND

Step 1: Select the cell or range of cells to be cleared.
Step 2: Choose Clear from the Edit menu.
Step 3: When Excel displays the Delete dialog box, select the All option button.
Step 4: Choose OK from the Delete dialog box.

Clearing the Entire Worksheet

Sometimes, everything goes wrong. If this happens you might want to **clear the worksheet** entirely and start over. To clear the worksheet, follow these steps.

TO CLEAR THE ENTIRE WORKSHEET

Step 1: Select the entire worksheet by clicking the **Select All button** (☐) which is just above row heading 1 and immediately to the left of column heading A.
Step 2: Press the DELETE key or choose the Clear command from the Edit menu.
Step 3: When Excel displays the Delete dialog box, select the All option.
Step 4: Choose the OK button from the Delete dialog box.

TO DELETE AN EMBEDDED CHART

Step 1: Click the chart.
Step 2: Press the DELETE key or choose the Clear command from the Edit menu.

An alternative to using the Select All button and the DELETE key or Clear command from the Edit menu to clear an entire worksheet is to choose the

Close command from the File menu. If you choose the Close command to erase a worksheet, choose the **New command** from the File menu to begin working on your next worksheet.

▶ EXCEL HELP FACILITY

At any time while you are using Excel, you can select the Help menu to gain access to the **Help facility** (Figure 1-78). The Excel Help menu provides a table of contents and a search command for navigating around the Help facility. Pressing function key F1 also allows you to obtain help on various topics.

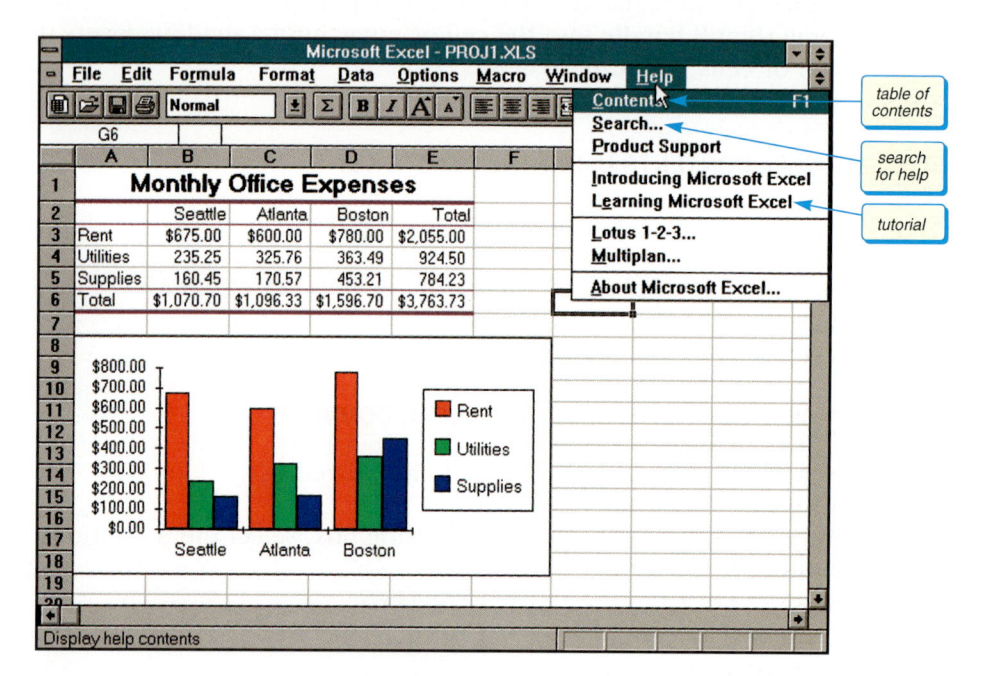

FIGURE 1-78

In many Excel dialog boxes you can click a Help button to obtain help about the current activity on which you are working. If there is no Help button in a dialog box, press function key F1 while the dialog box is on the screen.

Help Tool on the Standard Toolbar

To use the Excel Help facility, you can click the **Help tool** ( ) on the Standard toolbar (top screen of Figure 1-79). Move the arrow and question mark pointer ( ) to any menu name, tool, or cell, and click to get context-sensitive help. The term **context-sensitive help** means that Excel will display immediate information on the topic at which the arrow and question mark pointer is pointing. For example, clicking the Bold tool displays the Help window shown in the bottom screen of Figure 1-79.

You can print the Help information in the Help window by choosing the Print Topic command from the File menu in the Help window. You close a Help window by choosing Exit from the File menu in the Help window.

The Excel Help facility has features that make it powerful and easy to use. The best way to familiarize yourself with the Help facility is to use it.

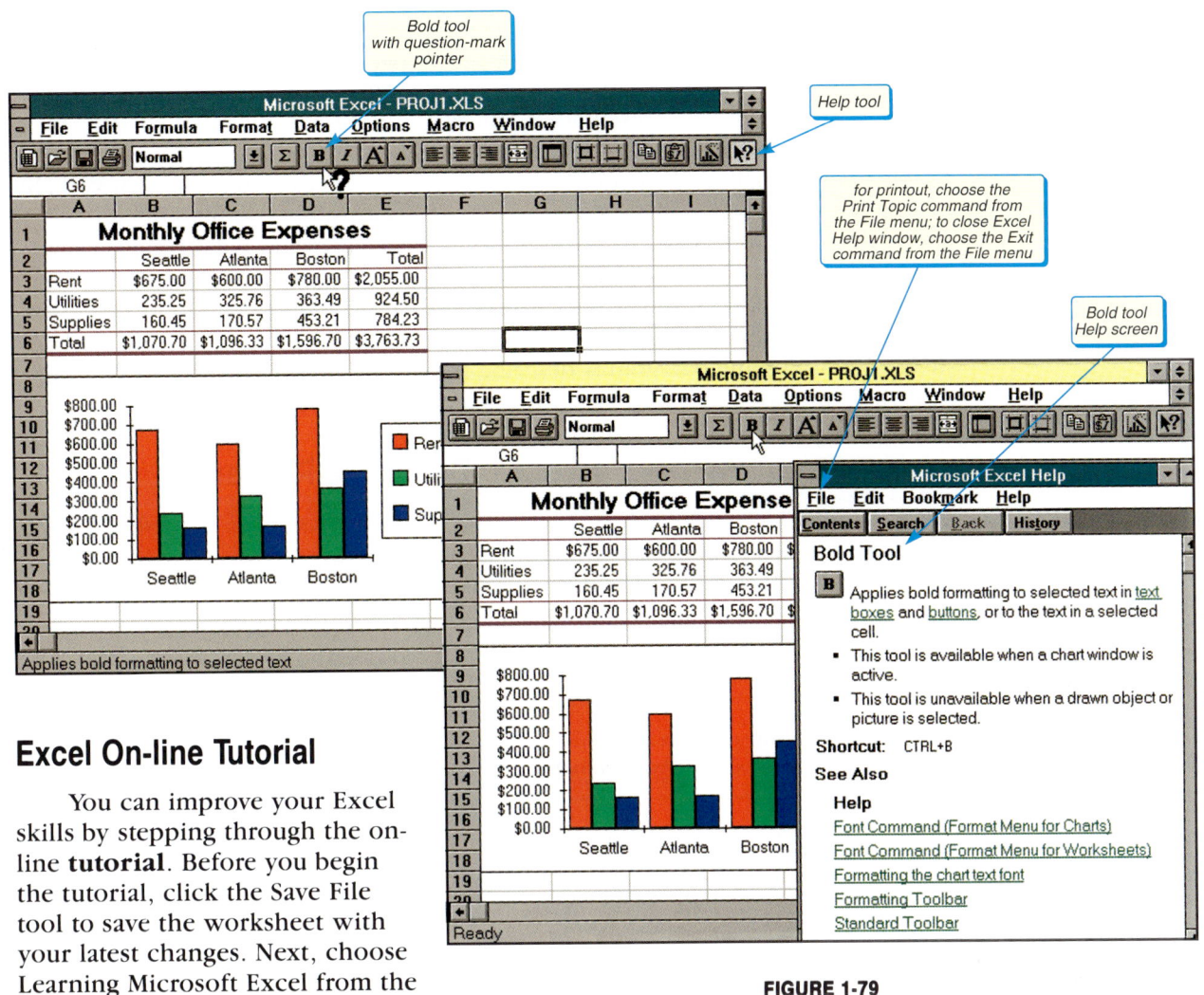

EXCEL HELP FACILITY **E43**

FIGURE 1-79

Excel On-line Tutorial

You can improve your Excel skills by stepping through the on-line **tutorial**. Before you begin the tutorial, click the Save File tool to save the worksheet with your latest changes. Next, choose Learning Microsoft Excel from the Help menu (Figure 1-78). Excel responds by displaying the screen shown in Figure 1-80. Select any of the eleven lessons. When you select one, Excel tells you approximately how long it will take to step through the tutorial (usually 10 to 15 minutes).

The lesson titled "Using Microsoft Excel Help" listed under Introduction is highly recommended to help you become familiar with Excel.

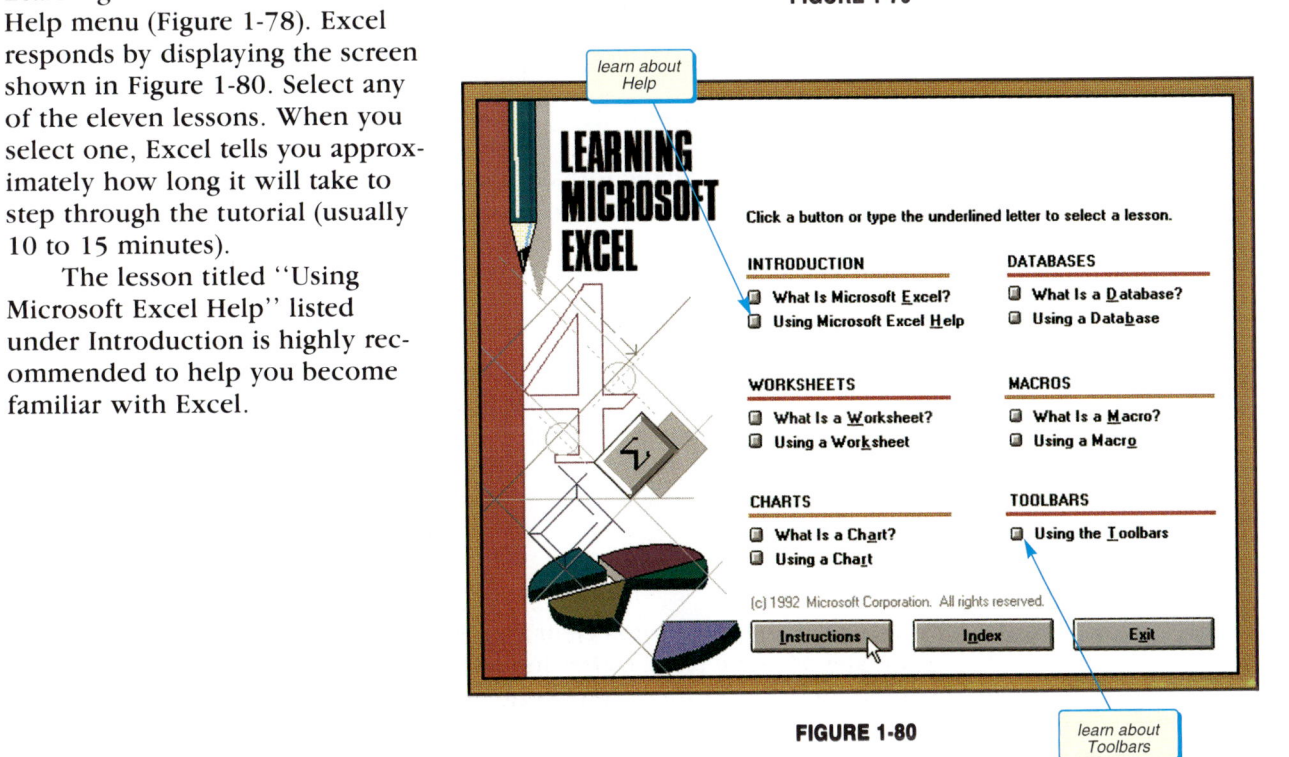

FIGURE 1-80

▶ Planning a Worksheet

At the beginning of this project, the completed monthly Office Expenses worksheet was presented in Figure 1-1 and then built step by step. In the business world, you are seldom given the worksheet specifications in this form. Usually, the specifications for a worksheet are given to you verbally or in paragraph form on paper, and it is your responsibility to plan the worksheet from start to finish. Careful planning can significantly reduce your effort and result in a worksheet that is accurate, easy to read, flexible, and useful.

In planning a worksheet, you should follow these steps: (1) Define the problem; (2) Design the worksheet; (3) Enter the worksheet; and, (4) Test the worksheet. The following paragraphs describe these four steps in detail and outlines how the Monthly Office Expenses worksheet in Figure 1-1 was planned.

FIGURE 1-81

> Purpose of Worksheet   Create a worksheet that determines and compares the total monthly expenses for the three offices.
>
> Expected Results   Display the total monthly expenses for each office, for each expense category, and for the company. Draw a column chart that compares the expenses within each office.
>
> Required Data   Obtain the monthly rent, utility, and supply expenses for the three offices.
>
> Required Calculations   Use the SUM function to calculate the total expenses for each office, each expense category, and the total expenses for the company.

Define the Problem

In this first step, write down on paper the following:

1. The purpose of the worksheet.
2. The results or output you want, including such items as totals and charts.
3. Identify the data needed to determine the results.
4. List the required calculations to transform the data to the desired results.

Figure 1-81 shows one way to define the Monthly Office Expenses problem.

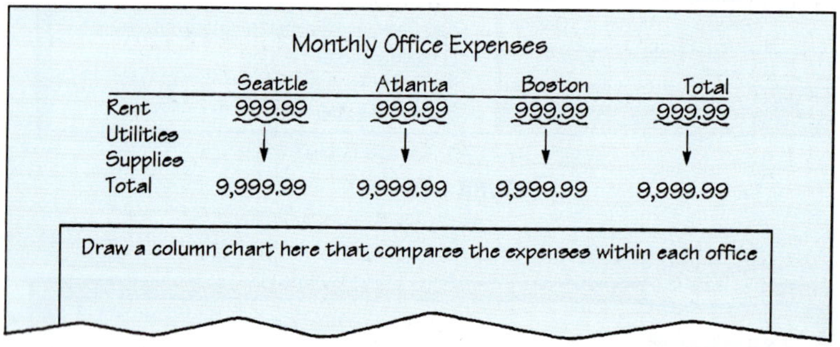

Design the Worksheet

In this second step, outline the worksheet on paper. Include the worksheet title, column titles, row titles, totals, and chart location if required.

FIGURE 1-82

>   Monthly Office Expenses
>
>   Seattle   Atlanta   Boston   Total
> Rent   999.99   999.99   999.99   999.99
> Utilities   ↓   ↓   ↓   ↓
> Supplies
> Total   9,999.99   9,999.99   9,999.99   9,999.99
>
> Draw a column chart here that compares the expenses within each office

Don't worry about the specific formats that will eventually be assigned to the worksheet. Figure 1-82 illustrates the outline for the Monthly Office Expenses worksheet. The series of 9s in Figure 1-82 indicates numeric entries.

Enter the Worksheet

After defining the problem and outlining the worksheet, start Excel and enter the worksheet. One technique that is used by spreadsheet professionals is to type, in order: (1) the worksheet title; (2) column titles; (3) row titles; (4) numeric data; (5) functions or formulas; (6) after the worksheet is entered, format it to make it easier to read; and, (7) finally, add any required charts.

Test the Worksheet

Test the worksheet until it is error free. You want to be sure that the worksheet generates accurate results. Develop test data that evaluates the functions and formulas in the worksheet. Verify the results using paper, pencil, and a calculator. Begin by entering numbers that are easy to compute by hand and move to more complex entries that test the limits of the worksheet.

KEY TERMS E45

▶ **PROJECT SUMMARY**

Project 1 introduced you to starting Excel and entering text and numbers into a worksheet. You learned how to select a range and how to use the AutoSum tool to sum numbers in a column or row. You also learned how to copy a cell to adjacent cells using the fill handle.

Once the worksheet was built, you learned how to change the font size of the title, bold the title, and center the title over a range using tools on the Standard toolbar. You formatted the body of the worksheet using the AutoFormat command. You used the ChartWizard tool to add a column chart to the worksheet. After the worksheet was complete, you saved it on disk and printed it. Finally, you learned how to edit data in cells and previewed the use of the Excel Help feature.

▶ **KEY TERMS**

active cell (*E5*)
active cell reference (*E5*)
arrow keys (*E8*)
AutoFormat command (*E25*)
AutoFormat dialog box (*E26*)
AutoFormat tool (*E27*)
AutoSum tool (*E15*)
BACKSPACE key (*E10*)
Bold tool (*E25*)
cancel box (*E9*)
cell (*E5*)
cell reference (*E5*)
cell gridlines (*E5, E6*)
Center Across Columns tool (*E23*)
chart toolbar (*E31*)
ChartWizard dialog box (*E31*)
ChartWizard tool (*E28*)
clear cells (*E41*)
clear chart (*E41*)
clear worksheet (*E41*)
Close command (*E42*)
column chart (*E5*)
column (*E5*)
context-sensitive help (*E42*)
copy (*E17*)
decimal numbers (*E15*)
Decrease-Font tool (*E24*)
documentation (*E42*)
Drives box (*E32*)
Edit menu (*E40*)
Edit mode (*E39*)
editing cells (*E39*)
embedded chart (*E28*)
empty cells (*E41*)

enter box (*E9*)
ENTER key (*E10*)
Enter mode (*E7*)
ESC key (*E10*)
Excel (*E2*)
File menu (*E35*)
fill handle (*E17*)
font size (*E22*)
font style (*E22*)
font type (*E22*)
footer (*E37*)
format (*E25*)
Format menu (*E26*)
formula bar (*E7*)
handle for charts (*E31*)
hard copy (*E35*)
header (*E37*)
Help facility (*E42*)
Help tool (*E42*)
Increase-Font tool (*E24*)
Insert mode (*E40*)
insertion point (*E9*)
keyboard indicators (*E8*)
left-justified (*E10*)
legend (*E31*)
loading a worksheet (*E38*)
menu bar (*E6*)
Microsoft Excel dialog box (*E4*)
mode indicators (*E7*)
mouse pointer shapes (*E5*)
New command (*E42*)
numbers (*E13*)
Open a worksheet (*E38*)
Open dialog box (*E38*)
Open File tool (*E38*)

Overtype mode (*E40*)
Page Setup Dialog box (*E36*)
paste area (*E17*)
point size (*E22*)
Print tool (*E36*)
printing a worksheet (*E35*)
Printing Dialog box (*E36*)
Printout (*E35*)
quitting Excel (*E37*)
range (*E17*)
Ready mode (*E7*)
relative reference (*E18*)
right-justified (*E15*)
row (*E5*)
Save As Dialog box (*E32*)
Save File tool (*E32*)
saving a worksheet (*E32*)
scroll arrow (*E6*)
scroll bar (*E6*)
scroll box (*E6*)
Select All button (*E41*)
select cell (*E8*)
Standard toolbar (*E7*)
starting Excel (*E4*)
status bar (*E7*)
SUM function (*E15*)
table formats (*E25*)
text (*E8*)
tutorial (*E43*)
Undo command (*E40*)
window (*E6*)
worksheet (*E5*)
worksheet window (*E6*)
.xls (*E34*)

QUICK REFERENCE

In Microsoft Excel you can accomplish a task in a number of ways. The following table provides a quick reference to each task presented in this project with its available options. The commands listed in the Menu column can be executed using either the keyboard or mouse.

Task	Mouse	Menu	Keyboard Shortcuts
AutoFormat	Click AutoFormat tool on Standard toolbar	From Format menu, choose AutoFormat	
Bold	Click Bold tool on Standard toolbar	From Format menu, choose Font	Press CTRL + P
Cancel an Entry in the Formula Bar	Click cancel box in formula bar		Press ESC
Center Across Columns	Click Center Across Columns tool on Standard toolbar	From Format menu, choose Alignment	
Chart	Click ChartWizard tool on Standard toolbar		
Clear Cell Gridlines from Printout		From File menu, choose Page Setup	
Clear Selected Cell or Range	Drag fill handle into cell or range	From Edit menu, choose Clear	Press DELETE
Clear Selected Worksheet		From Edit menu, choose Clear	Press DELETE
Complete an Entry in the Formula Bar	Click enter box in formula bar or click any cell		Press ENTER
Context-Sensitive Help	Click Help tool on Standard toolbar		Press SHIFT + F1
Copy Cell to Adjacent Cells	Drag fill handle across adjacent cells		
Decrease Font Size	Click Decrease Font Size tool on Standard toolbar	From Format menu, choose Font	Press CTRL + P
Delete Selected Chart		From Edit menu, choose Clear	Press DELETE
Edit Cell Contents	Click in formula bar		Press F2
Exit Excel	Double-click the Control-menu box	From File menu, choose Exit	Press ALT + F4
Help		Select Help menu	Press F1
Increase Font Size	Click Increase Font Size tool on Standard toolbar	From Format menu, choose Font	Press CTRL + P
Open a Worksheet on Disk	Click Open File tool on Standard toolbar	From File menu, choose Open	Press CTRL + F12
Print the Worksheet	Click Print tool on Standard toolbar	From File menu, choose Print	Press CTRL + SHIFT + F12
Save the Worksheet to Disk	Click Save File tool on Standard toolbar	From File menu, choose Save As	Press F12
Select Cell	Click cell	From Formula menu, choose Goto	Press ARROW
Select Entire Worksheet	Click Select All button		Press CTRL + SHIFT + SPACEBAR
Select Range	Drag mouse		Press SHIFT + ARROW
Start Excel	Double-click Microsoft Excel program-item icon	From File menu, choose Run and enter EXCEL.EXE	
Sum a Column or Row	Double-click AutoSum tool on Standard toolbar	From Formula menu, choose Paste Function	Press ALT + =
Undo Last Operation	Click Undo tool on Utility toolbar	From Edit menu, choose Undo	Press CTRL + Z

E46

STUDENT ASSIGNMENTS

STUDENT ASSIGNMENT 1
True/False

Instructions: Circle T if the statement is true or F if the statement is false.

T F   1. An Excel worksheet can contain up to 256 columns and 16,384 rows.
T F   2. One or more letters of the alphabet identify a worksheet column.
T F   3. Only rows numbered 0 through 18 are available for use when Excel begins.
T F   4. When Excel begins, it displays an empty worksheet titled Sheet1.
T F   5. To complete an entry and keep the same cell active, press an arrow key.
T F   6. The active cell has a heavy border around it.
T F   7. The active cell reference displays at the bottom of the screen in the status bar.
T F   8. The Increase Font Size tool increases the font size of the entry in the selected cell.
T F   9. To clear the entry in the active cell, press the DELETE key.
T F 10. If you have not yet clicked the enter box or pressed the ENTER key or an arrow key to complete an entry in the formula bar, use the ESC key to erase the entry from the formula bar.
T F 11. The Select All button that selects the entire worksheet is located on the standard toolbar.
T F 12. To copy a cell to adjacent cells, drag the fill handle on the lower right corner of the heavy border surrounding the active cell to adjacent cells.
T F 13. Numbers entered into a worksheet might not contain decimal points.
T F 14. Text that contains more characters than the width of the column will always occupy two or more cells.
T F 15. When a number is entered in an active cell, it is normally aligned to the right in the cell.
T F 16. If you make a mistake while typing a number in the formula bar, you can use the BACKSPACE key to delete unwanted characters.
T F 17. A number entered into an active cell cannot contain a dollar sign, comma, or percent sign.
T F 18. When you click the AutoSum tool, Excel proposes a range of cells to sum.
T F 19. Clicking the cancel box in the formula bar clears the entire worksheet.
T F 20. To open a worksheet, click the File Save tool.

STUDENT ASSIGNMENT 2
Multiple Choice

Instructions: Circle the correct response.

1. A _____ is at the intersection of a row and a column.
   a. window
   b. cell
   c. button
   d. range
2. To enter a number into a cell, the cell must be _____.
   a. blank
   b. defined as a numeric cell
   c. the active cell
   d. both a and c
3. Which of the following is a valid number you can enter on a worksheet?
   a. 3.25
   b. 3.25%
   c. $3.25
   d. all of the above

E47

4. When you enter text into the active cell, the text is _____ in the cell.
   a. aligned to the right
   b. aligned to the left
   c. centered
   d. decimal aligned
5. Keyboard indicators display in the _____ bar.
   a. status
   b. menu
   c. title
   d. tool
6. Excel uses the _____ between cell references to indicate a range.
   a. period (.)
   b. colon (:)
   c. semicolon (;)
   d. tilde (~)
7. To increase the font size of a worksheet title, select the cell containing the title and _____ one or more times.
   a. click the tool containing the large letter A on the tool bar
   b. click the tool containing the large letter I on the tool bar
   c. press the UP ARROW key on the keyboard
   d. press the PAGE UP key on the keyboard
8. The fill handle is located _____.
   a. on the menu bar
   b. on the toolbar
   c. on the heavy border that surrounds the active cell
   d. in the status bar
9. Which one of the following is a valid Sum function?
   a. =SUM(C3:C6)
   b. +SUM(C3:C6)
   c. @SUM(C3:C6)
   d. =SUM(C3.C6)
10. To select the entire worksheet, click the _____.
   a. Select All button
   b. ChartWizard tool
   c. Open File tool
   d. Save File tool

STUDENT ASSIGNMENT 3
Understanding the Excel Worksheet

Instructions: In Figure SA1-3, arrows point to the major components of an Excel worksheet. Identify the various parts of the worksheet in the space provided.

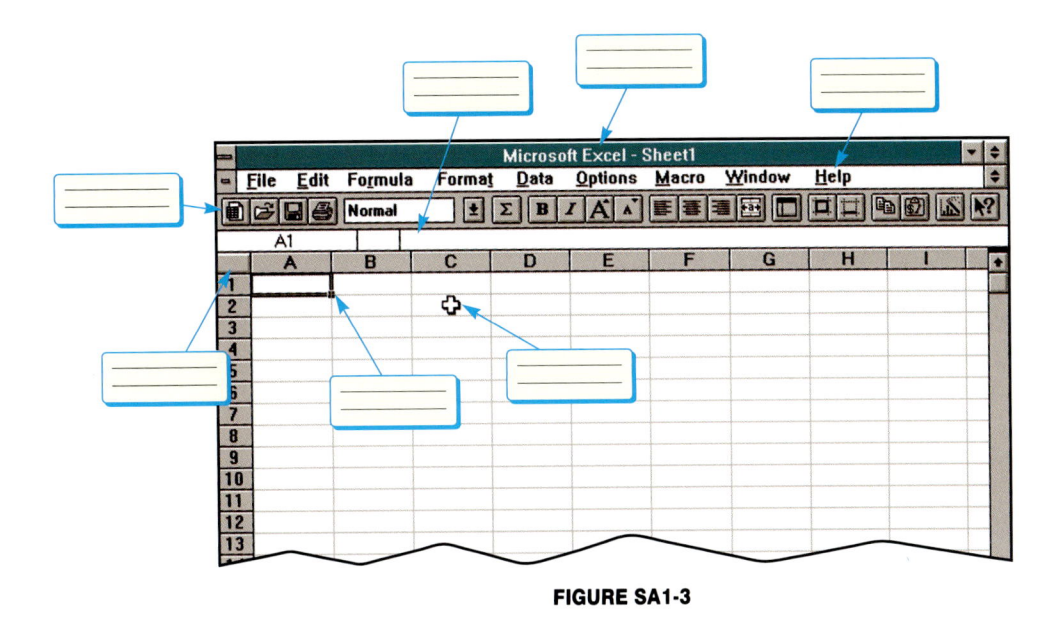

FIGURE SA1-3

STUDENT ASSIGNMENT 4
Understanding the Toolbar

Instructions: In the worksheet in Figure SA1-4, arrows point to several of the tools on the Standard toolbar. In the space provided, briefly explain the purpose of each tool.

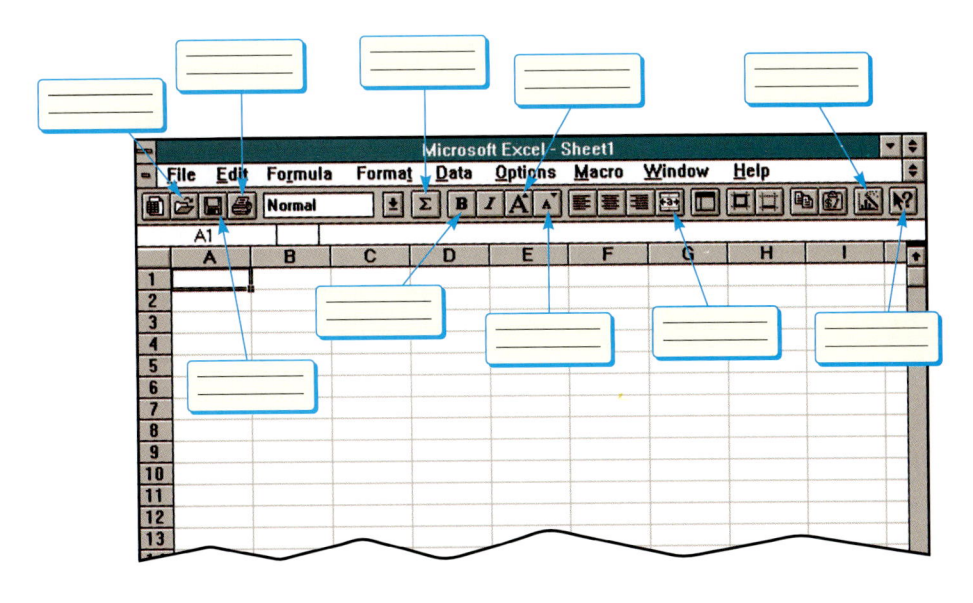

FIGURE SA1-4

E50   PROJECT 1   BUILDING A WORKSHEET

STUDENT ASSIGNMENT 5
Understanding the Formula Bar on the Worksheet

Instructions: Answer the following questions concerning the contents of the formula bar area in Figure SA1-5.

1. What does the A1 signify on the left side of the formula bar?
   _____

2. What is the purpose of the box that contains the letter x in the formula bar area?
   _____

3. What is the purpose of the box that contains the check mark in the formula bar?
   _____
   _____

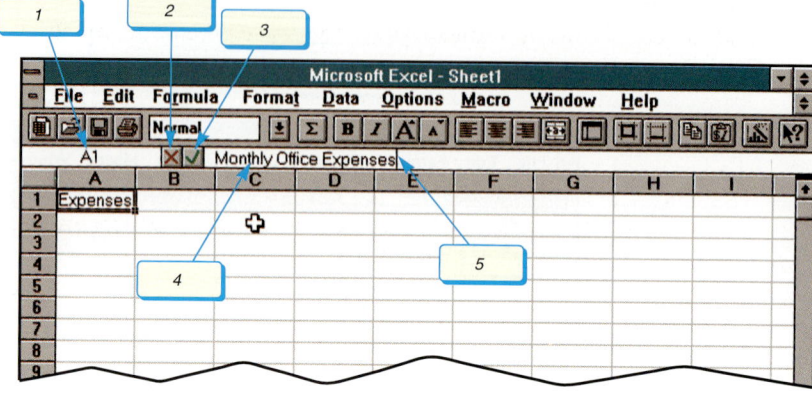

FIGURE SA1-5

4. How would you complete the entry into cell A1 of the text Monthly Office Expenses that is in the formula bar without using the mouse and maintain cell A1 as the active cell?
   _____

5. What do you call the vertical line that follows the text Monthly Office Expenses in the formula bar?
   _____

STUDENT ASSIGNMENT 6
Understanding the SUM Function

Instructions: Answer the following questions after reviewing the entries on the worksheet in Figure SA1-6.

1. List the steps to use the SUM function in cell B6 to sum the range B3:B5, sum the range C3:C5 and place it in cell C6, and sum the range D3:D5 and place it in cell D6.

   Steps: _____
   _____
   _____

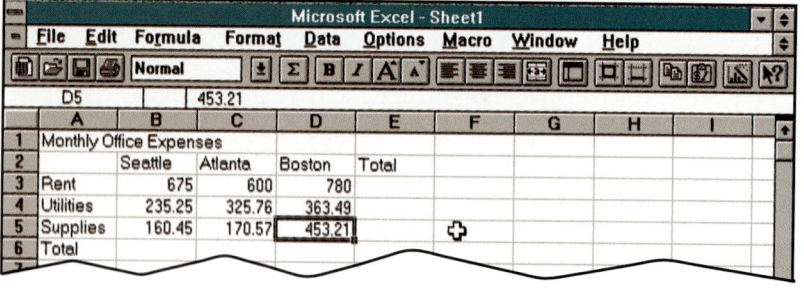

FIGURE SA1-6

2. List the steps that use the SUM function to sum the monthly rent expenses and place the sum in cell E3, sum the monthly utilities and place the sum in cell E4, sum the monthly supplies and place the sum in cell E5, and sum the total of all monthly expenses and place the sum in cell E6.

   Steps: _____
   _____

COMPUTER LABORATORY EXERCISES

COMPUTER LABORATORY EXERCISE 1
Using the Help Menu, Help Tool, and Excel Tutorial

Instructions: Perform the following tasks using a computer.

1. Start Excel.
2. Choose the Contents command from the Help menu on the menu bar.
3. Click Basic Concepts.
4. Read the paragraph. Use the scroll arrow in the lower right corner of the Help window to scroll through and read the rest of the document.
5. Click Worksheets in the Basic Concepts listing.
6. Read the contents of the screen.
7. Ready the printer and choose Print Topic from the File menu in the Help window to print a hard copy of the About Worksheets help message.
8. To return to the original Help screen, click the Contents button in the upper left corner of the Help window.
9. You can use the technique described in Steps 3 and 4 to display help on any other topic listed.
10. To close the Help window, choose Exit from the File menu in the Help window.
11. Click the Help button on the Standard toolbar.
12. Point at the AutoSum tool and click.
13. Ready the printer and choose Print Topic from the File menu in the Help window.
14. Close the Help window as described in Step 10.
15. Choose Learning Microsoft Excel from the Help menu.
16. Select these lessons: What is Microsoft Excel, Using Microsoft Excel Help, and Using the Toolbars.

COMPUTER LABORATORY EXERCISE 2
Formatting a Worksheet

Instructions: Start Excel. Open the worksheet CLE1-2 from the subdirectory Excel on the Student Diskette that accompanies this book. The worksheet CLE1-2 is shown in Figure CLE1-2. The worksheet resembles the Monthly Office Expenses worksheet created in Project 1.

Perform the following tasks:

1. Center the worksheet title in cell A1 across columns A through E.
2. Increase the font size of the worksheet title in cell A1 to 14 point by clicking the Font Increase Size tool twice.
3. Bold the worksheet title in cell A1.
4. Change the contents of cell B5 from 16o.45 to 160.45.
5. Move the chart from its current location to the location shown in Figure 1-66 on page E34.
6. Select the range A2:E6.

FIGURE CLE1-2

E51

COMPUTER LABORATORY EXERCISE 2 (continued)

7. Choose the AutoFormat command from the Format menu and review the fourteen formats in the Sample box by selecting each one using the mouse.
8. Select the Colorful 1 format and choose OK from the AutoFormat dialog box.
9. Choose Page Setup from the File menu and turn Cell Gridlines off. Choose OK from the Page Setup dialog box.
10. Click the Print tool to print the worksheet with the new format.
11. Select the column chart and delete it using the DELETE key.
12. Click the Print tool to print the worksheet with the new format.
13. Save the worksheet using the file name CLE1-2B.
14. Choose the Close command from the File menu to close the worksheet.

COMPUTER LABORATORY EXERCISE 3
Changing Data in a Worksheet

Instructions: Start Excel. Open the worksheet CLE1-3 from the subdirectory Excel on the Student Diskette that accompanies this book. As shown in Figure CLE1-3, the worksheet CLE1-3 is a semiannual income and expense worksheet.

Perform the following tasks:

1. Make the changes to the worksheet described in the table below the worksheet. As you edit the values in the cells containing numeric data, watch the total income (cells D6 and F6) and total expenses (cells D11 and F11). Each of the values in these four cells is based on the SUM function. When you enter a new value, Excel automatically recalculates the SUM functions. After you have successfully made the changes listed in the table, the total incomes in cells D6 and F6 should equal $126,882.00 and $127,811.00, respectively. The total expenses in cells D11 and F11 should equal $50,689.00 and $53,685.00, respectively.
2. Save the worksheet. Use the file name CLE1-3B.
3. Print the revised worksheet without gridlines.

FIGURE CLE1-3

CELL	CURRENT CELL CONTENTS	CHANGE CELL CONTENTS TO
A1	Sally's Gasoline Station	Sal's Gas Station
D3	48734	48535
F3	62785	61523
D5	6305	63005
F5	7301	47523
D8	14350	22357
F8	16225	19876

COMPUTER LABORATORY ASSIGNMENTS

COMPUTER LABORATORY ASSIGNMENT 1
Building and Modifying a College Cost Analysis Worksheet

Purpose: To become familiar with building a worksheet, formatting a worksheet, embedding a column chart, and printing and saving a worksheet.

Problem: As a student assistant working in the Financial Aid office you have been asked by the director to project the expenses for attending college for two semesters and a summer session. The estimated costs are shown in the table below:

	SEMESTER 1	SEMESTER 2	SUMMER
TUITION	720.00	670.00	370.00
BOOKS	250.00	300.00	100.00
LAB FEES	100.00	100.00	50.00

Instructions: Perform the following tasks:

1. Create the worksheet shown in Figure CLA1-1 using the numbers in the table. Enter the text and numbers into the cells described in the worksheet.
2. Direct Excel to determine the totals for Semester 1, Semester 2, Summer, Tuition, Books, Lab Fees, and a total for the three semesters.
3. Format the worksheet title Projected College Expenses as 14 point, bold, and centered over columns A through E.
4. Format the range A2:E6 using the table format Financial 2 as shown in the worksheet in Figure CLA1-1.
5. Use the ChartWizard tool to draw the column chart shown on the worksheet in Figure CLA1-1. Chart the range A2:D5.
6. Enter your name in cell A19. Enter your course, computer laboratory assignment number (CLA1-1), date, and instructor name below in cells A20 through A23.
7. Save the worksheet. Use the file name CLA1-1.
8. Print the worksheet with cell gridlines off.
9. Increase the tuition by $200.00 for Semester 1 and Semester 2. Increase the cost of books by $50.00 for all three semesters. Increase the Lab fees by $25.00 for Semester 2. The three semester totals should be $1,320.00, $1,345.00, and $570.00, respectively. Print the worksheet containing the new values with cell gridlines off.

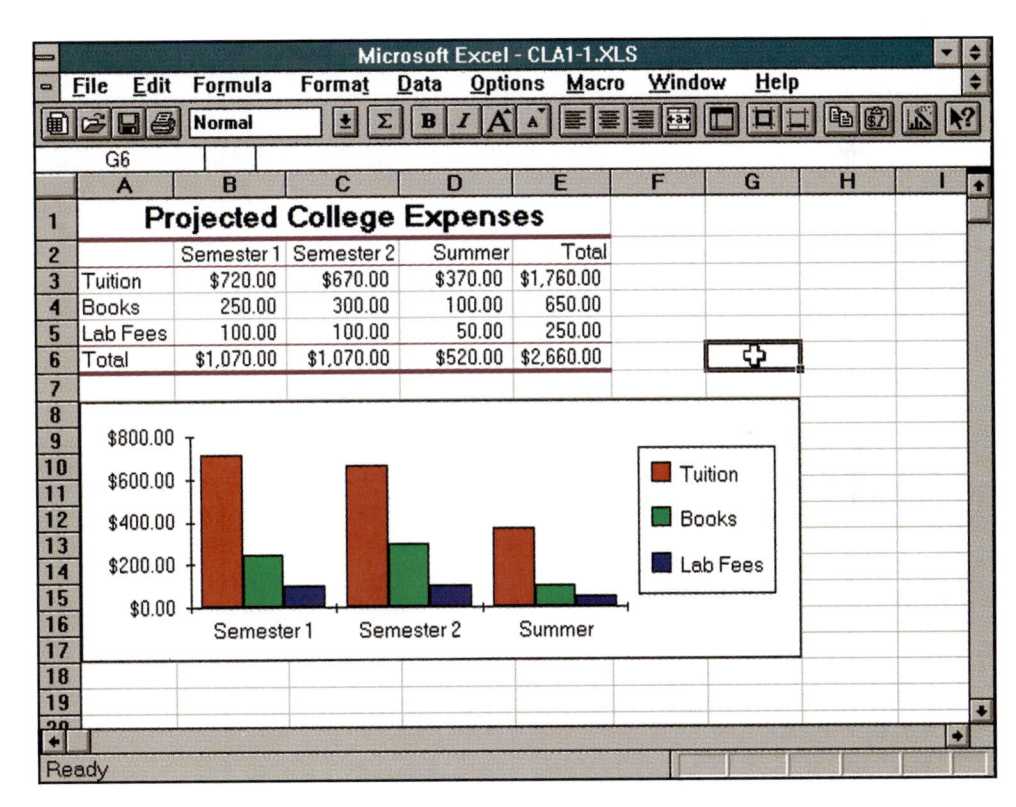

FIGURE CLA1-1

E53

COMPUTER LABORATORY ASSIGNMENT 2
Creating a Daily Sales Report Worksheet

Purpose: To become familiar with building a worksheet, formatting a worksheet, embedding a column chart, and printing and saving a worksheet.

Problem: The Music City company has hired you to work in its Information Systems Department as a part-time consultant. The president of the company has requested that a spreadsheet be created showing a daily sales summary report for the company's three stores. The request has been turned over to you to handle. The report is to list the daily sales in each store for compact disks (CDs), cassettes, and videos. The daily sales are shown in the table below:

	STORE 1	STORE 2	STORE 3
CDs	775.29	600.51	995.17
CASSETTES	550.38	425.43	605.24
VIDEOS	350.65	250.33	400.17

Instructions: Perform the following tasks:

1. Create the worksheet shown in Figure CLA1-2 using the numbers in the table. Enter the text and numbers into the cells described in the worksheet.
2. Direct Excel to determine the totals for Store 1, Store 2, Store 3, CDs, Cassettes, Videos, and all the stores.
3. Format the worksheet title Daily Sales Report as 14 point, bold, and centered over columns A through E.
4. Format the worksheet subtitle, Music City, as 12 point bold and centered over columns A through E.
5. Format the range A3:E7 using the table format Financial 1 as shown in Figure CLA1-2.
6. Use the ChartWizard tool to draw the column chart shown in the worksheet in Figure CLA1-2. Chart the range A3:D6.
7. Enter your name in cell A19. Enter your course, computer laboratory assignment number (CLA1-2), date, and instructor name below the chart in cells A20 through A23.
8. Save the worksheet. Use the file name CLA1-2.
9. Print the worksheet with cell gridlines on.
10. Print the worksheet with cell gridlines off.
11. Make the following changes to the daily sales: Store 1, CDs — $546.34, Store 2, Videos — $395.45, and Store 3, Cassettes — $943.67. The new three store totals should be $1,447.37, $1,421.39, and $2,339.01.
12. Select the chart and increase its width by one column.
13. Print the modified worksheet with cell gridlines off.

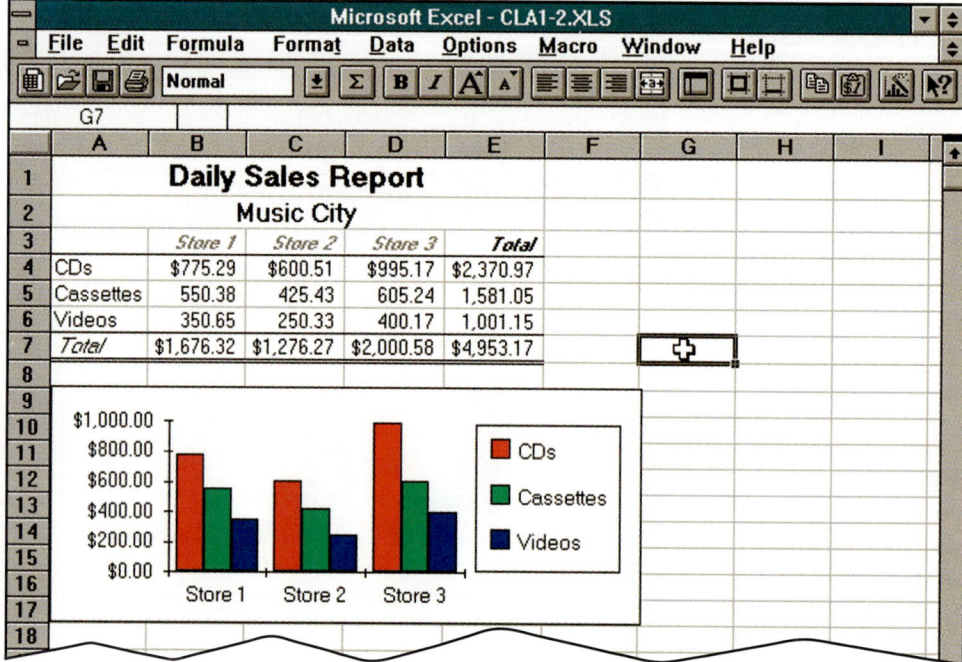

FIGURE CLA1-2

COMPUTER LABORATORY ASSIGNMENT 3
Creating a Personal Financial Statement

Purpose: To become familiar with building a worksheet, formatting a worksheet, embedding a column chart, and printing and saving a worksheet.

Problem: To obtain a bank loan the bank has requested you to supply a personal financial statement. The statement is to include your average monthly income for the last three years and all major expenses. The data required to prepare your financial statement is shown in the table below:

	1992	1993	1994
INCOME:			
Wages	1200.00	1450.00	1550.00
Tips	300.00	425.00	550.00
EXPENSES:			
Rent	650.00	700.00	850.00
Utilities	125.00	150.00	160.00
Insurance	125.00	140.00	200.00
Other	200.00	250.00	290.00

Instructions: Using the numbers in the table, create the worksheet shown in Figure CLA1-3, including the chart of expenses. Use the AutoSum tool to calculate the total income and total expenses for each of the three years. Enter your name in cell A19 and your course, computer laboratory assignment number (CLA1-3), date, and instructor name in cells A20 through A23.

To format the worksheet, use the table format Financial 1 for the Income table and then again for the Expenses table.

Save the worksheet using the file name CLA1-3. Print the worksheet without cell gridlines.

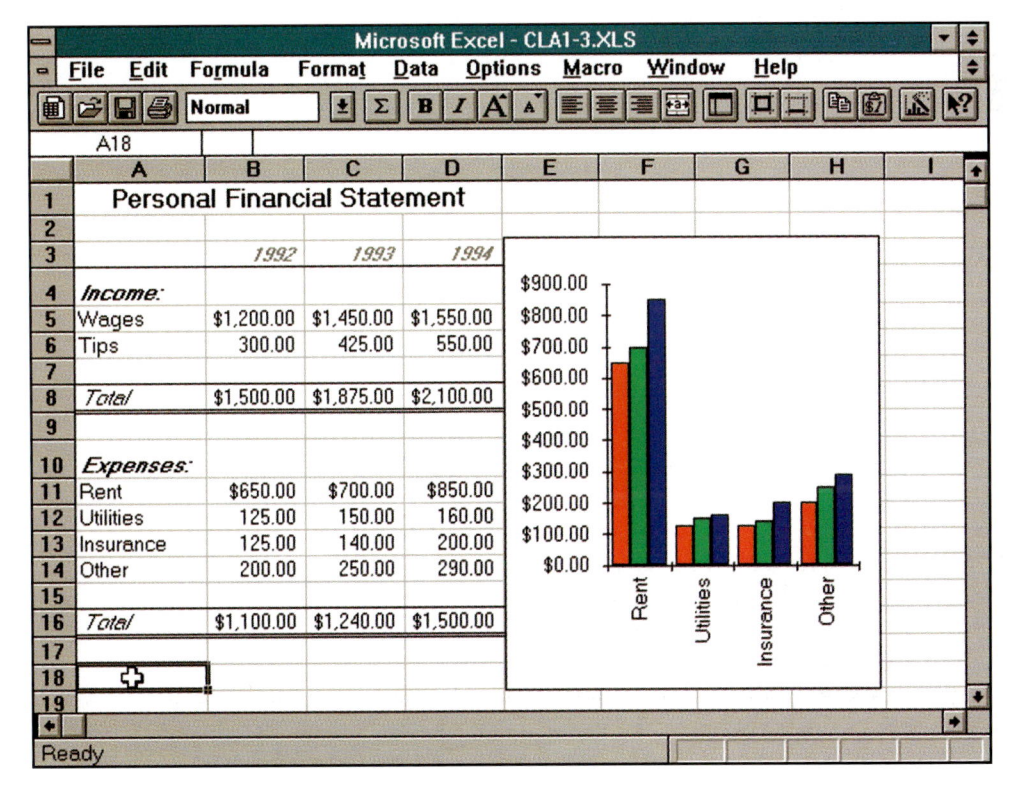

FIGURE CLA1-3

COMPUTER LABORATORY ASSIGNMENT 4
Planning a Weekly Expense Account Report

Purpose: To provide practice in planning and building a worksheet.

Problem: While in college, you are serving an internship in the Office Automation Department of the Academic Textbook Company (ATC). ATC is a publishing company that sells textbooks to high schools and colleges throughout the United States. The company has sales representatives that are reimbursed for the following expenses: lodging, meals, and travel.

You have been asked to create for distribution a worksheet that the sales representatives can use as a weekly expense report. Beginning next month, the weekly expense report must be submitted by each sales representative to the regional sales manager of the company by Wednesday of the following week. The worksheet should summarize the daily expenses and the total weekly expense. Expenses are only paid for Monday, Tuesday, Wednesday, Thursday, and Friday, the days on which the sales representatives can call upon teachers at the schools.

Instructions: Design and create the Weekly Expense Report. Develop your own test data. Submit the following:

1. A description of the problem. Include the purpose of the worksheet, a statement outlining the results, the required data, and calculations.
2. A handwritten design of the worksheet. This document should be approved by your manager (your instructor) before you build the worksheet.
3. A printed copy of the worksheet without cell gridlines.
4. A one-page, double-spaced typewritten description explaining to the sales representatives the purpose of the worksheet, how to retrieve the worksheet, enter data into the worksheet, save the worksheet, and print the worksheet.
5. Use the techniques you learned in this project to format the worksheet. Include a column chart that compares the daily costs.
6. Enter your name, course, computer laboratory assignment number (CLA1-4), date, and instructor name below the chart in column A. Save the worksheet using the file name CLA1-4.

Microsoft Excel 4 for Windows
PROJECT TWO

ADDING FORMULAS TO A WORKSHEET

OBJECTIVES You will have mastered the material in this project when you can:

- Align text in cells
- Enter a formula
- Identify the arithmetic operators +, –, *, /, %, and ^
- Determine a percentage
- Use Point mode to enter formulas
- Apply the AVERAGE function
- Add borders to a range of cells
- Use the Style box on the Standard toolbar to format numbers
- Use the shortcut menu to obtain a list of useful commands
- Use the Number command from the Format menu to format numbers
- Select the entire worksheet to change settings
- Change the font on the worksheet
- Select a best-fit column width or row height
- Change the width of a series of adjacent columns
- Change the height of a row
- Print a partial or complete worksheet
- Preview how a printed copy of the worksheet will look
- Print to fit
- Display and print the formulas version of a worksheet

▶ INTRODUCTION

In Project 1 you learned about entering data, summing values, how to make the worksheet easier to read, and how to draw a chart. You also learned about the Help facility and saving, printing, and loading a worksheet from disk into main memory. This project continues to emphasize these topics and presents some new ones.

The new topics include formulas, customized formatting, changing fonts, changing the widths of columns and heights of rows, and alternative types of worksheet displays and printouts. One alternative display and printout shows the formulas rather than the values in the worksheet. When you display the formulas in the worksheet, you see exactly what text, data, formulas, and functions you have entered into it.

▶ PROJECT TWO

The worksheet in Project 2 (on the next page in Figure 2-1) contains a sales report that shows the gross sales, returns, net sales, and percent returns by region. In addition, the worksheet includes totals in row 8 for the gross sales, returns, net sales, and percent returns and averages in row 9 of the gross sales, returns, and net sales. To improve the appearance of the worksheet and to make it easier to read, the numbers in the worksheet are formatted. The widths of columns A through E and the height of rows 2 and 9 are increased to add more space between the titles and numbers.

In Figure 2-1, the gross sales in column B and the returns in column C make up the data sent to the accounting department from the regional offices. You enter the numbers into the worksheet in the same fashion described in Project 1. Each regional net sales figure in column D is equal to the gross sales in column B minus the returns in column C and is calculated from a formula. Each regional percent return in column E is the quotient of the returns in column C divided by the gross sales in column B. Row 8 contains the total gross sales, total returns, total net sales, and percent returns for all sales. Finally, row 9 contains the average gross sales, average returns, and average net sales.

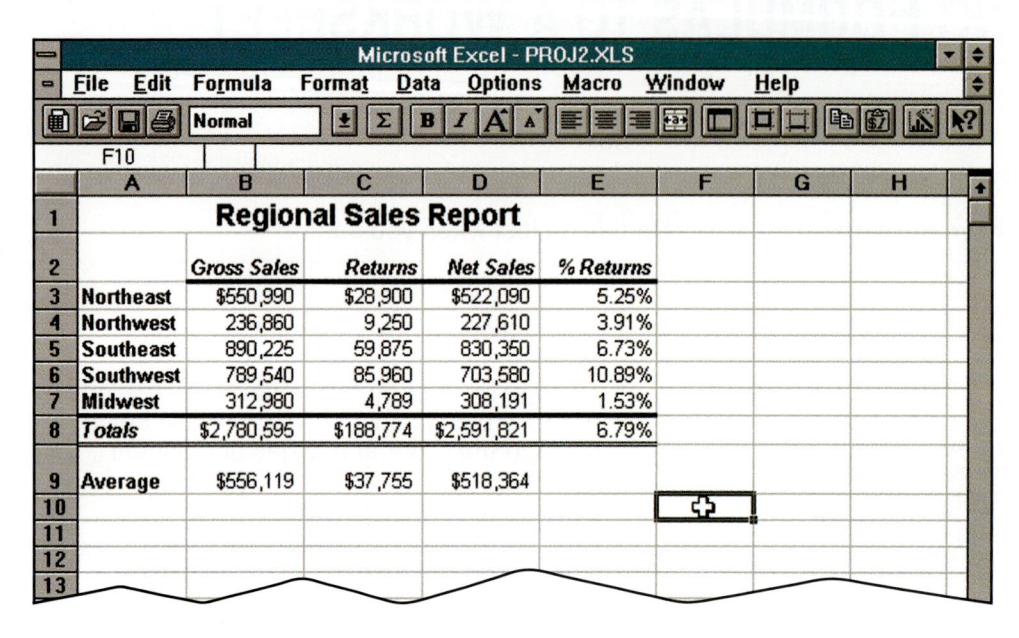

FIGURE 2-1

▶ **ENTERING THE TITLES AND NUMBERS INTO THE WORKSHEET**

The worksheet title in Figure 2-1 is centered over columns A through E in row 1. Because the centered text must first be entered into the leftmost column of the area over which it is centered, it will be entered into cell A1. The column headings in row 2 begin in cell B2 and extend through cell E2. The row titles in column A begin in cell A3 and continue down to cell A9. The numbers are entered into the range B3:C7. The steps required to enter the worksheet title, column titles, row titles, and numbers are outlined in the remainder of this section and are shown in Figure 2-2 on the next page.

TO ENTER THE WORKSHEET TITLE

Step 1: Select cell A1.
Step 2: Type the text Regional Sales Report.
Step 3: Click the enter box or press the ENTER key.

The worksheet title displays as shown in cell A1 of Figure 2-2.

TO ENTER THE COLUMN TITLES

Step 1: Select cell B2. Type Gross Sales and press the RIGHT ARROW key.
Step 2: Enter the column titles Returns, Net Sales, and % Returns in cells C2, D2, and E2 in the same fashion as described in Step 1.

The column titles display as shown in row 2 of Figure 2-2.

TO ENTER THE ROW TITLES

Step 1: Select cell A3. Type Northeast and press the DOWN ARROW key.
Step 2: Enter the row titles Northwest, Southeast, Southwest, Midwest, and Totals in cells A3 through A8 and enter Average in cell A9.

The row titles display as shown in column A of Figure 2-2.

TO ENTER THE NUMBERS

Step 1: Enter 550990 in cell B3 and 28900 in cell C3.
Step 2: Enter 236860 in cell B4 and 9250 in cell C4.
Step 3: Enter 890225 in cell B5 and 59875 in cell C5.
Step 4: Enter 789540 in cell B6 and 85960 in cell C6.
Step 5: Enter 312980 in cell B7 and 4789 in cell C7.

The numeric entries display as shown in the range B3:C7 of Figure 2-2.

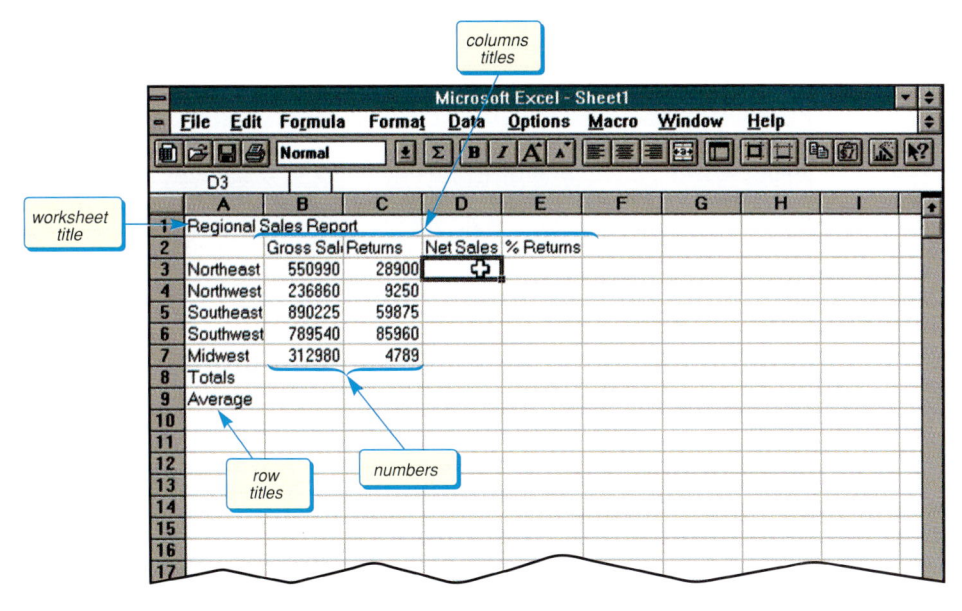

FIGURE 2-2

▶ ENTERING FORMULAS

The net sales for each region, which displays in column D, is equal to the corresponding gross sales in column B minus the corresponding returns in column C. Thus, the net sales for the Northeast region in row 3 is obtained by subtracting 28900 from 550990.

One of the reasons Excel is such a valuable tool is because you can assign a **formula** to a cell and Excel will calculate the result. In this example, the formula in cell D3 subtracts the value in cell C3 from the value in cell B3 and displays the result in cell D3. The steps to enter the formula using the keyboard are described on the next page.

TO ENTER A FORMULA THROUGH THE KEYBOARD

STEP 1 ▶

Select cell D3. Type the formula =b3 - c3 in the formula bar.

The formula displays in the formula bar and in cell D3 (Figure 2-3).

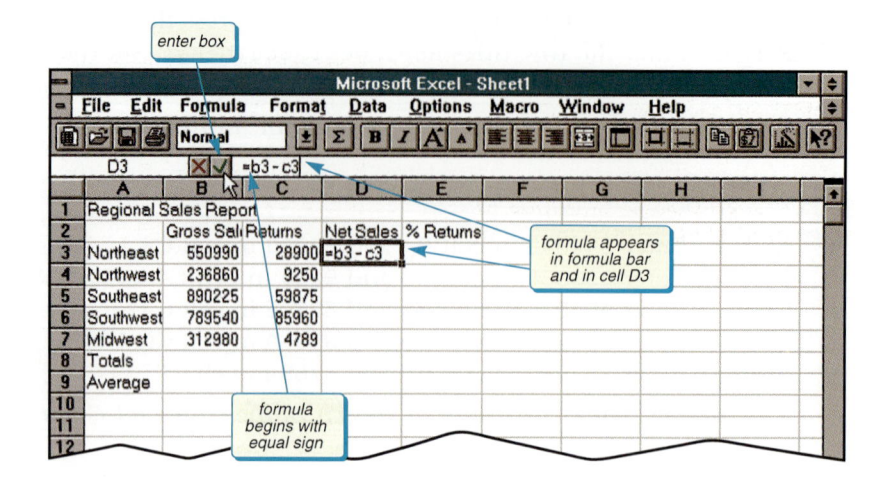

STEP 2 ▶

Click the enter box or press the ENTER key.

Instead of displaying the formula in cell D3, Excel completes the arithmetic indicated by the formula and displays the result, 522090 in cell D3 (Figure 2-4).

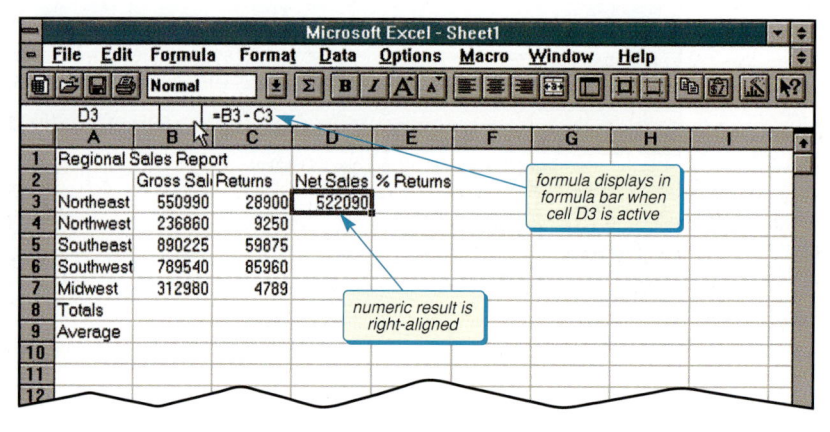

FIGURE 2-4

The equal sign (=) preceding b3 is an important part of the formula. It alerts Excel that you are entering a formula or function and not text, such as words. The minus sign (–) following b3 is the arithmetic operator, which directs Excel to perform the subtraction operation. Other valid Excel arithmetic operators include + (addition), * (multiplication), / (division), % (percentage), and ^ (exponentiation).

You can enter formulas in uppercase or lowercase and you can add spaces between the arithmetic operators to make the formulas easier to read. That is, =b3 – c3 is the same as =B3 – C3, =b3–c3 or B3 – C3. Notice in Figure 2-4 that Excel displays the formula in the formula bar in uppercase when cell D3 is the active cell even though it was entered earlier in lowercase.

Except for row references, the formulas required to compute the net sales for the other regions in column D are the same as the formula in cell D3. Hence, you can use the fill handle in the lower right corner of the heavy border that surrounds the active cell (Figure 2-4) to copy cell D3 down through the range D4:D7.

TO COPY A FORMULA IN ONE CELL TO ADJACENT CELLS DOWN A COLUMN

STEP 1 ▶

Select cell D3, the cell to copy. Point to the fill handle.

The mouse pointer changes to the small dark plus sign (Figure 2-5).

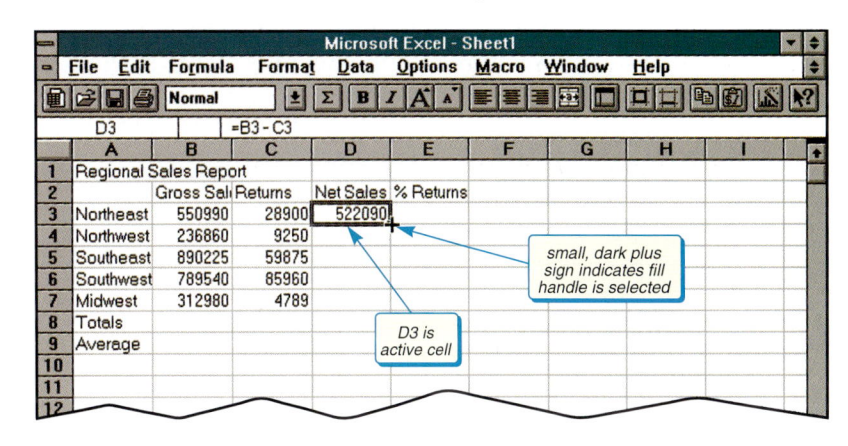

FIGURE 2-5

STEP 2 ▶

Drag the fill handle down to select the range D4:D7 and then release the left mouse button.

Excel copies the formula in cell D3 (= B3 – C3) to the range D4:D7 and displays the net sales for the remaining regions (Figure 2-6).

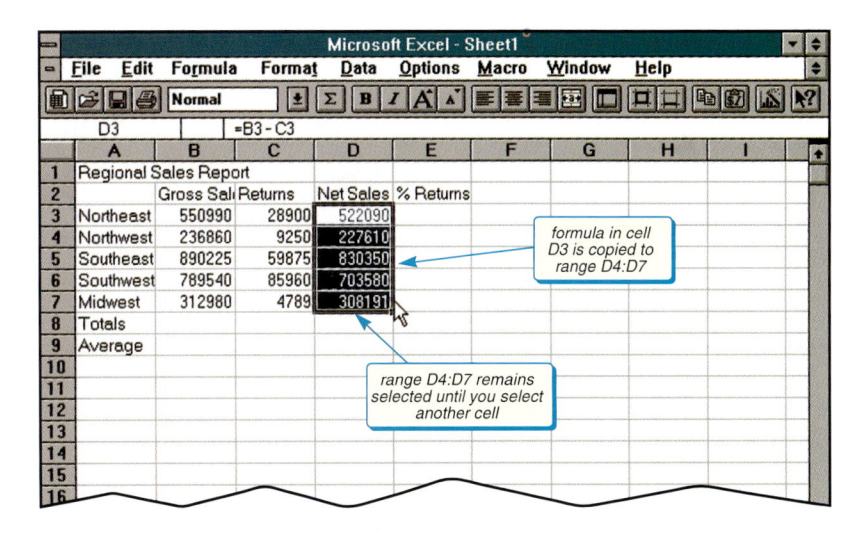

FIGURE 2-6

Select any cell to remove the selection from the range D4:D7.

When Excel copies the formula = B3 – C3 in cell D3 to the range D4:D7, the row references in the formula are adjusted as the formula is copied downward. For example, the formula assigned to cell D4 is = B4 – C4. Similarly, Excel assigns cell D5 the formula = B5 – C5, cell D6 the formula = B6 – C6, and cell D7 the formula = B7 – C7. When you copy downward, the row reference changes in the formula.

Order of Operations

The formulas in column D involve only one arithmetic operation, subtraction. But when more than one operator is involved in a formula, Excel uses the same **order of operations** as in algebra. Moving from left to right in a formula, the **order of operations** is as follows: first all **exponentiations** (^), then all **multiplications** (*) and **divisions** (/), and finally all **additions** (+) and **subtractions** (–). You can use parentheses to override the order of operations. For example, following the order of operations, 8 * 5 – 2 is equal to 38. However, 8 * (5 – 2) is equal to 24 because the parentheses instruct Excel to subtract 2 from 5 before multiplying by 8. Table 2-1 illustrates several examples of valid formulas.

▶ TABLE 2-1

FORMULA	REMARK
= E3	Assigns the value in cell E3 to the active cell.
= 7 * F5 or = F5 * 7 or = (7 * F5)	Assigns seven times the contents of cell F5 to the active cell.
= 525 * 15%	Assigns the product of 525 times 0.15 to the active cell.
= –G44 * G45	Assigns the negative value of the product of the values contained in cells G44 and G45 to the active cell.
= 2 * (J12 – F2)	Assigns the product of two times the difference between the values contained in cells J12 and F2 to the active cell.
= A1 / C6 – A3 * A4 + A5 ^ A6	From left to right: first exponentiation (A5 ^ A6), then division (A1 / C6), then multiplication (A3 * A4), then subtraction (A1 / C6 – A3 * A4), and finally addition (A1 / C6 – A3 * A4 + A5 ^ A6). If cells A1 = 10, A3 = 6, A4 = 2, A5 = 5, A6 = 2, and C6 = 2, then Excel assigns the active cell the value 18 (10 / 2 – 6 * 2 + 5 ^ 2 = 18).

▶ ENTERING FORMULAS USING POINT MODE

In the worksheet shown in Figure 2-1 on page E58, the percent returns for each region appear in column E. The percent returns for the Northeast region in cell E3 is equal to the returns (cell C3) divided by the gross sales (cell B3). Recall that the slash (/) represents the operation of division.

Rather than entering the formula = c3 / b3 in cell E3 completely through the keyboard as was done with net sales in cell D3, the following steps show how to use the mouse and Point mode to enter a formula. **Point mode** allows you to select cells for use in a formula by using the mouse.

TO ENTER A FORMULA USING POINT MODE ▼

STEP 1 ▶

Select cell E3. Type the equal sign (=) in the formula bar to begin the formula and click cell C3.

Excel responds by highlighting cell C3 with a moving border and by appending cell C3 to the equal sign in the formula bar and in cell E3 (Figure 2-7).

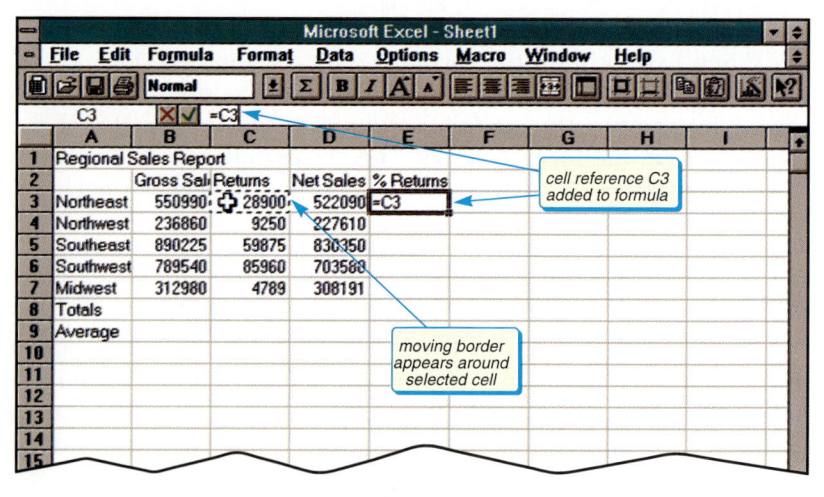

FIGURE 2-7

STEP 2 ▶

Type the slash (/) in the formula bar and click cell B3.

Excel highlights cell B3 with a moving border and appends cell B3 to the slash (/) in the formula bar and in cell E3 (Figure 2-8).

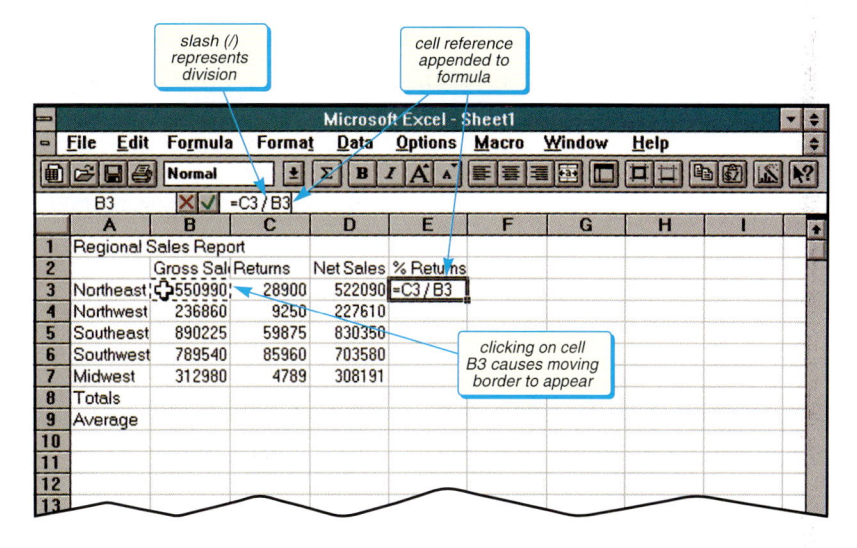

FIGURE 2-8

STEP 3 ▶

Click the enter box or press the ENTER key.

Excel determines the quotient of = C3 / B3 and stores the result, 0.052451, in cell E3 (Figure 2-9).

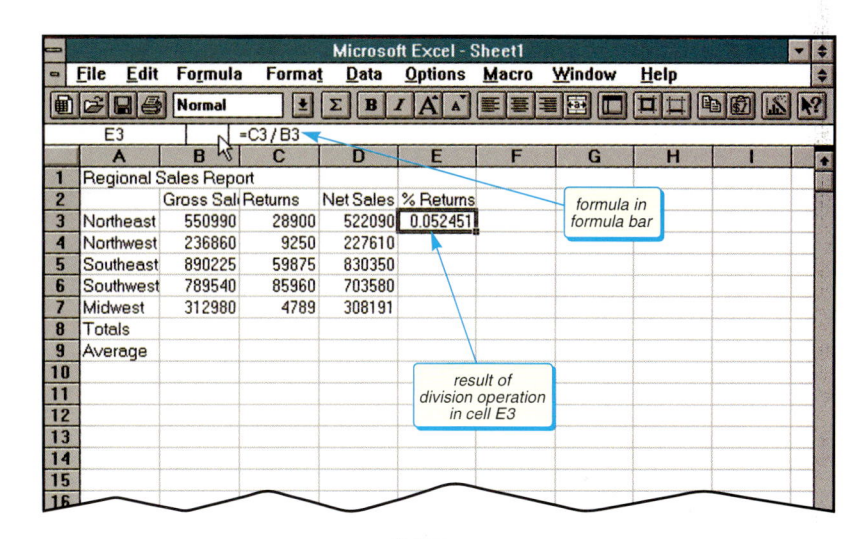

FIGURE 2-9

Later in this project the percent returns, 0.052451, will be formatted to 5.25%.

To complete the percent returns for the remaining regions and the total line in row 8, use the fill handle to copy cell E3 to the range E4:E8. Perform the steps on the next page to complete the copy.

TO COPY A FORMULA IN ONE CELL TO ADJACENT CELLS IN A COLUMN

STEP 1

Select E3, the cell to copy. Point to the fill handle.

STEP 2 ▶

Drag the fill handle down to select the range E4:E8 and then release the left mouse button.

Excel copies the formula in cell E3 to the range E4:E8 and displays the percent returns in decimal form for those cells (Figure 2-10).

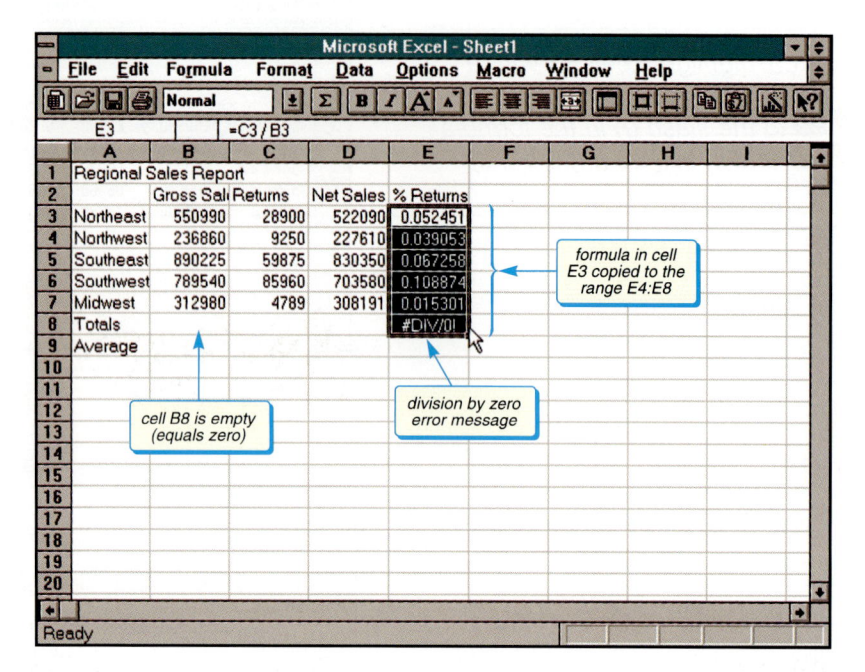

FIGURE 2-10

For the total percent returns in cell E8, Excel displays the error message #DIV/0! **#DIV/0!** means that the formula in the cell is trying to divide by zero. Recall that an empty cell is equal to zero and the denominator in the formula = C8 / B8 in cell E8 is cell B8, which is empty. In the next section, when the total gross sales and total returns are assigned to cells B8 and C8, the error message will change to a numeric value.

▶ SUMMING COLUMN TOTALS

The total gross sales, total returns, and total net sales display in row 8 (Figure 2-1 on page E58). To calculate these totals, the AutoSum tool will be used to sum the gross sales in the range B3:B7 and place the sum in cell B8. Then the SUM function will be copied to cells C8 and D8.

TO SUM A COLUMN OF VALUES ▼

STEP 1 ▶

Select cell B8. Click the AutoSum tool on the Standard toolbar.

Excel displays the SUM function in the formula bar and in cell B8. Excel highlights the proposed range to be summed (B3:B7) with a moving border (Figure 2-11).

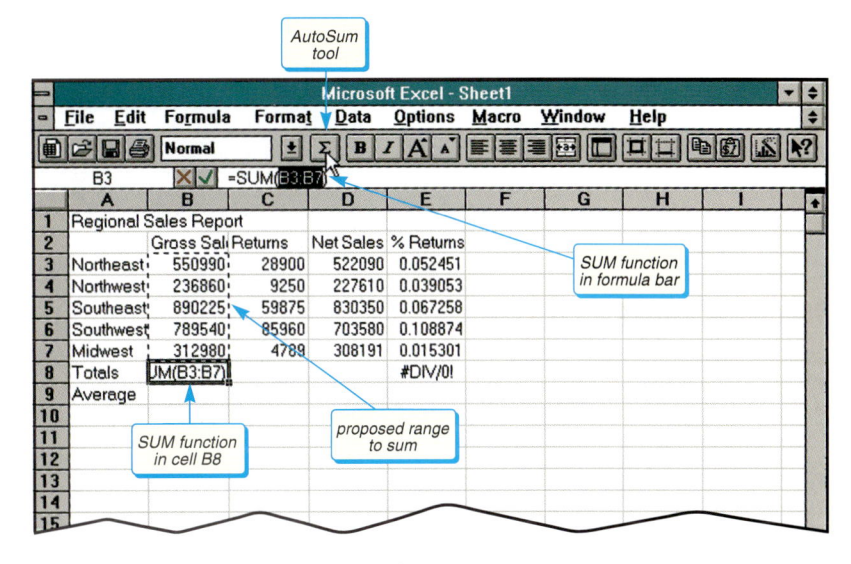

FIGURE 2-11

STEP 2 ▶

Click the AutoSum tool a second time.

Excel assigns =SUM(B3:B7) to cell B8 and displays the sum of the values in the range B3:B7, 2780595, in cell B8 (Figure 2-12).

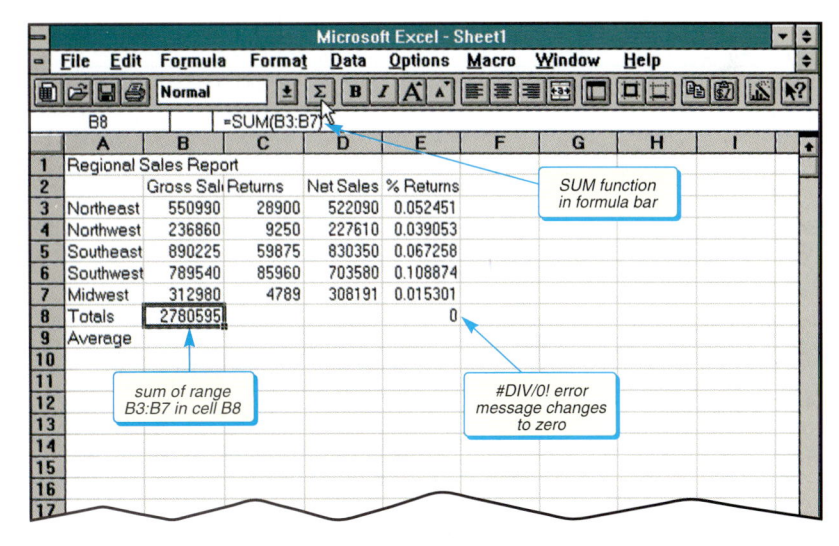

FIGURE 2-12

When you assign the function =SUM(B3:B7) to cell B8, Excel recalculates the entire worksheet. Thus, the error message #DIV/0! in cell E8 changes to zero because the denominator in the formula =C8 / B8 is no longer zero (Figure 2-12). That is, 0 / 2780595 is equal to zero.

The easiest way to complete the totals in row 8 is to copy the SUM function in cell B8 to the range C8:D8 using the fill handle. Follow the steps on the next page to complete the copy operation.

TO COPY A FUNCTION IN ONE CELL TO ADJACENT CELLS IN A ROW

STEP 1

Select cell B8, the cell to copy. Point to the fill handle.

STEP 2 ▶

Drag the fill handle across the range C8:D8 and then release the left mouse button.

Excel copies the SUM function in cell B8 to the range C8:D8 and displays the total returns and total net sales for the remaining regions (Figure 2-13).

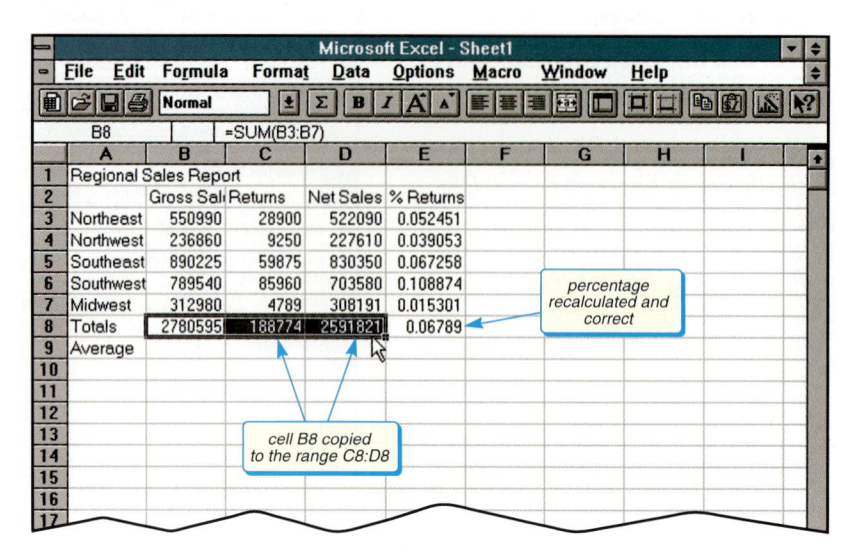

FIGURE 2-13

Select any cell in the worksheet to remove the selection from the range B8:D8. Because cell B8 was copied across a row, rather than down a column, Excel changes the column reference in the range for the SUM function. That is, Excel assigns cell C8 the function =SUM(C3:C7) and cell D8 the function =SUM(D3:D7).

▶ CALCULATING AN AVERAGE

The next step in creating the Regional Sales Report is to compute the average gross sales, place it in cell B9, and then copy it to the range C9:D9 to calculate the average returns and average net sales. The average gross sales can be computed by assigning to cell B9 the formula = (B3 + B4 + B5 + B6 + B7) / 5, but Excel includes an **AVERAGE function** that is much easier to use. Do the following to assign the AVERAGE function to cell B9.

TO FIND THE AVERAGE OF A GROUP OF NUMBERS

STEP 1 ▶

Select cell B9. Type =average(**in the formula bar.**

Excel displays the beginning of the AVERAGE function in the formula bar and in cell B9 (Figure 2-14).

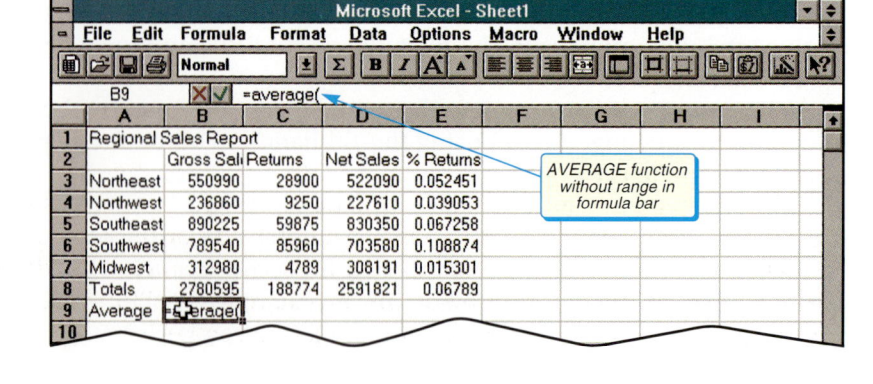

FIGURE 2-14

CALCULATING AN AVERAGE **E67**

STEP 2 ▶

Click cell B3, the first end point of the range to average.

Excel appends cell B3 to the left parenthesis in the formula bar and highlights cell B3 with a moving border (Figure 2-15).

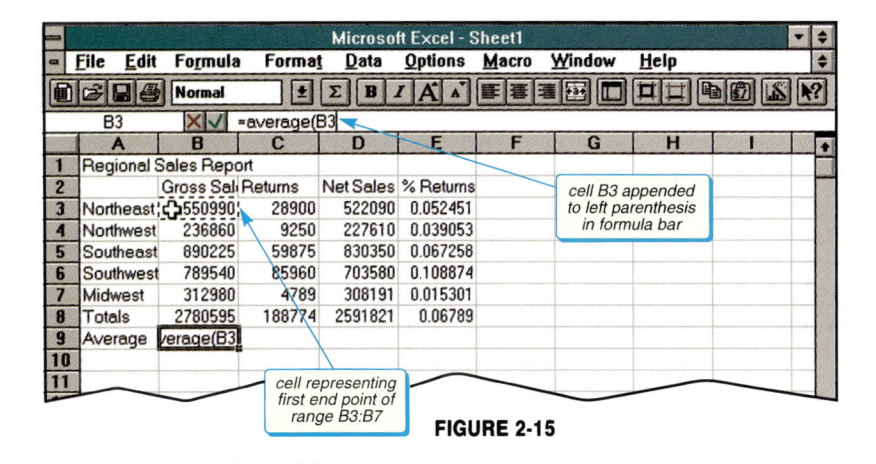

FIGURE 2-15

STEP 3 ▶

Drag the mouse pointer down to cell B7, the second end point of the range to average.

The moving border surrounds the range B3:B7. When you begin dragging, Excel appends a colon (:) and also the cell reference of the cell where the mouse pointer is to the function, =average(B3, in the formula bar (Figure 2-16).

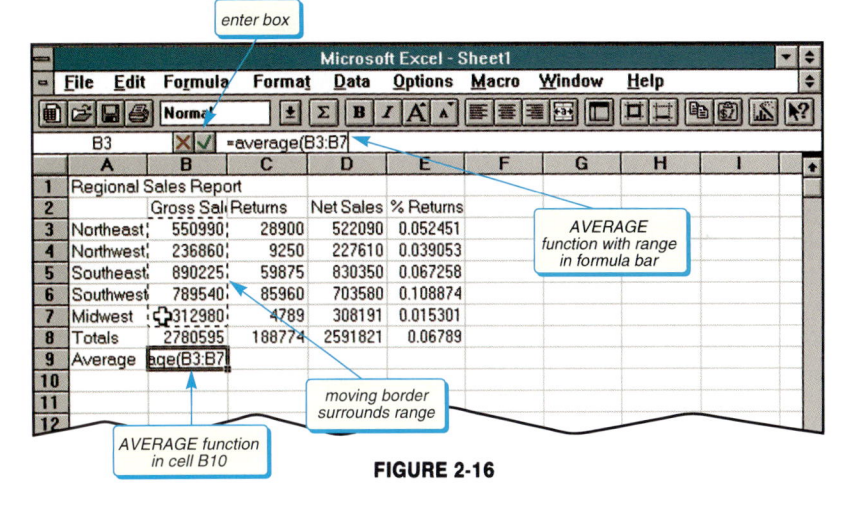

FIGURE 2-16

STEP 4 ▶

Release the left mouse button and then click the enter box or press the ENTER key.

Excel computes the average, 556119, of the five numbers in the range B3:B7 and assigns it to cell B9 (Figure 2-17).

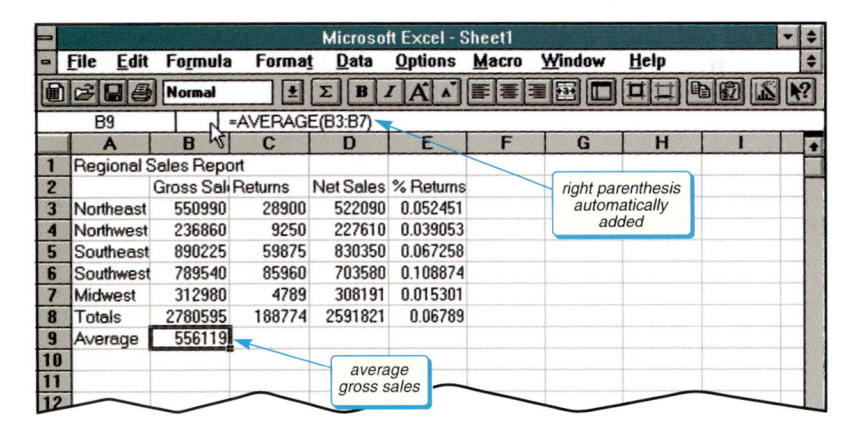

FIGURE 2-17

Notice that Excel automatically appends the right parenthesis to complete the AVERAGE function when you click the enter box or press the ENTER key.

The AVERAGE function requires that the range be included within parentheses following the function name. In the example just illustrated, Point mode was used to select the range following the left parenthesis.

E68　PROJECT 2　ADDING FORMULAS TO A WORKSHEET

Rather than use Point mode, you can type the range. If you decide to type a range, remember that the colon (:) separating the endpoints of the range is required punctuation.

The last two required entries are the average returns in cell C9 and the average net sales in cell D9. Except for the ranges, these two entries are identical to the AVERAGE function in cell B9. Thus, you can use the fill handle to copy cell B9 to the range C9:D9.

TO COPY A FUNCTION IN ONE CELL TO ADJACENT CELLS IN A ROW ▼

STEP 1

Select cell B9, the cell to copy. Point to the fill handle.

STEP 2 ▶

Drag the fill handle across the range C9:D9 and then release the left mouse button.

Excel copies the AVERAGE function in cell B9 to the range C9:D9 (Figure 2-18).

FIGURE 2-18

STEP 3 ▶

Select any cell to remove the selection from the range C9:D9.

The worksheet entries are now complete (Figure 2-19).

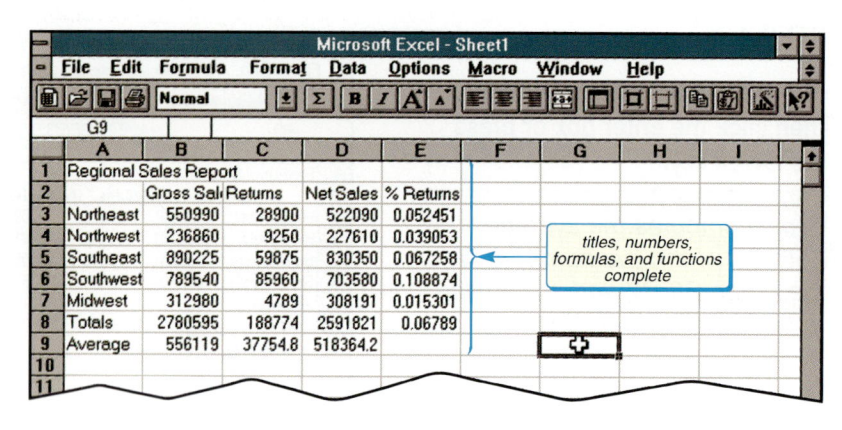

FIGURE 2-19

The average returns, 37754.8, and the average net sales, 518364.2, complete the entries in the Regional Sales Report worksheet. Thus far, you have seen the use of the SUM and AVERAGE functions. Besides these two functions, Excel has over 400 more that handle just about every type of calculation you can imagine. To obtain a list of the available functions, choose the Contents command from the Help menu, scroll down through the contents list, and select Worksheet Functions.

FORMATTING TEXT AND DRAWING BORDERS   **E69**

▶ SAVING AN INTERMEDIATE COPY OF THE WORKSHEET

A good practice is to save intermediate copies of your worksheet. That way, if your computer loses power or you make a serious mistake, you can always retrieve the latest copy from disk. It is recommended that you save an intermediate copy of the worksheet every 50 to 75 keystrokes. Use the Save File tool often, because you can save keying time later if the unexpected happens. For the following steps it is assumed you have a formatted disk in drive A.

TO SAVE AN INTERMEDIATE COPY OF THE WORKSHEET ▼

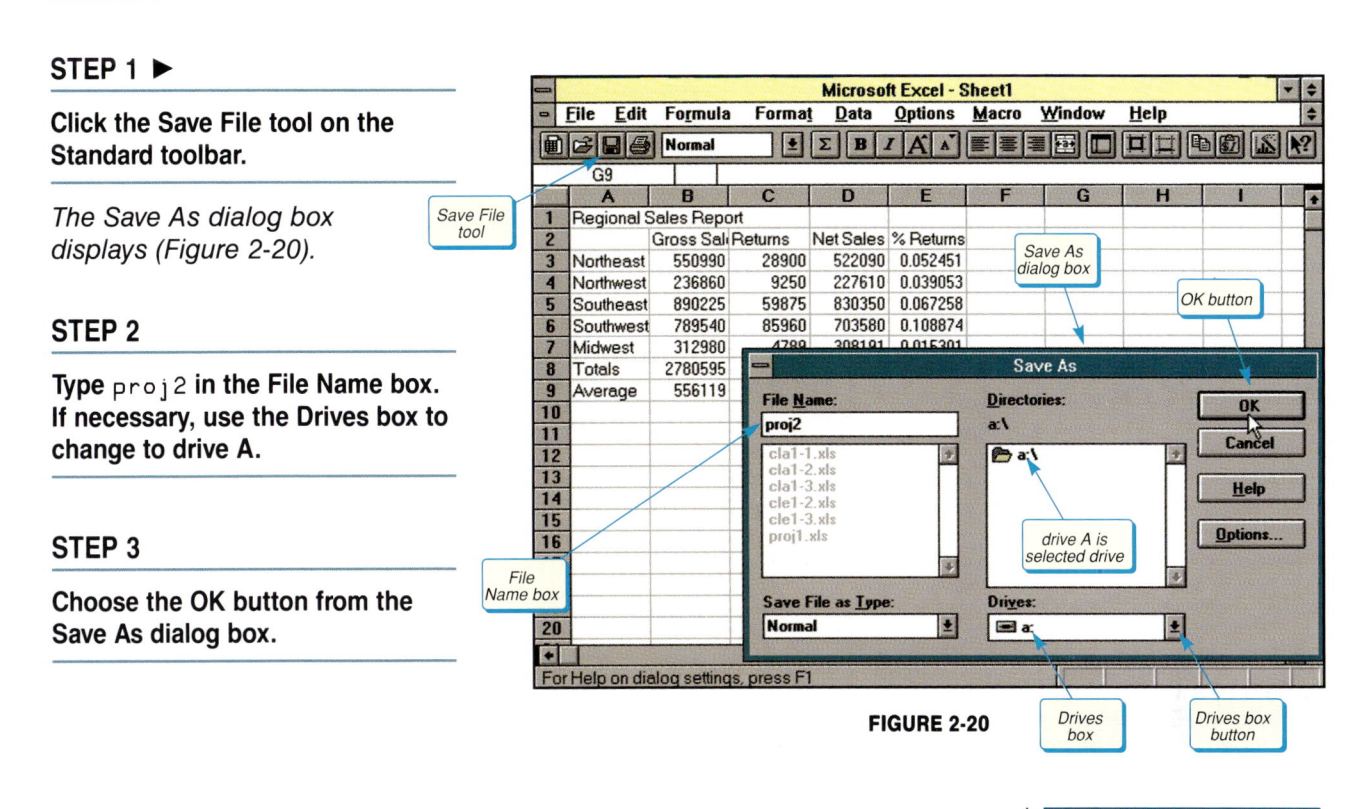

STEP 1 ▶

Click the Save File tool on the Standard toolbar.

The Save As dialog box displays (Figure 2-20).

STEP 2

Type `proj2` in the File Name box. If necessary, use the Drives box to change to drive A.

STEP 3

Choose the OK button from the Save As dialog box.

FIGURE 2-20

After Excel completes the save, the worksheet remains on the screen. You can immediately continue with the next activity.

▶ FORMATTING TEXT AND DRAWING BORDERS

Although the worksheet contains the data, formulas, and functions that make up the Regional Sales Report, the text and numbers need to be formatted to improve the appearance and readability of the worksheet.

In Project 1, you used the AutoFormat command to format the majority of the worksheet. However, you might not always find an acceptable Format Table layout to use. This section and the two sections that follow describe how to format the worksheet without using the AutoFormat command.

Formatting the Worksheet Title

In the worksheet shown in Figure 2-1, the worksheet title in cell A1 is centered across columns A through E, displays in bold, and has a larger point size than the rest of the text and numbers.

TO CENTER, BOLD, AND ENLARGE THE WORKSHEET TITLE ▼

STEP 1

Select cell A1. Drag the mouse pointer from cell A1 through E1.

STEP 2 ▶

Click the Center Across Columns tool on the Standard toolbar.

Excel centers the worksheet title across the range A1:E1 (Figure 2-21).

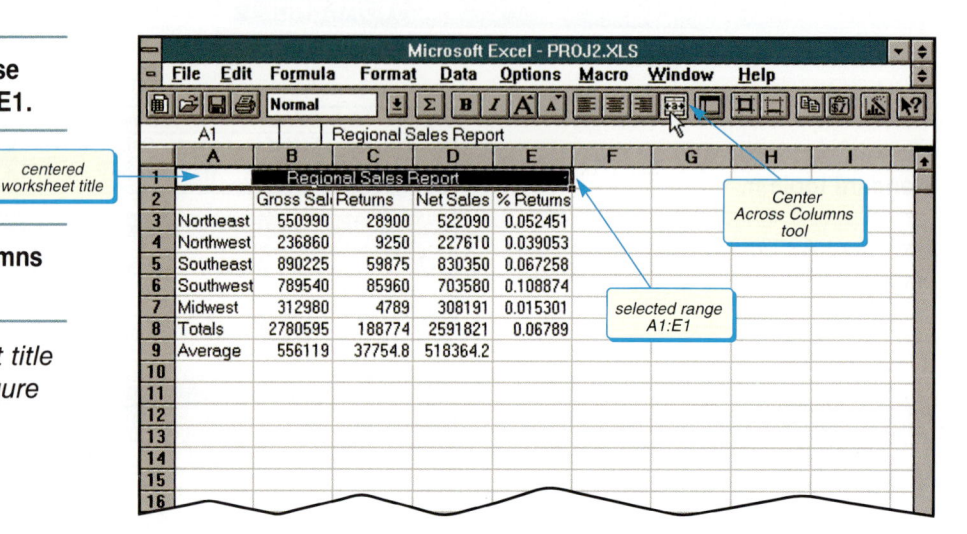

FIGURE 2-21

STEP 3 ▶

Click the Bold tool on the Standard toolbar to bold the title. Click the Increase Font Size tool on the Standard toolbar twice to increase the font size of the worksheet title.

The worksheet title, Regional Sales Report, is bold and larger (Figure 2-22).

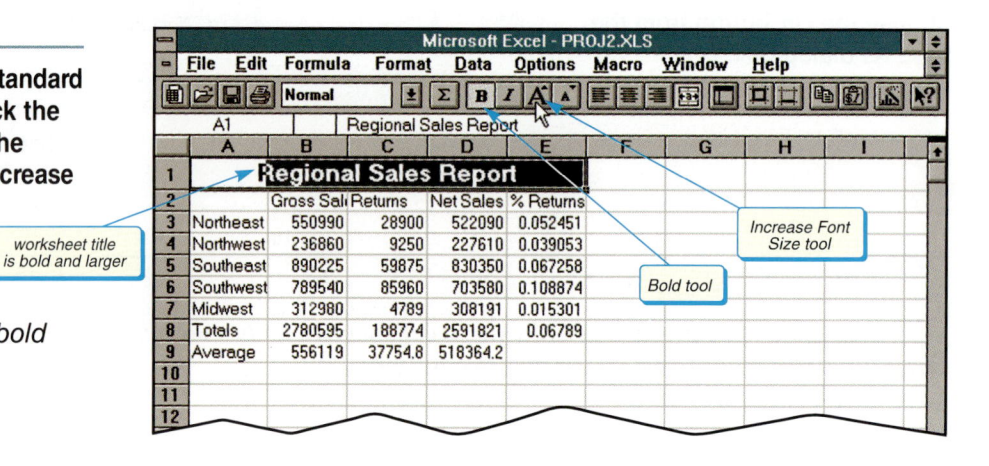

FIGURE 2-22

Recall that after you bold the contents of a cell, the Bold tool on the Standard toolbar is recessed whenever the cell is selected (Figure 2-22). If for some reason you want to remove the bold format in the active cell, click the recessed Bold tool.

Formatting the Column Titles

The column titles in row 2 are bold, italic, right-aligned, and underlined. To assign these formats to the column titles, you first must select the range B2:E2. The first three items, bold, italic, and right-aligned, can be assigned to the range using tools on the Standard toolbar.

TO BOLD, ITALICIZE, AND RIGHT-ALIGN COLUMN TITLES ▼

STEP 1

Select the range B2:E2.

STEP 2 ▶

Click the Bold tool, click the Italic tool, and click the Right Align tool, all on the Standard toolbar.

Excel makes the column titles bold, italic, and right-aligned (Figure 2-23).

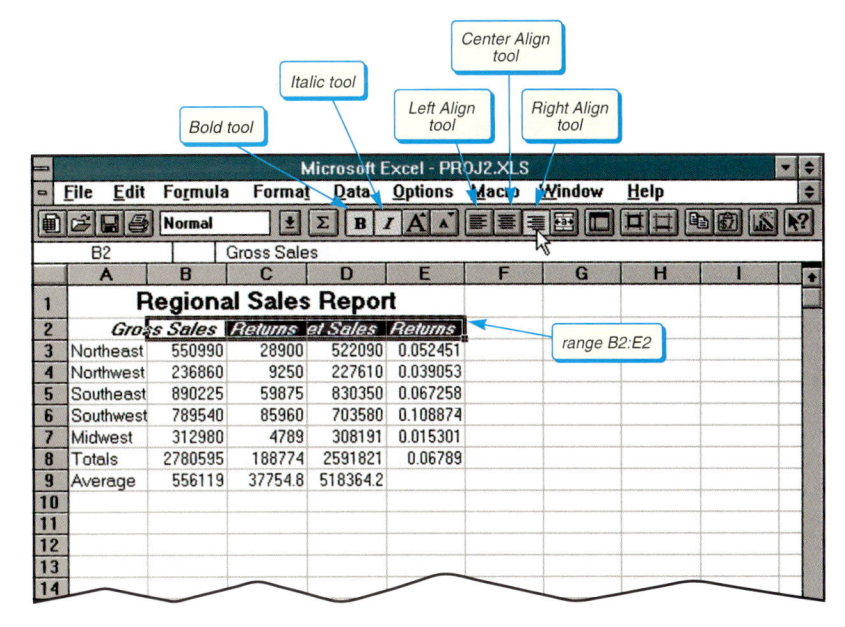

FIGURE 2-23

Notice when the column titles are right-aligned, those entries that are too long to fit in a column overlap into unused columns to the left, rather than to the right. If columns to the left are non-empty, then the characters on the left are hidden, such as in cell D2 (Figure 2-23). Later in this project, the widths of the columns will be increased so that the column titles fit in their corresponding columns.

The Standard toolbar includes three alignment tools — Left Align (▤), Center Align (▤), and Right Align (▤) (Figure 2-23). The pictures on the toolface indicate which way they align. The **Left Align** tool aligns the cell contents to the left in each cell of the selected range. The **Center Align** tool centers the cell contents within each cell of the selected range. The **Right Align** tool aligns the cell contents to the right in each cell of the selected range.

Drawing Borders

According to Figure 2-1 on page E58, the column titles are underlined. You use the **Border command** on the Format menu to draw lines on any side or all sides of a cell or range of cells.

TO DRAW A BORDER UNDER THE COLUMN TITLES

STEP 1 ▶

Select the range B2:E2. Select the Format menu and point to the Border command (Figure 2-24).

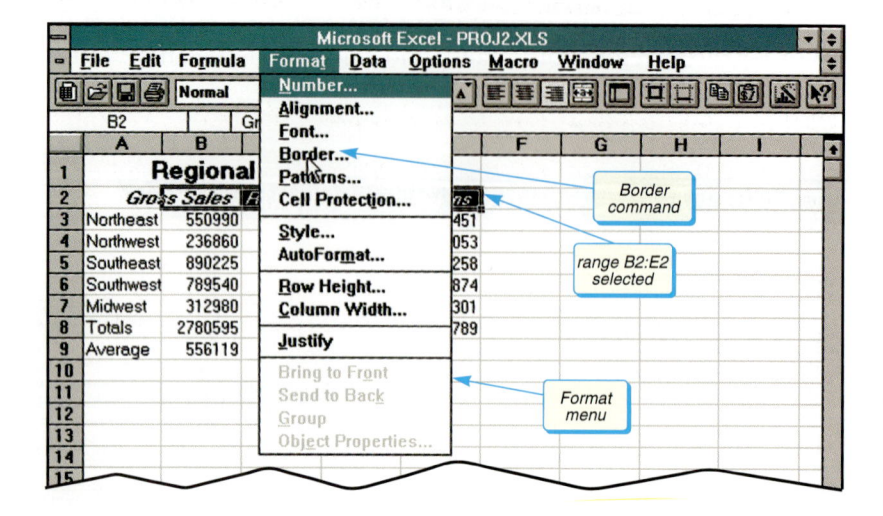

FIGURE 2-24

STEP 2

Choose the Border command.

*The **Border dialog box** displays.*

STEP 3 ▶

Click Bottom in the Border box. Next, click the bold line style in the Style box.

The bold line style displays in the Bottom box (Figure 2-25).

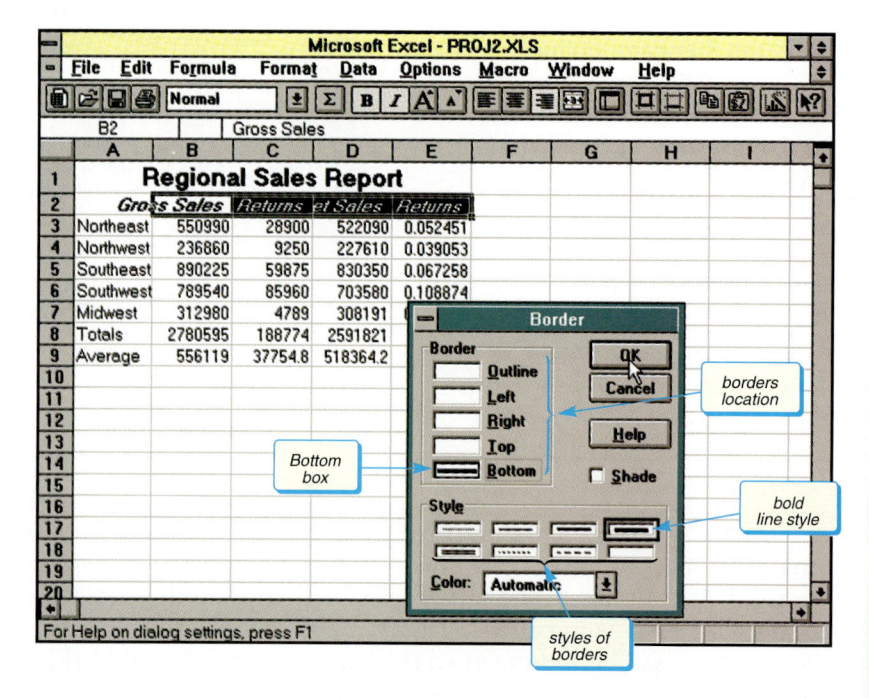

FIGURE 2-25

STEP 4 ▶

Choose OK from the Border dialog box.

Excel draws a bold border under the column titles in row 2 (Figure 2-26).

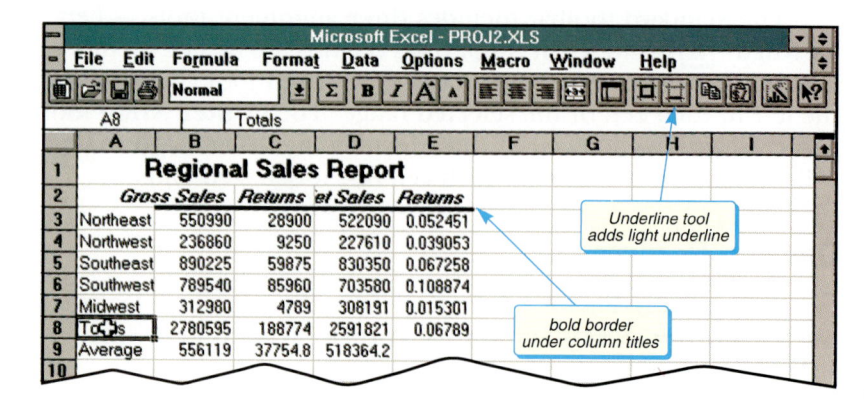

FIGURE 2-26

An alternative method for underlining is to select the range of cells to underline and click the **Underline tool** ( ) on the Standard toolbar (Figure 2-26). Clicking the Underline tool causes a light border to be drawn under the selected range of cells.

Using the Shortcut Menu to Access Excel Commands

Excel provides a **shortcut menu** (Figure 2-27) that contains the commands most often used for the current activity. You activate the shortcut menu by pressing the right mouse button.

The commands in the shortcut menu are no different than those on the menus listed on the menu bar. The major advantage is that the shortcut menu has the most likely used commands all on one menu. The list of commands in the shortcut menu changes depending on whether you are formatting a worksheet, editing a cell, or modifying a chart.

The next step in formatting the Regional Sales Report worksheet is to draw a bold line above and a double line below the totals in row 8. The shortcut menu will be used to carry out the border drawings. Before you click the right button to display the shortcut menu, make sure the mouse pointer is within the cell or range of cells you are affecting or you will select the cell where the mouse pointer is positioned when you press the right mouse button.

TO DRAW BORDERS ABOVE AND BELOW THE TOTALS ROW USING THE SHORTCUT MENU

STEP 1 ▶

Select the range A8:E8. With the mouse pointer within the selected range, click the right mouse button, and point to the Border command.

Excel displays the shortcut menu (Figure 2-27).

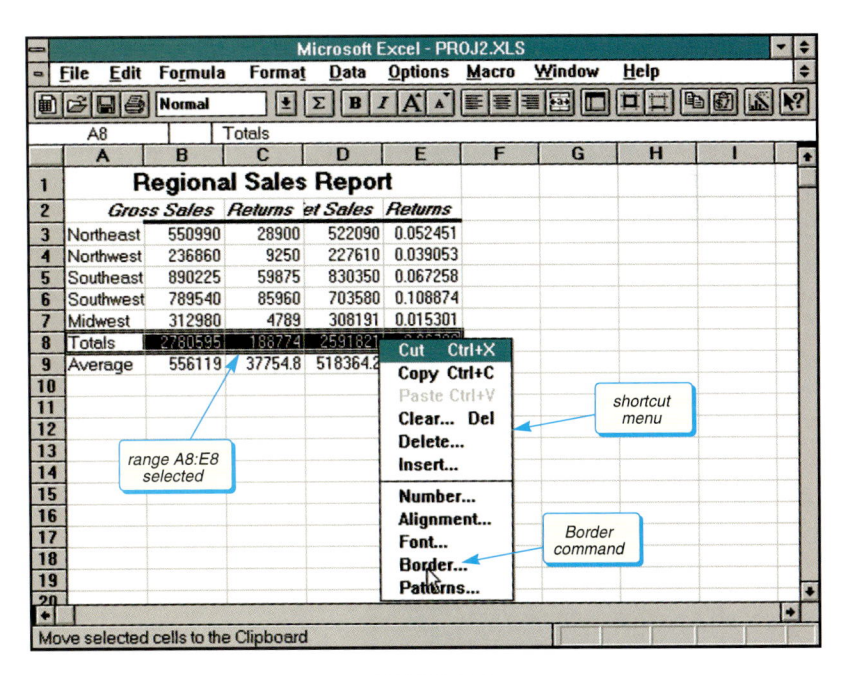

FIGURE 2-27

STEP 2

Choose the Border command from the shortcut menu.

Excel displays the Border dialog box.

STEP 3

Select Top in the Border box. Select the bold line style from the Style box.

The bold line style displays in the Top box of the Border box.

STEP 4 ▶

Select Bottom in the Border box. Select the double underline style from the Style box.

The double underline style displays in the Bottom box (Figure 2-28).

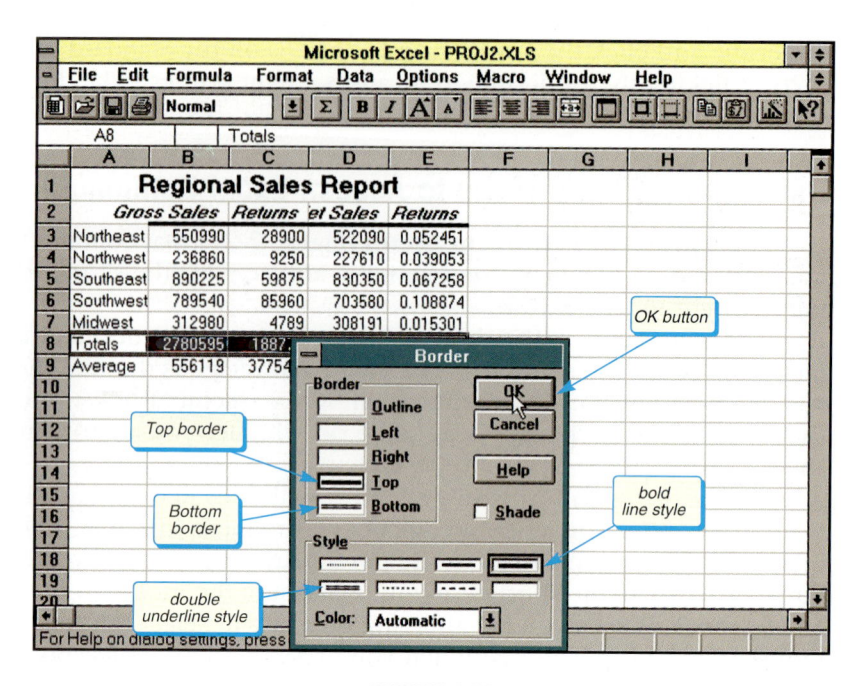

FIGURE 2-28

STEP 5 ▶

Choose OK from the Border dialog box and then select any cell in the worksheet.

A bold line displays immediately above and a double line displays immediately below the totals in row 8 (Figure 2-29).

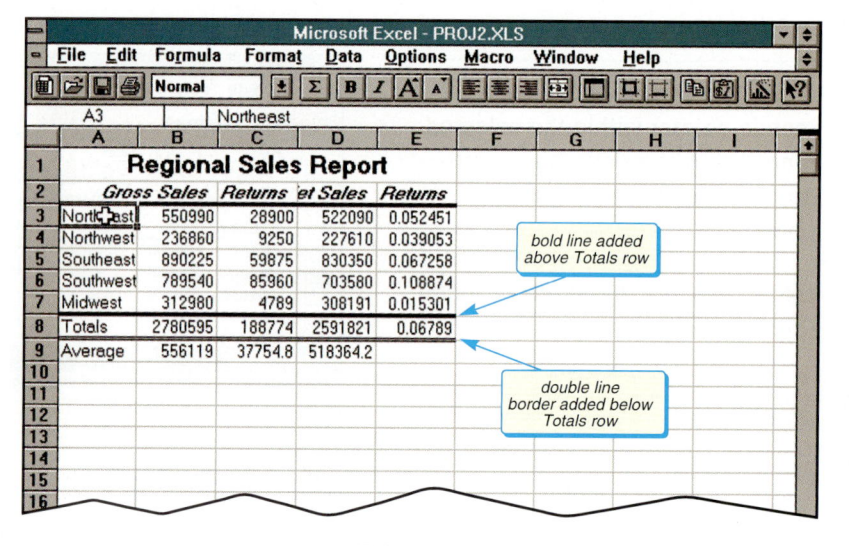

FIGURE 2-29

Formatting the Row Titles

The row titles in column A of the worksheet in Figure 2-1 on page E58 are bold. The row title Totals in cell A8 is also italicized.

TO FORMAT THE ROW TITLES ▼

STEP 1 ▶

Select the range A3:A9. Click the Bold tool on the Standard toolbar.

Excel bolds the row titles in the range A3:A9 (Figure 2-30).

because bold characters are wider, fewer display in cell

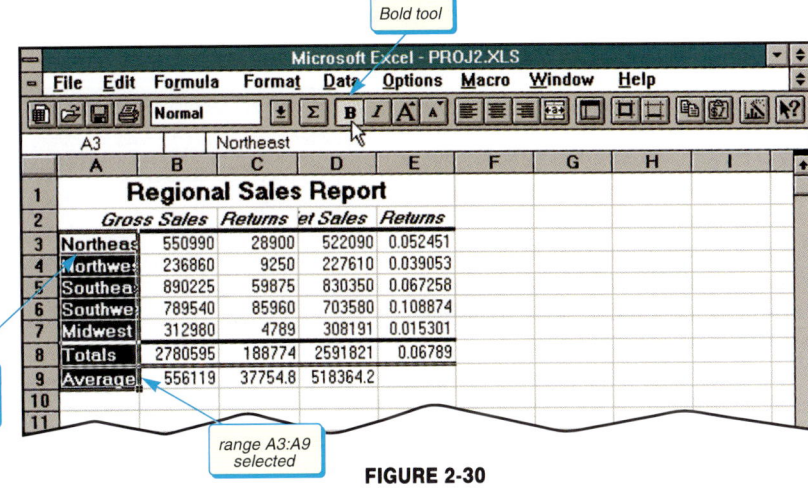

Bold tool

range A3:A9 selected

FIGURE 2-30

STEP 2 ▶

Select cell A8. Click the Italic tool on the Standard toolbar.

Excel displays the row title in cell A8 in italics (Figure 2-31).

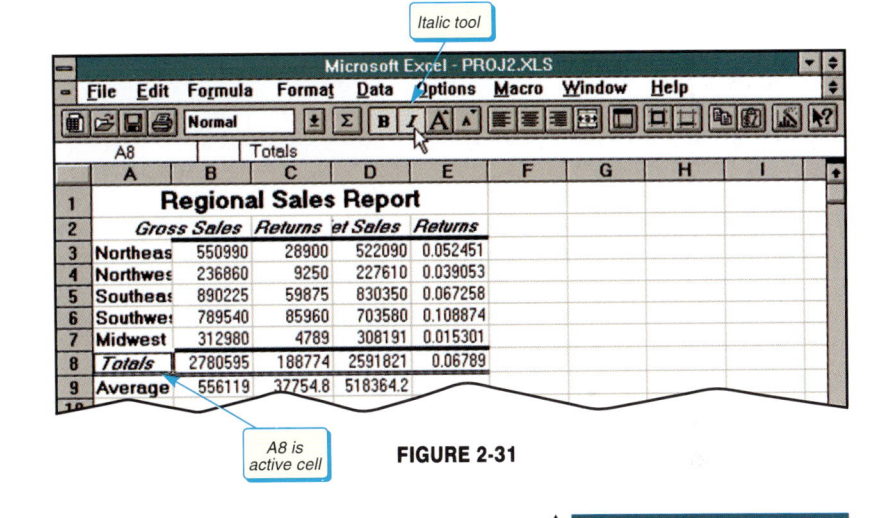

Italic tool

A8 is active cell

FIGURE 2-31

▶ FORMATTING NUMBERS

When using Excel, you can format numbers to represent dollar amounts, whole numbers with comma placement, percentages, and decimal numbers through the use of the **Style box** on the Standard toolbar.

Formatting Numbers Using the Style Box

The first three numbers in row 3 and the Totals and Average rows on the Project 2 worksheet are formatted so they display in dollar amounts with comma placement and no decimal places. The first three numbers in rows 4 through 7 are formatted so they display as whole numbers with comma placement. Formatting a worksheet so only the first row of numbers in a report and the totals have leading dollar signs is a common accounting practice.

The remainder of this section describes how to use the Style box tool to format the numbers in the Gross Sales, Returns, and Net Sales columns. Later, the decimal numbers in column E will be formatted to display as percents with two decimal places.

TO DISPLAY NUMBERS AS DOLLAR AMOUNTS USING THE STYLE BOX

STEP 1 ▶

Select the range B3:D3. Click the Style box arrow to the right of the Style box on the Standard toolbar.

Excel displays the drop-down list of format styles (Figure 2-32).

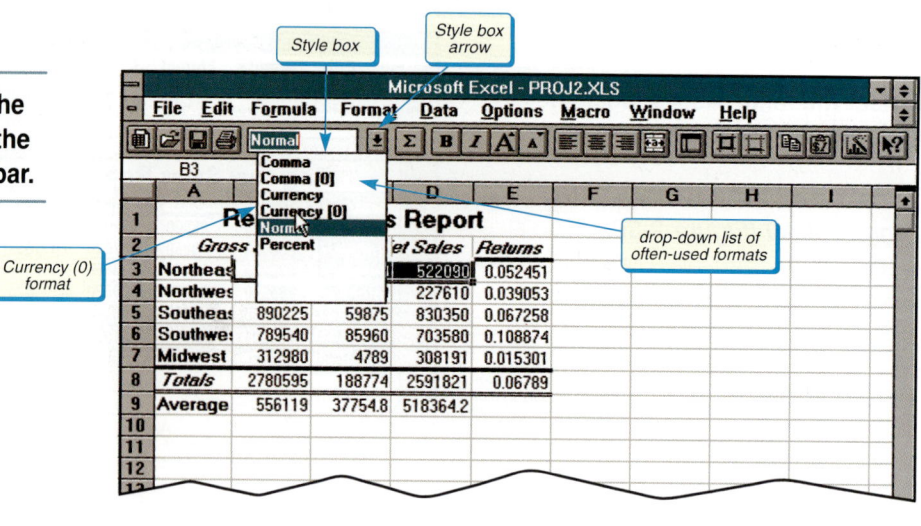

FIGURE 2-32

STEP 2 ▶

Select Currency (0) from the drop-down list of format styles.

The numbers in the range B3:D3 display as whole numbers with a leading dollar sign and a comma (Figure 2-33).

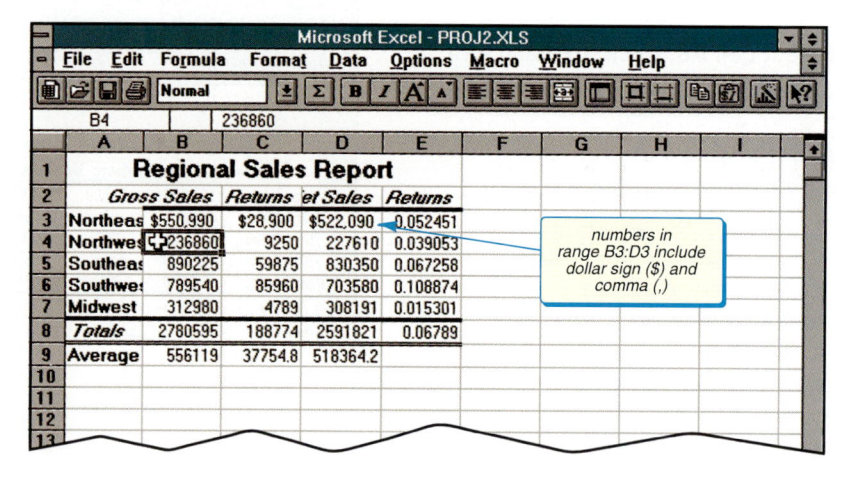

FIGURE 2-33

Notice in the drop-down list in Figure 2-32 that the third and fourth format styles are Currency and Currency (0). When the Currency style is applied to a cell, the number displays with a dollar sign, comma placement, and cents (two decimal places). The second one in the list, Currency (0), causes the number in a cell to display with a dollar sign, comma placement, and no cents. The zero in parentheses means *no decimal places*.

FORMATTING NUMBERS   E77

TO DISPLAY WHOLE NUMBERS WITH COMMA PLACEMENT USING THE STYLE BOX

STEP 1 ▶

Select the range B4:D7. Click the Style box arrow to the right of the Style box on the Standard toolbar.

Excel displays the drop-down list of format styles (Figure 2-34).

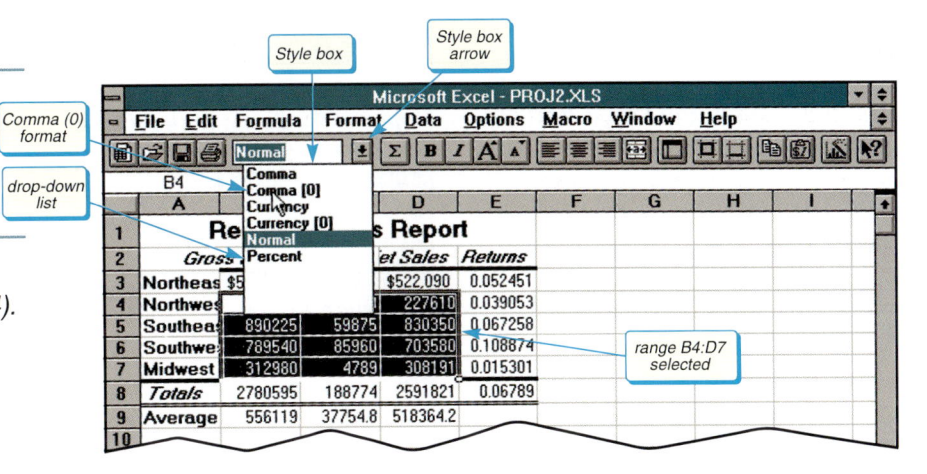

FIGURE 2-34

STEP 2 ▶

Select Comma (0) from the drop-down list box.

The numbers in the range B4:D7 display as whole numbers with comma placement (Figure 2-35).

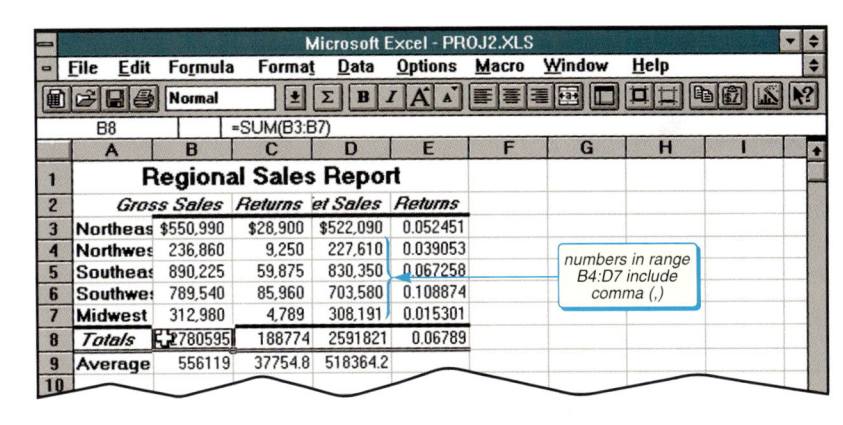

FIGURE 2-35

TO DISPLAY THE TOTALS AND AVERAGES AS DOLLAR AMOUNTS USING THE STYLE BOX

STEP 1 ▶

Select the range B8:D9. Click the Style box arrow on the Standard toolbar.

The drop-down list of format styles displays (Figure 2-36).

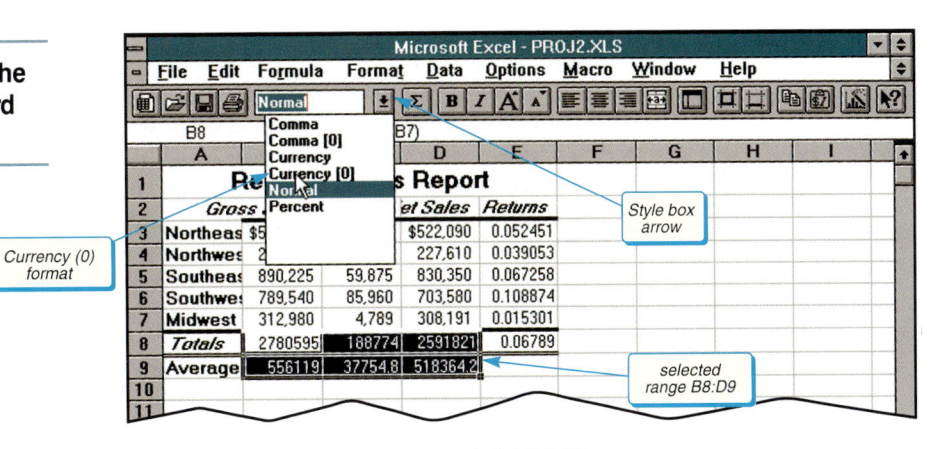

FIGURE 2-36

E78 PROJECT 2 ADDING FORMULAS TO A WORKSHEET

STEP 2 ▶

Select Currency (0) from the drop-down list box.

The numbers in the range B8:D9 are assigned the Currency (0) format style (Figure 2-37).

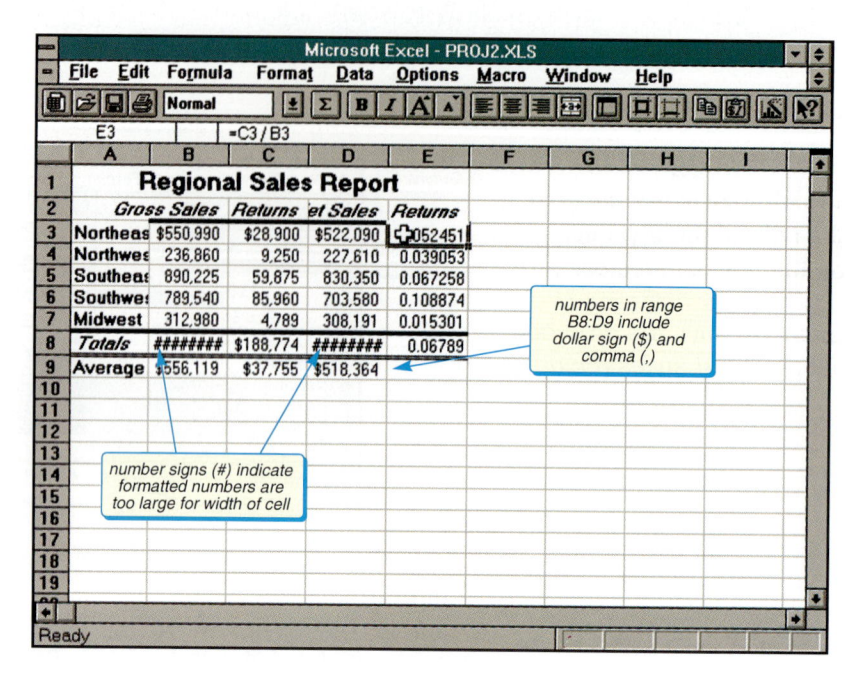

FIGURE 2-37

The **number signs (#)** that appear in cells B8 and D8 in Figure 2-37 indicate that the formatted numbers do not fit within the width of columns B and D. The cells still contain the correct values, 2780595 in cell B8 and 2591821 in cell D8, but because of the added format characters, Excel can't display them. Later in this project the column widths will be increased so the numbers in cells B8 and D8 display properly.

Notice in row 9 that Excel displays the returns average 37754.8 in cell C9 as 37755. Excel rounds the number to satisfy the format. It does the same with the net returns average 518364.2 in cell D9. However, be aware that if these cells are referenced in formulas or functions, Excel uses the actual values. It does not use the rounded values you see in the cells.

Formatting Numbers Using the Number Command

Thus far, you have been introduced to two ways to format numbers in a worksheet. In Project 1, you formatted the numbers using the AutoFormat command on the Format menu. In the previous section, you were introduced to using the Style box on the Standard toolbar as a means of selecting a format style. This section introduces you to a third way of formatting numbers using the **Number command** on the Format menu or the shortcut menu.

According to the worksheet in Figure 2-1 on page E58, each decimal number in column E is formatted as a percent with two decimal places. Neither the AutoFormat command nor the Style box tool allows for displaying a decimal number as a percent with two decimal places.

FORMATTING NUMBERS   **E79**

TO FORMAT NUMBERS AS PERCENTAGES USING THE NUMBER COMMAND ▼

STEP 1 ▶

Select the range E3:E8. Select the Format menu and point to the Number command (Figure 2-38).

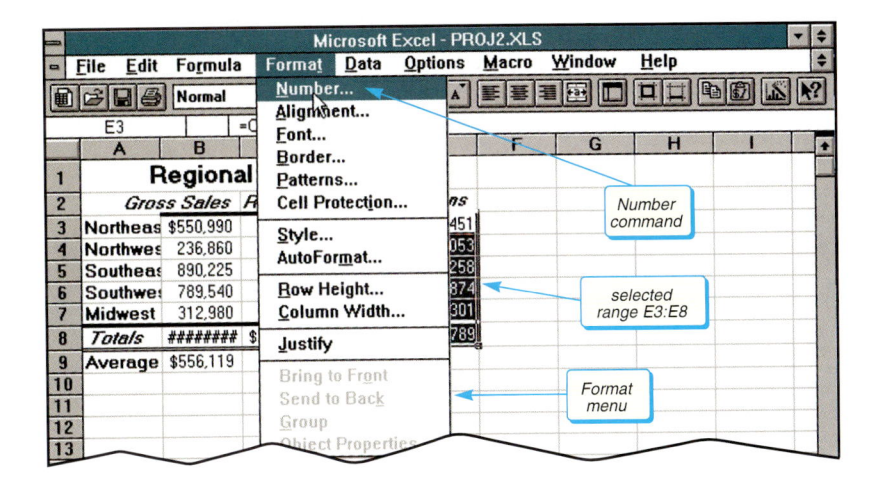

FIGURE 2-38

STEP 2

Choose the Number command.

The Number Format dialog box displays.

STEP 3 ▶

Select Percentage from the Category box and 0.00% from the Format Codes box.

The sample 5.25% at the bottom of the Number Format dialog box shows how the number 0.052451 will look in the first cell (E3) of the selected range (Figure 2-39).

FIGURE 2-39

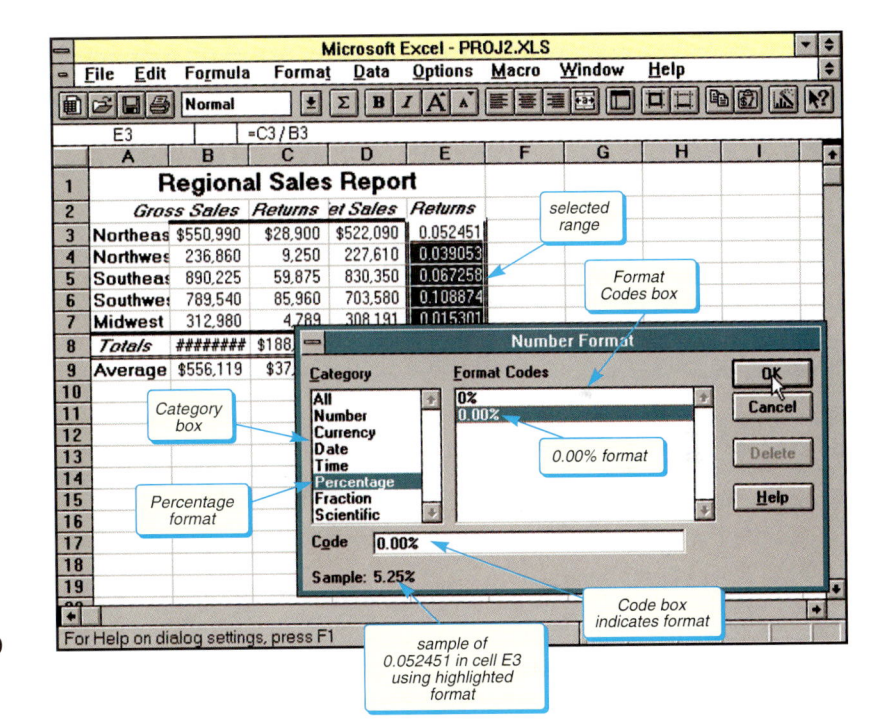

STEP 4 ▶

Choose OK from the Number Format dialog box.

The percent returns in the range E3:E8 display as percents with two decimal places (Figure 2-40).

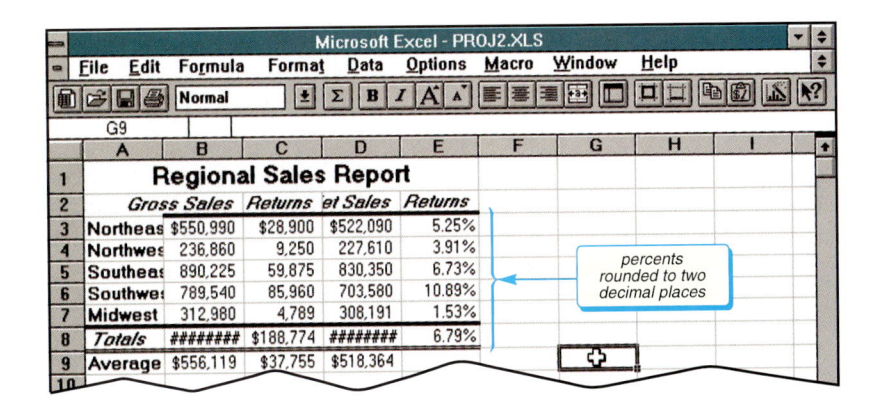

FIGURE 2-40

The Category box in the Number Format dialog box (Figure 2-39 on the previous page) shows several different types of formats. These formats allow you to display numbers in any desired format. You can also modify the Code box at the bottom of the Number Format box. For example, if you want to display three positions to the right of the decimal, rather than two as in the range E3:E8, you can add another zero in the Code box prior to choosing the OK button.

As mentioned earlier, Excel rounds a number to fit the format selected. For example, in cell E3 Excel rounds the actual value 0.052451 up to 5.25%. In cell E7, Excel rounds the actual value 0.015301 down to 1.53%.

▶ CHANGING THE FONT IN THE WORKSHEET

In Project 1 you learned that the default font Excel uses for a new worksheet is MS Sans Serif. This font as well as several others available with Windows products are called **screen fonts**. Screen fonts are *not* true **WYSIWYG** — **W**hat **Y**ou **S**ee on the screen **I**s **W**hat **Y**ou **G**et on the printer. That is, a worksheet does not always print the way it looks on the screen.

Windows includes several **TrueType fonts** that are WYSIWYG. That is, with TrueType fonts the same font outline you see on the screen is used with the printer. Characters in TrueType font are also clearer and crisper because the font is modified to match the resolution of your screen and monitor.

This project calls for changing the **font styles** of all the cells in the report from MS Sans Serif to TrueType Arial. One way to do this is to change the font of the range A1:E9. However, it is also more economical to change the font of the entire worksheet because when you save the worksheet, it will take up less disk space.

TO CHANGE THE FONT OF THE ENTIRE WORKSHEET ▼

STEP 1 ▶

Click the Select All button. Select the Format menu and point to the Font command.

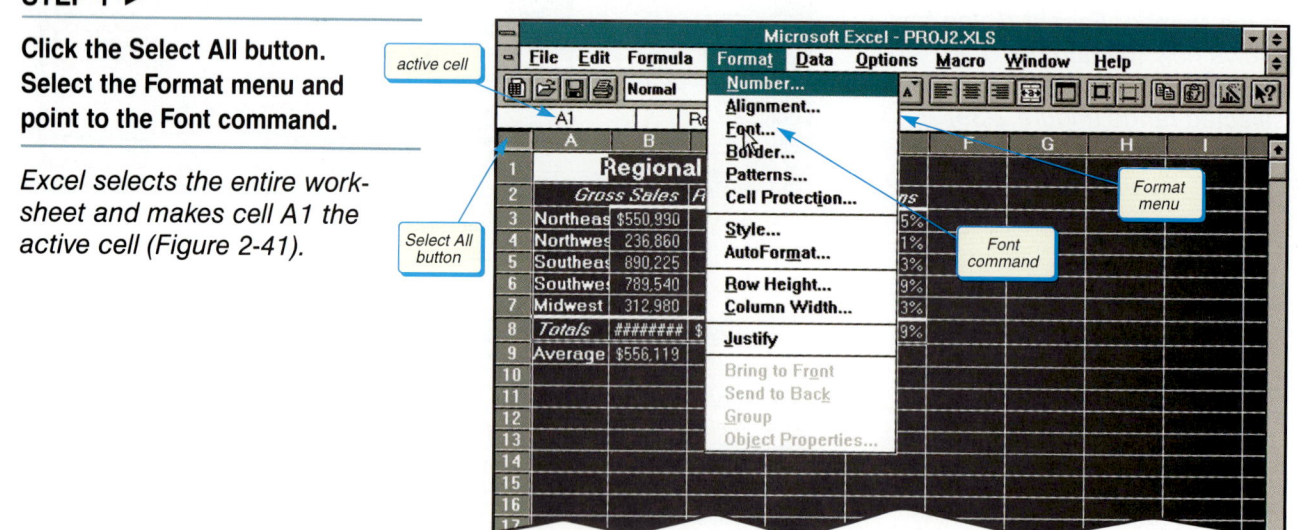

Excel selects the entire worksheet and makes cell A1 the active cell (Figure 2-41).

FIGURE 2-41

STEP 2 ▶

Choose the Font command.

*Excel displays the **Font dialog box** (Figure 2-42). Notice that MS Sans Serif is the default font for cell A1. Because the entire worksheet is selected and different font styles and font sizes are used in the worksheet, the **Font Style box**, **Size box**, and **Sample box** are empty.*

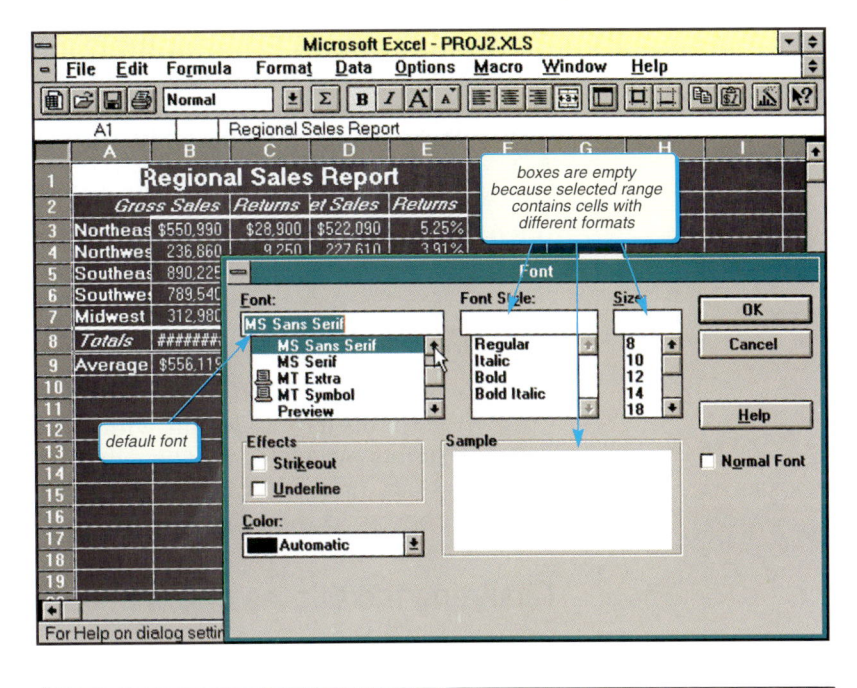

FIGURE 2-42

STEP 3 ▶

Use the Font scroll arrow to scroll to TT Arial. Select TT Arial (Figure 2-43).

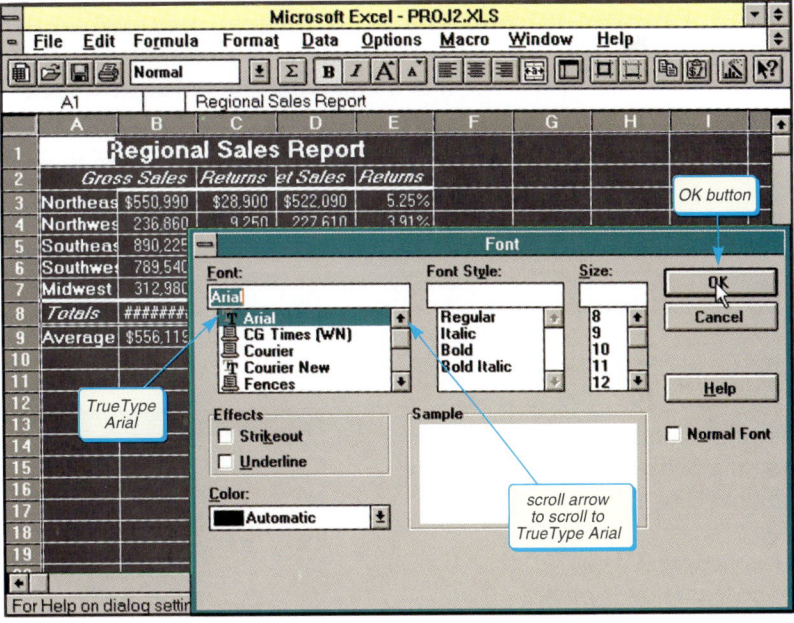

FIGURE 2-43

STEP 4 ▶

Choose OK from the Font dialog box and then select any cell in the worksheet.

The characters in the worksheet display using TrueType Arial font (Figure 2-44).

FIGURE 2-44

Excel allows you to change the font of a cell, a range of cells, or the entire worksheet. You can also change the font any time while the worksheet is active. For example, some Excel users prefer to change the font before they enter any data. Others change the font while they are building the worksheet or after they have entered all the data.

When developing presentation quality worksheets, several different fonts are often used in the same worksheet.

▶ Changing the Widths of Columns and Heights of Rows

When Excel begins and the blank worksheet appears on the screen, all the columns have a default width of 8.43 characters and a height of 12.75 points. At any time, you can change the width of the columns or height of the rows to make the worksheet easier to read or to ensure that entries will display properly in the cells to which they are assigned.

Changing the Widths of Columns

Excel provides two ways to increase or decrease the width of the columns in a worksheet. First, you can change the width of one column at a time. Second, you can change the width of a series of adjacent columns. This project demonstrates both methods.

When changing the **column width**, you can manually set the width or you can request that Excel size the column to best fit. **Best fit** means that the width of the column will be increased or decreased on the basis of the widest entry in the column.

TO CHANGE THE WIDTH OF A COLUMN FOR THE BEST FIT ▼

STEP 1 ▶

Move the mouse pointer to the border line between the column A and column B headings above row 1.

The mouse pointer becomes a dark plus sign with two arrowheads (↔) (Figure 2-45).

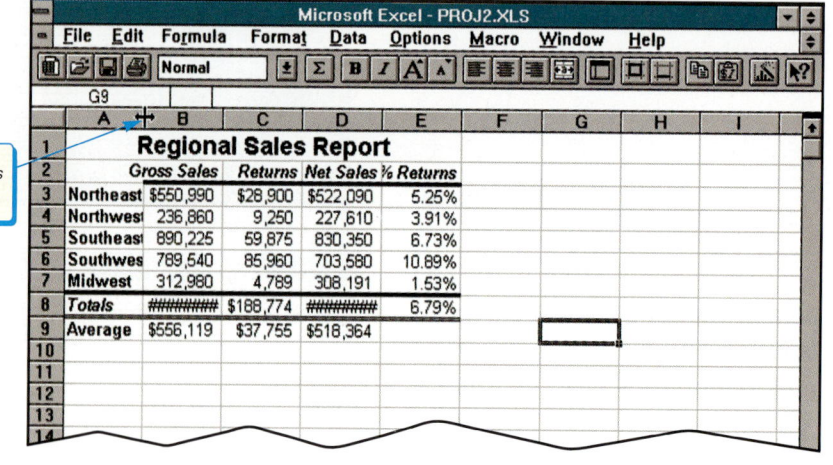

FIGURE 2-45

STEP 2 ▶

Double-click the left mouse button.

The width of column A increases just enough so the widest entry in column A, Southwest, fits in cell A6 (Figure 2-46).

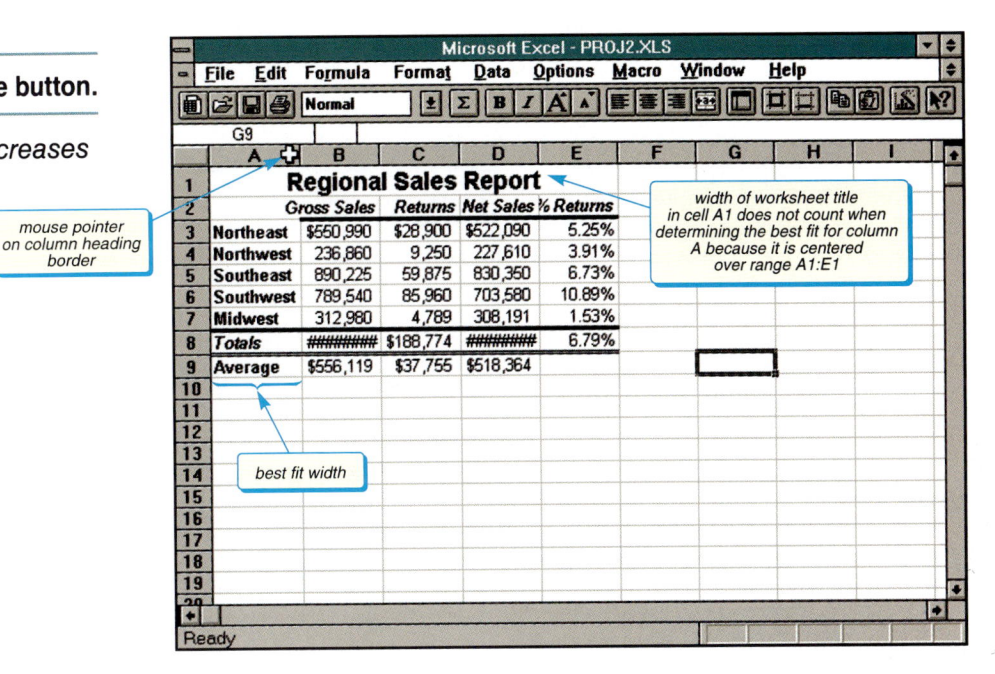

FIGURE 2-46

Compare the entries in column A of Figure 2-46 to Figure 2-45. Notice how Excel has increased the width of column A just enough so all the characters in the regional names display. To determine the exact character width of column A, you can move the mouse pointer to the border line between the column A and column B headings. When the mouse pointer changes to a dark plus sign with two arrowheads, hold down the left mouse button. Excel displays the new column width (9.71 for column A) in place of the cell reference in the formula bar.

Recall that the worksheet title, Regional Sales Report, is assigned to cell A1. Because it was centered earlier across columns A through E, Excel does not take the width of the title into consideration when determining the best fit for column A.

If you decide to undo a new column width prior to entering the next command or data item, you can choose the **Undo Column Width command** from the Edit menu.

The next step is to uniformly change the column widths of columns B through E from 8.43 to 10.57 characters. In this case the best fit will not be used because here more space is preferred between the columns to improve the appearance of the report.

E84　PROJECT 2　ADDING FORMULAS TO A WORKSHEET

TO CHANGE THE WIDTH OF A SERIES OF ADJACENT COLUMNS ▼

STEP 1

Move the mouse pointer to column heading B. Drag the mouse from column heading B across to column heading E, and then release the left mouse button.

Excel highlights the columns as you drag from column B through column E.

STEP 2 ▶

Move the mouse pointer to the line to the right of column heading E.

The mouse pointer becomes a dark plus sign with two arrowheads (Figure 2-47).

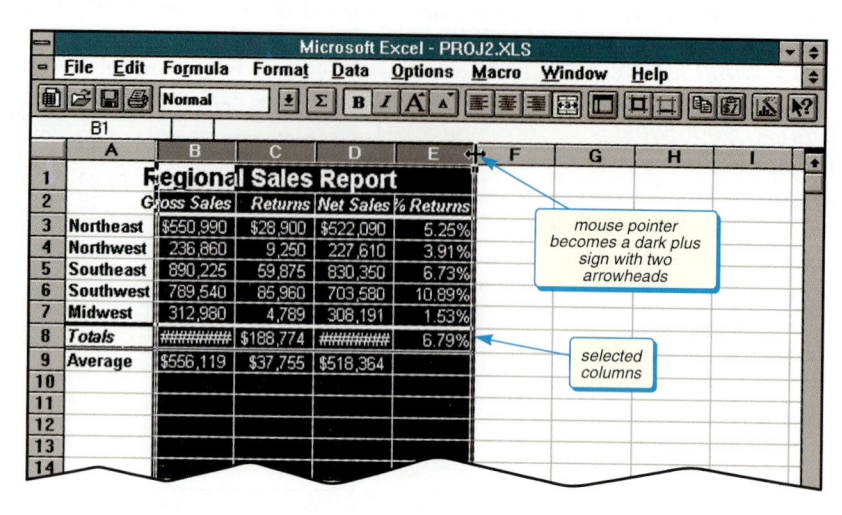

FIGURE 2-47

STEP 3 ▶

Drag the mouse to the right until the width displayed in place of the cell reference in the formula bar is equal to 10.57.

Excel displays a vertical dotted line that when added to the width of column E indicates the column width that will be assigned to columns B through E (Figure 2-48).

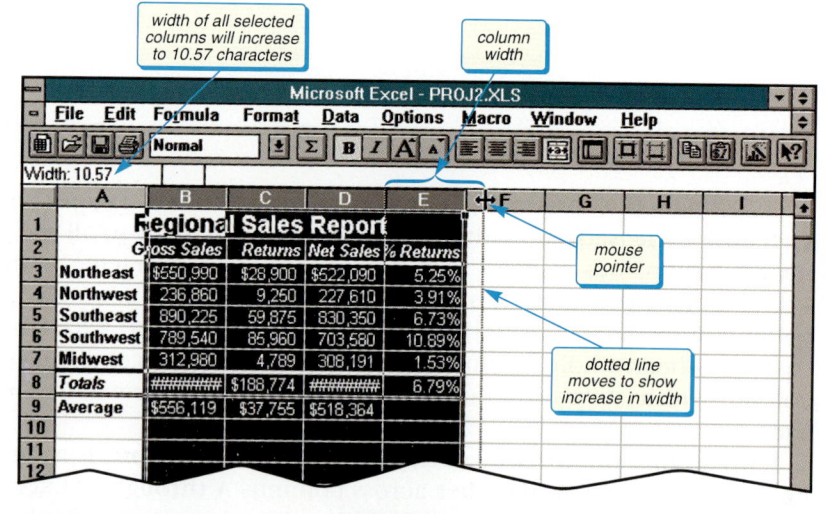

FIGURE 2-48

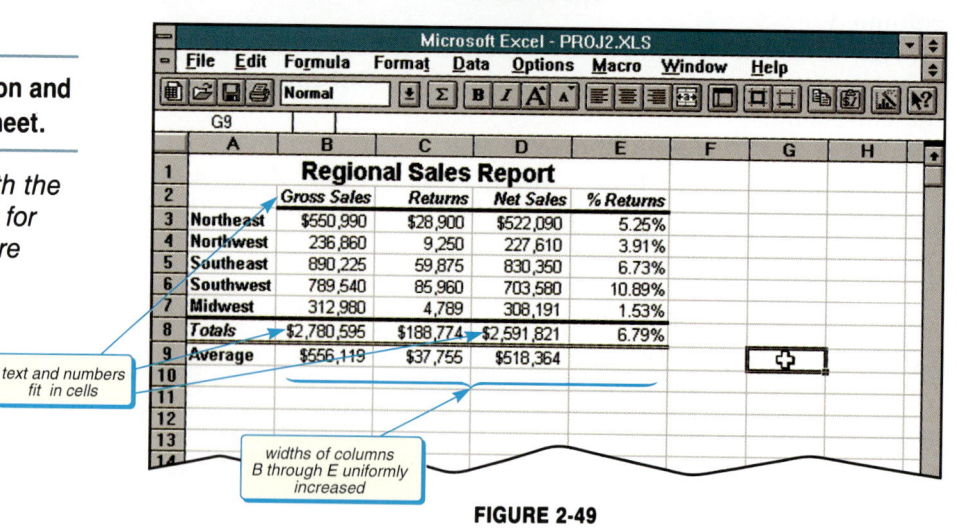

STEP 4 ▶

Release the left mouse button and select any cell in the worksheet.

The worksheet displays with the new column width settings for columns B through E (Figure 2-49).

FIGURE 2-49

CHANGING THE WIDTHS OF COLUMNS AND HEIGHTS OF ROWS **E85**

The column width can vary between zero and 255 characters. When you decrease the column width to zero, the column is hidden. Hiding columns is a technique you can use to hide sensitive data on the screen that you don't want other people to see. When you print a worksheet, hidden columns do not print.

If you prefer to use a dialog box rather than the mouse to change the column width, select any cell in the column or range of columns to be affected, choose the **Column Width command** in the Format menu or shortcut menu, and type in the desired width. The Column Width command only appears on the shortcut menu when one or more entire columns are selected. You select entire columns by dragging through the column headings.

Changing the Heights of Rows

When you change the font size of a cell entry, such as Regional Sales Report in cell A1, Excel automatically adjusts the **row height** to the best fit. You can also manually adjust the height of a row to add space that improves the appearance of the worksheet. The row height is measured in point size. The default row height is 12.75 points. The following steps show how to use the mouse to increase the height of row 2 from its normal height to 24 points so there is extra space between the worksheet title in row 1 and the column titles in row 2.

TO INCREASE THE HEIGHT OF A ROW BY DRAGGING THE MOUSE ▼

STEP 1 ▶

Move the mouse pointer to the border line between row headings 2 and 3.

The mouse pointer becomes a dark plus sign with two arrowheads (Figure 2-50).

FIGURE 2-50

STEP 2 ▶

Drag the mouse down until the height displayed in place of the cell reference in the formula bar is equal to 24.00.

Excel displays a horizontal dotted line (Figure 2-51). The distance between the dotted line and the top of row 2 indicates the new row height.

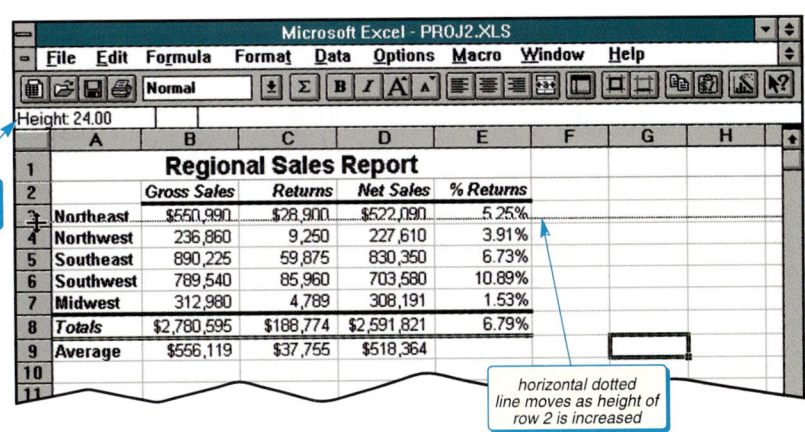

FIGURE 2-51

STEP 3 ▶

Release the left mouse button and select any cell in the worksheet.

The worksheet displays with the new height for row 2 (Figure 2-52).

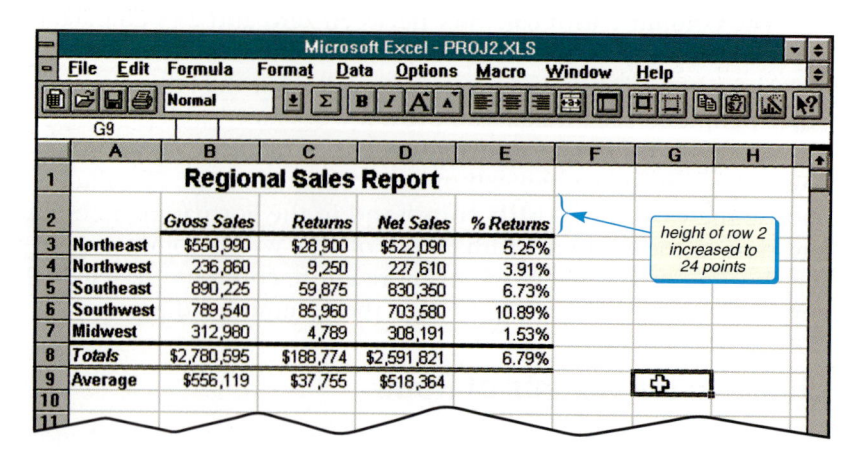

FIGURE 2-52

The row height can vary between zero and 409 points. When you decrease the row height to zero, the row is hidden.

To use a dialog box to change the row height, select any cell in the row or a series of cells down a column, choose the **Row Height command** in the Format menu or shortcut menu, and type the desired height. As with the Column Width command, the Row Height command only shows on the shortcut menu when one or more rows are selected.

The following steps show how to increase the height of row 9 to 24 points using the Row Height command in the Format menu.

TO INCREASE THE HEIGHT OF A ROW USING THE ROW HEIGHT COMMAND ▼

STEP 1 ▶

Select cell A9. Select the Format menu and point to the Row Height command (Figure 2-53).

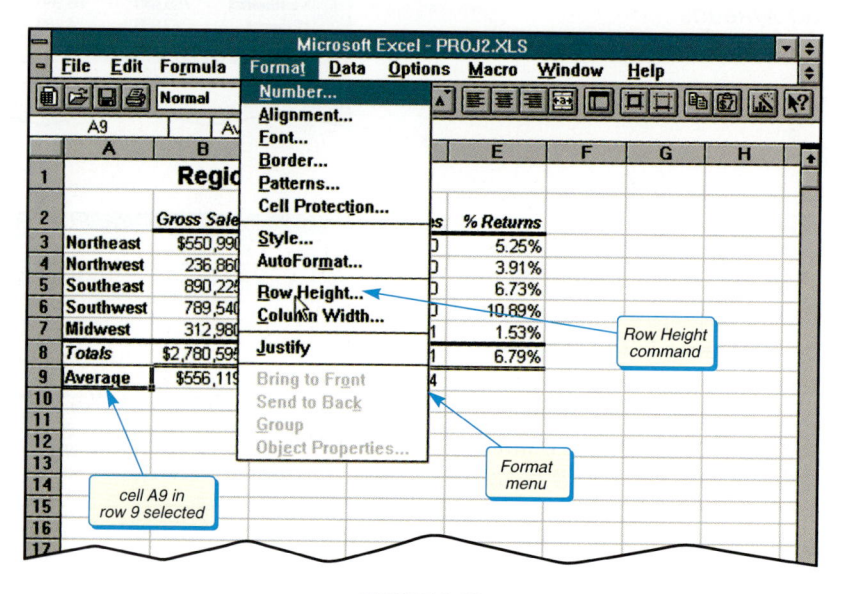

FIGURE 2-53

CHANGING THE WIDTHS OF COLUMNS AND HEIGHTS OF ROWS **E87**

STEP 2 ▶

Choose the Row Height command. Type 24 in the Row Height box.

Excel displays the Row Height dialog box with a row height of 24 points (Figure 2-54).

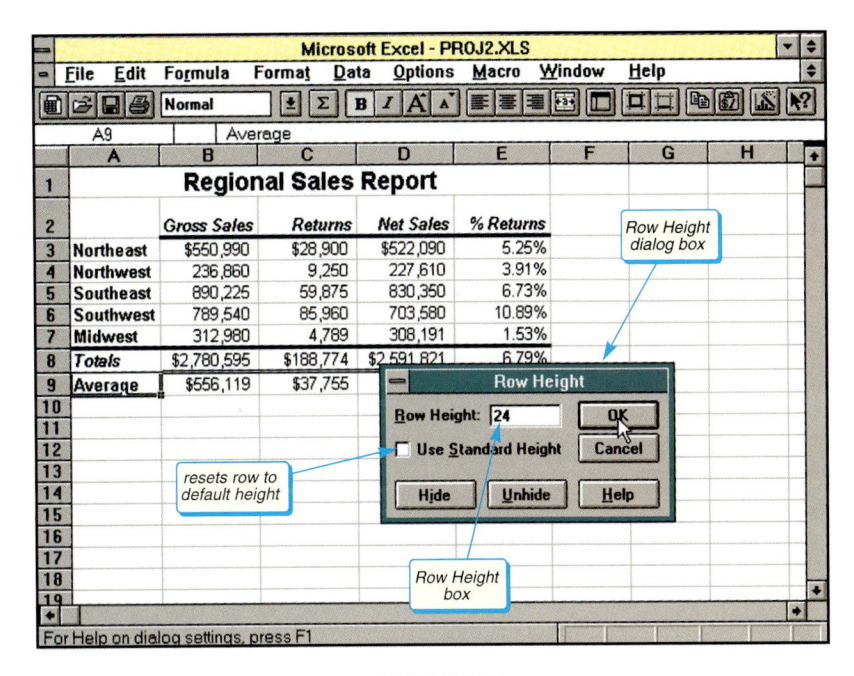

FIGURE 2-54

STEP 3 ▶

Choose OK from the Row Height dialog box.

Excel increases the height of row 9 from 12.75 to 24 points (Figure 2-55).

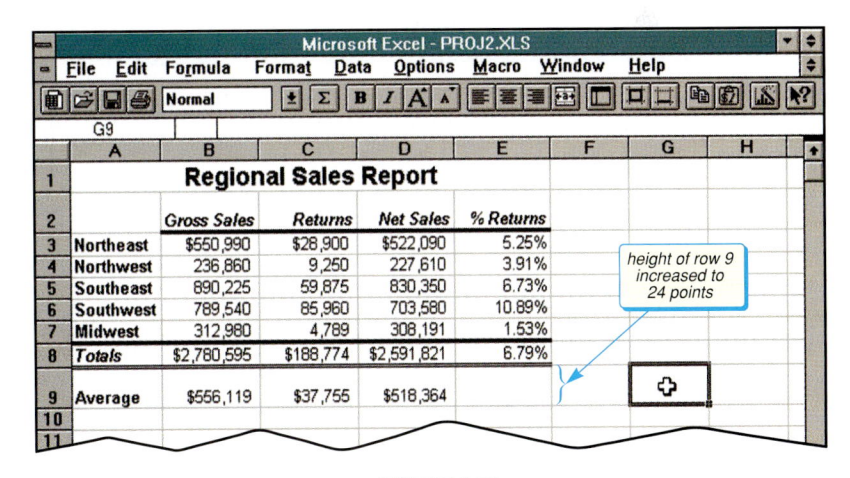

FIGURE 2-55

If you prefer to use the shortcut menu to change the height of a row, select row heading 9 in Step 1 rather than cell A9. When you click on the row heading, the entire row is selected and the row height command is available on the shortcut menu as well as the Format menu.

If for some reason you want to switch back to the default row height, simply click the Use Standard Height check box in the Row Height dialog box (Figure 2-54).

SAVING THE WORKSHEET A SECOND TIME USING THE SAME FILE NAME

Earlier an intermediate version of the worksheet was saved using the file name PROJ2.XLS. To save the worksheet a second time using the same file name, click the Save File tool on the Standard toolbar (Figure 2-56). Excel automatically stores the latest version of the worksheet under the same file name PROJ2.XLS without displaying the Save As dialog box as it did when you saved the worksheet the first time.

If you want to save the worksheet under a new name, choose the Save As command from the File menu. For example, some Excel users use the Save File tool to save the latest version of the worksheet to the default drive. They then use the Save As command from the File menu to save a second copy to another drive.

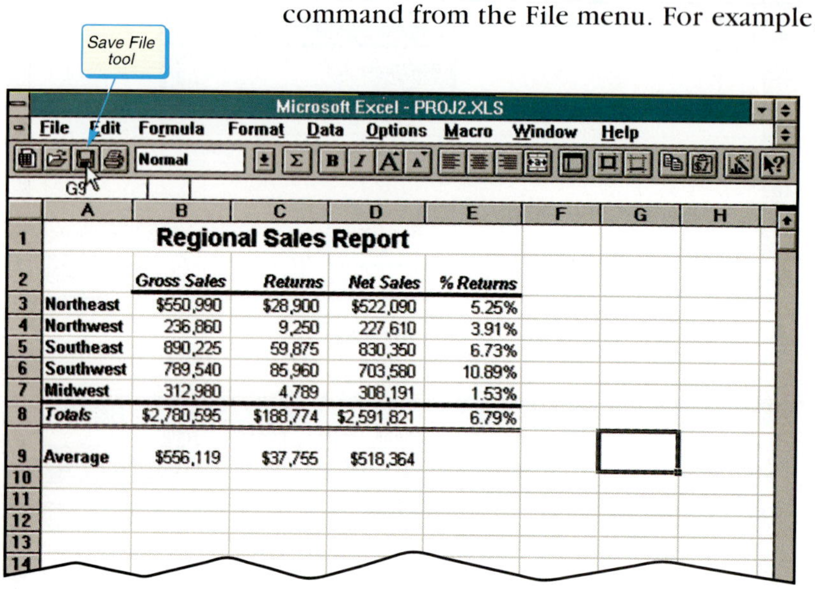

You can also instruct Excel to automatically create a backup of a worksheet on the default drive every time you save it by choosing the Options button in the Save As dialog box and clicking the Create Backup File check box. A **backup** copy is the previous version of the worksheet, renamed with a .BAK extension. Saving a backup copy of the worksheet is another form of protection against losing all your work.

FIGURE 2-56

PREVIEWING AND PRINTING THE WORKSHEET

In Project 1 you printed the worksheet without previewing it on the screen. By previewing the worksheet, you see exactly how it will look without generating a hard copy. **Previewing a worksheet** can save time, paper, and the frustration of waiting for a printout only to find out it is not what you want.

TO PREVIEW THE WORKSHEET AND PREPARE IT FOR PRINTING

STEP 1 ▶

Select the File menu and point to the Print Preview command (Figure 2-57).

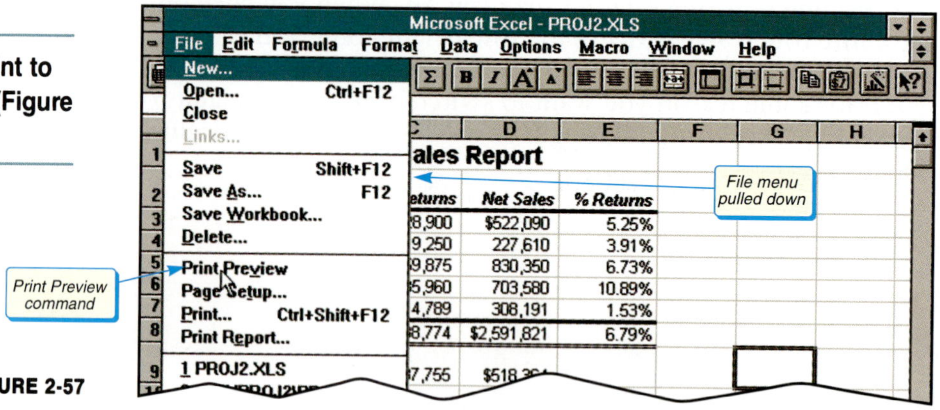

FIGURE 2-57

PREVIEWING AND PRINTING THE WORKSHEET **E89**

STEP 2 ▶

Choose the Print Preview command.

Excel displays a preview of the worksheet (possibly with cell gridlines) and the mouse pointer changes to a magnifying glass (🔍) (Figure 2-58). If number signs display for the totals, close the print preview and increase the column widths by one character.

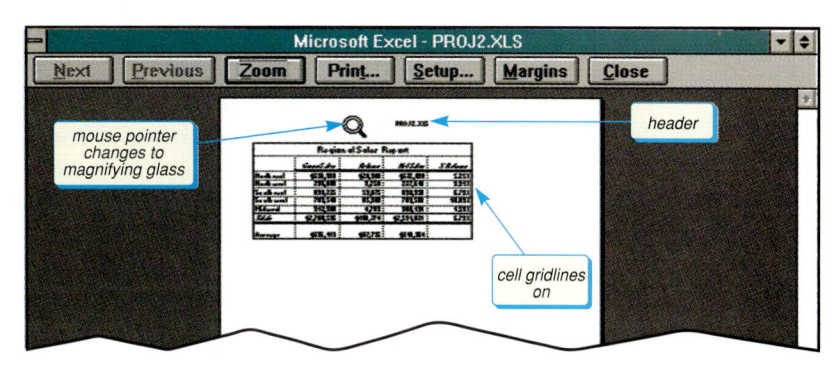

FIGURE 2-58

STEP 3

If the cell gridlines display in the preview, click the Setup button at the top of the print preview screen. Clear the Cell Gridlines check box so the cell gridlines in the preview do not print.

Excel displays the Page Setup dialog box with the Cell Gridlines check box empty (Figure 2-59).

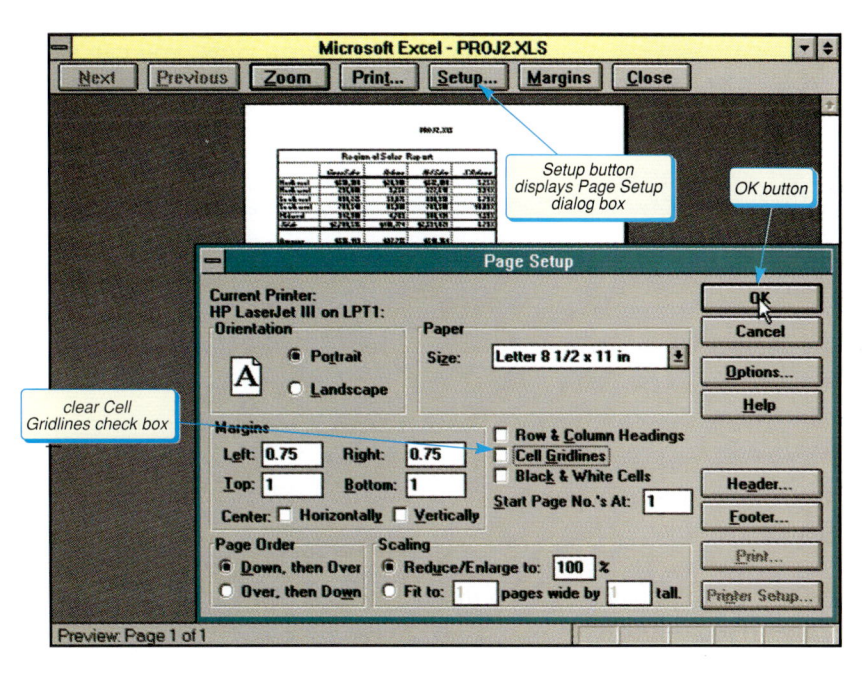

FIGURE 2-59

STEP 4 ▶

Choose the OK button from the Page Setup dialog box.

Excel displays the preview of the worksheet without cell gridlines (Figure 2-60).

STEP 5

Click the Close button in the Print Preview window to return to the worksheet.

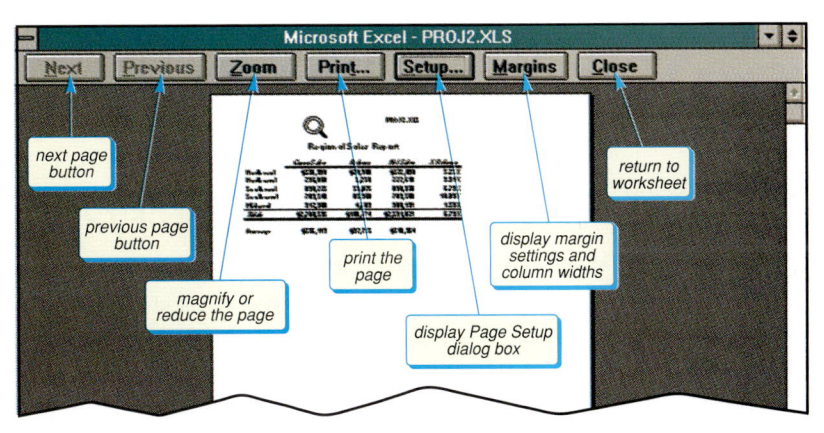

FIGURE 2-60

E90 PROJECT 2 ADDING FORMULAS TO A WORKSHEET

Excel displays several buttons at the top of the print preview screen (Figure 2-60 on the previous page). The first two buttons on the left allow you to page back and forth in a multiple-page worksheet. You use the Zoom button (Zoom) for magnifying or reducing the print preview. Clicking the mouse when the pointer displays as a magnifying glass on the worksheet carries out the same function.

When you click the Print button (Print...), Excel displays a Print dialog box that allows you to print the worksheet. The Setup button (Setup...) displays the same Print Setup dialog box that displays when you choose the Print Setup command from the File menu. The Margins button (Margins) allows you to adjust the top, bottom, left, and right margins, and the column widths. Whatever margin or column width changes you make with the Margins button remain with the worksheet when you close the Print Preview Window. The Close button (Close) closes the print preview screen and the worksheet reappears in the normal Excel window.

After closing the preview, you can print the worksheet using the Print tool (🖨) on the Standard toolbar as follows:

TO PRINT THE WORKSHEET AFTER PREVIEWING IT ▼

STEP 1

Ready the printer.

STEP 2 ▶

Click the Print tool on the Standard toolbar.

Excel prints the worksheet on the printer (Figure 2-61).

PROJ2.XLS

Regional Sales Report

	Gross Sales	Returns	Net Sales	% Returns
Northeast	$550,990	$28,900	$522,090	5.25%
Northwest	236,860	9,250	227,610	3.91%
Southeast	890,225	59,875	830,350	6.73%
Southwest	789,540	85,960	703,580	10.89%
Midwest	312,980	4,789	308,191	1.53%
Totals	$2,780,595	$188,774	$2,591,821	6.79%
Average	$556,119	$37,755	$518,364	

FIGURE 2-61

▶ PRINTING A SECTION OF THE WORKSHEET

You might not always want to print the entire worksheet. You can print portions of the worksheet by selecting the range of cells to print and then choosing the **Set Print Area command** from the **Options menu**. Once the print area is set, you can click the Print tool on the Standard toolbar. The following steps show how to print the range A2:B9.

TO PRINT A SECTION OF THE WORKSHEET

STEP 1 ▶

Select the range A2:B9. Select the Options menu and point to the Set Print Area command.

Excel highlights the selected range and displays the Options menu (Figure 2-62).

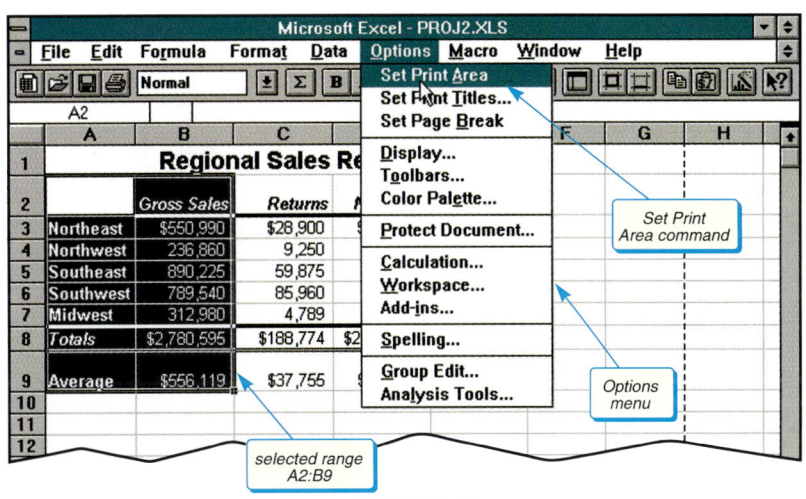

FIGURE 2-62

STEP 2 ▶

Choose the Set Print Area command.

Excel changes the print area from the entire worksheet to the selected range A2:B9 (Figure 2-63).

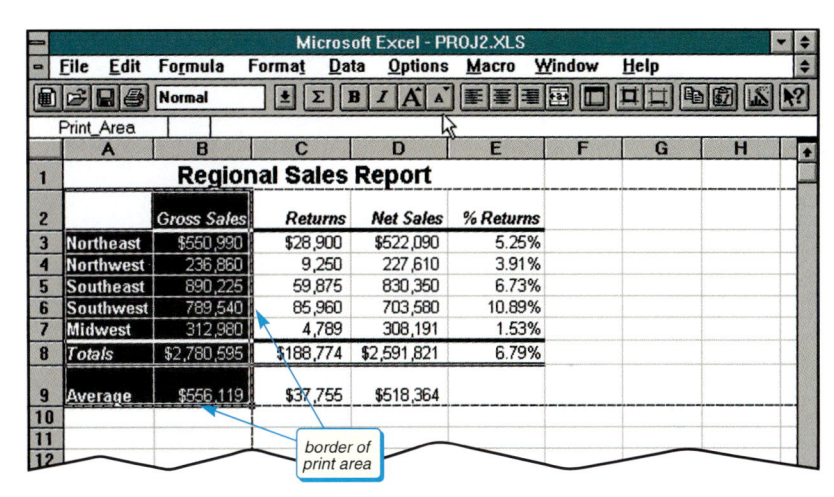

FIGURE 2-63

STEP 3 ▶

Ready the printer. Click the Print tool on the Standard toolbar.

Excel prints the selected range of the worksheet on the printer (Figure 2-64).

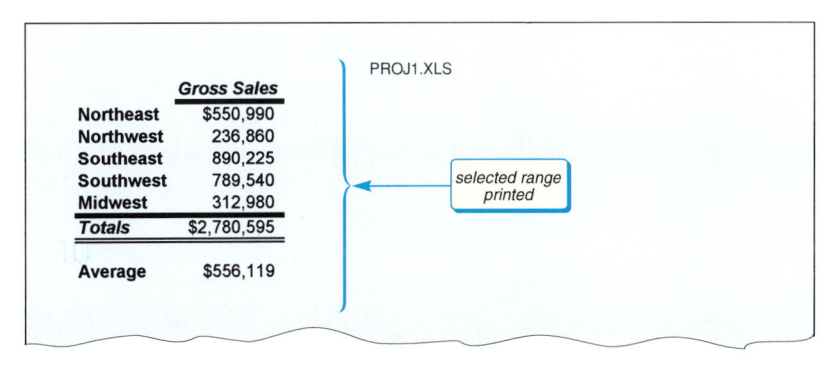

FIGURE 2-64

After the selected range of the worksheet prints, you will probably want to reset the print range to the entire worksheet. The following steps show you how to accomplish this task.

TO RESET THE PRINT AREA TO THE ENTIRE WORKSHEET

STEP 1

Click the Select All button. Select the Options menu and point to the Remove Print Area command.

STEP 2 ▶

Choose the Remove Print Area command.

Excel resets the print range to the entire worksheet (Figure 2-65). To remove the selection, select any cell in the worksheet.

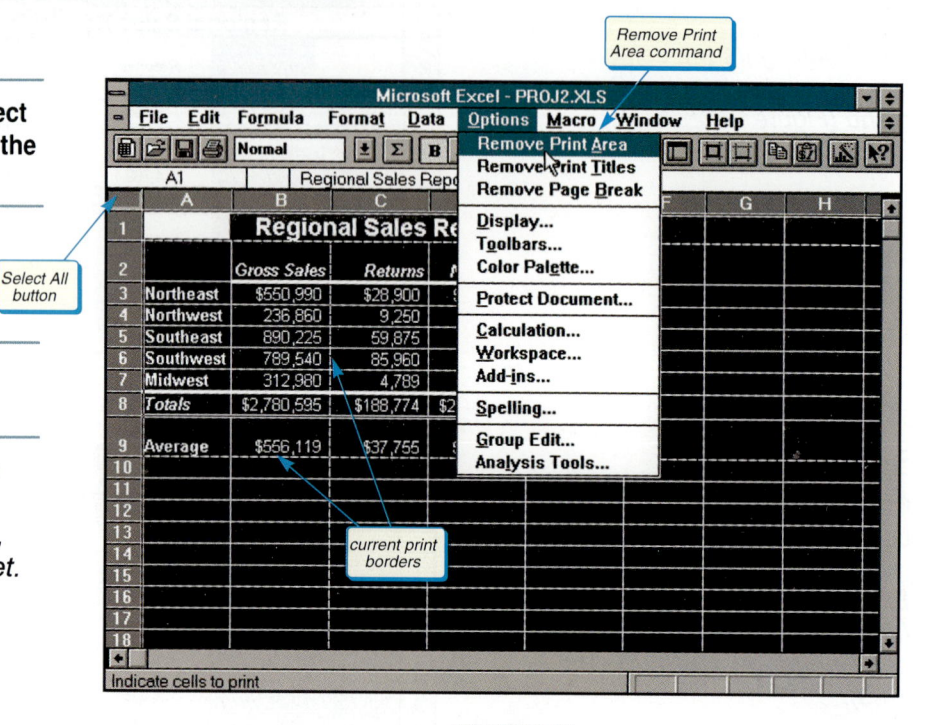

FIGURE 2-65

▶ DISPLAYING AND PRINTING THE FORMULAS IN THE WORKSHEET

Thus far, the worksheet has been printed exactly as it appears on the screen. This is called the **values version** of the worksheet. Another variation that you can display and print is called the formulas version. The **formulas version** displays and prints what was originally entered into the cells instead of the values in the cells. The formulas version is useful for debugging a worksheet because the formulas and functions display and print out, rather than the numeric results. **Debugging** is the process of finding and correcting errors in the worksheet.

When you change from values to formulas, Excel increases the width of the columns to best fit so the formulas and text do not overflow into adjacent cells on the right. Thus, the worksheet usually becomes significantly wider when the formulas display. To fit the wide printout on one page you can use the **Fit to: option** in the Page Setup dialog box from the File menu. To change from values to formulas and print the formulas on one page, do the following.

DISPLAYING AND PRINTING THE FORMULAS IN THE WORKSHEET   **E93**

TO DISPLAY THE FORMULAS IN THE WORKSHEET AND FIT THE PRINTOUT ON ONE PAGE ▼

STEP 1 ▶

Select the Options menu and point to the Display command (Figure 2-66).

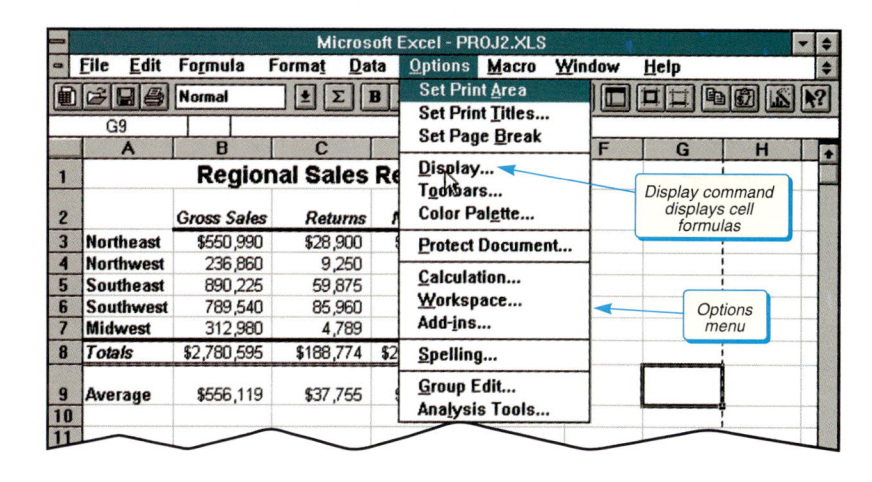

FIGURE 2-66

Choose the Display command. From the Display Options dialog box, select the Formulas check box in the Cells box.

The Display Options dialog box appears (Figure 2-67).

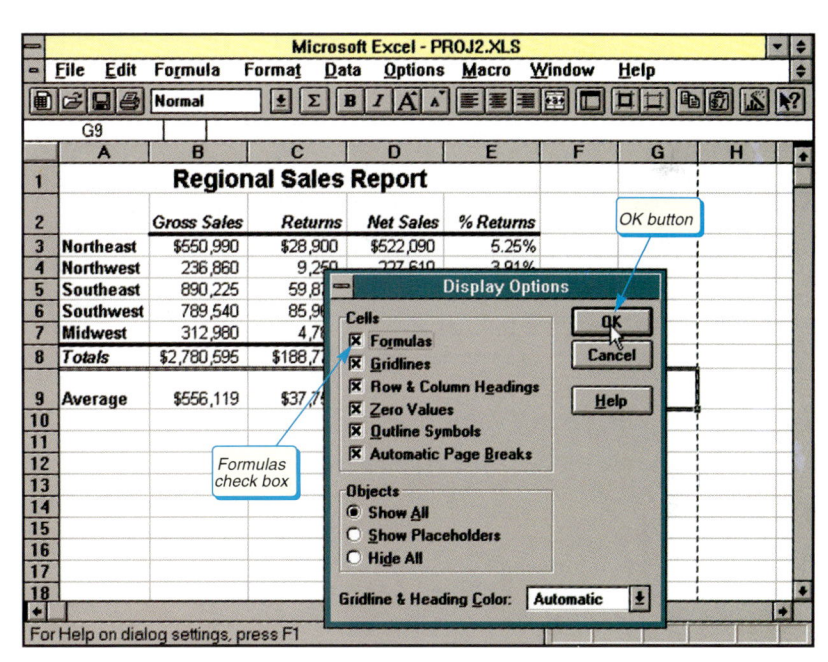

FIGURE 2-67

STEP 3 ▶

Choose OK from the Display Options dialog box.

The formulas in the worksheet display showing unformatted numbers, formulas, and functions that were assigned to the cells (Figure 2-68). Excel automatically increases the width of the columns.

FIGURE 2-68

E94 PROJECT 2 ADDING FORMULAS TO A WORKSHEET

STEP 4 ▶

From the File menu, choose the Page Setup command. From the Page Setup dialog box, select the Fit to option button to fit the wide printout on one page.

Excel displays the Page Setup dialog box with the Fit to option selected (Figure 2-69).

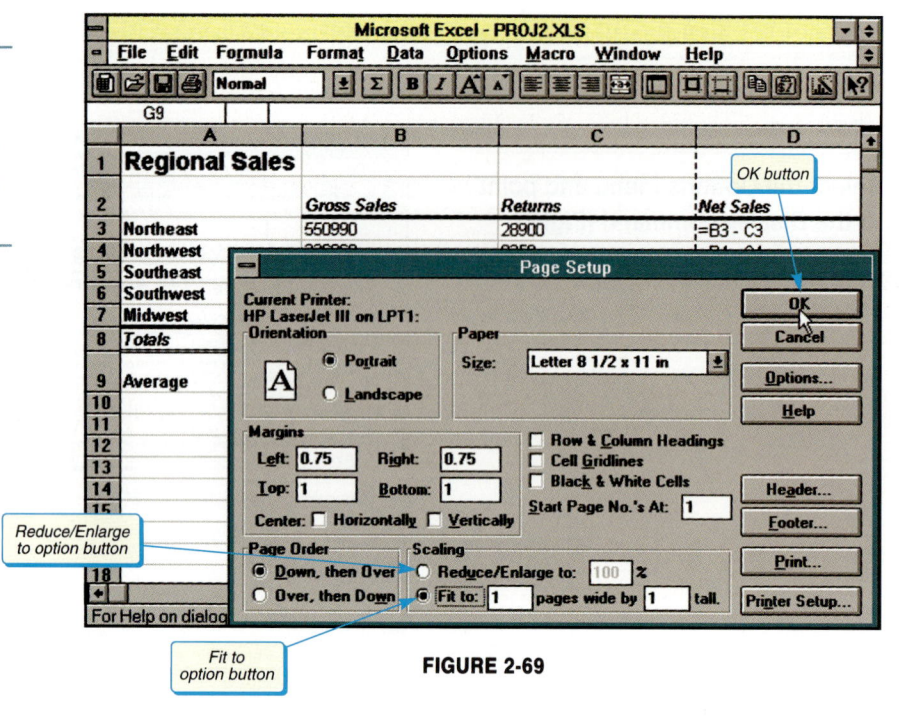

FIGURE 2-69

STEP 5 ▶

Choose the OK button from the Page Setup dialog box. Click the Print tool on the Standard toolbar.

Excel prints the formulas in the worksheet on one page (Figure 2-70).

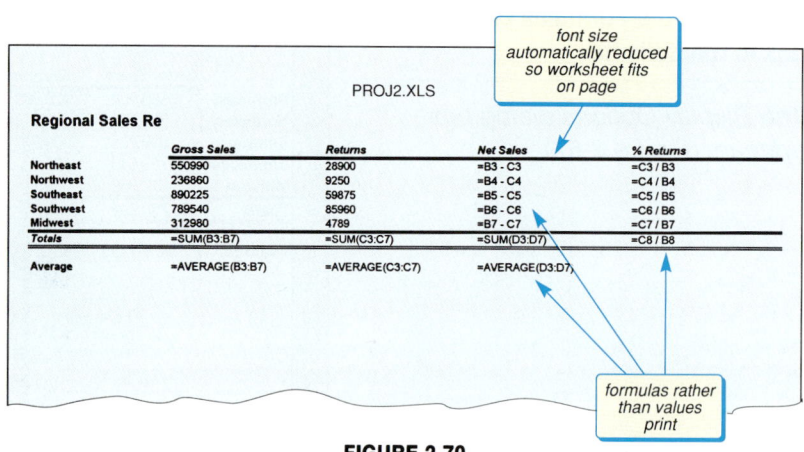

FIGURE 2-70

Although the formulas in the worksheet were printed in the previous example, you can see from Figure 2-68 that the display on the screen can also be used for debugging errors in the worksheet.

The formulas in the worksheet were printed using the fit to option so they would fit on one page. Anytime characters extend pass the dashed line that represents the rightmost edge of the printed worksheet (Figure 2-68), the printout will be made up of multiple pages. If you prefer to print the worksheet on one page, select the Fit to option button in the Page Setup dialog box (Figure 2-69) before you print.

Changing the Print Scaling Option Back to 100%

Follow the steps below to reset the **Scaling option** so future worksheets print at 100%, rather than being squeezed on one page.

TO CHANGE THE PRINT SCALING OPTION BACK TO 100%

Step 1: From the File menu, choose the Page Setup command.
Step 2: Select the Reduce/Enlarge to option button in the Scaling box.
Step 3: If necessary, type 100 in the Reduce/Enlarge to box.
Step 4: Choose OK from the Page Setup dialog box.

Through the Reduce/Enlarge to box you can specify the percentage of reduction or enlargement in the printout of a worksheet. The default percentage is 100%. The 100% automatically changes to the appropriate percent whenever you select the Fit to option.

▶ PROJECT SUMMARY

In Project 2 you learned how to enter formulas, calculate an average, draw borders, format numbers, and change column widths and row heights. You also learned how to preview a worksheet, print a section of a worksheet, and display and print the formulas in the worksheet using print to fit.

▶ KEY TERMS

#DIV/O! error message (*E64*)
addition (*E62*)
AVERAGE function (*E66*)
backup (*E88*)
best fit (*E82*)
Border command (*E73*)
Border dialog box (*E73*)
Center Align tool (*E71*)
Close button (*E89*)
Column width (*E82*)
Column Width command (*E85*)
debugging (*E92*)
Display command (*E93*)
division (*E62*)
drawing lines (*E73*)
exponentiation (*E61*)
Fit to option (*E92*)
Font dialog box (*E81*)

font size (*E70*)
font styles (*E80*)
Format (*E74*)
Formatting numbers (*E75*)
formula (*E59*)
formulas version (*E92*)
Italic tool (*E71*)
Left Align tool (*E71*)
multiplication (*E62*)
Number command (*E78*)
Number Format dialog box (*E79*)
number sign (*E78*)
Options menu (*E90*)
order of operations (*E61*)
parentheses in formulas (*E62*)
Point mode (*E62*)
previewing a worksheet (*E88*)
Print Preview command (*E88*)

Remove Print Area command (*E92*)
Right Align tool (*E71*)
row height (*E85*)
Row Height command (*E86*)
Row Height dialog box (*E87*)
Sample box (*E79*)
Screen fonts (*E80*)
Set Print Area command (*E90*)
shortcut menu (*E73*)
subtraction (*E62*)
TrueType fonts (*E80*)
Underline tool (*E73*)
Undo Column Width command (*E83*)
values version (*E92*)
WYSIWYG (*E80*)

QUICK REFERENCE

In Microsoft Excel you can accomplish a task in a number of ways. The following table provides a quick reference to each task presented in this project with its available options. The commands listed in the Menu column can be executed using either the keyboard or mouse.

Task	Mouse	Menu	Keyboard Shortcuts
Border		From Format menu, choose Border	Press CTRL + SHIFT + – (remove border)
Center Text	Click Center Align tool on Standard toolbar	From Format menu, choose Alignment	
Change Column Width	Drag column heading border; double-click column heading right border for best fit	From Format menu, choose Column Width	Press CTRL + 0 (Hide) Press CTRL + SHIFT +) (Unhide)
Fit to Print Across a Page		From File menu, choose Page Setup	
Font	Click Style box arrow on Standard toolbar	From Format menu, choose Font	Press CTRL + P
Format Numbers		From Format menu, choose Number	
Format Numbers Using Style Box	Click Style box arrow on Standard toolbar		Press CTRL + S
Italicize	Click Italic tool on Standard toolbar	From Format menu, choose Font	Press CTRL + I
Left-Align Text	Click Left Align tool on Standard toolbar	From Format menu, choose Alignment	
Normal Font	Click Style box arrow on Standard toolbar	From Format menu, choose Font	Press CTRL + 1
Print at 100%		From File menu, choose Page Setup	
Print Preview	Click Print Preview on Custom toolbar	From File menu, choose Print Preview	
Right-Align Text	Click Right Align tool on Standard toolbar	From Format menu, choose Alignment	
Row Height	Drag row heading border; double-click row heading bottom border for best fit	From Format menu, choose Row Height	Press CTRL + 9 (Hide) Press CTRL + SHIFT + ((Unhide)
Set Print Area to a Section of the Worksheet	Click Set Print Area tool on Utility toolbar	From Options menu, choose Set Print Area	
Set Print Area to the Entire Worksheet		From Options menu, choose Remove Print Area	
Shortcut Menu	Click right mouse button		
Switch Between Displaying Formulas and Values		From Options menu, choose Display	Press CTRL + `
Underline	Click Underline tool on Standard toolbar	From Format menu, choose Font	Press CTRL + U

STUDENT ASSIGNMENTS

STUDENT ASSIGNMENT 1
True/False

Instructions: Circle T if the statement is true or F if the statement is false.

T F 1. Click the right mouse button to display the shortcut menu.
T F 2. Use Currency (0) in the Style box on the Standard toolbar to change the entry in a cell to different international monetary values.
T F 3. The minimum column width is zero.
T F 4. If you assign a cell the formula = 8 / 4, the number 2 displays in the cell.
T F 5. When using the Number command in the Format menu, entire rows can be formatted; however, entire columns cannot be formatted.
T F 6. In the formula = 8 + 6 / 2, the addition operation (+) is completed before the division operation (/).
T F 7. The formulas = a2 – a3, = A2 – A3, and = A2-A3 result in the same value being assigned to the active cell.
T F 8. The error message #DIV/0! means that the cell was assigned a formula in which the numerator is zero.
T F 9. If you use the Point mode to enter a formula or select a range, you must click the enter box to complete the entry.
T F 10. Use the AVERAGE function to assign a cell the average of the entries in a range of cells.
T F 11. To save an intermediate copy of the worksheet to disk, you must choose the Save As command from the File menu.
T F 12. If you save a worksheet a second time using the Save File tool, Excel will save it under the same file name that was used the first time it was saved.
T F 13. If the function = SUM(B4:B8) assigns a value of 10 to cell B9, and B9 is copied to C9, cell C9 may or may not equal 10.
T F 14. Use the Border command in the Format menu to set the margins prior to printing the worksheet.
T F 15. When a number is too large to fit in a cell, Excel displays asterisks (*) in place of the number in the cell.
T F 16. MS Sans Serif is a WYSIWYG font.
T F 17. Use the Font command in the Format menu to change the font in a cell or range of cells.
T F 18. To increase or decrease the width of a column, use the mouse to point at the column heading name and drag it to the left or right.
T F 19. To select an entire row, click the row heading.
T F 20. When the formulas in the worksheet display, Excel displays numeric and text entries without the format assigned to them.

STUDENT ASSIGNMENT 2
Multiple Choice

Instructions: Circle the correct response.

1. Which one of the following arithmetic operations is completed first if they are all found in a formula with no parentheses?
   a. +
   b. –
   c. ^
   d. *

(continued)

STUDENT ASSIGNMENT 2 (continued)

2. The format Comma (0) in the Style box on the Standard toolbar causes 5000 to display as:
   a. $5,000
   b. 5000
   c. 5,000
   d. 5,000.00
3. Which one of the following formulas is valid?
   a. = C3 + b3
   b. = c3 + b3
   c. = C3 + B3
   d. all of the above
4. When you use the Print Preview command in the File menu, the mouse pointer becomes a _____ when it is pointed at the worksheet.
   a. small plus sign
   b. magnifying glass
   c. dark plus sign with two arrowheads
   d. block plus sign
5. The maximum height of a row is approximately _____ points.
   a. 100
   b. 200
   c. 300
   d. 400
6. A listing on the printer of the worksheet in which formulas display rather than numbers is called the _____ version of the worksheet.
   a. formulas
   b. displayed
   c. formatted
   d. content
7. If 0.052451 is assigned to a cell that is formatted to Percentage 0.00%, then the cell contents display as _____.
   a. 5.25%
   b. 5.24%
   c. 0.05%
   d. 5.00%
8. Which one of the following describes a column width whereby the user has requested that Excel determine the width to use?
   a. custom fit
   b. best fit
   c. close fit
   d. auto fit
9. The function = AVERAGE(B3:B7) is equal to _____.
   a. = b3 + b4 + b5 + b6 + b7 / 5
   b. = (b3 + b4 + b5 + b6 + b7) / 5
   c. both a and b
   d. none of the above
10. Which one of the following fonts uses the same outline to display type on the screen and on the printer?
    a. Courier
    b. MS Sans Serif
    c. TrueType Arial
    d. Preview

STUDENT ASSIGNMENT 3
Entering Formulas

Instructions: Using the values in the worksheet in Figure SA2-3, write the formula that accomplishes the task for each of the following items and manually compute the value assigned to the specified cell.

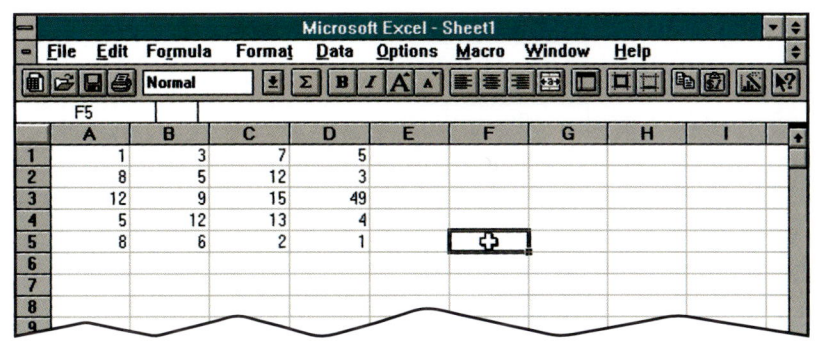

FIGURE SA2-3

1. Assign cell A7 the product of cells A2 and D2.

   Formula: _____

   Numeric result assigned to cell A7: _____

2. Assign cell F4 the product of cells B1, C1, and D5.

   Formula: _____

   Numeric result assigned to cell F4: _____

3. Assign cell D6 the sum of the range B1:C2, less cell A5.

   Formula: _____

   Numeric result assigned to cell D6: _____

4. Assign cell G2 five times the quotient of cell B2 divided by cell B1.

   Formula: _____

   Numeric result assigned to cell G2: _____

5. Assign cell E1 the sum of the range of cells D2:D5 minus the product of cells C1 and C3.

   Formula: _____

   Numeric result assigned to cell E1: _____

6. Assign cell G6 the result of cell A5 less cell A4 raised to cell B1.

   Formula: _____

   Numeric result assigned to cell G6: _____

7. Assign cell A6 the expression (X ^ 2 − 4 * Y * Z) / (2 * Y) where the value of X is in cell C2, the value of Y is in cell D2, and the value of Z is in cell D4.

   Formula: _____

   Numeric result assigned to cell A6: _____

STUDENT ASSIGNMENT 4
Understanding Formulas

Instructions: Figure SA2-4 displays the formulas in the worksheet. In the space provided, indicate in the fill-ins, the numeric value assigned to the cells if the numbers display rather than the formulas.

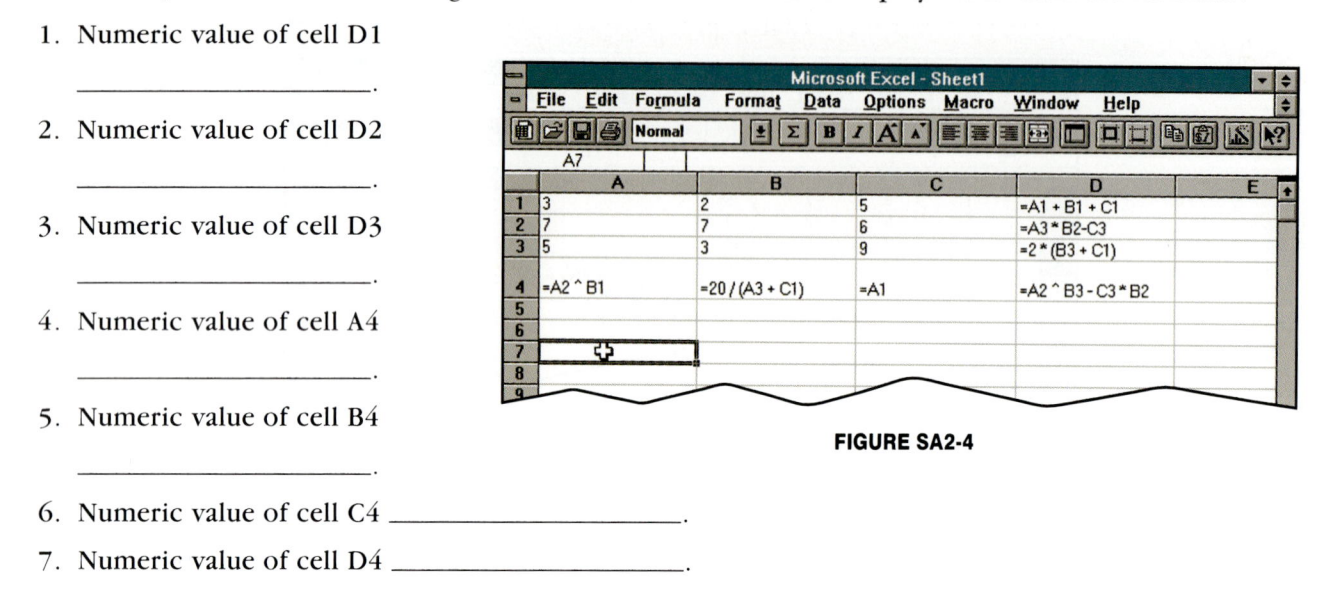

1. Numeric value of cell D1 _____.
2. Numeric value of cell D2 _____.
3. Numeric value of cell D3 _____.
4. Numeric value of cell A4 _____.
5. Numeric value of cell B4 _____.
6. Numeric value of cell C4 _____.
7. Numeric value of cell D4 _____.

Figure SA2-4 shows a worksheet with:
	A	B	C	D
1	3	2	5	=A1+B1+C1
2	7	7	6	=A3*B2-C3
3	5	3	9	=2*(B3+C1)
4	=A2^B1	=20/(A3+C1)	=A1	=A2^B3-C3*B2

FIGURE SA2-4

STUDENT ASSIGNMENT 5
Understanding Functions

Instructions: Figure SA2-5 displays the formulas in the worksheet. In the space provided, indicate the numeric value assigned to the cells if the numbers display rather than the functions.

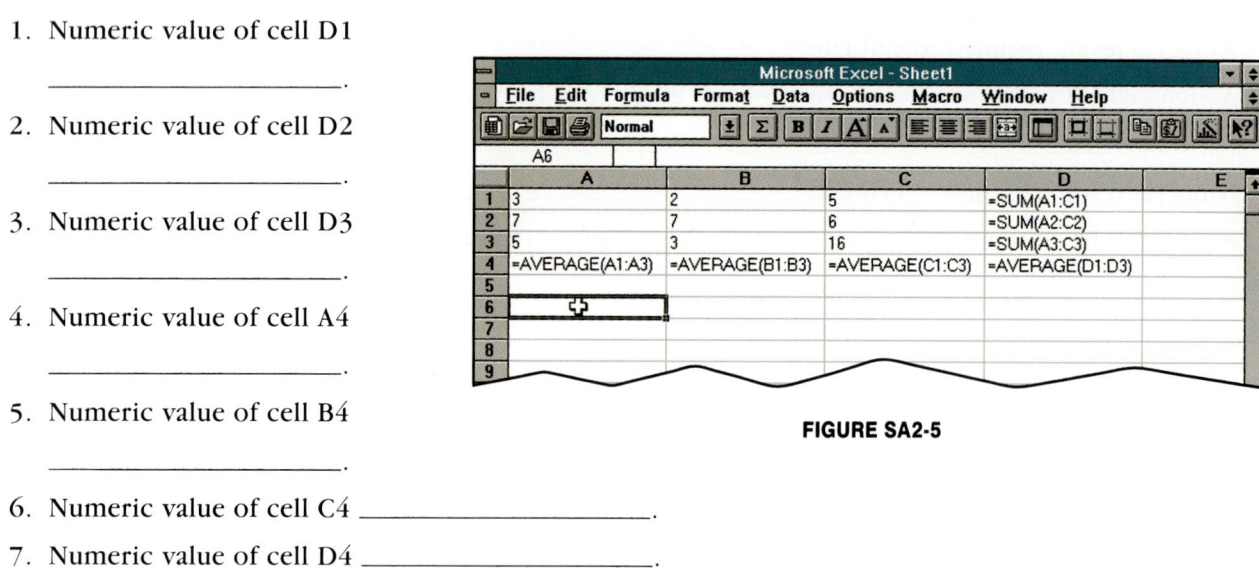

1. Numeric value of cell D1 _____.
2. Numeric value of cell D2 _____.
3. Numeric value of cell D3 _____.
4. Numeric value of cell A4 _____.
5. Numeric value of cell B4 _____.
6. Numeric value of cell C4 _____.
7. Numeric value of cell D4 _____.

Figure SA2-5 shows a worksheet with:
	A	B	C	D
1	3	2	5	=SUM(A1:C1)
2	7	7	6	=SUM(A2:C2)
3	5	3	16	=SUM(A3:C3)
4	=AVERAGE(A1:A3)	=AVERAGE(B1:B3)	=AVERAGE(C1:C3)	=AVERAGE(D1:D3)

FIGURE SA2-5

STUDENT ASSIGNMENT 6
Analyzing the Fonts in a Worksheet

Instructions: Use Figure SA2-6 to complete the statements below.

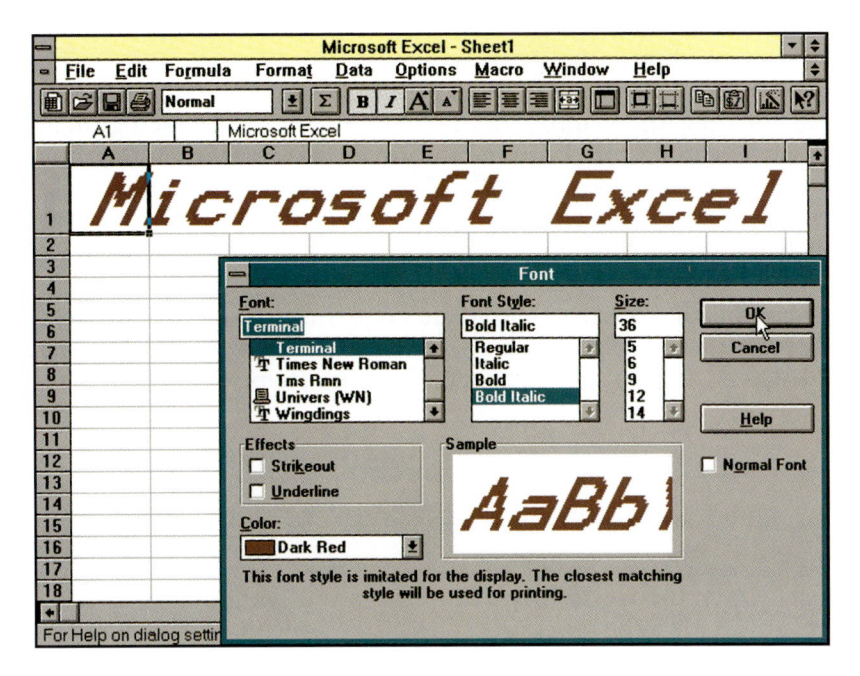

FIGURE SA2-6

1. To display the Font dialog box, choose the _____ command from the _____ menu.
2. Cell A1 uses a font called _____.
3. Cell A1 has a font style of _____.
4. Cell A1 uses a font size of _____.
5. Cell A1 uses a _____ color.
6. TrueType fonts are designated in the Font box by the symbol _____ before the font name.

COMPUTER LABORATORY EXERCISES

COMPUTER LABORATORY EXERCISE 1
Using the Search Command in the Help Menu

Instructions: Start Excel and perform the following tasks using a computer.

1. Choose the Search command from the Help menu.
2. Use the scroll arrows in the Search dialog box to show the column widths topic in the list. Select column widths and click the Show Topics button. With the topic Changing the width of columns highlighted, select the Go To button. Read the information displayed on the topic. Ready the printer. Choose the Print Topic command from the File menu in the Help window. Close the Help window.
3. Choose the Search command from the Help menu. Repeat step 2 for the term #DIV/0! and click the Go To button after Error Values is highlighted in the lower list. Read and print the information in the Help window titled Error Values. Close the Help window.
4. Choose the Search command from the Help menu. Type in the topic formulas and select the Show Topics button. Select Formula Tools Category from the lower list. Read and print the information in the Help window titled Formula Tools Category. Close the Help window.

COMPUTER LABORATORY EXERCISE 2
Correcting Worksheet Errors

Instructions: Start Excel. Open the worksheet CLE2-2 from the subdirectory Excel on the Student Diskette that accompanies this book. The worksheet CLE2-2 is shown in Figure CLE2-2. It resembles the Regional Sales Report created in Project 2. Perform the following tasks so the worksheet is identical to the one shown in Figure 2-19 on page E68, except for the centered worksheet title in row 1.

1. Correct the formula in cell E3 and copy it to the range E4:E8.
2. Correct the SUM function in cell B8 and copy it to the range C8:D8.
3. Correct the AVERAGE function in cell B9 and copy it to the range C9:D9.
4. Change the height of rows 2 and 9 from 24 points to best fit.
5. Enter your name, course, computer laboratory exercise number (CLE2-2), date, and instructor name in cells A14 through A18.
6. Preview the worksheet. Print the worksheet with cell gridlines.
7. Print the range A2:C9. Reset the print range to the entire worksheet.
8. Press CTRL + ` (SINGLE LEFT QUOTATION MARK) to change the display from values to formulas. Print the formulas in the worksheet. After printing the formulas, change the display back to values by pressing CTRL + ` (SINGLE LEFT QUOTATION MARK).
9. Hide columns B and C by changing their column widths to zero. Print the worksheet with cell gridlines off.

FIGURE CLE2-2

COMPUTER LABORATORY EXERCISE 3
Changing Formats and Fonts

Instructions: Start Excel and perform the following tasks.

1. Open the worksheet CLE2-3 from the subdirectory Excel on the Student Diskette that accompanies this book. The worksheet CLE2-3 is shown in Figure CLE2-3(a). After the worksheet displays on the screen, print it.
2. Perform the following modifications so the worksheet looks like Figure CLE2-3(b):
    a. Right-align and add a bold bottom border to the column headings.
    b. Assign these format styles from the Style box:
        1) Currency to the numbers in column A
        2) Currency (0) to the numbers in column B
        3) Comma to the numbers in column C
        4) Comma (0) to the numbers in column D
        5) Percent to the numbers in column E
        6) Normal to the numbers in column F
    c. Assign these fonts from the Font dialog box:
        1) TrueType Arial, bold, 12 point to column A
        2) MS Sans Serif, bold, 10 point to column B.
        3) TrueType Courier New, bold, 12 point to column C.
        4) Times New Roman, bold, 10 point to column D.
        5) System, bold, 10 point to column E.
        6) Modern, bold, 10 point to column F.
    d. Select columns A through F and double-click the right border of column heading E to change the column widths to best fit.
    e. Select rows 3 through 8 and change their heights to 24 points.
3. Enter your name, course, computer laboratory exercise number (CLE2-3), date, and instructor name in cells A14 through A18.
4. Save the modified worksheet. Use the file name CLE2-3B.
5. Preview the worksheet. Adjust column widths if number signs display in place of numbers. Print the worksheet.

FIGURE CLE2-3

COMPUTER LABORATORY ASSIGNMENTS

COMPUTER LABORATORY ASSIGNMENT 1
Building a Monthly Sales Analysis Worksheet

Purpose: To become familiar with building a worksheet that includes formulas, formatting a worksheet, using the recalculation features of Excel, and printing different versions of the worksheet.

Problem: The computer consulting firm you and a friend started recently on a part-time basis has received its first contract. The client has specified in the contract that you are to build a monthly sales analysis worksheet that determines the sales quota and percentage of quota met for the following salespeople:

NAME	SALES AMOUNT	SALES RETURN	SALES QUOTA
Harley Trapp	$15,789.00	$ 245.00	$12,000.00
Vance Lane	8,500.00	500.00	10,000.00
Mary Cicero	17,895.00	1,376.00	12,000.00
Tom Collins	12,843.00	843.00	11,000.00

Instructions Part 1: Perform the following tasks to build the worksheet shown in Figure CLA2-1 on the next page.

1. Enter the worksheet title Monthly Sales Report in cell A1. Center the title across columns A through F. Bold the title and increase its font size to 14 points.
2. Enter the column titles in row 2 as shown in Figure CLA2-1. Bold and right-align the column titles. Increase the height of row 2 to 24 points. Draw a bold bottom border in the range A2:F2.
3. Enter the names and row title in column A. Bold the entries in column A. Draw borders above and below the Totals in row 7 as shown in Figure CLA2-1.
4. Enter the sales data described earlier under Problem and also shown in Figure CLA2-1. Do not enter the numbers with dollar signs or commas.
5. Obtain the net sales in column D of the worksheet by subtracting the sales returns in column C from the sales amount in column B. Enter the formula in cell D3 and copy it to the range D4:D6.
6. Obtain the above quota amounts in column F by subtracting the sales quota in column E from the net sales in column D. Enter the formula in cell F3 and copy it to the range F4:F6.
7. Obtain the totals in row 7 by adding the column values for each salesperson. The averages in row 8 contain the column averages. Increase the height of row 8 to 24 points.
8. In cell A9, enter the % of Quota Sold title with equal signs and the greater than sign to create the arrow shown in Figure CLA2-1. Obtain the percent of quota sold in cell C9 by dividing the total net sales amount in cell D7 by the total sales quota amount in cell E7. Increase the height of row 9 to 24 points.
9. Enter your name, course, computer laboratory assignment number (CLA2-1), date, and instructor name below the entries in column A in separate cells.
10. Change the font in the worksheet to TrueType Arial.
11. Use the Style box on the Standard toolbar to format the numbers in row 3 and the range B7:F8 to Currency and the range B4:F6 to Comma. Use the Percentage 0.00% format in the Number Format dialog box to format cell C9.
12. Increase the widths of column A to 11.57 characters and column B through F to 12.71 characters.
13. Save the worksheet. Use the file name CLA2-1A.
14. Print the worksheet without cell gridlines. Print the formulas in the worksheet using the Fit to option button in the Page Setup dialog box. Reset the Scaling option to 100% by selecting the Reduce/Enlarge to option button in the Page Setup dialog box and changing the percent value to 100%. Change the display from formulas back to values.
15. Print only the range A2:B8. Reset the print area to the entire worksheet after the printer is finished.

FIGURE CLA2-1

	A	B	C	D	E	F
1			Monthly Sales Report			
2	Name	Sales Amt	Sales Returns	Net Sales	Sales Quota	Above Quota
3	Harley Trapp	$15,789.00	$245.00	$15,544.00	$12,000.00	$3,544.00
4	Vance Lane	8,500.00	500.00	8,000.00	10,000.00	(2,000.00)
5	Mary Cicero	17,895.00	1,376.00	16,519.00	12,000.00	4,519.00
6	Tom Collins	12,843.00	843.00	12,000.00	11,000.00	1,000.00
7	Totals	$55,027.00	$2,964.00	$52,063.00	$45,000.00	$7,063.00
8	Average	$13,756.75	$741.00	$13,015.75	$11,250.00	
9	% of Quota Sold ====>		115.70%			

red color and parentheses indicate negative number

Instructions Part 2: Increment each of the four values in the sales quota column by $1,000.00 until the percent of quota sold in cell C9 is below, yet as close as possible to, 100%. All four values in column E must be incremented the same number of times. The percent of quota sold in C9 should equal 98.23%. Save the worksheet as CLA2-1B. Print the worksheet without cell gridlines.

Instructions Part 3: With the percent of quota sold in cell C9 equal to 98.23% from Part 2, decrement each of the four values in the sales return column by $100.00 until the percent of quota sold in cell C9 is below, yet as close as possible to, 100%. Decrement all four values in column C the same number of times. Your worksheet is correct when the percent of quota sold in cell C9 is equal to 99.74%. Save the worksheet as CLA2-1C. Print the worksheet without cell gridlines.

COMPUTER LABORATORY ASSIGNMENT 2
Inflation Gauge

Purpose: To become familiar with entering and copying formulas, formatting a worksheet, and printing different versions of the worksheet.

Problem: You are employed as a summer intern by the State Budget department. One of the department's responsibilities is to report to the state legislature the expected inflation rate of food for the next year. They obtain their data by selecting a few often-used grocery items and they keep track of the prices over a period of time. They then determine and report the individual inflation rates and the expected prices in one year. As a summer intern with knowledge of Excel, they have asked you to create a worksheet for the following data:

Instructions: Perform the following tasks:

1. Create a worksheet similar to the one on the next page in Figure CLA2-2 using the above pricing information data and the formulas on the next page to determine the price change, inflation rate, and expected price.

ITEM	CURRENT PRICE	BEGINNING PRICE	NUMBER OF WEEKS
1 doz. eggs	$0.93	$0.92	13
1 lb. butter	2.59	2.50	15
1 gal. milk	1.92	1.85	18
1 loaf bread	1.10	1.07	6

(continued)

COMPUTER LABORATORY ASSIGNMENT 2 (continued)

Assign these three formulas to the first item — 1 doz. eggs in row 4 — and copy them to the rest of the items.

   a. Price Change = 52 * (Current Price − Beginning Price) / Weeks
   b. Inflation Rate = Price Change / Beginning Price
   c. Price in one Year = Current Price + Inflation Rate * Current Price

2. Assign regular, 10 point, TrueType Courier New font to the entire worksheet.
3. Assign the format style Comma from the Style box on the Standard toolbar to the ranges B4:C7, E4:E7, and G4:G7. Assign the Percentage format 0.00% from the Format Number dialog box to the range F4:F7.
4. Assign the worksheet title Inflation Gauge Report to cell A1 and center it across columns A through G. Bold and increase the font size of the worksheet title to 14 points.
5. Bold the column titles. Right-align the column titles in the range B2:G3. Draw a double-underline in the range A3:G3. Bold the row titles.
6. Increase the height of row 2 to 24 points. Select the columns A through G and change the width to best fit.
7. Enter your name, course, computer laboratory assignment number (CLA2-2), date, and instructor name below the entries in column A in separate but adjacent cells.
8. Save the worksheet as CLA2-2.
9. Print the worksheet.
10. Print the range A2:E7. Reset the print area to the entire worksheet after the printer is finished.
11. Press CTRL + ` to change the display from values to formulas. Print to fit on one page the formulas in the worksheet. After the printer is finished, reset the worksheet to display values by pressing CTRL + `. Reset the Scaling option to 100% by selecting the Reduce/Enlarge to option button in the Page Setup dialog box and setting the percent value to 100%.

FIGURE CLA2-2

COMPUTER LABORATORY ASSIGNMENT 3
Building a Biweekly Payroll Worksheet

Purpose: To become familiar with entering complex formulas.

Problem: You are employed by the Payroll department of a construction firm. You have been asked to prepare a biweekly payroll report for the following six employees:

EMPLOYEE	RATE PER HOUR	HOURS	DEPENDENTS
Col, Lisa	12.50	81.00	2
Fel, Jeff	18.00	64.00	4
Di, Marci	13.00	96.25	0
Sno, Niki	4.50	122.50	1
Hi, Mandi	3.35	16.50	1
Bri, Jodi	10.40	80.00	3

Instructions: Perform the following tasks to create a worksheet similar to the one in Figure CLA2-3 using the above employee information data:

1. Use the Select All button and assign regular 10 point TrueType Arial font to the entire worksheet.
2. Assign the worksheet title Biweekly Payroll File List to cell A1 and center it across columns A through H. Bold and increase the font size of the worksheet title to 12 points.
3. Bold the column titles and draw a bold border under them. Right-align the column titles in the range B2:H2. Bold the row titles in column A. Italicize the row title Totals in cell A9. Change the height of row 2 to 24 points and the width of columns A through H to best fit. Draw the borders above and below the total row as shown in Figure CLA2-3.
4. Use the following formulas to determine the gross pay, federal tax, state tax, and net pay:
    a. Gross Pay = Rate * Hours. (Hint: Assign the first employee in cell E3 the formula =B3 * C3, and copy the formula in E3 to the range E4:E8 for the remaining employees.)
    b. Federal Tax = 20% * (Gross Pay – Dependents * 38.46).
    c. State Tax = 3.2% * Gross Pay.
    d. Net Pay = Gross Pay – (Federal Tax + State Tax).
5. Show totals for the gross pay, federal tax, state tax, and net pay.
6. Assign the Comma format in the Style box to the entire worksheet.
7. Enter your name, course, computer laboratory assignment number (CLA2-3), date, and instructor name below the entries in column A in separate but adjacent cells.
8. Save the worksheet as CLA2-3.
9. Preview the worksheet. Adjust column widths if number signs display in place of numbers. Print the worksheet.

FIGURE CLA2-3

(continued)

COMPUTER LABORATORY ASSIGNMENT 3 (continued)

10. Press CTRL + ' to change the display from values to formulas. Print to fit on one page the formulas in the worksheet. After the printer is finished, reset the worksheet to display the numbers by pressing CTRL + '. Reset the Scaling option to 100% by selecting the Reduce/Enlarge to option button in the Page Setup dialog box and setting the percent value to 100%.
11. Increase the number of hours worked for each employee by 7.5 hours. Print the worksheet with the new values. Do not save the worksheet with the new values.

COMPUTER LABORATORY ASSIGNMENT 4
Determining the Monthly Accounts Receivable Balance

Purpose: To become familiar with planning a worksheet.

Problem: You are enrolled in a sophomore Office Information Systems course in which the students are given projects in the local business community. You have been assigned to Ron's Family Discount House. The project they have in mind is for you to generate a much needed report that summarizes their monthly accounts receivable balance. The following monthly information is available for test purposes:

CUSTOMER NUMBER	BEGINNING BALANCE	PAYMENT	PURCHASES	CREDIT
14376	$1,112.32	$35.00	$56.00	$0.00
16210	30.00	30.00	15.00	0.00
18928	125.50	25.00	0.00	12.50
19019	120.00	12.00	12.00	23.00
19192	10.00	7.00	2.50	1.50

Instructions: Include all five fields in the report plus the service charge and end-of-month balance. (Assume no negative unpaid monthly balances.) Use the following formulas to determine the service charge and the end-of-month balance:

Monthly Service Charge = 1.625% * (Beginning Balance − Payments − Credits)

End-of-Month Balance = Beginning Balance − Payments + Purchases − Credits + Monthly Service Charge

Final results for customer 14376 are a service charge of $17.51 and an end-of-month balance of $1,150.83.

Use the techniques you learned in this project to format the worksheet and to illustrate totals and averages. Submit the following:

1. A description of the problem. Include the purpose of the worksheet, a statement outlining the results, the required data, and calculations.
2. A handwritten design of the worksheet.
3. A printed copy of the worksheet without cell gridlines.
4. A printed copy of the formulas in the worksheet.
5. A short description explaining how to use the worksheet.

Enter your name, course, computer laboratory assignment number (CLA2-4), date, and instructor name below the entries in column A in separate but adjacent cells. Save the worksheet using the file name CLA2-4.

Microsoft Excel 4 for Windows
PROJECT THREE

ENHANCING A WORKSHEET AND DRAWING CHARTS

OBJECTIVES You will have mastered the material in this project when you can:

- Insert and delete cells
- Move cells
- Apply the MAX and MIN functions
- Copy the format of a cell to a range of cells
- Wrap text to enter multiple lines in a cell
- Use the IF function to enter one value or another in a cell on the basis of a logical test
- Copy absolute cell references
- Color the font and borders
- Create a three-dimensional (3-D) pie chart
- Rotate a chart
- Explode a 3-D pie chart
- Add an arrow and text to a chart
- Print a chart separately from the worksheet
- Print using landscape orientation

▶ INTRODUCTION

As you have seen in Projects 1 and 2, a worksheet is a powerful tool for organizing and analyzing data. Sometimes, however, the message you are trying to convey gets lost in the rows and columns of numbers. This is where the charting capability of Excel can be useful. With only a little effort, you can use Excel to create, display, and print professional looking charts and convey your message in a dramatic pictorial fashion.

▶ PROJECT THREE

This project enhances the Regional Sales Report created in Project 2. The original worksheet (Figure 3-1 on the next page) contains information on five regional offices. Management has decided to open two new Midwest regional office locations, Upper Midwest and Lower Midwest, and close the current Midwest office described in row 7.

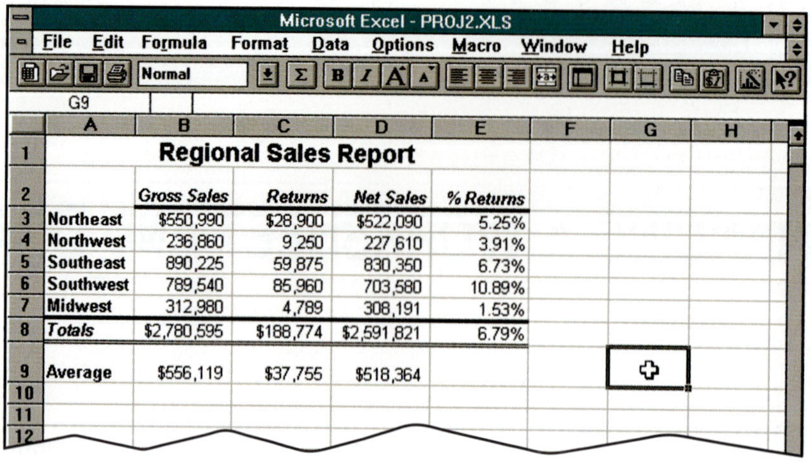

E110 PROJECT 3 ENHANCING A WORKSHEET AND DRAWING CHARTS

FIGURE 3-1

A new West regional office will take over many of the accounts handled by the Southwest office. Thus, one row (Midwest in row 7) of the worksheet completed in Project 2 must be deleted and new rows added (Figure 3-2).

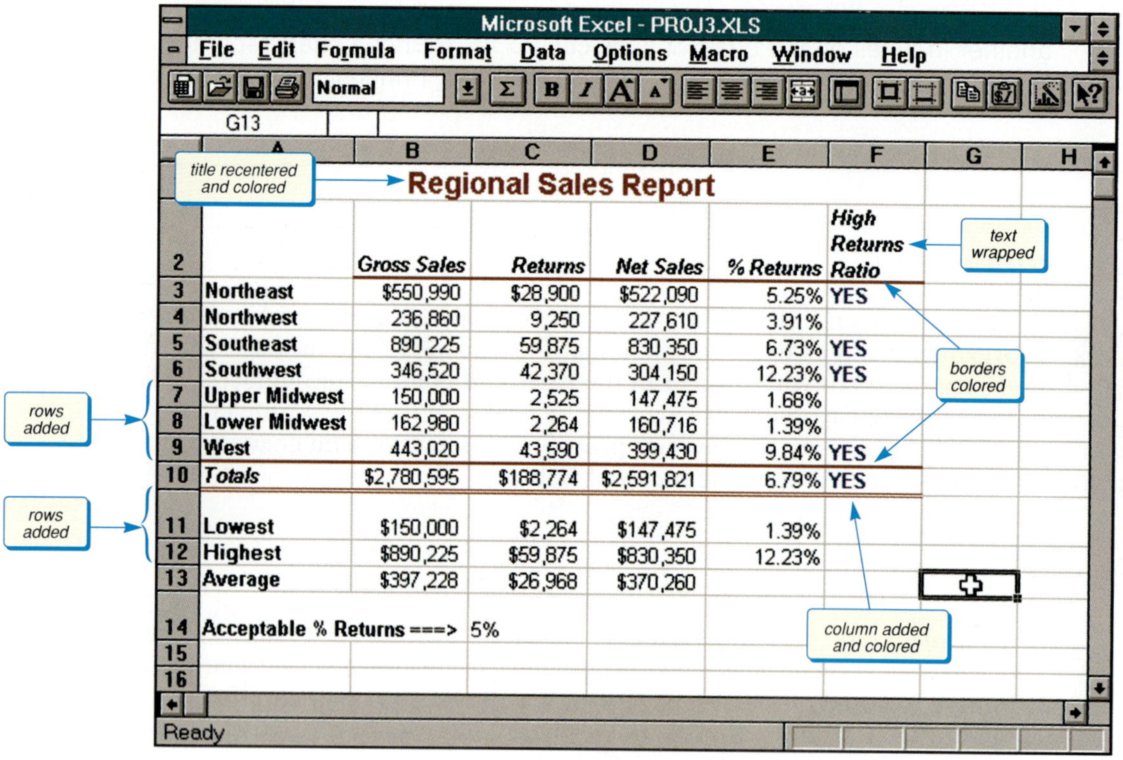

FIGURE 3-2

The revised Regional Sales Report will also include the lowest and highest gross sales, returns, and percent returns. Returns have become a major problem for the company, and therefore a new column (column F in Figure 3-2) will be added to indicate the regions exceeding the acceptable percent returns in cell C14. Because one column will be added, the title will be recentered. Color will also be added to enhance the worksheet.

PROJECT THREE **E111**

Finally, the president of the company will be making a presentation on gross sales by region. He has requested a three-dimensional (3-D) pie chart that highlights the region with the highest gross sales (Figure 3-3).

Opening a Worksheet

The Regional Sales Report was saved to disk in Project 2 using the filename PROJ2.XLS. Thus, the first step is to open PROJ2.XLS.

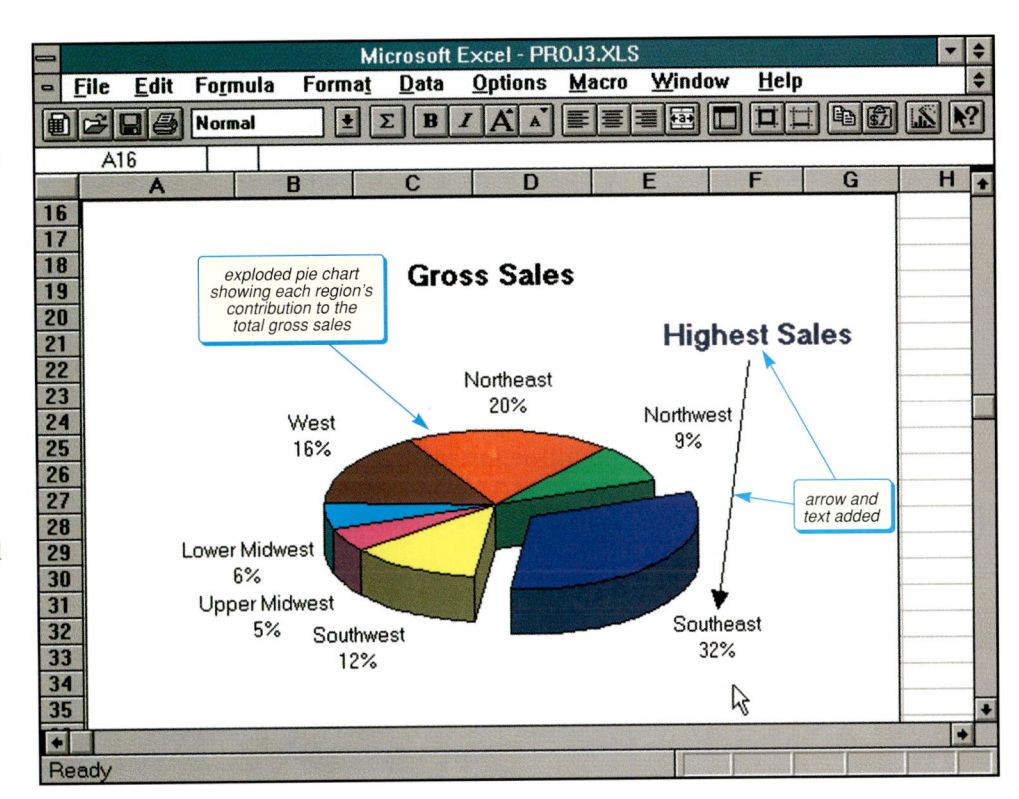

FIGURE 3-3

TO OPEN A WORKSHEET ▼

STEP 1 ▶

Click the Open File tool on the Standard toolbar.

Excel displays the Open dialog box (Figure 3-4).

STEP 2

If necessary, select drive A from the Drives box. Select the file name proj2.xls in the File Name box and choose the OK button.

Excel opens proj2.xls and displays it on the screen (Figure 3-1 on the previous page).

FIGURE 3-4

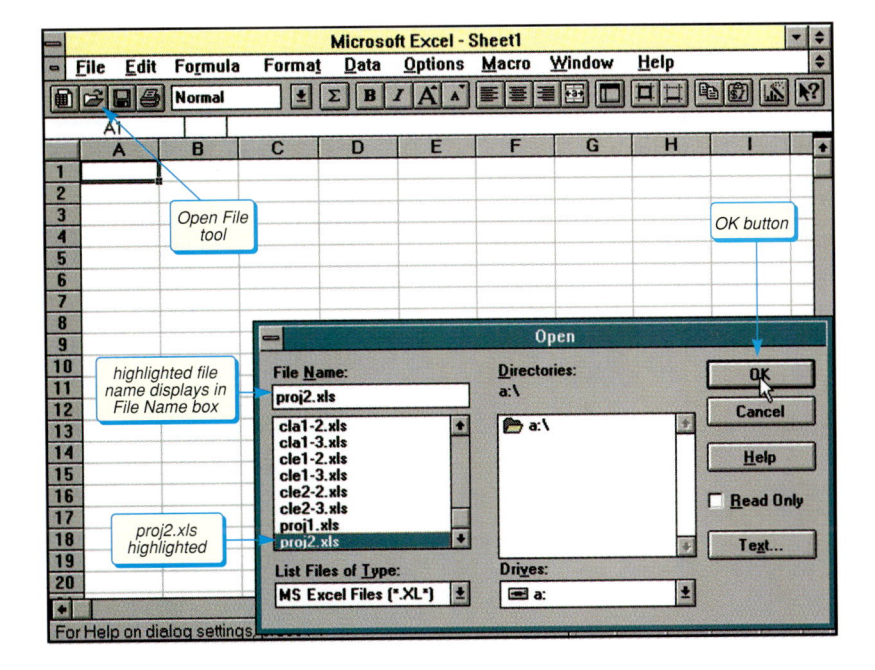

An alternative to Step 2 is to double-click the file name proj2.xls in the File Name box (Figure 3-4). When you double-click the file name proj2.xls, the Open dialog box disappears and Excel opens proj2.xls and displays it on the screen.

▶ DELETING AND INSERTING CELLS IN A WORKSHEET

At any time while the worksheet is on the screen, you can delete cells to remove unwanted data or add cells to insert new data. You can delete or insert individual cells, a range of cells, entire rows, or entire columns.

Deleting Rows

The **Delete command** on the Edit menu or shortcut menu removes cells (including the data and format) from the worksheet. Deleting cells is not the same as clearing cells. The **Clear command** described earlier in Project 1, clears the data out of the cell but the cells remain in the worksheet. The Delete command removes the cells from the worksheet and moves rows up when you delete rows or move columns to the left when you delete columns.

In the following example, the Delete command is used to delete the Midwest data in row 7 because the company has replaced this office with the two new ones that will be added later.

TO DELETE ROWS ▼

STEP 1 ▶

Select row 7 by clicking its row heading to the left of column A.

Excel highlights row 7 (Figure 3-5).

STEP 2 ▶

Select the Edit menu and point to the Delete command.

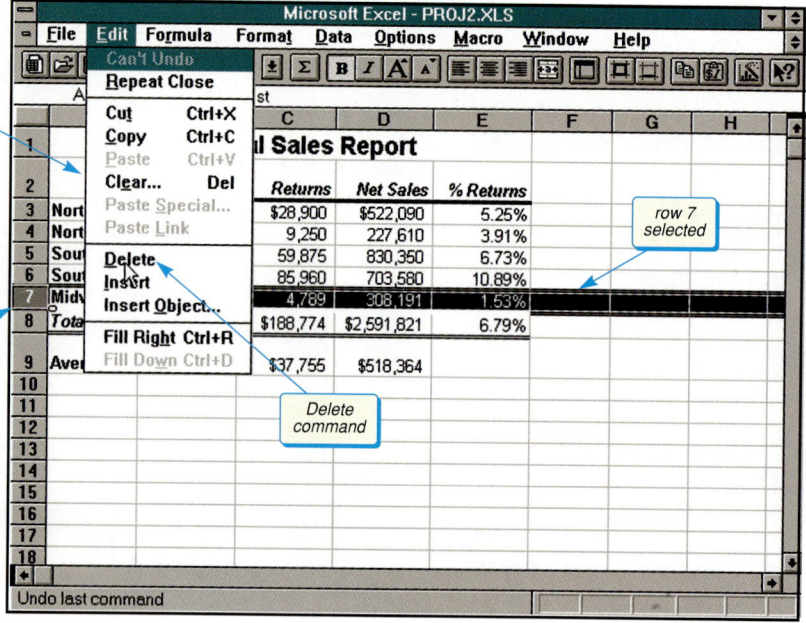

FIGURE 3-5

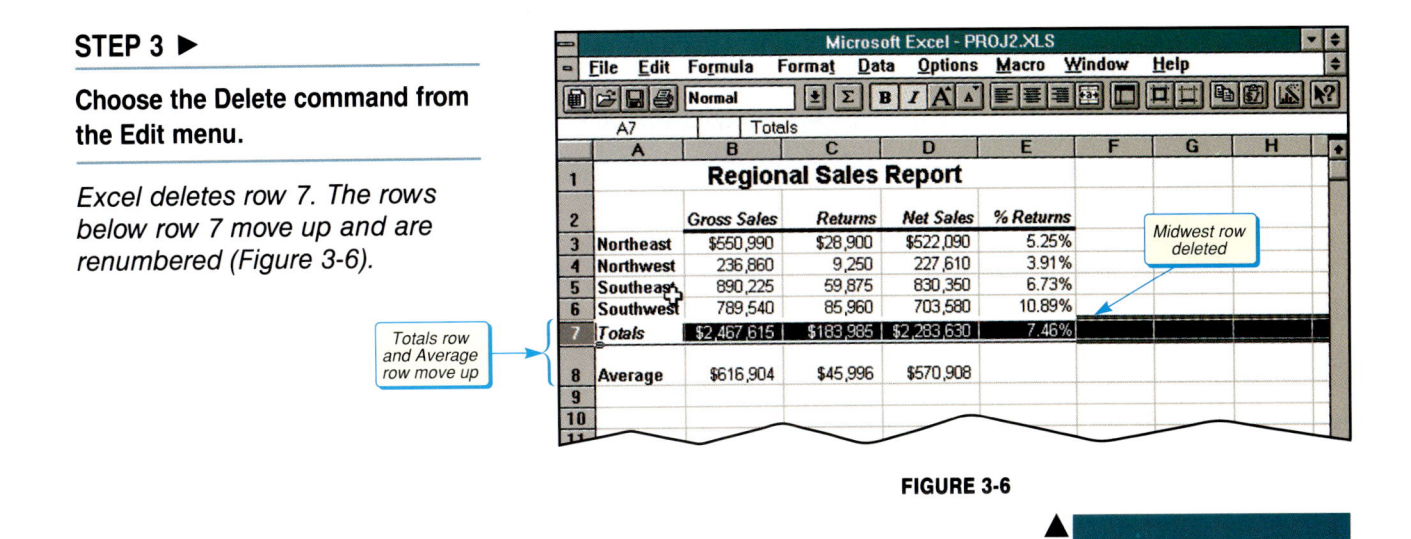

STEP 3 ▶

Choose the Delete command from the Edit menu.

Excel deletes row 7. The rows below row 7 move up and are renumbered (Figure 3-6).

FIGURE 3-6

Compare the location of the Totals row in Figure 3-5 on the previous page to Figure 3-6. Prior to deleting row 7, the totals were in row 8. After deleting row 7, the totals move up to row 7. Whenever you delete a row, the rows below it move up and are renumbered. Excel also changes the range referenced in the SUM function for the gross sales from the range B3:B7 to B3:B6 because the Gross Sales totals are now in cell B7. Excel makes similar adjustments to the SUM functions in cells C7 and D7. The percent returns formula = C8 / B8 in cell E7 changes to = C7 / B7.

Although Excel adjusts ranges in functions that reference the deleted row, it does not adjust cell references to the deleted row in formulas in the worksheet. Excel displays the error message **#REF!** (meaning cell reference error) in those cells containing formulas that reference cells in the deleted area. For example, if cell A7 contains the formula = A4 + A5 and you delete row 5, then Excel assigns the formula = A4 + #REF! to cell A6 (originally cell A7) and displays the error message #REF! in cell A6.

Deleting Columns

This project does not require you to delete columns. However, you should be aware that you can delete columns as well as rows. That is, select the columns to delete and choose the Delete command from the Edit menu or shortcut menu.

Deleting Individual Cells or a Range of Cells

Although Excel allows you to delete an individual cell or range of cells, you should be aware if you shift a cell or range of cells on the worksheet they may no longer be lined up with their associated cells. For this reason, it is recommended that you only delete entire rows or entire columns.

Inserting Rows

The **Insert command** on the Edit menu or the shortcut menu is used to insert a cell, a range of cells, entire rows, or entire columns anywhere in the worksheet. The Insert command allows you to insert rows between rows that already contain values. In the Regional Sales Report, room must be made between rows 6 and 7 to add the three regions, Upper Midwest, Lower Midwest, and West. The steps on the following page show how to accomplish the task of inserting rows in the worksheet.

TO INSERT ROWS

STEP 1 ▶

Click row heading 7 and drag through row heading 9.

Excel highlights rows 7, 8, and 9 (Figure 3-7).

STEP 2 ▶

Select the Edit menu and point to the Insert command.

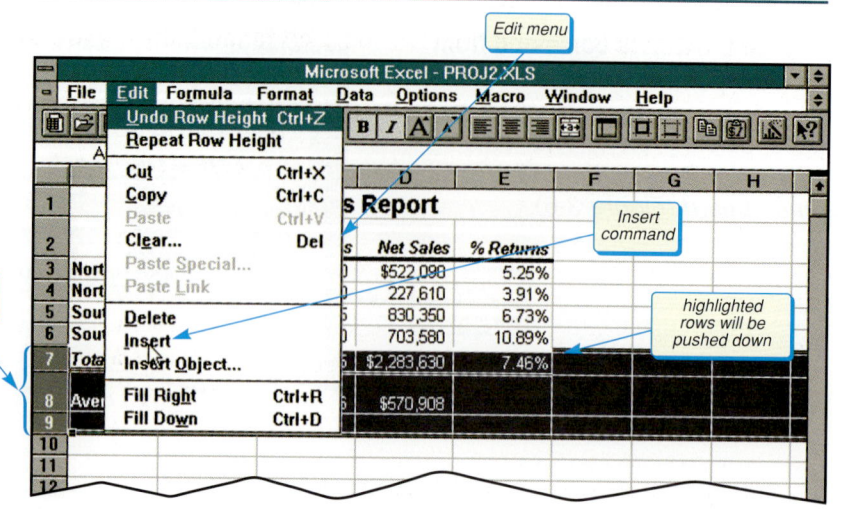

FIGURE 3-7

STEP 3 ▶

Choose the Insert command.

Excel inserts three blank rows — 7, 8, and 9 (Figure 3-8). To make room for the new rows, Excel opens up the worksheet by pushing down the rows below row 6.

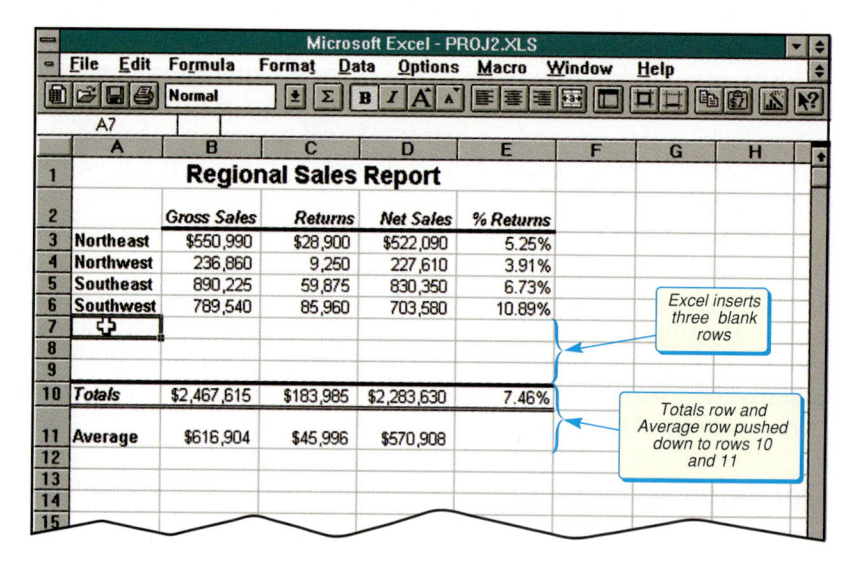

FIGURE 3-8

If the *pushed* rows include any formulas, Excel adjusts the cell references to the new locations. Thus, if a formula in the worksheet references a cell in row 7 before the insert, then after the insert, the cell reference in the formula is adjusted to row 10. Excel duplicates in rows 7, 8, and 9 the formats used in the corresponding cells in row 6. Hence, when you enter values into rows 7, 8, and 9, the values will be formatted the same as the values in row 6.

Inserting Columns

You insert columns into a worksheet in the same way you insert rows. To insert columns, begin your column selection immediately to the right of where you want Excel to insert the new blank columns. Select the number of columns you want to insert. From the Edit menu or shortcut menu, choose the Insert command. The inserted columns duplicate the format of the column to their left.

Inserting Individual Cells or a Range of Cells

Like the Delete command, the Insert command allows you to insert a single cell or a range of cells. However, you should be aware that if you shift a single cell or a range of cells, they may no longer be lined up with their associated cells. To ensure that the values in the worksheet do not get out of order, it is recommended that you only insert entire rows or entire columns.

▶ ADDING AND CHANGING DATA IN THE WORKSHEET

The next step is to modify the gross sales and returns for the Southwest region in row 6 because some of their accounts are being turned over to the new West region, and enter the data for the three new regions Upper Midwest, Lower Midwest, and West in rows 7 through 9.

TO ADD AND CHANGE DATA IN ROWS 6 THROUGH 9

Step 1: Enter 346520 in cell B6 and 42370 in cell C6.
Step 2: Enter Upper Midwest in cell A7, 150000 in cell B7, and 2525 in cell C7.
Step 3: Enter Lower Midwest in cell A8, 162980 in cell B8, and 2264 in cell C8.
Step 4: Enter West in cell A9, 443020 in cell B9, and 43590 in cell C9.

After entering the text and data, the range of cells A6:C9 displays as shown in Figure 3-9.

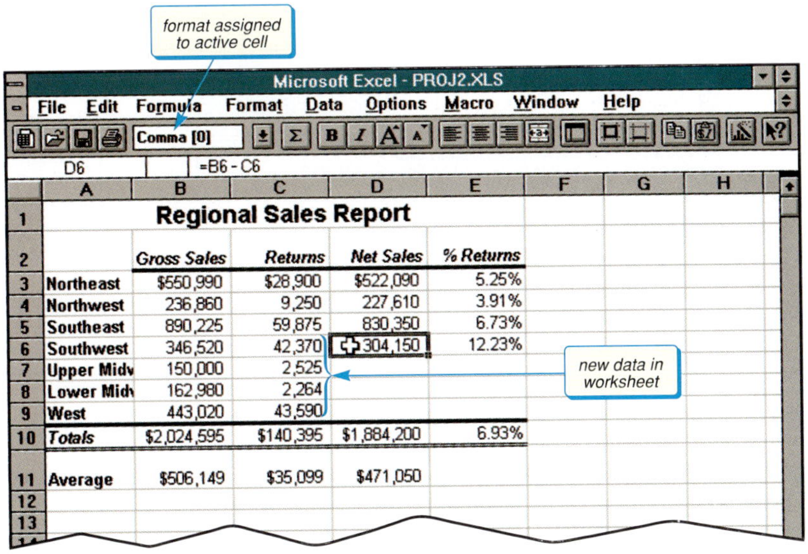

FIGURE 3-9

To Copy a Range of Cells to Adjacent Cells Using the Fill Handle

In Projects 1 and 2, you used the fill handle to copy a single cell to an adjacent paste area in the same column or row. The steps on the following page show how to use the fill handle to copy more than one cell (D6:E6) to an adjacent paste area (D7:E9).

TO COPY A RANGE OF CELLS USING THE FILL HANDLE

STEP 1

Select the range D6:E6, the range to copy. Point to the fill handle.

STEP 2 ▶

Drag the fill handle to select the range D7:E9 (Figure 3-10).

FIGURE 3-10

STEP 3 ▶

Release the left mouse button.

Excel copies the formulas and formats in the range D6:E6 to the paste area D7:E9. In addition, Excel evaluates the formulas and enters the results in the paste area (Figure 3-11).

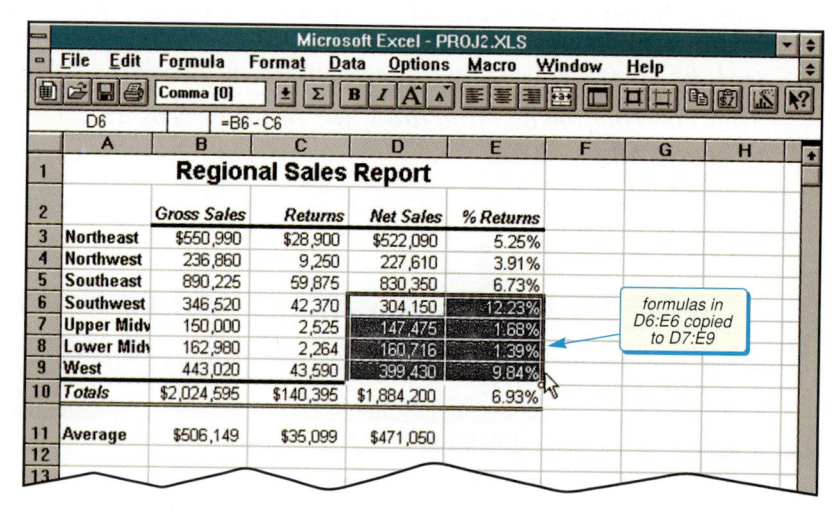

FIGURE 3-11

When you copy cells, Excel adjusts the cell references in any formulas copied to the paste area. Hence, the two copied formulas, = B6 – C6 in cell D6 and = C6 / B6 in cell E6, are modified as they are copied to the range D7:E9 so the formulas reference the gross sales and returns that correspond to the rows in which the formulas are placed.

Adjusting the Ranges in the SUM and AVERAGE Functions

After deleting and inserting rows, the ranges in the SUM functions in row 10 and the AVERAGE functions in row 11 no longer reflect the sums and averages of all the regions. For example, the SUM function in cell B10 sums the range B3:B6 and the AVERAGE function in cell A12 determines the average of the range B3:B6. Both functions should reference the range B3:B9, which encompasses all seven regions.

MOVING CELLS **E117**

As shown in the following steps, one efficient method of correcting the ranges is to use the AutoSum tool again in cell B10 and type the new range for the AVERAGE function in cell B11. Once the functions are changed, the fill handle is used to copy cells B10 and B11 to the range C10:D11.

TO EDIT FUNCTIONS AND RECOPY THEM TO ADJACENT CELLS ▼

STEP 1

Select cell B10 and double-click the AutoSum tool.

Excel calculates the sum of the numbers in the range B3:B9

STEP 2

Select cell B11. Click on the function in the formula bar. Change the range of the AVERAGE function from B3:B6 to B3:B9 and click the enter box or press the ENTER key.

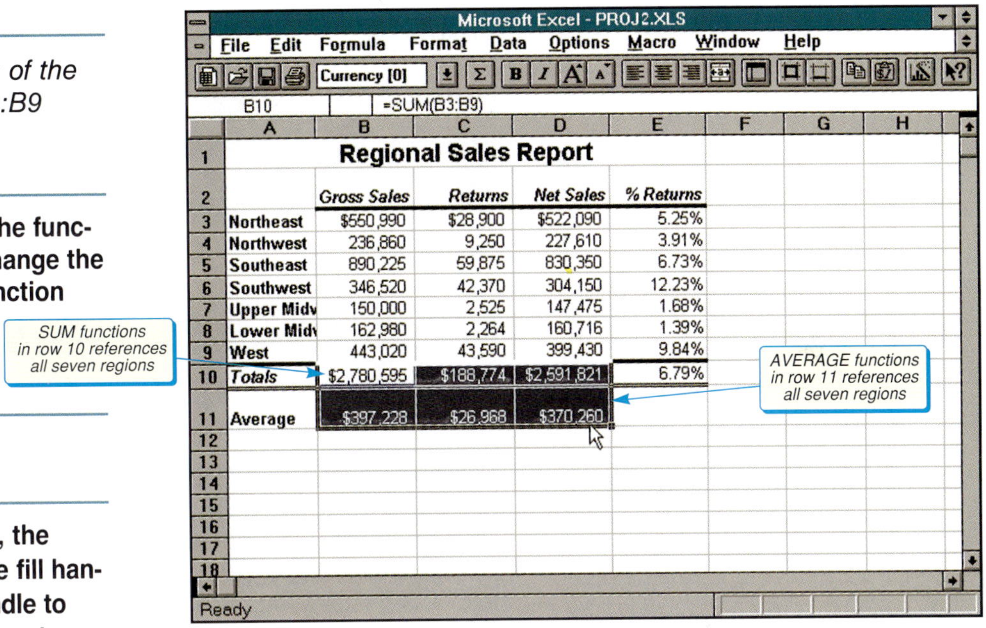

STEP 3 ▶

Select the range B10:B11, the range to copy. Point to the fill handle. Then drag the fill handle to select the range C10:D11 and release the left mouse button.

Excel copies the SUM function in cell B10 to the range C10:D10 and the AVERAGE function in cell B11 to the range C11:D11 (Figure 3-12).

FIGURE 3-12

Notice that the paste area C10:D11 was not empty prior to the copy and paste. When Excel copies one range to another, it replaces the previous values in the paste area with the new ones. If you make a mistake and accidentally copy over needed formulas, immediately choose the Undo command on the Edit menu.

▶ MOVING CELLS

The next step in revising the Regional Sales Report is to move the averages in row 11 to row 13 to make room for the lowest and highest values (see Figure 3-2 on page E110). Excel provides two ways to move cells: (1) drag the selection to its new location and drop it (also called **drag and drop**); or (2) choose the Cut and Paste commands from the Edit menu. The following steps illustrate the drag and drop method.

TO MOVE CELLS USING DRAG AND DROP ▼

STEP 1 ▶

Select row 11 by clicking its row heading to the left of column A. Position the mouse pointer on the bottom border of the highlighted range of cells.

The mouse pointer changes from a block plus sign to a block arrow (Figure 3-13).

	A	B	C	D	E
1		Regional Sales Report			
2		Gross Sales	Returns	Net Sales	% Returns
3	Northeast	$550,990	$28,900	$522,090	5.25%
4	Northwest	236,860	9,250	227,610	3.91%
5	Southeast	890,225	59,875	830,350	6.73%
6	Southwest	346,520	42,370	304,150	12.23%
7	Upper Midw	150,000	2,525	147,475	1.68%
8	Lower Midw	162,980	2,264	160,716	1.39%
9	West	443,020	43,590	399,430	9.84%
10	Totals	$2,780,595	$188,774	$2,591,821	6.79%
11	Average	$397,228	$26,968	$370,260	

row 11 heading
row 11 selected
mouse pointer changes to block arrow when pointed at edge

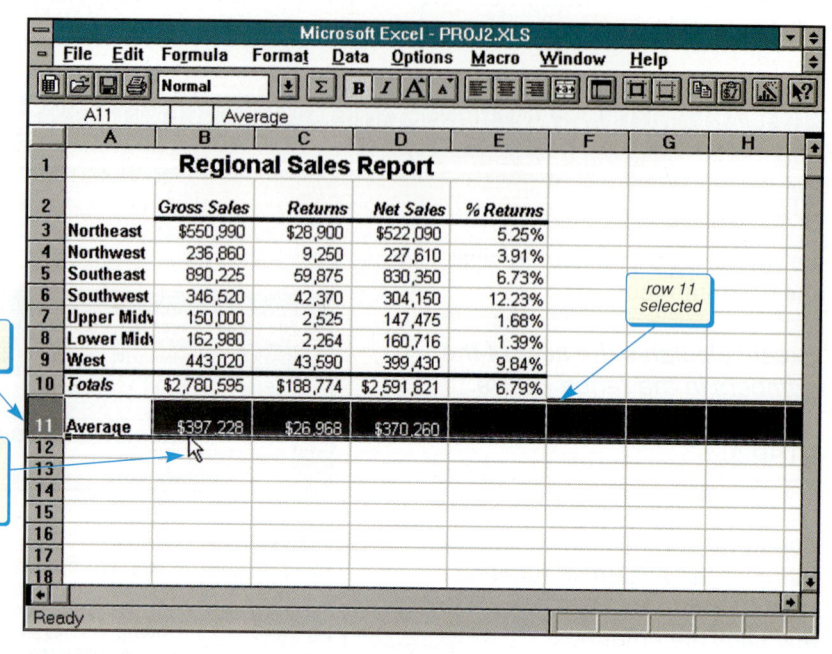

FIGURE 3-13

STEP 2 ▶

Drag the selected range down to row 13, the paste area.

Excel displays a light shaded border that moves as you drag the mouse (Figure 3-14). The light shaded border is the same size in terms of rows as the selected range to move.

as you drag, Excel displays a light shaded border to indicate the current location

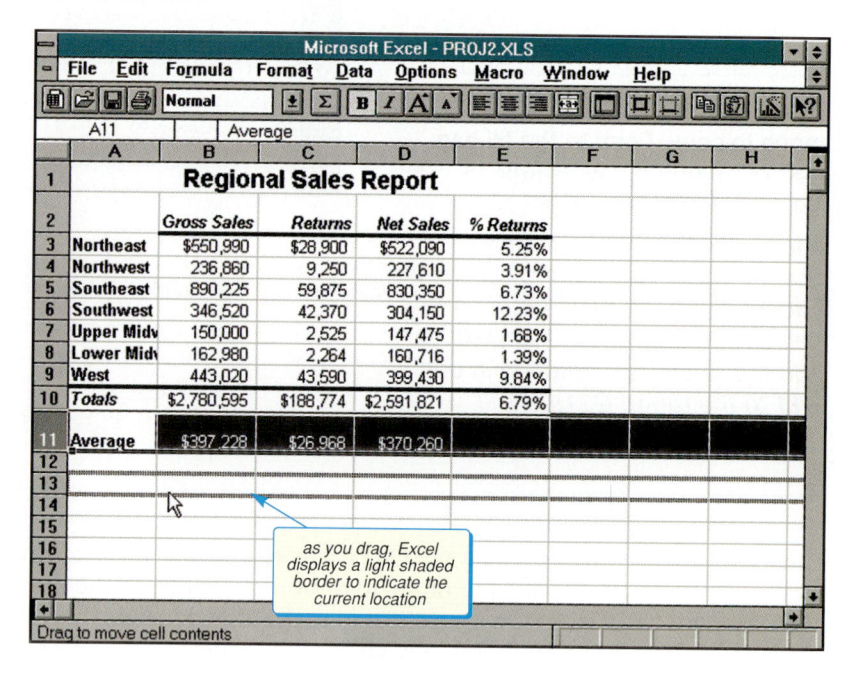

Drag to move cell contents

FIGURE 3-14

STEP 3 ▶

With the mouse pointer within the paste area, release the mouse button.

The averages and their corresponding formats including the row height are moved from row 11 to row 13 (Figure 3-15). Excel resets the height of row 11 to the default, 12.75 points.

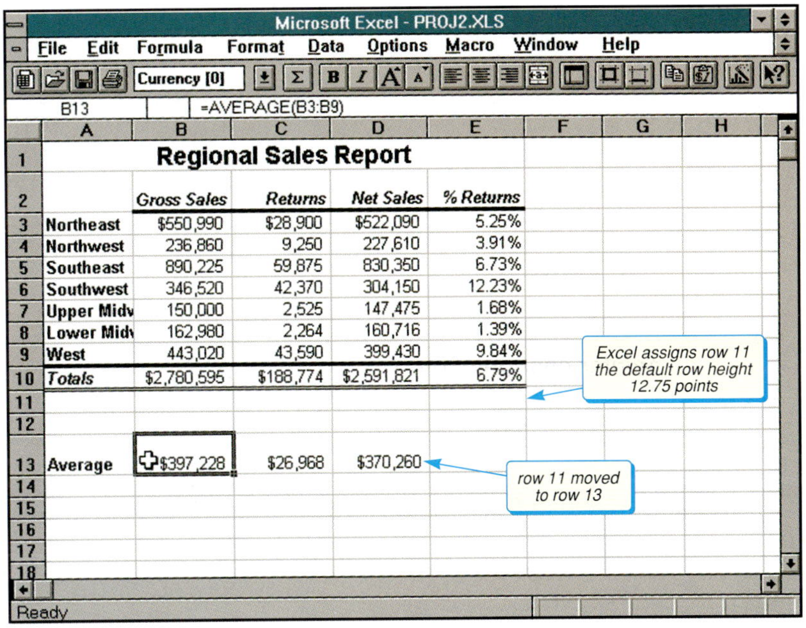

FIGURE 3-15

When you move a range of cells, the following occurs with respect to cell references: (1) Excel adjusts all cell references in formulas and functions in the worksheet so they are calculated using the same cell values they had before the move. Therefore, any formula or function that referenced row 11 before the move references row 13 after the move; and (2) formulas and functions that make reference to the paste area (row 13) as it was before the move, result in the error message #REF!

When you move cells, the original location (row 11) no longer contains the formats originally assigned to it. For example, all the cells in row 11 that were assigned TrueType Arial in Project 2, revert back to the Windows default font MS Sans Serif. The number format in row 11 changes back to the default General. And the height of row 11 changes from 24 points to the default height, 12.75 points. Anytime you move cells, check the formats assigned to the original location, especially if you plan to enter new values in these cells.

Using the Cut and Paste Commands to Move Cells

Rather than using the drag and drop method, you can use the Cut and Paste commands in the Edit menu to move cells. You will prefer these two commands when you want to move the cells to more than one area of the worksheet. The Cut command removes the selected cells from the worksheet and copies them onto the **Clipboard**. Once the selected cells are on the Clipboard, they can be pasted into the worksheet as often as required.

Moving Cells Versus Copying Cells

In Excel, moving cells is not the same as copying cells. When you copy cells, the copy range remains intact. When you move cells, the original location is blanked and the format is reset to the default. Copy cells to duplicate. Move cells to rearrange your worksheet.

▶ THE MAX AND MIN FUNCTIONS

According to Figure 3-2 on page E110, the lowest and highest gross sales, returns, net sales, and percent returns are to display in rows 11 and 12, just above the averages in row 13. The **MIN function** is used to display the lowest value in a range, and the **MAX function** is used to display the highest value in a range.

Before you enter the MAX and MIN functions, you must do the following: (1) change the height of row 13 from 24 points to the minimum height (best fit) needed to display a value in a cell; (2) enter the row titles Lowest in cell A11 and Highest in cell A12, and bold both titles; (3) change the height of row 11 to 24 points to add white space between rows 10 and 11; and (4) change the width of column A to best fit so the row titles in cells A7 and A8 fit in their cells. Perform the following steps to carry out these four activities.

TO ENTER BOLD ROW TITLES AND ADJUST THE ROW HEIGHT AND COLUMN WIDTH ▼

STEP 1 ▶

Move the mouse pointer to the border line between row headings 13 and 14 so the mouse pointer becomes a dark plus sign with two arrowheads (✥) (Figure 3-16).

STEP 2

Double-click the left mouse button.

Excel changes the height of row 13 from 24 points to best fit (Figure 3-17).

STEP 3

Move the mouse pointer to the border line below row heading 11 so the mouse pointer becomes a dark plus sign with two arrowheads.

STEP 4 ▶

Drag the mouse down until the height displayed in place of the cell reference in the formula bar is equal to 24.00.

Excel displays a horizontal dotted line. The distance between the dotted line and the top of row 11 indicates the new row height (Figure 3-17).

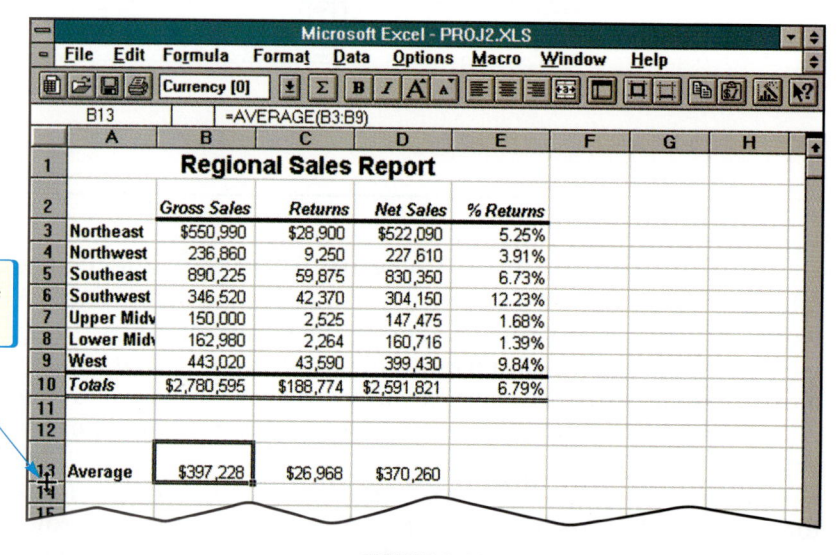

FIGURE 3-16

FIGURE 3-17

THE MAX AND MIN FUNCTIONS **E121**

STEP 5 ▶

Release the left mouse button.

Excel displays row 11 with a new height of 24 points (Figure 3-18).

FIGURE 3-18

STEP 6 ▶

Select cell A11 and enter `Lowest`. **Select cell A12 and enter** `Highest`. **Select the range A11:A12 and click the Bold tool on the Standard toolbar. Then move the mouse pointer to the border line between column heading A and column heading B above row 1.**

The mouse pointer becomes a dark plus sign with two arrowheads (Figure 3-19).

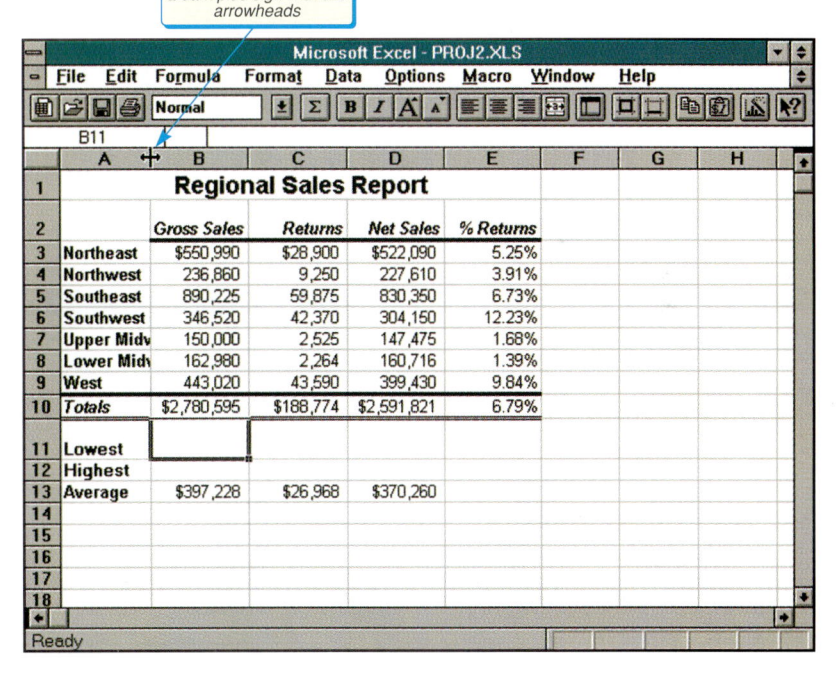

FIGURE 3-19

E122   PROJECT 3   ENHANCING A WORKSHEET AND DRAWING CHARTS

STEP 7 ▶

Double-click the left mouse button.

The width of column A is changed to best fit so the row titles in cells A7 and A8 display within the cells (Figure 3-20).

[Screenshot: Microsoft Excel - PROJ2.XLS. Callout: "width of column A changed to best fit". Worksheet contents:]

	A	B	C	D	E
1		Regional Sales Report			
2		Gross Sales	Returns	Net Sales	% Returns
3	Northeast	$550,990	$28,900	$522,090	5.25%
4	Northwest	236,860	9,250	227,610	3.91%
5	Southeast	890,225	59,875	830,350	6.73%
6	Southwest	346,520	42,370	304,150	12.23%
7	Upper Midwest	150,000	2,525	147,475	1.68%
8	Lower Midwest	162,980	2,264	160,716	1.39%
9	West	443,020	43,590	399,430	9.84%
10	Totals	$2,780,595	$188,774	$2,591,821	6.79%
11	Lowest				
12	Highest				
13	Average	$397,228	$26,968	$370,260	

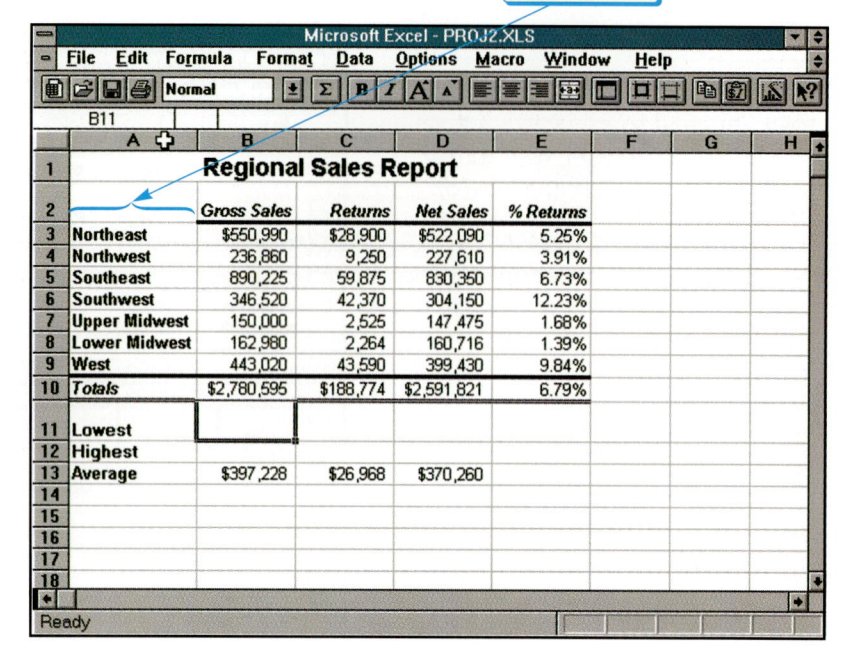

FIGURE 3-20

The next step is to enter the MIN and MAX functions in cells B11 and B12, respectively.

TO ENTER THE MIN AND MAX FUNCTIONS ▼

STEP 1 ▶

Select cell B11 and type `=min(` in the formula bar. Then move the mouse pointer to cell B3 and drag down to cell B9.

Excel surrounds the range B3:B9 with a moving border and appends B3:B9 to the open parenthesis in the formula bar (Figure 3-21).

[Screenshot: Microsoft Excel - PROJ2.XLS. Formula bar shows `=min(B3:B9`. Callouts: "active cell", "MIN function in formula bar", "range selected using Point mode". Status bar shows "Point".]

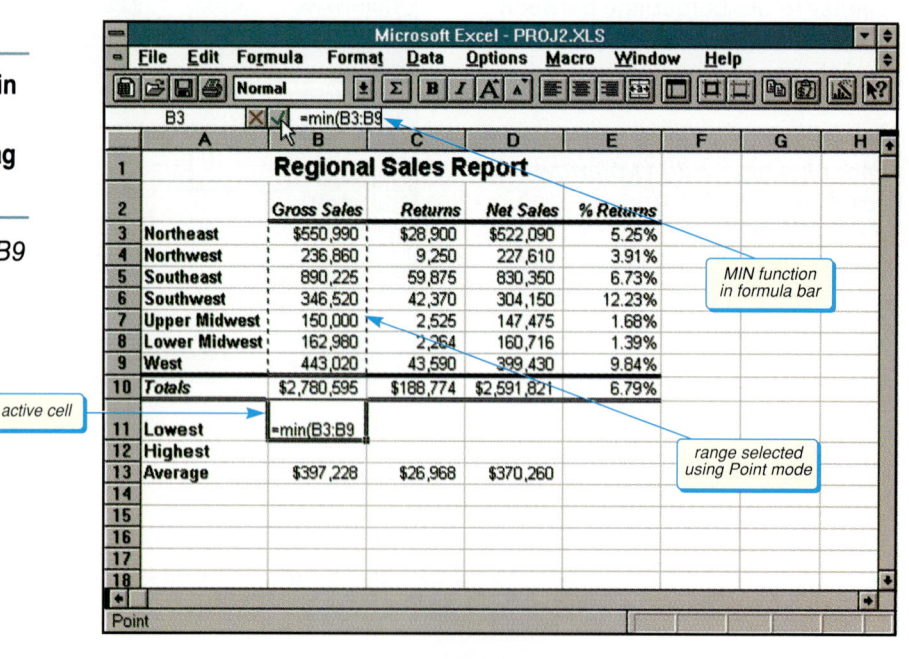

FIGURE 3-21

STEP 2 ▶

Release the left mouse button and click the enter box or press the ENTER key.

Excel assigns the MIN function to cell B12. The value $150,000 displays in cell B11 because it is the lowest number in the range B3:B9 (Figure 3-22). Excel assigns the Currency (0) format to cell B11 due to using Point mode to select the range B3:B9 for the MIN function. When you use Point mode, Excel assigns the number format of the first cell pointed to (cell B3). Thus, cell B11 is assigned the Currency (0) format.

FIGURE 3-22

STEP 3 ▶

Select cell B12 and type =max(in the formula bar. Then move the mouse pointer to cell B3 and drag down to cell B9. Release the left mouse button, and click the enter box or press the ENTER key.

Excel assigns the MAX function to cell B12. The value $890,225 displays in cell B12 because it is the highest number in the range B3:B9 (Figure 3-23). Here again, Excel assigns the Currency (0) format to cell B12 due to using the Point mode to select the range, and the first cell (B3) in the range has a Currency (0) format.

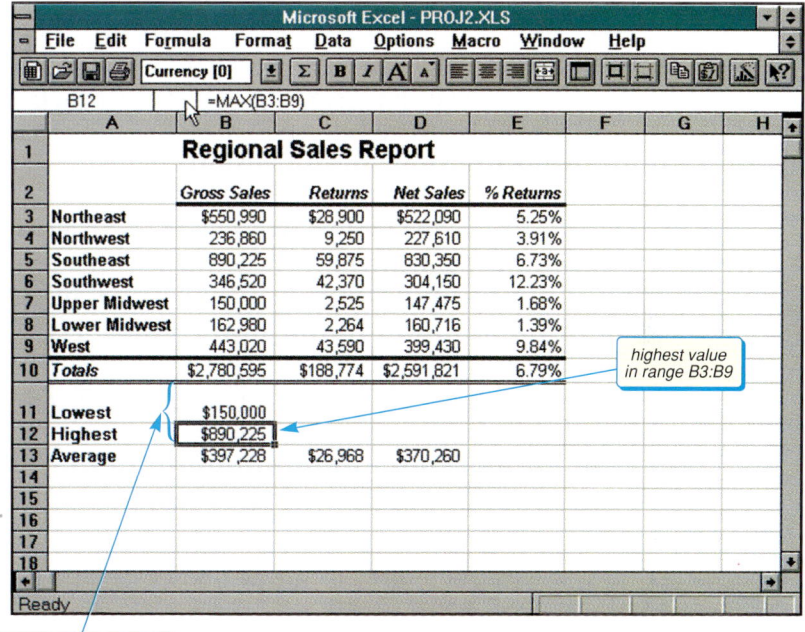

FIGURE 3-23

With the MIN and MAX functions entered into cells B11 and B12, the steps on the following page copy them to the range C11:E12.

TO COPY THE MIN AND MAX FUNCTIONS

STEP 1

Select the range B11:B12, the range to copy and point to the fill handle.

STEP 2 ▶

Drag the fill handle to select the paste area C11:E12, and release the left mouse button.

Excel copies the MIN and MAX functions in cells B11 and B12 to the range C11:E12 (Figure 3-24).

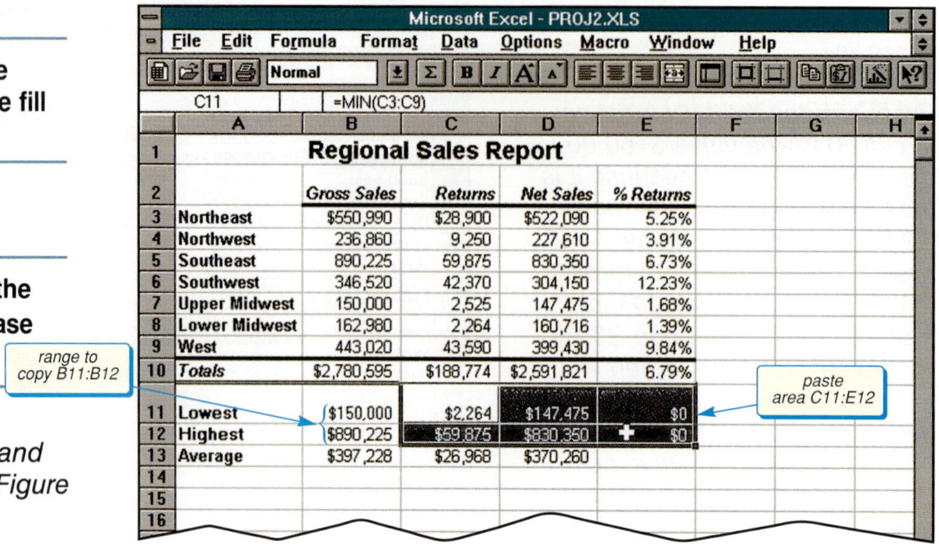

FIGURE 3-24

You can see in Figure 3-24 that each cell in row 11 contains the lowest values for the given range in its corresponding column. Likewise, row 12 contains the highest values. Cells E11 and E12, which contain the lowest and highest percent returns, need to be formatted to Percentage 0.00% to display properly. Rather than using the Number command in the Format menu to format these two cells, the next section introduces you to an alternative method of formatting a cell by copying the desired format from another cell.

▶ COPYING A CELL'S FORMAT

Notice in Figure 3-24 that two formatting problems have developed due to moving the averages from row 11 to row 13. First, the cells in row 11 are in a different font (MS San Serif) than the rest of the worksheet (TrueType Arial). Recall that the font of the cells in row 11 changed from TrueType Arial to the Windows default MS San Serif when row 11 was moved to row 13.

Second, Excel assigned the Currency (0) format to rows 11 and 12 due to using Point mode to select the ranges for the MIN and MAX functions in cells B11 and B12, which were copied to the range C11:E12. Therefore, the lowest percent returns .0139 in cell E11 and the highest percent returns .1223 in cell E12 display as $0.

If there is a cell in the worksheet that already uses the format you want to assign to another cell, you can use the **Copy tool** ( ) and the **Paste Formats tool** ( ) on the Standard toolbar to duplicate the format. Cell B12 uses TrueType Arial font and the Currency (0) format required in the range B11:D11. Cell E9 uses TrueType Arial font and the Percentage (0.00%) format required in the range E11:E12. The following steps illustrate the use of the Copy tool and Paste Formats tool to copy the format in cell B12 to the range B11:D11 and to copy the format in cell E9 to the range E11:E12.

TO COPY A CELL'S FORMAT TO A RANGE OF CELLS

STEP 1

Select cell B12, the cell with the desired format and click the Copy tool on the Standard toolbar.

Excel surrounds cell B12 with a moving border and copies the contents and format of cell B12 onto the Clipboard.

STEP 2 ▶

Select the paste area B11:D11 (Figure 3-25).

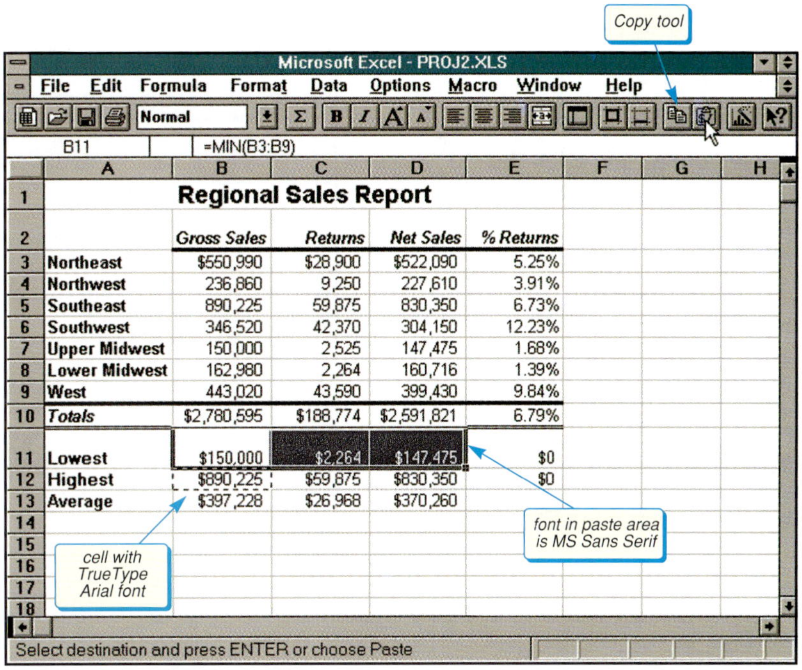

FIGURE 3-25

STEP 3 ▶

Click the Paste Formats tool.

Excel copies the format assigned to cell B12 to the range B11:D11 (Figure 3-26).

STEP 4

Press the ESC key to remove the moving border around cell B12, and select any cell to remove the selection from the range B11:D11.

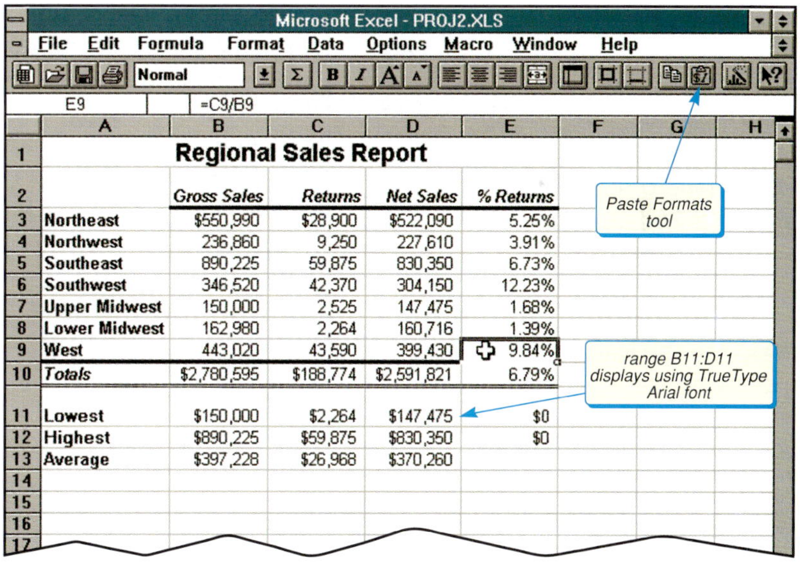

FIGURE 3-26

The Copy tool copies the format as well as the contents of cell B12 on the Clipboard. The Paste Formats tool instructs Excel to copy only the format on the Clipboard to the range B11:D11. Any cell with the TrueType Arial font and the Currency (0) format could have been used as the cell to copy.

To complete the formatting in rows 11 and 12, use the steps on the following page to copy the TrueType Arial font and Percentage 0.00% format assigned to cell E9 to the lowest and highest percent returns in cells E11 and E12.

TO COPY THE FORMAT ASSIGNED TO CELL E9 TO THE RANGE E11:E12

STEP 1 ▶

Select cell E9, the cell with the desired format and click the Copy tool on the Standard toolbar (Figure 3-27).

Excel surrounds cell E9 with a moving border and copies the contents and format of cell E9 onto the Clipboard.

STEP 2 ▶

Select the paste area E11:E12.

FIGURE 3-27

STEP 3 ▶

Click the Paste Formats tool.

Excel copies the format of cell E9 to the range E11:E12 and displays the lowest and highest percent returns using the Percentage 0.00% format (Figure 3-28).

STEP 4

Press the ESC key to remove the moving border around cell E9, and select any cell to remove the selection from the range E11:E12.

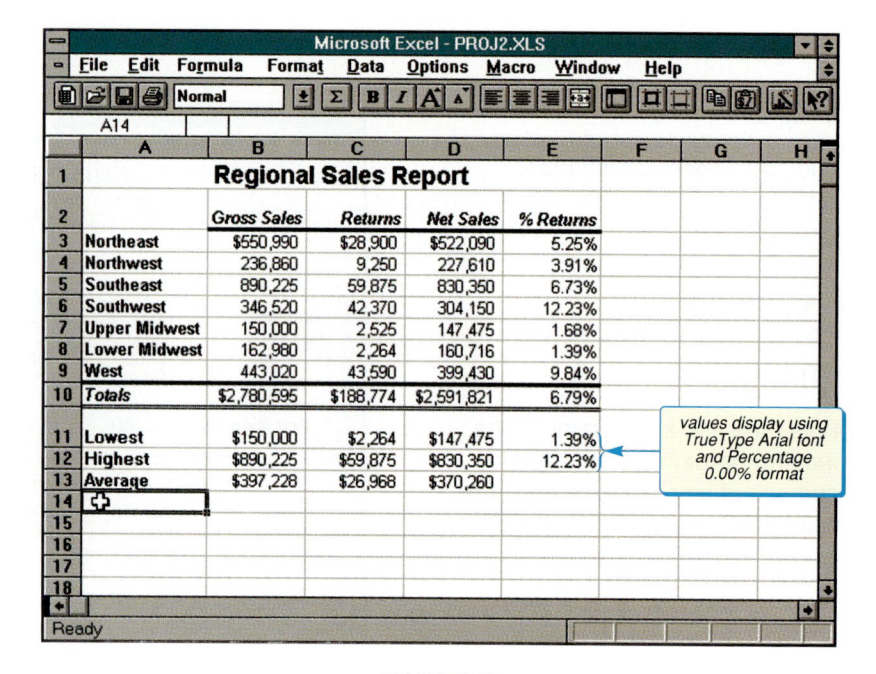

FIGURE 3-28

Notice that cell E10, the closest cell with the desired format to the range E11:E12, is not selected as the cell to copy because the borders above and below cell E10 would be copied as part of the format. Any of the other cells in the range E3:E9 have the desired format and, therefore, are acceptable as the cell to copy.

ENTERING NUMBERS WITH A FORMAT SYMBOL **E127**

▶ ENTERING NUMBERS WITH A FORMAT SYMBOL

The next step in modifying the Regional Sales Report is to enter the acceptable percent returns in row 14. The acceptable percent returns is 5%. You can enter this number as a decimal number (.05) and then format it to Percentage 0% or you can enter it as a whole number followed immediately by the percent sign (5%). When you enter a number with a percent sign, Excel assigns the cell a value of 0.05 and displays it using the Percentage 0% format. The following steps describe how to complete the entries in row 14.

TO ENTER A NUMBER WITH A PERCENT SIGN (%) ▼

STEP 1

Select cell A14 and enter the text `Acceptable % Returns ===>`. Then with cell A14 selected, click the Bold tool on the Standard toolbar.

STEP 2

Select cell C14 and enter `5%`. Then with cell C14 selected, click the Left Align tool on the Standard toolbar.

The 5% in cell C14 is left-aligned.

STEP 3 ▶

Adjust the height of row 14 to 24 points.

The text in cell A14 displays in bold, the number 5% displays left-aligned in cell C14, and the row height is increased from 12.75 points to 24 points (Figure 3-29).

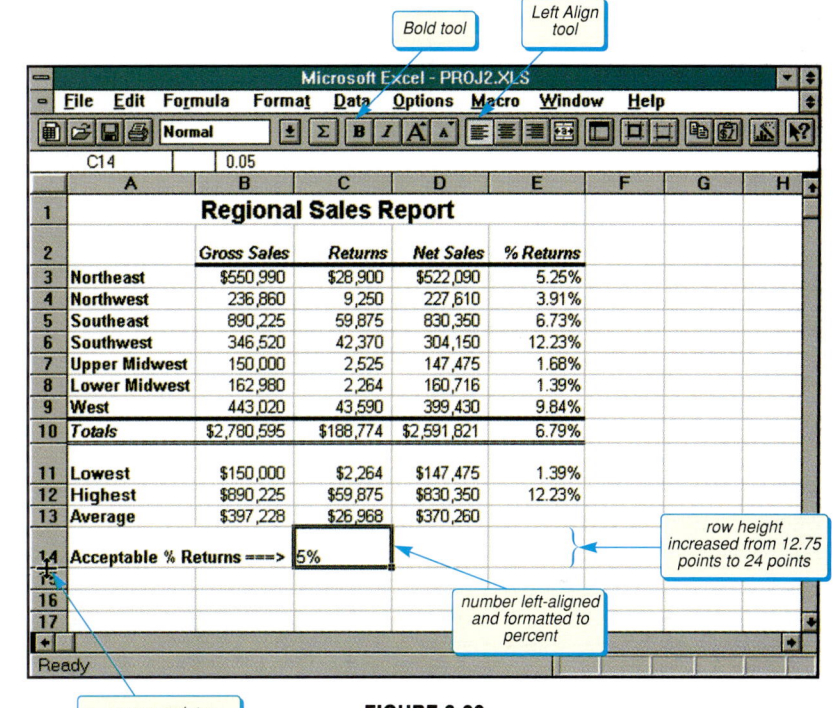

FIGURE 3-29

Summary of Format Symbols

Excel accepts three format symbols with numbers. They are the leading dollar sign ($), the comma (,), and the percent sign(%). Table 3-1 shows examples of the use of each format symbol.

▶ **TABLE 3-1**

FORMAT SYMBOL	ENTERED IN FORMULA BAR	DISPLAYS IN CELL	COMPARABLE FORMAT STYLE
$	$112	$112	Currency (0)
	$3798.12	$3,798.12	Currency
	$44,123.3	$44,123.30	Currency
,	7,876	7,876	Comma (0)
	4,913.6	4,913.60	Comma
%	4%	4%	Percentage 0%
	7.25%	7.25%	Percentage 0.00%

▶ WRAPPING TEXT IN A CELL

The next step is to enter the column title High Returns Ratio in cell F2. This column title is different from the others because even though it is longer than the width of cell F2, it displays within the cell on multiple lines rather than overflowing into an adjacent cell. Displaying text on multiple lines within a cell is called **wrap text**. The following steps show you how to wrap, bold, and italicize text in a cell.

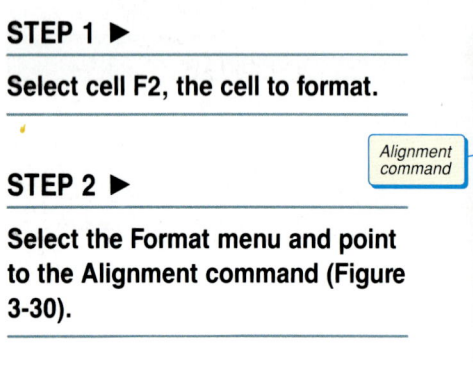

TO WRAP, BOLD, AND ITALICIZE TEXT IN A CELL ▼

STEP 1 ▶

Select cell F2, the cell to format.

STEP 2 ▶

Select the Format menu and point to the Alignment command (Figure 3-30).

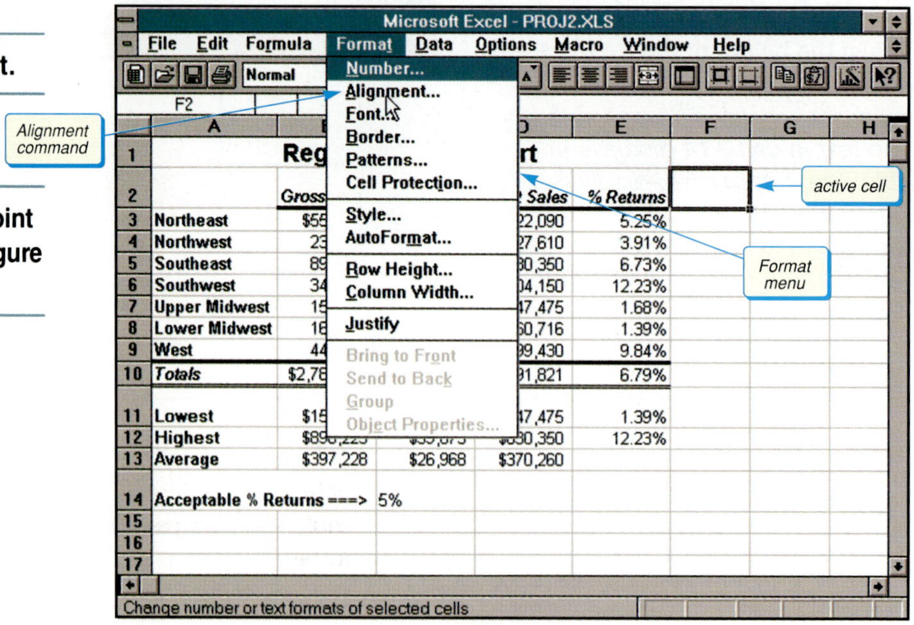

FIGURE 3-30

WRAPPING TEXT IN A CELL   E129

STEP 3 ▶

Choose the Alignment command from the Format menu.

Excel displays the Alignment dialog box.

STEP 4 ▶

Select Wrap Text and choose OK from the Alignment dialog box.

*Excel enters an x in the **Wrap Text box** when you select Wrap Text (Figure 3-31).*

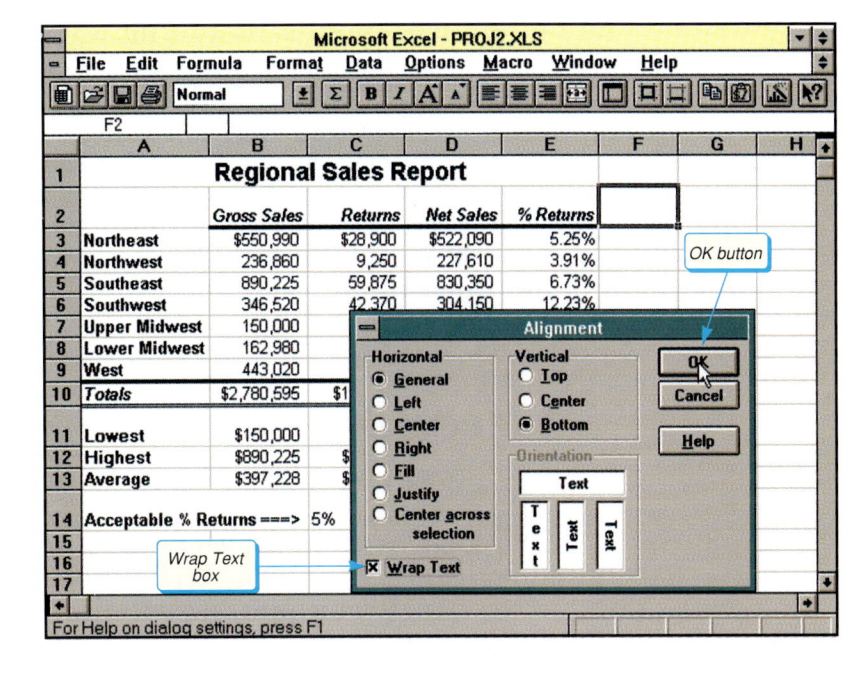

FIGURE 3-31

STEP 5 ▶

Type the column title `High Returns Ratio` in the formula bar (Figure 3-32).

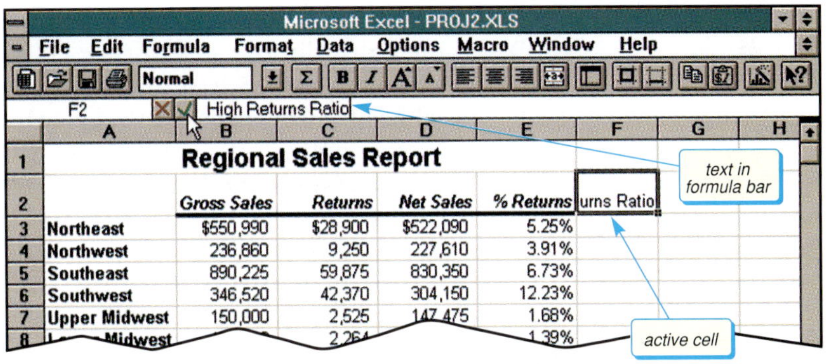

FIGURE 3-32

STEP 6 ▶

Click the enter box or press the ENTER key, and then click the Bold and Italic tools on the Standard toolbar.

Excel wraps the title on three lines in cell F2 and automatically increases the row height to best fit the three lines. The column title is bold, italicized, and wraps in the cell (Figure 3-33).

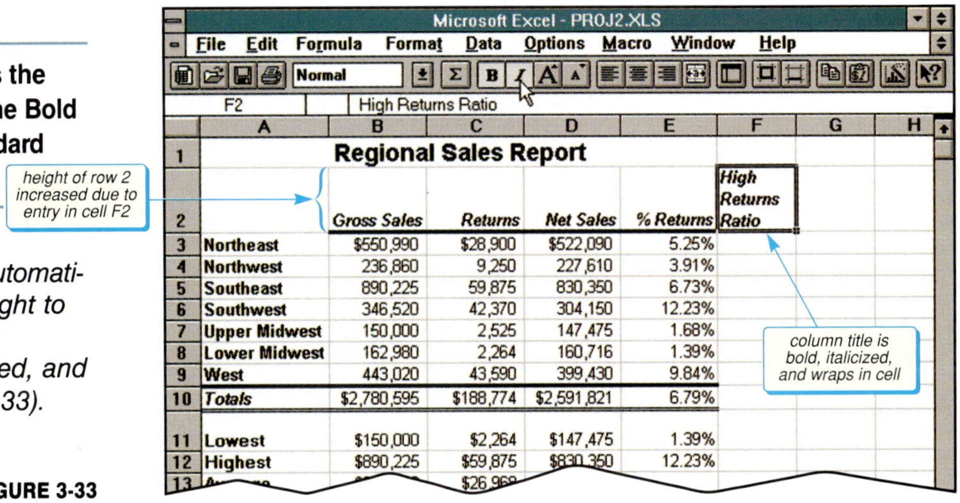

FIGURE 3-33

Recall that you can increase the width of a cell to 255 characters and the height of a cell to 409 points. This gives you plenty of room to enter entire paragraphs in a cell. If you want to control the number of words that go on each line, press ALT + ENTER after the last word you want entered on a line within a cell. Excel displays the next word in the text following the ALT + ENTER on the next line in the cell and adjusts the row height to best fit.

The cells containing the column titles in row 2 have a bottom border that should be extended to include cell F2, which contains the new column heading. The bottom border will be added to cell F2 later in this project as part of the steps to color the borders in row 2.

▶ MAKING DECISIONS — THE IF FUNCTION

If the percent returns in column E is greater than the 5% in cell C14, then the word YES displays in the corresponding cell in column F; otherwise, the cell is left blank. One way to add the word YES in column F is to manually compare the corresponding percent returns in column E to the acceptable percent returns in cell C14 and type the word YES when the corresponding percent returns in column E exceeds the acceptable percent returns in cell C14. However, because the data in the worksheet changes each time you prepare the report, you will find it preferable to automatically assign the word YES to the entries in the appropriate cells. What you need here is an entry for the cells in the range F3:F10 that displays either YES or leaves the cell blank.

Excel has the **IF function** that is useful when the value you want to assign to a cell is dependent on a logical test. A **logical test** is made up of two expressions and a relational operator. Each **expression** can be a cell reference, a number, text, a function, or a formula. A **relational operator** is one of the following: > (greater than), < (less than), = (equal to), > = (greater than or equal to), < = (less than or equal to), < > (not equal to). For example, assume you assign cell F3 the IF function:

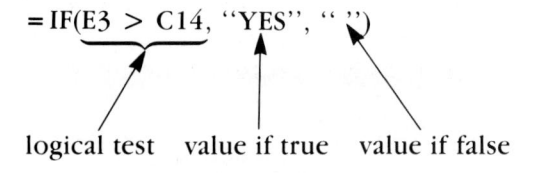

$$= \text{IF}(\underbrace{E3 > C14}_{\text{logical test}}, \underbrace{\text{``YES''}}_{\text{value if true}}, \underbrace{\text{`` ''}}_{\text{value if false}})$$

If the value in cell E3 is greater than the value in cell C14, then the word YES displays in cell F3. If the value in cell E3 is not greater than the value in cell C16, then cell F3 displays a blank character that makes the cell appear blank.

The general form of the IF function is:

= IF(logical_test, value_if_true, value_if_false)

The argument, value_if_true, is the value you want to assign to the cell when the logical_test is true. The argument, value_if_false, is the value you want to assign to the cell when the logical_test is false.

Table 3-2 lists the valid relational operators and examples of their use in IF functions.

▶ **TABLE 3-2**

RELATIONAL OPERATOR	MEANING	EXAMPLE
=	Equal to	=IF(A5 = B7, A22 - A3, G5 + E3)
<	Less than	=IF(E12 / D5 < 6, A15, B13 - 5)
>	Greater than	=IF(=SUM(A1:A5) > 100, 1, 0)
>=	Greater than or equal to	=IF(A12 >= E2, A4 * D5, 1)
<=	Less than or equal to	=IF(A1 + D5 <= 10, H15, 7 * A3)
<>	Not equal to	=IF(C5 <> B5, "Valid", "Invalid")

Absolute Versus Relative References

To complete the entries, it appears that in the range F3:F10 you enter the IF function =IF(E3 > C14, "YES", " ") in cell F3 and copy it to the range F4:F10. However, you know that when a function is copied down a column, Excel automatically adjusts the cell references in the function as it copies to reflect its new location. The first cell reference E3 should be adjusted to E4, E5, E6, E7, E8, and E9 as the IF function is copied down through the range F4:F10. But the second cell reference C14 must remain constant as the IF function is copied down the column.

Excel has the capability to keep a cell constant when it copies a formula or function by using a technique called **absolute referencing**. To specify an absolute reference in a formula, add a dollar sign ($) to the beginning of the column name, row name, or both. For example, C14 is an absolute reference and C14 is a relative reference. Both reference the same cell. The difference shows when they are copied. A formula using C14 instructs Excel to use the same cell (C14) as it copies the formula to a new location. A formula using C14 instructs Excel to adjust the cell reference as it copies. Table 3-3 gives some additional examples of absolute references. A cell reference with one dollar sign before either the column or the row is called a **mixed cell reference**.

▶ **TABLE 3-3**

CELL REFERENCE	MEANING
C14	Both column and row references remain the same when this cell reference is copied because they are absolute.
C$14	The column reference changes when you copy this cell reference to another column because it is relative. The row reference does not change because it is absolute.
$C14	The row reference changes when you copy this cell reference to another row because it is relative. The column reference does not change because it is absolute.
C14	Both column and row references are relative. When copied to another row and column, both the row and column in the cell reference are adjusted to reflect the new location.

The steps on the following page show how to enter the IF function into cell F3.

TO ENTER AN IF FUNCTION

STEP 1 ▶

Select cell F3 and type
`=if(e3 > $c$14, "YES", " ")`
(Figure 3-34).

FIGURE 3-34

STEP 2 ▶

Click the enter box or press the ENTER key.

Excel displays the text YES because cell E3 has a value greater than cell C14 (Figure 3-35).

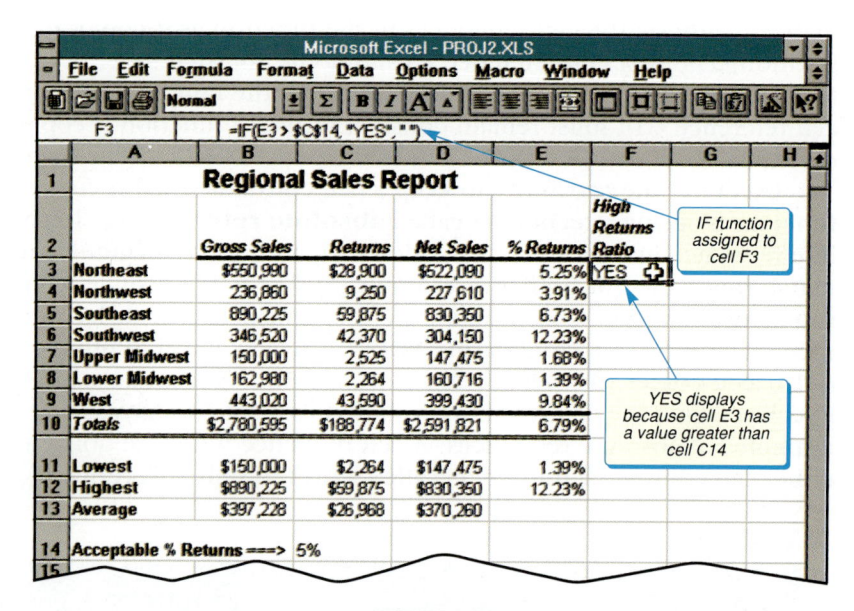

FIGURE 3-35

The value that Excel displays in cell F3 depends on the values assigned to cells E3 and C14. For example, if the returns in cell C3 are reduced by a few thousand dollars, then the IF function in cell F3 will change the display from YES to a blank cell. Changing the acceptable percent returns in cell C14 to a higher value (5.25% or greater) has the same effect.

When you enter or edit a formula that uses absolute references, you can type the $ in the appropriate position or you can use the function key F4 to cycle from relative to absolute to mixed the cell reference on which the insertion point is positioned, or immediately to the right of. Also, you are not required to add the right parenthesis for a function when you enter it in the formula bar. If you don't add the right parenthesis, Excel adds it when you click the enter box or press the ENTER key.

Copying the IF Function with an Absolute Reference

To complete the entries in column F, the steps that follow copy cell F3 to the range F4:F10 and bold the range F3:F10. As Excel copies the IF function in cell F3 to the range F4:F10, the absolute reference C14 remains constant. However, the relative reference E3 changes as the IF function is copied down through the range F4:F10. Table 3-4 illustrates the IF functions that will be copied from cell F3 to the range F4:F10.

The following steps use the fill handle to complete the copy of the IF function from cell F3 to the range F4:F10.

▶ **TABLE 3-4**

CELL	FUNCTION
F3	= IF(E3 > C14, "YES", " ")
F4	= IF(E4 > C14, "YES", " ")
F5	= IF(E5 > C14, "YES", " ")
F6	= IF(E6 > C14, "YES", " ")
F7	= IF(E7 > C14, "YES", " ")
F8	= IF(E8 > C14, "YES", " ")
F9	= IF(E9 > C14, "YES", " ")
F10	= IF(E10 > C14, "YES", " ")

TO COPY THE IF FUNCTION WITH AN ABSOLUTE REFERENCE ▼

STEP 1

Select cell F3, the cell to copy. Point to the fill handle

STEP 2 ▶

Drag the fill handle down through the range F4:F10 and release the left mouse button.

Excel copies the IF function in cell F3 to the range F4:F10. The word YES displays in the cells in the range F3:F10 whenever the adjacent cell in column E is greater than the value in cell C14, otherwise nothing displays in the cell (Figure 3-36).

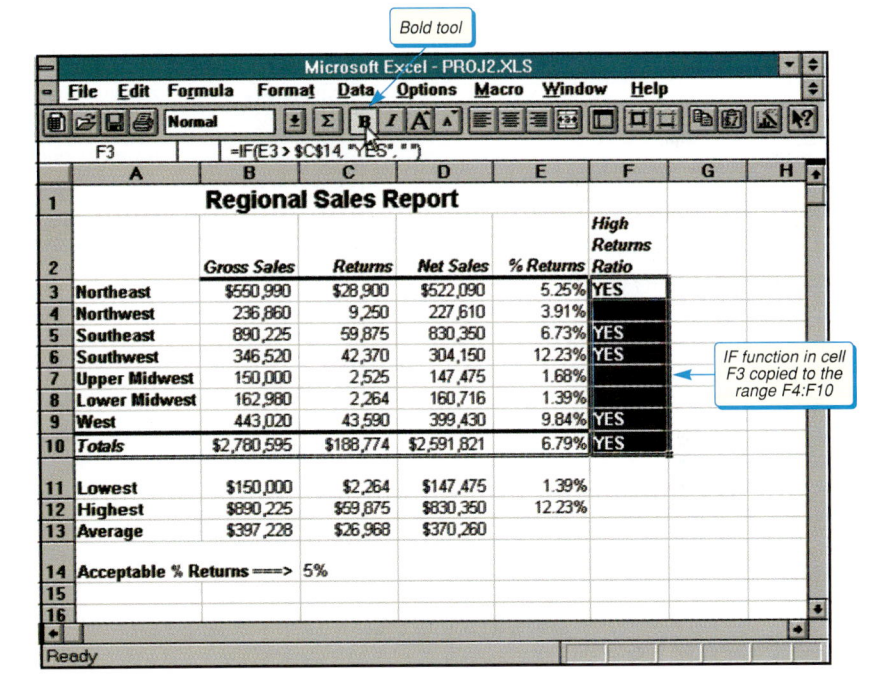

FIGURE 3-36

STEP 3

Click the Bold tool on the Standard toolbar.

Excel bolds the entries in the range F3:F10.

▶ RECENTERING THE WORKSHEET TITLE

In the previous steps, you added column F (High Returns Ratio) to the worksheet so the worksheet title is no longer centered across all the columns. In Figure 3-36 on the previous page, the worksheet title is centered across columns A through E. According to Figure 3-2 on page E110, the title is centered across columns A through F. Perform the following steps to recenter the worksheet title.

TO RECENTER THE WORKSHEET TITLE ▼

STEP 1

Select cell A1, the cell to which the centered worksheet title is assigned. Click the Center Across Columns tool on the Standard toolbar to undo the worksheet title centering.

STEP 2 ▶

Select the range A1:F1, the range to contain the title. Click the Center Across Columns tool.

Excel centers the worksheet title Regional Sales Report across the range A1:F1 (Figure 3-37).

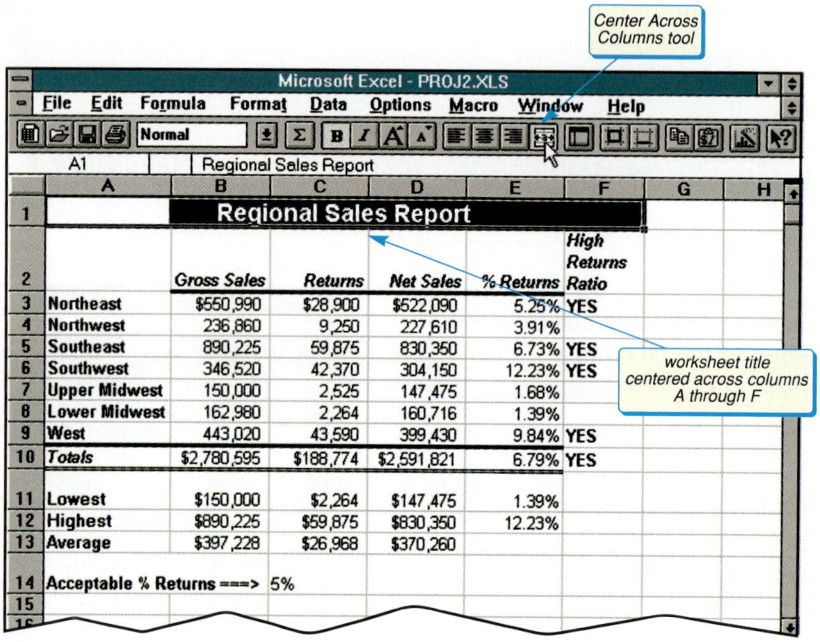

FIGURE 3-37

▶ ADDING COLOR TO A WORKSHEET

Microsoft Windows provides a basic color scheme that includes sixteen solid colors — black, white, red, green, blue, yellow, magenta, cyan, dark red, dark green, dark blue, light brown, purple, dark cyan, light gray, and gray. Excel automatically uses the colors established through the Windows Control Panel to display different parts of the screen, including the window background (white), the font (black), and the borders assigned to cells (black). You can change the color assigned to these parts of the screen to any of the other fifteen colors to enhance the display of the worksheet. If you have a color printer, you can also print the worksheet in the colors you select.

You color the font, background, and borders in a worksheet to emphasize entries or to make the worksheet appealing to the eye. In Figure 3-2 on page E110 the worksheet title is colored to highlight it, and the column titles border and the totals borders are colored to emphasize the rows in the worksheet with which they are associated. The high returns ratio entries in column F are colored because the column includes information to which you want to call attention. The colors dark red and dark blue are used because they stand out against a white screen background.

Changing the Color of the Font

The worksheet title, Regional Sales Report, in Figure 3-2 is assigned to cell A1 and centered over columns A through F and displays in dark red. The entries in column F under the title, High Returns Ratio, display in dark blue numbers. Follow these steps to change the color of the font in the worksheet title.

TO COLOR THE FONT IN THE WORKSHEET TITLE

STEP 1

Select cell A1, the cell to which the centered worksheet title is assigned.

STEP 2 ▶

From the Format menu, choose the Font command.

Excel displays the Font dialog box (Figure 3-38).

STEP 3 ▶

Click the Color box arrow and point to Dark Red in the drop-down list of colors.

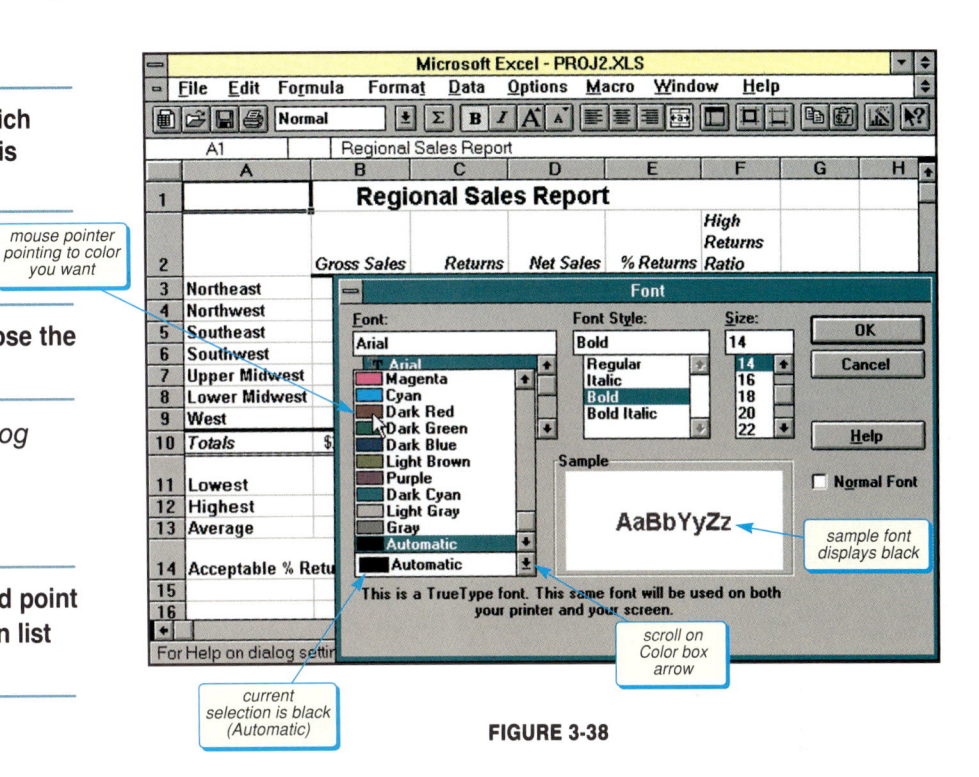

FIGURE 3-38

STEP 4 ▶

Select the color Dark Red.

The color in the Color box changes from Automatic (Black) to Dark Red, and the sample characters in the Sample box display in dark red (Figure 3-39).

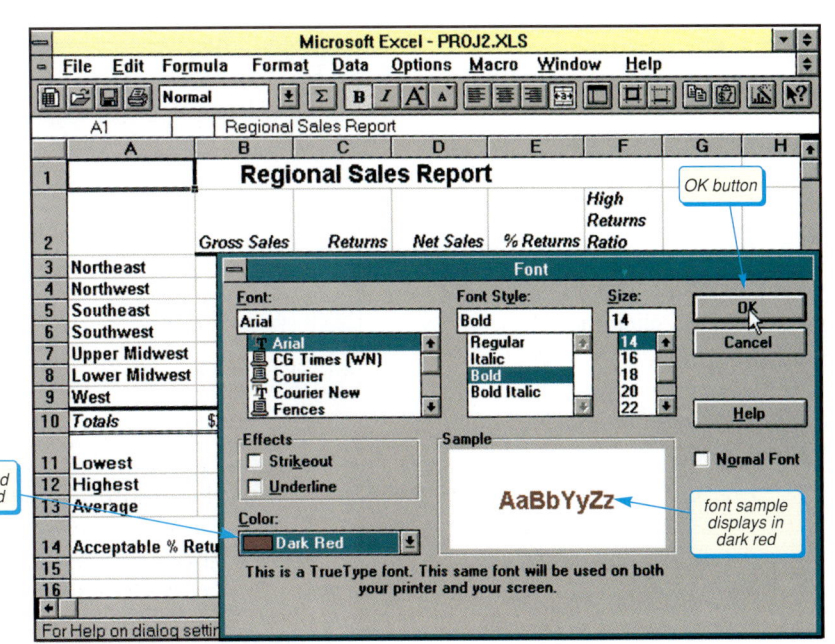

FIGURE 3-39

E136 PROJECT 3 ENHANCING A WORKSHEET AND DRAWING CHARTS

STEP 5 ▶

Choose the OK button from the Font dialog box.

Excel displays the worksheet title in dark red (Figure 3-40).

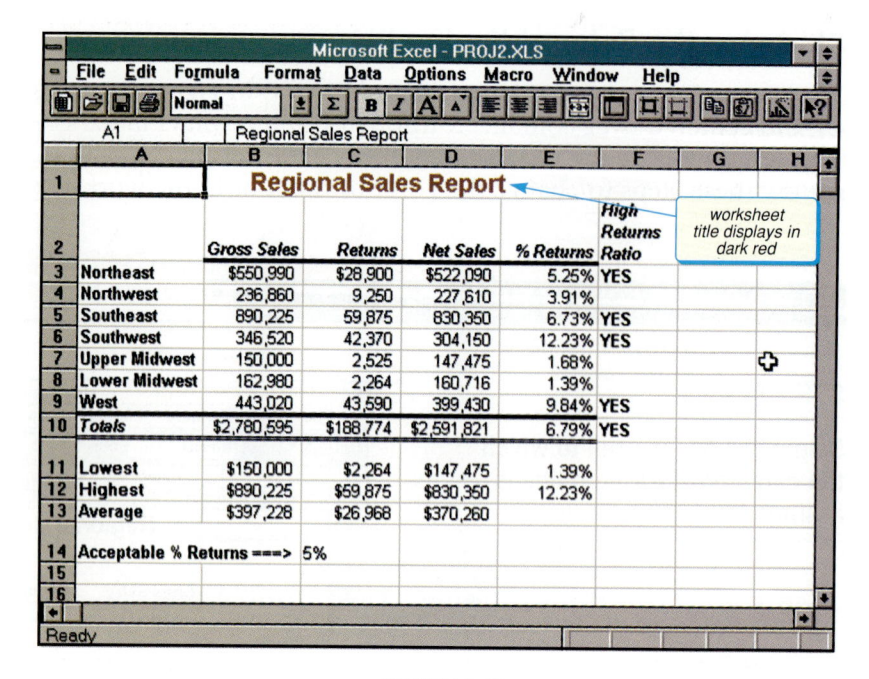

FIGURE 3-40

The steps for changing the color of the font below the column title, High Returns Ratio, in column F are the same as the previous set of steps except for the range and color selections. The following steps select the Font command from the shortcut menu instead of the Format menu.

TO COLOR THE FONT IN THE HIGH RETURNS RATIO COLUMN ▼

STEP 1 ▶

Select the range F3:F10, which includes the font to color.

STEP 2 ▶

With the mouse pointer within the range F3:F10, click the right mouse button.

Excel displays the shortcut menu (Figure 3-41).

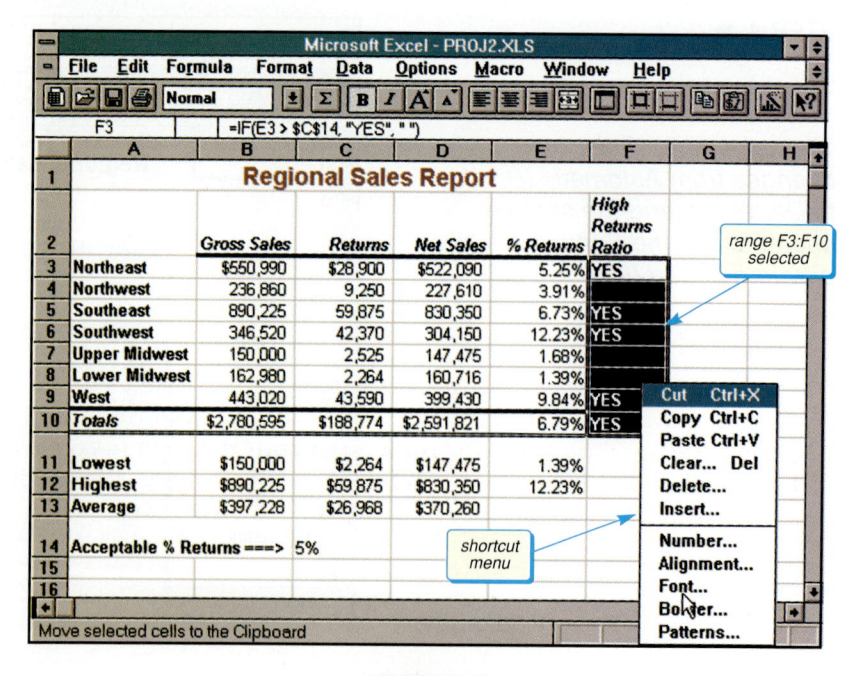

FIGURE 3-41

STEP 3

Choose the Font command from the shortcut menu.

Excel displays the Font menu.

STEP 4 ▶

Click the Color box arrow and point to Dark Blue in the drop-down list of colors. Then select Dark Blue.

The color in the Color box changes from Automatic (Black) to Dark Blue and the sample characters in the Sample box display in dark blue (Figure 3-42).

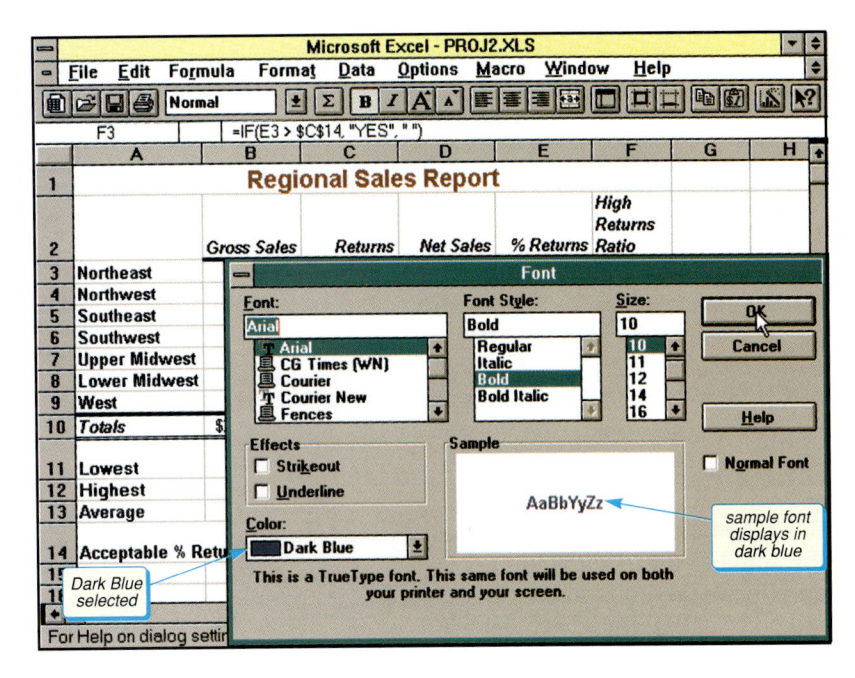

FIGURE 3-42

STEP 5 ▶

Choose the OK button from the Font dialog box. Select any cell in the worksheet.

Excel displays the word YES in the appropriate cells under the column title, High Returns Ratio, using a dark blue color (Figure 3-43).

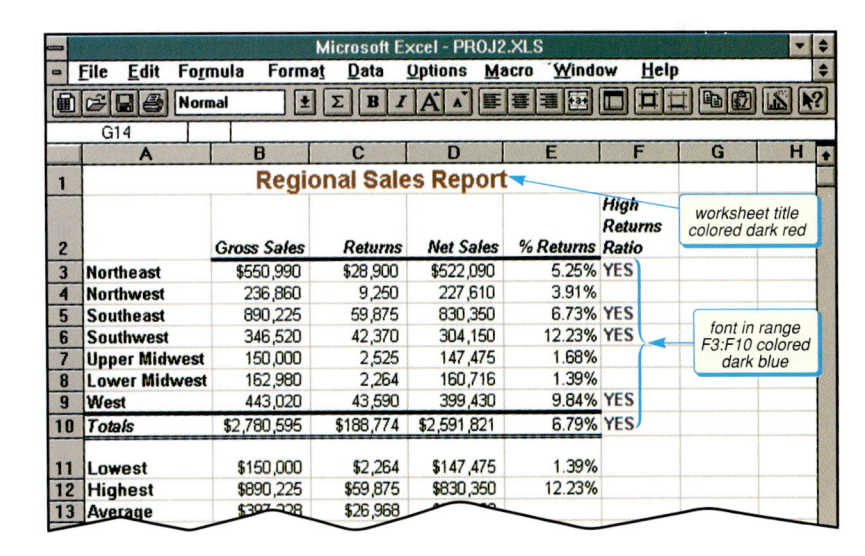

FIGURE 3-43

Changing the Color of the Borders

You change the color of the font using the Font command on the Format menu or shortcut menu. To change the color of the borders of cells, use the Border command on the Format menu or shortcut menu. In Figure 3-2 on page E110, the borders in the ranges B2:F2 and A10:F10 are colored dark red.

Perform the steps on the next page to color the borders in the range B2:F2 and A10:F10.

PROJECT 3 ENHANCING A WORKSHEET AND DRAWING CHARTS

TO CHANGE THE BORDER COLORS OF THE COLUMN HEADINGS

STEP 1 ▶

Select the range B2:F2, which contains the column headings. From the Format menu, choose the Border command.

Excel displays the Border dialog box (Figure 3-44).

STEP 2 ▶

Click the Color box arrow and use the scroll arrow to scroll to the dark red color. Point to the dark red color in the drop-down list of colors.

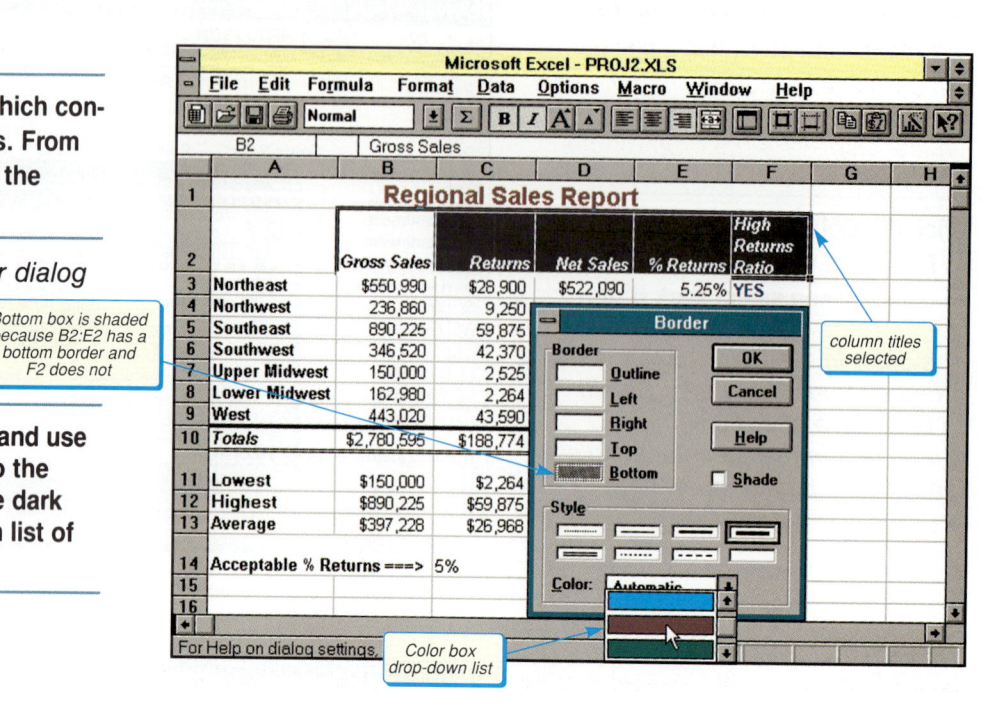

FIGURE 3-44

STEP 3 ▶

Select dark red by clicking the left mouse button. Select Bottom in the Border box. Select regular border style (third one in the top row) from the Style box.

The color in the Color box changes from Automatic to dark red (Figure 3-45).

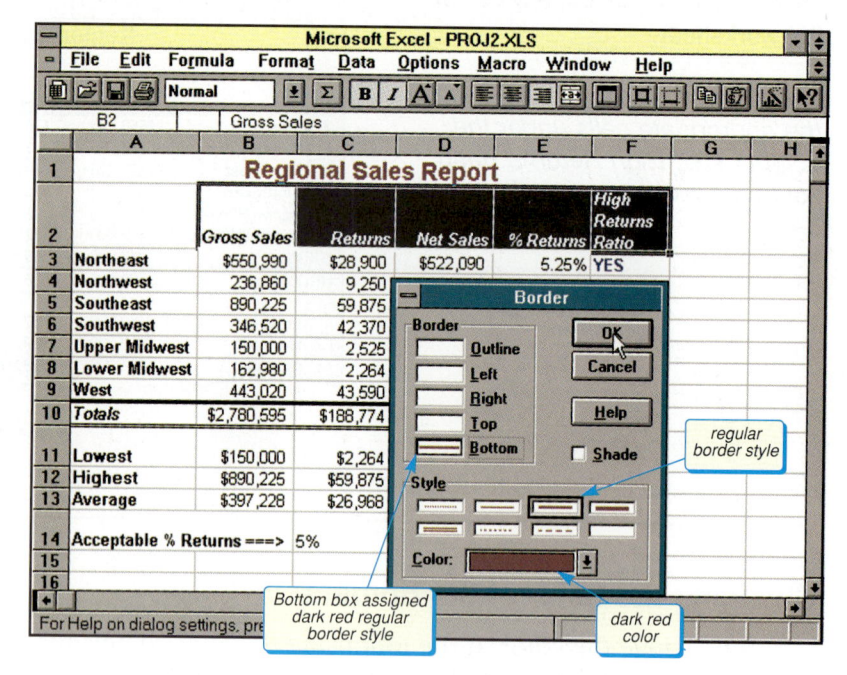

FIGURE 3-45

ADDING COLOR TO A WORKSHEET E139

STEP 4 ▶

Choose the OK button from the Border dialog box. Select any cell in the worksheet.

Excel displays a dark red regular border immediately below the column headings in the range B2:F2 (Figure 3-46).

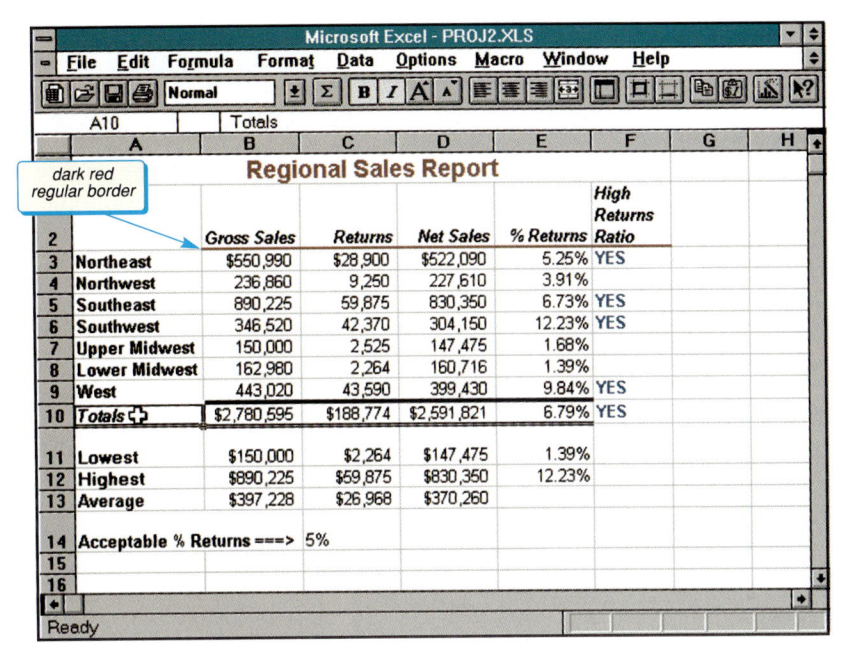

FIGURE 3-46

TO CHANGE THE BORDER COLOR OF THE TOTALS ROW ▼

STEP 1 ▶

Select the range A10:F10, the range to change. Then, from the Format menu, choose the Border command. Click the color box arrow and select the color dark red. Select Top in the Border box. Select the regular border style (third one in the top row) from the Style box. Select Bottom in the Border box. Select the double-line border style (first one in row two) in the Style box.

Excel displays the dark red line in the Top box and the dark red double-line in the Bottom box (Figure 3-47).

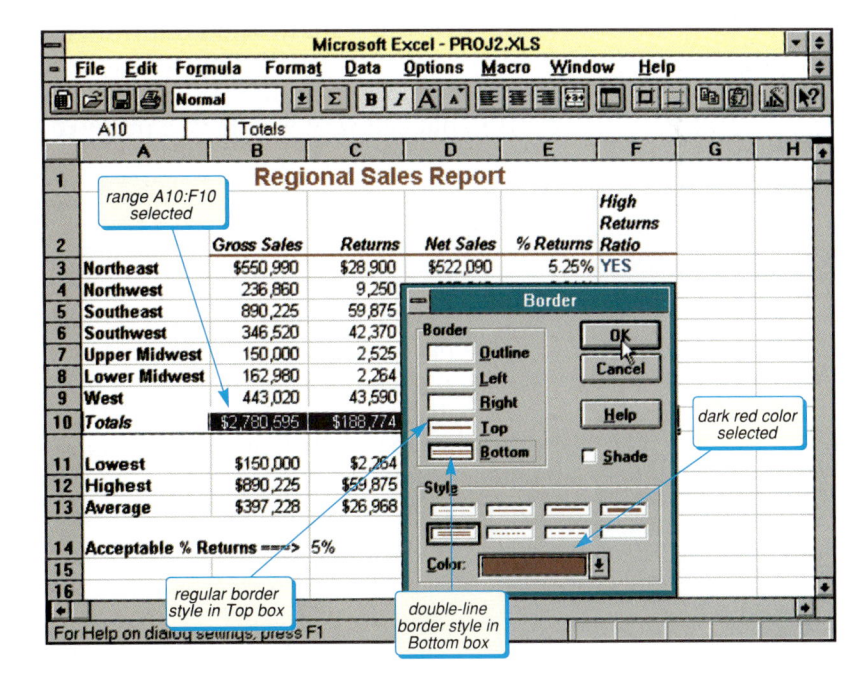

FIGURE 3-47

STEP 2 ▶

Choose the OK button from the Border dialog box. Select any cell in the worksheet.

Excel displays a dark red regular border above and a dark red double-line border below the Totals row in the range A10:F10 (Figure 3-48).

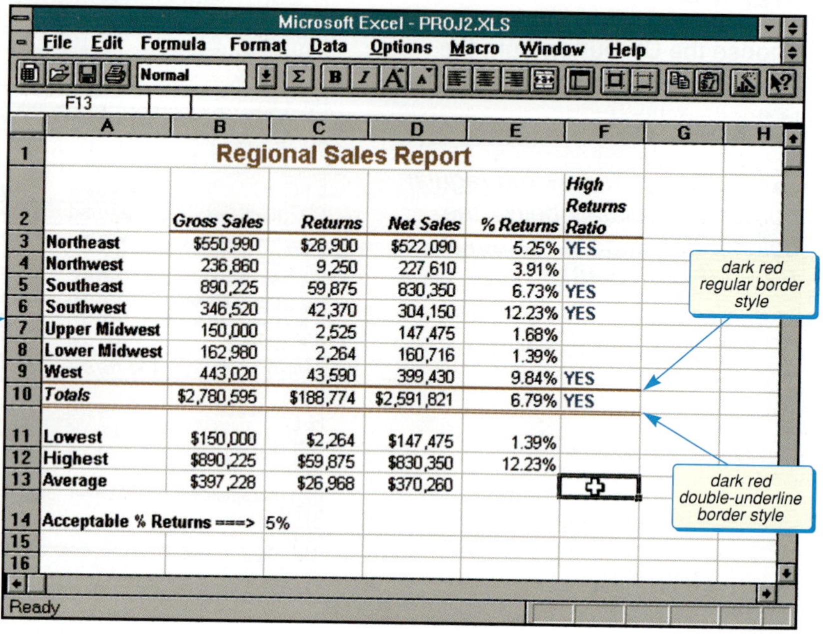

FIGURE 3-48

The formatting of the worksheet is complete. As you can see in Figure 3-48, you can use colors to enhance the appearance of the worksheet and highlight values that you want to stand out from the rest of the worksheet. However, be aware that too much coloring can adversely affect the appearance of the worksheet. Also keep in mind that certain color combinations look pleasing to one person, but can very well have a negative effect on another person.

▶ SAVING A WORKSHEET UNDER A DIFFERENT FILE NAME

This next step involves saving the worksheet under the file name PROJ3.XLS. Notice, however, the name of the worksheet in the title bar at the top of the screen in Figure 3-48 is PROJ2.XLS.

If you click the Save File tool on the Standard toolbar, the worksheet on the screen will replace PROJ2.XLS on disk because the Save File tool does not allow you to change the file name unless you're saving a new worksheet. An alternative save command that does allow you to change the file name is the Save As command on the File menu. Perform these steps to save a worksheet under a new file name.

ADDING A PIE CHART TO THE WORKSHEET   E141

TO SAVE A WORKSHEET USING A DIFFERENT FILE NAME ▼

STEP 1 ▶

From the File menu, choose the Save As command.

Excel displays the Save As dialog box (Figure 3-49). Drive A is the selected drive because PROJ2.XLS was retrieved from drive A at the beginning of this project.

STEP 2

Type `proj3` in the File Name box, and then choose the OK button from the Save As dialog box.

Excel saves the worksheet under the file name PROJ3.XLS.

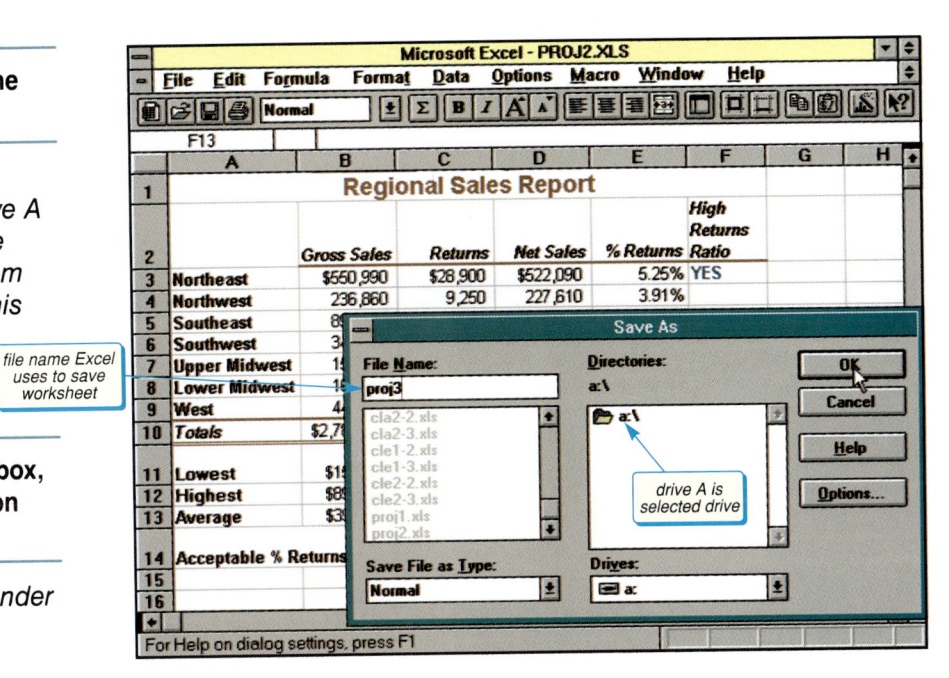

FIGURE 3-49

After the save operation is complete, Excel changes the worksheet name in the title bar at the top of the screen from PROJ2.XLS to PROJ3.XLS. You can immediately continue with the next activity.

▶ ADDING A PIE CHART TO THE WORKSHEET

The next step in this project is to draw the three-dimensional pie chart shown in Figure 3-50 on the next page. A **pie chart** is used to show how 100% of an amount is divided. Each slice (or wedge) of the pie represents a contribution to the whole. The pie chart in Figure 3-50 shows the contribution of each region to the total gross sales.

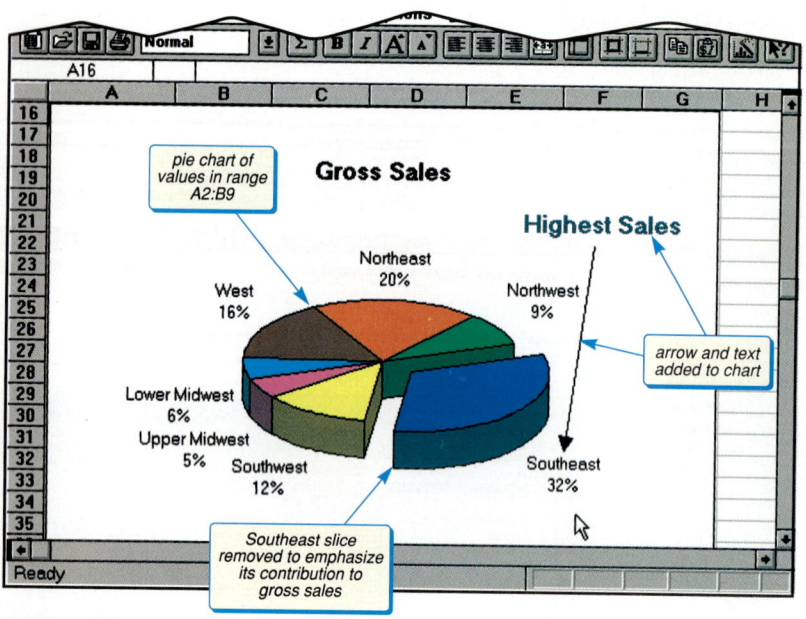

PROJECT 3 ENHANCING A WORKSHEET AND DRAWING CHARTS

FIGURE 3-50

The range in the worksheet to graph is A2:B9 (Figure 3-51). The region names in the range A3:A9 identify the slices. Column A is called **category names**. The range B3:B9 contains the data that will determine the size of the slices in the pie. Column B is called the **data series**. Because there are seven regions, the pie chart has seven slices. The cell immediately above the data series (cell B2) is used as the title of the pie chart.

This project also calls for emphasizing the Southeast region by offsetting its slice from the main portion and adding an arrow and the text Highest Sales. A pie chart with one or more slices offset is called an **exploded pie chart**.

Drawing the Pie Chart

The easiest way to draw a chart in Excel is to use the ChartWizard tool on the Standard toolbar. The ChartWizard tool creates the chart on the worksheet. Because the chart created is on the worksheet, it is called an embedded chart.

You can add an embedded chart anywhere on the worksheet and make the chart location any size you want. The following steps draw the chart directly below the values in the worksheet so that when the worksheet is printed the chart will print on the same page as the values. The chart location size A16:G37 will be used so that the pie chart is approximately the same size as the range of values in the worksheet.

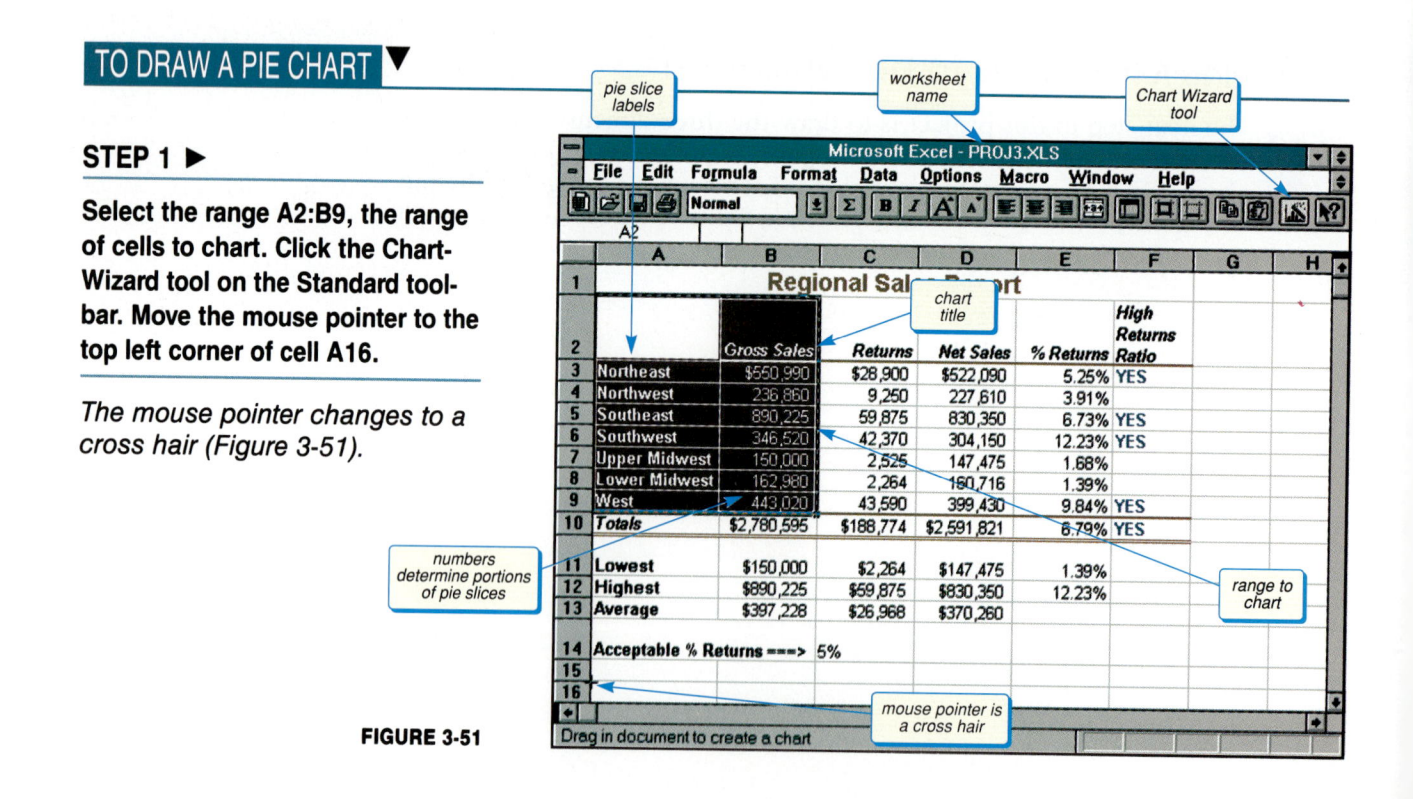

TO DRAW A PIE CHART

STEP 1 ▶

Select the range A2:B9, the range of cells to chart. Click the ChartWizard tool on the Standard toolbar. Move the mouse pointer to the top left corner of cell A16.

The mouse pointer changes to a cross hair (Figure 3-51).

FIGURE 3-51

ADDING A PIE CHART TO THE WORKSHEET **E143**

STEP 2 ▶

Drag to the lower right corner of cell G37.

The dotted line shows the proposed chart location in the worksheet (Figure 3-52).

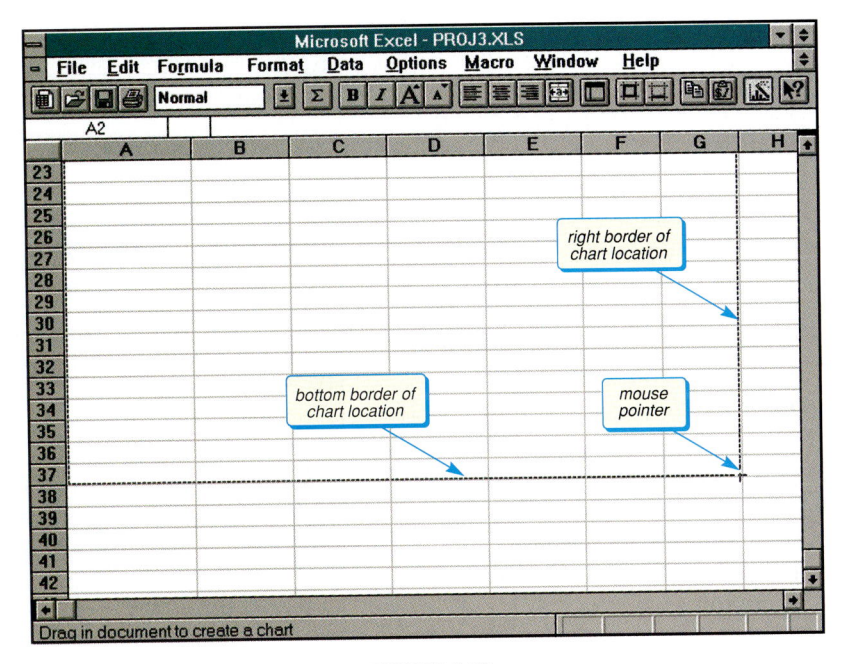

FIGURE 3-52

STEP 3 ▶

Release the left mouse button.

The ChartWizard – Step 1 of 5 dialog box appears (Figure 3-53).

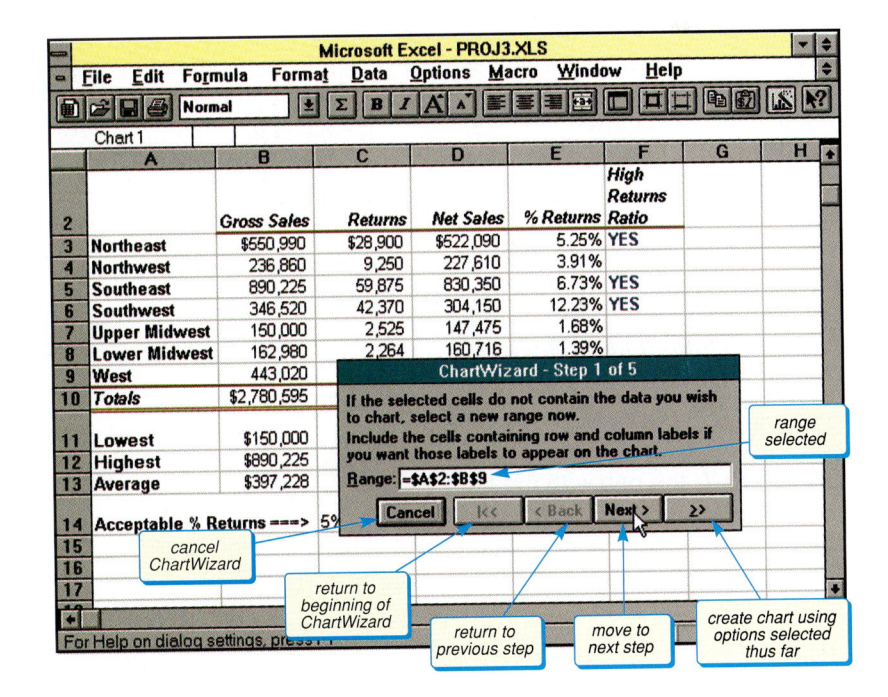

FIGURE 3-53

E144 PROJECT 3 ENHANCING A WORKSHEET AND DRAWING CHARTS

STEP 4 ▶

Choose the Next button from the ChartWizard — Step 1 of 5 dialog box.

The ChartWizard – Step 2 of 5 dialog box appears with fourteen charts to choose from (Figure 3-54). The first eight charts in the dialog box are two-dimensional. The last six charts are three-dimensional.

STEP 5 ▶

Select 3-D Pie, the three-dimensional pie chart in the bottom row.

Excel highlights the selected chart

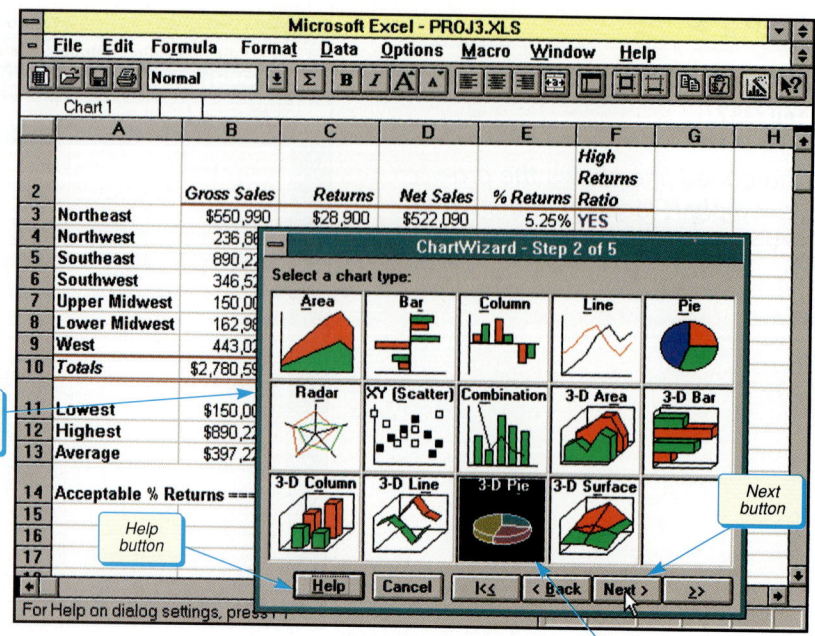

FIGURE 3-54

STEP 6 ▶

Choose the Next button from the ChartWizard — Step 2 of 5 dialog box.

The ChartWizard – Step 3 of 5 dialog box appears with seven different built-in pie chart formats to choose from (Figure 3-55).

STEP 7 ▶

Select box 7, the one with the letters A, B, C, and the percent signs.

Excel highlights the selected chart.

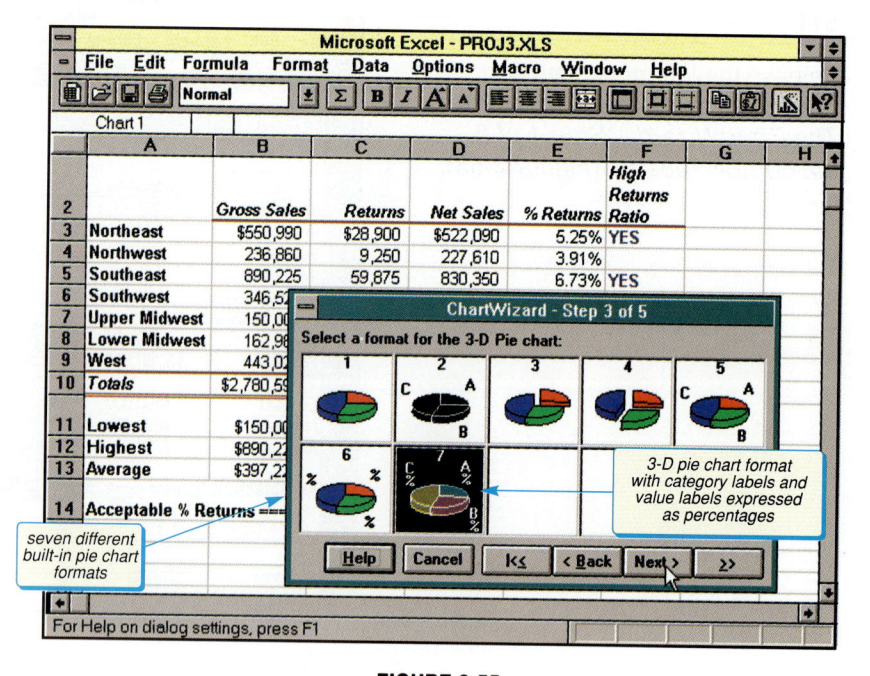

FIGURE 3-55

ADDING A PIE CHART TO THE WORKSHEET   E145

STEP 8 ▶

Choose the Next button from the ChartWizard — Step 3 of 5 dialog box.

The ChartWizard – Step 4 of 5 dialog box appears showing a sample of the proposed pie chart (Figure 3-56). The option buttons in this dialog box give you the opportunity to change the ChartWizard defaults.

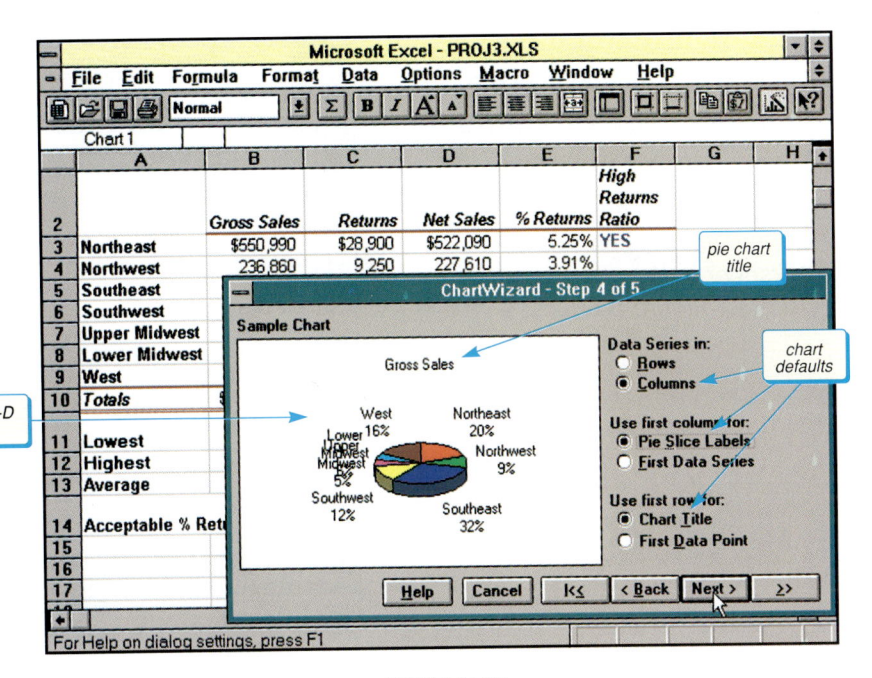

FIGURE 3-56

STEP 9 ▶

Choose the Next button from the ChartWizard — Step 4 of 5 dialog box.

The ChartWizard – Step 5 of 5 dialog box appears on the screen (Figure 3-57). The dialog box gives you the opportunity to add a legend and change the default chart title. The default chart title is cell B2, the one immediately above the data series (B3:B9)

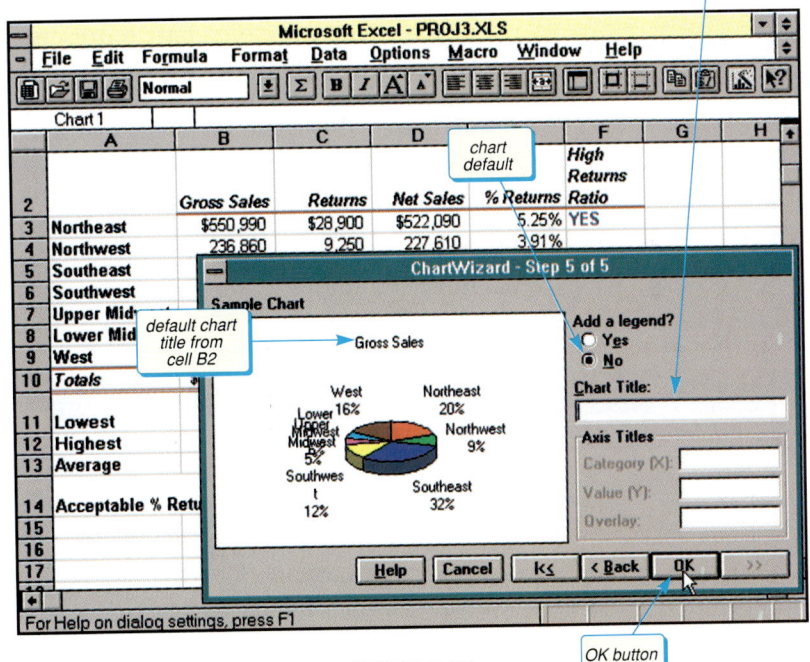

FIGURE 3-57

STEP 10 ▶

Choose the OK button from the ChartWizard – Step 5 of 5 dialog box.

Excel draws the three-dimensional pie chart on the worksheet in the chart location A16:G37 (Figure 3-58).

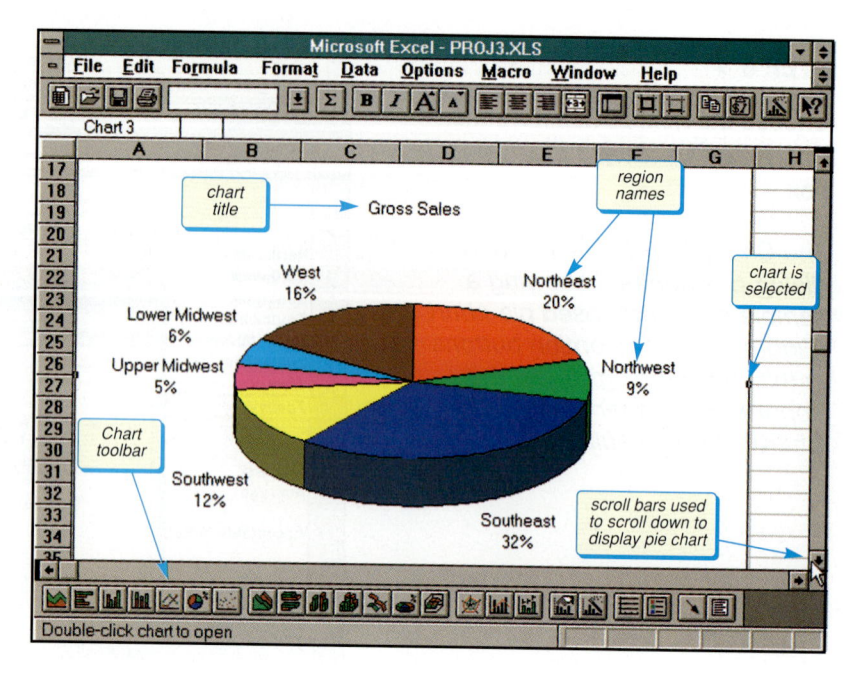

FIGURE 3-58

Each slice of the pie chart represents one of the seven regions. The names of the regions and the percent contribution to the total gross sales display outside the slices. The title Gross Sales at the top of the data series in cell B2 displays immediately above the pie chart as the chart title because of the chart default settings in Figure 3-56 on the previous page.

Excel determines the direction of the data series range (down a column or across a row) on the basis of the selected range. Because the selection for the pie chart is downward (range A2:B9), Excel automatically sets the Data Series in default to Columns as shown in Figure 3-56 on the previous page.

Notice in the five ChartWizard dialog boxes (Figures 3-53 through Figure 3-57) that you can return to the previous ChartWizard dialog box, return to the beginning of the ChartWizard, or create the chart with the options selected thus far while any one of the five ChartWizard dialog boxes is on the screen. Table 3-5 summarizes the functions of the buttons in the ChartWizard dialog boxes illustrated in those figures.

▶ **TABLE 3-5**

BUTTON	FUNCTION
Next >	Move to the next step.
< Back	Return to the previous step.
>>	Create the chart using the options selected thus far.
|<<	Return to the beginning of the ChartWizard.
Cancel	Cancel ChartWizard and return to the worksheet.
Help	Display help about the options and buttons.

▶ **ENHANCING THE PIE CHART**

Excel allows you to enhance (format and edit) any item in the pie chart, including the chart title, a slice, a slice title, and the chart itself. You can also add arrows and text to highlight those parts of the chart you want to emphasize.

Opening an Embedded Chart

To edit or format an embedded chart, you must first open it in its own window. Perform these steps to open a chart in its own window.

TO OPEN AN EMBEDDED CHART IN ITS OWN WINDOW ▼

STEP 1

Position the mouse pointer within the chart location in the worksheet.

STEP 2 ▶

Double-click the left mouse button.

Excel opens a window for the embedded chart (Figure 3-59).

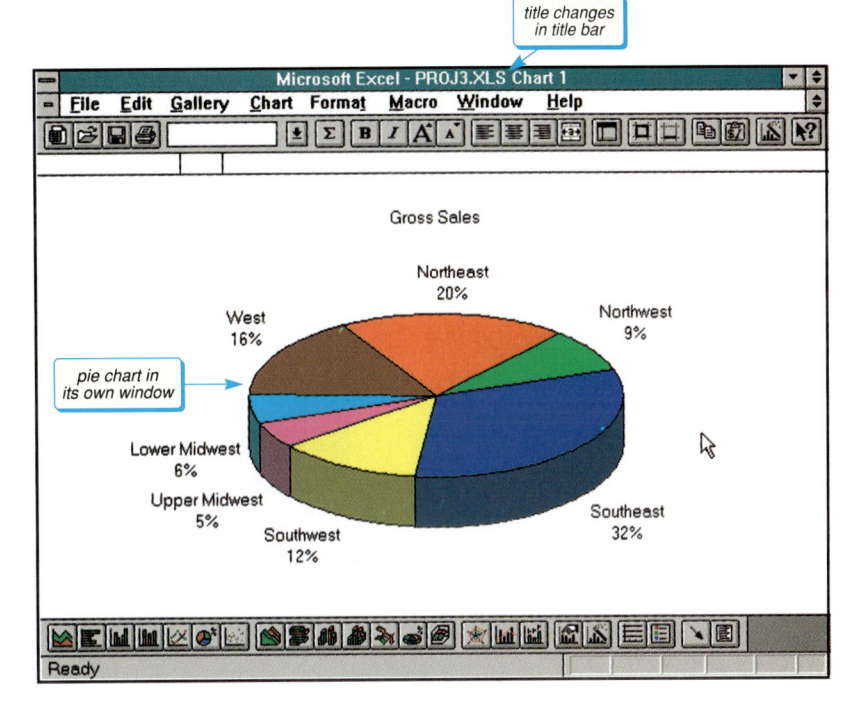

FIGURE 3-59

Compare Figure 3-59 to Figure 3-58. The makeup of the **chart window** has changed significantly. The title in the title bar is PROJ3.XLS Chart 1 rather than PROJ3.XLS. The menu bar includes new menu names such as Gallery and Chart. Where the active cell reference once displayed in the formula bar, a reference to the chart item selected displays. At the bottom of the window, the Chart toolbar displays. Finally, the worksheet is not directly accessible in this window. To access the worksheet, you must select PROJ3.XLS from the Window menu. An example of switching from the chart window back to the worksheet window follows shortly.

Bolding and Enlarging the Chart Title

Once the chart is in its own window, you can select those chart items you want to enhance. **Chart items** in the pie chart include the entire pie chart, the chart title, the pie slices, and the slice titles. Click the chart item or use the arrow keys to select the chart item you want to modify. When you use the arrow keys, Excel cycles through the chart items.

Perform the steps on the next page to bold and enlarge the chart title.

TO BOLD AND ENLARGE THE CHART TITLE

STEP 1

Click the chart title Gross Sales.

Excel surrounds the chart title with white selection squares (also called handles).

STEP 2 ▶

Click the Bold tool on the Standard toolbar, and click the Increase Font Size tool on the Standard toolbar twice.

Excel bolds and enlarges the title font size (Figure 3-60).

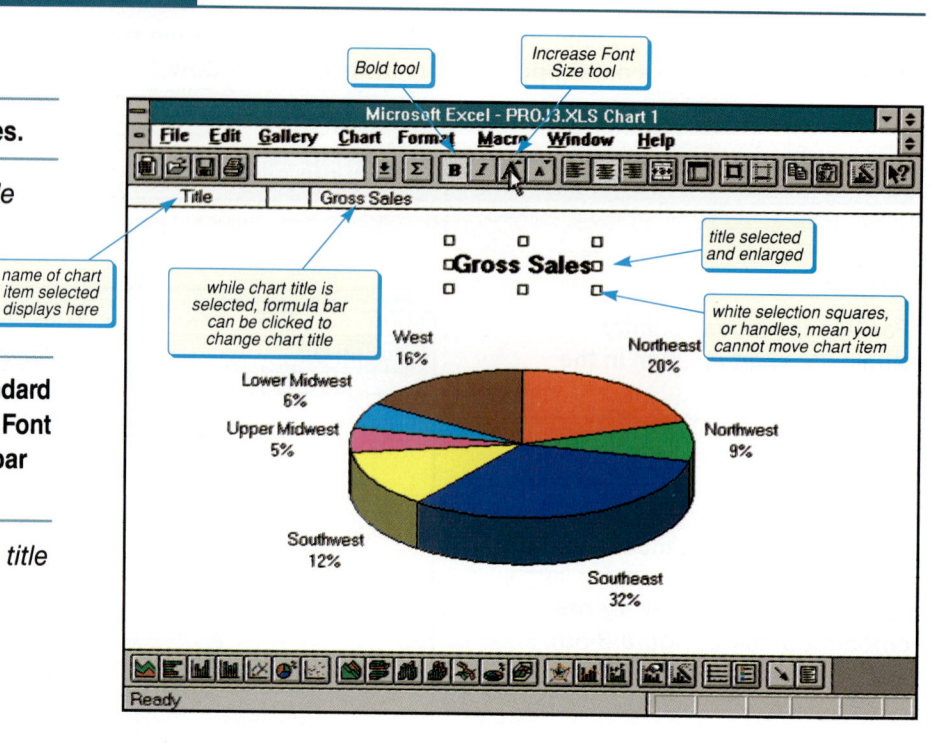

FIGURE 3-60

To remove the selection from the chart title, press the ESC key or click inside the chart window where there is no other chart item.

When you select a chart item, Excel surrounds it with white selection squares or black selection squares, also called **handles**. Chart items marked with **white selection squares** can be formatted with commands, but cannot be moved or resized. Chart items marked with **black selection squares** can be formatted, moved, and sized. If the chart item you select is text, such as the chart title in the previous example, then Excel displays the text in the formula bar in case you want to change the wording (Figure 3-60).

Exploding the Pie Chart

The next step is to emphasize the slice representing the Southeast region by offsetting it from the rest of the pie. This is called exploding the pie chart. Perform the steps at the top of the next page to offset a slice of the pie chart.

TO EXPLODE THE PIE CHART ▼

STEP 1 ▶

Click the dark blue Southeast slice to select it.

Excel surrounds the Southeast slice with black selection squares (Figure 3-61).

STEP 2 ▶

Drag the slice to the desired position, and release the left mouse button.

Excel redraws the pie chart with the Southeast region slice offset from the rest of the pie chart.

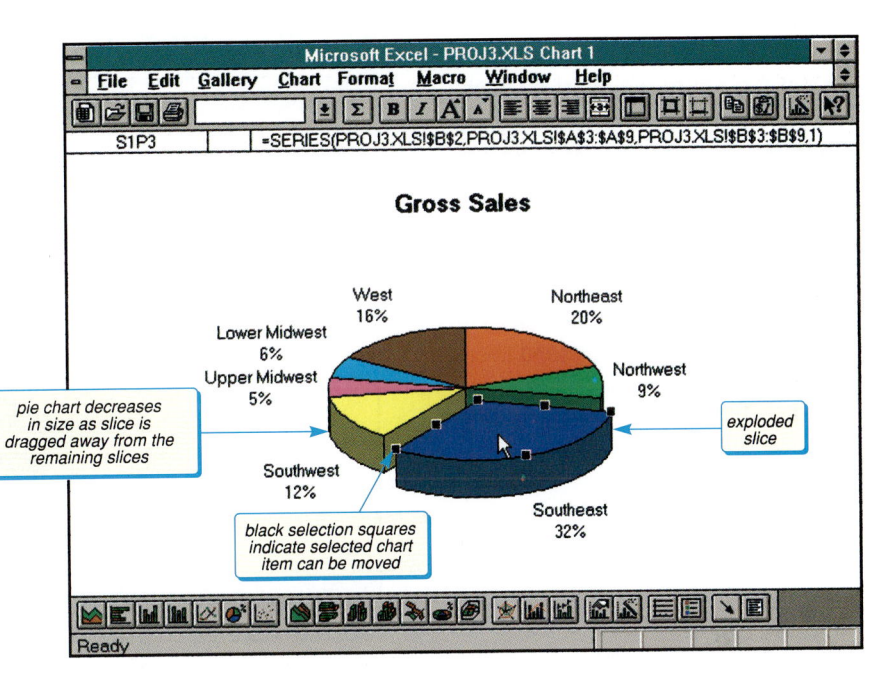

FIGURE 3-61

To remove the selection, press the ESC key or click inside the chart window where there is no other chart item.

Although you can offset as many slices as you want, notice that as you drag a slice away from the main portion of the pie chart, the slices become smaller. If you compare Figure 3-60 to Figure 3-61, you can see that by offsetting one slice, the pie chart becomes significantly smaller. If you offset additional slices, the pie chart becomes too small to have an impact on the reader.

Rotating the Pie Chart

In a three-dimensional chart, you can change the view to better display the section of the chart you are trying to emphasize. Excel allows you to control the rotation angle, elevation, perspective, height, and angle of the axes by using the **3-D View command** in the Format menu or shortcut menu.

To obtain a better view of the offset of the Southeast region slice, you can rotate the pie chart 30 degrees to the left. The **rotation angle** of a pie chart is defined by the line that divides the West and Northeast region slices (Figure 3-61). Excel initially draws a pie chart with one of the dividing lines pointing to 12:00 (or zero degrees).

TO ROTATE THE PIE CHART

STEP 1 ▶

Select the entire pie chart by clicking anywhere in the window where there is no chart item. Next, select the Format menu in the chart window.

You know the entire pie chart is selected when the white selection squares display around the border of the window (Figure 3-62).

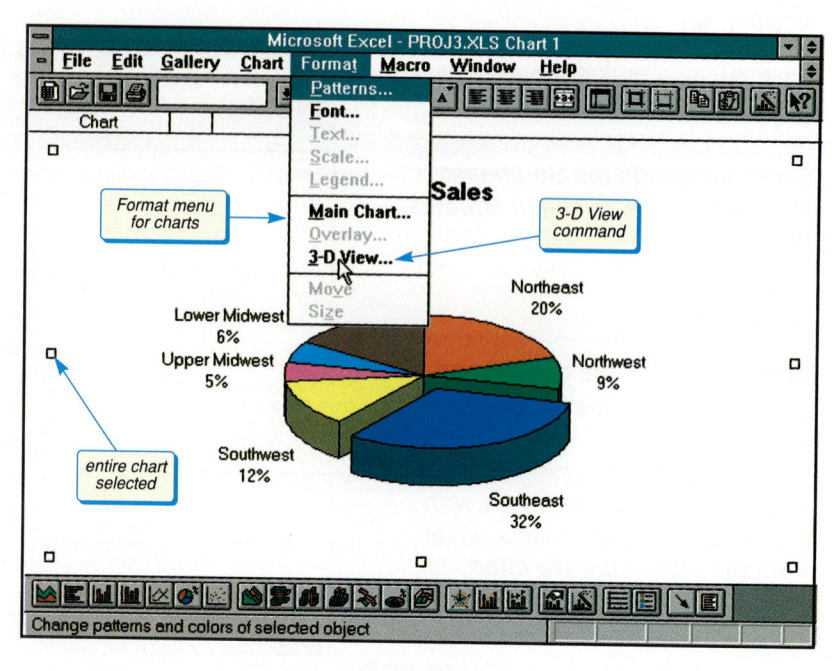

FIGURE 3-62

STEP 2 ▶

Choose the 3-D View command.

The 3-D View dialog box displays (Figure 3-63).

STEP 3 ▶

Click the Rotate left arrow button (the one with the arrow pointing to the left) until the Rotation box displays 330.

Excel displays a sample of the rotated pie chart in the dialog box (Figure 3-63).

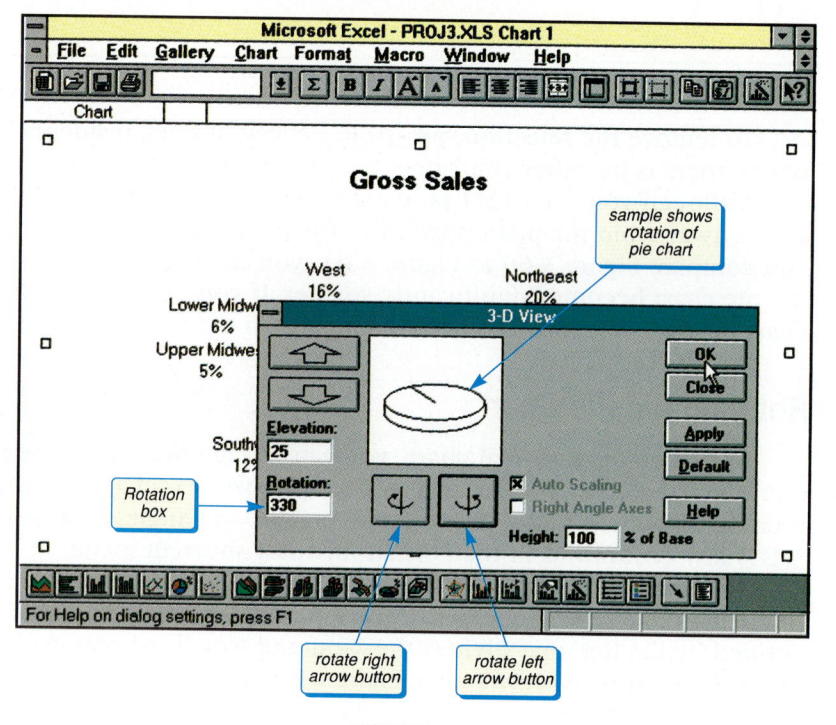

FIGURE 3-63

ENHANCING THE PIE CHART **E151**

STEP 4 ▶

Choose the OK button from the 3-D View dialog box.

Excel displays the pie chart rotated to the left (Figure 3-64).

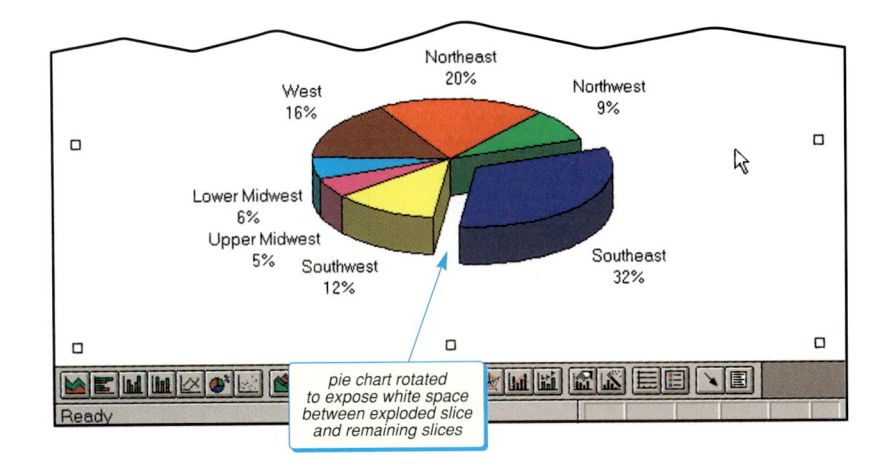

FIGURE 3-64

Compare Figure 3-64 to Figure 3-62 on the previous page. The offset of the Southeast region is more apparent in Figure 3-64 because the pie chart has been rotated to the left to expose the white space between the main portion of the pie and the Southeast slice.

Besides controlling the rotation angle, additional buttons and boxes in the 3-D View dialog box (Figure 3-63 on the previous page) allow you to control the elevation and height of the pie chart. When you change characteristics, Excel always redraws the pie chart in the small window of the 3-D View dialog box.

Adding a Chart Arrow

You can add an arrow to the chart and point it at any chart item to emphasize, or *call out*, a chart item. To add the arrow, you click the **Arrow tool** ( ) on the Chart toolbar at the bottom of the chart window. Excel immediately adds an arrow and points it at the center of the pie chart. To add a chart arrow, perform the steps listed below and on the next page.

TO ADD A CHART ARROW ▼

STEP 1 ▶

Click the Arrow tool on the Chart toolbar at the bottom of the chart window.

Excel adds an arrow and points it at the center of the pie chart. The arrow extends to the upper left corner of the window (Figure 3-65). Excel automatically adds black selection squares to both ends of the arrow, which means it can be moved to any location in the window.

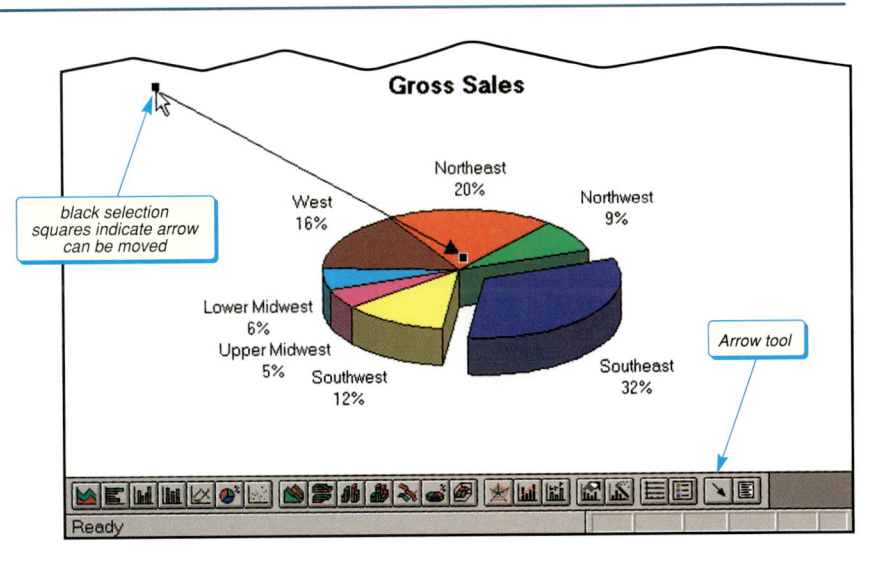

FIGURE 3-65

PROJECT 3   ENHANCING A WORKSHEET AND DRAWING CHARTS

STEP 2 ▶

Drag the handle at the left end of the arrow above and to the right of the pie chart (Figure 3-66).

STEP 3 ▶

Drag the handle on the arrowhead at the center of the pie chart to the title Southeast.

The arrow points to the slice title Southeast (Figure 3-66).

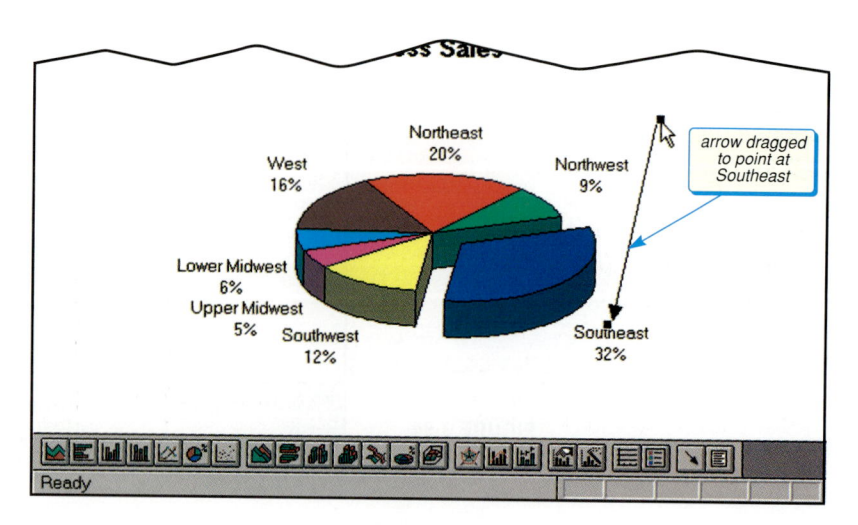

FIGURE 3-66

To remove the selection from the arrow, press the ESC key. You can add as many arrows as you want to a chart. However, more than two arrows tend to clutter the chart. There are also commands in the Format menu that allow you to control the color and **line weight** as well as the style, width, and length of the arrowhead.

Adding Chart Text

Excel automatically adds some text to a chart, such as the chart title, the slice titles, and percents. You can add even more text to clarify or emphasize a chart item. The next step in this project is to add the text, Highest Sales, immediately above the arrow. Follow these steps to add text to the chart and format the text.

TO ADD AND FORMAT TEXT ▼

STEP 1 ▶

Click the Text Box tool (📄) on the Chart toolbar at the bottom of the chart window.

Excel displays the word Text with black selection squares in the middle of the pie chart (Figure 3-67).

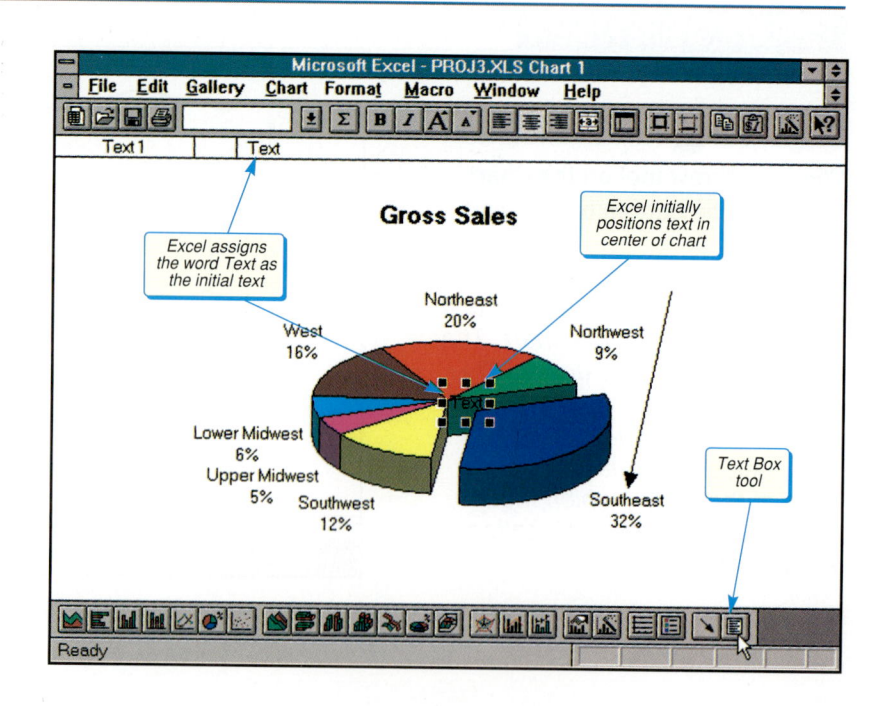

FIGURE 3-67

ENHANCING THE PIE CHART E153

STEP 2 ▶

Drag the text above the end of the arrow pointing at Southeast. Drag across the word Text in the formula bar and type `Highest Sales` to replace the word Text. Click the enter box or press the ENTER key.

Excel displays the text, Highest Sales, within the black selection squares (Figure 3-68).

STEP 3 ▶

Click the Bold tool on the Standard toolbar, and click the Increase Font Size tool on the Standard toolbar twice.

Excel bolds and enlarges the text, Highest Sales, to 14 points (Figure 3-68).

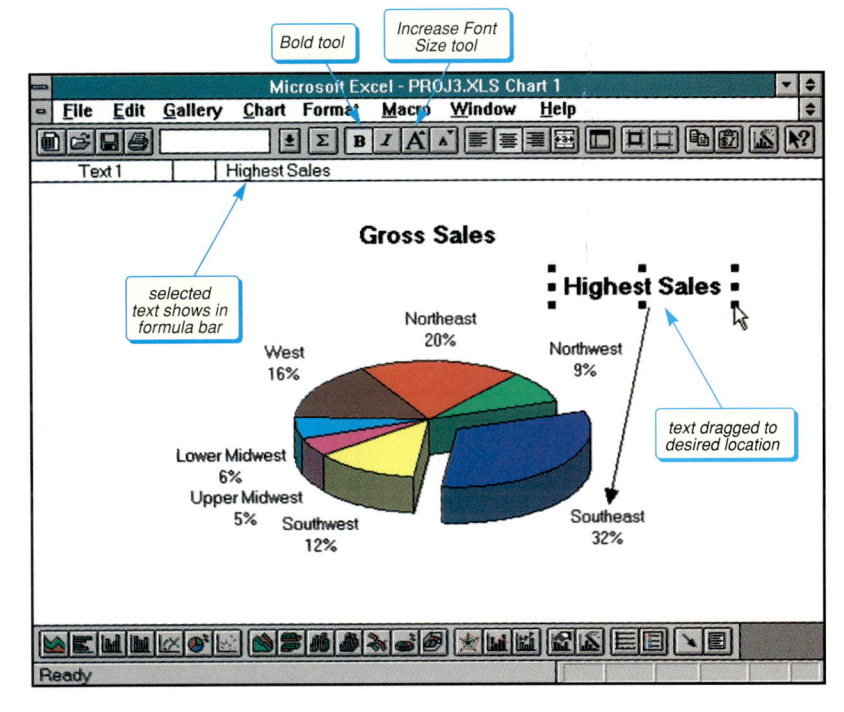

FIGURE 3-68

STEP 4 ▶

From the Format menu, choose the Font command.

The Font dialog box displays (Figure 3-69).

STEP 5 ▶

In the Font dialog box, select the color Dark Blue in the Color box.

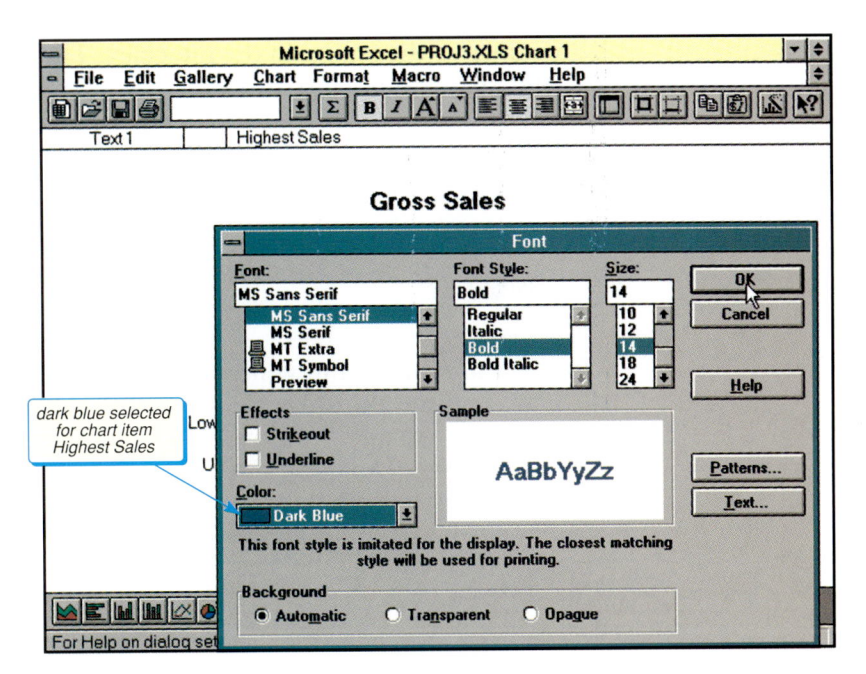

FIGURE 3-69

E154 PROJECT 3 ENHANCING A WORKSHEET AND DRAWING CHARTS

STEP 6 ▶

Choose the OK button. Press the ESC key to remove any selection.

Excel displays the bold and enlarged text, Highest Sales, in dark blue above the arrow (Figure 3-70).

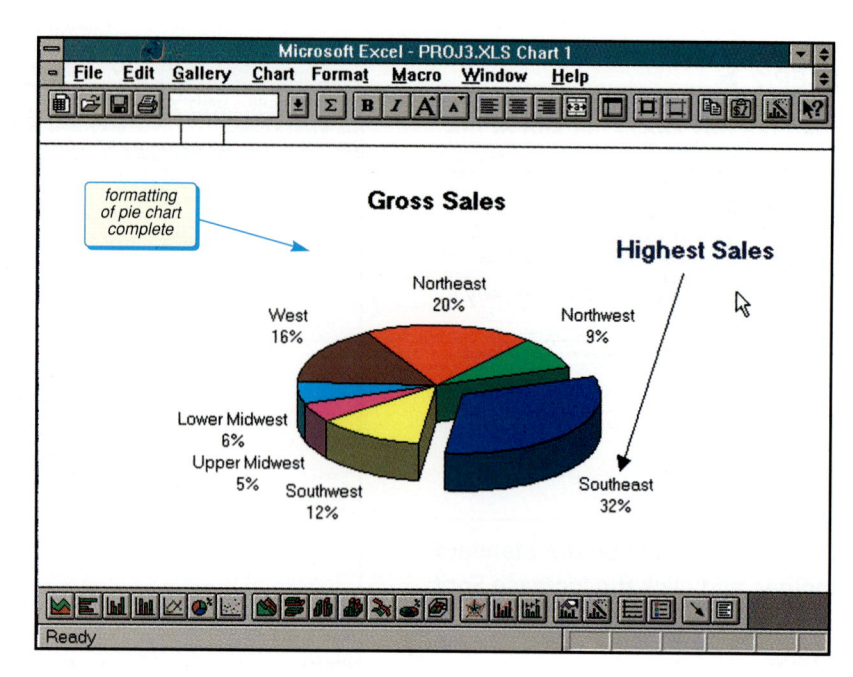

FIGURE 3-70

The offset of the slice, the text, and the arrow pointing at Southeast clearly emphasize the region in the pie chart. The dark blue color is used for the text, Highest Sales, because it is the same as the color of the Southeast slice.

▶ SWITCHING WINDOWS

With the pie chart complete, the next step is to switch from the chart window to the worksheet window. Excel allows you to switch from window to window, providing easy access to all windows developed for an Excel worksheet.

You switch from window to window by choosing the title you want to display from the **Window menu**. You should note that once you have created a chart in a separate window, you should not use the ChartWizard on the Standard toolbar to return to the chart. The ChartWizard is used to create new charts. Always use the Window menu to return to the chart.

To switch from the chart window to the worksheet window, perform the steps on the following page.

TO SWITCH WINDOWS

STEP 1 ▶

Select the Window menu, and point to PROJ3.XLS.

The check mark to the left of PROJ3.XLS Chart 1 indicates that it is the active window (Figure 3-71).

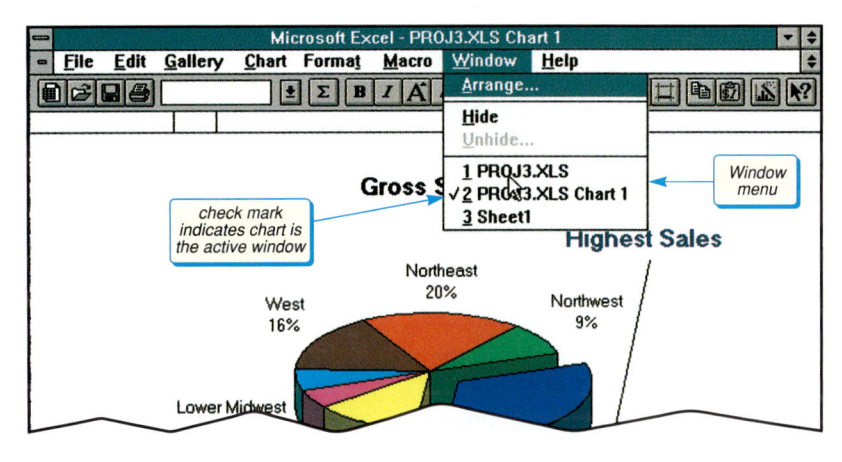

FIGURE 3-71

STEP 2 ▶

Choose PROJ3.XLS. If necessary, use the scroll arrow to scroll to the pie chart on the worksheet window.

Excel opens the PROJ3.XLS worksheet window with the embedded pie chart formatted (Figure 3-72).

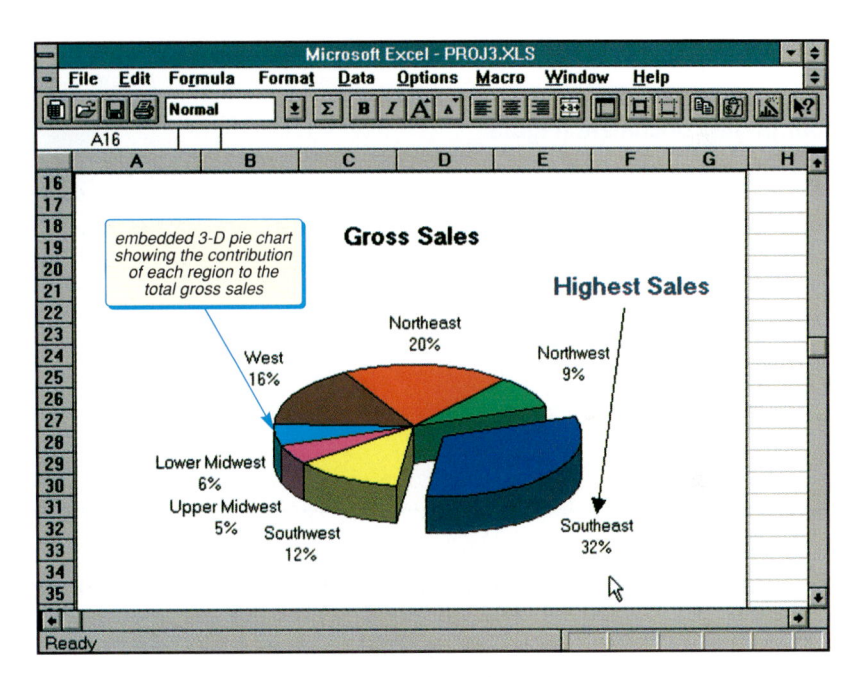

FIGURE 3-72

You can see from Figure 3-72 that all the changes made in the chart window are in the embedded pie chart. At any time, you can switch back to the pie chart document by double-clicking the embedded pie chart or by choosing the pie chart from the Window menu. This capability of being able to switch back and forth between the worksheet and the chart allows you to fine tune the pie chart until it meets with your approval. The next step is to save and print the worksheet.

TO SAVE AND PRINT THE WORKSHEET

STEP 1

Click the Save File tool in the Standard toolbar to save the worksheet with the embedded pie chart using the file name PROJ3.XLS.

STEP 2

With cell gridlines turned off in the Page Setup dialog box and the printer ready, click the Print tool on the Standard toolbar.

STEP 3 ▶

When the printer stops, retrieve your printed document (Figure 3-73).

Regional Sales Report

	Gross Sales	Returns	Net Sales	% Returns	High Returns Ratio
Northeast	$550,990	$28,900	$522,090	5.25%	YES
Northwest	236,860	9,250	227,610	3.91%	
Southeast	890,225	59,875	830,350	6.73%	YES
Southwest	346,520	42,370	304,150	12.23%	YES
Upper Midwest	150,000	2,525	147,475	1.68%	
Lower Midwest	162,980	2,264	160,716	1.39%	
West	443,020	43,590	399,430	9.84%	YES
Totals	$2,780,595	$188,774	$2,591,821	6.79%	YES
Lowest	$150,000	$2,264	$147,475	1.39%	
Highest	$890,225	$59,875	$830,350	12.23%	
Average	$397,228	$26,968	$370,260		

Acceptable % Returns ===>   5%

Gross Sales

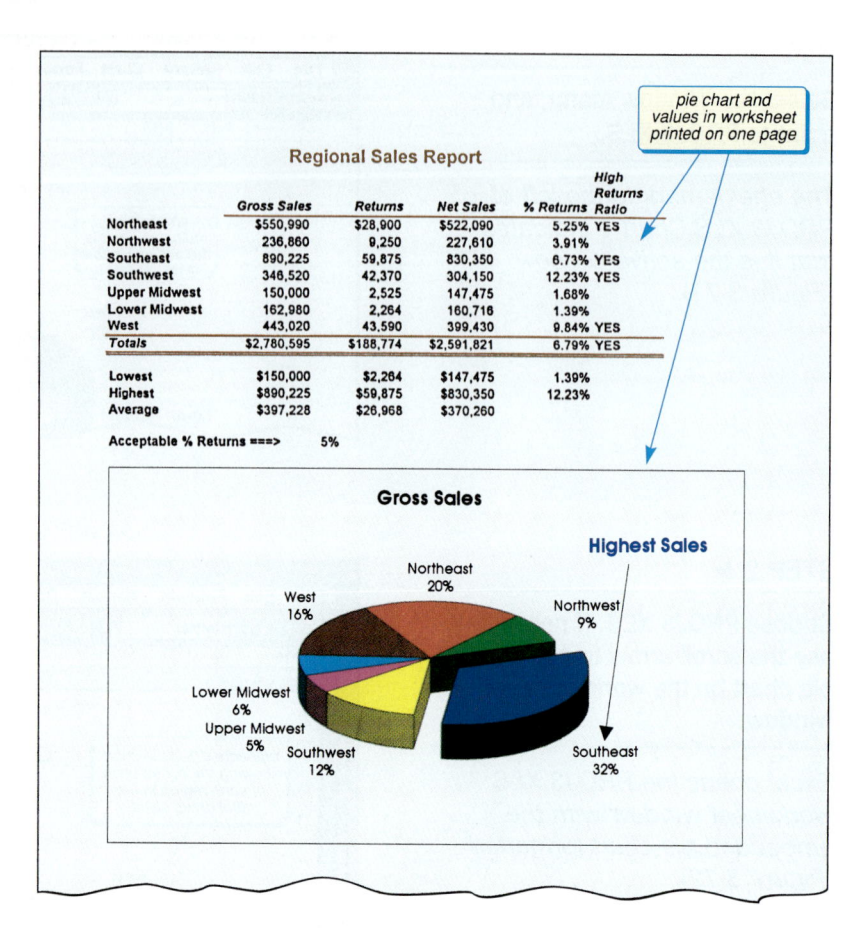

- Northeast 20%
- Northwest 9%
- Southeast 32% (Highest Sales)
- Southwest 12%
- Upper Midwest 5%
- Lower Midwest 6%
- West 16%

pie chart and values in worksheet printed on one page

FIGURE 3-73

The printout of the worksheet with the embedded pie chart in Figure 3-73 clearly shows that the Southeast region has the greatest gross sales. It is much easier to use the pie chart to describe the gross sales breakdown than it is to sort through the numbers in the second column of the worksheet.

▶ HIDING THE PIE CHART

With Excel you have the option of hiding the pie chart so that it does not display on the worksheet or print as part of a printout as shown in Figure 3-73. Once the pie chart is hidden, you can redisplay it when needed.

TO HIDE THE PIE CHART

STEP 1 ▶

From the Options menu, choose the Display command.

The Display Options dialog box displays (Figure 3-74).

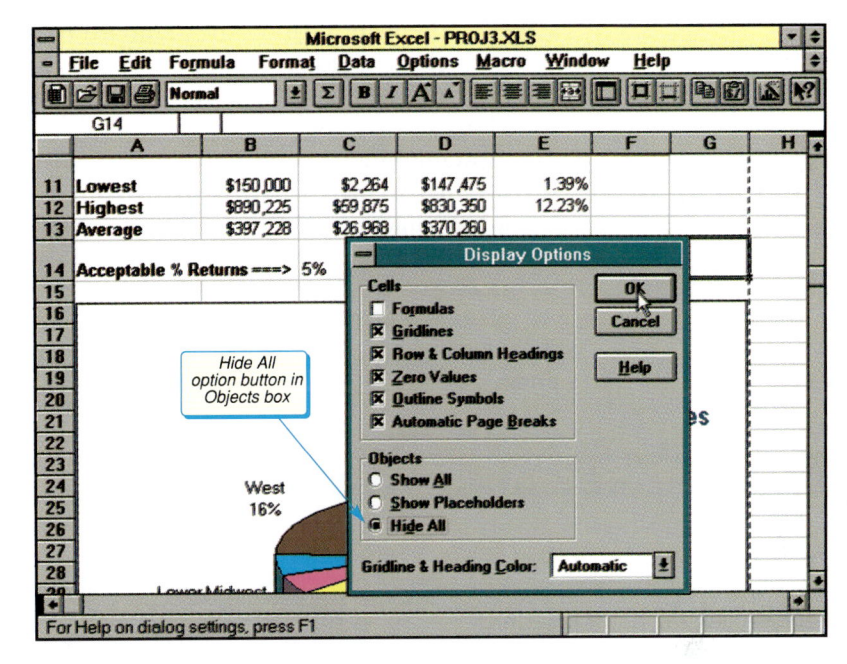

FIGURE 3-74

STEP 2 ▶

Select the Hide All option button in the Objects box, and choose the OK button from the Display Options dialog box.

The pie chart no longer displays on the worksheet (Figure 3-75).

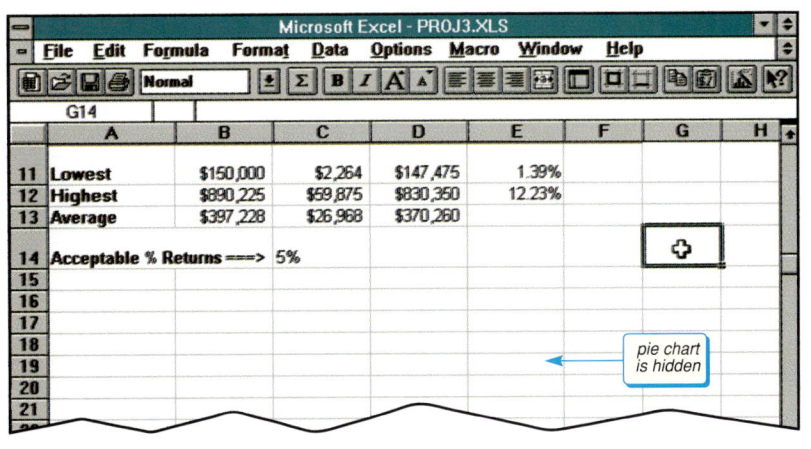

FIGURE 3-75

If you print the worksheet with the pie chart hidden, then the printout contains only the values (top half of Figure 3-73). If the pie chart is hidden and you want it to display and be included in printouts, select the Show All option button in the Display Options dialog box.

TO SHOW A HIDDEN CHART

Step 1: From the Options menu, choose the Display command.
Step 2: Select the Show All option button in the Objects box.
Step 3: Choose the OK button in the Display Options dialog box.

The chart displays in the worksheet as shown in Figure 3-72 on page E155.

▶ Printing the Pie Chart Separately from the Worksheet

You can print an embedded chart separate from the worksheet by using the Print tool on the Standard toolbar or the Print command from the chart window File menu when the chart is in a window by itself. You open an embedded chart in its own window by double-clicking within the chart location.

You might also want to print the chart in landscape orientation because the three-dimensional chart is wider than it is high. Thus far, all the printouts in this book have had a portrait orientation. **Portrait orientation** means the printout is across the page width of 8.5 inches. **Landscape orientation** means the printout is across the page length of 11 inches.

The following steps show how to open an embedded chart in its own window, change the page orientation from portrait to landscape, and print the chart.

TO PRINT A CHART SEPARATELY FROM THE WORKSHEET ▼

STEP 1

Double-click the chart location.

The pie chart displays in its own window.

STEP 2 ▶

Select the File menu.

The File menu displays (Figure 3-76).

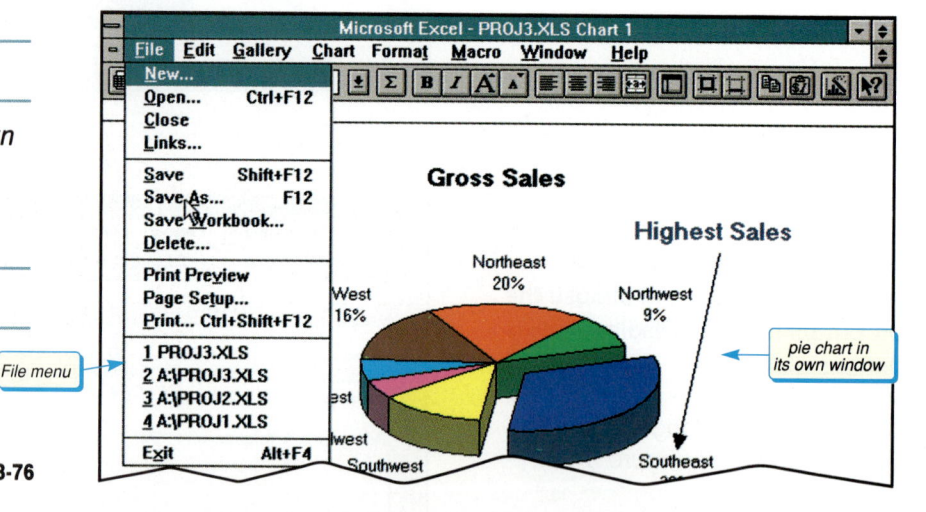

FIGURE 3-76

STEP 3 ▶

Choose the Page Setup command.

Excel displays the Page Setup dialog box (Figure 3-77).

STEP 4 ▶

Select the Landscape option button in the Orientation box.

STEP 5

Choose the OK button in the Page Setup dialog box.

FIGURE 3-77

STEP 6 ▼

Ready the printer according to the printer instructions, and click the Print tool on the Standard toolbar.

Excel sends the pie chart to the printer. When the printer stops, retrieve the printout (Figure 3-78).

landscape orientation

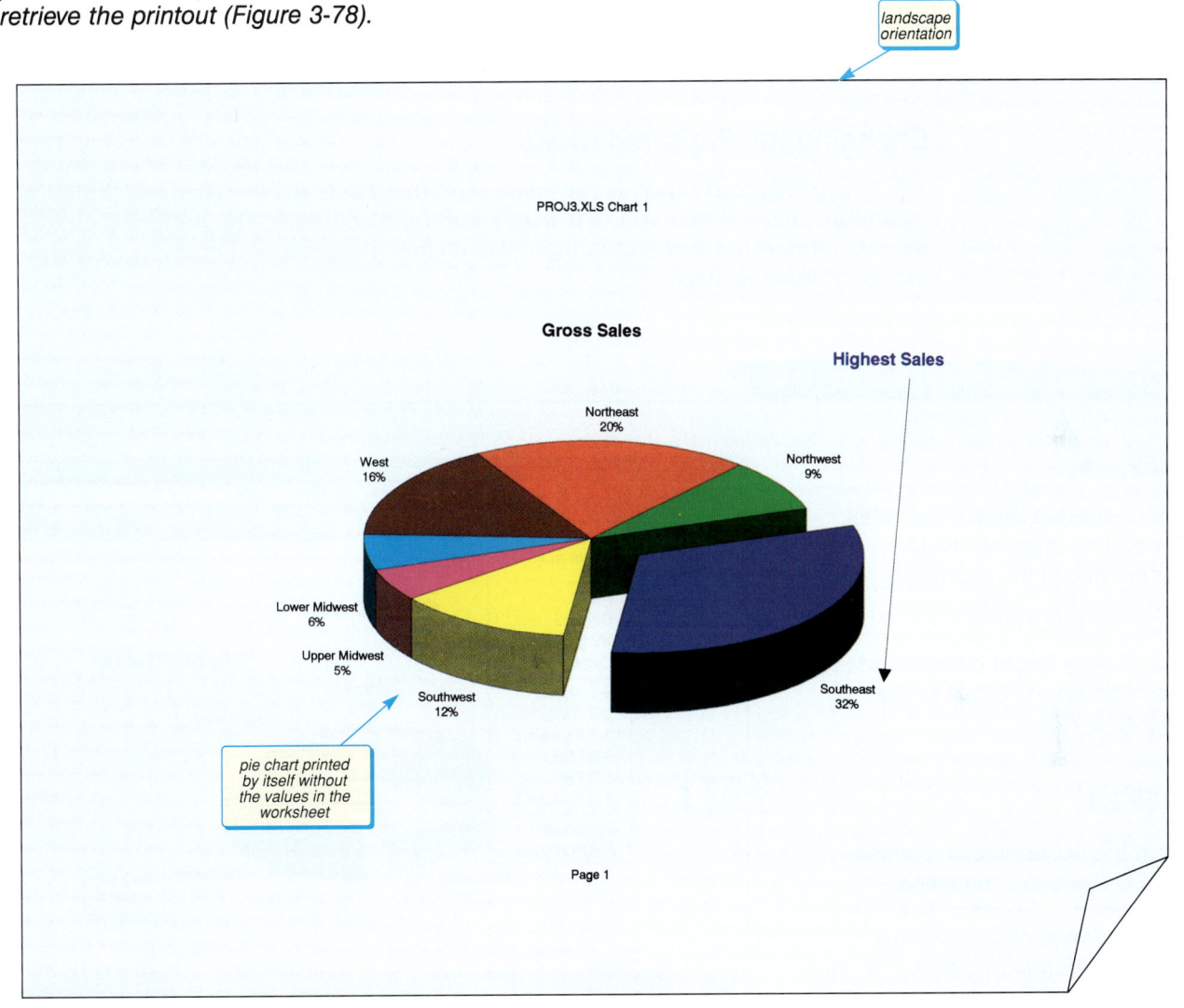

pie chart printed by itself without the values in the worksheet

FIGURE 3-78

▶ THE GALLERY AND CHART MENUS

When you have a chart open in its own window, the menu bar includes the Gallery and Chart menus. You use the **Gallery menu** to choose the type of chart you want. The charts listed in the Gallery menu correspond to the tools on the Chart toolbar. The major difference between using the Gallery menu and Chart toolbar is that if you choose a chart type from the Gallery menu, and a dialog box displays a pictorial list of the built-in formats. You can then choose the chart type built-in format you want to use. If you choose a chart type by using the Chart toolbar, Excel draws the chart using the built-in format selected the last time the chart type was drawn.

Changing the Preferred Chart

The **preferred chart** is the chart type that Excel draws when you initially create the chart. When you first load Excel on a computer, the preferred chart is the two-dimensional column chart. You change the preferred chart by performing the following steps.

TO CHANGE THE PREFERRED CHART ▼

STEP 1 ▶

With a chart in the window, click the desired chart on the Chart toolbar or choose the chart type you want from the Gallery menu.

The Gallery menu corresponds to the tools on the Chart toolbar (Figure 3-79).

STEP 2 ▶

From the Gallery menu, choose the Set Preferred command.

Excel changes the preferred chart to the one displaying on the screen.

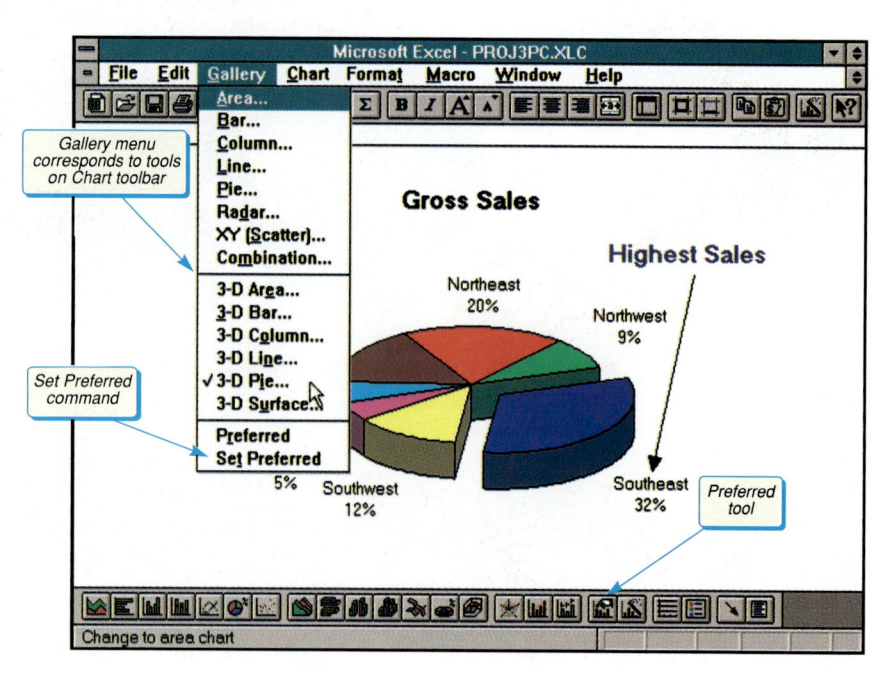

FIGURE 3-79

If you change to another chart after Excel draws the preferred chart, you can always switch back to the preferred chart by choosing the **Preferred command** from the Gallery menu or clicking the Preferred tool on the chart toolbar (Figure 3-79).

The Chart Menu

The **Chart menu** (Figure 3-80) includes commands that allow you to change the chart characteristics. This menu serves as an alternative to using the ChartWizard dialog boxes and some of the tools on the Chart toolbar at the bottom of the screen. However, if you prefer to use the ChartWizard dialog boxes to modify the chart, you can click the ChartWizard tool on the Standard toolbar or Chart toolbar and modify the active chart in a manner similar to the way you modified the pie chart earlier.

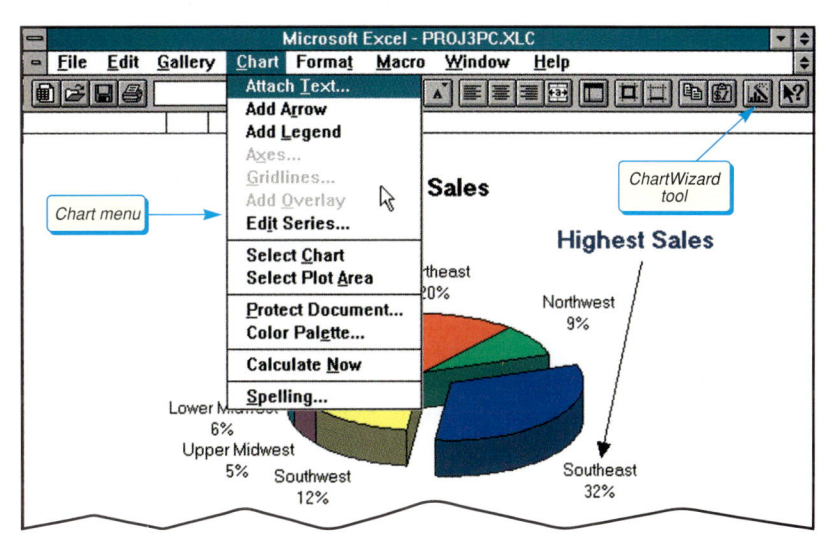

FIGURE 3-80

▶ PROJECT SUMMARY

In Project 3 you learned how to modify a worksheet, how to use the IF function and absolute referencing, and how to chart data. Modifying a worksheet usually involves deleting, inserting, copying, and moving cells. You also modified the worksheet by changing the type, size, and color of the font.

Excel has fourteen different charts from which to choose. To draw an embedded chart, use the ChartWizard tool. Excel has many tools that allow you to enhance the chart by formatting any chart item and adding arrows and text.

▶ KEY TERMS

#REF! (*E113*)
3-D View command (*E150*)
3-D View dialog box (*E150*)
absolute referencing (*E131*)
Alignment command (*E129*)
Alignment dialog box (*E129*)
Arrow tool (*E151*)
Automatic color (*E135*)
black selection squares (*E148*)
category names (*E142*)
chart items (*E146*)
Chart menu (*E161*)
chart window (*E147*)
ChartWizard dialog boxes (*E143–E145*)
Clear command (*E112*)
Clipboard (*E119*)
Copy tool (*E135*)

data series (*E142*)
Delete command (*E112*)
drag and drop (*E117*)
Edit menu (*E119*)
embedded pie chart (E147)
exploded pie chart (*E142*)
Format menu in chart window (*E150*)
format symbols (*E127*)
Gallery menu (*E160*)
IF function (*E130*)
handles (*E148*)
Insert command (*E113*)
landscape orientation (*E158*)
line weight (*E152*)
logical test (*E130*)
MAX function (*E120*)
MIN Function (*E120*)

mixed cell reference (*E131*)
moving cells (*E117*)
opening an imbedded chart (*E147*)
Orientation box (*E158*)
Paste Formats tool (*E124*)
pie chart (*E141*)
portrait orientation (*E158*)
preferred chart (*E160*)
Preferred command (*E160*)
relational operator (*E130*)
rotation angle (*E149*)
Set Preferred command (*E160*)
Text Box tool (*E152*)
white selection squares (*E148*)
Window menu (*E154*)
wrap text (*E128*)

QUICK REFERENCE

In Microsoft Excel you can accomplish a task in a number of ways. The following table provides a quick reference to each task presented in this project with its available options. The commands listed in the Menu column can be executed using either the keyboard or mouse.

Task	Mouse	Menu	Keyboard Shortcuts
Add Arrow to Chart	Click Arrow tool on Chart toolbar	From Chart menu in Chart window, choose Add Arrow	
Add Text to Chart	Click Text Box tool on Chart toolbar	From Chart menu, choose Attach Text	
Change to New Chart Type	Click specific chart type tool on Chart toolbar	From Gallery menu in Chart window, choose the chart type	
Change Orientation of Printout to Portrait or Landscape		From File menu, choose Page Setup	
Change to Preferred Chart	Click Preferred Chart tool on Chart toolbar	From Gallery menu in Chart window, choose Preferred	
Color Borders		From Format menu, choose Border	
Color Font		From Format menu, choose Font	
Copy Cells onto Clipboard	Click Copy tool on Standard toolbar	From Edit menu, choose Copy	Press CTRL + C
Delete Cells		From Edit menu, choose Delete	Press CTRL + – (minus sign)
Display Embedded Chart in a Chart Window	Double-click chart		
Explode Pie Chart	Click slice and drag		
Insert Cells		From Edit menu, choose Insert	Press CTRL + SHIFT + (plus Sign)
Move Cells	Position mouse pointer on border of selected range and drag to new location	From Edit menu, choose Cut From Edit menu, choose Paste	Press CTRL + X; Press CTRL + V
Paste Formats from the Clipboard	Click Paste Formats tool on Standard toolbar	From Edit menu, choose Paste Special	
Rotate or Change Perspective of Chart		From Format menu in Chart window, choose 3-D View	
Select Chart Item	Click chart item		Press ARROW KEYS
Select New Chart Type	Click appropriate chart type tool on Chart toolbar	From Gallery menu in Chart window, choose appropriate chart	
Set Preferred Chart		From Gallery menu in Chart window, choose Set Preferred	
Switch Documents		From Window menu, choose the document name	
Wrap Text		From Format menu, choose Alignment	

STUDENT ASSIGNMENTS

STUDENT ASSIGNMENT 1
True/False

Instructions: Circle T if the statement is true or F if the statement is false.

T F   1. You can open a worksheet by double-clicking the file name in the list of file names in the Open dialog box.
T F   2. When you insert rows in a worksheet, Excel *pushes down* the rows below the point of insertion to open up the worksheet.
T F   3. You must enter a percentage value like 5.3% as a decimal number (.053) in the formula bar.
T F   4. D23 is an absolute reference, and D23 is a relative reference.
T F   5. Although you can insert an entire row or entire column, you cannot insert a cell or range of cells within a row or column.
T F   6. Excel does not allow you to delete a row that contains a cell that is referenced elsewhere in the worksheet.
T F   7. If cell B7 contains the formula = B2 + B3 and you move row 7, Excel will maintain the formula = B2 + B3 in the new location of cell B7.
T F   8. The DELETE key is the shortcut key for the Delete command in the Edit menu.
T F   9. The Copy tool copies the contents of the Clipboard to the paste area and erases the contents on the Clipboard.
T F 10. The Paste Formats tool pastes the formats onto the Clipboard.
T F 11. When you copy cells, Excel adjusts the relative cell references in any formulas copied to the paste area.
T F 12. When you use the Insert command to insert rows, Excel inserts new rows by reducing the height of the cells below the insertion.
T F 13. Press the ESC key to remove the selection from a chart item.
T F 14. The preferred chart is the one you want Excel to draw.
T F 15. You cannot print a chart in its own window by clicking the Print tool.
T F 16. Although you can change the color of the font in the worksheet, you cannot change the color of borders added to cells.
T F 17. The term *wrap text* means that Excel will wrap data from the last cell in a row to the first cell in the next row.
T F 18. If you assign cell A4 the IF function = IF(A5 > A7, 1, 0) and cells A5 and A7 are equal to 7, then Excel displays the value 1 in cell A4.
T F 19. If you select a chart item and Excel surrounds it with black selection squares, then you can drag the chart item to any location in the window.
T F 20. Double-click an embedded chart to display it in its own window.

STUDENT ASSIGNMENT 2
Multiple Choice

Instructions: Circle the correct response.

1. Use function key _____ to change a relative reference in the formula bar to an absolute reference.
   a. F1
   b. F2
   c. F3
   d. F4

(continued)

STUDENT ASSIGNMENT 2 (continued)

2. Which one of the following functions returns the maximum value in a range?
   a. MIN
   b. IF
   c. MAX
   d. AVERAGE
3. To use the drag and drop method for moving a range of cells, the mouse pointer must point to the border of the range and change to the _____ shape.
   a. cross hair
   b. block arrow
   c. block plus sign
   d. cross with two arrows
4. Which one of the following commands in the Edit menu would you use to delete a row and move all the rows below it up without disturbing the Clipboard?
   a. Delete
   b. Insert
   c. Clear
   d. Cut
5. To change the color of the characters in a cell, select the cell and from the _____ menu, choose the Font command.
   a. File
   b. Format
   c. Options
   d. Edit
6. To paste a format on the Clipboard to the worksheet, select the paste area and click the _____ tool.
   a. Copy
   b. Center Alignment
   c. AutoFormat
   d. Paste Formats
7. If you assign cell A5 the value 10, cell B6 the value 3, and cell B7 the function =IF(A5 > 4 * B6, "Valid", "Invalid"), then _____ displays in cell B7.
   a. Valid
   b. Invalid
   c. #REF!
   d. none of the above
8. Which one of the following buttons in the ChartWizard dialog boxes instructs Excel to draw the chart using the options selected thus far?
   a. Next>
   b. Cancel
   c. |<<
   d. >>
9. The orientation of a printout that is across the page length is called _____ orientation.
   a. To fit
   b. portrait
   c. landscape
   d. Best fit
10. Which one of the following menus is used to switch between documents?
    a. File
    b. Edit
    c. Window
    d. Options

STUDENT ASSIGNMENT 3
Understanding the Insert and Delete Commands

Instructions: Fill in the correct answers.

1. Assume you want to insert four rows between rows 5 and 6.
   a. Select rows _____ through _____.
   b. From the Edit menu, choose the _____ command.
2. You have data in rows 1 through 6. Assume you want to delete rows 2 through 4 and move rows up to replace them.
   a. Select rows _____ through _____.
   b. From the Edit menu, choose the _____ command.
   c. In which row would the data from row 6 be located? _____
3. Which command on the Edit menu results in formulas receiving the error message #REF! from cells referenced in the affected range? _____

STUDENT ASSIGNMENT 4
Understanding Dialog Boxes

Instructions: Identify the menu and command that cause the dialog box to display and allow you to make the indicated changes.

	MENU	COMMAND
1. Enter the name of a worksheet you are saving.	_____	_____
2. Select landscape orientation for printing.	_____	_____
3. Select wrap text for a range of cells.	_____	_____
4. Select a file name to open.	_____	_____
5. Select a color for the font in a cell.	_____	_____
6. Select a color for the border of a cell.	_____	_____

STUDENT ASSIGNMENT 5
Understanding Functions

Instructions: Enter the correct answers.

1. Write a function that will display the highest value in the range F1:F13.

   Function: _____

2. Write a function that will display the lowest value in the range C18:F18.

   Function: _____

3. Determine the truth value of the logical tests, given the following cell values: E1 = 500; F1 = 500; G1 = 2; H1 = 50; and I1 = 40. Enter true or false.

   a. E1 < 400   Truth value: _____
   b. F1 = E1   Truth value: _____
   c. 10 * H1 + I1 < > E1   Truth value: _____
   d. E1 + F1 > = 1000   Truth value: _____
   e. E1 / H1 > G1 * 6   Truth value: _____
   f. 5 * G1 + I1 = H1   Truth value: _____

STUDENT ASSIGNMENT 5 (continued)

4. The cell pointer is at cell F15. Write a function that assigns the value zero (0) or 1 to cell F15. Assign zero to cell F15 if the value in cell B3 is greater than the value in cell C12; otherwise assign 1 to cell F15.

    Function: _____

5. The cell pointer is at cell F15. Write a function that assigns the value *Credit OK* or *Credit Not OK* to cell F15. Assign the label *Credit OK* if the value in cell A1 is not equal to the value in cell B1, otherwise assign the label *Credit Not OK*.

    Function: _____

STUDENT ASSIGNMENT 6
Understanding Absolute, Mixed, and Relative Referencing

Instructions: Fill in the correct answers. Use Figure SA3-6 for problems 2 through 5:

FIGURE SA3-6

1. Write cell D15 as a relative reference, absolute reference, mixed reference with the row varying, and mixed reference with the column varying.

    Relative reference: _____   Mixed, row varying: _____

    Absolute reference: _____   Mixed, column varying: _____

2. Write the formula for cell B8 that multiplies cell B1 times the sum of cells B4, B5, and B6. Write the formula so that when it is copied to cells C8 and D8, cell B1 remains absolute. Verify your formula by checking it with the values found in cells B8, C8, and D8.

    Formula for cell B8: _____

3. Write the formula for cell E4 that multiplies cell A4 times the sum of cells B4, C4, and D4. Write the formula so that when it is copied to cells E5 and E6, cell A4 remains absolute. Verify your formula by checking it with the values found in cells E4, E5, and E6.

    Formula for cell E4: _____

4. Write the formula for cell B10 that multiplies cell B1 times the sum of cells B4, B5, and B6. Write the formula so that when it is copied to cells C10 and D10, Excel adjusts all the cell references according to the new location. Verify your formula by checking it with the values found in cells B10, C10, and D10.

    Formula for cell B10: _____

5. Write the formula for cell F4 that multiplies cell A4 times the sum of cells B4, C4, and D4. Write the formula so that when it is copied to cells F5 and F6, Excel adjusts all the cell addresses according to the new location. Verify your formula by checking it with the values found in cells F4, F5, and F6.

   Formula for cell F4: _____

COMPUTER LABORATORY EXERCISES

COMPUTER LABORATORY EXERCISE 1
Using the Help Menu to Understand Charting

Instructions: Start Excel and perform the following tasks.

1. Choose the Contents command from the Help menu.
2. Click Charts. Click Creating a chart. Read the paragraph. Use the scroll arrow in the lower right-hand corner in the Help window to scroll through and read the rest of the document. Ready the printer and choose the Print Topic command from the File menu on the Help window to print a hard copy of the To create a chart Help message.
3. At the bottom of the Creating a chart Help message, click the ChartWizard tool. Print the Help message.
4. At the top of the ChartWizard Help message, click Chart toolbar. Print the Help message.
5. To exit Help, choose the Exit command from the File menu in the Help window.

COMPUTER LABORATORY EXERCISE 2
Switching and Modifying Chart Types

Instructions: You are an expense analyst for CBI Incorporated. Your supervisor has asked you to select and print various charts that illustrate the quarterly expenses shown in Figure CLE3-2.

Start Excel, open CLE3-2 from the subdirectory Excel on the Student Diskette that accompanies this book, and perform the tasks on the next page.

FIGURE CLE3-2

(continued)

COMPUTER LABORATORY EXERCISE 2 (continued)

1. Double-click within the chart location to open the embedded column chart in its own window. (If a two-dimensional embedded column chart does not display with the worksheet, click the Column Chart tool on the Chart toolbar — the third tool from the left.) Next, choose the Set Preferred command from the Gallery menu.
2. Beginning at the left side of the Chart toolbar at the bottom of the window, click the chart tools one by one. Notice how quickly Excel switches from one chart to another.
3. Select the Gallery menu. One by one, select the chart titles that begin with 3-D. When the Gallery dialog box displays, select one of the optional charts and choose the OK button.
4. Click the following tools on the Chart toolbar at the bottom of the window, preview each chart, and print each chart in landscape orientation:
   a. Bar Chart tool (second tool from the left on the Chart toolbar)
   b. 3-D Area Chart tool (eighth tool from the left on the Chart toolbar)
   c. 3-D Pie Chart tool (thirteenth tool from the left on the Chart toolbar)
5. Choose 3-D Column from the Gallery menu. Select the seventh optional chart in the Gallery dialog box. Click the Horizontal Gridlines tool (fourth tool from the right) on the Chart toolbar. If a legend is not part of the chart, click the Legend tool (third tool from the right) in the Chart toolbar. Preview the chart and print the chart in landscape orientation. Reset the page orientation to portrait in the Print Setup dialog box.
6. Click the Preferred Chart tool (sixth tool from the right) on the Chart toolbar. The original two-dimensional column chart displays. Choose CLE3-2.XLS from the Window menu. Print the worksheet with the embedded chart. Close CLE3-2 without saving the changes.

COMPUTER LABORATORY EXERCISE 3
Changing Values in a Worksheet

Instructions: This exercise uses the same worksheet as Computer Laboratory Exercise 2 (CLE3-2) shown in Figure CLE3-2. Your supervisor has asked you to select and print various charts that illustrate the quarterly expenses shown in Figure CLE3-2.

If the worksheet CLE3-2 is not opened, open it from the subdirectory Excel on the Student Diskette that accompanies this book. The following new expense figures have been given to you to enter into the worksheet:

	JANUARY	FEBRUARY	MARCH
Procurement	$25,349.56	$ 45,321.56	$123,781.72
Research	75,216.67	137,593.25	184,913.54
Marketing	56,173.43	22,123.27	203,876.23
Corporate	98,120.51	225,791.71	21,823.01
Fulfillment	10,340.15	12,310.33	78,501.42

As you enter the numbers, notice how Excel immediately recalculates the totals and redraws the column chart. Add your name, course, computer laboratory exercise number, date, and instructor name in column A, cells A37 though A41.

Save the worksheet. Use the file name CLE3-3. Print the worksheet with the new expense figures without gridlines.

COMPUTER LABORATORY ASSIGNMENTS

COMPUTER LABORATORY ASSIGNMENT 1
Modifying a Biweekly Payroll Worksheet

Purpose: To become familiar with using the IF function and adding, changing, and deleting values in the worksheet. Before you can begin this assignment, you must have first completed Computer Laboratory Assignment 3 in Project 2 on page E106.

Problem: Your supervisor in the Payroll department has asked you to modify the payroll worksheet you developed in Computer Laboratory Assignment 3 in Project 2. The major modifications include time-and-one-half for hours worked greater than 80 and no federal tax if the federal tax is greater than the gross pay. The worksheet (CLA2-3) created earlier in Project 2 is shown in Figure CLA3-1a.

FIGURE CLA3-1a

Instructions: Open the worksheet you created in Project 2, Computer Laboratory Assignment 3 (CLA2-3). Perform the following tasks:

1. Delete row 5 (Marci Di). Change Mandi Hi's number of dependents from 1 to 3. Insert 2 new rows immediately above the Totals row. Add the following new employees:

EMPLOYEE	RATE	HOURS	DEPENDENTS
Tie, Joe	$17.50	96.25	5
Webb, Jeff	21.95	80	3

2. For all employees, change the formulas to determine the gross pay in column E and the federal tax in column F. In cell E3, enter an IF function that applies the following logic:

   If Hours ≤ 80, then Gross Pay = Rate * Hours, otherwise Gross Pay = Rate * Hours + 0.5 * Rate * (Hours - 80)

   Copy the IF function in cell E3 to the range E4:E9.

   In cell F3, enter the IF function that applies the following logic:

   If (Gross Pay - Dependents * 38.46) > 0, then Federal Tax = 20% * (Gross Pay – Dependents * 38.46), otherwise Federal Tax = 0

   Copy the IF function in cell F3 to the range F4:F9.

(continued)

E169

COMPUTER LABORATORY ASSIGNMENT 1 (continued)

3. Copy the state tax and net pay formulas in the range G7:H7 to the range G8:H9.
4. Change the format of the range D3:D9 to Normal style. Do not redefine Normal style when Excel displays the dialog box. Use the Center Align tool to center the numbers in the range D3:D9.
5. Increase the height of rows 2 and 10 to 24 points. Increase the height of rows 3 through 9 to 18.75 points. Bold the Gross Pay and Net Pay columns. Change the width of columns A through H to best fit. Color the text and borders as shown in the worksheet results in Figure CLA3-1b.
6. Enter your name, course, computer laboratory assignment (CLA3-1), date, and instructor name in the range A14:A18.
7. Save the worksheet. Use the file name CLA3-1.
8. Preview the worksheet. Adjust column widths if number signs display in place of numbers. Print the worksheet without cell gridlines. Save the worksheet again by using the Save File tool.
9. Preview and print the formulas (CTRL + `) in landscape orientation using the Fit to option button in the Page Setup dialog box. Close the worksheet without saving the latest changes.

Biweekly Payroll File List

Employee	Rate	Hours	Dep.	Gross Pay	Fed. Tax	State Tax	Net Pay
Col, Lisa	12.50	81.00	2	1,018.75	188.37	32.60	797.78
Fel, Jeff	18.00	64.00	4	1,152.00	199.63	36.86	915.50
Sno, Niki	4.50	122.50	1	646.88	121.68	20.70	504.49
Hi, Mandi	3.35	16.50	3	55.28	0.00	1.77	53.51
Bri, Jodi	10.40	80.00	3	832.00	143.32	26.62	662.05
Tie, Joe	17.50	96.25	5	1,826.56	326.85	58.45	1,441.26
Webb, Jeff	21.95	80.00	3	1,756.00	328.12	56.19	1,371.68
Totals				7,287.46	1,307.98	233.20	5,746.28

FIGURE CLA3-1b

COMPUTER LABORATORY ASSIGNMENT 2
Building an Inventory Report

Purpose: To become familiar with the MIN and MAX functions, adding color to the text and borders, and wrapping text.

Problem: You are a management trainee employed by the Floor-Mart Corporation. Each month for the first six months of your employment you work in a different department. This month you are working in the Information Systems (IS) department. Your IS supervisor noticed from your resume that you learned Microsoft Excel in college and has requested that you build the worksheet for the Inventory department (Figure CLA3-2).

Instructions: Perform the following tasks to build the worksheet shown in Figure CLA3-2.

	A	B	C	D	E	F	G
1	\multicolumn{7}{c}{Floor-Mart Inventory Report}						
2	Stock Number	Warehouse Location	Description	Unit Cost	Selling Price	Quantity On Hand	Total Cost
3	C101	1	Roadhandler	$97.56	$125.11	25	$2,439.00
4	C204	3	Whitewalls	37.14	99.95	140	5,199.60
5	C502	2	Tripod	32.50	38.99	10	325.00
6	S209	1	Maxidrill	88.76	109.99	6	532.56
7	S416	2	Normal Saw	152.55	179.40	1	152.55
8	S812	2	Router	48.47	61.15	8	387.76
9	S942	4	Radial Saw	376.04	419.89	3	1,128.12
10	T615	4	Oxford Style	26.43	31.50	28	740.04
11	T713	2	Moc Boot	24.99	29.99	30	749.70
12	T814	2	Work Boot	22.99	27.99	56	1,287.44
13	*Totals*						$12,941.77
14	Lowest			$22.99	$27.99	1	$152.55
15	Highest			$376.04	$419.89	140	$5,199.60
16	Average			$90.74	$112.40	31	$1,294.18

FIGURE CLA3-2

1. Enter the worksheet title in cell A1. Bold, increase the font size to 14 points, and center the title across columns A through G.
2. Wrap the column headings in the range A2:G2. Bold and align the column headings. Adjust the column widths as follows: A = 8.43, B = 12, C = 11.14, D = 8.29, E = 10, F = 10, and G = 11.43.
3. Enter the data in the range A3:F12. Use the following formula in column G:

   Total Cost = Unit Cost * Quantity On Hand

   Enter the total cost formula = D3 * F3 in cell G3 and copy it to the range G4:G12.
4. Use the SUM function in cell G13 to calculate the sum of the range G3:G12.
5. The summaries in rows 14 through 16 apply to rows 3 through 12. Use the MIN function in row 14, the MAX function in row 15, and the AVERAGE function in row 16.
6. Format the entire worksheet to TrueType Arial. Format the numbers, and color the text and borders as shown in Figure CLA3-2.
7. Enter your name, course, computer laboratory assignment (CLA3-2), date, and instructor name in the range A18:A22.
8. Save the worksheet. Use the file name CLA3-2.
9. Preview and then print the worksheet without gridlines. Save the worksheet again by clicking the Save File tool on the Standard toolbar.
10. Change the display to formulas (CTRL + '). Preview and print the worksheet using the Fit to option button in the Page Setup dialog box. Close the worksheet without saving the latest changes.

COMPUTER LABORATORY ASSIGNMENT 3
Year-End Sales Analysis

Purpose: To become familiar with modifying the format of a worksheet that has been formatted with the AutoFormat command, and to understand embedding and formatting a chart.

Problem: King's Computer Outlet, with stores in six cities, has recently purchased Microsoft Windows and Microsoft Excel. Because of your experience with both Windows and Excel in college, they have hired you as a consultant to create worksheets that analyze the company's sales. High on the priority list is a year-end sales analysis worksheet (Figure CLA3-3a) that the president of the company has requested. She also wants a 3-D Area chart (Figure CLA3-3b) that describes the 1st Quarter sales among the cities. The following year-end sales data has been turned over to you:

	QUARTER 1	QUARTER 2	QUARTER 3	QUARTER 4
Chicago	$40,135	$52,345	$38,764	$22,908
Tampa	48,812	42,761	34,499	56,123
Atlanta	12,769	15,278	19,265	17,326
Dallas	38,713	29,023	34,786	23,417
Boston	34,215	42,864	38,142	45,375
Oakland	52,912	63,182	57,505	55,832

Instructions: Perform the following tasks to create the worksheet, embedded chart, and chart document:

1. Enter the worksheet titles, column titles, and row titles as shown in Figure CLA3-3a. Enter the year-end sales in the above table. Center, bold, and increase the font size of the two worksheet titles.
2. Use the AutoFormat command in the Format menu to format the range A3:F10. Select 3D Effects 1 from the Table Format list.
3. Bold and increase the font size of the column and row titles by two points. Bold the totals in row 10 and in column F.
4. Select the range A3:B9 and use the ChartWizard to draw the embedded 3-D Area chart in the chart location A19:G39. Double-click the chart to display it in its own window. Format the chart title and add the arrow and text shown in Figure CLA3-3b. Use the 3-D View command to rotate the chart into position and change its perspective and elevation so it approximates the chart shown on the next page in Figure CLA3-3b.
5. Return to the worksheet document through the Window menu. Enter your name, course, computer laboratory assignment (CLA3-3), date, and instructor name below the chart in the range A42:A46.
6. Save the worksheet. Use the file name CLA3-3.
7. Preview the worksheet. Adjust column widths if number signs display in place of numbers. Print the worksheet without cell gridlines. Save the worksheet by clicking the Save File tool on the Standard toolbar.
8. Print only the worksheet by hiding the chart.
9. Print the chart without the worksheet.

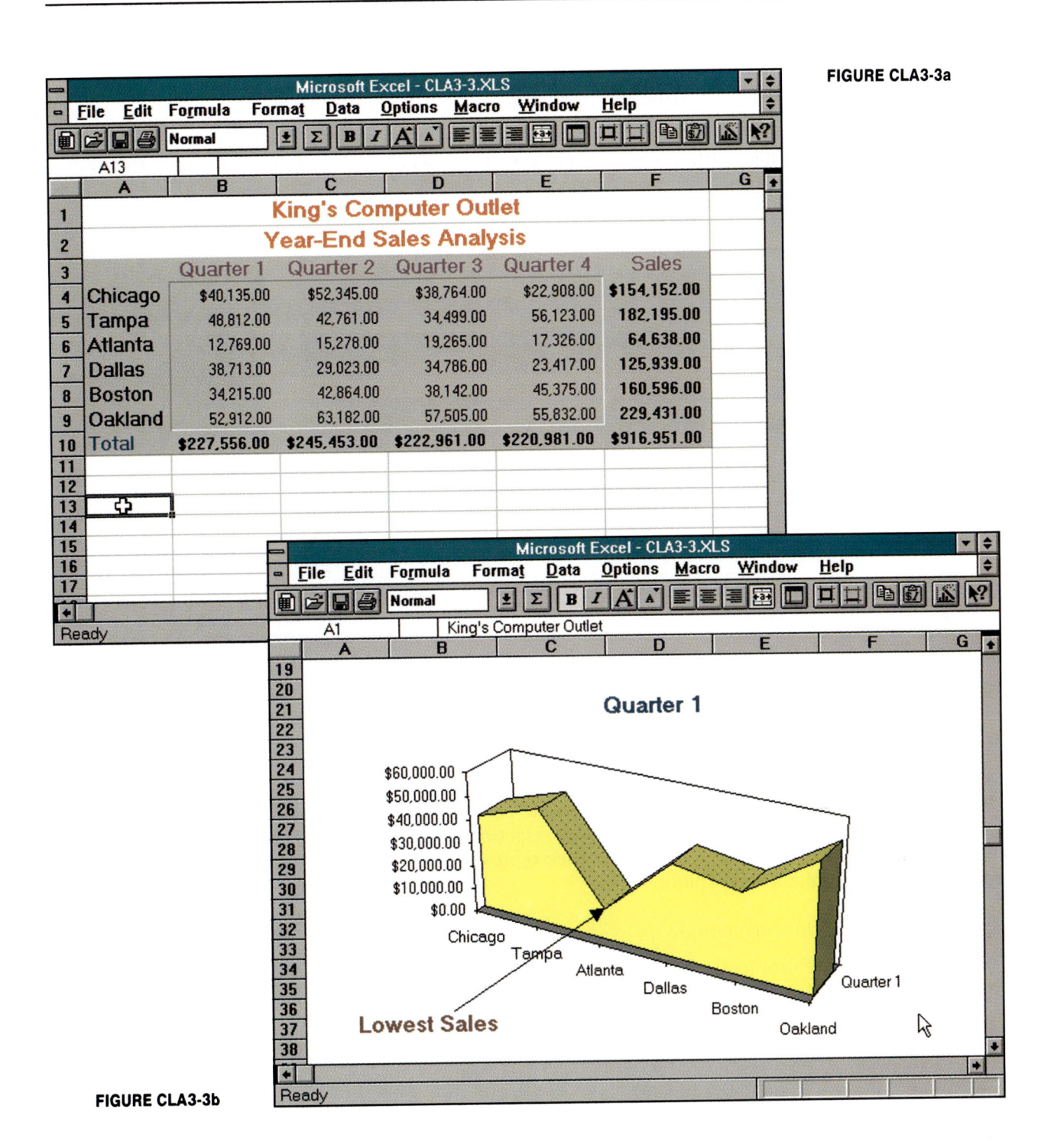

COMPUTER LABORATORY ASSIGNMENTS **E173**

FIGURE CLA3-3a

King's Computer Outlet
Year-End Sales Analysis

	Quarter 1	Quarter 2	Quarter 3	Quarter 4	Sales
Chicago	$40,135.00	$52,345.00	$38,764.00	$22,908.00	$154,152.00
Tampa	48,812.00	42,761.00	34,499.00	56,123.00	182,195.00
Atlanta	12,769.00	15,278.00	19,265.00	17,326.00	64,638.00
Dallas	38,713.00	29,023.00	34,786.00	23,417.00	125,939.00
Boston	34,215.00	42,864.00	38,142.00	45,375.00	160,596.00
Oakland	52,912.00	63,182.00	57,505.00	55,832.00	229,431.00
Total	$227,556.00	$245,453.00	$222,961.00	$220,981.00	$916,951.00

Quarter 1

Lowest Sales — Chicago, Tampa, Atlanta, Dallas, Boston, Oakland

FIGURE CLA3-3b

COMPUTER LABORATORY ASSIGNMENT 4
Week-Ending Department and Store Receipts

Purpose: To become familiar with planning a worksheet.

Problem: Businesses are usually subdivided into smaller units for the purpose of better organization. The Tri-Quality retail store by whom you are employed as an analyst is divided into ten departments. Each department submits its receipts at the end of the day to the store manager. The following daily receipts by department are available for test purposes:

DEPT.	MONDAY	TUESDAY	WEDNESDAY	THURSDAY	FRIDAY
1	$2,146	$6,848	$8,132	$8,912	$5,165
2	8,123	9,125	6,159	5,618	9,176
3	4,156	5,612	4,128	4,812	3,685
4	1,288	1,492	1,926	1,225	2,015
5	4,320	3,213	5,782	2,134	3,216
6	9,191	8,329	6,435	4,292	4,201
7	1,092	2,671	2,181	1,982	1,408
8	7,324	9,435	8,324	5,792	6,812
9	3,892	4,561	3,193	3,292	4,810
10	1,250	3,213	2,845	5,100	3,214

Instructions: You have been asked by your supervisor to develop a worksheet that shows the daily receipts and total receipts for each department, totals for each day, and the store total for the week. Also include averages for each day and averages for each department.

Use the techniques you learned in this project to enhance the worksheet. Color the borders, text, and numbers you want to emphasize.

Create an embedded chart that displays a 3-D pie chart that shows the total daily contributions to the store totals. (You select nonadjacent ranges by selecting the first range and then hold down the CTRL key and select the second range.) Explode the slice representing the day with the greatest sales. Use an arrow and text to highlight the exploded slice.

Submit the following documentation:

1. A description of the problem. Include the purpose of the worksheet, a statement outlining the results, the required data, and calculations.
2. A handwritten design of the worksheet.
3. A printed copy of the worksheet and embedded chart without cell gridlines.
4. A printed copy of the formulas in the worksheet.
5. A printed copy of the pie chart in landscape orientation.
6. A short description explaining how to use the worksheet.
7. Enter your name, course, computer laboratory assignment number (CLA3-4), date, and instructor name below the 3-D pie chart in column A in separate cells. Save the worksheet using the file name CLA3-4.

Microsoft Excel 4 for Windows
PROJECT FOUR

WORKING WITH LARGE WORKSHEETS

OBJECTIVES You will have mastered the material in this project when you can:

- Use the fill handle to create a series of month names
- Copy a range of cells to a nonadjacent paste area
- Freeze the column and row titles
- Shade cells
- Add a drop shadow to a range of cells
- Print the worksheet with print titles
- Add comments to a cell
- Move around a large worksheet
- Use tools on the Formatting and Utility toolbars
- Use Excel's spell checker
- Use the Zoom In and Zoom Out tools
- View different parts of the worksheet through window panes
- Outline your worksheet
- Use Excel to answer what-if questions

▶ INTRODUCTION

Worksheets are normally much larger than those presented in the previous projects. Worksheets that extend beyond the size of the window present a viewing problem because you cannot see the entire worksheet at one time. For this reason Excel provides several commands that allow you to rearrange the view on the screen to display critical parts of a large worksheet. These commands allow you to freeze titles so you can scroll through the document and maintain the row and column titles on the screen at all times, view different parts of a worksheet through window panes, and outline the worksheet. Outlining a worksheet allows you to hide detail rows and columns of numbers and display and manipulate subtotal and total lines.

Finally, this project illustrates using Excel to answer what-if questions like, *What if the budgeted percent expenses decrease by 1% each—how would the decrease affect the annual net income?* This capability of quickly analyzing the effect of changing values in a worksheet is important in making business decisions.

E175

PROJECT FOUR

The worksheet in Figure 4-1 contains a company's monthly budgeted revenue, budgeted expenses, and budgeted net income for a twelve-month period. In addition, the worksheet includes the annual total for all revenues and expenses in column N. The total budgeted revenue for each month in row 6 is determined by adding the corresponding monthly sales revenue in row 4 and other revenue in row 5.

Each of the monthly budgeted expenses in the range B8:M12 — manufacturing, research, marketing, administrative, and fulfillment — is determined by taking a percentage of the corresponding monthly total revenue in row 6. The budget percent values located in the range B16:C21 are as follows:

1. The monthly manufacturing expense is 38% of the monthly total revenue.
2. The monthly research expense is 11% of the monthly total revenue.
3. The monthly marketing expense is 16% of the monthly total revenue.
4. The monthly administrative expense is 17% of the monthly total revenue.
5. The monthly fulfillment expense is 8% of the monthly total revenue.

The total expenses for each month in row 13 of Figure 4-1 are the sum of the corresponding monthly budgeted expenses in rows 8 through 12. The net income for each month in row 14 is computed by subtracting the corresponding monthly total expenses in row 13 from the total revenue in row 6. Finally, the annual totals in column N are determined by summing the monthly values in each row.

	A	B	C	D	E	F	G
1		Budgeted Revenue and Expenses					
2		January	February	March	April	May	June
3	**Revenue**						
4	Sales Revenue	$232,897.95	$432,989.76	$765,998.61	$331,981.56	$567,912.56	$912,013.45
5	Other Revenue	1,232.93	3,265.81	2,145.99	17,210.25	41,023.56	32,100.45
6	Total Revenue	$234,130.88	$436,255.57	$768,144.60	$349,191.81	$608,936.12	$944,113.90
7	**Expenses**						
8	Manufacturing	$88,969.73	$165,777.12	$291,894.95	$132,692.89	$231,395.73	$358,763.28
9	Research	25,754.40	47,988.11	84,495.91	38,411.10	66,982.97	103,852.53
10	Marketing	37,460.94	69,800.89	122,903.14	55,870.69	97,429.78	151,058.22
11	Administrative	39,802.25	74,163.45	130,584.58	59,362.61	103,519.14	160,499.36
12	Fulfillment	18,730.47	34,900.45	61,451.57	27,935.34	48,714.89	75,529.11
13	Total Expenses	$210,717.79	$392,630.01	$691,330.14	$314,272.63	$548,042.51	$849,702.51
14	**Net Income**	$23,413.09	$43,625.56	$76,814.46	$34,919.18	$60,893.61	$94,411.39
15							
16		Budget % Expenses					
17		Manufacturing	38%				
18		Research	11%				
19		Marketing	16%				
20		Administrative	17%				
21		Fulfillment	8%				

January expenses are equal to monthly revenue (cell B6) times the budget % expenses range (C17:C21)

FIGURE 4-1

PROJECT FOUR **E177**

Because the monthly expenses in rows 8 through 12 are dependent on the budgeted percent expenses, you can use the what-if capability of Excel to determine the impact of changing these budgeted percent expenses on the total expenses and net income in rows 13 and 14.

Changing the Font of the Entire Worksheet

You begin this project by changing the font of the worksheet from the default MS Sans Serif to TrueType Arial so that the printout will be the same as what you see on the screen.

TO CHANGE THE FONT OF THE WORKSHEET TO TRUETYPE ARIAL

Step 1: Click the Select All button immediately above row heading 1 and to the left of column heading A.
Step 2: From the Format menu, choose the Font command.
Step 3: From the Font dialog box, select TT Arial in the Font box.
Step 4: Choose the OK button from the Font dialog box.
Step 5: Select any cell in the worksheet to remove the selection.

There is no immediate change on the screen. However, as you enter text and numbers into the worksheet, Excel will display them in the TrueType Arial font.

Entering the Worksheet Title

When working with a large worksheet that extends beyond the width of a window, it is best to display the worksheet title in the upper left corner in row 1.

H	I	J	K	L	M	N
July	August	September	October	November	December	Total
$151,768.34	$556,712.75	$874,245.65	$1,012,784.50	$156,120.45	$1,023,597.65	$7,619,023.23
3,923.67	3,516.78	14,789.86	17,614.00	9,458.54	5,461.75	151,743.59
$455,692.01	$560,229.53	$889,035.51	$1,030,398.50	$465,578.99	$1,029,059.40	$7,770,766.82
$173,162.96	$212,887.22	$337,833.49	$391,551.43	$176,920.02	$391,042.57	$2,952,891.39
50,126.12	61,625.25	97,793.91	113,343.84	51,213.69	113,196.53	854,784.35
72,910.72	89,636.72	142,245.68	164,863.76	74,492.64	164,649.50	1,243,322.69
77,467.64	95,239.02	151,136.04	175,167.75	79,148.43	174,940.10	1,321,030.36
36,455.36	44,818.36	71,122.84	82,431.88	37,246.32	82,324.75	621,661.35
$410,122.81	$504,206.58	$800,131.96	$927,358.65	$419,021.09	$926,153.46	$6,993,690.14
$45,569.20	$56,022.95	$88,903.55	$103,039.85	$46,557.90	$102,905.94	$777,076.68

projected annual net income

TO ENTER THE WORKSHEET TITLE

Step 1: Select cell B1.
Step 2: Type the text Budgeted Revenue and Expenses and press the ENTER key.

Excel responds by displaying the worksheet title in cell B1 in TrueType Arial font (Figure 4-2).

▶ USING THE FILL HANDLE TO CREATE A SERIES

In the previous projects, you used the fill handle to copy a cell or a range of cells to adjacent cells. You can also use the fill handle to automatically create a series of numbers, dates, or month names. Perform the following steps to enter the month name January in cell B2, create the remaining month names for the year in the range C2:M2, and enter the column title Total in cell N2 (see Figure 4-3).

TO CREATE A SERIES OF MONTH NAMES BY DRAGGING THE FILL HANDLE ▼

STEP 1 ▶

Select cell B2 and enter the text January. **Click the Right Align tool on the Standard toolbar. Point to the fill handle.**

The mouse pointer changes to a small dark plus sign (Figure 4-2).

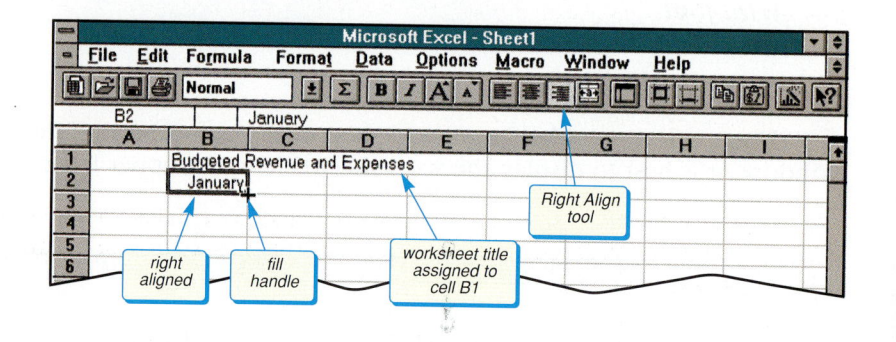

STEP 2 ▶

Drag the fill handle to the right to select the range C2:M2 and then release the left mouse button. Select cell N2 and enter the text Total. **With cell N2 selected, click the Right Align tool on the Standard toolbar.**

Excel creates the month name series February through December in the range C2:M2 and displays the column title Total in cell N2 (Figure 4-3).

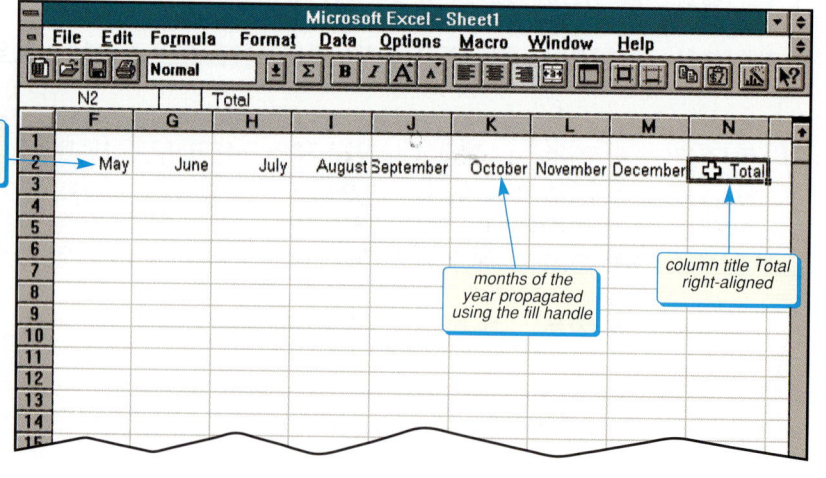

FIGURE 4-3

Besides creating a series of values, the fill handle also copies the format of cell B2 (right-align) to the range C2:M2. If you drag the fill handle past cell M2 in Step 2, after December, Excel logically repeats the months with January, February, and so on. You can create different types of series using the fill handle. Table 4-1 illustrates several examples. Notice in Examples 5 through 7 in Table 4-1 that if you use the fill handle to create a series of numbers, you are required to enter the first number in the series in one cell and the second number in the series in an adjacent cell. You then select both cells and drag the fill handle across the paste area.

If you want to use the fill handle to copy the same text, such as January, to each cell in the paste area without creating a series, hold down the CTRL key while you drag.

▶ **TABLE 4-1**

EXAMPLE	CONTENTS OF CELL(S) COPIED USING THE FILL HANDLE	NEXT THREE VALUES OF EXTENDED SERIES
1	6:00	7:00, 8:00, 9:00
2	Qtr3	Qtr4, Qtr1, Qtr2
3	Quarter 1	Quarter 2, Quarter 3, Quarter 4
4	Jul-93, Oct-93	Jan-94, Apr-94, Jul-94
5	1999, 2000	2001, 2002, 2003
6	1, 2	3, 4, 5
7	200, 195	190, 185, 180
8	Sun	Mon, Tue, Wed
9	Tuesday	Wednesday, Thursday, Friday
10	1st Part	2nd Part, 3rd Part, 4th Part
11	Number 1	Number 2, Number 3, Number 4

▶ ENTERING THE ROW TITLES AND INCREASING THE COLUMN WIDTHS

Perform the following steps to enter the row titles and increase the column widths to make the worksheet easier to read as shown in Figure 4-4 on the next page.

TO ENTER ROW TITLES AND INCREASE COLUMN WIDTHS

Step 1: Enter Revenue in cell A3, Sales Revenue in cell A4, Other Revenue in cell A5, and Total Revenue in cell A6. Enter Expenses in cell A7, Manufacturing in cell A8, Research in cell A9, Marketing in cell A10, Administrative in cell A11, Fulfillment in cell A12, Total Expenses in cell A13, and Net Income in cell A14.

Step 2: Move the mouse pointer to the border between column heading A and column heading B so the pointer changes to a plus sign with two arrowheads. Drag the mouse pointer to the right until the width displayed in place of the cell reference in the formula bar is equal to 17.57 and then release the left mouse button.

Step 3: Select columns B through N. Move the mouse pointer to the borderline between column headings N and O and drag the mouse to the right until the width displayed in place of the cell reference in the formula bar is equal to 12.57. Release the left mouse button.

The row titles display in column A as shown in Figure 4-4 on the next page.

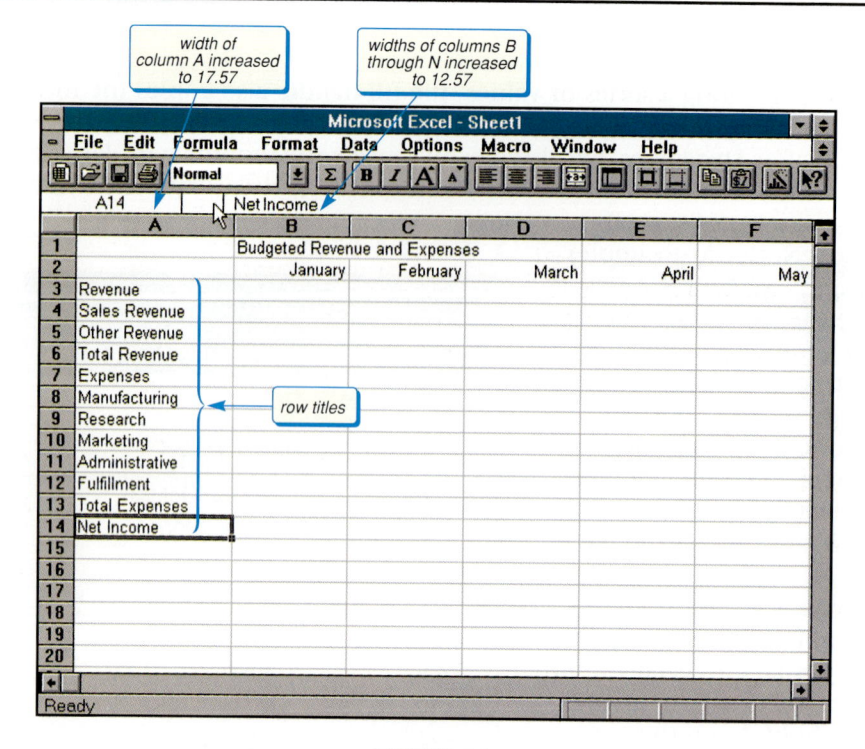

[Figure 4-4: Microsoft Excel worksheet showing "Budgeted Revenue and Expenses" with row titles in column A (Revenue, Sales Revenue, Other Revenue, Total Revenue, Expenses, Manufacturing, Research, Marketing, Administrative, Fulfillment, Total Expenses, Net Income) and month headings (January, February, March, April, May) in row 2. Callouts indicate: "width of column A increased to 17.57", "widths of columns B through N increased to 12.57", and "row titles".]

FIGURE 4-4

▶ COPYING A RANGE OF CELLS TO A NONADJACENT PASTE AREA

According to Figure 4-1 on pages E176 and E177, the row titles in the Budget % Expenses table in the range B17:B21 are the same as the row titles in the range A8:A12. Hence, the range A8:A12 can be copied to the range B17:B21. Notice, however, that the range to copy (A8:A12) is not adjacent to the paste area (B17:B21). In the first three projects, the fill handle worked well for copying a range of cells to an adjacent paste area, but you cannot use the fill handle to copy a range of cells to a nonadjacent paste area.

A more versatile method of copying a cell or range of cells is to use the Copy and Paste commands from the Edit menu or shortcut menu. You can use these two commands to copy a range of cells to an adjacent or nonadjacent paste area.

When the **Copy command** is invoked, it copies the contents and format of the selected range and places the entries on the Clipboard, replacing the Clipboard's contents. You can invoke the Copy command from the Edit menu or shortcut menu or by using the Copy tool (fourth from the right) on the Standard toolbar. The **Paste command** copies the contents of the Clipboard to the paste area. You can invoke the Paste command by selecting it from the Edit menu or shortcut menu or by pressing the ENTER key.

The following steps show how to use the Copy and Paste commands to copy the range A8:A12 to the range B17:B21. In the steps that follow, the Copy tool is used to invoke the Copy command, and the ENTER key is used to invoke the Paste command.

TO COPY A RANGE OF CELLS TO A NONADJACENT PASTE AREA

STEP 1 ▶

Select the range A8:A12 and click the Copy tool on the Standard toolbar. Scroll down until row 23 is visible and then select cell B17, the top cell of the paste area.

Excel surrounds the range A8:A12 with a moving border when the Copy tool is clicked (Figure 4-5). Excel also copies the values and formats of the range A8:A12 onto the Clipboard.

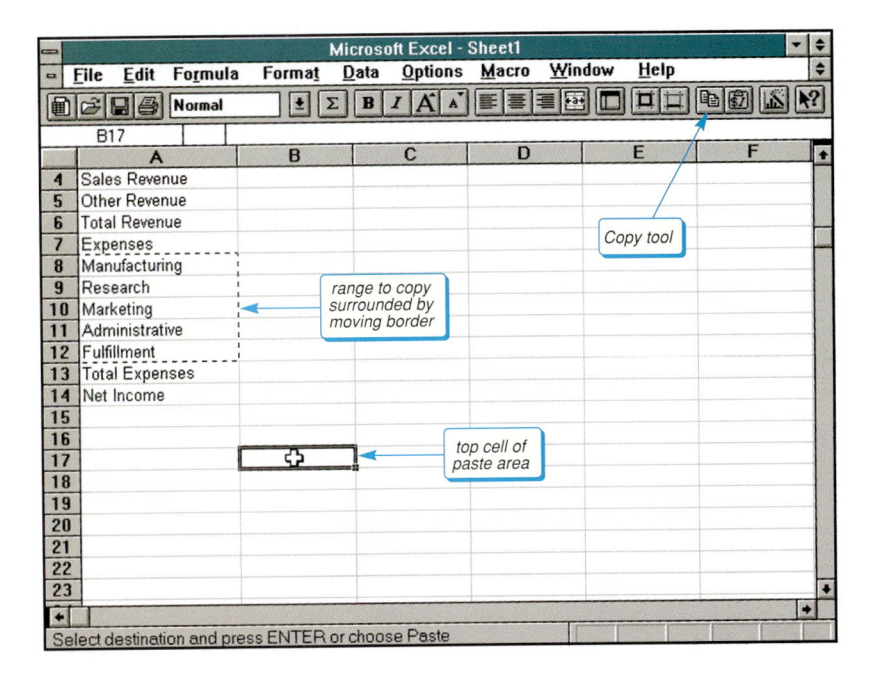

FIGURE 4-5

STEP 2 ▶

Press the ENTER key to invoke the Paste command.

Excel copies the contents of the Clipboard (range A8:A12) to the paste area B17:B21 (Figure 4-6).

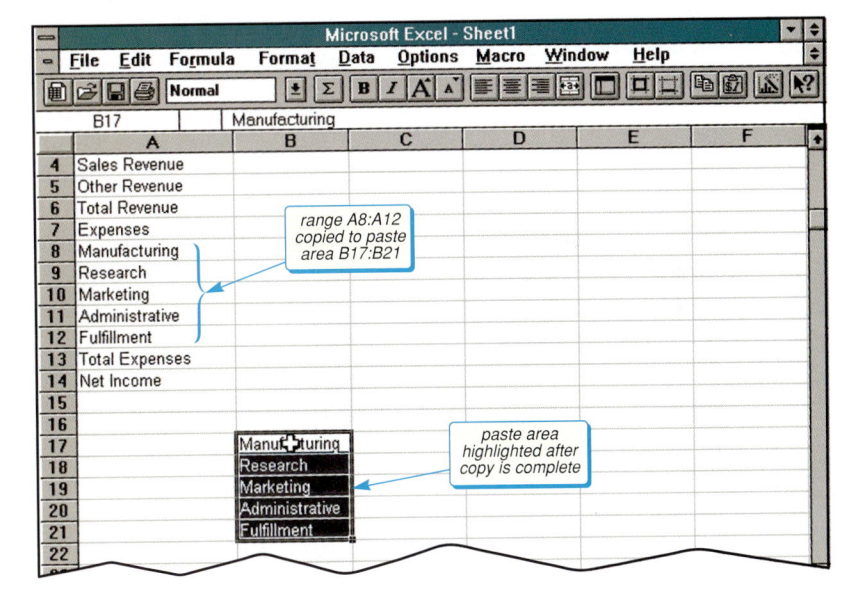

FIGURE 4-6

Notice in Figure 4-5 that you are not required to highlight the entire paste area (B17:B21) before invoking the Paste command. Because the paste area is exactly the same size as the range you are copying, you need only select the top left cell of the paste area. In the case of a single column range such as B17:B21, the top cell of the paste area (cell B17) is the upper left cell of the paste area.

The Paste command replaces the cells in the paste area with the copied cells on the Clipboard. Any data contained in the paste area prior to the copy and paste is lost. If you accidentally delete valuable data, immediately use the Undo Paste command from the Edit menu to undo the paste.

When you use the ENTER key to invoke the Paste command, the contents on the Clipboard are erased after the copy is complete. When you invoke the Paste command from the Edit menu or shortcut menu, the contents of the Clipboard remain available for additional copying. Thus, if you plan to copy the cells to more than one paste area, choose the Paste command from the Edit menu or shortcut menu rather than pressing the ENTER key. Then, select the next paste area and invoke the Paste command again. If you invoke the Paste command from the Edit menu or shortcut menu, the moving border around the range to copy remains to remind you that the copied range is still on the Clipboard. To erase the moving border, press the ESC key.

Completing the Entries in the Budget % Expenses Table

The Budget % Expenses table in the range B16:C21 includes a table title in cell B16, the row titles just copied in the last series of steps, and percent values. Follow these steps to complete the entries in the Budget % Expenses table.

TO ENTER THE BUDGET % EXPENSES TITLE AND PERCENTS

STEP 1 ▶

Enter Budget % Expenses in cell B16. Select the range B16:C16 and click the Center Across Columns tool on the Standard toolbar.

STEP 2 ▶

Enter the percent values 38% in cell C17, 11% in cell C18, 16% in cell C19, 17% in cell C20, and 8% in cell C21.

Excel displays the Budget % Expenses table as shown in Figure 4-7.

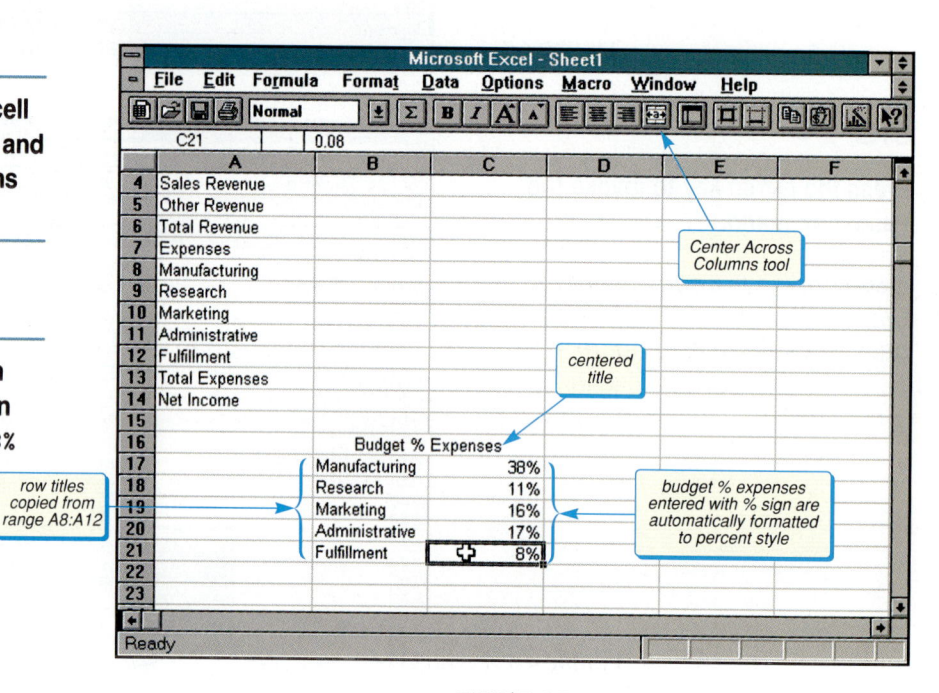

FIGURE 4-7

Entering the numbers in Step 2 with a percent sign automatically assigns the cells the Percent format.

▶ ENTERING THE REVENUE DATA AND USING THE FORMATTING TOOLBAR

The next step is to enter and format the revenue data in the range B4:N6. In the previous projects, you formatted numbers using one of three methods: (1) the Style box on the Standard toolbar; (2) the Copy tool and Paste Formats tool on the Standard toolbar; or (3) the Number command from the Format menu. This section describes another method for formatting numbers that involves displaying and using tools on the Formatting toolbar. The Formatting toolbar is one of seven built-in toolbars that provides tools to invoke often used commands.

Before displaying the Formatting toolbar, follow these steps to enter the revenue data and calculate the revenue totals (see Figure 4-8).

TO ENTER THE REVENUE DATA AND DETERMINE THE REVENUE TOTALS

Step 1: Select cell B4.
Step 2: Reading from left to right, enter the following numbers:

CELL	NUMBER	CELL	NUMBER	CELL	NUMBER	CELL	NUMBER
B4	232897.95	C4	432989.76	D4	765998.61	E4	331981.56
F4	567912.56	G4	912013.45	H4	451768.34	I4	556712.75
J4	874245.65	K4	1012784.50	L4	456120.45	M4	1023597.65
B5	1232.93	C5	3265.81	D5	2145.99	E5	17210.25
F5	41023.56	G5	32100.45	H5	3923.67	I5	3516.78
J5	14789.86	K5	17614.00	L5	9458.54	M5	5461.75

Step 3: Select cell B6 and click the AutoSum tool on the Standard toolbar twice. Copy the SUM function in cell B6 to the range C6:M6 by dragging the fill handle to select the paste area C6:M6 and releasing the left mouse button.

Step 4: Select cell N4 and click the AutoSum tool on the Standard toolbar twice. Copy the SUM function in cell N4 to the range N5:N6 by dragging the fill handle to select the paste area N5:N6 and releasing the left mouse button.

The revenue numbers and totals in the range B4:N6 display as shown in Figure 4-8.

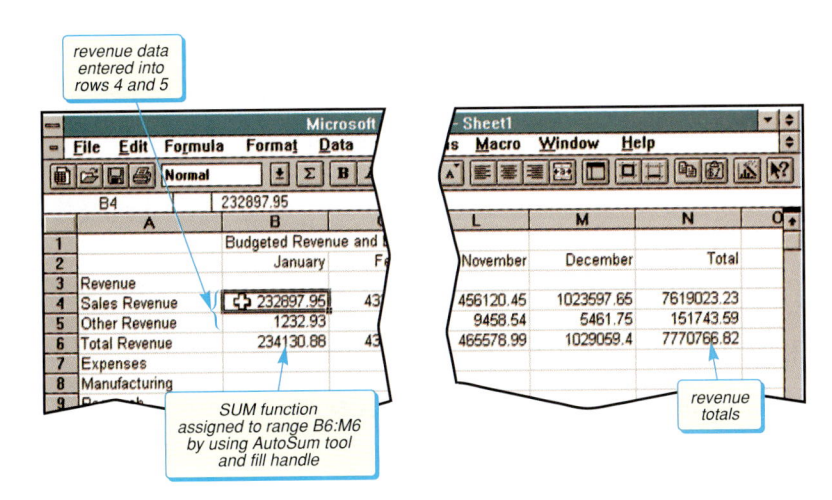

FIGURE 4-8

Displaying the Formatting Toolbar

Excel has more than 130 tools that you can display on toolbars. Most of the tools display on seven built-in toolbars, which can be activated at any time. One of the seven built-in toolbars is the Standard toolbar that usually displays at the top of the screen. Another built-in toolbar is the Formatting toolbar. The **Formatting toolbar** provides tools that can simplify formatting a worksheet. You display the Formatting toolbar by using the Toolbars command from the Options menu or by positioning the mouse pointer on the Standard toolbar and clicking the right mouse button to display the **Toolbar shortcut menu**. Perform the following steps to use the Toolbar shortcut menu to display the Formatting toolbar.

TO DISPLAY THE FORMATTING TOOLBAR ▼

STEP 1 ▶

Position the mouse pointer anywhere on the Standard toolbar and click the right mouse button.

Excel displays the Toolbar shortcut menu (Figure 4-9).

FIGURE 4-9

STEP 2 ▶

Choose the Formatting command.

The Formatting toolbar displays on the screen (Figure 4-10). Excel locates the Formatting toolbar on the screen wherever it displayed and in whatever shape it displayed, the last time it was used. Hence, it may display on your screen in a different location and in a different shape than in Figure 4-10.

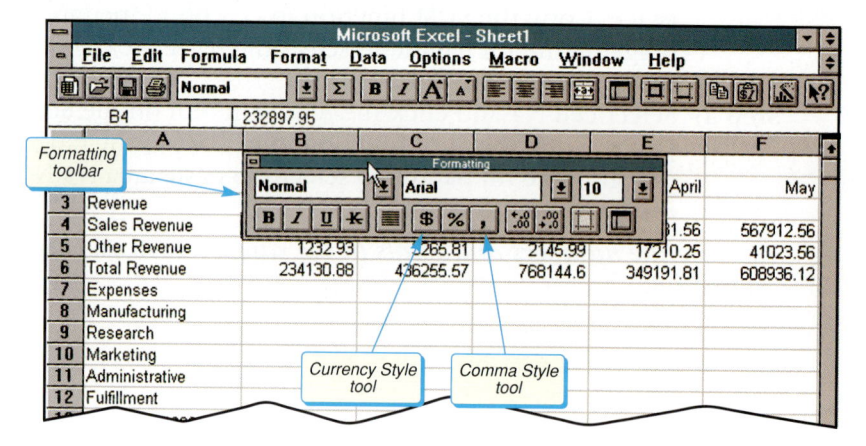

FIGURE 4-10

This project will use the **Currency Style tool** ($) and **Comma Style tool** (,) on the Formatting toolbar. For a description of the remaining tools on the Formatting toolbar, see page E222 or follow these steps:

TO LIST THE FUNCTIONS OF TOOLS ON A TOOLBAR

Step 1: From the Help menu, choose the Contents command.
Step 2: Scroll down to Tools under Reference and choose Tools.
Step 3: Choose Formatting Tools Category.

Excel lists the descriptions of all the tools on the selected toolbar.

Moving and Shaping a Toolbar

The Formatting toolbar in Figure 4-10 is called a **floating toolbar** because you can move it anywhere in the window. You move the toolbar by positioning the mouse pointer in a blank area within the toolbar (not on a tool) and dragging it to its new location. A floating toolbar always displays in its own window with a title bar and Control-menu box. As with any window, you can drag the toolbar window borders to resize it and you can click the Control-menu box in the title bar to hide a floating toolbar.

Sometimes a floating toolbar gets in the way no matter where you move it. Hiding the toolbar is one solution. However, there are times when you want to keep it active because you plan to use it. For this reason, Excel allows you to locate toolbars on the edge of its window. If you drag the toolbar close to the edge of the window, Excel positions the toolbar in a **toolbar dock**.

Excel provides four toolbar docks, one on each of the four sides of the window. You can add as many toolbars to a dock as you want. However, each time you dock a toolbar, the window decreases slightly in size to compensate for the room taken up by the toolbar. The following steps show how to dock the Formatting toolbar at the bottom of the screen below the scroll bar.

TO DOCK A TOOLBAR AT THE BOTTOM OF THE SCREEN

STEP 1

Position the mouse pointer in a blank area in the Formatting toolbar.

STEP 2 ▶

Drag the Formatting toolbar below the scroll bar at the bottom of the screen and release the left mouse button.

Excel docks the Formatting toolbar at the bottom of the screen (Figure 4-11).

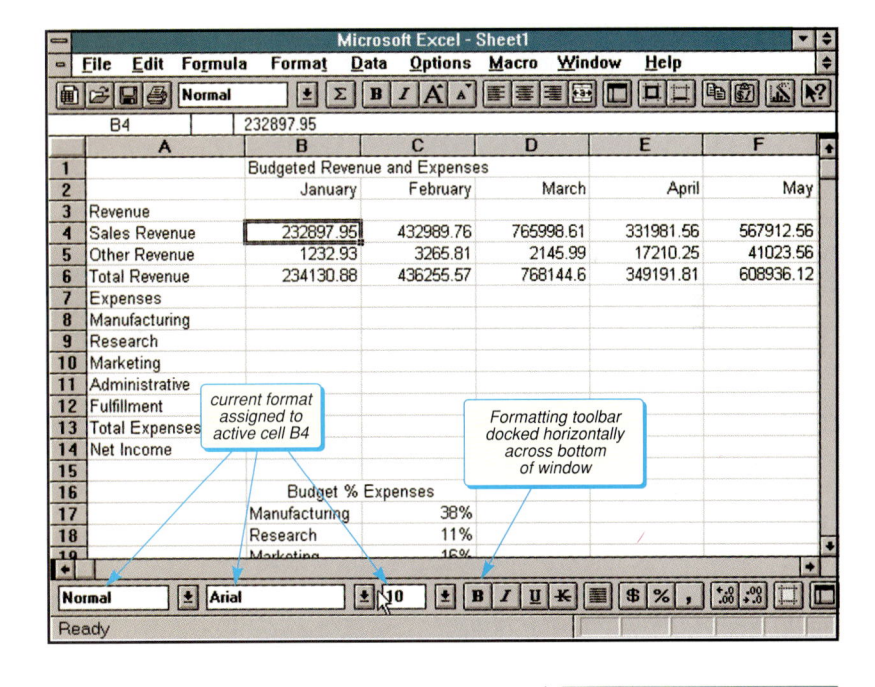

FIGURE 4-11

Compare Figure 4-11 to Figure 4-10. Notice how Excel automatically resizes the Formatting toolbar to fit across the window and between the scroll bar and status bar. Also, the heavy window border that surrounded the floating toolbar has changed to a thin border. To move a toolbar to any of the other three docks, drag the toolbar to the desired edge before releasing the left mouse button. A toolbar that has a drop-down list box such as the Font drop-down list box in the Formatting toolbar cannot be docked on the left or right edge of the window. To change a docked toolbar to a floating toolbar, double-click a blank area in the toolbar.

Selecting Nonadjacent Cells and Using the Formatting Toolbar

According to Figure 4-1 on pages E176 and E177, the numbers in rows 4 and 6 are formatted to the Currency style (dollar sign, comma placement, and cents) and the numbers in row 5 are formatted to the Comma style (comma placement and cents). The totals in row 6 are also bold. Rather than assigning the Currency style format to rows 4 and 6 separately, you can make the **nonadjacent selection** of the ranges B4:N4 and B6:N6 by using the CTRL key as described in Step 1 below.

TO SELECT NONADJACENT CELLS AND USE THE FORMATTING TOOLBAR ▼

STEP 1 ▶

Select the range B4:N4 by selecting cell B4 and dragging the mouse pointer to cell N4. With the range B4:N4 selected, use the left scroll arrow to scroll back to column B. Hold down the CTRL key and select the range B6:N6. Click the Currency Style tool on the Formatting toolbar.

The numbers in rows 4 and 6 display using the Currency style format (Figure 4-12).

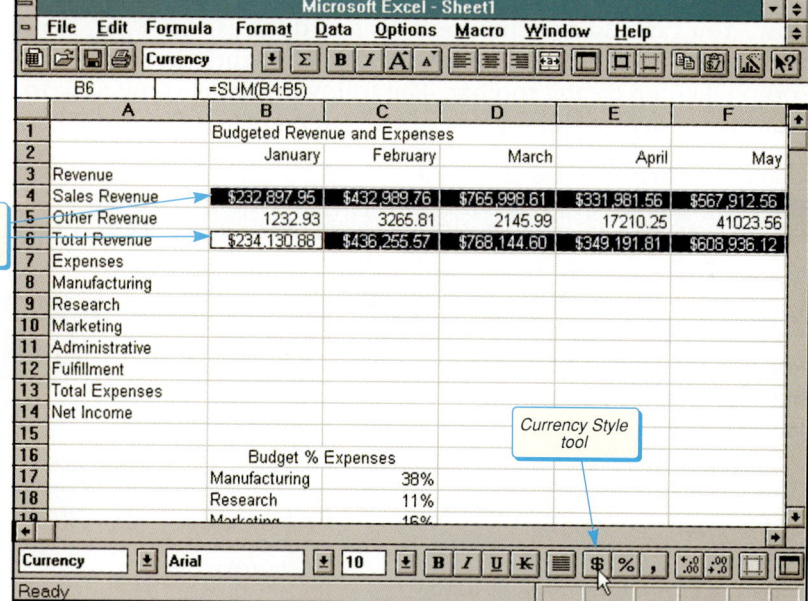

FIGURE 4-12

STEP 2 ▶

Select the range B5:N5. Click the Comma Style tool on the Formatting toolbar.

The numbers in row 5 display using the Comma format (Figure 4-13).

STEP 3

Select range B6:N6. Click the Bold tool on the Formatting toolbar.

The numbers in row 6 display in bold (Figure 4-14 on the next page).

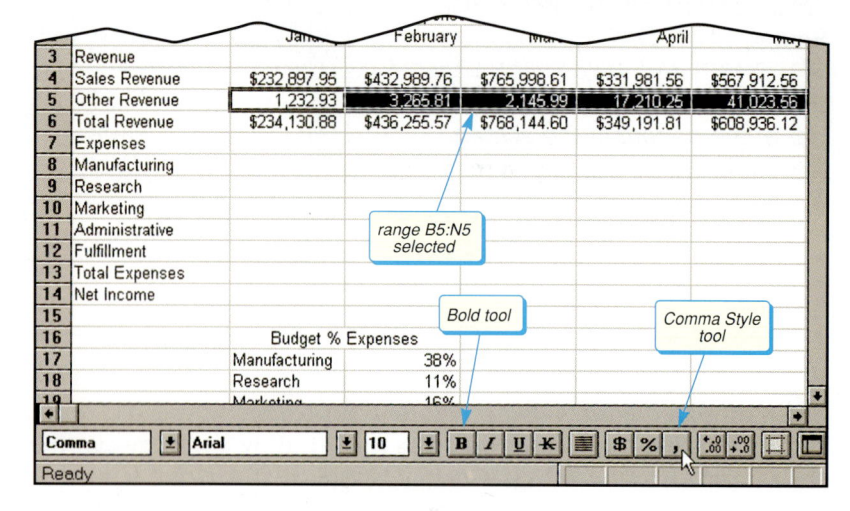

FIGURE 4-13

Saving an Intermediate Copy of the Worksheet

Before adding any more entries to the worksheet, follow these steps to save an intermediate copy of the worksheet.

TO SAVE AN INTERMEDIATE COPY OF THE WORKSHEET

Step 1: Click the Save File tool on the Standard toolbar.
Step 2: In the Save As dialog box, type the file name `proj4`. If drive A (or drive B) is not the selected drive, click the Drives box scroll arrow and select drive A (or drive B).
Step 3: Choose the OK button from the Save As dialog box.

Excel saves the partially completed worksheet to drive A (or drive B) under the name PROJ4.XLS.

▶ FREEZING WORKSHEET TITLES

Freezing worksheet titles is a useful technique for viewing large worksheets that extend beyond the window. For example, when you scroll down or to the right, the column titles in row 2 and the row titles in column A that define the numbers disappear off the screen. This makes it difficult to remember what the numbers represent. To alleviate this problem, Excel allows you to freeze the titles so that they remain on the screen no matter how far down or to the right you scroll.

Follow these steps to freeze the worksheet title and column titles in rows 1 and 2, and the row titles in column A.

TO FREEZE COLUMN AND ROW TITLES ▼

STEP 1 ▶

Select cell B3, the cell below the column headings you want to freeze and to the right of the row titles you want to freeze. Select the Window menu and point to the Freeze Panes command (Figure 4-14).

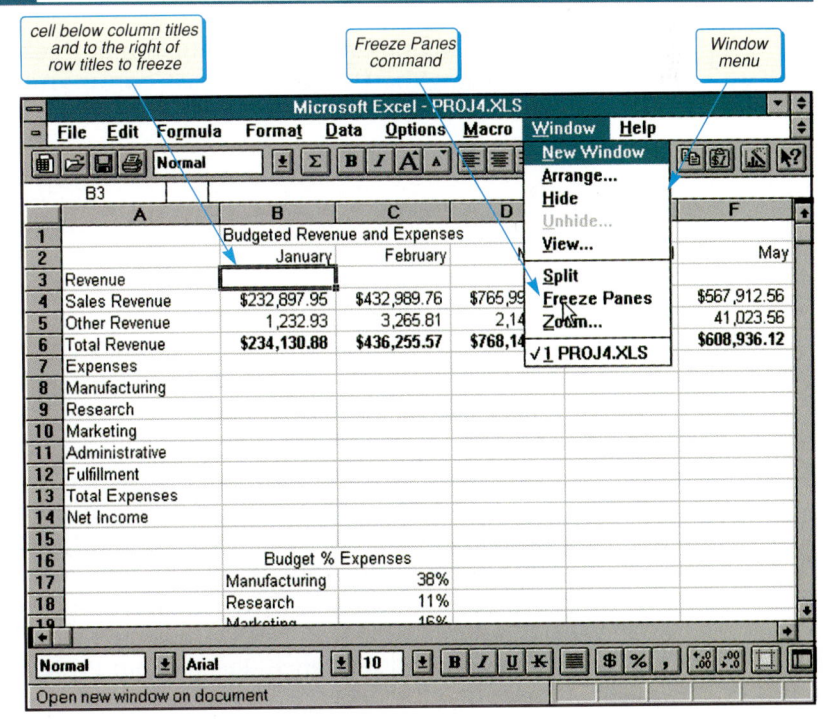

FIGURE 4-14

STEP 2 ▶

Choose the Freeze Panes command. Next, use the right scroll arrow to move the window so columns J through N display.

Excel splits the window into two parts. The right border along column A changes to a thin black line indicating the split between the frozen row titles in column A and the rest of the worksheet. The bottom border in row 2 is too thick to show the thin black line, but the titles in row 2 and above are also frozen (Figure 4-15).

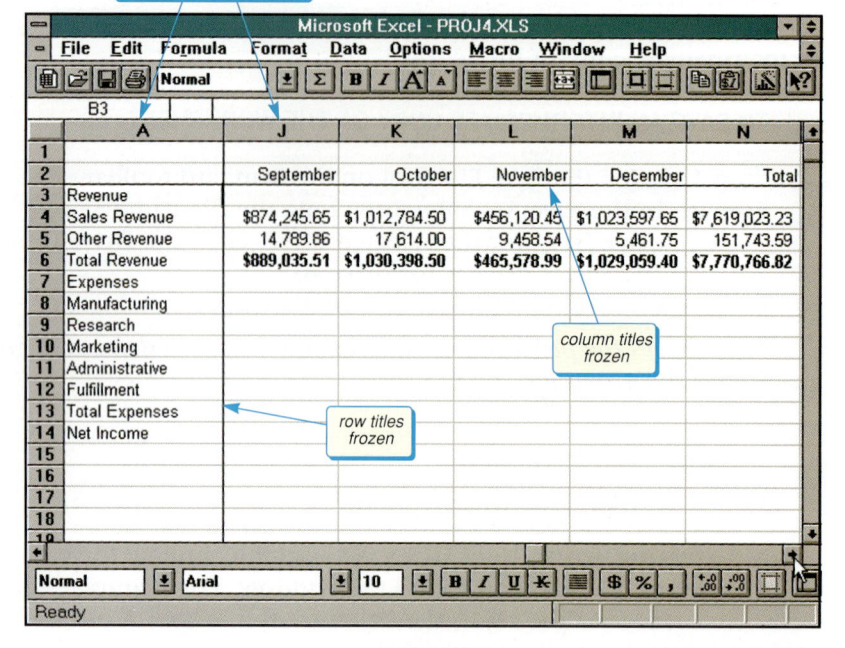

FIGURE 4-15

In Figure 4-15 the row titles in column A remain on the screen even when you use the right scroll arrow to move the window to the right to display the revenue for the months September through December and the total revenue in columns J through N. Without freezing the titles, column A would have scrolled off the screen.

The titles are frozen until you unfreeze them. You unfreeze the titles by choosing the **Unfreeze Panes command** from the Window menu. Later steps in this project show you how to use the Unfreeze Panes command.

▶ ENTERING AND COPYING THE EXPENSE FORMULAS AND TOTALS

The next step in this project is to determine the five monthly budgeted expenses in rows 8 through 12, the total monthly budgeted expenses in row 13, and the monthly net incomes in row 14 (see Figure 4-1 on pages E176 and E177). Each of the budgeted expenses in rows 8 through 12 is equal to the corresponding budgeted percent in the range C17:C21 times the corresponding monthly total revenue in cells B6 through M6. The expense formulas, the total expenses, and the net incomes, will be entered as follows: first, enter the formulas for January in the range B8:B14; and second, use the fill handle to copy the range B8:B14 to the range C8:M14.

The formulas for the January expenses, total expenses, and net income are shown in Table 4-2. Notice that the second factor in the expense formulas is an absolute cell reference. Recall from Project 3 that an absolute cell reference affects only a copy operation. The purpose of the absolute cell references in these formulas is to maintain the references to the percent expenses in the range C17:C21 while copying across the rows in the range C8:M14.

▶ TABLE 4-2

ROW TITLE	CELL	FORMULA	COMMENT
Manufacturing	B8	= B6 * C17	Multiply January expense (cell B6) by Manufacturing % expense (cell C17).
Research	B9	= B6 * C18	Multiply January expense (cell B6) by Research % expense (cell C18).
Marketing	B10	= B6 * C19	Multiply January expense (cell B6) by Marketing % expense (cell C19).
Administrative	B11	= B6 * C20	Multiply January expense (cell B6) by Administrative % expense (cell C20).
Fulfillment	B12	= B6 * C21	Multiply January expense (cell B6) by Fulfillment % expense (cell C21).
Total Expenses	B13	= SUM(B8:B12)	Use AutoSum tool on Standard toolbar.
Net Income	B14	= B6 – B13	Total revenue less total expenses.

To illustrate the entries for the month of January (B8:B14), the following steps change the worksheet display from values to formulas.

TO ENTER THE JANUARY EXPENSE FORMULAS AND TOTALS

Step 1: Press the CTRL + ` (single left quotation mark above the TAB key) keys to display formulas rather than values.

Step 2: Select cell B8 and enter =B6 * C17. Select cell B9 and enter =B6 * C18. Select cell B10 and enter =B6 * C19. Select cell B11 and enter =B6 * C20. Select cell B12 and enter =B6 * C21. Select cell B13 and click the AutoSum tool on the Standard toolbar twice.

Step 3: Select cell B14 and enter the formula =B6 – B13.

The formulas display as shown in Figure 4-16.

The steps on the next page change the display from formulas back to values and copy the formulas in the range B8:B14 in Figure 4-16 to the range C8:M14 using the fill handle.

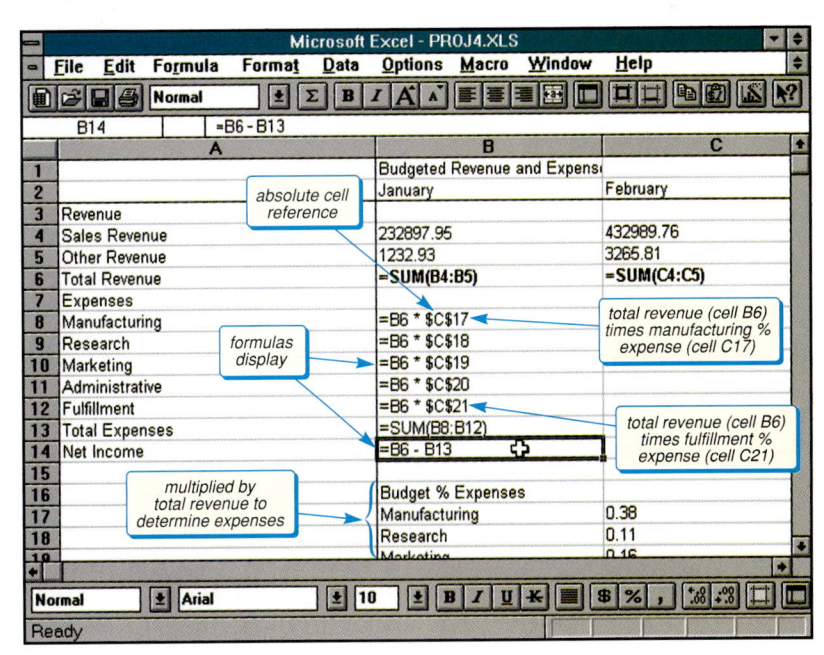

FIGURE 4-16

E190 PROJECT 4 WORKING WITH LARGE WORKSHEETS

TO COPY THE JANUARY EXPENSES AND TOTALS USING THE FILL HANDLE

STEP 1 ▶

Press the CTRL + ' (single left quotation mark above the TAB key) keys to display values rather than formulas.

STEP 2 ▶

Select the range B8:B14. Point to the fill handle near the lower right corner of cell B14.

The range B8:B14 is selected and the mouse pointer changes from a block plus sign to a small, dark plus sign (Figure 4-17).

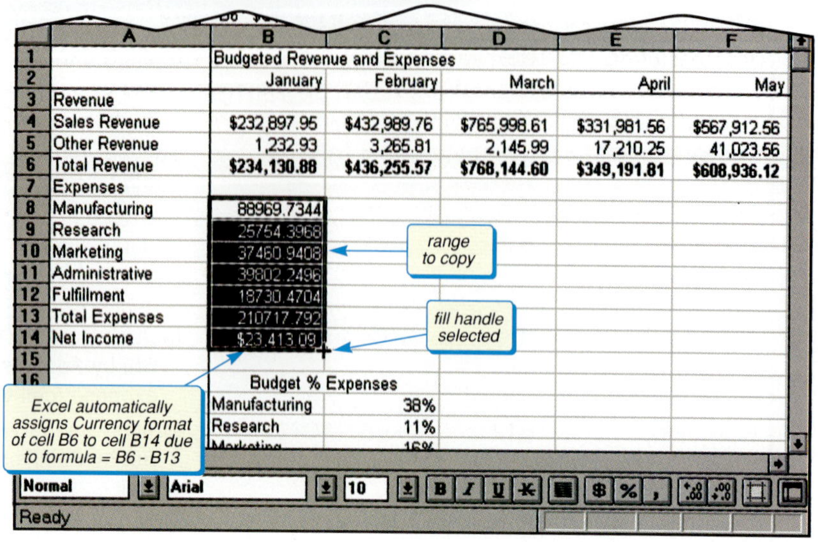

STEP 3 ▶

Drag the fill handle to select the paste area C8:M14 and then release the left mouse button.

Excel copies the formulas in the range B8:B14 to the paste area C8:M14 (Figure 4-18).

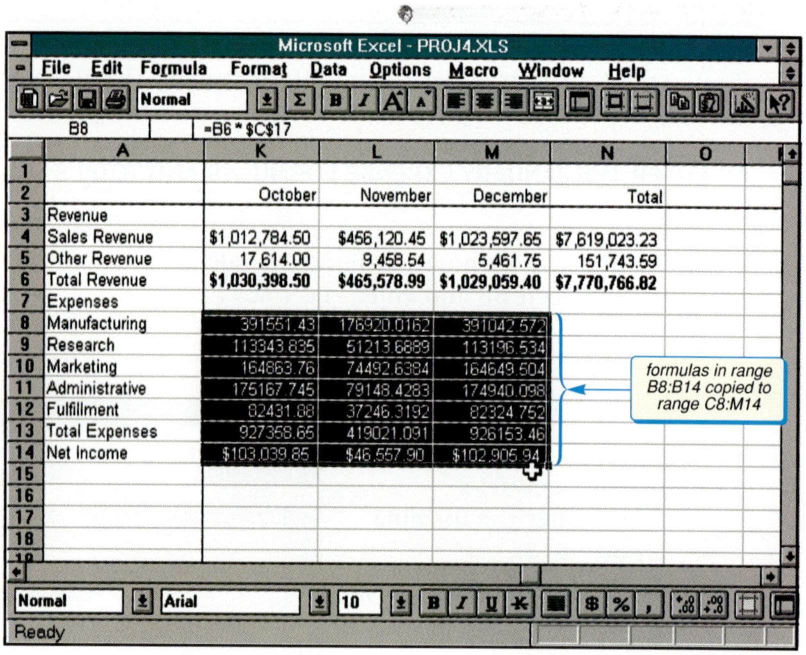

FIGURE 4-18

Notice that the monthly net incomes in row 14 in Figure 4-18 are formatted to Currency. When you enter a formula in which the first operator is a plus sign or minus sign, such as the minus sign (–) in = B6 – B13 in cell B14, Excel applies the format of the first cell in the formula (cell B6) to the cell assigned the formula (cell B14). Hence, the Currency format was automatically assigned to cell B14 earlier when the formula was entered (Figure 4-16). Excel assigned the Currency format to the range C14:N14 when the fill handle was used in Step 3 (Figure 4-18) to copy the net income in cell B14 to the range C14:N14.

Determining and Formatting the Expense Totals and Net Income

According to Figure 4-1 on pages E176 and E177, the final steps in completing the entries in the worksheet are to determine the expense totals in column N, the monthly expense totals in row 13, and the net income in row 14. Follow these steps to obtain the required totals in column N and row 13 through the use of the AutoSum tool on the Standard toolbar (see Figure 4-19).

TO DETERMINE THE EXPENSE TOTALS AND NET INCOME IN COLUMN N

Step 1: Select cell N8 and click the AutoSum tool on the Standard toolbar twice. Use the fill handle to copy cell N8 to the range N9:N13.
Step 2: Use the fill handle to copy the net income formula in cell M14 to cell N14.

The expense totals and net income display in column N as shown in Figure 4-19.

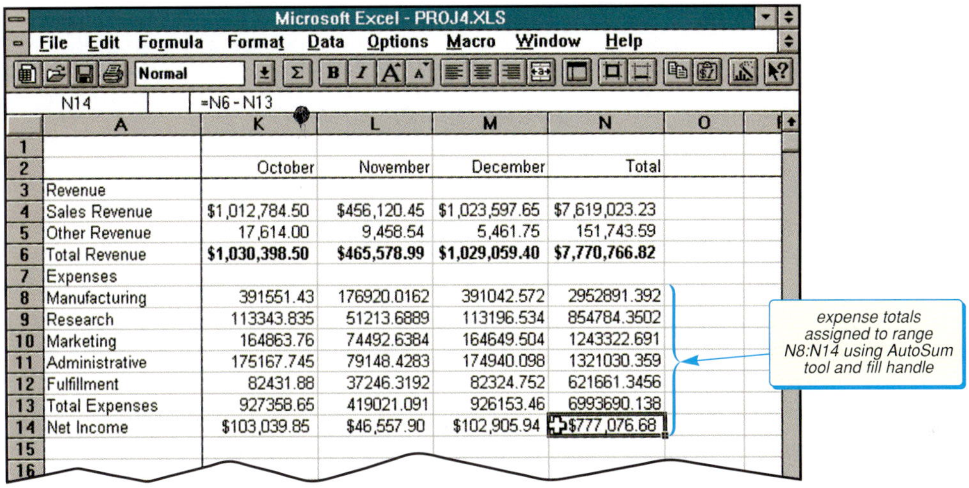

	A	K	L	M	N
2		October	November	December	Total
3	Revenue				
4	Sales Revenue	$1,012,784.50	$456,120.45	$1,023,597.65	$7,619,023.23
5	Other Revenue	17,614.00	9,458.54	5,461.75	151,743.59
6	Total Revenue	**$1,030,398.50**	**$465,578.99**	**$1,029,059.40**	**$7,770,766.82**
7	Expenses				
8	Manufacturing	391551.43	176920.0162	391042.572	2952891.392
9	Research	113343.835	51213.6889	113196.534	854784.3502
10	Marketing	164863.76	74492.6384	164649.504	1243322.691
11	Administrative	175167.745	79148.4283	174940.098	1321030.359
12	Fulfillment	82431.88	37246.3192	82324.752	621661.3456
13	Total Expenses	927358.65	419021.091	926153.46	6993690.138
14	Net Income	$103,039.85	$46,557.90	$102,905.94	$777,076.68

FIGURE 4-19

The next step is to format the budgeted expenses and total expenses in rows 8 through 13. According to Figure 4-1 on pages E176 and E177, the first row of expenses and the total expenses are formatted in the Currency style. Rows 9 through 12 are formatted in the Comma style. Also, the numbers in rows 13 and 14 are bold.

TO FORMAT THE EXPENSES IN ROWS 8–13 USING THE FORMATTING TOOLBAR

Step 1: Select the manufacturing expenses in the range B8:N8. Hold down the CTRL key and select the total expenses in the range B13:N13. Click the Currency Style tool on the Formatting toolbar.
Step 2: Select the range B9:N12. Click the Comma Style tool on the Formatting toolbar.
Step 3: Select the range B13:N14 and click the Bold tool on the Formatting toolbar.

Numbers in rows 8, 13, and 14 display using the Currency format. Numbers in rows 9 through 12 display using the Comma format (Figure 4-20 on the next page).

E192　PROJECT 4　WORKING WITH LARGE WORKSHEETS

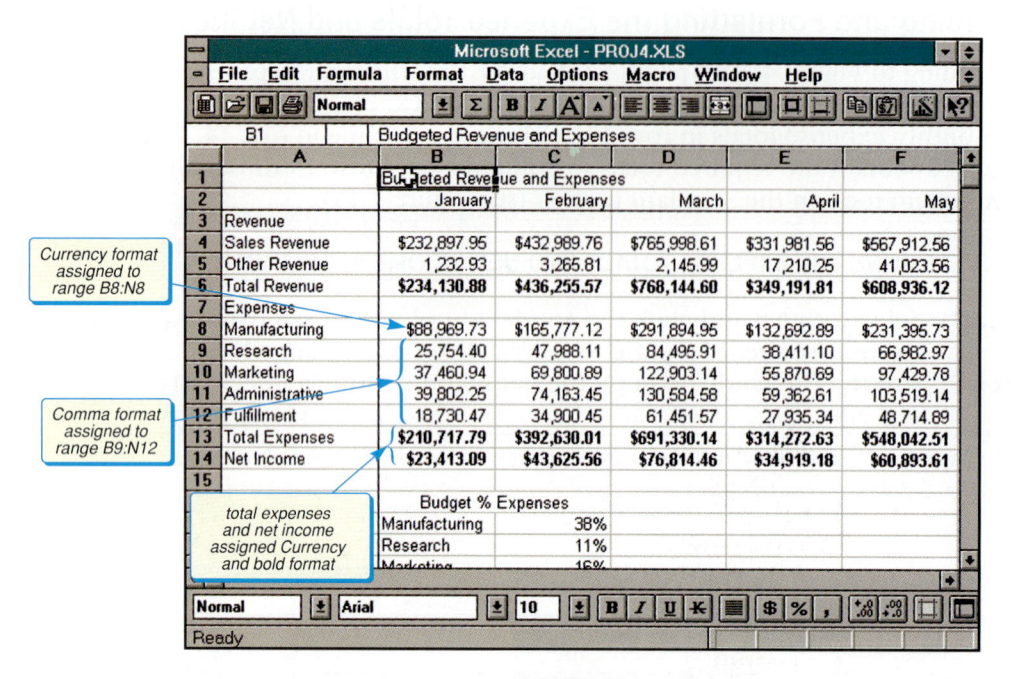

FIGURE 4-20

▶ HIDING A TOOLBAR

With the formatting of the worksheet complete, the next step is to hide the Formatting toolbar docked at the bottom of the screen. As shown in the following steps, you hide a toolbar by clicking its name in the Toolbar shortcut menu.

TO HIDE A TOOLBAR ▼

STEP 1 ▶

Position the mouse pointer in the Formatting toolbar and click the right mouse button.

Excel displays the Toolbar shortcut menu (Figure 4-21). Notice the check mark next to Formatting. The check mark means the toolbar is active.

STEP 2

Choose the Formatting command to hide the Formatting toolbar.

FIGURE 4-21

FORMATTING THE WORKSHEET, COLUMN, AND ROW TITLES   **E193**

You can also hide a docked toolbar by dragging it onto the screen and double-clicking its Control-menu box.

▶ FORMATTING THE WORKSHEET, COLUMN, AND ROW TITLES

If you compare Figure 4-20 to Figure 4-1 on pages E176 and E177, you can see the latter looks more professional and is easier to read. To change Figure 4-20 so that it appears as Figure 4-1, you have to modify the font of the worksheet, column, and row titles, increase the row heights, and add borders. The sections that follow accomplish these formatting tasks.

Changing the Font of the Worksheet, Column, and Row Titles

The following steps show how to change the format of the worksheet, column, and row titles (see Figure 4-22).

TO CHANGE THE FONT OF THE WORKSHEET, COLUMN, AND ROW TITLES

Step 1: Select cell B1. From the Format menu, choose the Font command. In the Font dialog box, select Bold in the Font Style box, 18 in the Size box, and Dark Red in the Color box. Choose the OK button from the Font dialog box.

Step 2: Select the column titles in the range B2:N2 and click the Bold tool and the Increase Font tool on the Standard toolbar.

Step 3: Select the row titles in the range A3:A14 and click the Bold tool.

Step 4: Select cell A3. Hold down the CTRL key and select cell A7 by clicking it. Hold down the CTRL key and select cell A14 by clicking it. From the Format menu, choose the Font command. From the Font dialog box, select 14 in the Size box and Dark Blue in the color box. Choose the OK button from the Font dialog box.

Step 5: Use the CTRL key and mouse to select the nonadjacent cells A6 and A13. Click the Italic tool and the Increase Font Size tool on the Standard toolbar. Select cell A2 to remove the selection from the nonadjacent cells A6 and A13.

The worksheet title, column titles in row 2, and the row titles in column A display as shown in Figure 4-22.

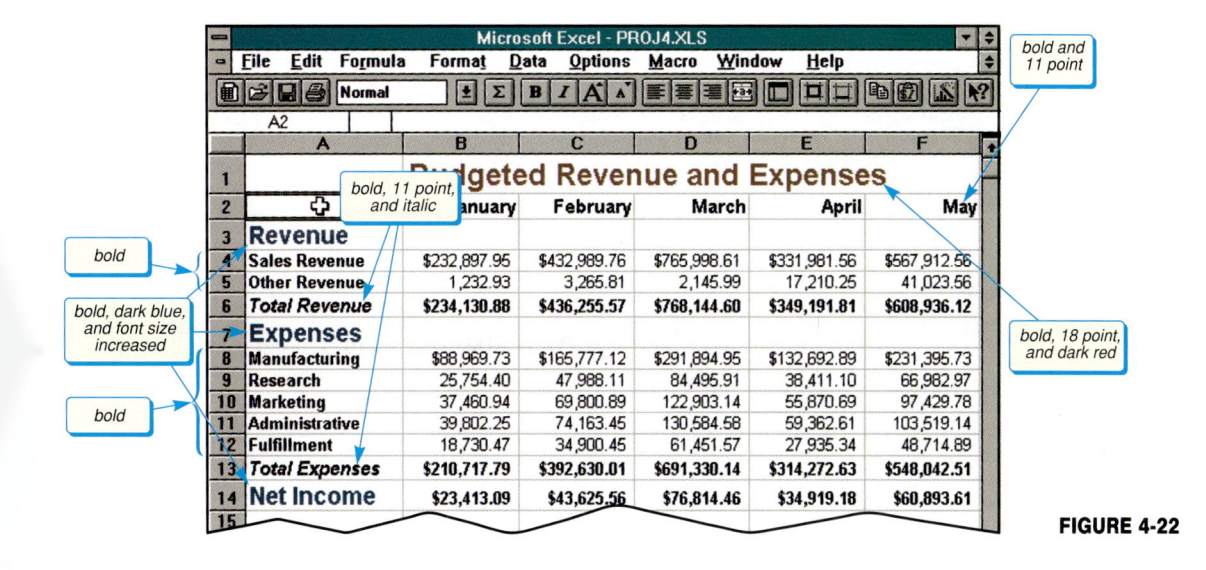

FIGURE 4-22

Increasing the Height of Nonadjacent Rows

You can use the CTRL key and mouse to make any nonadjacent selection in the worksheet, including nonadjacent rows. The next step selects the nonadjacent rows 2, 3, and 7 and increases the row heights to 24 points. Then the heights of rows 6 and 13 are increased to 18 points. The final step increases the height of row 14 to 36 points (see Figure 4-23).

TO INCREASE THE ROW HEIGHTS OF NONADJACENT ROWS

Step 1: Drag through row headings 2 and 3 on the left side of column A. Hold down the CTRL key and click row heading 7 on the left side of column A. Position the mouse pointer on the bottom border between row heading 7 and row heading 8. Drag the border of row heading 7 down until the height for row 7 on the left side of the formula bar is 24 points and then release the left mouse button.

Step 2: Click row heading 6 on the left side of column A. Hold down the CTRL key and click row heading 13 on the left side of column A. Position the mouse pointer on the border between row heading 13 and row heading 14. Drag the border of row heading 13 down until the height of row 13 in the formula bar is 18 points and then release the left mouse button.

Step 3: Click row heading 14 on the left side of column A. Position the mouse pointer on the bottom border between row heading 14 and row heading 15. Drag the border of row 14 down until the height of row 14 in the formula bar is 36 points and then release the left mouse button.

The row titles display in column A as shown in Figure 4-23.

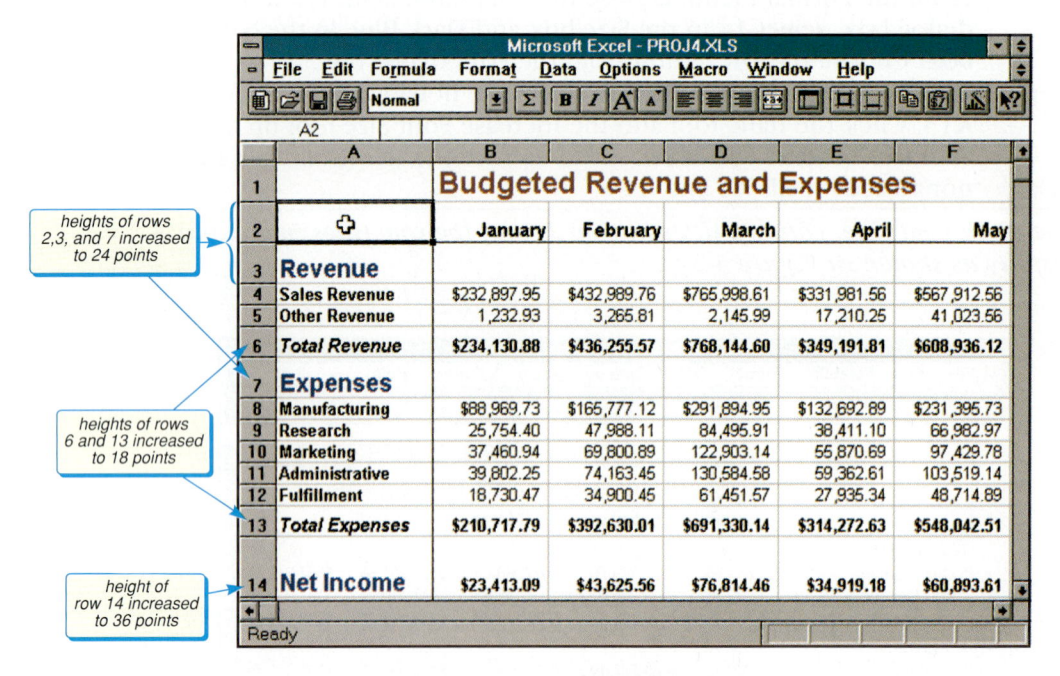

FIGURE 4-23

Drawing Borders in the Worksheet

Follow the steps below to add the red borders to the worksheet (see Figure 4-24).

TO DRAW BORDERS IN THE WORKSHEET

Step 1: Use the CTRL key and mouse to select the nonadjacent ranges A2:N2, A6:N6, and A13:N13. From the Format menu, choose the Border command. In the Border dialog box, select dark red in Color box, select Bottom in the Border box, and select the regular border style (third one in row one) in the Style box. Choose the OK button from the Border dialog box.

Step 2: Use the CTRL key and mouse to select the nonadjacent ranges A6:N6 and A13:N13. From the Format menu, choose the Border command. In the Border dialog box, select dark red in the Color box, select Top in the Border box, and select the light border style (second one in row one) in the Style box. Choose the OK button from the Border dialog box.

Step 3: Select the range A14:N14. From the Format menu, choose the Border command. In the Border dialog box, select dark red in the Color box, select Bottom in the Border box, and select the double-line border style (first one in row two) in the Style box. Choose the OK button from the Border dialog box.

Step 4: Select the range A3:A14. From the Format menu, choose the Border command. In the Border dialog box, select dark red in the Color box, select Right in the Border box, and select the light border style (second one in row one) in the Style box. Choose the OK button from the Border dialog box. Select cell A1 to remove the selection from the range A3:A14.

Excel displays the worksheet with the red borders. Notice that the light red border added to the right side of column A displays in black as long as the titles are frozen.

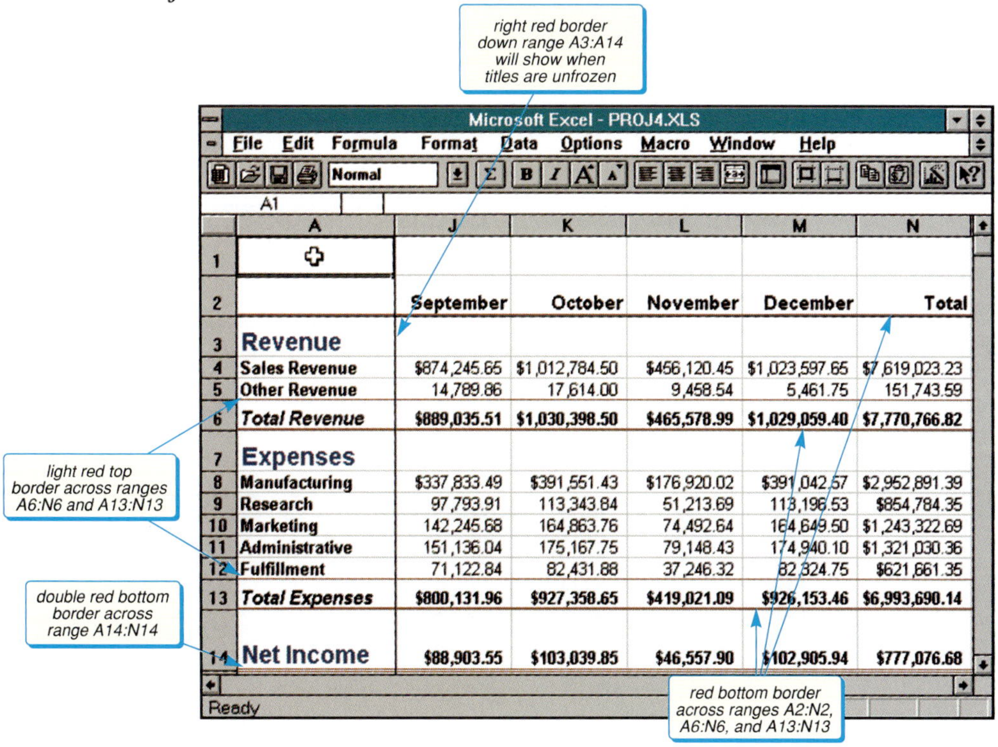

FIGURE 4-24

▶ FORMATTING THE BUDGET % EXPENSES TABLE

The Budget % Expenses table in the range B16:C21 includes a table title in cell B16, the row titles, and percent values. The table is also shaded and has a drop shadow. **Shaded cells** are cells that are colored differently than the screen background. A **drop shadow** gives the shaded cells a three-dimensional appearance. You can use both shading and a drop shadow to make a range of cells stand out in the worksheet.

Shading Cells

The following steps show how to use the Patterns command from the Format menu to shade a range of cells (see Figure 4-26).

TO SHADE A RANGE OF CELLS ▼

STEP 1

Scroll down and then select the Budget % Expenses table in the range B16:C21.

STEP 2 ▶

From the Format menu, choose the Patterns command. In the Cell Shading area, select None in the Pattern drop-down list box, dark red in the Foreground drop-down list box, and Automatic in the Background drop-down list box.

Excel displays a sample of the shading pattern in the Sample box (Figure 4-25).

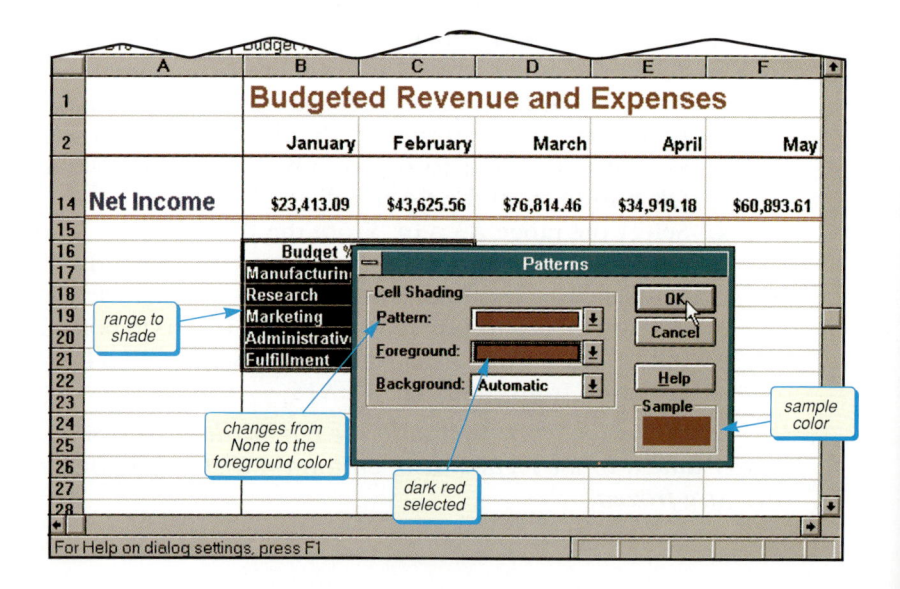

FIGURE 4-25

STEP 3 ▶

Choose the OK button from the Patterns dialog box. Select any cell outside the selected range.

Excel shades the range of cells B16:C21 dark red (Figure 4-26).

FIGURE 4-26

With the **Patterns command**, you can shade cells in any one of sixteen solid colors. You can also select one of eighteen patterns. A **pattern** includes designs made up of lines or dots. When you select a pattern, the Background box in the Patterns dialog box (Figure 4-25) determines the background color of the pattern. The Foreground box determines the colors of the lines or dots in the pattern.

Adding a Drop Shadow to a Range of Cells

The next step is to add the drop shadow to the Budget % Expenses table in the range B16:C21. As described in the following steps, you add a drop shadow by selecting a bold bottom border for cells B21 and C21, and bold right borders for cells C16 through C21 (see Figure 4-27).

TO ADD A DROP SHADOW TO A RANGE OF CELLS

Step 1: Select the range B21:C21. From the Format menu, choose the Border command. In the Border dialog box, select Bottom in the Border box and the bold border style (fourth one in row one) in the Style box. Choose the OK button from the Border dialog box.

Step 2: Select the range C16:C21. From the Format menu, choose the Border command. In the Border dialog box, select Right in the Border box and select the bold border style in the Style box. Choose the OK button from the Border dialog box. Select any cell outside the selected range.

The Budget % Expenses table displays with a drop shadow (Figure 4-27).

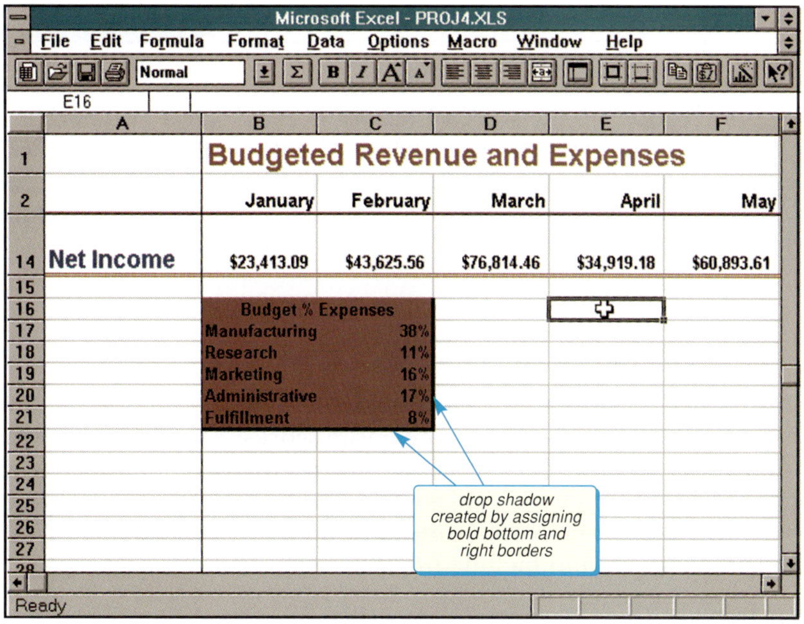

FIGURE 4-27

On Excel's Drawing toolbar (see page E222), you can use the Drop Shadow tool (▢) to add a drop shadow.

Changing the Color of the Font in the Budget % Expenses Table

Refer to the worksheet in Figure 4-1 on pages E176 and E177, and you will see that the font in the Budget % Expenses table is white. Perform the following steps to change the color of the font.

TO CHANGE THE COLOR OF THE FONT IN THE BUDGET % EXPENSES TABLE

STEP 1

Select the range B16:C21. From the Format menu, choose Font. In the Font dialog box, select white in the Color box.

STEP 2 ▶

Choose the OK button from the Font dialog box. Select any cell outside the selected range.

The font in the table in the range B16:C21 displays in white (Figure 4-28).

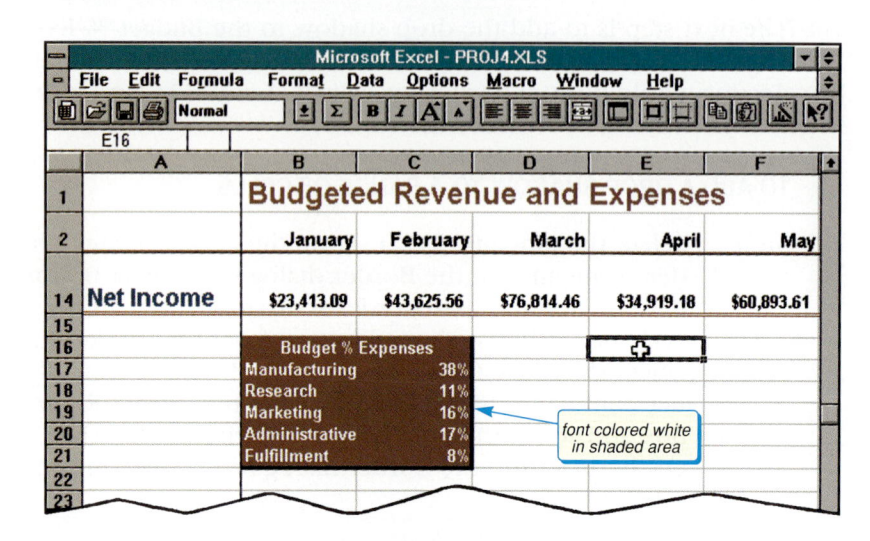

FIGURE 4-28

So the information on the screen is easier to read, select colors that help make the font stand out. For example, select a light color for the font when the cells have been shaded a dark color. Select a dark color font when the cells are shaded a light color. If you color the font the same color as the background, the entries in the cells are hidden.

▶ ADDING COMMENTS TO A WORKSHEET

Comments, or **notes**, in a worksheet are used to describe the function of a cell, a range of cells, or the entire worksheet. Comments are used to identify worksheets and clarify entries that would otherwise be difficult to understand. In Excel you can assign comments to any cell in the worksheet through the use of the **Note command** on the Formula menu. Overall worksheet comments should include the following:

1. Worksheet title
2. Author's name
3. Date created
4. Date last modified (use N/A if it has not been modified)
5. Short description of the purpose of the worksheet

Perform the steps on the next page to assign worksheet comments to cell A1.

ADDING COMMENTS TO A WORKSHEET E199

TO ASSIGN A NOTE TO A CELL

STEP 1

Select cell A1. From the Formula menu, choose the Note command.

*Excel displays the **Cell Note dialog box** with a blank Text Note box. The Cell box identifies the active cell (A1).*

STEP 2 ▶

Enter the note in the Text Note box as shown in Figure 4-29. To end a line prematurely, press ALT + ENTER.

Excel wraps text in the Text Note box.

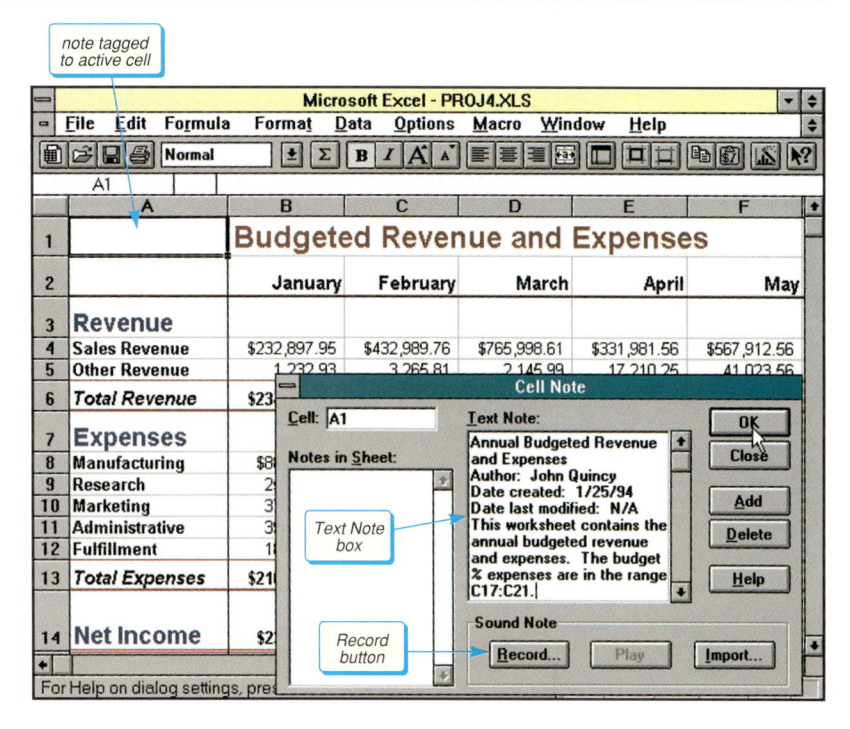

FIGURE 4-29

STEP 3 ▶

Choose OK from the Cell Note dialog box.

Excel adds a small red dot, called a note indicator, in the upper right corner of cell A1 to indicate that a note has been assigned to it (Figure 4-30).

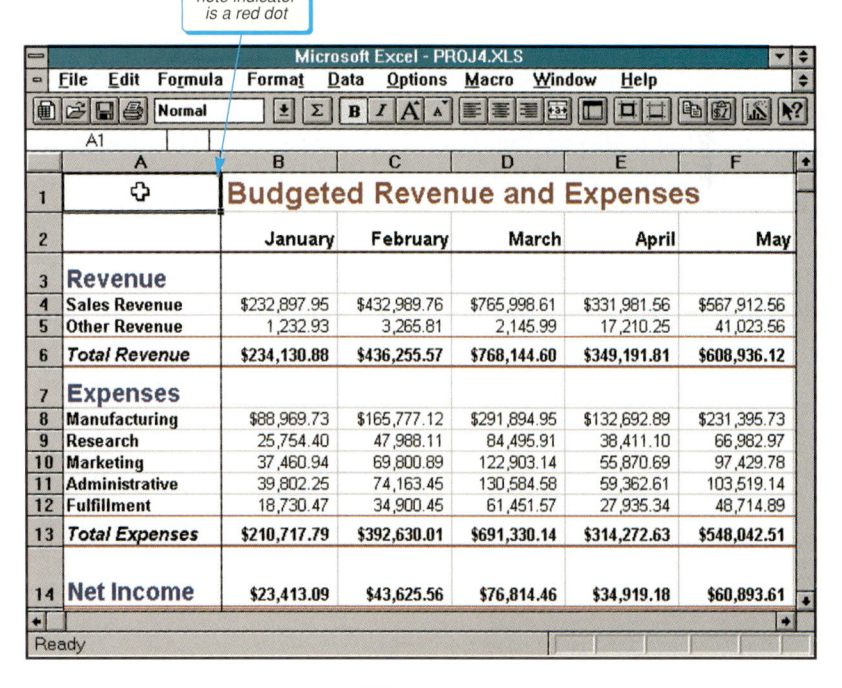

FIGURE 4-30

To read the comment or note any time the worksheet is active, double-click cell A1, the cell with the red dot. The red dot indicates the cell has a note attached to it. When you double-click cell A1, Excel immediately displays the message in the Cell Note dialog box as shown in Figure 4-29 on the previous page.

If you prefer that the note indicator (small red dot) not display in cell A1, choose the Workspace command from the Options menu and remove the x from the Note Indicator check box by clicking it. You can print notes assigned to cells by selecting the Notes option button from the Print dialog box.

Besides entering text comments, you can add an audio comment to a cell (up to two minutes) if you have an audio board and a microphone. You add the audio comment by selecting the Record button in the Cell Note dialog box (Figure 4-29). When an **audio comment** is added without a text note, the computer speaks the comment when you double-click the cell to which the audio comment is assigned.

▶ DISPLAYING AND DOCKING THE UTILITY TOOLBAR

The remainder of Project 4 uses several tools on the **Utility toolbar** that allow you to further enhance the worksheet. Perform the following steps to display the Utility toolbar.

TO DISPLAY AND DOCK THE UTILITY TOOLBAR ▼

STEP 1 ▶

Position the mouse pointer on the Standard toolbar. Click the right mouse button to display the Toolbar shortcut menu. Choose the Utility command.

The Utility toolbar displays on the screen (Figure 4-31).

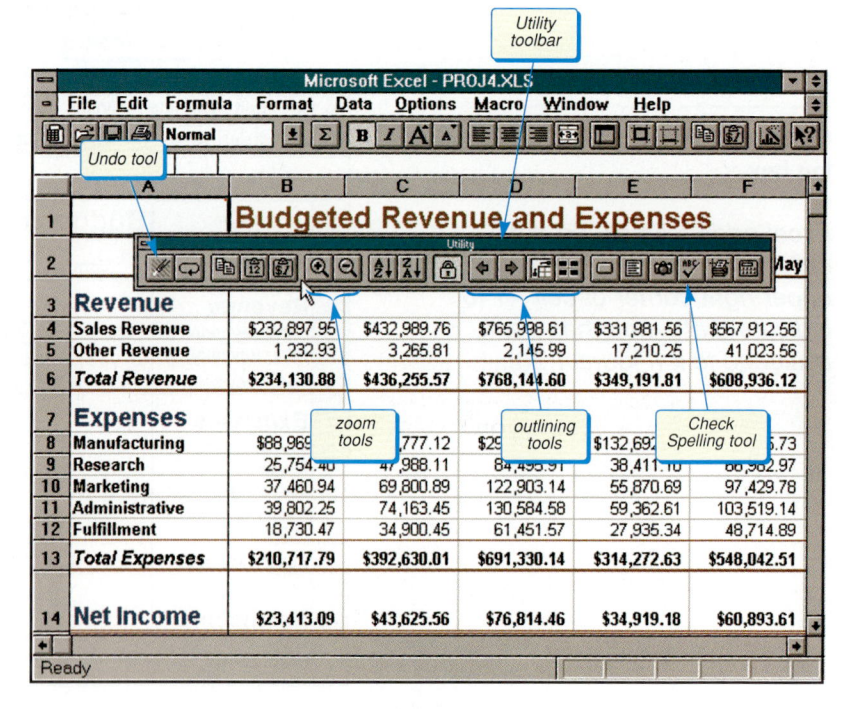

FIGURE 4-31

CHECKING SPELLING **E201**

STEP 2 ▶

Position the mouse pointer in a blank area on the Utility toolbar. Drag the Utility toolbar up above the formula bar and then release the left mouse button.

Excel docks the Utility toolbar between the formula bar and the Standard toolbar (Figure 4-32). If you drag the Utility toolbar above the Standard toolbar it will replace it.

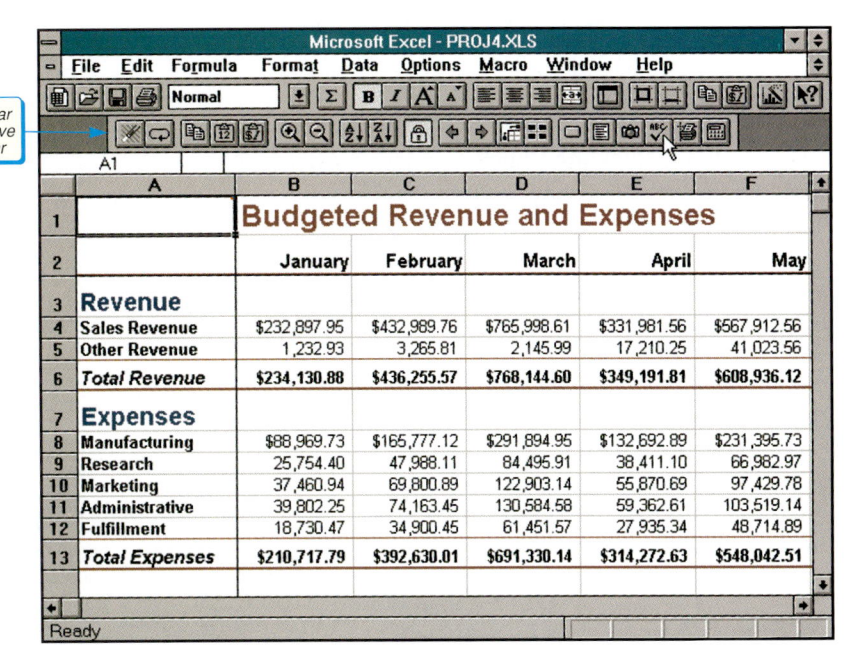

FIGURE 4-32

The Utility toolbar (Figure 4-32) includes several tools that are useful when working with large worksheets. For a complete description of the tools on the Utility toolbar, use the steps described earlier in this project on page E184 to display the functions of the tools or see page E222.

The first tool that will be used on the Utility toolbar is the **Check Spelling tool** ( ) to check the spelling of the text in the worksheet.

▶ CHECKING SPELLING

E xcel has a **spell checker** you can use to check your worksheet for spelling errors. The spell checker checks for spelling errors against its **standard dictionary**. If you have any specialized terms that are not in the standard dictionary, you can add them to a **custom dictionary** through the Spelling dialog box.

When the spell checker finds a word that is not in the dictionaries, it displays the word in the Spelling dialog box so you can correct it if it is misspelled.

You invoke the spell checker by choosing the **Spelling command** from the Options menu or by clicking the Check Spelling tool on the Utility toolbar. To illustrate Excel's reaction to a misspelled word, the month name January in cell B2 is spelled Jinuary, as shown in Figure 4-33 on the next page.

TO CHECK SPELLING IN THE WORKSHEET

STEP 1 ▶

Select cell A1. Click the Check Spelling tool on the Utility toolbar.

*The spell checker begins checking the spelling of the text and notes in the worksheet with the active cell (cell A1) and continues checking to the right and down row by row. If the spell checker comes across a word that is not in the standard or custom dictionaries, it displays the **Spelling dialog box** (Figure 4-33).*

STEP 2

When the spell checker displays a word in the Change To box, select one of the eight buttons in the Spelling dialog box.

For example, in Figure 4-33 the word January in cell B2 is misspelled as Jinuary. The spell checker displays its best guess of the word you wanted (January) in the Change To box. Because January is in fact the correct spelling, choose the Change button (Change).

STEP 3 ▶

Choose the OK button when Excel displays the Microsoft Excel dialog box to indicate the spell checking is complete (Figure 4-34).

STEP 4

Click the Save File tool on the Standard toolbar to save the corrected version of the worksheet to disk.

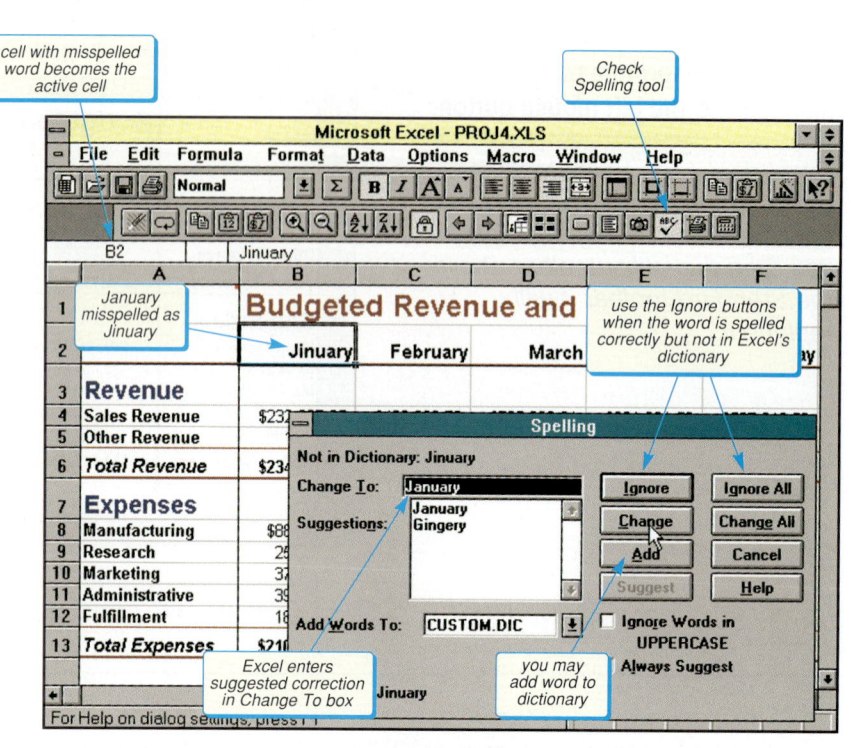

FIGURE 4-33

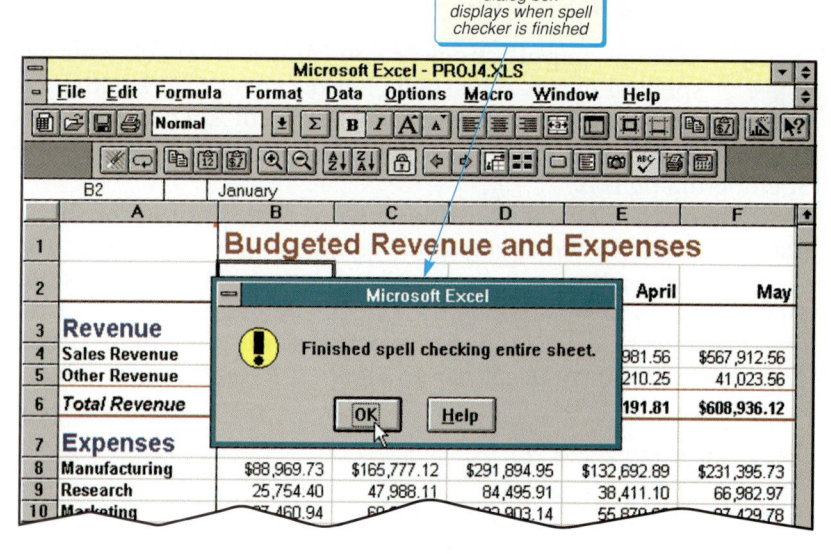

FIGURE 4-34

When the spell checker identifies a word not in the dictionaries, it changes the active cell to the cell containing the word not in the dictionaries. The Spelling dialog box (Figure 4-33) lists the word not in the dictionaries, a suggested correction, and a list of alternative spellings. If you agree with the suggested correction in the Change To box, choose the Change button. To change the word throughout the worksheet, choose the Change All button (Change All).

If one of the words in the Suggestions list box is correct, select the word and choose the Change button or double-click the word. If none of the listed words are correct, type the correct word and choose the Change button. To skip correcting the word, choose the Ignore button (Ignore). To have Excel ignore the word for the remainder of the worksheet, choose the Ignore All button (Ignore All).

Consider these additional points regarding the spell checker: (1) to check the spelling of the text in a single cell, select the cell, click in the formula bar as if you plan to edit the cell's contents, and click the Check Spelling tool on the Utility toolbar (or choose Spelling from the Options menu); (2) when you select a single cell and the formula bar is not active before invoking the spell checker, Excel checks the entire worksheet including notes and embedded charts; (3) if you select a range of cells before invoking the spell checker, Excel only checks the spelling of the words in the selected range; (4) if you select a cell other than cell A1 before you start the spell checker, a dialog box displays after Excel checks to the end of the worksheet asking if you want to continue checking at the beginning; and (5) to add words that are not in the standard dictionary to the custom dictionary, choose the Add button (Add) in the Spelling dialog box (Figure 4-33) when Excel identifies the word.

▶ PRINTING THE WORKSHEET WITH PRINT TITLES

With the worksheet complete and the text checked for misspelled words, the next step is to print the worksheet. When you print a large worksheet, you should specify print titles. **Print titles** are selected rows or columns that print on every page of the document. Print titles help identify numbers on a multipage report.

If you select a row in the worksheet such as row 1 for print titles, then row 1 prints at the top of every page. You choose a row for a print title when the worksheet is made up of rows of data that extend beyond the length of a page.

If you select a column for print titles such as column A, then column A prints on the left side of each page. You choose a column for a print title when the worksheet is made up of columns of data that extend beyond the width of a page.

In the case of Project 4 (Figure 4-1 on pages E176 and E177) the columns of numbers extend well beyond the width of a page. Thus, the row titles in column A should be chosen as print titles.

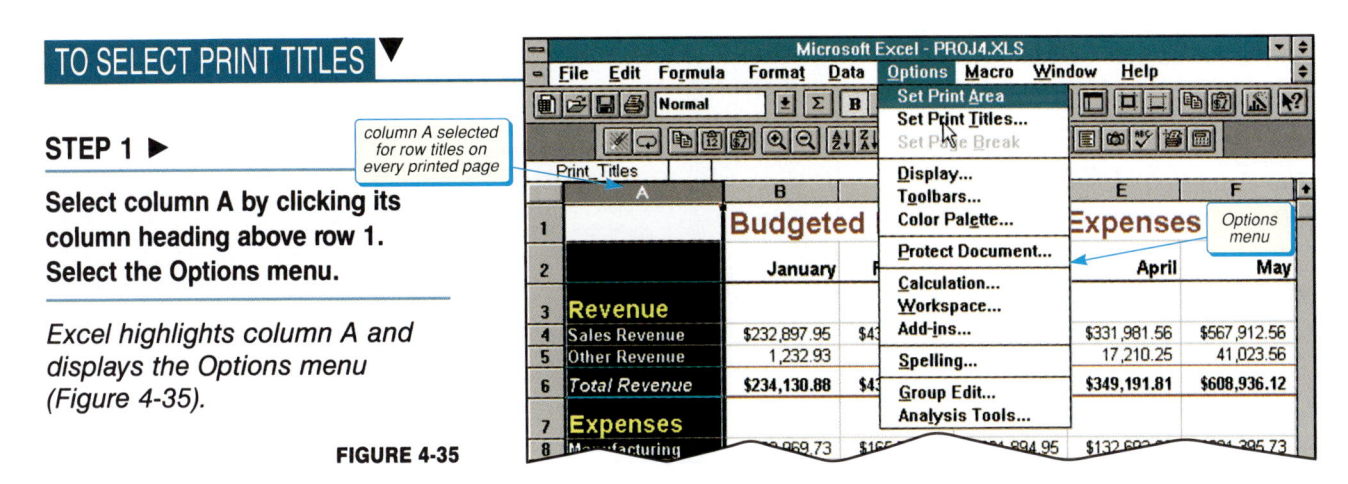

TO SELECT PRINT TITLES ▼

STEP 1 ▶

Select column A by clicking its column heading above row 1. Select the Options menu.

Excel highlights column A and displays the Options menu (Figure 4-35).

FIGURE 4-35

STEP 2 ▶

Choose the Set Print Titles command.

Excel displays the Set Print Titles dialog box (Figure 4-36). The range $A:$A in the Titles for Rows box indicates that column A will be used as print titles.

STEP 3

Choose the OK button from the Set Print Titles dialog box.

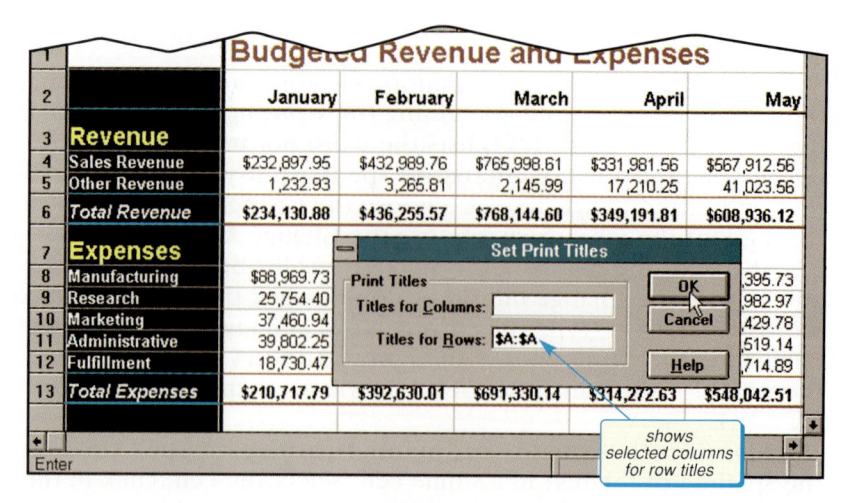

FIGURE 4-36

Before printing a large worksheet, you should consider other page setup characteristics, such as margins and page orientation.

Changing the Page Margins and Orientation

By default, a printed page has top and bottom margins of 1 inch and right and left margins of 0.75 of an inch. You can change the page margins to increase or decrease the amount of space that surrounds the printed worksheet. When you decrease the margins, Excel can fit more of the worksheet on a page. In the steps below, the right and left margins on the page will be changed from 0.75 inches to 0.5 inches.

Because the worksheet in Project 4 is wider than it is long, you can reduce the number of pages by changing the page orientation from portrait to landscape. Recall that a landscape orientation means the printout will print across the length of the paper.

TO CHANGE THE PAGE MARGINS AND ORIENTATION ▼

STEP 1 ▶

From the File menu, choose the Page Setup command. In the Page Setup dialog box, do the following: (a) in the Orientation box, select the Landscape option button; (b) in the Margins box, change Left from 0.75" to 0.5" and Right from 0.75" to 0.5"; and (c) remove the x from the Cell Gridlines box.

The Page Setup dialog box displays as shown in Figure 4-37.

STEP 2

Choose the OK button from the Page Setup dialog box.

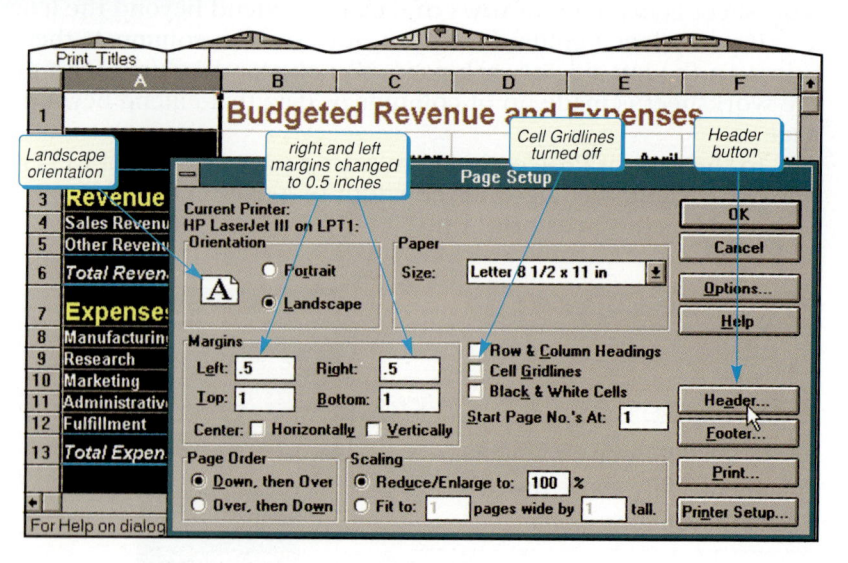

FIGURE 4-37

PRINTING THE WORKSHEET WITH PRINT TITLES **E205**

The row print titles, page margins, and orientation are now set. The next step is to print the worksheet and save it to disk with the print settings.

TO PRINT THE WORKSHEET AND SAVE IT WITH THE PAGE SETUP CHARACTERISTICS

Step 1: Use the Print Preview command on the File menu to preview the worksheet. If number signs (#) appear in the printout, increase the appropriate column widths.
Step 2: Ready the printer and print the worksheet.
Step 3: Click the Save File tool on the Standard toolbar.

The worksheet prints as a two-page printout (Figure 4-38). Excel saves the worksheet with the print titles and page setup characteristics to disk under the file name PROJ4.XLS.

FIGURE 4-38

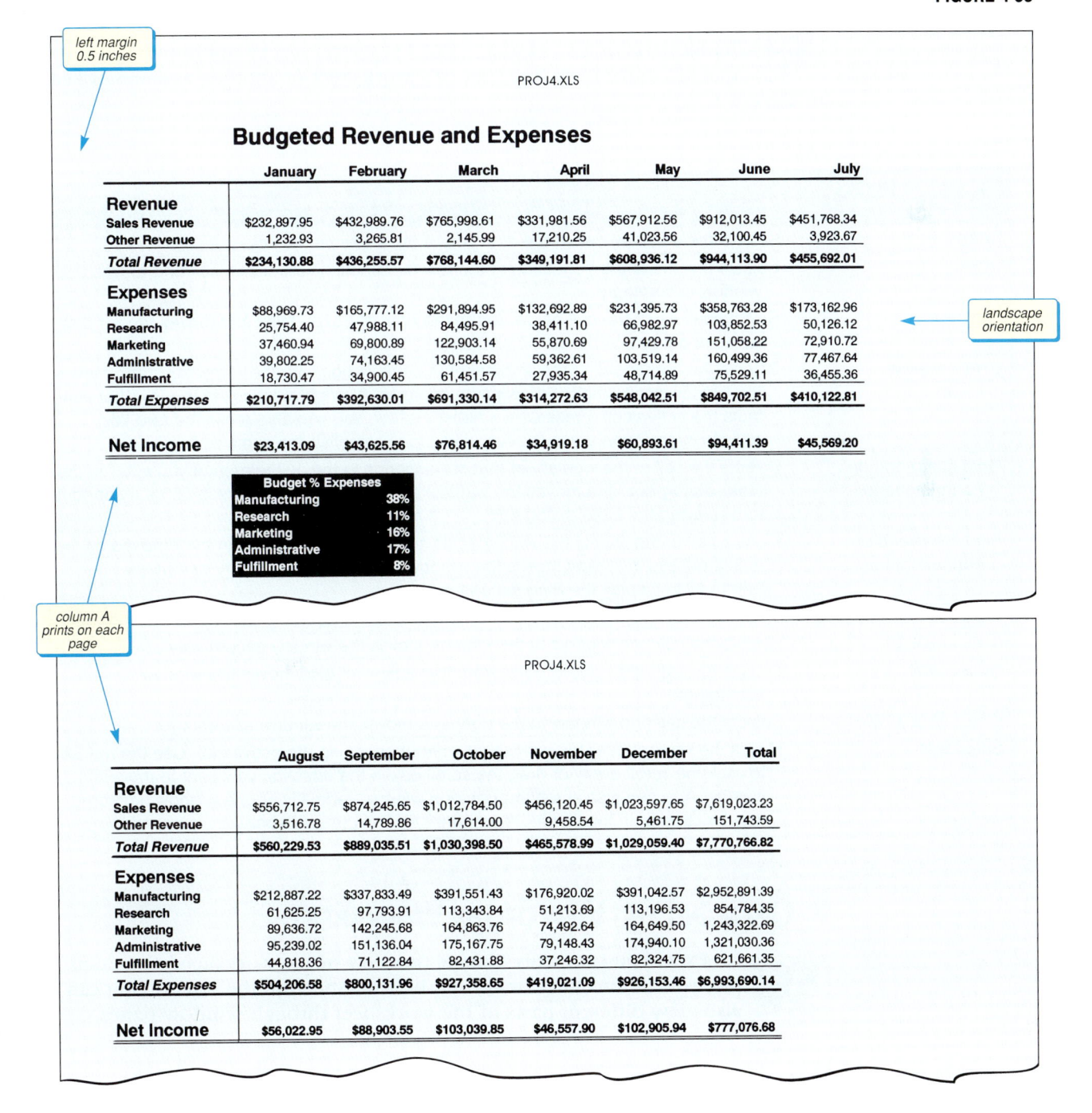

left margin 0.5 inches

PROJ4.XLS

Budgeted Revenue and Expenses

	January	February	March	April	May	June	July
Revenue							
Sales Revenue	$232,897.95	$432,989.76	$765,998.61	$331,981.56	$567,912.56	$912,013.45	$451,768.34
Other Revenue	1,232.93	3,265.81	2,145.99	17,210.25	41,023.56	32,100.45	3,923.67
Total Revenue	$234,130.88	$436,255.57	$768,144.60	$349,191.81	$608,936.12	$944,113.90	$455,692.01
Expenses							
Manufacturing	$88,969.73	$165,777.12	$291,894.95	$132,692.89	$231,395.73	$358,763.28	$173,162.96
Research	25,754.40	47,988.11	84,495.91	38,411.10	66,982.97	103,852.53	50,126.12
Marketing	37,460.94	69,800.89	122,903.14	55,870.69	97,429.78	151,058.22	72,910.72
Administrative	39,802.25	74,163.45	130,584.58	59,362.61	103,519.14	160,499.36	77,467.64
Fulfillment	18,730.47	34,900.45	61,451.57	27,935.34	48,714.89	75,529.11	36,455.36
Total Expenses	$210,717.79	$392,630.01	$691,330.14	$314,272.63	$548,042.51	$849,702.51	$410,122.81
Net Income	$23,413.09	$43,625.56	$76,814.46	$34,919.18	$60,893.61	$94,411.39	$45,569.20

landscape orientation

Budget % Expenses	
Manufacturing	38%
Research	11%
Marketing	16%
Administrative	17%
Fulfillment	8%

column A prints on each page

PROJ4.XLS

	August	September	October	November	December	Total
Revenue						
Sales Revenue	$556,712.75	$874,245.65	$1,012,784.50	$456,120.45	$1,023,597.65	$7,619,023.23
Other Revenue	3,516.78	14,789.86	17,614.00	9,458.54	5,461.75	151,743.59
Total Revenue	$560,229.53	$889,035.51	$1,030,398.50	$465,578.99	$1,029,059.40	$7,770,766.82
Expenses						
Manufacturing	$212,887.22	$337,833.49	$391,551.43	$176,920.02	$391,042.57	$2,952,891.39
Research	61,625.25	97,793.91	113,343.84	51,213.69	113,196.53	854,784.35
Marketing	89,636.72	142,245.68	164,863.76	74,492.64	164,649.50	1,243,322.69
Administrative	95,239.02	151,136.04	175,167.75	79,148.43	174,940.10	1,321,030.36
Fulfillment	44,818.36	71,122.84	82,431.88	37,246.32	82,324.75	621,661.35
Total Expenses	$504,206.58	$800,131.96	$927,358.65	$419,021.09	$926,153.46	$6,993,690.14
Net Income	$56,022.95	$88,903.55	$103,039.85	$46,557.90	$102,905.94	$777,076.68

Notice in the printout in Figure 4-38 on the previous page the reduced left margin. Because column A is repeated on the left side of page 2, it is much easier to identify what the numbers represent in the printout. Depending on the type of printer being used, you may have the August column on page 1 of the printout or on page 2 as shown in Figure 4-38.

Another way to control the number of columns and rows that print on a page is to set page breaks that instruct Excel to begin a new page. You set a page break by selecting the column in row 1 or the row in column A that begins the new page and then from the Options menu, choose the **Set Page Break command**.

▶ Moving Around the Worksheet

Up to this point, you have used the scroll bar and arrow keys to view different parts of a worksheet. Excel supports several additional ways to quickly move from one part of a worksheet to another, as summarized in Table 4-3.

▶ **TABLE 4-3**

KEY, BAR, OR COMMAND	FUNCTION
ARROW	Selects the adjacent cell in the direction of the arrow on the key.
HOME	Selects the cell at the beginning of the row that contains the active cell and moves the window accordingly.
CTRL + HOME	Selects cell A1 or the cell below and to the right of frozen titles and moves the window to the upper left corner of the worksheet.
CTRL + ARROW	Selects the border cell of the worksheet in combination with the Arrow keys and moves the window accordingly. For example, to select the rightmost cell in the row that contains the active cell, press CTRL + RIGHT ARROW. You can also press the END key, release it, and then press the Arrow key to accomplish the same task.
Goto command on Formula menu	Selects the cell in the worksheet that corresponds to the cell reference you enter in the **Goto dialog box** and moves the window accordingly. You can press F5 as a shortcut to displaying the Goto dialog box.
Find command on Formula menu	Finds a cell in the worksheet with specific contents that you enter in the Find dialog box. If necessary, Excel moves the window to display the cell. You can press SHIFT + F5 to display the Find dialog box.
PAGE UP	Selects the cell up one window from the active cell and moves the window accordingly.
CTRL + PAGE UP	Selects the cell one window to the left and moves the window accordingly.
PAGE DOWN	Selects the cell down one window from the active cell and moves the window accordingly.
CTRL + PAGE DOWN	Selects the cell one window to the right and moves the window accordingly.
Scroll Bar	Moves the window over the worksheet without changing the active cell. Use the mouse to click the scroll arrow or drag the scroll box in the direction you want to move the window. You can also scroll through one window vertically or one window horizontally by clicking in the scroll bar on either side of the scroll box.

▶ Changing the View of the Worksheet

With Excel you can easily change the view of the worksheet. For example, you can magnify or shrink the worksheet on the screen. You can also view different parts of the worksheet through window panes.

Magnifying or Shrinking the View of a Worksheet

You can magnify (zoom in) or shrink (zoom out) the display of a worksheet. When you magnify a worksheet, the characters on the screen become large and fewer columns and rows display. Alternatively, when you shrink a worksheet, more columns and rows display. Magnifying or shrinking a worksheet affects only the view; it does not change the window size or printout of the worksheet.

TO MAGNIFY AND SHRINK THE DISPLAY OF A WORKSHEET ▼

STEP 1 ▶

From the Window menu, choose the Zoom command. In the Zoom dialog box, select the 50% option button in the Magnification area.

The Zoom dialog box displays with the 50% option button selected in the Magnification box (Figure 4-39).

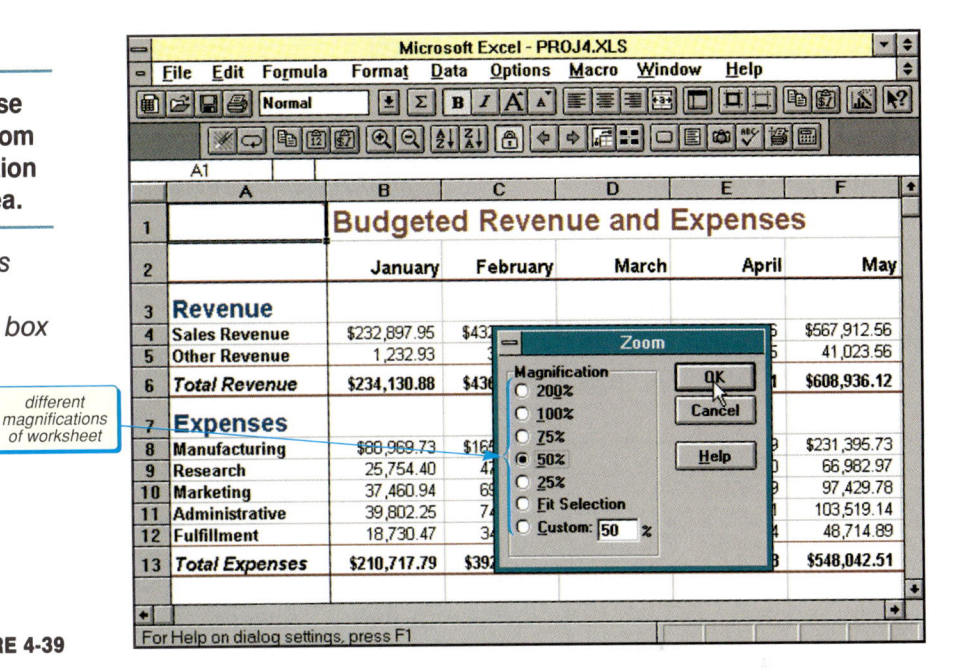

FIGURE 4-39

STEP 2 ▶

Choose the OK button from the Zoom dialog box.

Excel shrinks the display of the worksheet to a magnification of 50% of its normal display (Figure 4-40). This view displays nearly all of the Budgeted Revenue and Expenses worksheet in the window. Notice how you get a better view of the page breaks when you shrink the display of the worksheet. Depending on your printer driver, you may end up with different page breaks.

FIGURE 4-40

STEP 3 ▶

Click the Zoom In tool (🔍) on the Utility toolbar three times.

Each time you click the Zoom In tool, Excel increases the view of the worksheet to the next higher magnification percentage in the Zoom dialog box. Figure 4-41 shows the worksheet magnified to 200%.

STEP 4

Click the Zoom Out tool (🔍) on the Utility toolbar once.

Excel decreases the view of the worksheet from 200% to 100% magnification which is the default setting as shown in Figure 4-42 on the next page.

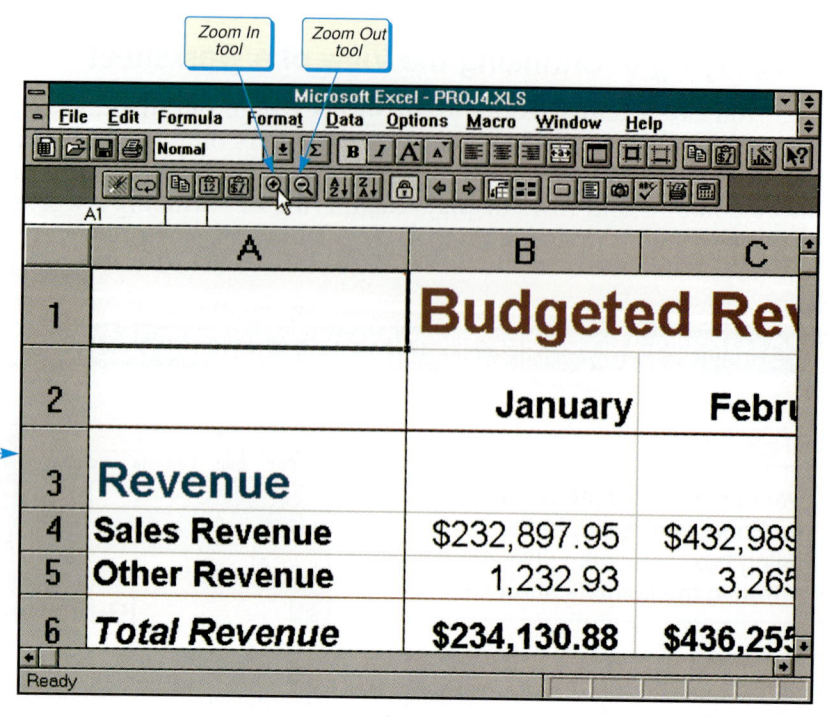

FIGURE 4-41

You can select the Custom option button in the Zoom dialog box and enter a magnification between 10% and 400% into the Custom box. You are not required to initially use the Zoom command on the Window menu. You can control the magnification by clicking the **Zoom In tool** (magnify) or **Zoom Out tool** (shrink) on the Utility toolbar.

Splitting the Window into Panes

In Excel, you can split the window into two or four **window panes** and view different parts of a large worksheet at the same time. Follow the steps below to split the window into four equal panes (see Figures 4-42 and 4-43).

TO SPLIT A WINDOW INTO FOUR PANES

Step 1: From the Window menu, choose the Unfreeze Panes command.
Step 2: Select cell D6, which is immediately to the right and below the center of the window. Select the Window menu.

Excel unfreezes the row and column titles that were frozen earlier in this project. Step 1 is required if you plan to divide the window into four equal panes because if titles are frozen, then Excel divides the window into panes on the basis of the frozen titles. Following Step 2, cell D6 is active and Excel displays the Window menu (Figure 4-42).

Step 3: From the Window menu, choose the **Split command**. Use the scroll arrows below and to the right of the panes to display the different parts of the worksheet.

Excel divides the window into four panes and the four corners of the worksheet display (Figure 4-43).

CHANGING THE VIEW OF THE WORKSHEET **E209**

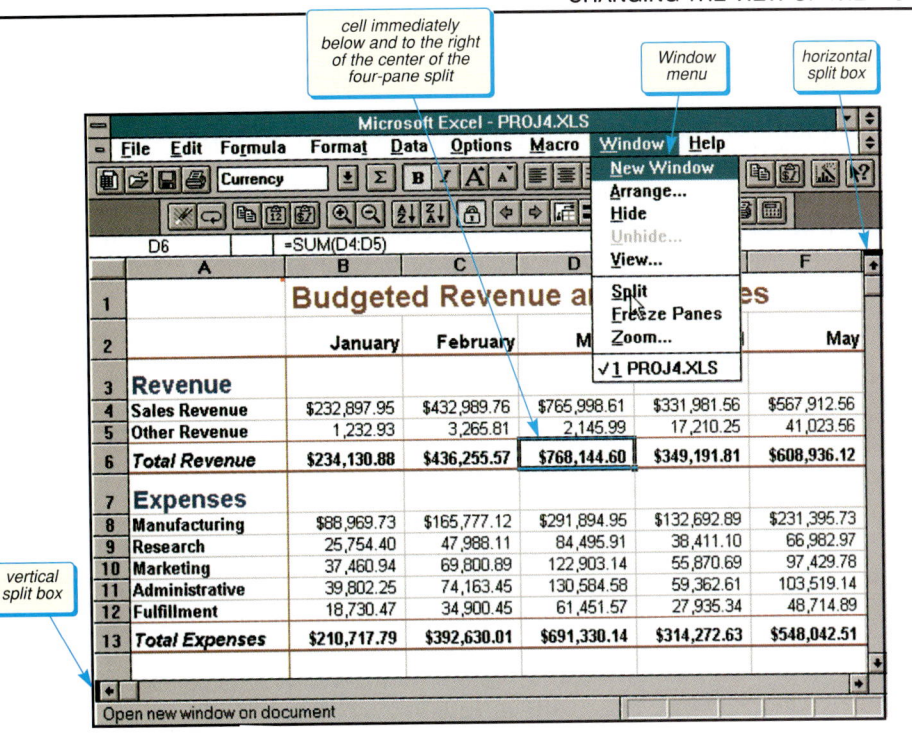

FIGURE 4-42

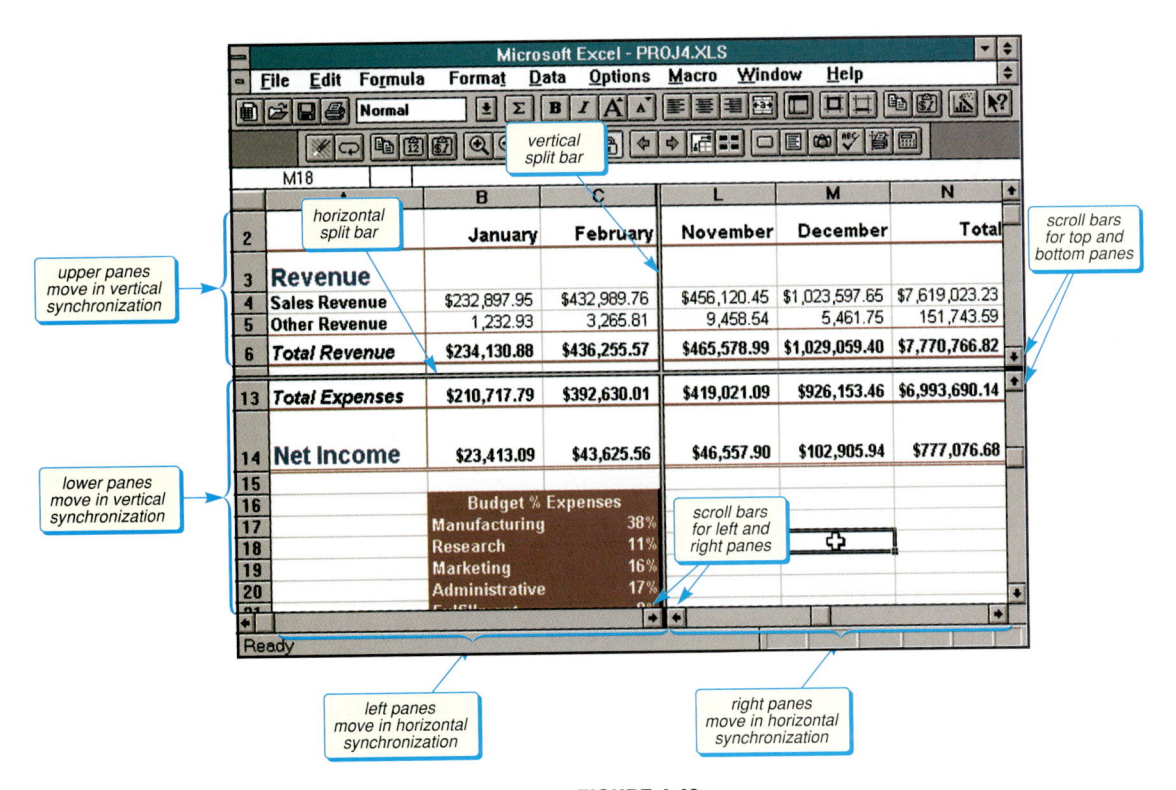

FIGURE 4-43

In Figure 4-43, the four panes are used to display the following: (1) the upper left pane displays the range A2:C6; (2) the upper right pane displays the range L2:N6; (3) the lower left pane displays A13:C20; and (4) the lower right pane displays the range L13:N20.

In Figure 4-43 on the previous page, the vertical bar going up and down the middle of the window is called the **vertical split bar**. The horizontal bar going across the middle of the window is called the **horizontal split bar**. If you look closely at the scroll bars below the window and to the right of the window, you will see that the panes split by the horizontal split bar scroll together vertically. The panes split by the vertical split bar scroll together horizontally. To resize the panes, drag either split bar to the desired location in the window.

You can change the values of cells in any of the four panes. Any change you make in one pane also takes effect in the other panes.

If you want to split the window into only two panes rather than four, replace the previous Steps 2 and 3 with the following: (1) position the mouse pointer on the **vertical split box** or the **horizontal split box** (Figure 4-42 on the previous page); and (2) drag either split box to where you want to split the window.

You can also use the split bars when four panes are on the window to resize the panes. To remove one of the split bars from the window, drag the split box back to its original location or double-click the split bar. Follow these steps to remove both split bars.

TO REMOVE THE FOUR PANES FROM THE WINDOW

Step 1: Position the mouse pointer at the intersection of the horizontal and vertical split bars.

Step 2: When the mouse pointer changes to a dark plus sign with four arrowheads (✥), double-click the left mouse button.

Excel removes the four panes from the window.

▶ OUTLINING A WORKSHEET

You can create an **outline structure** that allows you to collapse or expand rows and columns in a large worksheet. Outlining makes it easy to hide or collapse **detail rows**, such as rows 3 through 5 and 7 through 12, and display only **total rows**, such as rows 6, 13, and 14 (Figure 4-44). Likewise, you can collapse **detail columns**, such as columns B through M, and display the row titles in column A and a **total column**, such as column N.

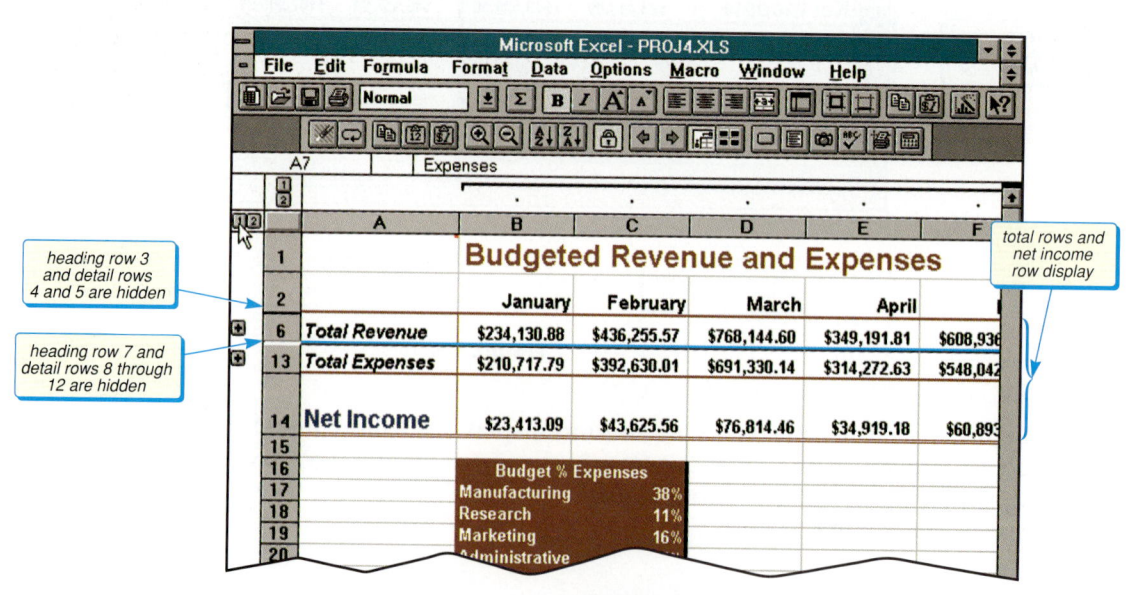

FIGURE 4-44

OUTLINING A WORKSHEET   E211

Once a worksheet is outlined, you can create charts and printouts from the total rows and total columns that describe similar levels of information but are not adjacent to one another when the worksheet displays in normal form. For example, you can treat the nonadjacent rows, 6, 13, and 14, in Figure 4-44 as if they were adjacent to one another when you chart or print the worksheet.

Creating an Outline

Excel provides two ways to create an outline from the active worksheet. First, you can use the **Outline command** from the Formula menu and have Excel create the outline automatically. Second, you can create an outline by using the **Demote tool** (▶) and **Promote tool** (◀) on the Utility toolbar.

When you use the Outline command, Excel creates the outline by inspecting ranges of cells that are used to compute totals. The Outline command does not take into consideration rows with only text such as rows 3 and 7 in the Project 4 worksheet. Thus, if you use the Outline command, you may not always end up with the outline you expect.

The Demote tool and Promote tool on the Utility toolbar allow you to choose exactly which rows or columns you want in each subordinate level. The following steps show how to create an outline of the worksheet using the Demote and Promote tools. In Project 4, the detail rows are 3 through 5 and 7 through 12. The detail columns are B through M.

TO CREATE AN OUTLINE OF YOUR WORKSHEET ▼

STEP 1 ▶

Select rows 3 through 5 by dragging the mouse pointer through their row headings to the left of column A and then releasing the mouse button. Point to the Demote tool.

Excel highlights rows 3 through 5 (Figure 4-45).

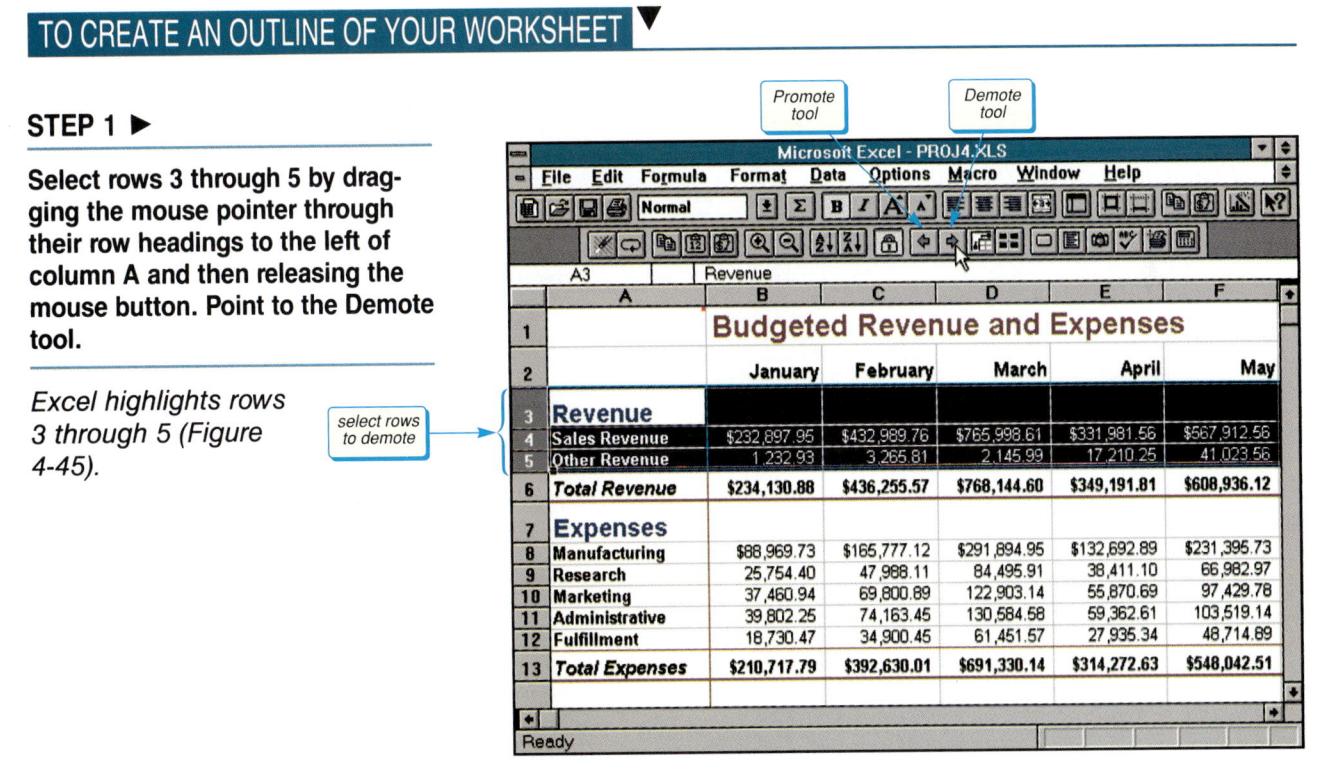

FIGURE 4-45

E212 PROJECT 4 WORKING WITH LARGE WORKSHEETS

STEP 2 ▶

Click the Demote tool on the Utility toolbar.

Excel displays a **row level bar** ([ ) with a **collapse symbol** (⊟) on the left side of the window which encompasses rows 3 through 5 (Figure 4-46). Next to the Select All button are **row level symbols** (1 2) that are used to collapse and expand rows 3 through 5.

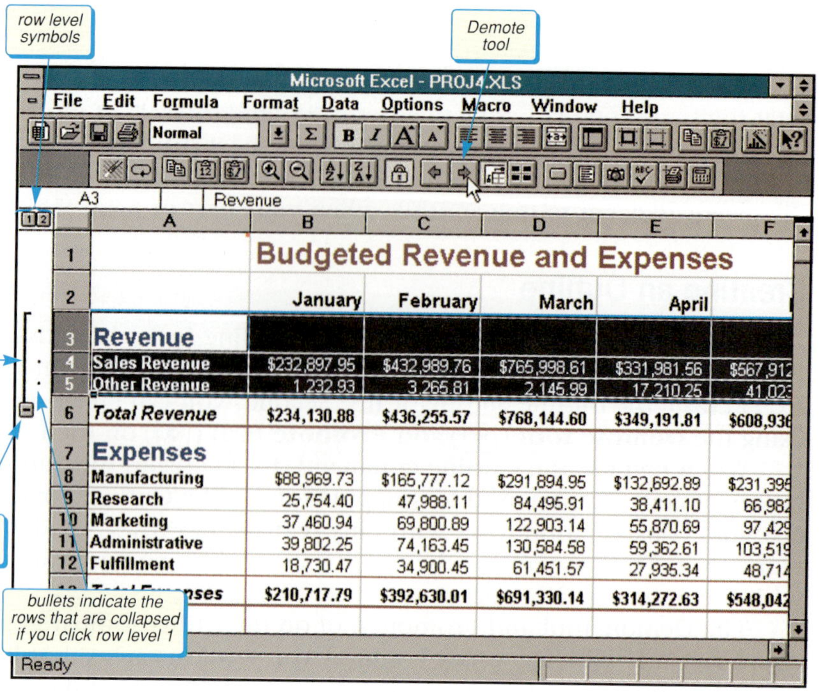

FIGURE 4-46

STEP 3 ▶

Select rows 7 through 12 by dragging the mouse pointer through their row headings to the left of column A and then releasing the left mouse button.

Excel highlights rows 7 through 12 (Figure 4-47).

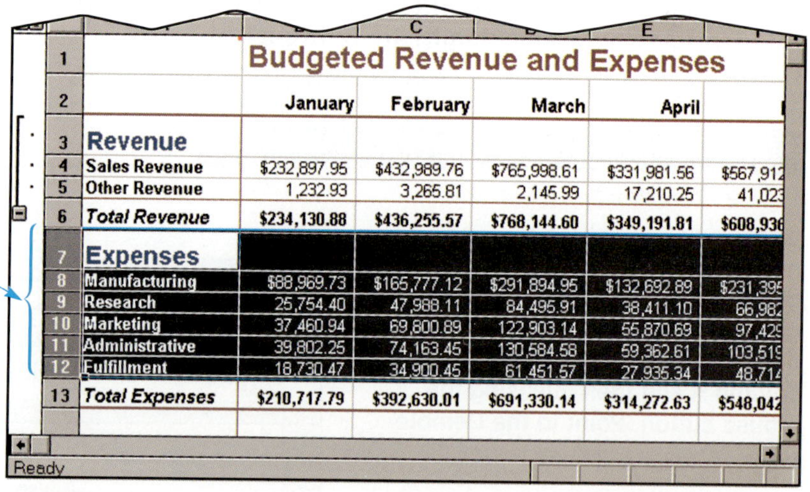

FIGURE 4-47

STEP 4 ▶

Click the Demote tool on the Utility toolbar.

Excel displays a row level bar with a collapse symbol on the left side of the window. The row level bar encompasses rows 7 through 12 (Figure 4-48).

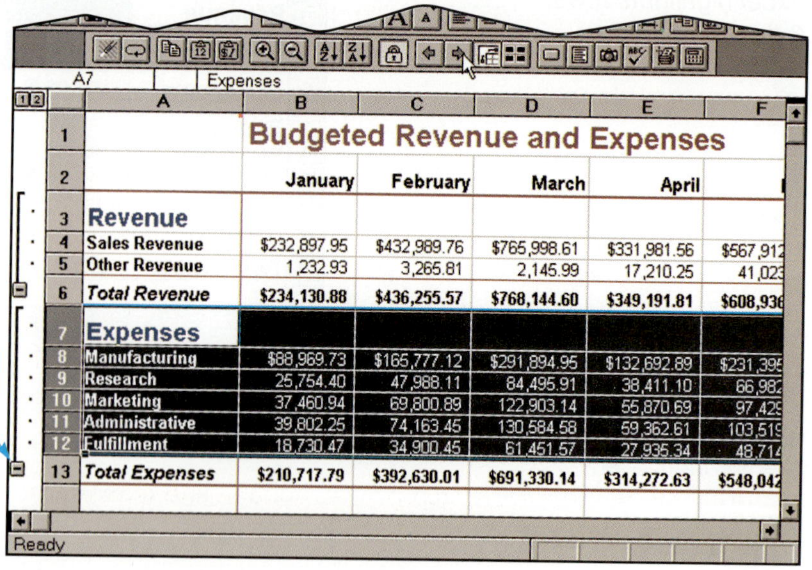

FIGURE 4-48

OUTLINING A WORKSHEET **E213**

STEP 5 ▶

Select columns B through M by dragging the mouse pointer through their column headings above row 1 and then releasing the left mouse button.

Excel highlights columns B through M (Figure 4-49).

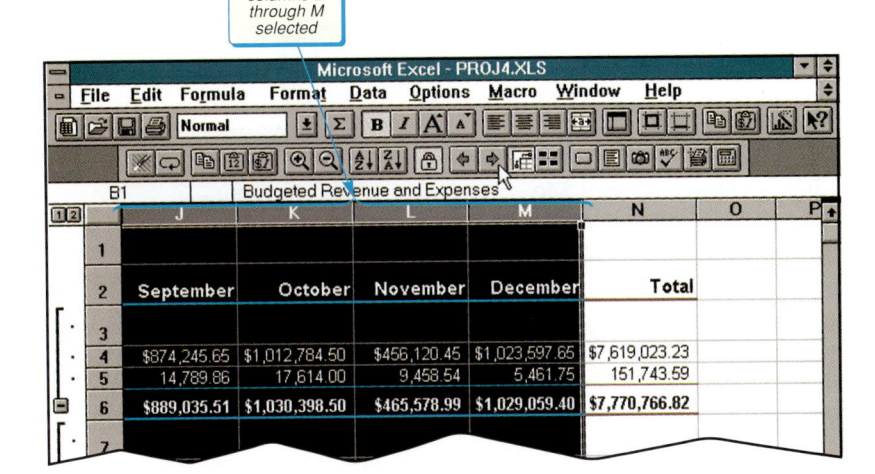

FIGURE 4-49

STEP 6 ▶

Click the Demote tool on the Utility toolbar.

*Excel displays a **column level bar** (▬) with a collapse symbol above the window that encompasses columns B through M (Figure 4-50). Above the Select All button are **column level symbols** ( ) that are used to collapse and expand columns B through M.*

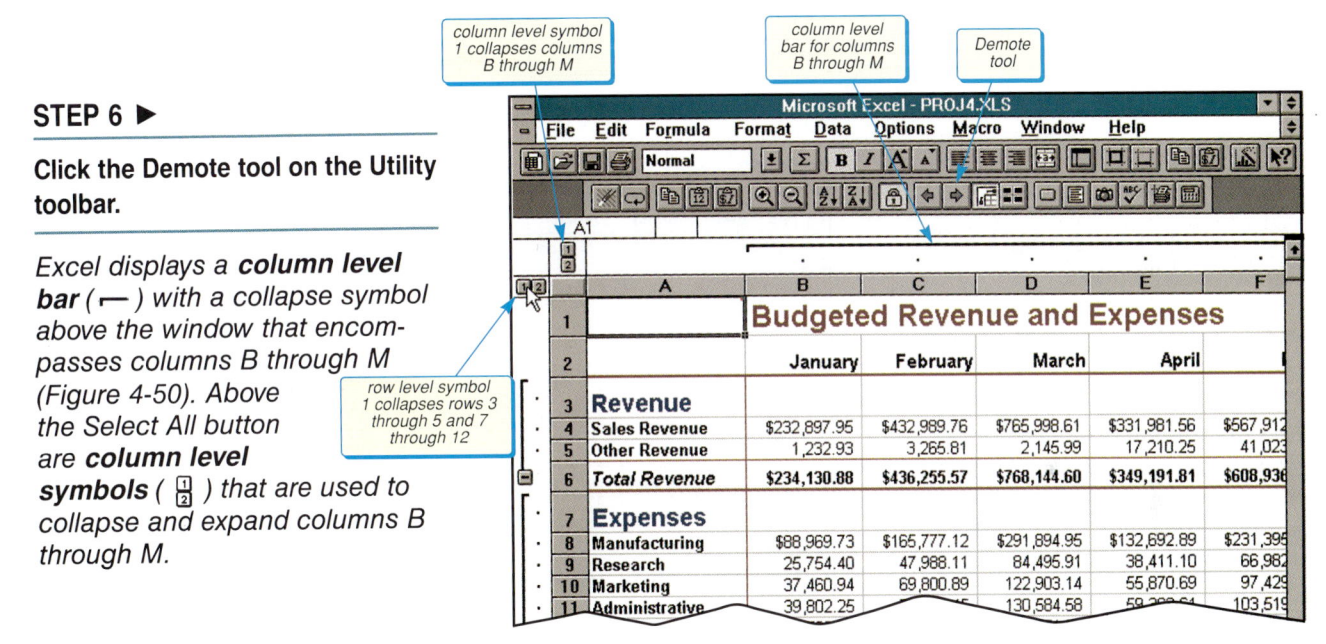

FIGURE 4-50

With the worksheet outlined, you can easily hide or display the subordinate rows (3 through 5 and 7 through 12) and columns (B through M) by collapsing or expanding them. You collapse all level 1 row subordinates by clicking the row level symbol 1, which is next to the Select All button (Figure 4-50). You collapse all column level subordinates by clicking the column level symbol 1 above the Select All button.

You can click the collapse symbols or the level bars to collapse individual detail rows or columns at the same level. When you collapse rows or columns, the collapse symbol changes to an **expand symbol** ( ) and the level bar disappears.

Perform the following steps to use the row and column levels next to the Select All button to collapse subordinate levels.

TO COLLAPSE DETAIL ROWS AND COLUMNS ▼

STEP 1 ►

Click row level symbol 1 to the left of the Select All button.

All detail rows (3 through 5 and 7 through 12) at the first level are hidden (Figure 4-51). Notice that the totals rows (rows 6, 13, and 14) are now adjacent to one another.

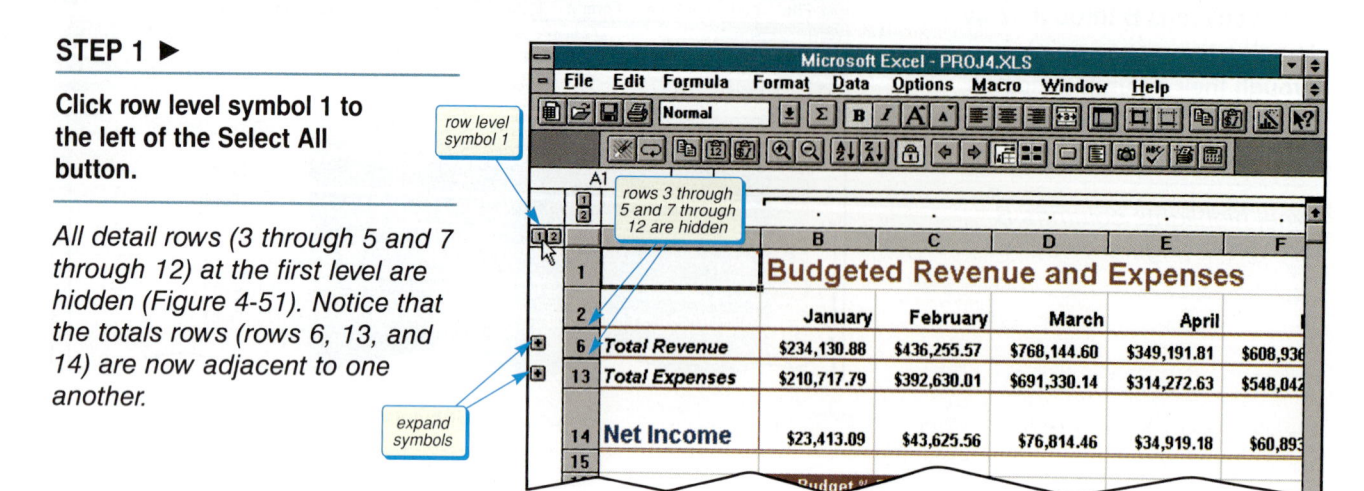

FIGURE 4-51

STEP 2 ►

Click column level symbol 1 above the Select All button.

The detail columns (B through M) at the first level are hidden (Figure 4-52). With all detail rows and columns hidden, the only visible information are the totals for the revenue, expenses, and net income.

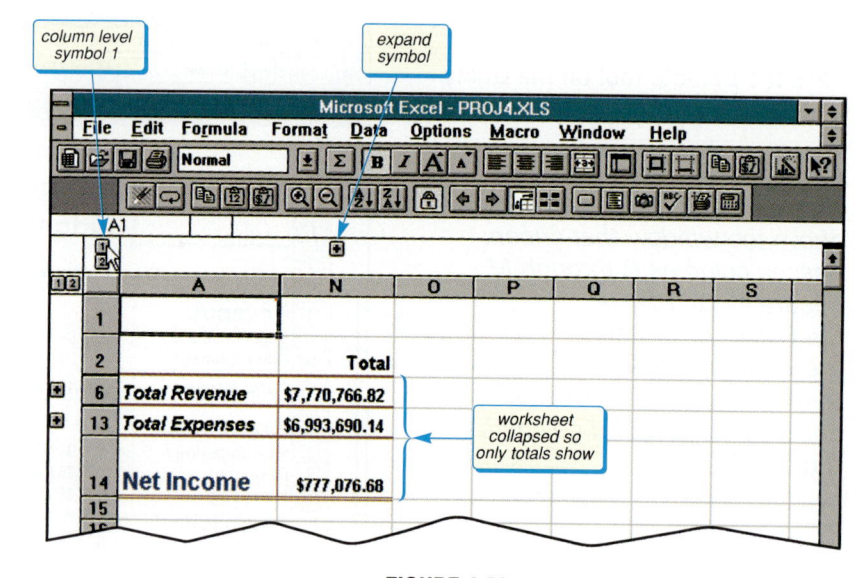

FIGURE 4-52

Working with the Visible Cells in an Outlined Worksheet

With the worksheet collapsed (Figure 4-52), you can print or chart the **visible cells**. For example, if you click the Print tool on the Standard toolbar after collapsing the subordinate rows and columns, Excel prints only the visible cells.

To chart the visible cells, you select them and then click the **Select Visible Cells tool** ( ) on the Utility toolbar. It is important that you click the Select Visible Cells tool or Excel will assume you want to chart both the visible and invisible cells. The following steps show how to create a three-dimensional column chart of the visible cells in Figure 4-52.

TO CHART VISIBLE CELLS

Step 1: Select the visible cells A2, N2, A6, N6, A13, N13, A14, and N14 as you would any range of adjacent cells. Click the Select Visible Cells tool on the Utility toolbar. Click the ChartWizard tool on the Standard toolbar. Drag the mouse down and across the chart location A15:R22. Release the mouse button to display the ChartWizard dialog box. In the ChartWizard dialog box, click the rightmost button with the two greater than signs.

Step 2: Click the 3-D Column Chart tool ( ) on the Chart toolbar at the bottom of the screen.

Excel draws a two-dimensional column chart comparing the total revenue, total expenses, and net income. Then, Excel changes the two-dimensional chart to a three-dimensional chart (Figure 4-53). After viewing the 3-D column chart, select it and press the DELETE key to clear it from the screen.

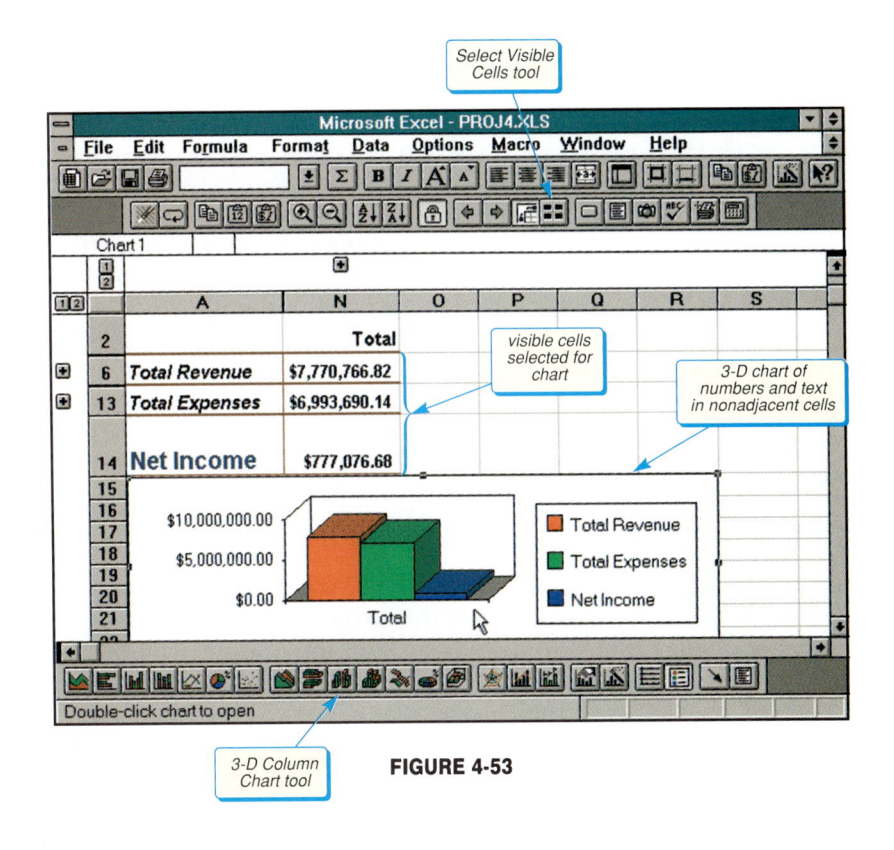

FIGURE 4-53

If you plan to expand the worksheet to show all the rows and columns, then you must delete the chart. If you don't delete the chart and then expand the rows and columns, Excel stretches the chart across the range selected in Step 1 as the chart location, A15:R22. If you click the Print tool on the Standard toolbar with the collapsed worksheet and embedded chart, Excel will print the worksheet and chart as it displays on the screen.

Expanding Collapsed Rows and Columns

To expand collapsed rows and columns and return the worksheet to its original form, click the row and column levels as described at the top of the next page.

TO EXPAND COLLAPSED ROWS AND COLUMNS ▼

STEP 1

Click row level symbol 2 to the left of the Select All Button to expand and display the subordinate rows — 3 through 5 and 7 through 12.

The greatest row and column level symbols always expand the worksheet to display all cells.

STEP 2 ▶

Click the column level symbol 2 above the Select All button.

Excel expands the subordinate columns — B through M (Figure 4-54).

FIGURE 4-54

▲

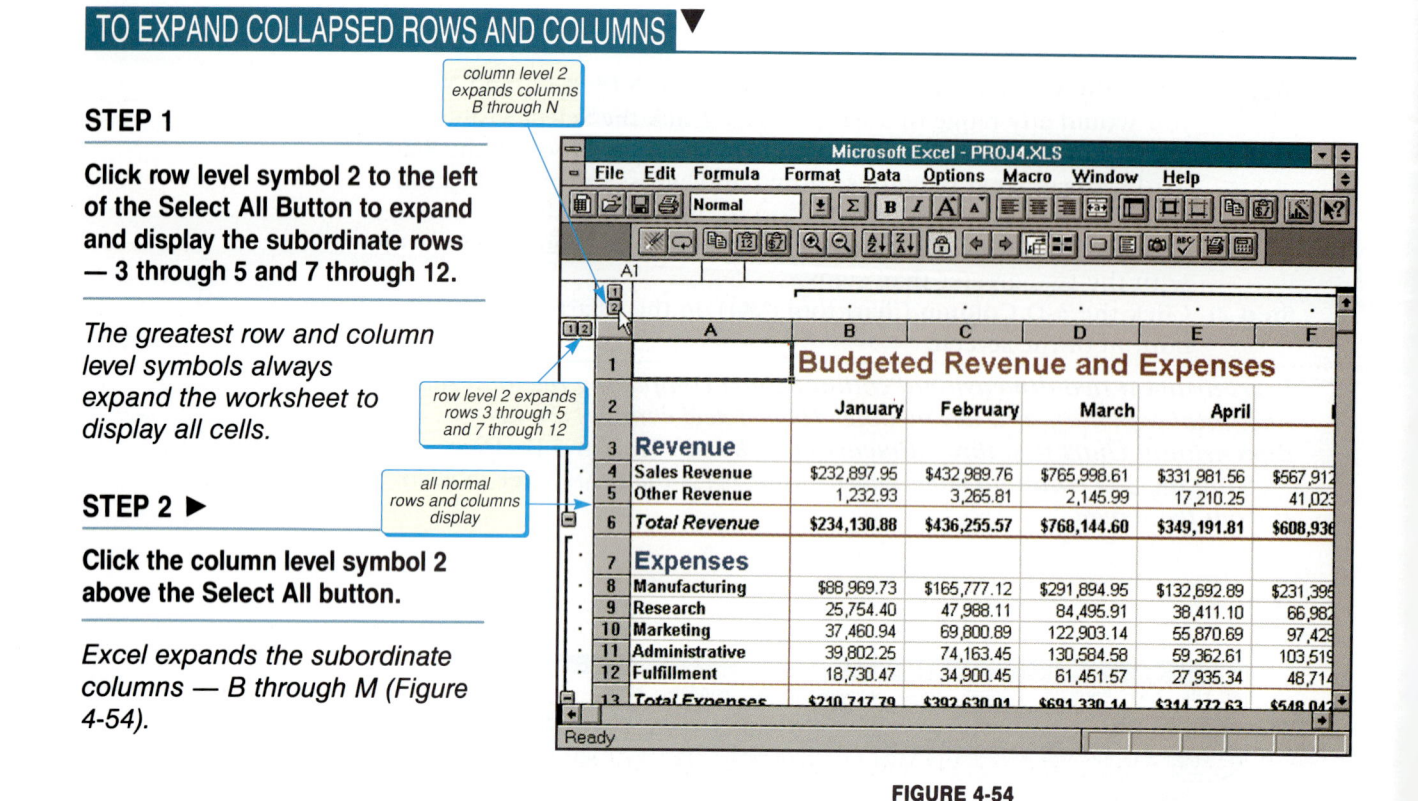

To display the hidden columns and rows, you can also click the expand symbols, one by one, rather than using the row and column level symbols.

Displaying and Hiding the Outline Symbols

When you're not using the outline symbols, you can hide them to increase the size of the window. When you need them to collapse rows and columns, you can quickly display them. To display or hide the outline symbols, you can use the **Show Outline Symbols tool** (📄) on the Utility toolbar or select the Outline Symbols check box in the Display dialog box. The Display command is on the Options menu.

The steps at the top of the next page illustrate the use of the Show Outline Symbols tool to hide and display the outline symbols.

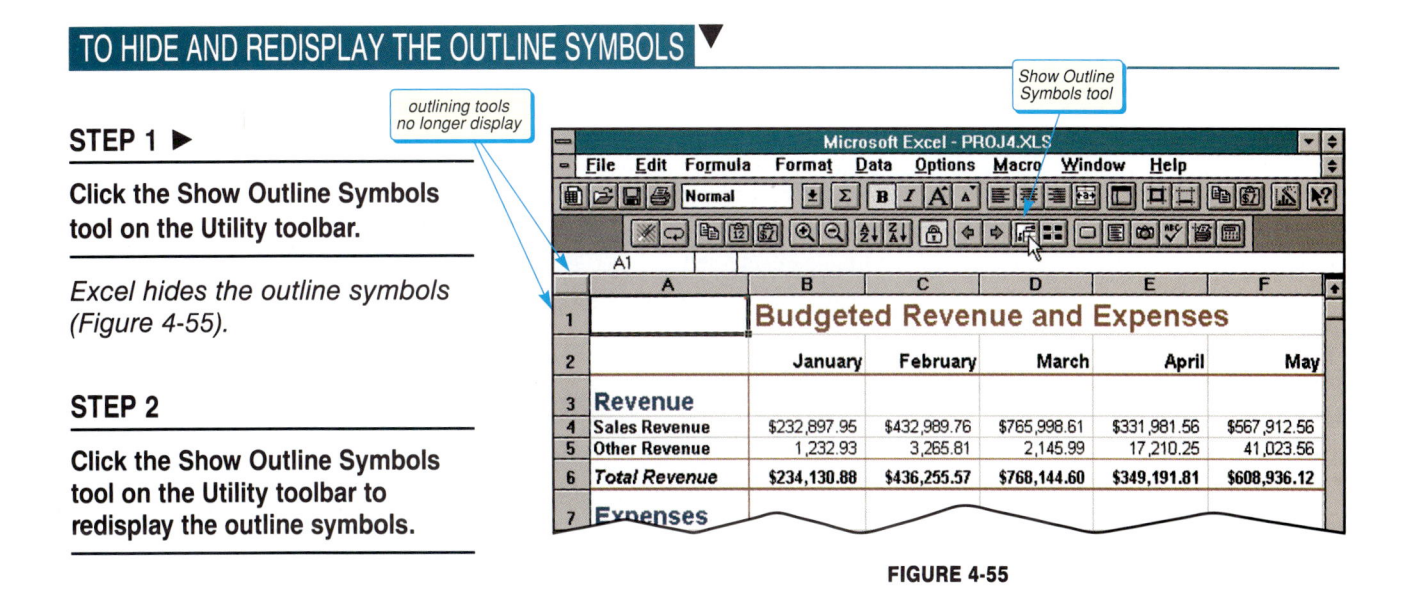

TO HIDE AND REDISPLAY THE OUTLINE SYMBOLS ▼

STEP 1 ▶

Click the Show Outline Symbols tool on the Utility toolbar.

Excel hides the outline symbols (Figure 4-55).

STEP 2

Click the Show Outline Symbols tool on the Utility toolbar to redisplay the outline symbols.

FIGURE 4-55

Saving the Worksheet with the Outline

The next activity in working with a large worksheet introduces you to deleting the worksheet outline. Before moving on to the next section, follow these steps to save the worksheet to disk with the outline.

TO SAVE THE WORKSHEET WITH OUTLINE SYMBOLS HIDDEN

Step 1: Click the Show Outline Symbols on the Utility toolbar to hide the outline symbols.
Step 2: Click the Save File tool on the Standard toolbar to save the worksheet using the file name PROJ4.XLS.
Step 3: Click the Show Outline Symbols on the Utility toolbar to redisplay the outline symbols.

The outlined worksheet is saved to disk with the outline symbols hidden. Step 3 redisplays the outline symbols in the worksheet on the screen in preparation for showing you how to delete an outline.

Changing Levels and Clearing the Outline Structure

Once you develop an outline structure, you can change it by demoting and promoting columns and rows from one level of the outline to another. Excel allows you to have up to eight levels in an outline. To change the outline, first select the columns or rows you want to move to another level. Next, depending on the direction of the move, use the Demote tool or Promote tool on the Utility toolbar.

To clear the outline structure from the worksheet, select the entire worksheet and use the Promote tool to move subordinate levels up to their superior levels. The steps at the top of the next page show how to remove the outline structure from the worksheet.

TO CLEAR AN OUTLINE STRUCTURE FROM A WORKSHEET

STEP 1

Click the Select All button to select and highlight the entire worksheet.

STEP 2 ▶

Click the Promote tool to display the Promote dialog box (Figure 4-56). With the Rows option button selected in the Promote box, choose the OK button.

STEP 3

Redo Step 2 until there are no more subordinate rows levels left. After all the rows levels are removed, select the Columns option button in the Promote box and repeat Step 2 in Figure 4-56.

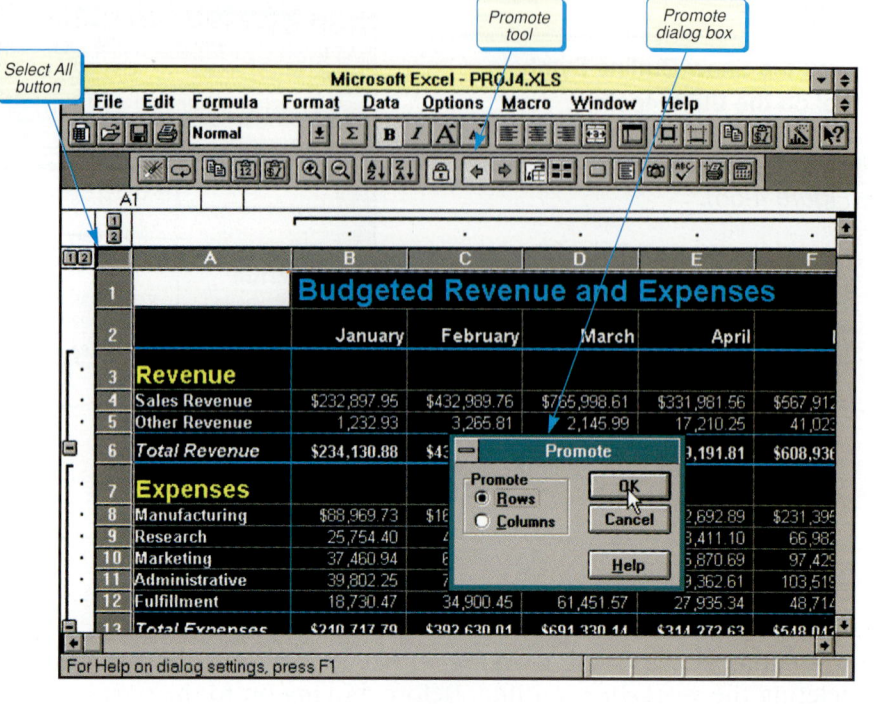

FIGURE 4-56

▶ Changing Values in Cells That Are Referenced in a Formula

The automatic recalculation feature of Excel is a powerful tool that can be used to analyze your worksheet data. Using Excel to scrutinize the impact of changing values in cells that are referenced by a formula in another cell is called **what-if analysis** or **sensitivity analysis**.

In Project 4, the monthly expenses in the range A8:M12 are dependent on the budget percent expenses in the range B16:C21. Thus, if you change any of the budgeted percent expenses, Excel immediately recalculates the monthly expenses in rows 8 through 12, the monthly total expenses in row 13, and the monthly net incomes in row 14. These new values in turn cause Excel to recalculate a new annual net income in cell N14.

A what-if question for the worksheet in Project 4 might be, *What if all the budgeted percent values in the range B16:C21 are decreased by 1% to the following: Manufacturing (37%); Research (10%); Marketing (15%); Administrative (17%); Fulfillment (7%)—how would these changes affect the annual expenses in cell N13 and the annual net income in cell N14?* To answer questions like this, you need only change these five percent values in the worksheet. Excel immediately answers the questions regarding the annual expenses in cell N13 and annual income in cell N14 by instantaneously recalculating these figures.

So that the Budget % Expenses table (range B16:C21) and the total expenses in cell N13 and net income in cell N14 show on the screen at the same time, the steps on the next page also divide the window into two vertical panes.

CHANGING VALUES IN CELLS THAT ARE REFERENCED IN A FORMULA E219

TO ANALYZE DATA IN A WORKSHEET BY CHANGING VALUES ▼

STEP 1 ▶

Drag the vertical split box from the lower left corner of the screen so that the vertical split bar is positioned immediately to the right of column E and then release the left mouse button. Use the right scroll arrow in the right pane to display the totals in column N.

Excel divides the window into two vertical panes and shows the totals in column N in the pane on the right side of the window (Figure 4-57).

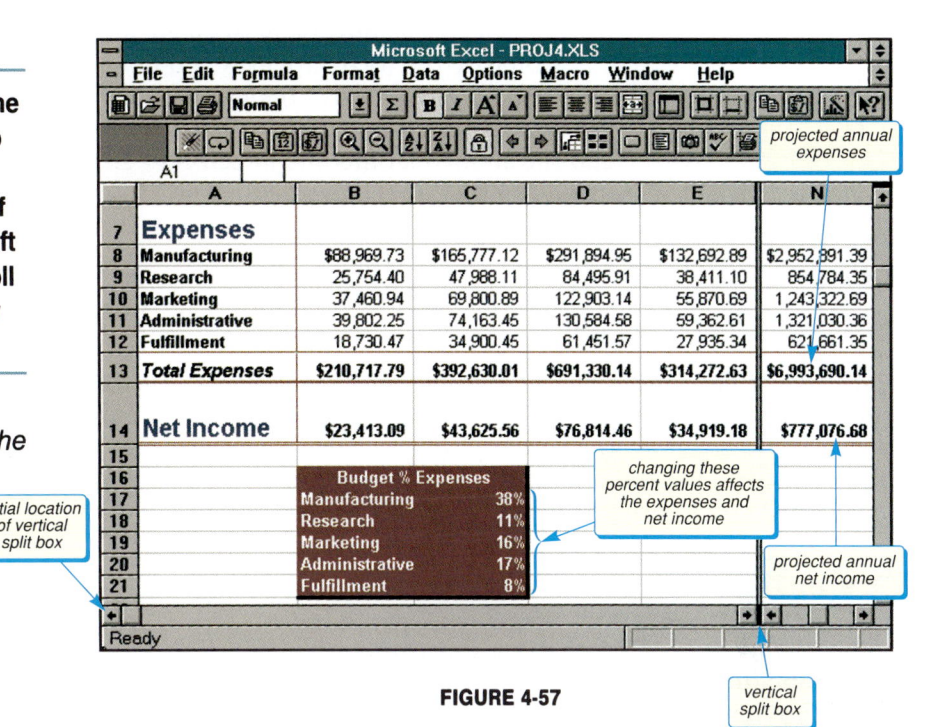

FIGURE 4-57

STEP 2 ▶

Enter 37% in cell C17, 10% in cell C18, 15% in cell C19, 16% in cell C20, and 7% in cell C21.

Excel immediately recalculates all the formulas in the worksheet, including the total expenses in cell N13 and annual net income in cell N14 (Figure 4-58).

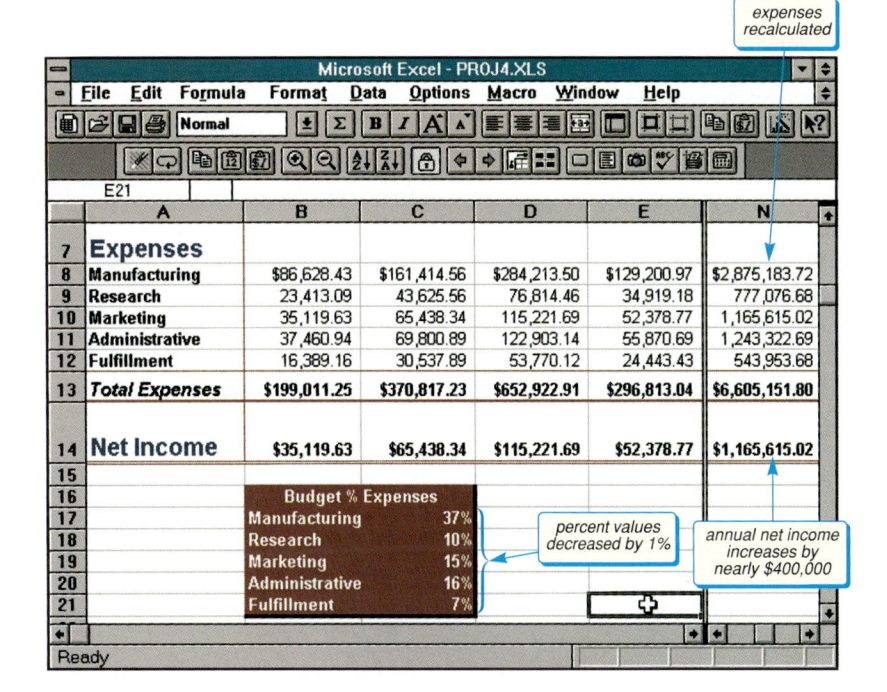

FIGURE 4-58

Each time you enter one of the new percent expenses, Excel recalculates the worksheet. This process usually takes less than one second, depending on how many calculations must be performed and the speed of your computer.

Compare the total expenses and net incomes in Figures 4-57 and 4-58. By reducing the original five budgeted percent expenses in Figure 4-57 by 1% each, the total expenses in cell N13 changes from $6,993,690.14 to $6,605,151.80 and the annual net income in cell N14 changes from $777,076.68 (Figure 4-57) to $1,165,615.02 (Figure 4-58). The 1% reduction in budgeted expenses translates into a net income gain of $388,538.34 for the year.

▶ Project Summary

This project introduced you to working with large worksheets. You learned how to freeze titles, change the magnification of the worksheet, and display different parts of the worksheet through panes. You also learned how to create an outline of the worksheet, add notes, check the spelling of the text in the worksheet, use the fill handle to create a series, and display hidden toolbars. Finally, this project introduced you to using Excel to do what-if analysis.

▶ Key Terms

audio comment (*E200*)
Check Spelling tool (*E201*)
collapse symbol (*E212*)
column level bar (*E213*)
column level symbol (*E213*)
Comma Style tool (*E184*)
comments (*E198*)
Copy command (*E180*)
Currency Style tool (*E184*)
custom dictionary (*E201*)
Demote tool (*E211*)
detail columns (*E210*)
detail rows (*E210*)
drop shadow (*E196*)
expand symbol (*E213*)
floating toolbar (*E185*)
Formatting toolbar (*E184*)
Freeze Panes command (*E187*)
freezing worksheet titles (*E187*)
Goto command (*E206*)
hiding a toolbar (*E192*)

horizontal split bar (*E210*)
horizontal split box (*E210*)
level bars (*E212, E213*)
nonadjacent selection (*E186*)
notes (*E198*)
Note command (*E199*)
Outline command (*E211*)
outline structure (*E210*)
Paste command (*E180*)
pattern (*E197*)
Patterns command (*E197*)
print titles (*E203*)
Promote tool (*E211*)
row level bar (*E212*)
row level symbol (*E212*)
Select Visible Cells tool (*E214*)
sensitivity analysis (*E218*)
Set Page Break command (*E206*)
Set Print Titles command (*E203*)
shaded cells (*E196*)

Show Outline Symbols tool
  (*E216*)
spell checker (*E201*)
Spelling command (*E201*)
Split command (*E208*)
standard dictionary (*E201*)
toolbar dock (*E185*)
Toolbar shortcut menu (*E184*)
total columns (*E210*)
total rows (*E210*)
Unfreeze Panes command (*E188*)
Utility toolbar (*E200*)
vertical split bar (*E210*)
vertical split box (*E210*)
visible cells (*E214*)
what-if analysis (*E218*)
window pane (*E208*)
Zoom command (*E207*)
Zoom In tool (*E208*)
Zoom Out tool (*E208*)

QUICK REFERENCE

In Microsoft Excel you can accomplish a task in a number of ways. The following table provides a quick reference to each task presented in this project with its available options. The commands listed in the Menu column can be executed using either the keyboard or mouse.

Task	Mouse	Menu	Keyboard Shortcuts
Copy Selection onto Clipboard	Click Copy tool on Standard toolbar	From Edit menu, choose Copy	Press CTRL + C
Demote Rows or Columns	Click Demote tool on Utility toolbar	From Formula menu, choose Outline	Press ALT + SHIFT + RIGHT ARROW
Drop Shadow	Click Drop Shadow tool on Drawing toolbar	From Format menu, choose Border	
Freeze Worksheet Titles	Click Freeze Panes tool (custom tool)	From Window menu, choose Freeze Panes	
Go to Specific Cell		From Formula menu, choose Goto	Press F5
Nonadjacent Selection	Select first range and hold down CTRL key to select additional ranges		
Note		From Formula menu, choose Note	Press SHIFT + F2
Page Break		From Options menu, choose Set Page Break	
Paste Selection from Clipboard	Click Paste Values tool on Utility toolbar	From Edit menu, choose Paste	Press CTRL + V
Print Titles		From Options menu, choose Set Print Titles	
Promote Rows or Columns	Click Promote tool on Utility toolbar		Press ALT + SHIFT + LEFT ARROW
Remove Splits	Drag split bars	From Window menu, choose Remove Split	
Series Creation	Drag fill handle	From Data menu, choose Series	
Shade Cells	Click Light Shading tool on Formatting toolbar	From Format menu, choose Patterns	
Show or Hide Outline Symbols	Click Show Outline Symbols on Utility toolbar		Press CTRL + 8
Spelling	Click Check Spelling tool on Utility toolbar	From Options menu, choose Spelling	
Split Windows into Panes	Drag vertical split box or horizontal split box	From Window menu, choose Split	
Toolbar Show or Hide	Position mouse pointer in toolbar and click right mouse button	From Options menu, choose Toolbar	Press CTRL + 7
Unfreeze Worksheet Titles	Click Freeze Panes tool (custom tool)	From Window menu, choose Unfreeze Panes	
Visible Cell Selection	Click Select Visible Cells tool on Utility toolbar		Press ALT + ;
Zoom In	Click Zoom In tool on Utility toolbar	From Window menu, choose Zoom	
Zoom Out	Click Zoom Out tool on Utility toolbar	From Window menu, choose Zoom	

TOOLBAR REFERENCE

The tools on the most often used toolbars are summarized below. Because you can use the Customize command on the Toolbar shortcut menu to add, delete, and relocate tools on a toolbar, the number and location of the tools that display on your toolbars may be different than those shown below.

Point to an active toolbar and click the right mouse button to display, hide, or customize any one of these toolbars. See page E190 for instructions as to how to list the functions of the tools on any toolbar.

Standard Toolbar

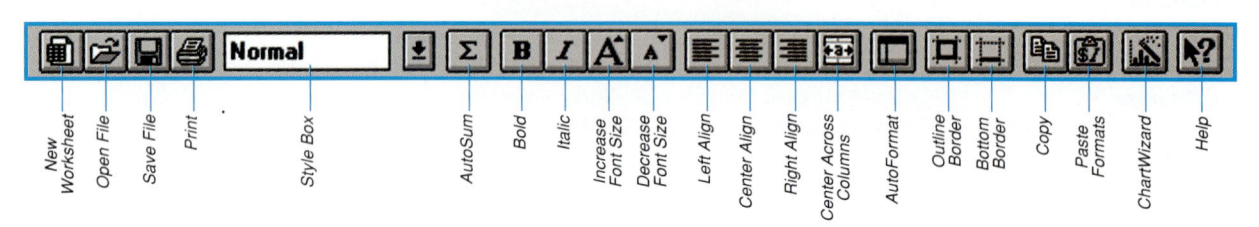

Tools (left to right): New Worksheet, Open File, Save File, Print, Style Box, AutoSum, Bold, Italic, Increase Font Size, Decrease Font Size, Left Align, Center Align, Right Align, Center Across Columns, AutoFormat, Outline Border, Bottom Border, Copy, Paste Formats, ChartWizard, Help

Formatting Toolbar

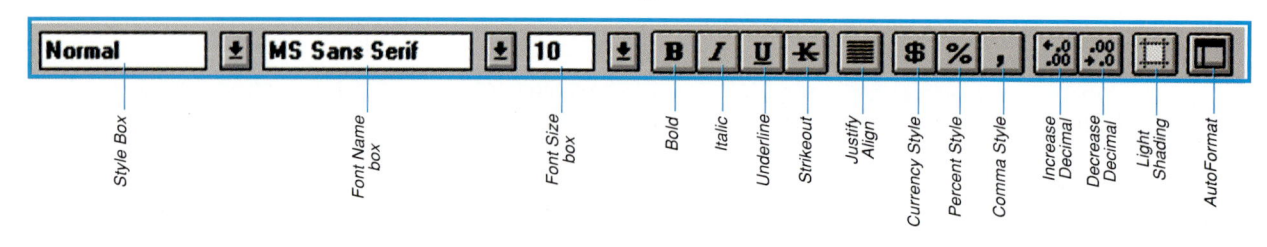

Tools (left to right): Style Box, Font Name box, Font Size box, Bold, Italic, Underline, Strikeout, Justify Align, Currency Style, Percent Style, Comma Style, Increase Decimal, Decrease Decimal, Light Shading, AutoFormat

Utility Toolbar

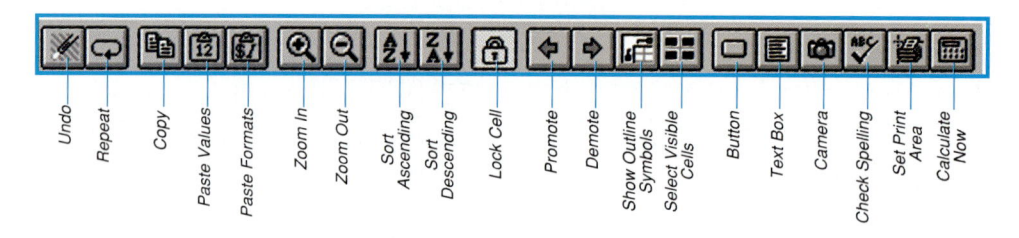

Tools (left to right): Undo, Repeat, Copy, Paste Values, Paste Formats, Zoom In, Zoom Out, Sort Ascending, Sort Descending, Lock Cell, Promote, Demote, Show Outline Symbols, Select Visible Cells, Button, Text Box, Camera, Check Spelling, Set Print Area, Calculate Now

Chart Toolbar

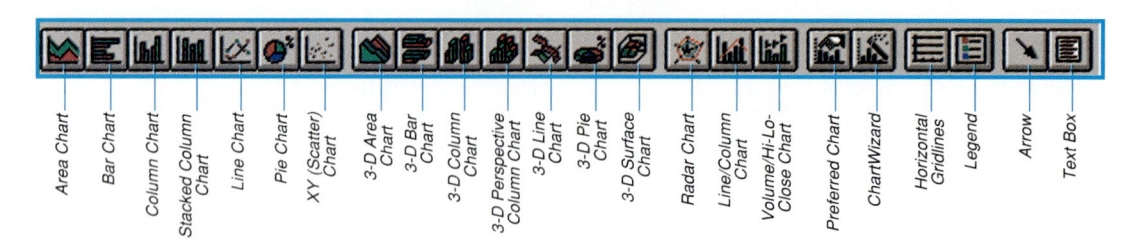

Tools (left to right): Area Chart, Bar Chart, Column Chart, Stacked Column Chart, Line Chart, Pie Chart, XY (Scatter) Chart, 3-D Area Chart, 3-D Bar Chart, 3-D Column Chart, 3-D Perspective Column Chart, 3-D Line Chart, 3-D Pie Chart, 3-D Surface Chart, Radar Chart, Line/Column Chart, Volume/Hi-Lo-Close Chart, Preferred Chart, ChartWizard, Horizontal Gridlines, Legend, Arrow, Text Box

Drawing Toolbar

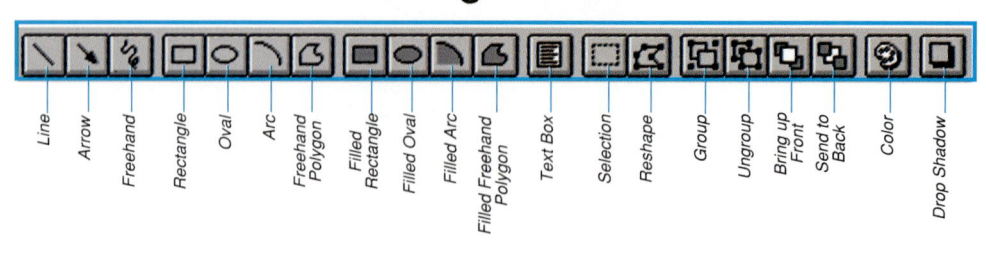

Tools (left to right): Line, Arrow, Freehand, Rectangle, Oval, Arc, Freehand Polygon, Filled Rectangle, Filled Oval, Filled Arc, Filled Freehand Polygon, Text Box, Selection, Reshape, Group, Ungroup, Bring up Front, Send to Back, Color, Drop Shadow

E222

STUDENT ASSIGNMENTS

STUDENT ASSIGNMENT 1
True/False

Instructions: Circle T if the statement is true or F if the statement is false.

T F 1. If you enter 1899 in cell B3, 1900 in cell B4, select B3:B4, and then drag the fill handle down to cell B10, Excel assigns cell B10 the value 1900.
T F 2. To copy the text January in cell B3 to all the cells in the range B4:B10, hold down the ALT key while you drag the fill handle from cell B3 to cell B10.
T F 3. To select nonadjacent cells, hold down the CTRL key to make additional selections after you make the first selection.
T F 4. The Copy tool on the Standard toolbar copies the selection onto the Clipboard.
T F 5. You can invoke the Paste command on the Edit menu by pressing the ENTER key.
T F 6. Use the Font command on the Format menu to shade cells a different color.
T F 7. To display the Toolbar shortcut menu, click the left mouse button with the mouse pointer positioned in a toolbar.
T F 8. You can move a floating toolbar anywhere in the window.
T F 9. Excel has toolbar docks on each of the four sides of the window.
T F 10. You can dock more than one toolbar at a toolbar dock.
T F 11. You can freeze vertical titles (columns) but you cannot freeze horizontal titles (rows).
T F 12. The $ in a cell reference affects only the Move command on the Edit menu.
T F 13. When you assign a note to a cell, Excel displays a small blue dot called the note indicator in the upper right corner of the cell.
T F 14. The spell checker's dictionary contains every word in the English language.
T F 15. Print titles are not the same as a header.
T F 16. You cannot dock a toolbar that contains a drop-down list box on the side of the window.
T F 17. If you save a worksheet after changing the page setup characteristics, the next time you open the worksheet the page characteristics will be the same as when you saved it.
T F 18. Press CTRL + HOME to select cell A1 or the cell below and to the right of frozen titles.
T F 19. If you shrink the display of a worksheet using the Zoom Out tool on the Utility toolbar and print the worksheet, the printout will be in normal size (100% magnification).
T F 20. You can split a window into eight panes.

STUDENT ASSIGNMENT 2
Multiple Choice

Instructions: Circle the correct response.

1. If you drag the fill handle to the right on cell A4, which contains Monday, then cell B4 will contain _____.
    a. Sunday
    b. Monday
    c. Tuesday
    d. #REF!
2. To skip correcting a word that the spell checker considers misspelled, select the _____ button.
    a. Cancel
    b. Ignore
    c. Change
    d. Delete

(continued)

E223

STUDENT ASSIGNMENT 2 (continued)

3. You can invoke the Goto command on the Formula menu to select a specific cell in the worksheet by pressing the _____ key.
   a. CTRL
   b. F5
   c. F7
   d. F9
4. You can split the window into _____.
   a. two horizontal panes
   b. two vertical panes
   c. four panes
   d. all of the above
5. The horizontal and vertical split boxes are located _____.
   a. on the Standard toolbar
   b. on the Utility toolbar
   c. next to the scroll arrows
   d. immediately to the left of the Select All button
6. Excel allows for up to _____ levels in an outline.
   a. 2
   b. 4
   c. 6
   d. 8
7. To select the cell at the beginning of the row that contains the active cell, press the _____ key.
   a. HOME
   b. CTRL + HOME
   c. CTRL + END
   d. TAB
8. To create subordinate levels in an outline of a worksheet, use the _____.
   a. Promote tool on the Utility toolbar
   b. Outline command on the formula bar
   c. Demote tool on the Utility toolbar
   d. both b and c
9. To collapse a level of an outline, use the _____.
   a. column or row level bar
   b. column or row level symbols
   c. collapse symbol
   d. all of the above
10. The Demote and Promote tools are located on the _____ toolbar.
    a. Standard
    b. Formatting
    c. Utility
    d. Chart

STUDENT ASSIGNMENT 3
Using the Utility Toolbar

Instructions: The Utility toolbar displays between the formula bar and the Standard toolbar in Figure SA4-3. Use Figure SA4-3 to answer the questions in this assignment.

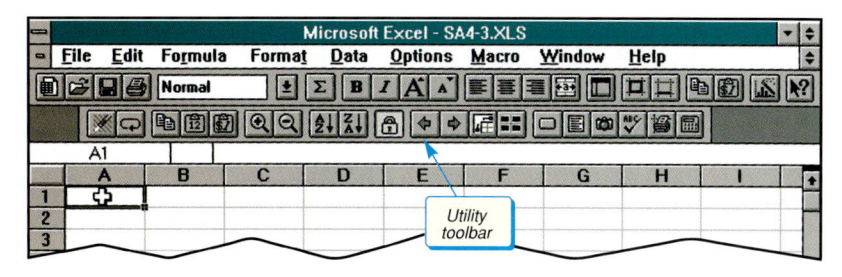

FIGURE SA4-3

1. Assume the Utility toolbar is hidden. Explain how you would display the toolbar without using the menu names on the menu bar.

    _____

2. How would you dock the Utility toolbar as shown in Figure SA4-3?

    _____

3. Describe the function of the following tools on the Utility toolbar.

    a. Demote tool ( ) _____

    b. Promote tool ( ) _____

    c. Zoom In tool ( ) _____

    d. Zoom Out tool ( ) _____

    e. Show Outline Symbols tool ( ) _____

    f. Select Visible Cells tool ( ) _____

    g. Check Spelling tool ( ) _____

4. Explain how you would hide the Utility toolbar.

    _____

STUDENT ASSIGNMENT 4
Understanding Excel Menus and Commands

Instructions: Identify the menu and command that displays the dialog box allowing you to make the indicated change.

		MENU	**COMMAND**
1.	Shade cells		
2.	Divide the window into panes		
3.	Change magnification		
4.	Set print titles		
5.	Change the margins		
6.	Activate a toolbar		
7.	Check spelling		
8.	Copy selected range		
9.	Paste Clipboard contents		

COMPUTER LABORATORY EXERCISES

COMPUTER LABORATORY EXERCISE 1
Using the Fill Handle and Mixed Cell Referencing

Instructions: Start Excel. Create the multiplication table shown in Figure CLE4-1:

Perform the following tasks:

1. Change the width of all the columns in the worksheet to 4.57 characters.
2. Use the fill handle to create the series of numbers between column B and column P in row 1 (2, 4, 6,..., 30) and the series of numbers between rows 2 and 20 in column A (1, 2, 3,...,19). Recall that the fill handle requires the first two entries to determine a numeric series. Add a bottom border to row 1 and a right border to column A.
3. Enter the formula = $A2 * B$1 in cell B2. Copy the formula in cell B2 to the range B2:P20. Bold the range A1:P20.
4. Enter your name, course, computer laboratory exercise number (CLE4-1), date, and instructor name in column A in separate but adjacent cells beginning in cell A22. Save the worksheet using the file name CLE4-1.
5. Print the worksheet without gridlines.
6. Press CTRL + ` (single left quotation mark) to change the display to formulas. Print the formulas version. Press CTRL + ` (single left quotation mark) to change the display to values.

FIGURE CLE4-1

COMPUTER LABORATORY EXERCISE 2
Creating a Series

Instructions: Start Excel. Open CLE4-2 from the subdirectory Excel on the Student Diskette that accompanies this book. The worksheet CLE4-2 (Figure CLE4-2a) contains the initial values for eight different series.

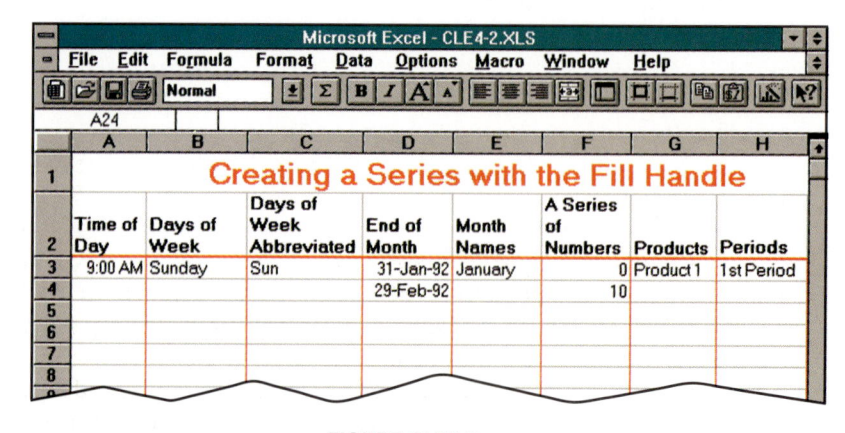

FIGURE CLE4-2a

Use the fill handle on one column at a time to propagate the eight different series as shown in Figure CLE4-2b through row 17. For example, in column A, select cell A3 and drag the fill handle down to cell A17. Your final result should be 11:00 PM in cell A17. In column D, select the range D3:D4 and drag the fill handle down to cell D17. Save the worksheet using the file name CLE4-2A. Print the worksheet on one page without cell gridlines.

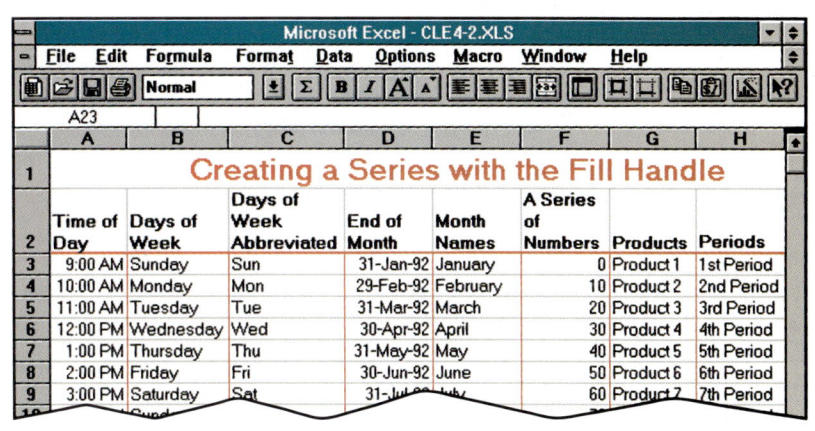

FIGURE CLE4-2b

COMPUTER LABORATORY EXERCISE 3
Working with Large Worksheets

Instructions: Start Excel and perform the following tasks:

FIGURE CLE4-3

1. Open the worksheet CLE4-3 from the subdirectory Excel on the Student Diskette that accompanies this book.
2. Display the Utility toolbar as shown in Figure CLE4-3.
3. Use the outline symbols to collapse the worksheet so that all detail rows and columns are hidden. Print the collapsed worksheet without cell gridlines.
4. With the worksheet collapsed, use the Show Visible Cells tools on the Utility toolbar to draw a 3-D column chart of the totals in the range A2:U18 in the chart location A21:W33. Print the worksheet with the embedded chart. Delete the 3-D column chart. Expand the worksheet completely by clicking row level 3 and column level 3 near the Select All button. Display the entire worksheet.
5. Click the Show Outline Symbols tool on the Utility toolbar to hide the outline symbols. Use the Zoom In and Zoom Out tools on the Utility toolbar to magnify and shrink the worksheet. Set the magnification back to 100% (normal magnification). Hide the Utility toolbar.
6. Select cell B3 and use the Freeze Panes command on the Window menu to freeze titles. Move around the worksheet using the keys, bars, and commands summarized in Table 4-3 on page E206. See if you can display the data in Group 4 and Quarter 4 while the titles are frozen.
7. Unfreeze the titles. Select cell E8. Choose the Split command from the Window menu to split the window into four panes. Use the scroll arrows to display the four corners of the worksheet. When you're finished, choose the Remove Split command from the Window menu.
8. Select column A and choose the Set Print Titles command from the Options menu. Change the right and left margins to 1''. Select Landscape orientation. Print the worksheet without cell gridlines. Save the worksheet using the filename CLE4-3A.

COMPUTER LABORATORY ASSIGNMENTS

COMPUTER LABORATORY ASSIGNMENT 1
Building a Large Worksheet

Purpose: To become familiar with building and printing a large worksheet.

Problem: You are employed as a spreadsheet specialist by the Unified Audio Center (UAC) Corporation. Their accounting department projects 2nd, 3rd, and 4th quarter revenues, expenses, and net incomes from the 1st quarter (Figure CLA4-1).

Column A includes the names of the audio and video equipment that UAC sells. The first quarter revenues for the items are shown in column B. All of the other numbers in the worksheet are determined from the 1st quarter revenues and the Projected Revenue and Projected Expenses tables in rows 28 through 31. The totals in rows 9, 16, 21, 25, 26, and column N are required as shown in the worksheet.

Instructions: Do the following to create the worksheet in Figure CLA4-1.

1. Change the font of the worksheet to TrueType Arial. Enter and format the worksheet title (cell B1), column titles (row 2), and row titles (column A) as shown in Figure CLA4-1. Set the width of column A to 18.14 characters and the width of columns B through N to 14.43 characters.
2. Enter the 1st quarter revenue numbers and corresponding SUM functions in column B. Use the formula = B9 + B16 + B21 + B25 to determine the total in cell B26.
3. Enter the Projected Revenue table (B28:C31) and Projected Expenses table (E28:F31).

	A	B	C	D	E	F	G
1		Projected Revenue and Expenses					
2	Audio and Video Merchandise	Qtr 1 Revenue	Qtr 1 Expenses	Qtr 1 Net Income	Qtr 2 Revenue	Qtr 2 Expenses	Qtr 2 Net Income
3	CD Players	$1,209,237.23	$778,748.78	$430,488.45	$1,236,445.07	$796,270.62	$440,174.44
4	CD Changers	875,340.97	563,719.58	311,621.39	895,036.14	576,403.28	318,632.87
5	Receivers	453,981.35	292,363.99	161,617.36	464,195.93	298,942.18	165,253.75
6	Tuners	987,145.23	635,721.53	351,423.70	1,009,356.00	650,025.26	359,330.74
7	Cassette Decks	745,392.45	480,032.74	265,359.71	762,163.78	490,833.47	271,330.31
8	Loudspeakers	1,598,234.87	1,029,263.26	568,971.61	1,634,195.15	1,052,421.68	581,773.48
9	Audio Total	$5,869,332.10	$3,779,849.87	$2,089,482.23	$6,001,392.07	$3,864,896.49	$2,136,495.58
10	Projection TVs	$2,198,345.99	$1,415,734.82	$782,611.17	$2,247,808.77	$1,447,588.85	$800,219.92
11	Picture Tube TVs	4,872,102.65	3,137,634.11	1,734,468.54	4,981,724.96	3,208,230.87	1,773,494.09
12	Portable TVs	254,019.05	163,588.27	90,430.78	259,734.48	167,269.00	92,465.47
13	Video Recorders	1,023,945.75	659,421.06	364,524.69	1,046,984.53	674,258.04	372,726.49
14	LaserDisc Players	154,098.34	99,239.33	54,859.01	157,565.55	101,472.22	56,093.34
15	Camcorders	845,928.12	544,777.71	301,150.41	864,961.50	557,035.21	307,926.29
16	Video Total	$9,348,439.90	$6,020,395.30	$3,328,044.60	$9,558,779.80	$6,155,854.19	$3,402,925.61
17	Decks	$321,854.00	$207,273.98	$114,580.02	$329,095.72	$211,937.64	$117,158.07
18	CD Players	451,981.54	291,076.11	160,905.43	462,151.12	297,625.32	164,525.80
19	Amplifiers	123,098.12	79,275.19	43,822.93	125,867.83	81,058.88	44,808.95
20	Speakers	453,629.21	292,137.21	161,492.00	463,835.87	298,710.30	165,125.57
21	Car Audio Total	$1,350,562.87	$869,762.49	$480,800.38	$1,380,950.53	$889,332.14	$491,618.39
22	CD Players	$654,019.38	$421,188.48	$232,830.90	$668,734.82	$430,665.22	$238,069.59
23	Cassette Players	71,820.60	46,252.47	25,568.13	73,436.56	47,293.15	26,143.42
24	AM/FM Radios	54,109.45	34,846.49	19,262.96	55,326.91	35,630.53	19,696.38
25	Portable Total	$779,949.43	$502,287.43	$277,662.00	$797,498.29	$513,588.90	$283,909.39
26	Total	$17,348,284.30	$11,172,295.09	$6,175,989.21	$17,738,620.70	$11,423,671.73	$6,314,948.97
27							
28		Projected Revenue			Projected Expenses		
29		Quarter 2	2.25%		Manufacturing	33.50%	
30		Quarter 3	-3.55%		Advertisement	21.25%	
31		Quarter 4	5.00%		Commission	9.65%	

FIGURE CLA4-1

4. To determine the 1st quarter expenses in cell C3, multiply the 1st quarter revenue in cell B3 times the sum of the projected expenses. That is, assign cell C3 the formula = B3 * (F29 + F30 + F31).
5. The net income in cell D3 is equal to the 1st quarter revenue (cell B3) minus the 1st quarter expenses (cell C3). That is, enter in cell D3 the formula = B3 – C3.
6. For the 2nd quarter revenue in cell E3 use the formula = B3 + B3 * C29. The same formula is used for the 3rd quarter revenue in cell H3 and the 4th quarter revenue in cell K3 except that the projected revenue cell reference is changed to cells C30 and C31, respectively. That is, enter in cell H3 the formula = B3 + B3 * C30 and in cell K3 the formula = B3 + B3 * C31.
7. Copy the formulas assigned to the 1st quarter expenses and net income in the range C3:D3 to the 2nd, 3rd, and 4th quarter expenses and net incomes in row 3. That is, copy the range C3:D3 to the ranges F3:G3, I3:J3, and L3:M3.
8. The total net income in cell N3 is equal to the sum of the net incomes for the four quarters (cells D3, G3, J3, and M3). That is, enter in cell N3 the formula = D3 + G3 + J3 + M3.
9. Use the Copy and Paste commands to complete the remaining entries in the worksheet.
10. Format the worksheet as shown in Figure CLA4-1. Assign a general worksheet comment to cell A1.
11. Enter your name, course, computer laboratory assignment number (CLA4-1), date, and instructor name below the entries in column A. Save the worksheet using the file name CLA4-1.
12. Set page breaks to begin printing columns E, H, K, and N on new pages by selecting the columns one at a time and choosing the Set Page Break command on the Options menu. Use the Page Setup command on the File menu to change the left and right margins to 1". Print the worksheet without cell gridlines lines in portrait orientation with column A as the print title on every page. Save the worksheet with the page setup settings. Each of the four quarters should print on a separate page.

H	I	J	K	L	M	N
Qtr 3 Revenue	Qtr 3 Expenses	Qtr 3 Net Income	Qtr 4 Revenue	Qtr 4 Expenses	Qtr 4 Net Income	Total Net Income
$1,166,309.31	$751,103.19	$415,206.11	$1,269,699.09	$817,686.21	$452,012.88	$1,737,881.89
844,266.37	543,707.54	300,558.83	919,108.02	591,905.56	327,202.45	1,258,015.53
437,865.01	281,985.07	155,879.94	476,680.42	306,982.19	169,698.23	652,449.28
952,101.57	613,153.4'	338,948.16	1,036,502.49	667,507.60	368,994.89	1,418,697.48
718,931.02	462,991.58	255,939.44	782,662.07	504,034.37	278,627.70	1,071,257.16
1,541,497.53	992,724.4'	548,773.12	1,678,146.61	1,080,726.42	597,420.19	2,296,938.40
$5,660,970.81	$3,645,665.20	$2,015,305.61	$6,162,798.71	$3,968,842.37	$2,193,956.34	$8,435,239.75
$2,120,304.71	$1,365,476.23	$754,828.48	$2,308,263.29	$1,486,521.56	$821,741.73	$3,159,401.30
4,699,143.01	3,026,248.10	1,672,894.91	5,115,707.78	3,294,515.81	1,821,191.97	7,002,049.51
245,001.37	157,780.88	87,220.49	266,720.00	171,767.68	94,952.32	365,069.07
987,595.68	636,011.62	351,584.06	1,075,143.04	692,392.12	382,750.92	1,471,586.16
148,627.85	95,716.33	52,911.51	161,803.26	104,201.30	57,601.96	221,465.82
815,897.67	525,438.10	290,459.57	888,224.53	572,016.59	316,207.93	1,215,744.21
9,016,570.28	$5,806,671.26	$3,209,899.02	$9,815,861.90	$6,321,415.06	$3,494,446.83	$13,435,316.07
$310,428.18	$199,915.75	$110,512.43	$337,946.70	$217,637.67	$120,309.03	$462,559.56
435,936.20	280,742.9'	155,193.29	474,580.62	305,629.92	168,950.70	649,575.21
118,728.14	76,460.92	42,267.22	129,253.03	83,238.95	46,014.08	176,913.17
437,525.37	281,766.34	155,759.03	476,310.67	306,744.07	169,566.60	651,943.20
$1,302,617.89	$838,885.92	$463,731.97	$1,418,091.01	$913,250.61	$504,840.40	$1,940,991.14
$630,801.69	$406,236.29	$224,565.40	$686,720.35	$442,247.90	$244,472.44	$939,938.34
69,270.97	44,610.50	24,660.46	75,411.63	48,565.09	26,846.54	103,218.56
52,188.56	33,609.44	18,579.13	56,814.92	36,588.81	20,226.11	77,764.59
$752,261.23	$484,456.23	$267,805.00	$818,946.90	$527,401.80	$291,545.10	$1,120,921.48
16,732,420.21	$10,775,678.61	$5,956,741.59	$18,215,698.52	$11,730,909.84	$6,484,788.67	$24,932,468.44

COMPUTER LABORATORY ASSIGNMENT 2
Outlining a Worksheet

Purpose: To become familiar with outlining a worksheet and printing and charting visible cells in a collapsed worksheet.

Problem: After building the worksheet in the previous assignment, your supervisor has requested that you create an outline of the worksheet and collapse the worksheet so that only the total rows and quarterly net incomes and total net incomes display (Figure CLA4-2a). Your supervisor also wants a 3-D column chart that compares the contribution of each category of merchandise to the total net income (Figure CLA4-2b). (**Note:** If you were not required to build the worksheet in Computer Laboratory Assignment 1, then ask your instructor for a copy of CLA4-1.)

FIGURE CLA4-2a

Instructions: Do the following to collapse the worksheet and chart the visible cells.

1. Open the worksheet CLA4-1. Remove the page breaks from the columns E, H, K, and N by selecting the columns one at a time and using the Remove Page Break command on the Options menu.
2. Create the outline and collapse the worksheet as shown in Figure CLA4-2a. To create the outline, use the Demote tool on the Utility toolbar with the following groups of detail rows: 3 through 8; 10 through 15; 17 through 20; and 22 through 24. Next, use the Demote tool with the following pairs of columns: B and C; E and F; H and I; and K and L. Finally, select columns B through M and use the Demote tool to create a second level column outline.
3. Click row level symbol 1 and column level symbol 2 next to the Select All button to collapse the worksheet as shown in Figure CLA4-2a. Print the visible cells in landscape orientation without cell gridlines. Expand the worksheet and save it using the file name CLA4-2A.
4. Click the row level symbol 1 and column level symbol 1 buttons near the Select All button to collapse the worksheet so that only columns A and N and the total rows display (Figure CLA4-2b). Hide the Outline symbols by clicking the Show Outline Symbols tool on the Utility toolbar.

5. Select cells A9 through N25. Click the Select Visible Cells tool on the Utility toolbar. Use the ChartWizard tool on the Standard toolbar to draw a chart in the chart location O1:U33. Use the Chart toolbar to change the chart to a 3-D column chart (Figure CLA4-2b).
6. Print the collapsed worksheet with the embedded chart in landscape orientation.
7. Save the collapsed worksheet with the chart using the file name CLA4-2B.

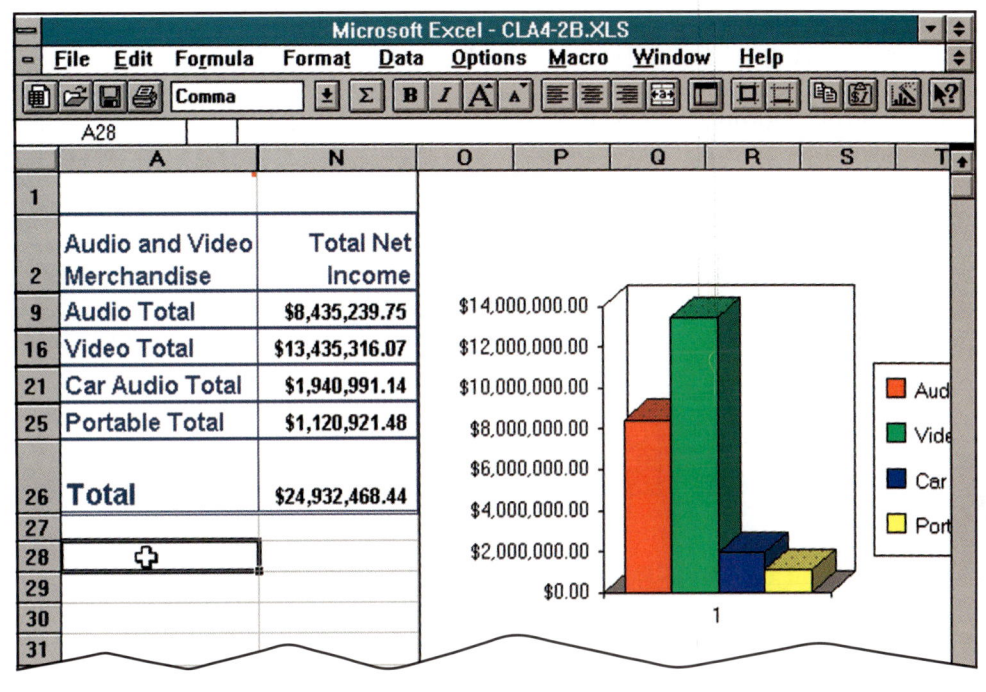

FIGURE CLA4-2b

COMPUTER LABORATORY ASSIGNMENT 3
Analyzing the Data in a Worksheet

Purpose: To become familiar with analyzing worksheet data by changing values in cells that are referenced by formulas in other cells.

Problem: Using the worksheet built in Computer Laboratory Assignment 4-1 (Figure CLA4-1), analyze the effect on the total net income in cell N26 by changing the projected revenue percents in the range C29:C31 and projected expense percents in the range F29:F31 to the values in the following table. (**Note:** If you were not required to build the worksheet in Computer Laboratory Assignment 1, then ask your instructor for a copy of CLA4-1.)

Case	PROJECTED REVENUE Q2%	Q3%	Q4%	PROJECTED EXPENSES Mfg.%	Ad.%	Comm.%	RESULT IN CELL N26
1	3	-2	6	30	25	6	$27,536,931.67
2	1.5	.5	2	32	12	8	33,641,792.91
3	2.25	-3.55	5	32.5	20	9.5	26,613,309.01
4	0	0	0	33.25	20.5	9	25,848,943.61
5	2.25	-3.55	5	35	23	10	22,411,207.59
6	1	2	3	33	20.75	9.45	25,919,724.61
7	2.25	-3.55	5	33.5	21.25	9.65	24,932,468.44

(continued)

COMPUTER LABORATORY ASSIGNMENT 3 (continued)

Instructions:

1. Open the worksheet CLA4-1.
2. Divide the window into two vertical panes and use the scroll arrows to display the worksheet as shown in Figure CLA4-3.
3. Enter each of the seven variations in the table at the bottom of the previous page, one at a time. With column A set as the print title, print column N for each variation without cell gridlines. Write the corresponding variation number on each of the seven printouts.

FIGURE CLA4-3

COMPUTER LABORATORY ASSIGNMENT 4
Stock Analysis Worksheet

Purpose: To become familiar with planning a worksheet.

Problem: You are rich and famous and own stock in many different companies. Your computer stock portfolio includes the companies listed in the table on the right. The number of shares you own in each company are in parentheses. Your investment analysts tell you that on average the computer industry will return 5% per year for the next ten years. Create a worksheet that organizes your computer stock portfolio and projects its annual worth for each of the next ten years.

HARDWARE	SOFTWARE	NETWORKING
Apple (5,000)	Autodesk (3,000)	3Com (2,500)
Compaq (11,500)	Borland (4,500)	Compaq (11,250)
DEC (6,550)	Lotus (11,250)	Novell (16,750)
IBM (22,500)	Microsoft (58,000)	
Intel (7,000)	Symantec (6,500)	

Instructions: Obtain the latest stock prices from the newspaper for your computer stocks. Using the figures in the table, compute the amount of your investment in each stock and list it under the current year. Next, use the 5% return per year to project the annual worth of these stocks for each of the next ten years. Group the companies in the worksheet by major segments (Hardware, Software, Networking). Show totals for each segment. Use the techniques developed in this project to manipulate the large worksheet. Submit the following:

1. A description of the problem. Include the purpose of the worksheet, a statement outlining the results, the required data, and calculations.
2. A handwritten design of the worksheet.
3. A printed copy of the worksheet without cell gridlines.
4. A printed copy of the formulas in the worksheet.
5. A short description explaining how to use the worksheet.
6. Enter your name, course, computer laboratory assignment number (CLA4-4), date, and instructor name below the entries in column A in separate but adjacent cells. Save the worksheet using the file name CLA4-4.

Microsoft Excel 4 for Windows
PROJECT FIVE

ANALYZING WORKSHEET DATA

OBJECTIVES You will have mastered the material in this project when you can:

- Assign a name to a cell and refer to the cell in a formula by using the assigned name
- Display the system date and system time in a worksheet using the NOW function
- Determine the monthly payment of a loan using the financial function PMT
- State the purpose of the FV and PV functions
- Enter a series of percents using the fill handle
- Build a data table to analyze data in a worksheet
- Write a command macro to automate data entry into your worksheet
- Analyze worksheet data by changing values and goal seeking
- Use Excel's Scenario Manager to record and save different sets of data values and the corresponding results of formulas
- Protect and unprotect cells

▶ INTRODUCTION

One of the more powerful aspects of Excel is its capability to analyze worksheet data or answer **what-if questions**. A what-if question regarding a loan might be "What if the interest rate on a loan increases by 1% — how would the increase affect the monthly payment?" Or "What if you know the result you want a formula in a worksheet to return, but you do not know the data required to attain that value?" Excel has the capability to quickly answer these types of questions and save you the time of performing trial-and-error analysis. This project describes four Excel what-if tools — automatic recalculation, data tables, goal seeking, and Scenario Manager.

This project also introduces you to the use of command macros and cell protection. You use a command macro to reduce a series of actions to the click of a button or a keystroke. Cell protection ensures that you don't inadvertently change values that are critical to the worksheet.

E233

PROJECT FIVE

Project 5 is made up of two parts: (1) a worksheet that determines the monthly payment, total interest, and total cost for a loan; and (2) a command macro that instructs Excel to accept new loan data from the worksheet user.

The worksheet (Figure 5-1) includes three distinct sections: (1) a loan analysis section in the range A1:B11; (2) a button, titled New Loan, that when clicked plays back the command macro in Figure 5-2; and (3) a data table that can be used to show the effect of different interest rates on the monthly payment, total interest, and total cost of the loan.

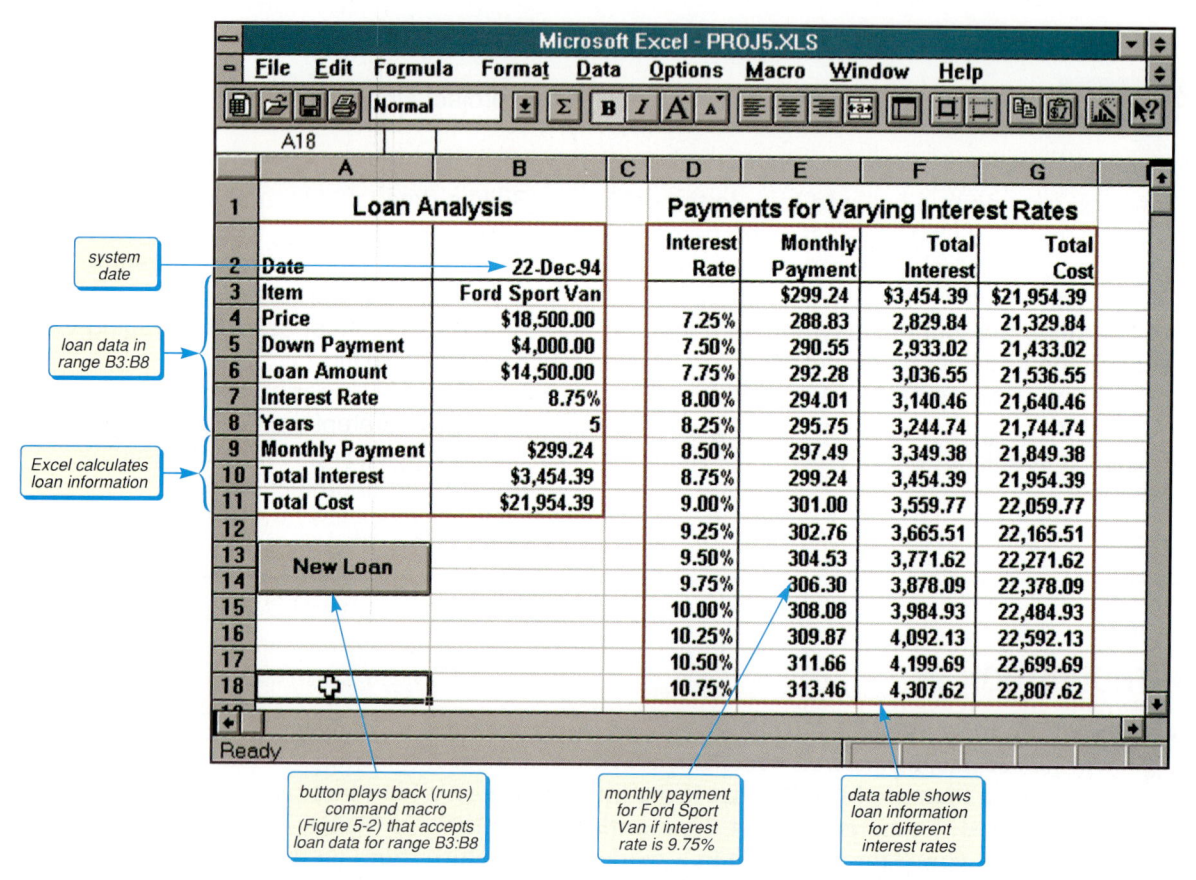

FIGURE 5-1

The Loan Analysis section on the left in Figure 5-1 answers the following question: What are the monthly payment (cell B9), total interest (cell B10), and total cost (cell B11) for a Ford Sport Van (cell B3) that costs $18,500.00 (cell B4), if the down payment is $4,000.00 (cell B5), the interest rate is 8.75% (cell B7), and the term of the loan is 5 years (cell B8)? As shown in Figure 5-1, the monthly payment is $299.24, the total interest is $3,454.39, and the total cost of the Ford Sport Van is $21,954.39. Excel determines the monthly payment in cell B9 through the use of the PMT function. Formulas are used to calculate the total interest and total cost in cells B10 and B11. The Loan Analysis section of the worksheet can determine the answers to loan questions as fast as you can enter the new loan data in the range B3:B8.

The function of the button titled New Loan in the range A13:A14 (Figure 5-1) is to automate the entry of loan data. The button plays back the command macro in Figure 5-2 which simplifies the loan data entry into cells B3 through B8. Using a button to enter the loan data is especially helpful for users who know little about computers and spreadsheets.

The third section of the worksheet in Figure 5-1 is the data table on the right side of the screen. Each time you enter new loan data into the worksheet, the data table recalculates new values for the monthly payment, total interest, and total cost for the different interest rates in column D. A **data table** is a powerful what-if tool because it can automate your data analyses and organize the answers returned by Excel. The data table in Figure 5-1 answers fifteen different what-if questions. The questions pertain to the effect the fifteen different interest rates in column D have on the monthly payment, total interest, and total cost. For example, what will the monthly payment for the Ford Sport Van be if the interest rate is 9.75% rather than 8.75%? The answer, $306.30, is in cell E14.

The **command macro** in Figure 5-2 is made up of a series of macro functions that are played back when you click the New Loan button (Figure 5-1). A **macro function** (also called an instruction) tells Excel to carry out an operation, such as select a range or clear the selection. Column B in Figure 5-2 includes comments that explain the purpose of the macro function in the same row in column A.

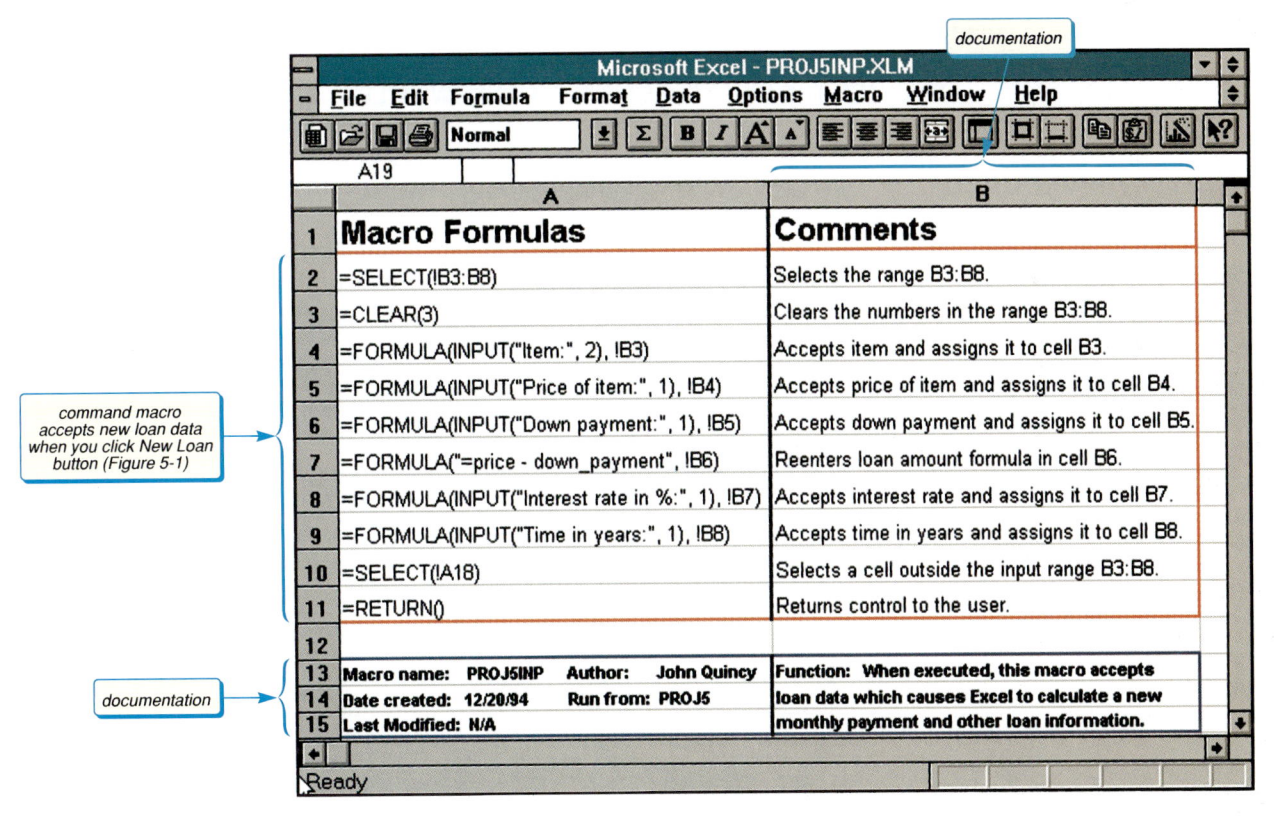

FIGURE 5-2

Changing the Font of the Entire Worksheet

The first step in this project is to change the font of the entire worksheet from Ms Sans Serif regular to TrueType Arial bold. With TrueType Arial, the printout will be the same as what you see on the screen. By bolding the font, the characters in the worksheet stand out.

TO CHANGE THE FONT OF THE ENTIRE WORKSHEET

Step 1: Click the Select All button immediately above row heading 1 and to the left of column heading A.
Step 2: From the Format menu, choose the Font command.
Step 3: In the Font dialog box, select TT Arial in the Font box.
Step 4: Select Bold in the Font Style box.
Step 5: Choose OK from the Font dialog box.

As you enter text and numbers on the worksheet, they will display in TT Arial bold.

Entering the Worksheet Title and Row Titles

The next step is to enter the Loan Analysis section title and row titles. To make the worksheet easier to read, the width of columns A and B and the height of rows 1 and 2 will be increased. The worksheet title will also be centered and made larger (see Figure 5-3).

TO ENTER THE WORKSHEET TITLE AND ROW TITLES

Step 1: Select cell A1 and enter Loan Analysis. Click the Increase Font Size tool on the Standard toolbar twice to increase the font size of the title to 12 points.
Step 2: Select the range A1:B1. Click the Center Across Columns tool on the Standard toolbar. Position the mouse pointer on the border between row headings 1 and 2 and drag until the height of row 1 in the formula bar is 21 points.
Step 3: Select cell A2 and enter the row title Date. Position the mouse pointer on the border between row headings 2 and 3 and drag until the height of row 2 in the formula bar is 27 points.
Step 4: Enter the following row titles:

CELL	ENTRY	CELL	ENTRY	CELL	ENTRY
A3	Item	A4	Price	A5	Down Payment
A6	Loan Amount	A7	Interest Rate	A8	Years
A9	Monthly Payment	A10	Total Interest	A11	Total Cost

Step 5: Select columns A and B. Position the mouse pointer on the border between column headings B and C and drag until the width of column B in the formula bar is 16 characters.

The worksheet title and row titles display as shown in Figure 5-3 on the next page.

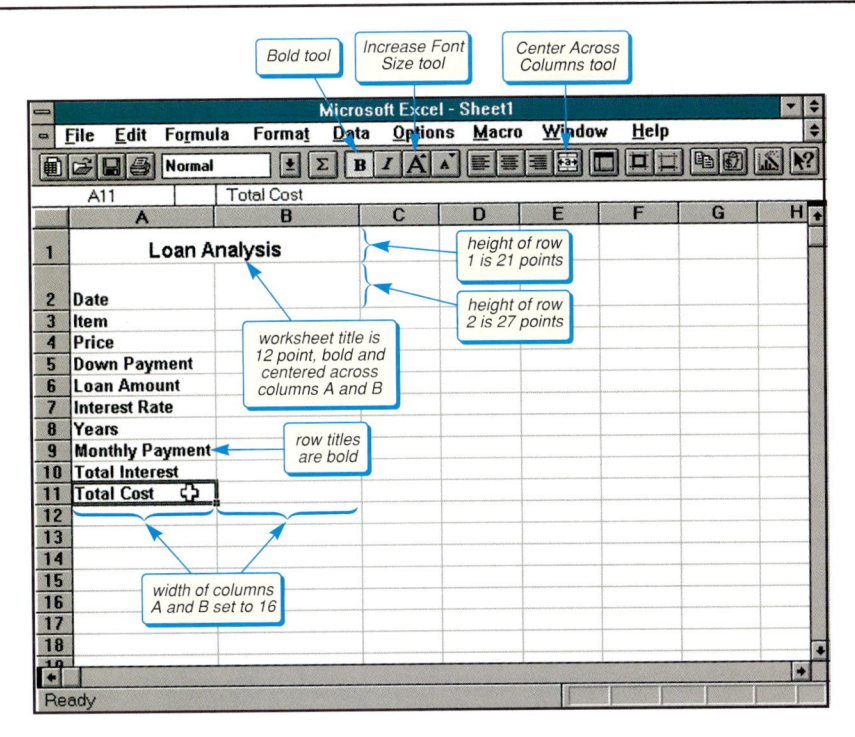

FIGURE 5-3

Displaying the System Date and System Time

The worksheet in Project 5 (Figure 5-1 on page E234) includes a date stamp in cell B2. A **date stamp** is the system date of which your computer keeps track. If the computer's system date is set to today's date, which it normally is, then the date stamp is equivalent to today's date.

In information processing, a report such as a printout of the worksheet is often meaningless without a date stamp. For example, in a banking environment a date stamp can be useful when the loan analysis is given to a potential customer in the form of a printout because it identifies the date the loan was discussed with the loan officer.

To enter the system date in a cell in the worksheet use the NOW function. The **NOW function** is one of nineteen date and time functions available in Excel. When assigned to a cell, the NOW function returns a decimal number in the range 1 to 65,380, corresponding to the dates January 1, 1900 through December 31, 2078 and the time of day. Excel automatically formats the number representing the system's date and time to the date and time format m/d/yy h:mm where the first m is the month, d is the day of the month, yy is the last two digits of the year, h is the hour of the day, and the mm is the minutes past the hour.

The steps on the next page show how to enter the NOW function and change the format from m/d/yy h:mm to dd-mmm-yy where dd is day of the month, mmm is the month name abbreviated, and yy is the last two digits of the year.

TO ENTER AND FORMAT THE SYSTEM DATE AND TIME

STEP 1 ▶

Select cell B2. Enter `=now()`

Excel displays the system date and system time in cell B2 using the default date and time format mm/dd/yy h:mm (Figure 5-4). Recall from Project 2, that you can enter functions, such as =now(), in uppercase or lowercase.

FIGURE 5-4

STEP 2 ▶

With cell B2 selected, choose the Number command from the Format menu. Select the date format d-mmm-yy in the Format Codes box.

Excel displays the Number Format dialog box with the Date category already selected because the NOW function was assigned to the active cell B2 (Figure 5-5).

FIGURE 5-5

STEP 3 ▶

Choose the OK button in the Number Format dialog box.

Excel displays the date in the form d-mmm-yy (Figure 5-6).

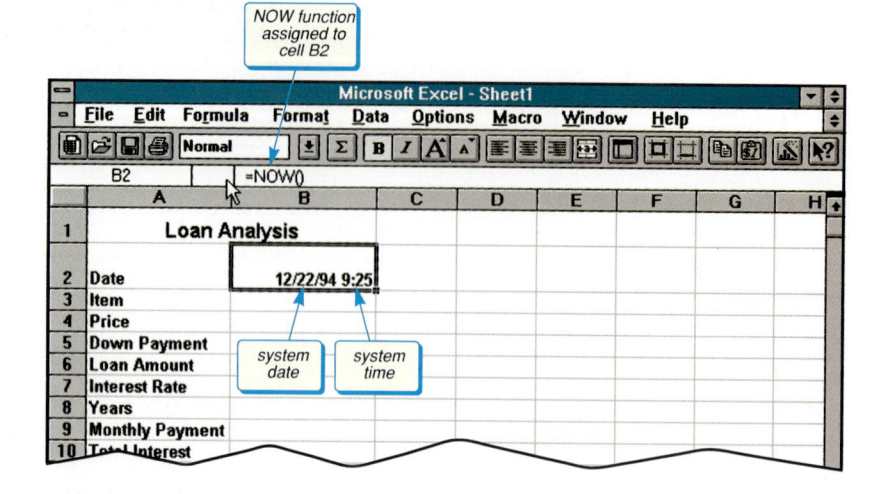

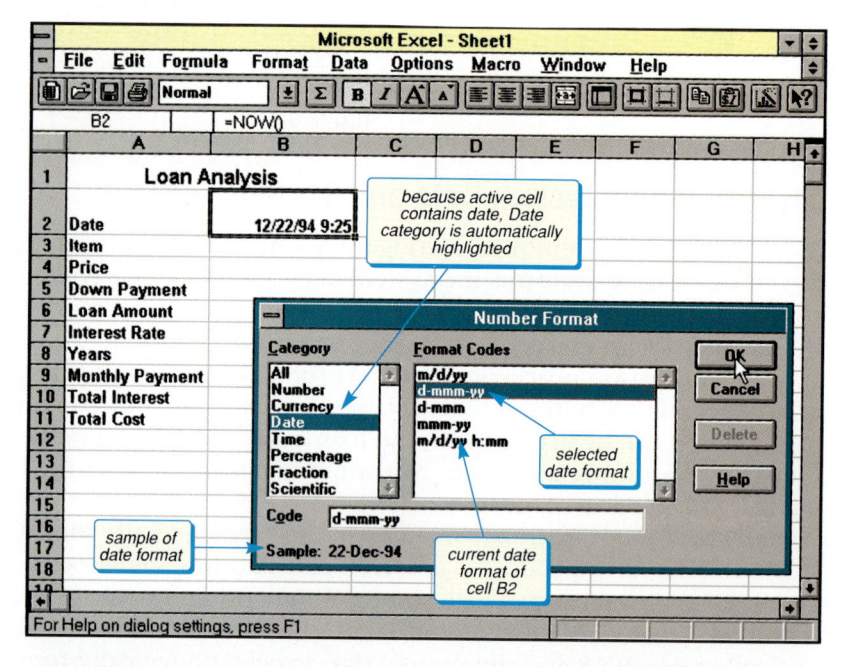

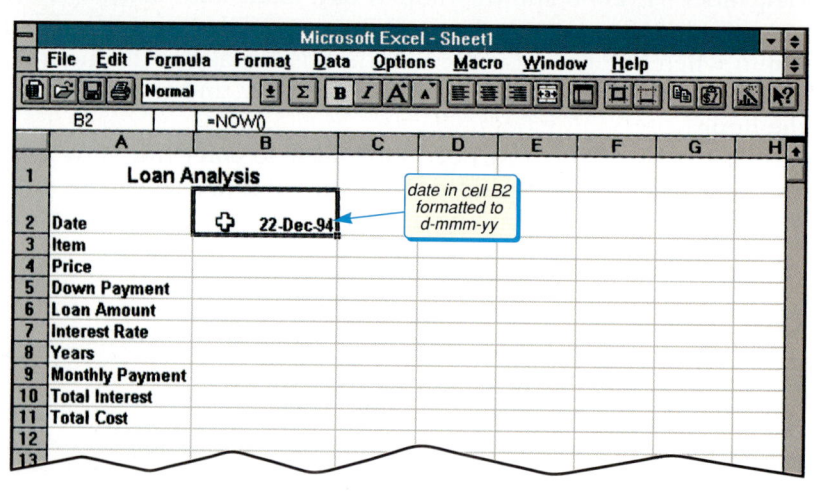

FIGURE 5-6

Notice in Figure 5-6 the date displays in the cell right-aligned because Excel treats a date as a number. If you format the date by applying the Normal style in the Style box on the Standard toolbar, the date displays as a number. For example, if the system time and date is 12:00 noon on December 22, 1994 and the cell containing the NOW function is assigned Normal style, then Excel displays the following number in the cell:

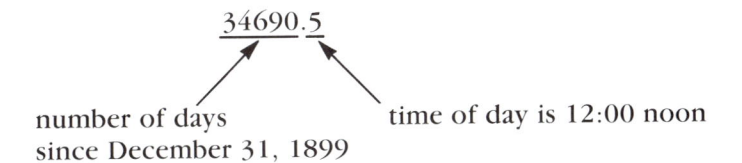

34690.5

number of days since December 31, 1899   time of day is 12:00 noon

The whole number portion of the number (34690) represents the number of days since December 31, 1899. The decimal portion (.5) represents the time of day (12:00 noon).

Outlining the Loan Analysis Section of the Worksheet

The next step is to outline the Loan Analysis section of the worksheet by drawing borders. An outline is used to separate the loan analysis in the range A1:B11 from the data table in the range D1:G18 and to separate the text in column A from the numbers in column B (see Figure 5-7).

TO DRAW AN OUTLINE

Step 1: Select the range A2:B11. From the Format menu, choose the Border command. In the Border dialog box, select dark red in the Color box, select Outline in the Border box, and select the regular border (third from left in row one) in the Style box. Choose the OK button in the Border dialog box.

Step 2: Select the range A2:B2. Click the Bottom Border tool ( ) on the Standard toolbar.

Step 3: Select the range A2:A11. From the Format menu, choose the Border command. In the Border dialog box, select Right in the Border box, and select the light border (second from left in row one) in the Style box. Choose the OK button in the Border dialog box.

The loan analysis section of the worksheet displays as shown in Figure 5-7. Notice the Bottom Border tool on the Standard toolbar used in Step 2 draws a light bottom border in the range A2:B2.

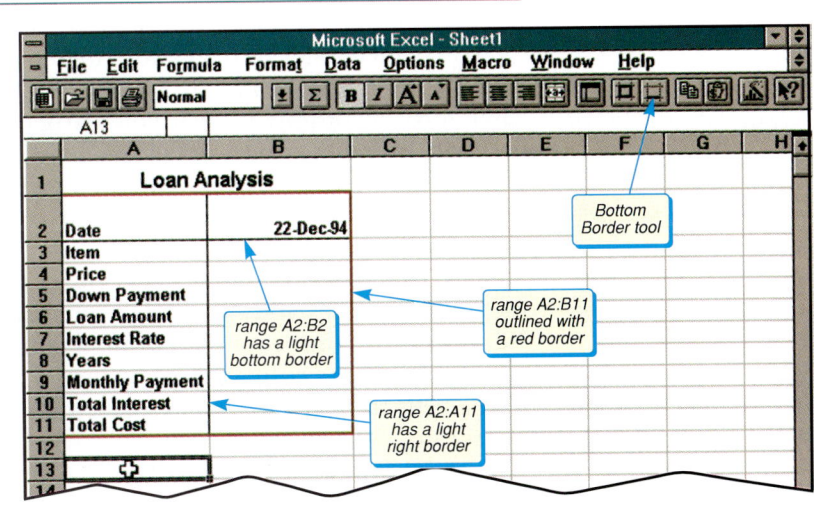

FIGURE 5-7

Entering the Loan Data

According to the worksheet in Figure 5-1 on page E234, the item to be purchased, the price of the item, the down payment, the interest rate, and the number of years until the loan is paid back are entered into cells B3 through B5 and cells B7 and B8. These five values make up the loan data (see Figure 5-8).

TO ENTER THE LOAN DATA

Step 1: Select cell B3 and enter `Ford Sport Van`. Click the right-align tool on the Standard toolbar. Select cell B4 and enter `18500`. Select cell B5 and enter `4000`.

Step 2: Skip cell B6 and select cell B7. Enter `8.75%`. Select cell B8 and enter `5`.

The loan data displays in the worksheet as shown in Figure 5-8. The interest rate is formatted to the Percentage 0.00% style because the percent sign (%) was appended to 8.75 when it was entered into cell B7.

The four remaining entries in the Loan Analysis section of the worksheet, loan amount (cell B6), monthly payment (cell B9), total interest (cell B10), and total cost (cell B11) require formulas that reference cells B4, B5, B7, and B8. The formulas will be entered referencing names assigned to cells rather than cell references because names are easier to remember than cell references.

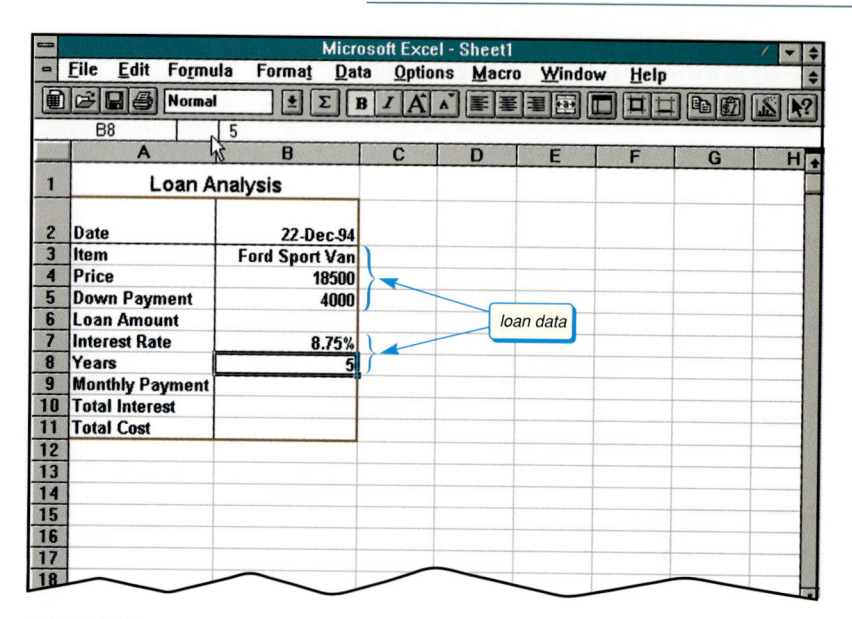

FIGURE 5-8

▶ CREATING NAMES BASED ON ROW TITLES

Naming a cell that you plan to reference in a formula helps make the formula easier to read and remember. For example, the loan amount in cell B6 is equal to the price in cell B4 less the down payment in cell B5. Therefore, according to what you learned in the earlier projects, you can write the loan amount formula in cell B6 as = B4 – B5. However, by assigning the corresponding row titles in column A as the names of cells B4 and B5 you can write the loan amount formula as = Price – Down_Payment which is clearer and easier to remember than = B4 – B5.

To name cells, you first select the range that encompasses the row titles that include the names and the cells to be named (A4:B11). Next, you use the **Create Names command** from the Formula menu. In the **Create Names dialog box**, you select row or column depending on where the names are located in relation to the cells to be named. In this case, the names are the row titles in column A. Therefore, you select columns.

In the following steps, each row title in the range A4 to A11 is assigned to the adjacent cell in column B. Because the data in cell B2 and the item in cell B3 will not be referenced in formulas, there is no need to include them in the range.

CREATING NAMES BASED ON ROW TITLES **E241**

TO CREATE NAMES

STEP 1 ▶

Select the range A4:B11. Select the Formula menu and point to the Create Names command.

The range A4:B11 is selected and Excel displays the Formula menu (Figure 5-9).

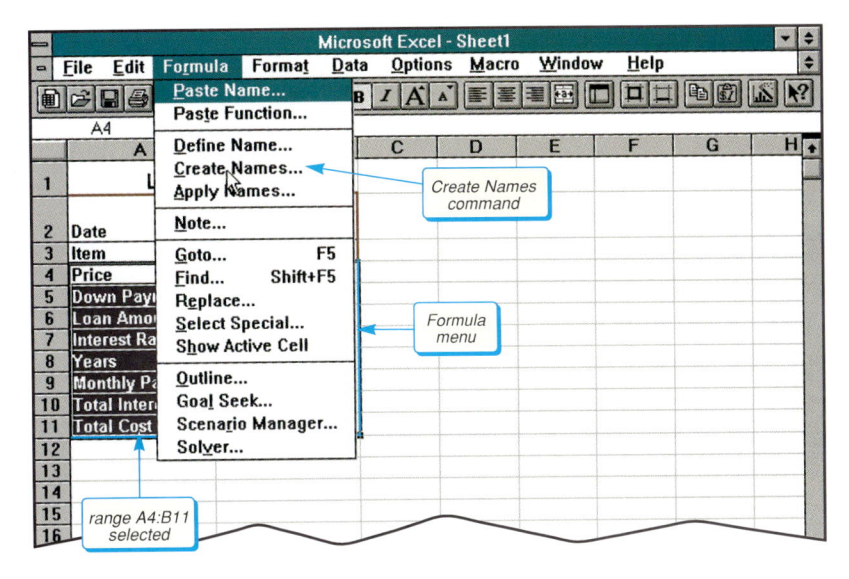

FIGURE 5-9

STEP 2 ▶

Choose the Create Names command from the Formula menu.

Excel displays the Create Names dialog box (Figure 5-10). Excel automatically selects the Left Column box because the general direction of the range in Step 1 is downward.

STEP 3

Choose OK from the Create Names dialog box.

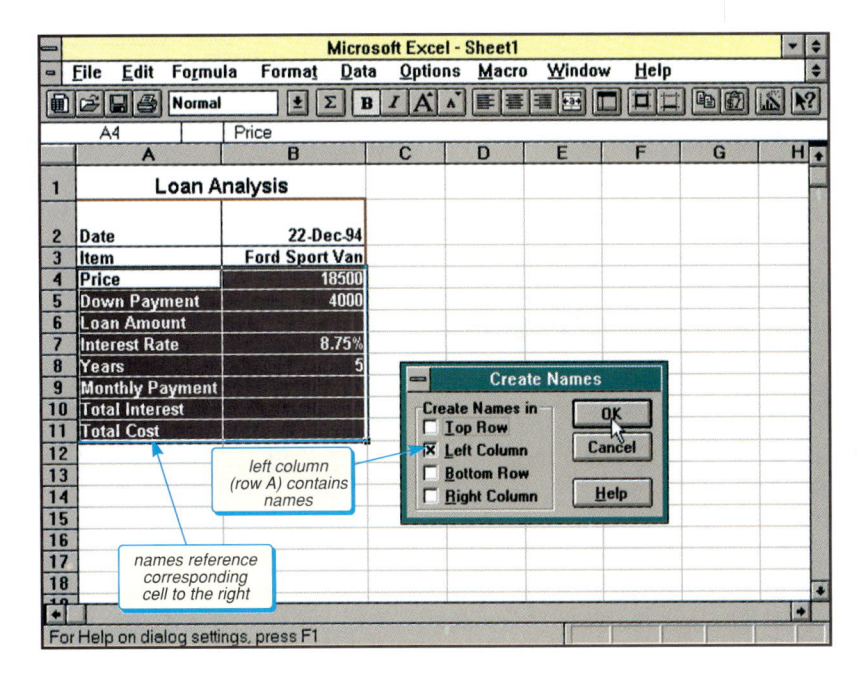

FIGURE 5-10

After Step 3, you can use the names in the range A4:A11 in formulas to reference the adjacent cells in the range B4:B11. Excel is not case-sensitive with respect to names of cells. Hence, you can enter the names in formulas in uppercase or lowercase. Some names, such as Down Payment in cell A5, include a space because they are made up of two words. To use a name in a formula that is made up of two or more words, you replace any space with the underscore character (_). For example, Down Payment is written as down_payment when you want to reference the adjacent cell B5.

Consider these two additional points regarding the assignment of names to cells: (1) a name can be a minimum of one character or a maximum of 255 characters; and (2) if you want to assign a name that is not a text item in an adjacent cell, use the Define Name command from the Formula menu.

The following steps use the formula = price – down_payment to determine the loan amount in cell B6. The steps also use the Style box on the Standard toolbar to format the nonadjacent cells B4:B6 and B9:B11 to the Currency style.

TO ENTER THE LOAN AMOUNT FORMULA USING NAMES AND APPLY THE CURRENCY FORMAT ▼

STEP 1 ▶

Select cell B6. Type the formula
=price - down_payment

STEP 2 ▶

Click the enter box, or press the ENTER key.

Excel displays the loan amount 14500 in cell B6 (Figure 5-11). Notice that when cell B6 is selected, Excel displays the name of the cell (Loan_Amount) on the left side of the formula bar rather than the cell reference B6.

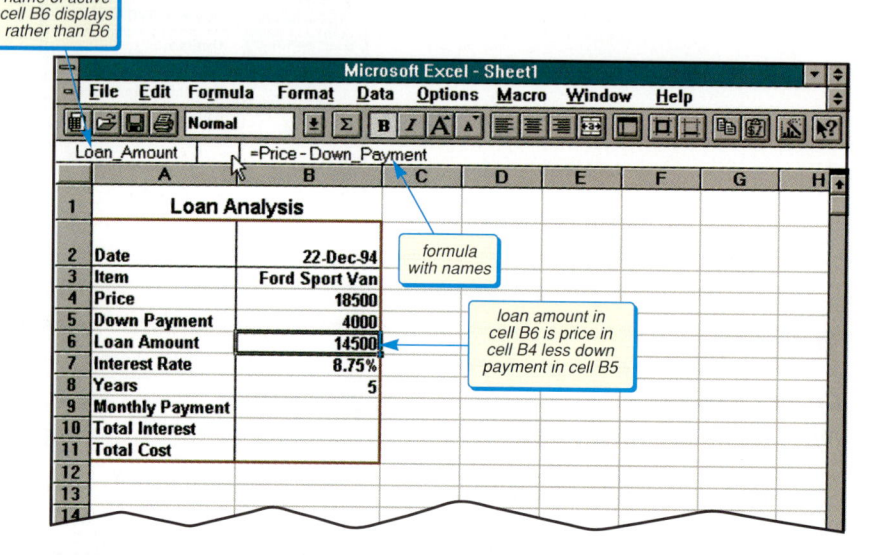

FIGURE 5-11

STEP 3 ▶

Select the range B4:B6. Hold down the CTRL key and select the nonadjacent range B9:B11. Click the Style box arrow on the Standard toolbar.

Excel displays the drop-down list of format styles (Figure 5-12a).

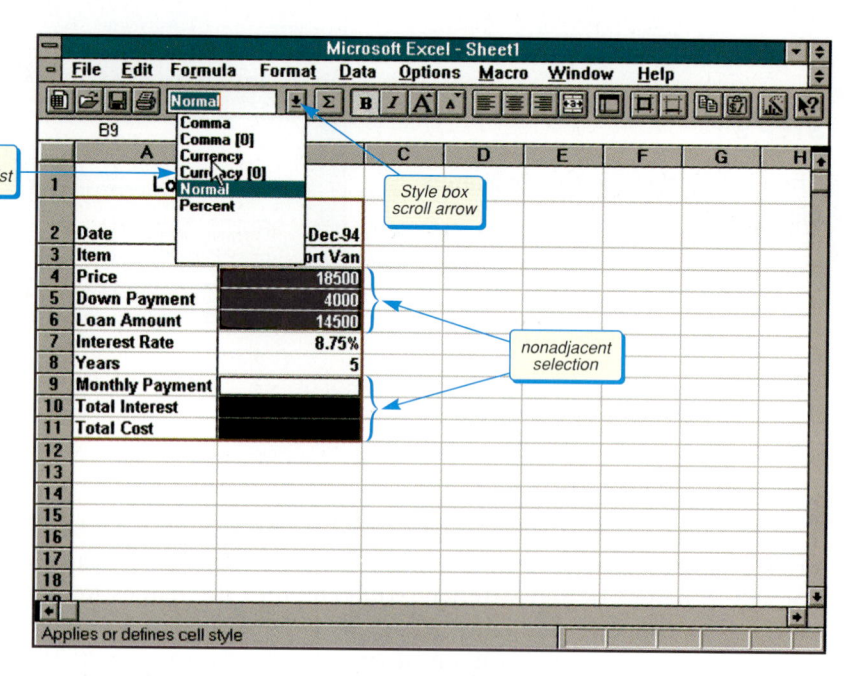

FIGURE 5-12a

STEP 4 ▶

Select the Currency style from the drop-down list. Select cell B9.

Excel assigns the Currency style format to the nonadjacent ranges B4:B6 and B9:B11 (Figure 5-12b). Later when numbers are assigned to cells B9:B11 they will display using the Currency style format.

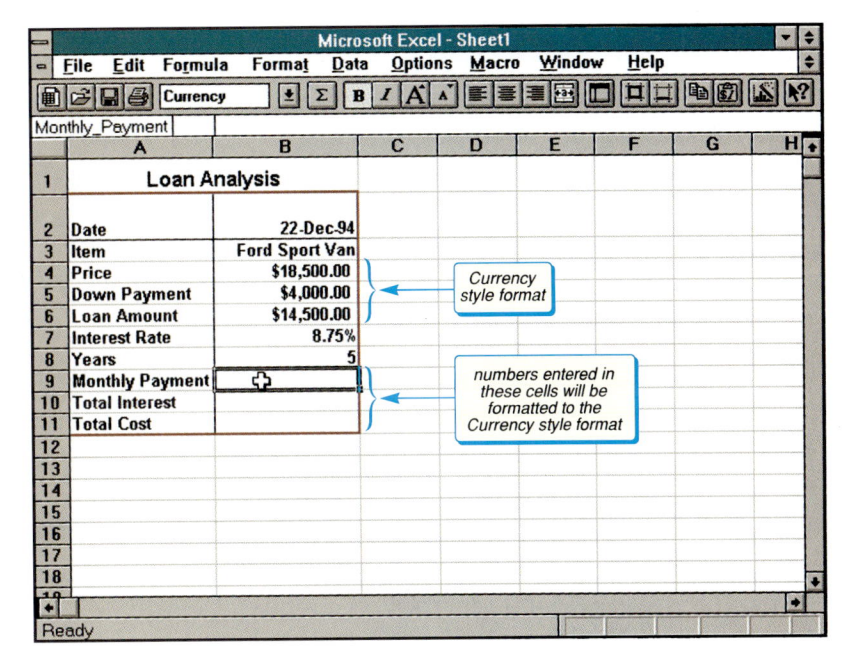

FIGURE 5-12b

▶ DETERMINING THE MONTHLY PAYMENT

You can use Excel's **PMT function** to determine the monthly payment (cell B9) on the basis of the loan amount (cell B6), the interest rate (cell B7), and the term of the loan (cell B8). The general form of the PMT function is

= PMT(rate, payments, loan amount)

where rate is the interest rate per payment period, payments is the number of payments, and loan amount is the amount of the loan.

In the worksheet in Figure 5-12b, cell B7 is equal to the annual interest rate. However, loan institutions calculate the interest, which is their profit, on a monthly basis. Thus, the first value in the PMT function is interest_rate / 12 rather than interest_rate. The number of payments (or periods) is equal to 12 * years (cell B8) because there are twelve months, or twelve payments, per year.

Excel considers the value returned by the PMT function to be a debit, and therefore returns a negative number as the monthly payment. To display the monthly payment as a positive number precede the loan amount with a negative sign. Thus, the loan amount is equal to –loan_amount.

The PMT function for cell B9 becomes the following:

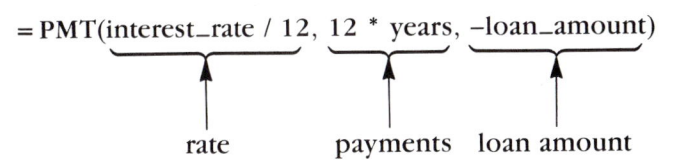

= PMT(interest_rate / 12, 12 * years, –loan_amount)

                 rate   payments loan amount

The steps at the top of the next page use the PMT function to determine the monthly payment in cell B7.

TO ENTER THE PMT FUNCTION

STEP 1 ▶

Select cell B9. Type the function `=pmt(interest_rate / 12, 12 * years, -loan_amount)`

STEP 2 ▶

Click the enter box in the formula bar or press the ENTER key.

Excel displays the monthly payment $299.24 in cell B9 (Figure 5-13) for a loan amount of $14,500.00 (cell B6) with an annual interest rate of 8.75% (cell B7) for five years (cell B8). Notice that with cell B9 selected, the PMT function displays in the formula bar.

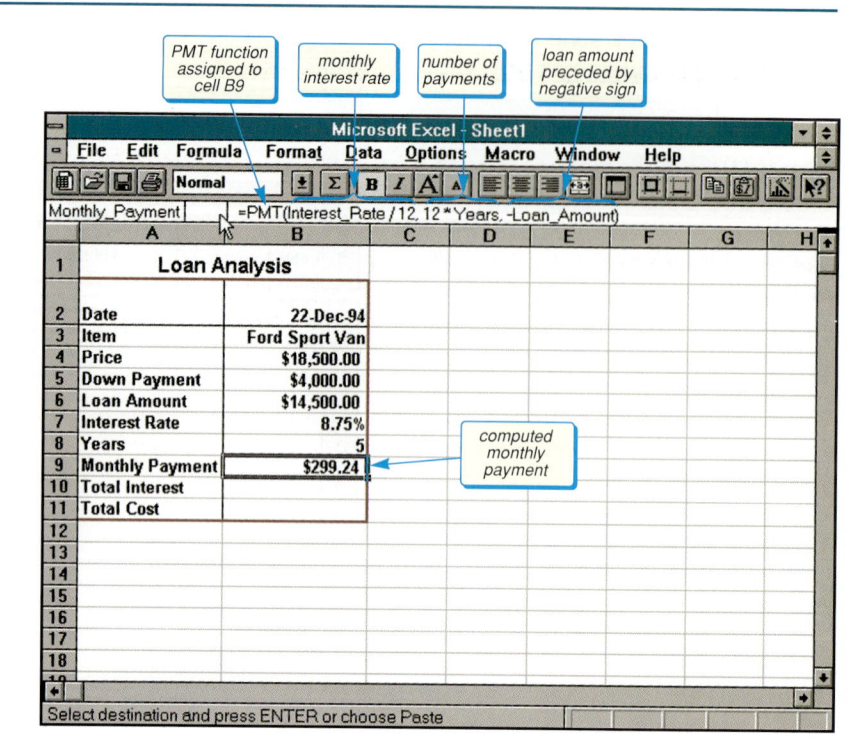

FIGURE 5-13

Besides the PMT function, Excel has forty-nine additional financial functions to help you solve some of the more complex finance problems. These functions save you from entering long, complicated formulas to obtain the results you require. Table 5-1 summarizes three of the most often used financial functions.

▶ **TABLE 5-1**

FUNCTION	DESCRIPTION
FV(rate, periods, payment)	Returns the future value of an investment based on periodic, constant payments and a constant interest rate.
PMT(rate, periods, loan amount)	Returns the periodic payment required to pay off a loan.
PV(rate, periods, payment)	Returns the present value of a series of payments.

DETERMINING THE TOTAL INTEREST AND TOTAL COST   E245

To view a complete list of Excel's financial functions, perform the following steps.

TO OBTAIN INFORMATION ON FINANCIAL FUNCTIONS

Step 1: Choose the Paste Function command from the Formula menu.
Step 2: Select Financial from the Function Category box when the Paste Function dialog box displays.
Step 3: Scroll through the list of financial functions in the Paste Function box.
Step 4: Choose Help from the Paste Function dialog box for a description of the financial functions. Scroll to the bottom of the Help window. Select Worksheet functions. Next, select Financial Functions. Click any financial function for additional information.
Step 5: After reviewing or printing the financial function information, double-click the Control menu box in the Help window to close it.
Step 6: Choose the Cancel button from the Paste Function dialog box.

▶ DETERMINING THE TOTAL INTEREST AND TOTAL COST

The next step is to determine the total interest (the loan institution's profit) and the borrower's total cost of the item being purchased. The total interest (cell B10) is equal to:

12 * years * monthly payment – loan amount

The total cost of the item to be purchased (cell B11) is equal to:

12 * years * monthly payment + down payment

To enter the total interest and total cost formulas, perform the following steps.

TO DETERMINE THE TOTAL INTEREST AND TOTAL COST ▼

STEP 1 ▶

Select cell B10. Enter the formula
`=12 * years * monthly-payment - loan-amount`

Excel displays the total interest $3,454.39 in cell B10 (Figure 5-14). With cell B10 selected, the formula displays in the formula bar.

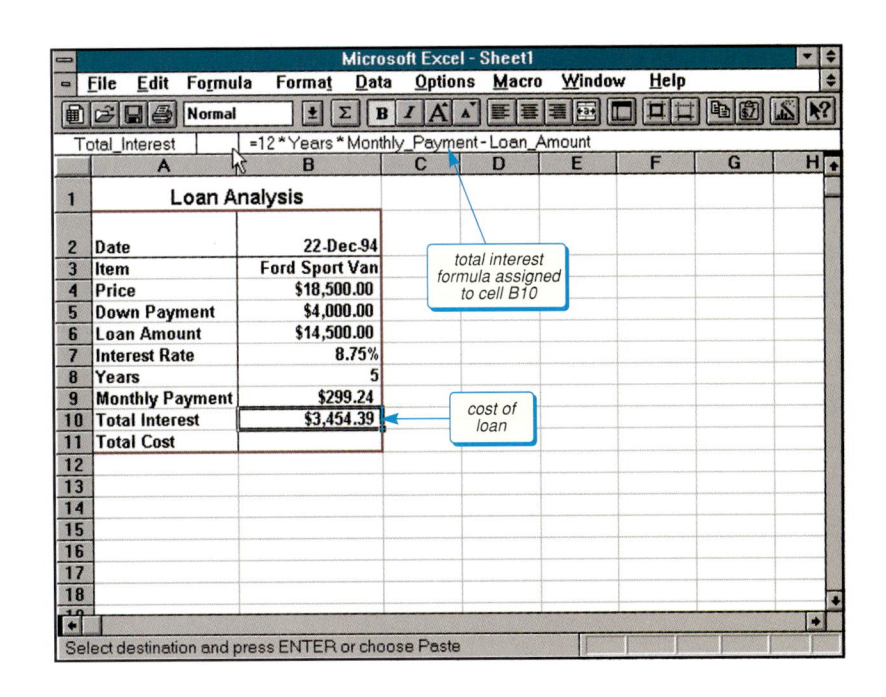

FIGURE 5-14

STEP 2 ▶

Select cell B11. Enter the formula
`=12 * years * monthly-payment + down-payment`

Excel displays the total cost of the item to be purchased in cell B11 (Figure 5-15). With cell B11 selected, the formula displays in the formula bar.

STEP 3

Click the Save File tool on the Standard toolbar and save the worksheet to drive A. Use the file name PROJ5.

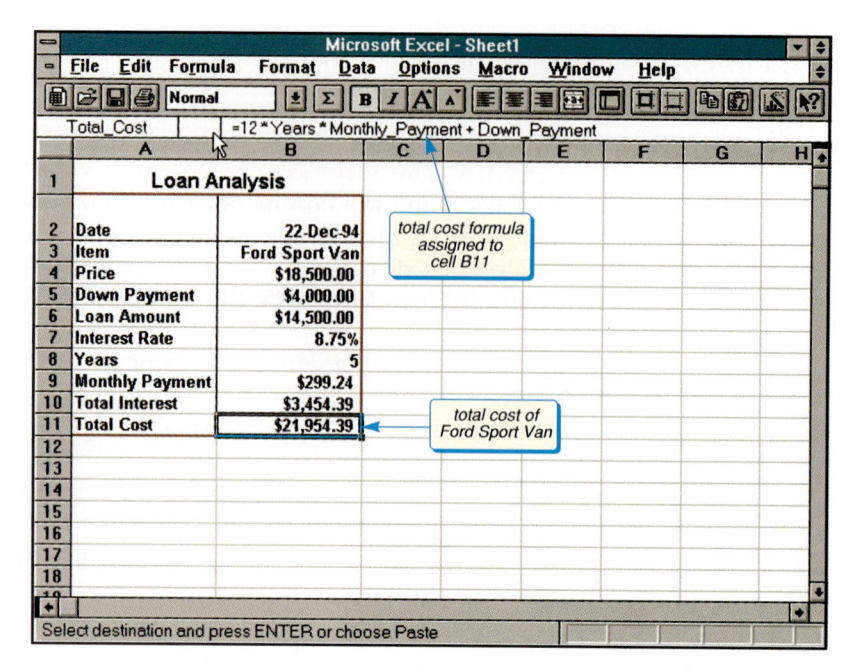

FIGURE 5-15

With the Loan Analysis section of the worksheet complete, you can determine the monthly payment, total interest, and total cost for any reasonable loan data. After entering the data table in the next section, alternative loan data will be entered to illustrate Excel's recalculation feature.

▶ USING A DATA TABLE TO ANALYZE WORKSHEET DATA

The next step is to build the Data Table section of the worksheet in the range D1:G18 (right side of Figure 5-16b on the next page). A data table is a range of cells that shows the answers to formulas in which different values have been substituted.

You have already seen that if a value is changed in a cell referenced elsewhere in a formula in the worksheet, Excel immediately recalculates and stores the new value in the cell assigned the formula. What if you wanted to compare the results of the formula for several different values? It would be unwieldy to write down or remember all the answers to the what-if questions. This is where a data table becomes useful because it will organize the answers in the worksheet for you automatically.

Data tables are built in an unused area of the worksheet. You may vary one or two values and display the results of the specified formulas in table form. The right side of Figure 5-16a illustrates the makeup of a one-input data table. With a **one-input data table**, you vary one cell reference (in this project, cell B7, the interest rate) and Excel fills the table with the results of one or more formulas (in this project monthly payment, total interest, and total cost).

The interest rates that will be used to analyze the loan formulas in this project range from 7.25% to 10.75% in increments of 0.25%. The data table (Figure 5-16b) illustrates the impact of varying the interest rate on three formulas: the monthly payment (cell B9), total interest paid (cell B10), and the total cost of the item to be purchased (cell B11).

USING A DATA TABLE TO ANALYZE WORKSHEET DATA **E247**

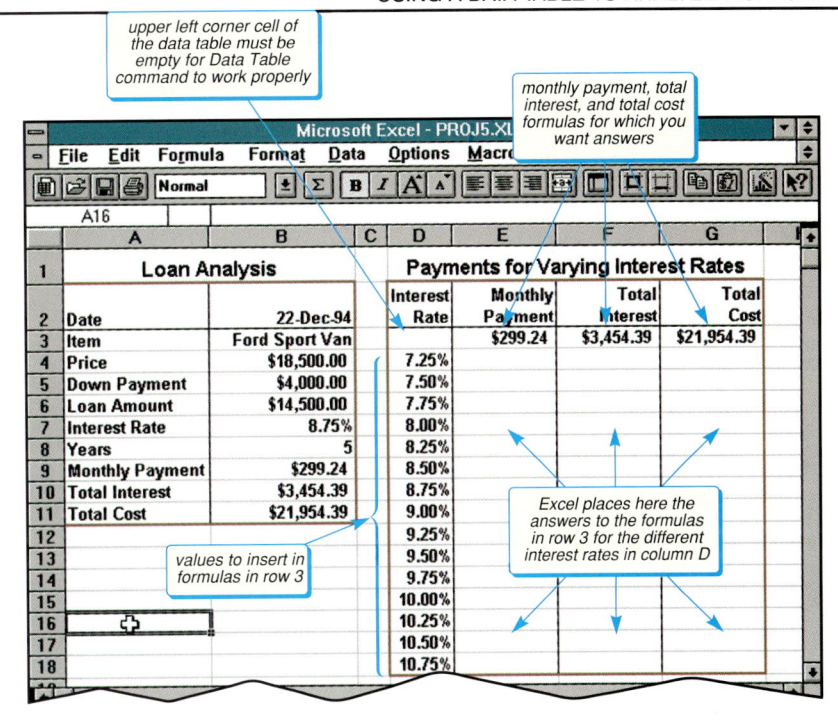

FIGURE 5-16a

Callouts:
- upper left corner cell of the data table must be empty for Data Table command to work properly
- monthly payment, total interest, and total cost formulas for which you want answers
- values to insert in formulas in row 3
- Excel places here the answers to the formulas in row 3 for the different interest rates in column D

Loan Analysis

	A	B
1	Loan Analysis	
2	Date	22-Dec-94
3	Item	Ford Sport Van
4	Price	$18,500.00
5	Down Payment	$4,000.00
6	Loan Amount	$14,500.00
7	Interest Rate	8.75%
8	Years	5
9	Monthly Payment	$299.24
10	Total Interest	$3,454.39
11	Total Cost	$21,954.39

Payments for Varying Interest Rates

Interest Rate	Monthly Payment	Total Interest	Total Cost
	$299.24	$3,454.39	$21,954.39
7.25%			
7.50%			
7.75%			
8.00%			
8.25%			
8.50%			
8.75%			
9.00%			
9.25%			
9.50%			
9.75%			
10.00%			
10.25%			
10.50%			
10.75%			

FIGURE 5-16b

Callout: data table filled with answers to formulas in row 3 for varying interest rates in column D

Payments for Varying Interest Rates

Interest Rate	Monthly Payment	Total Interest	Total Cost
	$299.24	$3,454.39	$21,954.39
7.25%	288.83	2,829.84	21,329.84
7.50%	290.55	2,933.02	21,433.02
7.75%	292.28	3,036.55	21,536.55
8.00%	294.01	3,140.46	21,640.46
8.25%	295.75	3,244.74	21,744.74
8.50%	297.49	3,349.38	21,849.38
8.75%	299.24	3,454.39	21,954.39
9.00%	301.00	3,559.77	22,059.77
9.25%	302.76	3,665.51	22,165.51
9.50%	304.53	3,771.62	22,271.62
9.75%	306.30	3,878.09	22,378.09
10.00%	308.08	3,984.93	22,484.93
10.25%	309.87	4,092.13	22,592.13
10.50%	311.66	4,199.69	22,699.69
10.75%	313.46	4,307.62	22,807.62

The following pages use these steps to construct the data table in Figure 5-16b: (1) adjust the widths of columns C through G; (2) enter the data table title and column titles in the range D1:G2; (3) use the data fill handle to enter the varying interest rates in column D; (4) enter the formulas in the range E3:G3 for which the data table is to determine answers; (5) use the Data Table command on the Data menu to define the range D3:G18 as a data table and identify the interest rate in cell B7 as the **input cell**, the one you want to vary; and (6) outline the data table to highlight it.

In the steps that follow, the columns are set to specific widths so the data table will fit in the same window with the Loan Analysis section. Keep in mind you may have to adjust the widths of columns after the numbers and text are assigned to the cells because large numbers that won't fit across a cell cause Excel to display number signs (#) in the cell. When you design a worksheet, you make the best possible estimate of column widths and then change them later as required.

TO ENTER THE DATA TABLE TITLE AND COLUMN TITLES

Step 1: Use the mouse to change the widths of columns C through G as follows: (a) C — 3; (b) D — 6.71; and (c) E, F, and G — 11.29.

Step 2: Select cell D1 and enter Payments for Varying Interest Rates. Click the Increase Font Size tool on the Standard toolbar twice to increase the table title. Drag from cell D1 to cell G1 and click the Center Across Columns tool on the Standard toolbar.

Step 3: Select the range D2:G2. From the Format menu, choose Alignment. Click the Wrap Text box so an x appears in it. Choose OK from the Alignment dialog box. With the range D2:G2 still selected, click the Right Align tool on the Standard toolbar.

Step 4: Enter the following in the range D2:G2: (a) in cell D2 enter Interest (ALT + ENTER) Rate; (b) in cell E2 enter Monthly (ALT + ENTER) Payment; (c) in cell F2 enter Total (ALT + ENTER) Interest; and (d) in cell G2 enter Total (ALT + ENTER) Cost.

The data table title and column headings display as shown in Figure 5-17.

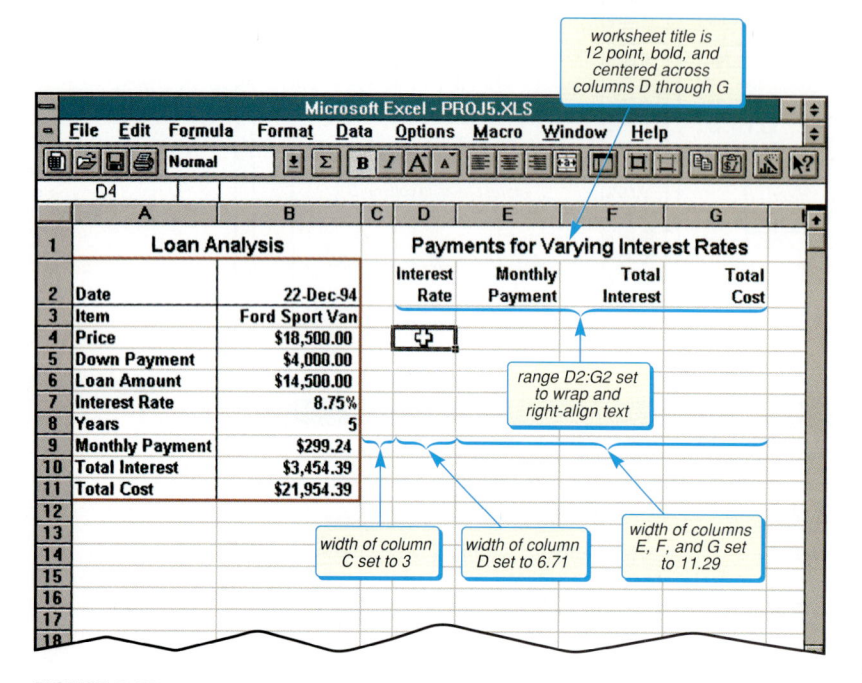

FIGURE 5-17

In Step 4 pressing ALT + ENTER instructs Excel to continue the entry on the next line of the cell.

The next step is to create the percent series in column D (see Figures 5-18a and 5-18b on the next page).

TO CREATE THE PERCENT SERIES IN COLUMN D

Step 1: Select cell D4 and enter 7.25%. Select cell D5 and enter 7.50%.
Step 2: Select the range D4:D5 and point to the fill handle. Drag the fill handle down to cell D18 (Figure 5-18a on the next page).
Step 3: Release the mouse button and select any cell to remove the selection from the range D4:D18.

Excel generates the series of numbers 7.25% to 10.75% in increments of 0.25% in the range D4:D18 (Figure 5-18b on the next page).

The percents in column D are the values Excel uses to compute the formulas entered at the top of the data table in row 3. Notice that the series beginning with 7.25% in column D was not started in cell D3 because the cell immediately above the series and to the left of the formulas in the data table must be empty for a one-input data table.

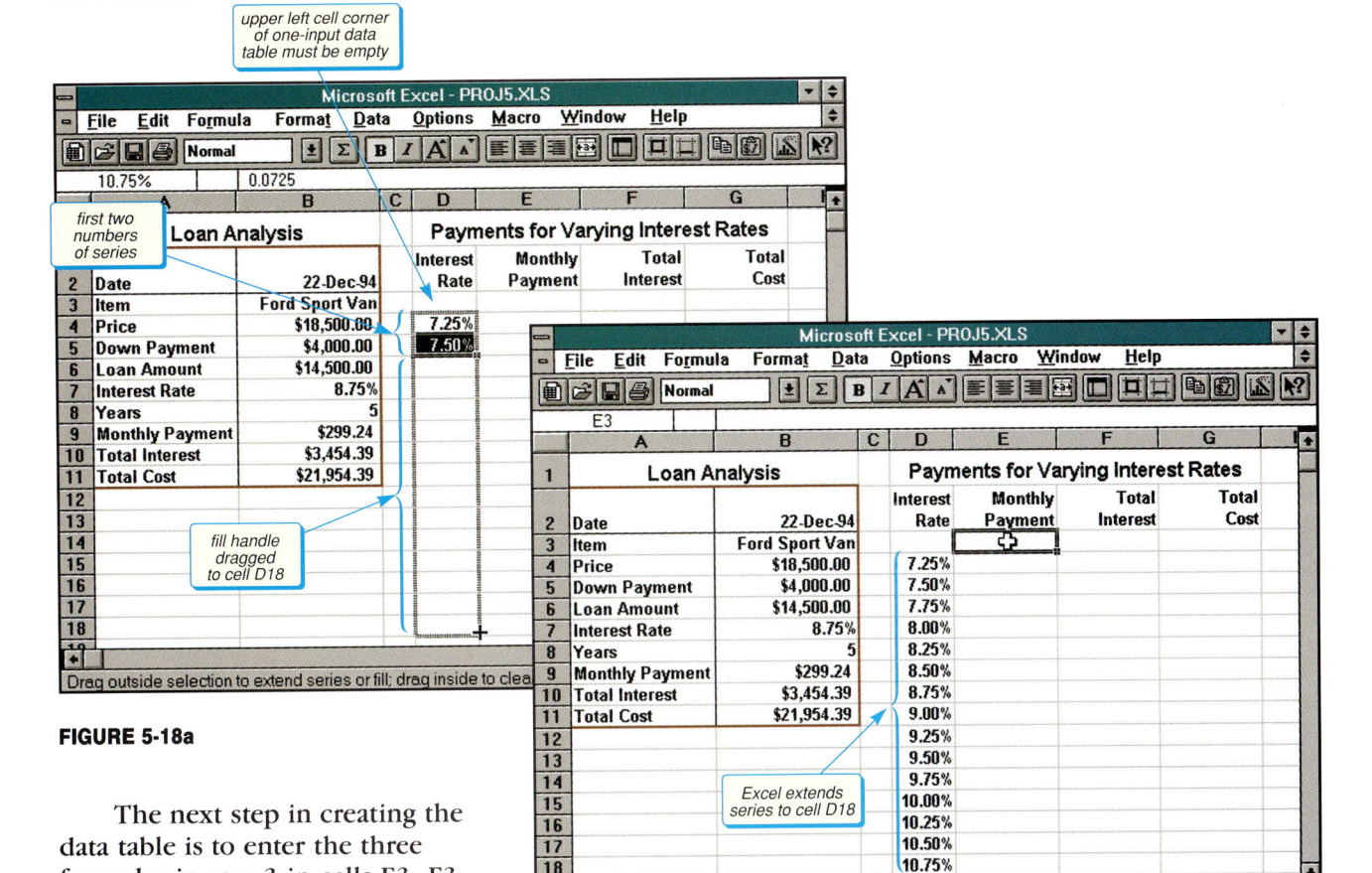

USING A DATA TABLE TO ANALYZE WORKSHEET DATA   **E249**

FIGURE 5-18a

FIGURE 5-18b

The next step in creating the data table is to enter the three formulas in row 3 in cells E3, F3, and G3. The three formulas are the same as the monthly payment formula in cell B9, the total interest formula in cell B10, and the total cost formula in cell B11.

Excel provides three ways to enter these formulas in the data table: (1) retype the formulas in cells E3, F3, and G3; (2) copy cells B9, B10, and B11 to cells E3, F3, and G3, respectively; or (3) enter the formulas =monthly_payment in cell E3, =total_interest in cell F3, and enter =total_cost in cell G3. Recall that earlier in this project cells B9 through B11 were assigned names.

Using the names preceded by an equal sign to define the formulas in the data table has two advantages: (1) it is more efficient; (2) if you change any of the formulas in the range B9:B11, the formulas at the top of the data table are automatically updated. The following steps use the names to define the formulas in the data table (see Figure 5-19 on the next page).

TO ENTER AND FORMAT THE FORMULAS IN THE DATA TABLE

Step 1: Select cell E3. Enter =monthly_payment
Step 2: Select cell F3. Enter =total_interest
Step 3: Select cell G3. Enter =total_cost
Step 4: Select the range E3:G3. Click the Style box arrow to the right of the Style box on the Standard toolbar. Select the Currency style. Select any cell in the worksheet to remove the selection from the range E3:G3.

Excel displays the values in row 3 that correspond to the formulas in cells B9, B10, and B11 (Figure 5-19 on the next page).

E250 PROJECT 5 ANALYZING WORKSHEET DATA

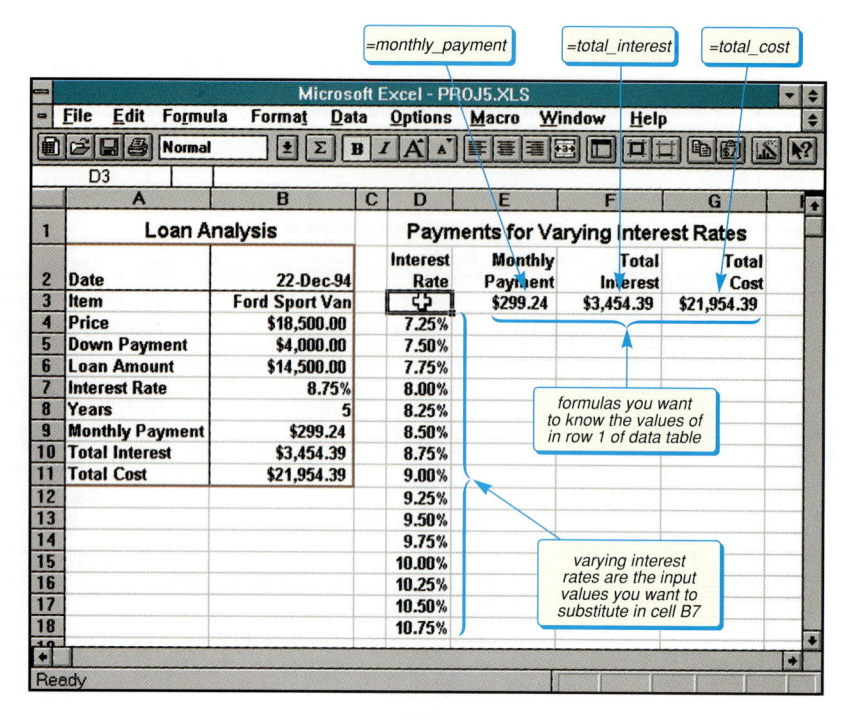

FIGURE 5-19

After creating the interest rates in column D and assigning the formulas in row 3, the next step is to define the range D3:G18 as a data table.

TO DEFINE A RANGE AS A DATA TABLE ▼

STEP 1 ▶

Select the range D3:G18. Select the Data menu and point to the Table command.

Excel displays the Data menu (Figure 5-20). Notice in the worksheet that the range D3:G18 does not include the data table title in row 1 and column headings in row 2. The column headings are **NOT** *part of the data table even though they identify the columns in the table.*

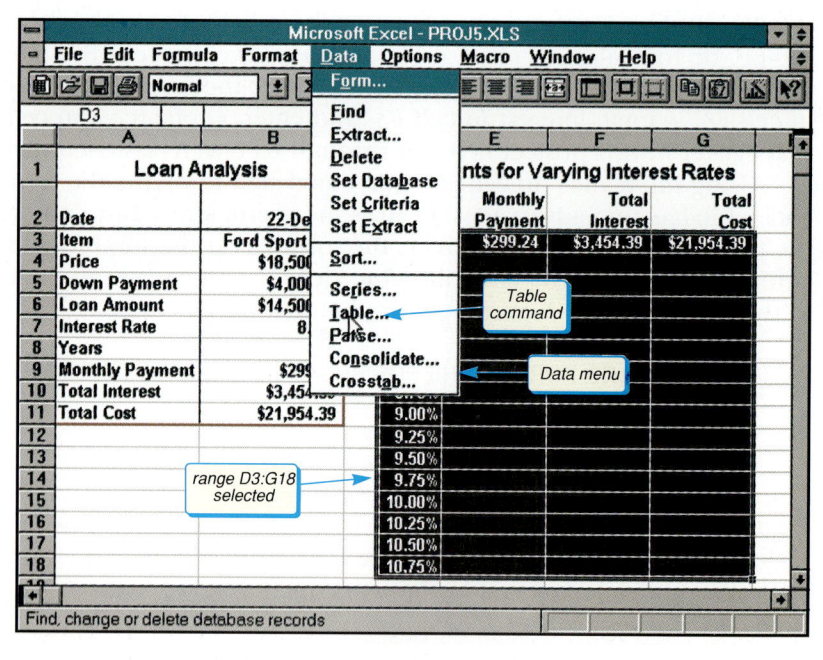

FIGURE 5-20

STEP 2 ▶

Choose the Table command from the Data menu. Select the Column Input cell box in the Table dialog box. Click cell B7, the input cell.

A moving border surrounds the selected input cell and Excel places the cell reference in the Column Input Cell box in the Table dialog box (Figure 5-21).

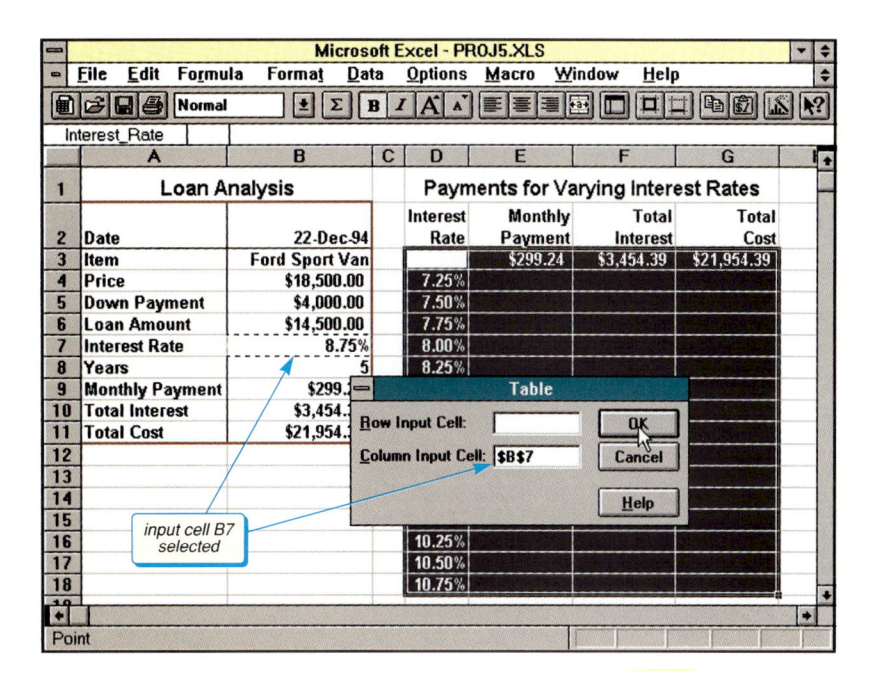

FIGURE 5-21

STEP 3 ▶

Choose the OK button from the Table dialog box.

Excel immediately fills the data table by calculating the three formulas at the top of the data table for each interest rate in column D (Figure 5-22).

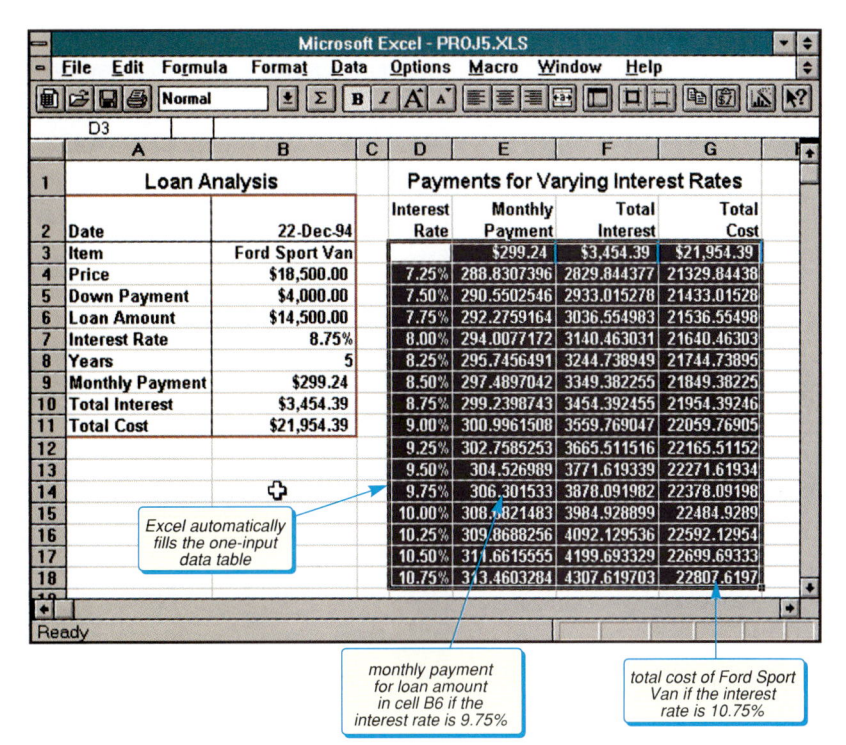

FIGURE 5-22

Notice in Figure 5-22 that the data table displays the monthly payment, total interest, and total cost for the interest rates in column D. For example, if the interest rate is 9.75% (cell D14) rather than 8.75% (cell B7), the monthly payment is $306.30 (cell E14) rather than $299.24 (cell B9). If the interest rate is 10.75% (cell D18) then the total cost of the Ford Sport Van is approximately $22,807.62 (cell G18) rather than $21,954.39 (cell B11). Thus, a 2% increase in the interest rate results in an $853.23 increase in the total cost of the Ford Sport Van.

TO OUTLINE AND FORMAT THE DATA TABLE AND SAVE THE WORKSHEET

Step 1: Select the range E4:G18. Click the Style box arrow to the right of the Style box on the Standard toolbar. Select the Comma style.

Step 2: Select the range D2:G18. From the Format menu, choose the Border command. In the Border dialog box, select dark red in the Color box, select Outline in the Border box, and select the regular border (third from left in row one) in the Style box. Choose the OK button from the Border dialog box.

Step 3: Select the range D2:G2. Click the Bottom Border tool on the Standard toolbar.

Step 4: Select the range D2:F18. From the Format menu, choose the Border command. In the Border dialog box, select Right in the Border box, and select the light border (second from left in row one) in the Style box. Choose the OK button from the Border dialog box.

Step 5: Click the Save File tool on the Standard toolbar to save the worksheet under the file name PROJ5.

The worksheet displays as shown in Figure 5-23.

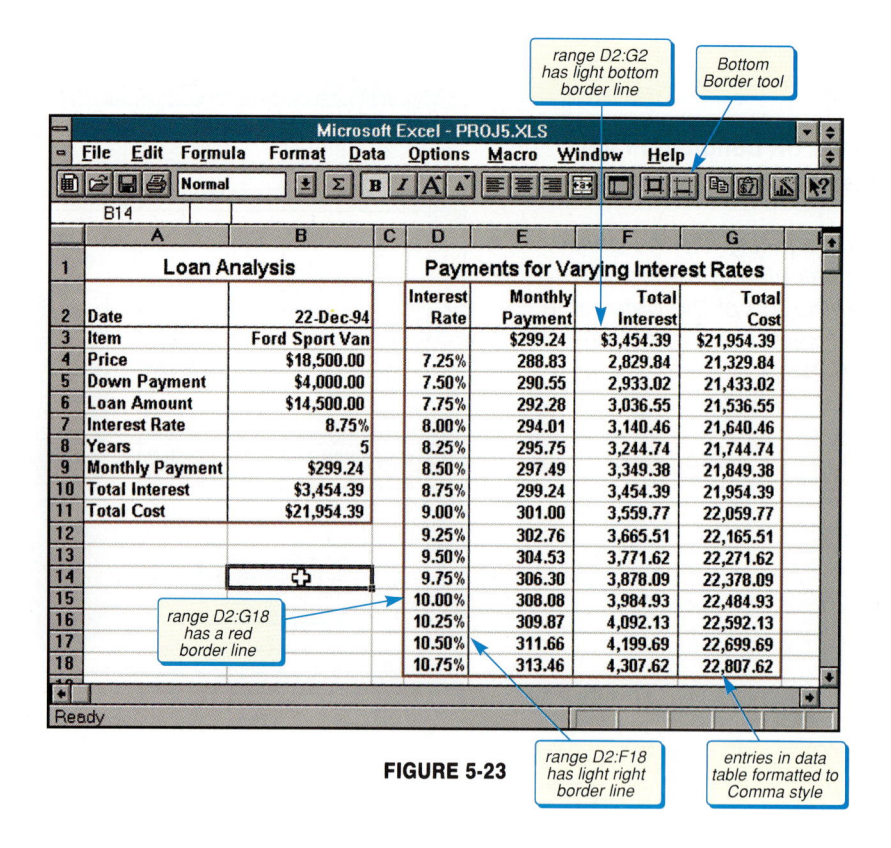

FIGURE 5-23

The following list details important points you should know about data tables:

1. You can have as many active data tables in a worksheet as you want.
2. You delete a data table as you would any other item on a worksheet.

3. For a data table with one varying value, the cell in the upper left corner of the table (cell D3 in Figure 5-23) must be empty.
4. To add additional formulas to a one-input data table, enter them in adjacent cells in the same row as the current formulas and define the entire range as a data table by using the Table command on the Data menu.
5. A one-input data table can vary only one value, but can analyze as many formulas as you want.

▶ ENTERING NEW LOAN DATA

With the Loan Analysis and Data Table sections of the worksheet complete, you can use them to generate new loan information. For example, assume you want to purchase a $178,500.00 house. You have $36,500.00 for a down payment and would like the loan for 15 years. The loan company is currently charging 8.75% interest for a 15-year loan. The following steps show how to enter the new loan data (see Figure 5-24).

TO ENTER NEW LOAN DATA

Step 1: Select cell B3. Enter House, the item to be purchased.
Step 2: Select cell B4. Enter 178500, the cost of the house.
Step 3: Select cell B5. Enter 36500, the down payment.
Step 4: Leave the interest rate at 8.75% in cell B7.
Step 5: Select cell B8. Enter 15, the number of years.

Excel automatically recalculates the loan information in cells B6, B9, B10, B11, and the data table (Figure 5-24).

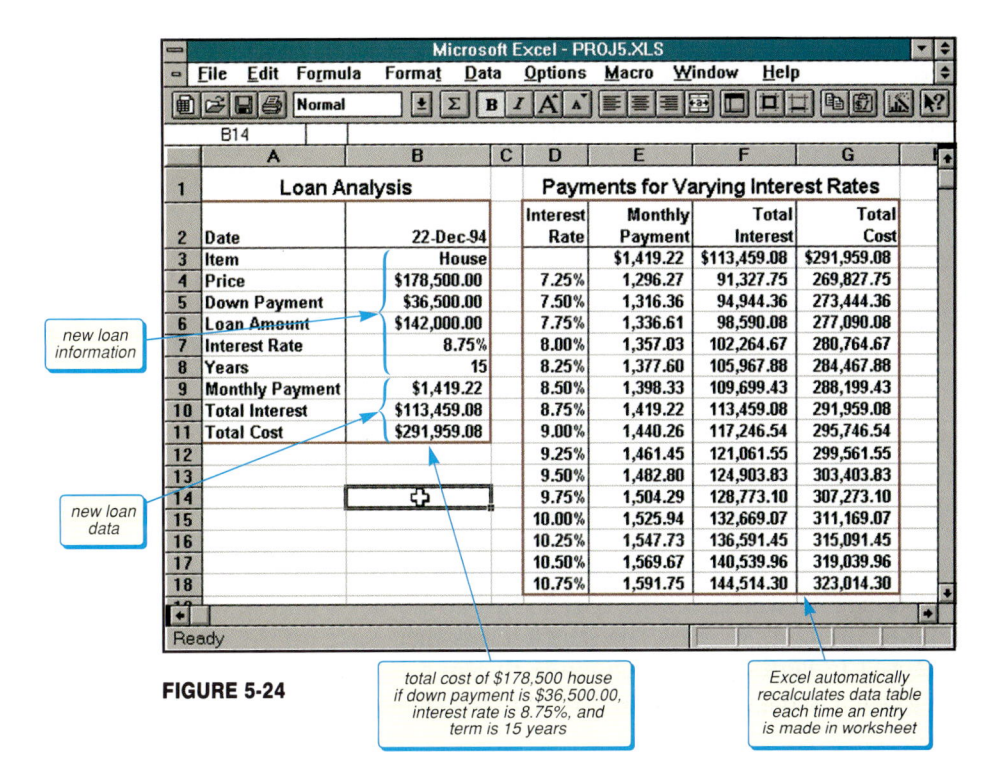

FIGURE 5-24

You can use the worksheet PROJ5 to calculate the loan information for any reasonable loan data. As you can see from Figure 5-24 on the previous page, the monthly payment for the house is $1,419.22. The total interest (loan institution's profit) is $113,459.08. The total cost of the house is $291,959.08.

▶ Building a Command Macro to Automate Loan Data Entry

A command macro is made up of a series of macro functions, or instructions, that tell Excel what to do to complete a task. A command macro such as the one in Figure 5-25 is used to automate routine worksheet tasks, like entering new data into a worksheet. Command macros are almost a necessity for worksheets that are built to be used by people who know little or nothing about computers and spreadsheets.

any cell entry that does not begin with an equal sign is considered a comment

comments explain the purpose of each macro function

a command macro is made up of macro functions on a macro sheet

macro sheet automatically displays formulas rather than values

macro functions begin with an equal sign (=)

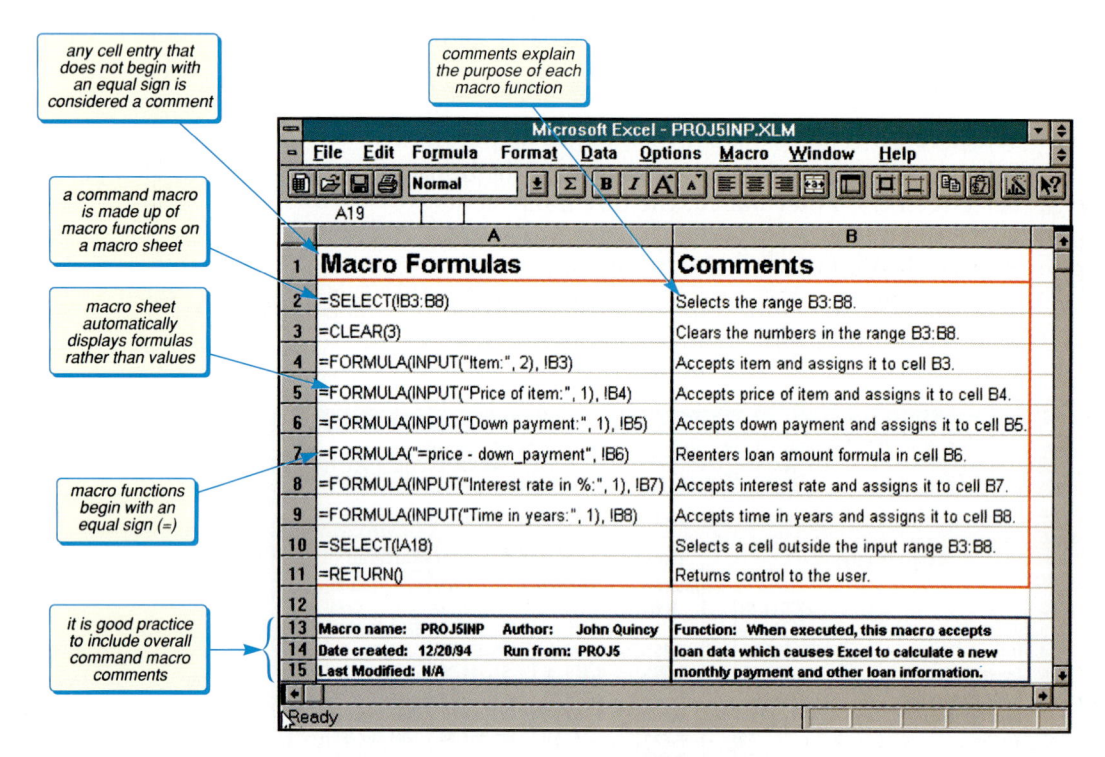

it is good practice to include overall command macro comments

	A	B
1	**Macro Formulas**	**Comments**
2	=SELECT(!B3:B8)	Selects the range B3:B8.
3	=CLEAR(3)	Clears the numbers in the range B3:B8.
4	=FORMULA(INPUT("Item:", 2), !B3)	Accepts item and assigns it to cell B3.
5	=FORMULA(INPUT("Price of item:", 1), !B4)	Accepts price of item and assigns it to cell B4.
6	=FORMULA(INPUT("Down payment:", 1), !B5)	Accepts down payment and assigns it to cell B5.
7	=FORMULA("=price - down_payment", !B6)	Reenters loan amount formula in cell B6.
8	=FORMULA(INPUT("Interest rate in %:", 1), !B7)	Accepts interest rate and assigns it to cell B7.
9	=FORMULA(INPUT("Time in years:", 1), !B8)	Accepts time in years and assigns it to cell B8.
10	=SELECT(!A18)	Selects a cell outside the input range B3:B8.
11	=RETURN()	Returns control to the user.
12		
13	Macro name: PROJ5INP Author: John Quincy	Function: When executed, this macro accepts
14	Date created: 12/20/94 Run from: PROJ5	loan data which causes Excel to calculate a new
15	Last Modified: N/A	monthly payment and other loan information.

FIGURE 5-25

For example, in the section on the previous page, new loan data was entered to calculate new loan information. However, the user who enters the data must know what cells to select and how much loan data is required to obtain the desired results. To simplify entering the loan data, a worksheet and command macro can be set up so that all the user has to do is click a button to **play back** (execute) the command macro. The instructions that make up the command macro (A2:A11 in Figure 5-25) then guide the user through entering the required loan data in the range B3:B8 while protecting against someone entering the loan data into the wrong cells.

Macro Functions

Excel has more than 200 macro functions from which you can choose to create a command macro. Many of the macro functions correspond to Excel commands on menus or to dialog box selections. For example, you can build a command macro to carry out most of the worksheet activity described thus far in this book. This project is concerned with using the five macro functions listed in Table 5-2.

▶ **TABLE 5-2**

MACRO FUNCTION	FUNCTION
CLEAR(type)	Clears the selected cell or range of cells. The type (1 = all, 2 = formats, 3 = formulas or numbers, 4 = notes) indicates what you want to clear in the selection.
FORMULA(formula_text, cell_reference)	Assigns formula_text to cell_reference. Formula_text can be text in quotation marks, a number, a formula in quotation marks, or another macro function.
INPUT("message",type)	Displays message in a dialog box and accepts a value from the user. The type (0 = formula, 1 = number, 2 = text) indicates how you want Excel to treat the value entered.
RETURN()	Ends the macro.
SELECT(selection)	Selects a cell or range of cells.

Macro functions look like formulas because they begin with an equal sign. Any entry in a command macro that does not begin with an equal sign is a comment. Thus, in Figure 5-25, only the entries in the range A2:A11 are macro functions. All the other entries are comments.

Planning a Command Macro

When you play back a command macro from the worksheet, Excel executes the macro functions one at a time beginning at the top of the command macro and working downward. Thus, when you plan a command macro you should remember that the order in which you place the macro functions in the command macro determines the sequence of execution.

Once you know what you want the command macro to do, you should write it out on paper. Before entering the command macro into the computer, put yourself in the position of Excel and step through the instructions and see how it affects the worksheet. Testing a command macro before entering it is an important part of the development process and is called **desk checking**.

You should add comments for each macro function (see right side of Figure 5-25) because they help you remember the purpose of the macro functions at a later date. For example, read the macro function in cell A2 in Figure 5-25. Then read the corresponding comment in cell B2. The comment in cell B2 explains the purpose of the macro function =SELECT(!B3:B8) in cell A2.

Opening a Macro Sheet and Naming the Command Macro

You write a command macro on a **macro sheet** which looks exactly like a worksheet. The steps on the next page show how to open a macro sheet and name the command macro.

E256　PROJECT 5　ANALYZING WORKSHEET DATA

TO OPEN A MACRO SHEET AND NAME THE COMMAND MACRO

STEP 1 ▶

From the File menu, choose the New command.

Excel displays the New dialog box (Figure 5-26).

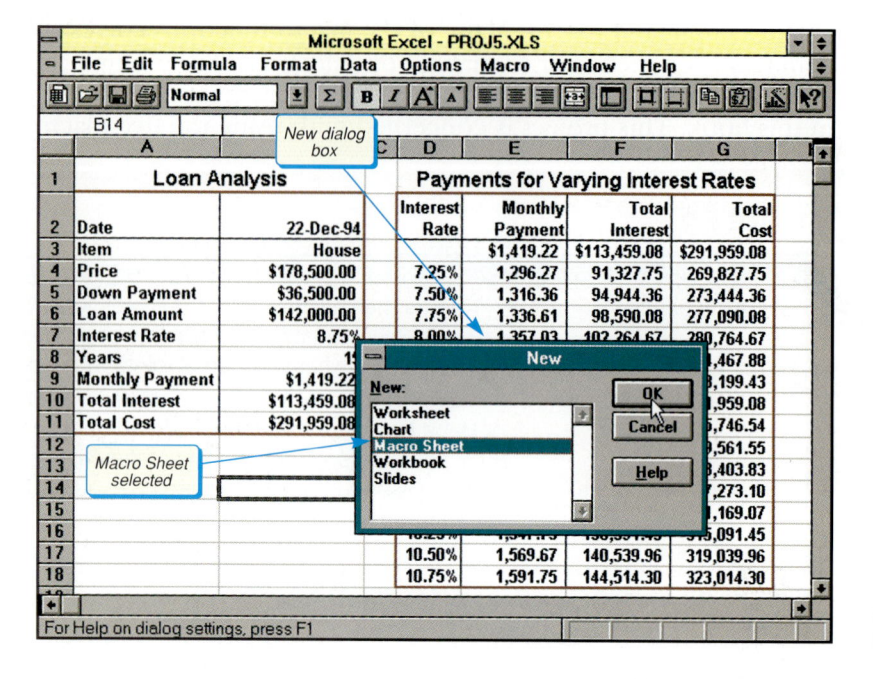

FIGURE 5-26

STEP 2 ▶

Select Macro Sheet in the New box and choose the OK button from the New dialog box.

Excel opens a macro sheet window that looks exactly like an empty worksheet except that the columns are wider.

STEP 3 ▶

With cell A1 selected in the macro sheet, choose the Define Name command from the Formula menu. In the Define Name dialog box, enter the name `proj5inp` in the Name text box, and select the Command option button in the Macro area.

Excel displays the name proj5inp in the Name text box of the Define Name dialog box (Figure 5-27).

STEP 4

Choose the OK button from the Define Name dialog box.

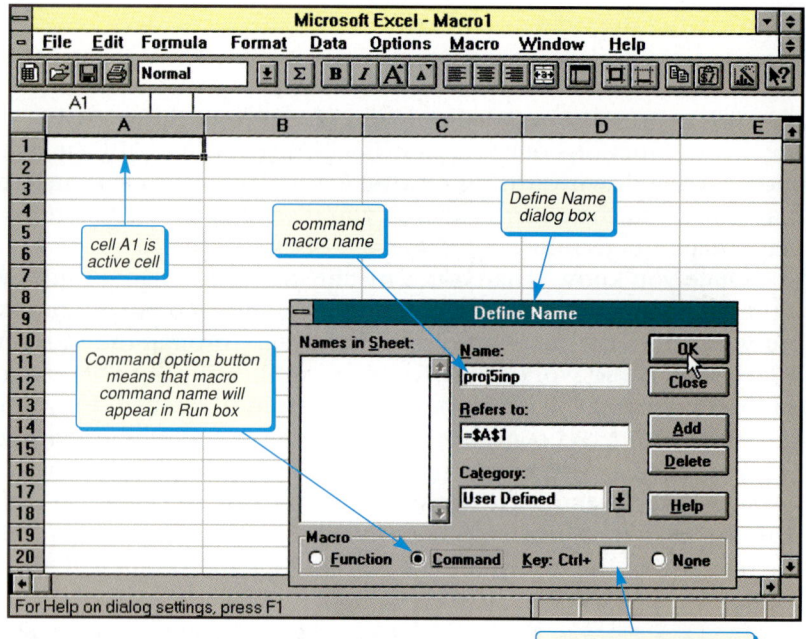

FIGURE 5-27

In Step 3 the name proj5inp was assigned to cell A1 because that is where the command macro begins. The name proj5inp will be used later as a reference to where Excel should begin the playback. Selecting the Command option button in the Macro box instructs Excel to display the name proj5inp in the Run box. The Run box displays when you choose Run from the **Macro menu** with the worksheet PROJ5 on the screen.

Entering the Command Macro on the Macro Sheet

After assigning cell A1 of the macro sheet the name proj5inp, the next step is to enter the command macro (see Figure 5-28 below and Figure 5-29 on the next page).

TO ENTER THE COMMAND MACRO ON THE MACRO SHEET

Step 1: Click the Select All button above row heading 1 and to the left of column A. Use the Font command on the Format menu to change the font of the worksheet to TT Arial. Use the mouse to increase the width of columns A and B to 19.86 so that the two columns nearly cover the entire width of the screen, yet fit on a one-page printout. Use the mouse to increase the height of row 1 to 21 points and the height of rows 2 through 12 to 18 points so that the macro functions are easier to read.

Step 2: Select cell A1 and enter Macro Formulas. Select cell B1 and enter Comments. Select the range A1:B1. On the Standard toolbar, click the Increase Font Size tool four times to increase the font size. Click the Bold tool on the Standard toolbar.

Step 3: Select cell A2 and enter the macro function =select(!b3:b8). Select cell B2 and enter the corresponding comment Selects the range B3:B8.

Step 4: Select cell A3 and enter the macro function =clear(3). Select cell B3 and enter the corresponding comment Clears the numbers in the range B3:B8 (Figure 5-28).

Step 5: Enter the remaining macro functions and comments in the range A3:B11 (see Figure 5-25 on page E254).

The macro functions display as shown in Figure 5-29 on the next page. Notice Excel capitalizes command macros even when you enter them in lowercase.

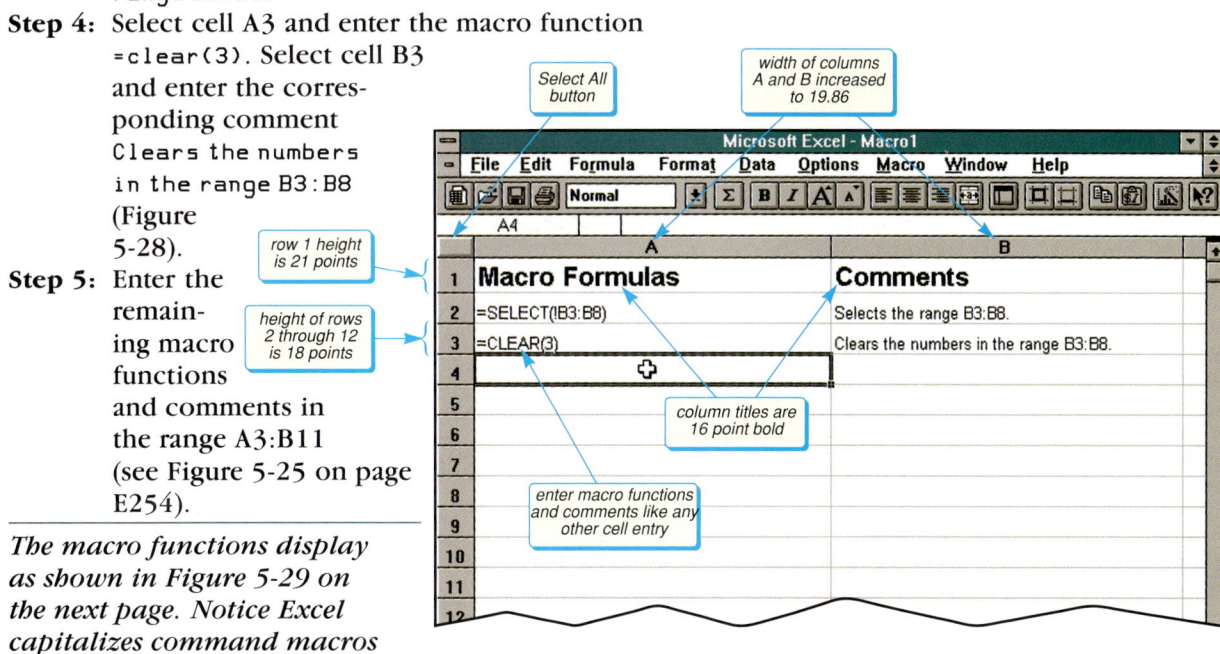

FIGURE 5-28

remainder of macro functions entered into macro sheet

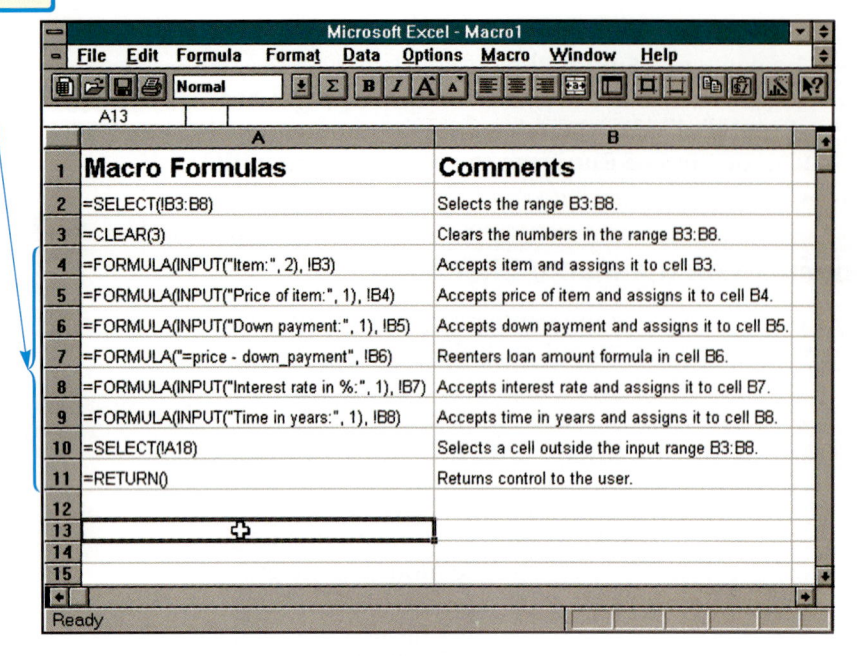

	A	B
1	Macro Formulas	Comments
2	=SELECT(!B3:B8)	Selects the range B3:B8.
3	=CLEAR(3)	Clears the numbers in the range B3:B8.
4	=FORMULA(INPUT("Item:", 2), !B3)	Accepts item and assigns it to cell B3.
5	=FORMULA(INPUT("Price of item:", 1), !B4)	Accepts price of item and assigns it to cell B4.
6	=FORMULA(INPUT("Down payment:", 1), !B5)	Accepts down payment and assigns it to cell B5.
7	=FORMULA("=price - down_payment", !B6)	Reenters loan amount formula in cell B6.
8	=FORMULA(INPUT("Interest rate in %:", 1), !B7)	Accepts interest rate and assigns it to cell B7.
9	=FORMULA(INPUT("Time in years:", 1), !B8)	Accepts time in years and assigns it to cell B8.
10	=SELECT(!A18)	Selects a cell outside the input range B3:B8.
11	=RETURN()	Returns control to the user.

FIGURE 5-29

Be aware of the following aspects of macro sheets and macro functions. First, Excel automatically displays the formulas version when a macro sheet is opened because it is more important to see the formulas than the values.

Second, to reference cells in the worksheet, you must begin a cell reference or range in a macro function with an exclamation point (!). Thus, in cell A2 the macro function =SELECT(!B3:B8) means select the range B3:B8 in the worksheet.

If the exclamation point is not appended to the front of the range, Excel selects the range B3:B8 in the macro sheet when the command macro is played back.

Third, according to Table 5-2 on page E255, the 3 in the macro function =CLEAR(3) in cell A3 instructs Excel to clear only the formulas (or numbers) from the selected cells B3:B8 in the worksheet. Thus, the CLEAR macro function does not delete the format in the range B3:B8.

Fourth, when a macro function is within a macro function, you do not begin it with an equal sign. For example, in cell A4 on the macro sheet, the macro function =FORMULA(INPUT("Item:", 2), !B3) includes the macro function INPUT, which does not start with an equal sign.

Fifth, cell B6 in the worksheet (Figure 5-11, page E242) is assigned the formula =price – down_ payment. Because the CLEAR macro function in cell A3 deletes this formula in cell B6, you need a macro function (cell A7 in the macro sheet) to place the formula back in cell B6 on the worksheet. The formula is required because Excel needs it to calculate the loan amount.

Sixth, due to the INPUT macro function within the FORMULA macro functions in cells A4, A5, A6, A8, and A9, Excel automatically displays a dialog box with the text within quotation marks as the prompt message.

Seventh, the =SELECT(!A18) macro function in cell A10 selects cell A18 in the worksheet, thus removing the selection from the range B3:B8. Finally, the =RETURN() macro function in cell A11 returns control of the worksheet back to the user.

Adding Overall Documentation to the Macro Sheet

The next step is to add the overall command macro documentation to the macro sheet in the range A13:B15 and draw borders to improve the appearance of the macro sheet as shown at the bottom of the screen in Figure 5-30. Finally, the macro sheet is saved to disk.

Follow the steps on the next page to add overall documentation, draw borders, and save the macro sheet.

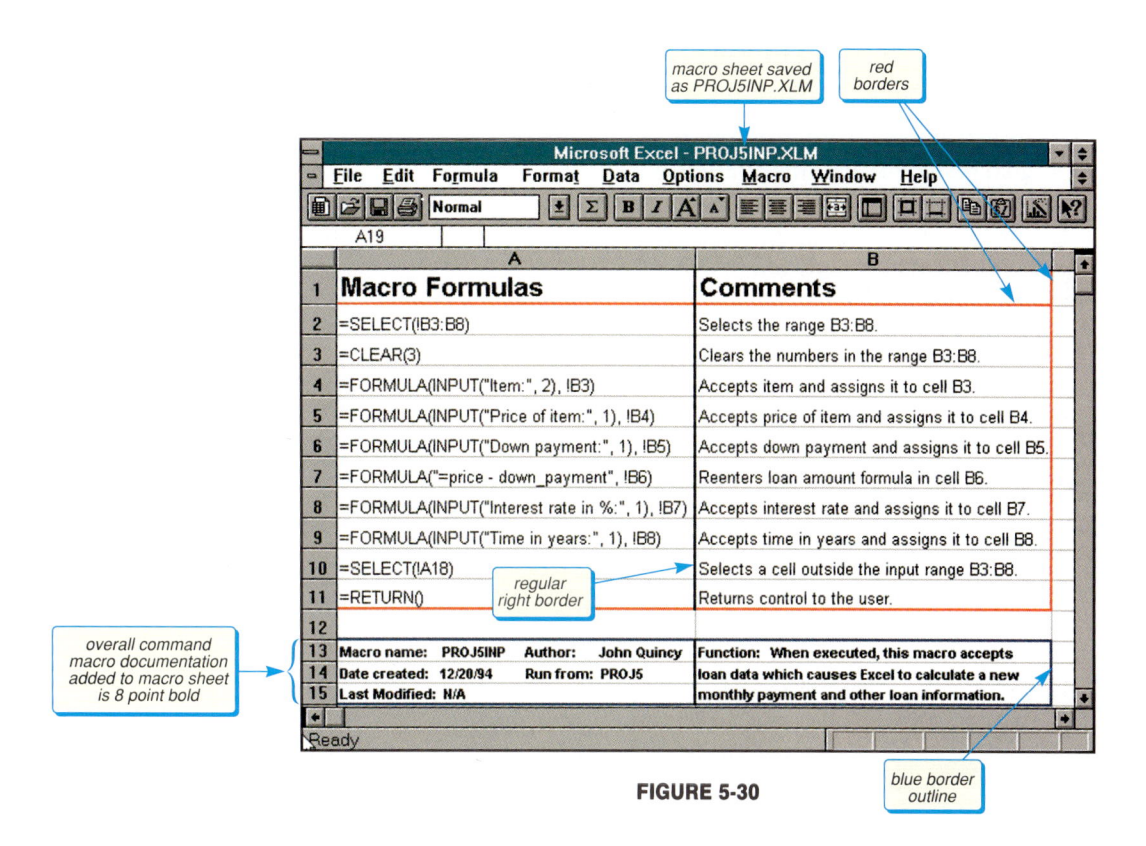

BUILDING A COMMAND MACRO TO AUTOMATE LOAN DATA ENTRY **E259**

macro sheet saved as PROJ5INP.XLM
red borders

	A	B
1	**Macro Formulas**	**Comments**
2	=SELECT(!B3:B8)	Selects the range B3:B8.
3	=CLEAR(3)	Clears the numbers in the range B3:B8.
4	=FORMULA(INPUT("Item:", 2), !B3)	Accepts item and assigns it to cell B3.
5	=FORMULA(INPUT("Price of item:", 1), !B4)	Accepts price of item and assigns it to cell B4.
6	=FORMULA(INPUT("Down payment:", 1), !B5)	Accepts down payment and assigns it to cell B5.
7	=FORMULA("=price - down_payment", !B6)	Reenters loan amount formula in cell B6.
8	=FORMULA(INPUT("Interest rate in %:", 1), !B7)	Accepts interest rate and assigns it to cell B7.
9	=FORMULA(INPUT("Time in years:", 1), !B8)	Accepts time in years and assigns it to cell B8.
10	=SELECT(!A18)	Selects a cell outside the input range B3:B8.
11	=RETURN()	Returns control to the user.
12		
13	Macro name: PROJ5INP Author: John Quincy	Function: When executed, this macro accepts
14	Date created: 12/20/94 Run from: PROJ5	loan data which causes Excel to calculate a new
15	Last Modified: N/A	monthly payment and other loan information.

regular right border

overall command macro documentation added to macro sheet is 8 point bold

blue border outline

FIGURE 5-30

TO ADD OVERALL DOCUMENTATION, DRAW BORDERS, AND SAVE THE MACRO SHEET

Step 1: Enter the comments shown in the range A13:B15 of Figure 5-30. Select the range A13:B15. Use the Font command on the Format menu to assign a font style of bold and a font size of 8 point to the selected range.

Step 2: With the range A13:B15 selected, use the Border command on the Format menu to assign a dark blue regular (third from left in row one) outline around the selected range. Select the range A13:A15. Use the Border command on the Format menu to assign a regular right border to the selected range.

Step 3: Select the range A1:B1. Hold down the CTRL key and select the range A11:B11. Use the Border command on the Format menu to assign a red regular bottom border to the nonadjacent selection. Select the range A1:A11. Use the Border command on the Format menu to assign a regular right border to the selected range. Select the range B1:B11. Use the Border command on the Format menu to assign a red regular right border to the selected range.

Step 4: Click the Save File tool on the Standard toolbar. When the Save As dialog box appears, enter the file name `proj5inp`. If necessary, select drive A. Choose the OK button from the Save As dialog box.

After you save the macro sheet, the name of the macro sheet, PROJ5INP.XLM, displays in the title bar (Figure 5-30).

Excel assigns the extension .XLM, which stands for Excel Macro Sheet, to the file name. Notice that the name PROJ5INP was used as the command macro name as well as the file name. The two names need not be the same. However, when there is only one command macro on the macro sheet, it is good practice to give both the command macro and the macro sheet the same name. Finally, the name PROJ5INP was selected because the trailing INP helps remind you that the command macro accepts *input* from the user.

Returning to the Opened Worksheet

After entering the command macro and saving the macro sheet, the next step is to display the window with the opened worksheet. Perform the following steps to display the opened worksheet.

TO RETURN TO THE OPENED WORKSHEET

STEP 1 ▶

Select the Window menu.

Excel displays the Window menu (Figure 5-31).

STEP 2

From the list of windows at the bottom of the Window menu, select PROJ5.XLS.

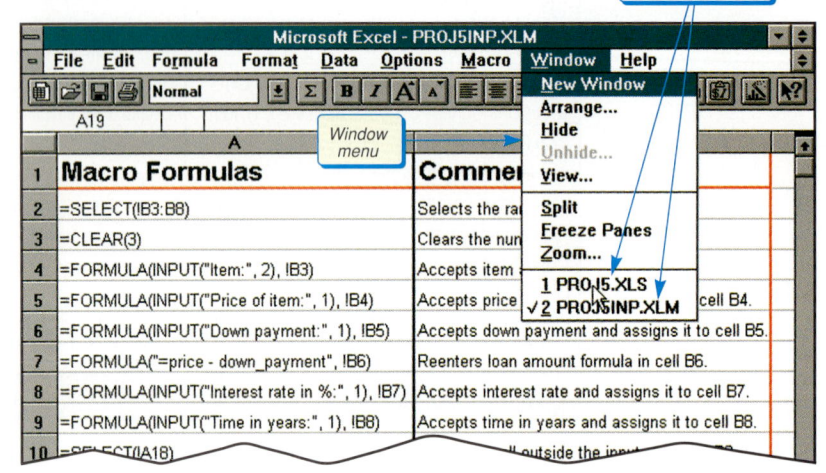

FIGURE 5-31

Following Step 2, Excel displays the worksheet PROJ5 rather than the macro sheet PROJ5INP. You can use the Window menu to switch back and forth between the two windows as often as required. However, if you exit Excel and then at a later time open PROJ5, you will also need to open PROJ5INP or play back the command macro to be able to use the Window menu to switch between the worksheet and macro sheet.

▶ ADDING A BUTTON TO THE WORKSHEET TO PLAY BACK A COMMAND MACRO

There are two ways to play back a command macro from the worksheet window. First, you can choose the Run command from the Macro menu and select the command macro name you want to play back. Second, you can add a **button** to the worksheet and assign it to play back a command macro. This project uses the second method. Assigning a command macro to a button makes it easier to play back the command macro.

You create the button by using the **Button tool** (□) on the Utility toolbar. You size and locate a button in the same way you did a chart in the earlier projects. You then change the name of the button by typing a new name. Finally, you use the **Assign to Object command** on the Macro menu to assign the command macro proj5inp to the button.

The following steps show how to create a button and assign to it a command macro.

TO ADD A BUTTON TO THE WORKSHEET AND ASSIGN TO IT A COMMAND MACRO

STEP 1 ▶

Position the mouse pointer in the Standard toolbar and click the right mouse button.

Excel displays the toolbar shortcut menu (Figure 5-32).

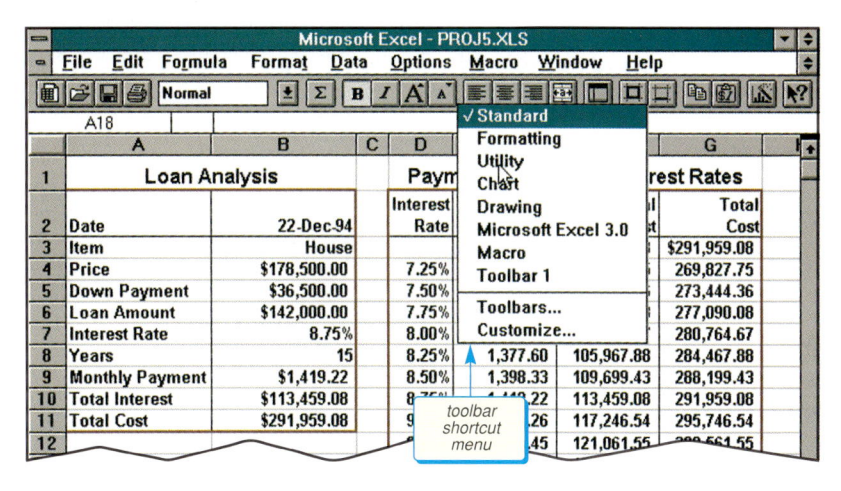

FIGURE 5-32

STEP 2

Choose the Utility command.

STEP 3 ▶

Drag the Utility toolbar to the dock above the formula bar.

Excel docks the Utility toolbar above the formula bar (Figure 5-33).

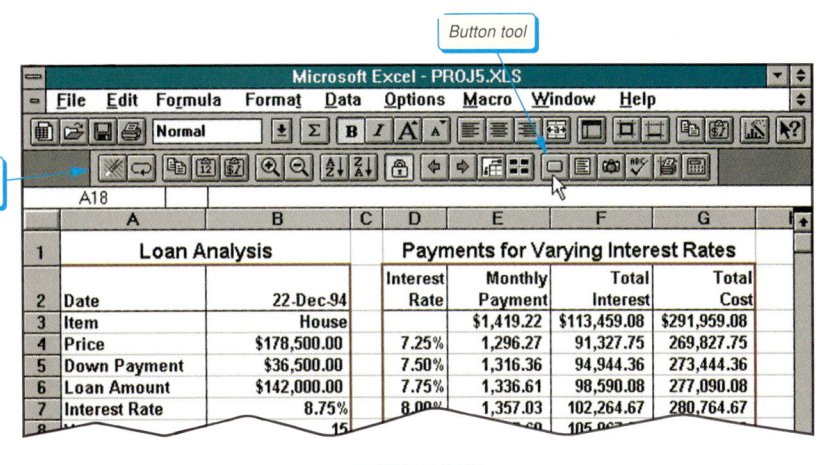

FIGURE 5-33

STEP 4 ▶

Click the Button tool on the Utility toolbar (Figure 5-33). Move the mouse pointer (a cross hair) to the upper left corner of cell A13. Drag the mouse pointer down and to the right to the lower right corner of cell A14.

Excel displays a border to show the size of the button location (Figure 5-34).

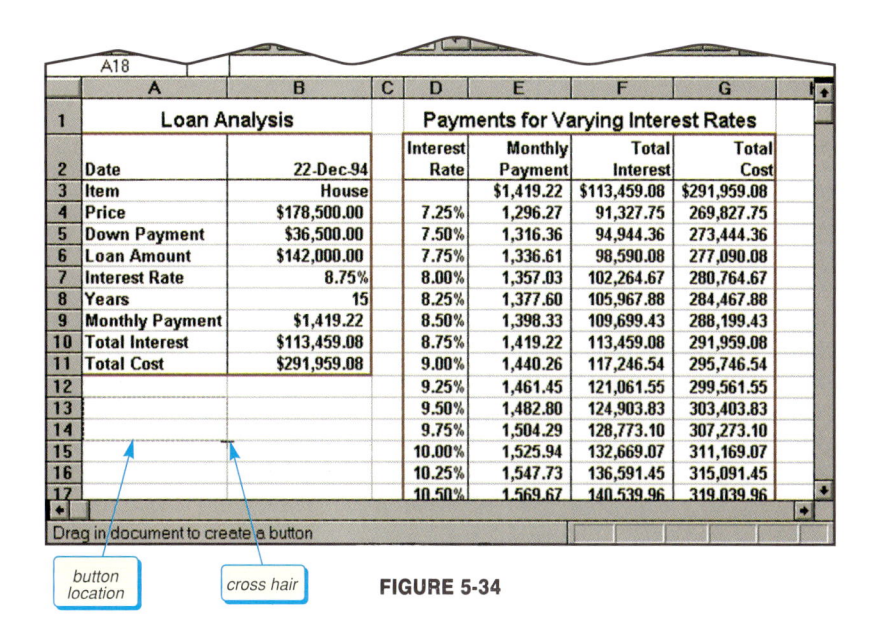

FIGURE 5-34

STEP 5 ▶

Release the left mouse button. In the Assign To Object dialog box, select the command macro -PROJ5INP.XLM!proj5inp.

Excel displays the button with the title Button 1 and also displays the Assign To Object dialog box (Figure 5-35). Notice that the button has handles on the sides and a shaded border. The handles and shaded border indicate you can resize and relocate the button on the worksheet after the Assign To Object dialog box is closed.

FIGURE 5-35

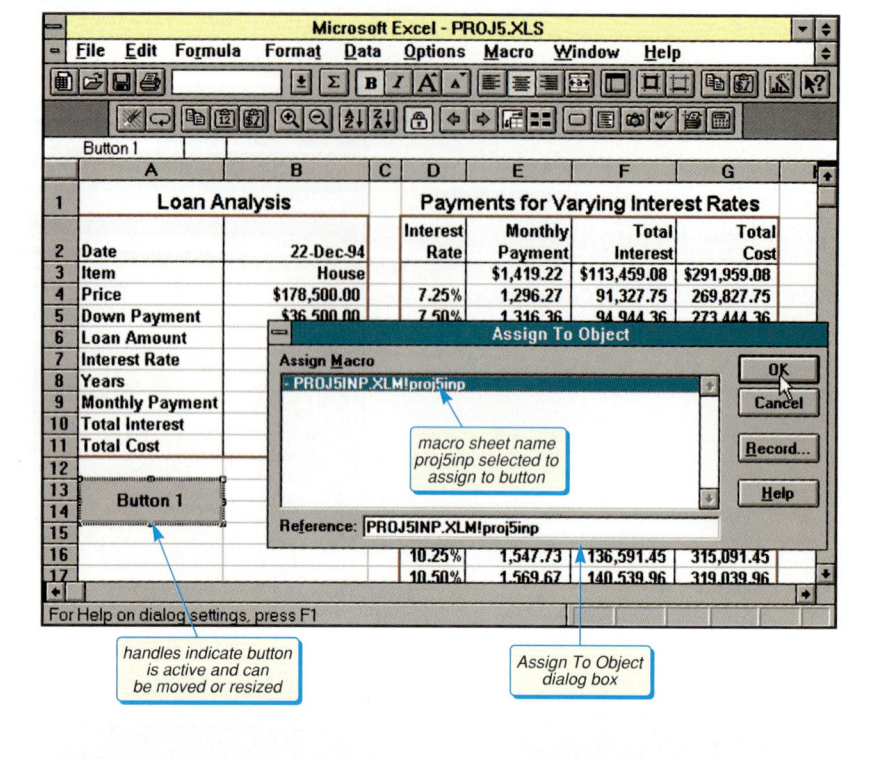

STEP 6 ▶

Choose the OK button from the Assign To Object dialog box. Click the button titled Button 1, drag across the button title Button 1, and type the new button title New Loan. Select any cell in the worksheet to lock in the button title.

The button with the title New Loan displays in the range A13:A14 of the worksheet (Figure 5-36).

STEP 7

Point to the Utility toolbar and click the right mouse button to display the toolbar shortcut menu. Select Utility to hide the Utility toolbar. Click the Save File tool on the Standard toolbar to save the worksheet with the button.

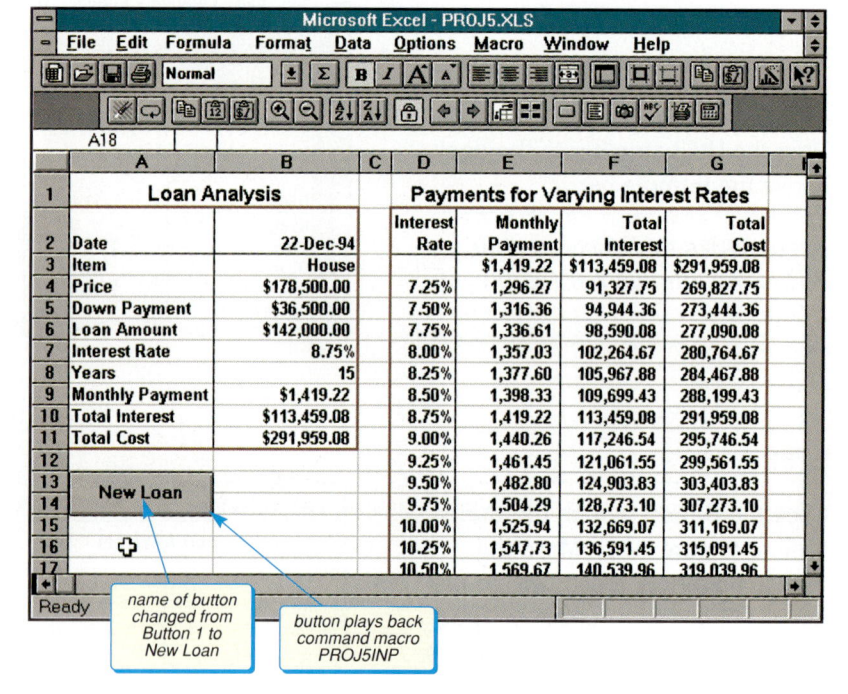

FIGURE 5-36

PLAYING BACK THE COMMAND MACRO **E263**

The first part of Step 6 assigns the command macro PROJ5INP to the button. In the dialog box in Figure 5-35, the name before the exclamation point (!) in -PROJ5INP.XLM!proj5inp is the file name of the macro sheet. The name following the exclamation point, proj5inp, is the name of the command macro.

If you want to resize, relocate, or change the name of the button anytime after Step 6, hold down the CTRL key and click the button. Once the button is surrounded by the shaded border and handles, you can modify it. You can also choose the Assign to Object command from the Macro menu to assign a different macro to the button. When you finish editing the button, you can remove the shaded border and handles from the button by selecting any cell in the worksheet.

▶ Playing Back the Command Macro

Follow the steps below to enter the loan data: Item — 25' Cabin Cruiser; Price — $32,550.00; Down Payment — $8,250.00; Interest Rate — 10.25%; Years — 7.

TO PLAY BACK A COMMAND MACRO AND ENTER NEW LOAN DATA ▼

STEP 1 ▶

Click the New Loan button. When Excel displays the Input dialog box with the prompt message Item:, type `25' Cabin Cruiser` (Figure 5-37).

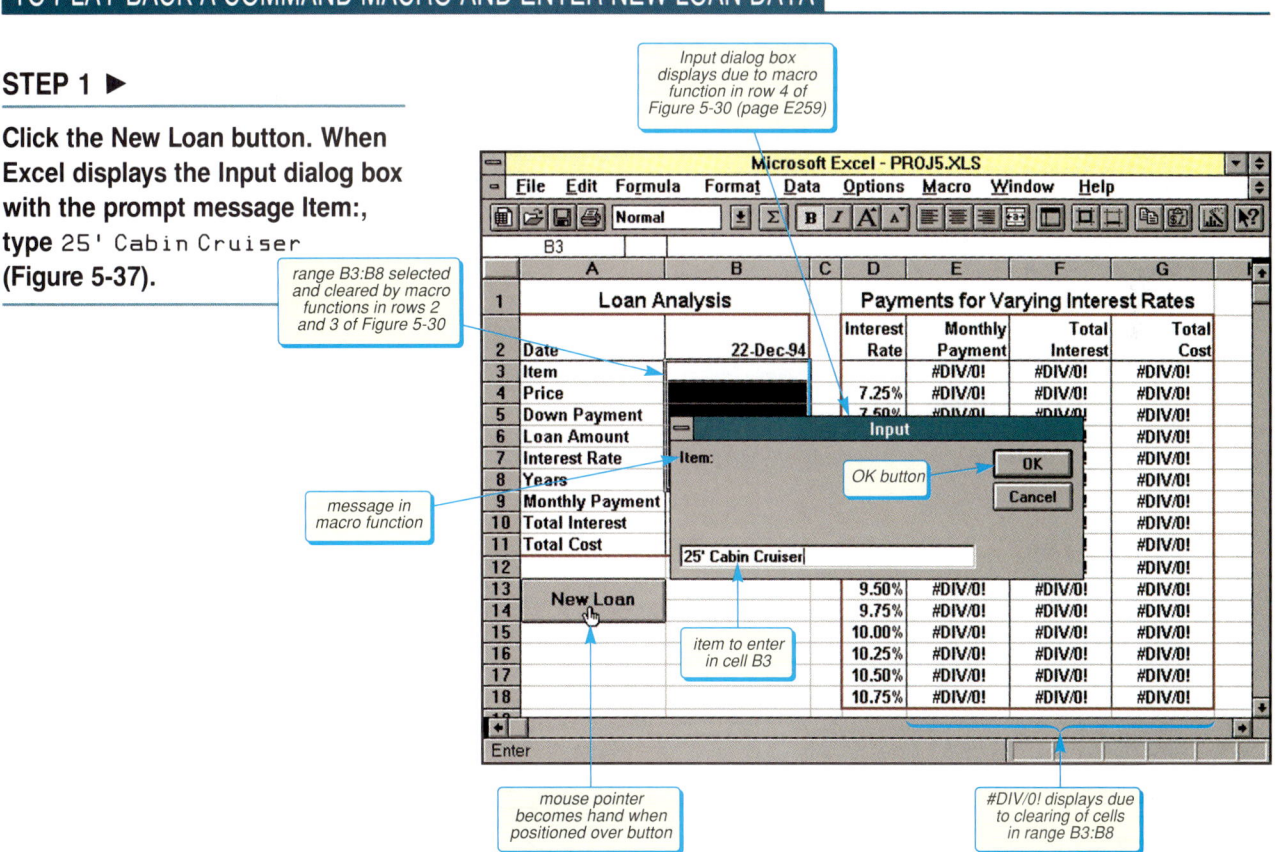

FIGURE 5-37

E264 PROJECT 5 ANALYZING WORKSHEET DATA

STEP 2 ▶

Choose the OK button in the Input dialog box. When Excel displays the Input dialog box with the prompt message Price of Item:, type `32,550` (Figure 5-38).

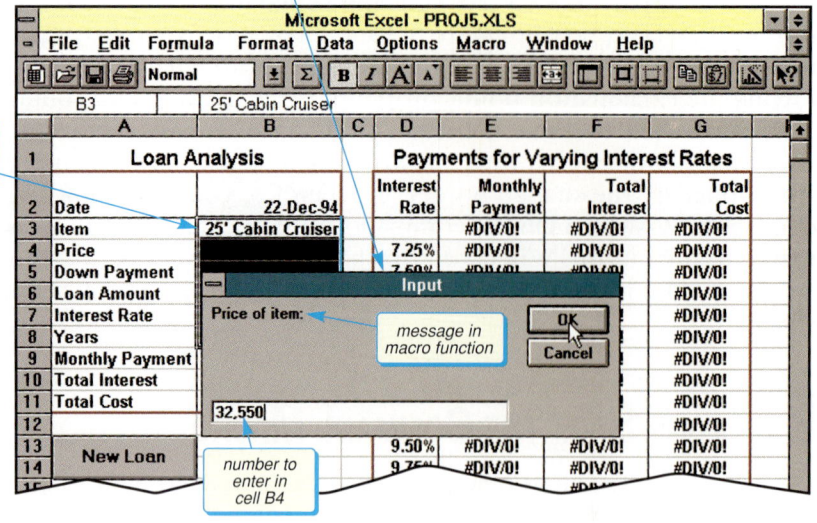

FIGURE 5-38

STEP 3 ▶

Choose the OK button in the Input dialog box. When Excel displays the Input dialog box with the prompt message Down payment:, type `8,250` (Figure 5-39).

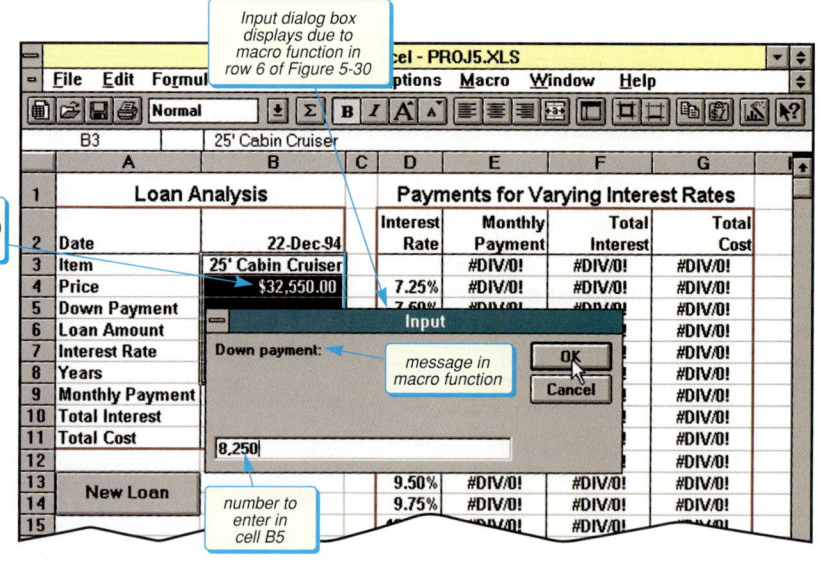

FIGURE 5-39

STEP 4 ▶

Choose the OK button from the Input dialog box. When Excel displays the Input dialog box with the prompt message Interest rate in %:, type `10.25%` (Figure 5-40).

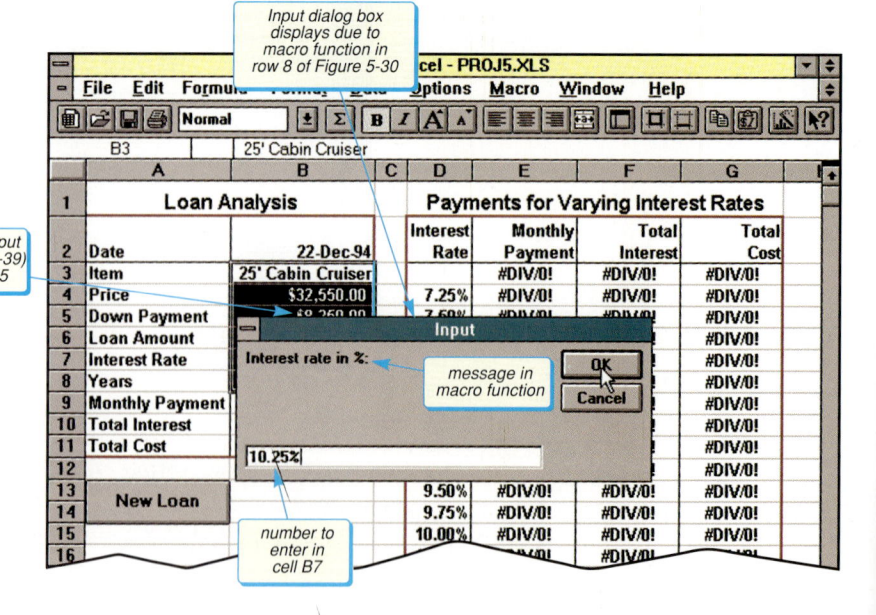

FIGURE 5-40

STEP 5 ▶

Choose the OK button in the Input dialog box. When Excel displays the Input dialog box with the prompt message Time in years:, type 7 (Figure 5-41).

Input dialog box displays due to macro function in row 9 of Figure 5-30 (page E259)

message in macro function

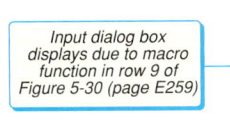

number to enter in cell B8

FIGURE 5-41

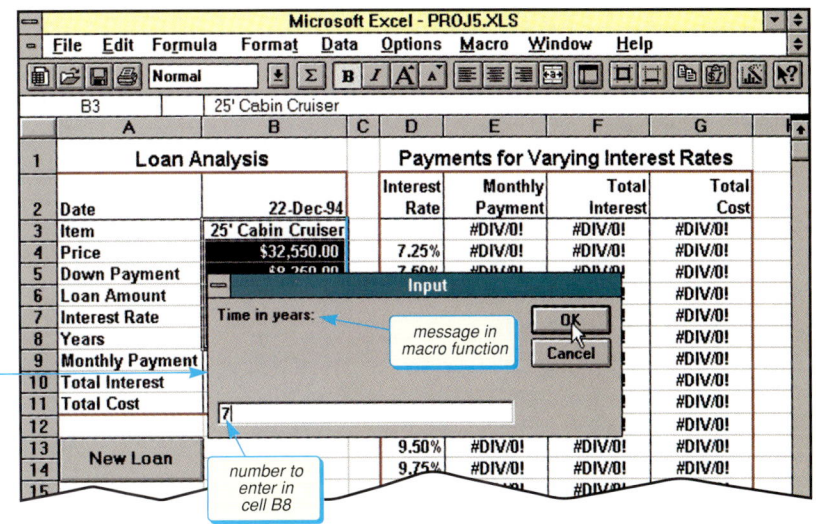

STEP 6 ▶

Choose the OK button from the Input dialog box.

Excel recalculates the loan information for the new loan data (Figure 5-42).

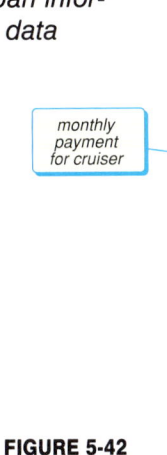

monthly payment for cruiser

monthly payment is $12.50 less if interest rate is 9.25%

FIGURE 5-42

Figure 5-42 shows that the monthly payment is $406.55 (cell B9), the total interest is $9,850.59 (cell B10), and the total cost is $42,400.59 (cell B11) for the 25' Cabin Cruiser. Furthermore, Excel automatically recalculates new results in the data table for the new loan data.

▶ GOAL SEEKING TO DETERMINE THE DOWN PAYMENT FOR A SPECIFIC MONTHLY PAYMENT

If you know the result you want a formula to produce, you can use goal seeking to determine the value of a cell on which the formula depends. The example on the next page uses the Goal Seek command to determine the down payment if the monthly payment for the 25' Cabin Cruiser is exactly $300.00.

TO DETERMINE THE DOWN PAYMENT FOR A SPECIFIC MONTHLY PAYMENT

STEP 1 ▶

Select cell B9, the cell with the monthly payment function. From the Formula menu, choose the Goal Seek command. When the Goal Seek dialog box displays, enter 300 in the To value box. Select the By changing cell box. In the worksheet, select cell B5.

The Goal Seek dialog box displays as shown in Figure 5-43. Notice in the dialog box that the first entry indicates the cell to seek a goal on (cell B9), the second box indicates the specific value you are seeking ($300.00), and the third box indicates the cell to vary (cell B5).

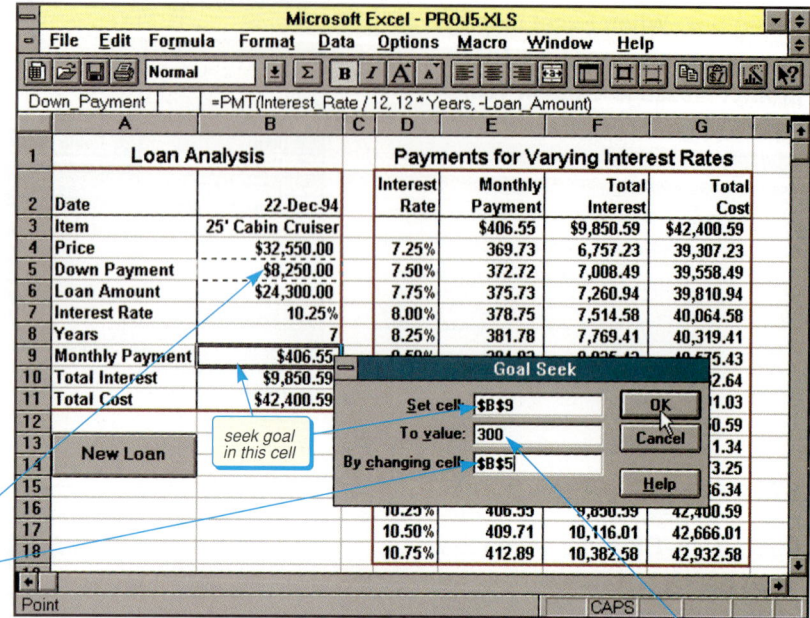

FIGURE 5-43

STEP 2 ▶

Choose the OK button from the Goal Seek dialog box. Next, choose OK from the Goal Seek Status dialog box.

Excel changes the monthly payment in cell B9 to the goal of $300.00 and sets the down payment in cell B5 to $14,618.83 (Figure 5-44).

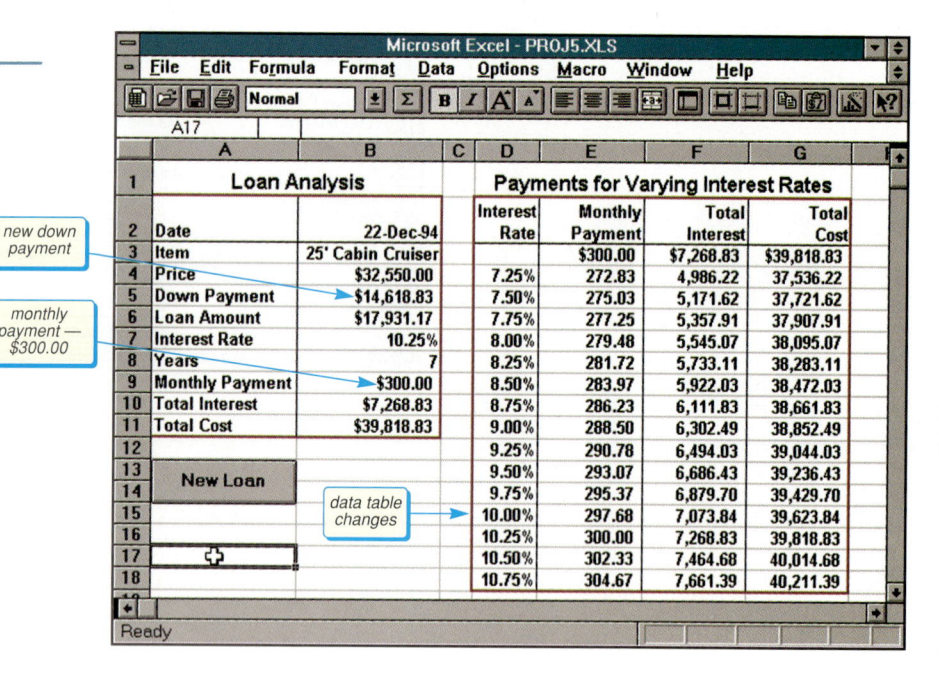

FIGURE 5-44

Thus, according to Figure 5-44, if the 25' Cabin Cruiser costs $32,550.00, the interest rate is 10.25%, the term is seven years, and you want to pay exactly $300.00 a month, then you must pay a down payment of $14,618.83.

USING SCENARIO MANAGER TO ANALYZE DATA **E267**

Notice in this goal seeking example that it is not required that the cell to vary be directly referenced in the formula or function. For example the monthly payment formula in cell B9 is = PMT(interest_rate / 12, 12 * years, loan_amount). There is no mention of the down payment in the PMT function. However, because the loan amount, which is referenced in the PMT function, is based on the down payment, Excel is able to goal seek on the monthly payment by varying the down payment.

▶ USING SCENARIO MANAGER TO ANALYZE DATA

An alternative to using a data table to analyze worksheet data is to use Excel's Scenario Manager. The Scenario Manager allows you to record and save different sets of input values called **scenarios**. For example, earlier in this project (Figure 5-24 on page E253) a monthly payment of $1,419.22 was determined for the following loan data: Item — House; Price — $178,500.00; Down payment — $36,500.00; Interest Rate — 8.75%; and Years — 15. Scenario Manager allows you to create a new worksheet with different scenarios of the loan. One scenario for the house loan might be: "What is the monthly payment, total interest, and total cost if the interest rate is the same (8.75%) but the number of years changes from 15 to 30?" Another scenario might be: "What is the monthly payment, total interest, and total cost if the interest rate is increased by 1% to 9.75% and the number of years remains at 15?"

The summary report that the Scenario Manager generates is actually an outlined worksheet (Figure 5-45) you can save, print, and manipulate like any other worksheet.

Before illustrating the Scenario Manager, click the New Loan button and enter the loan data for the house as described in Figure 5-24 on page E253.

The steps on the next page create the Scenario Summary Report worksheet with the three scenarios shown in Figure 5-45. The worksheet illustrates the monthly payment, total interest, and total cost for three scenarios. In Scenario 1, the interest rate is the same as the original loan data for the house (interest rate equals 8.75% and years equal 15). The second scenario sets the interest rate to 8.75% and the number of years to 30. The third scenario sets the interest rate to 9.75% and the number of years to 15.

	Scenario 1	Scenario 2	Scenario 3
Changing Cells:			
Interest_Rate	8.75%	8.75%	9.75%
Years	15	30	15
Result Cells:			
Monthly_Payment	$1,419.22	$1,117.11	$1,504.29
Total_Interest	$113,459.08	$260,161.25	$128,773.10
Total_Cost	$291,959.08	$438,661.25	$307,273.10

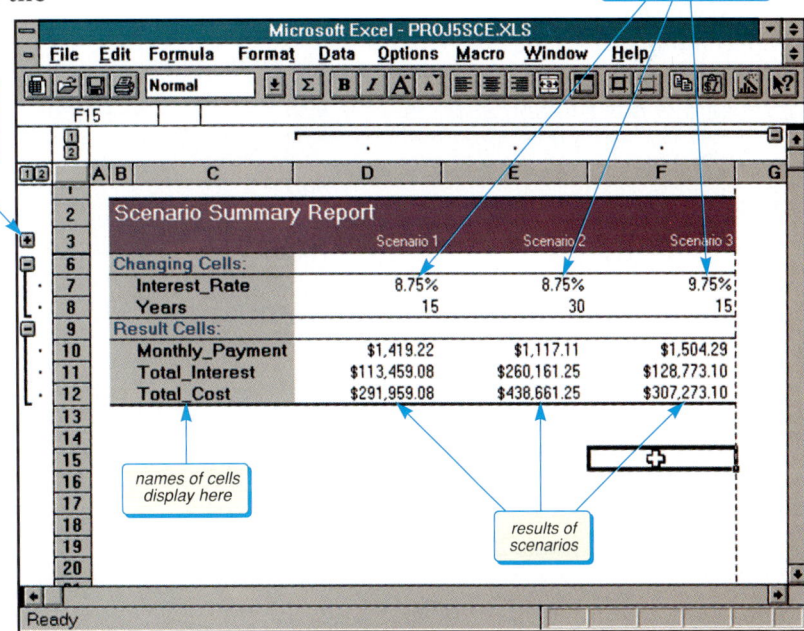

FIGURE 5-45

E268 PROJECT 5 ANALYZING WORKSHEET DATA

TO ANALYZE WORKSHEET DATA USING THE SCENARIO MANAGER ▼

STEP 1 ▶

Select the Formula menu and point to the Scenario Manager command.

The Formula menu displays (Figure 5-46).

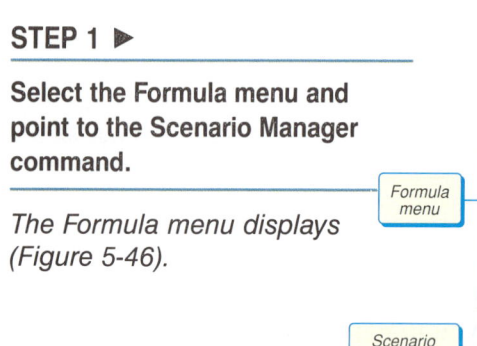

FIGURE 5-46

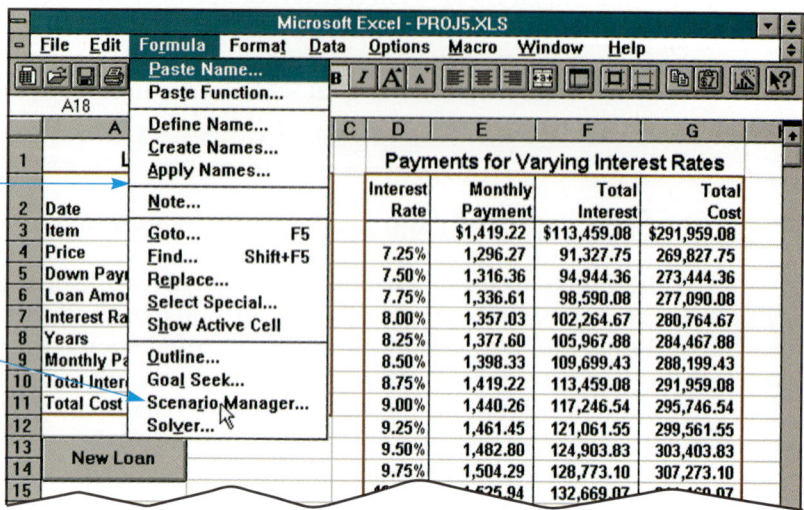

STEP 2 ▶

Choose the Scenario Manager command from the Formula menu. Use the mouse and drag across the range B7:B8 in the worksheet to select these cells in the Changing Cells box.

Excel displays a moving border around the cells in the worksheet to change (interest rate in cell B7 and years in cell B8) and assigns the range B7:B8 to the Changing Cells box in the Scenario Manager dialog box (Figure 5-47).

FIGURE 5-47

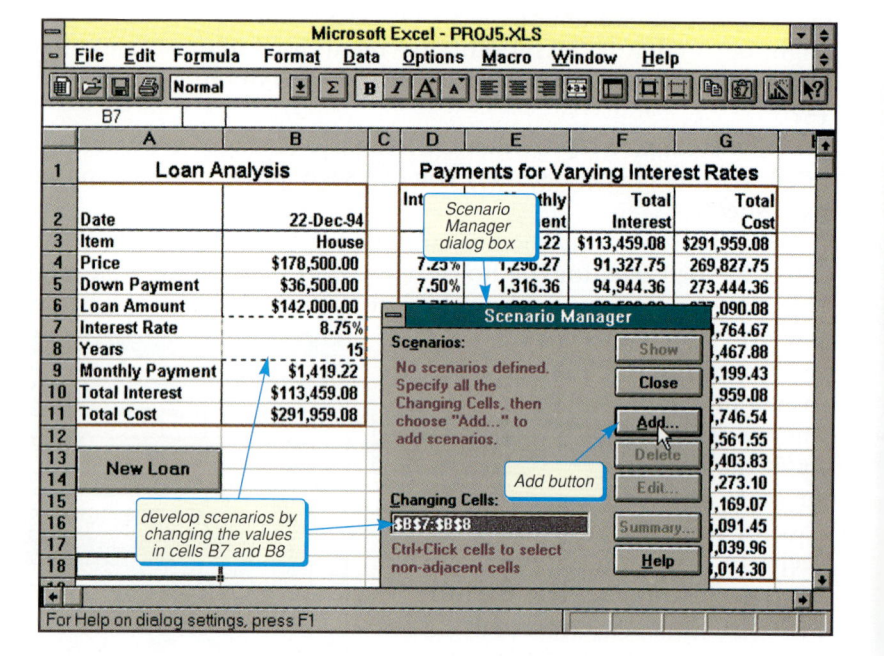

STEP 3 ▶

Choose the Add button (Add) from the Scenario Manager dialog box and then type the name `Scenario 1` in the Name box.

The Add Scenario dialog box displays with Scenario 1 as the name of the first scenario. The interest rate and years are automatically entered because of the selection of cells B7 and B8 in Step 2 (Figure 5-48).

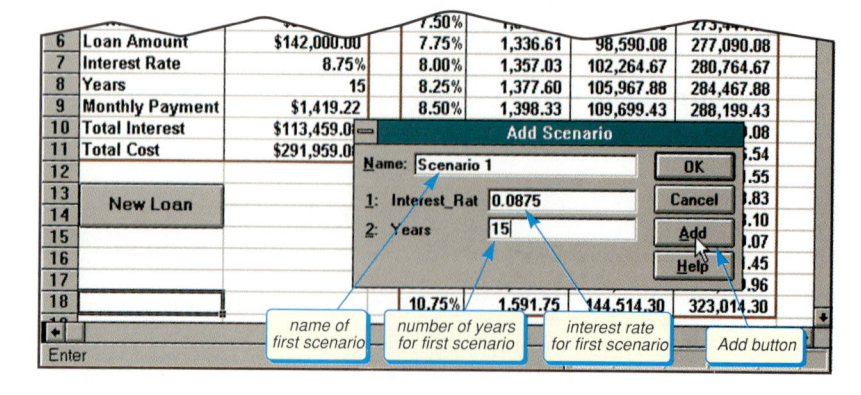

FIGURE 5-48

USING SCENARIO MANAGER TO ANALYZE DATA   **E269**

STEP 4 ▶

Choose the Add button from the Add Scenario dialog box and then type `Scenario 2` **in the Name box and** `30` **in the Years box.**

The Add Scenario dialog box displays with the second set of data (Figure 5-49).

FIGURE 5-49

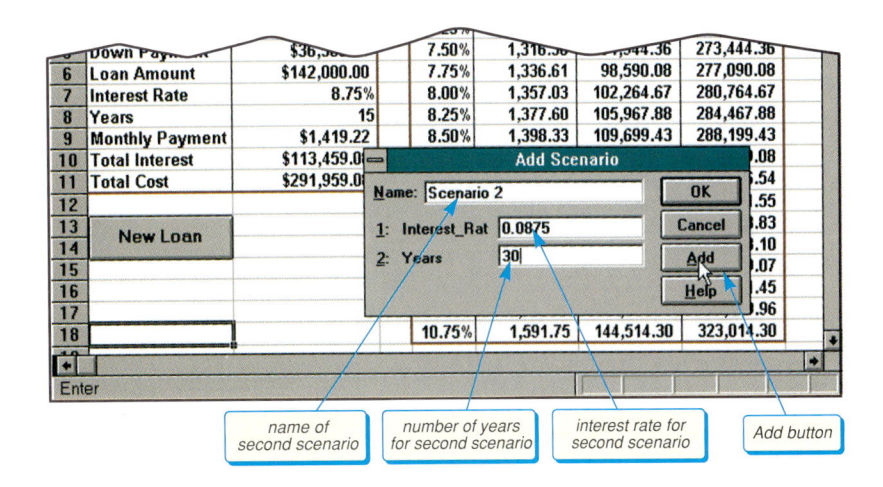

STEP 5 ▶

Choose the Add button from the Add Scenario dialog box. When the Add Scenario reappears, type `Scenario 3` **in the Name box,** `9.75%` **in the Interest_Rat box, and** `15` **in the Years box.**

The Add Scenario dialog box displays with the third set of data (Figure 5-50).

FIGURE 5-50

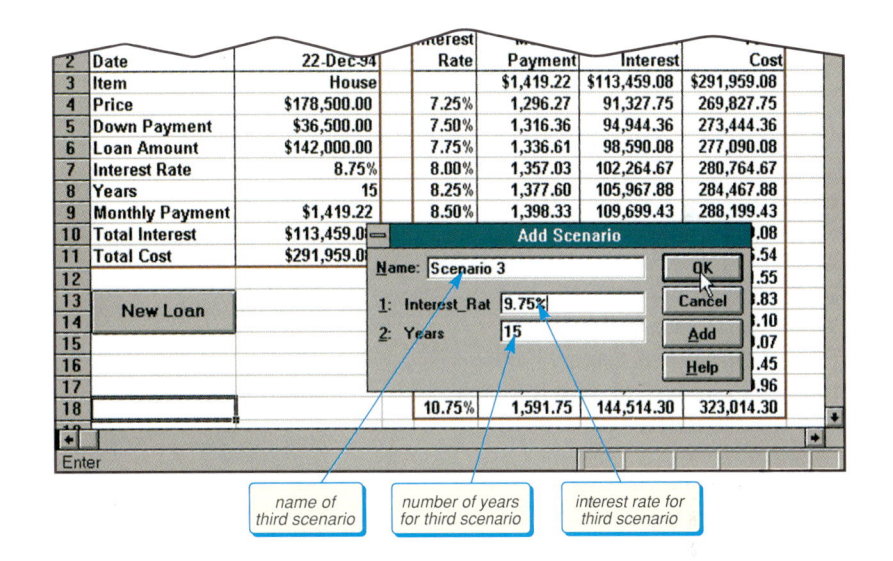

STEP 6 ▶

Because this is the last of the three scenarios, choose the OK button from the Add Scenario dialog box rather than the Add button.

Excel displays the Scenario Manager dialog box with the three named scenarios in the Scenarios box (Figure 5-51).

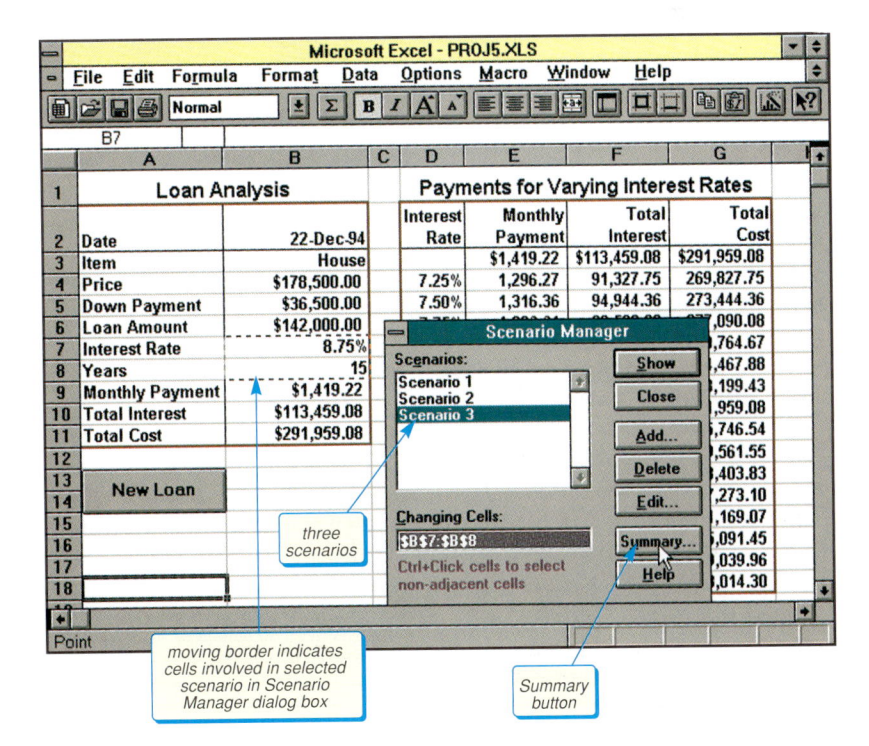

FIGURE 5-51

STEP 7 ▶

Choose the Summary button from the Scenario Manager dialog box. Use the mouse and drag across the range B9:B11 in the worksheet to select these cells in the Result Cells box.

Excel displays the Scenario Summary dialog box with the range B9:B11 selected in the Result Cells box (Figure 5-52).

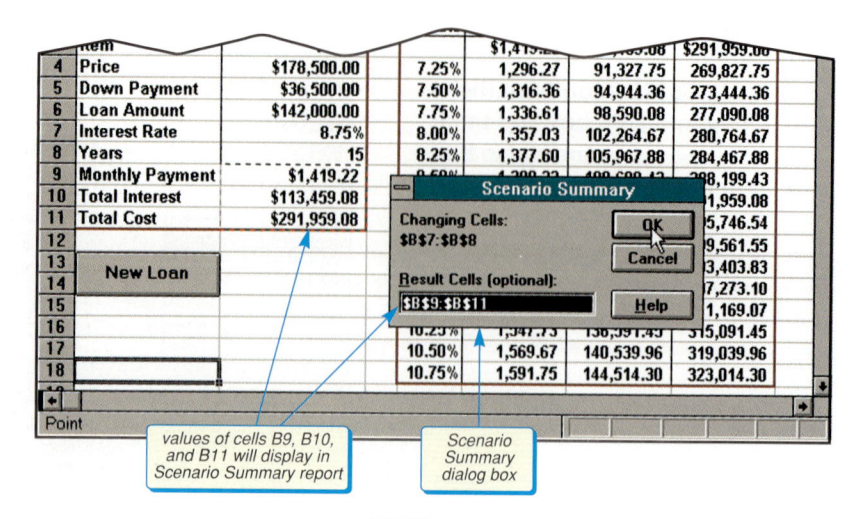

FIGURE 5-52

STEP 8 ▶

Choose the OK button from the Scenario Summary dialog box. When the Scenario Summary Report worksheet displays, click the Save File tool to save it to disk. Use the file name PROJ5SCE.

Excel displays the Scenario Summary Report worksheet with the name PROJ5SCE.XLS in the title bar (Figure 5-53).

STEP 9

When you have finished viewing the Scenario Summary Report worksheet, choose PROJ5.XLS from the Window menu to return to the original worksheet.

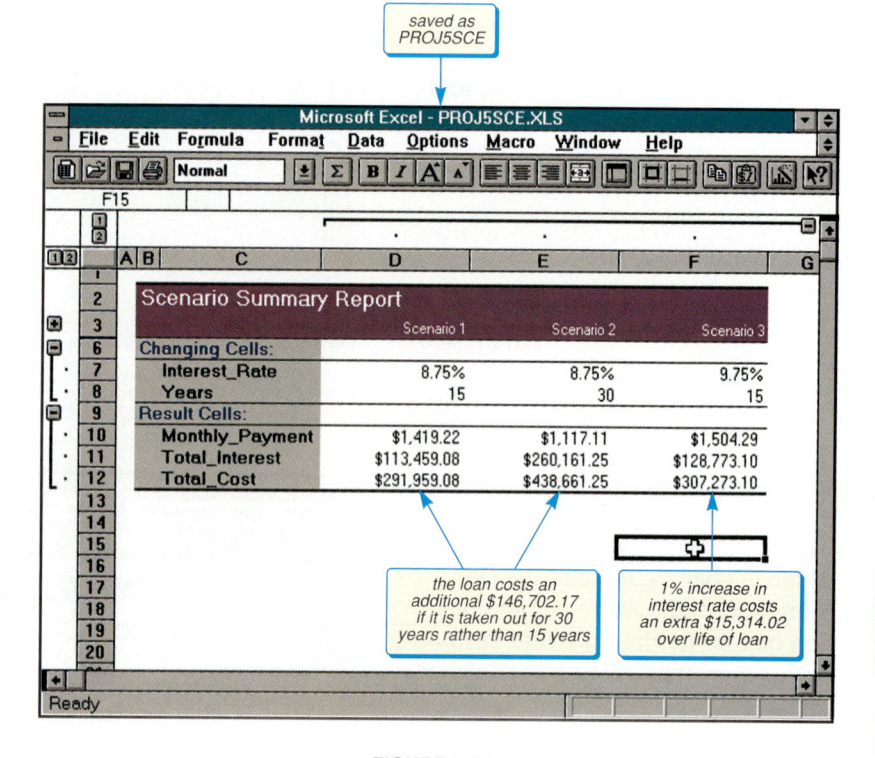

FIGURE 5-53

The Scenario Summary Report worksheet in Figure 5-53 shows the results of the three scenarios in rows 9 through 12. Compare Scenario 2 to Scenario 1. In Scenario 2 the interest rate is the same as in Scenario 1 but the length of time is 30 years rather than 15 years. Because the loan is for twice the length of time, the monthly payment is $302.11 less per month, but the total cost of the loan increases by $146,702.17 to $438,661.25. In Scenario 3, the number of years is the same as Scenario 1, but the interest rate is 1% greater. The 1% change increases the monthly payment by $85.07 per month and the total cost of the house to $307,273.10 or $15,314.02 more than the loan data in Scenario 1.

PROTECTING THE WORKSHEET

When you build a worksheet that will be used by people who know little or nothing about computers and spreadsheets, it is important that you protect the cells in the worksheet that you don't want changed, such as cells that contain text and formulas. In the loan analysis worksheet (Figure 5-54), there are only five cells that the user should be allowed to change: the item in cell B3, the price in cell B4, the down payment in cell B5, the interest rate in cell B7, and the years in cell B8. Also, because of the way the command macro assigned to the New Loan button works, cell B6 should be unprotected. The remaining cells in the worksheet should be protected so that they can't be changed by the user.

When you create a new worksheet, all the cells are unprotected. **Unprotected cells**, or **unlocked cells**, are cells whose values you can change at any time versus **protected cells**, or **locked cells**, that you cannot change. If a cell is protected and the user attempts to change its value, Excel displays a dialog box with a message indicating the cells are protected.

You should protect cells only after the worksheet has been fully tested and displays the correct results. Protecting a worksheet is a two-step process. First, select the cells you want to leave unprotected and change their cell protection settings to unprotected. Second, protect the entire worksheet. At first glance, these steps may appear to be backwards. However, once you protect the entire worksheet you cannot change anything including the protection of individual cells. Thus, you first deal with the cells you want to leave unprotected and then protect the entire worksheet.

The following steps show how to protect the loan analysis worksheet.

TO PROTECT A WORKSHEET

STEP 1 ▶

Select the range B3:B8, the range to unprotect. Select the Format menu and point to the Cell Protection command.

Excel displays the Format menu (Figure 5-54).

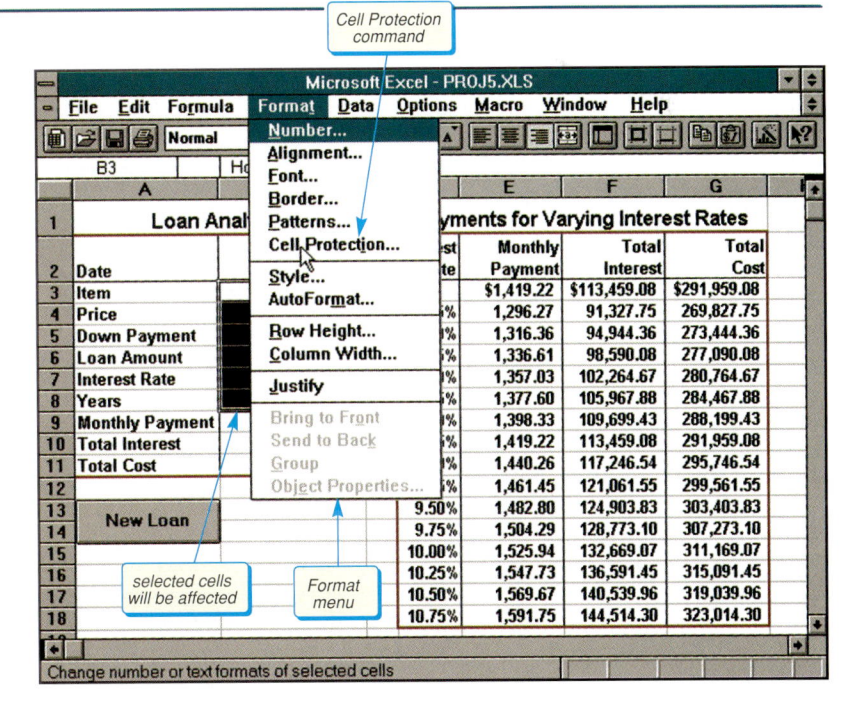

FIGURE 5-54

E272   PROJECT 5   ANALYZING WORKSHEET DATA

STEP 2 ▶

Choose the Cell Protection command from the Format menu. Click the Locked box to remove the x.

The Cell Protection dialog box displays with the x removed from the Locked box (Figure 5-55).

STEP 3

Choose the OK button from the Cell Protection dialog box.

FIGURE 5-55

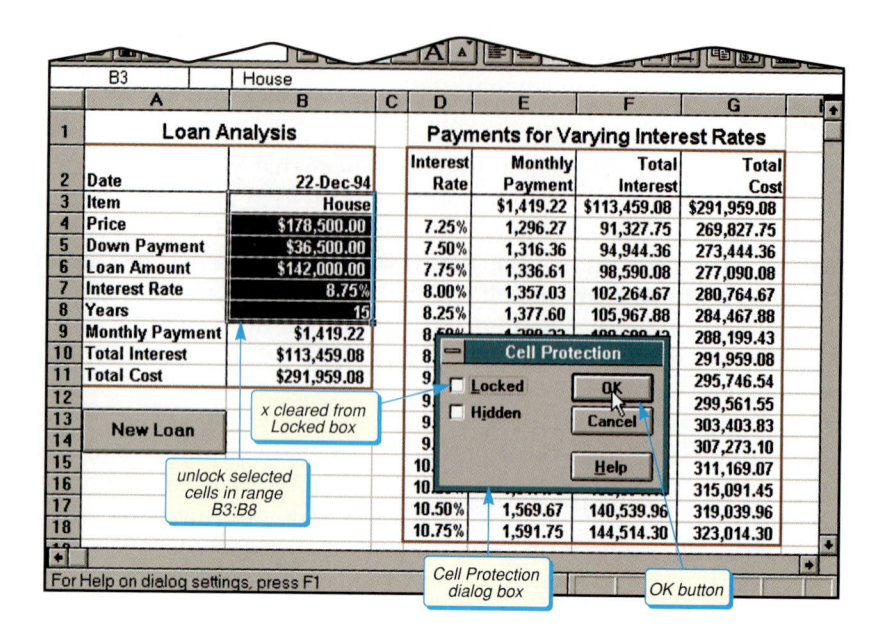

STEP 4 ▶

Select the Options menu and point to the Protect Document command.

Excel displays the Options menu (Figure 5-56).

FIGURE 5-56

STEP 5 ▶

Choose the Protect Document command from the Options menu.

Excel displays the Protect Document dialog box (Figure 5-57).

STEP 6

Choose the OK button from the Protect Document dialog box. Click the Save File tool on the Standard toolbar to save the protected worksheet.

All the cells in the worksheet are protected, except for the range B3:B8. The range B3:B8 includes the cells in which you enter new loan data.

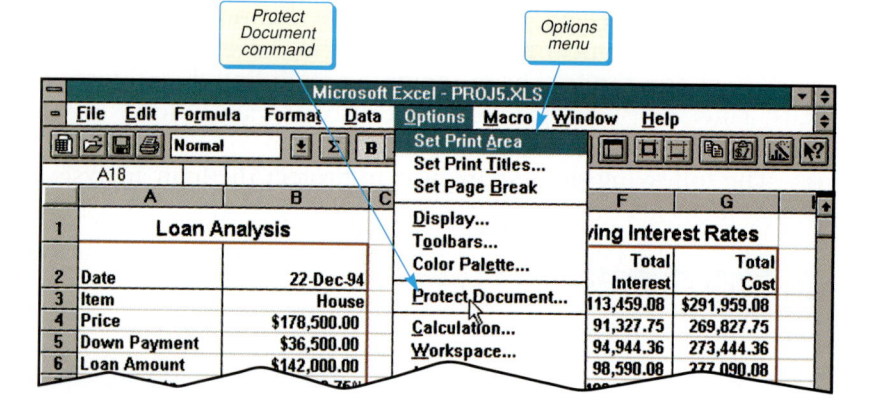

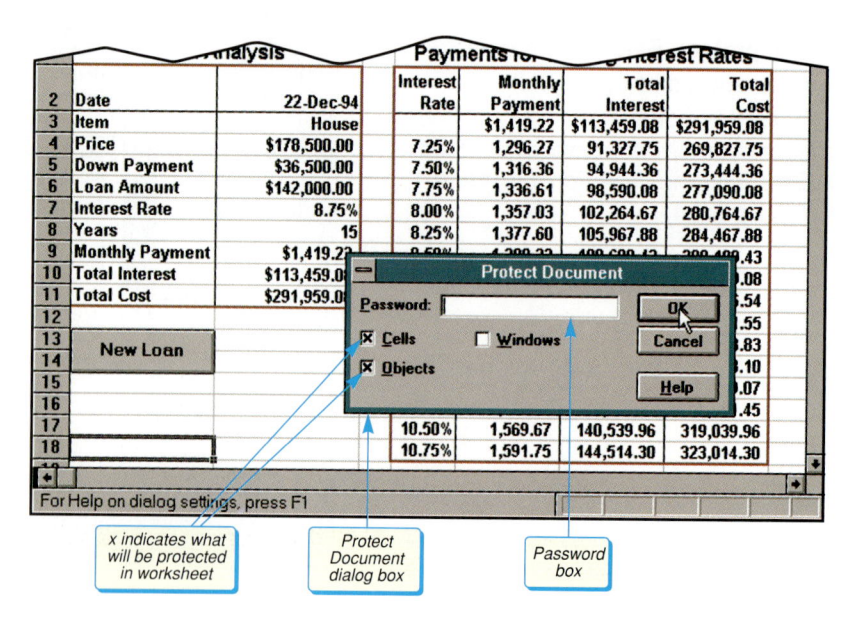

FIGURE 5-57

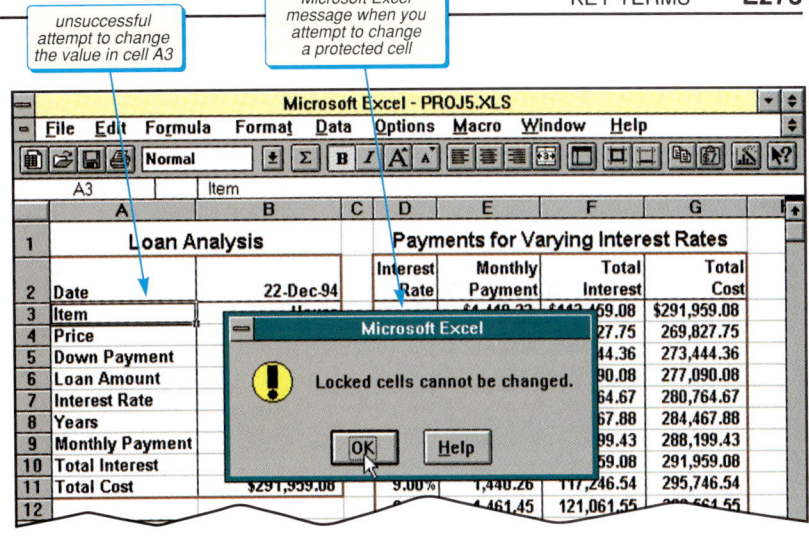

Notice in the Protect Document dialog box in Figure 5-57 that you can add a password. You add a password when you want to keep others from changing the worksheet from protected to unprotected.

With the worksheet protected, you can still play back the command macro PROJ5INP by clicking the New Loan button at any time because the cells referenced (B3:B8) by the command macro are unprotected. However, if you try to change any protected cell, Excel displays a dialog box with a diagnostic message. For example, try to change the row title Item in cell A3. When you type the first character with cell A3 selected, Excel responds by displaying the message shown in Figure 5-58. If you want to change any cells in the worksheet such as titles or formulas, unprotect the document by choosing the Unprotect Document command from the Options menu.

FIGURE 5-58

▶ Project Summary

In Project 5 you learned how to apply the PMT function to determine the monthly payment of a loan. You also learned how to analyze data by creating a data table and a Scenario Summary Report worksheet. This project explained that macros are used to automate worksheet tasks. You learned how to build a command macro that accepts loan data. Once the command macro was built, it was assigned to a button in the worksheet. The button was used to play back the command macro. Finally, you learned how to protect a document so a user can change only the contents of cells that you left unprotected.

▶ Key Terms

Assign to Object command (*E260*)
Bottom Border tool (*E239*)
button (*E260*)
Button tool (*E260*)
Cell Protection command (*E271*)
CLEAR macro function (*E258*)
command macro (*E235*)
Create Names command (*E240*)
data table (*E235*)
date stamp (*E237*)
Define Name command (*E242*)
desk checking (*E255*)
FORMULA macro function (*E258*)
FV function (*E244*)

input cell (*E247*)
Input dialog box (*E263*)
INPUT macro function (*E255*)
locked cells (*E271*)
macro function (*E235*)
Macro menu (*E257*)
macro sheet (*E255*)
naming a cell (*E240*)
naming a macro command (*E256*)
NOW function (*E237*)
one-input data table (*E246*)
outline range (*E259*)
play back (*E254*)
PMT function (*E242, E244*)

Protect Document command (*E272*)
protected cells (*E271*)
PV function (*E244*)
RETURN macro function (*E255*)
Scenario (*E267*)
Scenario Manager command (*E267*)
Scenario Summary Report worksheet (*E270*)
SELECT macro function (*E258*)
Table command (*E250*)
unlocked cells (*E271*)
unprotected cells (*E271*)

QUICK REFERENCE

In Microsoft Excel you can accomplish a task in a number of ways. The following table provides a quick reference to each task presented in this project with its available options. The commands listed in the Menu column can be executed using either the keyboard or mouse.

Task	Mouse	Menu	Keyboard Shortcuts
Create Button	Click Button tool on Utility toolbar		
Create Data Table		From Data menu, choose Table	
Create Scenario Summary Report Worksheet		From Formula menu, choose Scenario Manager	
Draw Bottom Border	Click Bottom Border tool on Standard toolbar	From Format menu, choose Border	
Edit Button	CTRL + click button		
Financial Functions		From Formula menu, choose Paste Function	Press SHIFT + F3
Name Cells		From Formula menu, choose Create Names	Press CTRL + SHIFT + F3
Open New Macro Sheet	Click New Macro Sheet tool on Macro toolbar	From File menu, choose New	Press ALT + CTRL + F1
Outline a Range	Click Outline Border tool on Standard toolbar	From Format menu, choose Border	Press CTRL + SHIFT + &
Protect Worksheet		From Options menu, choose Protect Document	
Unprotect Cells		From Format menu, choose Cell Protection	
Unprotect Worksheet		From Options menu, choose Unprotect Document	

STUDENT ASSIGNMENTS

STUDENT ASSIGNMENT 1
True/False

Instructions: Circle T if the statement is true or F if the statement is false.

T F 1. A macro function instructs Excel to carry out an operation, such as select a cell or clear the selection.

T F 2. The system date is always the same as today's date.

T F 3. The NOW function returns a number that is equal to the number of days since December 31, 1899. Assume the system date equals today's date.

T F 4. If cell B4 is named Balance and cell B5 is named Payment, then the formula = B4 – B5 can be written as = Balance – Payment.

T F 5. A data table is a cell that answers what-if questions.

T F 6. Excel allows for three different types of data tables.

T F 7. Use the Open command from the File menu to create a new macro sheet.

T F 8. A command macro is made up of a series of macro functions.

T F   9. The macro function CLEAR is used to clear the selected cell or range of cells.
T F 10. You end a command macro with the SELECT macro function.
T F 11. In a command macro to specify a range in the active worksheet, begin the cell reference or range with an ampersand (&).
T F 12. By default, a worksheet displays values and a macro sheet displays formulas.
T F 13. Any cell in a macro sheet that contains an entry that does not begin with an equal sign is a comment.
T F 14. The Button tool is on the Standard toolbar.
T F 15. To edit a button, hold down the CTRL key and click the button.
T F 16. When executed, the macro function INPUT causes a dialog box to display.
T F 17. The Scenario Manager is used to organize answers to what-if questions in a new worksheet.
T F 18. When you open a new worksheet it is unprotected.
T F 19. Select the cells to unprotect after you protect the entire worksheet.
T F 20. If you attempt to change the value of a protected cell, Excel immediately returns control to Windows.

STUDENT ASSIGNMENT 2
Multiple Choice

Instructions: Circle the correct response.

1. When the NOW function is assigned to a cell, the system date displays in the format _____.
   a. dd-mmm-yy
   b. m/d/yy h:mm
   c. mmm dd, yy
   d. yy-mm-dd
2. To name a cell, use the _____ command on the Formula menu.
   a. Create Names
   b. Paste Function
   c. Apply Names
   d. Paste Name
3. When a name of a cell is made up of two or more words, replace the spaces between the words with _____ when you use the name in a formula.
   a. minus signs (–)
   b. number signs (#)
   c. circumflexes (^)
   d. underscores (_)
4. Use the _____ function to determine a monthly payment on a loan.
   a. FV
   b. PMT
   c. PV
   d. NOW
5. You can view the list of Excel functions by choosing the _____ command from the Formula menu.
   a. Replace
   b. Solver
   c. Paste Function
   d. Find
6. Data tables are built _____.
   a. in an unused area of the worksheet
   b. on a macro sheet
   c. on an empty worksheet
   d. on a chart document

(continued)

STUDENT ASSIGNMENT 2 (continued)

7. In a one-cell data table, the input cell _____.
   a. must be referenced in the formula(s) at the top of the data table
   b. is the upper left corner cell of the worksheet
   c. is a range of cells
   d. must be defined on the macro sheet
8. In a command macro, use the _____ macro function to assign a value to a cell.
   a. INPUT
   b. RETURN
   c. SELECT
   d. FORMULA
9. In a command macro, to reference a cell on the worksheet rather than on the macro sheet, precede the cell reference with a(n) _____.
   a. number sign (#)
   b. exclamation point (!)
   c. vertical bar (|)
   d. slash (/)
10. After building a macro sheet, return to the worksheet window by selecting the _____ menu.
    a. Options
    b. File
    c. Window
    d. Macro

STUDENT ASSIGNMENT 3
Understanding Functions, Data Analysis, and Worksheet Protection

Instructions: Fill in the correct answers.

1. Write a function to determine the monthly payment (PMT function) on a loan of $75,000.00, over a period of 20 years, at an annual interest rate of 8.4%. Make sure the function returns the monthly payment as a positive number.

   Function: _____

2. Write a function to display the system date and system time.

   Function: _____

3. Write a function to determine the future value (FV function) of a $100.00 a month investment for 10 years if the interest rate is fixed at 6% and compounded monthly.

   Function: _____

4. Write a function to determine the present value (PV function) or how much it would cost for an annuity that pays $500.00 a month for 20 years and pays 8% compounded monthly. Display the cost of the annuity as a positive number by placing a minus sign before the monthly payment.

   Function: _____

5. Explain the purpose of a data table. What is the difference between a one-input data table and a two-input data table?

_____

_____

_____

6. Describe what Scenario Manager is used for.

_____

_____

_____

7. Explain the difference between a protected cell and an unprotected cell. How do you change the contents of a cell that is protected?

_____

_____

_____

STUDENT ASSIGNMENT 4
Understanding Excel Menus and Commands

Instructions: Identify the menu and command that displays the dialog box that allows you to make the change indicated.

		MENU	COMMAND
1.	Name cells	_____	_____
2.	Create a data table	_____	_____
3.	Create a macro sheet	_____	_____
4.	Change windows	_____	_____
5.	Assign a command macro to a button	_____	_____
6.	Format a date	_____	_____
7.	Change the margins	_____	_____
8.	Name a command macro	_____	_____
9.	Seek a goal for a cell assigned a formula	_____	_____
10.	Create a Scenario Summary Report worksheet	_____	_____
11.	Unprotect cells	_____	_____
12.	Protect cells	_____	_____

STUDENT ASSIGNMENT 5
Understanding Macro Functions

Instructions: Assume a macro sheet is open. In the space provided, write the macro function that completes the specified task.

1. Select the range A1:D23 on the worksheet: _____
2. Clear all from the selected range: _____
3. Assign the formula = B6 – B7 to cell A10 in the worksheet: _____
4. Accept a value from the user and assign it to cell G25 in the worksheet: _____
5. Return control to the user: _____
6. Select the range G10:G15 on the macro sheet: _____

STUDENT ASSIGNMENT 6
Understanding Worksheet Entries

Instructions: Indicate how you would make the suggested corrections.

Part 1: In the worksheet in Figure SA5-6a the monthly payment, total interest, total cost, and data table display in red within parentheses. The red color and parentheses indicate negative numbers. What would you do to display the results as positive numbers?

Change the formula in cell: _____ to _____

FIGURE SA5-6a

Part 2: In the worksheet in Figure SA5-6b, some or all of the loan data in the range B3:B8 was entered incorrectly. The loan data should be as follows: Item — House; Price — $178,500.00; Down Payment — $36,500.00; Interest Rate — 10.75%; and, Years — 15. Explain the error and method of correction.

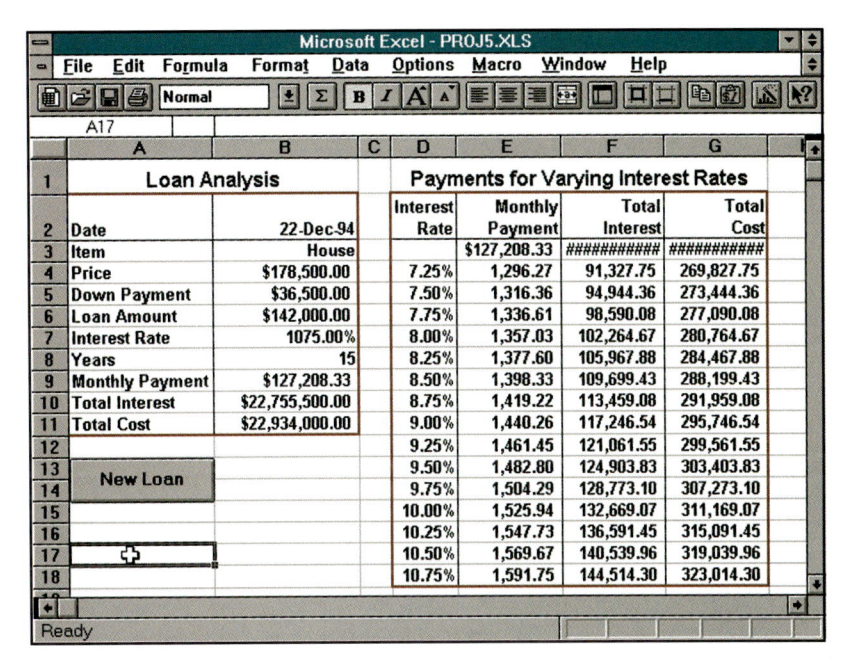

FIGURE SA5-6b

Error: _____

Method of Correction: _____

COMPUTER LABORATORY EXERCISES

COMPUTER LABORATORY EXERCISE 1
Using the Help Menu to Learn about Data Tables, Functions, and Command Macros

Instructions: Start Excel and perform the following tasks.

1. Choose the Contents command from the Help menu on the menu bar. Select Worksheets. Scroll down to the bottom of the list to the group titled Analyzing and Calculating a Worksheet. Select Filling in a one-input data table. Read and print the information. Click the Back button in the Help window. Select Filling in a two-input data table. Read and print the information. Click the Back button twice in the Help window. Scroll down and select Worksheet Functions from the Contents list. Select Financial Functions. Read and print the information. Close the Help window.
2. Select the Help menu on the menu bar. Choose Learning Microsoft Excel from the Help menu. Select and step through the following lessons: What is a Macro? and Using a Macro.

COMPUTER LABORATORY EXERCISE 2
Creating a One-Input Data Table

Instructions: Start Excel. Open the worksheet CLE5-2 from the subdirectory Excel on the Student Diskette that accompanies this book. As shown in Figure CLE5-2a, the worksheet computes the proposed annual salary (cell B4) from the proposed percent salary increase (cell B2) and the current annual salary (cell B3).

Perform the following tasks to create the one-input data table shown in Figure CLE5-2b.

1. Use the Create Names command from the Formula menu to assign the name in cell A4 to cell B4.
2. Enter and format the data table title and column titles in the range A6:B7 as shown in Figure CLE5-2b. Use the fill handle to create the series of numbers in the range A9:A15 (Figure CLE5-2b).
3. Assign cell B8 the formula =proposed_salary.
4. Create a data table in the range A8:B15. Use cell B2 as the input cell.
5. Draw borders around the data table as shown in Figure
6. Save the worksheet using the file name CLE5-2A. Print the worksheet without cell gridlines.
7. Use the goal seeking capabilities of Excel to determine the proposed percent increase in cell B2 if the proposed salary in cell B4 is set to $25,500,000. Your final result should be 0.59% in cell B2. Print the worksheet.

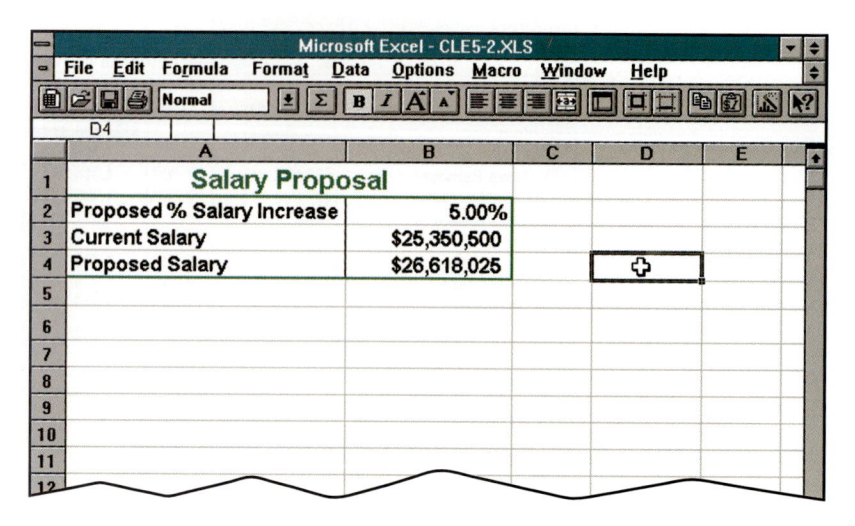

FIGURE CLE5-2a

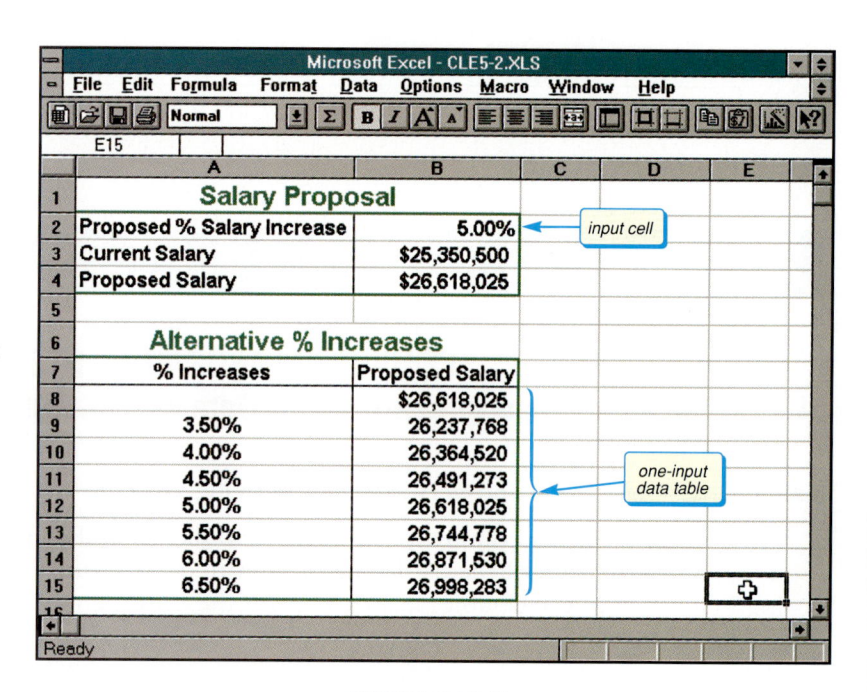

FIGURE CLE5-2b

COMPUTER LABORATORY EXERCISE 3
Assigning a Command Macro to a Button

Instructions: Start Excel and perform the following tasks:

1. Open the worksheet CLE5-3 from the subdirectory Excel on the Student Diskette that accompanies this book. Open the macro sheet CLE53INP from the same subdirectory.
2. Print the macro sheet without cell gridlines. Use the Window menu to display the CLE5-3 window. Display the Utility toolbar and add the button shown in Figure CLE5-3a. The command macro (Figure CLE5-3b) was assigned the name CLE53INP. Use the name CLE53INP to assign the command macro to the button.
3. Unprotect cell D9 and then protect the worksheet.
4. Click the Acceptable Total Parts button and enter 100,000. Print the worksheet without cell gridlines. Use the button to enter 79,000. Print the worksheet.
5. Save the worksheet as CLE5-3A.

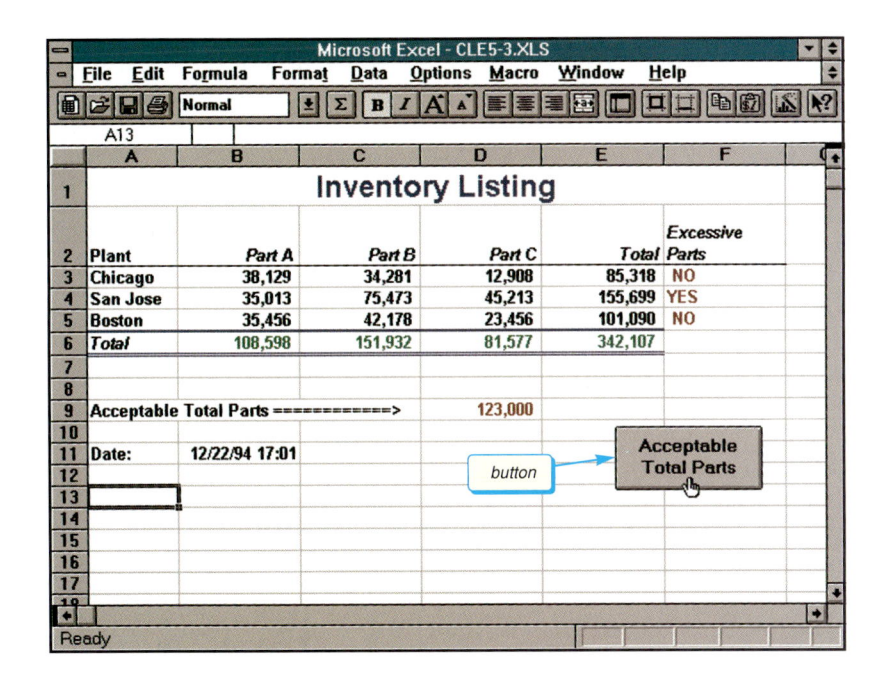

FIGURE CLE5-3a

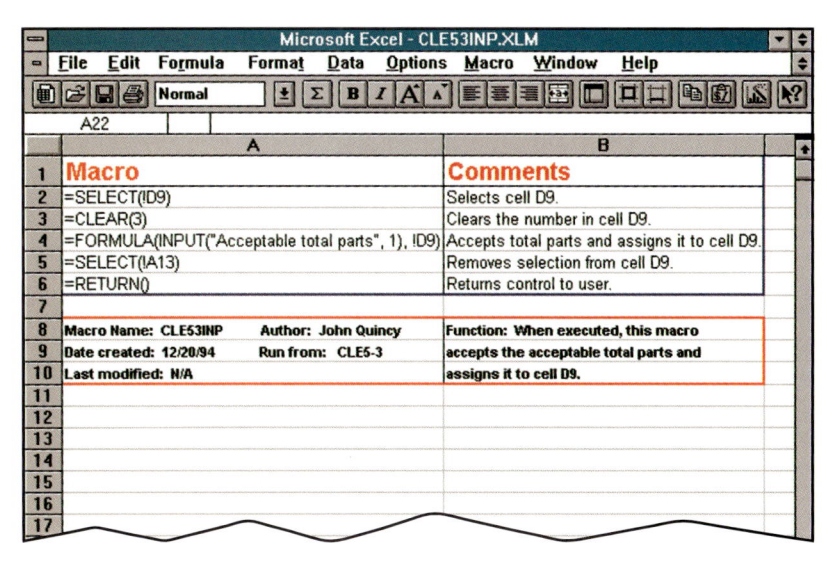

FIGURE CLE5-3b

COMPUTER LABORATORY ASSIGNMENTS

COMPUTER LABORATORY ASSIGNMENT 1
Determining the Monthly Mortgage Payment

Purpose: To become familiar with using the PMT function, names, one-input data tables, command macros, and buttons.

Problem: You are a part-time consultant for the Crown Loan Company. You have been asked to build a worksheet (Figure CLA5-1a) that determines the monthly mortgage payment and includes a one-input data table that shows the monthly payment, total interest, and total cost for a mortgage for varying years. The worksheet will be used by loan officers who know little about computers and spreadsheets. Thus, create a command macro (Figure CLA5-1b) that will guide the user through entering the mortgage data. Assign the command macro to a button.

Instructions: Perform the following tasks:

1. Change the font of the entire worksheet to TT Arial bold.
2. Enter the Mortgage Payment section of the worksheet. Assign cell B2 the NOW function so that it displays the system date and time. (It is not necessary that you display the exact date shown in Figure CLA5-1a.) Create names for the range B3:B6. Assign cell B6 the following formula:

   =PMT(interest_rate / 12, 12*years, –principal)

3. Enter the Payments for the Varying Years section of the worksheet. Assign cell E3 the formula, =monthly_payment, cell G3 the formula, =12*years*monthly_payment, and cell F3 the formula, =G3 – principal. Use the fill handle to create the series in the range D4:D15. Create a data table in the range D3:G15 using the Table command on the Data menu. Use cell B5 as the input cell.
4. Change the foreground pattern of the two sections (A1:B6 and D1:G15) to light gray. Next, display the Drawing toolbar, select the nonadjacent ranges, A1:B6 and D1:G15, and click the Drop Shadow tool. Hide the Drawing toolbar.
5. Add your name, course, computer laboratory assignment number (CLA5-1), date, and instructor name in column A beginning in cell A14. Save the worksheet using the file name CLA5-1. Print the worksheet without cell gridlines with the mortgage data in Figure CLA5-1a.
6. Use the New command on the File menu to create the command macro in Figure CLA5-1b. Select cell A1 and use the Define Name command to name the command macro CLA51INP. Save the macro sheet using the file name CLA51INP.
7. Use the Window menu to display the worksheet CLA5-1. Display the Utility toolbar. Create the button shown below the Mortgage Payment section in Figure CLA5-1a. Assign the command macro CLA51INP to the button. Hide the Utility toolbar. Unprotect the range B3:B5. Protect the worksheet. Click the Save File tool on the Standard toolbar to save the worksheet.
8. Use the button to determine the mortgage payment for the following mortgage data and print the worksheet for each data set: (a) principal — 63,500, interest rate — 7.75%, and years —15; (b) principal — 343,250, interest rate — 8.25%, and years — 30. The mortgage payment for (a) is $597.71 and for (b) $2,578.72.

COMPUTER LABORATORY ASSIGNMENTS   E283

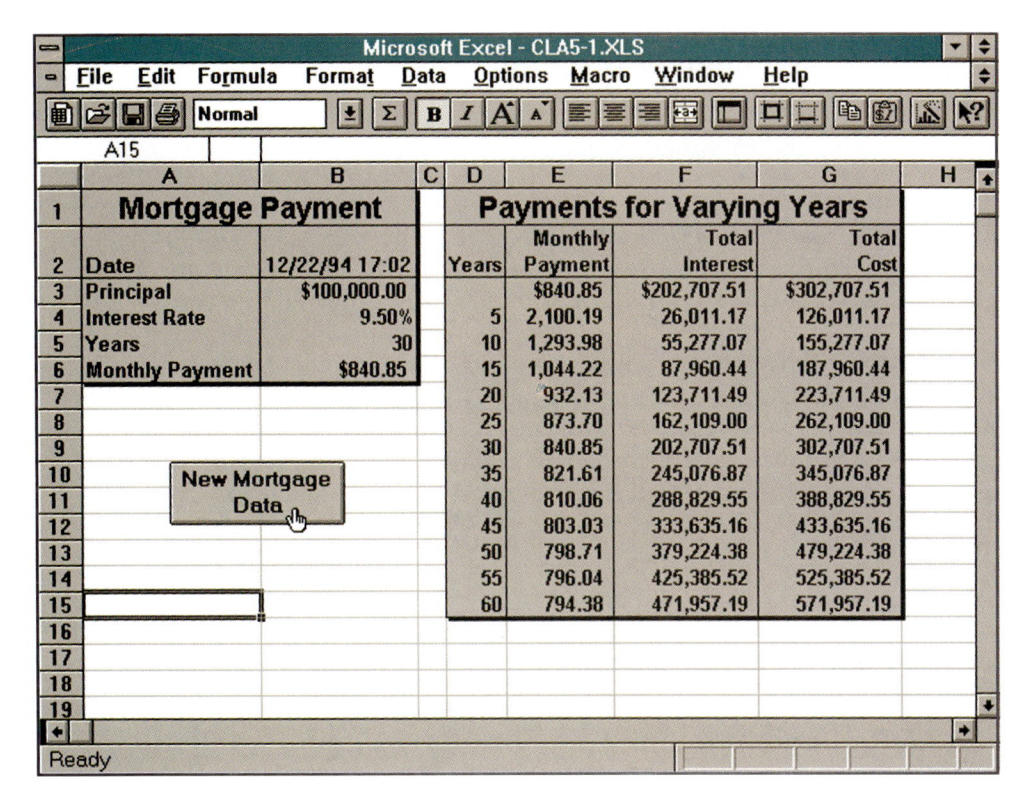

FIGURE CLA5-1a

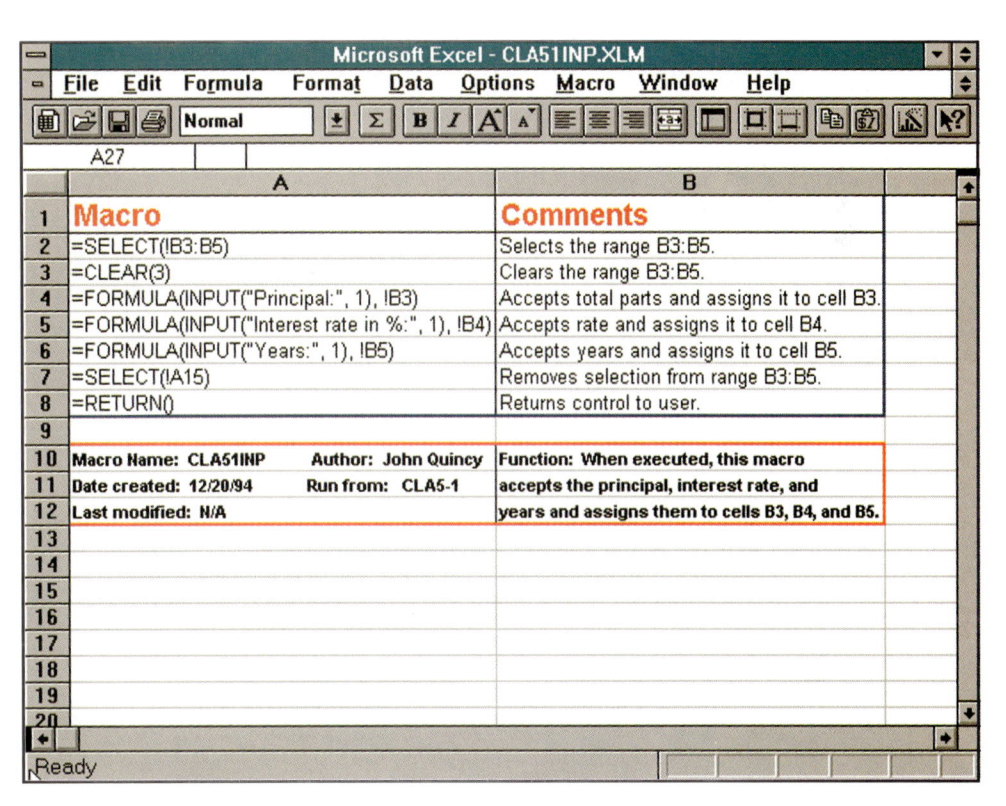

	A	B	C	D	E	F	G
1	Mortgage Payment				Payments for Varying Years		
2	Date	12/22/94 17:02		Years	Monthly Payment	Total Interest	Total Cost
3	Principal	$100,000.00			$840.85	$202,707.51	$302,707.51
4	Interest Rate	9.50%		5	2,100.19	26,011.17	126,011.17
5	Years	30		10	1,293.98	55,277.07	155,277.07
6	Monthly Payment	$840.85		15	1,044.22	87,960.44	187,960.44
7				20	932.13	123,711.49	223,711.49
8				25	873.70	162,109.00	262,109.00
9				30	840.85	202,707.51	302,707.51
10	New Mortgage Data			35	821.61	245,076.87	345,076.87
11				40	810.06	288,829.55	388,829.55
12				45	803.03	333,635.16	433,635.16
13				50	798.71	379,224.38	479,224.38
14				55	796.04	425,385.52	525,385.52
15				60	794.38	471,957.19	571,957.19

FIGURE CLA5-1b

	A	B
1	**Macro**	**Comments**
2	=SELECT(!B3:B5)	Selects the range B3:B5.
3	=CLEAR(3)	Clears the range B3:B5.
4	=FORMULA(INPUT("Principal:", 1), !B3)	Accepts total parts and assigns it to cell B3.
5	=FORMULA(INPUT("Interest rate in %:", 1), !B4)	Accepts rate and assigns it to cell B4.
6	=FORMULA(INPUT("Years:", 1), !B5)	Accepts years and assigns it to cell B5.
7	=SELECT(!A15)	Removes selection from range B3:B5.
8	=RETURN()	Returns control to user.
9		
10	Macro Name: CLA51INP Author: John Quincy	Function: When executed, this macro
11	Date created: 12/20/94 Run from: CLA5-1	accepts the principal, interest rate, and
12	Last modified: N/A	years and assigns them to cells B3, B4, and B5.

COMPUTER LABORATORY ASSIGNMENT 2
Determining the Future Value of an Investment

Purpose: To become familiar with using the FV function, names, two-input data tables, command macros, and buttons.

Problem: The Insurance company you work for is in need of a Future Value worksheet that its agents can use with a portable computer when they visit clients. A future value computation tells the user what a constant monthly payment is worth after a period of time if the insurance company pays a fixed interest rate.

An agent survey indicates they want a worksheet similar to the one in Figure CLA5-2a that includes not only a future value computation, but also a two-input data table that determines future values for varying interest rates and monthly payments. The survey indicates that the agents know little about computers and spreadsheets. Thus, you must create a command macro (Figure CLA5-2b) that will guide the agent through entering the future value data. Assign the command macro to a button.

Instructions: Perform the following tasks:

1. Change the font of the entire worksheet to TT Arial bold.
2. Enter the Future Value section of the worksheet. Assign cell B2 the NOW function so it displays the system date. (It is not necessary that you display the exact date shown in Figure CLA5-2a.) Create names for the range B3:B6. Assign cell B6 the following formula:

    = FV(interest_rate / 12, 12*years, −monthly_payment)

    Assign cell B7 the following formula:

    = 12*years*monthly_payment

3. Enter the Varying the Interest Rate and Monthly Payment data table. Assign cell A9 the entry, = future_value. Assign cells B9, C9, D9, and E9 the monthly payments, $50.00, $75.00, $100.00, and $125.00, respectively. Use the fill handle to create the series in the range A10:A19. Create a data table in the range A9:E19 using the Table command from the Data menu. Use cell B3 as the row input cell and cell B4 as the column input cell.
4. Add your name, course, computer laboratory assignment number (CLA5-2), date, and instructor name in column A beginning in cell A22. Save the worksheet using the file name CLA5-2. Print the worksheet without cell gridlines with the future value data shown in Figure CLA5-2a.
5. Use the New command from the File menu to create the command macro in Figure CLA5-2b. Select cell A1 and use the Define Name command to name the command macro CLA52INP. Save the macro sheet using the file name CLA52INP.
6. Use the Window menu to display the worksheet CLA5-2. Display the Utility toolbar. Create the button shown in the range D3:D4 in Figure CLA5-2a. Assign the command macro CLA52INP to the button. Hide the Utility toolbar. Unprotect the range B3:B5. Protect the worksheet. Click the Save File tool on the Standard toolbar to save the worksheet.
7. Use the button to determine the future value for the following data and print the worksheet for each data set: (a) monthly payment — $100.00, interest rate — 7.25%, and number of years — 30; (b) monthly payment — $300.00, interest rate — 9.25%, and number of years —10. The future value for (a) is $128,189.33 and for (b) $58,881.96.

COMPUTER LABORATORY ASSIGNMENTS **E285**

Microsoft Excel - CLA5-2.XLS

	A	B	C	D	E
1	**Future Value Computations**				
2	Date	22-Dec-94		New Future Value Data	
3	Monthly payment	$50.00			
4	Interest rate	8.75%			
5	Years	10			
6	Future value	$9,540.15			
7	Total investment	$6,000.00			
8	**Varying the Interest Rate and Monthly Payment**				
9	$9,540.15	$50.00	$75.00	$100.00	$125.00
10	7.00%	$8,654.24	$12,981.36	$17,308.48	$21,635.60
11	7.25%	8,774.34	13,161.50	17,548.67	21,935.84
12	7.50%	8,896.52	13,344.78	17,793.03	22,241.29
13	7.75%	9,020.83	13,531.24	18,041.65	22,552.06
14	8.00%	9,147.30	13,720.95	18,294.60	22,868.25
15	8.25%	9,275.99	13,913.98	18,551.97	23,189.97
16	8.50%	9,406.92	14,110.38	18,813.84	23,517.30
17	8.75%	9,540.15	14,310.22	19,080.30	23,850.37
18	9.00%	9,675.71	14,513.57	19,351.43	24,189.28
19	9.25%	9,813.66	14,720.49	19,627.32	24,534.15

Callouts: row input cell, column input cell, =future_value, row of different monthly payments, column of different percents, Excel fills data table

FIGURE CLA5-2a

Microsoft Excel - CLA52INP.XLM

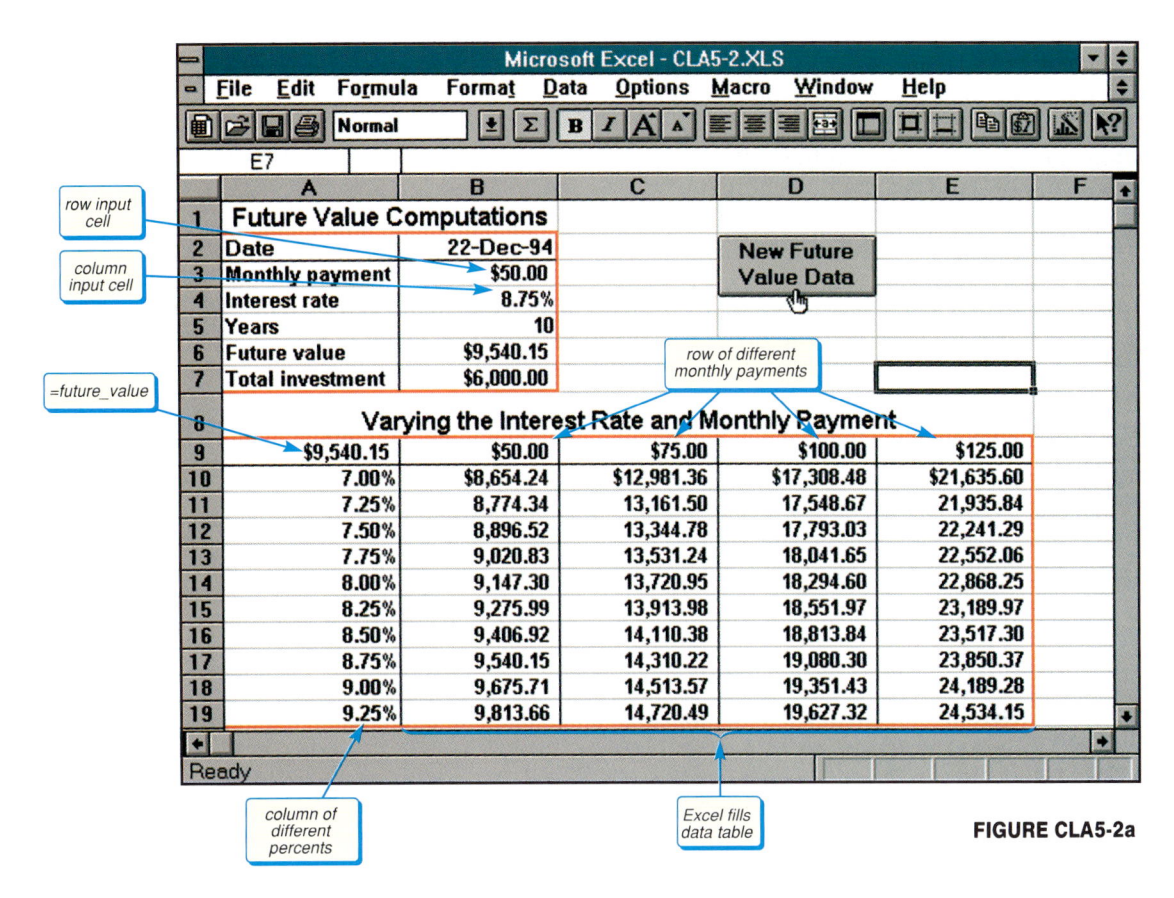

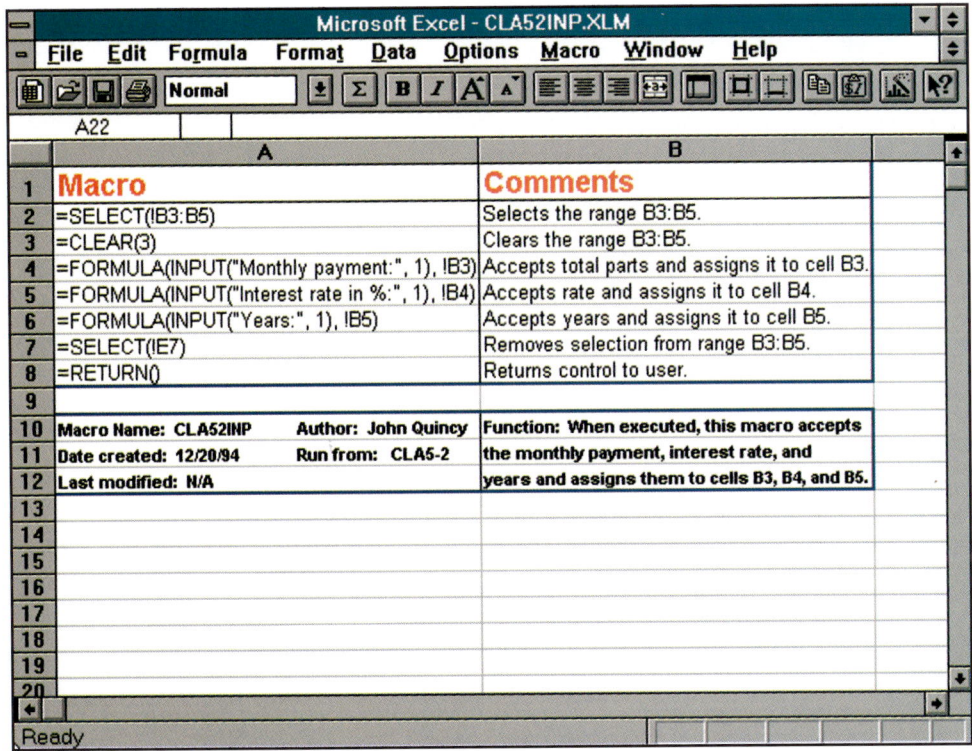

	A	B
1	**Macro**	**Comments**
2	=SELECT(!B3:B5)	Selects the range B3:B5.
3	=CLEAR(3)	Clears the range B3:B5.
4	=FORMULA(INPUT("Monthly payment:", 1), !B3)	Accepts total parts and assigns it to cell B3.
5	=FORMULA(INPUT("Interest rate in %:", 1), !B4)	Accepts rate and assigns it to cell B4.
6	=FORMULA(INPUT("Years:", 1), !B5)	Accepts years and assigns it to cell B5.
7	=SELECT(!E7)	Removes selection from range B3:B5.
8	=RETURN()	Returns control to user.
9		
10	Macro Name: CLA52INP Author: John Quincy	Function: When executed, this macro accepts
11	Date created: 12/20/94 Run from: CLA5-2	the monthly payment, interest rate, and
12	Last modified: N/A	years and assigns them to cells B3, B4, and B5.

FIGURE CLA5-2b

COMPUTER LABORATORY ASSIGNMENT 3
Building an Amortization Table and Analyzing Data

Purpose: To become familiar with the PMT and PV functions. To understand how to develop an amortization table and use goal seeking and the Scenario Manager to analyze data.

Problem: Each student in your Office Automation course is assigned a "live project" with a local company. You have been assigned to the Crown Loan Company to generate the loan information worksheet in Figure CLA5-3a and the Scenario Summary Report worksheet in Figure CLA5-3b. The president also wants you to demonstrate the goal seeking capabilities of Excel.

Instructions: Perform the following tasks to create the two worksheets:

1. Enter and format the text and numbers in the range A1:E4 (Figure 5-3a). Create names for the cells in the range B2:B4 and E2:E4 by using the names in the adjacent cells. In cell B4, enter the formula: = B2–B3. In cell E4, enter the PMT function:

    = PMT(rate / 12, 12*years, –loan_amount)

2. Enter the column titles for the amortization schedule in the range A5:E13. Use the data fill handle to generate the years in column A.
3. Assign the formulas and functions to the cells indicated in the table to the right.
4. Copy cell B7 to the range B8:B10. Copy the range C6:E6 to the range C7:E10. Draw the borders shown in Figure CLA5-3a.
5. Save the worksheet using the file name CLA5-3. Print the worksheet without cell gridlines with the loan data and loan information in Figure CLA5-3a.
6. Unprotect the ranges B2:B4 and E2:E3. Protect the worksheet. Save the worksheet.
7. Use Excel's goal seeking capabilities to determine the down payment required for the loan data in Figure CLA5-3a if the monthly payment is set to $200.00. The down payment that results in a monthly payment of $200.00 is $3,577.87. Print the worksheet. Change the down payment in cell B3 back to $2,300.00.

CELL	FORMULA OR FUNCTION
B6	= loan_amount
C6	= IF(A6 < = years, PV(rate / 12, 12 * (years – A6), – monthly_pymt), 0)
D6	= B6 – C6
E6	= IF(B6 > 0, 12 * monthly_pymt – D6, 0)
B7	= C6
D11	= SUM(D6:D10)
E11	= SUM(E6:E10)
E12	= down_pymt
E13	= D11 + E11 + E12

Crown Loan Company

	A	B	C	D	E
2	Price	$13,500.00		Rate	7.75%
3	Down Pymt	$2,300.00		Years	5
4	Loan Amount	$11,200.00		Monthly Pymt	$225.76
5	Year	Beginning Balance	Ending Balance	Paid On Principal	Interest Paid
6	1	$11,200.00	$9,292.08	$1,907.92	$801.17
7	2	9,292.08	7,230.93	2,061.15	647.94
8	3	7,230.93	5,004.24	2,226.69	482.41
9	4	5,004.24	2,598.72	2,405.52	303.57
10	5	2,598.72	0.00	2,598.72	110.38
11			Subtotal	$11,200.00	$2,345.48
12			Down Pymt		$2,300.00
13			Total Cost		$15,845.48

FIGURE CLA5-3a

8. Unprotect the worksheet by using the Unprotect Document command on the Options menu. Use the Define Name command from the Formula menu to name cell E11 total_interest. Use the same command to assign the name total_cost to cell E13. These names will show up in the Scenario Summary Report worksheet in the next step. Protect the worksheet.

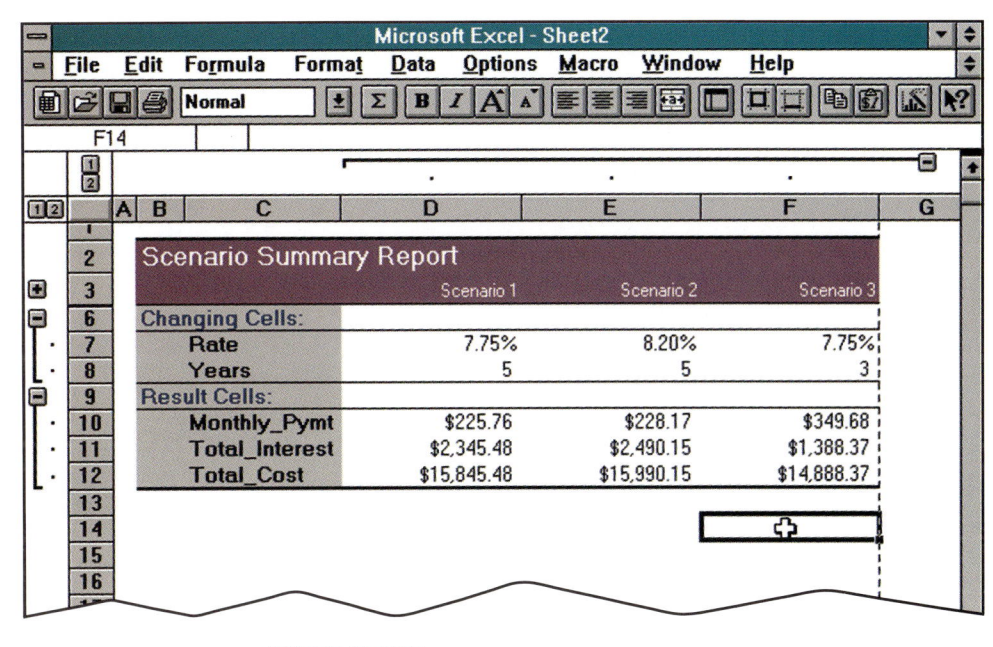

FIGURE CLA5-3b

9. Use Scenario Manager to create a Scenario Summary Report worksheet (Figure CLA5-3b) for the following scenarios: (1) Interest rate — 7.75% and Years — 5; (2) Interest Rate — 8.2% and Years — 5; and (3) Interest rate — 7.75% and Years — 3. Save the Scenario Summary Report worksheet as CLA53SCE and print it. Return to the worksheet CLA5-3 and save it.

COMPUTER LABORATORY ASSIGNMENT 4
Planning a Mortgage Payment Worksheet

Purpose: To become familiar with planning a worksheet.

Problem: You are a consultant working for Fair Loan Company. You have been assigned to create a worksheet similiar to the one in Figure CLA5-3a and a Scenario Summary Report worksheet similar to the one in Figure CLA5-3b. However, the amortization table should be extended to 30 years rather than 5 years. See Computer Laboratory Assignment 3 for the formulas to use.

Create a command macro to accept the loan data. Assign the command macro to a button in the worksheet. Create a Scenario Summary Report worksheet that shows the monthly mortgage payment, total interest, and total cost for a 30 year loan with three different interest rates. Add a one-input data table to the worksheet that analyzes the monthly mortgage payment, total interest, and total cost for varying interest rates between 5.00% and 10.00% in increments of .25%.

Instructions: Design and create the Mortgage Payment worksheet. Develop your own test data. Submit the following:

1. A description of the problem. Include the purpose of the worksheet, a statement outlining the results, the required data, and calculations.
2. A handwritten design of the worksheet.
3. A printed copy of the worksheet, command macro, and Scenario Summary Report worksheet.
4. A printed copy of the formulas in the worksheet.
5. A short description explaining how to use the worksheet.
6. Enter your name, course, computer laboratory assignment number (CLA5-4), date, and instructor name in column A in separate but adjacent cells. Save the worksheet using the file name CLA5-4.

MICROSOFT EXCEL 4 FOR WINDOWS
PROJECT SIX

SORTING AND QUERYING A WORKSHEET DATABASE

OBJECTIVES You will have mastered the material in this project when you can:

- Create a database
- Use a data form to display records, add records, delete records, and change field values in a database
- Sort a database on one sort key or multiple sort keys
- Use a data form to display records that pass a criteria
- Build a criteria area for finding, extracting, and deleting records in a database
- Apply database functions to generate information about the database
- Analyze a database using the Crosstab ReportWizard

▶ INTRODUCTION

In this project you will learn about the database capabilities of Excel. A **worksheet database**, also called a **database**, is an organized collection of data. For example, a telephone book, a grade book, and a list of company employees are databases. In these cases, the data related to a person is called a **record**, and the data items that make up a record are called **fields**. In a telephone book database, the fields are name, address, and telephone number.

A worksheet's row and column structure can easily be used to organize and store a database (Figure 6-1). Each row of a worksheet can be used to store a record and each column can store a field. Additionally, a row of column headings at the top of the worksheet are used as **field names** to identify each field.

Once you enter a database onto your worksheet, you can use Excel to (1) add and delete records; (2) change the values of fields in records; (3) sort the records; (4) find and extract records that pass comparison criteria; (5) analyze data using database functions; and (6) summarize information about the database. This project illustrates all six of these database capabilities.

PROJECT SIX   E289

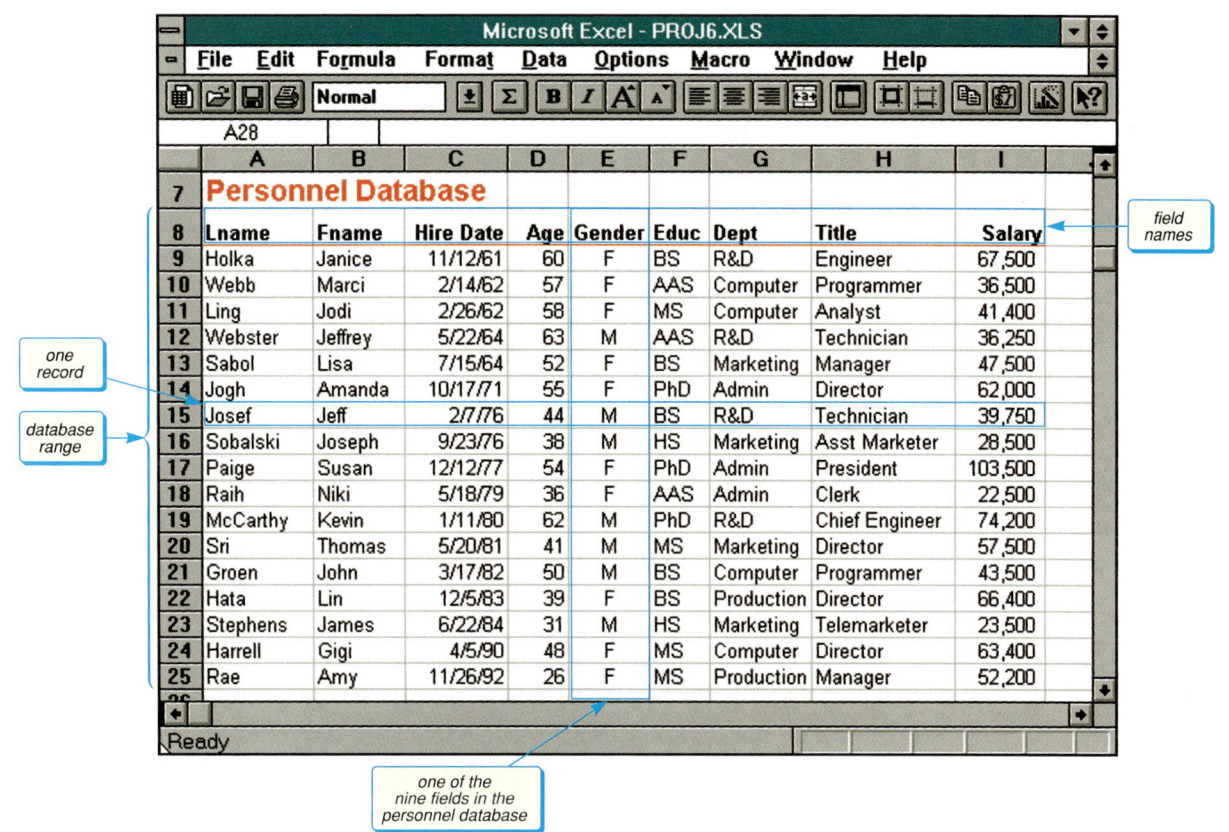

FIGURE 6-1

Personnel Database (Microsoft Excel - PROJ6.XLS)

	A	B	C	D	E	F	G	H	I
7	**Personnel Database**								
8	Lname	Fname	Hire Date	Age	Gender	Educ	Dept	Title	Salary
9	Holka	Janice	11/12/61	60	F	BS	R&D	Engineer	67,500
10	Webb	Marci	2/14/62	57	F	AAS	Computer	Programmer	36,500
11	Ling	Jodi	2/26/62	58	F	MS	Computer	Analyst	41,400
12	Webster	Jeffrey	5/22/64	63	M	AAS	R&D	Technician	36,250
13	Sabol	Lisa	7/15/64	52	F	BS	Marketing	Manager	47,500
14	Jogh	Amanda	10/17/71	55	F	PhD	Admin	Director	62,000
15	Josef	Jeff	2/7/76	44	M	BS	R&D	Technician	39,750
16	Sobalski	Joseph	9/23/76	38	M	HS	Marketing	Asst Marketer	28,500
17	Paige	Susan	12/12/77	54	F	PhD	Admin	President	103,500
18	Raih	Niki	5/18/79	36	F	AAS	Admin	Clerk	22,500
19	McCarthy	Kevin	1/11/80	62	M	PhD	R&D	Chief Engineer	74,200
20	Sri	Thomas	5/20/81	41	M	MS	Marketing	Director	57,500
21	Groen	John	3/17/82	50	M	BS	Computer	Programmer	43,500
22	Hata	Lin	12/5/83	39	F	BS	Production	Director	66,400
23	Stephens	James	6/22/84	31	M	HS	Marketing	Telemarketer	23,500
24	Harrell	Gigi	4/5/90	48	F	MS	Computer	Director	63,400
25	Rae	Amy	11/26/92	26	F	MS	Production	Manager	52,200

▶ PROJECT SIX

The database for Project 6 is illustrated in Figure 6-1. It consists of 17 employee personnel records. The field names, columns, types of data, and column widths are described in Table 6-1. Since the database is visible on the screen, it is important that it be readable. Therefore, some of the column widths in Table 6-1 are determined from the field names and not the maximum length of the data.

▶ **TABLE 6-1**

COLUMN HEADINGS (FIELD NAMES)	COLUMN	TYPE OF DATA	COLUMN WIDTH
Lname	A	Text	10
Fname	B	Text	8
Hire Date	C	Date	9
Age	D	Numeric	5
Gender	E	Text	7
Educ	F	Text	5
Dept	G	Text	9
Title	H	Text	13
Salary	I	Numeric	8

As you will see when creating a database, the column headings (field names) play an important role in the commands you issue to manipulate the data in the database. These column headings must be text and can contain a maximum of 255 characters. However, it's best to keep them short, as shown in row 8 of Figure 6-1 on the previous page.

One difference between the personnel database in Figure 6-1 and previous worksheets you have built is the location of the data on the worksheet. In all previous worksheets, you began the entries in row 1. When you enter a database onto a worksheet, you usually leave several rows empty, above the database, for adding entries that will be used to manipulate the database.

Setting Up the Worksheet

Before you create the database, there are some preliminary entries and modifications you should complete to set up the worksheet. The following steps change the font of the worksheet to TrueType Arial; the column widths to those specified in Table 6-1 on the previous page; the heights of rows 7 and 8 to 18 points; and enter and format the database title in cell A7. Although Excel does not require the database title in cell A7, it is a good practice to include one on the worksheet to identify the database area.

TO SET UP THE WORKSHEET

Step 1: Click the Select All button. Use the Font command on the Format menu to change the font of the worksheet from MS Sans Serif to TrueType Arial.

Step 2: Change the column widths as follows: A = 10, B = 8, C = 9, D = 5, E = 7, F = 5, G = 9, H = 13, and I = 8.

Step 3: Select cell A7 and enter `Personnel Database`. From the Format menu, choose the Font command. Select a font style of Bold, a size of 14 points, and the color red. Choose the OK button from the Font dialog box.

Step 4: Select rows 7 and 8 by clicking row heading 7 and dragging through row heading 8. With the mouse pointer on the border line between rows 8 and 9, increase the row height from 12.75 points to 18 points.

After setting up the worksheet, the next step is to create the personnel database.

▶ CREATING A DATABASE

To create the personnel database shown in Figure 6-1, you will enter the field names into row 8. Next, using the Database command on the Data menu, you will define the database range as A8:I9. The **database range** encompasses the field names (row 8) and one blank row (row 9) below the field names. The blank row is for expansion of the database.

After defining the database range as two rows long, you will use a data form to enter the personnel records. A **data form** is a dialog box in which Excel includes the field names in the database and corresponding boxes in which you enter the field values. The following steps create the personnel database shown in Figure 6-1 on the previous page.

CREATING A DATABASE **E291**

TO CREATE A DATABASE USING A DATA FORM ▼

STEP 1 ▶

Enter the field names in row 8 as described in Table 6-1 and shown in Figure 6-1 on page E289. Draw a light red bottom border below the field names. Use the tools and Style box on the Standard toolbar to do the following: (a) bold the field names; (b) right-align the field names in cells C8, D8, and I8; (c) center all column E entries (select column E and click the Center Align tool); and (d) assign the Comma (0) format style to column I.

The field names display in row 8 as shown in Figure 6-2.

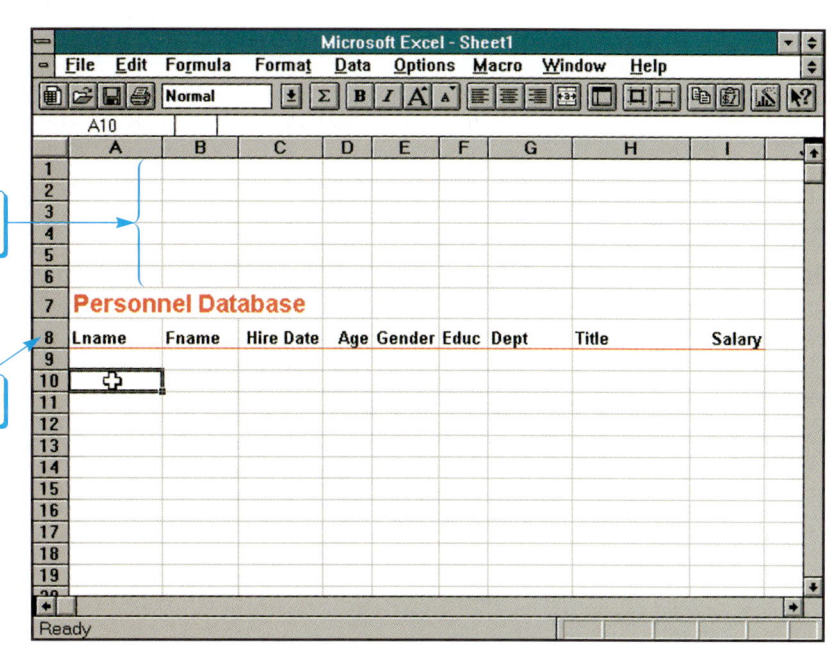

FIGURE 6-2

STEP 2 ▶

Select the range A8:I9. Select the Data menu and point to the Set Database command.

Excel displays the Data menu (Figure 6-3). The selected range includes the field names and an extra blank record. The blank record allows you to expand the database by adding records using the Form command.

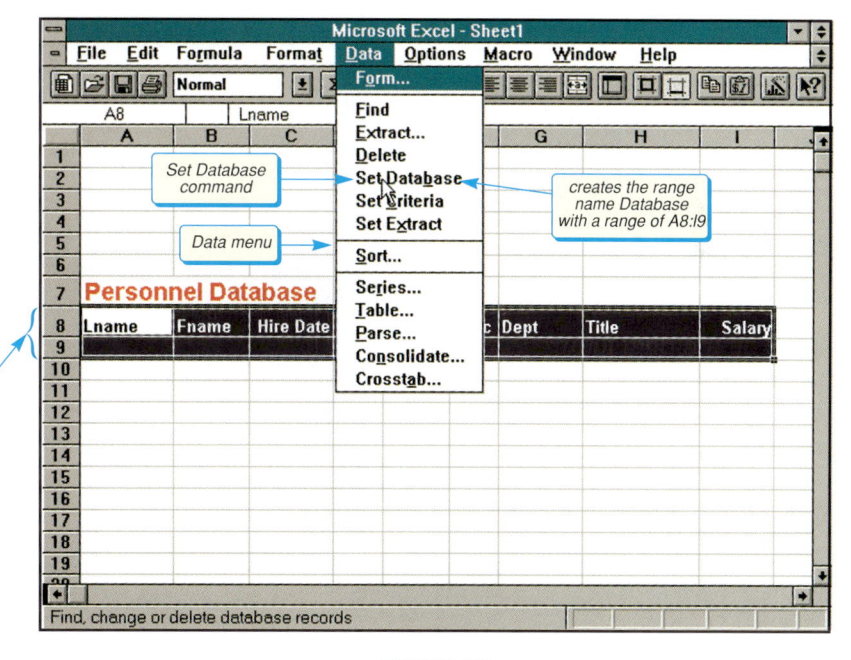

FIGURE 6-3

E292 PROJECT 6 SORTING AND QUERYING A WORKSHEET DATABASE

STEP 3

Choose the Set Database command from the Data menu.

Excel assigns the name Database to the range A8:I9.

STEP 4 ▶

Select cell A9. Select the Data menu and point to the Form command.

The Data menu displays (Figure 6-4).

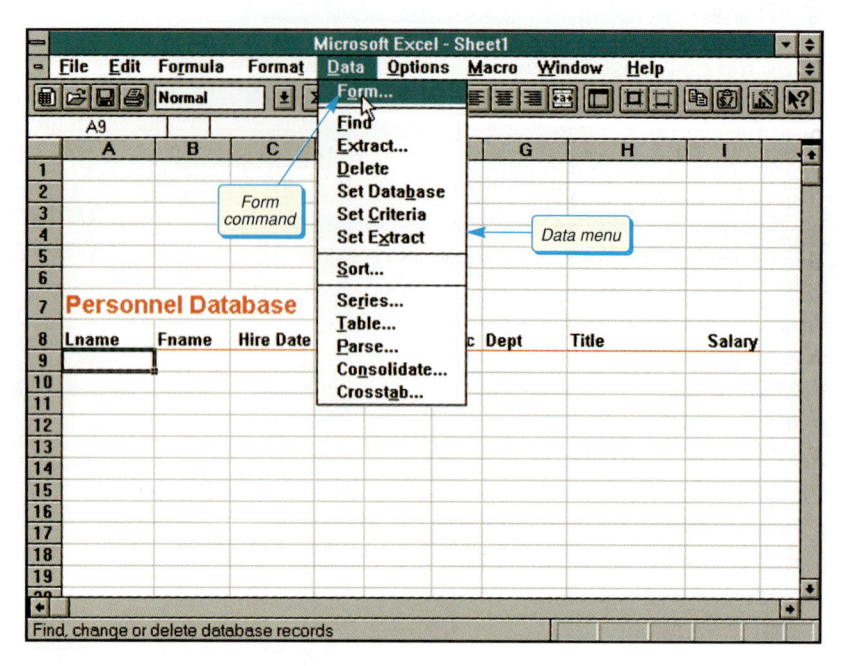

FIGURE 6-4

STEP 5 ▶

Choose the Form command from the Data menu.

Excel displays the data form (Figure 6-5) with the title Sheet1. The data form includes the field names and corresponding boxes for entering the field values.

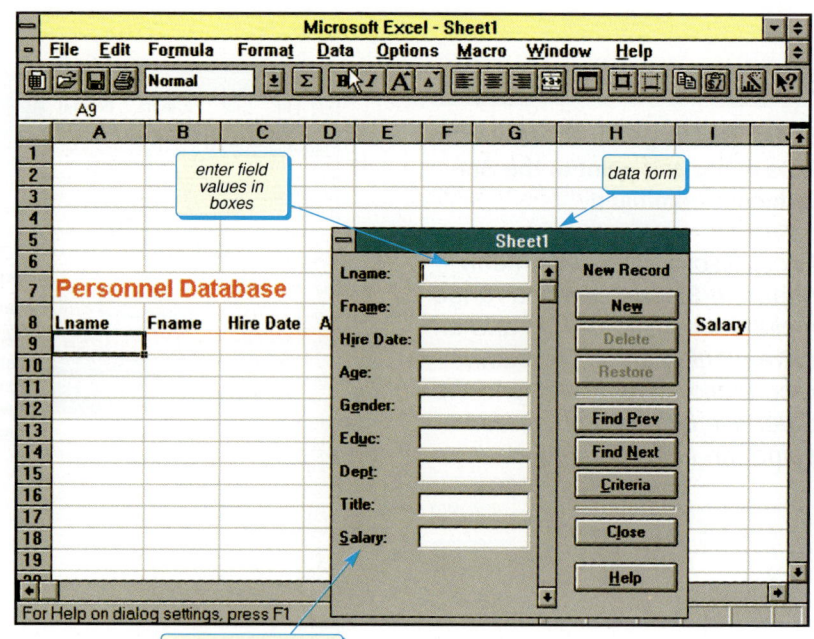

FIGURE 6-5

CREATING A DATABASE **E293**

STEP 6 ▶

Enter the first personnel record (row 9 of Figure 6-1 on page E289) onto the data form. Use the mouse or the TAB key to move the insertion point down to the next box and the SHIFT + TAB keys to move the insertion point to the previous box. After you have entered the first personnel record, point to the New button.

The first personnel record displays in the data form as shown in Figure 6-6.

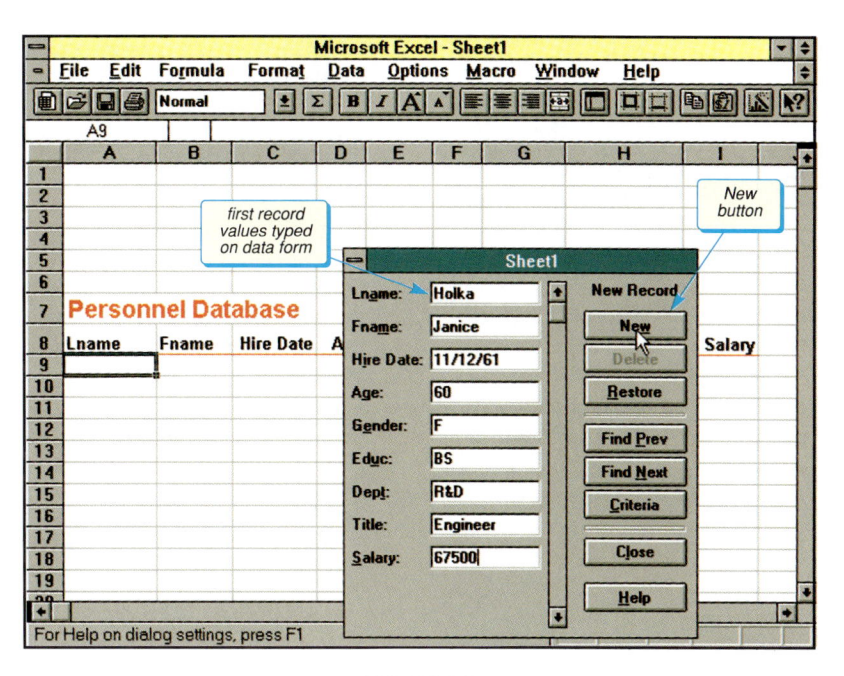

FIGURE 6-6

STEP 7 ▶

Choose the New button (New) from the data form. Type the second personnel record (row 10 of Figure 6-1 on page E289) onto the data form.

Excel adds the first personnel record to row 9 in the database range, and the second record displays on the data form (Figure 6-7).

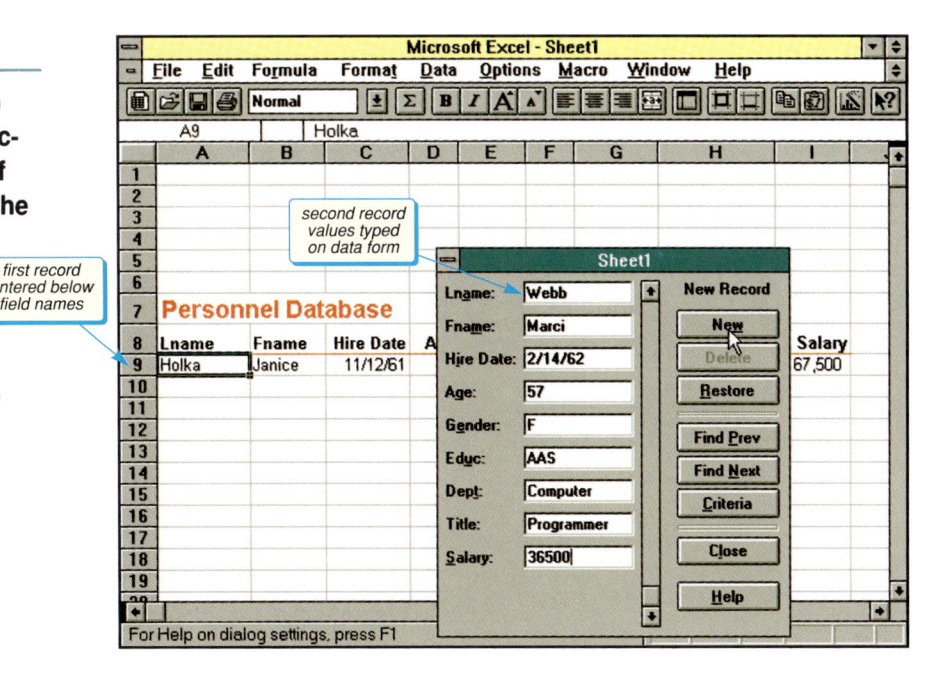

FIGURE 6-7

STEP 8 ▶

Choose the New button from the data form to enter the second personnel record. Enter the next fourteen personnel records in rows 11 through 24 of Figure 6-1 on page E289 using the data form. Type the last personnel record and point to the Close button (Close) on the data form.

Excel enters the records into the database range as shown in Figure 6-8. The last record displays on the data form.

FIGURE 6-8

STEP 9 ▶

With the last record typed on the data form, choose the Close button to complete the record entry. Save the worksheet using the file name PROJ6.

The personnel database displays as shown in Figure 6-9.

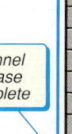

FIGURE 6-9

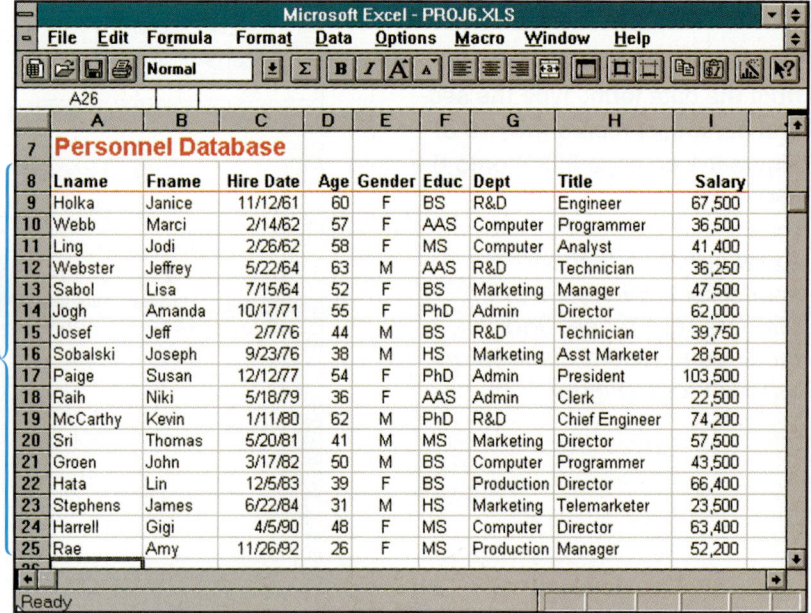

Rather than use a data form to build the personnel database, you could have entered the records in the same fashion as you entered data onto previous worksheets and then defined all the columns and rows (A8:I25) as a database range using the Set Database command on the Data menu. The data form was illustrated here because it is considered to be a more accurate and reliable method of data entry.

To move from field to field on a data form, you can use the TAB key as described earlier in Step 6 on page E293 or you can hold down the ALT key and press the key that corresponds to the underlined letter in the name of the field to which you want to move. Thus, to select the field titled Fname in Figure 6-8 you can hold down the ALT key and press the M key (ALT + M) because m is underlined in Fname.

With regard to the data shown in Figure 6-9, you should notice the following: (1) in column C, the dates are right-justified because Excel treats dates as numbers; (2) Excel formats the dates to the m/d/yy style because that is the format in which they were entered; (3) the Gender codes in column E are centered because in Step 1 on page E291 column E was assigned center-align; and (4) the salary entries in column I display using the Comma (0) format style because in Step 1 on page E291 column I was assigned this format.

Using the Data Form to View Records and Change Data

At any time while the worksheet is active, you can use the Form command on the Data menu to display records, add new records, delete records, and change the data in records. When a data form is initially opened, Excel displays the first record in the database. To display the sixth record as shown in Figure 6-10, you choose the Find Next button (Find Next) until the sixth record displays. Each time you choose the Find Next button, Excel advances to the next record in the database. If necessary, you can use the Find Prev button (Find Prev) to back up to a previous record. You can also use the UP ARROW key and DOWN ARROW key or the vertical scroll bar to the left of the buttons to move between records.

To change data in a record, you first display it on a data form. Next, you select the fields to change one at a time. Finally, you use the DOWN ARROW key or the ENTER key to confirm the field changes. If you change field values on a data form and then select the Find Next button to move to the next record, the field changes will not be made.

To add a new record, you choose the New button. A data form always adds the new record to the bottom of the database. To delete a record, you first display it on a data form and then choose the Delete button. Excel automatically moves all records below the deleted record up one row.

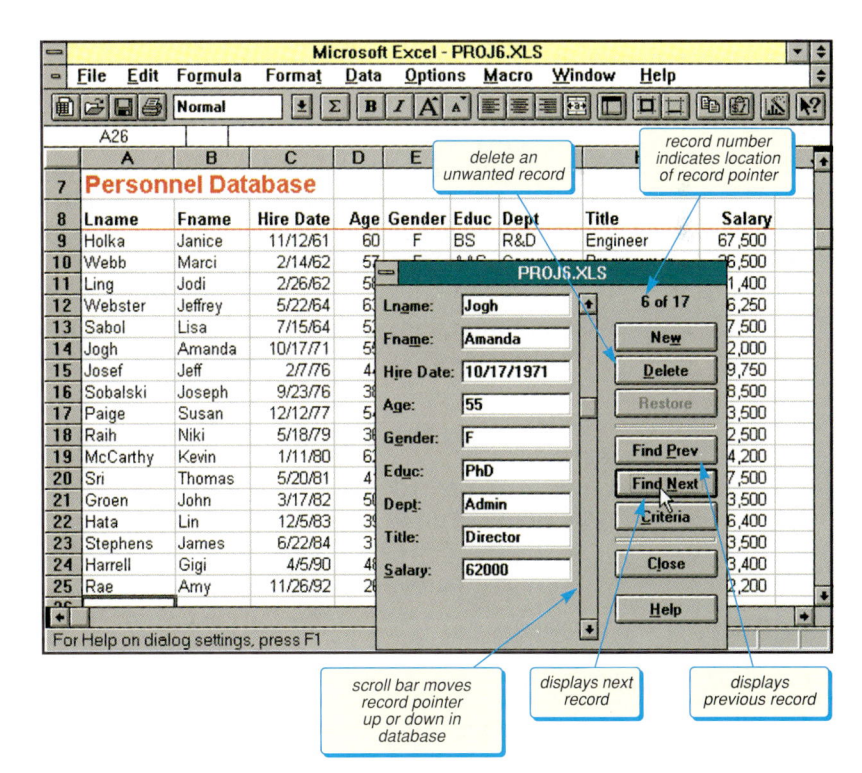

FIGURE 6-10

Printing a Database

You can print the database using the same procedures you followed in earlier projects to print a worksheet. If there is more to the worksheet than the database and you only want to print the database, then follow these steps.

TO PRINT A DATABASE

Step 1: From the Formula menu, choose the Goto command.
Step 2: When the Goto dialog box displays, select the name Database and choose the OK button. Excel responds by immediately selecting the database on the worksheet.
Step 3: Choose the OK button.
Step 4: From the Options menu, choose the Set Print Area command.
Step 5: Choose the Page Setup command from the File menu. Turn off cell gridlines in the Page Setup dialog box.
Step 6: Ready the printer and click the Print tool on the Standard toolbar.

▶ SORTING A DATABASE

The data in a database is easier to work with and more meaningful if the records are arranged in sequence on the basis of one or more fields. Arranging records in sequence is called **sorting**. Data is in **ascending sequence** if it is in order from lowest to highest, earliest to most recent, or in alphabetical order. For example, the records were entered into the personnel database beginning with the earliest hire date to the most recent hire date. Thus, the personnel database in Figure 6-9 on page E294 is sorted in ascending sequence by hire date.

Data that is in sequence from highest to lowest in value is in **descending sequence**.

You initiate a sort operation by selecting the records to sort. The selection should encompass all the fields in all the records below the field names, although it can be made up of fewer records and fewer fields. Be aware, however, that if you do not select all the fields (columns) in the database, the unselected fields will not remain with the records they belong to and the data will get mixed up. If you make a mistake and sort the records improperly, immediately choose the Undo Sort command from the Edit menu.

Sorting the Personnel Database by Last Name

To reorder the records in a database, use the Sort command on the Data menu. The field you select to sort the records on is called the **sort key**. The following steps show how to sort the personnel database into ascending sequence by last name (column A).

SORTING A DATABASE **E297**

TO SORT A DATABASE BY LAST NAME

STEP 1 ▶

Select all the records in the database (A9:I25). Select the Data menu and point to the Sort command.

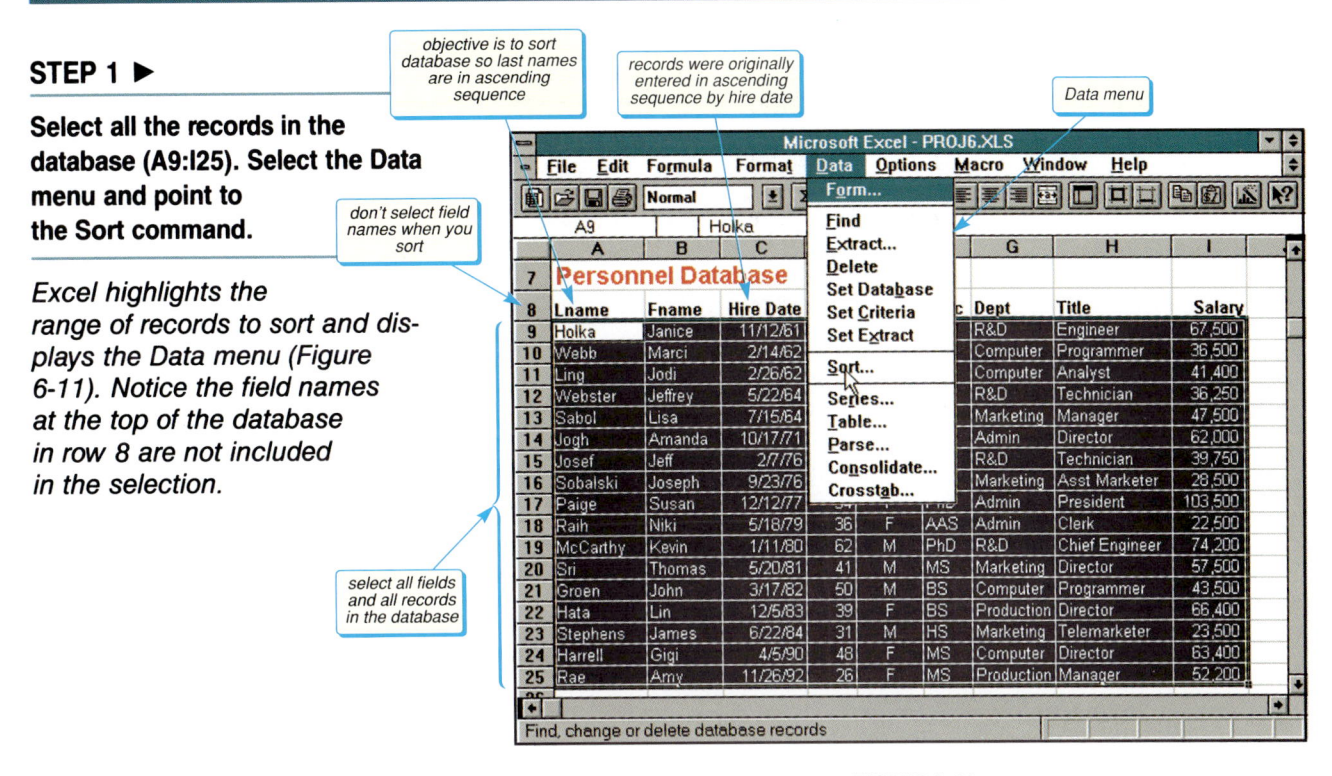

Excel highlights the range of records to sort and displays the Data menu (Figure 6-11). Notice the field names at the top of the database in row 8 are not included in the selection.

- objective is to sort database so last names are in ascending sequence
- records were originally entered in ascending sequence by hire date
- Data menu
- don't select field names when you sort
- select all fields and all records in the database

FIGURE 6-11

STEP 2 ▶

Choose the Sort command from the Data menu.

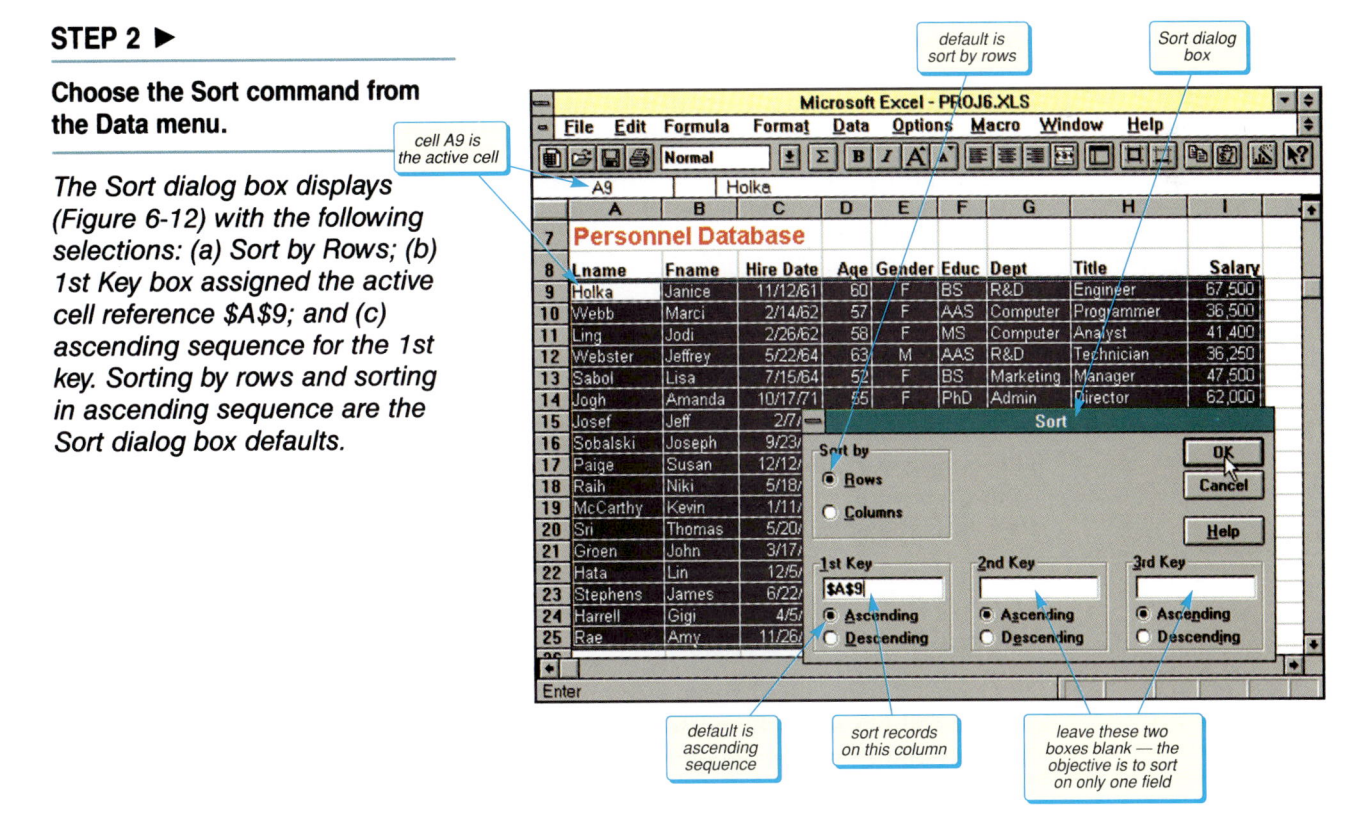

The Sort dialog box displays (Figure 6-12) with the following selections: (a) Sort by Rows; (b) 1st Key box assigned the active cell reference A9; and (c) ascending sequence for the 1st key. Sorting by rows and sorting in ascending sequence are the Sort dialog box defaults.

- default is sort by rows
- Sort dialog box
- cell A9 is the active cell
- default is ascending sequence
- sort records on this column
- leave these two boxes blank — the objective is to sort on only one field

FIGURE 6-12

STEP 3 ▶

Choose the OK button from the Sort dialog box. Select any cell in the worksheet.

Excel sorts the personnel database into ascending sequence by last name (Figure 6-13).

Callouts on figure:
- to undo sort, use Undo Sort command in Edit menu, or sort on hire date
- records no longer in ascending sequence by hire date
- records are in ascending sequence by last name

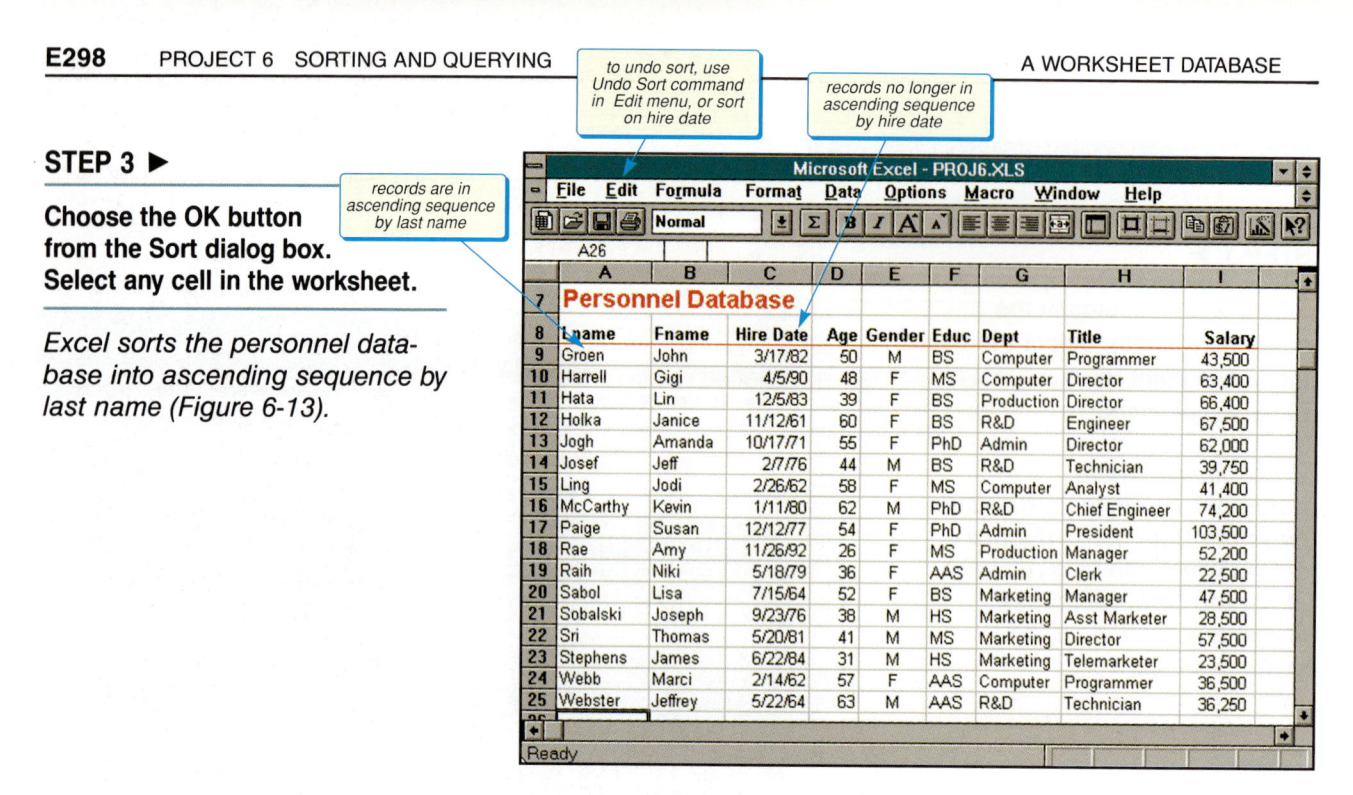

	A	B	C	D	E	F	G	H	I
7	Personnel Database								
8	Lname	Fname	Hire Date	Age	Gender	Educ	Dept	Title	Salary
9	Groen	John	3/17/82	50	M	BS	Computer	Programmer	43,500
10	Harrell	Gigi	4/5/90	48	F	MS	Computer	Director	63,400
11	Hata	Lin	12/5/83	39	F	BS	Production	Director	66,400
12	Holka	Janice	11/12/61	60	F	BS	R&D	Engineer	67,500
13	Jogh	Amanda	10/17/71	55	F	PhD	Admin	Director	62,000
14	Josef	Jeff	2/7/76	44	M	BS	R&D	Technician	39,750
15	Ling	Jodi	2/26/62	58	F	MS	Computer	Analyst	41,400
16	McCarthy	Kevin	1/11/80	62	M	PhD	R&D	Chief Engineer	74,200
17	Paige	Susan	12/12/77	54	F	PhD	Admin	President	103,500
18	Rae	Amy	11/26/92	26	F	MS	Production	Manager	52,200
19	Raih	Niki	5/18/79	36	F	AAS	Admin	Clerk	22,500
20	Sabol	Lisa	7/15/64	52	F	BS	Marketing	Manager	47,500
21	Sobalski	Joseph	9/23/76	38	M	HS	Marketing	Asst Marketer	28,500
22	Sri	Thomas	5/20/81	41	M	MS	Marketing	Director	57,500
23	Stephens	James	6/22/84	31	M	HS	Marketing	Telemarketer	23,500
24	Webb	Marci	2/14/62	57	F	AAS	Computer	Programmer	36,500
25	Webster	Jeffrey	5/22/64	63	M	AAS	R&D	Technician	36,250

FIGURE 6-13

In the previous set of steps, you were not required to select the sort key because Excel enters the active cell A9 (displays as A9) in the 1st Key box when the Sort dialog box displays. If you want to change the sort key to any other field in the database, you need only change the 1st Key box value by selecting any cell in the column to sort on. For example, if you want to sort the records into ascending sequence by the Title field in column H (Figure 6-13), you change the 1st Key box value in the Sort dialog box to any cell in column H.

You can use the Sort command to sort any range of data in a worksheet whether or not it is a database. In addition, you can sort columns as well as rows as indicated in the Sort dialog box in Figure 6-12 on the previous page.

Sorting Records Using the Sort Ascending and Sort Descending Tools

An alternative to using the Sort command on the Data menu is to use the Sort Ascending ( ) and Sort Descending ( ) tools on the Utility toolbar. These tools sort the selected range in sequence on the basis of the active cell. With these tools, you use the TAB and SHIFT + TAB keys to select the active cell after the range has been selected but before you click one of the sort tools.

Sorting a Personnel Database by Salary within Education within Gender

Excel allows you to sort a maximum of three fields at a time. The sort example that follows sorts the personnel database by salary (column I) within education (column F) within gender (column E). In this case, gender is the major sort key (1st key), education is the intermediate sort key (2nd key), and salary is the minor sort key (3rd key). In this sort example, the first two keys will be sorted in ascending sequence. The salary field will be sorted into descending sequence.

SORTING A DATABASE **E299**

The phrase "sort by salary *within* education *within* gender" means that the records are arranged in ascending sequence by gender code; within gender, the records are arranged in ascending sequence by education code; within education, the records are arranged in descending sequence by salary.

TO SORT A DATABASE BY SALARY WITHIN EDUCATION WITHIN GENDER

STEP 1 ▶

Select all the records in the database (A9:I25). From the Data menu, choose the Sort command. Select any cell in the Gender field (column E) for the 1st Key by clicking it. Select the 2nd Key box. Select any cell in the Education field (column F) by clicking it. Select the 3rd Key box. Select any cell in the Salary field (column I) by clicking it. Select the Descending option button in the 3rd Key area.

The Sort dialog box displays as shown in Figure 6-14.

FIGURE 6-14

STEP 2 ▶

Choose the OK button from the Sort dialog box.

Excel sorts the personnel database by salary within education within gender as shown in Figure 6-15.

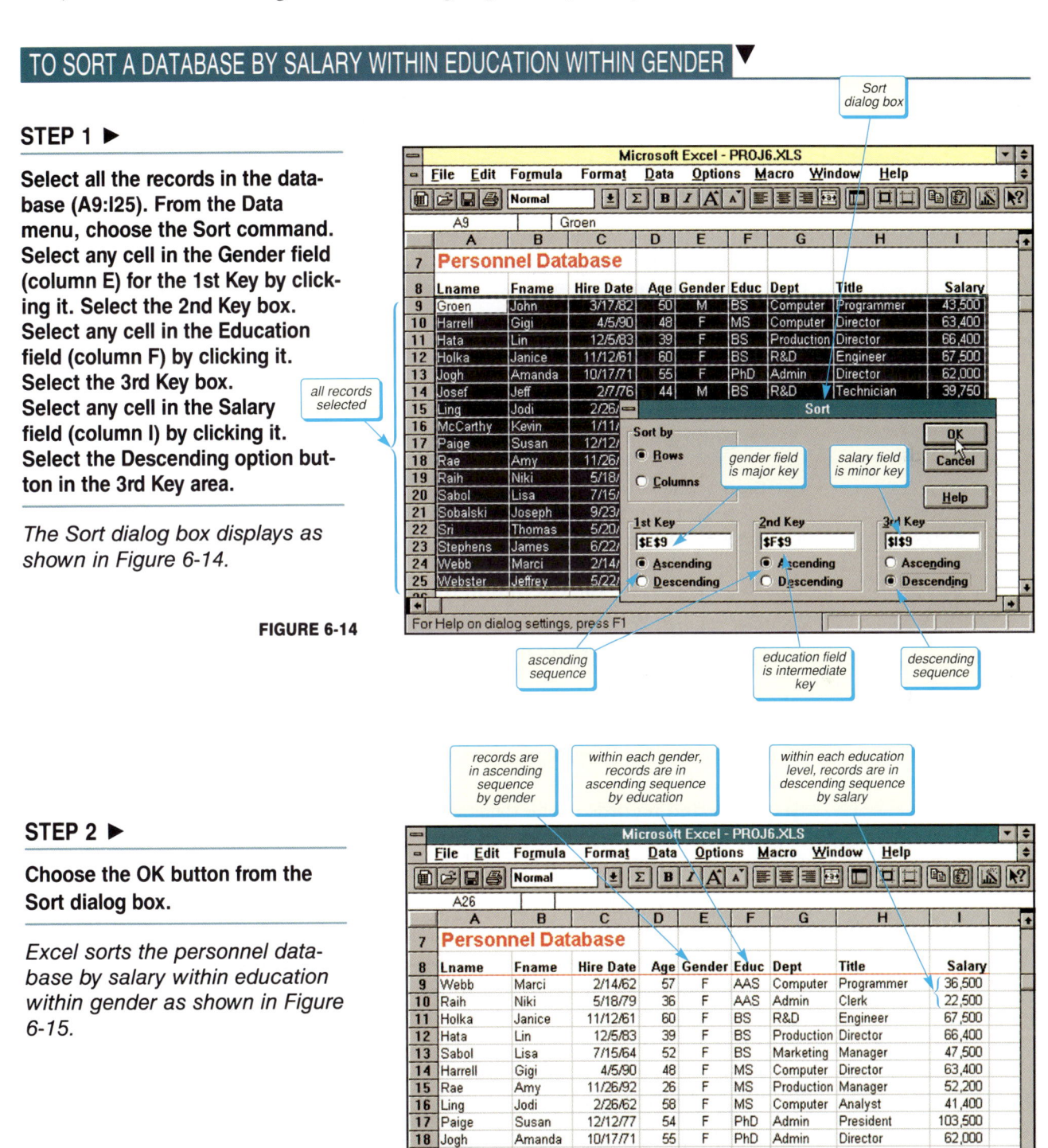

FIGURE 6-15

In Figure 6-15 on the previous page, the records are in ascending sequence by the gender codes in column E. Within each gender code, the records are in ascending sequence by the education codes in column F. Finally, within the education codes, the salaries are in descending sequence in column I. Remember, if you make a mistake in a sort operation, you can reorder the records into their original sequence by immediately choosing the Undo Sort command from the Edit menu.

Sorting with More than Three Fields

Excel allows you to sort with more than three keys by sorting two or more times. The most recent sort takes precedence. Hence, if you plan to sort on four fields, you sort on the three least important keys first and then sort on the major key. Thus, if you want to sort on fields, Lname within Title within Dept within Gender, you will first sort on Lname (3rd key) within Title (2nd key) within Dept (1st key). After the first sort operation is complete, you finally sort on the Gender field (1st key).

Before moving on to the next section, follow these steps to sort the personnel database into its original ascending sequence by the Hire Date field in column C.

TO SORT A PERSONNEL DATABASE BY HIRE DATE

Step 1: Select the range A9:I25.
Step 2: From the Data menu, choose the Sort command.
Step 3: When the Sort dialog box displays, select any cell in the Hire Date field (column C).
Step 4: Choose the OK button from the Sort dialog box.

The records in the personnel database are sorted into ascending sequence by hire date (see Figure 6-9 on page E294).

▶ FINDING RECORDS THAT PASS THE COMPARISON CRITERIA USING A DATA FORM

To find records in the database that pass a test made up of comparison criteria, you can use the Find Prev and Find Next buttons together with the Criteria button (Criteria) on the data form.

The **comparison criteria** are one or more conditions that include the field names and entries in the corresponding boxes on a data form. For example, you can instruct Excel to find and display only those records that pass the test: Hire Date < 1/1/80 and Gender = F and Age < 40. For a record to display on the data form, it has to pass all three parts of the test. Finding records that pass a test is useful for maintaining the database. When a record that passes the test displays, you can change the field values or delete the entire record from the database.

You use the same relational operators, =, <, >, >=, <=, and <>, to form the comparison criteria on a data form that you used to formulate conditions in IF functions in Project 3. The following steps illustrate how to use a data form to find records that pass the following test: Age >= 40 and Gender = M and Education <> AAS and Salary > $40,000.

FINDING RECORDS THAT PASS THE COMPARISON CRITERIA USING A DATA FORM **E301**

TO FIND RECORDS THAT PASS A COMPARISON CRITERIA USING A DATA FORM

STEP 1 ▶

From the Data menu, choose the Form command, and point to the Criteria button in the data form.

The first record in the personnel database displays on a data form (Figure 6-16).

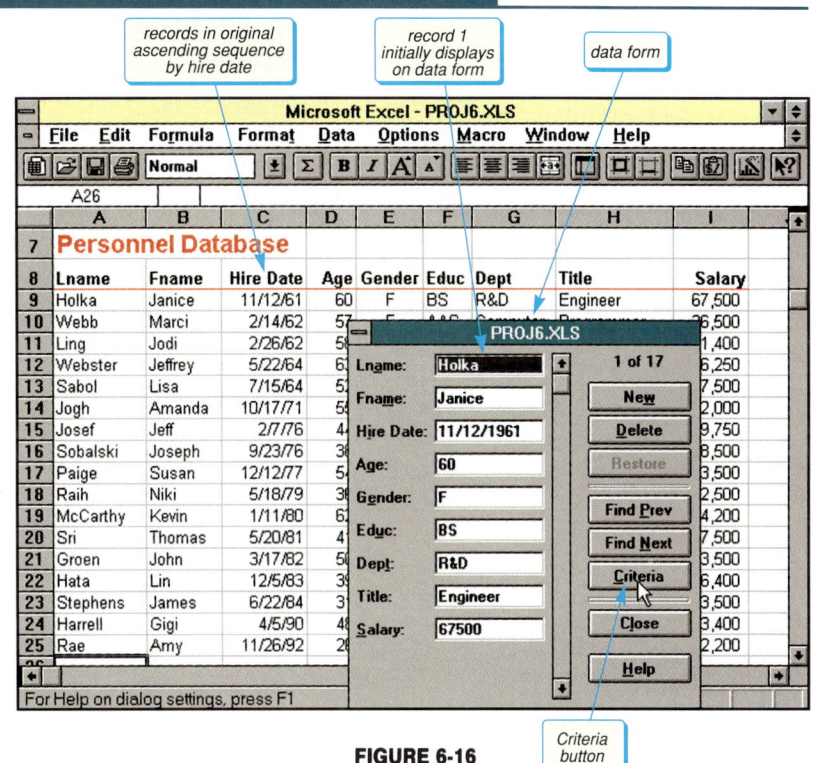

FIGURE 6-16

STEP 2 ▶

Choose the Criteria button from the data form.

Excel displays a data form with blank boxes (Figure 6-17).

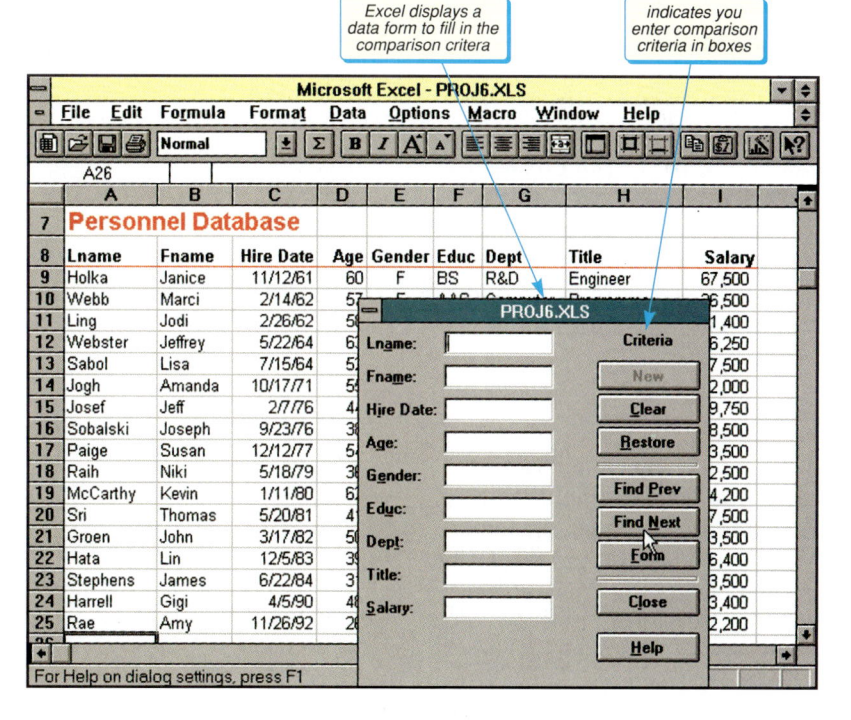

FIGURE 6-17

STEP 3 ▶

Enter >=40 in the Age box, =M in the Gender box, <>AAS in the Educ box, and >40000 in the Salary box.

The data form displays with the comparison criteria as shown in Figure 6-18.

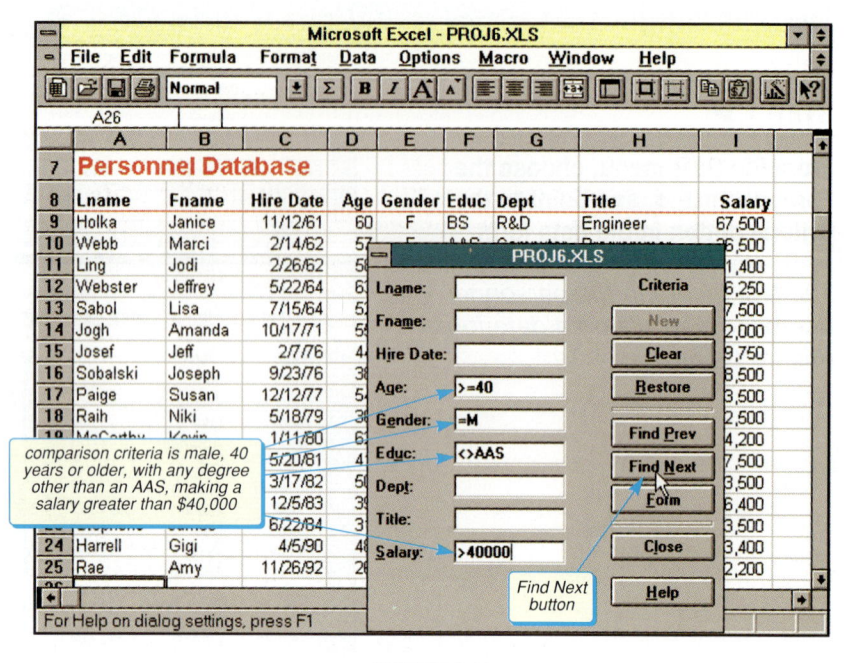

FIGURE 6-18

STEP 4 ▶

Choose the Find Next button from the data form.

Excel immediately displays the first record in the personnel database (record 11) that passes the test (Figure 6-19). Mr. Kevin McCarthy is a 62 year old male with a PhD who earns $74,200. The first 10 records in the personnel database failed the test.

STEP 5

Use the Find Next and Find Prev buttons to display other records in the database that pass the test. When you have finished displaying records, select the Close button from the data form.

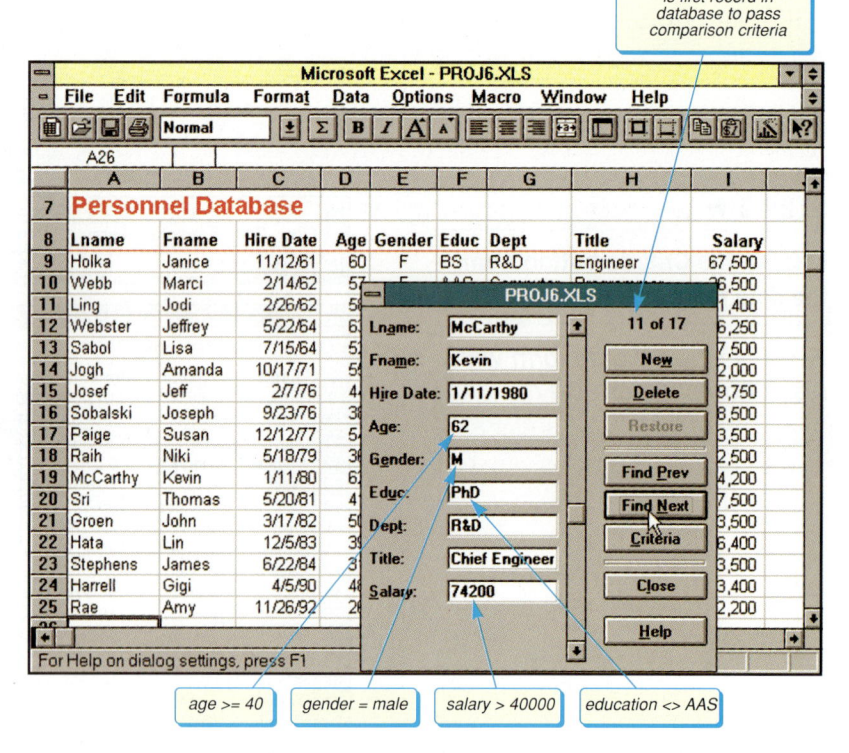

FIGURE 6-19

Three records in the personnel database pass the test: record 11 (Mr. Kevin McCarthy), record 12 (Mr. Thomas Sri), and record 13 (Mr. John Groen). Each time you choose the Find Next button, Excel displays the next record that passes the test. You can also use the Find Prev button to display the previous record that passed the test.

Notice in the comparison criteria established in Figure 6-18, no blank characters appear between the relational operators and the values. Leading or trailing blank characters have a significant impact on text comparisons. For example, there is a big difference between =M and = M.

Excel is not **case sensitive**. That is, Excel considers uppercase and lowercase characters in a criteria comparison to be the same. For example, =m is the same as =M.

Using Wildcard Characters in Comparison Criteria

In text fields you can use wildcard characters to find records that share certain characters in a field. Excel has two **wildcard characters**, the question mark (?) and the asterisk (*). The **question mark (?)** represents any single character in the same position as the question mark. For example, if the comparison criteria for Lname (last name) is =We?b, then any last name passes the test that has the following: We as the first two characters, any third character, and the letter b as the fourth character. Webb (row 10) passes the test.

Use the **asterisk (*)** in a comparison criteria to represent any number of characters in the same position as the asterisk. Jo*, *e, Web*r, are examples of valid text with the asterisk wildcard character. Jo* means all text that begins with the letters Jo. Jogh (row 14) and Josef (row 15) pass the test. The second example, *e, means all text that ends with the letter e. Paige (row 17) and Rae (row 25) pass the test. The third example, Web*r, means all text that begins with the letters Web and ends with the letter r. Webster (row 12) pass the test.

If the comparison criteria calls for searching for a question mark (?) or asterisk (*), precede either one with a tilde (~). For example, to search for the text What?, enter What~? in the comparison criteria.

Using Computed Criteria

A **computed criteria** involves using a formula in a criteria. For example, the computed criterion formula =Age <Salary / 1000 in the Age field on a data form for the personnel database would find all records whose Age field is less than the corresponding Salary field divided by 1000.

▶ CREATING A CRITERIA RANGE ON THE WORKSHEET

Rather than use a data form to establish criteria, you can set up a **criteria range** on the worksheet and use it to manipulate records that pass the comparison criteria. To set up a criteria range, you copy the database field names to another area of the worksheet (preferably above the database in case it is expanded downward or to the right in the future). Next, you enter the comparison criteria in the row immediately below the field names. You then use the Set Criteria command on the Data menu to define the field names and comparison criteria as a criteria range. The following steps show how to set up criteria in the range A2:I3 to find records that pass the test: Gender = M and Age > 40 and Salary <50000.

E304 PROJECT 6 SORTING AND QUERYING A WORKSHEET DATABASE

TO SET UP A CRITERIA RANGE ON THE WORKSHEET

STEP 1 ▶

Select the database title and field names in the range A7:I8. Click the Copy tool on the Standard toolbar. Select cell A1. Press the ENTER key to copy the contents on the Clipboard to the range A1:I2. Change the title in cell A1 from Personnel Database to Criteria Area. Enter >40 in cell D3. Enter M in cell E3. Enter <50000 in cell I3. Select the range A2:I3.

criteria range includes field names and comparison criteria

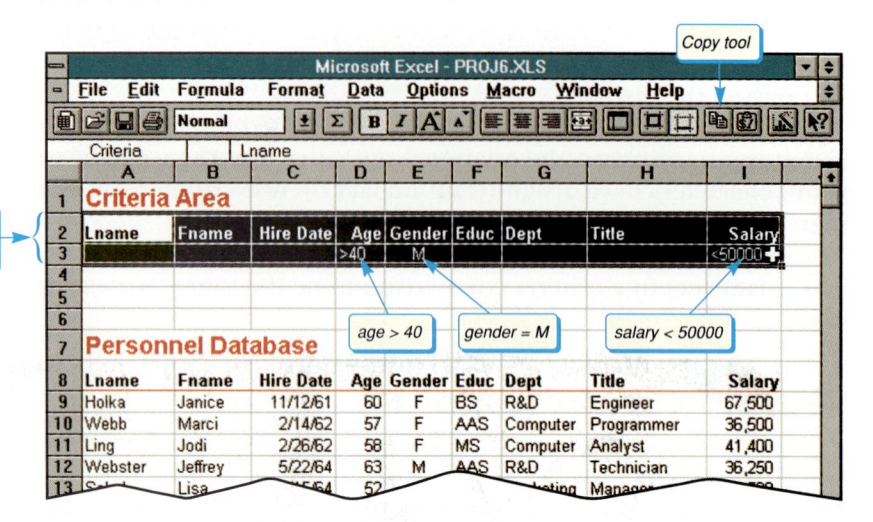

FIGURE 6-20

The worksheet in Figure 6-20 displays. Notice the criteria range title in cell A1 is not part of the criteria range.

STEP 2 ▶

Select the Data menu and point to the Set Criteria command.

The Data menu displays (Figure 6-21).

criteria range highlighted

STEP 3 ▶

Choose the Set Criteria command from the Data menu.

Excel defines the range A2:I3 as a criteria range and assigns it the name Criteria.

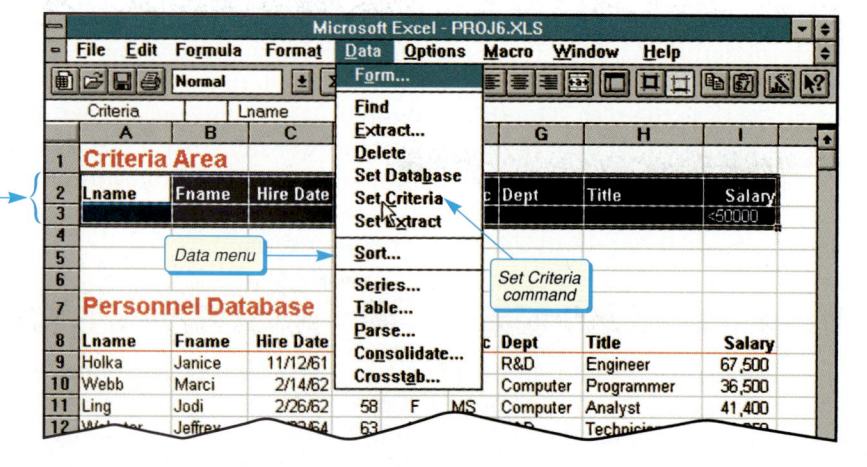

FIGURE 6-21

Here are some important points to remember about setting up a criteria range: (1) do not begin a test for equality involving text (Gender = M) with an equal sign because Excel will assume the text (M) is a range name rather than text; (2) if you include a blank row in the criteria range (for example, rows 2 and 3 and the blank row 4), all records will pass the test; (3) to ensure the field names in the criteria range are spelled exactly the same as in the database, use the Copy command to copy the database field names to the criteria range; (4) the criteria range is independent of the criteria set up in a data form; and (5) you can print the criteria range by using the Goto command in the same way here as discussed earlier for printing a database range (see page E296).

▶ FINDING RECORDS

The Find command on the Data menu is similar to the Find Next button on a data form. You use it to find records in the database (A8:I25) that pass the test established in the criteria range (A2:I3). Follow these steps to find the records that pass the test (Gender = M and Age > 40 and Salary < 50000) defined in the previous set of steps and shown in Figure 6-20.

TO FIND RECORDS USING A CRITERIA RANGE ▼

STEP 1

Select any cell (such as cell E5) above the database so the Find command begins with the first record.

STEP 2 ▶

Select the Data menu and point to the Find command.

The Data menu displays (Figure 6-22).

FIGURE 6-22

STEP 3 ▶

Choose the Find command from the Data menu.

Excel highlights the first record (top screen in Figure 6-23) that passes the test in the criteria range.

STEP 4 ▶

Press the DOWN ARROW key to find the next record.

Excel highlights the next record (middle screen in Figure 6-23) that passes the test in the criteria range.

STEP 5 ▶

Press the DOWN ARROW key to find the next record.

Excel highlights the next record (bottom screen in Figure 6-23) that passes the test in the criteria range.

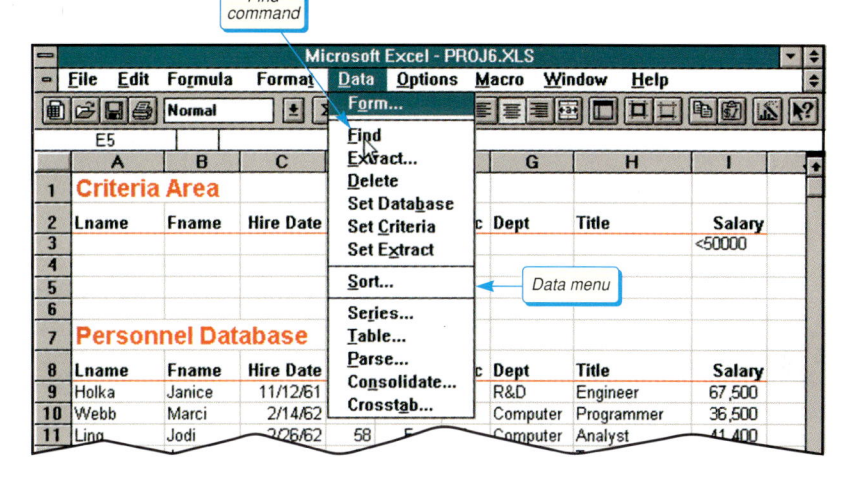

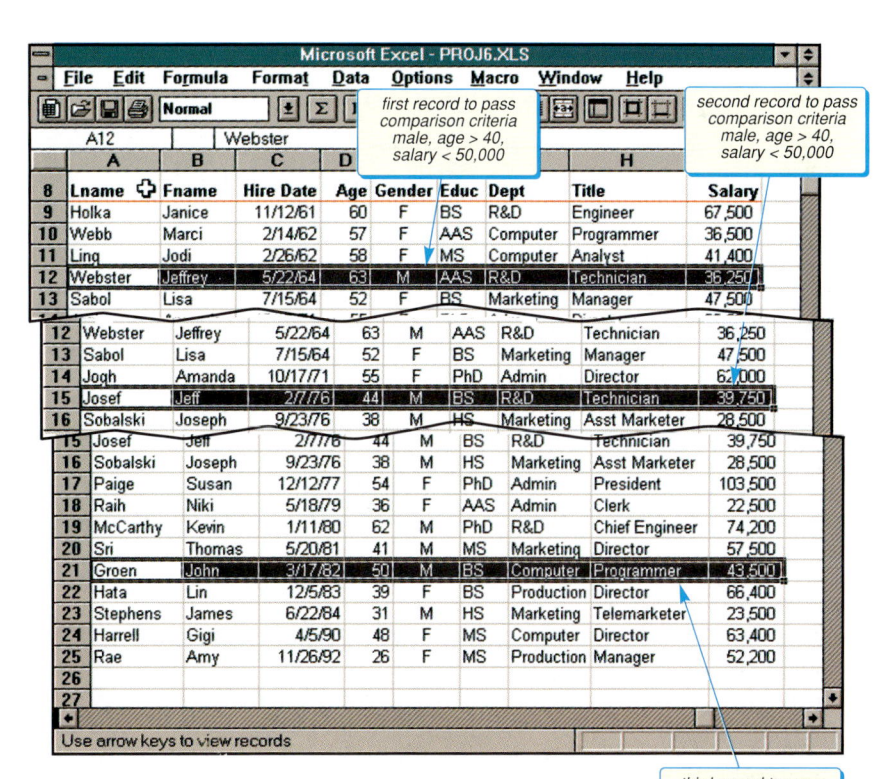

FIGURE 6-23

Continue with Step 5 until there are no more records in the database that pass the test in the criteria range. Use the UP ARROW key to display the previous record that passed the test. Choose the Exit Find command from the Data menu or press the ESC key to terminate the Find command.

When Excel highlights a record that passes the test in the criteria range, you can modify the record by choosing any command in the menus or you can change the field values. For example, you can insert a new row above the selected record, delete the selected record, reformat the selected record, or print the selected record. To move from field to field in a selected record, use the TAB and SHIFT+TAB keys or the mouse. If you select a field in the highlighted record or choose any command, Excel automatically terminates the Find command.

▶ EXTRACTING RECORDS

The Extract command on the Data menu copies records or individual fields from the database to another part of the worksheet called the **extract range**. The records that are copied must pass the test in the criteria range. As shown in Figure 6-24, you can extract those records (Gender = M and Age > 40 and Salary < 50000) that were individually selected in the steps on the previous page. Once the records that pass the test in the criteria range are extracted, you can manipulate and print them as a group by using the Goto and Set Print Area commands.

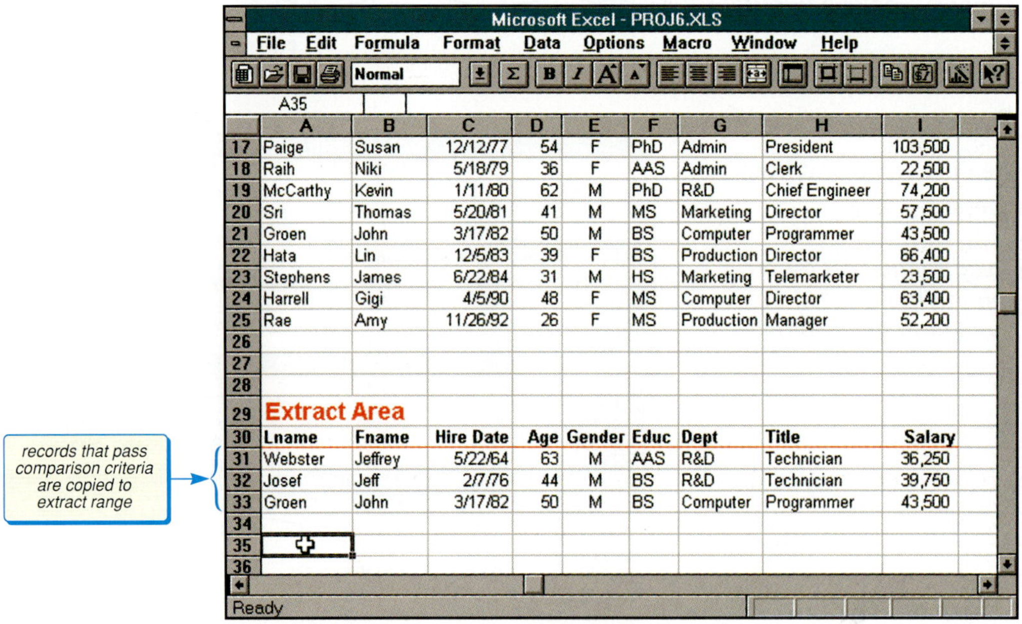

FIGURE 6-24

Creating the Extract Range

To create an extract range you perform the steps in the same manner shown earlier for a criteria range. That is, you copy the field names of the database to an area on the worksheet, preferably well below the database range. Next, you define the cells containing the field names as the extract range by using the Set Extract command on the Data menu. Finally, you use the Extract command on the Data menu to extract the records. The steps at the top of the next page show how to set up an extract range below the personnel database.

TO CREATE AN EXTRACT RANGE ON THE WORKSHEET

STEP 1 ▶

Select the database title and field names in the range A7:I8. Click the Copy tool on the Standard toolbar. Select cell A29. Press the ENTER key to copy the contents on the Clipboard to the range A29:I30. Change the title in cell A29 from Personnel Database to Extract Area. Select the range A30:I30. Select the Data menu and point to the Set Extract command.

The worksheet displays as shown in Figure 6-25. Notice that the extract range is defined as only the field names in row 30. Excel will automatically copy the records to the rows below the defined extract range.

STEP 2 ▶

Choose the Set Extract command from the Data menu.

Excel defines the range A30:I30 as the extract range and assigns it the name Extract.

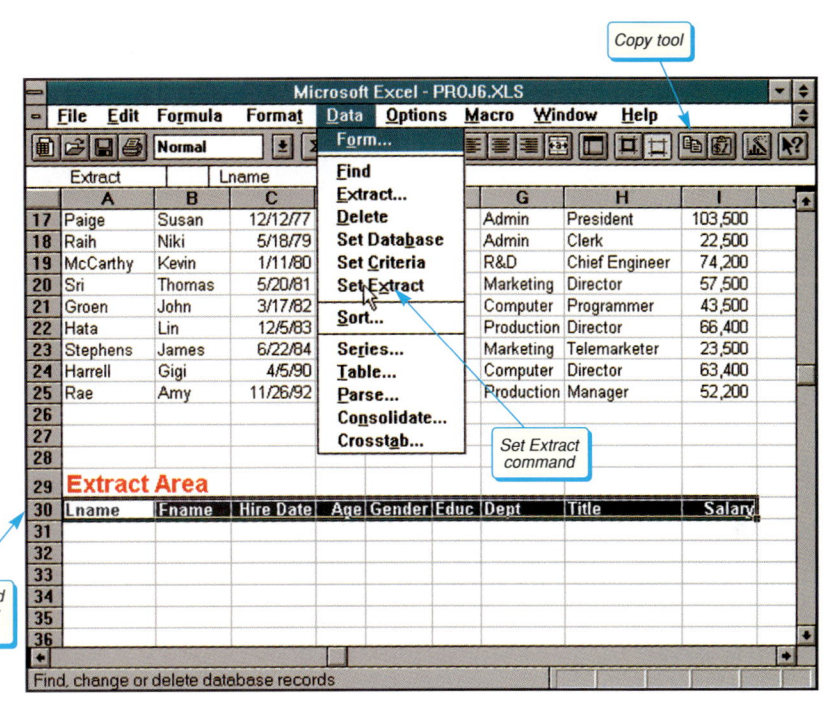

FIGURE 6-25

When you set up the extract range, you do not have to copy all the field names in the database to the proposed extract range. You can copy only those field names you want and they can be in any order. You can also type the field names rather than copy them, but it is not recommended.

Extracting Records to an Extract Range

The Extract command on the Data menu will work only if you have defined a database range, a criteria range, and an extract range. The following example uses the same database range (A8:I25) and criteria range (A2:I3) used earlier with the Find command. That is, in the example on the next page Excel will extract those records from the personnel database that pass the test: Gender = M and Age > 40 and Salary < 50000. The criteria range is shown in Figure 6-20 on page E304.

TO EXTRACT RECORDS

STEP 1 ▶

Select the Data menu and point to the Extract command.

The Data menu displays as shown in Figure 6-26.

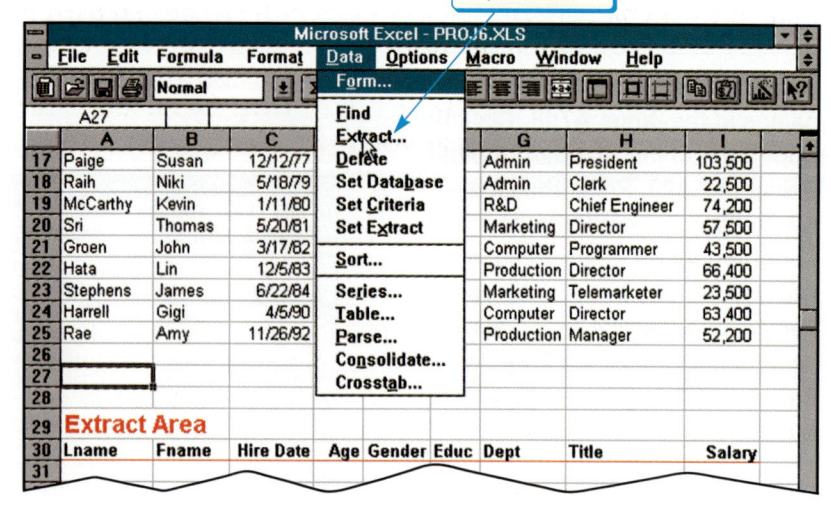

FIGURE 6-26

STEP 2 ▶

Choose the Extract command from the Data menu.

Excel displays the Extract dialog box (Figure 6-27).

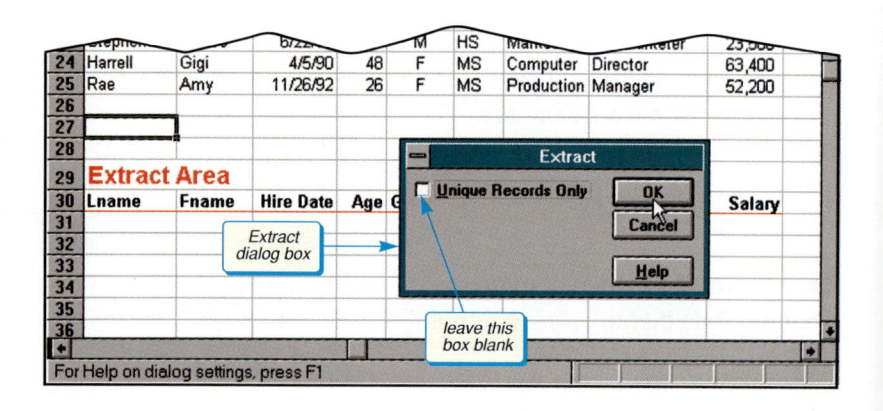

FIGURE 6-27

STEP 3 ▶

Choose the OK button from the Extract dialog box.

Excel copies the records from the personnel database that pass the test described in the criteria range to the extract range (Figure 6-28).

FIGURE 6-28

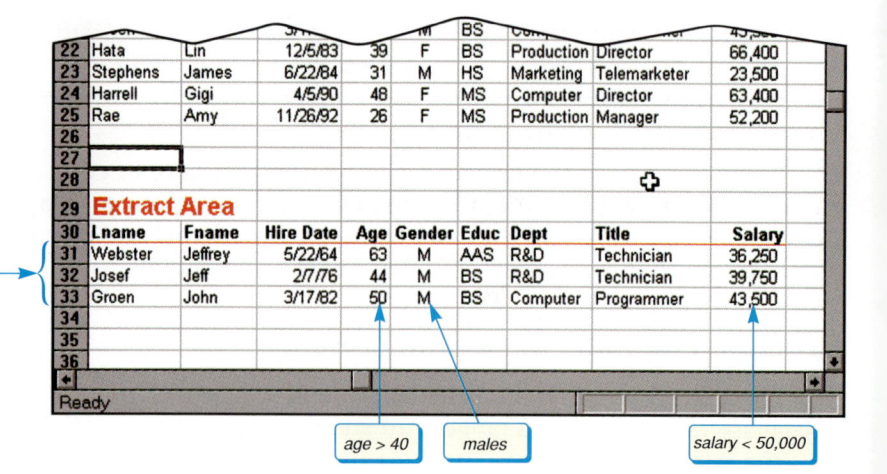

When you invoke the Extract command, Excel clears all the cells below the field names in the extract range. Hence, if you change the comparison criteria in the criteria range and invoke the Extract command a second time, Excel clears the original extracted records before it copies the records that pass the new test.

In the previous example, the extract range was defined as a single row containing the field names (A30:I30). When you define the extract range as one row long (the field names), any number of records can be extracted from the database because Excel will use all the rows below row 30 to the bottom of the worksheet. The alternative is to define an extract range with a fixed number of rows. However, if you define a fixed-size extract range and if more records are extracted than there are rows available, Excel displays a dialog box with the diagnostic message "Extract range is full."

▶ DELETING RECORDS

The **Delete command** on the Data menu deletes all records that pass the test established in the criteria range. Although this project does not involve the deletion of records, the following steps show you how to carry out the delete operation.

TO DELETE RECORDS

Step 1: Click the Save File tool to save the worksheet.
Step 2: With the database range and criteria range defined, choose the Delete command from the Data menu.
Step 3: When Excel displays the dialog box warning you that records that pass the test in the criteria range will be deleted, choose the OK button.

Excel immediately deletes the records that pass the test in the criteria range and moves up records to fill gaps. Excel does not allow you to undo a delete operation. Thus, the save operation in Step 1 protects you in case you make a mistake and delete records you don't want to delete.

▶ MORE ABOUT COMPARISON CRITERIA

The way you set up the comparison criteria in the criteria range determines the records that will pass the test when you use the Find command, Extract command, or Delete command. The following describes examples of different comparison criteria.

A Blank Row in the Criteria Range

If the criteria range contains a blank row, then all the records in the database pass the test. For example, the blank row in the criteria range in Figure 6-29 causes all records to pass the test.

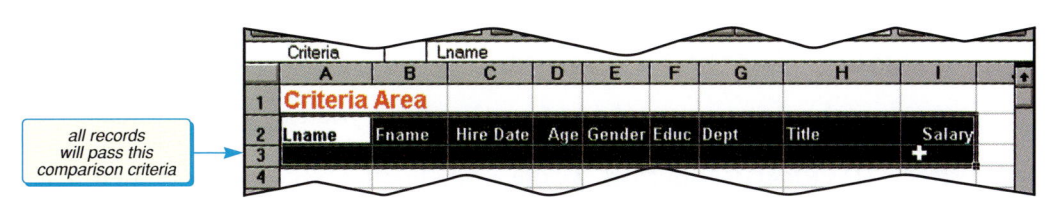

FIGURE 6-29

Using Multiple Comparison Criteria with the Same Field

If the criteria range contains two or more entries under the same field name, then records that pass either comparison criteria pass the test. For example, the criteria range in Figure 6-30 causes all records that represent personnel that have an AAS degree **or** a BS degree to pass the test.

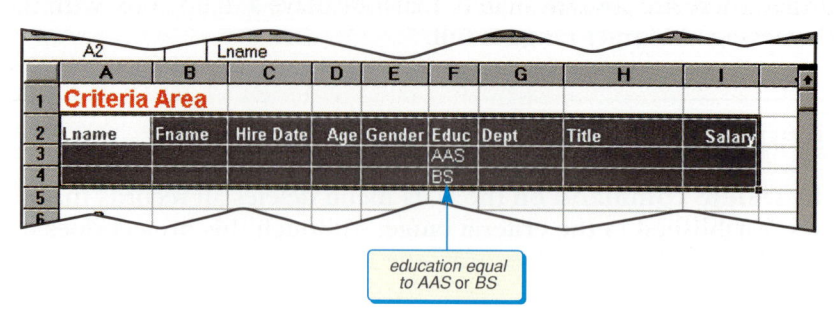

FIGURE 6-30

If an AND applies to the same field name (Age > 50 AND Age < 55) then you must duplicate the field name (Age) in the criteria range.

Comparison Criteria in Different Rows and Under Different Fields

When the comparison criteria under different field names are in the same row, then records pass the test only if they pass **all** the comparison criteria. If the comparison criteria for the field names are in different rows, then the records must pass only one of the tests. For example, in the criteria range in Figure 6-31, all records that represent personnel who are less than 40 years old **or** earn more than $70,000 pass the test.

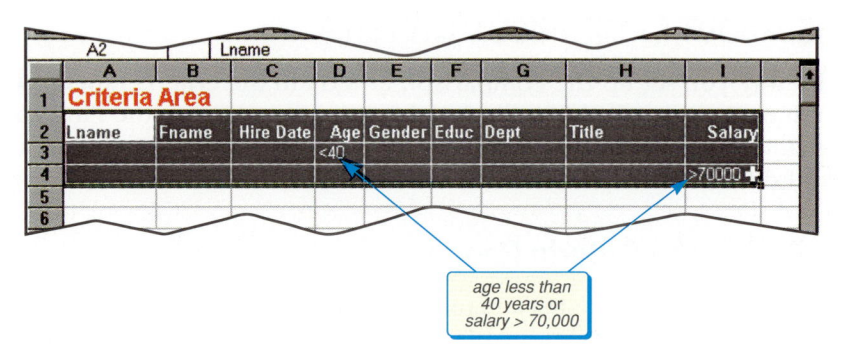

FIGURE 6-31

▶ Using Database Functions

Excel has twelve **database functions** that you can use to evaluate numeric data in a database. One of the functions is called the **DAVERAGE function**. As the name implies, you use the DAVERAGE function to find the average of numbers in a database field that pass a test. The general form of the DAVERAGE function is

=DAVERAGE(database, "field name", criteria range)

where database is the name of the database, field name is the name of the field in the database, and criteria range is the criteria or test to pass. In the following steps the DAVERAGE function is used to find the average age of the female employees and the average age of the male employees in the personnel database (see Figure 6-32).

TO USE THE DAVERAGE DATABASE FUNCTION

Step 1: Enter the field name `Gender` twice, once in cell K1 and again in cell L1. Enter the code for females `F` in cell K2. Enter the code for males `M` in cell L2.

Step 2: Enter `Average Female Age` in cell M1. Enter `Average Male Age` in cell M2.

Step 3: Enter the database function `=daverage(database, "Age", K1:K2)` in cell O1.

Step 4: Enter the database function `=daverage(database, "Age", L1:L2)` in cell O2.

Excel computes and displays the average age of the females in the personnel database in cell O1 and the average age of the males in the personnel database in cell O2 (Figure 6-32).

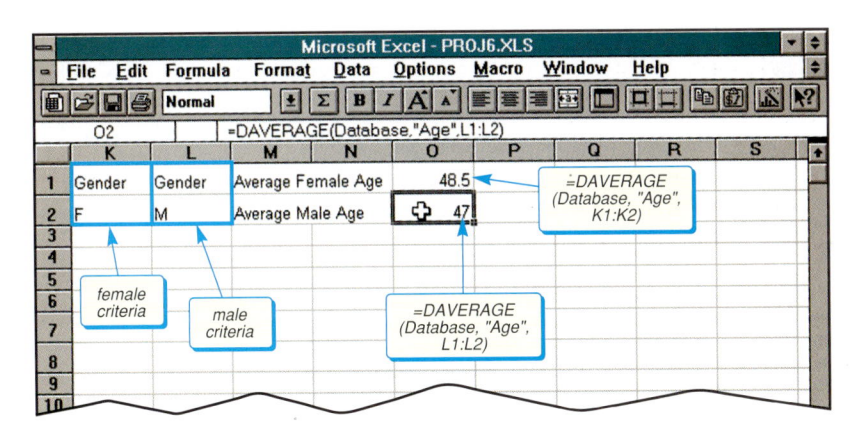

FIGURE 6-32

Notice in Figure 6-32 the first value (database) in the function references the personnel database defined earlier in this project (A8:I25). The second value ("Age") identifies the field on which to compute the average. Excel requires that you surround the field name with quotation marks unless the field has been assigned a name through the Define Name command. The third value (K1:K2 for the female average) defines the criteria range. Finally, the database functions do not require that you use the Set Criteria command because the third value in the database function carries out the task of defining the criteria range. However, if you want to use the defined criteria range (A2:I3), then use the name Criteria as the third value in the database function.

Other database functions that are similar to the functions described in previous projects include the DCOUNT, DMAX, DMIN, and DSUM functions. For a complete list of the database functions, choose the Paste Function command from the Formula menu and select the Database category.

USING THE CROSSTAB REPORTWIZARD TO SUMMARIZE DATABASE INFORMATION

A **crosstab table**, also called a **cross-tabulation table**, is a table that shows summaries for fields in the database. You can create the crosstab table on the same worksheet with the database or you can create it on a new worksheet.

The **Crosstab command** on the Data menu starts the **Crosstab ReportWizard**, which guides you through creating a crosstab table. The Crosstab ReportWizard does not modify the database in any way. It uses the data in the database to generate information.

The crosstab table that you will create in this section is shown in Figure 6-33. The table summarizes salary information by gender and department for the personnel database built earlier in this project (A8:I25). To create the crosstab table in Figure 6-33, you need to only enter three values when requested by the Crosstab ReportWizard: the row categories; the column categories; and the value field.

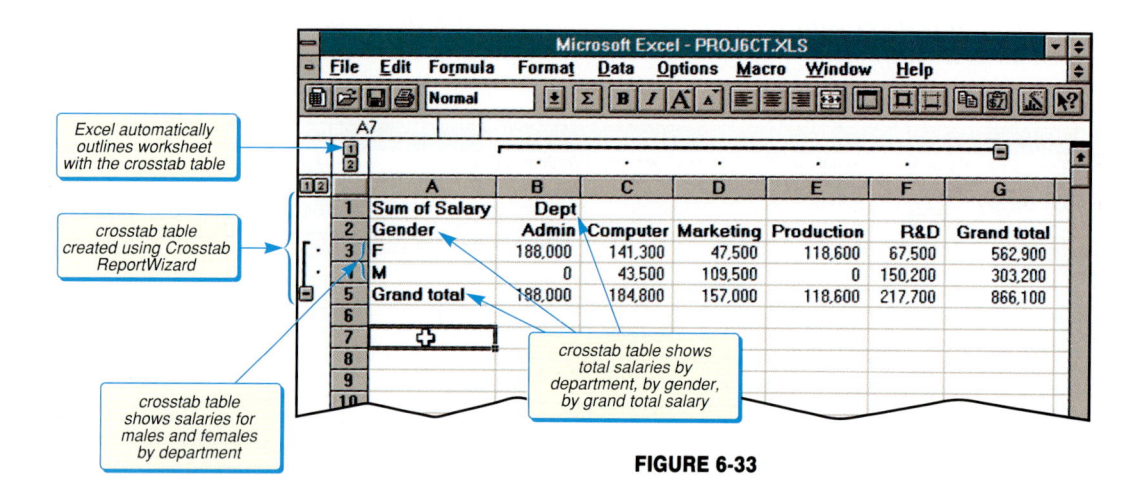

FIGURE 6-33

In Figure 6-33, the **row category** is the Gender field in the database — female (F) and male (M). The **column category** is the Dept field — Admin, Computer, Marketing, Production, and R&D. The **value field** is the Salary field. Grand total salaries automatically display for the row and column categories in row 5 and in column G. For example, from the table in Figure 6-33, you can see in the Computer department, the female employees are paid a total salary of 141,300, while the male employees are paid a salary of 43,500. Column G shows that all females in the company are paid 562,900 and all males are paid 303,200. The total company salary, 866,100, displays in cell G5.

Usually when you summarize a database, you want to process all the records. Like other database commands, the Crosstab ReportWizard uses the current criteria range to determine which records to process. Thus, before starting the Crosstab ReportWizard, it is important to check the criteria range in the worksheet to ensure all records will be processed. In the previous section, you were told that a blank row in the criteria range causes all records to pass the test in the criteria range. The comparison criteria in the criteria range (A2:I3) is still set to Age > 40 and Gender = M and Salary 50000 (Figure 6-20 on page E304). One way to create a blank row in the criteria range is to clear the cells in row 3.

To create the crosstab table shown in Figure 6-33, perform the steps on the following four pages.

USING THE CROSSTAB REPORTWIZARD TO SUMMARIZE DATABASE INFORMATION   **E313**

TO CREATE A CROSSTAB TABLE

STEP 1 ▶

Select the criteria range A3:I3. From the Edit menu, choose the Clear command to clear the comparison criteria. When the Clear dialog box displays, choose the OK button.

Excel clears the range A3:I3 in the criteria range (Figure 6-34).

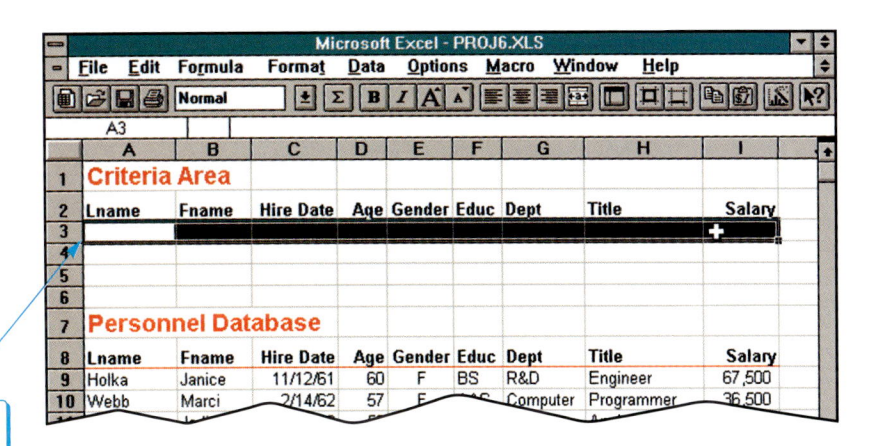

FIGURE 6-34

STEP 2 ▶

Select the Data menu and point to the Crosstab command.

The Data menu displays (Figure 6-35).

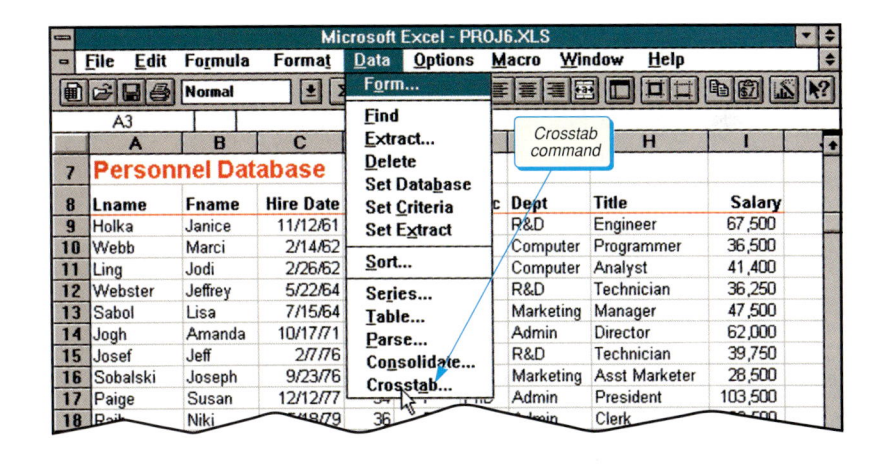

FIGURE 6-35

STEP 3 ▶

Choose the Crosstab command from the Data menu.

The Crosstab ReportWizard – Introduction screen displays (Figure 6-36). To obtain additional information on the Crosstab ReportWizard, you can choose the Explain button (Explain) in the lower left corner of the screen.

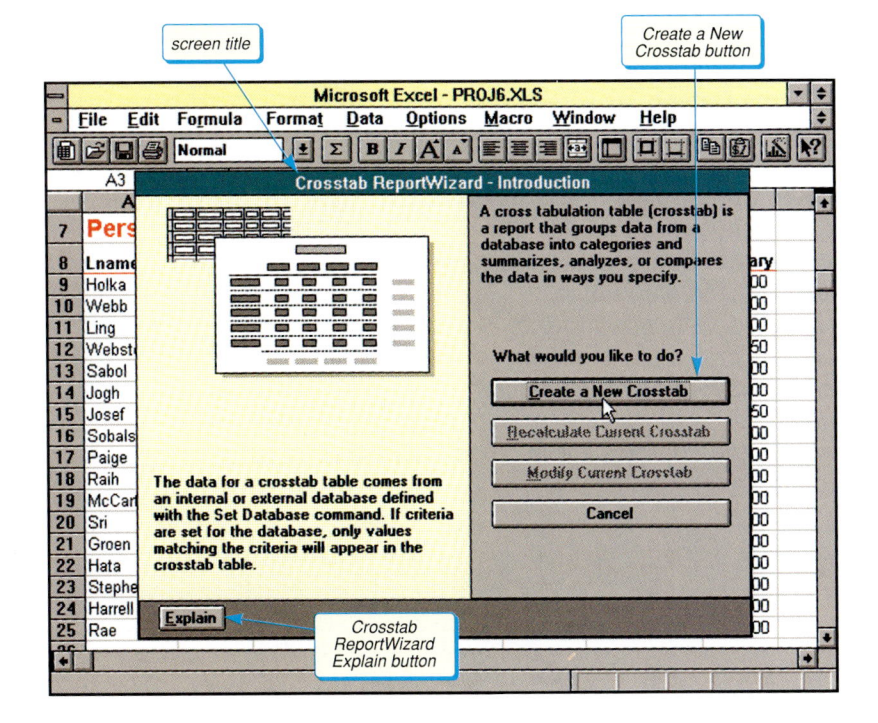

FIGURE 6-36

E314 PROJECT 6 SORTING AND QUERYING A WORKSHEET DATABASE

STEP 4 ▶

Choose the Create a New Crosstab button from the Crosstab ReportWizard – Introduction screen. Select the Gender field in the Fields in Database box. Choose the Add button (Add). Point to the Next> button.

Excel displays the Crosstab ReportWizard – Row Categories screen (Figure 6-37). When you choose the Add button, the Crosstab ReportWizard adds the Gender field to the Include as Row Categories box. The diagram in the upper left corner of the screen shows you that this screen is for entering the field name you want to categorize down the rows in the crosstab table.

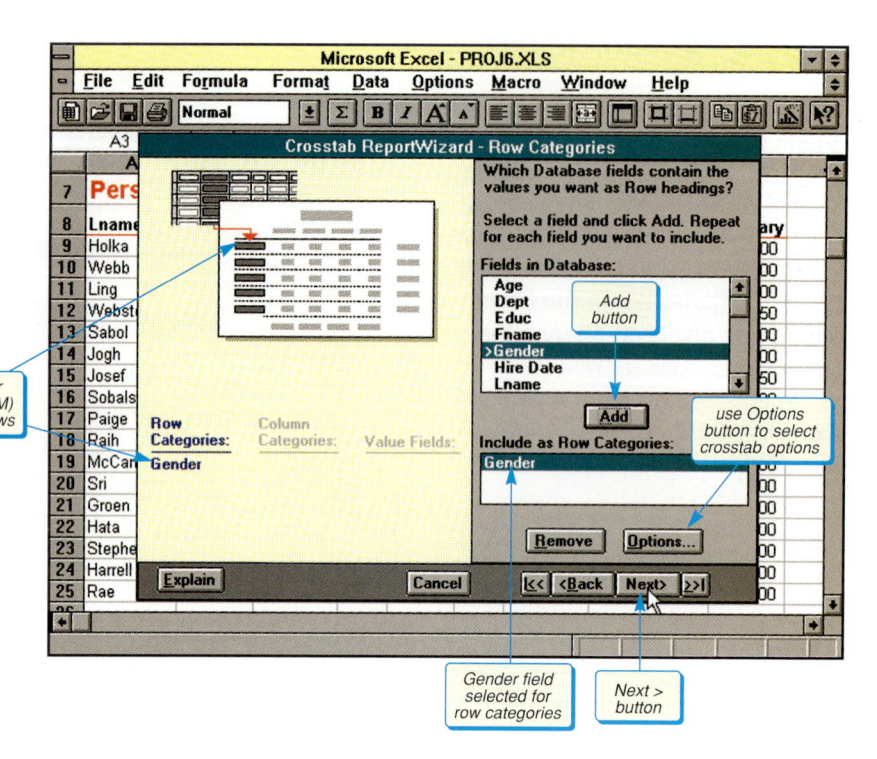

FIGURE 6-37

STEP 5 ▶

Choose the Next> button from the Crosstab ReportWizard – Row Categories screen. Select the Dept field in the Fields in Database box. Choose the Add button. Point to the Next> button.

The Crosstab ReportWizard – Column Categories screen displays (Figure 6-38). When you choose the Add button, the Crosstab ReportWizard adds the Dept field to the Include as Column Categories box. The diagram in the upper left corner of the screen shows you that this screen is for entering the field name you want to categorize across the columns in the crosstab table.

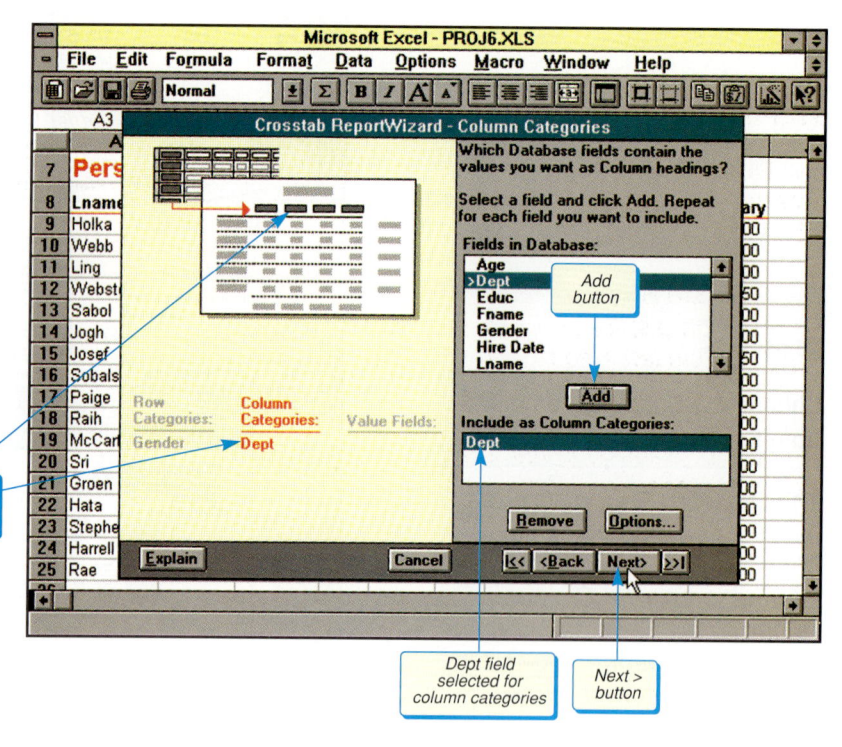

FIGURE 6-38

USING THE CROSSTAB REPORTWIZARD TO SUMMARIZE DATABASE INFORMATION **E315**

STEP 6 ▶

Choose the Next> button from the Crosstab ReportWizard – Column Categories screen. Select the Salary field in the Fields in Database box. Choose the Add button. Point to the Next> button.

The Crosstab ReportWizard – Value Fields screen displays (Figure 6-39). When you choose the Add button, the Crosstab ReportWizard adds the Salary field to the Calculate Values from box. The diagram in the upper left corner of the screen shows you that this screen is for entering the field name you want to summarize in the crosstab table.

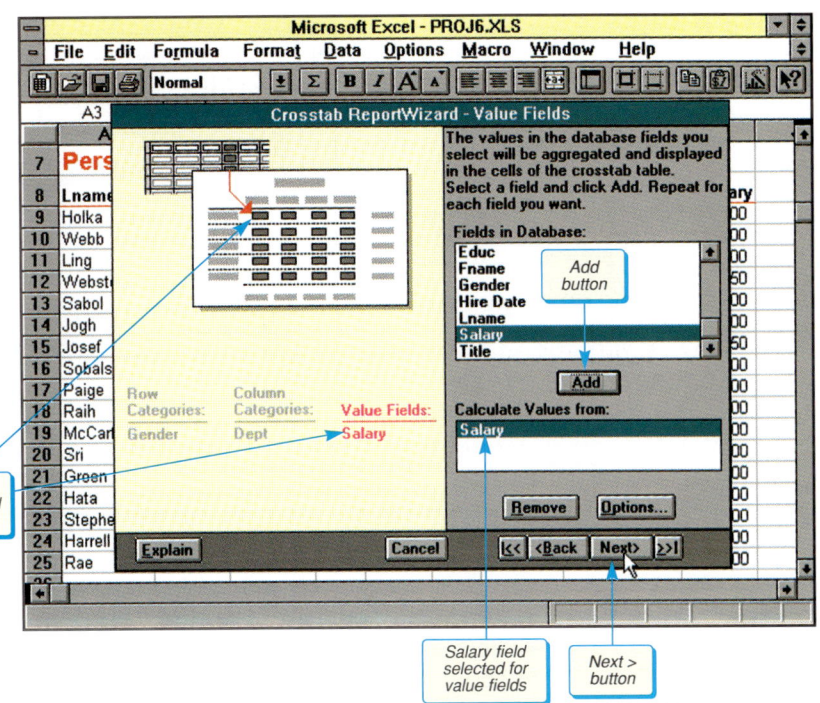

FIGURE 6-39

STEP 7 ▶

Choose the Next> button from the Crosstab ReportWizard – Value Fields screen.

The Crosstab ReportWizard – Final screen displays (Figure 6-40). On the left side of the screen, the Crosstab ReportWizard displays the field names selected in Steps 4, 5, and 6 for the row categories, column categories, and value fields.

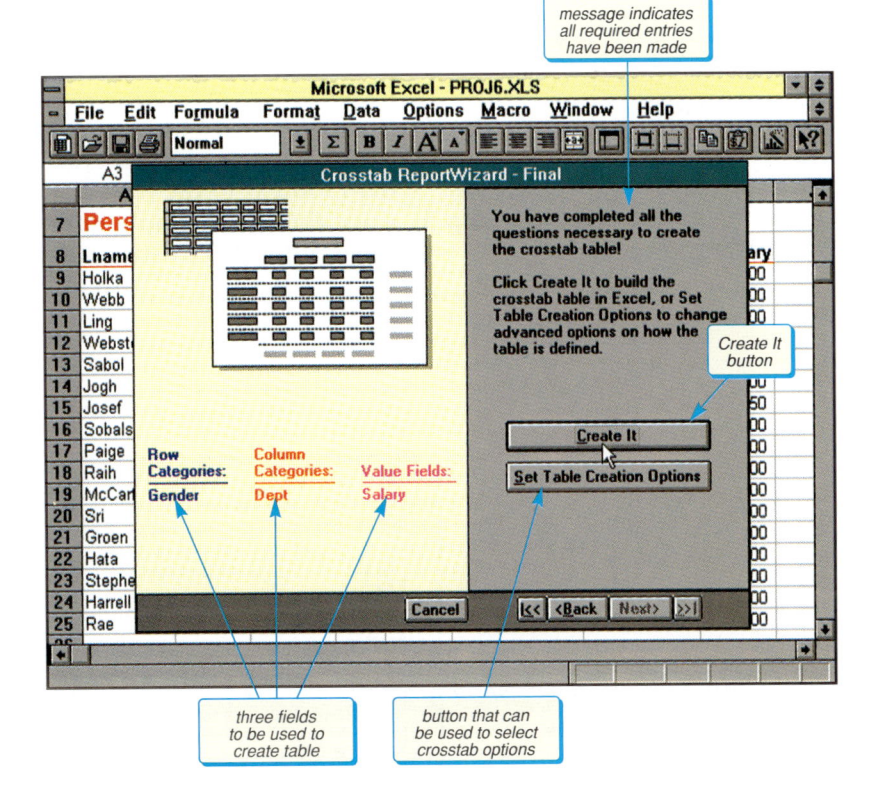

FIGURE 6-40

E316 PROJECT 6 SORTING AND QUERYING A WORKSHEET DATABASE

STEP 8 ▶

Choose the Create It button from the Crosstab ReportWizard – Final screen and select any cell.

The Crosstab ReportWizard creates and displays the crosstab table on a new worksheet (Figure 6-41).

FIGURE 6-41

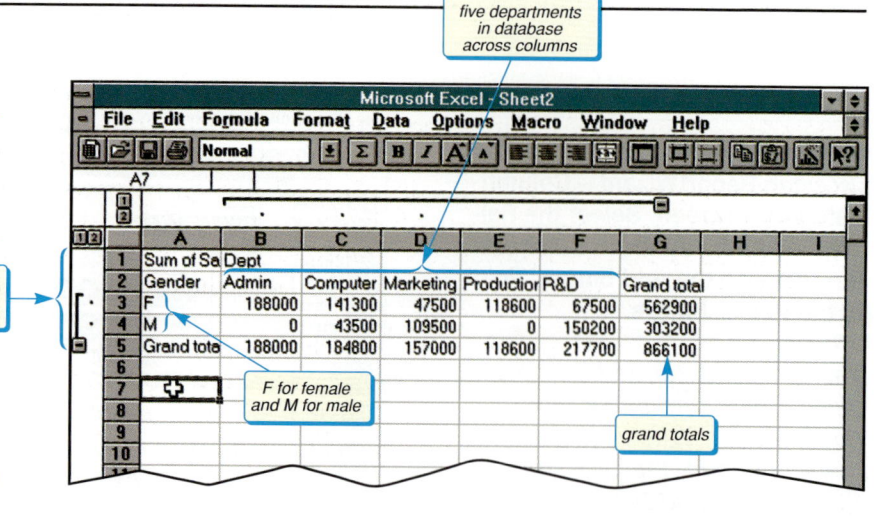

Because the crosstab table contains subtotals, the Crosstab ReportWizard automatically creates an outline based on row and column totals. Recall from Project 4 that the outline symbols allow you to expand and collapse the outline to show the detail lines or only the summary lines.

The final step is to format and save the crosstab table (see Figure 6-42).

TO FORMAT AND SAVE THE CROSSTAB TABLE

Step 1: Bold the ranges A1:A5 and B1:G2.
Step 2: Change the column widths as follows: A = 14.14, B = 9, C = 9.57, D = 10.57, E = 11.14, and G = 12. Leave column F at 8.43 characters.
Step 3: Right-align the headings in columns B through G.
Step 4: Assign the Comma (0) format style from the Style box on the Standard toolbar to the range B3:G5.
Step 5: Click the Save File tool on the Standard toolbar to save the worksheet with the crosstab table. Use the file name PROJ6CT.

The worksheet with the crosstab table displays as shown in Figure 6-42.

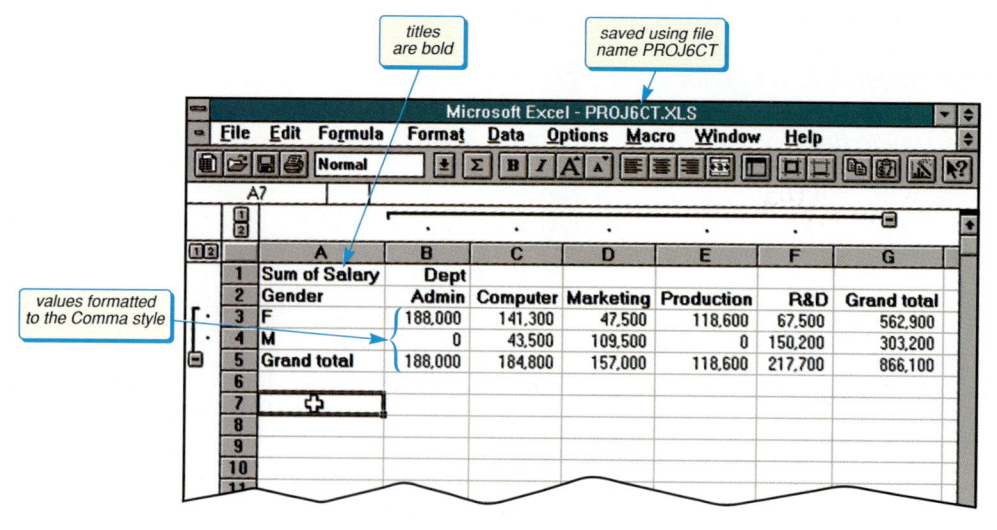

FIGURE 6-42

The following summarizes the important points regarding the CrossTab ReportWizard. First, before using the Crosstab ReportWizard, you must determine the field names in the database you want to use for: (a) the row category; (b) column category; and (c) field value. Second, any time you use a Data menu command that operates on the records in the database, Excel uses the current criteria range as a filter to process only those records that pass the test. Hence, if you want to process all the records in the database, make sure only a blank row exists in the criteria range.

Third, you can select Crosstab ReportWizard options on each of the Crosstab ReportWizard screens after the introductory screen. For example, the Set Table Creation Options button on the final screen (Figure 6-40) allows you to build the crosstab table in the same worksheet as the database. Fourth, you can use the Crosstab ReportWizard to create, recalculate after changing data in the database, or modify a crosstab table.

Fifth, the Crosstab ReportWizard screens have buttons at the bottom that allow you to back up to a previous screen, advance forward to the next screen, and create the crosstab table with the information given thus far. Table 6-2 summarizes the function of the buttons on the Crosstab ReportWizard screens.

▸ **TABLE 6-2**

BUTTON	FUNCTION
Explain	Displays more information about the current step.
Cancel	Closes the Crosstab ReportWizard without creating the crosstab table.
|<<	Returns back to the beginning of the Crosstab ReportWizard.
<Back	Goes back to the previous step.
Next>	Goes to the next step.
>>|	Goes to the final screen of the Crosstab ReportWizard using the selections made thus far.

▸ **PROJECT SUMMARY**

In Project 6 you learned how to create, sort, and query a database. Creating a database involves defining a section of the worksheet as a database range by using the Set Database command. You added, changed, and deleted records in a database through a data form. Querying a database involves finding, extracting, or deleting records that pass a test. You learned to use database functions and the Crosstab ReportWizard to generate information from the database.

▸ **KEY TERMS**

ascending sequence (*E296*)
asterisk (*) wildcard (*E303*)
case sensitive (*E303*)
column category (*E312*)
comparison criteria (*E300*)
computed criteria (*E303*)
criteria range (*E303*)
cross-tabulation table (*E312*)
Crosstab command (*E312*)
Crosstab ReportWizard (*E312*)
crosstab table (*E312*)
data form (*E290*)
Data menu (*E290*)
database (*E288*)
database function (*E310*)

database range (*E290*)
data type (*E289*)
DAVERAGE function (*E310*)
Delete command (*E309*)
descending sequence (*E296*)
Extract command (*E308*)
Extract dialog box (*E308*)
extract range (*E306*)
field (*E288*)
field name (*E288*)
Find command (*E305*)
Form command (*E292*)
question mark (?) wildcard (*E303*)

record (*E288*)
row category (*E312*)
Set Criteria command (*E304*)
Set Database command (*E290*)
Set Extract command (*E307*)
Sort Ascending tool (*E298*)
Sort command (*E297*)
Sort Descending tool (*E298*)
Sort dialog box (*E297*)
sort key (*E296*)
sorting (*E296*)
value field (*E312*)
wildcard characters (*E303*)
worksheet database (*E288*)

QUICK REFERENCE

The following table provides a quick reference to each task presented in this project with its available options. The commands listed in the Menu column can be executed using either the keyboard or mouse.

Task	Mouse	Menu
Create Criteria Range		From Data menu, choose Set Criteria
Create Database		From Data menu, choose Set Database
Create Extract Range		From Data menu, choose Set Extract
Crosstab Table		From Data menu, choose Crosstab
Data Form		From Data menu, choose Form
Delete Records		From Data menu, choose Delete
Extract Records		From Data menu, choose Extract
Find Records		From Data menu, choose Find
Sort	Click Sort Ascending tool or Sort Descending tool on Utility toolbar	From Data menu, choose Sort

STUDENT ASSIGNMENTS

STUDENT ASSIGNMENT 1
True/False

Instructions: Circle T if the statement is true or F if the statement is false.

T F 1. The series of numbers 1, 2, 3, 4, 5, 6 is in descending sequence.
T F 2. The column headings in a database are used as field names.
T F 3. When you create a database using the Set Database command, select only the row that contains the field names.
T F 4. A data form is not a dialog box.
T F 5. To add a new record to the database using a data form, select the New button.
T F 6. Excel treats dates as text.
T F 7. Excel allows you to sort on up to four sort keys at a time.
T F 8. A criteria range consisting of field names and empty cells below the field names will cause Excel to process all the records in the database.
T F 9. The wildcard character asterisk (*) can only be used at the end of text that is part of the comparison criteria.
T F 10. Excel allows you to sort rows or columns.

E318

T F 11. In the phrase "sort age within seniority within trade," age is the major key.
T F 12. To find records that pass a test using a data form, you first must set up a criteria range in the worksheet.
T F 13. To extract records, you must define a criteria range.
T F 14. Excel is not case sensitive when evaluating comparison criteria.
T F 15. When you use the Delete command to delete records in a database, Excel clears the cells but does not move records up.
T F 16. The DAVERAGE function is used to find the average of numbers in a database field that pass a test.
T F 17. Use the Crosstab command on the Data menu to start the Crosstab ReportWizard.
T F 18. Blank characters are significant in text-type comparison criteria.
T F 19. The criteria range in a worksheet is independent of the criteria set up in a data form.
T F 20. Each time you add a record to a database, Excel expands the database range by one row.

STUDENT ASSIGNMENT 2
Multiple Choice

Instructions: Circle the correct response.

1. Which one of the following commands on the Data menu highlights (selects) records that pass a test defined in a criteria range?
   a. Extract
   b. Find
   c. Crosstab
   d. Form

2. Which one of the following characters when used in comparison criteria represents *any character in the same position*?
   a. tilde (~)
   b. number sign (#)
   c. asterisk (*)
   d. question mark (?)

3. To copy all records that pass a test defined in a criteria range, use the _____ command on the Data menu.
   a. Extract
   b. Find
   c. Delete
   d. Form

4. When a data form is first opened, Excel displays the _____ record in the database.
   a. first
   b. last
   c. blank
   d. second

5. If you make a mistake and sort a database on the wrong field, immediately select the _____ command from the Edit menu.
   a. Clear
   b. Paste Special
   c. Undo Sort
   d. Fill Down

6. To select a field in a database to sort on when the Sort dialog box displays, enter the _____ in the 1st Key box.
   a. cell reference of the field (column) in the first record
   b. cell reference of the field (column) in the last record
   c. cell reference of any cell in the field (column)
   d. all of the above will work

(continued)

STUDENT ASSIGNMENT 2 (continued)

7. With a data form active and criteria defined, use the _____ to display the former record in the database that passes the test.
   a. Find Next button
   b. Find Prev button
   c. New button
   d. Close button
8. A database field name referenced in a database function must be surrounded by _____.
   a. quotation marks ('')
   b. apostrophes (')
   c. brackets ([])
   d. colons (:)
9. The Crosstab ReportWizard is used to create a _____.
   a. chart
   b. database
   c. summary table
   d. scenario
10. To set up a criteria range that will cause the Extract, Find, or Delete command to process all records, include a(n) _____ in the criteria range.
    a. blank cell under the first field name
    b. asterisk under all field names
    c. = " " under all field names
    d. blank row

STUDENT ASSIGNMENT 3
Understanding Sorting

Instructions: Write down the sort order of the records in the personnel database in Figure SA6-3. Use the term *within* to describe the sort order. For example, minor field within intermediate field within major field. Also indicate the sequence (ascending or descending) of each field.

Order: _____ within _____ within _____

Field(s) in ascending sequence:

_____

Field(s) in descending sequence:

_____

FIGURE SA6-3

STUDENT ASSIGNMENT 4
Understanding Dialog Boxes and Commands

Instructions: Identify the menu and command that carries out the operation or causes the dialog box to display and allows you to make the indicated changes.

		MENU	COMMAND
1.	Define the database range	_____	_____
2.	Define the criteria range	_____	_____
3.	Define the extract range	_____	_____
4.	Sort a database	_____	_____
5.	Undo a sort operation	_____	_____
6.	Delete records	_____	_____
7.	Extract records	_____	_____
8.	Find records	_____	_____
9.	Create a crosstab table	_____	_____
10.	Display a data form	_____	_____

STUDENT ASSIGNMENT 5
Understanding Comparison Criteria

Instructions: Assume that the figures that accompany each of the following problems make up the criteria range. Fill in the comparison criteria to select records from the database in Figure 6-1 on page E289 according to these problems. So that you better understand what is required for this assignment, the answer is given for the first problem.

1. Select records that represent male personnel who are less than 30 years old.

Lname	Fname	Hire Date	Age	Gender	Educ	Dept	Title	Salary
			<30	M				

2. Select records that represent personnel whose title is Manager or Director.

Lname	Fname	Hire Date	Age	Gender	Educ	Dept	Title	Salary

3. Select records that represent personnel whose last names begin with "Jo", education is BS, and are assigned to the R&D department.

Lname	Fname	Hire Date	Age	Gender	Educ	Dept	Title	Salary

(continued)

STUDENT ASSIGNMENT 5 (continued)

4. Select records that represent personnel who are at least 30 years old and were hired before 1/1/90.

Lname	Fname	Hire Date	Age	Gender	Educ	Dept	Title	Salary

5. Select records that represent male personnel or personnel who are at least 50 years old.

Lname	Fname	Hire Date	Age	Gender	Educ	Dept	Title	Salary

6. Select records that represent female engineer personnel who are at least 40 years old and whose last names begin with the letter H.

Lname	Fname	Hire Date	Age	Gender	Educ	Dept	Title	Salary

STUDENT ASSIGNMENT 6
Understanding Criteria

Instructions: Write down the row numbers of the records in the personnel database (Figure 6-1 on page E289) that pass the comparison criteria shown in Figure SA6-6.

Row numbers of records passing test: _____

FIGURE SA6-6

COMPUTER LABORATORY EXERCISES

COMPUTER LABORATORY EXERCISE 1
Using a Data Form to Maintain a Database

Instructions: Start Excel. Open the worksheet CLE6-1 from the subdirectory Excel on the Student Diskette that accompanies this book. The worksheet CLE6-1 is shown in Figure CLE6-1. It contains a database of union employees.

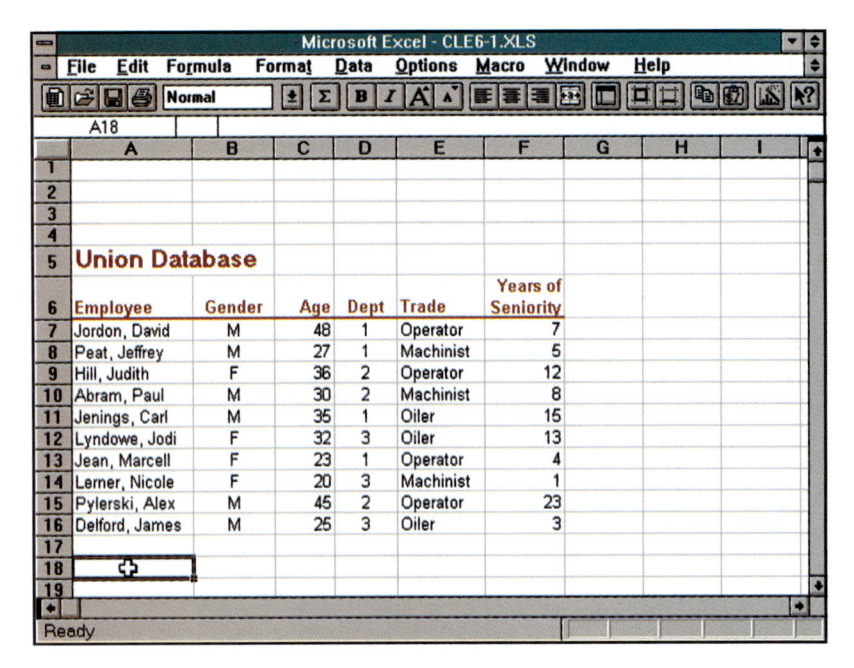

FIGURE CLE6-1

Perform the following tasks:

1. Invoke the Form command on the Data menu. Select the Find Next button and display each record.
2. The three types of maintenance performed on databases are: (1) change the values of fields, (2) add records, and (3) delete records. Use a data form to complete the type of maintenance specified in the first column of the following table to the records identified by employee name in the Union Database shown in Figure CLE6-1.

TYPE OF MAINTENANCE	EMPLOYEE	GENDER	AGE	DEPT	TRADE	YEARS OF SENIORITY
Change	Peat, Jeffrey		32	3		
Change	Delford, James				Machinist	7
Delete	Lerner, Nicole					
Delete	Abram, Paul					
Add	Daniels, Jacob	M	48	1	Oiler	0
Add	Beet, Sharon	F	22	2	Operator	0

E323

COMPUTER LABORATORY EXERCISE 1 (continued)

3. Add your name as the last record in the database. Enter an age of 35 and a department number of 3. Use your course number for the Trade field. Use your division number for the Years of Seniority field.
4. Save the worksheet using the file name CLE6-1A.
5. Use the Goto command on the Formula menu to select the Union Database. With the database selected, use the Set Print Area command on the Options menu to set the print area. Print the database with cell gridlines off. Click the Save File tool on the Standard toolbar to save the worksheet.
6. With a data form active, choose the Criteria button. Enter the following criteria: Age <32, Dept = 3. Select the Form button and display the records that pass the comparison criteria by using the Find Next and Find Prev buttons. When you are finished, choose the Close button.

COMPUTER LABORATORY EXERCISE 2
Sorting a Database

Instructions: Start Excel. Open the worksheet CLE6-2 (Figure CLE6-2) from the subdirectory Excel on the Student Diskette that accompanies this book. Sort the database according to the six sort problems below.

For each of the six sort problems, enter your name, course, computer laboratory exercise (CLE6-2x, where x is the sort problem number), date, and instructor name in the range A20:A24. Print the worksheet for each sort problem without cell gridlines. Save the worksheet with each sort solution using the file name CLE6-2x, where x is the sort problem number. For each sort problem, open the original worksheet CLE6-2.

FIGURE CLE6-2

1. Sort the database into descending sequence by division.
2. Sort the database by district within division. Both sort keys are to be in ascending sequence.
3. Sort the database by department within district within division. All three sort keys are to be in ascending sequence.
4. Sort the database into descending sequence by sales.
5. Sort the database by department within district within division. All three sort keys are to be in descending sequence.
6. Sort the database by salesperson within department within district within division. All four sort keys are to be in ascending sequence.

COMPUTER LABORATORY EXERCISE 3
Extracting Records from a Database

Instructions: Start Excel and perform the following tasks:

1. Open the worksheet CLE6-3 from the subdirectory Excel on the Student Diskette that accompanies this book. The criteria range, database range, and extract range are defined as shown in Figure CLE6-3.

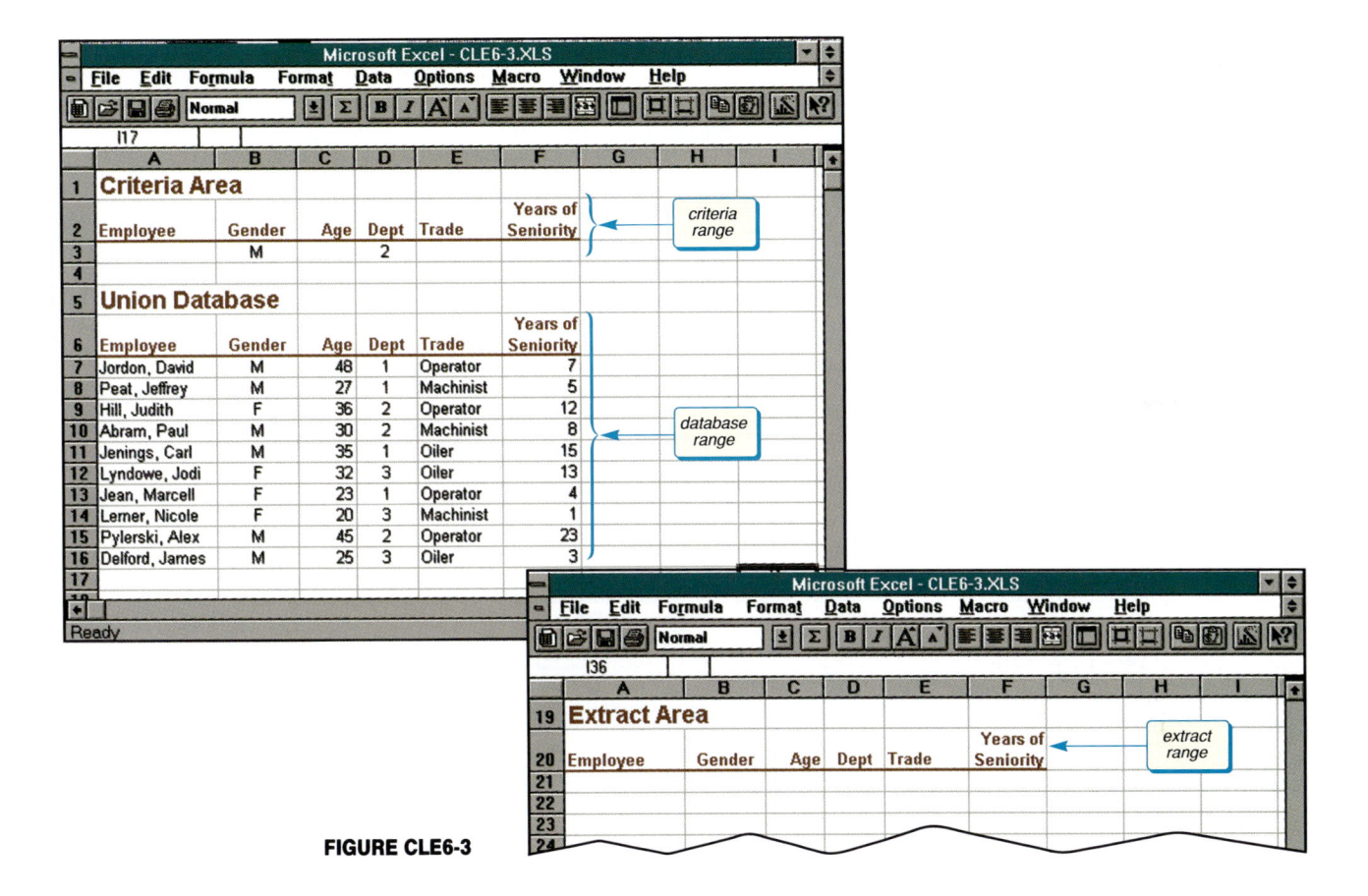

FIGURE CLE6-3

For each of the following problems, print the entire worksheet with cell gridlines off.

1. With the comparison criteria shown in Figure CLE6-3, use the Extract command on the Data menu to extract the records from the database that pass the test.
2. Delete the comparison criteria in row 3 and enter the comparison criteria Age > 30. Extract the records from the database.
3. Change the comparison criteria to Age > 32 and Age < 40. Extract the records from the database. You will have to add the field name Age in cell G2 and extend the criteria range. Enter > 32 under one field name Age and < 40 under the other one.
4. Reset the criteria range to A2:F3. Change the comparison criteria to a Trade that begins with the letter O. Extract the records from the database.
5. Change the comparison criteria to Gender = F, Trade = Operator, and Years of Seniority < 10. Extract the records from the database.
6. Change the comparison criteria to a blank row. Extract the records from the database.

COMPUTER LABORATORY ASSIGNMENTS

COMPUTER LABORATORY ASSIGNMENT 1
Building and Sorting a Database of Prospective Programmers

Purpose: To become familiar with building a database using a data form and sorting a database.

Problem: You are an Applications Software Specialist for Computer People, Inc. You have been assigned the task of building the Prospective Programmer database shown in Figure CLA6-1. Create the database beginning in row 7 of the worksheet. Use the field information shown in the following table.

COLUMN HEADINGS (FIELD NAMES)	COLUMN	TYPE OF DATA	COLUMN WIDTH
Name	A	Text	13
Gender	B	Text	8
Age	C	Numeric	5
Years	D	Numeric	7
QBasic	E	Text	8
COBOL	F	Text	8
C	G	Text	5
RPG	H	Text	6
Excel	I	Text	7
Paradox	J	Text	9

Prospective Programmer Database

Name	Gender	Age	Years	QBasic	COBOL	C	RPG	Excel	Paradox
Quinn, Jack	M	32	5	Y	N	N	Y	Y	N
Chab, Sarah	F	23	2	N	Y	N	N	Y	Y
Korman, Liz	F	26	4	Y	Y	N	Y	N	Y
Jones, David	M	24	2	Y	N	N	N	Y	N
Albe, James	M	38	15	Y	Y	Y	N	Y	N
Biag, John	M	29	7	N	Y	N	Y	N	Y
Holk, George	M	20	1	N	Y	Y	N	Y	Y
Lock, Nikole	F	42	12	Y	N	Y	N	N	N
Smyth, Fred	M	34	19	Y	Y	N	N	N	Y
Lave, Linda	F	49	16	N	N	N	N	Y	Y

FIGURE CLA6-1

Instructions: Perform the following tasks:

1. Change the column widths as described in the preceding table. Enter the database title and column headings as shown in Figure CLA6-1. Use the Set Database command to define the database range as A8:J9. Use a data form to enter the ten records.
2. Enter your name, course, computer laboratory exercise (CLA6-1), date, and instructor name in the range A30:A34. Print the worksheet without cell gridlines. Save the worksheet using the file name CLA6-1.
3. Sort the records in the database into ascending sequence by name. Print the sorted version.
4. Sort the records in the database by age within gender. Select ascending sequence for the gender code and ascending sequence for the age. Print the sorted version.

COMPUTER LABORATORY ASSIGNMENT 2
Finding and Extracting Records in the Prospective Programmer Database

Purpose: To become familiar with finding records and extracting records that pass a comparison criteria.

Problem: Use the Prospective Programmer database created in Computer Laboratory Assignment 1 (Figure CLA6-1) to complete the find and extract operations described in Part 1 and Part 2 of this assignment. (**Note:** If you were not required to build the worksheet in Computer Laboratory Assignment 1, ask your instructor for a copy of CLA6-1.)

Part 1 Instructions: Open worksheet CLA6-1. Use the Criteria button on a data form to enter the comparison criteria for the following tasks. Use the Find Next button on the data form to find the records that pass the comparison criteria. Write down and submit the names of the prospective programmers who pass the comparison criteria for tasks a through d.

a. Find all records that represent prospective programmers who are male and can program in COBOL.
b. Find all records that represent prospective programmers who can program in QBasic and RPG and use Excel.
c. Find all records that represent prospective female programmers who are at least 29 years old and can use Paradox.
d. Find all records that represent prospective programmers who know Excel and Paradox.
e. All prospective programmers who did not know Paradox were sent to a seminar on the software package. Use the Find Next button to locate the records of these programmers and change the Paradox field entry on the data form from the letter N to the letter Y. Make sure you press the ENTER key or press the DOWN ARROW key after changing the letter. Save and print the database. Use the file name CLA6-2A.

(continued)

E328 PROJECT 6 SORTING AND QUERYING A WORKSHEET DATABASE

COMPUTER LABORATORY ASSIGNMENT 2 (continued)

Part 2 Instructions: Open the worksheet CLA6-1 (Figure CLA6-1). For the Criteria range, copy the database title and field names (A7:J8) to A1:J2. Change cell A1 to Criteria Area. Use the Set Criteria command on the Data menu to define A2:J3 as the criteria range. For the Extract range, copy the database title and field names (A7..J8) to A21:J22. Change cell A21 to Extract Area. Use the Set Extract command on the Data menu to define A22:J22 as the extract range. Your worksheet should look similar to the top screen in Figure CLA6-2.

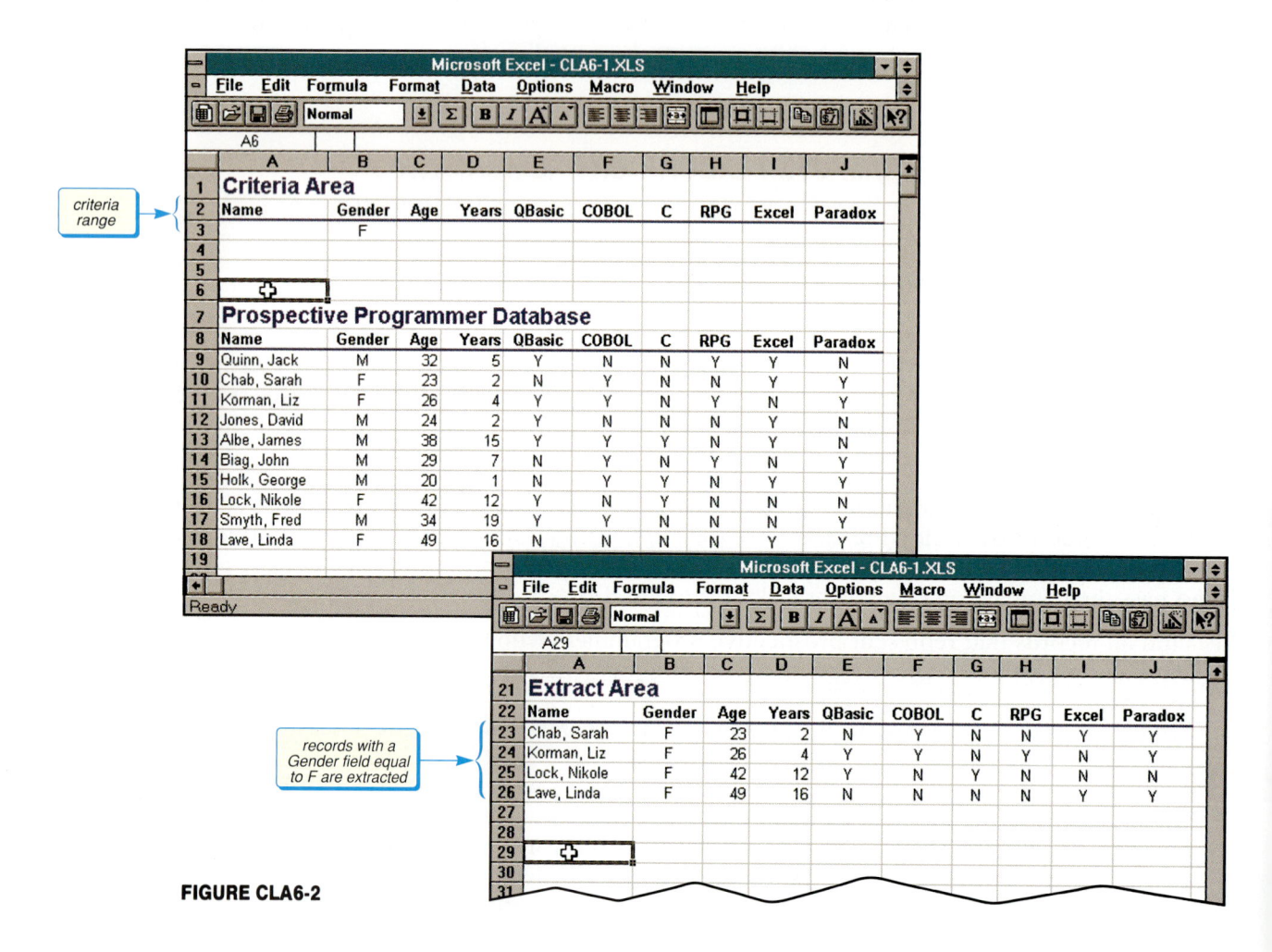

FIGURE CLA6-2

Use the criteria range and Extract command to extract records that pass the tests in tasks a through e below. Print the entire worksheet after each extraction.

a. Extract the records that represent prospective programmers who are female (see bottom screen in Figure CLA6-2).
b. Extract the records that represent prospective programmers who can program in QBasic and cannot program in RPG.
c. Extract the records that represent prospective male programmers who are at least 30 years old and can use Excel.
d. Extract the records that represent prospective programmers who know RPG and Paradox.
e. Extract the records that represent prospective programmers who do not know how to use any programming language. Save the worksheet. Use the file name CLA6-2B.

COMPUTER LABORATORY ASSIGNMENT 3
Building and Manipulating an Order Entry Database

Purpose: To become familiar with building a database using a data form, extracting records, and applying database functions to generate information.

Problem: You are employed as a spreadsheet specialist in the order entry department of JM Sports, Inc. You have been assigned to develop a database worksheet that keeps track of the outstanding orders (top screen in Figure CLA6-3). Besides developing the order database, include a criteria range and extract range for copying records that pass the comparison criteria.

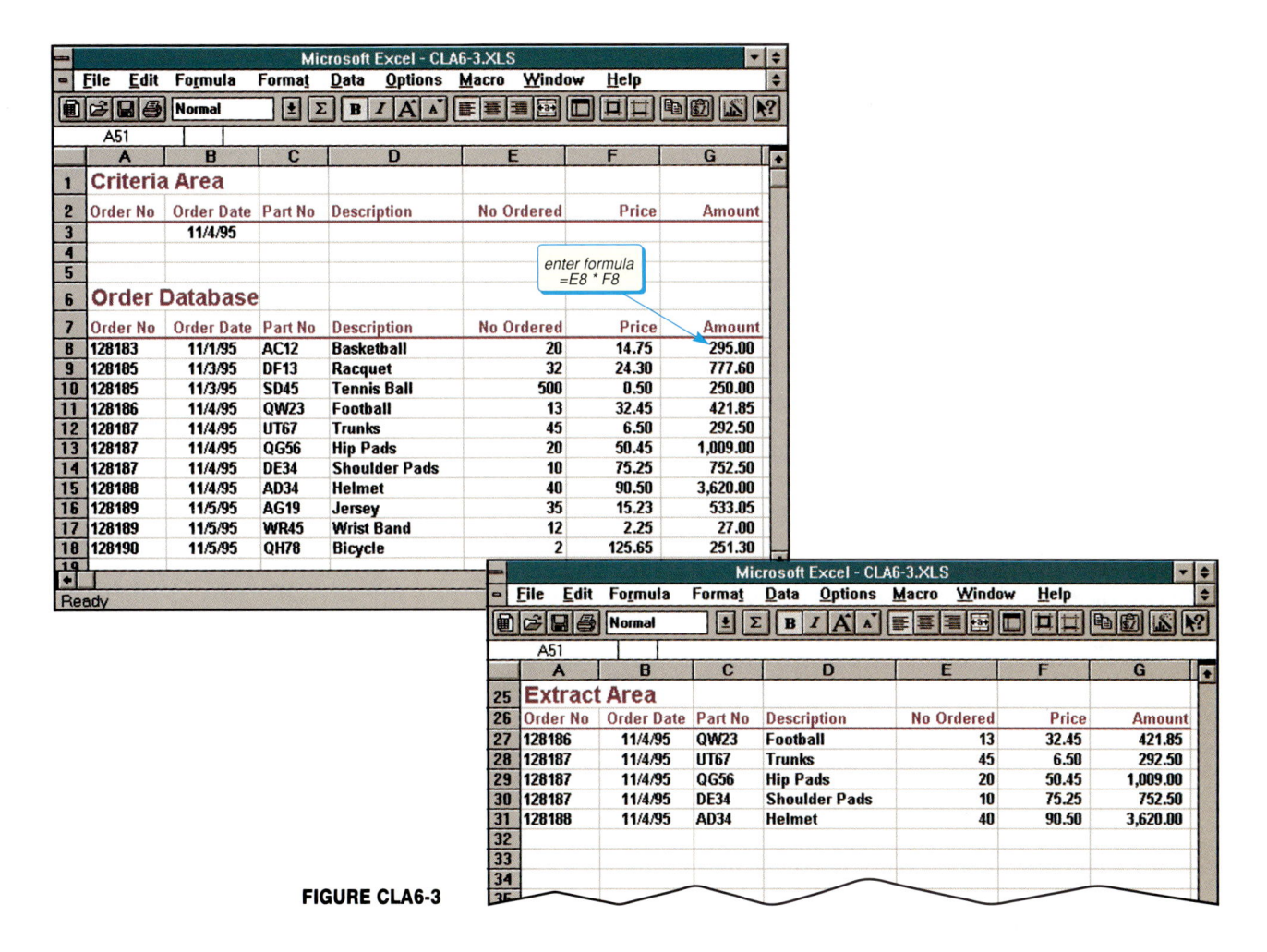

FIGURE CLA6-3

Instructions: Do the following to create the database shown in the range A6:G18 in Figure CLA6-3.

1. Change the font of the worksheet to bold TrueType Arial. Change the column widths to the following: A = 9, B = 11, C = 8, D = 16, E = 12, F = 11, G = 12. Enter the database heading and field names in the range A6:G7. Center entries in column B. Align the field names as shown in row 7 of the top screen in Figure CLA6-3. Color the font and draw a border under the column headings.
2. Define the range A7:G8 as a database. Enter the first record without using a data form. Enter the formula =E8 * F8 in cell G8. Use a data form to enter the remaining order records shown in the bottom screen of Figure CLA6-3.
3. Create the criteria area above the order database. Create the extract area beginning in row 25.
4. Save the worksheet. Use the file name CLA6-3.

(continued)

COMPUTER LABORATORY ASSIGNMENT 3 (continued)

5. Use the Page Setup command on the File menu to change both margins to 0.5 and turn off cell gridlines. Print the entire worksheet for each of the following extracts:
   a. Extract all records that have an order date of 11/4/95 (Figure CLA6-3).
   b. Extract all records that have a part number that begins with the letter Q.
   c. Extract all records that have an Amount field greater than $500.00.
6. Use the DSUM and DAVERAGE database functions to find the sum and average of the Amount field. Assign the database functions to cells I3 and J3. Blank the row under the criteria field names and use the name Criteria as the third value in the database functions. Your final result should be a sum of $8,229.80 and an average of $748.16. Use column titles to define the two cells. Print all entries in the worksheet in landscape orientation.
7. Use the Crosstab ReportWizard to generate a crosstab table that uses the following values: row category — order number; column category — order date; value field — amount. The grand total should equal $8,229.80. Format the crosstab table. For the date column headings, set the column width so that only the dates show (not the time). Print the crosstab table without cell gridlines. Save the worksheet with the crosstab table as CLA6-3CT. Switch to the database worksheet and use the Save File tool to save it.

COMPUTER LABORATORY ASSIGNMENT 4
Creating a Video Cassette Database

Purpose: To become familiar with planning, creating, and manipulating a database.

Problem: Obtain a list of at least fifteen movies from a nearby video store or library with the following information: movie title, year made, movie type (comedy, science fiction, suspense, drama, religious), director, producer, and number of academy awards. Create a video cassette database. Sort the database by movie title. Define a criteria range and extract range. Use the criteria range to query the database using different combinations of fields. For example, extract all movies that were produced prior to 1990 and have a movie type equal to comedy.

Instructions: Submit the following:

1. A description of the problem. Include the purpose of the database, a statement outlining the required data, and calculations.
2. A handwritten design of the database.
3. A printed copy of the worksheet without cell gridlines.
4. A short description explaining how to use the worksheet.
5. Enter your name, course, computer laboratory assignment number (CLA6-4), date, and instructor name well below the database in column A in separate but adjacent cells. Save the worksheet using the file name CLA6-4.

Index

#DIV/0 error message, **E64**
#REF! error message, **E113**, E119
AVERAGE function, E66–68
  adjusting ranges in, E116–117
Absolute references, **E131**
  copying IF function with, E133
  relative references versus, E131–132
Active cell, **E5,** E8
Active cell reference, **E5**
Adding data, E115–117
Addition (+), E60, **E62**
Alignment command, E128–129, E162
Analysis, *see* What-if tools
Arithmetic operator, E60
Arrow key, **E8**
Arrow tool, **E151**–152
Ascending sequence sort, **E296**
Assign to Object command, **E260,** E262, E263
Asterisk (*) wildcard character, **E303**
Audio comment, **E200**
Autoformat command, E25–27, E46
Autoformat dialog box, E26
Autoformat tool, **E27**
Automatic recalculation, E218–220, E253
AutoSum tool, **E15**–17, E46
  column totals and, E65
Averages, displaying as dollar amounts using Style box, E77–78

Background box, E197
BACKSPACE key, **E10**
Backup copy, **E88**
BAK extension, E88
Best fit, column width and, **E82**–83, E96
Black selection squares, **E148,** E151
Bold
  chart text, E153
  chart title, E147–148
  column titles, E71
  text in a cell, E128–129
  worksheet title, E70
Bold line style, E74
Bold tool, **E25,** 46
  recessed, E70
Border(s)
  color, E137–140, E162
  drawing, E71, E72–73
  large worksheet, E195
  macro sheet and, E259
  moving, E20
  using shortcut menu, E73–74
Border command, E71, E72, E96, E239, E274
  Color box arrow, E137–140
Border dialog box, E74
Bottom border, E239, E274
Bottom box, E72
Budget % Expenses table, E182
  font color, E198
  formatting, E196–198
Button
  adding to play back command macro, E260–263
  relocate, E263
  resize, E263
Button tool, **E260,** E274

Call out chart item, E151
Cancel box, **E9,** E10
Cancel entry, in formula bar, E46
"Can't Undo" message, E40

Capitalization, command macros and, E257
CAPS (Caps Lock), E8
Case sensitive, **E303**
Category box, E79
Category names, **E142**
Cell(s), **E5**
  active, E5, E8
  clearing, E41, E46, E112
  copying format, E124–126
  copying formulas to adjacent, E64
  copying to adjacent cell using fill handle, E17–21, E46
  deleting, E112–113, E162
  editing data in, E39–40, E46
  go to specific, E206
  input, E247
  inserting, E113–115, E162
  moving using drag and drop, E117–119, E162
  naming, E240–242, E274
  nonadjacent selection, E186, E221
  protected or locked, E271
  range of, *see* Cell(s), range of
  selecting, E8
  shading, E196–197, E221
  spell checking single, E203
  unprotected or unlocked, E271
  visible, E214–215, E221
  wrapping text in, E128–130, E162
Cell(s), range of, **E17**
  adjusting functions after copying, E116–117
  averaging, E67
  charts and, E29
  clearing, E41, E46
  colon separating endpoints, E68
  copying, E17–21
  copying cell's format to, E125–126
  copying to adjacent cells using fill handle, E115–116
  copying to nonadjacent paste area, E180–182
  defining as data table, E250
  deleting, E113
  endpoints, E68
  to graph, E142, E146
  inserting, E114
  moving, E117–119, E162
  nonadjacent selection, E186, E221
  outlining, E211, E239, E274
  printing, E90–92
  removing selection, E19
  selecting, E17, E46
  spell checking, E203
  to sum, E17
Cell contents, centering across columns, E23
Cell format, bold, E25
Cell gridlines, print preview and, E89
Cell Gridlines check box, empty, E36, E37, E46
Cell note dialog box, **E199**
Cell protection, E233
Cell reference, **E5**
  absolute versus relative, E131–132
  active, E5
  error message, E113
  macro function and, E258
  mixed, E131
  relative, E18

Center Across Columns tool, **E23,** E46
Center Align tool, **E71,** E96
Centering
  worksheet title, E70, E134
  worksheet title across columns, E23
Cents, E15, E76
Changes to worksheet, saving, E38
Character(s)
  blank, E41
  deleting in formula bar, E40
  overflow, E10
  special, E13
Chart(s), E2
  deleting selected, E46
  drawing, E141–161
  embedded, *see* Embedded chart
  Gallery menu and, E160, E162
  outlined worksheet and, E211
  pie, *see* Pie chart
  preferred, E160, E162
  selecting different types of, E31
  text, E152–154, E162
  title, E147–148
  type, E160, E162
  visible cells, E215
Chart arrow, E151–152, E162
Chart items, **E147,** E162
  call out, E151
Chart location size, E142
Chart menu, **E161**
Chart toolbar, Arrow tool, E151–152
Chart window, **E147**
  display embedded pie chart in, E155, E162
  switching to worksheet window from, E154–156
ChartWizard dialog box, E30, E143–146
ChartWizard tool, **E28**–29, E46, E142–146
Check Spelling tool, **E201**–203, E221
Clear command, **E112,** E41, E313
Clearing cell or range of cells, E41, E46
Clearing outline structure, E217–218
Clearing the worksheet, **E41**–42, E46
CLEAR macro function, E258
Clipboard, **E119,** E162, E180, E182, E221
Close button, E90
  data form, E294
Close command, **E42**
Collapse symbol, **E212**
Collapsed rows and columns, expanding, E215–216
Collapsing rows, E213
Colon (:)
  range of cells and, E17
  separating endpoint of range, E68
Color, E134–140
  borders, E137–140, E162
  chart arrow, E152
  font, E135–137, E162, E198
  patterns, E197
  shading with, E197
Column(s), **E5**
  best fit, E82–83, E96
  centering cell contents across, E23, E46
  copying cells in, E20–21
  copying formulas from one cell to adjacent cells, E64
  deleting, E113
  demote, E211, E221
  detail, E210

331

expanding or collapsing, E213, E215–216
hiding, E85
inserting, E114
number of, E6
print titles and, E203
sorting, E298
summing, E15–17, E46
total, E210
Column category, **E312**
Column chart, **E3**
  three-dimensional, E215
Column heading (column letter), E5
  border colors of, E138
Column level bar, **E213**
Column level symbols, **E213**
Column names, E6
Column references, absolute versus relative, E131
Column titles, E10–12
  bold, E71
  entering, E58
  formatting, E71–73
  italicized, E71
  large worksheet and, E193
  right-align, E71
Column totals, summing, E64–66
Column width, **E82**
  changing, E82–85, E96
  data table and, E247
  formulas version and, E92
  large worksheet and, E179–180
  print preview and, E90
  series of adjacent columns and, E84
  text longer than, E10
  undoing, E83
Column Width command, **E85**
Comma (,)
  dollar sign and, E76
  format symbol, E128
  whole numbers and, E77
Comma style, E191
Comma Style tool, **E184**
Command macros, E233, **E235**
  adding button to play back, E260–263
  automating loan data entry with, E254–265
  entering on macro sheet, E257–258
  naming, E255–257, E259
  planning, E255
  playing back, E263–265
  testing, E255
Comments, **E198–200**
  audio, E200
  macros and, E255
  red dot and, E200
Comparison criteria, **E300**–303, E309–310
  multiple, E310
  wildcard characters in, E303
Computed criteria, **E303**
Conditions, database comparison of, E300
Contents command, E68
Context-sensitive help, **E42**, E46
Control-menu box, floating toolbar and, E185
Copy command, **E180**
Copying
  cell's format, E124–126
  cells in a column, E20–21
  cells to adjacent cells, E17–21, E46
  cells, moving cells versus, E119
  onto clipboard, E119, E162
  formulas, E60–61
  formulas in one cell to adjacent cells, E64
  functions to adjacent cells, E66, E68, E116–117

MIN and MAX functions, E124
  range of cells to adjacent cells using fill handle, E115–116
  SUM function, E65–66
  to more than one paste area, E182
Copy selection onto clipboard, E180, E221
Copy tool, **E124–125**, E126, E180
Cost, total, E245
Create Backup file check box, E88
Create Names command, **E240–241**
Create Names dialog box, **E240–241**
Criteria range, **E303–304**, E318
  blank row in, E309, E312
Crosstab command, **E312**, E318
Crosstab ReportWizard, **E312–317**
Currency format, E190
Currency (0) format, E76, E78, E123
Currency style, E76, E243
Currency Style tool, **E184**
Custom dictionary, **E201**, E203
Customized format styles, E25–27
Custom toolbar, Print Preview, E88–90, E96
Cut command, E119, E162

Dashed rectangle, chart location and, E30
Data
  adding and changing, E115–117
  restoring, E40
  test, E44
Data analysis, E233–273
Database, E2, **E288–318**
  comparison criteria, E300–303
  creating, E290–296, E318
  criteria range, E303–304
  Crosstab ReportWizard, **E312–317**
  deleting records, E309
  extracting records, E306–309
  finding records, E305–306
  printing, E296
  sorting, E296–300
  summarizing, E312–317
  title, E290
Database functions, **E310–311**
Database range, **E290**
Data entry, command macro to automate, E254–265
Data form, **E290**, E318
  Close button, E294
  moving from field to field on, E295
  New button, E293–294
  records passing comparison criteria using, E300–303
  viewing records and changing data, E295
Data menu
  Crosstab, E312, E313
  Delete, E309
  Extract, E306, E318
  Find, E305, E318
  Form, E292, E295, E301
  Set Database, E291–292, E294
  Set Extract, E306
  Sort, E297, E299
  Table, E251
Data series, **E142**, E146
Data table, **E235**, E246–253, E274
  defining range as, E250
  formatting, E252
  formulas in, E249
  one-input, E246, E253
  with one varying value, E253
Date stamp, **E237**
Debugging, **E92**
Decimal numbers
  displaying as percentages, E79
  dollar sign and, E76

Decimal point, cents and, E15
Decision making, IF function and, E130–133
Decrease Font Size tool, **E24**
Define Name command, E242, E256
Delete command, **E112**, **E309**
Delete dialog box, All, E41
DELETE key, E41
Deleting
  cells, E112–113, E162
  columns, E113
  embedded chart, E41
  entire worksheet, E41–42
  range of cells, E113
  records, E295, E309, E318
  rows, E112–113
Demote tool, **E211–213**, E221
Descending sequence sort, **E296**
Desk checking, **E255**
Detail columns, collapsing, **E210**
Detail rows, hiding or collapsing, **E210**
Dialog boxes, Help button and, E42
Dictionary, E201
Disk
  opening worksheet on, E38, E46
  saving worksheet on, E33, E46
Display command, E93, E96, E157
  Outline Symbols, E216
Division (/), E60, **E62**
DMAX function, E311
DMIN function, E311
Documentation, macro sheet and, E258–259
Dollar amounts, displaying totals and averages as, E77–78
Dollar sign ($)
  absolute reference and, E131, E132
  leading, E75, E128
  Style box and, E76
Dot patterns, E197
Dotted line, row height and, E85
Double underline style, E74
Down payment, goal seeking to determine, E265–267
Drag and drop, moving cells using, **E117–119**, E162
Drawing borders, E71, E72–73
Drawing charts, E141–161
Drawing pie chart, E142–146
Drawing toolbar, E197
Drive, selected, E38
Drives drop-down list box, E33, E38
Drop shadow, **E196**, E197
Drop Shadow tool, E197, E221
DSUM function, E311

Edit button, E263, E274
Editing, functions, E117
Editing data, error correction and, E39–40, E46
Edit menu
  Clear, E41, E313
  Cut, E119, E162
  Delete, E112
  Insert, E113–115
  Paste, E119, E162, E180, E182
  Paste Special, E162
  Undo, E40, E117
  Undo Paste, E181
  Undo Sort, E297
Edit mode, **E39–40**
Elevation, pie chart, E151
Embedded chart, **E28–31**, E142
  deleting, E41
  opening, E147
  printing, E158

INDEX E333

Embedded pie chart
  changes and, E155
  display in chart window, E155, E162
Empty cell, equal to zero, E64
Enlarging
  chart title, E147–148
  worksheet title, E70
Enter box, **E9**
ENTER key, **E10**
  Paste command and, E182
Enter mode, E7
Equal sign (=), E60
  criteria range and, E304
  macro functions and, E255
Equal to (=) relational operator, E131
Error correction
  clearing a cell or range of cells and, E41, E46
  clearing entire worksheet and, E41–42
  debugging and, E92
  editing data and, E39–40, E46
  prior to data entry, E39
  text entry and, E10
  undoing last entry, E40
Error message (#DIV/0), E64
ESC key, **E10**
Excel 4.0
  exiting, E37–38, E46
  learning, E43
  starting, E4–5, E46
Exclamation point (!), cell reference in macro function and, E258
Exit command, E37–38
Exiting
  Excel, E37–38, E46
  Help information, E42
Expanding collapsed rows and columns, E215–216
Expand symbol, **E213**
Explode pie chart, E142, E148–149, E162
Exponentiation (^), E60, **E61**
Extract range, **E306**–309, E318

F1, Help, E42
F2, correcting error in formula line and, E40
F4, absolute references and, E132
F5, Goto command, E206, E221
Field(s), **E288**
  sorting on multiple, E298–300
Field names, **E288**
File
  opening, E38–39
  saving, E37
File Menu, Save As, E140–141
File Name list box, E38
File menu
  Close, E42
  Exit command, E37–38
  New, E42, E256
  Page Setup, E35–36, E94, E158, E204
  Print Preview command, E88–90, E96
  Save As, E88
File name, E32
  macro sheet, E259
  saving using same, E88
  saving worksheet under different, E140–141
File name extension, E34
Fill handle, **E18, E20**–21
  clearing cell contents using, E41, E46
  copying cell to adjacent cells using, E17–21, E46
  copying range of cells to adjacent cells using, E115–116
  creating a series with, E178–179, E221
Financial functions, E243–245, E274

Find command, E206, E305–306, E318
Find Next button, E295, E300, E302
Find Prev button, E295, E300, E302
Fit to: option, **E92**, E94
Fit to print across a page, E92, E94, E96
Floating toolbar, **E185**
Font
  changing for entire worksheet, E177, E236
  chart title, E147–148
  color, E135–137, E162, E198
  large worksheet and, E193
Font command, E153
  Color box arrow, E135–136
Font dialog box, TT Arial, E80–81
Font size, **E22**
  chart text, E153
  decreasing, E24, E46
  increasing, E24, E46
  row height and, E85
Font style, **E22, E80**
  bold, E25, E46
  changing, E80–82, E96
Font type, **E22**
Footer, **E37**
Foreground box, E197
Format/formatting, E22–27, E69–75
  Autoformat and, E25–27, E46
  bold, E25
  borders and, E71, E72–73
  chart text, E152–154
  color and, E134–140
  column titles, E71–73
  column width, E82–85
  copying, E124–126
  copying to range of cells, E125–126
  copying with fill handle, E179
  database, E295
  data table, E252
  expense totals, E191
  font change and, E80–82, E96
  font size, E22–25
  moving cells and, E119
  net income, E191
  row height, E85–87
  row titles, E74–75
  selection squares and, E148
  system date and time, E237–238
  worksheet title, E70
Format Codes box, E79–80
Format menu
  Alignment, E71, E96, E128–129, E162
  Autoformat, E26
  Border, E71, E72, E96, E137–140, E239, E274
  Column Width, E85
  Font, E73, E96, E135–137, E153
  Goto, E296, E304
  Number, E75–80, E237
  Protection, E271
  Row Height, E86–87, E96
  3-D View, E149–150
Format symbols
  entering numbers with, E127–128
  summary of, E128
Formatting numbers, E75–80, E96
  comma placement and, E77
  Formatting toolbar and, E183–186
  number signs, E78
  percentages, E79
  using Number command, E78–80
  using Style box, E75–78, E96
Formatting toolbar, **E184**
  displaying, E184
  formatting expenses using, E191
  hiding, E192–193

moving and shaping, E185
  selecting nonadjacent cells, E186
Form command, E292, E295, E301
Formula(s), **E59**–96
  averages, E66–68
  changing values in cells that are referenced in, E218–220
  copying, E60–61
  copying from one cell to adjacent cells in a column, E64
  data table and, E249
  displaying, E189–190
  displaying and printing, E92–95
  entering, E59–64
  entering using point mode, E62–63
  first operator as plus or minus sign, E190
  order of operations, E61–62
  summing column totals, E64–66
  switching to displaying values from, E93, E96
  testing, E44
Formula bar, **E7,** E46, E60
  cancel box, E10
  cancel entry in, E46
  worksheet title in, E9
Formula line, correcting error in, E40
FORMULA macro function, E258
Formula manager, Scenario Manager, E268
Formula menu
  Create Names, E240–241
  Define Name, E242, E256
  Find, E206
  Goal Seek, E266
  Goto, E206
  Note, E198–200
  Outline, E211
  Paste Function, E245
Formulas version of worksheet, **E92**–94
  macro sheet and, E258
Freeze Panes command, E187–188
Freezing worksheet titles, **E187**–188, E221
Functions
  AVERAGE, E66–68
  copying from cell to adjacent cells in row, E66, E68
  database, E310–311
  DAVERAGE, E310–311
  DCOUNT, E311
  DMAX, E311
  DMIN, E311
  DSUM, E311
  editing, E117
  financial, E243–245, E274
  list of available, E68
  macro, E255
  MAX, E120–124
  MIN, E120–124
  NOW, E237–239
  PMT, E243–245
  SUM, see SUM function
  testing, E44
FV (future value) function, E244

Gallery menu, **E160**
Goal Seek command, E265–267
Goto command (F5), **E206,** E221, E296, E304
Greater than (>) relational operator, E131
Greater than or equal to (> =) relational operator, E131
Greater than signs (> >), ChartWizard dialog box and, E31
Gridlines
  clearing from printout, E36, E46
  print preview and, E89

Handles, **E148**
  dragging on to resize chart, E31
  selected chart and, E31
Hard copy, **E35**
Header, **E37**
Height
  pie chart, E151
  row, *see* Row height
Help facility, **E42**–43, E46
Help menu, E42
Help tool, **E42**
Hidden chart, E156–157
Hide All option button, E157
Hiding
  outline symbols, E216–217, E221
  toolbar, E185, E192, E221
Horizontal split bar, **E210**
Horizontal split box, **E210**

IF function, **130**–133
  copying with an absolute reference, E133
Increase Font Size tool, **E24**, E148, E153
Input cell, **E247**
Input dialog box, E263–265
INPUT macro function, E258
Insert command, **E113**–115
Inserting
  cells, E113–115, E162
  columns, E114
  range of cells, E114
  rows, E113–114
Insertion point, **E9**
INSERT key, E40
Insert mode, **E40**
Interest, total, E245
Interest rate, E243
  data table and, E246, E251
Italicizing
  column titles, E71, E96
  text in a cell, E128–129

Keyboard, entering formulas through, E60
Keyboard indicators, **E8**

Landscape orientation, **E158**, E162
  large worksheet and, E204
Large worksheet, *see* Worksheet, large
Leading dollar sign ($), E128
Learning Microsoft Excel, E43
Left Align tool, **E71**, E96
Left-justified text, **E10**
Legend, **E31**
Less than (<) relational operator, E131
Less than or equal to (< =) relational
  operator, E131
Level bars, E213
Levels, outline, E217
Line patterns, E197
Line style, bold, E74
Line weight, chart arrow, **E152**
Loan amount, E243
Loan analysis, E234, E239
Loan data entry, command macro to
  automate, E254–265
Locked cells, **E271**

Macro, command, *see* Command macro
Macro(s)
  comments and, E255
  playback, E254
Macro function, **E235**, E255
  order placed in, E255
  within a macro function, E258
Macro menu, **E257**
  Run, E260
Macro sheet, **E255**
  documentation and, E258–259
  entering command macro on, E257–258

file name, E259
formulas version and, E258
opening, E255–257, E274
Macro windows, E260
Magnifying worksheet, E207–208
Margins, large worksheet, E204
Margins button, E90
MAX function, **E120**–124
Menu, macro, E257
Menu bar, **E6**
  chart window, E147
Menu names, E6
MIN function, **120**–124
Minus sign (–), E60
  formula in which first operator is, E190
  PMT function and, E243
Mixed cell reference, **E131**
Mode indicators, **E7**
Monthly payment, calculating, E243–245
Month names, creating series of by dragging
  fill handle, E178–179
Mouse
  cell selection and, E8
  entering formulas using point mode and,
    E62–63
  print preview and, E89, E90, E96
  row height and, E85–86
Mouse pointer
  block arrow, E5
  block plus sign, E5
  charts and, E142–143
  cross hair, E29
  dark plus sign, E18
  dragging over cells, E23
  floating toolbar and, E185
  magnifying glass, E89, E90, E96
  starting Excel, E4
Mouse pointer shapes, **E5**
Moving around worksheet, E206
Moving border, range to copy and, E182
Moving cells
  copying cells versus, E119
  using cut and paste commands, E119, E162
  using drag and drop, E117–119
Moving toolbar, E185
MS Sans Serif, E80
Multiple comparison criteria, E310
Multiplication (*), E60, **E62**

Naming
  button, E260, E263
  command macro, E255–257, E259
  macro sheet, E259
  See also File name
Naming a cell, referencing in a formula and,
  E240–242
Negative sign (–), PMT function and, E243.
  See also Minus sign
New button, data form, E293–294
New command, **E42**, E256
Next> button, E314–315
Nonadjacent cell selection, **E186**, E221
Normal style, E239
Note(s), **E198**–200, E221
Note command, **E198**–200
Note Indicator check box, E200
Not equal to (< >) relational operator, E131
NOW function, **E237**–239
NUM (Num Lock), E8
Number(s), E13
  comma placement and, E77
  entering, E13–15, E59
  entering with format symbol, E127–128
  formatting, E75–80, E96
  rounded, E78
  summing, E15–17, E46

Number command, **E78**–80
Number Format dialog box, E238
Number signs (#), **E78**
  large numbers and, E247

One-input data table, **E246**, E253
Open dialog box, E38–39
Open File tool, E38–39, E111
Opening
  embedded chart, E147
  macro sheet, E255–257, E274
  worksheet, E111
  worksheet, on disk, E38, E46
Options menu, **E90**
  Display, E93, E96, E157
  Protect Document, E272, E274
  Set Print Area, E91, E96
  Set Print Titles, E204
  Spelling, E201
  Toolbars, E184, E221
  Workspace, E200
Order of operations, for formulas, E61–62
Outline
  crosstab table and, E316
  range, E239, E274
  saving worksheet with, E217
  worksheet section and, E239, E274
Outline command, E211
Outlined worksheet, working with visible
  cells in, E214–215
Outline structure, **E210**–218
  clearing, E217–218
Outline symbols, displaying and hiding,
  E216–217, E221
Outline Symbols check box, E216
Overflow characters, E10
Overtype (OVR) mode, E8, **E40**

Page breaks, E206, E221
Page setup
  characteristics, E37
  large worksheet and, E204–206
Page Setup command, E35–36, E158, E204
  Fit to, E92, E94, E96
  Scaling box, E95
Page Setup dialog box, E35–36
  Fit to, E92, E94
Panes, splitting window into, E208–210,
  E221
Parentheses( )
  following function name, E16
  overriding order of operations with, E62
Password, E273
Paste, undoing, E181
Paste area, **E17**–18, E115–116, E119
  copying range of cells to nonadjacent,
    E180–182
Paste command, E119, E162, **E180**, E221
  ENTER command and, E182
Paste Formats tool, **124**–125, E126, E162
Paste Function command, E245
Pattern, **E197**
Patterns command, **E197**
Payments, number of, E243
Percentage 0.00% style, E240
Percentages, formatting using Number
  command, E79
Percent format, E127
Percent series, E248
Percent sign, E60, E128
  pie charts and, E144
Personnel database, E289–318
Pie chart, **E141**–159
  adding chart arrow, E151–152
  drawing, E142–146

INDEX

enhancing, E146–154
exploding, E142, E148–149, E162
font size, E147–148
hiding, E156–157
printing, E156, E158–159
rotating, E149–151, E162
saving, E156
text and, E152–154
3-D, E144
title, E142, E147–148
Planning a worksheet, E44
Play back command macro, E260–265
Play back macro, **E254**
Plus sign (+)
 addition and, E60, **E62**
 formula in which first operator is, E190
PMT (periodic payment) function, **E243**–245
Point mode, **E62**–63
 number format and, E123
Point size, row height and, E85
Portrait orientation, **E158**, E162, E204
Preferred chart, changing, **E160**, E162
Preferred command, **E160**, E162
Previewing worksheet, **E88**–90, E96
Print dialog box, E90
Printer, color, E134
Printing, E35–37, E46
 at 100%, E95, E96
 criteria range, E304
 database, E296
 embedded chart, E158
 extracted records, E306
 Help information, E42
 landscape orientation, E158, E162
 notes assigned to cells, E200
 outlined worksheet, E211
 pie chart, E156, E158–159
 portrait orientation, E158, E162
 range of cells, E90–92
 section of worksheet, E90–92, E96
Printing dialog box, E36
Printout, **E35**
 clearing cell gridlines from, E36, E46
Print Preview command, E88–90, E96
Print Scaling option, **E95**
Print Setup dialog box, E90
Print titles, **E203**–204, E221
Print tool, E36, E91
Problem definition, E44
Promote tool, E211, E217–218, E221
Protected cells, **E271**
Protecting worksheet, E271–273, E274
Pull-down menu, E6
Pushed rows, E114
PV (present value) function, E244

Question mark (?) wildcard character, **E303**
Questions, what-if, *see* What-if questions

Range
 database, E290
 extracting records and, E306–309
Range of cells, *see* Cell(s), range of
Ready mode, E7
Recalculation, E65
 automatic, E218–220, E235, E253
Record(s), **E288**
 adding new, E295
 deleting, E295, E309, E318
 extracting, E306–309
 finding, E305–306, E318
 selecting to sort, E296–297
 viewing, E295
Record button, E200

Red dot, comments and, E200
Region names, graphs and, E142
Relational operators, E131
 database and, E300
Relative reference, **E18**
 absolute reference versus, E131–132
Relocate, button, E263
Remove Print Area command, E92, E96
Report
 multipage, E203
 Scenario Manager and, E267, E270
Resize, button, E263
Restoring data, E40
Right-align column titles, E71
Right Align tool, **E71**, E96
Right-justified cells, numbers and, E14, E15
Rotation angle, of pie chart, **E149**–151, E162
Rounded values, E78
Row(s), **E5**
 border color and, E139
 deleting, E112–113
 demote, E211, E221
 detail, E210
 expanding or collapsing, E213, E215–216
 inserting, E113–114
 print titles and, E203
 pushed, E114
 sorting, E298
 storing record, E288
 subordinate, E212–213
 summing, E19–20, E46
 total, E210
Row category, **E312**
Row height, **E85**–87, E96
 increasing, of nonadjacent rows, E194
Row Height command, 86–87
Row level bar, E212
Row level symbols, **E212**
Row names, E6
Row number (row title), E5
Row references, absolute versus relative, E131
Row titles, E12–13, E236
 creating names based on, E240–243
 entering, E59
 formatting, E74–75
 large worksheet and, E179–180, E193
Row total, summing, E19–20

Sans Serif, E22
Save As command, E88, E140–141
Save As dialog box, E32, E34
Save File tool, E31–34, E37, E69, E140
Saving
 after spell checking, E202
 changes to worksheet, E38
 file, E37
 intermediate copy, E69, E187
 page setup characteristics, E205
 pie chart, E156
 using same file name, E88
 worksheet, E31–34
 worksheet on disk, E33, E46
 worksheet under different file name, E140–141
 worksheet with outline, E217
Scaling option, E95
Scenario Manager, E267–270, E274
Screen
 large worksheet and, E175
 previewing worksheet on, E88–90
 worksheet on, E6
Screen fonts, **E80**

Scroll arrows, **E6**
Scroll bars, **E6**, E206
Scroll boxes, **E6**
Scrolling, split bars and, E210
Section of worksheet, printing, E90–92, E96
Select a cell, **E8**, E46
Select All button, **E41**, E46
Selection squares
 pie charts and, E148, E151
 selected chart and, E31
Select Visible Cells tool, **E214**, E221
Sensitivity analysis, **E218**
Series, creating with fill handle, E178–179, E221
Set Database command, E291–292, E294
Set Extract command, E306
Set Page Break command, **E206**, E221
Set Preferred command, E160, E162
Set Print Area command, **E90**–91, E96
Set Print Titles command, E204, E221
Shaded cells, **E196**–197, E221
Shadow, drop, E196, E197
Sheet1 Maximize button, E4–5
Shortcut menu, **E73**, E96
 Border, E73–74, E137–140
 Column Width, E85
 Delete, E112
 Font, E135–137
 Insert, E113–115
 Number command, E78–80
 Paste, E180, E182
 Row Height, E86–87
 3-D View, E149
 Toolbar, E184
Show Outline Symbols tool, **E216**, E221
Shrinking worksheet, E207–208
Sort Ascending tool, E298
Sort command, E297, E299
Sort Descending tool, E298
Sorting, **E296**–300, E318
 more than three fields, E300
 three fields, E298–300
 using sort ascending and sort descending tools, E298
Sort key, E298
SPACEBAR, E41
Special characters, E13
Spell checker, **E201**–203, E221
Spelling command, **E201**
Spelling dialog box, **E202**, E203
Split bar, E210, E221
Split box, E210
Split command, **E208**
Spreadsheet, *see* Worksheet
Standard dictionary, **E201**, E203
Standard toolbar, **E7**
Starting Excel, E4–5, E46
Status bar, **E7**
Style box, **E75**
 displaying totals and averages as dollar amounts, E77–78
 dollar signs and, E76
 formatting numbers using, E75–78, E96
 Normal, E239
 whole numbers with comma placement and, E77
Subordinate rows, E212–213
Subtotals, crosstab table and, E316
Subtraction (−), E60, **E62**
Sum, calculating, E15–17
SUM function, **E15**–17, E46
 adjusting ranges in, E116–117

INDEX

column totals, E64–66
copying, E17–21, E65–66
Summarizing database information, E312–317
Summary report, Scenario Manager and, E267, 270
Summing
  columns, E15–17
  row total, E19–20
System date and time, E237–239

Table, crosstab, E312–317, E318
Table command, E251
Table formats, **E25–27**
Testing
  command macro, E255
  worksheet, E44
Text
  centering, E71, E96
  chart, E152–154, E162
  entering, E8–13
  formatting, E69–75
  left align, E71, E96
  right align, E71, E96
  wrapping, in a cell, E128–130, E162
Text Box tool, E152
Three-dimensional appearance, shaded cells and, E196
3-D Column Chart tool, E215
Three-dimensional pie chart, E144
3-D View command, **E149–150**
Tilde (~), comparison criteria and, E303
Time, system, E237–239
Title(s)
  chart, E147–148
  column, *see* Column titles
  database, E290
  pie chart, E142
  row, *see* Row titles
  worksheet, *see* Worksheet title(s)
Title bar, floating toolbar and, E185
Toolbar
  floating, E185
  hiding, E185, E192, E221
Toolbar dock, **E185**
Toolbars command, E184, E221
Toolbar shortcut menu, **E184**
Toolbar show or hide, E184–185, E221
Total(s)
  border color of, E139
  column, E64–66
  displaying as dollar amounts using Style box, E77–78
  row, E19–20, E139, **E210**
Total columns, **E210**
Total cost, E245
Total interest, E245
TrueType Arial, E80–81
TrueType font, **E80**
Tutorial, **E43**

Underline, double, E74
Underline tool, **E73**, E96
Underscore (_), name in a formula and, E241
Undo Column Width command, E83
Undo command, **E40**, E46, E117
Undo Paste command, E181
Undo Sort command, E297
Unfreeze Panes command, **E188**, E208, E221
Unlocked cells, **E271**
Unprotected cells, **E271**
Utility toolbar, **E200**
  Button tool, E260

Check Spelling tool, E201–202
Demote tool, E211–213
displaying, E201
docking, E200
Paste Values tool, E221
Promote tool, E211, E217–218, E221
Select Visible Cells tool, E214, E221
Sort tool, E298
Zoom In tool, E208
Zoom Out tool, E208

Value field, **E312**
Values
  changing in cells that are referenced in a formula, E218–220
  displaying, E189–190
  series of, E178–179
  switching to displaying formulas from, E93, E96
Values version of worksheet, **E92**
Vertical split bar, **E210**
Vertical split box, **E210**
View of worksheet, E206–210
Visible cells, **E214–215**, E221

What-if analysis, **E218**
What-if questions, E175, E218, **E233**
What-if tools
  automatic recalculation, E218–220
  data table, E246–253
  goal seeking, E265–267
  recalculation, E218–220, E235, E253
  Scenario Manager, E267–270
White selection squares, **E148**
Whole numbers, comma placement and, E77
Wildcard characters, **E303**
Window(s)
  chart, E147
  floating toolbar and, E185
  macro, E260
  macro sheet, E256
  opening embedded chart in its own, E147
  splitting into panes, E208–210, E221
  switching, E154–156, E162
Window menu, **E154–156**, E260
  Freeze Panes, E187–188
  Split, E208
  Unfreeze Panes, E188, E208, E221
  Zoom, E207
Windows Program Manager, E4
Worksheet, **E5**
  adding and changing data in, E115–117
  building, E2–56
  charts and, E28–31
  clearing entire, E41–42, E46
  color in, E134–140
  comments and, E198–200
  designing, E44
  enhancing, E109–141
  entering, E44
  entering numbers, E13–15
  entering text, E8–13
  font change and, E80–82, E96, E177
  formatting, E22–27
  formulas and, E57–96
  formulas version, E92–94
  intermediate copy of, E69, E187
  large, *see* Worksheet, large
  magnifying, E207–208
  opening, E38–39, E46, E111
  outlining, E210–218
  planning, E44
  preparation steps, E3
  previewing, E88–90
  printing, E35–37, E46

protecting, E271–273, E274
recalculating, E65
saving, E31–34
selecting cell, E8
shrinking, E207–208
sum calculations, E15–17
testing, E44
unprotecting, E271, E274
values version, E92
view, E206–210
Worksheet, large, E175–220
  borders, E195
  column widths, E179–180
  column titles, E193
  copying range of cells to nonadjacent paste area, E180–182
  creating series with fill handle and, E178–179
  displaying and docking Utility toolbar, E200–201
  entering and copying expense formula totals, E188–192
  entering revenue data, E183
  font, E177, E193
  font color, E198
  formatting Budget % Expenses table, E196–198
  formatting titles, E193
  Formatting toolbar, E184–186
  freezing worksheet titles and, E187–188
  increasing height of nonadjacent rows, E194
  moving around, E206
  outlining, E210–218
  page setup and, E204–206
  printing with print titles, E203–204
  row titles, E179–180, E193
  splitting windows and, E208–210
  worksheet title, E177–178, E193
Worksheet data, analyzing, E233–273
Worksheet database, *see* Database
Worksheet settings, restoring, E40
Worksheet title(s), E8–9, E22–25, E236
  centered across columns, E23
  centering, E134
  entering, E58
  formatting, E22–25, E70
  freezing, E187–188, E221
  large worksheet, E177–178, E193
  unfreezing, E188, E221
Worksheet window, **E6**
  switching from chart window to, E154–156
Workspace command, E200
Wrap text, **128–130**, E162
WYSIWYG (What You See Is What You Get), E80

X-axis, E31
XLM (Excel Macro Sheet) extension, E259
XLS extension, **E34**

Y-axis, E28, E29
YES, IF function and, E130

Zero(s)
  empty cell equal to, E64
  trailing, E15
Zoom button, E90
Zoom command, E207
Zoom In tool, **E208**, E221
Zoom Out tool, **E208**, E221

DATABASE

USING PARADOX 1.0 FOR WINDOWS

▶ PROJECT ONE

CREATING A DATABASE

Objectives **P2**
What Is a Database? **P2**
What Is Paradox for Windows? **P4**
Database Preparation Steps **P4**
Starting Paradox **P5**
The Paradox for Windows Desktop **P6**
Changing the Working Directory **P7**
Creating a Table **P8**
Saving a Table **P15**
Exiting Paradox for Windows **P17**
Adding Records to a Table **P17**
Adding Additional Records **P24**
Printing the Contents of a Table **P27**
Creating Additional Tables **P30**
Adding Records to a Table **P32**
Using a Form to View Data **P33**
Creating a Graph **P37**
Using the Help Facility **P43**
Designing a Database **P43**
Project Summary **P45**
Key Terms **P45**
Quick Reference **P45**
Student Assignments **P47**
Computer Laboratory Exercises **P52**
Computer Laboratory Assignments **P53**

▶ PROJECT TWO

QUERYING A DATABASE

Objectives **P59**
Introduction **P59**
The Answer Table **P60**
Opening a New Query Window **P61**
Including All Fields in the Answer Table **P62**
Running a Query to Create the Answer Table **P64**
Displaying Selected Fields in the Answer Table **P68**
Entering Conditions **P70**
Using Compound Conditions **P78**
Sorting Data in a Query **P80**
Joining Tables **P86**
Using Computed Fields **P92**
Calculating Statistics **P94**
Graphing the Answer to a Query **P96**
Saving a Query **P101**
Project Summary **P102**
Key Terms **P103**
Quick Reference **P103**
Student Assignments **P104**
Computer Laboratory Exercises **P109**
Computer Laboratory Assignments **P110**

▶ PROJECT THREE

MAINTAINING A DATABASE

Objectives **P113**
Introduction **P113**
Adding, Changing, and Deleting Records **P114**
Changing the Structure **P121**
Creating Validity Checks **P127**
Referential Integrity **P134**
Updating a Table That Contains Validity Checks **P137**
Mass Updates **P139**
Creating and Using Indexes **P142**
Project Summary **P152**
Key Terms **P152**
Quick Reference **P152**
Student Assignments **P153**
Computer Laboratory Exercises **P158**
Computer Laboratory Assignments **P159**

▶ PROJECT FOUR

PRESENTING DATA: REPORTS AND FORMS

Objectives **P163**
Introduction **P163**
Creating a Report **P166**
Grouping **P183**
Report Design Considerations **P188**
Creating and Using Custom Forms **P188**
Form Design Considerations **P209**
Project Summary **P210**
Key Terms **P210**
Quick Reference **P210**
Student Assignments **P212**
Computer Laboratory Exercises **P218**
Computer Laboratory Assignments **P219**

▶ PROJECT FIVE

ADVANCED TOPICS

Objectives **P221**
Introduction **P221**
Date, Memo, and OLE Fields **P222**
Restructuring the Slsrep Table **P223**
Updating the New Fields **P225**
Advanced Form Techniques **P235**
Using Date and Memo Fields in a Query **P256**
Project Summary **P258**
Key Terms **P258**
Quick Reference **P258**
Student Assignments **P259**
Computer Laboratory Exercises **P263**
Computer Laboratory Assignments **P265**

INDEX P270

PARADOX 1.0 FOR WINDOWS
PROJECT ONE

CREATING A DATABASE

OBJECTIVES You will have mastered the material in this project when you can:

- Describe databases and database management systems
- Start Paradox for Windows
- Describe the features of the Paradox for Windows desktop
- Change the working directory
- Create a table
- Define the fields in a table
- Open a table
- Add records to an empty table
- Close a table
- Add records to a nonempty table
- Print the contents of a table
- Use a form to view data
- Create a quick graph
- Use the help facility
- Understand how to design a database to eliminate redundancy

▶ WHAT IS A DATABASE?

Creating, storing, sorting, and retrieving data are important tasks. In their personal lives, many people keep a variety of records such as names, addresses, and phone numbers of friends and business associates, records of investments, records of expenses for tax purposes, and so on. These records must be arranged for quick access. Businesses must also be able to store and access information quickly and easily. Personnel and inventory records, payroll information, customer records, order data, and accounts receivable information are all crucial and must be readily available.

The term **database** describes a collection of data organized in a manner that allows access, retrieval, and use of that data. A **database management system**, like Paradox for Windows, allows you to use a computer to create a database; add, change, and delete data in the database; sort the data in the database; retrieve data in the database; and create forms and reports using the data in the database.

In Paradox, a database consists of a collection of tables. Figure 1-1 shows a sample database for an organization. It consists of two tables. The Customer table contains information about the customers of the organization. The Sales Rep table contains information about the organization's sales representatives.

CUSTOMER TABLE

Customer Number	Name	Address	City	State	Zip Code	Balance	Credit Limit	Sales Rep Number
AC12	Arend Corp.	21 Wilson	Muncie	IN	47303	$4,278.50	$6,000.00	03
AI53	Allied Industry	215 Raymond	Carmel	IN	46032	$203.00	$3,000.00	06
AX29	AAA Express	108 College	Muncie	IN	47303	$42.00	$3,000.00	06
CL67	Clark-White Ltd.	47 Chipwood	Moline	IL	61265	$3,206.00	$8,000.00	12
FC15	Ferguson Co.	602 Bridge	Mason	MI	48854	$6,704.00	$6,000.00	03
FY24	Farley-Young	19 Oak	Muncie	IN	47303	$2,504.00	$6,000.00	06
LW46	L. T. Wheeler	587 Rivard	Moline	IL	61265	$0.00	$6,000.00	06
NI34	Nelson Inc.	12 Bishop	Sumner	IL	62466	$2,011.50	$6,000.00	03
SH84	Shippers and Dale	208 Grayton	Carmel	IN	46032	$1,597.25	$8,000.00	12
SI84	Shelton Inc.	82 Harcourt	Niles	MI	49120	$7,020.00	$8,000.00	06

SALES REP TABLE

Sales Rep Number	Last Name	First Name	Address	City	State	Zip Code	Sales	Commission Rate
03	Harrison	Monica	12 LaGrange	Parkton	MI	48154	$52,348.00	0.07
06	Thompson	Charles	1564 Birchview	Auburn	IN	46706	$78,202.00	0.05
12	Juarez	Mara	722 Davison	Chicago	IL	60614	$28,222.00	0.07

FIGURE 1-1

The rows in the tables are called records. A **record** contains information about a given person, product, or event. A row in the Customer table, for example, contains information about a specific customer.

The columns in the tables are called fields. A **field** contains a specific piece of information within a record. In the Customer table, for example, the fourth field, City, contains the name of the city where the customer is located.

The first field in the Customer table is the Customer Number. This is a code assigned by the organization to each customer. Like many organizations, this organization calls it a "number" even though it actually contains letters and numbers. The customer numbers have a special form. They consist of two uppercase letters followed by a two-digit number.

These customer numbers are *unique*; that is, no two customers will be assigned the same number. Such a field can be used as a **unique identifier**. This simply means that a given customer number will appear in only a single record in the table. There is only one record, for example, in which the customer number is CL67. A unique identifier is also called a **primary key**. Thus, the Customer Number field is the primary key for the Customer table.

The next seven fields in the Customer table include the Name, Address, City, State, Zip Code, Balance, and Credit Limit. For example, customer AC12 is Arend Corp. It is located at 21 Wilson in Muncie, Indiana. The Zip Code is 47303. Its current balance (the amount it owes to the organization) is $4,278.50. Its credit limit (the amount its balance should not exceed) is $6,000.00.

Each customer has a single sales representative. The last field in the Customer table, Sales Rep Number, gives the number of the customer's sales representative.

The first field in the Sales Rep table, Sales Rep Number, is the number assigned by the organization to each sales representative. These numbers are unique, so the Sales Rep Number is the primary key of the Sales Rep table.

The other fields in the Sales Rep table are Last Name, First Name, Address, City, State, Zip Code, Sales, and Commission Rate. For example, sales representative 03 is Monica Harrison. She lives at 12 LaGrange in Parkton, Michigan. Her Zip Code is 48154. So far this year, she has sold $52,348.00 worth of product. Her commission rate is 7% (0.07).

The Sales Rep Number appears in both the Customer table and the Sales Rep table. It is used to relate customers and sales representatives. For example, in the customer table, you see the sales representative number for customer AC12 is 03. To find the name of this sales representative, look for the row in the Sales Rep table that contains 03 in the Sales Rep Number field. Once you have found it, you will see the name of the sales representative is Monica Harrison. To find all the customers for whom Monica Harrison is the sales representative, look through the Customer table for all the customers that contain 03 in the Sales Rep Number field. Her customers are AC12 (Arend Corp.), FC15 (Ferguson Co.), and NI34 (Nelson Inc.).

▶ WHAT IS PARADOX FOR WINDOWS?

Paradox for Windows is a powerful database management system (DBMS) that functions in the Windows environment and allows you to create and process data in a database. To illustrate the use of Paradox for Windows, this book presents a series of projects. The projects use the database of customers and sales representatives. In Project 1, the two tables that comprise the database are created, and the appropriate records are added to them. The project also uses a form to display the data in the tables, and prints a report of data in the tables. It also uses a form to display the data in the tables as well as a graph to visually represent the data. It also prints a report of data in the tables.

▶ DATABASE PREPARATION STEPS

To create the database consisting of the Customer table and the Sales Rep table shown in Figure 1-1 on the previous page, add data to the tables, display the data using a form or graph, and print the data, you will perform the following steps.

1. Start Paradox for Windows.
2. Change the working directory, the directory Paradox will use for all the files you create.
3. Begin the creation of the Customer table.
4. Define the fields in the Customer table.
5. Save the Customer table as a file on a diskette.
6. Add data records to the Customer table.
7. Print the contents of the Customer table.
8. Create and use a form to view the data in the Customer table.
9. Begin the creation of the Sales Rep table.
10. Define the fields in the Sales Rep table.
11. Save the Sales Rep table as a file on a diskette.
12. Add records to the Sales Rep table.
13. Create a graph that visually represents data from the Sales Rep table.

The following pages contain a detailed explanation of each of these steps.

STARTING PARADOX   **P5**

▶ STARTING PARADOX

To start Paradox, the Windows Program Manager must appear on the screen and the Paradox for Windows group window must be open. To accomplish these tasks, use the procedures presented earlier in *Introduction to Windows*. The remaining steps to start Paradox for Windows follow.

TO START PARADOX FOR WINDOWS ▼

STEP 1 ▶

Place a diskette in drive A unless you have already done so.

STEP 2 ▶

Use the mouse to point to the Paradox for Windows program-item icon in the Paradox for Windows group window (Figure 1-2).

Be sure you have a diskette in drive A. If you do not, you may see a System Error dialog box. To correct the problem, place a diskette in drive A and choose Retry.

FIGURE 1-2

STEP 3 ▶

Double-click the left mouse button. If the Paradox for Windows desktop is not already maximized, point to the Maximize button (▫).

Paradox displays the Paradox for Windows loading box for a few moments and then the Paradox for Windows desktop displays. If the desktop is not already maximized, the mouse pointer is pointing to the Maximize button (Figure 1-3).

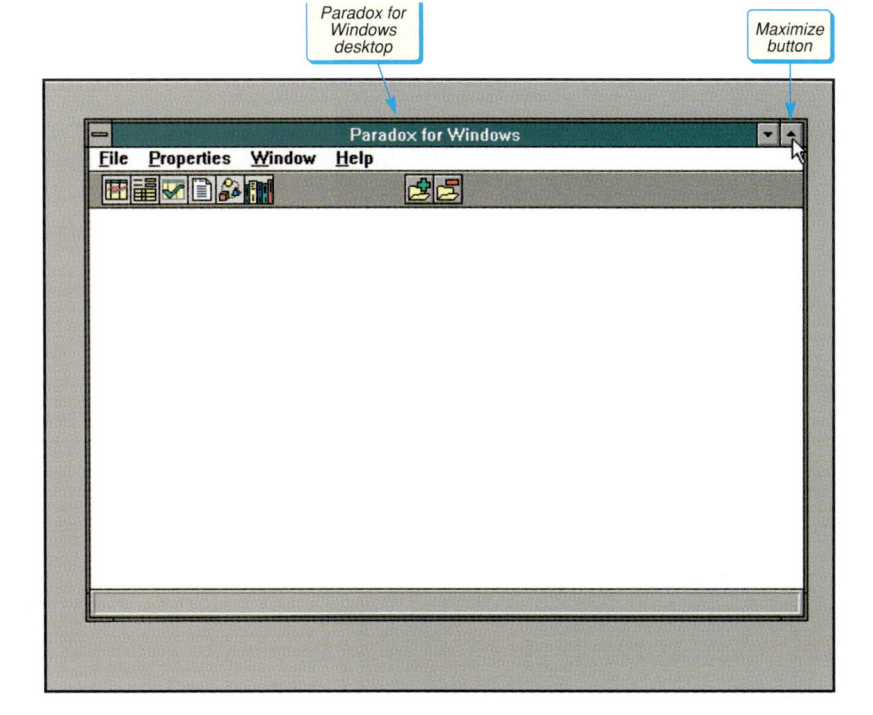

FIGURE 1-3

P6 PROJECT 1 CREATING A DATABASE

STEP 3 ▶

If the Paradox for Windows desktop is not maximized, click the Maximize button by pressing the left mouse button.

The maximized Paradox for Windows desktop displays on the screen (Figure 1-4).

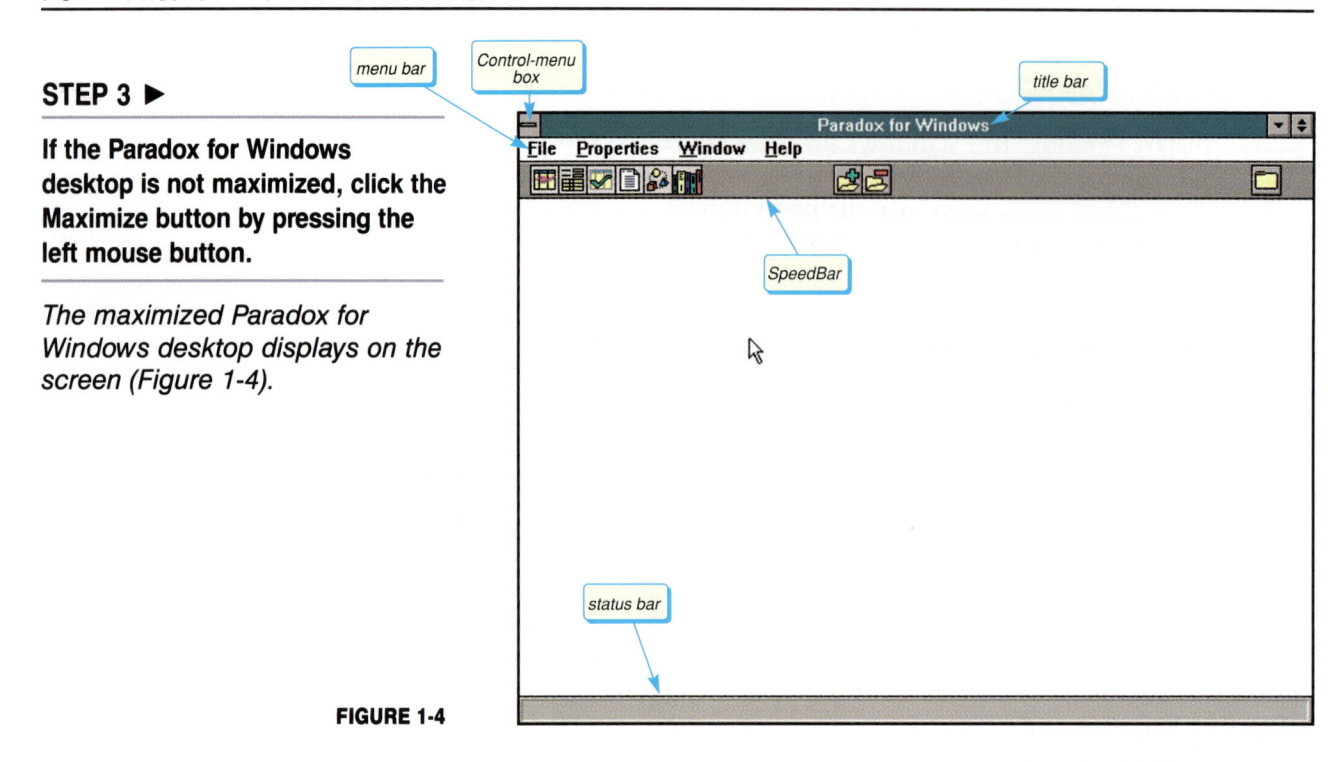

FIGURE 1-4

▶ THE PARADOX FOR WINDOWS DESKTOP

The first bar on the Paradox desktop is the **title bar** (Figure 1-4). It displays the title of the product, Paradox for Windows. The Control-menu box at the left end of the title bar is used to access the **Control menu**.

The second bar is the **menu bar**. It contains a list of menus. You select a menu from the menu bar using the method learned in *Introduction to Windows*.

The third bar is the **SpeedBar**. The SpeedBar contains buttons that allow you to perform certain tasks more quickly than using the menu bar. Each button contains a picture depicting its function. The specific buttons on the SpeedBar will vary, depending on the task you are working on. Figure 1-5 indicates the functions of the SpeedBar buttons on the Paradox desktop that you will find most useful. Buttons on other screens will be discussed as they are encountered.

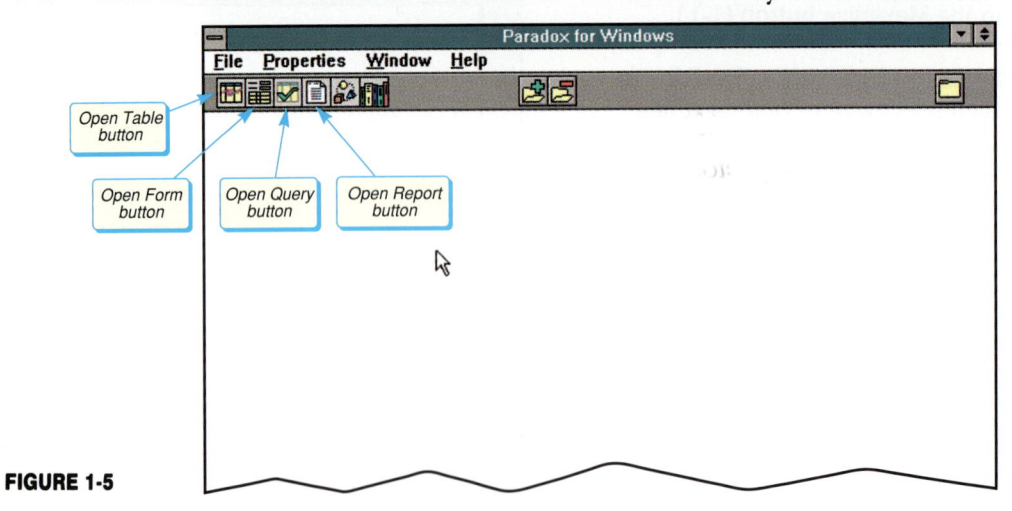

FIGURE 1-5

The bottom bar on the screen is the **status bar** (Figure 1-4). It contains special information that is appropriate for the task on which you are working. In addition, when you are pointing to a SpeedBar button, the status bar contains a description of the button.

▶ CHANGING THE WORKING DIRECTORY

Once you have started Paradox for Windows, you need to change the working directory. The **working directory** is the disk and directory where Paradox for Windows stores any files you create unless you specify otherwise. It is also the first place Paradox will look for files. Assuming you are placing your files on a diskette in drive A, you make the root directory on the diskette in drive A the working directory by performing the following steps.

TO CHANGE THE WORKING DIRECTORY ▼

STEP 1 ▶

Select the File menu by pointing to the word File on the menu bar and clicking the left mouse button. Then point to the Working Directory command.

Paradox displays the File menu, and the mouse pointer points to the Working Directory command (Figure 1-6).

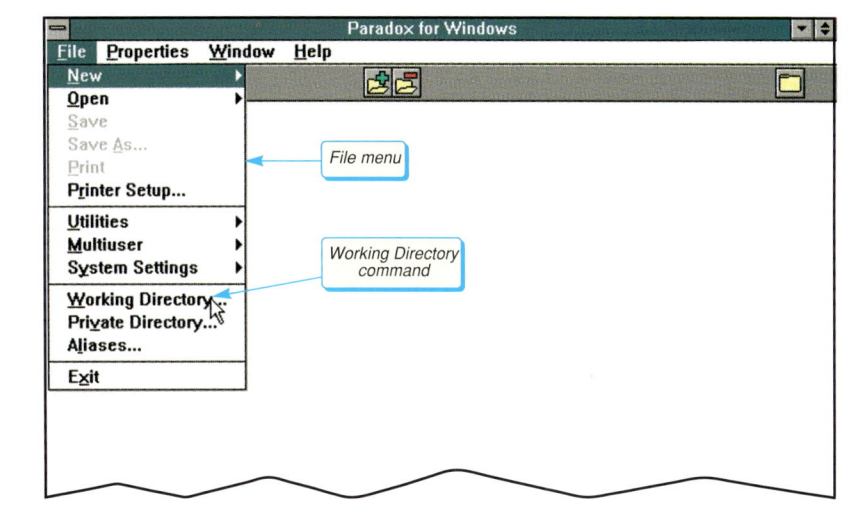

FIGURE 1-6

STEP 2 ▶

Choose the Working Directory command from the File menu by clicking the left mouse button.

The Set Working Directory dialog box displays on the screen (Figure 1-7). The name of the current working directory is highlighted in the Working Directory box. If it is already A:\, you can skip the next step.

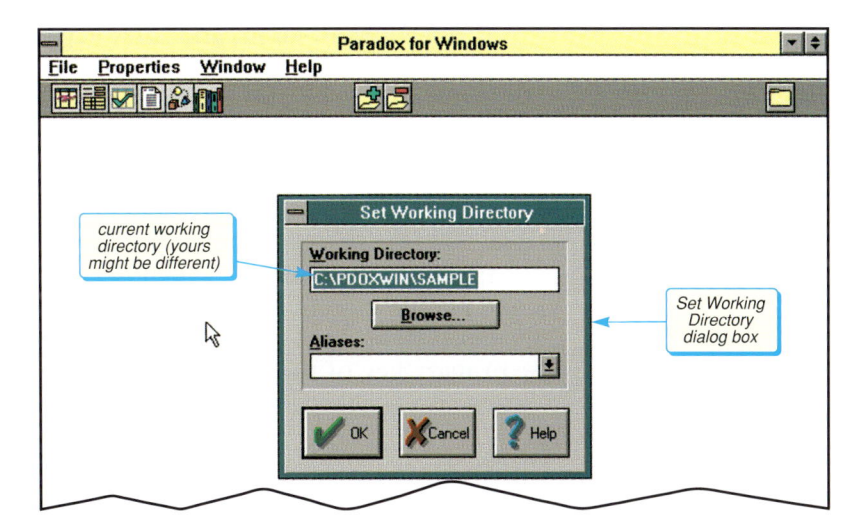

FIGURE 1-7

P8   PROJECT 1   CREATING A DATABASE

STEP 3 ▶

Type `a:\` and point to the OK button (✓ OK).

Paradox displays the entry in uppercase in the Working Directory text box (Figure 1-8).

STEP 4 ▶

Choose the OK button by clicking the left mouse button.

The dialog box will disappear, and the working directory is the root directory of the diskette in drive A.

FIGURE 1-8

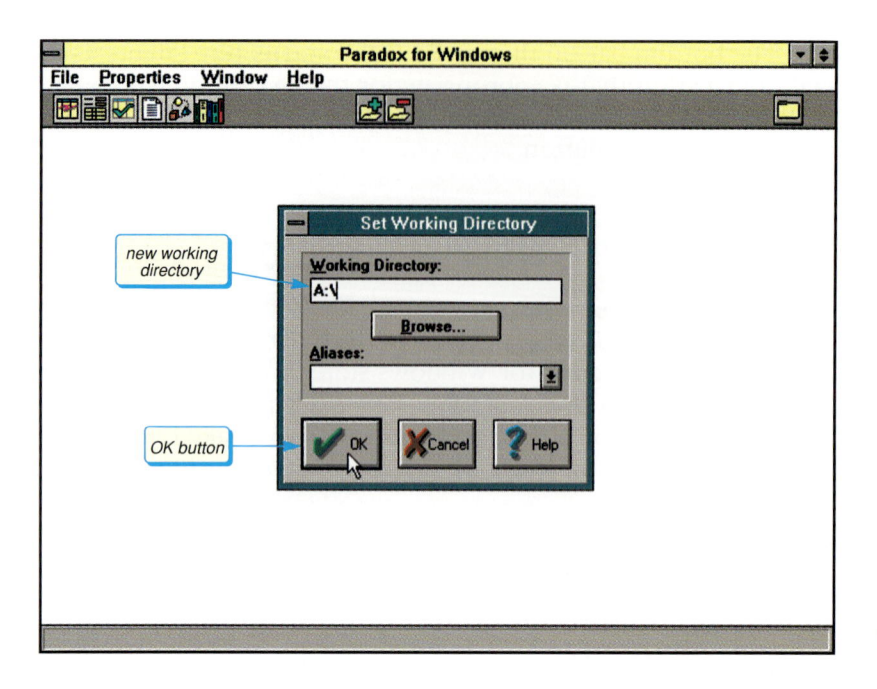

▶ CREATING A TABLE

A Paradox database consists of a collection of tables. To create a database, you must create each of the tables within it. In this project, for example, you must create both the Customer and Sales Rep tables shown in Figure 1-1 on page P3.

To **create a table**, you describe the **structure** of the table to Paradox by describing the fields within the table. For each field, you must indicate the following:

1. **Field name.** Each field in the table must have a unique name. In the Customer table (Figure 1-9 on the next page), for example, the field names are Customer Number, Name, Address, City, State, Zip Code, Balance, Credit Limit, and Sales Rep Number.
2. **Field type.** Field type indicates to Paradox the type of data that the field will contain. Some fields, such as Commission Rate, can contain only numbers. Others, like Balance and Credit Limit, can contain only numbers and dollar signs. Still others, such as Name, contain letters.
3. **Field size.** The field size specifies the maximum size value that can be placed in the field.

You must also indicate which field or fields make up the **primary key**, that is, the unique identifier, for the table. In the sample database, the Sales Rep Number is the primary key of the Sales Rep table and the Customer Number is the primary key of the Customer table. The only restriction on fields used as the primary key is that they be the first fields in the table.

▶ STRUCTURE OF CUSTOMER TABLE

Field Name	Type	Size	Key
Customer Number	A	4	*
Name	A	20	
Address	A	15	
City	A	15	
State	A	2	
Zip Code	A	5	
Balance	$		
Credit Limit	$		
Sales Rep Number	A	2	

▶ DATA FOR CUSTOMER TABLE

FIGURE 1-9

Customer Number	Name	Address	City	State	Zip Code	Balance	Credit Limit	Sales Rep Number
AC12	Arend Corp.	21 Wilson	Muncie	IN	47303	$4,278.50	$6,000.00	03
AI53	Allied Industry	215 Raymond	Carmel	IN	46032	$203.00	$3,000.00	06
AX29	AAA Express	108 College	Muncie	IN	47303	$42.00	$3,000.00	06
CL67	Clark-White Ltd.	47 Chipwood	Moline	IL	61265	$3,206.00	$8,000.00	12
FC15	Ferguson Co.	602 Bridge	Mason	MI	48854	$6,704.00	$6,000.00	03
FY24	Farley-Young	19 Oak	Muncie	IN	47303	$2,504.00	$6,000.00	06
LW46	L. T. Wheeler	587 Rivard	Moline	IL	61265	$0.00	$6,000.00	06
NI34	Nelson Inc.	12 Bishop	Sumner	IL	62466	$2,011.50	$6,000.00	03
SH84	Shippers and Dale	208 Grayton	Carmel	IN	46032	$1,597.25	$8,000.00	12
SI84	Shelton Inc.	82 Harcourt	Niles	MI	49120	$7,020.00	$8,000.00	06

To name a field, follow these rules:

1. The field name must be no more than 25 characters long.
2. The first character must not be a blank.
3. A field name should not contain the following characters: square brackets ([ ]), braces ({ }), parentheses, a number sign (#) by itself, or the combination of a hyphen followed by a greater than sign (–>). In this book, names will contain only letters and spaces.
4. The same name cannot be used for two different fields in the same table.

Each field has a field type. This indicates the type of data that can be stored in the field. The field types you will use in this project are:

1. **Alphanumeric (A)** – The field can contain any characters.
2. **Numeric (N)** – The field can contain only numbers. The numbers can be either positive or negative and can contain decimal places. Fields assigned this type can be used in arithmetic operations. Fields that contain numbers but will not be used for arithmetic operations, such as the Sales Rep Number field, should be assigned a field type of alphanumeric.
3. **Currency ($)** – The field can contain only dollar amounts. The values will be displayed with dollar signs, commas, and decimal points with 2 digits following the decimal point. Like numeric fields, you can use currency fields in arithmetic operations. Paradox automatically assigns a size to currency fields.
4. **Short number (S)** – The field can contain only whole numbers that are less than 32,767. Fields assigned this type can be used in arithmetic operations. This type is appropriate when the entries will not contain decimal places and will not exceed 32,767.

PROJECT 1 CREATING A DATABASE

The field names, types, sizes, and key information for the Customer table are shown in Figure 1-9 on the previous page. With this information, you are ready to begin creating the table. To create the table, use the following steps.

TO BEGIN THE TABLE CREATION

STEP 1 ▶

Select the File menu and point to the New command.

Paradox displays the File menu (Figure 1-10). The mouse pointer points to the New command.

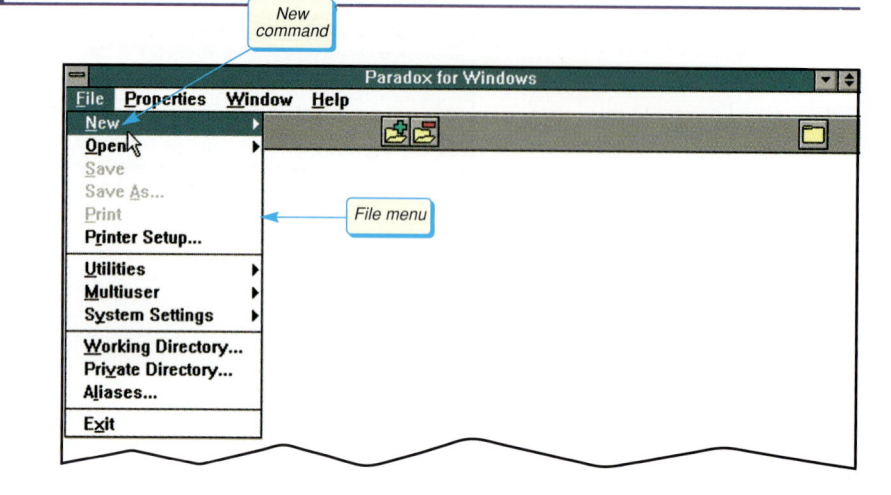

FIGURE 1-10

STEP 2 ▶

Choose the New command from the File menu by clicking the left mouse button and then point to the Table command.

A list of the types of files you can create displays in a cascading menu (Figure 1-11).

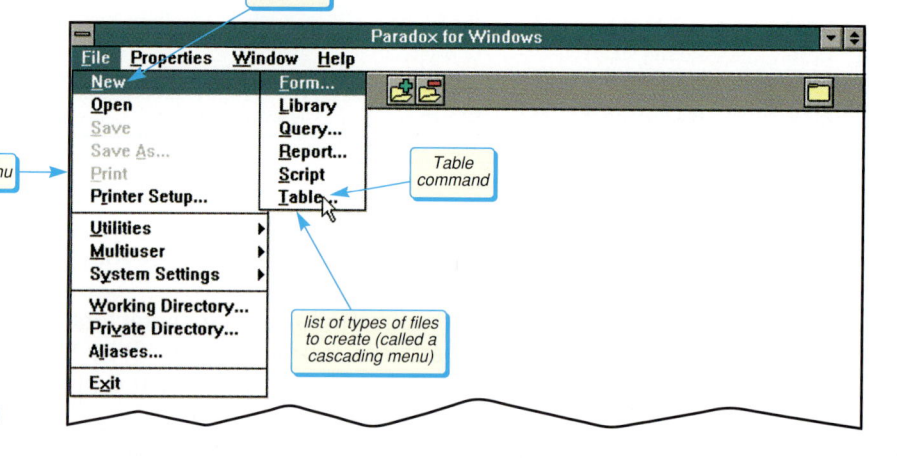

FIGURE 1-11

STEP 3 ▶

Choose the Table command from the New cascading menu by clicking the left mouse button and then point to the OK button in the Table Type dialog box.

The Table Type dialog box displays on the screen (Figure 1-12). The Table Type drop-down list box contains the highlighted value Paradox for Windows. This is the type of table you want to create.

FIGURE 1-12

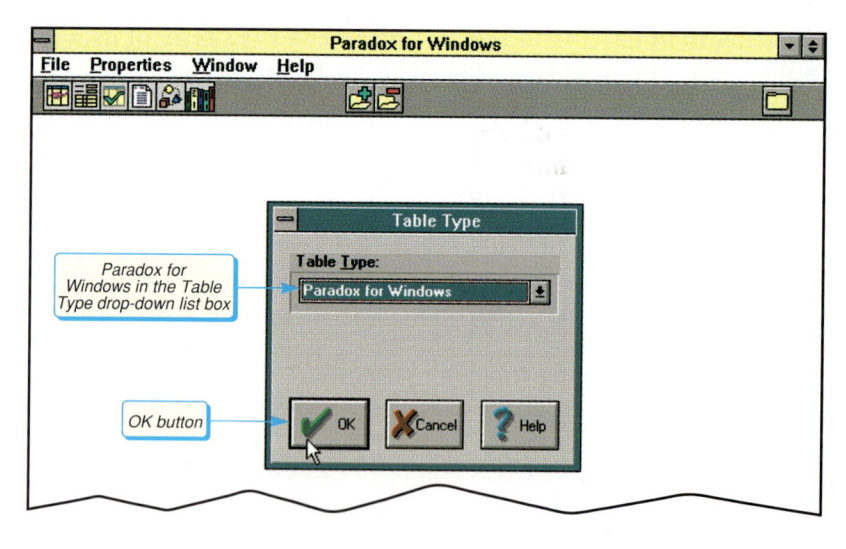

CREATING A TABLE **P11**

STEP 4 ▶

Choose the OK button in the Table Type dialog box.

The Create Paradox for Windows Table dialog box displays (Figure 1-13). To create the table, you will use the Field Roster area on the left side of this dialog box to define the fields. The dialog box contains space to enter the Field Name, the field Type, the field Size, and an indicator to show the field is a primary Key. The Field Name area is highlighted with a dark grey background, indicating Paradox is ready for you to enter information in the Field Name area.

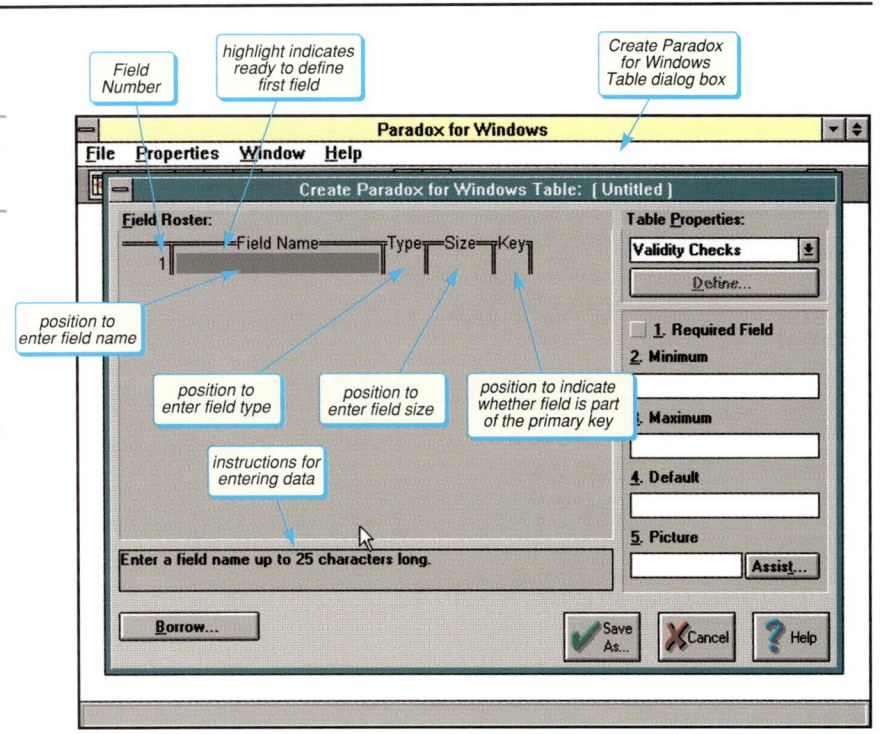

FIGURE 1-13

The next step in creating the table is to define the fields by specifying the required details in the Paradox for Windows Table dialog box. The steps to accomplish this are shown below and on the next three pages.

TO DEFINE THE FIELDS IN A TABLE ▼

STEP 1 ▶

In the Field Roster, type `Customer Number` **(the name of the first field) in the Field Name column and press the TAB key.**

The words Customer Number display in the Field Name column, and the highlight advances to the Type column indicating you can enter the field type (Figure 1-14).

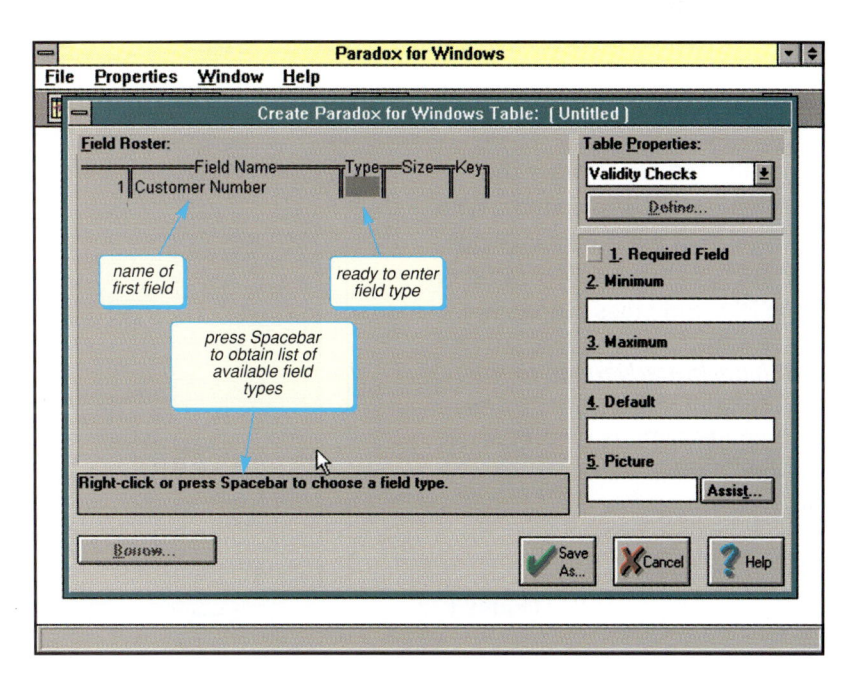

FIGURE 1-14

STEP 2 ▶

Press the SPACEBAR.

A list of available field types displays in the Type list box (Figure 1-15). To select a field type, type the underlined character. Alternatively, you can click the appropriate entry with the mouse, drag the highlight to the appropriate entry, or use the arrow keys to move the highlight to the entry and press Enter.

FIGURE 1-15

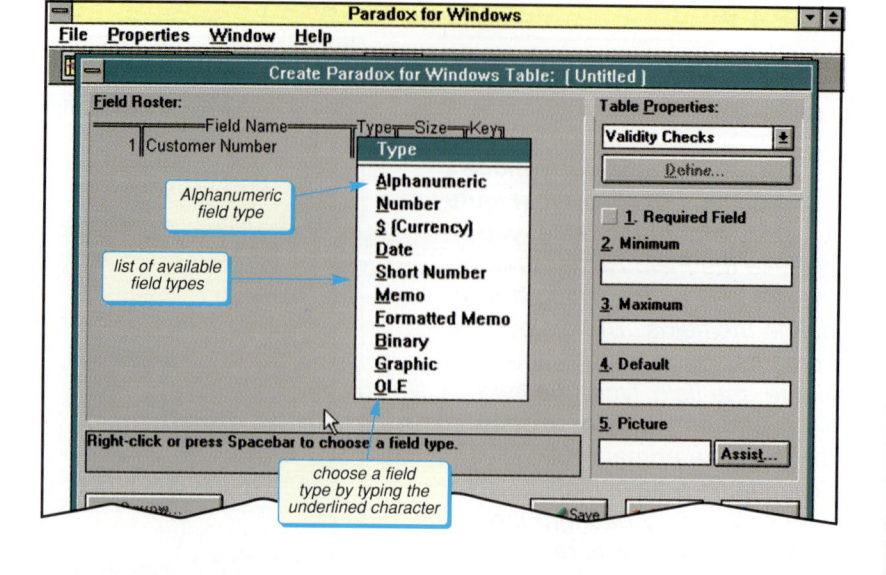

STEP 3 ▶

Because Customer Number is alphanumeric, type the letter A in either uppercase or lowercase.

The list of field types disappears, and the letter A displays in the Type column (Figure 1-16).

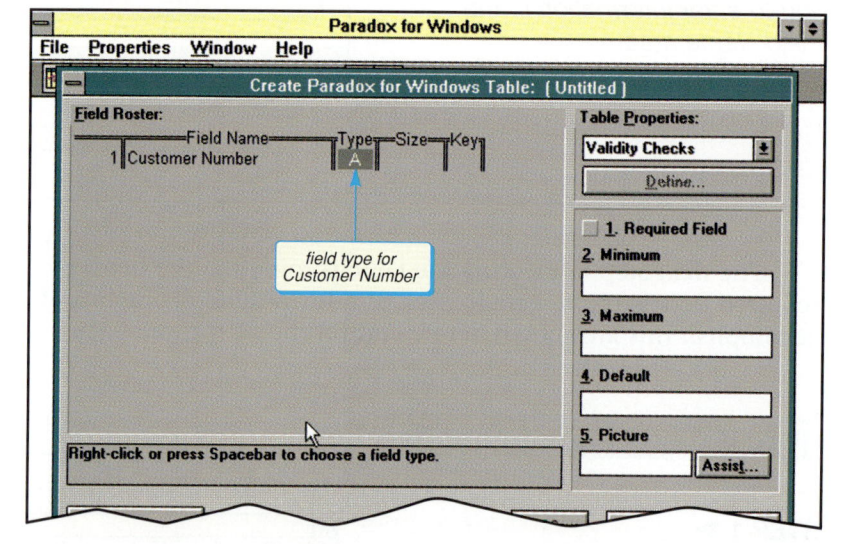

FIGURE 1-16

STEP 4 ▶

Press the TAB key to move the highlight to the Size column, type 4 (the size of the Customer Number field as shown in Figure 1-9 on page P9), and press the TAB key.

The highlight advances to the Key column (Figure 1-17). The size you entered is automatically right-aligned.

FIGURE 1-17

STEP 5 ▶

Because Customer Number is a key field, press any character and then press the TAB key.

Paradox inserts an asterisk in the Key column and the highlight advances to the Field Name column on the next row (Figure 1-18). The asterisk indicates the Customer Number is a key field.

FIGURE 1-18

STEP 6 ▶

Type `Name` **(Field Name), press the TAB key, type** `A` **(Type), press the TAB key, type** `20` **(Size), and press the TAB key.**

The name, type, and size for the second field are entered. The highlight is in the Key column (Figure 1-19).

FIGURE 1-19

STEP 7 ▶

Press the TAB key to indicate the Name field is not part of the key.

The highlight advances to the Field Name entry for the third field (Figure 1-20). For the remaining fields, the highlight will bypass the Key column.

FIGURE 1-20

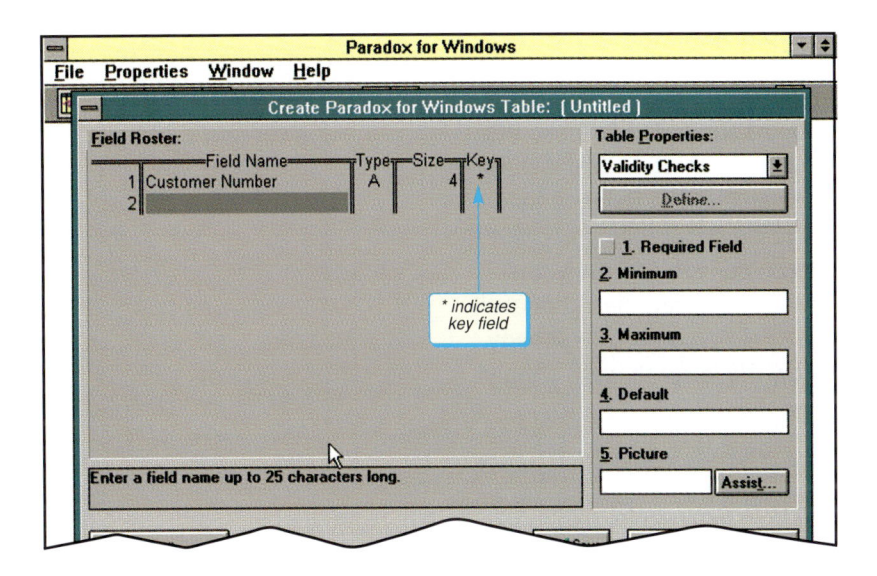

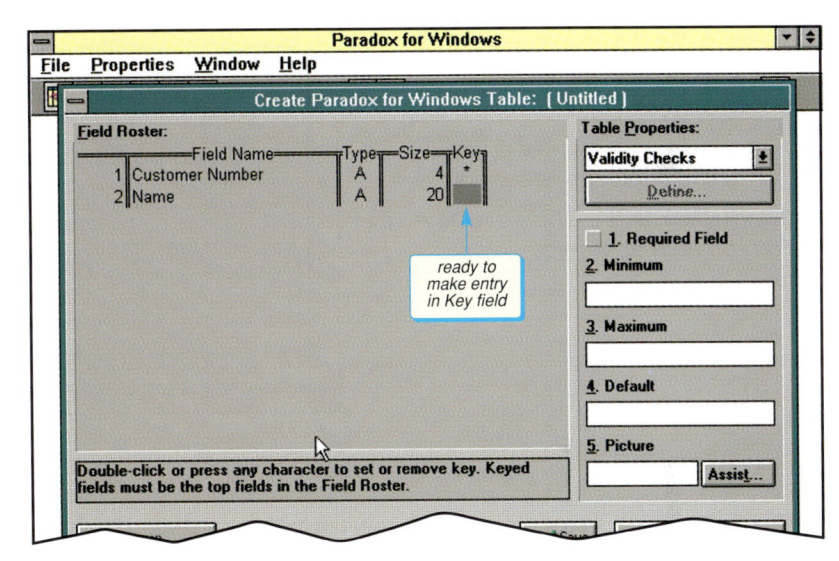

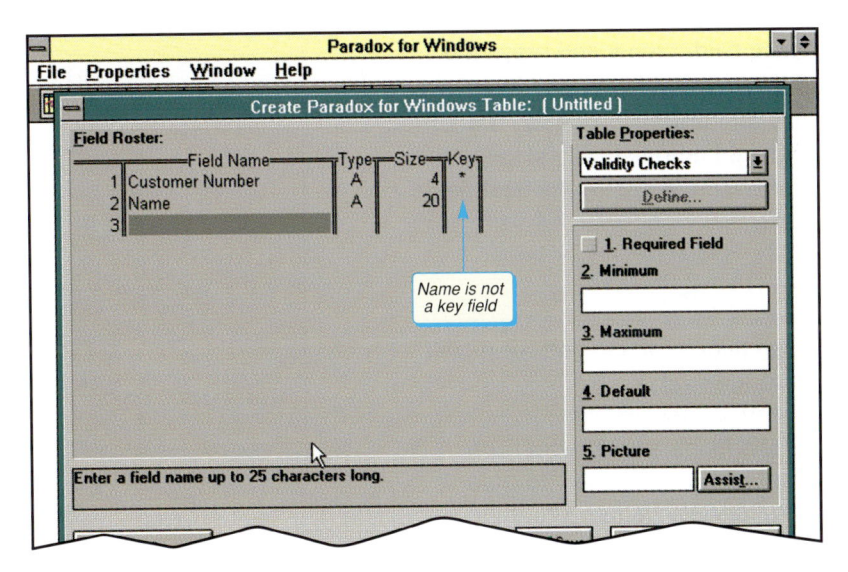

STEP 8 ▶

Use the techniques illustrated in Steps 1 through 7 to make the entries up through and including the name of the Balance field (Figure 1-21). When you enter the field type, you can press the SPACEBAR to see the list of available field types. If you already know the letter to type, simply type the letter.

Notice in Figure 1-21 that only the first field, Customer Number, is a key field.

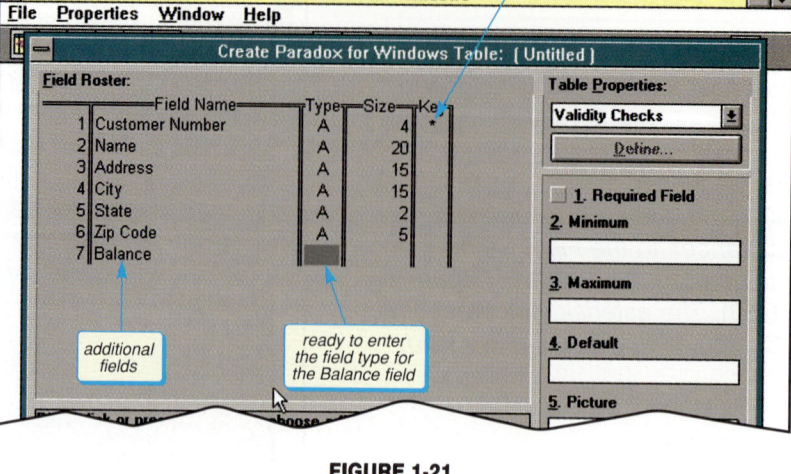

FIGURE 1-21

STEP 9 ▶

Press the SPACEBAR.

A list of available field types displays (Figure 1-22). The currency field type is indicated by a dollar sign ($).

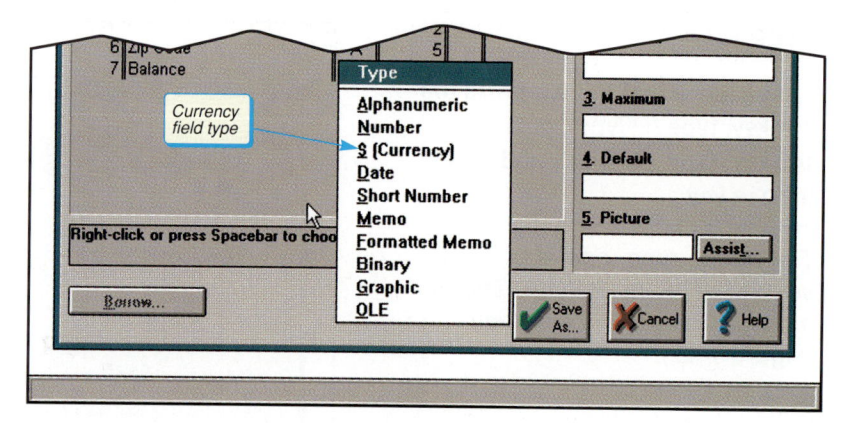

FIGURE 1-22

STEP 10 ▶

Because the Balance field is a currency field, type $ and press the TAB key. You do not need to enter a size for currency fields, so the highlight automatically skips to the Field Name entry for the next field.

STEP 11 ▶

Make the remaining entries shown in Figure 1-23.

All the fields are entered. The highlight is positioned to enter another field name. Since the table is complete, do not enter any more field names.

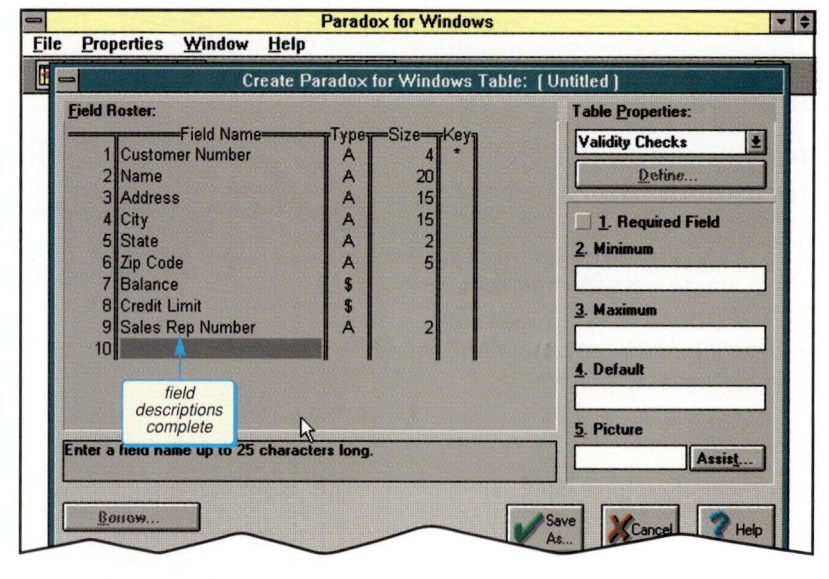

FIGURE 1-23

Correcting Errors in the Structure

When creating a table, check the entries carefully to ensure they are correct. If you make a mistake and discover it before you press the TAB key, you can correct the error by repeatedly pressing the BACKSPACE key until the incorrect characters are removed. Then, type the correct characters. If you don't discover a mistake until later, you can correct it by pointing to the entry with the mouse, clicking the left mouse button, typing the correct value, and then pressing the ENTER key.

If you accidentally add an extra field to the structure, point to the field name with the mouse, click the left mouse button, and then press CTRL+DELETE. This will remove the field from the structure.

If you forget a field, point to the Field Name column on the row where you would like to insert the field, click the left mouse button, and then press the INSERT key. The remaining fields move down one row, making room for the missing field. Make the entries for the field in the usual manner.

If you made the wrong field a key field, point to the Key entry for the field, click the left mouse button, and press any letter key to remove the asterisk.

As an alternative to these steps, you might want to start over. To do so, choose the Cancel button ( ) in the Create Paradox for Windows Table dialog box. The Paradox desktop displays and you can repeat the process you used earlier.

▶ SAVING A TABLE

You have now completely defined the structure of the table. The final step is to save the table as a file on disk. To do so, you must give the table a name.

Table names are from one to eight characters in length and must follow the rules for file names as specified in *Introduction to Windows*, because Paradox stores tables as files on disk. Paradox automatically adds its own extensions (DB for tables) to the file name. The two table names in this project are CUSTOMER and SLSREP.

To save the Customer table, complete the following steps.

TO SAVE THE TABLE ▼

STEP 1 ▶

Point to the Save As button in the Create Paradox for Windows dialog box ( ) (Figure 1-24).

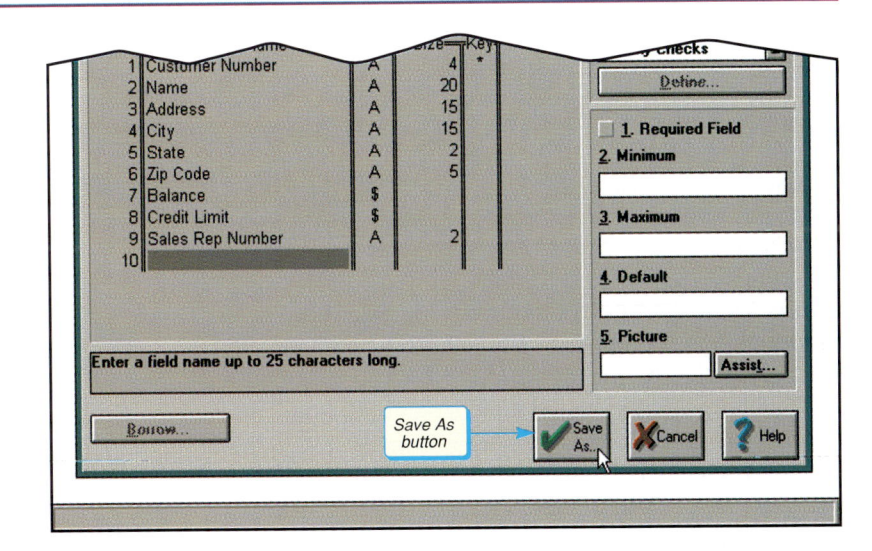

FIGURE 1-24

STEP 2 ▶

Choose the Save As button by clicking the left mouse button.

The Save Table As dialog box displays on the screen (Figure 1-25). Any tables already saved in the working directory are listed in the Tables list box. In Figure 1-25, no tables are currently stored in the working directory. The insertion point (a blinking vertical line) appears in the New Table Name text box. This is the position where you will specify a name for the table. The entry :WORK: *in the Path drop-down list box indicates the table will be stored in the working directory.*

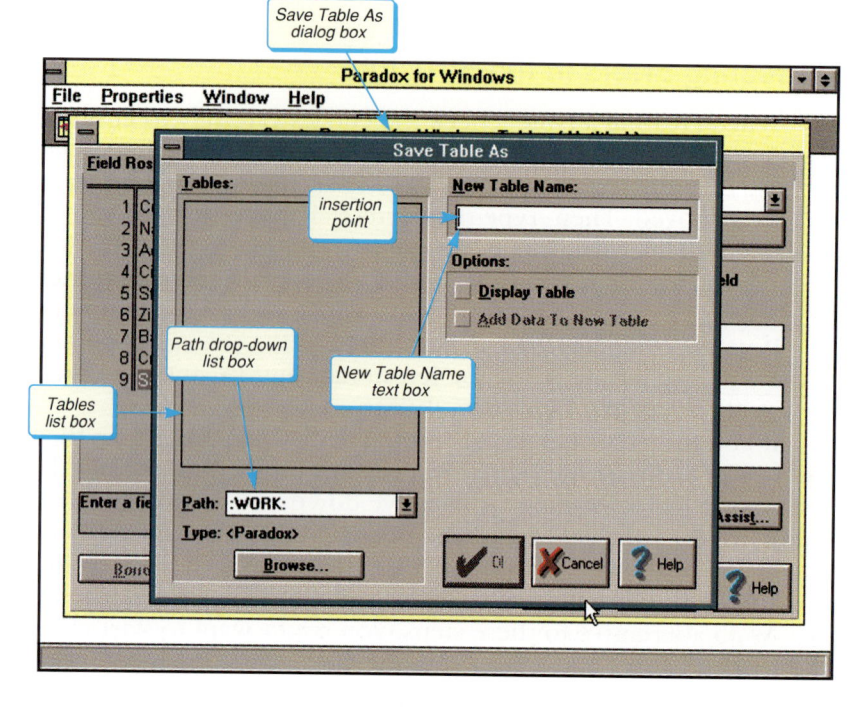

FIGURE 1-25

STEP 3 ▶

Type customer **and point to the OK button in the Save Table As dialog box.**

CUSTOMER displays in the New Table Name text box (Figure 1-26). Paradox displays the name in all uppercase letters regardless of how you type the name. The mouse pointer is pointing to the OK button.

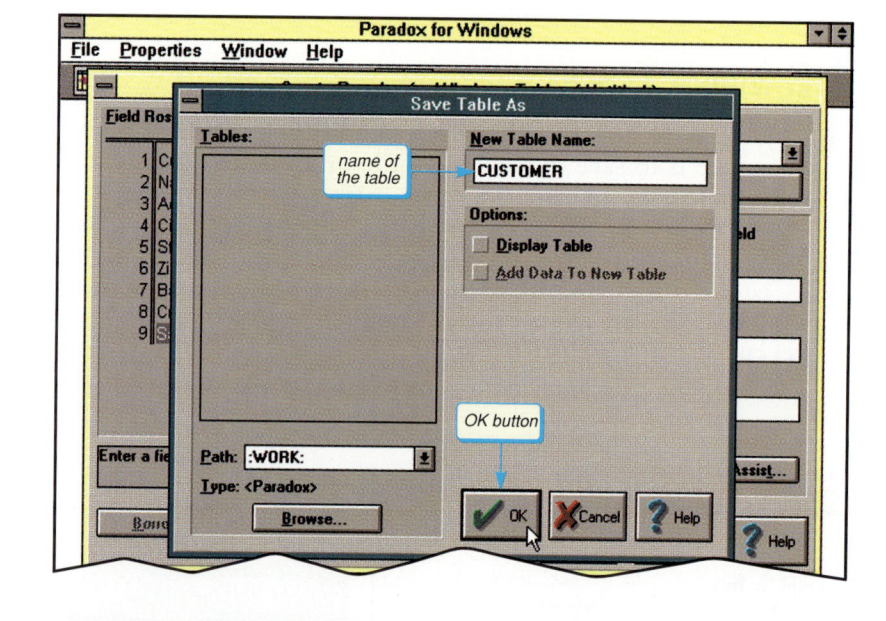

FIGURE 1-26

STEP 4 ▶

Choose the OK button.

Paradox stores the table using the name CUSTOMER and then returns to the Paradox desktop (Figure 1-27). The creation of the Customer table is now complete.

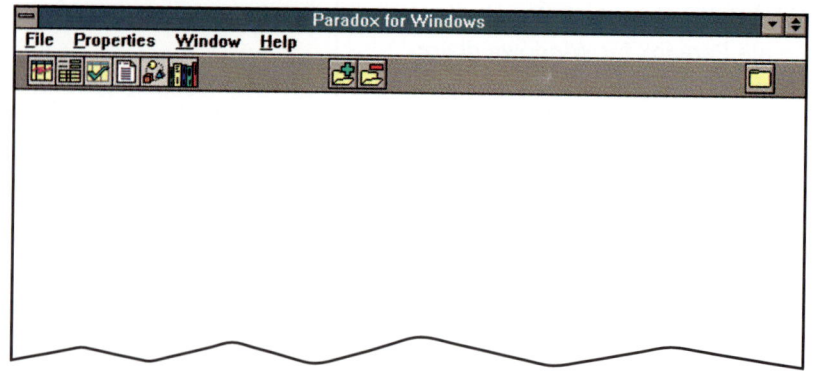

FIGURE 1-27

▶ EXITING PARADOX FOR WINDOWS

The creation of the Customer table is now complete. You can immediately begin adding records to the table. You may not, however, want to do this all in one session. If not, you can exit Paradox at this point.

TO EXIT PARADOX FOR WINDOWS ▼

STEP 1 ▶

Select the File menu and point to the Exit command (Figure 1-28).

STEP 2 ▶

Choose the Exit command.

Control returns to Windows Program Manager. After you exit Paradox, remove your diskette from drive A.

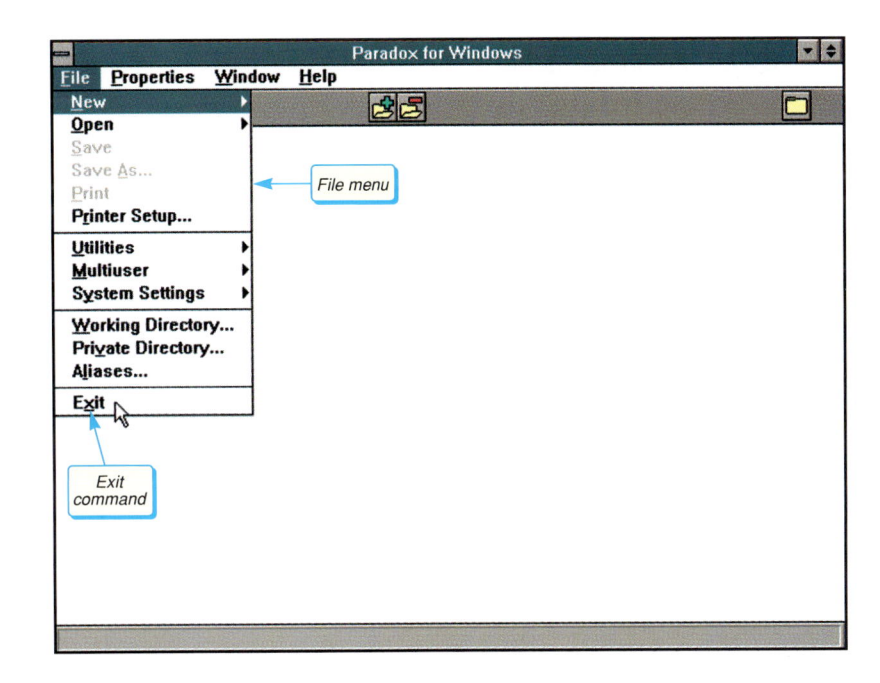

FIGURE 1-28

When you are ready to continue working, start Paradox for Windows using the method shown in Figure 1-2 through Figure 1-4 on pages P5 and P6. *Be sure you have inserted your diskette before you begin the process. Also be sure to choose the Working Directory command as shown in Figure 1-6 through Figure 1-8 on pages P7 and P8. If the working directory is not* A:\, *change it to* A:\.

▶ ADDING RECORDS TO A TABLE

Creating a table is the first step in a two-step process. The second step is to add records to the table. To add records to a table, the table must be open. It is also easiest to work if the window containing the table is maximized.

TO OPEN A TABLE

STEP 1 ▶

Point to the Open Table button (🔳) on the SpeedBar (Figure 1-29).

The function of the button to which the mouse pointer is pointing displays on the status bar.

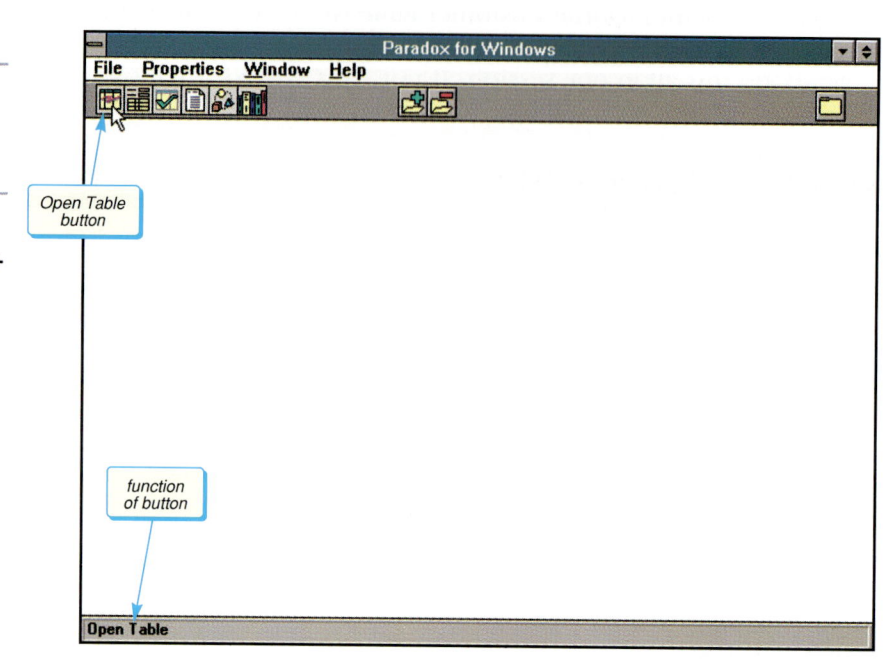

FIGURE 1-29

STEP 2 ▶

Click the Open Table button and then point to the name of the Customer table (CUSTOMER.DB) in the File Name list box.

The Open Table dialog box displays (Figure 1-30). A list of all the tables in the working directory appears in the File Name list box. CUSTOMER.DB is the table you saved in Figure 1-24 through Figure 1-27 on pages P15 and P16. If you did not exit Paradox, an extra table, called :PRIV:STRUCT.DB, will appear. This is a temporary table containing details of the structure of the table you just created (CUSTOMER.DB). It will be deleted when you exit Paradox.

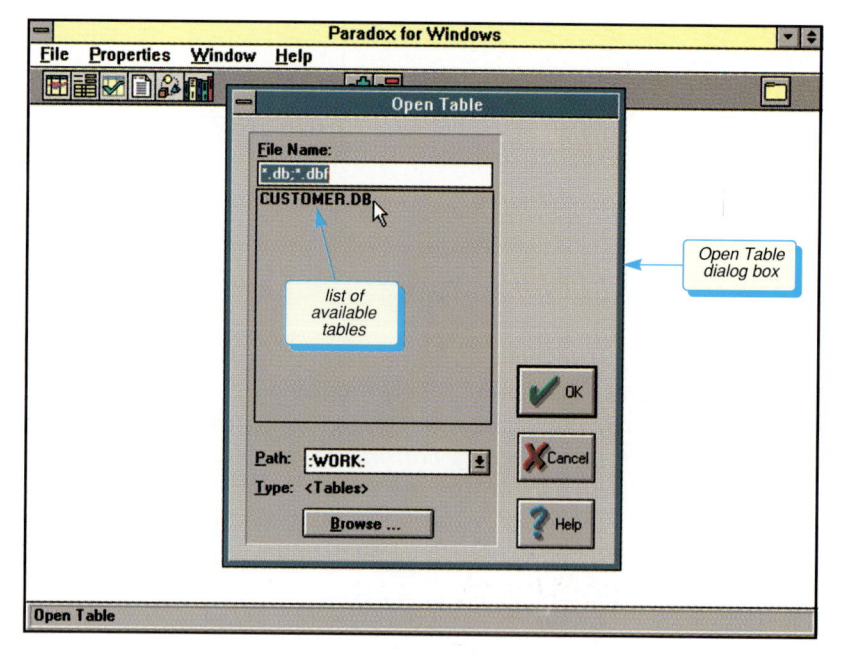

FIGURE 1-30

ADDING RECORDS TO A TABLE

STEP 3 ▶

Select the Customer table by clicking the left mouse button, and then point to the OK button.

Paradox highlights the CUSTOMER.DB name in the File Name list (Figure 1-31). The mouse pointer points to the OK button.

FIGURE 1-31

STEP 4 ▶

Choose the OK button in the Open Table dialog box and then point to the Maximize button.

Paradox opens the Customer table and displays the Table: CUSTOMER.DB window (Figure 1-32). The fields of the Customer table display in the window (as many as will fit). The mouse pointer is pointing to the Maximize button.

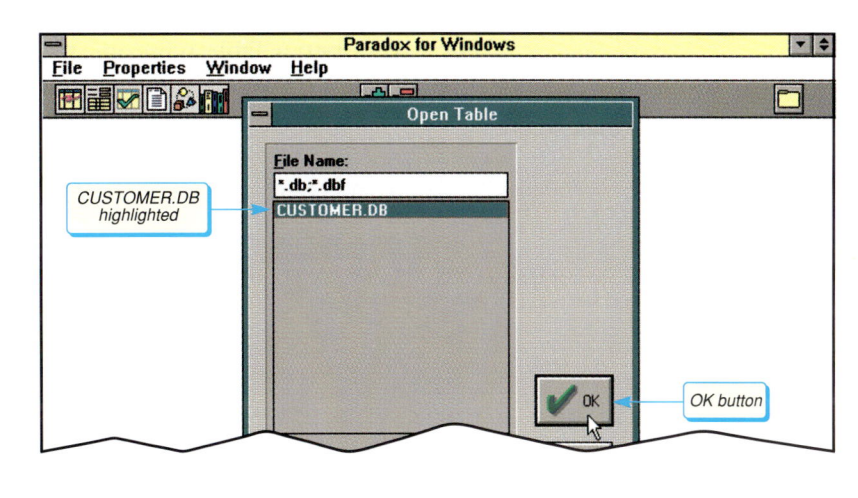

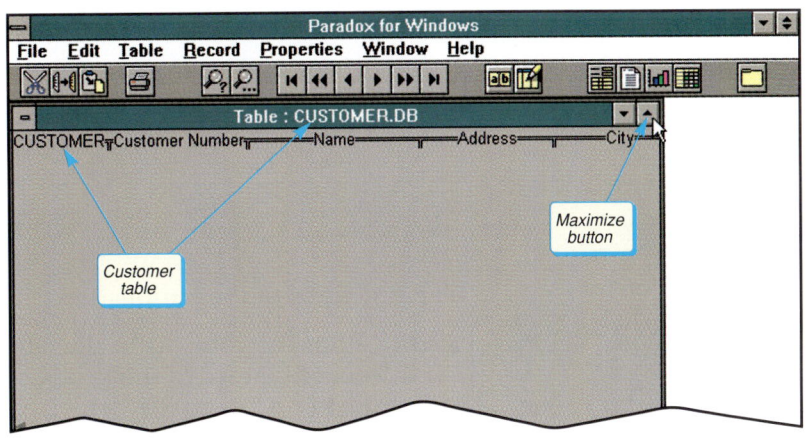

FIGURE 1-32

STEP 5 ▶

Click the Maximize button.

The window containing the Customer table is maximized (Figure 1-33). The mouse pointer has a different shape (⌐) because it is in the heading portion of the table. This shape indicates you can change certain characteristics of the look of the table. You will not make changes in this project. As soon as you move the pointer away from this portion of the screen, it once again becomes a block arrow. The message, 0 records, on the status bar indicates no records are in the table.

FIGURE 1-33

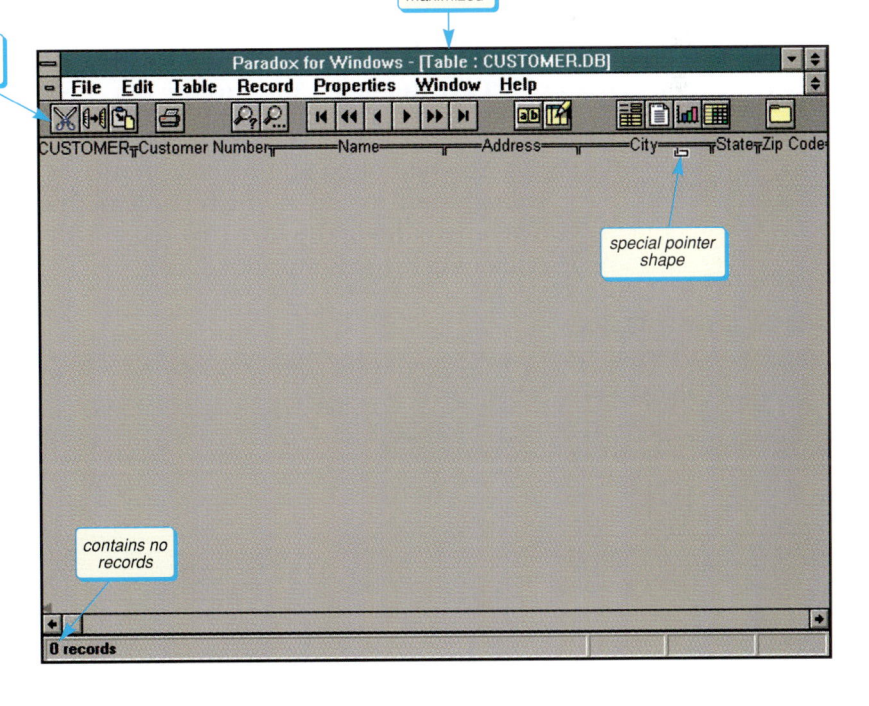

When you open a Table window, the SpeedBar contains a different set of buttons than the ones you saw earlier. The buttons you are most likely to use are shown in Figure 1-34.

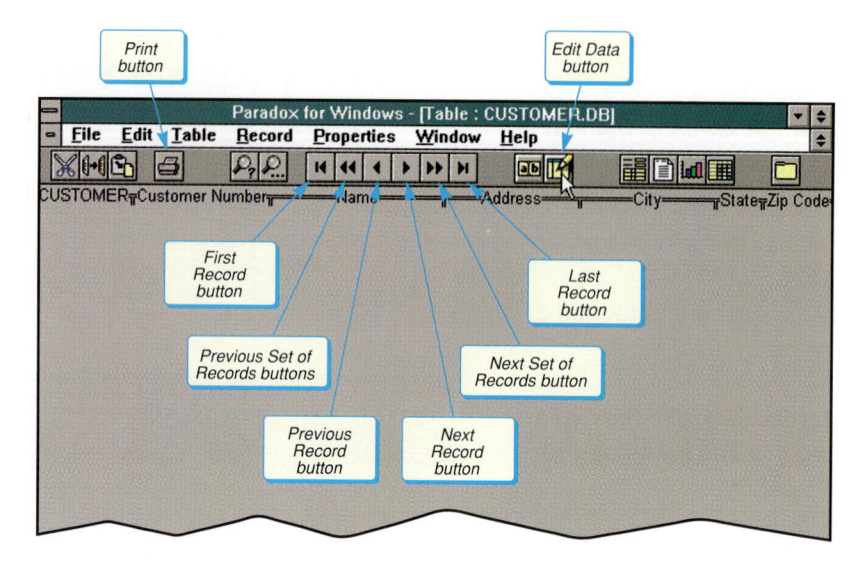

FIGURE 1-34

The functions of the buttons are as follows:

Print Print the contents of the table.
First Record Move to the first record in the table.
Previous Set of Records Move back one set (one screenful) of records.
Previous Record Move to the previous record; that is, move back one record from the current position.
Next Record Move to the next record; that is, move one record ahead from the current position.
Next Set of Records Move ahead one set of records.
Last Record Move to the last record in the table.
Edit Data Transfer to Edit mode.

You will often add records in phases. You may, for example, not have enough time to add all the records in one session. To illustrate, this project begins by adding the first two records in Figure 1-35 to the Customer table. The remaining records are added later.

FIGURE 1-35

▶ CUSTOMER TABLE

Customer Number	Name	Address	City	State	Zip Code	Balance	Credit Limit	Sales Rep Number
AC12	Arend Corp.	21 Wilson	Muncie	IN	47303	$4,278.50	$6,000.00	03
AI53	Allied Industry	215 Raymond	Carmel	IN	46032	$203.00	$3,000.00	06
AX29	AAA Express	108 College	Muncie	IN	47303	$42.00	$3,000.00	06
CL67	Clark-White Ltd.	47 Chipwood	Moline	IL	61265	$3,206.00	$8,000.00	12
FC15	Ferguson Co.	602 Bridge	Mason	MI	48854	$6,704.00	$6,000.00	03
FY24	Farley-Young	19 Oak	Muncie	IN	47303	$2,504.00	$6,000.00	06
LW46	L. T. Wheeler	587 Rivard	Moline	IL	61265	$0.00	$6,000.00	06
NI34	Nelson Inc.	12 Bishop	Sumner	IL	62466	$2,011.50	$6,000.00	03
SH84	Shippers and Dale	208 Grayton	Carmel	IN	46032	$1,597.25	$8,000.00	12
SI84	Shelton Inc.	82 Harcourt	Niles	MI	49120	$7,020.00	$8,000.00	06

ADDING RECORDS TO A TABLE **P21**

To add records to a table, Paradox must be in **Edit mode**. The following steps illustrate changing to Edit mode and then adding the first two records to the Customer table.

TO ADD RECORDS TO AN EMPTY TABLE ▼

STEP 1 ▶

Point to and click the Edit Data button ( ).

*Space for a first record displays on the screen (Figure 1-36). The mode is now Edit, meaning you can edit the table. This is the mode you use to add new records, change existing records, or delete records. The highlight displays in the Customer Number field, indicating you can enter a customer number. The status bar indicates that you are currently editing the first record in the table, you are in edit mode, and the record is **locked** (no other user can currently update the record).*

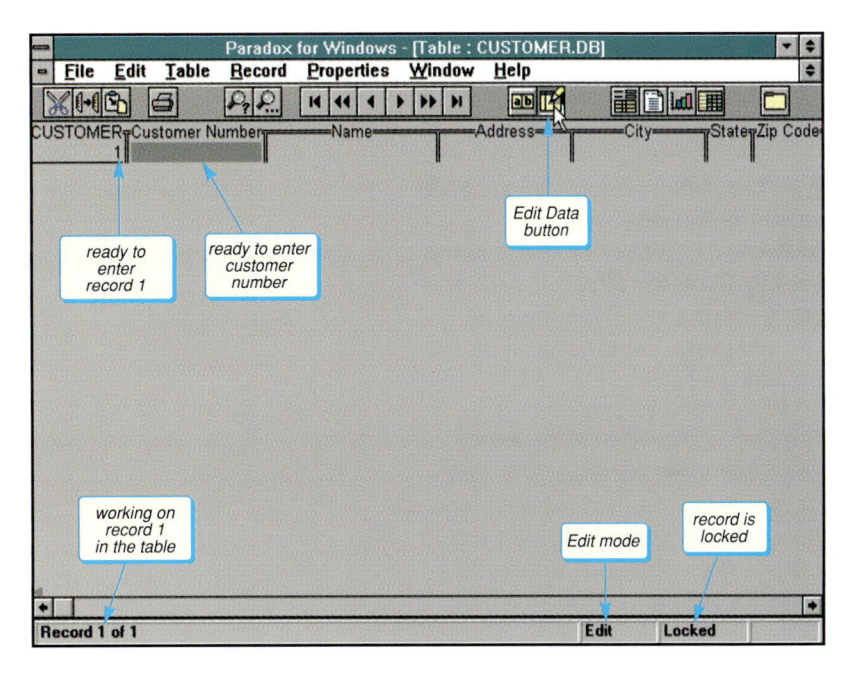

FIGURE 1-36

STEP 2 ▶

Type `AC12`, **the first customer number (Figure 1-37). Be sure you type both the A and the C in uppercase.**

The customer number is entered, but the insertion point is still in the Customer Number field.

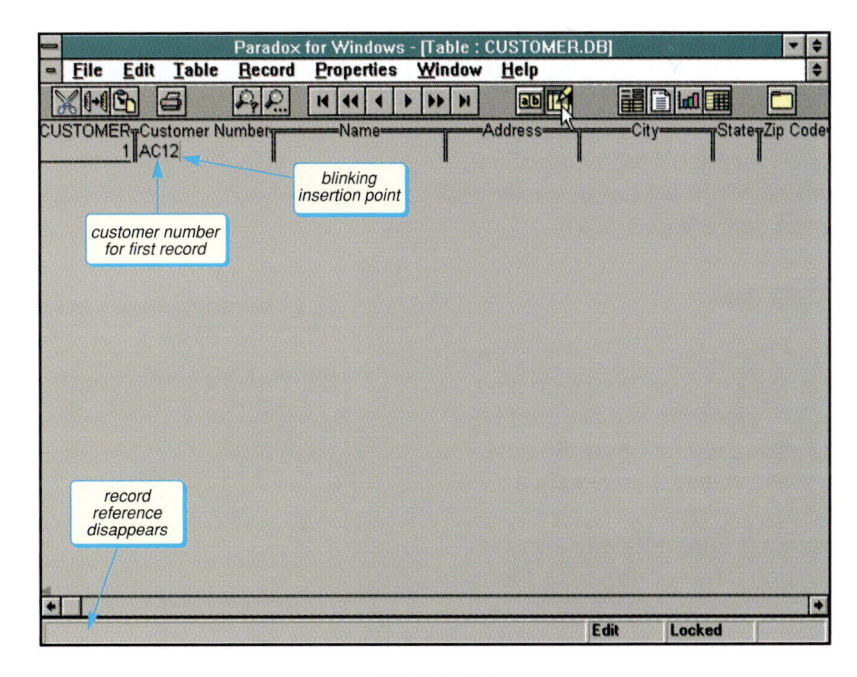

FIGURE 1-37

STEP 3 ▶

Press the TAB key.

The entry for the Customer Number field is now complete. The highlight moves to the Name field (Figure 1-38).

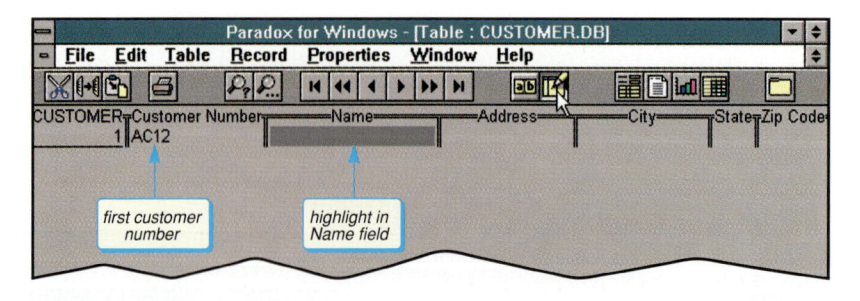

FIGURE 1-38

STEP 4 ▶

Type the name, `Arend Corp.`, **and press the TAB key. Type the address,** `21 Wilson`, **and press the TAB key. Type the city,** `Muncie`, **and press the TAB key. Type the state,** `IN`, **and press the TAB key. Type the zip code,** `47303`.

The Name, Address, City, and State fields are entered. The data for the Zip Code field displays on the screen (Figure 1-39), but the entry is not complete, since you have not yet pressed the TAB key.

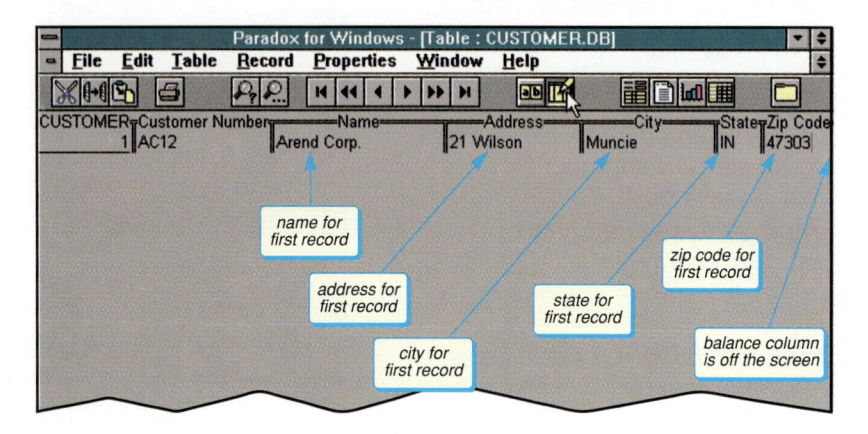

FIGURE 1-39

STEP 5 ▶

Press the TAB key.

The Zip Code is entered. The fields shift to the left so the Balance field and the Credit Limit field display on the screen, and the highlight advances to the Balance field (Figure 1-40).

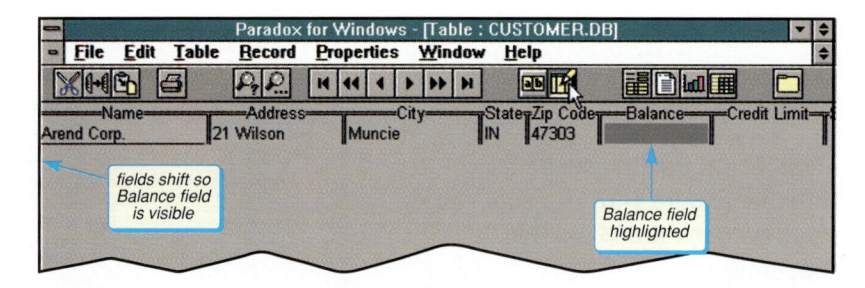

FIGURE 1-40

STEP 6 ▶

Type the balance, `4278.50`. **Press the TAB key, type the credit limit,** `6000`, **press the TAB key, and type** `03` **(sales rep number). Be sure you type** `03` **rather than simply** `3`.

Paradox automatically adds dollar signs and commas to the data in the Balance and Credit Limit fields because they are currency fields (Figure 1-41). The sales rep number has been typed but the insertion point is still positioned in the field.

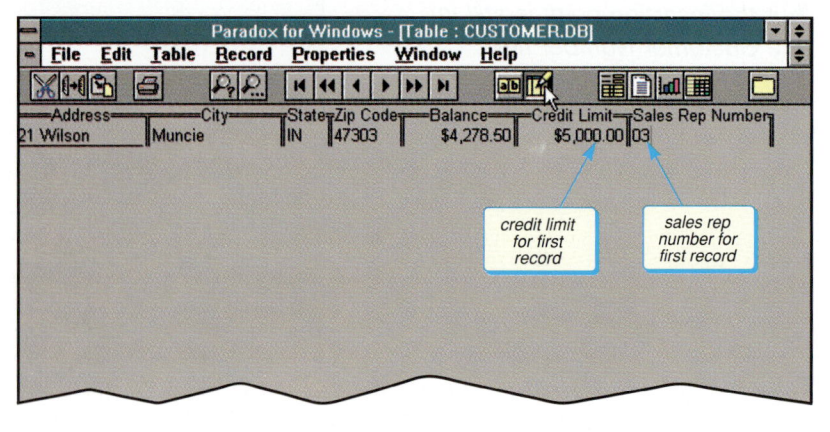

FIGURE 1-41

STEP 7 ▶

Press the TAB key.

The fields shift back to the right, the record is saved on disk, and the highlight moves to the Customer Number field on the next row (Figure 1-42). Asterisks in a field, such as those in the Balance field, indicate the number in the field does not fit in the space available on the screen.

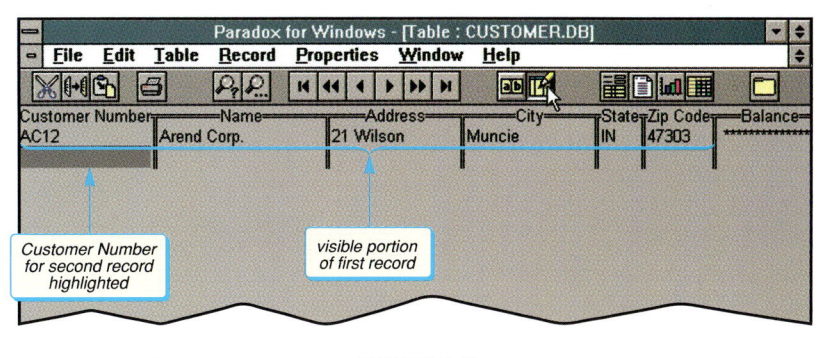

FIGURE 1-42

STEP 8 ▶

Use the techniques shown in Steps 2 through 7 to add the data for the second record shown in Figure 1-35 on page P20.

The two records are added, and the highlight is in the Customer Number field for a third record (Figure 1-43).

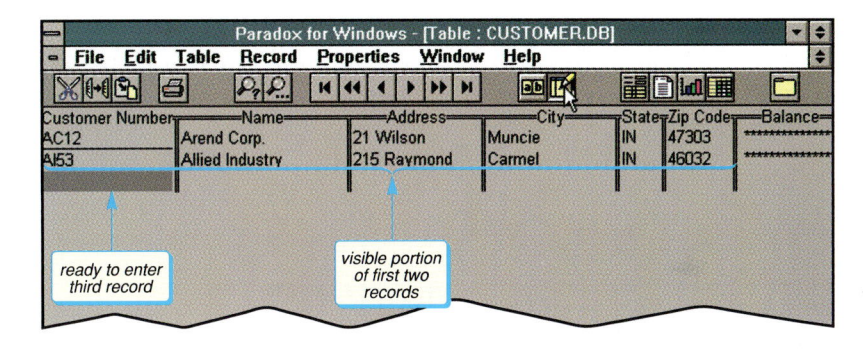

FIGURE 1-43

Each record is saved as soon as you have completely entered it and moved to the next record. No special Save step is required. When you are finished working on a table, close it using the Close command located on the Control menu in the menu bar, *not the title bar*. If you select Close from the title bar's Control menu, you will close Paradox for Windows.

It is a good idea to close a table as soon as you have finished working with it. It keeps the screen from getting cluttered and also prevents you from making accidental changes to the data in the table.

The process to close a table is shown in the following steps.

TO CLOSE A TABLE ▼

STEP 1 ▶

Select the Control menu on the menu bar and point to the Close command.

The Control menu displays on the screen (Figure 1-44). The mouse pointer points to the Close command.

FIGURE 1-44

P24 PROJECT 1 CREATING A DATABASE

STEP 2 ▶

Choose the Close command.

Paradox displays the desktop (Figure 1-45). The table and the window containing the table are both closed.

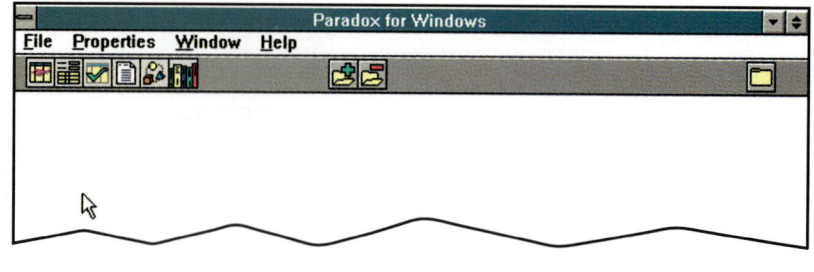

FIGURE 1-45

▶ ADDING ADDITIONAL RECORDS

You can add records to a table that already contains data using a process almost identical to that used to add records to an empty table. The only difference is that you place the highlight after the last data record before you enter the additional data. Complete the following steps to add the remaining records to the Customer table.

TO ADD ADDITIONAL RECORDS TO A TABLE ▼

STEP 1 ▶

Open the Customer table by clicking the Open table button, selecting the Customer table, and then choosing the OK button in the Open Table dialog box.

STEP 2 ▶

Maximize the table by clicking the Maximize button.

STEP 3 ▶

Point to the Edit Data button (Figure 1-46).

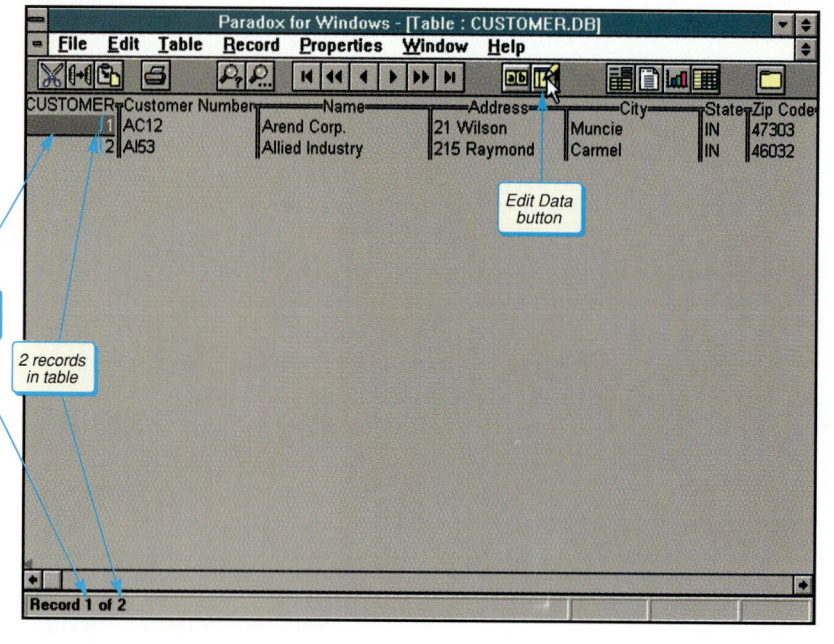

FIGURE 1-46

STEP 4 ▶

Click the Edit Data button.

Clicking the Edit Data button places Paradox in Edit mode as shown on the status bar (Figure 1-47). You can now add additional records to the table.

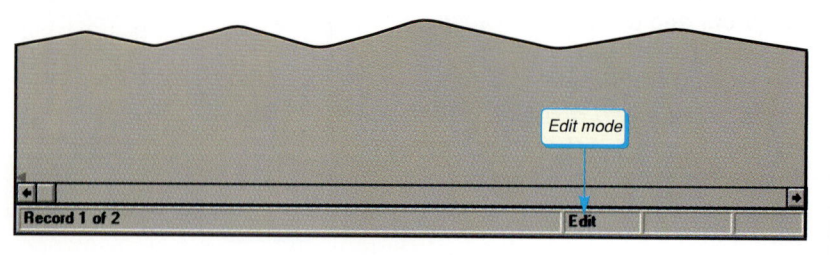

FIGURE 1-47

ADDING ADDITIONAL RECORDS **P25**

STEP 5 ▶

Point to the Last Record button
(▶|) on the SpeedBar
(Figure 1-48).

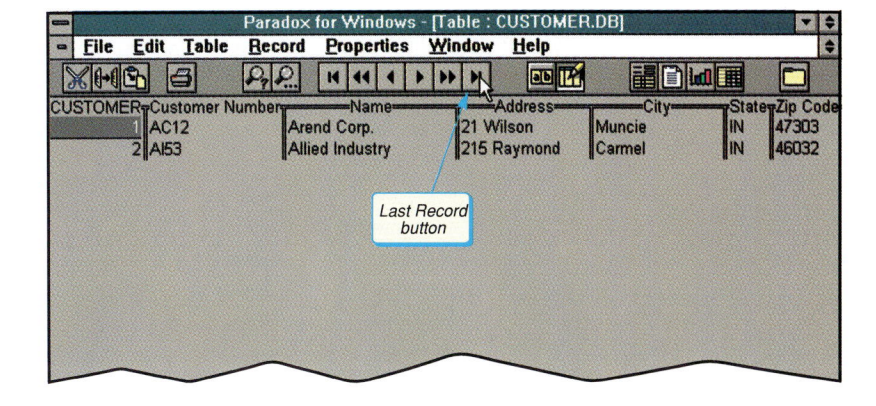

FIGURE 1-48

STEP 6 ▶

Click the Last Record button and
then point to the Next Record
button (▶).

*Paradox positions the highlight
on the last record in the table
(Figure 1-49). The mouse pointer
is pointing to the Next Record
button.*

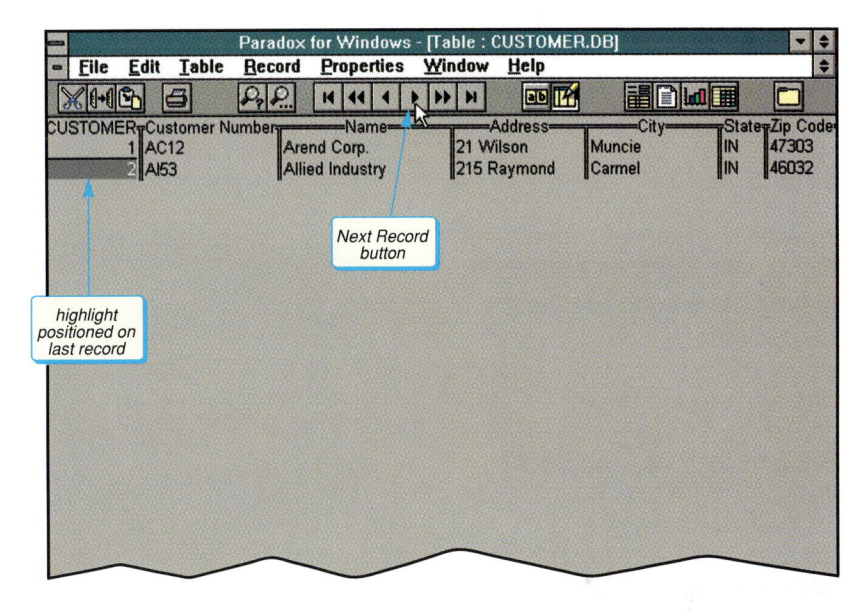

FIGURE 1-49

STEP 7 ▶

Click the Next Record button to
move to a new record.

*Paradox moves the high-
light to the position for a
new record (Figure 1-50).*

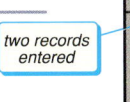

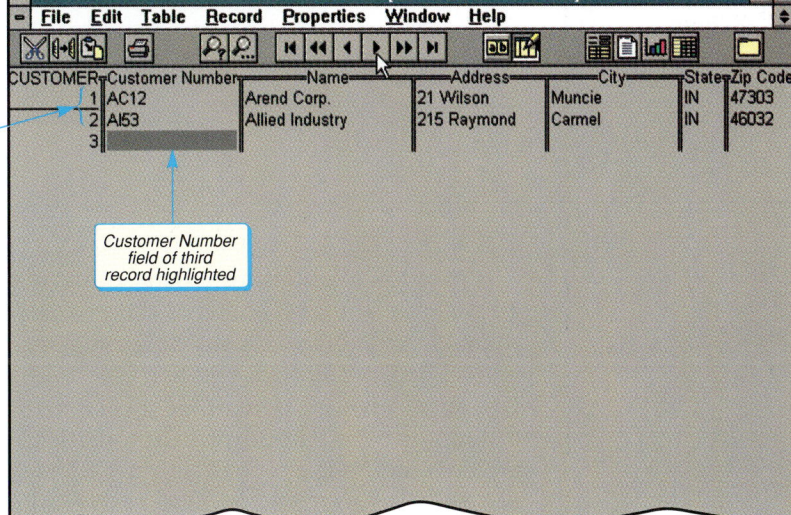

FIGURE 1-50

▸ CUSTOMER TABLE

Customer Number	Name	Address	City	State	Zip Code	Balance	Credit Limit	Sales Rep Number
AC12	Arend Corp.	21 Wilson	Muncie	IN	47303	$4,278.50	$6,000.00	03
AI53	Allied Industry	215 Raymond	Carmel	IN	46032	$203.00	$3,000.00	06
AX29	AAA Express	108 College	Muncie	IN	47303	$42.00	$3,000.00	06
CL67	Clark-White Ltd.	47 Chipwood	Moline	IL	61265	$3,206.00	$8,000.00	12
FC15	Ferguson Co.	602 Bridge	Mason	MI	48854	$6,704.00	$6,000.00	03
FY24	Farley-Young	19 Oak	Muncie	IN	47303	$2,504.00	$6,000.00	06
LW46	L. T. Wheeler	587 Rivard	Moline	IL	61265	$0.00	$6,000.00	06
NI34	Nelson Inc.	12 Bishop	Sumner	IL	62466	$2,011.50	$6,000.00	03
SH84	Shippers and Dale	208 Grayton	Carmel	IN	46032	$1,597.25	$8,000.00	12
SI84	Shelton Inc.	82 Harcourt	Niles	MI	49120	$7,020.00	$8,000.00	06

FIGURE 1-51

STEP 8 ▶

Add the remaining records from Figure 1-51 using the same techniques you used to add the first two records.

The ten records display on the screen and the highlight is in position for a new record (Figure 1-52).

STEP 9 ▶

Close the table using the technique shown in Figure 1-44 and Figure 1-45.

FIGURE 1-52

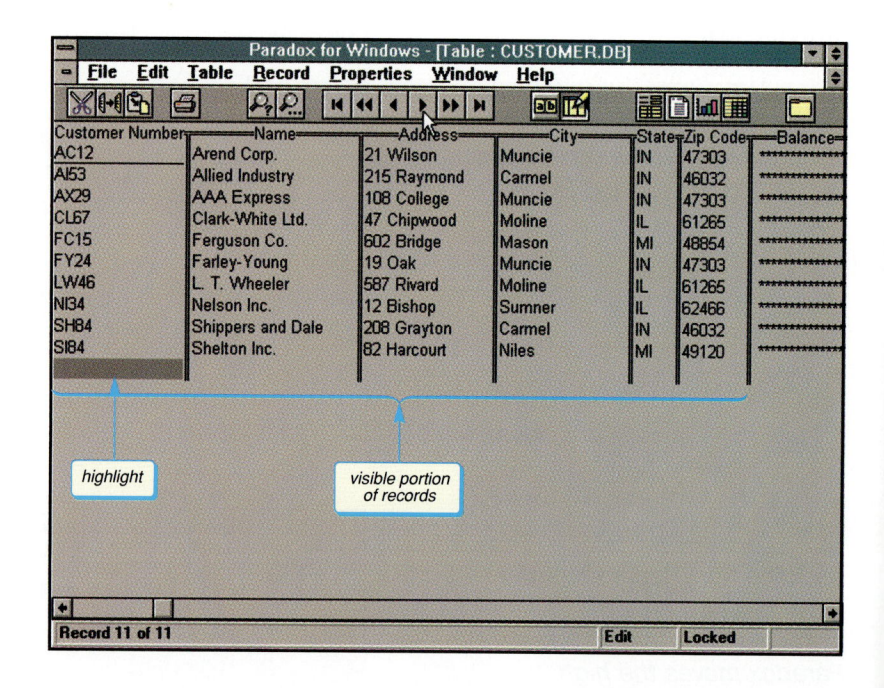

Paradox maintains the data so it is always ordered by the primary key. Because Customer Number is the primary key of the Customer table, the data in the table will automatically be arranged so the customer numbers are in alphabetical order. The data you just entered happened to be in the correct order. If you enter a record containing a customer number that is not in alphabetical order, however, Paradox will automatically place it in order once you have completely entered the record. For example, if you add a record with customer number PR29, as soon as you have entered the final field on the record and pressed the TAB key, Paradox will move the record so it appears between the record for customer NI34 and the one for customer SH84. In general, records are always ordered in ascending order by the key field.

Correcting Errors in the Data

Just as when you created the table, check the entries carefully to ensure they are correct. If you make a mistake and discover it before you press the TAB key, correct it by pressing the BACKSPACE key until the incorrect characters are removed and then typing the correct characters.

If you discover an incorrect entry later, correct the error by pointing to the entry with the mouse, clicking the left mouse button, and then typing the correct value. If the record you must correct is not on the screen, use the SpeedBar buttons (Next Record, Previous Record, and so on) (Figure 1-34) to move to it. If the field you want to correct is not visible on the screen, use the horizontal scroll bar along the bottom of the screen to shift all the fields until the one you want displays. Then make the correction.

If you accidentally add an extra record, point to any field in the record, click the left mouse button, and then press the CTRL + DELETE keys. This will remove the record from the table. If you forget a record, add it using the same procedure as for all the other records. Paradox will automatically place it in the correct location in the table.

Occasionally a record you thought you added is not in the table. In this case, you probably made a mistake entering the customer number. Suppose, for example, that when you typed the fifth record (Ferguson Co.), you accidentally entered the customer number for the sixth record (FY24). When you later tried to add the sixth record, Paradox for Windows rejected the addition, because a record with the same customer number (FY24) was already in the table. If this occurs, check the customer numbers carefully, make any necessary corrections, and then add the record.

▶ PRINTING THE CONTENTS OF A TABLE

When working with a database, you will often need to obtain a printed copy of the table contents. Figure 1-53 shows a printed copy of the contents of the CUSTOMER table. Since the CUSTOMER table is substantially wider than the screen, it will also be wider than the normal printed page. To overcome this difficulty you can print the database using Landscape orientation. If you are printing the contents of a table that fits on the screen, you will not need Landscape orientation.

FIGURE 1-53

Customer Number	Name	Address	City	State	Zip Code	Balance	Credit Limit	Sales Rep Number
AC12	Arend Corp.	21 Wilson	Muncie	IN	47303	$4,278.50	$6,000.00	03
AI53	Allied Industry	215 Raymond	Carmel	IN	46032	$203.00	$3,000.00	06
AX29	AAA Express	108 College	Muncie	IN	47303	$42.00	$3,000.00	06
CL67	Clark-White Ltd.	47 Chipwood	Moline	IL	61265	$3,206.00	$8,000.00	12
FC15	Ferguson Co.	602 Bridge	Mason	MI	48854	$6,704.00	$6,000.00	03
FY24	Farley-Young	19 Oak	Muncie	IN	47303	$2,504.00	$6,000.00	06
LW46	L. T. Wheeler	587 Rivard	Moline	IL	61265	$0.00	$6,000.00	06
NI34	Nelson Inc.	12 Bishop	Sumner	IL	62466	$2,011.50	$6,000.00	03
SH84	Shippers and Dale	208 Grayton	Carmel	IN	46032	$1,597.25	$8,000.00	12
SI84	Shelton Inc.	82 Harcourt	Niles	MI	49120	$7,020.00	$8,000.00	06

Monday, October 10, 1994 — CUSTOMER — Page 1

P28   PROJECT 1   CREATING A DATABASE

Complete the following steps to print the Customer table in Landscape orientation.

TO PRINT THE CONTENTS OF A TABLE ▼

STEP 1 ▶

Open the Customer table and maximize it using the techniques previously explained.

STEP 2 ▶

Select the File menu and point to the Printer Setup command (Figure 1-54).

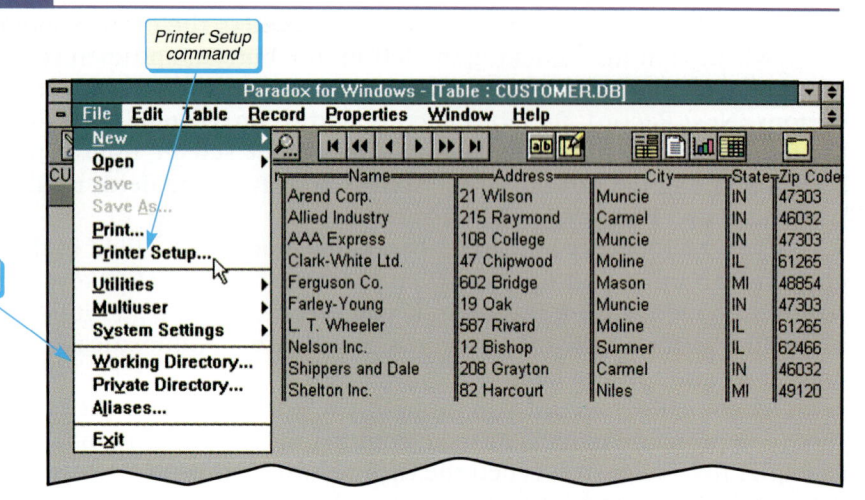

FIGURE 1-54

STEP 3 ▶

Choose the Printer Setup command from the File menu and then point to the Modify Printer Setup button.

Paradox displays the Printer Setup dialog box (Figure 1-55). The selected printer is the HP LaserJet Series II on LPT1:. Your printer may be different. The mouse pointer is pointing to the Modify Printer Setup button (Modify Printer Setup...).

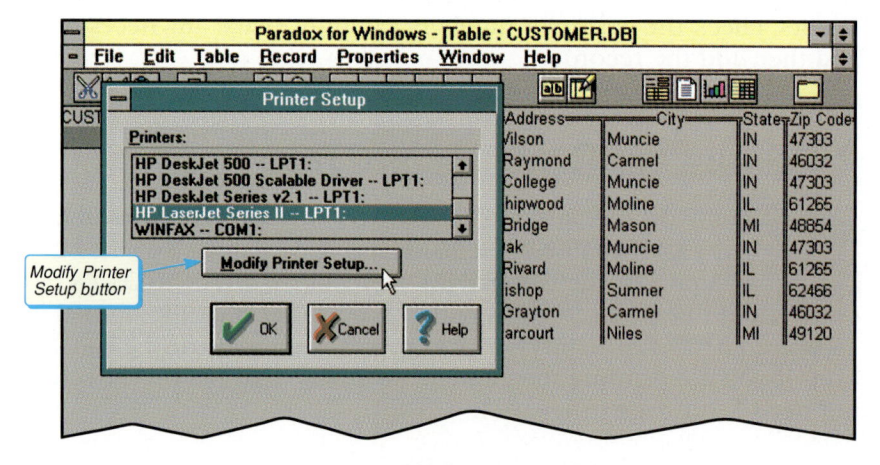

FIGURE 1-55

STEP 4 ▶

Choose the Modify Printer Setup button. Select the Landscape option button in the Orientation area by clicking it, and then point to the OK button.

Paradox displays the HP LaserJet Series II dialog box (Figure 1-56). When you select Landscape orientation, the Orientation icon (A) changes to Landscape.

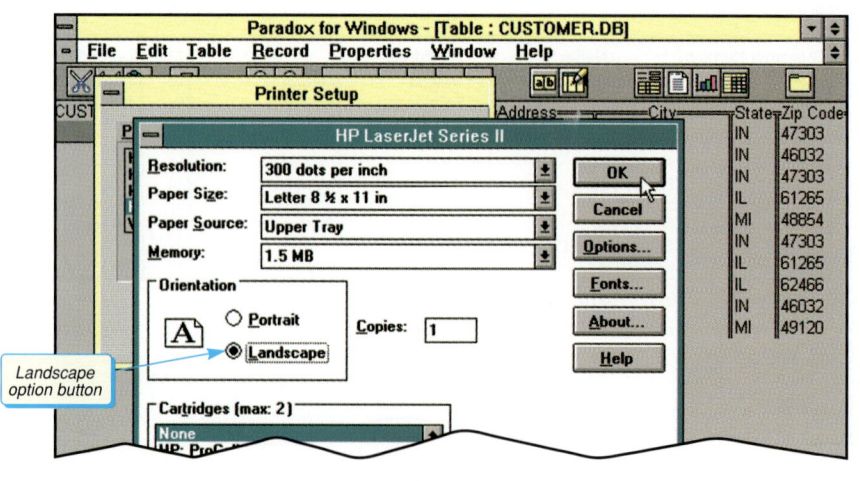

FIGURE 1-56

STEP 5 ▶

Choose the OK button in the HP LaserJet Series II dialog box. When Paradox displays the Printer Setup dialog box, also choose the OK button in that dialog box. Then point to the Print button (Figure 1-57).

STEP 6 ▶

Click the Print button.

Paradox displays the Print File dialog box (Figure 1-58). The Printer area contains the name of the default printer (HP LaserJet Series II — LPT1:) (yours may be different). In the Print area, you can change the range of pages to be printed. Enter the number of copies to print in the Copies text box. The Overflow Handling area contains three option buttons that indicate the method for handling **overflow** *(a report that does not fit on a single page).*

STEP 7 ▶

Choose the OK button in the Print File dialog box.

Paradox displays the Printing dialog box for a few moments and then prints the report shown in Figure 1-53 on page P27.

STEP 8 ▶

Close the table.

STEP 9 ▶

Convert the orientation back to portrait using the technique illustrated in Steps 1 through 5 except choose Portrait instead of Landscape in Step 4.

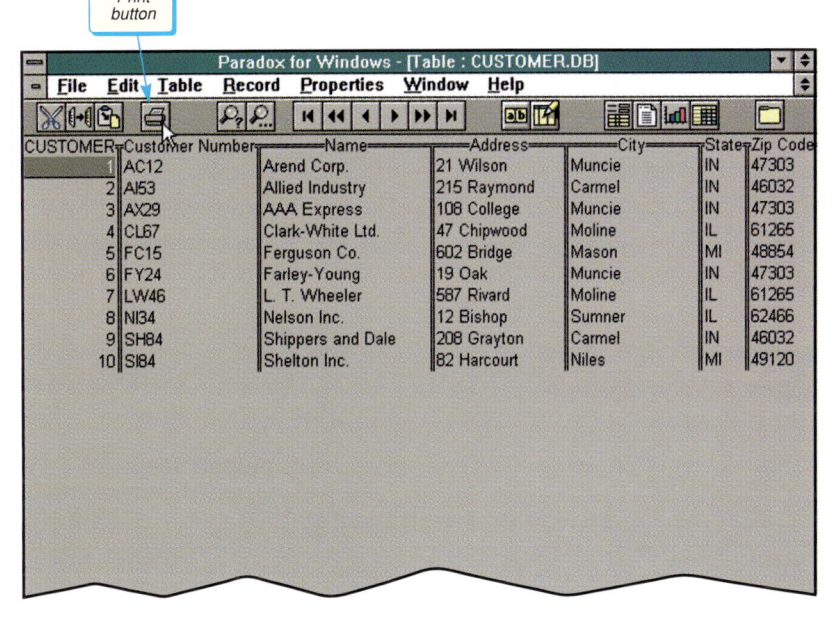

FIGURE 1-57

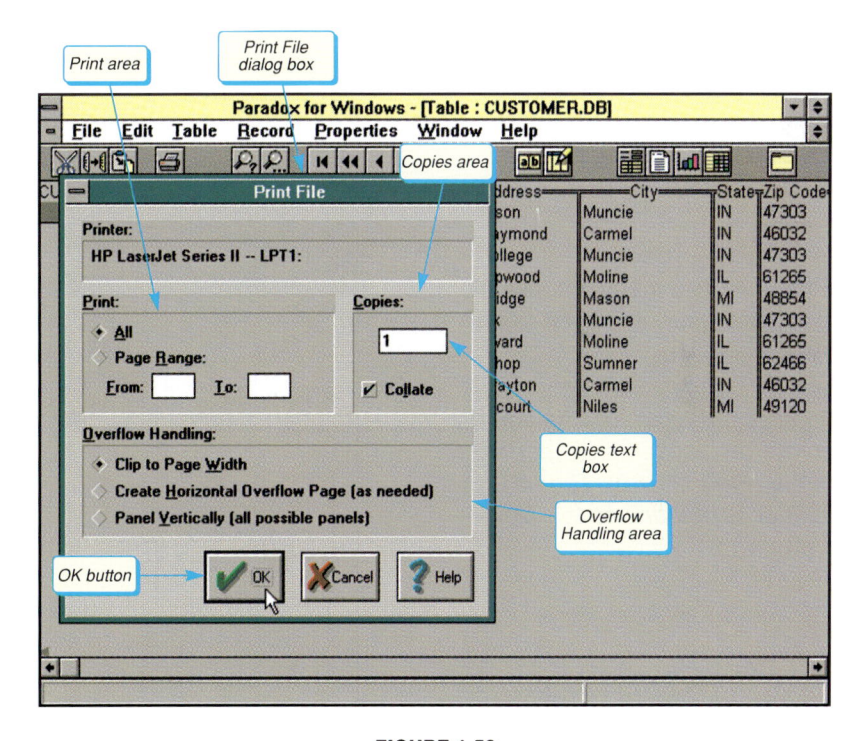

FIGURE 1-58

▶ STRUCTURE OF SALES REP (SLSREP) TABLE

Field Name	Type	Size	Key
Sales Rep Number	A	2	*
Last Name	A	12	
First Name	A	8	
Address	A	15	
City	A	15	
State	A	2	
Zip Code	A	5	
Sales	$		
Commission Rate	N		

▶ Creating Additional Tables

A database typically consists of more than one table. The sample database contains two, the Customer table and the Sales Rep table. You need to repeat the process of creating a table and adding records for each table in the database. In the sample database, you need to create and add records to the Sales Rep table. The structure and data for the table are given in Figure 1-59. The steps to create the table follow.

FIGURE 1-59

▶ DATA FOR SALES REP (SLSREP) TABLE

Sales Rep Number	Last Name	First Name	Address	City	State	Zip Code	Sales	Commission Rate
03	Harrison	Monica	12 LaGrange	Parkton	MI	48154	$52,348.00	0.07
06	Thompson	Charles	1564 Birchview	Auburn	IN	46706	$78,202.00	0.05
12	Juarez	Mara	722 Davison	Chicago	IL	60614	$28,222.00	0.07

TO CREATE A TABLE ▼

STEP 1 ▶

Select the File menu, choose the New command, and point to the Table command.

A list of the types of files you can create displays in a cascading menu (Figure 1-60). The mouse pointer is pointing to the Table command.

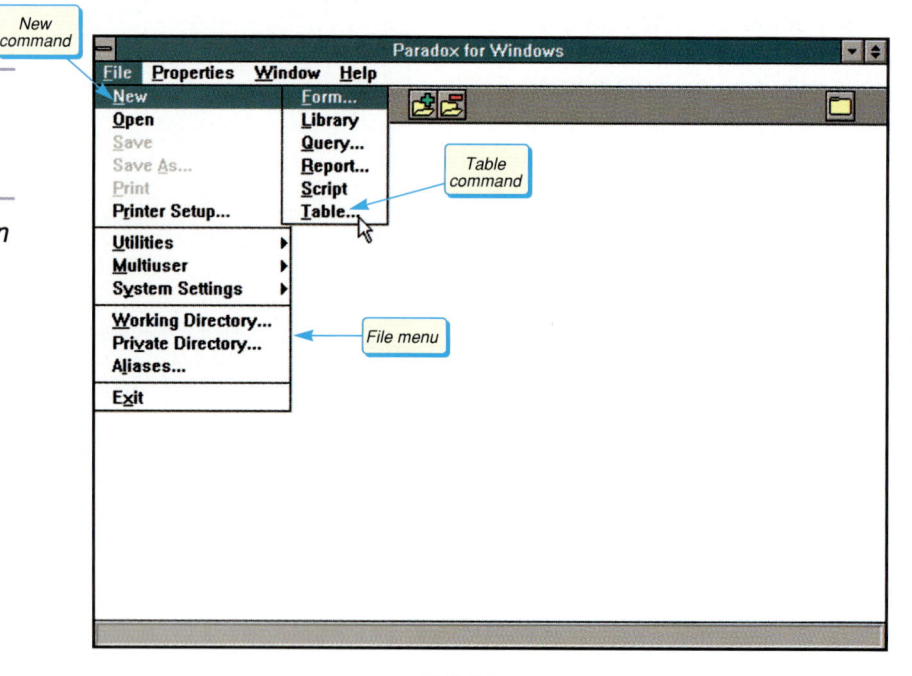

FIGURE 1-60

STEP 2 ▶

Choose the Table command, then choose the OK button in the Table Type dialog box. Make the appropriate entries to describe the fields. For the Commission Rate field, be sure to type N as the field type. When you have made all the entries, point to the Save As button.

Paradox displays the Create Paradox for Windows Table dialog box (Figure 1-61). The entries for the fields in the SLSREP table are in the Field Roster. The mouse pointer points to the Save As button.

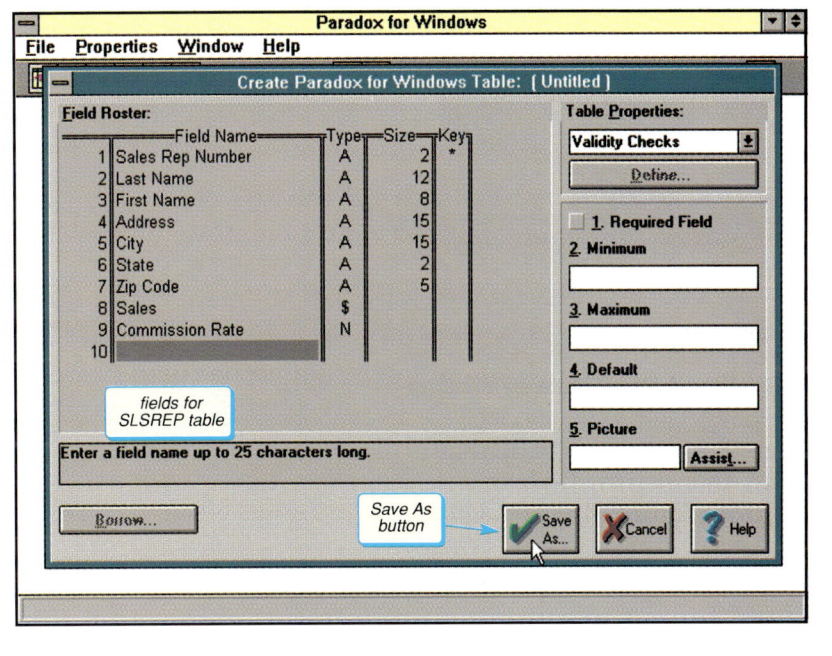

FIGURE 1-61

STEP 3 ▶

Choose the Save As button in the Create Paradox for Windows Table dialog box, then type `slsrep` (in uppercase or lowercase) as the name of the table in the New Table Name text box of the Save Table As dialog box. Point to the OK button.

The name of the new table, SLSREP, displays (Figure 1-62). The mouse pointer is pointing to the OK button.

STEP 4 ▶

Choose the OK button in the Save Table As dialog box.

The table is saved as a file in the working directory. Paradox displays the desktop.

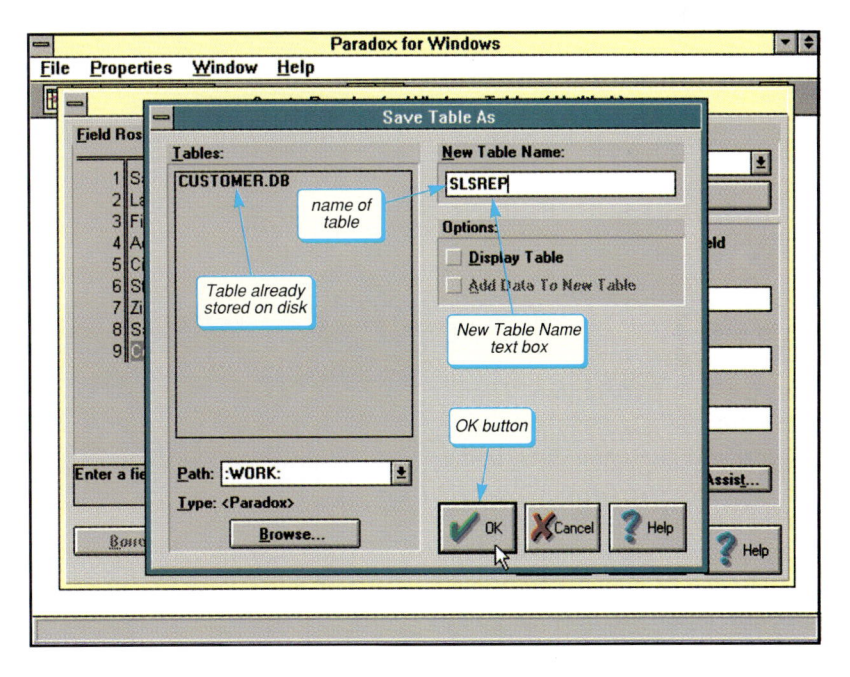

FIGURE 1-62

P32 PROJECT 1 CREATING A DATABASE

▶ ADDING RECORDS TO A TABLE

Now that you have created the SLSREP table, use the following steps to add records to it.

TO ADD RECORDS TO A TABLE ▼

STEP 1 ▶

Open the SLSREP table by clicking the Open Table button on the SpeedBar, selecting the SLSREP table, choosing the OK button in the Open Table dialog box, and then maximizing the table. Then point to the Edit Data button.

Paradox displays the SLSREP table and the mouse pointer points to the Edit Data button (Figure 1-63).

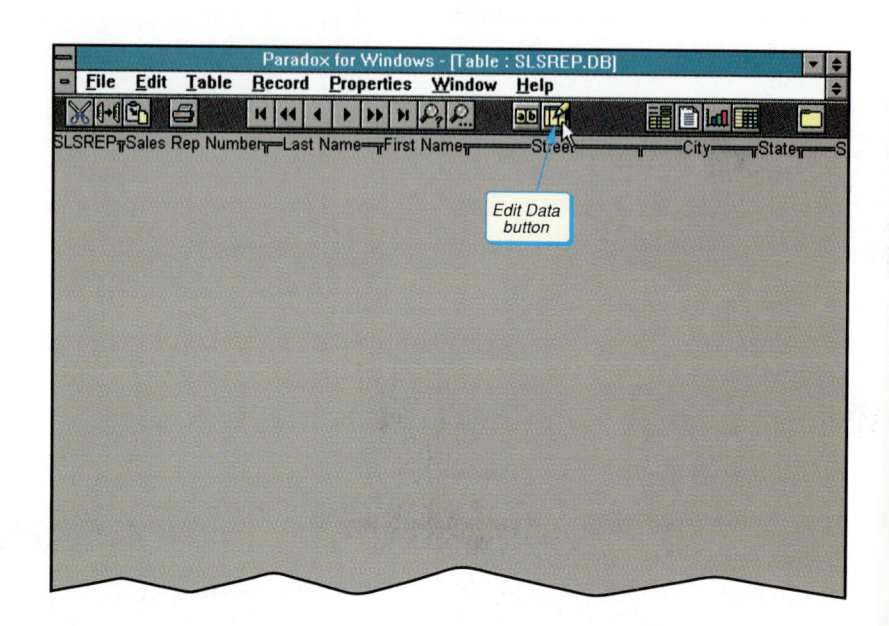

STEP 2 ▶

Click the Edit Data button. Then, using the same techniques you used to add customer data, add the sales representative data from Figure 1-59 on page P30. When entering the commission rate, you do not need to type the zero that appears before the decimal point.

The visible portion of the three records displays in the SLSREP table as data is added (Figure 1-64).

STEP 3 ▶

Close the table.

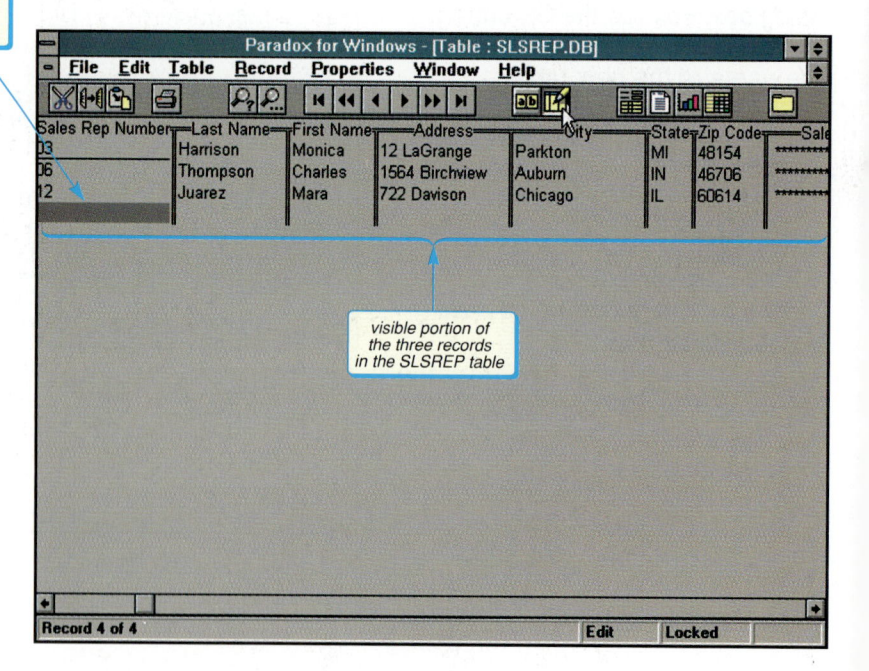

FIGURE 1-64

Using a Form to View Data

In creating tables, you have used **Table view**, that is, the data on the screen displayed as a table. You can also use **Form view**, in which you see a single record at a time.

The advantage of Table view is that you can see multiple records at once. It has the disadvantage that, unless you have few fields in the table, you cannot see all the fields at the same time. With Form view, you see only a single record, but you can see all the fields in the record. The view you choose is a matter of personal preference. It is easy to switch back and forth between views.

The **standard form** is a form that Paradox for Windows creates automatically. In a later project, you will create custom forms that you can use in place of the standard form. The following steps create the standard form.

TO CREATE A STANDARD FORM ▼

STEP 1 ▶

Open the CUSTOMER table (click the Open Table button, select the CUSTOMER table, choose the OK button in the Open Table dialog box, and click the Maximize button), and then point to the Quick Form button ( ) on the SpeedBar.

Paradox displays the CUSTOMER table and the mouse pointer points to the Quick Form button (Figure 1-65).

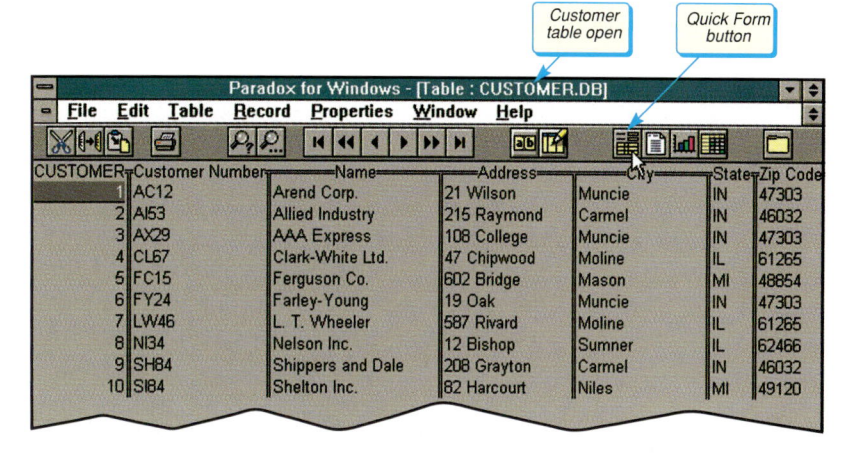

FIGURE 1-65

STEP 2 ▶

Click the Quick Form button.

The quick form for the CUSTOMER table displays on the screen (Figure 1-66). It contains all the fields in the table arranged vertically. In front of each field is the name of the field. Notice that when you switch from Table view to Form view, the Table window does not remain maximized.

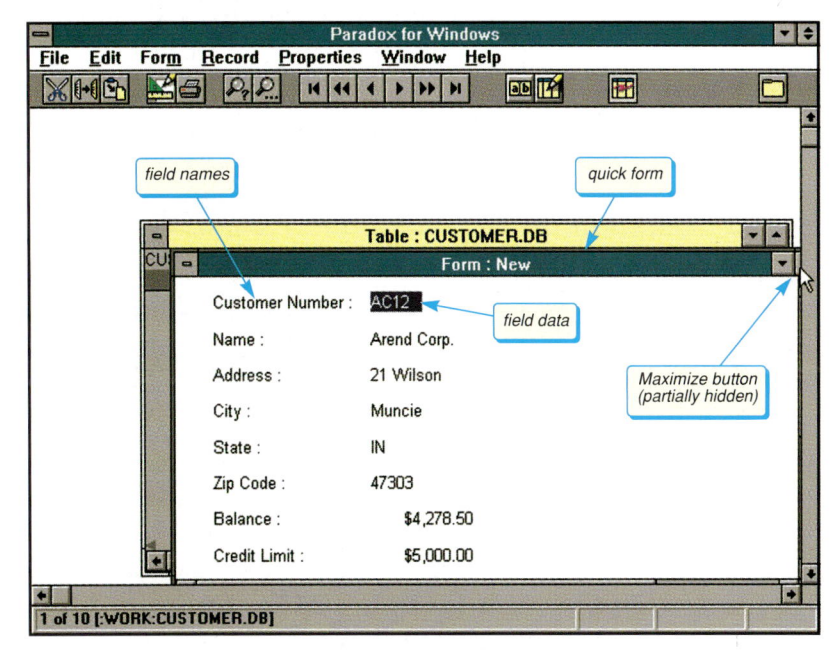

FIGURE 1-66

STEP 3 ▶

Click the Maximize button in the Form: New window.

The form is maximized (Figure 1-67). The status bar indicates Paradox is positioned on record 1. Since numbers are right-aligned, the values in the Balance and Credit Limit fields do not appear to line up with the other values.

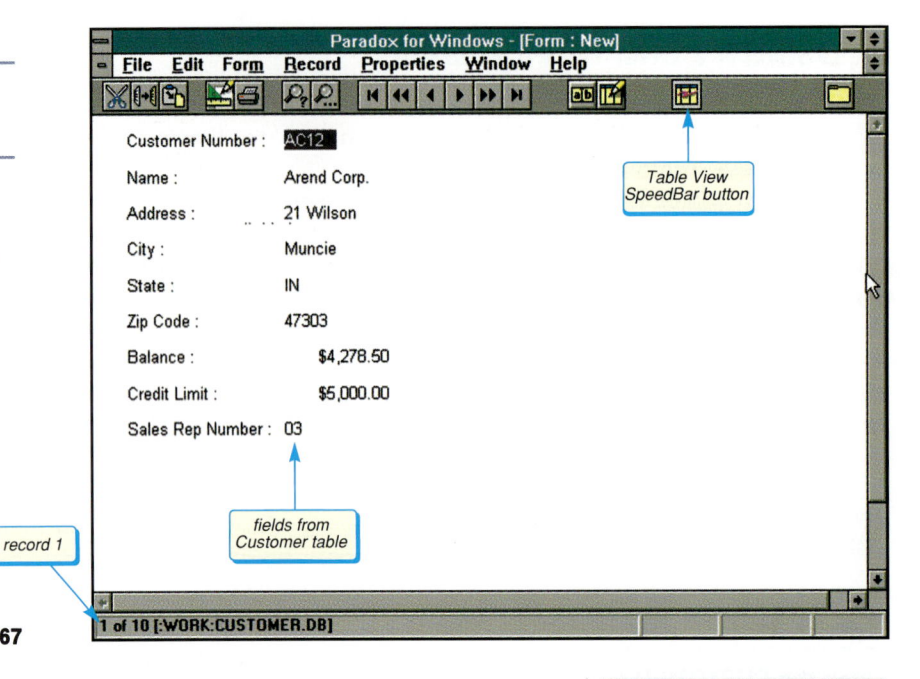

FIGURE 1-67

You can use Form view like you used Table view. Use the SpeedBar buttons to move between records. To change to Edit mode and update the data in the form, click the Edit Data button. Add new records or change existing ones. Press the CTRL+DELETE keys to delete the record on which you are positioned. In other words, you can perform database operations using either Form view or Table view.

Because you can see only one record at a time in Form view, to see a different record, such as the fifth record, use the SpeedBar buttons to move to it. In some cases, once you have seen a record in Form view, you will want to move to Table view to once again see a collection of records. To do so, click the Table View SpeedBar button ( ) (Figure 1-67). This button replaces the Quick Form button when in Form view and is located at the same position. To move from record to record in Form view and then return to Table view, perform the following steps.

TO MOVE FROM RECORD TO RECORD AND SWITCH TO TABLE VIEW ▼

STEP 1 ▶

Point to the Next Record button on the SpeedBar.

The first record displays on the form. The mouse pointer points to the Next Record button (Figure 1-68).

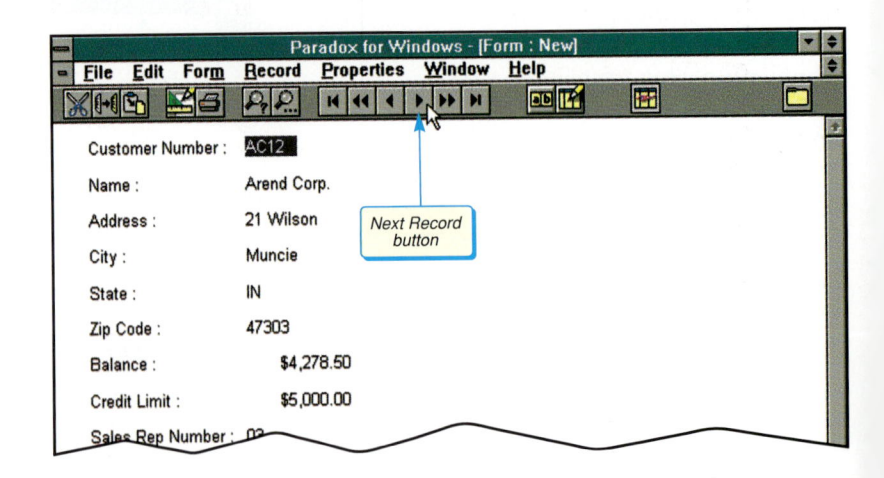

FIGURE 1-68

USING A FORM TO VIEW DATA   P35

STEP 2 ▶

Click the Next Record button four times.

The fifth record displays on the form (Figure 1-69).

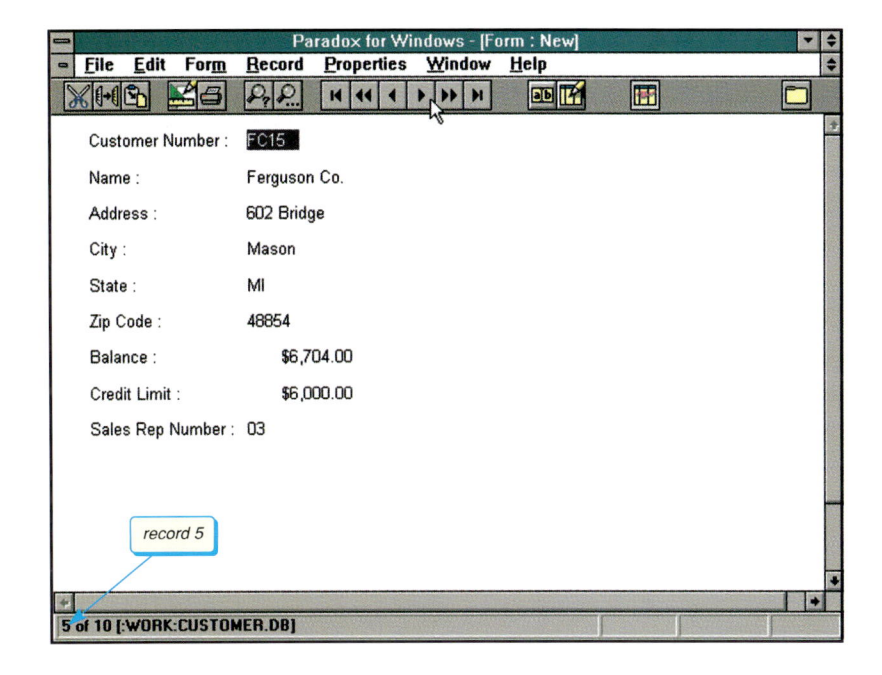

FIGURE 1-69

STEP 3 ▶

Point to the Table View button on the SpeedBar.

The mouse pointer points to the Table View button (Figure 1-70).

FIGURE 1-70

STEP 4 ▶

Click the Table View button.

The data again displays as a table (Figure 1-71). The position within the table is the same as it was on the form; that is, the highlight is positioned on the fifth record. Notice that the SpeedBar button has changed back to the Quick Form button. You can toggle back and forth between the two views by clicking this button.

STEP 5 ▶

Close the table.

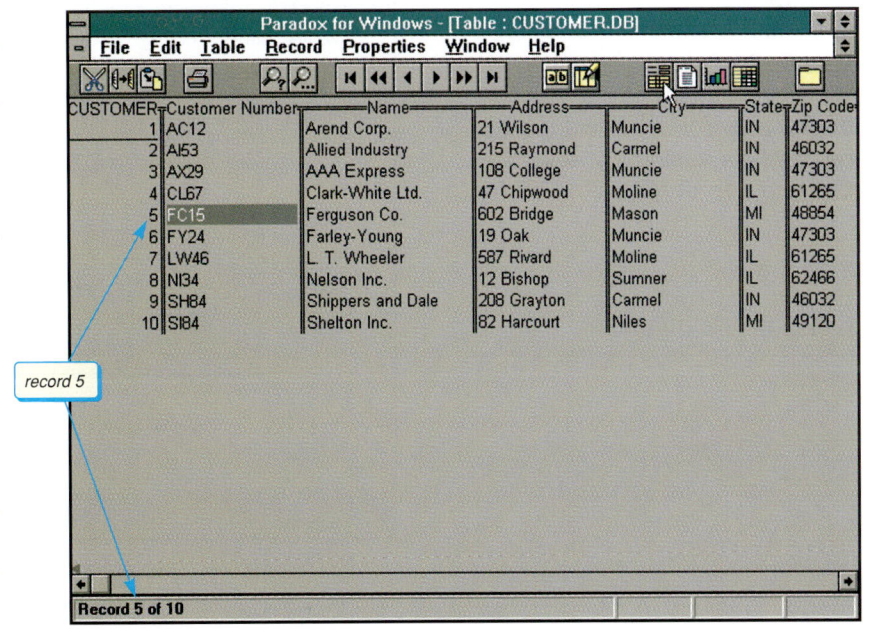

FIGURE 1-71

Closing a form is similar to closing a table. The only difference is that you will be asked if you want to save the form. If you are just using the quick form, there is no reason to save it because you easily can generate another one.

TO CLOSE A FORM

STEP 1 ▶

When in Form view, select the Control menu on the Menu bar and point to the Close command (Figure 1-72).

FIGURE 1-72

STEP 2 ▶

Choose the Close command from the Control menu and then point to the No button.

The Paradox for Windows dialog box displays asking if you want to save the form (Figure 1-73).

STEP 3 ▶

Choose the No button.

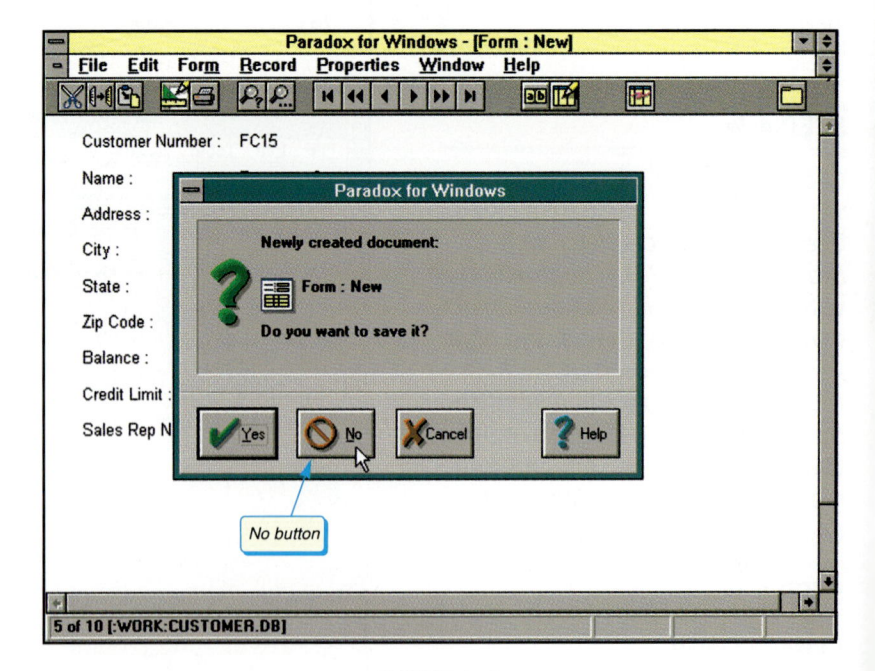

FIGURE 1-73

▶ CREATING A GRAPH

Sometimes the most effective way to present data in a database is graphically. Paradox for Windows contains a graphics tool that allows you to create and customize a wide variety of graphs.

The graph you will create is shown in Figure 1-74. It illustrates the sales figures of each of the three sales representatives. The sales representative numbers appear along the x- (horizontal) axis. The sales amounts are represented along the y- (vertical) axis. The height of each bar represents the sales amount for the corresponding sales representative.

The following steps illustrate the process of creating a initial graph.

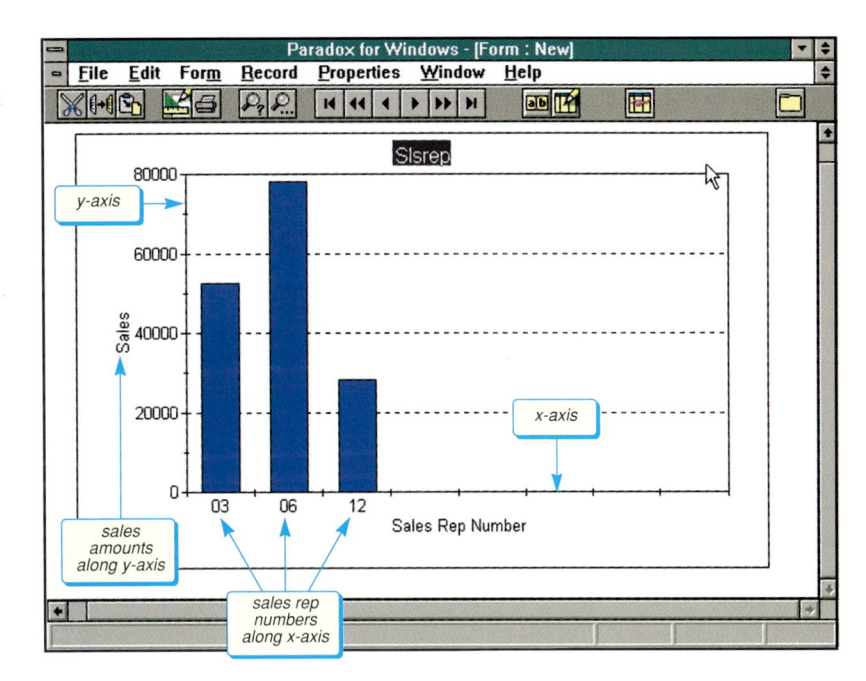

FIGURE 1-74

TO CREATE A GRAPH ▼

STEP 1 ▶

Open the SLSREP table and maximize the window.

STEP 2 ▶

Point to the Quick Graph button (📊) (Figure 1-75).

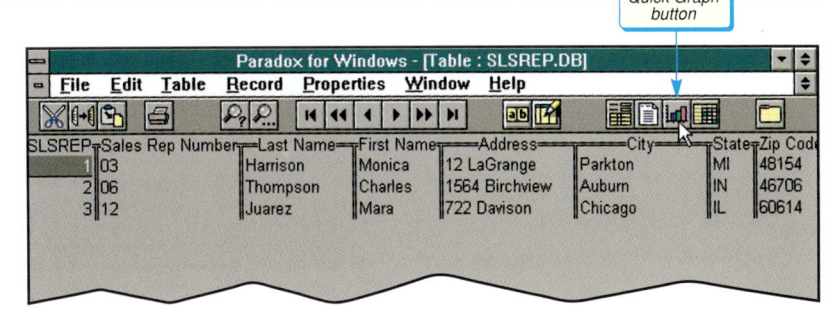

FIGURE 1-75

STEP 3 ▶

Click the Quick Graph button.

The Define Graph dialog box displays (Figure 1-76). X-axis is currently selected in the Field Used In box, which means that you can select the field for the x-axis. No fields are currently included for the x-axis.

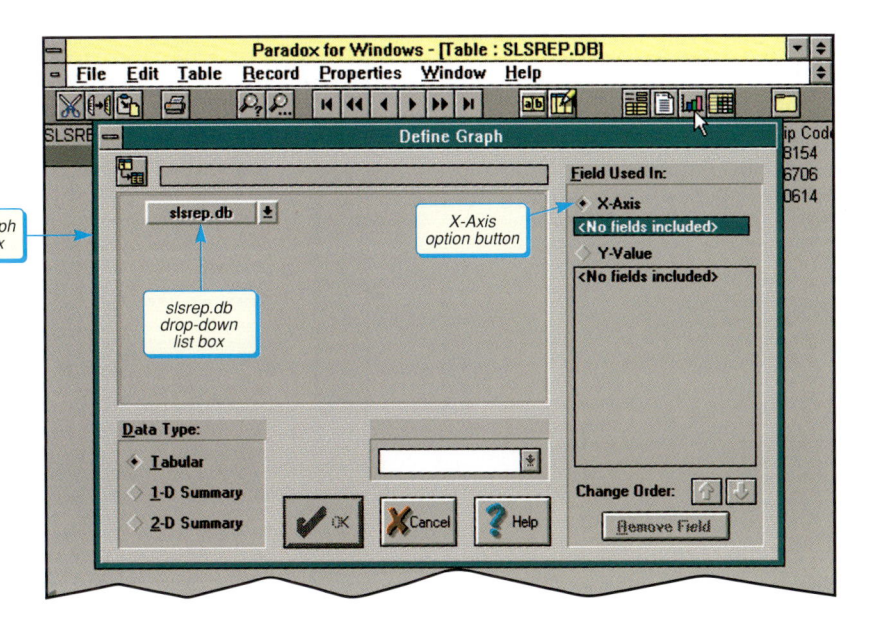

FIGURE 1-76

STEP 4 ▶

Point to slsrep.db drop-down list box arrow (Figure 1-77).

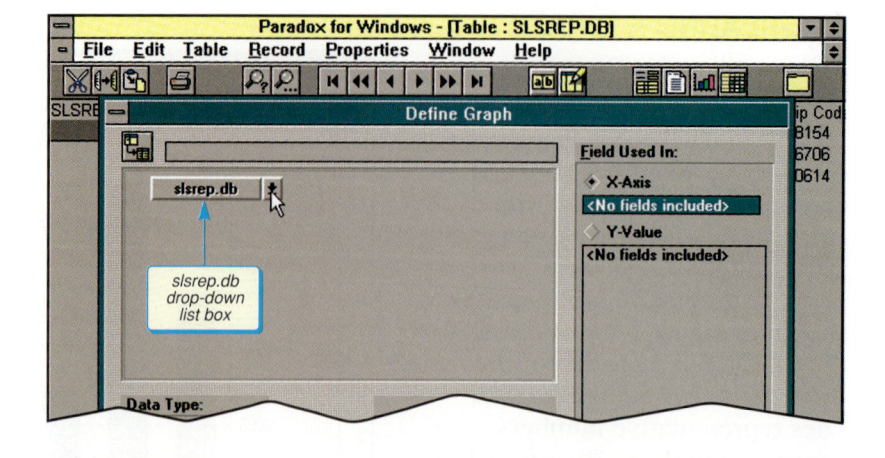

FIGURE 1-77

STEP 5 ▶

Click the slsrep.db drop-down list box down arrow.

A list of fields in the SLSREP table display in the list box (Figure 1-78).

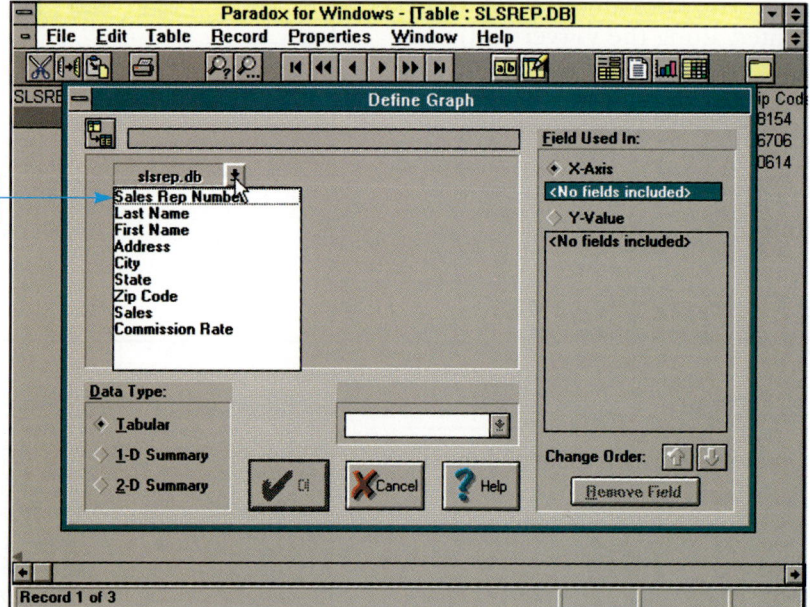

FIGURE 1-78

STEP 6 ▶

Select Sales Rep Number by pointing to it and clicking the left mouse button.

Sales Rep Number is selected as the field for the x-axis (Figure 1-79).

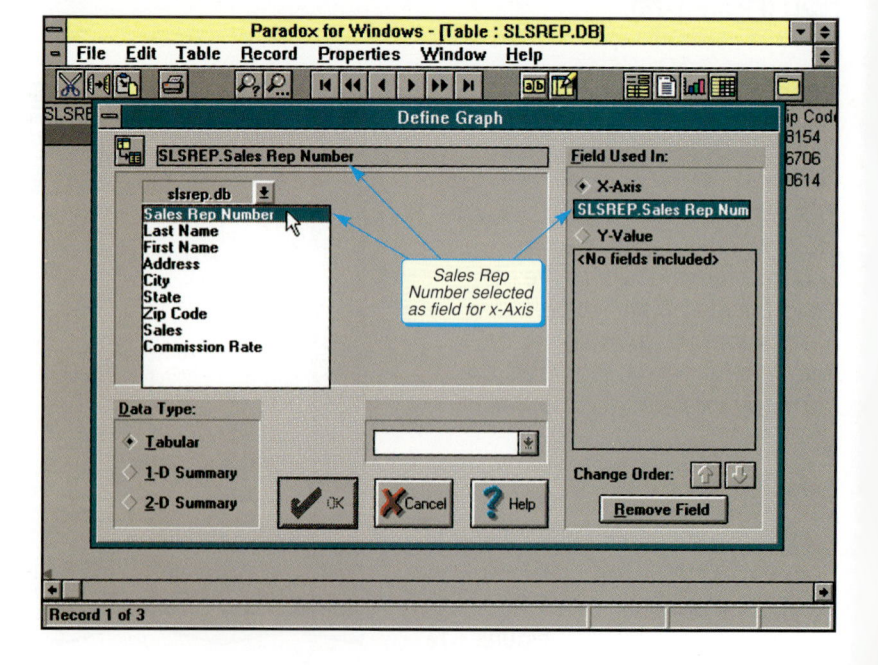

FIGURE 1-79

DESIGNING A DATABASE P39

STEP 7 ▶

Select Y-value in the Field Used In box by pointing to the Y-value option button and clicking the left mouse button.

Y-value is selected (Figure 1-80).

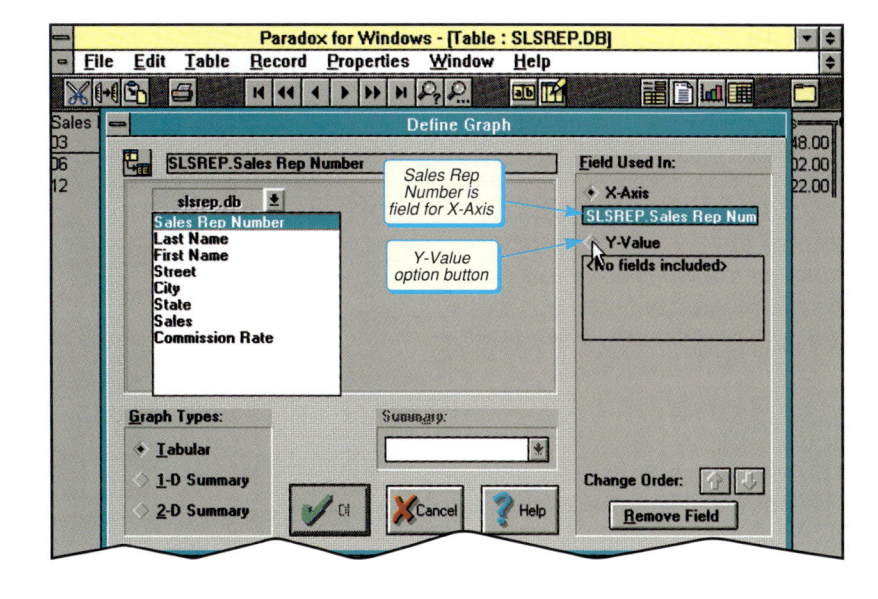

FIGURE 1-80

STEP 8 ▶

Click slsrep.db drop-down arrow.

A list of the possible fields displays in the list box (Figure 1-81). Only fields that contain numbers can be used for y-values. For the Slsrep table, only the Sales and Commission Rate fields are numeric. These two fields display in dark letters, indicating they can be used for y-values. The remaining fields display in gray, meaning they cannot be used.

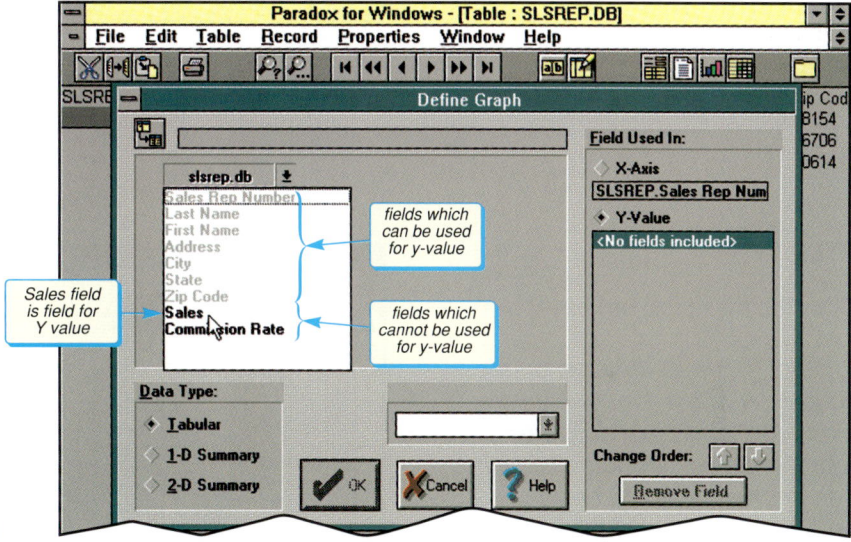

FIGURE 1-81

STEP 9 ▶

Select Sales by pointing to it and clicking the left mouse button.

The Sales field is selected as a field for y-values (Figure 1-82).

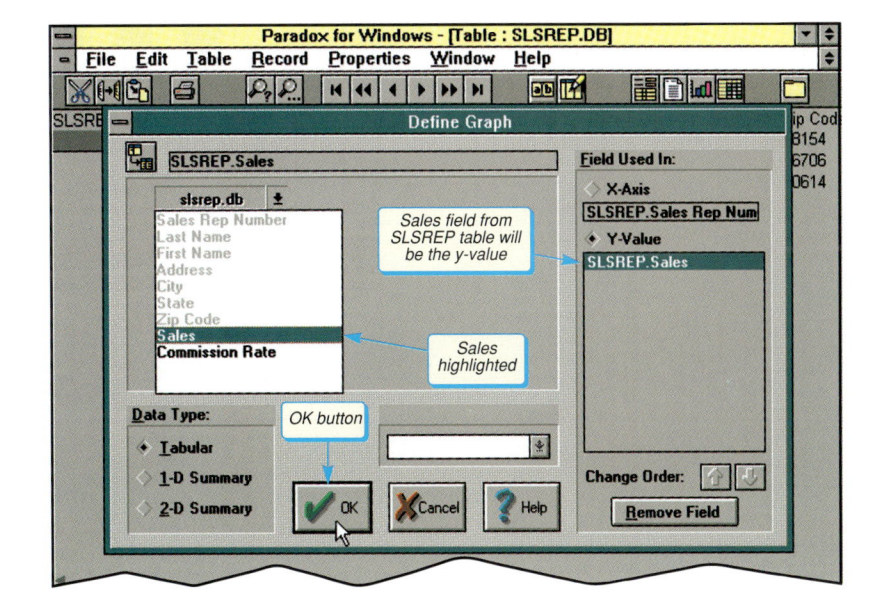

FIGURE 1-82

P40 PROJECT 1 CREATING A DATABASE

STEP 10 ▶

Choose the OK button.

The graph displays in a window (Figure 1-83). The graph is considered to be a special type of form so the title of the window contains the word Form. Since the graph was just created, the title also contains the word New.

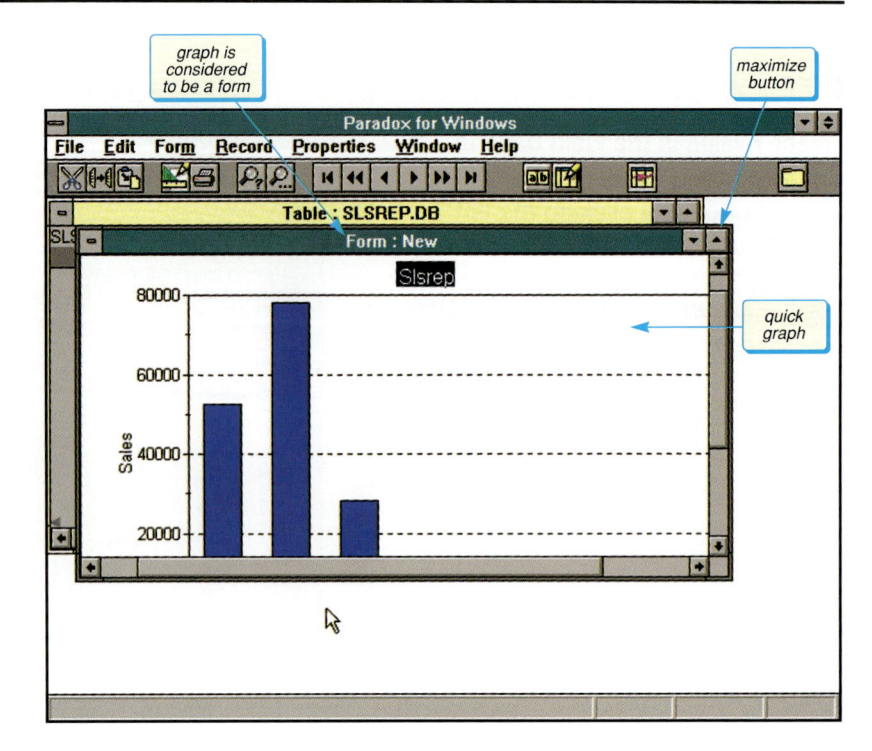

FIGURE 1-83

STEP 11 ▶

Click the maximize button.

The entire graph displays on the screen (Figure 1-84). The values along the x-axis are the sales representative numbers. The values on the y-axis are sales amounts. The title of the graph is the same as the name of the table.

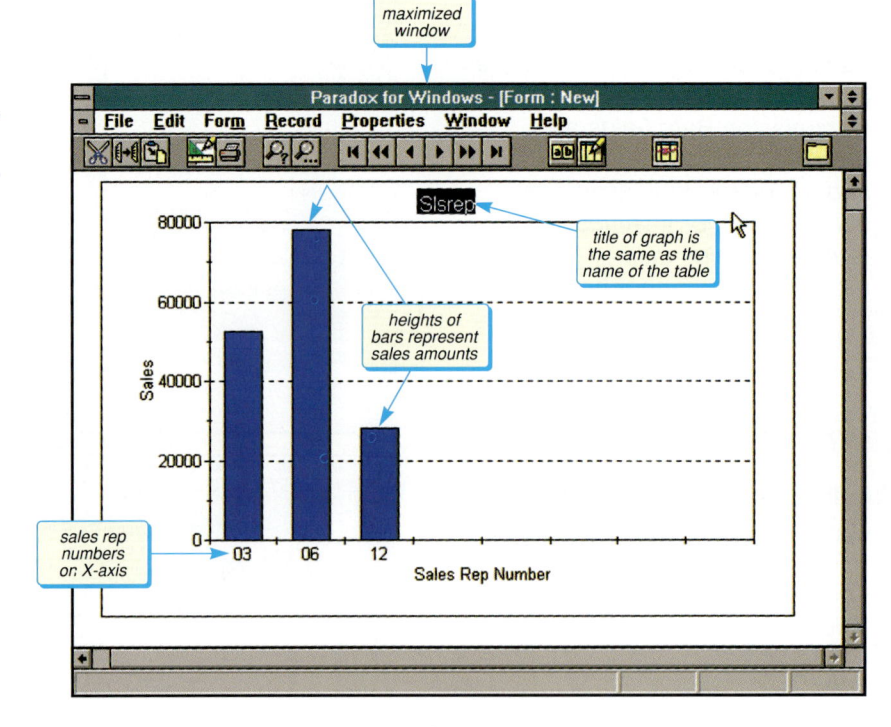

FIGURE 1-84

In addition to viewing the graph on the screen, you can also print the graph. The following steps will print the graph.

DESIGNING A DATABASE **P41**

TO PRINT THE GRAPH ▼

STEP 1 ▶

Point to the Print button (Figure 1-85).

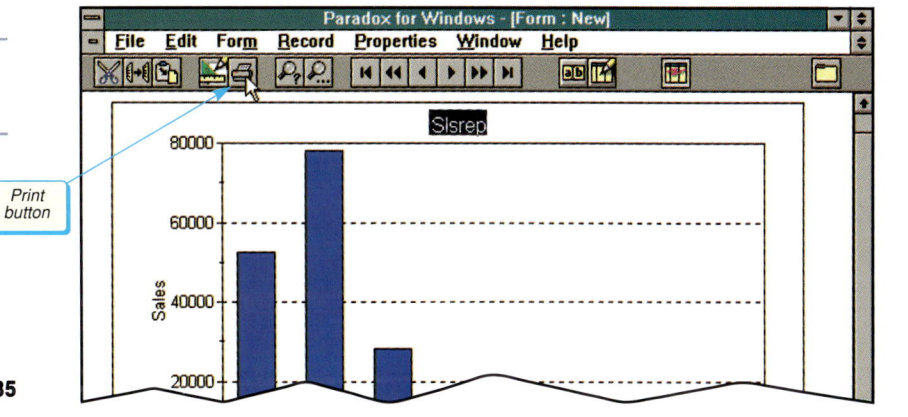

FIGURE 1-85

STEP 2 ▶

Click the Print button.

The Print File dialog box displays (Figure 1-86).

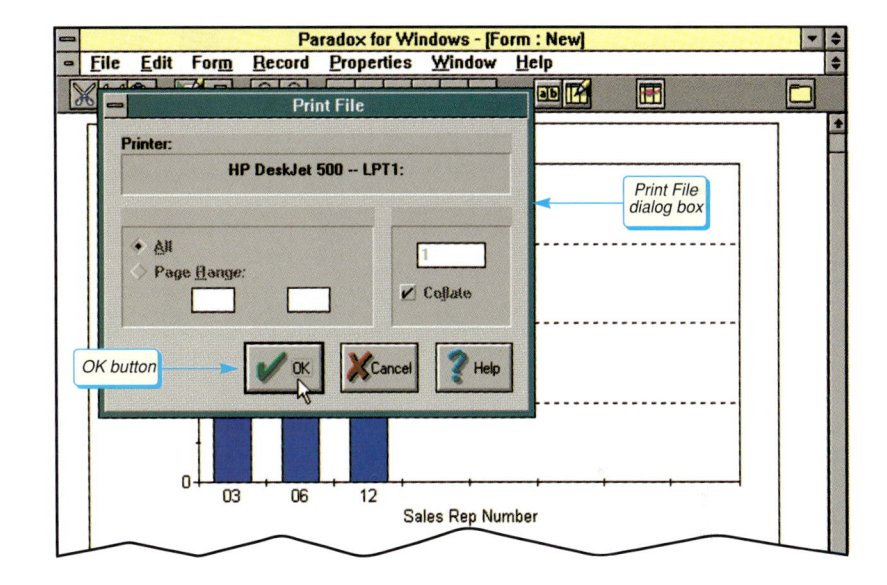

FIGURE 1-86

STEP 3 ▶

Choose OK.

The graph prints. The printed graph will look like the one in Figure 1-87.

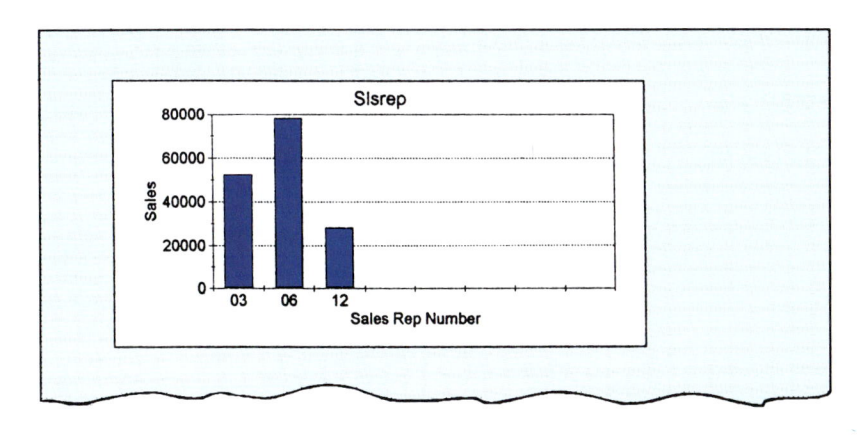

FIGURE 1-87

P42 PROJECT 1 CREATING A DATABASE

Closing a graph is similar to closing a form. Use the following steps to close a graph without saving it.

TO CLOSE A GRAPH ▼

STEP 1 ▶

Select the Control menu and point to Close (Figure 1-88).

FIGURE 1-88

STEP 2 ▶

Choose the Close command.

The Paradox for Windows dialog box displays (Figure 1-89).

STEP 3 ▶

Choose No.

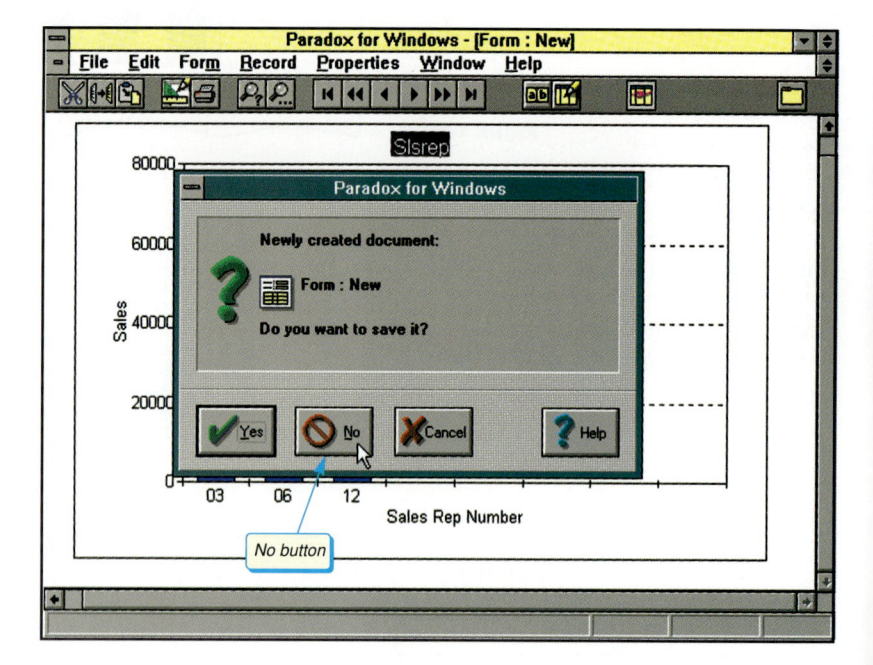

FIGURE 1-89

▶ Using the Help Facility

With Paradox for Windows, you can obtain help at any time by using the Help menu (Figure 1-90). For most information, choose Contents, which provides a variety of ways of finding the information you need. SpeedBar provides specific information about the buttons on the SpeedBar, while Keyboard gives information about special keys. Using Help displays information on the general use of the help facility. Support Info covers the different types of support available from Borland for Paradox for Windows. About... gives information about the version of Paradox for Windows and the user to whom the product is registered.

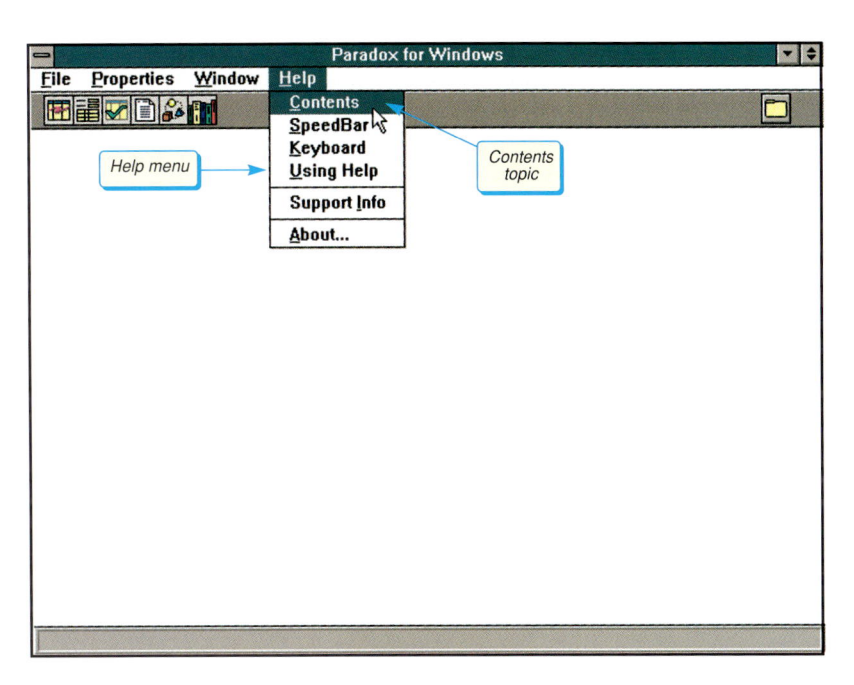

FIGURE 1-90

▶ Designing a Database

Database design refers to the arrangement of data into tables and fields. In the example in this project, the design is specified, but in many cases, you will have to determine the design based on what you want the system to accomplish.

With large, complex databases, the database design process can be extensive. Major sections of advanced database texts are devoted to this topic. Often, however, you should be able to design a database effectively by keeping one simple principle in mind: *Design to remove redundancy.* **Redundancy** means storing the same fact in more than one place.

To illustrate, you need to maintain the information shown in Figure 1-91. In the figure, all the data is contained in a single table. Notice that the data for a given sales representative (number, name, address, and so on) occurs in more than one record.

FIGURE 1-91

▶ CUSTOMER TABLE

Customer Number	Name	Address	City	State	Zip Code	Balance	Credit Limit	Sales Rep Number	Last Name	First Name	Address	City	State	Zip Code	Sales	Comm. Rate
AC12	Arend Corp.	21 Wilson	Muncie	IN	47303	4,278.50	6,000.00	03	Harrison	Monica	12 LaGrange	Parkton	MI	48154	$52,348.00	0.07
AI53	Allied Industry	215 Raymond	Carmel	IN	46032	203.00	3,000.00	06	Thompson	Charles	1564 Birchview	Auburn	IN	46706	$78,202.00	0.05
AX29	AAA Express	108 College	Muncie	IN	47303	42.00	3,000.00	06	Thompson	Charles	1564 Birchview	Auburn	IN	46706	$78,202.00	0.05
CL67	Clark-White Ltd.	47 Chipwood	Moline	IL	61265	3,206.00	8,000.00	12	Juarez	Mara	722 Davison	Chicago	IL	60614	$28,222.00	0.07
FC15	Ferguson Co.	602 Bridge	Mason	MI	48854	6,704.00	6,000.00	03	Harrison	Monica	12 LaGrange	Parkton	MI	48154	$52,348.00	0.07
FY24	Farley-Young	19 Oak	Muncie	IN	47303	2,504.00	6,000.00	06	Thompson	Charles	1564 Birchview	Auburn	IN	46706	$78,202.00	0.05
LW46	L. T. Wheeler	587 Rivard	Moline	IL	61265	0.00	6,000.00	06	Thompson	Charles	1564 Birchview	Auburn	IN	46706	$78,202.00	0.05
NI34	Nelson Inc.	12 Bishop	Sumner	IL	62466	2,011.50	6,000.00	03	Harrison	Monica	12 LaGrange	Parkton	MI	48154	$52,348.00	0.07
SH84	Shippers and Dale	208 Grayton	Carmel	IN	46032	1,597.25	8,000.00	12	Juarez	Mara	722 Davison	Chicago	IL	60614	$28,222.00	0.07
SI84	Shelton Inc.	82 Harcourt	Niles	MI	49120	7,020.00	8,000.00	06	Thompson	Charles	1564 Birchview	Auburn	IN	46706	$78,202.00	0.05

Storing this data in multiple records is an example of redundancy, which causes several problems:

1. Redundancy wastes space on the disk. The address of sales representative 03 (Monica Harrison), for example, should be stored only once. Storing this fact several times is wasteful.
2. Redundancy makes updating the database more difficult. If, for example, Monica Harrison moves, her address would need to be changed in several different places.
3. A possibility of inconsistent data exists. Suppose, for example, you change the address of Monica Harrison on customer FC15's record to 146 Valley, but don't change it on customer AC12's record. In both cases, the sales representative number is 03, but the addresses are different. In other words, the data is *inconsistent*.

The solution to the problem is to place the redundant data in a separate table, one in which the data will no longer be redundant. If, for example, you place the data for sales representatives in a separate table (Figure 1-92), the data for each sales rep will appear only once. Notice you need to have the sales rep number in both tables. Without it, there would be no way to tell which sales representative was associated with which customer. All the other sales rep data, however, was removed from the CUSTOMER table and placed in the SLSREP table. This new arrangement corrects the problems:

1. Because the data for each sales representative is stored only once, space is not wasted.
2. Changing the address of a sales representative is easy. You have only to change one row in the SLSREP table.
3. Because the data for a sales representative is stored only once, inconsistent data cannot occur.

Designing to omit redundancy will help you produce good and valid database designs.

FIGURE 1-92

▶ SLSREP TABLE

Sales Rep Number	Last Name	First Name	Address	City	State	Zip Code	Sales	Commission Rate
03	Harrison	Monica	12 LaGrange	Parkton	MI	48154	$52,348.00	0.07
06	Thompson	Charles	1564 Birchview	Auburn	IN	46706	$78,202.00	0.05
12	Juarez	Mara	722 Davison	Chicago	IL	60614	$28,222.00	0.07

▶ CUSTOMER TABLE

Customer Number	Name	Address	City	State	Zip Code	Balance	Credit Limit	Sales Rep Number
AC12	Arend Corp.	21 Wilson	Muncie	IN	47303	$4,278.50	$6,000.00	03
AI53	Allied Industry	215 Raymond	Carmel	IN	46032	$203.00	$3,000.00	06
AX29	AAA Express	108 College	Muncie	IN	47303	$42.00	$3,000.00	06
CL67	Clark-White Ltd.	47 Chipwood	Moline	IL	61265	$3,206.00	$8,000.00	12
FC15	Ferguson Co.	602 Bridge	Mason	MI	48854	$6,704.00	$6,000.00	03
FY24	Farley-Young	19 Oak	Muncie	IN	47303	$2,504.00	$6,000.00	06
LW46	L. T. Wheeler	587 Rivard	Moline	IL	61265	$0.00	$6,000.00	06
NI34	Nelson Inc.	12 Bishop	Sumner	IL	62466	$2,011.50	$6,000.00	03
SH84	Shippers and Dale	208 Grayton	Carmel	IN	46032	$1,597.25	$8,000.00	12
SI84	Shelton Inc.	82 Harcourt	Niles	MI	49120	$7,020.00	$8,000.00	06

QUICK REFERENCE **P45**

▶ **PROJECT SUMMARY**

Project 1 introduced you to starting Paradox for Windows and creating a database. You learned how to change the working directory, how to create the tables in a database by defining the fields within the tables, and how to add records to the tables. Once you created the tables, you learned how to print the contents of the table as well as how to use a form to view the data in the table. Finally, you created a graph that represented the data visually.

▶ **KEY TERMS**

Control menu (*P6*)	field name (*P8*)	redundancy (*P37*)
create a table (*P8*)	field size (*P8*)	SpeedBar (*P6*)
database (*P2*)	field type (*P8*)	standard form (*P33*)
database design (*P37*)	Form view (*P33*)	status bar (*P7*)
database management system (*P2*)	locked (*P21*)	structure (*P8*)
DBMS (*P4*)	menu bar (*P6*)	Table view (*P33*)
Edit mode (*P21*)	overflow (*P29*)	title bar (*P6*)
field (*P3*)	primary key (*P3, P8*)	unique identifier (*P3*)
	record (*P3*)	working directory (*P7*)

QUICK REFERENCE

In Paradox for Windows you can accomplish a task in a number of different ways. The following table provides a quick reference to each task presented in this project with its available options. The commands listed in the Menu column can be executed using either the keyboard or the mouse.

Task	Mouse	Menu	Keyboard Shortcuts
Assign a Field Name			Type name, press TAB
Change to Edit Mode	Click the Edit Data button on SpeedBar	From Table menu, choose Edit Data	Press F9
Change the Working Directory		From File menu, choose Working Directory	
Create a Quick Graph	Click Quick Graph button on SpeedBar	From Table menu, choose Quick Graph	
Create a Table		From File menu, choose New, then choose Table	
Enter Data in a Field			Type data, press TAB
Exit Paradox for Windows	Double-click Control-menu box on title bar	From File menu, choose Exit	Press ALT + F4
Indicate a Field Size			Type size, press TAB
Indicate a Field Type	Click field type entry with right mouse button to produce a menu of field types; click or drag desired type	Press SPACEBAR to produce menu of field types; type letter corresponding to desired type	Type appropriate letter

(continued)

QUICK REFERENCE (continued)

Task	Mouse	Menu	Keyboard Shortcuts
Indicate a Key Field	Double-click Key field entry		Type any character in Key field entry
Move from Form View to Table View	Click Table View button on SpeedBar	From Form menu, choose Table View	Press F7
Move from Table View to Form View	Click Quick Form button on SpeedBar	From Table menu, choose Quick Form	Press F7
Move to the First Record	Click First Record button on SpeedBar	From Record menu, choose First	Press CTRL+F11
Move to the Last Record	Click Last Record button on SpeedBar	From Record menu, choose Last	Press CTRL+F12
Move to the Next Field	Click field; if field is not on screen, use scroll bar to make field visible, then click field		Press TAB
Move to the Next Record	Click Next Record button on SpeedBar	From Record menu, choose Next	Press F12
Move to the Next Set of Records	Click Next Set button on SpeedBar	From Record menu, choose Next Set	Press SHIFT+F12
Move to the Previous Field	Click field; if field is not on screen, use scroll bar to make field visible, then click field		Press SHIFT+TAB
Move to the Previous Record	Click Previous Record button on SpeedBar	From Record menu, choose Previous	Press F11
Move to the Previous Set of Records	Click Previous Set button on SpeedBar	From Record menu, choose Previous Set	Press SHIFT+F11
Open a Table	Click Open Table button on SpeedBar	From File menu, choose Open, then choose Table	
Print the Contents of a Table	Click Print button on SpeedBar	From File menu, choose Print	Press SHIFT+F7
Save a Newly Defined Table	Choose Save As button in Create Paradox for Windows Table dialog box		
Start Paradox for Windows	Double-click Paradox for Windows program-item icon	First select Paradox program-item icon, then from File menu, choose Open	First select Paradox program-item icon, then press ENTER

STUDENT ASSIGNMENTS

STUDENT ASSIGNMENT 1
True/False

Instructions: Circle T if the statement is true or F if the statement is false.

T F 1. The term database describes a collection of data organized in a manner that allows access, retrieval, and use of that data.
T F 2. Table names can be from one to eight characters in length and can include blank spaces.
T F 3. The bottom bar on a Paradox for Windows desktop is called the information bar.
T F 4. The field or fields that make up the primary key can be located anywhere in a table.
T F 5. Field names can be no more than 25 characters in length and cannot include numeric digits.
T F 6. The only field type available for fields that must be used in arithmetic operations is Numeric.
T F 7. You can include blanks in a Paradox field name.
T F 8. To delete a field in a table structure, point to the field name with the mouse, click the left mouse button, and press the CTRL+D keys.
T F 9. To add a field, point to the field name column on the row where you would like to insert the field, click the left mouse button, and then press the INSERT key.
T F 10. You name a table before you define the field names, field types, and field widths.
T F 11. If you type the letter J in the Key column of the Create Paradox for Windows Table dialog box, an asterisk (*) will display.
T F 12. To add records to a table, change existing records, or delete records, Paradox must be in Edit mode.
T F 13. You use the TAB key to move to the next field in a record and the SHIFT+TAB keys to move to the previous field in a record.
T F 14. If you enter 10000 in a field that has been defined as a currency field type, then the value will display as $10,000.00.
T F 15. Records are always ordered in the sequence in which they are entered.
T F 16. To delete a record from a table, point to any field in the record, click the left mouse button, and then press CTRL+DELETE.
T F 17. You can change records using Form view but you can only add records using Table view.
T F 18. When you create a quick graph, only numeric fields can be used for the X axis.
T F 19. On the Table View screen, you change records in the Edit mode and add records in the Append mode.
T F 20. Controlling redundancy results in an increase in consistency.

STUDENT ASSIGNMENT 2
Multiple Choice

Instructions: Circle the correct response.

1. A database is _____.
   a. the same as a file
   b. a software product
   c. a collection of data organized in a manner that allows access, retrieval, and use of that data
   d. none of the above
2. Which of the following is not a benefit of controlling redundancy?
   a. greater consistency is maintained
   b. less disk space is occupied
   c. updating is easier
   d. all of the above are benefits
3. A field that uniquely identifies a particular record in a table is called a _____.
   a. foreign key
   b. secondary key
   c. primary key
   d. principal key
4. Paradox for Windows is a(n) _____.
   a. applications software package
   b. DBMS
   c. database
   d. both a and b
5. The bar on a Paradox desktop that gives information on the current position within a table and the number of records in a table is called the _____.
   a. title bar
   b. status bar
   c. SpeedBar
   d. menu bar
6. A record in Paradox is composed of a _____.
   a. series of databases
   b. series of files
   c. series of records
   d. series of fields
7. To add records to a table, you must be in the _____ mode.
   a. Table view
   b. Append
   c. Form view
   d. Edit
8. To remove a field from a table structure, press the _____ key(s).
   a. DELETE
   b. CTRL+D
   c. CTRL+DELETE
   d. CTRL+Y
9. If the status bar displays the message, locked, it means _____.
   a. no other user can access the record
   b. no changes can be made to the record
   c. changes cannot be made to the primary key
   d. you have made a mistake and locked the keyboard
10. To move from one field to the next in a record, use the _____ key(s).
    a. ALT+RIGHT ARROW
    b. TAB
    c. CTRL+RIGHT ARROW
    d. SHIFT+TAB

STUDENT ASSIGNMENT 3
Understanding the Paradox for Windows Desktop

Instructions: In Figure SA1-3, arrows point to the major components of the Paradox desktop. Identify the various parts of the desktop in the space provided.

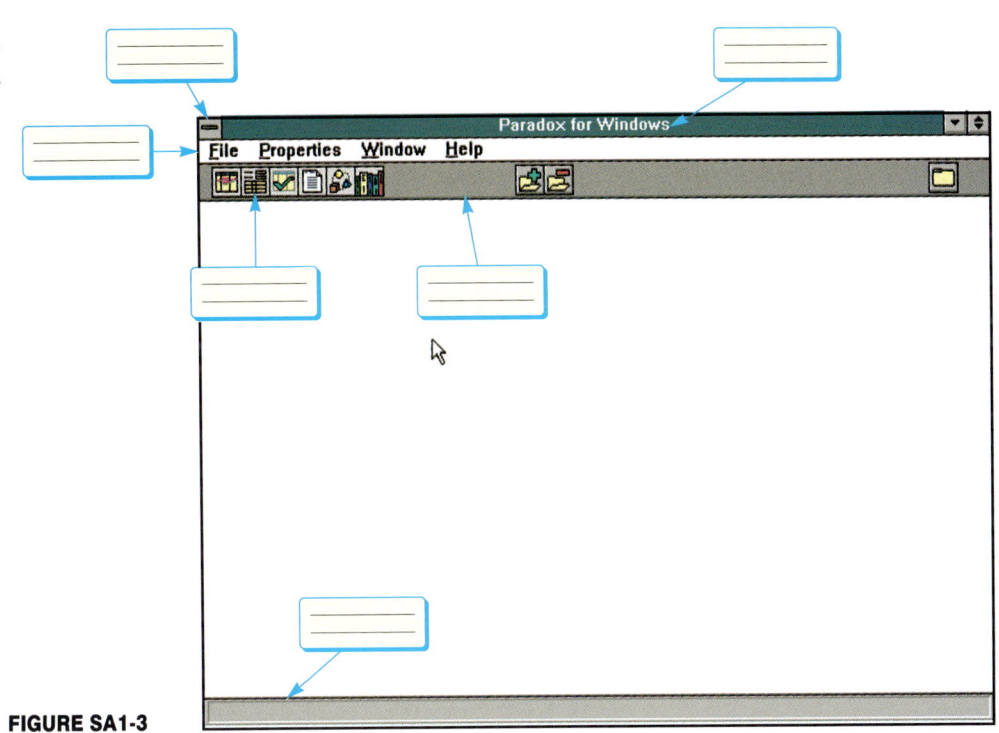

FIGURE SA1-3

STUDENT ASSIGNMENT 4
Understanding the Create Paradox for Windows Table Dialog Box

Instructions: Figure SA1-4 shows the Create Paradox for Windows Table dialog box. Use this figure to answer the questions on the next page.

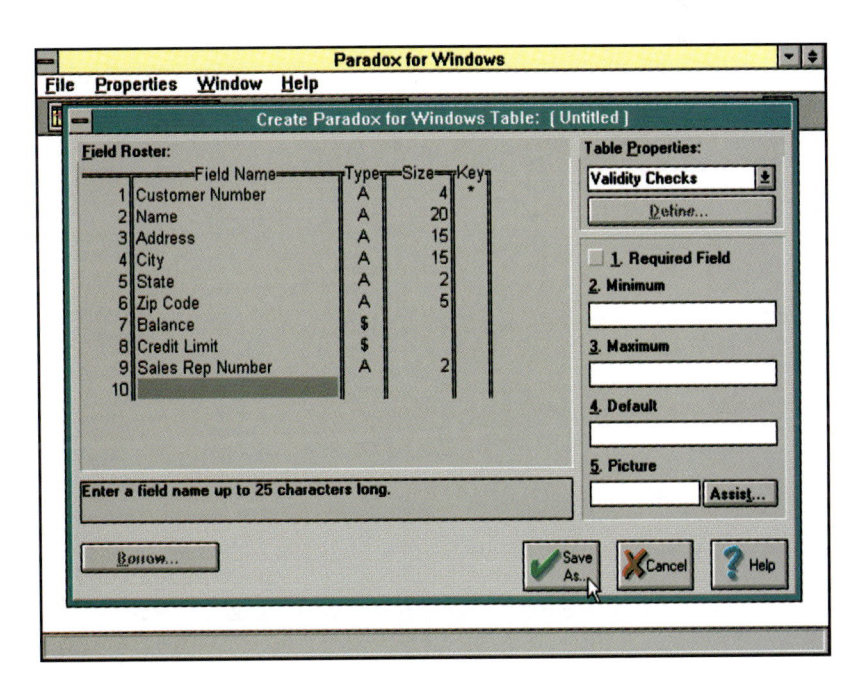

FIGURE SA1-4

STUDENT ASSIGNMENT 4 (continued)

1. Which fields can be used in mathematical operations?

2. What does the letter A in the Type column mean, and the $ in the Type column?

3. What does the asterisk (*) in the Key column mean? How did it get there?

4. Suppose you needed to insert a field for Customer Type immediately after the Zip Code field. The field is alphanumeric and is five characters in length. How would you accomplish this task?

5. Adding the Customer Type field was a mistake. The field needs to be deleted. How would you accomplish this task?

STUDENT ASSIGNMENT 5
Understanding the SpeedBar on the Paradox for Windows Table Window

Instructions: In Figure SA1-5, arrows point to various buttons on the SpeedBar. Identify the buttons in the space provided.

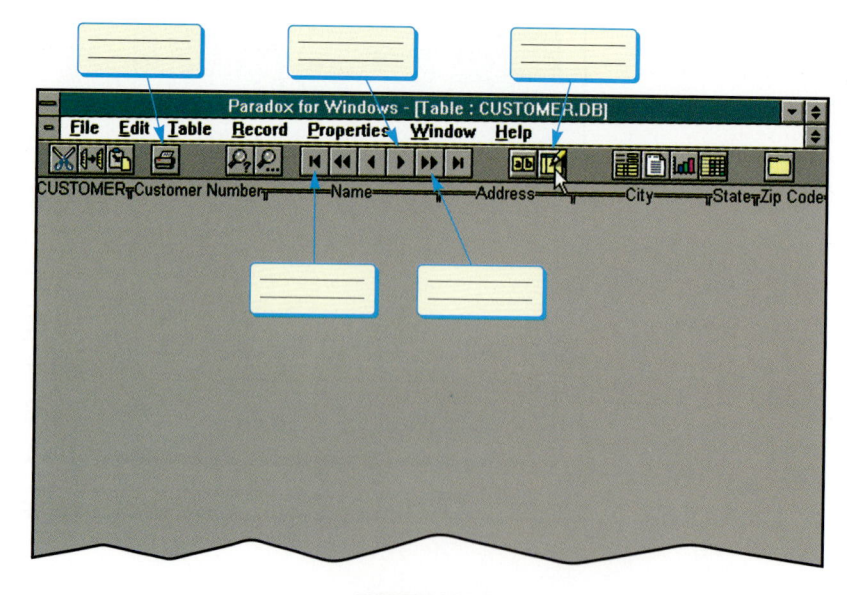

FIGURE SA1-5

STUDENT ASSIGNMENT 6
Using the Paradox for Windows Table screen

Instructions: The CUSTOMER.DB table is shown in Figure SA1-6. Use this figure to answer the questions following Figure SA1-6.

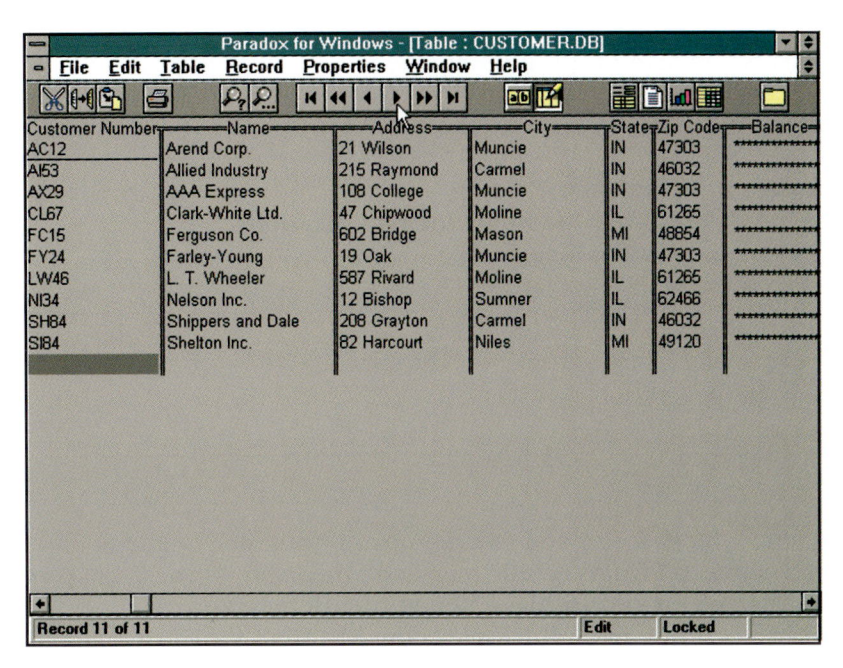

FIGURE SA1-6

1. Why does the Balance field contain asterisks?

2. Assume you have added the records to the table and maximized the window. You now want to change the address for customer FY24 in the CUSTOMER.DB table. What is the first step?

3. How can you change the customer name in record 1 from "Arend Corp." to "Arends Inc."?

4. You have just finished making the change in task 3 above and would like to change the amount in the Balance field for record 1 to $4,445.50. List the steps to accomplish this task.

COMPUTER LABORATORY EXERCISES

COMPUTER LABORATORY EXERCISE 1
Using the Help Menu

Instructions: Perform the following tasks using a computer.

1. Start Paradox.
2. Choose the Contents command from the Help menu.
3. Choose Search.
4. Type `create` in the Search dialog box and then select the phrase, Create Paradox Table dialog box, from the list.
5. Choose Show Topics and then choose Go To.
6. Read the information and answer the following two questions.
7. Name the two main panels in the dialog box.

_____

_____

8. How do you move between panels?

_____

_____

9. Exit the Help window by choosing the Exit command from the File menu in the Help window.
10. Choose the Open command from the File menu and then choose the Table command.
11. When the Open Table dialog box displays, choose the Help button.
12. Ready the printer and choose the Print Topic command from the File menu in the Help window to print a hard copy of the Open a Table help message.
13. Close the Help window by choosing the Exit command from the File menu in the Help window.
14. Choose the Cancel button to remove the Open Table dialog box from the screen.
15. Exit Paradox.

COMPUTER LABORATORY EXERCISE 2
Changing Data

Instructions: Start Paradox and open the SLSREP.DB table from the Paradox subdirectory on the Student Diskette that accompanies this book. Perform the following tasks:

1. Change the city for sales representative number 03 to Allendale.
2. Add the following record to the SLSREP table.

| 14 | Aldink | James | 35 Magee | Bedford | IN | 47421 | $45,564.00 | .05 |

3. Print the SLSREP table.
4. Change the city for sales representative number 03 back to Parkton. (This reverses the change you made in task 1 above.)
5. Delete the extra record that you added in task 2.
6. Print the SLSREP table.
7. Close the table and exit Paradox.

COMPUTER LABORATORY EXERCISE 3
Graphing Data

Instructions: Create a graph for the CUSTOMER.DB table and the SLSREP.DB table. Perform the following tasks.

1. Start Paradox.
2. Open the CUSTOMER.DB table from the Paradox subdirectory on the student diskette that accompanies this book.
3. On the SpeedBar, point to and click the Quick Graph button.
4. When the Graph dialog box displays, select the Customer Name field as the X-axis.
5. Select the Credit Limit field as the Y-axis.
6. Display the graph on the screen.
7. Are there any problems with this graph?

_____

_____

_____

8. Close the graph, then close the CUSTOMER.DB table.
9. Open the SLSREP.DB table from the Paradox subdirectory on the student diskette that accompanies this book.
10. On the SpeedBar, point to and click the Quick Graph button.
11. Select the Sales Rep Number field for the X-axis.
12. Select the Commission Rate field for the Y-axis.
13. Display the graph on the screen.
14. Are there any problems with this graph?

_____

_____

_____

15. Close the graph, then close the SLSREP table.
16. Exit Paradox.

COMPUTER LABORATORY ASSIGNMENTS

COMPUTER LABORATORY ASSIGNMENTS
Creating and Displaying a Database

Each project ends with four computer laboratory assignments. In each project, Computer Laboratory Assignment 1 involves a database of Parts, Computer Laboratory Assignment 2 involves a database of Employees, Computer Laboratory Assignment 3 deals with a database containing data about Movies, and Computer Laboratory Assignment 4 deals with a database containing information about the inventory of a bookstore.

    The computer laboratory assignments are cumulative. That is, the assignment for Computer Laboratory Assignment 1 in Project 2 builds on the assignment for Computer Laboratory Assignment 1 from Project 1. Thus, be sure to work through the computer laboratory assignment completely before proceeding to the next project. If not, you may encounter difficulty later on.

COMPUTER LABORATORY ASSIGNMENT 1
Creating a Parts Database

Purpose: To provide practice in creating and updating a database.

Problem: A wholesale distribution company needs to maintain information on the parts they sell to local retail stores. The database they will use for this purpose consists of two tables. The Part table contains information about items that the distributor has in stock. The Item Class table contains information about the item class to which each part belongs. You have been assigned to create and update this database.

Instructions: The structure and data for the Part table are shown in Figure CLA1-1a. The structure and data for the Item Class table are shown in Figure CLA1-1b. You are to create both tables.

▸ STRUCTURE OF PART TABLE

Field Name	Type	Size	Key
Part Number	A	4	*
Part Description	A	10	
Units On Hand	S		
Item Class Code	A	2	
Warehouse Number	A		
Price	$		

▸ DATA FOR PART TABLE

Part Number	Part Description	Units On Hand	Item Class Code	Warehouse Number	Price
AX12	IRON	104	HW	3	24.95
AZ52	DARTBOARD	20	SG	2	12.95
BA74	BASKETBALL	0	SG	1	24.95
BH22	CORNPOPPER	95	HW	3	29.95
BT04	GAS GRILL	11	AP	2	149.99
BZ66	WASHER	52	AP	3	399.99
CA14	GRIDDLE	78	HW	3	39.99
CB03	BIKE	44	SG	1	299.99
CX11	BLENDER	112	HW	3	22.95
CZ81	TREADMILL	68	SG	2	349.95

FIGURE CLA1-1a

Perform the following tasks using Paradox for Windows.

1. Create the Part table using the structure shown in Figure CLA1-1a. Use the name PART for the table.
2. Add the data shown in Figure CLA1-1a to the Part table.
3. Print the table.
4. Create the Item Class table using the structure shown in Figure CLA1-1b. Use the name CLASS for the table.
5. Add the data shown in Figure CLA1-1b to the Class table.
6. Print the table.
7. Create and print a graph. The x-values for the graph should be part numbers and the y-values should be units on hand.

▸ STRUCTURE OF ITEM CLASS TABLE

Field Name	Type	Size	Key
Item Class Code	A	2	*
Item Class Description	A	15	

▸ DATA FOR ITEM CLASS TABLE

Item Class Code	Item Class Description
AP	Appliances
HW	Housewares
SG	Sporting Goods

FIGURE CLA1-1b

COMPUTER LABORATORY ASSIGNMENT 2
Creating an Employees Database

Purpose: To provide practice in creating and updating a database.

Problem: A small manufacturing company has a database of employees. The database consists of two tables. The Employee table contains information about the employee. The Department table contains information about the department in which the employee works. You have been assigned to create and update this database.

Instructions: The structure and data for the Employee table are shown in Figure CLA1-2a. The structure and data for the Department table are shown in Figure CLA1-2b. You are to create both tables.

▸ STRUCTURE OF EMPLOYEE TABLE

Field Name	Type	Size	Key
Employee Number	A	4	*
Employee Last Name	A	12	
Employee First Name	A	8	
Department Code	A	2	
Pay Rate	$		

▸ DATA FOR EMPLOYEE TABLE

Employee Number	Employee Last Name	Employee First Name	Department Code	Pay Rate
1011	Rapoza	Anthony	04	8.50
1013	McCormack	Nigel	04	8.25
1016	Ackerman	David	01	9.75
1017	Doi	Chan	03	6.00
1020	Castle	Mark	04	7.50
1022	Dunning	Lisa	02	9.10
1025	Chaney	Joseph	01	8.00
1026	Bender	Helen	03	6.75
1029	Anderson	Mariane	04	9.00
1030	Edwards	Kenneth	03	8.60
1037	Baxter	Charles	01	11.00
1041	Evans	John	02	6.00

FIGURE CLA1-2a

Perform the tasks listed below and on the next page using Paradox for Windows.

1. Create the Employee table using the structure shown in Figure CLA1-2a. Use the name EMPLOYEE for the table.
2. Add the data shown in Figure CLA1-2a to the Employee table.
3. Print the table.
4. Create the Department table using the structure shown in Figure CLA1-2b. Use the name DEPT for the table.
5. Add the data shown in Figure CLA1-2b to the Department table.
6. Print the table.

▸ STRUCTURE OF DEPARTMENT TABLE

Field Name	Type	Size	Key
Department Code	A	2	*
Department Name	A	10	

▸ DATA FOR DEPARTMENT TABLE

Department Code	Department Name
01	Accounting
02	Marketing
03	Production
04	Shipping

FIGURE CLA1-2b

P56   PROJECT 1   CREATING A DATABASE

COMPUTER LABORATORY ASSIGNMENT 2 (continued)

7. Three new employees have just joined the company. Open the Employee table and add the three employees in Figure CLA1-2c.
8. Print the table.
9. Create and print a graph. The x-values for the graph should be employee numbers and the y-values should be pay rates.

FIGURE CLA1-2c

Employee Number	Employee Last Name	Employee First Name	Department Code	Pay Rate
1056	Andrews	Robert	02	9.00
1057	Dugan	Mary	03	8.75
1066	Castleworth	Mary	03	8.75

COMPUTER LABORATORY ASSIGNMENT 3
Creating a Movies Database

Purpose: To provide practice in creating and updating a database.

Problem: A family has a database of video tapes they have collected. This database consists of two tables. The Movie table contains information about the movies in the collection. The Director table contains information about the individuals who directed the movie. You have been assigned to create and update this database.

Instructions: The structure and data for the Movie table are shown in Figure CLA1-3a. The structure and data for the Director table are shown in Figure CLA1-3b on the next page. You are to create both tables.

▶ **STRUCTURE OF MOVIE TABLE**

Field Name	Type	Size	Key
Movie Number	A	3	*
Movie Title	A	18	
Year Made	S		
Movie Type	A	6	
Length	S		
Director Code	A	2	

▶ **DATA FOR MOVIE TABLE**

Movie Number	Movie Title	Year Made	Movie Type	Length	Director Code
001	Ann Thompson	1977	COMEDY	93	01
002	They Went Away	1964	COMEDY	93	04
003	A Crack in Time	1971	SCI FI	136	04
004	Too Late for Henry	1959	SUSPEN	136	03
005	The Dirty Car	1948	SUSPEN	80	03
006	They Know Too Much	1969	HORROR	109	03
007	Old House	1978	DRAMA	95	01
008	The Dervish	1963	HORROR	119	03
011	Winston's Dog	1979	COMEDY	96	01
012	Escape from Zero	1958	SUSPEN	128	03
014	The Ninth Planet	1968	SCI FI	141	04
021	A Single Bullet	1939	WESTER	99	02
022	Rear Window	1954	SUSPEN	112	03
023	No Sheriff	1953	WESTER	116	02
024	Just Like Me	1940	DRAMA	128	02

FIGURE CLA1-3a

STRUCTURE OF DIRECTOR TABLE

Field Name	Type	Size	Key
Director Code	A	2	*
Director Name	A	18	

DATA FOR DIRECTOR TABLE

Director Code	Director Name
01	Allward, Stacy
02	Markle, Amy
03	Rodriguez, Juan
04	DeNoyer, K. Z.

FIGURE CLA1-3b

Perform the following tasks using Paradox for Windows.

1. Create the Movie table using the structure shown in Figure CLA1-3a. Use the name MOVIE for the table.
2. Add the data shown in Figure CLA1-3a to the Movie table.
3. Print the table.
4. Create the Director table using the structure shown in Figure CLA1-3b. Use the name DIRECTOR for the table.
5. Add the data shown in Figure CLA1-3b to the Director table.
6. Print the table.
7. Open the Movie table and change the title for movie number 004 to *No Time for Henry*.
8. The Year entry for *The Dervish* is incorrect. Change it to 1960.
9. Delete the record for movie number 23.
10. Print the table.
11. Create and print a graph. The x-values for the graph should be movie numbers and the y-values should be lengths.

COMPUTER LABORATORY ASSIGNMENT 4
Creating a Books Database

Purpose: To provide practice in designing, creating and updating a database.

Problem: A small bookstore owner has a book inventory database. A report containing the data for this database is shown in Figure CLA1-4.

```
Monday, October 10, 1994                                                       Page 1
   Book    Title             Author          Publisher Name    Publisher  Book   Price    Units
   Code                                                        Code       Type            on Hand
   0189    The Old Hat       Frank Adams     Planars Books     PB         FIC    $4.95    2
   1351    The Box           Marybeth Sims   Stoyers-Insen     SI         HOR    $5.95    1
   138X    Death Becomes Her Maria Comio     Bantam Books      BB         MYS    $3.50    3
   2226    From the River    Joseph Loekse   Bantam Books      BB         SFI    $17.95   3
   2295    It Struck Twice   Marybeth Sims   Vanderlwand       VI         HOR    $22.95   0
   2766    The Black Tiger   Frank Adams     Planars Books     PB         FIC    $4.95    2
   3743    First and Last    Frank Adams     Planars Books     PB         FIC    $3.50    0
   3906    Whirlwind         Pamela Perry    Bantam Books      BB         SUS    $4.95    1
   6128    His Name Was Evil Maria Comio     Planars Books     PB         MYS    $3.95    3
   6171    One Last Chance   Pamela Perry    Samstra and Simons SS        SUS    $21.95   4
   6328    In Right Field    Pamela Perry    Bantam Books      BB         SUS    $4.95    2
   7405    Night Madness     Pamela Perry    Bantam Books      BB         SUS    $4.95    0
   7443    Ellen             Marybeth Sims   Stoyers-Insen     SI         HOR    $5.95    1
   9373    She Won't Shoot   Jodie Nichols   Samstra and Simons SS        FIC    $21.95   2
```

FIGURE CLA1-4

PROJECT 1 CREATING A DATABASE

COMPUTER LABORATORY ASSIGNMENT 4 (continued)

The owner has asked you to design the database for the bookstore; that is, you must determine the tables, fields, primary keys, and field characteristics. When you have finished designing the database, you are to create the tables and then update the database.

Instructions: Perform the following tasks using Paradox for Windows.

1. Using the data shown in Figure CLA1-4 on the previous page, determine the structure for the necessary tables.
2. Create the tables.
3. Determine the table names.
4. Add the data shown in Figure CLA1-4 to the tables.
5. Print the tables.
6. Create and print a graph. The x-values for the graph should be book codes and the y-values should be prices.

PARADOX 1.0 FOR WINDOWS
PROJECT TWO

QUERYING A DATABASE

OBJECTIVES You will have mastered the material in this project when you can:

- State the purpose of queries
- State the purpose and characteristics of the Answer table
- Create a new query
- Use a query to display all records and all fields
- Run a query
- Print the answer to a query
- Close the Answer table
- Close a query
- Clear a query
- Use a query to display selected fields
- Use character data in conditions in a query
- Use wildcards in conditions
- Use LIKE in conditions
- Use numeric data in conditions
- Use comparison operators
- Use compound conditions involving AND
- Use compound conditions involving OR
- Sort the answer to a query
- Join tables in a query
- Restrict the records in a join
- Use computed fields in a query
- Calculate statistics in a query
- Use grouping with statistics
- Graph the answer to a query
- Save a query
- Use a saved query

INTRODUCTION

A database management system like Paradox for Windows offers many useful features, among them the capability to answer questions. Figure 2-1 on the next page, for example, shows several questions regarding the Customer table created in Project 1.

- What is the balance of customer CL67?
- Which customers' names begin with Sh?
- Which customer's name sounds like Sheldon?
- How much available credit do the customers currently have?
- In which states does Sales Rep 03 have customers?

When you pose a question to Paradox, the question is called a query. A **query** is a question represented in a way that Paradox can understand.

First create a corresponding query using the techniques illustrated in this project. Once you have created the query, you **run the query**; that is, you perform the steps necessary to obtain the answer. When finished, Paradox displays the answer to your question in the format shown at the bottom of Figure 2-1.

PROJECT 2 QUERYING A DATABASE

QUERIES

- What is the balance of customer CL67?
- Which customer's name sounds like Sheldon?
- Which customers' names begin with Sh?
- In which states does Sales Rep 03 have customers?
- How much available credit (credit limit - balance) do the customers currently have?

▶ **CUSTOMER TABLE**

DATABASE

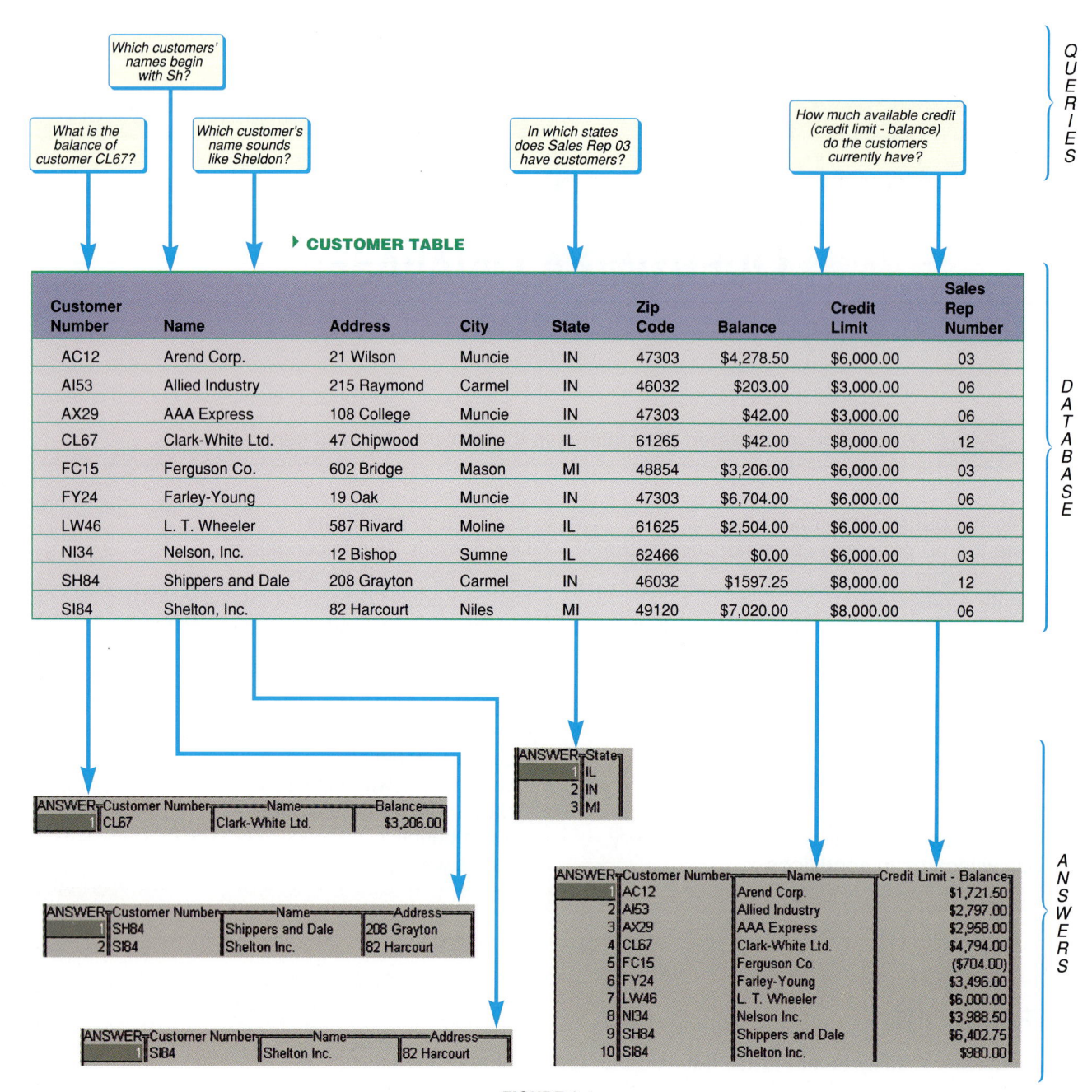

Customer Number	Name	Address	City	State	Zip Code	Balance	Credit Limit	Sales Rep Number
AC12	Arend Corp.	21 Wilson	Muncie	IN	47303	$4,278.50	$6,000.00	03
AI53	Allied Industry	215 Raymond	Carmel	IN	46032	$203.00	$3,000.00	06
AX29	AAA Express	108 College	Muncie	IN	47303	$42.00	$3,000.00	06
CL67	Clark-White Ltd.	47 Chipwood	Moline	IL	61265	$42.00	$8,000.00	12
FC15	Ferguson Co.	602 Bridge	Mason	MI	48854	$3,206.00	$6,000.00	03
FY24	Farley-Young	19 Oak	Muncie	IN	47303	$6,704.00	$6,000.00	06
LW46	L. T. Wheeler	587 Rivard	Moline	IL	61625	$2,504.00	$6,000.00	06
NI34	Nelson, Inc.	12 Bishop	Sumne	IL	62466	$0.00	$6,000.00	03
SH84	Shippers and Dale	208 Grayton	Carmel	IN	46032	$1597.25	$8,000.00	12
SI84	Shelton, Inc.	82 Harcourt	Niles	MI	49120	$7,020.00	$8,000.00	06

ANSWERS

ANSWER — Customer Number — Name — Balance
1 | CL67 | Clark-White Ltd. | $3,206.00

ANSWER — State
1 | IL
2 | IN
3 | MI

ANSWER — Customer Number — Name — Address
1 | SH84 | Shippers and Dale | 208 Grayton
2 | SI84 | Shelton Inc. | 82 Harcourt

ANSWER — Customer Number — Name — Credit Limit - Balance
1 | AC12 | Arend Corp. | $1,721.50
2 | AI53 | Allied Industry | $2,797.00
3 | AX29 | AAA Express | $2,958.00
4 | CL67 | Clark-White Ltd. | $4,794.00
5 | FC15 | Ferguson Co. | ($704.00)
6 | FY24 | Farley-Young | $3,496.00
7 | LW46 | L. T. Wheeler | $6,000.00
8 | NI34 | Nelson Inc. | $3,988.50
9 | SH84 | Shippers and Dale | $6,402.75
10 | SI84 | Shelton Inc. | $980.00

ANSWER — Customer Number — Name — Address
1 | SI84 | Shelton Inc. | 82 Harcourt

FIGURE 2-1

▶ THE ANSWER TABLE

When you run a query, Paradox places the answer in a special table called, appropriately enough, **Answer table** or **answer**. An image of the Answer table automatically displays in a window on the desktop. When you close this window, the Answer table continues to exist and can be used like any other table. Be aware of two special characteristics of this table:

1. When a new query is run, the answer will become the new Answer table. The new version of the Answer table will overwrite the old one.
2. When you exit Paradox, the Answer table will be deleted.

▶ OPENING A NEW QUERY WINDOW

To create a query you will use a special window called a **Query window**. To open a new query window, use the New command on the File menu as shown in the following steps. It is usually easier to work with the query window if it is maximized. Thus, as a standard practice, you should maximize the query window as soon as you open it.

TO OPEN A NEW QUERY WINDOW ▼

STEP 1 ▶

Select the File menu, choose the New command, and then point to the Query command (Figure 2-2).

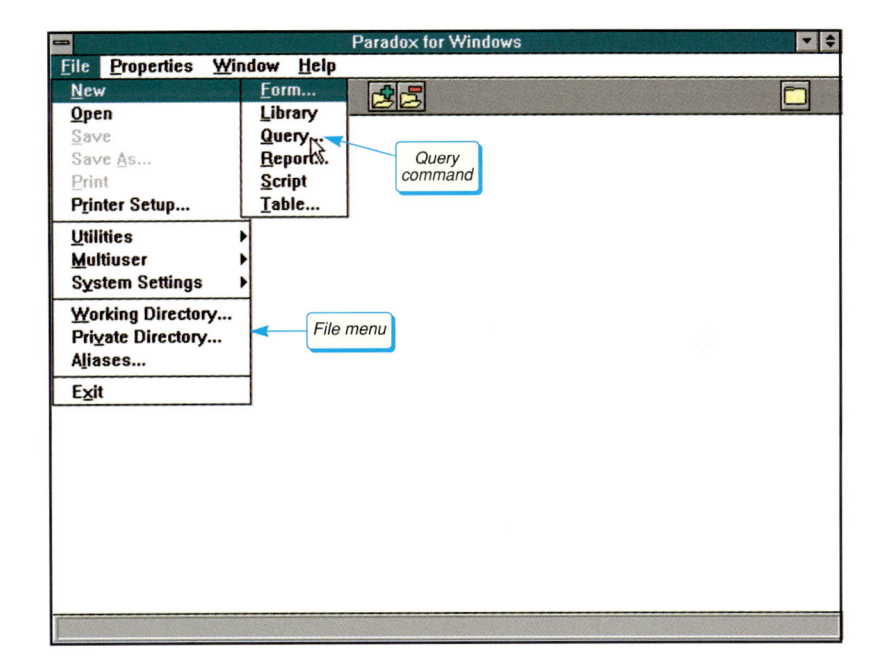

FIGURE 2-2

STEP 2 ▶

Choose the Query command, and then point to CUSTOMER.DB in the Select File dialog box.

The Select File dialog box displays on the desktop (Figure 2-3). The File Name list box contains a list of available tables. The mouse pointer points to CUSTOMER.DB.

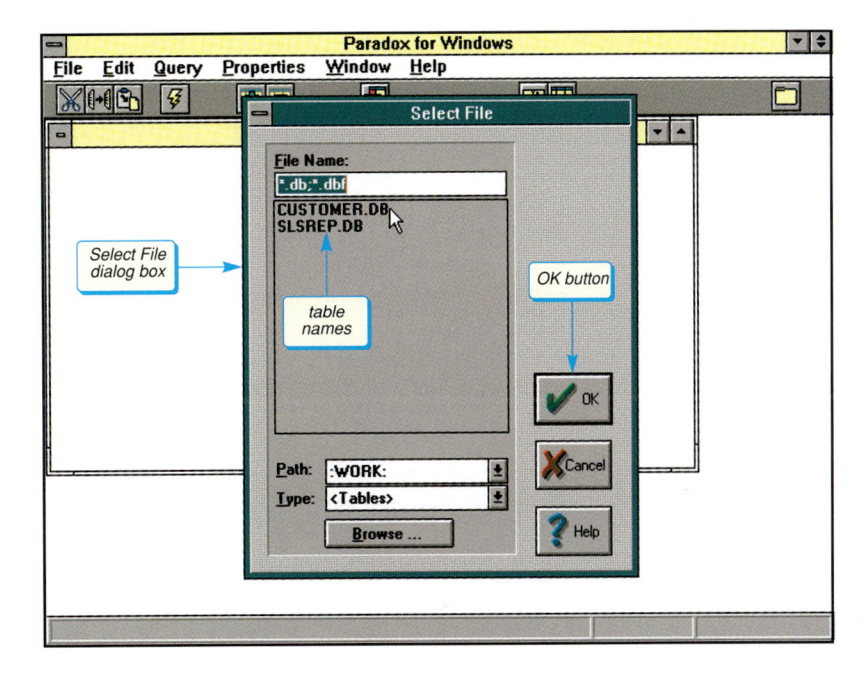

FIGURE 2-3

P62 PROJECT 2 QUERYING A DATABASE

STEP 3 ▶

Select CUSTOMER.DB and then choose the OK button. Point to the Maximize button in the Query window.

A Query window displays on the desktop (Figure 2-4). It contains a Query image of the Customer table. A **Query image** shows the field names in the table. Each field name has a corresponding check box that is used to indicate if a field should be in the Answer table. The mouse pointer is pointing to the Maximize button.

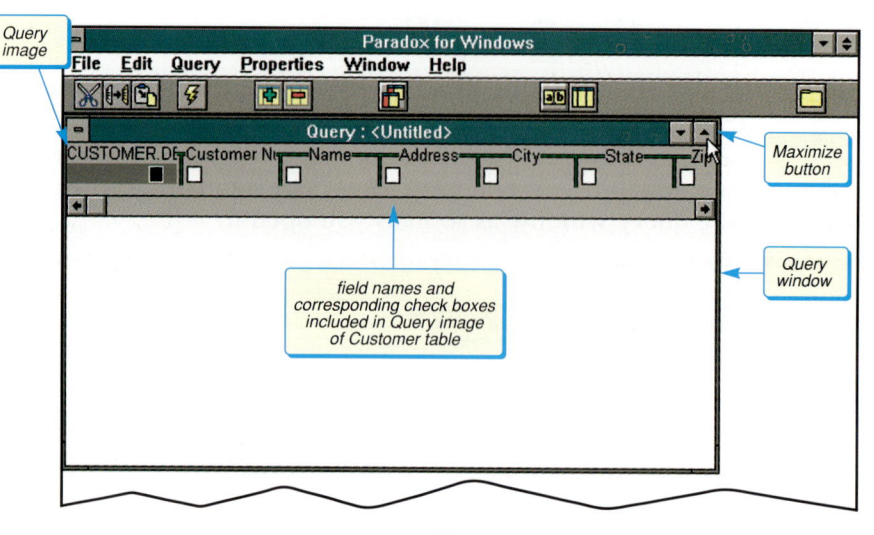

FIGURE 2-4

STEP 4 ▶

Click the Maximize button.

The Query window is maximized (Figure 2-5).

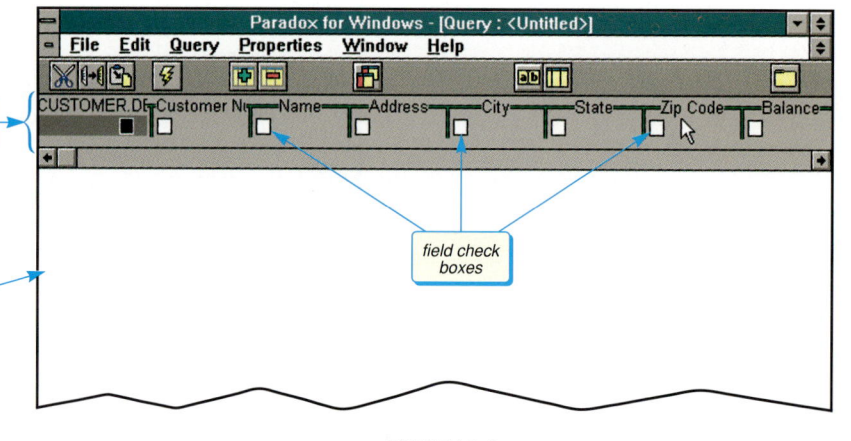

FIGURE 2-5

Once you have opened a new Query window, you are ready to create the actual query. Create the query by making entries in the Query image that displays in the window. Place check marks in the fields that you want to display in the Answer table. You can also enter **conditions** in the Query image, such as "the customer number must be CL67". When you enter conditions, only the record or records on which the condition is true will be included in the Answer table.

In the first query you will run, all the field values in the Customer table will be listed and no condition will be included. Hence, the fields in all the records will display in the Answer table (see Figure 2-10 on page P65).

▶ INCLUDING ALL FIELDS IN THE ANSWER TABLE

Under each field in a Query image is a small box (Figure 2-5), called a **field check box**. To indicate that a field is to be included in the answer to a query, you place a **check mark** in the **check box**. You place a check mark in a check box by pointing to the box and clicking the left mouse button.

INCLUDING ALL FIELDS IN THE ANSWER TABLE P63

If you point to a check box and then press and hold the left mouse button, you will see the **check menu** (Figure 2-7). This is a menu of the available types of check marks. Select a check mark type by dragging the highlight to it and releasing the mouse button. In this menu, the normal check mark, the one you will use most of the time, is the one that is initially highlighted. That is why you can simply click (press and immediately release) the left mouse button.

There is also a check box under the name of the table on the left side called the **table check box** (Figure 2-6). By clicking it, you place check marks in all fields. This is the quickest way to include all the fields in the answer to the query. The following steps create a query that results in all the fields in the Customer table displaying in the Answer table.

TO INCLUDE ALL FIELDS IN THE ANSWER TABLE ▼

STEP 1 ▶

Point to the table check box under CUSTOMER.DB (Figure 2-6).

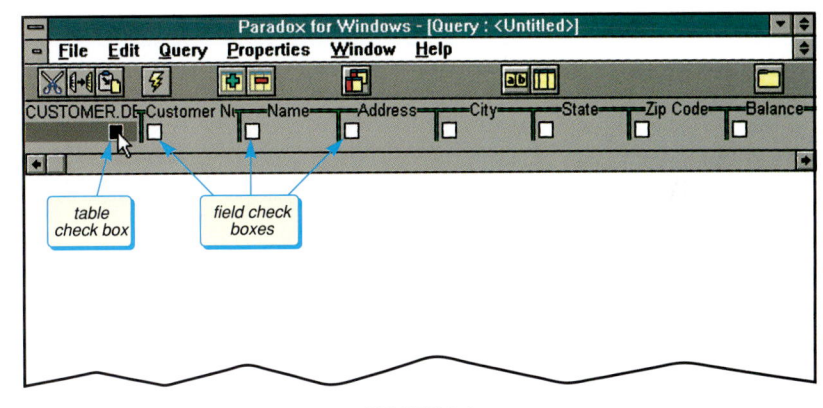

FIGURE 2-6

STEP 2 ▶

Press, but do not release, the left mouse button.

As long as you hold the mouse button down, the Check menu displays (Figure 2-7).

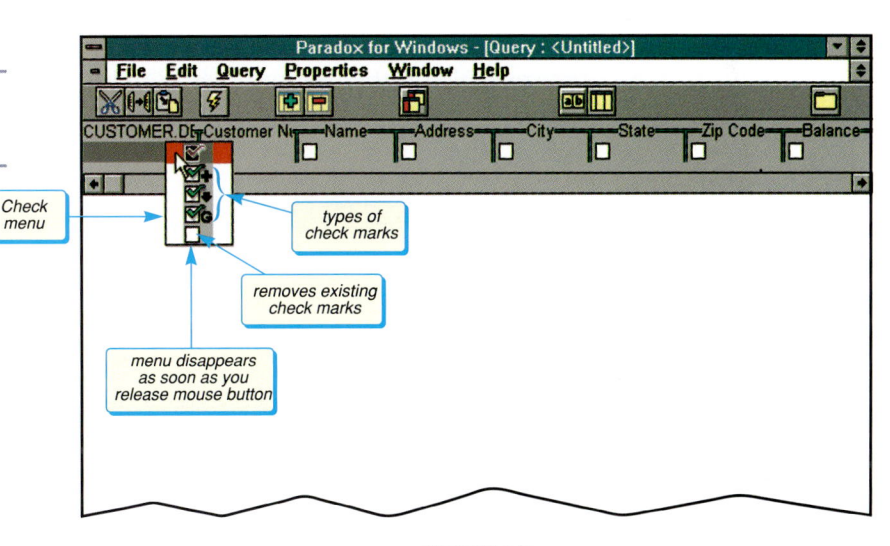

FIGURE 2-7

P64 PROJECT 2 QUERYING A DATABASE

STEP 3 ▶

Release the left mouse button.

All fields now have check marks (Figure 2-8). This indicates that all fields will be included in the answer.

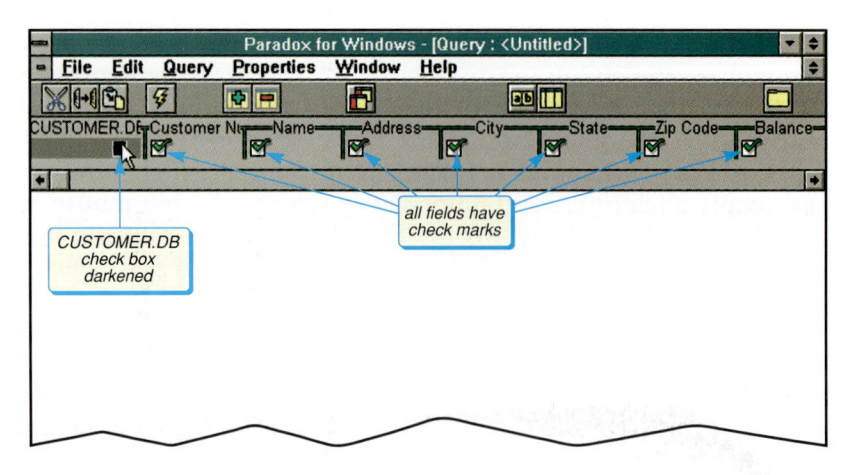

FIGURE 2-8

In some cases, you may find it more convenient to use the keyboard to place a check mark. To use the keyboard, you must first move the highlight to the field by repeatedly pressing the TAB key, which moves the highlight one field to the right, or the SHIFT + TAB keys, which moves it one field to the left. Once you have highlighted the correct field, press the F6 key.

▶ RUNNING A QUERY TO CREATE THE ANSWER TABLE

After you have created the query, you need to run it to display the Answer table. You run a query by clicking the **Run Query button** (𝟝) on the SpeedBar. Paradox then performs the necessary steps to obtain the answer, which it places in the answer table. It automatically displays the Answer table on the desktop. Recall that you will not enter a condition for this first query. Hence, all the customer records will display in the Answer table.

TO RUN A QUERY TO CREATE THE ANSWER TABLE ▼

STEP 1 ▶

Point to the Run Query button on the SpeedBar (Figure 2-9).

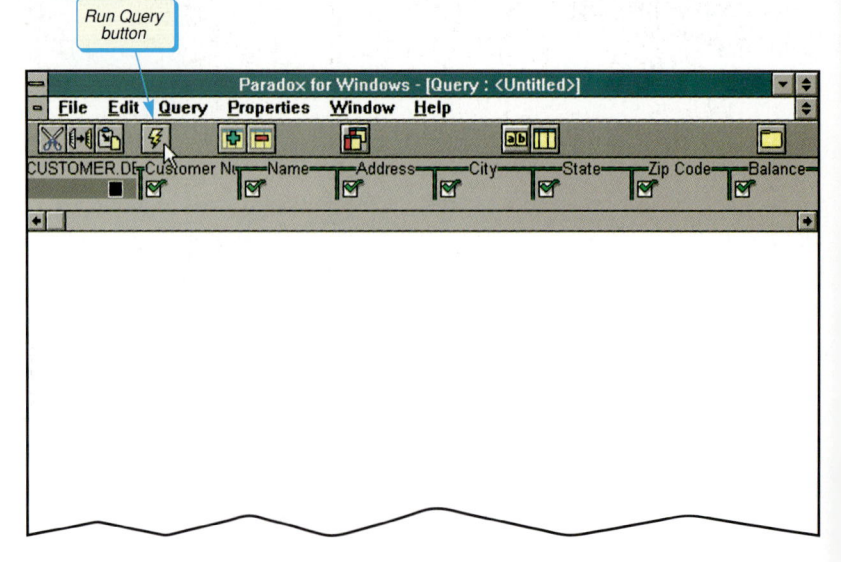

FIGURE 2-9

STEP 2 ▶

Click the left mouse button.

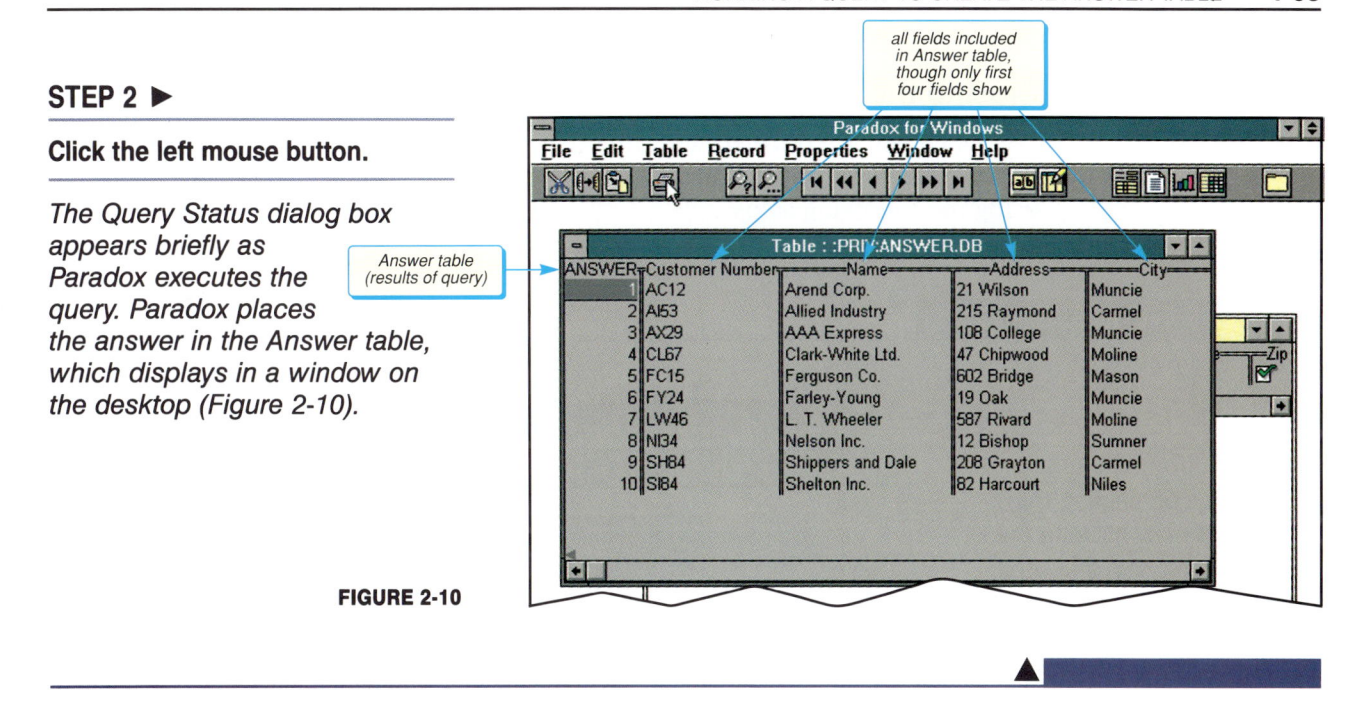

The Query Status dialog box appears briefly as Paradox executes the query. Paradox places the answer in the Answer table, which displays in a window on the desktop (Figure 2-10).

FIGURE 2-10

Examine the Answer table on the screen to see the answer to the query. You can scroll through the records, if necessary, just as you scroll through the records of any other table. You can also print a copy of the table.

Printing the Answer to a Query

The answer to a query is contained in the Answer table. Thus, to print the answer, use the same techniques you learned in Project 1 to print the data in the table. These steps are summarized below:

TO PRINT THE ANSWER TO A QUERY

Step 1: Click the Print button (🖨) (Figure 2-11).
Step 2: Choose the OK button in the Print File dialog box.

Paradox prints the Answer table.

If you need to switch to Landscape orientation, do so before clicking the Print button as indicated in Project 1 on page P28.

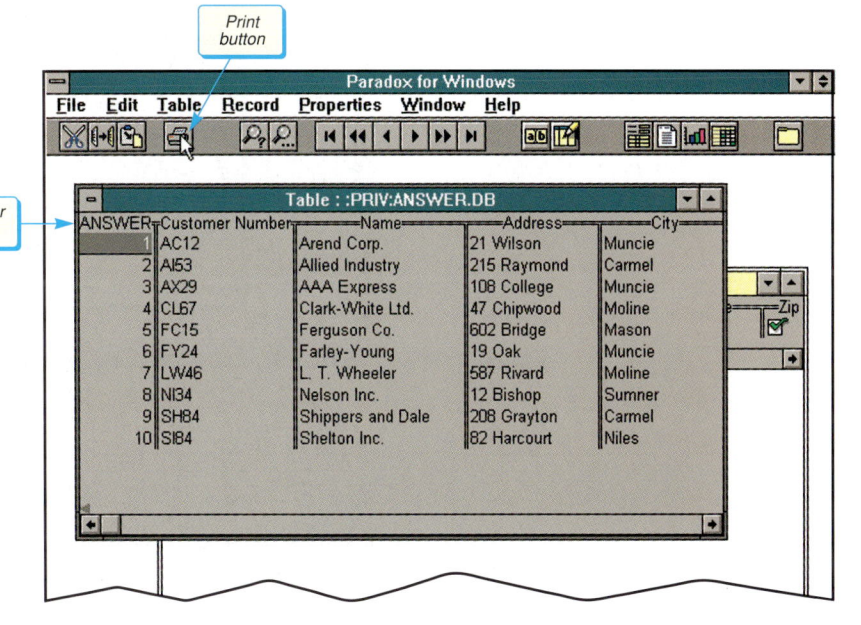

FIGURE 2-11

Closing the Answer Table

Once you are finished with the Answer table, you should remove it from the desktop. To remove the Answer table, close the window containing the table using the following steps.

TO CLOSE THE ANSWER TABLE

STEP 1 ▶

Select the Control menu for the window containing the Answer table by clicking the Control-menu box, and then pointing to the Close command (Figure 2-12).

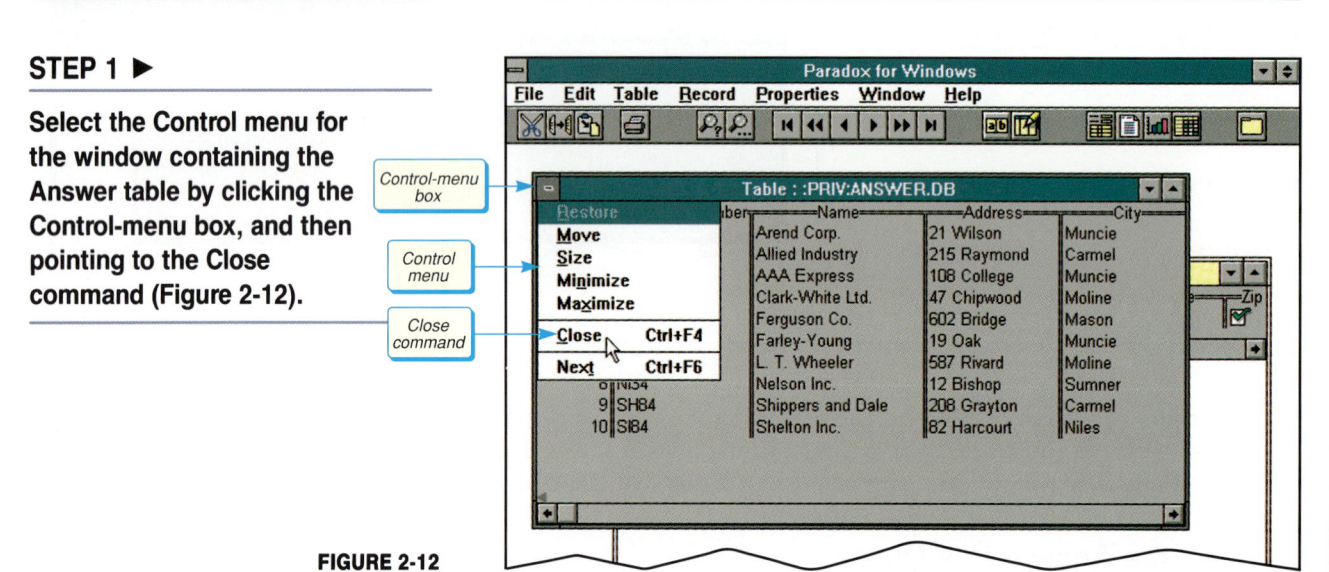

FIGURE 2-12

STEP 2 ▶

Choose the Close command by clicking the left mouse button.

The window containing the Answer table is removed from the desktop (Figure 2-13). The Query window remains on the desktop although it is no longer maximized.

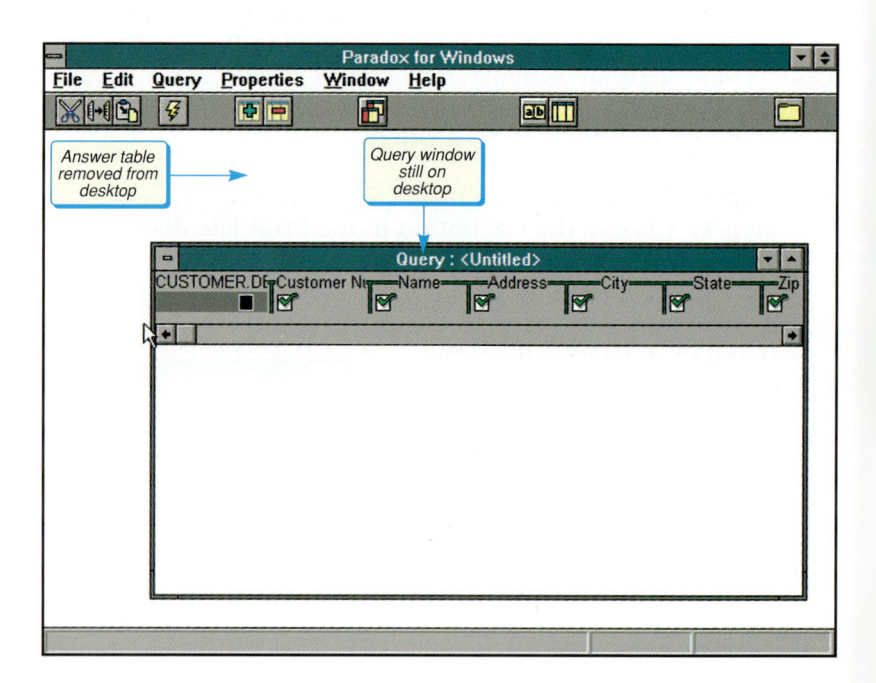

FIGURE 2-13

In the succeeding examples in this project, close the Answer table after you have finished with it.

RUNNING A QUERY TO CREATE THE ANSWER TABLE   **P67**

Closing a Query

To remove a Query window from the desktop, you close the Query window. When you close the Query window, a Paradox for Windows dialog box displays and asks if you want to save the query for future use. If you expect to make the same query often, you should save it. For now, you will not save any queries. How to save queries is shown later in the project. The following steps close a query without saving it.

TO CLOSE A QUERY ▼

STEP 1 ▶

Select the Control-menu box in the title bar of the Query window and point to the Close command (Figure 2-14).

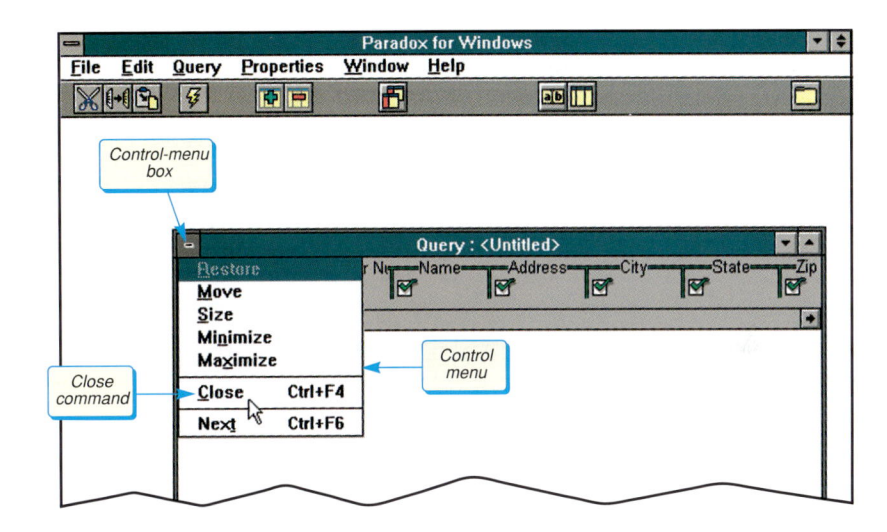

FIGURE 2-14

STEP 2 ▶

Choose the Close command and point to the No button ( ) in the Paradox for Windows dialog box.

The Paradox for Windows dialog box displays (Figure 2-15). The mouse pointer points to the No button.

STEP 3 ▶

Choose the No button.

The Query window is removed from the desktop.

FIGURE 2-15

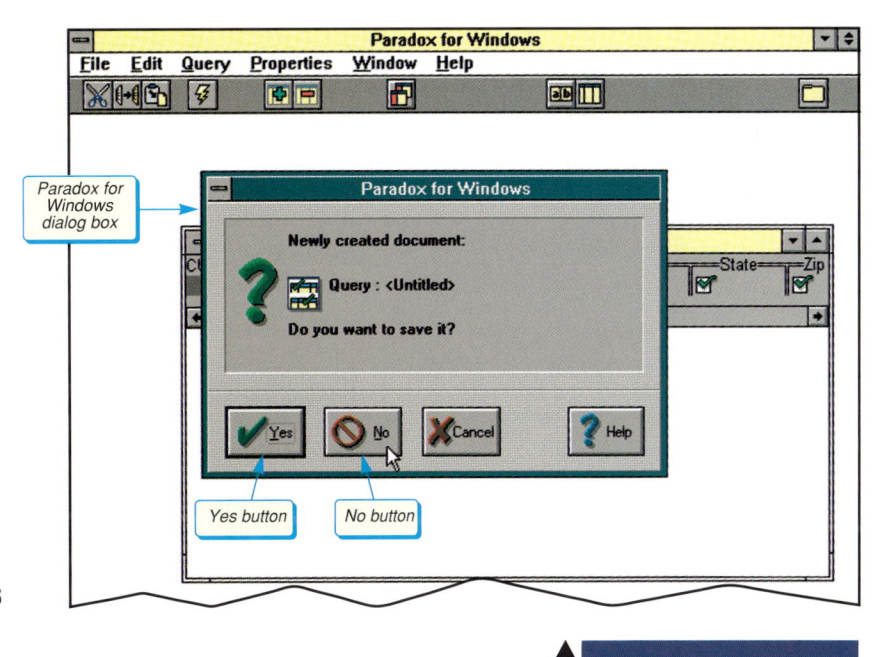

Another way to close a Query window is by double-clicking its Control-menu box in the title bar of the Query window (Figure 2-14).

Clearing a Query Image

If you make mistakes as you are creating a query, you can fix them individually. Alternatively, you might want to clear all the check marks and conditions in the Query image and start over. One way to clear the entries is to close the Query window and then start a new query just as you did earlier. A simpler approach, however, is to press the CTRL+DELETE keys. Pressing the CTRL+DELETE keys clears all entries from the Query image.

▶ DISPLAYING SELECTED FIELDS IN THE ANSWER TABLE

Only the fields that contain check marks in the Query window will be included in the Answer table. Thus, to display only certain fields, place check marks in those fields and no others. If you accidentally place a check mark in the wrong field, click the check box a second time to remove the check mark. Alternatively, you can press the CTRL+DELETE keys to clear the entire Query image and then start over.

The following steps create a query to show the customer number, name, and sales rep number for all customers by including check marks in only those fields.

TO INCLUDE SELECTED FIELDS IN THE ANSWER TABLE ▼

STEP 1 ▶

Select the File menu, choose the New command, choose the Query command, select the Customer table, choose the OK button, and then maximize the window. Point to the check box in the Customer Number field (Figure 2-16).

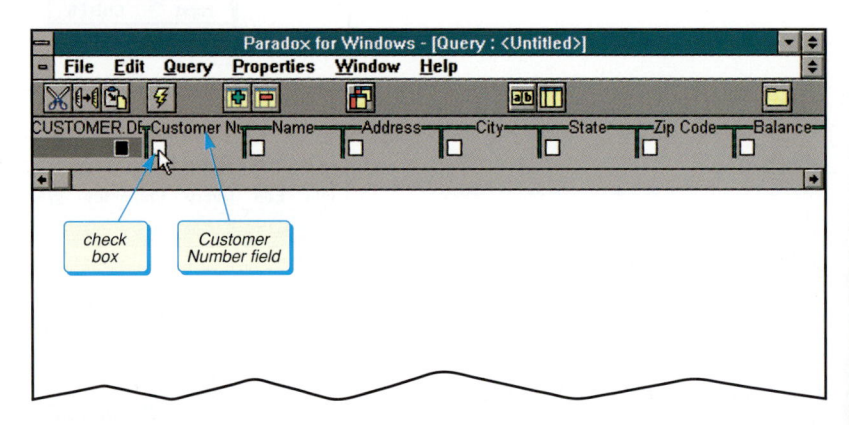

FIGURE 2-16

STEP 2 ▶

Press and hold down the left mouse button.

The Check menu displays (Figure 2-17). Because you want the basic check mark, do not move the highlight.

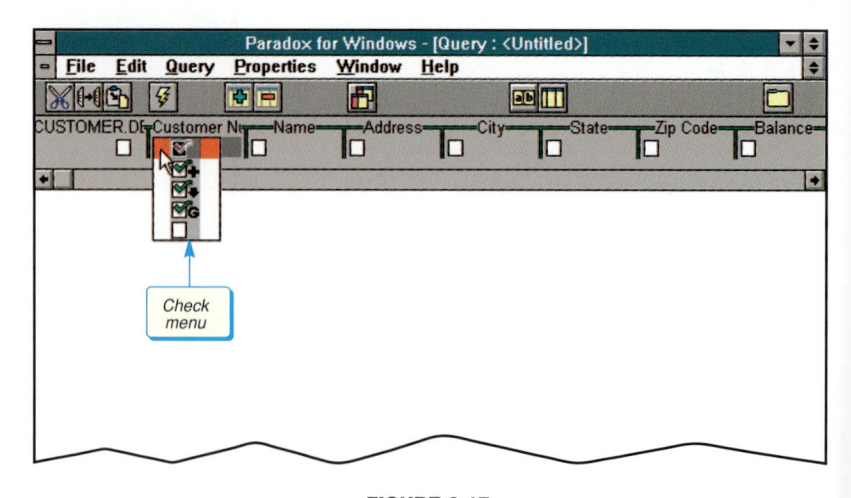

FIGURE 2-17

DISPLAYING SELECTED FIELDS IN THE ANSWER TABLE   **P69**

STEP 3 ▶

Release the mouse button, then point to the check box for the Name field and click the left mouse button. Point to the right scroll arrow at the right-hand edge of the scroll bar in the Query image.

The Customer Number and Name fields both have check marks (Figure 2-18). The mouse pointer points to the right scroll arrow.

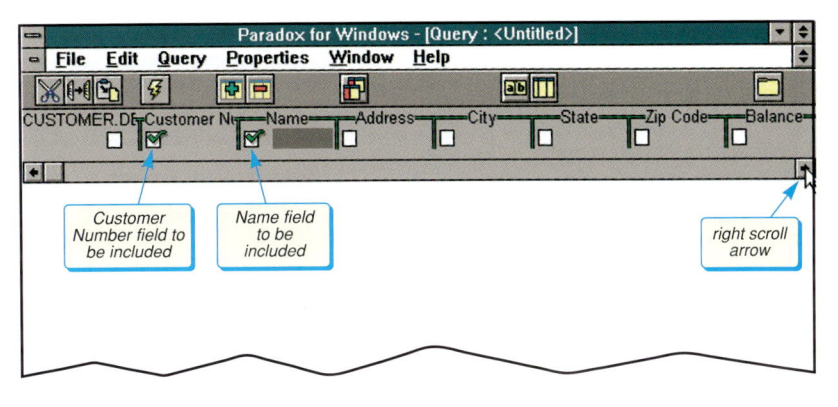

FIGURE 2-18

STEP 4 ▶

Click the right scroll arrow two times.

The fields in the Query image shift to the left (Figure 2-19).

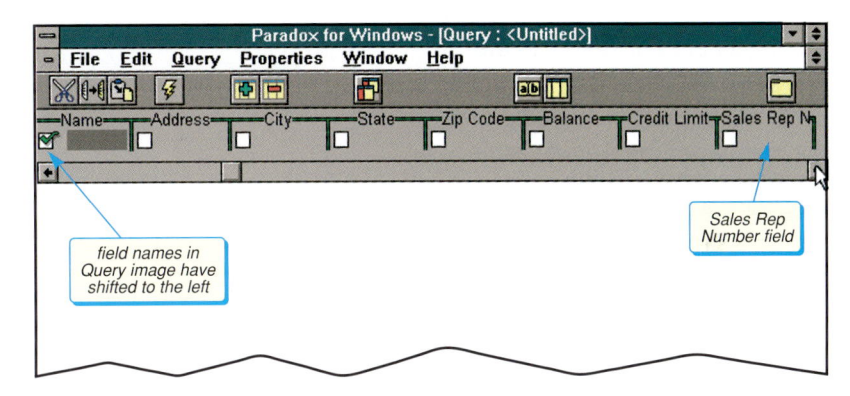

FIGURE 2-19

STEP 5 ▶

Point to the check box for the Sales Rep Number field and click the left mouse button. Point to the Run Query button on the SpeedBar (Figure 2-20).

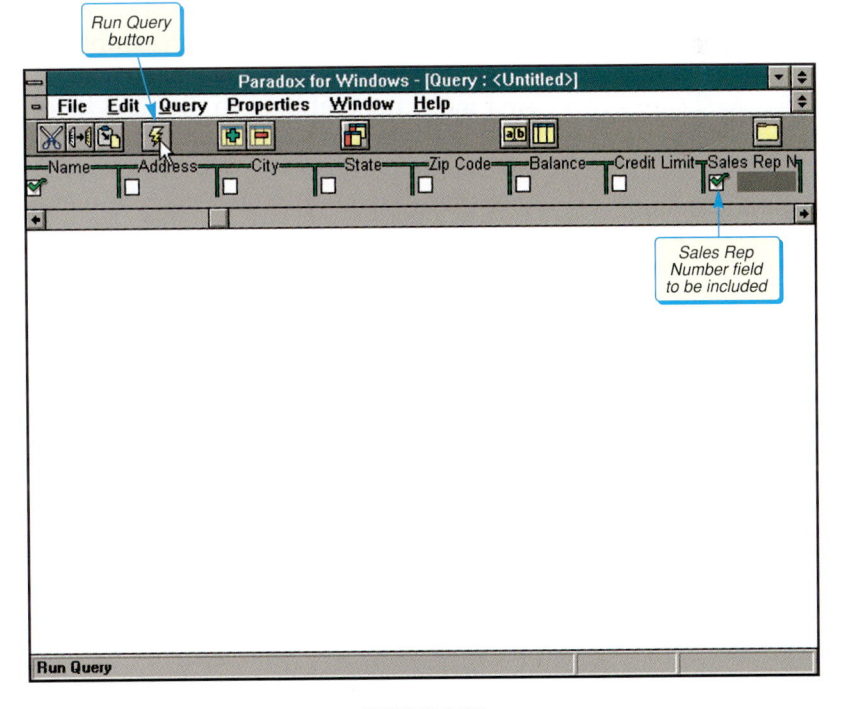

FIGURE 2-20

STEP 6 ▶

Click the Run Query button.

Paradox runs the query, producing the Answer table. The Answer table displays in a window on the desktop (Figure 2-21). Only the Customer Number, Name, and Sales Rep Number fields are included in the Answer table.

STEP 7 ▶

When you are finished with the Answer table close it by double-clicking the Control-menu box in the title bar of the Answer table window.

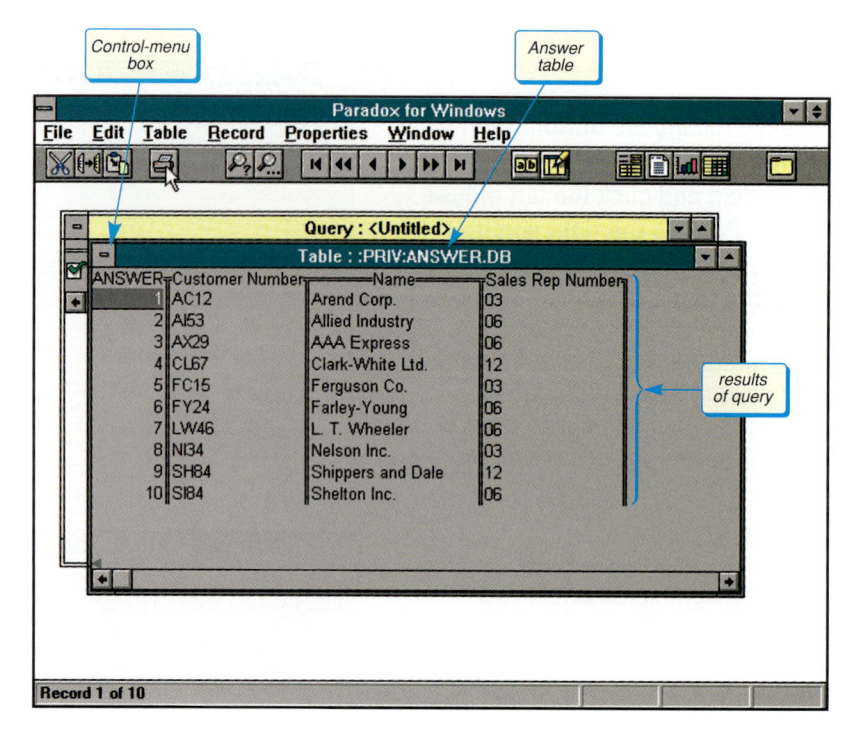

FIGURE 2-21

▶ ENTERING CONDITIONS

When you use queries, you usually are looking for those records that satisfy some condition. You might want the name of the customer whose number is CL67, for example, or the numbers, names, and addresses of those customers whose names start with the letters Sh. To enter a condition, first move the highlight to the field involved in the condition by pointing to the field with the mouse and clicking the left mouse button. It might be simpler to repeatedly press the TAB key, which moves the highlight one field to the right, or the SHIFT + TAB keys, which move it one field to the left.

Once you have moved the highlight to the correct field, type the appropriate condition. If you type a condition incorrectly, you can correct it by repeatedly pressing the BACKSPACE or DELETE keys to remove the incorrect entry and then typing the correct condition. You can also press the CTRL + DELETE keys to clear the entire Query image, and then start over.

The examples that follow illustrate the types of conditions that are available in Paradox for Windows.

Using Character Data in Conditions

When you are working with character data, you need to know two things about the conditions you enter in character fields (fields in the structure whose type is A) in a Query image. First, if there is any punctuation (like a comma) in the value, the value must be enclosed in quotation marks. Thus, if you were looking for a record in which the name is Nelson Inc., you could simply type `Nelson Inc`.

because there is no special punctuation. If, on the other hand, the name you are looking for is Nelson, Inc., you would need to type

`"Nelson, Inc."`

since the name contains a comma.

Second, you need to know that, with a few exceptions, conditions involving character fields are *case-sensitive*. This means that you must use the right combination of uppercase and lowercase letters. If, for example, the name is stored in the database as Nelson Inc. and you search for NELSON INC., you will not find the record.

In the following query, you are to find the customer whose number is CL67. Because there is no punctuation, you don't need quotation marks. It is important, however, for you to enter both an uppercase C and an uppercase L, because that is the way this entry appears in the database. The Answer table will display the selected fields, Customer Number, Name, and Balance, for customer CL67 (see Figure 2-24 on the next page).

TO USE CHARACTER DATA IN A CONDITION

STEP 1 ▶

Be sure you have a clear, maximized Query image for the Customer table on the desktop. (If you still have the Query image for the Customer table on the screen, press the CTRL+DELETE keys. If not, select the File menu, choose the New command, choose the Query command, select the Customer table, and then maximize the window.)

STEP 2 ▶

Press TAB to move the highlight to the Customer Number field, and then type CL67.

Customer number CL67 displays under Customer Number in the Query image (Figure 2-22).

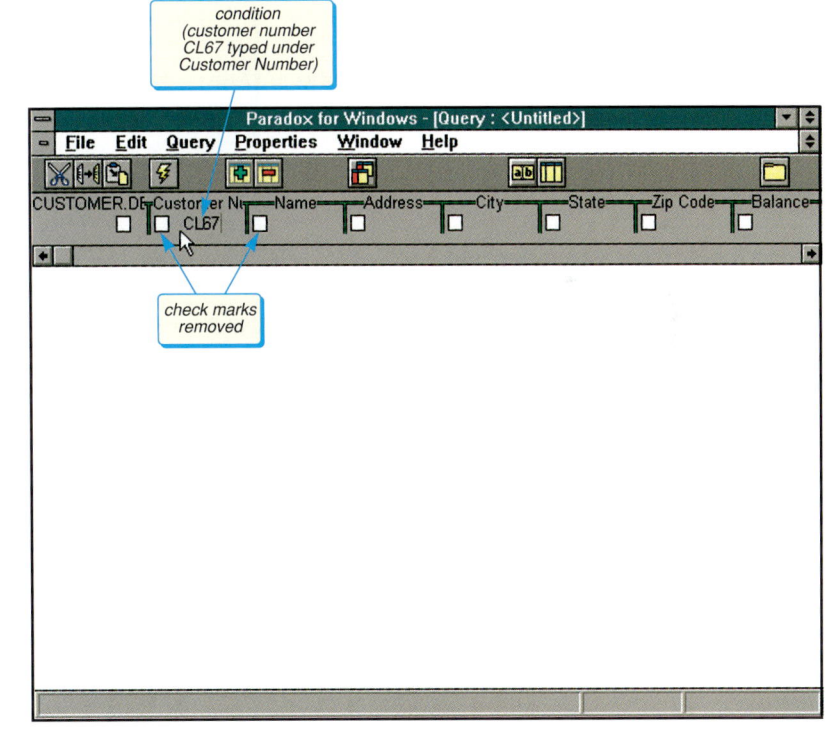

FIGURE 2-22

PROJECT 2 QUERYING A DATABASE

STEP 3 ▶

Place check marks in the Customer Number, Name, and Balance fields.

Check marks display in the field check boxes below the three field names (Figure 2-23).

FIGURE 2-23

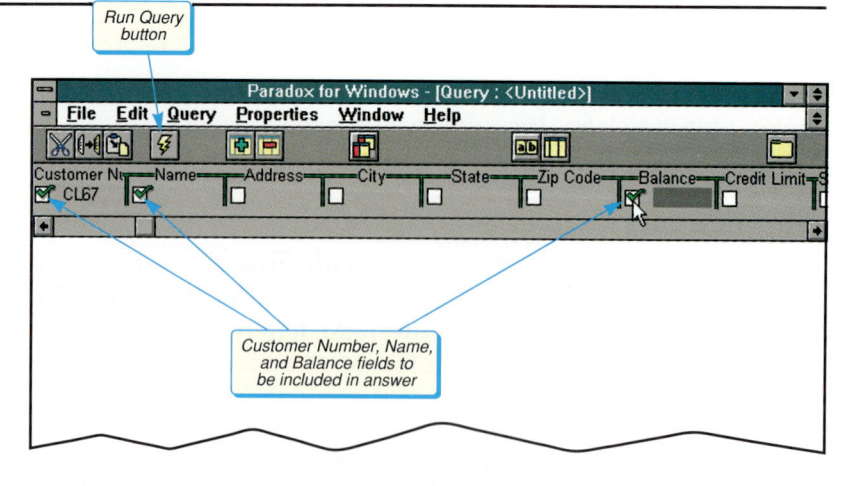

STEP 4 ▶

Run the query by clicking the Run Query button on the SpeedBar.

The number, name, and balance of customer CL67 display in the Answer table (Figure 2-24). The remaining records in the Customer table do not display in the Answer table because they do not have a customer number of CL67.

STEP 5 ▶

Close the Answer table after you are finished with it.

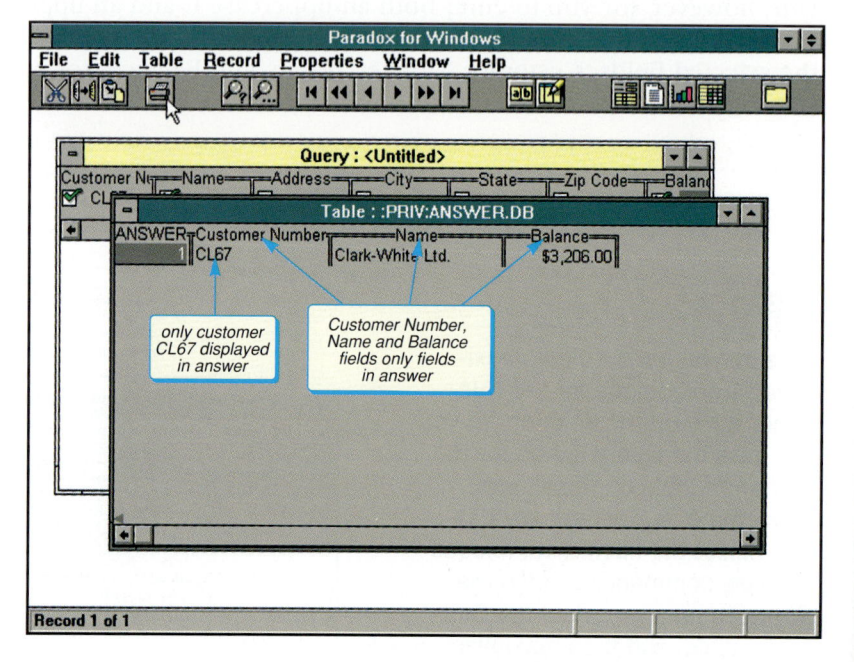

FIGURE 2-24

Using Special Character Conditions

Paradox has two special types of conditions available for character fields. The first involves the use of **wildcards**. Wildcards are useful when you know the value for which you are searching contains a certain pattern of characters. There are two special wildcard symbols.

The first of the two wildcards is the double period, which represents any collection of characters. Thus Sh.. represents an uppercase S followed by a lowercase h followed by any collection of characters. The other wildcard symbol is the @ sign, which represents any individual character. Thus T@m represents the letter T followed by any single character followed by the letter m.

The next query illustrates using a wildcard to display the number, name, and address of those customers whose names begin with Sh (see Figure 2-26). In this example, because you don't know how many characters will follow the Sh, the double period is appropriate.

TO USE A WILDCARD

STEP 1 ▶

Be sure you have a clear (CTRL + DELETE), maximized Query image for the Customer table on the desktop.

STEP 2 ▶

Place the highlight in the Name field and type Sh followed by two periods (Sh..). Place check marks in the Customer Number, Name, and Address fields. Point to the Run Query button on the SpeedBar.

The Name field contains Sh.., *and check marks display in the Customer Number, Name, and Address fields. The mouse pointer points to the Run Query button (Figure 2-25).*

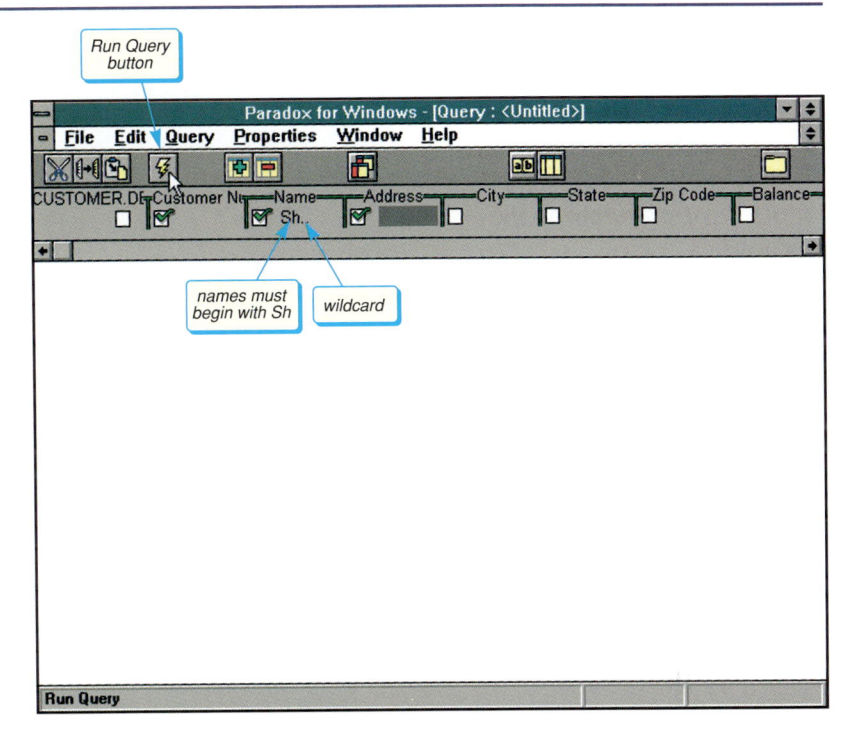

FIGURE 2-25

STEP 3 ▶

Run the query by clicking the Run Query button.

The Answer table contains the two customers whose names begin with Sh (Figure 2-26)

STEP 4 ▶

When you are finished with the Answer table, close it.

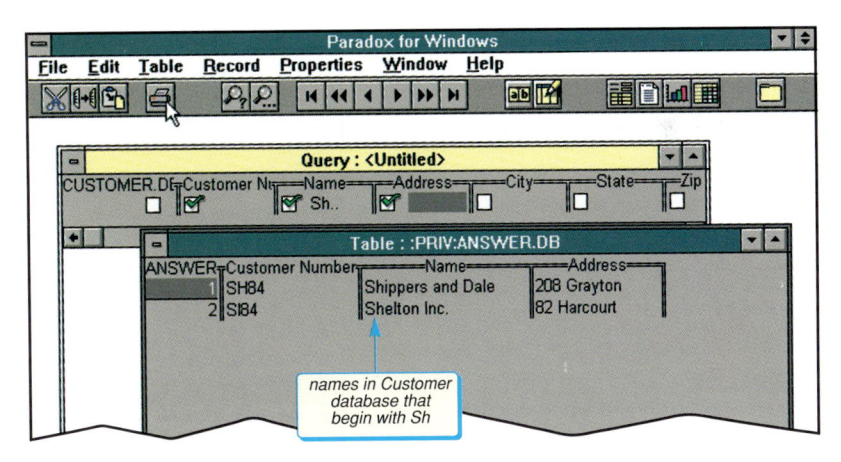

FIGURE 2-26

Querying by Sound Using the LIKE Operator

Sometimes you might not know the exact spelling of the name for which you are searching. You might only know what the name sounds like. In this case you can use the second special character condition. Paradox includes the special operator, LIKE, which indicates that the value must be like, that is, sounds like, a particular pattern rather than have to match it exactly. The following steps illustrate its use by displaying in the Answer table the number, name and address of any customer whose name is like Sheldon Inc. (see Figure 2-30 on page P75).

P74 PROJECT 2 QUERYING A DATABASE

TO USE LIKE

STEP 1 ▶

Be sure you have a clear (CTRL+DELETE), maximized Query image for the Customer table on the desktop.

STEP 2 ▶

Place check marks in the Customer Number and Name fields.

Check marks display in the field check mark boxes below the Customer Number and Name in the Query image (Figure 2-27).

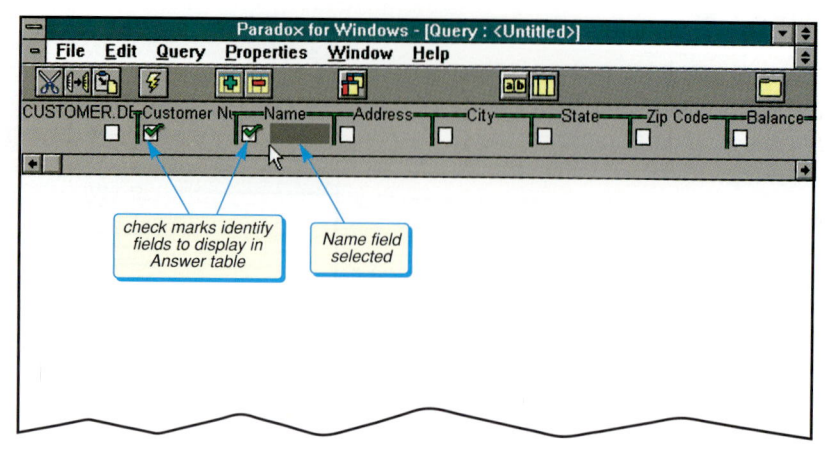

FIGURE 2-27

STEP 3 ▶

Type `LIKE Sheldon Inc.` in the Name field.

The width of the Name field expands to accommodate the entry (Figure 2-28).

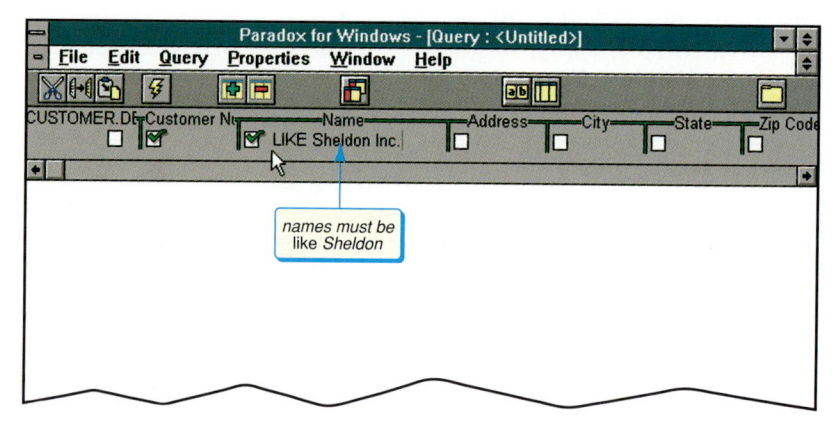

FIGURE 2-28

STEP 4 ▶

Place a check mark in the Address field (Figure 2-29), and point to the Run Query button on the SpeedBar.

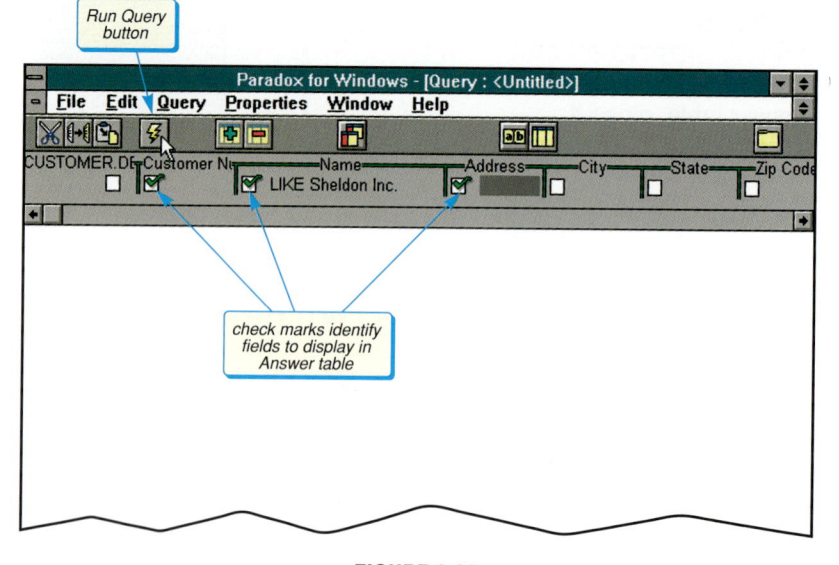

FIGURE 2-29

STEP 5 ▶

Run the query by clicking the Run Query button.

The Answer table contains customer Shelton Inc, whose name is like Sheldon Inc. (Figure 2-30).

STEP 6 ▶

When you are finished with the Answer table, close it.

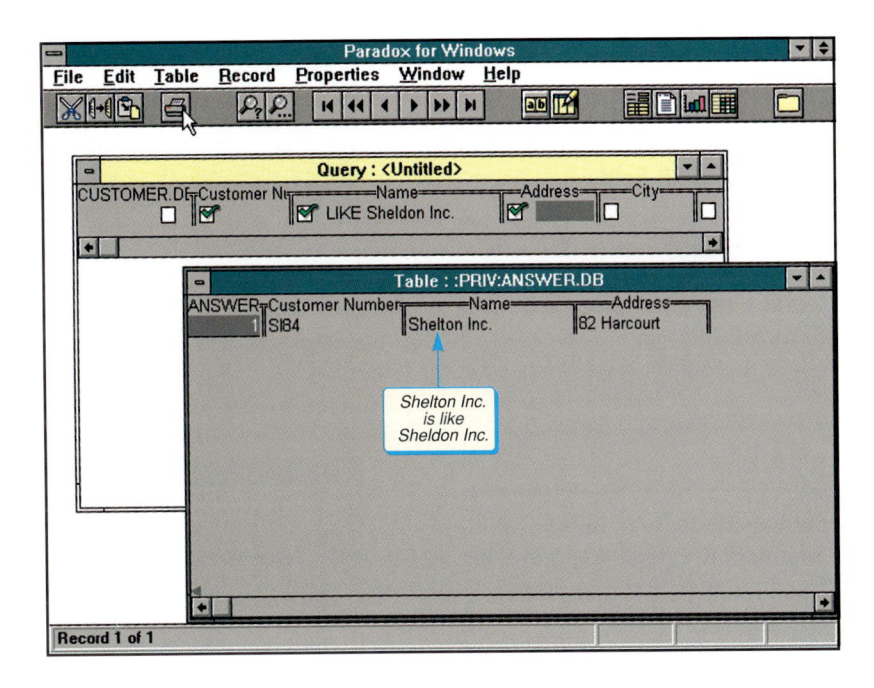

FIGURE 2-30

Using Numeric Data in Conditions

To use a number in a condition, you type the number without any dollar signs, commas, or quotation marks. In the next example, you will display in the Answer table the number, name, balance, and credit limit of all customers whose credit limit is 6,000 (see Figure 2-34 on the next page).

TO USE NUMERIC DATA IN A CONDITION ▼

STEP 1 ▶

Be sure you have a clear (CTRL + DELETE), maximized Query image for the Customer table on the desktop.

STEP 2 ▶

Place check marks in the Customer Number and Name fields. Point to the Balance field check box (Figure 2-31).

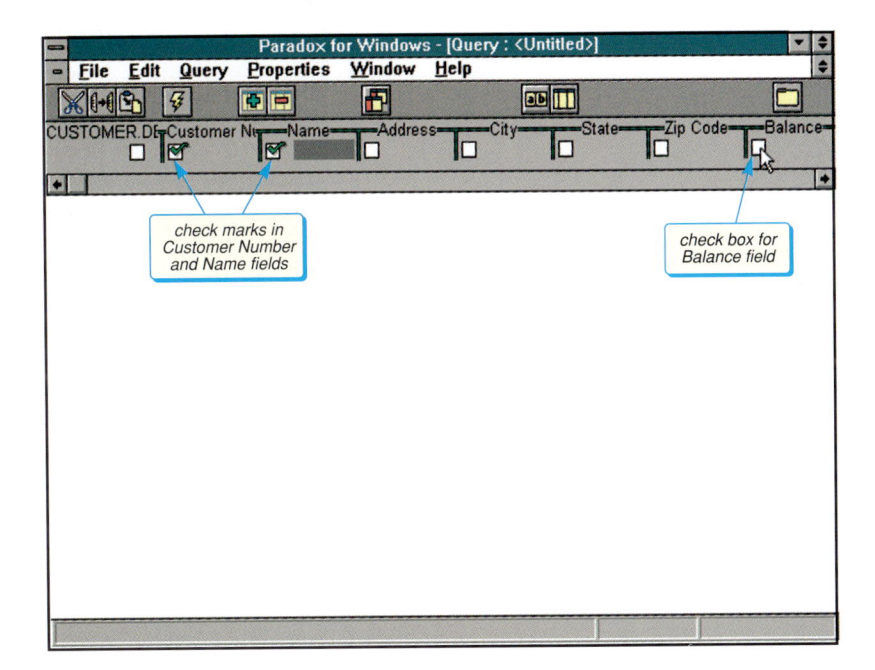

FIGURE 2-31

STEP 3 ▶

Place a check mark in the Balance field and point to the check box in the Credit Limit field.

The fields shift to the left. The mouse pointer is pointing to the Credit Limit field check box (Figure 2-32).

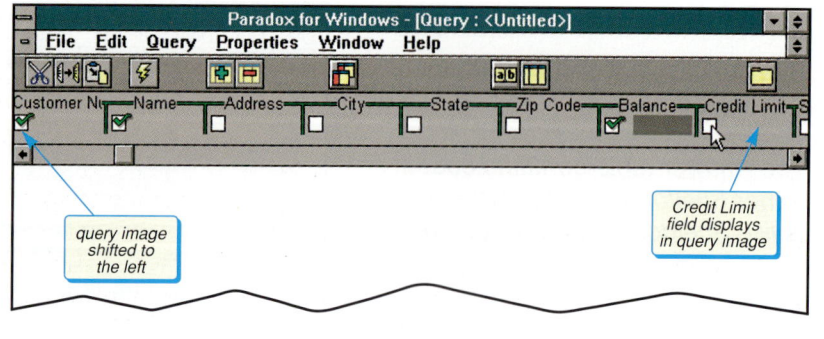

FIGURE 2-32

STEP 4 ▶

Place a check mark in the Credit Limit field and type 6000 in the Credit Limit field (Figure 2-33).

Paradox does not allow you to enter special characters such as the dollar sign ($) or comma (,) in the comparison value. However, you may use a decimal point (.).

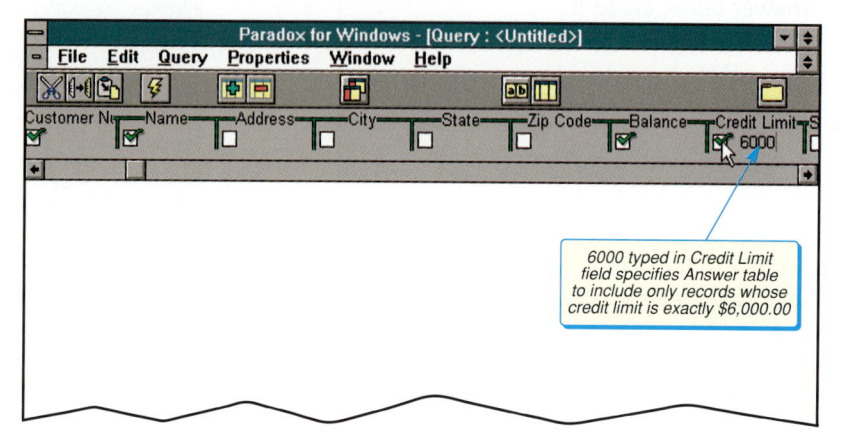

FIGURE 2-33

STEP 5 ▶

Click the Run Query button on the SpeedBar.

The answer contains only those customers whose credit limit is $6,000 (Figure 2-34).

STEP 6 ▶

When you are finished with the Answer table, close it.

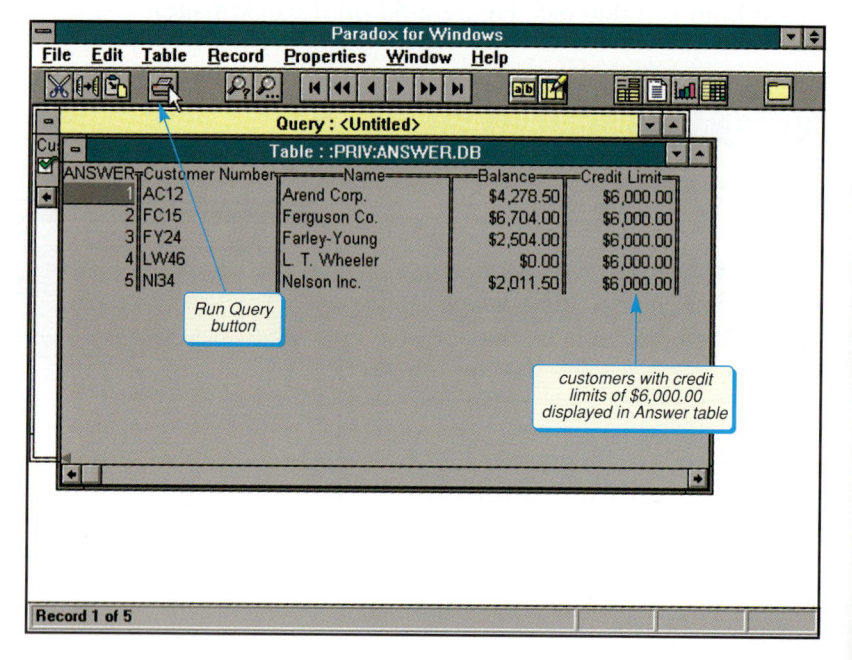

FIGURE 2-34

ENTERING CONDITIONS **P77**

Using Comparison Operators

Unless you specify otherwise, Paradox assumes the conditions you enter involve equality. In the last query, for example, you requested those customers whose credit limit was *equal to* 6000. If you want something other than equality, you must enter the appropriate **comparison operator**. The comparison operators are > (greater than, <(less than), > = (greater than or equal to), < = (less than or equal to, and NOT (not equal to).

The following steps use the > operator to display in the Answer table the number, name, balance, and credit limit for all customers whose balance is greater than $5,000 (see Figure 2-36).

TO USE A COMPARISON OPERATOR IN A CONDITION ▼

STEP 1 ▶

Be sure you have a clear (CTRL + DELETE), maximized Query image for the Customer table on the desktop.

STEP 2 ▶

Place check marks in the Customer Number, Name, and Balance fields. Type >5000 in the Balance field. Place a check mark in the Credit Limit field and point to the Run Query button on the SpeedBar (Figure 2-35).

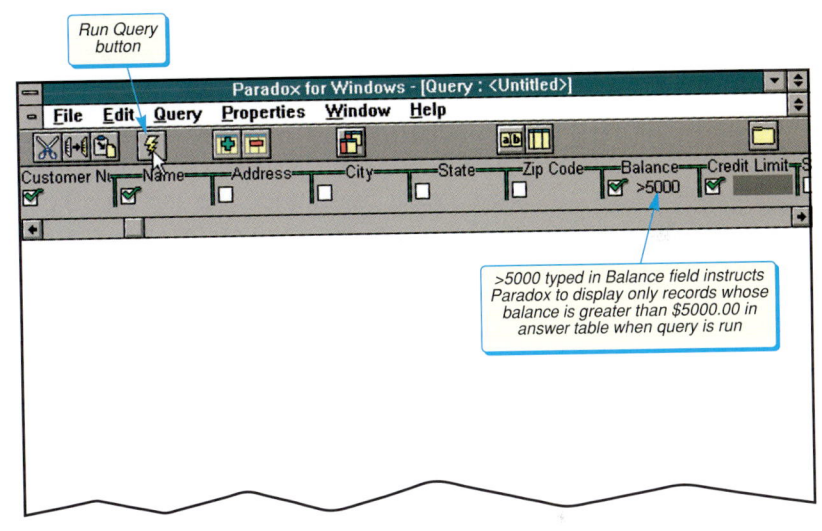

FIGURE 2-35

STEP 3 ▶

Click the Run Query button.

The Answer table contains only those customers whose balance is greater than $5,000 (Figure 2-36).

STEP 4 ▶

When you are finished with the Answer table, close it.

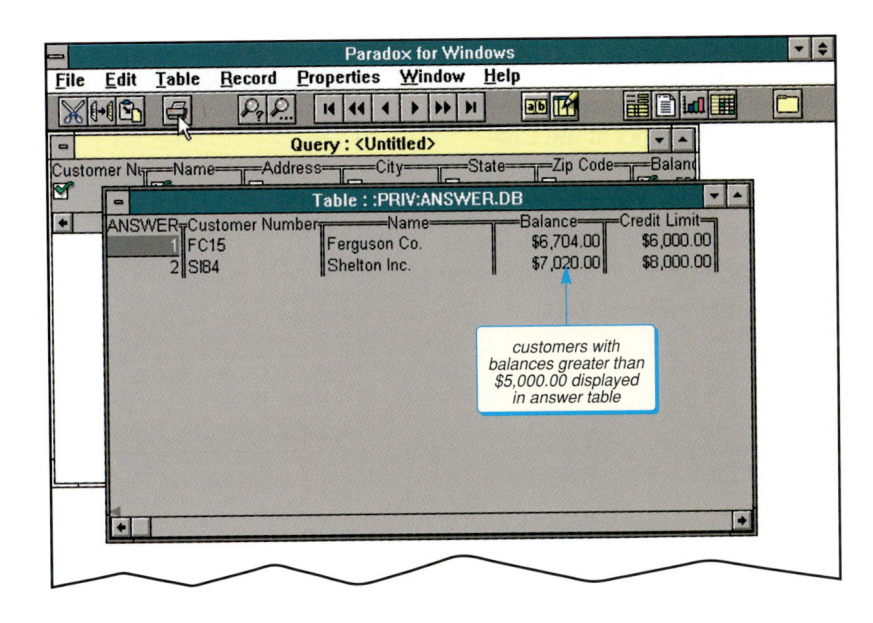

FIGURE 2-36

▶ Using Compound Conditions

Often you will have more than one condition that data for which you are searching must satisfy. This type of condition is called a **compound condition**. There are two types of compound conditions.

In **AND conditions** both individual conditions must be true for the compound condition to be true. For example, an AND condition would allow you to select those customers who have an $8,000 credit limit *AND* are represented by sales rep 12.

OR conditions, on the other hand, are true provided either individual condition is true or both conditions are true. An OR condition would allow you to select those customers who have an $8,000 credit limit *OR* are represented by sales rep 12. In this case, any customer whose credit limit is $8,000 would be included in the answer whether or not the customer was represented by sales rep 12. Similarly, any customer represented by sales rep 12 would be included whether or not the customer had an $8,000 credit limit.

AND Condition

To combine conditions with AND, place the conditions on the same line. The following steps use an AND condition to display the number, name, balance, credit limit, and sales rep for all customers whose credit limit is $8,000 AND who are represented by sales rep 12 (see Figure 2-37).

TO USE A COMPOUND CONDITION INVOLVING AND ▼

STEP 1 ▶

Be sure you have a clear (CTRL + DELETE), maximized Query image for the Customer table on the desktop.

STEP 2 ▶

Place check marks in the Customer Number, Name, Balance, Credit Limit, and Sales Rep Number fields. Type 8000 in the Credit Limit field and 12 in the Sales Rep Number field (Figure 2-37).

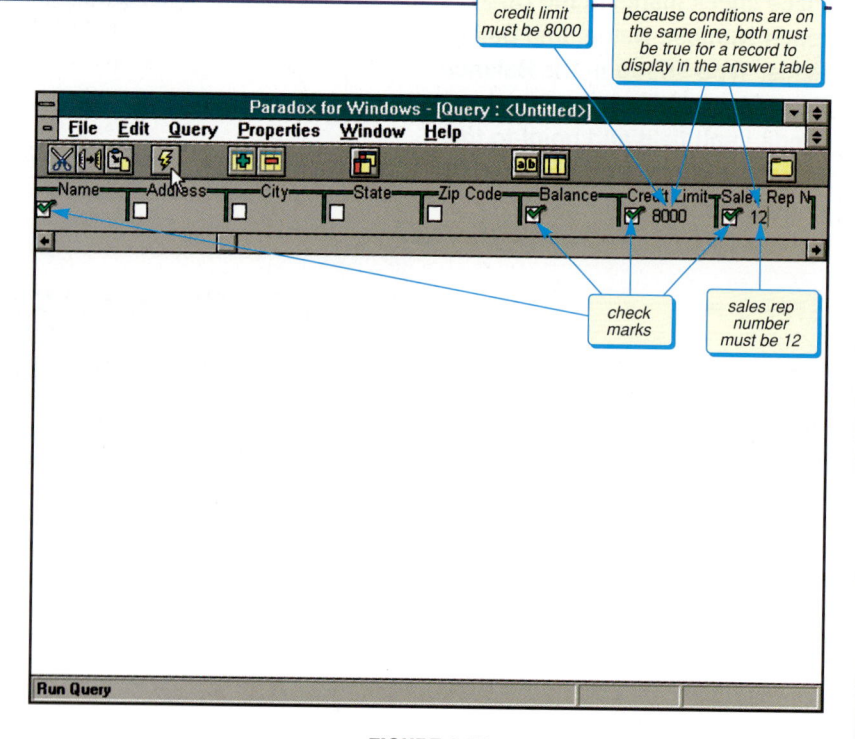

FIGURE 2-37

USING COMPOUND CONDITIONS P79

STEP 3 ▶

Click the Run Query button on the SpeedBar.

The answer contains only those customers who have an $8,000 credit limit and who are represented by sales rep 12 (Figure 2-38).

STEP 4 ▶

When you are finished with the Answer table, close it.

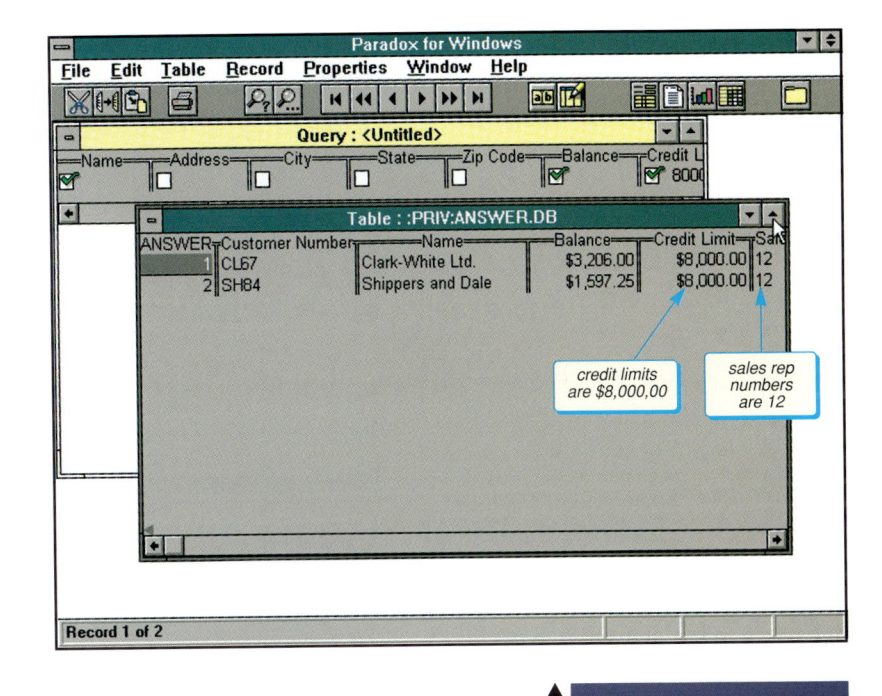

FIGURE 2-38

OR Condition

To combine conditions with OR, the conditions must go on separate lines in the Query image. To add a second line to the Query image, press the DOWN ARROW key. (If you accidentally add an extra line, you can remove it by pressing the CTRL + DELETE keys.) In addition to placing the conditions on separate lines, you must also be sure to place the same set of check marks on both lines.

The next steps use an OR condition to display the name, balance, credit limit, and sales rep for those customers who have an $8,000 credit limit OR who are represented by sales rep 06 (see Figure 2-42 on the next page).

TO USE A COMPOUND CONDITION INVOLVING OR ▼

STEP 1 ▶

Be sure you have a clear (CTRL + DELETE), maximized Query image for the Customer table on the desktop.

STEP 2 ▶

Place check marks in the Customer Number, Name, Balance, Credit Limit, and Sales Rep Number fields. Type 8000 in the Credit Limit field. Place a check mark in the Sales Rep Number field (Figure 2-39).

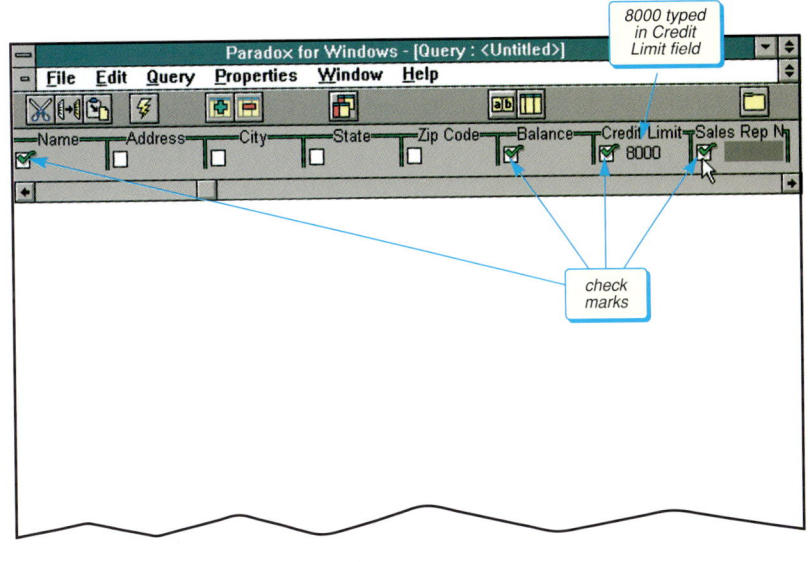

FIGURE 2-39

STEP 3 ▶

Press the DOWN ARROW key.

A second line displays in the Query image (Figure 2-40).

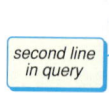

FIGURE 2-40

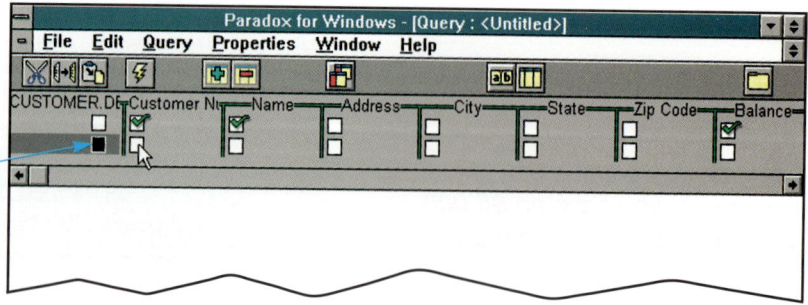

STEP 4 ▶

Place check marks in the Customer Number, Name, Balance, Credit Limit, and Sales Rep Number fields in the second line of the Query image. Type 06 in the Sales Rep Number field (Figure 2-41).

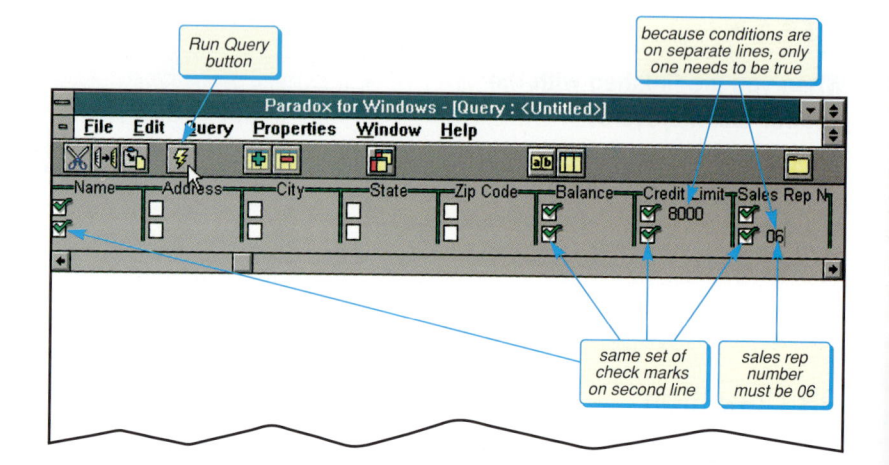

FIGURE 2-41

STEP 5 ▶

Click the Run Query button on the SpeedBar.

The answer contains those customers who have an $8,000 credit limit or who are represented by sales rep 06 (Figure 2-42).

STEP 6 ▶

When you are finished with the Answer table, close it.

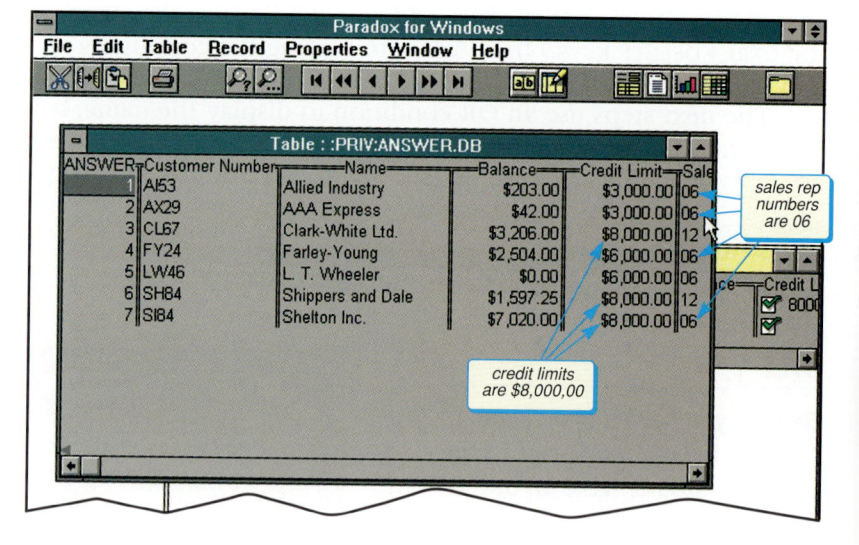

FIGURE 2-42

▶ SORTING DATA IN A QUERY

In some queries, the order in which the records in the answer are displayed really doesn't matter. All you are concerned about are the records that display in the Answer table. It doesn't matter which one is first or which one is last.

In other queries, however, the order can be very important. You might want to see customers' balances and want them arranged from the highest to the lowest. Perhaps you want to see customers' addresses and want them listed by state. Furthermore, for all the customers in a given state, you want them to be listed by city.

To order the records in the answer to a query in a particular way, you **sort** the records. The field on which the records are sorted is called the **sort key**. If you are sorting on more than one field (such as sorting by city within state), the more important field (state) is called the **major key** and the less important field (city) is called the **minor key**.

Some sorting happens automatically. Paradox considers the first field from the left with a check mark in the Query image the sort key. If there are two records with equal values in this first field, Paradox uses the second field with a check mark (assuming there is one) to further order these records. In other words, the first field would be the major key and the second would be the minor key. Another action Paradox takes automatically is to eliminate duplicates; that is, the Answer table will not contain two records that are identical.

There are two other check-mark options in the Check menu (Figure 2-7 on page P63) that you can use in connection with sorting. If you want to allow duplicates, use *check plus* on the Check menu. If you want to sort in descending order (highest to lowest) rather than ascending sequence (lowest to highest) use *check-descending* on the Check menu.

The following example uses a check mark to display in the Answer table the states where customers are located. The states are to be sorted and each state is to be listed only once (see Figure 2-44 on the next page). This is the way the standard check mark in the Check menu functions.

TO SORT DATA ▼

STEP 1 ▶

Be sure you have a clear (CTRL + DELETE), maximized Query image for the Customer table on the desktop.

STEP 2 ▶

Place a check mark in the State field and point to the Run Query button on the SpeedBar.

The State field contains a check mark (Figure 2-43). The mouse pointer points to the Run Query button.

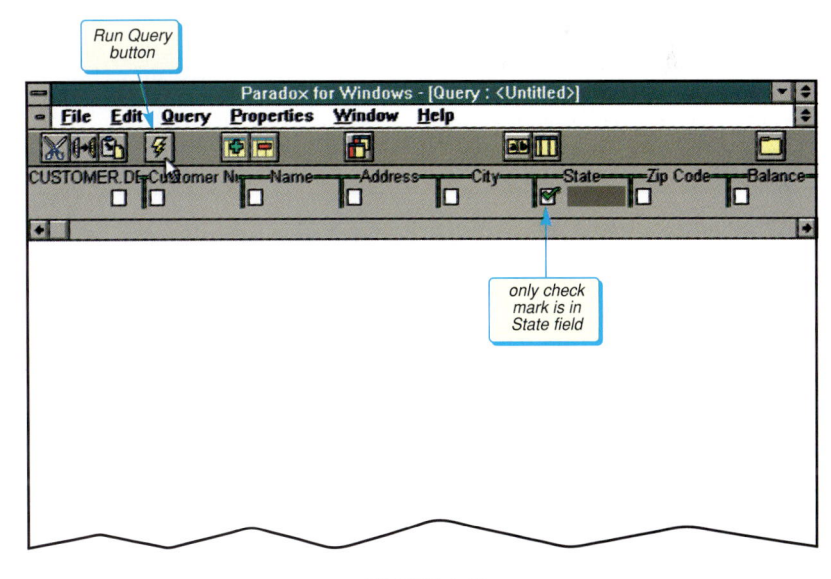

FIGURE 2-43

P82 PROJECT 2 QUERYING A DATABASE

STEP 3 ▶

Click the Run Query button on the SpeedBar.

The Answer table contains the state names from the Customer table (Figure 2-44). The names display in alphabetical order. Duplicates have been removed so each state is listed only once.

STEP 4 ▶

When you are finished with the Answer table, close it.

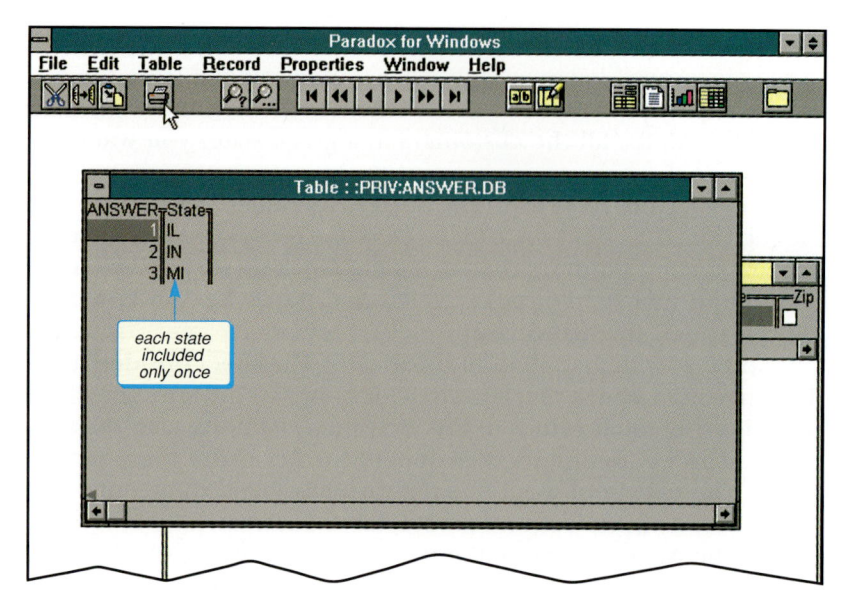

FIGURE 2-44

Another approach to sorting, the one that offers maximum flexibility is to sort the Answer table. To sort the Answer table, use the **Properties menu** *after* you have filled in the Query image, but *before* you run the query.

Including Duplicates in the Sorted Data

If you want to list the states for all the customers, including duplicates, you cannot use the check mark because using check marks eliminates any duplicates from the Answer table. Instead of the regular check mark in the Check menu, you need to use **check plus**. The following steps include duplicates in the Answer table (see Figure 2-46) by using check plus in the Check menu.

TO INCLUDE DUPLICATES ▼

STEP 1 ▶

Be sure you have a clear (CTRL+DELETE), maximized Query image for the Customer table on the desktop.

STEP 2 ▶

Point to the check box for the State field. Press, but do not release, the left mouse button. Drag the highlight to the check plus option.

The Check menu displays, and the check plus option is highlighted (Figure 2-45).

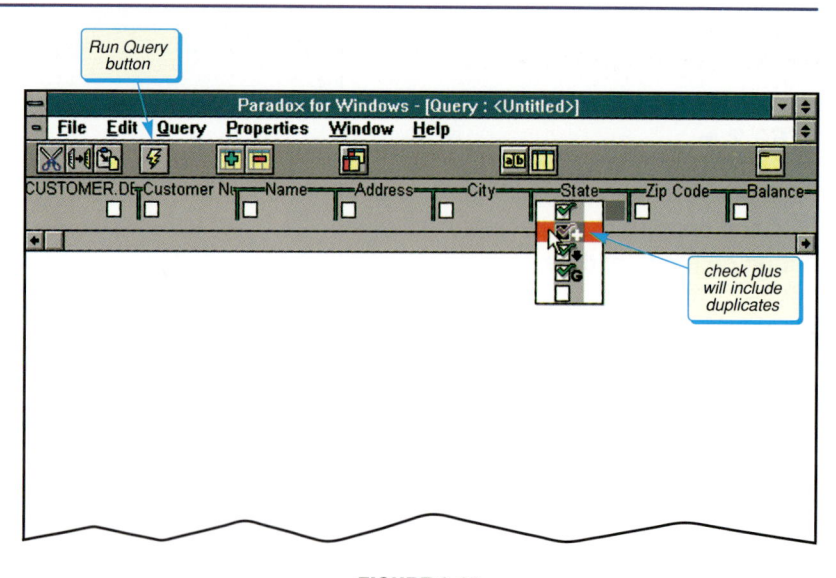

FIGURE 2-45

STEP 3 ▶

Release the left mouse button and then click the Run Query button on the SpeedBar.

The Answer table contains the state names from the database (Figure 2-46). Duplicates are included.

STEP 4 ▶

When you are finished with the Answer table, close it.

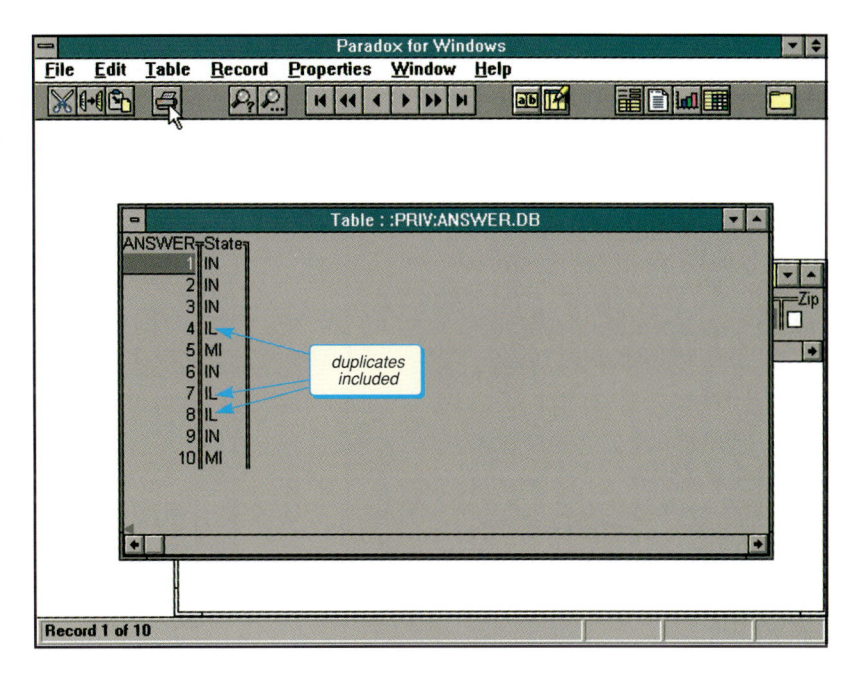

FIGURE 2-46

Sorting Data in a Query in Descending Sequence

In the final example of the use of check marks for sorting, the states are listed in reverse order (see Figure 2-48 on the next page). This requires **check descending** in the Check menu.

TO REVERSE THE ORDER ▼

STEP 1 ▶

Be sure you have a clear (CTRL + DELETE), maximized Query image for the Customer table on the desktop.

STEP 2 ▶

Point to the check box for the State field. Press, but do not release, the left mouse button. Drag the highlight to the check descending option.

The Check menu displays (Figure 2-47). The check descending option is highlighted.

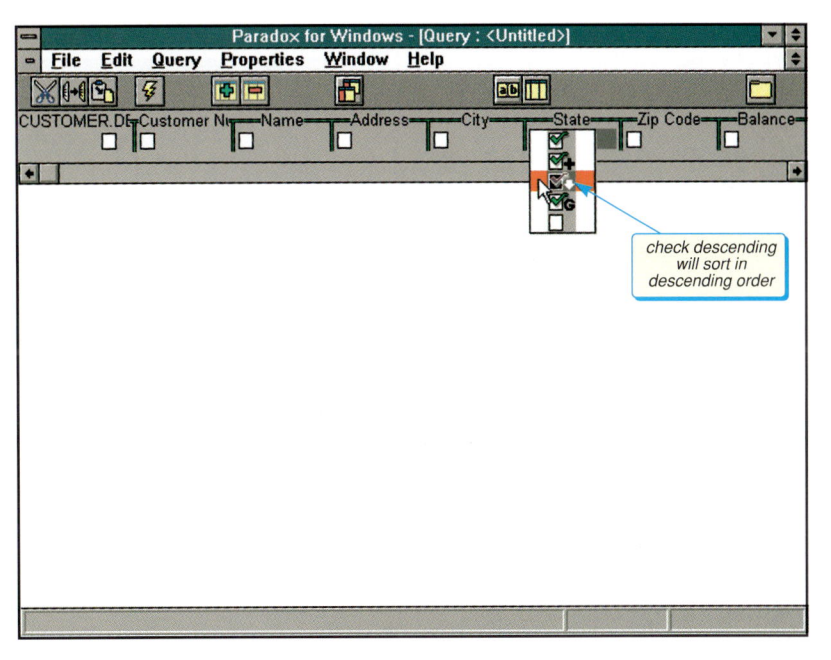

FIGURE 2-47

PROJECT 2 QUERYING A DATABASE

STEP 3 ▶

Release the left mouse button and click the Run Query button on the SpeedBar.

The Answer table contains the state names from the customer database (Figure 2-48). The state names are sorted in reverse order. Duplicates have been eliminated.

STEP 4 ▶

When you are finished with the Answer table, close it.

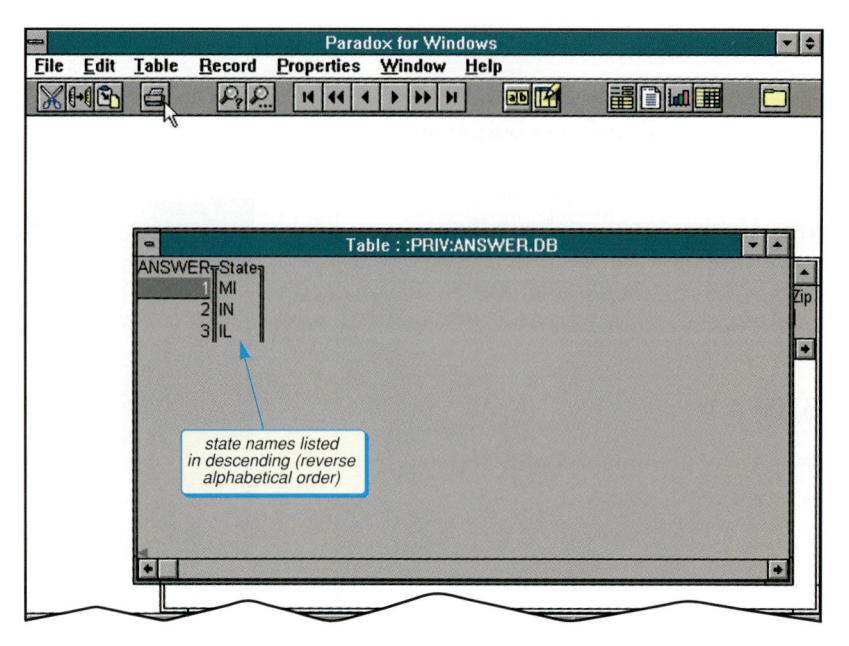

FIGURE 2-48

Sorting Data in a Query on Multiple Fields

The next example displays in the Answer table the number, name, address, city, and state for all customers. The data is sorted by city within state (see Figure 2-54 on page P86). The following steps override the normal sort order by using the Answer Table command on the Properties menu to sort the records in the Answer table.

TO SORT THE ANSWER TABLE ▼

STEP 1 ▶

Be sure you have a clear (CTRL + DELETE), maximized Query image for the Customer table on the desktop.

STEP 2 ▶

Place check marks in the Customer Number, Name, Address, City, and State fields. Select the Properties menu. Choose the Answer Table command and point to the Sort command.

The cascading menu for the Answer Table command displays (Figure 2-49). The mouse pointer points to the Sort command.

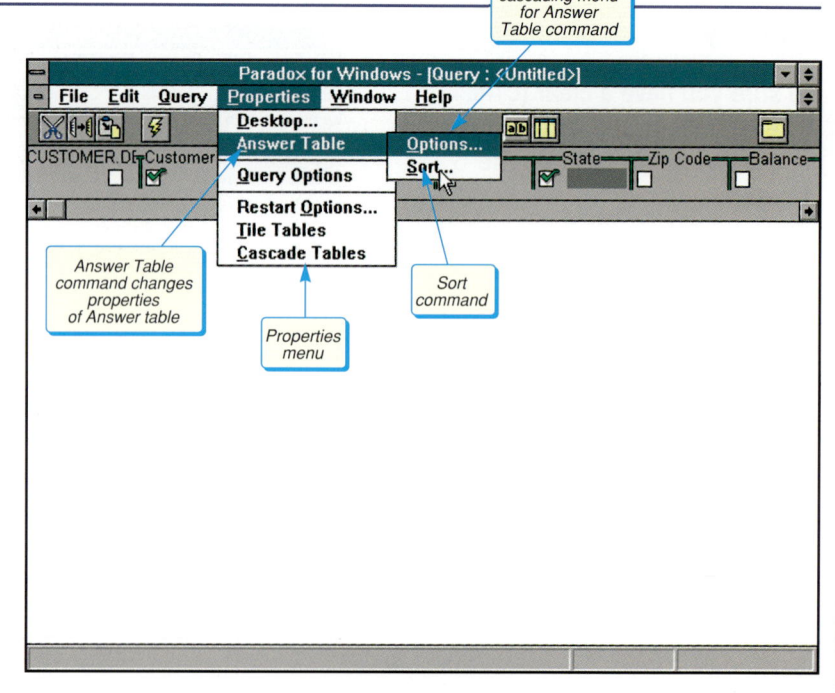

FIGURE 2-49

STEP 3 ▶

Choose the Sort command and then point to State.

The Sort Answer dialog box displays (Figure 2-50). You use this dialog box to specify the sort keys. The mouse pointer is pointing to State, the more important sort key.

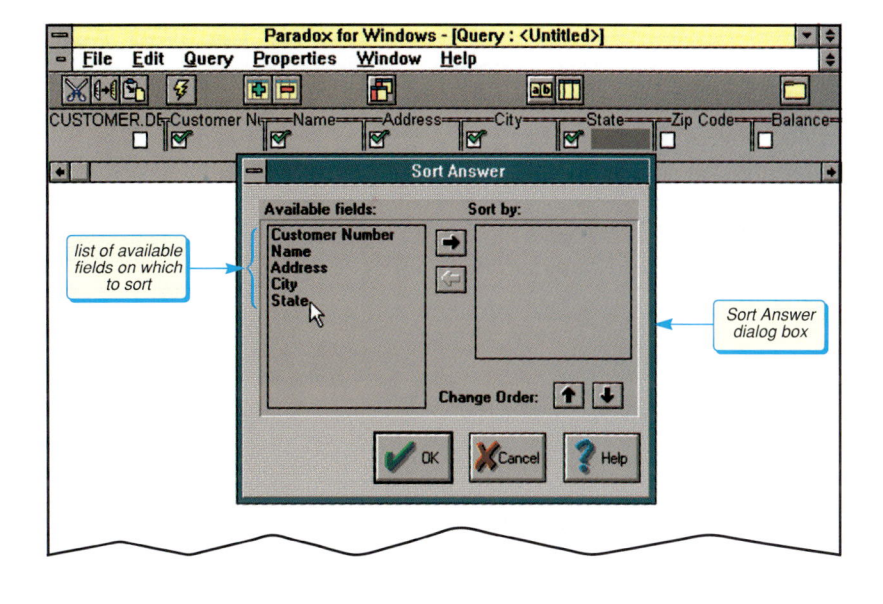

FIGURE 2-50

STEP 4 ▶

Select State and then point to the Add Field arrow (→) (Figure 2-51).

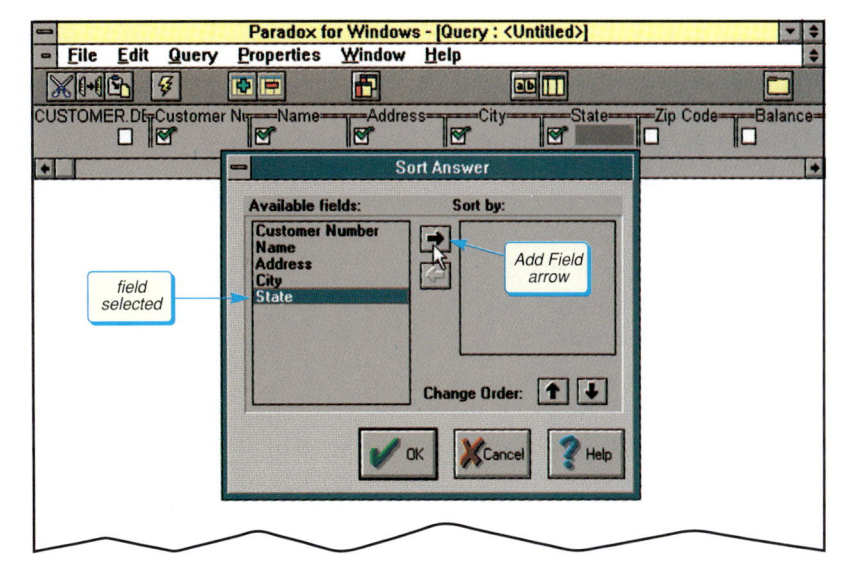

FIGURE 2-51

STEP 5 ▶

Click the Add Field arrow, select City, and then point to the Add Field arrow again.

State becomes the first sort key (Figure 2-52). The City field is selected, and the mouse pointer is pointing to the Add Field arrow.

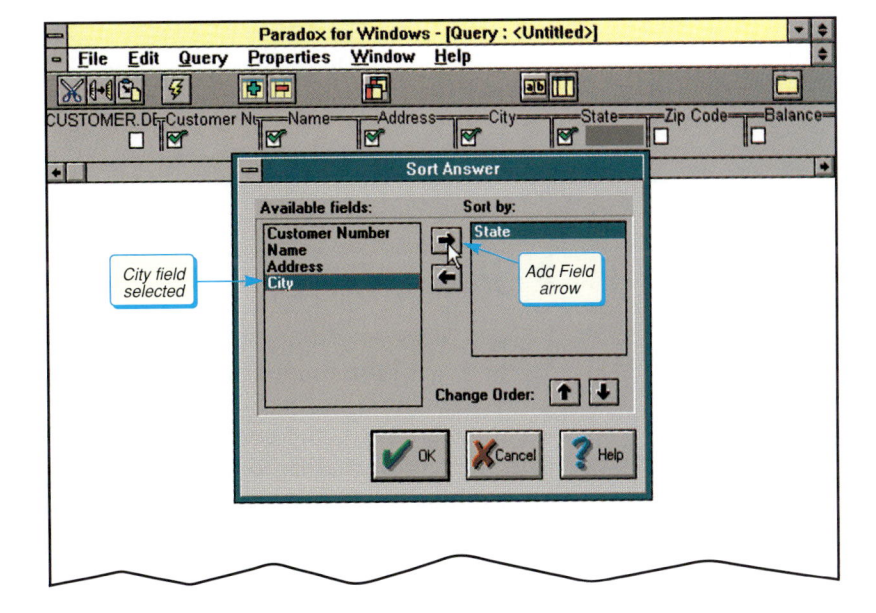

FIGURE 2-52

STEP 6 ▶

Click the Add Field arrow, choose the OK button on the Sort Answer dialog box, and click the Run Query button on the SpeedBar.

The Answer table displays (Figure 2-53). The State field is not visible.

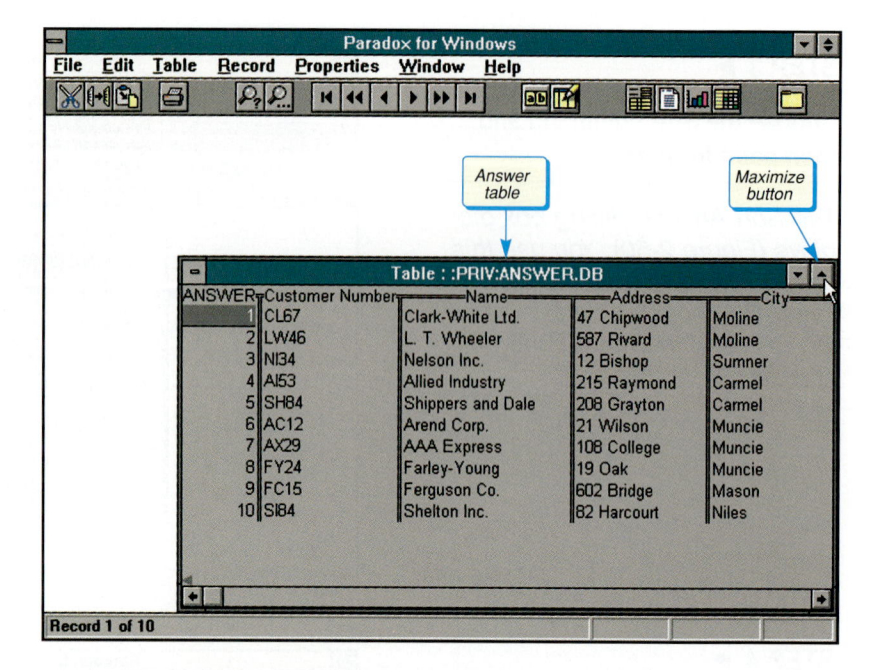

FIGURE 2-53

STEP 7 ▶

Maximize the window containing the Answer table.

The window is maximized (Figure 2-54). The records in the Answer table are sorted by state. Within each state, they are sorted by city.

STEP 8 ▶

When you are finished with the Answer table, close it.

FIGURE 2-54

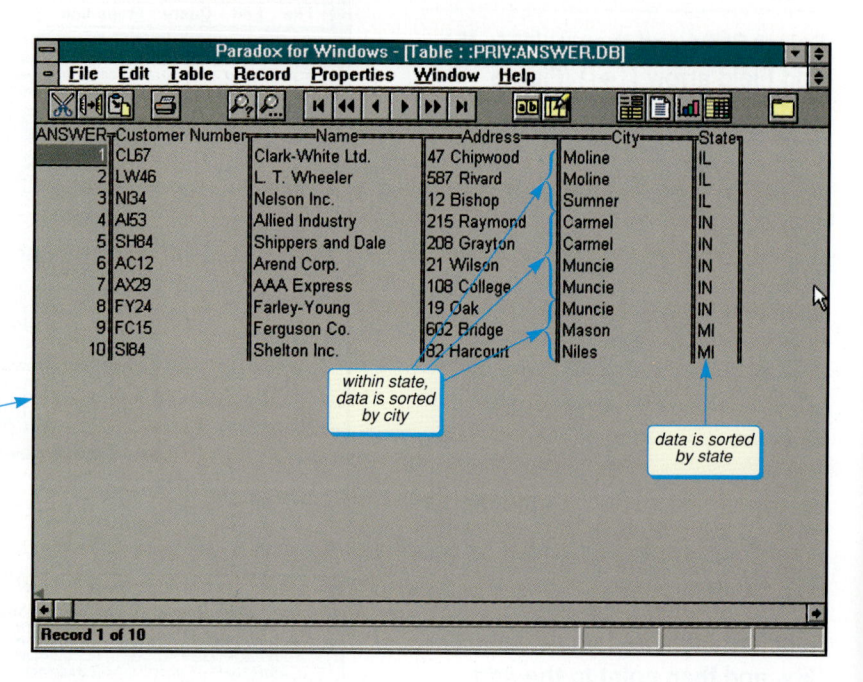

▶ JOINING TABLES

Suppose you want to list the number and name of each customer along with the number and name of the customer's sales rep. The customer name is in the Customer table, whereas the sales rep name is in the Slsrep table. Thus, the query cannot be satisfied using a single table. You need to **join** the tables; that is, to find records in the two tables that have identical values in matching fields (Figure 2-55). In this example, you need to find records in the Customer table and the Slsrep table that have the same sales rep number.

JOINING TABLES **P87**

▶ CUSTOMER TABLE

Customer Number	Name	Address
AC12	Arend Corp.	21 Wilson
AI53	Allied Industry	215 Raymond
AX29	AAA Express	108 College
CL67	Clark-White Ltd.	47 Chipwood
FC15	Ferguson Co.	602 Bridge
FY24	Farley-Young	19 Oak
LW46	L. T. Wheeler	587 Rivard
NI34	Nelson, Inc.	12 Bishop
SH84	Shippers and Dale	208 Grayton
SI84	Shelton, Inc.	82 Harcourt

Sales Rep Number
03
06
06
12
03
06
06
03
12
06

▶ SLSREP TABLE

Sales Rep Number	Last Name	First Name
03	Harrison	Monica
06	Thompson	Charles
12	Juarez	Mara

Give me the number and name of each customer along with the number and last name of the customer's sales rep.

Query requesting data from two tables

Join

ANSWER	Customer Number	Name	Sales Rep Number	Last Name
1	AC12	Arend Corp.	03	Harrison
2	AI53	Allied Industry	06	Thompson
3	AX29	AAA Express	06	Thompson
4	CL67	Clark-White Ltd.	12	Juarez
5	FC15	Ferguson Co.	03	Harrison
6	FY24	Farley-Young	06	Thompson
7	LW46	L. T. Wheeler	06	Thompson
8	NI34	Nelson Inc.	03	Harrison
9	SH84	Shippers and Dale	12	Juarez
10	SI84	Shelton Inc.	06	Thompson

Answers

FIGURE 2-55

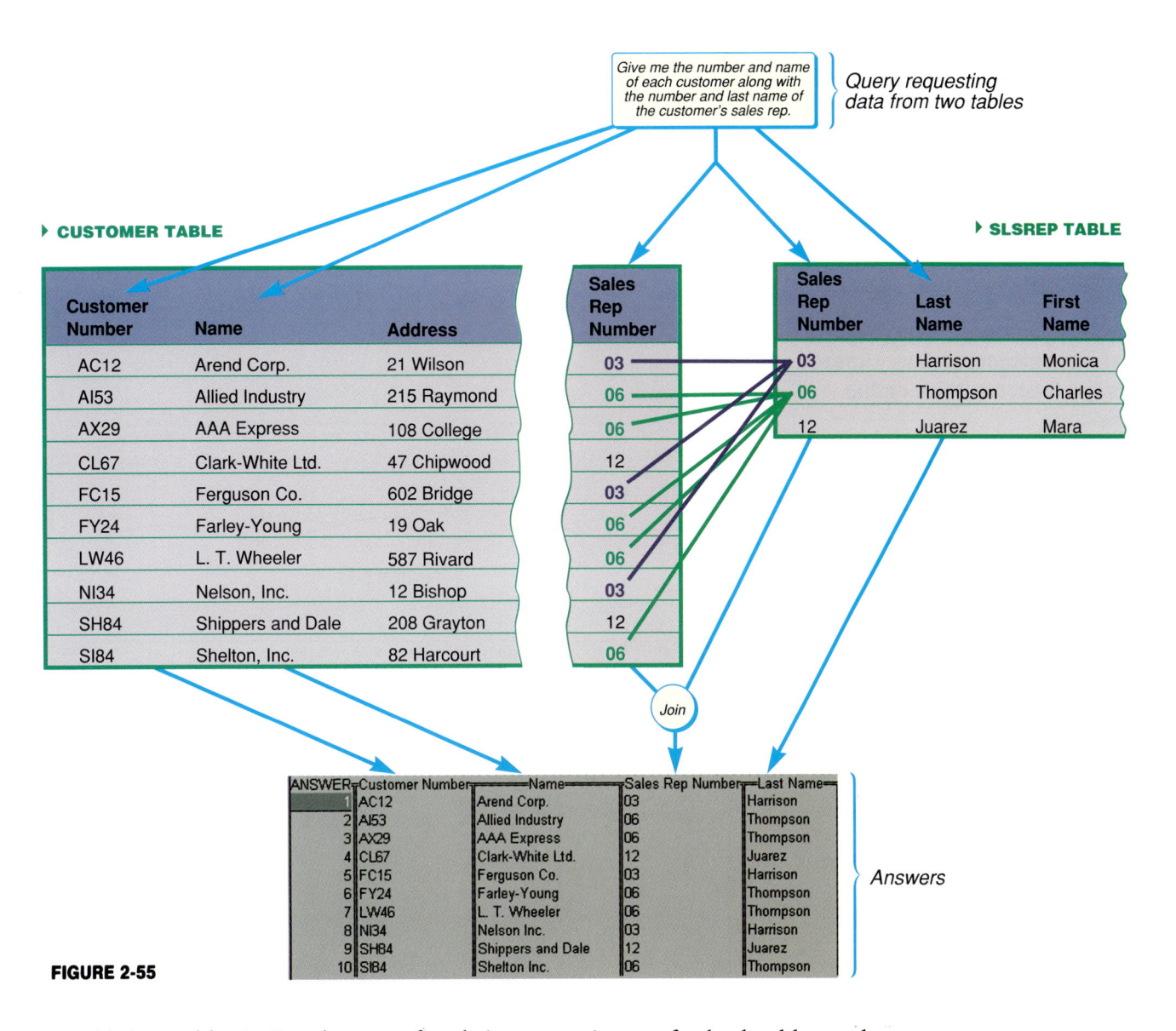

To join tables in Paradox, you first bring query images for both tables to the desktop (see Figure 2-58 on the next page). Select all the fields you want from both tables by placing check marks on the field check boxes in the Query image just like you do with a single table. Finally, you need to indicate how the tables are related; that is, which fields in the tables must match. In selecting data from the Customer and Slsrep tables, for example, you need to indicate that the Sales Rep Number fields in both tables must contain the same values.

To indicate that fields must match, use a special item called an example. An **example** is a sample value. You indicate you are entering an example, instead of a specific condition, by pressing the F5 key before you type the entry. Paradox visually indicates the entry represents an example by displaying it in a different color.

To indicate the matching fields, you must enter the *same* example in both fields. In the following steps, you will use 99 as the example in the Sales Rep Number fields. The choice of 99 is purely arbitrary. It really doesn't matter what number you choose for the examples, as long as you use the *same* number in both fields.

Adding a Second Table to the Query

The first step is to add an additional file to the query, that is, bring a query image for the additional table to the desktop.

TO ADD A TABLE TO A QUERY ▼

STEP 1 ▶

Be sure you have a clear (CTRL + DELETE), maximized Query image for the Customer table on the desktop.

STEP 2 ▶

Point to the Add Table button (▣) on the SpeedBar (Figure 2-56).

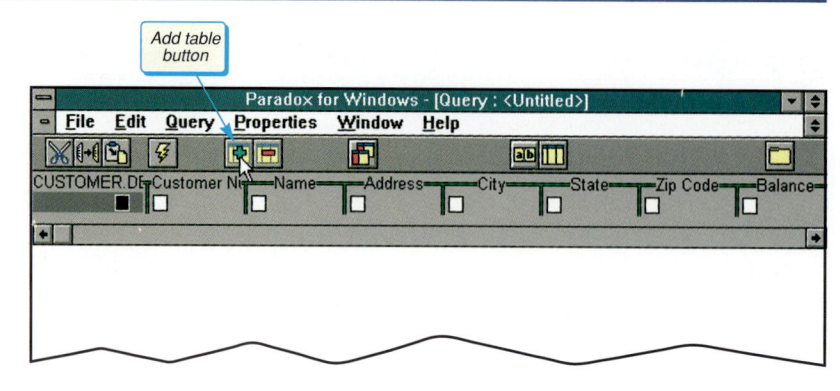

FIGURE 2-56

STEP 3 ▶

Click the Add Table button and point to SLSREP.DB.

The Select File dialog box displays on the desktop (Figure 2-57). The mouse pointer is pointing to SLSREP.DB (the Slsrep table).

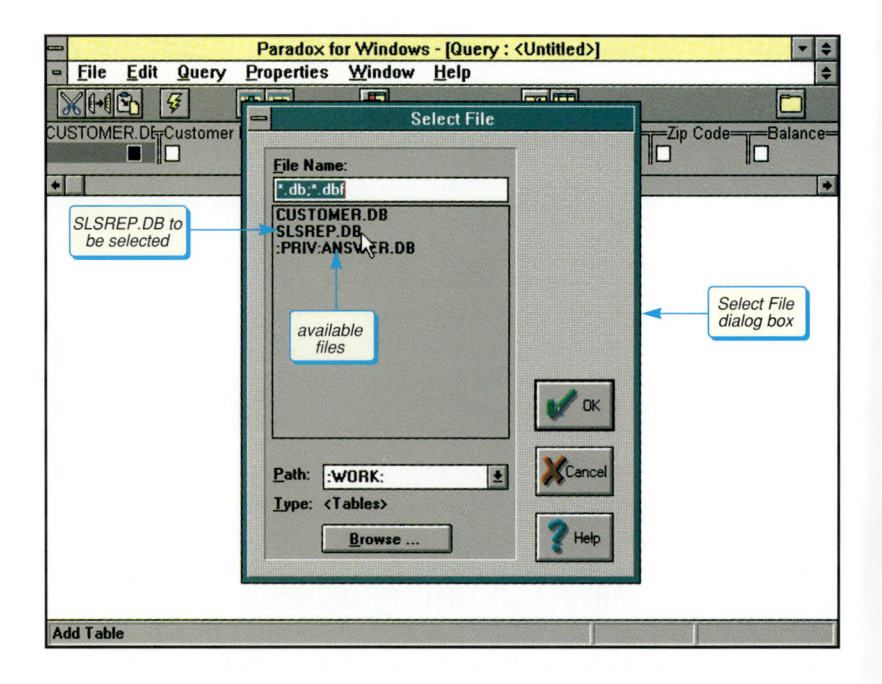

FIGURE 2-57

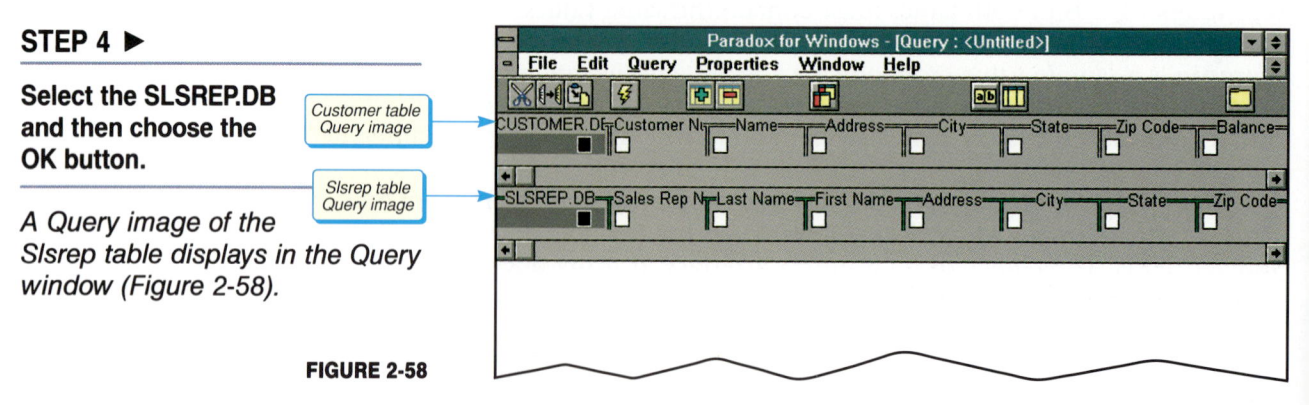

STEP 4 ▶

Select the SLSREP.DB and then choose the OK button.

A Query image of the Slsrep table displays in the Query window (Figure 2-58).

FIGURE 2-58

JOINING TABLES **P89**

Joining the Tables

Once you have both query images on the desktop, you need to fill them in appropriately to join the tables as the following steps illustrate.

TO JOIN THE TABLES ▼

STEP 1 ▶

Place check marks in the Customer Number and Name fields of the image for the Customer table (Figure 2-59).

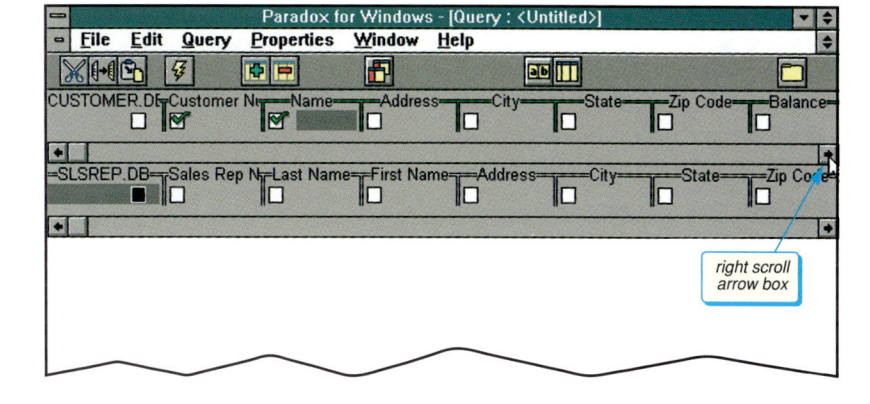

FIGURE 2-59

STEP 2 ▶

Repeatedly press the TAB key until the highlight has moved to the Sales Rep Number field. Press the F5 key and then type 99.

The example, 99, displays in the Sales Rep Number field (Figure 2-60).

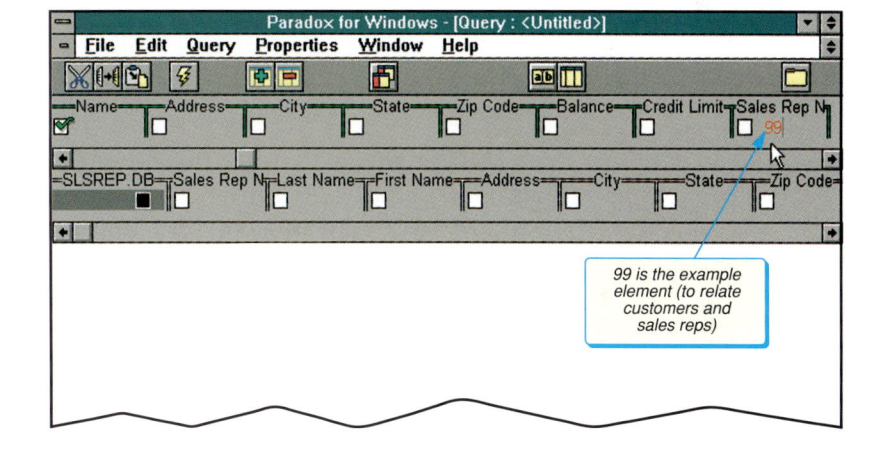

FIGURE 2-60

STEP 3 ▶

Place a check mark in the Sales Rep Number field of the Sales Rep query image. Press the F5 key and then type 99. Place a check mark in the Last Name field. Point to the Run Query button on the SpeedBar.

The example, 99, displays in both Sales Rep Number fields (Figure 2-61). The mouse pointer points to the Run Query button.

FIGURE 2-61

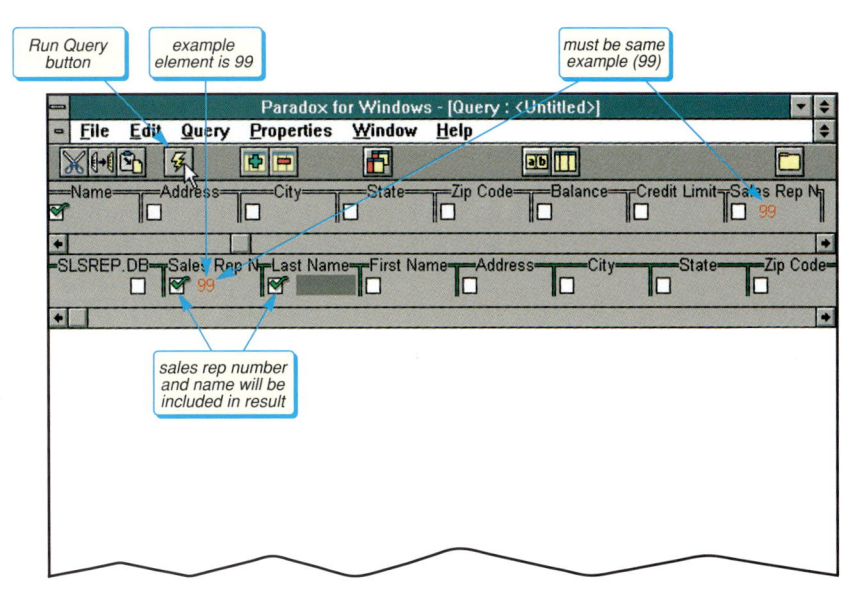

STEP 4 ▶

Click the Run Query button.

The answer contains the number, name and sales rep from the Customer table and Slsrep table (Figure 2-62).

STEP 5 ▶

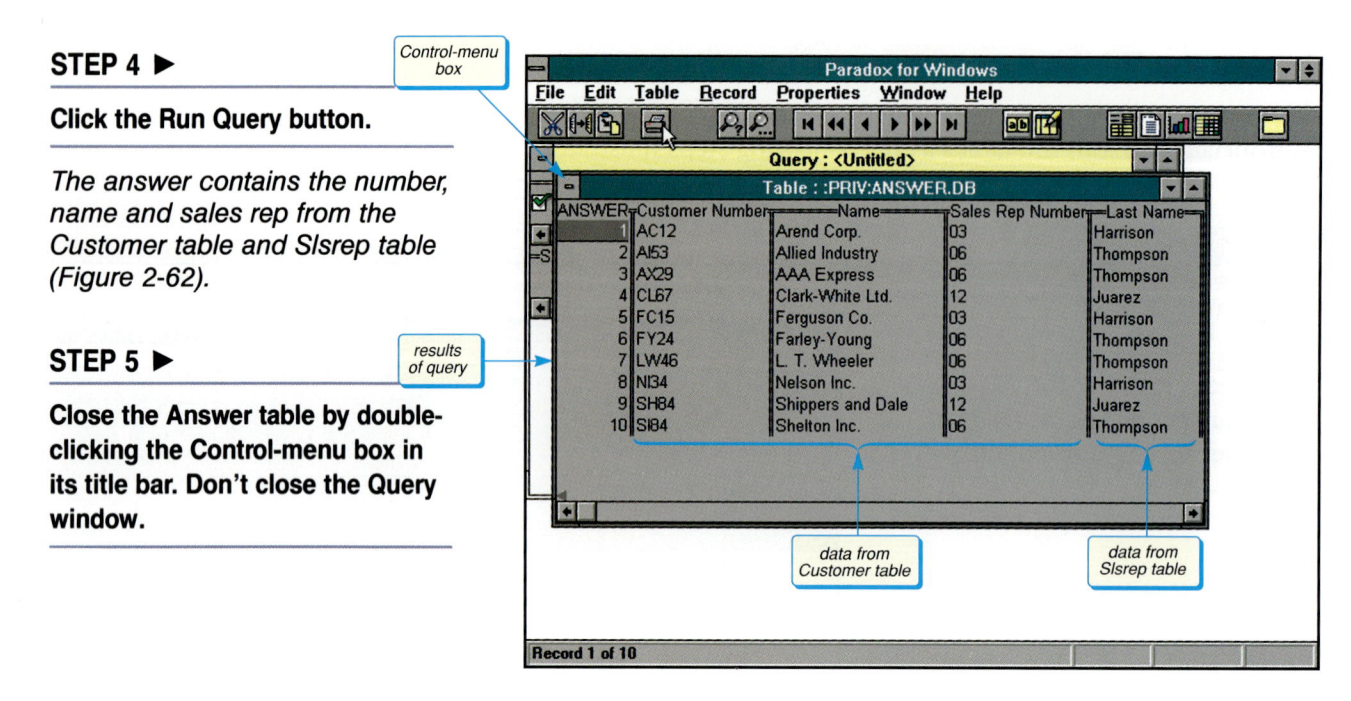

Close the Answer table by double-clicking the Control-menu box in its title bar. Don't close the Query window.

FIGURE 2-62

Use the mouse to move from one Query image to another (Figure 2-58 on page P88). Simply click the field in the Query image to which you want to move. If you are making entries with the keyboard, however, you might not want to move your hand from the keyboard to the mouse. In this case, you can use the F3 and F4 keys to move between images. Press the F3 key to move to the previous Query image or press the F4 key to move to the next Query image.

Restricting Records in a Join

Sometimes you will want to join tables, but you will not want to include all possible records. In such cases, you will include appropriate conditions in the queries to relate just like you did before. For example, to include the same fields as in the previous query, but only those customers whose credit limit is $8,000, you will make the same entries as before and then also enter the number 8000 in the Credit Limit field.

The following steps modify the query images from the previous example to restrict the records that will be included in the join (see Figure 2-64).

TO RESTRICT THE RECORDS IN A JOIN ▼

STEP 1 ▶

Press the F3 key to move up to the Query image for Customer. Press the SHIFT + TAB key to move back to the Credit Limit field and then type 8000 (Figure 2-63).

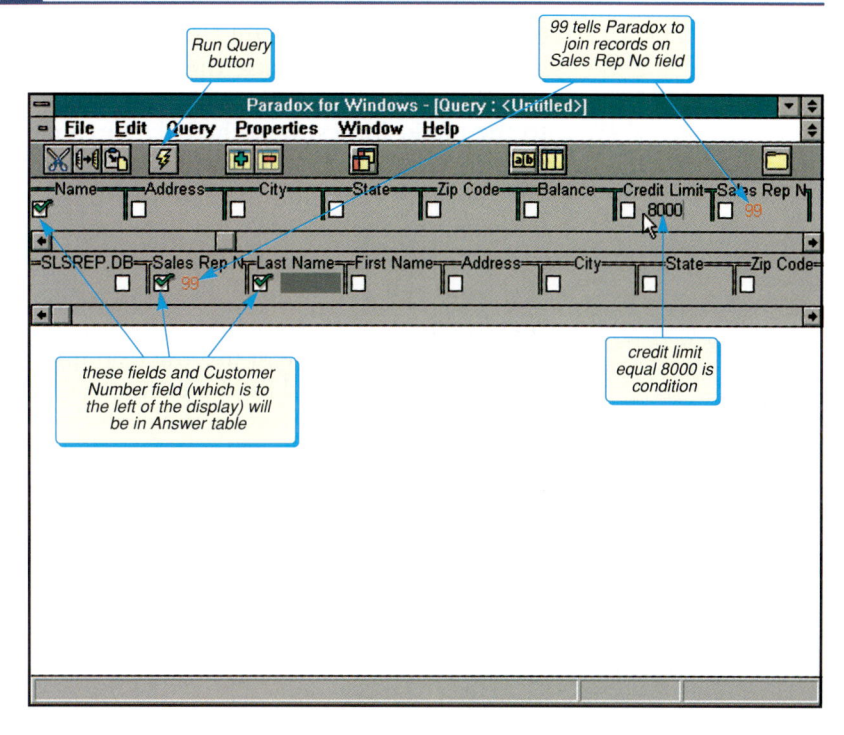

FIGURE 2-63

STEP 2 ▶

Click the Run Query button on the SpeedBar.

The Answer table now contains only those customers who have a credit limit of $8,000 (Figure 2-64).

STEP 3 ▶

Close the Answer table and Query image windows.

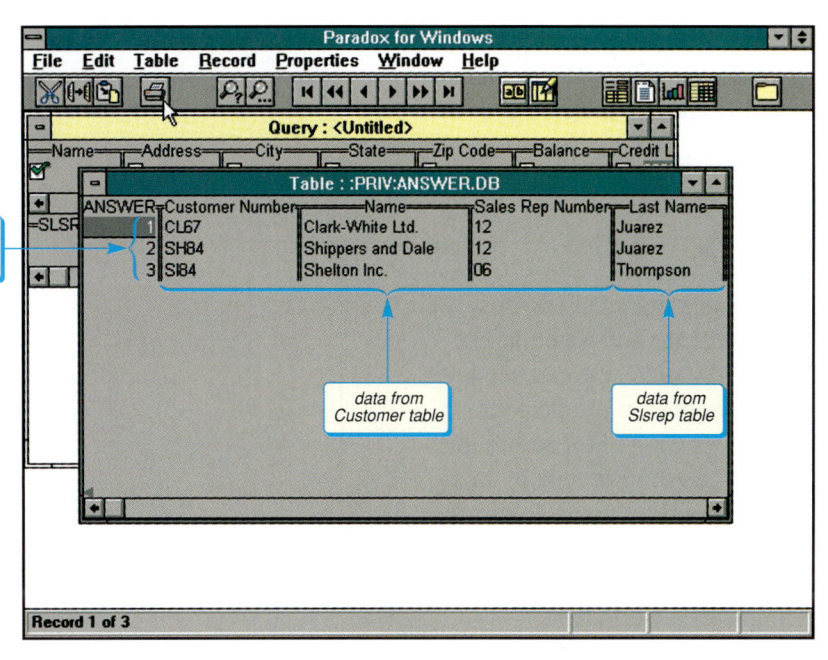

FIGURE 2-64

▶ Using Computed Fields

Suppose you want to find each customer's available credit. This poses a problem because there is no field for available credit in the Customer table. You can compute it, however, because the available credit is equal to the credit limit minus the balance. Such a field is called a **computed field**. To include computed fields in queries, you need to use examples.

To enter examples in each of the fields involved in the computation, enter an example, such as 100, for Balance and a *different* example, such as 200, for credit limit. Once you have entered the examples in each of the fields, you place the word calc followed by the appropriate expression in any field. (It doesn't matter which field you choose for this purpose.)

The expression will use the examples that you already created. In this case the expression would be the example you created for credit limits followed by a minus sign (–), followed by the example you created for balances.

Computations are not restricted to subtraction. Addition (+), multiplication (*), or division (/) are also available. You can also include parentheses in your computations.

The following steps use a computed field to display the customer number, name, and available credit of all customers (see Figure 2-68).

TO USE A COMPUTED FIELD ▼

STEP 1 ▶

Be sure you have a clear (CTRL + DELETE), maximized Query image for the Customer table on the desktop.

STEP 2 ▶

Place check marks in the Customer Number and Name fields. Repeatedly press the TAB key until the highlight is in the Balance field, press the F5 key, and then type 100 as the example of a balance. Press the TAB key to move to the Credit Limit field, press the F5 key, and then type 200 as the example of a credit limit.

Both the Balance field and the Credit Limit field contain examples (Figure 2-65).

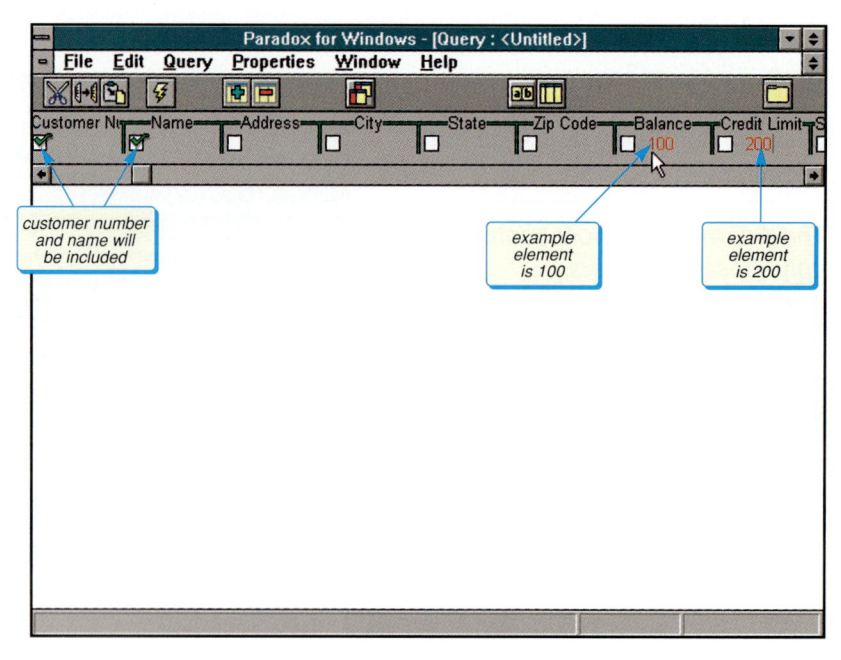

FIGURE 2-65

STEP 3 ▶

Press the TAB key to move to the Sales Rep Number field (Figure 2-66).

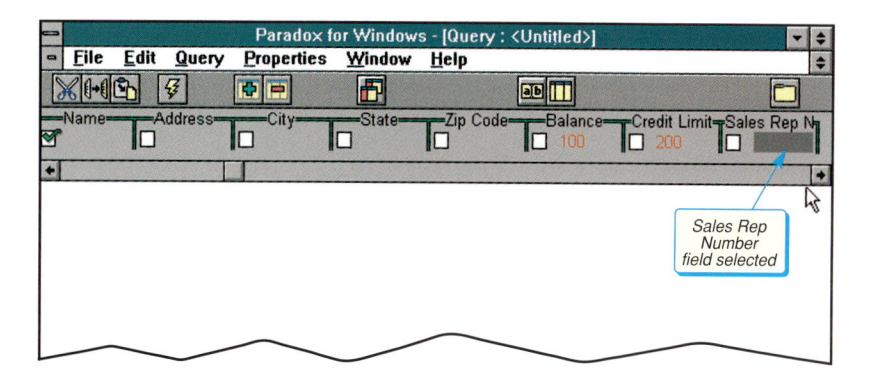

FIGURE 2-66

STEP 4 ▶

Type `calc` and press the SPACE-BAR. Press the F5 key and then type the number 200. Type a minus sign (-). Press the F5 key and then type the number 100. Point to the Run Query button on the SpeedBar.

The expression for calculating available credit displays in the Sales Rep Number field (Figure 2-67). The mouse pointer points to the Run Query button on the SpeedBar.

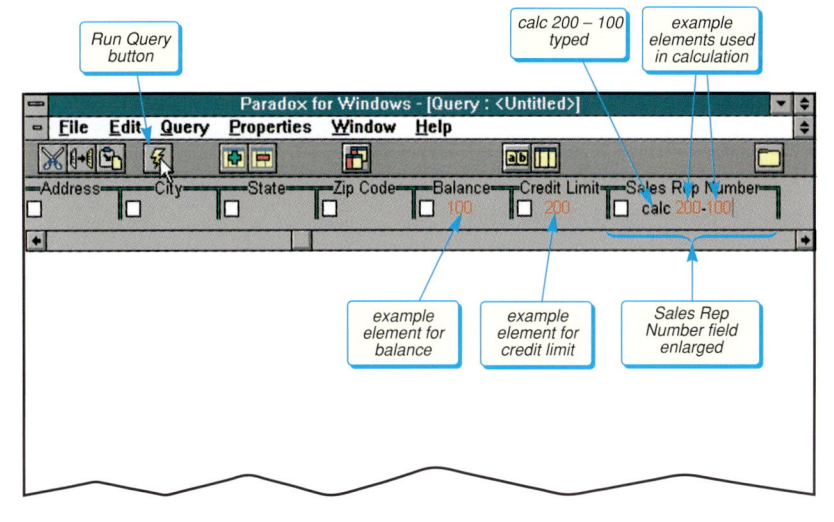

FIGURE 2-67

STEP 5 ▶

Click the Run Query button.

The Answer table contains the two checked fields as well as the calculation (Figure 2-68).

STEP 6 ▶

When you are finished with the Answer table, close it.

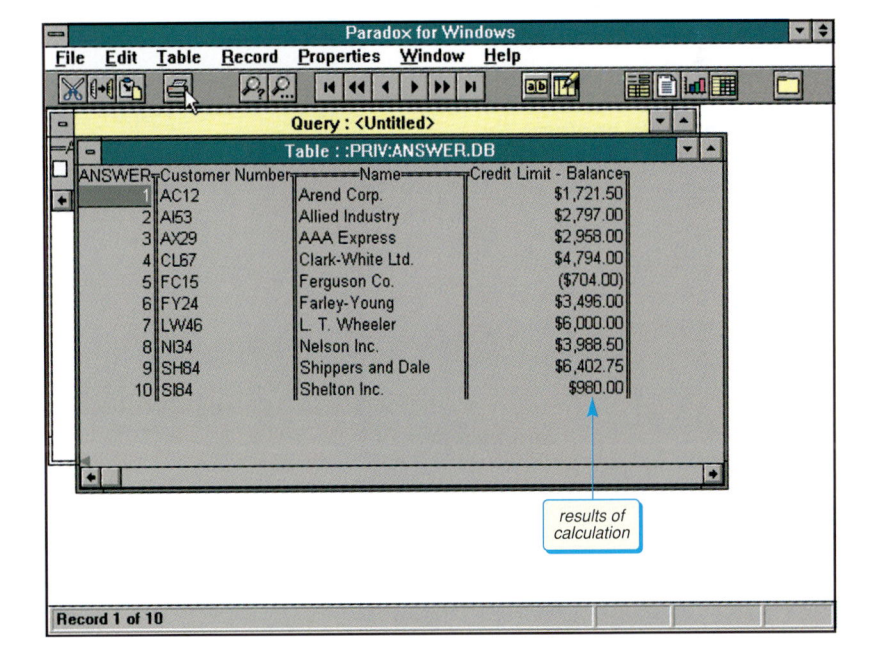

FIGURE 2-68

▶ Calculating Statistics

Paradox supports the built-in functions: COUNT, SUM, AVERAGE, MAX (largest value), MIN (smallest value), FIRST, and LAST. To use any of these functions in a query, precede it with the CALC operator, the same operator you used for computed fields on the previous page.

Calculating an Average

The following steps illustrate how you use these functions by calculating the average balance for all customers (see Figure 2-70).

TO CALCULATE AN AVERAGE

STEP 1 ▶

Be sure you have a clear (CTRL + DELETE), maximized Query image for the Customer table on the desktop.

STEP 2 ▶

Type `calc average` in the Balance field (Figure 2-69).

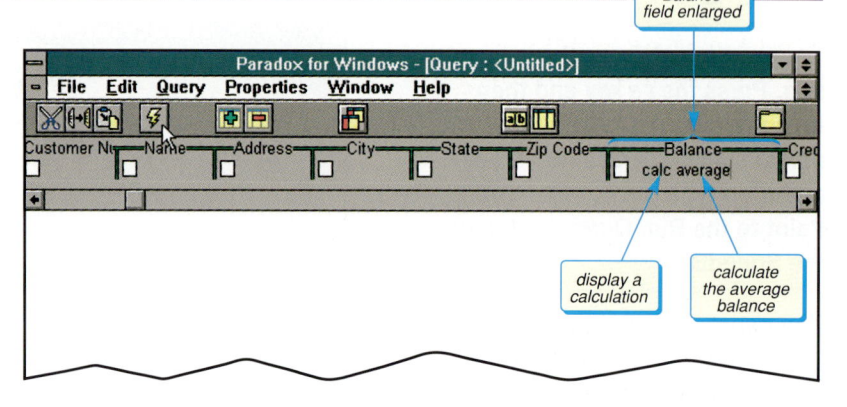

FIGURE 2-69

STEP 3 ▶

Click the Run Query button on the SpeedBar.

The Answer table contains the average balance of all customers (Figure 2-70).

STEP 4 ▶

When you are finished with the Answer table, close it.

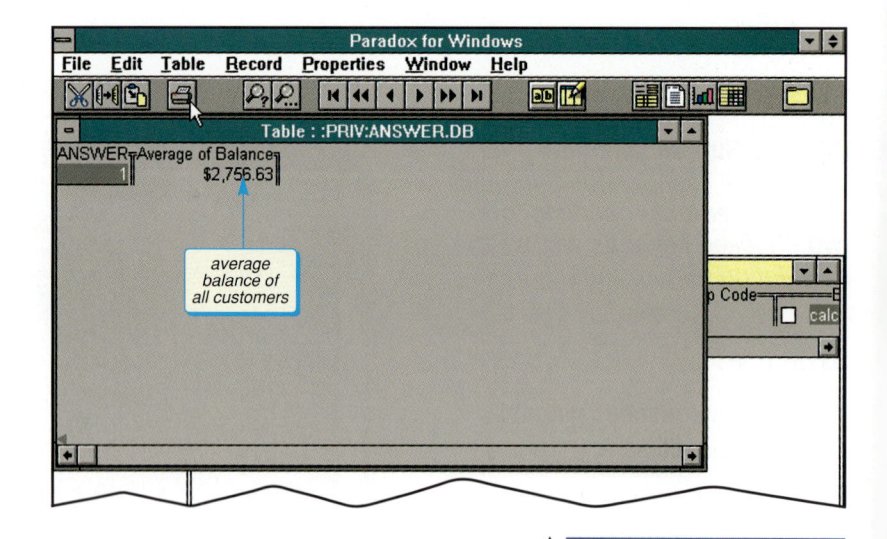

FIGURE 2-70

Grouping Similar Records

Sometimes calculating statistics for all the records in the table is appropriate. In other cases, however, you will need to calculate the statistics for groups of records. You might have to calculate the average balance for the customers of sales rep 03, the average for customers of sales rep 06, and so on.

This type of calculation involves **grouping**, which simply means creating groups of records that share some common characteristic. In grouping by sales rep number, the customers of sales rep 03 would form one group, the customers of sales rep 06 would be a second group, and the customers of sales rep 12 form a third group. The calculations are then made for each group. To indicate grouping in Paradox for Windows, place a check mark in the field to be used for grouping. Do not place check marks in any other fields.

The following steps calculate the average balance for customers of each sales rep (see Figure 2-72).

TO GROUP ▼

STEP 1 ▶

Be sure you have a clear (CTRL + DELETE), maximized Query image for the Customer table on the desktop.

STEP 2 ▶

Enter `calc average` in the Balance field. Place a check mark in the Sales Rep Number field and point to the Run Query button on the SpeedBar.

The calculation displays in the Balance field (Figure 2-71). There is a check mark in the Sales Rep Number field indicating records are to be grouped by sales rep number. The pointer points to the Run Query button.

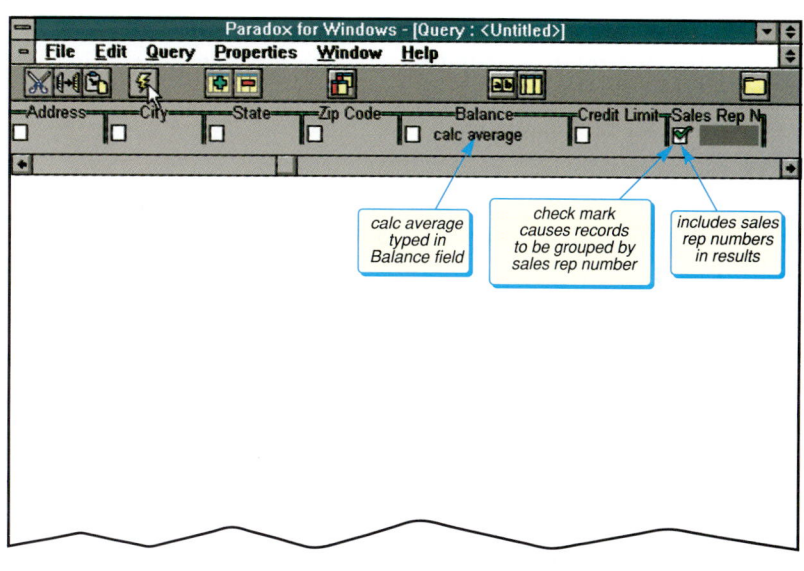

FIGURE 2-71

STEP 3 ▶

Click the Run Query button.

The Answer table shows each sales rep's number along with the average balance of the customers of that sales rep (Figure 2-72).

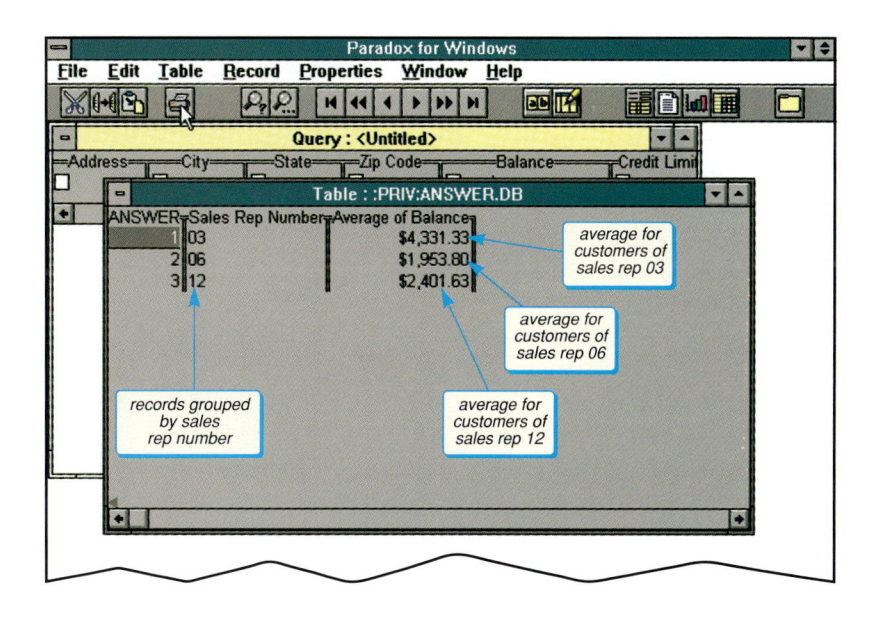

FIGURE 2-72

P96 PROJECT 2 QUERYING A DATABASE

▶ GRAPHING THE ANSWER TO A QUERY

A graph of the answer to a query can often be useful. Because the answer is stored in the Answer table, graphing the answer simply means graphing the contents of the table. To create an initial graph, you will use the same techniques you used in Project 1.

The following steps produce a graph that relates sales rep numbers to the average balance of customers of the sales rep (see Figure 2-76).

TO GRAPH THE ANSWER TO A QUERY ▼

STEP 1 ▶

Be sure the Answer table (Figure 2-72) is on the desktop. If it is not, rerun the query on the previous page.

STEP 2 ▶

Point to the Quick Graph button (Figure 2-73).

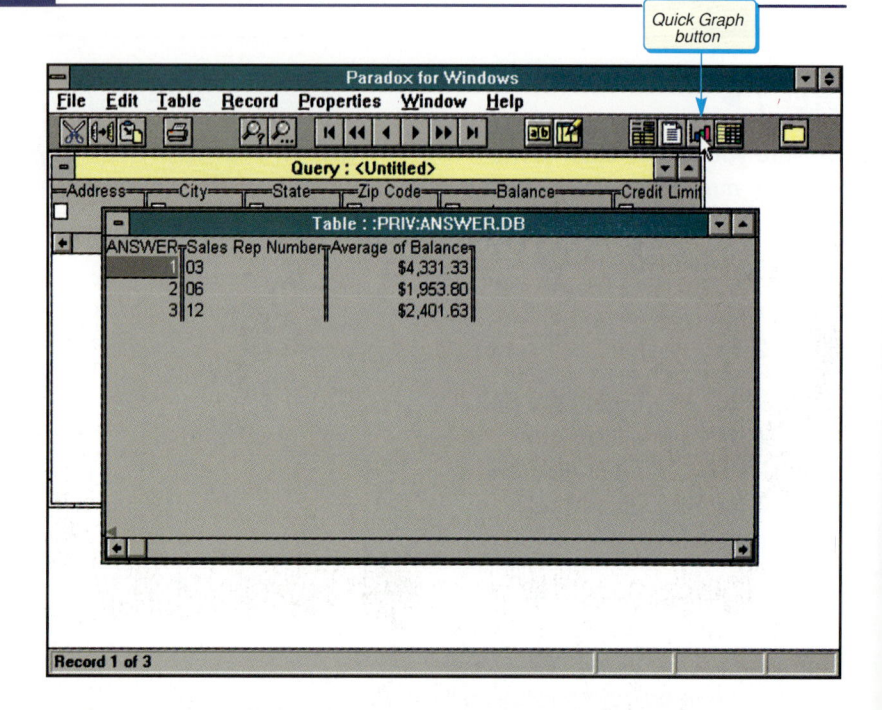

FIGURE 2-73

STEP 3 ▶

Click the Quick Graph button. Click the answer.db drop-down list box down arrow and select the Sales Rep Number field.

The Define Graph dialog box displays on the desktop (Figure 2-74). The Sales Rep Number field is selected as the field for the X-Axis (horizontal axis).

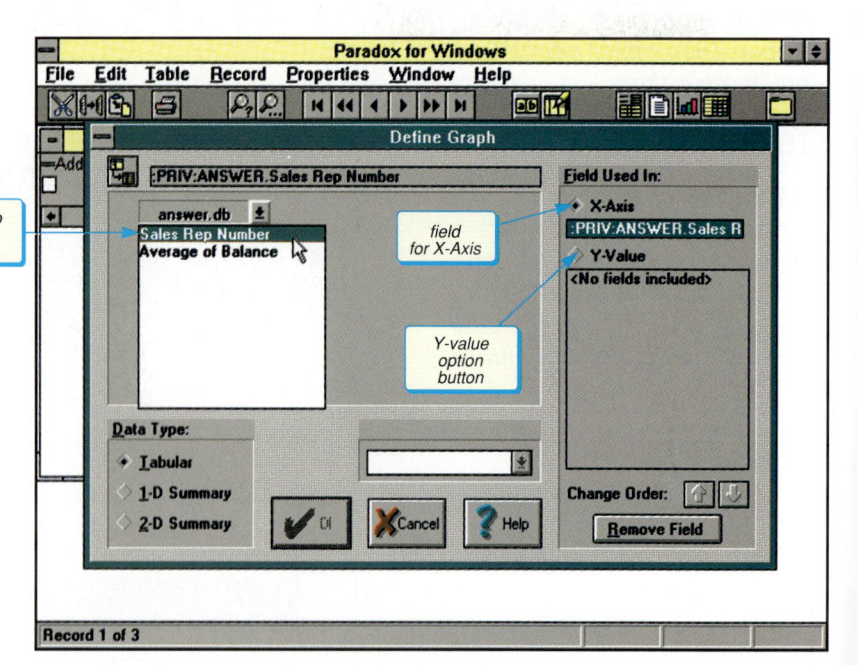

FIGURE 2-74

GRAPHING THE ANSWER TO A QUERY   **P97**

STEP 4 ▶

Click the Y-Value option button, click the answer.db drop-down list box down arrow, select Average of Balance, and then choose the OK button on the Define Graph dialog box.

The Quick Graph displays on the desktop (Figure 2-75). The entries along the X-axis are sales rep numbers and the Y-values represent average balances.

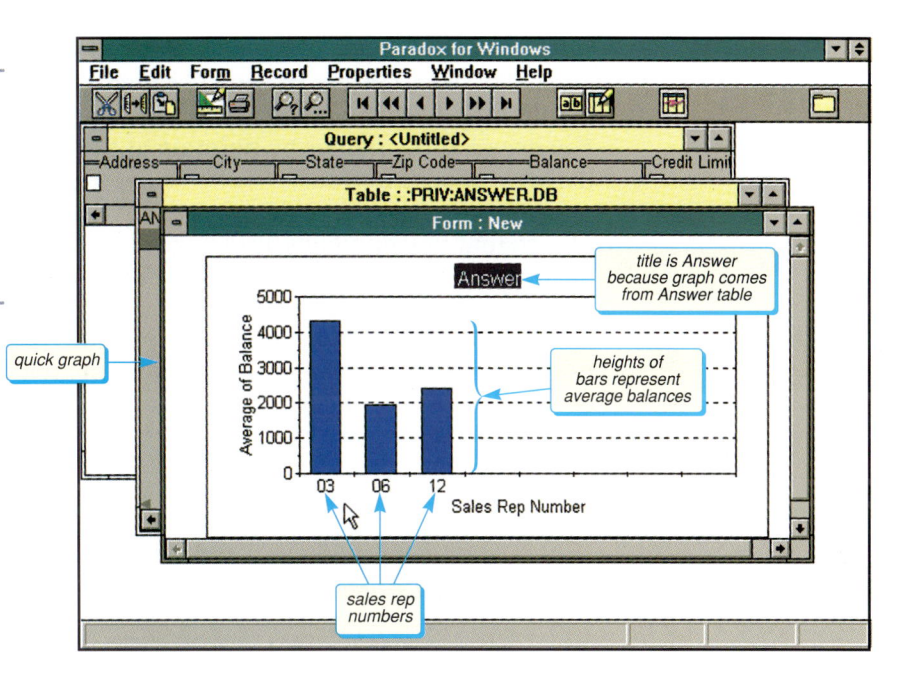

FIGURE 2-75

STEP 5 ▶

Maximize the window containing the graph.

A maximized version of the graph displays on the desktop (Figure 2-76).

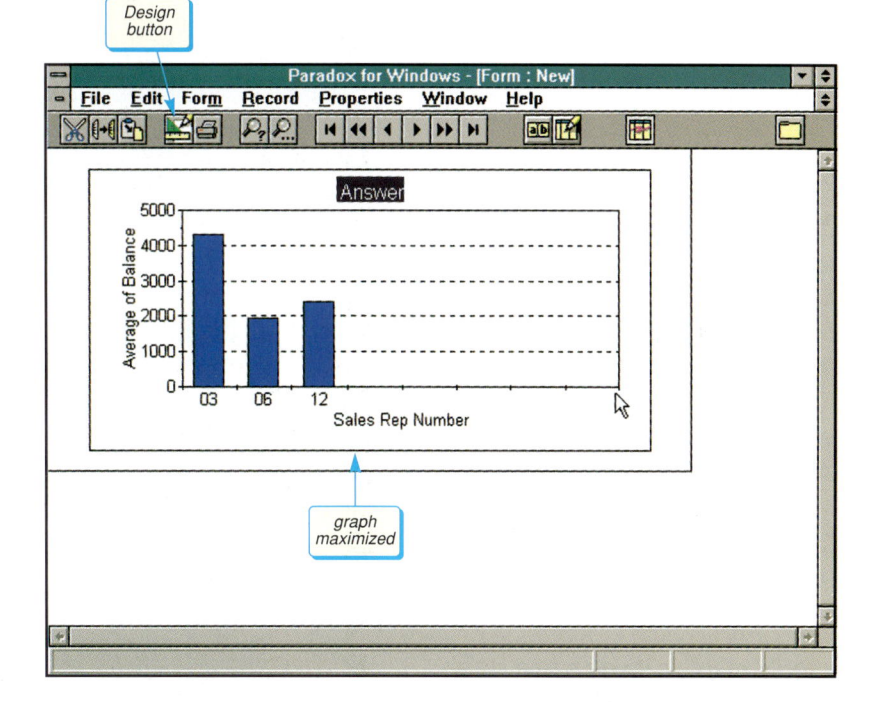

FIGURE 2-76

Changing the Bar Chart

Sometimes one type of graph will present the data more clearly than another. A pie chart, for example, indicates percentages better than a bar chart. Fortunately, changing the type of graph, as well as customizing the graph in a variety of ways, is a simple process in Paradox.

To make changes to the characteristics of a graph, you use a special type of menu called an **Object menu**. Throughout Paradox, many objects you see on the desktop have menus that you can use to change a variety of characteristics. You access these menus by pointing at the object and then pressing and releasing the *right* mouse button.

When you are changing the design of a graph, there are actually a number of different object menus available. The particular menu you will see depends on where you are pointing when you click the right mouse button. If you don't see the menu you expect to see, you were probably not pointing to the correct location. If this happens, remove the menu from the desktop by pointing to any position outside the menu and clicking the left mouse button. Then point to the correct location and click the right mouse button.

The following steps illustrate the process of changing the bar chart to a pie chart (see Figure 2-80).

TO CHANGE THE BAR CHART TO A PIE CHART ▼

STEP 1 ▶

Point to the Design button (🖼) shown in Figure 2-76 on the previous page.

STEP 2 ▶

Click the Design button to change to Form Design mode and then click the right mouse button in the approximate position shown in Figure 2-77. You need to be somewhere between the box that contains just the graph (the bars) and the box surrounding the graph, the title, and the labels for the axes.

The menu shown in Figure 2-77 should display. If you see a different menu, move the mouse pointer to a position outside the menu and click the left mouse button to remove the menu. Then move the mouse pointer to a slightly different position and click the right mouse button again.

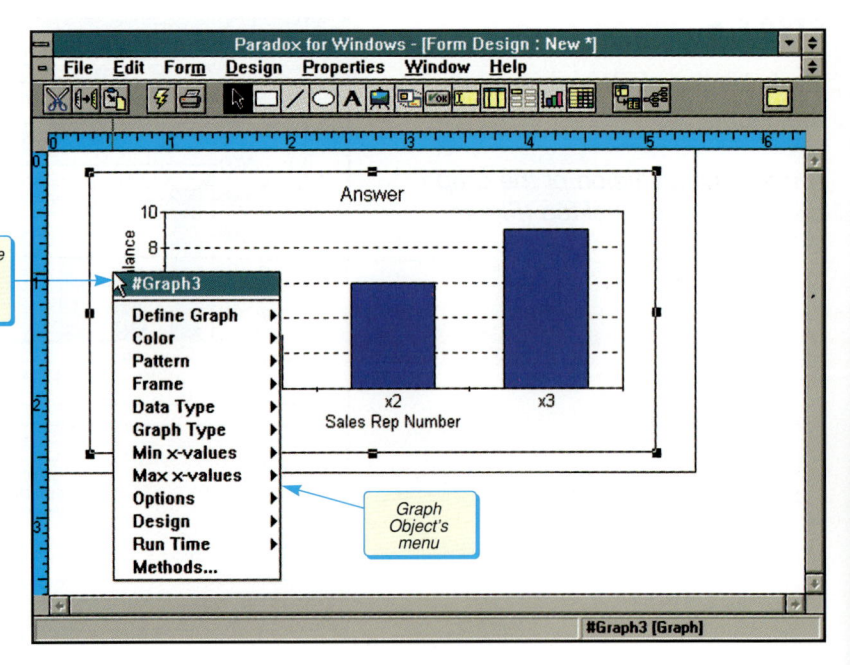

FIGURE 2-77

GRAPHING THE ANSWER TO A QUERY **P99**

STEP 3 ▶

Choose the Graph Type command and then point to 2D Pie (Figure 2-78).

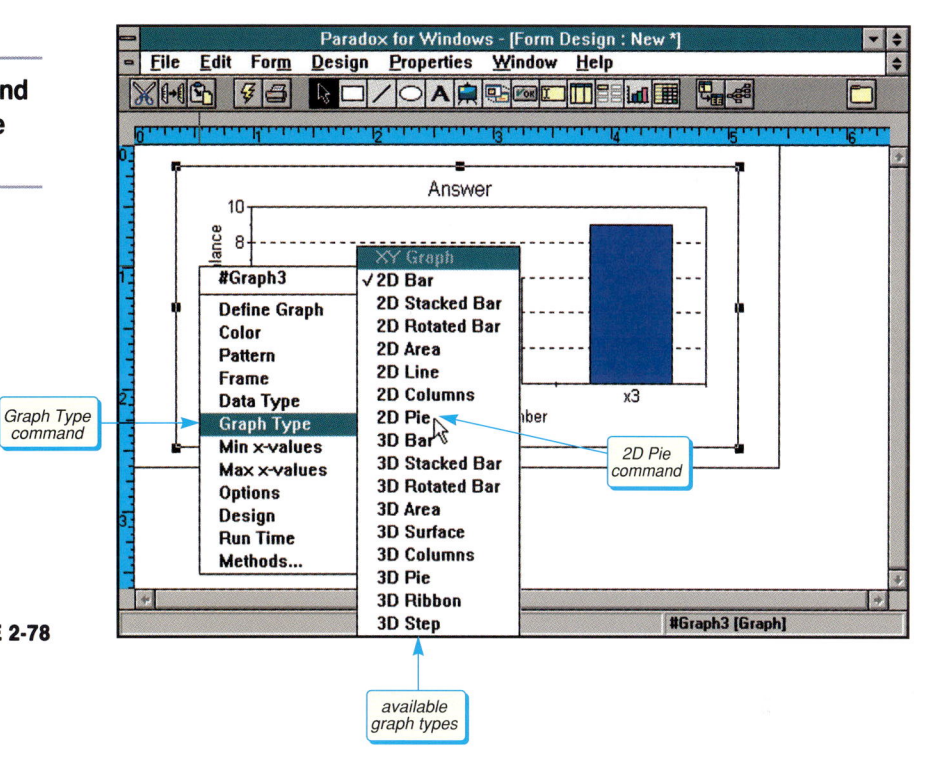

FIGURE 2-78

STEP 4 ▶

Choose the 2D Pie command.

A 2D pie graph example displays on the desktop (Figure 2-79). This illustration shows how a 2D pie graph generally looks but does not represent the actual data.

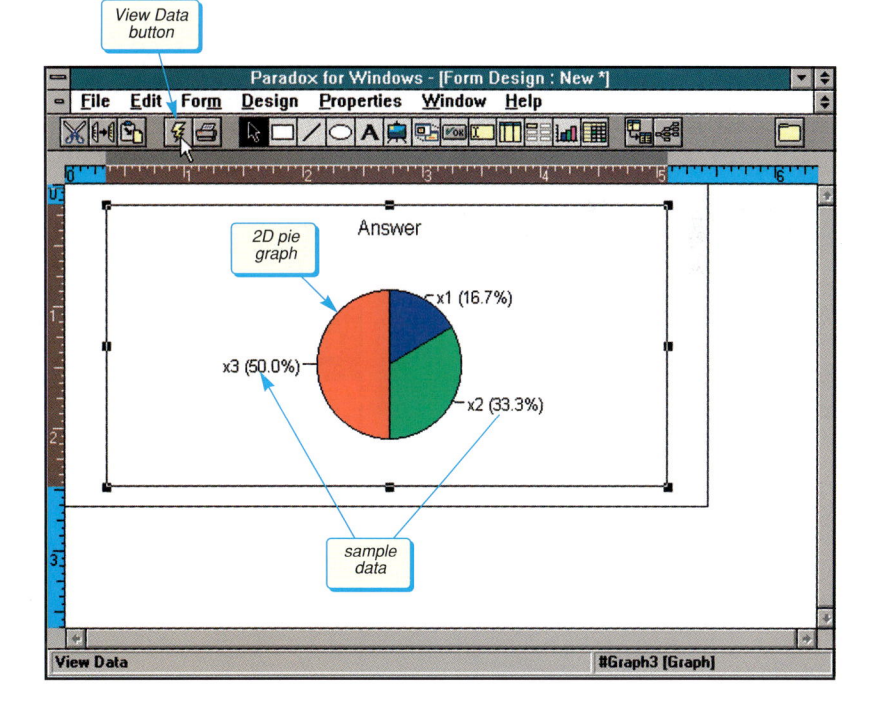

FIGURE 2-79

P100   PROJECT 2   QUERYING A DATABASE

STEP 5 ▶

Point to the View Data button on the SpeedBar (Figure 2-79).

STEP 6 ▶

Click the View Data button.

A 2D pie chart incorporating the data from the query displays on the desktop (Figure 2-80).

FIGURE 2-80

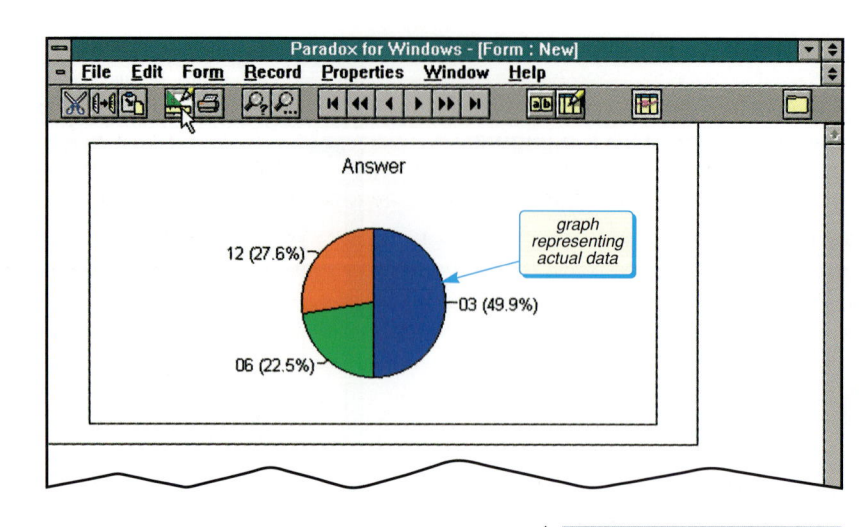

If you want to make any additional changes to the design of the graph, you can click the Design button. It is located at the same position on the SpeedBar on this screen as the View Data button on the design screen. This makes it easy to transfer back and forth between designing the graph and viewing data.

Closing the Graph Window

To remove a graph from the desktop, you need to close it. To close the graph, use the Close command on the Control menu. You will then be asked whether or not you want to save your work.

The following steps close the graph without saving it.

TO CLOSE A GRAPH WITHOUT SAVING IT ▼

STEP 1 ▶

Select the Control menu and point to Close (Figure 2-81).

STEP 2 ▶

Choose the Close command and then point to No.

A dialog box displays asking if you wish to save your work. The mouse pointer is pointing to the No button.

STEP 3 ▶

Choose the No button.

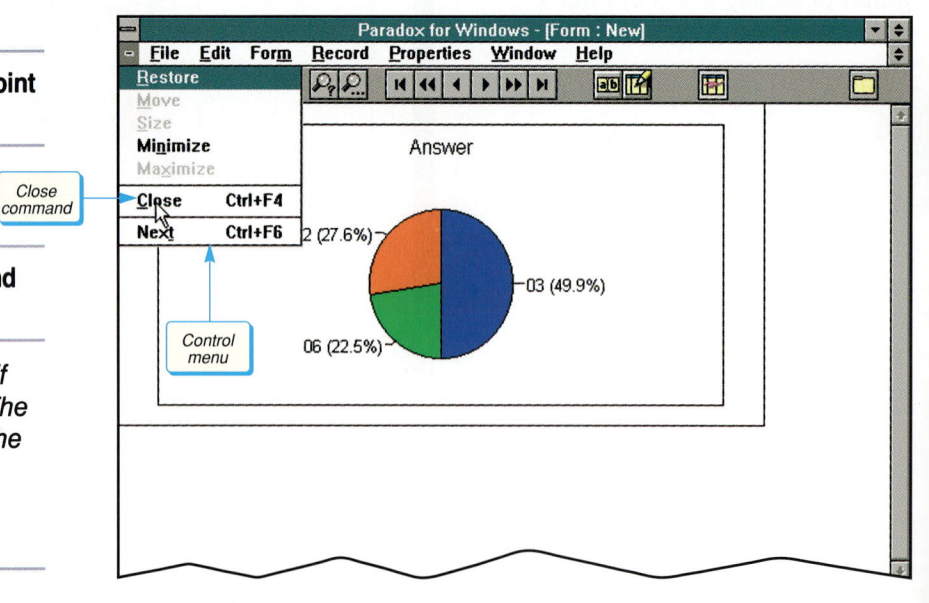

FIGURE 2-81

▶ Saving a Query

In the previous query examples in this project, you did not save the results of the queries. However, In some cases you will construct a query that you might want to use again. Avoid having to repeat all your entries by saving the query. To save the query, close the query as you did before. This time, however, indicate that you want to save your work. Then assign a name to the query. The following steps illustrate the process by saving the query currently on the desktop and calling it SLSAVG.

TO SAVE A QUERY ▼

STEP 1 ▶

Select the Control menu and point to the Close command (Figure 2-82).

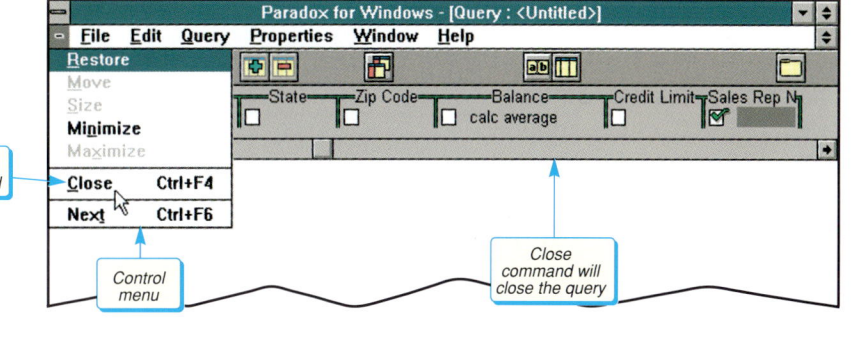

FIGURE 2-82

STEP 2 ▶

Choose the Close command, and then point to the Yes button (☑Yes).

The Paradox for Windows dialog box displays. The mouse pointer is pointing to the Yes button (Figure 2-83).

STEP 3 ▶

Choose the Yes button, type `slsavg`, and choose the OK button.

Paradox saves the query and removes it from the desktop.

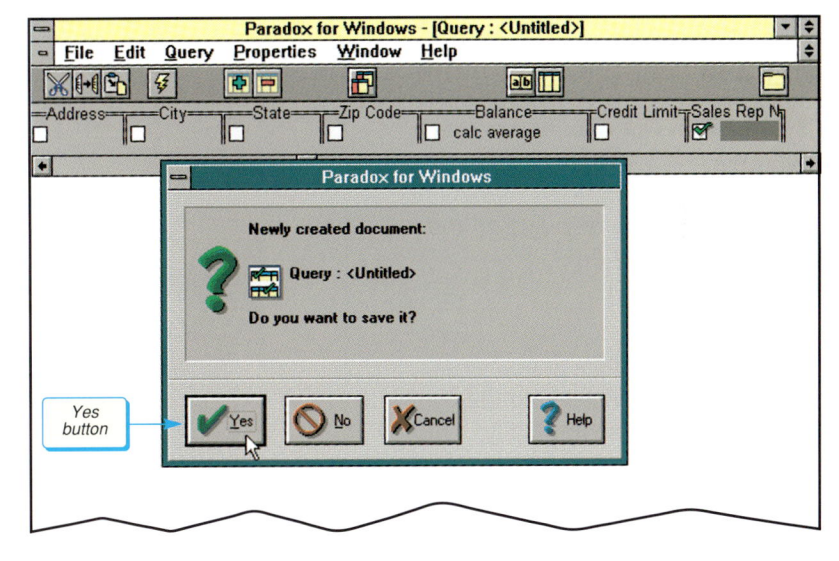

FIGURE 2-83

Using a Query

Once you have saved a query, you can use it at any time in the future by *opening* it, which brings the completed query image back to the desktop. You can then *run* it by clicking the Run Query button on the SpeedBar. You will then see the new Answer table.

TO USE A SAVED QUERY

STEP 1 ▶

Point to the Open Query button (📋) on the SpeedBar (Figure 2-84).

FIGURE 2-84

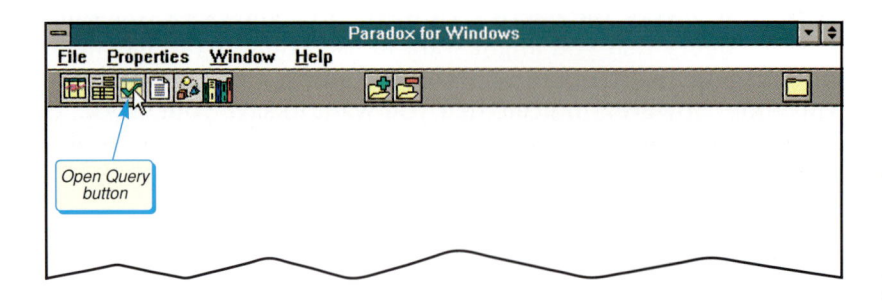

STEP 2 ▶

Click the Open Query button, select SLSAVG, choose the OK button, and maximize the window.

The Query image SLSAVG displays (Figure 2-85).

FIGURE 2-85

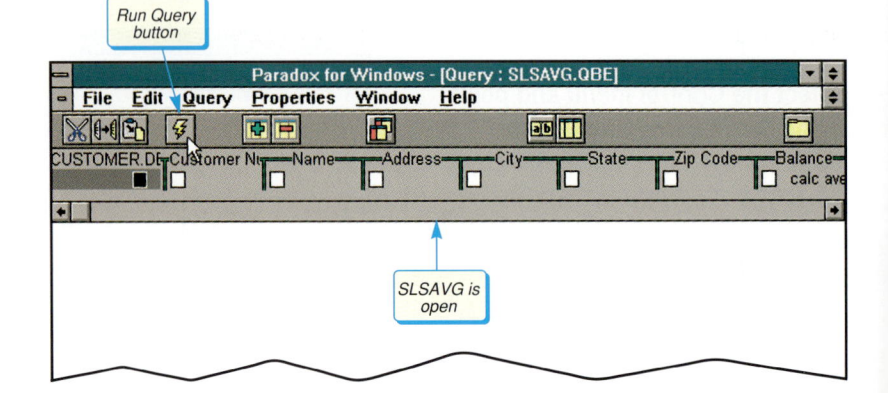

STEP 4 ▶

Click the Run Query button on the SpeedBar.

The Answer table displays on the desktop (Figure 2-86).

STEP 5 ▶

When you are finished with the Answer table, close it. Finally, close the Query image.

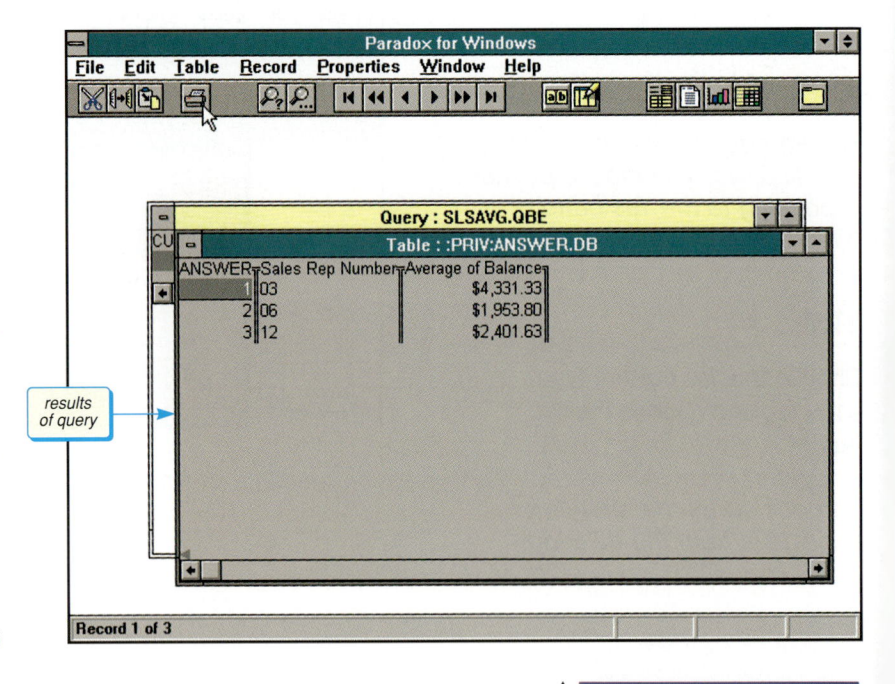

FIGURE 2-86

▶ PROJECT SUMMARY

Project 2 introduced you to querying a database using Paradox for Windows. You learned how to create and run queries. You used various types of conditions. You also learned how to join tables using queries. You used calculated fields and statistics, and you learned how to graph the answer to a query.

▶ Key Terms

Add Table button (*882*)
AND condition (*P78*)
Answer (*P60*)
Answer table (*P60*)
Answer Table command (*P84*)
check box (*P62*)
check descending (*P83*)
check mark (*P62*)
Check menu (*P63*)
check plus (*P82*)
Close command (*P100*)
comparison operator (*P77*)
compound condition (*P78*)
computed field (*P92*)

conditions (*P62*)
Design button (*P98*)
example (*P87*)
field check box (*P62*)
Graph Type command (*P99*)
grouping (*P95*)
join (*P86*)
major key (*P81*)
minor key (*P81*)
New command (*P61*)
Object's menu (*P98*)
OR condition (*P78*)
Properties menu (*P82*)

query (*P59*)
Query command (*P61*)
Query image (*P62*)
Query window (*P61*)
Quick Graph button (*P96*)
run the query (*P59*)
Run Query button (*P64*)
sort (*P81*)
Sort command (*P84*)
sort key (*P81*)
table check box (*P73*)
View Data button (*P100*)
wildcards (*P72*)

QUICK REFERENCE

In Paradox for Windows you can accomplish a task in a number of different ways. The following table provides a quick reference to each task presented in this project with its available options. The commands listed in the Menu field can be executed using either the keyboard or the mouse.

Task	Mouse	Menu	Keyboard Shortcuts
Add a Table to a Query	Click Add Table button on Speedbar	From Query menu, choose Add Table	
Clear a Query Image			Press CTRL + DELETE
Close a Query	Double-click Control-menu box	From Control menu, choose Close. Choose Yes to save query or No not to save query	
Close the Answer Table	Double-click Control-menu box	From Control menu, choose Close	
Create a New Query		From File menu, choose New, then choose Query	
Create an AND Condition			Place conditions on same line
Create an Example			Press F5
Create an OR Condition			Enter condition, press DOWN ARROW, and enter second condition
Enter a Condition	Click field for the condition, type condition		Press TAB or SHIFT + TAB to move to condition, type condition
Graph the Answer to a Query	Click Graph button on Speedbar	From Table menu, choose Quick Graph	
Include Duplicates	Click and hold check box for field, choose check plus		Press SHIFT + F6 with highlight under name of field
Join Tables			Place same example in matching fields

(continued)

QUICK REFERENCE (continued)

Task	Mouse	Menu	Keyboard Shortcuts
Move the Highlight to a Field in a Query Image	Click field		Press TAB and SHIFT + TAB
Print the Answer to a Query	Click Print button on Speedbar	From File menu, choose Print	
Place Check Marks in All Fields	Click check box under name of table		Press F6 with highlight under name of table
Place Check Mark in a Field	Click check box for field		Press F6 with highlight under name of field
Run a Query	Click Run Query button on Speedbar	From Query menu, choose Run	Press F8
Sort Data by Sorting the Answer Table		From Properties menu, choose Answer Table, then choose Sort	
Sort Data Using Check Marks and Excluding Duplicates	Click check box for field		Press F6 with highlight under name of field
Sort Data Using Check Marks in Descending Order	Click and hold check box for field, choose check descending		Press SHIFT + F6 with highlight under name of field until check descending is highlighted

S T U D E N T   A S S I G N M E N T S

STUDENT ASSIGNMENT 1
True/False

Instructions: Circle T if the statement is true or F if the statement is false.

T F 1. To include all the fields in a record in a query, place a check mark in the check box under the table name.
T F 2. To list only certain records in a table, use a query.
T F 3. To create a query in Paradox, open the table before selecting the query option.
T F 4. The answer to a query is placed in a special table called Answer.
T F 5. Press the TAB key to move the highlight to the next field in a query image.
T F 6. To run a query, click the Run Query button on the Toolbar.
T F 7. To clear all the entries in a query press the CTRL + Y keys.
T F 8. To indicate a field is to be included in a query, place a check mark in the check box under the field.
T F 9. In making comparisons, Paradox will consider the words Nelson and nelson equal even though a capital letter N is used in the first word.
T F 10. The wildcard symbols available for use in a query are .. and &.
T F 11. To create a condition involving equals, type the equals sign (=).
T F 12. To create a compound condition using AND, enter all conditions on the same line.
T F 13. To create a compound condition using OR, type the word OR before the second condition.
T F 14. To sort the records in the answer to a query, run the query and then use the Properties menu to specify the sort keys.

T F 15. To enter an example rather than an actual value in a field, press the F5 key before typing the entry.
T F 16. To join two or more tables, use a query.
T F 17. Press the F4 key to move from one Query image to the next.
T F 18. To obtain the average of the values in the Credit Limit field, type AVERAGE in the Credit Limit field of the Query image and run the query.
T F 19. To group all records that have like values in the same field, place a check mark in the field to be used for grouping and enter the word GROUP.
T F 20. To graph the answer to a query, be sure the Answer table is on the desktop and then click the Quick Graph button.

STUDENT ASSIGNMENT 2
Multiple Choice

Instructions: Circle the correct response.

1. To list only certain records in a table, use a _____.
   a. list
   b. query
   c. question
   d. answer
2. The answer to a query is placed in a special table called the _____ table.
   a. Query
   b. Solution
   c. Answer
   d. Result
3. To clear all the entries in a query, press _____.
   a. CTRL + D
   b. CTRL + DELETE
   c. CTRL + Y
   d. SHIFT + DELETE
4. The wildcard symbols available for use in a query are the _____ and the _____.
   a. double period (..), asterisk (*)
   b. question mark (?), ampersand (&)
   c. double period (..), at symbol (@)
   d. question mark (?), asterisk (*)
5. Equal to (=), Less than (<), and Greater than (>) are examples of _____.
   a. conditions
   b. comparison operators
   c. values
   d. compound conditions
6. When two or more conditions are connected with AND or OR, the result is called a _____.
   a. compound condition
   b. simple condition
   c. character condition
   d. pattern condition
7. To enter an example rather than a condition in a field, press _____ before typing the entry.
   a. F2
   b. F3
   c. F4
   d. F5

(continued)

P106   PROJECT 2   QUERYING A DATABASE

STUDENT ASSIGNMENT 2 (continued)

8. Use a query to _____ tables, that is, find records in two tables that have identical values in matching fields.
   a. merge
   b. match
   c. join
   d. combine
9. Press _____ to move from one Query image to the next.
   a. F2
   b. F3
   c. F4
   d. F5
10. To calculate the total of all balances in the Customer table, enter _____ in the Balance field of the Query image.
    a. sum
    b. sum all
    c. calc sum
    d. stat sum

STUDENT ASSIGNMENT 3
Understanding Query Images

Instructions: In Figure SA2-3, arrows point to the major components of the Paradox Query screen. Identify the parts of the Query screen in the space provided. Answer the following questions about the screen.

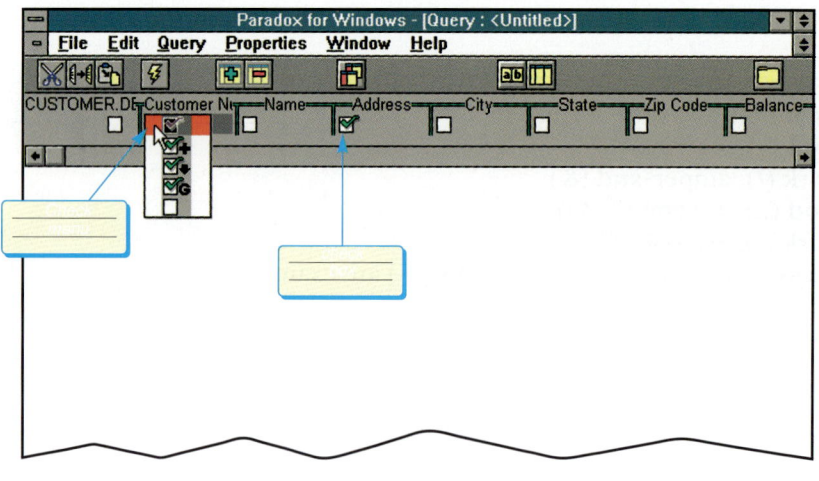

FIGURE SA2-3

1. What does the check mark mean in the Address field?
   _____
   _____

2. What does the check plus option do?
   _____

STUDENT ASSIGNMENT 4
Understanding Compound Conditions

Instructions: Figure SA2-4a shows a created query for the Customer table using a compound condition, and Figure SA2-4b lists the contents of the Customer table. In the space provided list the answer to this query.

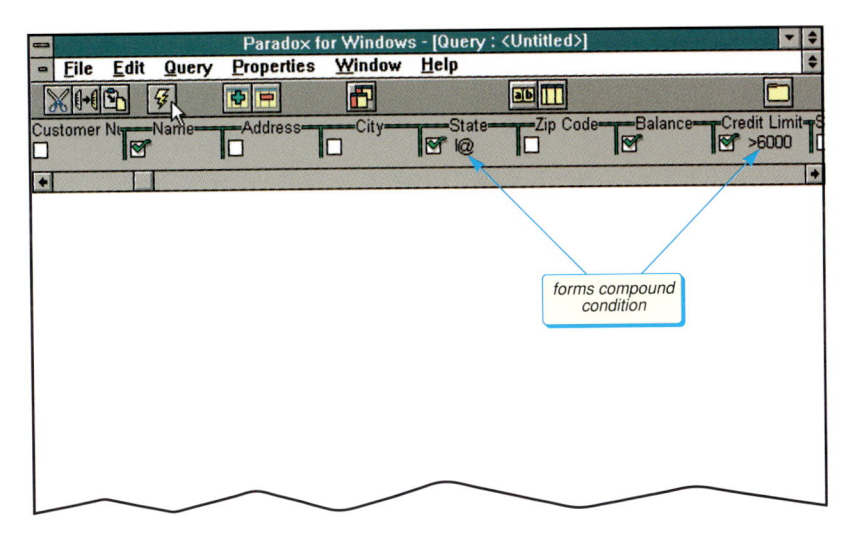

FIGURE SA2-4a

Customer Number	Name	Address	City	State	Zip Code	Balance	Credit Limit	Sales Rep Number
AC12	Arend Corp.	21 Wilson	Muncie	IN	47303	$4,278.50	$6,000.00	03
AI53	Allied Industry	215 Raymond	Carmel	IN	46032	$203.00	$3,000.00	06
AX29	AAA Express	108 College	Muncie	IN	47303	$42.00	$3,000.00	06
CL67	Clark-White Ltd.	47 Chipwood	Moline	IL	61265	$42.00	$8,000.00	12
FC15	Ferguson Co.	602 Bridge	Mason	MI	48854	$3,206.00	$6,000.00	03
FY24	Farley-Young	19 Oak	Muncie	IN	47303	$6,704.00	$6,000.00	06
LW46	L. T. Wheeler	587 Rivard	Moline	IL	61625	$2,504.00	$6,000.00	06
NI34	Nelson, Inc.	12 Bishop	Sumne	IL	62466	$0.00	$6,000.00	03
SH84	Shippers and Dale	208 Grayton	Carmel	IN	46032	$1597.25	$8,000.00	12
SI84	Shelton, Inc.	82 Harcourt	Niles	MI	49120	$7,020.00	$8,000.00	06

FIGURE SA2-4b

P108 PROJECT 2 QUERYING A DATABASE

STUDENT ASSIGNMENT 5
Understanding Sorting Data in a Query

Instructions: Figure SA2-5 shows a query created to sort data in a particular order. In the space provided, list the answer to this query. Refer to Figure SA2-4b for the contents of the Customer table.

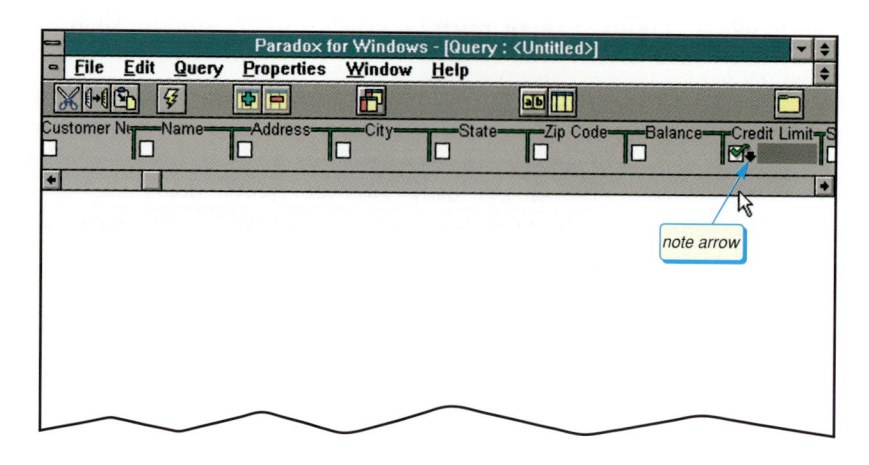

FIGURE SA2-5

STUDENT ASSIGNMENT 6
Understanding Statistics in Queries

Instructions: Figure SA2-6 shows a query created to calculate statistics. In the space provided, list the answer to this query. Refer to Figure SA2-4b for the contents of the Customer table.

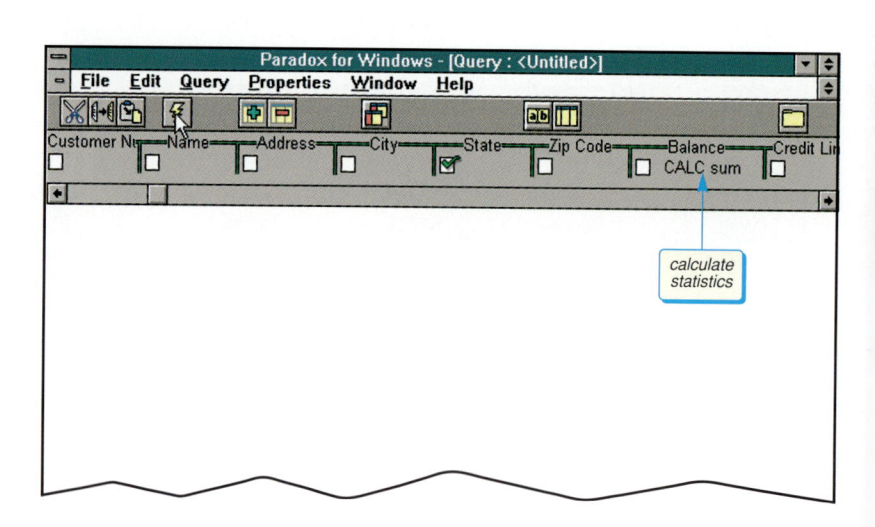

FIGURE SA2-6

COMPUTER LABORATORY EXERCISES

COMPUTER LABORATORY EXERCISE 1
Using the Help Menu

Instructions: Perform the following tasks.

1. Start Paradox.
2. Choose the Contents command from the Help menu.
3. Select Search.
4. Type queries in the Search dialog box, and then select the topic Function key actions in queries, from the list.
5. Read the information and answer the following two questions.
6. What does the F8 function key do?

_____

7. What does the SHIFT + F6 key combination do?

_____

8. Exit the Help window.
9. Exit Paradox.

COMPUTER LABORATORY EXERCISE 2
Sorting and Printing the Answer Table

Instructions: Perform the following tasks.

1. Start Paradox.
2. Create a new query and open the Customer table.
3. On the Query screen, place check marks in the Customer Number, Name, City, and Credit Limit fields.
4. Select the Properties menu, then choose the Answer Table and Sort commands.
5. Sort the data by state within credit limit.
6. Click Run query button.
7. Print the Answer table.
8. Close the Answer table and the query.
9. Exit Paradox.

COMPUTER LABORATORY EXERCISE 3
Performing Calculations in Queries

Instructions: The average balance for all customers is $2,756.63. Determine the difference between the actual balance and the average balance for each customer. Perform the following tasks.

1. Start Paradox.
2. Create a new query and open the Customer table.
3. Place check marks in the Customer Number, Name, and Balance fields.
4. Enter the example 5000 in the Balance field.
5. Move to the State field and enter the formula to calculate the difference between the actual balance and the average balance. (Hint: Enter 5000 as an example and 2756.63 as an actual value.)
6. Click Run query button.
7. Print the Answer table.
8. Close the Answer table and the query.
9. Exit Paradox

COMPUTER LABORATORY ASSIGNMENTS

COMPUTER LABORATORY ASSIGNMENT 1
Querying the Parts Database

Purpose: To provide practice in creating and using queries.

Problem: Query the Parts database in a variety of ways.

Instructions: Use the database created in Computer Laboratory Assignment 1 of Project 1 for this assignment. Execute each task on the computer and print the answer.

1. Create a new query and open the Parts table.
2. Display all the records in the table.
3. Display the Part Number, Part Description, and Price for all records in the table.
4. Display the records for all parts that are classified as Sporting Goods.
5. Display the records for all parts where the part description begins with the letter B.
6. Display the records for all parts that sound like Cornpupper.
7. Display the records for all parts that have a price greater than 29.95.
8. Display the records for all parts that are classified as Sporting Goods and have a price greater than 29.95.
9. Display the records for all parts that are classified as Housewares or have a price less than 24.95.
10. Display the average price of all parts.
11. Display the average price for each item class.
12. Graph the Answer table created in task 11.
13. Join the Parts table and the Item Class table and display the Part Description, Units On Hand, Item Class Description, and Price for all records.
14. Sort the Answer table created in task 13 in ascending order by part description within item class description.
15. Restrict the records retrieved in task 13 to only those parts located in warehouse 3.
16. Calculate and display the on-hand value (units on hand * price) for all records in the database.
17. Close the Answer table, close the query without saving, and exit Paradox.

COMPUTER LABORATORY ASSIGNMENT 2
Querying the Employee Database

Purpose: To provide practice in creating and using queries.

Problem: Query the Employee database in a variety of ways.

Instructions: Use the database created in Computer Laboratory Assignment 2 of Project 1 for this assignment. Execute the tasks on the computer and print the answer.

1. Create a new query and open the Employee table.
2. Display all the records in the table.
3. Display the Employee Number, Employee Last Name, Employee First Name, and Pay Rate for all the records in the table.
4. Display the records for all employees who work in the department with a code 01.
5. Display the records for all employees whose last names start with the letter E.
6. Display the records for all employees whose last names sound like Benter.
7. Display the records for all employees who have a pay rate less than $8.00.

8. Display the records for all employees who work in the department with a code 03 and have a pay rate less than $8.00.
9. Display the records for all employees who work in department code 01 or who have a pay rate less $8.00.
10. Display the pay rates for all employees in ascending order.
11. Determine the highest pay rate.
12. Determine the lowest pay rate.
13. Display the average pay rate for each department.
14. Create a graph from the Answer table you created in task 13.
15. Join the Employee table and the Department table and display Employee Number, Employee Last Name, Employee First Name, Pay Rate, and Department Name.
16. Sort the Answer table created in task 11 in ascending order by employee last name within department name.
17. Display the Employee Number, Employee Last Name, Employee First Name, Department Name, and Pay Rate for all employees who have a pay rate greater than $9.00.
18. Close the Answer table, close the query without saving, and exit Paradox.

COMPUTER LABORATORY ASSIGNMENT 3
Querying the Movie Database

Purpose: To provide practice in creating and using queries.

Problem: Query the Movie database in a variety of ways.

Instructions: Use the database created in Computer Laboratory Assignment 3 of Project 1 for this assignment. Execute the tasks on the computer and print the answer.

1. Create a new query and open the Movie table.
2. Display all the records in the table.
3. Display the Movie Title, Year Made, and Movie Type for all the records in the table.
4. Display the Movie Number, Movie Title, Year Made, and Length for all movies with a Movie Type of COMEDY.
5. Display all the records for movies made after 1969.
6. Display all the records for movies with a Movie Type of SUSPEN and length greater than 100.
7. Display all the records for movies that have a movie title that begins with Th.
8. Display all the records for movies made before 1950 or longer than 100 minutes.
9. Display all the records for movies that are longer than 100 minutes and are either SUSPEN or HORROR movie types.
10. Sum the lengths of all movies.
11. Count the number of movies each director has made.
12. Display the average movie length for each director.
13. Graph the Answer table created in task 12.
14. Join the Movie table and the Director table and display the Movie Number, Movie Title, Movie Type, and Director Name for all records.
15. Sort the Answer table created in task 14 in ascending order by movie title within director name.
16. Restrict the records retrieved in task 14 to only movies made after 1970 with a length longer than 100 minutes.
17. Display the Movie Title, Movie Type, Director Name, and the difference between the actual movie length and 100 minutes.
18. Close the Answer table, close the query without saving, and exit Paradox.

COMPUTER LABORATORY ASSIGNMENT 4
Querying the Book Database

Purpose: To provide practice in structuring, creating, and using queries.

Problem: You are the office manager for a local bookstore. The bookstore owner is gathering some facts to assist her in making plans for the next three months. She has sent you a memo outlining the type of information she needs. You must supply her with the correct information.

Instructions: Use the database created in Computer Laboratory Assignment 4 of Project 1 for this assignment. Provide the following:

1. An inventory list sorted by author within publisher name.
2. The average price of all books and then the average price for each publisher.
3. The price of the most expensive and least expensive book in the inventory.
4. A list of which books are currently not in stock.
5. A list of all books that need to be reordered. Books with less than two copies need to be reordered. For reordering purposes, she would like the book title, author, publisher name, and price. She expects to ask for this list on a weekly basis.
6. The on-hand value of each book.
7. A chart showing the average price for each publisher.
8. A list of titles by each different author in the inventory.
9. A count of the number of books grouped by book type.
10. The average price of books by book type.

Paradox 1.0 for Windows

PROJECT THREE

Maintaining a Database

OBJECTIVES You will have mastered the material in this project when you can:

- Add records to a table
- Change the contents of records in a table
- Delete records from a table
- Locate records
- Restructure a table
- Change field characteristics
- Add a field
- Save the changes to the structure
- Update the contents of a single field
- Make the same change to all records
- Specify a required field
- Specify a range
- Specify a default value
- Specify a picture
- Specify legal values
- Specify referential integrity
- Update a table with validity checks
- Delete groups of records
- Make changes to groups of records
- Create single-field and multiple-field secondary indexes
- Use a secondary index

▶ Introduction

After creating and loading a database, you must be able to maintain it. Maintaining the database means modifying the data to keep it up to date, such as adding new records, changing the data for existing records, and deleting records. Updating can include mass updates or mass deletions, that is, updating or deleting many records at the same time.

As the needs of an organization change, the database may need to be restructured. For example, an organization may decide that customers are to be categorized by customer type, requiring the addition of a field for customer type to the Customer table. Characteristics of existing fields may also need to be changed. For example, the Name field might be too short to contain the name of a new customer, so you need to change the field's width in the Customer table structure.

To improve the efficiency of certain types of database processing, you can create **secondary indexes**, which are similar to indexes found in the back of books. Figure 3-1 on the next page summarizes the various types of activities involved in maintaining a database.

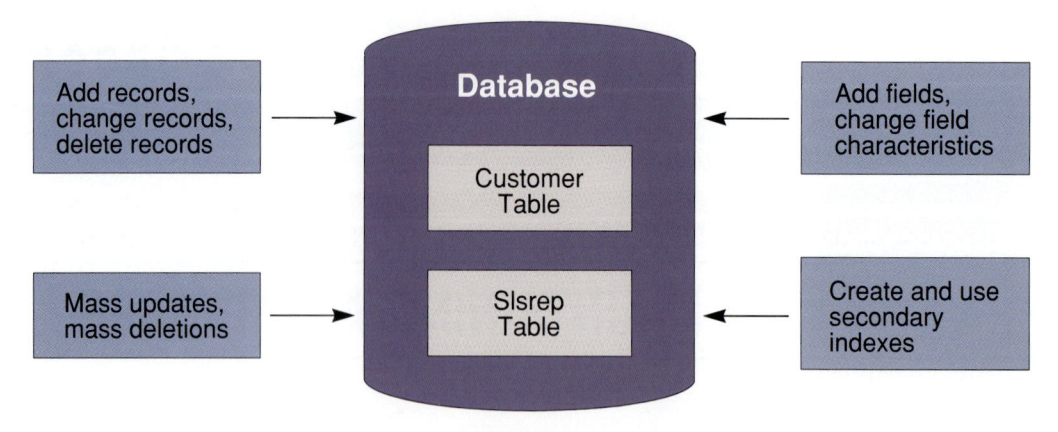

FIGURE 3-1

▶ Adding, Changing, and Deleting Records

Keeping the data in a database up to date requires three tasks: adding new records, changing the data in existing records, and deleting existing records.

Adding Records

In Project 1, you added records to a database using Table view; that is, as you were adding records, the records were displayed on the screen in the form of a table. When adding additional records, you can use the same techniques.

In Project 1, you viewed records using Form view. You can also use Form view to update the data in a table. Form view allows you to add new records, change existing records, or delete records. The same techniques used in Table view are used in Form view in the following steps to add a record to the Customer table.

TO USE A FORM TO ADD A RECORD ▼

STEP 1 ▶

Start Paradox. Open the Customer table and maximize its window. Point to the Quick Form button.

The Customer table is open (Figure 3-2) and the mouse pointer points to the Quick Form button.

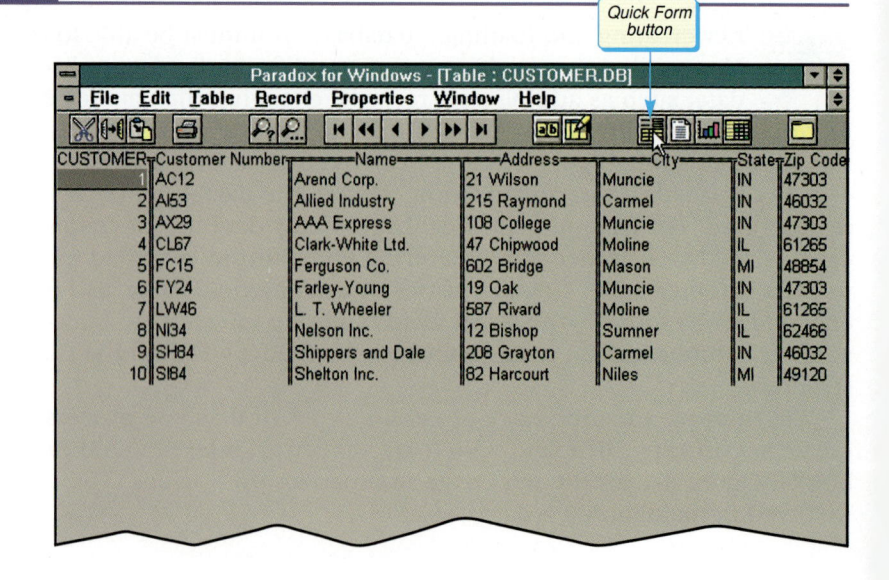

FIGURE 3-2

ADDING, CHANGING, AND DELETING RECORDS P115

STEP 2 ▶

Click the Quick Form button and maximize the form that displays on the screen. Point to the Edit Data button.

The screen contains a maximized version of the quick form (Figure 3-3). The mouse pointer points to the Edit Data button.

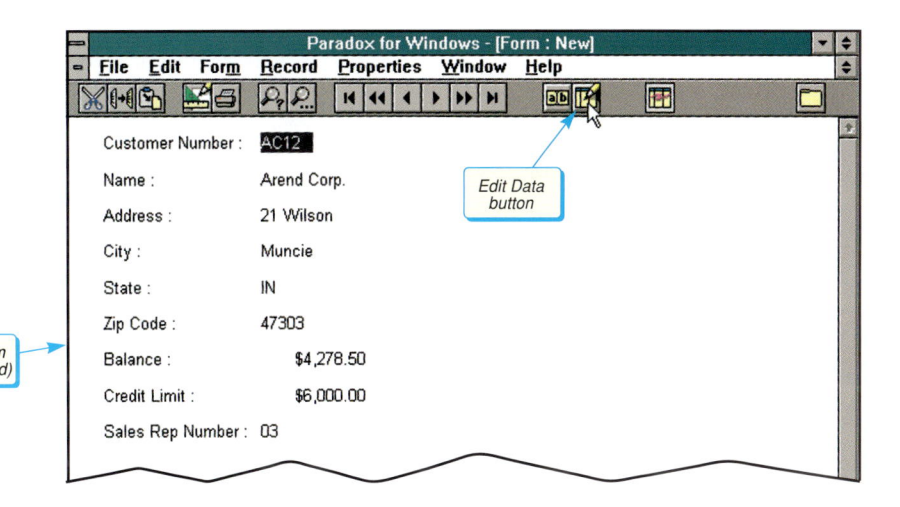

FIGURE 3-3

STEP 3 ▶

Click the Edit button and then point to the Last Record button.

The first record displays on the screen (Figure 3-4). The mouse pointer points to the Last Record button.

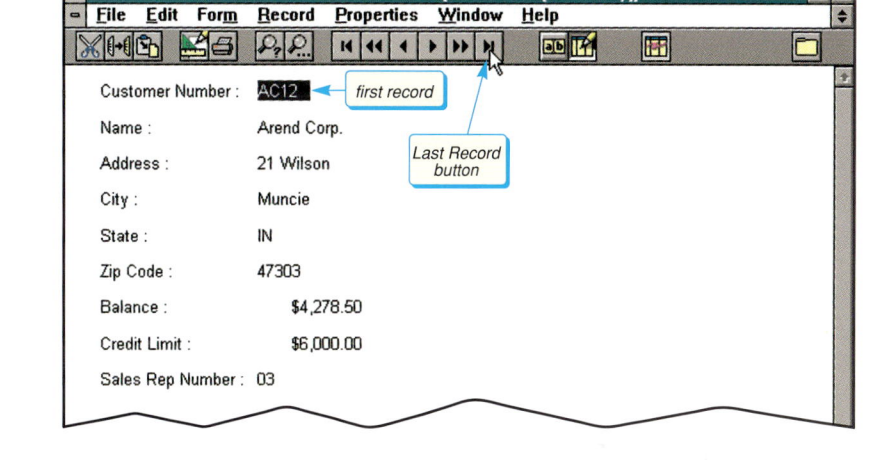

FIGURE 3-4

STEP 4 ▶

Click the Last Record button to move to the last record in the table and then point to the Next Record button.

The last record displays on the screen (Figure 3-5). The mouse pointer points to the Next Record button.

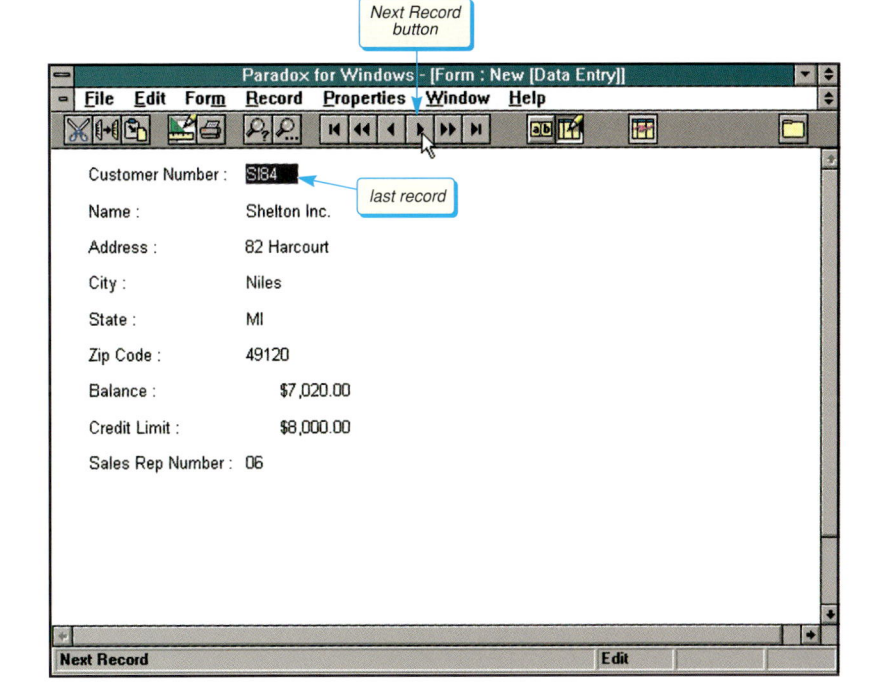

FIGURE 3-5

STEP 5 ▶

Click the Next Record button. Type the data for the new record as shown in Figure 3-6, and press the TAB key after entering each field.

STEP 6 ▶

Click the Next Record button to add the record.

STEP 7

Close the form by selecting the Control menu and then choosing the Close command. When you are asked if you want to save the form, choose No.

The record is now added to the Customer table.

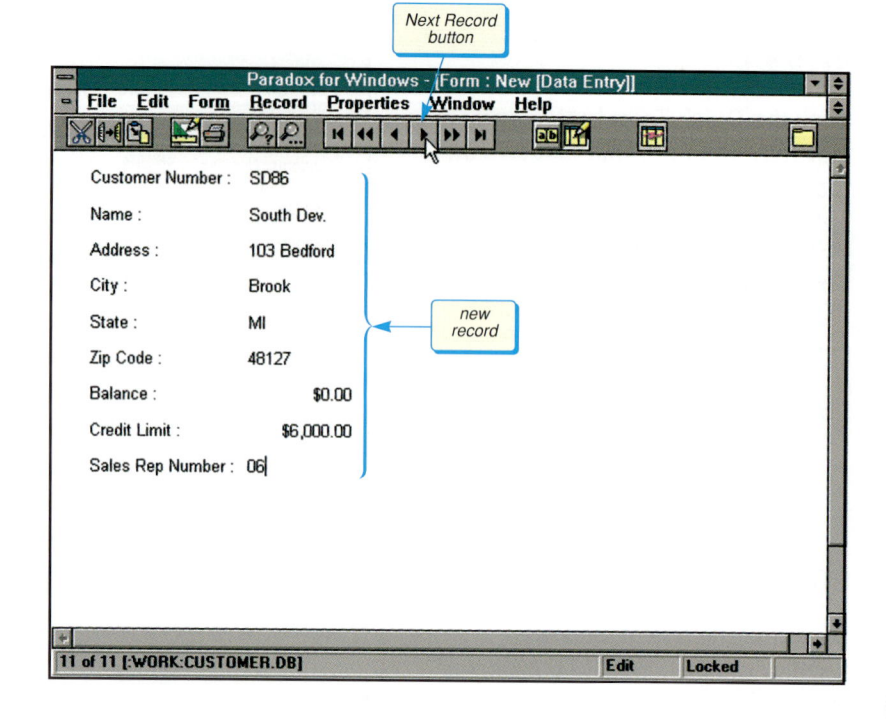

FIGURE 3-6

Originally, there were ten records in the Customer table. Now there are eleven records in the Customer table because of the addition of customer SD86.

Searching for a Record

In the database environment, **searching** means looking for records that satisfy some condition. Looking for all the customers whose sales rep number is 03 is an example of searching. The queries constructed in Project 2 were examples of searching. Paradox had to locate those records that satisfied whatever condition specified.

Searching is also required when using Form view or Table view. To update customer SD86, for example, you first need to find the customer. In a small table, repeatedly pressing the Next Record button until customer SD86 displays on the screen may not be particularly difficult. In a large table with many records, this would be extremely cumbersome. To go directly to a record just by giving the value in a field is the function of the **Locate command**. Use this command by first moving the highlight to the field in which you want to search.

The following steps move the highlight to the Customer Number field and then use the Locate command to find the customer whose number is SD86.

TO LOCATE RECORDS

STEP 1

Make sure the Customer table is open and the quick form for the Customer table is on the screen. Point to the First Record button (▐◀) and click it to make sure you are on the first record. If the Customer Number field is not currently selected (highlighted), select it by pointing to it and clicking the left mouse button.

STEP 2 ▶

Select the Record menu, choose the Locate command, and then point to the Value command in the cascading menu.

The Record menu and the Locate cascading menu display (Figure 3-7). The pointer points to the Value command.

STEP 3 ▶

Choose the Value command, type SD86 in the Value text box of the Locate Value dialog box, and then point to the OK button.

The Locate Value dialog box displays (Figure 3-8). The value, SD86, is entered in the Value text box and the pointer points to the OK button.

STEP 4

Choose the OK button.

Paradox locates the record for customer SD86.

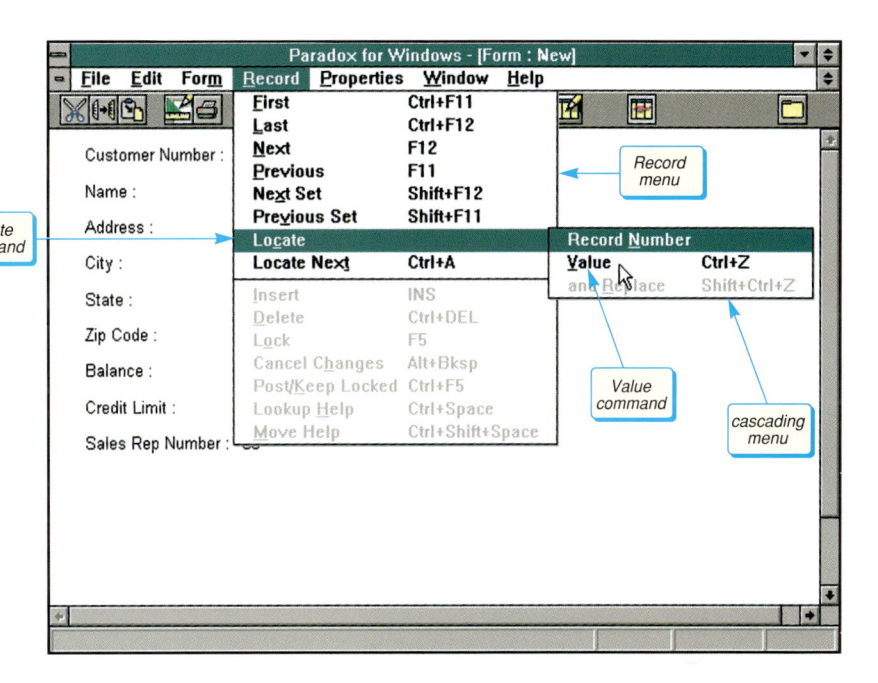

FIGURE 3-7

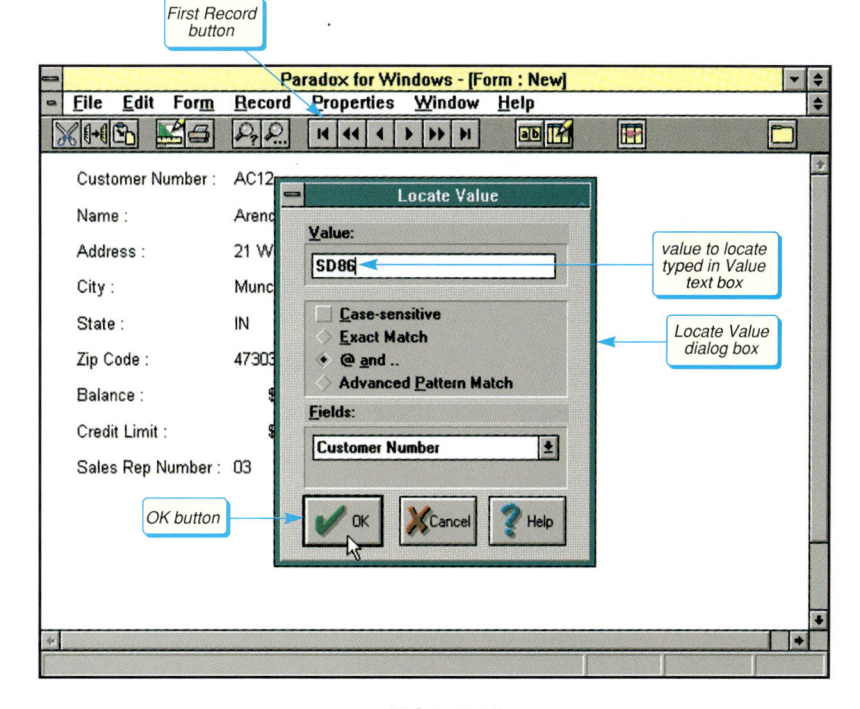

FIGURE 3-8

Sometimes, after locating a record that satisfies a condition, you will want to find the next record that satisfies the same condition. To accomplish this, simply select the Record menu and then choose the Locate Next command (see Figure 3-7).

Changing the Contents of a Record

After locating the record to be changed, move the highlight to the field you want to change by using the TAB key or clicking the field with the mouse. To make the change, you can simply type the new entry. Instead of retyping the entry in its entirety, however, you may prefer making changes to the existing entry. To make changes to an existing entry, first transfer to Field view by clicking the Field View button (▣).

Use Field view within either Table view or Form view. The steps are exactly the same. In Field view, you use the arrow keys to move within the field. When in Field view, you can also insert and delete individual characters. The following steps use Field view to change the name of customer SD86 from South Dev. to Southern Dev.

TO USE FIELD VIEW TO UPDATE THE CONTENTS OF A FIELD ▼

STEP 1 ▶

Make sure the quick form is on the screen and the record currently displayed is the record for customer SD86. Point to the field to be changed (the Name field) and select it by clicking the left mouse button. Point to the Edit Data button on the SpeedBar.

The field is selected (Figure 3-9). The mouse pointer points to the Edit Data button.

FIGURE 3-9

STEP 2 ▶

Click the Edit Data button to change to Edit mode and then point to the Field View button.

The mode is changed to Edit (Figure 3-10). The mouse pointer points to the Field View button.

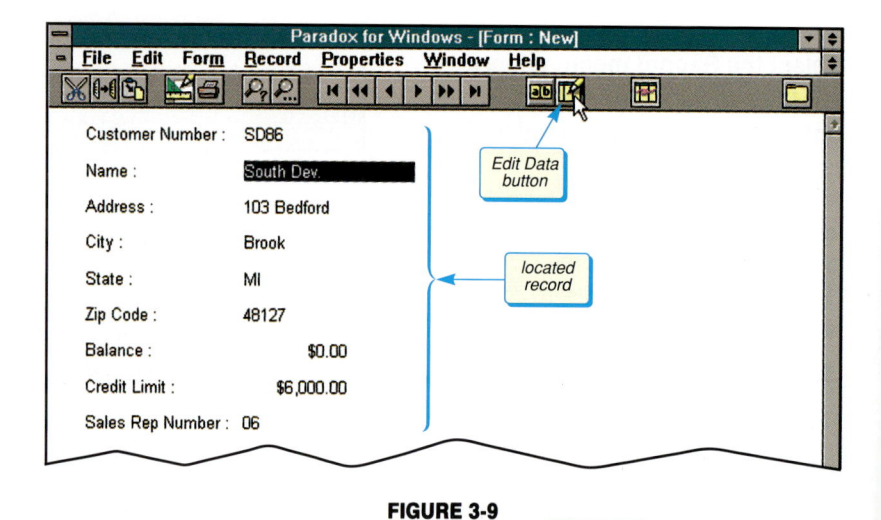

FIGURE 3-10

STEP 3 ▶

Click the Field View button.

An insertion point appears at the end of the current contents of the field (Figure 3-11).

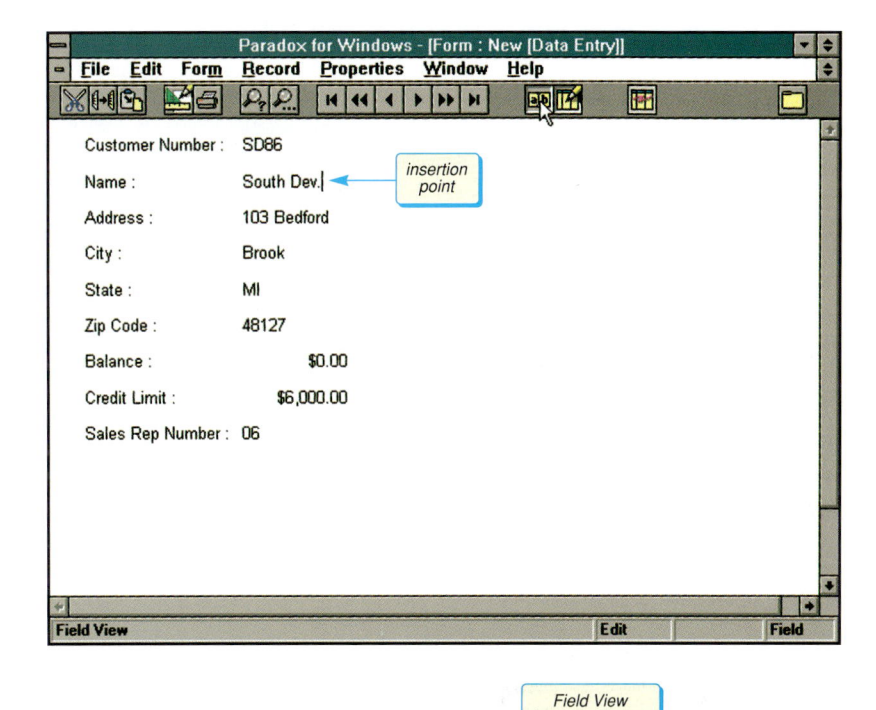

FIGURE 3-11

STEP 4 ▶

Press the LEFT ARROW key five times to move the insertion point immediately after the h in South, and then type ern. Press the TAB key to complete the entry.

The address is changed (Figure 3-12).

STEP 5

Select the Control menu and choose the Close command. When you are asked if you want to save the form, choose No.

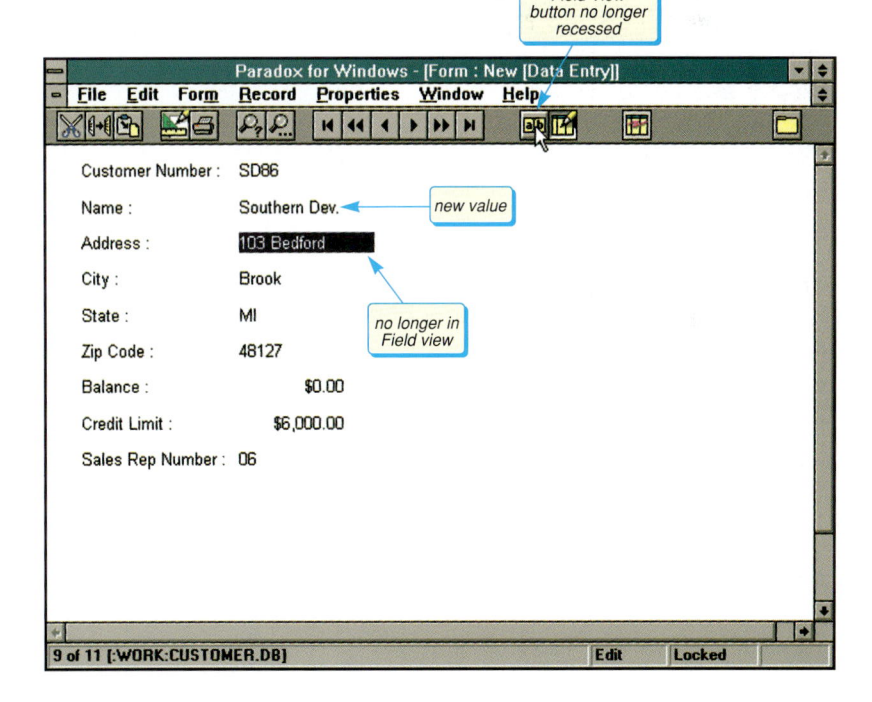

FIGURE 3-12

Deleting Records

When records are no longer needed, you should delete them from the table. If customer AI53 no longer does business with the organization, the customer record should be deleted. To delete a record, first locate it and then press CTRL + DELETE. The following steps delete Customer AI53.

TO DELETE A RECORD

STEP 1 ▶

Make sure the Customer table is open and the window containing the table is maximized. Locate the record for customer AI53. Be sure you are in Edit mode. If not, click the Edit Data button to transfer to Edit mode.

The Customer table is open (Figure 3-13). The mode is Edit and the highlight is on record 2.

FIGURE 3-13

STEP 2 ▶

Press CTRL + DELETE to delete the record.

The record is deleted (Figure 3-14).

STEP 3 ▶

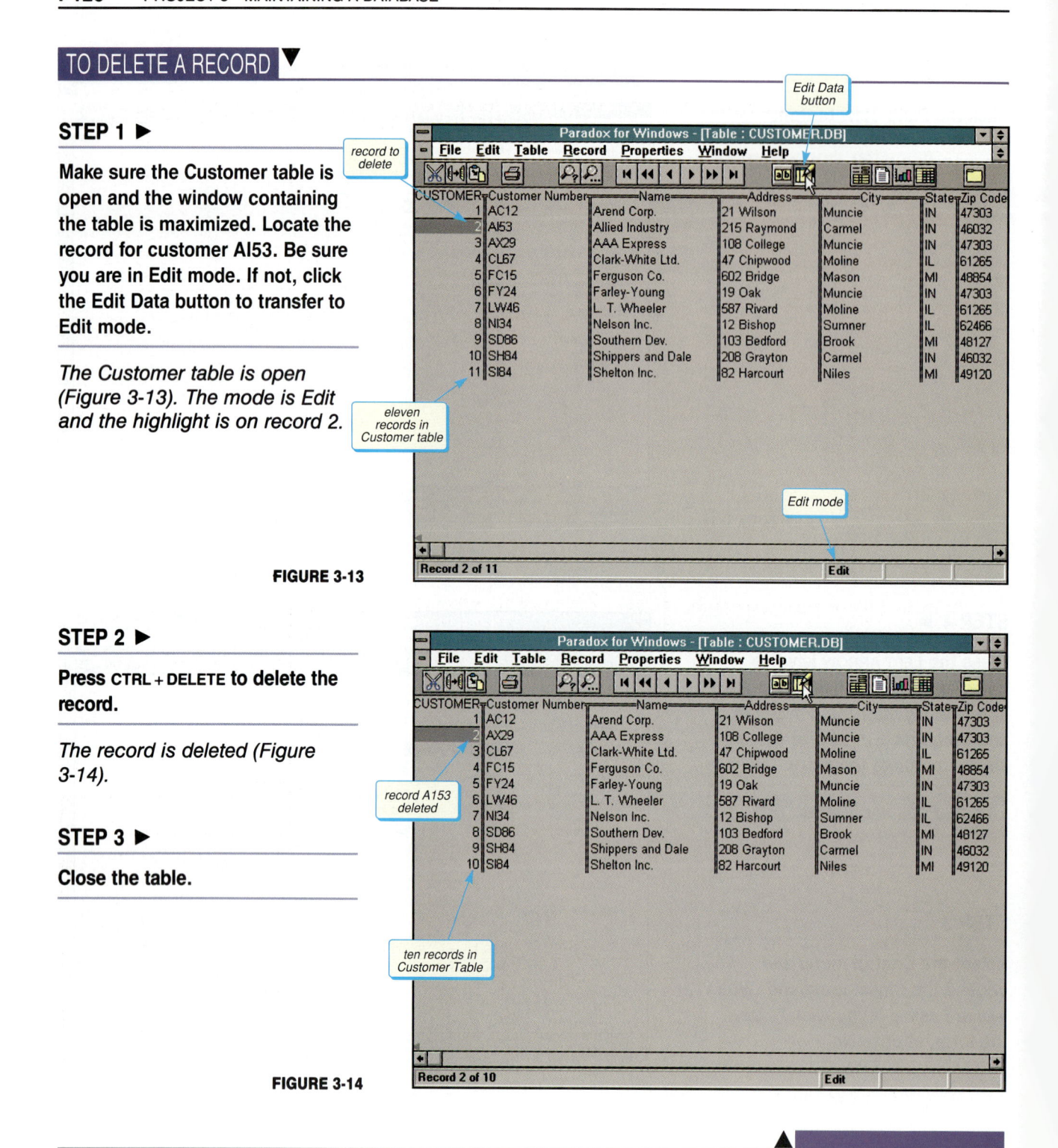

Close the table.

FIGURE 3-14

There are ten records in the Customer table because customer AI53 was deleted.

Changing the Structure

When you initially create a database, you define its **structure**; that is, you indicate the names, types, and widths of all the fields. If the structure you first defined would continue to be appropriate as long as you use the database, there would be no reason to restructure it. However, a variety of reasons cause the structure of a table to change. Changes in the needs of users of the database might require additional fields to be added. For example, if the database is to store customer types (regular, discount, or special), such a field would be added to the Customer table if it didn't already exist.

Characteristics of a given field might need to change. In the Customer table, Farley-Young's name is stored incorrectly in the database. It should be Farley-Young Industries. The Name field is currently not big enough to hold the correct name. To accommodate this change, you need to increase the width of the Name field.

Fields become obsolete when they are no longer necessary. When a field occupies space and serves no useful purpose, it should be removed from the table.

The steps to restructure the database to accommodate these changes are explained on the following pages.

Changing the Size of a Field

To make any of these structure changes, activate the table and then use the Restructure command. The following steps change the size of the Name field from 20 to 25.

TO CHANGE THE SIZE OF A FIELD

STEP 1 ▶

Make sure the Customer table is open and the window containing the table is maximized. Select the Table menu and choose the Restructure command. Point to the size field for the Name field.

The Restructure Paradox Table dialog box displays (Figure 3-15). The mouse pointer is pointing to the Size field for the Name field.

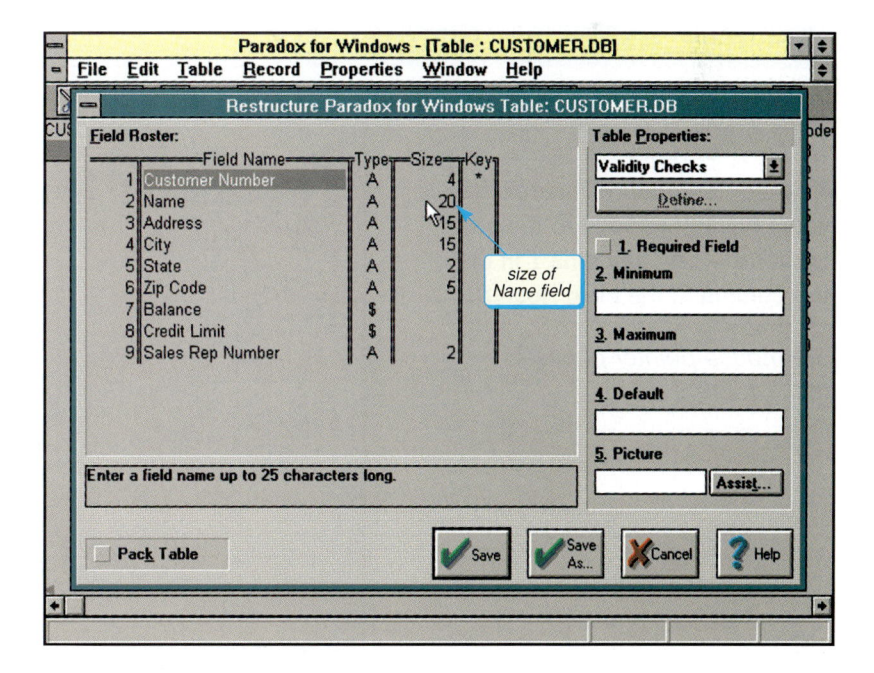

FIGURE 3-15

STEP 2 ▶

Select Size column for the Name field by clicking the left mouse button, and then type 25 (the new size).

The new size displays in the Size field (Figure 3-16).

STEP 3 ▶

Press the TAB key to complete the entry.

FIGURE 3-16

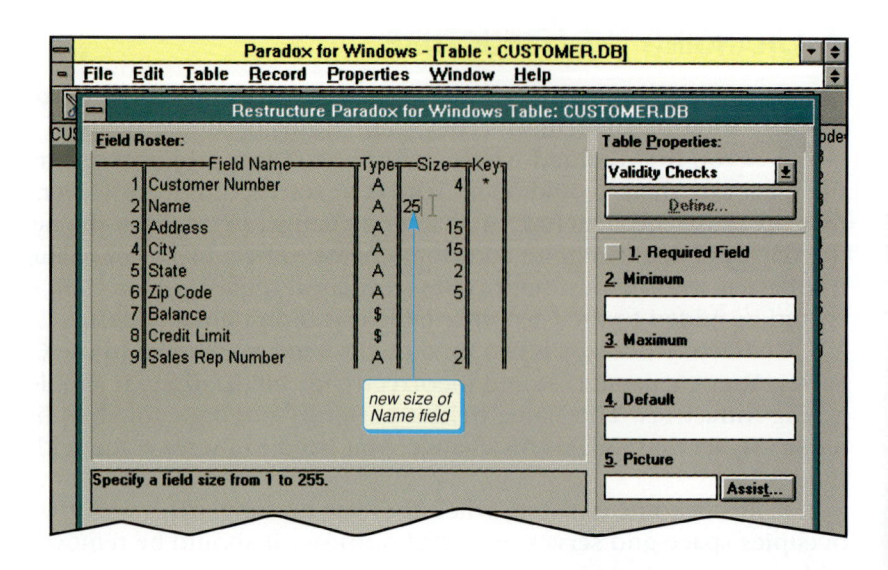

Adding a New Field

The next step is to add a new field to the table called Cust Type. The Cust Type field is used to indicate the type of the customer. The possible entries in this field are REG (regular customer), DSC (discount customer), and SPC (special customer). The new field will follow the Zip Code field in the list of fields, that is, it will be the *seventh* field in the restructured table. The current seventh field (Balance) will become the eighth field, Credit Limit will become the ninth field, and so on.

TO ADD A FIELD TO THE CUSTOMER TABLE ▼

STEP 1 ▶

With the Restructure Paradox Table dialog box open, point to the position for the new field (the 7 in the first column in the Field Roster).

The mouse pointer points to field 7 (Figure 3-17).

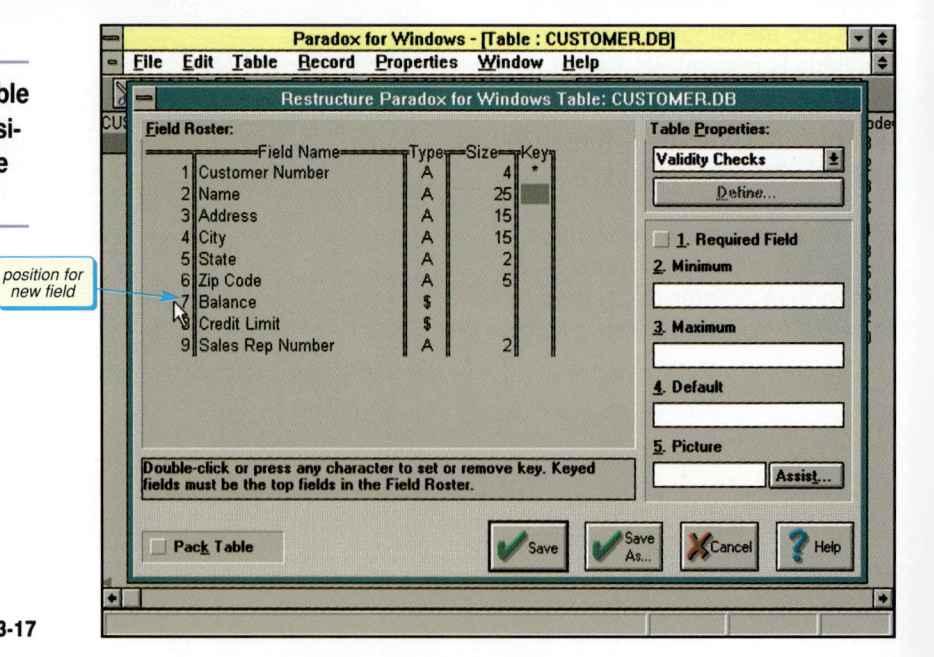

FIGURE 3-17

STEP 2 ▶

Click the left mouse button to select the position for the new field, and then press the INSERT key to insert a blank row.

A blank row displays in the position for the new field (Figure 3-18).

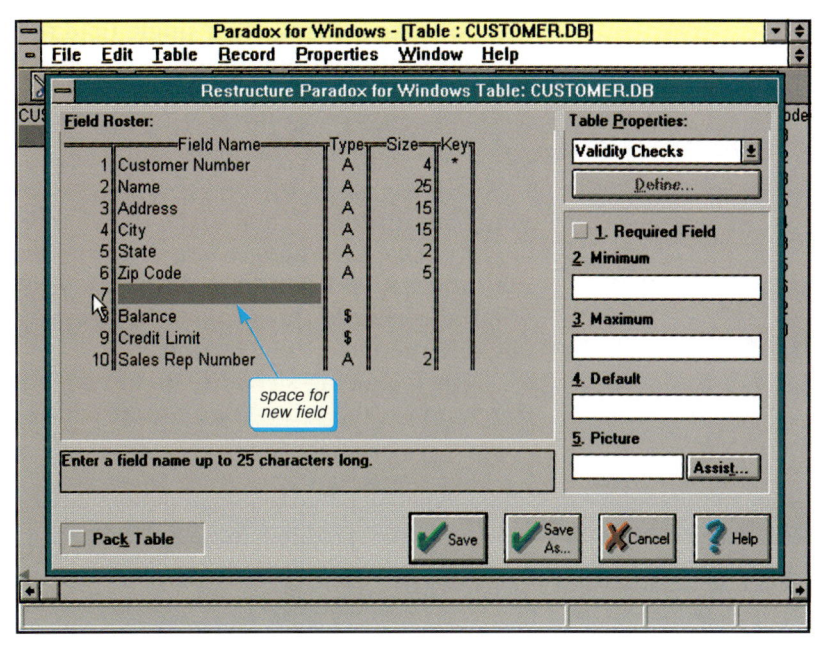

FIGURE 3-18

STEP 3 ▶

Type Cust Type **(field name) and press the** TAB **key. Type** A **(type) and press the** TAB **key. Type** 3 **(size) and press the** TAB **key.**

The entries for the new field are complete and the highlight advances to the next field (Figure 3-19).

STEP 4

Choose the Save button to save the changes to the Customer table structure.

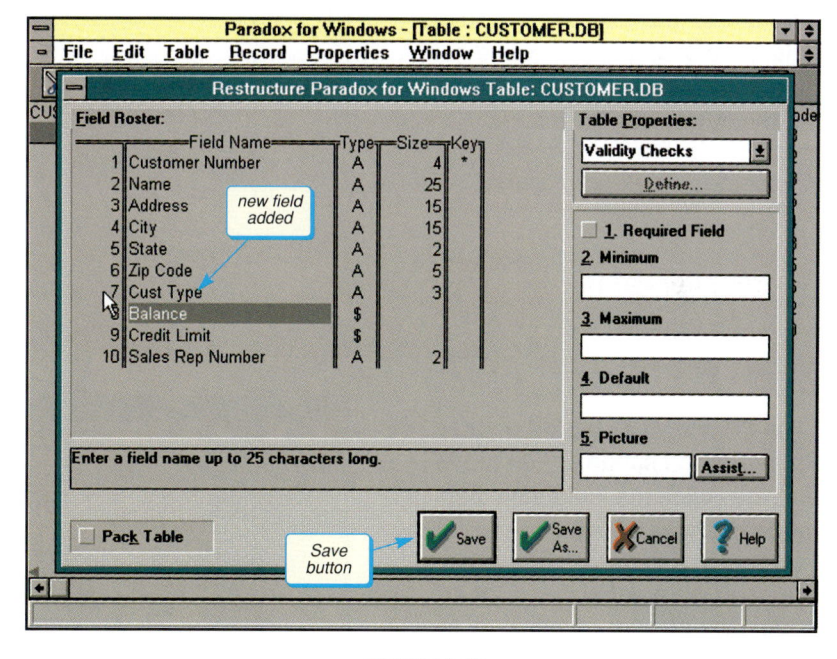

FIGURE 3-19

Updating the Restructured Database

As soon as you have changed the structure, the changes are immediately available. The customer name field is longer and the new customer type field is included.

PROJECT 3   MAINTAINING A DATABASE

To make a change to a single field (like changing the name from Farley-Young to Farley-Young Industries), point to the field to be changed, click the left mouse button, and then type the correct value. If the record you want to change is not displayed, use the Next Record and Previous Record buttons on the Speed-Bar to move to it. If the field you want to correct is not visible, use the horizontal scroll bar along the bottom of the screen to shift all the fields until the one you want displays. Then make the change.

To make the change, you can simply type the new entry. Rather than retyping the entry in its entirety, however, you might want to use **Field view**, just as you did earlier in this project. Remember that you transfer to Field view by clicking the Field View button.

The following steps use Field view to change the name from Farley-Young in record six to Farley-Young Industries.

TO USE FIELD VIEW TO UPDATE THE CONTENTS OF A FIELD ▼

STEP 1 ▶

Make sure the Customer table is open and the window containing the table is maximized. Point to the field to be changed (the Name field on record 6) and select it by clicking the left mouse button.

The field is selected (Figure 3-20).

FIGURE 3-20

STEP 2 ▶

Click the Edit Data button on the SpeedBar to change to Edit mode and then click the Field View button to change to Field view.

An insertion point appears at the end of the current contents of the field (Figure 3-21).

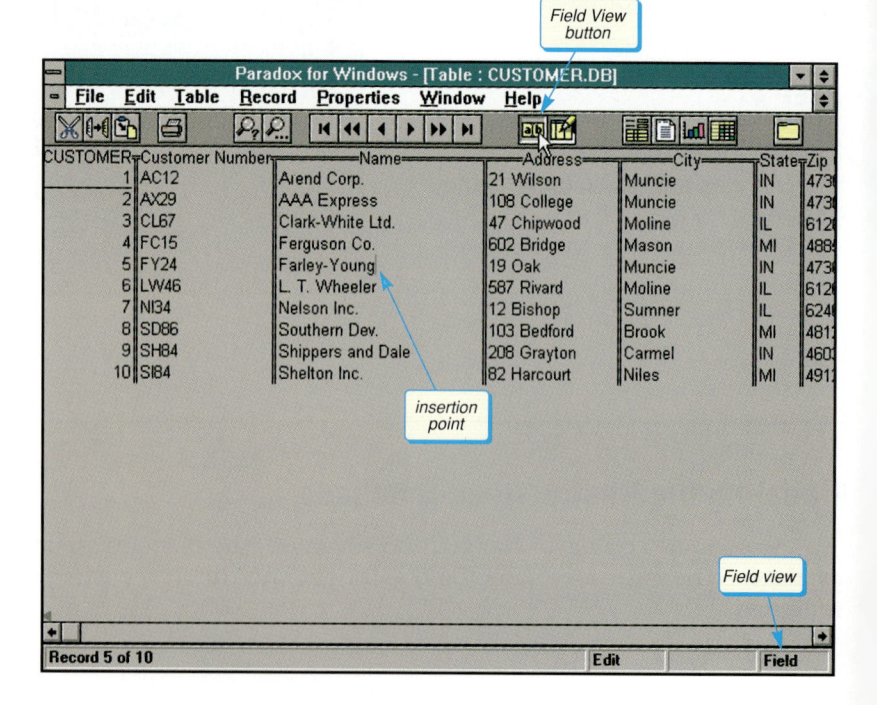

FIGURE 3-21

CHANGING THE STRUCTURE   **P125**

STEP 3 ▶

Press the SPACEBAR to insert a space, type `Industries` **and press the TAB key.**

The name is changed from Farley-Young to Farley-Young Industries (Figure 3-22).

STEP 4 ▶

Select the Control menu and choose the Close command.

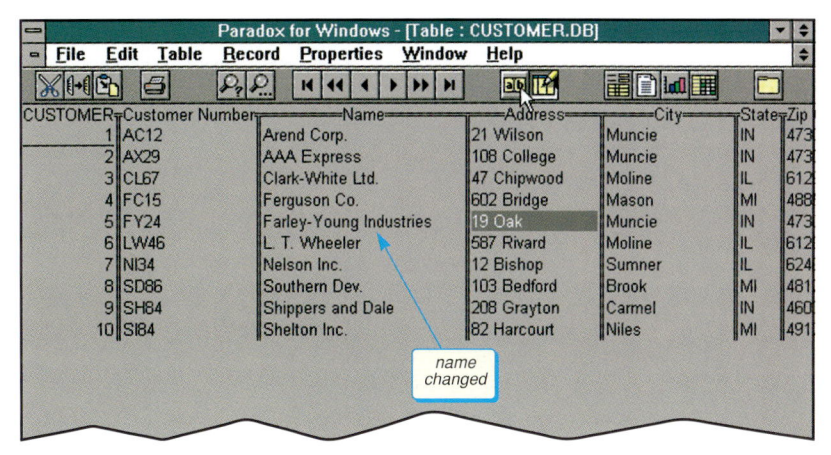

FIGURE 3-22

Updating the Contents of a New Field in a Table

The Cust Type field is blank on every record. One approach to updating the field would be to step through the entire table, and make the appropriate change to the value on each record. Given that most of the customers have the same type, there is a simpler approach.

Suppose, for example, that most customers are type REG (regular). The quickest and easiest way to initially set all the values to REG is to use a special type of query called an **update query**. Later, you will individually change the type for the special and discount customers.

When you run an update query, Paradox creates a special table, called the Changed table. It contains all the records that were changed by the query as they appeared *before* the changes. This table automatically displays on the desktop.

The following steps change the value to REG in the Cust Type field for all the records (see Figure 3-49 on page P137).

TO MAKE THE SAME CHANGE TO ALL RECORDS ▼

STEP 1 ▶

Select the File menu, choose the New command, and point to the Query command.

The cascading menu for the New command displays (Figure 3-23). The mouse pointer is pointing to the Query command.

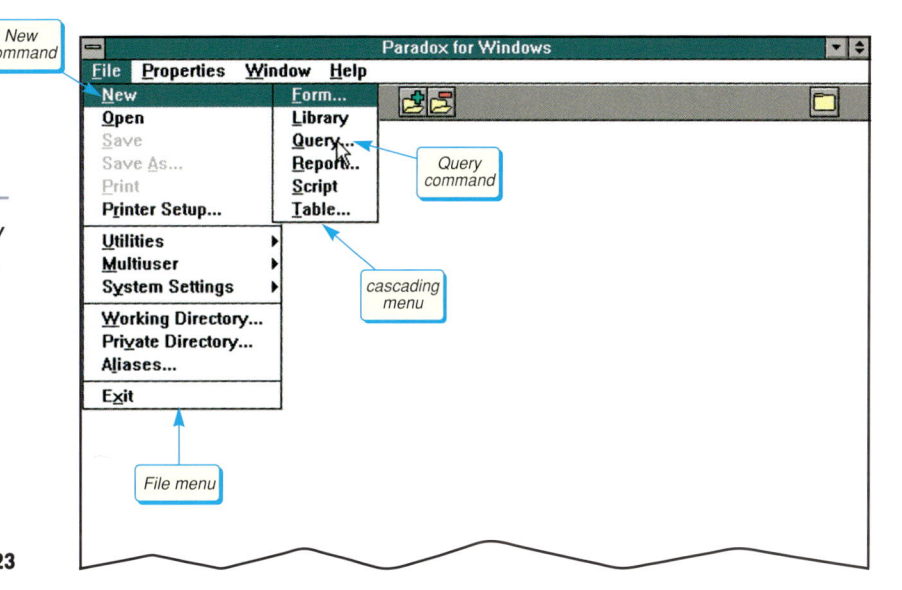

FIGURE 3-23

STEP 2 ▶

Choose the Query command by clicking the left mouse button.

The Select File dialog box displays (Figure 3-24).

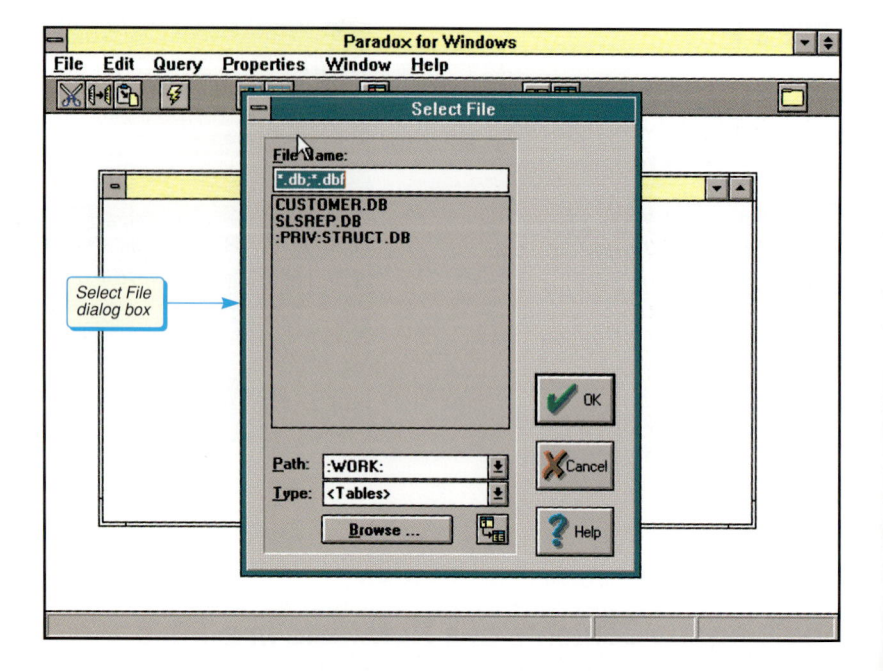

FIGURE 3-24

STEP 3 ▶

Select the Customer table and then choose the OK button. Maximize the Query image that displays on the screen.

A maximized Query image for the Customer table displays (Figure 3-25).

FIGURE 3-25

STEP 4 ▶

Press the TAB key until the Cust Type field is highlighted. Type `changeto REG` **and point to the Run Query button.**

The Cust Type field contains the appropriate entry and the mouse pointer points to the Run Query button (Figure 3-26).

FIGURE 3-26

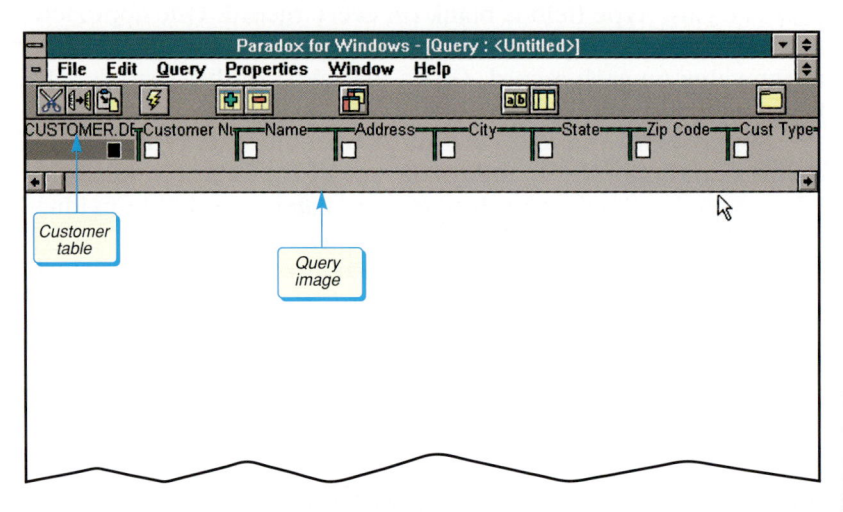

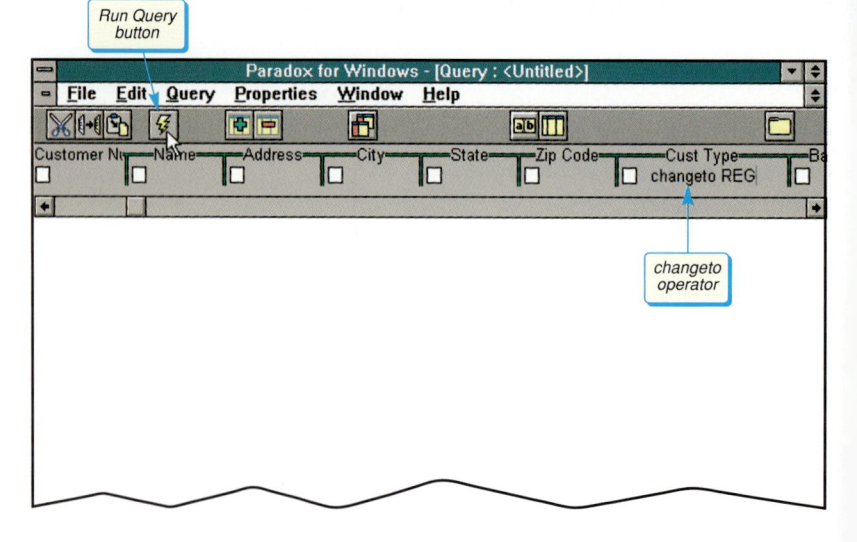

STEP 5 ▶

Click the Run Query button on the SpeedBar to run the query.

The Changed table displays on the screen (Figure 3-27). It contains all the records that were changed by the query. Because this query did not contain any conditions, the Changed table contains all the records from the Customer table.

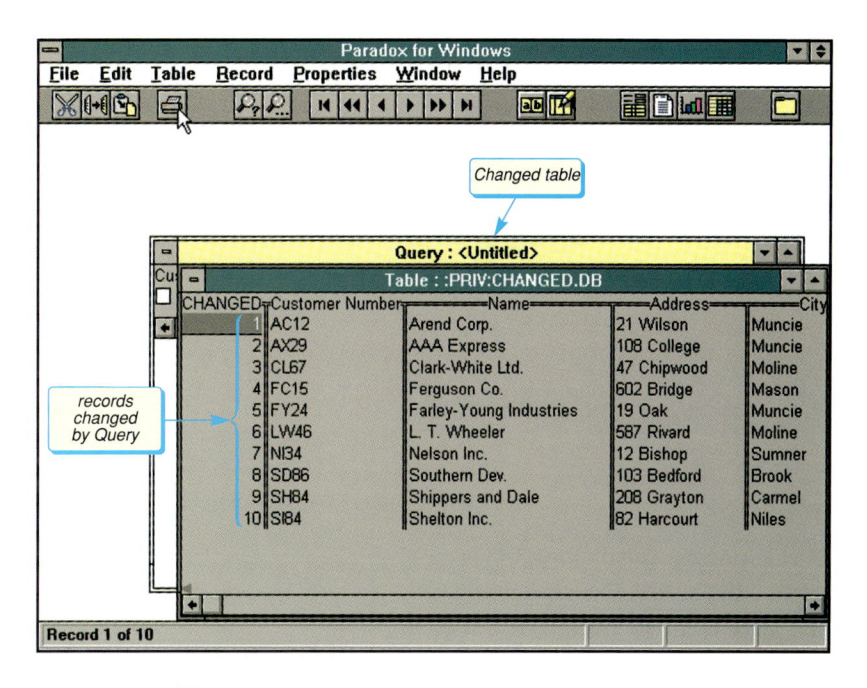

FIGURE 3-27

STEP 6 ▶

Close the Changed table and the query. Do not save the query. Open the Customer table and maximize the window. Press the TAB key until the Cust Type field is highlighted.

The Customer table shows that all entries in the Cust Type field are now REG (Figure 3-28).

FIGURE 3-28

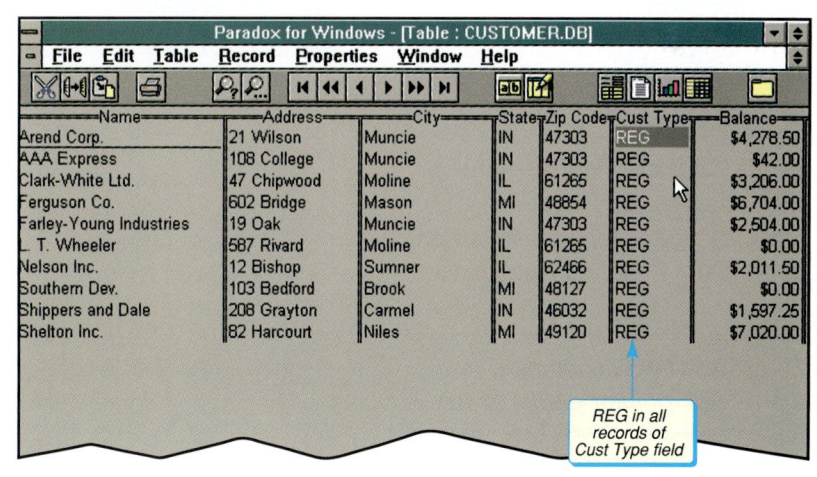

▶ CREATING VALIDITY CHECKS

In Project 3, so far you have created, loaded, queried, and updated a database. Nothing you have done, however, ensures that users enter only valid data. In this section, you will create **validity checks**, that is, rules a user must follow when entering data. As you will see, Paradox prevents users who do not follow the rules from entering data.

Using validity checks can force a user to make an entry in a particular field; that is, the user must not leave the contents of the field blank. Validity checks can ensure an entry lies within a certain range of values; for example, the values in the Balance field are between 0 and 20,000. Using Validity checks, you can specify a default value, that is, a value that Paradox will display on the screen in a particular field before the user begins adding a record. You can specify a format for an entry or that customer numbers must consist of two uppercase letters followed by a two-digit number.

To make data entry of customer numbers more convenient, you can also have lowercase letters converted automatically to uppercase. Finally, you can specify a collection of acceptable values, such as the only legitimate entries for Customer Type are REG, SPC, and DSC.

Specifying a Required Field

To ensure that the Name field is never left blank, perform the following steps make the Name field a required field.

TO SPECIFY A REQUIRED FIELD

STEP 1 ▶

Make sure the Customer table is open and the window containing the table is maximized. Select the Table menu and choose the Restructure command.

STEP 2 ▶

Select the Name field by pointing to the number that precedes it (2) and clicking the left mouse button. Point to the Required Field check box.

The Name field is selected and the mouse pointer points to the Required Field check box (Figure 3-29).

STEP 3 ▶

Click the Required Field check box to make the Name field a required field.

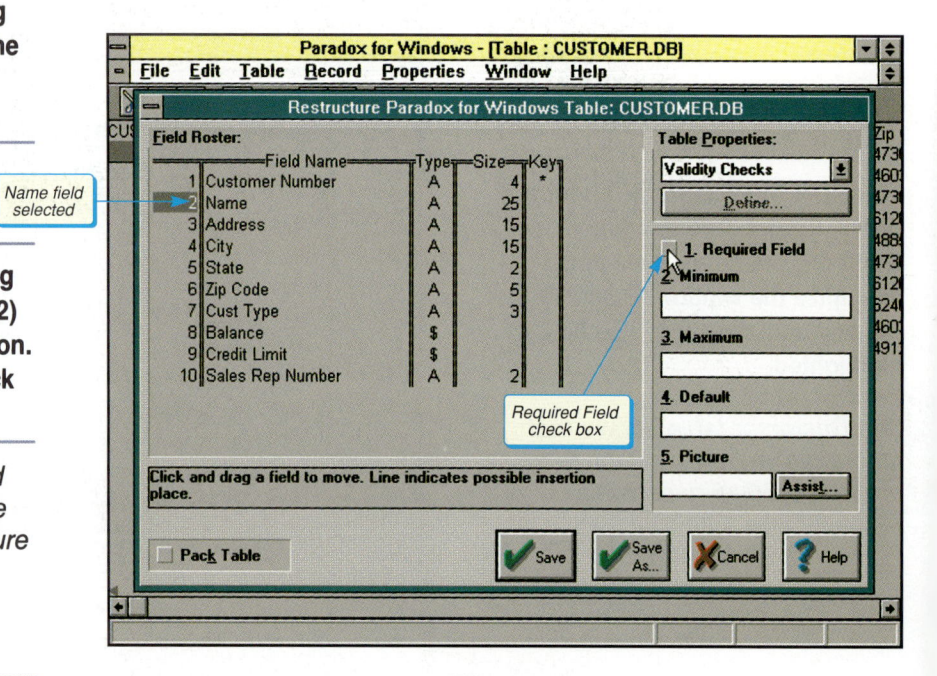

FIGURE 3-29

Paradox will now force a user to make an entry in the Name field. That is, it will not be possible to add a record with the Name field left blank.

Specifying a Range

To specify that entries in the Balance field must be between $0 and $20,000, perform the steps on the following page.

CREATING VALIDITY CHECKS **P129**

TO SPECIFY A RANGE ▼

STEP 1 ▶

Select the Balance field by clicking the number that precedes it (8). Point to the Minimum text box. The mouse pointer changes to an I-beam (I). Click the left mouse button.

The Balance field is selected (Figure 3-30). An insertion point displays in the Minimum text box.

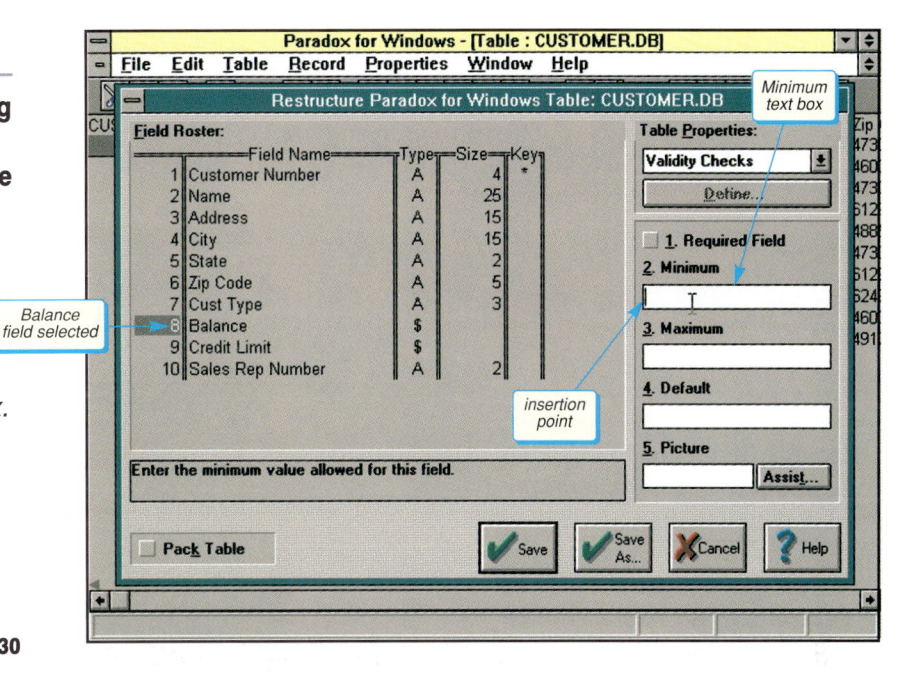

FIGURE 3-30

STEP 2 ▶

Type 0 (the minimum value). Point to the Maximum text box and click the left mouse button.

The number 0 displays in the Minimum text box (Figure 3-31). An insertion point displays in the Maximum text box.

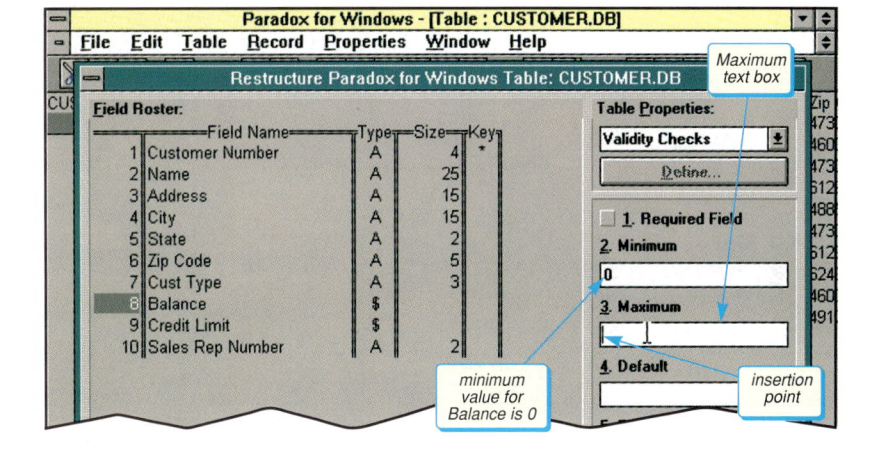

FIGURE 3-31

STEP 3 ▶

Type 20000 (the maximum value).

The number 20000 displays in the Maximum text box (Figure 3-32).

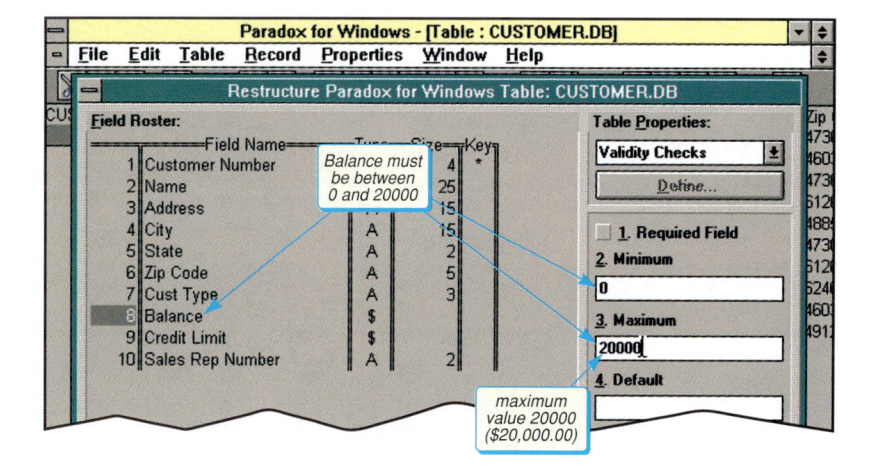

FIGURE 3-32

Users will now be prohibited from entering a balance that is either less than $0 or greater than $20000.

Specifying a Default Value

The following steps specify a default value of 6000 for the Credit Limit field. This simply means that if users do not enter a credit limit, the credit limit will be 6000.

TO SPECIFY A DEFAULT VALUE ▼

STEP 1 ▶

Select the Credit Limit field. Point to the Default text box and click the left mouse button.

The Credit Limit field is selected (Figure 3-33). An insertion point displays in the Default text box.

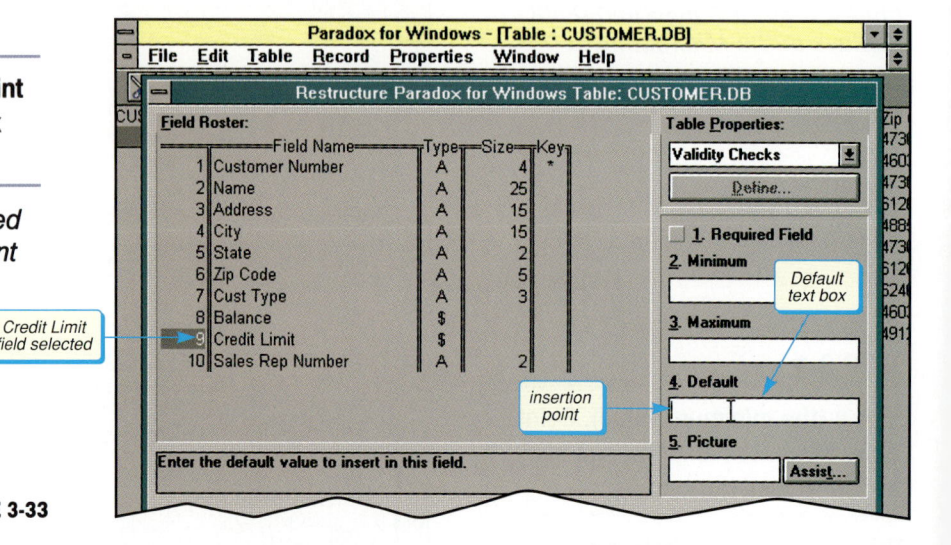

FIGURE 3-33

STEP 2 ▶

Type 6000 (the default value).

The number 6000 displays in the Default text box (Figure 3-34).

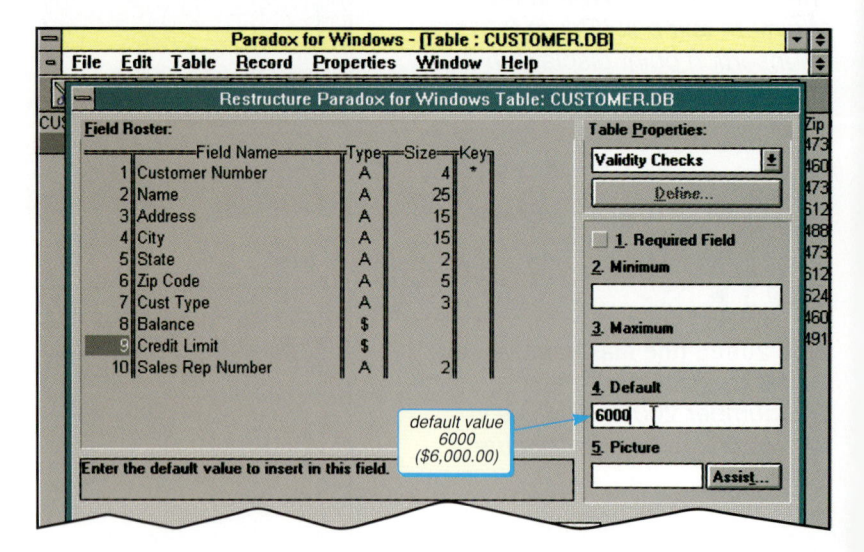

FIGURE 3-34

From this point on, if no entry is made in the Credit Limit field by a user, Paradox will automatically set the credit limit to 6000.

Specifying a Pattern

One way you can govern data entry is to create a **template**, or pattern, that the data must follow. Such a template is a series of characters, one for each position in the field, that indicates how data is to be entered into the field. The characters used are called **picture symbols**. Paradox picture symbols are shown in Table 3-1.

▸ **TABLE 3-1**

PICTURE SYMBOL	PURPOSE
@	Accepts any character
?	Accepts any letter in either uppercase or lowercase
&	Accepts any letter, but converts to uppercase
!	Accepts any character, but converts any letters to uppercase
#	Accepts only a numeric digit
{ }	Contains a list of acceptable entries
,	Separates entries within a list

In Table 3-1 you can see the @ symbol indicates that Paradox will accept any character. The ? indicates that Paradox will accept only alphabetic characters (letters). Thus, a template of ?????????? would prevent the user from entering numbers or special characters, such as a semicolon, in the field. The & symbol accepts any letter but indicates that letters are to be converted to uppercase. A template of &&&&&&&&& would cause any lowercase letters entered by the user to automatically be converted to uppercase letters. The ! is similar in that it also converts letters to uppercase. The difference is that & allows the user to only enter letters, whereas ! allows the entry of any characters. The # symbol indicates that the only acceptable entries are numeric digits.

These symbols can be mixed. Suppose, for example, the customer numbers must be two capital letters followed by a two-digit number (for example, XY18). You could force the data to be entered in the correct fashion by using a template of &&##.

Curly brackets({ }), also called **braces**, contain a list of acceptable entries. The entries in the list are separated by commas. Using such a list prevents a user from entering an item not in the list. In addition, if you make sure the first letters in the various items are unique, users need to type only the first letter of the particular item. Paradox will automatically fill in the rest. Use the { } picture symbols to force the user to enter REG, SPC, or DSC as the customer type.

The following steps specify a picture for the Customer Number field in the Customer table. The picture requires that the customer number consist of two letters followed by two digits.

P132 PROJECT 3 MAINTAINING A DATABASE

TO SPECIFY A PICTURE ▼

STEP 1 ▶

With the Restructure Paradox for Windows Table dialog box open, select the Customer Number field by selecting the number 1 that precedes it. Point to the Assist button (Assist...).

The Customer Number field is selected (Figure 3-35). The mouse pointer points to the Assist button.

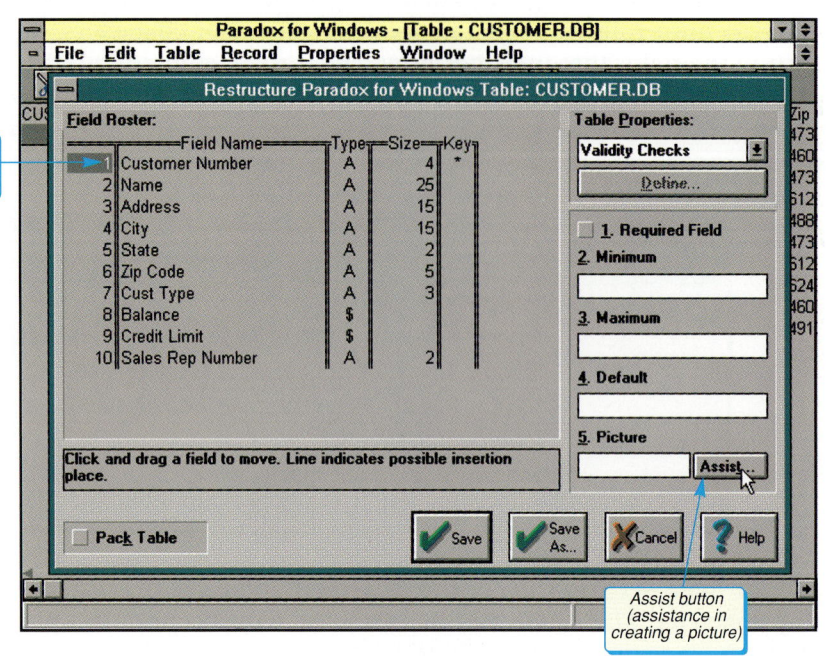

FIGURE 3-35

STEP 2 ▶

Choose the Assist button.

The Picture Assistance dialog box displays (Figure 3-36). The Picture text box is where you type the picture. The Sample Value text box allows you to enter a value to see if it satisfies the picture entered in the Picture text box. If you have a complicated picture, this can help you verify that you have entered the picture correctly. The Sample Pictures list box contains some frequently used sample pictures. If you want to use one of these, you can simply select it from the list.

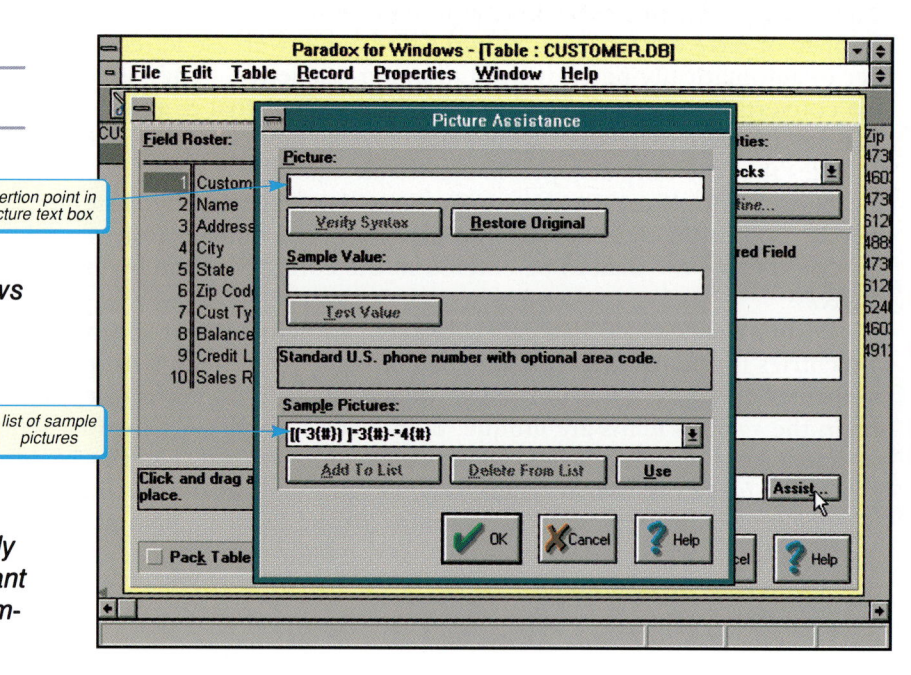

FIGURE 3-36

CREATING VALIDITY CHECKS   **P133**

STEP 3 ▶

In the Picture text box, type `&&##` (the picture for the Customer Number field) and point to the OK button.

The picture is entered (Figure 3-37) and the mouse pointer points to the OK button.

STEP 4 ▶

Choose the OK button.

FIGURE 3-37

Users will now be able to enter only customer numbers that consist of two uppercase letters, followed by a two-digit number.

Specifying a Collection of Legal Values

The only legal values for the Cust Type field are REG, SPC, and DSC. By using an appropriate picture for this field, you can make Paradox reject any entry other than these three possibilities. In other words, you can indicate to Paradox that these are the only three **legal values**. The following steps use a picture to specify the legal values for the Cust Type field.

TO SPECIFY LEGAL VALUES ▼

STEP 1 ▶

Select the Cust Type field and then choose the Assist button. In the Picture text box, type `{REG,SPC,DSC}` (the picture for the Cust Type field) and point to the OK button.

The Picture Assistance dialog box displays (Figure 3-38). The picture is entered in the Picture text box and the mouse pointer points to the OK button.

STEP 2 ▶

Choose the OK button.

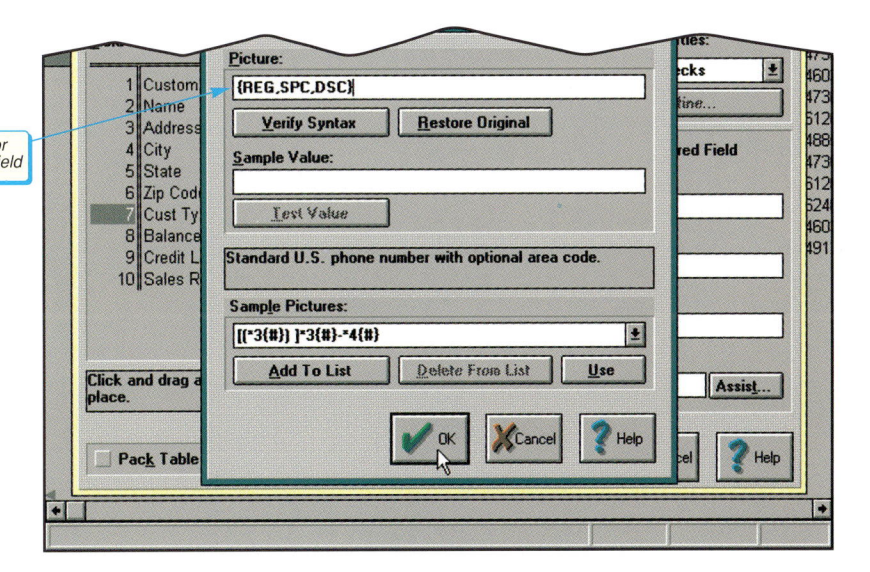

FIGURE 3-38

After specifying legal values, the next step is to save validity checks. Perform the following steps to save the validity checks.

TO SAVE THE VALIDITY CHECKS

Step 1: In the Restructure Paradox Table dialog box, choose the Save button. You will see the Restructure Warning dialog box. In this box you can indicate special action that Paradox should take in response to your changes. You can indicate, for example, whether the new validity checks are to be applied to existing records. In most cases you will simply choose the OK button.

Step 2: The Restructure Warning dialog box displays once for each validity check you have created. Thus, you should choose the OK button for each validity check until the dialog box no longer displays on the screen.

▶ REFERENTIAL INTEGRITY

A **foreign key** is a field in one table whose values are required to match the **primary key** of another table. For example, the sales rep number in the Customer table must match the primary key of the SLSREP table. That is, the sales rep number for any customer must be that of a real sales rep, or a sales rep currently in the SLSREP table. You should not store a customer whose sales rep number is 4, for example, if there is no sales rep 4. The property that the value in a foreign key must match that of another table's primary key is called **referential integrity**.

Specify any referential integrity you want Paradox to enforce by selecting Referential Integrity from the Table Properties list box, and then indicate the foreign key as well as the primary key it must match. To each referential integrity you create, you must also assign a name. Paradox will then forbid any updates to the database that violate the referential integrity you have specified.

The following steps specify referential integrity and assign it the name custsls.

REFERENTIAL INTEGRITY   **P135**

TO SPECIFY REFERENTIAL INTEGRITY ▼

STEP 1 ▶

With the Customer table open, choose the Restructure command from the Table menu. Click the Table Properties list box arrow and then point to Referential Integrity in the drop-down list.

The Table Properties list displays (Figure 3-39). The mouse pointer points to Referential Integrity.

FIGURE 3-39

STEP 2 ▶

Select Referential Integrity and then point to the Define button.

Referential Integrity is selected (Figure 3-40). The mouse pointer points to the Define button.

FIGURE 3-40

STEP 3 ▶

Choose the Define button and then point to Sales Rep Number.

*The Referential Integrity dialog box displays (Figure 3-41). Use it to indicate the foreign key, referred to in this box as the **Child Fields** and to indicate the table the foreign key is supposed to match, referred to as the **Parent's Key**.*

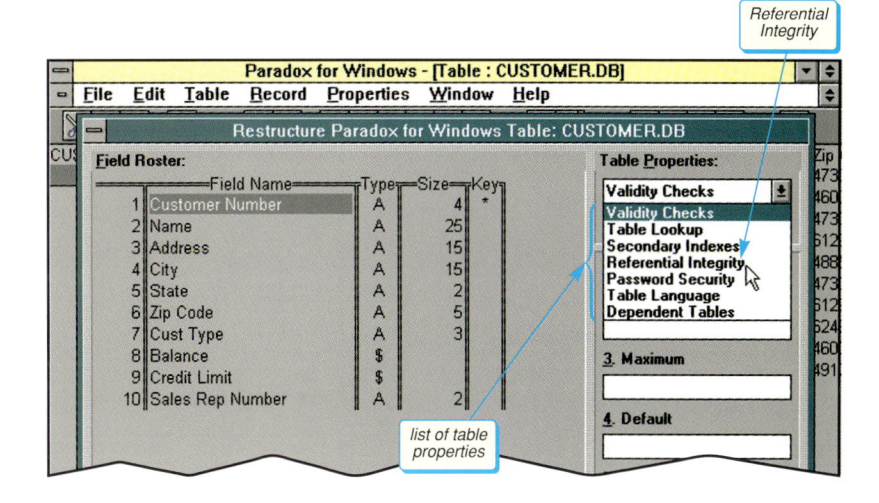

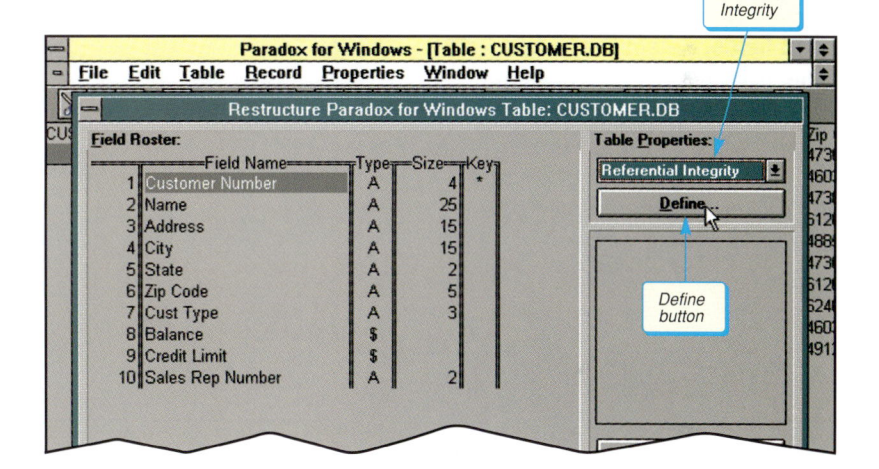

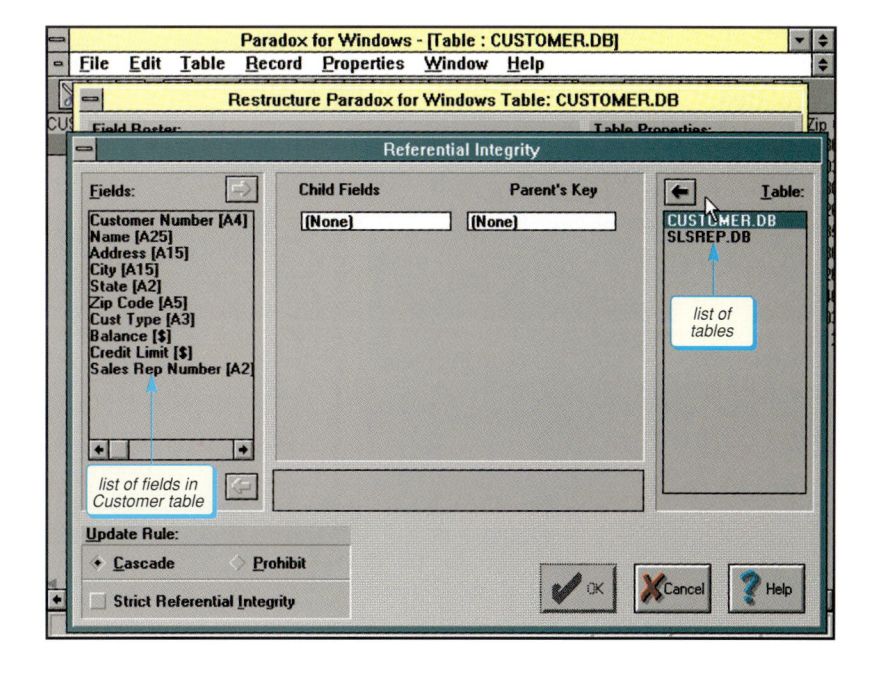

FIGURE 3-41

STEP 4 ▶

Select the Sales Rep Number field and then point to the Add Field arrow.

The Sales Rep Number field is selected (Figure 3-42). The pointer points to the Add Field arrow.

FIGURE 3-42

STEP 5 ▶

Click the Add Field arrow to add Sales Rep Number to the list of child fields. Select the SLSREP.DB table from the list of tables and then point to the Add Table arrow.

SLSREP.DB is selected (Figure 3-43). The mouse pointer points to the Add Table arrow.

FIGURE 3-43

STEP 6 ▶

Click the Add Table arrow to add the key of the Slsrep table to the Parent's Key column. Point to the OK button.

Sales Rep Number displays in the Parent's Key column (Figure 3-44). The mouse pointer points to the OK button.

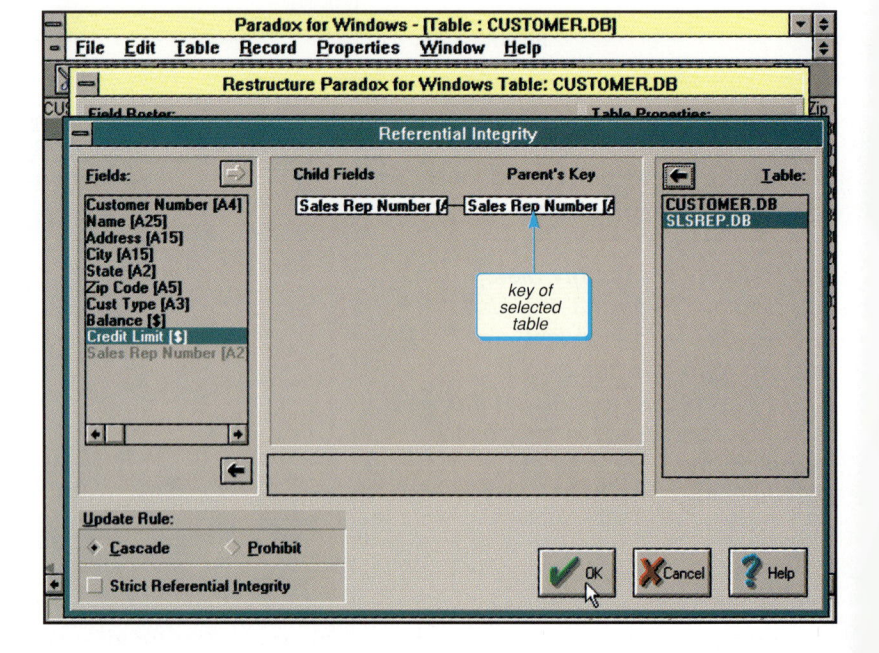

FIGURE 3-44

STEP 7 ▶

Choose the OK button. Then type `custsls` **(the referential integrity name) and point to the OK button in the Save Referential Integrity As dialog box.**

The Save Referential Integrity As dialog box displays (Figure 3-45). The name custsls is entered in the Referential Integrity Name text box. The mouse pointer points to the OK button.

STEP 8 ▶

Choose the OK button in the Save Refrential Integrity As dialog box.

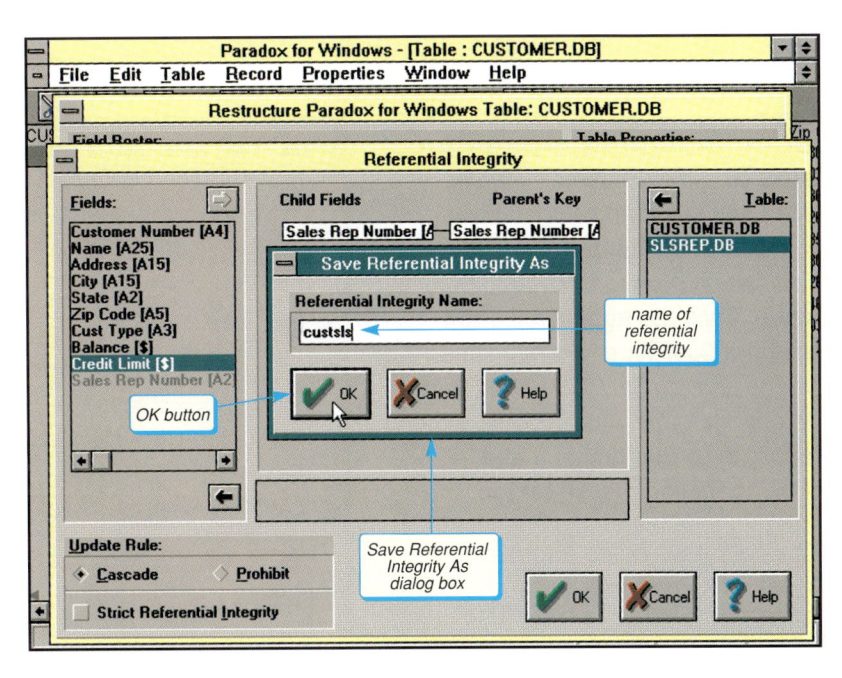

FIGURE 3-45

STEP 9 ▶

Save your changes.

Paradox will now reject any number in the Sales Rep Number field in the Customer table that does not match a sales rep number in the Slsrep table.

▶ UPDATING A TABLE THAT CONTAINS VALIDITY CHECKS

When you update a table that contains validity checks, Paradox will not let you enter invalid data. Attempting to leave a required field blank, entering a number that is out of the required range, entering a value that has an incorrect format, or entering a value that is not one of the possible choices will produce an error message. Until you fix the error, you will not be able to update the database.

When a table has validity checks, it is possible to get stuck in a field. You might forget the validity check you created, or the one you created was incorrect. In any case, if you have entered data that violates the validity check, you will not be able to leave the field. Pressing ESCAPE doesn't work, and you can't close the table.

The first thing you should try is to type an acceptable entry. If you find you cannot do this, repeatedly press the BACKSPACE key to erase the contents of the field. See if you can then leave the field. If, for some reason, this doesn't work either, your only recourse is to press CTRL+DELETE to delete the record on which you are working.

If you ever have to take such drastic action, you probably have a faulty validity check. In this case, use the techniques of the previous sections to correct the existing validity checks for the field.

The following steps update a table that contains validity checks by changing some of the values in the Cust Type field.

TO UPDATE A TABLE THAT CONTAINS VALIDITY CHECKS

STEP 1 ▶

Make sure the Customer table is open and the window containing the table is maximized. Click the Edit Data button to change to Edit mode. Click the right scroll arrow until the Cust Type field is visible on the screen. Select the field to be changed (the Cust Type field on record 3) by pointing to it and clicking the left mouse button.

The field is selected (Figure 3-46).

STEP 2 ▶

Type S and Paradox will automatically add PC.

STEP 3 ▶

Make the additional changes to customer types shown in Figure 3-47.

STEP 4 ▶

Close the table.

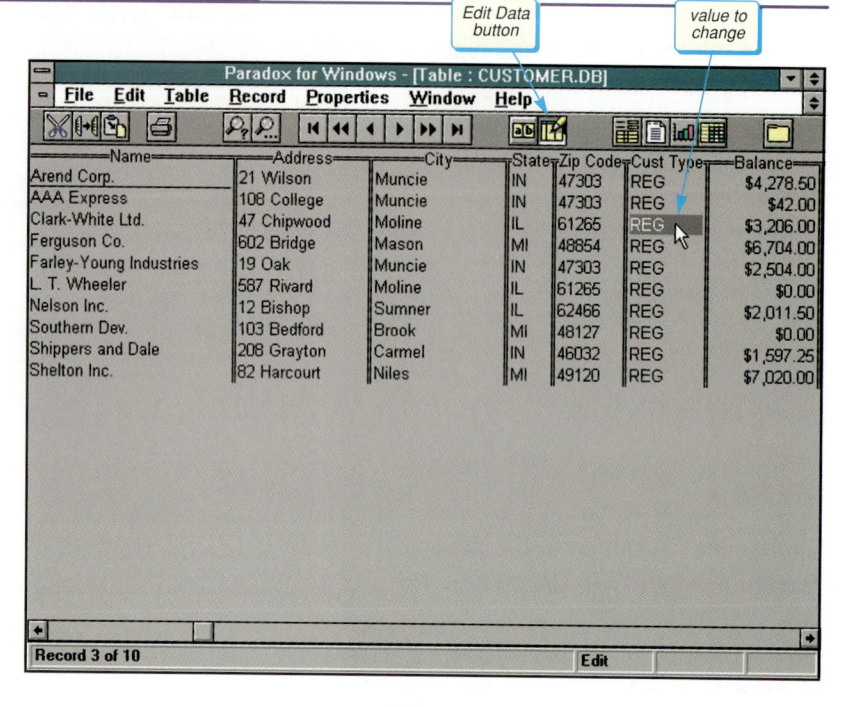

FIGURE 3-46

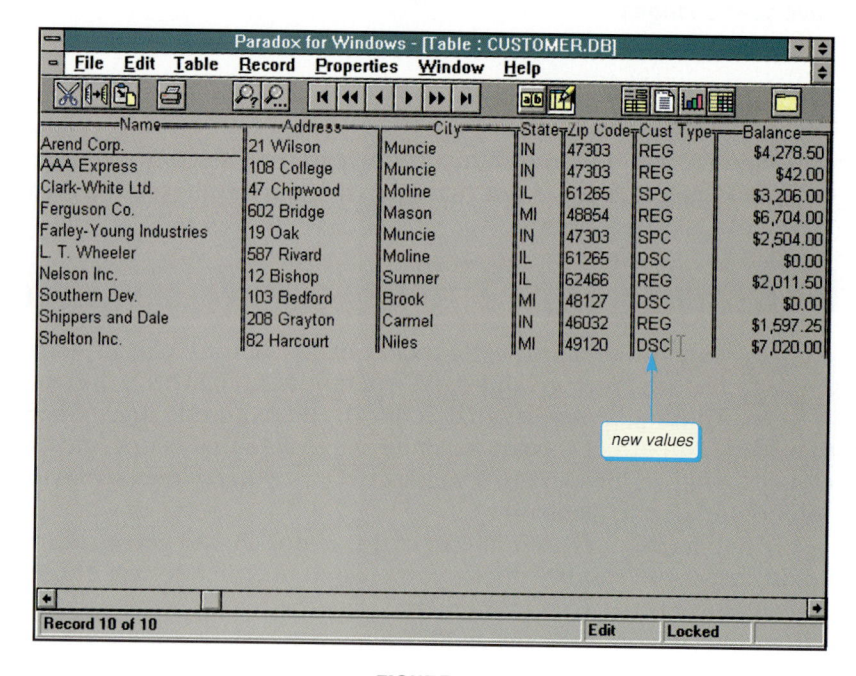

FIGURE 3-47

▶ Mass Updates

Earlier in this project, you used an update query to change all the entries in the Cust Type column to REG. When making mass changes with update queries, you can be more selective. You can delete all the records that satisfy some condition and also make the same change to all records satisfying a condition.

When you use an update query to make deletions, Paradox places the records that were deleted in a special table called the **Deleted table**. When you use an update query to make changes, Paradox places the records that were changed by the query as they appeared *before* the changes in the special table called the **Changed table**. These tables will automatically display on the screen. Both the Deleted table and the Changed table are temporary. Paradox automatically overwrites them whenever you perform another update query or deletes them when leaving Paradox.

Deleting Groups of Records

Many times in an organization territories change, affecting customers and their data. For example, certain zip codes may be assigned to a new territory. Instead of deleting these customers individually, which would be very cumbersome, you can delete them in one operation by using an update query. The following steps use an update query to delete all customers whose zip code is 46032.

TO DELETE GROUPS OF RECORDS ▼

STEP 1 ▶

Select the File menu, choose the New command, and point to the Query command.

The File menu and the cascading menu for the New command both display (Figure 3-48). The mouse pointer points to the Query command.

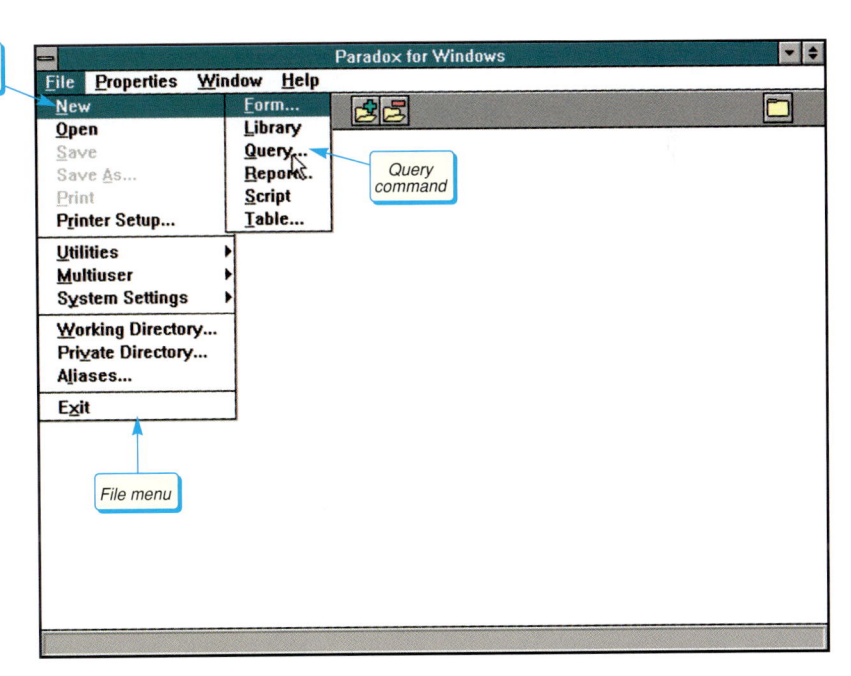

FIGURE 3-48

STEP 2 ▶

Choose the Query command. In the Select File dialog box, select the Customer table and choose the OK button. Maximize the Query window. Point to the highlight under the CUSTOMER.DB field in the Query image. Do not point to the check box. Press and hold the left mouse button.

The menu of query operations displays (Figure 3-49).

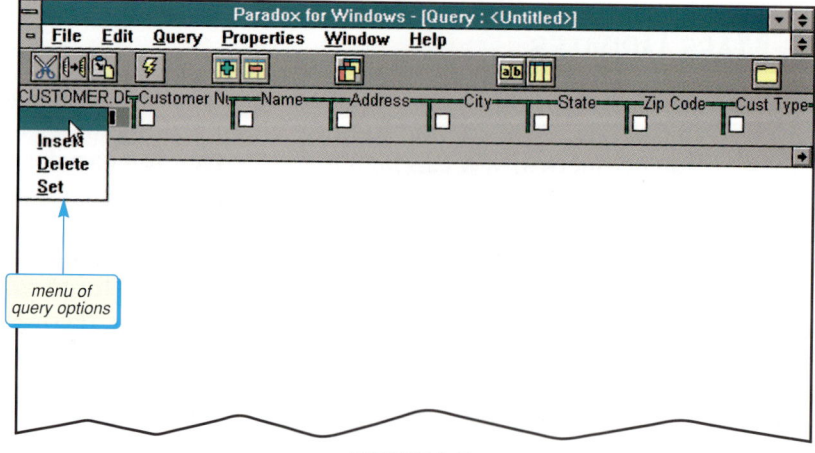

FIGURE 3-49

STEP 3 ▶

Select Delete by dragging the highlight to the Delete command in the menu and releasing the left mouse button.

The word Delete displays under the CUSTOMER.DB field (Figure 3-50).

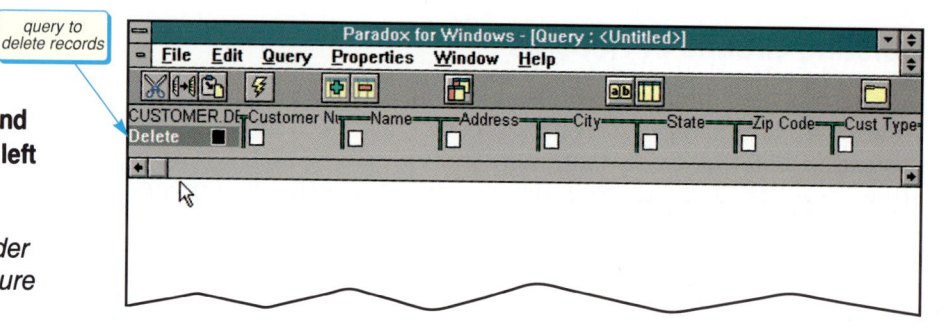

FIGURE 3-50

STEP 4 ▶

Press the TAB key until the highlight is in the Zip Code field, and then type 46032. Point to the Run Query button.

The condition is entered in the Zip Code field. The mouse pointer points to the Run Query button (Figure 3-51).

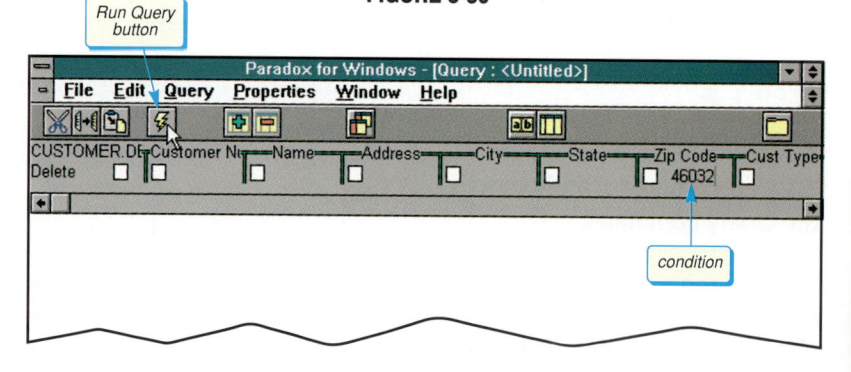

FIGURE 3-51

STEP 5 ▶

Click the Run Query button.

The query is executed. The record that was deleted by the query is placed in the DELETED table, which is displayed on the desktop (Figure 3-52).

STEP 6 ▶

Close the DELETED table and then close the Query window. Do not save the query.

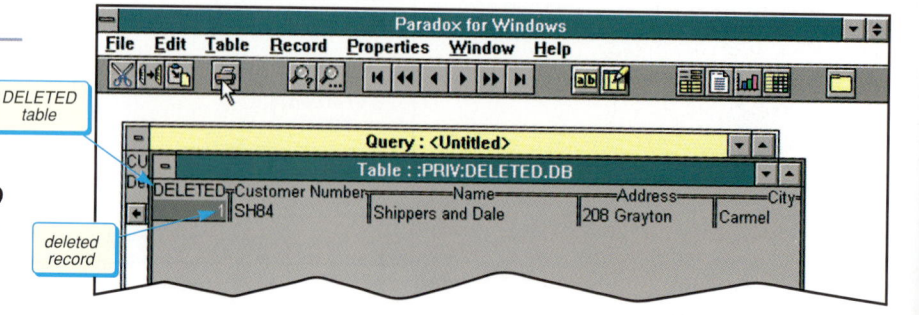

FIGURE 3-52

The customers whose zip code is 46032 have now been removed from the table. There are now nine records in the Customer table.

Changing Groups of Records

Just as you may need to delete several records at once, you may also need to change several records at a time. To individually change the credit limit of all customers whose credit limit is currently 3000 to 4000 is very time consuming. An update query simplifies this process. The following steps use an update query to change the credit limit of all customers whose credit limit is 3000 to 4000.

TO MAKE CHANGES TO GROUPS OF RECORDS ▼

STEP 1 ▶

Select the File menu, choose the New command, and choose the Query command. In the Select File dialog box, select the Customer table and choose the OK button. Maximize the Query window. Press the TAB key until the highlight is in the Credit Limit field and then type 3000, changeto 4000. **Point to the Run Query button.**

The condition and the changeto operator are both entered in the Credit Limit column. The mouse pointer points to the Run Query button (Figure 3-53).

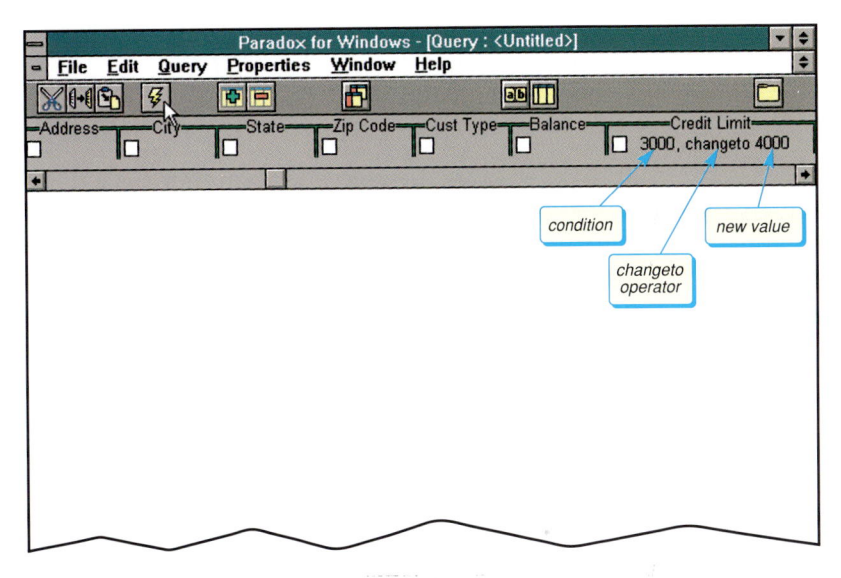

FIGURE 3-53

STEP 2 ▶

Click the Run Query button.

The query is executed. The list of records changed by the query is placed in the CHANGED table, which displays on the desktop (Figure 3-54).

STEP 3 ▶

Close the CHANGED table and then close the Query window. Do not save the query.

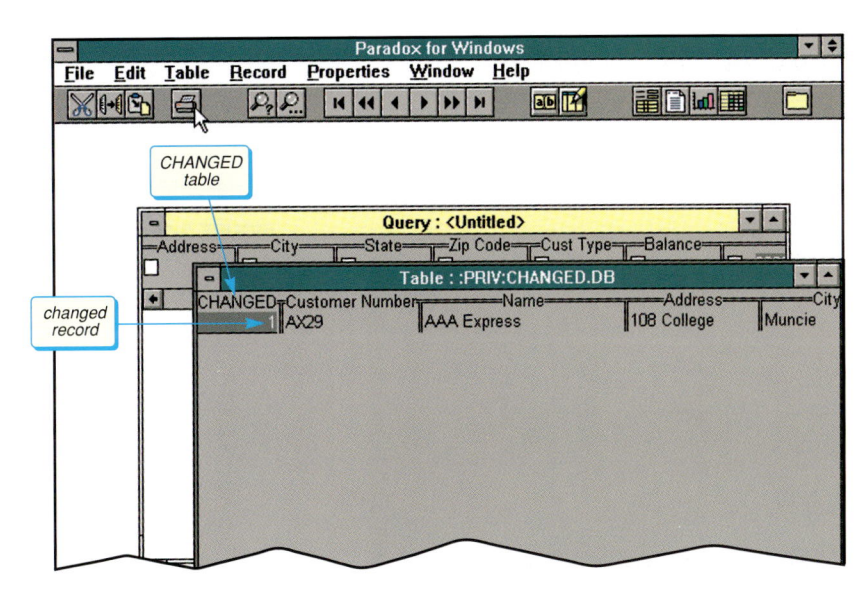

FIGURE 3-54

Undoing Mass Changes

If you accidentally enter the wrong condition when making mass deletions or changes, you could incorrectly delete or change a large number of records. If this happens, you can undo the change by performing the following steps in the Deleted or Changed tables.

TO UNDO A MASS DELETE OR CHANGE

Step 1: Select the File menu, choose the Utilities command, and then choose the Add command.
Step 2: In the Table Add dialog box, select the Deleted table (for a mass deletion) or the Changed table (for a mass change) in the Add Records From Source Table text box and select the table you updated in the To Target Table text box.
Step 3: Choose the ADD button (Add).

▶ CREATING AND USING INDEXES

The concept of an index is a familiar one. The index in the back of a book contains important words or phrases together with a list of pages on which the given words or phrases can be found. An index for a database table is similar. Figure 3-55, for example, shows the Customer table along with an index built on customer names. In this case, the items of interest are customer names instead of key words or phrases.

▶ INDEX ON NAME FIELD

Name	Record Number
AAA Express	2
Arend Corp.	1
Clark-White Ltd.	3
Farley-Young Industries	5
Ferguson Co.	4
L. T. Wheeler	6
Nelson Inc.	7
Shelton Inc.	9
Southern Dev.	8

▶ CUSTOMER TABLE

Record Number	Customer	Name	Address	City	State
1	AC12	Arend Corp.	21 Wilson	Muncie	IN
2	AX29	AAA Express	108 College	Muncie	IN
3	CL67	Clark-White Ltd.	47 Chipwood	Moline	IL
4	FC15	Ferguson Co.	602 Bridge	Mason	MI
5	FY24	Farley-Young Industries	19 Oak	Muncie	IN
6	LW46	L. T. Wheeler	587 Rivard	Moline	IL
7	NI34	Nelson, Inc.	12 Bishop	Sumne	IL
8	SD86	Southern Dev.	103 Bedford	Brook	IN
9	SI84	Shelton, Inc.	82 Harcourt	Niles	MI

FIGURE 3-55

Each customer name occurs in the index along with the number of the record on which the customer name is located. The names display in the index in alphabetical order. If you were to use this index to find Ferguson Co., for example, you would rapidly scan the names in the index to find Ferguson Co., look at the corresponding record number (5), and then go immediately to record 5 in the Customer table, thus finding this customer much quicker than if you had to look through the entire Customer table one record at a time. Paradox rapidly scans the records when it uses an index. Thus, indexes make the process of retrieving records very fast and efficient.

Another benefit of using indexes is that they provide an efficient alternative to sorting. That is, if you want the records to appear in a certain order, you can use an index instead of having to physically rearrange the records in the table. Physically rearranging the records in a different order, which is called sorting, can be a very time-consuming process.

To see how indexes can be used for this purpose, look at the record numbers in the index in Figure 3-55 and suppose you use these to list all customers. That is, you simply follow down the record number column, listing the corresponding customers as you go. In this example, you would first list the customer on record 2 (AAA Express), then the customer on record 1 (Arend Corp.), then the customer on record 3 (Clark-White Ltd.), and so on. You would be listing the customers in Name order without actually sorting the table.

To gain the benefits from an index, you must first create one. Paradox automatically creates an index on the primary key called the **primary index**. Other indexes, called **secondary indexes**, are indexes you create. To create the secondary index, you must indicate the field or fields on which the index is built and assign the index a name.

Usually you will create secondary indexes on a single field (like Name). In other words, the **index key** is usually a single field. Field names cannot be used for the name of the index because Paradox reserves field names for a special type of index, called a **case-sensitive** index. (In a case-sensitive index, all uppercase letters come before lowercase letters. In such an index, for example, DOG would come *before* cat because uppercase D comes before lowercase c. Usually you will not want this type of index.)

In naming a single-field index, the most obvious choice would be the name of the field, but Paradox prohibits using the field name unless you want the index to be case-sensitive. In most cases, however, you will not want the index to be case-sensitive. By naming the index the same as the name of the field followed by one additional character, you can easily identify the index. In this text, you will use the number 1 as the additional character. Thus, the name of the index built on the Name field will be Name1; the name of the index built on the Zip Code field will be Zip Code1; and so on.

Although the index key will usually be a single field, it can be a combination of fields. In Project 2, you sorted the Answer table by city *within* state. In other words, you ordered the records by a combination of fields: state and city. By using a combination of fields for the index key you can use an index for the same purpose. The steps in creating such an index are very similar to the steps used when the index is a single field. In this case, you should assign a name that represents the combination of fields. For example, for the index built on the combination of credit limit and balance, the name to be used is credbal.

Specifying secondary indexes, as well as changing the structure of a table, specifying validity checks, and specifying referential integrity are all considered to be part of the process called restructuring a table. To restructure a table, use the Restructure option as shown in the following steps.

TO RESTRUCTURE A TABLE

STEP 1 ▶

Open the Customer table and maximize the window.

STEP 2 ▶

Select the Table menu and point to the Restructure command.

The Table menu displays. The mouse pointer points to the Restructure command (Figure 3-56).

FIGURE 3-56

STEP 3 ▶

Choose the Restructure command by clicking the left mouse button.

The Restructure Paradox Table dialog box displays on the screen (Figure 3-57). The field roster contains the current structure of the Customer table.

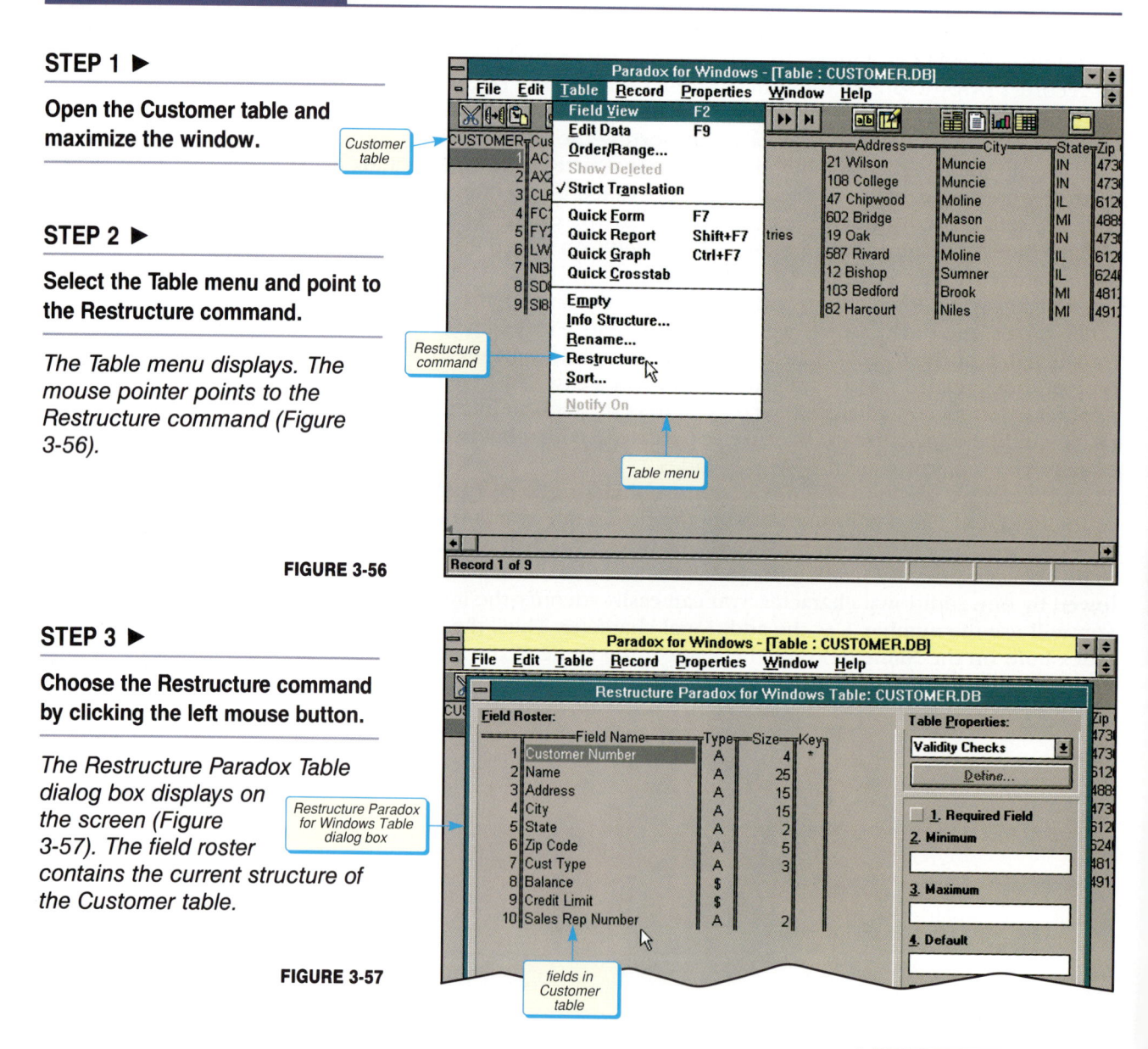

FIGURE 3-57

CREATING AND USING INDEXES   P145

Creating Single-Field Indexes

The next step is to create two **single-field secondary indexes**. In the first one, the index key will be the Name field. In the second, the index key will be the Zip Code field. After creating the two single-field secondary indexes, you then create a **multiple-field index**, in which the index key will be the combination of the Credit Limit field and the Balance field. Perform the following steps to create the indexes.

TO CREATE SINGLE-FIELD SECONDARY INDEXES

STEP 1 ▶

With the Restructure Paradox for Windows Table dialog box open, point to the Table Properties list box arrow (Figure 3-58).

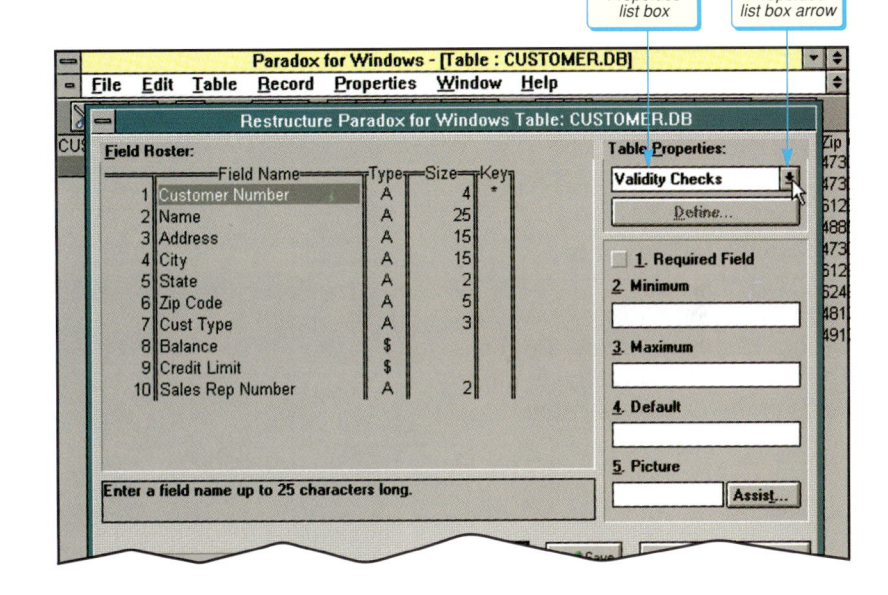

FIGURE 3-58

STEP 2 ▶

Click the arrow and point to Secondary Indexes.

The Table Properties drop-down list displays (Figure 3-59). The mouse pointer points to Secondary Indexes.

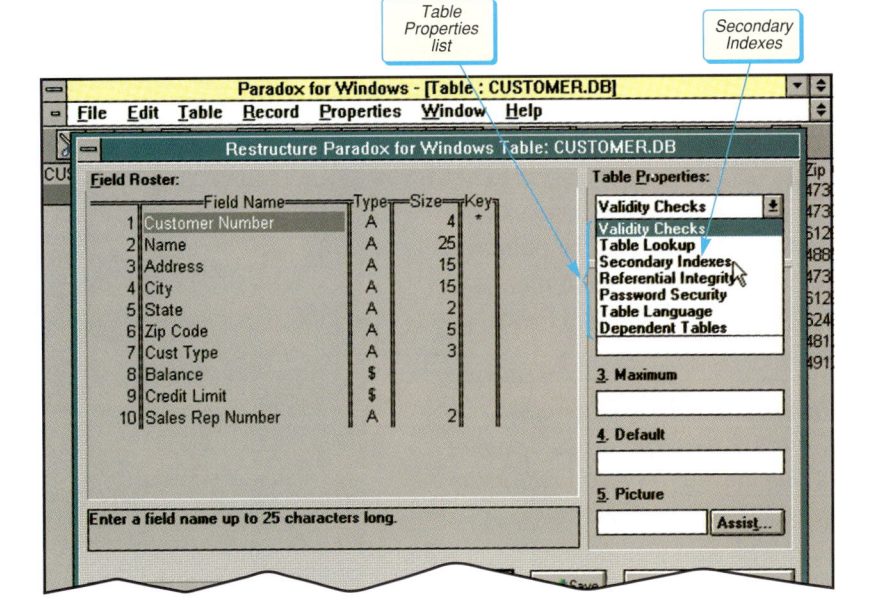

FIGURE 3-59

STEP 3 ▶

Click the left mouse button to select Secondary Indexes, and then point to the Define button (Define).

Secondary Indexes is selected (Figure 3-60). The mouse pointer points to the Define button. There is already a secondary index on Sales Rep Number. Paradox created this automatically when you specified referential integrity.

FIGURE 3-60

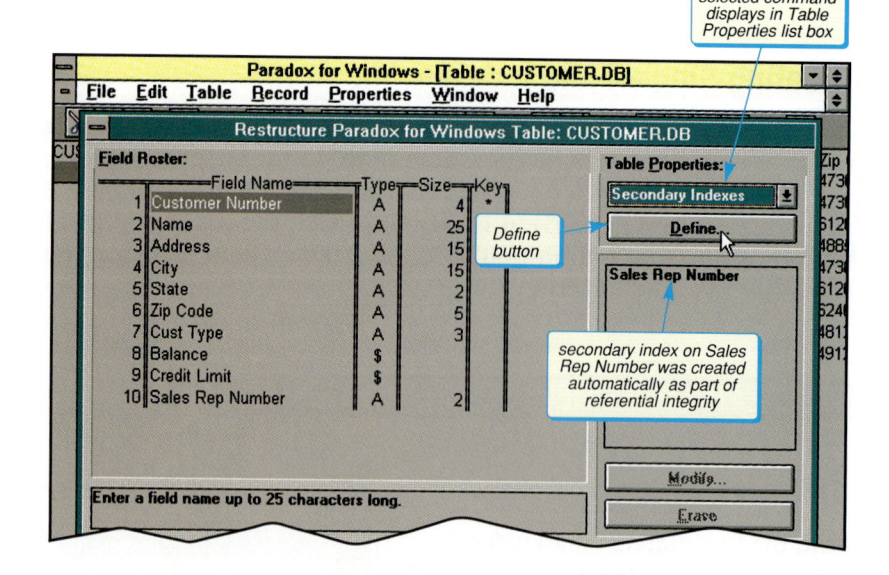

STEP 4 ▶

Choose the Define button.

The Define Secondary Index dialog box displays (Figure 3-61). The Fields list box contains the fields in the Customer table.

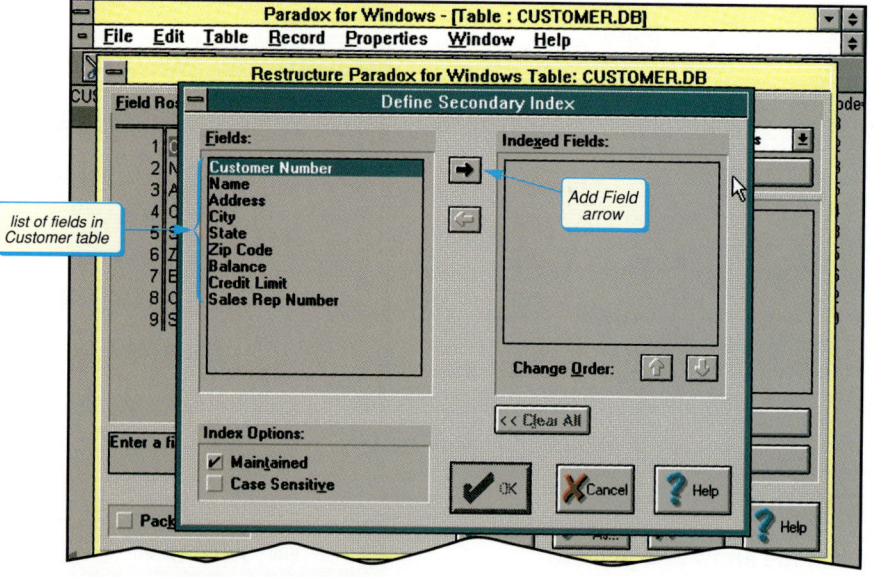

FIGURE 3-61

STEP 5 ▶

Select the Name field by pointing to it and clicking the left mouse button. Point to the Add Field arrow.

The Name field is selected (Figure 3-62). The mouse pointer is pointing to the Add Field arrow.

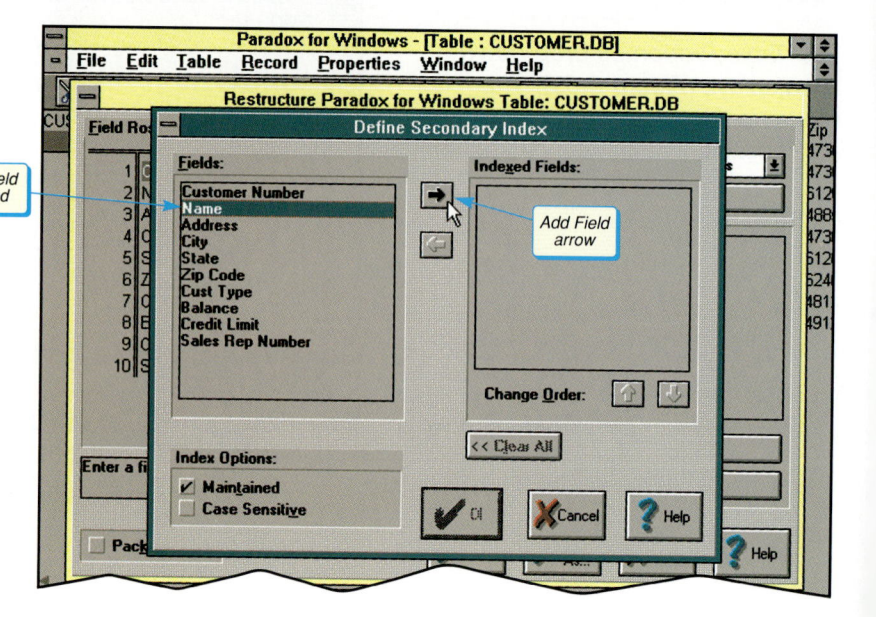

FIGURE 3-62

CREATING AND USING INDEXES • P147

STEP 6 ▶

Click the Add Field arrow and then point to the OK button.

The Name field is added to the list of indexed fields (Figure 3-63). The mouse pointer points to the OK button.

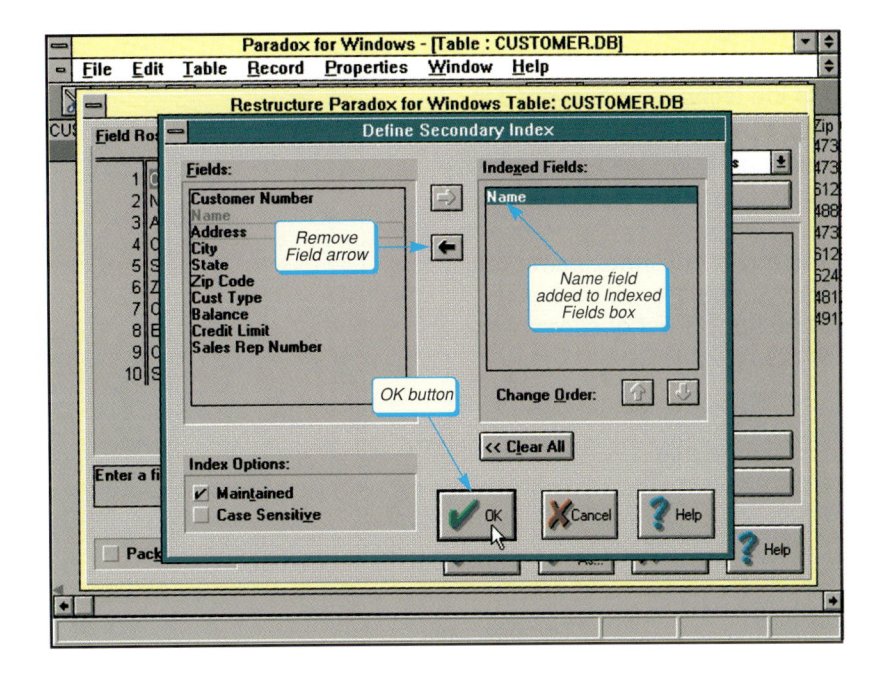

FIGURE 3-63

STEP 7 ▶

Choose the OK button, type Name1 in the Index Name box, and then point to the OK button in the Save Index As dialog box.

The Save Index As dialog box displays (Figure 3-64). Name1 is entered as the index name. The mouse pointer points to the OK button in the Save Index As dialog box.

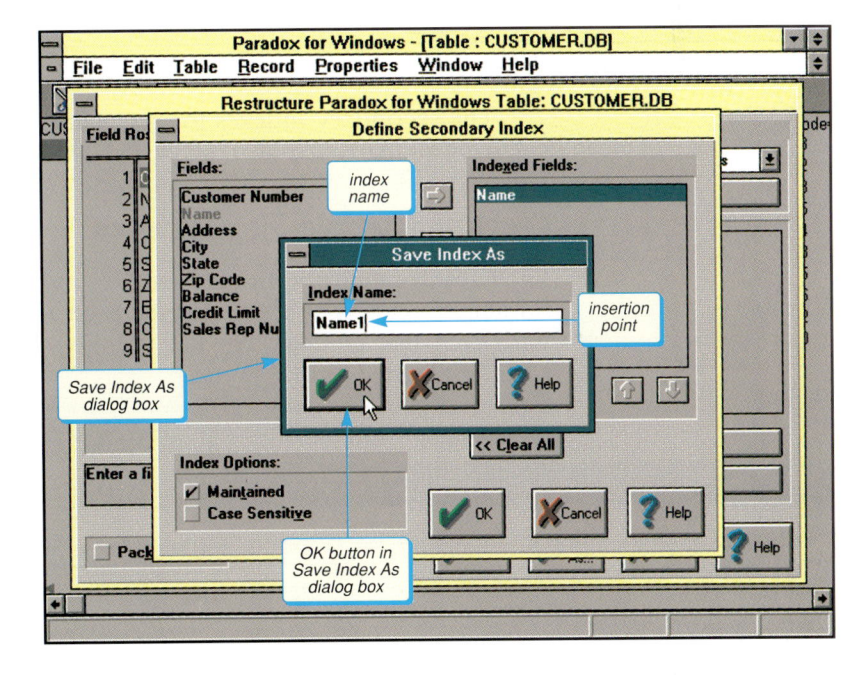

FIGURE 3-64

STEP 8 ▶

Choose the OK button in the Save Index As dialog box.

The secondary index for the Name field displays in the list of secondary indexes (Figure 3-65).

FIGURE 3-65

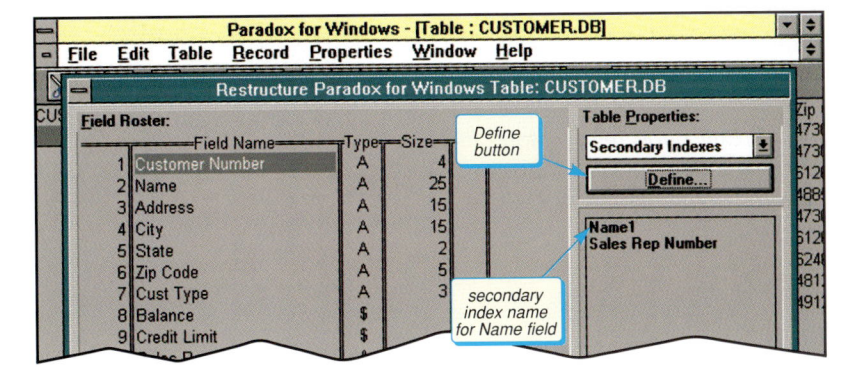

P148   PROJECT 3   MAINTAINING A DATABASE

STEP 9 ▶

Use the techniques described in Step 4 through Step 7 to create a secondary index with the name Zip Code1 for the Zip Code field.

The secondary index name Sales Rep Number1 displays below Name1 in the list of secondary indexes (Figure 3-66).

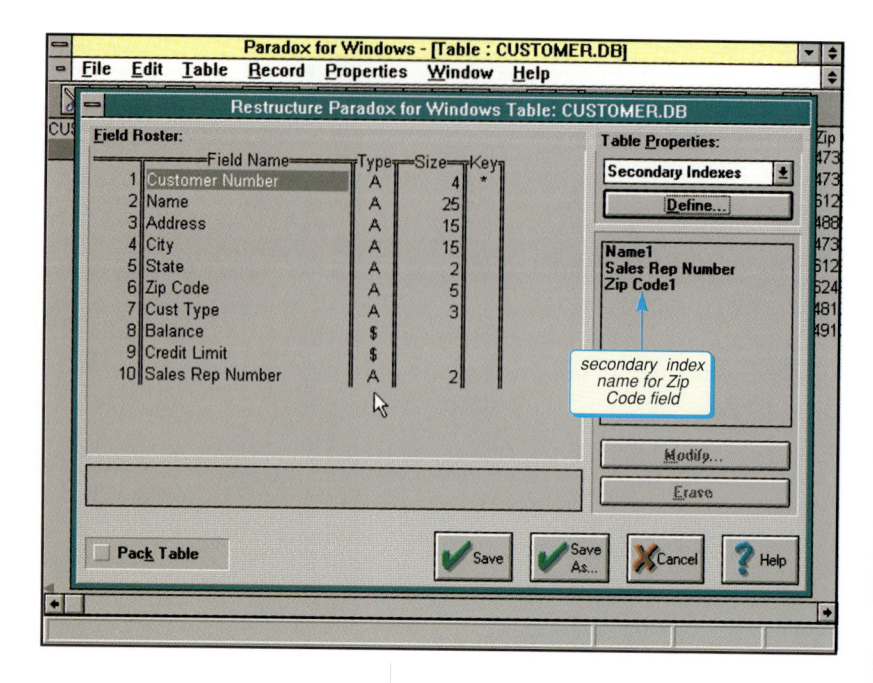

FIGURE 3-66

The secondary indexes for the Name and Sales Rep Number fields are now created and ready for use.

Creating Multiple-Field Indexes

Creating multiple-field secondary indexes is similar to creating the indexes for single fields. The following steps create a multiple-field secondary index with the name credbal. The key will be the combination of the Credit Limit field and the Balance field.

TO CREATE A MULTIPLE-FIELD SECONDARY INDEX ▼

STEP 1 ▶

In the Restructure Paradox for Windows Table dialog box, choose the Define button, select the Credit Limit field, and then point to the Add Field arrow.

The Credit Limit field is selected (Figure 3-67) and the mouse pointer points to the Add Field arrow.

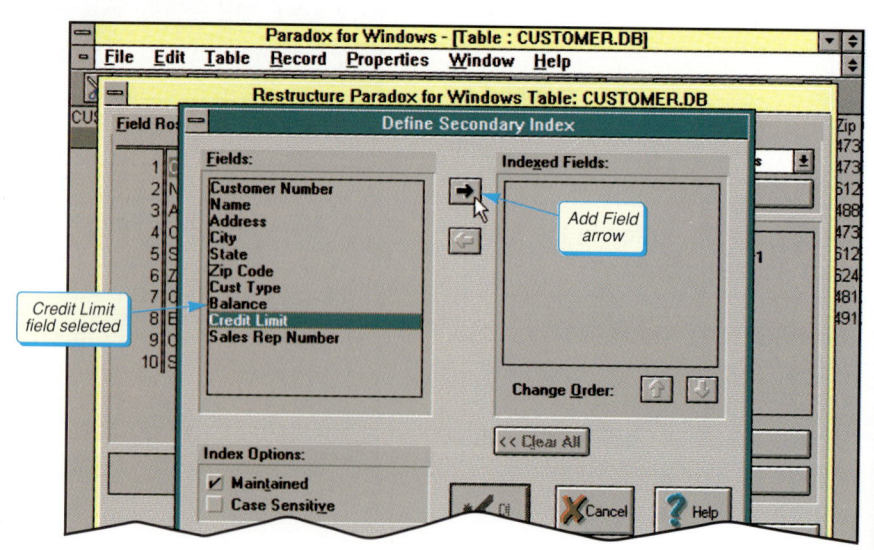

FIGURE 3-67

STEP 2 ▶

Click the Add Field arrow to add the Credit Limit field to the list of indexed fields. Select the Balance field and point to the Add Field arrow.

The Balance field is selected (Figure 3-68). The mouse pointer points to the Add Field arrow.

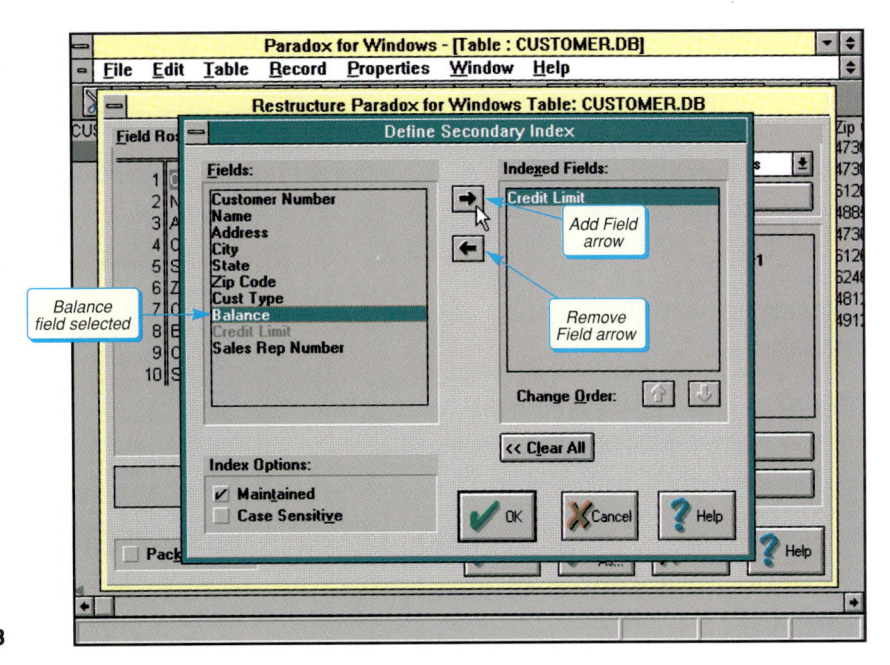

FIGURE 3-68

STEP 3 ▶

Click the Add Field arrow and then choose the OK button. Type `credbal` in the Index Name box and choose the OK button in the Save Index As dialog box.

The credbal index is added to the list of secondary indexes (Figure 3-69).

STEP 4 ▶

Choose the Save button to save your work.

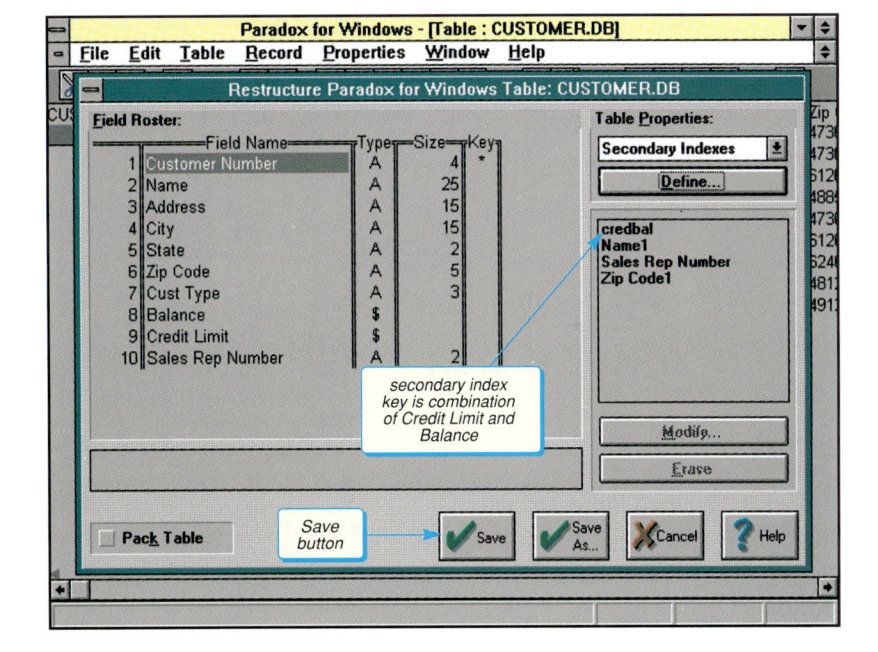

FIGURE 3-69

Using an Index to Order Records

Recall from previous discussions that Paradox sequences the records by customer number whenever you list them because customer number is the primary key. The steps on the following page use the Name1 secondary index created to change the order in which Paradox sequences the records so they are displayed alphabetically by customer name (see Figure 3-72 on the following page.

P150   PROJECT 3   MAINTAINING A DATABASE

TO SELECT A SECONDARY INDEX FOR ORDERING RECORDS

STEP 1 ▶

Make sure the Customer table is open and the window containing the table is maximized. Select the Table menu and point to the Order/Range command.

The Table menu displays and the mouse pointer is pointing to the Order/Range command (Figure 3-70).

FIGURE 3-70

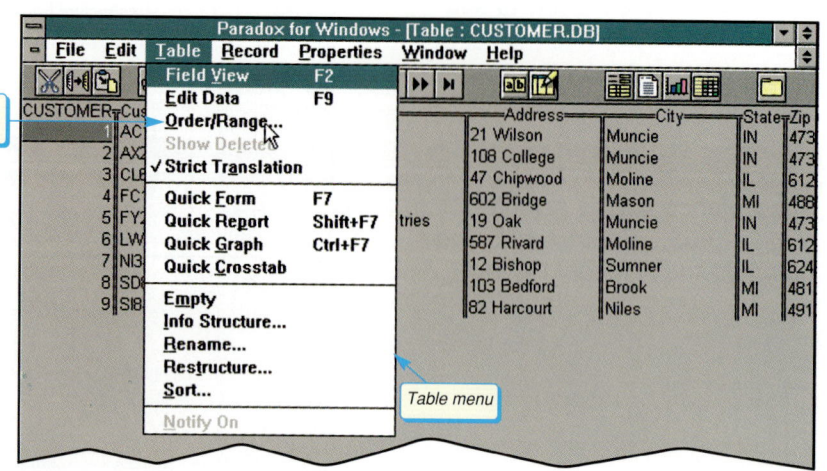

STEP 2 ▶

Choose the Order/Range command.

The Order/Range dialog box displays (Figure 3-71). The available indexes display in the Index List box.

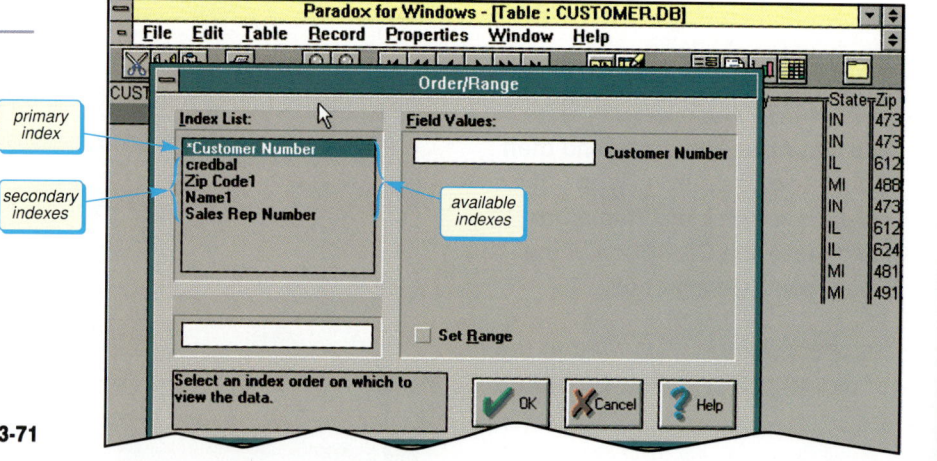

FIGURE 3-71

STEP 3 ▶

Select the Name1 index by pointing to it and clicking the left mouse button. Then choose the OK button.

The records in the Customer table display alphabetically by the customer name (Figure 3-72).

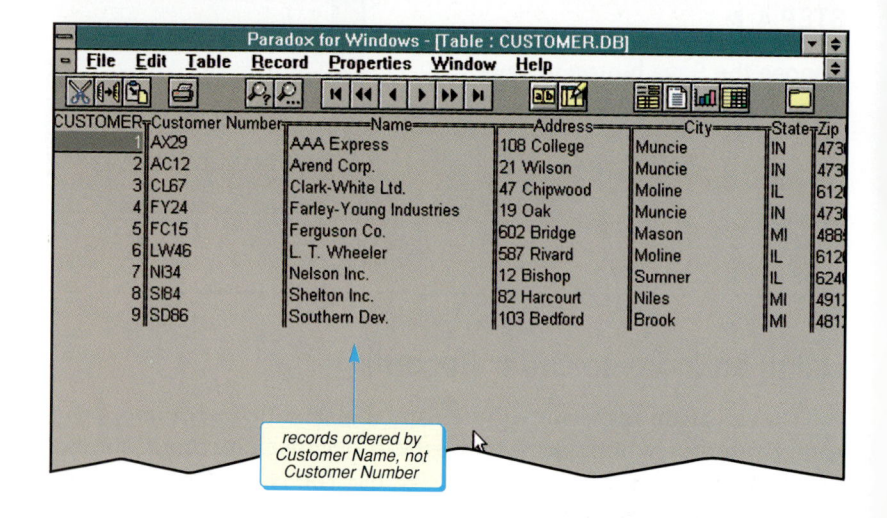

FIGURE 3-72

CREATING AND USING INDEXES **P151**

The following steps use the credbal secondary index to order the records by credit limit and balance.

TO CHANGE THE SECONDARY INDEX TO CREDBAL

STEP 1 ▶

With the Customer table open, choose the Order/Range command from the Table menu, choose the credbal index, and choose the OK button.

STEP 2 ▶

When Paradox redisplays the records in the Customer table, repeatedly press the TAB key until the highlight is in the Credit Limit field.

The records are ordered by credit limit (Figure 3-73). Within any group of customers who have the same credit limit, the records are ordered by balance.

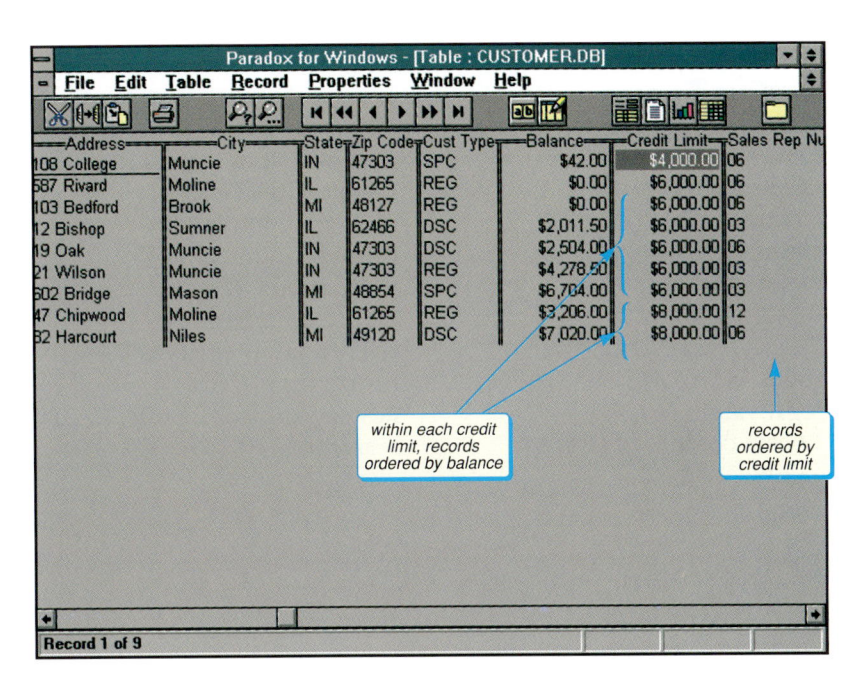

FIGURE 3-73

When you have finished viewing the Customer table, close it as described in the following steps.

TO CLOSE THE CUSTOMER TABLE

Step 1: Select the Control menu and point to the Close command (Figure 3-74).

Step 2: Choose the Close command.

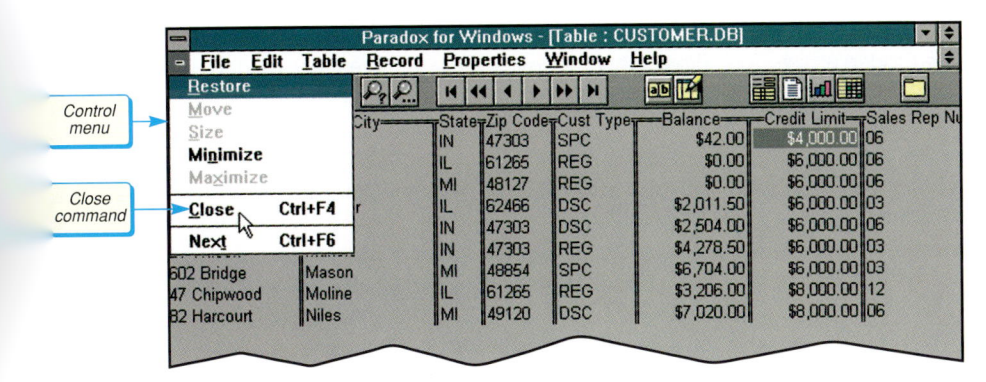

FIGURE 3-74

P152   PROJECT 3   MAINTAINING A DATABASE

▶ Project Summary

Project 3 covered the issues involved in maintaining a database and presented the steps on how to create and use both indexes and validity checks. The project explained how to change the structure of a table and how to specify referential integrity between two tables. In this project you learned to use Form view to add records and also how to search for the next record satisfying a certain condition. Finally, the project showed you how to make mass changes to a table.

▶ Key Terms

braces (*P131*)
case-sensitive (*P143*)
Changed table (*P139*)
Child Fields (*P135*)
Deleted table (*P139*)
foreign key (*P134*)
Field view (*P124*)
index key (*P143*)
legal values (*P133*)
Locate command (*P116*)

multiple-field index (*P145*)
Parent's Key (*P135*)
picture symbols (*P131*)
primary index (*P143*)
primary key (*P134*)
Query command (*P139*)
referential integrity (*P134*)
restructure (*P121*)
Restructure command (*P121*)
searching (*P116*)

secondary indexes (*P113, P143*)
single-field secondary indexes (*P145*)
structure (*P121*)
Table Utilities command (*P142*)
template (*P131*)
update query (*P125*)
validity check (*P127*)

QUICK REFERENCE

In Paradox for Windows you can accomplish a task in a number of different ways. The following table provides a quick reference to each task presented in this project with its available options. The commands listed in the Menu column can be executed using either the keyboard or the mouse.

Task	Mouse	Menu	Keyboard Shortcuts
Add a Field			Press INSERT
Change a Field Characteristic			Type new value, press TAB
Change a Group of Records			Type the word changeto followed by new value
Change to Field View	Click Field View button on SpeedBar	From Table menu or Form menu, choose Field View	Press F2
Create a Secondary Index	Click Table Properties list box arrow. Click Secondary Indexes option	From Table Properties list, choose Secondary Index	Press ALT + P, choose Secondary Index
Delete a Field			Press CTRL + DELETE
Delete a Group of Records	Click and hold and choose Delete from the menu of query options		Type DELETE under name of table in Query image
Delete a Record		From Record menu, choose Delete	Press CTRL + DELETE
Restructure a Table		From Table menu, choose Restructure	

Task	Mouse	Menu	Keyboard Shortcuts
Save a Table's Properties	Click Save button	From Restructure Warning dialog box, choose Save button	
Search for a Record	Click Locate Field Value button on SpeedBar	From Record menu, choose Locate, then choose Value	Press CTRL + Z
Select an Index Key	Click field. Click Add Field arrow		
Specify a Default Value	Click Default text box, and type value		Press ALT + 4, then type value
Specify a Picture	Click Assist button, type picture, and click OK button		Press ALT + T, type picture, press ENTER
Specify a Range	Click Minimum text box; type minimum value. Click Maximum text box; type maximum value.		Press ALT + 2, type minimum value. Press ALT + 3, type maximum value.
Specify a Required Field	Click Required Field option button		Press ALT + 1
Specify Legal Values			Create picture containing legal values between braces
Specify Referential Integrity	Click Table Properties list box arrow. Click Referential Integrity option.	From Table Properties list, choose Referential Integrity	Press ALT + P, choose Referential Integrity
Use an Index to Order Records		From Table menu, choose Order/Range	

STUDENT ASSIGNMENTS

STUDENT ASSIGNMENT 1
True/False

Instructions: Circle T if the statement is true or F if the statement is false.

T F 1. Paradox automatically sorts records by the primary index.
T F 2. Paradox allows secondary indexes on single fields only.
T F 3. Indexes provide an efficient alternative to sorting.
T F 4. To create a secondary index, choose Secondary Indexes from the Table Properties list of the Restructure Table dialog box.
T F 5. To arrange the data in a table in order by a secondary index, choose the Set Index command from the Table menu.
T F 6. The quickest and easiest way to make the same change to all records is to use a query.
T F 7. A template is a series of characters, one for each position in a field, that indicates how data is to be entered in a field.
T F 8. Only currency and numeric fields can be assigned default values.
T F 9. To force all letters in a field to display as uppercase, use the ? in the template.
T F 10. A field has the picture {HW,SG,AP}. To enter the value HW in the field, a user needs only to type the letter H.

STUDENT ASSIGNMENT 1 (continued)

T F 11. A foreign key is a field in one table whose values are required to match a primary key of another table.
T F 12. The property the value in a foreign key must match in another table's primary key is called entity integrity.
T F 13. To add records to a table in Form view, move to the last record in the table and click the Next Record button.
T F 14. You can add and change records using Form view but you can only delete records using Table view.
T F 15. To delete a record from a table, point to any field in the record, click the left mouse button, and then press CTRL+D.
T F 16. To search for a specific record in a table, use the Locate command from the Record menu.
T F 17. To delete a group of records that satisfy a condition, use a query.
T F 18. In a query to delete records, any deleted records are placed in a permanent table called Deleted.
T F 19. To delete records that satisfy some condition using a query, enter the word DEL followed by the condition in the appropriate column.
T F 20. In a query, use the changeto operator to replace one value with another in a field.

STUDENT ASSIGNMENT 2
Multiple Choice

Instructions: Circle the correct response.

1. Indexes _____.
   a. provide an efficient alternative to sorting
   b. allow rapid retrieval of records
   c. allow rapid retrieval of tables
   d. both a and b
2. To create secondary indexes, choose _____ from the Table Properties list of the Restructure Paradox Table dialog box.
   a. Secondary Index
   b. Define Secondary Indexes
   c. Create Indexes
   d. Create Secondary Indexes
3. To arrange the data in a table in order by a secondary index, choose the _____ command from the Table menu.
   a. Set Index   c. Order/Range
   b. Sort/Order   d. Reorder
4. A(n) _____ is a series of characters, one for each position in a field, that indicates how data is to be entered in a field.
   a. object   c. picture function
   b. template   d. character set
5. To force all letters in a field to display as uppercase, use the _____ picture symbol in the template.
   a. ?   c. @
   b. #   d. &
6. A(n) _____ is a field in one table whose values are required to match a primary key of another table.
   a. secondary key   c. foreign key
   b. auxiliary key   d. matching key
7. The property the value in a foreign key must match in another table's primary key is called _____ integrity.
   a. entity   c. relationship
   b. referential   d. inter-relation

8. To search for a specific record, use the Locate command from the _____ menu.
   a. Edit
   b. Record
   c. Search
   d. Select
9. The Referential Integrity dialog box uses the term _____ fields to indicate the foreign key in a table.
   a. parent
   b. child
   c. dependent
   d. connector
10. In a query, use the _____ operator to replace one value with another in a field.
    a. with
    b. by
    c. changeto
    d. replace

STUDENT ASSIGNMENT 3
Understanding the Restructure Paradox Table Screen

Instructions: Figure SA3-3 shows the Restructure Paradox for Windows Table dialog box for the Customer table. Validity check information for the Credit Limit field is displayed on the screen. Use this figure to answer the following questions.

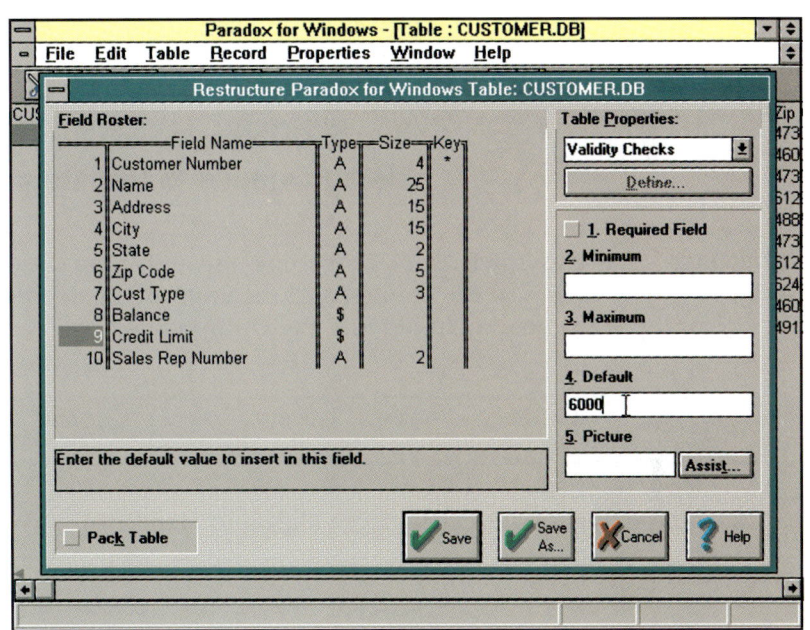

FIGURE SA3-3

1. Is Credit Limit a required field?

2. What is the default value for the field?

3. What range of values is acceptable for the field?

4. How can you create a secondary index on the Credit Limit field?

STUDENT ASSIGNMENT 4
Understanding Templates

Instructions: Indicate what the effect will be when the template in column 2 is applied to the data in column 1. If valid, write the corresponding value and if invalid, write INVALID in the space provided.

database	????????
database	&???&???
12ab45	##!!##
93	??
8934x	####?
8174x	####&
197a	####
FIC	@@@
mi	&&
346 Magee	!!!!!!!!

STUDENT ASSIGNMENT 5
Using Queries to Update a Table

Instructions: The Customer table needs to be updated using queries. For each of the following changes to the Customer table, list the column and the appropriate expression necessary to make the change. Use the following table to help identify the column headings.

CUSTOMER	Customer Number	Name	Address	City	State	Cust Type	Balance	Credit Limit	Sales Rep Number

1. Change the city for all records from Mason to Manitowc.

   _____

   _____

2. Change the sales rep number for all records from 03 to 06.

   _____

   _____

3. Change the credit limit for all records from $8,000 to $9,000.

   _____

   _____

4. Delete all records where the Cust Type is SPC.

   _____

   _____

STUDENT ASSIGNMENT 6
Understanding the Form View Screen

Instructions: Figure SA3-6 shows the Form view screen for the first record in the Customer table. Use this figure to help you perform the following tasks in Form view.

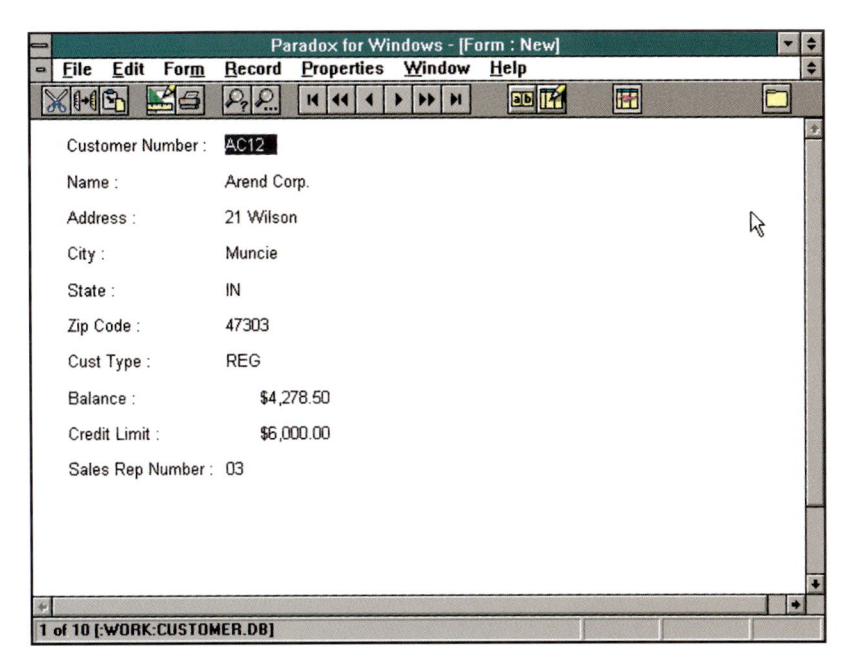

FIGURE SA3-6

1. Move from the first record to the second record.

2. Add a new record to the Customer table.

3. Move to the first record in the table.

4. Locate the first record that contains the value Moline in the City field.

5. Locate the next record that contains the value Moline in the City field.

COMPUTER LABORATORY EXERCISES

COMPUTER LABORATORY EXERCISE 1
Using the Help Menu

Instructions: Perform the following tasks.

1. Start Paradox.
2. Open the Customer table and choose Restructure from the Table menu.
3. Choose Secondary Index from the Table Properties list.
4. Choose the Help button (Help).
5. Scroll the screen contents until you reach the Secondary Index topic.
6. Point to the word key in the definition column of the topic and click. (The mouse pointer changes to a small hand.)
7. Read the information and answer the following question:
   What are the effects of establishing a key?
   _____
   _____
8. Exit the Help window.
9. Exit Paradox.

COMPUTER LABORATORY EXERCISE 2
Creating and Using Secondary Indexes

Instructions: Perform the following tasks.

1. Start Paradox.
2. Open the Customer table and choose Restructure from the Table menu.
3. Choose Secondary Index from the Table Properties list.
4. Create a multiple-field index on the combination of the state and city fields.
5. Name the index statcity.
6. Return to the Customer table.
7. Order the records by the statcity index.
8. Print the table.
9. Close the table.
10. Exit Paradox.

COMPUTER LABORATORY EXERCISE 3
Creating Validity Checks

Instructions: Perform the following tasks.

1. Start Paradox.
2. Open the Slsrep table.
3. Choose Restructure from the Table menu.
4. Assign a minimum value of .04 and a maximum value of .09 to the Commission Rate field.
5. Create a template for the State field to convert the two-character state code to uppercase.
6. Make the Last Name field a required field.
7. Save the changes to the structure and return to the Slsrep table.
8. Print the table.
9. Exit Paradox.

COMPUTER LABORATORY ASSIGNMENTS

COMPUTER LABORATORY ASSIGNMENT 1
Maintaining the Parts Database

Purpose: To provide practice in maintaining a database.

Instructions: Use the database created in Computer Laboratory Assignment 1 of Project 1 for this assignment. Execute each task on the computer and print the results.

1. Open the Part table and display the Restructure Paradox Table dialog box.
2. Create a secondary index for the Part Description field. Name the Index Part Description1.
3. Create a secondary index on the combination of the Item Class Code and Part Description fields. Name the index Classpart.
4. Order the records in the Part table by the Classpart index.
5. Print the table.
6. Change the field width of the Part Description field to 19.
7. Change the entry for Part Number, BZ66 from WASHER to WASHING MACHINE.
8. Print the table.
9. Create the following validity checks for the Part table and list the steps involved.
    a. Make Part Description a required field.

    _____
    _____

    b. Create a template so part numbers must be two capital letters followed by a two-digit number.

    _____
    _____

    c. Use picture symbols to force the user to enter HW, SG, or AP for the Item Class Code field.

    _____
    _____

    d. Enforce referential integrity between the Part and Class tables. Assign the name Partclss to this validity check.

    _____
    _____

10. Return to the Part table and change from Table view to Form view.
11. Using the Form view screen, add the following record to the Part table.

    | CP03 | POOL TABLE | 2 | SG | 1 | 299.99 |

12. Return to Table view and print the table.
13. Create a new query for the Part table.
14. Using the Query screen, delete all records in the Part table where the Part Description starts with the letter P.
15. Close the query without saving it.
16. Print the Part table.
17. Exit Paradox

COMPUTER LABORATORY ASSIGNMENT 2
Maintaining the Employee Database

Purpose: To provide practice in maintaining a database.

Instructions: Use the database created in Computer Laboratory Assignment 2 of Project 1 for this assignment. Execute each task on the computer and print the results.

1. Open the Employee table and display the Restructure Paradox Table dialog box.
2. Create a secondary index for the Employee Last Name field. Name the index Employee Last Name1.
3. Create a secondary index on the combination of the Department Code and Employee Last Name fields. Name the index Deptname.
4. Order the records in the Employee table by the Deptname index.
5. Print the table.
6. Create a secondary index on the combination of the Pay Rate and Employee Last Name fields. Name the index Payname.
7. Order the records in the Employee table by the Payname index.
8. Print the table.
9. Add the field Union Code to the Employee Table. Define the field as Alphanumeric with a width of 3. Insert the Union Code field after the Department Code field. This field will contain data on whether the employee is a union member (UNM) or is non-union (NON). Save the changes to the Employee table.
10. Create a new query for the Employee table.
11. Using this query, change all the entries in the Union Code field to UNM. This will be the status of most employees.
12. Return to the Employee table and print the table.
13. Create the following validity checks for the Employee table and list the steps involved.
    a. Make employee first and last names required fields.

    _____

    _____

    b. Create a template so employee numbers must be four digits.

    _____

    _____

    c. Use picture symbols to force the user to enter UNM or NON for the Union Code field.

    _____

    _____

    d. Enforce referential integrity between the Employee and Dept tables. Assign the name Empdept to this validity check.

    _____

    _____

14. Return to the Employee table and change from Table view to Form view.
15. Using the Form view screen, add the following record to the Employee table.

    | 1070 | Fisher | Ella | 02 | NON | 9.30 |

16. Locate the employees with Employee Numbers 1016, 1022, and 1037 and change the Union Code for each record to NON.
17. Return to Table view and print the table.
18. Create a new query for the Employee table.

19. Using the Query screen, delete all records in the Employee table where the employee's last name starts with the letter F.
20. Close the query without saving it.
21. Print the Employee table.
22. Exit Paradox

COMPUTER LABORATORY ASSIGNMENT 3
Maintaining the Movie Database

Purpose: To provide practice in maintaining a database.

Instructions: Use the database created in Computer Laboratory Assignment 3 of Project 1 for this assignment. Execute each task on the computer and print the results.

1. Open the Movie table.
2. Create a secondary index for the Movie Title field. Name the index Movie Title1.
3. Create a secondary index on the combination of the Movie Type and Movie Title fields. Name the index Typetitle.
4. Order the records in the Movie table by the Typetitle index.
5. Print the table.
6. Change the field width of the Movie Title to 20.
7. Change the title for the movie, *The Dervish*, to *The Whirling Dervish*.
8. Order the records by the Movie Title index.
9. Print the table.
10. Add the field Color Type to the Movie table. Define the field as Alphanumeric with a width of 5. Insert the Color Type field after the Length field. This field will contain data on whether the movie is in color (COLOR) or black and white (BW). Save the changes to the Movie table.
11. Create a new query for the Movie table.
12. Using this query, change all the entries in the Color Type field to COLOR. This will be the status of most movies.
13. Return to the Movie table and print the table.
14. Create the following validity checks for the Movie table and list the steps involved.
    a. Make the movie title a required field.

    _____

    _____

    b. Create a template so the movie numbers must be three digits.

    _____

    _____

    c. Use picture symbols to force the user to enter COLOR or BW for the Color Type field.

    _____

    _____

    d. Enforce referential integrity between the Movie and Director tables. Assign the name Movdir to this validity check.

    _____

    _____

    e. Assign a default value of COLOR to the Color Type field.

    _____

    _____

15. Return to the Movie table and change from Table view to Form view.
16. Using the Form view screen, add the following record to the Movie table.

| 023 | Mojave | 1937 | WESTER | 97 | BW | 02 |

17. Locate the Movies with Movie Numbers 024, 021, and 004 and change the Color Type for each record to BW.
18. Return to Table view and print the table.
19. Create a new query for the Movie table.
20. Using the Query screen, delete all records in the Movie table where the movie was made in 1937.
21. Close the query without saving it.
22. Print the Movie table.
23. Exit Paradox

COMPUTER LABORATORY ASSIGNMENT 4
Maintaining the Book Database

Purpose: To provide practice in maintaining a database.

Problem: The owner of the bookstore where you are employed is very pleased with the work you have done so far on the Book database. Because the business is expanding rapidly, she would like to make some changes to the database. She has sent you a list of recommended changes and asked if you can implement them.

Instructions: Use the database created in Computer Laboratory Assignment 4 of Project 1 for this assignment. Provide printed output and/or a written explanation that confirms the changes to the database.

The following are recommended changes to the Book database:

1. The title for book code 2295 is really *The Thing Struck Twice* not *It Struck Twice.* Change the size of the field to accommodate the correct title.
2. Customer queries can be answered more efficiently if the books can be displayed in various orders. List the books in author order. In order by title within publisher. In order by title within book type.
3. Most books in inventory are paperback but there are a few hardback books. Add a new field with values such as SOFT(paperback) and HARD (hardback) to indicate the cover type.
4. Currently, the only hardback books in stock are those books with a price greater than $14.99. Use a more efficient method than changing each record individually to make those corrections to the database.
5. Various personnel in the bookstore are updating the database. Improve the accuracy of the data entry process by adding some validity checks to the database. The following are examples.
   a. No book is priced at less than 1.99 or more than 49.99.
   b. All book type and publisher code entries are in uppercase.
   c. The book title, publisher, and author fields are required.
   d. Publisher code entries should match the entries in the Publish table.
   e. SOFT and HARD are the only choices for the cover type. Most books are paperback.
   f. Any letters entered in the book code field are in uppercase.
6. Three copies of a new paperback book (code 6781) have just arrived and should be added to the database. However, the book publisher is not in the Publish table. Add the book to the database. The publisher is Fraser Books (FR). The book title is *The Runaway*, a mystery by Megan Rust. The price is $5.95.
7. The store will no longer carry science fiction (SFI) books. Delete all science fiction books from the database.

PARADOX 1.0 FOR WINDOWS
PROJECT FOUR

PRESENTING DATA: REPORTS AND FORMS

OBJECTIVES You will have mastered the material in this project when you can:

- Create a report
- Select fields for a report
- Select a portion of a report
- Change column headings in a report
- Change the Zoom factor when viewing a report
- Adjust the widths of the columns in a report
- Add a total to the report footer in a report
- View a report on the screen
- Print a report
- Save a report
- Add a group band to a report
- Add a subtotal to a group footer
- Explain the principles of good report design
- Create a form
- Select the fields for a form
- Use a grid to help align objects in a form
- Move fields on a form
- View data using a form
- Add boxes to a form
- Add text to a form
- Change font sizes, styles, and colors on a form
- Change frame styles on a form
- Explain the principles of good form design

▶ INTRODUCTION

In the previous projects, you learned how to create a database, query a database, and maintain a database. Project 4 introduces you to presenting the data in a database in a pleasing and useful way, either on paper or on the screen.

Reports generated on a printer represent one way of presenting data. Figures 4-1 and 4-2 illustrate two types of reports you can prepare. Figure 4-1 on the next page shows a report that lists the customer number, name, address, city, state, zip code, credit limit, and current balance of all customers. In addition, the end of the report lists the total of all the balances. This report is similar to the one you produced earlier in Project 1 (Figure 1-53 on page P27) by simply clicking the Print button on the SpeedBar. The report in Figure 4-1 has some significant differences, however.

P163

Tuesday, October 04, 1994 ← system date CUSTOMER page number → Page 1

Customer Number	Name	Address	City	State	Zip Code	Credit Limit	Current Balance
AC12	Arend Corp.	21 Wilson	Muncie	IN	47303	$6,000.00	$4,278.50
AX29	AAA Express	108 College	Muncie	IN	47303	$4,000.00	$42.00
CL67	Clark-White Ltd.	47 Chipwood	Moline	IL	61265	$8,000.00	$3,206.00
FC15	Ferguson Co.	602 Bridge	Mason	MI	48854	$6,000.00	$6,704.00
FY24	Farley-Young Industries	19 Oak	Muncie	IN	47303	$6,000.00	$2,504.00
LW46	L. T. Wheeler	587 Rivard	Moline	IL	61265	$6,000.00	$0.00
NI34	Nelson Inc.	12 Bishop	Sumner	IL	62466	$6,000.00	$2,011.50
SD86	Southern Dev.	103 Bedford	Brook	MI	48127	$6,000.00	$0.00
SI84	Shelton Inc.	82 Harcourt	Niles	MI	49120	$8,000.00	$7,020.00

Balance Total: $25,766.00 ← sum of the current balances for all customers

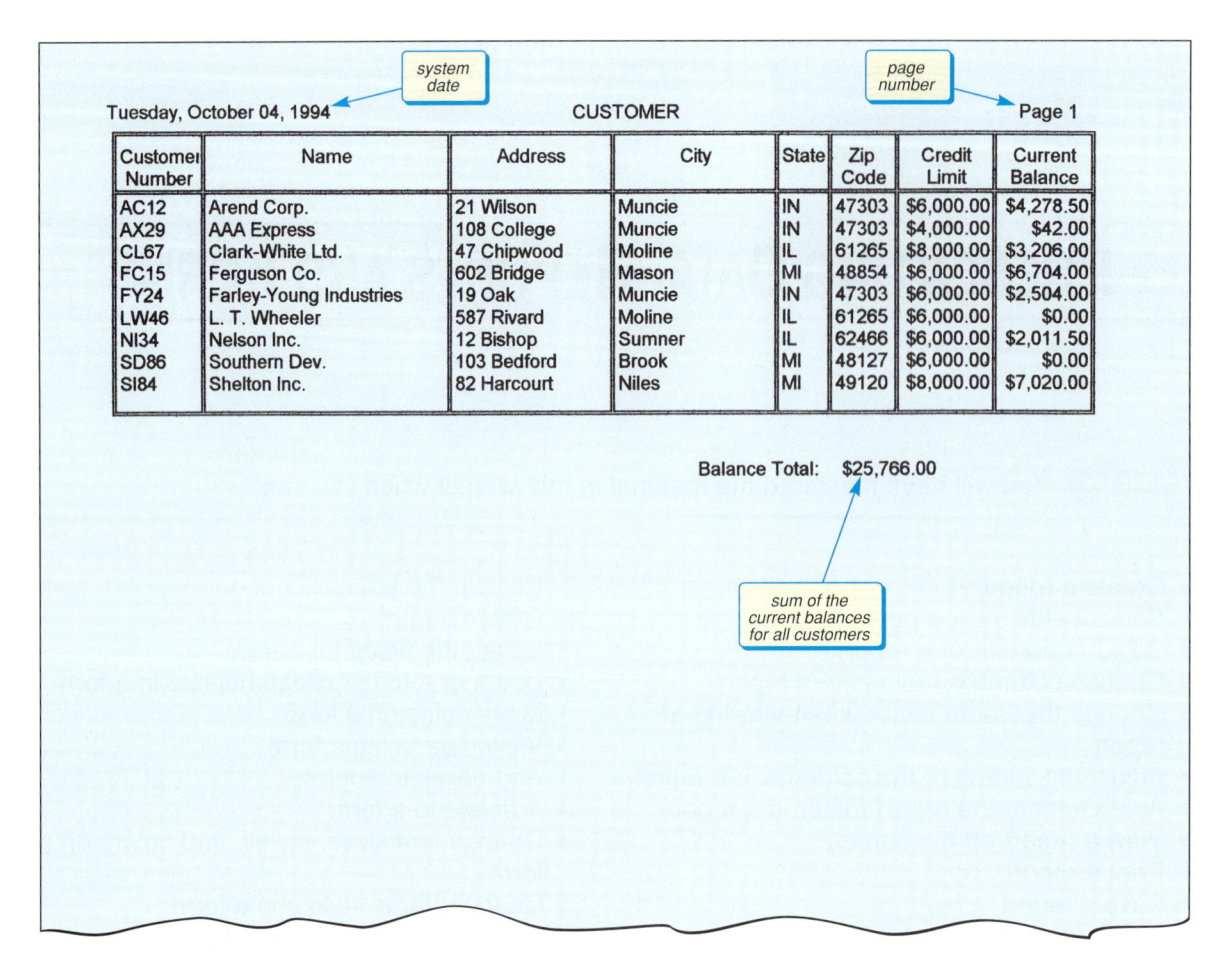

FIGURE 4-1

First, not all fields are included. The Customer table includes a Cust Type field (added in Project 3) and a Sales Rep Number field, neither of which appear on the report in Figure 4-1. Second, when compared to the report generated in Project 1, the order of Current Balance and Credit Limit is reversed in Figure 4-1 with Credit Limit coming first. Third, some column headings extend to two lines. Instead of Customer Number on a single line, for example, the word Customer displays on one line and the word Number displays on the next. Finally, the report in Figure 4-1 includes the total of the balances.

The report shown in Figure 4-2 is similar to the one in Figure 4-1 but contains an additional feature, grouping. **Grouping** means creating separate collections of records sharing some common characteristic. In the report in Figure 4-2, for example, the records have been grouped by sales rep number. There are three separate groups: one for sales rep 03, one for sales rep 06, and one for sales rep 12. The appropriate sales rep number appears before each group, and the total of the balances for the customers in the group (called a **subtotal**) appears after each group.

INTRODUCTION **P165**

Tuesday, October 04, 1994   CUSTOMER   Page 1

Sales Rep Number : 03 *← customers of sales rep 03*

Customer Number	Name	Address	City	State	Zip Code	Credit Limit	Current Balance
AC12	Arend Corp.	21 Wilson	Muncie	IN	47303	$6,000.00	$4,278.50
FC15	Ferguson Co.	602 Bridge	Mason	MI	48854	$6,000.00	$6,704.00
NI34	Nelson Inc.	12 Bishop	Sumner	IL	62466	$6,000.00	$2,011.50

Balance Subtotal: $12,994.00

Sales Rep Number : 06

Customer Number	Name	Address	City	State	Zip Code	Credit Limit	Current Balance
AX29	AAA Express	108 College	Muncie	IN	47303	$4,000.00	$42.00
FY24	Farley-Young Industries	19 Oak	Muncie	IN	47303	$6,000.00	$2,504.00
LW46	L. T. Wheeler	587 Rivard	Moline	IL	61265	$6,000.00	$0.00
SD86	Southern Dev.	103 Bedford	Brook	MI	48127	$6,000.00	$0.00
SI84	Shelton Inc.	82 Harcourt	Niles	MI	49120	$8,000.00	$7,020.00

Balance Subtotal: $9,566.00 *← sum of the current balances for customers of each sales rep*

Sales Rep Number : 12

Customer Number	Name	Address	City	State	Zip Code	Credit Limit	Current Balance
CL67	Clark-White Ltd.	47 Chipwood	Moline	IL	61265	$8,000.00	$3,206.00

Balance Subtotal: $3,206.00

Balance Total: $25,766.00 *← sum of the current balances for all customers*

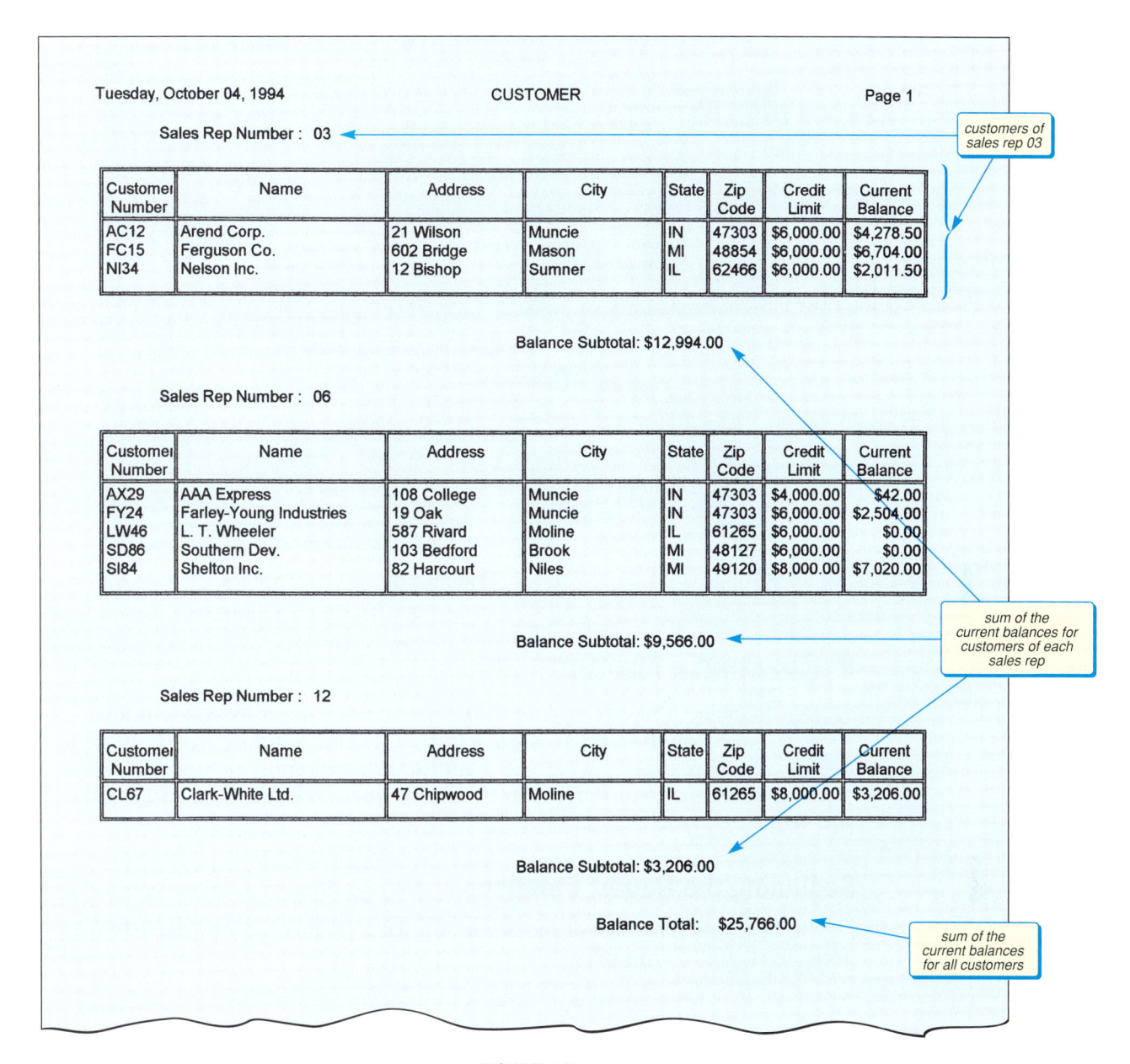

FIGURE 4-2

Another way of presenting data is by displaying custom forms on a screen. You have already used the Form view screen to view records in a table as well as to update records. When did, you used a standard display form automatically generated by Paradox. Rather than simply using the form Paradox creates, you can design and use your own custom forms like the one shown in Figure 4-3 on the next page.

This project covers the design and creation of reports and forms.

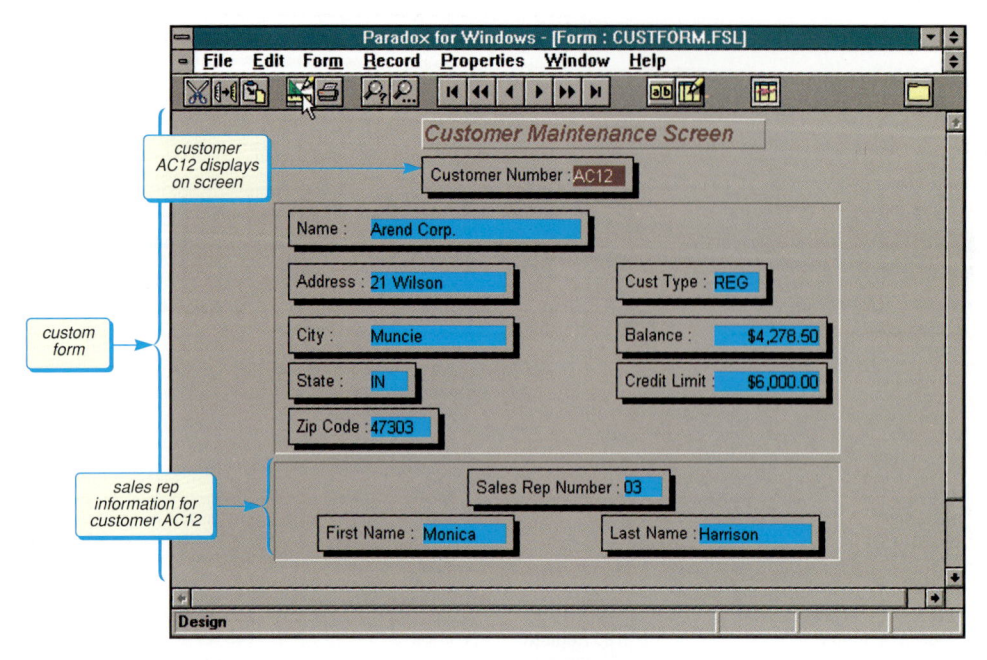

P166 PROJECT 4 PRESENTING DATA: REPORTS AND FORMS

FIGURE 4-3

▶ CREATING A REPORT

To create a report to send to the printer, you use a special window, called the **Report Design window**. In this window, you indicate to Paradox exactly what you want the printed report to look like. After creating the report, you can print the report whenever you want and as often as you want.

Beginning the Report Creation

To begin the creation of the report shown in Figure 4-1 on page P164, perform the following steps.

TO BEGIN CREATING A REPORT ▼

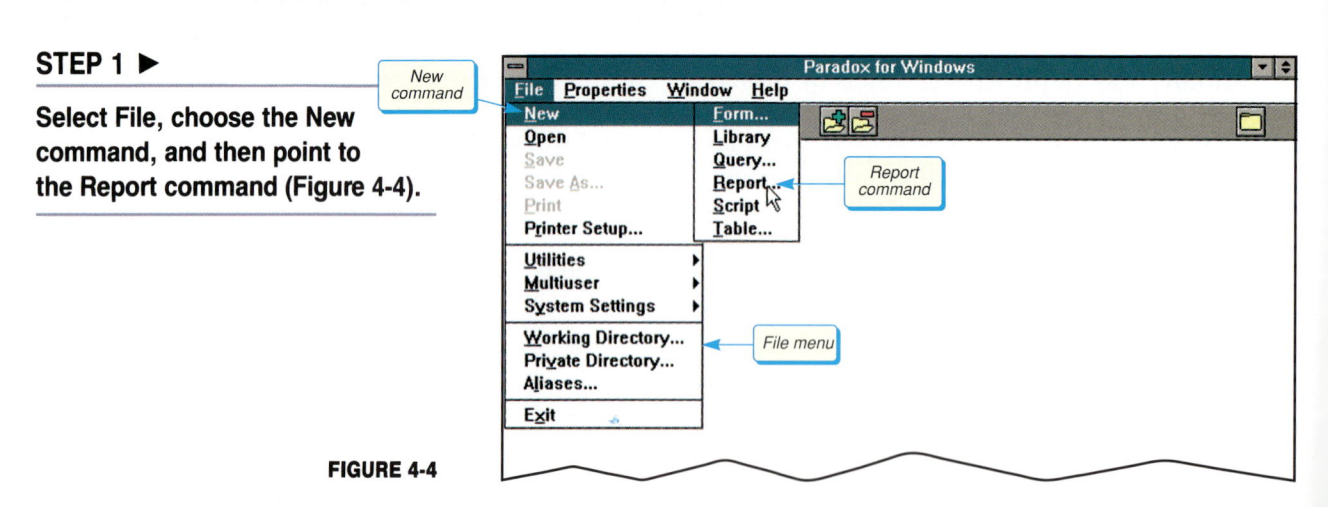

STEP 1 ▶

Select File, choose the New command, and then point to the Report command (Figure 4-4).

FIGURE 4-4

CREATING A REPORT **P167**

STEP 2 ▶

Choose the Report command and point to the Customer table (CUSTOMER.DB) in the File Name list box.

The Data Model dialog box displays (Figure 4-5). The mouse pointer points to the Customer table (CUSTOMER.DB).

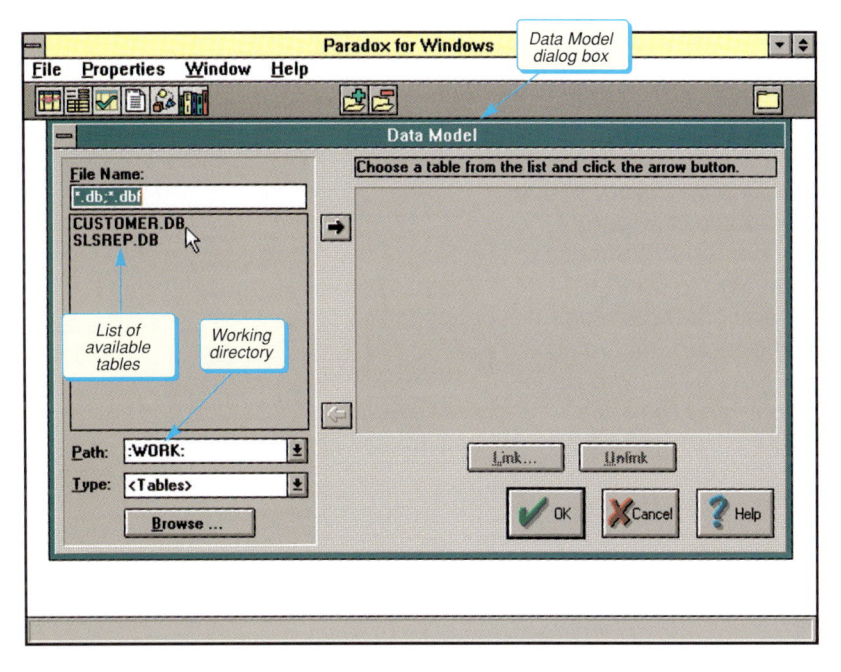

FIGURE 4-5

STEP 3 ▶

Select the Customer table by clicking the left mouse button and then point to the OK button.

The customer table is selected and displays in the data model (Figure 4-6). The mouse pointer points to the OK button.

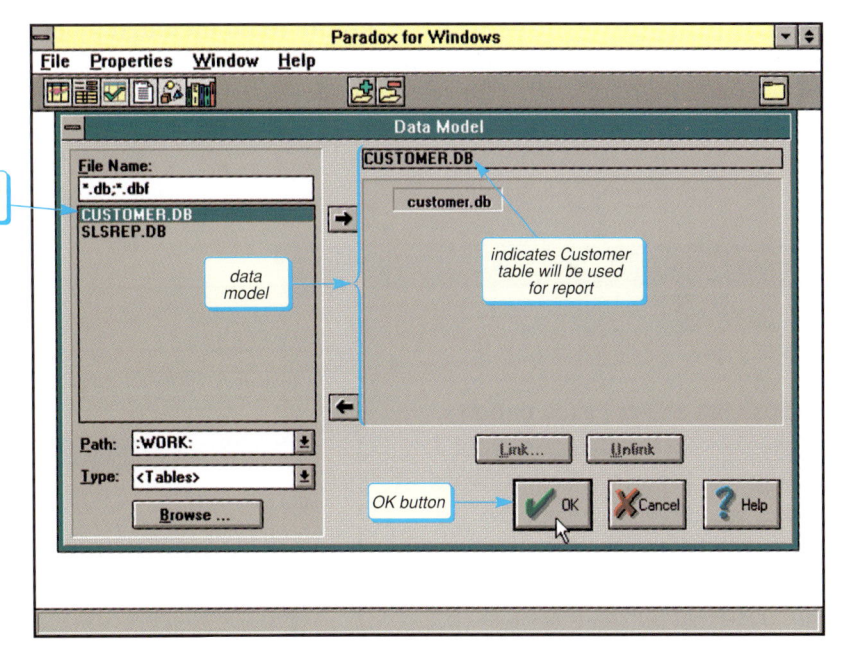

FIGURE 4-6

STEP 4 ▶

Choose the OK button in the Data Model dialog box.

The Design Layout dialog box displays (Figure 4-7). Options on this screen allow you to change several characteristics of the report, including the field layout, the page layout, and the style.

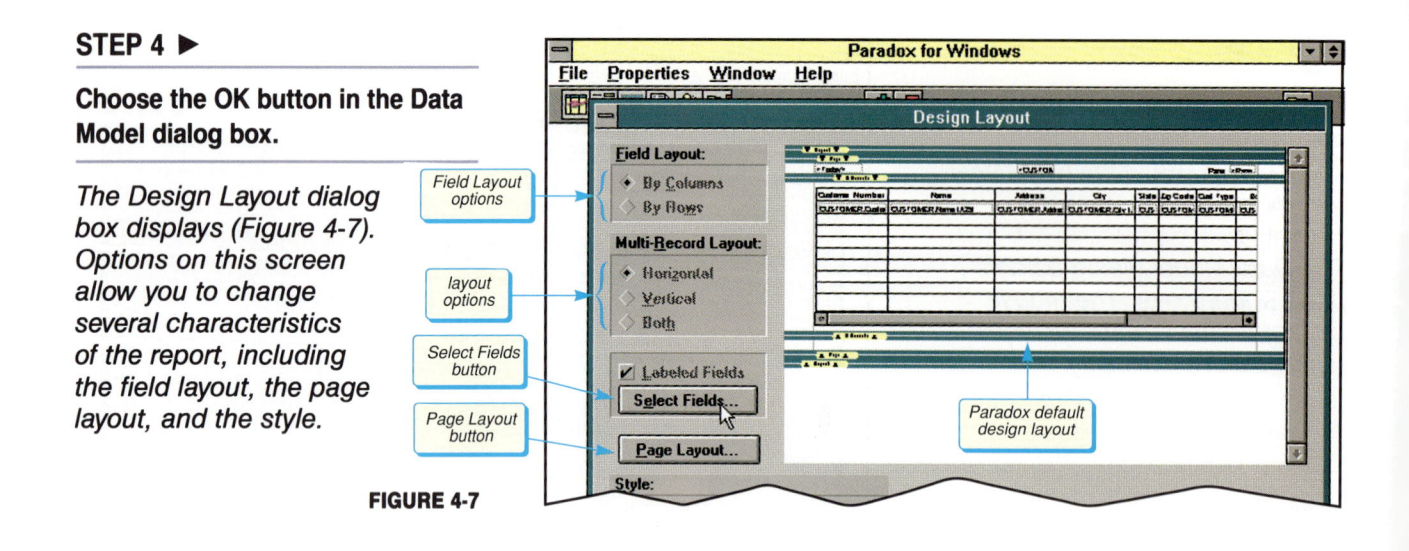

FIGURE 4-7

Selecting the Fields

The initial design shown on the screen includes all fields from the Customer table. Because the report being created does not include all fields, you must indicate which fields are to be included by using the Select Fields button. Further, you must indicate that Credit Limit should precede Balance.

To select the fields for the report, choose the Select Fields button and remove all the unwanted fields from the list of selected fields as shown in the following steps.

TO SELECT THE FIELDS FOR THE REPORT ▼

STEP 1 ▶

Choose the Select Fields button (Select fields) in the Design Layout dialog box. When the Select Fields dialog box displays, select the Cust Type field in the Selected Fields list box. Point to the Remove Field button (Remove field).

The Select Fields dialog box displays (Figure 4-8). The Cust Type field is selected. The mouse pointer points to the Remove Field button.

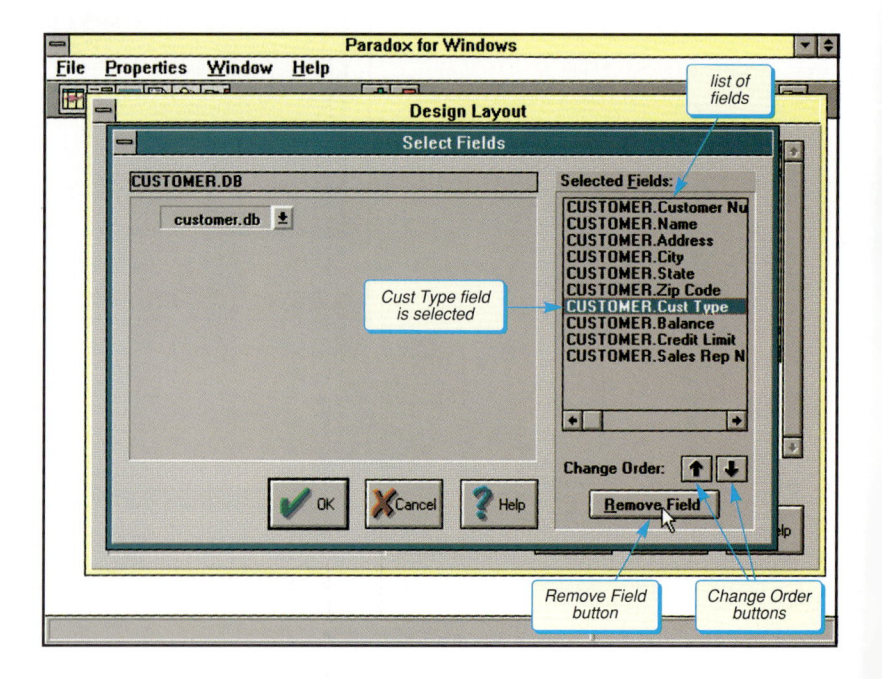

FIGURE 4-8

STEP 2 ▶

Choose the Remove Field button to remove the Cust Type field. Select the Sales Rep Number field and then remove it from the list by choosing the Remove Field button. Select the Credit Limit field and point to the Change Order Up button ([↑]).

The Cust Type and Sales Rep Number fields have been removed (Figure 4-9). The Credit Limit field is selected and the mouse pointer points to the Change Order Up button.

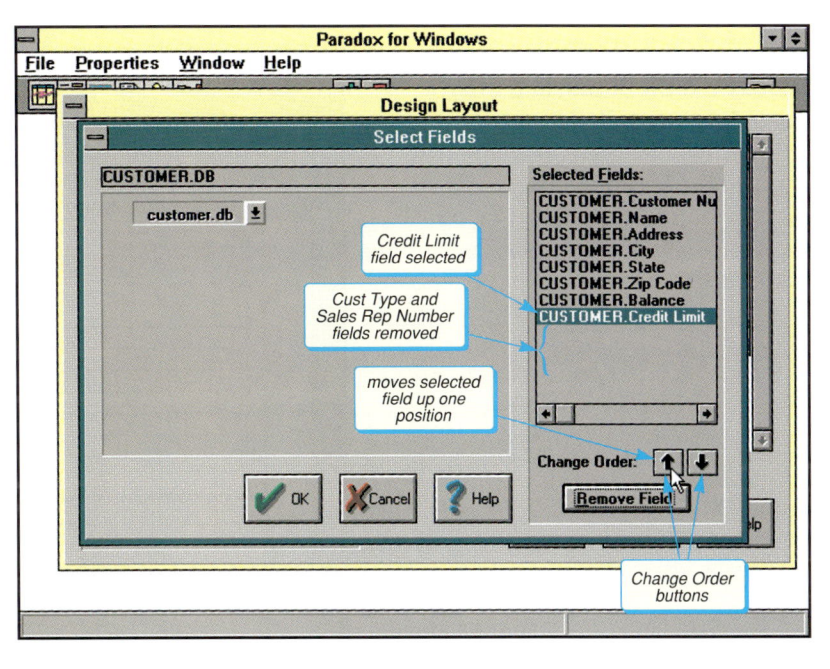

FIGURE 4-9

STEP 3 ▶

Click the Change Order Up button in the Select Fields dialog box to move the Credit Limit field before the Balance field and then choose the OK button to return to the Design Layout dialog box. Point to the OK button in the Design Layout dialog box.

The Design Layout dialog box displays (Figure 4-10). The list of fields in the report has changed. The mouse pointer points to the OK button.

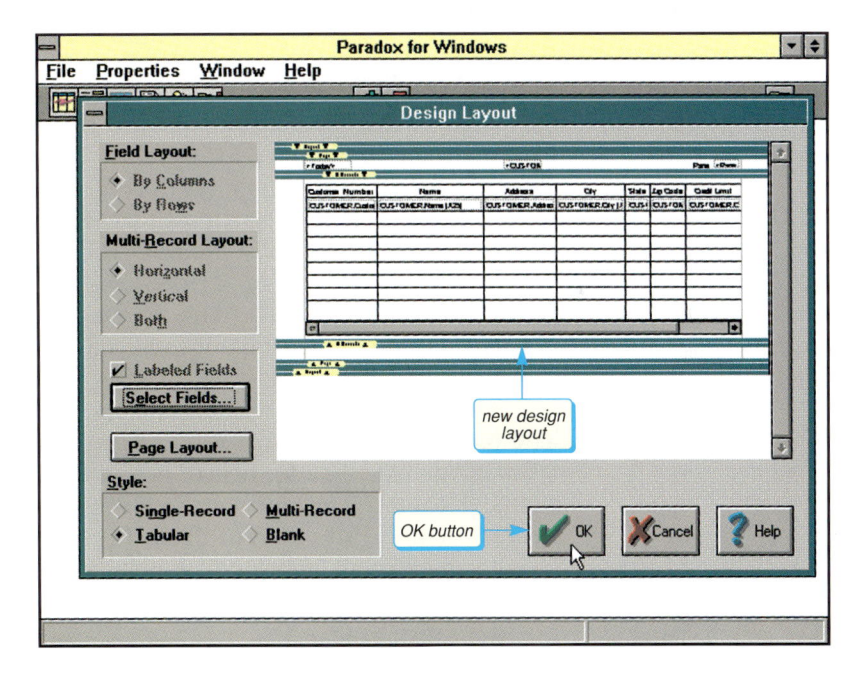

FIGURE 4-10

STEP 4 ▶

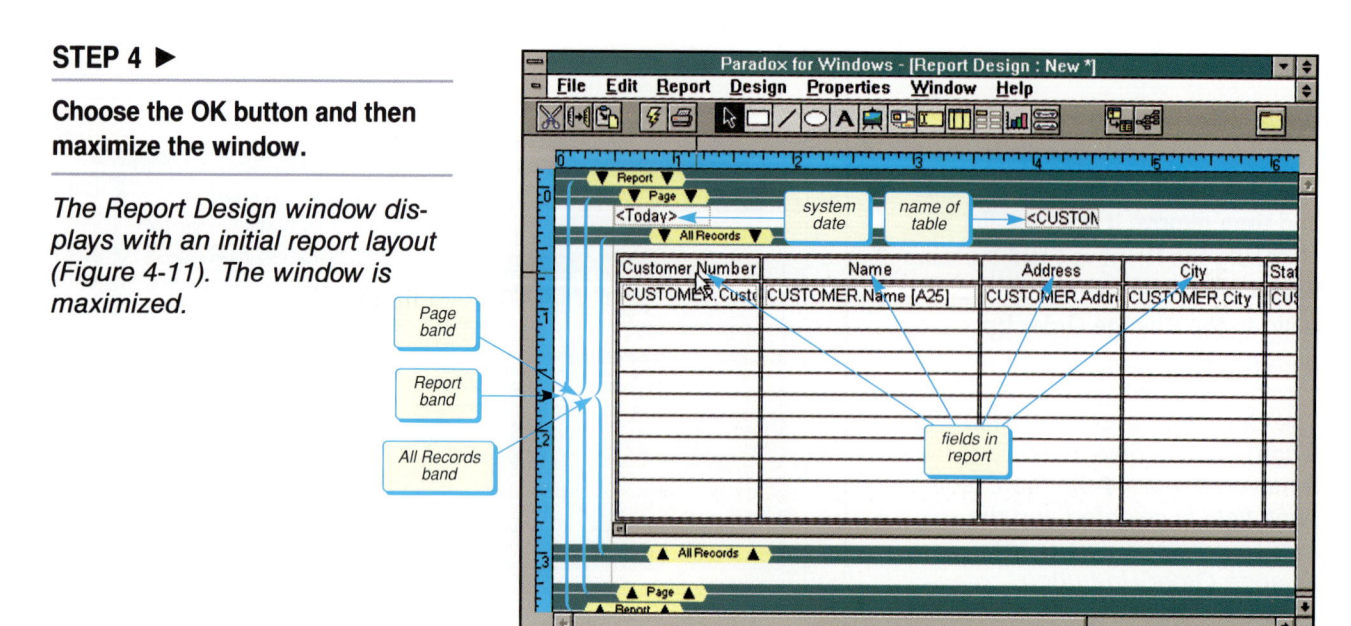

Choose the OK button and then maximize the window.

The Report Design window displays with an initial report layout (Figure 4-11). The window is maximized.

FIGURE 4-11

Report Bands

Each of the different portions of the report is described in what is termed a **band**. Notice in Figure 4-11 there is a **Report band**, a **Page band**, and an **All Records band**. The upper portion of the Report band is called the **report header** and the upper portion of the Page band is called the **page header**. The page header automatically includes the special names <Today> and <CUSTOM> (only a portion of <CUSTOMER> is currently visible), which will print as the system date and the table name CUSTOMER at the top of each page of the report. The lower portions of these bands are called the **report footer** and the **page footer**, respectively.

The contents of the report header print once, at the beginning of the report. The contents of the report footer print once, at the end of the report. The contents of the page header print once at the top of each page and the contents of the page footer print once at the bottom of each page. The contents of the All Records band print once for each record in the table.

To specify the layout of a report, you need to describe each of the bands you plan to include in the report. This means you need to indicate the precise position of each item that will appear in the band. In creating the report in Figure 4-1, the page header is already correct because Paradox automatically includes the system date and table name. Therefore, the report does not require either a report header or page footer. The All Records band requires changes to the column headings and the sizes of some of the columns. You also will need to add the total of the balances to the report footer (it should print once at the end of the report).

Changing Column Headings and Widths

Some of the columns in the initial design are too wide because the field name is longer than the data in the field. Customer numbers, for example, are only four characters. The Customer Number field name, however, is 15 characters, requiring the column width to be 15 characters. One way to change the width of the column heading is to split the heading into two lines; that is, to place Customer on one line and Number on the next.

To make a change to a column heading, you must first select the heading to be modified.

Selecting an Area of a Report

To select an area of a report, point to the area and then click the left mouse button. In many cases, you will need to click more than once because Paradox selects objects by starting with the largest object containing the mouse pointer and working inward. If the mouse pointer is pointing to the Customer Number column heading, for example, the first click selects the table, the second click selects the row of column headings, and the third click selects the Customer Number column heading. A fourth click produces an insertion point within the Customer Number column heading, allowing you to modify the heading.

It is easy to tell which portion is currently selected, because it will have small squares, called **handles** surrounding its border. If you accidentally select the wrong portion or click the mouse button too many times, simply point to a different portion of the report and click the left mouse button. You can then select the correct portion.

The following steps select the heading for the Customer Number field and then place the insertion point in front of the N in Number.

TO SELECT A PORTION OF THE REPORT ▼

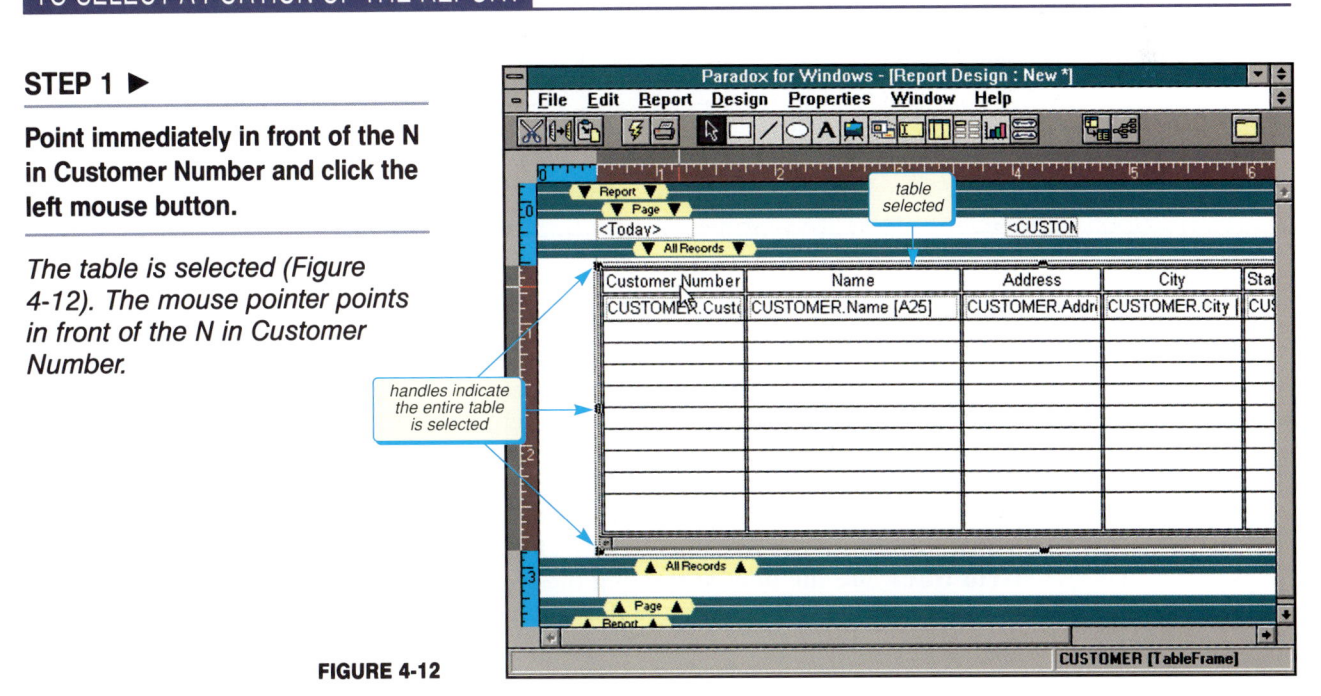

STEP 1 ▶

Point immediately in front of the N in Customer Number and click the left mouse button.

The table is selected (Figure 4-12). The mouse pointer points in front of the N in Customer Number.

FIGURE 4-12

P172 PROJECT 4 PRESENTING DATA: REPORTS AND FORMS

STEP 2 ▶

Click the left mouse button.

The entire row of column headings is selected (Figure 4-13).

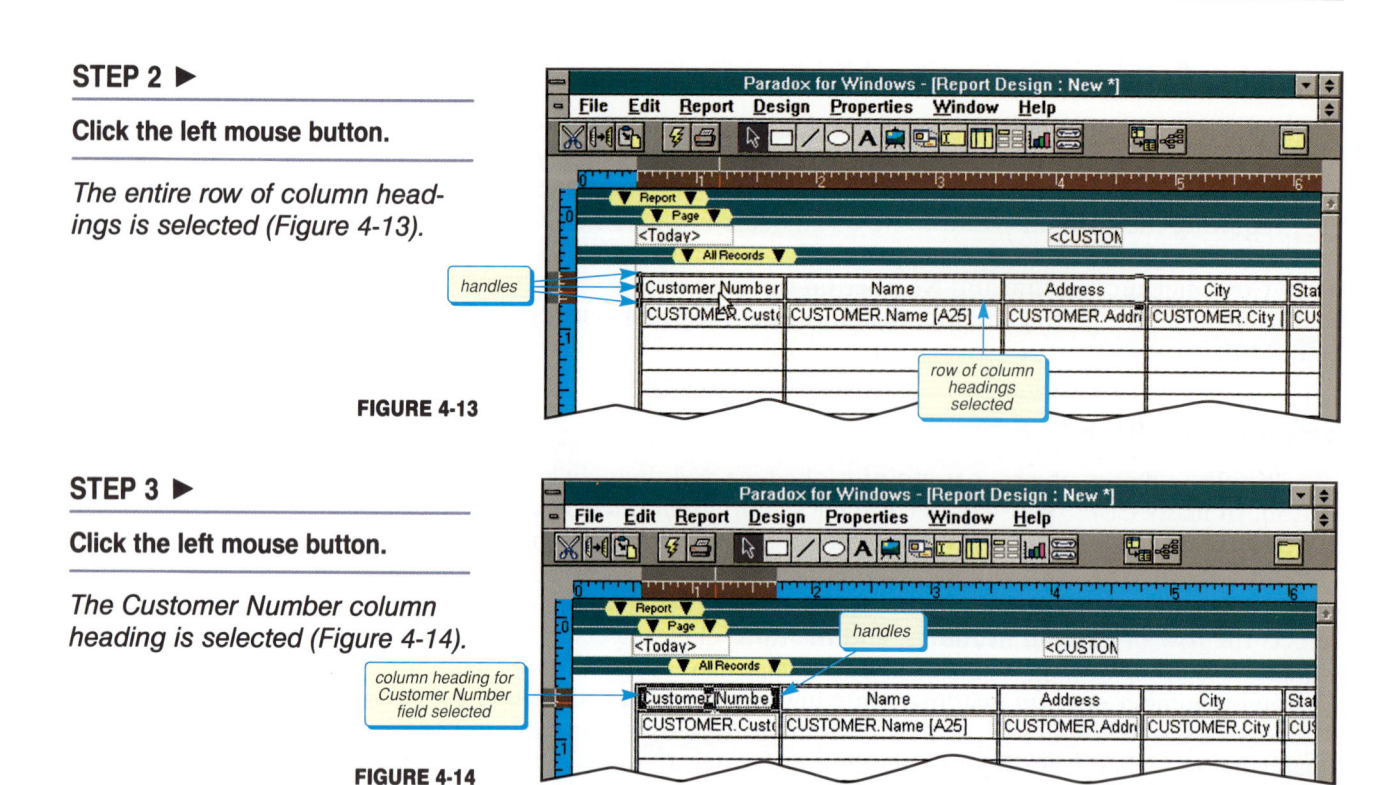

FIGURE 4-13

STEP 3 ▶

Click the left mouse button.

The Customer Number column heading is selected (Figure 4-14).

FIGURE 4-14

STEP 4 ▶

Click the left mouse button.

The insertion point appears at the position of the mouse pointer (Figure 4-15). When the mouse pointer is in the selected portion, it will appear as an I-beam.

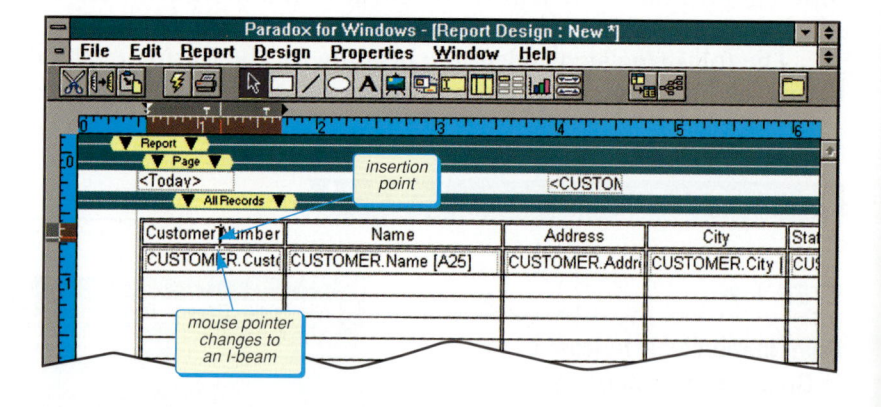

FIGURE 4-15

▲

Changing Column Headings

When changing the column headings, you can easily insert new text by simply typing the text at the appropriate location. You can delete a character by positioning the insertion point immediately in front of the character to be deleted and pressing the DELETE key. To split the heading into two lines, place the insertion point at the position where you want to split the heading and then press the SHIFT + ENTER keys. Once you have changed the headings, you can adjust the size of the columns by dragging one of the appropriate grid lines. **Grid lines**, are the lines separating the rows and columns.

The following steps change the column headings and column spacing in the report.

TO CHANGE COLUMN HEADINGS AND SPACING

STEP 1 ▶

Be sure the insertion point is located immediately before the N in Customer Number and then press the SHIFT+ENTER keys.

The heading splits into two lines. The word Customer appears on the first line and the word Number appears on the second. The words are centered in the column heading.

STEP 2 ▶

Point to an entry in the middle of the table and click the left mouse button to select the entire table. Then point to the vertical grid line to the right of the Customer Number heading. The mouse pointer changes to the horizontal double arrow (⇔) as shown in Figure 4-16.

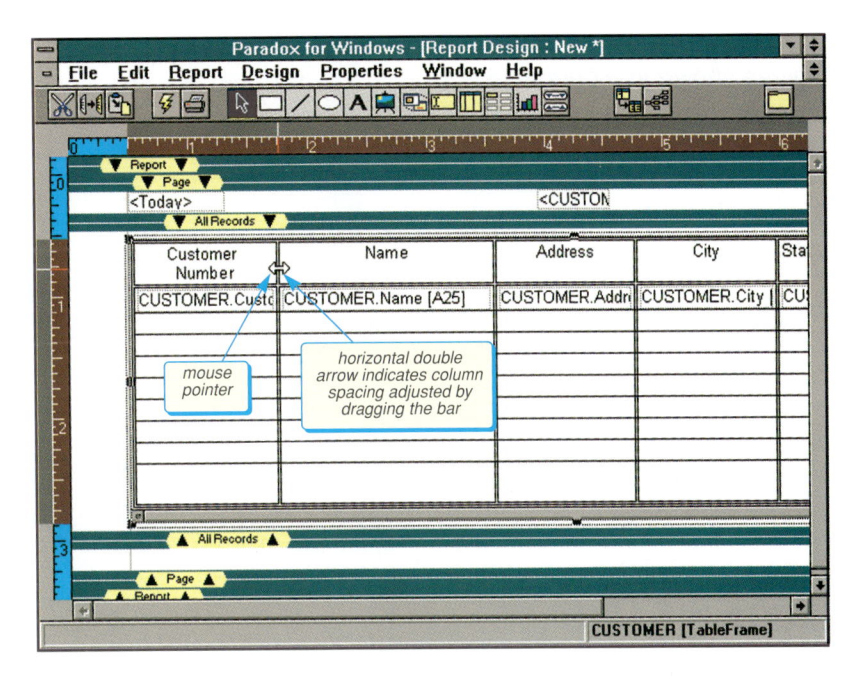

FIGURE 4-16

STEP 3 ▶

Drag the grid line to the left so there is no space on either side of the word Customer. Point to the right scroll arrow and click the scroll arrow to shift the columns to the left until the Balance column displays. Use the same techniques as you used in Step 1 and Step 2 to change the column headings and sizes for the Zip Code and Credit Limit fields to those shown in Figure 4-17 and then point immediately in front of the B in Balance.

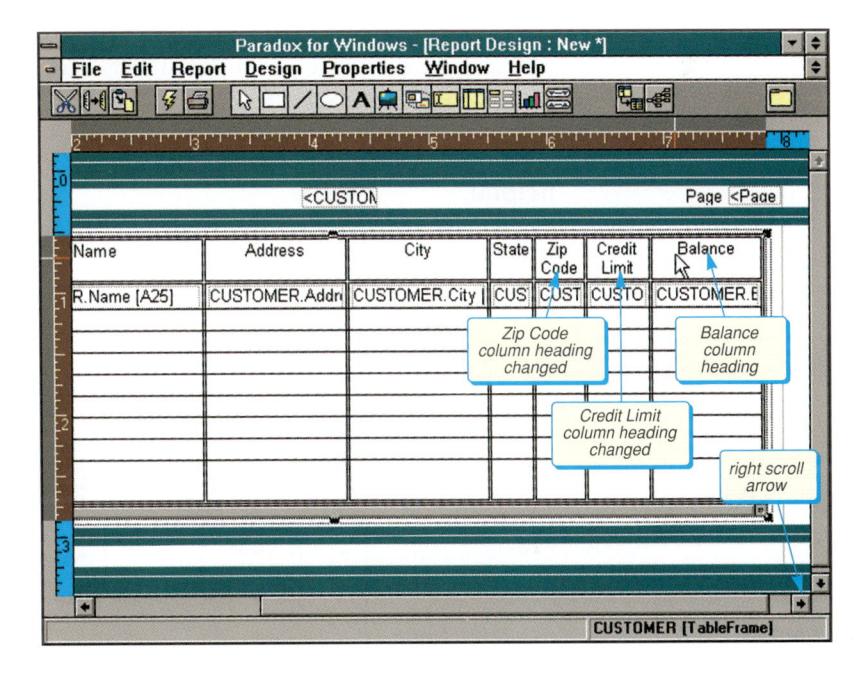

FIGURE 4-17

CREATING A REPORT   **P173**

STEP 4 ▶

Change the heading for the Balance field to Current Balance and change the field size to fit the new heading, and then point to the View Data button.

The heading and field sizes display as shown in Figure 4-18.

STEP 5 ▶

Click the View Data button to view the report on the screen.

The report displays on the screen as shown on the next page in Figure 4-20.

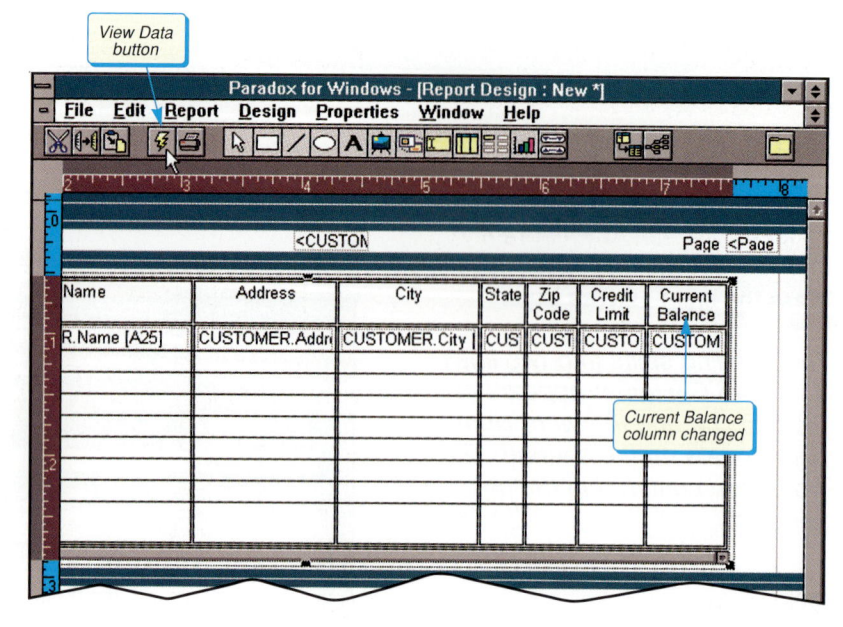

FIGURE 4-18

In many cases, a report will be too wide to fit on the screen. With Paradox, it is easy to adjust the magnification of the report, referred to as the **zoom factor**.

Changing the Zoom Factor

When designing or viewing a report, you can change the zoom factor (magnification) by using the **Zoom command** on the Properties menu. The magnification settings can vary between 25%, 50%, 100%, 200%, or 400%. Paradox can also be instructed to adjust the factor in such a way the entire width of the report fits on the screen (Fit Width), the entire height fits on the screen (Fit Height), or you can let Paradox determine the best way to fit the report on the screen (Best Fit). When designing a report, the Fit Width will be the most helpful.

Perform the following steps to change the Zoom factor for the report to Fit Width.

TO CHANGE THE ZOOM FACTOR ▼

STEP 1 ▶

Select the Properties menu, choose the Zoom command, and point to the Fit Width command.

The cascading menu for the Zoom command displays (Figure 4-19). The mouse pointer points to the Fit Width command.

FIGURE 4-19

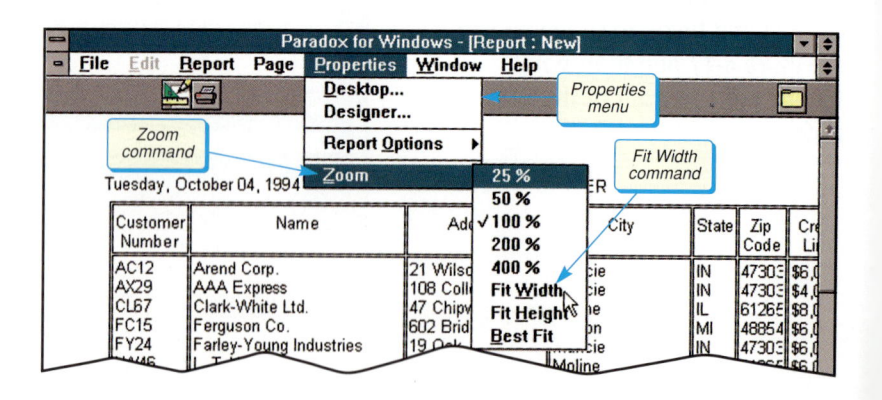

CREATING A REPORT **P175**

STEP 2 ▶

Choose the Fit Width command.

The zoom factor is adjusted so the entire width of the report displays on the screen (Figure 4-20).

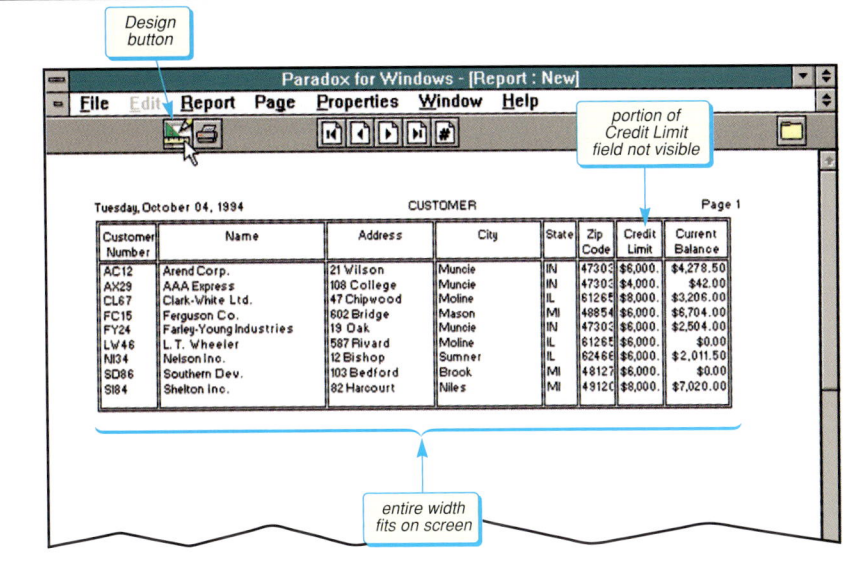

FIGURE 4-20

Once the report displays on the screen, it is evident that two columns, Zip Code and Credit Limit, should be enlarged so the data in the columns is more visible.

Adjusting Column Widths

To adjust the column widths in a report design, drag the column's right grid line. The following steps adjust the width of the Zip Code and Credit Limit columns.

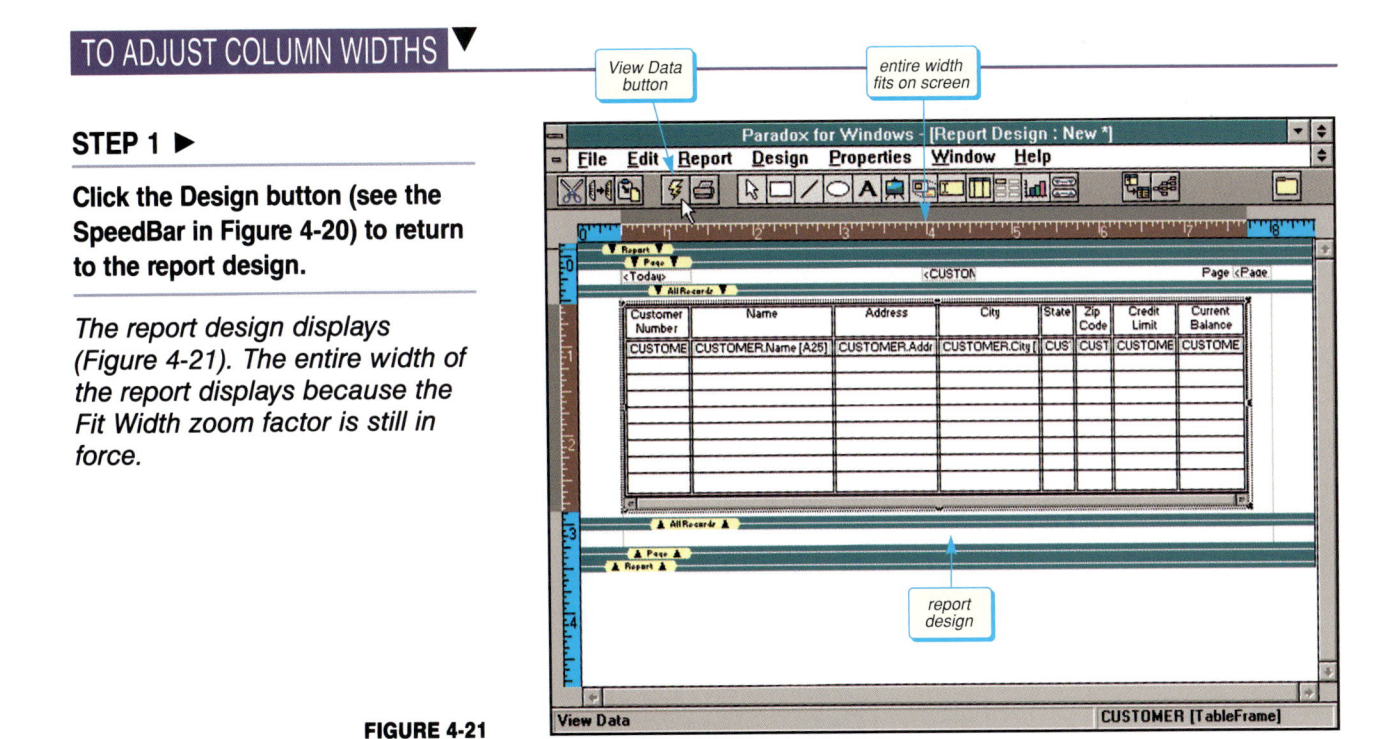

TO ADJUST COLUMN WIDTHS

STEP 1 ▶

Click the Design button (see the SpeedBar in Figure 4-20) to return to the report design.

The report design displays (Figure 4-21). The entire width of the report displays because the Fit Width zoom factor is still in force.

FIGURE 4-21

P176 PROJECT 4 PRESENTING DATA: REPORTS AND FORMS

STEP 2 ▶

Slightly increase the width of the Zip Code and Credit Limit fields. Click the View Data button (see the SpeedBar in Figure 4-21).

The report displays (Figure 4-22). The problem with the data not completely displaying in the Zip Code and Credit Limit fields has been corrected.

FIGURE 4-22

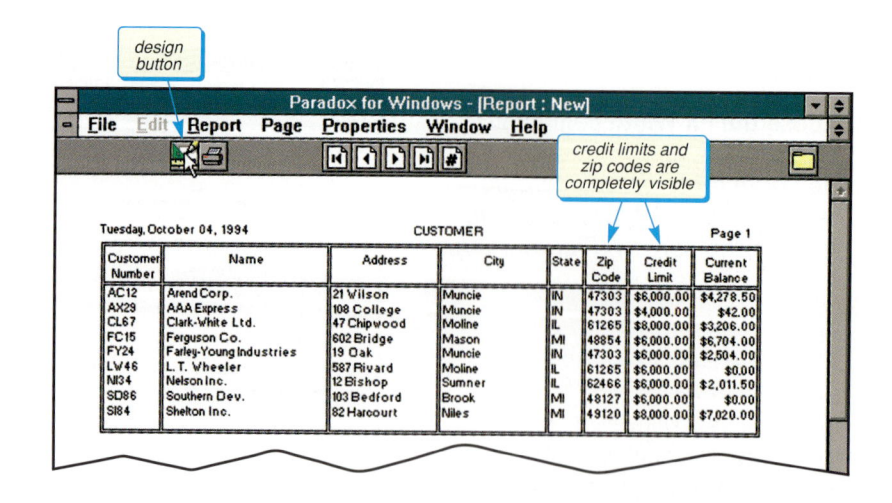

Resizing Bands

The next step in designing the report is to add the total of the Balance field to the report footer. Currently, however, the report footer is too small and it must be resized. To resize a band, first select it by pointing to it and clicking the left mouse button. Next, drag the upper or lower band line (the lines immediately above or below the band). To drag a band line, move the mouse pointer to the line until it changes to the vertical double arrow (⇕). Then drag the line.

Dragging the upper band line up increases the space at the top edge of the band. Dragging it down decreases the space. Dragging the lower band line down increases the space at the bottom edge of the band. Dragging it up decreases it.

Perform the following steps to enlarge the Report Footer by dragging the lower band line down.

TO ENLARGE THE REPORT FOOTER ▼

STEP 1 ▶

Click the Design button and then point to the Report footer.

The report design displays on the screen (Figure 4-23). The mouse pointer points to the report footer.

FIGURE 4-23

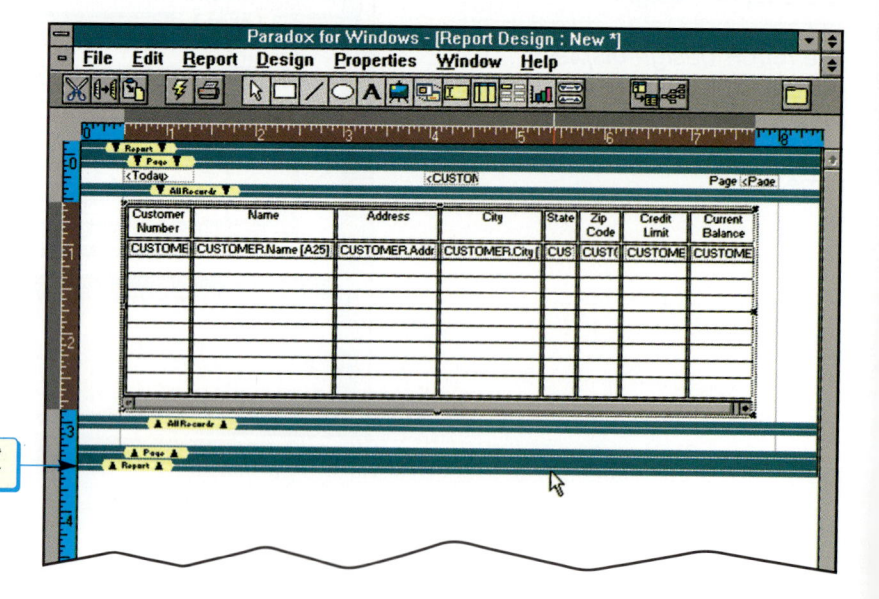

CREATING A REPORT **P177**

STEP 2 ▶

Select the report footer by clicking the left mouse button and then move the mouse pointer to the lower edge of the footer so it changes to the vertical double arrow.

The Report band changes color to indicate it has been selected (Figure 4-24). The mouse pointer points to the lower band line of the report footer. The mouse pointer has changed to the vertical double arrow (⇕), indicating you can resize the footer.

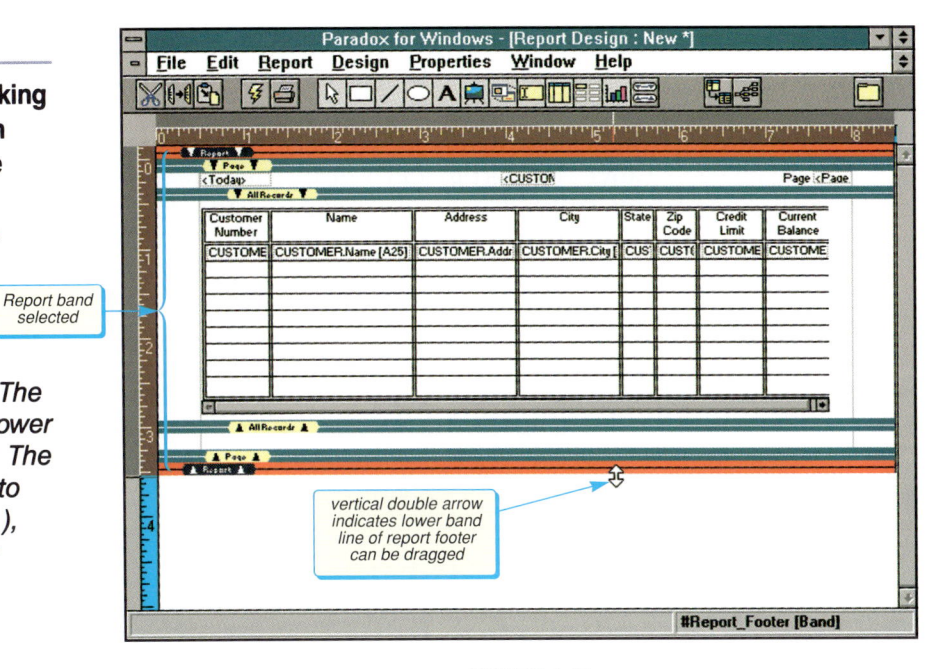

FIGURE 4-24

STEP 3 ▶

Drag the lower band line to the position shown in Figure 4-25 and then point to the Field tool button (▭) on the SpeedBar.

The footer has now been enlarged to make room for the field to be added.

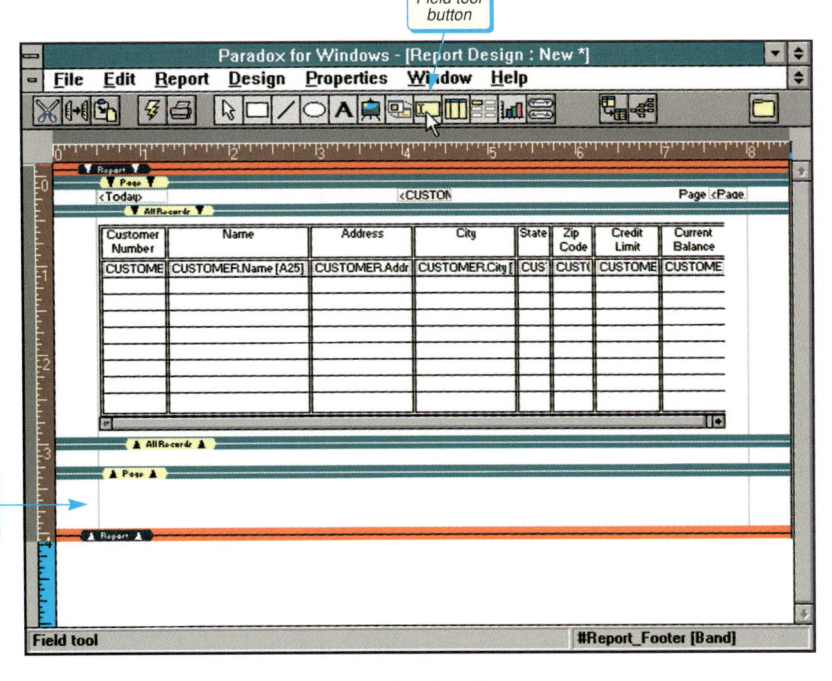

FIGURE 4-25

Adding a Field to the Footer

To add a field such as a total to the report footer, use the Field tool button on the SpeedBar. Then place a rectangle, called a **field object** on the report to indicate which field will occupy the rectangle. If you decide to end the process after you start to add a field, click the **Selection arrow button** ( ) on the SpeedBar. The mouse pointer returns to its normal shape and toggles off the Field tool.

Perform the following steps to add the sum of the balances to the report footer.

TO ADD A FIELD TO THE REPORT FOOTER ▼

STEP 1 ▶

Click the Field tool button and then move the mouse pointer to the position shown in Figure 4-26.

The Field tool button on the SpeedBar is darkened indicating the Field tool is selected. The mouse pointer shape (+) also indicates that the Field tool is selected.

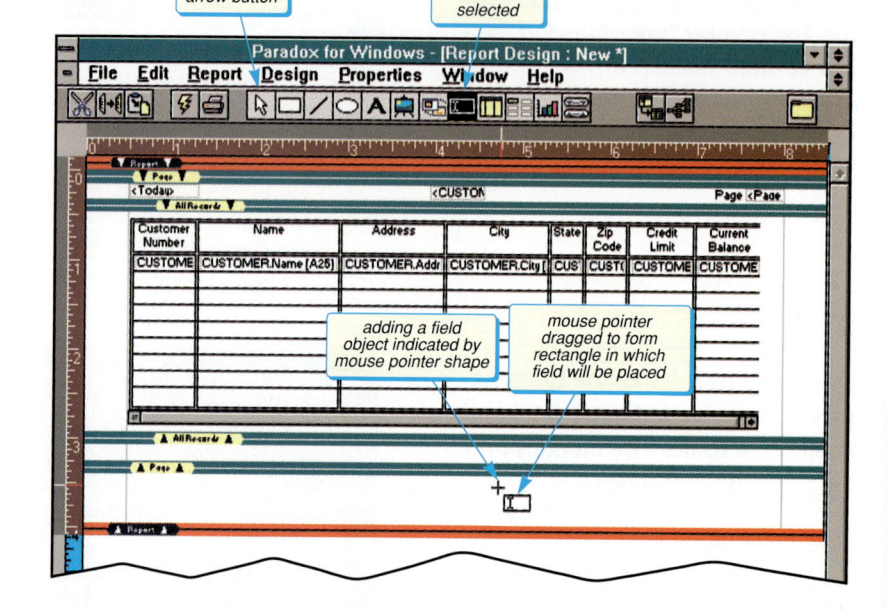

FIGURE 4-26

STEP 2 ▶

Click and hold down the left mouse button. Drag to the position shown in Figure 4-27 and then release the left mouse button.

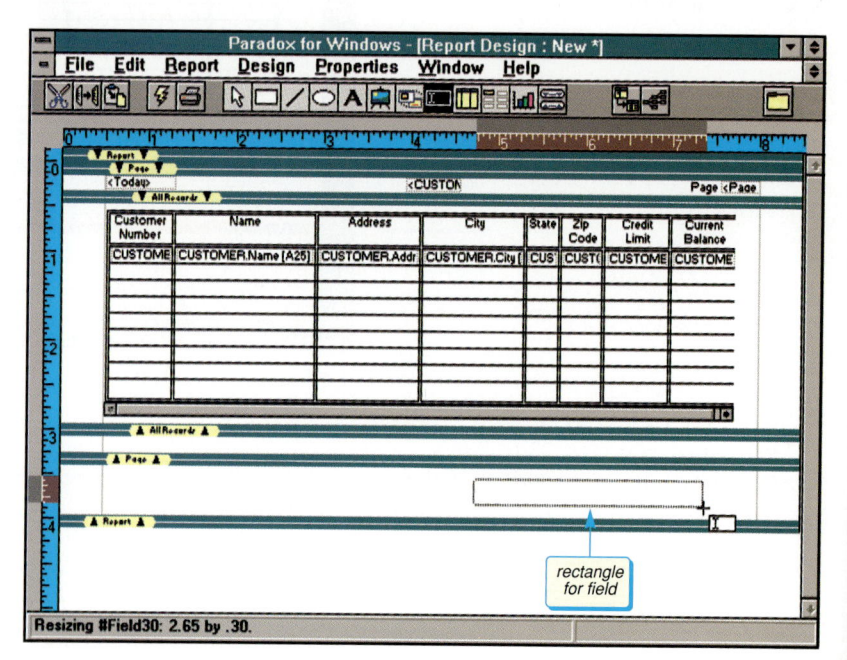

FIGURE 4-27

STEP 3 ▶

Point to the object you just created and click the right mouse button to display the object's menu. Choose the Define Field command from the field object's menu, and then point to the first entry in the cascading menu of available fields.

The cascading menu of available fields displays (Figure 4-28). The mouse pointer points to the first option (three dots), the option used to define a new field.

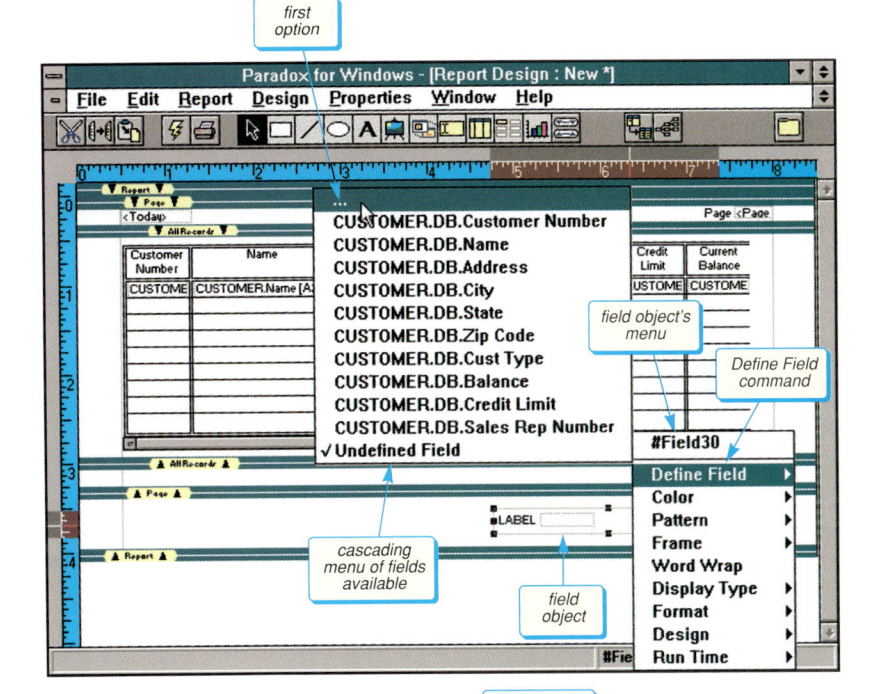

FIGURE 4-28

STEP 4 ▶

Choose the first option and then point to the customer.db list box arrow.

The Define Field Object dialog box displays (Figure 4-29). The mouse pointer points to the down arrow.

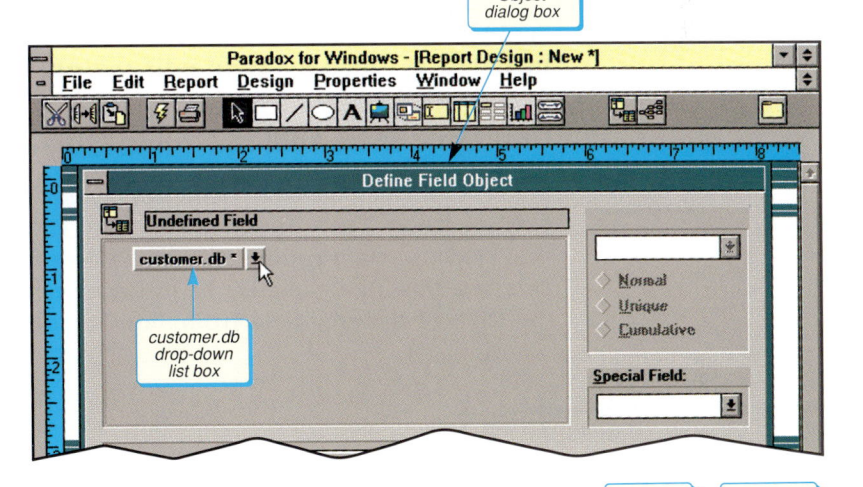

FIGURE 4-29

STEP 5 ▶

Click the customer.db list box arrow, choose the Balance field from the list, click the down arrow in the Summary list box, and point to Sum.

The Balance field is selected (Figure 4-30). The mouse pointer points to Sum in the Summary list box.

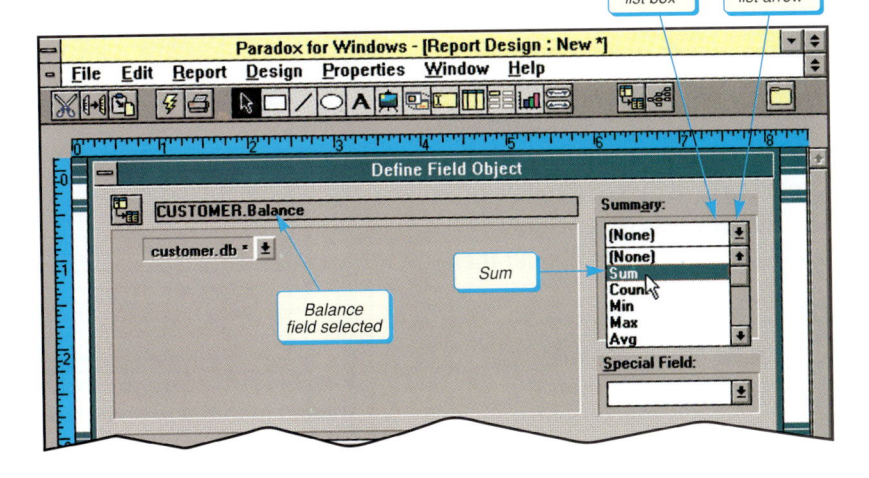

FIGURE 4-30

STEP 6 ▶

Select Sum and choose the OK button in the Define Field Object dialog box. Next, point to the beginning of the label Sum(Balance).

The field is added to the report footer (Figure 4-31). The mouse pointer points to the beginning of the label Sum(Balance).

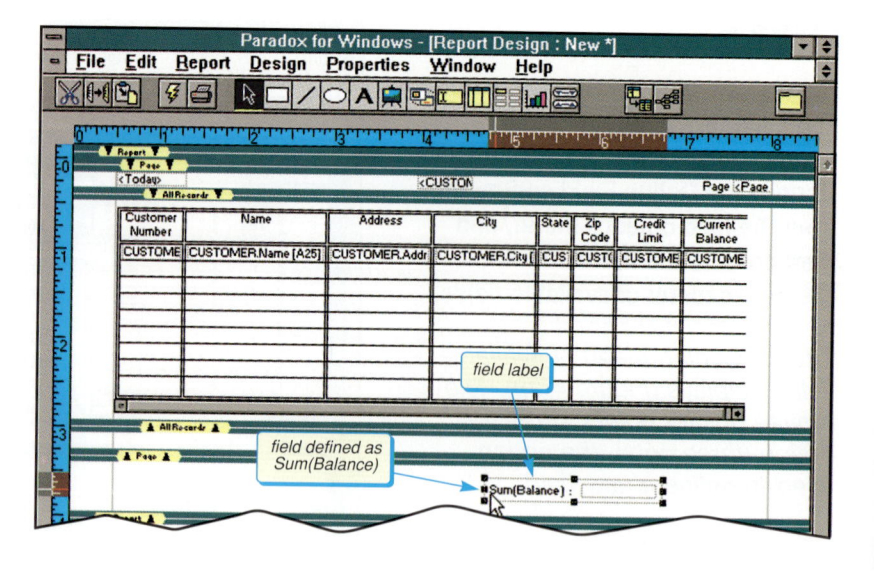

FIGURE 4-31

A field object contains two sections. The first section, which initially contains the field name, is called the **label**. The second section, which contains the field data, is called the **field edit region**.

Changing the Label in a Field Object

The label assigned by Paradox is Sum(Balance), which is not as descriptive as it might be. Thus, the next step is to change the label. To change the label, first select it, then produce an insertion point. You can change the label by deleting existing characters or inserting new ones. The following steps change the label of the new field from Sum(Balance) to Balance Total.

TO CHANGE A FIELD LABEL ▼

STEP 1 ▶

With the mouse pointer pointing to the letter S in Sum(Balance), repeatedly click the left mouse button until an insertion point appears before the S in Sum(Balance). Repeatedly press DELETE until Sum(Balance): is deleted and then type `Balance Total:`**.**

Sum(Balance): is replaced by Balance Total: (Figure 4-32).

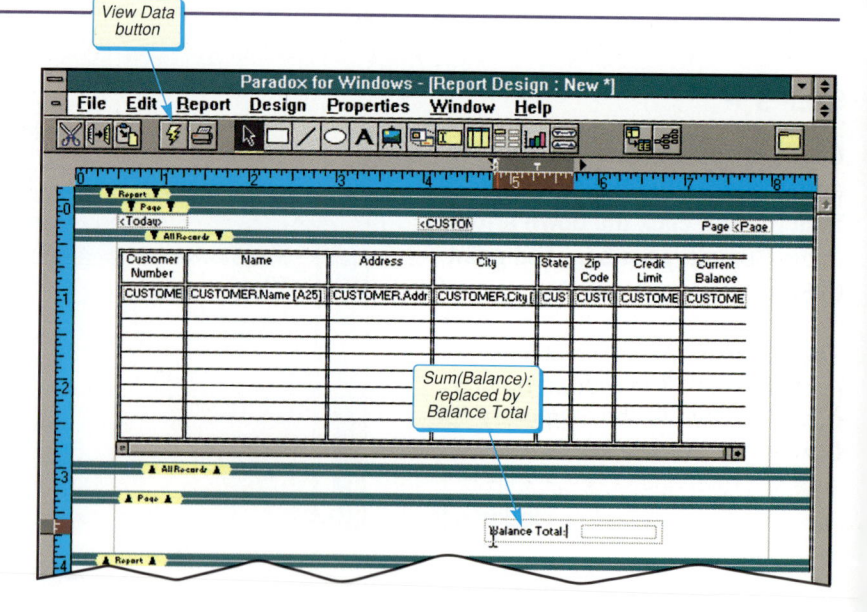

FIGURE 4-32

CREATING A REPORT **P181**

STEP 2 ▶

Click the View Data button (see the SpeedBar in Figure 4-32).

The report displays on the screen (Figure 4-33). The Balance Total and amount display at the end of the report.

STEP 3 ▶

Click the Design button to return to the report design.

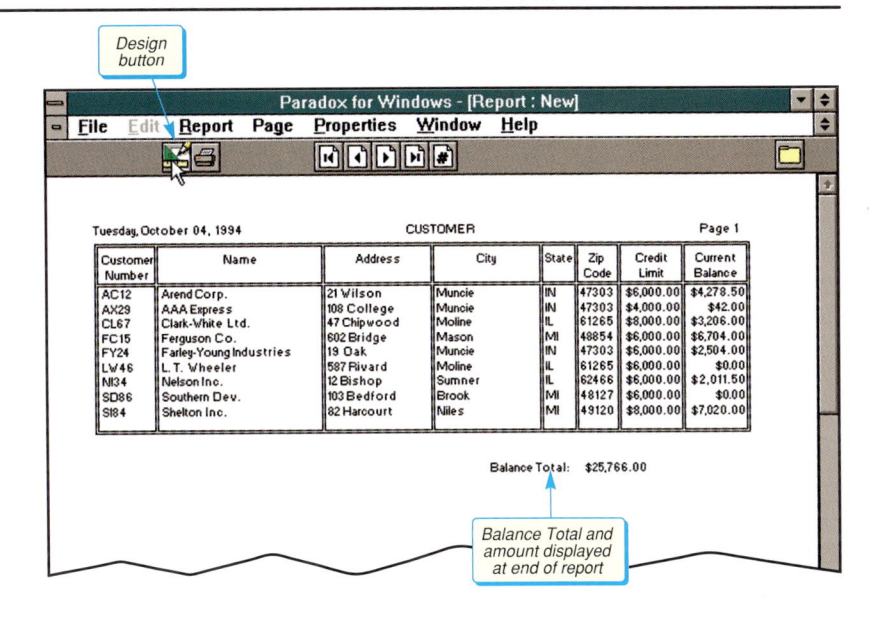

FIGURE 4-33

Saving a Report

Saving a report is accomplished by using the Save command on the File menu and assigning the file a name. If, for some reason, you do not want to save your work, do *not* choose the Save command. Instead, close the window containing the report and answer No when Paradox asks if you want to save your work.

Perform the following steps to save the report and assign it the name CUSTRPT1.

TO SAVE THE REPORT ▼

STEP 1 ▶

Select the File menu and point to the Save command.

The File menu displays (Figure 4-34). The mouse pointer points to the Save command.

STEP 2 ▶

Choose the Save command from the File menu. When the Save File As dialog box displays, type CUSTRPT1 (the name of the report) and choose the OK button.

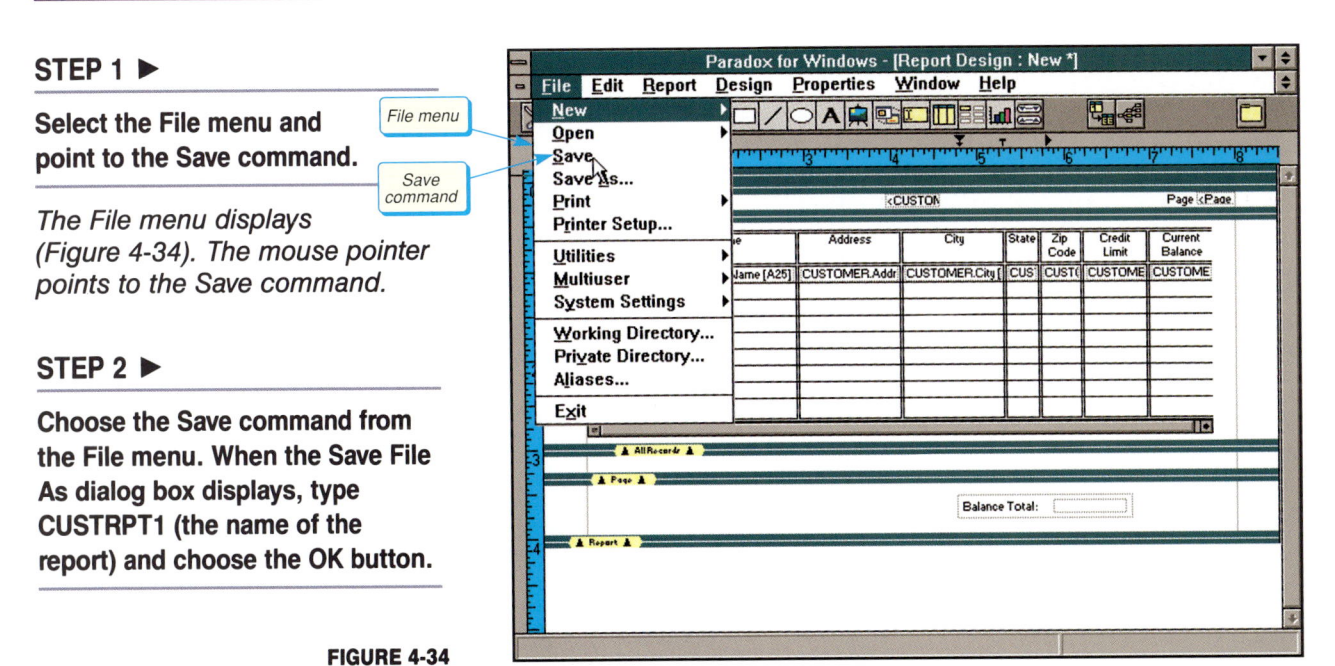

FIGURE 4-34

Closing a Report

Once you have finished designing the report, you should close the report by closing the window containing the report design. Perform the following steps to close the report.

TO CLOSE THE REPORT

Step 1: Make sure you are in the Report Design window. If not, click the Design button to return to the Report Design window. Then close the window by double-clicking its Control-menu box.

Printing a Report

While you are designing a report, you can send the report to the printer by clicking the Print button (🖨) on the SpeedBar. Usually, you will simply want to print the report from the Desktop. To print the report from the Desktop, click the Open Report button (📄) on the SpeedBar and then select the report you want to print.

Perform the following steps to print the report.

TO PRINT THE REPORT ▼

STEP 1 ▶

Point to the Open Report button on the SpeedBar (Figure 4-35).

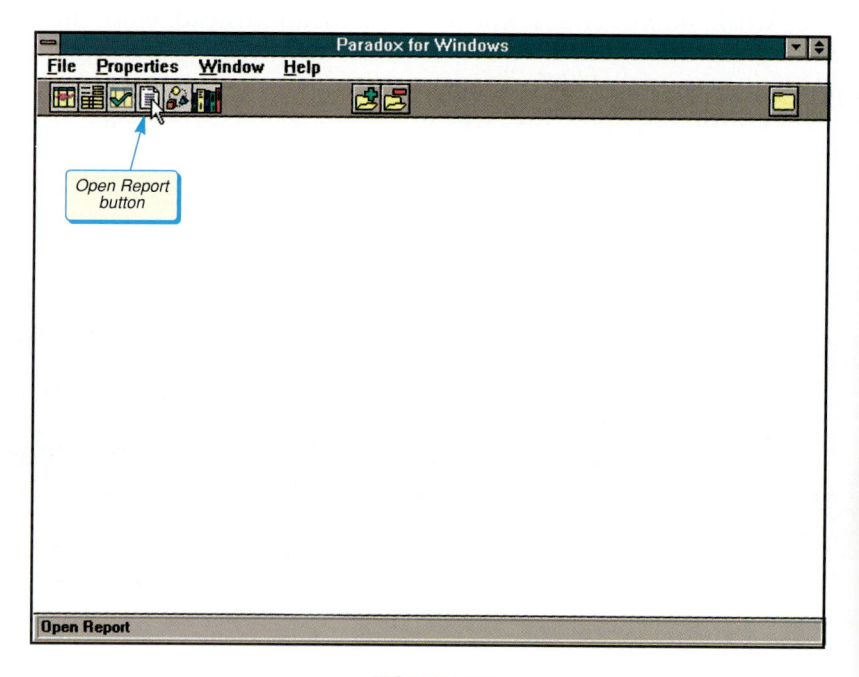

FIGURE 4-35

STEP 2 ▶

Click the Open Report button.

The Open Document dialog box displays (Figure 4-36). The File Name list box contains the list of reports that you have created. The Open Mode options are View Data (view the report on the screen), Design (return to the Report Design window), and Print (print the report).

STEP 3 ▶

Select the CUSTRPT1.RSL report, choose the Print option in the Open Mode area, and then choose the OK button in the Open Document dialog box. When the Print File dialog box displays, choose the OK button.

The report prints. It looks just like the report shown in Figure 4-1 on page P164.

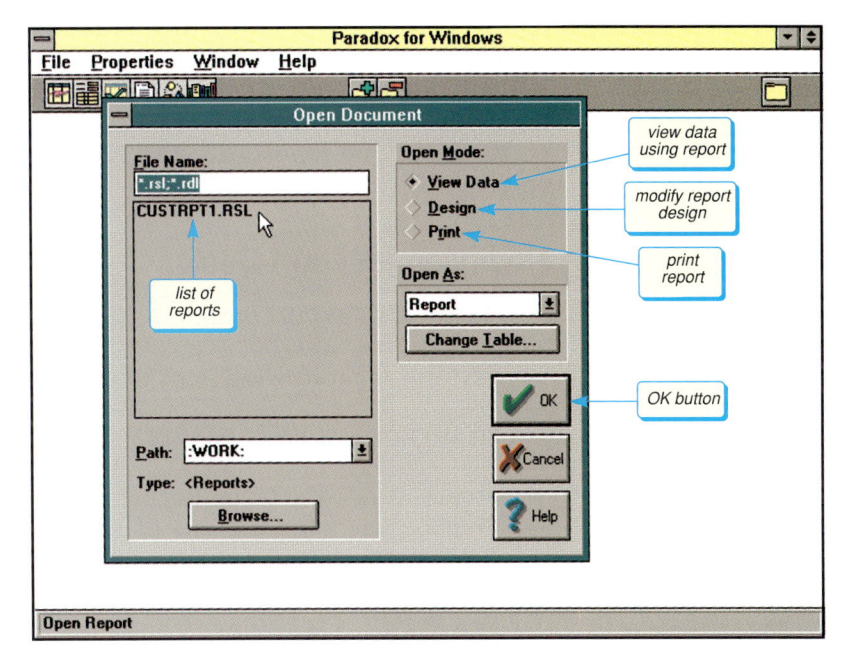

FIGURE 4-36

▶ GROUPING

Sometimes you want to **group** records in a report; that is, you want to create separate collections of records sharing some common characteristic. In the report in Figure 4-2 on page P165, for example, the records were grouped separately by sales rep: one group for each sales rep.

When you group, you typically include in the report two other types of field objects: a group header and a group footer. A **group header** is printed before the records in a particular group and a **group footer** is printed after the particular group. In Figure 4-2 the group header indicates the sales rep. The group footer includes the total of the balances for the customers of that sales rep. Such a total is called a **subtotal**, because it is a subset of the overall total of the balances.

To group records in Paradox, you need to add a special band, called a **group band** to the report design. The second report you are to create requires such a band.

Creating a New Report from an Existing Report

Sometimes a new report you want to create is very similar to an existing report. In such cases, rather than begin with a totally new report, it is easier to modify the design of an existing report and then *save it with a different name*. In the following sections you are to modify the design of CUSTRPT1 but save the modified version as CUSTRPT2. By modifying the existing report, you will create the second report (CUSTRPT2). The first report (CUSTRPT1) remains unchanged.

Modifying a Report Design

To modify a report design from the Desktop, click the Open Report button on the SpeedBar and then select the report whose design you want to modify. Perform the following steps to modify the design of the CUSTRPT1 report.

TO MODIFY A REPORT DESIGN

Step 1: Click the Open Report button.
Step 2: Select the CUSTRPT1.RSL report, choose the Design option in the Open Mode area, and then choose the OK button in the Open Document dialog box.

The design of the CUSTRPT1 report displays in the Report Design window.

Adding a Group Band

To group in a report in Paradox, you add a group band using the Add Band option. The following steps add a group band. The field used for grouping is the Sales Rep Number field.

TO ADD A GROUP BAND

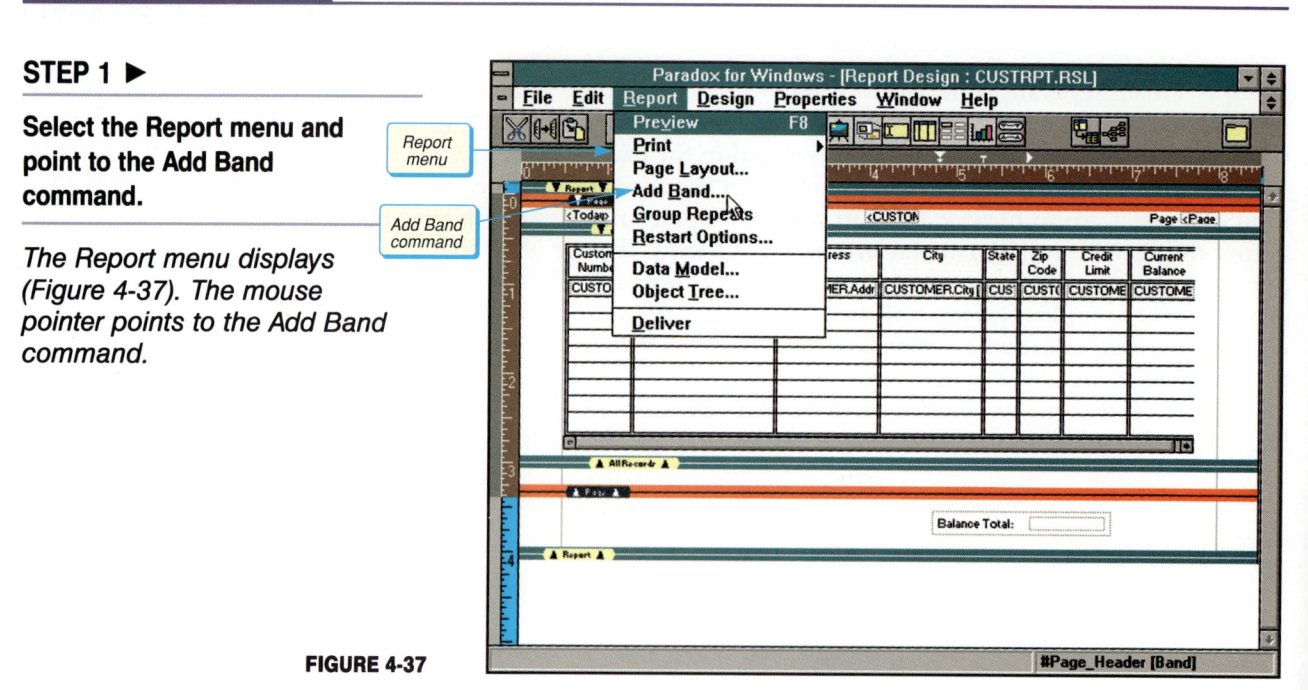

STEP 1 ▶

Select the Report menu and point to the Add Band command.

The Report menu displays (Figure 4-37). The mouse pointer points to the Add Band command.

FIGURE 4-37

GROUPING **P185**

STEP 2 ▶

Choose the Add Band command from the Report menu. When the Define Group dialog box displays, select the Sales Rep Number field, and point to the OK button.

The Define Group dialog box displays (Figure 4-38). The Sales Rep Number field is selected. The mouse pointer points to the OK button.

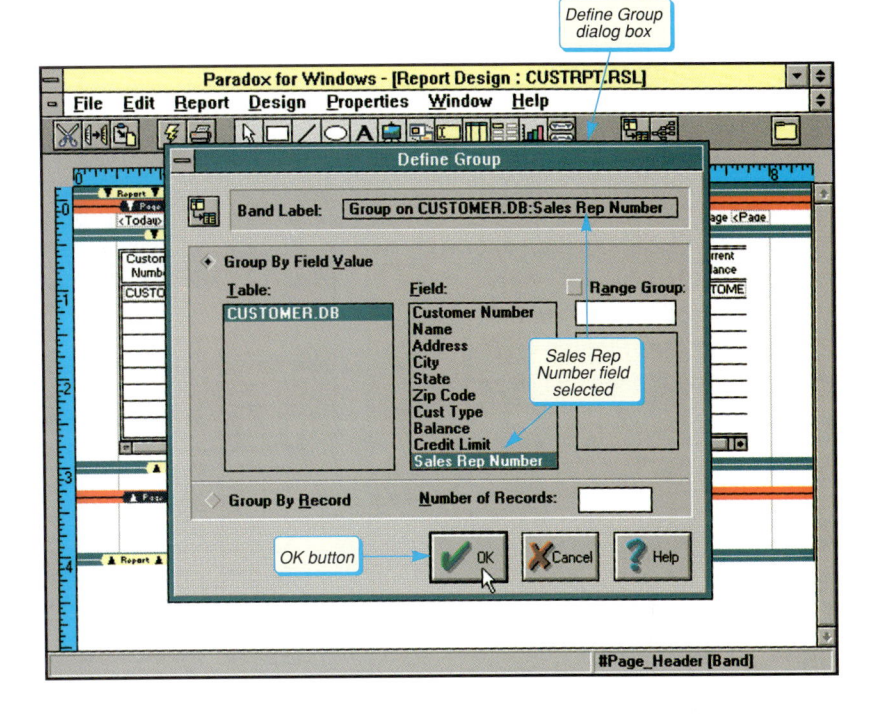

FIGURE 4-38

STEP 3 ▶

Choose the OK button.

Paradox adds a group band to the report design (Figure 4-39). It automatically places the Sales Rep Number field in the group header.

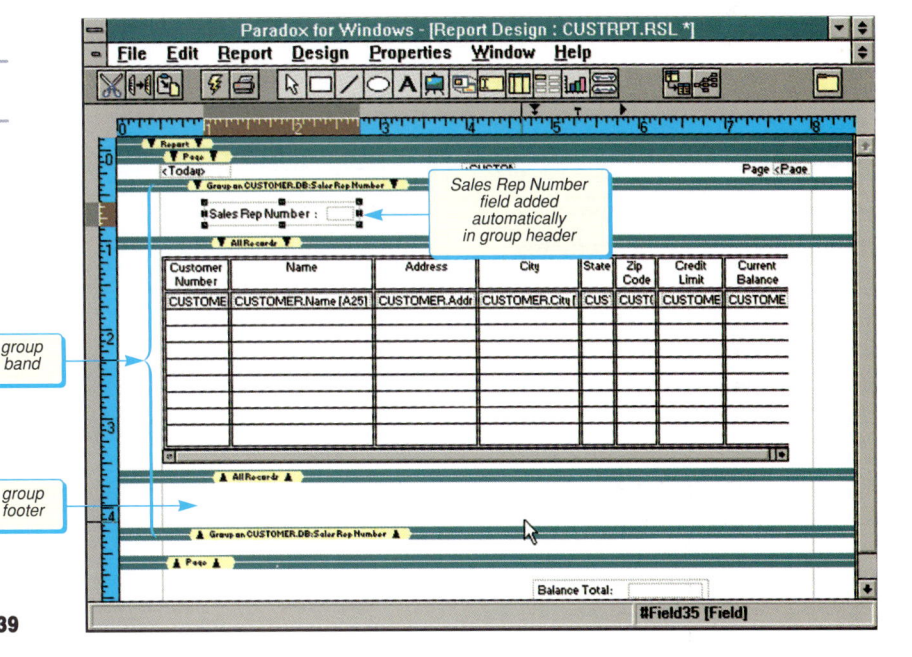

FIGURE 4-39

Adding a Subtotal

The process of adding a subtotal to a report is virtually identical to that of adding a total. The only difference is that the field is added to the group footer instead of to the report footer. The steps on the following two pages add a subtotal to the report.

TO ADD A SUBTOTAL

STEP 1 ▶

Add the sum of balances to the group footer in the position shown in Figure 4-40, using the same steps you used to add it to the report footer (see Figures 4-26 through 4-30 on pages P178 and P179).

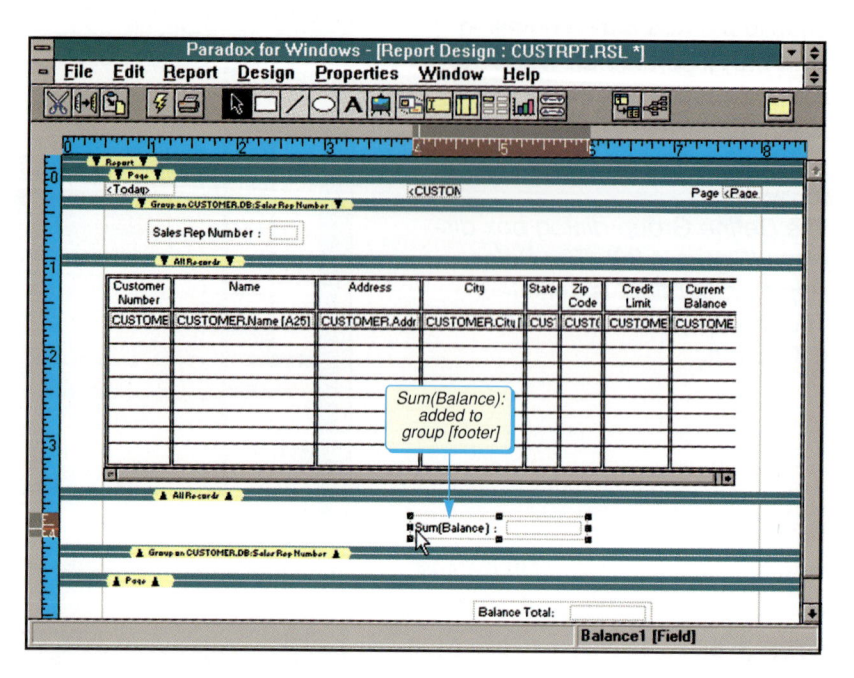

FIGURE 4-40

STEP 2 ▶

Replace the Sum(Balance): label in the field object you just created with `Balance Subtotal:` just as you replaced it with Balance Total: in the report footer (see Figure 4-32 on page P180).

Sum Balance: is replaced with Balance Subtotal: in the label portion of the field object (Figure 4-41). The colon overlaps the field edit region, so the field edit region needs to be moved.

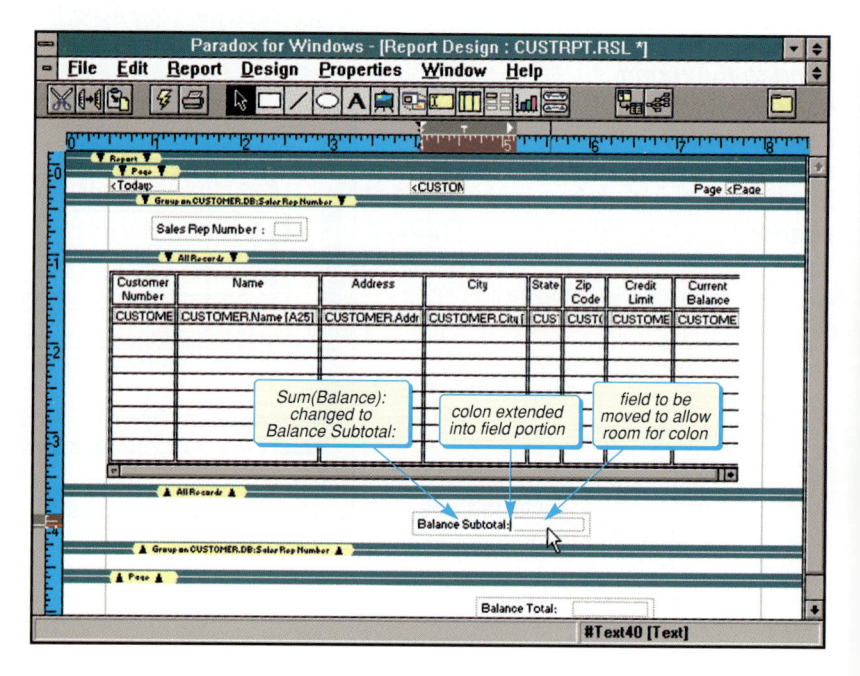

FIGURE 4-41

STEP 3 ▶

Point to the field edit region and select it by clicking the left mouse button.

The field edit region is selected (Figure 4-42).

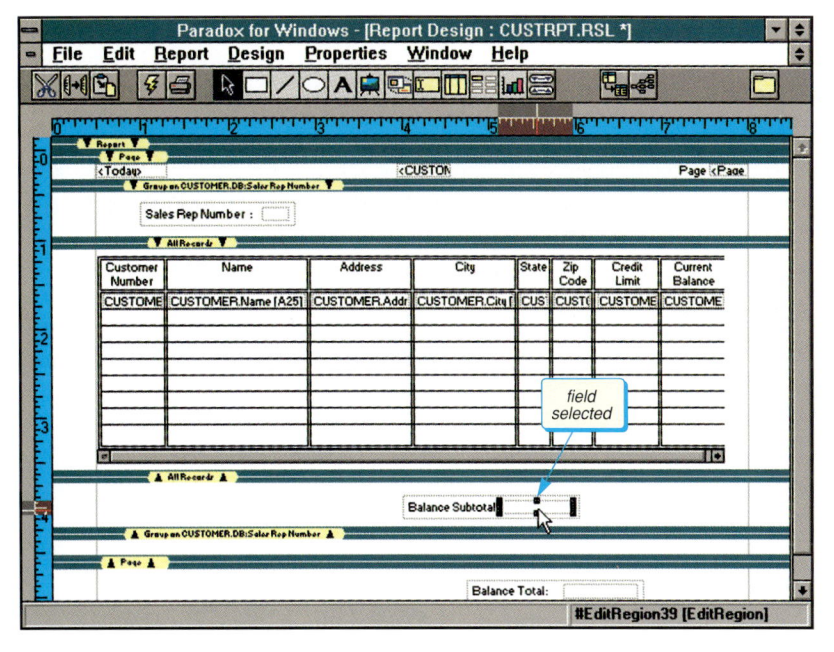

FIGURE 4-42

STEP 4 ▶

Drag the field edit region far enough to the right so the colon in the label no longer overlaps the field edit region.

The field edit region has been moved (Figure 4-43).

STEP 5 ▶

Click the View Data button to view the report.

The report shown in Figure 4-2 on page P165 displays on the screen. Records are grouped by sales rep number. After the records in each group, there is a subtotal.

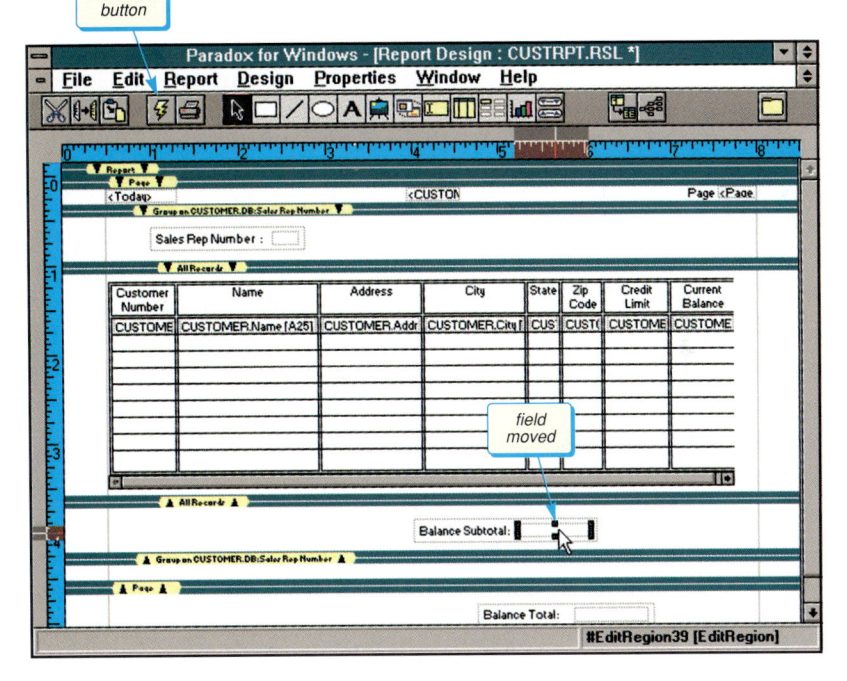

FIGURE 4-43

Saving the Report with a Different Name

To save the report with a different name, use the Save As command. The following steps use the Save As command to save the report as CUSTRPT2 and then close the Report Design window.

TO SAVE THE REPORT AND CLOSE THE WINDOW

Step 1: Select the File menu and choose the Save As command.
Step 2: When the Save File As dialog box displays, type CUSTRPT2 in the New File Name text box and choose the OK button.
Step 3: Close the Report Design window in the usual manner.

Printing the Report

To print the CUSTRPT2 report (see Figure 4-2 on page P165), use the steps outlined on pages P182 and P183.

▶ REPORT DESIGN CONSIDERATIONS

As you design and create reports, keep in mind the following guidelines.

1. The purpose of any report is to provide certain information. Ask yourself if the report you have designed conveys this information effectively. Is the meaning of the rows and columns in the report clear? Are the column headings easily understood? Are there any abbreviations on the report that would not be clear to those looking at the report?
2. Be sure to allow sufficient white space between groups. You can accomplish this by enlarging the group footer.
3. You can use different fonts and sizes, but do not overuse them. Using more than two or three different fonts and/or sizes often gives a cluttered and amateurish look to your report.
4. Be consistent in your reports. Once you have decided on a general style, stick with it.

▶ CREATING AND USING CUSTOM FORMS

Using the Form View screen, you added new records to a table and changed existing records. When you performed these tasks, you used a standard display form generated automatically by Paradox. Although the form did provide you with some assistance in the task, the form was not particularly pleasing. The standard form stacked fields on top of each other at the left side of the screen. This section covers **custom forms** you can use in place of those normally supplied by Paradox. To create a form, you use a special window, called the **Form Design window**. In this window, indicate to Paradox exactly what you want the form to look like. Once you have created the form, you can use the form to view or update data in place of the standard Paradox form whenever you want.

CREATING AND USING CUSTOM FORMS   P189

Beginning the Form Creation

The first step in creating a form is to choose the New command from the File menu, choose the Form command, and then select the tables that will be included. If you select more than one table, you also need to indicate how the tables are related.

The following steps begin the creation of the form shown in Figure 4-3 on page P166.

TO BEGIN CREATING A FORM ▼

STEP 1 ▶

Select File, choose the New command and then point to the Form command (Figure 4-44).

FIGURE 4-44

STEP 2 ▶

Choose the Form command. When the Data Model dialog box displays, point to the Customer table (CUSTOMER.DB) in the File Name list box.

The Data Model dialog box displays (Figure 4-45). The mouse pointer points to the Customer table.

FIGURE 4-45

STEP 3 ▶

Select the Customer table by clicking the left mouse button and point to the Add File arrow (➡).

The customer table is selected and displays in the data model (Figure 4-46). The mouse pointer points to the Add File arrow.

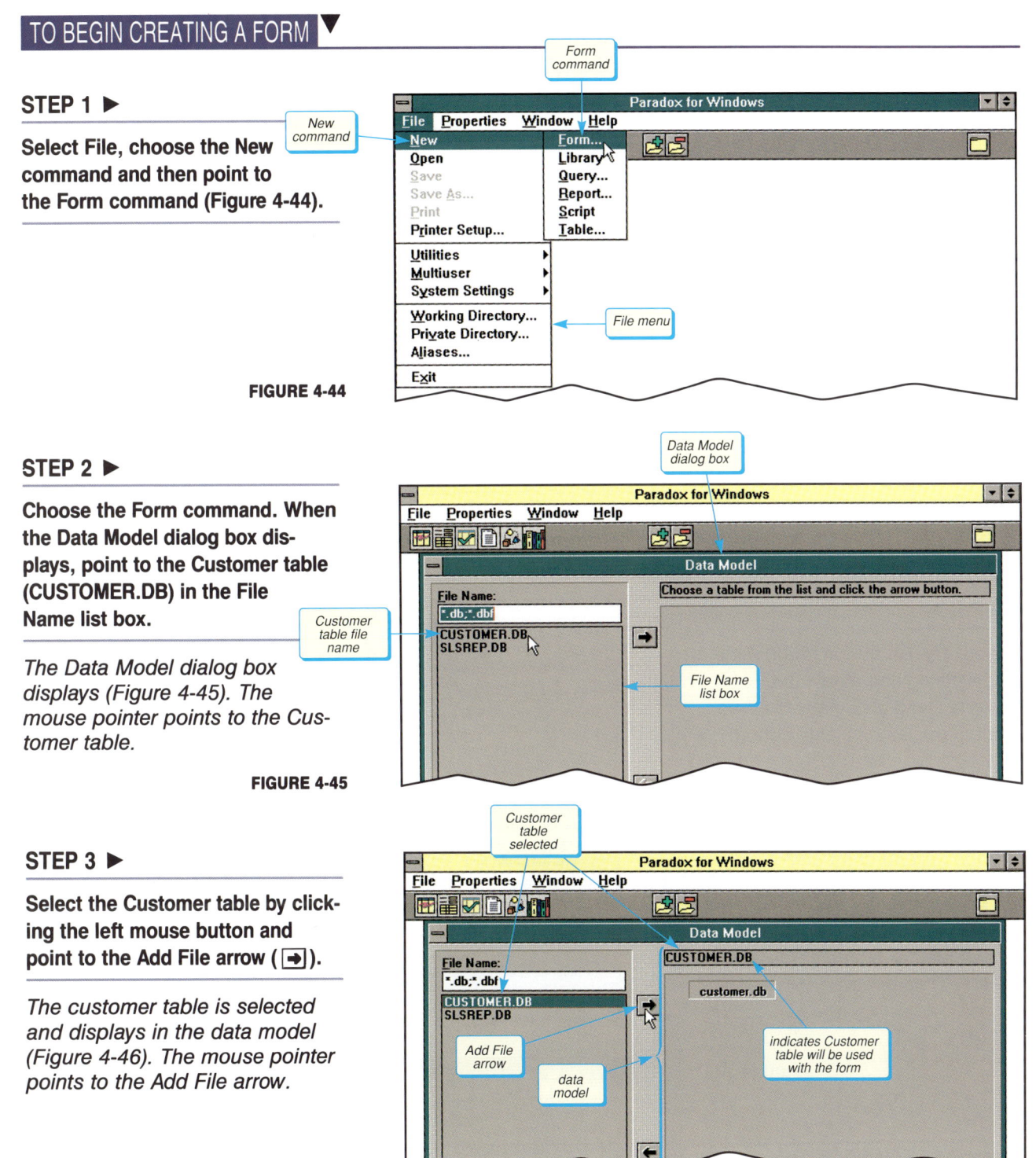

FIGURE 4-46

STEP 4 ▶

Click the Add File arrow, select the Slsrep table (SLSREP.DB), and point to the Customer table. Press and hold down the left mouse button.

The mouse pointer changes to the shape of the one shown in Figure 4-47.

FIGURE 4-47

STEP 5 ▶

Drag the mouse pointer to the Slsrep table, release the left mouse button, and point to the OK button.

The data model is complete (Figure 4-48) and the mouse pointer points to the OK button. The single-headed arrow from customer.db to slsrep.db indicates that each customer is related to a single sales rep.

FIGURE 4-48

STEP 6 ▶

Choose the OK button in the Data Model dialog box. When the Design Layout dialog box displays, point to the Select Fields button.

The Design Layout dialog box displays (Figure 4-49). Options in this dialog box allow you to change several characteristics of the form, including the field layout, the page layout, and the style. The mouse pointer points to the Select Fields button.

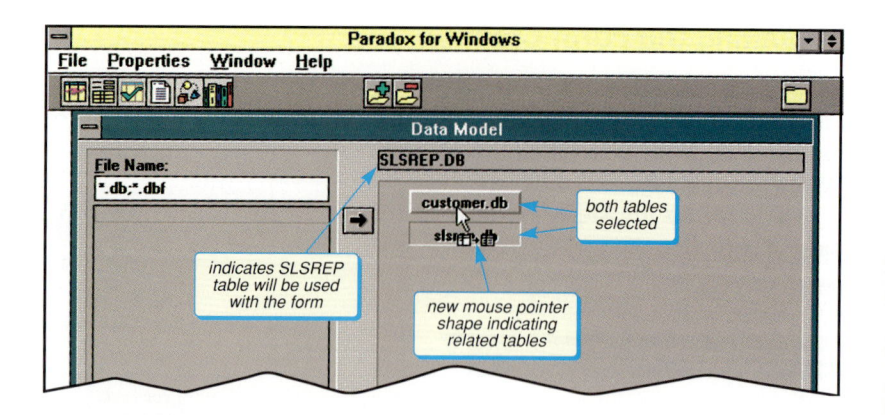

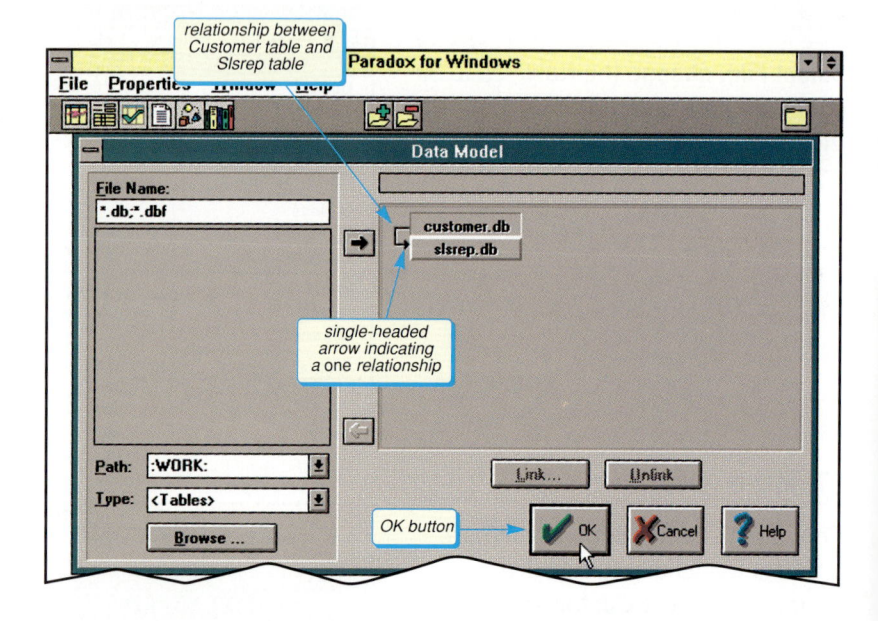

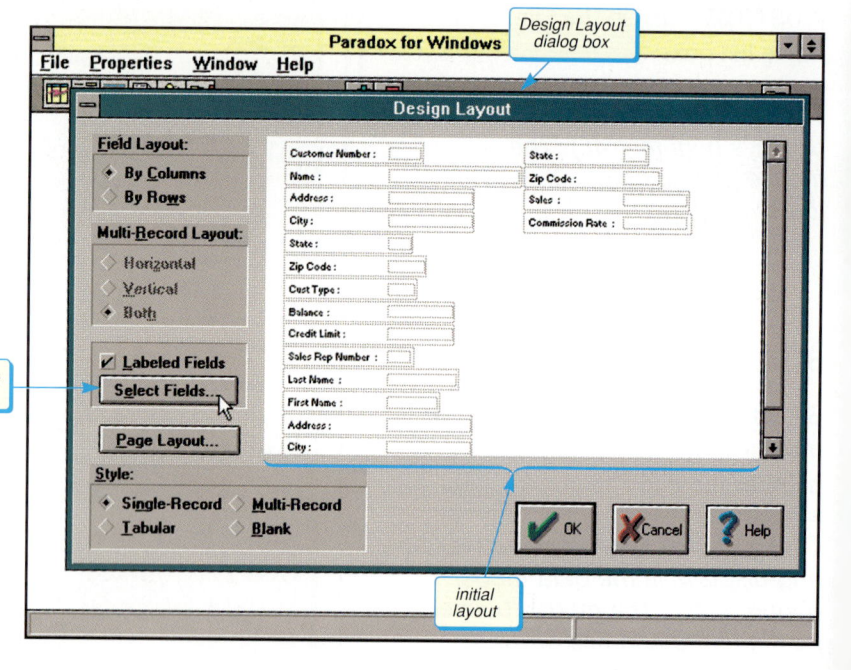

FIGURE 4-49

Selecting Fields for a Form

The initial design shown on the screen includes all fields from the Customer and Slsrep tables. Because the form being created does not include all fields, you must indicate which fields are to be included by using the Select Fields button. Perform the following steps to select the fields to be included.

TO SELECT THE FIELDS FOR THE FORM ▼

STEP 1 ▶

Choose the Select Fields button in the Select Fields dialog box, then remove all the SLSREP fields except Last Name and First Name. Point to the OK button.

The appropriate fields have been removed (Figure 4-50) and the mouse pointer points to the OK button.

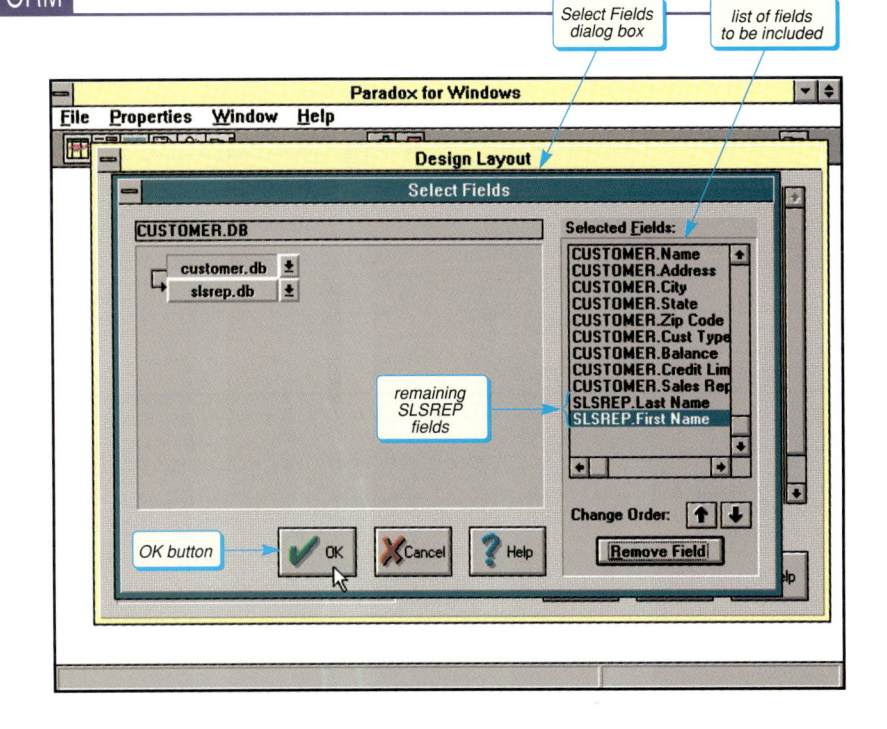

FIGURE 4-50

STEP 2 ▶

Choose the OK button to return to the Design Layout dialog box.

The Design Layout dialog box displays (Figure 4-51). The list of fields in the form has changed. The mouse pointer points to the OK button.

FIGURE 4-51

P192   PROJECT 4   PRESENTING DATA: REPORTS AND FORMS

STEP 3 ▶

Choose the OK button and then maximize the window.

The initial form layout displays (Figure 4-52). The window is maximized.

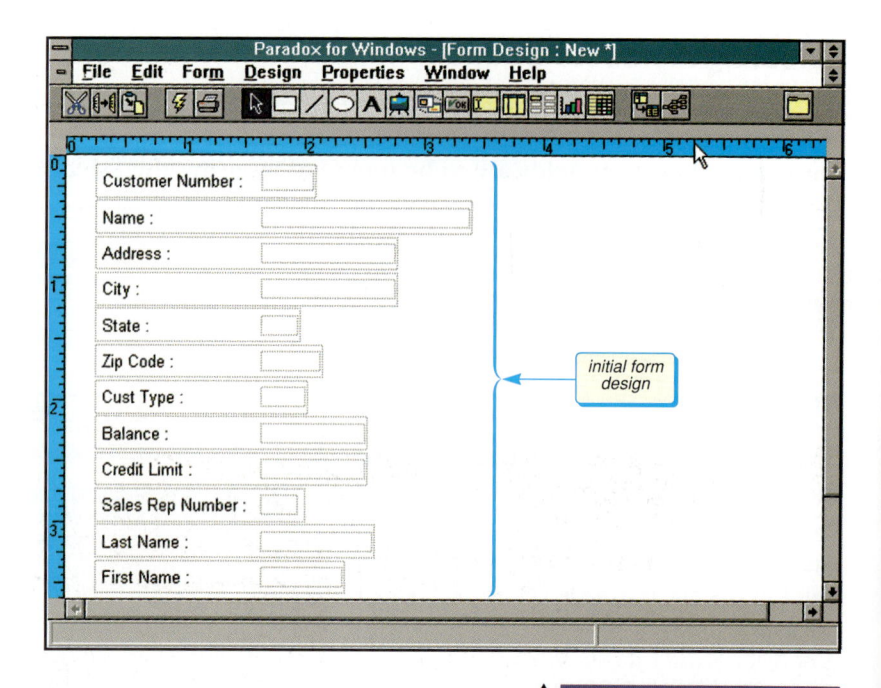

FIGURE 4-52

A problem you may encounter when working on the design of a form is ensuring that items line up properly. If, for example, you place two fields next to each other, it is difficult to make sure they are even. It is likely that you will place one slightly higher or slightly lower than the other. To address these difficulties, Paradox provides a **grid**, which is a series of horizontal and vertical lines covering the form surface. You can use the grid to help you align objects.

Using the Grid

To use the grid to align objects, perform two tasks. First, display the grid so it is visible on the screen. Second, you need to indicate to Paradox that items are to be snapped to the grid. **Snap to grid** means that when you place or move an item on the screen, Paradox will move it to the nearest grid lines.

Perform the following steps to display the grid and ensure the items placed or moved on the form will snap to the nearest grid location.

TO USE THE GRID ▼

STEP 1 ▶

Select the Properties menu and point to the Show Grid command (Figure 4-53).

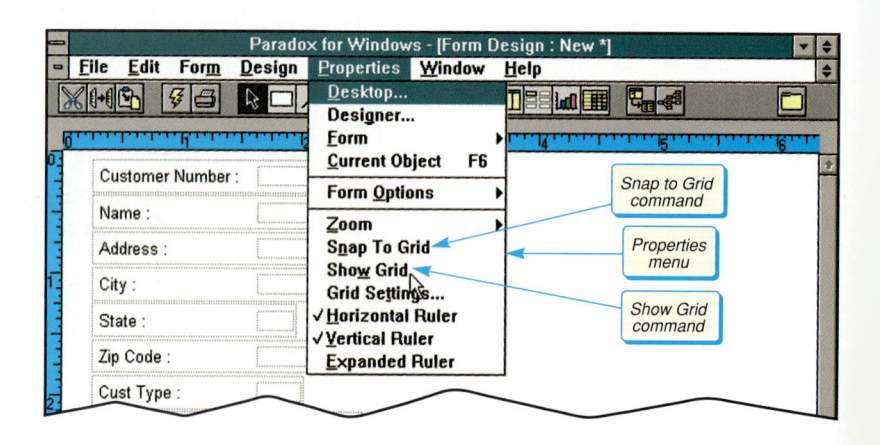

FIGURE 4-53

CREATING AND USING CUSTOM FORMS **P193**

STEP 2 ▶

Choose the Show Grid command.

The grid displays (Figure 4-54). To ensure that objects automatically snap to the nearest grid mark, you also need to choose the Snap To Grid command.

STEP 3 ▶

Select the Properties menu and then choose the Snap To Grid command.

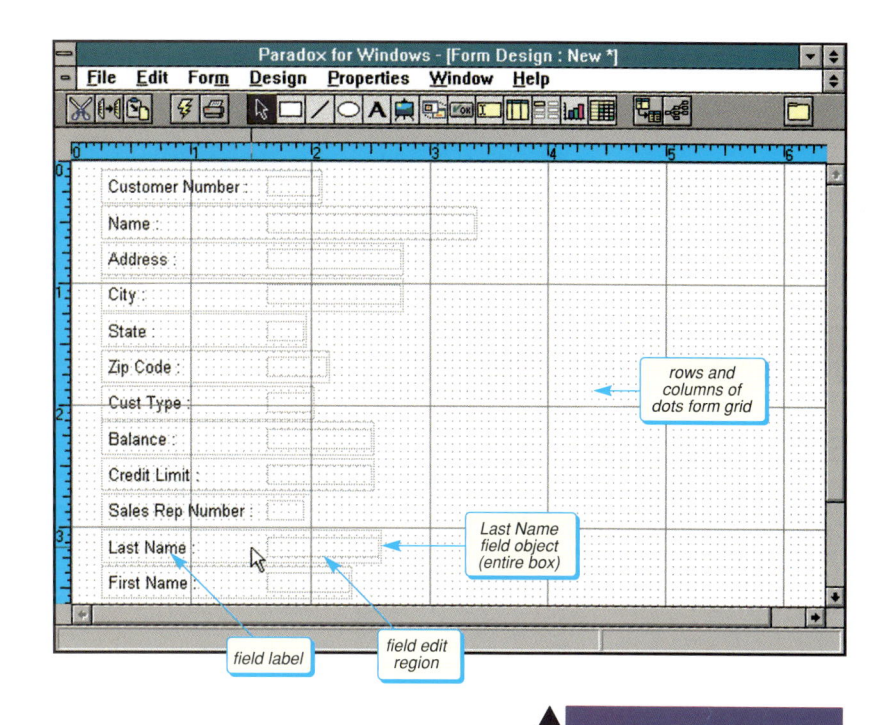

FIGURE 4-54

Selecting Fields

To move or resize a field on a form, you need to select it. To select the field, point to the inside of the field and click the left mouse button. Once you have selected the object, handles appear around the border of the object (see the Last Name field in Figure 4-55).

Perform the following step to select the Last Name field.

TO SELECT A FIELD ▼

STEP 1 ▶

Point to the Last Name field object and click the left mouse button.

The field is selected (Figure 4-55). Handles appear on the border of the box.

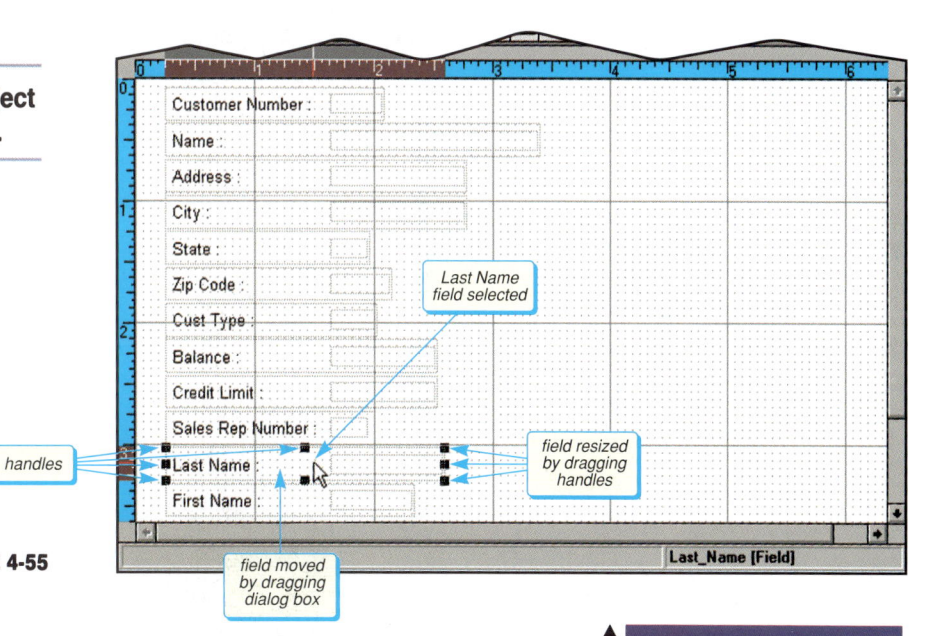

FIGURE 4-55

Once a field is selected, you can move it by dragging it or resize it by dragging one of its handles.

Moving Fields on a Form

To move a field on a form, first select it and then drag it to the new location. The following steps move the fields on the form.

TO MOVE FIELDS ON A FORM

STEP 1 ▶

Drag the Last Name field to the position shown in Figure 4-56.

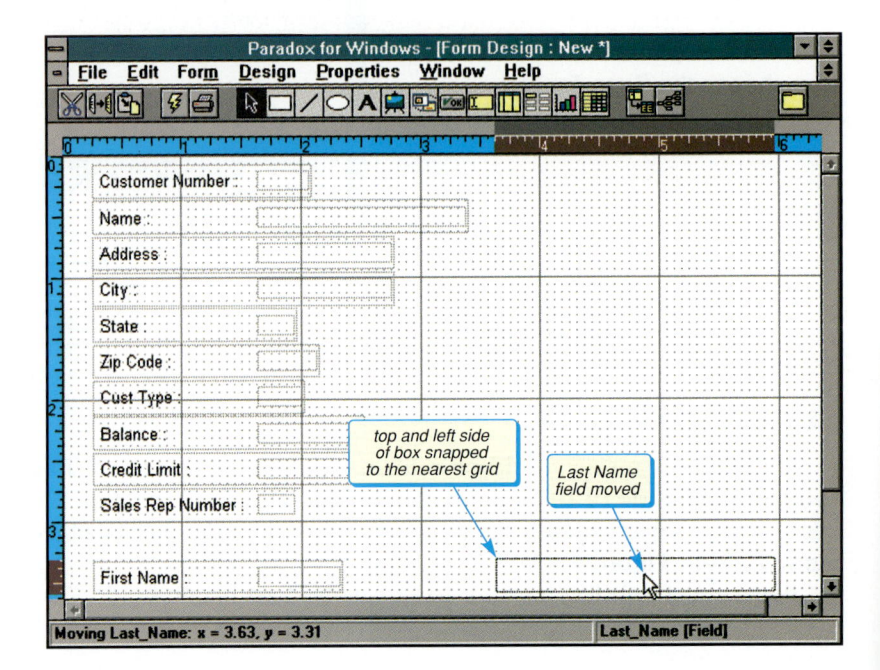

FIGURE 4-56

STEP 2 ▶

Move the remaining field objects to the positions shown in Figure 4-57. Point to the View Data button.

All fields have been moved. When selecting the order in which to move the boxes in this particular form, it is often easier to work from the bottom up. If not, you may find yourself needing to move one field to a position already occupied by another.

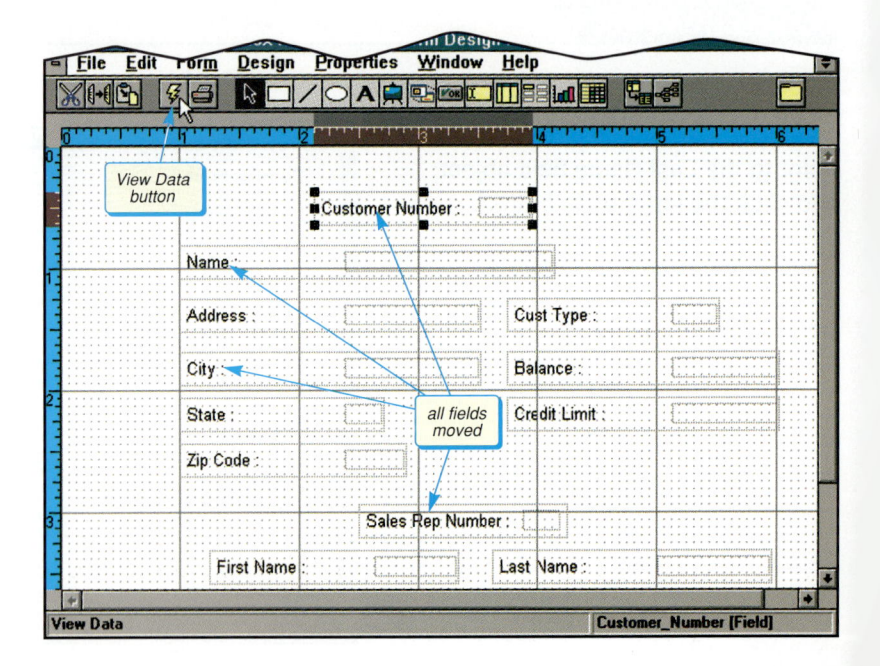

FIGURE 4-57

Saving a Form

To save a form, choose the Save command from the File menu and then assign the file a name. If, for some reason, you do not want to save your work, do *not* choose the Save command. Instead, close the window containing the form and answer No when Paradox asks if you want to save your work.

The following steps save the form, assigning it the name CUSTFORM.

TO SAVE THE FORM

Step 1: Select the File menu and choose the Save command.
Step 2: When the Save As dialog box displays, type CUSTFORM (the name of the form) in the File Name text box and choose the OK button.

Viewing Data Using a Form

When you want to view a form, click the View Data button. The following steps use the form to display the contents of the first record in the table.

TO VIEW DATA USING THE FORM

STEP 1 ▶

Click the View Data button.

The form displays (Figure 4-58). The data shown comes from the first record in the table.

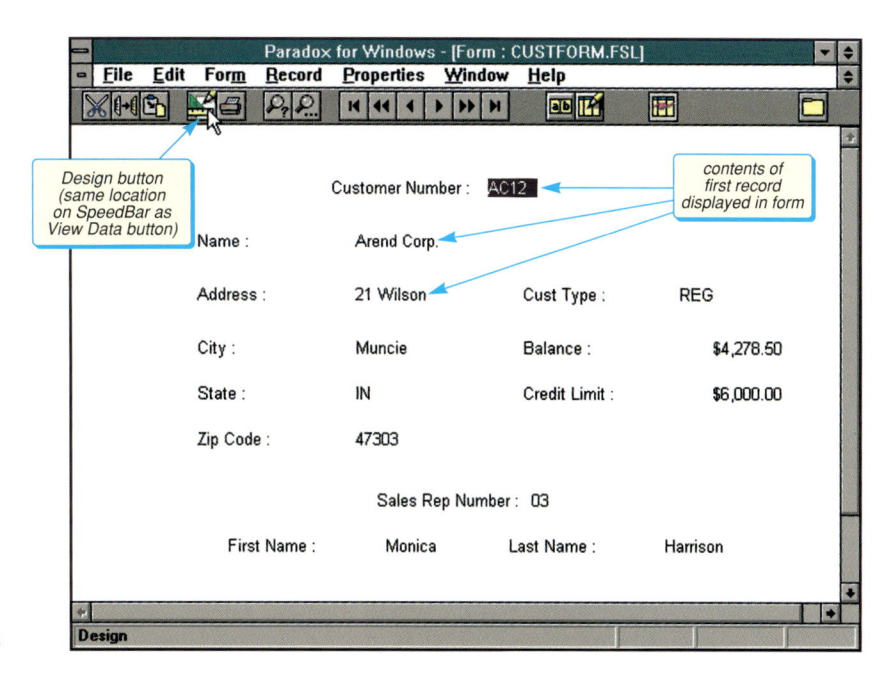

FIGURE 4-58

Adjusting the Position of the Field Edit Region

A great deal of space exists between the label for each field and the field edit region (the portion of the field object that contains the data). To make an adjustment, change the position of the field edit region within the field object to bring it closer to the label. The following steps adjust the positions of the field edit regions within the fields.

TO ADJUST THE POSITIONS OF THE FIELD EDIT REGIONS

STEP 1 ▶

Click the Design button in the SpeedBar and then point to the field edit region of the Customer Number field. Select the field object by clicking the left mouse and then click the mouse button again to select the field edit region.

The field edit region is selected (Figure 4-59).

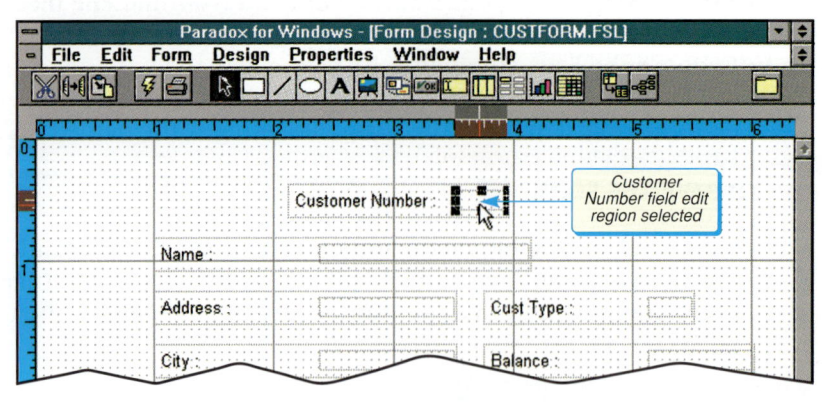

FIGURE 4-59

STEP 2 ▶

Move the field edit region to the position shown in Figure 4-60.

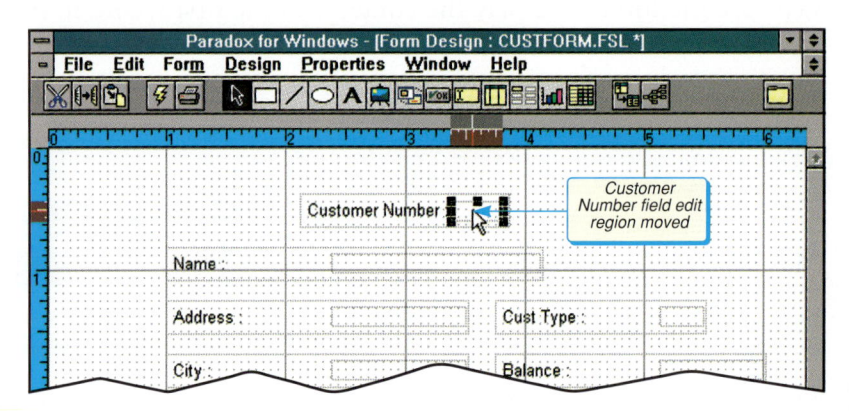

FIGURE 4-60

STEP 3 ▶

Move the remaining field edit regions to the positions shown in Figure 4-61.

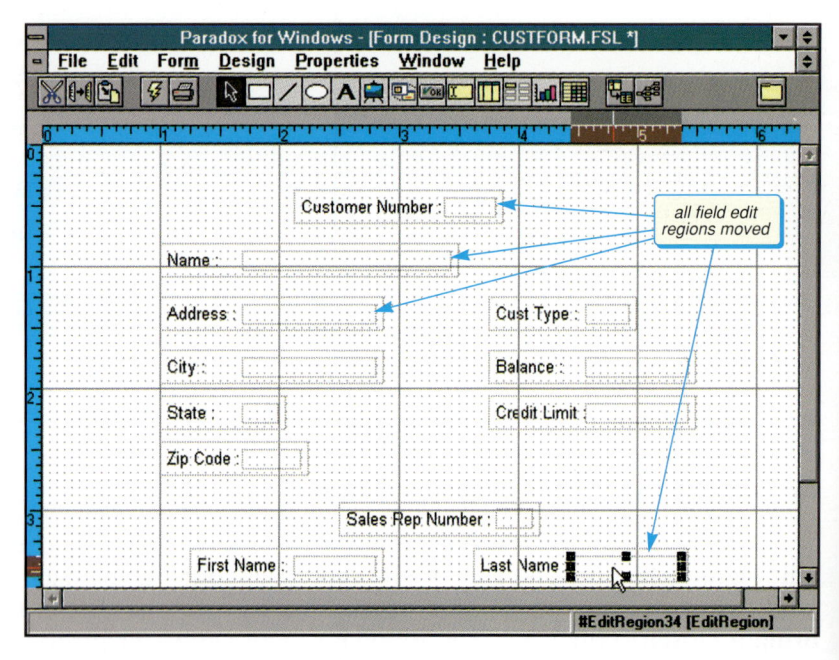

FIGURE 4-61

CREATING AND USING CUSTOM FORMS   **P197**

Adding Boxes to a Form

Boxes can improve the appearance of the form. To add a box, use the Box tool and then indicate the upper left and lower right corners of the box. Perform the following steps to add two boxes to the form.

TO ADD BOXES TO A FORM ▼

STEP 1 ▶

Point to the Box tool button (▢) on the SpeedBar (Figure 4-62) and click the left mouse button.

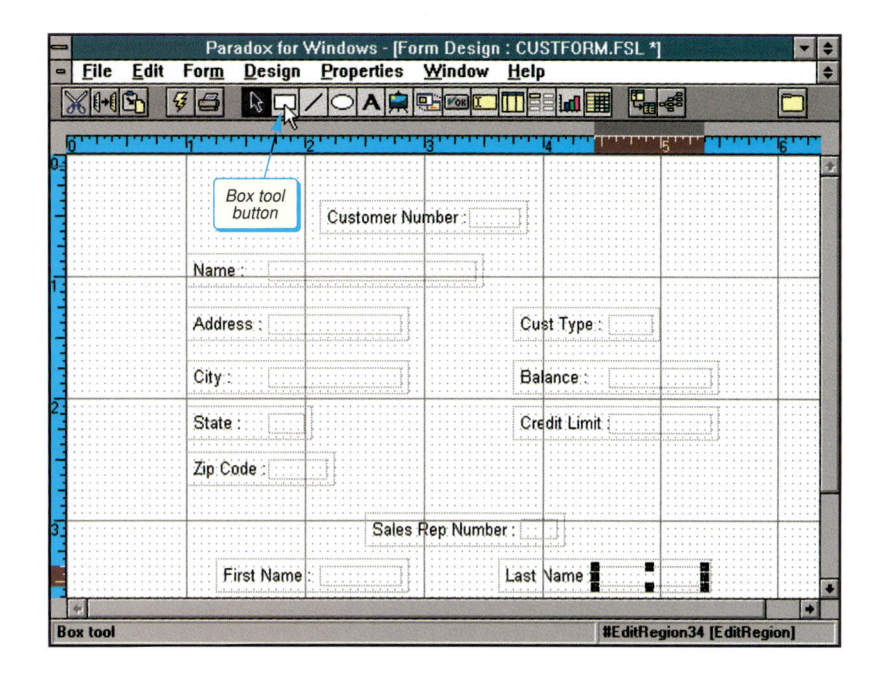

FIGURE 4-62

STEP 2 ▶

Move the mouse pointer, which has changed to a plus sign and a small box (⁺▢), to the position shown in Figure 4-63.

The Box tool button on the SpeedBar is darkened indicating the Box tool is selected. The mouse pointer shape also indicates the Box tool is selected.

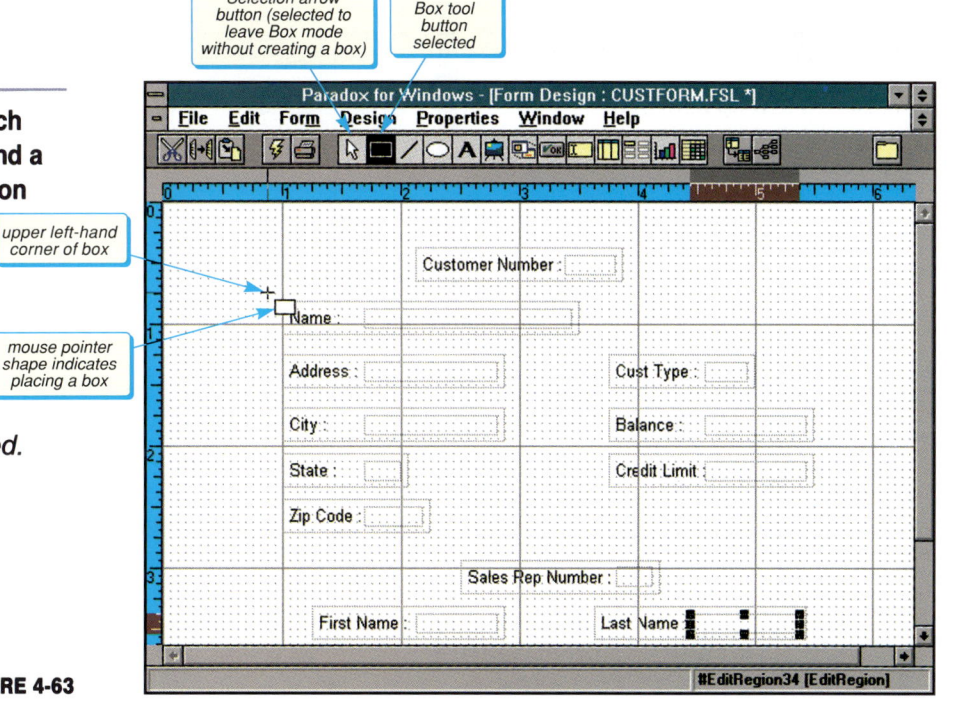

FIGURE 4-63

P198 PROJECT 4 PRESENTING DATA: REPORTS AND FORMS

STEP 3 ▶

Press and hold the left mouse button, drag the pointer to the position shown in Figure 4-64, and then release the left mouse button.

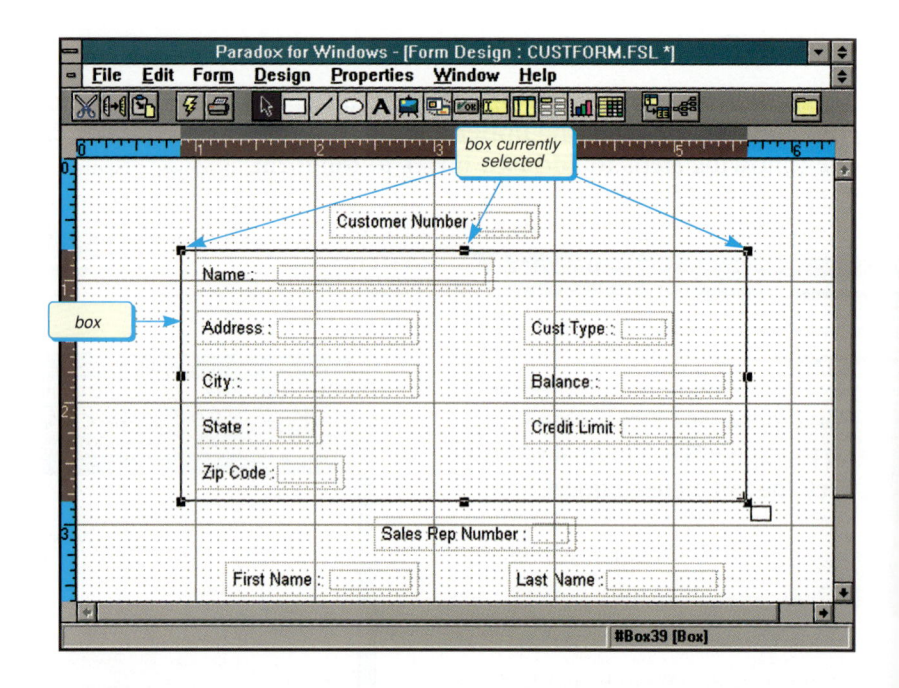

FIGURE 4-64

STEP 4 ▶

To allow room to add a second box, move to the bottom of the form by clicking the down scroll arrow on the vertical scroll bar. Then add a second box in the position shown in Figure 4-65. Point to the up scroll arrow.

A second box displays on the form. The mouse pointer points to the up scroll arrow.

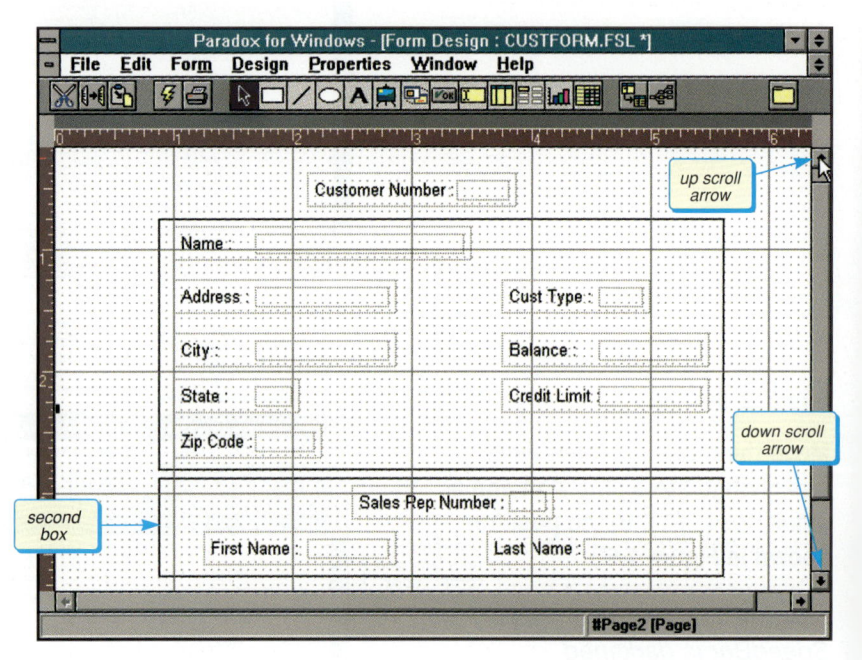

FIGURE 4-65

If after starting the process of adding a box you decide you don't want to complete the task, click the Selection arrow button on the SpeedBar. This will return the mouse pointer to its normal shape.

CREATING AND USING CUSTOM FORMS   P199

Adding Text to a Form

Adding text, such as a title, to a form is similar to adding a box. You click the Text tool button (A) instead of the Box tool button, and then add a box on the screen in the same way you added a box with the Box tool. Once you have added the box, an insertion point will appear inside the box and you can then type the text. The following steps use the Text tool to add a title to the form.

TO ADD TEXT TO A FORM ▼

STEP 1 ▶

Click the up scroll arrow to move to the top of the form and then point to the Text tool button on the SpeedBar.

The top of the form displays (Figure 4-66). The mouse pointer points to the Text tool button.

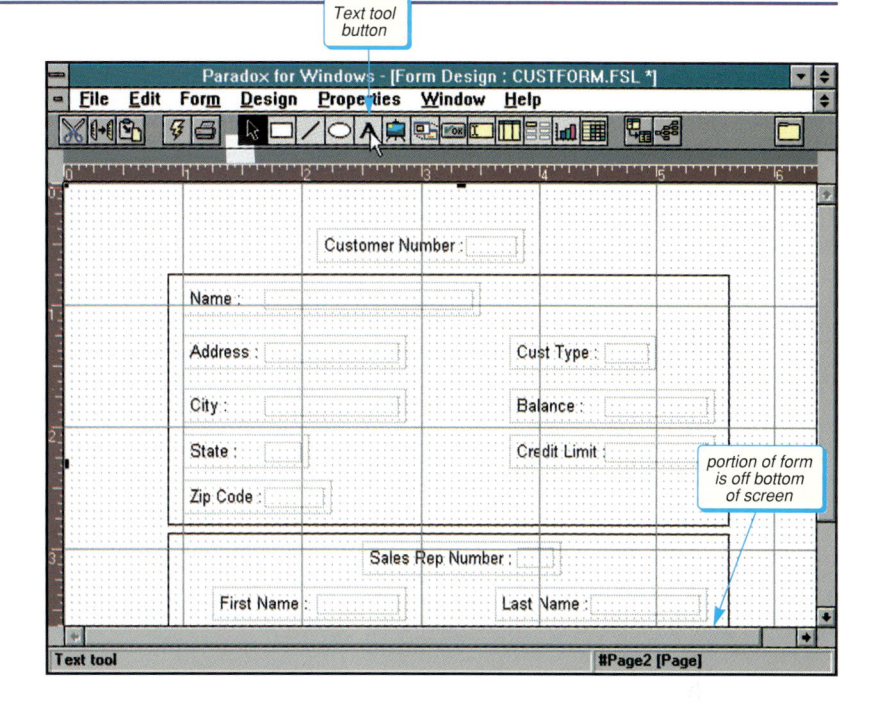

FIGURE 4-66

STEP 2 ▶

Click the Text tool button and then move the mouse pointer. The mouse pointer shape has changed (⁺A) and is in the position shown in Figure 4-67.

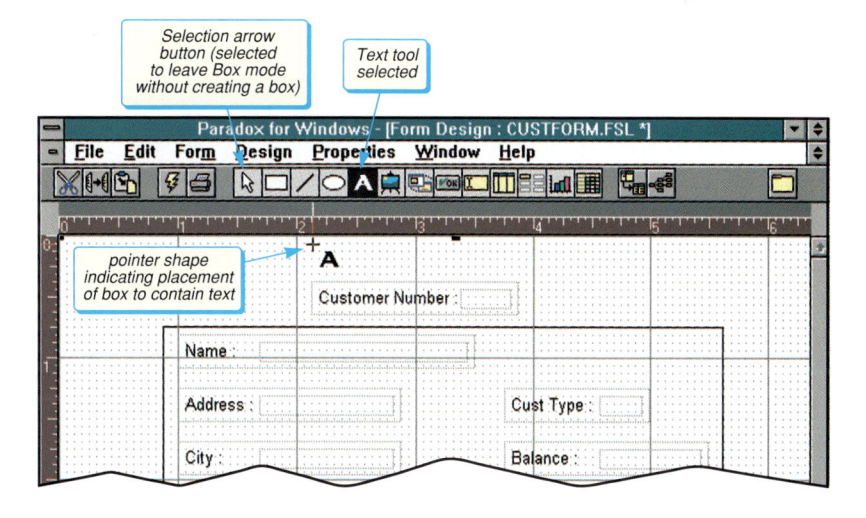

FIGURE 4-67

STEP 3 ▶

Press and hold the left mouse button. Drag the mouse pointer to the opposite corner of the rectangle shown in Figure 4-68 and then release the left mouse button.

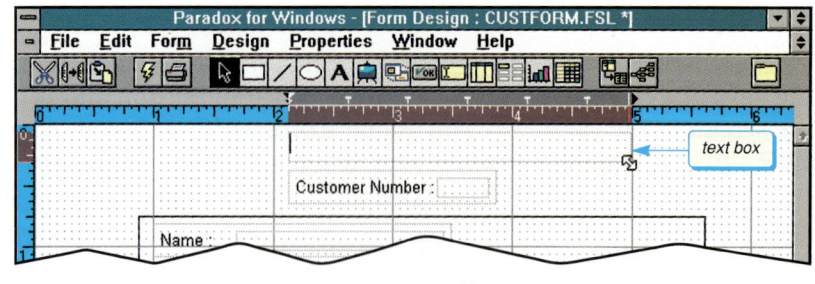

FIGURE 4-68

STEP 4 ▶

Type Customer Maintenance Screen and press ENTER.

Customer Maintenance Screen is entered in the text box (Figure 4-69). The mode returns to normal.

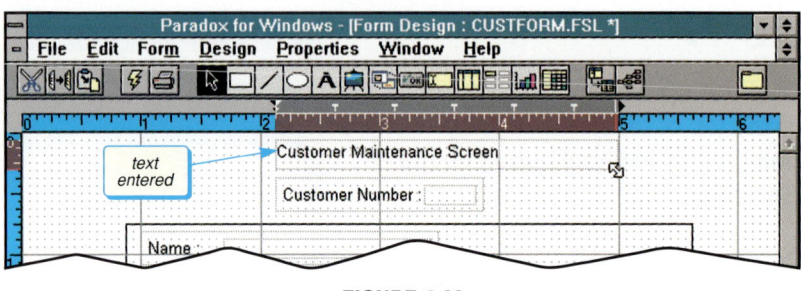

FIGURE 4-69

Changing Fonts

By using the **Font palette**, you can change several aspects of the way characters appear. You can change the typeface, the size, the style, and the color. The Font palette is accessible through the object's menu. The following steps change the font size, style, and color of the form title.

TO CHANGE THE FONT SIZE, STYLE, AND COLOR ▼

STEP 1 ▶

Point to the interior of the text box and click the right mouse button. Choose the Font command, choose the Size command, and point to 14.

The object's menu, the cascading menu of font options, and the list of font sizes display (Figure 4-70). The mouse pointer points to 14.

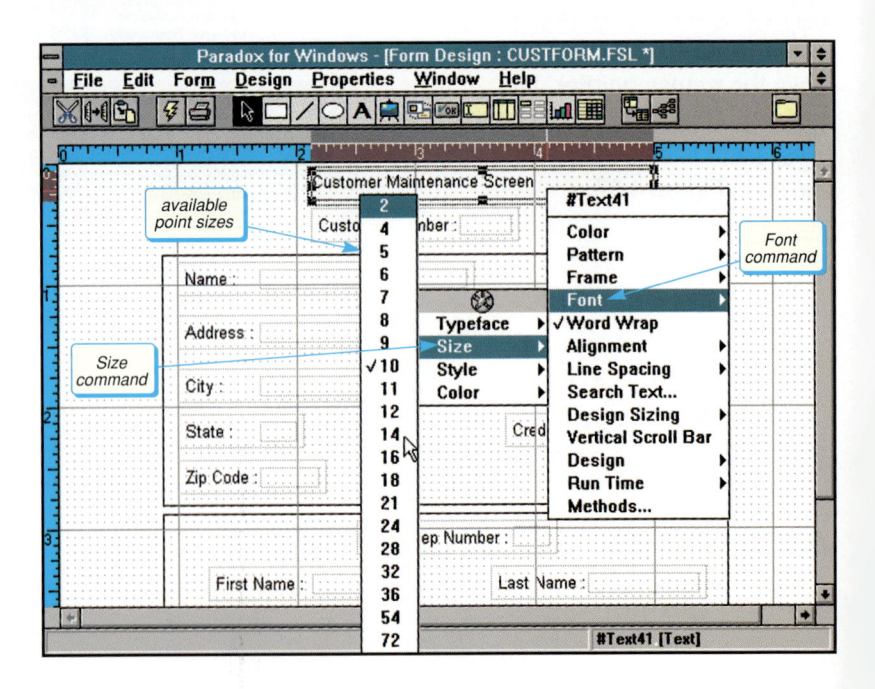

FIGURE 4-70

CREATING AND USING CUSTOM FORMS **P201**

STEP 2 ▶

Click the left mouse button to select size 14. Point to the interior of the text box and click the right mouse button. Choose the Font command, choose the Style command, and point to Italic.

The object's menu, the cascading menu of font options, and the menu of font styles display (Figure 4-71). The mouse pointer points to Italic.

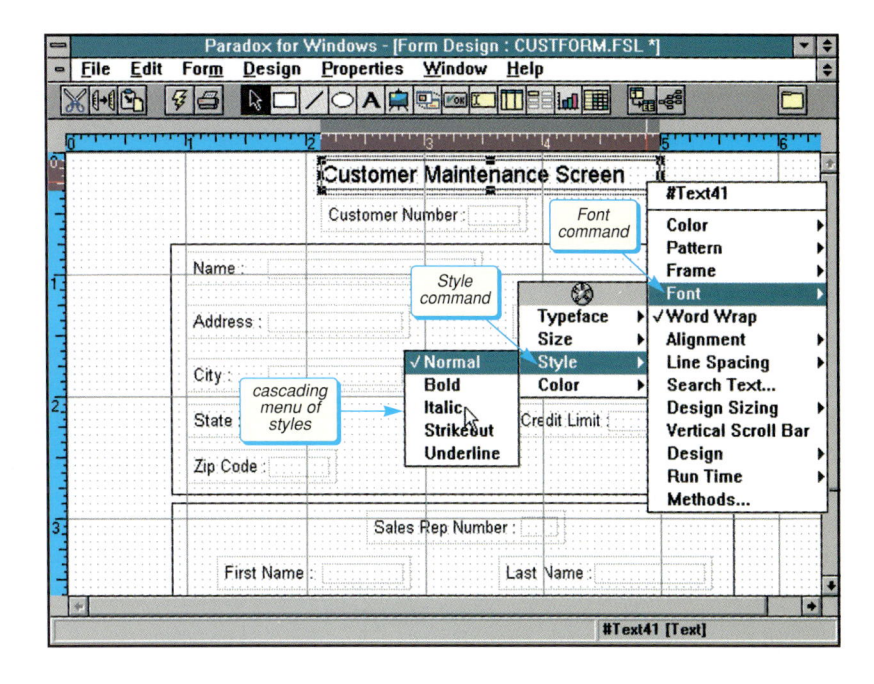

FIGURE 4-71

STEP 3 ▶

Click the left mouse button to select Italic. Point to the interior of the text box and click the right mouse button. Choose the Font command, choose the Color command, and point to the dark red color shown in the cascading color palette Figure 4-72.

STEP 4 ▶

Select the color by clicking the left mouse button.

FIGURE 4-72

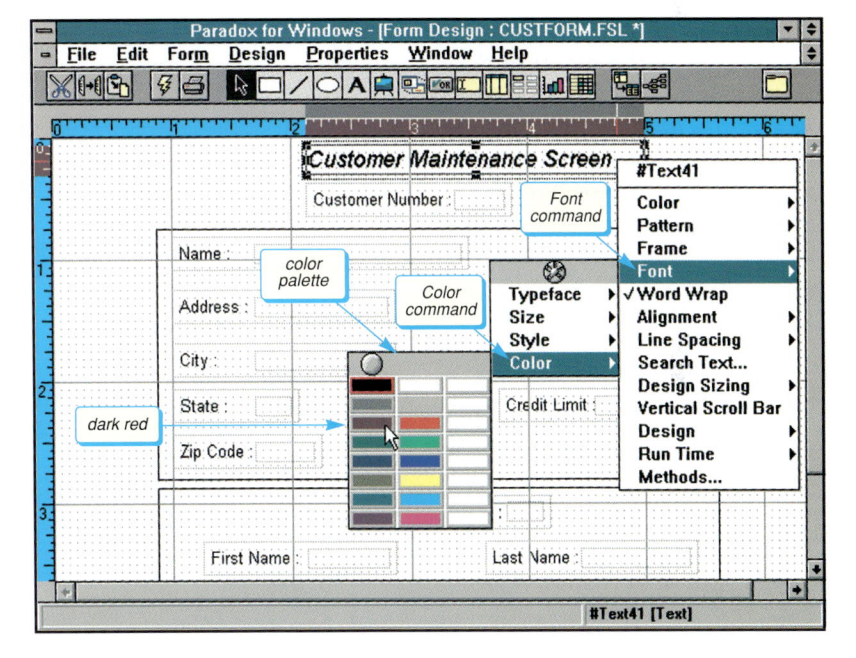

Removing the Grid

Once everything on the form has been moved to the correct position, you no longer need the grid. To make the screen look less cluttered, remove the grid. Use the same Show Grid option you used to initially display the grid. The following step summarizes removing the grid.

TO REMOVE THE GRID

Step 1: Select the Properties menu and choose the Show Grid command.

Changing the Background Color

Currently the color of the background of the form is white. You can change the color by using the background object's menu. The following steps assign light gray as the background color.

TO CHANGE THE BACKGROUND COLOR

STEP 1 ▶

Point to an open space on the form outside any of the boxes and then click the right mouse button. Select the Color command from the menu that displays and then point to the light gray color.

The menu shown in Figure 4-73 displays. (If you see a different menu, move the pointer to a position outside of the menu and click the left mouse button to remove the menu. Then move to a slightly different position and click the right mouse button again.) The color palette displays and the mouse pointer points to light gray.

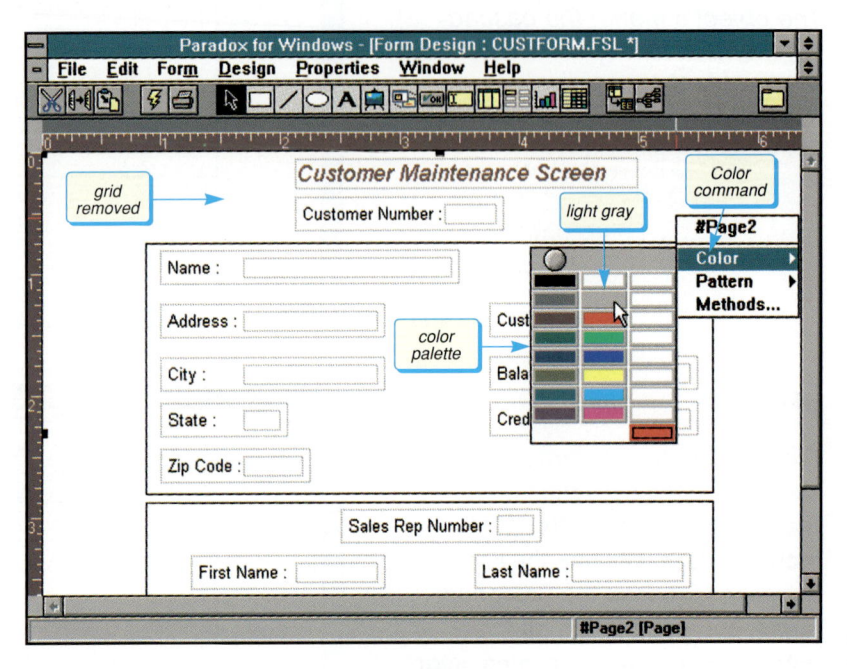

FIGURE 4-73

STEP 2 ▶

Select light gray by clicking the left mouse button.

The background color for the form is light gray (Figure 4-74).

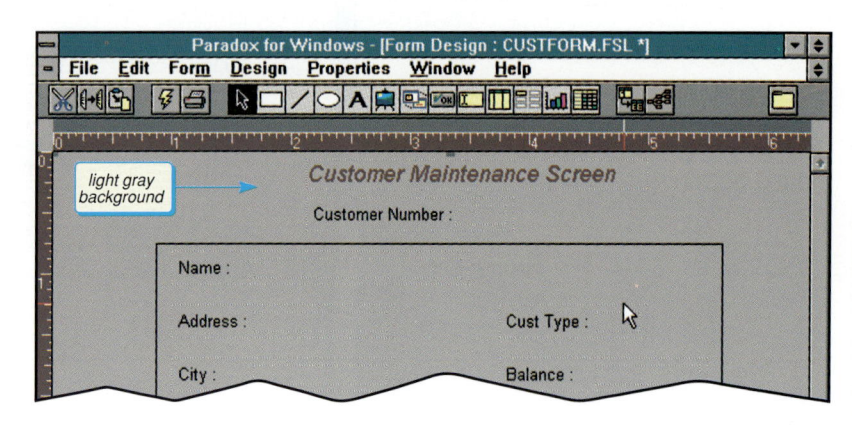

FIGURE 4-74

Changing Box Frame Styles

Boxes, fields, and text are all surrounded by a special kind of border called a **frame**. There are several frame styles available in Paradox. To change the style, color, or thickness of a frame, first select the object whose frame you want to modify. Then use the Frame command of the object's menu.

CREATING AND USING CUSTOM FORMS **P203**

Selecting More than One Object

In some cases, you will want to make the same change to several objects. Instead of making each individual change, you can select all the objects at once and then make a single change. To select more than one object at a time, hold down the SHIFT key as you select the additional objects. Perform the following steps to change the box frame styles.

TO SELECT THE BOXES AND CHANGE THE BOX FRAME STYLES ▼

STEP 1 ▶

Point to the inside of the upper box. Select it by clicking the left mouse button. Point to the inside of the lower box, hold down the SHIFT key, and click the left mouse button.

Both boxes are selected (Figure 4-75).

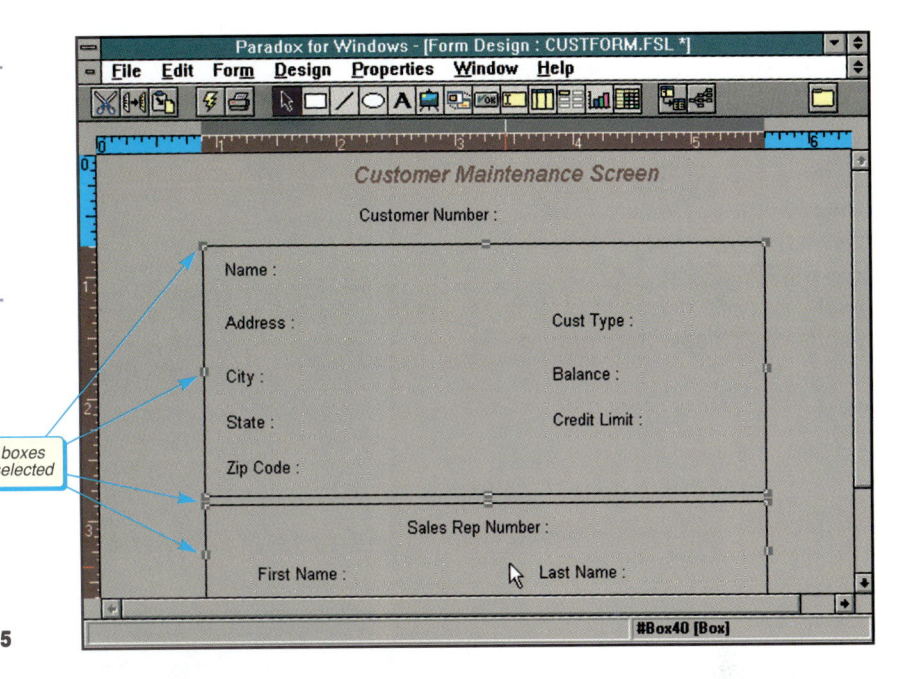

FIGURE 4-75

STEP 2 ▶

Click the right mouse button, choose the Frame command, choose the Style command, and point to the style shown in Figure 4-76.

STEP 3 ▶

Choose the style shown in Figure 4-76 by clicking the left mouse button.

The style of the box frames change to the selected style.

FIGURE 4-76

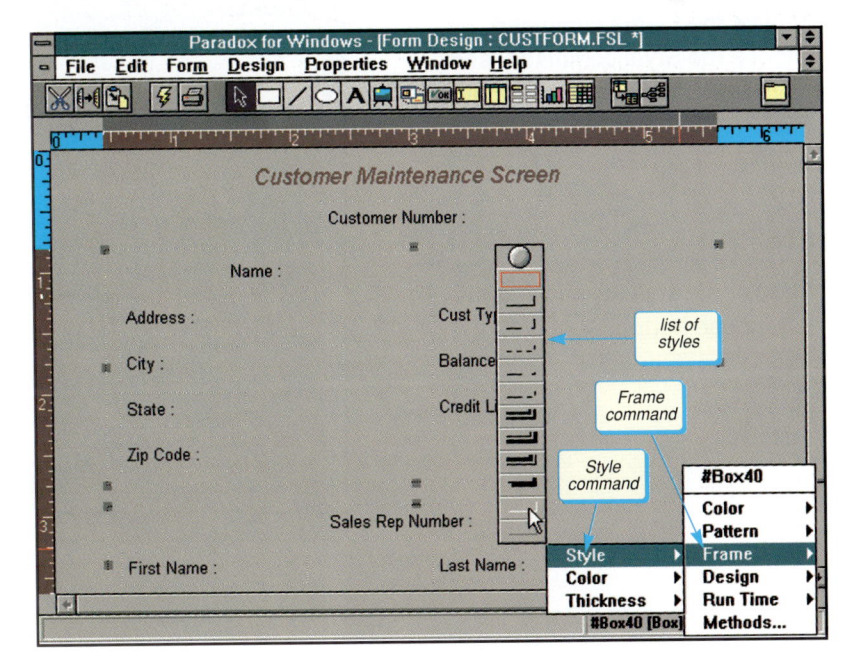

Changing the Field Frame Styles

Change the styles of the field frames just like you change the style of box frames. The following steps change the style of the field frames.

TO CHANGE THE FIELD FRAME STYLES

STEP 1 ▶

Select the Customer Number field object by pointing to it and clicking the left mouse button. Hold down the SHIFT key and select the remaining field objects by pointing to them and clicking the left mouse button. Be sure to hold down the SHIFT key as you select the other fields objects.

All fields are selected (Figure 4-77).

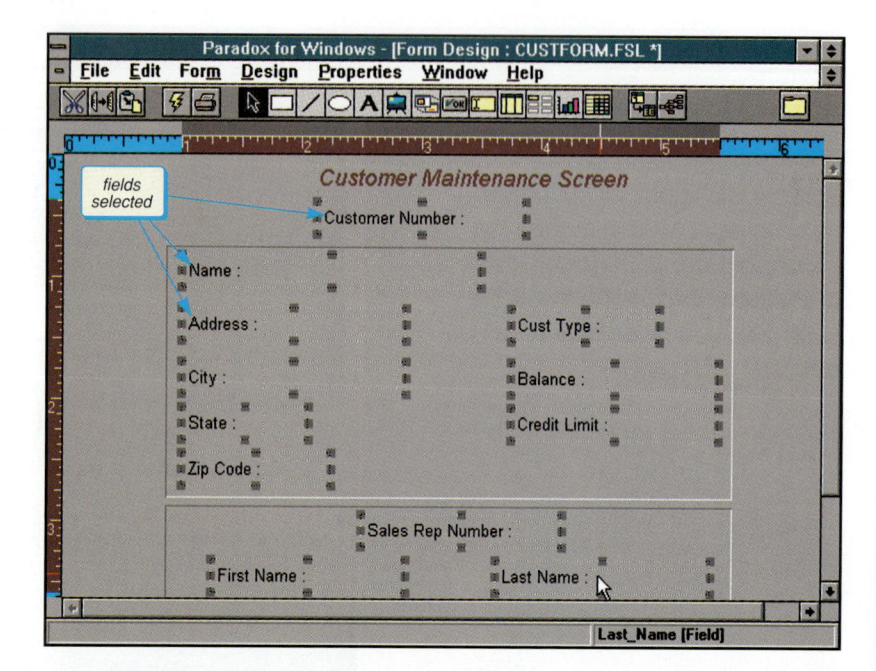

FIGURE 4-77

STEP 2 ▶

Click the right mouse button, choose the Frame command, choose the Style command, and point to the style shown in Figure 4-78.

STEP 3 ▶

Choose the style by clicking the left mouse button.

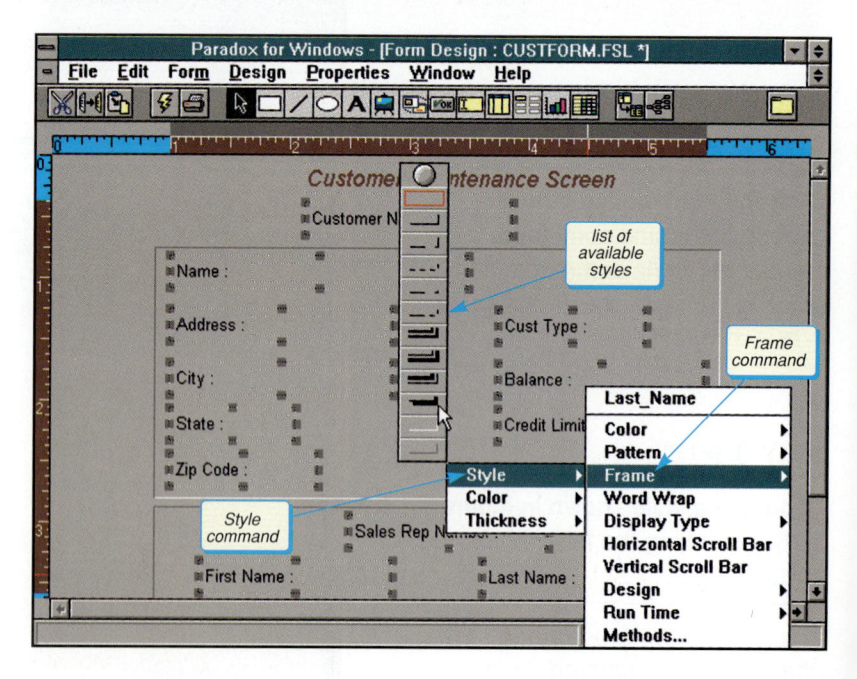

FIGURE 4-78

CREATING AND USING CUSTOM FORMS **P205**

Changing the Text Frame Style

Text frame styles are changed in the same way as other frame styles. Perform the following steps to change the style of the text frame surrounding the form title.

TO CHANGE THE TEXT FRAME STYLE ▼

STEP 1 ▶

Point to the text object containing the title, Customer Maintenance Screen, and select it by clicking the left mouse button. Click the right mouse button, choose the Frame command, choose the Style command, and point to the style shown in Figure 4-79.

STEP 2 ▶

Choose the style by clicking the left mouse button.

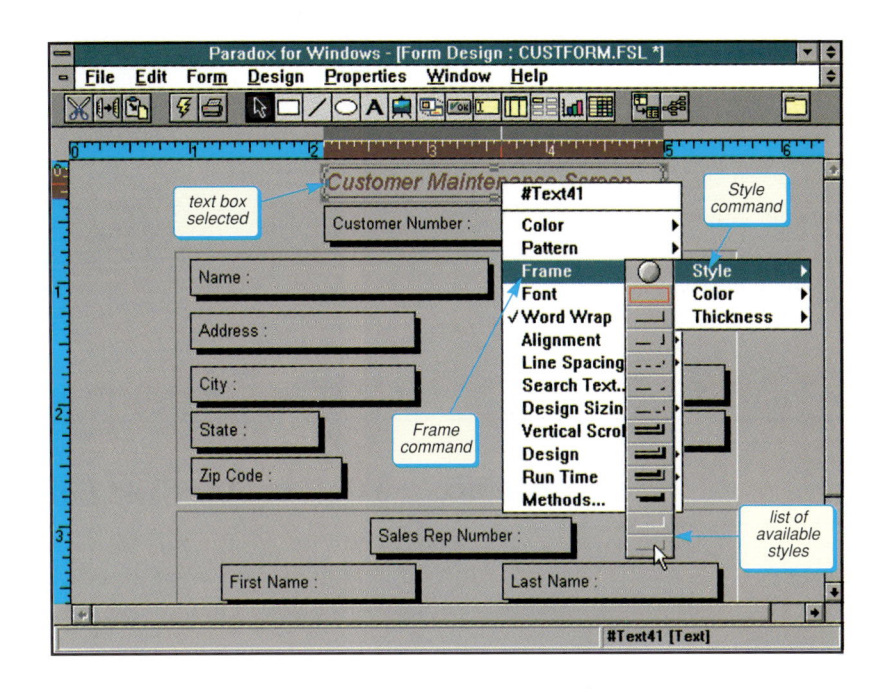

FIGURE 4-79

To see the effect of the changes, view data using the form as in the following steps.

TO VIEW DATA USING THE FORM ▼

STEP 1 ▶

Point to the View Data button.

The frames all have the newly selected styles (Figure 4-80). The mouse pointer points to the View Data button.

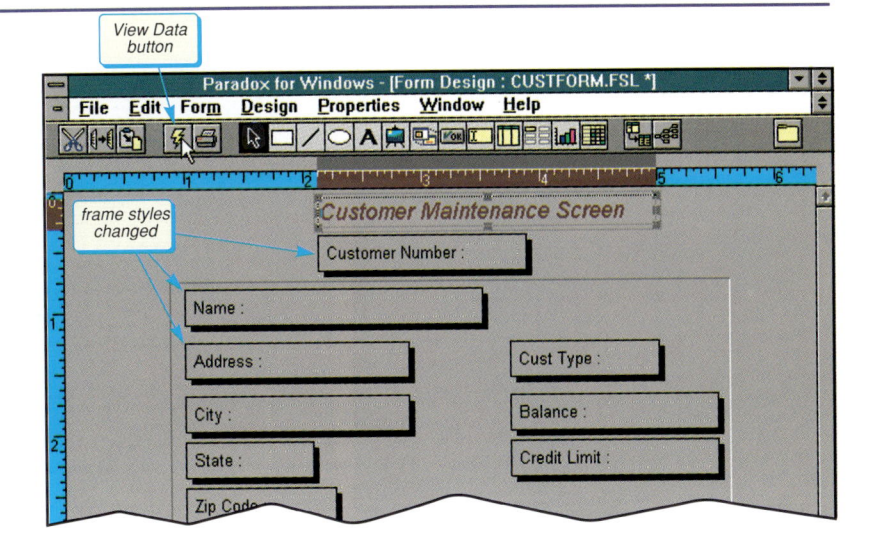

FIGURE 4-80

STEP 2 ▶

Click the View Data button.

The form displays on the screen (Figure 4-81). The data from the first record displays in the form. The mouse pointer points to the Design button because it is in the same position on the SpeedBar as the View Data button.

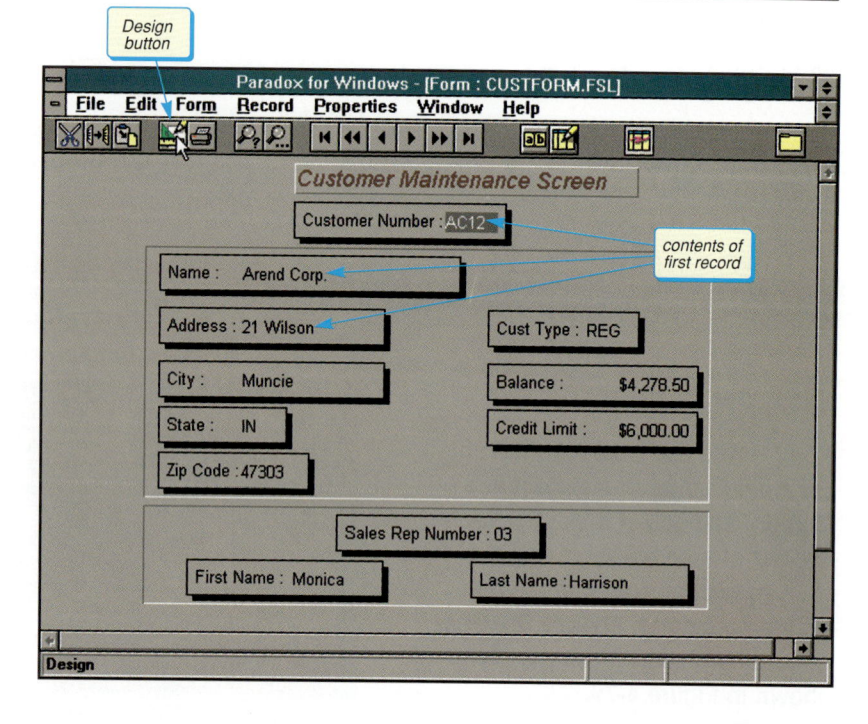

FIGURE 4-81

Changing the Color of the Field Edit Regions

One way to emphasize the position of the field edit regions is to change their color. To change the color of an edit region, use the edit region object's menu. The following steps change the color of the edit regions to light blue.

TO CHANGE THE COLOR OF THE FIELD EDIT REGIONS ▼

STEP 1 ▶

Click the Design button and then select all the field edit regions.

The fields are selected (Figure 4-82).

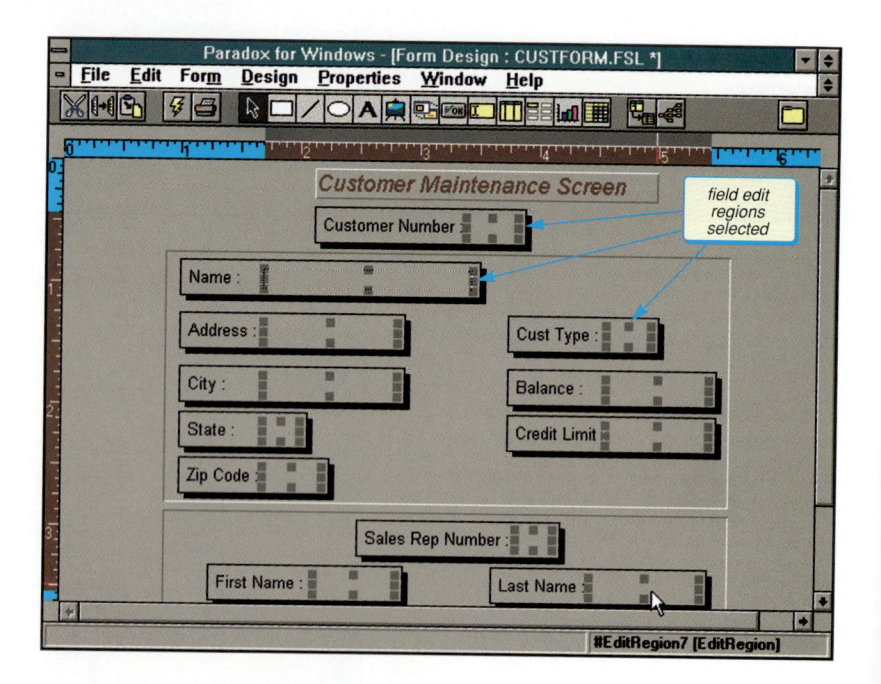

FIGURE 4-82

CREATING AND USING CUSTOM FORMS **P207**

STEP 2 ▶

Click the right mouse button, select the Color command, and point to light blue.

The color palette displays and the mouse pointer points to light blue (Figure 4-83).

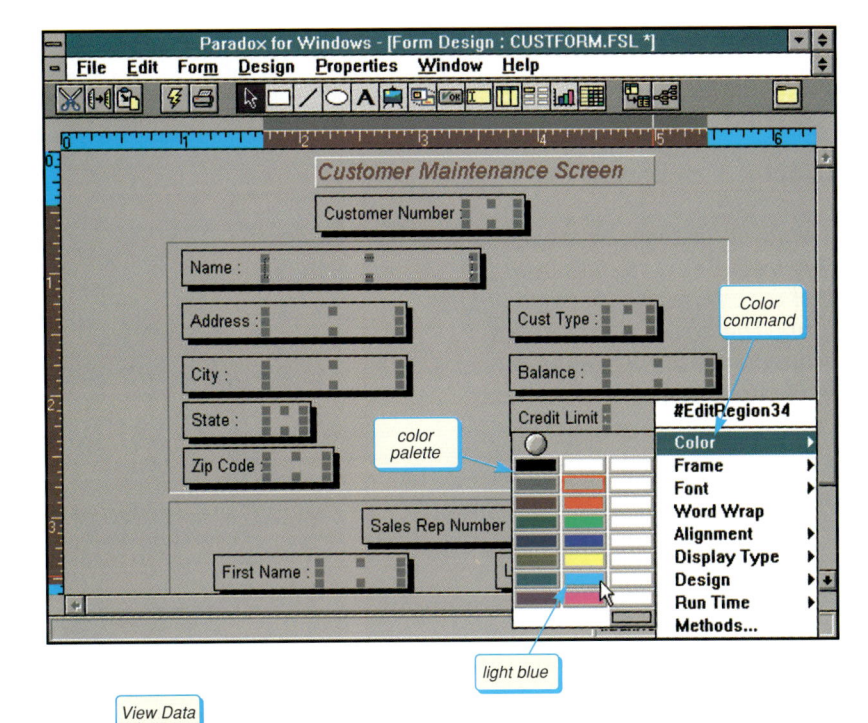

FIGURE 4-83

STEP 3 ▶

Select light blue by clicking the left mouse button and then point to the View Data button.

The field edit regions are light blue and the mouse pointer points to the View Data button (Figure 4-84).

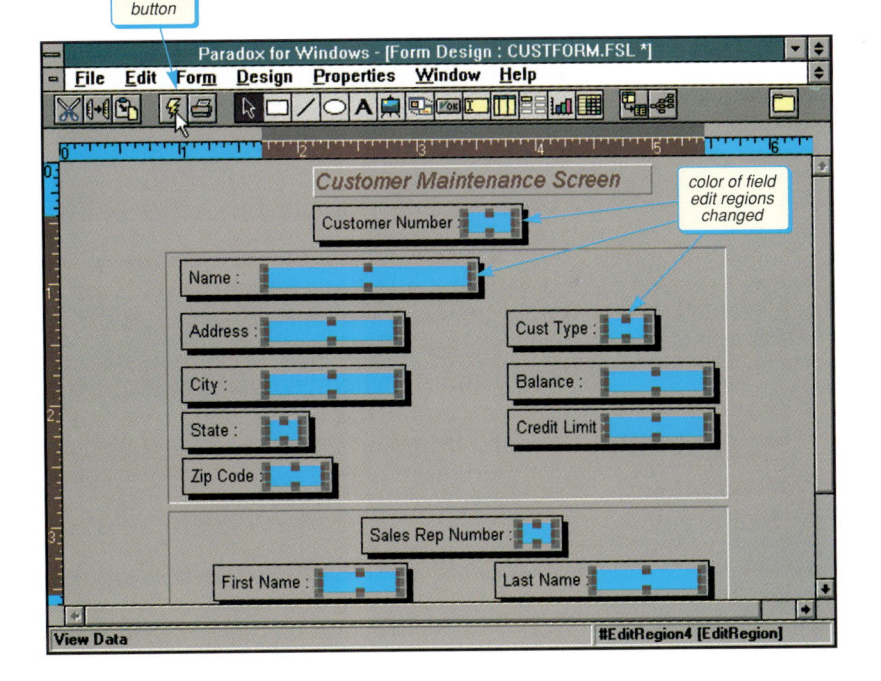

FIGURE 4-84

To see the effect of the changes, view the data using the form shown in the step on the following page.

P208   PROJECT 4   PRESENTING DATA: REPORTS AND FORMS

TO VIEW DATA USING THE FORM ▼

STEP 1 ▶

Click the View Data button.

The form displays on the screen (Figure 4-85). The data from the first record (AC12) displays in the form. The colors have changed. The color of the highlighted field is different from the other fields.

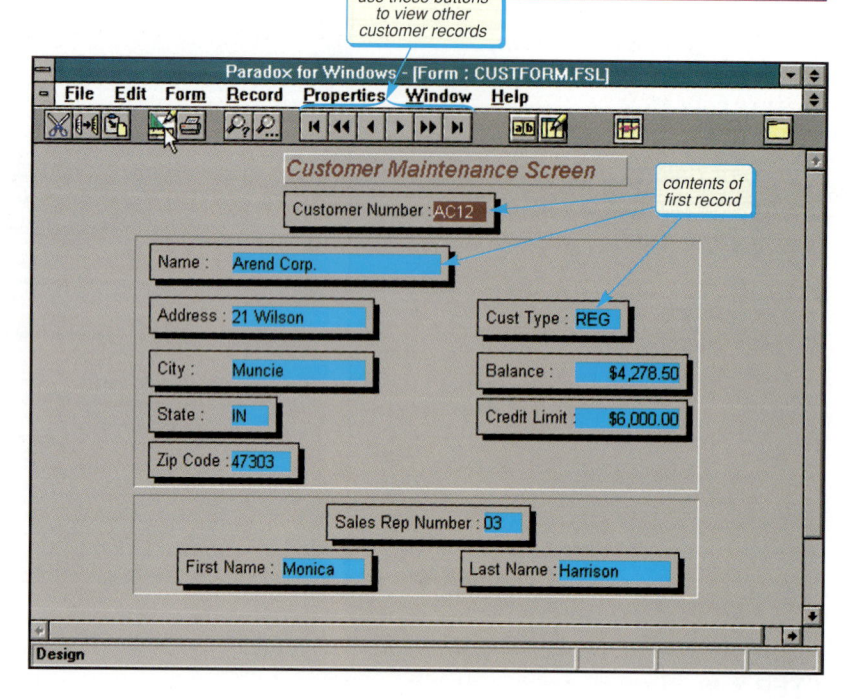

FIGURE 4-85

▲

Closing a Form

When you have finished designing the form, you should close the form by closing the window containing the form design. You also need to save your work. Answer Yes when Paradox asks if you want to save your work.

The two cases where you need to use one of the Save commands on the File menu are: (1) when you want to save the form and continue working, then use the Save command on the File menu; and (2) when you want to save the form under a different name, then use the Save As command on the File menu. Neither apply in this case, so you can simply close the window.

Perform the following step to close the form and save your work.

TO CLOSE THE FORM

Step 1: Click the Design button to return to the form design and then close the window. When Paradox asks you if you want to save the form, choose the Yes button.

Using the Form

To use a form to view or update data in a table, you click the Open Form button (📋) on the SpeedBar instead of the Open Table button. You then select the form you want to use. Just as when you used the Open Report button, you need to indicate an Open Mode in the Open Document dialog box. You want to use the View Data option, which allows you to use the form to view or update data. The Design option allows you to further modify the design of your form.

The following steps open the CUSTFORM form for use in viewing or updating the data in the Customer table.

TO USE A FORM

Step 1: Point to the Open Form button on the SpeedBar (Figure 4-86).
Step 2: Click the Open Form button and select the form.
Step 3: Choose the Open Mode (View Data to use the form or Design to modify the form).
Step 4: Choose the OK button.

The form shown in Figure 4-85 displays.

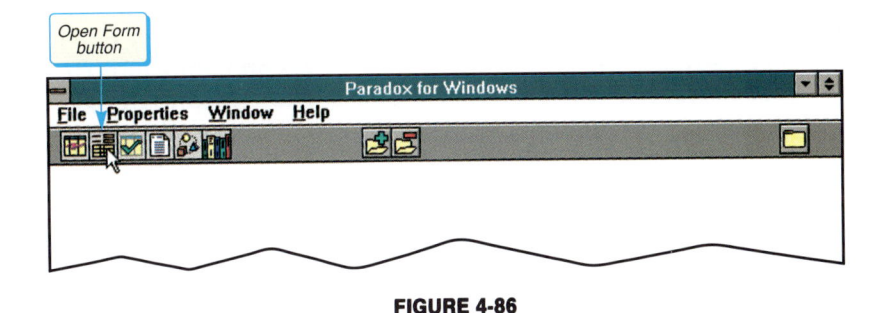

FIGURE 4-86

When you have finished working with a form, close it by closing the window containing the form in the usual manner.

▶ FORM DESIGN CONSIDERATIONS

As you design and create custom forms, keep in mind the following guidelines.

1. Remember that persons using a form may be looking at the form for several hours at a time. Forms that are excessively cluttered or that contain too many different effects (colors, fonts, frame styles, and so on) can become very difficult on the eyes.
2. Place the fields in logical groupings. Fields that relate to each other should be close to each other on the form. Consider using boxes to emphasize the groupings of related fields.
3. If the data a user enters comes from a paper form, make the screen form resemble the paper form as closely as possible.
4. Make sure the fields are reasonably close to the corresponding prompts.
5. Position the field edit regions clearly on the form. One way to do this is by making them a different color as you did in the form created in this project.

P210 PROJECT 4 PRESENTING DATA: REPORTS AND FORMS

▶ Project Summary

Project 4 covered the issues involved in presenting the data in a database. In the project, you learned how to create and print reports. You learned the purpose of the various bands and how to modify their contents. The project covered the steps illustrating how to group in a report by using group bands. You learned how to create and use custom forms, how to move fields, how to add boxes and text, and how to change the characteristics of various objects in a form. Project 4 showed you how to use a form to view or update data. Finally, you learned some general principles to help you design effective reports and forms.

▶ Key Terms

All Records band (*P170*)
band (*P170*)
Box tool button (*P192*)
custom forms (*P188*)
field edit region (*P180*)
field object (*P178*)
Field tool button (*P178*)
Font palette (*P200*)
Form Design window (*P188*)
frame (*P202*)
grid (*P192*)
grid lines (*P172*)

group (*P183*)
group band (*P183*)
group footer (*P183*)
group header (*P183*)
grouping (*P164*)
handles (*P171*)
label (*P180*)
Open Mode (*P183*)
Open Report button (*P182*)
Page band (*P170*)
page footer (*P170*)

page header (*P170*)
Properties menu (*P174*)
Report band (*P170*)
Report Design window (*P166*)
report footer (*P170*)
report header (*P170*)
Selection arrow button (*P178*)
Snap to grid (*P192*)
subtotal (*P164, P183*)
Zoom command (*P174*)
zoom factor (*P174*)

QUICK REFERENCE

In Paradox for Windows you can accomplish a task in a number of different ways. The following table provides a quick reference to each task presented in this project with its available options. The commands listed in the Menu column can be executed using either the keyboard or the mouse.

Task	Mouse	Menu	Keyboard Shortcuts
Add a Box Object	Click Box tool button on the SpeedBar		
Add a Field to a Report or Form	Click Field tool button on SpeedBar		
Add a Group Band to a Report	Click Add Band button on SpeedBar	From Report menu, choose Add Band	
Add Text	Click Text tool button on SpeedBar		
Change Background Color		From background object menu, choose Color	
Change Color of an Object		From the object's menu, choose Color	
Change Column Heading	Click heading until selected, then make change		Press TAB until heading selected, then make change
Change Column Width	Drag grid line		
Change Font Color		From object's menu, choose Font, then choose Color	

QUICK REFERENCE   P211

Task	Mouse	Menu	Keyboard Shortcuts
Change Font Size		From object's menu, choose Font, then choose Size	
Change Font Style		From object's menu, choose Font, then choose Style	
Change Frame Style		From object's menu, choose Frame, then choose Style	
Change Label in a Field Object	Click label until selected, then make change		Press TAB until label selected, then make change
Change Zoom Factor		From Properties menu, choose Close. Choose Yes to save the form or No to not save form	
Close Report		From Control menu, choose Close; choose Yes to save the report or No not to save report	
Create Form		From File menu, choose New, then choose Form	
Create Report		From File menu, choose New, then choose Report	
Modify Form Design	Click Form button on SpeedBar, select form, select report, select Design	From File menu, choose Open, choose Report, select report, select design	
Move Field Edit Region within a Field Object	Click field edit region until selected, then drag within field object		
Move Fields	Click field edit until selected, then drag		
Print Report	Click Print button on SpeedBar from Design window	From File menu, choose Report, select report, select Print	
Resize Band	Drag band lines		
Remove Grid		From Properties menu, choose Show Grid	
Return to Report or Form Design While Viewing Data	Click Design button on SpeedBar	From Form or Report menu, choose Design	Press F8
Save Form		From File menu, choose Save	
Save Report		From File menu, choose Save	
Save Report Under a Different Name		From File menu, choose Save As	
Select Fields for Report or Form	Choose Select Fields button		
Select Multiple Objects	Hold down SHIFT key and click each object until selected		
Select Object	Click object until selected		Press TAB until object selected

(continued)

P212   PROJECT 4   PRESENTING DATA: REPORTS AND FORMS

QUICK REFERENCE (continued)

Task	Mouse	Menu	Keyboard Shortcuts
Select Tables for Report or Form	Select table, click Add Table button, select additional table. Relate the tables by pointing to the table, then dragging pointer to another		
Show the Grid		From Properties menu, choose Show Grid	
Snap to Grid		From Properties menu, choose Snap To Grid	
Use a Form to View Data	Click Form button, select form, select View Data	From File menu, choose Form, select form, select View Data	
View Data When Designing a Form or Report	Click View Data button on SpeedBar	From Form or Report menu, choose View Data	Press F8

S T U D E N T   A S S I G N M E N T S

STUDENT ASSIGNMENT 1
True/False

Instructions: Circle T if the statement is true or F if the statement is false.

T   F   1. The first step in creating a report in Paradox is to select the table or tables to be included in the report.

T   F   2. The initial report design includes all the fields from a table.

T   F   3. To remove a field from a report, highlight the field on the Design Layout screen and press the DELETE key.

T   F   4. To reverse the order of two fields in a report, choose the Select Fields button in the Design Layout dialog box, select the second of the two fields to be reversed in the Select Fields dialog box, and then point to and click the Change Order Up arrow.

T   F   5. The contents of a report footer will appear only once on a report.

T   F   6. The Report Design screen uses small squares called handholds to indicate which portion of the report is currently selected.

T   F   7. To split a column heading between two lines, place the insertion point at the position where you would like to split the heading and then press CTRL-ENTER.

T   F   8. To view a report on the screen, point to and click the View Data button on the Report Design screen SpeedBar.

T   F   9. To adjust a report so the entire report fits on the screen, choose the Zoom command on the Properties menu.

T   F   10. On the Report Design screen, you can increase or decrease the width of a column by dragging the column's right grid line.

T   F   11. To add a field to a report, choose the Add Fields command from the Report menu on the Report Design screen.

T   F   12. To save a new report, choose the Save As command from the File menu and then assign a name to the report.

T F 13. Group bands are used to specify subtotals when you are using the Paradox report feature.
T F 14. The first step in creating a form is to choose the New command from the File menu, choose the Form command, and then select the tables to be included.
T F 15. To display a grid on the Form Design screen to help align objects on a form, choose the Show Grid command from the Design menu.
T F 16. To add boxes to a form, point to and click the Box tool button on the SpeedBar, and then drag the mouse pointer to place a box around the desired objects.
T F 17. To add text to a form, point to and click the Text tool button on the SpeedBar, type the text in the appropriate location, and then point to and click the Box tool button on the SpeedBar to place a box around the text.
T F 18. To change the size of characters in a text box on the Form Design screen, point to the interior of the text box, click the right mouse button, choose the Font command from the Object menu, and then choose the Size command.
T F 19. To select more than one object at a time on the Form Design screen, select the first object by pointing to and clicking the left mouse button and then select the other objects by holding down the CTRL key as you click the left mouse button.
T F 20. To use a custom form to view or update data in a table, click the Open Form button on the SpeedBar of the Paradox main screen.

STUDENT ASSIGNMENT 2
Multiple Choice

Instructions: Circle the correct response.

1. The process of creating separate collections of records sharing some common characteristic is known as _____.
   a. collecting
   b. matching
   c. grouping
   d. categorizing
2. To create a new report, choose the New command from the File menu and then _____.
   a. choose the Report command
   b. select the table or tables to include in the report
   c. enter a name for the new report
   d. choose the Report Design command
3. To remove a field from a report, highlight the field in the Select Fields dialog box and then _____.
   a. press the DELETE key
   b. point to and click the Remove Field button
   c. press the CTRL+DELETE keys
   d. click the right mouse button
4. The portions of the Report Design screen (such as report header and page header) are called _____.
   a. segments
   b. areas
   c. portions
   d. bands
5. The Report Design screen uses small squares called _____ to indicate which portion of the report is currently selected.
   a. handholds
   b. handles
   c. braces
   d. grippers

(continued)

STUDENT ASSIGNMENT 2 (continued)

6. To split a column heading between two lines, place the insertion point at the position where you would like to split the heading and then press the _____.
   a. SHIFT + ENTER
   b. CTRL + ENTER
   c. ENTER
   d. TAB + ENTER
7. To display a grid on the Form Design screen to help align objects on a form, choose the _____.
   a. Show Grid command from the Properties menu
   b. Show Grid command from the Design menu
   c. Snap To Grid command from the Properties menu
   d. Snap To Grid command from the Design menu
8. To select more than one object at a time on the Form Design screen, select the first object by pointing to and clicking the left mouse button and then select the other objects by holding down the _____ key as you click the left mouse button.
   a. CTRL
   b. TAB
   c. SHIFT
   d. ALT
9. To view a form with actual data, point to and click the _____ button on the SpeedBar.
   a. View Form
   b. View Data
   c. Display Data
   d. Display Form
10. To change characteristics such as color, typeface, style, and size, access the Font palette through the _____ menu on the Form Design screen.
    a. Properties
    b. Design
    c. Form
    d. Object

STUDENT ASSIGNMENT 3
Understanding the Report Design Screen

Instructions: In Figure SA4-3, arrows point to the major components of the Report Design screen. Identify the various parts of the Report Design screen in the space provided. Answer the following questions about the screen.

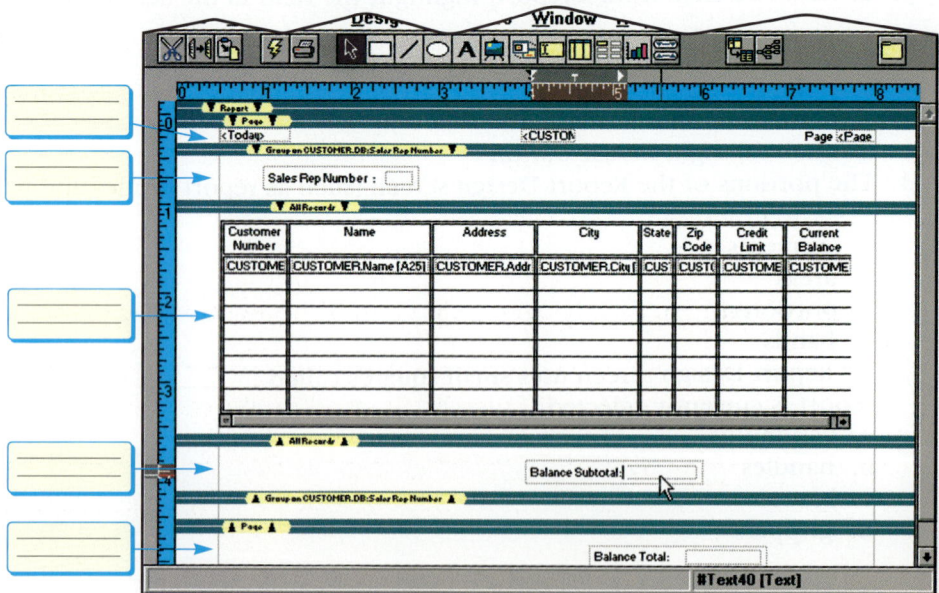

FIGURE SA4-3

1. How many times will the field with the label Balance Total: print?

2. How many times will the field with the label Balance Subtotal: print?

3. What values will print once at the top of every page?

STUDENT ASSIGNMENT 4
Understanding the Form Design Screen

Instructions: In Figure SA4-4, arrows point to various buttons on the SpeedBar on the Form Design screen. Identify these buttons in the space provided. Answer the following questions about the screen.

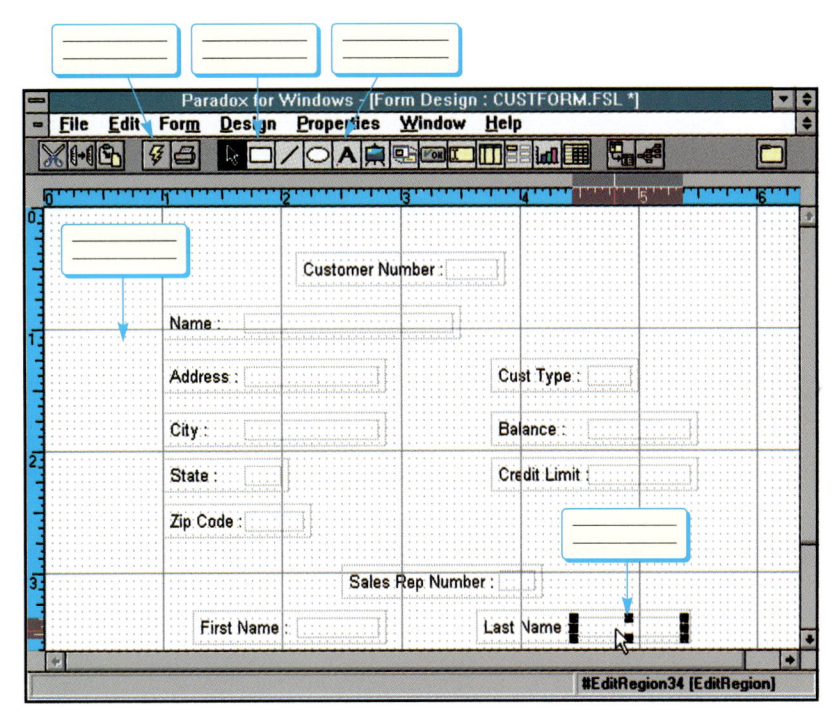

FIGURE SA4-4

1. What field is currently selected?

2. Why is one button on the SpeedBar significantly darker than the others?

3. What is the purpose of the grid-type background on the screen?

STUDENT ASSIGNMENT 5
Using the Report Design Screen

Instructions: Figure SA4-5 shows the initial Report Design screen for the Slsrep table. Use Figure SA4-5 to explain how to perform the following tasks on the Report Design screen.

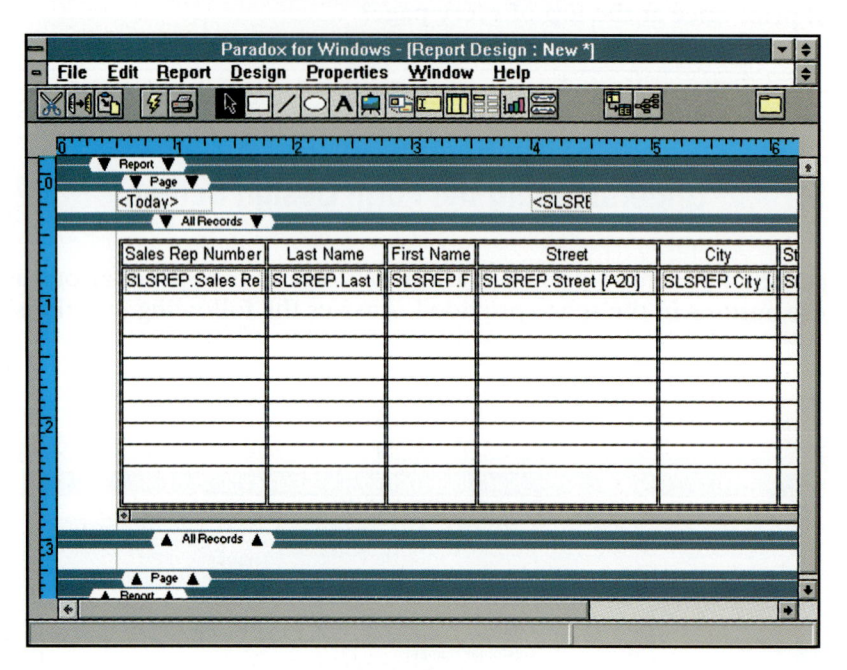

FIGURE SA4-5

1. Split the heading for Sales Rep Number so Sales Rep is on the first line and Number is on the second line.

   _____

   _____

2. Reduce the width of the Sales Rep Number field.

   _____

   _____

3. View the report on the screen.

   _____

   _____

4. Adjust the width of the report so it fits on the screen.

   _____

   _____

5. Add a field to the report footer band to total the sales for all sales reps.

   _____

   _____

STUDENT ASSIGNMENT 6
Using the Form Design Screen

Instructions: Figure SA4-6 shows the initial Form Design screen for the Slsrep table. Use Figure SA4-6 to explain how to perform the following tasks on the Form Design screen.

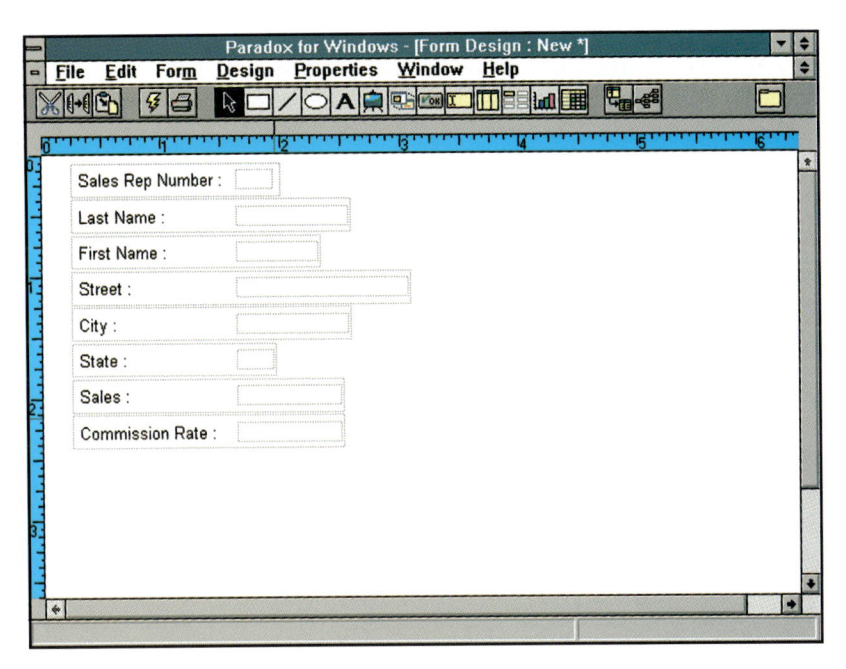

FIGURE SA4-6

1. Display a grid on the screen and make sure that objects are aligned with the nearest grid lines.

2. Move the First Name field so it is on the same line as Last Name.

3. Change the position of the contents of the First Name field to bring it closer to the field label.

4. Display the form on the screen.

5. Change the background color of the form.

COMPUTER LABORATORY EXERCISES

COMPUTER LABORATORY EXERCISE 1
Using the Help Menu

Instructions: Perform the following tasks using Paradox.

1. Start Paradox.
2. Open the report CUSTRPT1 in the Design mode and maximize the Report Design screen.
3. Select the Report menu and with the Report menu on the screen, and press the F1 key to access the Help system.
4. Read the information in the Help window and answer the following question:
   a. In addition to using the View Data button on the SpeedBar to view a report, what other methods are available for viewing a report?

   _____

   _____

5. Point to and click the Search button in the Help window.
6. Type group in the search box, choose the Show Topics button, and choose the ReportAdd Band topic from the group bands topics.
7. Read the information and answer the following question:
   a. In addition to using the Report menu for adding a group band to a report, what other method is available for adding a group band to a report?

   _____

   _____

8. Exit the Help system and then close the Report Design screen.
9. Exit Paradox.

COMPUTER LABORATORY EXERCISE 2
Creating a Report for the Slsrep Table

Instructions: Perform the following tasks using Paradox.

1. Start Paradox.
2. Create a report for the Slsrep table. Include all fields in the report.
3. Design the report using the guidelines and techniques presented in Project 4.
4. Include a report footer with a total of all sales.
5. Print the report.
6. Save the report as Slsrpt1.
7. Close the report and exit Paradox.

COMPUTER LABORATORY EXERCISE 3
Creating a Form for the Slsrep Table

Instructions: Perform the following tasks using Paradox.

1. Start Paradox.
2. Create a form for the Slsrep table. Include all fields on the form.
3. Design the form using the guidelines and techniques presented in Project 4.
4. Print the form.
5. Save the form as Slsfrm1.
6. Close the form and exit Paradox.

COMPUTER LABORATORY ASSIGNMENTS

COMPUTER LABORATORY ASSIGNMENT 1
Presenting Data in the Parts Database

Purpose: To provide practice in creating reports and forms.

Instructions: Use the database created in Computer Laboratory Assignment 1 of Project 1 for this assignment. Execute each task on the computer and print the results.

1. Create a report for the Part table. Include all fields in the report. Follow the design guidelines and procedures presented in Project 4 to produce an attractive report.
2. Display a total of the number of Units on Hand.
3. Print the report.
4. Save the report as Partrpt1.
5. Create a form for the Part table. Include the Item Class Description from the Class table.
6. Include the heading, Part Maintenance Screen on the form. Follow the design guideline and procedures presented in Project 4 to produce an attractive form.
7. Print the form
8. Save the form as Partfrm1.
9. Exit Paradox.

COMPUTER LABORATORY ASSIGNMENT 2
Presenting Data in the Employee Database

Purpose: To provide practice in creating reports and forms.

Instructions: Use the database created in Computer Laboratory Assignment 2 of Project 1 for this assignment. Execute each task on the computer and print the results.

1. Create a report for the Employee table. Include all fields except Union Code in the report. Follow the design guidelines and procedures presented in Project 4 to produce an attractive report.
2. Display the average pay rate of all employees.
3. Print the report.
4. Save the report as Emprpt1.
5. Modify Emprpt1 so the report groups records by department code. Display the average pay rate for each department.
6. Save the report as Emprpt2.
7. Create a form for the Employee table. Include the Department Name from the Dept table.
8. Include the heading, Employee Maintenance Screen, on the form. Follow the design guidelines and procedures presented in Project 4 to produce an attractive form.
9. Print the form.
10. Save the form as Empfrm1.
11. Exit Paradox.

COMPUTER LABORATORY ASSIGNMENT 3
Presenting Data in the Movie Database

Purpose: To provide practice in creating reports and forms.

Instructions: Use the database created in Computer Laboratory Assignment 3 of Project 1 for this assignment. Execute each task on the computer and print the results.

1. Create a report for the Movie table. Include all fields except Length and Director Code in the report. Place the Movie Type field before the Year Made field. Follow the design guidelines and procedures presented in Project 4 to produce an attractive report.
2. Print the report.
3. Save the report as Movrpt1.
4. Modify Movrpt1 so the report groups records by director code.
5. Save the report as Movrpt2.
6. Create a form for the Movie table. Include the Director Name from the Director table.
7. Include the heading, Movie Maintenance Screen, on the form. Follow the design guidelines and procedures presented in Project 4 to produce an attractive report.
8. Print the form
9. Save the form as Movfrm1.
10. Create a form for the Director table.
11. Include the heading, Director Maintenance Screen, on the form. Follow the design guidelines and procedures presented in Project 4 to produce an attractive report.
12. Print the form.
13. Save the form as Dirfrm1.
14. Exit Paradox.

COMPUTER LABORATORY ASSIGNMENT 4
Presenting Data in the Book Database

Purpose: To provide practice in creating reports and forms.

Instructions: Use the database created in Computer Laboratory Assignment 4 of Project 1 for this assignment. Execute each task on the computer and print the results.

The bookstore owner has asked you to prepare the following reports:

1. A report of all books in the database. The report need not include the cover type, but the owner would like to know the average price of all books in the database.
2. A report of all books grouped by publisher, and a report with books grouped by book type. She would like to know the average price of all books in the database and the average price by publisher and book type.

The owner is impressed with the improved accuracy in data entry resulting from the validity checks you added to the database but would now like to make the data forms more attractive for her employees. She has also asked you to provide her with attractive data screens for both the Book and the Publisher tables.

PARADOX 1.0 FOR WINDOWS
PROJECT FIVE

ADVANCED TOPICS

OBJECTIVES You will have mastered the material in this project when you can:

- Use date, memo, and OLE fields
- Enter data in date fields
- Enter data in memo fields
- Use the Paintbrush application to create graphic data
- Place graphic data in OLE fields
- Complete the display of memo fields
- Change the magnification of OLE fields
- Complete the display of OLE fields
- Save table properties
- Create a form with a one-to-many relationship
- Manipulate a table object on a form
- Add or remove scroll bars on a form
- Change magnification for OLE fields on a form
- Complete the display of memo fields on a form
- Use date and memo fields in a query

INTRODUCTION

In Project 5, you will create the form shown in Figure 5-1 on the next page. The form incorporates several new features that were not covered in Project 4. Three new types of fields that display on the form are added to the Slsrep table. (1) the Start Date field gives the date the sales representative began employment with the organization; (2) the Note field stores a note describing important characteristics of the sales representative. The note can be as long or as short as the organization desires; and (3) the Signature field holds the representative's signature.

The form shows not only data concerning the sales representative, but also the representative's customers. The customers are displayed as a table object on the form. The Note field contains a vertical scroll bar, which allows users to scroll through a note that is too lengthy to fit on the screen. The table of customer data also contains a vertical scroll bar. This scroll bar allows users to scroll through all the customers of the sales representative. To create this form, you first need to modify the structure of the Slsrep table by adding three new fields. Each new field uses a field type not previously encountered in the structure of the table. The way you fill these new fields with data depends on the field type. Finally, you will create the form including the table of customer data and the scroll bars shown in Figure 5-1 on the next page.

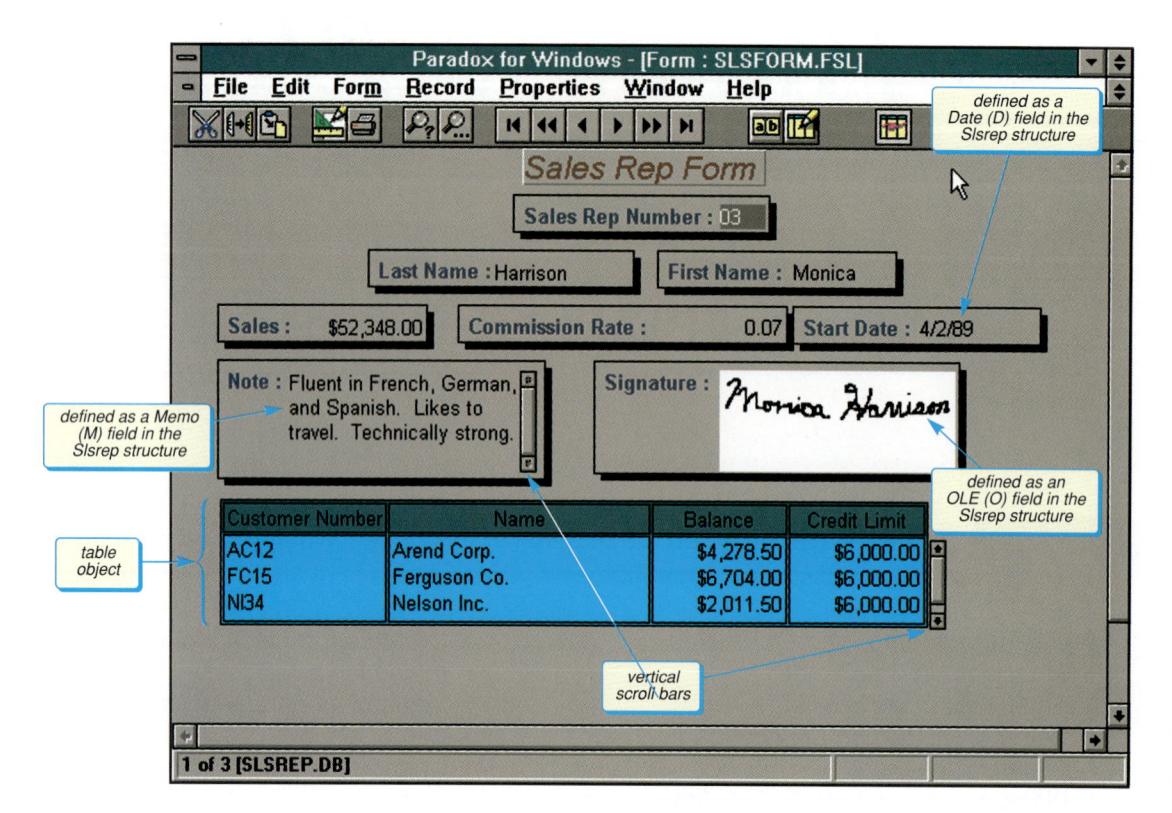

FIGURE 5-1

▶ DATE, MEMO, AND OLE FIELDS

The data shown in the form in Figure 5-1 incorporates the following additional field types not yet encountered when creating tables.

1. **Date (D)** – The field, titled Start Date, can contain only valid dates.
2. **Memo (M)** – The field, titled Note, can contain text that is variable in length. The length of the text stored in memo fields is virtually unlimited. You specify a size that indicates the number of characters the memo to be stored in the table will contain. Any additional text is stored in a separate file created and maintained automatically by Paradox.
3. **OLE (O)** – The field, titled Signature, can contain objects created by other applications, such as Windows Paintbrush, that support OLE (**Object Linking and Embedding**). In OLE fields you can edit the object in Paradox. When you do, Paradox transfers control to the application used to create the object. As soon as you finish making changes, control returns to Paradox.

An alternative to an OLE field is a **Graphic (G)** field. A graphic field can contain pictures. The pictures can be created by a graphics application. If you have a scanner, you can also scan existing pictures or photographs and store them in a graphic field.

Memo, graphic, and OLE fields are called BLOB fields. **BLOB** stands for Binary Large OBject. In certain cases, you may see the word BLOB on the screen in one of these fields. Take no special action. Paradox is simply indicating that the field is one of these types.

Graphic Versus OLE Fields

Graphics are stored using either graphic or OLE fields. The advantage to using OLE is that you can modify the graphics at any point. With a graphic field, you cannot change the graphic once it has been entered.

To illustrate the advantage of using OLE, suppose the Signature field (see Figure 5-1) is an OLE field. If a sales rep forgot to cross the T in his or her signature, it would be a simple matter to edit the field. The application in which the signature was first created would return to the screen and the sales rep could make the required change. If, on the other hand, the Signature field was a graphic field, the only way to make the change would be to recreate the signature and replace the existing signature with the new one.

Graphics fields are useful when you know that you will never need to edit a graphic once you have initially added it to the database. OLE fields are useful when you want to allow for future editing. In addition, OLE fields are useful for storing other specialized data. You can store such things as sounds and full-motion videos in OLE fields. You simply need to use appropriate Windows applications to create the sounds or the videos.

▶ **RESTRUCTURING THE SLSREP TABLE**

The following steps add the Start Date field, the Note field, and the Signature field to the Slsrep table. To allow editing of signatures, the Signature field type will be OLE. For both the Note and Signature field, the size will be 20, indicating 20 characters will be stored in the Slsrep table; the remainder will be stored in a separate file on disk.

TO RESTRUCTURE THE SLSREP TABLE ▼

STEP 1 ▶

Start Paradox and maximize the window if necessary. Open the Slsrep table, select the Table menu, and point to the Restructure command.

The Slsrep table is open (Figure 5-2). The Table menu displays and the mouse pointer points to the Restructure command.

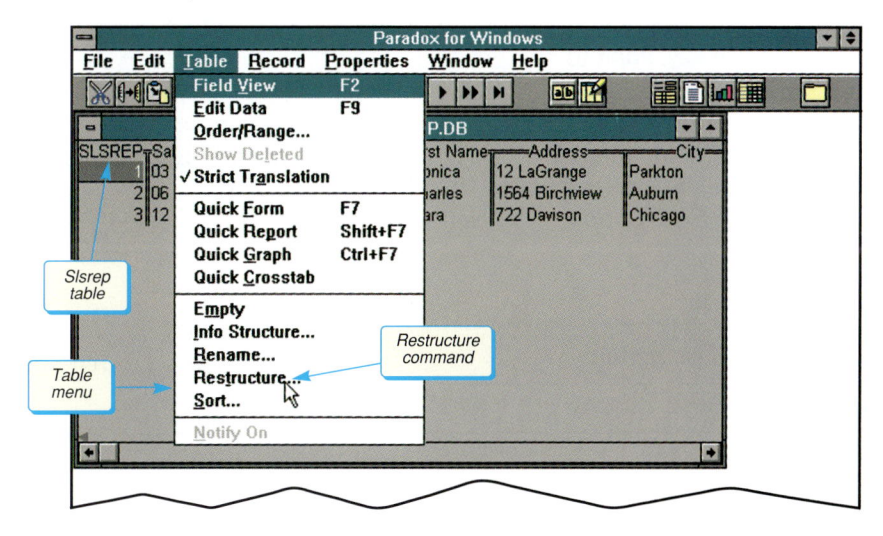

FIGURE 5-2

STEP 2 ▶

Choose the Restructure command. Press the DOWN ARROW key until the highlight is on the line below Commission Rate. Type Start Date, press the TAB key, and then press the SPACEBAR to display the Type menu of field types.

The Restructure Paradox for Windows Table dialog box displays (Figure 5-3). Start Date is entered as the name of a new field. The cascading menu of field types displays.

FIGURE 5-3

STEP 3 ▶

Type D (Date) as the field type and press the TAB key. Type Note as the name of the next field and press the TAB key. Type M (Memo) as the field type, and press the TAB key, type 20 as the size, and press the TAB key. Type Signature as the name of the final field, press the TAB key, type O (OLE) as the field type, press the TAB key, type 20 as the size, and press the TAB key. Point to the Save button.

The new fields are entered (Figure 5-4). The mouse pointer points to the Save button.

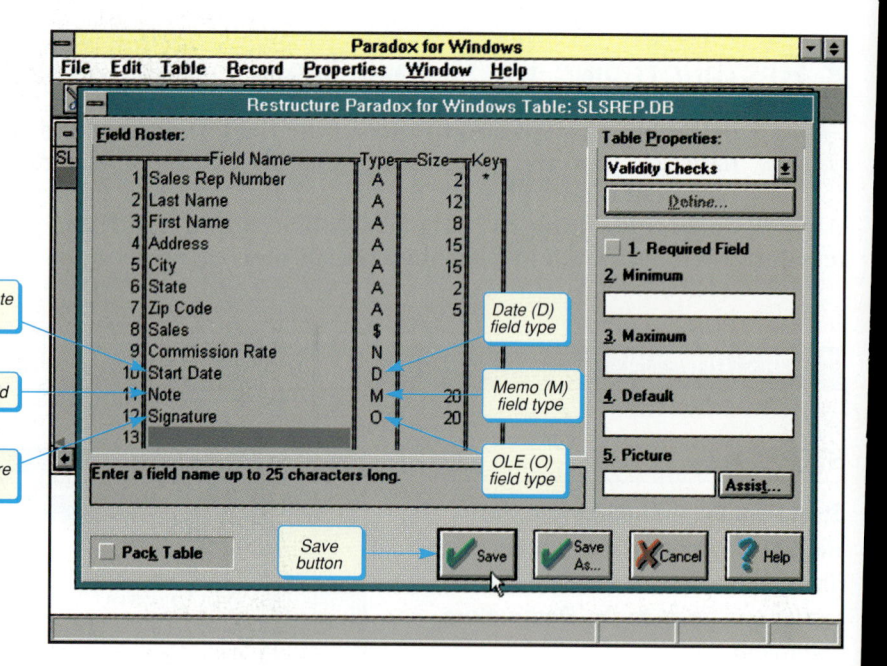

FIGURE 5-4

STEP 4 ▶

Choose the Save button.

The new fields are added to the structure of the Slsrep table. The updated Slsrep table is saved to disk.

▶ Updating the New Fields

The next step is to enter data into the new fields. The following sections cover the methods you use to update the date field, the memo field, and the OLE field in each record in the Slsrep table.

Updating Date Fields

To enter date fields, simply type the dates including slashes (/). The following steps add the start dates for all three sales representatives using Table view.

TO ENTER DATA IN DATE FIELDS ▼

STEP 1 ▶

Be sure the Slsrep table is open and the window containing the table is maximized. Click the right scroll arrow until the three new fields display on the screen. Select the Start Date field on the first record by clicking it and then point to the Edit Data button.

A portion of the Slsrep table displays (Figure 5-5). The Start Date field on the first record is selected. The mouse pointer points to the Edit Data button.

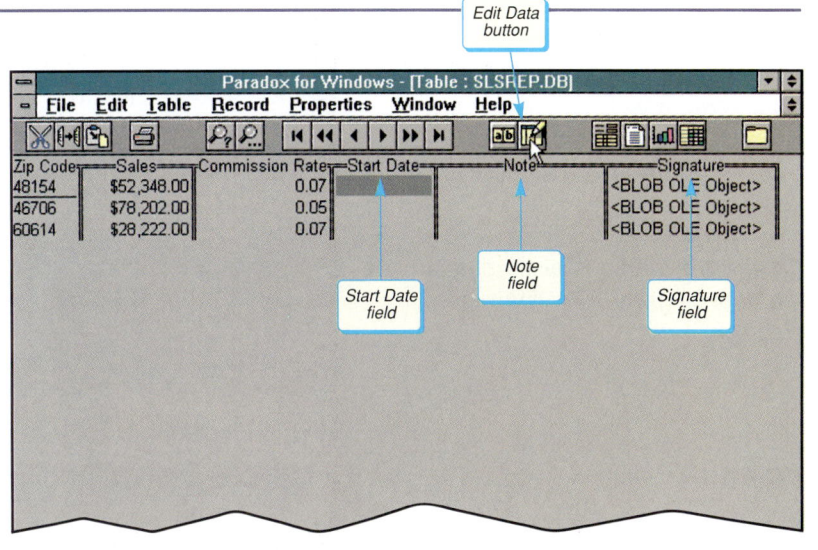

FIGURE 5-5

STEP 2 ▶

Click the Edit Data button. Type 4/2/89 as the start date on the first record and press the DOWN ARROW key. Type 10/2/90 as the start date on the second record and press the DOWN ARROW key. Type 6/6/88 as the date on the third record. Select the Note field on the first record by clicking it and then point to the Field View button.

The dates are entered (Figure 5-6). The Note field on the first record is selected. The mouse pointer points to the Field View button.

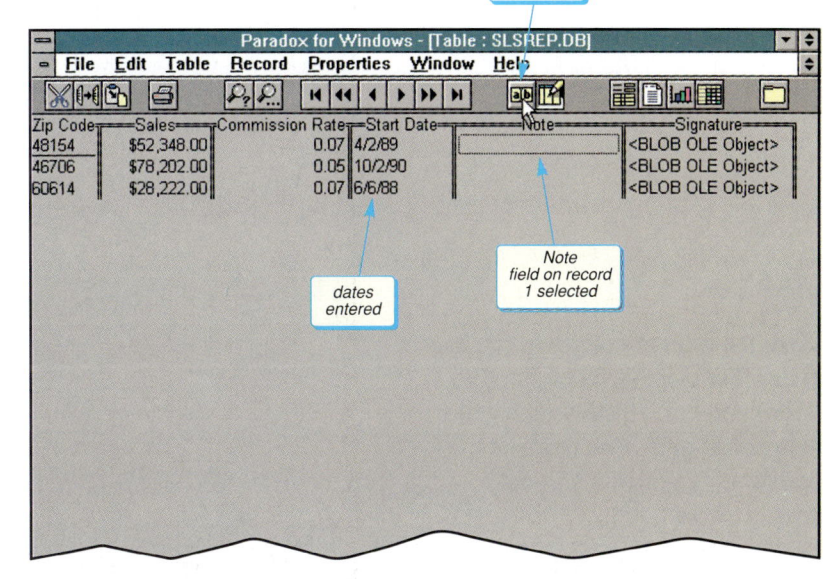

FIGURE 5-6

Updating Memo Fields

To update a memo field, you first select the field you want to update. You next click the Field View button to move to Field view. Paradox displays a full screen in which you can type the contents of the memo. When you have finished, click the Field View button again to return to Table view.

The following steps enter the notes concerning each sales rep using Field view.

TO ENTER DATA IN MEMO FIELDS ▼

STEP 1 ▶

Click the Field View button to enter Field view. Type `Fluent in French, German, and Spanish. Likes to travel. Technically strong.`

An entire window is available for the note (Figure 5-7). The note displays.

FIGURE 5-7

STEP 2 ▶

Click the Field View button to leave Field view and return to Table view.

The first portion of the note displays in the table (Figure 5-8). To see the entire note, you need to expand the space allowed for each row.

FIGURE 5-8

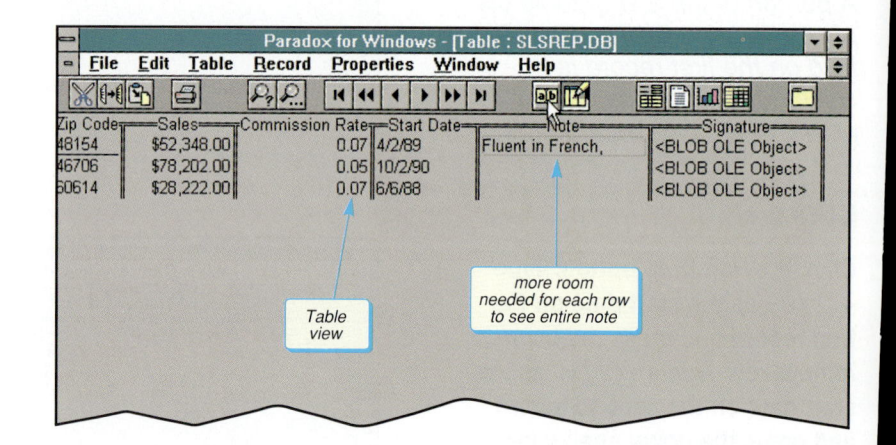

STEP 3 ▶

Move the mouse pointer to the line in the first displayed column (Zip Code) and immediately below the first row of data. The mouse pointer changes to a vertical double arrow (⇕).

The mouse pointer points to the line (Figure 5-9).

FIGURE 5-9

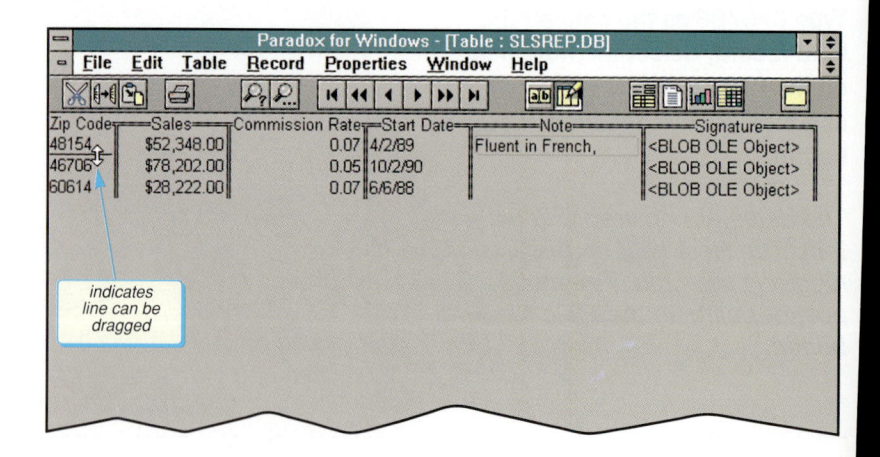

UPDATING THE NEW FIELDS **P227**

STEP 4 ▶

Drag the line to the position shown in Figure 5-10.

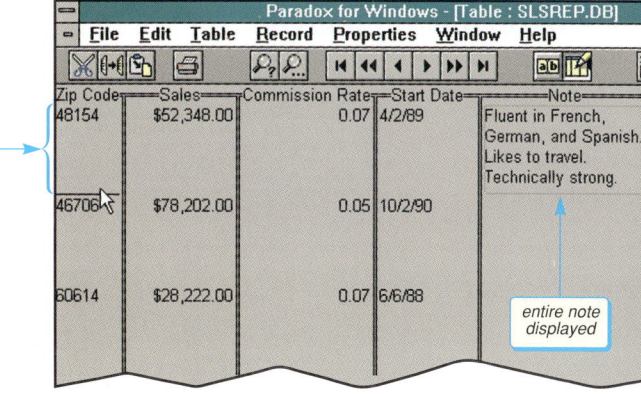

FIGURE 5-10

STEP 5 ▶

Select the Note field in the second record and click the Field View button. Type Somewhat fluent in Spanish. Willing to travel. Works well with new companies. Very innovative. **Click the Field View button again. Point to the Note field for the third record.**

Most of the note for the second customer displays (Figure 5-11). Only the first portion of the note for the first customer displays. The mouse pointer points to the Note field for the third record.

STEP 6

Click the Note field on the third record and then click the Field View button. Type Technically excellent. Good reputation among established customers. Advice is well-respected among customers. **Click the Field View button again to return to Table view.**

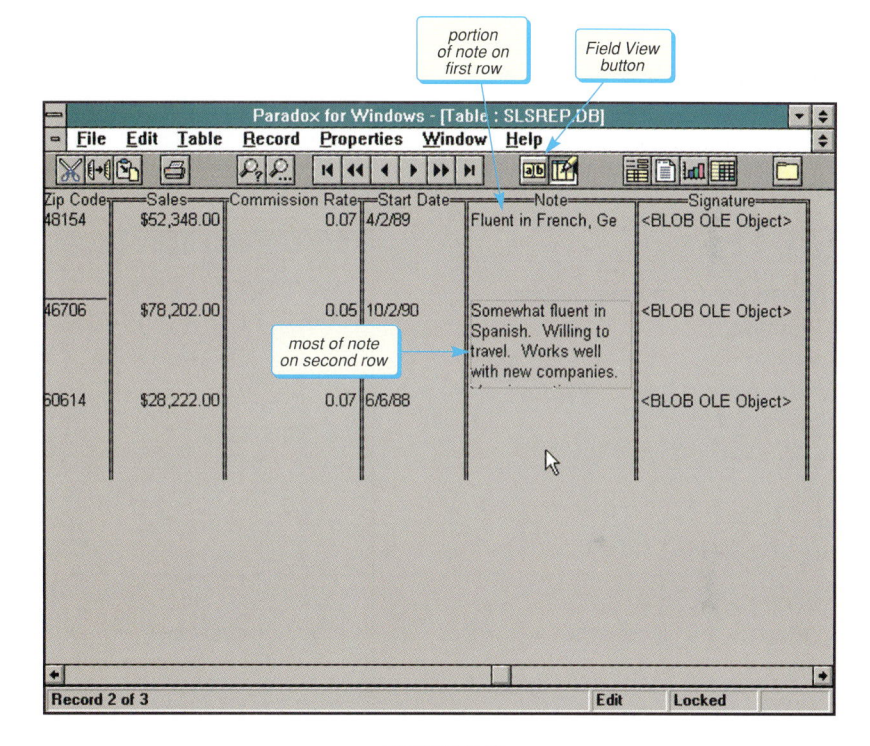

FIGURE 5-11

Completing the Display of Memo Fields

Only the selected memo displays. To have the memos for all the records on the screen display, you need to complete the display. **Complete the display** means the contents of the memo fields for all visible records should display. To accomplish this task, you need to choose the Complete Display command from the object's menu as described in the following steps on the next page.

P228 PROJECT 5 ADVANCED TOPICS

TO COMPLETE THE DISPLAY OF MEMO FIELDS ▼

STEP 1 ▶

Point to the Note field in any record and click the right mouse button.

The Note object's menu displays (Figure 5-12).

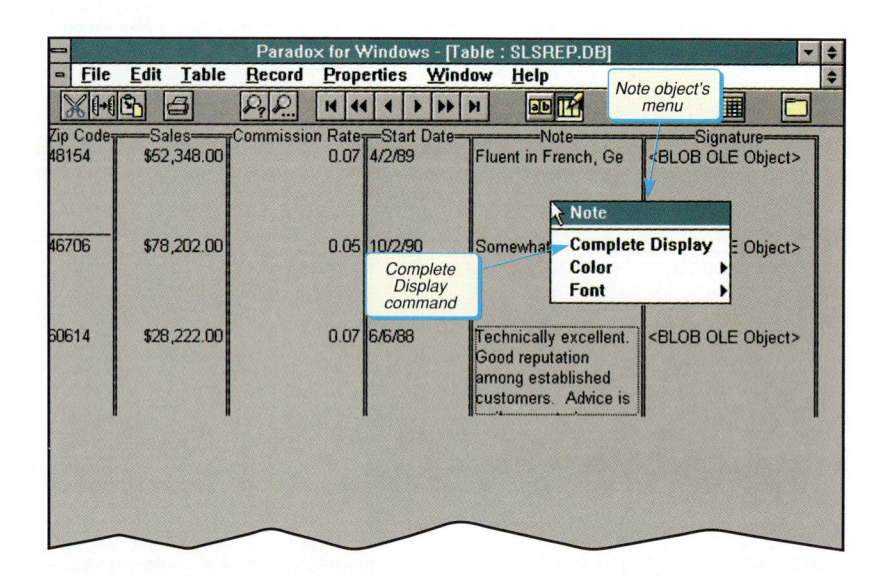

FIGURE 5-12

STEP 2 ▶

Choose the Complete Display command.

All the Note records display (Figure 5-13).

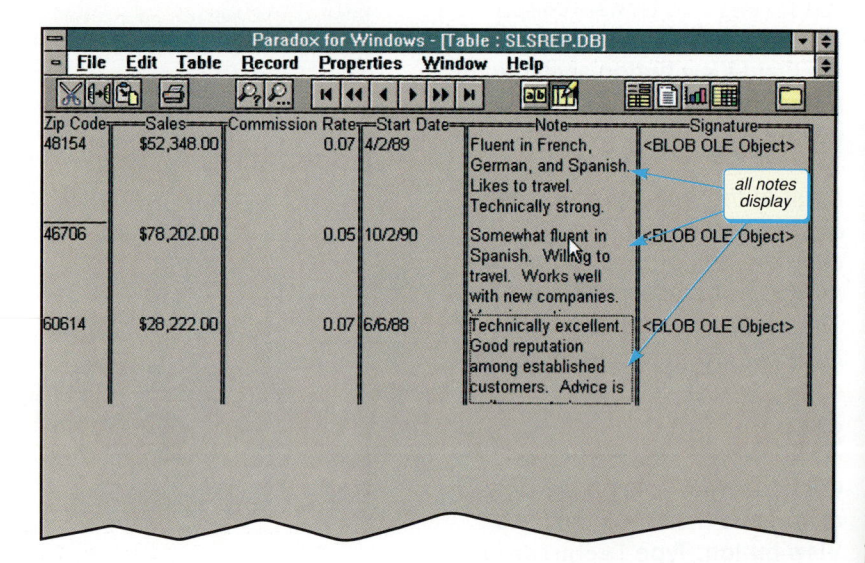

FIGURE 5-13

Updating OLE Fields

To update OLE fields, you can paste from files containing the picture. You can also transfer to a graphics application like Windows Paintbrush, load or create the picture, cut the picture to the clipboard, and then return to Paradox where you paste the contents of the clipboard into the field.

The following steps use the Paintbrush application described earlier in Project 1 of *Using Microsoft Windows 3.1* to enter the signature for the first sales rep.

TO ENTER DATA IN OLE FIELDS ▼

STEP 1 ▶

Select the Signature field on the first record and point to the Field View button.

The Signature field on the first record is selected (Figure 5-14). The mouse pointer points to the Field View button.

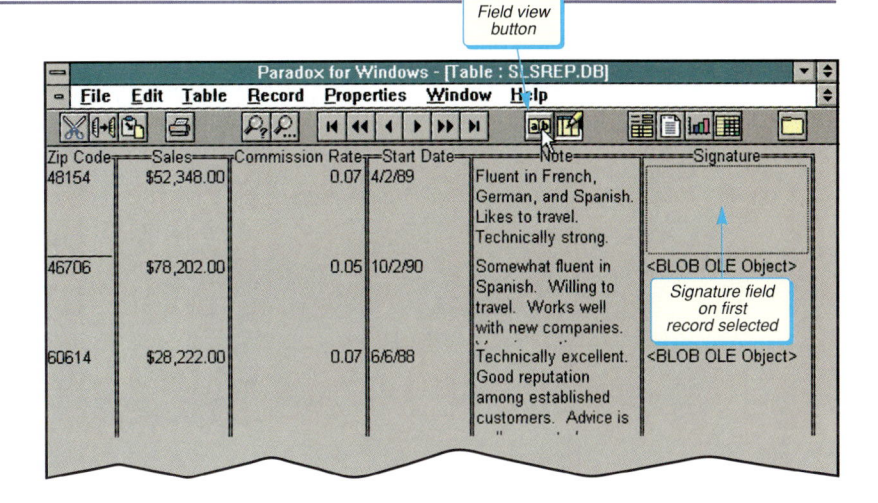

FIGURE 5-14

STEP 2 ▶

Click the Field View button to move to Field view. Hold down the ALT key and press the TAB key until the words Program Manager appear on the screen. Release the ALT key. Double-click the Paintbrush program-item icon in the Accessories group. Select the Brush tool ( ).

The Paintbrush window displays (Figure 5-15). The Brush tool is selected.

FIGURE 5-15

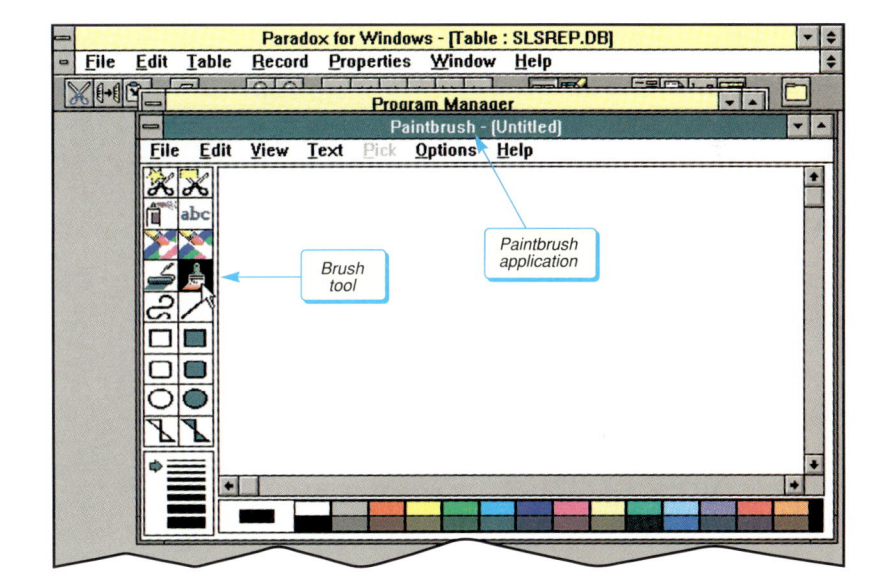

STEP 3 ▶

Use the mouse to draw the signature of Monica Harrison. Hold the left mouse button and move the mouse to create the signature. When you release the mouse button, you can move the mouse without drawing. Once you have finished drawing the signature, point to the Pick tool.

The signature displays (Figure 5-16). The mouse pointer points to the Pick tool ( ).

FIGURE 5-16

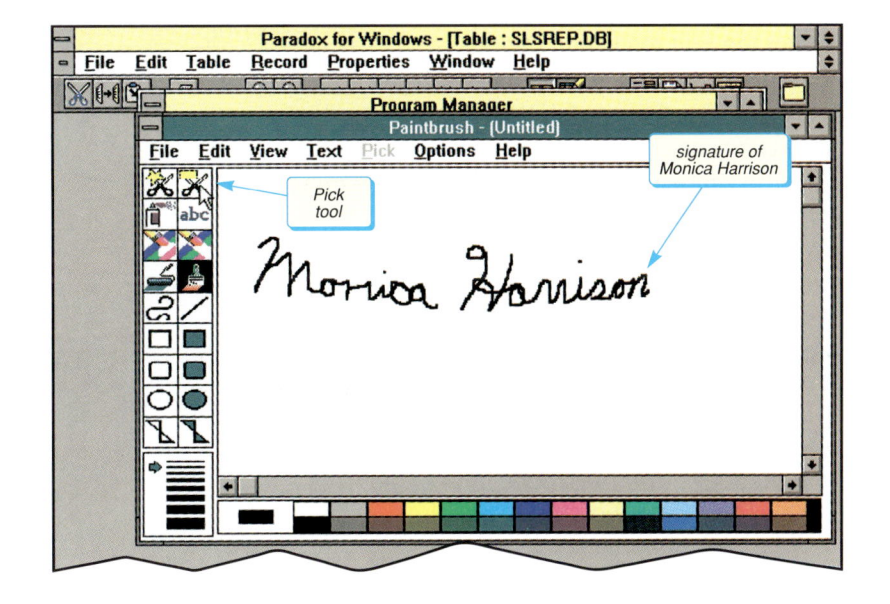

STEP 4 ▶

Click the Pick tool and then move the mouse pointer (a cross-hair shape) above and to the left of the signature (Figure 5-17).

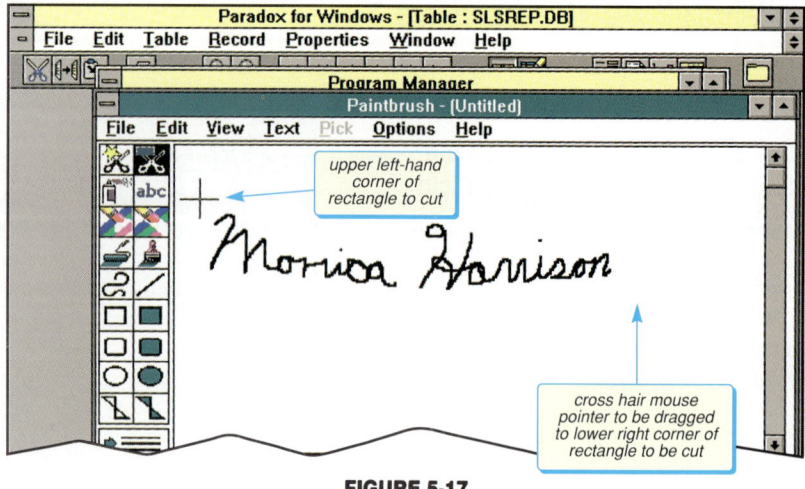

FIGURE 5-17

STEP 5 ▶

Press the left mouse button, drag the mouse pointer down and then to the right to the diagonally opposite corner of the signature and release the left mouse button.

A dashed line surrounds the signature (Figure 5-18).

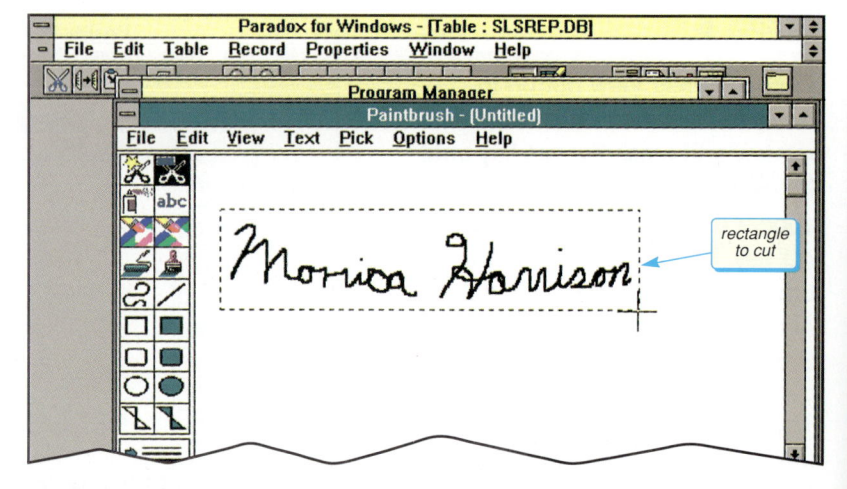

FIGURE 5-18

STEP 6 ▶

Select the Edit menu and choose the Cut command to place the signature on the clipboard. Hold down the ALT key and press the TAB key until the words Paradox for Windows [Table: SLSREP.DB] display on the screen, and then release both keys. Select the Edit menu in Paradox and point to the Paste command.

The Paradox for Windows Table window displays on the screen (Figure 5-19). The Edit menu displays. The mouse pointer points to the Paste command.

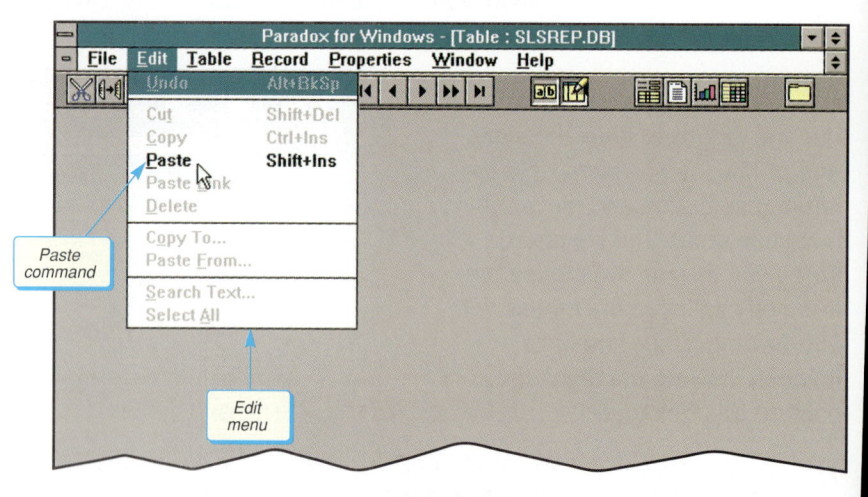

FIGURE 5-19

UPDATING THE NEW FIELDS **P231**

STEP 7 ▶

Choose the Paste command and then point to the Field View button.

The signature displays (Figure 5-20). The mouse pointer points to the Field View button.

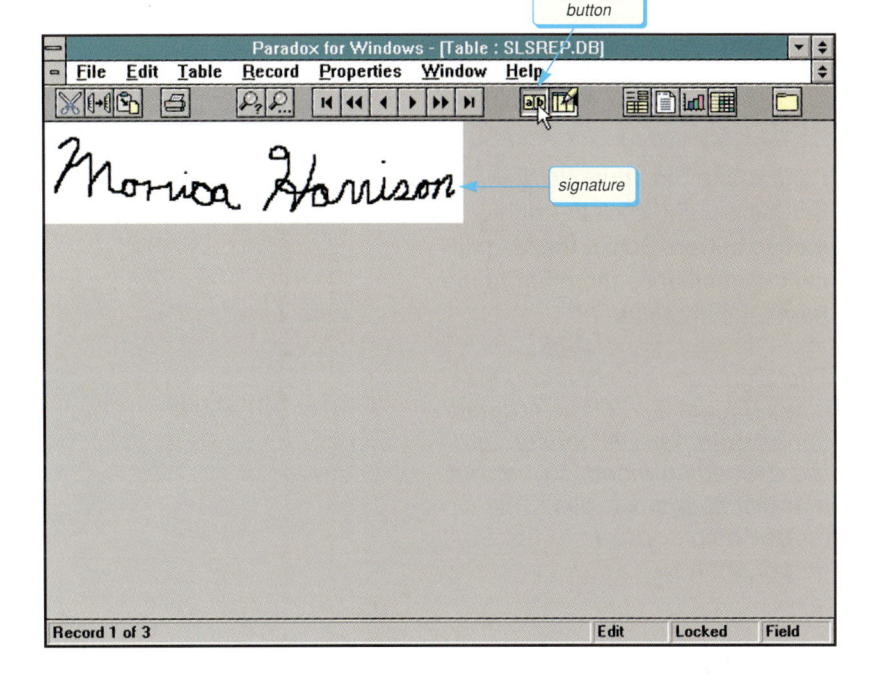

FIGURE 5-20

STEP 8 ▶

Click the Field View button to return to Table view and then point to the Signature field on the first record.

Paradox returns to Table view (Figure 5-21). Only a portion of the signature displays in the field.

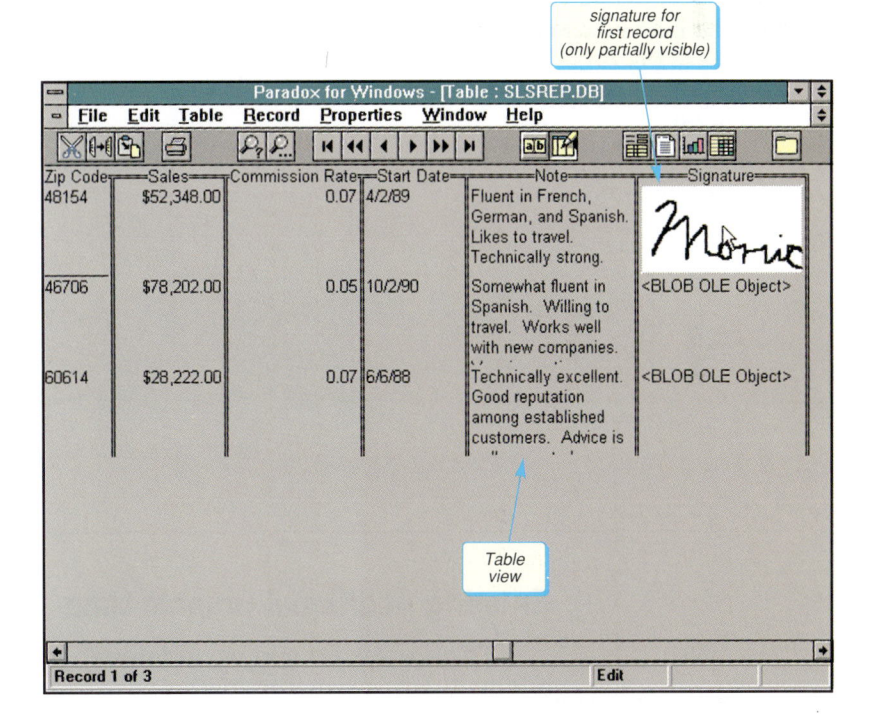

FIGURE 5-21

Changing the Magnification of OLE Fields

Only a portion of the signature displays in the Signature field. By changing the **magnification**, that is, the size of the signature, you can change how much displays on the screen. The steps on the next page change the magnification so the entire signature is visible.

TO CHANGE THE MAGNIFICATION ▼

STEP 1 ▶

Point to the Signature field on the first record and click the right mouse button. Select the Magnification command, and point to the Best Fit command.

The Signature object menu displays (Figure 5-22). The Magnification command is chosen and the cascading menu of possible magnifications displays. The mouse pointer points to the Best Fit command.

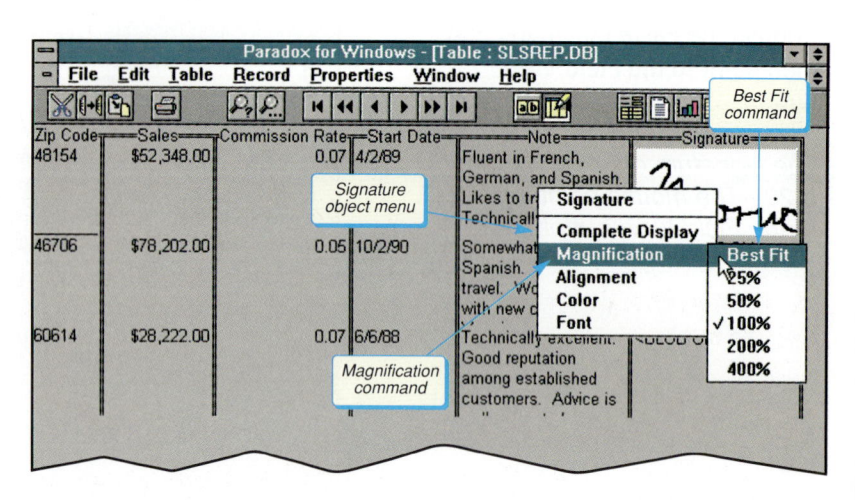

FIGURE 5-22

STEP 2 ▶

Choose the Best Fit command.

The entire signature displays (Figure 5-23).

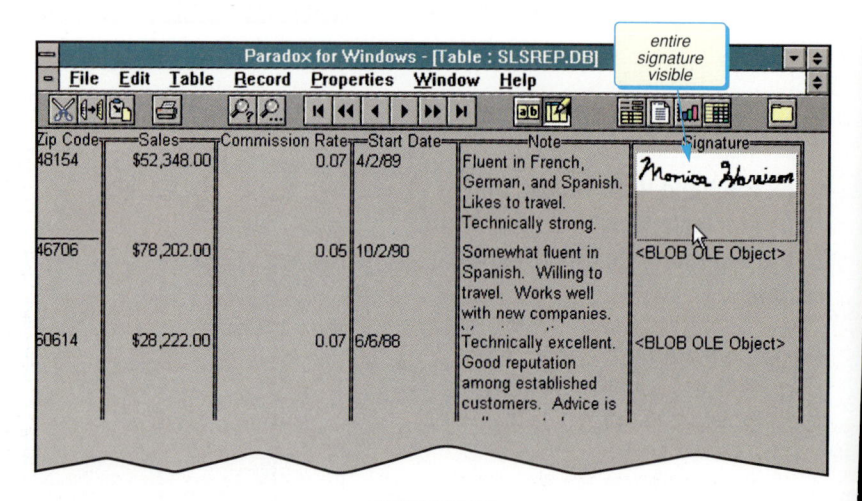

FIGURE 5-23

Entering Additional Graphic Data

The process for adding additional signatures is the same as the process for adding the first signature with one exception. Paintbrush is already active, so you need to transfer to it, rather than starting it. The following steps use the Paintbrush application to add the remaining signatures.

TO ENTER SIGNATURES IN THE REMAINING RECORDS

Step 1: Select the Signature field on the second record and click the Field View button. Hold down the ALT key, press the TAB key until the word Paintbrush appears, and then release the both keys.

Step 2: Using the same process you used earlier, create a signature for Charles Thompson.

Step 3: Repeat the process to place a signature for Mara Juarez in the Signature field on the third record.

You have finished using the Paintbrush application. Perform the following steps to close it.

TO CLOSE PAINTBRUSH ▼

STEP 1 ▶

Use the ALT + TAB keys to return to the Paintbrush application, select the File menu, and choose the Exit command. Point to the No button in the Paintbrush dialog box.

The Paintbrush dialog box displays (Figure 5-24). The mouse pointer points to the No button.

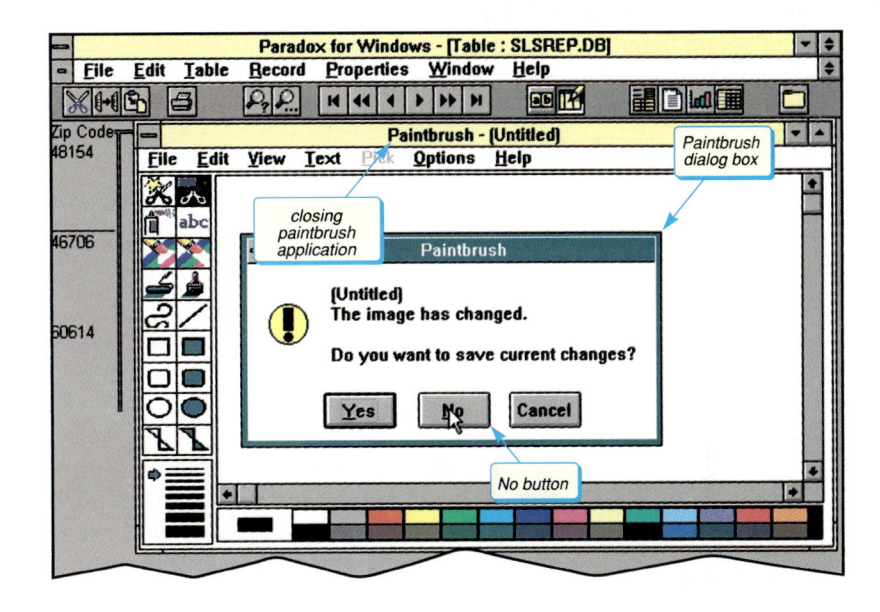

FIGURE 5-24

STEP 2 ▶

Choose the No button to exit Paintbrush without saving your work.

The Paradox for Windows Table window displays (Figure 5-25). Only the signature for the third record (Mara Juarez) displays.

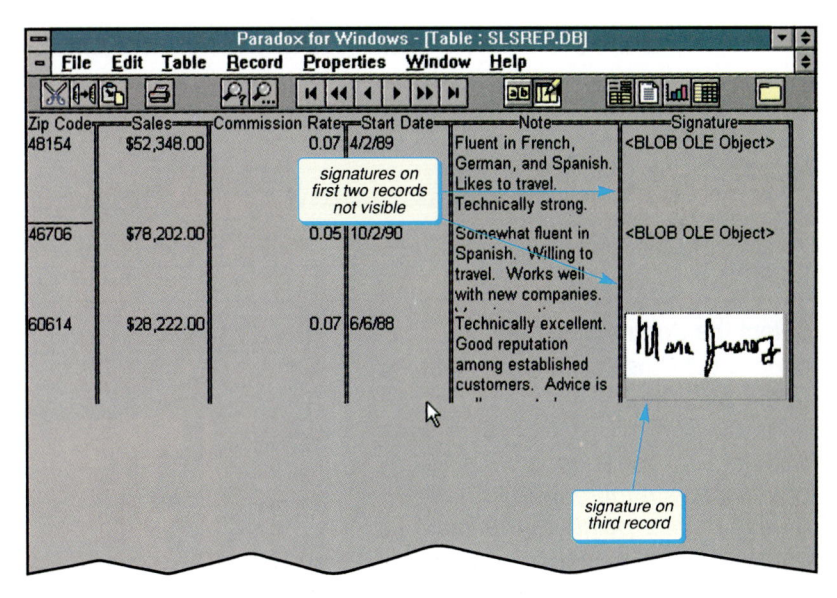

FIGURE 5-25

Completing the Display of an OLE Field

Just as with memo fields, only the selected OLE field displays. To display the contents of OLE fields for all the records, you need to choose the Complete Display command from the Signature object menu. Performing the step on the next page ensures that all the signatures for records on the screen will display simultaneously.

TO COMPLETE THE DISPLAY OF OLE FIELDS ▼

STEP 1 ▶

Point to the Signature field on one of the records and click the right mouse button to produce the Signature object menu. Choose the Complete Display command.

All signatures display (Figure 5-26).

FIGURE 5-26

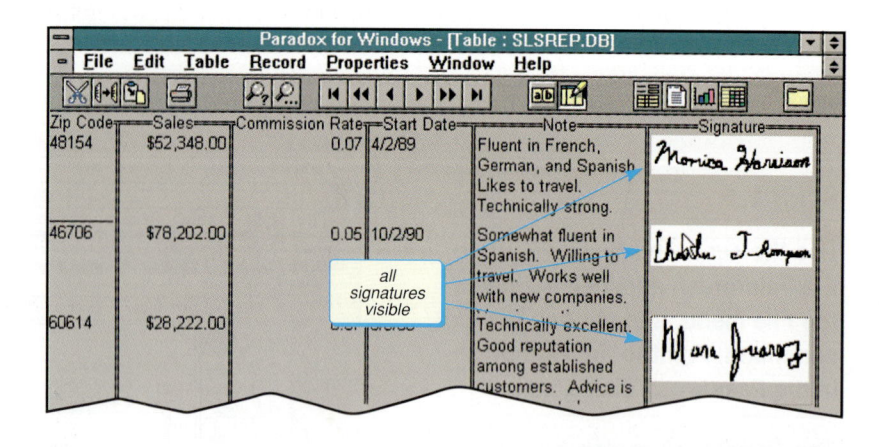

Saving the Table Properties

The row spacing, magnification, and complete display are all **table properties**. When you change any table properties, the changes apply only as long as the table is active *unless you save the table*. If you save the table, the table properties will apply every time you open it. To save the table, simply close the table. If any properties have changed, Paradox will ask if you want to save the changes. By answering Yes, the changes will be saved.

The following steps close the table and save the properties that have been changed.

TO CLOSE THE TABLE AND SAVE THE PROPERTIES ▼

STEP 1 ▶

Select the Control menu and choose the Close command. Point to the Yes button.

The Paradox for Windows dialog box displays (Figure 5-27). The mouse pointer points to the Yes button.

STEP 2 ▶

Choose the Yes button to save the table properties.

FIGURE 5-27

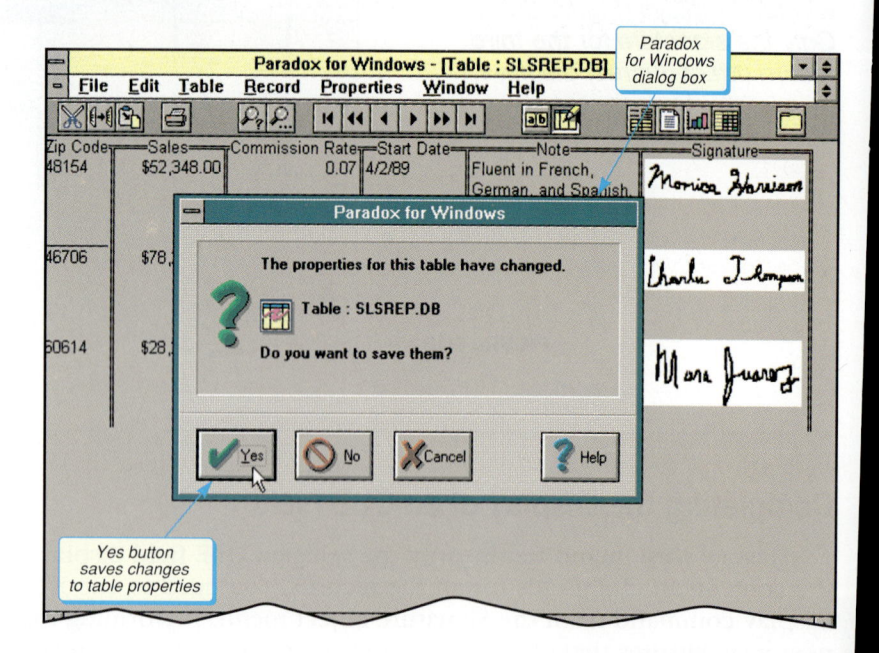

Advanced Form Techniques

Like the form you created in Project 4, the form in this project includes data from both the Slsrep and Customer tables. There is an important difference, however. In Project 4, the focus of the form was to display customer information including the name of the customer's sales rep. Because each customer has only a *single* sales rep, the form in Project 4 (Figure 4-3 on page P166) includes fields for only a single first and last name.

Creating a Form with a One-To-Many Relationship

The focus of the form in this project is sales reps, and each sales rep can have *many* customers. This relationship between sales reps and customers is called **one-to-many** (*one* sales rep has *many* customers). This can present a problem with the form because in addition to the basic data about a sales rep (number, name, address, and so on), the form also has to include data about the sales rep's many customers. To include the data, place the customer data as a table object in the form. You don't have to take any special action to do this, however. Paradox does it for you automatically. All you need to do is drag the mouse pointer *from* Slsrep *to* Customer when you create the data model. (In Project 4, where the form focused on customers, you dragged the mouse pointer from Customer to Slsrep.)

The following steps begin creating the form.

TO CREATE A FORM ▼

STEP 1 ►

Select File, choose the New command, and then choose the Form command. Select the Customer table (CUSTOMER.DB) and click the Add File arrow. Select the Slsrep table (SLSREP.DB) and then point to slsrep.db in the data model.

Both tables are selected in the data model box (Figure 5-28). The mouse pointer points to slsrep.db.

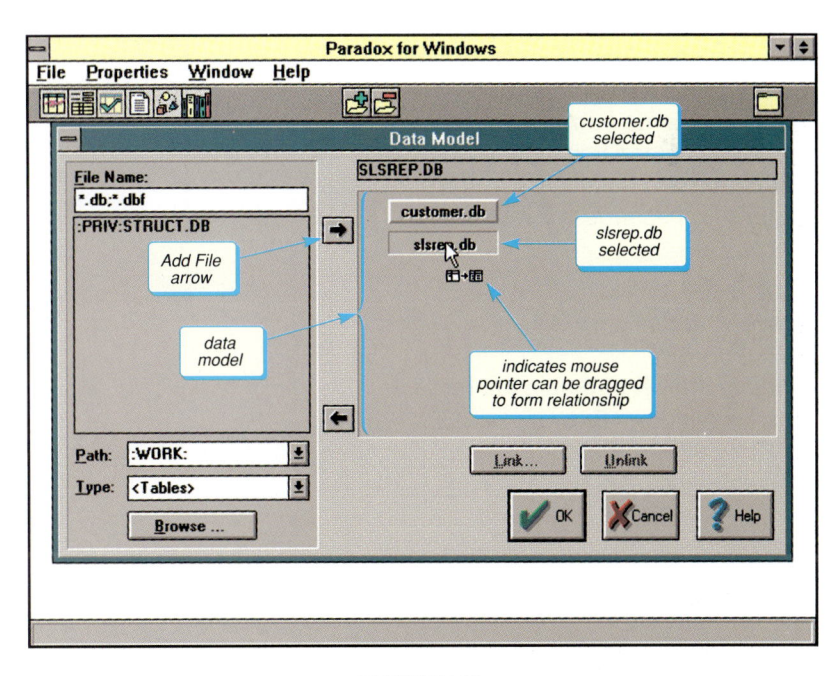

FIGURE 5-28

STEP 2 ▶

Drag the mouse pointer to the Customer table, release the left mouse button, and point to the OK button.

The data model containing the two database tables and an arrow indicating the one-to-many relationship is complete (Figure 5-29) and the pointer points to the OK button. The double-headed arrow from slsrep.db to customer.db indicates that each sales representative is related to many customers.

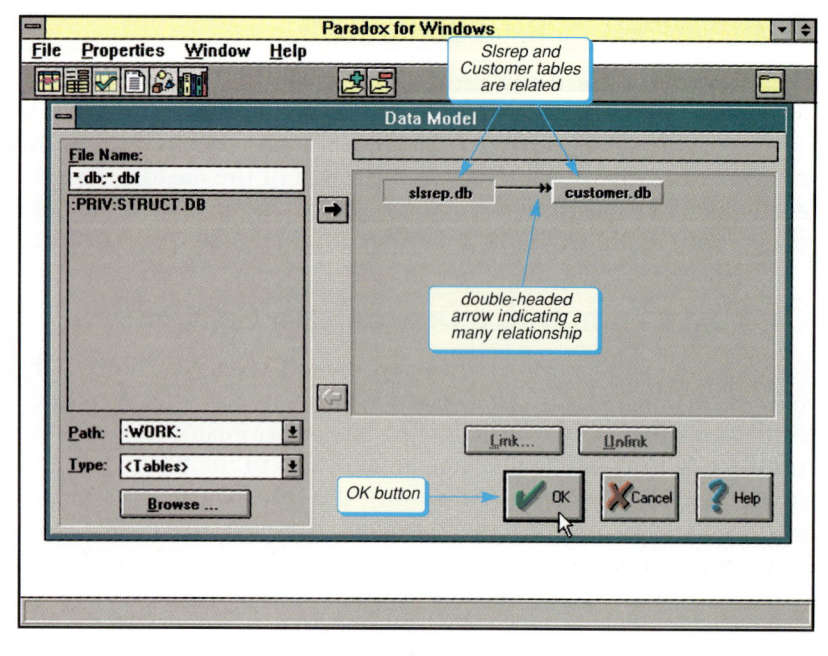

FIGURE 5-29

STEP 3 ▶

Choose the OK button.

The Paradox for Windows Error dialog box displays (Figure 5-30). The message indicates that there is not enough room on the form for all the fields from both tables to display. Once you select the fields that are necessary for this form, the message will no longer apply.

STEP 4 ▶

Choose the OK button in the Paradox for Windows Error dialog box.

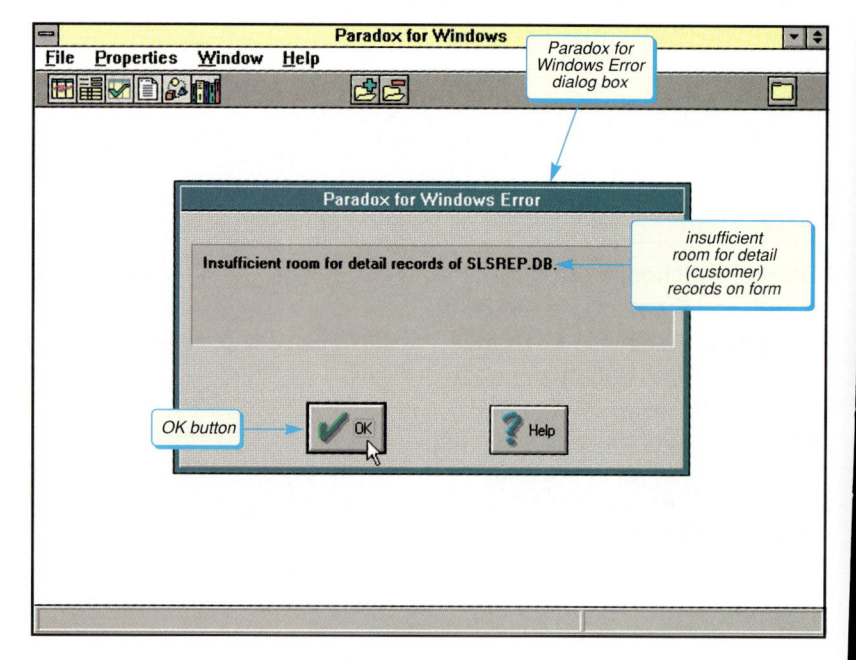

FIGURE 5-30

Selecting the Fields for the Form

To select the fields you want to display on the form, use the same technique you used in Project 4 with one modification. Select the fields for each of the two tables (Customer and Slsrep) separately. The following steps select the fields for the form.

TO SELECT THE FIELDS FOR A FORM ▼

STEP 1 ▶

Choose the Select Fields button on the left side of the Design Layout dialog box and point to the customer.db list box arrow in the Select Fields dialog box.

The Select Fields dialog box displays (Figure 5-31). The mouse pointer points to the customer.db list box arrow.

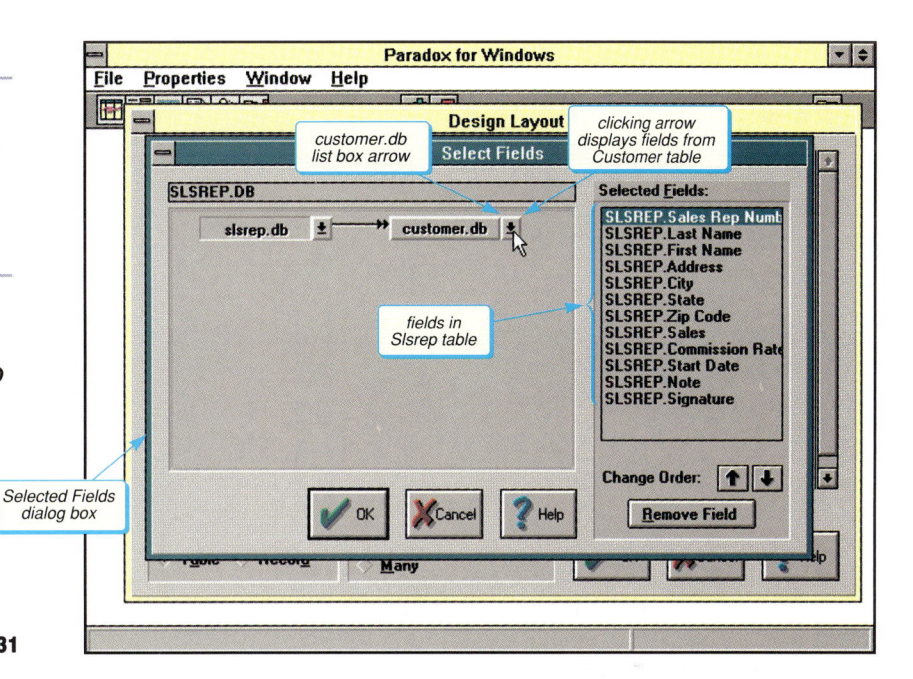

FIGURE 5-31

STEP 2 ▶

Click the customer.db list box arrow.

The list of fields in the Customer table displays (Figure 5-32).

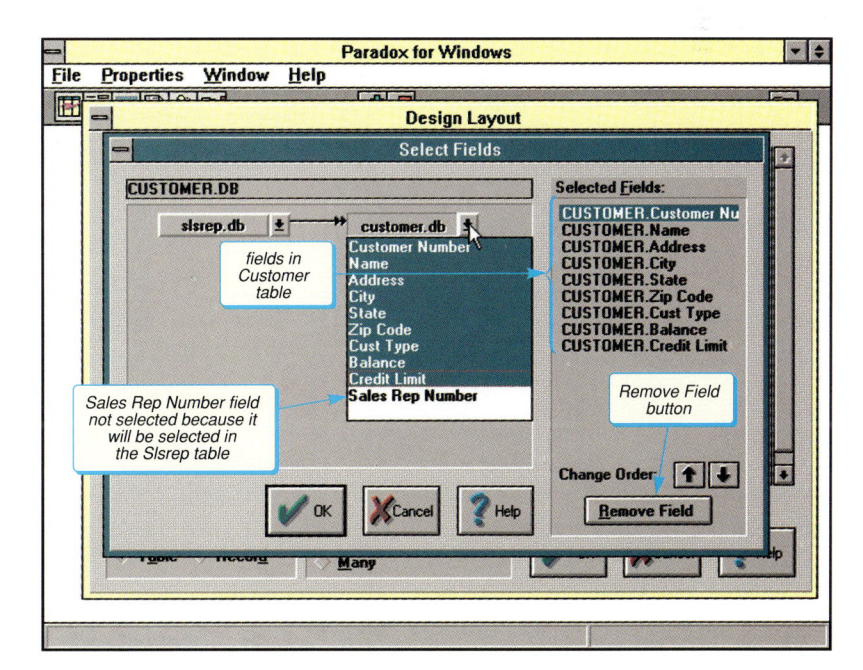

FIGURE 5-32

PROJECT 5 ADVANCED TOPICS

STEP 3 ▶

Remove all fields from the Customer table except Customer Number, Name, Balance, and Credit Limit (Figure 5-33) by selecting the field and then choosing the Remove Field button.

FIGURE 5-33

STEP 4 ▶

Click the slsrep.db list box arrow. Remove the Address, City, State, and Zip Code fields. Point to the OK button.

The Address, City, State, and Zip Code fields are removed (Figure 5-34). The mouse pointer points to the OK button.

FIGURE 5-34

STEP 5 ▶

Choose the OK button and then point to the OK button in the Design Layout dialog box.

The Design Layout dialog box displays (Figure 5-35), showing the Paradox default design for the fields selected. The mouse pointer points to the OK button.

STEP 6 ▶

Choose the OK button and then maximize the window containing the form.

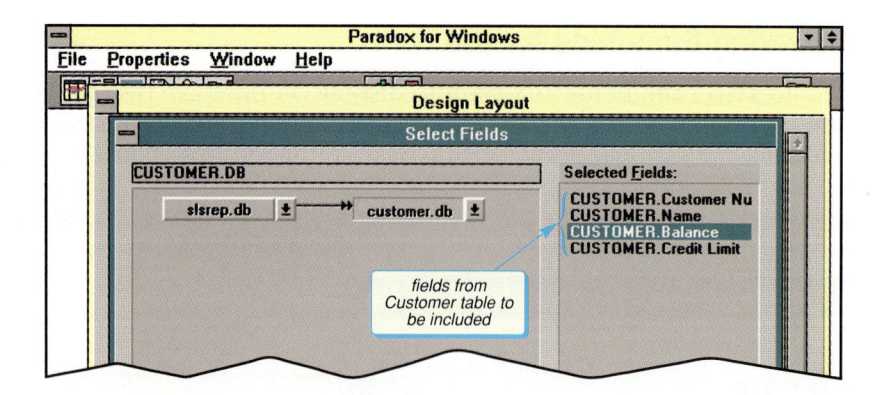

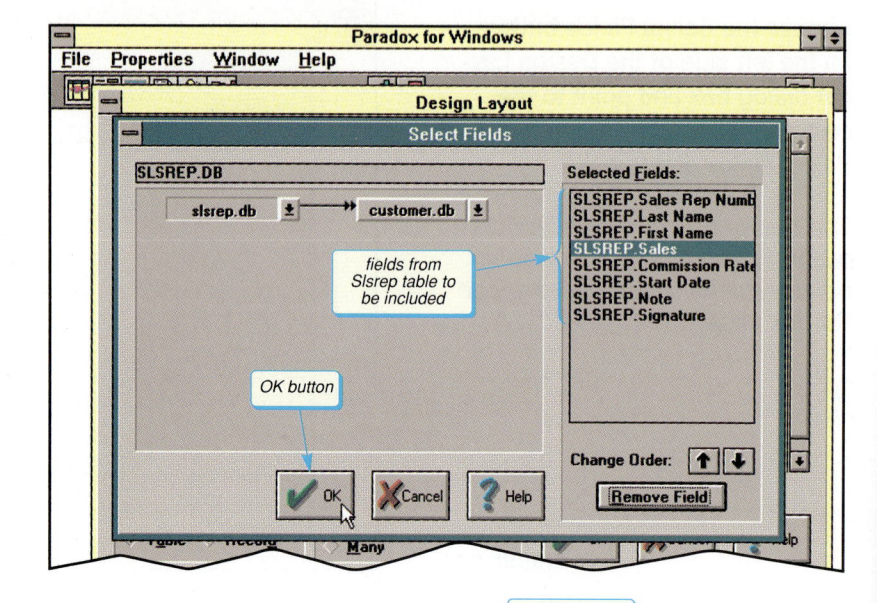

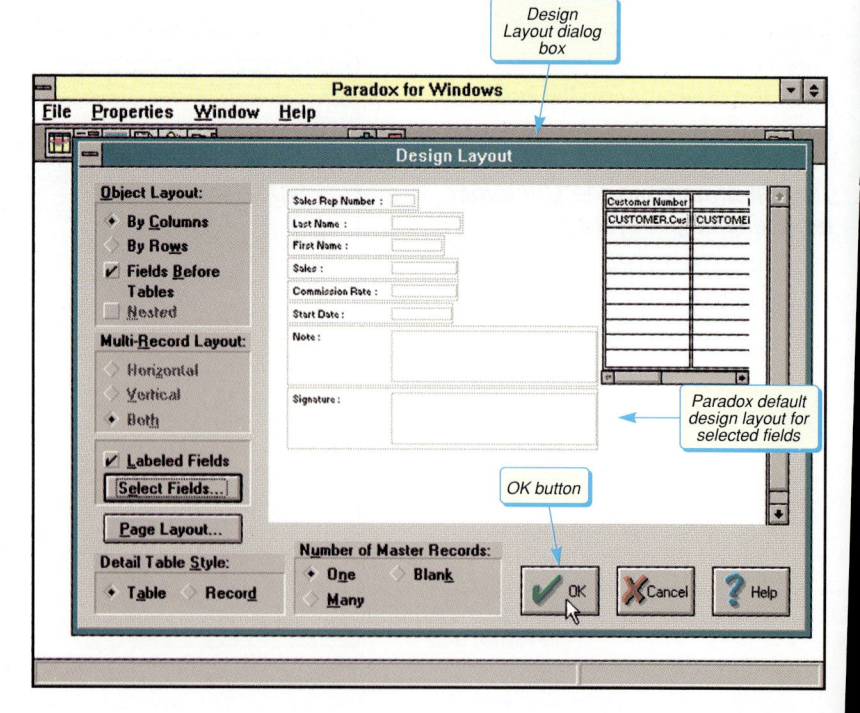

FIGURE 5-35

ADVANCED FORM TECHNIQUES   P239

Moving and Resizing Fields

Moving fields and resizing fields on the form are accomplished using the same techniques for moving and resizing fields on the form you created in Project 4. You begin by moving the object that contains multiple rows from the Customer table. Such an object, which resembles Table view, is called a **table object**. The following steps move the table object on the form and also change its size.

TO MOVE AND RESIZE THE TABLE OBJECT ON THE FORM ▼

STEP 1 ▶

Select the field edit region for the Note field by pointing to it and clicking the left mouse button twice. Point to the handle on the right-hand side of the field edit region.

The field edit region is selected (Figure 5-36). The mouse pointer points to the handle on the right-hand side. The mouse pointer shape changes to the horizontal double arrow (⇔) indicating that you can resize the region by dragging the handle.

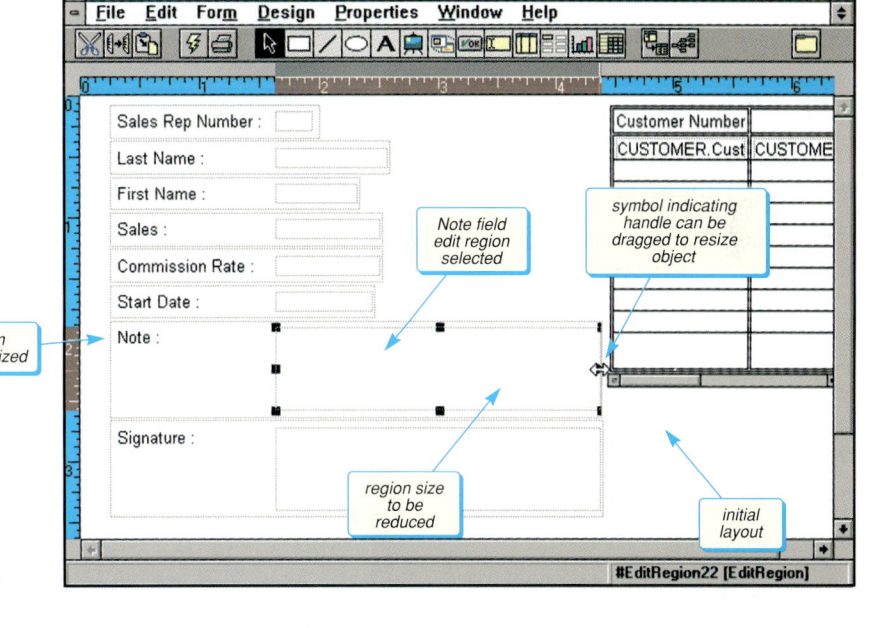

FIGURE 5-36

STEP 2 ▶

Resize the field edit region to the size shown in Figure 5-37. Select and resize the field edit region for the Signature field to the size shown in the figure.

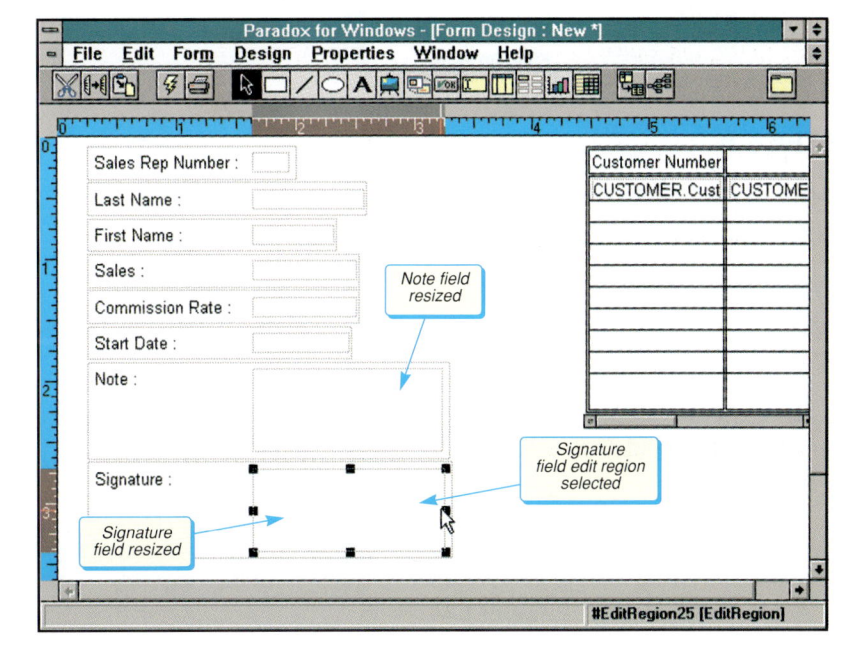

FIGURE 5-37

P240 PROJECT 5 ADVANCED TOPICS

STEP 3 ▶

Select the Customer table object by pointing to it and clicking the left mouse button.

The Customer table object is selected (Figure 5-38).

FIGURE 5-38

STEP 4 ▶

Drag the Customer table object to the position shown in Figure 5-39.

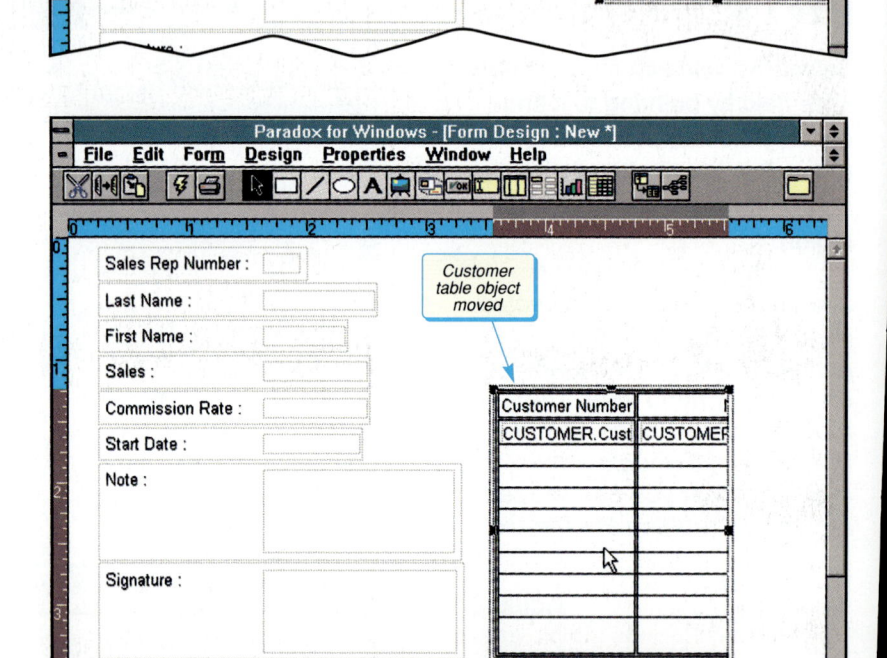

FIGURE 5-39

STEP 5 ▶

Point to the handle on the top edge of the Customer table object.

The mouse pointer points to the handle on the top of the Customer table object (Figure 5-40).

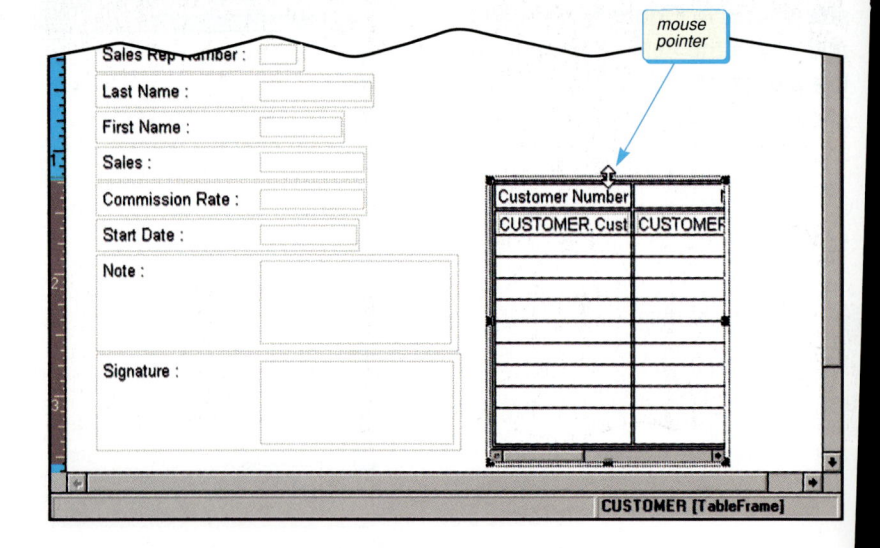

FIGURE 5-40

ADVANCED FORM TECHNIQUES **P241**

STEP 6 ▶

Resize the Customer table object to the one shown in Figure 5-41 by dragging the handle.

The Customer table object is resized.

FIGURE 5-41

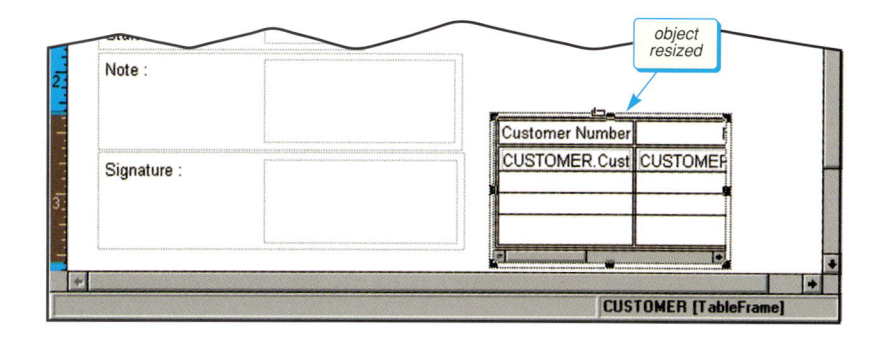

Showing and Working with the Grid

Recall from Project 4 that in creating a form, you learned how to display the grid and how to snap objects to the grid. The following steps display the grid and snap objects to the grid.

TO DISPLAY THE GRID AND SNAP OBJECTS TO THE GRID ▼

STEP 1 ▶

Select the Properties menu and choose the Show Grid command. Select the Properties menu and then choose the Snap To Grid command. Use the mouse to move the Field Edit regions within the fields so there is no excess space between the Field labels and the Field Edit regions. Use the mouse to move the fields to the positions shown in Figure 5-42.

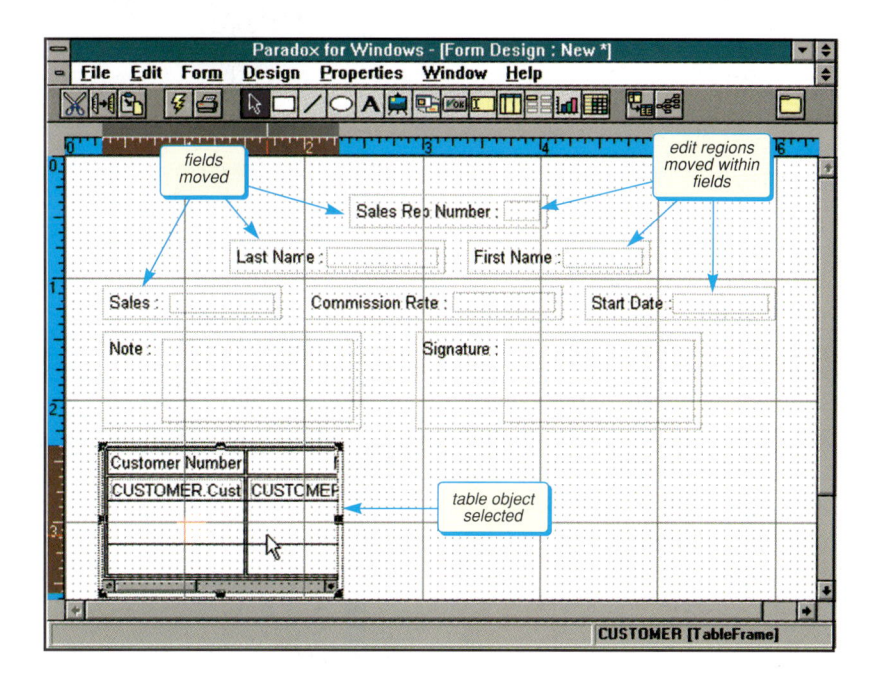

FIGURE 5-42

STEP 2 ▶

Select the Customer table object and then drag the handle on the right-hand edge to the position shown in Figure 5-43.

FIGURE 5-43

Adding or Removing Scroll Bars

The table object currently contains a **horizontal scroll bar**. This scroll bar is no longer necessary because all the fields are now visible. The table object does need a **vertical scroll bar**, however, because a sales representative may have more customers than will fit on the screen. The vertical scroll bar allows users to scroll through all the customers. Use the following steps to add a vertical scroll bar to the table object and remove the horizontal scroll bar.

TO ADD OR REMOVE SCROLL BARS ▼

STEP 1 ▶

Select the Customer table object. Point to it and click the right mouse button. Point to the Vertical Scroll Bar command.

The Customer table object's menu displays (Figure 5-44). The mouse pointer points to the Vertical Scroll Bar command.

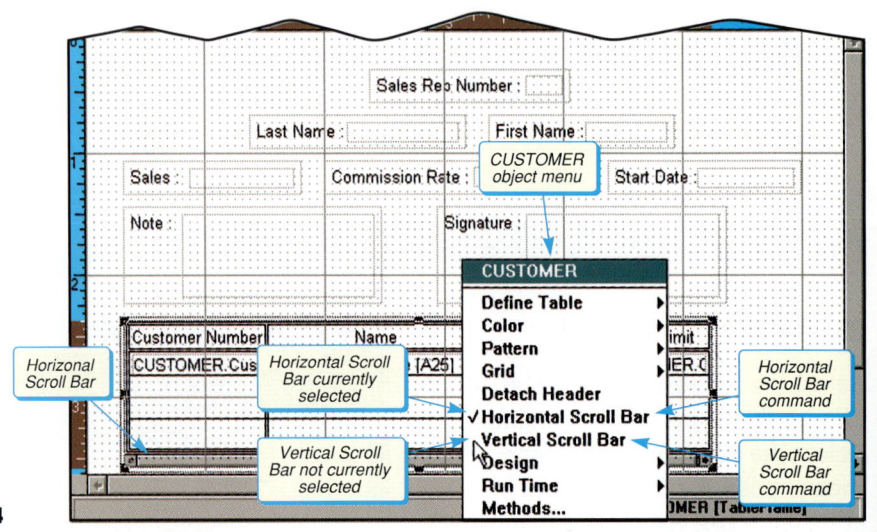

FIGURE 5-44

STEP 2 ▶

Choose the Vertical Scroll Bar command. Point to the Customer table object, click the right mouse button, and choose the Horizontal Scroll Bar command.

The vertical scroll bar displays and the horizontal scroll bar is hidden (Figure 5-45).

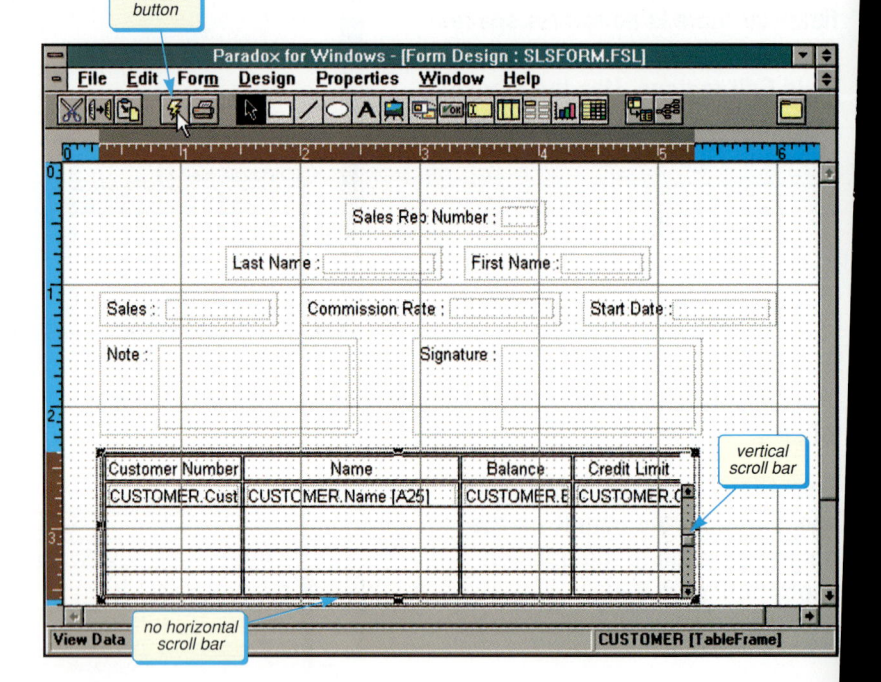

FIGURE 5-45

Saving the Form

Save the form by closing it. However, if you want to continue working on the form, you don't want to close it. To save the form without closing it, use the Save or Save As command on the File menu. The following steps save the form without closing it.

TO SAVE YOUR WORK

Step 1: Select the File menu and choose the Save command.
Step 2: Type slsform as the name of the form and choose the OK button.

Viewing Data Using the Form

To view data from the table using the form, click the View Data button on the SpeedBar. The following steps display data using the form.

TO USE THE FORM TO VIEW DATA ▼

STEP 1 ▶

Point to the View Data button shown at the top of Figure 5-45.

STEP 2 ▶

Click the View Data button.

The data from the first record displays in the form (Figure 5-46).

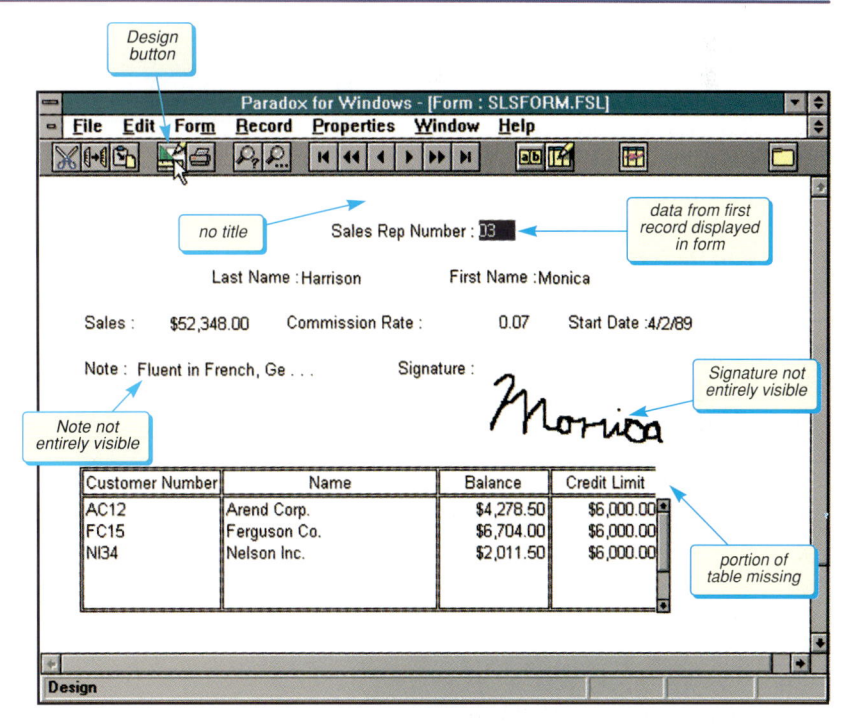

FIGURE 5-46

Changing the Background Color

The steps on the next page use the procedures developed in Project 4 (see page P202) to change the background color of the form and remove the grid.

P244 PROJECT 5 ADVANCED TOPICS

TO CHANGE THE BACKGROUND COLOR AND REMOVE THE GRID ▼

STEP 1 ▶

Click the Design button shown at the top of Figure 5-46.

STEP 2 ▶

Point to an open space on the form outside any of the boxes and then click the right mouse button. Select the Color command from the menu that displays and then point to the light gray color.

The menu shown in Figure 5-47 displays. The color palette displays and the mouse pointer points to light gray.

STEP 3 ▶

Choose light gray by clicking the left mouse button. Remove the grid by selecting the Properties menu and then choosing the Show Grid command.

The background color on the form changes to light gray and the grid is removed.

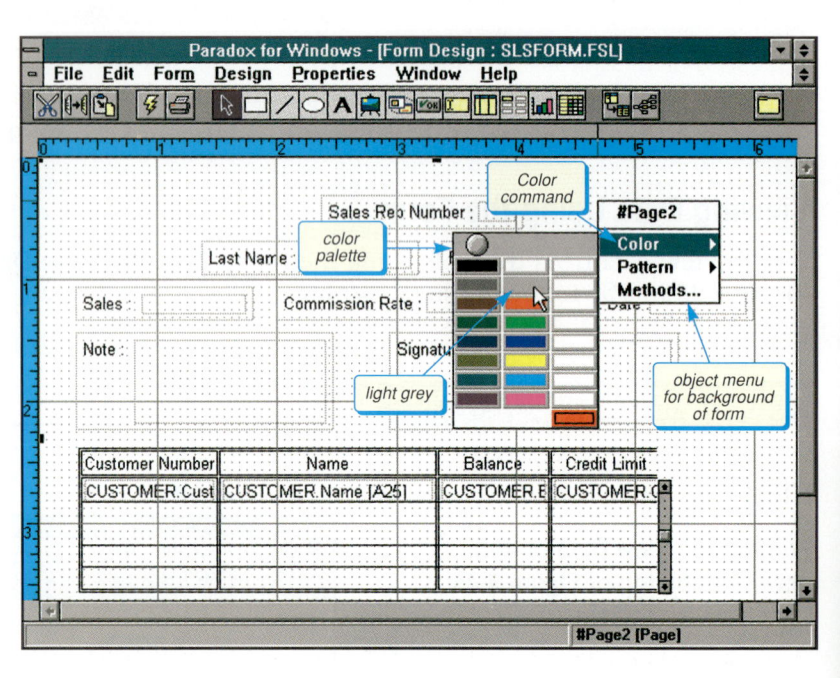

FIGURE 5-47

Changing Frame Styles

The following steps use the procedure developed in Project 4 (see page P204) to change the frame styles for the field objects on the form.

TO CHANGE THE FRAME STYLES ▼

STEP 1 ▶

Point to any field object on the form and click the left mouse button. Next, hold down the SHIFT key and select the field objects one at a time until you have selected all of them.

The field objects are selected (Figure 5-48).

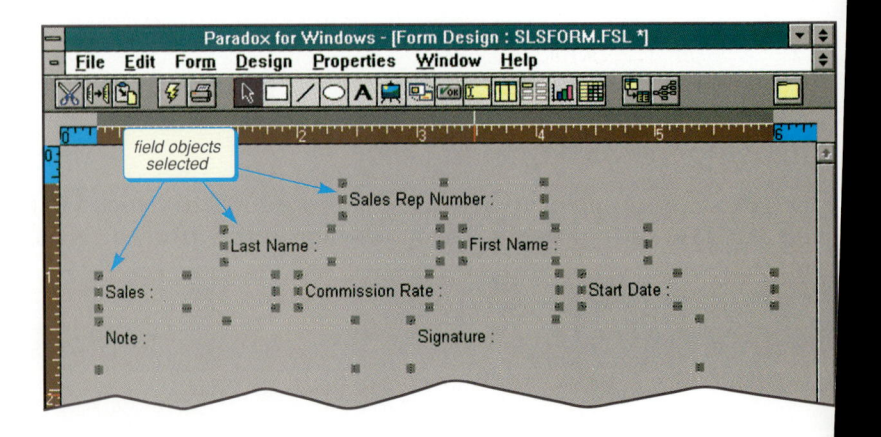

FIGURE 5-48

ADVANCED FORM TECHNIQUES **P245**

STEP 2 ▶

Click the right mouse button to display the object's menu, select the Frame command, select the Style command, and then point to the frame style shown in Figure 5-49.

STEP 3 ▶

Select the style by clicking the left mouse button. Point to a position outside all field objects and click the left mouse button to remove the selection from the fields.

The field objects display with a drop-shadow frame (see Figure 5-50 below).

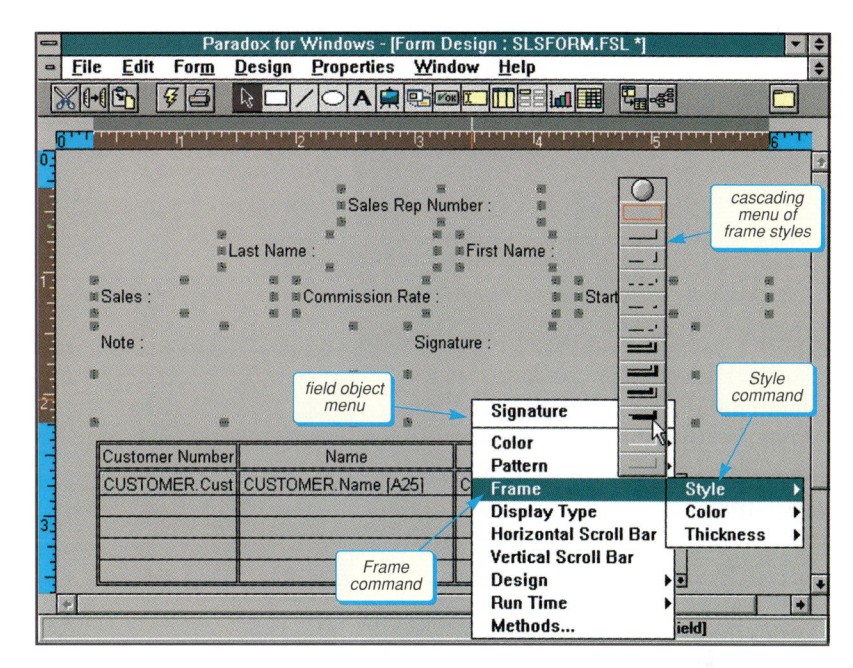

FIGURE 5-49

Changing Magnification

Earlier you changed the magnification for the Signature field in Table view so the entire signature displayed. You can make the same type of change on the Form. The following steps change the magnification of the Signature field so the entire signature displays.

TO CHANGE THE MAGNIFICATION OF AN OLE FIELD ▼

STEP 1 ▶

Select the field edit region of the Signature field, click the right mouse button to display the object's menu, select Magnification, and point to the Best Fit command.

The Signature object menu displays (Figure 5-50). The Magnification command is chosen and the mouse pointer points to the Best Fit command.

STEP 2 ▶

Choose the Best Fit command.

FIGURE 5-50

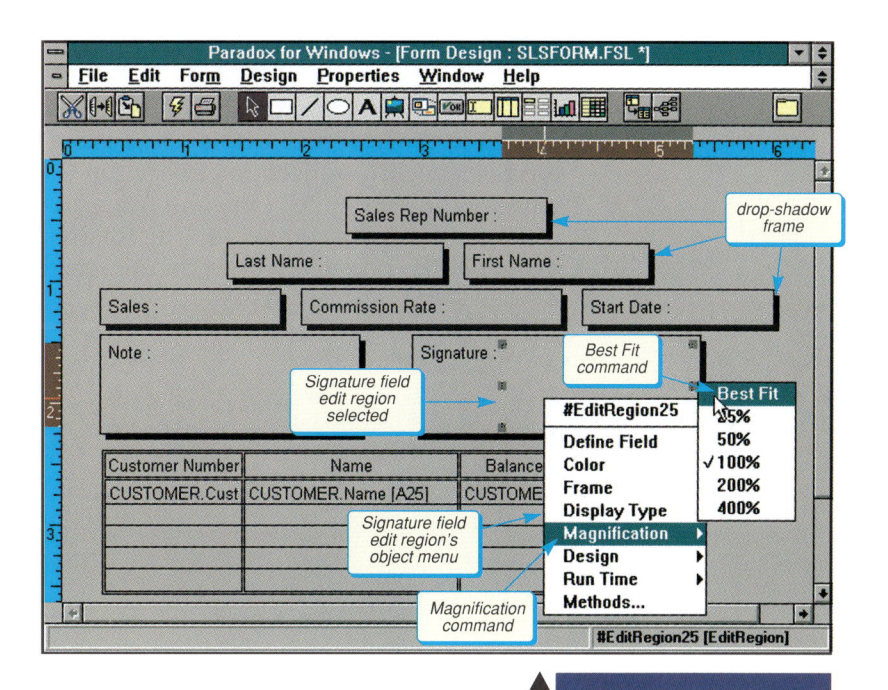

Resizing a Table Object

With the vertical scroll bar on the table object, a small portion of the object is not visible. Thus, you need to expand the size of the object slightly. The following step changes the size of the table object.

TO CHANGE THE SIZE OF THE TABLE OBJECT

STEP 1 ▶

Select the object and then drag the handle on the right-hand edge to the right so the table and scroll bar are both visible.

The table object is resized and both the table and scroll bar are visible (Figure 5-51).

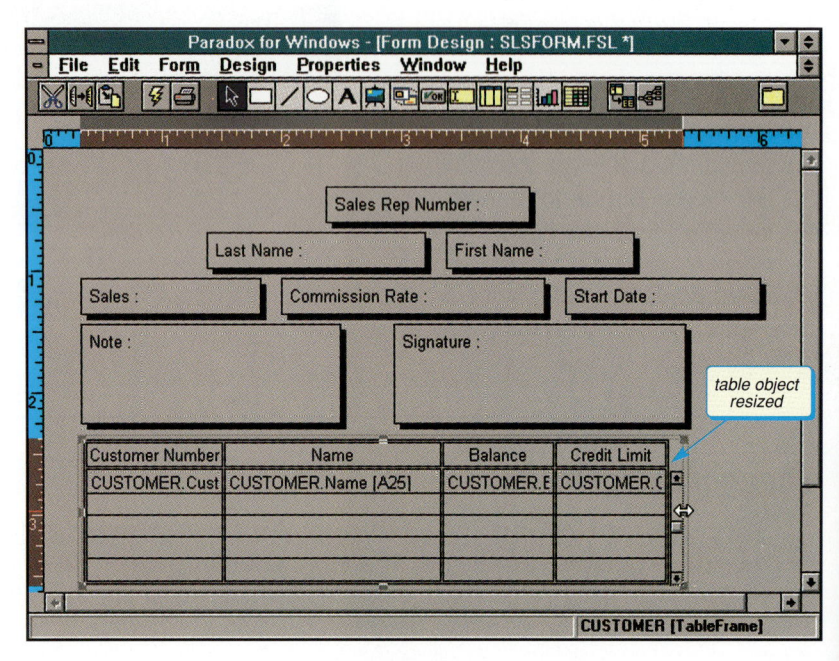

FIGURE 5-51

Completing the Display of the Note Field and Viewing Records

Only the portion of the Note field (titled Note on the form in Figure 5-51) stored in the table will display because of its size. To display as much as will fit on the screen, you need to choose the Complete Display command. First, choose the Run Time command from the Note object menu. Then choose the Complete Display command. The following step ensures that as much of the Note field as possible will fit on the screen and displays the first record.

ADVANCED FORM TECHNIQUES **P247**

TO COMPLETE THE DISPLAY OF THE NOTE FIELD AND VIEW A RECORD ▼

STEP 1 ▶

Select the field edit region of the Note object and click the right mouse button to produce the object's menu. Choose the Run Time command and point to the Complete Display command.

The Note object menu displays (Figure 5-52). The Run Time command is chosen and the mouse pointer points to the Complete Display command.

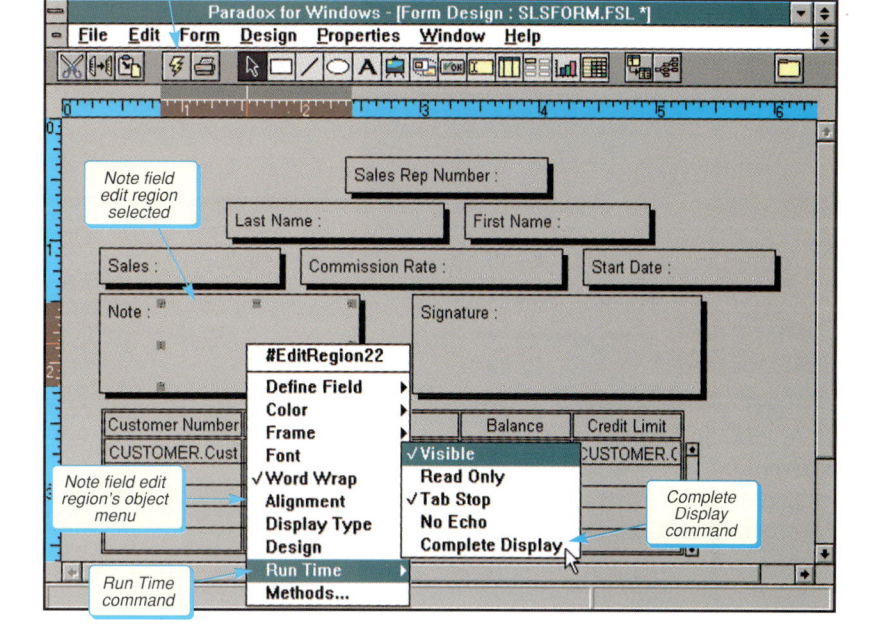

FIGURE 5-52

STEP 2 ▶

Choose the Complete Display command. Point to the View Data button shown at the top of Figure 5-52.

STEP 3 ▶

Click the View Data button.

The data from the first record displays in the form (Figure 5-53). The entire Note displays, as well as the Signature and Customers.

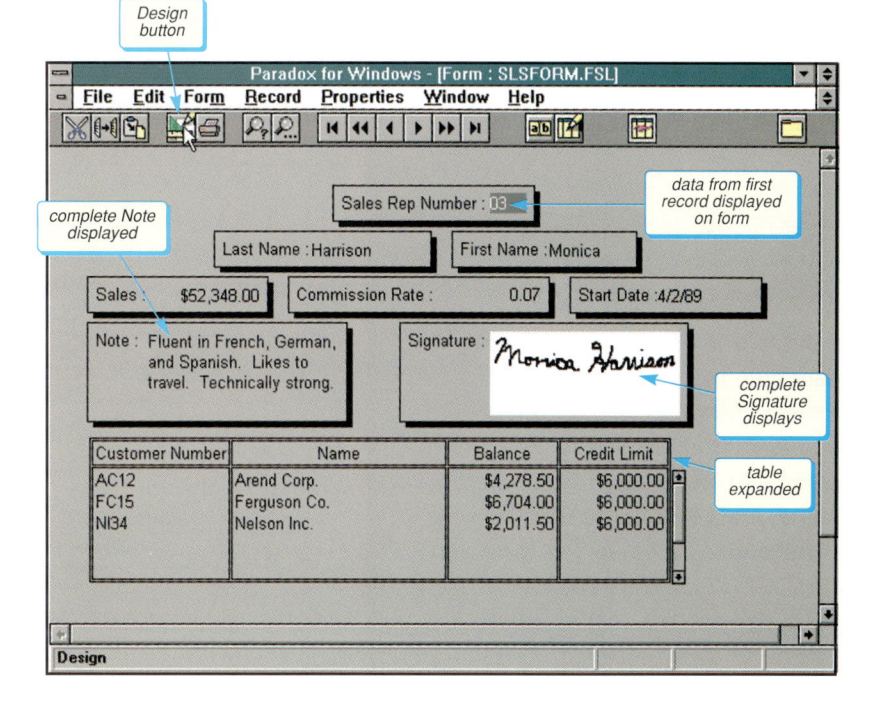

FIGURE 5-53

Changing the Characteristics of Field Labels

Several changes can be made to the characteristics of the field labels in the form. You make these changes by using the Field Label object's menu. Perform the following steps to change the color and style of the field labels.

TO CHANGE THE COLOR AND STYLE OF THE FIELD LABELS ▼

STEP 1 ▶

Click the Design button. Select all the field labels except those in the Customer table object. Click the right mouse button, choose the Font command, choose the Color command and point to the dark blue color.

The field labels are selected (Figure 5-54). The object's menu displays. The Font command is chosen, the Color command is chosen, and the mouse pointer points to dark blue.

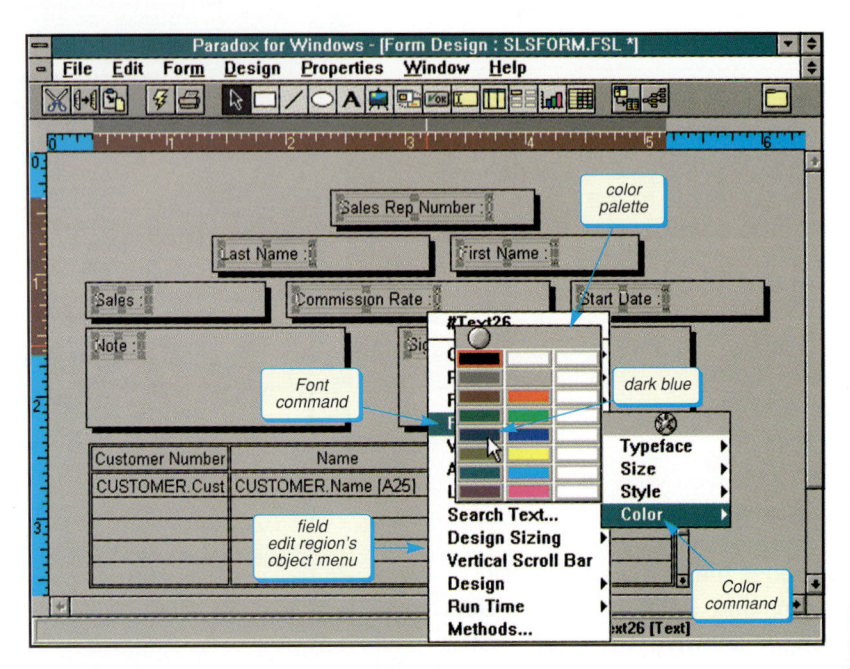

FIGURE 5-54

STEP 2 ▶

Point to one of the fields. Choose dark blue by clicking the left mouse button. Click the right mouse button, select the Font command, select the Style command, and point to the Bold command.

The Field Labels' object menu displays (Figure 5-55). The Font command is chosen, the Style command is chosen, and the mouse pointer points to the Bold command.

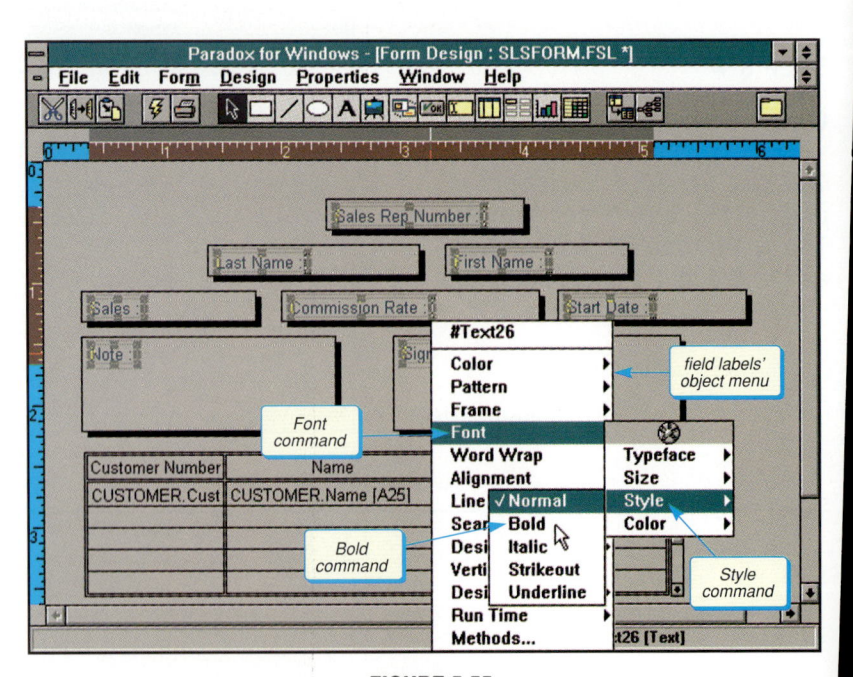

FIGURE 5-55

ADVANCED FORM TECHNIQUES   **P249**

STEP 3 ▶

Choose the Bold command by clicking the left mouse button.

The field labels are all dark blue and bold (Figure 5-56).

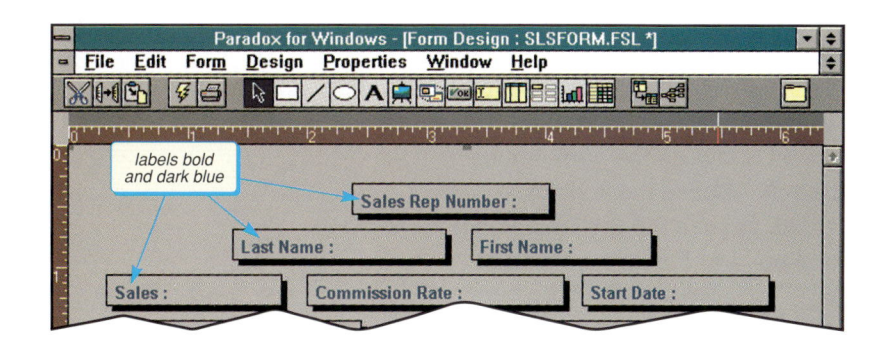

FIGURE 5-56

Placing a Title on a Form

The following steps use the procedures developed in Project 4 to place a title on the form (see To Add Text to a Form on page P199).

TO PLACE A TITLE ON THE FORM ▼

STEP 1 ▶

Click the Text tool button, place a rectangle at the top of the form, and type `Sales Rep Form`.

A text object containing `Sales Rep Form` is placed at the top of the form (Figure 5-57).

FIGURE 5-57

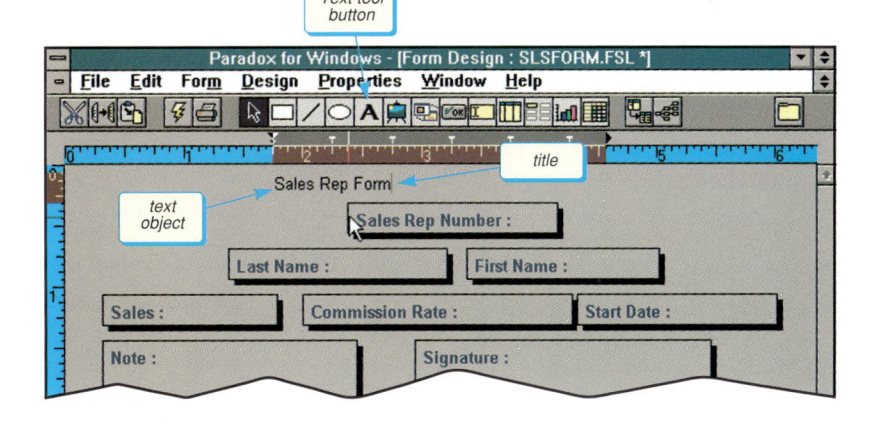

STEP 2 ▶

Point to the text object and click the right mouse button. Choose the Font command, choose the Size command, and point to 16.

The text object menu displays (Figure 5-58). The mouse pointer points to 16.

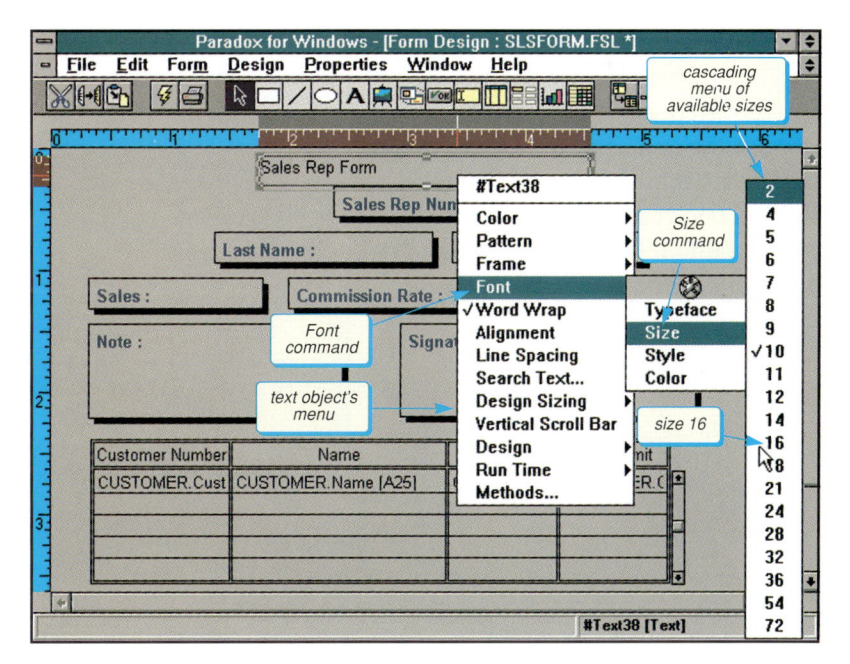

FIGURE 5-58

P250 PROJECT 5 ADVANCED TOPICS

STEP 3 ▶

Select size 16 by clicking the left mouse button. Point to the text object and click the right mouse button. Choose the Font command, choose the Style command, and point to the Italic command.

The text object's menu displays (Figure 5-59). The Font command is chosen, the Style command is chosen, and the mouse pointer points to the Italic command.

FIGURE 5-59

STEP 4 ▶

Choose the Italic command by clicking the left mouse button. Point to the text object and click the right mouse button. Choose the Font command, choose the Color command, and point to the dark red color.

The text object menu displays (Figure 5-60). The Font command is chosen, the Color command is chosen, and the mouse pointer points to dark red.

FIGURE 5-60

STEP 5 ▶

Choose the dark red color by clicking the left mouse button. Point to the text object and click the right mouse button. Choose the Frame command, choose the Style command, and point to the style shown in Figure 5-61.

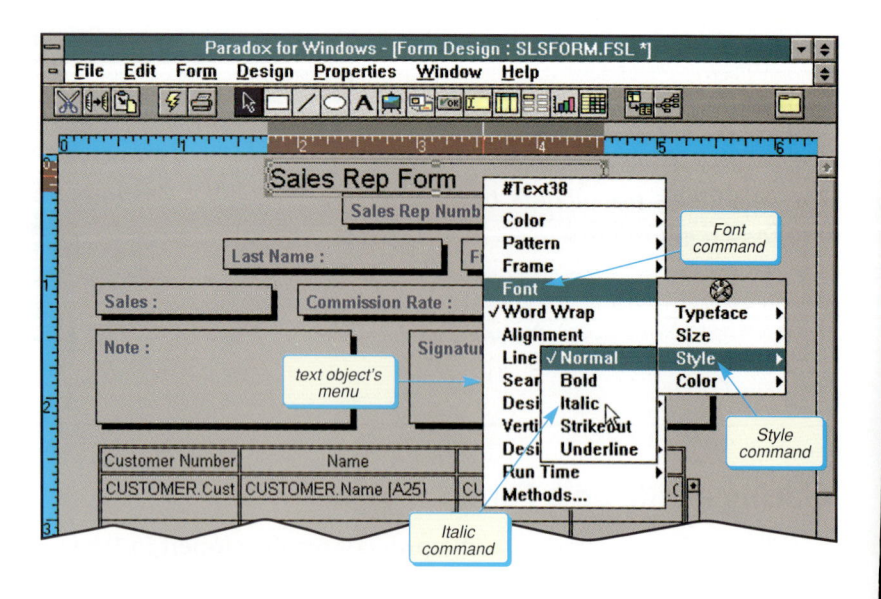

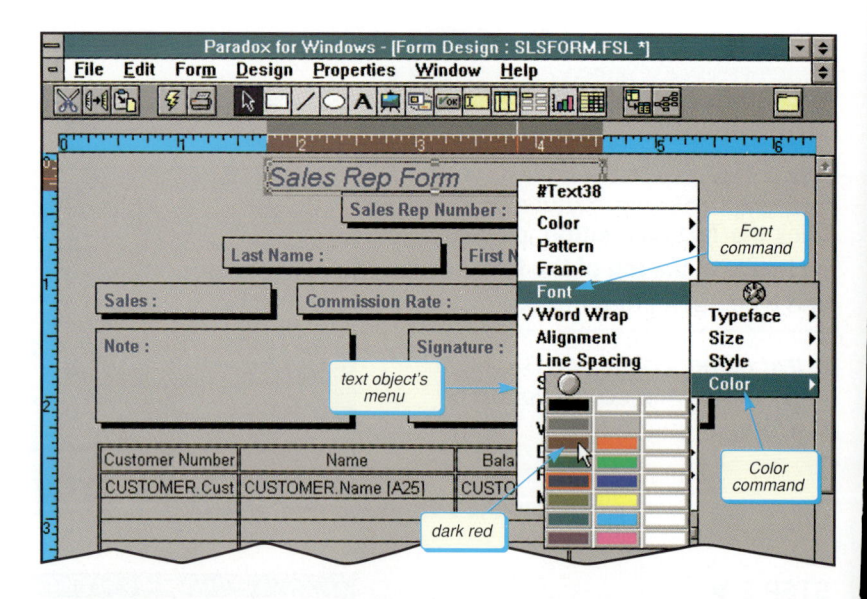

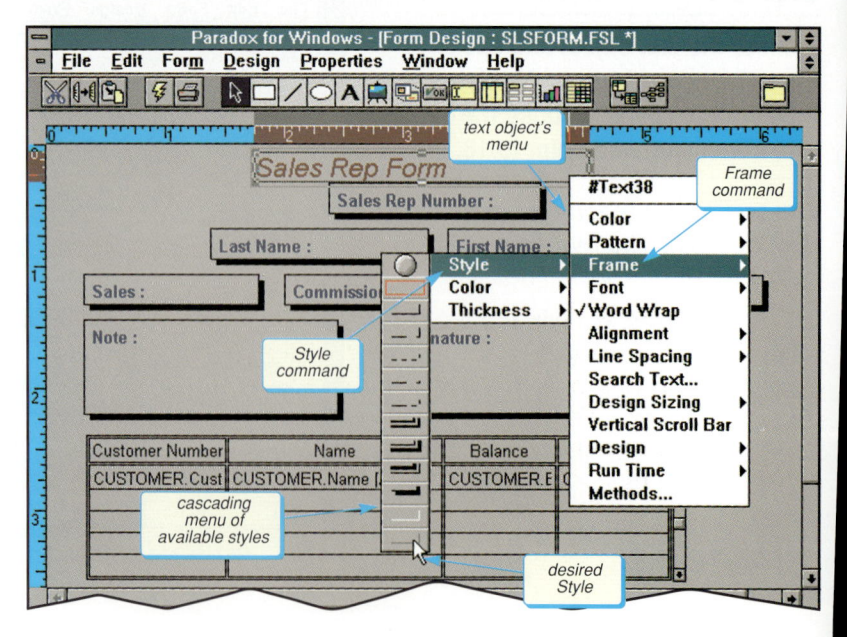

FIGURE 5-61

STEP 6 ▶

Choose the style by clicking the left mouse button and then point to the handle on the right-hand edge of the text box.

The size, style, and color of the text has changed (Figure 5-62). The mouse pointer points to the handle at the right-hand edge of the box.

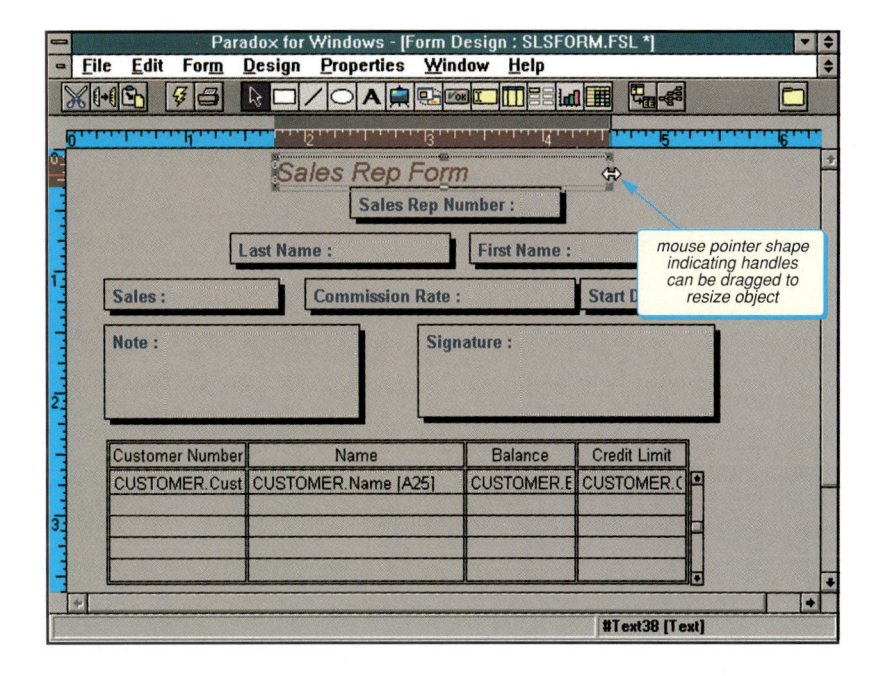

FIGURE 5-62

STEP 7 ▶

Drag the handle to the left so there is no extra space in the box following the word Form. Then point to the middle of the box and drag the box so it is centered.

The box size changes (Figure 5-63) and the box is centered.

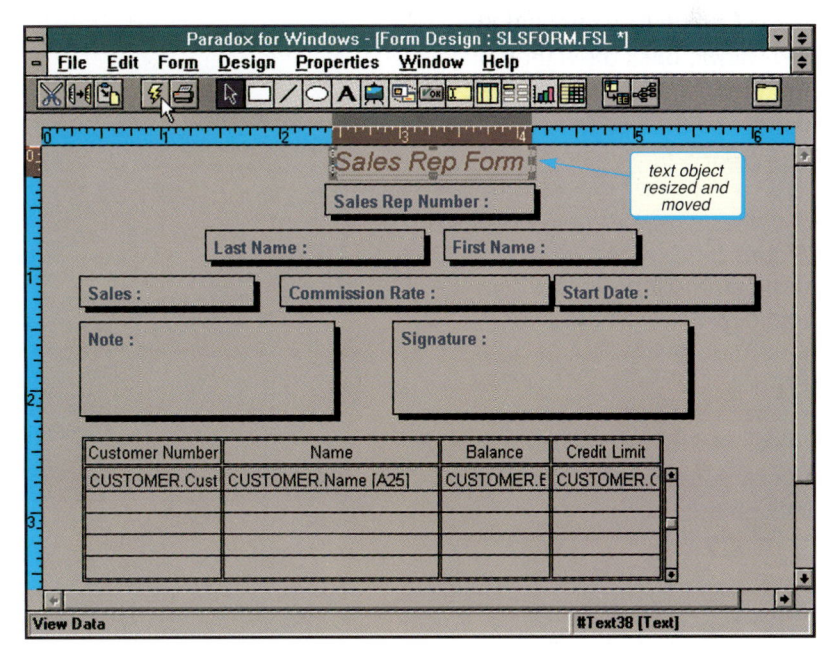

FIGURE 5-63

Changing the Color of the Table Object

By selecting the table object and then using its menu, you can change characteristics of the table that displays the Sales rep's customers. You can select the column headings separately and use their menu to change characteristics of the column headings. The steps on the next page change the color of the table object to blue and change the color of the column headings within the table object to dark blue.

TO CHANGE THE COLOR OF THE TABLE OBJECT

STEP 1 ▶

Select the table object in the lower portion of the form and then click the right mouse button. Choose the Color command and point to the blue color.

The table object menu displays (Figure 5-64). The Color command is chosen and the mouse pointer points to blue.

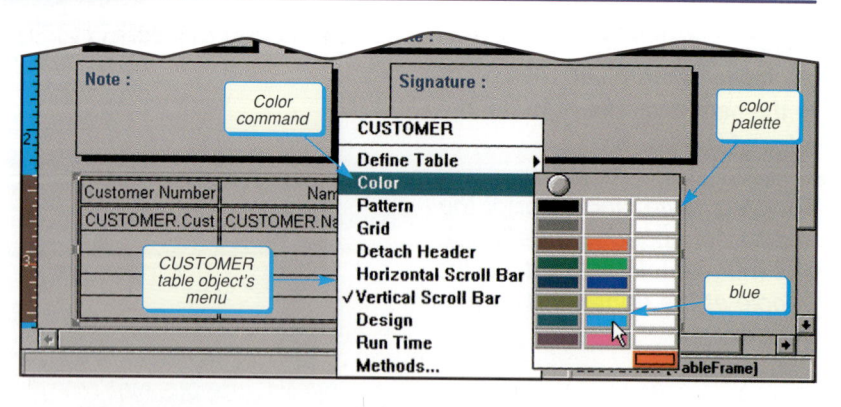

FIGURE 5-64

STEP 2 ▶

Select blue by clicking the left mouse button. Select the table header (the row containing the words Customer Number, Name, and so on). Click the right mouse button, choose the Color command, and then point to the dark blue color.

The header object menu displays (Figure 5-65). The Color command is chosen and the mouse pointer points to dark blue.

STEP 3

Select dark blue by clicking the left mouse button. Point to the View Data button.

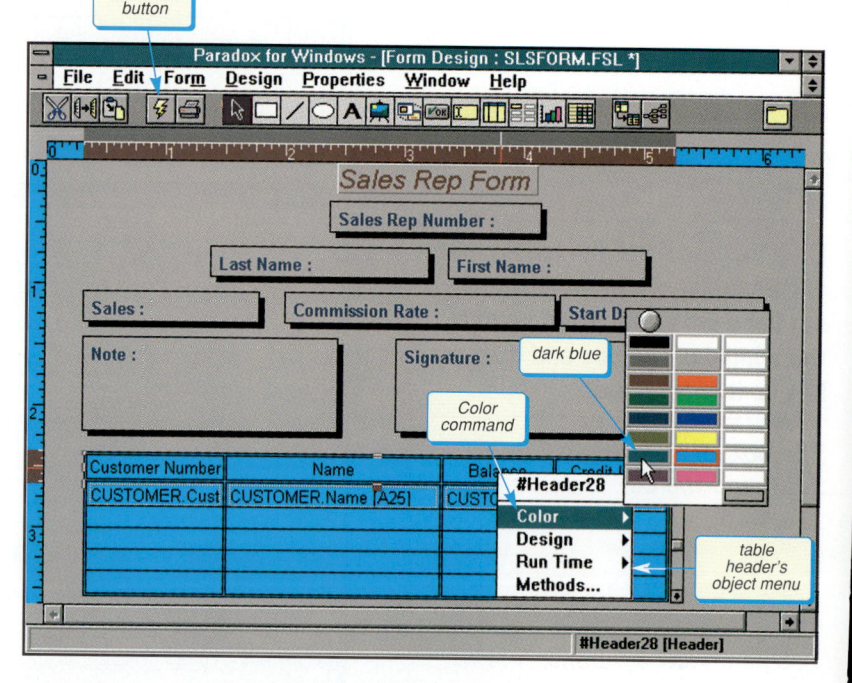

FIGURE 5-65

STEP 4 ▶

Click the View Data button to display the first record.

The data from the first record displays in the form (Figure 5-66). The colors, fonts, and frame styles have been changed.

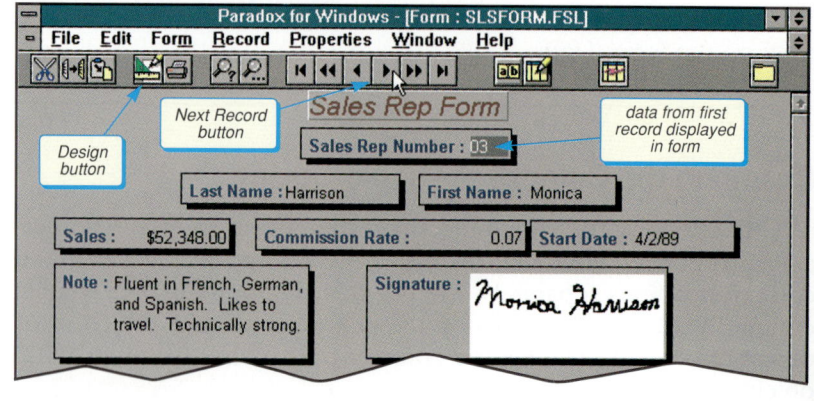

FIGURE 5-66

ADVANCED FORM TECHNIQUES **P253**

Resizing the Table Object

The table object does not require the number of rows currently displayed. Perform the following steps to reduce the number of rows that display in the table object.

TO CHANGE THE SIZE OF THE TABLE OBJECT ▼

STEP 1 ▶

Click the Design button. Select the table object, and then drag the handle on the bottom of the object to the position shown in Figure 5-67.

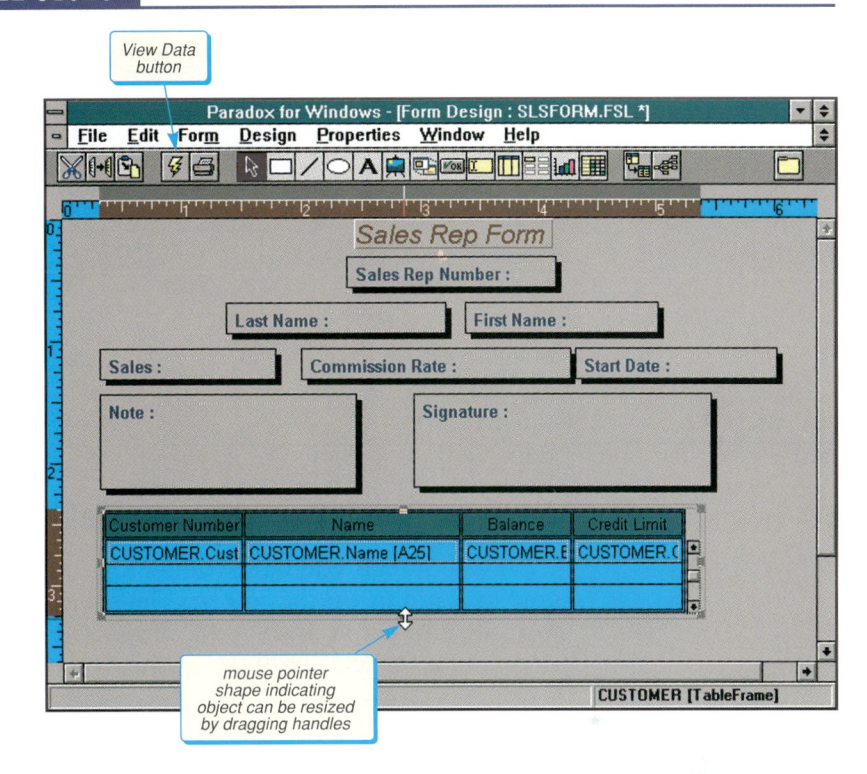

FIGURE 5-67

STEP 2 ▶

Click the View Data button to see the effect of the change and then point to the Next Record button.

Data from the first record displays in the form (Figure 5-68). The mouse pointer points to the Next Record button.

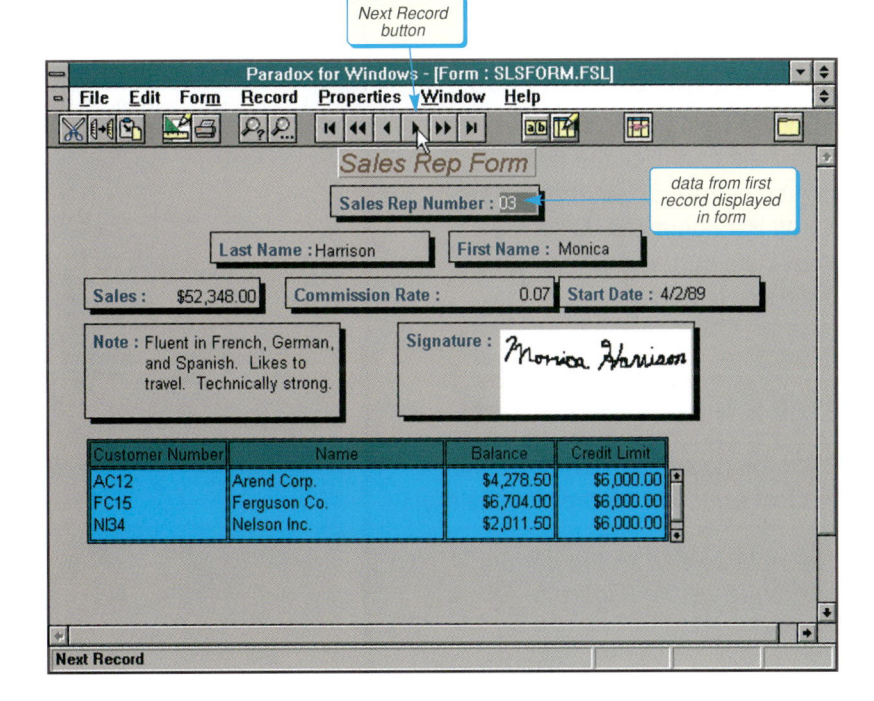

FIGURE 5-68

P254 PROJECT 5 ADVANCED TOPICS

STEP 3 ▶

Click the Next Record button.

Data from the second record displays in the form (Figure 5-69). A portion of the note is not visible because there is not enough room for it to fit in the Note field.

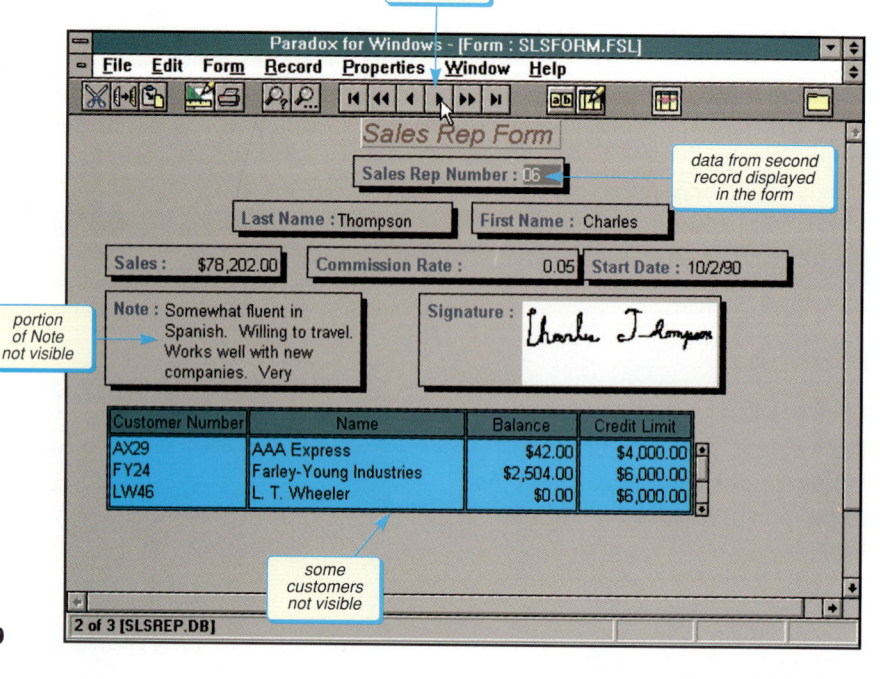

FIGURE 5-69

Adding a Scroll Bar to a Note Field

Even though you have completed the display of the Note field, a lengthy note may not fit on the screen. The simplest way to allow a user to be able to read the entire note is to add a vertical scroll bar to the field. The following steps add a vertical scroll bar to the Note field.

TO ADD A SCROLL BAR TO THE NOTE FIELD AND USE IT ▼

STEP 1 ▶

Click the Design button. Select the Note field and click the right mouse button. Select the Vertical Scroll Bar command. Click the View Data button and then click the Next Record button.

STEP 2 ▶

Click the down scroll arrow on the vertical scroll bar for the Note field.

The note scrolls so the bottom portion is visible (Figure 5-70).

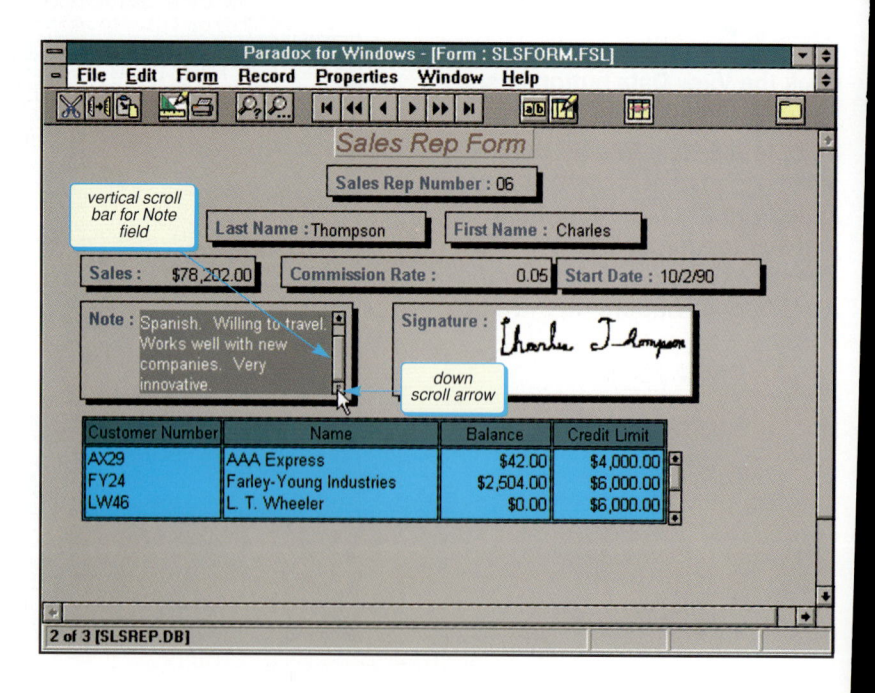

FIGURE 5-70

STEP 3 ▶

Click the down scroll arrow in the Customer table twice.

The records scroll so records 3, 4, and 5 are visible (Figure 5-71).

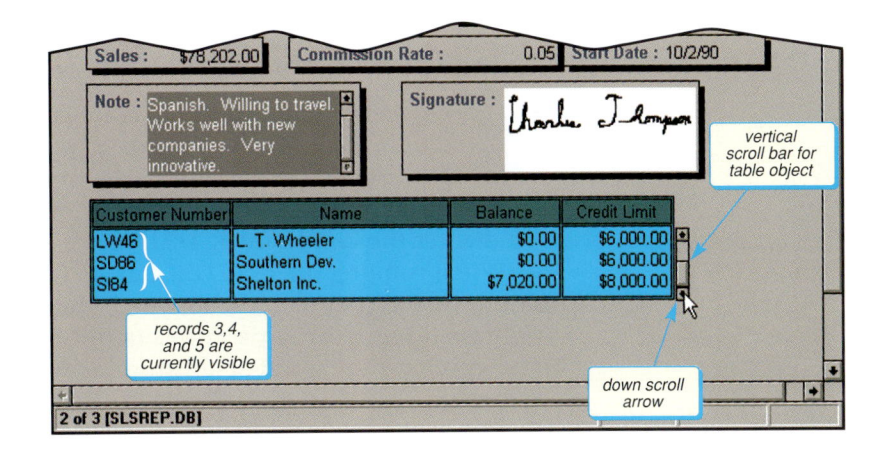

FIGURE 5-71

Closing the Form and Saving the Changes

The form design is now complete, so you can close the form and save the changes. The following steps close the form and also save the changes made to its design.

TO CLOSE THE FORM AND SAVE THE CHANGES

Step 1: Click the Design button to return to the form design.
Step 2: Close the window containing the form.
Step 3: Choose the Yes button in the Paradox for Windows dialog box (Figure 5-72) to save the changes.

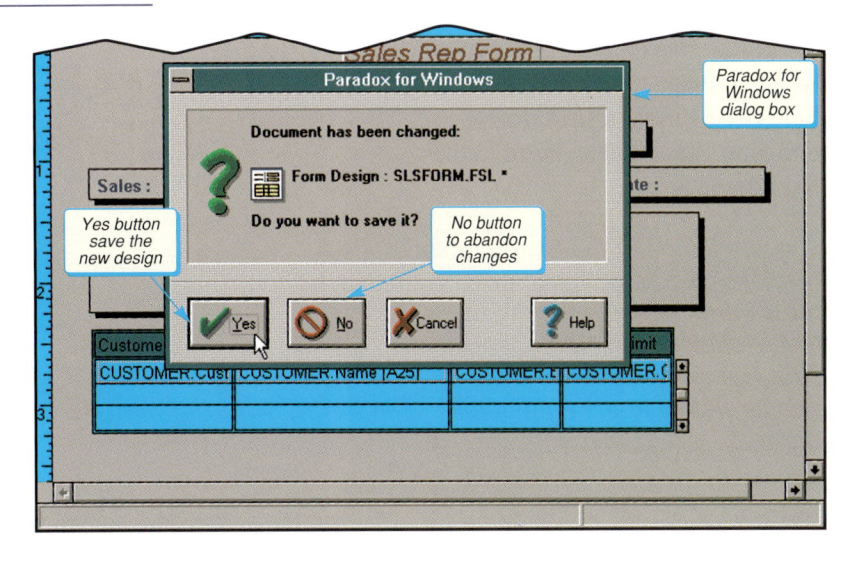

FIGURE 5-72

To Open a Form

To use a form you have created, perform the following steps.

TO USE A FORM

Step 1: Point to the Open Form button on the SpeedBar.
Step 2: Click the Open Form button and select the form.
Step 3: Choose the open mode (View Data to use the form or Design to modify the form).
Step 4: Choose the OK button.

When you have finished working with a form, close it in the usual manner by closing the window containing the form.

▶ Using Date and Memo Fields in a Query

In queries, you can use date fields by simply typing the dates (including the slashes). By typing a date, you can search for records with that specific date. You can also use comparison operators. To find all the sales representatives whose start date was prior to January 1, 1990, for example, you would enter the condition < 1/01/90.

When running queries, you can also use memo fields. Typically you will want to find all the records on which the memo field contains a specific word or phrase using wild cards, for example, you could find all the sales representatives who have the word Spanish in the Note field by entering the condition, ..Spanish.. .

The following steps create and run queries that use date and memo fields.

TO USE DATE AND MEMO FIELDS IN A QUERY ▼

STEP 1 ▶

Select the File menu, choose the New command and then choose the Query command. Select SLSREP.DB and then choose the OK button. Maximize the Query window. Place check marks in the Sales Rep Number, Last Name, and First Name fields. Point to the right scroll arrow.

A query image of the Slsrep table displays (Figure 5-73). Check marks are placed in the Sales Rep Number, Last Name, and First Name fields. The mouse pointer points to the right scroll arrow.

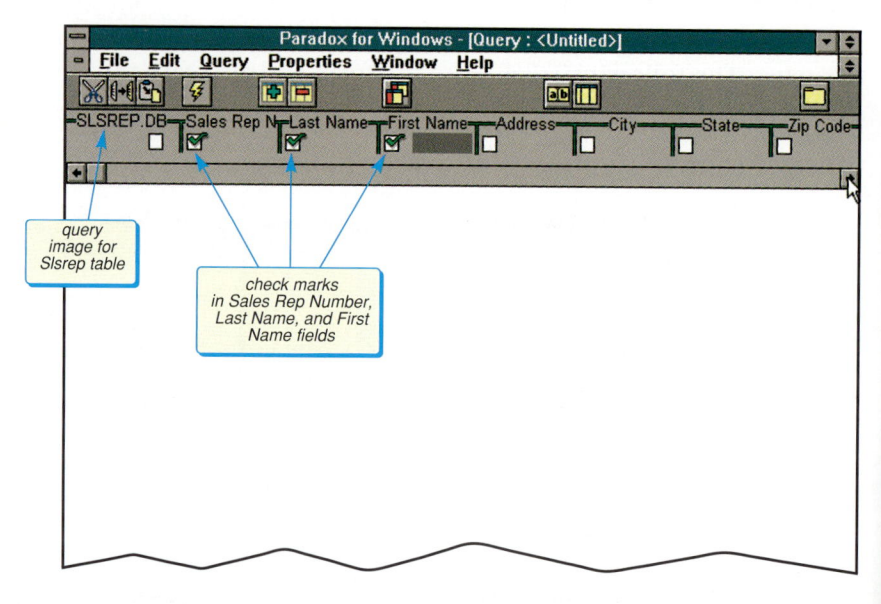

FIGURE 5-73

STEP 2 ▶

Click the right scroll arrow until the Note field displays. Place check marks in the Start Date and Note fields. Be sure the Note field is highlighted and type ..Spanish... Point to the Run Query button.

Check marks are placed in the Start Date and Note fields (Figure 5-74). The Note field contains ..Spanish... The pointer points to the Run Query button.

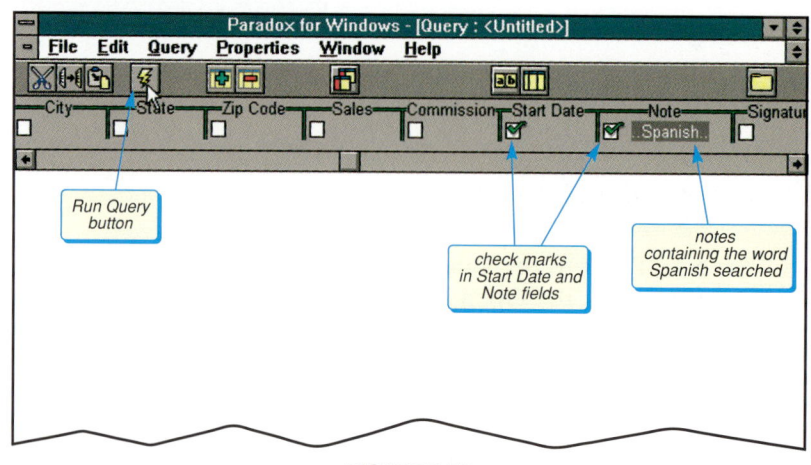

FIGURE 5-74

STEP 3 ▶

Click the Run Query button to run the query. Point to the Note field in the first record in the Answer table.

The Answer table displays (Figure 5-75). The results contain the two sales representatives who have the word Spanish somewhere within the Note field. The mouse pointer points to the Note field in the first record.

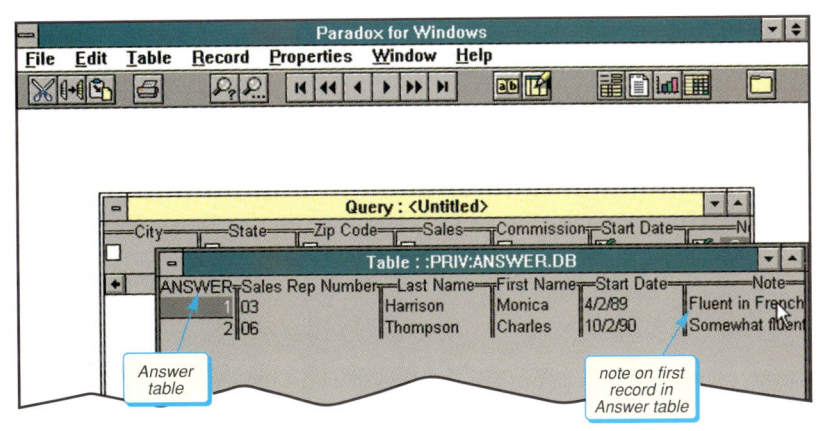

FIGURE 5-75

STEP 4 ▶

Double-click the Note field in the first record.

The entire note displays (Figure 5-76). The note contains the word Spanish.

FIGURE 5-76

STEP 5 ▶

Close the Answer table and maximize the query. Select the Start Date field and type <1/01/90. Point to the Run Query button.

The Query image contains <1/01/90 in the Start Date field and ..Spanish.. in the Note field (Figure 5-77). The mouse pointer points to the Run Query button.

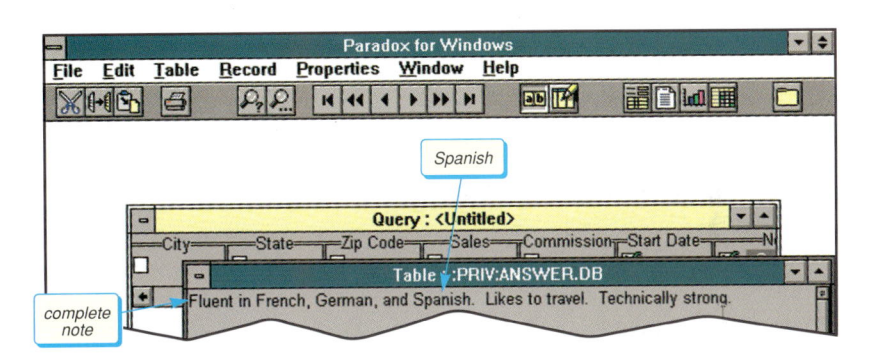

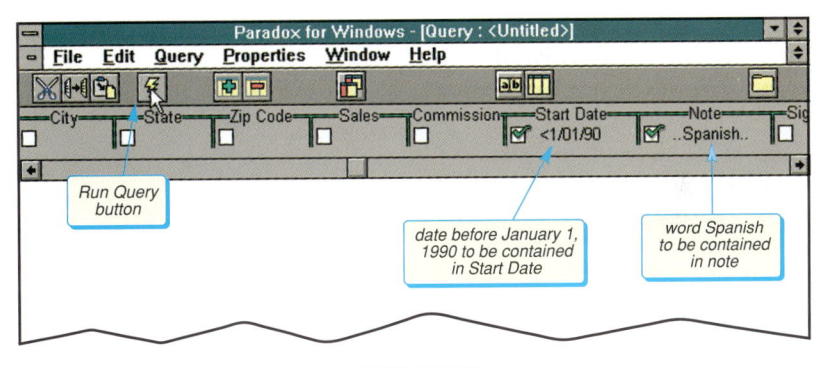

FIGURE 5-77

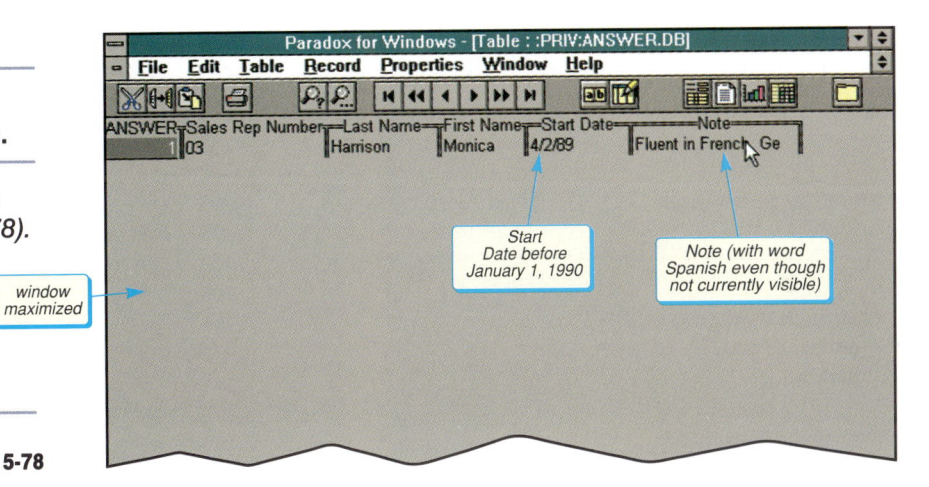

STEP 6 ▶

Click the Run Query button and then maximize the Answer table.

The Answer table displays in a maximized window (Figure 5-78).

STEP 7 ▶

Close the Answer table and the query without saving it.

FIGURE 5-78

PROJECT 5 ADVANCED TOPICS

▶ PROJECT SUMMARY

Project 5 introduced you to some additional field types. You learned how to create and work with date, memo, and OLE fields. In the project, you also learned how to use the new field types in a form. How to build a form on a one-to-many relationship in which several records from one of the tables displaying on the screen at the same time was presented to provide you with more experience using forms. Finally, you learned how to use date and memo fields in queries.

▶ KEY TERMS

Binary Large Object (BLOB) (P223)
clipboard (P230)
complete the display (P227)
cut (P230)
date field (P222)
graphic field (P222)

grid (P241)
horizontal scroll bar (P242)
magnification (P231)
memo field (P222)
Object Linking and Embedding (OLE) (P222)

one-to-many relationship (P235)
paste (P231)
snap to grid (P241)
table object (P239)
table properties (P234)
vertical scroll bar (P242)

QUICK REFERENCE

In Paradox for Windows you can accomplish a task in a number of different ways. The following table provides a quick reference to each task presented in this project with its available options. The commands listed in the Menu column can be executed using either the keyboard or the mouse.

Task	Mouse	Menu	Keyboard Shortcuts
Add Horizontal Scroll Bar to Table Object on Form		From object's menu, choose Horizontal Scroll Bar	
Add Vertical Scroll Bar to an Object		From object's menu, choose Vertical Scroll Bar	
Add Data to an OLE Field	Click Field View button on SpeedBar, press ALT + TAB, double-click graphic application icon, create graphic, cut graphic, press ALT + TAB, click Field View button	From Table or Form menu, choose Field View, press ALT + TAB to switch to graphic application, create graphic, cut graphic, ALT + TAB to switch to Paradox, past graphic, from Table or Form menu, choose Field View	Press F2 to switch to Field View, ALT + TAB to switch to graphic application, create graphic, cut graphic, ALT + TAB to switch to Paradox, past graphic, press F2 to leave Field View
Add Data to a Memo Field	Click Field View button on SpeedBar, type memo, click Field View button again	From Table or Form menu, choose Field View, type memo; from Table or Form menu, choose Field View	Press F2 to move to Field View, type memo, press F2 again
Change the Magnification of OLE Fields		From object's menu, choose Magnification, then choose desired magnification	
Complete Display of OLE Fields on Form		From object's menu, choose Complete Display	

Task	Mouse	Menu	Keyboard Shortcuts
Complete Display of Memo Fields on Form		From object's menu, choose Run Time, then choose Complete Display	
Complete Display of Memo, or OLE Fields in Table View		From object's menu, choose Complete Display	
Create a Data Model Using a One-to-Many Relationship	Select tables, then drag mouse pointer from "one" table to "many" table		
Remove Horizontal Scroll Bar from Memo Field or Table Object on Form		From object's menu, choose Horizontal Scroll Bar	
Remove Vertical Scroll Bar from Memo Field or Table Object on Form		From object's menu, choose Vertical Scroll Bar	
Save Table Properties	Click Control-menu box, choose Close, choose Yes	From Control menu, choose Close, then choose Yes button	
Update Memo Field	Click Field View button on SpeedBar, update memo, click Field View button	From Table or Form menu, choose Field View, update memo; from Table or Form menu, choose Field View	Press F2 to move to Field View, update memo, press F2 again
Update OLE Field	Click Field View button on SpeedBar to move to application that created data, modify data, exit application, then click Field View button	From Table or Form menu, select Field View, modify data, exit application; from Table or Form menu, choose Field View	Press F2 to application that created data, modify data, exit application, press F2 again
Use Date Field in Query			Type comparison operator, then type date, including slashes
Use Memo Field in Query			Type character string including any necessary wildcard symbols

STUDENT ASSIGNMENTS

STUDENT ASSIGNMENT 1
True/False

Instructions: Circle T if the statement is true or F if the statement is false.

T F 1. The term OLE means Object Linking and Encoding.
T F 2. You can store graphics in either Graphic or OLE fields.
T F 3. With an OLE field, you cannot change the graphic once it has been entered.
T F 4. You do not specify a field width for date type fields.

(continued)

STUDENT ASSIGNMENT 1 (continued)

T F 5. When you define a memo type field, you only need to specify a field width size that indicates the number of characters the memo to be stored in the table will contain.
T F 6. To restructure a table, open the table and choose the Restructure command from the Properties menu.
T F 7. Clicking the Field View button on the SpeedBar of the Table window, displays a full screen where data for a memo field can be entered.
T F 8. To change the properties of a graphics or memo field, click the right mouse button, and choose the appropriate command(s) from the object's menu.
T F 9. To save table properties permanently, choose the Save command from the Properties menu.
T F 10. To change the background color of a form, point to an open space outside any of the boxes, click the left mouse button, and choose the Color command from the object's menu.
T F 11. To remove a grid, choose the Show Grid command from the Properties menu.
T F 12. To change the color of a field label, select the field label, click the right mouse button, choose the Font command from the object's menu, and then choose the Color command.
T F 13. To use a form, click the Open Form button on the SpeedBar of the Paradox desktop.
T F 14. To use a date field in a query, enclose the date in single quotes.
T F 15. You cannot use comparison operators with date fields.
T F 16. The only difference between a graphic field and an OLE field is that you can scan photographs and store them in a graphic field.
T F 17. You can also store sounds and full-motion videos in OLE fields.
T F 18. To insert a field at the end of a table structure, press the DOWN ARROW key until the highlight is on the line below the last entry and then press the INSERT key.
T F 19. Paradox automatically inserts slashes (/) in date fields.
T F 20. To switch between the Paintbrush and the Paradox applications, use the ALT + TAB keys.

STUDENT ASSIGNMENT 2
Multiple Choice

Instructions: Circle the correct response.

1. The term OLE means _____.
   a. Object Linking and Encoding
   b. Object Linking and Embedding
   c. Object Locking and Encoding
   d. Object Locking and Embedding
2. To restructure a table, open the table and choose the Restructure command from the _____ menu.
   a. Table
   b. Properties
   c. File
   d. Utilities
3. To remove a grid from a Form Design window, choose the _____ command from the Properties menu.
   a. Remove Grid
   b. Display Grid
   c. Show Grid
   d. Grid
4. Clicking the _____ button on the SpeedBar of the Table window, displays a full screen where data for a memo field can be entered.
   a. Memo View
   b. Full View
   c. Field View
   d. Form View
5. To switch between the Paintbrush application and the Paradox application use the _____ keys.
   a. ALT + SPACEBAR
   b. ALT + CTRL
   c. ALT + SHIFT
   d. ALT + TAB
6. A sales rep may represent many customers, but a customer can be represented by only one sales rep. This is a _____ relationship.
   a. one-to-none
   b. one-to-one
   c. one-to-many
   d. many-to-many

7. To select all field objects on a form, select the first object by clicking the left mouse button and then hold down the _____ key as you select each of the others.
   a. left CTRL
   b. right CTRL
   c. SHIFT
   d. ALT
8. To change the size of a graphic or OLE field on a form, select the field edit region of the field, click the right mouse button to produce the object's menu, select _____, and choose the Best Fit command.
   a. Size
   b. Width
   c. Enlargement
   d. Magnification
9. The Slsrep table contains a Start Date field that contains the date a sales rep began with the organization. To find all sales reps who started after 1989, enter the condition _____ in the Start Date field of the Slsrep query image.
   a. >'12/31/89'
   b. > = 12/31/89
   c. >12/31/89
   d. > ='12/31/89'
10. The Slsrep table contains a Note field that contains notes describing important characteristics of the sales representatives. To find all sales reps who have technical abilities, enter the condition _____ in the Note field of the Slsrep query image.
    a. ..technical
    b. ..technical@
    c. ..technical..
    d. technical..

STUDENT ASSIGNMENT 3
Understanding Field Objects

Instructions: Figure SA5-3 shows the form design for the sales rep table. An object menu has been selected. Use this figure to answer the following questions.

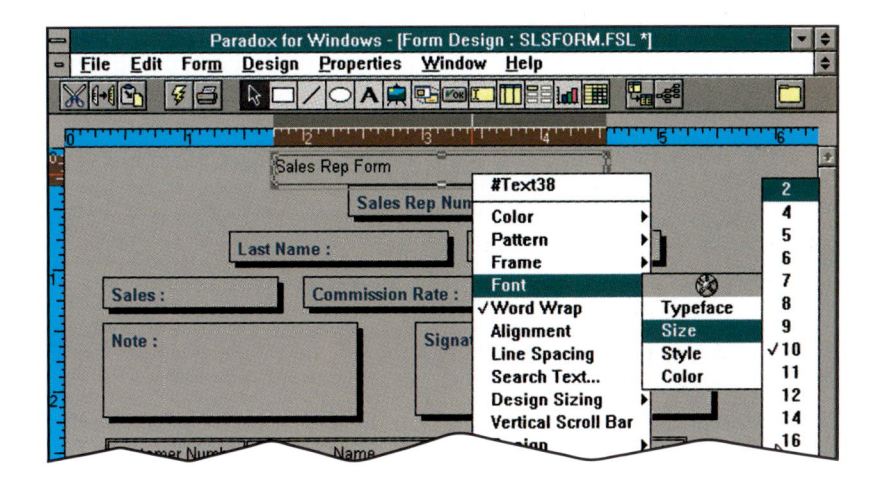

FIGURE SA5-3

1. What is the currently selected object? _____

2. What does the check mark in front of the Word Wrap command mean? _____

3. How do you select the menu for an object? _____

4. What does the Frame command do? _____

5. What does the Style command do? _____

P262   PROJECT 5   ADVANCED TOPICS

STUDENT ASSIGNMENT 4
Understanding Table Objects

Instructions: Figure SA5-4 shows the Form design for the sales rep table. The object menu for the Customer table has been selected. Use this figure to answer the following questions.

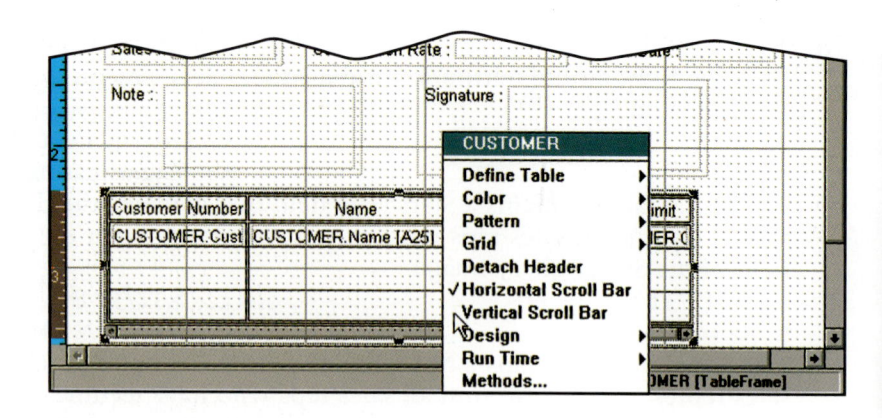

FIGURE SA5-4

1. What is a table object? _____

2. How can you remove the horizontal scroll bar from the Customer table object? _____

3. How can you add a vertical scroll bar to the Customer table object? _____

4. How can you change the color of the Customer table object? _____

5. How can you change the color of the Customer table heading? _____

STUDENT ASSIGNMENT 5
Using Date and Memo Fields in Queries

Instructions: In this assignment, you are to create queries for the Slsrep table. Use the table below to help identify column headings.

Sales Rep Number	Last Name	First Name	Address	City	State	Zip Code	Sales	Commission Rate	Start Date	Note	Signature

1. Explain the steps necessary to display the last name and first name of all sales reps who have some technical ability. _____

2. Explain the steps necessary to display the number, last name, first name, and sales of all sales reps who started after 1988 and have sales of more than $50,000. _____

3. Explain the steps necessary to display the last name, first name, and sales for all sales reps who either have some knowledge of French or started working before 1990. _____

STUDENT ASSIGNMENT 6
Understanding the Customer Database

Instructions: In Figure SA5-6, arrows point to various fields in the Slsrep table. Identify the field types for these fields in the space provided. Answer the following questions about the Customer database.

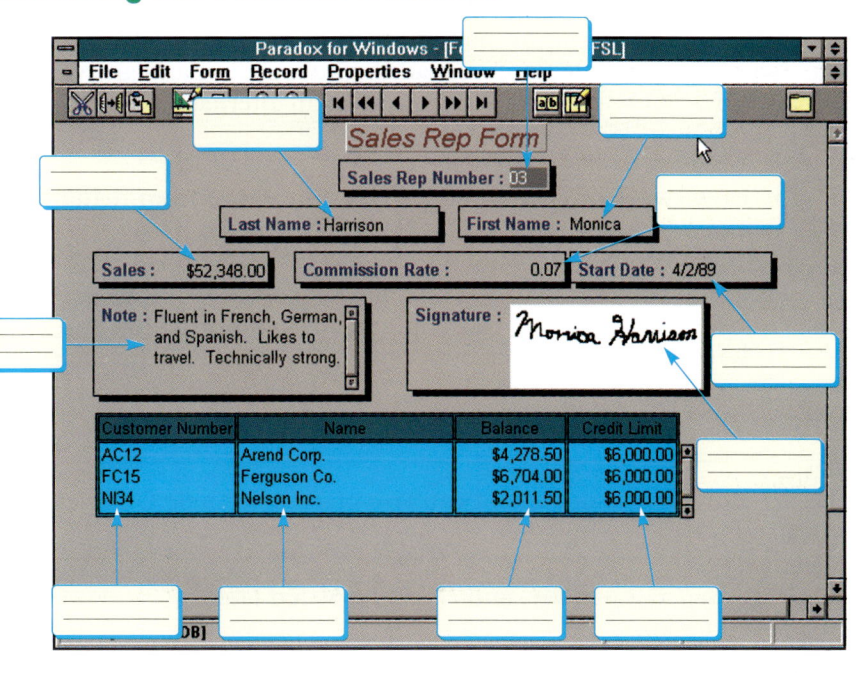

FIGURE SA5-6

1. The sales rep form depicts a one-to-many relationship between the Slsrep table and the Customer table. What is a one-to-many relationship? _____

   _____

2. Assume the highlight is on the first field of the record shown in Figure SA5-6. How would you add the phrase, Currently attending college, to the Note field? _____

   _____

3. Figure SA5-6 displays information on three customers represented by sales rep 03. Assume an additional customer is added to the Customer table and that customer is also represented by Monica Harrison. What would you need to do to display the information for the fourth customer?

   _____

   _____

COMPUTER LABORATORY EXERCISES

COMPUTER LABORATORY EXERCISE 1
Using the Help Menu

Instructions: Perform the following tasks using Paradox.

1. Start Paradox
2. Open the Slsrep table and maximize the Table window.
3. Choose the Contents command from the Help menu.

(continued)

COMPUTER LABORATORY EXERCISE 1 (continued)

4. Choose Search.
5. Type `field view` in the Search dialog box.
6. Go to the Field view topic, read the information and answer the following two questions.
   a. How can you enter field view? List all alternatives. _____

   _____

   b. How can you remain in field view and move from field to field? _____

   _____

7. Return to the Search dialog box and type `OLE`.
8. Go to the When to use OLE topic, read the information and answer the following two questions.
   a. What is the difference between DDE and OLE? What does the abbreviation DDE mean?

   _____

   _____

   b. How large a document can you place in a single OLE field? _____

   _____

9. Exit the Help window and close the Slsrep table.
10. Exit Paradox.

COMPUTER LABORATORY EXERCISE 2
Creating and Using Date Fields

Instructions: Start Paradox and open the Customer table. Perform the following tasks.

1. Choose the Restructure command from the Table menu.
2. Add a new field, Order Date to the Customer table. The field is a date field that contains the date the customer placed their most recent order.
3. Save the changes to the structure.
4. Enter the data shown in Figure CLE5-2.
5. Print the table.
6. Close the table.
7. Create a new query and select the Customer table.
8. For all queries, display the Customer Number, Customer Name, Balance, Credit Limit, Sales Rep Number, and Order Date and print the Answer table.
9. Find those customers who placed orders in 1994.
10. Find those customers who have not placed any orders since January 1, 1994.
11. Find those customers whose most recent orders were placed between June 1, 1994 and July 31, 1994. (Hint: Use the comma (,) as an AND operator in the Order Date field to find records where the date is greater than May 30, 1994 and less than August 1, 1994.)
12. Close the query without saving it.
13. Exit Paradox.

Customer Number	Order Date
AC!2	9/30/94
AX29	8/24/94
CL67	5/12/94
FC15	2/25/94
FY24	11/12/93
LW46	12/12/93
NI34	6/3/94
SD86	7/20/94
SI84	9/24/94

FIGURE CLE5-2

COMPUTER LABORATORY EXERCISE 3
Editing OLE Fields

Instructions: Start Paradox and open the Slsrep table. Perform the following tasks.

1. Enter edit mode. Select the Signature field for Sales Rep Number 03.
2. Press the SHIFT + F2 keys to access the Paintbrush application.
3. Underline the M in Monica Harrison's signature. Explain the steps to accomplish this.

   Steps: _____

   _____

4. Choose the Update command from the File menu in the Paintbrush application.
5. Choose the Exit and Return to Signature command from the File menu in the Paintbrush application.
6. Print the table. Close the table and exit Paradox.

COMPUTER LABORATORY ASSIGNMENTS

COMPUTER LABORATORY ASSIGNMENT 1
Improving the Part Database

Purpose: To provide practice in using date, memo, and OLE fields and to create forms containing table objects.

Instructions: Use the database created in Computer Laboratory Assignment 1 of Project 1 for this assignment. Execute each task on the computer and print the results.

1. Start Paradox and open the Part table. Choose Restructure from the Table menu.
2. Add the fields, Reorder Date and Reorder Notes to the table structure. Reorder Date is a date field and Reorder Notes is a memo field.
3. Save the changes to the structure. Add the data shown in Figure CLA5-1 to the Part table.

Part Number	Reorder Date	Reoder Notes
AX12	7/12/94	Blanket Purchase Order. Call in order to EJZ Mfr.
AZ52	7/24/94	Call in order to SG Unlimited. Minimum order required.
BA74	9/17/94	Call in order to SG Unlimited. Minimum order required.
BH22	9/15/94	Graduation item. Replenish stock in early April. Call in order to EJZ Mfg.
BT04	8/9/94	Summer item only. Reorder from ABC Supplies.
BZ66	6/30/94	Can single order. Requires written Purchase Order. Order from Whirlwind or ABC Supplies
CA14	10/1/94	Blanket Purchase Order. Call in order to EJZ Mfr.
CB03	8/28/94	Can single order. Requires written Purchase Order. Use SG Unlimited.
CX11	9/21/94	Blanket Purchase Order. Call in order to EJZ Mfr.
CZ81	9/19/94	Can single order. Requires written Purchase Order. Use SG Unlimited.

FIGURE CLA5-1

(continued)

COMPUTER LABORATORY ASSIGNMENT 1 (continued)

4. Close the Part table.
5. Create a form for the Class table. Include all the fields from the Class table. Also include the Part Number, Part Description, Units On Hand, and Price fields from the Part table. Follow the design guidelines and procedures presented in Project 5 to produce an attractive form.
6. Print the form.
7. Save the form as clssform.
8. Close the form and create a new query for the Part table.
9. Query the Part table to find all records where parts were ordered between July 1, 1994 and August 31, 1994. Display the Part Number, Part Description, Units on Hand, Price, and Reorder Date. (Hint: Use the comma (,) as an AND operator in the Order Date field to find records where the date is greater than June 30, 1994 and less than September 1, 1994.)
10. Print the Answer table.
11. Query the Part table to find all records where the part can be ordered from ABC Supplies. Display the Part Number, Part Description, Price, and Reorder Notes.
12. Print the Answer table.
13. Query the Part table to find all records where parts were ordered before September 1, 1994 and the number of units on hand is less than 20. Display the Part Number, Part Description, Units on Hand, Price, Reorder Date, and Reorder Notes.
14. Print the Answer table.
15. Close the query without saving it.
16. Exit Paradox.

COMPUTER LABORATORY ASSIGNMENT 2
Improving the Employee Database

Purpose: To provide practice in using date, memo, and OLE fields and to create forms containing table objects.

Instructions: Use the database created in Computer Laboratory Assignment 2 of Project 1 for this assignment. Execute each task on the computer and print the results.

1. Start Paradox and open the Employee table.
2. Choose Restructure from the Table menu.
3. Add the fields, Start Date, Notes, and Signature to the table structure. Start Date is a date field, Notes is a memo field, and Signature is an OLE field.
4. Save the changes to the structure.
5. Add the data shown in Figure CLA5-2 to the Employee table.
6. Add the signatures for the employees in the Accounting department using the techniques described in Project 5.
7. Close the Employee table.
8. Create a form for the Department table. Include all the fields from the Department table. Also include the Employee Number, Employee Last Name, Employee First Name, and Pay Rate fields from the Employee table. Follow the design guidelines and procedures presented in Project 5 to produce an attractive form.

9. Print the form.
10. Save the form as deptform.
11. Close the form and create a new query for the Employee table.
12. Query the Employee table to find all employees who started after 1989. Display the Employee Number, Employee Last Name, Employee First Name, Start Date, and Pay Rate.

Employee Number	Start Date	Notes
1011	7/1/87	Employee of the Year in 1990.
1013	6/15/89	Union Representative.
1016	6/1/88	Won safety award. Had CPR training.
1017	2/15/90	Eligible for promotion in 1993.
1020	8/15/90	Excellent computer skills. Trains co-workers.
1022	1/1/89	Had CPR training. Speaks Spanish.
1025	4/1/89	Eligible to sit for the CPA exam in 1993.
1026	1/15/91	Expert in Statistical Process Control.
1029	7/15/91	Had CPR training.
1030	1/1/92	CAD expert.
1037	6/1/92	Passed CPA exam. Had CPR training.
1041	9/1/92	Speaks Spanish and French. Set up marketing offices in Madrid, Spain.
1056	3/1/93	Marketing Intern.
1057	4/1/93	Engineering Intern.
1066	4/1/93	Engineering Intern.

FIGURE CLA5-2

13. Print the Answer table.
14. Query the Employee table to find all employees who have had CPR training. Display the Employee Number, Employee Last Name, Employee First Name, and Notes fields.
15. Print the Answer table.
16. Query the Employee table to find all employees who started before 1990 and have a pay rate greater than $9.00. Display the Employee Number, Employee Last Name, Employee First Name, Department Name, and Pay Rate. (Hint: Join the Employee and Department tables.)
17. Print the Answer table.
18. Close the query without saving it.
19. Exit Paradox.

COMPUTER LABORATORY ASSIGNMENT 3
Improving the Movie Database

Purpose: To provide practice in using date, memo, and OLE fields and to create forms containing table objects.

Instructions: Use the database created in Computer Laboratory Assignment 3 of Project 1 for this assignment. Execute each task on the computer and print the results.

1. Start Paradox and open the Director table.
2. Choose Restructure from the Table menu.
3. Add the fields, Birth Date, Notes, and Logo to the table structure. Birth Date is a date field; Notes is a memo field; and Logo is an OLE field.
4. Save the changes to the structure.
5. Add the data shown in Figure CLA5-3 to the Director table.

Director Code	Birth Date	Notes
01	10/21/15	Won three Academy Awards. Won awards at Cannes film festival in 1958 and 1963.
02	12/12/25	Won American Film Institute Award. Excels at Westerns.
03	2/15/32	Master of Suspense. Combines excellent photography with special effects.
04	5/14/41	Youngest director to ever win an Academy Award in 1964.

FIGURE CLA5-3

6. Each director uses a logo that includes his or her initials on the movie credits. Add a logo for each director using the techniques described in Project 5.
7. Close the Director table.
8. Create a form for the Director table. Include all the fields in the Director table. Include the Movie Number, Movie Title, Year Made, and Movie Type fields from the Movie table. Follow the design guidelines and procedures presented in Project 5 to produce an attractive form.
9. Print the form.
10. Save the form as dirform.
11. Close the form and create a new query for the Director table.
12. Query the Director table to find all records where the director was born before 1940. Display the Director Code, Director Name, and Birth Date.
13. Print the Answer table.
14. Query the Director table to find all records where the Director won an award at the Cannes film festival. Display the Director Code, Director Name, Birth Date, and Notes fields.
15. Print the Answer table.
16. Query the Director table to find all records where the Director was born after 1940 and won an Academy Award. Display the Director Code, Director Name, Birth Date, and Notes fields.
17. Print the Answer table.
18. Close the query without saving it.
19. Exit Paradox.

COMPUTER LABORATORY ASSIGNMENT 4
Improving the Book Database

Purpose: To provide practice in using date, memo, and OLE fields and to create forms containing table objects.

Problem: The bookstore owner has asked you to make some improvements to the Book database. She has sent you a memo outlining the improvements.

Instructions: Use the database created in Computer Laboratory Assignment 4 of Project 1 for this assignment. Provide the following:

1. Add fields to the Publisher table to store data on the date when the most recent order was placed with the publisher, and to store ordering information. The data for these fields is shown in CLA5-4.
2. Each publisher now uses a design symbol to draw attention to its books. The owner has sent you a list of these symbols and asked if there is any way to include them in the database. (Hint: Use abbreviations or first names as the design symbol.)
3. A form that shows information about the publisher and all its books. The only items the owner needs from the Book table are Book Code, Title, Author, and Price.
4. Two lists—one showing orders placed before September 1, 1994 and the other showing orders after September 1, 1994.
5. A list of all publishers who fill single orders.

Publisher Code	Order Date	Notes
BB	9/24/94	Will fill single orders and special requests. Ships daily.
FR	9/3/94	Will fill single orders. Ships twice a week.
PB	8/18/94	Will fill single orders on emergency basis only. Ships twice a week.
SI	8/31/94	Has minimum order requirement of 10 books. Ships orders when needed.
SS	9/27/94	Has minimum order requirement of 25 books. Ships weekly.
VI	10/3/94	Will fill single orders and special requests. Ships daily.

FIGURE CLA5-4

Index

@, P72, P131
About... help menu, P43
Add Band command, P184–185
Adding new fields, P122–123
Adding records, P114–116
Addition, P92
Add Table button, P88
All Records band, **P170**
Alphanumeric fields, **P9,** P12
Ampersand (&), P131
AND conditions, **P78**–79
Answer table, **P60**
   closing, P66
   creating, P64–65
   displaying selected fields, P68–71
   graphing, P96–100
   including all fields in, P62–64
   printing, P65
   sorting, P82–86.
   See also Query
Assist button, P132
Asterisk (*), P13, P23
AVERAGE function, P94

Background color, P202, P244
BACKSPACE key, P27
Band, **P170**
   group, **P183,** P184–185
   resizing, P176–177
Bar charts, P97–99
Best Fit command, P232, P245
Binary Large Object (BLOB), P223
BLOB, **P223**
Bold command, P248–249
Boxes
   adding to forms, P197–198
   frame styles, P202–203
   resizing, P251
Box tool, P197
Braces ({ }), P131
Brush tool, P229

Calc operator, P92, P93–94
Cancel button, P15
Case-sensitive conditions, P71
Case-sensitive index, **P143**
Changed table, P125, P127, P141
Change Order Up button, P169
Character fields
   conditions, P70–72
   wildcards, **P72**–73
Check-descending, P81, **P83**
Check mark, **P62**–64
   examples, **P87**
   sorting and, P81
Check Menu, **P63,** P68, P81
Check plus, P81, **P82**
Child Fields, **P135**
Clipboard, P230
Close command, P23, P36, P42, P66–67.
   See also Closing
Closing
   answer table, P66
   forms, P36, P208, P243, P255
   graphs, P42, P100
   Paintbrush application, P228–232
   query, P67, P101
   reports, P182
   tables, P23–24, P151, P234

Color
   field edit regions, P206–207
   field labels, P248–249
   form background, P202, P243–244
   table object, P251–252
Color command, P202, P207, P244, P250, P252
Color palette, P202, P207, P244
Columns, P3
   headings, P171–174
   widths, P171, P175–176
Comma (,), P131
   in character data conditions, P70
Comparison operators, **P77**
Complete Display command, P247
Complete the display, **P227**–228
   Note field, P246–247
   OLE field, P233–234
Compound conditions, **P78**–80
Computed field, **P92**–93
Conditions, **P62**
   AND, **P78**–79
   character data in, P70–72
   comparison operators, **P77**
   compound, **P78**–80
   entering, P70
   example, **P87,** P92
   LIKE operator, P73–75
   numeric data in, P75–76
   OR, **P78,** P79–80
   wildcards, **P72**–73
Contents help menu, P43
Control menu, **P6,** P23
Correcting errors, P15, P27
COUNT function, P94
Create Paradox for Windows dialog box, P11
CTRL + DELETE, P15, P27, P70, P119–120
Currency fields, **P9,** P14
Custom forms, P165, **P188.** *See also* Form(s)
Cut command, P230

Database, **P2**–4
   design, **P43**–44
   preparation steps, P4
Database management system, **P2**
Data entry validity, *see* Validity checks
Data Model dialog box, P167, P189, P235–236
Date field, P221, **P222**
   creation, P224
   in query, P256–257
   updating, P225
DB extension, P15
Default text box, P130
Default values, P127, P130
Define button, P146
Define Field command, P179
Define Field Object dialog box, P179
Define Graph dialog box, P37, P96
Define Group dialog box, P185
Define Secondary Index dialog box, P146
Delete command, P140
Deleted table, P140
Deletion
   fields, P15
   mass updates, P139–140
   records, P27, P119–120
   undoing, P142
Descending order, in sort, P81, P83

Design button, P98
Design Layout dialog box, P168, P169, P190, P191, P238
Desktop, P6–7
   maximizing, P5–6
Directory, working, **P7**–8
Disk drive A, P5
Diskette, P5
Division, P92
Dollar sign ($), **P9**
Double period (..), P72–73
Duplicate records, P81, P82–83

Edit Data button, **P20**–21, P24, P32, P115, P118, P225
Edit mode, **P21,** P24
Edit region, *see* Field edit region
Error correction, P15, P27
Error dialog box, P236
Examples, **P87,** P92
Exclamation point (!), P131
Exit command, P17
Exiting, Paradox for Windows, P17

F3, P90
F4, P90
F5, P87, P92
F6, P64
Field(s), **P3**
   adding, P122–123
   alphanumeric, **P9,** P12
   computed, **P92**–93
   currency, **P9,** P14
   defining, P11–14
   deleting, P15
   key, P13, P15, P26
   moving and resizing, P239–241
   name, **P8,** P9, P11, P13
   numeric, **P9**
   obsolete, P121
   required, P128
   selecting for forms, P191–192, P193–194, P237–238
   selecting for query, P62–64, P68–71
   selecting for reports, P168–169
   short number, **P9**
   size, **P8**
   type, **P8,** P9
   updating, P124–127
Field check box, **P62**
Field edit region
   color of, P206–207
   repositioning, P186–187, P195–196
   resizing, P239
Field frame styles, P204
Field labels, P248–249
Field object, **P178**
   changing label for, P180–181
Field range specification, P127–130
Field Roster, P11
Field size
   restructuring, P121–122
   selecting, P12
Field tool button, 78
Field types, selecting, P11–12
Field View button, P118–119, **P124,** P226–227, P229
   updating with, P124–125
FIRST function, P94

P270

First Record button, **P20**, P117
Fit Height, P174
Fit Width, P174-175
Font command, P249-250
Font palette, **P200**-201
Footers
　group, **P183**
　page, **P170**
　report, **P170**, 176-180
Foreign key, **P134**
Form(s), P33-34
　adding boxes to, P197-198
　adding text to, P199-200
　background color, P202, P243-244
　closing and saving, P36, P194, P208, P243, P255
　creating, P189-190, P235-236
　custom, P165, **P188**
　design considerations, P209
　field manipulation, P194
　fonts, P200-201
　frame styles, **P202**-205, P244-245
　graphs as, P40
　maximizing, P34
　object alignment, P192-193
　one-to-many relationships, P235
　selecting fields for, P191-192, P193-194, P237-238
　titles, P249-251
　using, P209, P255
　viewing, P195, P205-206, P208, P243. *See also* Form view
Form Design mode, P98
Form view, **P33**
　scrolling through records, P34-35
　switching to Table view, P35
Frames, **P202,** P244-245
　box frame styles, P202-203
　field frame styles, P204
　text frame styles, P205

Graph
　bar charts and pie charts, P97-100
　closing, P42, P100
　creating, P37-40
　maximizing, P97
　printing, P41
　query answer, P96-100
Graphic field, **P222**-223. *See also* OLE field
Graph Type command, P99
Greater than (>) comparison operator, P77
Greater than or equal to (> =) comparison operator, P77
Grid lines, **P172**-173
　custom form design, **P192**-193
　displaying, P241
　removing, P201, P244
　snap to, **P192**-193, P241
Group band, **P183,** P184-185
Group footer, **P183**
Group header, **P183**
Grouping records, P94-95, P164, P183, P184-185

Handles, **P171**
Header, P170
　group, **P183**
Header object menu, P252
Headings, P172-174
Help menu, P43
Horizontal axis, P37
Horizontal scroll bar, **P242**

Indexes, P113, P142-144
　case-sensitive, **P143**
　multiple field, **P145,** P148-149
　naming, P143
　record ordering, P149-151
　single field, **P145**-148
Index key, **P143,** P144
Inserting fields, P15
Italic font, P201, P250

Join, **P86**-91
　moving between tables, P90
　restricting records in, P90-91

Keyboard help menu, P43
Key field, P26
　changing, P15
　indicating, P13

Label, **P180**-181, P248-249
Landscape orientation, P27-28, P65
LAST function, P94
Last Record button, **P20,** P25, P115
Legal values, **P133**
Less than (<) comparison operator, P77
Less than or equal to (< =) comparison operator, P77
LIKE operator, P73-75
Locate command, **P116**-117
Locate Value dialog box, P117
Locked records, **P21**
Lowercase letters, character field conditions, P71

Magnification
　OLE fields, **P231**-232, P245
　Zoom command, **P174**
Major key, **P81**
Mass updates, P125-127, P139
　changes, P141
　deletions, 139-140
　undoing, P142
Mathematical operations, P92-94
MAX function, P94
Maximize, P5-6, P19, P24
　forms, P34
　graph, P97
　Query window, P62
Maximum text box, P129
Memo field, **P222**
　creation of, P224
　in query, P256-257
　See also Note field
Menu bar, **P6**
MIN function, P94
Minimum text box, P129
Minor key, **P81**
Modify Printer Setup button, P28
Mouse pointer shape, P19
Multiple field index, **P145,** P148-149
Multiplication, P92

Naming
　fields, **P8,** P9, P11, P13
　indexes, P143
New command, P10, P30, P61, P189
Next Record button, **P20,** P25, P34-35, P115-116, P253
Next Set of Records button, **P20**
NOT comparison operator, P77
Note field, P221, P222
　completing the display, P227-228, P246-247
　in query, P256-257

scroll bar for, P254-255
updating, P226-227
Numeric data, P75-76
Numeric fields, **P9**

Object Linking and Embedding (OLE), **P222**. *See also* OLE field
Object menus, P98
Object's menu, **P98,** P200
OLE field, **P222**- 223
　completing the display, P233-234
　creation, P224
　data entry, P229-231
　magnification modifications, **P231**-232, P245
　updating, P228
One-to-many relationship, **P235**
Open Document dialog box, P183
Open Mode options, P183
Open Query button, P102
Open Report button, P182-183
Open Table button, P32
Open Table dialog box, P18-19
OR conditions, **P78,** P79-80
Ordering records, P26
Order/Range dialog box, P150
Overflow, **P29**

Page band, **P170**
Page footer, **P170**
Page header, **P170**
Paintbrush application, P228-232
Paradox for Windows, P4
　exiting, P17
　starting, P5
Paradox for Windows dialog box, P67
Parent's key, **P135**
Paste command, P230-231
Period, double (..), P72-73
Pick tool, P229-230
Picture Assistance dialog box, P132
Picture symbols, **P131**-133
Picture text box, P132
Pie charts, P97-100
Portrait orientation, P29
Pound sign (#), P131
Previous Record button, **P20**
Previous Set of Records button, **P20**
Primary index, **P143**
Primary key, P3, **P8,** P26, **P134**
Print button, **P20**
Printer Setup command, P28
Print File dialog box, P29, P41
Printing
　answer to query, P65
　graphs, P41
　reports, P182-183, P188
　tables, P27-29
:PRIV:STRUCT.DB, P18
Properties menu, **P82**
Punctuation, in character data conditions, P70-P71

Query, **P59**
　closing and saving, P67, P101
　conditions, *see* Conditions
　creating, P61-64
　graphing answer for, P96-100
　joined tables, P86-91
　mass updates, P139-143
　memo and date fields in, P256-257
　multiple fields, P84-86
　printing answer, P65

running, P64–65
sorting data in, **P81–86**
update, **P125**
using, P101–102.
See also Answer table
Query command, P61, P140
Query image, **P62**
  clearing, P68
  joined tables, P87
Query Status dialog box, P65
Query window, **P61–62**
Question mark (?), P131
Quick Form button, P33, P114–115
Quick Graph button, P96
Quotation marks (" "), in character data conditions, P70–P71

Range specification, P127–130
Records, **P3**
  adding to table, P17, P21–23, P24–26, P32, P114–116
  changing, P118–119, P141–142
  deleting, P27, P119–120, P139–140
  global changes, P125–127
  grouping, P94–95, P141–142, **P164**, P183, P184–185
  locking, **P21**
  missing, P27
  moving through with Next Record, P34–35
  ordering, P26, P149–151
  searching for, **P116–**117
  sorting in query, P80–86
Redundancy, **P43–**44
Referential integrity, **P134–**137
Remove Field button, P169
Report(s), P163–165
  adding subtotal to, P185–187
  closing, P182
  column headings, P171–174
  column widths, P171, P175–176
  creating, P166–167, P184
  design guidelines, P188
  design modification, P184
  footers and headers, P170, P176–180
  printing, P182–183, P188
  record groupings, P164, P183, P184–185
  saving, P181, P188
  selecting fields for, P168–169
  selecting portions of, P171–172
Report band, **P170**
Report command, P166
Report Design window, **P166**
Report footer, **P170**
  adding fields to, P178–180
  resizing, P176–177
Report header, **P170**
Required fields, P128
Restructure command, P144, P223
Restructure Paradox for Windows Table dialog box, P121–124, P145, P148, P224
Restructure Warning dialog box, P134
Restructuring, P144, P223–224
  adding new fields, P122–123
  field size, P121–122
Rows, P3
Run Query button, **P64,** P140, P256–257
Run the query, **P59**
Run Time command, P247

Sample Pictures list box, P132
Sample Value text box, P132

Save As button, P15–16, P31, P208
Save Index As dialog box, P147
Save Referential Integrity As dialog box, P137
Save Table As dialog box, P16, P31
Saving
  forms, P194, P208, P243, P255
  query, P101
  reports, P181, P188
  table, P15
  table properties, P234
  validity checks, P134
Scroll bar, P221, P242, P254–255
Searching, **P116–**117
Secondary indexes, **P113, P143**
  multiple field, **P145,** P148–149
  ordering records with, P149–151
  single field, **P145–**148
Select Fields button, P191
Select Fields dialog box, P168–169, P237
Select File dialog box, P61, P88
Selection arrow button, **P178**
Set Working Directory dialog box, P7
SHIFT key, P203, P204
Short number fields, **P9**
Show Grid command, P201
Signature field, P221–224, P229–234, P245. *See also* OLE field
Single-field secondary index, **P145–**148
Snap to grid, **P192–**193
Sort Answer dialog box, P85
Sorting
  Answer table, P82–86
  descending order, P81, P83
  indexes vs., P143
  multiple fields query, P84–86
  in query, **P81–**86
Sort key, **P81**
Sounds like (LIKE) operator, P73–75
SpeedBar, **P6**
  button functions, P20
  help menu, P43
Standard deviation, P94
Standard form, **P33**
Start Date field, *see* Date field
Statistical calculations, P94
Status bar, **P7**
STD function, P94
Structure, **P8–**9, **P121.** *See also* Restructuring
Style command, P201, P245
Subtotal, **P164,** P185–187
Subtraction, P92
SUM function, P94
Support Info help menu, P43
System Error dialog box, P5

Table(s), P2–3
  adding records to, P17, P21–23, P24–26, P32
  Answer, **P60**
  Changed, P125, P127, P141
  closing, P23–24, P151, P234
  creating, **P8–**15, P30–31
  Deleted, P140
  joining, **P86–**91
  naming, P15
  opening, P18–20
  printing, P27–29
  restructuring, P223–224
  saving, P15, P234

Table check box, **P63**
Table command, P10, P30–31
Table object, **P239**
  color of, P251–252
  resizing, P246, P253–254
Table object menu, P252
Table properties, **P234**
Table Properties list, P135, P145
Table structure, **P8–**9. *See also* Restructuring
Table Type dialog box, P10–11
Table Utilities command, **P142**
Table view, **P33,** P35, P114
  switching from Form view, P35
Template, **P131**
Text frame styles, P205
Text object menu, P249–250
Text tool button, P199
Title, on forms, P249–251
Title bar, **P6**
2D Pie command, P99–100

Undoing mass changes, P142
Unique identifier, **P3,** P8
Update query, **P125**
Updating, P113–116
  date fields, P225
  Field View and, P119–120, P124–125
  mass changes, P125–127, P139–143. *See also* Mass updates
  memo fields, P226–227
  new (empty) fields, P125–127
  restructured database, P123–124
  tables containing validity checks, P137–138
Uppercase letters
  case-sensitive index, **P143**
  character field conditions, P71
  picture symbol, P131
Utilities command, **P142**

Validity checks, **P127**
  default values, P127, P130
  field range specification, P128–130
  legal values, P133–134
  pattern specification (pictures), P131–133
  required field specification, P128
  saving, P134
  table updating, P137–138
  violations of, P137
Value command, P117
Vertical axis, P37
Vertical scroll bar, P221, **P242,** P254–255
View Data button, P100, P195, P205–206, P208, P243, P252
Viewing forms, **P33,** P195, P205–206, P208, P243. *See also* Form view

Wildcards, **P172–**73, P256
Windows Program Manager, P5
Working directory, **P7–**8

X axis, P37, P38

Y axis, P37, P39

Zoom command, **P174**
Zoom factor, **P174–**175